W9-CRF-134

The Dictionary of Art · volume one

The Dictionary of Art

CONSULTING EDITOR Hugh Brigstocke

EDITOR Jane Turner

1

A
TO
Anckerman

GROVE

The Dictionary of Art

edited by JANE TURNER, in thirty-four volumes, 1996

This edition is distributed within the United Kingdom and Europe by Macmillan Publishers Limited, London, and within the United States and Canada by Grove's Dictionaries Inc., New York.

Text keyboarded by Wearset Limited, Sunderland, England
Database management by Pindar plc, York, England
Imagesetting by William Clowes Limited, Suffolk, England
Printed in the United States of America by RR Donnelley & Sons Company, Willard, Ohio

British Library Cataloguing in Publication Data

The dictionary of art
1. Art - Dictionaries 2. Art - History - Dictionaries
I. Turner, Jane
703

ISBN 1-884446-00-0

Library of Congress Cataloging in Publication Data

The dictionary of art / editor, Jane Turner.
p. cm.
Includes bibliographical references and index.
Contents: 1. A to Anckerman
ISBN 1-884446-00-0 (alk. paper)
1. Art—Encyclopedias.
I. Turner, Jane, 1956–
N31.D5 1996 96–13628
703—dc20 CIP

Contents

Preface

1. The Dictionary of Art. The title is deceptively simple. Yet when work began on the *Dictionary of Art* in the early 1980s, it was evident that it would not be a simple undertaking. Only after some time had elapsed, however, did we fully realize the enormity of the task on which we had embarked. The objective was clear enough: to produce, in 25 million words, an illustrated reference work that provided comprehensive coverage of the history of all the visual arts worldwide, from prehistory to the present. Like our renowned sister publication, the *New Grove Dictionary of Music and Musicians*, 20 vols (London, 1980), we aimed to present this comprehensive account using the highest possible standards of scholarship, while at the same time ensuring that entries were accessible to non-specialists. We have benefited enormously from the accumulated wisdom and experience of our Grove colleagues, but the preparation of these two publications has posed some quite different challenges. As Stanley Sadie, the editor of the *New Grove*, explained in his preface to the sixth edition of the music dictionary first prepared by Sir George Grove in the 1870s and 1880s, less than three percent of the entries in the *New Grove* were retained from earlier editions; the Grove editors did, however, have one distinct advantage over us—namely an existing product to revise and refine. We had to start more or less from scratch.

2. Contents and scope. From the outset, we intended that the *Dictionary of Art* would take an entirely different approach from that of existing art reference works. Architecture and photography were certainly to be included, and the decorative arts would be treated as seriously as the traditional 'fine arts' of painting, sculpture and architecture, as would such contemporary art forms as performance art and multimedia installations, which do not fit easily into conventional categories. The only visual art form deliberately excluded was the history of film making, a subject that in itself would require a major reference work. (There is, however, an entry on Experimental film, and the film making activities of other kinds of artists are treated in their biographies.)

More importantly, if the *Dictionary* were to be truly comprehensive, its coverage could not be limited to biographies. Most ancient cultures and most civilizations outside the Western world simply do not lend themselves to a biographical approach. It was decided therefore that the *Dictionary* should offer as many types of article as possible in order to accommodate the wide range of topics of interest to modern students and historians of art. These articles vary in length from a few lines to hundreds of pages. (Indeed, some entries could be considered substantial books in their own right.) Combined with extensive cross-references and alternative headwords and an index of some 750,000 items, this diversity of approach is designed to enable readers to find information quickly and easily, from numerous points of access. Entries are further supplemented by detailed bibliographies, which have been carefully selected by the *Dictionary*'s authors and editors to reflect the most important past and recent scholarship.

A reference work is bound to reflect the attitudes and methodologies of the era in which it is created, and the *Dictionary of Art* is no exception. But there can have been few other times as exciting as the 1980s and the early 1990s in which to produce a work intended to be used well into the 21st century. When we began, we had little idea how momentous the political changes of the 1990s would prove to be, and just as the political map of the globe has been redrawn, so, too, have the boundaries of art history. Exactly when the latter process began cannot be pinpointed as accurately as the fall of the Berlin Wall in 1989, but it is certainly true that in the last quarter of the 20th century the ways in which art is studied have changed more dramatically than at any other time since the origins of the discipline in the late 19th century. Old assumptions have been questioned, opinions revised, new facts brought to light and whole new areas explored for the first time.

At no other period in this century has there been so much new evidence to consider, a phenomenon often referred to by the media as the 'information explosion' of recent decades. In 1974, for instance, the astonishing army of 10,000 Chinese terracotta warriors and horses, now seen as the quintessential embodiment of Qin-period sculpture, was excavated after having been buried for over 2000 years. Four years later workmen in Mexico City unearthed sculptures that led to the rediscovery of the Templo Mayor (or Great Temple) of the Aztecs. Moreover, it is not only in archaeological contexts that new 'finds' are made. Information continues to come to light about even the best-known artists and their work. New evidence concerning the possible identity of the sitter in one of the world's most famous paintings, Leonardo da Vinci's *'Mona Lisa'*, was published as recently as 1991. Since 1968 the entire corpus of paintings traditionally ascribed to Rembrandt has been systematically re-evaluated by a team of Dutch scholars, and the findings of this project (published from 1982 onwards) have led, controversially, to the reattribution of many works to Rembrandt's lesser-known pupils.

Along with the discovery of new facts have come fundamental changes in attitudes and understanding. Questions of authorship, formal analysis and stylistic development are no longer sufficient to satisfy the curiosity of today's art historians. They want to know more—for whom and how a work of art was produced, for instance. It has become clear that art objects can be fully understood only within the complete social, cultural, historical and economic context in which they were created. Subject-matter, iconography and patronage, as well as issues of gender, sexuality, politics and race, have thus taken their place among the many methodological approaches that have broadened our understanding of the history of artistic endeavour. In addition, forms of art, cultures and artists once completely neglected now attract the same professional interest as those areas making up the traditional Eurocentric canon. The history of architecture, photography and the decorative arts appear increasingly alongside the history of painting and sculpture in university syllabuses. Women artists of the past now receive the recognition they deserve, and, increasingly, the other roles women have played in the creation of art, as patrons for example, have begun to be better documented.

Perhaps the most significant advance in art-historical studies of the past several decades has been in our increased understanding of artistic practices in traditions outside the West. As long ago as 1749, the enlightened Dr Samuel Johnson, in the *Vanity of Human Wishes*, said: 'Let observation with extensive view survey mankind, from China to Peru.' Yet when it comes to standard art history reference books, little serious scholarly attention has been paid, in the intervening two and a half centuries, to the arts of China and Pre-Columbian Peru, let alone to those of Africa, the Pacific Islands and Native Americans, to name but a few of the areas only now finding their rightful place in a more universal history of art.

3. TYPES OF ARTICLE. The headings under which readers of the *Dictionary of Art* can look for information, though they appear in alphabetical order, can be grouped into some 12 broad categories. The largest group (numerically but not in extent) is that of biographies, which total about 20,800 of the 45,000 entries. About 17,300 biographies have been allocated to artists of all kinds: painters, sculptors, architects, illuminators, draughtsmen, silversmiths,

cabinetmakers, potters, industrial designers and so on. As far as possible, every aspect of an artist's career is touched on, including, where relevant, the person's character and personality, as well as related activities, such as designs for prints and the decorative arts, and art theory, collecting and dealing. There are also some 3500 biographies devoted to patrons, collectors, dealers, theorists, writers, art historians, museum officials, critics and teachers.

The selection of biographies to be included was among the most contentious tasks undertaken by our advisers and editors. The *Dictionary of Art* was never intended as a directory: it is a critically organized repository of historically significant information. Therefore the decision to include (or to exclude) an artist was inevitably a matter of scholarly and editorial judgement. Naturally the criteria for inclusion vary from century to century. Compared with modern periods, a greater percentage of those medieval or Renaissance artists whose names are known appear in the *Dictionary*'s pages because far fewer artists from these early periods are documented. In more recent times, the criteria have necessarily to be more closely linked with critical judgement. We have tried to compensate for this by increasing the number of artists included for each subsequent century, while reducing the length of the individual entries. There are thus more biographies of 20th-century artists (for whom there was no official cut-off date) than for any previous period. We were greatly helped in this difficult exercise by two factors—the large number of biographies that we were able to accommodate in this multivolume work and the expert advice and guidance we were given by our numerous regional advisers. Although we realize that no one person will agree with all the judgements we have made, we can only hope that most readers will find the selection reasonably consistent and intelligent.

The allocation of space to biographies had to be balanced against the pages given over to the achievements of groups whose individual identities might not be known, but whose activities or works still occupy an important place in the history of art. We have thus included many entries on non-Western peoples, such as the Nazca of Peru, the Yoruba of Africa and the Liao of China. The contribution of specific peoples can also be studied within the context of the substantial articles on the art of ancient cultures and civilizations outside the West, such as Aboriginal Australia, China, ancient Egypt and the Indian subcontinent. This aspect of our coverage extends to many millions of words and constitutes, we believe, the most comprehensive coverage of the arts of Asia, Africa, Australasia and the Americas ever published in one source.

Supplementing our coverage of the world's civilizations and peoples are articles on every modern country recognized by the United Nations (though in some cases, e.g. China and Japan, this will be combined with the history of the ancient civilization). Following a summary of geography and history, the modern country articles provide detailed historical surveys of architecture, painting and graphic arts, sculpture and the decorative arts. Sections on patronage, collecting and dealing, art education, museums, art libraries and photographic collections and historiography are also generally included.

There are many entries on cities and towns with significant artistic traditions, from every continent of the world. Each article discusses the history and urban development of the city or town, its art life and institutions and, where appropriate, the local production of decorative arts. Many city articles also include individual discussions of important buildings when these are the creations of anonymous artists (e.g. medieval cathedrals) or the result of collaborative efforts extending over many decades or centuries.

Entries on sites form another important category of our coverage. Site articles discuss the significance of archaeological excavations, and the monuments and artefacts found at locations as wide-ranging as Ayutthaya, Babylon or Great Zimbabwe. Another kind of site entry documents monuments and buildings that are not located in a modern city and therefore cannot be discussed under such a heading—for example the French château of Chenonceaux; the Spanish royal monastery and palace of the Escorial; and Monticello, the house designed by Thomas Jefferson near Charlottesville, Virginia. This category of entry also affords the opportunity to include factories and centres of production, for example tapestries at Cadillac, porcelain at Capodimonte, glass at Waterford and jet at Whitby.

In line with the tradition of many art dictionaries, we have individual entries on artistic styles, schools, groups and movements. Over 500 articles of this type—from Abstract Expressionism, the Ashcan school, Baroque and Brutalism to Donkey's Tail, Egyptian Revival, Estridentismo and the Utrecht Caravaggisti—offer a general definition and history of the style, school, group or movement in question, frequently situating its development within the wider social and political sphere. The origins and historical use of the term itself are often explained, especially for headings considered conceptually outmoded by some modern scholars. In a few cases, however, it seemed more appropriate to consider a particular style in the broader historical context of the relevant country article; thus, for example, Japanese painting and printmaking styles such as *Nihonga*, *ukiyoe* and *Zenga* are discussed in the relevant sections of the article on Japan (and can also be found by consulting the index).

The general trend away from basing art history primarily on stylistic analysis has coincided with greater attention being paid to the forms, themes and subject-matter of art. These topics are addressed in some 800 articles in the *Dictionary*, including Bed, Book, Carpet, Garden, Marine painting, Photography, Portraiture and Stele. Where appropriate, such articles attempt to provide a global account of their development (Altar, Garden, Mirror and Tomb being good examples). These articles illuminate key issues: design, taste, intention and function, patronage and cultural context. In other cases, the history and development of certain art forms and themes play such an integral role in the development of the arts of a particular culture or civilization that they are best studied under the latter heading. In the survey of Islamic art, for instance, no account of the development of textiles would be complete without a detailed study of Islamic carpets, and it is there that the principal discussion will be found. In the Carpet entry, by contrast, the reader is given technical information that applies to carpets in all regions and cultures (e.g. knotting and weaving techniques); this is followed by a short historical overview of carpets worldwide and a detailed history of Western carpets. Cross-references and the index will guide the reader to equally detailed discussions under other headings.

A similar category of art form entry discusses the history of building types (e.g. Airport, Church, Mosque and Palace), as well as parts of buildings, decorative features and construction techniques (e.g. Arch, Cantilever, Dome, Frieze, Machicolation, Moulding, Orders, Pinnacle and Vault). There is also a variety of related entries essential to the understanding of architecture (e.g. Building regulations, Lighting and Property development).

Another area of our coverage that we believe to be unprecedented is the series of some 600 entries devoted to the materials and techniques of art. Rather than being directed at the practising specialist, these articles are included to enable curators, scholars, students and collectors to understand technical issues related to how, and from what, works of art are made. Until now, standard art reference books have tended to neglect the interrelation between design, medium and technique. Articles such as Acrylic painting, Aluminium, Aquatint, Brass, Brush, Fresco, Glass, Glaze, Jade, Lithography, Panel, Stone and Wood typically discuss the properties, sources and manufacture of the material or technique concerned, the history of its use and its conservation. We have made every effort to ensure that difficult and complex scientific information is explained in clear and accessible language. Conservation issues are also covered in general entries such as Conservation and restoration, Heritage, and Technical examination, the last of which includes, among many others, detailed discussions of scientific dating methods and techniques for analysing the macrostructure of a work (e.g. by infra-red photography).

The history of art patronage is another area in which our treatment of the subject is intended to extend the boundaries of what is currently available in other reference sources, especially when the thousands of additional names of patrons found in the index are taken into account. Besides the individual biographies of patrons and ruling dynasties who commissioned works of art and the surveys of patronage found under each country heading, there are entries for all the major religions of the world. Articles on specific religious orders treat the history, iconography and patronage of each order, exploring in detail how each has influenced the production of art. Finally, there are substantial articles on many theoretical and general issues, such as Abstraction, Aesthetics, Anthropology and art, Art legislation, Authenticity, Colour, Connoisseurship, Decadence and decline, Display of art, Dissemination, Feminism and art, Forgery, Iconoclasm, Mass production, Ornament and pattern, Perspective, Semiotics and Sociology and art.

4. AUTHORS. Never before has the work of so many art historians—often with widely differing perspectives—been brought together in a single endeavour. Modern communications and the sweeping political changes that occurred during the course of our work resulted in unparalleled international scholarly cooperation. It enabled us to cast our net for advisers and authors far wider than we would have dreamt possible only a few years ago. The 6700 scholars whose names appear in vol. 33 came from over 120 countries. Not only did we have contributions from authors from all the former republics of the USSR (which still existed as a political bureaucracy when we began), but we were also lucky to have the enthusiastic participation of local scholars throughout Central and Eastern Europe, South America, Korea and the Caribbean—to isolate just a few of the places often overlooked by publishers. In many cases, the material they contributed has never before been available in English. The result of this extraordinary collaborative effort is, we hope, a reference work of which the whole is greater than the sum of the parts and in which 'new things are made familiar, and familiar things are made new' (Alexander Pope: *The Lives of the Poets*, 1779-81). Most of all, it is an achievement that is a tribute to the scholarship of today's international community of art historians.

With more than 45,000 entries, written by 6700 people over a period of 12 years, the *Dictionary of Art*, like the *New Grove*, 'no doubt embodies many contradictions'. But as Stanley Sadie went on to explain in his preface to the *New Grove*, 'contradictions on matters of interpretation are not of course unwelcome; it is part of a dictionary's role to represent a variety of standpoints'. Like our Grove colleagues, we have made every effort to compare related articles and to resolve apparent discrepancies, although the results are not always conclusive. Where differences of opinion do occur, we have endeavoured to respect the views of the author whose signature appears at the end of each article or subsection, while calling the reader's attention to other interpretations by means of parenthetical editorial comments and/or cross-references. Errors of fact are another matter, and users of the *Dictionary of Art* are asked to write to the editorial office, c/o Macmillan Publishers, 25 Eccleston Place, London, SW1, to notify us of any such sins of commission (or omission) so that they may be corrected in the future.

Jane Turner
London, 1996

Introduction

I. Alphabetization and identical headings. II. Article headings and structures. III. Standard usages. IV. Cross-references. V. Locations of works of art. VI. Illustrations. VII. Bibliographies and other sources. VIII. Authors. IX. Appendices. X. Index.

I. Alphabetization and identical headings.

All main headings in this dictionary are distinguished by bold typeface. Headings of more than one word are alphabetized letter by letter as if continuous, up to the first true mark of punctuation, and again thereafter: the comma in **Stam, Mart** therefore breaks the alphabetization, and his biography precedes the article on **Stamford**, whereas the full point of an abbreviation such as in **Cornelisz. van Haarlem** is ignored. Parenthesized letters or words and square-bracketed matter are also ignored in alphabetization: for example, the article **Barlow, (James) Alan (Noel)** precedes that on **Barlow, Francis**, which would come before **Barlow, F(aye) W(inifred)**. The reader who searches in the wrong place for a prefixed or double surname will be led to the correct location by a cross-reference. Abbreviations of 'Saint' and its foreign equivalents (S, SS, St, Ste etc) are alphabetized as if spelt out in full. The prefixes Mc and Mac where occurring as the first two or three letters of a name are alphabetized under Mac. The modified vowels ä, ö and ü are read as a, o and u, not as ae, oe and ue, and Dutch names with ij are alphabetized according to English usage rather than under y. Acronyms are alphabetized by initial, as if words, rather than by the full name (**CIAM** follows **Ciaccono** rather than **Congregation of the Oratory**). Artists active largely before *c*. 1500 for whom the second part of the name indicates a place of origin, domicile or profession etc are entered under the first name, so that, for example, **Leonardo da Vinci** is under 'L' not 'V'. If two headings are identical except for spacing, the spaced version appears first. Accented letters are treated like unaccented ones, although for headings identical except for the accents the unaccented form appears first. Numerals, except roman numeral epithets of generation, are alphabetized as if spelt out (**291** precedes **Tworkov, Jack**). Rulers and popes with roman numeral epithets are arranged numerically after any unnumbered rulers with that name and before any individuals with that name as a surname, as is illustrated by the following (incomplete) sequence of headings and cross-references:

Charles, Duc de Berry
Charles, Duke of Orléans
Charles, Prince of Wales
Charles I, Duke of Savoy
Charles I, King of England and Scotland
Charles I, King of Spain
Charles II, King of Naples and Jerusalem
Charles II, King of Spain
Charles III, King of Spain
Charles III, Margrave of Baden-Durlach
Charles V, Holy Roman Emperor
Charles VIII, King of France
Charles X, King of France
Charles, Richard
Charles Albert, King of Sardinia
Charles Augustus, Duke of Saxe-Weimar
Charles II Augustus, Duke of Zweibrucken
Charles Borromeo
Charles Eusebius, Prince of Liechtenstein
Charles of France
Charles the Bald
Charles Theodore, Elector Palatine of the Rhine
Charles the Wise, King of France
Charleston

Article headings that are truly identical are distinguished by the use of parenthesized small roman numerals; such articles are entered according to the following hierarchy: place, material, technique, art form, object, family entry, individual biography, peoples. If there are two articles on places with identical names, they are entered in chronological order by date of foundation. Where two or more unrelated people have identical names, also distinguished by small roman numerals, they are arranged chronologically by date of birth.

The entry **Masters, anonymous, and monogrammists** contains articles on all anonymous masters except ancient Greek and Roman vase painters, who appear under the entry **Vase painters**. The former is subdivided into: ***I. Anonymous masters***; ***II. Dated masters***; and ***III. Monogrammists***. Anonymous masters are alphabetized ignoring the title 'Master' and such intervening words as 'of' or 'the'; dated masters are organized chronologically; and the monogrammists alphabetically by initials. Vase painters appear in alphabetical order, ignoring the words 'Painter of'.

II. Article headings and structures.

1. BIOGRAPHICAL. All biographies in this dictionary start with the subject's name and, where known, the places and dates of birth and death and a statement of nationality and occupation. In the citation of a name in a heading, the use of parentheses indicates parts of the name that are not commonly used, while square brackets enclose variant names or spellings:

Jones, Charles (Thomas): full name Charles Thomas Jones, referred to as Charles Jones
Jones, C(harles) T(homas): full name Charles Thomas Jones, referred to as C. T. Jones
Smith [Smythe]**, Betty** [Elizabeth]: usually referred to as Betty Smith but sometimes in the form of Betty Smythe, Elizabeth Smith or Elizabeth Smythe
Smith, Betty [Smythe, Elizabeth]: Betty Smith's name has the alternative version of Elizabeth Smythe only
Smith [née Johnson], **Betty**: Smith is Betty Johnson's married name, by which she is generally known
Jones, Charles [Brown, William]: William Brown is known chiefly by his pseudonym of Charles Jones
Brown, William [pseud. Jones, Charles]: William Brown is referred to as such and is also known by the pseudonym of Charles Jones

Places of birth and death are cited according to the name current during the subject's lifetime, followed by the modern name, where that is different:

(*b* Constantinople [now Istanbul], . . .)

Statements of places and dates of birth and death are given with as much precision as the evidence allows and may be replaced or supplemented by dates of baptism (*bapt*), burial (*bur*), canonization (*can*), feast day (*fd*) or regnal years (*reg*). Where information is conjectural, a question mark is placed directly before the statement that it qualifies. Where dates of birth and death are unrecorded but there is documentary evidence for the subject's activity between certain fixed dates, *floruit* (*fl*) dates are given; when such evidence is circumstantial, as for instance in the case of an anonymous master, this is cited as '*fl c.*'.

A subject's nationality is stated as current at the time:

(*b* Antwerp, 2 May 1560; *d* Antwerp, 12 Aug 1625). Flemish architect.
(*b* Antwerp, 16 Sept 1835; *d* Brussels, 24 Feb 1910). Belgian painter.

If the subject changed nationality or country of activity, this is stated where significant, as may also be the subject's ancestry; otherwise this information is evident from the parenthesized matter after the heading or is conveyed in the text. The subject's nationality is followed by a definition of occupation, that is to say the activity (or activities) of art-historical significance that justified inclusion in the dictionary; for non-artists, the subject's profession is also stated (e.g. 'American banker and collector').

Biographies are generally structured to present information in chronological order. Longer biographies usually begin with a brief statement of the subject's significance and are then divided into sections, under such headings as 1. Life and work. 2. Working methods and techniques. 3. Character and personality. 4. Critical reception and posthumous reputation.; within sections there may be further divisions to aid the reader in finding specific information. The biographies of two or more related artists or patrons and collectors are gathered in 'family' entries, alphabetized under the main form of the surname; monarchs, popes, rulers and aristocrats who were members of a family of patrons and collectors appear under their dynastic or family name, rather than under their given name or title. (The reader looking under the given name or title will be directed to the correct location of the entry by a cross-reference.) Within a family article, individual members of significance have their own entries, beginning with an indented, numbered bold heading; for the second and subsequent members of the family, a statement of relationship to a previous member of the family is included wherever possible:

> **Smith.** English family of sculptors.
> **(1) John Smith** (*b*. . .; *d*. . .).
> **(2) Richard Smith** (*b*. . .; *d*. . .). Son of (1) John Smith.
> **(3) Edward Smith** (*b*. . .; *d*. . .). Brother of (2) Richard Smith.

The numbers allocated to family members are used in cross-references from other articles:

> 'He commissioned the sculptor Richard Smith (*see* SMITH, (2)) . . .'

Members of the same family with identical names are usually distinguished by the use of parenthesized small roman numerals after their names. Synonymous family members commonly differentiated in art-historical literature by large roman numerals appear as such in this dictionary in two cases: where a family entry does not contain the full sequence (e.g. **Karel van Mander I** and **Karel van Mander III**); and where there are two or more identical families whose surnames are distinguished by parenthesized small roman numerals (e.g. **Giovanni Battista I Carlone (ii)** and **Giovanni Battista II Carlone (ii)**).

2. NON-BIOGRAPHICAL. As with biographies, the headings of all non-biographical articles provide variant spellings, transliterations etc in square brackets, where relevant, followed by a definition. Longer articles are divided as appropriate for the topic and are provided with contents lists after the heading, introductory paragraph or each new major subheading. In all articles the hierarchy of subdivisions, from largest to smallest, is indicated by large roman numerals (I), arabic numerals (1), small roman numerals (i) and letters (a). A cross-reference within a long survey to another of its sections takes the form '*see* §I, 2(iii)(b) above'. The most extensive surveys, such as those of **China** or of **Islamic art**, include a detailed table of contents of all sections and subsections.

III. Standard usages.

For the sake of consistent presentation in this dictionary, certain standard usages, particularly in spelling and terminology, have been imposed throughout. In general, the rules of British orthography and punctuation have been applied, except that wherever possible original sources are followed for quoted matter and for specific names and titles. Many of the conventions adopted in the dictionary will become evident through use, for example the general abbreviations (which are listed at the front of each volume); some of the other editorial practices are explained below.

1. PLACE NAMES. While the dictionary was in production, there were rapid and momentous global political changes, many of which have affected the names of countries and cities. Every attempt has been made to cite these correctly as at the time of going to press, the standard for which has been the United Nations policy for officially recognized names (except that the use of Burma has been retained over the use of Myan ma). Variant versions of place names—alternative spellings, transliterations, foreign-language equivalents—appear in square brackets in the headings of country, civilization, city and site articles; all such variants have been indexed (*see* §X below). Cities are cited by their commonly used English-language names (e.g. Antwerp has been used instead of the Flemish Antwerpen or the French Anvers), but where there is no English name the usage of *The Times Atlas of the World* (London, 1992) has been followed for most Western place names. For references within the text of any entry to places that have changed name in the course of history (often more than once), the name historically correct for the context has been used, followed, after its first mention, by its modern name, as in 'Constantinople (now Istanbul)'.

2. RULERS' NAMES AND TITLES. As with some place names, certain biographical names have been standardized to their anglicized versions. This applies in particular to European regal and papal names of earlier periods, whereas names tend to be given in the vernacular form for modern rulers. Almost without exception, the forms chosen are based on those in R. F. Tapsell's *Monarchs, Rulers, Dynasties and Kingdoms of the World* (London, 1983). Rulers' titles are always cited in English. By contrast, members of the lesser nobility in France, German-speaking areas, Italy and Spain have both their name and title in the vernacular (for other countries, English-language equivalents are generally used).

3. FOREIGN TERMS AND TRANSLITERATION SYSTEMS. For citations of foreign-language material, a basic reading knowledge of art-historical terms in French, German, Italian and Spanish has been assumed (although wherever there is an exact English equivalent of a foreign term this has been used). Foreign words that have gained currency in English are cited in roman type, whereas those that have not are italicized and are qualified with a brief definition, unless this is clear from the context. The conventions of capitalization in foreign languages are generally adhered to within italicized matter (e.g. book titles) but not in running, roman text for job titles (e.g. Peintre du Roi), for names of institutions, professional bodies and associations and for recurring exhibitions. Abbreviations for foreign periodical titles cited in bibliographies (*see* §VII below) are capitalized, despite the relevant foreign-language conventions.

In languages with non-roman characters, every attempt has been made to employ consistently a system of romanization generally accepted by scholars in the relevant field of art history. The particular transliteration system adopted for each area is sometimes indicated in the introduction to the appropriate survey (e.g. under **China**, where the circumstances under which the *pinyin* and the Wade–Giles systems are used are explained).

4. WORKS OF ART. Titles of works of art are generally cited in italics and by their English names, unless universally known by a foreign title. Some subjects, religious and mythological in particular, have been given standard titles throughout. The use of 'left' and 'right' in describing a work of art corresponds to the spectator's left and right. For locations of works of art *see* §V below.

5. CALENDARS AND DATES. Dates after 1582 are given according to new style, following the Gregorian calendar, for all countries, including Russia (which changed to new style only

in 1917); the only exception is for Britain, for which dates are given according to the Julian calendar up to the change in 1752. Absolute consistency cannot be guaranteed, since usage varied and it is often impossible to tell which calendar is applicable.

Where non-Christian calendars are cited, their Christian era dates are generally given first, except for BP (before present, i.e. before 1950). Citations of other calendars are qualified by the appropriate abbreviation (e.g. AH for *Anno Hegirae*; BE for Buddhist era); AD is generally omitted for Christian era dates after *c.* 1000.

Generally accepted dates for chronological periods have been inserted where appropriate to provide a context for the use of conventional period and dynastic labels. In many cases, especially with reference to those ancient cultures and civilizations understood primarily on the basis of archaeological evidence, such as ancient Egypt, the Aegean Bronze Age, Pre-Columbian America and prehistoric Europe, these dates are provisional and subject to greater or lesser scholarly agreement. The same is true of dates for dynastic labels, which may not always accurately reflect the historical situation, since different areas may have been conquered at different times. For the benefit of the non-specialist reader and to avoid confusion, every effort has been made to cite dates consistently, but it should not be assumed that the author whose name follows a particular article (or sequence of articles) accepts in detail the chronologies chosen by the editors for use in the dictionary.

We have also attempted, wherever possible, to provide biographical dates in parentheses in running text at the first mention of all art-historically significant individuals who do not have their own entries in the dictionary. (For the citation of conjectural dates of birth and death *see* §II, 1 above.) The presence of parenthesized regnal dates for rulers and popes, however, does not necessarily indicate the lack of a biography of that person. Where no dates are provided, the reader may assume that there is a biography of that individual in the dictionary (or that the person is so obscure that dates are not readily available). The use of a question mark, for example in the date of a work of art, queries an indistinct digit(s), as in 148(?7), or an illegible one, as in 148(?).

6. MEASUREMENTS AND DIMENSIONS. All measurements are cited in metric, unless within quoted matter or if the archaic form is of particular historical interest. Where two dimensions are cited, height precedes width; for three dimensions, the order is height by width by depth. If only one dimension is given, it is qualified by the appropriate abbreviation for height, width, length, diameter etc.

IV. Cross-references.

This dictionary has been compiled in the spirit of creating an integrated and interactive whole, so that readers may gain the widest perspective on the issues in which they are interested. The cross-referencing system has been designed and implemented to guide the reader easily to the information required, as well as to complementary discussions of related material, and in some cases even to alternative views. External cross-references (i.e. those to a different heading) take several forms, all of which are distinguished by the use of small capital letters, with a large capital to indicate the initial letter of the entry to which the reader is directed. Such cross-references appear exactly as the bold headings (excluding parenthesized matter) of the entries to which they refer, though in running text they are not inverted (e.g. 'He collaborated on the project with ANTHONY VAN DYCK . . .' The phrases 'see', 'see under' and 'see also' are always italicized when referring to another entry or another section of a multipartite article in the dictionary; where the word 'see' appears in roman type, the reference is to an illustration within the article or to another publication).

Given the comprehensiveness of the dictionary, cross-references are used sparingly between articles to guide readers to further discussions or to articles they may not have considered consulting; thus within a phrase such as 'He was influenced by Michelangelo' there is not a cross-reference to MICHELANGELO (though the reader can assume that there is a biography of Michelangelo, since there are no dates after his name), whereas 'Rosso Fiorentino and Francesco Primaticcio, through their work at FONTAINEBLEAU, introduced the Mannerist style into France (*see also* FRANCE, fig. 45)' alerts the reader to a useful description in the site entry and an illustration in the country survey. Cross-references have also been used to direct the reader to additional bibliography.

Another type of cross-reference appears as a main bold heading, to direct the reader to the place in the dictionary where the subject is treated:

> **Santi, Raffaello.** *See* RAPHAEL.
> **Holman Hunt, William.** *See* HUNT, WILLIAM HOLMAN.
> **Louis XIV.** *See* BOURBON, §I(9).
> **White, Stanford.** *See under* MCKIM, MEAD & WHITE.
> **Watches.** *See under* CLOCKS AND WATCHES.

Some cross-references of this type include a short definition and guide the reader to a fuller discussion or illustration:

> **Bimah** [bema]. Raised pulpit in a synagogue, from which the Torah is read (*see* JEWISH ART, §II, 1(iii) and fig. 8).

V. Locations of works of art.

For each work of art mentioned specifically, every attempt has been made to cite its correct present location. In general this information appears in an abbreviated form, in parentheses, directly after the first mention of the work. The standard abbreviations used for locations are readily understandable in their short forms and appear in full in Appendix A in vol. 33. Pieces that are on loan or on deposit are duly noted as such, as are works that are *in situ.* Works in private collections are usually followed by the citation of a published illustration or a catalogue raisonné number to assist in identification. Similarly, objects produced in multiples, such as prints and medals, are identified with a standard catalogue number. Works for which the locations are unknown are cited as untraced or are supplied with the last known location or, in the case of pieces that appeared on the art market, are given the city, auction house or gallery name and, when known, the date of sale and lot number or a reference to a published illustration; works that have been destroyed are so noted.

VI. Illustrations.

As often as permissible, pictures have been integrated into the text of the article that they illustrate, and the wording of captions has been designed to emphasize the subject to which the picture is related. For an article with a single illustration, the textual reference appears as '(see fig.)'; multiple illustrations are numbered. Colour plates appear in many of the volumes; references to these are in the form '(see colour pl. XII, fig. 2)' or '(*see* GLASS, colour pl. V, fig. 1)'. There are frequent cross-references to relevant illustrations appearing in other articles, and all captions have been indexed.

VII. Bibliographies and other sources.

All but the shortest of entries in the dictionary are followed by bibliographies and may also have sections on unpublished sources, writings, photographic publications or prints and video recordings or films. These function both as guides to selected further reading and viewing and as acknowledgments of the sources consulted by authors. In some family entries and in longer surveys, bibliographies may be located directly after the introduction and/or at the end of each section. All bibliographies are chronologically arranged by the date of first edition (thus providing an abstract of the topic's historiography); longer bibliographies are divided into categories, in which the items are also in chronological order. Items published in the same year are listed alphabetically by authors' names and, where by the same author, alphabetically by title; items with named authors or editors take precedence over exhibition catalogues, which are cited by title first. Abbreviated references to certain alphabetically arranged dictionaries and encyclopedias (listed in full in vol. 33, Appendix C, List A) appear at the head of the bibliography (or section) in alphabetical order. The title of the article in such reference books is cited only if the spelling or form of the name differs from that used in this dictionary or if the reader is being referred to a different subject. Some other frequently cited works (*see* Appendix C, List B) are given in an abbreviated form, but in their correct chronological position within the bibliography and usually with their volume and page numbers. Appendix C also includes a list of the abbreviations used for works from publishers' series.

For books that have appeared in several editions, generally the first and most recent have been cited (unless there was a particular reason to include an intermediate edition), and where page numbers are provided these refer to the most recent edition. Revisions are indicated by the abbreviation 'rev.', reprints with '*R*' and translations with 'trans.' prefaced by an abbreviation to indicate the language of the translation. Where the place or date of publication does not appear in a book this is rendered as 'n.p.' or 'n.d.' as appropriate; where this information can be surmised it appears in square brackets. Volume numbers usually appear in small roman numerals, both for citations from multi-volume publications and for periodicals; issue numbers of periodicals are in arabic numerals. The titles of periodicals are cited in abbreviated forms, a full list of which appears in Appendix B in vol. 33. Exhibition catalogues are provided with the name of the host location (not the place of publication) according to the list of location abbreviations (*see* Appendix A). Collected papers from conferences and congresses are arranged chronologically by date of their oral presentation rather than by the date of their publication in hard copy. Dissertations are included in the bibliography sections (rather than as unpublished sources), with an abbreviated form of the degree (diss., MA, MPhil) and awarding institution; if available on microfilm, this is noted.

Lists of unpublished sources, apart from dissertations, include such material as manuscripts, inventories and diaries. They are organized alphabetically by the location of the holdings, with an indication of the contents given in square brackets. Lists of selected writings are included in biographies of subjects who wrote on art; these are ordered according to the same principles as the bibliographies. Sections of photographic publications and prints list published books or collections of work by the subject of the article. If there is a significant collection of material on video or film, this is listed in its own section, in chronological order.

Throughout the production time of this dictionary authors were asked to submit important new bibliography for addition to their articles. Some contributors did so, while others left updating to be done by the editors. For the additions that were made by the editorial staff in the final days before going to press, this may have resulted in the text of an article apparently failing to take into consideration the discoveries or opinions of the new publications; it was nevertheless felt useful to draw readers' attention to significant recent literature.

VIII. Authors.

Signatures of authors, in the form of their choice, appear at the end of the article or sequence of articles that they contributed. In multipartite articles, a section (or sections) that is unsigned is by the author of the next signed section. Where two authors have jointly written an article, their names appear in alphabetical order:

CHARLES JONES, BETTY SMITH

If, however, Smith was the main author and was assisted or had her text amended by Jones, their signatures appear as:

BETTY SMITH, with CHARLES JONES

In the event that Jones assisted with only the bibliography to Smith's text, this would be acknowledged as:

BETTY SMITH (bibliography with CHARLES JONES)

Where an article or introduction was compiled by the editors or in the few cases where an author has wished to remain anonymous, this is indicated by a square box (□) instead of a signature.

IX. Appendices.

Readers' attention is directed to the appendices in vol. 33. These comprise full lists of: abbreviated locations of works of art (A); abbreviated periodical titles (B); standard reference books and series (C); and authors' names (D).

X. Index.

All articles and illustrations in this dictionary have been indexed not only to provide volume and page numbers of the main headings but also to pinpoint variant names and spellings and specific information within articles and captions. Full guidelines for using the Index, located in the final volume, can be found as its preface.

Acknowledgements

Projects of this magnitude inevitably incur a multitude of debts. As is clear from the preface, the preparation of the *Dictionary of Art* represents an enormous collective effort, one that took over 14 years and involved literally a cast of thousands, from every corner of the globe. Here I can name only a selection of those who participated in the project in some capacity and apologize to those who cannot be mentioned individually. No single group deserves greater thanks than the countless unnamed contributors (our unsung heroes and heroines) who submitted their entries and proofs on schedule and followed the house-style notes for contributors. There were also many authors whose advice and support went far beyond the writing of their articles, for example in helping us to plan and commission large, complex multi-author articles. Other contributors (including a small army of in-house writers) agreed at short notice to provide entries when the original commissions failed to arrive. I should also like to thank many others who assisted us in innumerable ways: recommending authors, providing information, alerting us to discoveries, checking bibliographical details, securing photographs etc. We are most grateful to them all. The formal acknowledgements are divided into three sections: outside advisers, in-house staff and other outside sources. Unfortunately, for reasons of space, none of the lists can be fully comprehensive, and the extent and duration of each person's involvement has had to be weighed against those of hundreds of other individuals. However, we should like to express our thanks to everyone who participated in the creation of the *Dictionary*, whether mentioned below or not, for all the efforts they have put into making it a success.

1. Outside advisers and consultants.

(i) Editorial Advisory Board. Our first debt of gratitude must go to the members of our distinguished Editorial Advisory Board for the guidance they provided on matters of general concept and approach.

Prof. Emeritus Terukazu Akiyama (formerly of the University of Tokyo)
Prof. Carlo Bertelli (Université de Lausanne)
Prof. Whitney Chadwick (San Francisco State University)
Prof. André Chastel (formerly of the Collège de France, Paris)†
Prof. Oleg Grabar (Institute for Advanced Study, Princeton)
Prof. Francis Haskell (University of Oxford)
Prof. Alfonso E. Pérez Sánchez (formerly of the Museo del Prado, Madrid)
Prof. Robert Rosenblum (New York University)
Dr Jessica Rawson (University of Oxford and formerly of the British Museum, London)
Prof. Willibald Sauerländer (formerly of the Zentralinstitut für Kunstgeschichte, Munich)
Mr Peter Thornton (formerly of the Sir John Soane's Museum, London)
Prof. Irene Winter (Harvard University, Cambridge, Massachusetts)

† deceased

In addition to informal advice over the years, a number of formal working seminars were arranged with advisory board members and other experts to examine particular areas of our coverage. I should like to thank, especially, Professor Akiyama for his continued advice on our coverage of Japanese art and art history; Whitney Chadwick for her help on contemporary and women artists; Francis Haskell for his assistance with patrons; Oleg Grabar for his advice on Islamic art, as well as on the balance of coverage between non-Western areas; and Peter Thornton for his constant support on matters pertaining to interior design and the decorative arts.

(ii) Area advisers. Once our general conceptual scheme had begun to take shape, outside experts were formally invited to develop plans for the coverage of the arts in their areas of specialization. Governed only by a general word allocation and suggestions for certain basic patterns of coverage, each was asked to prepare an outline (or report) with proposed headings, relative word lengths and names of potential authors. These area reports were then assigned to in-house area editors (see §2 below) to coordinate and supplement where necessary.

I. Ancient and non-Western cultures and civilizations.

Aboriginal art
Howard Morphy

Aegean Bronze Age art
Reynold Higgins†

Afghan art
David Macdowell

African art
John Picton

Ancient Cyprus
Nicolas Coldstream

Ancient Egyptian art
T. G. H. James

Ancient Greek and Roman jewellery
Reynold Higgins†

Ancient Greek and Roman sculpture
Geoffrey Waywell

Ancient Greek architecture
J. J. Coulton

Ancient Greek painting
Martin Robertson

Ancient Near Eastern art
Julian Reade

Ancient Roman architecture, painting and decorative arts
Margaret Lyttelton†

Armenian art
Lucy der Manuelian

Caribbean art
Dolores Yonker

Chinese and Korean art
Roderick Whitfield

† deceased

Chinese architecture
Nancy Shatzman Steinhardt

Chinese decorative arts
Jessica Rawson

Chinese general issues
Jonathan Hay

Chinese painting, sculpture and decorative arts
James Cahill

Early Christian and Byzantine art
Robin Cormack

Etruscan art
Tom Rasmussen

Indian art
Pramod Chandra
Vidya Dehejia
Robert Skelton

Islamic art
Robert Hillenbrand

Islamic carpets
Jon Thompson

Japanese art
David Waterhouse

Korean art and architecture
Youngsook Pak

Migration period art in Europe
John Mitchell

Mongolian art
Krystyna Chabros

Native North American art
Christian Feest
William Sturtevant
Richard Townsend

Nepalese art
Ian Alsop

Pacific Islands art
Peter Gathercole

Pre-Columbian Central and South American Art
Warwick Bray

Pre-Columbian Mesoamerican art
G. B. Nicholson

Prehistoric European art
Sara Champion
A. C. Renfrew

Pre-Islamic Arabian art
D. T. Potts

Sino-Central Asian art
Herbert Härtel

South-east Asian art
Robert Brown

Tibetan art
Jane Casey Singer
Frances Wood

Viking art
James Graham-Campbell

Western Central Asian art
Anatoly I. Ivanov

II. Medieval.

Architecture, sculpture and painting in Italy, 1200-1400
Julian Gardner

European medieval architecture
Paul Crossley

European medieval decorative arts and liturgical objects
Neil Stratford

European medieval stained glass
Jill Kerr

European medieval wall and panel painting
Paul Binski

Manuscript illumination in Italy, c. *800-1400*
Valentino Pace
Kay Sutton

Medieval architecture in Italy, 800-1200
Mario D'Onofrio

Medieval art in Scandinavia
Christopher Hohler

Painting and manuscript illumination in 15th-century France
Nicole Reynaud

Painting and mosaics in Italy, 300-1200
Caecilia Davis-Weyer

Sculpture in France, Spain, England and the Low Countries, 800-1500
Walter Cahn

Sculpture in Germany and Central Europe, 800-1200
Willibald Sauerländer

Sculpture in Italy, 800-1200
Dorothy Glass

Sculpture of the Holy Roman Empire, c. *1300-c. 1500*
Anton Legner

Western illuminated manuscripts
Christopher de Hamel

III. Regional surveys.

Albanian art
Gjergi Frashëri

American architecture, c. *1600-* c. *1914*
William Jordy

American decorative arts
Gerald Ward

American painting and sculpture, c. *1600-c. 1914*
Jules Prown

Art of the Holy Roman Empire in the 18th century
Alastair Laing

Arts of the (former) USSR
Mikhail N. Sokolov

Australian architecture
Conrad Hamann

Australian painting, sculpture and decorative arts
Patrick McCaughey
Terence Smith

Austrian and Hungarian sculpture in the 19th century
Walter Krause

Austrian art, 1500-1800
Kurt Woisetschläger

Austrian decorative arts
Elisabeth Scheicher

Belgian metalwork
Leo de Ren

Bohemian and Moravian painting and sculpture
Amanda Simpson

Bohemian Baroque architecture
Jirí Tomás Kotalík

British architecture, 1840-1914
J. Mordaunt Crook

British and early Netherlandish painting in the 16th century
Susan Foister

British and Irish painting in the 19th century
Marcia Pointon

British and Irish sculpture in the 18th and 19th centuries
Nicholas Penny

British painting in the 17th century
Sir Oliver Millar

British painting in the 18th century
John Hayes

British sculpture, 1500-1700
John Physick

Canadian archtitecture
Alan Gowans

Canadian painting, sculpture and decorative arts
Laurier Lacroix

Czech decorative arts
Dagmar Tucná

Dutch and Belgian architecture in the 19th century
Helen Searing

Dutch and Belgian painting, sculpture and the graphic arts in the 19th century
Ronald de Leeuw

Dutch and Flemish architecture and sculpture, 1550-1800
Kerry Downes

Dutch and Flemish ceramics
Mireille Jottrand

Dutch painting, drawing and graphic arts, 1550-1800
Christopher White

English and Welsh architecture, to c. *1840*
Howard Colvin

Flemish painting, drawing and graphic arts, 1550-1800
Kristin Belkin
Elizabeth McGrath

French and Italian architecture in the 18th and 19th centuries
Robin Middleton

French architecture in the 17th century
Neil MacGregor

French decorative arts
Pierre Ennès
Amaury Lefébure
Patricia Lemonnier

French furniture and interiors
Jean Nérée Ronfort

French painting, architecture and graphic arts in the 16th century
Jean Guillaume

French painting in the 17th century
Michael Kitson

French painting in the 18th century
Philip Conisbee

French painting, 1800-1870
Jon Whiteley

French painting and graphic arts, 1860-1900
Christopher Lloyd

French sculpture and decorative arts in the 16th century
Bertrand Jestaz

French sculpture in the 17th and 18th centuries
Geneviève Bresc

French sculpture in the 19th century
Anne Pingeot

German architecture, 1500-1700
Jürgen Zimmer

German architecture in the 19th century
Barry Bergdoll

German ceramics and glass
Walter Spiegl

German ivories and miniature sculpture, 1500-1800
Christian Theuerkauff

German painting and graphic arts in the 15th century
Kurt Löcher
Peter Strieder

German painting in the 16th and 17th centuries
Keith Andrews†

German painting in the 19th century
Will Vaughan

German sculpture in the 19th century
Peter Bloch
Sibylle Einholz

Greek art
Chrysanthos Christou

Icelandic art
Bera Nordal

Irish and Scottish architecture
Alistair Rowan

Italian architecture in the 15th and 16th centuries
Howard Burns

Italian architecture in the 17th century
Joseph Connors

Italian decorative arts
Renato Ruotolo

Italian painting in the 15th century
Jane Martineau

Italian painting in the 16th century
Martin J. Kemp

Italian painting in the 17th and 18th centuries
Hugh Brigstocke
Erich Schleier
Richard Spear

Italian painting and sculpture in the 19th century
Sandra Berresford

Italian sculpture in the 15th to 18th centuries
Charles Avery
Bruce Boucher
Anthony Radcliffe

Latin American art and architecture, to c. *1820*
John Bury

Netherlandish painting, 1400-1550
Lorne Campbell

† deceased

Polish art
Aleksander Gieysztor
Jerzy Pietrusinski
Andrezej Rottermund

Portuguese art, 1500-1800
Angela Delaforce
Hellmut Wohl

Portuguese art in the 19th century
José-Augusto França

Romanian art
Codruta Cruceanu

Russian and Soviet architecture from 1700
Catherine Cooke

Russian painting and sculpture from 1700
Larissa Haskell

Scandinavian architecture
Hakon Lund

Scandinavian painting and sculpture, 1400-1700
Torbjörn Fulton
Anna Nilsén

Scandinavian painting and sculpture, 1700-1900
Pontus Grate

Spanish architecture
Fernando Marías

Spanish architecture and decorative arts, 1490-1820
John Bury

Spanish architecture, c. *1820-*c. *1914*
Vicente Lleo Canal

Spanish painting in the 15th century
Santiago Alcolea

Spanish painting of the 16th to 18th centuries
Johnathan Brown

Spanish painting in the 19th century
Enrique Arias
Wifredo Rincón

Spanish sculpture
Juan José Martín González

Swedish decorative arts
Helena Dahlbäck-Lutteman

Swiss painting and sculpture, c. *1600-1900*
Hans A. Lüthy

Yugoslav art
Boris Vizintin

IV. 20th century.

Architecture after 1900
Gavin Stamp

Chinese art after 1900
Michael Sullivan

German and Austrian painting and sculpture since 1935
Richard Calvocoressi

Indian art after 1900
Geeta Kapur

Japanese art after 1900
Toru Asano
Shigeo Chiba
Yoshikazu Iwasaki
Kazu Kaido

Spanish art in the 20th century
Francisco Calvo Serraller

European, American and Japanese prints in the 20th century
Alexander Duckers

European, American and Russian painting and sculpture in the 20th century
Ronald Alley

European art, 1890-1920
Peter Vergo

V. Art forms and general issues.

Design and designers
Simon Jervis

Fans
Helene Alexander

Frames
Paul Mitchell

Gardens and garden design
John Dixon Hunt

Gems
Gertrud Seidmann

General Issues
David Freedberg
Henri Zerner

Jewellery
Diana Scarisbrick

Medals and plaquettes
Graham Pollard

Metalwork
Clare Le Corbeiller
Hannelore Müller
Anthony North

Painting materials and techniques
Joyce Plesters
Ashok Roy

Photography
Weston Naef

Printmaking
David Landau

Puppets
Henryk Jurkowski

Religion and art
Diane Apostolos-Cappadona

Sculpture and applied art materials and techniques
Jonathan Ashley-Smith

Tapestry
Candace Adelson

Wallpaper
Joanna Banham

2. EDITORIAL AND ADMINISTRATIVE STAFF. Among my colleagues, I must first acknowledge and express my gratitude to my predecessor as editor of the *Dictionary of Art*, Hugh Brigstocke, who was responsible for its overall plan. It was he who conceived the general intellectual framework, and, having argued the case in favour of an inclusive and broadly based theoretical approach (one that paid serious scholarly attention to architecture and the arts outside the West, among other things), he went on to establish the relative balance between the different areas of coverage. This basic plan, the result of four years of intensive work and consultation with many outside experts, was more or less finalized by the time of his departure in 1987, when the editing of the first texts got underway. It is a tribute to the coherence and intelligence of the plan that it has remained substantially unaltered since then. The task of planning the coverage and commissioning area reports was shared, in the early stages, with Jane Martineau, who joined the staff as Text Editor and was responsible for compiling the initial house-style rules based on those of the *New Grove*. In subsequent revisions to the house-style manual, I was greatly assisted by Ruth Thackeray, who, with Jane Martineau, was involved in the early training of desk editors.

In 1988 we reorganized the staff into editorial teams, as reflected in the list below. The success of this team approach to editing, in which copy editors and art historians worked together to prepare manuscripts for the typesetter, is due in large part to the support I received from our deputy editors. I should particularly like to thank Nicola Coldstream for her able supervision of the Classical and medieval teams; Marco Livingstone and, later, Samantha Roberts for ensuring that the coverage of 19th- and 20th- century art was thoughtful and well-balanced and that the articles themselves were free of unnecessary jargon; and, finally, Pat Barylski and, later, Diane Fortenberry for their sensitive guidance of the non-Western teams, who were grouped together (without an acceptable collective name) for reasons of the similar intellectual approach generally taken to their material rather than for any direct links between their areas. Besides contacting potential authors and preparing their articles for publication once they arrived, many members of the editorial staff, art historians in their own right, also contributed entries. Among our in-house writers, I should particularly mention the valuable contribution of Philip Cooper, who wrote more short biographies than any other author. After each article was edited for content and house-style, it was submitted to one of a small team of vetters before being sent to the typesetter; the *Dictionary* is undoubtedly a much more accurate and consistent work of reference due to their careful checking and high editorial standards.

The administration of a project this size is a formidable task. We are grateful to all those who played a part in the organization of commissions, contracts, payments, translations, illustrations, copyright permissions, proofs, author corrections, filing etc. The rules governing the compilation of the index were established by Ruth Levitt, who was succeeded by Gillian Northcott, under whose supervision a large team of indexers and checkers created some three quarters of a million index references. The final supervision of the illustrations database, which numbered some 15,000 items, was handled by Stephanie Farrow; she was ably assisted on matters of sizing and electronic digitization by Martyn Evans. Around 12,000 articles—over a quarter of the *Dictionary*—arrived in a language other than English, and among those involved in coordinating our team of outside translators, who had to cope with 30 different languages, were Paul Ratcliffe and Teresa Brown. For the proof stages of the project I am grateful to

Lucy Temperley, Jayne Bartholomew, Samantha Roberts and, most of all, Diane Fortenberry, who shared with me the task of checking the corrections to 30,000 page proofs in a period of just over ten weeks. On the production side, we greatly benefited from the expert experience of Macmillan's Production Director, John Peacock, who was assisted in our offices by Stephen Benaim. Among those involved in the typesetting at Pindar plc, special mention must be made of Vincent Loach, whose unstinting attention to technical details saved us much time and trouble; moreover, he and his colleagues managed to read enough of the *Dictionary of Art* in their spare time to compile the *Dictionary of Death: The Pindar Book of Bitter Ends*, an entertaining account of the often poignant but sometimes gruesome ways in which artists met their death.

(i) Editorial teams.

African and Australasian art
Jeremy Coote
Dunja Hersak

Ancient Egyptian art
Dominic Montserrat
Delia Pemberton
C. N. Reeves
Ian Shaw

Ancient Near Eastern art
Dominique Collon

Architecture
Val Clack (dep. ed.; vetter)
Paul Davies
David Hemsoll
Gordon Higgott
Charles Hind
Julian Honer (vetter)
Harold Meek
John Musgrove
Christine Stevenson
Alexandra Wedgwood
Robert Williams

British and French painting and northern European sculpture
Marc Jordan (dep. ed.)

Chinese, Korean and Mongolian art
Diane Fortenberry (dep. ed.; vetter)
Graham Hutt
Susan Pares
Susannah Perry
Sarah Waldram

Classical Greek and Roman art
Michael Bird (vetter)
David Hibler
Margaret Lyttelton†
Kim Richardson (vetter)

Decorative arts and materials and techniques
Michael Hall
Frankie Liebe (vetter)
Judith Neiswander
Alexandra Pel (dep. ed.; vetter)
Liz Stubbs (vetter)
Lucy Trench
Sarah Yates (vetter)

Early Christian and Byzantine art
Kara Hattersley Smith
Valerie Nunn

Eastern European art
Anne Charvet
Kevin Halliwell (vetter)
Jeremy Howard

General issues and theory
Kevin Halliwell (vetter)
Richard Wollheim

Holy Roman Empire and Central European art
Alistair Laing
Dorothy Limouze

Islamic art
Sheila Blair
Jonathan Bloom
Roderick Brown
Godfrey Goodwin (dep. ed.)
Tim Stanley
Stephen Vernoit

Italian painting
Lucinda Collinge
Helen Langdon
Jane Martineau (dep. ed.; vetter)
Margaret Walker

Italian sculpture and Scandinavian art
Antonia Böstrom

Japanese art
Elizabeth Bennett
Kendall Brown
Eric Chaline
Ingrid Cranfield
Christine Guth
Amy Newland

Medieval art
Tanya Alfillé (dep. ed.; vetter)
Nicola Coldstream (dep. ed.; vetter)
Jill Franklin
Delia Gaze (vetter)
David Rose (vetter)
Kay Sutton

Netherlandish, Dutch and Flemish painting
Jane Turner (ed.; vetter)

19th- and 20th-century art
Francesca Calvocoressi
Elizabeth Clegg
Oliver Garnett
Marco Livingstone (dep. ed.; vetter)
Samantha Roberts (dep. ed.; vetter)
Matthew Taylor (vetter)

Patronage
Tanya Harrod
Janet Southorn†

Pre-Columbian art
Orianna Baddeley
Elizabeth Baquedano
David Jones

Prints
Katharina Mayer Haunton

South Asian art
Pat Barylski (dep. ed.; vetter)
Dan Ehnbom
Elizabeth Errington
Jenny Marsh (vetter)
Rekha Morris (dep. ed.)
Michael Willis

South-east Asian art
Angela Hobart
John Villiers

Spanish and Portuguese art
Angela Delaforce

† deceased

(ii) Non-editorial departments.

Administration
Christianne Bakker
Jayne Bartholomew
Victoria Boyd
Ian Critchley
Sara Cunningham
Sophie Durlacher
Caroline Jackson
Lucy Temperley

Index
Teresa Brown
Ruth Levitt
Gillian Northcott

Picture Department
Martyn Evans
Stephanie Farrow
Caroline Hensman
Lorraine Mallon
Philippa Thomson

Translations
Teresa Brown
Paul Ratcliffe

3. OTHER OUTSIDE SOURCES. Many people and organizations outside the *Dictionary* have provided generous help to us and to our contributors. We are particularly grateful to librarians in London, especially at the British Library, the Courtauld Institute, the Royal Institute of British Architects (RIBA), the School of Oriental and African Studies (SOAS), the Tate Gallery, the National Art Library at the Victoria and Albert Museum and the Warburg Institute, who facilitated the work of our staff and local authors. I should like to thank Noël Annesley, Deputy Chairman of Christie's, for his official support of staff members carrying out research for us on decorative art topics. For the commissioning of a number of short biographies of Dutch artists, we benefited from the services of the Stichting Postuniversitair Kunsthistorisch Onderzoek (SPKO), based in the Netherlands. We have enjoyed cordial and helpful relations with the editorial offices of a number of London art publications, such as *Apollo Magazine*, the *Art Newspaper* and the *Burlington Magazine*, who have patiently endured and resolved many a bibliographical query. The generosity of Her Majesty Queen Elizabeth II in waiving the reproduction fees for all works illustrated from the British Royal Collection is hereby gratefully acknowledged. Special thanks are also owed to several other photographic sources and copyright-holders, who processed especially large orders from us, including: the Archivi Alinari, Florence; the Bildarchiv Foto Marburg; the British Museum, London; Giraudon, Paris; the Kunsthistorisches Museum, Vienna; the Metropolitan Museum of Art, New York; and the Service Photographique de la Réunion des Museés Nationaux, Paris. The colour plates were designed by Robert Updegraff. The specific sources for all images in the *Dictionary*, both black-and-white and colour, are acknowledged in the list of picture credits appended to each volume.

A number of publishers and individuals kindly granted us permission to reuse and adapt material from previously published sources:

Annenberg School for Communication, University of Pennsylvania, and Oxford University Press: *The International Encyclopedia of Communications*, ed. Erik Barnouw (New York and London, 1989): **Printing**

Boston Museum of Fine Arts and the Pierpont Morgan Library, New York: *Rembrandt: Experimental Etcher* (exh. cat., 1969-70): **Rembrandt van Rijn, §II, 3**

British Museum Press: *The British Museum Book of Chinese Art* by Jessica Rawson (London, 1992), pp. 14-19: **China, §I, 1 and 3**

Editions d'Art Albert Skira S.A.: *Félix Bracquemond, le réalisme absolu: Oeuvre gravé, 1849-1859, catalogue raisonné* by Jean-Paul Bouillon (Geneva, 1987): **Félix Bracquemond**

George Weidenfeld & Nicolson Ltd.: *Who's Who in Architecture*, ed. J. M. Richards (London, 1977): **Mies van der Rohe**

Flammarion, Paris: *Les Manuscripts à peinture en France, 1440-1520* (exh. cat. by François Avril and Nicole Reynaud, Paris, Bib. N., 1993), pp. 109-20; 293-305: **Jean Bourdichon; Master of Jouvenel des Ursins**

Jane Voorhees Zimmerli Art Museum, Rutgers University, New Brunswick, NJ: *Haarlem: The Seventeenth Century* (exh. cat. by Frima Fox Hofrichter and others, 1983): **Haarlem, §2(i)**

Larousse plc: *Chambers Biographical Dictionary*, ed. Magnus Magnusson (5th edn, Edinburgh, 1990): **Max Uhle**

Los Angeles County Museum of Art: *Shippo: The Art of Enameling in Japan* (exh. cat., 1987): **Japan, §XV, 8**

National Gallery, London: *Art in the Making: Rembrandt* (exh. cat. by David Bomford, Christopher Brown and Ashok Roy, 1988): **Rembrandt van Rijn, §II, 2**

National Gallery, London, the Rijksmuseum, Amsterdam, and the Staatliche Museen Preussischer Kulturbesitz, Berlin: *The Master and his Workshop: Paintings* (exh. cat. by Christopher Brown, Jan Kelch and Pieter van Thiel, 1991-2) and *The Master and his Workshop: Drawings and Etchings* (exh. cat. by Holm Bevers, Peter Schatborn and B. Welzel, 1991-2): **Rembrandt van Rijn, §II, 1-2 and 4**

National Gallery of Art, Washington, DC: *Guercino: Drawings from Windsor Castle* (exh. cat. by Nicholas Turner, 1991-2): **Guercino, §1**

Oxford University Press: *The Oxford Companion to Gardens*, ed. Sir Geoffrey Jellicoe, Susan Jellicoe, Patrick Goode and Michael Lancaster (Oxford, 1986): **Powerscourt; Pratolino**

Palumbo, Peter: *Proof of Evidence* (London, 1990): **Mies van der Rohe**

Penn State Press: *The Painting of Baciccio* by Robert Enggass (University Park, 1964): **Giovanni Battista Gaulli**

Phaidon Press Ltd: *Mies van der Rohe at Work* by Peter Carter (New York and London, 1974): **Mies van der Rohe**

Princeton University Art Museum: *Images of the Mind: Selections from the Edward L. Elliot Family and John B. Elliot Collections of Chinese Calligraphy and Painting at the Art Museum, Princeton University* (exh. cat. by Wen Fong, 1984): **Daoji; Ni zan**

Sharp, Dennis: *The Rationalists* (London, 1987): **Mies van der Rohe**

The Free Press, a division of Macmillan Publishing Co.: *Macmillan Encyclopedia of Architects*, ed. Adolf K. Placzek, 4 vols (New York, 1982): **Francesco del Borgo; Ernest Cormier; Cornelius Gurlitt; Edwin Lutyens; Albert Speer**

* * *

On a personal note, I should like to thank all of my former secretaries, many of whose names appear in §2 above since their able skills enabled them to be moved into other roles; these include my first, Jayne Bartholomew (proof collation), and later Gillian Northcott (index), Rosalind Thiro (copy editor) and Kate Jaeger (marketing) and, lastly, my present assistant, Sally Meen. I am grateful also to Denise Smith, for ensuring that my first two and a half years of motherhood were entirely uncomplicated and pleasurable, and to my husband, Nicholas Turner, for his advice on countless art-historical matters and for his continued support, especially during the final editorial stages of this project. Finally, I am pleased to acknowledge the support that we have received from Macmillan Publishers Ltd. Their unwavering commitment to this ambitious academic undertaking is due in no small measure to the courage and vision of their chairman, Nicholas Byam Shaw, whose enthusiasm for progress was matched only by his commitment to quality. Among the other company directors, I should also like to thank Adrian Soar and Brian Stonier, as well as Richard Garnett, whose guidance was much appreciated in the early days of the project. In the day-to-day management since 1985, I have enjoyed the full cooperation and support of the Dictionary's Publisher, Ian Jacobs. The journey was made easier—and certainly more pleasant— in the company of such a sympathetic and tireless professional.

J. T.

General Abbreviations

The abbreviations employed throughout this dictionary, most of which are listed below, do not vary, except for capitalization, regardless of the context in which they are used, including bibliographical citations and for locations of works of art. The principle used to arrive at these abbreviations is that their full form should be easily deducible, and for this reason acronyms have generally been avoided (e.g. Los Angeles Co. Mus. A. instead of LACMA). The same abbreviation is adopted for cognate forms in foreign languages and in most cases for plural and adjectival forms (e.g. A.= Art, Arts, Arte, Arti etc). Not all related forms are listed below. Occasionally, if a name, for instance of an artists' group or exhibiting society, is repeated within the text of one article, it is cited in an abbreviated form after its first mention in full (e.g. The Pre-Raphaelite Brotherhood (PRB) was founded...); the same is true of archaeological periods and eras, which are abbreviated to initial letters in small capitals (e.g. In the Early Minoan (EM) period...). Such abbreviations do not appear in this list. For the reader's convenience, separate full lists of abbreviations for locations, periodical titles and standard reference books and series are included as Appendices A–C in vol. 33.

A. Art, Arts
A.C. Arts Council
Acad. Academy
AD Anno Domini
Add. Additional, Addendum
addn addition
Admin. Administration
Adv. Advances, Advanced
Aesth. Aesthetic(s)
Afr. African
Afrik. Afrikaans, Afrikaner
A.G. Art Gallery
Agrar. Agrarian
Agric. Agriculture
Agron. Agronomy
Agy Agency
AH Anno Hegirae
A. Inst. Art Institute
AK Alaska (USA)
AL Alabama (USA)
Alb. Albanian
Alg. Algerian
Alta Alberta (Canada)
Altern. Alternative
a.m. ante meridiem [before noon]
Amat. Amateur
Amer. American
An. Annals
Anatol. Anatolian
Anc. Ancient
Annu. Annual
Anon. Anonymous(ly)
Ant. Antique
Anthol. Anthology
Anthropol. Anthropology
Antiqua. Antiquarian, Antiquaries
app. appendix
approx. approximately
AR Arkansas (USA)
ARA Associate of the Royal Academy
Arab. Arabic
Archaeol. Archaeology
Archit. Architecture, Architectural
Archv, Archvs Archive(s)
Arg. Argentine
ARHA Associate of the Royal Hibernian Academy
ARIBA Associate of the Royal Institute of British Architects
Armen. Armenian
ARSA Associate of the Royal Scottish Academy
Asiat. Asiatic
Assist. Assistance
Assoc. Association
Astron. Astronomy
AT&T American Telephone & Telegraph Company
attrib. attribution, attributed to
Aug August
Aust. Austrian
Austral. Australian
Auth. Author(s)
Auton. Autonomous
Aux. Auxiliary
Ave. Avenue
AZ Arizona (USA)
Azerbaij. Azerbaijani
B. Bartsch [catalogue of Old Master prints]
b born
BA Bachelor of Arts
Balt. Baltic
bapt baptized
BArch Bachelor of Architecture
Bart Baronet
Bask. Basketry
BBC British Broadcasting Corporation
BC Before Christ
BC British Columbia (Canada)
BE Buddhist era
Beds Bedfordshire (GB)
Behav. Behavioural
Belarus. Belarusian
Belg. Belgian
Berks Berkshire (GB)
Berwicks Berwickshire (GB; old)
BFA Bachelor of Fine Arts
Bibl. Bible, Biblical
Bibliog. Bibliography, Bibliographical
Biblioph. Bibliophile
Biog. Biography, Biographical
Biol. Biology, Biological
bk, bks book(s)
Bkbinder Bookbinder
Bklore Booklore
Bkshop Bookshop
BL British Library
Bld Build
Bldg Building

Bldr	Builder
BLitt	Bachelor of Letters/Literature
BM	British Museum
Boh.	Bohemian
Boliv.	Bolivian
Botan.	Botany, Botanical
BP	Before present (1950)
Braz.	Brazilian
BRD	Bundesrepublik Deutschland [Federal Republic of Germany (West Germany)]
Brecons	Breconshire (GB; old)
Brez.	Brezonek [lang. of Brittany]
Brit.	British
Bros	Brothers
BSc	Bachelor of Science
Bucks	Buckinghamshire (GB)
Bulg.	Bulgarian
Bull.	Bulletin
bur	buried
Burm.	Burmese
Byz.	Byzantine
C	Celsius
C.	Century
c.	*circa* [about]
CA	California
Cab.	Cabinet
Caerns	Caernarvonshire (GB; old)
C.A.G.	City Art Gallery
Cal.	Calendar
Callig.	Calligraphy
Cam.	Camera
Cambs	Cambridgeshire (GB)
can	canonized
Can.	Canadian
Cant.	Canton(s), Cantonal
Capt.	Captain
Cards	Cardiganshire (GB; old)
Carib.	Caribbean
Carms	Carmarthenshire (GB; old)
Cartog.	Cartography
Cat.	Catalan
cat.	catalogue
Cath.	Catholic
CBE	Commander of the Order of the British Empire
Celeb.	Celebration
Celt.	Celtic
Cent.	Centre, Central
Centen.	Centennial
Cer.	Ceramic
cf.	confer [compare]
Chap., Chaps	Chapter(s)
Chem.	Chemistry
Ches	Cheshire (GB)
Chil.	Chilean
Chin.	Chinese
Christ.	Christian, Christianity
Chron.	Chronicle
Cie	Compagnie [French]
Cinema.	Cinematography
Circ.	Circle
Civ.	Civil, Civic
Civiliz.	Civilization(s)
Class.	Classic, Classical
Clin.	Clinical
CO	Colorado (USA)
Co.	Company; County
Cod.	Codex, Codices
Col., Cols	Collection(s); Column(s)
Coll.	College
collab.	in collaboration with, collaborated, collaborative
Collct.	Collecting
Colloq.	Colloquies
Colomb.	Colombian
Colon.	Colonies, Colonial
Colr	Collector
Comm.	Commission; Community
Commerc.	Commercial
Communic.	Communications
Comp.	Comparative; compiled by, compiler
Concent.	Concentration
Concr.	Concrete
Confed.	Confederation
Confer.	Conference
Congol.	Congolese
Congr.	Congress
Conserv.	Conservation; Conservatory
Constr.	Construction(al)
cont.	continued
Contemp.	Contemporary
Contrib.	Contributions, Contributor(s)
Convalesc.	Convalescence
Convent.	Convention
Coop.	Cooperation
Coord.	Coordination
Copt.	Coptic
Corp.	Corporation, Corpus
Corr.	Correspondence
Cors.	Corsican
Cost.	Costume
Cret.	Cretan
Crim.	Criminal
Crit.	Critical, Criticism
Croat.	Croatian
CT	Connecticut (USA)
Cttee	Committee
Cub.	Cuban
Cult.	Cultural, Culture
Cumb.	Cumberland (GB; old)
Cur.	Curator, Curatorial, Curatorship
Curr.	Current(s)
CVO	Commander of the [Royal] Victorian Order
Cyclad.	Cycladic
Cyp.	Cypriot
Czech.	Czechoslovak
$	dollars
d	died
d.	denarius, denarii [penny, pence]
Dalmat.	Dalmatian
Dan.	Danish
DBE	Dame Commander of the Order of the British Empire
DC	District of Columbia (USA)
DDR	Deutsche Demokratische Republik [German Democratic Republic (East Germany)]
DE	Delaware (USA)
Dec	December
Dec.	Decorative
ded.	dedication, dedicated to
Democ.	Democracy, Democratic
Demog.	Demography, Demographic
Denbs	Denbighshire (GB; old)
dep.	deposited at
Dept	Department
Dept.	Departmental, Departments
Derbys	Derbyshire (GB)
Des.	Design
destr.	destroyed
Dev.	Development
Devon	Devonshire (GB)
Dial.	Dialogue
diam.	diameter
Diff.	Diffusion
Dig.	Digest
Dip. Eng.	Diploma in Engineering
Dir.	Direction, Directed
Directrt	Directorate
Disc.	Discussion
diss.	dissertation
Distr.	District
Div.	Division
DLitt	Doctor of Letters/Literature
DM	Deutsche Mark
Doc.	Document(s)
Doss.	Dossier
DPhil	Doctor of Philosophy
Dr	Doctor
Drg, Drgs	Drawing(s)
DSc	Doctor of Science/Historical Sciences
Dut.	Dutch
Dwell.	Dwelling
E.	East(ern)

EC	European (Economic) Community
Eccles.	Ecclesiastical
Econ.	Economic, Economies
Ecuad.	Ecuadorean
ed.	editor, edited (by)
edn	edition
eds	editors
Educ.	Education
e.g.	*exempli gratia* [for example]
Egyp.	Egyptian
Elem.	Element(s), Elementary
Emp.	Empirical
Emul.	Emulation
Enc.	Encyclopedia
Encour.	Encouragement
Eng.	English
Engin.	Engineer, Engineering
Engr., Engrs	Engraving(s)
Envmt	Environment
Epig.	Epigraphy
Episc.	Episcopal
Esp.	Especially
Ess.	Essays
est.	established
etc	*etcetera* [and so on]
Ethnog.	Ethnography
Ethnol.	Ethnology
Etrus.	Etruscan
Eur.	European
Evangel.	Evangelical
Exam.	Examination
Excav.	Excavation, Excavated
Exch.	Exchange
Excurs.	Excursion
exh.	exhibition
Exp.	Exposition
Expermntl	Experimental
Explor.	Exploration
Expn	Expansion
Ext.	External
Extn	Extension
f, ff	following page, following pages
F.A.	Fine Art(s)
Fac.	Faculty
facs.	facsimile
Fam.	Family
fasc.	fascicle
fd	feastday (of a saint)
Feb	February
Fed.	Federation, Federal
Fem.	Feminist
Fest.	Festival
fig.	figure (illustration)
Fig.	Figurative

figs	figures
Filip.	Filipina(s), Filipino(s)
Fin.	Finnish
FL	Florida (USA)
fl	*floruit* [he/she flourished]
Flem.	Flemish
Flints	Flintshire (GB; old)
Flk	Folk
Flklore	Folklore
fol., fols	folio(s)
Found.	Foundation
Fr.	French
frag.	fragment
Fri.	Friday
FRIBA	Fellow of the Royal Institute of British Architects
FRS	Fellow of the Royal Society, London
ft	foot, feet
Furn.	Furniture
Futur.	Futurist, Futurism
g	gram(s)
GA	Georgia (USA)
Gael.	Gaelic
Gal., Gals	Gallery, Galleries
Gaz.	Gazette
GB	Great Britain
Gdn, Gdns	Garden(s)
Gdnr(s)	Gardener(s)
Gen.	General
Geneal.	Genealogy, Genealogist
Gent.	Gentleman, Gentlemen
Geog.	Geography
Geol.	Geology
Geom.	Geometry
Georg.	Georgian
Geosci.	Geoscience
Ger.	German, Germanic
G.I.	Government/General Issue (USA)
Glams	Glamorganshire (GB; old)
Glos	Gloucestershire (GB)
Govt	Government
Gr.	Greek
Grad.	Graduate
Graph.	Graphic
Green.	Greenlandic
Gr.-Roman	Greco-Roman
Gt	Great
Gtr	Greater
Guat.	Guatemalan
Gym.	Gymnasium
h.	height
ha	hectare
Hait.	Haitian
Hants	Hampshire (GB)
Hb.	Handbook

Heb.	Hebrew
Hell.	Hellenic
Her.	Heritage
Herald.	Heraldry, Heraldic
Hereford & Worcs	Hereford & Worcester (GB)
Herts	Hertfordshire (GB)
HI	Hawaii (USA)
Hib.	Hibernia
Hisp.	Hispanic
Hist.	History, Historical
HMS	His/Her Majesty's Ship
Hon.	Honorary, Honourable
Horiz.	Horizon
Hort.	Horticulture
Hosp.	Hospital(s)
HRH	His/Her Royal Highness
Human.	Humanities, Humanism
Hung.	Hungarian
Hunts	Huntingdonshire (GB; old)
IA	Iowa
ibid.	*ibidem* [in the same place]
ICA	Institute of Contemporary Arts
Ice.	Icelandic
Iconog.	Iconography
Iconol.	Iconology
ID	Idaho (USA)
i.e.	*id est* [that is]
IL	Illinois (USA)
Illum.	Illumination
illus.	illustrated, illustration
Imp.	Imperial
IN	Indiana (USA)
in., ins	inch(es)
Inc.	Incorporated
inc.	incomplete
incl.	includes, including, inclusive
Incorp.	Incorporation
Ind.	Indian
Indep.	Independent
Indig.	Indigenous
Indol.	Indology
Indon.	Indonesian
Indust.	Industrial
Inf.	Information
Inq.	Inquiry
Inscr.	Inscribed, Inscription
Inst.	Institute(s)
Inst. A.	Institute of Art
Instr.	Instrument, Instrumental
Int.	International
Intell.	Intelligence
Inter.	Interior(s), Internal
Interdiscip.	Interdisciplinary
intro.	introduced by, introduction
inv.	inventory

Inven.	Invention
Invest.	Investigation(s)
Iran.	Iranian
irreg.	irregular(ly)
Islam.	Islamic
Isr.	Israeli
It.	Italian
J.	Journal
Jam.	Jamaican
Jan	January
Jap.	Japanese
Jav.	Javanese
Jew.	Jewish
Jewel.	Jewellery
Jord.	Jordanian
jr	junior
Juris.	Jurisdiction
KBE	Knight Commander of the Order of the British Empire
KCVO	Knight Commander of the Royal Victorian Order
kg	kilogram(s)
kHz	kilohertz
km	kilometre(s)
Knowl.	Knowledge
Kor.	Korean
KS	Kansas (USA)
KY	Kentucky (USA)
Kyrgyz.	Kyrgyzstani
£	libra, librae [pound, pounds sterling]
l.	length
LA	Louisiana (USA)
Lab.	Laboratory
Lancs	Lancashire (GB)
Lang.	Language(s)
Lat.	Latin
Latv.	Latvian
lb, lbs	pound(s) weight
Leb.	Lebanese
Lect.	Lecture
Legis.	Legislative
Leics	Leicestershire (GB)
Lex.	Lexicon
Lg.	Large
Lib., Libs	Library, Libraries
Liber.	Liberian
Libsp	Librarianship
Lincs	Lincolnshire (GB)
Lit.	Literature
Lith.	Lithuanian
Liturg.	Liturgical
LLB	Bachelor of Laws
LLD	Doctor of Laws
Lt	Lieutenant
Lt-Col.	Lieutenant-Colonel
Ltd	Limited
m	metre(s)
m.	married
M.	Monsieur
MA	Master of Arts; Massachusetts (USA)
Mag.	Magazine
Maint.	Maintenance
Malay.	Malaysian
Man.	Manitoba (Canada); Manual
Manuf.	Manufactures
Mar.	Marine, Maritime
Mason.	Masonic
Mat.	Material(s)
Math.	Mathematic
MBE	Member of the Order of the British Empire
MD	Doctor of Medicine; Maryland (USA)
ME	Maine (USA)
Mech.	Mechanical
Med.	Medieval; Medium, Media
Medic.	Medical, Medicine
Medit.	Mediterranean
Mem.	Memorial(s); Memoir(s)
Merions	Merionethshire (GB; old)
Meso-Amer.	Meso-American
Mesop.	Mesopotamian
Met.	Metropolitan
Metal.	Metallurgy
Mex.	Mexican
MFA	Master of Fine Arts
mg	milligram(s)
Mgmt	Management
Mgr	Monsignor
MI	Michigan
Micrones.	Micronesian
Mid. Amer.	Middle American
Middx	Middlesex (GB; old)
Mid. E.	Middle Eastern
Mid. Eng.	Middle English
Mid Glam.	Mid Glamorgan (GB)
Mil.	Military
Mill.	Millenium
Min.	Ministry; Minutes
Misc.	Miscellaneous
Miss.	Mission(s)
Mlle	Mademoiselle
mm	millimetre(s)
Mme	Madame
MN	Minnesota
Mnmt, Mnmts	Monument(s)
Mnmtl	Monumental
MO	Missouri (USA)
Mod.	Modern, Modernist
Moldav.	Moldavian
Moldov.	Moldovan
MOMA	Museum of Modern Art
Mon.	Monday
Mongol.	Mongolian
Mons	Monmouthshire (GB; old)
Montgoms	Montgomeryshire (GB; old)
Mor.	Moral
Morav.	Moravian
Moroc.	Moroccan
Movt	Movement
MP	Member of Parliament
MPhil	Master of Philosophy
MS	Mississippi (USA)
MS., MSS	manuscript(s)
MSc	Master of Science
MT	Montana (USA)
Mt	Mount
Mthly	Monthly
Mun.	Municipal
Mus.	Museum(s)
Mus. A.	Museum of Art
Mus. F.A.	Museum of Fine Art(s)
Music.	Musicology
N.	North(ern); National
n	refractive index of a medium
n.	note
N.A.G.	National Art Gallery
Nat.	Natural, Nature
Naut.	Nautical
NB	New Brunswick (Canada)
NC	North Carolina (USA)
ND	North Dakota (USA)
n.d.	no date
NE	Nebraska; Northeast(ern)
Neth.	Netherlandish
Newslett.	Newsletter
Nfld	Newfoundland (Canada)
N.G.	National Gallery
N.G.A.	National Gallery of Art
NH	New Hampshire (USA)
Niger.	Nigerian
NJ	New Jersey (USA)
NM	New Mexico (USA)
nm	nanometre (109 metre)
nn.	notes
no., nos	number(s)
Nord.	Nordic
Norm.	Normal
Northants	Northamptonshire (GB)
Northumb.	Northumberland (GB)
Norw.	Norwegian
Notts	Nottinghamshire (GB)
Nov	November
n.p.	no place (of publication)
N.P.G.	National Portrait Gallery
nr	near

Nr E. Near Eastern
NS New Style; Nova Scotia (Canada)
n. s. new series
NSW New South Wales (Australia)
NT National Trust
Ntbk Notebook
Numi. Numismatic(s)
NV Nevada (USA)
NW Northwest(ern)
NWT Northwest Territories (Canada)
NY New York (USA)
NZ New Zealand
OBE Officer of the Order of the British Empire
Obj. Object(s), Objective
Occas. Occasional
Occident. Occidental
Ocean. Oceania
Oct October
8vo octavo
OFM Order of Friars Minor
OH Ohio (USA)
OK Oklahoma (USA)
Olymp. Olympic
OM Order of Merit
Ont. Ontario (Canada)
op. opus
opp. opposite; opera [pl. of opus]
OR Oregon (USA)
Org. Organization
Orient. Oriental
Orthdx Orthodox
OSB Order of St Benedict
Ott. Ottoman
Oxon Oxfordshire (GB)
oz. ounce(s)
p pence
p., pp. page(s)
PA Pennsylvania (USA)
p.a. per annum
Pak. Pakistani
Palaeontol. Palaeontology, Palaeontological
Palest. Palestinian
Pap. Paper(s)
para. paragraph
Parag. Paraguayan
Parl. Parliament
Paroch. Parochial
Patriarch. Patriarchate
Patriot. Patriotic
Patrm. Patrimony
Pav. Pavilion
PEI Prince Edward Island (Canada)
Pembs Pembrokeshire (GB; old)
Per. Period
Percep. Perceptions
Perf. Performance, Performing, Performed
Period. Periodical(s)
Pers. Persian
Persp. Perspectives
Peru. Peruvian
PhD Doctor of Philosophy
Philol. Philology
Philos. Philosophy
Phoen. Phoenician
Phot. Photograph, Photography, Photographic
Phys. Physician(s), Physics, Physique, Physical
Physiog. Physiognomy
Physiol. Physiology
Pict. Picture(s), Pictorial
pl. plate; plural
Plan. Planning
Planet. Planetarium
Plast. Plastic
pls plates
p.m. post meridiem [after noon]
Polit. Political
Poly. Polytechnic
Polynes. Polynesian
Pop. Popular
Port. Portuguese
Port. Portfolio
Posth. Posthumous(ly)
Pott. Pottery
POW prisoner of war
PRA President of the Royal Academy
Pract. Practical
Prefect. Prefecture, Prefectural
Preserv. Preservation
prev. previous(ly)
priv. private
PRO Public Record Office
Prob. Problem(s)
Proc. Proceedings
Prod. Production
Prog. Progress
Proj. Project(s)
Promot. Promotion
Prop. Property, Properties
Prov. Province(s), Provincial
Proven. Provenance
Prt, Prts Print(s)
Prtg Printing
pseud. pseudonym
Psych. Psychiatry, Psychiatric
Psychol. Psychology, Psychological
pt part
Ptg(s) Painting(s)
Pub. Public
pubd published
Publ. Publicity
pubn(s) publication(s)
PVA Polyvinyl acetate
PVC polyvinyl chloride
Q. quarterly
4to quarto
Què. Québec (Canada)
R reprint
r *recto*
RA Royal Academician
Radnors Radnorshire (GB; old)
RAF Royal Air Force
Rec. Record(s)
red. reduction, reduced for
Ref. Reference
Refurb. Refurbishment
reg *regit* [ruled]
Reg. Regional
Relig. Religion, Religious
remod. remodelled
Ren. Renaissance
Rep. Report(s)
repr. reprint(ed); reproduced, reproduction
Represent. Representation, Representative
Res. Research
rest. restored, restoration
Retro. Retrospective
rev. revision, revised (by/for)
Rev. Reverend; Review
RHA Royal Hibernian Academician
RI Rhode Island (USA)
RIBA Royal Institute of British Architects
RJ Rio de Janeiro State
Rlwy Railway
RSA Royal Scottish Academy
RSFSR Russian Soviet Federated Socialist Republic
Rt Hon. Right Honourable
Rur. Rural
Rus. Russian
S San, Santa, Santo, Sant', S o [Saint]
S. South(ern)
s. solidus, solidi [shilling(s)]
Sask. Saskatchewan (Canada)
Sat. Saturday
SC South Carolina (USA)
Scand. Scandinavian
Sch. School
Sci. Science(s), Scientific
Scot. Scottish
Sculp. Sculpture

SD	South Dakota (USA)
SE	Southeast(ern)
Sect.	Section
Sel.	Selected
Semin.	Seminar(s), Seminary
Semiot.	Semiotic
Semit.	Semitic
Sept	September
Ser.	Series
Serb.	Serbian
Serv.	Service(s)
Sess.	Session, Sessional
Settmt(s)	Settlement(s)
S. Glam.	South Glamorgan (GB)
Siber.	Siberian
Sig.	Signature
Sil.	Silesian
Sin.	Singhala
sing.	singular
SJ	Societas Jesu [Society of Jesus]
Skt	Sanskrit
Slav.	Slavic, Slavonic
Slov.	Slovene, Slovenian
Soc.	Society
Social.	Socialism, Socialist
Sociol.	Sociology
Sov.	Soviet
SP	S o Paulo State
Sp.	Spanish
sq.	square
sr	senior
Sri L.	Sri Lankan
SS	Saints, Santi, Santissima, Santissimo, Santissimi; Steam ship
SSR	Soviet Socialist Republic
St	Saint, Sankt, Sint, Szent
Staffs	Staffordshire (GB)
Ste	Sainte
Stud.	Study, Studies
Subalp.	Subalpine
Sum.	Sumerian
Sun.	Sunday
Sup.	Superior
suppl., suppls	supplement(s), supplementary
Surv.	Survey
SW	Southwest(ern)
Swed.	Swedish
Swi.	Swiss
Symp.	Symposium
Syr.	Syrian
Tap.	Tapestry
Tas.	Tasmanian
Tech.	Technical, Technique
Technol.	Technology
Territ.	Territory
Theat.	Theatre
Theol.	Theology, Theological
Theor.	Theory, Theoretical
Thurs.	Thursday
Tib.	Tibetan
TN	Tennessee (USA)
Top.	Topography
Trad.	Tradition(s), Traditional
trans.	translation, translated by; transactions
Transafr.	Transafrican
Transatlant.	Transatlantic
Transcarpath.	Transcarpathian
transcr.	transcribed by/for
Triq.	Triquarterly
Tropic.	Tropical
Tues.	Tuesday
Turk.	Turkish
Turkmen.	Turkmenistani
TV	Television
TX	Texas (USA)
U.	University
UK	United Kingdom of Great Britain and Northern Ireland
Ukrain.	Ukrainian
Un.	Union
Underwtr	Underwater
UNESCO	United Nations Educational, Scientific and Cultural Organization
Univl	Universal
unpubd	unpublished
Urb.	Urban
Urug.	Uruguayan
US	United States
USA	United States of America
USSR	Union of Soviet Socialist Republics
UT	Utah
v	*verso*
VA	Virginia (USA)
V&A	Victoria and Albert Museum
Var.	Various
Venez.	Venezuelan
Vern.	Vernacular
Vict.	Victorian
Vid.	Video
Viet.	Vietnamese
viz.	*videlicet* [namely]
vol., vols	volume(s)
vs.	versus
VT	Vermont (USA)
Vulg.	Vulgarisation
W.	West(ern)
w.	width
WA	Washington (USA)
Warwicks	Warwickshire (GB)
Wed.	Wednesday
W. Glam.	West Glamorgan (GB)
WI	Wisconsin (USA)
Wilts	Wiltshire (GB)
Wkly	Weekly
W. Midlands	West Midlands (GB)
Worcs	Worcestershire (GB; old)
Wtrcol.	Watercolour
WV	West Virginia (USA)
WY	Wyoming (USA)
Yb., Y.-b.	Yearbook, Year-book
Yem.	Yemeni
Yorks	Yorkshire (GB; old)
Yug.	Yugoslavian
Zamb.	Zambian
Zimb.	Zimbabwean

A Note on the Use of the Dictionary

This note is intended as a short guide to the basic editorial conventions adopted in this dictionary. For a fuller explanation, please refer to the Introduction, pp. xiii–xx.

Abbreviations in general use in the dictionary are listed on pp. xxix–xxxiv; those used in bibliographies and for locations of works of art or exhibition venues are listed in the Appendices in vol. 33.

Alphabetization of headings, which are distinguished in bold typeface, is letter by letter up to the first comma (ignoring spaces, hyphens, accents and any parenthesized or bracketed matter); the same principle applies thereafter. Abbreviations of 'Saint' and its foreign equivalents are alphabetized as if spelt out, and headings with the prefix 'Mc' appear under 'Mac'.

Authors' signatures appear at the end of the article or sequence of articles that the authors have contributed; in multipartite articles, any section that is unsigned is by the author of the next signed section. Where the article was compiled by the editors or in the few cases where an author has wished to remain anonymous, this is indicated by a square box (□) instead of a signature.

Bibliographies are arranged chronologically (within section, where divided) by order of year of first publication and, within years, alphabetically by authors' names. Abbreviations have been used for some standard reference books; these are cited in full in Appendix C in vol. 33, as are abbreviations of periodical titles (Appendix B). Abbreviated references to alphabetically arranged dictionaries and encyclopedias appear at the beginning of the bibliography (or section).

Biographical dates when cited in parentheses in running text at the first mention of a personal name indicate that the individual does not have an entry in the dictionary. The presence of parenthesized regnal dates for rulers and popes, however, does not necessarily indicate the lack of a biography of that person. Where no dates are provided for an artist or patron, the reader may assume that there is a biography of that individual in the dictionary (or, more rarely, that the person is so obscure that dates are not readily available).

Cross-references are distinguished by the use of small capital letters, with a large capital to indicate the initial letter of the entry to which the reader is directed; for example, 'He commissioned LEONARDO DA VINCI . . .' means that the entry is alphabetized under 'L'.

A.A.A. *See* ALLIED ARTISTS' ASSOCIATION and AMERICAN ABSTRACT ARTISTS.

Aachen [Fr. Aix-la-Chapelle]. City in Nordrhein-Westfalia, Germany. It was the birthplace and residence of Charlemagne, ruler of the Frankish Kingdom, and remained associated with German rulers throughout the Middle Ages; most Holy Roman emperors were crowned there until 1531. It was founded by the Romans in the 1st century AD as a modest military settlement. Its Roman name, Aquae Granni ('Waters of Granus'), was derived from a local Celtic deity and the area's abundant hot springs: the remains of three bath complexes have been uncovered in the centre of the city. Despite the collapse of the Roman Empire, the therapeutic waters encouraged continued habitation, and during the early 790s Charlemagne chose Aquisgranum, as it was then called, as his capital. Until his death in AD 814, he spent part of almost every year there and built an elaborate palace, of which the chapel survives (*see* §2 (ii) below). He gathered scholars and artists from all over Europe in order to promote the cultural revival known as the Carolingian *renovatio*. Between 1172 and 1176, by order of Emperor Frederick Barbarossa, fortification walls were built around the palace and burgeoning town, and between 1334 and 1349 Charlemagne's audience hall was replaced by an elegant town hall.

After a disastrous fire in 1656, much of the city was rebuilt in the Baroque style. Ceasing to be a Free Imperial city in 1794, Aachen was taken into Prussia in 1815. Now an industrial and mining city, it was badly damaged in World War II.

BIBLIOGRAPHY

K. Faymonville: *Die Kunstdenkmäler der Stadt Aachen*, 2 vols (Düsseldorf, 1916–22)

W. Kaemmerer: *Geschichtliches Aachen: Von Werden und Wesen einer Reichsstadt* (Aachen, 1955, rev. 2/1957)

H. Cüppers, ed.: *Aquae Granni: Beiträge zur Archäologie von Aachen*, Rheinische Ausgrabungen, xxii (Cologne, 1982)

L. Falkenstein: 'Charlemagne et Aix-la-Chapelle', *Byzantion*, lxi (1991), pp. 231–87

CHARLES B. MCCLENDON

1. Centre of manuscript production. 2. Buildings.

1. CENTRE OF MANUSCRIPT PRODUCTION. Manuscripts produced at Aachen are those of a group of scribes of different origins and training rather than of a self-contained monastic scriptorium. The two groups of manuscripts associated with the royal court under Charlemagne, the 'Ada' and 'Coronation Gospels' groups, may well have been produced at Aachen itself, as could many of the liturgical, Classical and rare patristic texts produced for the court library. Under Louis the Pious (*reg* 814–40), on the other hand, evidence for the production at Aachen of legal manuscripts (the *leges* scriptorium group), of Classical and patristic texts (the Bamberg Pliny group) and of contemporary theology is substantial. As six extant manuscripts demonstrate, the court at Aachen continued to be a focus of fine book production in the reign of Emperor Lothair I (*reg* 840–55), but Aachen itself ceased for some decades thereafter to be a significant political or cultural focus.

See also CAROLINGIAN ART, §IV, 3.

BIBLIOGRAPHY

W. Koehler: *Die Karolingischen Miniaturen*, ii–iv (Berlin, 1958–82)

B. Bischoff: 'Die Hofbibliothek Karls des Grossen' and 'Die Hofbibliothek unter Ludwig dem Frommen', *Mittelalterliche Studien*, iii (Stuttgart, 1981), pp. 149–86

R. McKitterick: *The Carolingians and the Written Word* (Cambridge, 1989), pp. 57–9

——: 'Carolingian Uncial: A Context for the Lothar Psalter', *BL J.*, xvi (1990), pp. 1–15

ROSAMOND D. MCKITTERICK

2. BUILDINGS.

(i) Palace. (ii) Palatine chapel.

(i) Palace. Charlemagne maintained many residences throughout his realm, all of which could be termed palaces because of their royal status, but none rivalled that at Aachen in size and splendour. Attracted by the site's natural hot springs and its strategic location between the Rhineland and northern France, his father, Pepin the Short (*reg* 754–68), spent winters at Aachen in 765, and Charlemagne followed suit in 769 and 787. Construction of a new palace was sufficiently advanced by 794 to allow it to be used regularly. Periodic excavation since the mid-19th century has uncovered the core of the complex (see fig. 1). To the south, a polygonal chapel (a) was flanked at the east end by two small basilican structures (b) and approached from the west by a monumental atrium (c). An audience hall (*aula regia*) stood *c.* 125 m to the north (d); its axis ran parallel to that of the chapel, but its main apse was at the west instead of the east. The audience hall and atrium of the chapel were in turn connected by a narrow, two-storey walkway (e), which was intersected midway by a massive rectangular gate-house (f). The layout of the palace followed a grid that seems to have been based on a module of 12 Carolingian feet (1 ft=330 mm) and diverged

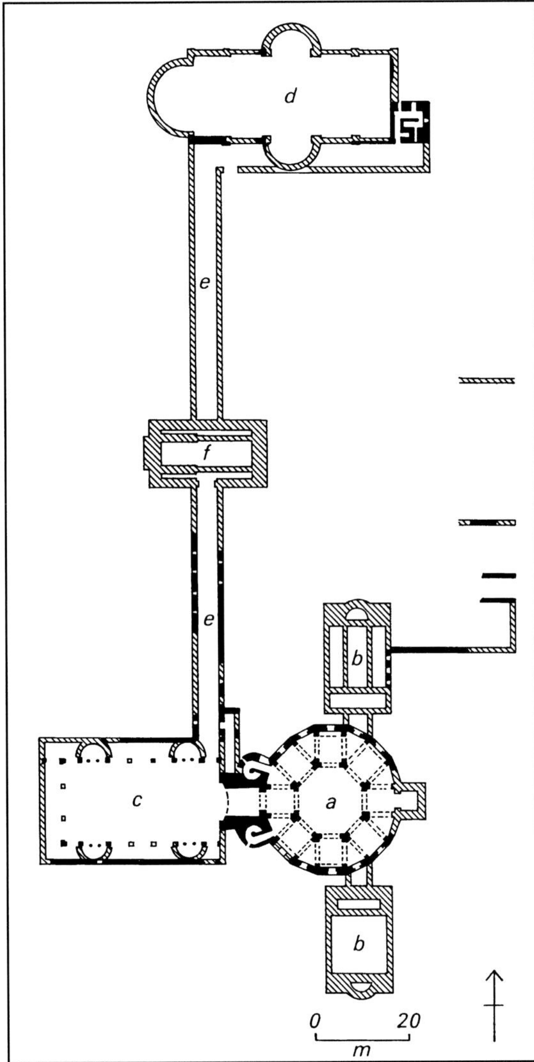

1. Aachen, plan of palace complex: (a) Palatine chapel; (b) basilican structures; (c) atrium; (d) audience hall; (e) walkway; (f) gate-house

from the Roman town's rectilinear street-plan by some 40°, in order to place the chapel on a strict east–west alignment. Around these ceremonial buildings of stone and mortar presumably stood subsidiary structures of wood—living quarters, workrooms and stables—but they have left no trace.

The audience hall was an aisleless building (47.42× 20.76 m) with three apses, the largest to the west, and smaller ones in the middle of the north and south sides. At the east end, a massive stair-tower provided access to catwalks for maintenance. The exterior elevation was articulated at wide intervals by a series of thick pilasters and arches that framed one or more superimposed rows of round-arched windows. The long passageway between the audience hall and chapel was barrel-vaulted on the ground-floor, with mere slits for windows, and timber-roofed above, with broadly spaced tripartite windows looking out on to the west range of the complex. The thick foundations of the gate-house (29.57×15.10 m) indicate that it, too, was vaulted at ground-level and possessed a second storey, reached by stairs in its western corners.

The main buildings of the palace reflected Charlemagne's acclamation of Aachen as a new or second Rome. The audience hall with its three apses took the form of a triclinium, a structure traditionally used in Roman villas for reception or dining. This building type seems to have gone out of fashion in the Latin West in the 6th century AD, but it was revived in Rome in the mid-8th century for the papal palace adjoining the Lateran basilica. The blind arcading of the elevation was inspired by the audience hall of Constantine the Great at Trier. The reasons for this reference seem obvious. Charlemagne was described by contemporaries as a 'new Constantine', and Trier had served as Constantine's capital before he marched on Rome in AD 312. The arrangement of the monumental gateway and narrow corridor ultimately derived from Constantinople, where the Chalke Gate, built by Emperor Justinian, led to a covered passage that linked the imperial palace to Hagia Sophia (*see* ISTANBUL, §III, 12). Pope Zacharias (*reg* 741–52) erected a similar entrance tower in Rome, with a bronze gate leading to an elevated corridor that joined various parts of the Lateran palace. Thus, the design of the palace at Aachen was not only utilitarian in nature but also symbolized Charlemagne's political ties with both northern Europe and the Mediterranean.

(ii) Palatine chapel.

(a) Architecture. The best-preserved portion of the palace is the chapel, which, although partially obscured by later additions, still dominates the city. Dedicated to the Virgin, the chapel was nearing completion in 798, according to a letter of Alcuin (*c.* 735–804; Mnmt Ger. Hist., Epistolae, iv/2, p. 244). A 12th-century reference in the *Annales Tielenses* (Mnmt Ger. Hist., Scriptores, xxiv, p. 22) states that it was consecrated by Pope Leo III in 805, and a lost inscription inside the building ascribed its construction to Odo of Metz, an individual otherwise unknown (see Schlosser, 1896). The chapel (see fig. 2) is a complex double-shell design, composed of a domed octagonal core (diam. 14.46 m), with an enveloping aisle and upper gallery, and enclosed within a 16-sided outer wall. The east end was marked by a projecting square apse, replaced by the Late Gothic choir, while at the opposite end stands a multi-storey entranceway or westwork. The broad planes of the exterior are pierced by three tiers of individual round-arched windows. A cornice with brackets caps the outermost wall, while the octagonal drum of the dome is articulated at the corners by paired pilasters with Corinthian capitals, now badly eroded. The central octagon dominates the interior space, defined by eight massive piers that rise to form superimposed arches, squat at ground-level and attenuated above. The predominant impression is one of compression and lift, created by the lateral splaying of the piers and the tall proportions of the upper storey, which together lead the eye to the eight-sided cloister vault. The gallery, covered by a series of transverse barrel vaults, is divided into rectangular and triangular bays by heavy diaphragm arches. The ambula-

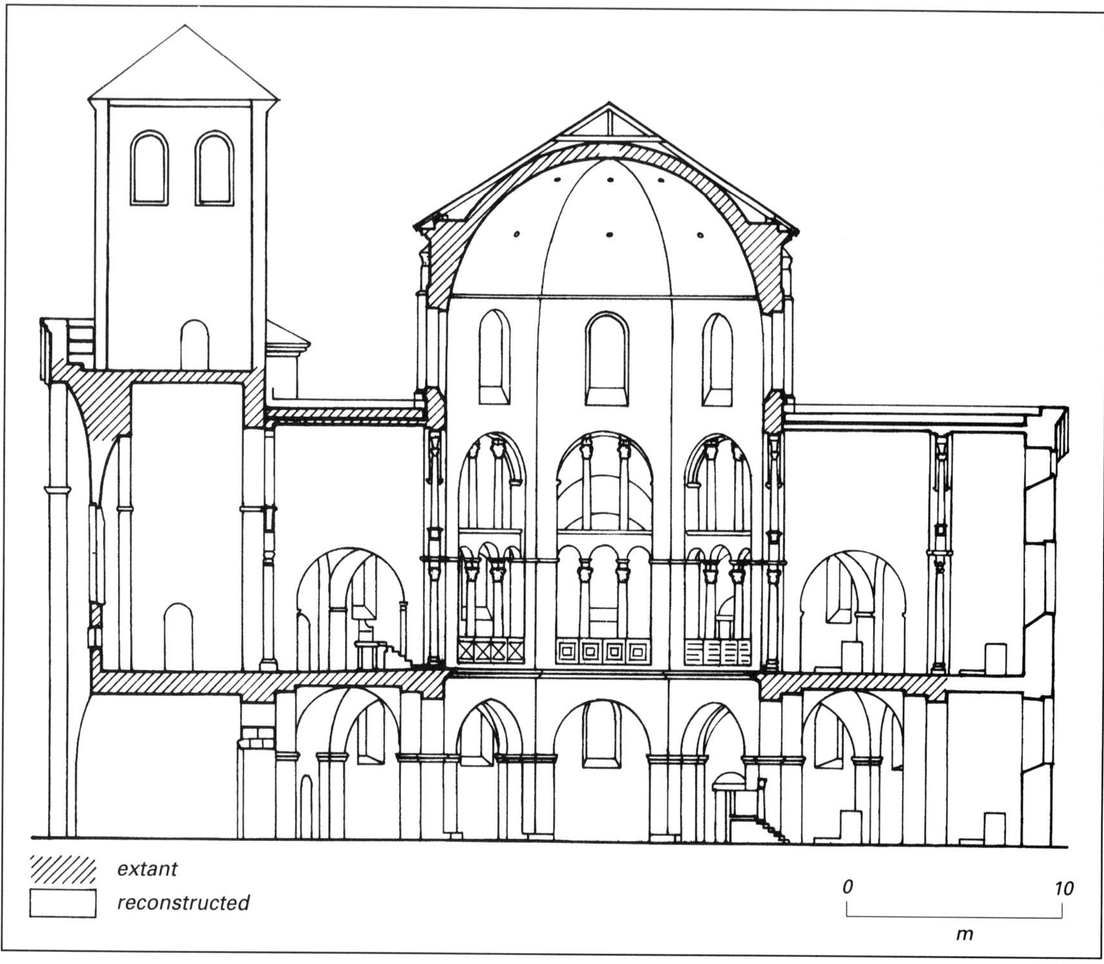

2. Aachen, section drawing of Palatine chapel

tory in contrast is low and dark, covered by an intricate sequence of groin vaults.

The current, resplendent interior decoration is not Carolingian but the result of a radical restoration carried out *c.* 1900 after late Baroque stucco had been stripped from the walls. It seems clear, nonetheless, that the walls were originally covered with rich marble revetment and the dome with mosaic (*see* CAROLINGIAN ART, §IV, 1), reviving the aesthetics of late antiquity. According to EINHARD, these luxurious materials, including marble columns, were imported from Rome and Ravenna. The current configuration of the throne in the gallery opposite the apse dates to the Ottonian period, but fragments of the original *opus sectile* floor show that this was a place of special prominence. From this vantage point, Charlemagne could look down to the main altar and up to the image of Christ in the dome, while the congregation below saw their king enthroned between heaven and earth.

The centralized design of the chapel, always rare in the West, also recalled Early Christian building traditions. Numerous models have been proposed, but the closest comparison, and the one most often cited, is S Vitale in Ravenna, dating from the reign of Justinian (*see* RAVENNA, §2(vii)). Their plans and elevations are strikingly similar, and Charlemagne's links with Ravenna are well known. Even so, the Early Christian model was not copied literally but transformed into a distinctly new and medieval form. The subtle interplay between curvilinear and angular patterns at S Vitale was replaced by a more ponderous and rectilinear approach. Billowing exedrae, framed by thin angular piers, became at Aachen flat screens sustained by massive, broad supports. In place of the undulating, free-flowing interior of S Vitale, that at Aachen is contained and defined through the compartmentalization of space, in keeping with the grid-like attitude toward planning that is characteristic of the layout of the whole palace. The construction techniques are also very different. S Vitale's brick-and-mortar masonry was translated at Aachen into the local idiom of rough-hewn stones and quoining. The WESTWORK, an element introduced to church architecture in Carolingian times, not only provided access to the gallery, as did the two stunted, cylindrical stair-towers flanking the entrance at S Vitale, but it also added a monumental vertical accent to the façade of the church (in place of a low narthex), marking the position of the king's throne by a great arch.

Like S Vitale and many other Early Christian churches, the chapel was preceded by an atrium, but one with its own distinctive characteristics. Long and low, the atrium was defined to the north and south by a solid outer wall, from which projected two large niches, screened off on the inside by rectangular piers and paired columns, forming a raised, covered platform that surrounded an open courtyard on three sides. Rather than a traditional quadriporticus, the atrium seems to have been designed as a place of assembly for the staging of such events as the annual gathering of nobles and the reception of foreign ambassadors. The remains of a water channel running diagonally across the courtyard indicate that a fountain stood at the centre, perhaps mounted by the bronze pine-cone that now stands in the vestibule of the chapel (*see* §(b) below). Two rectangular buildings set on a north–south axis either side of the chapel's east end were of similar dimensions (15×23 m), and each was connected to the gallery by a two-storey narthex, yet their exact functions remain unknown.

Charlemagne was buried in his chapel in 814. In 1165, through the instigation of Frederick Barbarossa, he was canonized, and his remains drew many pilgrims. From the start the palatine chapel was a focal-point of German kingship, and it inspired many copies until well into the 14th century. The gables were added to the roof in the 13th century and the dome rebuilt after the fire of 1656. Between 1355 and 1414 the eastern square apse was replaced by a double-bay apsed choir with extremely tall traceried windows and a quadripartite rib vault, the wall shafts of which are supported on angel-corbels. The chapel was designated the cathedral of a newly constituted diocese in 1802.

BIBLIOGRAPHY

Einhard: *Life of Charlemagne* (MS.; *c.* late 820s); ed. G. Pertz, Mnmt Ger. Hist., Scriptores, xxvi (Hannover, 1829), p. 457

J. von Schlosser: *Schriftquellen zur Geschichte der karolingischen Kunst* (Vienna, 1896), p. 28, n. 107 [Odo of Metz]

A. Haupt: *Die Pfalzkapelle Kaiser Karls des Grossen zu Aachen*, Monumenta Germaniae Architectonica, ii (Leipzig, 1913)

W. Braunfels and H. Schnitzler, eds: *Karl der Grosse: Lebenswerk und Nachleben*, 3 vols (Düsseldorf, 1965–7)

W. E. Kleinbauer: 'Charlemagne's Palace Chapel at Aachen and its Copies', *Gesta*, iv (1965), pp. 2–11

Karl der Grosse: Werk und Wirkung (exh. cat., Aachen, Rathaus, 1965)

F. Oswald, L. Schaeffer and H. R. Sennhauser: *Vorromanische Kirchenbauten: Katalog der Denkmäler bis zum Ausgang der Ottonen*, i (Munich, 1966), pp. 14–18

H. E. Kubach and A. Verbeek: *Romanische Baukunst an Rhein und Maas: Katalog der vorromanischen und romanischen Denkmäler*, i (Berlin, 1976), pp. 1–13

H. Belting: 'Das Aachener Münster im 19. Jahrhundert: Zur ersten Krise des Denkmal-Konzepts', *Wallraf-Richartz Jb.*, xlv (1984), pp. 257–90

CHARLES B. MCCLENDON

(b) Sculpture. Among the columns and marbles brought by Charlemagne from Rome and Ravenna to Aachen was probably the late Antonine Proserpina Sarcophagus in which, according to tradition, Emperor Charlemagne was entombed. Antique columns and capitals survive in the chapel alongside Carolingian imitations. Antique bronzes were set up to vie with the authority of monuments at the Lateran palace: a *She-bear* from southern Gaul, now in the vestibule of the chapel, was to emulate the Roman *She-wolf*, and an equestrian statue (untraced) from Ravenna, thought to represent Theodoric (*reg* 489–526), was to parallel that of *Marcus Aurelius* on the Capitoline in Rome, then believed to depict Constantine the Great. A foundry brought to Aachen before 796 cast bronze doors and railings for the chapel, completing the work sometime after 800. Four surviving pairs of doors follow antique models, and the railings, originally gilt, still enclose the galleries. Changes in their design demonstrate a progressive mastery of the classicizing styles also developed in manuscript illumination at Charlemagne's court. It remains uncertain, however, whether the large bronze pine-cone in the chapel vestibule was made by this foundry or is a Roman casting set on a Carolingian base, which bears the four Rivers of Paradise and a fragmentary inscription naming an otherwise unknown Abbot Udalrich as donor. Whatever the case, it served as a fountain like the pine-cone (Rome, Vatican, Cortile Pigna) then in the atrium of Old St Peter's, Rome.

BIBLIOGRAPHY

W. Braunfels: 'Karls des Grossen Bronzewerkstatt', *Karolingische Kunst* (1965), iii of *Karl der Grosse: Lebenswerk und Nachleben*, ed. W. Braunfels and H. Schnitzler (Düsseldorf, 1965), pp. 168–202

Karl der Grosse: Werk und Wirkung (exh. cat., Aachen, Rathaus, 1965), nos 3–4, 6–7

P. Lasko: *Ars Sacra, 800–1200*, Pelican Hist. A. (Harmondsworth, 1972), pp. 14–16

(c) Treasury. Einhard's *Life of Charlemagne* relates that Charlemagne endowed his chapel with a rich treasure of liturgical objects and willed it to be kept from dispersal after his death. Other sources record that many relics were brought from Jerusalem, Constantinople, Rome and elsewhere and placed as objects of veneration into and above altars, encased in costly reliquaries and exhibited on special occasions. The location of a space reserved for the early medieval church treasure remains uncertain. From the early 15th century to the mid-19th it was kept in a large cabinet in the St Matthew Chapel (1379), which was used as a sacristy at the south junction of the choir and palatine chapel. In 1873 it was moved to the Charles Chapel (on the north-east side, 1455–74), in 1881 to the Hungarian Chapel (at the south-west, 1367) and in 1931 to the present site in a vaulted passage north of the Poor Souls' Chapel.

Of six objects surviving from Carolingian times, only three remain at Aachen: the Aachen Gospels, an ivory diptych depicting epiphanies of Christ and an early Byzantine silk (*see* EARLY CHRISTIAN AND BYZANTINE ART, §VII, 8). The Coronation Gospels and the burse reliquary of St Stephen (*c.* 830) were transferred to the imperial treasury in Vienna in 1798 (Vienna, Schatzkammer) and the 'Talisman (or Amulet) of Charlemagne' containing hair of the Virgin was given to Empress Josephine Bonaparte in 1804 and subsequently to Reims Cathedral.

Grimme lists 210 later additions to the treasury, of which the most significant were offerings from rulers seeking to legitimize their aspirations by claiming the heritage of Charlemagne. The Lothar Cross (*c.* 985–91), the Gospels of Otto III (Munich, Bayer. Staatsbib., Clm. 4453) and several Byzantine silks were donated by Otto III. An ivory situla may also have been given by him or by Henry II. The latter certainly donated the magnificent pulpit and the altar antependium known as the Pala d'Oro (both still in the chapel) and a golden book cover for the Aachen Gospels. Frederick Barbarossa, King of Germany, was responsible for the large Romanesque candelabrum (*c.* 1166) still hanging from the apex of the dome and the sumptuous shrine into which his grandson Frederick II placed Charlemagne's remains in 1215. In 1238 the shrine of the Virgin received Aachen's most sacred relics, the Virgin's robe, the swaddling clothes and loincloth of Christ, and the shroud of the head of John the Baptist. The Luxembourg emperor Charles IV presented the bust reliquary of Charlemagne and another reliquary formed like a small chapel the windowed base of which was seen part of Charlemagne's arm. In the late Middle Ages there were three more gifts to justify entitlement from the Carolingian past: in 1475 the crown of Margaret of York (1446–1503), wife of Charles the Bold, Duke of Burgundy; in 1481 an arm reliquary of Charlemagne given by King Louis XI of France; and, during the first quarter of the 16th century, several works by the Aachen goldsmith Hans von Reutlingen (*fl* 1497–1522) were presented by Maximilian I and one by Charles V.

From the 17th century numerous objects came to the treasury, each fashioned in the style of its period, from the Baroque to the Gothic Revival, the Romanesque Revival and the contemporary, the latest to be recorded being a chalice made in 1960 by Ewald Mataré.

BIBLIOGRAPHY

E. G. Grimme: *Der Aachener Domschatz*, Aachener Kunstblätter, xlii (Düsseldorf, 1972, rev. 2/1973)

JOACHIM E. GAEHDE

Aachen [Aach; Ach; Acha]**, Hans** [Johann; Joan] **von** (*b* Cologne, 1552; *d* Prague, 4 March 1615). German painter and draughtsman, active also in Italy and Bohemia. One of the foremost painters of the circle gathered at the Prague court of Emperor Rudolf II (*see* HABSBURG, §I, (10)), he synthesized Italian and Netherlandish influences in his portraits and erudite allegories.

1. Hans von Aachen: *Bacchus, Ceres and Cupid*, oil on canvas, 1.63×1.13 m, *c.* 1600 (Vienna, Kunsthistorisches Museum)

1. CAREER. Hans's surname is derived from his father's native town. According to Karel van Mander, he probably studied *c.* 1567–73 with the portrait painter Georg Jerrigh, who had trained in Antwerp. Von Aachen subsequently became a member of the Cologne guild of painters. He travelled to Italy *c.* 1574, first working in Venice as a copyist and for the painter Gaspar Rem (1542–1615/17), before going in 1575 to Rome, where he copied antique sculptures and the works of Italian masters; he also painted an *Adoration of the Shepherds* for the church of Il Gesù in Rome (1580s; untraced, but known from an engraving (1588) by Aegidius Sadeler; Hollstein, no. 32). In Rome, von Aachen joined the circle of northern artists that included Otto van Veen, Joris Hoefnagel, Jan Speeckaert, Paul and Matthijs Bril and Joseph Heintz (i). From 1582–3 he worked in Florence, obtaining numerous portrait commissions, including some from the Medici family, and met the sculptor Giambologna. In 1585 he again settled in Venice.

In 1587 von Aachen went to Augsburg, painting portraits for the Fugger family, and to Munich, where he produced two altarpieces for the church of St Michael (*in situ*). In 1588 he revisited Cologne and may have visited Prague for the first time in the train of Duke William V of Bavaria; he also went back to Venice and gave up his home there. From 1589 he was working in Munich, where he produced portraits of the ducal family, altarpieces and allegories. Further portraits were painted for the Fuggers in Augsburg *c.* 1591–2. While based in Munich, Hans von Aachen was in contact with figures such as Friedrich Sustris, Peter Candid and Christoph Schwartz, as well as the engravers Jan and Raphael Sadeler.

On 1 January 1592 in Prague, Emperor Rudolf II appointed von Aachen 'Kammermaler von Haus aus'—a court painter who need not be present at court. In 1594 he made another journey to Prague, and after his marriage on 1 July 1596 to the daughter of Orlando di Lasso (*c.* 1530/32–1595), conductor of the Munich court orchestra, he finally settled there permanently. In Prague, von Aachen worked not only as a painter for Rudolf II, but also as an art agent, making frequent journeys abroad, for instance once to Besançon in 1597 to purchase pictures from the estate of Cardinal Antoine Perronet de Granvelle and again in 1600 to transport the collection, returning via Freiburg im Breisgau; in 1602 he travelled to Brunswick, Wolfenbüttel, Wittenberg and Dresden, and between 1603 and 1605 to Innsbruck, Venice, Turin, Mantua and Modena, partly in order to arrange the painting of portraits of possible future consorts for the Emperor. In 1604 he returned to Brunswick, and in 1605 he was in Vienna. Throughout these travels he worked not only as an art agent but also as a diplomat and envoy of the Emperor. He meanwhile continued to execute commissions for the

2. Hans von Aachen: *Triumph of Truth and Dominion* (*Allegory of the Truth of the Imperial Cause*), oil on copper, 560×470 mm, 1598 (Munich, Alte Pinakothek)

court in Munich, as well as for Augsburg clients. On 14 May 1605 Emperor Rudolf II conferred a knighthood on him. In 1610 von Aachen bought a house on the Hradčany.

After Rudolf's death in 1612, von Aachen was reappointed by his successor, Matthias, and given an estate in Raussnitz. The Emperor sent him to Dresden and Vienna in 1612, while 1613 saw him back in Augsburg, and 1614 again in Dresden. Von Aachen had several pupils, of whom Pieter Isaacsz. is the most famous—he was apprenticed to von Aachen while he was still in Italy. In Prague, Andreas Vogel (*b c.* 1588; *fl* 1638), Christian Buchner (*fl* 1600–20) and Hans Christoph Schürer (*fl* 1609–22) studied under him.

2. WORK. Along with Bartholomäus Spranger and Joseph Heintz (i), Hans von Aachen was the main representative of the late Mannerist, internationally influenced style of art at the court of Rudolf II in Prague *c.* 1600. His works—portraits, paintings of historical and religious subjects, genre pictures and allegories—veer between an idealized style of painting indebted to Roman and Florentine Mannerism as well as to Venetian models (Titian, Veronese, Tintoretto) and the newly emerging tradition of Dutch realism.

(i) Portraits and related work. Von Aachen's portraits are remarkable for their psychological sensitivity. One of the earliest, of his teacher in Venice *Gaspar Rem* (*c.* 1574–5; Vienna, Ksthist. Mus.), clearly shows the influence of Venetian portrait painting (e.g. Jacopo Bassano). In Munich and Augsburg he painted numerous formal court portraits in which Flemish and Italian influences were intermingled, as for example in *Octavian Secundus Fugger* and *Hans Fugger* (both 1592; Babenhausen, Fugger-Mus.). In 1586–8 he created a memorial altar with the *Discovery and Examination of the Holy Cross by Empress Helena* (priv. col.; preparatory drawing, Leiden, Rijksuniv. Prentenkab.) for the burial chapel of the Grafen von Schwarzenburg in the Franziskanerkirche in Munich. This early work was also clearly influenced by Venetian painting: areas in deep shadow are effectively contrasted with bright areas emphasized by applied highlights, thoroughly demonstrating his familiarity with the work of Tintoretto and Veronese. Otto Heinrich, Graf zu Schwarzenberg (1535–90), who commissioned the painting, and his wife are depicted in the Empress's retinue, and on the right-hand edge of the picture by way of signature there is a self-portrait of the painter.

At the court of Rudolf II a great many portraits of officers were painted in connection with the Turkish wars, such as von Aachen's full-length portrait of *Adolf von Schwarzenberg* (after 1599; Győr, János Xantus Mus.). He also painted several portraits of the Emperor, for example one in an allegorical framework, symbolizing both current political events and the apotheosis of the Emperor (known only through an engraving made by Aegidius Sadeler II in 1603; Hollstein, no. 68). On the back of another portrait of *Rudolf II* (*c.* 1603–4; Nuremberg, Ger. Nmus.), painted on alabaster, there is an *Allegory on the Wars against the Turks*, inspired by the Gemma Augustea, a famous antique gemstone in the Emperor's collection. Hans von Aachen also painted many portraits at the court in Prague, such as those of *Johannes Kepler* (1603–4; Rychnov nad Kněžnou, Château A.G.), one of the most important scientists of Rudolf II's reign, and his fellow painter *Bartholomäus Spranger* (*c.* 1608–9; Florence, Uffizi). Von Aachen also executed several portraits of *Emperor Matthias* (Vienna, Ksthist. Mus.).

(ii) History and genre paintings. Along with some genre scenes with Dutch colouring, Hans von Aachen's finest achievements in painting are undoubtedly his mythological and historical compositions, which represent Rudolfine court art at its most sublime. Pictures of the gods as lovers are subtly linked in meaning to the subject-matter and radiate sensuality. The figures of Minerva as protectress of the arts and sciences and Venus are often central. Frequently too Rudolf II's qualities as a ruler are emphasized: the arts, sciences and love prosper in the land of the sovereign who has prevailed against the Turks.

In *Bacchus, Ceres and Cupid* (*c.* 1600; Vienna, Ksthist. Mus.; see fig. 1) deities important for the existence of love are portrayed. The nude figure of a woman viewed from behind, a favourite motif in Rudolfine art, is represented here in a sensually suggestive way. The elongation of the female body is characteristic of the excessively refined Mannerist art and culture prevalent at the court in Prague *c.* 1600 and can also be found in the work of von Aachen's contemporaries at court, Bartholomäus Spranger and Joseph Heintz (i). From a series of what must originally have been twelve compositions of *Allegories on the Wars against the Turks* (1593–1606), painted on parchment and assembled in book form, seven oil sketches have been preserved (Vienna, Ksthist. Mus.; Budapest, Mus. F.A.), one composition is known from an engraving (Hollstein, nos 7–9) and four others from drawn copies of which there are eleven in all, likewise bound together as a book (Dresden, Kupferstichkab.).

Two allegories created in 1598 are tributes to Rudolf II: the *Triumph of Dominion over Time* (Stuttgart, Staatsgal.) and the *Triumph of Truth and Dominion* (or *Allegory of the Truth of the Imperial Cause*; Munich, Alte Pin.; see fig. 2). The first picture should be understood as an allegory on the rule of Rudolf II: if time conquers his enemies (the Turks), love, prosperity and the arts will flourish in his realm. In the second painting, personifications of fertility, peace and harmony symbolize the fruits of the just rule of Rudolf II. Again von Aachen features a strongly sensual nude female figure viewed from behind (Truth).

Hans von Aachen's allegorical paintings, with their often complicated encoding, carried an intellectual stamp, powerfully influenced by the personality of the Emperor and by his high level of culture. After Rudolf II's death, von Aachen continued to paint in a similar fashion, though the colouring became darker in his late works, as if he were trying to convey the slow decline of Rudolfine art. During the reign of Emperor Matthias he painted *Bathsheba Bathing* (1612–15; Vienna, Ksthist. Mus.), a tribute to the ideal of female beauty of Prague Mannerism; here again the naked female body is at the centre of the narrative. The boundary between mythological and religious painting is blurred in favour of extremely sensual eroticism. The objects surrounding Bathsheba, arranged in a still-life manner, are reminiscent of Netherlandish models, to which Hans von Aachen was also indebted in his few genre paintings, such as the *Brothel Scene with Two Ill-matched Lovers* (two versions, both *c.* 1600; Karlsruhe, Staatl. Ksthalle; Linz, Oberösterreich. Landesmus.) and a *Young Couple* (Vienna, Ksthist. Mus.).

BIBLIOGRAPHY

Hollstein: *Ger.*; Thieme–Becker

R. A. Peltzer: 'Der Hofmaler Hans von Aachen; Seine Schule und seine Zeit', *Jb. Ksthist. Samml. Allhöch. Ksrhaus.*, xxx (1911–12), pp. 59–182

——: 'Hans von Aachen: Eine Nachlese', *Wallraf-Richartz-Jb.*, v (1928), pp. 75–84

R. Chadabra: 'Die Gemma Augustea und die Rudolfinische Allegorie', *Umění*, xviii (1970), pp. 289–97

E. Fučíková: 'Über die Tätigkeit Hans von Aachens in Bayern', *Münchn. Jb. Bild. Kst*, xxi (1970), pp. 129–42

R. an der Heiden: 'Die Porträtmalerei des Hans von Aachen', *Jb. Ksthist. Samml. Wien*, lxvi (1970), pp. 135–226

E. Fučíková: 'Quae praestat invenis vix potuere viri: Hans von Aachens Selbstbildnis in Köln', *Wallraf-Richartz-Jb.*, xxxiii (1971), pp. 115–21

R. an der Heiden: 'Zu neu aufgefundenen Gemälden Hans von Aachens', *Pantheon*, xxii (1974), pp. 249–54

H. J. Ludwig: *Die Türkenskizzen des Hans von Aachen für Rudolf II* (diss., U. Frankfurt am Main, 1977)

Zeichnung in Deutschland: Deutsche Zeichner, 1540–1640, i (exh. cat., Stuttgart, Staatsgal., 1979–80), nos B14–19

T. daCosta Kaufmann: *L'Ecole de Prague: La Peinture à la cour de Rodolphe II* (Paris, 1985; trans. and rev. Chicago and London, 1988)

Prag um 1600: Kunst und Kultur am Hofe Kaiser Rudolfs II (exh. cat., Vienna, Ksthist. Mus., 1988), i, nos 89–110, 176–87; ii, nos 543–53, 608–15

J. Müller: *Concordia Pragensis: Die Stellung der rudolfinischen Hofkünstler im Schilder-Boeck Carel van Manders. Ein Beitrag zur Rhetorisierung von Kunst und Leben um 1600* (diss., U. Bochum, 1991)

C. HÖPER

Aagaard Andersen, Gunnar (*b* Ordrup, 14 July 1919; *d* Munkerup, nr Dronningmølle, Hillerød, 29 June 1982). Danish painter, sculptor, designer and writer. He studied at the Kunsthåndvaerkerskole (1936–9) and the Kongelige Danske Kunstakademi (1939–46), both in Copenhagen. He experimented with non-figurative forms of expression in numerous media. He was a co-founder of Groupe Espace in 1951, and his work was important for the development of Concrete art internationally.

From 1947 to 1950 Aagaard Andersen developed a new, pure pictorial dynamic, moving from fine-lined drawings and faceted landscapes towards an abstract formal language that explored form in terms of light, shadow and reflection. His 'picture boxes', in which various elements manifested rhythmic and dynamic growth, explored the concept of painting as object. He began to use the techniques of folding and pleating (e.g. *Black Picture Surface with Three Folded Sections*, 1964; Esbjerg, Kstpav.), and his work was dominated by his interest in light and shadow.

Besides paintings, Aagaard Andersen produced a number of sculptures, for example the abstract steel work *Interferences* (1972) for the platform of the railway station at Fredericia. He also executed decorative projects for buildings, for example the Koncerthus in Odense (1982), for which he produced a colossal copper sculpture in the foyer, 20 black-and-white marble reliefs and an acoustic ceiling. He also illustrated books and designed textiles, furniture and glass, and wrote many articles on art.

BIBLIOGRAPHY

Aagaard Andersen (exh. cat., Lyngby, Sophienholm; Århus, Kstmus.; 1977)

Thorsen and Mollerup: *Aagaard Andersen* (Copenhagen, 1985) [contains several articles by Aagaard Andersen]

J. J. Thorsen: 'Aagaard Andersen dans l'Art International: Aagaard le novateur', *ICSAC Cah.*, 5 (1986), pp. 49–52

——: *Modernisme i Dansk Malerkunst*, ii (Copenhagen, 1987), pp. 185–97

RIGMOR LOVRING

Aalto, (Hugo) Alvar (Henrik) (*b* Kuortane, 3 Feb 1898; *d* Helsinki, 11 May 1976). Finnish architect and designer. His success as an architect lay in the individual nature of his buildings, which were always designed with their surrounding environment in mind and with great attention to their practical demands. He never used forms that were merely aesthetic or conditioned by technical factors but looked to the more permanent models of nature and natural forms. He was not anti-technology but believed that technology could be humanized to become the servant of human beings and the promoter of cultural values. One of his important maxims was that architects have an absolutely clear mission: to humanize mechanical forms.

1. Training and early years, to 1927. 2. Influence of Rationalism, 1927–32. 3. International recognition, 1933–49. 4. Later years: the 1950s and after. 5. Influence.

1. TRAINING AND EARLY YEARS, TO 1927. His father was a government surveyor working in the lake district of central Finland and became a counterforce to his son's

strong artistic calling. Instead of becoming a painter, which tempted him for a long time, Alvar chose the career of architect as a possible compromise. He never became a planner dominated by technological thinking, however, but always gave his creations an artistic, humanistic character. He studied at the Technical College in Helsinki (1916–21), with one of the foremost proponents of National Romantic architecture, Armas Lindgren, as his principal teacher. This instilled in him not only the national fervour of Lindgren and his colleague Eliel Saarinen but also the tendency of the Art Nouveau school towards live, dynamic forms, and a striving to adapt architecture to the natural environment. During his period of study, however, another style became dominant, formally, in Scandinavia, namely a sophisticated neo-classicism associated with Scandinavia in the 18th century. The chief proponent of this school was the Swedish architect Gunnar Asplund, who soon became an admired model for Aalto and a close personal friend to him. In 1923 Aalto established a modest architects' office in the town where he grew up, Jyväskylä in central Finland. The buildings that he planned there bear the stamp not only of Asplund but also a powerful Italian influence, which he brought back with him from his first trip there in 1924. The early Renaissance of central and northern Italy, with masters such as Brunelleschi and urban environments such as Florence, Siena and Venice, remained a frequently visited source of inspiration for Aalto all his life. The most important works from Aalto's neo-classical period, which lasted until the summer of 1927, include the Workers' Club in Jyväskylä with the town's theatre of that time (planned in 1924), the Defence Corps building (1926) in the same town, the church in Muurame (1926), reminiscent of an Italian provincial church, and the Defence Corps building (1924) in Seinäjoki. He also took part in several of the architectural competitions that are common in Scandinavia and enable young, untried architects to receive important commissions. Though unsuccessful in the competition in 1923–4 for the Finnish Parliament building, in 1927 he won first prize in the competition for Viipuri City Library; this library was not, however, built until 1934–5, to entirely new plans bearing the stamp of Aalto's change-over to Rationalism. Another competition that Aalto won in 1927 was for a multi-purpose building, the Agricultural Co-operative building in Turku, which housed shops, offices, restaurants, hotels, private dwellings and, in particular, the town theatre. This great volume of building work caused Aalto to move his office to Turku in 1927.

2. INFLUENCE OF RATIONALISM, 1927–32. The new architecture launched from the beginning of the 1920s by Le Corbusier in France, the De Stijl group in the Netherlands and the Bauhaus in Germany reached Scandinavia in the late 1920s. However, in 1927 Aalto and his Swedish colleague Sven Markelius were drawn along with the new tendency, soon to be followed by Gunnar Asplund. Aalto's Agricultural Co-operative building shows the earliest signs of this innovation. In 1928 he was ready to design Finland's first completely Functionalist building, the newspaper group Turun Sanomat's building in Turku. It was completed in 1930 and fulfilled all of the criteria for a rationalist building that had been formulated by Le Corbusier, even though at that time Aalto knew Functionalism only through books and journals. With Erik Bryggman, he also planned the large open-air exhibition with pavilions, inspired by Soviet Constructivism and by modern typography, which was organized in the summer of 1929 in Turku to celebrate the 700th anniversary of the town. However, it was not so much the formal goals of the new architecture as its social goals to which Aalto and his Scandinavian colleagues were attracted. The Bauhaus and its programme of social reform, therefore, became a more important model for them to follow than the work of the French and Dutch Modernists.

In 1929 Aalto was invited to join CIAM. He went to Frankfurt to attend the second congress and established friendly relations, not only with older colleagues such as Le Corbusier and Walter Gropius but also with László Moholy-Nagy (who was the same age and who gave him important artistic inspiration) and with the group secretary Siegfried Giedion and the English architectural critic Philip Morton Shand who became a warm and influential supporter in the international arena. The same year Aalto made an international breakthrough when he won an architectural competition for the large tuberculosis sanatorium in Paimio outside Turku, a building commission that he completed in 1932 (*see* INTERNATIONAL STYLE, fig. 1). In it he broke away from the strict principles of early Rationalism, grouping the various building lengths in a non-geometrical, organic way and giving consideration more to the psychological needs of the users than to the functional aspects and technical and constructional factors. For the Paimio Sanatorium he designed buildings and all of the interior equipment, ranging from furniture and lamps to door handles, glassware and porcelain. His transformation of the newly invented tubular steel furniture into modern wooden furniture, manufactured by compression-moulding laminated wood, was particularly significant. In collaboration with master joiner Otto Korhonen (1884–1935) and his furniture factory in Turku, he had already created a chair in 1929, on which the press-moulded back and seat of plywood are supported by tubular-steel legs. For the sanatorium he invented a chair without any tubular steel at all, the so-called Paimio Chair, the back and seat of which are supported by a laminated wood frame that provides both arm supports and legs. This creation, perfect in form, competed successfully against Marcel Breuer's famous tubular steel construction, the so-called Wassili Chair, in realizing the dream of a modern lifestyle. The cantilevered tubular steel chair that the Bauhaus launched was also matched in 1932 by a corresponding Aalto-style product, the elegant armchair of curved wood, which was soon imitated by many other furniture designers but which remained most sought after in its original models with both hard or soft seat and high or low back. The basic design element for Aalto's standard furniture is the chair- or table-leg, which he jokingly called the 'column's little sister' and which was designed in three variants, the L-leg, the Y-leg and the X-leg.

3. INTERNATIONAL RECOGNITION, 1933–49. Aalto's international reputation was initially founded very much on the furniture that, in contrast to the buildings erected in Finland, could be exhibited to an international

public, for example at a show in London in 1933 that attracted attention, and at the Triennale exhibitions in Milan. In 1933 he moved to Helsinki, where two years later he erected his own residential and office building in the district of Munkkiniemi.

An important event for Aalto's career was meeting the factory-owning couple Maire and Harry Gullichsen in 1935. His friendship with them made possible the foundation of the Artek furniture design company, which began to sell Aalto's furniture in Finland and abroad and in general promoted a modern lifestyle, introducing modern international art into the country at the same time. Through Harry Gullichsen, Aalto soon received important large-scale planning and building commissions for Finnish industry. In 1937 he planned extensive residential areas and an industrial complex for the sulphate cellulose mill in Sunila near Kotka. Shortly afterwards he planned the paper mill and different types of dwellings for the industrial town of Inkeroinen. After World War II he was commissioned to build a complete industrial community on virgin land in Summa near Hamina on the south coast of Finland.

The commission of 1938 to design a private residence in Noormarkku near Pori for Maire and Harry Gullichsen was even more significant. The result, Villa Mairea, is one of the young Aalto's major works and shows his revolt against rigid Rationalism. On the one hand, he mixed folk traditions in Finnish building with the classical heritage of architectural history and with the formal concerns of Rationalism, producing a unique collage; on the other, he defined a new spatial concept that is related to both the forest as a felt environment and to the type of spatial openness that Cézanne introduced and that the Cubist painters developed further. Taking into account the experience of the materials' textures, the ceiling and floor of wood, walls of lime-washed tiles, slabs of natural stone and folkloric textiles, a better understanding is gained of the warm, harmonious atmosphere that characterizes this home, where everything is of exquisite quality without being ostentatious.

The first opportunity for an international public to become aware of Aalto's architecture was in 1937 at the Exposition Internationale des Arts et Techniques dans la Vie Moderne in Paris, where he was responsible for the Finnish Pavilion. Its ground-plan of structures freely grouped around an inner garden gave it a more open character than the Villa Mairea. The success of the pavilion led MOMA, New York, to invite Aalto to mount a one-man show there. In the following year (1939) he was given the responsibility for the Finnish Pavilion at the World's Fair in New York, although this involved fitting up a sector of the unit-hall shared by the small countries, in which Finland with her limited resources rented a stand. In the enclosed interior (see fig. 1) he created one of his most original works, raising a freely curving, forward-leaning 'auroral frontage' within the limited space, where the exhibits of Finland, a timber-exporting country, formed an assemblage. At both expositions Aalto also displayed the glassware he created during the 1930s, in particular the Savoy Vase with serpentine curved sides, all of which was influential on the international successes of Finnish arts and crafts during the post-war decades.

1. Alvar Aalto: interior of Finnish Pavilion, World's Fair, New York, 1939

In 1940 Aalto was appointed research professor in architecture at the Massachusetts Institute of Technology (MIT), Cambridge, but he managed to teach for only a short time in the USA before he was summoned back to his homeland. He was employed on the reconstruction of Finland's towns and cities after war damage. He had been occupied with urban and regional planning before World War II. Faced with the risk that reconstruction would be based, frighteningly, on a stereotyped technological standardization, he advocated the development of what he called 'flexible standardization'. It accepted large-scale industrialized building, since only this could remedy the housing shortage, but required the building elements to be made sufficiently flexible to be combined in innumerable different ways in accordance with the possibilities afforded by the environment and the individual users' needs.

In 1945 Aalto was commissioned to draw up a general plan for the province of Lappland and a new city plan for the totally destroyed provincial capital, Rovaniemi. His principles for urban and regional planning amounted to maintaining contact with nature and the countryside, favouring small-scale grouping of dwellings and, if possible, breaking down large industrial plants, office complexes, government departments and shopping centres into smaller interrelated units. For the new town of Imatra (also known as Vuoksenniska), which was founded after the cession of areas of land to the USSR, he drew up a general plan (1947–53; published in book form in 1957) with very sparse grouping of buildings. (For the same town he later, in 1955, designed one of his most notable works, the church of the Three Crosses, assymetrical and with variable dimensions.)

2. Alvar Aalto: town hall, Säynätsalo, 1949–52; view across the elevated courtyard

In 1946 Aalto resumed his teaching at MIT but confined his stays there to three or four months in a year. His most important contribution there was the building of Baker House Dormitory (1947–9). This building of red tiles, with its huge serpentine façade facing the river and steps rising in cascade form on the inner frontage, is the realization of Aalto's dream of flexible standardization, based on nature's principle of individualization: all 260 of the students' rooms with a view over the river have different shapes and therefore varied interior fixtures and furniture. However, the death of his wife and collaborator of many years, Aino Aalto (1894–1949), who devoted herself especially to tasks of interior equipment in conjunction with the couple's buildings, caused him deep depression, leading him to abandon all his work in the USA.

4. LATER YEARS: THE 1950S AND AFTER. The 1950s became a great, vital creative period in Aalto's life after he met the young architect Elissa Mäkiniemi (*b* 1922), his wife from 1952. The important monumental buildings that he was commissioned to design include the Kansaneläkelatos (National Pensions Insurance Institute) in Helsinki and the new buildings of the Technical College in Otaniemi outside Helsinki. These were two major tasks, which occupied him for a long time, and they were executed during 1952–6 and 1962–8 respectively. In both of them he used richly textured red tiles for the façades. In order to be able to build even more curved tile surfaces than in Baker House and in the main building of the Technical College in Otaniemi, he invented a triangular tile, which in 1955–8 enabled him to build the auditorium for Helsinki's House of Culture in the form of a gently rounded shell. In addition, the university in Jyväskylä (1951–6), with several buildings grouped around a campus, uses red tile-surfaces and offers various free-form interiors with the unlimited space characteristic of Aalto's work.

A key work of Aalto's architecture of the 1950s is the small civic centre for the industrial town of Säynätsalo outside Jyväskylä, where the moderate scale and grouping of the cubic structures around a small inner courtyard are reminiscent of Italian small towns such as San Gimignano. The synthesis between old building traditions of the Mediterranean countries and an uncompromising Modernism also characterizes the two buildings that Aalto built for himself in the 1950s, namely his summer holiday residence and studio in the wilderness of the island of Muuratsalo in the lake district of central Finland, rising like a Byzantine monastery on the rock-strewn shore, and his new office building in Munkkiniemi outside Helsinki, which combines the form of an ancient theatre auditorium with modern office premises.

It was during the 1950s that Aalto really began to receive commissions outside Finland. In 1953 he won the competition for the Vogelweidplatz sports hall in Vienna, with what was technically a very daring (and therefore unexecuted) project. In 1955 he and a dozen of the world's best-known architects were each invited to design a block of flats in the Hansaviertel in Berlin. When the project was formally opened in 1957 as the *Interbauausstellung*, Aalto's building was one of those that received most attention and praise. In 1959 he won the competition for an opera house in Essen, in which he combined his shell-like, asymmetrical auditorium, known from Helsinki's House of Culture, with a series of three-tiered, serpentine balconies that are mirrored in the tall foyer situated behind them. The opera house was eventually built between 1981 and 1988, but Aalto had already used its basic shape in his project for Helsinki's Finlandiatalo, which was completed in 1971. Between 1958 and 1962 he built a marble-clad, fan-shaped house of culture in Wolfsburg in Germany, where he also erected a church between 1960 and 1963. His Neue Vahr tower block in Bremen, fan-shaped in plan, was completed in 1962. Several of Aalto's best projects remained unrealized unfortunately, including the competition design of 1958 for a town hall in Kiruna in Sweden, which won first prize; his winning proposal from the same year for a museum of art in Ålborg, Denmark, was built ten years later, as was his church in Detmerode (1963–9), Germany.

In 1956 Aalto planned a very lavishly endowed residence in the village of Bazoches-sur-Guyonne outside Paris for the art dealer Louis Carré. The building's sloping roof covered with Normandy slate repeats the rhythm of the surrounding landscape, while every detail of the interior, which offers rooms of varying height, is specially designed. Nordens hus (1964–9) in Reykjavik, Iceland, can also be counted among Aalto's important works abroad. Its outline repeats the rhythm of the surrounding mountain ridges, while the interior, with a library and various assembly rooms, has a cosy, intimate character. For the Mount Angels Monastery in Oregon, USA, he designed in 1964 a small library in the form of a sloping theatre auditorium (completed 1968), and in the mountain village of Riola, south of Bologna in Italy, a church based on his designs, with stepped dormer windows and asymmetrical in plan, was built between 1975 and 1980.

One of Aalto's lasting ambitions was to build whole city centres with several public buildings grouped around squares. He planned such centres both for the place where he grew up, Jyväskylä, for Helsinki and for many other towns in Finland and abroad. In many instances he was commissioned to execute only a part of these projects: the town hall in Säynätsalo (1949–52; see fig. 2); a theatre

(1964–86) and a police station (1967–70) in Jyväskylä; the magnificent Finlandiatalo and its conference wing (1962–76) in Helsinki. In only two cases was Aalto's centre project fully implemented. Possibly Aalto's most beautiful library was erected around the central square of Rovaniemi between 1961 and 1966, with a crystal-like exterior and a bookpit inside. From 1969 to 1971 the theatre and radio building Lapponia was added, and from 1986 to 1988 the town hall, designed in 1963. However, the most richly endowed centre by Aalto was built in the town of Seinäjoki in central Finland, where the church (1951–60) was accompanied by a town hall (1958–62), a library (1960–65) and a theatre (1961–87), all of them grouped around a series of open spaces, testifying to the fact that Aalto welcomed the principle in the urban environment of unlimited space, more like the countryside than the city or town.

5. Influence. Aalto was an outgoing and spontaneous person with humour, charm and a great gift for relating to people, which contributed greatly towards his successes. Despite his bohemian living habits, lack of interest in financial gain and not very efficiently organized architect's bureau, during his career he managed to execute *c.* 1000 projects, always working with uninhibited pleasure and a wealth of ideas. Over the years he accepted more than 300 young architects from both Finland and abroad (particularly Switzerland, Italy, Scandinavia and the USA) as assistants for short or long periods of time. With his pronounced scepticism of theorizing, he refrained from writing books on architecture and from academic lecturing; however, he loved to converse about architectural matters that were at the same time social and cultural. He thought that the practical work in his office—which he called his 'academy'—was the best way to pass on professional knowledge: that is to say, a teaching method corresponding to what Renaissance painters and architects applied in their workshops where they were surrounded by apprentices and assistants.

BIBLIOGRAPHY

S. Giedion: *Space, Time and Architecture* (Cambridge, MA, 1944, rev. 3/1954), pp. 565–604
B. Zevi: *Storia dell'architettura moderna* (Turin, 1950), pp. 283–307
Archit. Aujourd'hui, xxix (1950) [special issue on Aalto]
E. Neuenschwander and C. Neuenschwander: *Finische Bauten: Atelier Alvar Aalto, 1950–51* (Zurich, 1954)
F. Gutheim: *Alvar Aalto*, Masters of World Architecture (New York and London, 1960)
Arquitectura [Madrid], ii (1960) [special issue on Aalto]
Quad. Arquit., xxxix (1960) [special issue on Aalto]
K. Fleig, ed.: *Alvar Aalto*, 3 vols (Zurich, 1963–78)
L. Mosso: *L'opera di Alvar Aalto* (Milan, 1965)
R. Venturi: *Complexity and Contradiction in Architecture* (New York, 1966)
Arkitekten [Stockholm], iv (1969) [special issue on Aalto]
B. Hoesli, ed.: *Alvar Aalto Synopsis: Painting Architecture Sculpture* (Zurich, 1970) [incl. writings, chronological list of works and bibliog., richly illus.; in Fr., Ger. and Eng.]
G. Baird: *Alvar Aalto* (New York, 1971) [photographs by Y. Futugawa]
G. Schildt, ed.: *Alvar Aalto luonnoksia* [Alvar Aalto sketches] (Helsinki, 1972; Eng. trans., 1978) [contains a selection of Aalto's articles and lectures]
C. Jencks: *Modern Movements in Architecture* (New York, 1973), pp. 167–83
C. Cresti: *Alvar Aalto*, Maestri del novecento, 25 (Florence, 1975; Eng. and Sp. trans., 1976)
Arkkitehti/Arkitekten, vii–viii (1976) [memorial issue on Aalto]
Archit. Aujourd'hui, cxci (1977) [special issue on Aalto]
Parametro, lxii (1977)
Prog. Archit., iv (1977) [special issue on Aalto]
Space Des., i–ii (1977) [special issue on Aalto]
A. Gozak: *Arhitektura i gumanizm* [Architecture and humanism] (Moscow, 1978)
P. D. Pearson: *Alvar Aalto and the International Style* (New York, 1978)
B. Zevi: *The Modern Language of Architecture* (Seattle, 1978)
Alvar Aalto, Architectural Monographs and Academy Editions, 4 (London, 1978) [texts by D. Porphyrios and R. L. Heinonen]
Alvar Aalto, 1898–1976 (exh. cat., ed. A. Ruusuvuori; Helsinki, Mus. Fin. Archit., 1978) [incl. writings]
Archit. Des., xii (1979) [special issue on Aalto]
K. Frampton: *Modern Architecture: A Critical History* (New York, 1980), pp. 192–202
L. Rubino: *Aino e Alvar Aalto: Tutto il disegno* (Rome, 1980)
W. Blaser: *Il design di Alvar Aalto* (Milan, 1981)
D. Porphyrios: *Sources of Modern Eclecticism: Studies on Alvar Aalto* (London, 1982)
G. Schildt: *Det vita bordet: Alvar Aaltos ungdom och grundlaggande konstnarliga ideer* (Helsinki, 1982); Eng. trans. as *Alvar Aalto: The Early Years* (New York, 1984) [biog. up to 1927]
M. Quantrill: *Alvar Aalto: A Critical Study* (London, 1983)
A & U, v (1983) [special issue on Aalto]
W. C. Miller: *Alvar Aalto: An Annotated Bibliography* (New York, 1984)
J. Pallasmaa, ed.: *Alvar Aalto Furniture*, Helsinki, Mus. Fin. Archit. cat. (Helsinki, 1984)
G. Schildt: *Moderna tider* (Helsinki, 1985); Eng. trans. as *Alvar Aalto: The Decisive Years* (New York, 1986) [biog. 1927–39]
——: *Den mänshliga fahtorn* (Helsinki, 1990); Eng. trans. as *Alvar Aalto: The Mature Years* (New York, 1991) [biog. 1940–76]
——: *Alvar Aalto: The Complete Catalogue of Architecture, Design and Art* (London and New York, 1994)

GÖRAN SCHILDT

Aaltonen, Wäinö (Waldemar) (*b* Marttila [Swed. St Mårtens], 8 March 1894; *d* Helsinki, 30 May 1966). Finnish sculptor and painter. He was the most significant sculptor of the early decades of Finnish independence (after 1917). His style combined classical tranquillity with a modern sensitivity and disclosed the beauty of granite as a sculptural material. He studied painting at the School of Drawing of the Turku Art Association between 1910 and 1915 but on graduation began to practise moulding techniques and to teach himself stone sculpting. In 1916 his firm instincts and talent for monumental sculpture were remarked on at a general exhibition. His *Granite Boy* (1917–20; Helsinki, Athenaeum A. Mus.) is one of the masterpieces of his youth, the timid austerity of the child's figure conveying an Egyptian quality. The marble sculptures *Little Wader* (1917–22; priv. col., see Okkonen, 1926) and *Wader* (1924; Helsinki, Athenaeum A. Mus.) are both good examples of Aaltonen's tonal carving. His main concerns were light and shadow and the atmosphere they create around the sculpture. In 1923 he made his first trip abroad, to Rome, followed by trips to France and England in 1925. In 1924 he was commissioned by the State to produce the statue of *Paavo Nurmi Running* (1925), although it was not erected outdoors until the 1950s (versions in Turku, outside the Olympic Stadium in Helsinki, Lausanne (1994)). As early as 1926 the influential critic Onni Okkonen published a book about Aaltonen's art that proposed his status as one of Finland's most important living artists.

The 1920s were Aaltonen's most effective period of creativity. Influenced by both Classical and modernist ideas, he captured incorporeality in gilded wooden sculptures such as *Girl's Head* (1925; Helsinki, Athenaeum A. Mus.) and experimented with Cubism, as in *The Dancer*

(1928; Turku, Aaltonen Mus.) and *Cubist Aleksis Kivi, Writer* (1927; Turku, Aaltonen Mus.). The memorial to Aleksis Kivi, the *Poet and his Genius* (1926–8; Tampere, Library Park), which symbolically depicts the poet's inspiration, also signified a breakthrough in Aaltonen's career. At this time he began to design Cubist book covers, as well as the sets for the avant-garde plays of Hagar Olsson. In exhibitions at that time he was noted for his sensuous interpretations in stone.

In the 1930s Aaltonen produced the figures for the Assembly Hall of the Parliament in Helsinki, the statue of *Aleksis Kivi* (1930–9; Helsinki, Railway Station Square) and the marble relief in Helsinki University, the *Goddess of Liberty Crowning Youth* (1938–40; damaged 1944). These, together with his many sculpted heads, such as that of *Jean Sibelius* (1935; Helsinki, Athenaeum A. Mus), strengthened Aaltonen's position as the creator of a national style of classicism. After the war, Aaltonen produced a number of memorials. The granite memorial to the war heroes in Lahti, entitled *Peace* (1950–52), conveys a tranquil nobility, and among the best works of his later period is the bronze statue of two horsemen *Establishing Friendship* (1951; Turku, Aninkainen Square). Before his death he produced a few abstract pieces, of which *Genius montanus I* (1961) was placed over his grave in the Maaria Cemetery, near Turku. Before World War II Aaltonen also painted a great deal, especially figure studies (e.g. *In the Concert*, 1926; priv. col., see 1988 exh. cat., p. 31). Apart from a few Cubist collages, he rarely attained the same standard as in his sculpture. His work covered a broad range, from medals to official portraits of presidents, book covers and theatre sets, which bears witness to his faith in his wide creative ability, apparently reinforced by the deafness he suffered from his youth. He was appointed a member of the Finnish Academy in 1948, and in 1967 the Wäinö Aaltonen Museum opened in Turku (*see* TURKU, §2).

BIBLIOGRAPHY

O. Okkonen: *Wäinö Aaltonen, 1915–1925: Tutkielma* [Wäinö Aaltonen, 1915–1925: a study] (Porvoo, 1926)
——: *Wäinö Aaltonen* (Porvoo, 1945)
Börje Sandberg, ed.: *Wäinö Aaltonen* (Helsinki, 1948)
G. Schildt: *Modern Finnish Sculpture* (New York, 1970)
L. Ahtola-Moorhouse: 'Review of Finnish Sculpture, 1910–80', *Suomalaista veistotaidetta—Finnish Sculpture*, The Association of Finnish Sculptors (Helsinki, 1980)
Wäinö Aaltonen vareissä: Maalauksia ja piirustuksia / Wäinö Aaltonen i färg: Målningar och teckningar [Wäinö Aaltonen in colour: paintings and drawings] (exh. cat., Helsinki, Acad. F.A., 1988)
Wäinö Aaltonen, 1894–1966 (exh. cat., ed. H. Pfäffli; Turku, Wäinö Aaltonen Mus., 1994)

LEENA AHTOLA-MOORHOUSE

Aarschot, Dukes of. *See* CRÖY, DE.

Aarts, Johannes Josephus (*b* The Hague, 18 Aug 1871; *d* Amsterdam, 19 Oct 1934). Dutch printmaker and painter. He trained at the Academie voor Beeldende Kunsten in The Hague, where he subsequently taught graphic art (1893–1911). In 1911 he succeeded Pieter Dupont as professor in graphics at the Rijksakademie in Amsterdam under the directorship of Antoon Derkinderen. In the early years of his career Aarts produced some paintings using the pointillist technique, mostly landscapes (The Hague, Gemeentemus.); he also carved some sculptures in wood. He is, however, best known for his graphic work. In technique and subject-matter, his prints have a great deal in common with those of Dupont. As the latter's successor he devoted himself to the revival of engraving, which his predecessor had reintroduced; his own experiments in this medium (in particular his scenes with diggers and beggars, all *c.* 1900) are considered milestones in early 20th-century Dutch printmaking. He also applied his skills to etching, lithography, woodcutting and wood-engraving; of the latter his *Dance of Death* series (*c.* 1915–20) is particularly well known. His subject-matter varies, from scenes from the lives of ordinary people to themes from literature and the Bible. An almost complete collection of his prints is housed in the Rijksmuseum in Amsterdam, and the Gemeentemuseum in The Hague holds some of his paintings.

BIBLIOGRAPHY

H. de Boer: 'J. J. Aarts', *Elsevier's Geillus. Mdschr.*, xvii (1907), pp. 34, 217–30 [with illus.]
Johannes Joseph Aarts (exh. cat., intro. G. Knuttel Willemszoon; The Hague, Gemeentemus., 1936)
A. J. Vernoorn: *Nederlandse prentkunst, 1840–1940* (Lochem, 1983), pp. 41, 70, 93 [with illus.]
M. Kersten: *De Nederlandse kopergravure, 1900–1975* (The Hague, 1989), pp. 26–33, 91–5 [with illus.]

JAN JAAP HEIJ

Aas, Nils (Sigurd) (*b* Inderøy, Nord-Trøndelag, 21 April 1933). Norwegian sculptor, designer and medallist. He became familiar with handicraft in his father's furniture workshop. In 1954 he began five years' study as a commercial artist at the Håndverks- og Kunstindustriskole in Oslo and from 1957 to 1963 he worked as an illustrator for a newspaper. He studied at the Kunstakademi in Oslo from 1959 to 1962 under the sculptor Per Palle Storm (1910–94) who advocated naturalism in sculpture. As an assistant to Arnold Haukeland from 1961 to 1964, Aas lost his apprehension of the untried and cultivated his sense of daring, as he gained experience with welding techniques. Highly imaginative and versatile, Aas worked in both abstract and figurative modes and is reckoned one of the foremost sculptors in Norway; in 1990 he was honoured with St Olav.

Aas's first sculpture was an equestrian monument in snow, made in Inderøy while he was a schoolboy. His first public project was the abstract steel figure *Bird* (1966–7), which is outside the Symra Cinema in Lambertseter, Oslo. The cinema and film suggested to Aas the subjects of the bird and flight. The sculpture, made of steel plates, stands on a concrete base 4 m high, the cinema's large brick wall forming a background. In 1967 he won the competition for a monument in Oslo to *King Haakon VII* (7 June Square). His unorthodox monumental bronze (h. *c.* 4.5 m including base, unveiled 1972) marked an artistic breakthrough for Aas. The King is shown standing, in a long coat, with his head raised and his right arm by his side: he holds his military cap in his left arm, bent in front of his breast. Although the sculpture was criticized for its non-militaristic posture, Aas wanted to convey the King's humility in the face of the people he was to serve. The tall, slender figure is simplified to grand lines of pivoting form, which convey the King's strong and steadfast character. At the same time, the sculpture reveals Aas's interest in the work of Alberto Giacometti. Aas was also influenced by the work of Constantin Brancusi, Giacomo Manzù, Marino Marini and Henry Moore.

Aas worked with a variety of materials and forms. In 1971 his sculpture *Beacon* was erected on Mølleråsen, north of Sandefjord. A stylized steel bird 3.5 m high on top of a 10 m base, it stands like a landmark on an elegantly formed column in light concrete. Aas got the idea for the wall sculpture *Northern light* (5×16.5 m, 1976–8) while sitting and twisting matchsticks between his fingers. It hangs in the Hall of the Council of Ministers in the Palais du Conseil de L'Europe in Strasbourg and consists of 100 pieces of Norwegian laminated spruce, each 150×200 mm in thickness. In 1981 a large granite monument to *Henrik Ibsen* (h. 3.6 m) was erected in Teaterparken (the theatre park) in Bergen. A life-size plaster model was made before the stone was cut; Aas worked on the granite and undertook the final polishing of this unorthodox sculpture, which was installed in three sections. Aas made Ibsen as he understood him to have been: a reserved, sensitive and timid person, short and stocky. It was particularly important for him to convey Ibsen's roles as a prophet and castigator of society. The character of the stone is thus brought forth in this highly stylized figure. A pen held in one lowered arm indicates the activity of the author. Aas has also made highly original sculptures in cut paper, steel thread or wood.

Aas began modelling busts in 1963. Bronze portraits of the author *Johan Borgen* (1965; Oslo, N.G.) and the government minister *Trygve Bratteli* (1982; Oslo, Norske Arbeiderparti) show his firm grasp of characterization. The surface planes have clear structures and show the traces of his work with tools and clay. A sculpture of Marilyn Monroe (1994) is situated in Haugesund. He is also internationally known for his engraved and cast commemorative medallions and in 1994 designed two Norwegian coins, the 10 and 20 kroner.

BIBLIOGRAPHY

Meissner; *NKL*

Fédération internationale de la médaille (exh. cats, Helsinki, 1973; Kraków, 1975; Budapest, 1977; Lisbon, 1979; Florence, 1983)

E. Dæhlin: 'Nils Aas', *Kst & Kult.*, iii/4 (1980), pp. 582–6

K. Berg and others, eds: *Inn i en ny tid* [Into a new era], vii of *Norges kunsthistorie* (Oslo, 1981–3), pp. 317, 323–7

B. Rostad: *Nils Aas: Et billedhuggerportrett* [Nils Aas: portrait of a sculptor] (Oslo, 1987)

INGEBORG WIKBORG

A(rt and) A(rchitecture) T(hesaurus). Ongoing American project, belonging to the Getty Art History Information Program (AHIP), intended as the first comprehensive thesaurus for the fields of art and architecture. Its aims are to promote consistency and compatibility among art-historical databases by providing a standardized, controlled vocabulary for use in bibliographic and visual databases and in the documentation of object collections. The AAT's terminology, arranged both alphabetically and hierarchically by concept, reflects the 'common usage' of scholars and cataloguers. Advisory boards composed of experts in the fields of architecture, decorative and fine arts, along with archivists and information managers in these fields, have reviewed and approved terminology for inclusion in the thesaurus.

The AAT was founded by Dora Crouch, Pat Molholt (*b* 19 Oct 1943) and Toni Petersen (*b* 13 May 1933) and was housed first at Rensselaer Polytechnic Institute in Troy, NY, and then at Bennington College in Bennington, VT. Initial work (1980–83) was funded by the Council on Library Resources, the National Endowment for the Humanities, the Andrew W. Mellon Foundation and the J. Paul Getty Trust. In 1983 the AAT became an AHIP project. In 1986 it moved to Williamstown, MA, under the directorship of Toni Petersen. The first edition of the AAT, published in 1990 by Oxford University Press in three volumes, received an award from the Association of American Publishers. The AAT was mounted as an online authority reference tool in the Research Libraries Information Network (RLIN) of the Research Libraries Group in 1990. An electronic edition on diskette, with accompanying browsing tool for use with personal computers, was developed in 1992; the complete second edition, in print and electronic form, was published in 1994 by Oxford University Press.

TONI PETERSEN

Abacco, Antonio. *See* LABACCO, ANTONIO.

Abacus. Uppermost element of a capital on a column or pilaster (*see* GREECE, ANCIENT, fig. 9n; ORDERS, ARCHITECTURAL, fig. 1xii). On the Doric, Ionic and Tuscan orders of architecture it is square in plan, but on the Corinthian each face is convex.

Abada, Tell. *See under* HAMRIN REGION.

Abadie, Paul (*b* Paris, 9 Nov 1812; *d* Chatou, 2 Aug 1884). French architect and restorer. He was the son of a Neo-classical architect of the same name (1783–1868), who was a pupil of Charles Percier and architect to the département of Charente. The younger Paul Abadie began studying architecture in 1832 by joining the atelier of Achille Leclère and then entered the Ecole des Beaux-Arts in 1835. While he was following this classical training, he participated in the rediscovery of the Middle Ages by going on archaeological trips and then, from 1844, in his capacity as attaché to the *Commission des Monuments Historiques*. He undertook his first restoration work at Notre-Dame de Paris, under the direction of Jean-Baptiste-Antoine Lassus and Viollet-le-Duc. Abadie was appointed deputy inspector at Notre-Dame in 1845, and in 1848, when the department responsible for diocesan buildings was created, he was appointed architect to the dioceses of Périgueux, Angoulême and Cahors. He subsequently completed about 40 restoration projects, mainly on Romanesque churches in Charente, in the Dordogne and the Gironde, and as a diocesan architect he was put in charge of two large cathedrals in his district: St Pierre d'Angoulême and St Front de Périgueux. In the former he undertook a huge programme of 'completion', returning to a stylistic unity that was in line with current episcopal policy (*see* ARCHITECTURAL CONSERVATION AND RESTORATION, fig. 2). He worked there from 1849 to 1880, rebuilding the upper levels of the north tower, restoring the central portal on the façade and building superstructures to replace those of the 16th century. He also undertook considerable restoration work on the rest of the building, suppressing post-Romanesque additions and constructing a new dome at the transept crossing. Abadie worked on St-Front de Périgueux from 1851 until his death. The project involved a difficult underpinning of the building (south wing, 1852–4), but work progressed rapidly towards an almost complete reconstruction that rationalized the architectural outline. In Bordeaux, where Abadie was appointed diocesan architect for the cathedral in 1862, he again took part in a sizeable programme of restoration work that was designed to symbolize the revival of Catholicism in the diocese. This included the restoration of the bell-tower of St Michel (1857–69) and the much-debated restoration of the façade of Sainte Croix (1859–65).

While he was carrying out this restoration work, Abadie planned or built around 40 new buildings, most of which were religious, including in Angoulême, the churches of St Martial (1849–56) and St Ausone (1856–68); in the Dordogne, the churches of Notre-Dame de Bergerac (1851–66), St Georges de Périgueux (1852–70) and Villefranche-de-Périgord (1855–70); and in Bordeaux, Ste Marie à La Bastide (1860–86) and St Ferdinand (1862–7). The church of St Martial in Angoulême is one of the first examples of 'archaeological' neo-Romanesque, while Notre-Dame de Bergerac is based on 13th-century Gothic examples and was inspired by a preceding project by Viollet-le-Duc. He also built a few residential properties (notably in the Rue Paul-Abadie in Angoulême) and several civic edifices. The most significant of the latter is Angoulême Town Hall (1854–69), where he used the remains of a former château and made stylistic reference to the town halls in medieval communes.

In 1874 Abadie won the competition to build the Eglise du Vœu National au Sacré-Coeur, the celebrated basilica in Montmartre, Paris. This was to be erected to fulfil a vow that had been made at the time of France's defeat in the Franco-Prussian war of 1870–71. Abadie's project, which has been rather hurriedly described as Romanesque Byzantine, represents, in the reworking of the Romanesque style of south-west France, the outcome of formal research by the restorer and the builder. Work began in 1875, the year in which Abadie was elected to the Institut de France. The basilica was not completed until around 1919, long after the architect's death, with modifications to the original plan that varied in significance according to the personalities of his successors, who included Honoré Daumet, Jean Charles Laisné, H.-P.-M. Rauline (*b* 1848), L. Magne (1849–1916) and L.-J. Hulot (1871–1959). With this monument, Abadie gave the Romanesque Revival its most notable expression and gave a decisive victory to the 'diocésains', a group composed mostly of rationalists that grew up under the influence of Viollet-le-Duc. Abadie was less militant and less of a theoretician than Viollet-le-Duc, however, and he produced at Montmartre and elsewhere a more equivocal achitecture that reflected his training, in which the rediscovery of the Middle Ages and the academic tradition existed side by side.

BIBLIOGRAPHY

C. Laroche: 'L'Oeuvre d'architecture de Paul Abadie (1812–1884): Situation culturelle et inventaire raisonné', *Bull. Soc. Hist. A. Fr.* (1981), pp. 219–38

Entre archéologie et modernité: Paul Abadie architecte, 1812–1884 (exh. cat., ed. C. Laroche; Angoulême, Mus. Mun., 1984)

Paul Abadie, architecte, 1812–1884 (exh. cat., ed. C. Laroche; Paris, Mus. Mnmts Fr., 1988)

J. Benoist: *Le Sacré-Coeur de Montmartre de 1870 à nos jours*, 2 vols (Paris, 1992)

CLAUDE LAROCHE

Abaj Takalik. Pre-Columbian MAYA site in Retalhuleu, in the Highland Maya region, near the Pacific coast of Guatemala. It is best known for its monumental stone sculptures, some of which were recorded in the 19th century. The site lies partly on the Finca San Isidro Piedra Parada, and it was known by this name when Eric Thompson published a description of some of the sculpture in 1943. 'Abaj Takalik' ('standing stone') is a translation of 'Piedra Parada' into Quiché Maya. It was occupied during the Pre-Classic (*c.* 2000 BC–*c.* AD 250) and Classic (*c.* AD 250–*c.* 900) periods. The site lies on a fertile slope between the mountains and the sea; there are remains of steep, manmade earthen terraces on which its structures were built. The earth removed to create the terraces may have been used to construct the various mounds at Abaj Takalik, a number of which were faced with stone cobbles. Adobe bricks were also used, and local volcanic material provided flooring. The site was covered in 1902 by volcanic ash, and much of the area is now used for growing coffee.

Abaj Takalik produced truly monumental stone sculptures, weighing between one and nearly twenty tons. Several hundred monuments, both plain and worked, and mostly of the abundant local andesite, are known. They include petroglyphs, a large number of boulder sculptures, 'potbelly' figures, sculptures in the round, silhouettes, and altars and stelae carved in low relief, the last two types often found in association. They vary greatly in their quality and degree of preservation. Style and iconography are also varied. Some monuments are finely carved with elaborate reliefs of human figures with symbolic paraphernalia, while others are simply incised boulders. Some of the sculptural styles and motifs are closely related to the late Olmec sculpture of the Mexican Gulf Coast (*see* MESOAMERICA, PRE-COLUMBIAN, §IV, 2(i)) and of CHALCATZINGO in central Mexico. During the Late Pre-Classic period (*c.* 300 BC–*c.* AD 250), Abaj Takalik was one of the most important centres in the Pacific region, together with KAMINALJUYÚ and IZAPA, sites with which its sculpture shows affinity. During the Early Classic period (*c.* AD 250–*c.* 600) the Abaj Takalik style closely resembled that of nearby SANTA LUCÍA COTZUMALHUAPA. Abaj Takalik Stele 2 has one of the earliest known dates of the Maya Long Count calendar (*see* MESOAMERICA, PRE-COLUMBIAN, §II), corresponding to the last half of the 1st century BC. The sculpture depicts two standing figures with feather headdresses facing a column of hieroglyphs. A similar composition appears on Stele 5, which has an inscription corresponding to AD 126. Hieroglyphs also appear on Stele 1 and on Altar 12.

There has been a degree of controversy over the dating of some Abaj Takalik sculptures. The resetting of some of the monuments during the Late Classic period (*c.* AD 600–*c.* 900) complicates the issue. John A. Graham of the University of California, Berkeley, who worked at the site from 1976, believed that the boulder and 'potbelly' sculptures of Abaj Takalik precede those of the Early Pre-Classic period (*c.* 2000–*c.* 1000 BC) OLMEC sites of the Gulf Coast; others consider that they belong to the Middle Pre-Classic period (*c.* 1000–*c.* 300 BC) or later.

BIBLIOGRAPHY

J. E. S. Thompson: *Some Sculptures from Southeastern Cevetzaltenango, Guatemala*, Notes on Middle American Archaeology and Ethnology, xvii, Carnegie Institution of Washington, DC, Division of Historical Research (Cambridge, MA, 1943), pp. 100–12

S. W. Miles: 'Sculpture of the Guatemala–Chiapas Highlands and Pacific Slopes, and Associated Hieroglyphs', *Hb. Mid. Amer. Ind.*, ii (1965), pp. 237–75

J. A. Graham, R. F. Heizer and E. M. Shook: 'Abaj Takalik 1976', *Studies in Ancient Mesoamerica*, iii, ed. J. A. Graham (Berkeley, 1978), pp. 85–110

J. A. Graham: 'Antecedents of Olmec Sculpture at Abaj Takalik', *Pre-Columbian Art History*, ed. A. Cordy-Collins (Palo Alto, 1982), pp. 7–22

L. A. Parsons: *The Origins of Maya Art*, Studies in Pre-Columbian Art and Archaeology, xxviii (Washington, DC, 1986)

J. A. Graham and L. Benson: 'Escultura olmeca y maya sobre canto in Abaj Takalik', *Arqueólogia*, iii (1990), pp. 77–84

ELIZABETH P. BENSON

Abakanowicz, Magdalena (*b* Felenty, nr Warsaw, 1930). Polish textile artist. She studied at the College of Fine Arts, Sopot, and graduated in 1955 from the Academy of Fine Arts, Warsaw. At the beginning of her career she was interested in drawing, painting and sculpture, but after 1960 she concentrated on textile arts in the broad sense of the term. Breaking with tradition, she initiated bold experiments with fibre and fabric. Her work contributed to the revolutionary textile movement known as FIBRE ART and finally entered the domain of modern sculpture.

Abakanowicz's début, with a composition of forms made of white fabrics, was in 1962 at the first Biennale Internationale de la Tapisserie in Lausanne. At that time she also experimented with tapestry, giving it three-dimensional relief by introducing non-woven shapes. In the late 1960s her development of three-dimensional textiles was fully realized in her 'abakans' (*see* TAPESTRY, fig. 15). These took various forms—winged, open or round—and were red, orange or white. She also created fifteen heavy, monolithic 'black forms' and three large 'black garments'. In 1971 she entwined Edinburgh Cathedral with rope, and the following year she repeated this happening with a fountain in Bordeaux. Ropes became a favourite material in various exhibition compositions. In the 1970s she experimented further with textile sculpture, using burlap, string and cotton gauze. She started with the *Deviations* series, followed by the *Alterations* series, featuring 'faces' and 'schizophrenic heads'. After this period her work concentrated on fragmented human figures (heads without trunks, bodies without heads, torsos without legs) placed singly or in large groups. The human body as a structure became her chief interest, and for her research she visited scientific laboratories and dissecting rooms, consulted the most advanced scientists and studied slides of the brain. She also travelled to Arizona for discussions with Paolo Soleri and to New Guinea to see the initiation ceremonies. Between 1976 and 1980 she created the *Human Backs* series of 80 figures, followed by the *Embryology* series (1980; oval forms made of linen, rags and cord) and the *Syndromes* series (16 brains made of clay). She made multiple casts of real human beings and individualized each form with a particular texture and pattern. The creases, ridges and veins of the resin-hardened fibre surface imitate organic characteristics, recalling the earth's rough surface or the cellular composition of human skin. The *Androgyn* series (1985) features torsos perched on low stretchers of wooden logs, which fill in for the missing legs; through such provocative images she expressed her view of the physical and spiritual condition of mankind. The *Catharsis* series (1986; 33 figures, each *c.* 3 m tall), made for the Fondazione Giuliano Gori, Florence, progressed a stage further and was cast in bronze.

Abakanowicz had more than 40 one-woman exhibitions all over the world, and her work is in many international museums, as well as in Poland (Warsaw, N. Mus.; Łódź, Cent. Mus. Textiles; Łódź, Mus. A.). In 1965 she was made a professor at the Stage College of Fine Arts, Poznań.

BIBLIOGRAPHY

Contemp. Artists

Polska tkanina awangardowa [Modern Polish art textiles] (exh. cat. by K. Kondratiuk, Poznań, 1969)

M. Constantine and J. L. Larsen: *Beyond Craft: The Art Fabric* (New York, 1973)

Magdalena Abakanowicz (exh. cat., Warsaw, Zachęta Gal., 1975)

Annu. Skira, i (1975)

Annu. Skira, ii (1976)

I. Huml: *Polska sztuka stosowana XX wieku* [20th-century Polish applied art] (Warsaw, 1978)

Annu. Skira, v (1979)

'Magdalena Abakanowicz: About the 1970s', *Annu. Skira*, vi (1980), pp. 130–31

Magdalena Abakanowicz, Polonia (exh. cat., Venice, Biennale, 1980)

Z. Żygulski jr: *An Outline History of Polish Applied Art* (Warsaw, 1987), p. 100

VIDEO RECORDINGS

Wytwórnia Filmów Oświatowych [Educational film workshop]: *Abakany* (Łódź, 1969)

Film Australia: *Abakanowicz in Australia* (Sydney, 1976)

——: *Division of Space* (Sydney, 1976)

Sydney Film and Television School: *Abakanowicz* (Sydney, 1976)

ZDZISŁAW ŻYGULSKI JR

Abaneri [anc. Abhānagari]. Temple site in north-eastern Rajasthan, India. It contains the fragmentary remains of two major monuments of the 8th century AD. The Chand Baori, a stepped ritual bathing tank *c.* 19 m deep, was probably built by Raja Chandra, from whom its name derives; an enclosing verandah dates to the 17th century. Although the Harshatmata Temple also dates to the 8th century, or early 9th, according to some scholars, a modern temple has been built over the original foundations, which include a broad platform and the lower walls of the original monument. A remarkable sequence of sculptures, showing primarily secular scenes, survives. These include kings with courtiers, musicians and couples (*see* INDIAN SUBCONTINENT, fig. 186). The figural scenes are framed by pilasters carved with floral motifs and capped by elaborate interlaced pediments employing the *gavākṣa* (Skt: 'cow's-eye') motif.

The sculpture of Abaneri extensively illustrates a phase of sculptural development midway between the Gupta style of the Mathura region and the abstracted linearized style adopted in northern India from the 10th century. Its style, often referred to as naturalistic, renders the figure with an energetic elasticity conveying both potential and actual movement. The profuse details, including facial expressions and gestures, are carved with great delicacy, and the high relief utilizes deep undercutting. Several of the ancient sculptures have been embedded into the walls of the modern temple, and numerous fragments—possibly from other temples no longer extant—lie about the site. Other pieces, including images of deities such as Ganesha, Durga and Gaja-Lakshmi and scenes from the life of Krishna, have been removed to the Archaeological Museum in Amer.

BIBLIOGRAPHY

R. C. Agrawala: 'Sculptures from Abaneri, Rajasthan', *Lalit Kala*, i–ii (1955–6), pp. 130–35

P. Jayakar: 'Notes on Some Sculptures *in situ* at Abaneri, Rajasthan', *Lalit Kala*, i–ii (1955–6), pp. 139–44

K. C. Jain: *Ancient Cities and Towns of Rajasthan* (Delhi, 1972)

S. Gupta: *Jaipur*, Rajasthan District Gazetteer (Jaipur, 1987)

WALTER SMITH

Aba-Novák, Vilmos (*b* Budapest, 15 March 1894; *d* Budapest, 29 Sept 1941). Hungarian painter, draughtsman and etcher. He trained as a drawing teacher at the College of Fine Arts, Budapest (1912–14). In 1913 he worked at the Szolnok colony and he served in World War I. He taught drawing for a while at the Technical University, Budapest. In 1922 he learnt etching from Viktor Olgyay at the College of Fine Arts. His early works show an affinity with the Group of Eight; later he moved closer to the work of the Activists, especially József Nemes Lampérth and Béla Uitz. He instinctively sought a dynamic and powerful form of expression. His pen-drawings and etchings are frequently based on biblical subjects and are characterized by a heroic conception, an illusory atmosphere and romantic associations. The etching *Savonarola* (1925; Budapest, N.G.) reveals his extraordinary compositional abilities, especially in the rendering of crowds, and his use of strong chiaroscuro. His landscapes are dominated by carefully composed, naturalist details and the exploitation of the dramatic effect of reflections. In his drawings, Cubist arrangements gradually gave way to a more diffuse composition. His nudes in the landscape (e.g. *Bathers*, pen-and-ink, 1922; Budapest, N.G.) evoke an air of serenity. He soon sought more emotional and dramatic themes, however, becoming preoccupied with the search for a psychologically authentic depiction of apocalyptic events and mass ecstasy, and looking to his more immediate environment for models and themes.

In 1929–30 he spent two years in Italy on a scholarship, which greatly contributed to the development of his mature style. He studied medieval and early Renaissance painters and decided to paint in tempera. Most of his major works were created between 1930 and 1936. He favoured bright colours, depicting Italian town squares, travelling circuses, village fairs, peasant festivals and church ceremonies. Typical characters reappear again and again. With this work he continued the tradition of Hungarian genre-painting. After receiving an award in 1932 at an exhibition of ecclesiastical art in Padua, he was offered large-scale commissions by the state and the church. His wall painting for the church of Jászszentandrás summarizes in its depiction of the blessed and the damned all his previous achievements in the drawing of space and the representation of character types. The composition is at once archaic and modern and there is drama and forcefulness in the exaggerated gestures and lively mimicry, and an emphasis on theatrical effects. The wall paintings of the *Heroes' Gate* (1934) in Szeged represent realistically the horrors of World War I. In the last part of his life he continued to work, although worsening health, growing demands, changes in his ambitions and new experiments in technique all affected his output. His wall paintings became increasingly like large-scale coloured drawings, for example the *Creation* cycle (1938) for the ceiling of the church in the Buda City Park, Budapest. He continued to depict in bright colours jovial characters bursting with vitality. From 1938 until his death he taught at the College of Fine Arts, Budapest.

WRITINGS

'Vallomás' [Confession], *Magyar Művészet* (1931), pp. 189–212

BIBLIOGRAPHY

E. Ybl: 'Aba-Novák Vilmos', *Magyar Művészet* (1931), pp. 137–46

T. Gerevich: 'Aba-Novák Vilmos', *Szépművészet* (1940–41), pp. 261–6

M. B. Supka: 'Aba-Novák Vilmos festészetének nemzeti sajátosságairól' [On the national characteristics of Vilmos Aba-Novák's painting], *Magyar nemzeti Gal. Közleményei* [Publications of the Hungarian National Gallery], ii (1961), pp. 175–7

——: *Aba-Novák Vilmos* (Budapest, 1971)

S. Kontha, ed.: *Magyar Művészet, 1919–1945* [Hungarian art, 1919–45] (Budapest, 1985), pp. 418–26

S. KONTHA

Abarca de Bolea, Pedro Pablo. *See* ARANDA.

Abarquh [Abarqūh]. Iranian town in northern Fars province. A prosperous centre in medieval times, by the 10th century it was fortified with a citadel and had a congregational mosque. The octagonal tower of mortared stone known as the Gunbad-i ʿAli was erected, according to its inscription, by a Daylamite prince in 1056–7 to contain the remains of his parents. The Masjid-i Birun, a mosque to the south of the town, may be slightly earlier, although it has many later additions. The congregational mosque (rest.), with four iwans around a rectangular court, dates mostly to the 14th century, although the base of the dome chamber probably belongs to the 12th-century mosque. The many mihrabs within the mosque include a particularly fine stucco example (1338). There are also several mud-brick tombs in the town. These square structures have plain exteriors and plastered and painted interiors. One of the earliest is the tomb of Pir Hamza Sabzpush (12th century); the finest was that of Hasan ibn Kay Khusraw (1318; destr.). In the 18th century, the town suffered first in the Afghan invasion and then in the fighting between the Zands and Qajars.

BIBLIOGRAPHY

Enc. Iran.

A. Godard: 'Abarḳūh (Province de Yazd)', *Āthār-ē Īrān*, i (1936), pp. 47–72

D. N. Wilber: *The Architecture of Islamic Iran: The Il Khānid Period* (Princeton, 1955)

I. Afshar: *Yādgārhā-yi Yazd* [Monuments of Yazd], 3 vols (Tehran, Iran. Solar 1348–54/1970–76)

S. S. Blair: *The Monumental Inscriptions of Early Islamic Iran and Transoxiana* (Leiden, 1992)

□

Abarshahr. *See* NISHAPUR.

Abate, Giulio Camillo dell'. *See under* MASTERS, ANONYMOUS, AND MONOGRAMMISTS, §I: MASTER OF FLORA.

1. Nicolò dell'Abate: *Card-players* (*c.* 1550; detail), frescoed frieze, Palazzo Poggi, Bologna

Abate [Abbate], **Nicolò** [Niccolò] **dell'** (*b* Modena, 1509–12; *d* ?Fontainebleau, 1571). Italian painter and draughtsman. He was one of the most important artists of the first FONTAINEBLEAU SCHOOL, which was developed at the French court by Rosso Fiorentino and Francesco Primaticcio, and he introduced the Italian Mannerist landscape into France.

1. ITALY, BEFORE 1552. He was almost certainly trained by his father, Giovanni dell'Abate (*d* 1559), a stuccoist, and by the sculptor Antonio Begarelli. Apparently after a period as a soldier, by 1537 he was working in Modena as a painter under Alberto Fontana (*fl* 1518–58). There the two artists decorated the façade of the Beccherie (Slaughterhouse) from which certain paintings survive (e.g. *St Geminian* and an allegory of the *Wine Harvest*; both Modena, Gal. & Mus. Estense). His early paintings clearly show the influence of Correggio and of such Ferrarese artists as Dosso Dossi. They also display a love of the picturesque and the pastoral, with frequent variations on the theme of the concert, as in the fragment of a concert scene (Reggio Emilia, Mus. Civ. & Gal. A.) from the façade decorations of the Palazzo Pratonieri in Reggio Emilia. Around 1540 he painted a series of frescoes based on Virgil's *Aeneid* in a study of a castle owned by the Boiardo family at Scandiano, near Modena. Some of these paintings survive (Modena, Gal. & Mus. Estense) but greatly altered by damage and restoration. Engravings after the paintings (published by G. B. Venturi, Modena, 1821) give some indication of their original state. The scheme of the room probably included 12 paintings, each representing a book of the *Aeneid*, many depicting several events. Below these were battle scenes; above them were lunettes containing landscapes. In the spandrels were eight female figures reaching up to the octagon of the ceiling, where dell'Abate painted portraits of members of the Boiardo family playing instruments and singing, a scene recalling the oculus of Andrea Mantegna's *Camera picta* (Mantua, Pal. Ducale). Although Dosso's *Aeneas* cycle (dispersed, U. Birmingham, Barber Inst.; Ottawa, N.G.; Washington, DC, N.G.A.), painted *c.* 1520 for Alfonso I d'Este, probably influenced dell'Abate, the Scandiano frescoes were the most extensive treatment of the Virgilian narrative in the period. They show dell'Abate's love of landscape, both for its own sake and to enhance narrative compositions. The figure style in these works suggests the influence of Parmigianino and Correggio.

The Scandiano project was undoubtedly instrumental in gaining other large commissions for dell'Abate. In 1546 he and Fontana were employed to decorate the Sala dei Conservatori of the Palazzo Pubblico in Modena. This decoration includes scenes from Roman history, once again set in idyllic landscapes. The treatment of landscape reflects Venetian and Emilian traditions, which in turn were shaped by those of northern European art. The decorations are restricted to a frieze under the cornice, a form often found in Emilian Renaissance palazzi. While this format is in the local tradition, the border of flowers and fruit underlining it shows an awareness of decorative schemes derived from those of Giulio Romano at the Palazzo del Te in Mantua or of Raphael at the Villa Farnesina in Rome.

Although dell'Abate was most influential for his contribution to large-scale decorative schemes, he executed a variety of other works, including altarpieces, for example that with a martyrdom of saints for SS Pietro e Paolo, Modena, in 1547 (ex-Gemäldegal., Dresden, destr.). In the same year he went to Bologna, where he encountered works by Lorenzo Costa, Francesco Salviati, Giorgio Vasari and, most importantly, Parmigianino. In Bologna he developed the decorative skills he later used in France. One of the most important schemes he worked on in Bologna was the Palazzo Torfanini (now Zucchini-Solomei), where his decorations included stories from Ludovico Ariosto's *Orlando furioso.* A series of arches frame the narrative scenes, which again have fantastical and elaborate settings, both natural and architectural. Garlands suspended between the arches are held by draped and nude figures sitting in the spandrels. Their poses recall figures by Michelangelo on the ceiling of the Sistine Chapel, Vatican, Rome, but they are treated with a more mannered

2. Nicolò dell'Abate: *Story of Aristaeus* (or *Death of Eurydice*), oil on canvas, 1.9×2.3 m, *c*. 1565 (London, National Gallery)

elegance. It is difficult to assess the effect of the scheme, as only two of the eight scenes are well preserved. Around 1550 dell'Abate was commissioned to decorate four rooms in the Palazzo Poggi, Bologna. These decorations, again limited to friezes (see fig. 1), include episodes from the *Life of Camilla*, from the *Aeneid*, as well as simple decorative landscapes and such ornamental devices as groups of putti playing with huge garlands. The landscapes are set in a fictive architectural structure, with garlands draped along the bottom cornice. The scheme is reminiscent of Baldassare Peruzzi's illusionistic decorations in the Sala delle Prospettive in the Villa Farnesina, Rome. Although the decorations are all painted, they appear to be composed of sculpted, painted and real elements. The scenes are separated by putti or larger figures, in rather disdainful poses, which are Mannerist in their elongation and refinement. The decorative works dell'Abate executed in Bologna were influential for future generations of artists there, including the Carracci family. They probably also helped him procure the appointment as assistant to the Bolognese artist Francesco Primaticcio in France, at the court of Henry II.

2. France, from 1552. Dell'Abate was in France from 1552 until his death in 1571, mainly working at the royal château of Fontainebleau. He was involved in major decorative projects there, following the precedent set by Rosso Fiorentino in the Galerie François I. Initially dell'Abate seems to have been subordinate to Primaticcio, whose influence on him is often noted. Writers, including Béguin (see 1969 exh. cat.), however, also stress dell'Abate's impact on Primaticcio, who increasingly concentrated on design, producing drawings for projects that dell'Abate executed. Dell'Abate's contributions to the schemes designed by Primaticcio have been identified mainly on stylistic grounds, as few are documented. Many of the large-scale projects do not survive or are in poor condition. Dell'Abate was largely responsible for the execution of the decoration of the Galerie d'Ulysse, for example, which was destroyed in 1738. The decorations, a complex programme of stories from the *Life of Ulysses*, are recorded in a series of preparatory drawings, mostly by Primaticcio (e.g. Florence, Uffizi; Paris, Louvre), and prints, notably Théodore van Thulden's *Les Travaux d'Ulysse* (Paris, 1633). It may have been dell'Abate's handling of paint and fine touch that provoked Vasari's comment that the Galerie seemed to have been painted in just one day. Another large-scale project on which dell'Abate worked was the decoration of the Galerie Henri II or Salle de Bal (1552–6). The theme of music appears

throughout the scheme, which has been heavily damaged and repainted. In the Chambre de la Duchesse d'Etampes (Escalier du Roi), the fresco of *Alexander Preserving the Works of Homer* is attributed to dell'Abate alone; no drawing for it by Primaticcio survives.

Dell'Abate's commissions apart from those at Fontainebleau included frescoes (before 1558) for the château of Fleury-en-Bière, for which drawings survive (e.g. Paris, Louvre). The constable, Anne, Duc de Montmorency, was a valuable patron, and dell'Abate's drawings (e.g. Paris, Louvre) for his Paris residence (destr.) show the artist's adoption of the rich decorative style developed at Fontainebleau by Rosso and Primaticcio. He also painted portraits in France, for example the enamelled double portrait of *Henry II and Catherine de' Medici* (1553; Paris, Louvre) for the Sainte-Chapelle in Paris. As a court artist, he designed tapestries and ephemeral decorations for court celebrations and for triumphal entries, such as that of Charles IX into Paris in 1571.

In addition, dell'Abate produced small-scale paintings, often of mythological subjects. In some examples the narrative is almost completely subordinated to the landscape, as in the *Story of Aristaeus* (or *Death of Eurydice*; *c.* 1565; London, N.G.; see fig. 2), in which the sky and the fantastical background, littered with figures derived from the Antique, appear agitated. In the *Continence of Scipio* (*c.* 1555; Paris, Louvre) the figures dominate the composition, their poses and attitudes interlocking across the picture plane. The elegant forms and the softness of the treatment are reminiscent of Salviati, who was in France in this period. The idyllic classical style, derived from Italian Mannerism, that dell'Abate brought to France greatly influenced the treatment of landscape in French art. After his death, painting at Fontainebleau was supervised by his son, Giulio Camillo dell'Abate (1552–82), who is one of those identified with the MASTER OF FLORA (*see* MASTERS, ANONYMOUS, AND MONOGRAMMISTS, §I).

BIBLIOGRAPHY

G. Vasari: *Vite* (1550, rev. 2/1568); ed. G. Milanesi (1878–85), vi, pp. 481–2; vii, pp. 410–11

L. Dimier: 'Niccolò dell'Abate et les tapisseries de Fontainebleau', *An. Soc. Hist. & Archéol. Gâtinais*, xiii (1895)

A. Venturi: 'Il Mauriziano. Casa Fioribelli: Affreschi di Nicolò dell'Abate', *L'Arte*, iv/9–10 (1901), p. 356

C. Gamba: 'Un ritratto e un paesaggio di Nicolò dell'Abate', *Cron. A.*, i (1924), pp. 77–89

G. Zucchini: 'La scoperta di affreschi di Nicolò dell'Abate in Bologna', *Com. Bologna* (June 1929)

G. Fabrizi: 'L'*Eneide* nei dodici quadri di Nicolò dell'Abate', *Capitolium*, vi/9 (1930), pp. 504–16

W. Bombe: 'Gli affreschi dell'*Eneide* di Nicolò dell'Abate nel Palazzo di Scandiano', *Boll. A.*, x (1931), pp. 529–53

E. Bodmer: 'L'attività artistica di Niccolò dell'Abate a Bologna', *Com. Bologna*, i–ii (1934), pp. 3–39

H. Tietze and E. Tietze Conrat: 'Some Drawings by Niccolò dell'Abate', *Gaz. B.-A.*, n. s. 5, xxviii (1945), pp. 378–9

S. Béguin: *L'Ecole de Fontainebleau: Le Maniérisme à la cour de France* (Paris, 1960)

——: 'Niccolò dell'Abbate en France', *A. France*, ii (1962), pp. 112–45

E. H. Langmuir: 'Nicolò dell'Abate at Bologna', *Burl. Mag.*, cxi (1969), pp. 635–9

A. Paolucci: 'Nicolò dell'Abate', *A. Illus.*, ii/23–4 (1969), pp. 90–93

Mostra di Nicolò dell'Abate (exh. cat., ed. S. Béguin; Bologna, Pal. Archiginnasio, 1969)

A. Mezzetti: *Per Nicolò dell'Abate, affreschi restaurati* (Modena, 1970)

A. Ottani Cavina: 'Il paesaggio di Nicolò dell'Abate', *Paragone*, 245 (1970), pp. 8–19

L'Ecole de Fontainebleau (exh. cat., ed. S. Béguin; Paris, Grand Pal., 1972)

Fontainebleau: L'Art en France, 1528–1610 (exh. cat., ed. S. Béguin; Ottawa, N.G., 1973)

G. Godi: *Nicolò dell'Abate e la presunta attività del Parmigianino a Soragna* (Parma, 1976)

I. Wardropper: 'Le Voyage italien de Primatice en 1550', *Bull. Soc. Hist. A. Fr.* (1981), pp. 27–31

S. Béguin, J. Guillaume and A. Roy: *La Galerie d'Ulysse à Fontainebleau* (Paris, 1985)

DORIGEN CALDWELL

ʿAbbās. *See* SAFAVID, (2).

ʿAbbasi, Shaykh. *See* SHAYKH ʿABBASI.

Abbasid [ʿAbbasid]. Islamic dynasty that ruled from several capitals in Iraq between AD 749 and 1258. The Abbasids traced their descent from al-ʿAbbas, the uncle of the Prophet Muhammad, and were thus able to claim a legitimacy that their predecessors had lacked (*see* UMAYYAD, §1). The Abbasids rose to power in north-east Iran by channelling disaffection with Umayyad rule, but they soon established their capitals in a more central location, founding BAGHDAD in 762. Although they initially encouraged the support of Shiʿites, the Abbasids quickly distanced themselves from their erstwhile allies to become champions of orthodoxy. Upon accession, each caliph adopted an honorific title, somewhat like a regnal name, by which he was later known. For the first two centuries, the Abbasids' power was pre-eminent, and their names were invoked from the Atlantic to western Central Asia. From the middle of the 10th century, however, real power was transferred to a succession of Persian and Turkish dynasts (*see* SAMANID, BUYID, GHAZNAVID and SALJUQ, §1), who paid lip-service to a series of puppet caliphs. After the fall of Baghdad to the Mongols in 1256, a nominal Abbasid caliphate was maintained in Cairo until 1517.

The shift in the centre of gravity from the Umayyad capital at Damascus to Baghdad involved not merely a geographical adjustment of 500 miles but had potent repercussions in politics, culture and art. Baghdad became, in a way that Damascus had not, an Islamic Rome. It absorbed ideas, artefacts and influences from the Islamic world, India, China and the Eurasian steppe and then exported them, transformed, throughout the Islamic world, stamped with its own unique cachet and glamour. Nine-bay mosques in Afghanistan and Spain, iridescent lustreware in Tunisia and Sind, Baghdadi textiles laboriously copied in Andalusia—even down to the inscription identifying the piece as made in Baghdad—and Iraqi stucco forms in Egypt and Central Asia all attest the unchallenged cultural dominance of Baghdad. The cumulative gravitational pull exerted by the eastern territories broke the grip of Mediterranean culture, and specifically of Greco-Roman Classicism and its Byzantine descendant, on Islamic art. Classical forms can still be dimly discerned on occasion—the triumphal arch underlies the portals of Abbasid palaces, and all three styles of Abbasid stucco-carving (*see* BEVELLED STYLE) are foreshadowed in early Byzantine art—but they have undergone a sea-change. New contexts and new functions transform them. In architecture (*see* ISLAMIC ART, §II, 4(i)(b)), the secluded, relatively small-scale splendours of the classically inspired Umayyad desert residences gave way to vast sprawling palaces or rather palace-cities at Baghdad, UKHAYDIR and Samarra' (*see* SAMARRA', §2), mostly urban and conceived on the Perso-Sasanian model, where massive scale is the dominant factor. Proportional ratios (often 3:2) and strict axiality hold these structures together. Inferior building materials—principally mud-brick—are disguised by lavish revetments, and acres of less important wall surface were cheaply and expeditiously covered with moulded and painted stucco featuring increasingly abstract vegetal and geometric patterns.

The figural iconography of these palaces (e.g. the Dar al-Khilafa or Jawsaq al-Khaqani at Samarra') attests the gradual consolidation and refinement of a cycle of princely pleasures (music, banqueting, hunting, wrestling, dancing and the like) to be interpreted not literally but as a sequence of coded references to a luxurious royal lifestyle (summarized by the 11th-century Persian poet Manuchihri in the rhyming jingle *sharāb u rabāb u kabāb* ('wine, music and meat'). This cycle was assiduously copied by Abbasid successor states or rival polities from Spain (Córdoba and Játiva: *see* UMAYYAD, §2) and Sicily (Palermo, Cappella Palatina) to Armenia (*see* AGHT'AMAR) and Afghanistan (*see* LASHKARI BAZAR). It occurs on marble troughs and ivory boxes (*see* ISLAMIC ART, §VIII, 7(ii)), on bronze buckets and ceremonial silks, on the exteriors and interiors of Christian churches, and of course in numerous palaces.

The immense financial resources of the early Abbasid empire generated luxury arts galore. Rock crystal workshops flourished in Basra (*see* ISLAMIC ART, §VIII, 13(i)). Gold and silver vessels with figural decoration including hunting scenes and dancing girls are described in the Bacchic poetry of the court laureate Abu Nuwas (*d c.* 813). Byzantine ambassadors marvelled at the 38,000 precious curtains displayed in a caliphal palace. Textiles bearing laudatory or benedictory inscriptions with the name of the ruling caliph (*see* TIRAZ) made the courtiers who wore them walking advertisements for their monarch. Moulded two-tone glass with relief inscriptions and lustre painting typified the technical advances achieved by Islamic craftsmen (*see* ISLAMIC ART, §VIII, 5(i)). Nearly all the objects in such precious materials as ebony, ivory or alabaster described in medieval texts have vanished, but they must be borne in mind when reconstructing the ambience of Abbasid art. It is all the more regrettable that the fullest sequence of any imperial Abbasid art form should survive in the humblest material of all—pottery (*see* ISLAMIC ART, §V, 2(ii)). Yet this material provides a paradigm of the radical innovation that characterizes this period. Pottery was suddenly promoted from largely domestic use to an art form. The impact of Chinese ceramics—porcelain, stoneware and glazed earthenware—was probably the galvanizing factor. Abbasid wares valiantly imitated Tang splashwares and celadons but with a diagnostic change: the Chinese emphasis on form, body, touch—even the sound a piece made when struck—was replaced, at least in part, by applied decoration not encountered in the prototype. This change of emphasis lays bare the profoundly different principles of Abbasid taste. The Islamic invention of the technically difficult craft of lustre painting transformed pottery and allowed for the vulgarization of more expensive art forms and materials that became characteristic of Islamic art.

The other art form that has survived in substantial quantity is calligraphy (*see* ISLAMIC ART, §III, 2(ii)). Under Abbasid patronage the somewhat haphazard penmanship of the earliest manuscripts of the Koran, expressed in irregular letter forms, skewed lines of taut spasmodic illumination and a general indifference to visual effect, was replaced by a solemn discipline appropriate to holy writ and redolent of epigraphy on paper. Horizontal parchment sheets often accommodated no more than four lines of text, so spaced and with letter forms subject to such extremes of stylization as to slow down recognition of the words themselves: an objective correlative to the awesome enigmas found in the text itself. A supple system of extension allowed calligraphers to balance words on a page with the utmost finesse and thus create striking visual harmonies. This style spread throughout the Abbasid dominions with only minor local variations. It thus typifies the prestige and paramount authority enjoyed by the art of Baghdad: a fact of life epitomized by the courtier Ziryab, the Baghdad *arbiter elegantiarum* who imported the lifestyle of the Iraqi capital in food, language, clothing and art to far-off Córdoba in the 10th century.

BIBLIOGRAPHY

A. Mez: *Die Renaissance des Islams* (Heidelberg, 1922); Eng. trans. by S. Khuda Bukhsh and D. S. Margoliouth as *The Renaissance of Islam* (Patna, 1938)

K. A. C. Creswell: *Early Muslim Architecture*, ii (Oxford, 1940/*R* New York, 1979)

R. Ettinghausen: 'The "Beveled Style" in the Post-Samarra Period', *Archaeologica Orientalia in Memoriam Ernst Herzfeld* (Locust Valley, NY, 1952), pp. 72–83

D. Sourdel: *Le Vizirat 'abbâside de 749 à 936*, 2 vols (Damascus, 1959–60)

D. Sourdel and J. Sourdel: *La Civilisation de l'Islam classique* (Paris, 1968)

L. Golombek: 'Abbasid Mosque at Balkh', *Orient. A.*, n. s., xv (1969), pp. 173–89

J. Lassner: *The Topography of Baghdad in the Early Middle Ages* (Detroit, 1970)

M. A. Shaban: *The 'Abbāsid Revolution* (Cambridge, 1970)

M. M. Ahsan: *Social Life under the Abbasids* (London, 1979)

J. Lassner: *The Shaping of 'Abbasid Rule* (Princeton, 1980)

H. Philon: *Early Islamic Ceramics: Ninth to Late Twelfth Centuries* (London, 1980)

H. Kennedy: *The Early Abbasid Caliphate* (London and Sydney, 1981)

R. Hillenbrand: "Abbasid Mosques in Iran', *Riv. Stud. Orient.*, lix (1985), pp. 175–212

T. Allen: *Five Essays on Islamic Art* (Sebastopol, CA, 1988)

J. Bloom: *Minaret: Symbol of Islam* (Oxford, 1989)

F. Déroche: *The Abbasid Tradition: Qur'ans of the 8th to the 10th Centuries AD* (1992), i of *The Nasser D. Khalili Collection of Islamic Art*, ed. J. Raby (London and Oxford, 1992–)

ROBERT HILLENBRAND

Abbate, Nicolò dell'. *See* ABATE, NICOLÒ DELL'.

Abbatini, Guido Ubaldo (*b* Città di Castello, *c.* 1600–05; *d* Rome, 1656). Italian painter and mosaicist. He trained in the Roman studio of Cavaliere d'Arpino. He is principally known for executing fresco decorations in several chapels in Rome to designs by Bernini. Independent commissions, such as the frescoes depicting the *Life of Charlemagne* (1635–7; Rome, Vatican, Sala di Carlo Magno), reveal, however, that despite his collaboration with Bernini and later with Cortona, his preference was for a restrained classical style, close to that of more conservative contemporaries such as Andrea Camassei and Giovanni Francesco Romanelli. He assisted Bernini with the vault of the Raimondi Chapel in S Pietro in Montorio (1642–4) and that of the Pio Chapel in S Agostino (*c*. 1644–5). He also painted the vision of clouds and angels in the vault above Bernini's marble group of *St Teresa in Ecstasy* (*c*. 1647; Rome, S Maria della Vittoria, Cornaro Chapel). In 1650 he executed independently the decorative frescoes on the ceiling and side walls of the sacristy of S Spirito in Sassia, Rome. He also executed mosaics in St Peter's, after his own designs and those of Cortona (e.g. 1654–6; chapel of S Sebastiano), as well as carrying out many modest artistic chores in St Peter's and the Vatican during Urban VIII's papacy, from gilding and marbling to painting topographical views (*see also* ITALY, fig. 104).

BIBLIOGRAPHY

G. B. Passeri: *Vite* (1679); ed. J. Hess (1934), pp. 234–40
O. Pollak: *Die Kunsttätigkeit unter Urban VIII*, 2 vols (Vienna, 1928–31)
E. K. Waterhouse: *Baroque Painting in Rome* (London, 1937, 2/1976), p. 49
B. Toscano: 'Il pittore del Cardinal Poli: Guidobaldo Abbatini', *Paragone*, 177 (1964), pp. 36–42
I. Lavin: *Bernini and the Unity of the Visual Arts* (New York, 1980), pp. 54, 56, 188, 189, 193, 200

ANN SUTHERLAND HARRIS

Abbaye de Créteil. Community of French writers, artists and composers in operation from November 1906 to February 1908, located in a villa on the banks of the Marne at Créteil, south-east of Paris. Their choice of name paid homage to François Rabelais, whose Gargantua had established the Abbey of Thelema as a model monastery, a self-supporting commune whose members devoted part of each day to group labour and the rest to perfecting the self intellectually. The Abbaye de Créteil numbered among its members the painters Albert Gleizes, Charles Berthold-Mahn and Jacques d'Otemar, the poets Charles Vildrac (*b* 1882), Georges Duhamel (1884–1966), René Arcos, Alexandre Mercereau, JULES ROMAINS, Henri-Martin Barzun (*b* 1881), the composer Albert Doyen, and the printer Lucien Linard, whom Gleizes had met while doing his military service. It was through Linard's trade of printing and publishing that the Abbaye hoped to secure its material future.

Only a few of the Abbaye's members lived there full-time, with cells available for associates who were only occasionally in residence. Until March 1907 Mercereau was in Russia, where as Eshmer Valdor he served as secretary to the review *Zolotoye Runo* (*see* GOLDEN FLEECE); Romains, still a medical student, may have particularly identified with the poet-physician Rabelais. Romains's collection of poems *La Vie unanime*, the first publication printed at the Abbaye, gave rise to the impression that all the members of the community subscribed to Unanimism, a belief that the reality of modern group life had permanently altered individual experience. In general the themes explored by the group's members did relate to the interconnected, epic qualities of modern life, to cities, crowds, machines, commerce, agriculture and shared emotions, especially in work done after the dissolution of the Abbaye, such as Gleizes's *Football Players* (1912–13; Washington, DC, N.G.A.). The multiplicity and simultaneity of experience, however, suggested not only new themes but also new methods in writing and painting, entailing a simplicity of imagery and a search for basic volumes. Filippo Tommaso Marinetti, who visited the Abbaye in the summer of 1907, drew much of his programme for Futurism from the thinking of Romains and the Abbaye circle.

Its radical nature notwithstanding, the Abbaye's programme nevertheless owed much to an older generation of late Symbolist poets, especially to Emile Verhaeren, Paul Adam and René Ghil (1862–1925), all of whom were active supporters of the Abbaye. Verharen's modern literary themes were borrowed by Romains, while Adam's idea of multiple perspectives, formulated as early as 1905, and Ghil's emphasis on elemental sounds, divorced from their customary linguistic meaning, were sources for abstract art and an influence on the subsequent work of Gleizes.

During its brief existence, the Abbaye published important works by Roger Allard, who later made his name as a supporter of Cubism, and Pierre-Jean Jouve. Its spirit survived in a circle around the review *Les Bandeaux d'or* in Paris, through which Gleizes met Henri Le Fauconnier in 1908. Gleizes and other former members later attained prominence as artists or men of letters. The group's influence was recognized in England in the lead article of the first issue of *Rhythm*, a review inaugurated by John Middleton Murray and Katherine Mansfield. The Abbaye idea, an optimistic mix of modernism and late medievalism, of Symbolism and ideas leading to Cubism, of individual creativity blended into group activity, continued to exert appeal until World War I.

BIBLIOGRAPHY

F. Goodyear: 'The New Thelema', *Rhythm*, i/1 (1911)
A. Gleizes: 'The Abbaye of Créteil: A Communistic Experiment', *The Modern School*, ed. C. Zigrosser (Stelton, NJ, 1918)
A. Mercereau: *L'Abbaye et le bolchevisme* (Paris, ?1922)
H. Clouard: *Histoire de la littérature française, du Symbolisme à nos jours, 1885–1914* (Paris, 1947), pp. 542ff
G. Duhamel: *Le Temps de la recherche* (1947), iii of *Lumières sur ma vie* (Paris, 1947)
D. Robbins: 'From Symbolism to Cubism: The Abbaye of Créteil', *A. J.* [New York], xxiii (Winter 1963–4), pp. 111–16
For further bibliography *see* GLEIZES, ALBERT, and ROMAINS, JULES.

DANIEL ROBBINS

Abbe, James (Edward) (*b* Alfred, ME, 17 July 1883; *d* San Francisco, 11 Nov 1973). American photographer. Self-taught, he started to produce photographs at the age of 12. From 1898 to 1910 he worked in his father's bookshop and then worked as a reporter for the *Washington Post*, travelling to Europe in 1910. Having earlier produced photographs of ships and sailors for tourist cards, from 1913 to 1917 he worked as a freelance photojournalist in Virginia. In 1917 he set up a studio in New York, where he produced the first photographic cover for the *Saturday Evening Post* as well as photographs for *Ladies Home Journal*, the *New York Times* and other publications. From 1922 to 1923 he worked as a stills photographer, actor and writer for film studios. Though this was mainly for Mack Sennett in Hollywood, he also worked for D. W. Griffiths as a stills photographer on *Way Down East* (1920) and accompanied Lilian Gish to Italy to provide stills for Griffiths's *The White Sister* (1923). After establishing a studio in Paris in 1924 he had his

Edwin Austin Abbey: mural from the cycle of the *Quest for the Holy Grail* (1890–1901), h. 2.44 m, delivery room of the Boston Public Library, Boston, Massachusetts

photographs published in such journals as *Harper's Bazaar*, *L'Illustration*, *New York Herald Tribune*, *The Tatler*, *Vanity Fair*, *Vogue* and *Vu*. He photographed film stars and the Moulin Rouge in Paris and also produced fashion pictures, such as *Natasha Rambova in Fortuny Gown* (*c*. 1924; see Hall-Duncan, p. 41).

From 1929 until 1932 Abbe travelled extensively in Europe, Mexico, the USA and the USSR as one of the first photojournalists, working for the *Berliner illustrierte Zeitung*. During this period he covered the Mexican Revolution of 1932 as well as crime and prohibition in Chicago. He photographed Hitler and Mussolini during their rise to power, and in 1932 he was the first foreign correspondent to photograph Stalin (among other images published in his book *I Photograph Russia*, 1934). In 1934 he returned to the USA, working in Larkspur, CO, as a freelance photojournalist until 1936. In the latter year he went to Spain as a war correspondent for the *Alliance* newspaper, covering the Civil War from General Franco's side. After this he ceased work as a photographer and became, in turn, a rancher, radio broadcaster and television critic.

PHOTOGRAPHIC PUBLICATIONS

I Photograph Russia (New York, 1934)

Stars of the '20s (London, 1975) [text by M. D. Early]

BIBLIOGRAPHY

C. Beaton and G. Buckland: *The Magic Image: The Genius of Photography from 1939 to the Present Day* (London, 1975), p. 185

N. Hall-Duncan: *The History of Fashion Photography* (New York, 1979), pp. 41, 43, 224

G. Walsh, C. Naylor and M. Held, eds: *Contemporary Photographers* (New York, 1982)

□

Abbey, Edwin Austin (*b* Philadelphia, PA, 1 April 1852; *d* London, 1 Aug 1911). American painter and illustrator, active in England. He began his artistic training in 1866, studying drawing with the Philadelphia portrait and landscape painter Isaac L. Williams (1817–95). In 1868 he attended evening classes in drawing at the Pennsylvania Academy of the Fine Arts under Christian Schussele (?1824–79). In the same year Abbey began to work as an illustrator for the Philadelphia publishers Van Ingen & Snyder. In 1870 *Harper's Weekly* published the *Puritans' First Thanksgiving*, and in 1871 Abbey moved to New York to join the staff of Harper & Brothers, thus inaugurating his most important professional relationship. Throughout the 1870s Abbey's reputation grew, both for his detailed exhibition watercolours and for his elegant line drawings, which, translated to wood-engravings in numerous periodicals, illustrated both factual and fictional events of the past and present. The influences on him were mainly English, in particular the works of the Pre-Raphaelite Brotherhood and illustrations in the English press, which he studied avidly. The success of his illustrations to some of Robert Herrick's poems, such as *Corinna's Going A-Maying* in *Harper's New Monthly Magazine* (May 1874), prompted Harper & Brothers in 1878 to send Abbey to England to do a complete series of drawings for an illustrated gift-book, *Selections from the Poetry of Robert Herrick* (New York, 1882). On his arrival in England, Abbey found his spiritual home, and except for a few trips, he never left.

Abbey, a small, handsome, athletic man, had a genius for forging long-lasting and often profitable friendships. In 1877 he helped to found the Tile Club, which included among its members the architect Stanford White, Augustus Saint-Gaudens and Winslow Homer, whose activities resulted in gift-books and lengthy magazine articles. Abbey's most intense friendship was with the English landscape painter and illustrator Alfred Parsons (1847–1920). The two artists shared studios and gallery exhibitions, travelled together widely and collaborated on several projects, most notably the gift-books *Old Songs* (New York, 1889) and *The Quiet Life* (New York, 1890). Abbey derived much of the inspiration for these from his long sojourns in the English countryside, especially, from 1885 to 1889, as one of the central figures in the artists' colony at Broadway (Hereford & Worcs), along with Parsons, Frank Millet (1846–1912) and John Singer Sargent.

Abbey undertook illustrative commissions throughout his life (his illustrations to Shakespeare's plays being especially noteworthy), but from 1889 on he devoted more time to mural projects and oil paintings. In 1890 he sent his first major oil, *May Day Morning* (New Haven, CT, Yale U. A.G.), based on one of the Herrick illustrations, to the Royal Academy Summer Exhibition, where it was favourably received. Until 1910 Abbey exhibited there frequently, and he was elected ARA in 1896 and RA in 1898. His exhibited works were usually based on Shakespearean, troubadour or Renaissance themes. Large and richly coloured, the paintings reflect Abbey's fascination with the stage, particularly in the arrangement of the figures, their poses and sumptuously coloured costumes (Abbey designed the costumes for John Hare's *Tosca* (1889) and Sir Henry Irving's *Richard II* (1898), among other productions). Although he received many honours and awards, the signal event of Abbey's career was the commission in 1902 to paint Edward VII's coronation (London, Buckingham Pal., Royal Col.).

The major projects of Abbey's later life were commissions for murals. He decorated the delivery room of McKim, Mead & White's Boston Public Library with a 15-panel series (1890–1901) based on the *Quest for the Holy Grail* (see fig.). Works for the Royal Exchange, London, and other commissions followed. In 1902 Abbey began the decorations for the Pennsylvania State Capitol at Harrisburg. An allegory of the state's history and its resources, Abbey's work here departed from the schematic narrative of his other murals and adopted a full-blown rhetorical style related to the work of Kenyon Cox and Edwin Blashfield.

BIBLIOGRAPHY

E. V. Lucas: *Edwin Austin Abbey, Royal Academician: The Record of his Life and Work*, 2 vols (London, 1921)

Edwin Austin Abbey (1852–1911) (exh. cat., ed. K. A. Foster and M. Quick; New Haven, CT, Yale U. A.G., 1973)

Unfaded Pageant: Edwin Austin Abbey's Shakespearean Subjects (exh. cat. by L. Oakley, New York, Columbia U., Miriam & Ira D. Wallach Gal., 1994)

MARC SIMPSON

Abbey, John Roland (*b* Brighton, 23 Nov 1894; *d* London, 24 Dec 1969). English collector. Educated privately, he was commissioned to the Rifle Brigade in 1914. He was invalided home in November 1916 and made a director in his family's brewing firm. He began his book collection in 1929, at first with an interest in modern bindings. In 1931 he commissioned Sybil Pye and R. de Coverley and Sons to produce a binding to his own design for Siegfried Sassoon's *Memoirs of an Infantry Officer*. Consistently stressing the importance of appearance and condition, Abbey began buying antiquarian books in 1933 and manuscripts (of which he ultimately owned 143) in 1946, with advice from Sydney Cockerell. After World War II he had the largest private collection of his time, including 1914 18th- and 19th-century books of watercolour prints.

Auctions of his collection were held between 1965 and 1967 (buyers included Paul Mellon and the Landesbibliothek, Stuttgart) and, after his death, between 1970 and 1975. He bequeathed books and manuscripts to the British Museum and Eton College.

WRITINGS

Travels in Aquatint and Lithography, 1770–1860 (London, 1953)

A Bibliographical Catalogue, 2 vols (London, 1956–7)

BIBLIOGRAPHY

DNB

J. J. G. Alexander and A. C. De la Mare: *The Italian Manuscripts in the Library of Major John Roland Abbey* (London, 1969)

JACQUELINE COLLISS HARVEY

Abbondi, Antonio. *See* SCARPAGNINO, ANTONIO.

Abbott, Berenice (*b* Springfield, OH, 17 July 1898; *d* 9 Dec 1991). American photographer. She spent a term at the Ohio State University in Columbus (1917–18) and then studied sculpture independently in New York (1918–21) where she met Marcel Duchamp and Man Ray. She left the USA for Paris in 1921 where she studied at the Académie de la Grande Chaumière before attending the Kunstschule in Berlin for less than a year in 1923. From 1924 to 1926 she worked as Man Ray's assistant and first saw photographs by Eugène Atget in Man Ray's studio in 1925. Her first one-woman show, at the gallery Le Sacre du Printemps in Paris in 1926, was devoted to portraits of avant-garde personalities such as Jean Cocteau, James Joyce and André Gide. She continued to take portraits until leaving Paris in 1929, such as that of *James Joyce* (1927; see *Berenice Abbott: Photographs*, p. 26). After Atget's death (1927) she bought most of his negatives and prints in 1928, and in 1929 she returned to New York. There she began a series of documentary photographs of the city and from 1935 to 1939 directed the 'Changing New York' project for the Works Progress Administration Federal Art Project, which resulted in the book of photographs *Changing New York* (1939). Like Atget's views of Paris these covered both the people and architecture of New York in a methodical and detached way. The images in *Greenwich Village Today and Yesterday* (1949) were motivated by a similar spirit. She also took various portrait photographs in the 1930s and 1940s, such as that of *Max Ernst* (1941; see O'Neal, p. 182).

From 1947 to 1958 Abbott ran the House of Photography, a firm established to develop and sell her photographic inventions, although it proved a financial failure. At a conference at the Aspen Institute for Humanistic Studies in Colorado (1951) she caused a storm by criticizing the Pictorialism of such photographers as Alfred Stieglitz, Edward J. Steichen and Paul Strand. Instead she advocated a documentary style, exemplified by her images of urban America, such as *American Shops* (1954; see O'Neal, p. 197). In 1956 she printed and published 100 sets of Atget's photographs in New York as *Eugène Atget Portfolio: Twenty Photographic Prints from his Glass Negatives.* Having experimented with scientific photography since 1939, from 1958 to 1961 she worked for the Physical Science Study Committee of Educational Services, taking photographs to illustrate the laws of physics. These were used in three books, published in Cleveland, OH, with texts by E. G. Valens: *Magnet* (1964), *Motion* (1965) and *The Attractive Universe* (1969). Continuing her championship of Atget, in 1964 she published *The World of Atget*, writing the text herself. In 1966 she moved to Abbot Village, ME, where she continued producing documentary photographs, such as those for *A Portrait of Maine* (1968). In later life she occupied herself increasingly with organizing and printing her earlier work, and from the late 1970s and into the 1980s several portfolios of earlier photographs were published by the Parasol Press in New York.

WRITINGS

A Guide to Better Photography (New York, 1941)
A New Guide to Better Photography (New York, 1953)

PHOTOGRAPHIC PUBLICATIONS

Changing New York, text by E. McCausland (New York, 1939)
Greenwich Village Today and Yesterday, text by H. W. Lanier (New York, 1949)
The World of Atget (New York, 1964)
Berenice Abbott: Photographs, text by D. Vestal and M. Rukeyser (New York, 1970, rev. Washington, DC, and London, 1990)
Berenice Abbott: The Red River Photographs, text by H. O'Neal (Provincetown, MA, 1979)

BIBLIOGRAPHY

Berenice Abbott: The 20's and 30's (exh. cat. by B. Shissler Nosanow, New York, Int. Cent. Phot.; Washington, DC, N. Mus. Amer. A.; 1981–2)
H. O'Neal: *Berenice Abbott: Sixty Years of Photography*, intro. by J. Canaday (New York and London, 1982)

□

Abbott, John White (*b* Exeter, 13 May 1764; *d* Exeter, 1851). English watercolourist, painter and apothecary. He was nephew of the prominent lawyer John White (1744–1825). An important patron of Francis Towne, he spent his entire career in Exeter as an apothecary and surgeon. Abbot was a keen amateur artist, taking lessons from Towne, but although he was an Honorary Exhibitor of landscape oils at the Royal Academy, London, from 1793 to 1805 and again in 1810 and 1812, he never sold a picture. His oil *Fordland* (1791; priv. col., see Oppé, pl. xxxii) is a *plein-air* study of woodland that owes much to Gainsborough's early work in its naturalism and broken, delicate handling.

In 1791 Abbott toured Scotland, the Lake District, Lancashire, Derbyshire and Warwickshire. He toured Monmouthshire in 1797, and again in 1827, as well as Gloucestershire and Wiltshire. He also made studies of Richmond, Surrey, in 1842, but the bulk of his work was done in the vicinity of Exeter. The *Mouth of the Exe* (priv. col., see Oppé, pl. xxxv, b) shows him adopting Towne's method of bold pen outline and monochrome wash to create a drawing that is topographically accurate and yet sensitive to the effects of light on foliage. The brightly coloured forest watercolour *Kerswell, Devon* (1813; London, V&A) has the classical grandeur of woodlands by Claude Lorrain. He made many imaginary Claudean-style landscapes, as well as watercolour copies of Towne's Italian drawings and a number of landscape etchings (London, BM). Watercolours such as *Exeter Cathedral* (Eton, Berks, Coll. Lib.) show an acute observation of figures that has more in common with Paul Sandby than with Towne. Abbott's watercolours are less bold in composition than Towne's but display a sensitivity to nature, particularly to tree formations, that is part of the intense exploration of landscape by English artists in the late 18th century and the early 19th. In 1825 Abbott inherited his uncle's property and retired to Fordland, near Exeter; in 1831 he was made Deputy Lieutenant of Devonshire.

BIBLIOGRAPHY

A. P. Oppé: 'John White Abbott of Exeter', *Walpole Soc.*, xiii (1924–5), pp. 67–84
I. A. Williams: 'John White Abbott: A Devonshire Artist', *Apollo*, xvii (1933), pp. 84–6
M. Hardie: *The Eighteenth Century* (1966), i of *Water-colour Painting in Britain* (London, 1965–9)
Paintings and Drawings by Francis Towne and John White Abbott (exh. cat., Exeter, Royal Albert Mem. Mus., 1971)

SUSAN MORRIS

Abbott, Lemuel Francis (*b* Leics, *c.* 1760; *d* London, 5 Dec 1802). English painter. He was the son of a clergyman and went to London to study with Francis Hayman shortly before the latter's death in 1776; he may have completed his studies in Derby with Joseph Wright of Derby. By the early 1780s Abbott had established a busy portrait practice in London. The formula he adopted for most of his head-and-shoulder portraits can be seen in *Sir William Herschel* (1785; London, N. Mar. Mus.): the body is parallel to the picture plane, and the sitter's head is moved into three-quarter profile, as if his attention has been suddenly distracted. In later portraits, such as those of fellow artists *Francesco Bartolozzi* (*c.* 1792; London, Tate) or *Joseph Nollekens* (*c.* 1797; London, N.P.G.), the sitter's hand or some attribute balances the movement of the head. Only male portraits by Abbott are known, and his patrons were mostly drawn from the professional classes, particularly the Navy; there are several versions of *Lord Nelson* (e.g. 1798; London, N. Mar. Mus.). His style is crisp but scratchy in technique, and often the anatomy of his figures is inaccurate. Paint is handled in a manner comparable with that of Gainsborough Dupont, but Abbott's sense of composition is superior. In 1798 he was certified insane, but he continued to exhibit at the Royal Academy in London for two further years. Several of his works were probably finished by another hand.

BIBLIOGRAPHY

Waterhouse: *18th C.*
A. C. Sewter: 'Some New Facts about Lemuel Francis Abbott', *Connoisseur*, cxxxv (1955), pp. 178–83
R. Walker: *Regency Portraits* (London, 1985)

HUGH BELSEY

Abd, Tell al-. *See* UBAID, TELL AL-.

'Abd al-Hayy [Khwāja 'Abd al-Ḥayy] (*fl c.* 1374; *d* Samarkand, 1405). Illustrator and painter. According to the Safavid chronicler Dust Muhammad, 'Abd al-Hayy trained under Shams al-Din at Baghdad during the reign of the Jalayirid sultan Uways I (*reg* 1356–74) and became the leading painter under his son Ahmad, who was also 'Abd al-Hayy's pupil. When Timur took Baghdad, 'Abd al-Hayy was sent to Samarkand, either in 1393 or in 1401, where he spent the rest of his life. He seems to have specialized in monochrome ink drawings: Dust Muhammad recorded that 'Abd al-Hayy's pupil, Ahmad Jalayir, contributed a black-and-white drawing to a manuscript of the *Abūsa'īdnāma* ('Book of Abu Sa'id'), and a number of examples attributed to the late 14th century and preserved in various albums (e.g. Berlin, Staatsbib. Preuss. Kultbes., Orientabt. Diez A. 70–73) bear the notation that they were copied from 'Abd al-Hayy's drawings by Muhammad ibn Mahmud Shah Khayyam. In his album (Istanbul, Topkapı Pal. Lib., H. 2154), Dust Muhammad attributed one painting (fol. 20*v*) to 'Abd al-Hayy. It was detached from a copy (London, BL, Add. MS. 18113) of the *Dīvān* ('Collected poems') of Khwaju Kirmani copied at Baghdad in 1396. The scene of a sleeping youth visited by angels is in the same style as the other paintings in the manuscript, one of which (fol. 45*v*) is signed by JUNAYD. Dust Muhammad may have attributed the painting to ʿAbd al-Hayy because it includes a drawing on the wall of a woman holding an infant and standing in a rocky landscape. According to the Timurid chronicler Ibn ʿArabshah (1392–1450), ʿAbd al-Hayy was a skilled painter who worked for Timur on wall paintings at Timurid palaces. The wall painting of the woman and child is similar to marginal drawings in a copy (Washington, DC, Freer, 32.30–37) of Ahmad Jalayir's *Dīvān*, which have also been attributed to ʿAbd al-Hayy. According to Dust Mohammad, one of ʿAbd al-Hayy's outstanding students was Pir Ahmad Baghshimali. After ʿAbd al-Hayy's death his work remained a source of inspiration, and his purity, delicacy and firmness of brush were considered unrivalled.

See also ISLAMIC ART, §III, 4(v)(c).

BIBLIOGRAPHY

Enc. Iran.
Dūst Muḥammad: 'Preface to the Bahram Mirza Album' (1544); Eng. trans., ed. W. M. Thackston, in *A Century of Princes: Sources on Timurid History and Art* (Cambridge, MA, 1989), p. 345
D. E. Klimburg-Salter: 'A Sufi Theme in Persian Painting: The Diwan of Sultan Ahmad Gala'ir in the Freer Gallery of Art, Washington, DC', *Kst Orients*, xi (1977), pp. 43–84
V. A. Prentice: 'A Detached Miniature from the *Masnavis* of Khwaju Kermani', *Orient. A.*, xxvii (1981), pp. 60–66

ʿAbd al-Jalil Čelebi. *See* LEVNI.

ʿAbdallah Khan [ʿAbdallāh Khān] (*fl c.* 1810–50). Persian painter. His major work was a large mural with 118 life-size figures covering three walls in the interior of the Nigaristan Palace at Tehran (destr.; *see* ISLAMIC ART, §VIII, 11(i)). On the end wall the Qajar monarch Fath ʿAli Shah (*reg* 1797–1834) was depicted enthroned in state surrounded by his sons; on the side walls he was attended by a double row of courtiers and foreign ambassadors, including the British ambassador Sir Gore Ouseley (1770–1844) and Napoleon's envoy C. M. Gardane (1766–1818). Most 19th-century European travellers attributed this mural to the painter MUHAMMAD HASAN KHAN, but in the late 1880s the scholar E. G. Browne read the inscription below the painting stating that it was done by ʿAbdallah Khan in 1812–13. The mural is known through several small-scale copies (e.g. London, India Office Lib., Add. Or. 1239–1242). A full-length portrait of Fath ʿAli Shah in a red robe and bejewelled astrakhan cap (London, V&A, 707–1876) has been ascribed to the artist. In 1813–14 he executed murals depicting the courts of the Qajar rulers Agha Muhammad (*reg* 1779–97) and Fath ʿAli Shah on the walls of the Sulaymaniyya Palace (destr.) at Karaj near Tehran, of which a few fragments were preserved in the library of the National School of Agriculture there.

BIBLIOGRAPHY

B. W. Robinson: 'The Court Painters of Fatḥ ʿAlī Shāh', *Eretz-Israel*, vii (1964), pp. 94–105
——: *Persian Paintings in the India Office Library* (London, 1976), pp. 250–53
——: 'Persian Painting in the Qajar Period', *Highlights of Persian Art*, ed. R. Ettinghausen and E. Yarshater (Boulder, 1979), pp. 331–62
M. A. Karimzada Tabrizi: *Aḥvāl u āthār-i naqqāshān-i qadīm-i īrān* [The lives and art of old painters of Iran] (London, 1985), no. 540
B. W. Robinson: 'Persian Painting under the Zand and Qājār Dynasties', *From Nadir Shah to the Islamic Republic* (1991), vii of *The Cambridge History of Iran* (Cambridge, 1968–91), pp. 870–90

S. J. VERNOIT

ʿAbdallah Sayrafi [ʿAbdallāh al-Ṣayrafī] (*b* ?Tabriz; *fl* 1310–44). Calligrapher. The son of Khwaja Mahmud Sarraf al-Tabrizi, he was a pupil of HAYDAR, one of the six followers of YAQUT AL-MUSTAʿSIMI. ʿAbdallah Sayrafi spent his life in the Ilkhanid capital of Tabriz where he designed inscriptions in glazed tile for two buildings, the Dimishqiyya Madrasa and the building called 'The Master and the Pupil' (both destr.). He wrote a short treatise on calligraphy (Berlin, Staatsbib. Preuss. Kultbes., Orientabt., MS. or. oct. 48); a page of calligraphy in *thuluth*, *naskh*, and *riqāʿ* (Baghdad, Iraq Mus., 1324) shows that he had mastered the six classical scripts (*see* ISLAMIC ART, §III, 2(iii)(c)). He penned several manuscripts of the Koran, including one in *naskh* (Mashhad, 1320; Imam Riza Shrine Mus.) and another in *muḥaqqaq* (1327; Dublin, Chester Beatty Lib., MS. 1468). His work was still renowned in the 15th century, and his style was followed by JAʿFAR (*see also* ISLAMIC ART, §III, 2(iv)(b)). When the Timurid prince Ibrahim Sultan restored the Friday Mosque at Shiraz in 1417–18, he had a stone with a Koranic inscription carved by ʿAbdallah Sayrafi transported there from Tabriz.

BIBLIOGRAPHY

Enc. Iran.
Qāżī Aḥmad ibn Mīr Munshī: *Gulistān-i hunar* [Rose-garden of art] (*c.* 1606); Eng. trans. by V. Minorsky as *Calligraphers and Painters* (Washington, DC, 1959), pp. 61–3
S. S. Blair: *The Ilkhanid Shrine Complex at Natanz, Iran* (Cambridge, MA, 1986), p. 13

NABIL SAIDI

ʿAbd al-Samad [(Khwāja) ʿAbd al-Ṣamad; ʿAbd as-Ṣamad; Abdus Ṣamad] (*fl c.* 1540–95). Iranian miniature painter and calligrapher, active also in India. Trained in Safavid Iran, ʿAbd al-Samad migrated to India, where he became director of the Mughal painting workshops under the emperor Akbar (*reg* 1556–1605). In this key position, he influenced the development of Mughal painting in the second half of the 16th century more than any other artist (*see* INDIAN SUBCONTINENT, §VI, 4(i)(b)).

1. IRAN AND WESTERN CENTRAL ASIA, BEFORE 1555. No inscribed works by ʿAbd al-Samad are known from the period when he worked in Safavid Iran, though attributions have been proposed. Already a mature painter, he paid homage in 1544 to Akbar's father, the Mughal emperor Humayun (*reg* 1530–40; 1555–6), when the exiled ruler was given refuge at the court of the Safavid shah Tahmasp I at Tabriz. In 1550 ʿAbd al-Samad joined Humayun in Kabul, where an interim capital had been established. During the immediately succeeding years, together with other painters, he regularly presented works to the Emperor on various occasions including Nawruz, the Persian New Year. *Two Young Men in a Garden*, dated 1551, is one such illustration by the artist later mounted in the *Muraqqaʿ-i gulshan* (Tehran, Gulistan Pal. Lib., MSS 1663–4), an album of pictures and calligraphic pieces of various dates formed by Humayun's grandson Jahangir (*reg* 1605–27). Several literary references to New Year's presentations can be matched with paintings included in

the *Muraqqaʿ-i gulshan*, all of which are in a conservative Persian style. In fact, it is primarily through the patron and subjects that the Mughal designation can be given; in style they remain strongly Safavid.

2. INDIA, 1555 AND AFTER. ʿAbd al-Samad travelled to India with the imperial party in 1555 and under Akbar became a leading member of the imperial workshops. The young Akbar himself studied painting with ʿAbd al-Samad, one of whose greatest works of this time is *Akbar Presenting a Painting to Humayun in a Tree House* (Tehran, Gulistan Pal. Lib., MSS 1663–4). In about 1569 ʿAbd al-Samad succeeded MIR SAYYID ʿALI as director of a 14-year project to copy and illustrate for the young Akbar the great *Dastan-i Amir Hamza* ('Legend of Amir Hamza') or *Ḥamzanāma* ('Tales of Hamza'; dispersed). In contrast to his predecessor, ʿAbd al-Samad oversaw the completion of ten volumes and one thousand illustrations in a seven-year period; Mir Sayyid ʿAli had directed the completion of only four volumes in the same length of time. Perhaps in part because of this organizational ability, ʿAbd al-Samad took on increasingly prominent administrative roles: director of the imperial mint (1577), overseer of commerce (1582), manager of the royal household (1583) and finance minister for the province of Multan (1586). His son, Muhammad Sharif, became a friend of the young Prince Salim, later Jahangir. Like his father, he too was an artist given important administrative responsibilities within the governmental hierarchy. No other painter's family is known to have held comparable power.

ʿAbd al-Samad was an extraordinary craftsman and his pictures are full of minute detail describing the patterns of architectural tilework, for example, or costumes and foliage. A contemporary account also praises his ability to paint elaborate scenes on grains of rice. All of this evidently appealed to Humayun, although Akbar, in his early years as Emperor, demanded lively narrative scenes rather than virtuoso displays of technique.

The earliest work made by ʿAbd al-Samad for Akbar may be *Prince Akbar Hunting* (Los Angeles, Benkaim priv. col.), datable to about 1556. The attribution is suggested by a comparison with the last work known by the artist, *Khusrau Hunting*, from a *Khamsa* ('Five poems') of Nizami manuscript (1595; London, BL, Or. MS. 12208, fol. 82a). That the paintings are so close in sensibility and style is evidence of the painter's tremendous conservatism. Yet, while his own style is not innovative, he clearly encouraged experimentalism and novelty among those painters whose work he directed. The *Ḥamzanāma* is the single most vital and inventive Mughal manuscript, and it is in the last ten volumes—the portion of the project that he oversaw—that this character is firmly established. Over 100 artists and craftsmen were involved in this effort, and in many cases they had been brought to the imperial studios from elsewhere. That a new and original style evolved during this process is testament as much to ʿAbd al-Samad's organizational skills as to his artistic abilities.

There are relatively few works attributable to ʿAbd al-Samad during the early years of Akbar's reign, perhaps because he was so involved with the completion of the *Ḥamzanāma*. Among works of his middle period in India is *Two Camels Fighting* (USA, priv. col.), an important copy and adaptation of a famous work by the great 15th-century Persian painter Bihzad. A popular motif in Mughal art, the work also bears an important inscription noting the painter's advanced age and paying homage to his son Muhammad Sharif.

ʿAbd al-Samad was clearly a strong personality who influenced both his son and other artists. When Akbar discovered the painter Daswanth, he sent him to ʿAbd al-Samad for training, and the younger artist's early works show that he initially adopted a style recognizably close to that of ʿAbd al-Samad, whose use of dark tonalities, especially for landscape, and lack of interest in adopting techniques drawn from European prints (widely available and highly influential with other painters) were personal characteristics. Also typical was ʿAbd al-Samad's insistence on the prime importance of the picture surface. This is shown in *Jamshid Writing on a Rock* (1588; Washington, DC, Freer; see fig.), in which the solid gold sky negates spatial depth. The gold also creates a sense of opulence and wealth, another important element of ʿAbd al-Samad's style. His figures, however, do not have the individualized personality so effortlessly created by such artists as Basawan or Bishan Das. Faces represent types.

This and ʿAbd al-Samad's other late works, such as the scene of *Khusrau Hunting*, were again in the mainstream

ʿAbd al-Samad (attrib.): *Jamshid Writing on a Rock*, opaque colour on paper, 420×265 mm; *verso* of single leaf from a Jahangir-period album, 1588 (Washington, DC, Freer Gallery of Art, MS. 63.4)

of Mughal art. This is not because he had changed, but because by the 1590s Mughal painting had come to have many of those values that he had so long championed. Just as the technical skills of Mughal artists developed and matured, so too imperial taste became more epicurean. Densely detailed, technically immaculate compositions in which no individual detail predominates became the rule and replaced the earlier taste for compositional excitement and strong colour.

On the other hand, painting at the end of the Akbar period (*c.* 1600) moved away from the style of ʿAbd al-Samad, presenting instead compositionally simple scenes that stress the definition and interaction of human personalities—a skill in which ʿAbd al-Samad showed little interest. That this could not happen until after his death is further evidence of the power he held over the imperial workshops.

See also INDIAN SUBCONTINENT, §VI, 4(i)(b).

BIBLIOGRAPHY

EWA: 'Abdu 's-Samad'

W. Staude: '"Abd us-Samad, der Akbar Maler, und das Millionenzimmer in Schönbrunn', *Belvedere*, x (1931), pp. 155–60

M. B. Dickson and S. C. Welch: 'Abdus Samad', *The Houghton Shahnameh* (Cambridge, MA, 1981), pp. 192–200

M. C. Beach: *Early Mughal Painting* (Cambridge, MA, 1987)

MILO CLEVELAND BEACH

Abdülaziz. *See* OTTOMAN, §II(7).

ʿAbdülcelil Çelebi. *See* LEVNI.

Abedin, Zainul (*b* Kishorganj, East Pakistan [now Bangladesh], 18 Nov 1914; *d* Dhaka, 28 May 1976). Bangladeshi painter and printmaker. He studied painting at the Government School of Art in Calcutta from 1933 to 1938, and then taught there until 1947. His work first attracted public attention in 1943 when he produced a powerful series of drawings of the Bengal famine. After the partition of India and Pakistan in 1947 he worked as chief designer in the Pakistan government's Information and Publications Division, and also became principal of the Institute of Fine Arts in Dhaka (later known as the Bangladesh College of Arts and Crafts), which he helped to found in 1948 and where he remained until 1967. From 1951 to 1952 he visited Europe and, in addition to exhibiting his work at several locations, worked at the Slade School of Art in London, and represented Pakistan at the UNESCO art conference in Venice in 1952. An exhibition of his work in Lahore in 1953 became the starting-point for a series of exhibitions aimed at promoting contemporary Pakistani art. In 1956–7 he travelled to Japan, the United States, Canada, Mexico and Europe on a Rockefeller Foundation fellowship and in 1960 visited the Soviet Union. Since Bangladesh became independent in 1971, he has been regarded as the founding-figure of modern Bangladeshi art. His works embraced a variety of styles (*see* BANGLADESH, fig. 3), from the realistic sketches of the Bengal famine to semi-abstract and abstract paintings. Examples are preserved in a number of collections including the Zainul Abedin Sangrahashala at Mymensingh, the Academy of Fine Arts in Calcutta and the Lahore Museum.

BIBLIOGRAPHY

Zainul Abedin [Pakistan art folios] (Karachi, 1968)

B. K. Jahangir: *Contemporary Painters: Bangladesh* (Dhaka, 1974), pp. 5–9, 57

M. S. Islam: *Zainul Abedin* (Dhaka, 1977)

□

Abeele, Pieter van (*b* Amsterdam, 1608; *d* Amsterdam, after 1677). Dutch medallist. One of the foremost Dutch medallists of the 17th century, he was influential in developing a style that was more sculptural than before. Most of his medals consist of two silver plates of repoussé work, chased and joined together at the rim to create a hollow medal. This novel technique allowed the artist to create portraits in very high relief. His medals date from the late 1640s to the 1670s. One of the earliest, probably of 1647, portrays on one side *Prince Frederick Henry of Orange* and on the other *Prince Maurice of Orange.* More usually, the reverses of his medals bear a coat of arms, as for example the medal commemorating the settlement of the disputes between William II of Orange and the States of Holland (1650). Here the reverse bears William's armorial shield, a crown, and the English garter. The ground of the obverse is covered with orange branches in the manner typical of van Abeele and demonstrates his mastery of chasing. On his medal of *Admiral Maarten Tromp* (1653) the armorial reverse incorporates a scene from a naval battle. On others, such as the well-known medals commemorating the departure of Charles II for Britain from Scheveningen (1660), with their grim portrait of the King on the obverse, the scene occupies the whole of the reverse. On these medals the reverse is usually of a small-scale figurative type popular in Dutch medals, but executed with a vigour that is van Abeele's own. He also devised allegorical reverses, such as the charming marriage medal in which a couple on the obverse and a figure of Motherhood on the reverse are surrounded by garlands of flowers.

BIBLIOGRAPHY

Forrer; Thieme–Becker

E. Hawkins, A. W. Franks and H. A. Grueber: *Medallic Illustrations of the History of Great Britain and Ireland* (London, 1885)

PHILIP ATTWOOD

Abel, Josef (*b* Aschach, 22 Aug 1764; *d* Vienna, 4 Oct 1818). Austrian painter. He studied at the Akademie der Bildenden Künste in Vienna under Jakob Matthias Schmutzer (1733–1811) from 1783. On the advice of his mentor, Heinrich Füger, Abel turned from landscape to history painting, winning a gold medal in 1794 for *Daedalus and Icarus* (Vienna, Akad. Bild. Kst.). He was invited to Poland in 1795 by Prince Adam Casimir Czartoryski, and he produced numerous family portraits for the prince in a variety of media. In 1797 he returned to Vienna, where he taught, as well as undertaking commissions for paintings and for prints (e.g. *Portrait of the Artist's Father*, see Aurenhammer, fig. 7).

Abel had a preference for Classical subject-matter during his early training, and this was reinforced by his stay in Rome from 1801 to 1807. During this period he painted his most important work, *F. G. Klopstock in Elysium* (1803–7; Vienna, Belvedere), in collaboration with his friend Johann Christian Reinhart, who painted the landscape background. In 1815 Abel was elected a member of the academy in Vienna on the strength of *Cato of Utica* (completed 1817; Vienna, Akad. Bild. Kst.). In addition to his portraits and history paintings, he also produced theatre curtains, for example the main curtain for the theatre in Pest (1810; drawing, Vienna, Albertina, 14611), as well as a curtain (1794; destr. 1945) for the Burgtheater in Vienna, based on Füger's designs.

BIBLIOGRAPHY

Meissner

H. Aurenhammer: 'Josef Abel, 1764–1818', *Mitt. Österreich. Gal.*, x (1966), pp. 3–26 [18 pict.]

ANDRZEJ RYSZKIEWICZ

Abela, Eduardo (*b* San Antonio de los Baños, nr Güines, 1889; *d* Havana, 1965). Cuban painter and caricaturist. He graduated from the Academia de S Alejandro in Havana in 1920 and lived in Paris from 1927 to 1929. There he studied at the Académie de la Grande Chaumière and abandoned academicism, developing a modernist 'Cuban' style, in which folkloric scenes of peasant life were depicted in a colourful, energetic, pseudo-naive manner reminiscent of Jules Pascin and Amedeo Modigliani. An outstanding work of this period is *Triumph of the Rumba* (*c.* 1928; Havana, Mus. N. B.A.). After a trip to Italy in the early 1930s, Abela began to paint canvases such as *Guajiros* ('peasants'; 1938; Havana, Mus. N. B.A.), in which the Classical sobriety and order is the result of his contact with Italian medieval and Renaissance art. His style underwent a radical change in the early 1950s, and from this time until his death he painted small works that recall the drawings of children as well as the works of Marc Chagall in their use of fantasy.

Abela was a noted caricaturist early in his career, which contributed to the informal, whimsical quality of his painting. His most famous cartoon series, *The Fool*, helped bring about the overthrow of the Machado regime in Cuba in 1933.

BIBLIOGRAPHY

L. de la Torriente: 'El mundo ensoñado de Abela', *Rev. Inst. N. Cult.*, i/1 (1956), pp. 41–56

O. Hurtado and others: *Pintores cubanos* (Havana, 1962)

Abela: Magic and Fable (exh. cat., ed. C. Luis; Miami, FL, Cub. Mus. A. & Cult., 1983)

J. A. Martínez: *Cuban Art and National Identity: The Vanguardia Painters, 1927–1950* (Gainsville, 1994)

GIULIO V. BLANC

Abel de Pujol, Alexandre [Abel, Alexandre-Denis] (*b* Douai, 30 Jan 1785; *d* Paris, 28 Sept 1861). French painter. He was the natural son of Alexandre de Pujol de Mortry, a nobleman and provost of Valenciennes, but did not use his father's name until after 1814. He trained first at the Académie de Valenciennes (1799–1803), then at the Ecole des Beaux-Arts, Paris, and in the studio of Jacques-Louis David. At the end of 1805 it seemed he would have to end his apprenticeship for lack of money but David let him continue free of charge, so impressed had he been by *Philopoemen. . . Splitting Wood* (1806; ex-Delobel priv. col., Valenciennes). The astonishing *Self-portrait* (Valenciennes, Mus. B.-A.), showing the artist as the very image of a romantic hero, dates from this period.

From 1808 Abel exhibited history paintings at the Salon, making his living, however, by painting shop signs. In 1811 he won the prestigious Prix de Rome and his father subsequently permitted him to adopt his name. Thus from 1814 he signed his pictures *Abel de Pujol.* His stay in Italy was brief; he returned to Paris in 1812 and painted portraits in a finely executed Neo-classical style (e.g. *Nicolas Legrand and his Grandson*, exh. Salon, 1817; ex-Heim Gal., London, see 1978 exh. cat., no. 14). He won the prize for history painting at the Salon of 1817, with *St Stephen Preaching* (Paris, St Thomas d'Aquin), a representative work, characterized by impeccable drawing, clear composition, broad light effects and an evident predilection for painting beautiful drapery. At the Salon of 1819 he won acclaim for the *Death of the Virgin* (untraced), commissioned for the cathedral of Notre-Dame, and the *Renaissance of the Arts*, a ceiling painting over the grand staircase at the Louvre (destr. 1855; fragments, Valenciennes, Acad.). These anticipate the two main aspects of his future work: religious paintings and ceiling paintings with allegorical (e.g. *Egypt Saved by Joseph*, 1827; Paris, Louvre) or mythological subjects (e.g. decoration for the Galerie de Diane, 1822–4; Fontainebleau, Château). The grisaille decoration he executed in collaboration with Charles Meynier in 1826 on the coving in the great hall of the Bourse, Paris, was much acclaimed and won him a reputation as a painter in grisaille.

The revival of the use of frescoes in churches was another aspect of his work, first realized in the chapel of St Roch in the church of St Sulpice (1819–22) in which he modified his palette and simplified his forms to obtain monumental effects. His technical inventiveness was demonstrated again in 1828 when he painted the antependium made from lava in the church of St Elisabeth, Paris, where he also designed three stained-glass windows. Further experimental work was his participation in research into encaustic techniques of decoration (King's staircase, 1835; Fontainebleau, Château). Meanwhile he continued to execute numerous large-scale decorations in public buildings, two examples being the *Apocalypse* (2.5×13 m, 1837; Paris, Notre-Dame de Bonne-Nouvelle) and *St Denis Preaching in Gaul* (3.5×14 m, 1838–40; Paris, St Denys du St Sacrement). These are linked to the Nazarenes in the austerity of their frieze composition and the choice of archaic subject-matter. More striking is his unusual use of grisaille in more intimate works, such as the portrait of *Mademoiselle de L* (exh. Salon, 1831; Valenciennes, Mus. B.-A.).

In 1835 Abel de Pujol was elected to a chair in the Académie. His studio, which was particularly popular between 1817 and 1830, was attended, among others, by Camille Roqueplan, Alexandre-Gabriel Decamps, Adrienne Grandpierre-Deverzy (*b* 1798)—his second wife—and Théophile Vauchelet (1802–73). His son, Alexandre (1816–84), was also a pupil and exhibited at the Salons of 1847 and 1850. Alexandre's works, particularly his portraits, have been attributed to his father, but his signature, 'Adre de Pujol', identifies them securely as his own.

BIBLIOGRAPHY

De David à Delacroix (exh. cat., Paris, Grand Pal., 1974)

Trésors des musées du Nord de la France, II: Peinture française, 1770–1830 (exh. cat., Calais, Mus. B.-A.; Arras, Mus. B.-A.; Douai, Mus. Mun.; Lille, Mus. B.-A.; 1975–6) [notes on Abel de Pujol by D. Vieville]

Forgotten French Art from the First to the Second Empire (exh. cat., London, Heim Gal., 1978)

P. Grunchec: *Le Concours des Prix de Rome, 1797–1863* (Paris, 1986)

B. Foucart: *Le Renouveau de la peinture religieuse en France, 1800–1860* (Paris, 1987)

ISABELLE DENIS

Abercrombie, Sir **(Leslie) Patrick** (*b* Ashton-upon-Mersey, 6 June 1879; *d* Aston Tirrold, Oxon, 23 March 1957). English urban planner, architect and writer. He was educated at Uppingham, Leics, and was an apprentice in architectural offices, first in Manchester and then in Liverpool. In 1907 Charles H. Reilly appointed him to the School of Architecture at the University of Liverpool, and in 1909, following the foundation of the School of Civic Design, the first urban planning school in Britain, he became deputy to its professor, S. D. Adshead. He helped found its publication, the *Town Planning Review*, and became a major contributor; he wrote a series of articles on American and European cities, giving a detailed account of his conception of history, architectural styles and the analysis of urban planning. In 1915 he became Professor of Civic Design and was nominated Librarian for the Town Planning Institute. He was active as an editor and conference organizer as well as a teacher and practising architect, involved in work stimulated by the Housing and Town Planning Act of 1909; for example he produced various schemes for low-cost housing in established and new towns in Yorkshire.

In 1916, with Arthur and Sidney Kelley, he won the international competition for a new city plan for Dublin; the jury included Patrick Geddes and John Nolen. Abercrombie's plan addressed the problems relating to such a large-scale project, utilizing working models previously employed by eminent urban planners such as Georges-Eugène Haussmann, Eugène Alfred Hénard and Camillo Sitte. Abercrombie's subsequent plan for Doncaster (1922), the first English regional plan to be published, also embodied the first complete application of Geddes's regional planning concepts (*see* GEDDES, PATRICK). This plan, and those for Deeside (1923; with Sidney Kelley and Theodore Fyfe) and Tees-side (1925; with Adshead) in the north of England reveal a marked increase in the scale of planning through the application of Geddes's principles of conurbation, and, in so doing, they forged a link between urban and economic planning.

Abercrombie refined and articulated his planning methodology in later schemes: for example, in his plan for Sheffield (1924; with R. H. Mattocks) he introduced an elaborate preliminary analysis that allowed him to test the effectiveness of civic surveys. He also became a defender of the environment, a pioneering activity that began with the plan for Stratford-on-Avon (1923; with Lascelles Abercrombie) and culminated with the foundation of the Council for the Preservation of Rural England (1926), of which he was chairman and president for life. His planning methodology revolved around analysis, preservation and development, retaining old structures where possible and making them workable under modern conditions, as seen in the plans for East Kent (1925–8; with John Archibald), Thames Valley (1929; with Walter Mayo), Bristol and Bath (1930; with Bertrand Brueton) and Cumberland (1932).

Abercrombie was regarded as one of the most important urban planners in the country. He was committed to comprehensive planning, seeing in the urban planner a new type of intellectual whose interdisciplinary skills enabled him to carry out painless social transformation. His *Town and Country Planning* (1933) reveals just such a vision, the roots of which can be traced back to the Utopias of William Morris and the industrial philanthropy of the 19th century. This manual formed a central point of reference in the English and international literature of urban planning, which had never before been taken seriously by architectural historians.

In 1935 Abercrombie replaced Adshead in the Chair of Town Planning at the University of London, and in 1937 he participated in the Barlow Commission, which thoroughly criticized the existing planning legislation. This gave him the opportunity to carry out the London County Plan (1943; with J. H. Forshaw), for which competing proposals were produced by the MARS Group and the Royal Academy, and the Greater London Plan (1944). In the first plan one can see traces of the ideas of Steen Eiler Rasmussen and Alker Tripp, but on the whole the two plans for London represent a synthesis of developments in English urban planning from the beginning of the century and reveal the extent that it had moved away from the schemes of Ebenezer Howard. It was not the garden city that would transform the London metropolis but the satellite towns and intervening green belts proposed by Charles B. Purdom and Raymond Unwin from the 1920s. With this technical and methodological inheritance, Abercrombie approached such later plans as those for Plymouth (1945), Edinburgh (1949; with Derek Plumstead) and, finally, Addis Ababa (1956; with Gerald Dix): what had become a proven language of urban planning could be exported anywhere, duly amended, as a universal concept recognizing no frontiers. Abercrombie was knighted in 1945; he received gold medals from the RIBA (1946), AIA (1949) and the Town Planning Institute (1955).

WRITINGS

'The Era of Architectural Town Planning', *Town Planning Rev.*, v/3 (1914), pp. 195–213

'The Preservation of Rural England: The Control of Development by Means of Rural Planning', *Town Planning Rev.*, xii/1 (1926), pp. 5–56

Town and Country Planning (London, 1933, rev. 3/1959)

Planning in Town and Country: Difficulties and Possibilities (Liverpool and London, 1937)

BIBLIOGRAPHY

G. E. Cherry: *The Evolution of British Town Planning* (Plymouth, 1974)

A. Manno: *Patrick Abercrombie: A Chronological Bibliography, With Annotations and Biographical Details* [Brunswick Environmental Papers] (Leeds, 1980)

——: *Patrick Abercrombie: Storia della pianificazione urbane e rurale in Inghilterra, 1909–40* (diss., Venice, Ist. U. Archit., 1980)

G. Dix: 'Patrick Abercrombie, 1879–1957', *Pioneers in British Planning*, ed. G. E. Cherry (London, 1981), pp. 103–30

ANTONIO MANNO

Aberdeen. Scottish city situated on the east coast of the estuary of the River Dee and River Don, with a rich agricultural hinterland. The city centre is divided into two historic parts of distinct character: Old Aberdeen, dominated by St Machar's Cathedral and King's College (est. 1495), part of the University, which grew up near the Don around the seat of the bishop (the bishopric was established in 1137), and New Aberdeen, a royal burgh beside the Dee (est. ?early 12th century), which was extended in the Neo-classical style in the late 18th century and early 19th and which forms the heart of the present commercial centre.

In Old Aberdeen, well established by the time of the earliest surviving royal charter of 1179 and enhanced by the founding of a royal mint soon after, the High Street leads south from the cathedral, which was started by the Don in 1164, rebuilt from *c.* 1370 and is dominated by distinctive sandstone 16th-century spires. Nearby, King's College Chapel (completed 1505) is all that survives of Bishop Elphinstone's original foundation (1495). The centre of the royal burgh was, by the time of the first map (1661), concentrated around a castle and Castle Gate (now Street), and Broad Street and Gallowgate ran north. Rebuilding, though no major physical expansion, to house the growing population took place until improvements were made to roads and to the navigation of the Dee in the late 18th century; the docks and quays were built in the 19th and early 20th century.

Union Street, a major new route to the west, was laid out after 1800 and carried on arches across the River Denburn and the medieval streets below. Its success led to the development of streets and squares north and south of it, such as Golden Square (1817) and Bon Accord Square (1823–6). Union Street (see fig.) is particularly fine, lined with many handsome Neo-classical buildings by ARCHIBALD SIMPSON and John Smith (i), built with the sparkling local granite, which was both used in Aberdeen and exported. Union Street was extended later in the 19th century as Queen's Road, the catalyst for generously planned, smart suburban development with such villas as the Baronial-style No. 50 (1886) by the original and roguish John Bridgeford Pirie (1852–90). The quality of the granite imparted a crisp, hard character even to the most ornate Victorian and Edwardian buildings, such as the Perpendicular-style façade of Marischal College (1906) by A. Marshall Mackenzie (1848–1933). Although the inevitable suburban growth of speculative bungalows and local authority tower blocks occurred throughout the 20th century, commercial rebuilding did not destroy the essential character of the city centre.

Aberdeen Art Gallery was founded in 1884 and was greatly boosted by the bequest in 1900 of the collection of the granite merchant Alexander Macdonald. From 1880 he had commissioned a unique series of portraits of British artists and also collected the work of living artists. The gallery's strength is British art of the 18th, 19th and 20th centuries. It has an especially fine representation of most major groups, styles and movements of the first half of the 20th century, such as the New English Art Club, the Glasgow Boys, the Camden Town Group and the Scottish Colourists. Local artists are well represented with works by William Dyce, John Philip, James Cassie (1819–79), James McBey (1883–1959), James Cowie and Joan Eardley.

BIBLIOGRAPHY

R. E. H. Mellor and J. S. Smith: *A Visitor's Guide to Aberdeen* (Aberdeen, n.d.)

W. A. Brogden: *Aberdeen: An Illustrated Architectural Guide* (Edinburgh, 1986)

MALCOLM HIGGS

Abergen, Antonis van. *See* OBBERGHEN, ANTONIS VAN.

Aberdeen, view down Castle Street and Union Street; from a photograph by George Washington Wilson, *c.* 1880

Aberli, Johann Ludwig (*b* Winterthur, 14 Nov 1723; *d* Berne, 17 Oct 1786). Swiss painter, draughtsman and engraver. In 1741 he moved to Berne, where he took drawing lessons with Johann Grimm (1675–1747), whose school of drawing he took over in 1747. He visited the Bernese Oberland with Emanuel Handmann, Christian Georg Schütz (1718–91) and Friedrich Wilhelm Hirt (1721–72) in 1759 and in the same year travelled to Paris with Adrian Zingg (1734–86). This was his only trip abroad, but it determined him to work exclusively as a landscape painter. After nine months he returned to Berne, where his landscape views became popular, particularly with foreign travellers, enamoured of 'Nature' and keen to retain souvenirs of their travels. He was one of the first artists to portray the beauties of the Swiss countryside; his favourite subjects were the Aare Valley and views of Swiss lakes (e.g. *View of Erlach on the Lake of Biel*; Berne, Kstmus.). He invented a technique known as the 'Aberli style', which consisted of watercolour washes added to an image in which slightly smudged outlines were achieved through a combination of engraving and etching. The prints were made from drawings taken from nature and finished in the studio. His style was characterized by delicate execution, an intimate narrative approach, refined colours and the ability to convey a light and vaporous atmosphere. Aberli's success was such that he had to employ assistants and pupils to aid him in the coloration process; his pupils included Erasmus Ritter, Johann Jakob Biedermann, Marquard Wocher (1760–1830), Gabriel Ludwig Lory the elder (1763–1840) and Peter Birmann. From 1773 to 1775 Aberli also painted a series of costumes in response to tourist demand.

BIBLIOGRAPHY

SKL

Johann Ludwig Aberli, 1723–86 (exh. cat. by C. König-von Dach, Berne, Kstmus., 1987)

JEANNE-MARIE HORAT-WEBER

Abhānagari. *See* ABANERI.

'Abid ['Ābid] (*fl c.* 1615–58). Indian miniature painter, son of AQA RIZA (i) and brother of ABU'L-HASAN. Both his father and his brother worked for the Mughal emperor Jahangir (*reg* 1605–27). Although 'Abid probably began working in the royal atelier *c.* 1615, all of his known signed works are datable to the reign of Shah Jahan (*reg* 1628–58). His style varied somewhat from that of his celebrated older brother, but 'Abid's work also stayed within the strict formalism of the Persian-derived courtly concerns for symmetry, technical perfection and minute detail. Within these constraints, 'Abid's portraits of court figures are injected with an animation that creates characterization of individual personalities and intensifies the narrative. 'Abid was an accomplished colourist, whose vivid use of colour seems to contrast with the realism of his subjects, primarily battle and court scenes. His known paintings are relatively few; most are from the *Padshāhnāma* of *c.* 1636–58 (Windsor Castle, Royal Lib., MS. HB.149, fols 94*v* [signed], 192*v* and at least two dispersed leaves elsewhere).

See also INDIAN SUBCONTINENT, §V, 4(i)(c) and (d).

BIBLIOGRAPHY

The Art of Mughal India: Paintings and Precious Objects (exh. cat. by S. C. Welch, New York, Asia House Gals, 1964)

The Grand Moghul: Imperial Painting in India, 1600–1660 (exh. cat. by M. C. Beach, Williamstown, MA, Clark A. Inst.; Baltimore, MD, Walters A.G.; Boston, MA, Mus. F.A.; New York, Asia Soc. Gals; 1978–9)

W. Komala: *The Windsor Castle 'Badshah-Nama' and its Place in the Development of Historical Painting during the Reign of Shah Jahan, 1628–58* (diss., Iowa City, U. IA, 1982)

JEFFREY A. HUGHES

Abildgaard, Nicolai Abraham (*b* Copenhagen, 11 Sept 1743; *d* Frederiksdal, Copenhagen, 4 June 1809). Danish painter, designer and architect. His paintings reveal both Neo-classical and Romantic interests and include history paintings as well as literary and mythological works. The variety of his subject-matter reflects his wide learning, a feature further evidenced by the broad range of his creative output. In addition to painting, he produced decorative work, sculpture and furniture designs, as well as being engaged as an architect. Successfully combining both intellectual and imaginative powers, he came to be fully appreciated only in the 1980s.

1. EARLY LIFE AND PAINTING, TO 1790. He studied at the Kongelige Danske Kunstakademi in Copenhagen (1764–72), and in 1767 he assisted Johan Edvard Mandelberg (1730–86) in painting the domed hall of the Fredensborg Slot with scenes from the Homeric epic the *Iliad.* In 1772 he was granted a five-year travelling scholarship from the Kunstakademi to study in Rome. During his Roman sojourn he extensively copied works of art from the period of antiquity up to that of the Carracci family. His friendships with the Danish painter Jens Juel, the Swedish sculptor Johan Tobias Sergel and the Swiss painter Johann Heinrich Fuseli placed him among artists who were in the mainstream of a widespread upheaval in European art. In these years Abildgaard developed both Neo-classical and Romantic tastes; his masterpiece of the period is *Philoctetes Wounded* (1774–5; Copenhagen, Stat. Mus. Kst; see fig. 1), a highly personal interpretation of the Belvedere *Torso* (Rome, Vatican, Mus. Pio-Clementino) and Michelangelo's *ignudi* in the Sistine Chapel in the Vatican, Rome. The pains of the wounded man are passionately expressed, yet the pathos is balanced by the heroic idealism of the muscular body. A revealing instance of the artist's reinterpretation of an antique source is *Ymer Suckling the Cow Audhumla* (*c.* 1777; Copenhagen, Stat. Mus. Kst). In the famous fresco from the 'basilica' of Herculaneum, representing Hercules' first meeting with his son Telephos, the latter is suckling a deer (1st century AD; Naples, Mus. Archeol. N.). Abildgaard transferred this compositional idea to a subject from Norse mythology. In his first sketch, however, he had modelled the figure of Ymer after Sergel's sculpture *Resting Faun* (1770–74; Stockholm, Nmus.). The final painting was probably completed after Abildgaard's return to Denmark.

In 1777 Abildgaard was elected a member of the Kunstakademi and commissioned to produce a series of history paintings of the Danish kings of the house of Oldenburg for the Banqueting Hall of Christiansborg Slot in Copenhagen, then the royal residence. From 1778 to 1791 he made ten monumental paintings, of which only three survived the fire of 1794, when the whole palace

1. Nicolai Abraham Abildgaard: *Philoctetes Wounded*, oil on canvas, 1.23×1.74 m, 1774–5 (Copenhagen, Statens Museum for Kunst)

was ruined. The rest are known only from sketches (Copenhagen, Stat. Mus. Kst). Although Abildgaard adopted a realist approach, the large canvases rely strongly on European Renaissance and Baroque traditions. Thus, in terms of composition, *Christian I Raises Holstein to the State of Duchy* (1778–9; Copenhagen, Christiansborg Slot) is similar to Rubens's *Wisdom of Solomon* (Copenhagen, Stat. Mus. Kst), then in the royal collection, and more generally to 15th-century Italian ceremonial representations and the works of Raphael.

In 1778 Abildgaard had been appointed professor at the Kongelige Akademi, and the demands of this post together with those due to his royal commission left little time for small-scale paintings. Nevertheless, he did paint some, such as *Socrates in Prison* (*c.* 1784; Copenhagen, Ny Carlsberg Glyp.), whose subject-matter reflects his Neo-classical tastes. Though fully dressed, the pose of the philosopher is again inspired by the Belvedere *Torso.* Abildgaard was a man of extremely wide reading, as is witnessed by his copious private library (now part of the library of the Kunstakademi), and he also drew on themes from Ossian and Shakespeare, as well as from ancient Danish mythology and history in his work.

A most original and enigmatic work from the same period is the *Temple of Fortune* (1785; Hillerød, Frederiksborg Slot), which is actually a painted fire-screen. Iconographically, it is a complex work and is based on a satirical essay (1764) of the same title by the Danish poet Johannes Ewald (1743–81). In 1780 Abildgaard had made drawings to illustrate the text, which were engraved by Johan Frederik Clemens. In the fire-screen, people from all classes are grouped around the stairs leading to the Templum Fortunae, all of them playing a part in the representation of human folly. From 1785 to 1789 Abildgaard worked on a series of drawings and paintings inspired by the satirical novel *Niels Klim* (Latin edn, 1741; Danish edn, 1742) by Ludvig Holberg (1684–1754). They were eventually turned into copperplates by Clemens for a new Danish translation of the novel published in Copenhagen in 1789. From 1789 to 1791 Abildgaard was Director of the Kunstakademi.

2. PAINTING AND SCULPTURE DESIGNS, 1790–1809. In the last decade of the 18th century, and especially after the tragic fire at the Christiansborg Slot, besides teaching, Abildgaard largely dedicated himself to the realization of a public monument to commemorate the abolition of serfdom in Denmark in 1788. Popularly called the Liberty Memorial (1792–7; Copenhagen, Vesterbrogade), it consists of an inscribed obelisk surrounded at the base by the allegorical statues of Fidelity, Agriculture, Courage and Patriotism (or Civic Virtue), with other allegories carved in relief between them. Although Abildgaard probably contributed very little to the actual execution of the monument, he was responsible for the iconographical programme and the overall architectural design (the alle-

gorical statues were in fact carved by the sculptors Johannes Wiedewelt, Andreas Weidenhaupt (1738–1805) and Nicolai Dajon (1748–1823)). Through this work and the above-mentioned fire-screen Abildgaard stands out as characteristic of the idealistic artists that appeared in the wake of the European Enlightenment, a sort of *peintre-philosophe*. During the same period he also designed a series of tombstones and monuments to commemorate illustrious Danes. The sarcophagi for the heir-presumptive Frederik (*d* 1805) and his consort Sophie Frederikke (*d* 1794) were also made after Abildgaard's designs (Roskilde Cathedral, Frederik V Chapel).

From 1801 to 1809 Abildgaard was again Director of the Kunstakademi, and by the beginning of the 19th century he had entered into a second bloom as a painter. The monumental—in form if not in size—allegorical paintings from 1800 of *Theology*, *Justice* (Copenhagen, Stat. Mus. Kst) and *Philosophy* (priv. col., see Skovgaard, fig. 48) may be afterthoughts from his work on the Liberty Memorial. They have highly learned, somewhat unorthodox compositions (e.g. Theology holds out a Medusa head, thus opposing enlightenment with terror), and possibly Abildgaard's intentions were satirical. His interest in Voltaire's tragedy *Le Triumvirat* (1767) further indicates that he was deeply engaged in political thought at this time. He painted at least five scenes from the play, the first ones probably begun as early as 1796. Some formed wall decorations for the house he designed at 5, Nytorv in Copenhagen, such as that illustrating Act 4, Scene 4 (1800), which shows an instance of the struggle for power following the assassination of Julius Caesar. Two of the female protagonists, Fulvie and Julie, are engaged in violent action, as one, dagger in hand, eagerly seeks vengeance against the triumvirs, while the other urges for peace and reconciliation. The dramatic style of the figures harks back to his Roman years, and particularly to the influence of Fuseli. The compositional scheme is the same as used by Alexander Runciman in his etching *Landing of St Margaret* (*c.* 1774), a work Abildgaard may have known. In the painting of the two women Abildgaard characterized their moral standing by way of colour: Fulvie's fluttering cape is purple, suggesting blood and vengeance, while Julie wears a pale blue dress, indicating composure and continence.

From 1802 to 1804 Abildgaard executed four large canvases (Copenhagen, Stat. Mus. Kst) using episodes from Terence's play *Girl from Andros* (see fig. 2). Helped by Sebastiano Serlio's theories of perspective and his own reminiscences of Roman architecture, he created a vision of the ideal city of antiquity. These cityscapes bear little historical or topographical authenticity, and in their static austerity, clearly inspired by Nicolas Poussin, they form a sharp contrast to the lively movements of the 'actors'. Nevertheless, the artist achieved a perfect unity of composition and colour within each and between all four of the paintings, mostly due to a delicate, sometimes dramatic handling of light and shadow. The paintings were conceived as pendants and presented to his second wife, Juliane Marie, whom he married in 1803. They decorated the walls of their home at the Kunstakademi in the Charlottenborg Slot.

2. Nicolai Abraham Abildgaard: *Scene from Terence: Girl from Andros, 2, iii*, oil on canvas, 1.57×1.28 m, 1802 (Copenhagen, Statens Museum for Kunst)

Abildgaard's late work is thematically centred around literary and historical scenes from Greek and Roman antiquity. Thus in 1808–9 he painted 33 scenes from Apuleius' *Metamorphoses, or the Golden Ass*, a Roman novel in which the young hero Lucius is changed into an ass through the witchcraft of his lover, the maidservant Fotis. In *Fotis Appalled at the Sight of Lucius' Metamorphosis* (1809; Copenhagen, Stat. Mus. Kst) the girl strikes a dramatic pose in front of the youth, who has the head of an ass. His body, however, is still human and reveals the strong influence of the style found in work by the circle around the Carracci. A subdued, lyrical tone emanates from many of his late genre-like pictures, and the mature artist showed his ability to convey a universally human range of sentiment and feeling. Thus *Papirius and his Mother* (1809) is ironic, *Anacreon and Amaryllis* (1808) idyllic, and *Sappho and the Mytilene Woman* (1809; all Copenhagen, Stat. Mus. Kst) elegiac. The latter two form part of a series on ancient love poetry.

3. OTHER ACTIVITIES. Throughout his life Abildgaard was commissioned to produce work of a more decorative nature. He painted overdoors for the Potentate Apartment at Christiansborg Slot (*Allegories of the State of Things in Europe during Four Ages* and *Allegory of the Sound*, destr. 1794; studies in Copenhagen, Stat. Mus. Kst) and for Count Adam Gottlob Moltke's town house (*Allegories of the Three World Religions*, 1780s; Copenhagen, Håndværkerforen.). From 1794 he worked for the heir-presumptive Frederick on the decorations of the latter's apartments at the Amalienborg Palace in Copenhagen. The State Room is a work of great integrity and originality,

one of the first in the Neo-classicist style in Denmark. The originally yellow walls were divided by white and gilt Ionic pilasters resting on a violet-blue panel base. The frieze, with gilt garlands on a royal blue ground, corresponded to the colouring of the furniture and curtains. In niches flanking the main door there were sculptures of the muses *Euterpe* and *Terpsichore*, probably modelled by the young Bertel Thorvaldsen after Abildgaard's design. In the Throne Room the walls were decorated with allegorical oval paintings and overdoors by Abildgaard himself (the Continents and the Elements). On the whole, as an interior decorator Abildgaard avoided the neatness of the Empire style for the sake of a more grandiose vision of antiquity, preferring strong simplicity and striking colours. To complete the general effect he designed furniture that came to influence several generations of the Danish Golden Age era and fell within that peculiar field called 'artist's furniture' (i.e. that designed by painters to furnish their own homes). Abildgaard used and reinterpreted ancient Greek and Roman models. For his own home he designed, among other things, eight gilt chairs of the *klismos* type, with wickerwork seats and a palmetto frieze on the top rail, of exquisite taste and elegance, albeit hardly functional for the user (*see* DENMARK, fig. 16). He tried his hand in almost every field within the applied arts. In 1779 he made costume designs for a production of Johannes Ewald's *Balder's Death* at the Kongelige Teater in Copenhagen. He designed various medals, and in his *Apis Clock* (Copenhagen, Kstindustmus.) a Renaissance-style bronze bull is integrated in the work, wearing a round clock on its back.

Abildgaard's output as an architect is limited to only a few works, but they nonetheless show his versatility in this field also. From 1799 to 1803 he built a private house at 5, Nytorv in Copenhagen for which some of the above-mentioned Triumvirat scenes were painted as wall decorations. It is a simple, well proportioned Neo-classicist construction, which still contributes to the architectural harmony of the square, although the top floor is a later addition. After 1805 he built a country house for himself, called Spurveskjul (Sparrow's Hide) near Frederiksdal. For the English-style landscape gardens at the manor houses of Frederiksberg near Copenhagen and Sorgenfri he designed such follies as the Apis Temple (1802; Copenhagen, Frederiksborg Have). This was a small temple derived from Roman models, and the Dionysian bull in the fronton was copied from an ancient intaglio.

BIBLIOGRAPHY

L. Swane: *Abildgaard: Arkitektur og dekoration* (Copenhagen, 1926)
B. Skovgaard: *Maleren Abildgaard* (Copenhagen, 1961)
T. Holck Colding: *Akademiet og Guldalderen, 1750–1850* [The Academy and the Golden Age, 1750–1850], Dansk Kunsthistorie (Copenhagen, 1972), pp. 143–57
P. Kragelund: 'The Church, the Revolution and the "Peintre Philosophe": A Study in the Art of Nicolai Abildgaard', *Hafnia*, ix (1983), pp. 25–65
E. K. Sass: *Lykkens Tempel: Et maleri af Nicolai Abildgaard* [The Temple of Fortune: a painting by Nicolai Abildgaard] (Copenhagen, 1986)
P. Kragelund: 'Abildgaard around 1800: His Tragedy and Comedy', *Anlct. Romana Inst. Dan.*, xvi (1987), pp. 137–85
M. Gelfer-Jørgensen, ed.: *Herculanum paa Sjælland: Klassicisme og nyantik i dansk møbeltradition* [Herculaneum on Zealand: classicism and Neo-antiquity in the Danish tradition of furniture] (Copenhagen, 1988), pp. 33–60
J. Andersen: *De år i Rom: Abildgaard, Sergel, Füssli* [Those years in Rome: Abildgaard, Sergel, Fuseli] (Copenhagen, 1989)

JENS PETER MUNK

Abingdon, Alexander of. *See* ALEXANDER OF ABINGDON.

Abiseo. *See* GRAN PAJATÉN.

Åbo. *See* TURKU.

Aboba. *See* PLISKA.

Āboliņš, Valdis (*b* Liepāja, 14 April 1939; *d* West Berlin, 14 Feb 1984). Latvian performance artist. He arrived in Germany at the age of five as a refugee and later triumphed over geopolitical circumstances to help revitalize artistic culture in his occupied homeland. While pursuing architectural studies at the Technische Hochschule in Aachen (1961–71), he grew interested in the interplay of progressive politics and innovative art forms, which prompted early collaborations with Wolf Vostell and Joseph Beuys, such as their performance *20 July '64*. In 1966 Āboliņš and Gerd Vorhoff founded the Neue Galerie in Aachen, where they organized happenings and performances by Beuys, Jörg Immendorff, Nam June Paik, Tomas Schmit and other key members of FLUXUS, the movement instigated by another exiled Balt, the composer George Maciunas (1931–78). At the same time, inspired by the New Left, Āboliņš combated artistic provincialism within the conservative Latvian émigré community by proposing a cultural rapprochement with Soviet Latvia. Advocating an international—rather than a narrowly nationalist—Latvian identity, Āboliņš helped to organize in 1973 the first major exhibition of art from Latvia to reach the West since the Soviet annexation. One year later he became the executive secretary of the Neue Gesellschaft für Bildende Kunst in West Berlin, under the auspices of which he promoted the rediscovery of the avant-gardist Gustav Klucis and the Western European début of the contemporary realist MAIJA TABAKA. In turn, Āboliņš exhibited in Riga, where his irreverence, kitsch aesthetics and experiments with CORRESPONDENCE ART were revelatory to the local audience. Ironically, it was his leftist orientation that enabled him to alleviate the isolation of Latvian artists under Communism.

BIBLIOGRAPHY

Valdis Āboliņš, Miss Vietnam mit rohem Hering im Mund: Oder Fluxus, Berlin und die Riga-Konnekschen (exh. cat., W. Berlin, Staatl. Ksthalle, 1988)

MARK ALLEN SVEDE

Abondio. Italian family of medallists and wax modellers, active in Central Europe. (1) Antonio Abondio worked first in Italy and later for the imperial courts in Vienna and Prague. He worked in an eclectic style drawn from Italian and northern sources. His oeuvre consists principally of some 60 medals, though he also produced some wax portraits (13 of which survive) and a few plaquettes of religious and mythological themes. His son and pupil, (2) Alessandro Abondio, continued his father's work at the imperial court, developing the genre of portraiture in wax. He also made figure subjects. Alessandro's output was highly regarded by collectors.

BIBLIOGRAPHY

H. Stoecklein: 'Urkunden und Regesten: Alessandro Abondio', *Archv Medaillen- & Plakettenknd.*, i (1913–14), pp. 42–7

□

(1) Antonio Abondio (*b* Riva del Garda, Trento, 1538; *d* Vienna, 22 May 1591). He and Leone Leoni were the only Italian medallists to be highly successful as court artists north of the Alps. Abondio's earliest dated medal is of *Jacopo Antonio Buoncompagni-Sora* (1561; Vienna, Ksthist. Mus.). No stylistic development for his medals has been proposed. His eclectic style reflects Italian, German and Netherlandish sources. In Italy he followed the Milanese court style exemplified in the work of Leoni; he was influenced by medals of the Venetian Alessandro Vittoria, and, most surprisingly, early in his career he was influenced by the charming works of Alfonso Ruspagiari and the school of wax modellers and medallists centred on Reggio Emilia. Abondio's signed medal of *Caterina Riva* (1565; e.g. London, BM) presents her almost as a painting, three-quarter length and three-quarter facing, with the voluminous drapery used to make a Mannerist decoration.

Abondio appears to have left Italy first in 1565–6 for employment by the Holy Roman Emperor Ferdinand II in Innsbruck and Ambras. He was called to Vienna by the Emperor Maximilian II in 1566, was sent to the Netherlands in April of that year and appointed court medallist at Prague in December. His work at Vienna between 1567 and 1571 included a commission for a new series of imperial portraits, which was paid for in Prague in 1570. He was in Spain in 1571–2 in the retinue of the imperial ambassador Baron Johann von Khevenhüller, of whom three medals were made (e.g. Vienna, Ksthist. Mus.). In 1574 Abondio received confirmation from Emperor Maximilian II of a family patent of nobility, and in 1577 he was given a house by Emperor Rudolf II and was commissioned to produce the models for the coinage of the new reign. The medals Abondio produced after leaving Italy show the influence of the Netherlandish school of such medallists as Jacques Jonghelinck. Abondio combined the Netherlandish handling of the portrait with the court style of Leoni in a superb medal of the *Holy Roman Emperor Maximilian II* (1575; Dworschak, p. 62). His medal of the Emperor's wife, *Empress Marie* (1575; Dworschak, p. 63), is in the simpler style of Leoni.

Abondio's principal surviving portraits in wax depict *Emperor Maximilian II*, *Empress Marie* (Munich, Bayer. Nmus.) and the Emperor's brother *Charles, Archduke of Austria* (ex-Gould Collection, New York). A large wax of *Maximilian II* (1575; Vienna, Ksthist. Mus.) has as a reverse an *Allegory of Victory over the Turks* (Dworschak, pp. 84–5). Of the Spanish Habsburgs there are wax portraits of *Philip II, King of Spain*, his consort *Elizabeth of France* (*d* 1568) and son *Charles* (*d* 1568; all ex-Spitzer Collection, Paris). The reverses of Abondio's medals draw on the several Italian traditions represented by the work of Leoni, Vittoria and Pietro Paolo Galeotti, but they are less convincing than the prototypes. In Germany, Abondio adopted the local tradition of using elaborate coats of arms as reverse types. His plaquettes are entirely German in character. There is a set of single figures of *Mars*, *Mercury* and *Venus* (Weber, no. 646, 1–3), a *Virgin and Child* (Weber, no. 651) and a beautiful *Head of Christ* with reverse of *Christ at the Column* (Weber, no. 652). The most remarkable and original of the plaquettes is a *Toilet of Venus* (Weber, no. 650; see fig.), with both the figure composition and the monogram signature in the style of Dürer: a compliment from an Italian artist to his German patrons. His normal form of signature was AN.AB.

Antonio Abondio: *Toilet of Venus*, lead plaquette, 93×73 mm, 1587 (Cambridge, Fitzwilliam Museum)

The variety of portrait types in the medals and the establishment of the wax portrait as an independent form of court portraiture give Abondio an important place in the history of medalmaking both in Italy and in Germany. The style of the wax portraits, with an over-elaborate attention to detail (for example in the use of seed pearls as decoration), tends to deaden the vitality of his images. His imperial portraits are more interesting in the medals than in the waxes. His principal pupils were his son (2) Alessandro Abondio, Raffaello Ranghieri (*fl* 1567–87) and Pietro de Pomis.

BIBLIOGRAPHY

DBI; Meissner; Thieme–Becker

A. Fiala: *Antonio Abondio: Keroplastik a medajlér* [Antonio Abondio: wax modeller and medaller] (Prague, 1909)

G. Habich, ed.: *Die deutschen Schaumünzen des 16. Jahrhunderts*, II/ii (Munich, 1934), pp. 486–507

F. Dworschak: *Antonio Abondio: Medaglista e ceroplasta (1538–1591)*, Collana di artisti trentini (Trento, 1958)

J. Pope-Hennessy and R. W. Lightbown: *Catalogue of Italian Sculpture*, London, V&A cat. (London, 1964), ii, pp. 556–9, nos 582–7 [six wax portraits]

E. J. Pyke: *A Biographical Dictionary of Wax Modellers* (Oxford, 1973), p. 3; *Supplement* (London, 1981), p. 3; *Supplement II* (London, 1983), p. 3

I. Weber: *Deutsche, niederländische und französische Renaissanceplaketten, 1500–1650* (Munich, 1975), pp. 284–8

Antonio Abondio und seine Zeit (exh. cat. by K. Schulz, Vienna, Ksthist. Mus., 1988)

Prag um 1600: Kunst und Kultur am Hofe Rudolfs II (exh. cat., ed. J. J. W. Evans and J. Spicer; Essen, Villa Hügel, 1988), pp. 575–94 [entry by R.-A. Schütte]

J. G. POLLARD

(2) Alessandro Abondio (*b c.* 1580; *d* Munich, *bur* 29 April 1648). Son of (1) Antonio Abondio. He is recorded in the 1606 household register of Emperor Rudolf II as a 'sculptor and picture engraver' with a monthly salary of 20 gulden. It is difficult to follow his working career, which began a few years earlier, because, unlike his father, he did not sign his medals. In the inventory of Rudolf II's *Kunstkammer*, drawn up between 1607 and 1611, Alessandro Abondio is noted as the maker of a large number of embossed wax pieces, mainly of mythological subjects. After the death of Rudolf II, Abondio entered the service of Emperor Matthias II (*reg* 1612–19) and then worked for his successor, Emperor Ferdinand II. In 1619 Abondio married Regina von Aachen, the widow of the painter Hans von Aachen. In that same year he obtained Munich citizenship and from then on was largely resident there. At first Abondio worked for Duke Albrecht VI (*d* 1666); the surviving records attest to a long personal relationship between the artist and his ducal patron. Alessandro made wax portraits of the Duke, which were used by an Augsburg die-cutter as models for the dies for *Gnadenpfennige* ('charity pennies'); precious versions of these were produced by the Munich goldsmiths Christoph Ulrich Eberl (before 1580–1634) and Hans Osinger.

From 1630 Abondio was in the service of Elector Maximilian I. An annual maintenance payment of 150 gulden made to Abondio by the Elector documented from 1630 until Abondio's death suggests that Abondio also worked for other patrons. From 1630, or possibly earlier, Abondio collaborated with the die-cutter Paul Zeggin who cut his wax models in iron. Abondio made sculptures in wax as well as wax portraits. In 1639 a 'Hercules embossed in wax' by 'Alexander Abundi' is mentioned and also in that year an 'epitaph for the Duchess embossed from wax'. Both wax models were cast by the bell-founder Bernhard Ernst (*fl* 1633–68) and engraved by the goldsmith Melchior Epstein (*d* 1659); both are untraced. Abondio is documented as having produced an embossed wax *Entombment* dated 1640, which was identified by some writers with the *Pietà* (destr. during World War II) formerly in the Dreifaltigkeitskirche in Munich. Works by Abondio were included in numerous contemporary *Kunstkammern*; his friend Sandrart mentioned that the wax portraits of *Dr Paul Freher and his Wife* were regarded as a 'wonderful rarity' and 'shown to those who loved art'. Only one wax medal can be attributed to Abondio through an inscription: it shows *Johann Manlich* from Augsburg and was made in 1635 (Vienna, Ksthist. Mus.). Alessandro is linked stylistically in his medalmaking with his father—both men modelled in a similarly subtle and delicate way. While Antonio favoured cast medals, however, Alessandro preferred the struck medal, usually intended as a *Gnadenpfennig*, forming a transition from the Renaissance medal to that of the Baroque period.

BIBLIOGRAPHY

Meissner; *NDB*; Thieme–Becker
J. von Sandrart: *Teutsche Academie* (1675–9); ed. A. R. Peltzer (1925)
F. Kenner: 'Bildnissmedaillen der Spätrenaissance', *Jb. Ksthist. Samml. Allhöch. Ksrhaus.*, xii (1891), pp. 155ff
G. Habich: 'Wachsbildnis des *Johannes Manlich* von Alessandro Abondio', *Schwäb. Mus.* (1928), pp. 57–60
G. Habich, ed.: *Die deutschen Schaumünzen des 16. Jahrhunderts*, II/ii (Munich, 1934)
R. Bauer and H. Haupt, eds: 'Das Kunstkammerinventar Kaiser Rudolfs II., 1607–1611', *Jb. Ksthist. Samml. Wien*, lxxii (1976), pp. 1–191
L. Börner: *Deutsche Medaillenkleinode des 16. und 17. Jahrhunderts* (Würzburg, 1981)
D. Diemer: 'Bronzeplastik um 1600 in München: Neue Quellen und Forschungen, 2. Teil', *Jb. Zentinst. Kstgesch.*, iii (1987), p. 158, fig. 100

RUDOLF-ALEXANDER SCHÜTTE

Aboriginal Australia. Culture of the original inhabitants of Australia and their descendants. This survey covers the traditional art forms of the Australian Aborigines, such as rock art, sculpture in wood, clay and sand, body decoration and bark painting, both before and after European colonization took place at the end of the 18th century. It also examines the interrelationships between the art of Aboriginal groups living in different regions on the continent. Traditional art forms have continued to be produced in most regions well into the late 20th century, but at the same time some contemporary Aboriginal artists, influenced by the dominant white culture in which they now live, have begun to explore new forms and media; this art, produced mainly for external markets, is discussed separately.

I. Introduction.

1. GEOGRAPHY AND EARLY SETTLEMENT HISTORY. Australia and New Guinea formed a single landmass, the prehistoric continent of Sahul, until *c.* 8000 years ago, when the rising sea-level separated them at the Torres Strait. This continent was first occupied at least 40,000 years ago, by people who arrived by boat from South-east Asia. By 30,000 BP people had spread across most of the continent, although the Central Desert remained largely unoccupied until 10,000 years ago (White and O'Connell). Until European colonization at the end of the 18th century Australian Aborigines were hunters and gatherers, even though they had been in contact with agriculturalists north of the Torres Strait for many thousands of years. According to the earliest European records, at the time of colonization in 1788 the population had reached a level variously estimated between 300,000 and 1,000,000 people, speaking some 200 separate languages with a great range of dialects (Dixon). Population density varied enormously according to environmental factors. Many of the well-watered coastal regions and the great inland river system of the Murray–Darling supported relatively dense populations for hunting and gathering societies, whereas the vast region of the Western Desert contained only a few thousand people in total (see fig. 1). Although there is considerable overlap in the environmental resources across the continent, populations in the richer tropical environments of the north and the well-watered temperate regions of the south-east were semi-sedentary with a predictable annual cycle of movement, whereas in some

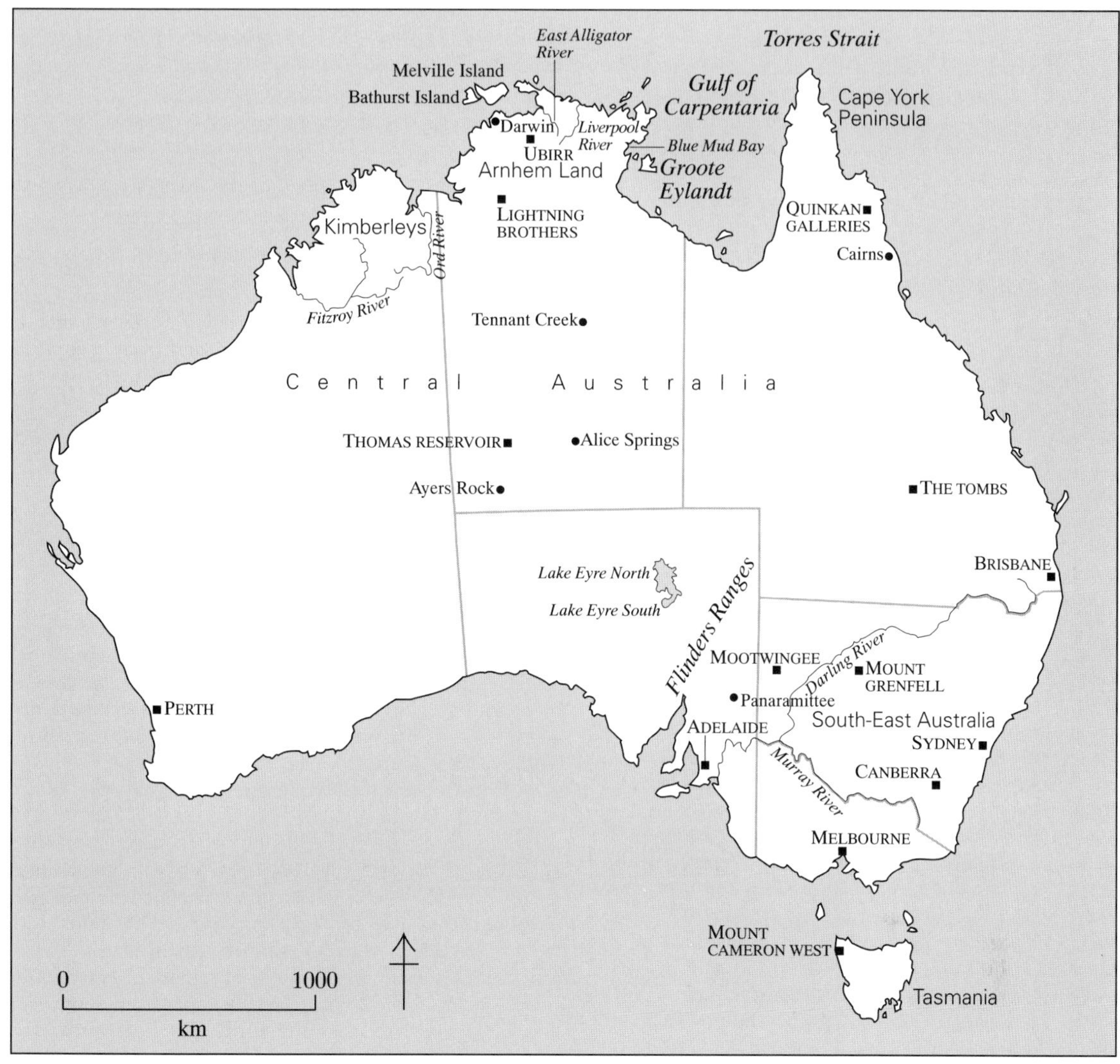

1. Map of Aboriginal Australia; those sites with separate entries in this dictionary are distinguished by CROSS-REFERENCE TYPE

of the less fertile and drier areas populations were nomadic and occupied vast tracts of land.

Aborigines have had a major impact on the Australian environment. Most profoundly, the use of fire both in hunting and in clearing the undergrowth has altered the flora and fauna of the continent in favour of a regime that tolerates, and in some cases benefits from, the regular burning of land. The archaeological record shows that changes occurred over time, including an increase in the systematic use of fire, the invention of polished stone axes *c.* 20,000 years ago, the introduction of the dog 4000 years ago and the general tendency towards the development of smaller stone tools and the production of composite hafted implements (Mulvaney; White and O'Connell). The correlation between social and technological changes is not precisely known, but by the time of European colonization Aborigines had developed a highly complex hunter-gatherer society involving the skilful management of land and resources, a predictable seasonal cycle and a system of social and religious organization centred on rights over land that ordered the relationship between people and the environment.

2. RELIGION. Despite considerable variation, Aboriginal religions throughout Australia share many common features. A central concept is the belief in a time of world-creation frequently referred to in English as the 'Dreaming' or 'Dreamtime' (Stanner). In the Dreaming, ancestral beings occupied the surface of the earth, emerging from beneath the ground or journeying from distant places. These ancestral beings varied in form, sometimes having the shape of animals or inanimate objects such as stones, at other times human characteristics. They travelled across the land, sometimes in groups, encountering others on the way and acting rather as humans do but on a grander scale. Through their actions they transformed the earth's surface, creating the form of the landscape: where they walked valleys were created, where they bled lakes were

formed and where they left their digging sticks in the ground, or splintered their spears against a rock, trees grew. Every action affected the landscape, which then took on mnemonic importance in their lives. At the end of the Dreaming, the ancestral beings withdrew from the surface of the earth, returning beneath the ground or simply transforming themselves into features of the landscape (Maddock; Charlesworth and others). They left behind human groups whom they had created and set in the landscape.

Although ancestral beings no longer occupied the earth, they continued to exist in another dimension necessary to the humans who succeeded them. They left behind a body of sacred law—songs, dances and paintings—that arose out of their world-creating acts and provided an account of them. The human groups used this sacred law to re-enact and preserve the memory of Dreamtime events in ritual, thus providing a source of spiritual power for subsequent generations. The songs and paintings, like the landscape itself, are considered to be not merely representations of the ancestral past but also manifestations of the ancestral beings themselves and a means of establishing contact with them.

People are linked with the ancestral past in a continuous cycle through the process of spirit conception, the performance of ritual and the return of the spirits of the dead to the ancestral domain. Within the landscape the ancestral beings created reservoirs of spiritual power, which provide the conception spirits that initiate each new existence. As people take part in ceremonies throughout their lives, they accumulate spiritual power progressively, moving closer to the ancestral domain towards the end of their lives. On death, their spirits return to the land or to certain lands of the dead, where they are reincorporated within the time-frame of the Dreaming, becoming a source of spiritual energy for subsequent generations. Religious practices are aimed at maintaining contact with the ancestral past and controlling the cyclical movement of spiritual power to ensure that the souls of the dead return to the land and that the fertility of people and land is maintained (Morphy, 1984).

There are important political dimensions to Aboriginal religion, in maintaining the relationship between groups of people, ancestral beings and land (Myers) and in reinforcing these relationships by means of a system of restricted knowledge. Through their journeys, ancestral beings are associated with particular areas of land, and in many parts of Australia rights to land are believed to have been entrusted by those ancestral beings to the founding human ancestors of patrilineal clans. The sacred law became a charter of rights for the continued ownership of the land by subsequent generations of the clan and a source of spiritual strength (Williams). Elsewhere, especially in the more sparsely populated desert regions, rights to land and membership of totemic cult groups are established on a wider basis, including kin ties through women and links to particular conception sites. Throughout Aboriginal Australia the system of restricted knowledge is associated with the segmentation of society based on age and gender. Religious knowledge is sometimes treated as secret, with certain objects and their meanings being revealed only within the closed context of the ceremonial ground to those who possess rights to such knowledge and have passed through previous stages of initiation. Usually it is the right to disseminate information and to be present in certain contexts that is controlled rather than the knowledge itself. In many parts of Australia, in particular towards the centre of the continent, ceremonies or phases of them may be restricted to men or women only. In general the authority of men and (to a lesser extent) women increases as they grow older and gain access to spiritual power by participating in ceremonies and acquiring knowledge.

3. Representational systems. Aboriginal art displays an enormous variety of styles, both regionally and over time. However, within this broad range of variation, it is possible to identify two contrasting systems of representation that each reflect formal similarities throughout the continent. One system consists mainly of figurative representations and has been referred to as 'iconic' or 'motivated', since there is a direct relationship between image and object. The other is characteristically geometric and has been called 'arbitrary' or 'unmotivated', since the same configuration can be attributed with various interpretations (Morphy, 1980, 1989; Munn). The distinction between the two systems is not an absolute one, and there are examples that do not fit neatly into either category; nevertheless it is a distinction that has proved useful. In most regions both systems are employed, often in different contexts, but sometimes in combination. For example, figurative representations in rock paintings are often thought to be the impressions of ancestral beings left behind on the rock surface, whereas geometric representations are believed to be designs that the ancestral beings painted on their bodies or that originated through ancestral action. The designs are both manifestations of ancestral beings, in that they are thought to be their creations or (like the landscape itself) an integral part of them, and representations of the ancestral past, in that they encode events that occurred in the Dreamtime.

In most cases the geometric art can be interpreted only by someone who already knows its meaning, as is appropriate for a system of restricted knowledge. Much of the sacred geometric art represents schematic relationships between topographic features, not entirely unlike maps. However these geometric configurations are multivalent and can encode a multiplicity of meanings, without giving priority to any single one. The same design can represent an area of land, marks on the body of an ancestral being or the 'crest' of a totemic cult group associated with that area of land. Thus geometric art can be used to encode the relationships and associations between particular places, the ancestral events that created them and the social groups that have rights in them.

4. Role of the artist. Since art mediates between the present and the ancestral past, the artist plays an important role in Aboriginal society and may possess significant status in ceremonial and political affairs. Paintings, sculptures, ground drawings and ceremonial constructions, like all other humanly produced expressions of the ancestral past, are forms of religious knowledge passed

on from one generation to the next. People can only reproduce works of art in which they have inherited rights. Moreover, art production is usually part of a ceremonial role that is defined by such factors as kinship relations to other participants, moiety affiliation and ritual status or seniority. Frequently only one or two people can perform the requisite act. On some occasions, however, when several individuals may be in the appropriate category, three factors are relevant in deciding who should produce the work: the right to produce it, knowledge of its correct form and the ability to produce it. Although there is no separate category of 'artists' in Aboriginal society, some people are recognized as being better at producing paintings and ceremonial objects than others; people who combine knowledge with skill are often given a major role in ceremonies.

With the exception of Tiwi artists of Melville and Bathurst Islands who produce *pukamani* funerary poles (*see* §II, 5 and fig. 8 below), artists seldom receive payment, but they may be fed and looked after while working. Although emphasis is placed on reproducing ancestral forms and there is a general denial of innovation, in reality considerable room for individual creativity exists. In rare cases, such as among the Tiwi, innovation is overtly encouraged in some contexts (Goodale and Koss), and throughout much of central Australia (*see* §III, 2 below) 'new' designs can enter the system through an individual's dreams, even though ideology will have it that this is simply the rediscovery of pre-existing forms.

BIBLIOGRAPHY

W. E. H. Stanner: *On Aboriginal Religion*, Oceania Monographs, 11 (Sydney, 1966/*R* 1990)

J. C. Goodale and J. D. Koss: 'The Cultural Context of Creativity among Tiwi', *Essays on the Verbal and Visual Arts: Proceedings of the Annual Spring Meeting of the American Ethnological Society: 1967*, pp. 175–91; also in *Anthropology and Art: Readings in Cross-Cultural Aesthetics*, ed. C. M. Otten (Garden City, NY, 1971), pp. 182–200

D. J. Mulvaney: *The Prehistory of Australia: Ancient People and Places* (London, 1969/*R* Ringwood, 1975)

K. Maddock: *The Australian Aborigines: A Portrait of their Society* (London, 1972)

N. D. Munn: *Walbiri Iconography: Graphic Representation and Cultural Symbolism in a Central Australian Society* (Ithaca, NY, 1973)

R. M. W. Dixon: *The Languages of Australia* (Cambridge, 1980)

H. Morphy: 'What Circles Look Like', *Canberra Anthropol.*, iii/1 (1980), pp. 17–36

J. P. White and J. F. O'Connell: *A Prehistory of Australia, New Guinea and Sahul* (Sydney, 1982)

M. Charlesworth and others: *Religion in Aboriginal Australia: An Anthology* (St Lucia, Queensland, London and New York, 1984)

H. Morphy: *Journey to the Crocodile's Nest* (Canberra, Washington, DC, and London, 1984)

F. R. Myers: *Pintubi Country, Pintubi Self: Sentiment, Place and Politics among Western Desert Aborigines* (Washington, DC, Canberra and London, 1986)

N. M. Williams: *The Yolngu and their Land: A System of Land Tenure and the Fight for its Recognition* (Canberra, 1986)

H. Morphy: 'On Representing Ancestral Beings', *Animals into Art*, ed. H. Morphy, One World Archaeology, 7 (London, 1989), pp. 144–60

W. Caruana: *Aboriginal Art*, World A. (London, 1993)

D. Horton, ed.: *Encyclopaedia of Aboriginal Australia*, 2 vols (Canberra, 1994)

II. Traditional art forms.

Aboriginal art is rich in the variety of its forms. The most durable art, and also that for which the earliest evidence exists, is rock art: examples of rock paintings and engravings, or petroglyphs (as they are also known), are found through the Australian continent. A wide variety of abstract and figurative sculptural forms is also produced across Australia, using a rich variety of materials—wood and stone, feathers, grasses and seeds, sand, clays and resins. Sand sculptures, though they sometimes occur separately, often provide the basis for more complex ceremonial constructions combining a variety of different media, such as painting, wooden objects and feather string, within the same overall creation. Perhaps the most widely used medium throughout Australia, however, is the human body. As with rock art, early evidence exists for ornaments and body decorations, both directly in the form of excavated artefacts and indirectly through representations on rock surfaces. Forms of art can also be defined according to their contexts of occurrence. Mortuary art is a particularly important category outside the desert regions. Architectural forms for the most part consisted of temporary constructions, occupied for part of the year only. But even so, bark huts, like most material culture objects, could become the subject or object of art. The use of bark and wood as supports for painting is now widely associated with Aboriginal art production, but it is a relatively recent development (since colonization) and occurs only in northern Australia.

1. INTRODUCTION. Aboriginal designs often exist independently of particular manifestations. The same design may be reproduced in such different art forms as body painting, sand sculpture and rock art. And because designs exist independently of particular objects and media, almost anything can be made into an art object. It may have a design produced on its surface, or it may be incorporated within a ceremonial construction. Producing the work of art often involves fitting the design to the shape of the surface and to the space available.

Most of the materials and techniques employed in the manufacture of everyday objects can be used in the production of art objects. Sculptures are frequently composite forms made from such naturally occurring materials as wood, plant fibres, animal fur, feathers, resins, seeds and beeswax. Numerous pigments are used, including mineral and vegetable dyes, which are combined with many different fixatives such as egg yolk, orchid juice and blood. Four colours (red, yellow, black and white) are most common, although the particular shade chosen may expand the range of variation. With mineral pigments, the source may be as significant as the colour, since particular ochre deposits are often transformations of the blood of specific ancestral beings.

Specialist equipment is limited to the woodworking tools available. Traditionally this would have included stone axes, shell or stone scrapers, engravers made from stone or teeth, and naturally occurring rasps such as the sharkskin employed in Arnhem Land. Pigments are applied by hand or sprayed on by mouth, although in many parts of Australia specialized brushes made from bark and various other fibres were and sometimes still are used.

HOWARD MORPHY

2. ROCK ART. Most regions of Australia have examples of rock art, which occur on outcrops or under the overhangs of rock shelters. Some regions, such as the Arnhem Land escarpment (*see* §III, 4–5 below) or the western Kimberleys (*see* §III, 3 below), are known for their high density of rock art sites and the distinctive character of the art. Images may be created by additive means, such as painting or drawing, or by extractive techniques, such as pecking, pounding or abrading the outer patinated layer of rock. Painting may be done in natural mineral pigments mixed with water; drawing, which occurs less frequently, uses lumps of dry pigment like crayons. Images created by extractive techniques are conventionally referred to as engravings, although the true engraving technique of incising the rock is uncommon in Aboriginal rock art. Engravings may be tens of millimetres deep or so shallow as to be imperceptible. Newly made engravings are visible due to colour differences between the freshly exposed rock and its patinated surround and in some cases due to the difference in depth. Many rock-engravings are difficult to see except in oblique light conditions, as the exposed rock has weathered back to the same patina as the original rock.

(i) Context and dating. (ii) Stylistic classification.

(i) Context and dating. Pigmented art is known only from rock shelters (usually sandstone or quartzite) where the walls are relatively well protected from rain and other destructive agents. Engravings may also be executed in rock shelters, but they are most abundant on other types of rock exposures. These range from broad, horizontal rock surfaces such as the ridge tops of the Sydney Basin region in south-east Australia to vertical walls of cliffs or boulders, such as those that characterize the massive screes of the Pilbara sites in Western Australia. Some rock art is closely associated with archaeological evidence of camping activities: stone artefacts, food debris and the ash of fires. Other rock art sites have clearly not been used for daily secular activities. In central Queensland, an extensive study of the relationship between paintings and other evidence of shelter use showed that in many cases these paintings were associated with burials (Morwood). There is, however, no consistent correlation between the visual characteristics of the art and the nature of related archaeological evidence.

Recent advances in radiocarbon dating provide new techniques for dating organic matter in pigments and in the patina formed on freshly exposed rock-engravings. Although results obtained to date are experimental, these techniques may eventually prove useful for dating rock art. The principal means of estimating the age of rock art in Australia remains to assess its relationship to other archaeological data. Only rarely has this been achieved by excavation of rock-engravings below archaeological deposits. More commonly, the postulated relationships are indirect, and only fairly broad estimates of the age of various rock art styles can be made. Excavated evidence from Cape York Peninsula (*see* §III, 6 below) suggests that the tradition of rock-engraving in Australia dates back to the late Pleistocene epoch (*c.* 13,000 BP; Rosenfeld, Horton and Winter; *see also* QUINKAN GALLERIES). Indirect evidence relating the fauna represented to past environments indicates that some rock paintings in Arnhem Land may be of similar age. Depictions relating to European contact, such as horses, ships or men with guns, show that both rock painting and engraving were carried out in early colonial times. At the end of the 20th century rock painting was still periodically, if rarely, practised in the Kimberleys and in areas in the Northern Territory.

(ii) Stylistic classification. In 1976 Lesley Maynard proposed a threefold classification for all Aboriginal rock art, which she believed showed its chronological development. Though later research has invalidated Maynard's chronological sequence her classifications have provided a framework for analysing the principal stylistic characteristics of Aboriginal rock art throughout the continent. She distinguished between Figurative styles, with images mainly of native fauna and humans (*see* §(b) below), and Non-figurative styles of circles, arcs and other motifs (*see* §(a) below), in which animals are indicated only by their tracks. She named the latter the Panaramittee style, after a locality in the Flinders Ranges. Panaramittee-style sites are most commonly found in the arid zones of the interior, where contemporary art in other media also relies heavily on Non-figurative patterns and tracks. The Figurative art styles are more widely distributed and these were classified by Maynard into the earlier Simple Figurative style and the more recent Complex Figurative style. This chronology was rejected when some of the art styles that she considered to be Complex Figurative were shown to be among the earliest known paintings. As a first guide to the geographical distribution of stylistic preferences, her schema still has value, but some rock art, notably the elaborate stencilled designs of the Carnarvon Ranges in central Queensland (*see* THE TOMBS), are excluded from this classification.

(a) Non-figurative styles. The arid-zone rock art sites comprise open rock exposures with engravings consisting of a fairly restricted range of motifs, principally circles, arcs, dots, meandering lines and the tracks of macropods, birds (probably emu) and humans, as well as rock shelters with similar motifs in paint. Distinctions between sites, however, can be established through a range of more complex designs, which tend to occur in relatively smaller numbers and vary significantly in form from area to area. Some of the most unusual are the elaborate but schematic, face-like designs of the Cleland Hills, 200 km west of Alice Springs (*see* THOMAS RESERVOIR), the large feathery patterns and stick humans with huge headdresses at N'Dahla Gorge, 90 km east of Alice Springs, and the maze design at Panaramittee in the Flinders Ranges. Most of these engravings are heavily patinated despite their location in arid environments in which rock weathers slowly. This, together with the absence of dingo tracks and a supposed similarity to Tasmanian rock engravings, led R. Edwards to argue for a Pleistocene age for these arid-zone, Non-figurative, Panaramittee-style engravings. Since Tasmania was cut off from the mainland at the end of the Pleistocene epoch, *c.* 12,000 years ago, Edwards considered that this tradition of rock-engraving must have flourished and reached the island before that event. However, a re-evaluation of the Tasmanian engravings has shown that all the known sites (*see* MT CAMERON WEST) are located

on the present, post-glacial shoreline of the west coast and that they are associated with shell-middens dating no earlier than *c.* 1000 BC, making them a recent development in Tasmanian prehistory. Moreover, the similarity between Tasmanian and Panaramittee-style engravings is of such a generalized nature that an ontogenetic relationship is open to question and difficult to substantiate. The Tasmanian engravings consist almost exclusively of circles, dots and diffuse peck marks, and only at Mt Cameron West are more complex motifs found: some of the circles contain linear infill and are themselves contained within a larger enclosing outline. Similarities with the arid-zone engravings are limited to the shared use of circular motifs and the absence of figurative motifs.

An age of *c.* 10,000 years obtained by radiocarbon dating from calcrete covering the patina of Panaramittee-style engravings at Sturt's Meadow, western New South Wales (*see under* MOOTWINGEE), has confirmed a near-Pleistocene age for the site, although the duration of the tradition as a whole remains unresolved. There are, for instance, striking similarities between the feathery motifs engraved at the Panaramittee-style site of N'Dahla Gorge and recent paintings in one of the shelters at Ayers Rock (Uluru) in the same region. In general, the recent rock-shelter paintings and other art works of the arid zone tend to use complex arrangements with the same range of motifs as those found on the earlier engravings. This seems to indicate a long and continuous artistic tradition.

(b) Figurative styles. Figurative art styles appear to be much more varied than the Panaramittee styles but, to some extent, this diversity results from regional elaborations of a shared body of basic motifs. In most Figurative art styles essentially the same schemata are used for the most commonly depicted animals and for the human form. Larger animals, such as the emu (see fig. 2), are depicted in profile; short-legged or low animals, such as goannas and echidnas, are shown in bird's-eye view. Human figures are generally shown frontally. Female figures are commonly indicated by a lateral displacement of the breasts under the arms, while male figures are distinguished by their genitalia. Sexual exaggeration or overtly sexual themes, however, are rare, except in some sites of the Pilbara in Western Australia. Figures of humans and animals are usually static, and the compositional relationship between figures is often difficult to discern.

In some cases, the repetition of formal arrangements is suggestive of intentional and meaningful composition. For instance, the representation of a long snake superimposed by a number of diverse human and animal figures arranged in a frieze is repeated several times in shelters of the Laura region of Cape York Peninsula. More commonly, painted figures appear to have been placed more or less haphazardly over suitable rock surfaces. In the rock shelters of the Cobar Plain, in south-east Australia, small-scale paintings show groups of seemingly related figures in action (*see* MT GRENFELL). Here groups of men 'dancing', playing clapsticks or spearing game can be identified. Movement is suggested primarily by the angle and positioning of the limbs of the stick human figures and the silhouetted animals. In contrast to this lively style, the larger-scale paintings, such as those in the Laura area (*see* QUINKAN GALLERIES), are striking in their anatomical and decorative elaboration and in the use of several colours, but their effect is static.

2. Figurative-style rock painting of an emu with eggs, Laura region, Cape York Peninsula

Essentially the same artistic devices as at Laura are reduced to simple outline in the large-scale engravings of the Sydney Basin. The multicoloured paintings of the LIGHTNING BROTHERS, in the north-west of the Northern Territory, are similar in style. In this case, the colourful elaboration is not mere embellishment: black, the colour of strength, highlights the backbone, feet, armpits, eyes and ears of the two mythological figures after whom the site is named, whose eyes must resist the brightness of lightning and whose ears resist the sound of thunder produced by the stamping of their feet.

Probably the most spectacular examples of Figurative rock art are the Wandjina-style paintings of the western Kimberley ranges (*see* §III, 3 and fig. 14 below) and the figures known as 'X-ray paintings' of Western Arnhem Land (*see* §III, 4 below). Both these types of rock paintings are relatively recent. They are still integral to the contemporary Aboriginal cultures of their respective regions. The most characteristic figures of the Kimberley paintings are large-scale human figures depicting ancestral heroes with large helmet-like headdresses that symbolize the storm clouds that herald the rainy season. The paintings are the transformations of the Wandjina spirits who created the land, the people and their laws. Wandjina paintings must be ritually maintained and repainted in order to ensure the continuance of the natural order, the seasons and the abundance of plants and animals. Many paintings in this region show evidence of superimposition, with variation in the details or even fairly substantial modification of the images.

In Western Arnhem Land a complex sequence of changing art styles has been uncovered. Authors differ on the details of the sequences identified but generally agree on the principal stages. The earliest is characterized by large-scale, but static, images of animals and humans painted in red. Some unusual figures among these have been identified as extinct animals and, on this basis, an antiquity of up to 25,000 years has been suggested (Murray and Chaloupka). These identifications, and hence the age of the paintings, are debated. The next recognized stage of paintings, known as the Dynamic style, constitutes the

3. X-ray style rock painting of a barramundi fish, Bala-uru, Deaf Adder Gorge, Western Arnhem Land, early 1900s

most detailed and controlled body of Aboriginal rock art known. The paintings are small-scale (200–300 mm high) and dominated by stylized, long-limbed human figures, whose exaggerated movements create an impression of frenetic activity (for illustration *see* UBIRR). They are adorned with huge headdresses, tassles, dancing skirts and other accessories and are shown carrying or using a range of weapons and other objects. The accompanying animal figures also show much detail of fur, feathers and other features, but their form and proportions are closer to reality. The absence of estuarine and wetlands animal species from this art style suggests that it pre-dates the establishment of the present environment following the post-glacial rise in sea-level *c.* 6500 years ago. The line-work is exceedingly delicate and must have required the use of a fine brush and thorough grinding of pigments to prepare the paints.

The Dynamic style gave way, through a series of less easily defined stages, to the style known as X-ray art. The distinguishing characteristic of this most recent rock art is the formalized depiction of internal organs and of skeletal traits in some animal figures (see fig. 3). Not all the figures in this style are shown with X-ray features. These paintings are considerably larger than those in the earlier Dynamic style, sometimes almost life-size. Fine line-work, intricate, almost geometric design for the X-ray features and the frequent use of a range of colours make this art visually very striking. This style appears to be the immediate precursor of contemporary bark paintings of Western Arnhem Land.

BIBLIOGRAPHY

F. D. McCarthy: *Australian Aboriginal Rock Art* (Sydney, 1958/*R* 1979)

I. M. Crawford: *The Art of the Wandjina: Aboriginal Cave Painting in Kimberley, Western Australia* (Melbourne, 1968)

R. Edwards: 'Art and Aboriginal Prehistory', *Aboriginal Man and Environment in Australia*, ed. D. J. Mulvaney and J. Golson (Canberra, 1972), pp. 356–67

E. J. Brandl: *Australian Aboriginal Paintings in Western and Central Arnhem Land* (Canberra, 1973)

V. Blundell: 'The Wandjina Cave Paintings of North-west Australia', *Arctic Anthropol.*, xi (1974), pp. 213–23

L. Maynard: 'Classification and Terminology of Australian Rock Art', *Australian Institute of Aboriginal Studies Biennial Conference: Canberra, 1974*

——: 'Classification and Terminology in Australian Rock Art', *Form in Indigenous Art: Schematisation in the Art of Aboriginal Australia and Prehistoric Europe*, ed. P. J. Ucko (Canberra, 1977), pp. 387–402

——: 'The Archaeology of Australian Aboriginal Art', *Exploring the Visual Art of Oceania*, ed. S. M. Mead (Honolulu, 1979), pp. 93–110

A. Rosenfeld, D. Horton and J. Winter: *Early Man in North Queensland: Art and Archaeology of the Laura Area* (Canberra, 1981)

E. Godden and J. Malnic: *Rock Paintings of Aboriginal Australia* (Sydney, 1982)

M. Morwood: 'The Prehistory of the Central Queensland Highlands', *Adv. World Archaeol.*, iii (1984), pp. 325–80

G. Chaloupka: 'Chronological Sequence in Arnhem Land Plateau Rock Art', *Archaeological Research in Kakadu National Park*, ed. R. Jones (Canberra, 1985), pp. 269–80

R. Layton: 'The Cultural Context of Hunter-Gatherer Rock Art', *Man*, xx/3 (1985), pp. 434–53

A. Rosenfeld: *Rock Art Conservation in Australia* (Canberra, 1985)

P. Murray and G. Chaloupka: 'The Dreamtime Animals: Extinct Megafauna in Arnhemland Rock Art', *Archaeol. Oceania*, xix (1986), pp. 105–16

R. Layton: *Australian Rock Art: A New Synthesis* (Cambridge, 1992)

G. L. Walsh: *Bradshaws: Ancient Rock Paintings of North-west Australia* (Geneva, 1994)

For earlier sources *see* the bibliography under §VII below.

ANDRÉE ROSENFELD

3. SCULPTURE. Using a broad definition of sculpture, most Aboriginal three-dimensional objects can be grouped into one of the following categories: carvings, moulded forms, constructions using several different media, assemblages and installations, and sand or ground sculpture. These categories should not be considered as exhaustive or closed: for example, a 'stuffed emu', recorded as having been used in an initiation ceremony in New South Wales in the 1870s, falls outside these groupings.

Most examples of Aboriginal sculpture found in permanent collections are sacred and depict ancestral beings, totemic heroes or mythological events. They thus refer either directly or obliquely to specific sites in Aboriginal religious geography and tend to express the association of specific groups of people with those places. Besides their mythological import, many also had ceremonial functions.

An increasing proportion of new Aboriginal sculpture, especially that produced since the 1950s, is non-sacred. The more secular works range widely, from those made for love magic to those that focus primarily on contemporary politics, for example *Maralinga* (1990; Perth, A.G. W. Australia; Crumlin, p. 106) by LIN ONUS. Many sculptures created specifically for the smaller artefact market have human or animal subjects, for example, the wooden figure of a *Darwin Policeman* (1964; Perth, U. W. Australia, Berndt Mus. Anthropol.) by MITHINARI (see Berndt, Berndt & Stanton, p. 130); a human-headed gypsum pipe bowl (*c.* 1920s; Adelaide, S. Austral. Mus.; see 1988–9 exh. cat., p. 198) by Jim Kite (*b c.* 1870s); birds made by Malangawa from buffalo horns (see Berndt and Phillips, p. 302); and the large number of wooden reptiles made in Central Australia and found widely in souvenir shops (see Brokensha).

(i) Carvings. (ii) Moulded forms. (iii) Constructions. (iv) Assemblages and installations. (v) Sand sculpture.

(i) Carvings. The most widespread category of Aboriginal sculpture is carving in wood. Such sculptures are frequently painted, incised or branded and sometimes complemented with fibre, feather or other symbolic attachments. Fragmentary records from the 19th century and the early 20th

indicate that wooden effigies of totemic and ancestral beings were used in ceremonies in both south-west and south-east Australia; carved sacred objects were also found in the latter region. But apart from the carved trees of New South Wales, with their highly varied geometric religious designs (*see* §III, 1(ii) below), and the cylindro-conical stones (or cylcons) of the Darling River area, few if any free-standing carved works survive from colonial or pre-colonial times in this region. Some affinity with sculpture in the round is exhibited by innovative relief-carving of implements, emu eggs and walking sticks from the Flinders Ranges, Adelaide and northern New South Wales, engraved pearl shells from the central and north-west regions and the extensive south-east Australian tradition of geometric incision of weapons (*see* §III, 1(i) and fig. 13 below).

Wooden figures of anthropomorphic ancestral beings, spirits, totemic animals and human beings are common in north-east Arnhem Land, as are sacred clan emblems (*rangga*), dancing-poles, memorial posts, representations of heads of deceased people and log bone-receptacles. Perhaps the most massive of all Aboriginal wooden sculptures are the poles used in the Kunapipi ceremonies of north-east Arnhem Land, which are up to 8 m high. The elongated Mimi figures of Western Arnhem Land are an energetic development in the adjacent region from the 1970s. Their impact is well matched by that of elaborately constructed ceremonial carvings from the Aurukun region in Cape York Peninsula, such as a totemic cult sculpture representing the culture hero Nhampa-Ngulpanh, which was photographed during a ceremonial performance in 1962 (Canberra, N. Mus.; see fig. 4; *see also* §III, 6 and fig. 17 below).

From Cape York in the east to the Kimberleys in the north-west, a basic commonality prevails of visual conventions, techniques and materials in wooden anthropomorphic sculpture. Somewhat culturally distinctive, the Tiwi of Bathurst and Melville Islands are noted for their tradition of monumental graveposts (see fig. 8 below), carved and painted in a vast variety of geometric and naturalistic designs, as well as for their powerful iron-wood figures of people and animals and their elaborately serrated spears. Carved stone works were first produced in the Kimberleys in the 1960s and consist principally of human heads.

Anthropomorphic carvings in wood from desert Australia are far rarer than in the tropical north but include remarkable engraved spirit-child figures from Jigalong, unpainted and smooth human figures from Docker River and Yuendumu (e.g. Adelaide, S. Austral. Mus.) and powerful painted figures produced in Utopia in the 1980s. The Central and Western Desert areas are better known for the sacred, non-public slabs of stone and wood (*tjurunga*), which bear highly schematic and geometric engraved representations of ancestral beings, sites and mythic events, and also for the way-markers (*toas*) of the Lake Eyre area, which appear to have had a public role but a similar iconography to that of more restricted objects (see fig. 5). Small ritual icons of painted wood have also been recorded from Kununurra in the north-west, Victoria River in north-central Australia and Groote Eylandt in the Gulf of Carpentaria.

(ii) Moulded forms. These include the small beeswax figures of north-east Arnhem Land and Cape York Peninsula; clay heads used for sorcery in Western Arnhem Land;

4. Carved totemic cult sculpture representing the culture hero Nhampa-Ngulpanh, wood with paint and other materials, from Aurukun, Cape York Peninsula, 1962 (Canberra, National Museum of Australia); from a photograph by Fred McCarthy taken during a ceremonial performance, 1962

5. Carved way-markers (*toas*), wood with paint and other materials, h. 150–450 mm, from the area of Lake Eyre, central Australia, *c.* 1905 (Adelaide, South Australian Museum)

early works in mud by the Kimberleys artist Dodo (*b* 1910); gypsum grave-markers of far western New South Wales; and many of the gypsum forms moulded on to way-markers in southern central Australia. In the early 19th century, images of totemic animals and human figures in clay or grass were observed at an initiation ceremony in south-east Queensland. This suggests that such forms were not restricted to the arid and tropical zones. The work of Thancoupie (*b* 1937) of Cape York Peninsula is one of few forays into ceramic sculpture by an Aboriginal artist (*see* §IV below).

(iii) Constructions. Among the most spectacular of Aboriginal religious sculptures are constructions, usually consisting of a wooden base or frame to which hair-string, twine, feathers, moulded wax or gypsum and a wide variety of other objects may be attached. These were frequently worn fixed to the bodies of ceremonial performers or were carried by them, the boundary between ritual apparel and sculpture being thus blurred. In central Australia the most notable of such constructions are the *waninga* (or *wanigi*) string crosses and decorated *tnatantja* poles. Up to 5 m high, these sculptures are of astonishing beauty and variety but are largely kept hidden from public view. Trees, 'fantastically crowned at the summit', which from their description sound similar, were observed at a ceremonial ground in south-east Queensland in 1824; and inverted trees topped with bark lacework were seen at an initiation in the same region a few years later.

Like *waninga*, small public ritual icons in north-east Arnhem Land also combine wood with string and feathers in their construction. The ritual body-masks of Princess Charlotte Bay, Lockhart River and Pennefather River, all in Cape York Peninsula, and the complex tin, string and wood mythic emblems (or 'portable scenery') of ceremonies at Mowanjum, Western Australia, are among the most elaborate and arresting constructions borne by ceremonial performers in Australia. By contrast, a simple Tasmanian model raft collected in 1843 (Oxford U., Pitt Rivers Mus.) is at the humbler end of the construction scale.

(iv) Assemblages and installations. These normally combine a set of different sculptures of the categories already discussed. Tiwi graveposts, for example, are clustered at the grave, and a number of Aurukun installations consist of a dozen or more individual sculptures suspended from a rail resting on forked posts. Large sacred objects were observed *c.* 1812 in a bower construction on an island in the Gulf of Carpentaria. The assemblage of carved skulls, bones and implements, known both as *Violent Death* and *Carving of Bones* (1982; Darwin, Museums & A. Gals N. Territ.), by the innovative Arnhem Land artist Njinawanga (*b* 1947) has a powerful narrative structure.

BIBLIOGRAPHY

U. H. McConnell: 'Native Arts and Industries on the Archer, Kendall and Holroyd Rivers, Cape York Peninsula, North Queensland', *Rec. S. Austral. Mus.*, xi (1953), pp. 1–42
C. P. Mountford and R. Tonkinson: 'Carved and Engraved Human Figures from North Western Australia', *Anthropol. Forum*, ii/3 (1969), pp. 371–90
R. M. Berndt and E. S. Phillips, eds: *The Australian Aboriginal Heritage: An Introduction through the Arts* (Sydney, 1973)
P. Brokensha: *The Pitjantjatjara and their Crafts* (Sydney, 1975)
Aboriginal Australia (exh. cat. by C. Cooper and others, Sydney, Austral. Gal. Directors Council, 1981–2)
R. M. Berndt, C. H. Berndt and J. E. Stanton: *Aboriginal Australian Art: A Visual Perspective* (Sydney, 1982)
J. Isaacs: *Thancoupie the Potter* (Sydney, 1982)
K. Akerman and P. Bindon: 'Love Magic and Style Changes within One Class of Love Magic Objects', *Oceania*, lvii/1 (1986), pp. 22–32
P. Jones and P. Sutton: *Art and Land: Aboriginal Sculptures of the Lake Eyre Region* (Adelaide, 1986)
J. Hoff: *Tiwi Graveposts* (Melbourne, 1988)
Dreamings: The Art of Aboriginal Australia (exh. cat., ed. P. Sutton; New York, Asia Soc. Gals; U. Chicago, IL, Smart Mus. A.; Melbourne, Mus. Victoria; Adelaide, S. Austral. Mus.; 1988–90)
B. J. Dodo, K. Akerman and K. McKelson: *Kimberley Sculpture* (exh. cat., Perth, 1989)
R. Crumlin, ed.: *Aboriginal Art and Spirituality* (exh. cat., Canberra, High Court of Australia, 1991)

PETER SUTTON

(v) Sand sculpture. Sand sculptures generally consist of engraved lines or ridges of sand or earth on a flat area of ground, or of shaped mounds forming simple bas-reliefs. Intimately linked to places, terrestrial and celestial, they form a focus for ritual and dance, and as such are not primarily a mode of personal expression but an aspect of religious practice. They sometimes incorporate holes, leaves, rocks, sticks or carved objects, and even fire or water at a certain stage of the ritual. The term 'sand sculpture' is used to refer to three-dimensional designs in contrast to ground paintings, which are two-dimensional. Since both forms exploit the same materials and occur in similar contexts, this distinction is somewhat arbitrary for Aborigines. However, sand drawings, used by the Walpiri people in central Australia (*see* §III, 2 below), are considered to be different despite their visual resemblance, as they are an informal improvisational aspect of story-telling. Sand sculpture is also closely related to other media of expression, especially paintings in ochres on the body and on bark (*see* §§4 and 7 below), and in the south-east on carved trees (*see* §III, 1(ii) below).

Many sand sculptures made by the Yolngu people of north-east Arnhem Land are formed from simple geometric shapes, such as circles and semicircles, squares and rectangles, parallel lines, lenses, diamonds and triangles. While all are 'iconic', albeit schematized, some are more obviously figurative, such as a depiction of the dugout canoe belonging to Dingo Ancestor. They are employed primarily in mortuary ceremonies (*see* §5 below), especially water, fire and smoke purification rites (see fig. 6), as well as in ceremonies in which the disinterred bones of the dead are crushed and placed in a hollow-log coffin. For example, the Bukulup (washing) ceremony is performed for the purification of the close relatives of a person who has recently died. Men of a patrilineal clan sing throughout the day in the camp while a man of the clan or the son of a woman of the clan makes a sand sculpture in a cleared area, usually *c.* 5 m or more across. Near sunset others begin to gather; a few at a time stand in the sand sculpture, which depicts a lagoon or spring at the clan's country, while others pour water over them as a clan leader calls out names of the ancestors. In this way an ancestral waterhole is recreated wherever the ceremony is enacted, perhaps far from the country represented. In other ceremonies a simple sand sculpture forms the arena for dances.

The sand sculptures of the Yolngu are simplified, geometric versions of painted ancestral designs. As such, they have many possible interpretations, of varying degrees of secrecy. Each is a kind of map of the clan's country and a depiction of its ancestral beings and sacred objects, which are transformations of some attribute of an ancestor. The design is also specific to the clan that owns the country, while being similar in form to the designs of clans with the same ancestral being. The design thus encodes the connection between ancestor, place, the sacred object that the ancestor put into the country and the group that he or she created, as well as connections with other countries and clans related to the ancestral journey.

Sand engravings formerly used in the Burbung initiation ceremonies of the Wiradjuri people of New South Wales were both figurative and geometric. Some depicted anthropomorphic spirit beings, while others took the form of animals such as kangaroos and emus. The dominant geometric forms were meandering parallel lines, concentric circles and squares, and combinations and elaborations of these figures. The designs that depicted various aspects of ancestral beings, such as the Sky Being Biame, were revealed to male initiates and formed the focus of dances. One design, for example, represented the mounds in which mound-building birds incubated their eggs.

6. Sand sculpture made in connection with a Yolngu smoke purification ceremony by the Daygurrgurr Gupapuyungu clan at Ngangalala, Eastern Arnhem Land; from a photograph by Ian Keen, 1975

BIBLIOGRAPHY

R. H. Mathews: 'The Burbung of the Wiradthuri Tribes', *J. Anthropol. Inst. GB & Ireland*, xxv (1896), pp. 295–318, pls xxv–xxviii; xxvi (1897), pp. 272–85

R. M. Berndt: *Australian Aboriginal Religion* (Leiden, 1974)

M. Clunies Ross and L. R. Hiatt: 'Sand Sculptures at a Gidjingali Burial Rite', *Form in Indigenous Art: Schematisation in the Art of Aboriginal Australia and Prehistoric Europe*, ed. P. J. Ucko (Canberra, 1977), pp. 131–46

I. Keen: 'Yolngu Sand Sculptures in Context', *Form in Indigenous Art: Schematisation in the Art of Aboriginal Australia and Prehistoric Europe*, ed. P. J. Ucko (Canberra, 1977), pp. 165–83

H. Morphy: 'Yingapungapu: Ground Sculpture as Bark Painting', *Form in Indigenous Art: Schematisation in the Art of Aboriginal Australia and Prehistoric Europe*, ed. P. J. Ucko (Canberra, 1977), pp. 205–9

IAN KEEN

4. Body decoration. Throughout Aboriginal Australia, adult men and women decorate their bodies and those of their children in many different ways. Decorative items that are worn include necklets, chaplets, waist- and armbands and pubic coverings. The naked body is a natural medium for painting. This is usually done by someone else for a particular reason, sometimes simply for enjoyment or enhancement of personal appearance, but more often it has some form of religious or magical significance, specifically identifying a person as a participant within a ritual or ceremony. Most parts of the body are decorated; designs cover the face, chest, thighs and upper legs and continue over the shoulders to the back.

A more permanent form of decoration, common in most Aboriginal areas, is scarring or cicatrization. Designs are usually arranged across the chest or arms and sometimes on the legs, to indicate the death of a close relative or spouse. On Melville and Bathurst Islands, for example, scarring called *miunga* covers both sides of the upper back as well as the upper and outer parts of the arms and thighs of men and women. Horizontal lines are also made across the chest and forehead. The V-shaped designs represent fronds of the zamia palm or barbs of spears. Such body decoration is apparently carried out in youth, but not as part of a formal rite. However, in north-central South Australia and some southern parts of the Western Desert, scarring constitutes part of the ritual process during the Wilyaru initiation of youths. Parallel cicatrices cut on the back of a novice are said to represent the marks on the mythic Lizard Man who instituted this ritual in the Dreaming.

Among the extensive range of body designs specific to any one region, each design or series of designs symbolizes particular mythic characters and relates to their activities in the creative era of the Dreaming. Moreover, the designs are usually linked directly to specific parts of the landscape. Often a highly stylized configuration is a shorthand statement of the topography associated with, or shaped by, these mythic beings. Men or women wearing these painted designs in ritual must be affiliated, by birth or in some other special way, to the body of myths concerned.

7. Body decoration of actors in the Djanba (mythical being) series of the Gadjari fertility ritual, Kalumburu, northern Kimberleys; from a photograph by J. E. Stanton, 1963

Since the aim of ritual is to bring about such events or conditions as the renewal of natural species, fertility of the land and the social well-being of the group, the actions of mythic beings must be replicated and the original scene of the Dreaming re-enacted as closely as possible. Actors, according to their ritual role and body painting, are believed to assume the character and quality of a Dreaming personage or natural species symbolizing that being. Body painting is therefore a means of ensuring the spiritual presence of these deities at a ritual.

In the secret–sacred rites the actual painting is part of the ritual itself, which is accompanied by songs or the retelling of the appropriate mythological accounts. The painting process can take several hours, especially in north-east Arnhem Land (see fig. 17 below) where the chest designs extend down the front of the legs to the knees. A person's body is prepared for painting by removing hair and smearing the skin with red ochre. The pigments used—red and yellow ochre, white pipeclay and black manganese or charcoal—are crushed on flat stones and mixed with water. They are applied with burred twigs, orchid roots or stems, sometimes with the fingers and, in Arnhem Land, with a brush made from human hair.

In central Australia and some other regions extensive use is made of birds' down, usually from eagle nestlings, although other white down and wild cotton are also used. Some of it is rubbed in red ochre while the rest is left in its natural colour (see fig. 7 for an illustration of this practice). After rubbing an initiate's body with red ochre, the basic design is lightly sketched, and the down or cotton is then superimposed, piece by piece, using human blood as an adhesive. The down covers the chest, back, shoulders and thighs. It often extends up the neck and the face and is integrated with an elaborate, usually conical headdress, decorated in the same way and tipped with feathers or a sacred object. In the central Australian area alone, thousands of patterns were used in the various ritual cycles, each clearly distinguishable and specifically related in meaning to a particular Dreaming character or place. For example, the design may refer to a Honey Ant place, the sun, or to some creature such as a bandicoot, emu or snake in the form of a human or natural species.

In northern Australia in the great Kunapipi fertility rituals feather down is also used in body designs together with elaborate extensions in the form of headdresses. The meanings of these relate to the great northern epic concerning the mythological travels of the two Wawilak Sisters, who were swallowed by the Yulunggul Snake, which eventually led to the onset of the monsoonal season. Among these designs, Yulunggul is referred to by cabbage trees associated with him as well as by lightning and by various creatures that became sacred by jumping into his watering-place. As the Kunapipi ritual spread south-westwards, it became known as Gadjari ('Old Woman' or 'Mother') and body painting resembling that of the Western Desert was incorporated (see fig. 7).

In Queensland, mainly in the Boulia area but also spreading into north-eastern South Australia, dancer–actors are painted to represent an unpredictable spirit, Molonga, in ceremonies witnessed by both men and women. They wear a bound and feathered conical headdress and their body designs consist of two red bands across the face and forehead with long bands down the body.

The body painting of women, although similar in many respects to men's, differs in meaning and sometimes in intention. Girls' puberty rites, while structurally comparable to the initiation of male youths, are shorter and generally less of a social occasion. The associated body painting is also less complex in most areas. In the Boulia area a girl is decorated with bands of charcoal and feather down: painted men and women dance to welcome her on her return to the main camp. Among the Aranda of central Australia, she is finally decorated with a headband, tips of bandicoot tails, necklets and string armlets, and her body is painted with a mixture of fat and red ochre. Actual body designs are apparently rare in female puberty rites: an example from Western Arnhem Land, however, is the painting of a crescent moon in white clay below the breasts, intended symbolically to regulate the girl's menstrual flow. On occasion, a naturalistic representation of Ngalyod, the Rainbow Serpent, is also used.

Body painting has particularly flourished within the sphere of women's secret–sacred rituals, especially in the west-central sector of the Northern Territory, west into the Kimberleys and throughout the Western Desert. In the Northern Territory there are two primary ritual–myth sequences: the Yawalyu and the Djarada (or Yilbindji). The Yawalyu, with wider connotations and more direct and powerful Dreaming implications, is concerned with the re-enactment and symbolic interpretation of mythological events and characters and with their territorial associations. In the Djarada the focus is on the supernatural powers of the two Dreaming Munga-munga women and on harnessing their powers for personal use (i.e. desirability to men, and healing). Indirectly, the concern is with fertility, since the Munga-munga are daughters of the great

8. Mortuary posts (*pukamani*) erected by the Tiwi, carved wood, h. *c.* 2–5.5 m, Snake Bay, Melville Island; from a photograph by M. Brandl, 1968

Gadjari (Kunapipi). In this ritual the bodies of participants are painted with ochre on a background of animal fat. Since the songs relevant to any Djarada ritual are arranged in series, distinctive sets of designs are correspondingly used. For example, rows of dots and bands with central, stylized configurations of genitalia represent the original patterns believed to have been worn by the Munga-munga. Other bands depict boomerangs and the grooves made by the Munga-munga's dancing feet. *Yawalyu* designs include representations of the Rainbow Serpent and the dangerous Djundagal snake; particular sites associated with mythic beings; clouds, water, rain and thunderbolts; red dust tossed about by a whirlwind; goanna tracks; stone spear-heads; and various creatures.

In almost all sacred ritual, whether for males or females, the most important of the mythic beings and the most elaborate and symbolically significant of these sacred designs are revealed only towards the end of a ritual sequence. Body painting and associated paraphernalia are essentially a kind of camouflage, intended to provide an extra dimension to the person painted, hiding his or her own human identity in the manifestation of a supernatural one—that of a Dreaming deity.

BIBLIOGRAPHY

W. E. Roth: *Ethnological Studies among the North-west-central Queensland Aborigines* (Brisbane, 1897)

W. B. Spencer and F. J. Gillen: *The Native Tribes of Central Australia* (London, 1899/*R* 1969)

T. G. H. Strehlow: *Aranda Traditions* (Melbourne, 1947)

C. H. Berndt: 'Women's Changing Ceremonies in Northern Australia', *L'Homme*, i (Paris, 1950)

C. P. Mountford: *The Tiwi: Their Art, Myth and Ceremony* (London, 1958)

R. M. Berndt, ed.: *Australian Aboriginal Art* (Sydney, 1964/*R* 1968)

R. M. Berndt and C. H. Berndt: *The World of the First Australians: An Introduction to the Traditional Life of the Australian Aborigines* (London and Canberra, 1964/*R* Canberra, 1988)

N. D. Munn: *Walbiri Iconography: Graphic Representation and Cultural Symbolism in a Central Australian Society* (Ithaca, NY, 1973, rev. Chicago, 1986)

R. M. Berndt: *Australian Aboriginal Religion* (Leiden, 1974)

H. Morphy: Ancestral Connections: Art and an Aboriginal System of Knowledge (Chicago, IL, 1991)

CATHERINE H. BERNDT

5. MORTUARY ART. In their concern about the fate of their dead, Aborigines generally believe that spirits eventually find their way to the land of the dead, where they are reunited with the Dreaming deities, or that they return to their own countries, perhaps to be reborn. Regional attitudes toward these beliefs and to related artistic expressions vary considerably. Highly developed and distinctive forms of mortuary art are characteristic of the northern coastal regions of Australia and to some extent the tablelands of New South Wales. In other areas, art forms clustered around the rites of death were and are less spectacular.

The Tiwi of Bathurst and Melville Islands prepare and erect wooden posts on and around a grave about two months after a death (see fig. 8). These posts, the rituals associated with them, the mourners and the corpse before burial are all termed *pukamani*, connoting a taboo condition. Rituals involving a wide range of dancing by men and women extend intermittently over three months or more. There is also ritual feeding of the 'workers' who cut, carve, decorate and erect the posts. Posts erected before the 1930s tend to be limited in their range of designs, with openings and projections at the apex. By the mid-1950s the designs had become more varied and innovative; many posts are surmounted by naturalistic human and spirit figures, as well as other creatures. Stylized designs are painted in ochres on their trunks. Apart from the more readily identifiable naturalistic representations, some of the upper parts of posts bear depictions such as limbs of trees, women's breasts, rocks, windows and doors. In their total conception most represent the deceased persons or their close relatives, while the designs, either carved or painted, refer to events in those persons' lives.

When the posts are brought to a graveside from the secluded places where they have been made, they are erected amid highly emotional scenes. Mourners throw themselves on the grave; men dance around the posts, while both men and women sing personal songs of grief. The posts are not only memorials to the dead, but are believed to house temporarily the dead person's spirit. Such spirits (*mopaditi*) are considered unpredictable. They remain at or near their graves both because they resent their death and are ready to blame the living for it and because they are attached to their relatives. On completion of the rituals, they leave for the land of the dead, or their particular countries. During the dancing, participants are decorated, some with ornate facial and body designs, and they wear various items, all of which are specifically named. Women wear chaplets of human-hair string with dog-tail tips. Men hold between their teeth a ball pendant of feathers, stained with mixed red and yellow ochres, and wear painted bark armlets with projecting decorations of feathers, sometimes ornamented with red seeds. Those dancing carry discs. Men also wave intricately carved and painted spears, made as gifts to the dead. At the conclusion of the rites the beards of the chief male mourners are plucked and the decorations are washed from their bodies, signifying that they are now released from their *pukamani* responsibilities and that the spirits of the dead have left the grave site. The posts are left to rot on the grave.

The mortuary art of the Yolngu of north-east Arnhem Land encompasses a wide variety of forms, easily differentiated from those of the Tiwi. They include decorated hollow logs, ground structures, wooden figures and flags. Although most corpses are now buried, traditionally a dead person was painted with his or her sacred clan designs and then exposed on a platform awaiting decomposition, so that the bones could be collected. After some months or even years, when the bones were ready for collection, they were covered in red ochre and placed temporarily in a painted bark coffin. The dead person's skull was cleaned and painted with its emblematic design and then worn as a shoulder-necklet by a widow or close female relative in memory of the dead person. Later, a tall hollow log (*laragidj*) was prepared and painted, and the bones broken up and placed inside. The log was then ritually erected in the main camp and left to disintegrate; finally its remains were scattered across the camp. The designs painted in ochre on the trunks of the logs represent the clan emblem of the dead man or woman. They vary according to the person's moiety affiliation and refer to his or her country and its mythological associations. Moreover, the logs themselves are often carved into highly conventionalized representations of a mythic creature such as a fish, an animal, a natural object or a feature related to the clan's mythology. Ground structures consisting of a complex patterning of sand mounds are topographic and mythological representations of the deceased's country.

Each of the two patrilineal intermarrying moieties, Dhuwa and Yirritja, has its own substantiating mythological repertory that sponsors not only the use of particular designs but also different objects. That relating to the Dhuwa moiety focuses mainly on the Banumbir 'Morning Star' song cycle in which spirits at Bralgu, the land of the dead, send out that star to their living relatives. In the actual mortuary rituals, long dancing-poles with lengths of feathered string and feather balls are used to signify this daily occurrence. The Yirritja moiety includes, among other things, a *wuramu* post figure representing either the deceased's image or a mythic or historical character. The *wuramu* tradition is usually associated with Indonesian ('Macassan') traders from the Celebes who visited the north Australian coast *c.* 1600–1900. During a delayed mortuary ritual, a carved wooden figure called a 'collection man', with feathered-string arms, is first carried through the camp and anything that is left lying around is collected to compensate the men responsible for making it. Afterwards it is erected near the deceased's camp to the accompaniment of songs and dancing relating to these early Indonesian visits. Masts and specially designed flags are used symbolically to bid farewell to the spirit of the dead. The figures represent Indonesians, the Dutch (*balanda*, now a general term for Europeans) or effigies of specific dead persons. The wide range of innovative designs of these sculpted figures often contrasted markedly with those produced by members of the Dhuwa moiety.

While in north-east Arnhem Land hollow logs are primarily of mortuary significance, in western and southern Arnhem Land their use in this context is combined with the initiation of young men. Mythologically, the ritual associated with this concerned Moon Man, who tried to persuade Red-Eyed Pigeon Man to do as he did—not to die permanently, but to return regularly to the world of the living; Pigeon Man was not convinced, and that is why human beings die physically. The Lorgun rites (the term refers to both the ritual and the actual hollow log) take place when the moon is waning, some time after a death. The log (*lorgun*) is relatively short compared with the north-east Arnhem Land variety; it has a V-shaped 'mouth' and is hung with lengths of feathered string. When people arrive for the rites, the deceased's mother or another close female relative prepares the dancing ground and then calls the men to paint themselves. Novices are brought forward to witness the dances and are told they must now observe a number of food taboos. Eventually the log is brought from its hiding place and the deceased person's bones are removed from their stringybark bundles and placed into the receptacle. As the last bones are put in, a song is sung whose words refer to the dead person's spirit diving into the sea. To the accompaniment of wailing, the log is erected in the main camp at sunrise and left there to disintegrate.

Among the people of the Wiradjuri and Kamilaroi language groups of the New South Wales tablelands carved trees feature in mortuary rites. Within a clearing where a grave has been dug, up to four adjacent trees are engraved boldly with geometrical, stylized designs arranged within a long oval of natural bark. These are said to be 'totemic' in significance, although their meanings have not been recorded. It seems that they symbolize the pathway that the spirit of the dead should take to its ultimate resting place in the Skyworld. According to reports, only important persons were given this form of burial and, like the Lorgun rites of the north, such rites were also relevant to male initiation.

Complex 'rituals of death' are observed in most areas of Aboriginal Australia, but they rarely involve the elaborate aesthetic manifestations common in northern Australia. This undoubtedly reflects the need felt in the north to retain an individual's personal identification after death, defining his or her role within the land of the dead. Aboriginal groups living in areas of northern Australia maintained complex forms of mortuary ritual into the late 20th century (*see* §III, 6 and fig. 17 below). In contrast, in New South Wales and other parts of Australia there is less emphasis on the aesthetic aspects and more on the social transformation, the depersonalization and merging of the deceased within the reservoir of the dead who are subject to being channelled back into the world of the living.

BIBLIOGRAPHY

H. Basedow: 'Anthropological Notes on the Western Coastal Tribes of the Northern Territory of South Australia', *Trans. Royal Soc. S. Australia*, xxxi (1907), pp. 1–62
W. B. Spencer: *Native Tribes of the Northern Territory of Australia* (London, 1914)
W. L. Warner: *A Black Civilization: A Social Study of an Australian Tribe* (New York and London, 1937, rev. 1958)
C. H. Berndt: 'Expressions of Grief among Aboriginal Women', *Oceania*, xx (1950), pp. 286–332
F. D. McCarthy: *Australia's Aborigines: Their Life and Culture* (Melbourne, 1957)
C. P. Mountford: *The Tiwi: Their Art, Myth and Ceremony* (London, 1958)
J. C. Goodale: 'The Tiwi Dance for the Dead', *Expedition*, ii/1 (autumn 1959), pp. 3–13
R. M. Berndt and C. H. Berndt: *The World of the First Australians: An Introduction to the Traditional Life of the Australian Aborigines* (London and Canberra, 1964/*R* Canberra, 1988)
——: *Man, Land and Myth in North Australia: The Gunwinggu People* (Sydney, 1970)
R. M. Berndt and E. S. Phillips, eds: *The Australian Aboriginal Heritage: An Introduction through the Arts* (Sydney, 1973, rev. 1978)
R. M. Berndt: *Australian Aboriginal Religion* (Leiden, 1974)
R. M. Berndt, C. H. Berndt and J. E. Stanton: *Aboriginal Australian Art: A Visual Perspective* (Sydney, 1982)
H. Morphy: *Journey to the Crocodile's Nest* (Canberra, 1984)
——: *Ancestral Connections: Art and an Aboriginal System of Knowledge* (Chicago, IL, 1991)

RONALD M. BERNDT

6. ARCHITECTURE. Indigenous Aboriginal architecture of north Australia has been well documented, but knowledge is sparse for the centre and the south. The dominant functional category was domestic shelter, the principal purpose of which was to protect against the weather. Separate shelters were used in settlements for diurnal activities, when men and women often congregated apart, and for nocturnal gatherings when nuclear families

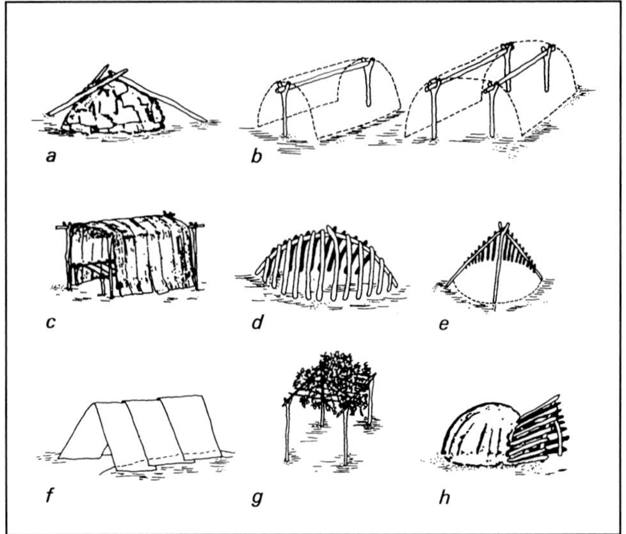

9. Types of Aboriginal shelter: (a) paperbark dome shelter; (b) single and double ridge vault types; (c) vaulted shelter with sleeping platform; (d) rigid bough structure for dome; (e) conical structure for dome; (f) folded plate shelter of stringybark; (g) shade shelter; (h) dome with porch

resided together. People either sat or lay inside shelters, so that these were consistently low (h. 1.2–1.5 m). There was also a wide distribution of common structural principles and forms, but materials and construction details were subject to regional variations. The mobile hunter–gatherer life style resulted in impermanent structures that were not technologically specialized and up to seven or eight shelter types might be employed during the changing seasons.

Two examples from the northern monsoonal coasts exemplify the influence of materials on form. The most suitable claddings were bark sheets from *Melaleuca leucadendron* (paperbark) and *Eucalyptus tetradontra* (stringybark). Paperbark is very flexible and thus suitable for making a dome over a structure of pliable saplings (see fig. 9a). At the start of the wet season, this coastal type was occupied with the opening sealed off and filled with smoke to repel mosquitoes. In contrast to paperbark, stringybark can bend in only one direction. As the wet season continued, the stringybark could be prised off its trunk and used in a range of vaulted forms supported on both single and double ridge-poles (9b). To avoid the boggy ground a further elaboration was a sleeping platform under which fires could be burnt to repel mosquitoes (9c).

In Arnhem Land the forked post and crosspole of this type of structure are still esteemed as religious objects rich in meaning. Their significance derives from the mythological activities of the Wawilak Sisters, ancestral heroines who built the first vaulted dwelling in the region. Among the many interpretations, one clan regards the horns of the fork as a personal totem representing red noses, fire, blood and the wet mud of a sacred well from which sacred objects emerged (Reser, 1977).

Domes covered either circular or elliptical ground-plans up to 3.6 m in diameter according to the size of the occupant group. A common type in the arid interior had a framework of rigid curved boughs (9d). Cladding was of thatched grass, foliage or reeds, sometimes with a coating of mud or clay, possibly for insulation against extremes of temperature or to keep off rain; examples have been recorded in all conditions. For the south-east of the continent there are reports of domes supported on low, circular stone walls. Conical forms were less common but nevertheless widely distributed (9e). A cubic wet-weather structure has been documented at two locations in the Gulf of Carpentaria (Biernoff; Memmott). A more complex architectural form was built by a sedentary group in the north Queensland rain-forest. Clusters of intersecting domes were clad with layers of palm-leaves plaited on to cane frames, covered with an outer skin of another type of leaf and overlaid with cane sticks for further stability. These domes were large enough to stand up in and were occupied by several families (Koettig).

Stringybark was also used for unsupported structures of both a folded plate (9f) and a barrel vault type. Other common seasonal shelters were windbreaks (linear and circular), open sleeping platforms and tree platforms for flood-prone areas. Shade was provided by implanting leafy boughs in the ground and erecting a horizontal roof structure (9g), or making a lean-to with a ridge-pole. Entry 'porches' were attached to some enclosed shelters (9h).

Apart from shelters, Aboriginal structures included rock-wall fisheries, hunting nets strung between posts, ground ovens, wells, storage platforms and posts, ceremonial stone arrangements and circular mounds, as well as foliage walls, trenches and pit traps for game. Various regional types of structure were used to house the dead: mounds, mounds inside huts, platforms, graves and cylindrical bark coffins (*see* §5 above). These were embellished by the various cultural groups with different types of symbolic markers and objects, including feathers, bones, painted wooden structures, cylindro-conical stones (cylcons), incised bark, carved tree trunks representing the dead person's chest cicatrices, the deceased's possessions and a fire laid ready for use at the time of reincarnation. Complex architectural symbolism was a product of the intellectual preoccupation with cosmology and cosmogony.

BIBLIOGRAPHY

R. B. Smyth: *The Aborigines of Victoria and Other Parts of Australia and Tasmania*, 2 vols (Melbourne and London, 1878)

W. E. Roth: *Ethnological Studies among the North-west-central Queensland Aborigines* (Brisbane, 1897)

T. Worsnop: *The Prehistoric Arts, Manufactures, Works, Weapons, etc. of the Aborigines of Australia* (Adelaide, 1897)

W. Roth: 'North Queensland Ethnography Bulletin No. 16: Huts and Shelters', *Rec. Austral. Mus.*, viii/1 (1910)

D. Thomson: 'The Seasonal Factor in Human Culture', *Proc. Prehist. Soc.*, n. s. 4 (1939), pp. 209–21 [West Cape York Peninsula]

P. Hamilton: 'Aspects of Interdependence between Aboriginal Social Behaviour and the Spatial and Physical Environment', *Aboriginal Housing*, ed. Royal Australian Institute of Architects (Canberra, 1972), pp. 1–13 [desert shelters and camps]

M. Koettig: *Rising Damp: Aboriginal Structures in Perspective* (diss., U. Sydney, 1976)

J. P. Reser: 'The Dwelling as Motif in Aboriginal Bark Painting', *Form in Indigenous Art: Schematisation in the Art of Aboriginal Australia and Prehistoric Europe*, ed. P. J. Ucko (Canberra, 1977), pp. 210–19 [Arnhem Land]

——: 'Values in Bark', *Hemisphere*, xxii/10 (1978), pp. 27–35 [Arnhem Land]

D. Biernoff: 'Traditional and Contemporary Structures and Settlement in Eastern Arnhem Land with Particular Reference to Nunggubuyu', *A Black Reality: Aboriginal Camps and Settlements in Remote Australia*, ed. M. Heppell (Canberra, 1979), pp. 153–79

P. Memmott: 'Lardil Artifacts and Shelters', *Occas. Pap. Anthropol.*, ix (1979), pp. 107–42

PAUL MEMMOTT

7. BARK PAINTING. Elaborately painted sheets of bark have gained appreciation in galleries, museums and private collections and for a while, in the 1960s and later, became almost synonymous with Aboriginal art. This type of bark painting, however, is relatively recent—the product of a gradually developing arts and crafts industry that began with European colonization—and the creation of such works is restricted to one main area, Arnhem Land (*see* §III, 4 and 5 below). In Arnhem Land bark painting is part of an active artistic tradition that continues to be expressed in other media such as body painting, sand sculpture and ceremonial carving, but bark has the advantage of being portable and therefore easily traded with Westerners. Before European colonization, bark painting was apparently carried out in varied traditional contexts over a more widespread area.

(i) Techniques. The bark for painting comes from the local species of stringybark tree and can be obtained most easily when the sap is flowing during the wet season and the following few months. The bark is removed by making two horizontal rings around the trunk with an axe, one close to the base, the second at the top of the trunk. A vertical line is then cut between the two and the sheet of bark is prised away using a pointed stick or lever. The bark is then straightened by laying its outer surface on a gently burning fire and allowing it to uncurl. Following this procedure the outer layer of stringybark is removed and the inner surface is sanded to a smooth finish in preparation for painting. The bark is then left flattened under heavy stones for a few weeks in order to be seasoned and to retain its shape.

Similar techniques are used for painting on bark as on other surfaces, although they vary somewhat according to area. Pigments are produced using natural ochres, pipe clay and charcoal, which are ground on stone palettes and applied with brushes of stringybark, human hair or palm fronds or with commercially made brushes. Natural fixatives, such as gulls' eggs or the juices of a tree orchid, are either added to the pigment or rubbed over the surface to preserve the painting and to add to its sheen. Since the 1960s, however, increasing use has been made of commercial wood glue for this purpose. In north-east Arnhem Land a split stick is fixed across the top and bottom and bound together at either end to keep the bark straight; while in Western Arnhem Land a series of holes are made at the top and bottom of the painting and sticks are bound to it using loops of string.

(ii) Early evidence. Early records for the colonial period suggest that bark may have been used for painting in parts of southern Australia, for example Tasmania, the eastern part of South Australia and Queensland, where there were suitable trees (Groger-Wurm). The reports refer to paintings or drawings on the inside of bark huts or, more rarely, to the use of bark painting in ceremonial contexts. François Péron (1775–1810) provided the earliest published reference (1807) to painted sheets of bark at the site of an

Aboriginal grave on Maria Island, off the east coast of Tasmania. There are other references to drawings in Tasmanian bark huts, including one depicting the bullock carts of an early European colonist, but no paintings survive and little detail has been recorded. Similarly only two works, both from Victoria, have survived from the rest of southern Australia (London, BM; Melbourne, Mus. Victoria). They depict scenes of Aboriginal life engraved on the fire-blackened inner surface of a bark sheet, but they may be atypical.

Traditional contexts for the use of bark painting are much better known from northern Australia. Painting on the inside of wet-season huts seems to have been a common practice in Western Arnhem Land, the region of Darwin and other parts of the tropical north. A few paintings survive from the 1870s and 1880s. The best known are those from the Port Essington region (collected before 1878; U. Sydney, Macleay Mus.) and those from the walls of a dismantled hut collected by Capt. James Carrington in 1887 (Adelaide, S. Austral. Mus.). In 1912 Sir W. Baldwin Spencer (1860–1929) started compiling a major collection of bark paintings from Oenpelli in Western Arnhem Land. He also dismantled wet-season huts but soon began commissioning paintings, resulting in the first commercial bark production. Painting on the inside of bark huts continues in those rare places where the huts are still made. In ceremonial contexts, bark paintings usually occurred on objects made from bark rather than on flattened bark 'canvases'. Among the main bark ceremonial objects in Arnhem Land were the cylindrical stringybark containers in which the remains of dead relatives were kept for several years until the final burial. The Tiwi of Melville and Bathurst Islands used elaborately painted baskets in burial ceremonies (*see* §5 above). There are, however, isolated accounts from as far apart as central Arnhem Land (Warner) and Victoria (Groger-Wurm) of painted bark sheets being used in initiation ceremonies.

(iii) Contemporary work. Bark paintings produced today reflect the range of stylistic characteristics of their region rather than, as formerly, the particular ceremonial context and set of subjects. Following European colonization, bark-painting imagery and styles became a product of the interaction between artists and purchasers. In Western Arnhem Land the emphasis has been on X-ray art (Taylor) with few geometric designs being produced other than those from the Port Keats region west of Darwin, which are predominantly geometric. In Eastern Arnhem Land the full range of regional art styles has been employed (Morphy), with a slight emphasis on the inclusion of a figurative component, as in the bark painting being completed by NARRITJIN MAYMURRU (see fig. 10). Groote Eylandt paintings are mainly figurative and often somewhat starkly outlined on a black background. Paintings from Melville and Bathurst Islands are often based on designs for the Pukamani mortuary ceremony (*see* §5 above).

Although Arnhem Land remains the main area for the production of contemporary bark paintings (see also fig. 15 below), works for sale are also produced by people living in the Kimberleys, where the figurative imagery is mainly of Wandjina ancestral beings (*see* §III, 3 below). The technique was briefly introduced on Mornington Island in north Queensland and in the Cape York Peninsula. In Arnhem Land, however, bark painting is an important economic activity, which also plays a vital role in the indigenous cultural system. It provides the main opportunity for the training of artists and for passing on knowledge about the artistic system. Also, since the imagery painted on bark and other surfaces can only be produced by those with an inherited right to it, bark paintings are used as a means of presenting Aboriginal culture to outsiders.

10. Bark painting being completed by the Yolngu artist Narritjin Maymurru, Yirrkala, Eastern Arnhem Land; from a photograph by Howard Morphy, 1973 (Canberra, National Museum of Australia)

BIBLIOGRAPHY

F. A. Péron and C. L. de Freycinet: *Voyage de découvertes aux Terres Australes . . . pendant les années 1800, 1801, 1802, 1803 et 1804*, 2 vols (Paris, 1807–16)

W. B. Spencer: *Native Tribes of the Northern Territory of Australia* (London, 1914)

W. L. Warner: *A Black Civilization: A Social Study of an Australian Tribe* (New York and London, 1937, rev. 1958)

C. P. Mountford: *Art, Myth and Symbolism* (1956), i of *Records of the American-Australian Scientific Expedition to Arnhem Land, 1948* (Melbourne, 1956)

H. M. Groger-Wurm: *Eastern Arnhem Land*, i of *Australian Aboriginal Bark Paintings and their Mythological Interpretations*, Australian Aboriginal Studies, 30; Social Anthropology Series, 5 (Canberra, 1973)

H. Morphy: 'Schematisation to Conventionalisation: A Possible Trend in Yirrkala Bark Paintings', *Form in Indigenous Art: Schematisation in the Art of Aboriginal Australia and Palaeolithic Europe*, ed. P. J. Ucko (Canberra, 1977), pp. 198–204

L. Taylor: 'Seeing the "Inside": Kunwinjku Paintings and the Symbol of the Divided Body', *Animals into Art*, ed. H. Morphy, One World Archaeology, 7 (London, 1989), pp. 371–89

HOWARD MORPHY

8. OTHER ARTS. The beauty of other Aboriginal artefacts, such as containers, ornaments, pipes and weapons, is largely due to the way natural resources are used. Ochres, charcoal, clay, plant and hair fibres, root dyes, woods, resins, feathers, teeth, skin and shells are fashioned into objects of simple elegance that contrast sharply with the better-known, bolder and more highly coloured artefacts produced by the Maori people of New Zealand to the east (*see* MAORI, §1) and by the peoples of PAPUA NEW GUINEA to the north. Despite pronounced similarities in the approach to design, much variation occurred throughout Australia, partly as a result of the diverse materials available for the process of manufacture in different locations and also because of the distinct artistic traditions of the various social groupings.

(i) Containers. (ii) Ornaments. (iii) Pipes. (iv) Weapons.

(i) Containers. Aboriginal people manufactured many types of containers, including baskets woven from various plant fibres, bags made of string produced from the root bark of particular trees and a range of receptacles of different shapes and sizes made from bark, skin and shell. In Arnhem Land and parts of Cape York Peninsula, women make softened bark from the stringybark tree and fig tree into lengths of string. This handspun string is woven into rectangular 'dilly' or 'string' bags, using a variety of stitches (e.g. knotted netting, single loop, hour-glass and loop, and twist). Sometimes, before weaving, the string is dyed red or yellow with the roots of such plants as *Haemodorum coccineum* or *Ceolospernum reticulatum.* Dyed string is also used to add contrasting, horizontal bands of colour to the natural string bag. For special occasions, tiny, brightly coloured feathers from the necks of parakeets or the delicate white feathers from the breasts of magpie geese are rolled into the string, so as to give the bags a soft, fluffy, outer surface.

Baskets, either flat-based or conical in shape, are made from the young, green fronds of pandanus (especially *Pandanus spiralus*). These are split into strips, dried in the sun and then either left their natural colour or dyed and used as weft threads of the woven pattern. Some conical baskets are woven so tightly that honey from the hives of wild bees and water can be carried in them. Sometimes, especially since the emergence of a tourist industry, several split strands of pandanus fibre dyed bright orange, yellow, brown, pink or purple are bound into cylindrical lengths, which are then coiled into basket shape and held in place with blanket stitch to create a container resembling a European shopping basket.

Crescent-shaped baskets are made in the rain-forest regions of north Queensland from lengths of split lawyer cane (*Calamus caryotoides*), a prolific climbing plant. The basket is made using two continuous strands of cane, with several straight strands extending the length of the base. The distinctive shape is formed by stringing the ends of the split cane like a bow and attaching it by top-stitching to the inner surface. Sometimes men paint the outer surface with red and yellow ochres, white clay and charcoal. Coiled baskets of reeds were formerly made in eastern Australia. The reeds were wound on a continuous spiral starting from the centre of the base and ending at the rim. In Tasmania, women made delicately shaped, globular baskets from *Juncus* reeds for carrying personal items and food. These resembled the baskets of Aboriginal women in Victoria. Nowadays European materials are sometimes used in the manufacture of bags and baskets. For example, commercial dyes are used to colour plant fibres and strips of brightly printed cloth are used as decoration on small round-bottomed baskets made of pandanus. Some bags, such as those normally made from bark string, are crocheted from coloured wool or nylon string.

The Tiwi people of Bathurst and Melville Islands make large rectangular containers for use in mortuary ceremonies (*see* §5 above). These comprise a long sheet of flattened and cleaned stringybark folded in half lengthwise and sewn together at the sides with pandanus strips threaded through punched holes. Striking and bold geometric designs are painted on the outer surface.

In the Kimberleys region of Western Australia two types of elegant bark containers are made for utilitarian purposes. One, unique to the region, is shaped like a European bucket with the bark base attached to the cylinder by seams of handspun bark-fibre string. It is waterproofed with a thick layer of resin. String handles are added and the outer surface is decorated with traditional symbols, stencilled hands and Wandjina figures (*see* §III, 3 below), using white clay, sometimes blown on to the surface. The other type, similar to those found in northern Queensland and Arnhem Land, is long and cylindrical. Bark's tendency to curl back into the form of the original tree trunk is exploited by Aboriginal women, and rough bark at the ends of the rectangular strip is thinned to enable it to be pleated and bound into place with stick handles and twine. The outer surface is also sometimes decorated with designs using white clay, often on a red ochre background.

Elegantly carved, elongate wooden dishes are made in the desert region of central Australia. After chipping, shaping and hollowing, these multipurpose containers are usually left plain and smooth or they are finely chiselled with fluted decoration and covered with red ochre. For ceremonial purposes, Warlpiri, Pintupi and Luritja women painted Dreamtime designs on both the inner and outer surface of these wooden containers, using ochres to make circular and dotted motifs. Some bowls are now made for sale and these are often decorated with a wide range of acrylic paints. Pitjantjatjara women use hot wire to incise swirling linear designs of Dreamtime motifs on such bowls (see fig. 11).

In several areas of Australia, large gastropod shells are used to carry food and water. In Arnhem Land, for example, water is carried in the large *Syrinx aruanus* shell, to which is attached a fig-string handle.

(ii) Ornaments. Aboriginal people adorn their bodies with a variety of materials. In the Kimberleys, pearl shell pendants are highly prized and often traded far afield. String, handspun from human hair and sometimes greased and heavily laden with red ochre, is attached to the apex of the shell, so that the pendant can be hung around a

11. Wooden container being decorated with incised swirling lines by a Pitjantjatjara woman, central Australia

man's neck or waist. The beauty of this pendant lies in the interlocking key design, incised into the pearly inner surface and filled with red ochre to highlight the pattern.

During mortuary ceremonies, Tiwi men wear various special ornaments (*see* §5 above), and in Arnhem Land male dancers wear delicate handspun bark-fibre cords or tiny entwined parakeet feathers suspended from bark-fibre waist- and headbands. Finely plaited pandanus-fibre strips may be worn around the upper arm.

Throughout most of northern and central Australia, men often dance with bunches of fresh green leaves tied around their ankles. In Arnhem Land the practice is restricted to certain ceremonies such as initiation and mortuary rites. Human hairstring belts, greased and thickly covered with red ochre, are also worn. In the rain-forests of northern Queensland, white and yellow feathers from sulphur-crested cockatoos were used in the past for men's headdresses. These were either arranged as a radiating flat crown, with the central shaft of feather spines held together by beeswax, or they were clustered into small feather bunches stabilized with beeswax and affixed to separate locks of hair or beard. Forehead bands were made of handspun bark-fibre or possum-fur string, from which eel bones, kangaroo teeth or seeds were suspended so as to hang over the temple.

Women in the Western Desert regions of central Australia use bright red and yellow seeds from the bean tree (*Erythrina vespertilio*), threaded on string handspun from human hair. They wrap these strings of seeds across their breasts, over their shoulders and around their waists and wear them as armbands. Strips of white sheeting are also sometimes worn as a headband with a bunch of white feathers just above the centre of the forehead.

Delicate reed necklaces, threaded on vegetable-fibre string, are worn by Aborigines in eastern Australia. In Tasmania, striking necklaces are made from possum fur or kangaroo sinew, raddled with red ochre, and from iridescent trochus shell. Similar shell necklaces are still made by Aboriginal women on Cape Barren Island, but these are now threaded with European sewing cotton or nylon thread. As part of daily attire, incised kangaroo bone and reed ornaments were worn through the nasal septum by men in the rain-forest region of north Queensland. Many were decorated with tiny, incised parallel lines and short dashes and rubbed over with charcoal to highlight the pattern.

(iii) Pipes. Drone pipes (*didjeridu*) are found in Arnhem Land and more recently in the Kimberleys and Mornington Island in the Gulf of Carpentaria. They are made from small tree trunks or branches, the cores of which have been eaten out by termites. They are between 1.2 and 1.8 m long and vary considerably in diameter. In some areas the mouthpiece is shaped with beeswax to suit the player. In the Kimberleys these drone pipes are painted black or deep red-brown and then incised with images of Dreamtime figures and handprints so as to allow the natural colour of the timber to show through. In Arnhem Land the drone pipes are painted with earth ochres or acrylic paints in designs similar to those found on bark paintings from the region. Mornington Island pipes are coated with black or red-brown commercial paint, and bands of red, black and/or white often adorn part of the surface. Suitable lengths of metal or plastic piping are also occasionally used.

The smoking pipe was introduced to Arnhem Land by Indonesian ('Macassan') traders. Macassan pipes have a slender, cylindrical shaft of softwood, about 500–600 mm in length, with a metal bowl. The softwood barrel is decorated with finely incised, cross-hatched and geometric designs and painted with earth ochres or with yellow, black, white and red acrylic paints. These continue to be used in Arnhem Land together with European pipes and those made from the claw of the large mud crab.

(iv) Weapons. Aboriginal peoples from all over Australia used similar groups of weapons for both hunting and combat (see fig. 12). These included clubs, shields, spears, spear-throwers and boomerangs. However, boomerangs were not used in Arnhem Land or Cape York, and neither boomerangs, shields nor spear-throwers were used in Tasmania. In the Kimberleys, distinctive elongated hardwood shields are decorated on the outer surface with multiple incised zigzag designs. Some are covered with red ochre and others are infilled with alternate red and white bands. Arnhem Land spears and spear-throwers are sometimes painted with cross-hatched ochre designs similar to those of the region's bark paintings. Those from Port Essington are light and elegant with a beeswax knob at the handheld end decorated with an impressed linear design, and subtle red and white ochre motifs on the shaft. Bathurst and Melville Islands ceremonial spears and clubs are highly decorated, echoing the bold geometric designs of the islands' baskets, bark paintings, burial poles and body painting.

In the desert regions of central and north-western Australia, the thin, leaf-shaped spear-thrower made of mulga-wood (*Acacia aneura*) was a multipurpose object of

12. Weapons and other objects, painted wood, bark and vegetable fibre, at a rain-forest camp in northern Queensland, *c.* 1880

great elegance. Besides being used to propel a spear, it also doubled as an adze, as it had a stone blade embedded in resin at one end. Water, pigments or blood could be collected in its concave surface.

There are two distinctive central Australian hardwood boomerangs. The first type is fluted, coloured with red ochre, gently curved, and is either returning or non-returning. The other is the hook boomerang, sometimes known from its shape as a 'number 7'. These are left plain or decorated with parallel bands of incised lines filled with red ochre; some also have white bands painted on the hook as well as on the handheld end. Often a small band of dots and circles, reminiscent of the Dreamtime designs found in ground paintings from this region, is painted on one end or both.

Light, oval-shaped shields, made from bean-wood (*Erythrina vespertilio*), were similarly embellished with parallel grooves on both surfaces. They were usually red from ochre and sometimes a dot, circle and line design depicting Dreamtime events was painted on the outer surface in red, yellow, white and black. Today acrylic paints and a wider range of colours are often used.

In eastern Australia, extremely large, heavy boomerangs were decorated with delicate linear incisions. The natural grain of the wood sometimes enhanced the design. Narrow parrying shields had similar incised markings covering the outer surface. In the past these markings were engraved with a possum tooth or stone tool. The most common incised design was a diamond figure set in a field of herringbone patterns, parallel chevrons and diagonal fluting. A fine 19th-century shield from the Darling River, NSW, is illustrated at fig. 13 below.

A unique one-handed sword was used in the north Queensland rain-forest. Made of heavy hardwood, it had a small handgrip and a long blade with plain, polished, convex surfaces. The sword was used only with a highly decorated, kidney-shaped shield that was cut from the buttress of a fig-tree, the natural curve determining its shape. Ornate linear patterns were painted on the shield's outer surface, using red and yellow ochres, white pipeclay and ground charcoal. Blood, either human or animal, was used as a fixative. Designs were painted with the fingers, brushes made from lawyer cane chewed at one end, or with commercially produced brushes. It is thought that the designs probably related to totems.

BIBLIOGRAPHY

F. A. Péron and C. L. de S. de Freycinet: *Voyage de découvertes aux Terres Australes . . . pendant les années 1800, 1801, 1802, 1803 et 1804*, 2 vols (Paris, 1807–16)

W. B. Spencer and F. Gillen: *The Native Tribes of Central Australia* (London, 1899/*R* 1969)

W. E. Roth: *North Queensland Ethnography*, Queensland Government Printer, Bulletins nos 1–8 (1901–6); *Rec. Austral. Mus.*, vi–viii (1907–10) [Bulletins nos 9–18]

U. H. McConnel: 'Native Arts and Industries on the Archer, Kendall and Holroyd Rivers, Cape York Peninsula, North Queensland', *Rec. S. Austral. Mus.*, xi/1 (1953), pp. 1–42, pls i–xvii

F. D. McCarthy: *Australia's Aborigines: Their Life and Culture* (Melbourne, 1957)

C. P. Mountford: *The Tiwi: Their Art, Myth and Ceremony* (London, 1958)

P. Brokensha: *The Pitjantjatjara and their Crafts* (Sydney, 1975)

C. C. Macknight: *'The Voyage to Marege': Macassan Trepangers in Northern Australia* (Melbourne, 1976)

J. Clark: *The Aboriginal People of Tasmania* (Hobart, 1983)

J. Isaacs: *Arts of the Dreaming: Australia's Living Heritage* (Sydney, 1984)

K. Khan: 'North Queensland Aboriginal Baskets', *Craft Australia*, iv (1985), pp. 18–22

KATE KHAN, BETTY MEEHAN

III. Regions.

Australia is here divided into a number of geographical regions that reflect broad variations in the cultural and artistic systems of their Aboriginal populations (see fig. 1 above). The south and south-east was the first region to be colonized by Europeans, and knowledge of its art is less detailed than that of other areas. Nevertheless, the region does seem to have considerable unity, especially in the widespread tradition of finely engraved and incised wooden artefacts. The central region, stretching from south-east Queensland in the east across to the coast of Western Australia, is an arid zone with low population densities and considerable cultural continuities. Across the northern coastal region there is greater linguistic variation and art styles can differ markedly between adjacent areas, making it possible to define a number of more precisely demarcated regions. From west to east these comprise the Kimberleys, characterized by paintings of the legendary Wandjina heroes, Western Arnhem Land with its X-ray paintings, and Eastern Arnhem Land with its intricate clan designs. Cape York Peninsula on the eastern side of the Gulf of Carpentaria has distinctive art forms that show some continuities with works from the TORRES STRAIT ISLANDS. Within each region there is considerable variation and in some cases, such as Melville and Bathurst Islands, Groote Eylandt and Lake Eyre, sub-regions exist that have their own distinctive art styles.

□

1. South-east Australia and Tasmania. 2. Central Australia. 3. Kimberleys. 4. Western Arnhem Land. 5. Eastern Arnhem Land. 6. Cape York Peninsula.

1. South-east Australia and Tasmania. This cultural and stylistic region can be defined as the area south and east of an arc drawn from near Adelaide in South Australia up through the great Murray–Darling River system of New South Wales and south-west Queensland to a point along the north-east coast just below Brisbane, together with the island of Tasmania. Over this entire area engraved linear designs display recognizable combinations of motif that typify the region's art. Within this overall style, variations on a theme have led to distinctive, localized designs. As in all Australian Aboriginal art, the designs are related to the land or country of their maker. They are primarily found incised on hunter's weapons, but variations occur on burial and ceremonial trees and on the richly decorated skin cloaks peculiar to some areas within the region. They even characterize the relatively sparse rock art of the region (*see* Mootwingee). A number of significant rock art sites exist in south-eastern Australia. Among the most notable are the Sydney-Hawkesbury sandstone engravings at Cobar in central western New South Wales. Rock-engravings fit in with sequences found elsewhere in Australia. Paintings in rock shelters in New South Wales seem to be a more recent development, though the situation may have been distorted by differential preservation. Most extant specimens of traditional south-east Australian art were made, used, bartered and collected in the 19th century. Representative examples of small-scale works are found in museums throughout the world. Since the 1990s, Aboriginal people from the region have sought to strengthen their identity, resulting in a revival of interest in traditional arts and crafts. In such areas as the Lower Murray River replicas of 'traditional' weapons have been made based on 19th-century material preserved in museums.

As a result of the devastating impact of European colonization, little survives of the art of Tasmania. The early records suggest that rich and varied traditions similar to those in the rest of Australia also existed in Tasmania (see Ruhe for a summary). The paintings of Thomas Bock (1790–1855) and early photographs reveal traditions of elaborate hair decoration and body adornment (see Morphy and Edwards).

(i) Weapons. The formal and graphic elements that are combined to produce the recognizable 'South-eastern' style are relatively few and simple. The several varieties of weapons, shields, clubs, boomerangs and spear-throwers that were made throughout the region were decorated with designs formed from repeated crosshatch, herringbone, zigzag, chevron, diamond, interlocking diamond and rhombic elements. In some localities red, white and black pigments were used to accentuate areas of design. Discrete motifs were relatively uncommon, but when they do occur they usually take the form of curvilinear or geometric shapes enclosing smooth, recessed, raised, infilled or coloured areas. Human, animal and other representational figures are rare on artefacts, though their use was greatly stimulated when artefacts were produced for barter and sale outside Aboriginal society. One example,

13. South-east Australian shield, wood, 1125×240 mm, from Darling River, New South Wales, 19th century (London, British Museum)

a club collected by R. B. Smyth from the Aborigines of Victoria (Rome, Mus. N. Preist. & Etnog.), is decorated on both surfaces with finely incised representations of an emu and iguanas. Smyth thought such figures represented the totems of their maker's tribe. Another club (Melbourne, Mus. Victoria) possesses a linear design that Smyth claimed represented a lagoon and an anabranch of a river, the space enclosed by the lines showing the country occupied by the tribe of the weapon's owner.

The workmanship displayed in some of the old weapons, especially the shields traditionally carved by stone or animal-tooth tools, is striking, as is seen in a rare and superbly decorated specimen from the Darling River region (London, BM; see fig. 13). Made of hardwood rather than bark, its handle was cut into the solid wood at the back of the shield with a stone tool. The finely carved design was executed with an engraving tool made from a possum's jawbone. Broad shields of this type were about 1 m long on average and were used throughout south-east Australia to deflect spears in general fights between warring parties. The shields' designs stressed both individual and group identity. Like their owners, they were often 'painted up' for fights, as ethnographic accounts record, though this example has no traces of pigment and appears to have relied instead on the striking nature of its complex incised design for its effect. The unusual inclusion on the shield of circular motifs, which are uncommon for the south-east, link this design with those of the Lake Eyre region further west.

Stylistic variation between the internal groupings within the larger region is discernible. Just as the excellence of the work of individual craftsmen or artists stands out, so do particular styles that suggest specific provenances. For instance, in the early years of the 19th century Aborigines living in the upper Darling River area, more specifically along the tributaries of the Bogan and Macquarie rivers, seem to have possessed a special inventiveness in wood-carving, which is revealed in many particularly unusual and beautiful pieces.

(ii) Carved trees and decorated cloaks. The greatest concentration of dendroglyphs or carved trees (associated with either burial or ceremonial grounds) is also found to the east of the Darling, on the Bogan and Macquarie rivers, in Kamilaroi tribal lands. This area is noted for the greatest variety of motifs and greatest skill in their execution. One particular carved tree (Sydney, Austral. Mus.) was recorded by Etheridge (1918) as being one of two trees that marked 'the grave of a celebrated boomerang-thrower of the Macquarie tribe, killed in a fight with the Bogan blacks'. Though the design is cut with a metal tool, the deterioration in workmanship and design integrity often associated with the introduction of metal tools is not evident here. Indeed, the introduction of European woodworking tools into this area appears to have stimulated wood-carving skills, resulting in the production of some particularly fine carved weapons and trees.

Possum-skin cloaks, the other major vehicle for linear designs in the region, are extremely rare. While there are many records of these beautiful objects being collected, few survive in museums. Two outstanding examples come from the region's coastal area. One (Melbourne, Mus. Victoria) consisting of 50 engraved possum pelts, still bears traces of red-ochre decoration; it was obtained in 1872 from Lake Condah Aboriginal station in coastal Victoria and is remarkably similar in design to one collected in 1838–42 from the Hunter River in eastern New South Wales (Washington, DC, N. Mus. Nat. Hist.).

The exact relationship of the designs on the cloaks to those on the trees and weapons is obscure. Early commentators had difficulty in obtaining information from local Aborigines, who were hesitant to discuss their traditional practices with Europeans. There are, however, indications that there were associations between body cicatrice designs and those on the cloaks, trees and artefacts, as well as with ephemeral ceremonial-ground drawings.

BIBLIOGRAPHY

R. B. Smyth: *The Aborigines of Victoria*, 2 vols (London, 1878)

R. Etheridge: *The Dendroglyphs, or 'Carved Trees' of New South Wales*, Memoirs of the Geological Survey of New South Wales: Ethnological Series, 3 (Sydney, 1918)

N. Peterson: 'The Natural and Cultural Areas of Aboriginal Australia: A Preliminary Analysis of Population Groupings with Adaptive Significance', *Tribes and Boundaries in Australia*, ed. N. Peterson, Australian Institute of Aboriginal Studies Social Anthropology Series, 10 (Canberra, 1976), pp. 50–71

Aboriginal Australia (exh. cat. by C. Cooper and others, Sydney, Austral. Gal. Directors Council, 1981–2), pp. 29–42, 82–120

D. Bell: *Aboriginal Carved Trees of Southeastern Australia: A Research Report* (Sydney, 1982)

H. Morphy and E. Edwards, eds: *Australia in Oxford*, Pitt Rivers Museum Monograph 4 (Oxford, 1988)

P. Sutton, P. Jones and S. Hemming: 'Survival, Regeneration, and Impact', *Dreamings: The Art of Aboriginal Australia* (exh. cat., ed. P. Sutton; New York: Asia Soc. Gals; U. Chicago, IL, Smart Gal.; Melbourne, Mus. Victoria; Adelaide, S. Austral. Mus.; 1988–90), pp. 180–212

E. L. Ruhe: 'The Bark Art of Tasmania', *Art and Identity in Oceania*, ed. A. Hanson and L. Hanson (Honolulu, 1990), pp. 129–48

C. Cooper: *Designs in Wood* (diss., Canberra, Austral. N. U.) (in preparation)

CAROL COOPER

2. CENTRAL AUSTRALIA. This extensive cultural region stretches from Tennant Creek in the north to the Flinders Ranges in the south, and from Queensland in the east to the west Australian coast. The main language groups are the Aranda, Warlpiri, Pintubi, Luritja and Pitjantjatjara. Most artists are based in the towns of Hooker Creek, Yuendumu, Papunya, Hermannsburg, Ayers Rock (Uluru), Ernabella, Utopia, Kintore and Balgo, although many live in smaller camps between these larger centres.

Throughout this vast area there is much stylistic continuity in the graphic designs used in sand drawings, body painting and the decoration of ceremonial objects. Patterns of circles, lines and dots characterize the designs, which are used in a variety of contexts to represent specific localities and events of ancestral importance. The indigenous symbolism and use of such designs has been thoroughly documented by Nancy Munn, who identified a set of 13 graphic elements regularly used in sand drawings; these include circles, arcs, dots, ovals and meandering or straight lines. Each element has a wide range of potential meanings: a simple circle can be used to indicate such varied items as a nest, water-hole, tree, hill or camp fire; a short, straight line may identify a spear, a digging stick, or an animal or person lying down or moving in a certain direction. The exact reference to each element is fixed within the accompanying narrative. The elements are combined into larger design units that build a broader picture of details about the daily activities of particular ancestral subjects.

While both men and women publicly engage in sand drawing to tell stories of ancestral times, they also control their own designs in different types of ceremonial contexts. Women's designs (*yawalyu*) are revealed to them in dreams by spirit children (*yinawuru*), acting as proxies for ancestral beings. The painting of such designs on the body in Yawalyu ceremonies is said to enhance the personal, sexual and procreative aims of the wearer. Although the accompanying stories are associated with specific ancestral figures and with a general locality, such locational references are not stressed by women (Munn). They tend rather to see in their dreams the ancestral precedent for their own hunting and gathering or food-consuming activities. *Yawalyu* body designs differ from those in sand drawings in that the basic elements are often outlined with one or more lines. Hence, circles become concentric and parallel lines are used instead of single straight lines.

Designs controlled exclusively by men (*guruwari*) are considered to be reproductions of marks originally created by the ancestral beings, although men also produce new designs from their dreams. They are painted on the body and on regalia such as shields and are incised on wooden or oval stone slabs known as *tjurunga*, as well as on waymarkers known as *toas* (see fig. 5 above). Larger and more elaborate designs may be constructed on the ground using white and ochred bird down or plant fibre. The ceremonies in which these designs are used include the Bulaba, a ritual that dramatizes ancestral events for the benefit of the whole camp, Guridji circumcision rituals and Banba or major fertility ceremonies that ensure the maintenance of different totemic species and of life sources as a whole. Since the standardized designs represent specific ancestral localities, their use during ceremonies is intended to tap the reserves of ancestral power left at these places and to communicate it to the participants and the objects. *Guruwari* designs are similar to women's *yawalyu* designs but generally larger. The concentric circle patterns are identified with sites created by ancestral beings when they stopped and the lines indicate the path of their travels. The designs help to create symbolic links between the hunting and ceremonial journeys undertaken by contemporary humans and the journeys and exploits of the ancestral beings. The prime underlying symbolic reference of concentric circles is to female sexuality, while parallel lines are associated with male sexuality.

For details concerning the Hermannsburg school of watercolourists, established in the area in the 1930s, and the contemporary production of acrylic paintings and batik textiles, *see* §IV below.

BIBLIOGRAPHY

W. B. Spencer and F. J. Gillen: *The Native Tribes of Central Australia* (London, 1899/*R* 1969)
C. P. Mountford: 'Aboriginal Crayon Drawings Relating to Totemic Places Belonging to the Northern Aranda Tribe of Central Australia', *Trans. Royal Soc. S. Australia*, lxi (1937), pp. 84–95
G. Roheim: *The Eternal Ones of the Dream: A Psychoanalytic Approach to Australian Myth and Ritual* (New York, 1945)
N. O. Munn: *Walbiri Iconography: Graphic Representation and Cultural Symbolism in a Central Australian Society* (Ithaca, NY, 1973, rev. Chicago, 1986)
G. Bardon: *Aboriginal Art of the Western Desert* (Adelaide, 1979)
L. Taylor: *Ancestors into Art: An Analysis of Pitjanjatjara Kulpidji Designs and Crayon Drawings* (diss., Canberra, Austral. N. U., 1979)
N. Peterson: 'Art of the Desert', *Aboriginal Australia* (exh. cat. by C. Cooper and others, Sydney, Austral. Gal. Directors Council, 1981–2), pp. 43–51
P. Jones and P. Sutton: *Art and Land: Aboriginal Sculptures of the Lake Eyre Region* (Adelaide, 1986)

LUKE TAYLOR

3. KIMBERLEYS. This cultural region between the Ord and Fitzroy rivers in Western Australia is occupied by speakers of a number of non-Pama-nyungan languages. The region is best known for its rock art (*see also* §II, 2 above), though Aboriginal communities have produced art in various media, including body painting (see fig. 7 above) and, in recent years, commercial paintings on board and bark. Two types of figures are characteristic of the region's rock paintings: Bradshaw and Wandjina figures. The first belong to a tradition that is no longer practised. They are known in the local languages as Giro-giro or Kiro-kiro but among archaeologists as 'Bradshaw figures', after their European discoverer, Joseph Bradshaw, who encountered them in 1892. These figures are caught in mid-action, often wear headdresses and other ornaments and sometimes occur in groups. Painted in red ochre, they are generally less than 300 mm high and in style are similar to the Mimi figures of the Oenpelli–Kakadu region of Western Arnhem Land (*see* §4 below). Bradshaw figures are found in both the western and eastern Kimberleys (though relatively little is known of the art of the eastern area). Welch (1993) considers that two phases can be detected within the 'Bradshaw' art, characterized by different headdresses, artefacts and poses. He tentatively equates the later Bradshaw art of the Kimberleys with the Lewis Stick period in the rock art of Western Arnhem Land.

Wandjina are legendary heroes depicted as mouthless human-like figures wearing semicircular headdresses (see fig. 14). The Wandjina are often accompanied by animals with which they are associated in legends; these are depicted in a twisted perspective: the body shown in

14. Kimberleys rock painting at Galvin's Gorge, head and shoulders of Wandjina (totemic clan hero) with two snakes depicted on right-hand side of head, red ochre on white background, diam. of head *c.* 400 mm

profile but the feet, anus and head seen from other angles. In the same caves as the Wandjina there are small, roughly drawn figures representing either malevolent and capricious beings that subvert the ancestral order established by the Wandjina, or the victims of sorcery. The latter were painted by people wishing to invoke the Wandjinas' power to cripple and kill their opponents (Layton). Indirect evidence suggests the Wandjina style is up to 3000 years old, since the earlier Dynamic 'Bradshaw' styles do not depict the use of stone-tipped spears, and Kimberley stone spear points are thought to appear *c.* 1000 BP (see Crawford, 1968, 1977; Welch, 1990). Confined to the western half of the Kimberleys, bounded roughly by the Drysdale River, the Wandjina tradition is later than that of the Bradshaw figures. It was first documented by Sir George Grey (1812–98) in 1838.

The Wandjina are seen as having established the Aboriginal social order by demarcating clan territories and instituting ceremonial exchanges (Blundell and Layton; Blundell). Each clan holds pre-eminent rights over an area containing one or more rock shelters bearing Wandjina and other paintings. The clans are totemic and in the western Kimberleys each is associated with a named Wandjina hero. Traditionally, the clan had a ritual responsibility for the increase of the particular animal species associated with its Wandjina, which was discharged at ceremonies in which the Wandjina paintings were retouched. This aspect of the cult ceased, probably during the 1930s, following the severe disruption caused by the attempts at white pastoral settlement and the relocation of Aboriginal groups on missions (Blundell). Senior men have nonetheless continued to repaint Wandjina whenever possible. A number of cases have been recorded between 1947 and 1986 (*see* WALL PAINTING, fig. 1). Rituals celebrating the Wandjina were being performed in the late 1980s–early 1990s, while commercial bark paintings of Wandjina heads are a popular modern art form. Pearl shell pendants, once exclusively produced for ceremonial exchange, are now also available commercially.

Little of the rock art in the eastern Kimberleys is directly associated with 'increase' ceremonies, although in one documented example the paintings are said to have been executed by an ancestral hero (Capell, 1972). Most paintings are placed in apparently random assemblages, not linked by the legendary associations of the site, and are more stereotyped than in the western zone. Only images of the spirits of unborn children are retouched, 'to replace a spirit-child born into the human world' (Kaberry, 1935, 1936; Capell, 1972).

Recent rock art styles are more static, and compositions are rarer. Figures are often more than 1 m high and are outlined and infilled in red, black and white on a white background. Among recent important contemporary developments in the region is the art from Turkey Creek in the East Kimberleys. The art developed as part of a renaissance of ritual that followed the death of a woman in a car accident, commemorated by the Krill Krill song cycle. Paintings on board made for rituals have become well known. The paintings of ROVER THOMAS with their stark geometricity have gained an international reputation (see 1994. exh. cat).

BIBLIOGRAPHY

A. P. Elkin: 'Rock-paintings of North-west Australia', *Oceania*, i (1930), pp. 257–79 [eye-witness accts of ptg tech.]

J. Love: 'Rock Paintings of the Worrora and their Mythological Interpretation', *J. Royal Soc. W. Australia*, xvi (1930), pp. 1–24

P. M. Kaberry: 'The Forrest River and Lyne River Tribes of North-west Australia', *Oceania*, v (1935), pp. 408–36

——: 'Spirit-children and Spirit-centres of the North Kimberley Division, West Australia', *Oceania*, vi (1936), pp. 392–400

J. Love: *Stone-age Bushmen of Today* (London, 1936) [eye-witness accts of ptg tech.]

A. Capell: 'Mythology in Northern Kimberley', *Oceania*, ix (1939), pp. 382–404

I. M. Crawford: *The Art of the Wandjina: Aboriginal Cave Paintings in Kimberley, Western Australia* (London and Melbourne, 1968) [colour photos]

A. Capell: *Cave Painting Myths: Northern Kimberley* (Sydney, 1972)

V. Blundell and R. Layton: 'Marriage, Myth and Models of Exchange in the Western Kimberleys', *Mankind*, xi (1978), pp. 231–45

V. Blundell: 'Symbolic Systems and Cultural Continuity in Northwest Australia: A Consideration of Aboriginal Cave Art', *Culture*, xi (1982), pp. 3–20

R. Layton: 'The Cultural Context of Hunter-gatherer Rock Art', *Man*, n. s., xx/3 (1985), pp. 434–53

D. Welch: 'The Bichrome Art Period in the Kimberley, Australia', *Rock A. Res.*, vii (1990), pp. 110–24

——: 'Early "Naturalistic" Human Figures in the Kimberley, Australia', *Rock A. R.*, x (1993), pp. 24–37

G. L. Walsh: *Bradshaws: Ancient Rock Paintings of North-west Australia* (Geneva, 1994)

Roads Cross: The Paintings of Rover Thomas (exh. cat. by R. Thomas, Canberra, N. G., 1994)

J. Schmiechen: *Survey of Aboriginal Rock Art and Cultural Sites: Drysdale River, East Kimberley, Western Australia: Report of Findings* (in preparation)

ROBERT LAYTON

4. WESTERN ARNHEM LAND. This cultural region is located in the Northern Territory of Australia and is bounded by the East Alligator and Liverpool rivers. Its landscape is dominated by spectacular escarpments, many containing caves decorated with rock paintings—among the most extensive and best-preserved of which are in the UBIRR complex in Kakadu National Park. The two other most important art forms are ceremonial body painting and bark paintings on stringybark produced for sale. Such bark paintings replaced the traditional painting of rock shelters and bark in wet-season huts as the arena for representing secular subjects, but in response to market demand, contemporary bark painters have been incorporating more sacred subject-matter relating to the creative actions of ancestral beings. Artists paint in recognizable local 'schools' or styles centred around the Aboriginal townships at Oenpelli, Maningrida and Bamyili, and at small bush camps throughout the region. Although the Aboriginal peoples of the region speak some ten different languages of the non-Pama-nyungan group, multilingualism is common, and this facilitates movement throughout the area and participation in major regional ceremonies. As a result artists share stylistic traits that emphasize their cultural distinctiveness from groups in Eastern Arnhem Land.

Among the large body of documented rock paintings in Western Arnhem Land, two characteristic styles are known: Dynamic Figurative, which was subsequently replaced by the X-ray style (*see* §II, 2(ii)(b) above). The term 'Dynamic Figurative' was introduced to describe the small, red, human-like figures (h. *c.* 200–300 mm) actively engaged in hunting, fighting and ceremonial scenes (for illustration *see* UBIRR). Neither the original meaning nor function of the Dynamic Figurative style paintings is known. Contemporary Aborigines describe them as representations of Mimi (rock country spirits), said to be long, thin, trickster spirits that live in the crevices of the rock caves. They also attribute the production of such paintings to the Mimi; hence some scholars refer to them as Mimi art. This type of painting has considerable antiquity, but direct evidence of its age is lacking. A Pleistocene date (*c.* 10,000 BP) has been suggested by relating the subject-matter of the paintings to geomorphological studies of environmental changes in the region (Chaloupka).

'X-ray' art, the term used to describe rock paintings of animals infilled with schematic representations of internal organs and skeletal features (see fig. 3 above), continued to be produced until recent times. The subject-matter reflects the changing economy of Aboriginal groups over a long period of environmental change, from pre-estuarine to estuarine (*c.* 7000–5000 BC) and finally to the present-day freshwater, wetland conditions (*c.* AD 1000). The region's Aborigines do not have a single term for all the different types of X-ray painting, although they acknowledge it as 'our way of painting' and its style is continuous with some paintings used in contemporary ceremonies.

The designs used in ceremonial body painting are believed to have been created by the ancestral beings and handed down through the generations. Figurative X-ray motifs are painted on the body during the most public stages of the Mardayin ceremony, performed to ensure the fertility of the natural world, to initiate young men and to settle the souls of the dead. During the more sacred stages of this ceremony, elaborate, geometric designs called *rarrk* are painted in natural ochres on the bodies of initiates and on sacred objects. *Rarrk* consist of geometric grids of dotted lines infilled with polychrome crosshatching patterns. These designs represent both features of the clan lands of the owner of the designs and the associated ancestral events. Since landscape is often conceived to be the transformed remains of ancestral beings, *rarrk* can also be interpreted as showing body parts. As ancestral creations, *rarrk* designs are considered to contain some of the power of the original beings, which can be transferred to the initiates who wear the designs. The Mardayin ceremony dramatizes the manner in which the power of the original ancestral beings is now controlled by the clan groups who own the designs.

Similar functions and interpretations are also ascribed to *buluk* designs, which are constructed from coloured cotton wool or kapok stuck to a dancer's torso. These designs are worn in the most important phases of the Kunapipi and Yabburdurrwa ceremonies, which are re-enactments of the Dreaming concerned with initiation and fertility. *Buluk* designs consist of either highly schematic figures or wholly geometric motifs.

Western Arnhem Land bark paintings are characterized by figurative subjects; the most common are representations of hunting scenes derived from stories of the Mimi spirits (see fig. 15). Such paintings generally show a relatively large X-ray representation of a common food species in combination with a much smaller Mimi figure in the act of spearing the animal. These paintings are associated with others that show the butchery or cooking of game. The characteristic body features that identify the distinct species of animal are carefully represented.

15. Western Arnhem Land bark painting by Robin Nganjmira: *Two Brolgas with Mimi Spirits*, natural ochres on bark, 1.20×0.67 m, 1981; from a photograph by Luke Taylor, 1981

To indicate the particular creative and transformable characteristics of ancestral beings, the artist may elaborate either the internal infill or the outline of the figure. For example, the use of crosshatching infill, combined with X-ray motifs, identifies the painting with *rarrk* ceremonial designs. Since ancestral beings are also thought to have transformed themselves freely into different animal types or into composite animal and human body forms, artists may also modify the outline of the figures, combining figurative elements from a number of distinct species to create monstrous configurations that embody these mythical figures. A common example is seen in the paintings of Ngalyod (the First Mother) or Rainbow Serpent, the original mythical creator of Western Arnhem Land. The latter has been painted with a body form that combines

16. Eastern Arnhem Land body painting, the Yolngu artist Larrtjinga painting a boy's chest before circumcision, Yirrkala; from a photograph by Howard Morphy, July 1973

elements from such diverse species as kangaroo, crocodile, snake or barramundi to indicate its status as the creator of all subsequent beings.

BIBLIOGRAPHY

W. B. Spencer: *Native Tribes of the Northern Territory of Australia* (London, 1914)

A. P. Elkin, R. M. Berndt and C. H. Berndt: *Art in Arnhem Land* (Melbourne, 1950)

C. P. Mountford: *Art, Myth and Symbolism*, i of *Records of the American-Australian Scientific Expedition to Arnhem Land, 1948* (Melbourne, 1956)

R. M. Berndt, ed.: *Australian Aboriginal Art* (Sydney, 1964/*R* 1968)

K. Kupka: *Un Art à l'état brut: Peintures et sculptures aborigènes d'Australie* (Lausanne, 1962); Eng. trans. as *Dawn of Art: Painting and Sculpture of the Australian Aborigines* (Sydney, 1965)

R. M. Berndt and C. H. Berndt: *Man, Land and Myth in North Australia: The Gunwinggu People* (Sydney, 1970)

E. J. Brandl: *Australian Aboriginal Paintings in Western and Central Arnhem Land: Temporal Sequences and Elements of Style in Cadell River and Deaf Adder Creek Art* (Canberra, 1973)

P. J. Carroll: 'Mimi from Western Arnhem Land', *Form in Indigenous Art: Schematisation in the Art of Aboriginal Australia and Prehistoric Europe*, ed. P. J. Ucko (Canberra, 1977), pp. 119–230

Kunwinjku Bim: Western Arnhem Land Paintings from the Collection of the Aboriginal Arts Board (exh. cat. by A. Brody, Melbourne, N.G. Victoria, 1984)

G. Chaloupka: 'Chronological Sequence of Arnhem Land Plateau Rock Art', *Archaeological Research in Kakadu National Park*, ed. R. Jones (Canberra, 1985), pp. 269–80

L. Taylor: 'Seeing the "Inside": Kunwinjku Paintings and the Symbol of the Divided Body', *Animals into Art*, ed. H. Morphy, One World Archaeology, 7 (London, 1989), pp. 371–89

LUKE TAYLOR

5. Eastern Arnhem Land. This cultural region in the Northern Territory stretches from Cape Stewart in the west to the Gulf of Carpentaria in the east, and as far south as Blue Mud Bay. The area is occupied by some 5000 speakers of the Yolngu family of languages. Intensive European contact in the region began in the late 1920s with the establishment of the mission stations of Milingimbi, Elcho Island (Galiwinku) and Yirrkala. These have become the main centres for the Aboriginal population and are associated with minor variations in the regional art style.

People belong to patrilineal clans, which are divided between two moieties, Dhuwa and Yirritja. Each clan owns an area of land, the sacred law and objects associated with it and the ancestral designs on which all Yolngu art is based. Designs are produced in various media and on different objects according to the needs of the ceremonial context. For example, the same basic design can occur as a sand sculpture or body painting, or on a flat surface such as a coffin lid; it can be painted on a memorial post, woven into the pattern of a sacred basket or incised on to the wooden core of a sacred object.

The most characteristic features of this regional style are the geometric rendering of the clan designs and the elaborate crosshatching that covers much of a painted surface. Each design is unique in its details, although those associated with the same ancestral being often have common features. For example, the Wild Honey/Fire set of ancestral beings is associated with an overall diamond design. Alternate diamonds are infilled in varying ways to represent different attributes of the ancestral beings. Their meaning depends partly on focus, as the designs are multivalent: a red infilled diamond could represent flames or the honey-filled cell of a honeycomb. Each clan along a particular ancestral track has its own variant of the respective design: diamonds, for example, might be equilateral, elongated or in varying sizes.

Paintings are often divided into segments that represent different areas of land and sometimes adjacent segments may contain different clan designs, reflecting the association of different ancestral beings with the land. In addition to clan designs, paintings include other geometric elements representing features of the landscape and the ancestral events that resulted in their creation. Thus each painting has an underlying geometric structure, which relates to the area's totemic geography, serving both as a guide to its interpretation and as an active agent in the process of generating new paintings (Morphy, 1989). Figurative representations can be used to represent ancestral events and natural species associated with particular geographical features, and because of the multivalency of the geometric art many alternative figurative realizations of a geometric design are possible. The most sacred paintings (*mardayin miny'tji*) consist largely of clan designs and other geometric elements, although they may also include some figurative representations of associated totemic species. Paintings produced in public contexts tend to have greater figurative content than those produced in more restricted contexts.

Crosshatching, the last component of a painting to be completed, is produced by drawing a long brush of human hair across the surface of the painting to produce alternating colour sequences of fine parallel lines. The resulting shimmering effect is highly valued by the Yolngu, for it represents the ancestral power within the painting.

Some paintings and sacred objects are highly restricted forms, integrated within a hierarchical system of knowledge and revealed only to initiated adult men (Morphy, 1991). Moreover, knowledge of the meaning of designs is revealed to an individual only gradually; women are ostensibly denied access to the most restricted levels of knowledge. In ceremonies, designs are used as a means of contacting the ancestral being represented or creating a source of power that can be directed towards particular ends. In a circumcision ceremony, for example, initiates have their bodies painted with designs that belong to their own or a closely related clan (see fig. 16). The painting reinforces an initiate's position as a clan member and is thought to endow his body with spiritual power. Individuals are thought to accumulate power throughout their lives by participating in ceremonies and becoming associated with sacred objects. On the individual's death, paintings are used as a means to return that power, in the form of the dead person's soul, back to the ancestral clan lands. The designs are painted on the dead person's body, or in recent years more commonly on the coffin lid, to place the deceased in contact with ancestral powers who will assist the soul on its journey.

Since World War II Eastern Arnhem Land paintings on bark and other surfaces have taken on new functions. They have become an important commodity for sale to white Australians, with individual artists such as Mawalan Marika (*see* MARIKA, (1)), NARRITJIN MAYMURRU (see fig. 10 above) and DAVID MALANGI gaining widespread reputations. They have also acquired new significance in the political arena as symbols of Yolngu identity. One of the best-known events of the struggle for Aboriginal land rights occurred in 1963, when the people of Yirrkala sent a bark petition to the Australian Federal Parliament. Since then paintings have been used in many land right cases to demonstrate the religious basis for Aboriginal rights, for the art of Eastern Arnhem Land is rooted in the relationship between people, ancestral beings and land.

See also fig. 6 above.

BIBLIOGRAPHY

A. P. Elkin, R. M. Berndt and C. H. Berndt: *Art in Arnhem Land* (Melbourne, 1950)

H. M. Groger-Wurm: *Eastern Arnhem Land*, i of *Australian Aboriginal Bark Paintings and their Mythological Interpretations* (Canberra, 1973)

H. Morphy: '"Now you Understand": An Analysis of the Way Yolngu Have Used Sacred Knowledge to Retain their Autonomy', *Aborigines, Land and Landrights*, ed. N. Peterson and M. Langton (Canberra, 1983), pp. 110–33

——: 'Maintaining Cosmic Unity: Ideology and the Reproduction of Yolngu Clans', *Property, Power and Ideology in Hunting and Gathering Societies*, ed. T. Ingold, D. Riches and J. Woodburn (Oxford, 1988), pp. 141–63

——: 'On Representing Ancestral Beings', *Animals into Art*, ed. H. Morphy, One World Archaeology, 7 (London, 1989), pp. 144–60

——: *Ancestral Connections: Art and an Aboriginal System of Knowledge* (Chicago, 1991)

HOWARD MORPHY

6. CAPE YORK PENINSULA. This cultural region stretches from the Mitchell River drainage basin in the south to the tip of Cape York Peninsula in the north. It is an area of great linguistic diversity including many speakers of languages of the Wik group. The best known art forms of the region are the extensive paintings in the rock shelters of the Laura and Princess Charlotte Bay areas (*see* §II, 2 above). The galleries of the Laura region Caves, in particular, are spectacular, numerous and frequently on a large and imposing scale (*see* QUINKAN GALLERIES). The subjects most frequently depicted are the animals, plants and ancestral beings that comprised the main totemic and ceremonial symbols of the region's Aboriginal religion. Many of the human-like figures have been identified as images created during the practice of sorcery and sexual magic. Much of the rock art appears to be ancient, and engraved designs in one shelter have been assigned a minimum age of 13,000 years (Rosenfeld, Horton and Winter). Works from the colonial period are readily identified by their depiction of such subjects as armed horsemen and pearling boats.

Such rock art cannot, however, be taken as typical of the whole region, most of which lacks rock shelters or rocky country of any description. In fact, the Cape York Peninsula peoples concentrated greater artistic efforts on decorating bags, spears, throwing-sticks and other useful artefacts, and on ephemeral ceremonial objects and body painting. All portable works were made of local organic materials and, typically and intentionally, had a short life. Family resemblances among these objects identify them as coming from the Peninsula region. Such resemblances include the use of red abrus beads as decorative finishes to adhesives on throwing sticks, fire-stick holders and umbilical-cord pendants; the use of shell—for example trochus shell pendants and baler shell counterbalances on the handles of throwing-sticks; and the geometric, linear, painted designs on spears and ceremonial objects.

Melanesian influences are manifest in the region's ceremonial art and in the designs on Cairns rain-forest shields, traditions that were well entrenched in mainland Aboriginal culture at the time of colonization. Elaborate painted masks, drums and such features of painting styles as linear enclosures of colour fields and the use of triangular forms suggest, even more strongly, artistic influence from Torres Strait and New Guinea.

Ceremonial masks, some of which have entered public collections, were often highly detailed, painted constructions that covered not only the face or head but often the whole body. Normally, they were associated with esoteric rituals of the highest order and were not made for sale. By the 1990s they had all but disappeared from the living cultures of the region. With the introduction of steel woodworking tools to Aurukun in the 1940s, the production of carved wooden representations of mythic beings increased dramatically. These were still being made in the 1980s and 1990s, their basic carving and painterly conventions being the same as they were at the time of the earliest European contact. A good example is provided by two figures known as the *Two Young Women of Cape Keerweer* (Adelaide, S. Austral. Mus.; see fig. 17), which were carved for a ceremony held to release the spirit of a young man who had died in Aurukun gaol. A similar sculptural tradition existed in the south-east of the region, near Cooktown in the Starcke River area, where two highly decorated sculptures of Crocodile totemic beings were produced in the early 20th century (Adelaide, S. Austral. Mus.).

The art of Cape York Peninsula has never attained the same degree of fame as that of its counterparts in Arnhem Land or central Australia. This is partly because the destruction of ritual traditions has been greater but also because the Aboriginal people of the region have not been much involved in the production of art aimed at a non-Aboriginal cash market.

In the 1970s and 1980s, most of the traditional Aboriginal works leaving the region were utilitarian artefacts—woven bags, fire-sticks, throwing-sticks and spears, intended for sale at relatively low prices in the 'crafts' market. With reproductions based on photographs and examples preserved in museum collections, the production of Cairns

17. Cape York Peninsula mortuary sculpture by Angus Namponan, Peter Peemuggina and Nelson Wolmby: *Two Young Women of Cape Keerweer*, wood, nails, ochre and eucalyptus bark, h. 700 mm (left), 730 mm (right), 1987 (Adelaide, South Australian Museum)

rain-forest shields resumed. With the encouragement of art teachers at a local college, some artists in the town of Cairns began to apply designs adopted from the region's art to intaglio printmaking. At the same time, some attempts were made to enter the fine arts market. A small number of sacred carvings from Aurukun and bark paintings from Aurukun and elsewhere were sold. The bark paintings were experiments in the use of a new medium, influenced by the example of Arnhem Land and encouraged by non-Aboriginal entrepreneurs. Neither sacred carvings nor bark paintings became a major medium of production for the market, and by the early 1990s few works of significance were being made within the artistic traditions of Cape York Peninsula, apart from those meant for private use.

BIBLIOGRAPHY

D. Thomson: 'The Hero Cult, Initiation and Totemism on Cape York', *J. Royal Anthropol. Inst. GB & Ireland*, lxiii (1933), pp. 453–537 and pls xxvii–xxxvii

U. H. McConnel: 'Inspiration and Design in Aboriginal Art', *A. Australia*, n. s. 2, lix (1935), pp. 49–68

I. Dunlop: *Dances at Aurukun, 1962* (Sydney, 1964) [film]

F. D. McCarthy: 'The Dancers of Aurukun', *Austral. Nat. Hist.*, xiv (1964), pp. 296–300

P. Trezise: *Rock Art of South-east Cape York* (Canberra, 1971)

——: 'Aboriginal Rock Art of Cape York Peninsula', *The Australian Aboriginal Heritage: An Introduction through the Arts*, ed. R. M. Berndt and E. S. Phillips (Sydney, 1973), pp. 118–28

H. Morphy: 'The Art of Northern Australia', *Aboriginal Australia* (exh. cat. by C. Cooper and others, Sydney, Austral. Gal. Directors Council, 1981–2), pp. 52–65

A. Rosenfeld, D. Horton and J. Winter: *Early Man in North Queensland: Art and Archaeology in the Laura Area* (Canberra, 1981)

Cultural Exhibition of Queensland (exh. cat. by J. Bartlett, Omiya, Saitama Prefect. Mus., 1989) [well-illus. overview]

PETER SUTTON

IV. Contemporary art.

Much of 20th-century Aboriginal art is 'transitional' in a number of ways. It is the art of people overwhelmed by an alien culture within which they have had to learn to live. It has also accepted and used new media of expression learnt from the dominant culture. Most of the new forms are made for sale to white tourists, collectors, museums and public and private art galleries. Equally, many white teachers, missionaries, anthropologists, artists, crafts- and art-advisers have supported the emergence of new forms of Aboriginal art. Whether consciously or unconsciously, they have influenced Aboriginal artistic expression in both form and content. For many contemporary Aboriginal artists, the content of their art still provides a link to the Dreamtime past of their ancestors and in particular their connection with ancestral lands. Yet the forms their art now takes are often commercially motivated, and the proceeds of its sale provide the only non-Governmental income for many communities.

1. Painting and drawing. 2. Other arts.

1. Painting and drawing. In central Australia in the 1930s Aranda children on the Finke River Lutheran Mission at Hermannsburg produced drawings in a 'European' manner under the influence of Arthur Murch (1902–89) and Frances Derham (1894–1987). In the same decade Albert Namatjira decided to develop the foundations of the still continuing Hermannsburg school of Aranda watercolourists after some instruction from the Western artist Rex Battarbee (1893–1969) of Victoria. After decades of disdain by white art critics, Namatjira's work has recently been more sympathetically reassessed. In the 1940s lively genre pictures were executed at the Carrolup Aboriginal School in Western Australia, now an Aboriginal controlled settlement and a flourishing centre for 'new' arts and crafts including textile printing and potterymaking.

But even before that, from the late 1920s, the regular production for sale of bark paintings (*see* §II, 7 above) was actively sponsored by missionaries in north-east Arnhem Land. Barks are now produced mainly in Arnhem Land but also by the Tiwi of Bathurst and Melville Islands and in the Kimberleys region of Western Australia. This commercial production has encouraged new techniques to preserve both bark and pigments, and, although the use of designs for ritual purposes has continued (Berndt, Berndt and Stanton), new, non-secret, designs have been used by artists willing to indulge Western tastes for more representative imagery. Women, who until recently in Arnhem Land were confined to weaving baskets, bags and mats, are also beginning to paint barks, for example at Yirrkala, using both traditional designs and portrayals of their everyday life or even Christian iconography. Most recently, the all-pervading use of acrylic paints has been extended to the 'translation' of bark painting subjects to canvas.

The acrylic paintings—or 'dot paintings' as they are popularly referred to—of the various communities of central and Western Australia represent the most innovative and—again in Western terms—most successful contemporary art movement in Aboriginal Australia. They are based on the traditional iconography of largely curvilinear motifs which are still employed in ritual body painting and on sacred objects such as the flat oval stone or wooden slabs (*tjurunga*) and ground designs, as well as in less 'restricted' forms on shields, spears, carrying dishes and boomerangs, and in the illustrating of stories told to children. The translation into the modern, saleable medium of paint, canvas and artist's board came about in 1971 at the instigation of an art teacher, Geoffrey Bardon (*b* 1940), then working at the government-established Papunya settlement west of Alice Springs. Such paintings, like their prototypes, are generally a formalized mapping of a particular geographical location associated with a specific mythological happening or individual (see fig. 18). In the early days of the movement, many Papunya paintings incorporated clearly recognizable figures and even secret–sacred objects, but since 1971 there has been an increasing abstraction of motifs, a recodifying that renders impossible precise interpretation by the uninitiated. Certain artists have used a restricted palette corresponding to the traditional earth colours of body and ground painting. Others,

18. Paddy Jupurrurla Nelson, Paddy Japaljarri Sims and Larry Jungarrayi Spencer, advised by Jimmy Jungurrayi Spencer: *Star Dreaming*, acrylic on canvas, 3.72×1.71 m, 1985 (Canberra, Australian National Gallery)

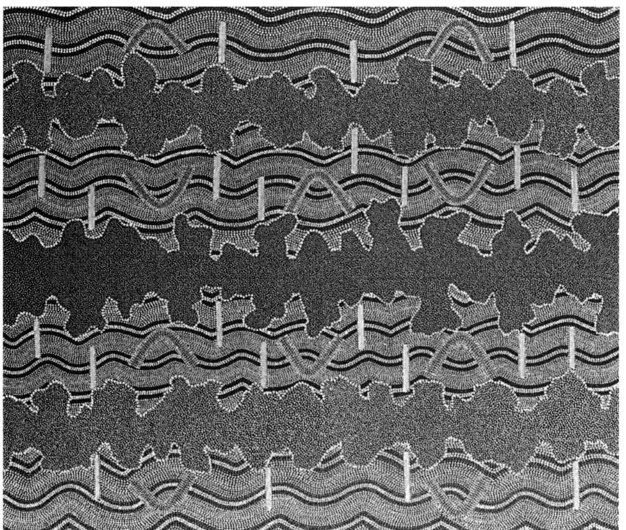

19. Clifford Possum Tjapaltjarri: *Water Dreaming*, acrylic on canvas, 1.52×1.83 m, 1983 (Bedford Park, Flinders University of South Australia, SA 150 Collection)

especially the newer artists in communities such as Balgo, Lajamanu and Utopia—who now include a significant number of women—continue to exploit the total chromatic freedom allowed by modern acrylic paints.

The success not only in Australia but also on the international art market of the work of such male artists as CLIFFORD POSSUM TJAPALTJARRI of the Anmatyerre/ Aranda language group (see fig. 19), the Pintupi Charlie Tjaruru Tjungarrayi, the first Papunya artist to have been the subject of a retrospective exhibition, held in 1987, as well as the younger Warlpiri MICHAEL NELSON TJAKAMARRA, who has worked closely with the Sydney-based former conceptual artist Tim Johnson (*b* 1947), has led to an escalation of prices. In 1971 Papunya paintings sold for £A30–40; in the early 1990s they frequently fetched £A5000–10,000. This rise in individual acclaim has put strain on some communities since paintings are often collaborative works. Recognition has also encouraged the establishment of other acrylic painting centres, for example in the Warlpiri community at Yuendumu, west of Papunya, where women form 70% of the painters. This may have resulted from the fact that both the anthropologist and the teacher who encouraged the new art form were themselves women, while at Papunya, Bardon had found relations with the older men easier in a strictly gender-defined society. Yuendumu painting uses a wider range of colours than that from Papunya. In the same way that several Papunya artists have painted Hermannsburg-style watercolours, some Aranda painters, notably Wenten Rubuntja (*b* 1926), now work almost exclusively in the Papunya manner.

At Mt Allan (Yuelumu) in central Australia the elders of the Warlpiri and Anmatyerre community took a conscious decision in the 1980s to allow all members, men, women and children, to paint in acrylics. Some of the most accomplished work technically has been by girls as young as 12, though ownership of the stories, and the cash generated by their sale, remain with their parents. In Western Australia, the Balgo community has also turned to acrylic painting for external sale, while other groups have continued to prefer to use ochres on board or canvas. At Turkey Creek in the eastern Kimberley Ranges an artistic community has emerged around the painter ROVER THOMAS.

2. OTHER ARTS. While the Tiwi (both men and women) of Bathurst and Melville Islands continue to carve and paint *pukamani* poles as part of their own ceremonial life, they are also now producing them for sale as well as other carvings of birds and mythical beings. For the 1988 Bicentennial, the Aboriginal art adviser Djon Scott Mundine of Ramingining Arts in north-east Arnhem Land persuaded the Australian National Gallery to commission and purchase 200 log coffins, which their Aboriginal creators regarded as a proper commemoration of 200 years of white occupation.

In the north-west desert regions of South Australia dedicated white teachers introduced a whole range of new art forms to the women of the Pitjantjatjara (see fig. 11 above) and Yunkuntjatjara communities. From 1954, largely under the guidance of Winifred Hilliard at Ernabella, spinning and rug-weaving were introduced, but from *c.* 1971 these gave way to the less labour-intensive batik-printing for fashion fabrics. Anmatyerre/Aliawarra women at Utopia (in the central region) and Pitjantjatjara and Yunkuntjatjara women at Indulkana also turned to batik. Skills acquired from Indonesian textile-workers were used to produce a range of swirling foliate designs, which have also recently been translated by these and other communities into silkscreen or linocut prints. Women in the far west of Australia and at Yuendumu in central Australia as well as much further north on Bathurst Island and at Yirrkala have also taken up batik. Figures like those on the *pukamani* carvings are being repeated as motifs in the fabric printing of the Tiwi Designs Cooperative. Woodblock and silkscreen printing was begun in 1969 under the supervision of Madeline Clear as a partnership between two young Tiwi, Bede Tungutalum (*b* 1948) and Giovanni Tipungwuti. Other fabric production in more urban settings includes that of Jumbana Designs in Adelaide, Bronwyn Bancroft in Sydney and the aggressive marketing of the fabrics and prints of JIMMY PIKE, born in the Great Sandy Desert of Western Australia. Some fabrics, like some of the craft pottery now produced by various Aboriginal communities, including the Tiwi, have met with considerable white sales resistance for not looking 'Aboriginal' enough. Almost unique in gaining wide recognition and in achieving a freedom of expression in ceramics, both small pieces and murals, is the work of Thancoupie (*b* 1937), who is from Weipa on Cape York Peninsula but was trained in Sydney.

Though many Aborigines object to the use of the word 'urban'—an alternative Aboriginal term, 'Koori', is preferred in the south-east—the adjective does serve to describe the current residence of many Aboriginal artists living outside the communities of central or northern Australia. Like Thancoupie, many of these are working exclusively in non-traditional media. They are more likely to work without community support and to have to deal more directly with Western society and its art world. Among them is Banduk Marika (*see* MARIKA, (3)), who until the late 1980s spent most of her adult life in Darwin and Sydney. Sister of one famous bark painter and daughter of another, she has used traditional images, though for linocuts and prints, not barks and refers to her work as 'contemporary traditional'. Those without tribal upbringing or their own inherited traditional imagery include art school-trained TREVOR NICKOLLS from Port Adelaide, who in his search for roots has used a wide range of subject-matter and styles, including the dotting techniques of acrylic paintings from central Australia, yet has also expressed a wish to be recognized as an artist and not 'merely' as an Aboriginal artist (Beier). Sally Morgan (*b* 1951, active in Perth) and Robert Campbell jr (*b* Kempsey, NSW, 1944, *d* 1993) have also used the dotting or hatching techniques of traditional art to tell their own autobiographies or make political statements. Byron Pickett (*b* 1955) has used his silkscreen prints to show the different worlds of traditional Aborigines and Western culture, though even his grandparents did not live traditional Aboriginal lives. 'Koori' artists of Sydney and Melbourne, such as Gordon Syron (*b* 1941), LIN ONUS (see fig. 20), Jeffrey Samuels (*b* 1956), Arone Raymond Meeks (*b* 1957) and Fiona Foley (*b* 1964), have consciously sought out and borrowed from their Aboriginal heritage. Aboriginal photographers and film makers are also gaining recognition, such as Polly Sumner (*b* 1952) in Adelaide and Tracey Moffatt (*b* Brisbane, 1960) in Sydney. Much of the art of this group is nonetheless deeply concerned with the questions of Aboriginal identity and the problems of Aboriginal poverty and deprivation and is often more obviously political than that of groups still living in the communities of central and northern Australia.

20. Lin Onus: *Where to now?*, linocut on bone paper, 418×297 mm, 1986 (Bedford Park, Flinders University of South Australia)

BIBLIOGRAPHY

N. H. H. Graburn, ed.: *Ethnic and Tourist Arts: Cultural Expressions from the Fourth World* (Berkeley, 1976)

G. Bardon: *Aboriginal Art of the Western Desert* (Adelaide, 1978)

R. Edwards, ed.: *Aboriginal Art in Australia* (Adelaide, 1978)

A. Crocker: *Mr Sandman Bring Me a Dream* (Sydney, 1981)

R. M. Berndt, C. H. Berndt and J. E. Stanton: *Aboriginal Australian Art: A Visual Perspective* (Sydney, 1982, rev. 1989)

J. Isaacs: *Thancoupie the Potter* (Sydney, 1982)

——: *Australia's Living Heritage: Arts of the Dreaming* (Sydney, 1984)

Koori Art '84 (exh. cat., ed. T. Johnson and V. Johnson; Sydney Artspace, 1984)

U. Beier: *Dreamtime–Machine Time: The Art of Trevor Nickolls* (Bathurst, New South Wales, 1985)

W. Caruana: *Contemporary Australian Aboriginal Art* (Canberra, 1986)

Dot and Circle: A Retrospective Survey of the Aboriginal Acrylic Paintings of Central Australia (exh. cat., ed. J. Maughan and J. Zimmer; Bedford Park, Flinders U. S. Australia; Melbourne, Royal Inst. Technol. A.G.; 1986)

The Dreamtime Today: A Survey of Contemporary Aboriginal Arts and Crafts (exh. cat., ed. J. Maughan and J. V. S. Megaw; Bedford Park, Flinders U. S. Australia; Adelaide, Royal S. Austral. Soc. A., Kintore Gal.; 1986)

Aboriginal Australian Views in Print and Poster (exh. cat., ed. J. Samuels and C. Watson; Melbourne, Prt Council Australia, 1987)

Australia—Art and Aboriginality 1987: Portsmouth Festival U.K. (exh. cat., ed. V. Johnson; Portsmouth, Aspex Gal.; Sydney, Aboriginal A.; 1987)

Charlie Tjaruru Tjungarrayi (exh. cat., ed. A. Crocker; Orange, Reg. A. G., Hist. Soc. Mus., 1987)

J. Davila: 'Aboriginality: A Lugubrious Game?', *A. & Text*, xxv/4 (1987), pp. 53–7

KARNTA: Aboriginal Women's Art (exh. cat., ed. C. McGuignan, 1987)

Dreamings: The Art of Aboriginal Australia (exh. cat., ed. P. Sutton; New York, Asia Soc. Gals; U. Chicago, IL, Smart Gal.; Melbourne, Mus. Victoria; Adelaide, S. Austral. Mus.; 1988–90)

J. Altman, C. McGuigan and P. Yu: *The Aboriginal Arts and Crafts Industry: Report of the Review Committee*, Department of Aboriginal Affairs (Canberra, 1989)

J. Isaacs: *Aboriginality: Contemporary Aboriginal Paintings and Prints* (St Lucia, Queensland, 1989, rev. 1992)

Mythscapes: Aboriginal Art of the Desert (exh. cat., ed. J. Ryan; Melbourne, N.G. Victoria, 1989)

Nothing to Celebrate? Australian Aboriginal Political Art & the Bicentennial (exh. cat., ed. M. Ruth Megaw; Bedford Park, Flinders U. S. Australia, 1989)

S. Britton, L. Dauth and F. Wright, eds: 'Contemporary Australian Aboriginal Art', *Artlink*, x/1–2 (1990)

Balance 1990: Views, Visions, Influences (exh. cat., ed. M. Eather and Marlene Hall; Brisbane, Queensland A.G., 1990)

East to West: Land in Papunya Painting (exh. cat., ed. J. Kean; Adelaide, Tandamya Aboriginal Cult. Inst., 1990)

G. Bardon: *Papunya Tula: Art of the Western Desert* (Melbourne, 1991)

M. Boulter: *The Art of Utopia: A New Direction in Contemporary Aboriginal Art* (Tortola, BVI, 1991)

R. Crumlin, ed.: *Aboriginal Art and Spirituality* (North Blackburn, Victoria, 1991)

T. Smith: 'From the Desert: Aboriginal Painting, 1970–90', *Australian Painting, 1788–1990*, by B. Smith with T. Smith (Melbourne, 1991), pp. 495–517

Aboriginal Women's Exhibition (exh. cat., ed. H. Perkins; Sydney, A.G. NSW, 1991)

J. Hardy, J. V. S. Megaw and M. Ruth Megaw, eds: *The Heritage of Namatjira: The Watercolourists of Central Australia* (Melbourne, 1992)

G. Bennett: 'Aesthetics and Iconography: An Artist's Approach', *Aratjara: Art of the First Australians—Traditional and Contemporary Works by Aboriginal and Torres Strait Artists* (exh. cat., ed. B. Lüthi; Düsseldorf, Kstsamml. Nordrhein-Westfalen; London, Hayward Gal.;

Humlebæk, Louisiana Mus.; Sydney, Mus. Contemp. A.; 1993–4), pp. 85–91

J. V. S. MEGAW, M. RUTH MEGAW

V. Collectors and dealers.

Over two centuries of European colonization, interest in Aboriginal art has attracted the attention of different types of viewers and collectors. Aboriginal objects have been collected as art rather than as ethnographic curios only since World War II. They were first collected during such voyages as those from 1768 by James Cook (1728–79) and in 1800–04 by François Péron (1775–1810), but little of this survives. Until the mid-19th century, when well-documented collections began, artefacts were collected by individuals as mementoes of Australia: many found their way into European museums, but documentation on these objects and on their collectors is largely lost. Much of this material in Europe returned to Australia in the 1970s as part of the Christensen collection loaned to the National Gallery of Victoria, Melbourne.

From the 1850s a more systematic approach to collecting began with the acquisition of artefacts for private collections or for museums in Australia and overseas. One of the great collectors of this period was the amateur naturalist R. E. Johns, who formed two large collections from south-east Australia, one of which was given to the Robert O'Hara Bourke Memorial Museum in Beechworth, Victoria in 1868, while the other was acquired by the Museum (formerly National Museum) of Victoria in 1910. Operating on a smaller scale were people such as Mary Bundock, who spent most of her life at an isolated sheep station on the Richmond River, New South Wales, and used her contact with Aboriginal groups to collect for several museums during the 1870s, including the Rijksmuseum voor Volkenkunde in Leiden, Kew Gardens, London, and the Australian Museum in Sydney. The development of Australian anthropology in the 1890s owed much to the work of such collectors and recorders of Aboriginal artefacts and customs.

Until well after World War II missionaries and anthropologists were responsible for the major collections for the study of Aboriginal society, the former including Karl Strehlow and R. G. Reuther, and the latter Sir W. Baldwin Spencer (1860–1929) and W. E. Roth. T. T. Webb and Wilbur Chaseling made large collections from Milingimbi and Yirrkala respectively and sold them to museums in Brisbane, Sydney and Melbourne. In the 1930s and 1940s Donald Thomson of Melbourne University compiled one of the best-documented Arnhem Land collections, which was transferred on his death to the then National Museum of Victoria. Ronald Berndt and his wife Catherine collected from the 1940s onwards and their holdings became the basis of the Berndt Museum of Anthropology (formerly the Anthropology Research Museum) at the University of Western Australia, Perth. C. P. Mountford developed collections based on his expeditions to Arnhem Land, Melville and Bathurst Islands and central Australia. During this period museum ethnographers such as Norman Tindale of the South Australian Museum, Adelaide, and Fred McCarthy of the Australian Museum, Sydney, took active roles in acquisitions, and in the 1960s Helen Groger-Wurm acquired a superb collection for the National Museum of Australia in Canberra and the Museums and Art Galleries of the Northern Territory in Darwin.

The activities of anthropologists and missionaries stimulated private collecting in two ways: they gradually increased awareness of Aboriginal art and helped make art a commodity. From the late 1950s the market in Aboriginal art began to expand rapidly and, although it was still largely based on local community enterprises, a few major collector/dealers began to emerge. Jim Davidson, a Melbourne businessman, made annual journeys to the Northern Territory to purchase Aboriginal art and, in addition to dealing in the works, established a large personal collection. Dorothy Bennet began collecting and dealing in the early 1960s, organizing exhibitions in Australia and Japan and establishing a shop in Darwin. Sandra Holmes also built up large collections of Arnhem Land and Tiwi art in particular, concentrating on the work of YIRAWALA, whose art she did much to promote. Outside Australia major collections were developed by Ed Ruhe and Louis Allen in the USA and Karel Kupka in France. In the 1980s Aboriginal art was sold through specialist galleries in all the major cities in Australia, supported by a government marketing organization, and many private collections had begun to emerge, of which the most prominent were those of Robert Holmes à Court (1937–90), Lord McAlpine of West Green (*b* 1942), Margaret (Mrs Douglas) Carnegie and Sir Roderick Carnegie (*b* 1932) and John Kluge. By the 1990s there had been a dramatic increase in the number of dealers in contemporary Australian Aboriginal art. For example, in 1993 there were more than 20 galleries specializing in Aboriginal art in Alice Springs and two in central London.

BIBLIOGRAPHY

I. McBryde: 'Museum Collections from the Richmond River District', *Records of Times Past: Ethnohistorical Essays on the Culture and Ecology of New England Tribes*, ed. I. McBryde (Canberra, 1978)

Aboriginal Australia (exh. cat. by C. Cooper and others, Sydney, Austral. Gal. Directors Council, 1981–2)

J. Altman and L. Taylor: *Marketing Aboriginal Art in the 1990s: Papers Presented to a Workshop in Canberra, 12–13 June 1990* (Canberra, 1991)

VI. Museums and exhibitions.

The term 'Aboriginal art', as distinct from Aboriginal ethnographic objects, was hardly used as a category until the 20th century. Indeed, until the 1950s Aboriginal objects were not displayed in Australian art galleries but in museums of natural history. Even today the vast majority of Aboriginal art works are still housed in ethnographic departments of state and national museums.

Within Australia the largest collections of Aboriginal art are in museums in the state capitals: the Australian Museum in Sydney; the Museum of Victoria, Melbourne; the South Australian Museum, Adelaide; the Queensland Museum, Brisbane; and the Western Australian Museum, Perth. These museums all began to establish collections in the 19th century, beginning with the Australian Museum (1827) and the then National Museum of Victoria (1854). Much of the best 19th-century material, however, left Australia for museums in Europe. The British Museum, London, the Pitt Rivers Museum, Oxford, the Manchester Museum, the Museum of Archaeology and Anthropology at Cambridge University and the National Museum of

Ireland, Dublin all have large collections, as do most of the major ethnographic museums in Europe, for example the Staatliches Museum für Völkerkunde in Munich and the Museum für Völkerkunde in Hamburg. Missionaries, in particular, continued to supply large collections to museums in their home countries until the beginning of the 20th century: as late as 1913 Otto Liebler, a Lutheran missionary, presented a collection of 606 Arrente objects to the Staatliches Museum für Völkerkunde (now Linden-Museum) in Stuttgart.

As the 20th century progressed, the development of public collections shifted from overseas to Australian museums, which now house nearly all the major collections made during the first half of the century. In the 1960s major new collections were developed in Darwin through the Museums and Art Galleries of the Northern Territory and in the National Ethnographic Collection in Canberra (now part of the National Museum of Australia). After World War II, Aboriginal art began to gain a place in the state art galleries, beginning with the paintings collected by C. P. Mountford during the 1948 Australian–American Scientific Expedition to Arnhem Land. By 1988 the Australian National Gallery in Canberra had the fastest growing collection of Aboriginal art and had begun to devote considerable space to its exhibition. The first major exhibition of its holdings was launched in 1989. In the 1970s and 1980s overseas museums, especially the British Museum in London, the Musée de l'Homme in Paris and the National Museum of Ethnology in Osaka, began again to expand their holdings of Aboriginal work.

Major exhibitions of Aboriginal art were not held until about the mid-20th century, although Aboriginal artefacts were displayed as examples of Australian crafts at many 19th-century Great Exhibitions and they were housed in museum ethnographic galleries. The first generally recognized exhibition, *Australian Aboriginal Art*, took place in 1929 at the National Museum of Victoria. A second exhibition, *Primitive Art*, was organized in Melbourne in 1943 by Leonhard Adam. This exhibition stimulated Australian interest in Aboriginal art, according to Tony Tuckson, the artist and gallery director, who in 1960 organized the next major exhibition, *Australian Aboriginal Art*, which toured the major state capitals.

The first exhibition of an individual Aboriginal artist's work (apart from that of the watercolourist Albert Namatjira) was that of Yirawala, the Kunwinjku artist, at the University of Sydney in 1971. This was followed in 1978 by the joint exhibition in Canberra of work by Banapana Maymurru and NARRITJIN MAYMURRU. The first individual exhibition in a commercial gallery was that of Johny Bulunbulum at Sydney's Hogarth Galleries in 1981, followed shortly afterwards by a show devoted to works by Peter Marralwanga in the Creative Native Aboriginal Art Gallery in Perth. Also held in 1981 was *Aboriginal Australia*, which was circulated by the Australian Gallery Directors Council and which by the mid-1990s was the largest exhibition of Aboriginal art so far organized. The frequency of exhibitions increased greatly in the 1970s and 1980s, going from less than one per year in the 1960s to more than 20 a year by the mid-1980s; overseas exhibitions similarly increased during this period. The Australian bicentennial in 1988 further stimulated interest in Aboriginal art; this resulted in a series of major exhibitions in Australia and the USA, including *The Inspired Dream* and *Dreamings: The Art of Aboriginal Australia*. These were followed in Europe by *Aratjara: Art of the First Australians*.

BIBLIOGRAPHY

Australian Aboriginal Art (exh. cat. by C. Barrett and A. S. Kenyon, Melbourne, Mus. Victoria, 1929)

Primitive Art (exh. cat., intro. L. Adam; Melbourne, Mus. Victoria, 1943)

J. A. Tuckson: 'Aboriginal Art and the Western World', *Australian Aboriginal Art*, ed. R. M. Berndt (Sydney, 1964/*R* 1968), pp. 60–68

Aboriginal Australia (exh. cat. by C. Cooper and others, Sydney, Austral. Gal. Directors Council, 1981–2)

Koori Art '84 (exh. cat., ed. T. Johnson and V. Johnson; Sydney Artspace, 1984)

Dot and Circle: A Retrospective of the Aboriginal Paintings of Central Australia (exh. cat., ed. J. Maughan and J. Zimmer; Bedford Park, Flinders U. S. Australia; Melbourne, Royal Inst. Technol. A.G., 1986)

The Inspired Dream (exh. cat., ed. M. West; Brisbane, Queensland A.G., 1988)

Dreamings: The Art of Aboriginal Australia (exh. cat., ed. P. Sutton; New York, Asia Soc. Gals; U. Chicago, IL, Smart Gal.; Melbourne, Mus. Victoria; Adelaide, S. Austral. Mus.; 1988–90)

Aratjara: Art of the First Australians–Traditional and Contemporary Works by Aboriginal and Torres Strait Artists (exh. cat., ed. B. Lüthi; Düsseldorf, Kstsamml. Nordrhein-Westfalen; London, Hayward Gal.; Humlebæk, Louisiana Mus.; Sydney, Mus. Contemp. A.; 1993–4)

For further bibliography *see* §IV above.

VII. Historiography.

The authors of the early literature on the Australian Aborigines, such as Thomas Worsnop (1821–98), Robert Brough Smyth (1830–89) and Edward Curr (1820–89), occasionally referred to art but provided little detailed information. Indeed the prevailing attitude throughout most of the 19th century was that Aborigines did not produce 'art'. Evolutionary theorists placed Aborigines at the lowest level of human development and their paintings and carvings were dismissed cursorily: the anthropologist Sir Edward Burnett Tylor (1832–1917), for example, described them as 'rude frescoes'. This attitude may partly have arisen because much Aboriginal art, restricted to the ceremonial ground, was unknown to Europeans, while certain forms, such as body painting and sand sculpture, are ephemeral. Yet even when the art was recorded and admired, its Aboriginal roots were denied: Sir George Grey (1812–98) wrote in 1841 of the Wandjina paintings of the Kimberleys: '. . . whatever may have been the age of these paintings, it is scarcely probable that they could have been painted by a self-taught savage'.

Sir W. Baldwin Spencer, F. J. Gillen and, to a lesser extent, Alfred Howitt (1839–1908), Robert Mathews (1841–1918) and W. E. Roth produced the first detailed accounts of Aboriginal art at the end of the 19th century. Although Spencer and Gillen shared the prevailing evolutionary paradigm (Morphy, 1988), they wrote extensive ethnographic accounts of Aboriginal art and its ritual contexts: the rock art and bark paintings of Western Arnhem Land, for example, are referred to in positive terms (Spencer). Few other anthropologists wrote about Aboriginal art until after World War II, although references to art appear in general descriptive accounts (e.g. Tindale) and catalogues were produced to accompany the few exhibitions of Aboriginal art that were held during the period (*see* §VI above). The diffusionist anthropologist

Daniel Sutherland Davidson (1900–52) produced some comparative papers on Aboriginal art, and this work strongly influenced the prehistorian Fred McCarthy, who began his study of rock art. One of the few to write on Aboriginal art before World War II was Margaret Preston, who saw Aboriginal design as a possible source of inspiration in her desire to create a uniquely Australian art, although she tended to interpret its positive qualities as the accidental product of inadequate technique.

From the 1940s, writings on the subject increased with the publication of both substantial exhibition catalogues and monographs on the art of particular regions. C. P. Mountford, Ronald Berndt and Catherine Berndt discussed the ceremonial context of art, illustrating and documenting the meanings of paintings and objects. This provided invaluable data but did not attempt to analyse the systems of representation or the integration of art within Aboriginal knowledge. Nancy Munn filled this gap in the 1950s and 1960s by revealing the iconography and symbolism of art in the context of socialization in Warlpiri and Pitjantjantjara society. Building on Munn's work, Howard Morphy and Luke Taylor produced detailed semiological studies of the artistic systems of the Yolngu and Kunwinjku respectively, focusing on the role of art in the reproduction of systems of knowledge and structures of authority.

Two schools developed in the flourishing study of rock art: some scholars, such as John Clegg and Lesley Maynard, saw rock art as primarily archaeological data, while others, including Robert Layton, Michael Morwood and Andrée Rosenfeld, integrated rock art within general anthropological approaches to art. Ethnographic accounts of rock art began to appear just as the practice of painting on rocks was dying out (Chaloupka; Taçon; Blundell).

With the increased recognition and commercial success of Aboriginal art in the 1970s, and its prominence in Australian consciousness, it began to be written about from various different perspectives by art historians, artists and journalists as well as anthropologists. A more extensive range of art-historical problems began to be considered, including questions relating to aesthetics and audience creation (Morphy, 1987; Jones). Other major themes concerned the commercialization of art (Altman), the development of continuing traditions (Bardon; Megaw) and the effects on art of the dialogue between Aboriginal and European societies (e.g. Morphy, 1983; Jones and Sutton; Loveday and Cooke). Concerns with cultural heritage and conservation became important issues (Edwards, 1972; Edwards and Stewart; Rosenfeld) and interests extended to consideration of the art of urban Aboriginal people and the role of art in the creation of identity in the post-colonial context (e.g. Johnson). By 1990 Aboriginal art was liberated from its previous isolation in ethnographic museums, having gained increasing relevance to several academic disciplines and audiences, and it featured strongly in discourse on Australian art, its definitions and directions.

BIBLIOGRAPHY

EARLY STUDIES

G. Grey: *Journals of Two Expeditions of Discovery in North-west and Western Australia during the Years 1837, 38 and 39* (London, 1841)

R. B. Smyth: *The Aborigines of Victoria and Other Parts of Australia and Tasmania*, 2 vols (Melbourne and London, 1878)

E. M. Curr: *The Australian Race: Its Origins, Language, Customs*, 4 vols (Melbourne, 1886–7)

E. B. Tylor: *Anthropology: An Introduction to the Study of Man and Civilization* (London, 1892)

R. H. Mathews: 'Rock Carvings and Paintings of the Australian Aborigines', *Proc. Amer. Philos. Soc.*, xxxvii (1897), pp. 466–78

W. E. Roth: *Ethnological Studies among the North-west-central Queensland Aborigines* (Brisbane, 1897)

T. Worsnop: *The Prehistoric Arts, Manufactures, Works, Weapons, etc of the Aborigines of Australia* (Adelaide, 1897)

W. B. Spencer and F. J. Gillen: *The Native Tribes of Central Australia* (London, 1899/*R* 1969)

A. W. Howitt: *The Native Tribes of South-east Australia* (London, 1904)

W. B. Spencer and F. J. Gillen: *The Northern Tribes of Central Australia* (London, 1904/*R* 1969)

W. B. Spencer: *Native Tribes of the Northern Territory of Australia* (London, 1914)

M. Preston: 'The Indigenous Art of Australia', *A. Australia*, xi (1925), pp. 32–45

N. Tindale: 'Natives of Groote Eylandt and the West Coast of the Gulf of Carpentaria', *Rec. S. Austral. Mus.*, iii (1925), pp. 61–134

D. S. Davidson: *Aboriginal Australian and Tasmanian Rock Carvings and Paintings*, Memoirs of the American Philosophical Society, v (Philadelphia, 1936)

F. D. McCarthy: *Australian Aboriginal Decorative Art* (Sydney, 1938/*R* 1962)

GENERAL

C. P. Mountford: *Aboriginal Paintings from Australia* (London, 1954, rev. Milan, 1964)

F. D. McCarthy: *Australian Aboriginal Rock Art* (Sydney, 1958, rev. 1979)

R. M. Berndt, ed.: *Australian Aboriginal Art* (Sydney, 1964/*R* 1968)

R. Edwards, ed.: *The Preservation of Australia's Aboriginal Heritage* (Canberra, 1975)

L. Maynard: 'Classification and Terminology in Australian Rock Art', *Form in Indigenous Art: Schematisation in the Art of Aboriginal Australia and Prehistoric Europe*, ed. P. J. Ucko (Canberra, 1977), pp. 387–402

R. Edwards and J. Stewart: *Preserving of Indigenous Cultures: A New Role for Museums* (Canberra, 1980)

J. Clegg: *Notes towards Mathesis Art* (Balmain, 1979, rev. 1981)

P. Loveday and P. Cooke, eds: *Aboriginal Arts and Crafts and the Market* (Darwin, 1983)

R. Layton: 'The Cultural Context of Hunter-gatherer Rock Art', *Man*, xx/3 (1985), pp. 434–53

A. Rosenfeld: *Rock Art Conservation in Australia* (Canberra, 1985)

Australia—Art and Aboriginality 1987: Portsmouth Festival U.K. (exh. cat., ed. V. Johnson; Portsmouth, Apex Gal.; Sydney, Aboriginal A.; 1987)

H. Morphy: 'Audiences for Art', *Australians from 1939*, ed. A. Curthoys, A. W. Martin and T. Rowse (Sydney, 1987), pp. 167–75

——: 'The Original Australians and the Evolution of Anthropology', *Australia in Oxford*, ed. H. Morphy and E. Edwards, Pitt Rivers Museum Monograph 4 (Oxford, 1988), pp. 48–61

P. G. Jones: 'Perceptions of Aboriginal Art: A History', *Dreamings: The Art of Aboriginal Australia* (exh. cat., ed. P. Sutton; New York, Asia Soc. Gals; U. Chicago, IL, Smart Gal.; Melbourne, Mus. Victoria; Adelaide, S. Austral. Mus.; 1988–90), pp. 143–79

P. Sutton, P. Jones and S. Hemming: 'Survival, Regeneration, and Impact', *Dreamings: The Art of Aboriginal Australia* (exh. cat., ed. P. Sutton; New York, Asia Soc. Gals; U. Chicago, IL, Smart Gal.; Melbourne, Mus. Victoria; Adelaide, S. Austral. Mus.; 1988–90), pp. 180–212

J. Altman: *The Aboriginal Arts and Crafts Industry* (Canberra, 1989)

H. Morphy: 'On Representing Ancestral Beings', *Animals into Art*, ed. H. Morphy, One World Archaeology, 7 (London, 1989), pp. 144–60

S. Britton and F. Wright, eds: 'Aboriginal Arts in Australia', *Artlink* (1990) [special issue, 11]

SPECIALIST STUDIES

A. P. Elkin, R. M. Berndt and C. H. Berndt: *Art in Arnhem Land* (Melbourne, 1950)

R. M. Berndt: *Kunapipi: A Study of an Australian Aboriginal Religious Cult* (New York, 1951)

C. P. Mountford: *Art, Myth and Symbolism*, i of *Records of the American–Australian Expedition to Arnhem Land* (Melbourne, 1956)

——: *The Tiwi: Their Art, Myth and Ceremony* (London, 1958)

N. Munn: *Walbiri Iconography: Graphic Representation and Cultural Symbolism in a Central Australian Society* (Ithaca, NY, 1973, rev. Chicago, 1986)

V. J. Blundell: 'The Wandjina Cave Paintings of North-west Australia', *Arctic Anthropol.*, xi (1974), pp. 213–23
G. Bardon: *Aboriginal Art of the Western Desert* (Adelaide, 1979)
R. Edwards: *Australian Aboriginal Art: The Art of the Alligator River Region of the Northern Territory* (Canberra, 1979)
A. Rosenfeld, D. Horton and J. Winter: *Early Man in North Queensland: Art and Archaeology of the Laura Area* (Canberra, 1981)
J. V. S. Megaw: 'Western Desert Acrylic Painting: Artefact or Art?', *A. Hist.*, v (1982), pp. 205–18
H. Morphy: '"Now You Understand": An Analysis of the Way Yolngu Have Used Sacred Knowledge to Retain their Autonomy', *Aborigines, Land and Landrights*, ed. N. Peterson and M. Langton (Canberra, 1983), pp. 110–33
M. Morwood: 'The Prehistory of the Central Queensland Highlands', *Adv. World Archaeol.*, iii (1984), pp. 325–80
G. Chaloupka: 'Chronological Sequence of Arnhem Land Plateau Rock Art', *Archaeological Research in Kakadu National Park*, ed. R. Jones (Canberra, 1985), pp. 269–80
N. Amadadio and others: *Albert Namatjira: The Life and Work of an Australian Artist* (Melbourne, 1986)
P. G. Jones and P. Sutton: *Art and Land: Aboriginal Sculptures of the Lake Eyre Region* (Adelaide, 1986)
Kuruwarri: Yuendemu Doors (Canberra, 1987) [works by Warlukurlangu artists]
H. Morphy: 'From Dull to Brilliant: The Aesthetics of Spiritual Power among the Yolngu', *Man*, xxiv/1 (1989), pp. 21–40; also in *Anthropology, Art and Aesthetics*, ed. J. Coote and A. Shelton, Oxford Studies in the Anthropology of Cultural Forms (Oxford, 1992/*R* 1994), pp. 181–208
P. Taçon: 'Art and the Essence of Being: Symbolic and Economic Aspects of Fish among the People of Western Arnhem Land', *Animals into Art*, ed. H. Morphy (London, 1989), pp. 236–50
L. Taylor: 'Seeing the "Inside": Kunwinjku Paintings and the Symbol of the Divided Body', *Animals into Art*, ed. H. Morphy (London, 1989), pp. 371–89
H. Morphy: *Ancestral Connections: Art and an Aboriginal System of Knowledge* (Chicago and London, 1991)

HOWARD MORPHY

About, Edmond(-François-Valentin) (*b* Dieuze, Meurthe, 14 Feb 1828; *d* Paris, 16 Jan 1885). French writer and critic. He had a brilliant scholastic career, and he was awarded a place at the Ecole Française d'Athènes in 1851, having shown, according to the jury, 'a strong appreciation of the great works of art'. He remained in Athens until 1853, when he returned to Paris to embark on a literary career. Although his first work, *La Grèce Contemporaine* (1855), was successful and was well received by the influential *Revue des Deux Mondes* (in which his novel *Tolla* was published in 1855), About was unsuccessful as a playwright. While he continued to write novels and political essays he contributed to several Parisian newspapers, such as *Le Figaro*, *L'Opinion Nationale*, *Le Constitutionnel*, *Le Gaulois* and *Le Soir*. Following the Franco-Prussian War of 1870, together with his friend Francisque Sarcey he founded his own newspaper, *XIXe Siècle*, a 'Conservative Republican' organ that was anticlerical and opposed to the restoration of the monarchy.

About quickly gained a reputation as an influential art critic. In 1855 he published his *Voyage à travers l'Exposition des Beaux-Arts*, a collection of apparently casual but extremely lively pieces on different sections of the Exposition Universelle of 1855 in Paris. In the following years he wrote a series of columns on the annual Salons in *Le Moniteur*, *Le Petit Journal*, *La Revue des Deux Mondes* and his own newspaper, which were sometimes collected in book form.

About was one of the last major French critics to uphold the supremacy of history painting and the hierarchy of the genres. He was particularly gripped by pictorial representation of dramatic historical events, to which he devoted long descriptions in his reviews, but he also appreciated paintings on contemporary social issues, for example *So That's What You Call Vagrancy* (exh. Salon 1855; Paris, Mus. d'Orsay) by Alfred Stevens (i). Violently hostile to Manet and dismissive of the Impressionists, he preferred to support young artists who expressed their originality within the French academic tradition, most notably Paul Baudry, whose Paris Opéra decorations he praised in several publications. About's newspaper columns reveal him as an articulate and brilliant journalist, eager to please the Parisian intelligentsia.

WRITINGS

Voyage à travers l'Exposition des Beaux-Arts (Paris, 1855)
Le Salon de 1864 (Paris, 1864)
Le Salon de 1866 (Paris, 1867)
Raphaël à l'exposition des Champs-Elysées (Paris, 1875)
Peintures décoratifs du grand foyer de l'Opéra par Paul Baudry (Paris, 1876)
Le Décameron du Salon de peinture pour l'année 1881 (Paris, 1881)
Quinze journées au Salon de peinture et de sculpture en 1883 (Paris, 1883)

For a full list of About's Salon criticism (1855–70), see M. Ward and C. Parsons: *A Bibliography of Second Empire Salon Criticism* (Cambridge, 1986).

BIBLIOGRAPHY

DBF
F. Sarcey: Obituary, *XIXe Siècle* (17 Jan 1885)
J. Barbey d'Aurevilley: *Journalistes et polémistes, chroniqueurs et pamphlétaires* (Paris, 1895)
'Edmond About: Ecrivain et critique d'art (1828–1885)', *Cah. Mus. A. & Essai*, 16 (Paris, 1985)

PAUL GERBOD

Abraham, Pol [Hippolyte] (*b* Nantes, 19 March 1891; *d* Paris, 20 Jan 1966). French architect and teacher. A student of Alfred-Henri Recoura (1864–1939), he graduated from the Ecole des Beaux-Arts, Paris, in 1920. He settled in Paris, and his first works were influenced by Art Deco. In 1923 he became one of the two architects of the new seaside resort of Sables-d'Or-les-Pins (Côtes-du-Nord). There, and in the nearby village of Val-André, Abraham began his analysis and rejection of the picturesque in such buildings as Villa Miramar (1928) and Villa Ramona (1929). In 1929, in partnership with Henry-Jacques Le Même (*b* 1897), he made his first design for a sanatorium, later executing three examples at Passy (Haute-Savoie), which are among his best works: Roc-de-Fiz (1931), Guébriant (1933) and Geoffroy de Martel de Janville (1939). Two blocks of flats built in Paris in 1931 (at 28 Boulevard Raspail and Square Albinoni) characterize the peak of his production in their precision and sobriety of composition, moderate use of the modernist vocabulary and use of new techniques and materials.

In 1934 at the Ecole du Louvre Abraham upheld a polemical thesis on Gothic contradicting Eugène Viollet-le-Duc. He subsequently undertook experiments on stone masonry. For several houses built in Brittany in 1939, he made use of a regionalism formerly despised, and in 1942 for the Etudes Provinciales competition, of which he was a prizewinner, he had recourse to historicism. Appointed architect-in-chief for the rebuilding of the Loiret, he returned to his former preoccupations there and in Orléans undertook remarkable works in which he tested his theories of the heavy wall and partial prefabrication. After World War II he was the consultant of numerous administrations, taught at the Ecole Spéciale d'Architecture, Paris, was on the jury of the Grand Prix de Rome and was nominated to the Inspection Générale des Bâtiments Civils et Palais Nationaux. He occupied himself by publishing designs and promoting his ideas, guided by the search for a constructive rationality, which, in his view, would transcend style.

WRITINGS

Quelques oeuvres réalisées, 1921–1923 (Strasbourg, n.d.)
Travaux d'architecture (Strasbourg, 1934)
Viollet-Le-Duc et le rationalisme médiéval (Paris, 1934)
Architecture préfabriquée (Paris, 1946)

BIBLIOGRAPHY

D. Le Couédic: 'Le Charme discret du mouvement moderne', *1919–1945: Bretagne, modernité et régionalisme* (Brussels, 1986), pp. 52–77

DANIEL LE COUÉDIC

Abraham ben Judah ibn Hayyim (*fl* 15th century). ?Portuguese writer of Jewish origin. A treatise on the preparation of colours and gold for use in manuscript illumination (Parma, Bib. Palatina, MS. De Rossi 945) has been attributed to him (for a contrary opinion see Metzger); it is the only extant book of this kind apparently written by a Jew. The Portuguese text is written in Hebrew characters. An ornate signature of Abraham ibn Hayyim appears on fol. 20*r*, and an inscription of fol. 1*r* states that the work was written by him in Loulé in 1262; the author was consequently believed to have lived in the 13th century, but the treatise is now generally accepted as being of the 15th century, when Portugal, especially Lisbon, was an important centre of Hebrew manuscript illumination. It has been suggested that JOSEPH IBN HAYYIM, the artist who illuminated the Kennicott Bible (1476; Oxford, Bodleian Lib., MS. Kenn. 1; *see* JEWISH ART, §IV, 1(ii)), was Abraham's son.

BIBLIOGRAPHY

D. S. Blondheim: 'An Old Portuguese Work on Manuscript Illumination', *Jew. Q. Rev.*, xix (1928–9), pp. 97–135
R. Vishnitzer: 'Note on "An Old Portuguese Work on Manuscript Illumination"', *Jew. Q. Rev.*, xx (1929–30), p. 89
T. Metzger: *Les Manuscrits hébreux copiés et décorés à Lisbonne dans les dernières décennies du XVe siècle* (Paris, 1977), pp. 4–6, note 5
H. J. Abrahams: 'A Thirteenth-century Portuguese Work on Manuscript Illumination', *Ambix*, xxvi/2 (1979), pp. 95–9
B. Narkiss: *The Kennicott Bible* (London, 1985), p. 79

EVELYN M. COHEN

Abrahams, Carl (*b* St Andrew, Jamaica, 1913). Jamaican painter. He began his career as a cartoonist for various local periodicals. In 1937 Augustus John, then working in Jamaica, encouraged him to begin painting. Unlike the majority of his contemporaries, he eschewed the 'official' classes of the Institute of Jamaica and virtually taught himself to paint through self-study courses and manuals and by copying masterpieces from art books. His cartoonist's wit and a sardonic humour became the most important ingredients in work that drew on numerous stylistic sources, from Renaissance painting to Cubism. He was a devout Christian, and produced a host of religious works of an undeniable sincerity, although he transformed many traditional Christian themes into witty contemporary parables. His *Last Supper* (1955; Kingston, Inst. Jamaica, N.G.) is the best known of these. Some of his finest work consists of ironic transformations of the great mythological themes of the past and intensely personal fantasies based on contemporary events. He was also one of the few painters to treat successfully historical Jamaican subjects, for example in paintings of the imagined daily lives of the extinct Arawaks, the landing of Columbus, and a series depicting the riotous living of 17th-century buccaneers in Port Royal. His *Destruction of Port Royal* (*c.* 1970; Kingston, Inst. Jamaica, N.G.) is a dramatic portrayal of that cataclysmic event. In 1985 he won a competition to create two murals for the Norman Manley Airport in Kingston. The murals successfully combine many of his thematic interests into a montage celebrating Jamaican life and history.

BIBLIOGRAPHY

Carl Abrahams: A Retrospective (exh. cat. by D. Boxer, Kingston, Inst. Jamaica, N.G., 1975)
Jamaican Art 1922–1982 (exh. cat. by D. Boxer, Washington, DC, Smithsonian Inst.; Kingston, Inst. Jamaica, N.G.; 1983)

DAVID BOXER

Abrahamstrup. *See* JÆGERSPRIS.

Abramo, Lívio (*b* Araraquara, 1903). Brazilian printmaker. He worked initially as a printmaker and painter until 1933 when, influenced by Lasar Segall's expressionism, he abandoned painting for wood-engraving, which he had first practised in São Paulo *c.* 1926. He initially treated social themes such as the São Paulo working class and between 1935 and 1938 produced a series of wood-engravings, *Spain*, based on the Spanish Civil War, for example *War* (1937; U. São Paulo, Inst. Estud. Bras.). In 1950 he won a trip abroad from the Salão Nacional de Belas Artes, Rio de Janeiro, and he visited Italy, Switzerland, France and the Netherlands. On his return he made the series of wood-engravings, *Rio*, with scenes and landscapes characterized by a frank lyricism. He was named best national engraver in the first São Paulo Bienal in 1951. His constant activity as a teacher influenced many younger engravers. In 1957 he founded the Julian de la Herreria engraving workshop in Asunción, Paraguay, and in 1960 the Estúdio Gravura in São Paulo. From 1962 he lived in Asunción, where he became director of the Centro de Estudos Brasileiros. In later years his work tended towards a geometrization of space as in the series on rain and on groups of Paraguayan houses, for instance *Paraguay* (1962; São Paulo, E. Wolf priv. col.; see exh. cat., pl. 112). He had a large retrospective in 1977 in the Museu de Arte Moderna in São Paulo.

BIBLIOGRAPHY

S. Milliet: *Pintores e pinturas* (São Paulo, 1940)
J. R. Teixeira Leite: *A gravura brasileira contemporânea* (Rio de Janeiro, 1965)
Art of Latin America since Independence (exh. cat. by S. L. Catlin and T. Grieder, New Haven, CT, Yale U. A.G.; Austin, U. TX, A. Mus.; San Francisco, CA, Mus. A.; La Jolla, CA, A. Cent.; 1966)

ROBERTO PONTUAL

Abramovitz, Max. *See under* HARRISON AND ABRAMOVITZ.

Abrams, Harry N(athan) (*b* London, 8 Dec 1904; *d* New York, 25 Nov 1979). American publisher and collector. He trained at the National Academy of Design and the Art Students League in New York before working in publishing. In 1950 he set up his own publishing company,

Harry N. Abrams Inc., one of the first American companies to specialize in art books. In 1968 he founded Abbeville Books. His collecting, which began in the mid-1930s, went through three distinct phases: his first interest was in such contemporary American painters as Milton Avery and Raphael Soyer. He continued to purchase such works into the 1950s, but from the mid-1940s his collecting began to be dominated by works by major 20th-century artists; he acquired, among other works, Marc Chagall's *Clock* (1948), Pablo Picasso's *Motherhood* (1921) and Georges Rouault's *Miserere* (1939).

Abrams's most notable period as a collector was the 1960s, when he became known as a major collector of new American art. His interest in this area was fuelled by the *New Realists* exhibition of 1962 at the Sidney Janis Gallery in New York, from which he acquired his first example of Pop art. He subsequently acquired such works as Morris Louis's *Pillar of Fire* (1961), a Robert Rauschenberg combine, *Third Time Painting* (1961), Lucas Samaras's *Chairs* (1965) and Wayne Thiebaud's *Football Player* (1963).

BIBLIOGRAPHY

Harry N. Abrams Family Collection (exh. cat., New York, Jew. Mus., 1966)

B. Kurtz: 'Interview with Harry N. Abrams', *Arts* [New York], xlvii/1 (Sept–Oct 1972)

A. DEIRDRE ROBSON

Abramtsevo. Russian estate near Sergiyev Posad, 57 km north of Moscow, and site of an artists' colony. It was first recorded in documents between 1584 and 1586 under the name Obramkovo. In the 18th century it became the village of Abramkovo, part of a private estate known by the mid-19th century as Abramtsevo. In 1843 the estate was acquired by the writer Sergey Aksakov (1791–1859). He wrote his most successful works there and had numerous artists and writers as visitors, including Taras Shevchenko and Vissarion Belinsky. In 1870 the estate was acquired by the prominent industrialist and patron SAVVA MAMONTOV, who made it a major Russian artistic colony from the 1870s to the 1890s. Here, as at Princess Tenisheva's estate at Talashkino, an interest in national culture and antiquities flourished, and there was a revival of Russian folk art. Various well-known Russian artists lived at Abramtsevo at that time, among them Il'ya Repin, Mikhail Vrubel', Valentin Serov, Konstantin Korovin, Mikhail Nesterov, Yelena Polenova, Vasily Polenov and Viktor Vasnetsov. They formed the Abramtsevo/Mamontov artistic circle—an association of representatives of the most advanced artistic intelligentsia, who were creatively involved in the construction and decoration of the estate.

A collection of items of everyday peasant life was started, and in 1884 a joiner's workshop was organized on the estate, soon headed by Yelena Polenova. It united local craftsmen from the villages of Kudrino, Akhtyrka and Mutovki and initiated the production at Abramtsevo of caskets, dishes and furniture, decorated primarily with bas-relief carving (Abramtsevo/Kudrinskaya carving), which employs vegetable and geometrical ornament with representations of birds and animals. A number of exceptional folk artists came from among the students in the workshop, including Vasily Vornoskov (1876–1940), who created his own original style of carving and who taught many other craftsmen. In 1890 a ceramics workshop was also set up at Abramtsevo, which instigated the production of maiolica, although this had never been traditional in Russia. Mikhail Vrubel' produced notable examples of maiolica at the Abramtsevo workshop.

Abramtsevo, main estate building, mid-18th century, rebuilt 1870–78

In what later became the Abramtsevo Museum-Estate are the main estate building, dating from the mid-18th century (rebuilt 1870–78; see fig.), buildings in the 'Russian style' by Viktor Gartman (e.g. the Studio, 1872), Ivan Ropet (e.g. the Terem, 'Tower Chamber', 1873), Viktor Vasnetsov (e.g. the Church, 1881–2, and the 'Hut on Hen's Legs', 1883). These contain exhibitions and information about the activities of the Abramtsevo circle. The nearby town of Khot'kovo contains a factory producing carved artistic items, its craftsmen continuing the traditions of Abramtsevo-Kudrinskaya carving. The wood-carvers are taught in the Vasnetsov Abramtsevo Art College in the same town.

BIBLIOGRAPHY

N. V. Polenova: *Abramtsevo* (Moscow, 1922)

N. Pakhomov: *Abramtsevo* (Moscow, 1969)

D. Z. Kogan: *Mamontovskiy kruzhok* [Mamontov's circle] (Moscow, 1970)

N. M. Beloglazova: *Abramtsevo* (Moscow, 1981)

O. I. Arzumanova and others: *Muzey-zapovednik v Abramtsevo* [The museum-estate at Abramtsevo] (Moscow, 1984)

ALEKSANDR U. GREKOV

Abrantes, Marquês de Fontes e. *See* FONTES E ABRANTES, Marquês de.

Abraq, Tell. *See under* ARABIA, PRE-ISLAMIC, §IV, 1, 3, 4, 6 and 8.

Abreu, José Francisco de (*b* Elvas, *fl* Elvas, 1753–9). Portuguese architect and master builder. His earliest known works are the six side altars (black-veined marble, 1753) in the small 15th-century chapel of S Bento in Vila Viçosa, where all his work is to be found. They are carved in a characteristic Late Baroque manner. In 1754 he designed and directed the installation of the high choir at the church of S Agostinho, with a baluster and handrail in white, black and pink marble. Also in 1754 he took charge of the reconstruction of the Paços do Concelho, fending off plans to open the work to public tender and undertaking to adhere to approved designs. He resumed work at S Agostinho in 1758, replacing the old retable of the high altar, thought unworthy by Joseph I, with a new design of coloured marble. He may also have directed work on the façade of the Matriz de Portel (1741–59). Abreu's chief work is the sanctuary of Nossa Senhora de Lapa (*c.* 1756). He probably designed its Latin-cross plan. A magnificent portico stands out from a building of great sobriety, which seems to herald Neo-classical taste in architecture.

BIBLIOGRAPHY

T. Espanca: *Inventário artístico do distrito de Evora, zonal sul*, i (Lisbon, 1978)

JOSÉ FERNANDES PEREIRA

Abreu, Mario (*b* Turmero, nr Maracay, 22 Aug 1919). Venezuelan painter and sculptor. From 1943 to 1947 he studied drawing and painting in the Escuela de Artes Plásticas y Aplicadas, Caracas. He was a founder-member of the Taller Libre de Arte, taking part in its activities from 1949 to 1952. His paintings, always within a figurative framework, are marked by a pursuit of the magical and of indigenous roots. In his early work he was interested in the themes of roosters and flowers, using the surrounding environment as a source of inspiration. He expressed human, animal and vegetable existence in strong, warm colours (e.g. *The Rooster*, 1951; Caracas, Gal. A. N.). In 1952 Abreu moved to Europe, visiting Spain and Italy and living in Paris until 1962, when he returned to Venezuela. In Europe his contact with the Musée de l'Homme in Paris and with Surrealism produced a profound transformation in his work. He created his first *Magical Objects* in 1960, and he continued to make these throughout the 1960s, in circular and rectangular forms, and with varied subject-matter made out of domestic and industrial materials, including refuse. The best-known of these objects are *Souvenir of Hiroshima* (*c.* 1965) and *I, Mario, the Planet Hopper* (1966; both Caracas, Gal. A. N.).

BIBLIOGRAPHY

A. Boulton: *Historia de la pintura en Venezuela*, ii (Caracas, 1972)

J. Calzadilla: *Pintura venezolana de los siglos XIX y XX* (Caracas, 1975)

Pinturas y objetos: Mario Abreu (exh. cat., ed. Binev; Maracay, Gal. Mun. A., 1990)

MARÍA ANTONIA GONZÁLEZ-ARNAL

Abreu do Ó. Portuguese family of wood-carvers. Manuel Abreu do Ó and his brother Sebastião Abreu do Ó (both *fl* Évora *c.* 1728–*c.* 1770) worked in collaboration, carving some of the finest and most influential Joanine and Rococo altarpieces in southern Portugal. They carved in delicate flat relief using patterns similar to those found in Spain, a style contrasting with the dramatic plastic effects seen in contemporary wood-carving in northern Portugal.

An example of the Abreu do Ó brothers' early work is the main retable of the Cartuxa, the Charterhouse, Évora, gilded in 1729. It is composed on one level, and a sense of movement is suggested by the projection of the outer columns. They created one of the finest ensembles of 18th-century carving in southern Portugal in the chancel and transept of the Carmelite church of Nossa Senhora dos Remédios, Évora (*c.* 1760–70). On the main retable the areas between the column shafts are decorated with leaves and roses scattered asymmetrically, creating the impression of a lace covering. The votive tablet crowning the arch of the retable is carved with great delicacy. The lateral retables have curving double pediments whose undulating movement is echoed by large canopies above. The design of the pulpit was important in southern Portugal, because although it was in the Joanine style and inspired by developments in Lisbon it was also Rococo in spirit. The interior of the church emphasizes the importance of the role that gilt wood-carving played in the decoration of Portuguese churches during the 18th century.

BIBLIOGRAPHY

T. Espanca: 'Artes e artistas em Évora no século XVIII', *Bol. Mun. Turismo*, vii (Évora, 1950), pp. 25, 128

R. C. Smith: *A talha em Portugal* [Wood-carving in Portugal] (Lisbon, 1963), pp. 74, 138, 162

NATALIA MARINHO FERREIRA ALVES

Abrugia, Niccolò di Bartolomeo dell'. *See* NICCOLÒ PISANO.

Absidiole [apsidiole]. Small apse-like chapel, usually projecting from the eastern side of a transept (*see* CHURCH, fig. 2).

Absolon, John de Mansfield (*b* London, *c.* 1843; *d* Perth, Western Australia, 8 May 1879). Australian watercolourist, soldier, colonist and businessman of English descent. The son of the watercolour painter John Absolon (1815–95), he served in the Queen's Rifles and exhibited paintings and sketches with the Society of British Artists before first visiting Western Australia in 1869. Shipboard watercolour sketches and many studies of the bushland environs of Perth, such as *From the Verandah at Northam*, (1869–70; see Kerr, p. 5) recorded this first journey. He returned to England to marry Sarah Bowles Habgood, the niece of Thomas Habgood, an influential colonist, and daughter of Robert Mace Habgood, who divided his business and shipping interests between London, Fremantle and Geraldton. The couple returned to Perth, Western Australia, where Absolon helped manage the family's mining and mercantile interests. The firm of R. W. Habgood & Co. of Fremantle and London was known thereafter as Habgood Absolon & Co. He adapted his painting methods to an impressionistic manner that captured the harsh light and sparsely vegetated antipodean landscape. He also represented the London Art Union in Western Australia from November 1871. Absolon's watercolour sketches of Western Australia demonstrate, like those of a former associate, the watercolourist John Skinner Prout, a keen eye and rare sensitivity to the appearance of his new surroundings. These he documented in a *plein-air* style that pre-dated works by members of Melbourne's Heidelberg school. His paintings depart, quite radically, from European prototypes. The handling of light, colour and atmosphere learnt during early painting trips with his father to the coast of Brittany probably assisted this process. He died, aged thirty-six, after only ten years in the colony.

BIBLIOGRAPHY

B. Chapman: *The Colonial Eye: A Topographical and Artistic Record of the Life and Landscape of Western Australia, 1798–1914* (exh. cat. by B. Chapman, Perth, A. G. W. Australia, 1979)

R. Erickson: *The Bicentennial History of Western Australia, Pre-1829–1888* (Nedlands, 1988)

J. Kerr: *The Dictionary of Australian Artists: Painters, Sketchers, Photographers and Engravers to 1870*, (Melbourne, 1992), pp. 4–5

□

Abstract art. Term applied in its strictest sense to forms of 20th-century Western art that reject representation and have no starting- or finishing-point in nature. As distinct from processes of abstraction from nature or from objects (a recurring tendency across many cultures and periods that can be traced as far back as Palaeolithic cave painting), abstract art as a conscious aesthetic based on assumptions of self-sufficiency is a wholly modern phenomenon. *See also* ABSTRACTION.

1. Origins and early experiments, to *c.* 1913. 2. Pioneers, 1912–20. 3. European movements of the 1920s. 4. Concrete art and geometric abstraction, 1930–45. 5. Abstract Expressionism, *Art informel* and related tendencies, mid- to late 1940s and 1950s. 6. Geometric and monochrome abstractions of the 1950s. 7. Post-painterly Abstraction, Op art, Minimalism and other objective forms of the 1960s. 8. Abstract art after the emergence of conceptual art, 1970s and after.

1. ORIGINS AND EARLY EXPERIMENTS, TO *c.* 1913. In the late 19th century, and particularly in Symbolist art and literature, attention was refocused from the object to the emotions aroused in the observer in such a way that suggestion and evocation took priority over direct description and explicit analogy. In France especially this tradition contributed to the increased interest in the formal values of paintings, independent of their descriptive function, that prepared the way for abstraction. In his article 'Définition du néo-traditionnisme', published in *L'Art et critique* in 1890, Maurice Denis proclaimed, in words that have since been much quoted, that 'It is well to remember that a picture, before being a battle horse, a nude woman or some anecdote, is essentially a flat surface covered with colours assembled in a certain order.' This definition of painting, which stresses the independence of form from its descriptive function while stopping short of a complete severing of links with perceived reality, continued to characterize the moves towards a more fully abstract art in France in the early 20th century.

A combination of circumstances helped lead a number of European artists towards abstract art in the years preceding World War I. The opening of ethnographic museums furthered an interest in art from other cultures and civilizations (*see* PRIMITIVISM, §2), which in turn encouraged artists to free themselves from conventional methods of representation. By looking to the arts of Africa and Oceania as much as to Cézanne, the major figures associated with CUBISM were among the first to rethink the approach both to figure and space. In Picasso's *Female Form* (1910; Washington, DC, N.G.A.), for example, multiple views of the figure are incorporated in such a way that forms are fractured, and the surface is fragmented to the point where any link to the subject is so tenuous that it can be reconstructed only with the aid of the title. Although Picasso, like Braque, retained his commitment to subject-matter, other artists took the formal implications of Cubism to an even more abstract conclusion: around 1913 Giacomo Balla in Italy and Mikhail Larionov and Natal'ya Goncharova in Russia combined Cubist fragmentation of form with a representation of movement derived from Futurism to create abstract paintings. Certain artists associated with Dada, notably Hans Arp and Kurt Schwitters, later applied Cubist collage techniques to abstract compositions.

The first abstract paintings in the strict sense, dating from *c.* 1910, were underpinned by a strong philosophical undercurrent derived from 19th-century German Idealist thought, which posited the supremacy of mind over matter. Such beliefs were especially important to two of the earliest practitioners of abstract art, Vasily Kandinsky and František Kupka, and to other influential figures of the period such as Piet Mondrian and Theo van Doesburg. Kupka, who as early as 1911 in France was producing abstract paintings such as *Nocturne* (Vienna, Pal. Liechtenstein), was also among the first to elaborate theories about abstract art; in unpublished notebooks written between 1910 and 1914, he expressed a belief in the capacity of abstract form and colour to embody an 'idea' of universal significance beneath the surface of appearance. In Munich by 1910, the contested date of his first abstract watercolour, Kandinsky was formulating the theoretical possibility of abstract art in a text published in 1912, *Über das Geistige in der Kunst.* This proved to be one of the most influential and widely read theoretical treatises on the subject over the next 30 years and beyond.

The ground for abstract art was also prepared by 19th-century scientific theories. The descriptions of optical and prismatic effects of pure, unmixed colour initiated by Johann Wolfgang von Goethe in his *Farbenlehre* (1810) and extended by colour theorists such as Michel-Eugène Chevreul and Ogden Rood had a direct impact on such artists as Robert Delaunay, who extended Chevreul's term 'simultaneous contrasts of colour' to suggest that colour could be the means by which not only form but also the illusion of movement could be created in abstract paintings. In *Simultaneous Windows on the City* (1912; Hamburg, Ksthalle; see fig. 1) and related works, and in the *Circular Form* series, for example *Circular Forms: Sun and Moon* (1913; Amsterdam, Stedel. Mus.), Delaunay reduced the emphasis on representing objects so as to increase the impact of colour and light; both his work and his writings, which were quickly made available in German translation, influenced the Blaue Reiter artists Franz Marc and August Macke. It was the Italian artists associated with FUTURISM, however, whose development of an abstract language was most clearly conditioned by the challenge of representing speed and motion. Gino Severini, for example, developed the associative power of abstraction by fusing remembered experience with current sensation in paintings such as *Dynamic Hieroglyphic of the Bal Tabarin* (1912; New York, MOMA; for illustration *see* SEVERINI, GINO). During the same period in England, similar ideas were explored within the movement known as VORTICISM. In his drawings and prints of 1912, for example, Wyndham Lewis transformed machine parts into cylindrical and geometric shapes in order to capitalize on the associations provoked by machinery independent of their forms. Around 1913 two American painters working in Paris, Stanton Macdonald-Wright and Morgan Russell, the instigators of a movement labelled SYNCHROMISM, created colour abstractions concerned with the twisting movement of form. Marcel Duchamp and Francis Picabia, two of the leading painters in a variation on Cubism christened ORPHISM by Guillaume Apollinaire, produced mechanomorphic paintings that transmuted vaguely mechanical and sexual parts into abstract forms. Duchamp's *The Bride* (1912; Philadelphia, PA, Mus. A.) and Picabia's *Udnie* (1913; Paris, Pompidou) invited the spectator to interpret the forms imaginatively from clues provided by their titles. During the same period another painter associated with Orphism, Fernand Léger, used abstract pictorial equivalents to capture the dissonant contrast of manmade machines set against the natural landscape. In spite of the central position of Paris in the development of a modernist avant-garde aesthetic, the continued devotion among French artists to recognizable subject-matter, combined with the absence of a firm metaphysical or theoretical basis for their experiments, ultimately restrained them from developing a full abstract language.

1. Robert Delaunay: *Simultaneous Windows on the City*, oil on canvas, 460×400 mm, 1912 (Hamburg, Hamburger Kunsthalle)

2. PIONEERS, 1912–20. By the end of World War I such artists as Kandinksy, Mondrian and Kazimir Malevich were creating paintings that were less reliant on appearances, perception and physical sensation and that instead obeyed their own laws of colour and form. Stylistically, this encompassed a wide range from a loose, free-form approach, as in Kandinsky's *Improvisations*, to a tight geometric abstraction as practised by Mondrian and the DE STIJL group. In spite of their differences, however, these artists shared an interest in esoteric doctrines that underpinned their commitment to abstract art.

Kandinsky's early writings were particularly influential for their analysis of colour, notably in *Über das Geistige in der Kunst*, and of form, which was the subject of an essay, 'Über die Formfrage', published in *Der Blaue Reiter Almanach* in 1912. Basing his approach to colour on the empirical theories of Goethe, Kandinsky went further in suggesting that colour, like music, can evoke certain emotional and psychological responses even when used non-representationally in a painting. Similarly, he argued that formal content was determined not by external appearances but by the 'inner necessity' of the artist's emotional response. In providing a theoretical justification for expressive abstraction, Kandinsky developed the notion of the affective purpose of art, basing this on the assumption that art must possess 'soul' in order to elicit a response from the spectator, and that this soul, manifested in the balance of colours and composition, is in turn dependent on the integrity of the artist. While Kandinsky's pictures of this period generally continued to combine apparently abstract forms with shapes suggestive of figures, animals and landscapes, in certain works, such as *Composition VII* (1913; Moscow, Tret'yakov Gal.), he approached pure abstraction.

The spiritual and moral dimensions of Kandinsky's art and theory, grounded in part on his understanding of THEOSOPHY, were shared by Mondrian even before World War I. It was not until 1917, however, that Mondrian developed the basis of his geometric abstraction and a theoretical justification for it. In his essay 'Natuurlijke en abstracte realiteit' (1919), Mondrian followed the mystic philosopher M. H. J. Schoenmaekers, whom he had met in 1916–17, in elaborating a theory of universal beauty by renouncing the 'particulars of appearance' and embracing the 'abstraction of form and colour' within the precise formulation of the 'straight line and the clearly defined primary colour'. For Mondrian, as for Schoenmaekers and the Theosophists, the orthogonal, in line with a long history of divine geometry, was cosmically pre-eminent, as it expressed the mystical concept of life and immortality in a harmonious relationship. By 1921 Mondrian had conceived the basis of a style that he termed NEO-PLASTICISM, which was based on the use of a black linear grid and on asymmetrically placed zones of primary colour. In such paintings as *Composition with Red, Yellow and Blue* (1921; The Hague, Gemeentemus.), 'dynamic equilibrium' is achieved by the juxtaposition of lines, planes and narrow bands of flat colour held in taut relation to each other.

The development by Malevich of a form of abstract painting known as SUPREMATISM was also stimulated by topical esoteric concerns. He first exhibited 35 such paintings, each consisting of flat shapes such as quadrangles against light grounds, at the exhibition *Poslednaya futuristicheskaya vystavka kartin: 0.10* ('The last Futurist exhibition of paintings: 0.10'), held at the Dobychina Gallery in Petrograd (now St Petersburg) in 1915. The titles of many of the works referred to the concept of the FOURTH DIMENSION, which was evolved partly in response to Russian mystical philosophy, as a new form of consciousness that provided an escape into the world of the spirit (for illustration *see* SUPREMATISM). To effect cosmic integration, Malevich, following the philosopher Pyotr Uspensky, affirmed the necessity of venturing into a new space–continuum by replacing the forms derived from nature with 'non-objective'—that is to say completely abstract—forms. The rectilinear planes featured in such paintings as *Untitled* (1915; Amsterdam, Stedel. Mus.) make no reference to things external to the picture, other than to mathematical figures such as parallelograms, yet despite this resolute flatness and expunction of associations, the disposition of overlapping forms against a white ground inevitably creates a sense of ebb and flow. In 1919, immediately after painting his *White on White* series of 1917–18 (*see* MALEVICH, KAZIMIR, fig. 2), Malevich wrote about the use of white in terms of space travel, and in 1920 he even suggested the possibility of building a Suprematist satellite. During this period other artists in Russia, such as Il'ya Chashnik (1902–29), El Lissitzky and Gustav Klucis, began to develop their own variants of Suprematism. After the Revolution of 1917, Suprematism quickly came to be regarded as one of the major new artistic tendencies to challenge the conservative traditionalism of the old Tsarist order, leading abstract art to gain official support, if only temporarily, for the first time in its history.

Other artists, especially those based in central Europe, sought to counter the barbaric realities of World War I through abstraction. Both Hans Arp and Sophie Taeuber (later Taeuber-Arp) sought to approach eternal values and to deny human egotism in a series of *Duo-collages* made as collaborations in 1918. They hoped that the impersonal technique employed in these works made with paper-cutters, together with the geometric rigour of presentation, would help to transcend human imperfections and in so doing 'cure' people of the frenzy of the period. In common with other Dadaists, such as Kurt Schwitters in the pictures and reliefs he called *Merzbilder*, from 1916 to 1919 Arp also produced more random arrangements that championed chance as the governing factor.

Artists working in France in the 1920s, such as Joan Miró and André Masson, came under the influence of Surrealism (and in particular its elevation of irrational forces) and began to explore 'pure psychic automatism', as defined in André Breton's *Manifeste du surréalisme* (Paris, 1924), employing such techniques as psychic improvisation, BIOMORPHISM and AUTOMATISM. Conceiving of their pictures as reflections of the workings of the subconscious mind, in works such as Miró's *Birth of the World* (1925; New York, MOMA) they created a form of improvised abstract painting that anticipated the gestural aspects of Abstract Expressionism referred to as action painting.

3. EUROPEAN MOVEMENTS OF THE 1920S. The dissemination of the theory and practice of abstract art in Europe after World War I was greatly aided by the banding together of artists into associations and by the establishment of schools and periodicals. Notable among them were De Stijl (1917–31) in the Netherlands, Vkhutemas (1920–30) and Inkhuk (1920–26) in Russia and the Bauhaus (1919–33) in Germany. Most of these were formed in a spirit of reconstruction after the devastation of war, with abstract art, like the machine, coming to be equated with both modernity and progress as a rejection of the old order and an embrace of a new future. The French periodical *L'Esprit nouveau* (1920–25), established by Le Corbusier and Amédée Ozenfant as the official organ of their movement, Purism (*see* PURISM, §1), conveyed a new aesthetic based on mathematics and geometry and inspired other artists to take up abstraction. In Europe, in response to debates concerning the role of art in effecting changes in society, abstract art came to be seen as an instrument with which to improve the quality of life. For artists who conveyed these views, including Theo van Doesburg in the Netherlands, Aleksandr Rodchenko in Russia and László Moholy-Nagy at the Bauhaus, abstract art became as important an issue for design as for painting. These developments, coupled with a concern for broadening their audience, led to an expanding of definitions of abstract art and to the introduction of new terms, such as CONSTRUCTIVISM and CONCRETE ART, to describe forms of abstract art based on the rigorous and non-referential use of geometric forms. Van Doesburg's insistence that the principles of De Stijl, also referred to as Neo-plasticism, be applied not only to easel painting, as exemplified by Mondrian, but also to architecture, furniture and interior design was symptomatic of this wider definition of abstract art. Van Doesburg urged collaboration between the practitioners of different disciplines in the hope of creating total environments capable of reaching a wide audience. However, the poor reception given to the Café de l'Aubette project in Strasbourg, on which van Doesburg collaborated in 1926–8 with Hans Arp and Sophie Taeuber-Arp, showed that the public was not to be easily persuaded.

Disagreements about how best to reach a general audience were vividly exemplified in Russia just after the

Revolution of 1917. Artists such as Malevich, Kandinsky (who had returned to Russia in 1914) and the sculptor Naum Gabo strongly believed that abstract art had a vital contribution to make to society in raising human consciousness and that this transformation could be effected in the traditional media of painting and sculpture. Gabo's work, for example, demonstrated that sculpture could be reinvented by using new materials to represent space and movement so as to concentrate attention on effects of light and on the apparent dissolution of solid mass. By contrast, Vladimir Tatlin and Rodchenko, both of whom had conducted important experiments with abstract forms in the pre-revolutionary period, came to regard the continuation of traditional fine art after the Revolution as contrary to the spirit of the urgent requirements of the day, judging that it should be replaced by self-evidently utilitarian forms of construction. By the time Tatlin exhibited his maquette for the *Monument to the Third International* (1919–20; destr.; *see* TATLIN, VLADIMIR, fig. 2) the notion of the 'artist' was giving way to that of the 'artist–technician' among Soviet Constructivists, with abstraction channelled largely through posters, textiles, ceramics and stage designs rather than through paintings. While the education system before the introduction of the first Five-year Plan in 1928 could allow the two factions to exist simultaneously for a time, increasing political opposition to what were deemed the obfuscations of abstract art led to arguments for a more easily understood and propagandistic realist art, culminating in the adoption of Socialist Realism as the official style in 1934.

In Germany an almost parallel sequence of events took place at the Bauhaus, albeit under different political circumstances. Paul Klee and Kandinsky, who had joined the teaching staff in 1920 and 1922 respectively, both rationalized further their theory and practice of abstract art. In *Punkt und Linie zu Fläche* (Munich, 1926) Kandinsky complemented his earlier theories about colour with an analysis of composition, retaining a belief in emotional expressiveness but acknowledging the need for intellectual control that was a major factor in his adoption at this time of a geometric idiom. Klee's *Pädagogisches Skizzenbuch* (1925) is a methodical study of compositional methods that reflects the increasingly 'scientific' bias of the Bauhaus at this stage; in the later 1920s his paintings became more overtly abstract, although he never fully severed his links with representational subject-matter. Kandinsky's affirmation in 1932 that both he and Klee were 'painters of spiritual essence', coupled with Klee's belief in intuition, were pitted against the cool rationalism of Hannes Meyer, who as the Bauhaus's director from 1927 introduced rigid Constructivist principles along Soviet lines; he asserted that form was a product of arithmetic and that no aesthetic factor was involved in design. In the event, neither view triumphed: with the ascendancy to power of the Nazis, the Bauhaus was closed in 1933, and abstract art in Germany came to be suppressed, if only temporarily, as 'degenerate art' (*see* ENTARTETE KUNST), while a largely neo-classicist-inspired realism became the officially promoted style.

4. CONCRETE ART AND GEOMETRIC ABSTRACTION, 1930–45. The ideological opposition to abstract art that developed in Germany and the USSR led many abstract artists to gravitate to Paris, which gradually became the most important centre for abstract art, despite the antipathy of the French art establishment to its stricter forms. Even before Kandinsky's arrival in 1933, a great range of Europeans had already established themselves in and around Paris, including the Russians Lissitzky, Gabo, Antoine Pevsner and Jean Pougny; Dutch artists associated with De Stijl, such as Mondrian, van Doesburg (who died in 1931), Georges Vantongerloo and César Domela; Hans Arp and Sophie Taeuber-Arp; the Poles Henryk Stażewski, Władysław Strzemiński and Katarzyna Kobro; and the Italian Enrico Prampolini. Most of these artists were among those who formed the nucleus of new groups and periodicals established in Paris during the 1930s to promote abstract art. Taeuber-Arp's *Composition with Rectangles and Circles on Black Ground* (1931; Basle, Kstmus.; see fig. 2) was typical of the geometric rigour of their work. One of the most important sculptors working in Paris during this period was Constantin Brancusi, who favoured forms of extreme simplicity abstracted from nature; although he was not identified with any movement, he had a lasting influence on the development of abstract sculpture well into the 20th century.

Arguments for the total autonomy of abstract art, which had gathered momentum during the 1920s, were vehemently expressed in a manifesto formulated by van Doesburg and published in April 1930 in the only issue of a new periodical based in Paris, *Art concret.* In it van Doesburg argued that a picture should be 'constructed entirely from purely plastic elements, that is to say planes and colours' and that as 'a pictorial element has no other significance than itself' the picture as a whole similarly has 'no other significance than itself'. This formalist emphasis reflected van Doesburg's familiarity with Constructivist tenets during the 1920s and illustrates the extent to which he had departed from Mondrian's mystical justifications. This rationale for Concrete art quickly gained followers, who used the term in preference to abstract because they agreed with van Doesburg that 'nothing is more real than a line, a colour, a surface'. Jean Hélion, who also signed the manifesto, sought in his *Equilibrium* series (1932–4) to express the effects of space and movement on geometric elements, while during the same decade Domela and Vantongerloo developed an impersonal, severe, mathematically based art; Arp, Strzeminski, Kobro and Max Bill were among those who proposed their own interpretations of Concrete art at this time, with Bill popularizing the concept in Switzerland and South America.

More catholic tendencies were embraced in the 1930s by an association based in Paris, ABSTRACTION-CRÉATION, which promoted its ideas through a magazine of the same name, and by another group and periodical, CERCLE ET CARRÉ, which flourished only briefly. The very diversity of Abstraction–Création, however—its members included Arp, Delaunay, Albert Gleizes, Hélion, Auguste Herbin, Kupka, van Doesburg and Vantongerloo—was also its weakness. Disagreements arose over exhibition policy: the dominant faction supported only 'pure' abstraction and would accept no painting containing any suggestion of an outside reference; those who resisted were eventually compelled to resign over what they considered

2. Sophie Taeuber-Arp: *Composition with Rectangles and Circles on Black Ground*, oil on canvas, 645×920 mm, 1931 (Basle, Kunstmuseum)

an excessively rigid approach. Debates also raged in their magazine over how abstract art could best serve society in the face of political events abroad. Some left-wing contributors argued that abstract art was too remote from the general population to succeed in such aims, while others argued for aesthetic freedom on the basis that the objective of Communism was to liberate the individual. If the two sides of the argument seemed irreconcilable, the editorial stance of the magazine at least promoted the view that commitment to abstract art represented independence and opposition to totalitarianism.

With the increasing threat of war in Europe, many European artists were forced to uproot themselves again. Towards the end of the 1930s England was perceived as a safer refuge. For a brief period after the arrival of Walter Gropius, Marcel Breuer, Moholy-Nagy, Gabo and Mondrian, the north London suburb of Hampstead and St Ives in Cornwall became centres of abstract and especially Constructivist art; English artists such as Ben Nicholson and Barbara Hepworth moved in their own work towards a greater degree of abstraction, while the cause of international abstract art was publicized through the touring exhibition *Abstract and Concrete Art* in 1936 and through the publication in 1937 of the collection of essays *Circle: International Survey of Constructive Art*. However, the British public showed little interest in abstract art, and with the outbreak of World War II many of the Europeans decided in any case to leave for the USA, where they continued to encourage the development of abstract art.

5. ABSTRACT EXPRESSIONISM, ART INFORMEL AND RELATED TENDENCIES, MID- TO LATE 1940S AND 1950S. After World War II the geometric abstraction of artists such as Albers, Arp and Bill was shown widely in Europe, notably at the exhibition *Art concret* in 1945 (Paris, Gal. Denise René), organized with the help of Theo van Doesburg's widow, Nelly van Doesburg, and at the Salon des Réalités Nouvelles, which over the following ten years became the largest exhibiting forum in Paris. After the traumas of World War II, however, many other artists found the geometric order too limiting to reflect their particular psychological experiences; in their search for a more immediate expression, they turned to a looser and often more gestural form of abstract painting. Inspired partly by influential exhibitions at the Galerie René Drouin and the work of Jean Fautrier, Jean Dubuffet and Wols, the painting that resulted was exhibited and promoted in Paris under a plethora of names, including lyrical abstraction, ART INFORMEL, MATTER PAINTING and TACHISM. Expressive abstraction soon became an international phenomenon, encompassing ZEN 49 (founded 1949) and QUADRIGA (founded 1952) in Germany, the painters associated with COBRA (1948–51) and a group of younger English painters based primarily in ST IVES, such as Patrick Heron and Peter Lanyon, while related developments also

took place in Italy, Spain, South America and in Japan with the GUTAI group. In the USA a separate but related phenomenon, ABSTRACT EXPRESSIONISM, flourished at this time.

These groups shared several characteristics: an emphasis on impulsiveness and spontaneity that rejected predetermined composition and that frequently equated drawing with painting; a concentration on the individual mark or 'tache', as opposed to the straight line or carefully circumscribed shape; a concern for the expressive potential of paint and its textured or optical effect; and a sense of immediacy in the execution. Qualities of freshness and urgency led to a physical awareness of the artist's contact with the picture surface and of the act of painting itself, manifested in the USA by ACTION PAINTING.

In spite of the common features, there were significant differences among the various post-war groups and problems even in naming them. For example the terms *Art informel* and Tachism are often used interchangeably, even though the painters associated with *Art informel*, such as Jean Fautrier, Jean-Paul Riopelle, Antoni Tàpies and Jean Dubuffet (who approached abstraction in his *Texturologies*), generally preferred to use thick accretions of layers of paint, hence the term matter painting (for illustration *see* TÀPIES, ANTONI); whereas the Tachists, such as Georges Mathieu (who coined the word), Hans Hartung and Henri Michaux, concentrated on the swift execution of the painted stroke or gesture. The degree or type of abstraction varied from group to group. Artists associated with St Ives, such as Lanyon and Terry Frost, produced atmospheric abstractions of the Cornish landscape, whereas many of the Cobra artists tended to create hybrid forms reminiscent of the mythological animals they admired in Nordic art and legend. Even within groups, the degree of abstraction was seldom clearcut, depending more on the individual proclivities of each artist. During this period, especially in Paris, tendencies were often named and promoted by critics and writers rather than by the artists themselves, thus helping to disseminate the work but also bracketing tendencies into a rather amorphous, international expansion of *Art informel* and Tachism from around 1956.

Confusion also arises from the application of the term Abstract Expressionism to American artists, as it has been used to encompass both the gestural action painting of artists such as Jackson Pollock, Willem de Kooning and Franz Kline and the COLOUR FIELD PAINTING of Mark Rothko, Barnett Newman and Ad Reinhardt; it is also used to describe paintings by artists who do not fit strictly into either category, such as Clyfford Still, Robert Motherwell and Hans Hofmann, or those whose work contains residual figuration, such as Adolph Gottlieb, William Baziotes and Arshile Gorky. Given this disparity, some critics and historians have preferred to refer to the New York school (as in the title of a major exhibition at Los Angeles, CA, Co. Mus. A., 1965), in response to the term Ecole de Paris, and to the role played by these American artists in transferring the centre of power from Paris to New York; even this term, however, is not wholly accurate, since most of the major painters originated from outside New York and in many cases continued to work in other places. Whatever name is given to these developments, the fact remains that they emerged not only as a reaction against dominant trends of realism within American painting but also from a knowledge and assimilation of European models, particularly Cubism and the Surrealist technique of automatism, and (in the case of Pollock and others) from Native American and Mexican art. The psychoanalytic theories of Sigmund Freud and Carl Gustav Jung provided an intellectual context for their search for a new subject-matter underpinning the raw and impressive physical presence of their paintings (*see* PSYCHOANALYSIS AND ART).

While the Abstract Expressionists made reference to shared influences and intentions, great formal differences nevertheless underlie such works as Pollock's *Autumn Rhythm* (1950; New York, Met.) and Newman's *Vir heroicus sublimis* (1950–51; New York, MOMA). Pollock placed his unstretched canvas on the floor and literally poured paint on to the surface to produce weaving, linear arabesques that create an 'all-over' effect. Newman and other artists associated with colour field painting, on the other hand, evenly covered the canvas with a flat application of paint so that the viewer's field of vision is saturated with colour; no allowance is made for individual 'gesture' within this unmodulated surface. Like the Surrealists, Pollock believed that the basic artistic impulse was grounded in the unconscious, and it was this concept, interpreted in Existentialist terms, that led the critic Harold Rosenberg to devise his definition of action painting. For Newman, as for Rothko, painting was a means of expressing the sublime, of creating a transcendent art that had its origins in Old Testament theology. Thus Rothko's zones of colour were conceived not as decoration but as a means of effecting a revelatory and emotional experience for the spectator. Such levels of meaning, however, were not taken into account by formalist criticism, especially as promoted by Clement Greenberg, who vaunted the new painting for its supercession of Cubist space. Abstract Expressionism came to be seen as essentially different from European painting because of its vitality, use of large scale, intense physicality and holistic quality, by which the entire picture surface pre-empted its segmentation into parts. A case was soon made by American critics for the superiority of this art, which was promoted internationally through exhibitions and publications in such a way that New York came to be generally recognized as the most important centre of artistic production after World War II.

6. GEOMETRIC AND MONOCHROME ABSTRACTIONS OF THE 1950S. Just as the various forms of expressive abstraction became established as an international style in the late 1950s, the weakening of the original impetus had led towards a certain mannerism. In New York, for example, de Kooning's many imitators, labelled the 10th Street school because of the preponderance of galleries representing them in that area, used the techniques of Abstract Expressionism more as surface embellishments than as signs of underlying content. Inevitably there was a reaction against this lapse of a once avant-garde style into a new kind of academicism. In its wake, artists developed styles that eschewed the personal touch, such as Minimalism,

hard-edge painting and Post-painterly Abstraction as well as Pop art.

In Europe geometric abstraction remained a force to be reckoned with. The Groupe Espace was formed in 1949 after the success of the *Art concret* exhibition of 1945 and the founding of the Salon des Réalités Nouvelles in Paris in 1946. The Groupe Espace sought to promote Constructivism as an influence on the urban environment. Their anti-expressive bias was shared by an international network of other groups such as MOVIMENTO ARTE CONCRETA (MAC) in Milan (1948), ART ABSTRAIT in Belgium (1952), LES PLASTICIENS (1955, from 1959 Les Nouveaux Plasticiens) in Canada and Equipo 57 in Spain (1957), all of which promoted alternatives to *Art informel* and pursued a programme of geometric abstraction. Josef Albers explored perception and the illusory aspects of colour from 1950 in his *Homages to the Squares* (for illustration *see* ALBERS, JOSEF), a series he worked on until his death. In Switzerland Karl Gerstner (*b* 1930) and Richard Paul Lohse continued the teachings of Max Bill in their investigation into the mathematical aspects of colour programming, which they called KALTE KUNST in 1954, while in Britain ties with Dutch Constructivism were established through the magazine *Structure* (1958–64) and through a shared interest in the theories of the American Charles Biederman.

During the 1950s a number of artists experimented with single-colour abstractions, including Lucio Fontana in his *Spatial Concepts* (from 1948), Piero Manzoni in his *Achromes* (exhibited from 1957), Yves Klein in blue monochromes (exhibited from 1956), Robert Rauschenberg in series of monochromes, including white paintings (exhibited in 1951) and Ad Reinhardt in his blue, red and ultimately 'black' paintings (*c*. 1954–67). Such works constituted the ultimate reduction of painting, but the artists' intentions were varied. To Rodchenko in 1921 the monochrome had represented the last venture in painting before he turned to Constructivism. By contrast, Rauschenberg wished to create an empty screen against which the moving shadows of spectators could be projected, while Fontana established the flat uniform surface only to pierce it spatially with holes and later slits; Manzoni seems to have been motivated by more purely nihilistic purposes; while for Klein blue was so potent and mysterious a hue that the canvas surface needed to be covered only in paint of that colour. Reinhardt's intention with his 'black' canvases was to make the 'first paintings which cannot be misunderstood'. Whatever the motive, the monochrome experiments of the 1950s offered a severe form of abstraction that both paved the way for Minimalism in the 1960s and for the ongoing critical debates concerning the 'end of painting'.

7. POST-PAINTERLY ABSTRACTION, OP ART, MINIMALISM AND OTHER OBJECTIVE FORMS OF THE 1960S. Abstract art enjoyed its greatest success in terms of support in the 1960s, in major exhibitions staged in Europe and the USA and through international art magazines. Broadly speaking, European artists explored scientific discoveries and experimentation, while Americans developed a more purely formal language. Both directions were characterized by a more objective and impersonal approach that transcended the individual imprint of the artist.

In Europe these new developments were encompassed largely by KINETIC ART, OP ART and art using electric light sources. All these were among the trends referred to as NOUVELLE TENDANCE, an umbrella term used in the early 1960s to describe the diverse Constructivist tendencies and movements that opposed expressive abstraction. Artists working with light, and kinetic and Op artists, all tended to depersonalize the art object, using materials and techniques borrowed from industrial science, exploiting direct stimuli such as light, sound and real movement, encouraging spectator involvement and generally subverting traditional aesthetic standards. Among the groups to develop these interests within *Nouvelle tendance* were the GROUPE DE RECHERCHE D'ART VISUEL (GRAV) in Paris, ARTE PROGRAMMATA, GRUPPO N and GRUPPO T in Italy, ZERO Group in Germany, NUL in the Netherlands and Equipo 57 in Spain. One of the most influential pioneers of Op art, however, was an English painter, Bridget Riley, and GRAV included Victor Vasarely as well as Jésus Soto and other South Americans among its members.

In the USA the direction towards a more objective abstract art was restricted largely to painting and sculpture, although there were also important American Op artists such as Richard Anuszkiewicz and at least one major artist working with light, Dan Flavin. Various exhibitions of American painting held in the USA during the 1960s, such as *Toward a New Abstraction* (1963), *Post-painterly Abstraction* (1964) and *Systemic Painting* (1966), brought together works that shared an ordered and structured composition, clearly defined edges and linear clarity. The two most commonly used terms for these developments are POST-PAINTERLY ABSTRACTION and HARD-EDGE PAINTING. Morris Louis, Kenneth Noland, Ellsworth Kelly and Frank Stella, who were included in all these exhibitions, may be taken as paradigms of this new direction (for illustrations *see* KELLY, ELLSWORTH and NOLAND, KENNETH).

Louis and Noland worked in Washington, DC (*see* WASHINGTON COLOR PAINTERS), not in New York, and they were inspired by the stain paintings of HELEN FRANKENTHALER rather than by Pollock. Both used acrylic paint for a kind of painting that allowed for no reworking. Louis, for example, in his *Unfurleds* series (1960–61), poured thinned paint on to unprimed or selectively sized canvas so that it sank into and stained the weave, making the image and its support inseparable and eliminating the gestural marks and tactile surface of action painting, thereby concentrating attention on the purely visual experience of colour. Similar techniques were employed by Noland but applied to more structured motifs of concentric circles or parallel bands of colour. Kelly, who had spent his formative years in Europe from 1948 to 1954, took his hard-edge shapes from nature or architecture and abstracted them to the point of unrecognizability. Stella was the most extreme of all in stressing the flatness of the picture plane, denying illusionism and other levels of meaning; he insisted that there were no suggestions in his paintings beyond the structure expressed on their surface. This emphasis on the work of art as a physical object was a reaction against the values of the previous generation but also part of a wider interest at the time in PHENOMENOLOGY.

MINIMALISM emerged in the 1960s as a highly influential development in abstract sculpture, especially in the USA. The *Primary Structures* exhibition (1966) brought together British and American artists, many of them trained as painters, who had begun to produce objects of extreme formal simplicity largely after the example of Brancusi. The Americans, notably Carl André and Donald Judd, used rigidly geometrical prefabricated industrial units often displayed according to serial principles; Judd's *Untitled* (1968; Toronto, A.G. Ont.; see fig. 3) is a characteristic example. They renounced what they considered to be a European preference for relational methods of composition, as Stella used in his paintings, favouring instead the use of regular grid structures or centralized formats so that the shape of the work as a whole could be apprehended at once. Along with Judd, Robert Morris (ii) provided a theoretical premise for Minimalist sculpture by stressing the presence or factuality of the work itself, the object's autonomy and the mind's powers of perception. In Britain a group of sculptors associated with the St Martin's School of Art, London, under the tutelage of Anthony Caro, explored new forms of abstract sculpture that were witty in conception and painted in bright colours. Phillip King, Tim Scott and William Tucker were among those who established their reputations at the exhibition *New Generation: 1965* (1965). Like the American Minimalists, they used industrially manufactured and synthetic materials, including sheet metal, glass, plastic and fibreglass, but unlike them they maintained a referential quality in their choice of both motifs and titles. In spite of the growing internationalism, national tendencies continued to be discernible.

3. Donald Judd: *Untitled*, stainless steel and green perspex, nine of ten units, each 229×1016×788 mm, with 229 mm intervals, 1968 (Toronto, Art Gallery of Ontario)

8. ABSTRACT ART AFTER THE EMERGENCE OF CONCEPTUAL ART, 1970S AND AFTER. By the end of the 1960s the boundaries between abstract and representational art, as with so many other categories, began to break down. The international developments encompassed by the term CONCEPTUAL ART, which emerged in part as a reaction against the marketable art object, were closely related to movements important in the development of abstract art. LAND ART and ARTE POVERA, for example, drew attention to the environment and sought to transcend the distinction between sculpture and object and between abstraction and representation, while artists involved with PROCESS ART took as their main theme the methods by which their work was made. Land artists such as Robert Smithson, Richard Long and Jan Dibbets favoured abstract patterns or primary forms similar to those employed by the Minimalists, using nature as their raw material and often documenting their ephemeral or large-scale works in photographs. Smithson's *Spiral Jetty* (1970; for illustration *see* LAND ART)—a coil 457 m long of mud, salt crystals, rocks and water at the Great Salt Lake in Utah—is typical of this synthesis. The work was seen directly by few people other than the artist, but it was recorded in photographs and film, undercutting traditional expectations and resisting categorization. In Germany the most influential figure, both as an artist and teacher, was Joseph Beuys, who emphasized the largely personal associations of particular natural materials such as fat and felt, with form as their by-product rather than as a predetermined factor.

Conceptual attitudes, especially in the USA, revived in abstract art a concern for mental constructs and logic. As with artists of the *Nouvelle Tendance*, planning and programming became essential, and the work of art itself was frequently the fulfilment of a verbal construct or mathematical formula. Sol LeWitt, as a general principle, used written instructions as the starting-point of his art. In LeWitt's abstract *Wall Drawings*, for example, which consist of pencilled lines or coloured shapes, the impersonality of the idea logically entailed the collaboration of assistants for their execution. The client was often sold only the instructions, thus again calling into question the uniqueness of both the creator and the work itself. Although such strategies were not new to art, given the earlier example of artists such as Duchamp and Moholy-Nagy, their alliance in the 1970s with contemporary developments in critical theory and linguistics gave them a particular weight.

The challenge presented by conceptual art during the 1970s to traditional forms of painting and sculpture was met by a number of artists who continued to work in these media. In the context of these largely individual investigations, SUPPORTS-SURFACES, a group of painters based in France, was unusual in emerging as a cohesive movement; they were not alone, however, in their concern with material structure, physical attributes and use of decorative patterns, since these were shared by other Europeans such as Gillian Ayres and by Americans such as Miriam Schapiro and Robert Zakanitch (*b* 1936), loosely referred to as 'dekor' or 'pattern painters'. Agnes Martin, Robert Ryman and Brice Marden, three American abstract painters tangentially related to Minimalism, showed that formalism and metaphysical concerns could be intertwined, while a rearticulation of the compositional and relational tradition of Constructivism was to be found in the work of Beuys's pupils Blinky Palermo and Imi Knoebel.

The pluralism that increasingly dominated the evolution of art during the 1970s and 1980s created a climate in which abstract and representational forms were equally acceptable and sometimes even interchangeable. Many artists, such as Georg Baselitz, used referential imagery but conceived of their paintings as abstract, while others, such as the American sculptor Joel Shapiro (*b* 1941), took as their starting-point forms associated with abstract art but endowed them with suggestions of objects and of the human figure. Cy Twombly extended the language and meaning of gestural Abstract Expressionism by adding scrawled words embued with poetic and mythic associations to the other marks contained in his non-figurative canvases and drawings, while Gerhard Richter produced both figurative and abstract paintings, which by the particular nature of their painted surface and reference to the ambiguities of photography, seemed to call into question what is abstract and what is 'real': both lines of pursuit have since influenced and exercised many other artists. The pluralism of the period found numerous outlets even within the bounds of wholly non-referential work, and these could each be traced to earlier 20th-century movements as diverse as Constructivism and Abstract Expressionism. The relationship to earlier models could be as sincere as the emulation of Hans Hofmann by John Hoyland or as ironic in its appropriation of Op art and hard-edge painting as the parodies by American painters labelled Neo-Geo, such as Philip Taaffe (*b* 1955) or Peter Halley (*b* 1953). A widespread loss of faith in the concept of the avant-garde during this period brought with it a move away from the candour and utopian optimism that characterized abstraction in early modernism, to the extent that modernism itself was seen by some to have run its course and to have given way to the more eclectic impulses of Post-modernism. In this context, abstract art has generally changed both its meaning and its function while continuing to exploit the diverse forms and approaches associated with its history. Increasing access to information concerning art made outside western Europe and America prompts the need also for a greater awareness of other traditions and of new perspectives on abstraction that might be offered. In terms of the art discussed to date, it still remains to be resolved whether Post-modernism marked a moment of clear and decisive rupture in the history of abstract art, as proposed by much of the North American, English and French literature, or alternatively, whether the same moment was characteristic of a shift from a high to a late modernism in art, a position often argued for in German literature of the same period. While the Post-modern arguments of rupture lead to a discontinuous and variable problematization of abstract art and its history, the latter narrative offers the positive and diachronic advantages of an unfolding critical model and of continuous period histories into early–high–late types of abstract art production.

BIBLIOGRAPHY

PERIODICALS AND REVIEWS

De Stijl, i/1–viii/90 (1917–32)
Veshch–Gegenstand–Objet, 1–3 (1922)
Z. Elem. Gestalt (1923)
Bauhaus: Z. Bau & Gestalt. (1926–31)
A. Concr. (1930)
Cerc. & Carré (1930)
Abstraction, Création, A. Non-Fig., i–v (1932–6)
Axis, 1–8 (1935–7)
Réalités Nouv., 1–9 (1947–55)
Cobra: Rev. Int. A. Expermntl (1948–51)
Structure (1958–64)
Zero, 1–3 (1958–61)

ARTISTS' WRITINGS AND STATEMENTS

V. Kandinsky: *Über das Geistige in der Kunst* (Munich, 1912)
——: 'Über die Formfrage', *Der Blaue Reiter Almanach* (Munich, 1912, 2/1914), pp. 74–100
——: 'Rückblicke', *Kandinsky, 1901–1913* (Berlin, 1913), pp. iii–xxix
K. Malevich: *Ot kubizma i futurizma k suprematizmu: Novyy zhivopisnyy realizm* [From Cubism and Futurism to Suprematism: the new realism in painting] (St Petersburg, 1915, rev. Moscow, 3 and 4/1916)
P. Mondrian: 'Natuurlijke en abstracte realiteit', *De Stijl*, ii (1919), no. 8, pp. 85–9; no. 9, pp. 97–9; no. 10, pp. 109–13; no. 11, pp. 121–5; no. 12, pp. 133–7; iii (1919), no. 2, pp. 15–19; iii (1920), no. 3, pp. 27–31; no. 5, pp. 41–4; no. 6, pp. 54–6; no. 7, pp. 58–60; no. 8, pp. 65–9; no. 9, pp. 73–6; no. 10, pp. 81–4; repr. and Eng. trans. in *The New Art—The New Life: Collected Writings of Piet Mondrian* (London, 1987), pp. 82–123
Desyataya gosudarstvennaya vystavka: Bespredmetnoye tvorchestvo i suprematizm [Tenth state exhibition: non-objective creation and Suprematism] (exh. cat., essay by K. Malevich, Moscow, 1919)
P. Mondrian: *Le Néo-plasticisme: Principe général de l'équivalence plastique* (Paris, 1921); repr. in *The New Art—The New Life* (London, 1987), pp. 132–47
P. Klee: *Pädagogisches Skizzenbuch*, ed. W. Gropius and L. Moholy-Nagy (Munich, 1925; Eng. trans., New York, 1944, 2/1953)
V. Kandinsky: *Punkt und Linie zu Fläche* (Munich, 1926) [pubd as a Bauhaus bk]
P. Klee: 'Exakte Versuche im Bereich der Kunst', *Bauhaus: Z. Bau & Gestalt.*, ii/2–3 (1928)
N. Gabo: 'The Constructive Idea in Art', *Circle: International Survey of Constructive Art* (London, 1937), pp. 1–10
P. Mondrian: 'Plastic Art and Pure Plastic Art (Figurative Art and Non-Figurative Art)', *Circle: International Survey of Constructive Art* (London, 1937), pp. 41–56
G. Mathieu: 'La Liberté, c'est le vide' (exh. cat., Paris, Gal. Colette Allendy, 1947)
H. Arp: *Dadaland* (Paris, 1948)
A. Calder: 'What Abstract Art Means to Me', *MOMA Bull.*, xviii/3 (1951), p. 8
W. de Kooning: 'What Abstract Art Means to Me', *MOMA Bull.*, xviii/3 (1951), pp. 4–8
R. Motherwell: 'What Abstract Art Means to Me', *MOMA Bull.*, xviii/3 (1951), pp. 12–13
K. Gerstner: *Kalte Kunst* (Teufen, 1957)
J. Albers: *The Interaction of Color* (New Haven and London, 1963)
G. Mathieu: *Au-delà du tachisme* (Paris, 1963)
——: *Le Privilège d'être* (Paris, 1963)
'Conversation with A. Caro, K. Noland and J. Olitski', *Monad* (Jan 1964), pp. 18–22 [interview with D. Thompson]
'Questions to Stella and Judd', *ARTnews* [New York], lxv (1966), no. 5, pp. 55–61 [rev. transcript of original radio broadcast, New York, Feb 1964]
A. Hill, ed.: *Data-directions in Art, Theory and Aesthetics* (London, 1968)
G. Rickey: *Constructivism: Origins and Evolution* (London, 1968)
Art in Progress IV (exh. cat. by R. Ryman, New York, Finch Coll. Mus. A., 1969)
G. Mathieu: *De la révolte à la renaissance* (Paris, 1973)

G. de Vries, ed.: *Über Kunst/On Art: Artists' Writings on the Changed Notion of Art after 1965* (Cologne, 1974)
D. Judd: *Complete Writings, 1959–1975* (Halifax, NS, and New York, 1975)
A. Reinhardt: *Art as Art: The Selected Writings of Ad Reinhardt* (New York, 1975/*R* 1991) [intro. by B. Rose]
Fundamenteele schilderkunst/Fundamental Painting (exh. cat., Amsterdam, Stedel. Mus., 1975) [incl. statements by R. Mangold, B. Marden, A. Martin and R. Ryman, among others]
K. Noland: 'Color, Form and Abstract Art', *A. America*, lxv (1977), pp. 99–105 [interview with Diane Waldman]
N. Holt, ed.: *The Writings of Robert Smithson* (New York, 1979)
M. Poirier and J. Necol: 'The '60s in Abstract', *A. America*, lxxi (1983), no. 3, pp. 122–37 [13 statements and an essay]
P. Halley: *Collected Essays, 1981–1987* (Zurich and New York, 1987)
R. Weil, ed.: 'Talking Abstract', *A. America*, lxxv (1987), no. 7, pp. 80–97; no. 12, pp. 112–29 [interviews with American artists in two parts]
B. Newman: *Selected Writings and Interviews* (New York, 1990)
Collected Writings of Robert Motherwell (Oxford, 1993)

For further writings *see* individual biographies.

EXHIBITION CATALOGUES

Cubism and Abstract Art (exh. cat. by A. Barr, New York, MOMA, 1936)
Le Mouvement (exh. cat. by V. Vasarely, Paris, Gal. Denise René, 1955)
Situation (An Exhibition of British Abstract Painting) (exh. cat. by R. Coleman, London, RBA Gals, 1960)
American Abstract Expressionists and Imagists (exh. cat. by H. H. Arnason, New York, Guggenheim, 1961)
Toward a New Abstraction (exh. cat. by B. Heller, New York, Jew. Mus., 1963)
Post-painterly Abstraction (exh. cat. by C. Greenberg, Los Angeles, CA, Co. Mus. A., 1964)
The New Generation: 1965 (exh. cat., preface B. Robertson, intro. and notes I. Dunlop; London, Whitechapel A.G., 1965)
Primary Structures: Younger American and British Sculptors (exh. cat. by K. McShine, New York, Jew. Mus., 1966)
Systemic Painting (exh. cat. by L. Alloway, New York, Guggenheim, 1966)
Geometric Abstraction, 1926–1942 (exh. cat. by M. Seuphor and J. Elderfield, Dallas, TX, Mus. F.A., 1972)
Robert Ryman (exh. cat., London, Whitechapel A.G., 1977)
Abstraction–Création, 1931–1936 (exh. cat., Paris, Mus. A. Mod. Ville Paris; Münster, Westfäl. Landesmus.; 1978)
Origini dell'astrattismo: Verso altri orizzonti del reale (exh. cat. by G. Ballo and others, Milan, Pal. Reale, 1979)
Abstraction: Towards a New Art, Painting, 1910–1920 (exh. cat., London, Tate, 1980)
Arte astratta italiana, 1909–1959 (exh. cat., Rome, G.N.A. Mod., 1980)
The Avant-garde in Russia, 1910–1930: New Perspectives (exh. cat. by S. Barron and M. Tuchman, Los Angeles, CA, Co. Mus. A., 1980)
Brice Marden (exh. cat., London, Whitechapel A.G., 1981)
Abstract Painting and Sculpture in America, 1927–1944 (exh. cat., Pittsburgh, PA, Carnegie Inst., 1983)
Beyond the Plane: American Constructions, 1930–1965 (exh. cat., Trenton, NJ State Mus., 1983)
Kosmische Bilder in der Kunst des 20. Jahrhunderts (exh. cat., ed. S. Holsten; Baden-Baden, Staatl. Ksthalle, 1983)
Action Precision: The New Direction in New York, 1955–60 (exh. cat. by R. Rosenblum and others, Newport Beach, CA, Harbor A. Mus., 1984)
Carte Blanche to Denise René: Geometric and Kinetic Adventure (exh. cat. by A. Glibota and others, Paris, A. Cent., 1984)
Os grandes mestres do abstracionismo brasileiro (exh. cat. by M. R. Rathsam and A. F. Beuttenmuler, São Paulo, Sociedade de Amigos dos Museus do Brasil, [1984–5])
Contrasts of Form: Geometric Abstract Art, 1910–1980 (exh. cat. by M. Dabrowski, New York, MOMA, 1985)
Abstraction Abstraction (exh. cat. by E. A. King and D. Carrier, Pittsburgh, PA, Carnegie–Mellon U.A.G., 1986)
Arte astratta nelle Marche, 1935–1985 (exh. cat. by C. Melloni, Ascoli Piceno, Pin. Civ., 1986)
Konstruktion und Geste: Schweizer Kunst der 50er Jahre (exh. cat. by W. Rotzler and H. Walter-Dressler, Karlsruhe, Städt. Gal. Prinz-Max-Pal., 1986)
Neo-geometry (exh. cat., Munich, Kstver., 1986)
Nuove geometrie (exh. cat. by F. Caroli, Milan, Rotunda Besana, 1986)
The Spiritual in Art: Abstract Painting, 1890–1935 (exh. cat., Los Angeles, CA, Co. Mus. A., 1986)
L'Art en Europe: Les Années décisives, 1945–1953 (exh. cat., Saint-Etienne, Mus. A. Mod., 1987)
New York Art Now: The Saatchi Collection (exh. cat. by D. Cameron, London, Saatchi Col., 1987)
Astratta: Secessioni astratte in Italia dal dopoguerra al 1990 (exh. cat., Verona, Pal. Forti, 1988)
The Image of Abstraction (exh. cat. by K. Brougher, Los Angeles, CA, Co. Mus. A., 1988)
The Presence of Painting: Aspects of British Abstraction, 1957–1988 (exh. cat. by M. Tooby, Sheffield, Mappin A. G., and elsewhere; 1988)
Contemporary Perspectives I: Abstraction in Question (exh. cat. by R. Smith, J. Simm and W. Ferguson, Sarasota, FL, Ringling Mus. A., 1989)
Espagne arte abstracto, 1950–1965 (exh. cat. by J. M. Bonet, Paris, Artcurial, 1989)
The New Sculpture, 1965–75: Between Geometry and Gesture (exh. cat., ed. R. Armstrong and R. Marshall; New York, Whitney, 1990)
Paris 1930: Arte abstracto, arte concreto, Cercle et Carré (exh. cat. by G. Fabré and R. Stanislowski, Valencia, IVAM Cent. Julio González, 1990)
Aparición de lo invisibile: Pintura abstracta contemporánea en Mexico (exh. cat. by M. A. Alamilla and others, Mexico City, Mus. A. Mod., 1991)
Wille zur Form ungegenständliche Kunst, 1910–1938 in Österreich, Polen, Tschechoslowakei und Ungarn (exh. cat., Vienna, Messepalast, 1993)

GENERAL

W. Worringer: *Abstraktion und Einfühlung* (Munich, 1908; Eng. trans., London, 1948)
J. L. Martin, B. Nicholson and N. Gabo, eds: *Circle: International Survey of Constructive Art* (London, 1937)
S. Janis: *Abstract and Surrealist Art in America* (New York, 1944)
C. Estienne: *L'Art abstrait, est-il un académisme?* (Paris, 1950)
M. Seuphor: *L'Art abstrait, ses origines, ses premiers maîtres* (Paris, 1950)
T. B. Hess: *Abstract Painting: Background and American Phase* (New York, 1951)
H. Rosenberg: 'The American Action Painters', *ARTnews*, li/8 (1952), pp. 22–3, 48–50
M. Tapié: *Un Art autre, où il s'agit de nouveau d'évidages du réel* (Paris, 1952)
A. Heath: *Abstract Painting, its Origins and Meaning* (London, 1953)
M. Seuphor: *Dictionnaire de la peinture abstraite* (Paris, 1957)
P. Soulages: *Au-delà de l'informel* (Paris, 1959)
C. Greenberg: *Art and Culture* (Boston, MA, 1961)
J. MacTruitt: 'Art Arid, DC, Harbor's Touted "New" Painters', *Washington Post* (21 Dec 1961), p. 20
R. Rosenblum: 'The Abstract Sublime', *ARTnews*, lix/10 (1961), pp. 38–41, 56, 58
C. Gray: *The Russian Experiment in Art, 1863–1922* (London, 1962, rev. 1986)
C. Greenberg: 'After Abstract Expressionism', *A. Int.*, vi/8 (1962), pp. 24–32
J. Paulhan: *L'Art informel* (Paris, 1962)
D. Vallier: *L'Art abstrait* (Paris, 1967)
G. Battcock, ed.: *Minimal Art: A Critical Anthology* (New York, 1968)
G. Celant, ed.: *Arte Povera, Conceptual, Actual or Impossible Art?* (London and Milan, 1969)
S. Ringbom: *The Sounding Cosmos: A Study of the Spiritualism of Kandinsky and the Genesis of Abstract Painting* (Åbo, 1970)
I. Sandler: *The Triumph of American Painting: A History of Abstract Expressionism* (New York, 1970); repr. as *Abstract Expressionism: The Triumph of American Painting* (London, 1970)
M. Tuchman: *The New York School: Abstract Expressionism in the '40s and '50s* (London, [1970])
J. Leymarie and others: *Abstract Art since 1945* (London, 1971)
M. Ragon and M. Seuphor: *L'Art abstrait*, 4 vols (Paris, 1971–4)
C. Blok: *Geschichte der abstrakten Kunst, 1900–1960* (Cologne, 1975)
G. Levin: *Synchromism and American Color Abstraction, 1910–1925* (New York, 1978)
H. Osborne: *Abstraction and Artifice in Twentieth-century Art* (Oxford, 1979)
Towards a New Art: Essays on the Background to Abstract Art, 1910–20, preface M. Compton (London, 1980)
J. Gallego: *Arte abstracto español en la colección de la Fundación Juan March* (Madrid, 1983)
L. D. Henderson: *The Fourth Dimension and Non-Euclidean Geometry in Modern Art* (Princeton, 1983)
C. Lodder: *Russian Constructivism* (New Haven and London, 1983)

R. Pincus-Witten: *Entries (Maximilism): Art at the Turn of the Decade* (New York, 1983); rev. as *Postminimalism into Maximilism: American Art, 1966–1986* (Ann Arbor, 1987)
A. B. Nakov: *Abstrait/Concret: Art non-objectif russe et polonais* (Paris, 1984)
M. A. Prat: *L'Abstraction en France, 1919–1939* (Paris, 1984)
D. Vallier: *L'arte astratta* (Milan, 1984)
R. Krauss: *The Originality of the Avantgarede and other Modernist Myths* (Cambridge, MA, and London, 1986)
J. O'Brian: *The Collected Essays and Criticism*, 4 vols (Chicago and London, 1986, rev. 1993) [Clement Greenberg]
M. Ragon: *25 ans d'art vivant: Chronique vécue de l'art contemporain de l'abstraction au Pop art, 1944–1969* (Paris, 1986)
F. Whitford: *Understanding Abstract Art* (London, 1987)
D. J. Clarke: *The Influence of Oriental Thought on Postwar American Painting and Sculpture* (New York and London, 1988)
J. L. Duval: *Histoire de la peinture abstraite* (Paris, 1988; Eng. trans., London, 1989)
D. Kuspit and others: *Abstrakte Malerei aus Amerika und Europa/ Abstract Painting from America and Europe* (Vienna, 1988)
M. Pleynet and M. Ragon: *Art abstrait, 1970–1987* (Paris, 1988)
M. Auping: *Abstraction, Geometry, Painting: Selected Geometric Abstract Painting in America since 1945* (New York, 1989)
D. Anfam: *Abstract Expressionism* (London, 1990)
Y. A. Bois: *Painting as Model* (New Haven, 1990)
G. Boudaille and P. Javault: *L'Art abstrait* (Paris, 1990)
A. E. Gibson: *Issues in Abstract Expressionism: The Artist-run Periodicals* (Ann Arbor and London, 1990)
S. Guilbaut, ed.: *Reconstructing Modernism: Art in New York, Paris and Montreal, 1945–1964* (Cambridge, MA, and London, 1990) [esp. essay by T. de Duve]
A. Moszynska: *Abstract Art* (London, 1990)
R. Paulson: *Figure and Abstraction in Contemporary Painting* (New Brunswick, 1990)
D. Shapiro: *Abstract Expressionism: A Critical Record* (Cambridge, 1990)
A. C. Chave: 'Minimalism and the Rhetoric of Power', *Power: Its Myths and Mores* (exh. cat., Indianapolis, IN, Mus. A., 1991)
M. Cheetham: *The Rhetoric of Purity: Essentialist Theory and the Advent of Abstract Painting* (Cambridge, 1991)
C. Millet: *Conversations avec Denise René* (Paris, 1991)
S. Polcari: *Abstract Expressionism and the Modern Experience* (Cambridge, 1991)
U. Ruberti: *Il post-informale in Europa* (Rome, 1991)
D. Leclerc and M. H. Barclay: *The Crisis of Abstraction in Canada: The 1950s* (Ottawa, 1992)
M. Ragon: *Journal de l'art abstrait* (Geneva, 1992)
C. Harrison, F. Frascina and G. Perry: *Primitivism, Cubism, Abstraction: The Early Twentieth Century* (New Haven and London, 1993)
E. Strickland: *Minimalism: Origins* (Indianapolis, 1993)
A. Kagan: *Absolute Art* (St Louis, 1995)

ANNA MOSZYNSKA

Abstract Expressionism. Term applied to a movement in American painting that flourished in the 1940s and 1950s, sometimes referred to as the New York School or, very narrowly, as ACTION PAINTING, although it was first coined in relation to the work of Vasily Kandinsky in 1929. The works of the generation of artists active in New York from the 1940s and regarded as Abstract Expressionists resist definition as a cohesive style; they range from Barnett Newman's unbroken fields of colour to Willem de Kooning's violent handling of the figure. They were linked by a concern with varying degrees of abstraction used to convey strong emotional or expressive content. Although the term primarily denotes a small nucleus of painters, Abstract Expressionist qualities can also be seen in the sculpture of David Smith, Ibram Lassaw and others, the photography of Aaron Siskind and the painting of Mark Tobey, as well as in the work of less renowned artists such as Bradley Walker Tomlin and Lee Krasner. However, the majority of Abstract Expressionists rejected critical labels and shared, if anything, only a common sense of moral purpose and alienation from American society. Abstract Expressionism has nonetheless been interpreted as an especially 'American' style because of its attention to the physical immediacy of paint; it has also been seen as a continuation of the Romantic tradition of the Sublime. It undeniably became the first American visual art to attain international status and influence.

1. BACKGROUND, ORIGINS AND EARLY PHASE. The roots of Abstract Expressionism lie in the social and artistic climate of the 1920s and early 1930s. Apart from Hans Hofmann, all its major exponents were born between 1903 and 1915 and grew up during a period of American isolationism. Although Europe remained the traditional source of advanced culture, American efforts during the 1920s to develop an aesthetic independence culminated in the direct, homespun realism of Regionalism. Consequently, the development of the art of Willem de Kooning, Arshile Gorky, Jackson Pollock and Clyfford Still, for example, illustrates a complex interaction between tradition, rebellion and the individual talent. European modernism stimulated them deeply, while their desire to retain the impact of personal experience recalled the aims of American Scene painting. Pollock, Still, Smith and Franz Kline were all affected by their native backgrounds in the rural West and in the steel- and coal-producing regions respectively. In other cases Jewish or European origins contributed to an unusual gamut of ethnic, intellectual and private sources of inspiration.

Between the wars New York offered some notable opportunities to assimilate comparatively recent artistic developments. Its galleries included the Museum of Non-objective Art, which housed the impressive Kandinsky collection, and the Museum of Modern Art, which mounted exhibitions throughout the 1930s and 1940s covering many aspects of 20th-century painting.

Much of the creative intellectual ferment of the time was focused in the theories of the Russian émigré painter and writer John Graham who befriended Gorky, Pollock and others. His book *Systems and Dialectics of Art* (1937) justified abstraction as distilling the essence of reality and traced its roots to primitivism, the unconscious and the painter's empathy with the brushstroke. The younger American artists thus seem to have become highly conscious of their historical position and dictates. Most felt that they had to reconcile Cubist spatial organization with the poetic subject-matter of Surrealism and realized that original art would then need to go beyond both.

The development of Arshile Gorky's art from the late 1920s exemplified the cross-currents in the matrix of Abstract Expressionism. He progressively assimilated the main phases of modern European painting in order to explore his own identity until in *The Artist and his Mother* (*c.* 1926–34; New York, Whitney) the private world of Gorky's Armenian origins merged with his contemporary stance as heir to the space and forms of Synthetic Cubism, Picasso and Miró. This mood of transition is especially apparent in technical paradoxes, such as the strange contrasts of carefully finished areas with unresolved passages of paintwork that make this double portrait appear as if it were suspended in a process of change. By the early 1940s this tendency (which can be traced back to Paul Cézanne and to Futurism) provided new means of incorporating the tensions of the artist's immediate circumstances into the actual picture. De Kooning, for example, deliberately allowed successive efforts to capture volume and contour to overtake the stability of his figures, as in *Queen of Hearts* (*c.* 1943; Washington, DC, Hirshhorn); such figures typify one aspect of early Abstract Expressionism in retreating into a dense, ambiguous visual fabric.

At an early stage Pollock, Still and Mark Rothko established a similar polarity between the figure (or other signs of existence) and external forces. The 'realism' of their early landscapes, interiors and urban scenes undoubtedly reflected the emphasis on locale in American Scene painting, but the expressive symbolism was prophetic. A sense of isolation and gloom probably derived in part from the context of the Depression allied with personal factors. They combined highly sensitive, romantic temperaments with left-wing or radical views so that the social circumstances of the period naturally suggested an approach to art that explored the human predicament. This had already been anticipated by some literature of the 1920s and 1930s, notably the novels of William Faulkner (1897–1962), that placed the self against an inimical environment; contemporary American art, however, offered few successful precedents. On the contrary, the weaknesses of depicting human themes literally had already surfaced in Thomas Hart Benton's anecdotal brand of Regionalism that Pollock, a former pupil of Benton, later described as 'something against which to react very strongly'. Despite the wagons, cowboy and mules in Pollock's *Going West* (*c.* 1934–5; Washington, DC, N. Mus. Amer. A.), it remains more elemental than anything by Benton. A feeling of almost cosmic tumult is countered by an overall vortex-like unity.

As Pollock's work became more abstract during the 1930s it nonetheless retained an underlying conflict between impulsive chaos and the need to impose some overall sense of order. Yet the common problem of the 1930s was not just evolving a formal language for what Rothko subsequently termed 'pictures of the human figure—alone in a moment of utter immobility' ('The Romantics were prompted': *Possibilities*, 1, winter 1947–8, p. 84) and other contrasting psychological states; the controversy in the USA focused instead upon the definition and priorities of an authentic avant-garde art.

Several future Abstract Expressionists were employed on the Works Progress Administration's Federal Art Project (WPA/FAP). Alongside the practical benefits of financial support and official endorsement, the WPA/FAP allowed opportunities to experiment with new techniques and to tackle the problems of working on a large scale. It also acted as a catalyst for a more cohesive New York community. But the advocacy of Social Realism on the project alerted many to its academic nature, which Gorky summarized as 'poor art for poor people'. From a visual rather than literary standpoint, the humanitarian imagery of a leading Social Realist such as Ben Shahn seemed as barren as the reactionary equivalents in Regionalism. David Smith's *Medals for Dishonor* series (15 plaster models, 1939; e.g. *No. 9—Bombing Civilian Populations*, ex-artist's priv. col., see G. McCoy, ed.: *David Smith*, New York, 1973, fig. 15) and the early paintings of Philip Guston not only engaged anti-Fascist ideas but also revealed a legacy of the radicalism of the 1930s that was never abandoned, despite largely unfounded claims that later the movement was on the whole 'de-politicized'. Smith and Guston, rather, subsequently sought to show how their respective media could signify and not merely illustrate their beliefs about freedom, aggression and constraint. Similarly, Pollock drew almost nothing from the overt Socialism of the Mexican José Clemente Orozco's murals but a great deal from their capacity to embody human strife in the objective pictorial terms of rhythm and surface pattern.

Another alternative in the 1930s was the tradition of 'pure' abstraction, stemming from Piet Mondrian and upheld by the AMERICAN ABSTRACT ARTISTS group (AAA) to which Ad Reinhardt belonged. Reinhardt's eventual divergence from mainstream Abstract Expressionism can be traced to this initial assumption that the liberating potential of non-objective and specifically geometric art lay in its very independence from the social sphere. A more moderate approach was adopted by the painters Hans Hofmann and Milton Avery. Hofmann, born in Bavaria in 1880, provided a link with an earlier phase of European modernism and, through his own school, which he founded in New York in 1934, taught the synthesis of Cubist structure (emphasizing the unity of the picture plane) with the brilliant colours of Fauvism. Avery's more lyrical approach suffused a simple, flat handling of space with light and atmosphere. This inspired Rothko and Adolph Gottlieb, with its Matisse-like balance between observation and the artist's feelings. Moreover, the growing popularity among an emergent New York avant-garde of theories originated by Leon Trotsky tended to discourage strict orthodoxy by stressing the autonomy of art over social and political restrictions. Out of this amalgam of diverse sources and beginnings, Abstract Expressionism during the 1940s sought to integrate the inner world of emotions with the realities of the picture-making process.

2. THE 1940S: PATHS TO ABSTRACTION. The exhibition *Fantastic Art, Dada, Surrealism* (1936–7; New York, MOMA) heralded a phase when Surrealism and its affinities changed the course of American painting. Furthermore, the arrival of several leading European Surrealists including André Breton, André Masson and Max Ernst in the USA after the outbreak of World War II allowed stimulating personal contacts, Robert Motherwell being one of the first to benefit in this way. This brought an international note to the art scene and reinforced a sense of historical moment: the hegemony of the Ecole de Paris had shifted to New York. As the war continued it also seemed that new subject-matter and accompanying techniques were necessary to confront what was perceived as the tragic and chaotic zeitgeist. Surrealism had partly satisfied such needs by unleashing the disruptive forces of the unconscious, but its tendency towards pure fantasy now appeared irrelevant. In a statement made in 1943 in the *New York Times* (13 June, p. 9), Rothko and Gottlieb declared the new gravity of intent: 'There is no such thing as good painting about nothing. We assert that the subject

is crucial and only that subject-matter is valid which is tragic and timeless.'

The pursuit of universal themes continued Surrealist artists' fascination with the omnipotent force of sexuality and explained much apparently Freudian imagery in paintings of the earlier 1940s. Erotic motifs occur in Gorky's *The Liver is the Cock's Comb* (1944; Buffalo, NY, Albright–Knox A.G.). Interpenetrating or phallic elements characterized Smith's sculptures at times, as well as the paintings of Pollock, Rothko, Still and Theodoros Stamos; the living figure in Motherwell's *Pancho Villa Dead and Alive* (1943; New York, MOMA) is distinguished by his genitalia. Such inconography in fact derived less from Freud than from a more universal symbolism invoking regeneration, fertility and primitive impulses. These themes in twin stemmed from the Abstract Expressionist's overriding concern with subjectivity. To this end the Surrealist use of biomorphism, a formal language of organic curves and similar motifs, was variously exploited. For Gorky it evolved into a metamorphic realm where tendrils, spikes and softer masses referred simultaneously to nature and to human anatomy. Pollock's version was less specific, and in *Pasiphaë* (1943; New York, Met.) it implied womb-like enclosure versus whirling activity. Even de Kooning, the least sympathetic towards Surrealism, reiterated organic contours in his claustrophobic canvases of the mid-1940s as reminders of a strong yet cryptic eroticism. Thus biomorphism served to bridge the figurative modes of the 1940s with a manifold path to abstraction.

Another catalyst in the 1940s was a preoccupation with the concept of myth, especially as interpreted by the Swiss psychologist Carl Gustav Jung, whose writings had gradually gained an American readership. According to Jung, myths gave universal form to basic human truths and related to a profound level of experience that he identified as the 'collective unconscious'. These theories helped several Abstract Expressionists attain more reductive styles because myth, Jung claimed, had a dramatic simplicity expressed through 'archetypes', that is, primal figures and symbols. Primitive art often dealt with myth and became a secondary source at this stage, particularly in the aftermath of exhibitions at the Museum of Modern Art in New York, ranging from prehistoric rock pictures in Europe and Africa (1937) to American Indian art (1941). The totem was a frequently used primitive motif, aptly fitted to personify the Jungian archetype in the guise of a mysterious, upright entity. In Pollock's *Guardians of the Secret* (1943; San Francisco, CA, MOMA) sentinels at either side of the picture seem to guard a central maze of lines and markings that suggests the chaotic recesses of the collective unconscious. Similarly, Still, Smith and others turned the totem into a visual cipher halfway between a figure and a non-representational emblem.

The great potential of the abstract sign soon became clear: it embodied a kind of terse pictorial shorthand, provocative in itself or, rather like individual script, imbued with the physical impetus of its creator. In 1941 Gottlieb began a series known collectively as *Pictographs* (e.g. *Voyager's Return*, 1946; New York, MOMA). Enigmatic details, including body parts and geometric motifs, were set within a rough gridwork that recalled an archaic sign system or petroglyph. By 1947 Rothko, Stamos and others had created sparse schematic images marked by a shallow, post-Cubist space, and defined in the *Ideographic Picture* exhibition, organized by Barnett Newman for the Betty Parsons Gallery, New York, in 1947, as 'a symbol or character painted, written or inscribed representing ideas'.

Newman's own works of this period reflected the theory that abstraction could convey awesome meanings. Their breakthrough was analogous to that in Aaron Siskind's contemporary photographs, such as *Iron Work I* (1947; see C. Chiarenza: *Aaron Siskind: Pleasures and Terrors*, Boston, 1982, fig. 77), which gained impact from a calculated ambiguity. Their syntax of vertical elements, quivering edges and voids retained the dramatic aura associated with figuration but no longer conformed to either a biomorphic style or to the geometry of Mondrian. Rothko's paintings also progressed in a similar direction already anticipated in 1943 when he wrote, 'We favor the simple expression of the complex thought' (letter to the *New York Times* Art Editor, Edward Alden, 7 June 1943), which was to be achieved through the 'large shape' that could impose its monumentality upon the viewer.

This reduction to essentials had widespread consequences during the 1940s. It shifted attention away from relatively graphic symbolism towards the capacities of colour and space to acquire an absolute intensity, not bound to describe events and forms within the picture but free to embody extremes of light and darkness, enclosure, liberation and so on. The dynamics of the act of painting assumed a central role. Gorky's use of very fluid washes of pigment in 1942, under the influence of the Chilean Surrealist Matta (Echaurren), foreshadowed both tendencies. The resultant veils, billows and liquid runs of colour created an unusually complex space, as in *Water of the Flowery Mill* (1944; New York, Met.) that changed from one area to another with the same spontaneity that had previously been limited to Gorky's organic shapes.

Still, Gottlieb, Stamos and Richard Pousette-Dart pursued a different course in the 1940s by stressing tangible paint layers with heavy or unconventional textures. These methods altered their works from the traditional concept of a discrete easel picture to more palpable images whose presence confronted the actual world of the spectator. Dimensions grew in order to accentuate psychological and physical rapport with the viewer. Inevitably, the search for heightened immediacy, for a charged relationship between surface and viewer, meant that a number of artists would regard the painting as an incarnation of the process—the energy, tensions and gestures—that had created it.

The Surrealist technique AUTOMATISM again unlocked possibilities for incorporating immediacy with a vivid record of manual activity, and the impulses behind it, into the final work. Automatism had supposedly allowed Surrealists like Miró and Masson to paint without full conscious control and so essentially stimulated the discovery of unorthodox forms. In contrast, Abstract Expressionism elevated Automatist procedures into a means of reorganizing the entire composition. Hofmann was among the first to pour and drip paint in the early 1940s in order to achieve increased liveliness, but Pollock took the technique to revolutionary limits. By the mid-1940s he painted with such urgency that the remnants of figures and other symbolic details were almost dismembered and lost within the great arcs and whorls formed by his sweeping gestures, for example *There were Seven in Eight* (1945; New York, MOMA). A climax came in 1947 when the restrictions of brushes and the upright format of the easel picture were abandoned as Pollock took to working directly on the floor, dripping paint either straight from the can or with the aid of an implement such as a stick or a trowel. Consequently, in works of this period an astonishing labyrinth of paint traces expand, oscillate and hurtle back upon themselves resembling, as the artist described it, 'energy and motion made visible'. Pollock had reconciled two long-standing though divergent impulses, an obsession with chaotic force and the desire for order, into the vibrant unity of a field, for example *Number 2, 1949* (Utica, NY, Munson–Williams–Proctor Inst.; see fig. 1).

This synthesis was unique at the time, but Abstract Expressionist painting in the late 1940s generally approached a threshold where restlessness and flux predominated. The composition dissolved into a seething field of fragments dispersed with almost equal intensity throughout the picture, hence the term 'all-over' was sometimes used to describe this tendency. A type of space evolved that was dense and unstable beyond even that of Analytical Cubism, as in de Kooning's *Painting* (1948; New York, MOMA). This probably owed something to the doubt-ridden anxieties of the post-war years and perhaps the pressures of fast-moving urban life. It certainly also stemmed from the consequences of Automatism, which took even less overtly Abstract Expressionist painters like Reinhardt and Tobey to the stage where a teeming, calligraphic field of brushstrokes predominated. By the end of the decade the need to reassert meaningful content in unprecedented ways had again become imperative.

3. THE 1950S: CLIMAX, REACTION AND LATER WORK. Newman's essay 'The Sublime is Now', published in the *Tiger's Eye* (i/6, 1948), called for a new art stripped to its formal essentials that still dealt with 'absolute emotions'. He concluded, 'The image we produce is the self-evident one of revelation, real and concrete.' Within two years Newman, Rothko and Still fulfilled these aims, primarily through a total concentration on colour, a pictorial element loaded with dramatic connotations, simultaneously palpable and metaphysical insofar as its total effect transcends analysis. The deep redness of Newman's *Onement I* (1948; New York, MOMA) no longer describes forms since it comprises an absolute continuum, punctuated, though not broken, by a central vertical band of a brighter hue. Encompassing fields of colour tended to minimize internal pictorial relations and so invite the onlooker's participation, especially when enlarged to the mural scale sometimes adopted in the early 1950s. Small incidents acquired an uncanny prominence; the luminous rifts that escaped from Still's essays in black or the slight haloes around Rothko's rectangles implied the numinous behind the apparently monolithic façades. By 'telling little', as Rothko described it in 1958, these works in fact managed to express more.

COLOUR FIELD PAINTING was championed, using narrow stylistic criteria, by the critic Clement Greenberg as a breakthrough in modernist painting's attitude to space because it superseded the shallow figure-ground relationships found in Cubism. Another interpretation has concentrated upon its elemental conflicts of light and scale, and of void and presence, as extending the Romantic tradition of the Sublime with its predilection for epic revelations. Both readings are valid but overlook the fact that the artists had essentially lifted the symbolic extremes and states of consciousness depicted in their earlier works on to an abstract plane. Moreover, the primal field of colour, accentuating the viewer's isolation and sense of self, may equally have reflected a need for strong emotional experience in the barrenness of the Cold War during the late 1940s and the 1950s in the USA. Indeed its imagery was not confined to Abstract Expressionist painting and recurred in the photographs of Siskind and Harry Callahan as well as in the expanses of space that engulfed the solitary figures painted by Ben Shahn and Andrew Wyeth.

In 1950 de Kooning abruptly abandoned his increasingly hermetic all-over compositions, such as *Excavation* (1950; Chicago, IL, A. Inst.; see fig. 2), to begin a number of female subjects, the first being *Woman I* (1950–52; New York, MOMA). Paradoxically, this return to the figure vied with de Kooning's painting style, where the furious tumult of brushstrokes seemed to possess independence and velocity. The poet and critic Harold Rosenberg traced similarities in the work of Pollock, de Kooning and Franz Kline, who had begun black-and-white abstractions *c.* 1949 that aggrandize the individual brushstroke into enormous vectors appearing to continue beyond the picture's edges (for illustration *see* KLINE, FRANZ). Rosenberg had assimilated the existentialism popular among the New York intelligentsia of the late 1940s and claimed that this art represented the physical traces of its creator's spontaneous working methods. He characterized it as Action painting. Subsequent histories have tended to maintain the consequent division into 'action' or 'gestural' styles and 'colour field painting', although these rather

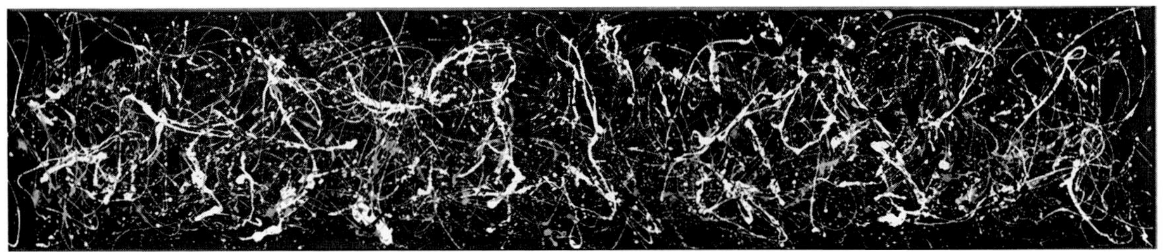

1. Jackson Pollock: *Number 2, 1949*, oil, duco and aluminium paint on unsized canvas, 375×1950 mm (Utica, NY, Munson–Williams–Proctor Institute)

2. Willem de Kooning: *Excavation*, oil and enamel on canvas, 2.03×2.54 m, 1950 (Chicago, IL, Art Institute of Chicago)

simplistic critical categories were disowned by the artists and overrode many subtle connections.

Newman's *Onement* paintings (which date from *c.* 1948 to 1953) and de Kooning's *Woman* paintings, a theme to which he repeatedly returned, stand at opposite poles of technique and mood, ranging from the exalted to the grotesque. Both nonetheless juxtapose a centralized presence against an ambience, whether of colour or urban chaos. Still's *1957-D-No1* (1957; Buffalo, NY, Albright–Knox A.G.; for illustration *see* STILL, CLYFFORD) further demonstrates the shortcomings of critical categories by conferring the graphic contours and energy associated with gestural painting upon grandiose and otherwise almost homogeneous walls of pigment. Alongside Pollock's 'drip' paintings and the large, linear steel sculptures by Smith of the late 1940s onwards, it established a radical type of Abstract Expressionist work where any static or conventional background ceased to exist and all parts interacted as if galvanized into a network of forces. The viewer's perceptual process had to integrate the pictorial incidents actively, the far-flung extremes of scale, colour and focus and, in Smith's sculptures, the great disparities when seen from different viewpoints. This meant that they had a 'life' beyond what was contained in any one aspect. The dynamic encounter between the work and its audience became a hallmark of Abstract Expressionism.

National recognition increased during the 1950s. The role of dealers, critics and institutions such as the Museum of Modern Art, New York, in this development encouraged the theory that the movement was promoted at home and abroad as a weapon of Cold War ideology to stress the USA's superior freedom of expression. While the claim may be just, the artists themselves were not actively responsible. In fact several challenged such control by avoiding contact with the art establishment or taking their work to conclusions that almost defied critical commentary, such as the progression towards hypnotic monochrome painting by Reinhardt and Rothko in the 1960s.

While Abstract Expressionism's intensity depended partly on its very stylistic terseness, as in Newman's work, or singularity, as in Pollock's, its latter phases tended to pivot around a search to avoid defined limits or to extract the greatest range of meanings from a strictly limited idiom. The notion of working in series allowed nuances and variations to register most forcefully against a fairly constant visual syntax: Newman's group of 14 paintings, *Stations of the Cross* (1958–66; *see* NEWMAN, BARNETT, fig. 1), or Smith's *Cubi* series (1961–5) show a creative impulse transcending the parameters of a single act. Themes and images from the 1940s also returned on a grandiose scale. Thus Gottlieb's *Bursts* (which he painted from 1957) refashioned pictograph symbols into newfound explosive gestures and calmer fields of colour. It was Pollock's last period, however, that encapsulated the movement's overall dilemma. At best he summoned earlier mythic imagery, through methods such as black paint soaked into bare canvas in the remarkable, nightmarish compositions of 1951 and 1952. More often the sheer fusion of audacity and control attained in the 'drip' paintings pre-empted further innovation, and Pollock's death in 1956 reinforced suspicions that a vanguard was now in decline.

In this later phase a community of younger artists emerged to adopt the tenets of spontaneity, improvisation and the importance of process. They included the painters Helen Frankenthaler and Joan Mitchell, poet Frank O'Hara (1926–66) and the sculptors associated with assemblage. However, they replaced the basic urgency and existential vision of their models with a more lyrical and relatively decorative stance, (that could indeed suggest a feminist revision of 'masculine' premises), characterized for example by Frankenthaler's *Mountains and Sea* (1952; artist's col., on loan to Washington, DC, N.G.A.; for illustration *see* FRANKENTHALER, HELEN). By then Abstract Expressionism had nonetheless transformed the fundamentals of painting and sculpture in the mid-20th century, and its influence in terms of style and aesthetics extended over a vast spectrum of subsequent art.

BIBLIOGRAPHY

C. Greenberg: *Art and Culture* (Boston, 1961)
H. Rosenberg: *The Tradition of the New* (New York, 1961)
Artforum, iv/1 (1965) [issue ded. to Abstract Expressionism]
M. Tuchman, ed.: *New York School* (Greenwich, NY, 1965)
B. Rose: *Readings in American Art Since 1900* (New York, 1968)
W. Rubin: *Dada and Surrealist Art* (London, 1969), pp. 342–410
I. Sandler: *The Triumph of American Painting: A History of Abstract Expressionism* (New York, 1970)
D. Ashton: *The Life and Times of the New York School* (Bath, 1972)
S. Hunter: *American Art of the Twentieth Century* (New York, 1972)
C. Harrison: 'Abstract Expressionism', *Concepts of Modern Art* (London, 1974/1988, ed. N. Stangos), pp. 169–211
W. Andersen: *American Sculpture in Process: 1930–1970* (Boston, MA, 1975)
R. Rosenblum: *Modern Painting and the Northern Romantic Tradition* (London, 1975)
K. McShine, ed.: *The Natural Paradise* (New York, 1976)
J. Wechsler: *Surrealism and American Painting* (New Brunswick, 1977)
E. Carmean jr: *The Subjects of the Artist* (Washington, DC, 1978)
R. Hobbs and G. Levin: *Abstract Expressionism, the Formative Years* (New York, 1978)
I. Sandler: *The New York School* (New York, 1978)
B. Rose: *American Painting* (London, 1980)
A. Cox: *Art-as-politics: The Abstract Expressionist Avant-garde and Society* (Ann Arbor, 1982)
S. Guilbaut: *How New York Stole the Idea of Modern Art* (Chicago, 1983)
W. Seitz: *Abstract Expressionist Painting in America* (Cambridge, MA, 1983)
M. Baigell: *A Concise History of American Painting and Sculpture* (New York, 1984)
P. Turner, ed.: *American Images: Photography, 1945–80* (London, 1985)
M. Auping, ed.: *Abstract Expressionism: The Critical Developments* (New York, 1987)
D. Shapiro and C. Shapiro, eds: *Abstract Expressionism: A Critical Record* (Cambridge, 1989)
D. Anfam: *Abstract Expressionism* (London, 1990)
C. Ross: *Abstract Expressionism: Creators and Critics* (New York, 1990)
S. Polcari: *Abstract Expressionism and the Modern Experience*, (Cambridge, 1991)
D. Thistlewood, ed.: *American Abstract Expressionism* (Liverpool, 1993)

DAVID ANFAM

Abstraction. Term used in an art context in several ways: in general for processes of imagemaking in which only some of the visual elements usually ascribed to 'the natural world' are extracted (i.e. 'to abstract'), and also for the description of certain works that fall only partially, if at all, into what is commonly understood to be representational. Differing ideas and manifestations of abstraction appeared in artists' works in the successive modern movements of the 20th century (*see* ABSTRACT ART). As the notion of abstraction in the second sense is always dependent on what the parameters of representation are thought to be, the two terms can be contiguous in definition, raising interesting points for the general theory of reference. For instance, an abstract work is often defined as one that does not represent anything, but not every work that does not represent anything is necessarily abstract. A painting that has a fictitious subject, for example a painting of Don Quixote or Camelot, does not represent anything (for there is no such person or place) but is not therefore abstract. A Zeus-picture or a Paradise-picture is no more abstract than a Napoleon-picture or a Paris-picture. An abstract work neither represents anything nor is representational.

This runs close to paradox. Does it amount to saying that an abstract picture pictures nothing and indeed is not a picture? It is perhaps better to speak of works rather than pictures. Still, to say that a work is abstract if it is non-representational does not hold in general. Most architectural and musical works are non-representational, yet are not thereby classed as abstract. Something is missing in the equation of 'abstract' with 'non-representational'.

What is missing in such qualifications is that 'abstract' as applied to works of art is not a merely passive negative characterization, but has a further privative force. A non-representational painting is abstract in that it lacks a certain function or feature that is usual for and expected of paintings in general, while representationality (or more generally, denotationality) is not usual in or expected of architectural or musical works, and its absence in such a work does not constitute a lack or deprivation, or the classification of the work as abstract. Likewise, while it seems feasible to call a fish without fins 'finless', and a dog that doesn't bark 'barkless', it would seem odd to call fish 'barkless' or dogs 'finless', or birds and horses either 'finless' or 'barkless'. In spirited discussion among artists and critics, abstraction, that is, absence of representation, is sometimes presented in a more positive light—not as a lack or deprivation but as a purification. Not only does representation, incessantly before us in practical and commercial contexts on postcards, billboards and screens, come to be disparaged as having little or no aesthetic import, but furthermore, the argument runs, representation relates a work to something outside it, whereas an abstract work keeps entirely to itself with no distraction or detraction from its own functions and features.

It still remains, however, that abstraction, whether deprivation or purification, is a matter of what a work does not do or what features it does not have. To say that a work is abstract is to say only that it does not represent and is not even representational, so 'Abstract' is often combined with another term that indicates a primary function or feature of a work, as for example in 'Abstract

Expressionist'. Other combinations may be contemplated, such as 'abstract allusionist'. 'Abstract representational' would, of course, be self-cancelling, and, strictly, so would 'abstract portrait' and 'abstract landscape'. These latter terms, however, can be regarded as indicating that representation, though not altogether absent from the work, is subordinated to other symbolic functions such as exemplification, expression or allusion.

Since an abstract work is one without representation, or more generally denotation, the question naturally arises what an abstract verbal or linguistic work may be, a text that says nothing, a story that does not tell a story, a poem that does not speak of anything. Like a picture that does not picture, these works are deprived of a normal denotative function and refer directly by showing rather than saying, as by exemplifying patterns or expressing feelings. A curious anomaly arises here. Through the ambiguity in the use of 'abstract', extreme cases of this kind, such as a page of miscellaneous and irregularly distributed words, are sometimes called not 'abstract' but 'concrete'! For example, in CONCRETE POETRY, 'concrete' is used as opposed not to 'abstract' as 'non-representational' but to 'abstract' as 'repeatable' or 'universal'. For a normal denotative text, whatever is spelt the same way in the same language, regardless of differences in fount, hand, size, colour etc, is another instance of the same work. On the other hand, a Concrete poem, an alphabet painting by Jasper Johns or an example of Chinese calligraphy is unrepeatable—the particular concrete object is the functioning symbol. Other objects, even if spelt the same way (where that term is applicable), are not instances of the same work but are different works.

See also REPRESENTATION.

BIBLIOGRAPHY

N. Goodman: *Languages of Art* (Indianapolis, 1968, 2/1976)

C. Z. Elgin: *With Reference to Reference* (Indianapolis, 1983)

N. Goodman: *Of Mind and Other Matters* (Indianapolis, 1984) [esp. chap. 3]

N. Goodman and C. Z. Elgin: *Reconceptions in Philosophy and Other Arts and Sciences* (Cambridge, MA, 1988)

NELSON GOODMAN

Abstraction-Création. International group of painters and sculptors, founded in Paris in February 1931 and active until 1936. It succeeded another short-lived group, CERCLE ET CARRÉ, which had been formed in 1929 with similar intentions of promoting and exhibiting abstract art. Its full official title was Abstraction-Création: Art non-figuratif. The founding committee included AUGUSTE HERBIN (president), Georges Vantongerloo (vice-president), Hans Arp, Albert Gleizes, Jean Hélion, Georges Valmier and František Kupka.

Membership of Abstraction-Création was in principle open to all abstract artists, but the dominant tendency within the group was towards the geometric formality championed by Theo van Doesburg and by other artists

Jean Hélion: *Ile-de-France*, oil on canvas, 1454×2000 m, 1935 (London, Tate Gallery)

associated with De Stijl. Works such as Jean Hélion's *Ile-de-France* (1935; London, Tate; see fig.), which came to typify the group's stance, owed more to the post-war 'rappel à l'ordre' interpreted by the Purists in terms of a 'classic' and 'architectonic' ordering of art, design and architecture, than to the biomorphic abstraction derived from Surrealism. During its brief existence the group published annual *cahiers*. The first issue, edited by Hélion and published in 1932, offered some definitions:

> Non-figuration, that is to say cultivation of pure plasticity, to the exclusion of any explanatory, anecdotal, literary or naturalistic element . . . ; abstraction because certain artists have arrived at the conception of non-figuration through progressive abstraction from the forms of nature; creation because artists have achieved non-figuration directly through a conception of purely geometric order.

Over 40 artist-members, including the members of the committee, were represented by reproductions of their non-figurative works, in some cases with accompanying statements. Among them were Willi Baumeister, Alexander Calder, Robert Delaunay and Sonia Delaunay, Otto Freundlich, Naum Gabo, Jean Gorin, László Moholy-Nagy, Piet Mondrian, Antoine Pevsner, Kurt Schwitters, Henryk Stazewski, Theo van Doesburg, Jacques Villon and Edward Wadsworth. It was acknowledged that the Russian artists El Lissitzky, Malevich and Tatlin were 'unable to join'.

If Abstraction-Création had a dominant theme at the outset, this was the idealist tendency in late Cubism (represented by Gleizes, Hélion and Herbin). To this was added the geometrical tendency of De Stijl, represented by Mondrian, van Doesburg and Vantongerloo, and an émigré version of Constructivism (represented by the expatriates Gabo and Pevsner). A commitment to the rationalization of design went hand in hand with a tendency to spiritualize geometry.

By 1935 the association had 'about 50' members, of whom 32 contributed to the annual *cahier*. In the same year a broader category of 'Members and Friends' numbered 410. A breakdown of these by countries was published in the fourth *cahier*. The majority were resident in France, with 209 based in Paris; Switzerland, the Netherlands, Great Britain, Germany, Poland and Italy and a further 10 countries provided the remaining members. Among those who had joined by this time were Josef Albers, Lucio Fontana, Julio González, Arshile Gorky, Barbara Hepworth, Vasily Kandinsky and Ben Nicholson. From December 1933 an exhibition of members' work was held for about a year at an address on the Avenue de Wagram, Paris.

The diverse members of Abstraction-Création were united by their commitment to the identification of abstract art with liberation. Although the association between aesthetic and political freedom was generally idealistic in character, it gained significance from the suppression of modern artistic practice under various totalitarian governments during the 1930s. The following editorial statement was published in 1933:

> The second issue of *Abstraction-Création* appears at a time when, under all régimes, in some countries more effectively than others, but everywhere, free thought is fiercely opposed. . . . We place this issue under the banner of a total opposition to all oppression, of whatever kind it may be.

The last *cahier* appeared in 1936 after much deliberation. It must by then have been clear to many of the contributors that abstract art was not the means of saving the world from the forces of oppression. During the prelude to World War II, many of those who had gathered in Paris in the late 1920s and early 1930s travelled to the USA in pursuit of security, their migrations partly encouraged by the network of contacts that Abstraction-Création had established.

WRITINGS

Abstraction-Création: Art non-figuratif, 1–5 (1932–6)

BIBLIOGRAPHY

Abstraction-Création, 1931–36 (exh. cat., Paris, Mus. A. Mod. Ville Paris, 1978)

□

Abu (i). *See* MT ABU.

Abu (ii). *See* ASWAN.

Abu ʿAli Muhammad ibn ʿAli ibn Muqla. *See* IBN MUQLA.

Abu Dhabi. *See under* UNITED ARAB EMIRATES.

Abu Ghurab. Site of the ancient Egyptian sun temple of King Neuserre (*reg c.* 2416–*c.* 2392 BC), on the western bank of the Nile north-west of Abusir, almost opposite the southernmost suburbs of modern Cairo. The temple, called Shesepib re ('joy of the sun god Re'), is situated at the edge of the Libyan Desert, in the area of the Memphite necropolis.

Six sun temples were built for the state sun god Re-Horakhty by the kings of the 5th Dynasty, but by the late 20th century only two had so far been located. The sun temple of Neuserre was excavated by Friedrich Wilhelm von Bissing in 1898–1901. Nearly all the reliefs were removed, mostly to German collections, and many perished during World War II. The temple was built mainly of limestone. It consists, from east to west, of the valley temple, causeway and upper temple. This arrangement is similar to that of pyramid complexes and suggests a generally accepted concept of a purpose-built temple during the Old Kingdom. A brick-built bark of the sun god was discovered near by.

The main features of the upper temple (about 110×80 m; see fig.) are an entrance passage; a large court open to the sun with a covered corridor round its three sides; a massive platform on which stood a masonry-built obelisk symbolizing the sun god; a one-room chapel; and the Room of the Seasons connected with an ascending corridor leading on to the obelisk-platform. A large alabaster altar stands in the centre of the court.

The painted raised reliefs (bas-reliefs) are skilfully designed but less carefully executed than those of the 4th and early 5th dynasties. Some of the reliefs show the sun god's beneficent attitude towards the king's reign through episodes of the *sed*-festival (a celebration of the royal jubilee) and represent the most detailed treatment of this theme known from the Old Kingdom. The reliefs from the Room of the Seasons illustrate the sun's life-giving influence in nature. The panorama of Egyptian country

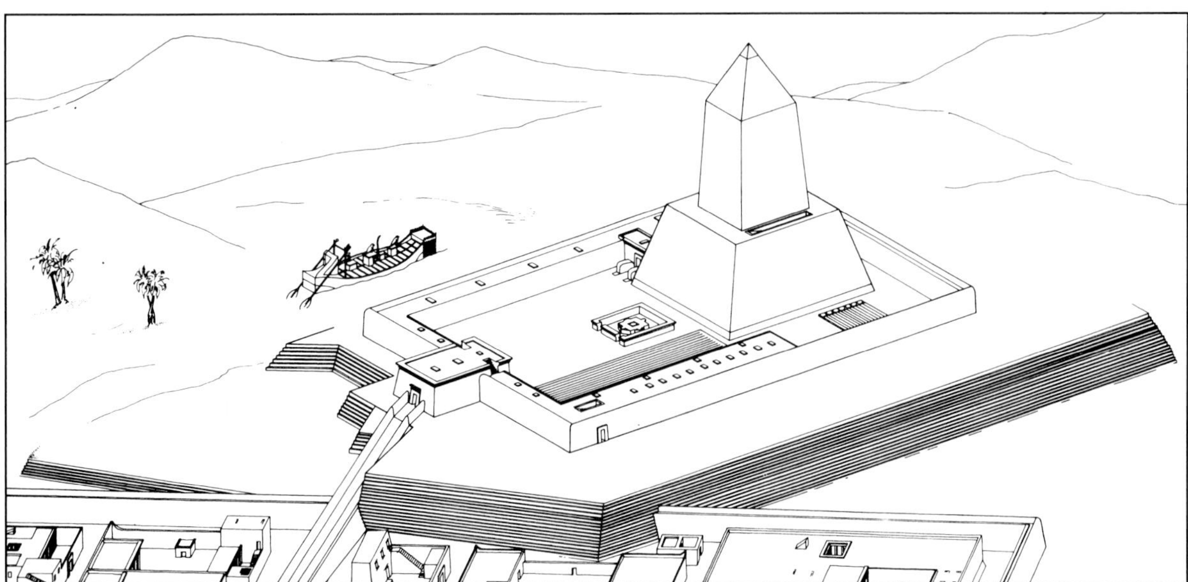

Abu Ghurab, upper temple of the sun temple of King Neuserre (*reg c.* 2416–*c.* 2392 BC); reconstruction drawing

scenes is divided into two periods, *akhet* (inundation, or autumn/winter) and *shemu* (spring/summer). The most characteristic images of animal, bird and plant life are represented, as well as man's typical outdoor activities. This is the earliest extensive corpus of such scenes, accurately observed and realistically portrayed, from Egypt.

BIBLIOGRAPHY

LÄ

F. W. von Bissing, ed.: *Das Re-Heiligtum des Königs Ne-woser-re (Rathures)*, i, L. Borchardt: *Der Bau* (Berlin, 1905); ii, F. W. von Bissing and H. Kees: *Die kleine Festdarstellung* (Leipzig, 1923); iii, H. Kees: *Die grosse Festdarstellung* (Leipzig, 1928)

E. Edel and S. Wenig: *Die Jahreszeitenreliefs aus dem Sonnenheiligtum des Königs Ne-user-re* (Berlin, 1974)

JAROMIR MALEK

Abu Habba. *See* SIPPAR.

Abularach, Rodolfo (*b* Guatemala, 7 Jan 1933). Guatemalan painter and printmaker. From 1954 to 1957 he studied at the Escuela Nacional de Artes Plásticas in Guatemala City while researching folk art for the Dirección de Bellas Artes, but he was virtually self-taught and began as a draughtsman and painter of bullfighting scenes. In 1958 he travelled to New York on a Guatemalan government grant, prolonging his stay there with further grants, studying at the Arts Students League and Graphic Art Center and finally settling there permanently. He was influential in Guatemala until *c.* 1960, but because of his long residence abroad his work did not fit easily in the context of Central American art. Before leaving Guatemala he had painted landscapes and nudes in a naturalistic style, but he soon adopted a more modern idiom partly inspired by aboriginal Guatemalan subjects. After moving to New York, and especially from 1958 to 1961, his art underwent a profound transformation as he sought to bring together elements of abstract art and Surrealism and experimented with textures, for example in cross-hatched pen-and-ink drawings such as *Fugitive from a Maya Lintel* (1958; Washington, DC, MOMA Latin America). Later he simplified his art and turned his attention to light as a substance emanating from within his works. In the 1980s he began to paint large landscapes characterized by a magical symbolism.

BIBLIOGRAPHY

L. Méndez Dávila: *Arte vanguardia Guatemala* (Guatemala City, 1969), pp. vii–viii

R. Cabrera: *Rodolfo Abularach: Artista testimonial* (Guatemala City, 1971)

JORGE LUJÁN MUÑOZ

Abu'l-Hasan (*b* 1588; *fl* 1600–30). Indian painter. In 1618 the Mughal emperor Jahangir (*reg* 1605–27) wrote in his memoirs that Abu'l-Hasan's 'work was perfect...At the present time he has no rival or equal... Truly he has become *Nadir al-Zaman* ("Wonder of the age")'. Some of this artist's paintings are among the greatest in Mughal art. He was born in Jahangir's household in 1588, the son of the erstwhile Safavid artist AQA RIZA (i). Abu'l-Hasan's earliest known work, a drawing based on Albrecht Dürer's *St John* and executed when he was only 12 (Oxford, Ashmolean), already shows in its naturalism the trend of his mature work. A single painting in a manuscript of the fable-book *Anvār-i Suhaylī* ('Lights of Canopus'), probably done in 1604 (London, BL), develops the naturalism of his portraiture but still contains a Safavid landscape based on his father's work; his sense of respect for the latter is indicated by his signing himself here 'the dust of Riza's threshold'. He maintained throughout his career the meticulous finish of the Safavid style.

The most famous painting of his youthful maturity is his *Squirrels in a Plane Tree* (1605-7; London, India Office Lib.), depicting 12 squirrels gambolling in a plane tree while a hunter below tries to climb the trunk. The painting combines his new mastery of volume, shown in the squirrels, the hunter and the tree trunk, with homage to the Safavid masters in the landscape background with its gold sky and mauve hills. The general composition seems to have been based on a page executed by ʿAbd al-Samad in 1555–6 in the *Muraqqaʿ-i gulshan* or Gulshan Album (Tehran, Gulistan Pal. Lib.). This youthful masterpiece seems to have earned Abu'l-Hasan the privilege of being portrayed before 1608 with a select group of other masters on a page by Daulat in the Gulshan Album.

There are few pictures attributable to Abu'l-Hasan between the *Squirrels* and the remarkable group of paintings produced in the ten years after 1615, which shows his powers at their height. Some of these were intended for the *Jahāngīrnāma*, the imperial copy of Jahangir's memoirs. It was Abu'l-Hasan's presentation in 1618 of the *Celebrations at Jahangir's Accession* (St Petersburg, Acad. Sci.) that induced Jahangir to write so fulsomely about his favourite artist. It was also to Abu'l-Hasan that Jahangir turned for pictorial expression of his moods, whether political wish-fulfilment or his preoccupation with the poet Saʿdi's idea of a 'dervish-oriented kingship' in which the king put away from himself the cares of state but came to Paradise because of his love for holy men: the Emperor may have been seduced by Abu'l-Hasan's increasing powers of realism into attributing to these fantasies power to heal what he thought of as his wounded spirit. Two of Abu'l-Hasan's finest paintings illustrate Jahangir's regard for dervishes and increasing contempt for kingship. A double page (one half 1615, the other possibly slightly later; Washington, DC, Freer, and Baltimore, MD, Walters A.G.) shows Jahangir with his sons and surrounded by his chief noblemen, his feet resting on a globe; court officials usher into his presence the long-dead Saʿdi and other mystics while the Ottoman and Persian emperors stand rejected. In another painting (1619; Geneva, Prince Sadruddin Aga Khan priv. col.) Jahangir shows himself to his people at the *jharokā* window in the Agra Fort from which early in his reign he had let down a golden chain hung with bells to be rung by those seeking justice; however, in the painting officials drive suppliants away while the Emperor gazes at a holy man who has taken up residence in a hut below.

Abu'l-Hasan also painted the most important political paintings of Jahangir's reign. In one example (1616–17; Dublin, Chester Beatty Lib.) Jahangir is depicted as an archer standing on a globe shooting an arrow at the severed head of the black Malik ʿAmbar, the general of the Ahmadnagar army. Since Malik ʿAmbar lived until 1626, this painting is pure wish-fulfilment, as is Abu'l-Hasan's painting of 1618–20 showing *Jahangir Embracing Shah ʿAbbas I of Iran* (Washington, DC, Freer; see fig.). This is Abu'l-Hasan's supreme representation of his master and one of the greatest of political pictures. Whereas *Jahangir Shooting the Head of Malik ʿAmbar* is weighed down by symbolism and quotation, the new picture speaks for itself. Ostensibly a representation of the friendship between Jahangir and Shah ʿAbbas, it shows the two rulers standing on a globe on their respective countries; in fact the powerful Jahangir is pushing the deferential figure of Shah ʿAbbas off into the Mediterranean. Jahangir's head is encircled by the sun and moon, a reference to his title of Nur al-Din ('Light of religion'). A later picture (1623; Washington, DC, Freer) adds yet another dimension to imperial iconography: Jahangir, fully armed, stands on top of a segment of the globe in remote, godlike isolation

Abu'l-Hasan: *Jahangir Embracing Shah ʿAbbas I of Iran*, colour and gold on paper, 238×154 mm, *c.* 1618–20 (Washington, DC, Freer Gallery of Art)

from a battle being fought between his forces and those of his rebellious son Shah Jahan (*reg* 1628–58) represented by tiny figures in the vast green plain below.

There is no further evidence of Abu'l-Hasan's work apart from a few accession portraits executed early in the reign of Shah Jahan. As he was so closely identified with Jahangir, he is unlikely to have found much favour with the new ruler. Abu'l-Hasan remained in many respects a deeply conservative artist. Although he consciously adopted European naturalism in portraiture, he refrained from experimenting with expanding the background of his pictures, which are remarkable for their flatness. This seems to have been a conscious decision, since it serves to highlight his powers of realistic portraiture. More than any other Mughal artist, his fame rests on his status as a portrait painter to Jahangir, the portrayer of the Emperor's moods and innermost desires. In this he was unequalled, both in his portrayal of Jahangir's gradual imaginative withdrawal from the world and in the iconographic imagery that accompanied this spiritual progress.

BIBLIOGRAPHY

A. Rogers, trans.: *The Tūzuk-i-Jahāngīrī or Memoirs of Jahāngīr*, ed. H. Beveridge (London, 1909–14)

R. Ettinghausen: 'The Emperor's Choice', *De artibus opuscula XL: Essays in Honor of Erwin Panofsky*, ed. M. Meiss (New York, 1961), pp. 98–107

——: *Paintings of the Sultans and Emperors of India in American Collections* (New Delhi, 1961)
A. K. Das: *Mughal Painting during Jahangir's Time* (Calcutta, 1978)
The Grand Moghul: Imperial Painting in India, 1600–1660 (exh. cat. by M. C. Beach, Williamstown, MA, Clark A. Inst., 1978)
The Imperial Image: Paintings for the Mughal Court (exh. cat. by M. C. Beach, Washington, DC, Freer, 1981)
J. P. Losty: 'Abu' l Hasan', *Master Artists of the Imperial Mughal Court*, ed. P. Pal (Bombay, 1991), pp. 69–86

J. P. LOSTY

Abu'l-Hasan ʿAli ibn Hilal al-bawwab. *See* IBN AL-BAWWAB.

Abu'l-Hasan Ghaffari. *See* GHAFFARI, (2).

Abu'l-Hasan Mustawfi Ghaffari. *See* GHAFFARI, (1).

Abu'l-Qasim [Abū'l-Qāsim] (*fl c.* 1816). Persian painter. His only known work is a long composition depicting the Qajar monarch *Fath ʿAli Shah* (*reg* 1797–1834) entertained by female musicians and dancers. The only surviving fragments of it are a painting of the Shah (London, B. W. Robinson priv. col.) and three paintings of the entertainers (Tehran, Nigaristan Mus., ex-Amery priv. col.). The paintings of a woman playing a drum and of a woman playing a stringed instrument are signed *raqam-i kamtarīn Abū'l-Qāsim* ('painted by the most humble Abu'l-Qasim') and dated 1816, but the third painting showing a woman dancing is half-length and damaged. All the fragments share the same continuous architectural background and scale (a little less than life-size). Robinson has suggested that this mural might be the one described in the mid-19th century by the traveller Robert Binning, who reported that the house he occupied in Shiraz contained a painting of Fath ʿAli Shah seated in state attended by ten women. The composition extended around three sides of the room and the figures were almost life-size. This identification suggests that Abu'l-Qasim might have been a native of Shiraz.

BIBLIOGRAPHY

B. W. Robinson: 'The Court Painters of Fatḥ ʿAlī Shāh', *Eretz-Israel*, vii (1964), pp. 94–105
S. J. Falk: *Qajar Paintings: Persian Oil Paintings of the 18th and 19th Centuries* (London, 1972)
B. W. Robinson: 'The Amery Collection of Persian Oil Paintings', *Stud. Iran.*, i (1972), pp. 43–53
——: 'Persian Painting in the Qajar Period', *Highlights of Persian Art*, ed. R. Ettinghausen and E. Yarshater (Boulder, 1979), pp. 331–62
M. A. Karimzada Tabrizi: *Aḥvāl u āthār-i naqqāshān-i qadīm-i īrān* [The lives and art of old painters of Iran] (London, 1985), no. 66
B. W. Robinson: 'Persian Painting under the Zand and Qājār Dynasties', *From Nadir Shah to the Islamic Republic* (1991), vii of *The Cambridge History of Iran* (Cambridge, 1968–91), pp. 870–90

S. J. VERNOIT

Abu Mina [Abū Mīnā]. Site of a Christian city and pilgrimage centre in the Maryūt Desert, *c.* 45 km south-west of Alexandria, Egypt. It grew up around the shrine of St Menas, who was martyred during the persecution of the Christians instigated by Diocletian (*reg* 285–305). The ancient name of the site is not known, and the position of the saint's grave had been long forgotten until, according to legend, several miracle cures led to its rediscovery. The place then quickly developed into an increasingly major centre of pilgrimage where, among other things, the so-called Menas ampules were manufactured as pilgrim flasks and achieved particular renown. The first excavations of the site were undertaken by Kaufmann in 1905–7. Further excavations have been directed successively by the Coptic Museum in Cairo (1951), Schläger (1963 and 1964), Wolfgang Müller-Wiener (1965–7) and Peter Grossmann (since 1969).

The earliest archaeological remains date to the late 4th century, although the grave itself was in an older hypogeum. The first martyrium basilica erected over the grave dates to the first half of the 5th century and was rapidly enlarged by various reconstructions and extensions. Around the turn of the 5th and 6th centuries, the Great Basilica was added to the east in the form of a transept-basilica, making it the largest church in Egypt (see fig.). Some decades later a small baptistery was replaced by an octagonal baptistery with niches, a dome and a large piscina, suitable for mass baptisms (a).

During the reign of Justinian I (*reg* 528–65), the first basilica was replaced by a double-shell tetraconch church similar to a type current in Syria (*see* EARLY CHRISTIAN AND BYZANTINE ART, §II, 2(i)(d)) but with a slightly elongated east–west axis and with straight outer walls that do not follow the curves of the conches (b). Only the eastern conch, because of its significantly firmer foundation, appears to have had a semi-dome, while the remaining conches were covered by half-vaulted wooden roofs. A bi-apsidal narthex (c) was also constructed between the tetraconch church and the Great Basilica (d).

From the last quarter of the 5th century onwards, the site became a pilgrimage centre. An ecclesiastical district developed around the sanctuary area with colonnaded streets, courtyards and squares, as well as pilgrims' hostels, baths, church administration buildings and storage structures. It was enclosed by a surrounding wall with its own gates. Beyond lay the civilian settlement, with housing distributed in a markedly disorganized fashion. Interpersed among the houses were a few small burial areas that most likely belonged to individual, probably Alexandrian, families. In the late 6th century, the whole area was surrounded by a defensive wall, of which *c.* 600 m, including two gates, survived in the north-west of the city. The North Gate, situated on the main urban thoroughfare, was constructed as a gate of state with three passageways and a portico positioned on the city side. A colonnaded street, which was never completed, connected this gate with the inner ecclesiastical district. It intersected an older residential area.

Of the two ecclesiastical complexes that lie outside the city, the one to the north comprises a well-proportioned basilica with a narthex and an atrium-like courtyard, surrounded by a triclinium and several lodging rooms. There is also a baptistery to the south of the church. Presumably this complex was used by Monophysites, who were regarded as heretics by the city's inhabitants. About 1.5 km east of the city is a community of *c.* 100 small hermitages, in the middle of which stands the Eastern Church, a double-shell tetraconch structure of the 6th century, which replaced a small basilica built of unfired bricks. The outer walls of the later structure also have a tetraconch shape, which is more in keeping with the Syrian model for this building type.

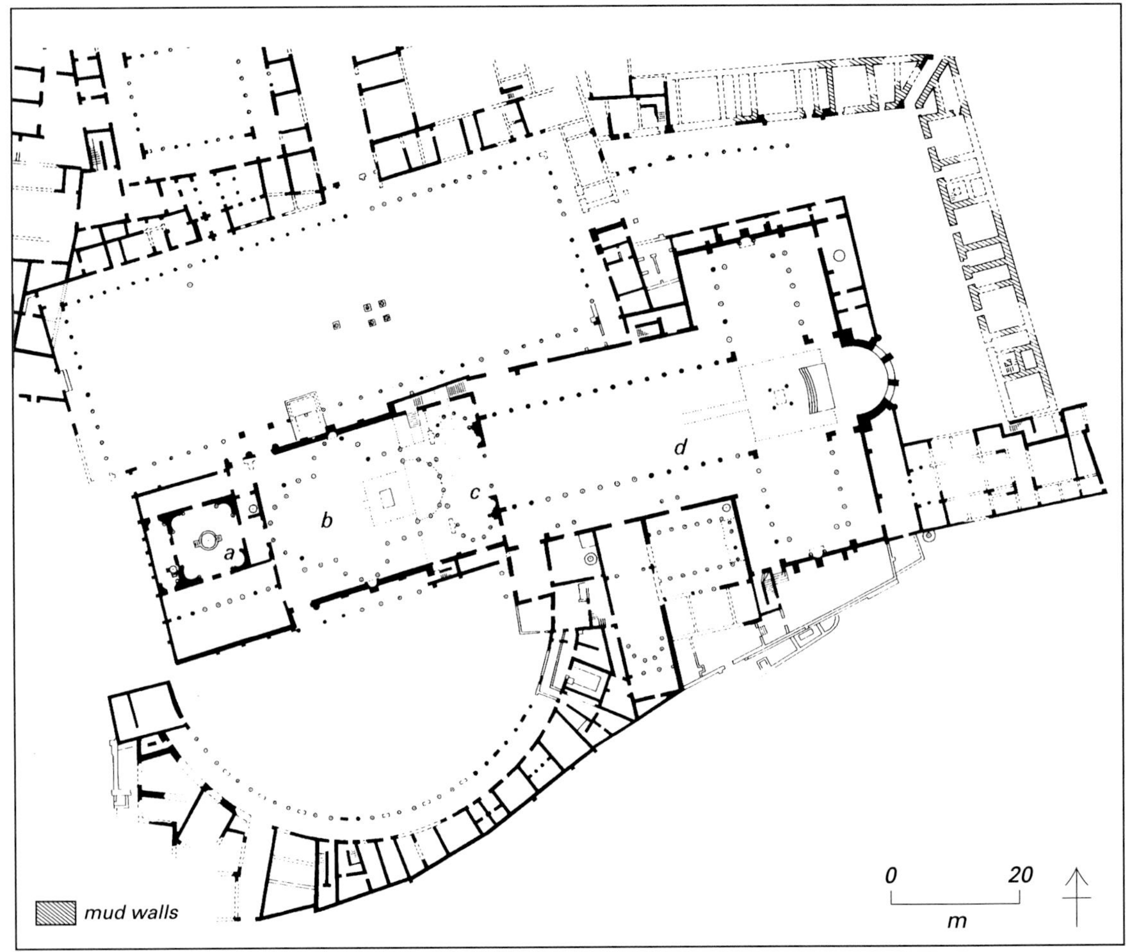

Abu Mina, church complex, remodelled late 5th century AD to mid-6th, ground-plan: (a) octagonal baptistery; (b) martyr's tetraconch church; (c) bi-apsidal narthex; (d) cross-transept basilica

In AD 619, the city was destroyed by the Persians. After only perfunctory reconstruction, it was conquered by the Arabs in 639–41, and it fell into the hands of the Coptic Church, which presumably led to the emigration of a large proportion of the original Greek population. The subsequent inhabitants had a totally different understanding of architecture, and only rubble was used for the newly constructed areas. Streets and courtyards were built over, and the formerly large rooms of the hostels were subdivided into smaller units. Several small commercial winepresses and pottery kilns were established.

In the 8th century, only the tetraconch martyr's church was renovated and transformed into a five-aisled basilica. The city flourished briefly, and the quantity of discernible housing indicates a considerable population; select people were entrusted with its administration. By the early 9th century, however, the nomads had begun to attack the city, forcing its inhabitants to leave.

BIBLIOGRAPHY

K. M. Kaufmann: *Die Menasstadt*, i (Leipzig, 1910)
F. W. Deichmann: 'Zu den Bauten der Menas-Stadt', *Archäol. Anz.* (1937), pp. 75–86
J. Drescher: *Apa Mena: A Selection of Coptic Texts Relating to St Menas* (Cairo, 1946)
J. B. Ward-Perkins: 'The Shrine of St Menas in the Maryût', *Pap. Brit. Sch. Rome*, xvii (1949), pp. 26–71
P. Labib: 'Fouilles du Musée Copte à Saint Ménas', *Bull. Inst. Egypte*, xxxiv (1951/2), pp. 133–8
P. Grossmann: *Abu Mina: A Guide to the Ancient Pilgrimage Center* (Cairo, 1986)
G. Severin and H.-G. Severin: *Marmor vom heiligen Menas*, Liebieghaus Monographie, x (Frankfurt am Main, 1987)
P. Grossmann: *Die Gruftkirche und die Gruft* (1989), i of *Abū Mīnā* (Mainz, 1989–)

PETER GROSSMANN

Abu Rawash [now Abū Ruwāsh]. Site of necropolis in Egypt, 9 km north of Giza, which flourished *c.* 2925–*c.* 2450 BC. Mud-brick mastaba tombs of 1st Dynasty nobles are the earliest buildings at Abu Rawash. The largest mastaba (26×14 m) has eight large recesses in its long walls and is flanked by eight servants' burials on its eastern side. Two funerary boats are associated with Tomb M25. The pyramid of King Radjedef of the 4th Dynasty dominates the site. Reached by a gigantic causeway, it is spectacularly situated at a height of *c.* 157 m above the level of the Nile Valley. It was originally *c.* 67 m high and

105 m square. The 1500 m causeway originally supported a stone corridor, which, with its side walls, measured 14 m wide, while the embankment below widened to 31.5 m at its base and reached a height of 12 m in places. Most of the stone has been quarried away, but the burial-chamber pit (now open to the sky) gives a good impression of the pyramid's former splendour. The pyramid stood in a large enclosure (267×217 m) on levelled rock. The funerary temple was never completed as designed, but a boat trench (37×9 m) lies beside the pyramid, and a smaller ritual pyramid stood near by. The easternmost promontory of the mountain range was thought by the German Egyptologist Karl Richard Lepsius to be the rock core of an enormous mud-brick pyramid.

Over 20 fragments of fine statues of Radjedef and his family were found at Abu Rawash, including red quartzite heads of the King (Cairo, Egyp. Mus., and Paris, Louvre), a limestone bust of his daughter Neferhetepes and a pink granite statuette of his son Sitka (both Paris, Louvre).

BIBLIOGRAPHY

F. Bisson de La Roque: *Rapport sur les fouilles d'Abu-Roasch*, 3 vols (Cairo, 1924–5)

B. Porter and R. L. B. Moss: *Topographical Bibliography* (1927–), III/i pp. 1–10

P. Montet: 'Tombeaux de la Ière et de la IVe dynasties à Abu-Roach', *Kêmi: Rev. Philol. Archéol. Egyp. & Copt.*, vii (1938), pp. 11–69

A. Klasens: 'The Excavations of the Leiden Museum of Antiquities of Abu-Roash', *Oudhdknd. Meded. Rijksmus. Ouden Leiden*, xxxviii (1957), pp. 58–68

V. Maragioglio and C. Rinaldi: *L'architettura della piramidi Menfite*, v (Rapallo, 1966), pp. 7–41

E. P. UPHILL

Abu Simbel, the Great Temple of Ramesses II (*reg c.* 1279–*c.* 1213 BC), before its removal to higher ground

Abu Simbel. Site in Egypt, on the west bank of the Nile in Lower Nubia, 280 km south of Aswan. With the construction of the Aswan Dam in the early 1960s, the temple complex was one of a number of ancient monuments saved by being moved to a new site. Having been cut into pieces and reassembled, it now stands on the shores of Lake Nasser, 64 m higher and 180 m west of its ancient site. It is not known whether any small rock-cut chapels already existed at Abu Simbel, but inscriptions from the Middle Kingdom show that it was already an ancient sacred site when Ramesses II (*reg c.* 1279–*c.* 1213 BC) chose it for his most grandiose, and most famous, Nubian monument.

The construction of the Great and Small Temples of Abu Simbel began in the early years of Ramesses II, and they were completed by around the 25th year of his reign. The Great Temple (see fig. and §1 below) is the first of four temples that were dedicated to the King himself in association with the chief gods of Egypt, Amun-re, Re-Horakhty and Ptah. The other temples, at Wadi es-Sebua, ed-Derr and Gerf Hussein, were completed in the middle and later years of the reign (*see* NUBIA, §III). The Small Temple (see §2 below) is situated a little way to the north of the Great Temple. The temples were rediscovered by Jean-Louis Burckhardt, who, in 1813, was the first European to visit and describe them in modern times.

1. THE GREAT TEMPLE. Any forecourt preceding the temple has disappeared, although, by analogy with others, a dromos and perhaps brick pylon would be expected. All that survives in front of it is a brick wall with a gateway leading towards the Small Temple. Flanking the ramp-stairway leading to the terrace are two stelae mounted in stone niches. The terrace is lined with statues of falcons alternating with statues of the King as Osiris and as living ruler. These statues, although on a large scale, are dwarfed by the rock-cut façade of the temple (30 m high and 35 m long). At the northern end of the terrace is a solar chapel with an altar. The altar originally incorporated four statues of baboons and had obelisks on its north and south sides, but these are now in the Egyptian Museum, Cairo. At the southern end of the terrace is a copy of the 'Marriage Stele' of the 34th Year of Ramesses II's reign, recording his marriage with a Hittite princess.

South of the terrace is a small rock-cut chapel, the function of which is not clear, although it may be a MAMMISI or 'birth house'. The main façade is carved in the form of a single pylon, the cavetto cornice of which is crowned with a frieze of baboons in the attitude of adoration. The whole is dominated by four colossi of Ramesses II, each 22 m high (*see* PHOTOGRAPHY, fig. 11). The King is seated, wearing the *nemes* headcloth and double crown. Smaller figures, representing his chief wife, his mother and some of his children, are carved in front of the throne and between his legs (as in the case of the Colossi of Memnon; *see* THEBES (i), §V). The bases of the statues are carved with the King's name and figures of a religious official known as the iun-mwt.f (Egyp.: 'pillar of his mother') priest.

Over the doorway, in a large rectangular niche, a figure of the King as the hawk-headed god Re-Horakhty emerges. This large image is flanked by smaller figures of the goddess Maat and the *was* sceptre, thus creating a rebus of the King's throne name, User-maat-Re. Two sunk-relief figures of the King (possibly added at a later stage) make offerings to the rebus within the niche.

The temple is entirely hewn from the rock; therefore the conventional Egyptian temple plan has been adjusted. The first hall is analogous with the statue-lined courtyards of the royal mortuary temples at Thebes (*see* THEBES (i), §§VI and VII) and the small temple of Ramesses III in the first courtyard at Karnak. It consists of a central nave and two aisles rather than an open peristyle court. The hall (h. 8 m) is supported by eight square piers, each accompanied by a colossus of the King (of the 'Osirid' or mummiform type) wearing the *shendyt* kilt (the 'royal pleated kilt'), with arms crossed on the chest holding crook and flail. The colossi on the northern side wear the double crown, and those on the southern side wear the white crown. Two chambers open from the northern side of the hall, while two suites (consisting of three rooms each) are entered through doors flanking the central axis of the hall. These were temple storerooms and possibly the resting places of certain cult images.

A second hall supported by four square piers precedes the sanctuary. The dominant feature of the sanctuary, occupying the whole of the back wall, is a statue group of the presiding deities, which is designed to be illuminated by the rising sun on two days each year. Ptah and Re-Horakhty flank the King and Amun-Re in the centre. When the sun enters the sanctuary, it completely illuminates only the image of the King. These statues and the altar in front are carved from the rock. The decoration of the temple interior is in sunk relief of quite good workmanship, with paint surviving in many places. Among the most important reliefs is the large scene of the Battle of Qadesh (between Ramesses II and the Hittite king Muwatallis), on the north wall of the first hall. This relief, unusually, has been signed by the chief sculptor, Piaay, son of Khanefer. The temple contained other statuary, including two hawk-headed sphinxes (London, BM) and a statue dedicated by the Viceroy of Nubia, Paser II (London, BM).

2. THE SMALL TEMPLE. Its façade is dominated by six colossi (h. 10 m), four of Ramesses II and two of his chief wife Nefertari, to whom the temple is dedicated. Smaller statues of the royal children (princes with the King, princesses with the Queen) flank the larger ones. The doorway leads into a square hall supported by six square piers. The sides of the piers facing inwards towards the aisle have been carved into the form of sistra with heads of the goddess Hathor. The entrance hall is decorated with two scenes of Ramesses II smiting his enemies, accompanied by Nefertari. This type of scene is usually found as decoration of the façade, but due to the unusual nature of the temple has here been placed inside (as also in the Great Temple). The remainder of the scenes in this hall are well-executed depictions of standard types of offering and ritual. Three doors give access to a narrow hall. An unusual scene depicts the coronation of Nefertari by the goddesses Hathor and Isis. Two statue groups may originally have been placed in this room. The sanctuary has a large statue of Hathor in the form of a cow emerging from the wall, protecting a small figure of the King in front of her (as in the Hathor chapel of Tuthmosis III at Deir el-Bahri). The wall reliefs show Ramesses II worshipping himself and Nefertari (who in this temple was identified with a local form of Hathor). The relief work throughout the temple is of good quality (considering the poor sandstone) with rather attenuated figures. The colouring used is predominantly yellow, which adds to the delicate effect.

BIBLIOGRAPHY

LÄ

L. Christophe: *Abou-Simbel et l'épopée de la découverte* (Brussels, 1965) [a history of the temple since the earliest European visitors]

C. Desroches-Noblecourt and C. Kuentz: *Le Petit Temple d'Abou Simbel*, 2 vols (Cairo, 1968)

T. Säve-Söderbergh, ed.: *Temples and Tombs of Ancient Nubia* (London, 1987) [account of the campaign for the salvage of Abu Simbel and other Nubian monuments]

R. G. MORKOT

Abusir [Egyp. Per-Usir; Gr. Busiris]. Ancient Egyptian royal necropolis that flourished during the 5th Dynasty (*c.* 2465–*c.* 2325 BC). The site is 25 km south-west of the centre of Cairo and has been intermittently excavated since the beginning of the 19th century by teams of English, French, German, Egyptian and Czech archaeologists.

In the 5th Dynasty the sun cult reached its climax, and, according to legend, the first kings of that dynasty were considered the direct descendants of the sun god Re. Sahure (*reg c.* 2458–*c.* 2446 BC), the first king who established his pyramid complex at Abusir, presumably wished to be buried in the vicinity of the sun temple of his predecessor, Userkaf, which stood at the northern outskirts of the necropolis. Sahure's pyramid was small, and its core was built of poor quality limestone. His pyramid temple, however, was carefully executed in different kinds of stone and richly decorated with reliefs, the whole representing a new stage in the evolution of this type of monument. A small subsidiary pyramid, an enclosure wall, a causeway and a valley temple also originally belonged to the pyramid complex.

Sahure's brother, Neferirkare (*reg c.* 2446–*c.* 2426 BC), started to build his pyramid complex a little further to the south and at a higher level than Sahure's. His pyramid, initially *c.* 74 m high, still dominates the necropolis. In the pyramid temple, which was hastily finished in mud-brick, were found remains of papyrus archives with invaluable data about the function of the pyramid complex, the organization of the royal mortuary cult and the state administration in general. Raneferef (*reg c.* 2419–*c.* 2416 BC), the elder son of Neferirkare, died at the very beginning of the construction of his pyramid, which was hastily changed into a *mastaba* and completed by his younger brother Neuserre. The mortuary temple attached to the *mastaba* included a columned hall (unique in the 5th Dynasty), another papyrus archive (similar to that of Neferirkare) and rare royal sculptures (Cairo, Egyp. Mus.) that constitute the richest collection of such statuary from the 5th Dynasty. A ritual slaughterhouse was built in front of the unfinished pyramid of Raneferef.

Neuserre (*reg c.* 2416–*c.* 2392 BC) also completed a third pyramid complex, adjacent to the south side of his father's pyramid (*see* PYRAMID, fig. 1(d)). This small but very important structure was begun for Khentkaus, the 'king's wife' to Neferirkare, who was buried at Giza; Neuserre completed it as a cenotaph where she was worshipped as 'the King's mother'. Despite the lack of a convenient building site on the desert plateau, Neuserre decided to construct his burial complex there. He took over a part of his father's causeway, modified the standard form of his mortuary temple and built his pyramid next to the north wall of his father's pyramid temple.

The foundations of a second unfinished pyramid on the Abusir plateau can be seen to the north-west of the pyramid of Sahure. This tomb can be tentatively attributed to Shepseskare (*reg c.* 2426–*c.* 2419 BC). The tombs of the members of royal families and high state officials of that time are clustered around the pyramids. Of the few tombs unearthed to date, the *mastaba* of Ptahshepses (*c.* 2400 BC), the vizier and son-in-law of Neuserre, ranks highest. Approximately 1 km north of the pyramid of Sahure, the remains of two sun temples out of six known to have been built by the 5th Dynasty kings have been found: those of Userkaf and Neuserre (*see* ABU GHURAB). From the papyrus archives found in the Abusir mortuary temples, the sun temples, which were dominated by an obelisk, were closely connected both in their religious cult and economically with the pyramid complexes of their builders.

On the south-western outskirts of the site, large and very sophisticated complexes of shafts dating from the end of the Late Period have been discovered. The necropolis was abandoned by the last kings of the 5th Dynasty, presumably because of the lack of a suitable building site. From the Middle Kingdom, it became a cemetery for common people that flourished particularly in the Late Period, under the influence of the cults in nearby North Saqqara. In the New Kingdom, the pyramid temple of Sahure became the centre of the cult of the goddess Sakhmet.

BIBLIOGRAPHY

L. Borchardt: *Das Grabdenkmal des Königs Ne-user-rʿ* (Leipzig, 1907)
——: *Das Grabdenkmal des Königs Nefer-ír-ke'-re* (Leipzig, 1909)
——: *Das Grabdenkmal des Königs Sa'ḥu-rʿ*, 2 vols (Leipzig, 1910–13)
F. W. von Bissing: *Das Re-Heiligtum des Königs Ne-woser-re (Rathures)*, 3 vols (Leipzig, 1905–28)
B. Porter and R. L. B. Moss, eds: *Topographical Bibliography* (1927–), III/i, pp. 314–48
H. Ricke and others: *Das Sonnenheiligtum des Königs Userkaf*, 2 vols (Cairo, 1965, 2/Wiesbaden, 1969)

MIROSLAV VERNER

Abu Tahir [Abu Ṭāhir]. Persian family of potters. The family is sometimes known, somewhat improperly, by the epithet Kashani [al-Kashani, Qashani], which refers to their home town, Kashan. It was a major centre for the production of lustre pottery in medieval Iran, and they were among the leading potters there, working in both the Monumental and the Miniature styles (*see* ISLAMIC ART, §V, 3(iii)). As well as the lustre tiles for many Shiʿite shrines at QUM, MASHHAD, Najaf and elsewhere, they made enamelled and lustred vessels. Three other families of Persian lustre potters are known, but none had such a long period of production. At least four generations of the Abu Tahir family are known from signatures on vessels and tiles, including dados, large mihrabs and grave covers. The family may be traced to Abu Tahir ibn Abi Husayn, who signed an enamelled bowl (Cairo, Mus. Islam. A.). A lustre bowl in the Monumental style (London, N.D. Khalili priv. col.), signed by Abu Tahir ibn Muhammad Hamza ibn al-Hasan, may also be his work, but the genealogy is slightly different. The first clearly documented member of the family is (1) Muhammad ibn Abi Tahir, who worked with another potter ABU ZAYD on the most important projects of the pre-Mongol period. Muhammad ibn Abi Tahir's son (2) ʿAli worked in the mid-13th century and ʿAli's son (3) Yusuf in the early 14th. Dated works by these three thus span more than a century (1205–1334), although there are surprisingly long gaps between generations. In the 14th century the family turned to other professions, for one of Yusuf's brothers, (4) Abu'l-Qasim, became a scribe and accountant in the Ilkhanid bureaucracy, and another brother, ʿIzz al-Din Mahmud, became a Sufi who entered the Suhrawardi *khānaqāh* at Natanz and wrote a spiritual guide, the *Miṣbāh al-Hidāya wa Miftāḥ al-Kifāya* ('Light of Divine Guidance and Key to Completeness').

BIBLIOGRAPHY

O. Watson: *Persian Lustre Ware* (London and Boston, 1985)
S. S. Blair: 'A Medieval Persian Builder', *J. Soc. Archit. Historians*, xlv (1986), pp. 389–95

(1) Muhammad ibn Abi Tahir [Muḥammad ibn Abī Ṭāhir] (*fl* 1206–15). His earliest work is a large (2.9×1.2 m) panel of 15 tiles that covers the top of the cenotaph of Fatima in the shrine at Qum. It is composed of large central panels enclosing arch motifs filled with the finest of arabesques in relief, framed by multiple borders of blue-glazed relief inscriptions; all these relief elements are set against a background of lustre scrolls. The narrow inscription bands, fine detail and flat modelling distinguish this piece from later works and show its somewhat experimental style. Muhammad apparently collaborated on the project with Abu Zayd, who signed the frieze dated 1206 around the sides of the cenotaph. A decade later Muhammad again collaborated with Abu Zayd on a more ambitious programme of lustre decoration for the shrine of Imam Riza at Mashad (*see* SHRINE, colour pl. IV, fig. 1). Muhammad was responsible for the framing around the entrance and perhaps for an unsigned mihrab and the dado frieze tiles, while Abu Zayd signed a mihrab dated 1215 and a number of star and octagonal tiles. Muhammad must have worked on other large-scale projects, for his signature is found on other high-quality pieces, such as a fragment from a large mihrab (ex-Kelekian priv. col.; see Ettinghausen, fig. 25). His work represents the artistic and technical peak achieved by the Kashan lustre potters, in which calligraphy and background decoration are carefully balanced and arabesque mouldings are elaborate yet lively and uncluttered.

(2) ʿAli [ʿAlī ibn Muḥammad ibn Abī Ṭāhir] (*fl* 1242–65). Son of (1) Muhammad ibn Abi Tahir. His earliest work is a large mihrab (1242) in the shrine at Meshed. It uses the same types of decoration seen in the work of his father but is more coarsely executed. Within a few years ʿAli made another large mihrab, fragments of which have been found in a tomb tower at Gurgan. He apparently used the same mould for his signature tile as he had in the earlier mihrab, although the other sections are different. In the 1260s, when the Kashan potteries revived after half a century of stagnation, ʿAli's virtuosity was revealed. He made a series of stars and crosses (Oct–Dec 1262; see fig.) set in dado panels and a large mihrab (May 1265) for the Imamzada Yahya in Varamin. He also signed the mihrab dated November 1264 in the Imamzada Ahmad Qasim at Qum. By stylistic analogy, the large mihrab in the shrine at Najaf must be his work of the same period. He is the only lustre potter in this period to sign his wares, and, although his work is not as sophisticated as the best work done earlier in the century, the quality of design and drawing remains high.

(3) Yusuf [Yūsuf ibn ʿAlī ibn Muḥammad ibn Abī Ṭāhir] (*fl* 1305–34). Son of (2) ʿAli. In 1305 he finished his father's work in the Imamzada Yahya at Varamin, collaborating with ʿAli ibn Ahmad ibn ʿAli al-Husayni on a medium-sized arched tile (St Petersburg, Hermitage). In the following years he produced several sets of frieze tiles. One dated January 1310 is remarkable for its high technical quality and clean drawing; another is dated January 1311. His work soon declined in quality, for his modest (460×760 mm) moulded tile recording repairs undertaken some time between 1316 and 1327 to the Qalʿa Mosque in the nearby village of Quhrud is mediocre. Its importance lies in its technique (it is underglaze painted in blue and black), for it shows that in the 14th century the family worked in cheaper techniques as well as lustre. The final lustre piece produced by the family (Tehran, Archaeol. Mus., 3270) is a large (1.29×2.12 m) mihrab made in May 1334 for the Imamzada ʿAli ibn Jaʿfar at Qum. Although it is larger than any other mihrab, the moulded decoration is clumsy and the painting sketchy. Its poor quality was a harbinger of the demise of Kashan lustre potteries, which apparently ceased production by 1340.

ʿAlī ibn Muhammad ibn Abī Tāhir: panel of star-shaped tiles from the Imamzada Yahya, Varamin, 2.9×1.2 m, each tile diam. 310 mm, 1262 (London, Victoria and Albert Museum)

(4) Abu'l-Qasim Jamal al-Din ʿAbdallah (*d* 1337–8). Brother of (3) Yusuf. On the orders of the Ilkhanid vizier Rashid al-Din (*reg* 1295–1316), Abu'l-Qasim wrote a biography of the sultan entitled *Tārīkh-i Uljaytū* ('History of Uljaytu'). His treatise on minerals and precious substances, including precious stones, composed in 1303, belongs to a recognized genre of Islamic scientific literature descending from classical prototypes, but Abu'l-Qasim appended a technical description of pottery manufacture. This appendix is perhaps the only document of its sort to survive from the pre-modern Islamic world. In it Abu'l-Qasim described the potter's raw materials, where they might be found in the Kashan area and their properties. They included various stones, clay and metals in mineral form. He discussed the processing of these materials by means of grinding, sifting and smelting, as well as the proportions in which they should be compounded to produce the frit body of ceramic vessels and tiles and to make the glazes and colourings applied to the frit body. He also described the firing of fine ceramic vessels in clay cases provided with lids (saggars), the design and furnishing of the kiln in which the firing occurred, and the sorts of wood used to fire kilns in Kashan, Baghdad and Tabriz. Finally he discussed the application of 'enamel' glazes and gilding, for which a special gilding kiln was required.

WRITINGS

ʿArāʾis al-Jawāhir wa Nafāʾis al-Aṭāʾib [Brides of gems and delicacies of amenities], (1303); ed. I. Afshar (Tehran, 1967); part. ed. and German trans. by H. Ritter, J. Ruska and R. Winderlich as 'Orientalische Steinbücher und persische Fayencetechnik', *Istanbul. Mitt.*, iii (1935) [whole issue]; Eng. trans. by J. W. Allen as 'Abū'l-Qāsim's Treatise on Ceramics', *Iran*, xi (1973), pp. 111–20

BIBLIOGRAPHY

R. Ettinghausen: 'Evidence for the Identification of Kashan Pottery', *A. Islam.*, iii (1936), pp. 44–70

SHEILA S. BLAIR

Abu Zayd [Abū Zayd ibn Muḥammad ibn Abī Zayd] (*fl* Kashan, 1186–1219). Persian potter. At least 15 tiles and vessels signed by Abu Zayd are known, more signed works than are known for any other medieval Iranian potter. He frequently added the phrase 'in his own hand' (*bi-khāṭṭihi*) after his name, so that it has been misread as Abu Zayd-i Bazi or Abu Rufaza. His earliest piece is an enamelled (Pers. *mīnāʾī*) bowl dated 4 Muharram 583 (26 March 1186; ex-Tabbagh priv. col.), but he is best known for his lustrewares. A fragment of a vase dated 1191 (ex-Bahrami priv. col., see Watson, pl. 53) is in the Miniature style, but most of his later pieces, such as a bowl dated 1202 (Tehran, priv. col., see Bahrami, pl. 16a) and a dish dated 1219 (The Hague, Gemeentemus.), are in the Kashan style, which he is credited with developing (*see* ISLAMIC ART, §V, 3(iii)). He collaborated with Muhammad ibn Abi Tahir (*see* ABU TAHIR, (1)) on the two most important lustreware projects of the period, the decoration of the tomb chambers in the

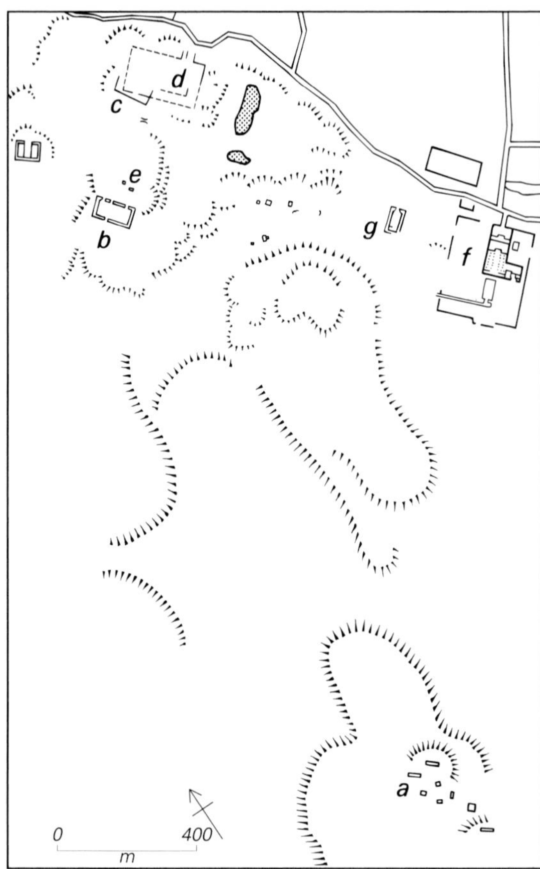

1. Abydos, general plan: (a) Umm el-Qaab; (b) Shunet el-Zebib; (c) Kom el-Sultan; (d) Temple of Osiris; (e) Middle Kingdom tombs and cenotaphs; (f) temple of Sethos I; (g) temple of Ramesses II

shrines of Fatima at Qum and Imam Riza at Mashhad. Abu Zayd's signature on pieces in the two most important techniques of overglaze luxury ceramics is one of the main reasons that enamelled ware, like lustreware, can be attributed to Kashan.

BIBLIOGRAPHY

M. Bahrami: 'A Master Potter of Kashan', *Trans. Orient. Cer. Soc.* (1944–5), pp. 35–40

O. Watson: *Persian Lustre Ware* (London and Boston, 1985)

——: 'Documentary Mīnā'ī and Abū Zaid' Bowls', *The Art of the Saljūqs in Iran and Anatolia: Proceedings of a Symposium Held in Edinburgh in 1982*, ed. R. Hillenbrand (Cosa Mesa, 1994), pp. 170–80

□

Abydos [anc. Egyp. Abdjw]. Egyptian site, *c.* 50 km south of Sohag, and necropolis of the ancient city of This (perhaps modern Girga), which was briefly the capital of the newly united Egypt in the Late Predynastic period (*c.* 3000–*c.* 2925 BC). As the country's most ancient capital, it remained significant throughout Egyptian history, becoming the principal cult centre of Osiris, a funerary deity who embodied the tradition of kingship. From the later Middle Kingdom (*c.* 1750 BC), the Early Dynastic period (*c.* 2925–*c.* 2575 BC) royal necropolis was believed to contain the tomb of Osiris; because of this, it was visited by pilgrims until Roman times (30 BC–AD 395). Large cemeteries continued to accumulate, and they were characterized in the latest period by a distinctive Greco-Egyptian type of stele. These merged Egyptian and Classical styles with a largely Egyptian decorative repertory and were increasingly inscribed in Greek. Thus for two millennia Abydos was an important centre of non-royal art, as well as the location of major temples.

1. EARLY DYNASTIC PERIOD–MIDDLE KINGDOM (*c.* 2925–*c.* 1630 BC). Many kings of the 1st and 2nd dynasties (*c.* 2925–*c.* 2650 BC) were buried in the cemetery of Umm el-Qaab (see fig.1a), set in the low desert near a cleft in the rock escarpment, which contained the cemetery of the latest Predynastic kings of Egypt. These tombs had little, if any, superstructure, but their occupants were buried with abundant grave goods of high quality, such as stone vases, ivory furniture and jewellery (e.g. Paris, Louvre; Oxford, Ashmolean). They were marked by mortuary stelae giving the kings' Horus names (the first part of the royal titulary); the limestone stele of Wadj (Paris, Louvre, E 11007; see fig. 2) is a masterpiece of carving. The tombs were complemented by sacred areas, surrounded by élite graves that were located near the cultivation. The later areas were enclosed by massive, richly decorated mud-brick walls: one, the Shunet el-Zebib (1b), stands more than 6 m high. These structures were

2. Abydos, stele of Wadj, limestone, Early Dynastic period, 1st Dynasty, *c.* 2925–*c.* 2775 BC (Paris, Musée du Louvre)

3. Abydos, temple of Sethos I, relief carving of Sethos I offering to Nefertem and Sakhmet on the south wall of the hall of Ptah-Sokar and Nefertum, *c.* 1290–*c.* 1279 BC

probably the forerunners of the step-pyramid enclosures at Saqqara.

Kom el-Sultan (1c), near the Shunet el-Zebib, is the site of the early town of Abydos. Its temple was probably dedicated originally to the local funerary gods Khentiamentiu and Wepwawet; later it became the Temple of Osiris (1d). The temple may have been founded before the 1st Dynasty, and early votive objects have been recovered from the site; most later periods are attested by fragments of architecture and sculpture, including a tiny ivory statuette of Cheops (h. 75 mm; Cairo, Egyp. Mus., JE 36143), which may be archaistic. Little of the temple's structure has been preserved. In the Middle Kingdom the area became a focus of pilgrimage: extensive cemeteries grew up (1e), while near the temple were cenotaphs in the form of chapels with mortuary stelae, offering tables and statues, but without burials. The cenotaphs, which were set up for individuals or groups, secured for the deceased perpetual participation in the festivals of Osiris. The site has yielded *c.* 2000 Middle Kingdom private stelae, ranging from excellent works to crude objects resembling ostraca, but very few belonged to members of the core élite. The larger cenotaphs were vaulted mud-brick chambers set in small enclosures and flanked by trees; they imitated the form and context of temple sanctuaries and are therefore significant as evidence for lost architectural types, while their massive construction has parallels among other Middle Kingdom tombs. The small temple of Ramesses II (*see* §2 below) later covered part of the cenotaph area.

2. NEW KINGDOM (*c.* 1540–*c.* 1075 BC). From the 12th Dynasty (*c.* 1938–*c.* 1756 BC) some rulers built cenotaph or temple complexes in the low desert south of Kom el-Sultan. A chapel of Queen Tetisheri of the 17th Dynasty (*c.* 1630–*c.* 1540) has yielded a fine stele (Cairo, Egyp. Mus., CG 34002), and fragmentery reliefs of Ahmose (*c.* 1540–1514), the founder of the New Kingdom, were discovered in the early 1990s. The only substantial standing remains, however, are from early 19th Dynasty temples: a chapel of Ramesses I (*reg c.* 1292–*c.* 1290 BC), dedicated after his death and known only from superb relief blocks (New York, Metropolitan); a temple and cenotaph of Sethos I (*reg c.* 1290–*c.* 1279 BC); and a temple of Ramesses II (*reg c.* 1279–*c.* 1213 BC). These monuments display a striking unity of style.

The complex of Sethos I (see fig. 1f) is an unfinished architectural and artistic masterpiece constructed on a broad, uneven site. The limestone temple is approached from a quay with an 'esplanade' through two ruined open courts; the portico of the second court had seven doorways, four of which were subsequently blocked by Ramesses II, leading through two hypostyle halls to seven chapels roofed with false vaults and respectively dedicated to Sethos himself, Ptah, Re-Harakhty, Amun-Re, Osiris, Isis and Horus. Behind these chapels is a suite of rooms dedicated to the local divine triad of Osiris, Isis and Horus, while to the south of them is a unique extension incorporating chapels for the Memphite gods Ptah-Sokar and Nefertum, along with corridors, stairways, a repository for divine barks and suites of service rooms. Parallel to the first two courts is a complex of mud-brick storage magazines surrounding a central stone hall. The entire area was surrounded by an enclosure wall, with a brick pylon on the desert side pointing towards the supposed tomb of Osiris.

In its architecture and dedication, the temple forms a national cult centre with an emphasis on Osiris and Sethos. Apart from its grand yet compact conception, it is outstanding for its sophisticated articulation of space and light, especially in the second hypostyle hall, where a change in levels and column forms signals a change in context. Subtle distinctions in the design of doorways indicate their relative importance, while niches provide transitions between each deity's axis and the next. The wall reliefs of Sethos I, which fill the rear portion and part of the southern extension, are 'classicizing', perhaps looking back to the mid-18th Dynasty (*c.* 1400 BC), and are relatively stiff and formal (see fig. 3). The quality of line and detail is remarkable, and the composition of larger areas is free and inventive. The texts are fuller than in most temples, and the space around the figures is elegantly arranged to allow for this. Text and relief complement and comment on each other in rich patterns. The excellent preservation of colour in a number of places demonstrates an extra dimension of decoration and meaning. The unpainted reliefs in the southern extension, which are among the finest, date to the end of Sethos' reign. Further south are faded paintings in a restricted range of colours, which demonstrate that much of the temple was completely decorated in paint before carving; in the hall of barks, most of the paintings were later used as drafts for carving reliefs. The adjacent corridor was carved in the early reign of Ramesses II with a vigorous relief of the King and his heir lassoing a bull. All the reliefs in the first hypostyle hall and courts are also from the time of

Ramesses II, but many of these, some of inferior quality, may represent designs of Sethos I executed during his son's reign.

The underground cenotaph of Sethos I at the rear of the temple is commonly known as the Osireion. It was constructed by Sethos, but most of its decoration dates to the reign of his grandson Merneptah (*reg c.* 1213–*c.* 1204 BC). It is approached from the north by a descending corridor leading into a sequence of rooms. Its central hall consists of an open space with eight square granite pillars surrounded by a water-filled moat and enclosed by an outer wall with seventeen niches. Beyond this hall is a transverse room with a pitched ceiling, which seems to have been inaccessible when complete; it had been decorated with underworld and astronomical scenes in the reign of Sethos. The style of the granite pillars in the cenotaph recalls the architecture of the 4th Dynasty (*c.* 2575–*c.* 2465 BC), but analogies for most of its features are nearer at hand in the royal tombs of the Valley of the Kings (*see* THEBES (i), §IX), on which the general design of this remarkable structure is based. The choice of granite and sandstone (not local stones) for its construction is probably symbolic. The central hall was open to the sky, and rites of the resurrection of Osiris may have been performed there.

The limestone temple of Ramesses II (see fig. 1g), which dates to the earliest years of his reign, is smaller than his father's; only the lower parts of the walls are preserved. It is less original in design and has a single axis. The first court is lost; the second retains a fine register of reliefs showing the presentation of offerings. The inner areas are unusual in having pillared octostyle halls, as well as two corner rooms, each with a pair of pillars, surrounding benches and wall niches. In its present unroofed state, the most striking feature of the temple is the preservation of the brilliant polychromy of the reliefs, which are sunk as far as the first octostyle hall and raised beyond. Complex patterns of colour symbolism can be identified, for example on the fecundity figures in the first octostyle hall. The reliefs are probably the finest non-military carvings of Ramesses II; they are close to those of the temple of Sethos I in technique and quality, but livelier and denser, and were perhaps executed by the same sculptors.

BIBLIOGRAPHY

LÄ

A. Mariette: *Abydos: Description des fouilles exécutées sur l'emplacement de cette ville*, 2 vols (Paris, 1869–80)

W. M. F. Petrie: *The Royal Tombs of the Earliest Dynasties*, 2 vols (London, 1900–01)

A. M. Calverley and others: *The Temple of King Sethos I at Abydos* (London and Chicago, 1933–)

H. E. Winlock: *The Temple of Ramesses I at Abydos* (New York, 1937)

B. J. Kemp: 'The Egyptian 1st Dynasty Royal Cemetery', *Antiquity*, xli (1967), pp. 22–32

——: 'The Osiris Temple at Abydos', *Mitt. Dt. Archäol. Inst.: Abt. Kairo*, xxiii (1968), pp. 138–55

W. Kaiser: 'Zu den königlichen Tabelzirken der 1. und 2. Dynastie in Abydos und zur Baugeschichte des Djoser-Grabmals', *Mitt. Dt. Archäol. Inst.: Abt. Kairo*, xxv (1969), pp. 1–21

W. K. Simpson: *The Terrace of the Great God at Abydos: The Offering Chapels of Dynasties 12 and 13* (New Haven and London, 1974)

K. P. Kuhlmann: 'Der Tempel Ramses II in Abydos: Vorbericht über eine Neuaufnahme', *Mitt. Dt. Archäol. Inst.: Abt. Kairo*, xxxv (1979), pp. 189–93

A. R. David: *A Guide to Religious Ritual at Abydos* (Warminster, 1981)

W. Kaiser and G. Dreyer: 'Umm el Qaab: Nachuntersuchungen im frühzeitlichen Königsfriedhof, 2. Vorbericht', *Mitt. Dt. Archäol. Inst.: Abt. Kairo*, xxxviii (1982), pp. 211–69

Z. Hawass: 'The Khufu Statuette: Is it an Old Kingdom Sculpture?', *Mélanges Gamal eddin Mokhtar*, i (Cairo, 1985), pp. 379–94

D. O'Connor: 'The "Cenotaphs" of the Middle Kingdom at Abydos', *Mélanges Gamal eddin Mokhtar*, ii (Cairo, 1985), pp. 161–77

A. Abdalla: *Graeco-Roman Funerary Stelae from Upper Egypt*, Liverpool Monographs in Archaeology and Oriental Studies (Liverpool, 1992)

JOHN BAINES

Academy. Association or school of artists organized as a professional institution with a view to providing training, theoretical debate and exhibiting opportunities, and to mediate between its members and patrons or public. The word 'academy' derives from the ancient Greek 'akademeia', the name of the grove near Athens where Plato taught his pupils philosophy. In early modern times the term was first used in 15th-century Italy to describe meetings of literati, but from the 16th century it was adopted by those artists' corporations that included teaching as one of their main purposes, particularly teaching with an intellectual as opposed to a purely manual content. Drawing after antique statuary and from the live model (*see* ACADEMY FIGURE) played a preponderant part in this teaching, although anatomy, geometry, perspective, history and other disciplines were variously included in the curricula of academies. From around 1600 the academic idea spread from Italy to France, Spain and the Netherlands. It was in France under Louis XIV, however, that an artists' academy first became an effective and integral part of state arts policy and commanded sufficient authority to affect materially the training, aspirations and career structure of artists (*see* FRANCE, §XV, 2). Many academies of art established in the 18th century took the Académie Royale de Peinture et de Sculpture (founded 1648), Paris, as a model, and its teaching methods remained current in most art schools until the middle of the 20th century. With the decline in the 20th century of the prestige of the academic idea and the concomitant growth of alternative institutions devoted to art education, some academies dropped their teaching function and concentrated on their honorific, administrative and exhibiting roles.

This article is concerned primarily with the history and development of the academy in the Western tradition. Further information on specific academies is given in this dictionary within the relevant articles on cities (where subdivided, under the headings 'Art life and organization' or 'Institutions') and on countries (under 'Art education').

See also EDUCATION.

1. ORIGINS AND EARLY DEVELOPMENT. The earliest known Renaissance use of the word 'academy' occurs in a letter of 1427 from the humanist scholar Poggio Bracciolini (Eng. trans. in P. W. G. Gordan: *Two Renaissance Book Hunters*, New York, 1947, p. 118). This recounts his wish to decorate his villa near Florence with a collection of Antique sculpture, which he described figuratively as 'my "Academy" in Val d'Arno'. It is clear from the context

that he intended the word to be taken as meaning a place for contemplation and discussion away from the everyday business of the world. It was this usage that was applied in the 15th century to informal gatherings of literati for discussion of literary or philosophical topics. There is evidence of the existence, but not of the nature, of an 'Academia Leonardi Vincii' run by Leonardo in Milan around 1490; this may have been an informal group discussing questions of art theory rather than an institution with a clear didactic intention. Nevertheless, the fact that such philosophical enquiries could take place would have supported the arguments aimed at raising painting from the status of craft to that of a liberal art presented in Leonardo's writings. In these Leonardo advised beginners first to acquire knowledge and only then to practise painting, and he suggested that perspective and proportion be taught, and that drawing be mastered before undertaking (the more material procedures of) painting. Such an intellectualization of the processes of painting, which emphasized conceptual over manual skills, is connected with artists' attempts to promote their status. Thus, though Leonardo's Academia was probably not a teaching institution, the link between the idea of 'academy' and a more intellectual approach to painting was significant in the light of later developments.

In Florence at about the same time Lorenzo de' Medici appointed the sculptor Bertoldo di Giovanni as head of a 'school and academy' for the education of painters and sculptors. The exact nature of this institution (*see* FLORENCE, §V, 2) is not clear. According to Vasari, writing 70 years later (*Vite*, 2/1568), Lorenzo's purpose was to remedy the shortage of sculptors in Florence, and he offered to educate Domenico Ghirlandaio's apprentices 'in such a way that it would do credit to himself and Ghirlandaio and the city of Florence'. It would seem that the 'students' had access to the Medici collection of antiquities in a garden opposite the convent of S Marco. If Vasari's account is accurate, Bertololo's school was independent of the craft guilds. It also pursued educational methods (drawing after the Antique) that, if Ghirlandaio was representative, Florentine artists could not offer in their workshops; in so doing they enhanced the prestige of a supportive political authority.

Another similarly ambiguous piece of evidence in the early history of the art academy is Agostino dei Musi's engraving of 1531 inscribed *Academia di Bacchio Bandin in Roma in luogo detto Belvedere*, which shows a group of artists drawing a small statue in the studio of the sculptor Baccio Bandinelli. Apart from the inscription itself, there is no evidence to suggest that it represents more than a group of friends gathered to draw from the Antique and to discuss questions of art.

2. THE FIRST OFFICIAL ACADEMIES. Vasari's account of the Medici academy occurs in his *Vite* (2/1568) of Michelangelo and of Pietro Torrigiani. Michelangelo considered sculpture to be a 'scienza studiosa', and he also said that 'One paints with the brain and not with the hand'. Although Vasari recognized the need for practical training, he endorsed this image of the learned artist not only in his *Vite* but also in his promotion of the Accademia del Disegno (*see* FLORENCE, §V, 1), the constitution of which was formally granted in 1563. It is, perhaps, in this context that his description should be read. At all events, the Accademia del Disegno shared certain important characteristics with Lorenzo's academy as it appears in Vasari's account. First it enjoyed political protection and control in that the Grand Duke Cosimo I de' Medici was (with Michelangelo) joint head of the institution; effective control was vested in Cosimo's representative, Vincenzo Borghini. Second, and related to this, the Accademia itself was independent of the trade guilds, albeit that its members who were practising artists were not released from the obligation to join the appropriate guild until 1571. Thereafter the Accademia began to assume guild functions, becoming itself officially incorporated as a guild in 1584. Third, the Accademia's regulations of 1563 contained mandatory provisions for the education of young artists: arithmetic, geometry and anatomy lectures were envisaged; masters were to be elected to teach the art of *disegno* and to visit artists' workshops to correct students' work before it was allowed to leave the shop. While the last regulation may imply a continuing guild-like concern with quality control, it can be interpreted as an attempt to substitute criteria for judging art that acknowledged intellect as superior to craft.

Borghini instituted discourses on artistic matters in 1563. Such discourses are recorded as still occurring in 1591. However, the Accademia del Disegno's educational programme as a whole seems never to have been carried out with any degree of continuity. In the later 1570s the painter Federico Zuccaro drafted proposals intended to revitalize the programme, including the teaching of mathematics, henceforth taught more or less continuously for the rest of the century and through that following. The incorporation of mathematics reflected the belief that the external world was to be understood in terms of mathematical structures. In his other reform proposals, Zuccaro made two suggestions that would become significant features of later academies—a room for life drawing and students' prizes. Life classes may have been held at the Accademia in the 1590s and it seems likely that during the same period there were classes in physiognomy and other branches of natural philosophy. The proposals for life drawing and prizes were incorporated into the rules of the Accademia di S Luca (*see* ROME, §VI), founded in 1593 under Zuccaro's presidency. (In 1577 and 1588 Gregory XIII and Sixtus V had failed in their attempts to establish an academy with an education programme for young artists that would have regard to Tridentine dogma.) Rules in the statutes of the new institution provided for regular debates on art-theoretical matters, and for twelve visiting teachers annually (one per month) to decide from among the students who should draw from casts, who from life. All these proposed features of the Accademia di S Luca—a rotating academic staff, prizes, life drawing, debates on questions of art—would in due course be adopted by the Académie Royale de Peinture et de Sculpture in Paris, as would the rule that no academician was to sell his work from an open shop because this was not an 'opera intellettuale'. Zuccaro's fellow artists seem to have found the theoretical debates tedious, and the Accademia's teaching programme foundered after only a few years, not to be securely revived until after Carlo Maratti became its

1. Bartolomeo Passarotti: *Anatomy Lesson*, ink and wash, 385×540 mm, late 16th century (Paris, Musée du Louvre)

principal in 1664 and Giovanni Pietro Bellori its secretary in 1671; although there was no regular life class in Rome outside the Académie de France (*see* §4 below), established in 1666, until the Accademia's affiliate, the Accademia del Nudo, opened in 1754.

Besides the officially recognized academies of Florence and Rome, the other notable 16th-century academy was that established privately by the artists Ludovico Carracci and his cousins Agostino Carracci and Annibale Carracci (*see* CARRACCI) in Bologna, probably in 1582; it soon became known as the Accademia degli Incamminati, where, according to Malvasia (*Felsina pittrice*, 1678, i, pt 3), it was 'expected ... with admirable frequency to draw living persons, nude entirely or in part, weapons, animals, fruits, and, in short, all things in Creation'. Besides the stress on drawing after nature, in conscious reaction to the prevailing Mannerist style, which the Carracci saw as too much based on imagination rather than observation, lectures on perspective, architecture and anatomy were held and drawing competitions organized. By combining the programme of an academy with that of an active studio, the Carracci were better able to promote their aesthetic ideals, which sought to create a synthesis of the draughtsmanship of the Roman school, exemplified by Raphael and Michelangelo, with the colourism of northern Italian art, exemplified by Titian and Correggio. Just as the Carracci took as models different masters of the past, they seem also to have encouraged their pupils to learn from Bolognese artists other than themselves. Following the departure of Annibale and Agostino for Rome in the mid-1590s, Ludovico tried to have the Incamminati put on a more official footing and it seems that around 1603 they became associated with Bologna's Company of Painters. The Carracci academy closed in 1620, the year following the death of Lodovico: it had included among its pupils Francesco Albani, Guido Reni and Domenichino, painters widely admired in 18th-century artistic academies.

3. THE SPREAD OF THE ACADEMIC IDEA. Few further public academies were founded before the 18th century. An academy modelled on that of Florence was opened at Perugia in 1573, but by 1600 it seems to have stopped operating. In 1637 the city of Modena assigned rooms for an academy, which, however, ceased operating in 1646 with the death of its principal, Lodovico Lana. In Milan the archbishop Federico Borromeo (*see* BORROMEO, (2)), who had been the first Cardinal Protector of the Accademia di S Luca in Rome, founded an academy in 1620 with a view to revitalizing religious art. He donated to the academy paintings and sculptures from his own collection for the students to use as models. The Accademia Ambrosiana ceased operating in 1625, but was reactivated between 1669 and 1690. In 1678 an academy was successfully founded in Turin with rules modelled on those of Rome and under the protection of Mary Joanna, Duchess and Regent of Savoy, widow of Charles-Emanuel II. A class at a late 16th-century Italian academy is depicted in *Anatomy*

Lesson (Paris, Louvre; see fig. 1) by the 16th-century artist Bartolomeo Passarotti.

From around 1600 some private patrons made rooms available in their residences and provided models for artists to draw from. An example of such a life class is that of Prince Gian Carlo Doria in Genoa in the second decade of the century. Other private academies were run by artists in their own studios: Pietro Paolini ran an academy at Lucca, as did Camillo Procaccini and Giulio Cesare Procaccini in Milan. The main activity of these 17th-century academies seems to have been life drawing, thus enabling a number of artists to share the costs of the model, light and heating, but it is not clear how much teaching was done. Paolini is said to have given instruction in life drawing and drawing after casts, but Malvasia's description (*Felsina pittrice*, 1678, ii, pt 4) of a number of painters in the Ghislieri academy in Bologna as 'maestri' is ambiguous.

Outside Italy public academies were rare in the 17th century. In Seville the house of the painter and writer Francisco Pacheco was referred to as an academy, but it seems to have been more in the nature of an informal, literary academy that included artists and amateurs among its members. The activities of the academy which existed in Seville during the years 1660–74 were limited to life drawing. In 1606 a group of painters in Madrid agreed to rent premises for 'an academy of the art of painting', but this may have been to conduct no more than life drawing in common. A more ambitious plan of around 1600 for a teaching academy that would include not just life drawing-classes but also lectures on perspective, anatomy, physiognomy and mathematics was not realized in Madrid until 1744. Such efforts were connected with the concern of Spanish artists to raise the status of their profession and with a desire to avoid tax and military service by being practitioners of a recognized liberal art.

In Haarlem around 1600 Karel van Mander I set up a private academy for life drawing in conjunction with Hendrick Goltzius and Cornelis Cornelisz. van Haarlem. Van Mander's concern with painting as a liberal profession is indicated in his *Schilder-boek* (Haarlem, [1603]–1604), in which he wrote of the 'shameful laws and narrow rules' by which in nearly all cities save Rome 'the noble art of painting has been turned into a guild'. The concern with status was transformed into more concrete terms in 1631, when the Haarlem guild's rules were altered to give artist painters (as opposed to house painters and gilders who were also members) the highest rank within the corporation. At the same time a rule was adopted providing joint sessions in drawing and anatomy, and public lectures. Life drawing was not, however, referred to explicitly.

Elsewhere in the Netherlands the pattern was for painters to establish their own life classes and there is no record of a guild life class being held before that introduced in 1682 at the guild of painters and sculptors of The Hague founded 26 years previously. Probably most life drawing and related instruction was conducted in artists' studios. Rembrandt, for example, corrected his pupils' drawings, and Joachim von Sandrart called Gerrit van Honthorst's studio at Utrecht an academy (*Teutsche academie*, Nuremberg, 1675). Sandrart himself was involved in an academy in Nuremberg in the mid-1670s, in which for a short time architecture lessons were also given. In Antwerp an academy was founded by royal decree in 1663 and put under the direction of David Teniers II. The Antwerp academy, however, remained under the control of the painters' guild. In England some kind of academy for the study of the nude model existed in 1673; in 1692 a drawing-class was established at Christ's Hospital attached to the Writing School; and in 1697 a school of drawing started under the direction of Bernard Lens (ii). Elsewhere in northern Europe the guild remained the dominant social and economic group structure for artists until well into the 18th century. The major exception to this situation was in Paris, where the Académie Royale de Peinture et de Sculpture had been established in 1648 (*see* PARIS, §VI, 1).

4. THE INFLUENCE OF THE ACADÉMIE ROYALE DE PEINTURE ET DE SCULPTURE. The foundation document of Teniers's life class referred to an 'academy . . . like those of Rome and Paris'. This provides evidence of the early influence abroad of the Académie Royale and acknowledges its similarity to that of Rome. The Académie Royale's regulations and its aim of raising the status of painting and painters followed Zuccaro's original conception for the Roman academy. Thus, provision was made for professors rotating on a monthly basis to supervise the life class, for prizes for students, and for members' debates on all questions of art, which students could attend. Additionally, regular lectures on perspective, anatomy and geometry were conducted, developing the rules of the Académie's other model, Vasari's Accademia. Such an ambitious programme was not always followed consistently. By 1662 the students were complaining of a lack of teaching—evidence that the academic idea had taken firm hold among the rising generation. Nevertheless, the Académie Royale's educational programme was the most consistently applied hitherto and the most widely followed henceforth, in both its curriculum and its method. The prescribed progress of drawing from drawings, drawing from casts and drawing from life (as depicted by Charles-Nicolas Cochin II; see fig. 2) formed, with local variations, the basis of the training of artists in the European tradition until well into the 20th century.

Further regulations promulgated in 1663 and adopted by the Académie Royale in 1664 contained certain features that contributed to the nature of academies in general. First, provision was made for members' works to be exhibited annually—this was complied with only intermittently until 1737 and shortly thereafter changed to a biennial privilege rather than an annual obligation. The regular exhibitions organized by the Académie Royale in the 18th century quickly became major artistic and social events, and they were widely copied, notably by the Royal Academy in London, which continued to exhibit members' works into the late 20th century. Second, the Académie Royale's regulations provided in effect that no one could be appointed a professor who had not been received as a history painter or sculptor. It was this rule that institutionalized the precedence of history painting and that created a self-perpetuating oligarchy within the academic membership, because the higher officers of the institution could come only from the professorate. Hence the precedence

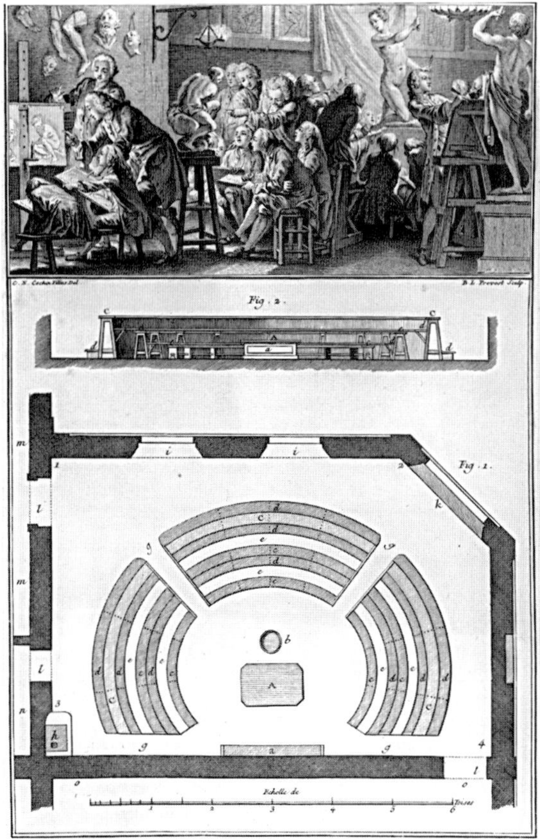

2. Charles-Nicolas Cochin II: *School of Drawing*, engraving, pl. 1 for the article 'Dessein' in Diderot's *Encyclopédie*, iii (Paris, 1763), showing the stages of academic instruction rather than an actual drawing school (London, British Library)

of history painting and of history painters became mutually reinforcing, a concept that was scarcely questioned for the next 200 years wherever the academic idea had been adopted. Third, although the regulations did not expressly refer to a PRIX DE ROME, in practice (funds permitting) the top prizes for students in painting and sculpture were scholarships to study in Rome. With the opening of the Académie de France in Rome in 1666 (*see* PARIS, §VI, 1) the prevalent view of the superiority of the art of ancient Rome and of the masters of the Renaissance as models for the young artist was institutionalized in a form broadly accepted throughout Europe until the later 19th century. Fourth, in granting to the Académie Royale a state grant to cover its costs and (until 1705) a monopoly in holding life classes, and to academicians a monopoly of royal commissions, as well as in the designation of the Académie as 'Royale', the idea that the state had a role in art education and production became firmly established.

One characteristic of the Académie Royale that was less often followed elsewhere was the separation of painting and sculpture from architecture. In Paris the latter had a separate academy founded in 1671, the Académie Royale d'Architecture (*see* PARIS, §VI, 1). Nevertheless, in many material respects the academies established outside France modelled themselves on that of Paris, with which they often had a personal connection. The Accademia di S Luca in Rome formally amalgamated with the Académie Royale in 1676, although the merger did not last long; and a French painter on occasion became principal of the Accademia, for example Charles Errard in 1672 and Jean-François de Troy in 1744. In 1726 Jacob van Schuppen (1670–1751), who had belonged to the Académie Royale, introduced rules closely modelled on those of Paris for the academy in Vienna, now known as the Akademie der Bildenden Künste, which had been first established in 1692. The rules provisionally adopted by the academy in Madrid in 1744 were modelled on those of Paris and Rome—most of its founder-members were French or Italian, or, if Spanish, trained in France or Italy, and its professor of painting was Louis-Michel van Loo, the Paris academician. In 1762, inspired by the model of the Académie Royale, the students of the Brussels academy, founded in 1711 by the municipality and now the Académie Royale des Beaux-Arts, successfully petitioned Duke Charles of Lorraine to become its protector. In Copenhagen, Stockholm and St Petersburg rules that followed the Paris model were adopted (in 1754, 1768 and 1757 respectively) when the academies were directed by the Paris academicians Jacques Saly, Pierre-Hubert L'Archevêque (1721–78) and Louis-Joseph Le Lorrain. These examples indicate the geographic spread of academies, which extended to Mexico in 1785. Their quantitative expansion also accelerated in the later 18th century so that by 1800 over 100 public academies existed, including those at Berlin (founded 1697, reorganized 1786), Dresden (founded 1705, reorganized 1762), Naples (1755) and Venice (1756). This number also includes provincial academies in Spain and France, such as those at Valencia (1768) and Dijon (1767), dependent on their respective central institutions in Madrid and Paris.

No single factor explains this growth. The conviction of artists that art was subject to teachable rules, albeit then mutable by individual genius, was not new, nor was their concern with their status as artists as opposed to craftsmen. Further, the artists of Madrid had invoked a mercantilist argument (unsuccessfully) to persuade Philip IV to open an academy in 1620: it would, they said, train Spanish artists and so avoid the employment of foreigners. As befitted the optimism of the 18th century, that argument was later put more positively. Thus Christian Ludwig von Hagedorn, who reorganized the Dresden Kunstakademie in 1762, wrote, 'Art can be looked at from a commercial point of view . . . while it redounds to the honour of a country to produce excellent artists, it is no less useful to raise the demand abroad for one's industrial products.' In Prussia, Friedrich Anton von Heinitz, who reorganized the Berlin Akademie der Künste, said in 1788, 'We pursue no other aim than to enhance national industry', and he cited art as an important source of income in France, England and Italy. Similar arguments were used in connection with the reorganization of the academies in Copenhagen in 1771 and The Hague and Stockholm in 1779, and all envisaged that the teaching of drawing would have a beneficial effect on the craft industries. Increasing nationalism and positive assessment of art's role in commerce, and of the State's role in art, combined with artists' aspirations to produce the enormous growth in the number of academies.

The corollary of state subvention for the academies was state control to a greater or lesser degree. The academies at St Petersburg and (under its 1757 rules) Madrid were seen as organs of state. The position of the Royal Academy of Arts (*see* LONDON, §VI), founded in 1768, was different. It had evolved from the wish of artists to have a state-sponsored, formally run academy on the continental model in contrast to the St Martin's Lane Academy, which was the main training ground for artists in England from 1720 to 1768, and which had been run on informal, democratic lines. (Sir Godfrey Kneller had earlier run a private academy in London, which operated from 1711 to *c.* 1720, also on democratic lines.) The Royal Academy's declared aims were to conduct a free school for students and annual exhibitions of contemporary art, the profits of the latter to be used mainly to pay the costs of the former. These aims were soon realized, resulting in financial independence and freedom from overt political pressure and in this respect providing a model for Edinburgh's Royal Scottish Academy (1826) and New York's National Academy of Design (1825). By the time of the foundation of the Royal Academy, the exhibition of members' works had a well-established precedent in the biennial Salons of the Académie Royale; its training curriculum and methods were also similar to those of Paris, complete with prizes and travelling scholarships to Rome.

Unlike the Académie Royale, the London academy included architects. In Paris the teaching of architects was not combined with that of painters and sculptors until 1795. The Académie Royale d'Architecture was founded in 1671 essentially as a school, but without the monopoly of teaching enjoyed by the painter and sculptor academicians. The curriculum included lectures on architecture, mathematics and mechanics. In the middle years of the 18th century students registered at the Académie only to enter the annual competition, the winning of which usually, but not automatically, conferred a scholarship for study in Rome; many trained at the private school run by Jacques-François Blondel (*see* BLONDEL, (2)) from 1740 until he became a professor at the Académie in 1762. Although recommended styles of architecture changed with changes of teacher and the times, the Académie's programme was geared to producing highly finished drawings of grand architectural projects. From the end of the 18th century its curriculum began to be criticized for producing architects who could invent designs but did not know how to build, and, notwithstanding numerous institutional changes, the teaching of architecture remained broadly the same in France for another 150 years, and in most other centres for almost as long.

5. ACADEMIC IDEALS VERSUS PRACTICAL CONCERNS. Architectural academic training was not alone in being criticized. From around the end of the 18th century the existing academic method was increasingly challenged. Some Romantic writers, and then artists, questioned whether art could be taught at all, since, as Johann Wolfgang von Goethe put it in 1772 in his essay *Von deutscher Baukunst* (published in 1773 in J. G. Herder's *Von deutscher Art und Kunst*), a good work of art should be more experienced than calculated. Some German artists in particular reacted against what they saw as neglectful teachers, and against mechanical copying exercises of parts of bodies, or of schematically rendered gestures and expressions. The engravings of facial expressions in Charles Le Brun's *Conférence sur l'expression générale* (numerous posthumous editions; the most complete being that of Etienne Picart, Amsterdam and Paris, 1698), which must have seemed a great pedagogic advance to artists concerned with differentiating states of emotion, would a century later appear tyrannical to artists concerned with invention, individual genius and self-expression. Hence in place of rules these artists proposed advice, and in place of formal teaching they proposed a more friendly relationship between master and pupil. In 1818 the Prussian architect Karl Friedrich Schinkel recommended replacing academic classes with workshops. Ten years earlier the revived constitution of the Munich Akademie der Bildenden Künste had declared: 'The teacher shall not suffer any uniform mechanism, but leave to the pupil as much freedom as possible to show his particular talent and the special qualities of his manner of looking at objects and imitating them.' In practice, however, copying from drawings and casts was usually retained in German academies in the elementary classes. Only from the 1840s did the most advanced students enjoy relative freedom in master classes where they could work on their own projects with the benefit of guidance.

In the 19th century, German academies also adopted from the French ateliers the inclusion of the teaching of painting, in addition to drawing. These ateliers were artists' studios with a stock of casts and models for life drawing and painting, in effect private academies. The best known was that of Jacques-Louis David, which was taken over by Antoine-Jean Gros when David fled Paris in 1816. It was subsequently run by Paul Delaroche and then by CHARLES GLEYRE. Artists trained in such establishments, which were separate from the proprietor's working studio, followed a curriculum that revolved around the requirements of the Prix de Rome competition and its qualifying competitions. Michel-Martin Drolling and Delaroche, for example, ran competitions for painted compositional sketches (*esquisses*) probably because the Académie des Beaux-Arts (*see* PARIS, §VI, 3), administrative successor of the *ancien régime* academies, had decided in 1817 on the oil sketch as a means of weeding out entrants for the Prix de Rome competition. Painting was not taught at the Ecole des Beaux-Arts (which had taken over the teaching functions of the old academies) before 1863. On the other hand, formal lectures on anatomy, perspective and, from 1819, ancient history (and for architectural students mathematics and descriptive geometry) were available only at the Ecole, whose curriculum, except for a few years after the reforms of 1863, stayed largely unchanged until 1968. The ateliers were therefore providing teaching supplementary to that available at the Ecole, but whereas artists had always learnt to paint in artists' studios, previously this had been in the course of helping the master on actual commissions. Now the great majority of pupils did not assist the master in any way but devoted their time to academic exercises. Although the Académie Julian (*see* FRANCE, §XV), founded in 1868, made much of its undogmatic teaching methods, its teaching was geared to Ecole des Beaux-Arts requirements, its visiting professors included many Prix de Rome winners, and its publicity (it was a commercially run art school) advertised student successes in terms of the academic system. It did, however, provide tuition for women, who were excluded from the Ecole until 1897.

There was one major change in the academic curriculum in France in the 19th century, namely the recognition of landscape as an academic subject, with the first Prix de Rome for historic landscape taking place in 1817. Initially, however, entries were judged by reference to the execution of the figures within the landscape and the depiction of the character of the site in relation to the given, Classical, theme. Furthermore, from 1839 candidates had to pass a perspective test to be eligible to compete. All this reflected the traditional concerns of history painters. Nevertheless, the criteria for judging entries changed over the decades, the overall effect becoming important from the 1830s, and, significantly, neither historical theme nor figure was required in the subject for the Prix Troyon of 1869 (the landscape prize administered by the Académie des Beaux-Arts in place of the Prix de Rome for historic landscape). Landscape painting was not, however, taught at the Ecole, although it was introduced at the Düsseldorf Kunstakademie in 1830 and a few other academies subsequently.

Thus, in spite of the Romantic attack on the academies, the academic system remained intact and the curriculum almost unchanged conceptually. Another potential agent for change had, however, been developing, namely discussions of the relationship between the fine arts and design for commercial purposes. Many late 18th-century academies were established or, like those at Dresden (1762), Stockholm (1779) and Berlin (1786), reorganized, in part to raise standards of draughtsmanship within craft industries. Since the previous century academic artists had been put in charge of the French national tapestry works, the Gobelins, where, moreover, some apprentices were given drawing-lessons by members of the Académie Royale. Elsewhere art schools were established for craftsmen, as at Naples in 1741 and Geneva ten years later, a Manufakturschule in Vienna in 1758 and the Trustees' Academy of Design in Edinburgh in 1760. In 1767 the Ecole Royale Gratuite de Dessin opened in Paris under the flower painter Jean-Jacques Bachelier. Its 1500 pupils copied drawings and prints of figures, animals, flowers and ornament, and they took lessons in geometry and architecture. The trend in central Europe, however, was for trades classes to be incorporated as elementary classes within fine arts academies. In the 19th century this trend was reversed by the establishment of separate trade schools, for example the Berlin Gewerkschule in 1809, a trade school in Augsburg in 1836 and in Copenhagen in 1857. The courses they offered were, however, drawing courses, without teaching of working processes, and their function was to enable craftsmen to translate the designs provided by academically trained artists into their particular media more accurately. Both the trade schools and the trades classes can be distinguished from the academies by their lack of provision for training of the intellect, which, at least in theory, was what gave academies their particular status. Implicit in this distinction was a view of a clear demarcation between the fine arts and the applied arts, with the academies, or at least the 'advanced' classes within them, catering only for the former.

This divorce between conception and execution, between art and craft, was especially marked in Great Britain, where in the early 19th century machines were increasingly taking over working processes, and where, save in Edinburgh, no drawing schools for craftsmen had been set up. By mid-century criticism of the standards of industrial design was being voiced in France and England. The solution adopted was the setting up of more drawing schools, this time, however, in conjunction with museums of applied art, notably the South Kensington Museum (later the Victoria and Albert Museum), London, founded after the Great Exhibition of 1851, which would furnish models of taste to copy. Workshop practice remained outside the curriculum. It was William Morris who from 1861 cooperated with major British artists to design and produce articles for everyday use in a practical demonstration of his belief in the unity between the material, working process, function and aesthetic form (*see* ARTS AND CRAFTS MOVEMENT). In questioning the functioning of the fine arts Morris was also questioning the special, and exclusive, role of the academies of art as teaching institutions. By the end of the 19th century craft instruction was being taught in a few British art schools.

Around the beginning of the 20th century there appeared in German art schools a new emphasis on making, rather than just designing. The inspiration derived indirectly from Morris, but with the difference that in Germany the aim was unity between art and industrial production, not art and craft. With this aim in mind some German academies established craft workshops, such as that at the academy at Breslau (now Wrocław in Poland), around 1903. The Leipzig academy, founded in 1764 as a traditional fine arts institution, became an academy of the art of printing. On the other hand, the trade school, the Kunstgewerbeschule, in Hamburg began to include fine arts courses. Such an amalgamation between conception and production was alien to the traditional concept of the academy of arts, in which the only material process of painting, sculpture and architecture that was taught was drawing, a process that was, moreover, intellectualized by reference to the Antique. It is with this 'clean hands' approach of the academies that the programme of the BAUHAUS, founded by Walter Gropius at Weimar in 1919, may be contrasted.

Gropius's central concern was 'the unified work of art . . . in which there is no distinction between monumental and decorative art'. Thus craft training was seen as essential for architects, painters and sculptors. Moreover, Gropius was concerned that art should have a practical end: from 1923 the Bauhaus was directed towards marrying art with the technology of the machine age. It aimed at a thorough craft, technical and formal training with the aim of collaboration in building, practical research into problems of house construction and furnishing, and the development of standard prototypes for industry and the crafts. The later Bauhaus thus operated as a quasi-commercial organization selling an increasing number of licences to industry to manufacture Bauhaus-designed products. Although the Bauhaus included fine arts courses within its programme, it was totally different in concept from the traditional fine arts academy, first because of its commerciality, second because it produced actual items for use, albeit prototypes, and third because, in producing prototypes, it acknowledged that the ultimate product of its teaching was not the unique result of individual genius, but the machine-made, and so repeatable, result of collective ideas and practical design.

6. 20TH-CENTURY DEVELOPMENTS. By the middle of the 20th century the ossification of the academic system was complete. The Accademia di S Luca had ceased to be responsible for teaching in 1873, and erosion of the financial value of legacies intended for student prizes resulted in its administering only one important competition. Its continuing prestige resides in its archives and its collection of works of art by past members. The Royal Scottish Academy's school, started in 1839, closed in 1931. The Royal Academy in London became associated for a long period with conservative opposition to avant-garde art. Sir Alfred Munnings, appointed President in 1944, used his office as a platform for his reactionary views on modern art, causing embarrassment and controversy in a broadcast speech in 1949. In Paris the academic courses of the Ecole des Beaux-Arts were modernized only after the student protests of 1968.

Elsewhere, art schools have increasingly become part of larger educational institutions offering degree courses. This is the case in the USA and to some extent in Britain, for example with the Slade School of Fine Art, which is part of University College in the University of London. The role of the academies of art in the education of artists has thus become marginalized. In 1977 the Royal Academy in London began charging fees to students, contrary to its original purpose; the National Academy of Design, New York, had done so 100 years earlier. The Royal Academy's better known functions are as a venue for loan exhibitions and retrospectives, as well as for the annual exhibition of the works of members and others. All these developments reflect particular historical, political and social circumstances, although the separation of the teaching of architecture from that of painting and sculpture, now standard, additionally reflects a late 20th-century perception that the teaching of architecture should be as much concerned with function and technical problems as with form.

BIBLIOGRAPHY

G. Vasari: *Vite* (1550, rev. 2/1568); ed. G. Milanesi (1878–85), iv, p. 256; vii, pp. 141–2

C. C. Malvasia: *Felsina pittrice* (1678); ed. M. Brascaglia (1971)

A. de Montaiglon, ed.: *Procès-verbaux de l'Académie Royale de Peinture et de Sculpture, 1648–1793*, 10 vols (Paris, 1875–92)

J. Guiffrey: 'L'Histoire de l'Académie de St Luc', *Archv A. Fr.*, n. s., ix (1915) [whole vol.]

N. Pevsner: *Academies of Art Past and Present* (Cambridge, 1940/*R* New York, 1973)

D. Mahon: *Studies in Seicento Art and Theory* (London, 1947)

H. M. Wingler: *The Bauhaus: Weimar, Dessau, Berlin, Chicago* (Cambridge, MA, and London, 1969)

A. Boime: *The Academy and French Painting in the Nineteenth Century* (Oxford, 1971)

E. Taverne: 'Salomon de Bray and the Reorganization of the Haarlem Guild of St Luke in 1631', *Simiolus*, vi/1 (1972–3), pp. 50–59

C. Bédat: *L'Académie des Beaux-Arts de Madrid, 1744–1808* (Toulouse, 1974)

A. Blaugrund: *The National Academy of Design: A Brief History* (New York, n. d.) [after 1975]

J. Brown: *Murillo & his Drawings* (Princeton, 1976)

E. Gordon: *The Royal Scottish Academy of Painting, Sculpture and Architecture, 1826–1976* (Edinburgh, 1976)

R. Chafee: 'The Teaching of Architecture at the Ecole des Beaux-Arts', *The Architecture of the Ecole des Beaux-Arts*, ed. A. Drexler (London, 1977), pp. 61–109

A. Sutherland Harris: *Andrea Sacchi* (Oxford, 1977)

R. A. Moore: 'Academic *Dessin* Theory in France after the Reorganization of 1863', *J. Soc. Archit. Hist.*, xxxvi/3 (1977), pp. 144–74

J. H. Rubin: *Eighteenth-century French Life Drawing* (Princeton, 1977)

J. Brown: *Images and Ideas in Seventeenth-century Spanish Painting* (Princeton, 1978)

M. Crawford Volk: 'On Velázquez and the Liberal Arts', *A. Bull.*, lx (1978), pp. 69–86

——: 'The Madrid Academy', *A. Bull.*, lxi (1979), p. 627

C. Dempsey: 'Some Observations on the Education of Artists in Florence and Bologna during the Later Sixteenth Century', *A. Bull.*, lxii (1980), pp. 552–69

V. Kemenov: *The USSR Academy of Arts* (Leningrad, 1982)

C. Fehrer: 'New Light on the Académie Julian and its Founder (Rodolphe Julian)', *Gaz. B.-A.*, 6th ser., ciii (1984), pp. 207–16

'France's New Design School', *Indust. Des.*, xxxi/3 (May–June 1984), p. 80

E. Levy: 'Ideal and Reality of the Learned Artist: The Schooling of Italian and Netherlandish Artists', *Children of Mercury: The Education of Artists in the Sixteenth and Seventeenth Centuries*, ed. J. M. Muller (Providence, RI, 1984), pp. 20–27

J.-M. Pérouse de Montclos: *'Les Prix de Rome': Concours de l'Académie Royale d'Architecture au XVIIIe siècle* (Paris, 1984)

L. Olmstead Torelli: 'Academic Practice in the Sixteenth and Seventeenth Centuries', *Children of Mercury: The Education of Artists in the Sixteenth and Seventeenth Centuries* (Providence, RI, 1984)

L. Richard: *Encyclopédie du Bauhaus* (Paris, 1985)

P. Grunchec: *Les Concours d'esquisses peintes, 1816–1863* (Paris, 1986)

S. C. Hutchison: *The History of the Royal Academy, 1768–1986* (London, 1986)

C. Dempsey: 'The Carracci Reform of Painting', *The Age of Correggio and the Carracci* (exh. cat., Washington, DC, N.G.A.; New York, Met.; Bologna, Pin. N.; 1986–7), pp. 237–54

G. Mayer and others: *Académie Royale des Beaux-Arts de Bruxelles: 275 ans d'enseignement* (Brussels, 1987)

A. W. Boschloo and others, eds: *Academies of Art between Renaissance and Romanticism* (The Hague, 1989), pp. 14–60, 77–104, 302–19, 434–50

G. Feigenbaum: 'Practice in the Carracci Academy', *The Artist's Workshop*, ed. P. M. Lukehart, Stud. Hist. A., xxxviii (Washington, DC, 1993), pp. 58–76

HUMPHREY WINE

Academy figure. Term applied to a drawn or painted representation of the human figure, most commonly made as part of the instruction in an academy or art school. Although the practice of making drawings from nude models had developed during the Renaissance and was commended by such theorists as Alberti, it was only with the foundation of academies of painting in the 17th century that such drawing became formalized as part of a rigorous programme of training. Indeed, by the mid-18th century, the word 'académie' was defined in Diderot's *Encyclopédie* as 'a public school where painters go to draw or paint, and sculptors to model, after a nude man called the model'. In France one of the principal means by which the Académie Royale de Peinture et de Sculpture asserted its predominance was by maintaining a monopoly on life classes. After the student had mastered the difficulties of copying engravings and plaster casts, he was set to draw from the nude figure under the supervision of the professor. The model was almost invariably male because female models were forbidden at the Académie Royale, and elsewhere they were extremely expensive to hire. Classes lasted two hours, and the pose was usually changed twice a week. The student began by drawing with red chalk on white paper and later progressed to black chalk on tinted papers, applying white chalk for highlights. Such drawing was an exercise in shading, hatching, graining and stumping, and increasingly the results became so homogeneous in style that unsigned examples are almost impossible to attribute. Painted academy figures (*académies*) were made by more advanced students and were sent to Paris by *pensionnaires* at the Académie de France in Rome as indicators of their progress. As the art academies gradually lost their prestige towards the end of the 19th century, their mainstay also fell into disrepute, although the practice of making academy figures has never been entirely abandoned.

See also ACADEMY; FRANCE, §XV; and PARIS, §VI, 1.

BIBLIOGRAPHY

A. Boime: *The Academy and French Painting in the Nineteenth Century* (New Haven and London, 1971)

Eighteenth-century French Life-drawing: Selections from the Collection of Mathias Polakovits (exh. cat. by J. H. Rubin, Princeton U., NJ, A. Mus., 1977)

M. Roland Michel: *Le Dessin français au XVIIIe siècle* (Paris, 1987), pp. 47–76

The Artist's Model: Its Role in British Art from Lely to Etty (exh. cat. by I. Bignamini and M. Postle, U. Nottingham, A.G.; London, Kenwood House; 1991)

□

Acanthus. Ornamental motif based on the leaves of the acanthus plant, an evergreen shrub native to the Mediterranean area. Two species have been proposed as likely models for different forms of decorative leaf motifs: *Acanthus mollis*, with broad, blunt tips to the leaves, and *Acanthus spinosus*, with comparatively narrow leaves and pointed lobes terminating in spines. Acanthus leaves added to a lotus and palmette border gave rise to a motif known as ANTHEMOIN. The acanthus was described by ALOIS RIEGEL as a variant of the palmette motif (for discussion and illustration *see* PALMETTE). The acanthus leaf's spiky form and scrolling growth made it highly suitable for both ornamental and architectonic use, although, after its initial introduction in Greek art and architecture, the motif rarely corresponded closely to a particular species of plant; throughout its long history the leaf ornaments known as acanthus were imaginary designs adapted variously with no reference to any living plant. In various forms, it was one of the most widely used types of foliage motif from antiquity until the late 19th century.

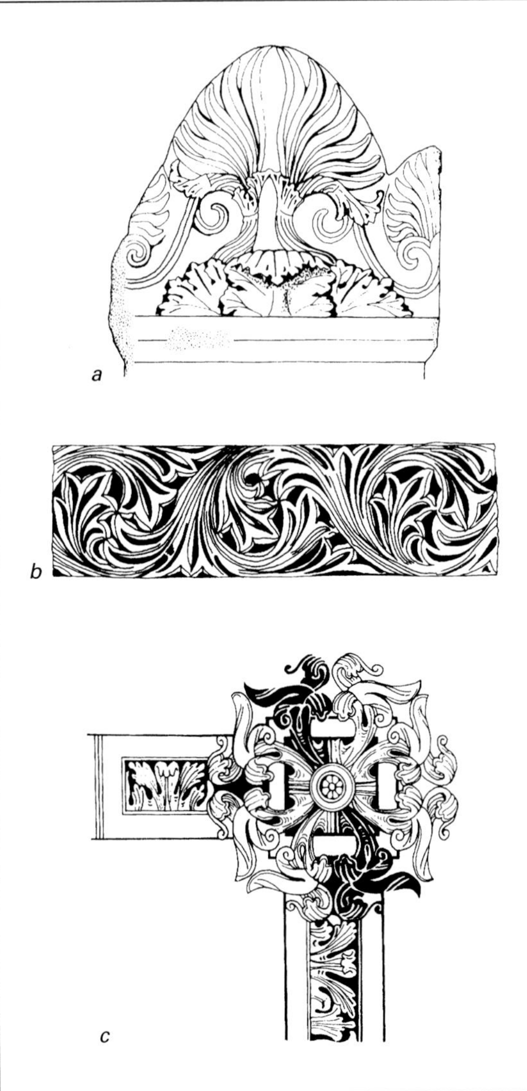

1. Acanthus motifs (from top to bottom): (a) carved ornament at the top of a marble stele, from Athens, *c.* 390–*c.* 365 BC (London, British Museum, Sculpture 605); (b) stone relief from the church of SS Sergios and Bakchos, Istanbul, AD 527–36; (c) detail of a border and corner rosette from the Benedictional of St Aethelwold, Winchester, Old Minster, *c.* AD 980 (London, British Library, Add. MS. 49598, fol. 25)

1. EARLY DEVELOPMENT, BEFORE *c.* 1600. The earliest, most notable and most enduring use of the acanthus is in the capital of the Corinthian order (*see* ORDERS, ARCHITECTURAL, §I, 1(iii), 2(i)(a) and fig. 4), first adopted in Greece in the late 5th century BC as a variation on capitals of the Ionic order, the earliest example being a free-standing column (untraced) from the interior of the Temple of Apollo at Bassai (*c.* 430–*c.* 400 BC; for a later example see fig. 1a). The Roman architect Vitruvius, writing in the 1st century BC, attributed the origins of the Corinthian capital to acanthus leaves growing round a basket of toys left in a cemetery (*On Architecture* IV.i.9–10). The story, though clearly an invention, shows the early connection between the ornamental leaf and this plant. The essentially ornamental nature of the Corinthian order was further developed by the Romans in the ornate Composite order (*see* ORDERS, ARCHITECTURAL, §I, 1(iv)), with elaborate, heavily foliate capitals using fleshy, florid acanthus leaves with looser, bolder curves and blunter tips. The richer, scrolling form of the Roman acanthus provided an adaptable motif that was used throughout the Greco-Roman world. Acanthus, ivy and vine scrolls were disseminated as enrichments on buildings and in designs on wall paintings and mosaics (for scrollwork on the frieze of the Ara Pacis *see* ROME, ANCIENT, fig. 23).

In Byzantine art the acanthus became a supporting decorative motif apparently without any specific symbolic associations. It developed away from Classical realism to a linear style, in which it took on a spiky, highly stylized form that owes nothing to the acanthus plant in nature

2. Byzantine acanthus leaf motif on a capital, AD 532–7, Hagia Sophia, Istanbul

(see fig. 1b and fig. 2; *see also* EARLY CHRISTIAN AND BYZANTINE ART, fig. 49). In the course of the 6th and 7th centuries, in those areas of Europe where animal ornament had dominated, the Church introduced plant ornament, one element of which was the acanthus leaf in its Byzantine form.

In Carolingian art the acanthus was part of the classical revivals initiated by Charlemagne (*see* ORNAMENT AND PATTERN, §III, 2). Byzantium rather than Rome was the source for the re-introduction of the motif, which was employed in such buildings as the palatine chapel at Aachen (late 8th–early 9th century; *see* AACHEN, §2(ii) and fig. 2), which had Corinthian capitals. In secular and religious metalwork the acanthus ranged from classical forms and spikier, harsher Byzantine forms to richer and more elaborate designs that were combined with other motifs (e.g. baldric mounts with acanthus design, 9th century; Stockholm, Stat. Hist. Mus.; *see* ORNAMENT AND PATTERN, fig. 4). In the 10th century the acanthus scroll was introduced to Scandinavian art, where animals were depicted entwined in its leafy scrolls, particularly in the Ringerike style (*see* VIKING ART, §II, 1(vii)). In northern Europe the acanthus, in a modified and more naturalistic form, was one of the most commonly used motifs in the Romanesque style. It is used prolifically in the west façade (early 12th century) of Notre-Dame-La-Grande, Poitiers (11th century; *see* POITIERS, §2(iii)). The lobed leaf, the half leaf and the leaf collar served many purposes, such as supporting or repeat patterns. These motifs remain stylized and non-specific alongside the naturalistic leaves that were introduced in later Gothic architecture. The acanthus played a prominent part in manuscript illumination, in particular the art of the Winchester school (e.g. Benedictional of St Aethelwold, see fig. 1c; *see also* WINCHESTER, §II and ANGLO-SAXON ART, fig. 9), and appears on such objects as manuscript covers (e.g. whalebone manuscript cover, early 12th century; London, V&A; *see* ORNAMENT AND PATTERN, fig. 5).

During the early Renaissance in Florence the Classical acanthus was used in both architectural and non-architectural contexts. Several of the trade guild statue niches on the Orsanmichele, Florence, have columns with acanthus capitals, notably those for Nanni di Banco's *Four Crowned Saints* (1416; *in situ*; for discussion and illustration *see* NANNI DI BANCO) and Donatello's *St Mark* (1411–13; *in situ*) and *St George* (*c.* 1414; Florence, Bargello). Brunelleschi employed the archaeologically accurate Corinthian order in the church of S Lorenzo, Florence, where the tomb of *Piero I and Giovanni de' Medici* (completed 1472; Florence, S Lorenzo, Old Sacristy; *see* VERROCHIO, ANDREA DEL, fig. 2) by Andrea del Verrochio is decorated with large bronze acanthus leaves on the lid of the sarcophagus. As a non-architectural motif, the acanthus was applied to furniture, woodwork and ceramics, frequently in a hybrid acanthus/palmette form (e.g. Faienza maiolica dish, showing the *Arrival of Aeneas at Delos*, 1497; Sèvres, Mus. N. Cér.). The invention of printing radically changed the means by which patterns and motifs were dispersed in Europe. From the late 15th century onwards individual decorative motifs were transmitted through engravings and pattern books, which were published in large numbers in Italy, Germany, France and the Netherlands (*see* PATTERN BOOK, §I, 2). In these designs, which generally originated in Italy, ornamental foliage of all kinds was prominent, drawn from naturalistic Gothic and classicizing Renaissance as well as Islamic forms, and variations on the acanthus were numerous. Alessandro Vittoria (1525–1608) used the acanthus in the stucco fireplace (1552–3) in the Palazzo Thiene, Vicenza, and WENDEL DIETTERLIN in his book *Architectura* (Stuttgart, 1593, rev. ed. 1598) used the motif in a purely decorative way, with only brief consideration for its Classical architectural function.

2. *c.* 1600 AND AFTER. Drawing the acanthus was an essential skill for 17th- and 18th-century craftsmen, as the motif was one of the leading decorative elements in the Baroque style. It was used extensively on mouldings and cornices by such designers as Daniel Marot (*see* ORNAMENT AND PATTERN, fig. 7); on *boiseries*; in ormolu furniture decoration by the workshop of André-Charles Boulle in such pieces as the two commodes (1708–9; Versailles, Château; *see* FRANCE, fig. 54) commissioned by Louis XIV; and in the marquetry commode (1739; London, Wallace; for illustration *see* COMMODE) designed by Antoine-Robert Gaudreaus for the bedroom of Louis XV at Versailles, Jacques Caffiéri used acanthus decoration in heavily cast and chased bronze mounts. In England from the 1660s until the early 18th century it appeared on silverware in many forms: embossed in bands, chased and engraved, used in running scrolls and applied to handles, candlesticks and church plate (e.g. silver-gilt ewer and communion cup, 1683; London, V&A). It was often used to hide joins in metalwork (e.g. candle sconces, mid-18th century; London, V&A). *Eléments d'orfèvrerie* (1748) by Pierre Germain II (1703–83), a collection of engraved designs for metalwork, helped to popularize a form of the motif that was used in metalwork and also adapted for ceramics, such as Sèvres porcelain (e.g. pair of vases, *c.* 1761; London, Wallace) and Josiah Wedgwood's Queen's ware (e.g. vase, *c.* 1785–7; London, V&A).

The acanthus was employed as a motif in Neo-classical interiors in France by Charles Percier and Pierre-François-Léonard Fontaine, in England by Thomas Hope and

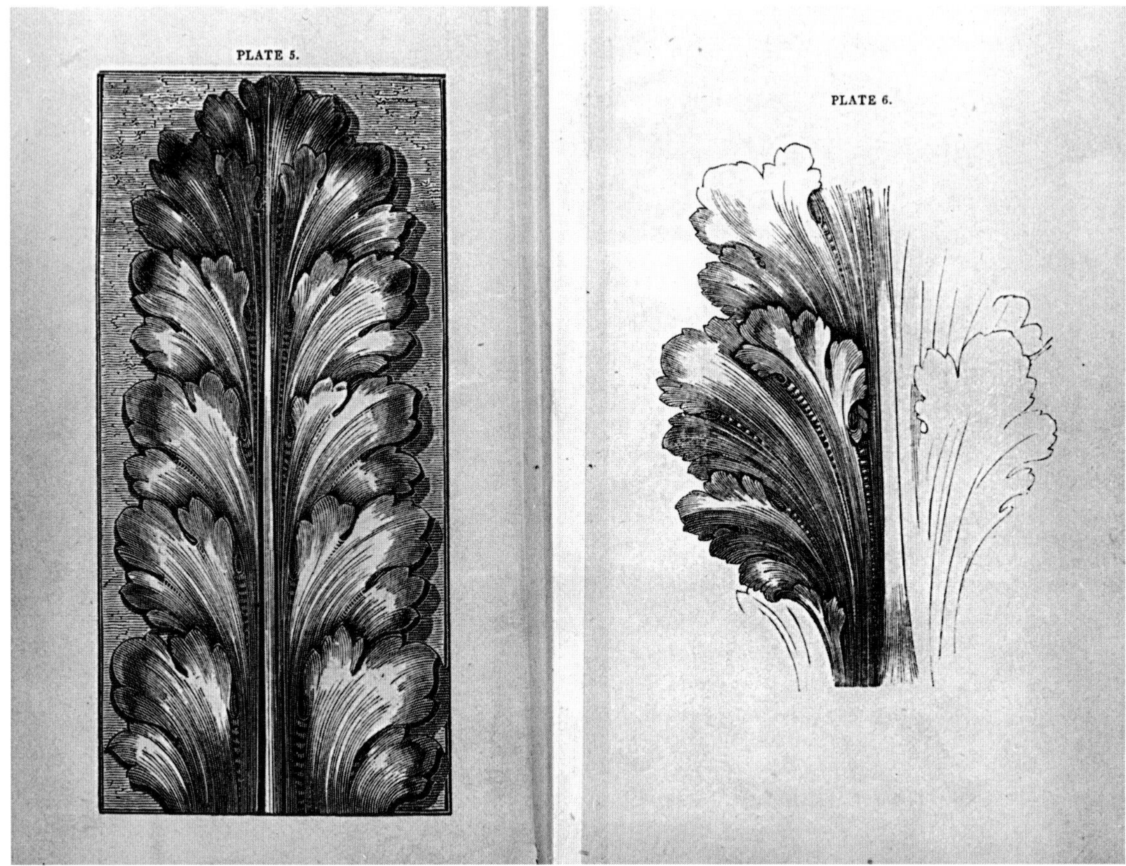

3. James Pope: *A Guide for Drawing the Acanthus and Every Description of Ornamental Foliage* (London, 1850), pls 1 and 6

Robert Adam (for example at Kenwood House, London) and in Russia by Charles Cameron, for example at the Roman Baths in the garden of the summer palace of Catherine II at Tsarskoye Selo (1749–56; now Pushkin Palace-Museum). A series of influential designs that made extensive use of the acanthus were published by Michelangelo Pergolesi (*d* 1801), who may have come to England at the invitation of Robert Adam, in his *Designs for Various Ornaments* (London, 1777–1801). In furniture and metalwork the motif was used in an upright rather than a curved form, in keeping with the restraint of the Neo-classical style (e.g. console table designed by William Kent, 1727–32; London, V&A). In late Regency England the acanthus motif had become commonplace and unrestrained and was used indiscriminately, without regard for its classical associations (e.g. porcelain teapot, Spode, *c.* 1830; London, V&A). In the USA it was applied to furniture both as a decorative motif, for example as freehand painted scrolling leaves (e.g. couch, 1810–25), and with an acknowledgement of its classical origins, for example on the capitals of columns used as supports for a pier table (1820–35; both Winterthur, DE, Du Pont Mus.). Throughout the 19th century pattern books were produced devoted solely to varieties of the representation of the acanthus leaf and stalk, a notable example being James Page's *A Guide for Drawing the Acanthus and Every Description of Ornamental Foliage*, which appeared in several editions, including one of 1850 (see fig. 3). By the mid-19th century A. W. N. Pugin was railing against its debasement in such publications as *The True Principles of Pointed or Christian Architecture* (London, 1841) and *Contrasts* (London, 1856). Although it was included in Owen Jones's *Grammar of Ornament* (London, 1856) in both its natural and stylized form, Jones complained of acanthus leaves being applied 'to any form and in any direction'. William Morris, however, revitalized the motif by studying early examples and the behaviour of real plants (e.g. 'Acanthus' wallpaper, 1875; London, V&A), and Christopher Dresser, a botanist and designer, not only studied the growth patterns of the acanthus but also formalized it into a design called 'Power', which was applied to a number of Wedgwood cane-ware vases and wine-coolers (e.g. pair, *c.* 1880; Barlaston, Wedgwood Mus.).

Although the scrolling foliage motif was an important component in Art Nouveau, the acanthus rarely appears in a recognizable form. Notable exceptions are the decorative plasterwork in the Karlsplatz Underground Station (1898) designed by Otto Wagner and the architecture of Louis Sullivan, who used the motif in stuccowork on the Auditorium Building (inaugurated 1889), Chicago, and decorated the Getty tomb (1890) in Graceland Cemetery, Chicago, with bronze acanthus leaves that may have been influenced by Verrochio's Medici Tomb. In the early 20th century René Lalique employed the acanthus motif on such pieces as the Amiens vase, a rhomboidal frosted vase in which four stylized coiled acanthus leaves protrude from each side (e.g. Paris, Mus. A. Déc.), and Jacques-Emile Ruhlmann used acanthus-derived motifs, often in delicate fillets of ivory, on a small roll-top desk (Paris, Mus. A. Déc.) exhibited in 1923 and on furniture exhibited at the Exposition International des Arts Décoratifs et Industriels Modernes in Paris in 1925. With the advent of modernism and the consequent reduction in ornament and decoration, the acanthus motif was little used in the mid- and late 20th century.

BIBLIOGRAPHY

H. Shaw: *The Encyclopedia of Ornament* (London, 1842)
G. Ebe: *Akanthus* (Berlin, 1883)
A. Riegl: *Stilfragen: Grundlegungen zu einer Geschichte der Ornemantik* (Berlin, 1893)
J. Evans: *A Study of Ornament in Western Europe* (New York, 1975)
E. Temple: *Anglo-Saxon Manuscripts, 900–1066: A Survey of Manuscripts Illuminated in the British Isles* (London, 1976)
E. H. Gombrich: *The Sense of Order: A Study of the Psychology of Decorative Art* (Oxford, 1979)
R. Peesch: *The Ornament in European Folk Art* (New York, 1983)
J. Rawson: *Chinese Ornament: The Lotus and the Dragon* (London, 1984), pp. 9–89
J. Onians: *Bearers of Meaning: The Classical Orders in Antiquity, the Middle Ages and the Renaissance* (Princeton, NJ, 1988)
L. Burn: *The British Museum Book of Greek and Roman Art* (London, 1991)
E. Wilson: *8000 Years of Ornament: An Illustrated Handbook of Motifs* (London, 1994), pp. 125–41

BRUCE TATTERSALL, EVA WILSON

Accardi, Carla (*b* Trápani, 9 Oct 1924). Italian painter. After training at the Accademie di Belle Arte in Palermo and Florence, she moved to Rome in 1946, where she met the Sicilian artists Pietro Consagra, Ugo Attardi (*b* 1923) and Antonio Sanfilippo (1923–80), the last of whom she married in 1949. Together with Giulio Turcato, Mino Guerrini (*b* 1927), Piero Dorazio and Achille Perilli (*b* 1927), the group established FORMA in 1947 to promote an abstract Marxist art distinct from social realism. Accardi participated in the *Forma* exhibition (October 1947; Rome, A. Club) with work still indebted to post-Cubism (e.g. *Decomposition*, 1947; U. Parma, Cent. Studi & Archv Communic.). After one-woman shows in Rome (Lib. Age Or, 1950) and Milan (Lib. Salto, 1951), and having established contact with the Movimento Arte Concreta, Accardi visited Paris. There the contrasting static and energetic work of Alberto Magnelli and Hans Hartung initiated a crisis of direction, and she abandoned painting in 1952–3. On resuming, her dynamic and calligraphic marks in the largely black-and-white *Integrazione* series (e.g. *Negative-Positive*, 1956; artist's col., see 1986–7 exh. cat., p. 28) achieved a balance between sign and ground, surface and space. Their spontaneity as traces of existential experience brought her wide recognition in Italy and France. After joining the Continuità group in 1961 in reaction to *Art informel*, she reintroduced colour, applying repeated rhythmic strokes to transparent plastic, which afforded an open ground (e.g. *Red–Black*, 1967; artist's col., see 1986–7 exh. cat., p. 44). In the 1970s she mounted plastic on shaped stretchers with which she created fragile environments that influenced the practitioners of Arte Povera. When she subsequently reverted to painting on canvas, she adopted greater variety in her mark-making.

BIBLIOGRAPHY

Carla Accardi (exh. cat. by C. Levi, Milan, Padiglione A. Contemp., 1983)
Accardi: Il campo del togliere (exh. cat. by A. Bonito Oliva, Acireale, Pal. Città, 1986–7)

MATTHEW GALE

Acceptus (*fl* Apulia, *c.* 1039–41). Italian sculptor. His name occurs in inscriptions on a marble pulpit in Canosa Cathedral and on the beams of similar pulpits at S Maria, Siponto, and the Sanctuary of S Michele at Monte Sant'Angelo. The inscription on the Canosa pulpit (PER IUSSIONEM DOMINI MEI GUITBERTI VENERABILIS PRESBITERI, EGO ACCEPTUS PECCATOR ARCHIDIACONUS FECI[?T] HOC OPUS) identifies Acceptus as an archdeacon who made the pulpit on the orders of the priest Guitbertus. The inscription on the beam at Siponto refers to Acceptus (DMITTE CRIMINA ACCEPTO) and gives the date 1039; the lectern at Monte Sant'Angelo is dated 1041, and the inscription on one of the beams identifies Acceptus as sculptor ([SC]ULPTOR ET ACCEPTUS BULGO). The workshop evidently included more than one sculptor, since another beam at Siponto is signed DAVID MAGISTER. Fragments of choir screens at Monte Sant'Angelo and Siponto, and the lion support and crossbeam of a throne at Siponto, indicate that the Acceptus workshop made several kinds of liturgical furniture.

The original form of the pulpits at Siponto and Monte Sant'Angelo can be reconstructed on the basis of the Canosa pulpit (total h. 2.74 m), which consists of a rectangular box raised on columns and archivolts, with a semicircular projection for the lectern, which is in the form of an open book decorated with a lion mask, supported by a displayed eagle resting on a human head. The pulpit box is constructed of panels of marble slotted into beams and uprights, suggesting origins in wooden furniture. The beams are decorated with foliage scrolls and the uprights with geometric motifs and terminal knobs. The remains at Monte Sant'Angelo include the lectern, eagle support, three beams with inscriptions and foliage scrolls, two uprights and three capitals; those from Siponto include the eagle and two uprights of a pulpit, as well as seven beams with foliage scrolls and inscriptions, some from the pulpit and some probably from a ciborium.

The sculpture is stylized but of high quality. There is some difference between the smoother and more simplified forms of the Canosa pulpit and the more finely detailed carving of the Siponto and Monte Sant'Angelo fragments, suggesting either a difference in date or that the Canosa pulpit may have been carved by assistants. It is also possible that the rigid style of the Canosa pulpit was influenced by a local metalworking tradition. Acceptus's workshop may have carved the upper parts of the archbishop's throne in Canosa Cathedral (*see* ROMOALDUS), which are very like the pulpit box; there are also similar lion and human masks on the transept capitals of the cathedral. The workshop was also active in Bari, where the door jambs of Bari Cathedral (begun under Archbishop Bisantius, 1025–35) are decorated with foliage scrolls identical to those on some of the Siponto beams. Bari, which formed a joint see with Canosa, may have been the main centre of production.

The sculpture of Acceptus represents the earliest phase of Romanesque sculpture in Apulia and formed the basis of its subsequent development. Influenced by Byzantine and Islamic art, and by small-scale objects in precious materials, it established a distinctive style and iconography.

BIBLIOGRAPHY

E. Bertaux: *L'Art dans l'Italie méridionale*, 3 vols (Paris, 1904/*R* Rome, 1968)
M. Wackernagel: 'La bottega dell'arcidiacono Acceptus, scultore pugliese dell'XI secolo', *Boll. A.*, ii/4 (1908), pp. 143–50
——: *Die Plastik des XI. und XII. Jahrhunderts in Apulien* (Leipzig, 1911)
F. Schettini: *La scultura pugliese dall'XI al XII secolo* (Bari, 1946)
J. R. Gaborit: 'L'Ambon de Sainte Marie de Siponte et les origines de la sculpture romane en Pouille', *Mélanges offerts à René Crozet*, i (Poitiers, 1966), pp. 253–8
H. Schäfer-Schuchardt: *Die Kanzeln des 11. bis 13. Jahrhunderts in Apulien* (Wurzburg, 1972)
Alle sorgenti del romanico: Puglia XI secolo (exh. cat., ed. P. Belli D'Elia; Bari, Pin. Prov., 1975)
A. Prandi, ed.: *Aggiornamento dell'opera di Emile Bertaux*, v (Rome, 1978), pp. 644–7, 649, 694–5, 795, 803, 991
P. Belli D'Elia: 'Il Romanico', *La Puglia fra Bisanzio e l'occidente* (Milan, 1980), pp. 117–253
T. Garton: *Early Romanesque Sculpture in Apulia*, Outstanding Diss. F.A. (New York, 1984)
P. Belli D'Elia: *La Puglia* (Milan, 1986)

TESSA GARTON

Accolti, Pietro (di Fabrizio) (*b* ?Arezzo, 1579; *d* Florence, 1642). Italian writer, painter and architect. He was descended from an illustrious Aretine family (his grandfather was Cardinal Benedetto Accolti (1497–1549), Archbishop of Ravenna and Secretary to Pope Clement VII). He was librarian and architect in the service of Cardinal Carlo Medici, and a member of the Florence Accademia and the Accademia di Disegno. He is known for *Lo inganno degli occhi* (1625), a three-part treatise (on plane figures, solids and shading) in which he showed how perspective practice derived from principles of visual perception. In this he examined classical and modern theories of vision, including those by Euclid (*fl c.* 300 BC), Witelo (*c.* 1230–80), Franciscus Aguilonius (1567–1617) and Guidobaldo del Monte, and criticized contemporary writers on perspective for underestimating the importance of light and shadow. He emphasized the need to distinguish parallel solar rays from diverging point sources of light, such as candlelight, and presented some original ideas on arranging compositions with multiple vanishing points and on foreshortening pictures within pictures. Chapters on anamorphosis and *quadratura* ceiling painting represent contemporary interest in these topics. Accolti's attitude towards perspective rules was remarkably flexible; he cited them only to 'open the eyes and minds' of students without intending to set restrictions. Cropper compares his ideas on *unione* and *sfumamento* (the transitions between light and shadow) to those of Pietro Testa and interpreted them as a product of the Carracci reform of colour and chiaroscuro. As with Matteo Zaccolini's four-volume treatise on perspective (1618–22), his writings testify to the 17th-century revival of Leonardo's ideal of scientific painting. In fact, the 'Discorso intorno al disegno', dedicated to young academicians, in *Lo inganno* is a paraphrase of the latter's *Trattato della pittura*. None of Accolti's painted or architectural works has been identified.

UNPUBLISHED SOURCES

Florence, Bib. N., MS. Passerini 158 bis (Accolti)
Arezzo, Biblioteca Consortile, MS. 34, fol. 92*v*, 103, 118*v* ['Memorie di casa Accolti', 1623–1628, by Lionardo di Jacopo Accolti]

WRITINGS

Lo inganno degli occhi (Florence, 1625)
'Delle lodi di Cosimo II, Granduca di Toscana' [oration to the Accademia di S Luca, 1621], *Prose fiorentine raccolte dallo Smarrito accademico della Crusca*, ed. C. Dati and G. G. Bottari (Florence, 1661 and 1716–45), vi (1716), pp. 111–33

BIBLIOGRAPHY

C. Pedretti: 'Il *Trattato della pittura* di Leonardo plagiato da Pietro Accolti nel 1625', *Rac. Vinc.*, xix (1962), pp. 292–4
E. Cropper: *Ideal of Painting: Pietro Testa's Düsseldorf Notebook* (Princeton, 1984)
M. Kemp: *Science of Art* (New Haven and London, 1990)

JANIS CALLEN BELL

Acconci, Vito (Hannibal) (*b* New York, 24 Jan 1940). American sculptor, performance artist and video artist. He worked for an MFA degree at the University of Iowa from 1962 to 1964. He initially devoted himself to poetry and writing but began to produce visual work in 1969, most of which incorporates subversive social comment. The works of 1969 were photographic records of actions such as bending and throwing, as in *Toe-Touch* (1969; see 1980 exh. cat., p. 12). From 1970 until 1974 he staged a series of activities and performances, such as *Broad Jump '71*. This took place at the Convention Hall in Atlantic City, NJ, and was a jumping competition for men, with a woman as the prize: the work was designed to expose the conventions of male ownership of women.

After 1974 and for the remainder of the 1970s Acconci's presence was only registered at most through recorded tapes of his voice. In *Tonight We Escape from New York* (1977) he installed a rope ladder in the Whitney Museum; alongside this were four loudspeakers, through which fragments of a racist dialogue were played, sounding as if they rose and fell along the ladder. He also used video and film in his work, as in the installation *VD Lives/TV Must Die* (1978) at the Kitchen in New York. This consisted of two TV monitors through which erotic images and sounds were played and in front of which were metal balls on stretched elastic bands, poised to smash the monitors. In the 1980s Acconci turned to permanent sculptures and installations, as in *Instant House* (1980; La Jolla, CA, Mus. Contemp. A.), in which the four sides of a house were pulled together by ropes by the viewer inside. He also produced sculpture and furniture made from natural and incongruous mass-produced objects, as in *Garbage Seating* (1986; see 1987 exh. cat., p. 39), made from dustbins, earth and tree branches.

BIBLIOGRAPHY

Vito Acconci: A Retrospective, 1969–1980 (exh. cat. by J. R. Kirshner, Chicago, IL, Mus. Contemp. A., 1980)
Vito Acconci: Domestic Trappings (exh. cat. by R. J. Onorato, La Jolla, CA, Mus. Contemp. A., 1987)

□

Acemhöyük. Site in central Turkey that flourished in the first half of the 2nd millennium BC, in a fertile plain watered by the River Karasu. The oval mound of Acemhöyük, measuring 700×600 m, and 20 m high, rises in the

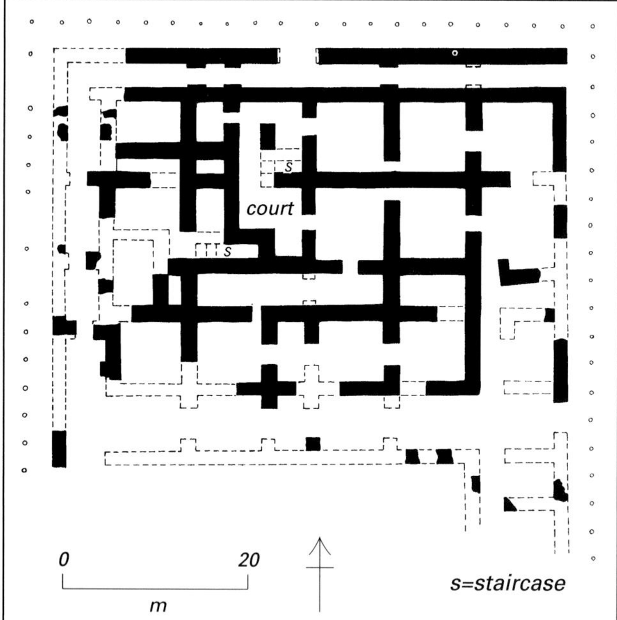

Acemhöyük, plan of central building of the Sarıkaya Palace, first quarter of the 2nd millennium BC

centre of the town of Yeşilova, 18 km north-west of Aksaray; it was surrounded by a lower city 600 m wide, now covered by the modern town. Acemhöyük was thus the largest ancient settlement in this agricultural region, and excavations were begun in 1962 by a Turkish team led by Nimet Özgüç. Some of the objects from the excavations are in the Museum of Anatolian Civilizations, Ankara; most are in the archaeological museums at Niğde and Aksaray; and a fine collection of ivories from the site is in the Metropolitan Museum of Art, New York.

Occupation of the mound began at least as early as 3000 BC and the surviving architectural remains and artefacts from the Early Bronze Age settlements (levels IX–VI) testify to the existence of a distinctive local culture that nevertheless maintained close links with contemporary settlements in central Anatolia and Cilicia. The lower town was first occupied in *c.* 2000 BC, and during the first quarter of the 2nd millennium BC Acemhöyük developed into a great city, and the mound and lower town were occupied to their fullest extent. This city is probably to be identified as ancient Burushhanda, the capital of one of the great kingdoms of Anatolia during the period of the Old Assyrian trade colonies, mentioned in cuneiform texts of the first quarter of the 2nd millennium BC (*see* ANATOLIA, §I, 2(ii)(a)), and celebrated for copper-working and trade. Large areas of level III (19th and 18th centuries BC) were investigated, and private and public buildings have been uncovered. Although the rectangular plans of the private dwellings resemble those of Kültepe, the building techniques were not the same. Because of the scarcity of stone in this area, mud-brick and wood formed the basic construction materials, generally on stone foundations. Houses each contained a kitchen, storerooms and a large room, with a hearth in the form of a wide platform in the middle.

Three public buildings have been investigated: two are referred to for convenience as the Sarıkaya Palace, at the highest point on the south side of the mound, and the Hatipler Palace, on the eminence on the north side of the city, while the third is a large but heavily damaged structure on the west side of the mound. Identical construction techniques and similar artefacts show that these buildings all belong to level III, which was destroyed by an extremely fierce conflagration *c.* 1700 BC. The Acemhöyük palaces were constructed on 4 m-wide foundations of huge stones laid on level ground. Across these stones 4 m wooden cross beams were set side by side to cover the entire surface. A second layer of thick wooden beams was laid at right angles to the first (i.e. along the line of the stone foundations) to act as bonding beams. Mud-brick walls 1.5 m thick were placed in the centre of this composite foundation. Since mud-brick walls are not very durable, vertical wooden posts were placed at 0.9 m intervals within the thickness of the wall. The wall intersections and the doorways were further reinforced with a lattice of timber poles cut to the thickness of the mud-brick walls and laid horizontally one on top of the other for the entire height of the wall. The lowest layer of this reinforcing lattice was extended across the bottom of the doorways to form a threshold. This building technique differs significantly from those found in contemporary palaces elsewhere in Anatolia, although wood was frequently used in buildings (e.g. at BEYCESULTAN) to give added elasticity in the event of an earthquake.

The central building of the Sarıkaya Palace (see fig.) has a portico of wooden columns, set on stone bases that supported a roof on its north façade. The east and west sides of the palace were probably surrounded by the same construction, while the south façade looked out on to the River Karasu. It is assumed that subsidiary buildings, such as the kitchen and archive, were situated around adjacent courtyards that have not been excavated. The ground floor of the central building survives, but the massive foundations and the collapsed remains of upper floors suggest that the building had two storeys. A depiction of the building found on the walls of a large bathtub from the palace implies that the second storey had balconies. The area covered by ruins makes it probable that the ground floor of the palace consisted of at least 50 rooms. By the 1990s the Hatipler Palace had not been fully excavated, but it had at least 76 rooms. Only its south-east façade had a portico, supported on six mud-brick piers 3.0×0.5 m.

Although much was lost in the fire that destroyed the city, Acemhöyük has proved one of the richest sites in Anatolia, both for luxury goods and everyday artefacts. Ivory was used for figurines to adorn furniture, for relief plaques decorated with figures or geometric designs and covered with gold leaf, and for other ornaments; there are gaming boards, the bead decoration from items of dress, vessels made of obsidian and rock crystal, bronze weapons, a large number of copper ingots, the remains of a four-wheeled chariot and pottery. Clay bullae, impressed with the designs from cylinder and stamp seals, have been found in private storerooms and in all the rooms of the palaces. The designs illustrate the contemporary styles of

Assyria, Babylonia and Syria, as well as Anatolia. Seal impressions on some of the bullae are identified by their cuneiform inscriptions as belonging to Shamshi-Adad I, King of Assyria (*reg* 1813–1781 BC), the daughter of Iahdun-Lim, King of Mari, and Aplahanda, King of Carchemish in the early 18th century BC.

After the destruction of level III, there was some reoccupation of the site until *c.* 1650 BC (level II). Much later, in the Hellenistic period (level I, 4th century BC), a village was founded on the southern and western parts of the site with houses, some of them two storeys high, constructed according to central Anatolian architectural traditions. Earlier strata were levelled and built over, stones quarried from older structures were broken up and used to prepare the foundations, and, upon these, walls of sun-dried brick were erected. Among the artefacts found in these houses were figurines, rhyta, moulds for decorated clay plaques, and pottery, both Hellenistic and local.

BIBLIOGRAPHY

K. Emre: 'The Pottery from Acemhöyük', *Anatolia*, x (1966), pp. 99–153
N. Özgüç: 'Excavations at Acemhöyük', *Anatolia*, x (1966), pp. 38–52
——: 'An Ivory Box and a Stone Mould from Acemhöyük', *Turk Tarih Kurumu: Belleten*, xl/160 (1976), pp. 555–60
——: 'Some Contributions to Early Anatolian Art from Acemhöyük', *Belleten*, xliii/170 (1979), pp. 289–305
A. Özten: 'Two Stone Plates from the Sarıkaya Palace at Acemhöyük', *Belleten*, xliii/170 (1979), pp. 385–8
N. Özgüç: 'Seal Impressions from the Palaces at Acemhöyük', *Ancient Art in Seals*, ed. E. Porada (Princeton, NJ, 1980), pp. 61–80
——: 'Seals of the Old Assyrian Colony Period and Some Observations on the Seal Impressions', *Ancient Anatolia: Aspects of Change and Cultural Development. Essays in Honor of Machteld J. Mellink* (Wisconsin, 1986), pp. 48–53
A. Özten: 'Acemhöyük taş kapları' [Stone vessels from Acemhöyük], *Belleten*, lii/203 (1988), pp. 393–406
N. Özgüç: 'An Early Bronze Age Pot Grave of a Child from Acemhöyük', *Between the Rivers and Over the Mountains*, ed. M. Frangipane and others (Rome, 1993), pp. 517–20

NIMET ÖZGÜÇ

Acevedo, Alonso de Fonseca y, Archbishop of Toledo. *See* FONSECA Y ACEVEDO, ALONSO DE.

Acevedo y Zúñiga, Manuel de. *See* MONTERREY, 6th Conde de.

Aceves Navarro, Gilberto (*b* Mexico City, 24 Sept 1931). Mexican painter. He studied at the Escuela Nacional de Pintura y Escultura 'La Esmeralda' under Enrique Assad Lara and Carlos Orozco Romero. His work reflects a concern for the negative effects of industrialization and modernization on cities and displays a nostalgia for more humane urban conditions. His large-scale paintings, for example the *Boots of the Gran Solar* (oil on canvas, 1.60×1.80 m, 1982; artist's col.), convey a sense of urgency through the use of light and colour, with broad lines and chromatic tones creating dynamic forms that show the influence of Abstract Expressionism.

BIBLIOGRAPHY

Siete pintores contemporáneos: Gilberto Aceves Navarro, Luis López Loza, Rodolfo Nieto, Brian Nissen, Tomás Parra, Vlady, Roger von Gunten (exh. cat., Mexico City, Pal. B.A., 1977)
R. Tibol: *Aceves Navarro, Durero y las variaciones* (Mexico City, 1978)
M. Idalia: 'Más libertad y menos barroquismo en la nueva pintura de Aceves Navarro' [Greater freedom and less extravagance in the new painting of Aceves Navarro], *Excelsior* (13 Sept 1979), p. 1-B
S. Alatriste: *La intuición primitiva* (Mexico City, 1986)

JULIETA ORTIZ GAITÁN

Achaemenid. Name given to a people of Persian origin, who founded an empire that flourished *c.* 550–331 BC.

1. Introduction. 2. Official art. 3. Private art. 4. Regional styles.

1. INTRODUCTION. The Achaemenid Persian empire was founded *c.* 550 BC by Cyrus the Great. At its greatest extent under Darius the Great (*reg* 522–486 BC), it stretched from the Indus into northern Greece and across Egypt. The Macedonian Alexander the Great (*reg* 336–323 BC) was able to defeat the Achaemenids in 331 BC only after prolonged military campaigns.

This vast Persian hegemony was rich in legacies of administrative expertise and cultural heritage. Its dynastic name was derived from an 8th-century BC ancestor who ruled as a Persian vassal of the Iranian kingdom of the Medes, who were to inherit great power by conquering the Assyrians in the late 7th century BC. Both the Median overlords and Persian vassals enjoyed access to the Mesopotamian/Iranian artistic heritage. Annals of the Assyrian kings describe the Medes and the Persians living in fortified cities as early as the 9th century BC, while 7th-century BC paylists state that Persians worked alongside Egyptians, Ionians, Lydians, Medes and Elamites at the court of Nebuchadnezzar II of Babylon (*reg* 604–562 BC).

The artistic traditions fostered within the Achaemenid empire cover a complex system of influences presented in a full range of media: monumental stone and brick architecture, applied and free-standing sculpture in stone, moulded brick and metal, wall painting, coins, seals, vessels of glass, alabaster and metal, metal jewellery, horse trappings and decorated weaponry, ornamental woodwork, ivory carving and textiles. An official court art was created under the patronage of the early Achaemenid kings that was acutely aware of the propaganda value of reflecting the geographical diversity of the realm as well as the ancient artistic heritage that persisted in these locales. At the same time, art was also created for private use both within and outside the court circle. In order to understand the art of the Achaemenid empire it is necessary to distinguish between official and private art, both within the Persian heartland of south-west Iran and in the far-flung administrative provinces, with their strongly individual traditions.

Textual documentation on Achaemenid society is very limited. The surviving official imperial texts need careful interpretation. They do not, for example, contain explicit narrative accounts of court ceremonies that might explain some of the iconographical intricacies of official representations. Similarly there are no anecdotal, religious or poetic texts from which to gather information relevant to the interpretation of Achaemenid art. Commentary on monuments, which is available for ancient Greece, for example, through the travelogues of Pausanias, is lacking. Much of the textual documentation on the Achaemenids actually derives from the Greek world, notably the *Histories* of Herodotus (5th century BC) and the *Anabasis* of Xenophon (4th century BC), but these sources, as well as the later ones describing Alexander's conquests, provide only an external view of the Persian empire. An understanding of Achaemenid art has been further hampered by the fact that much historical discussion on the Persians has

1. Rock relief and inscription of Darius the Great, w. *c.* 6 m, Bisitun, Iran, *c.* 520–519 BC

emerged from analysis of Greek texts by scholars steeped in Classical rather than Near Eastern traditions.

Most of the surviving art is derived from the imperial cities of Pasargadae, Persepolis and Susa in south-west Iran. Elsewhere in the empire there is little evidence that has been systematically excavated, partly because only recently has interest been shown in the later levels of long-inhabited sites. The ephemeral natures of wall painting, metalwork and textiles have led to few examples surviving.

2. OFFICIAL ART. Official Achaemenid art was produced under the king's direct authority. This applies to the palatial architecture and monumental sculpture commissioned by the Persian rulers in their capitals and to the series of imperial coins of royal issue. Less straightforward, but of prime importance, are the many seals used by court officials, which provide a bridge between the public and private spheres of artistic production. The Persian kings were informed patrons, selectively adapting antique and foreign images and styles of architecture and sculpture to serve specific new purposes. This may be seen most clearly in the two newly founded Achaemenid capitals, PASARGADAE and PERSEPOLIS. Pasargadae was founded by Cyrus the Great, probably after his victory over Croesus of Lydia in 547 BC, and its buildings exhibit a blend of Near Eastern and Western techniques and forms. The palaces display characteristic Lydian and Ionian stone-working techniques and styles, such as the methods of joining masonry and column drums and the profiles of column base mouldings. However, they also display decidedly Eastern architectural decoration, as in the colossal Assyrianizing guardian bulls at the main doors of the Gatehouse. This mixture of approaches reflects both the use of craftsmen from throughout the empire and the harmonious assimilation of rituals and visual ideas from the conquered lands.

One relief, carved on the sole preserved doorjamb of the twin secondary entrances to the Gatehouse (for illustration *see* PASARGADAE), indicates the importance of viewing Achaemenid art against earlier Near Eastern traditions of kingship, diplomacy and art. It depicts a composite creature wearing the quadripartite wings commonly associated with Assyrian guardian genii, the 'atef' war crown of Egypt and an elaborate Elamite royal robe. The figure faces into the Gatehouse and seems to symbolize access to the interior by privileged invitation rather than its defence. The relief reflects Cyrus's ideological embracing and acquisition of critical Near Eastern traditions, joining together the cultural and administrative traditions of the Elamite civilization and his aspirations towards Egypt, although the actual conquest of Egypt was not effected until after his death. In the context of the Pasargadae Gatehouse, the Elamite robe and the Egyptian crown suggest eastern and western limits of civilization brought together into a new union. The wings evoke the rich legacy of Mesopotamian palatial art. In the Achaemenid context they may also have alluded allegorically to the four quarters of the empire. Herodotus reports that Cyrus had a prophetic dream in which Darius had wings shadowing both Asia and Europe. This story may preserve a vestige of a Persian interpretation of the winged figure as symbol of defined domain.

The ideological and stylistic roots of official Achaemenid art were refined under Darius the Great. The city of Persepolis, which he founded in the last quarter of the 6th century BC, epitomized an international expression of imperialism. Its architecture was laden with symbolism, drawing upon Egyptian, Mesopotamian/Iranian and East Greek traditions to produce an elaborate syncretism of style and iconography. The overall message is of a harmonious world order in which the virtues of kingship have resolved all conflict. Significantly, official Achaemenid art is not historical in the annalistic sense, for representations of the king stress dynastic identity rather than the individual.

One monument alone is a historical record in the usual sense: the rock relief and text (see fig. 1) carved at the beginning of Darius's reign high up on the cliff face of Mount BISITUN in western Iran. The main text describes a series of battles fought by various generals, while the relief presents the ideological basis of these historical victories. Darius stands with his foot upon the squirming figure of one rival claimant to the throne (Gaumata), while the bound figures of other rebels are lined up before him. Two Persian weapon-bearers stand behind the king. Hovering over the scene is the image of Ahura Mazda, the patron deity of the Achaemenids, who is constantly invoked in imperial texts as the divine collaborator of the king in all things. Ahura Mazda wears a crown of divinity and holds the ring, an ancient Mesopotamian symbol of divine authority. His torso emerges from a winged disc. The human figures on the relief are rendered according to the principles of social perspective, clearly establishing the relative status of the king, his helpers and his foes. The basic composition is directly modelled upon a rock relief of the late 3rd millennium BC at Sar-i Pul-Zuhab, *c.* 100 km east of Bisitun on the same ancient road to Babylon, that is itself a somewhat provincial version of an Akkadian royal relief. Stylistically, however, the Bisitun monument reflects a conscious reworking of Assyrian art of the reign of Assurbanipal (*reg* 668–627 BC). The selection of these prototypes was not fortuitous, for both possess different but compatible formal elements. The Achaemenid synthesis reveals a preference for the visual experience rather than episodic narrative. In this aspect it draws upon a whole category of Akkadian period monuments such as the Victory stele of Naram-Sin (*reg* 2254–2218 BC; Paris, Louvre; *see* AKKADIAN, fig. 1).

Such conscious evocations may seem too elaborate for Achaemenid Persia, yet similar forms of intricate allusion are documented in literary construction. In a famous edict recovered at Babylon, Cyrus the Great had himself cast in the role of pious king, preserver of the ancient line of worthy rulers. The edict specifically describes Cyrus as a follower in the tradition of the Assyrian king Assurbanipal, who had conquered Babylon, rebuilt the temples and restored its institutions. Cyrus deliberately echoed the archaizing phraseology of Assurbanipal's pronouncements in Babylon. Achaemenid official art was thus the visual expression of this well-informed, adaptive emulation of earlier expressive modes.

Under the patronage of Darius a distinctly Achaemenid sculptural style developed, best seen in the extensive architectural reliefs at Persepolis, though it is also apparent in other media, particularly seals and metalwork. On the natural forms of men and animals this style contrasts flowing contours with intricate and often abstract patterned elements of coiffure, dress and ornament. The Achaemenid court style has often been described as cold or even deadly, but viewed positively it achieves a formal harmony and discretion, which complements an iconographic programme describing dynastic control and world order.

Official representations of the king have been found in stone reliefs at Pasargadae, Persepolis and neighbouring Naqsh-i Rustam, the site of several of the royal tombs. At Susa, due to the scarcity of local stone, the palaces were mainly decorated with moulded-brick relief. Fragments of palace wall paintings have also been discovered there. A colossal gateway statue of Darius the Great was excavated by the French mission at Susa in 1972. This is made of Egyptian stone and was originally intended to stand before a temple in Egypt; its secondary usage at Susa emphasizes the ability of ancient monarchs to harness manpower and transport technology to royal demand. In all the extant representations of the king (except the Bisitun relief and a copy set up in Babylon) the dynastic image is presented in static, timeless mode. The king appears in audience, stands (bow in hand) before Ahura Mazda and a blazing fire altar, or passes in stately splendour with servants close behind. In each case the figure is crowned and wears royal shoes without straps. Interestingly, in the numerous representations of a heroic figure slaying lions, bulls and fantastic creatures, the personage wears a headdress and strapped shoes, which are characteristic of non-royal figures on other reliefs. For this reason the heroic figure is often called a Royal Hero—as distinct from a king *per se*. Although he surely represents the king in some sense, he is best understood as depicting the king in his aspect as the archetypal embodiment of 'a Persian man'.

The image of kingship preserved on Achaemenid coins of centralized royal issue offers yet another aspect of dynastic identity. Darius the Great commissioned the development of a distinctive coinage in gold and silver (*see* ANCIENT NEAR EAST, §II, 8(i)). Four types are known, all variations on the theme of the crowned king as warrior/hunter. On the first two types the royal figure is either half-length holding his bow and arrows (type I), or full-length and drawing his bow (type II). The coins bear no inscriptions, and the dating of individual issues has relied upon the evidence of hoard contexts and presumed stylistic development. The use of a type II archer coin as a stamp seal on a dated administrative tablet from Persepolis has proved that this type, at least, had been issued by 500 BC.

Achaemenid coins provide the earliest known types bearing representations of a personage rather than a divinity. The depictions of the ruler are not likenesses in any naturalistic sense, but idealized visions, and present a dynastic portrayal of the ruler as warrior and hunter. Individualized portraiture developed on coins produced by satraps within the western reaches of the empire, and these early ruler portraits are generally considered part of the Greek tradition. Formally they certainly reflect Greek style, but they emulated an idea devised originally by Darius of using coins as a vehicle for representation of the ruler.

Official Achaemenid coinage was minted mainly for use in the western parts of the empire, where payment in coin (especially to engage mercenaries) was expected, and the image chosen for this coinage was designed to advertise the Persian king in a quintessentially Persian mode. Commentary on Achaemenid art frequently presumes a rigid division in the system of workshop production and market destination of portable goods. Items which look predominantly Greek are presumed to have been made for a Hellenic or Hellenized clientele, while items that look essentially Persian or eastern are presumed to have been made for an eastern market. In fact, the imperial coins relate in style and iconography to well-documented schools of seal production in the heartland of the empire. It is likely that the coin dies were made in the busy seal workshops at the Persian court, even though they were used to mint currency to pay westerners far from the imperial centre.

The Achaemenid empire inspired the culmination of a great Near Eastern heritage in the art of seals. During this period the cylinder seal enjoyed a revival, alongside the continued use of the stamp. Analysis of several thousand seals known through their impressions on imperial administrative documents from Persepolis (the Treasury and the Fortification Tablets) has provided much information on the complexities of seal production within the empire. Many of the documents are dated and give extensive information on the users of the seals. It is thus possible to distinguish between official and private seal art. The court style was formulated in an official workshop near Persepolis. Evidence from the Fortification Tablets indicates that, for example, the rendering of the Achaemenid court robe had reached a standard style several years before the end of the 6th century BC. An important group of seals, some known through actual seals and more through impressions, are cylinders bearing an inscription panel with the name and titles of the Persian king. All bear representations of a royal figure in court robe, royal beard and crown, and include framing palm trees that may have alluded to royal authority through reference to a specific royal grove of palms. The Persians were famous for their

2. Lobed phiale inscribed with name and titles of Artaxerxes I, silver, diam. 295 mm, *c.* 464–424 BC (Washington, DC, Freer Gallery of Art)

'paradise' gardens, and architectural remains at Persepolis and Susa have revealed hypostyle audience halls designed to symbolize groves in which the soaring columns resembled stylized palm trees. The seals bearing royal names seem to have been official seals owned by specific court offices rather than by persons holding those offices, and they may have been commissioned directly by the named king. These official seals offer a restricted range of imagery: the king before an altar; the king hunting lions from a chariot; the king as heroic vanquisher of beasts; and the king with defeated enemies.

3. PRIVATE ART. Many seals that are known to have been owned by specific court individuals may be considered examples of private art, and the Fortification Tablet seal impressions from the reign of Darius display the richness of artistic vocabulary available to high-status patrons at the Persian court (*see* ANCIENT NEAR EAST, fig. 23). Sometimes this was closely linked to the established court style, but very often it was responsive to other influences. A superb example is the seal of Parnaka, the most powerful man in the Persepolis bureaucracy under Darius. After losing his seal, he had a new one made in the 22nd regnal year of the king (500 BC). This new seal, commissioned after the Achaemenid court style was well established, is a blatant return to the modelled style of Neo-Assyrian seals, but the archaizing element must be understood as being a positive quality rather than a sign of creative poverty.

Vessels and jewellery are an important, if problematic, source of information on the Achaemenid court style and the social and economic functions of its relations to private art. Few of these objects have been found in context, making precise dating and workshop relationships elusive. Nevertheless, the extant examples can be compared with representations on architectural reliefs and wall paintings. Those made of precious metals (*see* METAL, colour pl. II, fig. 1) conform to the court-style preference for graceful animal forms and abstract ornamental refinement, confirming Greek accounts of the lavish use of gold and silver plate and jewellery by the Persian court. A characteristic vessel form, both in silver and bronze, was the phiale (a shallow bowl with offset rim and lobed patterns hammered out in full relief). Several examples incorporate a royal-name inscription (see fig. 2), suggesting, coupled with a remark by Aelianus (*Varia Historia* 1.22), that such inscribed silver phialai may have been given as gifts of state to ambassadors. Beautifully crafted as these objects were, they seem to have been assessed by weight rather than by aesthetic criteria and were an important means of accumulating and dispersing wealth within the empire.

4. REGIONAL STYLES. A large category of art produced within the Persian empire—so-called 'Greco-Persian' art—is familiar mainly from hundreds of unprovenanced stamp seals. It seems to blend the characteristics of Greek and Persian court style and imagery in a distinctive way, and presumably emerged in regional workshops of the western empire. The Greek contribution may be seen in elements such as smooth, fully modelled forms, free-field compositions, the depiction of women and of genre scenes (e.g. non-heroic hunts); but in order to assess the Achaemenid contribution a wider knowledge of the Persepolis seal impressions must be awaited.

In the 5th and 4th centuries BC the impact of internationalism had a major effect upon expressive interchange. Greco-Persian art is but one manifestation of this environment. Imported Persian textiles found in the Siberian tombs of Scythian chieftains on the eastern fringe of the empire suggest a largely lost medium that must have played a major part in the transmission of visual ideas across the empire and beyond its borders. The wealth of gold objects from the OXUS TREASURE and the BLACK SEA COLONIES demonstrates another area within the greater empire that was attuned to a creative blend of local and exotic traditions. The tomb paintings discovered at Karaburun in Anatolia (for illustration *see* ELMALI) are yet more examples of regional art in the empire; they combined local modes of representation and funeral custom with elements of the court style from the heart of the empire.

While discussion of Achaemenid art ought perhaps to be confined to manifestly official examples, it is becoming apparent that it possessed different styles and levels of execution, which made it a fertile ground for creative encounters between Western and Eastern artistic traditions.

BIBLIOGRAPHY

E. Porada: *Alt-Iran: Die Kunst in vorislamischer Zeit* (Baden-Baden, 1962); Eng. trans. as *Ancient Iran: The Art of Pre-Islamic Times*, A. World (London, 1965); *The Art of Ancient Iran: Pre-Islamic Cultures*, A. World (New York, 1965)

R. Ghirshman: *Perse: Proto-Iraniens, Mèdes, Achéménides*, A. Mankind (Paris, 1963); Eng. trans. as *The Art of Ancient Iran from its Origins to the Time of Alexander the Great* (London, 1964)

J. Boardman: *Greek Gems and Finger Rings* (London, 1970), pp. 303–57

C. Nylander: *Ionians in Pasargadae: Studies in Old Persian Architecture* (Uppsala, 1970)

P. Amiet: 'La Glyptique de la fin d'Elam', *A. Asiat.*, xxviii (1973), pp. 3–32
C. Starr: 'Greeks and Persians in the Fourth Century BC', *Iran. Antiq.*, xii (1977), pp. 49–115
M. C. Root: *The King and Kingship in Achaemenid Art: Essays on the Creation of an Iconography of Empire*, Acta Iranica, 19 (Leiden, 1979)
P. R. S. Moorey: 'Deve Hüyük II in Context: The Archaeological Evidence for Persian Occupation of the Near East *c.* 550–330 BC', *Cemeteries of the First Millennium BC at Deve Hüyük*, Brit. Archaeol. Rep., Int. Ser., 87 (1980), pp. 128–42
M. C. Root: 'The Parthenon Frieze and the Apadana Reliefs at Persepolis: Reassessing a Programmatic Relationship', *Amer. J. Archaeol.*, lxxxix (1985), pp. 103–20
M. B. Garrison: *Seal Workshops and Artists in Persepolis: A Study of Seal Impressions Preserving the Theme of Heroic Encounter on the Fortification and Treasury Tablets* (diss., U. Michigan, 1988)
M. C. Root: 'Evidence from Persepolis for the Dating of Persian and Archaic Greek Coinage', *Numi. Chron.*, cxlviii (1988), pp. 1–12
H. Sancisi-Weerdenburg and A. Kuhrt, eds: *Achaemenid History*, 4 vols (Leiden, 1988–)
M. C. Root and M. B. Garrison: *Seal Impressions on the Persepolis Fortification Tablets: A Catalogue Raisonné* (Chicago, in preparation)

MARGARET COOL ROOT

Achenbach, Oswald (*b* Düsseldorf, 2 Feb 1827; *d* Düsseldorf, 1 Feb 1910). German painter. He studied at the Kunstakademie in Düsseldorf, as did his elder brother, the painter Andreas Achenbach (1815–1910), who was the main influence on him other than his teacher, Johann Wilhelm Schirmer. At a very early stage he began to prepare studies for landscapes in the area around Düsseldorf, sketching boulders, rocks, bushes, trees and people. From 1843 he went on many study tours, visiting Bavaria in 1843 and northern Italy and Switzerland in 1845. The Bavarian and Italian Alps stimulated him to create a unified approach to landscape painting. In such early works as *Landscape* (1846; Düsseldorf, Kstmus.) his receptiveness to atmospheric values can be seen, even if the precise detail and clear articulation into foreground, middle ground and background still clearly show his debt to Schirmer.

In 1850 Achenbach travelled to Rome and the Campagna, where he met Arnold Böcklin, who was also studying in Düsseldorf, and Heinrich Dreber. This journey was very significant for Achenbach; from then on Italian landscape and the southern way of life became his main subjects. Numerous drawings and oil sketches bear witness to his intensive study of nature. The warm ochre tones, attention to detail and the severe form of his works at this period still show Schirmer's influence, but after another journey to Italy in 1857, when he visited Rome, Naples and Capri, these traits were almost completely eliminated. In contrast to Schirmer's rational compositional methods, atmospheric elements became crucial to Achenbach's work. His study of light and colour had shown him that the best way of conveying the sensation of a *plein-air* landscape was by blending one area of the picture into the next to create an atmospheric haze of colour, as in *Landscape in the Campagna* (1855; Düsseldorf, Kstmus.). Achenbach's taste for the picturesque and his ability as a colourist enabled him to depict landscapes with conviction and unity. His liking for using his fingers and palette knife to distribute colour and model form was typical of his method of painting, with its broad outlines and wide variety of approaches.

Achenbach achieved international recognition early in his career: in 1852 he was made a member of the Rijksakademie van Beeldende Kunsten in Amsterdam. In 1863 he succeeded Schirmer as professor of landscape painting at the Kunstakademie in Düsseldorf. He used the local Rhine scenery as the basis of his teaching, and also increasingly devoted his own work to it. He travelled to Paris and Normandy in 1859, and to Kissingen, Marienbad and Heidelberg in 1866 and 1870, but neither these journeys nor subsequent visits to Belgium and the Netherlands in 1873 made a deep impact on his work. A further stay in Rome and Naples in 1871 did produce changes. If his earlier drawings and oil sketches had enabled him to familiarize himself with the details of a particular locale, the studies he made at this time were aimed increasingly at clarifying composition.

Achenbach also became more intensively concerned with architecture. As well as paintings of Roman monuments and the colourful city life of Rome and Naples, such as *By the Porta Capuana in Naples* (1875; Munich, Neue Pin.), he continued to produce landscapes, but in the following decade his interest was concentrated less on the Campagna and more on the area round Naples, Sorrento and Capri. His liking for architecture led him to paint architectural views, but this resulted in a repetitious over-use of certain motifs. In his later pictures he quite often enhanced genre scenes by adding figures in fashionable dress, as in *Social Gathering on a Garden Terrace* (1889; Berlin, Neue N.G.). Achenbach attempted to depict landscape naturalistically in all its possible manifestations; colour effects and light phenomena were of particular importance to him in his work, although this often gives his pictures a theatrical effect. He was one of the most important landscape painters of the Düsseldorf school.

BIBLIOGRAPHY

Meissner
J. H. Schmidt: *Oswald Achenbach* (Düsseldorf, 1944)
W. Hütt: *Die Düsseldorfer Malerschule, 1819–1869* (Leipzig, 1964), pp. 136–8
J. Markowitz: *Die Düsseldorfer Malerschule*, ii, Düsseldorf, Kstmus. cat. (Düsseldorf, 1969), pp. 28–40
Die Düsseldorfer Malerschule (exh. cat., ed. W. von Kalnein; Düsseldorf, Kstmus., 1979), pp. 247–56

JOSEF STRASSER

Achilles Painter. *See* VASE PAINTERS, §II.

Achmim. *See* AKHMIM.

Achtermann, (Theodor) Wilhelm (*b* Münster, Westphalia, 15 Aug 1799; *d* Rome, 26 May 1884). German sculptor. He first trained with his father as a joiner, and in 1829 he won a scholarship to Berlin. From 1830 to 1836 he studied at the Akademie der Künste, Berlin, with the sculptors Friedrich Tieck and Christian Daniel Rauch. He was deeply religious and during these years he concentrated almost exclusively on religious themes, for example a *Christ on the Cross* (1830), a *Hovering Angel* for a font (1831), a *Resurrection* relief (1834) and a *Virgin and Child* (1836). In 1838 the Prussian Minister of Culture, Bethmann Hollweg, commissioned Achtermann to make a marble crucifix for Burg Rheineck bei Niederbreisig (*in situ*) and this enabled Achtermann to travel to Italy, initially to Carrara for marble for his work, and subsequently to

Rome, where he later settled. In Rome the main influences on his work derived from artists in the circles around Bertel Thorvaldsen and Friedrich Overbeck. Affinities with the work of the Lukasbrüder characterized his principal sculpture for Münster Cathedral: an over life-size *Pietà* (1843–9; destr. World War II; small marble version in Rome, S Prassede) and a large-scale *Deposition* group (1850–58; destr. World War II; plaster cast in Rome, Trinità dei Monti). Achtermann's preoccupation with the theme of the Crucifixion continued throughout his life with, for example, a work of *c.* 1821 in the Mausoleum, Charlottenburg, Berlin, and in 1857 a work for Achtermann's tomb in the Campo Santo Teutonico, Rome. Although his work was limited stylistically and veered between self-quotation and sentimentality, Achtermann was one of the most consistent representatives of 19th-century German religious sculpture. His work, however, derived from his training as a craftsman and his deeply felt Catholicism, and Achtermann thus remained an outsider within the Rauch school.

BIBLIOGRAPHY

J. M. Strunk: *Wilhelm Achtermann: Ein westfälisches Künstlerleben* (Vechta, 1931)
P. Bloch and W. Grzimek: *Das klassische Berlin: Die Berliner Bildhauerschule im 19. Jahrhundert* (Frankfurt am Main, Berlin and Vienna, 1978, 2/1994)
Abbilder—Leitbilder: Berliner Skulptur von Schadow bis heute (exh. cat., ed. H. Börsch-Supan; W. Berlin, Schloss Charlottenburg, 1978)
H. Börsch-Supan: *Die Kunst in Brandenburg-Preussen* (Berlin, 1980)
Rheinland Westfalen und die Berliner Bildhauerschule des 19. Jahrhunderts (exh. cat., ed. P. Bloch; Bottrop, Mod. Gal.; Cappenberg-Salm, Schloss Cappenberg; Aachen, Suermondt-Ludwig-Mus.; 1984)
D. Kaiser-Strohmann: *Theodor Wilhelm Achtermann (1799–1884) und Carl Johann Steinhäuser (1813–1879): Ein Beitrag zu Problemen des Nazarenischen in der deutschen Skulptur des 19. Jahrhunderts* (Frankfurt am Main, Berne and New York, 1985)
R. Thiele: 'Achtermann', *Allgemeines Künstlerlexikon*, i (Munich and Leipzig, 1992)

PETER SPRINGER

Acker, Hans [Hans von Ulm] (*fl* Ulm, 1413–61). German painter. He belonged to an artist family of which several generations were documented in 15th-century Ulm. According to municipal tax lists, 'Ackerlin, painter' was a master by 1413. He received payments from the masons' lodge of Ulm Cathedral from 1415. In 1441 the cathedral lodge in Berne paid 'Master Hans of Ulm' for the production and delivery of stained-glass windows: this Hans is identified with Acker (*see also* GOTHIC, §VIII, 5). The Berne *Passion* window (1441; Berne Cathedral, chancel), his only surviving documented work, demonstrates the capabilities of mid-15th-century German glass painting in dealing with box-shaped hall-church interiors. Its Apostle figures still belong to the tradition of the 'Soft style', inspired by Bohemian art, while the style of their robes is reminiscent of those in the chancel windows of Ulm Cathedral. The appearance of a landscape background reveals the influence of the glass paintings (*c.* 1420) in the cathedral's Besserer Chapel.

However, as the latter are no longer assumed to be the product of Acker's workshop, related windows in Ulm Cathedral (Kuttel window, *c.* 1413; *Day of Judgement* window, 1431; *Passion* cycle windows, 1440) must be removed from the workshop's oeuvre. Nor can the former upper windows of the Margarethenkapelle of Konstanz Cathedral (1430; Freiburg im Breisgau Cathedral since 1820) be definitely identified as a product of the workshop. It is fairly certain that there was an Acker workshop, though not that Lukas Moser was a member of it or even Acker's teacher. However, stylistic similarities between figures in the Berne *Passion* windows and a *St Jerome* window (*c.* 1447–50; Ulm Cathedral, Neithardt Chapel), as well as the direct transposition of facial features, affirm workshop attribution, and a payment made by the Ulm Cathedral lodge in 1449 is generally connected with the workshop's repairs on the chancel windows. It cannot be conclusively proved that Acker worked as a panel painter.

BIBLIOGRAPHY

W. Lehmbruck: *Hans Acker: Maler und Glasmaler von Ulm* (Ulm, 1968)
N. Werner: 'Zu den Glasgemälden der Bessererkapelle des Münsters zu Ulm', *Giessen. Beitr. Kstgesch.*, i (1970), pp. 29–49
R. Becksmann: Corp. Vitrearum Med. Aevi: Deutschland, ii/1 (Berlin, 1979), pp. 102–10
C. Reisinger: *Flandern in Ulm: Glasmalerei und Buchmalerei—Die Verglasung der Bessererkapelle am Ulmer Münster* (Worms, 1985)
R. Becksmann: 'Der Mann aus Brügge: Eine Fiktion', *Kstchronik*, xliv (1988), pp. 315–21

WERNER BRODA

Ackermann, Max (*b* Berlin, 5 Oct 1887; *d* Bad Liebenzell, nr Stuttgart, 14 Nov 1975). German painter. He studied under Henry Van de Velde at the School of the Fine Arts and Arts and Crafts of the Grand Duchy of Saxony (later the Bauhaus, Weimar) (1906–7), and under Franz von Stuck at the Akademie der Bildenden Künste, Munich (1909–10). He worked under Adolf Hölzel at the Staatliche Akademie der Bildenden Künste in Stuttgart from 1912, and by 1918 he had produced his first non-objective works under the influence of the latter. Although primarily an abstract painter he was briefly involved with Magic Realism in the 1920s. He devised a type of colour abstraction, which he called 'Absolute Painting', and in 1930 he founded a 'Seminar for Absolute Painting' at the Volkshochschule in Stuttgart. Works such as *Painting XII* (1949; Berlin, Alte N.G.) relied heavily on a body of theory derived mainly from Hölzel and the colour theories of Goethe.

BIBLIOGRAPHY

L. Langenfeld, ed.: *Max Ackermann: Aspekte seines Gesamtwerkes* (Stuttgart, 1972)

COLIN RHODES

Ackermann, Rudolph [Rudolf] (*b* Stollberg, Saxony, 20 April 1764; *d* Finchley, London, 30 March 1834). English publisher and patron of German birth. He trained as a carriage designer in Paris and moved to England between 1783 and 1786. He established his own business as a carriage maker, undertaking major commissions in London and Dublin. In 1804 he designed Pius VII's carriage for the coronation of Napoleon and in 1805 the funeral carriage of Horatio, Viscount Nelson. By 1800 Ackermann had built up a unique business at 101 The Strand, London, known as 'The Repository of Arts'. This encompassed a drawing school with 80 pupils, the sale and loan of Old Master paintings and watercolour drawings, the publication of decorative prints and illustrated books and the manufacture of watercolour paints including a number of new chemical pigments.

In the early 19th century, Ackermann was an important and regular patron of English watercolour painters, employing William Henry Pyne, Augustus Charles Pugin, Thomas Heaphy, Frederick Mackenzie (1787–1854), Thomas Uwins and John Gendall. Much of the later work of Thomas Rowlandson was commissioned by Ackermann; the prolific association of the author William Combe and Rowlandson began in 1810 in the third volume of Ackermann's *The Microcosm of London* and flourished in the three *Tours of Doctor Syntax* (1811, 1820, 1821), *The Dance of Life* (1817), *The English Dance of Death*, 2 vols (1815–16) and *The History of Johnny Quae Genus* (1821–2).

Ackermann was fascinated by scientific and technological advances as they related to the fine and decorative arts. He published many of the first backlit transparencies (1796–8), patented a waterproof paper (1801) and was the first to employ gas lighting in a manufactory (1811). In 1817 he patented Alois Senefelder's process of lithography in England, operating his own lithographic press until 1822. He was active in the search for an unforgeable note for the Bank of England (1819) and recommended a new steel plate engraved on a cylindrical die.

Between 1794 and 1832 Ackermann published over 300 books, many with hand-coloured plates, and tens of thousands of copies of decorative prints in aquatint, mezzotint, stipple, lithography, steel plate engraving and soft-ground etching, all produced to the highest technical standards. His principal publications included: *The Microcosm of London*, 3 vols (1808–10; 104 aquatints); *The History of the Abbey Church of St Peter's Westminster*, 2 vols (1812; 80 aquatints); *A History of the University of Oxford* (1814; 64 aquatints); *A History of the University of Cambridge* (1815; 80 aquatints); *The History of the Colleges* (1816; 44 aquatints); and *The Repository of Arts*, a monthly magazine published from 1809 to 1828 (1432 coloured plates). His younger sons succeeded him in 1830 as Ackermann & Co., and the business of his eldest son, Rudolph Ackermann jr, established in 191 Regent Street in 1822, continues as Arthur Ackermann & Son Ltd at 33 New Bond Street, London.

BIBLIOGRAPHY

DNB
J. Ford: *Ackermann, 1783–1983: The Business of Art* (London, 1983)
S. Jervis: 'Rudolph Ackermann', *London, World City, 1800–1840* (exh. cat., ed. C. Fox; Essen, 1992)
R. Hill: 'Bankers Boards & Beau Monde', *Country Life*, clxxxviii (1994), pp. 64–7

JOHN FORD

Ackersloot [Akersloot], **Willem (Outgertsz.)** (*b* Haarlem, *fl* 1620–34; *d* The Hague, ?1634). Dutch engraver. He was the son of Outgert Arisz. Ackersloot (*fl* 1631). In 1624 he became the brother-in-law of the artist Cornelis van Kittensteyn (1600–38). After a stay in Paris in 1620, he was back in his native Haarlem by 1624. His oeuvre comprises 18 engravings, dating from 1624 to 1633. He eventually became a skilful reproductive engraver; among his best works are the portraits of *Frederik Hendrik* and *Amalia van Solms* after Adriaan van de Venne (both 1628), the *Ceres Changing Stellio into a Lizard* after Jan II van de Velde (i) and the book illustrations after Pieter Jansz. Saenredam's early drawings for Samuel Ampzing's *Beschryvinge en de lof der stad Haerlem* ('Description and praise of the city of Haarlem'; Haarlem, 1628). He is last documented in The Hague in 1634.

BIBLIOGRAPHY

Hollstein: *Dut. & Flem.*; *NKL*; Thieme–Becker
F. G. Waller: *Biographisch woordenboek van Noord Nederlandsche graveurs* (The Hague, 1938), p. 2

CHRISTIAAN SCHUCKMAN

Acmeism [Rus. Akmeizm, from Gr. akmĕ: 'perfection']. Russian poetic movement established in St Petersburg in 1913, which flourished until the early 1920s and was associated with the journal *Apollon*. The leaders and theoreticians of this movement were Nikolay Gumilyov (1886–1921) and Sergey Gorodetsky (1884–1967), and the movement's poets included Anna Akhmatova (1888–1966) and Osip Mandel'shtam (1891–1938). In general terms Acmeism professed a conservatism and a dedication to 'world art' and its preservation in the turbulent period of the October Revolution of 1917, when other literary trends, such as Futurism, were denouncing the past. The primary links between this literary movement and art were forged through Gumilyov and his relationship with Natal'ya Goncharova and Mikhail Larionov. Both artists made portraits of him as well as illustrating his poems.

In the early part of his career Gumilyov wrote three pieces of art criticism for Russian journals, discussing the work of Paul Gauguin and Paul Cézanne, among others. He also wrote an article (unfinished) on African art. During visits to London and Paris, Gumilyov met Roger Fry, worked with the Russian sculptor Boris Anrep (1883–1969) and discussed collaborations with Larionov and Goncharova on a production for Diaghilev. Gumilyov's late Acmeist work shows the probable influence of Rayism. The enthusiasm shared by Gumilyov, Goncharova and Larionov for ethnography and Eastern art forms is felt in their work from the period of their friendship in 1917.

Acmeism also had much in common with the poetic movement Imagism, which rejected Romanticism. The Acmeists were opposed to the mystical vagueness of the Russian Symbolists, and they emphasized craftsmanship and earthly reality. Their poetry was characterized by clarity of language and a visual orientation, some of the best describing objects from the natural world or timeless objects of man's creativity. More concerned with grounding their work in the systems of art and verbal culture than in social reality, the Acmeists filled their verse with allusions to other artistic systems, justifying Mandel'shtam's definition of the movement as 'the yearning for world culture'.

BIBLIOGRAPHY

S. Driver: 'Acmeism', *Slav. and E. Eur. Rev.*, xii (1968), pp. 141–56
D. Mickiewicz: 'The Problem of Defining Acmeism', *Rus. Lang. J.*, suppl. (Spring 1975), pp. 1–20
E. Rusinko: 'Russian Acmeism and Anglo-American Imagism', *Ulbandus Rev.*, i (1978), pp. 37–49
——: 'Acmeism, Post-symbolism and Henri Bergson', *Slav. Rev.*, xli (1982), pp. 494–510
A. Parton: 'Goncharova and Larionov—Gumilev's Pantum to Art', *Nikdaj Gumilev, 1886–1986: Papers from the Gumilev Centenary Symposium* (Berkeley, 1987), pp. 225–42

ELAINE RUSINKO

Acosta, Wladimiro [Konstantinovsky, Wladimir] (*b* Odessa, Russia, 23 June 1900; *d* Buenos Aires, 11 July 1967). Argentine architect. He studied architecture at the

Istituto di Belle Arti in Rome, graduating in 1919. From 1922 he worked in Germany, gaining experience in building engineering and urban design, before moving to Argentina in 1928. He worked in Chile, Uruguay, Brazil, Venezuela, Guatemala and, from 1954 to 1957, in the USA, where he taught (1956) at Cornell University, Ithaca, NY. On his return to Argentina he was appointed Professor of Architectural Composition (1957–66) at the Universidad de Buenos Aires. Acosta was an early exponent of an approach to architecture through environmental design and engineering, which he promoted through his book *Vivienda y clima* (1937) and his 'Helios' buildings. These were based upon correct orientation, cross-ventilation, and the control of solar radiation by means of *brises-soleil*, with a minimum of mechanical inputs. Like the architects of the Modern Movement in Europe, he saw architecture as a social phenomenon and became dedicated to the provision of mass housing for rapidly growing urban populations. His early work included individual houses in Buenos Aires, for example the Casa Stern, Ramos Mejia (1939), the 'Helios' villa (1943) at La Falda and others elsewhere in Argentina, at Rosario, Córdoba, Bahia Bianca and Bariloche. He also designed a psychiatric hospital (1942) at Santa Fé, but he is principally known for his multi-storey 'Helios': Departmentos de Figueroa Alcorta y Tagle (1942–3) and Co-operativa El Hogar Obrero workers' housing (1954; with Fermin Bereterbide and A. Felici), Avenida Rivadavia y Riglos, Buenos Aires, a slim 24-storey slab block on a two-storey podium. Acosta's buildings are simple and astylar in the early Modern Movement genre, although expressive of the principles of solar control.

WRITINGS

Vivienda y clima (Buenos Aires, 1937)
Vivienda y ciudad (Buenos Aires, 1947)
'Villa à La Falda', *Archit. Aujourd'hui* (Sept 1948), pp. 62–3

BIBLIOGRAPHY

F. Bullrich: *Arquitectura Argentina contemporánea* (Buenos Aires, 1963)
S. Borghini, H. Salama and J. Solsona: *1930–1950: Arquitectura moderna en Buenos Aires* (Buenos Aires, 1987), pp. 30–37, 99–101

LUDOVICO C. KOPPMANN

Acoustics. Sound can be defined as audible vibrations within a relatively steady medium, and in buildings sound may be air-borne or structure-borne. The science of architectural acoustics is divisible into noise control and room acoustics. The following article is mainly concerned with the latter and the 'desired' sound generated within a space, because its design has had a significant impact on architectural form; it concentrates on examples of Western architecture.

For an extended discussion of acoustics see *Grove 6*.

1. The science of room acoustics. 2. Types of acoustic space.

1. THE SCIENCE OF ROOM ACOUSTICS. Different acoustical conditions are preferable for listening to the spoken word as compared with different types of music. The shape, size and construction of halls and theatres—and to some extent other building types, including churches—developed historically in response to acoustical requirements. Room-acoustic design, however, is a relatively recent subject of study. Until the 20th century this relationship between acoustical requirements and the building form resulted from trial and error, involving the architect's intuition and awareness of precedent rather than scientific knowledge. Acoustically inadequate halls were usually demolished within about 50 years, so that most surviving older halls are probably among the best that were built.

From 1895 the American physicist Wallace Clement Sabine (1868–1919) carried out experiments on reverberation time. Three years later he was asked to apply his knowledge of room acoustics to the planning of the auditorium at Symphony Hall (opened 1900–01), Boston, MA, designed by McKim, Mead & White. Reverberation is the sound that lingers in a space when the sound source has stopped, as the sound energy reflects off the enclosing surfaces of the room before gradually escaping from the room or becoming absorbed; the time taken for the reverberant sound to disappear beyond audibility was standardized for scientific purposes as a reduction in sound level of 60 decibels. Reverberation time depends on the cubic volume of the room and the amount of sound-absorption present. Sabine evolved a simple formula for its calculation, and for many years this remained practically the only easily measurable aspect of room acoustics. Accordingly until *c.* 1960 much effort was focused on prescribing an exact reverberation time for various types of room.

The reverberation-time calculation, however, is independent of a room's shape. Sound is assumed to be analogous to a gas filling a room and then gradually escaping: for a room of given cubic volume the rate of escape of gas remains the same regardless of its shape. For several decades halls were constructed with reverberation characteristics that were similar to the admired historic halls, yet their acoustics were invariably inferior. It became apparent that the shape of a room—or, more precisely, the position of sound-reflecting surfaces—is important in determining its acoustical character, especially the clarity and loudness of music played in the room, and the acoustical 'scale' of the space.

When a musical sound is produced in a hall, the sound arriving at the listener's ears is a combination of sound direct from the musicians' instruments and sound reflected off the wall, balcony and ceiling surfaces. The sound continues to reflect many times, and the same acoustic information continues to reach the ear in sequence according to the number of times the sound has reflected. The sound strength and tonal fullness are determined by the density and arrival time of these reflections, especially with regard to those arriving within about 200 milliseconds of the direct sound. It is the shape of the room that determines this pattern and the degree to which the reflections are sustained and guided to the listener.

Sound that is reflected laterally is particularly important in a concert hall, since the listener feels enveloped by the music and involved in the performance when sound arrives from different directions. This effect is especially exciting when the orchestra plays forte and reflections from the surfaces of the room are strong. Tall, narrow room proportions—as in the traditional 19th century, rectangular concert halls—are more desirable than the low, wide proportions of most 20th-century auditoria. In the former, multiple cross-reflections of sound are generated, so that sound energy is retained as long as possible, and music played in the hall has great fullness and strength.

Each element of the hall can be studied and made optimal using the modelling techniques available to the acoustician. The pattern of sound distribution in a hall is affected by the angle in three dimensions of each section of wall, ceiling and floor, together with its position in space. The angle and position in plan of the side walls are particularly critical at the mid-section of the hall for encouraging the lateral reflection of sound. Various methods may be adopted to simulate the pattern of sound distribution in a room. Light-reflection, or sound of a suitably scaled pitch, may be used with an architectural model, or sound reflections may be simulated graphically by computer. Modelling is especially useful for identifying potential acoustical faults, such as long-delayed echoes.

2. TYPES OF ACOUSTIC SPACE. The history of auditoria may be divided into those buildings where speech intelligibility should not be obscured by late-arriving reflected sound, and concert halls for the performance of instrumental music, where fullness of tone and a longer reverberation time are desirable. Leonardo da Vinci projected these acoustic criteria into sketches depicting two buildings of contrasting form, one containing 'theatres for hearing mass' (Paris, Inst. France, Codex B, fol. 55*v*) and another labelled 'place for preaching' (Paris, Inst. France, MS. B.N. 2037, fol. 5*v*; see fig. 1).

(i) Churches. (ii) Theatres. (iii) Opera houses. (iv) Rooms for speech. (v) Concert halls.

(i) Churches. In the Middle Ages churches were the first large-scale enclosures for public assembly. The stone walls and vaults, and the large cubic volume relative to the number of occupants, resulted in a relatively long reverberation time—some 12 seconds in the largest cathedrals, much less in village churches. The strength of long-delayed reflected sound is increased by the extreme height-to-width ratio of many Gothic churches. The reverberation is predominantly of low frequency because there are no bass absorbers except the windows, and stonework can absorb high-frequency sound. The acoustics of these buildings did much to encourage the development of Western music, especially the choral tradition. Music drama was also much performed, and, although speech intelligibility was poor, this was overcome by the audience following the performers around the building as the scene of the action changed. In Baroque churches, however, the ample wooden furnishings are efficient bass absorbers, and the reverberation tends to be strongest at middle frequencies. Such acoustic conditions are excellent for the instrumental music that developed during the Baroque era.

Church design after the Reformation illustrates a conscious adaptation from one type of acoustic environment to the other. When the sermon became a major element in Protestant services, Gothic churches in northern Europe—for instance the Thomaskirche, Leipzig, where Johann Sebastian Bach (1685–1750) was Cantor—were remodelled by hanging curtains and by inserting new galleries near the pulpit. This reduced reverberance and increased speech clarity. When designing the 50 new parish churches for the City of London, Christopher Wren (in a letter of 1711) emphasized that they should be small enough for everyone to see and hear the preacher.

(ii) Theatres. According to Vitruvius, however, the earliest attempt at acoustic control in buildings was in Classical theatres. In *On Architecture* (V.5) he claimed that bronze acoustic vases were commonly built into seating risers to act as resonators for amplifying the sound; yet their actual effect must have been negligible. (Many similar vessels can be seen built into the walls of such widely scattered churches as the parish church (12th century), Bjäresjö, near Ystad, Sweden; St Nicholas (13th century), Leeds,

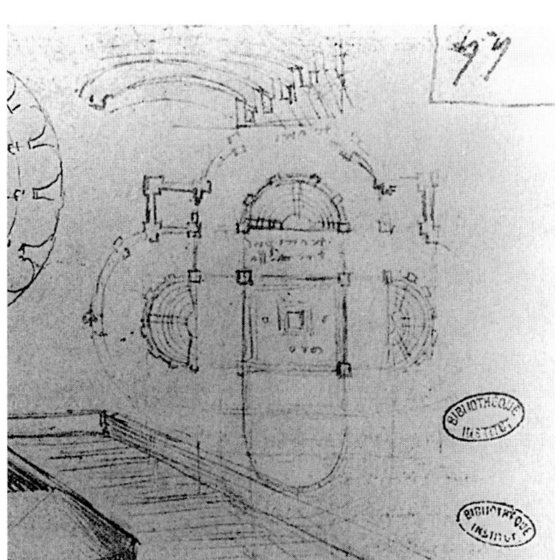

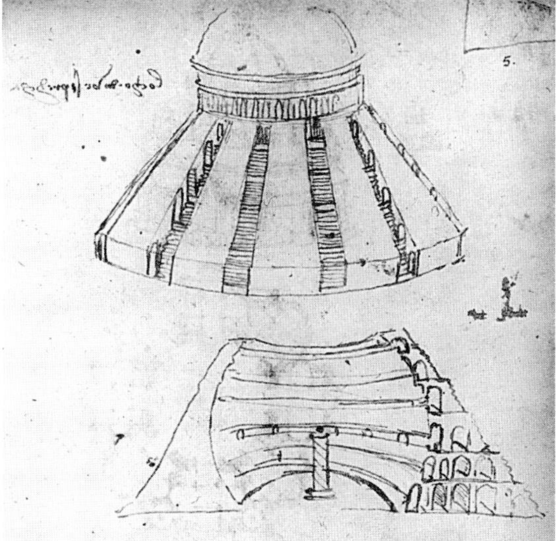

1. Acoustic designs by Leonardo da Vinci, pen and ink, *c.* 1488: (left) 'theatre for hearing mass', Cod. B, fol. 55*v*; (right) 'place for preaching', MS. B.N. 2037, fol. 5*v* (Paris, Institut de France)

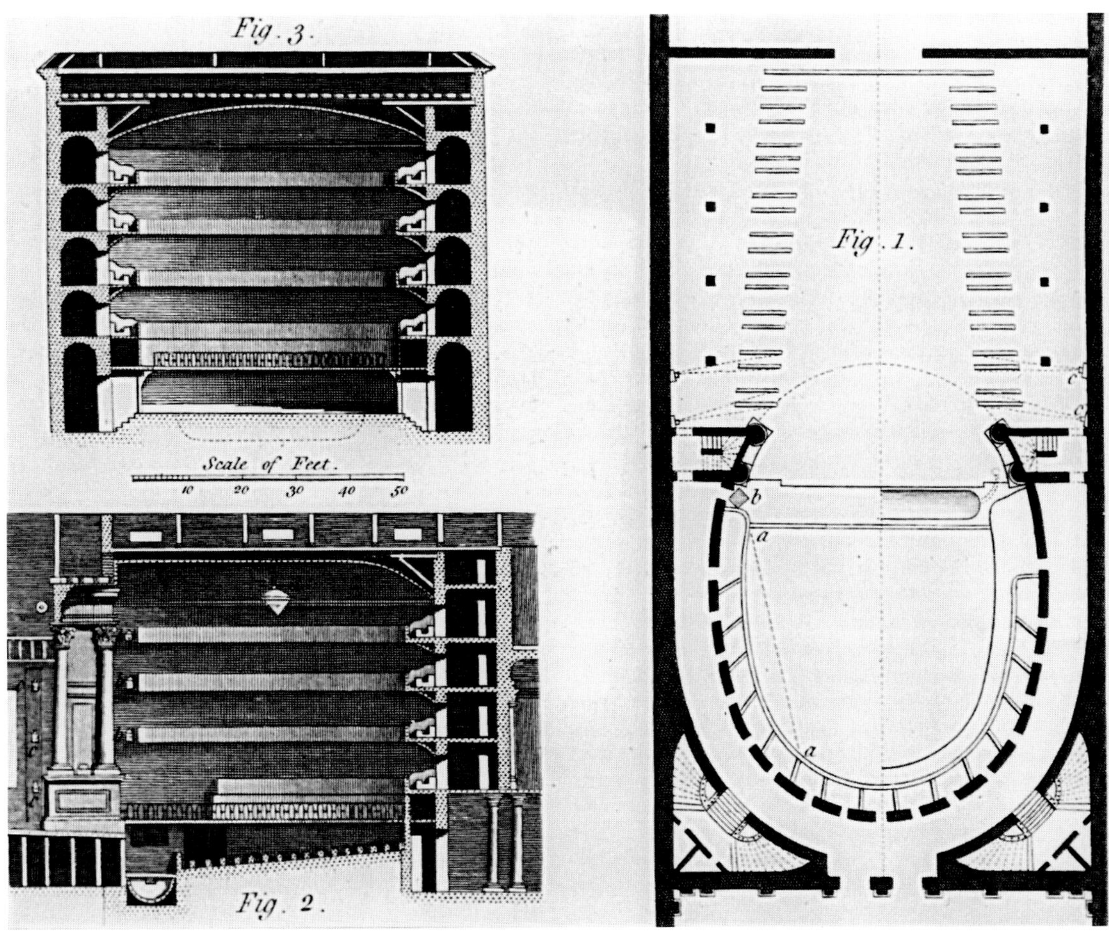

2. Acoustic theatre design of truncated elliptical plan by Pierre Patte, engraving, 1782; from George Saunders: *A Treatise on Theatres* (London, 1790)

Kent; and Hagios Mamas (17th century), Korakov, Cyprus. These were presumably intended for the opposite purpose, that of absorbing sound, like the modern Helmholtz resonator.)

Following the Renaissance revival of the Classical theatre, for example at Andrea Palladio's Teatro Olimpico (1580) at Vicenza, the enclosing colonnade around the auditorium gradually evolved into tiers of boxes, developing by the later 17th century into the Italian Baroque form of theatre (*see* THEATRE, §III, 2(i)(a) and 3(i)(a)). Although designed principally around social and theatrical rather than acoustical needs, such theatres proved acoustically suited to their purpose. The boxes around the walls, crowded with an audience in full costume, would have reduced the reverberation time, helping to provide the acoustical clarity necessary for revealing the detail of both the elaborate aria and *recitativo secco.* The ceiling and box fronts at the same time provided the sound-reflecting surfaces essential for tonal liveliness and strength. The interior surfaces were frequently lined with thin wood panelling, which absorbed the bass frequencies but reflected the middle and upper frequencies, further enhancing speech clarity. Contemporary writers, such as Fabrizio Carini Motta, Francesco Algarotti, Pierre Patte and George Saunders, stressed the importance of wood, though invariably stating wrongly that it acts as a resonator analogous to a musical instrument, rather than as a low-frequency sound-absorber.

(iii) Opera houses. The truncated ellipse was a common plan shape for opera houses, favoured on acoustical grounds by contemporary architectural theorists. Patte recommended concave surfaces in general, especially the double-focus ellipse, for 'concentrating' the sound (see fig. 2). He considered the ellipse especially appropriate for theatres, believing that speech propagates in ellipsoidal waves. (In reality convex, diffusing surfaces are preferable, and the relief surface decoration used in Baroque-style theatres and concert halls helps to achieve a diffuse, or evenly scattered, sound field.) The hallmark of theatres decorated by the Galli-Bibiena family was their bell- or trumpet-shaped plan, for example the Markgräfliches Opernhaus (1744–8), Bayreuth. This shape was also traditionally supposed to have been adopted for acoustic reasons, but unfortunately there is no surviving statement by the Galli-Bibienas on acoustics. Many 18th-century opera houses were designed with curious acoustic devices

to help amplify and project the orchestra's sound. In Italian theatres an airspace was often incorporated below the orchestra pit to help the wooden floor resonate, for example at the Teatro Regio (1738–40; destr.), Turin, designed by Benedetto Innocente Alfieri, while at the Teatro Nuovo in Parma the entire parterre was built over a great semi-elliptical masonry saucer connected with passages from the orchestra pit.

An important acoustical advantage of 18th-century theatres and playhouses was that with the projecting forestage the relationship of actor and audience was acoustically intimate. Advances in theatre lighting in the 19th century and the consequent exploitation of spectacular theatre, however, caused the actor to retreat behind the proscenium arch, which placed him, acoustically speaking, in a different space from the audience. At the Festspielhaus (1872–6), Bayreuth, Richard Wagner further distanced his performers by creating a sunken and hooded orchestra pit. Although intended for visual rather than acoustic reasons, the sound reaching the audience is entirely reflected, giving a mysterious distant quality. In the 20th century reaction away from the proscenium stage towards various forms of open stage, for example in the auditorium designed by Tanya Moiseiwitsch (*b* 1914) for the Shakespeare Festival Theater (1957) at Stratford, Ont., enabled a more intimate style of performance suited to the age of radio and television.

(iv) Rooms for speech. Several other building types require clear acoustics for speech, including parliament buildings, debating chambers, lecture and conference halls and courtrooms. Historically, acoustical considerations usually influenced their architectural form and layout, although, even in the present day, rooms with up to about 100 seats may be satisfactory for natural speech without the use of electronic sound reinforcement. The distance from the chairman to the farthest speaker should be minimal. Also, because sound is attenuated as it passes across successive rows of seats, audibility is improved when the seating is raked. The press galleries in such debating chambers as the House of Commons, Westminster, are often located high up to gain sound reflection from the walls and ceiling surfaces, while in churches the traditional canopy over the pulpit is useful for projecting the voice of the preacher. Before the invention of the electroacoustic public-address system, acoustical considerations occasionally resulted in elegantly expressive interior forms. For example, Le Corbusier's competition design (1926–7; unexecuted) for the Palace of the League of Nations, Geneva, contains a parabolic ceiling in the assembly hall for projecting speech from the stage, while Alvar Aalto's lecture hall at the Viipuri (now Vyborg) City Library, built in 1934–5 (destr. 1940–41), had an undulating, sound-reflective timber ceiling intended to diffuse sound as it travelled from either end of the hall, so that during debates audience members could be heard equally as well as speakers on the platform.

(v) Concert halls.

(a) Before the 20th century. Unlike theatres, only a few purpose-built concert halls were built before the mid-19th century (*see* CONCERT HALL). The earliest, such as the elliptical St Cecilia's Hall (1762), Edinburgh, designed by Robert Mylne the younger, the concert hall at the Hanover Square Rooms (1774–5), London, which were sponsored by Giovanni Andrea Battista Gallini (1728–1805), Johann Christian Bach (1735–82) and Carl Friedrich Abel (1723–87), and the Altes Gewandhaus (1794; destr. 1894), Leipzig, designed by Johann Friedrich Carl Dauthe (1749–1816), must have had clear, intimate acoustics on account of their small size; with a full audience crowded within, however, they would have been much less reverberant than is now regarded as optimal.

The numerous larger symphony halls that were built in the second half of the 19th century were based on the form of the palace ballroom, being rectangular in shape and roughly a double cube in volume. These (the Musikvereinsgebäude, 1867–9, Vienna, by Theophilus Hansen being the most celebrated) remain acoustically the most admired concert halls in the world. Their excellence is due to several factors. They are still relatively small, containing typically 1500–2000 seats within a floor area that, if replanned to present-day standards of safety and comfort, would accommodate about 1100. They are constructed of hard, dense materials (masonry, plaster or occasionally thick, closely fastened wood panels), which sustain strong, multiple reflections of sound from the enclosing surfaces. The tall, narrow shape encloses a large cubic volume relative to the sound-absorptive audience area, providing substantial reverberance. The parallel side walls ensure that strong, lateral sound reflections (from the junction of the wall with the balcony and ceiling soffits) are directed into the centre of the main floor. Their narrow width provides a short travel path for reflected sound, with a consequently small 'time delay gap' between the direct and early reflected sound, so that the reverberance is combined with a clear, strong sound in the hall.

(b) 20th century. These attributes were not understood at the time, and with the early 20th-century demand for greatly increased audience capacities, architects and acousticians sought principally to direct the sound efficiently towards the rear of the hall. (In reality, the rear seats are seldom problematic in this respect, even in very large halls.) Designs were modelled around graphic 'ray diagrams' of sound distribution, but the resulting flared profile ensured that the sound, directed into the seating area, is quickly absorbed by the audience. Music produced in such halls, most notoriously the Salle Pleyel (opened 1927), Paris, designed by Aubertin, Granel and Mathon, with Gustave Lyon, has a thin, directional quality.

The fan-shaped plan introduced at this time to accommodate ever-larger audiences caused reflected sound to be channelled along the side to the rear of the hall, leaving most of the main floor without the benefit of reflected sound. To compensate, the ceiling was lowered to become the principal sound-reflecting element, but the smaller cubic volume relative to the sound-absorptive area of audience renders such halls acoustically 'dead'. Music played in many 20th-century halls was further weakened because of the use of thin wood panelling, owing to the myth that the walls of a hall could be made to vibrate and strengthen (rather than in reality absorbing) low-frequency reflected sound.

The acoustics of numerous auditoria of the early- to mid-20th century, especially in North America, were also compromised by their intended use for both speech events and music, with the result that the halls were seldom acoustically optimal for either purpose. Several techniques for varying a hall's suitability for different types of performance have since been developed. Chamber music, for example, and music of the classical period require more intimate, less reverberant acoustics, and large-scale choral and symphonic music of the Romantic period may require near church-like acoustics. Motorized fabric banners may be introduced into a basically reverberant space, either to reduce the reverberation time, as at Roy Thomson Hall (1976–82), Toronto, by Arthur Erickson, or to reduce side wall reflections when used in conjunction with electronic sound amplification, for example at Pikes Peake Center (1980), Colorado Springs, CO, by Artec Consultants Inc. The reverberation time of an auditorium may be varied by altering the cubic volume, either by means of openable 'reverberation chambers', such as one used at the International Convention Centre Concert Hall (1991), Birmingham, by Percy Thomas Partnership and Artec Consultants Inc., or, less usually, a movable ceiling, for example at IRCAM (1977), Paris, by Piano and Rogers. The position of sound-reflective surfaces may be varied, by the use of a motorized suspended canopy, for example at the Royal Concert Hall (1982), Nottingham, by the Renton Howard Wood Levin Partnership. Alternatively, the impression of added sound reflections and increased reverberation time can be created electronically. Electronic 'assisted resonance' was developed in the 1960s as a remedial measure at London's Royal Festival Hall (1948–51), designed by Leslie Martin and Robert Matthew (1906–75), but it has since been applied by design at various halls, for example the Kremlin Palace of Congresses (1959–61), Moscow, designed by a team headed by Mikhail Posokhin and Ashot Mndoyants, and the Hult Center for the Performing Arts (1978–82), Eugene, OR, by Hardy Holzman Pfeiffer Associates.

Acquarossa, painted roof-tile from a house, terracotta, 595×530 mm, 6th century BC (Viterbo, Museo Civico)

The positioning of sound-reflective surfaces (as against the simple calculation of reverberation time) became especially important in Hans Scharoun's design for the Philharmonie (1956–63), Berlin (for illustration *see* SCHAROUN, HANS). With its centralized concert platform, the lack of sound-reflective side walls is overcome by stepping the seating into terraces, providing a successful mixture of sound-reflective and sound-absorptive surfaces. Studies made since the 1960s have provided a clearer understanding of the attributes of the traditional rectangular hall, in particular on the value of lateral sound reflection to the sensation of acoustic envelopment. This has been applied in, for example, Christchurch Town Hall (1972), New Zealand, by Warren and Mahoney; the National Theatre and Concert Hall (1987), Taipei, by Yang Chüeh-cheng; the Dr Anton Philips Concert Hall (1987), The Hague, by D. van Mourik; and the Eugene McDermott Concert Hall (1989) of the Morton H. Meyerson Symphony Center, Dallas, designed by I. M. Pei.

BIBLIOGRAPHY

Grove 6

F. Carini Motta: *Trattato sopra la struttura de' theatri e scene che a nostri tempi si costumano* (Guastalla, 1676/*R* Milan, 1972)

C. Wren: *Parentalia, or Memoirs of the Family of the Wrens: Viz. of Mathew Bishop of Ely, Christopher Dean of Windsor, etc, But Chiefly of Sir Christopher Wren, in which is Contained, besides his Works, a Great Number of Original Papers and Records* (London, 1750), p. 130

F. Algarotti: *Saggio sopra l'opera in musica* (Livorno, 1763; Eng. trans., London, 1917)

P. Patte: *Essai sur l'architecture théâtrale* (Paris, 1782); ed. C.-N. Cochin in *Projet d'une salle de spectacle pour un théâtre de comédie* (Geneva, 1974)

G. Saunders: *A Treatise on Theatres* (London, 1790/*R* 1968)

W. C. Sabine: *Collected Papers on Acoustics* (Cambridge, MA, 1924/*R* New York, 1964)

L. L. Beranek: *Music, Acoustics and Architecture* (New York, 1962/*R* Huntingdon, NY, 1979)

V. L. Jordan: *Acoustical Design of Concert Halls and Theatres: A Personal Account* (London, 1980)

L. Cremer and H. A. Muller: *Principles and Applications of Room Acoustics*, 2 vols (London and New York, 1982)

M. Forsyth: *Buildings for Music: The Architect, the Musician, and the Listener from the Seventeenth Century to the Present Day* (Cambridge, MA, 1985)

P. Lord and D. Templeton: *The Architecture of Sound* (London, 1986)

M. Forsyth: *Auditoria: Designing for the Performing Arts* (London, 1987)

MICHAEL FORSYTH

Acquarossa [It.: 'red water']. Modern name of an Etruscan settlement near Viterbo, Italy. It is situated on a small tufa plateau bounded on three sides by streams, one of which runs red. Excavations conducted by the Swedish Institute of Classical Studies during the 1960s and 1970s uncovered the tufa foundations of buildings that comprised various sectors of an ancient town. These provide some of the most extensive archaeological evidence relating to Etruscan domestic architecture and urban organization. The site was already inhabited in the 8th century BC and grew considerably during the following two centuries. Its main economic activity was apparently agriculture. Throughout its history the settlement had close links both with the coastal Etruscan cities and with those inland, in particular Tarquinia and Volsinii Veteres (Orvieto). It was permanently abandoned at the beginning of the 5th century BC, and the absence of any overlay of Roman or later material contributes to its archaeological importance.

Acquarossa does not display a regular overall plan, although in the area considered to have been the centre of political and social life the buildings seem to have been arranged according to a rational system. The remains of 6th-century BC houses reveal the use of several different standard plans, notably the 'broad house' type, which consists of two or three parallel rooms fronted by an elongated vestibule with a fireplace (*see* ETRUSCAN, fig. 8c); they show close similarities with some contemporary rock-cut tombs at Cerveteri (Caere). The final phase of a later, complex structure in Zone F may have been the religious or administrative centre of the settlement (*see* ETRUSCAN, fig. 8d). Its L-shaped plan shows two wings, each comprising several rooms and facing a colonnaded courtyard, apparently with both private and public areas. In addition to foundations, finds at Acquarossa include many architectural terracottas, some with white painted designs (see fig.). With the terracottas from Poggio Civitate (Murlo), they are among the earliest Etruscan examples of this kind of roof decoration in a domestic, rather than religious, context.

BIBLIOGRAPHY

E. Wetter, M. Moretti and C. E. Östenberg: *Med kungen på Acquarossa* [With the king at Acquarossa] (Malmö, 1972)
C. E. Östenberg: *Case etrusche di Acquarossa* (Rome, 1975)

MARCO RENDELI

Acquaviva d'Aragona, Andrea Matteo III, Duca d'Atri (*b* Conversano, Puglia, Jan 1458; *d* Conversano, 9 Jan 1529). Italian patron. He was the son of Giulio, Duca d'Atri (*d* 1481), and Caterina Orsini, Contessa di Conversano (Apulia), a cousin of Queen Isabella of Castile; in 1477 he married Isabella Piccolomini of Aragon (*d* 1504). His extensive territories included much of the Abruzzo and Apulia, and through his second marriage to Caterina della Ratta, Contessa di Caserta, he gained lands in Campania, Lucania and Calabria. Andrea Matteo led a tumultuous political and military career, alternately supporting the Aragonese and the Angevins and losing and regaining his lands several times. From 1505, however, he settled in Naples, devoting himself increasingly to cultural activities. He was one of the most important humanist princes in southern Italy, and a member of Giovanni Pontano's Neapolitan academy; Pontano (1422–1503) dedicated his *De magnanimitate* to the Duca, whom he saw as the incarnation of Renaissance man, while Paolo Giovio praised him as '*heros antiquae virtutis*'.

Andrea Matteo had a thorough knowledge of Greek literature, writing a commentary on Plutarch's *De virtute morali* (1526), which he published in his own press, installed in 1518–19. He also took an interest in astrology and music. His rich library (MSS in Vienna, Österreich. Nbib.; Naples, Bib. Girolamini, and various European and North American collections) must have possessed the most important Classical works. He collected manuscripts from his early youth and commissioned such illuminators as Cola Rapicano, CRISTOFORO MAJORANA, Gioacchino di Gigantibus de Rottenburg and REGINALDO PIRAMO DA MONOPOLI to decorate his books. He also employed illuminators from Ferrara and Siena, as well as some showing the influence of Antonello da Messina and Bramante. His manuscripts have complex iconographic schemes, revealing Andrea Matteo to have been a man of broad culture, and they also illustrate the evolution of taste during the period. The earliest examples, illuminated during the 1470s and 1480s, contain the popular white-scroll decoration. These are followed by books with classicizing architectural frontispieces in the Paduan style, while the later manuscripts bear elegant frames with grotesque decoration. In 1506–7 Andrea Matteo had a votive chapel built in Atri Cathedral, for which he commissioned panels of the *Nativity* and *Flagellation*. The artist, Pedro de Aponte, a Spaniard in the entourage of Ferdinand II, also illuminated a copy of Pliny for the Duca (Naples, Bib. Girolamini, MS. C FIII 6).

BIBLIOGRAPHY

DBI
A. Putaturo Murano: *Miniature napoletane del rinascimento* (Benevento, 1973)
M. Santoro: 'La cultura umanistica', *Storia di Napoli*, iv/2 (Naples, 1974), pp. 317–400
F. Bologna: *Napoli e le rotte mediterranee della cultura da Alfonso il Magnanimo a Ferdinando il Cattolico* (Naples, 1977), pp. 215–36
F. Tateo: *Chierici e feudatari del Mezzogiorno* (Bari, 1984)
E. Cassec: 'La miniatura italiana in Olanda: Risultati di ricerche nella collezione della Biblioteca dell'Università di Leida', *La miniatura italiana tra gotico e rinascimento. Atti del II congresso di storia della miniatura: Firenze, 1985*, pp. 155–74
P. Giusti and P. Leone de Castris: *'Forastieri e regnicoli': La pittura moderna a Napoli nel primo cinquecento* (Naples, 1985), pp. 103–4
A. Putaturo Murano, A. Perricciolí Saggese and A. Locci: 'Reginaldo Piramo da Monopoli e i miniatori attivi per Andrea III Acquaviva', *Monopoli nell'età del rinascimento. Atti del convegno internazionale di studio: Monopoli, 1985*, pp. 1102–68

GIOVANNA CASSESE

Acrocorinth. *See* CORINTH.

Acrolith [Gr.: 'high stone']. Ancient Greek statue with the limbs and head made of marble or stone and the body of wood, sometimes covered with a layer of gold.

□

Acropolis, Athenian. *See* ATHENS, §II, 1.

Acropolis 606, Painter of. *See* VASE PAINTERS, §II.

Acroterion. Decorative finial crowning the apex and lower angles of the pediments of ancient Greek and Roman buildings. Acroteria were normally made of terracotta, poros, limestone or marble, although bronze acroteria are mentioned in the literary sources: Pausanias (*Guide to Greece* V.x.4) noted gilded Victories framed by bronze cauldrons at the lower angles of the pediments of the Temple of Zeus at Olympia. The bronze Victories framing *Bellerophon and the Chimaera* on the Temple of Athena Nike on the Acropolis at Athens are recorded in inscriptions, and traces of their bases survive.

The stylistic development of acroteria begins in the 7th century BC. The earliest surviving examples are the frequently enormous terracotta discs that crowned Lakonian-tiled roofs, such as that from the Temple of Hera at Olympia (Archaeol. Mus.; *c.* 600 BC; *see* OLYMPIA, fig. 3). This type continued in the 6th century BC, and it was also sculpted in marble with relief decoration—rosettes, gorgoneia and gorgons—mainly in regions under Lakonian influence. Terracotta acroteria became highly decorative in the course of the 6th century, thanks to the potential of the more flexible Corinthian system of tiling and the advanced coroplastic tradition of the Corinthian workshops. The evolution of acroteria into increasingly sophisticated compositions based on floral, animal and mythological themes and the development of great plasticity and spectacular polychromy are recorded in a series of fragmentary examples from Greece, Magna Graecia and Sicily. Floral elements appear quite early on in variations of the palmette motif and predominate as central acroteria even after the establishment of marble as the standard sculptural material. Hybrid figures of fantastic beasts, such as sphinxes and griffins, were popular as lateral acroteria, initially in terracotta and later in marble; these did not persist after the 6th century BC, however, except in certain 4th-century BC funerary reliefs, which included depictions of Sirens and birds. Acroteria with mythological themes that included groups of figures usually crowned small buildings and expressed the same anthropocentric spirit as that found in the pedimental compositions.

Terracotta acroteria continued to be produced until the end of the 5th century BC, although because of the fragility of the clay, complete groups have not survived. Thus the central subject framed by the fragmentary sphinxes at the lower pedimental angles on the Temple of Artemis Laphria at Kalydon (*c.* 580–570 BC) remains elusive. Nevertheless, it is possible in many instances to form a very general picture of the impressive acroteria of the Archaic and Classical periods (*c.* 750–323 BC). At Olympia, for example, the central group of *Silenus Attacking a Maenad* is framed by fleeing Maenads (*c.* 530 BC), and the central acroterion showing *Athena Fighting a Giant* is framed by Victories (*c.* 490 BC). Later examples include the group of *Zeus Abducting Ganymede* (Olympia, Archaeol. Mus.; *c.* 480–470 BC; *see* OLYMPIA, §2(ii) and fig. 6), although there is no evidence for the framing acroteria. Also unknown are the lateral acroteria that complemented the central compositions of *Theseus with Skiron* and the *Abduction of Kephalus by Eos* on the Stoa Basileios in the Athenian Agora (Pausanius, *Guide to Greece* I.iii.1), of which only sparse fragments have been recovered.

Marble acroteria, which began replacing terracotta ones from the 6th century BC, are better preserved. This does not mean, however, that the reconstruction of complete compositions is always possible. It is certain that the Siphnian Treasury at Delphi (*c.* 525 BC) was crowned by flying Victories framed by sphinxes in the lower angles, as was the Alkmaionid Temple of Apollo (*c.* 520 BC). On the other hand, the context of the Victories associated with the Giantomachy pediment on the Athenian Acropolis is still uncertain, as is that of the remnants of a battle scene that surmounted the Amazonomachy pediment on the Temple of Apollo Daphnephoros at Eretria (*c.* 500–490 BC).

The central acroteria above both pediments on the Temple of Aphaia on Aigina (*c.* 500–*c.* 490 BC) were large floral compositions with palmettes and lyre-shaped volute motifs, flanked heraldically by two female figures; the acroteria in the lower angles were sphinxes. An evolved version of this scheme appeared on the Temple of Poseidon at Sounion towards the middle of the 5th century BC, where a single anthemion dominated the apex, framed by two probably female figures as lower-angle acroteria. Compositions with central anthemion elements framed by, as a rule, female figures at the lower angles crowned both the Parthenon at Athens and the Temple of Hera at Argos, as well as the Temple of Athena Alea at Tegea, the Temple of Artemis at Epidauros and Temple of the Sanctuary at Samothrace.

In the Ionic temple at Lokroi Epizephyrioi in southern Italy (last quarter of the 5th century BC) the central floral acroterion evidently enveloped a female figure in its tendrils, while the lateral acroteria depicted the Dioskuroi slipping on to the backs of their horses, supported on Tritons. The precursors of these are the early 5th-century BC mounted Amazons that crowned the Athenian Treasury at Delphi (*c.* 490 BC). Other elaborate groups appear as lateral acroteria in the closing years of the 5th century BC: *Nereids Riding Dolphins* on the Athenian Temple of Ares, *Nereids Riding Whales* (from Formia, *c.* 400 BC) and the equestrian female figures on the west pediment of the Temple of Asklepios at Epidauros (first quarter of the 4th century BC; *see* EPIDAUROS, fig. 2). In the last case the central element of the composition represented an abduction. There are also depictions of abductions framed by running female figures, such as the representations of *Boreas and Orithyia* and of *Eos and Kephalos*, which surmounted the Temple of the Athenians on Delos (*c.* 425–420 BC), or the two comparable representations on the Nereid Monument from Xanthos (London, BM; *c.* 400 BC; for illustration *see* XANTHOS).

Acroterial figures that are frequently thought to personify forces of nature probably represent specific mythological figures whose identity may be deciphered only when evidence of the representations they frame (undoubtedly mythological) is brought to light. Nevertheless, it is reasonably certain that a more or less direct thematic correspondence between the compositions of the acroteria and those of the pediments always existed. It is virtually impossible to distinguish acroterial sculptures from pedimental figures, except that the former tend to be larger.

Floral acroteria, often in impressively elaborate compositions, also crowned funerary monuments in the 4th century BC, although from Hellenistic times (331–23 BC) onwards these gradually degenerated into conventional ornaments. The Temple of Artemis Leukophryene at Magnesia on the Maeander (2nd century BC), as well as that of Despoina at Arcadian Lykosoura (2nd century BC), had tripartite compositions in which both the lateral and apex elements were floral, a pattern that dominated the architecture of the Roman period.

BIBLIOGRAPHY

H. Gropengiesser: *Die pflanzlichen Akrotere klassischer Tempel* (Mainz, 1961)

A. Delivorrias: *Attische Giebelskulpturen und Akrotere des 5. Jhs. v. Chr.* (diss., U. Tübingen, 1974)

M. Y. Goldberg: *Types and Distribution of Archaic Greek Akroteria* (diss., Bryn Mawr Coll., PA, 1977; microfilm, Ann Arbor, 1980)

A. Gulaki: *Klassische und klassizistische Nikedarstellungen: Untersuchungen zur Typologie und Bedeutungswandel* (diss., U. Bonn, 1981)

P. Danner: 'Westgriechische Akrotere', *Röm. Hist. Mitt.*, xxx (1988), pp. 17–40

——: 'Griechische Akrotere der archaischen und klassischen Zeit', *Riv. A.* (1989) [suppl. 5]

A. DELIVORRIAS

Acrylic painting. Although 'acrylic' has become a generic term for any synthetic paint medium, acrylics are a specific type of manmade polymer that has become standard in the commercial paint industry as well as widely used by artists from the mid-20th century; most synthetic paint media in contemporary artistic use are based on acrylic emulsions. Acrylics are thermoplastic, have great optical clarity and excellent light stability, good adhesion and elasticity and resist ultraviolet and chemical degradation. Their unique surface properties, transparency and brilliance of colour, together with the possibilities they offer for indeterminacy, immediacy, randomness and the ability to rework immediately and to achieve extremely thin or thick surfaces, are qualities that have been exploited fully by such painting movements as Abstract Expressionism in the 1950s, and, subsequently, colour field painting, hard-edge painting and Pop art.

See also PAINT, §§I and II; POLYMER COLOUR; and PLASTIC, §2(ii).

1. HISTORY AND USES. Acrylics were first prepared in 1880 as acrylate by Otto Rohm. He patented it in 1915, and its suggested use was as a substitute for drying oils in industrial paints and lacquers. Polymethyl methacrylate, a rigid form of acrylic, was first marketed in Germany in 1927, but large-scale production of it in the form of Plexiglass (Perspex) began in 1936 in the USA, where acryloid—an acrylic resin surface coating—was first marketed in 1931. Thus the early development of acrylics was for industrial purposes. In the 1920s, however, the Mexican muralists experimented with synthetic media developed for industrial use, including pyroxylin (nitro-cellulose) automobile lacquers and ethyl silicate (an organic/silicon compound) when looking for a durable material for outdoor use (*see* WALL PAINTING, §I). In 1936 David Alfaro Siqueiros held an experimental workshop in New York City, where artists, among them Jackson Pollock, experimented with the latest synthetics and paints, trying new methods of application such as spray-guns. Subsequently Siqueiros used pyroxylin for *Echo of a Scream* (1937; New York, MOMA; *see* SIQUEIROS, DAVID ALFARO, fig. 1) and for *Portrait of the Bourgeoisie* (1939; *see* SIQUEIROS, DAVID ALFARO, fig. 2) in the stairwell of the Electricians' Union Building in Mexico City; and from the late 1940s Jackson Pollock used a pyroxylin lacquer tradenamed Duco in many of his works (e.g. *Number 2, 1949*; Utica, NY, Munson–Williams–Proctor Inst.; *see* ABSTRACT EXPRESSIONISM, fig. 1). The disadvantage of Duco and lacquer-based paints, however, is their toxic solvent base which may be damaging to the artist's health.

The alkyd resins (a type of polyester) were discovered in 1902 and marketed as Glyptal from 1926. Many WPA artists experimented with alkyd-based paints in the 1930s. (In the late 20th century they have been used to manufacture artists' paints that have faster drying properties and a higher gloss than oil paints; *see* PAINT, §I). In 1946 Bocour Artists Colours Inc. first marketed Magna, an oil-like painting medium comprising acrylic resin (n-butyl methacrylate) dissolved in an organic solvent, which could be thinned with turpentine or mineral spirits and combined with oil paints. Magna colours were used in the 1950s by Morris Louis, Helen Frankenthaler and later by Roy Lichtenstein (e.g. *Whaam!*, 1963; London, Tate; see fig.). They were also used extensively by Mark Rothko, who employed them to originate a form of colour field painting that strongly resembled the effect of watercolour stain.

After World War II the vinyl polymers—polyvinyl acetate (PVA) and polyvinyl chloride (PVC)—superseded the alkyd-based paints in industrial use but were never widely used by artists. Acrylics and vinyls were developed simultaneously, but the former superseded the latter because of their extensive handling and colour properties. There was a major breakthrough in the 1950s with the introduction of aqueous emulsion acrylics or latex paints. In 1953 Rohm and Haas Co. introduced Rhoplex, the first acrylic emulsion specially designed for paint. Rhoplex

Roy Lichtenstein: *Whaam!*, acrylic on canvas, 1.73×4.06 m, 1963 (London, Tate Gallery)

resists aging, is exceptionally fast drying and has good adhesion and intermixing properties, including a tolerance for a wide variety of pigments; it is also alkaline, non-yellowing and resistant to ultraviolet and most mild acids. It has become the base for all contemporary artists' acrylic emulsions and was instrumental in the development of HARD-EDGE PAINTING, COLOUR FIELD PAINTING and stain painting. Notable exponents of acrylic painting in the USA include Helen Frankenthaler (e.g. *Cape (Provincetown),* 1964; Melbourne, N.G. Victoria; *see* UNITED STATES OF AMERICA, fig. 18), Kenneth Noland (e.g. *Trans West*, 1965; Amsterdam, Stedel. Mus.; for illustration *see* NOLAND, KENNETH), Morris Louis (*see* LOUIS, MORRIS and fig.), Sam Francis, Jules Olitski, who used a spray-gun to create subtle variations of colour, and Larry Poons, who at first used acrylics to produce dot Op art paintings and later poured layers of acrylic into one another to create a heavy, craggy surface.

Acrylic painting was an integral part of Pop art, where its adhesive qualities and brilliant colour were exploited in such collage paintings as Peter Blake's *Got a Girl* (1960–61; Manchester, Whitworth A.G.; for illustration *see* BLAKE, PETER). By the mid-1970s there had been a thorough investigation of acrylic painting media, in particular thickeners, gels, dispersants (to ensure uniform pigment dispersion), wetting agents and preservatives to prevent bacterial contamination through water or other additives (*see* PAINTING MEDIUM). Acrylic paint could be used in a wider variety of techniques than oil paint and with much more primitive tools, for example brooms and razors, as it tends to retain the integrity of the colour with manipulation. Such techniques as pouring, splashing, blowing and adding other materials to the paint made the entire painting process more fluid and accelerated painterly experimentation from the mid-1970s. In the late 1970s and early 1980s fluorescent colours (Day-glo paints) became popular but proved ephemeral as the dyes fade in a few years. They were used by Frank Stella in such paintings as *Darajerd III* (1967; Washington, DC, Hirshhorn). More recently, painters such as Paula Rego have abandoned oil in favour of acrylic, partly because of its quick drying properties but also because of an aversion to the smell of turpentine.

2. PROPERTIES. The properties of acrylic paints include durability, good flexibility and brushing properties, and a range of transparent to opaque covering qualities. The advantages include ease of use, quick drying time, easy mixture with other media and with elements to create body and texture (e.g. sand, plaster, twigs, diatomaceous earth, glitter, modelling paste and spackling paste). Their good adhesive qualities allow the medium to be used as a glue in collage and permit much more flexibility than the brittle surface of an oil painting. They can be thinned with water or with an acrylic base painting medium such as gloss, matt, or gel, without becoming granulated. In hard-edge, colour field and stain painting, acrylic paint (unlike oil paint) produces no halo and is therefore ideal for the fresh watercolour effect and matt surface of these styles. Alternatively, acrylic may be thickened with additives to make a 'stiffer' paint that can be used to imitate oil techniques. Other advantages include easy cleaning (soap and water as opposed to thinner and soap and water with oils) and the absence of hazardous (or simply unpleasant) fumes. Large amounts of acrylic mixed colour may be combined with water, or medium or texture, and stored in a tightly closed container for long periods of time for later use.

Acrylics can be used with wax or oil crayons in a resist technique or mixed with chalk, which will partially resist and partially blend with the acrylic, causing unpredictable results, a combination used in situations where the artist wishes to work with little control of the medium for 'fresh' results. These methods are too new to permit proper assessment for longevity and colourfastness by conservators, however, and for conservation purposes the artist should employ only the family of acrylic paints and gels developed for artists' use; it is also helpful if all the materials used, along with brand names, are recorded on the reverse of the support. Although conservators discourage the use of oil over an acrylic underpainting as a more rapid way of building a painting, suggesting that mixtures of oils and acrylics are probably not permanent, many artists do use acrylic in combination with oils for underpainting (*see* GROUND). Acrylic paint can be glazed over with oils, allowing the saturated acrylic colour to 'glow' through. This method has been employed by photorealist artists such as Richard Estes and Audrey Flack. As acrylic paint is easily soluble in relatively weak solvents, acrylic paintings should not be varnished with a traditional varnish; even 'Soluvar' varnish, formulated specifically to address this problem, is not safe in all cases. Acrylic is useful in multimedia art objects such as painted sculpture, ceramics or wood because, if a medium other than water is used, acrylic paint does not sink into the material or damage it as oil would.

Acrylics can be used with multiple supports of varying texture as they are not abrasive or deleterious to either raw canvas or paper. Rigid supports, such as masonite, can be used and are preferable for thickly applied paint or a heavily laden mixed-media work. The high flexibility of acrylics makes them particularly suitable for use on fabrics, as the fabric can be stretched and pulled without cracking the paint; it also enables their use with heavy texturizing elements and allows scraping, scratching and modelling into the surface.

BIBLIOGRAPHY

H. T. Neher: 'Acrylic Resins', *Indust. & Engin. Chem.*, xxviii (1936), pp. 267–71
'Methacrylate Resins', *Indust. & Engin. Chem.*, xxviii (1936), pp. 1160–63
R. L. Wakeman: *The Chemistry of Commercial Plastics* (New York, 1947)
G. Allyn: *Basic Concepts of Acrylic Resin Emulsion Technology* (Philadelphia, 1956)
A. Duca: *Polymer Tempera Handbook* (Somerville, MA, 1956)
J. Gutierrez: *From Fresco to Plastics, New Materials for Easel and Mural Painting* (Ottawa, 1956)
B. Chaet: *Artists at Work* (New York, 1960)
A. M. Reed: *The Mexican Muralists* (New York, 1960)
Amer. Artist (1962–77) [technical page]
J. Charlot: *The Mexican Mural Renaissance, 1920–25* (New Haven, 1963)
L. N. Jensen: *Synthetic Painting Media* (Englewood Cliffs, NJ, 1964)
C. R. Martens: *Emulsions and Water-soluble Paints and Coatings* (New York, 1964)
J. Gutierrez and N. Roukes: *Painting with Acrylics* (New York, 1965)
R. O. Woody: *Painting with Synthetic Media* (1965)
J. A. Brydson: *Plastics Materials* (London and New Jersey, 1966/*R* London, 1975)
R. J. Gettens and G. L. Stout: *Painting Materials* (Dover, 1966)

A. Rodriguez: *A History of Mexican Mural Painting* (London, 1969)
R. Mayer: *The Artists' Handbook* (New York, 1970)
R. O. Woody: *Polymer Painting* (New York, *c*. 1970)
R. Kay: *The Painter's Guide to Studio Methods and Materials* (New York, 1972)
C. R. Martens: *Technology of Paints, Varnishes and Lacquers* (New York, 1974)
B. Chaet: *An Artist's Notebook: Materials and Techniques* (London and New Jersey, 1979)
R. Mayer: 'The Alkyd Generation', *Amer. Artist* (1979)

CARMEN BRIA, CELIA RABINOVITCH, with MICHAEL SICKLER

Action painting. Term applied to the work of American Abstract Expressionists such as Jackson Pollock and Willem de Kooning and, by extension, to the art of their followers at home and abroad during the 1950s. An alternative but slightly more general term is gestural painting; the other division within ABSTRACT EXPRESSIONISM was colour field painting.

The critic Harold Rosenberg defined action painting in an article, 'The American Action Painters' (1952), where he wrote: 'At a certain moment the canvas began to appear to one American painter after another as an arena in which to act.... What was to go on canvas was not a picture but an event'. This proposition drew heavily, and perhaps crudely, upon ideas then current in intellectual circles, especially in the wake of Jean-Paul Sartre's essay *L'Existentialisme est un humanisme* (Paris, 1946; Eng. trans., 1948), which claimed that 'there is no reality except in action'. In the 1940s Herbert Ferber, Barnett Newman and others had already characterized their creative process in similar terms; Rosenberg was probably also inspired by photographs of Pollock at work (rather than the actual paintings) that emphasized his apparent psychological freedom and physical engagement with materials. 'Action painting' became a common critical term to describe styles marked by impulsive brushwork, visible pentiments and unstable or energetic composition (for illustration *see* ABSTRACT EXPRESSIONISM, fig. 1), which seemed to express the state of consciousness held by the artist in the heat of creation. Action painting thereby shared the spontaneity of Automatism. Although this implicit, direct synthesis of art and consciousness is questionable, the spontaneous methods associated with the concept were paralleled in European movements such as TACHISM and ART INFORMEL.

BIBLIOGRAPHY

H. Rosenberg: 'The American Action Painters', *ARTnews*, li/8 (1952), pp. 22–3, 48–50
——: 'The Concept of Action in Painting', *New Yorker*, xliv (25 May 1968), pp. 116–28
F. Orton: 'Action, Revolution and Painting', *Oxford A. J.*, xiv/2 (1991), pp. 3–17
For further bibliography *see* ABSTRACT EXPRESSIONISM.

DAVID ANFAM

Activists [Hung. Aktivizmus]. Hungarian artistic, literary and political group that emerged *c*. 1914, after the disintegration of the group THE EIGHT (iii) in 1912. Though not a cohesive group, the Activists were stylistically united by their reaction to the predominantly Post-Impressionist aesthetic of the Eight. Instead they turned for inspiration to Cubism, Expressionism, Futurism, Dada and Constructivism, and although some of these had previously influenced the Eight, the Activists made most consistent and profound use of these modern movements. The most notable Activists were Sándor Bortnyik, Péter Dobrović (*b* 1890), János Kmetty, János Máttis Teutsch, László Moholy-Nagy, Jószef Nemes Lampérth, Lajos Tihanyi and Béla Uitz, of whom only Tihanyi had previously been a member of the Eight. Many Activists were at some time members of the MA GROUP, which revolved around the writer and artist Lajos Kassák, the main theoretical, and later artistic, driving force behind Hungarian Activism.

Both artistically and politically the Activists were more radical and international than the Eight, a reflection of both the turbulent atmosphere caused by World War I and the revolutionary fervour within Hungary itself. The Activists saw themselves as giving a voice to the working classes and, like the Eight, as agitators for a Utopian, Socialist society. Unlike the members of the Eight, however, many of the Activists were of working-class origin, and while not intellectuals themselves, they received many of their ideas from the Galilei Circle of young Hungarian intellectuals, which organized debates and lectures in Budapest. One of the earliest artistic stimuli on the Activists was the exhibition of Expressionist and Futurist art in the Nemzeti Szalon (National Salon) in Budapest at the beginning of 1913. This show had previously been in Berlin and included work by the Expressionists Oskar Kokoschka, Alexei Jawlenski and Ludwig Meidner, as well as Futurist works by Umberto Boccioni, Carlo Carrà, Luigi Russolo and Gino Severini. This affected both the style and aesthetic of the Activists and, in place of the Eight's call for order and harmony, they posited the tortured, emotional disorder of Expressionism.

On 1 November 1915 the first issue of Kassák's periodical *A tett* ('The deed') appeared in Budapest, modelled on Franz Pfemfert's *Die Aktion*. *A tett* included works by Uitz and Dobrović among others, and in such works as Dobrović's linocut *The Lamentation* (1915; see Szabó, 1971, pl. 13) the rough angularity, medium and subject-matter reveal the debt to German Expressionism. The same influence in painting can be found in such works by Tihanyi as the portrait of *Lajos Kassák* (1918; see 1973 exh. cat., pl. 168). *A tett* also had a strong social message and, as its name suggests, called for individual action as a means of broad social change. This attitude contrasted with the passive nostalgia that marked *Nyugat*, the formerly radical literary forum of the Eight. The subversive, outspoken tone of *A tett* ensured the confiscation of several editions by the authorities; it was banned after 17 issues, on 20 September 1916, accused of publishing 'propaganda hostile to the nation'. Soon after this, Kassák founded the journal *MA* ('Today'), which became the central forum and organizing body for most of the Activists even after its move to Vienna in 1920.

In April 1916 and again in June 1917 a group of Activists called the Fiatalok ('The young'), including Dobrović, Kmetty, Nemes Lampérth and Uitz, exhibited in the Nemzeti Szalon in Budapest. The catalogue for the second exhibition stated that, while starting from Cubism, they aimed at a 'great monumental art of the 20th century'. Nemes Lampérth, for example, was at this time painting highly coloured, near abstract works such as *Landscape* (1917; Pécs, Pannonius Mus.), which, while using Fauvist colour, showed a Cubist-influenced composition from flat planes. During the brief Communist regime of Béla Kun in 1919, the Activists assumed a central role in the country's culture, in particular as teachers of art: Uitz, for example, was made head of the Proletarian Fine Arts workshop. They also produced posters to propagate government messages, as in Uitz's *Red Soldiers, Forward!* (1919; Budapest, N.G.), designed to rouse the army in defence of the unstable Communist regime. On 25 March 1919 some Activists signed a manifesto calling for the establishment of a mass Communist culture. Following the fall of the Kun government, the aesthetic of the Activists began to be subsumed under the Constructivist aesthetic of *MA*, by then exiled in Vienna. Uitz, for example, visited Moscow in 1921 and after leaving the MA group, in autumn 1922 founded, with Aladár Komját, the journal *Egység* ('Unity'), which published Naum Gabo and Antoine Pevsner's *Realistic Manifesto* and other important documents on avant-garde Soviet art.

BIBLIOGRAPHY

L. Neméth: *Modern Art in Hungary* (Budapest, 1969)

J. Szabó: *A magyar Aktivizmus története* [History of Hungarian Activism] (Budapest, 1971) [with Fr. summary]

Magyar Aktivizmus (exh. cat. by J. Szabó, Pécs, Pannonius Mus., 1973)

K. Passuth: *Magyar müvészek az európai avantgarde-ban, 1919–1925* [Hungarian artists in the European avant-garde, 1919–25] (Budapest, 1974)

The Hungarian Avant Garde: The Eight and the Activists (exh. cat. by J. Szabó and others, London, Hayward Gal., 1980)

J. Szabó: *A magyar Aktivizmus müvészete, 1915–1927* [Hungarian Activist art] (Budapest, 1981)

S. A. Mansbach: 'Revolutionary Events, Revolutionary Artists: The Hungarian Avant-Garde until 1920', *'Event' Arts and Art Events*, ed. S. C. Foster (Ann Arbor, 1988), pp. 31–60

□

Acudoğu [Acudoğlu]**, Ratip Aşir** (*b* Istanbul, 1898; *d* Istanbul, 1957). Turkish sculptor. After military service in World War I he went in 1918 to the Fine Arts Academy in Istanbul, where he studied under the sculptor Ihsan Özsoy (1867–1944). With the help of his father he then went to Germany, where he studied at the Akademie der Bildenden Künste in Munich. From Munich he went to Paris, where, after failing to get lessons from Aristide Maillol, he worked independently, inspired by the work of Maillol and Emile-Antoine Bourdelle. After returning to Turkey in 1925 and passing an examination he was able to go back to Paris, where he entered the Académie Julian and worked under the sculptors Henri Bouchard (1875–1960) and Paul Landowski (1875–1961). He returned to Turkey in 1928 and worked first as an art teacher at Edirne Teachers' College and then at various middle schools in Istanbul until his death. His principal works included the monument in Menemen to *Mustafa Fehmi Kubilây*, a young officer who was shot in the city in 1930 while ordering crowds to disperse; the monument to *Ismet Inönü* in Erzincan; and the monument to *Atatürk* at the Faculty of Agriculture in Ankara. He also worked on portrait busts, that of *Fahriye Yen* (Istanbul, Mimar Sinan U., Mus. Ptg & Sculp) being particularly successful.

BIBLIOGRAPHY

S. Tansuğ: *Çağdaş Türk sanatı* [Contemporary Turkish art] (Istanbul, 1986)

□

Adalbertus. *See* TYLKOWSKI, WOJCIECH.

Adam (i). French family of sculptors. Originally from Lorraine, the earliest known members of the family to be involved with the arts were Sigisbert Adam, a sculptor, and Lambert Adam, a metal-founder (both *fl* late 17th century). Lambert's son (1) Jacob-Sigisbert Adam spent most of his working life in Nancy, where he undertook the early training of his sons (2) Lambert-Sigisbert Adam, (3) Nicolas-Sébastien Adam and (4) François-Gaspard-Balthazar Adam. His daughter Anne married Thomas Michel (*d* before 15 May 1751), a sculptor from Metz; among their children were the sculptors Sigisbert-François Michel (1727–after 1785) and Claude Michel (known as CLODION). The three Adam brothers went to Rome at the start of their careers, Lambert-Sigisbert and Nicolas-Sébastien returning to France to work on the outdoor sculpture at Versailles, among other projects, and François-Gaspard-Balthazar going on to Sanssouci, Potsdam.

(1) Jacob-Sigisbert Adam (*b* Nancy, 28 Oct 1670; *d* Nancy, 6 May 1747). He is said to have been a pupil of César Bagard. He worked for Leopold, Duke of Lorraine, both on the decorative sculpture at the Palais Ducal at Nancy and at the château of Lunéville, and his small bronzes and terracottas were much admired by contemporary collectors. Typical of his small-scale work are the terracotta statuettes of *Bacchus* and *Jupiter* (Nancy, Mus. B.-A.). They are attractive but without marked character.

(2) Lambert-Sigisbert Adam [Adam *l'aîné*] (*b* Nancy, 10 Oct 1700; *d* Paris, 12 May 1759). Son of (1) Jacob-Sigisbert Adam. He was a pupil of his father and finished his training in the Paris workshop of François Dumont. In 1723 he won the Prix de Rome. During his period in Rome, at the Académie de France, he was patronized by the influential Cardinal Melchior de Polignac, the French Ambassador to the Holy See, for whom he restored and copied antique sculpture. He contributed a relief of the *Virgin Appearing to St Andrew Corsini* to Clement XII's Corsini Chapel at S Giovanni in Laterano (marble, *c.* 1732; *in situ*) and became a member of the Accademia di S Luca, presenting a bust of *Sorrow* (marble, 1732; *in situ*). He also entered the competition for the Trevi Fountain, but although his elaborate Baroque design (1731) was selected as the winner, Clement XII eventually commissioned the fountain from Nicola Salvi. After his return to Paris in 1733, Adam produced reclining statues personifying *The Seine* and *The Marne* rivers for the cascade at Saint-Cloud (1733–4; *in situ*). In 1737 he was received (*reçu*) as a member of the Académie Royale de Peinture et de Sculpture in Paris on presentation of the marble group *Neptune Calming the Waves* (1737; Paris, Louvre), sculpted in the manner of Bernini. In collaboration with his brother Nicolas-Sébastien he created the vast and riotous lead group the *Triumph of Neptune and Amphitrite* for the Bassin de Neptune in the park at Versailles (1735–40; *in situ*; see fig.); this is considered the most flamboyant Baroque sculpture to have been executed in 18th-century France, and it represents an eloquent testimony to Lambert-Sigisbert Adam's interest in the art of Bernini.

In spite of difficulties caused by his rebarbative personality, Adam's official career was brilliant and productive.

In 1752 his large groups representing *Fishing* and *Hunting* (marble; Potsdam, Schloss Sanssouci) were given by Louis XV to Frederick II of Prussia; he received many other state commissions, including those for statues of *Plenty* for the Château de Choisy, Val-de-Marne (now priv. col.), *Lyric Poetry* for Mme de Pompadour's château at Bellevue (marble, 1752; now Paris, Louvre) and *St Jerome* for the Dôme des Invalides, Paris (marble, 1752; now Paris, St Roch). Among his works for private clients were busts of *Neptune* and *Amphitrite* (marble, 1724; Berlin, Schloss Charlottenburg) for Cardinal de Polignac, and bas-reliefs at the Hôtel de Soubise, Paris (1735–6; *in situ*) for the Rohan family. He also produced some portrait busts (most destr.) and groups with light-hearted themes, including *Child with its Hand Gripped by a Lobster* (plaster, exh. Salon 1740; bronze reductions, Detroit, MI, Inst. A., and London, V&A).

In his attempt to introduce the pathos of Italian Baroque art into French sculpture in the 18th century, Adam became an increasingly isolated figure, clinging to the style of his youth and already criticized in his lifetime for the rhetorical extravagance of his work. Nevertheless, much of his sculpture demonstrates his virtuosity as a marble carver. He exercised an influence not only over his two younger brothers, Nicolas-Sébastien and François-Gaspard-Balthazar, but also over his nephews Sigisbert-François Michel and Clodion.

(3) Nicolas-Sébastien Adam (*b* Nancy, 22 March 1705; *d* Paris, 27 March 1778). Son of (1) Jacob-Sigisbert Adam. He was trained by his father and then joined his eldest brother (2) Lambert-Sigisbert in Paris. Failing to win the Prix de Rome, he travelled to Italy at his own expense, working on the way in the Château de La Mosson, near Montpellier, and arriving in Rome in 1726. There he was introduced by Lambert-Sigisbert to Cardinal Melchior de Polignac, for whom he restored a number of antique marbles. He returned to Paris in 1734 and pursued what was to be a busy career. Although he was not received (*reçu*) as a member of the Académie Royale de Peinture et de Sculpture in Paris until 1762, his reception piece, a marble statue of *Prometheus* (Paris, Louvre), is one of the best of the century. He collaborated with Lambert-Sigisbert on the flamboyant lead group of the *Triumph of Neptune and Amphitrite* for the Bassin de Neptune in the park at Versailles (1735–40; *in situ*; see fig.) and also worked for the Rohan family at the Hôtel de Soubise, Paris, executing bas-reliefs of the *Loves of the Gods* (1736) in the Salon de la Princesse. He was employed by the Bâtiments du Roi at the Chambre des Comptes in Paris, at the abbey of St Denis and at Versailles, where he produced a bronze relief of the *Martyrdom of Ste Victoire* for the chapel (1747; *in situ*). Among his other works were a marble vase with the attributes of *Autumn* for the park at the Château de Choisy, Val-de-Marne (1745; now New York, Met.); a statue of *Iris Attaching her Wings* (marble, 1775–6; Versailles, Château), finished after his death by his nephew Clodion; *Religion Welcoming a Convert* (plaster, 1745; Paris, St Paul-St-Louis); and bas-reliefs of the *History of Apollo* for the Hôtel de la Boexière, Paris (*c.* 1753; now Paris, Château de Bagatelle). However, his most accomplished work is the funerary monument to

Lambert-Sigisbert Adam and Nicolas-Sébastien Adam: *Triumph of Neptune and Amphitrite*, lead group for the Bassin de Neptune, château of Versailles, 1735–40

Catharina Opalinska, wife of Stanislav I Leszczyński, Grand Duke of Lorraine (coloured and white marbles and bronze, 1749; Nancy, Notre-Dame-de-Bon-Secours). This white marble group shows the deceased being guided heavenwards by an angel silhouetted against a pyramid of dark marble; executed with great technical refinement, it is considered one of the finest and most genuinely pathetic French funerary monuments of the 18th century. The art of Nicolas-Sébastien, though equally influenced by the Roman Baroque and just as versatile and polished, is more delicate and subtle than that of Lambert-Sigisbert. It was to have a marked influence on the work of Clodion.

(4) François-Gaspard-Balthazar Adam (*b* Nancy, 23 May 1710; *d* Paris, 18 Aug 1761). Son of (1) Jacob-Sigisbert Adam. He was a pupil of his father and followed his brothers (2) Lambert-Sigisbert and (3) Nicolas-Sébastien to Rome in 1730, later establishing himself in Paris. In 1740 he won second place in the Prix de Rome competition and returned to Rome in 1742, to the Académie de France. From 1747 to 1760 he was in the service of Frederick II of Prussia, who made him his principal sculptor. He executed numerous sculptures for the decoration of the park of Sanssouci at Potsdam, including marble statues of *Apollo* (1748), *Urania* (1748), *Zephyrus and Flora* (1749), *Cleopatra and the Asp* (1750), *Vulcan* (1756) and *Cybele* (1758; all *in situ*). He was succeeded at Sanssouci by his nephew Sigisbert-François Michel. His work, though unoriginal, helped to spread the French Rococo style in northern Europe.

BIBLIOGRAPHY

Lami; Meissner

A.-N. Dezallier d'Argenville: *Vie des fameux sculpteurs depuis la renaissance des arts* (Paris, 1787/*R* Geneva, 1972), pp. 339–52
P.-J. Mariette: 'Abecedario', *Archvs A. Fr.*, ii (1851–3), pp. 7–8
H. Thirion: *Les Adam et Clodion* (Paris, 1885)
F. Souchal: *Les Artistes à la cour des ducs de Lorraine Léopold et François III* (diss., Paris, Ecole Chartes, 1950)
M. Levey: *Art and Architecture of the 18th Century in France*, Pelican Hist. A. (Harmondsworth, 1972), pp. 62–7
F. Souchal: 'L'Inventaire après le décès du sculpteur Lambert-Sigisbert Adam', *Bull. Soc. Hist. A. Fr.* (1974), pp. 181–91
P. Fusco: 'Lambert-Sigisbert Adam's "Bust of Neptune"', *Bull. LA Co. Mus. A.*, xxi (1975), pp. 13–24
L. Seelig: 'François-Gaspard Adam Standbild des Feldmarschalls Schwerin', *Münchn. Jb. Bild. Kst*, xxvii (1976), pp. 155–98

FRANÇOIS SOUCHAL

Adam (ii). Scottish family of architects and designers. (1) William Adam had four sons, three of whom, (2) John Adam, (3) Robert Adam and (4) James Adam, were also architects. On William's death, John assumed control of his father's practice in Scotland; he took first Robert and then James into partnership, and together they completed some of their father's projects as well as taking on new commissions. In 1758 Robert, who was among the leading architects and designers in Europe in the second half of the 18th century, opened his own practice in London, where James joined him in partnership in 1763. William's fourth son, also called William Adam (1738–1822), was active in the London partnership from 1763, but his concern was primarily with its business dealings.

(1) William Adam (*b* Kirkcaldy, Fife, 30 Oct 1689; *d* Edinburgh, 24 June 1748). Architect and landscape designer. He was the leading architect in Scotland during the second quarter of the 18th century and had an extensive practice. An important contractor for the Government, serving from 1730 to his death as Master Mason to the Board of Ordnance for North Britain, he also pursued various business enterprises, including ownership of a brickworks. Apparently self-taught as an architect, he was involved with building country houses from the early 1720s. His early patron, Sir John Clerk, 2nd Baronet of Penicuik, made his own library available to Adam, and in 1727 they made a joint trip to England. Adam developed a style that was influenced by Sir John Vanbrugh, James Gibbs and the English Palladianism of Richard Boyle, 3rd Earl of Burlington and 4th Earl of Cork, and his circle. Thus, Baroque and Palladian forms co-existed in his work, although he handled them in a very personal and inventive way.

Among Adam's country houses were such villas and smaller houses as Mavisbank (1723–39; gutted 1973), Clerk's own house on which the two collaborated; The Drum (begun *c.* 1724); and Arniston (begun *c.* 1726), all in Lothian. His larger houses included Hopetoun House, Lothian (begun 1721; completed by his sons, *c.* 1750–60), and Duff House, Grampian (*c.* 1730–43). At Duff House he was involved in a law suit with William Duff, Lord Braco, afterwards 1st Earl of Fife (*d* 1763), over costs and his fee, but otherwise his relations with clients appear to have been good. His public buildings included Robert Gordon's Hospital, Aberdeen (1730–32); the Town House, Dundee (1731–4; destr.); the University Library, Glasgow (1732–45; destr.); and the Royal Infirmary, Edinburgh (1738–48; partially destr. 1884). He was involved as a landscape designer at several estates (e.g. Newliston, Lothian, 1731), had responsibility for constructing forts in the Highlands and supervised initial building work at Inveraray Castle, Strathclyde, begun in 1745 to Roger Morris's designs.

As early as 1727 Adam conceived the idea of producing a volume of engraved illustrations depicting his own as well as earlier Scottish architecture. A number of plates were engraved and subscriptions sold, but this project was brought to fruition only in 1810 with the publication of *Vitruvius Scoticus* by his grandson, William Adam (1751–1839), the son of John Adam.

UNPUBLISHED SOURCES

Edinburgh, Register House, Clerk of Penicuik Papers, GD 18/4981 [J. Clerk of Eldin: 'Draft Notes of a Life of Robert Adam' (?1790s)]

BIBLIOGRAPHY

W. Adam: *Vitruvius Scoticus* (Edinburgh, 1810); repr. with intro. by J. Simpson (Edinburgh, 1980)
R. Fleming: *Robert Adam and his Circle in Edinburgh and Rome* (London, 1962)
J. Gifford: *William Adam, 1689–1748* (Edinburgh, 1989)

(2) John Adam (*b* Kirkcaldy, Fife, *bapt* 5 March 1721; *d* Blair Adam, Tayside, 25 June 1792). Architect, son of (1) William Adam. He was trained by his father and worked with him until the latter's death in 1748. He succeeded to the family's architectural practice and contracting business, including the post of Master Mason to the Board of Ordnance for North Britain. He brought his brother Robert into partnership immediately, and James shortly after. During the late 1740s and the 1750s all three brothers were active as contractors on the Highland forts, especially Fort William, and at Inveraray Castle, Strathclyde, as well; but they also continued their father's architectural projects, for example Hopetoun House, Lothian (*c.* 1750–60), and took on new commissions, including Dumfries House, Strathclyde (1753–9), and Arniston, Lothian (1753–8). Since his partnership with Robert was dissolved in 1758, and that with James two years later, during the 1760s Adam practised alone in Edinburgh, though he was increasingly active in other business interests. After *c.* 1770 he seems to have ceased working as an architect, though he retained a strong interest in the London activities of his two brothers.

BIBLIOGRAPHY

W. Adam: *Vitruvius Scoticus* (Edinburgh, 1810); repr. with intro. by J. Simpson (Edinburgh, 1980)
R. Fleming: *Robert Adam and his Circle in Edinburgh and Rome* (London, 1962)
I. Lindsay and M. Cosh: *Inveraray and the Dukes of Argyll* (Edinburgh, 1973)

(3) Robert Adam (*b* Kirkcaldy, Fife, 3 July 1728; *d* London, 3 March 1792). Architect and designer, son of (1) William Adam. He and his rival William Chambers were the leading British architects in the second half of the 18th century. After training under his father, he embarked on a Grand Tour in 1754; this ended early in 1758 when he settled in London rather than Edinburgh. There he established a practice that was transformed into a partnership with his younger brother James after the latter's return in 1763 from his own Grand Tour. By then, however, the Adam style was formed, and Robert remained the partnership's driving force and principal designer until his death. He not only developed a distinctive and highly influential style but further refined it through his large number of commissions, earning fame and a certain amount of fortune along the way. Eminently successful, he left an indelible stamp on British architecture and interior decoration and on international Neo-classicism.

1. Life and work. 2. Working methods. 3. Sources and influence.

1. Life and work.

(i) Early work in Scotland, to mid-1754. (ii) Grand Tour, mid-1754–1757. (iii) Early work in London, 1758–mid-1760s. (iv) Mature work, mid-1760s–mid-1780s. (v) Late work, late 1780s and after.

(i) Early work in Scotland, to mid-1754. Born into a close-knit Lowlands family, Adam grew up in Edinburgh surrounded by intellectuals and the architectural and building affairs of his father, from whom he learnt both the art and business of his future profession. He attended the High School in Edinburgh and matriculated in 1743 at Edinburgh University, though he does not appear to have graduated. Joining his father's architectural office, where his older brother, John, was already at work, he participated in the activities then underway. These included not only buildings designed by his father but also very profitable contracting work, both for the Board of Ordnance and for private individuals. In this latter category was Inveraray Castle, Strathclyde, begun in 1745 in the Gothic Revival style to Roger Morris's designs. Following the death of their father in 1748, John took over both sides of the work and established a partnership with Robert. In addition to Inveraray, their contracting work included a number of forts, including Fort George, Highland, built after the failed Jacobite rising of 1745; this aspect of their business was supplemented by various other commercial enterprises, all of which contributed to the family's wealth and enabled both Robert and James to make the Grand Tour to Italy.

In the 1750s the partnership—which by now included James—gradually increased the number of its commissions. Among them were Hopetoun House, Lothian (*c.* 1750–60), where they completed the exterior their father had begun and designed and executed the interiors; a new wing at Arniston, Lothian (1753–8), where their father had worked earlier; and a totally new building, Dumfries House, Strathclyde (1753–9). At all three they followed current English fashion. Thus on, and to a substantial extent in place of, their father's robust Anglo-Baroque manner, the brothers (but primarily Robert, who seems to have been the chief designer) introduced Rococo and even chinoiserie decorative details along with Palladian formats their father had employed. Adam learnt these styles from engravings and books but also from a trip to England that he made in 1749–50. He recorded the things that interested him on this tour in a sketchbook (London, RIBA); these include fanciful Gothick buildings and landscaped parks and gardens, as well as Palladian structures.

(ii) Grand Tour, mid-1754–1757. In October 1754 Adam left Edinburgh for a tour in Italy, an experience that was to alter radically not only his style but also his career, though aspects of his Scottish experiences were to colour both. Stopping briefly in London, he met the painter and archaeologist Gavin Hamilton. He then travelled to Brussels to join up with Charles Hope, the younger brother of John Hope, 2nd Earl of Hopetoun (*d* 1781), who was to share expenses and, hopefully, introduce Adam to various aristocrats. Travelling via Paris and southern France, they reached Florence in February 1755, where Adam met Charles-Louis Clérisseau, a French architect and draughtsman of ruins. Clérisseau was a former *pensionnaire* at the Académie de France in Rome and had, in Adam's words (letter to James Adam, 19 Feb 1755; Edinburgh, Register House):

> the utmost knowledge of Architecture of perspective & of Designing & Colouring I ever saw, or had any Conception of; He rais[e]d my Ideas, He created emulation and fire in my Breast. I wish[e]d above all things to learn his manner, to have him with me at Rome, to Study close with him & to purchase of his works. what I wish[e]d for I obtain[e]d.

Clérisseau agreed to accompany him to Rome, to live with him there and to teach him 'all these Knacks, so necessary to us Architects'. He became, in effect, Adam's instructor, friend, employee and guide to the marvels of antiquity and techniques of drawing. From him, from the painter Laurent Pécheux (1729–1821) and from Giovanni Battista Piranesi, whom he met shortly after his arrival in Rome, Adam imbibed the excitement and variety of antique sources, a sense of scale and a manner of rendering them in drawings. These influences mingled with and overlaid those he had brought with him from Scotland, and together they formed the seeds of the Adam style.

During his two-year sojourn in Rome (Feb 1755 to May 1757), Adam sketched antique ruins, as well as Renaissance and Baroque buildings. He developed his skill at drawing and prepared for a career in London. For by now his aim had changed, and he was determined to play a central role in British architecture. He set about meeting important noblemen who might further his career and planned a variety of publications that would ensure his fame and success. Among them was a revision of Antoine Desgodetz's *Les Edifices antiques de Rome* of 1682, which he proposed to correct by underlining in red the author's errors, in order to demonstrate his own knowledge of 'Antiquitys to an Inch'. Although this particular scheme was not realized, Adam did manage to initiate work on the *Ruins of the Palace of the Emperor Diocletian at Spalatro in Dalmatia*, a grand folio volume that commemorated his five-week trip to Spalato (now Split). The drawings were executed by Clérisseau and two Italian draughtsmen, the plates were produced by various English and Italian engravers (including Francesco Bartolozzi), and the text was written anonymously by his cousin, the Edinburgh University principal William Robertson. Published in London in 1764, this impressive volume certainly demonstrated to the world Adam's familiarity with the monuments of antiquity. By the time it appeared, however, he had already established himself as one of the leading figures in London's architectural scene.

(iii) Early work in London, 1758–mid-1760s. Arriving in London on 17 January 1758, Adam set about the development of his career. In this he was enormously successful. Within two weeks he was elected a member of the Society of Arts, and he soon began to meet potential clients. In 1761 he was elected a fellow of the Royal Society and was appointed, with William Chambers, joint Architect of the

King's Works. Although obtaining commissions was initially perhaps slower than he had hoped, in his first three years in London he was engaged on 25 projects, the majority of which were executed; in January 1763 he informed Henry Home, Lord Kames, that he had 'business all over England, which I am with difficulty able to get managed with Honour to myself & Satisfaction to my Employers' (Abercairny Papers; Edinburgh, Register House). His brothers James and William joined him in London that year, and during the 1760s and into the 1770s Adam and Chambers were the leading architects in Britain.

In his early work (i.e. to *c.* 1765), Adam was assimilating a variety of sources, though from the first he was introducing into Britain new Neo-classical ideas and stylistic effects from Italy. These turn up in the series of country houses he remodelled or completed and in his occasional commissions for original undertakings. These included garden buildings, London town houses and small public edifices, such as the Admiralty Screen, Whitehall, London (1759–60). In his earliest projects (e.g. the interiors for Hatchlands, Surrey, NT, 1758–61), the mélange of sources is still quite evident, as is the relative heaviness of the relief; but, shortly after, he began to blend the elements and soften the relief. From the beginning, the results of his Roman studies were displayed. Thus, his ceilings at Hatchlands show the influence of 17th-century decoration at the Villa Pamphili (now Doria-Pamphili), Rome, and he had planned to introduce grotesque panels there derived from antique decorations recovered during excavations and from Renaissance adaptations of them. Although these were not carried out, they were at Shardeloes, Bucks (1761–4), and at a host of later houses, but flatter and more refined in form than those intended for Hatchlands. For the garden façade (see fig. 1) at Kedleston Hall, Derbys (a house completed by him *c.* 1760–71), he drew on two Roman monuments—the Arch of Constantine and the Pantheon (for its low saucer dome)—to transform a typical Palladian composition, but again cleaning up, flattening and refining his sources.

At Syon House, London, between 1760 and 1769, Adam took a quadrangular Tudor nunnery with a later Jacobean long gallery, which had been somewhat adapted for greater aristocratic comfort, and transformed it into what Horace Walpole was to describe as 'another Mount Palatine' (see fig. 2). He created a series of rooms of varied and unusual shapes, partially derived from Roman Baths; these he ornamented with lively decoration, also reflecting Classical influences, ranging from apses screened by columns to statuary, grotesques and trophy panels. Responding to the demands of fashionable society, these were spaces intended for various functions that not only were appropriate for those functions but delighted the eye by their variation and ornamentation. This would have been carried even further had he been allowed to fill Syon's interior courtyard with a great circular saloon, as he had intended.

Adam's remodellings, interior decoration and completion of projects begun by others was only partly the result of an enormous amount of recent country-house building in England. In the first volume to appear of their *Works in Architecture* (1773), Robert and his brother James not only claimed to have brought about 'a kind of revolution in the whole system of this useful and elegant art' but cited specifically their accomplishments in interior decoration: 'We have introduced a great diversity of ceilings, freezes, and decorated pilasters, and have added grace and beauty to the whole, by a mixture of grotesque stucco, and painted ornaments, together with the flowing rainceau, with its fanciful figures and winding foliage' (i/1, pp. 3, 5-6). Nevertheless, Robert yearned to build grand external elevations and made many designs, though relatively few were carried out. When they were, as at Kedleston, they

1. Robert Adam: Kedleston Hall, Derbyshire, south (garden) façade, *c.* 1760–61

too left their mark. Even there, however, he was unable fully to execute his plans, for the absence of the wings he had wished to add partially deprives the elevation of that sense of movement both brothers cherished, derived ultimately from Vanbrugh. They defined this in the *Works* as 'the rise and fall, the advance and recess, with other diversity of form, in the different parts of a building, so as to add greatly to the picturesque of the composition' (i/1, p. 3).

(iv) Mature work, mid-1760s–mid-1780s. By the middle of the 1760s Adam had realized his mature manner, having synthesized his various sources into an effective personal style. Although he further refined that manner over the next three decades, flattening and attenuating its decorative components and making the style ever more elegant, the basic ingredients and their compositional effects were by now established. There were some new influences, especially the ETRUSCAN STYLE for interiors and the use of broad, complex chimney-pieces, both inspired by Piranesi's *Diverse maniere d'adornare i cammini* (1769); but these contributed to those general tendencies evident from the 1770s on, and they did not materially alter the basic style that was set within the first seven or eight years of his London career.

In 1765 Adam became Surveyor of Chelsea Hospital and in 1769 MP for Kinross-shire, at which time he resigned his position as joint Architect of the King's Works, which passed to his brother James. He never became a member of the Royal Academy, no doubt because of the enmity of Chambers, who was then Treasurer and the institution's dominating force.

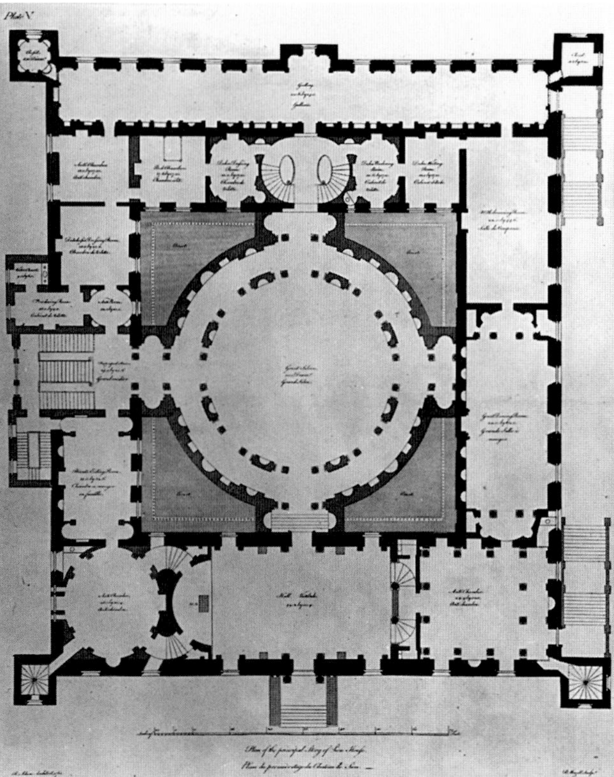

2. Robert Adam: plan of Syon House, London, 1760–69; from Robert and James Adam: *Works in Architecture*, ii (London, 1778)

(a) Country houses. These continued to provide a highly important source of work. Adam built some major new houses of this type, from Luton Hoo, Beds (1766–74), to Gosford House, Lothian (1790–*c.* 1800), as well as a number of smaller villas, among them Brasted Place, Kent (1784–5), and Walkinshaw House, Strathclyde (*c.* 1791–3). But, as before, some of his greatest accomplishments involved remodelling existing houses and completing others. Of these, perhaps the most impressive are Osterley Park House, Middx (1765–80); Kenwood House, London (1767–9); Harewood House (1759–71) and Nostell Priory (1765–85), both W. Yorks; Newby Hall, N. Yorks (1767–*c.* 1780); and Saltram, Devon (1768–79) (*see also* SCOTLAND, fig. 15).

At Osterley Park, Adam again took a quadrangular Tudor house and transformed it, this time by breaking through one of the sides with a dramatic double-columned portico, raising the level of the courtyard and ornamenting the rooms in spectacular fashion. The entrance hall is dominated by designs based on Roman sources, featuring coffered apses, trophy panels and pilasters, the capitals of which were derived from the relatively unusual ones Adam had seen in the peristyle at Spalato. He decorated the dining-room with his mature grotesque panels, here complex, refined and flat. The Etruscan Dressing-room (for illustrations *see* ETRUSCAN STYLE) is the finest surviving example of this style, inspired by Piranesi and 'Etruscan' vases (they were probably Greek), but developed by Adam into the height of elegant, brittle and flat Neo-classical decoration. At Kenwood House, Adam ornamented his flat garden façade with delicate attenuated pilasters, their shafts converted into decorative panels using Liardet's cement, a newly invented patent stucco, of which the Adams bought the patent; he also designed a grand tunnel-vaulted library (see fig. 3). In this space, intended for fashionable entertaining as well as for the books of his patron, William Murray, 1st Earl of Mansfield (*d* 1793), Adam produced perhaps his finest room. Inserting the bookshelves within screened apses at either end, he employed large columns, grotesque panels and a variety of ornaments on the ceiling and walls and in the frieze. In the last, he combined the insignia of his client with a motif derived from the Temple of Antoninus and Faustina in Rome, an imaginative adaptation of antiquity characteristic of Adam's approach.

In addition to the smaller classical villas that Adam designed in the last two decades of his career, he also built a number of castellar houses, especially in Scotland. Among these are Wedderburn Castle, Borders (1771–5); Culzean Castle, Strathclyde (1777–92); and Seton Castle, Lothian (1789–91). Although he employed turrets and battlements for these, he also drew on Roman, Early Christian and later buildings which he had seen in Italy and Germany. He arrived at a picturesque synthesis, rather than a nostalgic re-creation of a long-lost era; a generally symmetrical composition; and interiors that were as classical as those of his other country houses.

3. Robert Adam: library, Kenwood House, London, 1767–9

(b) Town houses. From the outset of his career in London, Adam received commissions for town residences, but these increased substantially from the later 1760s. Among the earliest were Coventry House, Piccadilly (1764–6), and Shelburne (later Lansdowne) House, Berkeley Square (1761–8), the former involving interior remodelling, where the latter was a large new house. In the early to mid-1770s his London houses provided perhaps the most striking demonstration of his talent; these included Wynn House, 20 St James's Square (1772–6); Derby House, 23 Grosvenor Square (1773–4; destr.); and Home House, 20 Portman Square (1773–7). This continued into the early 1780s, typified by Cumberland House, Pall Mall (1780–82, 1785–8). As with the country houses, Adam moved from his early mature synthesis, as at Lansdowne House, to the elegant attenuation and refinement of Derby House or Home House. In some ways his accomplishment is even more marked here, because he was creating appropriate settings for fashionable society within the tight confinements of relatively narrow terrace houses. At Derby House the variety of spaces and their juxtaposition vied with the refined delicacy of the ornamentation to achieve Adam's most brittle and rarefied manner. The splendour of the Great Drawing-room was complemented by the novel motifs and colouring of Etruscan decoration elsewhere.

(c) Urban planning. In addition to individual town houses, Adam engaged in a number of urban-planning schemes. He often introduced varied shapes, including squares, crescents and circuses, although his long terraces of juxtaposed houses or unified façades on the sides of a square were more common. As early as his stay in Italy he drew up designs for rebuilding Lisbon, a city devastated by earthquake in 1755. This was not taken up; nor were his later schemes for the expansion of Bath beyond the River Avon (1777–82) and of Edinburgh beyond the Cowgate across a new South Bridge (*c.* 1785–6). He was, however, able to carry out such London developments as the Adelphi (1768–72), Mansfield Street (1770–75), Portland Place (1776–*c.* 1780 and later) and Fitzroy Square (1790–94), as well as Charlotte Square in Edinburgh (1791–1807). For these, he took the principles of his individual town-house compositions and adapted them to large and more complex groupings, often applying the delicate ornamentation in Liardet's cement.

The grandest of Adam's schemes was the Adelphi, built on leased land between the Strand and the Thames. He embanked the Thames, raising the Royal Terrace's houses (destr.) above vaulted warehouses that he hoped the Government would lease. For this, and for the rest of this H-shaped development, he employed his favourite decorative elements, but in a composition without an obvious central emphasis. Though aesthetically satisfying, the Adelphi was a failure financially. The Government declined to lease the warehouses, and the troubles of the Adam brothers were compounded by a run on Scottish banks. Placed thus in dire financial straits, they were forced to dispose of the Adelphi by lottery.

(d) Public buildings. Adam never ceased to yearn for grand commissions, and his unexecuted projects include major buildings designed for Lincoln's Inn, London (1771–2), and King's College (1784–7) and the University (1788–9) at Cambridge (designs for all three, London, Soane Mus.). In Edinburgh he was able to erect the Register House (1774–92) and at least the beginning of the University (1789–93), though it was completed long after his death and to a different design. These buildings characteristically relate to his country houses in composition and exterior decoration, with rusticated lower floors, shallow domes, emphasis on the centres and ends of buildings, and such recurring motifs as Palladian windows within relieving arches and modified triumphal arches.

Two especially interesting examples of Adam's small semi-public buildings are the Society of Arts (1772–6) and the Theatre Royal, Drury Lane (1775–6; destr.), both in London. The Society of Arts was incorporated within his Adelphi development and, as with the central pavilion of his Edinburgh Register House, employed a temple-front arrangement of large attached columns supporting a pediment (see fig. 4). Once again Adam departed from traditional rules; he combined the Ionic order with a Doric frieze and incorporated both Classical roundels and a Palladian window within a relieving arch, the latter featuring a delicate velarium filled with bell-flower ornamentation. The overall effect refashioned a variety of sources into a flat, refined and attenuated style. For the Theatre Royal, remodelled for the actor-manager David Garrick, he combined a temple-front façade with a refined and elegant interior. Ornamented by arabesque pilasters whose gilded decoration was set on glass, behind which was red and green foil, this was an effect Adam had employed a few years earlier in the Glass Drawing-room at Northumberland House, London (1773–5; destr.).

(e) Churches, mausolea and monuments. The largest and most impressive of Adam's churches was St Mary, Mistley,

Essex (1775; partially destr.). There he transformed an early 18th-century church into one that echoed his own spatial and decorative manner—dramatically accentuated by the twin towers, which are all that survive. He made a number of designs for small churches, a few of which were executed, including St Andrew, Gunton, Norfolk (completed 1769), the façade of which was conceived as a Classical pedimented temple.

The mausoleum thrived as a building type during the second half of the 18th century, providing another form of building in which Adam could experiment. Among his earliest mausolea was that for Bowood, Wilts (1761–4), which devolved from a cylindrical design to a square. Others included the cylindrical tomb for his friend, the philosopher David Hume, in Edinburgh's Old Calton Burying Ground (1777–8), and one on a square plan at Castle Upton, Co. Antrim, Ireland (1789–91). Related to these mausolea, though not independent structures, are church memorials, and Adam designed a number of them during his career. Among the earliest is the *Lt-Col. Roger Townshend* monument in Westminster Abbey, London (designed 1759); a later example is that in Warkton, Northants (1775), dedicated to *Mary, Duchess of Montagu*.

(f) Furniture and decorative objects. Adam designed a multitude of decorative objects for his domestic interiors, from furniture, carpets, door-knobs and escutcheons to stove-grates (for illustration *see* FIREPLACE FURNISHINGS), candelabra, silverware, ink wells and (even) sedan chairs. This is not to say he designed everything that was included in any one commission or that Neo-classical furniture made for an Adam house was necessarily made to his designs. For many clients he designed only wall furniture—pier-tables, mirrors, bookcases—or a decorative object or two. In some cases he did design a great deal. For Robert Child (*d* 1782) at Osterley Park House, for example, this included chairs for the dining-room, a commode and carpet for the drawing-room, a bed for the State Bedroom (*see* ENGLAND, fig. 92) and chairs and a chimney-board for the Etruscan Dressing-room. But even there, most of the furniture was designed and executed by such professional cabinetmakers as John Linnell (i); this was also true of Adam's other commissions. Those pieces that he did design—delicate, refined and ornamented with elegantly flattened Classical motifs in relief—were all in the Adam style.

(g) Gothic Revival. Although his architectural and decorative style was predominantly Neo-classical, Adam occasionally produced Gothic Revival designs if clients insisted. This differed from his castellar manner, which conveyed a picturesque impression by effects of massing drawn from a variety of sources, for his Gothic Revival buildings emulated a more playful and frivolous Gothick. Examples include the exterior of St Mary Magdalene at Croome d'Abitot, Hereford & Worcs (1763), and Brizlee Tower at Alnwick Castle, Northumb. (1777–83). But his Gothic Revival work was primarily for interiors, as at Strawberry Hill, Middx (1766–8), and Alnwick Castle itself (late 1760s–*c.* 1780). At Strawberry Hill, Horace Walpole, the revival's leading promoter, not only commissioned a chimney-piece and ceiling for the Round Tower there, but

4. Robert Adam: elevation of the Society of Arts, London, 1772–6; from Robert and James Adam: *Works in Architecture*, ii (London, 1778)

supplied Adam with medieval models from which to design. Nevertheless, the result was as delicate and refined as Adam's Neo-classical decoration. At Alnwick the result was apparently similar (his work there has since been obliterated). His Gothic Revival decorations for the interiors of Hulne Abbey on the Alnwick estate survive (1778); these reveal how delightful, if fanciful and unauthentic, Adam's essays in this manner were.

(v) Late work in Scotland, late 1780s and after. In the early and mid-1780s Adam was less busy, perhaps due to the building recession brought about by the American Revolution. But at the end of the decade and in the early 1790s, during which there was a phenomenal building boom, he was once again very active, especially in Scotland. At Gosford (1790–*c.* 1800) and Archerfield (1789–91), two Lothian houses, Edinburgh University (1789–93) and Glasgow's Royal Infirmary (1791–5; destr.), his powers and his style continued unabated. The exteriors retained the attenuated proportions and staccato emphases, and the interiors, though sometimes employing certain plainer passages, displayed the delicate and elegant refinement of his most rarefied manner.

2. WORKING METHODS. Adam was the dominating figure in the partnership with his brother James. It was he who generally met with clients, created the initial sketches

and retained ultimate control over the commissioned work. This can be seen in the large collection of almost 9000 drawings, both sketches and renderings, preserved in Sir John Soane's Museum in London. Even the drawings made for clients by the office staff can often be related to sketches in Adam's hand. His initial effort for an interior was often directed to its ceiling, with the design for a carpet or pavement frequently related to, yet different from, its counterpart above. He worked quickly, as can be seen from the quantity of designs that issued from his office. In 1762 James commented that 'I think from what I can perceive he makes plans much faster than I can make Cornishes.'

Adam's speed in designing was materially assisted by a number of draughtsmen or office assistants and a 'regiment of artificers', as Elizabeth Montagu called his craftsmen in 1779. In Italy he had assembled a group of draughtsmen to help him; on his return to England, Augustin Brunais (*fl* 1763–7) and one other (most probably Laurent-Benoît Dewez) accompanied him. George Richardson, who had accompanied James on his Grand Tour, also joined the office. Other Italians arrived subsequently, among them Giuseppe Manocchi (*d* 1782) and Joseph Bonomi. The latter (after four years measuring and drawing antiquities for the Adam brothers in Rome) was employed from 1767 to 1781 as a draughtsman, during which time he was prohibited by contract from doing any other drawings, even for himself, under a penalty of £200. Robert's fame was such that even after his death architects continued to identify themselves in advertisements as his former draughtsmen.

Those craftsmen responsible for executing Adam's designs included plasterers, decorative painters, wood- and stone-carvers, metalworkers (notably Matthew Boulton), locksmiths, cabinetmakers, carpet manufacturers and every type of artisan from bricklayers to glaziers. The principal stuccoists were Joseph Rose (*c*. 1723–80) and his nephew, also called Joseph Rose (1746–99). Adam's decorative painters included Antonio Zucchi, who arrived about 1766 and remained until 1781, when he returned to Italy. Although Zucchi was relied upon to supply inset decorative paintings that were independent of specific designs by Adam, in almost all other cases craftsmen followed his designs extremely closely.

3. Sources and influence. The most significant source for the Adam style was Roman antiquity. A good part of this was the result of Adam's years spent in Italy, but it was supplemented by studying books, engravings and drawings. Through them he learnt of such Roman monuments as those at Palmyra. They also provided sources for his occasional use of Greek motifs. Complementing these ancient sources were those of the Renaissance and Baroque eras. Although the Adam brothers claimed these were employed primarily as a means of elucidating ancient ones, in fact they had significant influence in their own right, providing, for example, inspiration for Robert's grotesque decoration (e.g. his design for the Breakfast Room at Kedleston Hall, 1768).

Three aspects of 18th-century architectural design were also influential. Most significant was the Palladian style of the Burlington circle, inherited by Adam from his father and used by the brothers in their early work in Scotland. It remained important throughout Robert's career for compositional effects and for a variety of detailing, ranging from rustication and modillion cornices to the ubiquitous Palladian-window motif within a relieving arch. Second was Piranesi, who, from his formative influence during Robert's Grand Tour and through his *Diverse maniere d'adornare i cammini* (1769), left an indelible mark on the Adam manner. Finally, there was a French influence that can be seen in Adam's planning, as in his use of the *enfilade* and in his courtyard screens.

Although Adam had an army of assistants, he took no pupils. Nevertheless, his influence was enormously widespread. This he accomplished through both his executed work and published designs. By the 1760s such older architects as Robert Taylor and James Paine were beginning to change or at least modify their styles in response to Adam's innovations. In addition, from the later 1760s on, a whole host of younger architects, including George Dance (ii), Thomas Leverton, Henry Holland, James Wyatt and John Soane, began their careers in the Adam mould. Though some, for example Wyatt, were to retain this style while others changed dramatically, Adam's influence was an important aspect of their early development. Lesser architects were even more influenced by his work, as were scores of pattern-book authors. Among these was William Pain, whose conversion can be seen by comparing his early *Builder's Companion and Workman's General Assistant* (1758) with his Adam-influenced *Practical Builder* of 1774. Adam's effect was also strong in the decorative arts, and Thomas Chippendale's Neo-classical furniture after *c*. 1763 is one excellent example of this.

The Adam influence extended far beyond Britain. In Russia it can be seen in the work of Charles Cameron at the palaces of Tsarskoye Selo (1779–84) and Pavlovsk (1782–5), both near St Petersburg. In the USA examples range from the work of such established architects as Charles Bulfinch and Samuel McIntire in Massachusetts to numerous anonymous buildings as far south as Georgia, as far west as Indiana, and as late as the 1820s.

UNPUBLISHED SOURCES

Edinburgh, Register House [family letters from Robert and James Adam, from the 1740s on; Clerk of Penicuik Papers]

WRITINGS

Ruins of the Palace of the Emperor Diocletian at Spalatro in Dalmatia (London, 1764)

with J. Adam: *The Works in Architecture of Robert and James Adam*, i–ii (London, 1773–8), iii (London, 1822); repr. in 1 vol. (London, 1975)

BIBLIOGRAPHY

J. Swarbrick: *Robert Adam and his Brothers* (London, 1915)

A. T. Bolton: *The Architecture of Robert and James Adam*, 2 vols (London, 1922)

J. Lees-Milne: *The Age of Adam* (London, 1947)

J. Fleming: 'Robert Adam, the Grand Tourist', *Cornhill Mag.*, clxviii/1004 (1955), pp. 118–37

G. Beard: 'Robert Adam's Craftsmen', *Connoisseur Yb.* (1958), pp. 26–32

D. Stillman: *The Genesis of the Adam Style* (diss., New York, Columbia U., 1961)

G. Beard: 'New Light on Adam's Craftsmen', *Country Life*, cxxxi (10 May 1962), pp. 1098–1100

J. Fleming: *Robert Adam and his Circle in Edinburgh and Rome* (London, 1962)

E. Harris: 'Robert Adam and the Gobelins', *Apollo*, lxxvi (1962), pp. 100–06
——: *The Furniture of Robert Adam* (London, 1963)
A. Rowan: *The Castle Style in British Domestic Architecture in the 18th and Early 19th Century* (diss., U. Cambridge, 1965)
R. Rowe: *Adam Silver* (London, 1965)
G. Beard: *Georgian Craftsmen and their Work* (London, 1966)
D. Stillman: *The Decorative Work of Robert Adam* (London, 1966)
——: 'Robert Adam and Piranesi', *Essays in the History of Architecture Presented to Rudolf Wittkower* (London, 1967), pp. 197–206
J. Fleming: '"Retrospective View" by John Clerk of Eldin with Some Comments on Adam's Castle Style', *Concerning Architecture*, ed. J. Summerson (London, 1968), pp. 75–84
——: 'Robert Adam's Castle Style', *Country Life*, cxliii (23 May 1968), pp. 1356–9; (30 May 1968), pp. 1443–7
E. Croft-Murray: *Decorative Painting in England, 1537–1837*, ii (London, 1971)
M. Tomlin: *Catalogue of Adam Period Furniture* (London, 1972)
A. Rowan: 'After the Adelphi: Forgotten Years in the Adam Brothers' Practice', *J. Royal Soc. A.*, cxxii (1973–4), pp. 659–78
G. Beard: *Decorative Plasterwork in Great Britain* (London, 1975)
——: *The Work of Robert Adam* (New York, 1978)
——: *Craftsmen and Interior Decoration in England, 1660–1820* (Edinburgh, 1981)
M. Sanderson: 'Robert Adam's Last Visit to Scotland', *Archit. Hist.*, xxv (1982), pp. 33–46
City Dwellings and Country Houses: Robert Adam and his Style (exh. cat., New York, Cooper-Hewitt Mus., 1982)
A. A. Tait: 'Reading the Ruins: Robert Adam and Piranesi in Rome', *Archit. Hist.*, xxvii (1984), pp. 524–33
A. Rowan: *A Catalogue of the Architectural Drawings of Robert Adam in the Victoria and Albert Museum* (London, 1985)
——: *Designs for Castles and Country Villas by Robert and James Adam* (Oxford, 1985)
J. Rykwert and A. Rykwert: *Robert and James Adam: The Men and the Style* (London, 1985)
I. Bristow: 'The Room in the Context of Robert Adam's Work', *Philadelphia Mus. A.: Bull.*, lxxxii (1986), pp. 13–19
D. Stillman: *English Neo-classical Architecture*, 2 vols (London, 1988)
——: 'The Neo-classical Transformation of the English Country House', *Stud. Hist. A.*, xxv (1989), pp. 75–93
D. N. King: *The Complete Works of Robert and James Adam* (Boston, 1991)
J. Bryant: *Robert Adam, 1728–92: Architect of Genius* (London, 1992)
S. Parissien: *Adam Style* (Washington, DC, 1992)
A. A. Tait: *Robert Adam: Drawings and Imagination* (New York, 1993)

(4) James Adam (*b* Edinburgh, 21 July 1732; *d* London, 20 Oct 1794). Architect, son of (1) William Adam. In the 1750s he was taken into partnership in Edinburgh with his older brothers John and Robert, and from 1760 to 1763 he was on a Grand Tour in Italy. Accompanied by an architectural draughtsman, George Richardson, James was guided by Charles-Louis Clérisseau, Robert's teacher, employee and friend during his time in Italy. In 1763 James joined Robert in a London partnership, remaining his brother's associate and subsidiary designer until Robert's death in 1792. He then continued alone until his own death two years later.

In 1769 James succeeded Robert as joint Architect of the King's Works, remaining in that post until its dissolution in 1782. Most of his architectural work was subsumed within the Adam partnership, whose chief designer was Robert, but James executed a few independent designs, among them the Shire Hall at Hertford, Herts (1767–71); façades for Portland Place, London (1776); and late works in Scotland in the two years between Robert's death and his own. These included St George's Episcopal Church, Edinburgh (1792–4), and College Houses (1793) and the Tron Church (1794) in Glasgow.

WRITINGS

with R. Adam: *The Works in Architecture of Robert and James Adam*, i–ii (London, 1773–8), iii (London, 1822); repr. in 1 vol. (London, 1975)
Practical Essays on Agriculture, 2 vols (London, 1789, 2/1794)

BIBLIOGRAPHY

A. T. Bolton: 'The Shire Hall, Hertford', *Archit. Rev.* [London], xliii (1918), pp. 68–73
——: *The Architecture of Robert and James Adam*, 2 vols (London, 1922)
J. Fleming: *Robert Adam and his Circle in Edinburgh and Rome* (London, 1962)
A. Rowan: 'After the Adelphi: Forgotten Years in the Adam Brothers' Practice', *J. Royal Soc. A.*, cxxii (1973–4), pp. 659–78

DAMIE STILLMAN

Adam (iii). German family of painters. (1) Albrecht Adam had four sons who were artists: Benno Adam (1812–1892), Franz Adam (1815–1886), Eugen Adam (1817–1880), and Julius Adam (1826–1874). Albrecht's brother Heinrich Adam (1787–1862) was also an artist. (2) Richard Benno Adam was the grandson of Benno Adam.

(1) Albrecht Adam (*b* Nördlingen, 16 April 1786; *d* Munich, 28 Aug 1862). He trained under Christoph Zwinger (1744–1813) in Nuremberg, and in 1807 he moved to Munich to continue his studies. From 1809 he worked in Milan, following his appointment as court painter to Eugène de Beauharnais, viceroy of Italy, whom he accompanied to Russia in 1812. After returning to Munich in 1815, he executed a series of 83 small battle-pieces in oil on paper, based on sketches made in 1812. His Russian exploits also provided the material for a set of 100 lithographs entitled *Voyage pittoresque et militaire de Willenberg en Prusse jusqu'à Moscou* (1827–33), produced with the assistance of his sons Franz and Benno, which helped to establish his contemporary reputation. In Munich, Albrecht's patrons included Maximilian I and his successor, Ludwig I of Bavaria, at whose behest Albrecht painted the *Battle of Borodino* for the Munich Residenz. For the palace in St Petersburg of Maximilian, Duc de Leuchtenberg, he executed 12 large battle-pieces. Other commissions took him to Stuttgart in 1829 and to Mecklenburg in 1838. After 1848 he was employed as a battle painter by Marshal Radetzky and by Emperor Francis Joseph of Austria, of whom he also produced several portraits during his residence in Vienna from 1855 to 1857. In 1859 he followed the army of Napoleon III during the Italian campaign against the Austrians, which he recorded in a series of drawings and sketches. On his return to Munich he painted the *Battle of Landshut* (1858–9) for Archduke Charles Ludwig and the *Battle of Zorndorf* (1859–62; Munich, Maximilianum) for King Maximilian II. In his later years, many of his pictures were painted in collaboration with his sons.

WRITINGS

H. Holland, ed.: *Aus dem Leben eines Schlachtenmalers: Selbstbiographie* (Stuttgart, 1886)

COLIN J. BAILEY

(2) Richard Benno Adam (*b* Munich, 5 March 1873; *d* Munich, 20 Jan 1937). Great-grandson of (1) Albrecht Adam. He studied in Munich with Nicolas Gysis at the Akademie der Bildenden Künste, with Sigmund Strähuber and Ludwig von Langenmantel (1854–1922), and in the private school run by Heinrich Knirr (*b* 1862). Between

1892 and 1894 he studied at the Staatliche Akademie der Bildenden Künste in Karlsruhe. From 1896 he painted his first equestrian portraits of the German, Austrian, Bohemian and Hungarian nobility. In 1899 he painted the *Budapest Hunting Society*, which included 47 equestrian portraits. He was a war artist during World War I in Galicia and in the Imperial Headquarters in France. Between 1928 and 1931 he made several commission-related journeys to the USA, producing such works as the *American Sportsmen*.

UNPUBLISHED SOURCES

Munich Stadtarchv [letters and diaries]

BIBLIOGRAPHY

Albrecht Adam und seine Familie: Zur Geschichte einer Münchner Künstlerdynastie im 19. und 20. Jahrhundert (exh. cat. by U. v. Hase-Schmundt and others, Munich, Stadtmus., 1987)

U. V. HASE-SCHMUNDT

Adam, Henri-Georges (*b* Paris, 14 Jan 1904; *d* La Clarté, Brittany, 27 Aug 1967). French sculptor, printmaker and tapestry designer. His father was a jeweller, and after his return from World War I in 1918 Adam worked in his studio and learnt how to engrave. At the same time he studied drawing at the Ecole Germain-Pilon and read Charles Baudelaire's *Les Fleurs du mal*, which was to have a great influence on him. In 1925 he attended evening classes at a school of drawing in Montparnasse. From 1928 to 1934 he started to produce prints and became associated with André Breton, Louis Aragon and Paul Eluard, although he was never greatly influenced by them. His early prints, reminiscent of the work of George Grosz, were mostly designed as social satire, mocking the myths surrounding patriotism, the family and religion, as in *When Papa is Patriotic* (1935). In 1933 he designed the costumes and scenery for Hans Schlumberg's *Miracle à Verdun* performed at the Théâtre des Bouffes du Nord in Paris. His first exhibition of prints was held in 1934 at the Galerie Billiet-Vorms in Paris.

The Spanish Civil War (1936–9) prompted Adam to create a cycle of engravings entitled *Disasters of War*, which included such works as the *Horse and the Plough* (1941; Y. Adam priv. col., see 1968 exh. cat., p. 106). In 1937 he participated in the exhibition *Artistes de ce temps* at the Petit Palais in Paris, and the following year he was awarded the Blumenthal prize for engraving. After being mobilized in 1939 and taken prisoner in 1940, he then worked as a hospital attendant in Besançon. His experiences led to a series of 120 drawings evoking the horrors of war. In 1943 he produced costume and stage designs for Jean-Paul Sartre's *Les Mouches*, performed at the Théâtre de la Cité in Paris. He began producing sculpture in 1942 and the following year executed his first important work *The Effigy* (Y. Adam priv. col., see 1966 exh. cat., p. 7), based on medieval tomb figures. It was exhibited at the Salon de la Libération, Paris, in 1944 through the intervention of Picasso and caused a considerable stir at the exhibition, André Lhote being its strongest defender. Adam's friendship with Picasso led to the latter offering him his studio in the Rue des Grands-Augustins, where Adam worked for the next seven years. In 1945 he was one of the co-founders of the Salon de Mai in Paris, at which he exhibited his *Burnt Man* (1945; Y. Adam priv. col.). In 1947 he engraved a series of plates to illustrate Gérard de Nerval's *Les Chimères*, although they were never published (see Gheerbrant, pls 52–61, 70–83). The same year he produced the first of many tapestry cartoons, for *Danae*, which was woven at Aubusson. His tapestry *Meridian* was hung in the UNESCO Palace in Paris in 1958.

In 1956 Adam began his series of sculptures *Vegetable and Marine Mutations*, which were designed to expand the subject-matter of sculpture beyond the tradition of the human form, as in *Large Shell* (1956; Y. Adam priv. col., see George, pl. 31). The same year he began the series of engravings *Flagstones, Sand and Water*, which included such works as *Flagstone, Sand and Water, No. 1* (1956; Y. Adam priv. col., see Gheerbrant, pl. 109). He produced a number of large public sculptures, the first of which was *The Signal* (1959–61; Le Havre, Mus. B.-A.), a vast geometric work whose aspect radically alters from different viewpoints. One of his most impressive public works is *The Wall* (1965–6; Chantilly, Lycée), a series of unevenly sized and shaped stones with a network of deep incisions. From 1963 to 1967 he provided sculptural decoration for the church at Moutier in Switzerland.

BIBLIOGRAPHY

B. Gheerbrant: *Henri-George Adam: Oeuvre gravé, 1939–1957* (Paris, 1957)
Adam (exh. cat. by B. Dorival and others, Paris, Mus. N. A. Mod., 1966)
W. George and I. Jianou: *Adam* (Paris, 1968)
A la rencontre d'Adam (exh. cat. by Y. Goldenberg, Paris, Hôtel de la Monnaie, 1968)

□

Adam, Paul (*b* Paris, 7 Dec 1862; *d* Paris, 1 Jan 1920). French writer and critic. His fictional work developed rapidly from a naturalist concept of the novel (e.g. *Chair molle*, Paris, 1885) to a symbolist one (e.g. *Etre*, Paris, 1888). As an art critic, he played an important role in the first years of Neo-Impressionism. The few pieces that he wrote between 1886 and 1889 placed him in the top rank of contemporary critics and were of considerable influence. He was less interested in analysing the theoretical bases of Neo-Impressionism than in deciphering their implications, stressing the relationship of this new method of painting to Symbolism. He felt that the use by Seurat and his followers of a body of scientific theories on which to base their art was not only an indication of their adherence to the modernity that pervaded the century but also revealed an underlying tendency towards abstraction. At the same time fundamental visual concepts or 'preconceived sensorial notions' that had served as the basis of western art were called into question. In this regard, the 'pictorial concern to interpret the pure phenomenon' corresponded to the aspiration towards synthesis that marked Symbolism and was 'in close correlation to contemporary philosophy, biology and physics in denying the existence of objects, declaring matter to be the mere appearance of vibratory movement that is the source of our impressions, our sensations, our ideas' (*Dix ans d'art français*, p. 38). In this collection of his articles that had appeared between 1896 and 1907, his opinions evolve from the intransigent approach he took during the years when Symbolist art was prominent, to a more eclectic one. He continued, however, to see Seurat as the dominant artist of his time.

WRITINGS

'Peintres impressionnistes', *Rev. Contemp.* (April–May 1886)

'Les Artistes indépendants', *La Vogue*, viii (Sept 1886)

'Les Impressionnistes à l'exposition des Indépendants', *Vie Mod.*, x (15 April 1888)

preface: G. Vanor: *L'Art symboliste* (Paris, 1889)

Dix ans d'art français (Paris, 1909)

BIBLIOGRAPHY

J. Huret: *Enquête sur l'évolution littéraire* (Paris, 1891, rev. Vanves, 1982)

C. Mauclair: *Paul Adam* (Paris, [1921])

F. Jean-Desthieux: *Le Dernier des encyclopédistes, Paul Adam* (Paris, 1928)

P. Smith: 'Paul Adam, "Soi" et les "Peintres impressionnistes": La Genèse d'un discours moderniste', *Rev. A.* [Paris], 82 (1988)

R. Rapetti: '"Ce mode neuf de voir": Neo-impressionismo e simbolismo in Francia', *L'età del divisionismo* (exh. cat., ed. G. Belli and F. Rella; Trent, Mus. A. Mod. & Contemp. Trento & Rovereto, 1990), pp. 56–74

M. F. Zimmermann: *Les Mondes de Seurat* (Anvers-Paris, 1991)

RODOLPHE RAPETTI

Adami, Valerio (*b* Bologna, 17 March 1935). Italian painter, draughtsman and printmaker. He was given a rigorous training as a draughtsman between 1951 and 1954 in Achille Funi's studio at the Accademia di Belle Arti di Brera, Milan, which provided the basis for his mature work. Before developing his characteristic contour line and flat surfaces, he experimented briefly with an expressionistic style that combined violent and humorous imagery inspired by the explosive forms in space favoured by Roberto Matta and by strip cartoons; typical of this phase is one of his earliest large canvases, *L'ora del sandwiche* (1963; Camilla Adami priv. col., see Damisch and Martin, pl. 42). He settled in Paris in 1957 but divided his time between France and Italy. In such paintings as *Stanze a cannocchiale* ('Telescoped rooms', 1965; Pittsburgh, PA, Carnegie Mus. A.) he began to develop a highly decorative idiom of stylized images outlined in black on a surface of interlocking areas of intense, unmodulated colour. His usual starting-point was a photograph or several associated images, which he reworked, fragmented and presented in a schematic form. This remained Adami's system of working in later years, although his subject-matter changed.

From 1968 to 1970 he favoured everyday themes, such as shop-windows, hotel rooms or bathroom interiors of a clinical and disturbing cleanliness. In the early 1970s he turned to recent political events and to literary and philosophical themes for inspiration. He produced paintings of representatives of modern European culture, such as *Sigmund Freud Journeying to London* (1973; Saint-Paul-de-Vence, Fond. Maeght). In the mid-1970s he introduced mythological and metaphysical themes. Adami conceived of his painting as a synthesis of Western memory, a humanist quest infused with nostalgia.

BIBLIOGRAPHY

H. Damisch and H. Martin: *Adami* (Paris, 1974)

M. Le Bot: *Valerio Adami, essai sur le formalisme critique* (Auvers-sur-Oise, 1975)

Adami (exh. cat., Paris, Pompidou, 1985)

ALFRED PACQUEMENT

Adams, Ansel (Easton) (*b* San Francisco, CA, 20 Feb 1902; *d* Carmel, CA, 22 April 1984). American photographer. He trained as a musician and supported himself by teaching the piano until 1930. He became involved with photography in 1916 when his parents presented him with a Kodak Box Brownie camera during a summer vacation in Yosemite National Park. In 1917–18 he worked part-time in a photo-finishing business. From 1920 to 1927 he served as custodian of the LeConte Memorial in Yosemite, the Sierra Club's headquarters. His duties included leading weekly expeditions through the valley and rims, during which he continued to photograph the landscape. He considered his snapshots of Yosemite and the Sierra Nevada Mountains, taken during the early 1920s, to be a visual diary, the work of an ardent hobbyist. By 1923 he used a $6\frac{1}{2}\times8\frac{1}{2}$-inch Korona view camera on his pack trips, and in 1927 he spent an afternoon making one of his most famous images, *Monolith, the Face of Half Dome, Yosemite National Park* (Chicago, IL, A. Inst.; see fig.). Adams planned his photograph, waited for the exact sunlight he desired and used a red filter to darken the sky against the monumental cliff. He later referred to this image as his 'first true visualization' of the subject, not as it appeared 'in reality but how it *felt* to me and how it must appear in the finished print' (*Ansel Adams: An Autobiography*, p. 76).

With the assistance of Albert Bender (1866–1941), one of San Francisco's foremost patrons of the arts, Adams published his first portfolio, *Parmelian Prints of the High Sierras* (San Francisco, 1927), and his first illustrated book, *Taos pueblo* (San Francisco, 1930). In 1930 he met Paul Strand and decided to devote himself to photography. Strand's photographic vision made Adams realize the potential of the medium as an expressive art form. Adams abandoned textured photographic paper, his last vestige of Pictorialism, for glossy stock and experienced a liberation in his creative direction as well. In 1932 he and several San Francisco Bay Area photographers formed GROUP f.64 to promote 'straight' unmanipulated photography.

Adams visited Alfred Stieglitz at his New York gallery, An American Place, in 1933 and exhibited there in 1936, his contact with Stieglitz giving him more confidence in the medium. He wrote his first technical manual, *Making a Photograph* (London & New York, 1935), and subsequently published several others, along with collections of photographs.

Adams used all types of camera and experimented constantly with new techniques. He developed a 'zone system', which divided the gradations of light into ten zones from black to white, allowing the photographer, with the help of an exposure meter, to correlate areas of different luminosity in the subject with the approximate value of grey in the final print. Adams's technical mastery, his complete control of the final image, was a necessary stage of development in achieving his full creative vision. His photographs transcend the simple description of objects and landscape: they depict transient aspects of light, atmosphere and natural phenomena.

In 1940 Adams helped to establish the Department of Photography at the Museum of Modern Art in New York and co-curated its first exhibition. He also established the Department of Photography at the California School of Fine Arts (now the San Francisco Art Institute) in 1946. He moved to Carmel, CA, in 1961 and was one of the founders of the Friends of Photography in 1966.

Ansel Adams: *Monolith, the Face of Half Dome, Yosemite National Park*, 1927 (Chicago, IL, Art Institute of Chicago)

WRITINGS

with V. Adams: *Illustrated Guide to Yosemite Valley* (San Francisco, 1946, rev. 2/1963)
with E. Land, D. McAlpin and J. Holmes: *Ansel Adams: Singular Images* (New York, 1974)
Ansel Adams: An Autobiography (Boston, 1985)

PHOTOGRAPHIC PUBLICATIONS

Sierra Nevada: The John Muir Trail (Berkeley, CA, 1938)
Born Free and Equal: Photographs of the Loyal Japanese-Americans at Manzanar Relocation Center, Inyo County, California (New York, 1944)
Camera and Lens (New York, 1948)
The Negative (New York, 1948)
My Camera in Yosemite Valley (Yosemite, CA, 1949)
My Camera in the National Parks (Yosemite, CA, 1950)
The Print (New York, 1950)
Natural Light Photography (New York, 1952)
Artificial-Light Photography (New York, 1956)
These we Inherit (San Francisco, 1962)
Polaroid Land Photography Manual (New York, 1963, rev. 1978)
Examples: The Making of 40 Photographs (Boston, 1983)

BIBLIOGRAPHY

J. Muir: *Yosemite and the High Sierra* (Boston, 1948)
M. Austin: *The Land of Little Rain* (Boston, 1950)
N. Newhall: *Death Valley* (Redwood City, CA, 1954)
——: *Mission San Xavier del Bac* (Redwood City, CA, 1954)
——: *The Pageant of History in Northern California* (San Francisco, 1954)
N. Newhall, ed.: *Yosemite Valley* (San Francisco, 1959)
E. Corle: *Death Valley and the Creek Called Furnace* (Los Angeles, 1962)
N. Newhall: *The Eloquent Light*, i of *Ansel Adams* (San Francisco, 1963) [only vol.]
E. Joesting: *An Introduction to Hawaii* (Redwood City, CA, 1964)
N. Newhall: *Fiat Lux: The University of California* (New York, 1967)
——: *The Tetons and the Yellowstone* (Redwood City, CA, 1970)
L. de Cock, ed.: *Ansel Adams* (New York, 1972)
W. Stegner: *Ansel Adams: Images, 1923–1974* (Boston, 1974)
L. C. Powell: *Photographs of the Southwest* (Boston, 1976)
J. Szarkowski: *The Portfolios of Ansel Adams* (Boston, 1977)
J. Alinder and M. S. Alinder: *Ansel Adams: A San Francisco Heritage* (San Francisco, 1978)
P. Brooks: *Yosemite and the Range of Light* (Boston, 1979)
J. Alinder: *The Unknown Ansel Adams* (Carmel, 1982)
A. Gray: *Ansel Adams: An American Place, 1936* (Tucson, 1982)
H. M. Callahan, ed.: *Ansel Adams in Color* (Boston and London, 1993)

RICHARD LORENZ

Adams, Clinton (*b* Glendale, CA, 11 Dec 1918). American painter, printmaker, art historian, writer and teacher. His appointment to the art faculty of the University of California, Los Angeles, in 1942 was interrupted by military service, and it was not until 1946 that he resumed his career as a teacher of the practice and theory of art. This took him to the universities of Kentucky (Lexington), Florida (Gainesville) and finally New Mexico (Albuquerque), where he served as Dean (1961–76). Despite academic demands, Adams always found time to paint and showed his work in over 50 solo exhibitions. Equally at home in oil, acrylic, watercolour and egg tempera, he was initially inspired by the abstracted cityscapes of Stuart Davis. Later he absorbed the lessons of Matisse, achieving particularly radiant paintings during the 1980s. In 1993 he was elected an Academician by the National Academy of Design.

In 1948, at Stanton Macdonald-Wright's suggestion, Adams began to make lithographs with the Los Angeles printer, Lynton Kistler. Early in his use of colour, he exhibited at the *1st International Biennial of Color Lithography* (1950) in Cincinnati, OH. During 1960 Adams helped JUNE WAYNE set up the Tamarind Lithography Workshop, which transformed printmaking in the USA. When the Workshop moved to Albuquerque as the Tamarind Institute, Adams became its Director (1970–85; *see* LITHOGRAPHY, §II, 2(ii)(c)).

During the 1970s Adams entered an intensive period as a writer, founding the exemplary research journal *The Tamarind Papers* in 1974, and editing and contributing to it until 1996. The author of more than 100 articles about lithography, he co-authored the 'bible' of the process in 1971 and went on to write an outstanding history (1983) of lithography in America. In 1985, Adams received the Governor's Award for 'Outstanding Contributions to the Arts of New Mexico'. In fact, through his many activities, his impact on the knowledge and practice of lithography has been world-wide.

WRITINGS

with G. Antreasian: *The Tamarind Book of Lithography: Art and Techniques* (New York, 1971)
Fritz Scholder Lithographs (Boston, 1975)
'The Prints of Andrew Dasburg: A Complete Catalogue', *Tamarind Pap.*, iv (1980–81), pp. 18–25
American Lithographers, 1900–1960: The Artists and their Printers (Albuquerque, 1983)
'Adolf Dehn: The Lithographs', *The Prints of Adolf Dehn: A Catalogue Raisonné* (St Paul, 1987), pp. 26–42
'The Nature of Lithography', *Lasting Impressions: Lithography as Art*, ed. P. Gilmour (Canberra, London, Philadelphia, 1988), pp. 24–41
Printmaking in New Mexico, 1880–1890 (Albuquerque, 1991)
Crayonstone: The Life and Work of Bolton Coit Brown, with a Catalogue of his Lithographs (Albuquerque, 1993)
Regular contributions to *Tamarind Pap.* (1974–95)

BIBLIOGRAPHY

Tamarind: Homage to Lithography (exh. cat. by V. Allen, New York, MOMA, 1969), pp. 10, 13, 27, 60
Clinton Adams (exh. cat. by V. D. Coke, Albuquerque, U. NM, A. Mus., 1971)
J. Watrous: *A Century of American Printmaking, 1880–1980* (Madison, WI, 1984)
Clinton Adams: Paintings and Watercolours, 1945–1987 (exh. cat. by V. D. Coke and P. Walch, Albuquerque, U. NM, A. Mus., 1987)
P. Gilmour: 'Lithographic Collaboration: The Hand, the Head, the Heart', *Lasting Impressions: Lithography as Art*, ed. P. Gilmour (Canberra, London and Philadelphia, 1988), pp. 264, 344–5, 347–9, 358
Spectrum of Innovation: Color in American Printmaking, 1890–1960 (exh. cat. by D. Acton, Worcester, MA, A. Mus., 1990–91), pp. 33–9, 246–8

PAT GILMOUR

Adams, Mark (*b* Fort Plain, NY, 27 Oct 1925). American tapestry artist, painter and stained-glass designer. He studied painting at Syracuse University and with Hans Hoffmann in New York, where he was influenced by the medieval tapestries in the Cloisters and also by the work of Matisse. In the 1950s Adams was apprenticed to the influential French tapestry designer Jean Lurçat, from whom he learnt the bold colours and clear imagery that characterize his work. He also studied at the Ecole Nationale d'Art Décoratif in Aubusson before beginning to use a series of workshops, notably that of Marguerite and Paul Avignon, who wove his first nationally acclaimed tapestry, *Phoenix and the Golden Gate* (1957). *Flight of Angels* (1962) was exhibited at the first Biennale Internationale de la Tapisserie in Lausanne. In 1976 his cartoon of *California Poppies* (San Francisco, CA Pal. Legion of Honor; see fig.) was woven for the *Five Centuries of Tapestry* exhibition at the California Palace of the Legion of Honor, San Francisco, as a demonstration piece. Later tapestries, for example *White Block* (1977) and *Sunset with Palms* (1979), were woven by the San Francisco Tapestry Workshop, with which he was associated. Public

Mark Adams: *California Poppies*, cotton and wool, 1.37×0.86 m, 1976 (San Francisco, CA, California Palace of the Legion of Honor); woven by graduate students of the Fine Arts department of San Francisco State University under the direction of Jean-Pierre Larochette

commissions included a series of panels depicting garden scenes for the San Francisco International Airport (1981–3) as well as designs for stained-glass windows, notably two for the Temple Emanu-El in San Francisco (*Fire* and *Water*, 1971–4). He painted a self-portrait in 1982 (artist's col., see Johnson, Mills and Price, p. 25).

BIBLIOGRAPHY

Mark Adams: An Exhibition of Tapestries, Paintings, Stained Glass Windows and Architectural Designs (exh. cat. by W. H. Elsner, San Francisco, CA Pal. Legion of Honor, 1970)

Mark Adams (exh. cat. by H. T. Hopkins, San Francisco, CA, John Berggruen Gal., 1980)

R. F. Johnson, P. Mills and L. Price: *Mark Adams* (San Francisco, 1985)

COURTNEY ANN SHAW

Adams, Maurice B(ingham) (*b* Burgess Hill, Sussex, 1849; *d* London, 17 Aug 1933). English architect, editor and draughtsman. After completing his articles with H. N. Goulty of Brighton, he became assistant to William Ralph Emerson, and Architect to Brighton Council. Between 1872 and 1923 he was Editor of *Building News*. He instituted the Building News Designing Club, which enabled young architects to submit designs for his criticism. He contributed largely to the paper's illustrations, redrawing designs for lithographic reproduction, and covered a wide range of subjects in a skilful and accurate, if somewhat dull, linear style. He also published several architectural books. Through the owner of *Building News* he obtained his major architectural commissions, notably Camberwell Polytechnic and Art Gallery (1902). He also designed country houses near London, for example Queensmead Cottage, Kings Road, Windsor, Berks (1883), for Reginald Talbot, as well as in Australia (e.g. Bellevue Hill, Double Bay, for Charles B. Fairfax in the mid-1880s) and America, where he designed timber houses in New Jersey for E. S. Wilde in *c.* 1890. By 1878 he had settled in Bedford Park, the pioneering London garden suburb, which he helped to publicize. There he completed R. Norman Shaw's church of St Michael and All Angels, adding the north aisle and parish hall (1887), and the chapel of All Souls (1909). He also designed the School of Art in 1882 (destr.) and two houses with a studio for the artist J. C. Dollmann (1851–1934) in 1880. Adams was a practical planner and his style varied from domestic QUEEN ANNE REVIVAL to a cheerfully inventive Jacobean eclecticism.

WRITINGS

with R. N. Shaw: *Sketches for Cottages* (London, 1878)

Artists' Homes (London, 1883)

Modern Cottage Architecture (London, 1904)

Cottage Housing (London, 1914)

BIBLIOGRAPHY

T. A. Greeves: 'London's First Garden Suburb', *Country Life*, cxlii (7 Dec 1967), pp. 1524–9

——: 'The Making of a Community', *Country Life*, cxlii (14 Dec 1967), pp. 1600–02

——: *Bedford Park: The First Garden Suburb* (London, 1975)

——: 'London's First Garden Suburb: 100 Years of Bedford Park', *Country Life*, clviii (27 Nov 1975), pp. 1446–8

A. S. Gray: *Edwardian Architecture: A Biographical Dictionary* (London, 1985)

T. AFFLECK GREEVES

Adams, Robert (i) (*b* Northampton, 5 Oct 1917; *d* Gt Maplestead, Essex, 5 April 1984). English sculptor and painter. He studied at the Northampton School of Art from 1933 to 1944. During World War II he was employed as an engineer, and after the war he spent two years teaching himself to sculpt in wood. Though he had participated in various group exhibitions during the war, it was not until 1947 that he had his first one-man show, of sculpture, at the Gimpel Fils Gallery in London. He also produced abstract paintings, but soon came to specialize in sculpture. His early sculpture of this period, such as *Figure* (1949–51; London, Tate), showed the influence of Henry Moore, whose works he knew from photographs. These comprised forms abstracted from natural objects, executed in wood, plaster and stone. After his one-man show he made several extended trips to Paris, where he became interested in the work of Brancusi and Julio González. In 1950 he received a Rockefeller award from the Institute of International Education to visit the USA. Having by then an established reputation, he was also commissioned to produce a 3-m high carving for the Festival of Britain in 1951.

In 1949 Adams had begun to work with metal and the same year was given a teaching post in industrial design at the Central School of Art and Design in London, which he held until 1960. While there he came into contact with Victor Pasmore and with the group of artists around him, which included Adrian Heath (*b* 1920), Anthony Hill, Kenneth Martin and Mary Martin. The group acted as a forum for Constructivist ideas in Britain and Adams exhibited with them from 1951 to 1956. Unlike the rest of the group, however, he rejected both mathematical formulae and new materials in sculpture. Many of his works were in wood and were based on organic forms, as in *Growing Forms* (1954; see 1962 exh. cat., pl. D). He was nevertheless sympathetic to the group's aim of forging a link between art and architecture, and this was reflected in his vast mural relief for the Municipal Theatre at Gelsenkirchen in Germany, constructed in 1959 from reinforced concrete.

While teaching at the Central School Adams learnt how to weld and in 1955 began to produce constructions of sheet and rod elements, as in *Tall Spike Forms* (1956; see 1962 exh. cat., pl. L), which showed the influence of González and a move towards non-figuration. In 1962, together with Hubert Dalwood (1924–76), Adams represented British sculpture at the Venice Biennale. His work of the 1960s often used welded steel sheets, sometimes perforated, as in *Large Screen Form* (1962; London, Tate). These were ideally to be displayed against a well-lit background so as to allow light to shine through. In 1966 he produced a large steel sculpture for the British Petroleum building in London, made from welded geometrical elements formed into a relief arrangement.

In the 1970s and until his death Adams concentrated on bronze casts, which though still non-figurative were softer and less geometrical than before, as in *Ovoid Variations* (1980; see 1988 exh. cat., pl. 27). Among his later public works was the large steel sculpture for Kingswell in Hampstead (1973), designed from a simple, Minimalist form.

BIBLIOGRAPHY

Robert Adams (exh. cat. by A. Hill, London, Gimpel Fils, 1951)
L. Alloway: *Nine Abstract Artists* (London, 1954), pp. 21–2
Ceri Richards, Robert Adams, Hubert Dalwood: British Pavilion (exh. cat. by J. P. Hodin, Venice Biennale, 1962)
Robert Adams, Retrospective Exhibition (exh. cat. by C. Spencer, London, Camden A. Cent., 1971)
P. Curtis: *Modern British Sculpture from the Collection* (Liverpool, Tate, 1982)
Robert Adams: Late Bronzes (exh. cat., London, Gimpel Fils, 1988)

□

Adams, Robert (ii) (*b* Orange, NJ, 8 May 1937). American photographer. After teaching English literature for several years, Adams turned to photography in the late 1960s, studying with Minor White. In his black-and-white photographs of the American West, such as his series *From the Missouri West* (1980), he emphasized man's presence in nature and the tension between the beauty of the landscape and man's effect upon it. His landscapes include such features as telephone poles and wires, mountains edged by highway guard-rails, parking lots and housing complexes. In 1975 Adams took part in the group exhibition *New Topographics: Photographs of a Man-altered Landscape* (*see* NEW TOPOGRAPHICS). As a photographer and an articulate writer on photography, he has published *Summer Nights* (1985) and important essays on 19th- and 20th-century photography.

BIBLIOGRAPHY

Mirrors and Windows: American Photography since 1960 (exh. cat., ed. J. Szarkowski; New York, MOMA, 1978)
J. Z. Grover: 'The Sublime and the Anachronistic: Robert Adams' American Landscape', *After image* (1981), pp. 6–7

MARY CHRISTIAN

Adams, Tate (*b* Holywood, County Down, Ireland, 26 Jan 1922). Australian painter, printmaker, book designer, lecturer, collector, gallery director and publisher of limited edition artists' books, of Irish decent. He worked as a draughtsman before entering war service in the British Admiralty from 1940 to 1949, including five years in Colombo, where he made sketching trips to jungle temples with the Buddhist monk and artist Manjsiro Thero. Between 1949 and 1951 Adams worked as an exhibition designer in London and studied wood-engraving with Gertrude Hermes in her evening class at the Central School of Arts and Crafts (now Central St Martin's College of Art and Design). In 1951, after moving to Melbourne, Adams began a 30-year teaching commitment at the Royal Melbourne Institute of Technology (RMIT), where he instructed many of the younger generation of Australian printmakers, including George Baldessin and Jan Senbergs. A brief return to Britain and Ireland in 1957–8 provided experience with Dolmen Press, Dublin, which published his first book of engravings, *The Soul Cages* (1958). Returning to Melbourne, Adams established a specialized printmaking diploma at the RMIT and, from 1959, undertook nine journeys to Japan, making contact with contemporary printmakers there. His Crossley Gallery, the first in Australia devoted exclusively to prints, opened in 1966. Located in Melbourne, it became the active hub of Australian contemporary printmaking, showing such artists as Fred Williams, Roger Kemp, Leonard French and John Brack. In 1974 Adams and Baldessin opened the Crossley Print Workshop to publish artists' prints. Subsequently the Lyre Bird Press, established in 1977, published fine-quality limited-edition books, among them the award-winning *John Brack Nudes* (1982). In 1989, shortly before his election to Fellowship of the Royal Society of Painter-Etchers and Engravers, Adams moved to northern Queensland, re-establishing the Lyre Bird Press at James Cook University of North Queensland, Townsville, where it continues to publish.

WRITINGS

The Lyre Bird Speaks (Townsville, 1994)

BIBLIOGRAPHY

J. Zimmer: *Recent Australian Prints* (Melbourne, 1984)
A. McCulloch and S. McCulloch: *The Encyclopedia of Australian Art* (Sydney, 1994), pp. 27–8

□

Adam-Salomon, Antoine-Samuel (*b* La Ferté-sous-Jouarre, Seine-et-Marne, 9 Jan 1818; *d* Paris, 1881). French photographer and sculptor. He originally worked as a sculptor, and he turned to portrait photography under the influence of the Munich photographer Franz Hanfstaengel. Adam-Salomon's antique poses, making much use of light and shade to give painterly effects, were inspired by Classical sculpture and painting and incorporated expensive fabrics and settings. He also favoured heavy retouching of the negatives, for which he was criticized by some contemporaries. He was, however, much admired for the imposing character of many of his portraits (e.g. *Portrait of a Man*, *c.* 1865; see Berger and Levrault, no. 1). He continued his sculpture as well, producing portrait busts (many still extant), generally based on photographs. Subjects included Rossini and the poet Lamartine, as well as a monument in Les Invalides, Paris, to the Duke of Padua. Some of those hostile to photography, such as Lamartine, were persuaded to consider it as an art by the work of Adam-Salomon. He founded his studio in Paris in 1859, working on reproductions of works of art as well as portraits of the rich bourgeoisie, and he proposed working on a portrait gallery of European notables. He was made a member of the Société Française de Photographie in 1870 and received the Légion d'honneur the same year. He held exhibitions of his work in Paris in 1859, 1867 and 1869, in London in 1867 and in Boston, MA, in 1869. His style is typified by the late *Self-portrait as Dr Faust*, where he portrays himself in velvet robe, seated on a carved throne with his hand resting on a skull.

BIBLIOGRAPHY

A. de Lamartine: *Cours familier de littérature* (Paris, 1859) [interview]
R. Lecuyer: *Histoire de la photographie* (Paris, 1945), pp. 99–100
Berger and Levrault, eds: *Regards sur la photographie en France au XIXe siècle* (Paris, 1980)

PATRICIA STRATHERN

Adamson, Amandus [Amand (Ivanovich)] (*b* Uuga Rätsepa, nr Paldiski, 12 Nov 1855; *d* Paldiski, 26 June 1929). Estonian sculptor. From childhood he excelled in wood-carving. His first serious work after graduating from the St Petersburg Academy of Arts, where he studied (1876–81) under Alexander Bock (1829–95), was a carved frame for Johann Köler's painting *Tribute to Caesar* (1883; Tallinn, A. Mus.), commissioned by several Estonian art associations on the occasion of the coronation of Alexander III (*reg* 1881–94). This work was inspired by Adamson's impressions of altars in 17th-century churches in Tallinn. Baroque motifs became an important feature of his work, as in his allegorical miniatures *Dawn* and *Dusk* (1895; Tallinn, A. Mus.), carved from pear wood. Adamson completed his studies in Paris, where he was influenced by the works of Jean-Baptiste Carpeaux and Jules Dalou. A theme that runs through his smaller works is the sea, as in the *Boat's Last Breath* (wax, 1899; biscuit, 1901, executed at the Imperial Porcelain Factory, St Petersburg, Rus. Mus.; marble, 1926, Tallinn, Salme Cult. Cent.). He also sculpted monumental works on the Baltic and Black Seas, such as the monument to the *Sailors of the Battleship Rusalka* (1902; Tallinn) and a monument to *Boats Lost at Sea* (1904; Sevastopol'). Alongside his romantic interpretation of the sea, Adamson also depicted the sea as a workplace, as in *Fisherman from the Island of Muhu* (plaster, 1892) and *In Anxious Expectation* (bronze, 1897; both Tallinn, A. Mus.).

In 1907 Adamson became an academician of the Academy of Arts in St Petersburg. He created models for several multifigural monuments that can be compared with works by Mikhail Mikeshin. Adamson sculpted a composition for the 300th anniversary of the Romanovs in Kostroma (1911–17; destr.) and was also involved in the decoration of several important buildings in St Petersburg, including a frieze for the Russian Museum of Alexander III (1900–1911; now the Museum of Ethnography) and ornamentation for the Singer Company building (1902–4; architect Pavel Syuzor) and the Yeliseyev trading house (1902–6; architect Gavriil Baranovsky), both on Nevsky Prospect.

After Estonia proclaimed its independence in 1917, Adamson lived in Paldiski. His allegorical works of this period show the drama of post-war life, as in *Hunger, 1918–20* (Tallinn, City Mus.). In 1922–3 in Italy, he reworked many of his earlier creations in marble and sculpted a group for the altar of St Paul's, Tartu. He had earlier taken up painting, as in *Women from the Island of Capri Repairing Nets* (1896; Tallinn, priv. col.). He also taught at the Baron Stieglitz Institute of Technical Drawing (1901–4) and the drawing school of the Society for the Encouragement of the Arts (1881–7) in St Petersburg.

BIBLIOGRAPHY

T. Nurk: *Amandus Adamson, 1855–1929* (Tallinn, 1960)

SERGEY KUZNETSOV

Adamson, John (*b* Fife, 1809; *d* St Andrews, Fife, 1870). Scottish photographer. He studied medicine in Edinburgh (1829) and Paris, but returned to St Andrews in the 1830s. A member of the St Andrews Literary and Philosophical Society, he associated with the circle interested in photographic experimentation and theory. Adamson experimented with Talbot's calotype process, introduced to Scotland by Sir David Brewster (1781–1868), and made the first calotype portrait in Scotland, of *Miss Melville Adamson* (*c.* 1842; Edinburgh, Royal Mus. Scotland; see Morrison-Low, p. 20). He taught several of the early Scottish photographers, including his younger brother, Robert (*see* HILL AND ADAMSON), and Thomas Rodger (1833–83) of St Andrews. Most of Adamson's surviving work is in the Royal Museum of Scotland, Edinburgh, and St Andrews University Library.

BIBLIOGRAPHY

A. D. Morrison-Low: 'Dr John and Robert Adamson: An Early Partnership in Scottish Photography', *Phot. Col*, iv/2 (1983), pp. 198–214

JULIE LAWSON

Adamson, Robert. *See under* HILL AND ADAMSON.

Adamson Associates. Canadian architectural partnership established in 1934 in Toronto by Gordon Sinclair Adamson (1904–86), who practised in the city for 20 years. The firm has been prominent internationally for many decades, and responsible for major, multi-complex modern building projects in Canada, North America and England. In 1949 Adamson Associates was the first architectural group in Ontario to establish an in-house consultancy for the interior design and furnishing of their buildings. In 1962 the company expanded into large-scale structural and site planning. By the 1970s the firm was recognized for its expertise in curtain-wall and cladding techniques, and for state-of-the-art, energy-saving heating and cooling systems. The company's notable projects include the North York Municipal Building (1974–8), Toronto, Gulf Canada Square (1977–9; now Canada Crescent Corporation; associate architects), Calgary, Alta, and North American Life Centre (1986–8), North York, Ont. Adamson Associates was the architectural company responsible for coordinating all the buildings that comprise New York's World Financial Center, and architects for the pyramidal-roofed Three World building (1985) and the Winter Garden (1988), both designed by Cesar Pelli. The latter is a glazed, barrel-vaulted public promenade, lined with shops and cafés and decorated with tall palm trees brought from California. The company also acted as executive architects for the Canary Wharf scheme in London's docklands (from 1987) in association with Cesar Pelli and others. Adamson Associates built the 50-storey Canary Wharf tower, which is clad in stainless steel, and designed the Docklands Light Railway Station there.

BIBLIOGRAPHY

'Hydro Place, Toronto', *Can. Architect*, xxi (April 1976), pp. 26–9

J. Hix: 'Learning from Hydro Place', *Can. Architect*, xxi (April 1976), pp. 30–38

'C. D. Howe Building, Ottawa', *Can. Architect*, xxv (March 1980), pp. 19–27

L. Whiteson: *Modern Canadian Architecture* (Edmonton, Alta, 1983), pp. 188–91, 270

□

Adam van Düren. *See* DÜREN, ADAM VAN.

Adán, Juan (*b* Tarazona, 1741; *d* Madrid, 1816). Spanish sculptor. He was trained in Saragossa with José Ramirez. In 1765 he went to Rome, where he won a scholarship from the Spanish Academia de Bellas Artes and was appointed Director of the Accademia di S Luca, Rome. Adán's early work became known in Spain through the drawings and sculptures he sent from Rome, the finest being a *Lamentation.* He returned to Spain in 1776 and worked in Lérida, Granada and Jaen, finally settling in Madrid in 1786. In 1793 he was appointed court sculptor (Escultor de Cámara) by Charles IV (*reg* 1788–1808). He made many carvings in wood, such as a *St Joseph* and a *Virgin of the Sorrows*, for churches in Madrid. Other characteristic works are the portrait busts of leading contemporary figures such as *Manuel Godoy, the Prince de la Paz*, and *José Monino, the Conde de Floridablanca.* The busts of *Charles IV* and *Queen Maria Luisa* (Madrid, Pal. Real) recall their portraits by Goya. Adán's *Venus* (1793) at the Alameda, Osuna, is one of the finest works of Spanish Neo-classicism. During the French invasion of 1808 he refused to cooperate with the enemy, and after the war he was elected Director of Sculpture at the Real Academia de S Fernando, Madrid.

BIBLIOGRAPHY

E. Pardo Canalís: *Escultores del siglo XIX* (Madrid, 1951)

F. J. Sánchez Cantón: *Escultura y pintura del siglo XVIII*, A. Hisp., xvii (Madrid, 1965)

JUAN NICOLAU

Adaro Magro, Eduardo (*b* Madrid, 6 Feb 1848; *d* Madrid, 27 March 1906). Spanish architect. In 1872 he graduated from the Escuela de Arquitectura of the Real Academia de Bellas Artes de S Fernando, Madrid, and began his long service with the Banco de España. He belonged to the generation of Spanish architects active after the restoration of Alfonso XII in 1874. Adaro Magro favoured a variant of eclectic classicism, embellishing the academic designs of his façades with ornament drawn from Renaissance models and in a style not far removed from that of the Beaux-Arts. He was elected a member of the Real Academia de Bellas Artes de S Fernando in 1903 but was unable to take his place there.

Adaro Magro's principal work was the Banco de España (begun 1884; inaugurated 1891) in the Paseo del Prado, Madrid. He received the commission after a national competition failed to produce an entry. Severiano Sáinz de la Lastra (*d* 1884) contributed to the plans, Lorenzo Alvarez Capra (1836–1901) and José María Aguilar collaborated on its execution, while Alejandro Herrero, José Amador de los Ríos and Aníbal Alvarez (1806–70) were engaged in the decoration. The building is designed in a classicist aesthetic, in which Italian and French influences are intermingled. Adaro Magro was also active in the construction of elegant country houses, luxury residences and penitentiary buildings. He designed memorial monuments and took part in the reconstruction of buildings destroyed by the earthquake in Upper Andalusia in 1884.

BIBLIOGRAPHY

P. Navascués: *Arquitectura y arquitectos madrileños del siglo XIX* (Madrid, 1973)

Guía de arquitectura y urbanismo de Madrid, Colegio Oficial de Arquitectos de Madrid, 2 vols (Madrid, 1982–3)

ALBERTO VILLAR MOVELLÁN

Addaura. Cave site in the northern slope of Monte Pellegrino 8 km north of Palermo on the north coast of

Addaura, engraved figures on the cave wall, *c.* 12,000 BP

Sicily. It contains a number of prehistoric figures engraved in the surface of a smooth slab of rock on the left-hand side (see fig.), which were revealed when a layer of stalagmite was detached by exploding ammunition in the 1940s. The earliest, lightly incised group includes horses, cattle, a hind and a woman carrying a bundle. The main group consists of ten male figures, each about 250 mm high, and a larger figure of a deer. The outlines of the former are bold and assured, though the heads are invariably crude, often animal- or bird-like; hands and feet were simply omitted. Later two bovids were added; these are much more roughly drawn. All had been covered by the stalagmite, which must have taken many centuries, if not millennia, to form. A date of *c.* 12,000 BP seems likely, since flints of this period were found in an adjacent cave. However, the scenes cannot be matched closely in comparable painted and engraved caves of France and Spain (*see* PREHISTORIC EUROPE, §II, 2). Even the rarer Italian examples, such as those at Romanelli, near Lecce, and Genovesi, Levanzo, contain nothing quite like them. The interpretation of the figures at Addaura is particularly controversial. The human figures stand, walk, crouch or lie on their faces, apparently painfully trussed; but it is not clear whether the artist intended them to be viewed as a single scene, perhaps of dancing or sacrifice, or as individual unrelated figures. The effect is powerful, but nevertheless it remains puzzling.

BIBLIOGRAPHY

I. Marconi Bovio: 'Incisioni rupestri all' Addaura (Palermo)', *Bull. Paletnol. It.*, viii/5 (1953), pp. 5–22

L. Bernabò Brea: *Sicily* (London, 1957), pp. 32–3

J. Hawkes: *Atlas of Ancient Archaeology* (London, 1974), p. 98

DAVID TRUMP

Addis, Sir **John M(ansfield)** (*b* London, 11 June 1914; *d* Pembury, Kent, 31 July 1983). English diplomat, collector and art historian. In 1947, as a member of the British Diplomatic Service, he was posted to Nanjing, Jiangsu Province, then the capital of the Nationalist Chinese government. He became interested in Chinese art and history and began a collection of porcelain, furniture and textiles at a time of political and economic uncertainty, when Chinese collectors were forced to sell. When he moved to the British embassy in Beijing in 1954 he continued his research into Chinese ceramic history with the help of specialists from the Palace Museum. In 1963 he became British ambassador to the Philippines and was largely responsible for organizing the Manila Trade Pottery Seminar (1968), to which he also contributed five of the nine discussion monographs. From 1972 to 1974, as British ambassador to China, he played an important part in promoting the Chinese archaeological exhibition *The Genius of China*, held in London at the Royal Academy in 1973–4, the first comprehensive exhibition of Chinese archaeological discoveries to be held in Europe. He contributed a number of valuable papers on underglaze copper red decorated wares to the Oriental Ceramic Society, London, of which he was president from 1974 to 1977. He gave most of his important collection of Chinese blue-and-white porcelain to the British Museum, London, together with a bequest that was used to establish the John Addis Islamic Gallery, and bequeathed his valuable textile collection and unique pieces of Chinese furniture to the Victoria and Albert Museum, London. He was a trustee of both the British Museum and the Victoria and Albert Museum, where he also served on the advisory council.

WRITINGS

'Some Buddhist Motifs as a Clue to Dating', 'Shu fu Type Wares Excavated in the Philippines', 'Some Ch'ing pai and White Wares Found in the Philippines', 'Early Blue and White Excavated in the Philippines', 'Underglaze Red Discovered in the Philippines', *Manila Trade Pottery Seminar: Manila, 1968*, nos 1–5

Exhibition of Chinese Blue and White Porcelain and Related Underglaze Red (exh. cat., Hong Kong, City A. Mus. & Gal., 1975)

Chinese Ceramics from Datable Tombs and some other Dated Material (London, 1978)

Chinese Porcelain From the Addis Collection: 22 Pieces of Jingdezhen (Chingtechen) Porcelain Presented to the British Museum (London, 1979)

MARGARET MEDLEY

Addison, Joseph (*b* Milston, Wilts, 1 May 1672; *d* London, 17 June 1719). English writer and politician. He was educated at Charterhouse School and Queen's College, Oxford, receiving his MA in 1693. Between 1699 and 1703 he travelled on the Continent; in his *Remarks upon Several Parts of Italy* (1705) he noted that Italy was 'the great school of Musick and Painting', and a primary purpose of his tour was 'to compare the natural face of the country with the Landskips the [classical] Poets have given us of it'. His *Remarks* became a *vade-mecum* on artistic matters for 18th-century British travellers.

Although he was active as a politician (he was appointed Under-Secretary of State in 1706 and was an MP, 1708–19), Addison's greatest influence was as an educator and popularizer of ideas on taste and culture, which he achieved through the periodical essay. He contributed to *The Tatler*, a thrice-weekly half-sheet founded by his friend Richard Steele (1672–1729), which ran from 1709 to 1711. Its successor, *The Spectator* (1711–12, 1714), was largely co-written with Steele; although first published as a daily periodical essay, it appeared soon after in book form and remained in print throughout the 18th century. As an arbiter of English taste in manners, literature and the arts for the age that followed him, Addison was without rival. His influence on aesthetic theory derives from such essays in *The Spectator* as the one on English gardens (no. 477), another on literature and art (no. 166) and, most importantly, from a series of 11 essays on the 'Pleasures of the Imagination' (nos 411–21), loosely indebted to John Locke's *An Essay Concerning Human Understanding* (1690). Though lacking complexity, Addison's judgements were frequently based on the pragmatic assumption that the arts should 'deduce their Laws and Rules from the general Sense and Taste of Mankind, and not from the Principles of those Arts themselves' (no. 29). The short fictional tales with which his essays abound can be seen as literary prototypes for the engraved moral tableaux of William Hogarth. Around 1712 Addison's kit-cat portrait was painted by Sir Godfrey Kneller (London, N.P.G.).

WRITINGS

Remarks upon Several Parts of Italy (London, 1705)

essays in *The Tatler* (1709–11); ed. D. F. Bond, 3 vols (Oxford, 1987)

essays in *The Spectator* (1711–12, 1714); ed. D. F. Bond, 5 vols (Oxford, 1965/*R* 1987)

Dialogues upon the Usefulness of Ancient Medals (London, 1721)

BIBLIOGRAPHY
S. Johnson: 'Addison' [1779], *Lives of the English Poets*, ed. G. B. Hill, 3 vols (Oxford, 1905), ii, pp. 79–158
P. Smithers: *The Life of Joseph Addison* (Oxford, 1954)
M. G. Ketcham: 'The Arts of Gesture: The *Spectator* and its Relationship to Physiognomy, Painting, and the Theater', *Mod. Lang. Q.*, xlii (1981), pp. 137–52
W. H. Youngren: 'Addison and the Birth of Eighteenth-century Aesthetics', *Mod. Philol.*, lxxix (1982), pp. 267–83

FRANK FELSENSTEIN

Adelaide. Australian city and capital of the state of South Australia. It is situated on the banks of the River Torrens, between the Mt Lofty Ranges and Gulf St Vincent in the south-eastern part of the continent. The city (population *c.* 1 million) is noted for its fine colonial urban plan. Adelaide was founded in 1836 as an exercise in planned settlement, jointly controlled by the British Government and a London committee whose members were influenced by Edward Gibbon Wakefield's ideas on systematic colonization. The final site for the city, *c.* 8 km from the sea, with a suitable inlet for a harbour (Port Adelaide) *c.* 11 km to the north-west, was selected amid considerable controversy by Surveyor-General Colonel William Light (1786–1839). Light's urban plan (see fig.) is remarkable for its public squares and parkland, features not included in Governor Darling's regulations (1829) for New South Wales, which dominated 19th-century urban planning in most parts of Australia. Light planned Adelaide in two parts, north and south of the river. The grid of the southern part, the principal commercial area, was orientated to the cardinal directions, with two main streets (King William Street and Grote/Wakefield streets) intersecting at a central square (Victoria Square). Four smaller squares were also included, and the outer streets on all four sides were planned as broad terraces, with North Terrace, bordering the river, intended for the best residences: Government House, a stuccoed Regency villa by GEORGE KINGSTON, was built there in 1838–9 (extended 1855 by E. A. Hamilton). A wide belt of parkland bisects the city along the river and surrounds it on all sides, separating it from its suburbs. North Adelaide, also with a public square, was orientated to the contours of the sloping land north of the river and was designed as the city's principal residential area.

A Board of Commissioners supervised the sale of land in the colony, cash purchasers receiving a town allotment of one acre (0.405 ha) and another 80 acres (*c.* 35.5 ha) in the country. By 1850 the growth of wheat production and the discovery of silver, lead and copper in the surrounding region had provided an influx of wealth and new migrants to Adelaide, among them German settlers who established the wine industry in the Barossa Valley, north of the city. South Australia received self-government in 1856, and its first parliament house was built in North Terrace, Adelaide, in the 1850s (rebuilt 1883–1939 by Edmund Wright and Lloyd Taylor). North Terrace subsequently became the cultural centre of the city and the site of such institutions as the South Australian Museum (founded 1856), which has the world's largest collection of Aboriginal artefacts, the University of Adelaide (1874) and the State Library (1879). In the vicinity of Victoria Square are the principal

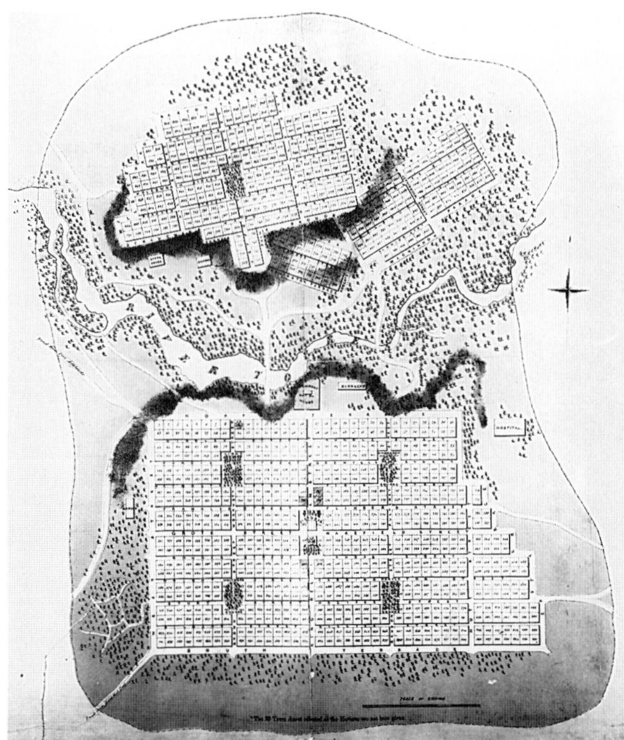
Adelaide, city plan by Colonel William Light, 1837 (Adelaide, South Australian State Archives)

government buildings, including the Greek Revival Magistrates' Court (1847–50; by Richard Lambeth) and several Renaissance Revival buildings: the Treasury (1858–76, by E. A. Hamilton), Town Hall (1863–6; by EDMUND WRIGHT and E. J. Woods), General Post Office (1867–72; by Wright and Hamilton) and Supreme Court (1869; by R. G. Thomas). Nearby is the Roman Catholic cathedral of St Francis Xavier (begun 1856 by Charles Hansom, completed 1889 by Edward Pugin), in Spanish Gothic style, while the Anglican cathedral of St Peter (begun 1869; by William Butterfield) was built in North Adelaide in a French Gothic style. Suburban development around the city centre was greatly stimulated by a speculative land boom in the 1870s and early 1880s, leading to large-scale construction of single-storey houses and some fine mansions built in fashionable styles.

Modern planning techniques were introduced to Adelaide with the Town Planning and Development Act of 1920, when garden suburbs (e.g. Colonel Light Gardens) were established to help meet the housing shortage created by a new influx of migrants after World War I. Expansion continued after World War II, when the satellite city of Elizabeth, north of Adelaide, was founded (1954–5), accompanied by the development of regional shopping and administrative centres. Population growth had slowed by the 1970s, however, and the following decades were marked by urban consolidation and inner-city renewal. Significant, mainly medium-rise commercial construction cycles took place in the city centre in the 1960s and 1980s, the latter including the development of a casino, hotel and conference centre over the railway station in North Terrace.

Notable artists active in Adelaide included George French Angas (1822–86), who recorded early views of the city, and HANS HEYSEN, who later rendered the landscape of the Adelaide Hills with great intensity (*see* AUSTRALIA, fig. 10). Adelaide boasts Australia's oldest art society, the Royal South Australian Society of Arts (1856), initiated by painter and teacher Charles Hill (1824–1916). In 1861 the School of Design (now Adelaide College of Arts and Education) was founded, laying the foundations for public art teaching in South Australia. Adelaide's principal gallery is the Art Gallery of South Australia (founded 1881), while Flinders University Art Museum (founded 1966) was one of the first in Australia to function in conjunction with art-historical studies. The Adelaide Festival Centre (1970–77; by Hassell & Partners) in the North Terrace parklands provides a focus for the prestigious biennial Adelaide Arts Festival (initiated 1960).

See also AUSTRALIA, especially §§II, III and XI–XIII.

BIBLIOGRAPHY

A. Grenfell Price: *Foundation and Settlement of South Australia* (Adelaide, 1924)

E. J. R. Morgan and S. H. Gilbert: *Early Adelaide Architecture, 1836–1886* (Melbourne, 1969)

C. Bond, ed.: *Preserving Historic Adelaide* (Adelaide, 1978)

E. Jensen and R. Jensen: *Colonial Architecture in South Australia* (Adelaide, 1980)

D. L. Johnson and D. Langmead: *The Adelaide City Plan* (Adelaide, 1986)

D. Whitelock: *Adelaide, 1836–1986: A History of Difference* (Adelaide, 1986)

G. Dutton and D. Elder: *Colonel William Light: Founder of a City* (Melbourne, 1991), pp. 137–276

VALERIE A. CLACK

Adelcrantz, C(arl) F(redrik) (*b* Stockholm, 3 Jan 1716; *d* Stockholm, 26 Feb 1796). Swedish architect. His father, Göran Josuae Adelcrantz (1668–1739), was a pupil and associate of Nicodemus Tessin (ii) and had studied in France and Italy before assisting in the building of the Kungliga Slott in Stockholm. He became City Architect of Stockholm and created the splendid Baroque cupola (1724–44) on Jean De la Vallée's Katarinakyrka, but he had been pushed aside during the political crisis that followed the death of Charles XII in 1718. He advised his son not to become an architect but nevertheless let him attend the drawing school at the palace. After his father's death, Adelcrantz went abroad for architectural study in Paris and Italy, returning in 1743 to assist Carl Hårleman in the interior work on the Kungliga Slott. In 1757 he became Superintendent and in 1767 President of the Royal Academy of Arts, which he reorganized by instituting schools of drawing and painting, sculpture and architecture. He was made a baron in 1766.

The Kina Slott (1763) in the gardens of Drottningholm Slott, near Stockholm, is the major work of Adelcrantz's Rococo period and a gem of sophisticated chinoiserie. The façades are in oxblood and ochre rendering, under gently curved, green copper roofs with bells and dragons on the corners. The interiors combine original Chinese material with painted pastiche ornaments of Rococo character and wainscoting painted in strong blue, green and red. Also at Drottningholm, Adelcrantz was responsible for the Court Theatre (1764–6; *see* THEATRE, fig. 16), which survives in its original state, as do the 18th-century costumes and stage machinery (*see* STOCKHOLM, §4(ii)). His main work as a theatre architect was the Royal Opera House (1775–82; destr. 1892) in Gustav Adolfs Torg, Stockholm, which had a horseshoe auditorium with balconies and a sloping stage incorporating machinery of the type established by Jacques-Germain Soufflot in Lyon. The interiors, like his contemporary palace interiors, were in the Swedish variant of the Louis XVI style, known as Gustavian, after Gustav III (who was assassinated in this opera house in 1792). The exterior (whose identical counterpart is mirrored in Erik Palmstedt's Sophia Albertina Palace on the opposite site) was Neo-classical with a giant order of Corinthian pilasters. This vocabulary was also used in Adelcrantz's Court of Appeal (1776) at Vaasa in Finland.

As Superintendent for almost 40 years, Adelcrantz strengthened his office's control of ecclesiastical and civic building. Among his own church projects, the Adolf Fredrikskyrka (1767–83) in Stockholm is of a centralized type on a slightly elongated Greek-cross plan and with a tower surmounted by a cupola over the crossing. For parish churches he preferred a longitudinal type with a simple, rectangular layout. In his mansions and country houses, he developed Hårleman's model, with simple, rectangular layouts and symmetrical arrangements of detached wings, as at Sturehof (1778) near Stockholm. Adelcrantz's work continued the French influence favoured by Hårleman, developing from Rococo into Neo-classicism. Later works demonstrate his awareness of the archaeologically severe early Greek revivalism that was coming into fashion at the end of his life.

BIBLIOGRAPHY

S. Fogelmarck: *Carl Fredrik Adelcrantz, arkitekt* (diss., Stockholm U., 1957)

H. O. Andersson and F. Bedoire: *Swedish Architecture: Drawings, 1640–1970* (Stockholm, 1986)

□

Ademollo, Carlo (*b* Florence, 9 Oct 1824; *d* Florence, 15 July 1911). Italian painter. He was the nephew of the painter Luigi Ademollo (1764–1849) and studied under Giuseppe Bezzuoli at the Accademia dei Belle Arti in Florence. He initially specialized in history painting, turning to genre painting and *vedute* in the 1850s. In about 1854 he joined the Scuola di Staggia, a group of painters who painted *en plein air* in the Sienese countryside near Staggia. He also frequented the Caffè Michelangelo in Florence, an important centre of artistic life at the time.

Ademollo was a volunteer in the campaigns of the Risorgimento in 1859 and 1866 and made many sketches and drawings of them, finally being appointed official painter to Garibaldi's army. He thus established himself as a popular painter of patriotic scenes, such as the monumental *Last Onslaught at the Battle of San Martino* (Florence, Pitti), the *Death of the Cairoli Brothers* (Pavia, Mus. Risorgimento) and the *Breach of Porta Pia* (Milan, Mus. Risorgimento). As well as these quasi-official activities, he produced successful portraits of contemporary politicians and the Florentine nobility, such as *Benedetto Cairoli* (1890; Pavia, Mus. Risorgimento).

BIBLIOGRAPHY

Thieme–Becker

A. De Gubernatis: *Dizionario degli artisti italiani viventi* (Florence, 1889)

ETTORE SPALLETTI

Adena Mound. Prehistoric site in North America. It is the largest of several mounds along the Scioto River north of Chillicothe, OH. Although it is the eponym of the Early Woodland-period Adena culture of the Upper Ohio River Valley (*c.* 1000–*c.* 100 BC), the date of the mound itself is unknown. No stylized engraved palettes, characteristic of Adena culture, were found. The mound comprises a penannular earthwork built in several stages to a height of 8 m. A circular structure with sloping sides and double-set wooden post walls was constructed on a floor from which numerous fires had been cleared. Next, burials were placed centrally in rectangular tombs dug into the floor of the structure, a low mound was heaped over them and the funerary structure was burned. The entire area was then covered by layers of black sand incorporating several new cremations and burials outside the central tombs. For some considerable time after this, additional cremated human remains and extended burials were placed in further layers of sand and gravel. The cremation and inhumation burials, and occasionally clay-covered bundles of bones, were accompanied by annular and penannular copper bracelets and rings; cut river mussel shell animal effigies; cut mica headbands; expanded centre gorgets, ground, polished and drilled, of schist and chlorite; and a human effigy carved in the round on an Ohio pipestone tube (see fig.).

BIBLIOGRAPHY

W. C. Mills: 'Excavation of the Adena Mound', *OH State Archaeol. Hist. Q.*, x (1902), pp. 451–79

W. S. Webb and C. E. Snow: *The Adena People*, University of Kentucky Reports in Anthropology and Archaeology, vi (Lexington, KY, 1945)

W. S. Webb and R. S. Baby: *The Adena People 2* (Columbus, OH, 1957)

D. S. Brose, J. A. Brown and D. W. Penney: *Ancient Art of the American Woodland Indians* (New York, 1985)

K. B. Farnsworth and T. E. Emerson: *Early Woodland Archaeology*, Center for American Archaeology, Kampsville Seminars in Archaeology, ii (Kampsville, IL, 1986)

DAVID S. BROSE

Adeodato. *See under* GRUAMONTE.

Aders, Carl (*b* Elberfeld, nr Wuppertal, 1780; *d* Italy, before 10 July 1846). German merchant and collector. He played a key role in the introduction of early Netherlandish art to British writers and artists during the reign of George IV. In 1806, Aders and an Englishman, William Jameson, co-founded a counting house—sources suggest it was an accounting firm serving the shipping industry—in Elberfeld, Germany. Business often called him to the commercial centres of Europe, and in the 1810s he began to frequent art dealers and to make purchases. His only adviser in this appears to have been his fiancée (later his wife), Elizabeth Smith, whom he met *c.* 1816. She was the daughter of the mezzotint engraver John Raphael Smith and was herself an amateur artist.

Aders bought prints and paintings of the Italian and Dutch schools, but the core of his collection was early Netherlandish painting. Few northern artists were known at the time, and little attempt had been made by scholars to sort out and identify various oeuvres. Art dealers

Adena Mound, human effigy, Ohio pipestone, late 1st millennium BC

attached a few recognizable names, such as Dürer, van Eyck and Memling, to almost any work that came into their possession, and many of Aders's paintings were falsely attributed to these artists. His collection, mainly purchased by the mid-1820s, was divided between his London house in Euston Square and a summer retreat in Godesberg, Germany. Alexander Gilchrist described the London establishment: 'The walls of drawing-room, bedroom, and even staircase, were all closely covered; with gallery railings in front to protect the pictures from injury.'

Aders owned a copy of Hubert and Jan van Eyck's *Adoration of the Lamb* (attributed to a 17th-century Netherlandish master and now in Antwerp, Kon. Mus. S. Kst.) that was celebrated during the 19th century as the only intact version of the altarpiece, the original having been dismantled and dispersed. (It is now reunited in Ghent, St Bavo's Cathedral; for illustration *see* EYCK, VAN, (1).) He also owned an exquisite *Virgin and Child* by Rogier van der Weyden (Lugano, Col. Thyssen-Bornemisza), believed to be part of a diptych with *St George and the Dragon* (Washington, DC, N.G.A.); a *Rest on the Flight into Egypt* by Memling (Paris, Baron Guy de Rothschild priv. col.); the *Virgin and Child with SS Jerome and Francis* by Petrus Christus (Frankfurt am Main, Städel. Kstinst. & Städt. Gal.); and many paintings now in the National Gallery, London, among them *Portrait of a Man* by Dieric Bouts I and a *Deposition* and *Adoration of the Magi* from an altarpiece by Gerard David.

Word of Aders's collection spread among contemporary artists, and many were invited to view it, including William Blake, Thomas Lawrence, George Beaumont, John Linnell, Francis Danby, Samuel Palmer, James Ward, Thomas Stothard, John Flaxman and the German Jakob Götzenberger. Samuel Coleridge, William Wordsworth and Charles Lamb were also friends of the Aderses; Lamb dedicated a charming poem to the collection, 'To C. Aders, Esq. On his collection of paintings by the Old German masters'. Three art critics, Johanna Schopenhauer, Johann David Passavant and Gustav Waagen, wrote about the paintings. Around 1830, 'a terrible reverse in trade' (Gilchrist) forced Aders to dissolve his business partnership and to sell the collection. First to go were books and engravings, including copies of Blake's *Canterbury Pilgrims* and *Songs of Innocence* bought from the artist. In May 1833 the barrister Henry Crabb Robinson reported that the prints were sold 'very, very cheap'. The next year the paintings were shown at the Gallery of British Artists, Pall Mall East, and on 1 August 1835 they were auctioned by E. Foster & Son, Pall Mall. Records indicate all lots were sold; but more than half, having been bid on by friends, reappeared in the Christie and Manson sale on 26 April 1839. A great portion of the Netherlandish collection was bought by the surgeon, Joseph H. Green, and donated to the National Gallery, London, by his family in 1880. Proceeds from the sale amounted to less than £650.

UNPUBLISHED SOURCES

Cambridge, MA, Harvard U., Houghton Lib. [album of Elizabeth Aders]

BIBLIOGRAPHY

J. Schopenhaeur: *Ausflug an den Niederrhein und nach Belgien* (Leipzig, 1830)

J. D. Passavant: *Tour of a German Artist in England*, 2 vols (London, 1836)

G. Waagen: *Works of Art and Artists in England*, 2 vols (London, 1838/*R* 1970)

A. Jameson: *Companion to the Most Celebrated Private Galleries of Art in London* (London, 1844)

G. Waagen: *Treasures of Art in Great Britain*, 3 vols (London, 1854)

A. Gilchrist: *Life of William Blake*, 2 vols (London, 1863)

H. C. Robinson: *Diary, Reminiscences, and Correspondence*, ed. T. Sadler (London, 1869)

M. K. Joseph: 'Charles Aders', *Auckland U. Coll. Bull.*, xliii/6 (1953)

S. Sulzberger: 'La Réhabilitation des primitifs flamands, 1802–1867', *Bull. Cl. B.-A., Acad. Royale Sci., Lett. & B.-A. Belgique*, xii/3 (1959)

K. Bonomi: *The Karl and Eliza Aders Collection of Early Netherlandish Paintings* (MA thesis, New York U., Inst. F.A., 1987)

KATHRYN BONOMI

Adharbayjan. *See* AZERBAIJAN.

Adhémar, Jean (*b* Paris, 1908; *d* Paris, 20 June 1987). French art historian. He came from a distinguished Provençal family and studied art history first at the Ecole des Chartes, Paris, under Marcel Aubert and then at the Sorbonne, Paris, under Henri Focillon. At the invitation of Julien Cain (*d* 1974), in 1932 he joined the staff of the Cabinet des Estampes et de Photographie in the Bibliothèque Nationale, Paris. As Director of the department (1961–77) he made a significant contribution to the collection, acquiring numerous old and contemporary works. He also recognized the importance of the photographic collection and oversaw its expansion. Adhémar was involved in organizing over 20 exhibitions at the library; in 1935 he organized a major exhibition of the prints of Francisco de Goya. During the 1930s Adhémar was the Paris correspondent for Fritz Saxl and the Warburg Institute in London. His first book (1939) showed the inspiration of the Warburg on his approach. His principal interest was the arts and patronage of the French Renaissance. He edited important catalogues on 16th-century engravers (1938) and the drawings of François Clouet (1970). Adhémar was equally familiar with the 19th century and published important contributions to the study of the graphic work of Honoré Daumier, Edgar Degas and Henri de Toulouse-Lautrec. He became increasingly interested in the relationship between the arts and literature. He studied the writings of Diderot, Baudelaire, Flaubert and Zola and arranged exhibitions devoted to, among others, Racine, Rousseau and Balzac. From 1956 Adhémar was editor of the *Gazette des Beaux-Arts.* He expanded the scope of the journal to include such topics as the history of caricature and collecting. During his long career, he was involved with over 100 exhibitions, covering the works of such diverse artists as Pablo Picasso, Max Ernst, Brassaï, Man Ray, Robert Doisneau and Roger Vieillard (1907–89). His wide-ranging interests are attested to in his prolific list of publications, which appeared in *Nouvelles de l'estampe* (1978), which he had founded in 1965.

WRITINGS

Goya: L'Oeuvre gravé, les peintures, les tapisseries et 110 dessins du Musée du Prado (exh. cat., Paris, Bib. N., 1935)

Inventaire du fonds français: Graveurs du XVIe siècle, Bib. N. cat. (Paris, 1938)

Influences antiques dans l'art du moyen âge français (London, 1939/*R* Liechtenstein, 1968)

ed., with J. Seznec: D. Diderot: *Salons, 1759–81*, 4 vols (Oxford, 1957–67, rev. 1983)

BIBLIOGRAPHY

'Essai de bibliographie des travaux de Jean Adhémar', *Nouv. Est.*, xxxvii (1978), pp. 20–35

'Hommage à Jean Adhémar', *Gaz. B.-A.*, cxi (1988) [whole issue; with full bibliog.]

See also bibliographies of the articles on the individual artists cited.

□

Adhesives. Substances used to bond two surfaces. The surfaces may consist of the same material, as when mending a broken object, or of different materials, for example a collage. When applied to pigments the adhesive is called a FIXATIVE, when applied to a crumbling solid a CONSOLIDANT.

1. Types. 2. Uses.

1. TYPES. The earliest adhesives used in the making of works of art and decorative objects were such natural products as proteins, resins, juices of plants, waxes and fats. In the 20th century the development of synthetic polymer adhesives has made it possible to join any two materials.

(i) Natural.

(a) Animal-derived adhesives. 'Glue' is a general term for adhesives based on gelatine, that is degraded collagen (the major connective protein in animals). Skin and bone waste products are the most generally used source of collagen but yield contaminated products, for example glue made from tannery waste is likely to contain both metal and organic tanning agents and be of low quality. Purer forms of collagen provide better products, for example the swim-bladders of fish, especially sturgeon, yield isinglass, while parchment yields parchment glue. The glue is made by slow cooking of the source-material in water, then clarifying the resulting solution and concentrating or drying the gelatine. Mammal-derived glues are soluble only in hot water, while fish glues dissolve to form liquids at room temperature. Skin glues tend to be stronger than other types. Terms such as 'rabbit-skin glue' (Europe) and 'deer-skin glue' (Japan) do not now define the source-material but indicate the grade. CASEIN, a protein obtained from milk, can be converted to very strong adhesive by mixing with lime (calcium hydroxide) suspension; the calcium cross-links the protein to form a strong, water-resistant film. Albumin, a protein derived from egg white or blood, has been used in the same way as casein or by hot pressing to denature and cross-link the molecules while drying the adhesive to a film. All proteins are susceptible to bacterial attack in damp conditions. Two other animal-derived adhesives are beeswax (*see* WAX) and shellac (*see* RESIN, §1).

(b) Plant-derived adhesives. Starch pastes are some of the oldest adhesives. Starch occurs in roots or seeds as granules, which can be separated and purified by milling. Pastes can be made from the purified starch or the crude flour, which contain proteins and oils. The granules must be heated in water to break down their structure and dissolve the starch. Starch occurs in two main forms: branched amylopectin and straight-chained amylose. The amylopectin is soluble in cold water, but an amylose solution will gel or precipitate on standing. The composition and proportions of the two components in different starches determines the resultant working and adhesive properties of the paste. Starch is a polysaccharide and can be degraded to make semi-synthetic gums. In Mexico, after the Spanish conquest of 1519, Christian 'stalk' sculptures were constructed from plant stems, held together by the mucilage extracted from an orchid root (*Sobralia citrina*). The alginates obtained by heating seaweeds in water are a different class of polysaccharide. Polysaccharides are susceptible to fungal attack in damp conditions. Tree exudations, resins such as rosin, dammar and rubber, and GUM, such as gum arabic, are also used in adhesives.

(c) Mineral-derived adhesives. The major natural mineral adhesive is bitumen, a mixture of solid and semi-solid hydrocarbons derived from crude oil; it is soluble in solvents but was mostly applied molten. Hydrocarbon waxes purified from bitumen can be classified as micro-crystalline (branched molecules) and paraffin (straight chain molecules) waxes (*see* PIGMENT, §IV, 2)

C. V. HORIE

(ii) Synthetic.

(a) Solvents. Materials that dissolve in organic solvents can be stuck by applying the appropriate SOLVENT to the surfaces to be joined. The material will then swell or even dissolve, and when the surfaces are pressed together the molecules of one surface will merge with those of the other, leaving a strong bond once the solvent has evaporated. The strength of the bond depends primarily on the polarity of the materials: if the materials are of identical polarity the surfaces will merge completely and it is hardly appropriate to speak of a glued joint. If, however, different materials are joined, polarity and solubility will have a crucial influence on the final result—for example, in the bonding of polymethyl methacrylate (perspex) with toluene.

(b) Polymer solutions. The most frequently used adhesives are made by dissolving polymers in a highly volatile solvent. In this way the polymer can be applied as a liquid film. The solvent evaporates, leaving a polymer film that bonds the two surfaces. Because the evaporation is accompanied by a reduction of volume, air bubbles may appear between the adhesive and the surface to which it is applied. This will weaken the adhesion. The bonding is chiefly brought about by electrostatic attractions and by the mechanical adhesion of the glue to the irregularities of the surface. In order to get the highest possible concentration of solid material, low-molecular polymers are used. In many cases the temperature at which these polymers will turn into glass lies below room temperature, which may cause problems with cohesion. Typical adhesives of this kind are contact adhesives such as polyvinyl acetate (PVA), nitrocellulose and chloroprene.

(c) Dispersants. A high-molecular substance (i.e. one with a high relative molecular mass) can be combined with a larger volume of solid material and given lower viscosity by using dispersants. This means that the monomer is dispersed in a non-solvent. After polymerization the viscosity of the mixture is determined primarily by the size of the polymers and no longer by their molecular volume. Water is invariably the vehicle used for these glues so that the adhesion is mostly of a mechanical nature. Nevertheless they contain another 40% to 50% water, which has to evaporate after the surfaces have been pressed together. This means that they are suitable only for joining porous materials. Typical adhesives of this kind include white-wood glues and acrylate dispersants.

(d) Heat sealing. Thermoplastics can sometimes be used as adhesives without the need for a solvent. The solid polymer is applied between two surfaces and then heated to above its melting point. When liquid, the polymer flows into the irregularities of the surfaces to be joined and holds these together mechanically once it has solidified again. Because melted polymers have a high viscosity and surface tension it may be difficult to achieve good adhesion. This can be remedied by using a mixture of high-molecular and low-molecular polymers: when heated the low-molecular polymer will melt and the high-molecular polymer will then dissolve in it. After solidification the low-molecular polymer secures adhesion and the high-molecular polymer cohesion. A typical example of this type of adhesive is polyvinyl acetate (PVA).

(e) Reactive adhesives. Liquid substances consisting of monomers and pre-polymerized monomers can be polymerized into thermosetting or thermoplastic polymers after they have been applied between two surfaces. Because this involves no evaporation of solvents, and shrinkage tends to be limited with polymerization, good adhesion can be achieved. By adjusting the viscosity of the basic liquid it is possible to join smooth as well as rough surfaces. Typical adhesives are epoxy resins and polyesters.

See also PLASTIC, §I, and RESIN, §2.

EDDY DE WITTE

2. USES.

(i) Natural adhesives. All the water-soluble adhesives (glue, albumin, starch and alginates) have been used more or less interchangeably in lightweight, non-critical applications. Glue is an excellent adhesive for wood, and its use in furniture production has been documented from the earliest records over 3000 years ago (*see* WOOD (i), §III, and MARQUETRY, §1). The solution is applied hot to warmed surfaces and the parts are closed quickly. A join that can be handled forms rapidly by the cooling and jelling of the glue, which dries to create a joint frequently stronger than the wood itself, although over time, and particularly in damp conditions, the join deteriorates. This defect ensures that gluing wood is reversible and that the process has as a result been retained as the major technique in conservation of both structural and decorative repairs. Glue is the binding agent in GESSO, a coating used as a ground for painting and gilding since antiquity. Glue has long been used for sizing fibres for textiles and paper (*see* SIZE). The drying of glue from a jelly causes considerable shrinkage, and glass can be decorated by glue etching in which the surface is pulled off in the required design and texture by the shrinking film (*see* GLASS, §III). Glue is widely used as a paper adhesive, for instance in COLLAGE, paper tapes and cardboard. Shrinkage damages objects by detaching surfaces or disturbing shapes, and the gradual delamination of aging ephemeral paper objects is a considerable problem (*see* PAPER, §VI). Both parchment glue and egg white have been used traditionally as the adhesive for gold leaf (*see* GILDING, §I, 1(i)).

Casein adhesives have similarly been used for millennia, primarily for wood where some water resistance was required. Until the late 20th century much plywood was constructed using casein. Beeswax was used as a medium in encaustic painting (*see* ENCAUSTIC PAINTING, §1), and shellac is widely used as a heat-set adhesive for photographs but may prove impossible to detach. Starch pastes are the traditional adhesives for paper and generally facilitate conservation (*see* PAPER, §VI). Resin and bitumen have been used since antiquity as adhesives and waterproofing agents for masonry constructions. Genesis (11:3) states that bitumen was employed as a mortar and adhesive in the construction of the Tower of Babel. Molten sulphur, which sets to a rigid solid, holds interlocking parts together, in a similar fashion to the use of molten lead for securing iron clamps in stonework, and has been used both for constructing and repairing ceramics. The technique was used as porcelain increasingly became more sculptural. An example is the Sèvres centrepiece presented to the Duke of Wellington.

C. V. HORIE

(ii) Synthetic adhesives. With the development of synthetic adhesives it is now possible to join any two materials. Two major factors are the choice of the right type of glue—one that is adapted to the chemical composition of the materials to be joined—and the preparatory treatment of the surfaces. The actual adhesion of the glue and the surface to be bonded takes place at a molecular level, and every alteration in the surface condition, no matter how small, has an influence on the final result. Metal surfaces, for example, may be covered with a thin layer of grease or rust, or with inhibitors, used to prevent corrosion during storage, which change the surface structure. Plastic surfaces may be contaminated with the remains of stripping agents or by the diffusion of softeners. Any surface to be bonded should therefore be degreased with a suitable solvent. In order to improve the mechanical aspects of the adhesion the surface may be roughened with sandpaper or a sandblaster, by etching with acids or alkalis, or by means of a bombardment of ions or electric discharge. Immediately after the preparatory treatment the surfaces must be covered with a film of glue to avoid new corrosion or the deposition of contaminants.

The physical characteristics of commercial glues can be adapted to specific needs, bearing in mind the following basic principles. In order to avoid the evaporation of solvents and to slow down chemical reactions, adhesives are best stored at a low temperature. Before use, however, they must be brought up to room temperature in their sealed container, as opening the container at a low temperature causes condensation of water on the adhesive. The viscosity of adhesives dissolved in organic solvents can be reduced by adding quick solvents. Slow-evaporating solvents will sometimes improve the penetration and can increase the flexibility of the glued joint for a long time. In the case of soluble adhesives both surfaces are covered with a thin film of glue. Before pressing the surfaces together time should be allowed for most of the solvent to evaporate, thus achieving almost instant bonding. The optimal adhesive power, however, will not occur until after several hours or days, depending on the nature of the solvents and the porosity of the materials joined. The viscosity of dispersants can be either increased or reduced. It is increased by adding small quantities of water-soluble polymers (carboxymethyl cellulose, polyvinyl alcohol) of an aromatic hydrocarbon (toluene, xylene) or of an acrylic acid dispersant. To improve the moistness of the surfaces to be joined, small quantities of tensioactive substances may be added. These are also necessary when fillers (sawdust, stone dust, pigments) are added to dispersants in order to fill bigger gaps or to colour the glued joint. Dispersants contain a high proportion of water, which makes them suitable only for joining porous materials.

A slightly raised temperature can help to accelerate the evaporation of water or solvents. When using reactive adhesives (epoxys, polyesters) it is important to measure the various components carefully before mixing them. In the case of polyesters an increased quantity of initiator will influence the setting time. With epoxy resins, however, the setting time is influenced not by the mixture but by the chemical composition of the hardener. Because of the reaction mechanism, an incorrect mixture will in this case invariably result in weaker adhesion. The adhesive powers of reactive glues can be strongly increased by using linking agents. These are products that combine various reactive groups in one molecule (vinyl and epoxy materials). One of the reactive groups will react chemically with the surface to be bonded while the other will react with the adhesive. Pressure-sensitive adhesives are used to join close-fitting surfaces quite rapidly. The glue consists of a highly reactive monomer (cyanoacrylate), which is stabilized with an acid. When the adhesive is spread out over a large surface the acid is neutralized and the glue polymerizes instantly. Because the inhibitor is destroyed at the contact surface only, and because the monomer is highly liquid, these adhesives are suitable only for joining tightly fitting, non-porous materials.

(iii) Conservation. In conservation it is never the intention to bring about an adhesion that is stronger than the original materials; thus when a glued joint is exposed to pressure or stretched or bent, the bond must break first to avoid damage to the original. Another fundamental rule is the principle of reversibility; when choosing an adhesive it is again necessary to be able to break the seal without damaging the original. This may cause problems, especially when liquid glue flows into porous surfaces. The choice of adhesive for a specific conservation task depends primarily on the object to be treated. Further information on the use of adhesives in the conservation of a specific material will be found in the relevant section of that article.

EDDY DE WITTE

BIBLIOGRAPHY

A. Lucas and J. R. Harris: *Ancient Egyptian Materials and Industries* (London, 1962)
H. Lee and K. Neville: *Epoxy Resins* (London, 1967)
J. T. Martin: *Adhesion and Adhesives* (Amsterdam, 1967)
B. Parkyn, F. Lamb and B. V. Clifton: *Polyesters* (New York, 1967)
C. V. Cagle: *Adhesive Bonding: Techniques and Application* (New York, 1968)
Hoechst, ed.: *Manuel sur la Mowilith* (Frankfurt, 1970)
J. Shields: *Adhesives Handbook* (London, 1970)
J. F. Kohlwey: *Kunststoffen* [Artificial materials] (Amsterdam, 1971)
W. J. Roff and J. R. Scott: *Fibres, Film, Plastics and Rubbers* (London, 1971)
E. De Witte and M. Goessens-Landries: 'The Use of Synthetic Resins in Conservation: An Annotated Bibliography, 1932–1974', *A. & Archeol. Tech. Abstr.*, xiii/2 (1976), supplement, pp. 279–354
N. S. Brommelle and G. Thomson: *Science and Technology in the Service of Conservation* (London, 1982)
Science for Conservators Book 3: Adhesives and Coatings, Crafts Council Conservation Science Teaching Series, ed. H. Wilks (London, 1983)
Adhesives and Consolidants, Paris Congress 1984, Reprints, International Institute for Conservation of Historical and Artistic Works [IIC]
P. Mora, L. Mora and P. Philippot: *Conservation of Wall Paintings* (London, 1984)
L. Masschelein-Kleiner: *Ancient Binding Media, Varnishes and Adhesives*, International Centre for the Study of the Preservation and Restoration of Cultural Property, Rome (ICCROM), Technical Notes Series (Rome, 1985)
C. V. Horie: *Materials for Conservation: Organic Consolidants, Adhesives and Coatings* (London, 1990)

C. V. HORIE, EDDY DE WITTE

Adhicchatra. *See* AHICHCHHATRA.

Adılcevaz. *See* KEFKALESI.

ʿAdil Shahi [ʿĀdil Shāhī]. Dynasty that ruled portions of southern India from 1489 to 1686. Its founder, Yusuf ʿAdil Shah (*reg* 1489–1509), had come to India from Persia and was appointed governor of BIJAPUR under the BAHMANI rulers. He declared his independence when that dynasty declined. Yusuf had a prolonged conflict with the Portuguese, who were able to secure Goa in 1510. The ʿAdil Shahis and their rival states in the Deccan formed a series of alliances and counter-alliances in the struggle for hegemony. For example, in 1543 a confederacy of Ahmadnagar, Golconda and Vijayanagara attacked the ʿAdil Shahi capital Bijapur, but Ibrahim ʿAdil Shah (*reg* 1534–57) maintained control. His successor ʿAli ʿAdil Shah (*reg* 1557–79) joined an alliance that destroyed Vijayanagara in 1565. ʿAli ʿAdil Shah was an enlightened prince who built a large number of public works, including the Jamiʿ Mosque at Bijapur. The dynasty reached its zenith under Ibrahim ʿAdil Shah II (*reg* 1579–1627), a great patron of art, music and letters; fine surviving paintings include a number of his portraits. One of the most outstanding architectural achievements of his reign is the Ibrahim Rauza, the mausoleum of Ibrahim II and his family, which is set in a walled garden with tomb and mosque on a common plinth. While Ibrahim was able to avert confrontation with the MUGHAL rulers, who were slowly expanding into the Deccan, his successor Muhammad ʿAdil Shah (*reg* 1627–56) was forced to agree to a 'Deed of Submission' in 1636. Muhammad's tomb, the Gol Gumbaz, is a gigantic domed structure (*see* INDIAN SUBCONTINENT, fig. 110). In the reign of Sikandar ʿAdil Shah (*reg* 1672–86) Bijapur fell to the Mughal emperor Aurangzeb.

See also INDIAN SUBCONTINENT, §§III, 7(ii)(a) and V, 4(vi)(b).

BIBLIOGRAPHY

W. Haig: 'The Five Kingdoms of the Deccan, 1527–1599', *The Cambridge History of India*, iii (Cambridge, 1928/*R* Delhi, 1965), pp. 433–66
H. K. Sherwani and P. M. Joshi, eds: *History of the Medieval Deccan (1295–1724)*, 2 vols (Hyderabad, 1973)
D. C. Varma: *History of Bijapur* (New Delhi, 1974)

R. NATH

Adler, Dankmar (*b* Stadtlengsfeld, nr Eisenach, 3 July 1844; *d* Chicago, 16 April 1900). American architect and engineer of German birth. His family moved to the USA in 1854, and he trained in Detroit, in the architectural offices of John Schaefer, E. Willard Smith and others. After his family moved from Detroit to Chicago, Adler

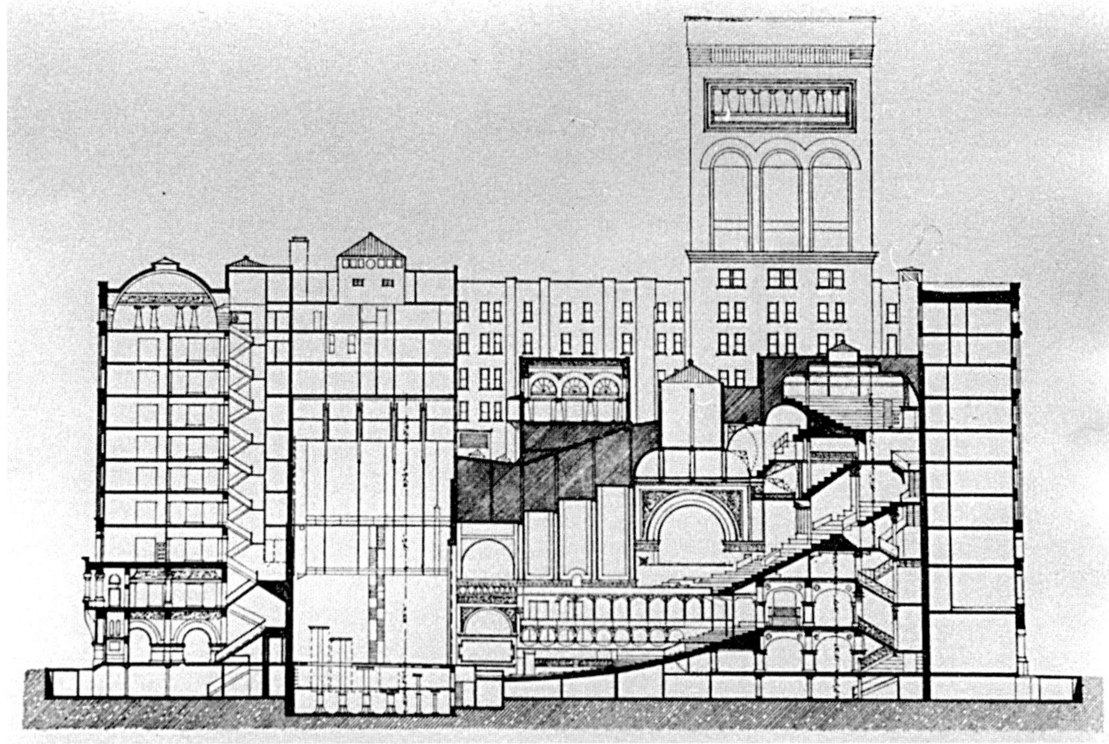

Adler & Sullivan: longitudinal section of the Auditorium Building, Chicago, 1886–9

worked under a German émigré architect, Augustus Bauer (1827–94), and gained valuable training in an engineering company during his military service in the American Civil War. After the war, he worked with O. S. Kinney (*d* 1868), and later Ashley Kinney, building educational and civic structures in the Midwest. Adler's ability soon brought him to the attention of an established practitioner, Edward Burling (1818–92), who needed assistance in the aftermath of the Chicago fire of 1871. Burling & Adler's many buildings include the First National Bank (1871) and Mercantile (1873) buildings and the Methodist Church Block (1872), all designed in Chicago by Adler and all demolished. In 1879 he and Burling parted.

Adler's first independent commission was the Central Music Hall (1879; destr. 1900), Chicago, which integrated an office-block, a multipurpose auditorium and shops, a successful formula that Adler later repeated. Other early commissions in Chicago were houses for John Borden (1880; destr. 1955) and Henry Leopold (1882; destr. before 1932), and a number of commercial buildings: the Borden Block (1881; destr. 1916), Jewelers' Building (1882), the Brunswick and Balke Factory (1882–91; destr. 1989) and the Crilly & Blair Complex (1881; destr. *c.* 1970). By 1881 Adler's employees included Louis Sullivan, as is evident from the style and placement of the ornament on the Borden Block. Adler made Sullivan a full partner in 1883, by which time the office was designing factories, stores, houses, office-blocks and especially theatres. The early success of Adler & Sullivan was due to Adler's planning and engineering innovations and his reputation as a careful builder and businessman of integrity. He could recognize and guide talent in others, and the firm also benefited from his many social connections. A founder of the Western Association of Architects, he led its merger into the American Institute of Architects, of which he was secretary in 1892.

Between 1879 and 1889 Adler executed many commissions for theatres and concert halls, ranging from remodellings to enormous multipurpose complexes. He was recognized as a leading expert in acoustics and served as acoustics consultant during the construction (1890–91) of Carnegie Hall, New York. Adler & Sullivan's records do not survive, and the contribution of the partners and their employees can only be inferred; for the Auditorium Building, Chicago (1886–9; see fig.), Sullivan, Paul Mueller and Frank Lloyd Wright, who was employed as a draughtsman, all contributed to the building complex, but the commission and the overall design were Adler's. Among the innovations Adler adapted for the Auditorium Building were caisson foundations (*see* SKYSCRAPER), huge trusses to support the rooms above the theatre space and hydraulic machinery to raise and lower sections of the stage. The plan of the concert hall, with its excellent provision for sight and sound, evolved from early Adler designs; Sullivan was engaged on the ornamental decoration, and Mueller contributed to the engineering. The result was a true synthesis of acoustics, aesthetics and technical innovation, with colour and ornament, science and technology harnessed in the service of art. Wright called it 'the greatest room for music and opera in the world'. Other theatre commissions carried out by Adler & Sullivan include the Schiller Theatre (1891–3; destr. 1961), Chicago, which—

like the Auditorium Theatre—was part of a tall office building. Several influential early skyscrapers were also produced by the firm, notably the Wainwright Building, St Louis (1890–91; *see* UNITED STATES OF AMERICA, fig. 7), the Chicago Stock Exchange (1893; destr. 1971) and the Guaranty Building, Buffalo (1894–6; *see* SULLIVAN, LOUIS, fig. 1).

The financial crash of 1893–4, a shift in architectural taste and irreconcilable aesthetic and economic arguments between Adler and Sullivan led to the partnership being acrimoniously dissolved in 1895. That year Adler became a consultant for a company manufacturing lifts for new skyscrapers, mostly in New York. He left after six months, returning to architecture and to Chicago, taking his son Abraham (1876–1914) into partnership. Adler and Sullivan now became competitors—but not implacable enemies—in a shrinking market. Between 1896 and 1900 Adler's offices in Chicago and New York had fewer than a dozen commissions, whereas in 1886 Adler & Sullivan had had 18 jobs in addition to the Auditorium. Of the edifices built after the split with Sullivan, Adler's Morgan Park Academy dormitories (1896; destr. *c.* 1970) for a college preparatory school and Isaiah Temple (1898), both in Chicago, were architecturally the most interesting. The temple contains many elements he had used in the Central Music Hall, but the overall style is more historically derived than any Adler & Sullivan designs.

Adler spent much of his later life writing and working successfully for state licensing of architects. He was particularly interested in two causes: recognition for architecture as a learned profession and the education of both the public and the practitioners on how to design for modern society. There were some unbuilt projects, but after his death the firm he left behind did not flourish. A brilliant and conscientious architect and engineer, Adler's work was dominated by the idea of the building as a synthesis, in which 'form and function are one' and in which 'there must be throughout, from foundation to roof, in the arrangement of all the parts, in the design of every line, the imprint and all-pervading influence of one master mind'. He solved practical problems creatively and literally put a firm foundation under the skyscraper and a solid skeleton under its skin. Adler opposed height limitations and slavish obedience to historical precedents, and he was unusual in his willingness to experiment with new materials and relatively untried structural and foundation techniques, as well as in the breadth of building type undertaken. With Sullivan he provided a model for the modern, multi-specialist architectural office, providing also a creative and productive milieu, in which some of the 20th century's leading architects began their careers.

UNPUBLISHED SOURCES

Chicago, IL, Newberry Lib., Dankmar Adler Archv [journals, letters, autobiography]

Chicago, IL, Richard Nickel Cttee [architectural photographs and archv, 1972]

WRITINGS

'Foundations of the Auditorium Building', *Inland Architect & News Rec.*, xi (1888), pp. 31–2

'The Auditorium Tower', *Amer. Architect & Bldg News*, xxxi (1891), pp. 15–16

'Tall Office Buildings—Past and Future', *Engin. Mag.*, iii (1892), pp. 765–73

'Theater-Building for American Cities', *Engin. Mag.*, vii (1894), pp. 717–30; viii, pp. 814–29

'The Influence of Steel Construction and of Plate Glass upon the Development of Modern Style', *Inland Architect & News Rec.*, xxviii (1896), pp. 34–7

BIBLIOGRAPHY

M. Schuyler: 'Architecture in Chicago: Adler & Sullivan', *Archit. Rec. Suppl.*, 3 (1895), pp. 3–48

L. Sullivan: *Autobiography of an Idea* (New York, 1924)

F. Lloyd Wright: *Genius and the Mobocracy* (New York, 1949)

C. Condit: *American Building Art: Nineteenth and Twentieth Century* (New York, 1961)

R. Elstein: *The Architectural Style of Dankmar Adler* (MA thesis, U. Chicago, 1963)

R. Baron: 'Forgotten Facets of Dankmar Adler', *Inland Architect & News Rec.*, vii (1964), pp. 14–16

C. Condit: *The Chicago School of Architecture* (Chicago, 1964)

R. Elstein: 'The Architecture of Dankmar Adler', *J. Soc. Archit. Historians*, xxvi (1967), pp. 242–9

J. Saltzstein: 'Dankmar Adler: The Man, the Architect, the Author', *Wisconsin Architect*, xxxviii (1967): (July), pp. 15–19; (Sept), pp. 10–14; (Nov), pp. 16–19

N. Menocal: *Architecture as Nature: The Transcendentalist Idea of Louis Sullivan* (Madison, 1981) [with complete list of Adler's pubd writings, pp. 206–07]

C. Grimsley: *A Study of the Contributions of Dankmar Adler to the Theater Building Practices of the Late Nineteenth Century* (diss., Evanston, IL, Northwestern U., 1984)

L. Doumato: *Dankmar Adler, 1844–1900* (Monticello, IL, 1985)

R. Twombly: *Louis Sullivan: His Life and Work* (New York, 1986) [with full list of Adler & Sullivan commissions]

C. Gregersen: *Dankmar Adler: His Theatres and Auditoriums* (Athens, OH, 1990)

ROCHELLE BERGER ELSTEIN

Adler, (Johann Heinrich) Friedrich (*b* Berlin, 15 Oct 1827; *d* Berlin, 15 Sept 1908). German architect, archaeologist and writer. He was one of the leading figures of Berlin's architectural establishment in the latter half of the 19th century. On completion of his studies in 1852, he was given the prestigious post of Bauleiter at the Neues Museum in Berlin, designed by Friedrich August Stüler. He subsequently became a lecturer and in 1861 a professor of architectural history at the Bauakademie in Berlin. Many of his church buildings used medieval motifs and elements, for example the Christuskirche (1862–8) in Berlin and the Elisabethkirche (1869–72) in Wilhelmshafen. He followed Karl Bötticher in his attempts to merge medieval and classical elements, best illustrated in his design for the Thomaskirche (competition 1862; built 1865–70), Berlin. There, Adler used Gothic structural devices embellished with rich Renaissance detail, a tendency that was also present in many of the entries for the Berlin Cathedral competition (1869). The Thomaskirche became something of a prototype for Protestant churches in Germany. A keen archaeologist, Adler participated in the excavations by Ernst Curtius (1814–96) in Olympia (1875–81). He also designed the Archaeological Museum at Olympia in 1883. After entering the civil service in 1877, he quickly rose to an influential position in the Ministerium für Öffentliche Arbeiten, where he was responsible for church building until his retirement in 1903. He also restored Schleswig Cathedral (1888–94), and the Schlosskirche at Wittenberg in 1892 as a monument to the Reformation. Adler was a member of several national and foreign academic institutes and scholarly societies. He travelled widely in Greece, Palestine and Asia Minor and published numerous articles and books on archaeology and architectural history.

WRITINGS

Die mittelalterlichen Backstein-Bauwerke des preussischen Staates, 2 vols (Berlin, 1859–69)
Baugeschichtlichen Forschungen in Deutschland, 2 vols (Berlin, 1870–79)
with E. Curtius: *Olympia: Die Ergebnisse*, 5 vols (Berlin, 1890–97/*R* 1966)
[autobiographical contrib. to] *Das geistige Deutschland am Ende des XIX. Jahrhunderts*, i (Leipzig and Berlin, 1898), p. 8

BIBLIOGRAPHY

Thieme–Becker; Wasmuth
V. Hammerschmidt: *Anspruch und Ausdruck in der Architektur des späten Historismus in Deutschland, 1860–1914* (Frankfurt am Main, 1985)

□

Adler, Jankel (*b* Tuszyn, nr Łódź, 26 July 1895; *d* Aldbourne, Wilts, 25 April 1949). Polish painter. He underwent an apprenticeship in engraving in 1912 and in 1913 moved to Barmen (now Wuppertal) in Germany, where he studied under Gustav Wiethüchter at the Kunstgewerbeschule during World War I. In 1918 he came into contact with Das Junge Rheinland, a group of artists based in Düsseldorf. In the same year he visited Poland, where he was one of the founders of the Ing Idisz (Young Yiddish) group, an association of painters and writers in Łódź dedicated to the expression of their Jewish identity. The few surviving works produced by Adler during this period, all in an Expressionist style, with the human figure subjected to elongated and distorted proportions, reveal his own response to these concerns. *The Rabbi's Last Hour* (1919; Łódź, Mus. A.), in which the influence of El Greco has been discerned, is a good example. His inventory of images included motifs from Jewish folk art and Hebrew calligraphy.

In 1920 Adler returned to Barmen, moving later to Düsseldorf, where he remained in contact with the Junge Rheinland group. He played a major role in the Rheinische Sezession, joined the Rheingruppe and the Gruppe Progressiver Künstler in Cologne and in 1922 helped organize a congress of the Union of Progressive International Artists. From 1922 to 1933 he participated in major German and international exhibitions of progressive art; in 1926 he was awarded first prize for *Wall Painting* (mixed media on canvas, 3.08×4.6 m, 1926; Düsseldorf, Tonhalle), representing three women against an abstract faceted background, and in 1928 he won a gold medal for his painting *Cats* (1927; Cologne, Mus. Ludwig). Adler's paintings of this period, such as *Three Women* (1926; Düsseldorf, Kstmus.), dominated by static human figures with an overpowering presence and heavy facial features and limbs, are restrained and monumental. They incorporate formal, stylistic and technical elements derived from a variety of sources including German Expressionism, Picasso and Cubism, and Constructivism. In order to explore the tension between abstraction and naturalism he borrowed Cubist devices such as multiple viewpoints, the tilting of the picture plane and the isolation and reintegration of decorative elements and details. Unlike the Cubists, however, he used these elements in pictures such as *Still-life (Tea)* (oil, ink and sand on paper, 1928; Düsseldorf, Kstmus.) to add a mystical dimension to his work. His concern with the formal design of his compositions, with their carefully balanced tonal contrasts, and the variations of texture achieved by mixing sand and other substances into the paints, can be linked to Constructivism. His approach to imagery in the early 1930s, on the other hand, indicates an affinity with Neue Sachlichkeit.

Adler was forced to leave Germany in 1933, at the height of his success there, because of the rise to power of the Nazis. His paintings were removed from German museums and appeared on the lists of 'degenerate art' (*see* ENTARTETE KUNST). He settled in France in 1934, living first in Paris and later in Argèles-sur-Mer and Cagnes-sur-Mer. In 1940 he joined the Polish Army, with which he travelled in 1941 to Glasgow, where he had a strong influence on young painters such as Robert Colquhoun and Robert MacBryde. He made direct reference to the suffering occasioned by World War II in *The Mutilated* (1942; London, Tate) and continued to explore his Jewish identity, for example in *Two Rabbis* (1942; New York, MOMA). He settled permanently in London in 1943, taking an active role in the circle of European refugee artists and also making contact with British painters and poets. The images in his paintings became more ambiguous, turning into ideograms or abstract symbols, and his figures became more abstract and geometrical, more delicate and refined in their proportions and at the same time more expressive of movement and vitality. In these works, such as *Woman with Raised Hands* (1948–9; Jerusalem, Israel Mus.), abstract symbolism merges with a sense of impending destiny and respect for the human experience.

BIBLIOGRAPHY

P. Fierens: *Jankel Adler* (London, 1948)
S. W. Hayter: *Jankel Adler* (London, 1948)
A. Klapheck: *Jankel Adler* (Recklinghausen, 1966)
N. Guralnik: 'Jankel Adler's "Purim Spiel": An Encounter between Picasso and Chassidism', *Ann. Rev.: Tel Aviv Mus.*, 2–3 (1984), pp. 20–29
Jankel Adler (exh. cat., ed. N. Guralnik; Tel Aviv Mus., 1985) [retro.]
Jankel Adler (exh. cat., ed. U. Krempel and K. Thomas; Düsseldorf, Städt. Ksthalle, 1985) [retro.]

NEHAMA GURALNIK

Admont Abbey. Benedictine abbey in Styria, Austria. It was founded in the mid-11th century by Bishop Gebhard from Salzburg, endowed by Saint Henna von Gurk, Gräfin von Friessach (*d* 1045), and settled by Benedictine monks from St Peter's, Salzburg. The Romanesque minster (consecrated 1074), which was famous for its marble columns, was rebuilt after a fire in 1152; a Gothic choir was added in 1276–86. The abbey became an important cultural centre with a renowned scriptorium. From 1121 to the 16th century a convent was attached to the abbey. Under the abbots Mathias Preininger (1615–28) and Urban Weber (1628–59) the whole establishment was transformed in the Baroque style, and the church was rebuilt (1615–26). In 1742 Gotthard Hayberger submitted to Abbot Anton II von Mainersberg (1718–51) a huge plan for the rebuilding of the complex, although only a fraction was undertaken owing to its cost. Hayberger's most important building was the library in the east wing, which was completed in 1776 by Josef Hueber (*d* 1787). The room is two storeys high and 70 m long, with a domed, longitudinal ellipse in the centre, bounded by piers faced with pairs of colossal half columns. At either side is a three-bay wing, each bay sail-vaulted. The main impact is made by the

Rococo bookcases, with gilt decoration sparingly applied, and by the galleries that run along the wings at first-floor level. In 1774–6 Bartolomeo Altomonte painted allegories of the *Arts and Sciences under the Patronage of the Church and Religion* on the side and central vaults. The library contains 14 bronzed limewood sculptures by JOSEF STAMMEL, of which the most important are the 'Four Last Things' (*Death, Judgement, Hell, Heaven*) under the central dome. Except for the library, the abbey buildings burnt down in 1865 and were rebuilt (1866–9) in a Gothic Revival style by Wilhelm Bücher (1824–88).

BIBLIOGRAPHY

K. Woisetschlager: *Steiermark (ohne Graz)*, Dehio-Handbuch, iv (Vienna, 1982), pp. 3–6

M. Mannewitz: *Stift Admont* (Freiburg im Breisgau, 1987)

Kunstschatten uit de Benediktijnerabdij Admont (exh. cat., Europalia; Tienen, 1987)

A. GERHARDT

Adoian, Vosdanig Manoog. *See* GORKY, ARSHILE.

Adriaenssen [Adrieanssen], **Alex(ander)** (*bapt* Antwerp, 16 Jan 1587; *d* Antwerp, 30 Oct 1661). Flemish painter. He was the son of the composer Emanuel Adriaenssen and brother to the painters Vincent Adriaenssen (1595–1675) and Niclaes Adriaenssen (1598–1648/9). In 1597 he was apprenticed to Artus van Laeck (*d* 1616) and in 1610 became a master in the painters' guild. In 1632 he took on Philips Milcx as apprentice, and in 1635 he painted the coats of arms of the 17 provinces on the triumphal arches in honour of the new governor. Adriaenssen's many signed and often dated oil paintings on wood and canvas are all still-lifes, mainly of food on tables with copper- and tinware, glass and pottery (e.g. *Still-life with Fish*, 1660; Amsterdam, Rijksmus.). There are four paintings of vases of flowers, but vases of flowers, as well as single flowers on the table, also appear in other still-life combinations. Only two canvases are known in which he worked with figure painters: a garland of flowers around a painting of the *Holy Family* (Ghent, Paul Boterdaele priv. col.) by Simon de Vos and a porcelain bowl of fruit beside a *Virgin and Child* (ex-Gal. 'Den Tijd', Antwerp, 1982) attributed to a follower of Rubens. His compositions are graceful and balanced but somewhat stereotyped, and they are bathed in a soft chiaroscuro. Adriaenssen depicted with great skill the moist waxiness of fish and oysters, the luminous transparency of drops of water and glasses filled with liquid, as well as crisp, juicy fruit, downy feathers and velvety fur.

BIBLIOGRAPHY

Bénézit; *BNB*; *NBW*; Thieme–Becker; Wurzbach

P. Rombouts and T. van Lerius: *De Liggeren (1453–1794) en andere historische archieven der Antwerpsche Sint Lucasgilde* (Antwerp, 1864–76/*R* Amsterdam, 1961), i, pp. 399, 460, 471; ii, pp. 41, 44, 58

T. van Lerius: *Biographies d'artistes anversois* (Antwerp, 1880), i, pp. 12–24

M. L. Hairs: *Les Peintres flamands de fleurs au XVIIe siècle* (Brussels, 1955, rev. 3/1985), pp. 361, 364–6

E. Greindl: *Les Peintres flamands de nature morte au XVIIe siècle* (Brussels, 1956, rev. 2/1983), pp. 55–7, 178–9, 333–4

E. Duverger: *Antwerpse kunstinventarissen uit de zeventiende eeuw*, I/ii (Brussels, 1985), p. 153; I/iv (Brussels, 1989), nos 899, 1031; I/v (Brussels, 1991), p. 79; I/vi (Brussels, 1992), no. 1719, pp. 268, 297, 343, 348, 351, 354; I/vii (Brussels, 1993), p. 163

G. Spiessens: *Leven en werk van de Antwerpse schilder Alexander Adriaenssen (1587–1661)* (Brussels, 1990)

J. de Maere and M. Wabbes: *Illustrated Dictionary of 17th-century Flemish Painters* (Brussels, 1994), i, p. 28; ii, pp. 14–16

G. SPIESSENS

Adrian-Nilsson, Gösta [GAN] (*b* Lund, 2 April 1884; *d* Stockholm, 29 March 1965). Swedish painter. After studying at Zahrtmanns Skole, Copenhagen, in 1914 he went to Berlin; both Kandinsky and Franz Marc were of great importance to his development at this time of a semi-abstract style with deep, glowing colours. He developed his own style of expressive Cubism (e.g. *Sailors' War Dream*, 1917; Malmö, Kstmus.). He was captivated by modern technology and masculine strength, and this was often reflected in his work. In 1919 he began producing purely non-objective work, and he made numerous collages *c.* 1920 in a Dadaist spirit. Between 1920 and 1925 he lived in Paris, coming into contact with Alexander Archipenko and Fernand Léger. Léger's influence can partly be seen in his depiction of figures as robotic human shapes in the form of sportsmen, seamen and soldiers. Adrian-Nilsson also produced geometric abstract work in the late 1920s. In the 1930s he developed a personal approach to Surrealism, participating in exhibitions such as Kubisme-Surrealisme in Copenhagen (1935). During the 1940s his work again became purely abstract. He was influential to the members of the Halmstad group, particularly during their Surrealist phase. His later work was nearer to Romantic painting, inspired by the Swedish landscape painter Marcus Larson. He signed his works 'GAN'.

WRITINGS

Den gudomliga geometrien [The divine geometry] (Stockholm, 1922)

BIBLIOGRAPHY

N. Lindgren: *GAN* (Halmstad, 1949)

GAN (exh. cat.; Stockholm, Liljevalchs Ksthall; Malmö, Ksthall; 1984)

J. T. Ahlstrand: *GAN: Gösta Adrian-Nilsson* (Arlöv, 1985)

JACQUELINE STARE

Adriano Fiorentino [Adriano di Giovanni de' Maestri] (*b* ?Florence, *c.* 1450–60; *d* Florence, before 12 June 1499). Italian sculptor. Like his collaborator Bertoldo di Giovanni, he may have started his working life as a servant in the house of Lorenzo de' Medici. An 'Adriano nostro' is recorded delivering letters for Lorenzo in 1483 and again in March 1484, when Lorenzo referred to him as 'Adriano formerly our groom' (*staffiere*).

Adriano's best-known enterprise is the bronze statuette of *Bellerophon and Pegasus* (Vienna, Ksthist. Mus.; *see* BERTOLDO DI GIOVANNI, fig. 2), which he cast after a model of Bertoldo's. Its underside is signed *Expressit me Bertholdus. Conflavit Hadrianus.* Marcantonio Michiel, who saw the piece in a Paduan collection, took this to mean that Adriano was Bertoldo's assistant in casting. Bertoldo's influence is certainly apparent in Adriano's signed bronze statuette of *Venus* (Philadelphia, PA, Mus. A.; see fig.). The nude *Hercules* (J. W. Frederiks priv. col., on loan to Rotterdam, Mus. Boymans–van Beuningen), formerly attributed to Bertoldo, matches the *Venus* in both its facture and its stance. A signed *Venus and Cupid*, reproduced by Fabriczy (1886), has since disappeared. Important evidence of Adriano's activity in the production of small bronzes was provided by the discovery of his signature

Adriano Fiorentino: *Venus*, bronze, h. 422 mm, *c.* 1490 (Philadelphia, PA, Museum of Art)

beneath a leering *Pan* with tautly flexed legs (Vienna, Ksthist. Mus.); this is the finest example in the group of statuettes attributed to him and the one most likely to have been made in Florence. He also signed a marble statuette of a *Sleeping Satyr* (Berlin, Skulpgal.).

According to a deposition of May 1499, Adriano served for a time with Buonaccorso Ghiberti, a fortifications expert and founder of artillery who worked for over two years under Virginio Orsini, the condottiere commander of the Aragonese army. Buonaccorso's service ended in June 1488. The hardy simplicity of Adriano's *Venus* and *Hercules* statuettes perhaps reflects his experiences with the casting of cannonry during this period.

In 1493 Adriano is recorded living in the household of King Ferdinand in Naples and the following year in the house of the Duke of Calabria, where his brother Amadeo wrote to him with the news of Michelangelo's flight from Florence. The three medals of *Ferdinand II* (Hill, *Corpus*, nos 335–7) and the portrait medals of the Neapolitan writers *Pietro Compatre*, *Giovanni Pontano* and *Jacopo Sannazaro* (Hill, *Corpus*, nos 339–43) probably date from this time. The heads of the writers are shown in striking, classical profile, while the faintly sketched figures on the reverses are reminiscent of antique encaustic painting. The *Pontano* medal prompted the attribution to Adriano of a bronze bust of that humanist (Genoa, Gal. Pal. Bianco), a balding, staring head set at an ungainly angle in a Roman tunic. The medal and bust in turn determined his authorship of a slightly more classical marble relief portrait of *Pontano* (New York, Met., since 1991).

Adriano's search for work took him northward; in a letter of May 1495 Elisabetta Gonzaga, Duchess of Urbino, urged her brother Francesco II, Marquis of Mantua, to employ Adriano. She had been sufficiently impressed by his talents during his three-month stay in Urbino to praise him as 'a good sculptor' who 'has made here some very beautiful medals', adding that he was 'a good composer of sonnets, a good player of the lyre, and he also improvises rather outstandingly'. Adriano's medal of the *Duchess of Urbino* (Hill, *Corpus*, no. 344) dates from this time. He then worked in Germany, where he made a bust of *Frederick the Wise of Saxony* in bell-metal, signed and dated 1498 (Dresden, Grünes Gewölbe). This owlish portrait with carefully studied details of costume has more in common with the spirit of contemporary German painting than with Italian sculpture.

BIBLIOGRAPHY

Thieme–Becker

C. von Fabriczy: 'Ein bisher unbeachtetes Werk des Adriano Fiorentino', *Kst & Gew.*, xx (1886), p. 7

——: 'Adriano Fiorentino', *Jb. Kön.-Preuss. Kstsamml.*, xxiv (1903), pp. 71–98

G. F. Hill: *Corpus* (1930), pp. 82–7

G. L. Hersey: *Alfonso II and the Artistic Renewal of Naples, 1485–1495* (New Haven, 1969), pp. 29–30

J. D. Draper: *Bertoldo di Giovanni, Sculptor of the Medici Household* (Columbia, MO, 1992), pp. 44–52, 69, 181

The Currency of Fame: Portrait Medals of the Renaissance (exh. cat., ed. S. K. Scher; New York, Frick, 1994)

JAMES DAVID DRAPER

Adrianople. *See* EDIRNE.

Adsett, Sandy (*b* Wairoa, Hawke's Bay, NZ, 27 Aug 1939). Maori painter, carver, weaver, costume and stage designer. His involvement with art began at Te Aute Maori Boys' College (1954–7), Hawke's Bay, Waipawa County, and continued with formal art training at Ardmore Teachers' College (1958–9) and at Dunedin Teachers' College (1960), where he trained as an art specialist. He subsequently worked for the Department of Education as an arts and crafts adviser and served on committees for national art education policies, the Historic Places Trust (with particular reference to Maori sites), art museums and tribal committees (dealing with traditional and customary art forms and architecture). He helped to promote contemporary developments in Maori arts for community buildings, meeting houses, churches and public sites, serving on private and governmental commissions. In his own work he maintains a balance between the conservation of older traditional materials and forms of Maori arts and the experimental use of new materials, such as composite chipboard, synthetic dyes, plastic-coated basketry fibres and composite, laminated board. His painted and woven-fibre works are notable for their rich but subtle colours and controlled sense of line. They vary in size from complex architectural installations or stage designs for the Royal New Zealand Ballet to designs for postage stamps. At Te Huki Meeting House (1982), for example, the carved figures supporting the walls and the house-posts, as well as the painted rafter patterns of the ceiling and woven wall panels are all linked by style, motif and colour to relate intricate tribal narratives.

JOHN HOVELL

BIBLIOGRAPHY

D. Nicholas and K. Kaa: *Seven Maori Artists* (Wellington, 1986), pp. 16–19 and pls 6–10 [interviews]

Adshead, S(tanley) D(avenport) (*b* Bowdon, Cheshire, 1868; *d* London, 11 April 1946). English architect and urban planner. The son of a landscape painter, he was apprenticed to an architect in Manchester in 1885. He went to London in 1890, where he built up experience in well-known architectural offices, notably with George Sherrin (*d* 1909) and William Flockhart (*d* 1913). His brief and shrewd recollections of these years are a valuable record of prosperous London practice in the 1890s. He gradually gained a reputation as a perspectivist but his architectural career was slow to develop. The library and assembly rooms at Ramsgate, Kent (1904), and offices for the Bennett Steamship Co., Southwark, London (1908), show his preference for an individual, refined Georgian-revival style.

In 1909 Adshead became Professor of Town Planning at Liverpool University and inaugurated the Department of Civic Design, the first town-planning school in Britain, with Patrick Abercrombie as his deputy. In 1910 they founded the *Town Planning Review*, which called for a crisper, more formalized and more internationally conscious approach to urban design than that which had hitherto found favour with Raymond Unwin and the pioneers of the garden city. Adshead became Professor of Town Planning at University College, London, in 1914 but remained loyal to the tenets of 'Liverpool-school' planning. After Unwin's, his was the most articulate architectural voice in the implementation of the national housing programmes of the 1920s. Between 1911 and 1931 Adshead was in partnership with Stanley C. Ramsey (1882–1968) and their projects included housing on the Duchy of Cornwall Estate, Kennington, London (from 1911), a wartime housing scheme for Dormanstown, Middlesbrough, and a series of consultancies for British local authorities in the 1920s. In due course Adshead moved on to develop a number of regional planning schemes of which the earliest and most important was for the Middlesbrough area, made with Abercrombie in 1925. A later scheme of significance was his layout for Lusaka, Zambia (1930–31), developed and carried out by others.

Adshead's approach to urban planning remained that of the artist rather than the social scientist, but he was always open to ideas. His passion for orderly, simplified appearances helped to curb the more picturesque tendencies in British planning and national housing programmes of the 1920s. Although none of his great projects was carried out *in toto*, the Duchy of Cornwall Estate admirably shows the refinement of his sober, neo-Georgian style, which influenced the plans of others, notably Louis de Soissons's layout for Welwyn Garden City.

BIBLIOGRAPHY

C. H. Reilly: *Representative British Architects of the Present Day* (London, 1931), pp. 15–27

S. Pepper and M. Swenarton: 'Neo-Georgian Maison-type', *Archit. Rev.* [London], clxviii (1980), pp. 87–92

A. Powers, ed.: '"Architects I have known": The Architectural Career of S. D. Adshead', *Archit. Hist.*, xxiv (1981), pp. 103–23

M. Swenarton: *Homes Fit for Heroes* (London, 1981)

□

Adygey region. *See under* RUSSIA, §XII, 1.

Adyton [Gr. 'not to be entered'; Lat. *adytum*]. Most sacred inner part of a temple, accessible only to the priests (*see* GREECE, ANCIENT, fig. 7g).

□

Adzhina Tepe. Buddhist monastery of the 7th century AD to first half of the 8th, in the valley of the Vakhsh River, 12 km east of Kurgan-Tyube, southern Tajikistan. During this early medieval period it belonged to Vakhsh (U-sha in Chinese sources), one of the 27 domains of Tokharistan. Excavations between 1960 and 1975 by the Academy of Sciences, Tajikistan, and the Hermitage Museum, St Petersburg, exposed the entire site; most of the finds are on loan to the Hermitage Museum, St Petersburg. The buildings, which covered an area of 100×50 m, were constructed of mud-bricks (*c.* 490×250×110 mm) and rammed earth, with walls surviving to a height of 5.5 to 6.0 m. The site comprised two square complexes linked by an enfilade of three rooms (see fig. (a)). The south-eastern complex or monastery (b) had domed cells (c) for monks, a hall or refectory (d), service quarters, store-rooms and a small sanctuary (e). An open courtyard in the centre had a fired brick path across it, linking the enfilade to the sanctuary. A corridor around the perimeter of the courtyard was divided into four right-angled sections by a deep iwan, or vestibule, in the middle of each side. One of these vestibules led into the sanctuary, the second into the meeting-hall, the third into the enfilade and the fourth to the monastery exit (j) and also on to a vaulted ramp (k) that originally gave access to the roof and the now lost second storey.

The north-western or main stupa complex had a similar plan. In the centre of the courtyard was a large terraced cruciform stupa (f). Subsidiary stupas (g) were located in the corners of the courtyard. Small platforms or pedestals with sculpture were found in small domed sanctuaries (h) facing the main stupa. Sculpture (e.g. a *parinirvāṇa* scene (i) with a 12 m reclining Buddha) was also found in the right-angled corridors, either in specially built niches or on pedestals. Polychrome clay images of the Buddha, *bodhisattvas*, various divinities and demonic beings were used in compositions juxtaposing statues in the round on pedestals with wall reliefs of images, leaves, flowers,

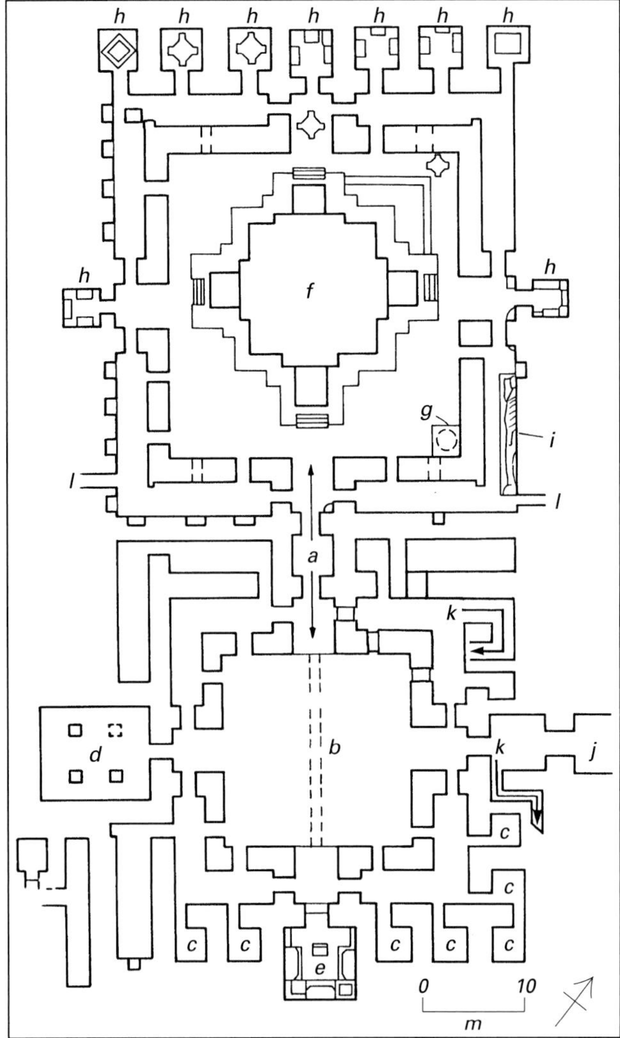

Adzhina Tepe, 7th century AD–first half of the 8th, plan: (a) enfilade of three rooms; (b) monastery courtyard; (c) domed cells; (d) hall or refectory; (e) sanctuary; (f) stupa; (g) subsidiary stupas; (h) small domed sanctuaries; (i) statue of Buddha in *parinirvāṇa*; (j) entrance to monastery; (k) ramp to first floor; (l) gates

tendrils and intertwining patterns. When any damaged sculpture had to be replaced, the remains were carefully bricked up in the walls, pedestals, floors and courtyard around the main stupa (*see also* CENTRAL ASIA, §I, 3(iii)(b)).

The main stupa complex and the sanctuary in the monastery were also richly painted. The paintings in the vaulted corridors of the stupa complex, as reconstructed, seem to illustrate the 'Thousand Buddhas', with rows of seated Buddhas, each differing in pose and gesture, and in the colour of their robes, haloes and mandorlas. There were probably several versions of the 'Preaching Buddha' and also scenes of local Tokharistan nobles bearing gifts and flowers (*see* CENTRAL ASIA, fig. 34).

During the spread of Islam to Tokharistan (*c.* 750 onwards), the sculpture and murals were destroyed. In several rooms the resulting rubble was *c.* 1 m in depth, and it is thus impossible to reconstruct fully the original scheme. Chinese authors related that in the Vakhsh region Hinayana teachings were followed, but archaeological data are not sufficient to determine whether Adzhina Tepe was a Hinayanist or Mahayanist monastery.

BIBLIOGRAPHY

B. A. Litvinsky and T. I. Zeymal': *Adzhina-tepe: Arkhitektura, zhivopis', skul'ptura* [Adzhina Tepe: architecture, painting, sculpture] (Moscow, 1971)

T. I. Zeymal': 'Raskopki na Adzhina-tepe v 1975' [Excavations at Adzhina Tepe in 1975], *Arkheol. Raboty Tadzhikistane*, xv (1975), pp. 147–56

T. I. ZEYMAL'

Aech'un. *See* SIN, (2).

Aedicula. Columnar niche or shrine applied decoratively to a larger building. The word is a diminutive from the Latin word *aedes* ('temple'). Summerson traced its application to Gothic architecture and drew attention to the importance of playing at being in a house for all small children; he claimed that this kind of play has much to do with the aesthetics of architecture and leads ultimately to the use of the aedicula. The earliest surviving examples of aediculae are shop-signs from Pompeii, such as that showing Mercury or Hermes emerging from a small building. Later aediculae appear extensively in wall paintings of the Fourth Style (*c.* AD 20–*c.* 90; *see* ROME, ANCIENT, §V, 2). Later still, aediculae were often used in the architecture of the eastern provinces of the Roman Empire; they consisted of columns or pilasters flanking a niche for statuary, with a pediment above, as in the stage-building of the theatre at ASPENDOS (later 2nd century AD). Aediculae were also used in the interior of the 'Temple of Bacchus' at BAALBEK (2nd century AD) and the nymphaeum and propylaea at Gerasa (later 2nd century AD). The aediculae of the 'Temple of Bacchus' consist of alternating triangular and segmental pediments framing the statues that articulate the upper part of the walls, between the giant order of engaged columns. An aedicula at the far end of the temple has been restored as a broken pediment supported on small columns; this example may be over-ripe and complex, reflecting a late stage in a long tradition.

The term is also applied to the architectural framing of doors and windows with columns or pilasters supporting a lintel or an entablature and pediment. This type of aedicular opening was adapted from Roman use and became a common feature of classical architecture in the Renaissance and after, as seen, for example, in the interior of the Old Sacristy (commissioned 1419), S Lorenzo, Florence (*see* BRUNELLESCHI, FILIPPO, fig. 2). It was also used as a design element on façades, as at S Giuseppe, Milan, where the façade (1629–30; *see* RICCHINI, FRANCESCO MARIA, fig. 1) is composed of two tall aediculae, one superimposed on the other. This type of 'aedicular façade' became the most popular type for churches in the Italian Baroque. Another well-known example of the use of the aedicula in the Renaissance can be seen in the vestibule of the Biblioteca Laurenziana (commissioned 1523), S Lorenzo, Florence (*see* MICHELANGELO, fig. 10).

BIBLIOGRAPHY

J. Summerson: *Heavenly Mansions: An Interpretation of Gothic* (London, 1949), pp. 1–28

R. Wittkower: *Art and Architecture in Italy, 1600–1750*, Pelican Hist. A. (Harmondsworth, 1958, rev. 2/1973)

MARGARET LYTTELTON

Aegean Bronze Age civilizations. For the art produced during the Greek Bronze Age (*c.* 3600–*c.* 1100 BC) on Crete *see* MINOAN, in the Cyclades *see* CYCLADIC, and on the Greek mainland *see* HELLADIC. The Mycenaean civilization is covered under the last phase of Helladic.

□

Aegeri, Carl. *See* EGERI, CARL VON.

Aegina. *See* AIGINA.

Aelst, Pieter Coecke van, I. *See* COECKE VAN AELST, PIETER, I.

Aelst, Pieter van (*b* ?Alost; *fl* 1509–55). Flemish tapestry-maker. He was the son of Pieter van Edingen Aelst, also a weaver of tapestries, and a member of his father's workshop in Brussels. In 1509 he was cited as a restorer of Margaret of Austria's collection of tapestries. In 1517 he was paid for tapestries of David and John the Baptist made for Henry VIII, and in 1547 and 1548 he was still listed as a tapestry maker for the court of Charles V. His mark, PVA, has been found on four tapestry series, all made in collaboration with others: on five of eight *History of Noah* tapestries (Kraków, N.A. Cols), part of a series made by six Brussels workshops for the King of Poland; on seven of ten *History of Abraham* tapestries, after Bernard van Orley (Vienna, Ksthist. Mus.); on two of eight *History of Odysseus* tapestries (Hardwick Hall, Derbys, NT); and on three of six *History of Moses* tapestries (San Francisco, CA Pal. Legion of Honor).

BIBLIOGRAPHY

Thieme–Becker

L. Baldass: *Die Wiener Gobelinssammlung* (Vienna, 1920)

M. Roethlisberger: 'Deux tentures bruxelloises du milieu du XVIe siècle', *Oud-Holland*, lxxxvi (1971), pp. 88–115

——: 'The Ulysses Tapestries at Hardwick Hall', *Gaz. B.-A.*, lxxix (1972), pp. 111–25

J. Szablowski, ed.: *The Flemish Tapestries at Wawel Castle in Cracow* (Antwerp, 1972)

A. Bennett: *Five Centuries of Tapestry from the Fine Arts Museum of San Francisco* (San Francisco, 1976)

ELISE L. SMITH

Aelst, Willem van (*b* Delft, 1627; *d* ?Amsterdam, after 1687). Dutch painter. He specialized in still-lifes, as did his uncle and teacher Evert van Aelst of Delft (1602–57), whose name survives only in inventories and who died in poverty. Willem's earliest known work, a *Still-life with Fruit* (1642; destr., ex-Suermondt-Ludwig-Mus., Aachen), is likely to have been influenced by his uncle's style. On 9 November 1643 he enrolled in the Delft painters' guild and from 1645 to 1649 was in France, where he painted the *Still-life with Fruit* (1646; Stockholm, E. Perman priv. col.). From 1649 to 1656 he worked in Florence as court painter to Ferdinando II de' Medici, Grand Duke of Tuscany. There he met his fellow countrymen Matthias Withoos and Otto Marseus van Schrieck, the latter also a still-life painter, who probably influenced van Aelst's detailed and smooth style, and with whom van Aelst returned to the Netherlands in 1656—first briefly to Delft before settling in Amsterdam in 1657. Van Aelst's usual signature on paintings, *Guill*[er]*mo van Aelst*, recalls his stay in Italy, as does the (occasional) use of his bent-name 'Vogelverschrikker' (scarecrow), which appears, for example, on a *Still-life with Poultry* (1658; Amsterdam, Rijksmus.).

Van Aelst became famous for his ornate still-lifes with fine glassware, precious silver goblets, fruit and flowers. They are unparalleled in the rendering of surfaces and characterized by a bright, sometimes rather harsh colour scheme. His *Still-life with Shell* (1659; Berlin, Bodemus.) demonstrates that, although he was influenced by Willem Kalf, he preferred sharply outlined forms and more striking colour contrasts. His connection with Amsterdam is especially evident in the flower still-lifes painted between 1659 and 1663, such as *Still-life with Flowers in a Niche* (1662; Rotterdam, Boymans–van Beuningen) and *Still-life with Flowers and a Watch* (1663; The Hague, Mauritshuis; see fig.), in which the ear-shaped vases can be recognized as the work of Johannes Lutma (i), a famous Amsterdam silversmith. As well as a subtle combination of bright colours and the use of striking light effects, the Mauritshuis painting is remarkable for its asymmetrical arrangement of the bouquet, a new idea in flower painting, and one soon taken up by many other painters.

Van Aelst also specialized in still-lifes with game, at least 60 of which survive, painted between 1652 and 1681. A comparison between one of the earliest dated examples

Willem van Aelst: *Still-life with Flowers and a Watch*, oil on canvas, 625×490 mm, 1663 (The Hague, Koninklijk Kabinet van Schilderijen 'Mauritshuis')

(1653; destr. World War II, ex-Kaiser-Friedrich Mus., Berlin, see Sullivan, fig. 100) and his latest known work, *Still-life with Dead Cocks* (1681; sold The Hague, Van Marne & Bignall, 27 Jan 1942, lot 2; see Sullivan, fig. 105), shows that his successful formula was established early and remained virtually unchanged for over 30 years. At the centre of both is a marble tabletop on which birds and hunting accessories are displayed, the vertical element provided by a bird hanging down over the table. Certain items associated with hunting (game bag, bird net, hunting horn, falcon's hoods and quail pipes) are always included, yet the compositions are individually varied, and the skilful style of painting makes each one a pleasure to look at (e.g., 1664, Stockholm, Nmus.; 1668, Karlsruhe, Staatl. Ksthalle; 1671, The Hague, Mauritshuis). His pupils included Maria van Oosterwijck in Delft and Rachel Ruysch in Amsterdam.

BIBLIOGRAPHY

S. A. Sullivan: *The Dutch Gamepiece* (Totowa and Montclair, NJ, 1984), pp. 52–4, 97

Great Dutch Paintings from America (exh. cat.; The Hague, Mauritshuis; San Francisco, F.A. Museums; 1990–91), pp. 130–33, no. 1

B. P. J. BROOS

Aerial perspective. *See under* PERSPECTIVE, §III.

Aerograph. *See* AIRBRUSH.

Aeropittura. Italian movement that emerged in the late 1920s from the second wave of Futurism (*see* FUTURISM, §1), which it eventually supplanted. It was announced by the publication on 22 September 1929 of the *Manifesto dell'Aeropittura*, signed by Giacomo Balla, Benedetta (Marinetti's wife, the painter and writer Benedetta Cappa, 1897–1977), Fortunato Depero, Gerardo Dottori, Fillia, Filippo Tommaso Marinetti, Enrico Prampolini, the painter and sculptor Mino Somenzi (1899–1948) and the painter Tato (pseud. of Guglielmo Sansoni, 1896–1974). This text became the key document for the new adherents of Futurism in the 1930s. Although Marinetti had written the first Futurist manifestos, and Balla, Depero and Prampolini were senior figures within the movement, it was Dottori and younger painters who developed the new form most impressively. Building on earlier concerns with the speeding automobile, both Marinetti and the Fascist government gave particular importance to aeronautics in the 1920s, extolling the pilot as a type of Nietzschean 'Superman'.

There were various applications of the new tendency. Painters such as Tato, Ugo Pozzo (1900–1981), Tullio Crali (*b* 1910) and Renato Di Bosso (*b* 1905), who was also active as a sculptor, engaged in a naturalistic representation of the pilot's new perceptions of landscape seen from extreme angles of perspective. Other painters, such as Prampolini in *The Cloud Diver* (1930; Grenoble, Mus. Peint. & Sculp.), evolved a more abstract language of circles, spirals and intersecting shapes to evoke mood and the symbolism of flight. Other exponents of this approach included Fillia, Benedetta and Pippo Oriani (1909–72). Dottori also tended to abstract from reality, while Bruno Munari favoured geometrical abstraction. A third aspect of Aeropittura involved the movement of the pencil, brush or spray as an analogy for the movement of the aeroplane, as in Di Bosso's *Spiralling towards the Island of Garda* (1934; see G. Lista, *Futurismo*, Paris, 1985, p. 96), in which the giddy plunge to earth is represented by rotating circular forms.

The first exhibition of Aeropittura, held in 1931 at the Galleria Pesaro in Milan, included works by Dottori, Tato, Munari and Fillia. It was followed by an exhibition in Paris in 1932 and in 1934 by one in Berlin sponsored by Joseph Goebbels. By the late 1930s there were manifestos of Aeropoesia and Aeromusica, Prampolini had created Aerodanza Futurista, and manifestations related to Aeropittura had been proposed even for photography, sculpture and architecture. The movement fragmented on Marinetti's death in 1944 and dissolved completely with the collapse of Fascism at the end of World War II.

BIBLIOGRAPHY

E. Crispotti: *Il mito della macchina e altri temi del Futurismo* (Trapani, 1969; rev. 1971)

Aeropittura futurista (exh. cat., Milan, 1970)

Aeropittura (exh. cat., London, Accad. It. A. & A. Applic., 1990)

For further bibliography *see* FUTURISM, §1.

KENNETH G. HAY

Aertgen van Leyden [Aert Claessoon; Aernt Claesz.] (*b* Leiden, 1498; *d* Leiden, 1564). Dutch painter, draughtsman and designer of stained glass. Van Mander's extensive biographical account forms the basis of knowledge of the life and work of this otherwise elusive artist. According to him, Aertgen was the son of a Leiden 'fuller' or cloth finisher, but in 1516 he chose to become a painter and apprenticed himself to Cornelis Engebrechtsz. Van Mander describes the uneven quality and vast stylistic changes within Aertgen's work: at first he painted in the style of his master, then he was influenced by Jan van Scorel and later by Maarten van Heemskerck. Van Mander further reports that Aertgen's paintings represented mainly biblical stories from the Old and New Testament and that they were often beautifully composed, though painted in a 'loose and unpleasant manner'. Leiden city records confirm that a painter called Aert Claesz. was working in Leiden between 1521 and 1564 and living, as van Mander states, on the Zijdegracht (at least in 1561 and 1564). Van Mander also mentions that he made hundreds of designs for 'glass engravers' and lists a number of his paintings. One of these was rediscovered in 1969: a late triptych with the *Last Judgement* including donor portraits of the Montfoort family (1555; Valenciennes, Mus. B.-A.). This has proved the only undisputed work by Aertgen van Leyden, to whom a good many anonymous early 16th-century Leiden school drawings and paintings have been ascribed.

Attributions to Aertgen were made partly on the basis of old inscriptions on drawings and partly from references to paintings in 17th-century inventories. Relying on van Mander's description of the artist's eclectic style, scholars have tended to emphasize the stylistic differences between the works making up Aertgen's hypothetical oeuvre, notwithstanding the improbability that one artist made all the work. Taking Aertgen's rediscovered late triptych as a starting point, it is not easy to determine which of the paintings and drawings attributed to Aertgen in the past might be regarded as works from an earlier period. There is a small group of paintings grouped around the *Church Sermon* (*c*. 1530–35; Amsterdam, Rijksmus.), which, with

Aertgen van Leyden (attrib.): *Christmas Night*, oil on panel, 450×580 mm, *c*. 1511 (Paris, Musée du Louvre)

its cool palette, Italian Renaissance ornamental details in the architecture and fine portrait heads among the members of the congregation, suggests the influence of Lucas van Leyden (to whom it was long attributed, later being given to the eponymous Master of the Church Sermon).

Another group is centred around a triptych with the *Raising of Lazarus* (*c*. 1530–35; Amsterdam, Rijksmus.), which shows a completely different style and manner of painting: the figures are more stylized and elongated, but better organized within an attractive landscape. The underdrawing in the triptych reveals similarities with the exaggerated figure types in a group of drawings in chalk and ink, some of which are designs for stained-glass windows. These were attributed by Wescher to the Master of the Miracle of the Apostles after the drawing of *SS Peter and John Healing the Lame Man* (Berlin, Kupferstichkab.). The style of the figures in this last group is most closely related to that of the *Last Judgement* from 1555.

A third group of works attributable to Aertgen comprises primarily drawings in pen and ink and wash, some of which were also intended as designs for stained-glass windows. Distinguished by thick parallel brushstrokes for shading, these were assigned by Wescher to the Master of 1527, after the drawing of *Christ among the Children* (Paris, Louvre) bearing that date. With their more crowded compositions of sturdy figures placed close to the picture plane, these drawings resemble the painting *Christmas Night* (various copies, e.g. Paris, Louvre, see fig.; and Cologne, Wallraf-Richartz-Mus.), which as early as the beginning of the 17th century was thought to be by Aertgen van Leyden.

The two separate groups of drawings assembled by Wescher were discussed together for the first time under Aertgen's name by van Regteren Altena, who used the painting of *Christmas Night* as one of the starting points for the proposed reconstruction of the artist's work. Bruyn added substantially to this assembled oeuvre, but in the 1986 Amsterdam exhibition Wescher's division of the drawings was reinstated and the attributions of the paintings left open to question. Despite certain resemblances between the various groups, it seems reasonable to assume that more than one artist lies behind the works provisionally assigned to Aertgen van Leyden, especially since dozens of other painters are recorded working in Leiden at that time.

BIBLIOGRAPHY

C. van Mander: *Schilder-boeck* ([1603]–1604), fols 236v–238r

P. Wescher: 'Höllandische Zeichner zur Zeit des Lucas van Leiden', *Oud-Holland*, xlv (1928), pp. 245–54

I. Q. van Regteren Altena: 'Aertgen van Leyden', *Oud-Holland*, lvi (1939), pp. 17–25, 74–87, 129–38, 222–35

J. Bruyn: 'Twee St Antonius-panelen en andere werken van Aertgen van Leyden' [Two panels of St Anthony and other works by Aertgen van Leyden], *Ned. Ksthist. Jb.*, xi (1960), pp. 36–119

J. D. Bangs: *Cornelis Engebrechtsz.'s Leiden: Studies in Cultural History* (Assen 1979), pp. 128–43

F. Scholten: 'Technische aspecten van de *Kerkprediking* en twee andere werken uit de Aertgen van Leyden-groep' [Technical aspects of the *Church Sermon* and two other works from the Aertgen van Leyden group], *Ned. Ksthist. Jb.*, xxxvii (1986), pp. 53–74

Kunst voor de beeldenstorm [Art before the iconoclasm] (exh. cat., ed. J. P. Filedt Kok, W. Halsema-Kubes and W. Th. Kloek; Amsterdam, Rijksmus., 1986), pp. 153–72, 328–30

J. P. FILEDT KOK

Aert Ortkens [Aert de Glaesmakere]. *See* ARNOULT DE NIMÈGUE.

Aertsen [Aertsz.], **Pieter** [Lange Pier] (*b* Amsterdam, 1507/8; *d* Amsterdam, *bur* 3 June 1575). Dutch painter and draughtsman, active also in the southern Netherlands. He probably trained in his native Amsterdam but early on moved to Antwerp, where he enrolled in the Guild of St Luke as a master in 1535. In 1542 he was granted citizenship of the city. Among his pupils in Antwerp were Johannes Stradanus and later Joachim Beuckelaer, a cousin of the artist's wife and his most loyal follower. The earliest known work by Aertsen is a triptych with the *Crucifixion* (*c.* 1545–6; Antwerp, Maagdenhuismus.) for the van den Biest Almshouse in Antwerp. From 1550 Aertsen's development can be traced through a large number of signed and dated paintings. Religious works, mostly intended for churches, must have formed an important part of Aertsen's output. His early paintings seem to have been strongly influenced by other Antwerp artists, as can be seen in the van den Biest triptych, where the figures are close to those in Jan Sanders van Hemessen's background scenes. Van Hemessen's influence is also strong in the pair of triptychs showing the *Seven Sorrows of the Virgin* and the *Seven Joys of the Virgin* (the latter dated 1554; both Zoutleeuw, St Leonard).

Aertsen returned to Amsterdam in or shortly before 1557, probably in connection with important commissions for churches there. He took up residence permanently in the city and repurchased his burghership in 1563. The paintings from his Amsterdam period show a more personal character, although they form a highly fragmented group since all the large altarpieces were destroyed during the subsequent religious iconoclasm. The inner panels of a triptych showing the *Adoration of the Magi*, which was probably made for a church in Delft and of which only two wings survive (Amsterdam, Rijksmus.), form a continuous scene with a monumental figure group, which is close to the powerful naturalism of Aertsen's secular work. Other fragments surviving from this period are also large in scale and their subjects are executed in a similarly direct manner, for example the fragment from the *Adoration of the Shepherds* (Amsterdam, Hist. Mus.), which presumably formed part of Aertsen's altarpiece (finished 1559) for the Nieuwe Kerk in Amsterdam. The same is true of a number of religious pieces apparently intended for domestic interiors rather than churches (e.g. *Adoration of the Shepherds*, 1559; Rouen, Mus. B.-A.).

Aertsen's fame, however, is primarily based on his monumental genre paintings, which introduced a number of new themes into Dutch painting. The earliest examples date from the beginning of the 1550s. The *Country Feast* (1550; Vienna, Ksthist. Mus.) is the first in an extensive series of scenes of country life, mainly festivals, scenes of social gatherings (e.g. *Country Gathering*, 1557; Antwerp, Mus. Mayer van den Bergh) and popular customs (the *Egg Dance*, 1552; Amsterdam, Rijksmus.); these themes had previously been restricted to prints and drawings before Aertsen introduced them as suitable subject-matter for paintings. There were no precedents at all for his kitchen scenes (e.g. *Kitchen Scene with Christ in the House of Martha and Mary*, 1553; Rotterdam, Mus. Boymans–van Beuningen; see fig.) nor for his market scenes in which peasants offer their goods for sale (e.g. *Market Scene with Christ and the Adulteress*, 1559; Frankfurt am Main, Städel. Kstinst. & Städt Gal.). All these works are closely related in style and composition. Large half-length or full-length figures, surprisingly naturalistic in appearance, fill the canvas, while much importance is attached to still-life elements, which are rendered with unusual precision. These images are also related thematically; the frivolous, at times overtly erotic, character of the gatherings suggests that the country scenes were probably intended as a warning against excess and voluptuousness. In the kitchen and market scenes Aertsen made his intentions explicit by adding biblical scenes in the background, which form an appropriate contrast to the abundance of the main scene. Aertsen continued to make monumental genre paintings throughout his career. During his Amsterdam period he extended his repertory to include the single full-length figure (e.g. the *Kitchen Maid*, 1559; Genoa, Pal. Bianco) and the harvest scene, which he seems to have favoured in the 1560s (e.g. *Harvest Scene*; Stockholm, Hallwylska Mus.).

A special group within Aertsen's oeuvre is formed by a small group of paintings from the early 1550s that have no large foreground figures so that they resemble more closely a still-life (e.g. the *Butcher's Stall*, 1551; Uppsala, U. Kstsaml.; *see* THE NETHERLANDS, fig. 15; and the *Still-Life with Christ Visiting Martha and Mary*, 1552; Vienna, Ksthist. Mus.). Although these scenes were important for the development of the still-life as a form in itself, it must be emphasized that their significance was still determined by small biblical scenes in the background.

An important example for Aertsen must have been the scenes in brothels or in notaries' offices painted by van Hemessen during the 1530s and 1540s; these are similar to Aertsen's genre paintings in composition as well as their extremely naturalistic style. However, compared with van Hemessen, who painted in a satirical manner typical of early 16th-century Flemish genre painting, Aertsen was much more restrained in his approach. His combination of biblical and genre motifs is prefigured in the work of landscape painters such as Herri met de Bles and the Brunswick Monogrammist, whose compositions and subjects were copied by Aertsen in a number of smaller, more traditional scenes, with a high viewpoint and large numbers of small figures; these are undated, but it is possible some may have been executed in the 1540s (e.g. *Market Square with Ecce homo*; Utrecht, Catharijneconvent). Aertsen also painted several images of this type during the last year of his life, achieving a more striking structure and composition by setting his biblical subjects in idealized townscapes based on illustrations from Sebastiano Serlio's treatise on architecture (Dut. trans. by Pieter Coecke van Aelst, 1539–50).

Pieter Aertsen: *Kitchen Scene with Christ in the House of Martha and Mary*, oil on panel, 1.26×2.00 m, 1553 (Rotterdam, Museum Boymans–van Beuningen)

A number of Aertsen's drawings have been preserved, some showing designs for altarpieces or parts of altarpieces, for instance *St Martin and the Beggar* (Munich, Staatl. Graph. Samml.), a design for one of the outer panels of the triptych with the *Seven Sorrows of the Virgin*. Others show idiosyncratic designs for monumental church windows, the compositions of which seem barely restricted by the patterns of the window tracery, as in *Christ Washing the Disciples' Feet* (Bergues, Mus. Mun. Mont-de-Piété).

Initially the new possibilities introduced by Aertsen for genre and still-life painting as independent forms were not followed up by other artists in Antwerp, with the exception of Joachim de Beuckelaer. In the northern Netherlands the artist's sons Pieter Pietersz. (1540–1603) and Aert Pietersz. (1550–1612) remained strongly indebted to their father's style and imagery. It was not until about 1600 that a younger generation of Netherlandish painters developed an interest in market and kitchen scenes. By that time the genre had also become popular in Italy, Spain and the German-speaking countries, so it must really be considered a European phenomenon.

BIBLIOGRAPHY

Thieme–Becker; Wurzbach

van Mander: *Schilder-boeck* ([1603]–1604), ii, fols 238*r*, 243*r*–4*v*

F. J. van den Branden: *Geschiedenis der Antwerpsche schilderschool* (Antwerp, 1883), pp. 163–72

G. J. Hoogewerff: *De Noord-Nederlandsche schilderkunst*, iv (The Hague, 1941–2), pp. 488–580

T. H. Lunsingh Scheurleer: 'Pieter Aertsen en Joachim Beuckelaer en hun ontleeningen aan Serlio's architectuurprenten' [Pieter Aertsen and Joachim Beuckelaer and their borrowing from Serlio's architectural prints], *Oud-Holland*, lxii (1947), pp. 123–34

J. Bruyn: 'Some Drawings by Pieter Aertsen', *Master Drgs*, iii (1965), pp. 355–68

D. Kreidl: 'Die religiöse Malerei Pieter Aertsens als Grundlage seiner künstlerischen Entwicklung', *Jb. Kstwiss.*, lxviii (1972), pp. 43–108

J. A. Emmens: '"Eins aber ist nötig": Zu Inhalt und Bedeutung von Markt- und Küchenstücken des 16. Jahrhunderts', *Album amicorum J. G. van Gelder* (The Hague, 1973), pp. 93–101

A. Grosjean: 'Toward an Interpretation of Pieter Aertsen's Profane Iconography', *Ksthist. Tidskr.*, xliii (1974), pp. 121–43

M. Braman Buchan: *The Paintings of Pieter Aertsen*, 2 vols (diss., New York U., Inst. F.A., 1975) [with further bibliog.]

R. Genaille: 'Pieter Aertsen: Précurseur de l'art rubénsien', *Jb.: Kon. Mus. S. Kst.* (1977), pp. 7–96

K. P. F. Moxey: *Pieter Aertsen, Joachim Beuckelaer, and the Rise of Secular Painting in the Context of the Reformation* (New York, 1977) [with further bibliog.]

K. M. Craig: 'Pieter Aertsen and *The Meat Stall*', *Oud-Holland*, xcvi (1982), pp. 1–15

——: '*Pars ergo Marthae transit*: Pieter Aertsen's "Inverted" Paintings of *Christ in the House of Martha and Mary*', *Oud-Holland*, xcvii (1983), pp. 25–39

J. Bruyn: 'De Meester van Paulus en Barnabas (Jan Mandijn ?) en een vroeg werk van Pieter Aertsen', *Rubens and his World: Bijdragen opgedragen aan prof. dr. ir. R.-A. d'Hulst* (Antwerp, 1985), pp. 17–29

G. Irmscher: '*Ministrae voluptatum*: Stoicizing Ethics in the Market and Kitchen Scenes of Pieter Aertsen and Joachim Beuckelaer', *Simiolus*, xvi (1986), pp. 219–32

H.-J. Raupp: *Bauernsatiren: Entstehung und Entwicklung des bäuerlichen Genres in der deutschen und niederländischen Kunst, ca. 1470–1570* (Niederzier, 1986), pp. 214–23

Art before the Iconoclasm: North Netherlandish Art, 1525–1580, 2 vols (exh. cat., ed. J. P. Filedt Kok, W. Halsema-Kubes and W. Th. Kloek; Amsterdam, Rijksmus., 1986)

R. L. Falkenburg: 'Iconographical Connections between Antwerp Landscapes, Market Scenes and Kitchen Pieces', *Oud-Holland*, cii (1988), pp. 114–26

Ned. Ksthist. Jb., xl (1989) [whole issue]

HANS BUIJS

Aertsz., Jan. *See* AMSTEL, JAN VAN.

Aeschbacher, Hans (*b* Zurich, 18 Jan 1906; *d* Russikon, Zurich, 27 Jan 1980). Swiss sculptor, painter and draughtsman. He was self-taught as a draughtsman and only turned to sculpture in 1936. His early sculptural work (1936–45) mainly comprises heads and torsos in addition to heavy, life-size female nudes. These works, mainly in marble and bronze, emphasize volume and were influenced by Aristide Maillol, Charles Despiau and Wilhelm Lehmbruck. During the 1940s Aeschbacher gradually subordinated the human form to a study of the stone's own biomorphic structure. A series of amorphous *Bumps* heralded the final departure from naturalism. In 1952–3 Aeschbacher started to produce *Stelae*, a series of colossal but slender vertical structures that were influenced by the tectonic quality of Archaic Greek masonry. This new emphasis on verticality led after 1960 to the production of lighter, more airy works. Notable examples of work from this period are *Figure IV* (granite, h. 3.92 m, 1967; Bregenz, Kultzent. Schendlingen); *Figure I* (granite, h. 3.05 m, 1969; Hakone-machi, Hakone Open Air Mus.); *Figure I* (granite, h. 3.60 m, 1970; Zurich, Spital Triemli); and *Figure I* (concrete, h. 5.89 m, 1973; Zurich, Überbauung Utohof). In 1975 Aeschbacher returned to earlier themes by producing compositions using parabolic curves and concentric circles. On the other hand, however, he turned to new materials such as concrete, lava and acrylic glass. During his career Aeschbacher also executed a large number of paintings and drawings, which illustrate the same development from naturalism to abstraction.

BIBLIOGRAPHY

H. H. Holz, ed.: *Hans Aeschbacher* (Zurich, 1976) [excellent bibliog.]
B. A. Miesch-Müller: *Hans Aeschbacher (1906–1980): Eine Studie zum Gesamtwerk eines aussergewöhnlichen Schweizer Plastikers* (Zurich, 1990)

CHRISTINA MAURER

Aesslinger, Hans (*b* ?Munich, *fl* 1535; *d* Munich, 1567). German sculptor, mason and medallist. In 1536 he became a master sculptor in Munich and shortly afterwards entered the service of Ludwig X, Duke of Bavaria. He moved to Landshut in 1537 to work on the construction of the Italian wing of the ducal Stadtresidenz. In 1555 he travelled to Neuburg an der Donau to oversee the shipment of stone for the palace's chimneys. He was influenced by and may have assisted Thomas Hering, the sculptor of these chimneys. Also in 1555 he reverted to Munich citizenship.

The few surviving examples of his sculpture show him to have been an accomplished if somewhat derivative artist. Many seem to have been commissioned by Duke Albrecht V of Bavaria, who paid him an annual salary from 1558 (and perhaps as early as 1551) to 1567. Aesslinger's limestone reliefs (both 1550) of the *Massacre of the Innocents* (Berlin, Skulpgal.) and the *Judgement of Paris* (Munich, Bayer. Nmus.) are based on prints by Marcantonio Raimondi after Raphael. In addition to his carving of reliefs, Aessingler's activities as a court artist were varied. He also worked as a portraitist, identified by Habich (1932) as the Monogrammist HA of the *Albrecht V* medals of 1554 and 1558, and as the sculptor of the related life-size limestone portrait relief of *Albrecht V* (ex-Munich, Staatl. Münzsamml.). Aesslinger also worked for the Archiepiscopate of Salzburg. Between 1559 and 1561 he carved the *Resurrection* relief for the epitaph of *Archbishop Michael von Kuenburg* (Franziskanerkirche). A portrait medal (*c.* 1562) of Archbishop Johann Jakob Khnen von Belasi is attributed to Aesslinger.

BIBLIOGRAPHY

NDB; Thieme–Becker
W. Vöge: *Königliche Museen zu Berlin: Beschreibung der Bildwerke der christlichen Epochen*, iv (Berlin, 1910), pp. 167–8
E. F. Bange: *Die Kleinplastik der deutschen Renaissance in Holz und Stein* (Leipzig, 1928), pp. 94–5
O. Hartig: 'Münchner Künstler und Kunstsachen', *Münchn. Jb. Bild. Kst*, n. s. 1, vii (1930), pp. 365, 367–71; viii (1931), pp. 322–4, 327, 329, 331, 333–4, 336–7, 340, 343
G. Habich: *Die deutschen Schaumünzen des XVI. Jahrhunderts*, ii (Munich, 1932), pp. 457–60
V. Liedke: 'Die Landshuter Maler- und Bildhauerwerkstätten von der Mitte des 16. bis zum Ende des 18. Jahrhunderts', *A. Bavar.*, xxvii/xxviii (1982), pp. 34–5, 96–7
J. C. Smith: *German Sculpture of the Later Renaissance, c. 1520–1580: Art in an Age of Uncertainty* (Princeton, 1994), pp. 51–2, 288, 312, 334–5, 360, 363–4

JEFFREY CHIPPS SMITH

Aesthetic Movement. Term used to describe a movement of the 1870s and 1880s that manifested itself in the fine and decorative arts and architecture in Britain and subsequently in the USA. Reacting to what was seen as evidence of philistinism in art and design, it was characterized by the cult of the beautiful and an emphasis on the sheer pleasure to be derived from it. In painting there was a belief in the autonomy of art, the concept of ART FOR ART'S SAKE, which originated in France as a literary movement and was introduced into Britain around 1860.

The Aesthetic Movement was championed by the writers and critics WALTER PATER, Algernon Charles Swinburne and Oscar Wilde. In keeping with Pater's theories, the artists associated with it painted pictures without narrative or significant subject-matter. Dante Gabriel Rossetti took his inspiration from Venetian art because of its emphasis on colour and the decorative. This resulted in a number of half-length paintings of female figures, such as the *Blue Bower* (1865; U. Birmingham, Barber Inst.). James McNeill Whistler came closest to the ideals of the Aesthetic Movement. In such paintings as *Nocturne in Blue and Gold: Old Battersea Bridge* (*c.* 1872–5; London, Tate), he did not intend to achieve topographical accuracy: truth to nature was not one of the aims of the Aesthetic Movement. At the famous libel trial between John Ruskin and Whistler in 1878, Whistler said of this work, 'The thing is intended simply as a representation of moonlight. My whole scheme was only to bring about a certain harmony of colour' (Spencer, p. 85). Albert Joseph Moore used formalized Classical settings for his languorous female figures, which seduce the viewer by the harmonies of colour and form as well as the latent eroticism, as in *A Venus* (York, C.A.G.; for illustration *see* MOORE, (1)). The neutral titles of his pictures serve to distract from the content and discourage narrative readings. Frederic Leighton leaned even more heavily on the Classical past, and he often adopted mythological figures (e.g. *Bath of Psyche*, exh. 1890; London, Tate).

The formal arrangement of Whistler's *Nocturne in Blue and Gold* was derived from Japanese art (*see* JAPONISME), which was an important influence on designers (see fig.) as well as painters. The furniture of E. W. Godwin, for

Aesthetic Movement interior by Walter Crane; from C. Cook: *The House Beautiful* (New York, 1881) (London, Victoria and Albert Museum)

example, is simple and elegant—solid balanced by void—occasionally with painted decoration. His preferred material was ebonized mahogany, which he used for the buffet that he designed originally for himself in 1867 (e.g. London, V&A), inset with panels of embossed Japanese leather paper. In the house in London that he decorated for himself there were Japanese fans on the ceiling and skirting, and Japanese vases. Such items were imported and sold at Liberty & Co. in London and could be found in fashionable 'Aesthetic' interiors of the 1870s and 1880s.

In 1876 F. R. Leyland commissioned Thomas Jeckyll to design the dining-room (now in Washington, DC, Freer) of 49 Princes Gate, London, which was to be the setting for his collection of porcelain and Whistler's painting *La Princesse du pays de la porcelaine* (1863–4). The walls behind Jeckyll's elaborate shelving were covered with Spanish leather, which Whistler overpainted in 1877 in gold on a blue ground with motifs based on the eye and tail-feathers of the peacock; opposite his picture, which hung over the fireplace, he painted two peacocks in full plumage. In the fireplace stands a pair of wrought-iron fire-dogs designed by Jeckyll in the form of sunflowers. With the peacock, the sunflower was a characteristic motif of the Aesthetic Movement, appearing in tiles painted by William De Morgan, embroidery designed by C. R. Ashbee, chintz and wallpaper designed by Bruce J. Talbert and in the painted face of a clock (1880; London, V&A) that was probably designed by Lewis Foreman Day.

The principal link between 'art' furniture, ceramics, metalwork and textiles of the Aesthetic Movement and the QUEEN ANNE REVIVAL style of architecture favoured by Godwin (for illustration *see* GODWIN, E. W.) and Richard Norman Shaw, among others, is the fact that their creators were, in the sophistication of their designs, elevating the form of their work to the status of fine art. They were creating 'artistic' objects and buildings. They were both reforming and informing taste, a matter that was of great concern to William Morris, who, though at odds with much of the philosophy of the Aesthetic Movement, helped to extend its influence to the USA. By 1870 Morris's wallpapers were on sale in Boston, and two years later *Hints on Household Taste* (1868) by Charles Locke Eastlake was produced in an American edition. This was important to the dissemination of the notion that art should be applied to all types of decoration. In 1876 the Centennial Exposition in Philadelphia did much to familiarize Americans with reformed taste in England, and in 1882–3 Wilde made a lecture tour of the USA. Though satirized for his effeteness and posturing, he increased awareness of the Aesthetic Movement.

In the USA Christian Herter produced his own version of Godwin's 'Anglo-Japanese' style (e.g. wardrobe, 1880–85; New York, Met.), and Ott & Brewer of Trenton, NJ, made ceramics in the Japanese taste. Louis Comfort Tiffany designed jewellery and silver (e.g. vase, 1873–5; New York, Met.), as well as glass and interiors, and must be regarded as one of the principal American exponents of the Aesthetic Movement, as he was to be of Art Nouveau. John La Farge contributed decorations to the Japanese Parlor (1883–4) of the house (destr.) of William Henry Vanderbilt in New York, which was the epitome of fashionable taste. In the fine arts Whistler's influence made a brief impact on the work of Winslow Homer (e.g. *Promenade on the Beach*, 1880; Springfield, MA, Mus. F.A.) and Elihu Vedder.

BIBLIOGRAPHY

W. Pater: *Studies in the History of the Renaissance* (London, 1873, rev. 4/1893); rev. as *The Renaissance: Studies in Art and Poetry* (Berkeley, 1980)

W. Gaunt: *The Aesthetic Adventure* (London, 1945)

E. Aslin: *The Aesthetic Movement: Prelude to Art Nouveau* (London, 1969)

R. V. Johnson: *Aestheticism* (London, 1969)

R. Spencer: *The Aesthetic Movement* (London, 1972)

M. Gironard: *Sweetness and Light: The Queen Anne Movement, 1860–1900* (Oxford, 1977/*R* New Haven and London, 1984)

I. Small, ed.: *The Aesthetes: A Sourcebook* (London, 1979) [excellent intro. and reprints of texts]

In Pursuit of Beauty: Americans and the Aesthetic Movement (exh. cat., New York, Met., 1986)

□

Aesthetics. Branch of Western philosophy concerned primarily with the arts, especially the fine arts, although it often treats the concepts of natural beauty and appreciation of nature as well. The notion of fine art and that of a corresponding branch of philosophy are of relatively recent origin, dating from the 18th century, although historical antecedents of many of the particular issues now recognized as belonging to aesthetics go back to antiquity. The present usage of the term stems from its adoption in 1735 by Alexander Gottlieb Baumgarten, who employed the Greek *aisthesis* (perception) to distinguish the study of sensory, perceptual concerns, such as beauty, from logic, the study of reason and intellect.

I. Introduction. II. Western survey.

I. Introduction.

The primary subject-matter of aesthetics is the complex cultural institution in which works of art are embedded, including artistic creation, performance, appreciation, interpretation, criticism, judgement, and the various roles the arts play in people's lives and in society. The aesthetician steps back from this institution and examines it from the outside (although the line between participating in the institution and studying it is somewhat arbitrary). In the 20th century the term has come to embrace an enormously diverse collection of particular issues, with no very definite central core. However, several frequently occurring themes can be identified.

1. Defining art. 2. Objectivity and subjectivity. 3. Values. 4. Art and art-making. 5. Aesthetics and practice.

1. DEFINING ART. The central question of aesthetics, according to some, is what art is, what works of art have in common and how they differ from non-art (*see* ART). Plato and Aristotle have inspired definitions in terms of mimesis or imitation. Benedetto Croce and R. G. Collingwood took art to be essentially expression of a certain sort. Tolstoy emphasized the communication of emotion. Clive Bell and others focused on formal properties. Some definitions are based on intrinsic features of works of art themselves (*see* ART, WORK OF). According to others, whether something is art depends rather on how it was created, the effects it does, or might, have on those who experience it, how people use it or think of it, or its role or status in society. Some aestheticians understand a concept of aesthetic experience, aesthetic emotion, aesthetic attitude, artistic creation or aesthetic objects (including natural objects) to be more fundamental than that of works of art and define the latter in terms of one or another of the former.

There has been considerable scepticism about the possibility of defining art, or of defining it in a useful and illuminating way. The diversity of what is commonly called art, as well as the variety of definitions that have been suggested, the often striking similarities between some kinds of art and some things, or activities, that are not usually considered art, the absence of a clear correlation between the notion of art in non-Western and pre-18th-century cultures, and also the dramatic shifts in uses of the term in recent Western culture, can easily make it seem that any definition will be arbitrary and pointless. Whether it is worth worrying about what art means rests in large part on how important that notion is within the cultural practices being investigated. If the creation, appreciation, understanding or value of such things as paintings, novels and musical works essentially involves thinking of them as instances of art, aestheticians will want to explain what it is to think of them in that way; but if art is a category imposed on these practices from above in an attempt to understand them, there is always the possibility that another way of understanding them might be more perspicuous, one that does not classify certain things as art or certain objects, activities, emotions or attitudes as aesthetic. If the notion of art is intrinsic to the practices of one particular society but not to others, examining it will be necessary in order to understand that society; but the fact that the notion is merely a local one may suggest that it is not very fundamental, even in that society.

Uncertainties about how to define art translate into uncertainties about the scope of aesthetics. But many issues traditionally classified under that heading can be pursued independently of a definition. Rather than making and defending generalizations about art, the nature and importance of works of specific media, periods, genres or styles can be investigated. Concepts of imitation, expression and communication can be examined without troubling over whether they apply to everything properly called art. Pictorial representation, metaphor, fiction and other notions, which appear to be important outside the realm of art as well as within it, can be explored without deciding where to draw the line.

2. OBJECTIVITY AND SUBJECTIVITY. Much discussion has focused on questions about the objectivity or subjectivity of aesthetic judgements. Some speak of a 'science' of criticism whose task is to ascertain objective facts about works of art and regard aesthetic judgements, when true, as expressing such facts. There are, in contrast, various more subjective conceptions of aesthetic judgement, some of them encapsulated in the idea that 'beauty is in the eye of the beholder'. Such judgements are said to be descriptions not of the work but of the speaker's response to it, or claims about how the work does or would affect people of certain sorts, or projections on to the work of the ideas or feelings of the person who judges it. Some take judgements to be mere expressions of the speaker's feelings or responses, not allowing for truth or falsity at all. Criticism is sometimes regarded as a creative enterprise, not unlike that of an artist, rather than anything like a search for knowledge or truth.

David Hume articulated a dilemma that vexed Immanuel Kant and many others: aesthetic judgements seem to be mere matters of taste, there being nothing in the object to make them correct or incorrect; so no-one has a right to demand the agreement of others. Nevertheless, in some particular instances it seems entirely reasonable to demand agreement—it may simply seem obvious that works by Rembrandt (or Homer or Bach) are superior to those of many 'lesser' artists. More recently some have argued that multiple incompatible interpretations of a work may be equally reasonable and hence that no interpretation can be considered correct or true (even if some can be ruled out as definitely incorrect); the best that can be said about an interpretation, it is argued, is that it is 'valid', or 'interesting', or more plausible than various alternatives (*see* HERMENEUTICS). These issues are analogous to ones about the objectivity or subjectivity of moral judgements, of judgements about colours and other secondary properties, and even of hardcore scientific propositions. The status of aesthetic judgements needs to be investigated in the context of more general theories of language and truth.

3. VALUES. Aesthetics is sometimes classified as a branch of value theory, along with ethics. This ignores the

many significant issues of aesthetics that are related only indirectly, if at all, to questions of value, and it begs questions about how fundamental judgements of value are. It may be more important to understand a work than to decide how good it is. Nevertheless, questions about value have been central in the work of many aestheticians.

The most obvious ones concern evaluative judgements of particular works: judgements that a work is good, great, successful, mediocre, or better or worse than another. There are discussions of the grounds on which such evaluations are made and, of course, disputes about their objectivity or subjectivity. Some have attempted to formulate general criteria of aesthetic value, to specify what characteristics of a work or natural object constitute aesthetic merits. Some definitions of art are in effect specifications of such criteria. Only good art counts as art at all, on some accounts, and to be good art is, for instance, to be expressive or to possess 'significant form'. Those who distrust generalizations about the arts may deny that there is a single kind of value that might be called aesthetic. The fact that questions of comparative value seem so often to make little sense (e.g. which is better, the Sistine Chapel or the Taj Mahal?) may suggest that works of different kinds are valuable in very different and incommensurable ways. Some argue that no useful rules or criteria can be given for judging aesthetic value, and some consider the whole enterprise of assessing the value of a work irredeemably subjective and pointless. There are fundamental questions about how aesthetic value is related to other kinds of value, especially moral value: do moral virtues or defects in a work have any bearing on its aesthetic value or are the two entirely independent? Is there an aesthetic component to moral values—do or should distinctively aesthetic considerations play a part in determining whether someone is a good or a virtuous person or lives a good life?

In addition to questions about the merit of particular works, one can ask about the value of the institution of art as a whole, the reasons why people engage in it and the benefits they derive from it—or the ills that it is responsible for. Questions about the importance of the institution in people's lives and in society remain even for those who reject estimations of the value of particular works (*see also* PSYCHOANALYSIS AND ART; PSYCHOLOGY AND ART; and SOCIAL HISTORY OF ART).

Some consider the values of the arts—either of particular works or of the institution—to be primarily cognitive; others consider them primarily emotive. The former emphasize the role of art in expressing or communicating knowledge, understanding or insight, in its capacity to edify or instruct; the latter focus on the evocation of emotional experiences in appreciators or the expression of emotions by artists, or simply the pleasure of appreciating and creating art. However, the distinction between emotive and cognitive conceptions of art is not very clearcut. A cognitivist may hold that the insights art provides are primarily about emotions or that art promotes understanding of a special intuitive or emotive kind, perhaps one involving empathy. Appreciators' emotional experiences may be important because of their contributions to understanding—understanding either of emotions or of their objects. Emotions themselves, on some accounts, are partly cognitive or even constitute ways of knowing.

There are sharp differences among aestheticians about how special the arts are, how closely they are linked to other interests and integrated into the rest of life. For theorists influenced by Plato, Aristotle, Freud, Darwin and Marx, for instance, the importance of the arts consists in their bearing on other aspects of our lives. Art is said to provide a safe outlet for dangerous emotions, to contribute to emotional catharsis, to promote understanding and empathy. It is praised for its capacity to reveal truths about ourselves and the human condition or to improve people morally—or it is damned for obscuring the true nature of reality or for its contributions to moral depravity (*see also* IDEOLOGY). It is an effective tool of PROPAGANDA, some say, a means of achieving political domination or fomenting revolution, or a means of deepening religious faith (*see also* CENSORSHIP and RELIGION AND ART). Even when art serves as an escape from the cares of life, its benefits may be thought to consist in its capacity for psychic renewal.

There has been a strong tendency, however, deriving partly from Kant but especially prominent in the late 19th century and early 20th, to regard art as essentially autonomous from the rest of life, to think of the arts as inhabiting a separate domain with its own distinctive intrinsic values. Some recognize a special 'aesthetic emotion', stressing the disparity between it and the emotions of life (Clive Bell and Roger Fry). Some regard the representational content of visual art as being not truly aesthetic and resist works with messages or morals, or ones that are 'merely' informative or interesting. The notions of 'disinterest' as a crucial ingredient of the aesthetic attitude (Kant), of the advisability of 'distancing' works from personal needs and ends (Edward Bullough) and of 'art for art's sake' emphasize what is distinctive about the arts or the aesthetic and their separation from other aspects of life.

4. ART AND ART-MAKING. There is a nest of traditional problems concerning whether and to what extent what is important about art is located in works of art themselves, whether the artist and his act of creation, or more broadly the manner and circumstances in which the work came about, come into play, and in what ways they do. Some of these problems are discussed under the rubric of the 'intentional fallacy', but the issues are much larger than that of the relevance of artists' intentions. According to Monroe Beardsley and the 'New Critics', all that matters aesthetically about a work are its intrinsic properties, what is perceptible in it and the effects its perceptible properties have on appreciators; the artist is important only as a means whereby the work is produced.

Contrary views take many forms. Some have regarded art as essentially a matter of communication between the artist and appreciators, with the work serving as a vehicle of such communication. The appreciator's primary interest is in the person who made the work, in something like what he meant by it, rather than in properties of the work itself. The communication theorist (*see* COMMUNICATION THEORY) recognizes a fundamental difference between works of art and aesthetically regarded natural objects, since the latter seem not to be vehicles of anyone's acts of communication. According to Richard Wollheim, the task of the critic is to reconstruct the artist's creative process as it appears in the work. Some recognized fictive or apparent communicators (which arguably are to be found in the work itself)—what Wayne Booth called 'postulated authors', for instance—rather than actual ones. Nietzsche, Benedetto Croce and R. G. Collingwood emphasized the artist's creative act rather than the product of his action but did not think of it especially as an act of communicating with appreciators.

Ernst Gombrich and Nelson Goodman, among others, contend that a work of art is to be understood in a certain language or in terms of certain conventions, and that identifying the relevant language or conventions requires going beyond a work's intrinsic properties (*see also* ICONOGRAPHY AND ICONOLOGY; SEMIOTICS; and SYMBOL). Communication may involve such conventions, but in some views what an appreciator is primarily interested in is what the work itself means, given the relevant conventions, rather than what the artist meant by it or communicated by means of it. Others have claimed that works need to be understood against the background of the circumstances in which they were produced but in ways that may not involve conventions; Michael Baxandall, for instance, argued that appreciation requires awareness of the problems the work was designed to solve.

5. AESTHETICS AND PRACTICE. Many important questions of aesthetics are specific to particular genres, media or styles of art, and many of them grow naturally out of the concerns of artists and critics. In some cases aestheticians aim to provide theoretical backing for one or another side of a critical dispute or attempt to justify a particular kind of art. Assessing the significance of various techniques for representing reality in the visual arts requires consideration of what may be meant by realism and the ways in which realism of various sorts may be desirable or undesirable. These interests—and also disputes about non-objective or abstract art—lead quickly to fundamental questions about the very notion of REPRESENTATION: questions about what it is to represent something and how pictorial representation differs from verbal description; about the point or purpose of pictorial representation or of the portrayal of reality by any means. There are lively disputes concerning what might be special about the medium of photography: whether the supposedly automatic manner of their genesis makes photographs inherently more realistic than paintings and drawings; whether photographs are merely mechanical reproductions of reality lacking in artistic value. Many aestheticians have been especially intrigued by the Dadaists and Surrealists and avant-garde figures such as John Cage, Marcel Duchamp and Robert Rauschenberg—by their ready-mades, happenings, Minimalism, performance art and conceptual art. Some worried whether, for example, Duchamp's *Fountain* (1917; editioned replica, 1964; Ottawa, N.G.; for illustration *see* READY-MADE) qualifies as art, but many issues are independent of this one. Critical disputes about whether to regard such works, events or activities as frauds perpetrated on a gullible public or as refreshing escapes from stodgy tradition, or something in between, need to be adjudicated. What is the point of using indeterminate or aleatoric means in the production of works of art? What significance is there in the breakdown of traditional genre, in the extreme emphasis on newness and originality, in the blurring of the lines between artist, performer, work and audience and in the apparent disdain for value judgements and the lack of interest in 'greatness'? Avant-garde works are sometimes said to be about art itself, and many of them inevitably raise fundamental issues of aesthetics.

Other practical matters that lead quickly to larger theoretical concerns for aestheticians include questions about AUTHENTICITY and FORGERY. If it is only a work's intrinsic properties that are important aesthetically, a forgery indistinguishable from the original will be no different from it aesthetically. The communication theorist, however, can argue that the forgery and the original are vehicles of very different acts of communication, even if they are indistinguishable. There are related questions about how, and whether, to repair or reconstruct damaged works and archaeological sites—whether the aim should be to restore the appearance of the original as nearly as possible or to avoid disturbing the remains.

Other practical matters that lead quickly to larger theoretical concerns include questions about relations between form and function in architecture and design, about pornography and censorship, about public support for the arts, about choices between 'high art' and popular art, and about the nature and validity of the 'test of time' for greatness in art.

BIBLIOGRAPHY

A. G. Baumgarten: *Meditatione philosophicae de nonnulis ad poema pertinentilous* (Halle, 1735); trans. by K. Aschenbrenner and W. Holther as *Reflections on Poetry* (Berkeley, 1954)
K. Gilbert and H. Kuhn: *A History of Aesthetics* (New York, 1939)
E. Cassirer: *The Philosophy of the Enlightenment* (Princeton, 1951)
P. O. Kristeller: 'The Modern System of the Arts', *J. Hist. Ideas*, xii (1951), pp. 465–527; xii (1952), pp. 17–46
M. H. Abrams: *The Mirror and the Lamp* (Oxford, 1953)
R. Arnheim: *Art and Visual Perception: A Psychology of the Creative Eye* (Berkeley, 1966)
G. Dickie: *Art and the Aesthetic* (Ithaca, 1974)
G. Dickie and R. Sclafani, eds: *Aesthetics: A Critical Anthology* (New York, 1977, 3/1989)
R. Scruton: *The Aesthetics of Architecture* (Princeton, 1979)
J. Margolis: *Art and Philosophy* (Brighton, 1980)
N. Wolterstorff: *Works and Worlds of Art* (Oxford, 1980)
A. Savile: *The Test of Time: An Essay in Philosophical Aesthetics* (Oxford, 1982)
F. Sparshott: *The Theory of the Arts* (Princeton, 1982)
M. Baxandall: *Patterns of Intention: On the Historical Explanation of Pictures* (New Haven and London, 1985)
R. Wollheim: *Painting as an Art* (Princeton, 1987)
K. L. Walton: *Mimesis as Make-believe: On the Foundations of the Representational Arts* (Cambridge, MA, 1990)

For further bibliography *see* §II below.

KENDALL L. WALTON

II. Western survey.

Certain Classical, medieval and Renaissance concepts related to visual culture have sometimes been characterized as being part of the history of aesthetics, but this notion of aesthetic history is argued by some historians to be misleading. However, as some of the major issues of aesthetics, particularly beauty, were also discussed in earlier periods, it is reasonable at least to examine these antecedents as well as modern developments.

1. Classical. 2. Medieval. 3. Renaissance and Baroque. 4. Modern.

1. Classical. Any approach to ancient Greek thought about the arts must begin by stressing how different Greek conceptions of the aesthetic were from some influential modern conceptions. In modern aesthetics it is common to think of the aesthetic as a domain clearly bounded off from the ethical and practical, aesthetic interest as clearly distinct from practical interest. For the ancient Greeks, this was not the case. Poetry, visual art and music were all taken to have an ethical role, in virtue of their form as well as in virtue of their content, and a citizen's interest in them was understood to be an interest in pursuing questions about how best to live. Aesthetic innovations were to be assessed for their contribution to human action and practical (usually communal) self-understanding. This attitude was reinforced by the civic institutions in which the arts were embedded; the major dramatic festivals of Athens were civic religious festivals at which citizens gathered together. Looking at the staged action and across the amphitheatre at one another, they characteristically saw in the performance an occasion both for the moral education of the young and the communal exploration of tensions and complexities in civic norms of excellence. Because of this view of the goal of art, aesthetic assessment was, like Athenian social assessment, a democratic business; every citizen was encouraged to engage in aesthetic/ethical reflection.

One sign of the thoroughgoing unity of the aesthetic with the ethical can be seen in the Greek word *kalon*. Usually translated as 'beautiful' in some contexts, as 'noble' or 'fine' in others, it is in reality a univocal word, giving evidence of the Greek belief that only what is ethically fine is pleasing to behold and that visible beauty is a sign of excellence.

The ancient Greeks are frequently described as coolly contemplative, devoted to ideals of perfect symmetry and proportion. Although there is an element of truth in this portrayal, as the Pythagorean theories of cosmic mathematical harmony did have influence on Greek thought about the arts, far more central to the Greek experience of the arts was the activity of the emotions. Most Greek thinkers about art emphasized the powerfully emotive effects of music, dance, drama, even painting and sculpture. They did not, however, hold that emotions are unintelligent, mere bodily drives or surges of affect. They tended to think of grief, fear, anger, love etc as involving (or even as being) value judgements, and as educable through the alteration of those judgements. This is one reason why they believed that works that arouse and shape emotion can have such a profound effect on moral development.

A central concept in ancient Greek aesthetic thought has often been seriously misunderstood. The crucial word *mimesis* has frequently been translated as 'imitation', and it has been assumed that a thinker who described the function of art as *mimesis* meant that the goal of art is the literal copying of natural reality through the production of objects that are as similar as possible, in all respects, to some concrete model. In fact an interest in *mimesis* implies no such view. The word is closely linked to the verb *mimeisthai*, which denoted the behaviour of actors in the dramatic performance of the mimes and meant simply 'to behave like a mime actor'. A study of the early evidence shows that, through this comparison, *mimeisthai* came to mean 'to represent something by conveying some of its characteristic traits'. *Mimesis*, then, is usually better translated as 'representation', and in the context of a view of representation that does not insist on literal naturalistic similarity. In no case was there an interest in the literal copying of all characteristics or on the use of a particular, rather than a generic, model. The emphasis was on the (usually very stylized) displaying of some features that were conventionally allowed to signify the sort of thing that the artist wished to represent, and the object was almost always a type of thing rather than a concrete particular.

Aesthetic thought in the Greek world began with the Homeric poems, in which the poet/speaker ascribes the origins of his art to the Muses, claiming that his art can educate because it embodies divine knowledge. The didactic poet Hesiod (*fl c.* 8th century BC) told a more complex story. His poet/speaker draws attention to the elusive character of poetic information by ascribing to his Muses the claim that they can make lies look like truth, but they can also tell the truth, if they so choose. These influential passages set the stage for a debate about the reliability of the poets as educators that continued throughout the history of Greek aesthetic theory and was broadened to take in mimetic art as a whole.

A particularly rich source of early reflection about art and education is the work of the comic poet Aristophanes (*c.* 450–385 BC), who commented at length on his own art and poetic art in general. His work *Frogs*, produced in 405 BC, shows a competition in the underworld between the shades of the poets Aeschylus and Euripides; the winner will return to help the city in its political crisis. Poetic statements, formal and metrical devices, and even musical choices—all arts are assessed for their ethical contribution, as all participants agree that poets are the city's primary teachers and guides. The play's defence of the morality of poetry gains force from the fact that sophists and rhetoricians had recently been drawing attention to the subversive and potentially deceptive powers of literary speech. The Aristophanic victor, Aeschylus, argued successfully that the poet is a much needed source of ethical truth and that the emotionally stirring features of poetic art are themselves ethically valuable.

Philosophers of the 4th century BC undertook a newly detailed examination of artistic techniques, always with a view to art's ethical and social role. The popular thought of the early 4th century on these subjects is probably well exemplified in a passage from the *Memorabilia* of Xenophon, in which Socrates is shown advising painters and sculptors how to render visually the characteristic signs of different sorts of souls. As usual, it is stressed that the artist will truly please only if he represents what is admirable. The passage gives a good example of the concept of *mimesis* at work.

The two greatest aesthetic thinkers of ancient Greece, Plato and Aristotle, agreed with their tradition that the function of art is to promote the ethical education of citizens and that formal and stylistic devices should be assessed with that end in view. They also agreed that most great art, and especially dramatic poetry, reveals a passionate interest in the mutable and undependable things of this world, teaching the beholder to cultivate such attachments. They differed sharply, however, in their assessment of the value of these attachments and therefore concerning their judgement on art. Plato's *Republic* argues that, since we wish citizens to believe that the good person is sufficient unto him or herself for good living, we should rule out works that represent or arouse emotions such as grief, fear and pity, which presuppose that things beyond our control do matter greatly. Aristotle's *Poetics* replies, arguing that the reversals displayed in the great tragic plots, and the pity and fear they arouse in their audience, are educational in a good sense, conducive to a true understanding of the relationship between the good human life and the goods of fortune.

The Hellenistic era in both Greece and Rome was especially rich in high-level aesthetic reflection. The two major philosophical schools, Epicureans and Stoics (*see* STOICISM), agreed that philosophers concerned with the 'therapeutic' education of the passions of the soul must also be concerned with the aesthetic form in which philosophical teaching is expressed. They reflected in complex ways about the contribution of visual art, music and, above all, literary forms to that education. Although Epicurus preferred to write in a plain non-literary style, the great Epicurean poet Lucretius (*c.* 99–55 BC) defended the importance of a certain type of poetry in education. The Stoics found in all the arts signs of nature's purpose, praising tragic poetry above all for its insight into the violence of passion. Meanwhile, literary and rhetorical theorists of many types, writing in both Greek and Latin, advanced the detailed study of literary form and style; and specialized works such as *De architectura* by VITRUVIUS promoted the understanding of aesthetic structure in the plastic arts.

See also NEO-PLATONISM.

BIBLIOGRAPHY

H. Koller: *Die Mimesis in der Antike* (diss., U. Berne, 1954)
G. Sörbom: *Mimesis and Art* (Uppsala, 1966)
J. Pollitt: *Art and Experience in Classical Athens* (Cambridge, 1972)
D. Russell and M. Winterbottom, eds: *Ancient Literary Criticism* (Oxford, 1972)
D. Russell: *Criticism in Antiquity* (London, 1981)
M. C. Nussbaum and S. Halliwell: *The Fragility of Goodness: Luck and Ethics in Greek Tragedy and Philosophy* (Cambridge, 1985)
S. Halliwell: *Aristotle's Poetics* (Chapel Hill, 1986)

MARTHA C. NUSSBAUM

2. MEDIEVAL. Evidence for medieval aesthetics may arguably be sought in the sophisticated, reflective discussions, mostly of theologians, about the concept of beauty. These formed a minor part of investigations into God's attributes and his relation to the created world. They were stimulated by one particular text, *De divinis nominibus* by Pseudo-Dionysius (*c.* AD 500), which included 'Beauty' and 'Beautiful' among the various names denoting God's attributes (chapter 4). Medieval readers believed Pseudo-Dionysius' works were the products of Dionysius, the Areopagite converted by St Paul (Acts xvii.34). As such, they had enormous prestige and were discussed in great detail by 13th-century theologians. Pseudo-Dionysius stated that not only does all beauty derive from God but also that, like goodness, beauty is a quality possessed by all things that exist. This presented the commentators with two main problems—in what way can all things be said to be beautiful and what is the relationship between this universal sense of 'beautiful' and the normal meaning of the word, by which some things are described as 'beautiful' and some not? Among the four medieval theologians who discussed the concept of beauty most acutely, Robert Grosseteste (*c.* 1170–1253) and Albert the Great (*c.* 1200–80) attempted to answer only the first of these questions, whereas Ulrich of Strasbourg (*d*?1278) and THOMAS AQUINAS tried also to answer the second.

In order to explain Pseudo-Dionysius' text, the theologians turned to an ancient Greek definition, according to which beauty results from symmetry together with colour. They found this definition in Cicero and Augustine (AD 345–430), but whereas Cicero and Augustine saw it as a criterion for deciding which particular things are beautiful or not, Grosseteste and Albert turned it into a way of explaining how all things are beautiful. Grosseteste's metaphysics made it easy for him to assert that all things possess colour and symmetry. Colour, most medieval thinkers held, is an effect of light, and Grosseteste saw the whole universe in terms of the irradiation of light from its primal source. Grosseteste also considered that the universe is designed according to the laws of geometry and so was happy to allow that everything in it is symmetrically proportioned. In his view light and symmetry are not different, contrasting requirements for beauty; light, he explained, is 'the most unitary of things and, by its equality to itself, the most fittingly proportioned'.

Grosseteste's metaphysics of light found few adherents. Albert the Great chose rather to use the Aristotelian concepts of matter and form to explain how all things combine colour or, more generally, the resplendence of light, with proportion and so are beautiful. Commenting (*c.* 1250) on *De divinis nominibus* , he proposed that the beautiful is 'the resplendence of a substantial or accidental form over proportioned and bounded parts of matter'. A well-proportioned, coloured body provides an obvious example of beauty: it is beautiful by the 'resplendence' of its colour, an accidental form, over its proportionate parts. Less obviously, everything made of matter and form must be beautiful. Matter is pure potentiality; a substantial form makes it actual by delimiting it and proportioning it to itself. For example, it is the form of a table that delimits matter into the proportions of a table. The form could be said, in Albert's terms, to be 'resplendent' over the parts of the table proportioned and delimited by it, and the table therefore to be beautiful.

Ulrich of Strasbourg was Albert's pupil and, in explaining how all things are beautiful, he followed his master closely. In his *De summo bono* (*c.* 1262–72)—a commentary on Pseudo-Dionysius in the form of a treatise—he devoted a section (ii/4) to the concept of beauty. Like Albert, he defined beauty as 'form . . . resplendent like light over that which is formed', and argued that, in one sense, matter is always proportioned to its form. All things, therefore, are beautiful. Unlike his teacher, however, Ulrich went on to explain the way in which 'beautiful' is said of some things but not of others. There are a number of senses in which matter can be more or less well-proportioned to its form: by its disposition, its quantity, the number of its parts and the relation of each part's size to that of the whole. It is this variation that accounts for differences in bodily beauty. So, for example, a man whose humours are well-balanced is more beautiful than one in whom a particular humour, such as melancholy, prevails; a body that is too small is not beautiful, nor is a man who has lost a limb, nor someone whose head is disproportionate to his body.

Unlike Ulrich, Aquinas did not devote a whole chapter or article to the concept of beauty, and his views must be gathered from a passage in his commentary (*c.* 1267) on *De divinis nominibus* and from isolated remarks in his *Summa theologiae* (I and IaIIae). Sometimes when Aquinas referred to beauty he was following the tradition of Pseudo-Dionysius and meaning the beauty that all things possess. For him, as for Albert and Ulrich, this beauty results from the combination of form with matter proportionate to it. More often, however, the context shows that he was speaking about the beauty that belongs only to some things, which, according to him, 'are pleasing when they are seen' or 'heard'. He explained that beauty is like goodness in that both attributes make things desirable, but whereas the desire towards something good is to obtain it, the desire for something beautiful is to see or know it. Beauty gives pleasure just by the disinterested awareness of it. Yet, although beauty is connected with cognition, there are objective criteria for it. At one point (ST I.q.39, a.8), Aquinas listed wholeness, proportion and brightness, although initially (ST I.q.5,a.4ad 1) he mentioned only proportion and explained that our senses, being themselves (according to Aristotle) 'a sort of proportion', take delight in proportioned things.

An interesting, but isolated, contrast to all these theories of beauty is found in the work of the Polish writer Witelo (or Erazm Ciołek; *c.* 1233–78), who discussed beauty not in the context of theology but in the course of his treatise on optics, the *Perspectiva* (early 1270s; IV. 148–50). He considered only visual beauty and took it for granted that some things are beautiful and some ugly. Instead of trying to provide a single definition for beauty, he set about listing some of the aspects that, individually or in appropriate combination, make an object's beauty manifest to the sight. He included colour, size and setting but also a number of pairs of contraries, such as continuity and discontinuity, transparency and opacity, similarity and dissimilarity. For, as he explained, the continuity of a green meadow is pleasing to the eyes, but stars that are separate and distinct are more beautiful than those very close together. Witelo also allowed that often 'custom makes beauty': for example, the shape and colour of the human body that the Moors might find pleasing are different from those that would please a Dane. However, although he considered beauty to be multiform and relative to the perceiver, Witelo nonetheless treated it as an objective feature of things—for example, beautifully painted workmanship is beautiful even when the onlooker, hindered by darkness, fails to see the painting and recognize its beauty.

It is open to question, however, whether these medieval theories about beauty were, as many historians believe, aesthetic theories. Although many aestheticians, especially in the 19th century, made beauty a central concept in their theories, there is an important difference between such philosophers and the medieval thinkers. Nineteenth-century aestheticians argued or assumed that there is a close relation between the concept of beauty and the products of such arts as music, painting, sculpture, architecture and literature. By contrast, no such relation was envisaged by medieval thinkers. Some were concerned only with beauty as an attribute of all things; for others, who examined beauty as an attribute that some things have and some lack, there was no special connection between beauty and human artifice. Ulrich of Strasbourg thought of visible beauty solely in terms of the human body, while Aquinas's only illustration of a beautiful thing is the Son of God. Even Witelo, who included among his examples of beautiful objects such products of artifice as smooth silks, regular handwriting and rounded columns, declared that while well-painted or well-sculpted figures are beautiful, 'the works of nature are more so'.

In the Middle Ages 'art' (Lat. *ars*) was a term with a very wide range of meaning: any productive skill from making shoes to making cathedrals was an 'art', and a number of non-productive intellectual disciplines such as grammar, arithmetic, physics and biology were also sometimes called 'arts'. Medieval treatises on some of these individual arts exist, including those arts that now interest aestheticians, but these were designed to be strictly practical handbooks, and conceptual reflection on their subjects is almost entirely absent. It is therefore still debatable whether a concept of art close to the modern one was implicit within medieval culture and can be discerned from the artefacts of the period. Although historians have combined theories derived from medieval artefacts with the theories about beauty that medieval scholars developed, often including medieval comments and technical discussion about various arts, the resulting mixture, presented to the reader as a homogeneous 'medieval aesthetics', can mislead rather than enlighten.

BIBLIOGRAPHY

Pseudo-Dionysius: *De divinis nominibus* (early 6th century AD), iii of *Patrologia Graeca*, ed. J.-P. Migne (Paris, 1857; Eng. trans., 1920)

Albert the Great: *Super Dionysium de divinis nominibus* (*c.* 1250), ed. P. Simon (Münster, 1972)

Ulrich of Strasbourg: *De summo bono* (*c.* 1262–72), II.1–4, ed. A. de Libera (Hamburg, 1987)

T. Aquinas: *In librum beati Dionysii de divinis nominibus expositio* (*c.* 1267), ed. C. Pera (Turin and Rome, 1950)

——: *Summa theologiae* (1268–72); Eng. trans., ed. T. Gilby and others (London and New York, 1964–80)

C. Baumker, ed.: *Witelo: Ein Philosoph und Naturforscher des XIII. Jahrhunderts* (Münster, 1908) [with extracts of *Perspectiva*]

E. de Bruyne: *Etudes d'esthétique médiévale*, 3 vols (Bruges, 1946)

H. Pouillon: 'La Beauté, propriété transcendentale chez les scolastiques (1220-1270)', *Archives d'histoire doctrinale et littéraire du moyen âge*, xv (1946), pp. 263–329 [with extracts of R. Grosseteste]

E. de Bruyne: *L'Esthétique du moyen âge* (Leuven, 1947; Eng. trans., New York, 1969)

U. Eco: *Il problema estetico in Tommaso d'Aquino* (Milan, 1954); Eng. trans. as *The Aesthetics of Thomas Aquinas* (London and Cambridge, MA, 1988)

——: 'Sviluppo dell'estetica medievale', *Momenti e problemi di storia dell'estetica* (Milan, 1959); Eng. trans. as *Art and Beauty in the Middle Ages* (New Haven and London, 1986)

W. Czapiewski: *Die Schöne bei Thomas von Aquin* (Freiburg, Basle and Vienna, 1964)
W. Tatarkiewicz: *History of Aesthetics*, ii (The Hague and Paris, 1970)

JOHN MARENBON

3. RENAISSANCE AND BAROQUE. Three main themes were developed and repeated in aesthetic thought between 1400 and 1600: synthetic beauty, a theme with literary origins; spiritual beauty, a notion ultimately derived from NEO-PLATONISM; and physical beauty, a type based on measurements and proportions that stem from Aristotelian philosophy. To these should be added the feminine ideal of the Renaissance, as exemplified in Petrarchan poetry. These ideas, formulated in the 16th century, remained the main basis for discussion until the end of the 17th.

(i) Synthetic beauty. Pliny relates that the painter Zeuxis, in order to represent Helen of Troy, selected the five most beautiful maidens of the town of Crotona and synthesized their most striking features into a perfect image. This idea that in order to produce a perfect image the artist must select and combine the best parts of everything belongs to a topos that permeated other disciplines such as rhetoric and ethics. In Renaissance art theory the notion appears in Leon Battista Alberti's treatise *De pittura* (1435) and it was repeated in every art treatise of the 16th century. Indeed, it affected art education, as the young artist was expected to distil his own style from the study of nature and the great masters, as well as the Antique. The notion of synthetic imitation developed further, giving rise to what was later called eclecticism. This doctrine is prefigured by Giulio Camillo in his treatise on imitation (1544), which suggests that, since the best art has already synthesized the best of nature, artists need only look at other works of art to gather a synthesis of the perfect visible. A few years later Paolo Pino in his *Dialogo di pittura* (1548) wrote that the best painting would be drawn by Michelangelo and coloured by Titian; but the culmination of this view is to be found in a sonnet attributed to Agostino Carracci, describing the best art as a synthesis of the talents of the best painters.

(ii) Spiritual beauty. It is through Marsilio Ficino's commentary (1469) on Plato's *Symposium*, rather than the original text, that Plato's doctrine of love became increasingly popular in the 16th century. Platonic love is a spiritual journey. It begins with the visual or auditory perception of beauty and ends with the ecstatic vision of God (Ficino, *Commentary*, VII, 14). Given the incorporeal nature of true beauty, it can only be perceived by incorporeal senses—sight and hearing (V. 2). In Baldassare Castiglione's *Il libro del Cortegiano*, Pietro Bembo speaks of this type of love whose strength 'guides the soul from the particular beauty of one body to the universal beauty common to all bodies' (IV, 68). This spiritual ascent begins with visual perception. These texts were influential, in so far as they led to an emphasis on spiritual love at the expense of physical love and beauty. They explain the emergence of an aesthetics based on the appreciation of incorporeal qualities perceived through the eye or the ear. From this emerged a vocabulary suited to describe purely visual qualities, which, in turn, were easily transferable to works of art.

Agnolo Firenzuola in his *Dialogo delle bellezze delle donne* (Florence, 1548) offers a good example of this phenomenon of transposition. This author fully agreed with Ficino on the effect of beauty, as a reflection of divine beauty, although he limited its field to beautiful women. While he defined physical *bellezza* (beauty) in terms of measurements and proportions (fols 73ff), he opposed it to spiritual *bellezza*, of which he identified six qualities: *leggiadria*, *venustà*, *grazia*, *vaghezza*, *aria* and *maestà*. English approximations to these are, consecutively, 'prettiness', 'beauty', 'grace', 'charm', 'demeanour' and 'dignity', but they remain beyond the reach of any verbal definition. Blended in ideal proportions, these features will produce a likeness of the idea of the perfect woman, capable of plunging man into a mystic state of divine ecstasy.

In the field of the visual arts, where categories such as *venustà*, *grazia* and *aria* were currently applied, these notions never implied that images could lead the soul to the contemplation of God through the graphic expression of divine beauty. Notions such as *bellezza* and *grazia*, however, became the mundane criteria through which writers spoke about the style and qualities of painting in an empirical, if not intuitive, fashion. Their use is connected to another theme, introduced by Castiglione, the concept of *sprezzatura*, i.e. the specific quality emerging from something difficult done with ease and elegance. It is precisely this criterion, used in conjunction with the notion of grace, that Lodovico Dolce, in his *Dialogo della pittura* (1557), invoked in order to praise Raphael and Titian and to attack Michelangelo's *Last Judgement* (1536–41; Rome, Vatican, Sistine Chapel), not only for its lack of decency but also, from a stylistic point of view, for the affectation and absence of grace of the figures that 'display all the difficulty of the art'.

(iii) Physical beauty and the Petrarchan ideal. The Renaissance ideal of feminine beauty is inspired by the love poetry of Petrarch. The physical features of Laura, Petrarch's mistress and muse—long blond hair, fine eyebrows, dark sparkling eyes, slightly rosy cheeks, long and slender neck, firm and white breasts, well-proportioned arms on which no veins can be seen and small, delicate white hands, together with perfect proportions—were paired with spiritual qualities in the appreciation of paintings of beautiful women. Pino confirmed this when referring to the 'true beauty' (*vaghezza*) of his art in his *Dialogo di pittura*: 'The painter is not worthy of praise for depicting all his [feminine] figures with pink cheeks and blond hair . . . but true beauty is nothing else than *venustà* and *gratia*; it is generated through a deep understanding of things as well as a proportion in things.' The opposition set by Pino between physical characteristics and painterly qualities is exemplified in Benedetto Varchi's *Della beltà e grazia* (*c.* 1550), which opposes a 'spiritual and platonic beauty' (*grazia*) to an Aristotelian beauty 'which consists in the proportion of the limbs'. This notion is further developed by the sculptor Vincenzio Danti, in his *Trattato delle perfette proporzioni* (1567), with the Aristotelian addition that beauty lies not only in perfect proportions but

also in the harmony between the shape of an object or a limb and the function it is intended to fulfil.

(iv) Later modifications. Towards the end of the 16th century there is a slight shift in ecclesiastical writers such as Gabriele Paleotti, writing in 1582, or Gregorio Comanini in 1592, who seem to favour naturalism. This coincides with the Counter-Reformation belief that more realistic representation in religious art, especially in scenes of martyrdom, would inspire strong religious emotions in the viewer. The naturalistic ideal, adopted by painters such as Caravaggio—who pointed to Nature as his only master—was severely criticized by most 17th-century writers on both sides of the Alps. They favoured instead a careful and discerning blend of naturalism and idealism. This is, in Italy, Giovanni Pietro Bellori's conception, expressed in his *L'idea del pittore, dello scultore e dell'architetto* (Rome, 1672; preface to his *Vite*), or in France the theory of the *beau idéal* expressed by writers such as Roland Fréart (*Idée de la perfection de la peinture* . . ., Le Mans, 1672) or André Félibien (*Entretiens*, 1666–88), both of whom shared an intense admiration for Raphael and Poussin. They defined *le beau idéal* as a golden mean between visual appearances and conceptual beauty.

The main problem for Renaissance and Baroque aesthetics is that its basis in a philosophical, if not theological, conception of beauty—a divine beauty, originally meant to induce divine ecstasy—was treated in a purely rhetorical way to express intuitions and empirical perceptions. As a result aesthetic thought always oscillated between fictively invoking painting as a representation of divine ideas and conceiving representation as a synthetic transcription of visual perceptions. In the late 17th century Roger de Piles addressed this dilemma in writings given final expression in the *Cours de peinture par principes* (Paris, 1708). His notions of 'truth in painting' led him to explore the link between the state of mind of the artist—the *enthousiasme*—transposed in the work and that felt by the viewer: a new kind of aesthetic, based on the work of art itself.

BIBLIOGRAPHY

D. Mahon: *Studies in Seicento Art and Theory* (London, 1947)
E. Panofsky: *Idea* (Eng. trans. by J. S. Peake, New York, 1968)
E. Cropper: 'On Beautiful Women, Parmigianino, *Petrarchismo* and the Vernacular Style', *A. Bull.*, 58 (1976), pp. 374–94
C. Dempsey: *Annibale Carracci and the Beginnings of Baroque Style* (Munich, 1977) [on the notion of eclecticism]
D. Summers: *Michelangelo and the Language of Art* (Princeton, 1981)
T. Puttfarken: *Roger de Piles' Theory of Art* (London, 1985)

FRANÇOIS QUIVIGER

4. MODERN. Aesthetics was conceived as a philosophical discipline within European rationalist and empiricist thought of the 17th and 18th centuries, the term being invented by the German philosopher Alexander Gottlieb Baumgarten. In the late 18th century Immanuel Kant formulated a highly influential, rigorous aesthetic theory about judgements of beauty and the sublime. In the 19th century Georg Wilhelm Friedrich Hegel's important writings were instrumental in moving aesthetic theories away from a concern with beauty to an emphasis on art and its cognitive significance. In the 20th century aesthetic theories of many different kinds were developed by American and European thinkers as diverse as John Dewey, Benedetto Croce and Martin Heidegger, and within such different intellectual traditions as phenomenology, semiotics, structuralism and hermeneutics.

(i) 17th–18th centuries. (ii) 19th century. (iii) 20th century.

(i) 17th–18th centuries.

(a) The Cartesian rationalist tradition. Although RENÉ DESCARTES himself wrote very little about the arts, the spirit of Cartesian rationalism pervaded classical writing on poetry and painting in France and England in the 17th and early 18th centuries, with its emphasis on system and rules and its praise of reason. The actual rules of poetry and painting defended, however, derived from Aristotle, Horace (65–8 BC) and other Classical sources. In such treatises as *De arte graphica* (1668) by CHARLES-ALPHONSE DU FRESNOY and *Cours de peinture par principes avec une balance des peintres* (1708) by ROGER DE PILES, the central idea is that the aim of painting is to please and instruct by means of the imitation of nature. These theorists distinguished different genres of painting and established canonical styles for each, the 'firm' style for heroic painting, the 'polished' for pastoral and so on. The greatest exponent of this type of art theory was JOSHUA REYNOLDS, whose *Discourses* to the Royal Academy (delivered between 1769 and 1790) summarize the Classical ideal with elegance, clarity and authority. Reynolds formulated a hierarchy of styles and genres, each with its own rules of composition, the 'grand style' of Raphael and Michelangelo being the highest. He urged the painter to imitate Nature, by which he meant Nature under the influence of great painters. Being true to nature meant representing the general rather than the particular, the ideal rather than the actual. When, in *Les Beaux Arts réduits à un même principe* (1746), Abbé CHARLES BATTEUX first articulated the modern system of the fine arts, he united poetry, painting and the other arts under the principle of the imitation of beautiful nature.

In Germany rationalism had a further, different effect on the development of thought about art. ALEXANDER GOTTLIEB BAUMGARTEN, writing in 1735, distinguished two spheres of cognition, that of thought or intellect and that of perception. Just as logic is the science of intellect, so, Baumgarten proposed, there should be a science of sensory perception or *Ästhetik*, a term he coined from the Greek *aisthesis* (perception), which would establish rules governing 'concrete sensory discourse' in general (i.e. the realm of paintings, poetry, music etc). Among Baumgarten's successors in the rationalist tradition was GOTTHOLD EPHRAIM LESSING, who argued in his celebrated essay *Laokoon* (1766) that poetry and painting are not analogous as the UT PICTURA POESIS doctrine had suggested, because the 'signs' utilized in poetry and painting are of radically different sorts. Since the medium of poetry is a temporal sequence of sounds, it can express only temporal objects, namely actions, whereas the medium of painting is spatial and can therefore express only spatial objects, namely bodies. Like Baumgarten, Lessing used a deductive method to establish his conclusions.

(b) The British empiricists. While the rationalists provided the term 'aesthetics' as well as the method and some of the assumptions governing classical criticism, it was the British empiricists who established aesthetics as an

independent philosophical field. The empiricists by and large accepted the Classical doctrines that art is an imitation of nature, that it pleases us by instructing us, and that it should imitate the general rather than the particular. The questions they asked concerned not the work of art itself but the experience of the spectator or critic of art, in particular the nature of good taste and aesthetic pleasure. ANTHONY ASHLEY COOPER, 3rd Earl of Shaftesbury, thought that we have a special intuitive insight or 'inward eye' that enables us to distinguish in an immediate way between the good and the bad, the beautiful and the ugly. In his *Inquiry Concerning Beauty, Order, Harmony, Design* (1725) FRANCIS HUTCHESON echoed this idea but reconstructed the 'inward eye' in empiricist terms as a type of sense perception: we have an internal sense of beauty much like the external senses of sight, hearing and so on. Moreover, while for Shaftesbury beauty is a property actually inhering in things, for Hutcheson it is a pleasant experience or feeling, which he called a pleasant 'idea', and the sense of beauty is 'our power of receiving this idea'. By contrast, other theorists such as Archibald Alison (1757–1839), in his *Essays on the Nature and Principles of Taste* (1790), explained beauty as arising from the pleasant associations an object or a scene may evoke in us.

In general, the empiricists recognized two kinds of beauty or 'pleasures of the imagination': the beauty of nature, often identified in terms of proportion and symmetry, and the beauty of imitations in literature, painting and the other 'imitative' arts. Beauty, however, is not the only recognized source of aesthetic pleasure. The category of the PICTURESQUE applies to landscapes and pictures exhibiting intricacy, roughness, variety and irregularity, and in his *Philosophical Inquiry into the Origin of our Ideas of the Sublime and Beautiful* (1757) EDMUND BURKE identified THE SUBLIME as whatever delights us yet is associated with pain and danger, such as the obscure, the powerful or the infinite. Burke's treatise influenced DENIS DIDEROT, whose *Salon* writings from 1759 to 1781 stress emotional effect rather than imitative accuracy and foreshadow Romanticism.

The empiricist view that aesthetic experience is a subjective feeling of pleasure caused by our perception of certain qualities in things raised the problem of how there can be an objective standard of taste. This problem was particularly acute for associationist theories of beauty. By contrast, Hutcheson and Burke thought that a standard of taste was assured because we are so constituted biologically that we naturally perceive all the same things as beautiful. For DAVID HUME, taste, or the faculty whereby we discriminate beauty, is simply the sophisticated exercise of our ordinary faculties of judgement and sensitivity. In his essay 'Of the Standard of Taste' (1757), Hume argued that the standard of taste is set by a particular group of people, the 'true judges', who are characterized as those who are particularly sensitive, disinterested and experienced in judging. Ultimately, however, Hume was sceptical about how absolute the standard would turn out to be.

(c) Kant and Romanticism. The aesthetic theory of the late 18th century and the early 19th was largely conditioned by two influences: one was the philosophy of the German philosopher IMMANUEL KANT and the other was the rather amorphous body of ideas and attitudes that constituted ROMANTICISM. Kant gave a new and more sophisticated answer to Hume's questions concerning the aesthetic judgement, the beautiful and the standard of taste and thereby furthered Baumgarten's project of founding a rational science of aesthetics. In his *Kritik der Urteilskraft* (1790) Kant argued that the judgement of taste is subjective, since it is a feeling of pleasure, but that nevertheless it can justifiably lay claim to universal acceptance, since the pleasure is both disinterested, i.e. unconcerned with personal practical goals, and also derived from the harmonious interaction of the imagination and the understanding, which are faculties shared by all knowing subjects. However, since to ascribe beauty to something is not to ascribe a concept to it, there can be no objective canons of beauty as envisaged by the rationalists. In his discussion of the aesthetic judgement, Kant, like his predecessors, took his examples as readily from nature as from art, and his emphasis on harmony of design ('purposiveness without purpose') as the source of a disinterested aesthetic delight tended to demote the importance of subject-matter in art as opposed to form. However, in his discussion of fine art, Kant gave a central place to 'aesthetic ideas': the artist tries to communicate through sensuous representations something that goes beyond the world of sense.

Romantic artists exalted the importance of art, seeing it as a source of insight and a means of self-expression. Art was no longer thought of as the mere imitation of an inert nature but as the expression of feeling and imagination. The mind has creative powers beyond both sensuous perception and reason; the imagination in particular is a source of intuitive insight into the true nature of reality. Furthermore, this insight into reality is possible because nature is an organic whole, imbued with spirit, and Man is a part of that whole. For the Romantics the artistic genius is the man of insight who can effect the union of real and ideal, nature and freedom, conscious and unconscious.

Some of these Romantic ideas had their source in Kant's philosophy, in particular the emphasis on the constructive powers of the mind and the importance attributed to the imagination as a source of human knowledge. However, the Romantics were critical of several elements in Kant's philosophy. JOHANN GOTTFRIED HERDER and FRIEDRICH SCHILLER, for example, criticized Kant's sharp division between reason and sense, thought and feeling. For Schiller, man arrives at a true 'harmony of the faculties' through a synthesis of impulses that is achieved in aesthetic experience. JOHANN WOLFGANG VON GOETHE and the English poet and essayist Samuel Taylor Coleridge (1772–1834), among others, objected to Kant's conception of man as rational and free in opposition to brute nature, which is governed by the categories of space, time and causality: instead they conceived of nature as an organic unity, with man expressing his sense of this unity through the creation of organically unified works of art.

(ii) 19th century. For the post-Kantian idealists, GEORG WILHELM FRIEDRICH HEGEL and FRIEDRICH SCHELLING, art was capable of revealing important insights about man and his relation to the universe. According to Hegel, art, religion and philosophy are three different modes of

consciousness whereby man arrives at an awareness of Absolute Spirit, i.e. of the rational necessity that governs the universe. For Hegel art, religion and philosophy are different ways in which Absolute Spirit reflects upon and becomes aware of its own activity. Individual human minds are the vehicle of self-awareness for Absolute Spirit. Hegel had much in common with the Romantics: both thought of nature and spirit as one, of art as a mode of self-expression and self-realization, and of the artist as one who seeks the infinite through the finite. However, in one crucial respect Hegel was a successor to Kant rather than the Romantics, for his entire system is based on the idea of reason, of the way in which rational necessity comes to self-awareness.

According to Hegel's *Vorlesungen über die Ästhetik* delivered in the 1820s (pubd posthumously, 1835), art is that particular mode of consciousness whereby ideas are presented in a 'sensuous' form rather than through myth or theology (religion) or through conceptual thought (philosophy). Like Schelling and the Romantic theorists, Hegel argued forcefully that art is not the mere imitation of an inert nature. Instead he adopted Kant's idea that the fine arts express 'aesthetic ideas', arguing that 'the work of art stands in the middle between immediate sensuousness and ideal thought'. Hegel's discussion of fine art powerfully asserts the cognitive importance of art, the importance of theme or subject-matter, and the way in which theme cannot be abstracted from the sensuous medium that conveys it. Hegel also emphasized art's historicity; his idea that art develops teleologically influenced several generations of art historians such as ALOIS RIEGL, HEINRICH WÖLFFLIN and ERWIN PANOFSKY.

Although ARTHUR SCHOPENHAUER was a contemporary of Hegel, his influence was not felt until much later. In *Die Welt als Wille und Vorstellung* (1819) Schopenhauer argued that underlying the world of appearances or 'representations' is a terrible, aimless force or energy, which he called the 'Will' and which is the basis of reality. Art is one of the few ways in which we can achieve temporary release from our subjection to the Will. When we experience a work of art (with the exception of music, which is the direct manifestation of the Will), we are contemplating the Platonic Ideas instantiated in that work of art, such as mass and extension in architecture. In Schopenhauer the disinterested Kantian aesthetic judgement becomes an aesthetic experience, in which we are 'outside' ordinary experience, lost in rapt contemplation of the art object. Schopenhauer's ideas influenced FRIEDRICH NIETZSCHE, writing in the 1870s and 1880s, who, however, thought that art is an affirmation of life rather than a means of withdrawing from it.

Hegel's emphasis on history gave support to the contemporary rediscovery of the art of the past, particularly that of the Middle Ages. In *The Stones of Venice* (1851) and elsewhere, the Victorian art critic JOHN RUSKIN glorified the Middle Ages as a period in which Christian faith and morality were expressed in both art and social arrangements. Ruskin saw in art a means of moral salvation in a mechanistic, scientific age dominated by the crisis in faith, the philosophy of utilitarianism, Darwin's evolutionary theory and the overwhelming social changes brought about by the Industrial Revolution. WILLIAM MORRIS and the ARTS AND CRAFTS MOVEMENT were greatly indebted to Ruskin, as were the Pre-Raphaelite painters whom he defended (*see* PRE-RAPHAELITISM). A similarly idealized view of art as a means of moral salvation and a way of promoting Christianity and human brotherhood is to be found in *Chto takoye isskustvo?* ('What is art?'; 1898), by LEO TOLSTOY.

The ART FOR ART'S SAKE movement, initiated by JAMES MCNEILL WHISTLER and OSCAR WILDE and taking its inspiration from WALTER PATER, together with the closely linked AESTHETIC MOVEMENT, expressed the reaction to the scientific spirit of the age in a different form. By contrast, the scientific spirit in aesthetics itself can be seen in the birth of experimental aesthetics, in the psychological theory of empathy of THEODOR LIPPS, which influenced Wölfflin and BERNARD BERENSON, and in evolutionary aesthetic theories such as that of Herbert Spencer (1820–1903), which claimed that art is a form of play resulting from excess energy generated in the human struggle for survival.

(iii) 20th century.

(a) Early 20th-century aesthetic theories. The Sense of Beauty (1896) by GEORGE SANTAYANA is a naturalistic, psychological theory of aesthetics that studies the aesthetic experience of spectators as they contemplate beautiful art or nature. Beauty itself is defined as 'pleasure regarded as a quality' of the object contemplated. Beauty of expression occurs when the associations we have to an object are experienced as one of its pleasant qualities. For Edward Bullough, writing in 1912, the aesthetic experience is no longer mere pleasure but a special psychic act of 'distancing'. To adopt the aesthetic attitude to a fog at sea, for example, is to ignore its practical implications and to focus on its 'aesthetic qualities'. These turn out to be not Schopenhauerian essences but qualities of the sensuous surface before us. Thus began a new empiricist tradition, in which aesthetic experience was analysed as awareness of qualities in their sensuous immediacy together with their sensuously grasped formal relations, and in which expression was reduced to immediately experienced expressive qualities (*see* FORMALISM). These ideas owed much to the art critics ROGER FRY and CLIVE BELL, the heirs of the Art for Art's Sake movement and propagandists for Cézanne and the Post-Impressionists. Fry and Bell argued that representational content in painting is of aesthetic interest only as form and that only form can produce the 'aesthetic emotion'.

The Italian idealist philosopher BENEDETTO CROCE had a very different view. In his *Estetica come scienza dell'espressione e linguistica generale* (1902) Croce defended the view that art is 'intuition', by which he meant a type of non-conceptual knowledge that contrasts with 'logic' understood as knowledge of general concepts. According to Croce, intuition is identical to expression, since the articulation of a cognition is its expression. However, expression does not entail embodiment in a medium; as soon as the artist has formulated the intuition completely in his mind the work of art is complete. The audience can grasp the work only by imaginatively recreating the artist's intuition for themselves. R. G. Collingwood (*see*

COLLINGWOOD, (2)) adopted many of Croce's ideas and developed them into his own theory of art (1938) as the expression of emotion, in which expression is defined as a cognitive process of clarifying and articulating a hitherto inchoate emotion.

Others also argued that art gives us a special intuitive insight into reality: both HENRI BERGSON and the later Santayana followed Schopenhauer in claiming that the artist can penetrate essences in a way that the discursive intellect cannot, while for JACQUES MARITAIN, who based his theories on Aristotle and Thomas Aquinas, the artist's non-conceptual knowledge is to be achieved through a type of mystical 'affective union' between artist and world.

By contrast, *Art as Experience* (1934) by the American philosopher JOHN DEWEY is a materialist, instrumental theory of art that emphasizes the important role of art in any good, productive life and condemns the rigid separation between art and life characteristic of formalism. In making a work of art the artist expresses an emotional experience in a medium. To understand the work, the audience recreates this experience. However, for Dewey, unlike Croce, the art object is a sensuous thing, imbued with meanings and values. Monroe Beardsley's *Aesthetics: Problems in the Philosophy of Criticism* (1958) combines an empiricist view of the aesthetic object as essentially perceptual with a Deweyan conception of aesthetic quality.

(b) The influence of linguistics. New developments in logic and linguistics in the 20th century led Charles Morris and SUSANNE K. LANGER to articulate different versions of a semiotic aesthetics. Following the work of Charles Sanders Peirce (*see* SEMIOTICS), Morris described the situation of signification or communication as one in which an 'interpreter' takes a 'sign' or 'sign vehicle' to refer to a 'referent' or 'designatum'. Morris followed Dewey in claiming that the expressive art object has what Peirce called 'iconic' meaning, since the expressive work of art displays its values and meanings in the medium itself. Susanne Langer distinguished between 'discursive' symbolic forms such as language, which have a syntax, a vocabulary and semantic rules for combining meaningful elements into meaningful wholes, with 'presentational' forms that lack these features but instead refer in a global way like Morris's iconic signs. In *Feeling and Form* (1953) she claimed that the forms in a work of visual art, considered abstractly, present an image or 'virtual object' that is apparent only to sensory perception and which symbolizes virtual space (pictures), virtual kinetic volume (sculpture) or virtual place (architecture).

Whereas Langer assumed that pictures symbolize iconically or presentationally, the art historian Ernst Gombrich argued that even the literal representational content of a picture is not entirely iconic but that art is in part, like language, a conventional symbol system. Gombrich argued in *Art and Illusion* (1960) that representation always begins with the making of a more or less conventional 'schema', which is then matched against reality. The most rigorous and systematic investigation of the idea that art is a language is Nelson Goodman's *Languages of Art* (1968), which considers each art form as a type of symbol system. Goodman attacked the notion that pictures are iconic and claimed that what counts as a picture is a function of the kind of symbol system to which it belongs. Thus pictures are symbols in systems that are syntactically and semantically dense and relatively replete.

The French structuralists, beginning with the work of the Swiss linguist Ferdinand de Saussure (1857–1913), also thought of works of art as operating like a language in the sense that their meaning is a function of the symbol system or 'langue' to which they belong (*see* STRUCTURALISM). According to Saussure, different sign systems or 'langues' carve up the set of 'signifiers' (sound patterns) and 'signifieds' (concepts) in quite different ways, so that different 'langues' define different systems of sound patterns and different systems of concepts that can only be understood in terms of other concepts in the system. JACQUES DERRIDA took this idea of language as a 'system of differences' and maintained that, consistently pursued, it leads to the 'post-structuralist' conclusion that meaning is never stable and that the 'fixed centres' or central concepts used to anchor a philosophical system or the meaning of a work of art can always be 'deconstructed' or shown to undermine themselves. There have been some attempts at 'deconstructivist' architecture in which the building is viewed as a palimpsest, a multi-layered collage of meanings with no central 'truth', and in which even the most basic architectural assumptions (such as that buildings exist for human use) are deconstructed (*see* DECONSTRUCTION and POST-STRUCTURALISM).

(c) The influence of phenomenology and Existentialism. In continental Europe PHENOMENOLOGY produced theories about the nature of the aesthetic object. According to the Polish philosopher Roman Ingarden, there is a distinction between the physical work of art and the phenomenological, intentional aesthetic object, which has no physical properties, only qualities directly given to sense perception. JEAN-PAUL SARTRE had a somewhat different view according to which the aesthetic object is an unreal object, which is both constituted and apprehended by the imagination (*see* EXISTENTIALISM). By contrast, Mikel Dufrenne's *Phénomenologie de l'expérience esthétique* (1953) argues that the aesthetic object is a phenomenal object, rather like Langer's 'virtual' image, which nevertheless has 'worlds': a represented world of persons, places and things and an expressed world of qualities that give the work its unified, person-like character.

For MARTIN HEIDEGGER and MAURICE MERLEAU-PONTY art had a metaphysical significance. For Heidegger, as for Derrida, there are no fixed centres or concepts such as 'self' or 'world' to which we can anchor our philosophical systems. *Dasein* (literally: 'being-there') consists in an active engagement in the world conceived of as primarily a world of equipment or tools to use rather than a world of objects to know. Throughout his career Heidegger attacked the notion of truth as correspondence between an inner and an outer world, claiming that the dichotomy made no sense, as we are necessarily 'in-the-world'. In his later essays on aesthetics Heidegger talked of truth as 'disclosure' or 'revelation' and claimed that this is the primary function of works of art. Thus van Gogh's picture *Old Boots with Laces* (Amsterdam, Rijksmus.), of peasant boots, discloses what the boots are in truth: there is a 'happening of truth at work', the revelation of a 'world' (the peasant's mode of being).

Like Heidegger, Merleau-Ponty saw no dichotomy between self and object, only a world of tools and tasks, but he differed from the other phenomenologists in thinking of consciousness as necessarily embodied: the body is the 'in-between realm' through which consciousness interacts with the world. Merleau-Ponty claimed that paintings function as emanations from this perceiving body.

(d) Other developments. The idea that a work of art is a cultural artefact whose meaning is determined by its role in society and history is implicit in Heidegger and also appears in the work of the analytic philosophers Arthur Danto and Richard Wollheim. In *The Transfiguration of the Commonplace* (1981) Danto argued that a work of art cannot be identified independently of an 'artworld', that is, independently of a historical context of art theory through which it achieves meaning. Wollheim borrowed the notion from the later writings of Ludwig Wittgenstein (*see* WITTGENSTEIN, (2)) of a 'form of life' and in *Art and its Objects* (1968) claimed that art itself is a form of life essentially embedded in institutions and practices. This view is to be sharply distinguished from the idea that art should serve as a means of promoting a particular form of society, as is suggested, for example, by the Marxist critics György Lukács (1885–1971) and WALTER BENJAMIN (*see also* MARXISM). It should also be distinguished from the Institutional Theory of art, which claims that what counts as an artwork is determined not by its having a meaning or by formal or expressive qualities, but solely by its playing the right kind of role in the right kind of social and artistic institutions.

Interest in the somewhat passive idea of 'aesthetic experience' has given way to a focus on the concept of interpretation, conceived of as an active search for the meaning of a work of art. HERMENEUTICS, the tradition stemming from Heidegger and his pupil Hans-Georg Gadamer (*b* 1900) treats interpretation as a linguistic process of translation from the author's 'language' to that of the audience. However, since a work of art cannot transcend its historical context, the artist's original intentions can never be fully recovered. The art object necessarily has 'gaps' that need to be filled in by the interpreter. By contrast, for semiotic and structuralist theories, interpretation is not a process of recovering artists' intentions but a matter of focusing on the work of art itself and the structures to which it belongs.

BIBLIOGRAPHY

A. A. Cooper (Shaftesbury): *Characteristics of Men, Manners, Opinions, Times*, 3 vols (London, 1711); ed. J. M. Robertson, 2 vols (New York, 1900)

F. Hutcheson: *An Inquiry concerning Beauty, Order, Harmony, Design* (London, 1725); ed. P. Kivy (The Hague, 1973)

A. G. Baumgarten: *Meditationes philosophicae de nonnulis ad poema pertinentilous* (Halle, 1735); trans. by K. Aschenbrenner and W. Holther as *Reflections on Poetry* (Berkeley, 1954)

E. Burke: *A Philosophical Inquiry into the Origin of our Ideas of the Sublime and Beautiful* (London, 1757); ed. J. Boulton (Notre Dame, IN, 1968)

D. Hume: *Of the Standard of Taste* (Edinburgh, 1757); ed. J. Lenz in *Of the Standard of Taste and Other Essays* (Indianapolis, 1965)

G. E. Lessing: *Laokoon: Oder über die Grenzen der Malerei und Poesie* (Berlin, 1766); Eng. trans. as *Laocoon*, ed. E. A. McCormick (Indianapolis, 1962)

J. Reynolds: *Discourses on Painting and the Fine Arts Delivered at the Royal Academy* (London, 1778); ed. S. Mitchell as *Discourses on Art* (Indianapolis, 1965)

I. Kant: *Kritik der Urteilskraft* (Berlin, 1790); Eng. trans. by J. C. Meredith (Oxford, 1952)

F. Schiller: *Über die ästhetische Erziehung des Menschen—in einer Reihe von Briefen* (Stuttgart, 1793); Eng. trans. by E. M. Willoughby and L. A. Willoughby as *On the Aesthetic Education of Man* (Oxford, 1967)

F. W. J. Schelling: *Über das Verhältniss der bildenden Künste zu der Natur* (Munich, 1807); Eng. trans. by D. Stott (Minneapolis, 1989)

A. Schopenhauer: *Die Welt als Wille und Vorstellung* (Leipzig, 1818, rev. 1844); Eng. trans. by E. F. J. Payne, 2 vols (Colorado, 1958)

G. W. F. Hegel: *Vorlesungen über die Ästhetik* (Berlin, 1835, rev. 1842); Eng. trans. by T. M. Knox as *Lectures on Fine Art*, 2 vols (Oxford, 1975)

F. Nietzsche: *Die Geburt der Tragödie aus dem Geiste der Musik* (Leipzig, 1872; Eng. trans., New York, 1968)

G. Santayana: *The Sense of Beauty* (New York, 1896/*R* 1955)

L. Tolstoy: *Chto takoye isskustvo?* (Moscow, 1898); Eng. trans. by A. Maude (Indianapolis, 1960)

B. Croce: *Estetica come scienza dell'espressione e linguistica generale* (Bari, 1902); Eng. trans. by D. Ainslie (London, 1922; rev. 3/Boston, MA, 1978)

G. Santayana: *Reason in Art* (New York, 1905)

E. Bullough: '"Psychical Distance" as a Factor in Art and as an Aesthetic Principle', *Brit. J. Psychol.*, v (1912), pp. 87–98

J. Maritain: *Art et scolastique* (Paris, 1920)

R. Ingarden: *Das literarische Kunstwerk: Eine Untersuchung aus dem Grenzgebeit der Ontologie, Logik und Literaturwissenschaft* (Halle, 1931; Eng. trans., 1973)

J. Dewey: *Art as Experience* (New York, 1934)

R. G. Collingwood: *The Principles of Art* (Oxford, 1938)

M. Dufrenne: *Phénoménologie de l'expérience esthétique*, 2 vols (Paris, 1953; Eng. trans., Evanston, 1973)

S. K. Langer: *Feeling and Form* (New York, 1953)

M. Beardsley: *Aesthetics: Problems in the Philosophy of Criticism* (New York, 1958, Indianapolis, 2/1981)

H.-G. Gadamer: *Wahrheit und Methode* (Tübingen, 1960; Eng. trans. rev. 2/New York, 1989)

E. H. Gombrich: *Art and Illusion* (London, 1960)

J. Derrida: *De la grammatologie* (Paris, 1967); Eng. trans. by G. C. Spivak (Baltimore, 1976)

N. Goodman: *Languages of Art* (Indianapolis, 1968)

R. Wollheim: *Art and its Objects* (New York, 1968, rev. 1980)

M. Heidegger: *Poetry, Language, Thought*, trans. and ed. by A. Hofstadter (New York, 1971) [selection of writings]

A. Danto: *The Transfiguration of the Commonplace* (Cambridge, MA, 1981)

For general bibliography *see* §I above.

JENEFER ROBINSON

Aethelwold [Æthelwold; Ethelwold], Bishop of Winchester (*b* Winchester, *c.* AD 908; *d* Beddington, Surrey, 1 Aug 984; *fd* 1 Aug). Anglo-Saxon saint, Church leader and patron. With Dunstan, Archbishop of Canterbury (*reg* 959–88), and Oswald, Archbishop of York (*reg* 972–92), he was the moving spirit behind the English monastic revival of the late 10th century.

Aethelwold's career began at the court of King Athelstan (*reg* 924–39). After ordination he joined Dunstan's reformed monastic community at Glastonbury. About 954 he established his own monastic house at Abingdon. According to later tradition, he was a skilled worker in metals and personally contributed to the embellishment of the abbey church. Appointed Bishop of Winchester in 963, he introduced reformed communities into both Old and New Minsters and established a regular monastic life in several other centres, notably Ely, Peterborough and Thorney. He was an enthusiastic patron: the masterpiece of the Winchester School of illumination, the Benedictional of St Aethelwold (London, BL, Add. MS. 49598; *see* ANGLO-SAXON ART, fig. 9), was made for his personal use by his chaplain, the monk Godeman, later Abbot of Thorney. He ordered major additions to his cathedral church, consecrated with great splendour in 980. He was also responsible for the translation of the relics of St Swithin to a new shrine within the cathedral in 971.

See also WINCHESTER, §§II and III, 1(i).

BIBLIOGRAPHY

F. Wormald: *The Benedictional of St Ethelwold*, Faber Library of Illuminated Manuscripts (London, 1959)

M. Winterbottom, ed.: *Three Lives of English Saints* (Toronto, 1972)

B. Yorke, ed.: *Bishop Æthelwold: His Career and Influence* (Woodbridge, 1988)

JANET BACKHOUSE

Aetion (*fl* late 4th century BC). Greek painter. Pliny (*Natural History*, XXXV.78) placed Aetion in the 107th Olympiad (352–349 BC) and (XXXV.50) included him in a list of painters who used a palette restricted to four colours: white, yellow, red and black. Cicero (*Brutus* xviii.70), however, listed him among those painters who used a wider palette. It is likely that the four-colour palette was a restriction adopted occasionally by many artists who, in other works, used more than four colours. None of Aetion's work survives, but Pliny ascribed to him pictures of *Dionysos*, *Tragedy and Comedy*, *Semiramis Rising from Slavery to Royal Power* and an *Old Woman Carrying Lamps and Attending a Bride*, whose modesty was apparent. His most famous painting depicted the *Wedding of Alexander the Great and Roxane*, and it was perhaps painted to celebrate it (327 BC). It was described by Lucian of Samosata (*Aetion* iv–vi), who saw it in Italy. Lucian added that when the painting was shown at Olympia, Proxenides, one of the chief judges of the games, was so impressed by it that he gave his daughter to Aetion in marriage. Alexander the Great stood best man. The painting included erotes playing with Alexander's armour, a motif repeated in several Roman wall paintings with reference to Mars and Hercules. Another Aetion, also assigned to the 107th Olympiad, appears in a list of bronze sculptors drawn up by Pliny (XXXIV.50); this is probably an interpolation from XXXV.78.

BIBLIOGRAPHY

W. Helbig: *Wandgemälde der vom Vesuv verschütterten Städte Campaniens* (Leipzig, 1868), nos 320 and 1137–9

J. Overbeck: *Die antiken Schriftquellen zur Geschichte der bildenden Künste bei den Griechen* (Leipzig, 1868/*R* Hildesheim, 1959), nos 1067, 1073, 1728(2), 1754, 1937–41

O. Elia: *Pitture murali e mosaici nel Museo Nazionali di Napoli* (Rome, 1932), no. 121

C. HOBEY-HAMSHER

Afạmiya. *See* APAMEIA.

Affecter. *See* VASE PAINTERS, §II.

Affleck, Ray(mond Tait) (*b* Penticton, BC, 20 Nov 1922; *d* Montreal, 16 March 1989). Canadian architect. He graduated in architecture from McGill University, Montreal, and began post-graduate studies at the Eidgenössische Technische Hochschule in Zurich. Between 1949 and 1953 he worked for various Montreal-based architectural firms before setting up his own practice in the city in 1953; it later became Affleck, Desbarats, Dimakopoulos, Lebensold, Sise (1955–69). The group worked with I. M. Pei and Partners on Place Ville Marie (1958–63), then, with Affleck as principal designer, on the Stephen Leacock Building (1961–5) and the Place Bonaventure (1964–8), all in Montreal. Another notable work was the National Arts Centre complex, Ottawa (completed 1969), in which Affleck and company devised a handsome, low-rise group of buildings, including a 2300-seat opera house, an 800-seat theatre and a 300-seat studio workshop. Affleck also taught for many years at the School of Architecture, McGill University (1954–8; Visiting Professor from 1965). Affleck is judged to be one of the few major Canadian architects to establish a reputation abroad. His concerns were tied less to a building's ultimate appearance than to people's experience of and movement through its internal spaces. His ideas for internal 'streets' were emulated by a generation of Canadian architects: he thought that indoor and outdoor systems should be interconnected and punctuated by 'events', which could take the form of garden areas or terrace restaurants, with shopping and office levels adjacent, all woven together with easy pedestrian access up, down or through the complex. His schemes were often gigantic, multipurpose buildings, and from the late 1960s Affleck and his partners (reorganized as Arcop Associates in 1969–70) were responsible for many substantial projects in Canada. In later years Affleck, sensitive to conservation movements, designed Maison Alcan (1980–83), Montreal, in which he preserved *in toto* a venerable 19th-century residence and two commercial buildings (1894 and 1928), all of differing heights, linking them at the rear with a full-length modern atrium; its long, pedestrian mall is lined with cosmopolitan-style cafés and boutiques.

BIBLIOGRAPHY

A. Schouvaloff: *Place for the Arts* (Liverpool, 1970)

'Centre National des Arts, Ottawa, Canada', *L'Archit. Aujourd'hui*, 169 (Sept–Oct 1973), p. 31

L. Whiteson: *Modern Canadian Architecture* (Edmonton, Alta, 1983), pp. 214–17, 254–7, 270

□

Affleck, Thomas (*b* Aberdeen, 1740; *d* Philadelphia, PA, 5 March 1795). American cabinetmaker of Scottish birth. He trained as a cabinetmaker in London. In 1763 John Penn, Governor of Pennsylvania, invited Affleck to Philadelphia, where the latter opened a shop on Second Street in the Society Hill area. He made stylish mahogany furniture (sold 1788; e.g. Philadelphia, PA, Cliveden Mus.; armchair, Winterthur, DE, Mus. & Gdns) for the governor's mansion at Lansdowne, PA, and for many of the most prominent families in the city, including the Mifflins, the Whartons and the Chew family at Cliveden.

A Quaker and Loyalist, Affleck refused to participate in the Revolution (1775–83), and he was banished for several months to Virginia in 1777. By the end of the war, however, he was the most prosperous cabinetmaker in the city. His Loyalist sympathies seem to have been forgiven because he was given a number of important commissions, including furniture, for the Pennsylvania Hospital, Congress Hall and the first Supreme Court Chamber in the City Hall, all in Philadelphia.

The large body of surviving furniture attributed to Affleck, which includes wall-brackets, chairs (New York, Met.), grand chest-on-chests and elaborately carved tallboys or high chests-of-drawers, confirms his reputation as the leading cabinetmaker in Philadelphia in the 18th century. Much of his furniture was derived from designs in his personal copy of *Gentleman and Cabinet-maker's Director* by Thomas Chippendale (i). He also made furniture in the Neo-classical style. After his death his son Lewis G. Affleck carried on the business for a short time until he went bankrupt.

BIBLIOGRAPHY

W. Hornor: *Blue Book, Philadelphia Furniture: William Penn to George Washington* (Philadelphia, 1935/*R* Washington, DC, 1977)

OSCAR P. FITZGERALD

Affry, Adèle d'. *See* MARCELLO.

Afghanistan. Country of some 647,500 sq. km in the middle of the steppe and desert zone of Eurasia. It is bounded on the north by the Amu (Oxus) River and the republics of Central Asia, on the west by Iran and on the south and east by the Indian subcontinent. In the Pamir Mountains to the north-east, a narrow tongue of land known as the Wakhan corridor links the country with China (see fig. 1). Located at the crossroads of major trade and migration routes between the Mediterranean, Central Asia, India and China, the region has been subjected to diverse cultural influences throughout its history.

I. Introduction. II. Historical survey. III. Historiography. IV. Museums and collections.

I. Introduction.

1. Geography and climate. 2. History. 3. Language and ethnic groups. 4. Religion and iconography.

1. GEOGRAPHY AND CLIMATE. The physical geography of Afghanistan is very varied and includes formidable mountain ranges, fertile valleys and barren deserts. The dominant mountainous core is the Hindu Kush, an extension of the Karakoram and Pamir mountains that stretches south-west for some 965 km and has peaks rising to some 5180 m in height. To the north, between the Hindu Kush and the Amu River lie the semi-desert plains of Turkestan. South of the Hindu Kush is a transitional zone of plateaux with broad mountain valleys. To the west and south-west the mountains gradually descend to the stony and sandy deserts of the Iranian plateau. North of Kabul the Kuh-e-Baba range ('Grandfather Mountains') of the Hindu Kush is the watershed for four great Afghan rivers: the Kabul River flowing east to the Indus, the Kunduz flowing north into the Amu River, the Hari Rud flowing west to Herat and the Helmand, which flows southwards into the marshy lake of Hamun Helmand in Sistan. There are several passes through the mountainous core of the country linking north to south and east to west, and traffic is also channelled along the rivers or round the mountain mass. The low-lying plains and deserts between Herat and Kandahar provide an easy route for traders and invaders travelling eastwards into the Indus Valley.

The climate is generally dry, with wide variations in temperature. Snow falls in the mountainous areas above *c.* 1830 m from October onwards and blocks the passes for much of the winter. In the plains of Turkestan most of the rain falls as spring thunderstorms, and there are sometimes disastrous floods when this water combines with melting snow from the mountains. In winter there is rain in the Herat area and the rivers are swollen with melt water in the spring, but in the Helmand basin there is virtually no rainfall in any season. The Jalalabad Valley has a winter rainfall and can, with irrigation, grow rich crops.

2. HISTORY. The limited documentation of prehistoric sites in Afghanistan has produced evidence of a small Palaeolithic hunter–gatherer population, part of which was established by about 20,000–15,000 BP in the northern foothills of the Hindu Kush at cave sites such as Aq Kupruk II (Ghar-i Mar). The domestication of sheep, goats and possibly cattle seems to have taken place by about the 9th millennium BC. Some of the Neolithic sites produced pottery, but there are no architectural remains associated with this phase of the transition from hunter-gathering to food production. Knowledge of bronze technology and embossing by the late 6th millennium BC is indicated by finds of sheet metal from Aq Kupruk II. From about 3500 BC onwards there is evidence of trade links associated with the export of lapis lazuli, particularly at Shahr-i Sokhta in Sistan. The lapis lazuli, which seems to have derived from the Badakhshan region in north-east Afghanistan, especially the Kokcha Valley, was exported all over the Near East. Mundigak and the related sites of Deh Morasi and Said Qala in southern Afghanistan show the development of urbanization from around the early 4th millennium BC to the 2nd.

From the *Ṛg veda* (*see* INDIAN SUBCONTINENT, §I, 2(i)), it appears that the Aryans passed through Afghanistan *c.* 1500 BC. Later Aryan migrants from Transoxania settled on the Iranian plateau and established the Achaemenid empire in the regions between the Mediterranean and the Indus River by the 6th century BC. In 330 BC the last Achaemenid, Darius III (*reg c.* 336–330 BC), was defeated by Alexander the Great, who went on to conquer the eastern satrapies in Afghanistan, bringing them into direct contact with Hellenism from the west. Alexander's successors, the SELEUCIDS, retained control in Bactria (the Amu River region north of the Hindu Kush and east of Merv and Herat) but lost the territories of Kabul and Kandahar *c.* 305 BC to the Mauryans from India.

About 250 BC Diodotus, the governor of Bactria, declared independence from the Seleucids. Subsequent Greco-Bactrian kings extended their territory south of the Hindu Kush to Kabul and Kandahar and invaded India (*see* BACTRIAN AND INDO-GREEK MONARCHIES). After the initial successes of Menander (*reg c.* 170 BC), the kingdom became fragmented under several rulers, partly as a result of increasing pressure from nomadic Sakas or Scythians migrating southwards from Central Asia. One group, the Yueh-chih, occupied Bactria *c.* 130 BC. The remaining Indo-Greek kings to the south were replaced by Indo-Scythian rulers of the house of Azes in the 1st century BC and by INDO-PARTHIANS under Gondophares (*reg c.* AD 20–50) in the 1st century AD.

In the 1st century AD the KUSHANA tribe united the Yueh-chih confederacy and established a powerful empire that expanded from Central Asia across Afghanistan to north-west India. The extent and stability of this empire

1. Map of Afghanistan; those areas with separate entries in this dictionary are distinguished by CROSS-REFERENCE TYPE

encouraged the growth of international trade along the silk route from China across Afghanistan to the Indus River ports and thence by sea to Alexandria and Rome. Under the third king, Kanishka I, the Kushanas patronized Buddhism, stupas and monasteries were established throughout Afghanistan, and missionaries followed Kushana traders across Central Asia to China. The chronology of this period is still disputed, the era of Kanishka being attributed to various dates between AD 78 and the 3rd century (*see also* INDIAN SUBCONTINENT, §IV, 5(ii)). What is clear is that the Kushanas were defeated by the rising power of the SASANIANS (*c.* 224–651) in the 3rd century. Afghanistan suffered again in the 5th century from the invasions of the Hephthalites (White Huns), who in turn were overthrown in the mid-6th century by the Turki Shahis, allied to the Sasanians. Raids into western Afghanistan in the late 7th century gave the Arabs control of Sistan and HERAT. From the 9th century, western Afghanistan was ruled by local Islamic dynasties: the SAMANIDS (*reg* 874–999) based in Bukhara and the Saffarids (*reg* 867–1495) based in Sistan. Eastern Afghanistan remained an independent non-Muslim kingdom, centred at Kabul, under the Turki Shahis and their successors the Hindu Shahis, until conflicts with the GHAZNAVIDS (*reg* 977–1186), an Islamic dynasty originating from GHAZNA, forced a transfer of the Hindu Shahi capital to Hund, on the Indus River east of Peshawar.

The first Ghaznavid, Sebüktigin (*reg* AD 977–97), governed on behalf of the Samanids, but his son Mahmud (*reg* 998–1030) established an independent empire over Samanid territories south of the Amu River and expanded eastwards into India. By the mid-11th century, western Afghanistan had been relinquished to the Saljuqs (*see* SALJUQ, §1), Turkish nomads originating from the steppelands north of the Caspian and Aral seas, but the Ghaznavids retained control of eastern Afghanistan and northern India. In 1151 Ghazna was sacked by GHURID chieftains from the inaccessible mountainous region east of Herat. Turkish tribes from the lower Syr (Jaxartes) River region overthrew the Saljuqs in 1153 and occupied Ghazna in 1163. In the next decades, the Ghurids gained control of Afghanistan and finally defeated the last Ghaznavid principality at Lahore in 1186.

Internal dynastic struggles and confrontation on the northern borders with the Khwarazmshahs resulted in the breakup of the Ghurid empire. From 1215–16 Ghurid territories were ruled by the Khwarazmshah Muhammad b. Takash (*reg* 1200–21), until the entire region was overrun in 1221 by the Mongols under Genghis Khan (*reg* 1206–27). Herat was restored in 1236 by his third son Ogedey (*reg* 1227–41), while Ghazna and Kabul became military bases for Mongol raids into India. From 1250 onwards the different Afghanistan regions were controlled by independent Mongol rulers, such as the Neguderis at Ghazna.

Timur extended his Transoxanian steppe empire southwards into Afghanistan with the capture of Herat in 1380. Under his son Shahrukh, Herat became the TIMURID capital. From 1469 Afghanistan was divided into two Timurid principalities, one based at Herat, the other at Kabul. In the 16th century incursions by the Uzbek tribal confederacy of the Amu River region meant that frontier towns such as Herat frequently changed hands.

Following the loss of his Central Asian Timurid principality of Ferghana to the Uzbeks, Babur (*reg* 1526–30), the founder of the MUGHAL dynasty, occupied Kabul in 1504. He began raids into India and captured Delhi in 1526. Afghan chiefs led by Sher Shah Sur (*reg* 1540–45; *see* SUR (ii)) forced Babur's son Humayun (*reg* 1530–40, 1555–6) into exile in 1540. The capture of Kabul in 1545 gave Humayun a base from which to reconquer India in 1555. During the reign of Akbar (*reg* 1556–1605) boundaries between Afghanistan and the Uzbek territories to the north were demarcated, but control of Kandahar remained disputed with the Safavid dynasty (*reg* 1501–1732; *see* SAFAVID, §1) to the west. Succeeding Mughals retained Kabul, but western Afghanistan came increasingly under Safavid control. In the early 18th century the Safavid governor, Mir Ways, declared independence. The Afghans occupied most of Iran from 1722 until expelled in 1727 by Nadir Shah (*reg* 1736–47), a Turkoman chieftain from Khurasan in service with the Safavids, who subsequently founded the Afsharid dynasty (*reg* 1736–95) of Iran. When Nadir was assassinated in 1747, Afghan soldiers in his army elected one of his leading commanders, Ahmad Khan of the Afghan Sardozay tribe, as Shah (*reg* 1747–73). The Durrani dynasty (*reg* 1747–1842), which Ahmad Shah founded, derived its name from his title *Dur-i Durrān* ('Pearl of pearls'). He established an empire comprising Afghanistan and north-west India, including Sind, Baluchistan, part of the Punjab and Kashmir, but most of the Indian territories were lost during the reign of Zaman Shah (*reg* 1793–1800).

In 1819 Dost Muhammad of the Barakzay tribe (*reg* 1819–62) took Kabul and retained control of Afghanistan despite pressures from Iran, Russia and the British. The kingdom of Afghanistan survived as a political entity until overthrown by leftist urban groups in 1978. The ensuing civil war was not halted by Soviet military intervention in 1979 or by the withdrawal of Soviet troops in 1987–9.

BIBLIOGRAPHY

C. E. Bosworth: *The Islamic Dynasties: A Chronological and Genealogical Handbook* (Edinburgh, 1967, rev. 1980)

F. R. Allchin and N. Hammond, eds: *The Archaeology of Afghanistan: From Earliest Times to the Timurid Period* (London and New York, 1978)

L. Dupree: *Afghanistan* (Princeton, 1980)

A. B. Delmas and M. Casanova: 'The Lapis Lazuli Sources in the Ancient East', *South Asian Archaeology, 1987*, ed. M. Taddei (Rome, 1990), pp. 493–505

3. LANGUAGE AND ETHNIC GROUPS. The earliest official inscriptions date from the Mauryan period. These comprise Aramaic inscriptions from Laghman and two bilingual inscriptions of Ashoka (*reg c.* 269–*c.* 232 BC) from Kandahar, one combining Aramaic with Greek and the other Aramaic with Indian Prakrit. Under the Greco-Bactrians at AI KHANUM, official inscriptions were in good Classical Greek. Under the Kushanas, inscriptions at Surkh Kotal, north of the Hindu Kush, were in Bactrian; inscriptions at Dasht-i-Nawar, 60 km west of Ghazna, were in Bactrian, Prakrit and an undeciphered local language, while the inscriptions of south-eastern Afghanistan were in Prakrit.

Afghanistan is not a single ethnic unit. In the pre-Muslim period, the Hindu Kush ('Death to the Hindu') Mountains formed a natural divide between the Hindu-dominated areas of the south and the Zoroastrian peoples of the north. The largest racial group in modern Afghanistan consists of the Pathans, a people of Turko-Iranian origin who speak Pushtu and are probably the descendants of the original inhabitants of the south. The Tajiks, who live north and east of Kabul, are of Iranian origin, speak Farsi and are thought to be descendants of the original northern inhabitants. The Hazaras who inhabit the central massif are thought to be descendants of the Mongols. There are also many minority groups, such as the Turkomans, Uzbeks and Nuristanis, who all speak their own dialects.

4. RELIGION AND ICONOGRAPHY. The terracotta female figures from Mundigak (*see* §II, 1(ii)(a) below) suggest that a fertility goddess resembling the great mother goddess of Mesopotamia was worshipped in the prehistoric period (*c.* 2000 BC). Zoroastrianism played an important role in Iranian lands such as Bactria before the conquest of Alexander the Great in 330 BC, but many remains of a pre-Zoroastrian religion also survived. The Sakas and Yueh-chih in Central Asia probably worshipped the sun and regarded Ahuramazda (the Zoroastrian supreme Good Spirit) as a god with a strong solar function (*see also* CENTRAL ASIA, §I, 1(v)(a)).

The coins of the Greek rulers of Bactria showed a typical range of Greek divinities, with the same attributes and iconography as found throughout the Hellenistic world: Zeus with his thunderbolt, Artemis with her bow and Pallas Athena with her shield. According to Herodotus (*Histories* IV.lviii–lxix), the Scythians worshipped Greek gods but called them by Scythian names, and this also reflects the Greek approach to foreign deities. Native divinities were syncretized with Greek gods and represented in Greek iconographic forms. The votive pedestal at TAKHT-I SANGIN, dedicated by the Iranian priest Atrosokes to the deity of the Oxus (Amu River) in the 2nd century BC, supported a statue of the Classical deity Silenus Marsyas, playing a double flute. Rare coins of Agathokles (*c.* 180 BC) from Ai Khanum follow the Classical tradition by depicting the Hindu deity Samkarshana in iconic form as a male figure in Oriental dress and winged headdress holding a plough, while his younger brother Vasudeva Krishna is similarly shown bearing the attributes of a conch shell (*saṅkha*) and wheel (*cakra*) (Kabul Mus.; see Allchin and Hammond, fig. 4.13). The enthroned and radiate Zeus on Indian tetradrachms of Hermaios (*c.* 90–70 BC) represents Zeus syncretized with Mithra, an Iranian pre-Zoroastrian solar deity (see 1992 exh. cat., p. 61, no. 24).

There were similar developments when the Kushanas extended their empire across Afghanistan in the 1st century AD. The first ruler, Kujula Kadphises, used Herakles, the Greek form of the Iranian war god and personification of victory, Verethragna. King Soter Megas used the rayed head of Mithra. All the gold and copper coins of his successor Vima Kadphises use the type of Shiva and his bull Nandi, showing the king's personal devotion to the war god, appropriate to his campaigns of conquest and to the support he required from his new Indian subjects. Kanishka was more eclectic, and his coins show a pantheon of primarily Iranian gods. Initially he used Greek legends, even to the extent of using the female name Selene for the male Iranian moon god. The Greek names were subsequently replaced by Bactrian ones, such as Mao (moon god), Mioro (sun god), Athsho (fire god) and Nana (water goddess, the Bactrian Anahita).

The Mauryan ruler Ashoka (*reg c.* 269–*c.* 232 BC) promoted Buddhism in Afghanistan as elsewhere, and inscriptions giving his edicts have been found in Laghman and at Kandahar; but it was only from the late 1st century BC onwards, under the Indo-Parthians and Kushanas, that Buddhism spread widely and numerous stupas were built in Afghanistan. During this period there were some remarkable developments in Buddhist iconography. Whereas previously the Buddha's presence had simply been indicated by symbols, such as a footprint or vacant throne, a new school of Buddhist thought stressing the miraculous life of the Buddha led to the representation of the Buddha in human form. A gold medallion from Tillya Tepe (see Sarianidi, pp. 188–9, no. 131), dated *c.* 50 BC–*c.* AD 50, has a reverse design of a lion and a *triratna* ('three jewels' symbol representing Buddha, the Law and the Buddhist community). The Kharoshthi inscription *siho vigatabhayo* ('the lion who chased away fear') refers to the Buddha, as does the obverse *dharmacakrapravatako* ('he who sets in motion the Wheel of the Law'; see Fussman, pp. 71–2), which is inscribed beside a bearded image of Herakles, complete with lion skin, pushing a wheel. The equation of a Classical deity with the Buddha suggests that the token was made in the aniconic period of Buddhist art, but within the Greco-Bactrian milieu, where religious images were traditionally represented in human form.

The gold reliquary from Bimaran Stupa 2 (*see* §II, 1(iv)(c) and fig. 14 below) also belongs to an early phase and has niches containing the standing images of the Buddha, Indra, Brahma and a fourth figure, variously thought to represent a *bodhisattva* or a donor. The billon coins found with the reliquary were issued posthumously in the name of Azes and date from the time of Kujula Kadphises (*c.* mid-1st century AD). Kanishka, who convened a Buddhist council in Kashmir to settle doctrinal disputes, issued coins in both gold and copper bearing an image of the Buddha. It was, however, a rare coinage, perhaps intended simply to commemorate the council. In spite of Kanishka's patronage of Buddhism, his dynastic shrine at SURKH KOTAL provides evidence of an indigenous religion associated with the cult of fire. His successor, Huvishka, shows the same eclectic approach in his coinage, but later Kushanas reverted to the more limited representation of the Hindu god Shiva with his mount Nandi and the enthroned Ardochsho, the Iranian goddess of good fortune, increasingly represented as her Hindu equivalent, Lakshmi. Kushana and Kushano-Sasanian kings are often depicted on coins with flames issuing from their shoulders, a divine symbol in Iranian terms of a universal ruler. A relief of the 3rd century AD from SHOTORAK similarly depicts the Dipankara Buddha (the first of 24 predecessors of the historical Buddha) as a substantially larger figure with flames rising from his shoulders (see Snellgrove, fig. 137; *see also* §II, 1(ii)(c) and fig. 6 below).

The two colossal images (h. 55 m and 38 m) in rock-cut niches at Bamiyan were clearly intended to inspire respect and show the Buddha as Lord of the world. Paintings in the niche containing the 38 m figure depict Sasanian donors and Buddhas, with a solar divinity in a quadriga above to indicate Buddha's solar character (see Tarzi, pls B8–27). The larger figure (see fig. 8 below) is set in a niche decorated with a pantheon of *bodhisattvas* encircling the cosmic Buddha (see Tarzi, pls B119–129). A late 7th-century AD Buddha statue from the monastery at FONDUKISTAN (see fig. 9 below) is depicted wearing heavy earrings and a jewelled chasuble over his monastic garment, i.e. the ascetic Buddha transformed into the glorified transcendent form also seen in India in the later iconography of Maitreya (the future Buddha; *see also* §II, 1(ii)(d) and (iii) below).

The ascendancy of Hinduism in the 7th–8th centuries AD, associated with the Hindu Shahi kings of Kabul, is represented by statues of the elephant god Ganesha from Koh Daman and Gardez; fragments of sculpture representing Shiva and his consort Durga killing the buffalo demon from Sa'robi; and two Surya images from Khair Khana near Kabul. Islam, brought by the advancing Muslim armies from the 8th century AD onwards, became the dominant religion of Afghanistan by the 10th century.

BIBLIOGRAPHY

B. Rowland: *The Evolution of the Buddha Image* (New York, 1963)

B. Y. Stavisky: *Kushanskaya Baktriya: Problemy istorii i kul'tury* (Moscow, 1977); Fr. trans. as *La Bactriane sous les Kushans: Problèmes d'histoire et de culture* (Paris, 1986)

Z. Tarzi: *L'Architecture et le décor rupestre des grottes de Bāmiyān*, 2 vols (Paris, 1977)

F. R. Allchin and N. Hammond, eds: *The Archaeology of Afghanistan: From Earliest Times to the Timurid Period* (London and New York, 1978)

D. L. Snellgrove, ed.: *The Image of the Buddha* (London, 1978)

V. Sarianidi: *The Golden Hoard of Bactria from the Tillya-tepe Excavations in Northern Afghanistan* (New York and Leningrad, 1985)

G. Fussman: 'Numismatic and Epigraphic Evidence for the Chronology of Early Gandharan Art', *Investigating Indian Art*, ed. M. Yaldiz (Berlin, 1987), pp. 67–88

The Crossroads of Asia: Transformation in Image and Symbol in the Art of Ancient Afghanistan and Pakistan (exh. cat., ed. E. Errington and J. Cribb; Cambridge, Fitzwilliam, 1992)

J. Harmatta: 'Religion in the Kushan Empire', *The Development of Sedentary and Nomadic Civilizations, 700 BC to AD 250*, ed. J. Harmatta, G. F. Etemadi and B. N. Puri (1993), ii of *UNESCO History of Civilizations of Central Asia* (Paris, 1992–)

D. W. MACDOWALL

II. Historical survey.

The study of art in Afghanistan can conveniently be divided into three broad periods. The rich and varied traditions of early historic Afghanistan gave way in the late 1st millennium AD to the influence of Islam, which dominated artistic output for 1000 years. Twentieth-century art has tended to imitate Western styles.

1. Before *c.* AD 900. 2. *c.* AD 900–*c.* 1900. 3. After *c.* 1900.

1. BEFORE *c.* AD 900.

(i) Architecture. (ii) Sculpture. (iii) Painting. (iv) Other arts.

(i) Architecture. At different periods in its history, Afghanistan has been subject to Harappan, Greek, Persian, Indian, Central Asian, Chinese, Islamic and Russian influences. The architecture of Afghanistan is the syncretic fusion of these divergent traditions, the origins of which can be traced in the prehistoric, Achaemenid and Hellenistic periods, culminating in the 1st millennium AD in the predominantly Buddhist architecture of GANDHARA (*see also* INDIAN SUBCONTINENT, §III, 3(ii)(a)).

2. Mundigak, 'Palace', north-west façade, *c.* 2500–*c.* 2000 BC

(a) Prehistoric. (b) *c.* 4th–*c.* 1st century BC. (c) *c.* 1st–*c.* 5th century AD. (d) *c.* 6th–*c.* 9th century AD.

(a) Prehistoric. Excavations at the Bronze and Iron Age town of Mundigak (founded *c.* 4000 BC) near Kandahar revealed a long history of simple mud and mud-brick domestic architecture. Monumental town walls were constructed in Period IV (later 3rd millennium BC), a date contemporary with the Urban Phase of the Harappan civilization at the great Indus Valley cities of MOHENJO-DARO and HARAPPA to the east. Two buildings, tentatively identified as a 'Palace' and a 'Temple', have massive exterior walls and buttresses built of fired brick with a surface coating of plaster. The 'Palace', located on the highest point of the site, has a façade on the north-west side, surviving some 35 m in length and nearly 3 m in height (see fig. 2). The line of semicircular buttresses or 'colonnade of pilasters' fronting this façade was capped by a frieze of stepped merlons. The interior plan, in contrast to the regularity and solidity of the exterior, appears haphazard and comprises small rooms of flimsy mud-brick construction around a central courtyard. Much, however, had been lost through erosion, particularly since the building was first excavated in the 1950s. The 'Temple' is more regular in plan, with a façade of decorative triangular buttresses traceable on three sides, although erosion had reduced the height of the building almost to foundation level.

When extant, these buttressed façades must have presented a very impressive aspect. This type of structure appears to have been a favourite form of architectural adornment, as even the ramparts are distinguished by more closely spaced, square buttresses than would be required for either structural or defensive reasons. The Late Bronze Age palace at Dashli 3 in Bactria (northern

Afghanistan) is similarly decorated with regular lines of square buttresses, on both the interior and exterior façades. The form recalls late 4th-millennium BC monumental architecture at Uruk (*see* MESOPOTAMIA, §II, 3), where semicircular, triangular and square buttressing were all used to decorate exterior façades. The semicircular buttresses of the 'Palace' at Mundigak seem to have a particularly close affinity with the 'Pillar Hall' at Uruk, while the merlons perhaps recall Mesopotamian prototypes.

The tradition of monumental building continued in the 1st millennium BC. Massive structures, usually on immense brick platforms, include Nad-i Ali in Sistan, south-west Afghanistan, the citadels at Maiwand and Kandahar in the south-east, and fortifications at Altin 1, Altin Dilyar Tepe, Kutlug Tepe, DILBERDJIN and Dashli in Bactria to the north (*see* CENTRAL ASIA, §I, 2(i)(a)). The same monumentality is also found in Iron Age and Achaemenid buildings of Pakistan (e.g. Bannu) and Iran (e.g. Tureng Tepe and the immense palace platform of PERSEPOLIS).

Altin 1 and Altin Dilyar Tepe in Bactria are both fortified towns with a high citadel surrounded by a town and massive outer defensive walls. This type of urban layout was to characterize Central Asian town planning for several millennia. The ramparts of Altin Dilyar are, furthermore, in the form of an immense circle, a feature of subsequent Parthian and Sasanian town planning that was still utilized in AD 762 at BAGHDAD. The Achaemenid citadel at Dilberdjin is also circular (though the surrounding town is largely later), as is a building at Kutlug Tepe, tentatively identified as a temple, that comprises three massive concentric mud walls pierced by embrasures.

Altin 1 was probably the administrative centre for a group of settlements. The most significant settlement was Altin 10, which contained two buildings, probably palaces, the one consisting of two porticoed courtyards with roofs supported by massive brick pillars, the other comprising a single courtyard dominated by a wide central entrance on one side. Both features subsequently evolved into two important architectural elements of the Middle East: the columned hall and the monumental portal.

The 1st millennium BC, therefore, was one in which the prototypes of certain basic architectural features were established: monumental buildings, the circular form, the columned hall and the monumental portal. That so many standard architectural elements of Afghanistan and neighbouring Iran were formulated in Afghanistan assumes significance in the light of the Central Asian origins of the Iranians themselves: when they arrived on the Iranian plateau, they already had a developed and vigorous architectural tradition.

(b) c. *4th*–c. *1st century* BC. New architectural traditions from the west arrived with the conquests of Alexander of Macedon and his Seleucid successors in the 4th–3rd century BC. The survival of the subsequent Greco-Bactrian and Indo-Greek kingdoms in the Central Asian and Indo-Iranian borderlands ensured the continuation and development of an independent Hellenistic artistic and architectural tradition that was open to more Oriental influences.

The only Greek city that has been excavated in Afghanistan is AI KHANUM (probably anc. Alexandria Oxiana). The city, founded at or soon after the time of Alexander's conquest (329–325 BC), occupies a naturally fortified position at the confluence of the Amu and Kokcha rivers. A low ridge on the third side is further reinforced by ramparts and, in places, a ditch. A north–south main thoroughfare divided the upper and lower town. The upper town has a necropolis and a citadel and is separated from the lower town by a main thoroughfare running from north to south. The lower town consists of three distinctive parts: an almost empty area to the north; a central administrative quarter and a palace; and living quarters to the south. The adjacent plain has an extensive irrigation system. The remains belong well within standard Hellenistic architectural traditions.

The earliest building is the temple dedicated to Kineas (*c.* 325–*c.* 300 BC), a leading citizen and probably one of the founders of the city. Other excavated buildings include a gymnasium, theatre, monumental mausoleum, propylaeum, monumental fountain, arsenal, several temples and some houses. The architectural decoration is typically Hellenistic, with stone columns bearing Corinthian, Ionic and Doric capitals throughout. A number of Oriental architectural features were nevertheless retained. Mud-brick was the primary building material, with stone used only for important structural purposes, such as columns. Even many of the Corinthian columns are Asiatic variations of the form, rather than true Greek. The great courtyard of the palace is dominated in the centre of one side by a monumental opening and reception hall supported by three rows of six columns each, in which it is easy to see the local elements of monumental portal and columned hall. While the mausoleum is a standard peripteral style temple, the Temple of Kineas and the temple 'à redans' or 'à niches indentées' are each situated in a large enclosure, or temenos. Such large temple enclosures are typical Asian features (*see also* CENTRAL ASIA, §I, 2(i)(a)). The layout of Ai Khanum conforms to standard Hellenistic town planning principles, with its grid system of streets and main north–south thoroughfare, though the division into citadel and lower town might be seen as a local influence. But elsewhere in Hellenistic Bactria, the Iranian circular plan remained popular: for example Jiga Tepe is a circular fortification, while Emshi Tepe is an entire circular city, like the earlier site of Altin Dilyar.

Evidence of major conflagrations at Ai Khanum in about 130 BC and again in 90 BC point to the final destruction of the city by invaders, possibly the Kushanas. But the unique blend of western and eastern elements found at the site continued to influence the subsequent cultures of Afghanistan for almost a millennium. Before the discovery and excavation of Ai Khanum in the 1960s, knowledge of this important formative period when the two cultures first became fused was almost non-existent.

(c) c. *1st*–c. *5th century* AD. The arrival of the originally nomadic KUSHANAS from Central Asia added a new element to the already eclectic nature of the architecture of Afghanistan. The establishment of the Kushana empire invigorated existing traditions and re-asserted international connections, particularly with the Indian subcontinent,

thereby encouraging the spread of Buddhism into Afghanistan. Under the Kushanas, the widely divergent traditions of architecture in Afghanistan became a cultural and political whole. The first Kushana political capital was at BEGRAM, north of Kabul. Subsequently the capital was moved to TAXILA in Pakistan and eventually to MATHURA in India. The site of KHALCHAYAN in Tajikistan has been identified by its excavators as an early Kushana dynastic shrine. The Kushanas established a similar dynastic cult centre at SURKH KOTAL, north of the Hindu Kush. The complex, dated *c.* 1st–*c.* 4th century AD, is reached by a monumental mud-brick and masonry staircase, flanked by four massive terraces cut from the hillside (see fig. 3). The main temple has a cella facing east, which is enclosed by a corridor on the three other sides and contains a square masonry platform with the remains of four Hellenistic column bases at each corner. The building was first thought to be a fire temple, but more recent research suggests that it may have had a more public ceremonial function. Abutting the south side of the temple is a later complex of two small fire temples linked by a courtyard. These each have a square central sanctuary enclosed by corridors. A Greek-letter inscription in the Bactrian language describes the construction of a well and the restoration of the complex by an official called Nokonzok in the year 31 of the Kanishka era (*c.* first half of the 2nd century).

The great staircase of Surkh Kotal is unique in the architecture of the region. The only contemporary parallel occurs at Wadi Hadhramaut in southern Arabia, where the monumental staircase approaches to a series of shrines bear many similarities to Surkh Kotal, although there is no apparent connection between the two sites. The associations with fire worship at Surkh Kotal have obvious Zoroastrian affinities, while the ambulatory in the form of corridors around the sanctuary is an essential feature of Buddhist architecture at sites such as ADZHINA TEPE. The syncretic fusion of different religious ideas and elements into a cult focused on the person of the emperor was apparently intended to symbolize the unity of different regions of the empire and the cultural tolerance of the Kushanas.

During the Kushana period Buddhism was the dominant religion in Afghanistan. The main architectural manifestation of Buddhism, the STUPA, is one of the most distinctive architectural features of eastern Afghanistan. In the long, complex evolution of the stupa form, Afghanistan played a major role, not least because contact with Hellenism gave rise to the distinctive art and architectural style of Gandhara. Many new forms of Buddhist architecture evolved, the Buddha image was given artistic and architectural expression, and numerous monastic complexes were built in the regions east of Kandahar in the south to Balkh in the north. Most importantly, it was during this formative period that Buddhism and its associated architecture spread from Afghanistan northwards into Central Asia and ultimately eastwards to China, Japan and South-east Asia, rather than directly from the Indian heartland.

The stupa, originally built to house relics associated with the Buddha, became both the centre for great monastic communities and the symbol of far-reaching philosophical ideas. In eastern Afghanistan the stupas number in hundreds, if not thousands. A well-preserved and architecturally outstanding example of the stupa form is found at GULDARA, south-east of Kabul (see fig. 4). The stupa consists of a dome and two drums positioned on a high, square platform and socle with a stairway on the south-west side. The core of the structure is faced with the distinctive 'diaper masonry' that is the hallmark of architecture of the Gandharan period throughout the region: large stones, dressed on one side with small, flat stones filling the interstices. The platform and both stupa drums are decorated with blind arcades of Indo-Corinthian pilasters (an Oriental variation of the Greek prototype). A

3. Surkh Kotal, fortified terraced enclosure and monumental stairs to the dynastic shrines on the acropolis, *c.* late 1st century AD to *c.* 4th

4. Guldara, main stupa, north-east façade, *c.* 2nd–*c.* 4th centuries AD

fortified monastery to the north comprises a central unexcavated courtyard, which possibly contained a central stupa and smaller votive stupas surrounded on four sides by an ambulatory and cells for monks. To the south of the principal stupa stands a second stupa of similar style also constructed of diaper masonry. The complex is dated on stylistic, epigraphic and numismatic grounds to the 2nd–4th century.

The Buddhist sites of HADDA, near Jalalabad in eastern Afghanistan, comprise numerous stupas, monasteries and artificial cave complexes extending over an area of approximately 39 sq. km. The major monastic complexes often have more than one large stupa and always have numerous votive stupas. The stupas, shrines and caves were decorated with a wealth of clay, stone and stucco sculptural decoration and wall paintings (*see* §§(ii)(c)–(d) and (iii)(b) below). The most spectacular sites were Tepe Kalan (three main stupas surrounded by dozens of decorated votive stupas) and Tepe Shotor (one main stupa with many votive stupas, richly decorated niches and shrines). All the excavated sites at Hadda have been destroyed, either soon after excavation in the 1920s or during fighting in the 1980s.

Although Afghanistan was incorporated into the SASANIAN empire in the 3rd century AD, under the Kushano-Sasanian rulers local cultural forms continued uninterrupted, albeit evincing increasing Sasanian influence. The Hephthalites who migrated southwards from Central Asia in the 5th century are often associated with great destruction, but in Afghanistan the Buddhist civilization not only continued but flourished following their invasion. Indeed, it is often difficult to distinguish any differences in the material culture of the Kushana, Sasanian and Hephthalite periods.

(d) c. *6th–*c. *9th century* AD. The numerous minor principalities that emerged in eastern Afghanistan during the 7th century AD were often little more than city states ruled by Hephthalite or Turkish lords who enjoyed considerable independence and frequently encouraged the religious arts. Although there was no great central unifying power, Buddhism imposed a cultural unity throughout, and some of the greatest Buddhist monuments were built during this period. At FONDUKISTAN, for example, the monastery contains a courtyard with niches that were elaborately decorated with painted clay sculptures and frescoes (*see* §§(ii)(d) and (iii)(c) below). Near Ghazna (probably the site of a minor principality), excavations also revealed a stupa and monastery complex at TEPE SARDAR that was almost Baroque in the richness of its sculptural decoration. The main stupa, the largest in Afghanistan, is surrounded by many votive stupas and chapels, richly decorated in clay reliefs. The remains in the sanctuary include clay fragments of several colossal Buddha statues. Most significantly, there is also a Brahmanical shrine in the Tepe Sardar complex, where a statue of Durga Mahishasuramardini was found. Following the establishment of the Hindu Shahis at Kabul in the 8th century AD, many significant Hindu works of art were created, but there are no great works of architecture belonging to this period, except perhaps the controversial Minar-i Chakri, a stone pillar on a mountain overlooking the Kabul valley.

By far the most spectacular Buddhist site in Afghanistan is BAMIYAN, in the central Hindu Kush. The cliffs on the north side of the valley are honeycombed for a length of about 1800 m by some 750 artificial caves, forming part of a Buddhist centre. Among the caves are two colossal, almost free-standing statues of the Buddha (55 m and 38 m high) and a smaller, seated Buddha, carved out of niches in the cliff face in high relief. Details of the robes are applied in stucco over a framework of ropes (representing the folds) attached to the bedrock with wooden pegs. The top halves of the faces have been destroyed by iconoclasts. In the niches surrounding the two standing Buddhas are the remains of frescoes. Frescoes and sculptures also decorate many of the caves, and plaster applied to the bedrock to represent architectural details often imitates wooden prototypes. Indeed, rock-cut architecture is characteristic of Bamiyan, in contrast with other eastern regions of Afghanistan, where architectural structures, particularly stupas, predominate. The only stupa discovered at Bamiyan was excavated to the east of the 38 m Buddha, though mounds of debris might indicate other examples.

In the architecture and art generally of Bamiyan there exists a surprising paradox. For Bamiyan was only a minor principality of the federation known as the Empire of the Western Turks, the capital of which was at Qunduz in north-eastern Afghanistan, where no monuments on such a scale exist. It has been suggested that Bamiyan may have been a dynastic centre for the Western Turks, in much the same way as Surkh Kotal functioned for the Kushanas. Whether or not this is true, Buddhist architecture reached a peak at Bamiyan. The caves cut out of the mountainside housed thousands of devotees; the colossal statues were the ultimate embodiment of the Buddha image, while the painting and sculpture combined Hellenistic, Iranian and Indian elements that influenced subsequent Chinese and Islamic art.

BIBLIOGRAPHY

J. Barthoux: *Les Fouilles de Haḍḍa*, 2 vols, Mém.: Dél. Archéol. Fr. Afghanistan, iv–v (Paris and Brussels, 1930–33)

J. Hackin and J. Carl: *Recherches archéologiques au col de Khair Khaneh près de Kâbul*, Mém.: Dél. Archéol. Fr. Afghanistan, vii (Paris, 1936)

J. Meunié: *Shotorak*, Mém.: Dél. Archéol. Fr. Afghanistan, x (Paris, 1942)

J. Carl, J. Hackin and J. Meunié: *Diverses recherches archéologiques en Afghanistan, 1933–1940*, Mém.: Dél. Archéol. Fr. Afghanistan, viii (Paris, 1959)

J.-M. Casal: *Fouilles de Mundigak*, 2 vols, Mém.: Dél. Archéol. Fr. Afghanistan, xvii (Paris, 1961)

S. Mizuno, ed.: *Haibak and Kashmir-Smast: Buddhist Cave Temples in Afghanistan and Pakistan Surveyed in 1960* (Kyoto, 1962)

B. Dagens, M. Le Berre and D. Schlumberger: *Monuments préislamiques d'Afghanistan*, Mém.: Dél. Archéol. Fr. Afghanistan, xix (Paris, 1964)

S. Mizuno, ed.: *Durman Tepe and Lalma: Buddhist Sites in Afghanistan Surveyed in 1963–1965* (Kyoto, 1968)

——: *Chagalag Tepe: Fortified Village in North Afghanistan Excavated in 1964–1967* (Kyoto, 1970)

——: *Basawal and Jelalabad-Kabul: Buddhist Cave Temples and Topes in South-east Afghanistan Surveyed Mainly in 1965* (Kyoto, 1971)

P. Bernard and others: *Fouilles d'Aï Khanoum*, 9 vols, Mém.: Dél. Archéol. Fr. Afghanistan, xxi, xxvi–xxxi, xxxiii (Paris, 1973–92)

I. T. Kruglikova: *Dil'berdzhin (raskopki 1970–1972 gg.)* [Dilberdjin (excavations 1970–1972)], i (Moscow, 1974)

G. Fussman and M. Le Berre: *Monuments bouddhiques de la région de Caboul, I: Le Monastère de Gul Dara*, Mém.: Dél. Archéol. Fr. Afghanistan, xxii (Paris, 1976)

I. T. Kruglikova, ed.: *Drevnyaya Baktriya* [Ancient Bactria], 3 vols (Moscow, 1976–84)

Z. Tarzi: 'Hadda à la lumière des trois dernières campagnes de fouilles de Tapa-é-Shotor (1974–1976)', *Acad. Inscr. & B.-Lett.: C. R. Séances* (1976), pp. 381–410; Eng. trans. by A. A. Motamedi with C. Grissman as 'Hadda after the Three Last Seasons of Excavations at Tepe Shotor (1974–1976)', *Afghanistan Q.*, xxxii/2 (Sept 1979), pp. 60–89

I. T. Kruglikova and G. Pugachenkova: *Dil'berdzhin (raskopki 1970–1973 gg.)* [Dilberdjin (excavations 1970–1973)], ii (Moscow, 1977)

Z. Tarzi: *L'Architecture et le décor rupestre des grottes de Bāmiyān*, 2 vols (Paris, 1977)

F. R. Allchin and N. Hammond, eds: *The Archaeology of Afghanistan: From Earliest Times to the Timurid Period* (London and New York, 1978)

H. G. Franz: 'Das Chakri Minar als buddhistische Kultsäule', *Afghanistan J.*, v/3 (1978), pp. 96–101

M. Taddei and G. Verardi: 'Tapa Sardār: Second Preliminary Report', *E. & W.*, xxviii (1978), pp. 33–136

H.-P. Francfort: *Les Fortifications en Asie centrale de l'âge du bronze à l'époque kouchane* (Paris, 1979)

W. Ball: *Archaeological Gazetteer of Afghanistan/Catalogue de sites archéologiques d'Afghanistan*, 2 vols (Paris, 1982)

D. Schlumberger, M. Le Berre and G. Fussman: *Surkh Kotal en Bactriane, I: Les Temples, architecture, sculpture, inscriptions*, 2 vols, Mém.: Dél. Archéol. Fr. Afghanistan, xxv (Paris, 1983)

T. Higuchi, ed.: *Bamiyan: Art and Archaeological Researches on the Buddhist Cave Temples in Afghanistan, 1970–1978*, 4 vols (Kyoto, 1983–4)

S. Kuwayama: 'Tapa Shotor and Lalma: Aspects of Stupa Court at Hadda', *AION*, xlvii (1987), pp. 153–76

For further bibliography *see* §§(ii) and (iii) below.

W. BALL

(ii) Sculpture. The sculpture of Afghanistan reflects the diverse cultural traditions brought by trade and a series of foreign invaders to the region. Stylistic links with Iran and the Indian subcontinent are already evident in the prehistoric period. From the late 4th century BC onwards, the predominant Hellenistic and subsequent Buddhist influences formed the basis of Gandharan art (*c.* 1st–5th century AD); later sculptures provide increasing evidence of the resurgence of Hinduism. Apart from a few free-standing statues, the sculpture primarily comprises friezes and relief images that were designed to be placed against a wall. Stone, particularly schist and limestone, was used until *c.* 3rd century AD; stucco and particularly unbaked clay were also used extensively throughout all periods, later to the almost total exclusion of stone. A proportion of the finds from the French excavations at Bamiyan, Begram, Hadda, the Kapisa sites and Fondukistan are in Paris, Musée Guimet. Tepe Shotor, Hadda, was enclosed as a protected archaeological site, with the sculptures retained *in situ* (since destroyed). The Bamiyan rock-cut images and large items such as the columns and capitals at Ai Khanum were also left *in situ*, but the majority of sculptures were placed in the Kabul Museum (destroyed by bombing in 1993).

□

(a) Prehistoric. (b) *c.* 4th–*c.* 1st century BC. (c) *c.* 1st–*c.* 3rd century AD. (d) *c.* 4th–*c.* 9th century AD.

(a) Prehistoric. A carving of a human head (*c.* 635×381 mm) on a soft limestone pebble was found during the 1965–6 excavation of the cave Aq Kupruk II (Ghar-i Mar or 'Horse Cave') on the Balkh River, south of Mazar-e Sharif (see Dupree, 1968, 1972; Marshak, figs 138–40). Despite the crude carving, the eyes are clearly depicted and the curve of a distorted mouth can also be seen. This object is associated with an Upper Palaeolithic blade industry (Kuprukian A) and can tentatively be dated 20,000–15,000 BP. The site of Mundigak on the upper

reaches of the Helmand River near Kandahar became a major centre in Period IV (*c.* 2500–*c.* 2000 BC; *see* §(i)(a) above). Finds from this period include terracotta figurines, compartmented seals and copper or bronze tools (see Shaffer, figs 3.39–40). A male head of white limestone (h. 915 mm; see fig. 5), broken high at the neck and assigned to Period IV, 3, was found in a complex of rooms associated with a niched wall (see Casal, pp. 76–7, 255; pls XLIII–XLIV). It is a rather colourless representation of a beardless man with a full (now broken) nose. The chin has been defaced and only faint traces remain of a mouth. Ears are shown as simple 'C' shapes, much like those on Mohenjo-daro sculptures. The eyes are oval and rather large, could not have accommodated inlays and have prominent eyebrows above which a hairline is indicated. There is a slight indication that the hair may have been parted in the middle and worn wide and full at the shoulders. There is also a fillet around the forehead, extending down the back of the head in twin flat bands, just as with the 'Priest-King' (*see* INDIAN SUBCONTINENT, fig. 137). This piece of sculpture fits well within the corpus of Harappan material in terms of size, material and some stylistic features.

An Afghan tribal leader from Sistan owns a small stone head said to come from the environs of the village of Khwabgah (see Dales, p. 219). This is also broken at the neck and survives to a height of 94 mm. It is fashioned from a soft, creamy buff stone, with many pits and white veins. The beardless head has a small, tight mouth above a small chin and lacks vivacity. The nose comes from a steeply slanted forehead in a rather direct way and is slightly broken. Large, ovate eyes, capped by distinctive eyebrows, seem to have been without inlay. There is a prominent hairline, which could denote the original existence of a cap or some other headgear. A slight indentation towards the front of the top of the head may indicate a central parting. Details are lacking, but the hair seems to have been worn wide and full at the shoulders, as on the Mundigak head. A fillet goes around the forehead and extends down the back of the head in twin flat bands.

5. White limestone head, h. 915 mm, from Mundigak, *c.* 2500–*c.* 2000 BC (Kabul, Kabul Museum)

A team of Italian archaeologists exploring Iranian Sistan in 1977 found a small limestone head on the surface of the small site of Chah-i Torogh, *c.* 15 km south of SHAHR-I SOKHTA (see Jarrige and Tosi, pp. 131–3). Chah-i Torogh is a Shahr-i Sokhta IV site, dating to the earliest centuries of the 2nd millennium BC. The head, broken at the neck, survives to a height of 35 mm and is thus significantly smaller than the stone sculptures from the Indus sites or Mundigak. The expressionless countenance has a full but broken nose. The ears seem to be oval rather than 'C' shapes. The hair appears to have been parted in the middle and held in place with a fillet that hangs down the back in a pair of flat bands as in other examples.

BIBLIOGRAPHY

J.-M. Casal: *Fouilles de Mundigak*, 2 vols, Mém.: Dél. Archéol. Fr. Afghanistan, xvii (Paris, 1961)

L. Dupree: 'The Oldest Sculptured Head?', *Nat. Hist.*, lxxvii/5 (1968), pp. 26–7

——: 'Prehistoric Research in Afghanistan (1959–1966)', *Trans. Amer. Philos. Soc.*, lxii/4 (1972), pp. 3–84

A. Marshak: 'Aq Kupruk: Art and Symbols', in L. Dupree: 'Prehistoric Research in Afghanistan (1959–1966)', *Trans. Amer. Philos. Soc.*, lxii/4 (1972), pp. 66–72

P. Basaglia and others: *La città bruciata del deserto salato* (Venice, 1977)

J. G. Shaffer: 'The Later Prehistoric Periods', *The Archaeology of Afghanistan: From Earliest Times to the Timurid Period*, ed. F. R. Allchin and N. Hammond (London and New York, 1978), pp. 71–186

C. Jarrige and M. Tosi: 'The Natural Resources of Mundigak: Some Observations on the Location of the Site in Relation to its Economic Space', *South Asian Archaeology, 1979*, ed. H. Härtel (Berlin, 1981), pp. 115–42

V. M. Masson: *Altyn Depe* (Leningrad, 1981); Eng. trans. by H. N. Michael (Philadelphia, 1988)

G. F. Dales: 'Stone Sculpture from the Protohistoric Helmand Civilization, Afghanistan', *Orientalia Iosephi Tucci memoriae dicta*, ii (Rome, 1985), pp. 219–24

P. Amiet: *L'Age des échanges interiraniens, 3500–1700 avant J.-C.* (Paris, 1986)

GREGORY L. POSSEHL

(b) c. *4th–*c. *1st century* BC. The earliest historical sculptural production from the Afghanistan region is remarkably Hellenistic in both style and content. Until the 1960s Greco-Bractrian art was known only from large numbers of coins, as all attempts to locate the Greek cities of the region had been unsuccessful. The discovery of Ai Khanum (Alexandria Oxiana) at the confluence of the Kokcha and Amu (Oxus) rivers and subsequent excavations at the site by the Délégation Archéologique Française en Afghanistan (1965–78) dramatically increased knowledge of the period from 330 to *c.* 100 BC. Apart from a few metalwork pieces (*see* §(iv)(c) below), the most impressive sculptures from Ai Khanum are of limestone or marble.

A hermlike bust of a bearded man (*see* AI KHANUM, fig. 2) from the northern square of the gymnasium is dated archaeologically to Phase II (*c.* 150 BC), although the palaeographic characteristics of the dedicatory inscription point to an earlier date (see Veuve, pls 52–3). Though the bust resembles images of Herakles or the bearded Hermes, the strong individual characterization of the facial features suggests an actual portrait, perhaps of a gymnastic master, a typical Hellenic character.

The largest number of sculptures came from the temple 'à redans' (or 'à niches indentées') and its sanctuary. These sculptures included the colossal left foot of an acrolithic cult image; the unfinished statuette of a naked young athlete that is Lysippan in its posture and treatment of volumes (*see* LYSIPPOS); an unbaked clay female head and a stucco male head from statues that stood on either side of the cella entrance; an unbaked clay mould of a female bust (see Francfort, pl. XVII); and two ivory or bone figurines of an unknown naked goddess, one of which was perhaps a puppet, with movable jointed forearms (see Francfort, pl. V). The naked athlete and foot from the cult image (see Stavisky, pls VIIIb–IXa) are unmistakably Hellenistic in style and typology. The evidence provided by the athlete is particularly important, since the piece is unfinished and therefore certainly a local product. Even the two stucco and clay heads and the female bust are definitely in the Hellenistic tradition, though the treatment of their features, especially the rather heavy chins and eyelids, display local characteristics that survived until *c.* 5th century AD, at such sites as Tepe Sardar (Tapa Sardar) and Tepe Shotor, Hadda. The two ivory goddesses, although presumably derived from Mesopotamian prototypes, appear most closely comparable to Indian examples.

A lion-head gargoyle, perhaps from a fountain in the same sanctuary, is Greek in type but shows such pronounced 'provincial' features that it may be linked stylistically with Gandharan lion heads and protomes (see Francfort, p. 91, pl. XL). Other gargoyles from Ai Khanum are the comedy mask (see Stavisky, pl. IXb) and the dolphin and lion *protomai* that decorated a fountain on the bank of the Amu River (see Leriche and Thoraval, figs 19–21). Although the latter gargoyles more closely resemble Greek prototypes than the lion-head example from the sanctuary, they are certainly local products and not of such a high quality.

The use of ivory in the Greco-Bactrian period was probably much wider than the finds at Ai Khanum indicate. It has also been suggested that the famous rhyta from NISA in Turkmenistan were produced in Greek Bactria or in the Indo-Greek region. Afghanistan at the end of the 1st millennium BC was also greatly receptive to surrounding cultures, and it appears that Indian ivories in the BEGRAM treasure may have been imported into the region during the Greco-Bactrian or Indo-Greek period (*see also* §(c) below and CENTRAL ASIA, §I, 8(iv)).

(c) c. *1st*–c. *3rd century* AD. Only a few sites in Afghanistan are associated with the art production of the Kushana period, but the archaeological potential of the country is too little exploited for the apparent paucity of finds to be meaningful. The underlying culture is naturally Bactrian Greek, but the region certainly remained open to western influences even in the Kushana period, so that the presence of stylistic or iconographic elements of Hellenistic derivation cannot always be explained as Greco-Bactrian art. At the same time the region received ideas (and, in some instances, perhaps even artefacts) from the eastern Gandharan area, where some of the most vital centres of the 'Greco-Buddhist' art were situated: TAXILA, the monasteries of Peshawar, Mardan and Swat (e.g. SHAH-JI-KI-DHERI, SAHRI BAHLOL, BUTKARA). From India came not only new artistic stimuli but also luxury goods destined for customers of high rank. Symbolic of this receptiveness is the treasure from Begram (anc. Kāpishī), north of Kabul, which probably has a terminus date of the 3rd century AD. The hoard includes Indian ivories, Chinese lacquers, Hellenistic bronzes and plaster casts of metalware and Roman glass, which range in date between the 1st century BC and the beginning of the 3rd century AD. The princely owner of the collection seems to have had exquisite artistic interests, for some of the objects, especially the plaster casts (see Hackin and others, figs 274–320), would have had little intrinsic value or worth as status symbols, but great value as models for reproduction, or inspiration for locally manufactured pieces. The most ancient objects of the treasure are almost certainly those from India. It has been suggested that some of the ivories might be the produce of a local Indo-Parthian school. However, although an intermingling of Indian and, to a much lesser extent, Iranian motifs is certainly recognizable in the ivories, it is far more likely that they were all made in an Indian environment (see Hackin and others, figs 1–239). Perhaps the only object really posing a difficult problem of interpretation is the glazed *kinnarī*-shaped askos, the stylistic details of which are purely Indian (presumably of the first half of the 1st century BC), though the technique of glazing definitely refers to the Parthian world (see Hackin and others, figs 241–2).

In the Jalalabad region of eastern Afghanistan, Gandharan sculpture in stone, presumably attributable to the Kushana period, is indistinguishable from the more widely documented Gandharan output of the north-west Indian subcontinent (present-day north-west Pakistan). Dark grey schist reliefs were discovered at HADDA by the Délégation Archéologique Française en Afghanistan (1926–8), but the stratigraphic context and even the precise site provenance (either Tepe Kafariha or Bagh Gai) of the sculptures are unfortunately unknown (see Dagens, Le Berre and Schlumberger, pp. 11–34, pls I–XXI). Hadda is more famous for later stuccowork, but the discovery of this group of schist sculptures is important because it documents a substantial stylistic unity in the regions to the east and west of the Khyber Pass. However, the question of whether the schist sculptures at Hadda were produced locally or were imported from the Peshawar region, as certain circumstances suggest, is still open to debate. It should be noted that the so-called 'toilet trays' that abound in Pakistani sites of the 2nd century BC to at least the 1st century AD are almost completely missing from Afghanistan (*see* INDIAN SUBCONTINENT, §IV, 5(ii)).

It is certain, however, that the few limestone reliefs discovered at Hadda were locally produced, and they do not show any marked differences in style from the schist group. The formal elements taken from the late Hellenistic repertory can be clearly identified, while the architectural structures that frame the scenes are those of the mature phase of Gandharan sculpture. Nor are any stylistic links missing between the limestone reliefs and the stuccowork, even though the latter is mostly attributable to a later period (from the 4th century onwards).

Another more consistent group of schist sculptures was discovered during excavations at Paitava, SHOTORAK and Kham-e Zargar in Kapisa province, north of Kabul. The work from Kapishi is distinguished by a large number of images of the Buddha standing with flames on his shoulders and water flowing from his feet. The iconography has been related to the so-called Miracle of Shravasti (see fig. 6). It has also been suggested that the area was one of localized Iranian influence and was therefore strongly receptive to religious phenomena of a luminous nature. There is, however, no reason to consider a specifically Iranian origin for the iconography, since India provides an equally natural ideological context. Another characteristic element of these sculptures is the high occurrence of stiff, frontal compositions, with figures that stand out against the background of the relief, thus eschewing superimpositions and perspective effects, and suggesting a close link with works belonging to the so-called dynastic art of the Kushanas at SURKH KOTAL, near Pul-i Khumri, Baghlan province (see Schlumberger, Le Berre and Fussman, pls 58–64). This dynastic art is characterized by images of Kushana kings that are absolutely un-Indian from an iconographic point of view but are connected rather with the nomadic tradition of Central Asia whence the dynasty itself originally emerged. Such royal images (Kabul Mus., see Allchin and Hammond, fig. 5.37) have counterparts in the coinage, the Kushana images of MATHURA (Uttar Pradesh, India) and in a few other examples.

6. Schist relief of the Miracle of Shravasti, from Paitava, *c.* 2nd–*c.* 3rd centuries AD (Paris, Musée Guimet)

Stylistic affinities with this 'dynastic' production, confirmed by the frequent presence of figures in 'Kushana' dress, occur in another group of sculptures that are nevertheless wholly Gandharan in their choice of themes and composition. The sculptures comprise greyish limestone reliefs from the temple of Surkh Kotal (almost exclusively architectural elements, see Schlumberger, Le Berre and Fussman, pls 53–5, 66–8), Sham Qala near Baghlan, Chaqalaq Tepe near Kunduz and from other sites in the same region. The same stylistic characteristics and materials are shared by sculptures from beyond the Amu River in present-day Uzbekistan at such sites as AYRTAM, Kara Tepe and Fayaz Tepe (*see* TERMEZ, §2). The small sample of clay sculptures from Surkh Kotal seems to be contemporary with the limestone work, even if it is not really possible to date either category with any precision.

Widely diffused stucco and unbaked clay production, belonging at least in part to the Kushana period, is documented from numerous sites at Hadda (e.g. Tepe Kalan, Tepe Kafariha, Bagh Gai, Tepe Shotor), the site of Lalma, due south of Hadda, and Basawal on the Kabul River east of Jalalabad. At Tepe Sardar near Ghazna there is some stuccowork that perhaps dates to the 3rd century AD. Stucco from Afghanistan, particularly the eastern regions, exhibits the same iconographic and stylistic characteristics as work in the same medium from north-west Pakistan. The narrative scenes tend to disappear and isolated images of the Buddha and *bodhisattvas* predominate, repeated on the walls of the stupas to signify the multiplication of both historical and transcendental Buddhas, a visual expression of the divine experience as professed in the doctrine of Mahayana Buddhism.

Excavations from the 1960s onwards have revealed unbaked clay sculptures, especially at the Buddhist sites of Tepe Sardar, Tepe Maranjan near Kabul and Tepe Shotor II–IV at Hadda. Minor discoveries have also been made at Basawal, Guldara, Bamiyan and DILBERDJIN. Only a part of this production falls within the 2nd and 3rd centuries AD, but some of the early clay sculptures are real masterpieces. The same stylistic tendency already encountered in stucco is also visible in the clay images, but coupled with a genuine revival of the Hellenistic style. The immediate impression is that the Mediterranean 'sources' are more cultured and courtly than those that formed the earlier basis for so many Gandharan images in schist. The Vajrapani–Herakles (see fig. 7) and the Tyche of Niche V2 in the 'Great *Vihārā*' of Tepe Shotor (2nd–3rd century), for example, exhibit the reappearance after many centuries of iconographic types and stylistic forms that seem to have their roots in the Hellenism of the Greco-Bactrian and Indo-Greek kingdoms.

(d) c. *4th*–c. *9th century* AD. The quantity of Gandharan stuccowork, discovered particularly at Hadda in the 1920s,

7. Relief of Vajrapani–Herakles, unbaked clay, Niche V2, Tepe Shotor monastery, Hadda, *c.* 2nd–*c.* 3rd centuries AD

has been studied in detail, but no satisfactory chronological classification has yet been reached. It is, however, generally held that the majority of these stuccos must be later than the 3rd century AD. The fragments of stucco ornamentation, mainly from stupas, depict images of the Buddha, *bodhisattvas* and, more rarely, narrative scenes. The images were made by applying progressively refined layers of plaster to an inner core. Colour applied to surface details is still preserved on many examples.

The earliest phase of stucco production reworked images derived from Hellenistic stylistic prototypes, but there was a simultaneous development towards a greater idealization of the human figure. The Buddha image in particular lost many realistic traits in order to make room for an elegantly balanced play of simplified volumes, but certain subsidiary figures still retained the vivacity of Hellenistic naturalism. Clay images from the Buddhist sites follow the same stylistic trend, but display a greater preference for stylistic conventionalization and are often more 'Indianized'. Meaningful stylistic comparisons can be made with late examples from Taxila and the random collection of heads from Akhnur in Kashmir (see INDIAN SUBCONTINENT, §IV, 6(ii)). A relatively late date for the work is affirmed not only by the archaeological evidence but also by the appearance of many iconographic and stylistic elements reflecting the ideal of serenity that formed the basis of Indian art in the Gupta period: the facial features of the Buddha image, for example, show a strong reduction to geometric forms, in marked contrast to the fluent richness of the drapery.

Some sculptural groups at Tepe Shotor that also seem to belong to this period on the basis of their technical characteristics demonstrate a capacity for stylization of the human figure that anticipates the solutions of successive centuries. In particular, the 'aquatic niche' (?4th century AD), one of the greatest masterpieces of the region, shows a group of figures modelled in the round, including a Buddha (now missing) standing on a lotus flower, against a highly effective and dramatic background of fantastic fish and other aquatic animals amid the eddies of a pool. A date of the 4th–6th century has been suggested for Tepe Shotor V–VII, while the 6th–7th century has been proposed for the few sculptures from Tepe Maranjan. Excavations at SARDAR TEPE, however, tend to confirm that this production of unbaked clay work took place between the 4th and the 6th century.

The Tepe Sardar excavations are also important for showing conclusively that the so-called school of terracotta sculpture of the north-west Indian subcontinent and Afghanistan never existed. The sculptures were always, in origin, unbaked clay, any terracotta characteristics being merely the result of a later conflagration of the entire monument. The Tepe Shotor and Tepe Sardar excavations have also permitted a detailed analysis of the techniques employed in the manufacture of clay sculptures. In certain respects the process was similar to that used for stucco. The clay sculptures were often supported by a wooden framework, were also coloured and, occasionally, perhaps during the 5th and 6th centuries AD, gilded. Decorative details, such as jewellery, architectural motifs, curls of hair, and also the heads of small figures, were produced in moulds and then applied to the sculptures.

The period also marks the beginning of a trend towards gigantism in images of the Buddha. Tepe Sardar, in particular, provides eloquent examples; but the phenomenon was not exclusive to sites in Afghanistan, even if it was destined to become more important there (*see also* ADZHINA TEPE, TAKHT-I-BAHI). Representations of the Buddha increasingly appeared between two or more *bodhisattvas* of smaller size: an iconographic scheme that was perpetuated even in the most complex representations of the next period. Also perhaps assignable to the 4th–6th century AD is the small head of 'plâtre au grain grossier, de qualité médiocre' (i.e. ?stucco, see Hackin, in Carl, Hackin and Meunié, 1959, pp. 19–21, fig. 60) discovered in a monastery near Kunduz, a beautiful example of the working of Hellenistic motifs, which were subsequently destined to merge into more refined solutions such as those at the 7th-century site of Fondukistan. At Qul-i Nader, Kapisa province, some fragments show the use of yet another technique, also seen at Tepe Shotor, of raw earth covered with painted stucco. Fragments of stucco sculpture from Kama Dakka, between Jalalabad and the Pakistani border, perhaps dating from the 6th–7th century, provide possibly the latest evidence for this phase of artistic production in Afghanistan.

In the second half of the 6th century AD, political and military struggles, including the decline of the Hephthalites, undermined the north-west territories of the Indian subcontinent, formerly the heartland of Gandharan architectural and artistic production. Conversely, Kapisa and the Bamiyan region acquired greater importance, due to the opening of a new road, and thus assumed the function of artistic vanguard. The travel diary of the Buddhist Chinese pilgrim Xuanzang gives some idea of the importance of the kingdom of Bamiyan *c.* AD 632. The two colossal images of the Buddha (55 m and 38 m high), sculpted out of the rockface at BAMIYAN and finished in stucco, are without doubt the most famous works in Afghanistan. For a long time it was thought that the 55 m Buddha (considered the younger of the two; see fig. 8) was made between the 5th and 6th centuries, partly because paintings in the surrounding niche recalled subjects also present at Ajanta (*see* INDIAN SUBCONTINENT, §V, 3(i)(a)). The 38 m Buddha was variously thought to date from the 2nd–3rd century or the 4th. A more recent hypothesis suggests that the two Buddhas, whatever the time difference between them, should not be dated much before Xuanzang's visit, i.e. in the second half of the 6th century, for an undertaking of such importance and influence would only be justified after Bamiyan had emerged as a major centre on an important traffic route.

The 7th century was a turning-point in the artistic production of Afghanistan, both architecturally and in sculpture. Tepe Sardar is a typical example: following the destruction of the ancient sanctuary a partial reconstruction took place, using building techniques that are to a certain degree innovative and sculptural decoration that is also new in its conception. Stratigraphical evidence and stylistic comparisons with FONDUKISTAN place the beginning of these activities in the second half of the 7th century, presumably following one of the Arab raids that began shortly after the middle of the century. Both Fondukistan and Tepe Sardar have yielded a remarkable quantity of unbaked clay sculptures of very high quality and distinctive technique: a core of common clay, prepared round a wooden stick or pole, was covered with an outer layer of modelled red clay, on which colour and/or gilding were applied. The sculptures are innovative in both technique and style, though whether there was an actual gap between this phase of production and the sculptures of the earlier period is uncertain. The use of moulded details greatly increased, not only for parts of the jewellery and clothing but also, ever more prevalently, for curls, locks and tresses of hair and for architectural features such as small pilasters and scroll patterns. Moulds were also commonly used for architectural figural decoration, particularly the small atlantids and numerous small Buddha figures in various postures that decorated the unbaked clay stupas and row of 'thrones' along two sides of the main stupa. Stylistically, some patterns drawn from the late Gupta repertory became more flamboyant and the human figures more elongated, the Buddha image being practically the only one occasionally to show an archaizing trend. The sculptural compositions within the niches or chapels are generally more complicated: paradise scenes at Tepe Sardar, for example, comprise colossal images of the Buddha and *bodhisattvas* in the midst of myriad minor figures. Colour increasingly became an integral part of the sculpture. Although only a few fragments preserve their original polychromy (including gilding), both Fondukistan and Tepe Sardar have yielded enough specimens to provide some idea of the original overall effect, which was presumably closer to the strong contrasts of the earliest known works from the Himalayan regions than to the more elementary chromatism of Gandharan stucco and clay examples of the earlier periods.

8. Rock-cut image of the Buddha in a painted niche, h. 55 m, Bamiyan, *c.* 5th–*c.* 6th centuries AD

In the field of Buddhist iconography, besides the ever-increasing importance of representations that can be labelled 'paradise' scenes, there was a greater occurrence, both in sculpture and painting at Tepe Sardar, Fondukistan and Bamiyan, of image types unknown or at least unusual in the earlier period, such as the so-called 'Buddha paré' (bejewelled Buddha; see fig. 9), and the introduction into Buddhism of deities taken from the Hindu pantheon, such as Durga Mahishasuramardini at Tepe Sardar. Colossal images such as the *Parinirvāṇa* Buddha at Tepe Sardar (l. 16 m) were constructed by modelling unbaked clay around a brick core, a technique that continued from the preceding period. As the cores of votive stupas were also brick, it is apparent that the sculptures employed a masonry technique derived from architecture, while architectural structures (chiefly the stupas) were finished using typical modelling techniques. Since the discovery in 1934 of the Surya seated in a chariot from Khair Khana (Kabul Mus.), several marble sculptures have come to the light in Afghanistan, chiefly in the areas of Kabul, Tagao and Gardez, as well as in the North-west Frontier Province of Pakistan. The marble sculptures, while showing affinities with Buddhist clay images from Fondukistan and Tepe Sardar, also exhibit some idiosyncratic features, such as more rigidly conventionalized details of hair and clothing (usually Sasanian in origin), while the subjects represented

9. Painted clay image of the bejewelled Buddha, from Niche D, Fondukistan, late 7th century AD (Paris, Musée Guimet)

belong, almost without exception, to the Hindu and not the Buddhist repertory. Sculptures in this category include a standing Surya, also from Khair Khana, Kabul; the inscribed Umamaheshvara from Tepe Skandar, *c.* 30 km north of Kabul; two images of Durga Mahishasuramardini, one from Gardez (Kabul Mus.), the other known as the 'Scorretti marble' after its former owner (Rome, Pal. Brancaccio); the Ganesha image with an inscription referring to a *Khiṃgāla Uḍḍiyāna Śāhi* from Gardez in the Dargah Temple at Pir Rathan Nath, Kabul; another Ganesha, originally from Shakar Dara, in a Hindu temple in the Shur Bazaar, Kabul; and a third seated on a lion-*vāhana* (vehicle), allegedly from somewhere near Tagao, an area from which other cognate sculptures have also been found.

It has been convincingly suggested that this group of sculptures should be assigned to the period of the Turki Shahi dynasty (7th–8th century AD), while the closely linked marble sculptures primarily from the area of Hund, Pakistan, should be dated later (9th–10th century). It is interesting to observe that the Ghazna area appears to have remained outside the boundaries of this politico-cultural entity, for no Turki Shahi coins were found at Tepe Sardar, nor have any marble sculptures been reported from the region apart from the Brahma stele in the palace of the Ghaznavid ruler Masʿud III (*reg* 1099–1115) and the Jaina stele (Kabul Mus.), presumably from the same site, which were taken as war booty from elsewhere. The production of these sculptures apparently came to an abrupt end during the 9th century, perhaps with the conquest of Ghazna by the Saffarid Yaʿqub b. Layth in 869–70. As the heads from Akhnur were the eastern counterparts of the earlier clay sculptures from such sites as Tepe Sardar and Tepe Maranjan, so also do fragments from Ushkar, again in Kashmir, provide the closest comparisons for the later works from Afghanistan. The stylistic and iconographic elaborations that took place both in the 4th–5th and the 7th–8th centuries in Afghanistan were, moreover, of great importance for contemporary and later developments in Central Asia and China.

See also CENTRAL ASIA, §§I, 3(iii) and II, 3.

BIBLIOGRAPHY

GENERAL

D. Schlumberger: 'Les Descendants non-méditerranées de l'art grec', *Syria*, xxxvii (1960), pp. 131–66, 254–318

J. M. Rosenfield: *The Dynastic Arts of the Kushans* (Berkeley, 1967)

M. Hallade: *The Gandhara Style and the Evolution of Buddhist Art* (London, 1968)

D. Schlumberger: *L'Orient hellénisé* (Paris, 1970)

B. Rowland: *The Art of Central Asia* (New York, 1974)

S. Gaulier, R. Jera-Bezard and M. Maillard: *Buddhism in Afghanistan and Central Asia*, 2 vols, Iconography of Religions, xiii/14 (Leiden, 1976)

B. Y. Stavisky: *Kushanskaya Baktriya: Problemy istorii i kul'tury* (Moscow, 1977); Fr. trans. as *La Bactriane sous les Kushans: Problèmes d'histoire et de culture* (Paris, 1986)

G. A. Pugachenkova: *Iskusstvo Baktriy epokhi Kushan* [The art of Bactria in the Kushana period] (Moscow, 1979)

B. Stawiski: *Mittelasien: Kunst der Kuschan* (Leipzig, 1979)

S. L. Huntington and J. C. Huntington: *The Art of Ancient India: Buddhist, Hindu, Jain* (New York and Tokyo, 1985), pp. 125–62

L. Nehru: *Origins of the Gandhāran Style: A Study of Contributory Influences* (New Delhi, 1989)

S. Kuwayama: *Kāpishī–Gandāra shi kenkyū* [Studies in the history of Kāpishī–Gandhāra] (Kyoto, 1990)

ARCHAEOLOGICAL REPORTS

J. Barthoux: *Les Fouilles de Haḍḍa, III: Figures et figurines*, Mém.: Dél. Archéol. Fr. Afghanistan, vi (Paris and Brussels, 1930)

J. Hackin and others: *Nouvelles recherches archéologiques à Begram (ancienne Kâpicî), 1939–1940*, 2 vols, Mém.: Dél. Archéol. Fr. Afghanistan, xi (Paris, 1954)

J. Hackin, J. Carl and J. Meunié: *Diverses recherches archéologiques en Afghanistan, 1933–1940*, Mém.: Dél. Archéol. Fr. Afghanistan, xiii (Paris, 1959)

B. Dagens, M. Le Berre and D. Schlumberger: *Monuments préislamiques d'Afghanistan*, Mém.: Dél. Archéol. Fr. Afghanistan, xix (Paris, 1964)

S. Mustamandi and M. Mustamandi: 'The Excavation of the Afghan Archaeological Mission in Kapisa', *Afghanistan Q.*, xxi/4 (1968), pp. 67–79

P. Bernard: 'Quatrième campagne de fouilles à Aï Khanoum (Bactriane)', *Acad. Inscr. & B.-Lett.: C. R. Séances* (1969), pp. 313–55

M. Mustamandi and S. Mustamandi: 'Nouvelles fouilles à Haḍḍa (1966–1967) par l'Institut afghan d'archéologie', *A. Asiatiques*, xix (1969), pp. 15–36

P. Bernard: 'Fouilles de Aï Khanoum (Afghanistan): Campagnes de 1972 et 1973', *Acad. Inscr. & B.-Lett.: C. R. Séances* (1974), pp. 280–308

G. Fussman: 'Nouvelle découverte à Bamiyan', *Afghanistan Q.*, xxvii/2 (1974), pp. 57–78

P. Bernard: 'Campagne de fouilles 1975 à Aï Khanoum (Afghanistan)', *Acad. Inscr. & B.-Lett.: C. R. Séances* (1976), pp. 287–322

P. Leriche and J. Thoraval: 'La Fontaine du rempart de l'Oxus à Aï Khanoum', *Syria*, lvi (1979), pp. 170–205

V. M. Sokolovsky: 'Rekonstruktsiya dvukh skul'pturnykh izobrazheniy iz Dil'berdzhina (raskop X)' [A reconstruction of two sculptural images from Dilberdjin (excavation 10)], *Materialy sovetsko–afganskoy arkheologicheskoy ekspeditsii* [Findings of the Soviet–Afghan archaeological expedition], ii of *Drevnyaya Baktriya* [Ancient Bactria] (Moscow, 1979), pp. 113–19

D. Schlumberger, M. Le Berre and G. Fussman: *Surkh Kotal en Bactriane, I: Les Temples, architecture, sculpture, inscriptions*, 2 vols, Mém.: Dél. Archéol. Fr. Afghanistan, xxv (Paris, 1983)

H.-P. Francfort: *Le Sanctuaire du temple à niches indentées, II: Les Trouvailles*, Mém.: Dél. Archéol. Fr. Afghanistan, xxvii (1984), iii of *Fouilles d'Aï Khanum* (Paris, 1973–92)

M. Taddei and G. Verardi: 'Clay Stūpas and Thrones at Tapa Sardār, Ghazni', *Zinbun*, xx (1985), pp. 17–32

S. Veuve: *Le Gymnase: Architecture, céramique, sculpture*, Mém.: Dél. Archéol. Fr. Afghanistan, xxx (1987), vi of *Fouilles d'Aï Khanum* (Paris, 1973–92)

Z. Tarzi: 'Tapa-e-Top-e-Kalān (TTK) of Haḍḍa', *South Asian Archaeology, 1987*, ed. M. Taddei (Rome, 1990), pp. 707–26

——: *Haḍḍa à la lumière des fouilles afghanes de Tapa-é-Shotor et Tapa-é-Top-é-Kalan* (diss., U. Strasbourg II, 1991)

SPECIALIST STUDIES

J. Hackin: 'Sculptures gréco-bouddhiques du Kapiça', *Mnmts Piot*, xxviii (1925–6), pp. 35–44

A. C. Soper: 'Aspects of Light Symbolism in Gandharan Sculpture', *Artibus Asiae*, xii (1949), pp. 252–83, 314–30; xiii (1950), pp. 63–85

K. Fischer: 'Gandharan Sculptures from Qunduz and Environs', *Artibus Asiae*, xxi (1958), pp. 231–49

S. Kuwayama: 'The Turki Śāhis and Relevant Brahmanical Sculptures in Afghanistan', *E. & W.*, xxvi (1976), pp. 375–407

M. M. Rhie: 'Some Aspects of the Relation of 5th-century Chinese Buddha Images with Sculpture from N. India, Pakistan, Afghanistan and Central Asia', *E. & W.*, xxvi (1976), pp. 439–61

G. Verardi: 'Gaṇeśa Seated on Lion: A New Śāhi Marble', *E. & W.*, xxvii (1977), pp. 277–83

P. Bernard and F. Grenet: 'Découverte d'une statue du dieu solaire Surya dans la région de Caboul', *Stud. Iran.*, x (1981), pp. 128–46

M. Taddei and G. Verardi: 'Buddhist Sculptures from Tapa Sardâr, Ghazni', *Parola Passato*, cxcix (1981), pp. 251–66

G. Verardi: 'Osservazioni sulla coroplastica di epoca kuṣāṇa nel nord-ovest e in Afghanistan in relazione al materiale di Tapa Sardâr', *AION*, xliii (1983), pp. 479–504

——: 'The Kuṣāṇa Emperors as *Cakravartins*: Dynastic Art and Cults in India and Central Asia, History of a Theory, Clarifications and Refutations', *E. & W.*, xliii (1983), pp. 225–94

C. Mustamandy: 'Herakles, Ahnherr Alexanders, in einer Plastik aus Hadda', *Aus dem Osten des Alexanderreiches*, ed. J. Ozols and V. Thewalt (Cologne, 1984), pp. 176–80

M. Taddei: 'Neue Forschungsbelege zur Gandhāra-Ikonographie', *Aus dem Osten des Alexanderreiches*, ed. J. Ozols and V. Thewalt (Cologne, 1984), pp. 154–75

K. Tanabe: 'Iranian Origin of the Gandharan Buddha and Bodhisattva Images', *Bull. Anc. Orient Mus.*, vi (1984), pp. 1–27

G. Verardi: 'Gandharan Imagery at Tapa Sardâr', *South Asian Archaeology, 1981*, ed. B. Allchin (Cambridge, 1984), pp. 257–62

Z. Tarzi: 'La Technique du modelage en argile en Asie centrale et au nord-ouest de l'Inde sur les Kouchans: La Continuité malgré les ruptures', *Ktema*, xi (1986), pp. 57–93

S. Kuwayama: 'Literary Evidence for Dating the Colossi in Bāmiyān', *Orientalia Iosephi Tucci memoriae dicata*, ii, ed. G. Gnoli and L. Lanciotti (Rome, 1987), pp. 703–27

D. Klimburg-Salter: 'Bāmiyān: Recent Research', *E. & W.*, xxxviii (1988), pp. 305–12

M. M. Rhie: 'Interrelationships between the Buddhist Art of China and the Art of India and Central Asia from 618–755 AD', *AION*, suppl. no. liv (1988)

D. Klimburg-Salter: *The Kingdom of Bāmiyān: Buddhist Art and Culture of the Hindu Kush* (Naples, 1989)

S. Kuwayama: 'L'Inscription du Gaṇeśa de Gardez et la chronologie des Turki-Ṣāhīs', *J. Asiat.*, cclxxix (1991), pp. 267–87

M. Taddei: 'The Bejewelled Buddha and the Mahiṣāsuramardinī: Religion and Political Ideology in Pre-Muslim Afghanistan', *South Asian Archaeology, 1989*, ed. C. Jarrige (Madison, 1992), pp. 457–64

——: 'La plastica buddhistica in argilla in Afghanistan e nel nordovest del subcontinente indiano', *Oxus: Tesori dell'Asia Centrale* (exh. cat., Rome, Pal. Venezia, 1993–4), pp. 118–22

For further bibliography *see* §§(i) above and (iii) below.

(iii) Painting. Apart from a few remnants of the Greco-Bactrian period (*c.* 4th–*c.* 1st century BC), most of the evidence for painting in Afghanistan dates from the 3rd century AD onwards and comes from the sites of Hadda and Bamiyan. The medium used throughout is tempera. A large proportion of the paintings at Bamiyan was retained *in situ*; unless otherwise specified, the remaining finds were placed in the Kabul Museum. Following the bombing of the museum in 1993, their fate is uncertain.

(a) *c.* 4th–*c.* 1st century BC. (b) *c.* 1st–*c.* 5th century AD. (c) *c.* 6th–*c.* 9th century AD.

(a) c. 4th–c. 1st century BC. The excavations at Ai Khanum, so rich in architecture and sculpture, provide little direct evidence of figural painting. There is, however, clear evidence that the technique of painting was extensively used. Several architectural pieces, mostly from Rooms 6 and 9 of the Administrative Quarter's southern complex (mid-2nd century BC), still preserve traces of paint on their whitewashed stone surfaces. These traces show that heart-and-dart motifs were painted on mouldings and different artists' 'hands' are even recognizable (see e.g. Bernard and others, i, pl. 80). Another precious relic of painting, found in the sanctuary of the temple 'à niches indentées' (or 'temple à redans') at Ai Khanum, is attributed to the earliest phase of the city (4th century BC). The few fragments of painted canvas, pasted on a wooden frame (a typical Greek technique), depict a frieze of walking lions that presumably constituted the background scene for a cult image.

More substantial evidence of painting in Afghanistan only occurs at the end of the Greco-Bactrian period. Flanking either side of the entrance to the 'temple of the Dioscuri' at DILBERDJIN, north of the Hindu Kush, are the remains of a two-tiered wall painting defined at the bottom by a band of Greek fretwork. The scene depicts two naked young men, one on either side of the door and each accompanied by a horse. The painting, identified by its excavators as a representation of the Dioscuri, belongs to the first phase of the sanctuary (founded *c.* 150 BC), though it is not necessarily contemporary with the period of construction of the temple. The painting is in a very poor state of preservation; nevertheless it is apparent even from the published line drawings and watercolours that the painter's cultural background was intensely Greek. According to the excavation reports, the Dioscuri remained visible during the second phase of the sanctuary (dated to the period of Kujula Kadphises, 1st century AD) but were immured behind a new wall during the third phase (period of Kanishka, *c.* late 1st century to early 2nd). This important point suggests that the Greek religious tradition was not abandoned in this part of the Kushana empire until the time of Kanishka. There is no reason to think of a Vedic connection (the Ashvins) for the two young heroes. The painting technique consisted of the preparation of a loess surface, a sketch of the whole composition in diluted red colour, the use of a comparatively poor range of colours (no blue or green pigments) without chiaroscuro and finally the outlining of the faces and naked bodies in black or brown.

(b) c. 1st–c. 5th century AD. Afghanistan has yielded a fairly large number of wall paintings of the Kushana period. Close stylistic and technical comparisons are possible between these examples and other specimens found in Pakistan and north of the Amu River, for example at Kara Tepe. Although dating the various paintings is extremely difficult, all these remains bear witness to a highly sophisticated technique, and it is clear that the use of painting was far from exceptional in this period.

If the use of colour on stucco sculpture is not taken into consideration, painting of the Kushana period at

Buddhist sites is only known from very poorly preserved fragments at Hadda. Some examples in *Vihāra* B. 56 at Bagh Gai, Hadda, were ochre sketches that were never completed: the most impressive is a representation of the story of Angulimala, which follows the same iconographic models employed by Gandharan artists in stone reliefs. Another sketch in ochre of a moustached head was found on a stupa at Tepe Shotor, Hadda, in 1966–7. A niche from Tepe Kalan (TK.17; Paris, Mus. Guimet) is a good example of symbiosis of sculpture and painting: a modelled Buddha image is flanked by painted images of donors and surmounted by winged cupids who hold a wreath above his head. The typically Greco-Roman iconography, somewhat reminiscent of 3rd-century AD painting at Palmyra, underwent what might be called a Buddhist interpretation: a certain parallelism is noticeable in the paintings from MIRAN, Chinese Turkestan, which are also attributed to the 3rd century.

In the 'temple of the Dioscuri' at Dilberdjin a painting belonging to the fourth period of the sanctuary depicts a standing, high-ranking official beside a divine pair seated on a crouching bull. Since the male divine figure is ithyphallic, the pair can be identified as Shiva and his spouse Parvati. Though it is often doubtful whether this and other 'Hindu' images from Central Asia and Afghanistan (e.g. the Durga Mahishamardini figure at Tepe Sardar) should actually be interpreted as purely Hindu subjects, the derivation from an Indian iconographic model is clear and suggests a date for the painting not earlier than the 4th century AD, though the excavators attribute it to the time of Vasudeva I (3rd century). The painting technique differs from that of the Dioscuri, particularly since it includes the use of chiaroscuro in drapery and perhaps also in the naked parts of the human bodies.

The later north-east religious complex at Dilberdjin contained three rooms with important remains of wall paintings. The painting technique is closer to that of the wall paintings from Central Asia and of the contemporary sites in Afghanistan (e.g. Bamiyan, FONDUKISTAN, Tepe Sardar) insofar as the preparation of the mud-plaster coating and whitewash are concerned. The colour range includes lapis lazuli blue, which also occurs in the Shiva and Parvati painting in the 'temple of Dioscuri'.

The most problematic painting, in Room 12 of the complex, depicts a helmeted character between attendant figures (see fig. 10). It has been suggested that the main figure, seated front view with knees apart in a posture strongly reminiscent of the iconography of Sasanian kings, is a victorious 'hero' to whom homage is paid, but others have labelled this character a 'goddess'. Though the excavators suggest that Dilberdjin was abandoned immediately after the Hephthalite invasion in the 5th century AD, the helmeted figure may be attributed to the 6th–7th century or, if compared with the *bodhisattva* Maitreya in the soffit of Cave K3 at Bamiyan, late 7th century, or even, if compared with Maitreya in the soffit of Niche E at Bamiyan, dated to the 8th century.

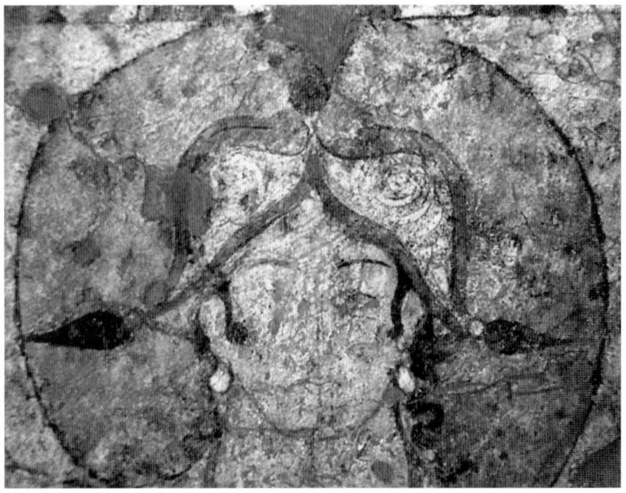

10. Wall painting (fragment) of a helmeted figure between attendants, from Room 12, Dilberdjin, *c.* 5th century AD or later (Kabul, Kabul Museum)

11. Wall painting of disciples of the Buddha flanking a skeleton, from meditation cave, Tepe Shotor, Hadda, *c.* 6th century AD

(c) c. *6th*–c. *9th century* AD. A discovery in 1976 at Tepe Shotor, Hadda, provided the first impressive document of Buddhist painting south of the Hindu Kush: in a meditation cave at the site, ten disciples of the Buddha are shown seated cross-legged on either side of a skeleton (see fig. 11). The exact meaning of this representation is unclear, though the presence in the scroll frieze below the monks of what appear to be floral elements resembling phalli, seems to suggest a Tantric reading of the whole composition. The style can still be placed in the Greco-Buddhist tradition that gave rise to such compositions as the Buddha with monks and trees from Kara Tepe (Uzbekistan; *see* CENTRAL ASIA, fig. 28), attributed to the 2nd–3rd century. The scroll frieze is also very 'Hellenistic' in its free naturalism; nevertheless many details show signs of evolution: the heads are comparatively smaller, the drapery more elaborate, the faces less naturalistic and the shape of the eyes reminiscent of late works such as the manuscript covers from Gilgit (Pakistan). The archaeological evidence confirms a 6th-century date.

In the 6th century AD there was a westward shift of the main roads connecting India to Central Asia. The importance of the sites in Gandhara declined while those in the Hindu Kush flourished. The main archaeological centre in the Hindu Kush is Bamiyan, with four minor centres:

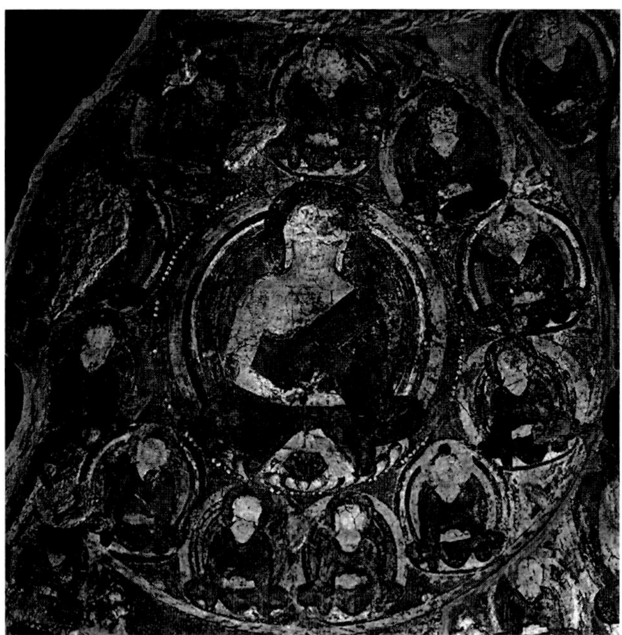

12. Wall painting (fragment) of seated Buddha images, from Cave K.10, Kakrak, *c.* late 7th century AD–*c.* early 8th (Paris, Musée Guimet)

Foladi and Kakrak, quite close to Bamiyan, Fondukistan, *c.* 130 km to the east, and Nigar (Dukhtar-i Nushirwan) to the north beyond the Kara Kotal Pass in the direction of Haibak (Samangan). Both Bamiyan and Fondukistan were investigated by the Délégation Archéologique Française en Afghanistan. In the 1960s and 1970s the wall paintings at Bamiyan were surveyed by scholars chiefly from Afghanistan and Japan and extensively restored by an Indian team.

The chronology of Bamiyan has often been the subject of controversy, also in connection with the formative process of various styles of painting, such as Gandharan, Syrian, Iranian (chiefly Sasanian) and Indian (Gupta). The early dating (Kushana period to the 4th–5th century AD) for the colossal Buddhas has now been abandoned, and most scholars are inclined to believe that neither image is earlier than the second half of the 6th century (*see* §(ii)(d) above). The paintings decorating their huge niches cannot therefore be any earlier in date. Research (see Klimburg-Salter, 1989) suggests the following working hypotheses: firstly, that the art of the Hindu Kush belongs to a single cultural period (7th–9th century); secondly, that it probably resulted from a consistent form of patronage; and thirdly, that the formal development indicates a possible movement towards a later Mahayana perspective.

The painting technique is common to Buddhist sites throughout Afghanistan and Central Asia. Like the wall paintings in India, those from Bamiyan and other sites in Afghanistan are not frescoes (as they are often unduly styled even in scientific literature), but rather tempera paintings. The wall surface first received a dressing of clay mixed with vegetable fibres (*kâhgel*), which functionally corresponds to the *arriccio* of the Italian medieval and later wall paintings. This dressing was coated with a thin white ground layer of burnt gypsum or plaster of Paris, on which the pigments were directly applied in a binding of animal glue. At other sites, such as Tepe Sardar, the ground layer was made of clay mixed with fibres obtained from the inflorescences of a kind of marsh reed (*simgel*); at DUNHUANG kaolin was employed for the same purpose.

A chronological classification of the wall paintings in the Hindu Kush has been attempted (see Klimburg-Salter, 1989) on the basis of style (morphology and representational conventions) and iconography. Phase Ia (mid- to second half of 7th century AD) is represented by paintings in the niche of the 38 m Buddha of Bamiyan; Phase Ib (*c.* second half of the 7th century) by the niche of the 55 m Buddha; Phase IIa–b (late 7th century–early 8th) by Bamiyan Cave K, Niches H and 'i', Fondukistan and Kakrak (see fig. 12); Phase IIc–d (8th century or later) by Bamiyan Niche E and Foladi.

Phase Ia appears to be linked to the 7th-century AD Sogdian paintings at PENDZHIKENT (*see also* CENTRAL ASIA, §I, 4(iv)(a)). Compositions are rather two-dimensional: there is no indication of shading and contours are obtained by using bands of colour separated by brown or black lines. Phase Ib, though essentially a linear style, is richer in shading and sometimes, at least in some subjects, even reflects conventions elaborated at Ajanta in India (*see* INDIAN SUBCONTINENT, §V, 3(i)(a)), though the most significant parallels are with the art of KIZIL and KHOTAN in Chinese Turkestan (*see also* CENTRAL ASIA, §II, 4(ii)(b)).

Phase II can be considered as the typical Bamiyan style, with such clear links with eastern Central Asia, especially Kizil and Kucha, as to suggest that after the Chinese invasion of Kucha *c.* AD 647, painters from there migrated to Bamiyan. The concurrent Chinese conquest of Kizil (647–8), the subsequent Tibetan conquest and Chinese reconquest perhaps also induced Kizil artists to flee their former large, cosmopolitan and free town. The tendency in Phase II is towards a high conventionalization of forms that abandons all interest in realism and develops into a somewhat linear elegance reminiscent of contemporary sculpture at Fondukistan. Characteristic features are thin double lines employed to define drapery, a swirl under the arms, and the use of contrasting black and white figures. At the end of the development, the human form is reduced to diagrammatic patterns.

Among the most interesting compositions at Bamiyan is one in the niche of the 38 m Buddha, which represents a *Pañcavārṣika* ceremony (as described by the Chinese Buddhist pilgrim Xuanzang in about AD 632), at precisely the point when the king presents the Buddha with all his worldly possessions. The ideological value of this ceremony is highly significant for understanding the role assumed by the kings of Bamiyan and the relationship between political and religious power. In the vault of the same niche a solar deity (possibly Surya) is also depicted.

The *Parinirvāṇa* in Cave K3, although poorly preserved, is one of the most impressive representations of this central scene of Buddhist devotion, with an abundance of detail that makes it and the companion painting in the soffit of Maitreya encircled by fifteen roundels, each containing six Buddhas, a rich source of information concerning jewellery, metalwork and (royal) garments (see Tarzi, figs 3–4, 6–12). Presumably the *Parinirvāṇa* was a 'reproduction' of the colossal reclining Buddha *c.* 300 m long that Xuanzang saw at Bamiyan (see Tarzi). The other *Parinirvāṇa* scenes at Bamiyan (Caves F, J and 222; see Miyaji, 1978) are not so rich or complicated and are rather reminiscent of traditional Gandharan representations of the same episode.

The remains of painting from more minor sites include the 'hunter king' in Sasanian style from Kakrak (Kabul Mus.) and the seated *bodhisattva* Maitreya from Niche E at Fondukistan. The Maitreya, together with a considerable number of modelled sculptures in unbaked clay in the same sanctuary, provide one of the most reliable links between sculpture and painting in the Hindu Kush region.

Various sites in other parts of Afghanistan preserve the remains of wall paintings. Those found by the Archaeological Mission of Kyoto University in Cave 130 at Basawal near Jalalabad depict a row of pairs of Buddhas facing each other. A similar setting is found in a painting excavated by the Italian Archaeological Mission in Room 52 at Tepe Sardar, Ghazna, where a row of alternating Buddhas and richly bejewelled *bodhisattvas* is perhaps intended to represent the revelation of Buddhas to *bodhisattvas*. Stylistically, these and other wall paintings from Tepe Sardar are close to those from Fondukistan, but comparisons are also possible with Khotan, Kizil and Pendzhikent. A dating in the 8th century AD seems quite reasonable.

The painting of pre-Muslim Afghanistan and Iran, even after the sanctuaries had been abandoned or (more rarely) destroyed, had a great impact on both art and literature of the subsequent period. At the end of the 10th century, the anonymous *Ḥudūd al-ʿālam* refers to the existence at Bamiyan of wall paintings 'in the Indian style' (see Melikian-Chirvani, p. 23). Even in the 13th century, Arab travellers still showed a lively interest in Bamiyan and its paintings: a description by Yaqut, of wall paintings depicting birds and other animals, is copied from an earlier account written by Samʿani in the mid-11th century (see Melikian-Chirvani, pp. 25–6).

BIBLIOGRAPHY

A. Godard, Y. Godard and J. Hackin: *Les Antiquités bouddhiques de Bāmiyān*, Mém.: Dél. Archéol. Fr. Afghanistan, ii (Paris, 1928)

J. Hackin and J. Carl: *Nouvelles recherches archéologiques à Bāmiyān*, Mém.: Dél. Archéol. Fr. Afghanistan, iii (Paris, 1933)

R. Gettens: 'Materials in the Wall Paintings of Bāmiyān, Afghanistan', *Tech. Stud.*, vi (Jan 1938), pp. 186–93

B. Rowland and A. Coomaraswamy: *The Wall Paintings of India, Central Asia and Ceylon* (Boston, 1938)

J. Hackin: 'Le Monastère bouddhique de Fondukistân: Fouilles de J. Carl, 1937', in J. Hackin, J. Carl and J. Meunié: *Diverses recherches archéologiques en Afghanistan, 1933–1940*, Mém.: Dél. Archéol. Fr. Afghanistan, xiii (Paris, 1959), pp. 49–58

U. Scerrato: 'A Short Note on Some Recently Discovered Buddhist Grottoes near Bāmiyān', *E. & W.*, xi (1960), pp. 94–120

K. Yamasaki: 'Saiiki hekiga no ganryo ni tsuite' [Pigments in the wall paintings of Central Asia], *Bijutsu Kenkyū*, 212 (1960), pp. 31–3

M. Bussagli: *Painting of Central Asia* (Geneva, 1963)

B. Dagens: 'Monastères rupestres de la vallée de Foladi', in B. Dagens, M. Le Berre and D. Schlumberger: *Monuments préislamiques d'Afghanistan*, Mém.: Dél. Archéol. Fr. Afghanistan, xix (1964), pp. 41–8

P. Bernard and others: *Fouilles d'Aï Khanoum, I: Campagnes 1965, 1966, 1967, 1968*, 2 vols, Mém.: Dél. Archéol. Fr. Afghanistan, xxi (Paris, 1973)

A. S. Melikian-Chirvani: 'L'Evocation littéraire du bouddhisme dans l'Iran musulman', *Monde Iran. & Islam*, ii (1974), pp. 1–72

V. P. Buryzh: 'Tekhnika zhivopisi' [Painting technique], *Materialy sovetsko-afganskoy ekspeditsiy, 1969–1973 gg.* [Findings of the Soviet-Afghan expedition], i of *Drevnyaya Baktriya* [Ancient Bactria] (Moscow, 1976), pp. 111–24

I. T. Kruglikova: 'Nastennye rospisi Dil'berdzhina' [The wall paintings of Dilberdjin], *Materialy sovetsko-afganskoy ekspeditsiy, 1969–1973 gg.* [Findings of the Soviet-Afghan expedition], i of *Drevnyaya Baktriya* [Ancient Bactria] (Moscow, 1976), pp. 87–110

A. Miyaji: 'Wall Paintings of Bāmiyān: A Stylistic Analysis', *Japan–Afghanistan Joint Archaeological Survey in 1974* (Kyoto, 1976), pp. 17–31

S. Sengupta: 'Preservation and Conservation of Bamiyan', *Bamiyan: Crossroads of Culture*, ed. A. Miyaji (Tokyo, 1976), pp. 9–15

A. Miyaji: 'The Parinirvāṇa Scenes of Bāmiyān: An Iconographical Analysis', *Japan–Afghanistan Joint Archaeological Survey in 1976* (Kyoto, 1978), pp. 13–22

P. Bernard and H.-P. Francfort: 'Nouvelles découvertes dans la Bactriane afghane', *AION*, xxxix (1979), pp. 119–48

V. P. Buryzh: 'Tekhnika rospisey pomeshcheniya 16' [The technique of the paintings of site 16], *Materialy sovetsko-afganskoy arkheologicheskoy ekspeditsiy* [Findings of the Soviet-Afghan archaeological expedition], ii of *Drevnyaya Baktriya* [Ancient Bactria] (Moscow, 1979), pp. 146–65

I. T. Kruglikova: 'Nastennye rospisi v pomeshcheniy 16 severo-vostochnogo kul'tovogo kompleksa Dil'berdzhina' [The wall paintings of site 16 at the north-eastern cultic complex of Dilberdjin], *Materialy sovetsko-afganskoy arkheologicheskoy ekspeditsiy* [Findings of the Soviet-Afghan archaeological expedition], ii of *Drevnyaya Baktriya* [Ancient Bactria] (Moscow, 1979), pp. 120–45

Z. M. Zhelninskaya and others: 'Analisy krasok nastennykh rospisey Dil'berdzhina' [An analysis of the colours of the wall paintings of Dilberdjin], *Materialy sovetsko-afganskoy arkheologicheskoy ekspeditsiy* [Findings of the Soviet-Afghan archaeological expedition], ii of *Drevnyaya Baktriya* [Ancient Bactria] (Moscow, 1979), pp. 166–72

A. Miyaji: 'The Wall Paintings of Bamiyan Caves (Continued): Stylistic Analysis', *Japan–Afghanistan Joint Archaeological Survey in 1978* (Kyoto, 1980), pp. 16–26

D. Klimburg-Salter: 'Ritual as Interaction at Bamiyan', *Systems of Communication and Interaction in South Asia*, ed. P. Gaeffke and S. Oleksiw (Philadelphia, 1981), pp. 65–9

C. Silvi Antonini and M. Taddei: 'Wall Paintings from Tapa Sardār, Ghaznī', *South Asian Archaeology, 1979*, ed. H. Härtel (Berlin, 1981), pp. 429–38

D. E. Klimburg-Salter, ed.: *The Silk Route and the Diamond Path: Esoteric Buddhist Art on the Trans-Himalayan Trade Routes* (Los Angeles, 1982)

Z. Tarzi: 'La Grotte K3 de Bâmiyân', *Arts Asiatiques*, xxxviii (1983), pp. 20–29

I. T. Kruglikova: *Dil'berdzhin: Khram Dioskurov* [Dilberdjin: the temple of the Dioscuri] (Moscow, 1986)

F. Grenet: 'L'Athéna de Dil'berdžin', *Cultes et monuments religieux dans l'Asie centrale préislamique*, ed. F. Grenet (Paris, 1987), pp. 41–5

D. Klimburg-Salter: 'Dukhtar-i Nushirwan: An Ideology of Kingship', *Kusumañjali: Sh. C. Sivaramamurti Commemoration Volume*, i, ed. N. Rao (New Delhi, 1987), pp. 62–76

——: *The Kingdom of Bāmiyān: Buddhist Art and Culture of the Hindu Kush* (Naples, 1989) [with app. on conservation by R. Sengupta]

M. Mode: 'The Great God of Dokhtar-e Noshirwān (Nigār)', *E. & W.*, xlii (1992), pp. 473–83

For further bibliography *see* §§(i) and (ii) above.

MAURIZIO TADDEI

(iv) Other arts.

(a) Coins. (b) Jewellery. (c) Metalwork. (d) Pottery.

(a) Coins. The official coinage of the Achaemenid (*see* ACHAEMENID, §2) period (550–331 BC) was the Persian gold Daric and silver siglos based on a gold:silver ratio of 13.3 to 1, but these coins are rarely found in Afghanistan (*see* ANCIENT NEAR EAST, §II, 8(i)). Normal currency during the 4th century BC consisted of worn Greek silver coins and their copies. The earliest of these coins had been exported from Athens and other cities of the Greek world as bullion. The hoard discovered in 1966 at Balkh comprised 170 old Greek silver coins of this category, 150 Athenian tetradrachms and coins from 13 other Greek states down to *c.* 380 BC. The group of Greek coins in the OXUS TREASURE had a similar composition. The 1933

13. Silver tetradrachm of Demetrios I of Bactria, obverse showing the king wearing an elephant headdress, diam. 33 mm, issued *c.* 200–*c.* 190 BC (London, British Museum); the reverse shows Herakles

hoard from Chaman-i-Hazuri, Kabul, dating from the mid-4th century BC, contained worn Greek silver with subsidiary denominations of bent bar silver coins weighing *c.* 11.7 gm and punch-marked silver (see Curiel and Schlumberger, pp. 31–45). Other hoards of similar bent bar silver coins with a wheel or sun symbol at each end of the bar have been found at Jalalabad and at Mir Zakah near Gardez (see Curiel and Schlumberger, pp. 65–91), as well as at sites in the Indus Valley such as TAXILA. Double the weight of a silver siglos and possibly derived from the bar coinage of Media, they appear to have constituted the silver coinage of the Achaemenid satrapies in north-west India before the invasion of Alexander the Great in 331 BC.

The fine coinage bearing the head of Herakles that Alexander issued was apparently based on a gold:silver ratio of 10 to 1. Another major change was the introduction of an Attic weight silver tetradrachm tariffed at 20 drachmae per gold stater that ensured the circulation of the new silver issues throughout the east as coins, not bullion. After Alexander's death in 323 BC, Bactria, as a Seleucid province, had a typically Hellenistic coinage with fine obverse portraits of the kings in gold and silver. The Greco-Bactrian kings who subsequently governed Bactria as an independent state after about 250 BC inherited this tradition. The tetradrachms of the first ruler Diodotos and his successor Eukhydemos are well engraved and show the king with a diadem. Demetrios, who invaded India in the early 2nd century BC, is shown with an elephant headdress (see fig. 13). Antimachos Theos is depicted with a Greek travelling cap (*petasos*) and Eucratides with a helmet. The reverse types of the coins show Greek divinities such as Zeus, Herakles, Artemis and the Dioscuri.

South-east Afghanistan was initially part of the Mauryan empire and used the Mauryan square silver punch-marked coinage and square copper coins. When the Greeks extended their rule to the south (*c.* 180 BC), they struck a distinctive coinage incorporating features from the existing Mauryan currency for their new Indian provinces. Pantaleon, Agathokles and their successors struck square copper coins with a reverse legend, initially in Brahmi and subsequently in Kharoshthi, which repeated the information given on the Greek obverse. Apollodotos I issued square silver drachms modelled on the Mauryan silver denomination, and all the Greek rulers of the regions south of the Hindu Kush struck a bilingual silver coinage on the reduced Indian weight standard. More than 80,000 coins collected in the 1830s by Charles Masson (*see* §III below) at BEGRAM, 60 km north of Kabul, and the hoard found in 1947 at Mir Zakah, 73 km north-east of Gardez, provide excellent evidence for the currency of this period in these regions. The Yueh-chih successors to the Greeks in Bactria from *c.* 130 BC onwards struck crude copies in base metal of the tetradrachms of Heliokles, the last Greco-Bactrian king, while the invaders of the Kabul Valley struck increasingly crude copies in copper of Hermaios, the last Indo-Greek king of the region. About AD 20 the Indo-Parthian king Gondophares established a powerful empire extending from Sistan across south Afghanistan to the Punjab. His coinage in Arachosia (Kandahar region) combined a striking portrait bust of the king with the Classical figure of Victory on the reverse. Successors to Gondophares in Arachosia and Sistan continued to strike copper tetradrachms until the Sasanian conquest by Ardashir and Shapur I (mid-3rd century AD).

The establishment of the Kushana empire in the 1st century AD led to the introduction of a standard coinage throughout Bactria and the Punjab. The nameless king Soter Megas struck a copper coinage with the radiate head of Mithra (*see* §I, 4 above) on the obverse and the mounted king on horseback on the reverse. His successor Vima Kadphises introduced the Kushana gold dinar and a large copper tetradrachm with the distinctive obverse motif of the king standing, sacrificing at a low fire altar. During the 2nd century Kanishka and Huvishka introduced a wide range of reverse types, such as Miiro (sun god), Mao (moon god), Oado (wind god) and Oesho (an Iranian wind god associated with the Hindu god Shiva). Under the later Kushanas the range of divinities was reduced to Shiva and Ardochsho, in an increasingly stylized form.

In the absence of an indigenous silver coinage, Sasanian silver drachms came to play an increasing role in the currency of Afghanistan during the 3rd century AD. The Sasanian coins have a portrait of the king on the obverse and a fire altar flanked by two attendants on the reverse, as do some associated Kushano-Sasanian gold and copper issues of Bactria and Gandhara. During the 4th century Hephthalite invaders of Bactria copied the types of the Sasanian king Shapur II (*reg* 309–79). Several Sasanian silver drachms from Afghanistan have Hephthalite countermarks and seem to have been coins paid in tribute in the time of Firuz (*reg* 457/9–84), which were countermarked to serve as Hephthalite currency. Rulers in the Turki Shahi period (early 7th century) followed the same tradition, as can be seen by the silver and copper drachms of Napki Malka and the coins of Vrahitigin. The silver currency of the Hindu Shahis of Kabul (750–1000) used a bull on the obverse and a horseman on the reverse. Most of the coins have an obverse legend in Sharada script, either *Sri Spalapati Deva* or *Sri Samanata Deva* (which are titles rather than personal names), and a letter or symbol in the field. The later debased coins of the currency, struck in billon, were extensively copied by the Islamic dynasties of Ghazna, Kanauj, Ajmer and Delhi (*see* INDIAN SUBCONTINENT, §VII, 6(ii)).

BIBLIOGRAPHY

H. H. Wilson: *Ariana Antiqua: A Descriptive List of the Antiquities and Coins of Afghanistan* (London, 1841/*R* Delhi, 1971)

R. Curiel and D. Schlumberger: *Trésors monétaires d'Afghanistan*, Mém.: Dél. Archéol. Fr. Afghanistan, xiv (Paris, 1953)

D. W. MacDowall and M. Taddei: 'The Early Historic Period: Achaemenids and Greeks'; 'The Pre-Muslim Period', *The Archaeology of Afghanistan: From Earliest Times to the Timurid Period*, ed. F. R. Allchin and N. Hammond (London and New York, 1978), pp. 201–14, 245–55

D. W. MacDowall: 'The Hazrajat Hoard of Indo-Greek Silver Drachms', *Pakistan Archaeol.*, xxvi/1 (1991), pp. 188–98

The Crossroads of Asia: Transformation in Image and Symbol in the Art of Ancient Afghanistan and Pakistan (exh. cat., ed. E. Errington and J. Cribb; Cambridge, Fitzwilliam, 1992)

D. W. MacDOWALL

(b) Jewellery. Northern Afghanistan has produced the richest finds of jewellery from the Achaemenid to the early Kushana period. The wealth of gold material suggests that during this time (*c*. 5th century BC–1st century AD) the region may have been a centre for goldwork of high artistic quality, but the lack of comprehensive excavation evidence makes the precise distinction between imported and indigenous wares unclear. Ornaments in the OXUS TREASURE, discovered near the Amu River, depict male figures, animals or mythical beasts. Prototypes for the stylized figures of fantastic animals occur in Achaemenid art, but the more vigorous appearance of the Oxus Treasure examples links them to the ANIMAL STYLE of the Central Asian steppes (*see* ANCIENT NEAR EAST, §II, 4(ii)(a)). Insets for stones on the haunches of the animals take the form of a dot between two curved triangles, a design that probably derives from the dot and comma motif on animal representations at Persepolis (*see* ACHAEMENID, §§2 and 4).

Six tombs of the 1st century BC–1st century AD at TILLYA TEPE yielded more than 20,000 gold objects, particularly buckles, clasps, collars, pendants and clothing plaques (*see also* §(c) below). The material shows that a local artistic tradition with roots in Achaemenid art continued until the beginning of the 1st century AD. The jewellery further reveals the co-existence of two other trends, the one influenced by the Animal style of the steppes, the other by Greek culture. Borrowed images are rather debased, as they usually lack the characteristic elegance and vitality of their sources of inspiration. A further distinct group shows a new stylistic development that combines Oriental, Greek and nomadic traditions. Elements borrowed from the decorative repertories of India and China appear on some items, while indigenous traditional motifs occur on others. Small drop-shaped insets of turquoise decorate the objects. Jewellery found in tombs on the opposite bank of the Amu River, in Uzbekistan, are, by contrast, all executed in a homogeneous style that follows well-defined local artistic traditions.

Jewellery of the 2nd–3rd century AD, recovered in excavations of the Kushana levels at Begram (see Ghirshman, pl. XVI.1–11), shows an increasing preference for polychromy and for ornaments encrusted with coloured, geometrically cut stones. Similar jewellery has also been found at Palmyra, Hatra and in south Russia (*see* ANCIENT NEAR EAST, §II, 4(ii)(b)). Although few extant examples have been found in Afghanistan, the wealth of ornaments depicted on the *bodhisattva* statues of Gandhara provide a comprehensive record of the jewellery of the Kushana period (*see* INDIAN SUBCONTINENT, §IV, 5(ii)(d)).

BIBLIOGRAPHY

O. M. Dalton: *The Treasure of the Oxus with Other Examples of Early Oriental Metalwork* (London, 1905, rev. 3/1964)

R. Ghirshman: *Bégram: Recherches archéologiques et historiques sur les kouchans*, Mém.: Dél. Archéol. Fr. Afghanistan, xii (Cairo, 1946), pp. 58–65

J. Hackin, J. Carl and J. Meunié: *Diverses recherches archéologiques en Afghanistan, 1933–40*, Mém.: Dél. Archéol. Fr. Afghanistan, viii (Paris, 1959), figs 228–55

A. M. Mandel'shtam: *Kochevniki ha puti v Indiya: Tradui tadzhikskoi arkheologicheskoi ekspeditsii* [The nomads on the Indian routes: results of the Tajik archaeological expedition] (Moscow, 1966)

——: 'Archäologische Bemerkungen zum Kuschana-Problem', *Beiträge zur alten Geschichte und deren Nachleben: Festschrift für Franz Altheim*, 2 vols, ed. R. Stiehl and H. E. Stier (Berlin, 1969–70), pp. 525–34

G. Pugachenkova: *Les Trésors de Dalverzine-tepe* (Leningrad, 1978), p. 47, pls 63–79

B. A. Litvinsky and I. R. Pichikyan: 'The Temple of the Oxus', *J. Royal Asiat. Soc. GB & Ireland* (1982), no. 2, p. 163

V. Sarianidi: *The Golden Hoard of Bactria from the Tillya-tepe Excavations in Northern Afghanistan* (New York and Leningrad, 1985)

C. FABRÈGUES

(c) Metalwork.

Prehistoric. In September 1966, a hoard of gold and silver vessels was uncovered near Sad Hazard village, between Kunduz and the lapis lazuli mines of Badakhshan, north-east Afghanistan. The hoard apparently came from an archaeological mound known as Fullol or Khosh Tapa ('happy mound'). The exact circumstances of discovery are not known; it is likely, however, that the hoard came to light while villagers were collecting earth from the site for their fields. Some of the vessels were cut up and sold to local goldsmiths and jewellers. Five gold and twelve silver vessels, almost all fragmentary and weighing *c*. 2 kg and 1 kg respectively, were placed in the Kabul Museum. Incised designs on the vessels include the stepped cross, so prevalent on Quetta ware and ceramics from Turkmenistan. Incised snakes recall examples from TEPE SIALK, Iran, and those on Anjira ware from Baluchistan. Two vessels have boars. Also present are the bearded bull, shown turned with a full face, as in finds from the Royal Cemetery of UR, and rows of romping bulls. One vessel has an eight-armed curl pattern and confronted bulls. None of the bovids depicted is of the humped Indian zebu type. The general conclusion of those who have handled the material is that the objects seem to come from diverse localities and different periods. Dupree, Gouin and Omer even entertain the possibility that the villagers assembled materials from several different find spots. Tosi and Wardak suggest that a local chieftain assembled the materials in antiquity. The bearded bulls suggest a date of

14. Reliquary decorated with repoussé images of the Buddha between Brahma and Indra, gold inset with garnets, h. 65 mm, from the relic deposit of Stupa 2 at Bimaran, 1st century AD (London, British Museum)

c. 2500 BC; other motifs place the date somewhat later, even extending into the early centuries of the 2nd millennium BC.

BIBLIOGRAPHY

L. Dupree, P. Gouin and N. Omer: 'The Kosh Tapa Hoard from North Afghanistan', *Afghanistan*, xxiv/1 (1971), pp. 44–54

M. Tosi and R. Wardak: 'The Fullol Hoard: A New Find from Bronze-Age Afghanistan', *E. & W.*, xxii/1 (1972), pp. 9–17

K. R. Maxwell-Hyslop: 'The Khosh Tapa–Fullol Hoard', *Afghan Stud.*, iii–iv (1982), pp. 25–37

GREGORY L. POSSEHL

Later periods. Excavated material from Greco-Bactrian and early Kushana sites (*c.* 3rd century BC–2nd century AD) provides most of the information on metalwork in the historical periods before *c.* AD 900, supplemented by a few stray finds from other periods. The material fits broadly into three categories: imported wares, local imitations (principally of contemporary Near Eastern and Iranian wares) and indigenous items.

The OXUS TREASURE, a hoard of primarily Achaemenid gold and silver objects, dated *c.* 550–*c.* 330 BC, was found in the banks of the Amu River, perhaps at Takht-i Kubad, in 1877. Achaemenid metal artefacts have also been excavated at TAKHT-I SANGIN, the fortress on the opposite bank of the river in Tajikistan. The earliest objects in the Oxus Treasure are in an assyrianizing style: a gold acinaces sheath decorated with hunting scenes and a gold phiale with addorsed lions. The hoard includes vessels (one in the form of a fish), a model of a chariot, human and animal figurines (deer, a goose, a silver handle in the form of an ibex), a silver disc with horsemen hunting reindeer, ibex and a hare depicted in ANIMAL STYLE, jewellery, coins and numerous votive plaques. The wide diversity of objects suggests the treasure may have been a temple hoard, but details concerning its precise context and original composition are lacking (*see also* §(b) above).

Excavated finds from the Greco-Bactrian city of AI KHANUM (*c.* 330–*c.* 100 BC) include a bronze cauldron handle with two female busts emerging from vine leaves and a copper crescent (probably a pectoral) with a female face (see Francfort, pp. 56–8, pl. XX.IV, nos 27–8). A bronze statuette of a thickset, wreathed Herakles is iconographically correct, but disproportionate, and was probably made locally (see Bernard, p. 302, fig. 13). A 3rd-century BC gilded silver medallion, thought to be imported from northern Syria, depicts Cybele and a winged Nike in a chariot pulled by two lions facing a figure on a stepped altar, with Helios, a crescent moon and star above (see Francfort, pp. 93–104, pl. XLI).

More than 20,000 metalwork objects, displaying a rich diversity of styles (e.g. Hellenistic, Greco-Bactrian, Animal style) and variously dated *c.* 1st century BC or early 1st century AD, were discovered in the royal burials at TILLYA TEPE. Most of these finds were pieces of gold jewellery (*see also* §I, 4 above), but also included were Chinese mirrors, a gold fluted phiale and a cylindrical container, both inscribed in Greek, several bowls and pots, some decorated with bands of Hellenistic vegetal motifs, a gold figure of a goat and, in the male grave, a gold handled dagger and two sheaths, inset with turquoise and decorated with animals, mythical winged beasts and dragons in Animal style.

At BEGRAM, bronze balsamaria or unguent vases in the form of busts of Athena, Hermes and Ares were probably imported from the west *c.* 1st century BC–*c.* 1st century AD, as were a bronze Harpokrates and an unusual syncretic image combining Serapis with Herakles. The bronze finds (Kabul Mus. and Paris, Mus. Guimet; see Ghirshman, pl. XII; Hackin and Hackin, figs 47–59; Hackin and others, figs 322–5) also include statuettes of a monk, a winged Eros and two horsemen, one Greek, the other of Scythian type, a cockerel with a human head, a mask of Silenus and a shield decorated with a gorgon head encircled by repoussé dolphins. Imported 1st–2nd century AD Alexandrian plaster mouldings of Hellenistic subjects are thought to have served as a source of reference for silversmiths at Begram. Several small bronze figurines of uncertain Afghan provenance (see 1992 exh. cat., nos 102–3, 105–6, 108, 110–12, 117) exhibit a similar range of Classical influences and subjects (e.g. a herm, Herakles, Demeter).

A quantity of metalwork was uncovered in the relic deposits of stupas near Kabul and Jalalabad in the 19th century (*see* §III below). Most famous is the Bimaran gold reliquary (see fig. 14), which is decorated with standing images of the Buddha, Indra, Brahma and perhaps a *bodhisattva* (London, BM; see 1992 exh. cat., pp. 186–92; *see also* §I, 4 above and INDIAN SUBCONTINENT, §IV, 5(ii)). These are the earliest datable Buddha images in Gandharan art, for which coins of *c.* mid-1st century AD included in the stupa deposit provide a *terminus ante quem.* Other reliquaries important for dating purposes are the gold amulet case from Ahinposh that contained Roman aurei of AD 100–136 and the inscribed bronze Wardak vase, which is dated year 51 of the Kushana king Kanishka and mentions his successor Huvishka (London, BM; see 1992 exh. cat., nos 170–71).

Two silver pateras, heirlooms of the Mirs of Badakshan, were acquired by a British officer, Dr P. Lord, in 1838. One is decorated with embossed and gilded sheet silver figures depicting the Triumph of Dionysos (London, BM; see Dalton, no. 196). Certain misunderstood details suggest a non-western, possibly local workshop of *c.* 1st century AD. The second patera, a Sasanian piece of *c.* mid-4th century, depicted a prince on horseback attacking a lion but was lost during the British retreat from Kabul in 1840 and is now known only from a drawing (see Harper, p. 134, pl. 11). A number of bronze Buddha and *bodhisattva* statues, purported to be principally from the eastern Afghanistan Hindu Kush region and variously dated *c.* 4th–*c.* 7th century (see von Schroeder, pl. V, figs 3a, 5a–b), are closely related to images from the Swat and Peshawar valleys, Pakistan. While Afghanistan is the most likely source of copper, tin and zinc for all these figures, preliminary technical analysis suggests there are identifiable regional variations in composition and manufacturing techniques (see 1992 exh. cat., pp. 241–56).

BIBLIOGRAPHY

O. M. Dalton: *The Treasure of the Oxus with Other Examples of Early Oriental Metalwork* (London, 1905, rev. 3/1964)

J. Hackin and J.-R. Hackin: *Recherches archéologiques à Begram*, 2 vols, Mém.: Dél. Archéol. Fr. Afghanistan, ix (Paris, 1939)

R. Ghirshman: *Bégram: Recherches archéologiques et historiques sur les kouchans*, Mém.: Dél. Archéol. Fr. Afghanistan, xii (Cairo, 1946)

J. Hackin and others: *Nouvelles recherches archéologiques à Begram, 1939–1940*, 2 vols, Mém.: Dél. Archéol. Fr. Afghanistan, xi (Paris, 1954)

P. Bernard: 'Fouilles de Aï Khanoum (Afghanistan): Campagnes de 1972 et 1973', *Acad. Inscr. & B.-Lett.: C. R. Séances* (1974), pp. 280–308

P. Harper: *Royal Imagery*, i of *Silver Vessels of the Sasanian Period* (New York, 1981)

U. von Schroeder: *Indo-Tibetan Bronzes* (Hong Kong, 1981)

H.-P. Francfort: *Le Sanctuaire du temple à niches indentées, II: Les Trouvailles*, Mém.: Dél. Archéol. Fr. Afghanistan, xxvii (1984), iii of *Fouilles d'Aï Khanoum* (Paris, 1973–92)

V. Sarianidi: *The Golden Hoard of Bactria from the Tillya-tepe Excavations in Northern Afghanistan* (New York and Leningrad, 1985)

G. Fussman: 'Numismatic and Epigraphic Evidence for the Chronology of Early Gandharan Art', *Investigating Indian Art*, ed. M. Yaldiz (Berlin, 1987), pp. 67–88

G. A. Pugachenkova and L. I. Rempel: 'Gold from Tillia-tepe', *Bull. Asia Inst.*, v (1991), pp. 11–25

The Crossroads of Asia: Transformation in Image and Symbol in the Art of Ancient Afghanistan and Pakistan (exh. cat., ed. E. Errington and J. Cribb; Cambridge, Fitzwilliam, 1992) [technical analysis app. by C. Reedy, pp. 241–63]

E. ERRINGTON

(d) Pottery. Prehistoric pottery (*c.* 4000–1000 BC) is characterized by painted decoration, which develops from simple curvilinear designs towards bolder and more complex geometric motifs and finally includes representations of stylized animals towards the end of the period. There are considerable stylistic links with southern Turkmenistan and Baluchistan throughout the prehistoric period. Burnishing, a distinctive new style of surface treatment, first appeared in the Achaemenid period (*c.* 530–330 BC) and soon became predominant. The initial simple wavy line or radial burnishes were superseded in the Hellenistic period (*c.* 3rd–1st century BC) by 'red spiral-burnished ware', that is spiral or horizontal line burnishing, usually on red/orange fabrics. Achaemenid and Hellenistic pottery shapes share some characteristics with Middle Eastern pottery of the same date, and Greek influence in the Hellenistic period can be seen with local imitations of Greek black-polished wares. Thereafter, foreign influences seem to recede, and the indigenous spiral-burnished wares predominate.

Red spiral-burnished ware was used almost exclusively in the Kushana period (*c.* 1st–3rd century AD). The ware occurs all over Afghanistan, much of Pakistan and in adjacent Parthian areas as far west as Khorasan in Iran. Although often considered a 'hallmark' for the Kushana period, it cannot be associated exclusively with the Kushanas, as was once thought, but is also found in the subsequent Sasanian, Hepthalite and Turki Shahi periods. Red spiral-burnished ware thus remained the most important pottery style, showing very little variation, throughout the 1st millennium AD until the beginning of the Islamic period (*c.* early 10th century).

BIBLIOGRAPHY

J.-C. Gardin: *Ceramiques de Bactres* (Paris, 1957)

L. Dupree: *Shamshir Ghar: Historic Cave Site in Kandahar Province, Afghanistan* (New York, 1958)

J.-M. Casal: *Fouilles de Mundigak*, 2 vols, Mém.: Dél. Archéol. Fr. Afghanistan, xvii (Paris, 1961)

A. W. McNicoll and W. Ball: *Excavations at Kandahar* (Oxford, 1995)

W. BALL

2. *c.* AD 900–*c.* 1900. Afghanistan was of particular importance for the arts of Islam between the 10th century and the 16th. Western Afghanistan was often included in the province of Khurasan (now limited to Iran). Although NISHAPUR was the provincial capital in early Islamic times, HERAT became increasingly important after the Mongol conquests in the 13th century and served as a capital of the TIMURID empire in the 15th. In the 11th–12th century, southern Afghanistan became important under the GHAZNAVID dynasty, which had capitals at GHAZNA and LASHKARI BAZAR. Eastern Afghanistan, with its centre at KABUL, flourished from the early 16th century under the patronage of the Mughal emperors of the Indian subcontinent. Northern Afghanistan, particularly the region of BALKH, became important from the 16th century under the SHAYBANID dynasty and their Uzbek successors.

The earliest Islamic buildings in Afghanistan date from the 9th century AD, when builders already employed materials, techniques and styles associated with the metropolitan centres of the Abbasid caliphate in Iraq. The nine-bay mosque at Balkh (9th century; *see* ISLAMIC ART, §II, 4(i)(c)), for example, was built of brick following a plan also found in North Africa and Spain and was decorated with carved stucco in the BEVELLED STYLE. Under the Ghaznavids and Ghurids (*reg* *c.* 1000–1215) there developed a progressive style of architecture distinguished by massive scale, occasional use of stone, distinctive arch profiles, new types of glazed tilework, terracotta decoration and inscriptions written in angular and cursive scripts (*see* ISLAMIC ART, §II, 5(i)(c)). Perhaps the most evocative example of this style is the towering late 12th-century minaret at Jam (*see* MINARET, fig. 3) in a remote valley in the centre of the country. Herat flourished under the Timurids, when the city and its environs were graced with splendid brick buildings enveloped in glittering webs of glazed tile (*see* ISLAMIC ART, §II, 6(i)(b)). Many of the most important monuments, however, were destroyed in the 19th century when the region was contested by the Russians and the British. The complex of Abu Nasr Parsa at Balkh exemplifies how shrines developed in the later period with the addition of madrasas and hospices around the grave of an earlier saint.

Many types of Islamic decorative art were produced in Afghanistan from early times. A group of hemispherical basins made of high-tin bronze is associated with the Ghaznavids because of the bifurcated hats worn by the courtiers depicted on them. Herat was a major centre of metalworking for centuries, to judge from the inlaid Bobrinski Bucket (*see* ISLAMIC ART, fig. 140) made in 1163, the huge cast bronze basin (dated 1374–5) in the congregational mosque, and the inlaid jugs made for the Timurid ruler Husayn Bayqara and other 15th-century patrons (*see* ISLAMIC ART, fig. 149). The arts of the book also flourished from an early date. Some idea of early manuscript illumination can be gained from a book (Leiden, Rijksuniv. Bib., MS. 437) formerly in the library of the Ghaznavid amir ʿAbd al-Rashid (*reg* 1049–51) and a copy of the Koran made at Bust in 1111–12 (Paris, Bib. N., MS. arab. 6041; *see* ISLAMIC ART, fig. 101). The apogee of the arts of the book in Afghanistan, and one of the great moments in all Islamic art, occurred in Herat under the patronage of the Timurid princes Baysunghur and Husayn Bayqara (*see* ISLAMIC ART, §III, 4(v)(d)). Splendid calligraphy by such masters as MIR ʿALI HUSAYNI HARAVI was embellished with beautiful illumination and paintings by such artists as BIHZAD and contained within sumptuous bindings (*see* ISLAMIC ART, fig. 138). After the collapse of Timurid power in the early 16th century, Herat ceased to be a major centre of patronage, but some painters worked in Kabul, temporary home of the Mughal court, in the middle of the century.

For bibliography see the individual articles cited in the text.

□

3. AFTER *c.* 1900. Creative expression in 20th-century Afghanistan resides in the artistry of diverse ethnic and tribal groups living mainly in rural villages and semi-nomadic camps. Western art styles, popularized during the early years of the 20th century by educated urban élites, tend to be imitative rather than innovative.

(i) Architecture. (ii) Painting and sculpture. (iii) Other arts.

(i) Architecture. The introduction of a more Western style of domestic architecture was accompanied by innovations in interior décor, furniture making, painting, landscape gardening and dress styles. When Amir Abdur Rahman (*reg* 1880–1901) acceded to the throne after living in exile in Central Asia for over a decade, he abandoned the traditional house plan with its interior courtyards and personally designed vaulted and domed palaces that faced outwards on to English gardens adorned with fountains.

The first 'European' home was built according to the same specifications as Dorchester House of Park Lane, London, in Kabul. This building heralded a period characterized by British Indian designs. These verandahed colonial styles fell out of fashion after the short 1919 war between Afghanistan and England, and King Amanullah (*reg* 1919–29) turned for inspiration to 18th-century European grand styles with their exuberant and eclectic mix of Neo-classical and pseudo-Rococo elements. By the mid-20th century this ebullience gave way to the utilitarian Soviet and Central European models that still dominate both domestic and public buildings.

Interior transformations mirrored changing lifestyles. In traditional homes each room served several purposes. White walls were decorated with floral ornamentation in pressed, moulded or carved stucco. Furnishings comprised richly coloured Afghan carpets and embroidered door hangings. There was no need for furniture, as mattresses and bolsters doubled for sitting and sleeping, fabric runners were spread on the floor for dining, and traditional clothing folded easily for storage in wall niches or decorated boxes.

Rooms in modern homes in Kabul, on the other hand, were set aside for specific purposes and filled accordingly with massive, ornately carved furniture, including commodious wardrobes to accommodate European clothes. While carpets were retained, stuccowork gave way to flocked and textured wallpaper, or stencilled approximations and daubed simulations of luxurious wood and marble wainscoting that provided a backdrop for a wealth of imported Victorian clutter.

(ii) Painting and sculpture. From the late 19th century onwards artists experimented with novel Western techniques, yet their landscapes and vivid abstract paintings incorporated no recognizable Afghan characteristics; even when the scenes were Afghan, the styles were clearly derivative. Sculpture, an innovation introduced many years later by students returning from Italy and the Soviet Union, was coolly received by this Muslim society. However, birds and animals carved from marble and lapis lazuli by artisans trained in Kabul by Chinese masters became popular with tourists.

Contemporary Afghan artists and sculptors have yet to enjoy either private patronage or public support despite official promotion by the government since the 1970s. In 1978 leftist urban leaders overthrew the élites who had set trends for almost 100 years. Their rise, closely followed by Soviet military intervention, ushered in a period dominated by socialist realism. Devastation caused by ground and air offensives forced more than a third of the Afghan population into exile in neighbouring Pakistan and Iran. Nevertheless, since 1989 an intrepid group of young artists has attracted growing numbers of students in their attempts to revive the Herati traditions of miniature painting and calligraphy renowned in Afghanistan during the 15th century.

Within the public domain, stylized floral mural painting (see fig. 15) enjoys a certain popularity in the decoration of mosques and teahouses. The most distinctive painting tradition in this genre, however, is displayed on truck bodies completely embellished with a wide range of themes including Swiss chalets, lovely ladies, trains, boats, telephones, animal combat scenes, birds and contemporary battle scenes.

(iii) Other arts. Of all Western innovations, dress probably had the most far-reaching, durable influence upon society. In the late 19th century hoops, bustles and wide-brimmed plumed and beribboned hats were introduced for the

ladies, along with splendid emblazoned uniforms, frock coats and tweeds fancied by the gentlemen at court. As fashions closely followed European changes, including mini-skirts and the ubiquitous T-shirt and jeans, Western dress became a measure of modernity throughout the educated urban populations and, for women, it symbolized emancipation.

More enduring indigenous examples of art and craftsmanship are found among the diverse creative traditions brought to Afghanistan over many centuries by artisans travelling to this pivotal Central Asian land from east, west, north and south along the routes of conquest and commerce. From 1978 onwards, however, the disruptions of war hastened the decline of crafts already affected by the introduction of modern materials, production methods, imports and commercialization. The art of ornamental stucco has all but disappeared; ikat weaving from an already limited number of northern workshops suffers equally; Nuristani wood-carving, Pushtun painted and lacquered wood decoration, tilemaking, copperwork and pottery and Herati glassblowing, silversmithing and silk weaving are all threatened. Nevertheless, since few items produced in Afghan villages and semi-nomadic camps are purely decorative and since most express personal and/or group identification and status, there is reason to hope for a craft revival once peace permits life to return to normal. The exquisite embroidery made by refugees for their personal use, in contrast to the lamentable pieces seen for sale, allows this note of optimism.

(a) Carpets and textiles. The richness of form and colour of the flat-woven, hand-knotted and felt carpets made by the Turkomen, Uzbek, Hazara, Aimaq, Kirghiz and Baluch place them among Afghanistan's most renowned artistic products. Ranking fifth among the country's exports before 1978, the carpet trade has continued on a reduced scale throughout the war, although the difficulties in obtaining quality raw materials coupled with local market demands on design and pricing have adversely affected the production of Afghan carpets by refugees in Pakistan and Iran. Carpet production contributes significantly to family income and is highly valued. Quality products are more particularly esteemed because they add to individual status. A bride gains heightened respect from her husband's family when her dowry includes fine examples of her own handiwork; a man's wealth and status is gauged by the quantity and quality of his household's production. Furthermore, since distinctive structures, designs, symbols and colours are proudly associated with specific groups, the excellence of the work of its individual producers enhances the reputation of the entire community.

While carpets represent a major portion of woven articles for sale, an inexhaustible variety of other items are made for both utilitarian and decorative use within the household. Long narrow woven bands both strengthen and decorate the wooden lattice framework of round felt-roofed yurts (*see* TENT, §II, 2(ii)). The Kirghiz, among others, entwine the reeds forming the skirting of yurts and interior partition screens with yarn in variegated designs. Almost all semi-nomadic groups use hand-knotted, often fringed, door hangings.

15. Floral mural painting

Furniture in most sedentary and semi-nomadic homes scarcely extends beyond an occasional wooden stool, one or two wooden chests and perhaps a cradle (*see* §(d) below). Possessions from clothing to food supplies are stored in flat-woven or knotted bags of various shapes and sizes. Uzbeks distinctively wrap bedding and clothing in flat-woven squares (2×2 m), which are stacked on top of chests. Finely embroidered V-shaped pieces and beaded tassels hung against these bundles provide the final adornment. Elsewhere, strings of pompoms and woollen tassels are used as cornices and wall hangings. By the mid-20th century, hand-woven textiles for clothing had largely given way to imported and locally manufactured materials. Exceptions are prized silk turbans, a speciality of the Herat area, and the popular striped cottons used for long-sleeved robes throughout the north.

Embroidery motifs and stitches serve to distinguish ethnic and regional goups. Embroidered items are made for family use and only rarely offered for sale. This handicraft is most importantly associated with marriage. Each male family member attending a wedding is presented with a finger-woven trouser drawstring with silk tassels and an intricately embroidered cummerbund. In addition to embroidered clothing, the bride's dowry typically includes up to 20 types of embroidered household items, from spoon bags, tray covers, sachets for money and make-up to dust covers for Korans and radios. Soft, knee-high leather boots embellished with fine embroidery by Turkic-speaking women of the north are especially prized. Every woman in the family takes part in spinning wool and silk, weaving, stitching and embroidering in order to amass this extensive collection. Kin-related girls often work together on the large embroidered and patchwork pieces. Mothers devise baby bonnets festooned with feathers, pompoms and protective charms. Intricately embroidered and beaded hats worn under men's turbans and women's headscarves are distinctive symbols of group identity. Ornaments, mirrorwork, gold braid, elaborate beading and fine embroidery decorate the high-waisted bodices, elbow-length cuffs and deep hems of women's dresses, the skirts of which may, among some groups, contain as much as 12 m of velvet or flowered cotton.

Among semi-nomadic groups, individual artistry is publicly displayed during their annual migrations in a variety of ornamental trappings for camels, donkeys and horses. In addition to saddle bags and blankets there are decorated leather harnesses, silver-studded saddles and neckpieces. A bridal camel, bedecked with a heavy, glass-beaded headdress and reins takes pride of place in any caravan. These sumptuous accoutrements proclaim wealth, status and power.

(b) Jewellery. Items for personal adornment have been zealously developed by all groups. Distinctive patterns distinguish each ethnic group, place of origin and, particularly among the Pushtun, tribe and sub-tribe. The most popular jewellery is made of silver, at times fire-gilded, a technique most employed by the Turkomen. Heavy, embossed torques of twisted silver are a speciality of Nuristan, but all bracelets, armlets, earrings, temple pendants and headdress ornaments tend to be massive and liberally hung with pendants. Insets of coloured glass or hardstones, including carnelian, turquoise and lapis lazuli, are frequently embued with symbolic meaning to avert sorrow, danger and disease or bring joy, serenity and marital bliss. Generous sprinklings of silver beads, discs, coins, medallions, dress fastenings, amulets and talismans are also sewn on to clothing in great profusion.

(c) Pottery. The shapes and designs of the primarily utilitarian pottery have survived unchanged for 5000 years. Glazes are rare, except for those found at Istalif, a hillside village just north of Kabul. The clear, bright blue pottery with black incised floral decorations and the bird and animal figurines from Istalif are unique. The Istalif double-headed horse must surely represent a tradition of considerable antiquity, although the potters themselves attribute their creations simply to 'custom'.

(d) Woodwork. Lacquered wooden boxes, stools, bedlegs and cradles are regional specialities, most notably in the east. Lacquerwork is normally restricted to colourful banding, but some artisans have developed a technique of applying several layers of different colours, which are then cut away to reveal intricate floral designs. The art of woodcarving in general is largely applied to such architectural elements as window-frames and panels, doorframes, lintels and pillars in homes and mosques. Much of this work exhibits affinities to Kashmiri floral, geometric and curvilinear traditions; unique motifs from Nuristan include animistic symbols that pre-date the conversion of this area to Islam in 1895. Distinctive snuff-boxes, made from small gourds, are traditionally shaped in wooden moulds as they ripen on the vine and are then highly polished, painted or adorned with silver stoppers and decorative collars.

BIBLIOGRAPHY

M. Kohzad: 'L'Inauguration du salon d'automne à Kaboul', *Afghanistan Q.*, i/4 (1946), pp. 30–34

B. Dupaigne: 'Aperçus sur quelques techniques afghans', *Obj. & Mondes*, viii (1968), pp. 41–84

A. Friedman: 'The Handicrafts of Afghanistan', *Afghanistan Q.*, xxv/2 (1972), pp. 11–12

N. Dupree: 'Archaeology and the Arts in the Creation of a National Consciousness', *Afghanistan in the 1970s*, ed. L. Dupree (New York, 1974), pp. 203–38

C. Naumann: 'Pamir und Wakhan', *Afghanistan J.*, i/4 (1974), pp. 91–104

G. O'Bannon: *The Turkoman Carpet* (London, 1974)

P. Centlivres: 'Les Uzbeks du Qattagnan', *Afghanistan J.*, ii/1 (1975), pp. 28–36

M. Centlivres-Demont: 'Les Peintures sur camions en Afghanistan', *Afghanistan J.*, ii/2 (1975), pp. 60–64

J.-C. Blanc: *Afghan Trucks* (London, 1976)

M. Centlivres-Demont: *Popular Art in Afghanistan: Paintings on Trucks, Mosques and Tea-houses* (Graz, 1976)

L. Dupree: *Afghan Women* (Hannover, 1976) [film; Afghanistan Ser., iv]

N. Dupree: 'Early Twentieth-century Afghan Adaptations of European Architecture', *A. & Archaeol. Res. Pap.*, xii (1977), pp. 15–21

R. Dor and C. Naumann: *Die Kirghisen des afghanischen Pamir* (Graz, 1978)

A. Janata: 'Ikat in Afghanistan', *Afghanistan J.*, v/4 (1978), pp. 130–39

A. Stucki: 'Horses and Women', *Afghanistan J.*, v/4 (1978), pp. 140–49

N. Dupree: 'A Building Boom in the Hindukush (Boom edilizio nell'Hindukush)', *Lotus Int.*, xxvi (1980), pp. 115–21

M. Klimburg: 'A Collection of Kafir Art from Nuristan', *Tribus*, xxx (1981), pp. 155–202

J. Kalter: 'Die Sammlungen des Linden-Museums aus Afghanistan und der Nachbargebieten', *Afghanistan J.*, ix/3 (1982), pp. 76–85

I. Rittmeyer: 'Die Sammlung Rittmeyer', *Afghanistan J.*, ix/4 (1982), pp. 112–14

R. Parsons: *The Carpets of Afghanistan* (Woodbridge, 1983)

N. Dupree: 'National Museum of Afghanistan', *Art Museums of the World*, i (Westport, 1987), pp. 26–30

——: 'Victoriana Comes to the Haremserai in Afghanistan (Viktorianischer Stil erobert den Haremserail)', *Bauen und Wohnen am Hindukush*, Stiftung Bibliotheca Afghanica, vii, ed. P. Bucherer-Dietschi (Liestal, 1988), pp. 111–49

The Decorative Arts of Central Asia (exh. cat., ed. J. Graham and H. Sandys; London, Zamara Gal., 1988)

J. Frembgen: *Naswar: Der Gebrauch von Mundtabak in Afghanistan und Pakistan*, Stiftung Bibliotheca Afghanica, viii (Liestal, 1989)

A. Szabo and T. Barfield: *Afghanistan: An Atlas of Indigenous Domestic Architecture* (Austin, 1991)

B. Dupaigne and R. Paiva: *Afghan Embroidery* (Lahore, 1993)

N. HATCH DUPREE

III. Historiography.

In the first centuries AD under KUSHANA rule, Afghanistan became established as a major centre of Buddhism, with many monasteries and stupas. Between the 5th and 8th centuries, a number of these Buddhist sites were visited and described by Chinese pilgrims such as Faxian (*c.* 400) and Xuanzang (*c.* 630).

Western interest in Afghanistan stems from the discovery in the 18th century by numismatists such as Theophilus Bayer, J. Pellerin and M. Mionnet that some fine portrait coins could be attributed to several Greek kings of Bactria (*see* BACTRIAN AND INDO-GREEK MONARCHIES) who were mentioned in Classical texts (see Wilson, pp. 3–4). At the beginning of the 19th century, the British in India became increasingly interested in Afghanistan, initially in order to forestall any potential designs of Napoleon I, and later for fear of Russian expansion in Central Asia. Various travellers who visited the country and recorded the monuments they saw were William Moorcroft and George Trebeck, on an ill-fated journey in 1825; Alexander Burnes and J. G. Gerard, who travelled to Bukhara in 1831; and

Martin Honigberger, a Transylvanian doctor, formerly in the service of the Sikh emperor Ranjit Singh, who explored several stupas in the neighbourhood of Kabul and Jalalabad in 1833. A major contributor was Charles Masson, a deserter from the East India Company army, who from 1826 onwards travelled extensively in the regions to the north of British India. He spent six years in Afghanistan (1832–8), during which time he surveyed and explored the archaeological remains near Kabul, Jalalabad and HADDA. The East India Company granted him a pardon in 1834 and funding to continue his investigations. He amassed a collection of more than 80,000 coins, primarily from BEGRAM, while his excavations of numerous stupas produced such remarkable objects as the Bimaran casket (see fig. 14 above; *see also* §IV below). His principal discoveries were published in *Ariana Antiqua* (see Wilson, pp. 55–118). He was also an early contributor to the journal (*J. Asiat. Soc. Bengal*) published from 1832 onwards by the Asiatic Society of Bengal (founded 1784), which under the editorship of JAMES PRINSEP became a principal source of information on the antiquities of India and neighbouring regions. Work on coins and their inscriptions, particularly by Prinsep and the German scholar Christian Lassen, resulted in the decipherment of the Kharoshthi script. But after the first Anglo-Afghan War (1839–42), little further fieldwork or research was undertaken, other than William Simpson's excavation of the Ahinposh Stupa near Jalalabad at the beginning of the second Anglo-Afghan War (1878–9) and incidental reports by members of the British border commissions in 1896–7 and 1903–5.

In the early 20th century the leading art historian in the field was undoubtedly ALFRED CHARLES AUGUSTE FOUCHER, who, fascinated by the extension of Hellenism in the east, contributed the monumental study, *L'Art gréco-bouddhique du Gandhâra.* The Franco-Afghan cultural convention of 1922 gave the French a virtual monopoly of archaeological research in Afghanistan for 30 years and a permanent institute in Kabul, with Foucher as first director. The Délégation Archéologique Française en Afghanistan has undertaken a major series of excavations and studies of the art and archaeology of Afghanistan. The results, published in more than 30 volumes (Mém.: Dél. Archéol. Fr. Afghanistan), include comprehensive excavation reports on Hadda, Begram, SURKH KOTAL and AI KHANUM. From the 1960s until 1978 Afghan archaeologists conducted extensive excavations at Tepe Shotor and Tepe Kalan, two important monastic complexes at Hadda. Since the 1960s other foreign missions have been allowed to work in Afghanistan: the Italian Istituto per il Medio ed Estremo Oriente at Ghazna (*see* SARDAR, TEPE), German and American teams in Sistan, a Japanese team from Kyoto University at Tepe Skandar, a Russian mission at TILLYA TEPE and the British Institute at Kandahar. This has led to much wider international interest in the art history of Afghanistan.

BIBLIOGRAPHY

A. Burnes: 'On the Colossal Idols of Bamian', *J. Asiat. Soc. Bengal*, ii (1833), pp. 561–4, pl. XIX

——: *Travels into Bokhara*, 3 vols (London, 1834/*R* Karachi, 1973)

J. G. Gerard: 'Memoir on the Topes and Antiquities of Afghanistan: From Jelalābād, 4th December 1833', *J. Asiat. Soc. Bengal*, iii (1834), pp. 321–9

E. Jacquet: 'Sur les découvertes archéologiques faites par M. Honigberger dans l'Afghanistan', *J. Asiat.*, n. s. 2, ii (1836), pp. 234–77; iv (1837), pp. 401–40; v (1838), pp. 163–97; vii (1839), pp. 385–404

W. Moorcroft and G. Trebeck: *Travels in the Himalayan Provinces of Hindustan and the Panjab from 1819 to 1825*, 2 vols, ed. H. H. Wilson (London, 1841); intro. G. J. Alder (*R* Karachi, 1979)

H. H. Wilson: *Ariana Antiqua: A Descriptive List of the Antiquities and Coins of Afghanistan* (London, 1841/*R* Delhi, 1971)

W. Simpson: 'Buddhist Architecture of the Jelalabad Valley', *Trans. RIBA* (1879–80), pp. 37–58

A. Foucher: *L'Art gréco-bouddhique du Gandhâra*, 2 vols (Paris, 1905–18)

M. Taddei and G. Verardi: 'The Italian Archaeological Mission in Afghanistan: Brief Account of Excavation and Study, 1976–1981', *Studi di storia dell'arte in memoria di Mario Rotili* (Naples, 1984), pp. 41–70

G. Whitteridge: *Charles Masson of Afghanistan* (Warmington, 1986)

For further bibliography *see* §II, 1(i), (ii) and (iii) above.

D. W. MACDOWALL

IV. Museums and collections.

The collections of material from Afghanistan are few in number but well published. The majority of pieces are located in the Kabul Museum and the Musée Guimet, Paris. The earliest collections date from the 19th century, when, notwithstanding political unrest and wars, a number of primarily British travellers and pioneers visited Afghanistan and sent a few stray finds, principally coins, to the British Museum, London. A major collection of coins and stupa relic deposits, made by Charles Masson in the 1830s (*see* §III above), was initially deposited in the East India Company Museum, London, then in 1880 divided between the British Museum and the Indian Museum, Calcutta.

After World War I cultural co-operation between the khan (later king) Aman-Allah (*reg* 1919–28) and France resulted in 1922 in the creation of the Délégation Archéologique Française en Afghanistan. The Délégation received exclusive rights to survey and excavate in Afghanistan for a period of 30 years. Following initial surveys by ALFRED CHARLES AUGUSTE FOUCHER at Balkh and Hadda (1922–3), finds from these investigations were shared between the Kabul Museum and the Musée Guimet, under the respective control of the king and the director of the Délégation. Even during World War II the scheme continued to benefit both countries. The majority of discoveries thus preserved were of outstanding importance, such as the well-known series of schist reliefs from Paitava (see fig. 6 above) and SHOTORAK, the stucco reliefs from HADDA, fragments of wall paintings, reliefs and clay statues from BAMIYAN, Kakrak and FONDUKISTAN (see figs 12 and 9 above), the famous hoard from BEGRAM and finds from the prehistoric city of Mundigak (see figs 2 and 5 above) and the large dynastic temple of SURKH KOTAL.

The French finally lost their exclusive rights to excavation in 1962, and from 1964 onwards no archaeological finds were legally allowed out of Afghanistan. Foreign teams worked under the control of the newly created Archaeological Survey of Afghanistan. The finds from British, American, German and Japanese excavations of prehistoric and historic sites, the French at AI KHANUM, the Italians at Ghazna (*see* SARDAR, TEPE) and Afghan and Soviet teams at Emshi Tepe and TILLYA TEPE were all placed in the Kabul Museum. In addition, site museums were created at Bamiyan, following restoration of the site

(1974–8), and at the Buddhist monastery of Tepe Shotor, Hadda (destroyed during bombing in 1979).

While Joseph Hackin was Director of the Musée Guimet in the 1930s, groups of 20 selected sculptures from the Hadda collection were distributed on permanent loan to various museums worldwide, in order that the material might become better known (Brussels, Musées Royaux A. & Hist.; Kansas City, MO, Nelson–Atkins Mus. A.; London, BM; Luxembourg, Mus. N. Hist. & A.; New Haven, CT, Yale U. A.G.; St Petersburg, Hermitage; Stockholm, Östasiat. Mus.; Tokyo, Ueno Royal Mus.; and a few others). In addition, about 12 ivory pieces from Begram were sent to India in 1960–63 as an exchange loan for some rare pieces of ancient Indian art. These ivories, the only examples outside Kabul or Paris, are in the National Museum, New Delhi. In the 1990s a programme was launched to expand the exhibit of Afghan material in the Musée Guimet beyond the original two galleries, in order to display additional, newly restored pieces from the reserve collection. Many other museums worldwide have Gandhara stucco pieces of uncertain provenance that are stylistically attributable to Afghanistan or Pakistan. It is to be hoped that the site origin of many of these pieces may be determined through the use of highly sophisticated methods of technical analysis that are increasingly available.

The Kabul Museum ranked among the most opulent depositories in the world, with a collection that recorded 50,000 years of the cultural history of Afghanistan. Although the artefacts were all boxed in 1991 for safekeeping during the civil war, the museum building was extensively damaged during bombing in 1993. Soon afterwards artefacts from the museum began to appear on the international art market and the ultimate fate of the collection is uncertain.

BIBLIOGRAPHY

O. Monod-Brühl: *Guide to the Musée Guimet* (Paris, 1966)
J. Auboyer: *L'Afghanistan et son art* (Prague, 1968)
N. Hatch Dupree and others: *The National Museum of Afghanistan: An Illustrated Guide* (Kabul, 1974)
F. R. Allchin and N. Hammond, eds: *The Archaeology of Afghanistan: From Earliest Times to the Timurid Period* (London and New York, 1978)
W. Ball and J. C. Gardin: *Archaeological Gazetteer of Afghanistan / Catalogue des sites archéologiques d'Afghanistan*, 2 vols (Paris, 1982)

F. TISSOT

Afinger, Bernhard (*b* Nuremberg, 6 May 1813; *d* Nuremberg, 25 Dec 1882). German sculptor. After an apprenticeship as a metal worker, having spent seven years as a journeyman in a silver-plating factory and having taught himself drawing and sculpting, he received a scholarship that allowed him to attend art school. In 1840 he met Christian Daniel Rauch who invited him to Berlin as his pupil, and there he was influenced by the prevalent Neo-classical style. However, his early works, such as the colossal figure of *Christ* that he carved in 1842 for the church in Dinkelsbühl, Mittelfranken, owe much to the tradition of the medieval sculptors of Nuremberg. In 1846 he founded his own workshop and in 1850 sculpted the much admired marble statuette of the actress *Elisa Rachel* (Berlin, Pfaueninsel). At the Great Exhibition in London in 1851 he won a commendation for his two medallions of the Prince and Princess of Prussia. During his long career Afinger produced 116 portraits in the form of medallions, busts and statuettes. He also carved a series of saints in sandstone for the castle church of Sagan. He received many public and private commissions for monuments of various kinds, such as the *Ernst Moritz Arndt* monument (1865) and the Christ Fountain (1878), both in Bonn. In 1873 he visited Italy, joined the Senat of the Königliche Akademie der Künste in Berlin in 1875 and in 1877 received a professorship there.

BIBLIOGRAPHY

Thieme–Becker
P. Bloch and W. Grzimek: *Das klassische Berlin: Die Berliner Bildhauerschule im neunzehnten Jahrhundert* (Berlin, Frankfurt am Main and Vienna, 1978), cols 149–50
Ethos und Pathos: Die Berliner Bildhauerschule, 1786–1914, 2 vols (exh. cat., ed. P. Bloch, S. Einholz and J. von Simson; Berlin, Staatl. Museen Preuss. Kultbes., 1990), esp. *Ausstellungskatalog*, pp. 11–12

HANNELORE HÄGELE

Aflalo, Roberto. *See under* CROCE, AFLALO AND GASPERINI.

Afonso, João (*fl* first half of the 15th century). Portuguese sculptor. He probably trained in the workshops of Batalha Abbey, where he absorbed the traditions of Coimbra, and he was the leading Portuguese sculptor of his time. In 1439–40 he worked on the tomb of *Fernão de Góis* in the church at Oliveira do Conde, where a Gothic inscription says that the work was carried out in 12 months by *João Afonso, mestre de Sinos*. The tomb is in the 14th-century tradition of MESTRE PÊRO and somewhat archaic in structure, comprising a chest borne by lions, with a recumbent figure on the cover and figures within aedicules at the sides. The treatment is more delicate than in most carving of the time; the arches and columns are slender and elegant, while the figures, with their animated poses and gracefully arranged drapery, are well modelled and show individual character. The same movement is found in the serene angels bearing the chalice in the *Corpus Domini* retable (1433; Coimbra), probably by the same hand. Many other works with similar characteristics are attributed to his workshop, albeit without documentary evidence. Numerous images of the Virgin and Child are considered to be by Afonso, including those at Tentúgal and Tábua (Dias); two figures of *St Michael* (Coimbra, Mus. N. Machado de Castro) and various figures in the Vilhena Collection (Lisbon, Mus. N. A. Ant.) have also been ascribed to him. If these attributions are correct, Afonso is the first Portuguese artist to have combined the sculptural tradition of Coimbra with that of Mestre Pêro's workshop and of the figure-carvers of Batalha Abbey; he in turn established a school that produced the fine sculptor Diogo Pires the elder.

BIBLIOGRAPHY

R. dos Santos: *A escultura em Portugal* (Lisbon, 1948), pp. 42–3, 46–7
V. Correia: *Obras*, iii (Coimbra, 1953), pp. 57–9
P. Dias: 'O gótico', *História da arte em Portugal*, iv (Lisbon, 1986), pp. 133–4
Sculpture et orfèvrerie: Aux confins du moyen âge (exh. cat. by L. Cardoso, Ghent, Sint-Pietersabdij, 1991), p. 91

MARIA ADELAIDE MIRANDA

Afonso, Jorge (*b* ?1470–75; *d* Lisbon, before 23 June 1540). Portuguese painter. He held a key position in

Portuguese art of the first half of the 16th century. He was the brother-in-law of Francisco Henriques, uncle of Cristóvão de Figueiredo and Garcia Fernandes, father-in-law of Gregório Lopes, and friend of the leading painter of Viseu, Vasco Fernandes. In his workshop, painters of the succeeding generation served their apprenticeships and completed their training, interpreting Afonso's Renaissance ideas in Mannerist style. By 1504 Afonso was living in Lisbon with a workshop close to the Monastery of S Domingos. In 1508 Manuel I appointed him *pintor régio* (court painter) and *examinador de todas as obras de pintura do reino* (examiner of all work in painting in the kingdom), appointments that were re-confirmed by John III in 1529. In this capacity he surveyed and evaluated work carried out at Tomar and various churches in Lisbon. Documents refer also to the execution of banners (1515) and to paintings (?1519–21; destr.) for the altarpiece of the church of the Conceição, Lisbon. In 1514 Afonso was ennobled and given the title of *araute Malaca* (Malacca Herald). In 1516 he received a substantial annuity from the Casa da Mina trading company for his services. The high valuation of his possessions and his will (1540) indicate the esteem in which his work was held.

All documented works by Afonso are untraced. Attributed to him is the group of paintings, formerly designated as by the Master of the Madre de Deus or the Master of 1515 (ii), from the polyptych executed for the Convent of Madre de Deus, Lisbon, and completed *c.* 1515, the date discovered during restoration of the panel of *Christ Appearing to the Virgin* (Lisbon, Mus. N. A. Ant.). The polyptych also included the *Annunciation* (Lisbon, Mus. N. A. Ant.), the *Adoration of the Shepherds*, the *Adoration of the Magi*, the *Ascension*, *Pentecost*, the *Assumption of the Virgin* and *St Francis Giving the Rules of the Order to St Clare* (all Lisbon, Convent of the Madre de Deus). This polyptych and the one painted for the Convent of Jesus, Setúbal, comprising fourteen panels (all Setúbal, Mus. Setúbal) divided in three series—the *Passion*, the *Childhood of Christ and Joys of the Virgin* and *Franciscan Saints*—were commissioned by Queen Eleanor, widow of John II, and probably executed (especially the second) with the assistance of artists in his workshop, Cristóvão de Figueiredo, Gregório Lopes and Garcia Fernandes, with whom he often worked. Both series of paintings show richer and more elaborate forms and pictorial clarification of the narrative, together with an adherence to the values of the northern Renaissance that is seen in the broad landscapes and use of aerial perspective. The iconography was often dependent on engravings and was influenced by texts that were close to the spirit of *devotio moderna*. An awareness of Italian art is seen in the monumental scale of the human figures, the knowledge of anatomy and the serene atmosphere of the settings. Afonso brought together these elements in a synthesis that is essentially Portuguese and that formed one of the strands in the development of early Portuguese painting.

BIBLIOGRAPHY

F. M. de Sousa Viterbo: *Noticia de alguns pintores portugueses e de outros que, sendo estrangeiros, exerceram a sua arte em Portugal*, 1 (Lisbon, 1903), pp. 8–25
A. de Gusmão: *O Mestre da Madre de Deus* (Lisbon, 1960)
L. R. Santos: *Jorge Afonso* (Lisbon, 1966)
D. Markl and F. A. Baptista Pereira: *O renascimento: História da arte em Portugal*, vi (Lisbon, 1986), pp. 123–38

F. A. BAPTISTA PEREIRA

Afonso V, King of Portugal. *See* AVIZ, (3).

Africa. Continent second only to Asia in size with a total area of 29,800,000 sq. km and a total population of 628 million (UN estimate, 1989). This survey focuses on the art traditions of Sub-Saharan Africa (i.e. south of the Sahara Desert), especially those of pre-colonial times as they continued into colonial and post-colonial times. It should be noted here that, while the major interest of scholars has been the study of unacculturated traditions, the fieldwork that makes such studies possible has been conducted many years, even centuries, after the time of first European contact. Furthermore, the notion of 'Sub-Saharan' Africa as a cultural entity, although still useful, is to some extent an arbitrary generalization: there has been both a high degree of internal diversity within the continent and much greater economic and political exchange between Africa and the outside world than was previously thought. Africa in the late 20th century comprises more than 50 independent nation states (see fig. 1); separate entries on most of these are found elsewhere in this dictionary. Other entries discuss specific civilizations, archaeological sites, cities and individual artists, as well as the art traditions of particular peoples.

For information on art produced in Africa *see also* EGYPT, ANCIENT, ISLAMIC ART and NUBIA.

BIBLIOGRAPHY

F. Willett: *African Art: An Introduction* (London, 1971, rev. 1993)
R. Brain: *Art and Society in Africa* (London, 1980)
Smithsonian Institution Libraries, National Museum of African Art Library, Library Acquisitions List (1981–)
W. Gillon: *A Short History of African Art* (London, 1984)
J. Vansina: *Art History in Africa: An Introduction to Method* (London and New York, 1984)
J. Kerchache, J.-L. Paudrat and L. Stéphan: *L'Art africain* (Paris, 1988; Eng. trans. by M. de Jager, New York, 1993)

□

I. Introduction. II. Art and aesthetics. III. Contexts of production and use. IV. Imagery and iconography. V. Materials, techniques and uses. VI. Art forms. VII. Regions. VIII. Diaspora. IX. Contemporary developments. X. Forgery. XI. Historiography. XII. Museums. XIII. Exhibitions. XIV. Collectors and dealers. XV. Art libraries and photographic collections.

DETAILED TABLE OF CONTENTS

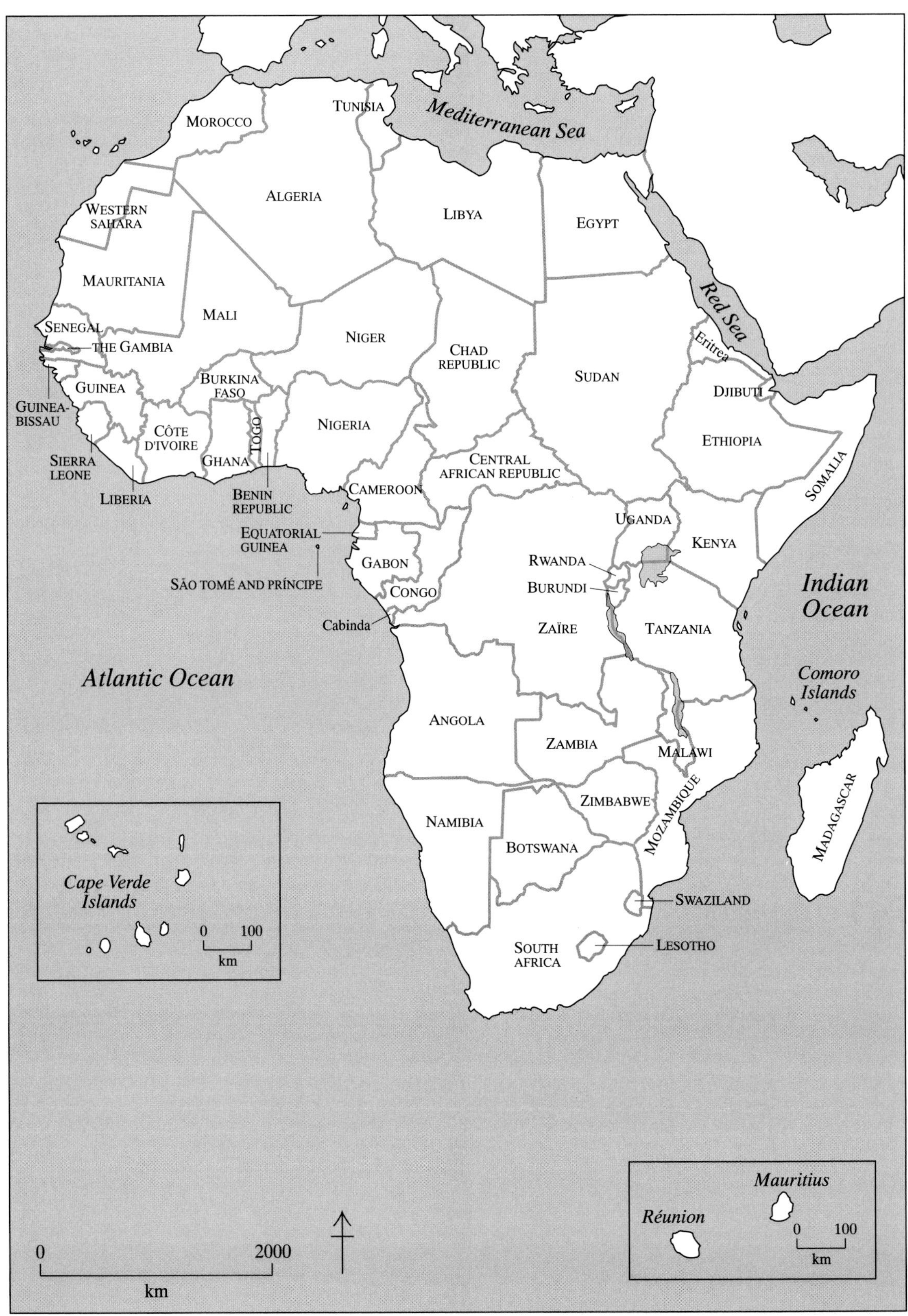

1. Map of Africa; those countries with separate entries in this dictionary are distinguished by CROSS-REFERENCE TYPE

I. Introduction.

1. Geography. 2. Ethnic and language groups. 3. History. 4. Religion.

1. Geography.

(i) Physical geography and climate. Much of Africa is plateau. The coastal plain is generally limited and backed by an escarpment where rivers break up into rapids and waterfalls, marking the limit for coastal shipping. Further upstream the great rivers are often navigable for long stretches by canoes and barges. Because the African coast is relatively lacking in estuaries or safe harbours, few African peoples developed ocean-going technologies or pursued overseas trade. Historically rivers were important for intra-continental contact, with the Nile being only one of several cases where major cultural and political developments took place around a riverine axis. A notable Sub-Saharan instance is the clustering of ancient bronze-casting technologies in the basin of the lower Niger. The interconnections between Nok, Nupe, Idah, Igbo-Ukwu, Ile-Ife and Benin are still obscure, but the proximity of all these places to the lower Niger and the intra-coastal network of creeks and lagoons linking the Niger Delta with Lagos to the west and Calabar to the east seems significant.

The interior plateau landscapes of Africa are diversified by bare-rock mountains (inselberge), upstanding tablelands and volcanic chains. In East Africa the landscape is diversified by a major sequence of intercontinental fault lines, responsible for the Rift Valley and its lakes. True mountain topographies are found in the Drakensberg of Natal, the Atlas Mountains in North Africa, the Ethiopian Highlands, parts of East Africa and the isolated massifs of the central Sahara. These areas are often characterized by considerable cultural and political distinctiveness—the result of specialized ecologies, isolation and freedom from invasion.

Seasonality in Africa is marked by a contrast between the rains and the dry season. At the northern and southern extremes of the continent a Mediterranean climatic regime (warm wet winters, hot dry summers) prevails. In the inter-tropical zone summer is the period of maximum rainfall, and here farming strategies are adapted to conditions of high humidity and extensive cloud cover in the growing season. Annual rainfall in the inter-tropical zones varies from over 3 m in the wettest districts to a few hundred mm on the edges of the Kalahari in the south and the Sahara in the north. Below 600 mm a settled agricultural way of life based on grain cultivation ceases to be viable, so drier districts have continued to be occupied by nomadic pastoralists. Except for a narrow band along the Equator, the contrast between wet and dry season is important throughout the greater part of the inter-tropical zone, even in high-rainfall districts. Parts of the upper Guinea coast in West Africa with over 3 m of rainfall still experience a severe dry season lasting from four to six months. In most cases rainfall follows a single maximum distribution, but in a band stretching from southern Ghana to Cameroon and in parts of East Africa there is a double maximum distribution pattern, in which the main rains and a second shorter period of rain are interrupted by a mid-season dry period. This rainfall pattern allows for double cropping of such short-duration grains as maize and is especially conducive to yam cultivation.

The importance of the dry and wet seasons is such that yearly variation in the start and end of the rains and the attendant uncertainty is socially and agriculturally disruptive. It is not surprising, therefore, that elaborate procedures for invoking or halting the rains are widespread, and in parts of Central Africa political authority is based on the perceived capacity to ensure the orderly progression of the seasons.

Seasonal rhythms affect pastoralists and settled cultivators differently. Pastoralists may follow the rains north and south, balancing the better grazing in wetter districts during the dry season against the reduced risks of disease for their animals in low-rainfall districts during the rainy season. For settled cultivators the rainy season is the time to stay at home and concentrate on agriculture, but during the dry season there may be scope to pursue a craft, join a hunting party, undertake a trading venture or take up seasonal work in towns. Festivals and major social occasions are concentrated in the dry season, when granaries

2. Hausa cushion-cover, leather, cotton and paint, 1.34×0.70 m, from Kano, Nigeria, *c.* 1920 (Edinburgh, Royal Museum of Scotland)

are full, people free of agricultural responsibilities and the paths and tracks more readily passable.

In addition to the normal irregularities connected with the passage of the seasons, account must also be taken of the phenomenon of long-term climatic change. There is much argument about whether the major droughts of the 1970s and 1980s represent a general trend. While available data are not yet adequate to settle the point, there is no disagreement that Africa entered a markedly drier phase *c.* 6000 years ago. This led to the dessication of the Sahara, which had been before then a favoured region for human habitation. The desertification of this area effectively separated the greater part of Africa from Europe. The cultural division this caused was offset to a limited degree by the expansion of cross-desert trade following the introduction of the camel *c.* AD 200.

(ii) Flora and fauna. The vegetation map of Africa is largely determined by rainfall, though in places topography also plays a part. North of the Sahara and at the Cape of Good Hope winter rainfall regimes are responsible for a Mediterranean-type vegetation (deciduous woodlands grading to scrub in low rainfall districts). On the Equator side of the Kalahari and Sahara deserts, savannah grassland gives way to savannah–woodland mosaic, semi-deciduous closed-canopy forest and full lowland humid rain-forest as rainfall totals increase towards the Equator.

About four-fifths of tropical Africa is savannah grassland that, left to itself, would mature into woodland. Where population pressure is high, however, the natural savannah vegetation has largely been replaced by farmland and grassy fallows. Wood is often very scarce, and remaining trees are largely such locally conserved economic species as the baobab, locust-bean and shea. Savannah is well suited to the production of cotton, which can only be grown with great difficulty in wetter districts, and to the raising of cattle, sheep and goats, especially where high population densities have eliminated the tsetse-fly. The relative scarcity of timber, combined with the ready availability of cotton yarn and animal hides, has influenced such arts and crafts of the savannah regions as the 'Morocco' leather and cotton cloth of the Hausa city states (see fig. 2).

The main belt of tropical rain-forest, much modified by cultivation and logging, centres around the Zaïre River basin and extends west towards southern Nigeria, with a western outlier running from Ghana to Sierra Leone. It is likely that the rain-forest presented an obstacle to initial settlement and that agricultural groups penetrated into the forest zone only at a relatively late date. Indeed, even in heavily farmed districts, islands of forest are carefully maintained for ritual activities.

The tropical rain-forest's species diversity makes it the richest and most complex of all ecosystems, and forest peoples have a vast store of knowledge concerning trees and plants, including how to obtain pigments and dyes for colouring the body, dyeing cloth and painting walls and carvings. Forest trees often have cultural as well as practical associations. In these respects, few African forest species surpass kola and the oil palm. Kola is an important stimulant, comparable to coffee or tea, and is an item of long-established commercial importance between the forest and the savannah. The oil palm provides oil for cooking and lighting and produces an important alcoholic beverage, palm wine. Both kola nuts and palm kernels are of importance in divination and ritual, and they often figure as decorative and symbolic motifs in the art of the forest zone.

The pastoral peoples of Africa are as interested in the aesthetics of living animals as in their artistic representation. Settled agriculturalists in drier savannah districts, where cattle are commonplace, think of domestic animals as sources of raw materials for artistic expression, but in the wetter savannahs and in the forest zone, where large domestic livestock are less common owing to disease, horses, cattle and sometimes even goats and sheep assume greater iconographic significance. In southern Nigeria, for example, rulers and title-holders kept horses and trypanosomiasis-resistant dwarf cattle more for prestige and sacrifice than for their economic utility, and these animals sometimes figure as motifs in the bronzework of the region.

The creatures that appear most often in African art are those that embody unusual mystical powers and confer the greatest prestige upon the hunter. Part of ivory's prestige derives from the difficulty and danger faced by the hunter of an elephant. Among other animals considered to possess particular mystical and symbolic force are antelopes, pythons, crocodiles, leopards and lions, which are frequently rendered in artistic terms (see fig. 3).

(iii) Minerals. Africa is a mineral-rich continent, with a long and widespread tradition of mineral-working. The African Iron Age may date back 2500 years, and until the colonial period iron was smelted from local deposits

3. Benin leopard figures, ivory, copper and mirrors, h. 815 mm, ?19th-century copies of earlier originals (London, British Museum)

throughout the continent and worked into agricultural implements, weapons and other items of domestic and ornamental hardware by a village blacksmith, who may also have served as gunsmith, goldsmith and jeweller. In some localities blacksmiths belonged to feared but socially inferior castes or clans. Although little ore has been smelted locally since the 1930s, the village blacksmith is as active as ever, using scrap metal as standard raw material.

Africa has long been famous for its gold. Until the opening up of New World sources in the 16th century, West Africa was the major supplier of gold to Europe and the Middle East. Gold from Central Africa was also important in the Indian Ocean trade and was a factor in the rise of Great Zimbabwe, while 20th-century output was dominated by mines in Southern Africa. Gold jewellery has long been appreciated in African societies, both for its aesthetic properties and as portable wealth. There are major deposits of copper in Central Africa, although these are not thought to have been the source of copper for the bronze of southern Nigeria. The exploitation of Africa's rich reserves of diamonds is a modern phenomenon, and diamonds have had little or no part to play in the story of African decorative arts.

Stone and brick have been used as building materials in North Africa since ancient times, for the monumental architecture of Egypt and of the Romans and Carthaginians. South of the Sahara, use of stone for building was uncommon in pre-colonial times (with such notable exceptions as Great Zimbabwe). Rapid chemical weathering in the tropical zone produces abundant supplies of lateritic mud, which provides a cheap, cool and flexible alternative to building in stone (*see also* §VI, 1 below).

BIBLIOGRAPHY

J. F. Griffiths: *Climates of Africa* (Amsterdam, 1972)
J. I. Clarke: *An Advanced Geography of Africa* (Amersham, 1975)
C. Buckle: *Landforms in Africa* (London, 1978)
P. Richards: *Indigenous Agricultural Revolution: Ecology and Food Production in West Africa* (London, 1985)

2. LANGUAGE AND ETHNIC GROUPS. By comparison with Europe or Asia, Africa is not a densely populated continent. The distribution, however, is very uneven. The major population concentrations are to be found in the Nile valley, Nigeria, the Kenyan and Ethiopian highlands, the Maghrib and in parts of South Africa. Nigeria alone accounts for perhaps one-fifth of the total population of the continent. Parts of the Sahel, east-central Africa and the Equatorial forest region are especially thinly peopled. Although there are few reliable population data before about 1950, it seems likely that this broad pattern of distribution is long established, since it correlates well with the general pattern of regional variation in soil fertility and rainfall reliability.

Africa is characterized by extraordinary linguistic diversity. Estimates vary, but it appears that the continent may have between 1000 and 1500 distinct languages. Of these perhaps 250 are spoken in just one country: Nigeria. Arabic is the main language of North Africa, and other important regional languages include Swahili in Central and East Africa and Hausa and Mandinka over much of the Sahel. Colonial languages (English, French and Portuguese) remain important for education and government

4. Rock painting of a pastoral scene, Tassili N'Ajjer, Algeria, ?*c.* 7000–*c.* 3000 BC

administration. Language classification is always a contentious issue and nowhere more so than in Africa. One widely accepted approach (see Greenberg) groups African languages into four major families (phyla): Niger-Kordofanian, Khoisan, Afro-Asiatic and Nilo-Saharan. (Malagasy, the language of Madagascar, belongs to Malayo-Polynesian, another language family altogether.)

Although it has long been conventional to identify pieces of African art by 'tribe', to produce a map of ethnic units is as contentious a task as producing a language map and will not be attempted here. It has been argued that ethnic consciousness was a phenomenon heightened or even created by the social and political conditions associated with colonialism. Furthermore, ethnic units are defined according to different criteria in different cases. In some parts of the continent ethnicity denotes membership of a linguistic community. Elsewhere it equates with class, occupational caste, regional origin, religious identity or even membership of a trading diaspora. Any generalization is likely to prove misleading, therefore, and the reader seeking further guidance must refer to specialist ethnographic publications, where such caveats are often dealt with in detail.

This complexity was made even greater in the 19th and 20th centuries through the immigration into Africa of Europeans (especially into Southern Africa), Asians (especially into East and Southern Africa) and freed black slaves and their descendants from the Americas.

BIBLIOGRAPHY

G. P. Murdock: *Africa: Its People and their Culture* (New York, 1959)
J. G. Greenberg: *The Languages of Africa* (The Hague, 1970)
J. Hiernaux: *The People of Africa* (London, 1974)
S. L. Kasfir: 'One Tribe, One Style? Paradigms in the Historiography of African Art', *Hist. Afr.*, xi (1984), pp. 163–93

PAUL RICHARDS

3. History.

(i) Before *c.* AD 600. (ii) *c.* AD 600–*c.* 1885. (iii) After *c.* 1885.

(i) Before c. AD *600.* The relatively late advent of indigenous literacy in many parts of Africa, especially south of the Sahara, means that there are very few documentary sources for African history and that archaeology is a prime source of knowledge about events, processes and developments in even the comparatively recent past. On the world stage, African archaeology is of major importance, not least because there is a strong probability that it was in Africa that humans first evolved. In addition the African experience provides an opportunity for interpreting major developments in human behaviour in the context of a landscape that has changed relatively little and is thus analogous to that exploited by past human populations.

Despite such potential, archaeological research in many parts of Africa remains in its infancy, being a low priority for the governments of recently independent nations. While intensive investigations have been undertaken in such areas as South Africa, Kenya and parts of the Nile Valley, huge regions remain almost completely unexplored.

(a) Human origins. Discoveries relating to the earliest periods of human activity have been made both in East Africa (from Ethopia southwards to Tanzania and inland as far as the western branch of the Rift Valley) and in Southern Africa, where conditions have favoured not only the preservation of the earliest hominids' bones and their stone tools but also their subsequent discovery by natural erosion or by quarrying. The concentrations of archaeological discoveries thus do not necessarily reflect the distribution of the earliest hominids. Precisely when modern man first appeared is not yet proven, but it may have been *c.* 200,000–100,000 BP. With the development of fully modern man, the African archaeological record indicates several features of particular relevance to the study of art. Formal disposal of the dead by burial is indicated, and graves and living sites provide evidence for personal adornment and clothing. Natural pigments, notably ochre, as well as bone and shell were frequently employed, probably with other more perishable substances. Particular interest attaches to the development of rock art, both painting and engraving (*see* §VI, 15 below), which was practised in Africa at least as long ago as in Europe (*see* PREHISTORIC EUROPE, §II, 2) and which, in its later phases in Southern Africa, may be closely linked with socio-religious practices of the SAN peoples.

(b) Development of agriculture. Between *c.* 10,000 and *c.* 6000 BC, in what is now the southern Sahara and in parts of East Africa, greatly increased rainfall resulted in the formation or enlargement of lakes and rivers in an area previously too arid to support human habitation. Beside these waters previously nomadic groups established semi-permanent habitations, identified by finds of pottery and barbed bone heads of harpoons. Between *c.* 5000 and *c.* 3000 BC the climate in the southern Sahara once again became more arid. It was at this time that people in this part of Africa began to control their plant and animal food supplies; this led ultimately to the development of farming.

The extent to which the domestication of animals and plants was an indigenous African development, rather than one caused by stimuli from outside that continent, has for long been a matter of controversy. Rock paintings in the Sahara, tentatively dated *c.* 7000–*c.* 3000 BC, provide numerous representations of domestic cattle indicating, among other features, the importance that was attached to body markings and the configuration of horns (see fig. 4). Later art in the Nile Valley and undated examples in the eastern Sahara show that attempts were made to tame such other species as giraffe and ostrich. Large numbers of heavily used grindstones on 4th-millennium BC sites in the Sudanese Nile Valley and parts of the Sahara probably indicate use of cereals, but the extent of their cultivation is still uncertain. By *c.* 1200 BC, if not before, bulrush millet was being intensively cultivated in the western Sahara of Mauritania.

5. Terracotta head, h. 155 mm, from Katsina Ala, Nok, Nigeria, *c.* 900 BC–*c.* AD 200 (Jos, National Museum)

The initial stages of African farming development almost certainly took place in the same general area as was occupied by the harpoon-fishers and at the time when established lifestyles were subject to stress from the lowering of water levels. It is easy to visualize how, in such circumstances, settled people might have controlled herds of formerly wild cattle and begun to protect and then to cultivate plant foods in order to maintain their supply in the face of reduced availability of fish.

It is reasonable to conclude, therefore, that during the last two millennia BC the peoples of the northern savannah belt between the southern fringes of the Sahara and the northern margin of the Equatorial forest turned increasingly to settled life and food production. To the south of the forest, however, the hunter-gatherer lifestyle of previous millennia continued.

(c) Discovery of metallurgy. During the 1st millennium BC, ironworking began in settlements south of the Sahara. The evidence for this comes primarily from the Jos Plateau of Nigeria, from sites that have also yielded the remarkable Nok terracottas (see fig. 5). Further evidence for ironworking rather more than 2000 years ago has been

6. Lydenburg head (no. 1), terracotta, h. 380 mm, from near Lydenburg, eastern Transvaal, South Africa, *c.* AD 500–700 (University of Cape Town, on loan to Cape Town, South African Museum); reconstruction

recovered around Lake Victoria, notably on its western shore in north-western Tanzania. In both areas the smelting technology used shows little sign of local antecedents, leading to suggestions that it was introduced from the north; however, no clear evidence for such long-distance connection has been cited. It is noteworthy that Sub-Saharan Africa generally lacked a distinct 'Bronze Age' when the softer metals were worked but techniques of ironworking had not yet been developed.

In the southern half of Africa the beginnings of farming and of metalworking seem to have been broadly concurrent. During the first few centuries AD, in territory previously inhabited by stone tool-using, mobile hunter–gatherer peoples, there were established villages of settled farmers, who worked metals and made pottery. Their pottery has a stylistic uniformity that, along with the apparent speed with which the lifestyle began over an enormous area and its marked contrast with what had gone before, led archaeologists to postulate rapid population migration, possibly of Bantu speakers.

By about the 3rd century AD farming peoples had begun to absorb and replace the hunter–gatherer populations of most of Southern Africa wherever environmental conditions were suitable for the cultivation of African cereal crops. Artefacts from this period other than pottery are scarce, but mention should be made of the remarkable series of seven life-size terracotta human heads of *c.* AD 500–700, reconstructed from fragments found at Lydenburg in the Transvaal (see fig. 6), which share many technological and stylistic features with the contemporary domestic pottery. In the south-westernmost regions pottery and domestic animals are attested by the 1st century AD, but metallurgy and crop cultivation remained unknown.

(d) Early settlements. During the 1st millennium AD peasant societies in several parts of Africa showed signs of increasing complexity and centralization. Indeed excavations at Jenne-Jeno, beside the inland Niger Delta in Mali, provide evidence for incipient urbanization 2000 years ago, probably supported by rice cultivation and by trade from an extensive hinterland. By the time that Arabic-speaking traders from North Africa crossed the Sahara in the 8th century AD, large centralized states had developed in the northern savannah. The most important of these was Ghana, centred on what is now southern Mauritania and south-western Mali. Although ancient Ghana and its successor, Mali, reached maximum prosperity through control of the gold production of the Bambuk area and by exploiting their intermediary position between the trans-Saharan Muslim traders and the rich savannah and forest lands of West Africa, their origin predates such long-distance links.

Within the forest itself states tended to be smaller because of restrictions on communication, but they included dense populations supported by yam cultivation. Information is largely derived from excavation at such sites as IFE and BENIN. The outstanding artistic works discovered here reveal the development of technological and artistic expertise together with a concentration of material resources. Although they reached a peak at these sites between the 13th and 18th centuries, at IGBO-UKWU in eastern Nigeria these developments may be traced back as far as the late 1st millennium AD. In East and Southern Africa broadly parallel developments occurred, again probably influenced by long-distance trade links, here involving the Indian Ocean coast, although its importance in African political centralization should not be exaggerated. Ivory, gum, spices, wood and slaves were exported together with, in later times, gold, in exchange for such luxury items as glass, beads, porcelain and textiles. Islam was introduced from a relatively early period. Despite the strong African roots of these maritime towns, it seems that their direct influence did not extend far inland. The interlacustrine kingdoms of East Africa, for example, seem to have arisen during the first half of the 2nd millennium AD, having virtually no contact with the Indian Ocean coast some 800–1200 km distant, but deriving their wealth primarily from large herds of cattle.

BIBLIOGRAPHY

C. Ehret and M. Posnansky: *The Archaeological and Linguistic Reconstruction of African History* (Berkeley, 1982)

T. H. Huffmann: 'Archaeology and Ethnohistory of the African Iron Age', *Annu. Rev. Anthropol.*, xi (1982), pp. 133–50
D. W. Phillipson: *African Archaeology*, Cambridge World Archaeology (Cambridge, 1985, rev. 1993)
——: 'An Archaeological Reconsideration of Bantu Expansion', *Muntu*, ii (1985), pp. 69–84
G. Connah: *African Civilizations* (Cambridge, 1987)
M. Hall: *The Changing Past: Farmers, Kings and Traders in Southern Africa* (Cape Town, 1987)
S. K. McIntosh and R. J. McIntosh: 'From Stone to Metal: New Perspectives on the Later Prehistory of West Africa', *J. World Prehist.*, ii (1988), pp. 89–133
J. Lewis-Williams and T. Dowson: *Images of Power* (Johannesburg, 1989)
T. Shaw, ed.: *The Archaeology of Africa: Food, Metals and Towns* (London, 1993)
D. E. Miller and N. J. van der Merwe: 'Early Metal Working in Sub-Saharan Africa: A Review of Recent Research', *J. Afr. Hist.*, xxxv (1994), pp. 1–36

DAVID W. PHILLIPSON

(ii) c. *AD 600–*c. *1885.* The diversity of societies, languages and cultures in the African continent is far too great to support generalizations about artistic and cultural trends. Some scholars have long recognized this and have attempted to group different cultural traditions by area. By 'culture' is understood not just the arts but whole distinctive ways of life, and by using the term 'tradition' the claim is made that cultures as they existed before the colonial period had been stable or even invariant for many generations. Classification by cultural area, however, has remained unsatisfactory, not only because it has proved impossible to apply the same set of criteria to different areas but also because this approach denies the existence of history, treating human cultures as if they were invariant geological strata or animal species. G. P. Murdock remedied this by focusing on the ways in which cultures had arisen, providing an early attempt at a genuine culture history of Africa. Since then, the main historical outlines of a cultural history have emerged.

The cultural map of Africa as it existed in the late 19th century took shape between *c.* AD 600 and 1100, and its traditions can be divided into four main cultural provinces: the *oikoumene*, the West African urban tradition and the western and eastern Bantu traditions. In addition there are other traditions of lesser geographic extent: several occur in the heart of the continent between the *oikoumene* and the cultures of the Bantu speakers, but they also include the Khoi-San traditions in south-western Africa and the Malagasy tradition.

(a) *Oikoumene.* (b) West African urban tradition. (c) Western Bantu tradition. (d) Eastern Bantu tradition. (e) Other traditions.

(a) Oikoumene.This term is derived from the Greek for 'inhabited world' and designates that part of Africa the cultures of which were polarized by the acceptance of Christianity or Islam and the peoples of which remained in continual contact with the old world. Encompassing almost half of the continent, the *oikoumene* includes all peoples north of a line linking the mouth of the Senegal River to the top of the Niger Bend to Lake Chad to the Nilotic Sudd, near Malakal, around the highlands of Ethiopia to the Somalia–Kenya border and then south to near the Indian Ocean following the shore inland to Mozambique. It also takes in the Comoro Islands and small parts of Madagascar.

The *oikoumene* grew out of many strands. First there was the civilization of ANCIENT EGYPT that developed in the Nile Valley, culminating in Pharaonic Egypt from *c.* 3200 BC onwards. Painting there shows influences from styles developed by the herders of the Sahara from *c.* 6000 BC, when Egypt was part of an intercommunicating zone that encompassed the Middle East. Its civilization did not spread widely to the west, although it interacted with older local traditions in the adjacent Nile Valley, perhaps as far south as present Khartoum. It was left to Phoenician (after *c.* 1000 BC) and Greek colonies (after *c.* 700 BC) to implant the cultures of the eastern Mediterranean on the northern shores of Africa. With the emergence of the Roman Empire, which incorporated Egypt in 30 BC, institutions of government, law and trade became more unified, although most aspects of indigenous culture remained relatively untouched. The Empire did not greatly influence Sudan, Ethiopia or even the peoples of the Sahara. More fundamental changes in culture and world view followed the spread of Christianity into Africa from the 1st century AD. In the next 500 years it unified all of North Africa as well as the Sudan south to the Sudd and highland Ethiopia. Christian artistic expression shows a striking uniformity over the whole area.

Islam was the core of the second *oikoumene.* By AD 640 Muslim armies had overrun Egypt before sweeping westwards, rapidly conquering the Maghrib. By *c.* 800 Muslim traders had reached the African shores of the Indian Ocean as well as towns south of the Sahara in West Africa. Islam did not, however, overrun Christian Sudan or Ethiopia, and the unification of the various branches of Islam took a long time, even in North Africa. By *c.* 1100 a single school of Muslim law dominated the Maghrib, while Sunni orthodoxy was regaining the heartland of Egypt. At this time the first West African rulers were beginning to convert, and Islam began to gain ground in the East African coastal towns. Between the 13th and 16th centuries northern Sudan also became Muslim, but highland Ethiopia remained Christian. After *c.* 1100 further Islamic advances were limited and slow. Inroads were made into West Africa, but the area retained its own character. In East Africa, Muslim traders made some converts as far south as Zimbabwe, but their advance had been lost by 1600.

Christianity and, later, Islam were extremely powerful forces, and persons from any part of the *oikoumene* shared, at least generally, the concerns, reasoning and customs of any other part. The practice of pilgrimage—to Mecca and Jerusalem—reinforced this unity. Nevertheless, within the Muslim tradition different cultural profiles developed. By 1100 this was evident in Egypt, Tunisia, Morocco, the Saharan desert cultures and the lowlands of the Horn of Africa. But, while Ethiopia redefined its cultural profile in reaction to Islam, and Sudan developed its own Muslim culture, such developments never threatened the fundamental unity of the culture of the *oikoumene.*

(b) West African urban tradition. Despite the vast linguistic and ethnic diversity of West Africa, there is an underlying unity based on an urban network linked by trade. The region also has a common tradition of state government and ideology that can be labelled sacred

kingship. This single ideology, once believed to have spread from one point to all the others, is not all-encompassing and probably evolved from a number of local village-based religions, becoming unified through centuries of mutual exchanges. The diversity of West African cultures stems from the strength of villages, which offered creative input into the urban cultures, taking only what was useful in return and resisting assimilation.

West Africa's cultural characteristics developed over a long period. Settlement in the savannah and on the desert fringe increased following the desertification of the Sahara from *c.* 2500 BC to *c.* AD 1. As population densities rose, trade based on the exchange of varying regional resources became important, and centres of trade developed. The first known city of the region, Djenné, illustrates this pattern of development. It was probably established *c.* 250 BC by peoples from the Sahara; by AD 400 its hinterland reached from the desert edge in Mauritania to the Atlantic Ocean to southern Mali. Some Hellenistic beads have even been found in Djenné. In this period other towns developed, so that by *c.* AD 700 a network of trade was taking shape in the western half of West Africa. Thus urbanization here should not be attributed to Muslim influences; indeed the first known large-scale states, with capitals located near the desert fringe, also pre-date Muslim trading contacts. One or two of them had begun to trade in gold with North Africa by the 7th century AD at the latest.

The trans-Saharan trade developed into a major trading network after the arrival of Islam in the Maghrib, spurring on the processes of urbanization and thus unifying West Africa. The earliest known trading centre in Nigeria, IGBO-UKWU, dates from *c.* 800, and the site shows evidence of intensive contact not only with North Africa but also with the ocean shore to the south. By *c.* 900 other cities were appearing, and by *c.* 1100 there was a town linked to the West African gold trade at Nyarko in southern Ghana. By this time the basic unity of West Africa was a reality: trading networks existed, and cities acted as crucibles of ideas, values and practices from afar that were then disseminated to the rural hinterlands.

An example of these processes is the history of terracotta art in West Africa. The earliest known centres of terracotta production were in northern Nigeria, where they had appeared by 900 BC. By AD 700 terracotta art was found all over the Sahel from Lake Chad to the Atlantic, with common stylistic features appearing from Nigeria to the Upper Niger and the coast. The tradition of building with sun-dried bricks also developed during the last centuries BC, so that by *c.* AD 1100 there were major monumental buildings in similar styles from Lake Chad to the Middle and Upper Niger. Finally, a common technique of metal-casting using the lost-wax process was established all over the West African savannah by *c.* 1000.

By *c.* 1100 a common cultural tradition linked all of West Africa (outside the forest areas between Sierra Leone and southern Ghana), and in the following centuries a gradual percolation of Islam and the expansion of specialized cattle herders, the Fulani, from Senegal to Sudan along the desert edge further strengthened common cultural features.

At the same time more localized cultural blocks were emerging in northern Nigeria, the area within the Niger Bend, the Upper Niger area, the area south of the River Senegal, southern Ghana and western Nigeria especially. These were urban, linked to the others and dominated by states but remaining culturally distinct.

(c) Western Bantu tradition. South of a line from the Atlantic Ocean near the border between Nigeria and Cameroon to the Indian Ocean in southern Somalia is an area occupied for the most part by Bantu-speaking peoples. These peoples migrated from their homelands in two directions. Western Bantu speakers settled most of Central Africa, while the eastern Bantu directly affected the cultural history of East and Southern Africa (*see* §(d) below).

The western Bantu speakers entered the rain-forests of Equatorial Africa *c.* 1800 BC, reached the savannah of Central Africa by 500 BC and arrived in southern Angola, the Middle Zambezi and eastern Zambia by *c.* the early 1st century AD. Their social organization was adapted to very low population densities. The basic units, 'houses', were led by 'big men'; several of them might group together for defensive purposes in ephemeral villages. The largest and most permanent social unit was the district, which consisted of a set of houses linked by alliance and marriage; this was the locus of ethnic identity. Ideologies of the big man and of kinship meshed well with religious beliefs and practices centring on the propitiation of spirits and the fear of witchcraft.

Cultural variation within the western Bantu tradition developed between the forest and the savannah peoples as a result not only of their physical separation and the difference of their physical environments but of varying degrees of interaction with autochthones and a later (*c.* AD 1–500) immigration of eastern Bantu speakers to the southern savannah. Despite the emergence of such localized cultural variants, a common core of beliefs and practices within the tradition remained. Evidence of early art in this area is sparse. Excavation of huge cemeteries found in the Upemba Depression of Zaïre and in the Shaba Province have revealed that wealth here was based on copper produced near by. Only a few objects in wood and pottery dating from before *c.* 1000 have survived in the savannah area, not enough as yet to speculate about common formal features for this early period. In south-eastern Zaïre (after *c.* 800) and in northern Angola (after *c.* 1500) enough works of art have survived to show a basic continuity.

(d) Eastern Bantu tradition. The earliest eastern Bantu speakers had moved from Cameroon to the Great Lakes by *c.* 1000 BC. There they met herders and farmers from the upper Nile and Ethiopia, and a stable, shared way of life developed, with world views and value systems that had become quite different from that of the western Bantu. By *c.* AD 400 the eastern Bantu had expanded both along the coast and inland from the Great Lakes as far south as Natal. The common culture that developed corresponds in part to that of the 'East African cattle area' designated by M. J. Herskovits; its best known works are terracotta masks from the Transvaal (see fig. 6 above).

Between *c.* 750 and *c.* 1000 a set of regional cultures, adapted to specific local conditions, grew out of the common tradition. In Southern Africa three main regional cultures can be discerned. Some farmer/herders moved back from Transvaal, first to the Limpopo River (*c.* 800) and then beyond to Zimbabwe (*c.* 900). These groups developed a centralized government based around hierarchical settlements, the largest of which were located on defensible hill-top positions, at which substantial herds of cattle were maintained. These sites, especially those in the Limpopo, show evidence of extensive ivory-working, apparently to produce items for export. Large quantities of glass beads were also produced and traded inland. From about the 11th century gold replaced ivory as the principal export, although it was also used locally, as is attested by élite graves at Mapungubwe, Transvaal. The layout of these central sites, the presence of dry-stone architecture and some aspects of the associated material culture are clearly ancestral to those of GREAT ZIMBABWE, which flourished during the 13th and 14th centuries and represents the culmination of this process of political centralization. At the same time the inhabitants of Botswana developed a different system based on more intensive herding and involving the creation of chiefdoms and structured interaction with the local hunter-gatherers, the San. In south-east Africa proper the Sotho–Nguni peoples retained more of the original culture, although their environments and autochthonic influences also helped to produce new cultural variants.

Beginning *c.* 750, four new major East African cultures emerged. Along the coast Swahili-speaking peoples adapted to the marine environment by founding fishing villages and becoming involved in overseas trade. Town sites on the coasts of Somalia, Kenya and Tanzania provide abundant evidence that by the 8th century maritime connections extended to at least as far south as Vilanculos Bay in Mozambique. In the Great Lakes new ceramics confirm immigration by non-Bantu-speakers from the north after *c.* 750. Well before *c.* 1400 this led to the creation of small states culminating in major kingdoms after *c.* 1500. In northern Tanzania and central Kenya a variety of foreign influences produced a highland variant of the original eastern Bantu culture, probably before 1000. A fourth variant of that heritage arose from *c.* 750 in south-eastern Zaïre, where eastern and western Bantu speakers had mixed. Chiefdoms and then states appeared in the area, and the culture expanded into all of Zambia and portions of Malawi after *c.* 1000.

(e) Other traditions. Several cultural traditions of lesser geographic extent must be mentioned. In south-western Africa the Khoi–San tradition derives from the cultures of the hunters and gatherers who have inhabited the area for thousands of years. As the Khoi expanded from their homeland in Botswana, cultural unification occurred as cattle were acquired and the new herders interacted with the hunters and gatherers.

During the early centuries AD, MADAGASCAR was settled by rice-growers from South-east Asia speaking Austronesian languages. Interaction with the eastern Bantu traditions followed, and a new cultural tradition arose. Later influences from all over the Indian Ocean contributed to Malagasy culture and arts without profoundly altering them. Unfortunately a lack of archaeological data means that a detailed chronology and cultural history for the island before *c.* 1500 have yet to be determined.

The cultural history of the peoples between the edge of the *oikoumene* and the Bantu traditions also remains obscure. The northern savannahs of Central Africa were settled by sedentary populations well before the 1st millennium BC. Where different cultural traditions confronted each other, as in the Ubangi–Uele basin, they fused, producing new variants. Further study is required to determine the age and stability of these traditions. Herders, farmers and hunter-gatherers from the southern Sudan, northern Uganda, Kenya and northern Tanzania have been better studied. Several traditions are involved, and their confrontations led to complex interactions and the creation of many local cultures. Many of the peoples concerned were highly mobile and left few archaeological traces. Several traditions (e.g. that of the Nilotic herders) can be traced, but, especially in Kenya and Tanzania, the dynamics of cultural interaction have been so intensive, complex and unstable for so long that the overall patterns remain unclear.

BIBLIOGRAPHY

J. Devisse: 'L'Apport de l'archéologie à l'histoire de l'Afrique occidentale entre le Vème et le XIIe siècle', *Acad. Inscr. & B.-Lett.: C. R. Séances* (1982), pp. 156–77

S. K. McIntosh and R. J. McIntosh: 'The Early City in West Africa: Towards an Understanding', *Afr. Archaeol. Rev.*, ii (1984), pp. 73–98

J. Vansina: 'Western Bantu Expansion', *J. Afr. Hist.*, xxv (1984), pp. 129–45

JAN VANSINA

(iii) After c. *1885.* From the end of the 19th century the colonial conquest and the intensive propagation of Christianity and Islam that attended it began to threaten Africa's cultural traditions and ways of life on a scale vastly exceeding the effects of the arrival of Europeans on the coasts after *c.* 1450 or the massive slave trade from *c.* 1660 to 1850. After 1885 five European powers (Belgium, Britain, France, Germany and Portugal) divided up the greater part of the continent between them. Colonial rule and expanded trade with Europe greatly increased the rate of urbanization and the power of the central institutions of the state. Although full colonial rule lasted for only 50 years (*c.* 1900–*c.* 1950), it was nevertheless largely through colonialism and the cultural and aesthetic climate of the colonial metropoles that the world developed its awareness of African art. From the African perspective, such metropolitan collections as the bronzes looted from Benin in the aftermath of the British military expedition of 1898 are particularly prone to stir up memories of injustices suffered under colonialism. It will be some time yet before the field of African art can be fully separated from the political geography of colonialism.

As far as post-colonial developments are concerned, the vigourous independence of rural African populations has kept alive many old art forms as well as adding new ones, often as elements in new religious cults. In addition, the growth of towns has led to the massive expansion of such popular arts as photography (see fig. 7), tourist art and 'bar art'. If measured by volume and brash, inventive vigour, then the surviving court arts of the old urban centres pale into insignificance beside these new forms of

7. Double portrait by an unknown photographer, 240×170 mm, Yamoussoukro, Côte d'Ivoire, 1970s (private collection)

artistic expression. As yet, however, the scholarly community has paid relatively little attention to popular arts in Africa's rapidly expanding urban centres.

BIBLIOGRAPHY

M. J. Herskovits: 'A Preliminary Consideration of the Culture Areas of Africa', *Amer. Anthropologist*, xxvi/1 (1924), pp. 50–64

L. Frobenius: *Kulturgeschichte Afrikas* (Zurich, 1934)

H. Baumann and D. Westermann: *Les Peuples et les civilisations de l'Afrique* (Paris, 1948)

G. P. Murdock: *Africa: Its Peoples and their Culture History* (New York, 1959)

J. Maquet: *Afrique: Les Civilisations noires* (Paris, 1962)

J. D. Fage and R. Oliver, eds: *The Cambridge History of Africa*, 8 vols (London, 1975–86)

J. Murray, ed.: *Cultural Atlas of Africa* (Oxford and New York, 1981)

UNESCO General History of Africa, 8 vols (Paris and London, 1981–)

C. Ehret and M. Posnansky: *The Archaeological and Linguistic Reconstruction of African History* (Berkeley, 1982)

D. Birmingham and P. Martin, eds: *History of Central Africa*, i (London, 1983)

W. Gillon: *A Short History of African Art* (London and New York, 1984)

J. Vansina: *Art History in Africa: An Introduction to Method* (London and New York, 1984)

Africa Explores: 20th Century African Art (exh. cat. by S. Vogel with I. Ebong, New York, Cent. Afr. A., 1991)

PAUL RICHARDS

4. RELIGION. By the late 20th century the religious map of Africa had become complex. In much of Sub-Saharan Africa 'traditional', often local, religions have continued to have many followers, especially in rural areas. In some areas, however, either Islam or Christianity has many adherents. Western Nigeria, for example, has a large Muslim population, while eastern Nigeria and such other areas as Uganda, Kenya and parts of Southern Africa have significant Christian populations. In addition, the East African coast and much of north-east Africa have been Islamic for centuries, although there is a long-established Christian Church in Ethiopia. Similarly, North Africa is predominantly Muslim, although a minority Coptic Christian Church exists in Egypt.

This section can provide only a brief introduction to religion in Africa. Further information on the many and complex links between religion and art in Africa will be found throughout the rest of this survey, in the entries on individual peoples and in the country entries.

BIBLIOGRAPHY

J. Relig. Africa (1967–)

Face of the Gods: Art and Altars of Africa and the African Americas (exh. cat. by R. F. Thompson, New York, Mus. Afr. A., 1993)

T. D. Blakely, W. E. A. van Beek and D. L. Thomson, eds: *Religion in Africa: Experience and Expression* (London and Portsmouth, NH, 1994)

(i) Indigenous religions. (ii) Christianity. (iii) Islam. (iv) Modern developments.

(i) Indigenous religions. Each 'traditional' or indigenous African religion is unique to a particular society. Each has its own 'high' God or Creator, often referred to as 'Divinity' in the anthropological literature. Each such Divinity is responsible for the creation of the world and for its protection. Divinity is all-powerful, while mankind is puny and helpless. In most indigenous African religions, people do not claim to know or understand Divinity or to know what Divinity looks like; Divinity is rarely if ever represented in art. Such qualities as compassion, anger, mercy and vengeance are, however, often attributed to Divinity. Much African myth is concerned with Divinity's creation of the world and with the activities of the first creatures, often half-human, half-divine, and with the actions of the first humans.

Divinity is typically remote and otiose. Once the world had been created, Divinity retired from any concern with everyday matters. Rather than being in any sort of contact with Divinity, therefore, the living communicate regularly with lesser forces. Generally these comprise ancestors, often referred to as ghosts, shades or ancestral spirits, and spirits, often referred to as deities or lesser divinities. These figures tend to be specific to individual societies, and they may be seen as symbolic representations of each society's experience of the world.

Ancestors are essentially the souls or spiritual essences of once-living people that have been transformed by the performance of mortuary rites into spiritual entities (*see* §III, 5(ii) below). They may be given shrines where they can be contacted by the living. Usually the ancestors are linked to lineages and kin-based groups and are concerned only with the affairs of their descendants. The senior members, those closest to the ancestors in life and who will join them soonest, are responsible for communication with them through prayer, sacrifice and ritual.

Spirits may be best understood as refractions of Divinity. They are aspects of Divinity as concerned with particular problems, such as illness, or with particular places. Generally spirits are not tied to lineages or other human groups but are free to wander where they will. The configuration of spirits with which any social group is concerned varies with their changing circumstances. People seek to control the power of spirits over them through sacrifice.

Communication with the ancestors and spirits is generally not sought haphazardly but rather undertaken in response to particular problems. The major forms of communication are prayer, sacrifice, possession, visions and dreams. Those mainly responsible for these forms of communication are often referred to as priests, prophets and diviners. Sacrifice to spirits tends to be more important in pastoralist societies, where the ancestors play a less significant role, while sacrifice to the ancestors is more important in agricultural societies. The great agricultural kingdoms place great emphasis on ritual for the royal ancestors.

Priests are generally regarded as possessing attributes of sacredness, often inherited, that enable them to make sacrifices and to act as repositories of divine truth and knowledge unknown to ordinary people. The elders of lineages and local groups share in these qualities of priests, at least in respect of the group's ancestors. Diviners are often held to be able to leave the immanent world and to enter that of the spirits and ancestors. They return from such trances with knowledge of the causes of misfortune or with knowledge of the future. Prophets bring messages from Divinity and often arise at times of disaster or of great stress (*see* §(iv) below).

In all traditional African societies a central problem is the occurrence of evil and misfortune, both to explain it and to cope with it. While the actions of Divinity, the spirits and the ancestors are one form of explanation, a belief in the human capacity to bring about misfortune through witchcraft and/or sorcery is widespread. Witchcraft involves an innate power to harm others merely by wishing to, while sorcery consists in the manipulation of substances. Beliefs in both witchcraft and sorcery are best understood as aspects of philosophies of misfortune. They are often part of sophisticated and complex belief systems that allow personal misfortune to be understood and dealt with. The term 'magic' has also been often used in accounts of African religion, especially by travellers and missionaries. Essentially it is an ethnocentric and derogatory term applied to the religious activities of indigenous practitioners. It has no defined meaning that can be usefully applied to the beliefs and practices of African religion and is best dispensed with.

BIBLIOGRAPHY

E. E. Evans-Pritchard: *Witchcraft, Oracles and Magic among the Azande* (Oxford, 1935; rev. and abridged 1979)
D. Forde, ed.: *African Worlds* (London, 1954)
M. Fortes: *Oedipus and Job in West African Religion* (Cambridge, 1959)
P. Tempels: *Bantu Philosophy* (Paris, 1959)
J. Middleton: *Lugbara Religion: Ritual and Authority among an East African People* (London, 1960)
R. G. Lienhardt: *Divinity and Experience: The Religion of the Dinka* (Oxford, 1961)
J. Middleton and E. Winter, eds: *Witchcraft and Sorcery in East Africa* (London, 1963)
M. Fortes and G. Dieterlen, eds: *African Systems of Thought* (London, 1965)
E. W. Smith: *African Ideas of God* (London, 1966)
J. Beattie and J. Middleton, eds: *Spirit Mediumship and Society in Africa* (London, 1969)
G. Parrinder: *Religion in Africa* (Harmondsworth, 1969)
J. Mbiti: *African Religions and Philosophy* (New York, 1970)
M. Douglas, ed.: *Witchcraft Confessions and Accusations* (London, 1971)
B. Ray: *African Religions: Symbol, Ritual and Community* (Englewood Cliffs, 1976)
J. W. Fernandez: *Bwiti: An Ethnography of the Religious Imagination in Africa* (Princeton, 1982)
T. Beidelman: *Moral Imagination in Kaguru Modes of Thought* (Bloomington, 1986)
J. Gray: *Àshe: Traditional Religion and Healing in Sub-Saharan Africa and the Diaspora—A Classified International Bibliography*, Bibliographies and Indexes in Afro-American and African Studies, 24 (Westport, CT, 1989)
R. Horton: *Patterns of Thought in Africa and the West* (Cambridge, 1993)

JOHN MIDDLETON

(ii) Christianity. By the late 20th century Christianity was probably the majority religion of Sub-Saharan Africa. This was especially so in such areas as eastern Nigeria, Uganda, Lesotho and parts of South Africa. In such areas, indeed, Christianity could be said to be the traditional religion, with some families having been Christian since the early 19th century. Like Islam (*see* §(iii) below), Christianity generally has more adherents in urban areas, while in rural areas it is more likely to exist side by side with other traditional beliefs. It is not uncommon for self-defining Christians to have recourse to pagan practices, and even Islamic ones, in response to particular problems or misfortunes.

Christianity in Africa is virtually as old as Christianity itself. In the very early Christian period, Egypt and North Africa were part of the Greco-Roman Mediterranean world and were thus visited by the early followers of the new religion. Churches were established in Egypt by the 2nd century AD, and Alexandria and Carthage became centres of Christian learning. Christianity was taken up the Nile, so that Christian churches flourished in Nubia into the 12th century. The Arab–Muslim advance into North Africa in the 7th century led eventually to the disappearance of Christianity from all the area, except for the Coptic Church in Egypt, which has continued to the present. Islam did not, however, affect the Christian Church in Ethiopia, which, with its links to the Christian Churches of Egypt and Syria, has maintained its rich and distinctive liturgical, architectural and painting traditions to the present day (*see* ETHIOPIA, §§I and II).

A second phase of the history of Christianity in Africa began with the European, especially Portuguese, contact with the West African coast from the late 15th century on. Missionary work began soon after and was spectacularly successful in the kingdom of the Kongo, where the king and many of his followers converted in 1491. Over the following centuries statues of saints with haloes were produced, as were crucifixes (see fig. 8) and other examples of Christian iconography. Given the almost archetypal status of the Kongo power figures (often erroneously referred to as 'nail fetishes') as primitive 'African' art, it is salutary to realize that there is a strong possibility that the very idea of driving nails into figures was derived by Kongo artists from Christian crucifixes and statues of martyrs (Jongmans; Thornton).

As trade with and, later, colonization of Africa increased, Christianity continued to make an impact in local areas.

8. Crucifix, copper alloy, h. 510 mm, from Kongo, Zaïre, ?17th century (Berlin, Museum für Völkerkunde, III C 44073)

Trading stations often had chaplains, and some local children received a partial Christian education. These developments had little effect on the interior until the late 18th century and the early 19th, when a new evangelism in Europe and America and the return of freed, and Christian, slaves to Africa combined to give Christianity in Africa a new impetus. With the partition of Africa by the colonial powers at the end of the 19th century and the development of road and rail transport, missionaries were able to establish themselves more securely, leading to the adoption of Christianity, in its myriad imported and local forms, as the major religion of Sub-Saharan Africa.

Christianity's effects on the visual arts in Sub-Saharan Africa have been mixed. They have often been negative, with members both preaching and practising the destruction of 'idols' and objects connected to traditional beliefs and practices. The cumulative effect of such attitudes and actions is difficult to judge, but thousands of objects must have been destroyed and whole art traditions, including those of body adornment and figure sculpture, wiped out. Presumably related knowledge and skills also disappeared. In discussing such questions, however, one must not forget that many of those who converted, as well as many of their descendants, probably came to share the world-view that encouraged the destruction of the 'pagan' traditions.

In many cases too, the abandonment, forcible or otherwise, of an art tradition presaged the adoption of new ones. Among the Baluyia of western Kenya, for example, the introduction of Christianity led to the abandonment of traditions of body painting but brought about the development of a vibrant tradition of mural painting in the later 20th century (Burt). Throughout the continent one of the most visible new art traditions is that of church and church-related architecture. By the late 20th century, however, the traditions (other than those of Ethiopia) had still not been widely studied, though the Angolan churches of the 16th, 17th and later centuries have received some attention (*see* ANGOLA, §2). Some works of the late 20th century, such as the basilica in Yamoussoukro, Côte d'Ivoire—a copy of St Peter's, Rome—have little architectural quality, being grandiose and uninspired monuments to political power rather than works of art.

In general by the late 20th century, however, the iconoclastic attitudes of earlier times had been replaced in many areas by new and more positive attitudes. A leading exemplar of these attitudes was the Roman Catholic priest Kevin Carroll (1920–93), who both studied and commissioned work by Yoruba artists, including sculptures and murals for churches and other buildings from the 1950s on. For example, he commissioned the Muslim Yoruba sculptor Lamidi Fakeye (*b c.* 1925) to carve panels with New Testament scenes for the doors of the Catholic church of the University of Ibadan in 1954 (Carroll, pls 85–6). (Examples of the work commissioned by Carroll and fellow priests are held by the African Art Museum at Tenafly, NJ.) By the early 1990s churches and other Christian buildings throughout the continent were decorated with African Christian art, and a related literature had begun to appear (e.g. Thiel and Helf; Harmsen).

BIBLIOGRAPHY

D. J. Fleming: *Heritage of Beauty: Pictorial Studies of Modern Christian Architecture in Asia and Africa Illustrating the Influence of Indigenous Cultures* (New York, 1937)

——: *Each with His Own Brush: Contemporary Christian Art in Asia and Africa* (New York, 1938)

D. G. Jongmans: 'Nail Fetish and Crucifix', *The Wonder of Man's Ingenuity*, Mededelingen van het Museum voor Volkenkunde, Leiden, xv (Leiden, 1962), pp. 50–62

A. Lehmann: *Afroasiatische christliche Kunst* (Berlin, 1966); Eng. trans. as *Christian Art in Africa and Asia* (St Louis, MO, and London, 1969)

K. Carroll: *Yoruba Religious Carving: Pagan and Christian Sculpture in Nigeria and Dahomey* (London, Dublin and Melbourne, 1967)

E. C. Burt: 'Mural Painting in Western Kenya', *Afr. A.*, xvi/3 (1983), pp. 60–63, 80

J. F. Thiel and H. Helf: *Christliche Kunst in Afrika* (1984)

Zimbabwe Christian Art: The First Collected Exhibition (exh. cat., Harare, Anglican Cathedral, 1986)

J. B. Waite: 'The African Art Museum of the S.M.A. Fathers', *Afr. A.*, xxi/1 (1987), pp. 64–7, 88

F. Harmsen: *The Way to Easter: Stations of the Cross in South Africa* (Pretoria, 1989)

J. Thornton: 'The Regalia of the Kingdom of Kongo, 1491–1895', *Kings of Africa: Art and Authority in Central Africa—Collection Museum für Völkerkunde Berlin* (exh. cat., ed. E. Beumers and H.-J. Koloss; Maastricht, Exh. & Congr. Cent., 1992), pp. 57–63 [see also figs 58–61 and captions]

JEREMY COOTE

(iii) Islam. As early as AD 640, followers of Islam had begun their conquest of Egypt. Further west and south,

Islam was probably first introduced into the western Sudan in the 8th and 9th centuries AD through the agency of Muslim merchants and scholars. The merchants exchanged goods from the Mediterranean lands and salt from the Sahara for gold, slaves, ivory and gum. Islam was introduced from North Africa along western routes, linking the Maghrib with the gold-trading centres of western Sudan, and along eastern routes that brought Tripoli, Tunis and Egypt into contact with such kingdoms of the central Sudan as Kanem, Bornu and the Hausa states. After Islam had been disseminated in the Sudan, partly by Berber armies, it was pushed further south by West African Muslim traders, who took it to the southern savannah and the Guinea Coast forest and to northern and central Nigeria. The growth of many towns was encouraged by the arrival of enterprising Muslim traders.

The Islamic colonization of the East African coast, meanwhile, began in the 8th century AD. Most of the early settlers were Arab or Persian merchants and clerics from southern Arabia and the Gulf. They intermarried with the indigenous populations and created numerous trading towns and city-states along the coastal strip. In these settlements Arab, Somali and, further south, SWAHILI cultures flourished, the latter being a synthesis of Bantu African and Islamic traits. Over the centuries these settlements maintained contacts with Arabia, the Gulf and western India.

The history of Islam in Sub-Saharan Africa has been one of interaction with the indigenous cultures it encountered. This interaction led to the development of a diversity of artistic traditions. In addition to the regions where the population converted to orthodox Islam, there were areas where pluralistic societies emerged or where Islamic beliefs and practices merged with the traditional culture in a syncretic pattern. In general, however, Islam became associated with processes of political centralization and urbanization. The construction of congregational mosques at fixed locations, for example, encouraged settlement. Notions of private property and private space were also encouraged and new working practices introduced. Skills and crafts that had traditionally been practised by women in nomadic societies often became the occupations of men as the societies became sedentary.

Many architectural and craft techniques were retained or reinvigorated. In this respect Islam had the ability to adapt itself region by region to the demands of the physical environment. In those regions where Islam was adopted, several new types of building were constructed, the most important being the congregational mosque. The arrival of Islam also led to the introduction of new building techniques. In the African savannah, for example, this is suggested by the continued use of indigenous terms for simple building techniques, while Arabic-derived terms are used for brick shapes.

The adoption of Islam also stimulated a number of other crafts. For example, Islamic prescriptions regarding body covering and the requirement for burial shrouds encouraged the textile crafts (see fig. 9). Islamic charms, talismans and similar items were also in great demand. Military exploits, meanwhile, stimulated a demand for the products of metalwork and leatherworking techniques.

9. Cotton tunic, embroidered with patterns derived from the Koran, l. 890 mm, from northern Nigeria, before 1940 (London, British Museum)

Despite the common Islamic constraints on the representation of living beings, in many well-established Islamic communities in West Africa masking and figurative traditions were able to continue, either because they function at a level not treated by Islamic ritual or because they proved effective. As Islam recognized witchcraft and magic, the use of traditional methods of control when Muslim methods failed was not felt to be incompatible with the faith. The 14th-century Moroccan traveller Ibn Battuta, for example, recorded the use of masks and figurative art forms among the Muslim Mande élite of Mali. Such practices continued into the late 20th century. For example, of the various Bedu masks in use in the area of Bondoukou, Côte d'Ivoire, many were carved in the 1960s by the Muslim Hwela artist Sirikye (*b c.* 1925). Gbain masks have also been carved by Muslims, and evidence suggests that the Gbain cult, for protection against witchcraft, was originally a Muslim Mande tradition. Belief in the power of amulets is also very strong among Islamized Mande. The Do masking tradition, meanwhile, is exclusively Muslim. It follows Muslim procedures and is never used in a non-Muslim context, the ownership and custody of Do masks being invariably vested in the ulema. Masking traditions probably also exist in other Islamized regions of West Africa.

For an account of Islamic architecture in Sub-Saharan Africa, *see* §VI, 1(v) below.

BIBLIOGRAPHY

J. S. Trimingham: *Islam in West Africa* (London, 1959)
——: *A History of Islam in West Africa* (Oxford, 1962)
I. M. Lewis, ed.: *Islam in Tropical Africa* (London, 1966)
J. Kritzek and W. H. Lewis: *Islam in Africa* (New York, 1968)
J. S. Trimingham: *The Influence of Islam upon Africa* (New York, 1968)

R. A. Bravmann: *Islam and Tribal Art in West Africa*, African Studies Series (London and New York, 1974)
——: *African Islam* (Washington, DC, and London, 1983)
L. Prussin: *Hatumere: Islamic Design in West Africa* (Berkeley, 1986)
A. A. Mazrui: 'Islam and African Art: Stimulus or Stumbling Block', *Afr. A.*, xxvii/1 (1994), pp. 50–57

S. J. VERNOIT

(iv) Modern developments. The period of high European colonialism in the 19th and 20th centuries and the consequent opening up of the African interior to world trade and governmental systems encouraged Christian missionary endeavour throughout Africa. Moreover this has continued into post-colonial times. Islam also spread more widely in the same period and for similar reasons. In the late 20th century indigenous and 'intrusive' faiths exist side by side within the same society, within the same community, within the same family, and even within the same individual.

Virtually everywhere the spread of Christianity has been accompanied by the rise of prophets. These have tended to appear in opposition to the racially inegalitarian practices of most early mission churches. Some of these prophets have established their own breakaway or 'separatist' churches, free of European control, although many of these have been shortlived, rent by dissension and competition. Other churches have grown into large organizations in their own right. The Zaïrean Church of Jesus Christ on Earth through the Prophet Simon Kimbanqu is one example, as are the many churches of the Zambian Watch-Tower movement, which grew out of the Jehovah's Witnesses movement. In western Africa many churches with Christian antecedents have developed into faith-healing, often Pentecostalist-type churches with recreated 'traditional African' elements. The Aladura churches of Nigeria are an example. Other prophetic movements that began in opposition to mission churches have turned their backs on Western Christianity altogether and have adopted supposed original African symbols. They have also emphasized polygyny as an 'African' institution, descent from the Christian kings of Ethiopia, taboos on European-type foods, clothing and hairstyles and so on.

Modern reformist movements in Islamic societies in Africa have been similar, although they have not arisen in response to racial issues. The best known are the great Fulani *jihad* of the early 19th century, which was directed against what the Fulani leaders considered the lax practices of the more established Islam of the region, and the Mahdist movement in late 19th-century Sudan, which was directed against the presence of European and Egyptian power. The effects of such movements and developments on the visual art and architecture of Africa have yet to be fully explored.

BIBLIOGRAPHY

B. Sundkler: *Bantu Prophets in South Africa* (London, 1961)
F. Welbourn: *East African Rebels* (London, 1961)
J. D. Y. Peel: *Aladura: A Religious Movement among the Yoruba* (London, 1969)
W. MacGaffey: *Modern Kongo Prophets* (Bloomington, 1983)
——: *Religion and Society in Central Africa* (Chicago, 1986)
S. Barnes, ed.: *Africa's Ogun: Old World and New* (Bloomington, 1989)

JOHN MIDDLETON

II. Art and aesthetics.

The art-historical and aesthetic categories applied to African art are in a constant state of flux. The history of their usage has been dogged by misapprehensions and misrepresentations, although this is hardly surprising, given that they often represent the inappropriate application of Western intellectual and aesthetic concepts. This article provides an overview of the history of scholarly research into and discussion of African art and in particular figure sculpture (*see* §1 below), followed by an account of the vast increase in studies of indigenous systems of aesthetic evaluation since the 1960s (*see* §2 below).

1. Critical and scholarly approaches. 2. Aesthetic evaluation.

1. CRITICAL AND SCHOLARLY APPROACHES. The perception and identity of African art in universal art history are profoundly marked by two categories of art objects: wooden masks and figurative sculpture. In 1926 Paul Guillaume and Thomas Munro in *Primitive Negro Sculpture* went so far as to present a map of 'The Country of Negro Art' that drew a closed line around the regions of West and Central Africa and effectively limited African art to the mask and figurative art traditions that characterize these regions. Truly, however, the importance of figurative art to an understanding of African art history cannot be overestimated. Frank Willett (p. 27) stated that 'the greatest contribution Africa has made ... to the cultural heritage of mankind is its richly varied sculpture'. More recently, Susan Vogel (see 1986 exh. cat. *African Aesthetics*, p. xiv), in asserting the moral basis of much African art, in which 'beautiful' is intended and perceived also to be 'good', has argued that this conflation of beauty and goodness may explain why, in African art 'as in Greek art, the principal subject is the human figure—to the almost total exclusion of nature in the form of landscape, or plant motifs'. Consequently, while this discussion attempts a historical overview of scholarly understandings of African art as a whole, it is inevitably focused primarily on understandings of figure sculpture.

(i) Historical attitudes. (ii) Style and canon. (iii) Context and meaning. (iv) Appreciation of form.

(i) Historical attitudes. The predominance of figuration in African art traditions and in the history of Western collecting has left a legacy of countless thousands of African figures dispersed throughout the world in ethnographic and art museums as well as in private collections. These figures have been little understood in terms of the original intentionality and socio-historical context that brought them into being. The 'discovery' of primitive art, including African sculpture, in the early 20th century was a 'discovery' of its perceived formal qualities accompanied by an almost total, and indeed often wilful, ignorance of its cultural content. Figures acquired in Africa 'as curios rather than art, and as evidence of what [Europeans] considered to be the primitive barbarity of Africans' (see MacGaffey, p. 32) were taken back to Europe as 'found objects'; little or no documentation was acquired with them, and they survived as 'mute objects, themselves damaged in the processes of collection and storage' (MacGaffey, p. 33). The meanings subsequently attributed to these silent objects were invented ideas that reveal more about Western history than about African art history.

Looking back at common Western perceptions of African religion and art, Leon Siroto (p. 7) argued that one constant and fundamental assumption has been that 'representations of the human form fell into one or the other of two categories of iconographic identity. One kind of representation was thought to be positive: the ancestor figure. The other was thought to be negative: an impersonal image intended to hold combined substances capable of projecting magical force'. Each of these paired, common misperceptions of African figurative art is based on profoundly erroneous constructions of African thought and religion. The simplistic notion of 'magic', for example, has been based on a 'whole theory of African civilization, or the supposed lack of it, [that] has been developed under the term "fetishism"', according to which 'Africans were incapable of abstract and generalizing thought; instead their ideas and actions were governed by impulse' (see MacGaffey, p. 32). Likewise, the Western assumption that '"ancestor worship" was the prevailing religious and iconographic concern in traditional Africa' (Siroto, p. 7) has led to the idea that the highest form of artistic expression in Africa was the 'ancestor figure', interpreted as an 'imposing, finely worked depiction of the deceased parent', characterized by 'large size, dignified posture, a seemingly grave and aloof expression and the signs of social and political status, such as a beard, a prestigious stool, a headdress and one or more children' (Siroto).

Other historically determined notions that have continued to have a deleterious influence on Western understanding of African figurative traditions are the idea of the imagined 'expressiveness' of African sculpture and the related idea that African art results from cultural imperative rather than intellectual impulse. It is because 'much African art is extremely stylized compared to Western realism, [that] African art has been regarded as expressionistic and exaggerated' (see 1986 exh. cat. *African Aesthetics*, p. xvii). African figures have been perceived simultaneously as powerfully expressive works of creative invention and yet as almost accidental in their form, as though they were the result of some unleashed primal 'energy'. These seemingly opposed notions have in common a fundamental denial of any intentionality on the part of the artist. Close examination and appreciation of individual works, however, leads to the proper acknowledgement that 'African artists had complete mastery over their tools and materials', and thus 'we may assume that their work looks just as they intended, and that [any] irregularity and roughness were intentional' (see 1986 exh. cat. *African Aesthetics*, p. xii).

The notion that African art is simply a cultural product also denies the particular artistic intentionality of individual works of art and sees them as 'tribal' products, 'natural', or predictable outcomes of a certain world view or cultural system. The literature on African art commonly situates the production of art at the level of specific cultural systems (i.e. the 'tribe'), thus implicitly equating art with a collective activity. In this view, the production of art is almost always by 'artists', in the plural, and works are interpreted in generic cultural terms in which a gloss is given to entire genres of figurative art, for example 'the Baule other-world figure', 'the Dogon ancestor' or 'the Yoruba twin figure'. Such generic characterizations, however, have often been well-intentioned, constituting a necessary step in the understanding of art as a cultural product in their attempt to move beyond 'African' art as a totality to the art of particular cultural traditions. It is not surprising, therefore, that many studies of the cultural dimensions of specific African sculptural traditions were undertaken by anthropologists (e.g. Himmelheber, 1935; Olbrechts, 1946; Gerbrands, 1956; Horton, 1965; Ottenberg, 1975; Ben-Amos, 1980) and that, when art historians began to undertake field studies of African art, they borrowed the methodologies of anthropology (e.g. Sieber, 1961; Thompson, 1974; Vogel, 1977; Glaze, 1981; Cole, 1982; Ezra, 1986; McNaughton, 1988).

(ii) Style and canon. According to Leon Siroto (p. 7), 'the time-lag between academic and commercial interest in African art has led to a massive immigration of unidentified objects into the West', resulting in a plethora of objects whose place in the world had to be determined in some manner. In order to come to grips with, classify and posit cultural and geographical provenances to these otherwise anonymous objects, Western museum curators and scholars, as well as art dealers, have relied upon certain formal criteria of differentiation that collectively fall under the rubric of 'style'.

In African sculpture, it has been argued, style 'includes in essence: the total appearance of an object; the expressive effect of its subject matter; and the creative methods or techniques used to produce these effects' (Wingert, 'Style . . .', p. 38). 'Style' ultimately became a normative and essentialist framework in the categorization of African sculpture. It has been assumed that 'the essential properties involved in the characteristics of a style' could be readily identified (Wingert, 'Style...', p. 37). For example, in enunciating acquisition criteria for the collection of the National Museum of African Art, Washington, DC, Roy Sieber advanced the ideas that each object 'should be central to its style' and that it 'should be significant within that style', ideas that presuppose the possibility of establishing common denominators of style for each style and genre of traditional African art. The idea that style is culturally determined, however, potentially conflicts with the appreciation and acknowledgement of the creativity of individual artists as manifested in their work. The question of the relationship between 'cultural style' and 'individual creativity' has thus led African art scholars to investigate through field research 'the traditional artist in African societies' (the title of a compendium edited by Warren L. d'Azevedo and published in 1973). Within the culturally defined genre, what latitude does the artist have in expressing his own style? The push-and-pull contradictions of the paired opposites of cultural style and individual artistry are nicely captured in Vogel's commentary (see 1986 exh. cat. *African Aesthetics*, p. 129) on a Fang figure: 'some of its power comes from its size and bulk. Its formal complexity and ineffable expression place it at the summit of African artistic achievement. It both crystallizes and extends the canon of Fang art' (see fig. 10).

'Style' has been the critical framework for formal analysis of morphological form in African figurative art, even though, according to Paul Wingert ('Further Style Analysis...', p. 35), the term '"style" approaches the inexplicable, by virtue of its inclusion of practically every facet

10. Fang reliquary guardian figure, wood and metal, h. 700 mm (Paris, Musée Dapper)

of an art object'. The method of style analysis is based upon 'the separation of a design into its constituent parts so as to examine these elements and to determine their significance in the expressive and aesthetic character of the work as a whole' or in terms of common denominators within specific artistic traditions. In an attempt to systematize the study of style in Fang figurative sculpture, Louis Perrois examined a corpus of figures and measured proportions, such as the height of the head in relation to that of the torso, and described the positions of arms and legs, the style of coiffure and a number of specific details, such as the shape of eyes, nose, mouth, ears, navel and breasts. From his investigation he deduced that Fang style could be divided into the northern 'hyper- and longiform' styles and the southern 'equiform and breviform' styles. At one level Perrois' work can be seen as a somewhat obsessive attempt to codify the denominators of substyles, as if thereby to prove that artists necessarily work within culturally predetermined styles, albeit perhaps unconsciously.

Style analysis as objective description has resulted in the establishment of the canon of 'African art': the differentiation of styles in terms of their genres and their ethnic provenance. Some scholars, such as William Fagg, have made major contributions to the field of African art studies by advancing studies of 'tribal styles' (see Willett, p. 29). As Sidney Kasfir has argued, the approach has often been limited to an implicit 'one tribe, one style' paradigm, in which the framework of analysis is implicitly or explicitly the tribal unit with its attendant stylistic denominators. Tribal styles have also been seen, in turn, as building blocks to larger entities, the larger 'style regions' of African art (see 1968 exh. cat.; Roy), a version of which approach has been adopted in this survey (*see* §VII below). Jan Vansina has argued, however, that a distributional approach to African art is insufficient and that 'the historical evolvement of the [African] art forms, even the sculptural forms, has not been a subject of sustained research' (p. 1). He argues for a study of 'art in Africa and its history' rather than an 'art history of Africa', the latter not being possible owing to the lack of monographs as well as the fact that 'too many scholars in the field of "African art" have been allergic to historical pursuits'. It is unclear what place 'style regions' will occupy in the future development of an African art history. They have been a convenient way to explore and group larger stylistic tendencies of African sculpture, especially figurative, but as the study of African art develops to include the areas of Africa north of the Sahara and the relatively neglected art traditions of East and Southern Africa, the inadequacy and profound limitations of the 'style region' approach become more and more evident. The regional geographic paradigm allows for an examination of artistic traits and comparative cultural phenomena, but it has yielded little in terms of history, concentrating as it has on space rather than time.

(iii) Context and meaning. The classificatory approach to types of African figurative sculpture has resulted in incomplete understandings of questions of meaning in African sculpture as well as of the relationship between the form of an image and its original efficacy. Leon Siroto (p. 6) has argued that in field research 'the type-oriented question "What does this image (or object) represent?" can lead to crucial misunderstandings' and that 'equally crucial misunderstandings of imagery have resulted from failure to ask the person-oriented question "Whom does this image (or object) represent?"' (p. 7). A hypothetical exchange between an investigator and a field informant may be illustrative. In a Baule village in Côte d'Ivoire, a field

11. Baule figure sculpture of an 'other-world man' (*blolo bian*), wood and pigments, *c.* 1950s (Washington, DC, National Museum of African Art)

worker seeing a sculpted figure and asking, 'What is this?', may receive the reply, 'It is a wooden figure' (*waka sran*), or 'It is a figure of an "other-world man"' (*blolo bian*; see fig. 11). If, however, a further question were to be asked, 'Whom does this figure represent?', the answer would be the name of a specific individual, such as Gbaflin Kwami, 'Kwami the dandy'.

Approaches to African art that concentrate too much on the shared parameters and components of style in objects removed from their context have often overlooked the significance of the subtle differences in form that created the individuality and power of a specific work. Leon Siroto remarked (p. 7) that '[African] images often show great care in their sculptural rendering and seem individual enough to carry specific information about their personal identity'. He argued for a connection between a belief in animism—'belief in personalized, man-like supernaturals' (p. 8)—and the artistic interpretation of form, such that 'the carver's recognition of the spirit as a distinct individual compelled him to use its form as a way of differentiating it from all other spirits, and, in some cases, from humans as well' (p. 20). Wyatt MacGaffey argued convincingly for the 'personhood' of such ritual objects as Kongo power figures (*minkisi*; sing. *nkisi*; see fig. 12), claiming that they incarnate specific, named persons who are invoked, addressed and negotiated with in speech. Part of the identity of such figures is in their form and the accumulated materials or medicines added to it in use.

Arnold Rubin argued that 'the content of African sculpture has clearly not received the attention it deserves' (see 1974 exh. cat., *African Accumulative Sculpture*, p. 36).

12. Kongo figure sculpture, *nkisi nkondi*, mainly wood, glass and iron, h. 423 mm, from Congo or Zaïre (Washington, DC, National Museum of African Art)

In using the term 'content', Rubin described 'one dimension of the affective power and complex of multiple meanings embodied in a work of art'. In his consideration of the media of African sculpture, Rubin focused on 'accumulation'. The work of art is not just the original form fresh from the hands of the African artist; it also includes the embellishments or traces of use added to the work by its owner(s). He argued that, in visual terms, the substances and elements added to African works of art may provisionally be divided into two broad categories of 'power' and 'display'. According to Rubin:

> Display materials (beads, bells, fabrics, mirrors, etc) are primarily oriented toward enhancement of the splendor of the objects to which they are attached. They usually carry associations of prosperity and cosmopolitan association for the individual or group on whose behalf such sculpture is created . . . The second category of materials—horns, skulls, and sacrificial accumulations, for example—is connected with the organization and exploitation of power.

Although Rubin claimed to use the notions of power and display as a 'neutral frame of reference' to explore relationships between meaning and form in African art, these two notions are not in fact polar opposites, and much African sculpture combines attributes of both. All African figurative sculptures, for example, were created for specific uses, and their intended use necessarily had an effect on form, whether originally or as it changed through time. Sculpture used and displayed in public, for instance, is often larger than that intended for use in private shrines or in the context of a consultation between diviner and client. Within a specific cultural tradition there may well be stylistic relationships between different types of figures that differ in scale. Among the Senufo of Côte d'Ivoire and Mali, one genre of sculpture, known as 'the children of Poro' (see Glaze), is used in public displays by the men's or women's Poro society. These figures are large (h. 1 m or more), whereas the stylistically similar figures that represent the bush-spirits, sometimes equestrian, that empower diviners of the Sandogo society and are used in consultations are small (h. 150–350 mm; see fig. 44 below; *see also* SENUFO, §2).

(iv) Appreciation of form. Discussion of style in African art is based on formal qualities and relationships. For example, in 1926 Guillaume and Munro wrote (p. 35):

> Every part in a typical, fully-realized negro statue functions as an element in plastic design: an embodiment, a repetition in rhythmic, varied sequence, of some theme in mass, line, or surface . . . The figure must be dissociated into its parts, regarded as an aggregate of distinct units: the head, limbs, breasts, trunk, and so on, each by itself.

Such stylistic analysis, which represents subjective appreciation of individual works of art as aesthetic creations rather than as ethnographic documents, has a long history in African art studies. From Carl Einstein (1915) to Susan Vogel (1986) the fascination with the sculptural richness of African art has led to an often celebratory literature that asserts the universal value of African art. At times hostile to the contextualization of African sculpture (e.g. Einstein), at times sensitive to contextual information (e.g. Vogel), this literature is far more conclusive as art appreciation than art history. It fits into the larger historical context of the discovery of 'tribal art' or 'primitive art', the terms of convenience that have been used to link the arts of Africa, Oceania and the Americas. The 1984 exhibition *'Primitivism' in 20th Century Art: Affinity of the Tribal and the Modern* explored the crucial influence of 'tribal' art on modern painters and sculptors in the West. Kirk Varnedoe, co-director of the exhibition, stresses that 'modernist primitivism ultimately depends on the autonomous force of objects—and especially on the capacity of tribal art to transcend the intentions and conditions that first shaped it' (see 1984 exh. cat., p. x). It is these allied ideas of 'autonomy' and 'transcendence' that have made possible a history of stylistic appreciation of African art in which artistic meaning is posited by a direct reading of form. Such appreciation is also undertaken by Africanist art historians who seek to articulate the reasons for our response to particular works of art. Paul Wingert, for example, while arguing that 'sculpture from the Central Cameroon Grasslands area has one of the most distinctive styles in all of Black Africa' (see 'Further Style Analysis. . .', p. 35), analyses one particular figure as follows:

> It is apparent at first glance that the paramount importance in this carving is the expression of vigorous movement that is held in a state of momentary suspension. . . . all of the component parts of the figure have a strongly declared autonomy in space. . . . The figure has a compact organic unity of expression.

Such analyses are purely formal and take little, if any, note of the rich traditions of indigenous aesthetic evaluation that scholarship has begun to explore (*see* §2 below).

BIBLIOGRAPHY

C. Einstein: *Negerplastik* (Leipzig, 1915, rev. Berlin, 1992)

P. Guillaume and T. Munro: *Primitive Negro Sculpture* (London, 1926)

H. Himmelheber: *Negerkünstler* (Stuttgart, 1935)

F. M. Olbrechts: *Plastiek van Kongo* (Antwerp, 1946)

A. A. Gerbrands: *Kunst aus cultuur-element, in het bijzonder in Neger-Afrika* (Leiden, 1956); Eng. trans. by G. E. van Baaren-Pape, Mededelingen van het Rijksmuseum voor Volkenkunde, Leiden, 12 (Leiden, 1957)

The Sculpture of Northern Nigeria (exh. cat. by R. Sieber, New York, Mus. Primitive A., 1961)

R. Horton: *Kalabari Sculpture* (Lagos, 1965)

Sculpture of Black Africa (exh. cat. by R. Sieber and A. Rubin, Los Angeles, CA, Co. Mus. A., 1968)

F. Willett: *African Art: An Introduction*, World A. (London and New York, 1971/*R* 1993)

L. Perrois: *La Statuaire Fang* (Paris, 1972)

P. S. Wingert: 'Style Determinants in African Sculpture', *Afr. A.*, v/3 (1972), pp. 37–43

——: 'Further Style Analysis in African Sculpture', *Afr. A.*, vi/1 (1972), pp. 35–41

W. L. d'Azevedo, ed.: *The Traditional Artist in African Societies* (Bloomington and London, 1973/*R* 1992)

African Accumulative Sculpture: Power and Display (exh. cat. by A. Rubin, New York, Pace Gal., 1974)

African Art in Motion: Icon and Act (exh. cat. by R. F. Thompson; Washington, DC, N.G.A.; Los Angeles, UCLA, Wight A.G.; 1974)

S. Ottenberg: *The Masked Rituals of Afikpo: The Context of an African Art* (Seattle, 1975)

L. Siroto: *African Spirit Images and Identities* (New York, 1976)

S. M. Vogel: *Baule Art as the Expression of a Worldview* (diss., New York U., 1977; microfilm, Ann Arbor, 1977)

C. Roy: *African Sculpture: The Stanley Collection* (Iowa City, 1979)

P. Ben-Amos: *The Art of Benin*, Tribal A. (London, 1980)

A. J. Glaze: *Art and Death in a Senufo Village*, Trad. A. Africa (Bloomington, 1981)

H. M. Cole: *Mbari: Art and Life among the Owerri Igbo* (Bloomington, 1982)
S. L. Kasfir: 'One Tribe, One Style: Paradigms in the Historiography of African Art', *Hist. Afr.*, xi (1984), pp. 163–93
J. Vansina: *Art History in Africa: An Introduction to Method* (London and New York, 1984)
K. Varnedoe: 'Preface', *'Primitivism' in 20th Century Art: Affinity of the Tribal and the Modern*, 2 vols (exh. cat., ed. W. Rubin; New York, MOMA, 1984), p. x
African Aesthetics: The Carlo Monzino Collection (exh. cat. by S. Vogel, New York, Cent. Afr. A., 1986)
The Human Ideal in African Art: Bamana Figurative Sculpture (exh. cat. by K. Ezra, Washington, DC, N. Mus. Afr. A., 1986)
P. R. McNaughton: *The Mande Blacksmiths: Knowledge, Power, and Art in West Africa*, Trad. A. Africa (Bloomington, 1988)
W. MacGaffey: 'The Eyes of Understanding: Kongo Minkisi', *Astonishment and Power* (exh. cat., Washington, DC, N. Mus. Afr. A., 1993–4), pp. 21–103

PHILIP L. RAVENHILL

2. AESTHETIC EVALUATION. Aesthetics is here taken to be the valued formal qualities in things or experiences expressed as canons of taste or qualitative judgements. Broadly, visual aesthetics may be understood as a philosophy of form concerned both with objects and with activities and performances. These are evaluated by individuals whose judgements may be shared, to varying degrees, within and across cultures.

(i) Introduction. (ii) Cross-cultural criteria. (iii) Case-studies. (iv) Conclusion.

(i) Introduction. The presence of finely crafted images in ancient central Sahara, early Egypt and Nubia, as well as early works in other parts of the continent, suggests that aesthetic evaluation is ancient in Africa. We can, however, only conjecture about the criteria used. Western aesthetic evaluations of African cultural phenomena were first made at the end of the 19th century in the publications of the German scholar F. Ratzel and of E. Grosse. These authors focused on objects (primarily figure sculpture) that most closely resembled 'art' as then conventionally defined in the West. The interest in African art displayed a few years later by such artists as Vlaminck, Picasso, Derain, Matisse and Braque helped to validate its study (*see* PRIMITIVISM). At the same time, however, their personal, ethnocentric and formalist perspectives ignored consideration of indigenous African views and aesthetic judgements. Unfortunately, such an approach has continued to be adopted in some quarters.

Similar attitudes shaped the appreciation of African art in the USA. There, however, the emerging African consciousness among African Americans during the Black Renaissance of the 1920s led to the aesthetic value of African art receiving glowing praise from such writers as C. S. Johnson and, especially, Alain Locke. Locke urged African American artists to use African art as a source of inspiration, not simply because of its aesthetic qualities but also because its ancestral forms possessed both spiritual and cultural relevance for them.

It was only in the 1930s and 1940s, however, that African aesthetic evaluations began to be documented in detail. Moreover, the most sustained work has taken place since the 1970s. The limits of present knowledge and the vastness and cultural diversity of the continent make attempts to generalize about African aesthetics inevitable, although it is not always clear what they achieve. Pan-African and cross-cultural studies may be contrasted with cultural case-studies. While many are still based on the unverified observations and interpretations of a single authority, in some cases, for example that of the Akan- and Yoruba-speaking peoples of West Africa, there is an extensive literature by both African and non-African scholars. A 'critical mass' of scholarship has emerged that suggests the depth and richness of aesthetic thought in Africa.

BIBLIOGRAPHY

F. Ratzel: *Völkerkunde*, 3 vols (Leipzig, 1885–8; rev. as 2 vols, 1894–5); Eng. trans. of rev. by A. J. Butler as *The History of Mankind*, 3 vols (London, 1896–8)
E. Grosse: *The Beginnings of Art*, The Anthropological Series (New York, 1897)
C. S. Johnson: 'The Creative Art of the Negroes', *Opportunity*, i (1923), pp. 240–45
A. Locke: 'A Note on African Art', *Opportunity*, ii (1924), pp. 134–8
A. Locke, ed.: *The New Negro: An Interpretation* (New York, 1925)
A. Locke: *Negro Art: Past and Present*, Bronze Booklet, 3 (Washington, DC, 1936)
W. L. d'Azevedo: 'A Structural Approach to Esthetics: Toward a Definition of Art in Anthropology', *Amer. Anthropol.*, lx/4 (1958), pp. 702–14
J. Coote: 'The Anthropology of Aesthetics and the Dangers of "Maquetcentrism"', *J. Anthropol. Soc. Oxford*, xx/3 (1989), pp. 229–43

(ii) Cross-cultural criteria. Whether cross-cultural, pan-African or perhaps even universal criteria of aesthetic evaluation exist remains a largely unanswered question. For example, in specific comparisons between Baule and Yoruba aesthetic evaluations such criteria as resemblance, balance and youthfulness were shared, but there were also some significant divergences, such as in the evaluation of asymmetry (see Vogel). R. F. Thompson has suggested that there is a definable pan-African aesthetic, which he derived from widespread cultural ideas about composure and collectedness of mind and which he termed 'the cool'. In one case at least, however, among the Asante, it appears that, while works from a wide variety of African cultures are easily and willingly evaluated, this is done with Asante, not pan-African, criteria (see Silver).

The other elements of a supposed general African aesthetic that have been proposed include: the avoidance of straight lines and the use of exponential curves (see Fagg); a moral basis, such as among the Twi of Ghana where the word *fe* means both 'beautiful' and 'fitting' (see Appiah), which may explain why the human figure is so prevalent throughout African art; skill in the transformation of media, that is, technical excellence or workmanship; the attributes admired in sculpture being those admired in people; moderation; and innovation and invention within set cultural parameters (see 1986 exh. cat.). Perhaps another is the importance of the secular, artful and playful aspects of African arts (see Okpewho; Drewal).

As for the question of universal aesthetic criteria, through formal experiments some researchers have found substantial agreement among the responses to art between Africans and non-Africans. However, the reasons for the similar judgements (i.e. the evaluative criteria) differed significantly (see Child and Siroto; Child).

BIBLIOGRAPHY

W. B. Fagg: 'On the Nature of African Art', *Mem. & Proc. Manchester Lit. & Philos. Soc.*, xciv (1952–3), pp. 93–104
I. L. Child and L. Siroto: 'BaKwele and American Esthetic Evaluations Compared', *Ethnology*, iv/4 (1965), pp. 349–60; repr. in *Art and*

Aesthetics in Primitive Societies: A Critical Anthology, ed. C. F. Jopling (New York, 1971), pp. 271–89

I. L. Child: 'The Expert and the Bridge of Judgement that Crosses Every Cultural Gap', *Psychol. Today* (Dec 1968), pp. 24–9

R. F. Thompson: 'An Aesthetic of the Cool', *Afr. A.*, vii/1 (1973), pp. 40–43, 64–7, 89–91; also abridged in *Arts of Africa, Oceania, and the Americas: Selected Readings*, ed. J. C. Berlo and L. A. Wilson (Englewood Cliffs, 1993), pp. 22–35

African Art in Motion: Icon and Act (exh. cat. by R. F. Thompson; Washington, DC, N.G.A.; Los Angeles, UCLA, Wight A.G.; 1974)

I. Okpewho: 'Principles of Traditional African Art', *J. Aesth. & A. Crit.*, xxxv/3 (1977), pp. 301–13

S. M. Vogel: 'Baule and Yoruba Art Criticism: A Comparison', *The Visual Arts: Plastic and Graphic*, ed. J. M. Cordwell (The Hague, 1979), pp. 309–25

H. R. Silver: 'Foreign Art and Asante Aesthetics', *Afr. A.*, xvi/3 (1982), pp. 64–7, 79–80

A. Appiah: 'An Aesthetics for the Art of Adornment in Africa', *Beauty by Design: The Aesthetics of African Adornment* (exh. cat., ed. M.-T. Brincard; New York, Afr.-Amer. Inst., 1984), pp. 15–19

African Aesthetics: The Carlo Monzino Collection (exh. cat. by S. M. Vogel, New York, Cent. Afr. A., 1986)

M. T. Drewal: *Yoruba Ritual: Performers, Play, Agency*, African Systems of Thought (Bloomington, 1992)

K. Welsh-Asante: *The African Aesthetic: Keeper of the Traditions*, Contributions in Afro-American and African Studies, 153 (Westport, CT, 1993)

(iii) Case-studies.

(a) Survey. (b) Akan-speaking peoples. (c) Yoruba-speaking peoples.

(a) Survey. This survey is organized both geographically, to highlight possible cross-cultural interactions that may have helped shape aesthetic evaluations, and thematically.

The DAN and related peoples of Côte d'Ivoire value highly such features as finished and polished surfaces, colour, symmetry about the vertical axis, balance, rhythm and harmony among volumes, and carefully rendered linear patterns. For masks, there is also their suitability for seeing and breathing well. Such evaluations are often expressed by Dan artists not so much in words as in gestures, for example in the ways they handle works-in-progress, turning them upside-down, holding them at arm's length and so on (see Vandenhoute). For the Dan, form is meant to be evocative; specific emotions and reactions are for specific contexts and are evoked by a 'symbolism of forms' (see 1976 exh. cat., rev. 1984, p. 182). Thus, a mask that successfully conveys awe or terror (*gbuze*) is angular in form with a large mouth, tubular eyes, black feathers and red colouring. One expressive of grotesqueness or ugliness (*ya*) often has a low forehead, pendulous lips, a short flat nose and brown colouring. In contrast, a beautiful or fine (*se*) mask has a high forehead, slitted eyes, a narrow nose, full-lipped mouth and white paint about the eyes conveying gentleness. Other evaluative terms in the Dan vocabulary are *li* ('beautiful'), *yeiya* ('hateful'), *manyene* ('splendid') and *ga pe mu* ('something to look at'). Among the GURO, who are neighbours of the Dan to the north, the artists who make masks seem to take particular pleasure in smooth, subtle transitions from convex to concave shapes, and they also prize profile views. They have an extensive evaluative vocabulary based around such concepts as *ezima* ('beauty') and *nee* ('ugliness'; see 1986 exh. cat., p. 10).

Among the MENDE of Sierra Leone ideals of feminine beauty are guarded and passed on by the female elders (*sowei*) of the female initiation society, Sande; they are closely related to the attributes in terms of which sculptures and Sande headdresses (*sowo-wui*) depicting women are evaluated (see fig. 13). These attributes include three fundamental features and associated aesthetic ideas: a high, broad, smooth forehead, expressive of intelligence, good fortune and social responsibility; a full head of thick hair, neatly braided and decorated and expressive of energy, fertility and abundance; and 'rainbow' neck rings, expressive of high status, vitality, well-being, divine munificence and the beauty that benefits communities. Additional features include *ngakpango-jo*: completeness, correctness; *a gulo nya ma leke kinein*: comfortable to wear or danceable, suggesting useful, efficacious beauty; *gbongbongo-bowobowo*: smoothness that epitomizes health; *mbema*: balance and symmetry connoting collectedness, composure; *ma ya-sahein*: clarity of form; *neku*: freshness, newness suggesting vitality; and *yengele*: delicacy, especially of the mouth, which is expressive of circumspection and good judgement. Sande headdresses thus embody a complex cluster of Mende social, aesthetic and spiritual aspirations (see Boone).

The Gola of Liberia, neighbours of the Mende, have an aesthetic preference for an air of nonchalance, for the ability 'to act as though one's mind were in another world . . . to do difficult tasks with an air of ease and silent disdain'. Women are particularly admired for 'a detached expression, and somnambulistic movement and attitude during the dance or other performance'; this 'is considered very attractive' (see d'Azevedo, pp. 63–4).

The IDOMA of Nigeria focus on evaluations of the skill and technical proficiency demonstrated by artists (see Sieber). Among the Tiv of Nigeria people in general take an active role in aesthetic evaluation. Few art works are created by specialists, and thus most Tiv consider themselves both artists and critics. Expressing their appraisals both during and after the creation of a work, they explicitly judge its quality by such criteria as balance, symmetry and 'tasteful' asymmetry (see Bohannan). Among the Edo-speaking Okpella of Nigeria discussions revolve around the pleasing embellishments (*ene*) of form that make objects beautiful (*osombotse*) as opposed to ugly (*oyembosue*). The latter term is used for something that is broken, marred or flawed or that is frightful/grotesque (*ulishi*). The concept of beautiful overlaps with that of good (*ti*) but is not synonymous with it (see Borgatti, p. 19).

Among the KONGO peoples of central Africa the term *umbanqu* means the fusion of 'tradition and creation' and connotes 'creativity'. This suggests a preference for a dynamic, processual invention of tradition in aesthetic production (see Maesen). Knowing the reasons why persons may suspend aesthetic evaluations in certain circumstances can also reveal aesthetic preferences. Thus among the Lega (*see* LEGA AND RELATED PEOPLES) of Zaïre people refuse to comment on the objects of the Bwami society except to say that they are all 'good', which has been interpreted to mean that they fulfil their didactic and initiatory purposes (see Biebuyck, p. 17).

In several African cultures moral and aesthetic values intersect. Among the Chokwe of Angola and Zaïre (*see* CHOKWE AND RELATED PEOPLES), the concepts of 'good' and 'beautiful' (*chibema*) in relation to 'art' are shaped by such issues as colour preferences, age, craftsmanship,

13. Members of the Mende female initiation society, Sande, with Sowo mask, Sierra Leone; from a photograph by Rebecca Busselle

correctness, smoothness and precision of technique (see Crowley, 1966, 1973). Aesthetic comments by the Anang IBIBIO people of Nigeria identify an 'aesthetic feeling tone' (*mfon*) related to notions of beauty and moral goodness (see Messenger, p. 124). Among the FANG of Gabon aesthetic values also resonate with allusions to moral order. According to J. W. Fernandez (1966), important Fang aesthetic principles are the notions of vitality, the 'capacity to survive' (*enin*) and balance (*bibwe*), which together comprise 'a vitality of balanced opposites' that emerges in discussions of reliquary figures (*bieri*). Similar concepts are also seen in the spatial organization of villages whose survival depends on balancing the tensions between different sections of the community (see Fernandez, 1973).

Among nomadic or semi-nomadic pastoralists whose minimal material culture contains few objects that might be termed 'art', aesthetic evaluations focus on other things. For example, in Rwanda there is a concentration on performance arts (see Smith). Among some of the NUBA peoples of Sudan aesthetic evaluation centres around judgements of embellishment through cicatrization and painting of young, strong, healthy bodies. Evaluation concerns such visual attributes as symmetry, balance, colour, focus and the reinforcing impact of two-dimensional imagery on three-dimensional forms (see Faris).

According to H. K. Schneider, the Nilotic Pokot (Pakot) define 'art' from 'non-art', or rather aesthetic from non-aesthetic objects, on the basis of pleasing and non-utilitarian embellishment termed *pachigh*, 'beautiful, pleasant to look at'. A headrest that might be seen as a sculpture by Westerners is for the Pokot only art in its decorative aspects, the incised designs or smooth, shiny surfaces. Often the most highly prized, aesthetically valued embellished objects are the rare, novel or unusual ones. Among the Nuer, Dinka and other Nilotic-speaking cattle-keepers of southern Sudan aesthetic evaluations concentrate on their cattle, on the colour configurations, hide textures, horn shapes and the size and condition of the bovine body (see Coote). For example, cattle with variegated hides are highly valued and are set aside as display animals. The valued attribute of contrast in such cattle constitutes a maximizing of aesthetic satisfaction in an environment generally characterized by a colourless landscape and vast herds of off-white, greyish cattle (see fig. 14).

BIBLIOGRAPHY

P. J. L. Vandenhoute: *Classification stylistique du masque Dan et Guéré de la Côte d'Ivoire occidentale (A.O.F.)*, Mededelingen van het Rijksmuseum voor Volkenkunde, Leiden, 4 (Leiden, 1948)

H. K. Schneider: 'The Interpretation of Pakot Visual Art', *Man*, lvi (Aug 1956), pp. 103–6; repr. in *Art and Aesthetics in Primitive Societies: A Critical Anthology*, ed. C. F. Jopling (New York, 1971), pp. 55–63

R. Sieber: 'The Aesthetics of Traditional African Art', *Seven Metals of Africa* (exh. cat. by F. Rainey, Philadelphia, U. PA, Mus., 1959); repr. in *Art and Aesthetics in Primitive Societies: A Critical Anthology*, ed. C. F. Jopling (New York, 1971), pp. 127–31

A. Maesen: *Umbangu: Art du Congo au Musée Royale du Congo Belge* (Tervuren, 1960)

14. Dinka ox with bold black-and-white markings, near Pacong, southern Sudan; from a photograph by Jeremy Coote, 1991

P. Bohannan: 'Artist and Critic in an African Society', *The Artist in Tribal Society: Proceedings of a Symposium Held at the Royal Anthropological Institute*, ed. M. W. Smith, Royal Anthropological Institute Occasional Paper, 15 (London, 1961), pp. 85–94; repr. in *Anthropology and Art: Readings in Cross-cultural Aesthetics*, ed. C. M. Otten (New York, 1971/*R* Austin, TX, 1976), pp. 172–81
W. L. d'Azevedo: *The Artist Archetype in Gola Culture*, Desert Research Institute Preprint, 14 (Nevada, 1966, rev. 1970)
D. J. Crowley: 'An African Aesthetic', *J. Aesth. & A. Crit.*, xxiv/4 (1966), pp. 519–24; repr. in *Art and Aesthetics in Primitive Societies: A Critical Anthology*, ed. C. F. Jopling (New York, 1971), pp. 315–27
J. W. Fernandez: 'Principles of Opposition and Vitality in Fang Aesthetics', *J. Aesth. & A. Crit.*, xxv/1 (1966), pp. 53–64; repr. in *Art and Aesthetics in Primitive Societies: A Critical Anthology*, ed. C. F. Jopling (New York, 1971), pp. 356–73
D. Biebuyck: 'Introduction', *Tradition and Creativity in Tribal Art*, ed. D. Biebuyck (Berkeley, 1969/*R* 1973), pp. 1–23
J. C. Faris: *Nuba Personal Art*, A. & Soc. Ser. (London, 1972)
D. J. Crowley: 'Aesthetic Value and Professionalism in African Art: Three Cases from the Katanga Chokwe', *The Traditional Artist in African Societies*, ed. W. L. d'Azevedo (Bloomington, 1973), pp. 221–49
J. Fernandez: 'The Exposition and Imposition of Order: Artistic Expression in Fang Culture', *The Traditional Artist in African Societies*, ed. W. L. d'Azevedo (Bloomington, 1973), pp. 194–220
J. C. Messenger: 'The Carver in Anang Society', *The Traditional Artist in African Societies*, ed. W. L. d'Azevedo (Bloomington, 1973), pp. 101–27
Die Künste der Dan (exh. cat. by E. Fischer and H. Himmelheber, Zurich, Mus. Rietberg, 1976; Eng. trans. and rev., Zurich, 1984)
J. M. Borgatti: *From the Hands of Lawrence Ajanaku* (Los Angeles, 1979)
P. Smith: 'Aspects de l'esthétique au Rwanda', *L'Homme*, xxv/1 (1985), pp. 7–21
S. A. Boone: *Radiance from the Waters: Ideals of Feminine Beauty in Mende Art* (New Haven, 1986)
Masks in Guro Culture, Ivory Coast (exh. cat. by E. Fischer and L. Homberger, Zurich, Mus. Rietberg, 1986)
J. Coote: '"Marvels of Everyday Vision": The Anthropology of Aesthetics and the Cattle-keeping Nilotes', *Anthropology, Art, and Aesthetics*, ed. J. Coote and A. Shelton, Oxford Studies in the Anthropology of Cultural Forms (Oxford, 1992), pp. 245–73

(b) Akan-speaking peoples. The AKAN themselves have an elaborate taxonomy of art forms and an extensive aesthetic vocabulary. For example, they have categories of non-utilitarian forms termed *afefedee* or 'items of beauty' and of utilitarian forms, *adehunu* or 'things empty', many of which are regarded as *agyapadee*, treasured items or heirlooms. Among the Akan set of positive evaluative terms (given here without their prefixes) are *bere*: beautiful, delicate; *bereye*: fineness; *adwenemtew*: clearness of thought, intention; *fe/efe*: fine, pretty, beauty; *hare*: light, quick; and *ahoofe*: elegance. Among the set of negative terms are *kusuu*: unclear; *hima/kyea*: unbalanced, crooked; *kyim*: twisted; *omum*: ugliness; *tawee/bawee*: rough, shapeless, ugly; and *basa-basa*: unskilful (see Warren and Andrews, pp. 6, 33–8).

The BAULE comment critically on the morphology of their figural sculpture in evaluating such physical attributes of persons as the fullness and roundness of the head, arms and calves. Formal evaluations include such aspects as balance and appropriate asymmetry, segmentation and composition/placement (see Vogel). In the tourist arts of the Asante (*see* ASANTE AND RELATED PEOPLES) the distorted and grotesque works created for an external audience exaggeratedly violated indigenous aesthetic norms, thus serving to reinforce Asante aesthetic and cultural values (see Silver, 1979).

BIBLIOGRAPHY

D. Warren and J. K. Andrews: *An Ethnoscientific Approach to Akan Arts and Aesthetics*, Working Pap. Trad. A., 3 (Philadelphia, 1977)
H. R. Silver: 'Beauty and the "I" of the Beholder: Identity, Aesthetics, and Social Change among the Ashanti', *J. Anthropol. Res.*, xxxv/2 (1979), pp. 191–207
P. L. Ravenhill: *Baule Statuary Art: Meaning and Modernization*, Working Pap. Trad. A., 5 (Philadelphia, 1980) [pubd with S. M. Vogel, 1980, as special issue on Baule aesthetics]
S. M. Vogel: *Beauty in the Eyes of the Baule: Aesthetics and Cultural Values*, Working Pap. Trad. A., 6 (Philadelphia, 1980)

H. R. Silver: 'Calculating Risks: The Socioeconomic Foundations of Aesthetic Innovation in an Ashanti Carving Community', *Ethnology*, xx/2 (1981), pp. 101–14

(c) Yoruba-speaking peoples. YORUBA aesthetics are expressed in what is known as *oro ijinle* ('deep discourse'). This draws on such concepts as *jijora*: resemblance; *ifarahon*: visibility, clarity of line and form; *didon*: luminosity, shining smoothness of surface; *idogba*: balance; *gigun*: straightness; *odo*: ephebism, youthfulness; *itutu*: an expression of composure or 'cool'; *kekere*, *tinrin* and *we*: delicacy; *yo*: roundness/pleasing protrusions; *wiwu*: sinister swellings; and *sonso*: pleasing angularity (see Thompson, 1973). *Iwa l'ewa* ('essence/truth is beauty') refers to the criterion of capturing the essential character of a thing or person. This reflects an artist's *oju-inu*: inner-eye or insight; his *oju-ona*: design-consciousness, sensitivity to design and composition; his *yiye*: appropriateness (sense of propriety); his *imoju-mora*: appropriate innovation, inventiveness; his *ifarabale*: possession of a sense of disciplined authority; his *pipe*: correctness, which ensures that the work is *laaye*: alive; *tito*: enduring; and *dahun*: responding or evocative (see Abiodun; 1991 exh. cat.). These are some of the concepts and criteria that underlie the appreciation and evaluation both of sculpture and of masks and masquerade performances by their spectators (see fig. 15).

The carving process is divided into a number of stages: *ona lile*: blocking out the main volumes; *aletunle*: dividing the main volumes; *didon*, rounding and smoothing surfaces; and *fifin*, incising lines, linear details. These reveal some of the conceptual models of Yoruba art, such as a dynamic and ongoing view of creative activity, as well as the aesthetic preferences of Yoruba artists for such characteristics as completeness (see Carroll; 1980 exh. cat.). Close analysis of works by individual masters has shown how many of these aesthetic principles are manifested in their work (see Fagg; Thompson, 1969; Bascom; Abiodun, Drewal and Pemberton). A form of seriate or segmented composition, explained as *letoleto, l'ese ese* ('one by one, step by step'), is widespread in and fundamental to Yoruba sculpture, body arts and performance, as well as in Yoruba social organization. It seems to be linked with fundamental ontological concepts and a belief in *ase*: performative power or life-force (see M. T. Drewal and H. J. Drewal; H. J. Drewal; M. T. Drewal).

15. Yoruba Gelede masker surrounded by cheering spectators, Ilaro, Nigeria; from a photograph by Henry John Drewal, 1978

BIBLIOGRAPHY

W. B. Fagg: 'De l'art des Yoruba', *Présence Afr.*, x–xi (1951), pp. 103–35
K. Carroll: *Yoruba Religious Carving: Pagan and Christian Sculpture in Nigeria and Dahomey* (London, 1967)
R. Thompson: 'Abatan: A Master Potter of the Egbado Yoruba', *Tradition and Creativity in Tribal Art*, ed. D. Biebuyck (Berkeley, 1969/*R* 1973), pp. 120–82
W. Bascom: 'A Yoruba Master Carver: Duga of Meko', *The Traditional Artist in African Societies*, ed. W. L. d'Azevedo (Bloomington, 1973), pp. 62–78
R. F. Thompson: 'Yoruba Artistic Criticism', *The Traditional Artist in African Societies*, ed. W. L. d'Azevedo (Bloomington, 1973), pp. 19–61
African Artistry: Technique and Aesthetics in Yoruba Sculpture (exh. cat. by H. J. Drewal, Atlanta, GA, High Mus. A., 1980)
R. A. Abiodun: 'Identity and the Artistic Process in the Yoruba Aesthetic Concept of *Iwa*', *J. Cult. & Ideas*, i/1 (1983), pp. 13–30
M. T. Drewal and H. J. Drewal: 'Composing Time and Space in Yoruba Art', *Word & Image*, iii/3 (1987), pp. 225–51
H. J. Drewal: 'Beauty and Being: Aesthetics and Ontology in Yoruba Body Art', *Marks of Civilization: Artistic Transformations of the Human Body*, ed. A. Rubin (Los Angeles, 1988), pp. 83–96
Yoruba Art and Aesthetics (exh. cat. by R. Abiodun, H. J. Drewal and J. Pemberton III, Zurich, Mus. Rietberg, 1991)
M. T. Drewal: *Yoruba Ritual: Performers, Play, Agency*, African Systems of Thought (Bloomington, 1992)
R. A. Abiodun, H. J. Drewal and J. Pemberton, eds: *The Yoruba Artist: New Theoretical Perspectives in African Art Studies* (Washington, DC, 1994)

(iv) Conclusion. A few studies have attempted to document changes in aesthetic evaluation. A study of tourist art among the Edo people of southern Nigeria, that is, of the ebony sculptures made at Benin City, has revealed some of the factors shaping the changing dynamics of aesthetic judgements. Transformations in scale, motif and style show the ways in which artists have responded to new economic conditions and formulated new aesthetic preferences (see Ben-Amos, 1977). Other producers of African tourist arts have responded to the demand for instant recognition through the adoption of naturalistic styles and the manufacture of convenient portable objects (see Bascom). A study of economic factors in three African tourist art markets has illustrated other changes in aesthetic evaluations of skill, creativity and cultural expression (see Jules-Rosette).

In addition to further studies of aesthetic change it is hoped that future research will include fuller documentation of the commentaries and aesthetic terminologies of indigenous critics. Such studies would deepen and enrich an understanding of aesthetic evaluation in Africa. The development of video technology makes it possible for artists and performers to review and comment immediately on works they made or in which they participated. The interaction of members of a culture, the interplay of attitudes and opinions, seems to be at the very heart of the formulation of taste within cultures, and the study of it must therefore be essential to understanding aesthetic evaluation in Africa. Also, most scholarly discussions have concentrated on what object types are viewed as having aesthetic value rather than exploring why they have it, that is, they are concerned more with a category of object (art) than with a category of thought (aesthetics; see Coote, p. 250). Making such a distinction should help future understandings.

BIBLIOGRAPHY

W. Bascom: 'Changing African Art', *Ethnic and Tourist Arts: Cultural Expressions from the Fourth World*, ed. N. H. H. Graburn (Berkeley, 1976/*R* 1979), pp. 303–19

P. Ben-Amos: '"A la recherche du temps perdu": On Being an Ebony-carver in Benin', *Ethnic and Tourist Arts: Cultural Expressions from the Fourth World*, ed. N. H. H. Graburn (Berkeley, 1976/*R* 1979), pp. 320–33

——: 'Pidgin Languages and Tourist Arts', *Stud. Anthropol. Visual Communic.*, iv/2 (1977), pp. 128–39

B. Jules-Rosette: 'Aesthetics and Market Demand: The Structure of the Tourist Art Market in Three African Settings', *Afr. Stud. Rev.*, xxix/1 (1986), pp. 41–59

J. Coote: '"Marvels of Everyday Vision": The Anthropology of Aesthetics and the Cattle-keeping Nilotes', *Anthropology, Art, and Aesthetics*, ed. J. Coote and A. Shelton, Oxford Studies in the Anthropology of Cultural Forms (Oxford, 1992), pp. 245–73

HENRY JOHN DREWAL

III. Contexts of production and use.

1. Patronage. 2. Artists. 3. Trade. 4. Commercial production. 5. Ritual.

1. PATRONAGE. In Africa as elsewhere the patron is often the link by which the artist is made aware of society's demands and needs for art. This role has often been neglected in studies of artistic production in Africa. Although creative interpretation originates with the artist, it is the patron who sanctions such interpretation, thereby playing a critical role in supporting artistic production and championing artistic creativity. The final art object is the product of the patron–artist relationship and of the interacting factors of the artist's creativity, the patron's demands and the existing prototypes. The patron–artist relationship is often mediated by the role of the trader (*see* §3 below).

(i) General. (ii) Political. (iii) Religious.

(i) General. Within each act of patronage, the rules of interaction, the kinds of information exchanged and the form of the contract are affected by a number of factors. These include the type of art form, the socio-cultural context in which the art object functions, the patron's position in the local art world, the nature of the dominant social roles played by patron and artist during and after interaction and the degree of cultural understanding shared by patron and artist. Patrons commission, pay for and use art objects. As a consumer, the patron is the economic motivator who stimulates artistic production and thus not only influences stylistic continuity within a tradition but can also function as an agent of change. Of equal importance is the key role the patron plays in introducing the object into the social context where it may be evaluated by the wider community.

Patronage determines the range of art styles that develop and flourish in a society. For example, among the BAMANA of West Africa such men's socio-religious associations as N'tomo, Kore, Chi-wara and Komo commission stylistically distinct forms of wooden masks and headdresses. Moreover multiple art traditions, such as the production of wood and metal sculpture, architecture, textiles and ceramics, can co-exist in a single society if there is sufficient patronage to support them. Conversely, long-standing art traditions decline and disappear if patronage is withdrawn. The patron's impact is most clearly seen where patron and artist interact face-to-face. The patron's influence is most direct when the interaction takes place prior to production. During a pre-production transaction in the African context, artist and patron agree a verbal contract in which the patron's desires concerning materials, iconographic and decorative motifs and the time to be taken are articulated. Such specifications may be general, indicating only the type of object desired, or they may be precise, with detailed instructions given. In turn, the artist informs the patron about his requirements concerning materials, the rituals necessary for production and payment. The artist does not always wait for a patron but may build up a stock of objects ready for visits from patron-consumers. Non-ritual textiles, pottery, leatherwork and carved household utensils are often stockpiled in this way. In these cases the choices made from the artist's stock by patron-consumers have a delayed effect on subsequent production.

Most frequently patrons belong to the same ethnic group as the artists they support, and this may be labelled in-group patronage. Thus, patron and artist share a common artistic tradition and vocabulary as well as shared expectations about the degree of acceptable stylistic variation. For example, FULANI weavers in Mali must adhere to traditional patterns, colours and materials in their wool blankets, since their patrons demand conformity, choosing weavers on the basis of their ability to adhere to specific designs (Imperato, 1973). On the other hand, innovation in subject-matter at least is encouraged by the traditional patrons of brass-smiths among the ASANTE AND RELATED PEOPLES, who order distinctive forms of goldweights to display as prestige objects (McLeod, 1971).

An interesting form of in-group patronage is the phenomenon of self-patronage, when artist and patron are the same person. Among the Gurensi of northern Ghana, for example, women act as their own patrons when embellishing their house walls with painted designs (Smith, 1978). A senior woman of a compound organizes the necessary activities and solicits the help of other female relatives who together select the design motifs, divide the house wall into sections and paint them (see fig. 20 below). Similarly, young male initiates among the YAKA of Zaïre create highly original masks to be worn and judged by the community during their initiation ceremony (Adelman).

Where patron–artist interactions cross ethnic boundaries, in what may be labelled out-group patronage, a common cultural understanding may not exist. Prior to production, therefore, there may be a detailed exchange of information. Shared expectations are less important when the patron chooses from stockpiled goods. When out-group patronage becomes institutionalized, it can have long-term effects, even leading to the development of a distinctive new style. For example, an Afro-Portuguese ivory tradition emerged in the 16th century when Portuguese sailors commissioned Bulom (Sherbro) ivory-carvers from what is now Sierra Leone to produce intricate pedestal bowls with European motifs (*see* § 2(iii) below).

In general, it is the patron who takes the praise for the successful work of art or the blame for its failure. For this reason the creative process does not necessarily end when an artist finishes an object. Changes in its appearance may be demanded by the owner due to aesthetic preferences or for some other reason. Sometimes a ritual object's potency and efficacy need to be enhanced. For example, some KONGO figures (*nkisi*) are not considered complete until a ritual specialist acting on behalf of a patron has applied magical ingredients to them. Some are activated by having nails and blades driven into them; thus their appearance is continually transformed.

Some objects are subjected to a continual process of decorative embellishment by patrons or other artists. For example, among the YORUBA, patron-owners of Gelede masks repainted them before each public appearance (see fig. 16). Masks may also be enhanced with the application of cloth, beads, feathers and even attached carvings. Similarly, SENUFO patrons alter the appearance of their carved masks and figures by applying polychrome, decorative patterns to them (Glaze, 1981, p. 16).

The reactions to and evaluations of art objects by audiences and critics influence the future decisions of both artists and patrons. For example, the huge upstanding ears of Yoruba Egungun Erin masks were introduced when a patron demanded more imposing ears than usual. When the mask attracted favourable attention at a festival, other patrons asked for similar masks, and local carvers added the type to their repertories (Wolff, 1981).

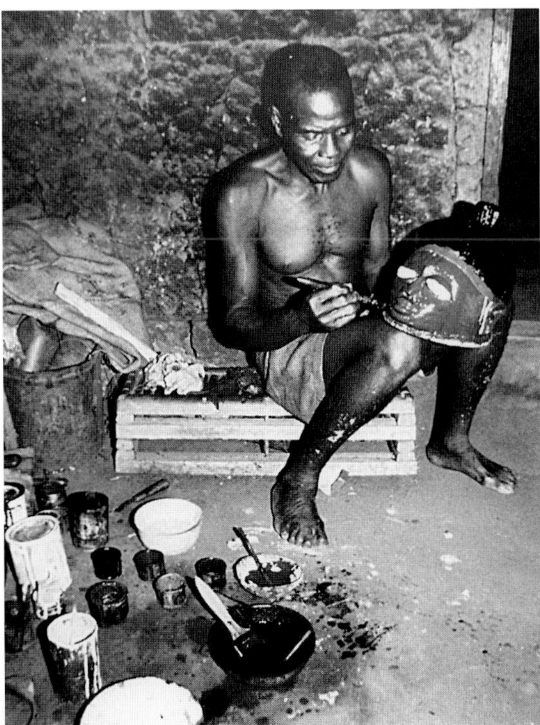

16. Yoruba patron–owner of a Gelede mask repainting it before a public performance, Ilaro, Nigeria; from a photograph by Henry John Drewal, 1978

Societies vary in the degree to which patron–artist interactions are formalized. In centralized societies with a high degree of social stratification and developed trade systems, for example among the Asante, NUPE, HAUSA and Kuba (*see* KUBA (iii)), the arts flourish. Here artists are needed to produce a wide range of products to meet the society's commercial, prestige and everyday needs, and patron–artist relations are direct, regular and tightly structured. Patrons are often traders, chiefs or leaders of some sort, and artists are often full-time specialists organized into structured workgroups. For example, in the 19th century the Nupe of central Nigeria were conquered by Muslim FULANI who imposed a guild system to ensure that artists would produce a wide range of trade and prestige objects. In this way the patronage of the Fulani ruling class, channelled through titled guild-heads, shaped the direction taken by Nupe crafts, bringing into existence, for example, a tradition of hammered brass vessels for Muslim ceremonies of protocol and gift exchange.

A less formal type of patronage, where contact between patron and artist is occasional and relatively unstructured, takes place in all societies but dominates where there is no centralized political system, for example among the DAN, SENUFO, FANG and IGBO. In such societies artists tend to be part-time, independent specialists, and it is the patron who takes the initiative by commissioning or purchasing objects. For instance, during the dry season in north-eastern Nigeria, Bata, Ungal and Fulani women decorate gourds that are used as gifts and dowry goods, but only on demand.

Patrons may operate both as individuals, motivated by their own needs, and as representatives of kinship, religious, leadership or age groups. Once displayed publicly art objects enhance the prestige and power of both the individual patron and the group. For example, the Yoruba mask Egungun Erin is known as 'the rich man's Egungun' because of its aesthetic quality and cost. To commission such a mask and costume often requires the resources of a whole kinship group, whose prestige is enhanced by its public appearances, as is that of the individual owner.

(ii) Political. Kings, emirs and chiefs of the centralized societies of West Africa (e.g. ASANTE AND RELATED PEOPLES, FON, YORUBA, NUPE, HAUSA), the Cameroon Grassfields (e.g. BAMUM) and the southern savannah of Central Africa (e.g. KONGO, KUBA, CHOKWE AND RELATED PEOPLES) are particularly important patrons in Sub-Saharan Africa. They exercise monopolies over scarce resources used in art production, have exclusive control of particular forms and motifs and control the labour and organization of craft workers. As patrons, such people largely control the production and distribution of highly valued prestige and leadership arts (Fraser and Cole). Prestige arts are those artistically embellished items of everyday life (household utensils, furniture, jewellery and clothing) that are used by persons of rank to display their wealth and special status. Leadership arts are more exclusive and include such items of regalia as dress and

17. Hausa emir in Sallah procession, dressed in ceremonial regalia and surrounded by retainers, Kano, Nigeria

accessories, sceptres, swords, thrones and ancestral sculptures. They function to stimulate loyalty to an office by instilling awe in beholders.

Items of regalia are commissioned by the emir and other Hausa nobility from local and regional craftsmen and figure prominently in public, ceremonial and political contexts where the very body of the leader becomes a focus of artistic elaboration. The appearance of the Hausa emir during the Sallah procession at the end of the Ramadan fast is such an event. Hand-embroidered gowns, layered one on top of the other, silver horse trappings, sceptres and a huge state umbrella draw attention to and magnify the importance of the emir (see fig. 17).

Such palace architecture as that of the Asante, the Yoruba and the Bamum also set rulers apart from the rest of the population. The massiveness and elaboration of the architecture express the special status of the leader (*see* §VI, 1(iii) below; *see also* PALACE, §VIII). Within the palace, art further enhances his special status. For example, the royal treasuries of the kings of the Cameroon Grassfields hold sculpture depicting royal ancestors, elaborately carved stools and thrones, drums, serving bowls, embroidered clothing, jewellery, tobacco pipes, drinking horns, fly-whisks, staffs and ceremonial swords. The leader is the guardian of such regalia and emblems of office and is responsible for the continuity of the various traditions, directly influencing the quality and quantity of objects produced. For example, after the emergence of the Asante kingdom in 18th-century Ghana, each king was required to commission two new, decorated swords, thereby assuring the continued vitality of the tradition (Ross, p. 25). Among the Kuba of Zaïre since the 17th century each king was required to commission a commemorative statue that functioned as his spiritual double.

To control production efficiently, leaders frequently have artists, whether freeborn or slave, who work in the vicinity of the palace, where they can be closely supervised. They may live in the palace complex itself, as in Bamum; in wards in the capital city, as in Benin and among the Nupe and Hausa; or in craft villages, as among the Asante, where shelter, board, financial support and regular employment are offered. The *Óbas* of BENIN, for example, established 40 to 50 guilds in wards near the palace. Members of these craft guilds were full-time specialists producing embroidered cloths, leather fans and sculpture in brass, ivory and wood for the *Óba* and for his chiefs and cult priests, if the *Óba* allowed. The kings (*fons*) of the larger kingdoms of the Cameroon Grassfields control wood-carving in a similar way, so that if a neighbouring ruler with no resident carvers wants a sculpture, he must commission and pay the local *fon*, not the artist (1984 exh. cat., pp. 61–2). Artists under royal patronage usually consider it a great honour to work for a leader and rarely request payment. Leaders, however, frequently reward artists with gifts.

The ability of leaders to recruit artists from a wide area, sometimes from different ethnic groups, is important in contributing to the mobility and spread of art styles. For instance, after the 19th-century Nupe conquest of northern Yoruba territories, the Fulani–Nupe emir settled Yoruba slaves, including weavers, in Bida, the capital city. Male Yoruba weavers introduced new cloth types and had a great impact on increasing textile production for the cloth trade, while female Yoruba weavers introduced weaving technology and new cloth types and designs to Nupe women (Perani, 1979). The patronage of leaders may encourage artists to be itinerant as, for example, in some 19th-century Liberian chiefdoms where weavers and wood-carvers attached themselves to households of wealthy chiefs in neighbouring or even distant chiefdoms, producing carvings and textiles in exchange for shelter and board.

The link between patron leaders and the origins of specific art forms is sometimes retained in a group's oral history. For example, Muhammadu Rumfa, a 15th-century Kano leader, is remembered for introducing red and green livery for retainers and leather sandals adorned with ostrich feathers as a royal prerogative. King Njoya of Bamum is credited with introducing weaving and tailoring to his court in the late 19th century and is said to have woven sample lengths so that his palace weavers could copy them (Geary, 1983). These attributions of royal artistic genius add legitimacy to the art traditions and, simultaneously, enhance the perceived qualities of the leader patrons.

(iii) Religious. Priests, diviners and members of religious associations and masquerade societies commission costumes, masks, shrine sculptures and prestige arts to honour and control supernatural beings and forces. The production of ritual art often involves calling upon supernatural forces to produce or activate masks or figures that then become receptacles for extraordinary powers. In this potentially dangerous activity the contract between patron and artist is both an economic agreement and a pledge of ritual cooperation. Patron–artist transactions regarding ritual carving are often highly structured. The interactions of male Gola artists and female Sande society officials in south-western Liberia offer an example. A transaction begins when the women commission a mask from a carver who thus becomes privy to the secret knowledge of Sande. While carving the mask the artist is supported by his Sande patrons who attempt to direct his work by insisting upon such details as specific coiffure designs and the form and

placement of neck rings. The patron–artist interaction is conceived here as a struggle: the carver may resist directives and, in extreme cases, destroy an unfinished work because of the continuous criticism of the patrons. Tension between the carver and the Sande officials may continue throughout the production period and sometimes, after the mask has been completed and performed, the artist may destroy it if he finds that it is treated with disrespect (d'Azevedo, 1973, pp. 145–7).

Occasionally whole communities may commission ritual objects from an artist. This is the case with the *ikoro* slit-drums of the IGBO of Nigeria. These huge signal drums, embellished with carved images of animals and humans, serve as symbols of village unity. Complex rituals are carried out before a giant tree is cut, and the lengthy carving process takes place in secret. Rituals of consecration have to be carried out at village expense to activate the drum before it can be used (see 1984 exh. cat., pp. 87–8).

In many cases of ritual patronage, the ultimate patron is a spirit with whom an individual makes a contract to act as mediator. The spirit often makes its demands known to an individual through a dream or vision or through a divination process. For example, among the DAN of Côte d'Ivoire masks are commissioned when a forest spirit appears in a person's dreams and requests the creation of a mask to allow that spirit to participate in the human world (Fischer, 1978). Similarly, BAULE nature spirits and spirit spouses, identified by a diviner as the source of an individual's misfortunes, may appear in dreams or trances to demand that figures be carved to portray them and act as a focus for offerings. The spirit then appears to the commissioning individual, diviner or carver to make its desires known, and a carving is prepared (Vogel, 1980). Illness and infertility are often taken to be signals that a spirit desires to be appeased with an act of art patronage. Among the CHOKWE AND RELATED PEOPLES of Zaïre, for example, if a man who has inherited a Pwo dance mask falls ill, a diviner may determine that the *pwo*, a female ancestor, is causing the sickness. The man must then reactivate the mask or have a new one carved (Bastin, p. 92).

BIBLIOGRAPHY

M. D. McLeod: 'Goldweights of Asante', *Afr. A.*, v/1 (1971), pp. 8–15
D. Fraser and H. Cole, eds: *African Art and Leadership* (Madison, 1972)
W. L. d'Azevedo: 'Sources of Gola Artistry', *The Traditional Artist in African Societies*, ed. W. L. d'Azevedo (Bloomington, 1973/*R* 1975), pp. 282–340
P. J. Imperato: 'Wool Blankets of the Peul of Mali', *Afr. A.*, vi/3 (1973), pp. 40–47, 84
K. L. Adelman: 'The Art of the Yaka', *Afr. A.*, ix/1 (1975), pp. 40–43
T. J. H. Chappel: *Decorated Gourds in North-eastern Nigeria* (Lagos, 1977)
D. Ross: 'The Iconography of Asante Sword Ornaments', *Afr. A.*, xi/1 (1977), pp. 16–25, 90–91
E. Fischer: 'Dan Forest Spirits: Masks in Dan Villages', *Afr. A.*, xi/2 (1978), pp. 16–23, 94
F. T. Smith: 'Gurensi Wall Painting', *Afr. A.*, xi/4 (1978), pp. 36–41, 96
P. R. McNaughton: *Secret Sculptures of Komo: Art and Power in Bamana (Bambara) Initiation Associations*, Working Pap. Trad. A., 4 (Philadelphia, 1979)
J. Perani: 'Nupe Costume Crafts', *Afr. A.*, xii/3 (1979), pp. 52–7, 96
P. Ben-Amos: *The Art of Benin*, Tribal A. (London, 1980)
——: 'Patron–artist Interactions in Africa', *Afr. A.*, xiii/3 (1980), pp. 56–7, 92
S. L. Kasfir: 'Patronage and Maconde Carvers', *Afr. A.*, xiii/3 (1980), pp. 67–70, 91–2
J. Perani: 'Patronage and Nupe Craft Industries', *Afr. A.*, xiii/3 (1980), pp. 71–5, 92
S. M. Vogel: *Beauty in the Eyes of the Baule: Aesthetics and Cultural Values*, Working Pap. Trad. A., 6 (Philadelphia, 1980)
A. J. Glaze: *Art and Death in a Senufo Village*, Trad. A. Africa (Bloomington, 1981)
N. H. Wolff: 'Headdress (Egungun Erin)', *For Spirits and Kings: African Art from the Tishman Collection* (exh. cat., ed. S. M. Vogel; New York, Met., 1981), pp. 110–12
——: 'Egungun Costuming in Abeokuta', *Afr. A.*, xv/3 (1982), pp. 66–70, 91
C. Geary: *Things of the Palace: A Catalogue of the Bamum Palace Museum in Foumban (Cameroon)*, Studien zur Kulturkunde, lx (Wiesbaden, 1983)
M.-L. Bastin: 'Ritual Masks of the Chokwe', *Afr. A.*, xvii/4 (1984), pp. 40–44, 92–3
J. Vansina: *Art History in Africa: An Introduction to Method* (London, 1984), esp. pp. 44–7
The Art of Cameroon (exh. cat. by T. Northern, Washington, DC, Smithsonian Inst. Traveling Exh. Serv., 1984)
Igbo Arts: Community and Cosmos (exh. cat. by H. M. Cole and C. C. Aniakor, Los Angeles, UCLA, Mus. Cult. Hist., 1984–6)

JUDITH PERANI, NORMA H. WOLFF

2. ARTISTS. The perceived role of artists in African society varies widely, depending on the nature and purpose of the work being produced and the traditions of a particular people or region. A major factor in the making of many types of art is that of gender (*see* §(ii) below). In general, the concept of an individual artist being associated with a personal style and oeuvre is a 20th-century development, following the introduction of Western views of art and teaching practices (*see* §IX below).

(i) Role and status. (ii) Gender.

(i) Role and status. In Africa the role of the artist ranges

18. *Mbari* master builder or 'man of skill' Akakporo, directing the construction of a *mbari* house at Umuedi Nworie, near Owerri, Igbo, Nigeria; from a photograph by Herbert M. Cole, 1967

from being the producer of ritual objects to the organizer of entertainments and rites of passage. He or she contributes to the establishment and maintenance of royal legitimacy as well as to new and emergent senses of identity. As for the artist's status, this ranges from being nobody of any importance to being of necessity a king, or, alternatively, a deviant. These variables are still insufficiently understood by scholars to enable the establishment of any precise correlation between role and status. For the moment, we have to be satisfied with the discussion of a few varied examples. This will give the reader an idea of the complexity of questions of artists' roles and statuses in 'traditional' African society. Some of the developments of colonial and post-colonial times are also addressed.

(a) Traditional examples. In the small-scale social groupings of traditional Africa it is not always obvious who the artist is. For example, for the building of a *mbari* house among the Owerri IGBO, a 'man of skill' is employed (see fig. 18). Such a man will already have a reputation for the successful direction of the construction of these buildings with their complex painting and sculpture. Similarly, in Afikpo Igbo communities, the 'play-leaders' who direct the performances of Okumkpa masked plays have established reputations for the successful direction of performances (see fig. 19). However, whereas the 'man of skill' is in essence affirming the authority of elders, whose responsibility it is to maintain appropriate relationships between people and deities, the subject-matter of Okumkpa plays is frequently derogatory of the elders who sanction the performances and are obliged to take the front-row seats. Perhaps not surprisingly, the status of 'play-leader' is adverse, and, for as long as one is directing plays that criticize and ridicule the elders, one is denied promotion within the local title system.

It is also useful to compare the Afikpo 'play-leader' with the 'preceptor', the senior man charged with the responsibility of organizing initiations into Bwami, the all-encompassing organization of the LEGA people of eastern Zaïre. Their roles are identical, yet in Afikpo the principle of the authority of the elders is confirmed by the criticism of those who are, in practice, in authority. In contrast, the successive phases of Bwami initiation entail a revelation of a philosophy. The Afikpo Igbo Okumkpa entails a revelation of practice, whereas Lega Bwami initiations entail a revelation of principle. If failure on the part of individual incumbents of senior office is enacted by Lega people, it is not within the context of Bwami. It is hardly surprising to learn that, in contrast to the Afikpo 'play-leader', the Lega 'preceptor' is a man of high regard.

This discussion suggests a perhaps obvious correlation between the purpose of the art work and the status of its producer, but other examples caution us against assuming such a necessary correlation. Thus, among the FANG people of Gabon, the carving of the figures that are placed with apotropaic intention upon boxes of ancestral bones

19. Afikpo Igbo 'play-leaders' directing the performance of an Okumkpa masked play, Amorie village, Afikpo, Nigeria; from a photograph by Simon Ottenberg, 1952

is, notwithstanding the ritual necessity of these figures, considered on a par with making fish-traps and is carried out in the public gaze of the men's club house. Here the role of producer attracts no particular esteem or status. Similarly, among the Tiv of Nigeria, sculptors attract no marked esteem, notwithstanding the social and ritual necessity of their work. In any case, for the Tiv, sculpture is something anyone can try, and, while some are better at it than others, no particular status attaches to this. The tradition of body-painting among some NUBA in Sudan might provide another example. A relevant factor is the extent to which, as determined within a received tradition of practice, an art form is considered to demand specialist knowledge. It is possible to suggest contrasts between contexts in which the practice of an art may broadly be categorized as commonplace (attracting no particular status), or specialist and clear-cut within an established order, or specialist but ambivalent, either because of the subject-matter of the art or because of the necessary circumstances of its making.

This is not a matter of the contrast between artists who support and those who subvert a political status quo; for the Afikpo 'play-leader' is not engaging in Okumkpa in an attempt to subvert chiefly authority but in its affirmation via the critique of the current incumbents of chiefly office. Among the Gola of Liberia, the wood-carver is perhaps an even more ambivalent character. While the status of a Gola chief is enhanced by the mere fact of having a famous sculptor within his retinue, success in sculpture is achieved through a relationship with a spirit mentor that encourages or entails behaviour that is locally regarded as deviant, to the extent that parents will take disciplinary action against a son whom they consider to be taking too much interest in the art. More to the point, the most significant artefact within a Gola sculptor's repertory is the mask worn by women of the Sande association in the relevant stage of the initiation of girls into adulthood (*see also* §VII, 4 below). The Sande association, however, is an institution the inner workings of which are secret and from which men are excluded except at the very highest levels of rank within Sande and the male equivalent association, Poro. The Gola carver thus is not a man of any particular authority, and yet in order to carve the mask the sculptor is the one man with access to the secret domain of women.

In contrast to the Gola carvers, and indeed those of the Tiv and Fang, the sculptors of Benin work within a hierarchical order of guilds, with the brass-casters at the top, followed by the ivory-carvers. Within each guild, there is a series of titled offices having responsibility for, among other things, negotiating the production of works of art. Moreover, guild titles are structured within an overall hierarchy of titled offices, and, while their status therein might be considered merely middle-ranking, the important point is that status is established and esteemed to the extent permitted within the title system. The role of the guilds is the production of artworks that participate in the enactment and definition of royal legitimacy, whether as ivory regalia worn by the king or brass regalia worn by titled men, or as ivory and brass furniture for altars within the royal palace (*see also* BENIN, §3). Even more marked is the contrast with the kingdoms of the Cameroon Grassfields, where sculptural expertise is an expected attribute of kings; even though much of the sculptural output is the work of palace servants, the king is nevertheless identified as its author (*see* BAMILEKE AND RELATED PEOPLES, BAMUM and BANGWA).

(b) Modern developments. By the early 1990s probably half the artists in any African country were working for an urban-based élite. Most of these were associated with an art gallery, having been trained in the fine art department of a university or college of higher education. While such institutions are colonial in origin, by the 1990s so many colonial elements had been either discarded or domesticated that they were thoroughly African. In particular, the subject-matter, the artists' intentions and the discourse of local historians and critics suggest that local cultural traditions and both local and national identities are dominant concerns.

In Nigeria, for example, some art movements have arisen out of pre-colonial decorative traditions. The Uli traditions of the Igbo were drawn on in the work of Uche Okeke and his followers, as they emerged from fine-art training at the time of Nigerian independence, determined to convey a sense of Nigerian identity by using forms associated with local traditions. Ibrahim El Salahi of Sudan drew upon both Islamic calligraphic and local craft patterns in his work. Moreover, in such countries as Kenya and Zaïre, such concerns have been manifested in work that can be seen as critical of the current state of political affairs. In South Africa, of course, artists took an often overt role in opposing apartheid. In the struggle for liberation from colonial rule in Mozambique, artists were prominent among the leaders of the Frelimo government in exile.

Thus, throughout Africa artists have taken up the role of mediator in a range of local and national concerns. The artist's status then depends upon his or her position *vis-à-vis* the élite and the position from which the status is being judged.

BIBLIOGRAPHY

P. Bohannan: 'Artist and Critic in an African Society', *The Artist in Tribal Society: Proceedings of a Symposium Held at the Royal Anthropological Institute*, ed. M. W. Smith, Royal Anthropological Institute Occasional Paper, xv (London, 1961), pp. 85–94; repr. in *Anthropology and Art: Readings in Cross-Cultural Aesthetics*, ed. C. M. Otten (New York, 1971/*R* Austin, TX, 1976), pp. 172–81

W. L. d'Azevedo: *The Artist Archetype in Gola Culture*, Desert Research Institute Preprint, xiv (Nevada, 1966, rev. 1970)

R. Brain and A. Pollock: *Bangwa Funerary Sculpture*, A. & Soc. Ser. (London, 1971)

D. Fraser and H. M. Cole, eds: *African Art and Leadership* (Madison, 1972)

W. L. d'Azevedo: 'Mask Makers and Myth in Western Liberia', *Primitive Art and Society*, ed. A. Forge (London, 1973), pp. 126–50

W. L. d'Azevedo, ed.: *The Traditional Artist in African Societies* (Bloomington and London, 1973/*R* 1993)

D. P. Biebuyck: *Lega Culture: Art, Initiation, and Moral Philosophy among a Central African People* (Berkeley, 1973)

P. J. C. Dark: *An Introduction to Benin Art and Technology* (Oxford, 1973)

S. Ottenberg: *Masked Rituals of Afikpo: The Context of an African Art* (Seattle, 1975)

R. Layton: *The Anthropology of Art* (Frogmore, 1981, rev. Cambridge, 1991)

H. M. Cole: *Mbari: Art and Life among the Owerri Igbo* (Bloomington, 1982)

Africa Explores: 20th Century African Art (exh. cat. by S. Vogel with I. Ebong, New York, Cent. Afr. A., 1991)

JOHN PICTON

(ii) Gender. Throughout Africa the division of labour by gender not only determines the everyday work of growing crops and trade but also strongly affects the production, use and imagery of visual art forms. This entry provides an overview of the role of women in the visual arts in Africa, both traditionally and in the modern situation.

(a) Traditional practices. In Africa generally men and women practise different arts, or at least different techniques. In many areas explicit rules restrict women from participation in wood-carving and metallurgy. Thus the wood sculptures and brass-castings for which Africa is most famous are the exclusive product of male artists. Beyond these two restricted pursuits, the division of artistic labour by gender varies from community to community. In North Africa, for example, women weave, while in the whole of Sub-Saharan Africa, apart from Nigeria and Madagascar, only men weave. Usually women are the potters, though there are a few communities, such as among the HAUSA of Niger, in which men are the potters. Although women modelled figures in clay or other soft materials among a number of peoples, for example the Dakakari and IGBO of Nigeria and the Kuba (*see* KUBA (iii)) of central Zaïre, it was more common that women's art comprised schematic forms or geometrical designs while the men produced the human and animal imagery.

Generally, where men and women engage in the same craft, whether for local use or for trade, there are clear distinctions between the equipment or materials they use or between the styles. In southern Nigeria, for example, where both men and women weave, men use a narrow, horizontal loom, while women weave on a broad, vertical loom. In the Fungom district of Cameroon, men produce tall, tapering baskets affixed to wooden slats with which to carry their burdens, while women plait a variety of bowl-shaped containers. In some instances the gender distinction lies in the type of imagery produced. For example, in mural painting in western Côte d'Ivoire and northern Ghana women paint schematic designs (see fig. 20), while men depict figurative scenes. Often efforts are complementary: men build house structures, and women shape the walls; men weave cloth, women decorate it by dyeing or embroidery. It was typical that both genders shared in the rewards of such complementary efforts, the initiating party retaining a claim on a share of the eventual profit.

Distinctions in production between the genders are reinforced in numerous ways, perhaps most obviously by social organization. For example, among the TUAREG, FULANI, BAMANA and Malinke in the populous Sahelian and light savannah region below the Sahara, where the social order prior to the rise of the modern state was explicitly hierarchical, with ranked status groups of nobles, freemen and servants, such artisans as smiths and leatherworkers belonged to named occupational groups ranked at the bottom of the status hierarchy. The wives of craftsmen often also pursued a craft. For example, smiths' wives among the HAUSA and Songhai of Niger usually engaged in tasks that, like smithing, were segregated from residential areas. Pottery, for example, was fired in open pits away from the town or village, and both tanning and indigo dyeing, with their offensive odours, also had their own areas. In the populous Yoruba cities of Nigeria, members of the women's weaving, dyeing and pottery guilds controlled their membership just as the male craftsmen did. Taboos or the possession of protective 'medicines' served to protect artists from encroachment in their field of expertise by members of the opposite gender. Sometimes also legends assigned the ownership of particular techniques to men or women within particular families; possession of the techniques by a particular gender could even be divinely authorized.

20. Kahnyno Thérèse of Medibli village painting a house, 1985; from a photograph by Monni Adams

Considerations of gender also entered into the actual production process. These are best known for male carvers and smelters/smiths, who must refrain from sexual activity prior to and during the work and whose workplace potentially fertile women must not approach. Taboos prevented men from entering the women's work area in a Kamba potting village in Kenya (see Gill). Also the work area was separated from the places where sexual relations took place, and the women potters had to refrain from sex for three days prior to their work. These Kamba potters produced cooking pots for the region and were held in high esteem for their skill. They were also feared, however, by other potters as well as by non-potters. These attitudes of fear and respect are similar to those towards male artisans in the West African Sahel. If reports on the social relations of women artisans were not so fragmentary, the basis for these ambivalent attitudes might be better understood.

In many parts of Africa rituals involving figures or featuring masked dancers were conducted solely by men, with women being prohibited from attending on pain of death or sterility. Where women were participants, they contributed in less spectacular fashion by lending costume elements, providing ceremonial containers, by repainting house walls or by singing and dancing to honour the spirits. In only one region of Africa, among the MENDE, Temne, Bullom and Gola of Sierra Leone and Liberia, did women organize public mask performances.

In spite of the general phenomenon of male leadership, in many contexts women did have formal public roles and responsibilities. Women were court officials, heads of urban markets and organizers of girls' initiation rites. Sometimes such women called attention to their achievements through art. Decorated pottery, painted houses, body and personal adornment and fashionable clothes silently convey success in a form that does not contradict the verbal leadership by which men demonstrate their superior authority.

(b) Modern developments. In spite of a tradition that only men work with metal, HAUSA Muslim women near Kano in Nigeria have been engraving designs on aluminium spoons used for daily and ceremonial use and for the tourist market. This relaxation of a rule was due to three factors: the lessening of sanctions surrounding metalwork; the relatively recent adoption of aluminium in the 1920s; and the spread of purdah in the area, which has prevented women from pursuing their former economic pursuits. Efforts to find a way to increase their earning power encouraged groups of women in Sierra Leone and Mali to learn weaving, a technique formerly reserved for men. To meet the expanded demands of the international tourist trade in Lusaka, Zambia, men took up the previously female activity of pottery-making, while women entered the formerly male activity of carving.

In the late 20th century some African women began to gain international recognition as contemporary artists. Perhaps because they were accustomed to producing surplus crafts in the market, in contrast to men producing only on commission, African women readily accepted the role of individual artists producing for sale. Among these were Kadiato Kamara (*b c.* 1933) of Sierra Leone who practised a traditional art of designing tie-dyed cloth; Nike Olaniyi Davis (*b* 1951) from northern Nigeria who used the imported technique of wax batik, which she learnt in a local art school, to express her own inspirations derived from dreams and books; and Ladi Kwali, a potter from Gwari, Nigeria, who learnt glazing at a pottery training centre. A number of women also trained as professional artists outside Africa. The Igbo potter Kate Ifejike-Obukwelu (*b* 1945) was educated in New York and produced both rounded pots of traditional shape and decorative ceramics, including paired male and female figures. Perhaps the outstanding example of an internationally trained, successful woman sculptor is the Kalabari Ijo artist Sokari Douglas Camp (*b* 1958), whose work includes large metal figures of women and children and male maskers (see fig. 21).

21. Sokari Douglas Camp: *Kalabari Masquerader with Boat Headdress*, steel and wood, mirror, bells and cloth, h. 2.18 m, 1987 (artist's collection)

BIBLIOGRAPHY

A. J. Glaze: 'Women, Power and Art in a Senufo Village', *Afr. A.*, viii/3 (1975), pp. 24–9, 64–8, 90–91

M. Etienne: 'Women and Men, Cloth and Colonization: The Transformation of Production–Distribution Relations among the Baule (Ivory Coast)', *Cah. Etud. Afr.*, xvii/1, no. 65 (1977), pp. 41–64

P. Ben-Amos: 'Owina n'Ido: Royal Weavers of Benin', *Afr. A.*, xi/4 (1978), pp. 48–53, 95–6

J. Teilhet: 'The Equivocal Role of Women Artists in Non-literate Cultures', *Heresies* (Winter 1978), pp. 96–102

M. Wahlman and E. Chuta: 'Sierra Leone Resist-dyed Textiles', *The Fabrics of Culture: The Anthropology of Clothing and Adornment*, ed. J. M. Cordwell and R. A. Schwarz, World Anthropology (The Hague, 1979), pp. 447–66

M. J. Adams: 'Afterword: Spheres of Men's and Women's Creativity', *Ethnol. Z. Zürich* (1980), no. 1, pp. 163–7

R. Richter: *Art, Economics and Change: The Kulebele of Northern Ivory Coast* (La Jolla, 1980)

M. Gill: *The Potter's Mark: Contemporary and Archaeological Pottery of the Kenyan Southeastern Highlands* (diss., Boston U., 1981)

L. Aronson: 'Popo Weaving: The Dynamics of Trade in Southeastern Nigeria', *Afr. A.*, xv/3 (1982), pp. 43–7, 90–91

S. Brett-Smith: 'Symbolic Blood: Cloths for Excised Women', *Res*, 5 (1982), pp. 15–51

22. Gourd stall at the daily market, Gombe, north-eastern Nigeria; from a photograph by Marla C. Berns, 1982

U. Wagner: *Catching the Tourists: Women Handicraft Traders in The Gambia* (Stockholm, 1982)
S. Ottenberg: 'Artistic and Sex Roles in a Limba Chiefdom', *Female and Male in West Africa*, ed. C. Oppong (London, 1983), pp. 76–90
L. Aronson: 'Women in the Arts', *African Women South of the Sahara*, ed. M. J. Hay and S. Stichter (London, 1984), pp. 119–38
B. Jules-Rosette: *The Messages of Tourist Art: An African Semiotic System in Comparative Perspective*, Topics in Contemporary Semiotics (New York, 1984)
R. Roberts: 'Women's Work and Women's Property: Household Social Relations in the Maraka Textile Industry of the Nineteenth Century', *Comp. Stud. Soc. & Hist.*, xxvi/2 (1984), pp. 229–50
M. Adams: 'Women and Masks among the Western Wè of Ivory Coast', *Afr. A.*, xix/2 (1986), pp. 46–55, 90
S. Afonja: 'Women, Power and Authority in Traditional Yoruba Society', *Visibility and Power: Essays on Women in Society and Development*, ed. L. Dube, E. Leacock and S. Ardener (Delhi, 1986/*R* 1989), pp. 136–57
P. Ben-Amos: 'Artistic Creativity in Benin Kingdom', *Afr. A.*, xix/3 (1986), pp. 60–63, 83–4
M. C. Daly, J. B. Eicher and T. V. Erekosima: 'Male and Female Artistry in Kalabari Dress', *Afr. A.*, xix/3 (1986), pp. 48–51, 83
W. J. Dewey: 'Shona Male and Female Artistry', *Afr. A.*, xix/3 (1986), pp. 64–7, 84
A. J. Glaze: 'Dialectics of Gender in Senufo Masquerades', *Afr. A.*, xix/3 (1986), pp. 30–39, 82
J. Perani: 'Hausa Calabash Decoration', *Afr. A.*, xix/3 (1986), pp. 45–7, 82–3
F. T. Smith: 'Compound Entryway Decoration: Male Space and Female Creativity', *Afr. A.*, xix/3 (1986), pp. 52–9, 83
——: 'Male and Female Artistry in Africa', *Afr. A.*, xix/3 (1986), pp. 28–9, 82
N. H. Wolff: 'A Hausa Aluminium Spoon Industry', *Afr. A.*, xix/3 (1986), pp. 40–44, 82
C. Geary: 'Basketry in the Aghem–Fungom Area of the Cameroon Grassfields', *Afr. A.*, xx/3 (1987), pp. 42–53, 89–90
B. Messick: 'Subordinate Discourse: Women, Weaving, and Gender Relations in North Africa', *Amer. Ethnol.*, xiv/2 (1987), pp. 210–25
B. La Duke: *Africa Through the Eyes of Women Artists* (Trenton, NJ, 1991)

MONNI ADAMS

3. TRADE. Scholarly knowledge is limited about the amount and extent of trade both within Africa and between Africa and the outside world. It is clear, however, that African societies have in general been far from isolated from one another or from the outside world. Trade has been an important factor in furthering and maintaining relations between local groups, between different geographical regions and between the continent and Europe, Asia and the Americas. Trade in both the raw materials out of which art is made and in finished art objects has played an important part in this. Moreover, trade has had important effects on art itself. The most obvious has been the introduction into communities of new objects to be adopted, adapted or copied. For example, North African goods and local imitations of them are found in Muslim areas of West Africa, Indian and Arab goods are found all over East Africa, and European goods are found throughout the continent. Often, though not always, these introductions have been at the expense of local production. This section can offer no more than a glimpse of the important relationship between art and trade in Africa.

(i) Local trade. (ii) Long-distance trade. (iii) External trade. (iv) Traders.

(i) Local trade. In many areas the village market is the place to which are brought not only foodstuffs but also such local craft products as iron hoes, wooden stools, baskets, mats, pots and gourds (see fig. 22). In larger markets some craftsmen may work in the market-place

itself, and in all but the smallest markets there are often non-local goods brought by enterprising local traders. In general, local exchanges provide markets for local craft production and encourage the emergence of specialist craft-workers. Tools made by one specialist, for example the smith, can be obtained by other specialists, for example the carvers, either for money or in exchange for their own product. Such craft products as cloth strips or hoes became forms of local currency, accepted even in the long-distance trade. Cloth strips were used over a wide area of the western and central savannahs of West Africa, and hoes were important on some East African trade routes.

(ii) Long-distance trade. In addition to providing wider markets for local crafts, long-distance trade brought in non-local raw materials. For example, the magenta-dyed silk favoured as an embellishment to Hausa gowns was waste silk from Mediterranean looms, dyed in North Africa and carried across the desert by camel. Historically, there were two major forms of long-distance trade in Africa: caravans, covering very long distances and stopping over at points on the route; and trade over shorter distances, from one major market to the next, never taking the merchants very far from their home base. In its most developed form the caravan trade followed circuits hundreds of miles long that took months or even years to complete, examples being some of the Saharan routes and the routes across East Africa. A well-documented West African caravan route led from the great Kola market in present-day Ghana to the Hausa cities of northern Nigeria (see Lovejoy). In west Central Africa, caravans travelled to Luanda in Angola from the Lake Mweru area of Zambia and Zaïre, an area that also traded with Mozambique. Traders from Omdurman in Sudan travelled to Hausaland in Nigeria along the ancient pilgrimage route from West Africa to Mecca; the same traders sought slaves and ivory as far away as the northern part of present-day Uganda. There was also a famous 'forty-day route' through the desert from the western part of present-day Sudan to Egypt.

In West Africa there were often traders' settlements along the trade routes, established by agreement with local chiefs who collected market tolls and 'gifts' from the merchants. Such towns became recognized stopping-places on the trade routes, with semi-permanent populations of resident traders from the same groups as the caravan traders. Such peoples as the Hausa and Dyula in West Africa and the Yao, Nyamwezi and coastal Swahili in East Africa established trading outposts far from their home areas. The markets of towns along the trade routes also attracted shorter-distance traders from nearby markets.

In addition to carrying raw materials, long-distance trade carried local crafts to markets far from their points of origin as well as providing markets en route that attracted local traders and craftsmen. The larger and more important markets themselves became significant centres of craft production, rivalled only by the courts of the major monarchs and the most important cult centres.

The trans-Saharan trade is the best-known long-distance caravan trade in Africa. The peculiar requirements of desert travel itself, for example for water storage, influenced the development of such crafts as leatherworking. In addition North African fashions, forms and motifs were introduced into northern West Africa where they were copied, often by different techniques. In Hausaland in northern Nigeria the North African burnous was adopted alongside shawls brought back from Mecca by pilgrims and garments made from local and imported cloth. Other developments that may be regarded as by-products of this trade include the way in which Hausa palaces and mosques imitate North African arch forms by an ingenious cantilever system in sun-dried mud reinforced with split palm trunk. Also, Hausa water-coolers can be seen as imitations of North African wheel-thrown pots. The export of West African cloth to the peoples of the desert was paid for from the proceeds of the desert trade. Much of the fine, indigo-dyed cloth produced in the area of Kano in northern Nigeria was made for export northwards (see fig. 23). A similar type of cloth was manufactured on the Senegal River, largely for sale to the Moors.

The Swahili trading empire stretched across East Africa to the Great Lakes and beyond. Some Swahili merchants even established political control over areas as far from their coastal base as present-day eastern Zaïre. Much of this trade was conducted by caravan, although some traders' towns were established, for example Tabora in present-day Tanzania. Until *c.* 1950 there was a Swahili village in the middle of Maasai country, a survival of one of the long-distance East African trade routes. Swahili villages also survived in Northern Rhodesia (now Zambia) into the 1950s. In addition to the Swahili, a number of other African peoples carried on long-distance trade in ivory and slaves across eastern Africa, the best known being the Yao. Earlier long-distance traders had carried ornaments made from conch shells; these have been found in excavations far inland.

(iii) External trade. The slave trade was probably the most significant external trade in African history. For centuries before Europeans reached Africa's Atlantic coasts slaves were exported by way of the Sahara and down the Nile to the Arab world. This trade continued in a small way into the 20th century. The Indian Ocean trade, though probably ancient, did not become large until the later 18th century and then only for *c.* 100 years. The Atlantic slave trade began when the Europeans reached the West African coast in the late 15th century, but it was not until the late 17th century, when the Dutch and the British became involved in sugar production in northern Brazil and the Caribbean, that there was large-scale export of slaves. This trade reached its peak in the late 18th century but did not finally end until towards the end of the 19th century. It has been estimated that *c.* 10 million or 11 million people were transported out of Africa, mainly between the 1660s and the 1860s. There has been much dispute as to the effects in Africa of the slave trade. It certainly caused great disruption in west Central Africa; but in West Africa the effects are much less certain. Many of the slaves came from areas already densely populated, and only in limited areas was there depopulation. Some small states disappeared in the course of attempting to obtain slaves for export, while other states became rich and powerful from

23. Indigo dyeing pits, Kano, Nigeria; from a photograph by H. Turner

the proceeds of the trade; along the coast, African merchants and merchant houses flourished.

The slave trade led to the introduction of many foreign goods into West Africa. The most important were textiles, for example cottons and silks from Asia and linens and woollens from Europe, and metals, including iron for tools and weapons, copper and brass largely for decoration and, in the form of bowls and basins, for domestic and ritual use of all kinds. A good part of these and other items were imported for direct consumption. There was, however, some recycling of raw materials: cloth was unwoven, brass melted down, and beads were ground up to form the raw materials for local industries. Only iron-smelting seems to have suffered seriously from competition with imports, although it survived in less accessible parts of West Africa until long after the end of the slave trade.

It is unlikely that many craftsmen were transported, since in many areas they belonged to a class that, while not wholly free, were not slaves and could not be sold. A craftsman could generally avoid being sold overseas, even if captured in war. Among the Asante, for example, he would be sent to one of the villages devoted to the making of ceremonial and domestic objects for the king's household. There was thus little transfer of African craft technology to the Americas. Weaving is a partial exception to this, since in some areas slaves were employed as weavers.

There appears to have been remarkably little transfer of technology into Africa either from Europe or from America in the slave-trade era. Claims have been made for the European origin of Benin and Ife brass-casting, but this can be discounted on chronological grounds (although it is just possible that certain refinements may have been contributed by European gunsmiths). It has been suggested that certain groupings found on Benin plaques may owe something to Christian iconography, but this seems very doubtful, although the art form of the plaque itself, so exceptional in African art, may possibly owe something to the influence of Portuguese traders. Even more improbable, on chronological and other grounds, is the suggestion that the West African loom owes anything to European technology. It is basically similar to the cotton looms of the eastern Sudan, the Yemen and India and was probably introduced originally by traders following the ancient trade route (marked by the use of cloth strips as currency) along what may be termed 'the cloth strip', where cotton and indigo can be grown, between the desert and the Middle Belt (see Johnson). There seems little or no indication of any transfer of technology from the Americas. It is just possible that the pedals and reed of the tripod loom of the Mende of Sierra Leone, described by one early traveller as 'worked entirely by hand', were inspired by the Portuguese.

In the 19th century trade patterns changed, with the export of slaves being increasingly replaced by trade in oil and oil-seeds, groundnuts from Senegambia and palm oil from Sierra Leone to the Niger Delta and thence overseas. By the later part of the century such areas as Gabon and the Congo were being opened up by traders in search of these and other goods; rubber became increasingly important. In East Africa ivory had long been one of the principal exports; it then went increasingly to Europe and America as well as to India. Ostrich feathers were for a time a major export across the Sahara and thence to Italy and France. Towards the end of the century, South Africa began exporting diamonds and then gold in addition to wool and ostrich feathers. Imports to Africa came increasingly from Europe and to a smaller extent from the USA. Indian hand-woven textiles, for example, were no longer competitive. Surprisingly, local weaving industries survived in West Africa, and efforts to persuade the people to export cotton and import cloth were still largely unsuccessful, though the simplest and poorest quality of local cloth was replaced by imported Lancashire cottons.

Generally, local crafts continued to be cheaper than their imported alternatives until the railways were built, and it was not until the coming of the motor lorry in the 1920s that European imports began to penetrate the remotest areas. By the 1930s Africans were again wearing Indian cottons, machine-made, often from cotton grown and exported from East Africa. Some local weaving industries survived, however, largely using imported machine-spun cotton yarn.

The world depression of the 1930s and import shortages during World War II led to revival of local industries in the villages. Generally, however, it is local industrialization and development in various forms that have caused the decline in local crafts rather than competition from imported goods. A craftsman can often earn more in shorter hours as a factory worker or a clerk than he can at his craft. It is thus mainly the most highly skilled craftsmen, producing prestige products for courts and wealthy commoners, who survive. These, however, are vulnerable to such trade crises as a decline in oil revenues or the failure of an export crop.

By the late 20th century it was generally impossible legally to export older works of art from Africa. No such prohibition existed in earlier times, and many pieces owe their preservation to the almost accidental trade that took thousands of objects, particularly figure sculptures and masks, to Europe (see Paudrat). During the 20th century the trade in African art became more organized and, in some contexts, commercialized.

MARION JOHNSON

(iv) Traders. The role of traders as both intermediaries between consumers and artists and as consumers and patrons in their own right is important in the African context.

(a) As intermediaries. In the complex network of supply and demand, traders communicate the needs and demands of art patrons and consumers to the artists. Traders in Africa tend to be conservative, but, as public tastes shift, they may take the lead in encouraging changes in art production. In the early 1970s, for example, urban market traders in Mali, in response to contemporary tastes, bought fewer traditional Bamana and Maninka cloths and encouraged local weavers to use modern dyes and new patterns (see Imperato). Similarly, in the 1960s Songye entrepreneurial traders in Zaïre encouraged changes in the forms and colours of raffia baskets to make them more appealing to European buyers (see Merriam).

Traders also act as agents of diffusion, carrying art objects over a broad geographical area and stimulating local demand for non-indigenous art forms. The traders' impact on the quantity, quality and distribution of goods produced is similar to that of leader-patrons (*see* §1 above). This can lead to a diaspora of artists, for example, as in the settlement of Hausa tailors, embroiderers, tanners, leatherworkers and other craftsmen throughout West and North Africa in the 19th and 20th centuries. Wood sculpture has become a 'market-driven' commodity only in the 20th century. Not only do trader-patrons encourage the fabrication of new forms to appeal to the tourist trade, they also promote the continuity of indigenous ritual carving styles that are redefined as commodities. For example, in the 1960s a flourishing Yoruba carving industry supported by trader-patrons emerged in Abeokuta, south-west Nigeria. Yoruba, Hausa and Ghanaian traders revived a lineage carving tradition that had largely disappeared for lack of ritual patronage. Stylistically, the carvings produced for trader-patrons adhered to the indigenous forms and aesthetics, but they were produced as commodities. As patrons, the traders encouraged a higher level of production than at any time in the past, and they spread the products across a wide geographical area. A similar industry occurred among the Senufo Kulebele of northern Côte d'Ivoire (Richter, 1980). Alternatively, traders may encourage local artists to copy foreign prototypes. This is particularly evident in the proliferation of such Western forms as salad bowls and servers, toothpicks and ashtrays offered by the purveyors of tourist arts (*see* §4 below). Hausa weavers and dyers of the Kano emirate produce a type of cloth known as *turkudi*, made up of narrow indigo-dyed strips, for leader-patrons and for the market-place. Although the cloth is used on ceremonial occasions by Hausa nobility, the most important consumers of it are the Tuareg. The production and distribution of *turkudi* for export involves a complex division of labour and a chain of economic interactions controlled by market agents. After buying cloth from the weavers, the agents commission cloth sewers to sew the bands together, dyers to dye the cloth a deep indigo colour and cloth beaters to pound it with powdered indigo to give it a glossy shine. The finished product is known as *yan kura* cloth and is sold to long-distance traders who carry it to Tuareg patrons in Niger and the Sahara.

JUDITH PERANI, NORMA H. WOLFF

(b) As consumers. Some African states grew rich from trade. Kings established elaborate courts and became patrons of all manner of court arts, for which they provided rich and exotic materials. However, not all the wealth passed into the hands of the kings and chiefs. There were wealthy merchants, too, and it was they who were largely responsible for the wealth and sophistication of the walled cities of Hausaland and the Swahili towns of the East African seaboard. Within established monarchies wealthy traders were not always able to display their wealth openly, although generally they did so when they could, often in the form of imported dress and other equipment. In the colonial period, many of the old sumptuary restraints were lifted, and there was an outburst of artistic elaboration in dress and, more recently, in such other consumer items as cars. Indeed, wealthy Swahili were once known as the Wana-Benzi, people of the Mercedes-Benz. Perhaps the most significant contribution of merchants to art patronage has been the development of the decorated houses of the Hausa cities in the colonial period.

MARION JOHNSON

BIBLIOGRAPHY

P. T. Bauer: *West African Trade: A Study of Competition, Oligopoly and Monopoly in a Changing Economy* (London, 1954/*R* 1965)

24. Kamba souvenir carvings, wood, female bust, h. 240 mm; warrior figure h. 250 mm; salad servers: l. 370 mm and 380 mm; mid-20th century (Berkeley, CA, University of California, Phoebe A. Hearst Museum of Anthropology)

K. O. Dike: *Trade and Politics in the Niger Delta, 1830–1885* (Oxford, 1956)

E. W. Bovill: *The Golden Trade of the Moors* (London, 1958, rev. 1970)

G. I. Jones: *The Trading States of the Oil Rivers* (London, 1963)

A. P. Merriam: 'Basongye Raffia Basketry', *Afr. A.*, ii/1 (1968), pp. 14–17, 73

The Development of Indigenous Trade and Markets in West Africa: Studies Presented and Discussed at the Tenth International African Seminar at Fourah Bay College: Freetown, December 1969

R. Gray and D. Birmingham, eds: *Pre-Colonial African Trade: Essays on Trade in Central and Eastern Africa before 1900* (London, 1970)

P. Martin: *The External Trade of the Loango Coast, 1576–1580: The Effects of Changing Commercial Relations on the Vili Kingdom of Loango* (Oxford, 1972)

P. J. Imperato: 'Bamana and Maninka Covers and Blankets', *Afr. A.*, vii/3 (1974), pp. 56–67, 91

E. J. Alpers: *Ivory and Slaves in East Central Africa: Changing Patterns of International Trade to the Later Nineteenth Century* (London, 1975)

P. Shea: *The Development of an Export Oriented Dyed Cloth Industry in Kano Emirate in the Nineteenth Century* (diss., U. WI, 1975)

M. Johnson: 'Cloth Strips and History', *W. Afr. J. Archaeol.*, vii (1977), pp. 169–78

D. Northrup: *Trade without Rulers: Pre-Colonial Development in South-Eastern Nigeria* (Oxford, 1978)

K. Arhin: *West African Traders in Ghana in the Nineteenth and Twentieth Centuries*, Legon History Series (London, 1979)

T. F. Garrard: *Akan Weights and the Gold Trade* (London, 1980)

B. W. Hodder: 'Indigenous Cloth Trade and Marketing in Africa', *Textile Hist.*, xi (1980), pp. 203–10

P. E. Lovejoy: *Caravans of Kola: The Hausa Kola Trade, 1700–1900* (Zaria, 1980)

D. Richter: *Art Economics and Change* (La Jolla, 1980)

R. W. Harms: *River of Wealth, River of Sorrow: The Central Zaire Basin in the Era of the Slave and Ivory Trade, 1500–1891* (New Haven, 1981)

J. E. Inikori: *Forced Migration: The Impact of the Export Slave Trade on African Societies* (London, 1981)

P. Shea: 'Approaching the Study of Production in Rural Kano', *Studies in the History of Kano*, ed. B. Barkindo (Ibadan, 1983), pp. 93–115

P. D. Curtin: *Cross-cultural Trade in World History* (Cambridge, 1984)

J.-L. Paudrat: 'From Africa', *'Primitivism' in 20th Century Art: Affinity of the Tribal and the Modern*, ed. W. Rubin (New York, 1984), pp. 125–75

J. Hogendorn and M. Johnson: *The Shell Money of the Slave Trade*, African Studies Series, 49 (Cambridge, 1986)

J. Perani: 'The Cloth Connection: Patrons and Producers of Hausa and Nupe Prestige Strip-Weave', *History, Design, and Craft in West African Strip-Woven Cloth* (Washington, DC, 1992), pp. 95–112

C. B. Steiner: *African Art in Transit* (Cambridge, 1993)

MARION JOHNSON, JUDITH PERANI, NORMA H. WOLFF

4. COMMERCIAL PRODUCTION. Much traditional African art has always been 'commercial production'. That is, it has been executed by master craftsmen in return for honours and/or bartered for livestock and farm produce. Traditionally, however, African artists do not commonly support themselves exclusively by their art. On the contrary, most make their living through subsistence agriculture, augmented by what they can obtain through the exercise of their art. This situation has altered with changing economic circumstances and particularly in response to the colonial presence, to tourism and to the arrival of the wage economy in many areas. These developments have led to an increase in commercial production, both of traditional and of non-traditional arts.

A major factor has been the artists' attempt to respond to Western tastes. Understanding has grown considerably more acute since the waning of colonialism and the arrival of political independence. The colonialists were replaced as potential consumers by tourists, who often have a positive attitude to Africa and a desire to take home art objects as evidence of their visit. The response has frequently been to produce what has been termed 'airport art', since so much of it has been made for sale in airport tourist shops. Understandably, such 'airport art' has usually been finest and most varied in those countries that attract the largest number of tourists, for example Kenya and Côte d'Ivoire. It has, however, also developed in virtually every other nation, even such less visited countries as Gabon and Rwanda.

(i) Chokwe. Since the late 19th century Chokwe people of north-eastern Angola have been immigrating into neighbouring Zaïre and Zambia. They went in search of economic opportunity and took with them their distinctive art style. Most Chokwe men practised a simple carving technique that they had learnt during their initiation. They used this to make small wooden amulets for their wives, and some also made small sculptures of humans and animals to be used in hunting magic. With the building of the Benguela Railway through their territory in the 1920s, however, Chokwe discovered an unexpected market for their arts. Portuguese and Belgian colonists and miners, as well as civil servants and their families, had time and money to spend in the various depots *en route* to and from their assignments. Chokwe artists began to produce baskets, wooden boxes, ashtrays and bowls with pyrographic decorations and, soon after, mask plaques, small wooden busts and figures in realistic European styles.

(ii) Kamba. Perhaps the most successful example of African 'airport art' is that produced by the Kamba people of Kenya, who like most East African peoples had no previous tradition of carving. Soon after World War II, Icelandic Lutheran missionaries encouraged some young Kamba male students to make carvings out of an attractive streaky tan-and-yellow local wood of such African animals as elephants and hippopotamuses, using European tools.

When these small carvings proved popular with tourists and expatriates on the streets of Nairobi, they broadened their subject-matter to include female busts, figures of warriors, letter openers and salad servers (see fig. 24) The latter had handles representing Maasai women, their long necks wrapped with imported steel wire to simulate the Maasai women's giant beaded necklaces. The carvings sold so well that local Kamba and East Indian entrepreneurs began exporting them. To cater to the growing market, factory-like 'production lines' were set up. Individual carvers were trained to specialize in a single operation, either adzing out the basic form, completing the figure, cutting in the details, sanding the surface or adding such extras as wire necklaces. But in spite of this process, usually so deadening to creativity, the Kamba have continued to change and modify their designs to assure their continued share of the market.

(iii) Makonde. Probably the second most successful 'airport art' also comes from East Africa, from Dar-es-Salaam, Tanzania. Here MAKONDE immigrant labourers from northern Mozambique, inspired in part by the Kamba example, began carving small human figures for the expatriate community and for the booming post-war tourist market. A more interesting genre featuring fantastic figures called *shetani* developed over time. *Shetani* had distorted bodies and weird, misshapen faces; sometimes several figures were entwined in one sculpture. Another development, also a uniquely Makonde expression, was the 'tree of life'. This comprised a number of small figures, not necessarily distorted or entwined, but clustered around a chunk or rough cylinder of hard wood. These complex sculptures are little understood but apparently represent mythological and lineage themes. Some seem to represent a family, with the founder of the lineage perhaps portrayed in the large head at the top (see fig. 25).

Later developments include the use of whole segments of a tree trunk, a metre or more high, and the exploitation of both the dark core of the wood and the softer yellow outer ring. Some such Makonde sculptures are spectacular, with small, finely carved and polished figures clambering over each other and seemingly struggling to emerge from the surface of the log. By the later 20th century such complex sculptures were no longer properly classifiable as 'airport art', although a few were still to be found in airport shops. More commonly, however, they were sold in elegant hotel shops and commercial art galleries, with prices often around US$1000. Heartening for the future of the arts in Africa, discriminating travellers have broadened their taste beyond wood sculpture to include African jewellery in brass, silver and gold; textiles such as batiks, 'mud-resist' *bokolonfini* and tie-dyes (using imported dyes), to say nothing of Manjaco and Asante narrow-strip weave cloths in non-traditional imported yarns or copied in print fabrics; furniture, hair combs, musical instruments, such long-overlooked crafts as baskets, carved gourds and even home-pictorial signboards.

25. Makonde *ujaama* ('tree of life') sculpture from Tanzania, wood, h. 305 mm, collected Cape Town, 1977 (USA, private collection)

BIBLIOGRAPHY

R. Dick-Read: *Sanamu: Adventures in Search of African Art* (London, 1964)

M. Shore-Bos: 'Modern Makonde: Discovery in East African Art', *Afr. A.*, iii/1 (1969), pp. 46–51, 80–81

D. J. Crowley: 'The Contemporary–Traditional Art Market in Africa', *Afr. A.*, iv/1 (1970), pp. 43–9, 80

——: 'The West African Art Market Revisited', *Afr. A.*, vii/4 (1974), pp. 54–9

J. A. Stout: 'The Eloquent Body...Sculptural Fantasy of Contemporary Makonde Tribesmen', *Cultural Resistance: Art from Guinea-Bissau, Mozambique and Angola* (exh. cat. by I. Hersey and others, New York, Afr.–Amer. Inst., 1975)

W. Bascom: 'Changing African Art', *Ethnic and Tourist Arts: Cultural Expressions from the Fourth World*, ed. N. H. H. Graburn (Berkeley, 1976), pp. 303–19

P. Ben-Amos: '"A la recherche du temps perdu": On Being an Ebony-Carver in Benin', *Ethnic and Tourist Arts: Cultural Expressions from the Fourth World*, ed. N. H. H. Graburn (Berkeley, 1976), pp. 320–33

B. H. Sandelowsky: 'Functional and Tourist Art along the Okavango River', *Ethnic and Tourist Arts: Cultural Expressions from the Fourth World*, ed. N. H. H. Graburn (Berkeley, 1976), pp. 350–65

U. Wagner: *Catching the Tourist: Women Handicraft Traders in The Gambia* (Stockholm, 1982)

B. Jules-Rosette: *The Messages of Tourist Art: An African Semiotic System in Comparative Perspective*, Topics in Contemporary Semiotics (New York, 1984)

J. Coote: 'Modern Makonde Carving: The Origins and Development of a New African Art Tradition', *Makonde: Wooden Sculpture from East Africa from the Malde Collection* (exh. cat.; Oxford, MOMA; Plymouth,

City Mus. & A.G.; Preston, Harris Mus.; and elsewhere; 1989–90), pp. 13–22
C. B. Steiner: *African Art in Transit* (Cambridge, 1994)

DANIEL J. CROWLEY

5. RITUAL. Art is an integral aspect of ritual throughout Africa. In puberty rituals in particular the arts of the body, adornment and dress are often highly elaborated and symbolically significant. In funerary rituals and others connected with death, body arts may also play a role, although sculpture is important. Masks and masquerades are common features of rituals throughout Africa, for it is frequently the masking societies that are responsible for organizing ritual ceremonies. A discussion of the ritual contexts of art illustrates the close relationship between art and life that is common in Africa.

This section can give only an indication of ritual as a context for art in Africa. Further discussion on art and ritual will be found throughout the rest of this survey and in the entries on the art traditions of individual peoples. □

(i) Puberty. (ii) Funerary.

(i) Puberty.

(a) Introduction. (b) Body arts. (c) Mask and masquerade. (d) Other arts.

(a) Introduction. In most African societies individuals are required to undergo certain rites before they can participate fully in adult society. Although the form, scale and duration of the ceremonies vary considerably from one society to another, the arts customarily play a central role in even the most modest events. Because these rites are concerned with social as well as biological maturation, their timing often does not coincide with the onset of physiological puberty. Depending on the particular African society, youths may undergo 'puberty' rituals when as young as eight or as old as twenty or more.

With few exceptions, separate rituals are held for boys and for girls. In some areas the rites are performed for an individual, while in societies with institutionalized age-sets youth of the same sex and relatively the same age are initiated together as a group. In female rites much of the art and its related symbolism and instruction concentrate on domestic life, fertility, marriage and maternity. The emphasis in male rites tends to focus less on domestic life and more on men's roles in the more public spheres of politics, economics and ritual.

Most male rites and some female rites are organized into three phases of varying elaborateness. During the first phase, the novices are physically separated from their families and either taken to an initiation camp outside the village or sequestered inside it in specially designated areas. The second or transitional phase may last only a day or continue for many months. The ritual enactment of the death of the initiate as a child and his or her rebirth as an adult is a prominent symbolic theme in this transition. Often during this phase special rules and regulations apply to interactions between the initiates and other members of the community; the novices also receive instruction in practical and esoteric matters. In some societies the bodies of the initiates are subjected to permanent alteration through scarification or circumcision. The final phase of the ritual process almost always involves a public celebration at which the initiates' new status is acknowledged by the community at large.

(b) Body arts. Throughout Africa initiates decorate their bodies, don special costumes and ornaments or wear special hairstyles to proclaim their transformation into adults. Dress and adornment are simultaneously aesthetic statements and means of validating ethnic, age and gender identities. In a number of cultures, initiates begin the ritual process wearing children's costumes and emerge from their seclusion dressed in clothing and ornaments reserved for adults. Among the Herero of Southern Africa, for example, where the puberty ritual for a young girl is a small family affair, it is the girl's donning of a woman's headdress during the puberty ritual that symbolizes her transition to womanhood. Traditionally, a woman's headdress was a three-horned leather cap (*ekori*), often decorated with strands of metal beads, and her dress was a leather apron and cloak. In Christianized Herero households, the horned cap has been replaced by a cloth headtie (*ocikaeva*) and the leather apron and cloak by a long-sleeved, ankle-length cotton dress. Despite these substitutions, the ritual donning of the headdress remains one of the central symbolic acts of Herero puberty rituals.

Among the Ga'anda of north-eastern Nigeria, an elaborate programme of scarification, the *hleeta*, was the defining feature of girls' puberty rites until 1978. The full rites consisted of a series of six biennial ceremonies beginning when a girl was five or six years old and ending just before her marriage around the age of sixteen. Identical patterns were used throughout the dispersed Ga'anda communities, graphically proclaiming the ethnic identity of the initiates. The artful and intricate patterns made by specialists were closely placed cuts that scarred to form small, delicate dots slightly lighter than the surrounding skin (see fig. 26). The first patterns were cut on the stomach. Two years later the forehead was scarified. The third set was placed on the neck and forearm and the fourth set on the waist, buttocks and back of the neck. The fifth set filled in areas on the stomach and arms, and the sixth and final set decorated the thighs and filled in areas on the chest, back and abdomen. Ga'anda scarification constituted the permanent transformation through artistic means of a girl's body into that of a woman's. Traditionally, the various Ga'anda communities held an annual seven-day festival to honour all the young women who had completed the *hleeta* during the preceding year. The young women, their *hleeta* patterns enhanced by red camwood, danced with ornamental iron axes over their left shoulders and carried gourds decorated with incised patterns in their left hands to symbolize their new domestic and economic responsibilities as married women.

Elaborate coiffures and other forms of body adornment are part of everyday appearance among pastoralist groups in East Africa. Specific hairstyles, ornaments and modes of dress distinguish children from young adults and young adults from elders. The transition from boy to junior 'warrior' results in the most dramatic change in dress and ornament among young MAASAI, Samburu, Turkana and Pokot men. All these groups have highly articulated age-set systems through the different stages of which men pass in a gradual process of social maturation. The stages

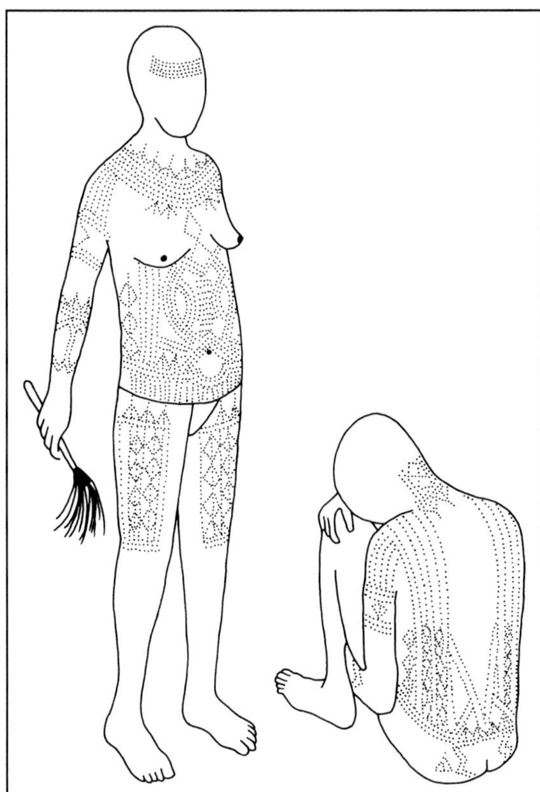

26. Ga'anda *bleeta* scarifications; after drawings by T. J. H. Chappel and Marla C. Berns

are marked by rituals. The first of these ceremonies transforms boys into young 'warriors' who thus acquire the right to wear certain coiffures and to use certain ornaments and colours. The young men invest great time and effort in the arts of personal adornment, and a man's dress is an emphatic statement of his personal aesthetic. The forms and types of ornamentation, however, also reflect and communicate ethnic affiliation and serve to manifest visually their bearer's position within the age-set system.

Many African puberty rites involve a series of elaborate and dramatic transformations in the form and style of costume and ornamentation as boys or girls move through the various ceremonies. Among the Okiek of Kenya, for example, girls are initiated as a group sometime between the ages of 13 and 17. Their puberty rites involve a series of ceremonies that last over a number of weeks. For the first ceremony, the girls appear wearing special dance costumes that consist of strands of beads wrapped around their wrists and forearms, bells on their calves, a beaded leather cloak on their shoulders, black-and-white colobus-monkey skins fitted on their arms and falling from their waists, and a decoratively painted headdress fitted over a tall mitre-like hat. The most elaborate of these headdresses are appliquéd with metal foil, and some even have battery-operated torch bulbs attached to them. The girls perform in full costume in the opening ceremonies of the ritual, after which they are taken to a house in the village where they are circumcised.

Following circumcision the girls are stripped of their elaborate costumes and jewellery and wrapped in blankets. They retire into the house for a period of healing, and during this phase their movements are greatly restricted. After they have healed sufficiently, their instruction in women's affairs and women's secret songs begins in earnest. The initiates are now dressed by their ritual leaders in calf-length skin skirts and skin cloaks. They wear a plain metal-band necklace and a chain with a round ring of yellow metal hanging from it. Each initiate also wears a beaded headband consisting of a single strand of dark blue beads, from the centre of which four pieces of chain hang down, reaching to the bridge of the nose. A bead of either red, white, yellow or black is fastened to the end of each chain. While in seclusion, the girls daily smear their arms, legs and faces with white clay and decorate each other's faces by drawing decorative lines in the clay. The girls may now venture out of the initiation house to visit female relatives living near by, to collect firewood and so on, but they are still expressly forbidden to have any contact with adult men.

On the morning of their coming-out ceremony, the initiates go to the river to bathe, their bodies are oiled, and they are dressed in a cloth sheet tied over one shoulder, a beaded leather skirt around the waist and a beaded leather cloak on the shoulders. Each young woman wears an elaborate array of beaded necklaces, bracelets and earrings. At the conclusion of the public festivity, the girl's beaded headband is removed and replaced by a beaded tiara that has two chain loops circling the eyes and a long beaded extension rising from the top of the head symbolizing the girl's transformation into a woman (see fig. 27). The young women return to their homes, put aside their ceremonial costumes and rejoin the daily life of their community. The next occasion when they will appear so elaborately dressed and adorned will be on their wedding day.

Among the BAMANA of the Baninko in southern Mali, boys' manhood rites take place once every seven years. The initiates into the men's Jo association range in age from 15 to 21. The various ceremonies take place over a period of eight or nine months. The novices are first taken to a bush camp, and, during the ritual called the Jo Faga (Jo killing), they enter the *sama so* (elephant house), a large mud plaster construction at whose summit is an enormous carved wooden horizontal mask representing an elephant. While they are in the belly of the beast the initiates are ritually killed as children and then reborn out of the beast as men. Following this ceremony, the novices spend a week in the bush in isolation, and they are stripped of all clothing and ornaments. (A mask symbolizing the principles of order and disorder protects the novices from harm. The masker is encased in a baglike form made from fibre or mud-dyed cloth that sports on its head a spread of porcupine quills.)

When the initiates emerge from the woods they cover themselves with unworked red fibres, which they gradually shed as they make their way to the outskirts of the village. There they each don a cache-sexe and bandoliers of red and white beans worn diagonally across their upper bodies; this comprises their daily dress for the period of their

27. Okiek woman wearing beaded tiara symbolizing her new status, Narok District, Kenya, 1983; from a photograph by Corinne A. Kratz

initiation. During the next few months the initiates wear more elaborate costumes and headdresses for a series of public ceremonies. Some groups of initiates may choose to devise their own distinctive costumes, but all are constructed from an array of bush materials in a variety of colours and textures, underscoring the initiates' association with the world of the bush. During their public performances the young men dance and sing special songs and often carry carved wooden statues of females that are decorated with strands of multicoloured beads. At a final ceremony of reincorporation, the young men discard the elaborate ritual costumes and put on plain country-cloth shirts, pants and caps made of handwoven unbleached cotton, the traditional everyday wear of adult men.

(c) Mask and masquerade. Puberty rituals are often the responsibility of mask-owning societies, and masks thus often feature in them. This is so, for example, in the male initiation complex known as Mukanda, which is found from south-western Zaïre into south-eastern Zambia among such peoples as the Ndembu, Suku, YAKA, KUBA (ii), PENDE and Chokwe (*see* CHOKWE AND RELATED PEOPLES). Most of these groups use a variety of fibre and wooden masks, both in the initiation camp and in the final coming-out ceremonies that take place in the village. Among the southern Kuba groups certain masks are created specifically for men's initiation and are intended to intensify the symbolic association between adult men, the forest and hunting. The masks are constructed from uncultivated forest palms, in contrast to the cultivated palm fibres used for weaving Kuba raffia textiles. Bird beaks, feathers and animal skins are often attached, and the masker carries bows and arrows and various hunting paraphernalia when performing in the forest camp. Among the Suku, the most important mask, the Kakunga, is worn by the ritual master. It is a large wooden mask with massive features including a bulbous forehead and cheeks. Kakunga appears on the day of the boys' circumcision to protect them, and in the final phase of the initiation cycle it leads the young men out of seclusion back to the village (*see also* YAKA, §1).

Masks appear in a large number of male initiation ceremonies throughout West and Central Africa. In West Africa they are central to BAGA, Diola, Bassari, BAMANA, Malinke, IGBO and IBIBIO rites, as well as appearing in the initiations of the Poro men's association among groups living in Liberia, Sierra Leone and Côte d'Ivoire. In Central Africa numerous peoples regularly use masks during male puberty rites. Besides those practising a form of Mukanda, the Lwalwa, Luluwa, Mbole and Bembe among others also use masks and figures in puberty rites.

Masks appear with less frequency during male initiations in East and Southern Africa, although the MAKONDE of Tanzania and Mozambique and the Chewa of Malawi are notable exceptions. During Chewa boys' initiation, a large fibre mask, Kisiyamaliro, is created. This representation of a mythical beast, resembling a bush cow or other large antelope, stands nearly 3 m high. It is constructed from dried maize leaves woven over a flexible wooden frame. The head of the beast has woven fibre horns and a large projecting snout. The boys are symbolically devoured by Kisiyamaliro and reborn out of it as men. In the final coming-out ceremony the mask leads the initiates back into the village and performs in a public ceremony. Following the initiation cycle, the mask is left to decay in the bush.

Masks and masquerades are less important in women's puberty rituals, although among the Ngbandi of Zaïre and the Makonde of Mozambique and Tanzania masks danced by males feature in both male and female puberty rites. Several Tanzanian Makonde masks collected in the early decades of the 20th century have fully carved, seated female figures attached to the crown of the mask. This motif seems to refer directly to the female puberty ritual itself, during which the initiates were carried on the backs of their adult sponsors.

One of the rare instances in Africa where masquerades are danced by women is during girls' initiation into the Sande association among the Vai, Gola, Temne and Mende of Liberia and Sierra Leone. The helmet mask, portraying a beautiful young woman with finely carved features, eyes modestly downcast, shining black skin and an elaborate coiffure, represents the Sande water spirit and symbolizes fertility and increase (*see* §II, 2(iii)(a) above; *see also* MENDE, §2).

(d) Other arts. Among the Bemba of Zambia, women's initiation traditionally involved a series of 18 different ceremonies and lasted for over a month. An initiation hut was built on the edge of the village, and its walls were

painted with a series of emblems. Some 40 or more clay images, painted white, black and red, were made by women potters for the initiation. These images represented a range of historical characters, common domestic objects, animals and birds as well as emblematic designs regularly found on pottery vessels. Each character or emblem had a name and was associated with a particular song.

During the various ceremonies, the girls were shown the figures, learnt their names and the songs and the multiple meanings associated with them. The pottery sculptures served as one of the primary means of instruction; through them the initiates learned the appropriate behaviour, values and beliefs associated with their future roles as Bemba wives and mothers. Among the Pedi, Tsonga and VENDA of Southern Africa free-standing carved wooden figures were once regularly used as didactic devices in boys', and occasionally girls', initiations. In south-central Zaïre, Kuba groups constructed an 'initiation' wall of raffia palm, to which they attached a variety of sculptures, masks and assorted objects in a graphic representation of men's secret lore and symbols.

BIBLIOGRAPHY

A. Van Gennep: *Les Rites de passage* (Paris, 1909; Eng. trans. by M. B. Vizedom and G. L. Caffee, London, 1960/*R* 1977)

J. Vansina: 'Initiation Rituals of the Bushong', *Africa*, xxv/2 (1955), pp. 138–53

A. I. Richards: *Chisungu: A Girls' Initiation Ceremony among the Bemba of Northern Rhodesia* (London, 1956); *R* as *Chisungu: A Girls' Initiation Ceremony among the Bemba of Zambia* (London, 1982)

G. D. Gibson: 'Herero Marriage', *Rhodes-Livingstone J.*, 24 (1959), pp. 1–37

J. Dias and M. Dias: *Os Macondes de Moçambique*, 3 vols (Lisbon, 1964–70)

P. Spencer: *The Samburu: A Study of Gerontocracy in a Nomadic Tribe* (London, 1965)

H. M. Cole: 'Vital Arts in Northern Kenya', *Afr. A.*, vii/2 (1974), pp. 12–23, 82

J. Buxton: 'Initiation and Bead-sets in Western Mandari', *Studies in Social Anthropology: Essays in Memory of E. E. Evans-Pritchard by his Former Oxford Colleagues*, ed. J. H. M. Beattie and R. G. Lienhardt (Oxford, 1975), pp. 310–27

H. M. Cole: 'Living Art among the Samburu', *The Fabrics of Culture: The Anthropology of Clothing and Adornment*, ed. J. M. Cordwell and R. A. Schwarz, World Anthropology (The Hague, 1979), pp. 87–102

M. Kecskesi: 'The Pickaback Motif in the Art and Initiation of the Rovuma Area', *Afr. A.*, xvi/1 (1982), pp. 52–5, 94–5

D. Biebuyck: *The Arts of Zaire*, 5 vols (Berkeley, 1985–)

J. S. La Fontaine: *Initiation: Ritual Drama and Secret Knowledge across the World* (Harmondsworth, 1985)

A Human Ideal in African Art: Bamana Figurative Sculpture (exh. cat. by K. Ezra, Washington, DC, N. Mus. Afr. A., 1986)

D. A. Binkley: *A View from the Forest: The Power of Southern Kuba Initiation Masks* (diss., Bloomington, IN U., 1987; microfilm, Ann Arbor, 1989)

M. C. Berns: 'Ga'anda Scarification: A Model for Art and Identity', *Marks of Civilization: Artistic Transformations of the Human Body*, ed. A. Rubin (Los Angeles, 1988), pp. 57–76

L. B. Faulkner: 'Basketry Masks of the Chewa', *Afr. A.*, xxi/3 (1988), pp. 28–31, 86

C. A. Kratz: 'Okiek Ornaments of Transition and Transformation', *Kenya Past & Present*, 20 (1988), pp. 21–6

A. Nettleton: 'History and the Myth of Zulu Sculpture', *Afr. A.*, xxi/3 (1988), pp. 48–51, 86–7

R. Sieber and R. A. Walker: *African Art in the Cycle of Life* (Washington, DC, 1988) [pubd in conjunction with exh., Washington, DC, N. Mus. Afr. A., 1987–8]

G. Meurillon: *Initiations septiennales et institutions du Jo bamanan du Baninko (Mali)* (Paris, 1992)

MARY JO ARNOLDI

(ii) Funerary.

(a) Introduction. (b) Sculpture. (c) Display.

(a) Introduction. In many African societies, burial and funerary celebration provide the stage for ritual action and the use and display of works of art that enact and reaffirm beliefs and societal values. Funerals conclude a person's passage through life, and death may be accompanied by elaborate ritual extending over many months or even years. The actual burial or interment of the remains is usually very brief and takes place immediately after the individual's demise, while subsequent commemorative funerary celebrations are carefully planned and prepared long in advance.

Although the content and form of funerary rites differ greatly from one African society to another, there are general principles underlying their structure. When death occurs, the community faces the upheaval of the biological and social order, for an important member has been lost. During the course of the funeral, this order needs to be re-established and asserted. Mortuary rituals also provide the setting for a symbolic discourse on life, death and the afterlife. In this context, works of art may be created to mediate between the living and the dead and to commemorate the deceased. Funerary rites facilitate the transition of the deceased into the afterlife, creating the conditions necessary for becoming an ancestral being. The living believe that the ancestors secure health and fecundity for those who attend to them, whether in the form of many offspring or in rich crop and animal yields. Dissatisfied and neglected ancestors may threaten their descendants for generations. They may bring misfortune, disease and death. Descendants therefore find it necessary to honour and propitiate the ancestors continuously.

Other concerns may be manifested during the public part of the mortuary ritual. Funerals sum up the social persona of the deceased, his or her conduct and achievements, and thus not all the deceased are accorded equal treatment. Age, sex and wealth determine the length and elaboration of the funerary process. Only important men and women who have lived a long life and gained respect and admiration in the community become ancestors.

(b) Sculpture. In West and Central Africa in particular, funerary celebrations and commemorations for important individuals are often accompanied by the commissioning and display of works of art. Among the better-known figurative funerary art forms are the terracottas of the AKAN of Ghana, which were first produced as early as the early 18th century. Made for display during formal funerary ceremonies, they represent deceased leaders and their retinues. Stylistically, the terracottas range from abstract forms, representing the head of the deceased only, to fully formed portrait heads and figures. In subsequent memorial ceremonies the terracottas were accorded the treatment befitting the deceased. Other forms of sculpture linked with mortuary ritual include the *nduen fobara* screens of the Kalabari Ijo (*see* IJO, §3). These complex constructions, made from wood and fabric and brightly painted, commemorated the leaders of big trading houses and became the surrogate residence for the spirit of the deceased. They

were kept in the group's meeting-houses and were propitiated when the living sought the protection of the powerful ancestral being.

Similar notions found expression in several of Nigeria's ancient traditions of funerary art. In and around NOK archaeologists have uncovered numerous terracotta sculptures dating back to *c.* 500 BC–AD 200. Terracotta heads with elaborate coiffures, headdresses and adornments, as well as other fragments, may have formed part of life-size sculptures used in a funerary context. Commemorative bronze and terracotta portraits of the rulers and other important male and female leaders in the ancient kingdom of IFE, which flourished from the 12th century AD to the 16th, are certainly conceptually, if not historically, linked to the Nok sculptures. In the Kingdom of Benin, whose dynasty can be traced back to the 14th century AD, the commissioning of brass heads portraying the kings and queen mothers was reminiscent of practices in both Nok and Ife (*see* BENIN). Upon succession, each new Benin king created an altar with numerous art works commemorating his predecessor, a place where the new king could communicate with the deceased.

Not all African funerary sculpture aspires to physical likeness or even takes representational form. The memorial effigies (*vigango*) of the Mijikenda of Kenya are distinguished by their minimalist elegance and clarity of design and only suggest the human form (see fig. 28). They were created and erected for important deceased members of the Chama ya Gohu, a men's secret society. Their particular characteristics, including the representation of such anatomical features on the planklike torso as the umbilicus, pectoral muscles or an indication of the waist, as well as the size of the head and their varying scale, indicate that they were 'personalized' sculptures and represented particular deceased individuals. The larger the effigy, the more important was the dead person's role in society.

28. Ritual installation of a Mijikenda memorial effigy (*vigango*), Kenya; from a photograph by Ernie Wolfe III

(c) Display. Funerary celebrations not only stimulate the creation of sculpture but also are often accompanied by spectacular displays of dances and masquerades. Different genres of performance may be enacted, among them dirges, laments and lyric songs, following a prescribed sequence. Their performance is a religious act as well as an aesthetic one, and they are often judged critically by the audience. Mortuary rites are both dramaturgical and aesthetic events. Such art forms as masquerade, dance, music and sculpture have a role to play in the discourse on life and the afterlife. The arts used in the mortuary rituals of many African societies express and enhance these societies' understanding of the person, the community and the cosmos. Besides mirroring these concepts, arts in the funerary context enact them and through repetitious enactment become instrumental in the constant process of constructing and consolidating the world of which death is very much a part.

Senufo. In her study on art and death in a SENUFO village in northern Côte d'Ivoire, A. J. Glaze discusses funerals as syntheses in which crucial components of social interaction manifest themselves. Most importantly, there is the interaction of man and spirit, then of male and female and lastly of the generations. Such art forms as figurative sculpture, masquerade, dance, music and song are vital parts of the funerals that the Senufo employ when dealing with the potential dangers of the spirits of the dead.

The death of an important elder sets into motion a prescribed chain of events. For a person who has lived a complete and full life, the burial and the funerary ceremony may take place on consecutive days. The corpse is wrapped in colourful and expensive funeral cloths, an expression of the riches he was able to accumulate through his hard work as a farmer. During his lifetime, he had purchased large quantities of finely woven cloth, which his kin now distribute as part of the inheritance. The mourners also contribute cloth to the funerary ceremony. The size and beauty of these cloths reflect upon the status of the dead member of the community and on the generosity of the givers. Social ties and obligations find their tangible and visible expression in this cloth-giving.

Among the main protagonists for the funeral ritual are the secret societies of which the deceased was a member. In the case of a man, the Pondo (Poro) society will be involved; in the case of a woman, the Sandogo (Sande) society will officiate. The maskers wear full raffia skirts and zoomorphic helmet masks with antelope horns, painted in bold black and white bands. The maskers execute their stunning dances in a prescribed sequence, and secret-society members carry out the ritual facilitating the transformation of the deceased into an ancestral being. The flow of events and the overall design of the funerary ritual has led Glaze to view the complete process as an orchestrated work of art.

Cameroon Grassfields. In the Grassfields of the Republic of Cameroon, burial and commemorative funerary ceremonies provide an ideal arena for the display of wealth. The Grassfields kingdoms and chiefdoms are hierarchically organized. Chiefs, office-holders and elders participate in a prestige economy in which each man strives to accumulate wealth in material goods and in people who follow and support him. The size of the funerals—participants may number thousands—and their duration visually express the deceased's importance. The grandeur not only serves to display the prestige and wealth acquired in this world but also ensures that the departed will secure a prominent position among the ancestors.

During his lifetime, a man also becomes a member of secret societies, warrior associations and dancing groups, which command high fees for admission. All these societies and associations have roles to perform at his funeral. In the north-western Cameroon Grassfields, the most important secret society for men is Kweifo, which wields political power. During burials and subsequent funerary celebrations for one of their own, Kweifo maskers give sinister and threatening performances. One mask, Nko, has a voluminous black raffia headdress with a stuffed monkey on its back. When Nko enters the funeral compound, all the women and the non-initiates flee in horror. Women who glance at Nko might bear deformed children. Nko destroys the dwelling of the deceased, throws stones, threatens the mourners and must be physically restrained and appeased by two attendants who 'cool' him down by sprinkling him with ritual substances prepared by an expert. Nko's appearance and actions mark the separation of the deceased from this world; his power lies in the visual expression of the anti-aesthetic, and he will ultimately carry the corpse to the grave and lay it to rest. The sombre messenger of dark, powerful forces disappears until he is called upon for the next funeral. Other masks and dance groups follow in the funerary process, providing entertainment.

Women who have led responsible lives, produced numerous offspring and grown food in abundance are accorded large funerals. While their funerals follow the general structure of the men's, the protagonists differ. Women of the female secret society Kefab, whose membership is open only to successful, wealthy women who have borne children, perform a solemn, slow dance at a woman's funeral, as will all the other associations of which the deceased was a member. Also, her husband may invite a single masker from a society to which he belongs to perform in the deceased's honour. After final farewells, she is laid to rest by the men of the compound.

The funerary rituals for a chief among the BANGWA of the southern Grassfields were observed (see Brain and Pollock). When a chief dies, men of the Night Society secretly perform the last rites before the death has even been announced to the public. The Night Society members, whose duties resemble those of the Kweifo, prepare the corpse for burial. The deceased's successor, a son who had been selected by the departed, anoints the body with medicines. It is then shrouded and buried. Until the day of the public funeral, the fiction is maintained that the chief is still alive. This lavish feast needs weeks, sometimes months, of preparation. Masks are cleaned and repainted, sometimes even newly carved, and costumes repaired. The royal sculptures, including carved wooden portraits of the former chiefs, musical instruments and elaborate objects of daily use, are publicly displayed in the dancing field, where the celebrations take place. The chief's palace is decorated with beautiful and rare cloths. Mourners in their finest attire assemble on the first day of the celebration. They present a stark contrast to the widows, who have smeared their naked bodies with mud. The women wail and lament the death of their husband, a reminder that this splendid celebration is one of death. Neighbouring chiefs bring the colourful masks of their chiefdoms to perform in honour of the deceased.

Bwende. The funerals of the chiefs of the Bwende and their neighbours on the Lower Congo River in the People's Republic of Congo and Zaïre have attracted much attention owing to their stunning visual aspects. In the past the Bwende used to honour departed chiefs with lavish sacrificial gifts of mats and cloths, out of which specialist artists created huge red anthropomorphic funerary bundles known as *niombo* (corpse) that enveloped the dried corpse (see fig. 29). The artist first built a frame for the torso, then constructed the limbs and added a head. The form of the *niombo* itself serves as a medium for communication with the people in the other world. Its open mouth alludes to this communication as does its colour, for red is the colour of mediation among the Bwende and their neighbours. On the day of burial, which followed days of dancing and celebration, the enormous figure was paraded to its grave. An orchestra of large figurated trumpets, slit-gongs and root trumpets accompanied the slow procession of hundreds of mourners. Women wailed and touched the figure one last time, while men carried it to its final resting-place. When the massive figure was lowered into the grave, the mourners leapt into the air simultaneously, thus marking the passage of one of their own. They resumed dancing and feasting and later returned to everyday life.

BIBLIOGRAPHY

A. Van Gennep: *Les Rites de passage* (Paris, 1909; Eng. trans. by M. B. Vizedom and G. L. Caffee, London, 1960/*R* 1977)

J. Goody: *Death, Property and the Ancestors: A Study of the Mortuary Customs of the LoDagaa of West Africa* (London, 1962)

R. Widman: *The Niombo Cult among the Babwende* (Stockholm, 1967)

V. W. Turner: *The Ritual Process: Structure and Anti-structure* (London, 1969/*R* 1974)

R. Brain and A. Pollock: *Bangwa Funerary Sculpture*, A. & Soc. Ser. (London, 1971)

R. Sieber: 'Kwahu Terracottas, Oral Tradition, and Ghanaian History', *African Art and Leadership*, ed. D. Fraser and H. M. Cole (Madison, 1972), pp. 173–83

The Arts of Ghana (exh. cat. by H. M. Cole and D. Ross, Los Angeles, UCLA, Mus. Cult. Hist., 1977–8)

R. Huntington and P. Metcalf: *Celebrations of Death: The Anthropology of Mortuary Ritual* (Cambridge, 1979)

Rites de la mort (exh. cat., Paris, Lab. Ethnol. Mus. Hist. Nat., 1979)

P. Ben-Amos: *The Art of Benin*, Tribal A. (London, 1980)

S. P. Blier: 'The Dance of Death: Notes on Architecture and Staging of Tamberma Funeral Performances', *Res*, 2 (1981), pp. 107–43

A. J. Glaze: *Art and Death in a Senufo Village*, Trad. A. Africa (Bloomington, 1981)

29. Bwende anthropomorphic funerary bundle (*niombo*), Kingoyi, with attendant orchestra, People's Republic of Congo; from a missionary's photograph, *c.* 1900

The Four Moments of the Sun: Kongo Art in Two Worlds (exh. cat. by R. F. Thompson and J. A. Cornet, Washington, DC, N.G.A., 1981–2)

M. Bloch and J. Parry, eds: *Death and the Regeneration of Life* (Cambridge, 1982)

L.-V. Thomas: *La Mort africaine: Idéologie funéraire en Afrique noire* (Paris, 1982)

Vigango: Commemorative Sculpture of the Mijikenda of Kenya (exh. cat., ed. E. Wolfe III; Williamstown, MA, Williams Coll. Mus. A., 1986)

Afr. A., xxi/1 (1987) [incl. 7 essays on 'Death, Ritual and Art in Africa']

N. Barley: *Foreheads of the Dead: An Anthropological View of Kalabari Ancestral Screens* (Washington, DC, 1988) [pubd in conjunction with exh., *Kalabari Ancestral Screens: Levels of Meaning*, Washington, DC, N. Mus. Afr. A., 1988–9]

R. Sieber and R. A. Walker: *African Art in the Cycle of Life* (Washington, DC, 1988) [pubd in conjunction with exh., Washington, DC, N. Mus. Afr. A., 1987–8]

C. M. Geary: 'Männerbünde in Kameruner Grasland', *Männerbande, Männerbünde: Zur Rolle des Mannes im Kulturvergleich*, 2 vols, ed. G. Völger and K. v. Welck; Ethnologica, n. s., 15 (Cologne, 1990), i, pp. 295–300

Likeness and Beyond: Portraits from Africa and the World (exh. cat., New York, Cent. Afr. A., 1990)

Niombo: Begräbnisrituale in Zentralafrika, Ethnologica, n. s., 16 (exh. cat. by A. Reikat, Cologne, Rautenstrauch-Joest-Mus.; Mannheim, Städt. Reiss-Mus.; 1990)

CHRISTRAUD M. GEARY

IV. Imagery and iconography.

1. Symbolism and ritual. 2. Gesture. 3. Portraiture. 4. Physical anomalies. 5. Mother-and-child imagery. 6. Animal imagery. 7. Equestrian imagery. 8. Tricksters.

1. SYMBOLISM AND RITUAL. The overall purpose of African ritual is to promote increase; that is, to stimulate (for example) the fecundity of mothers, the potency of fathers, the fertility of domesticated animals and of the land, spiritually guided sharpness of mind, physical dexterity in both earthly and spiritual contexts, social harmony in the community and good leadership. Symbols have an important role in ritual practices, and sexual symbolism in African art assumes an extremely wide range of expressive forms.

(i) Introduction. (ii) Human increase. (iii) Agricultural increase. (iv) Transition.

(i) Introduction. Africans frequently attribute the decline of particular communities to the neglect of ritual life and can hardly conceive of an existence without children; in addition to being a source of parental pride, children bring status to a family, they enlarge the labour force and the capacity for increase, and they serve after the death of the parent in paying ritual tribute to the deceased and, consequently, in ushering his or her spirit into a cycle of reincarnation and participation in the world of the living. There are overtly sexual sculptures and performances, as well as rituals that specifically address impotence and infertility (see Turner, 1967, pp. 12–14), but references to sexuality are more often embedded symbolically in ritual that appeals to a larger framework. This is because the universe functions as a body, and if one unit (e.g. man's realm) malfunctions, the whole must be treated. Ritual of increase generally functions by connecting the person and the community with fertile functions throughout the cosmos, in order to effect a holistic momentum that results in reproductivity in such specific areas as sexual performance.

The manmade environment often reflects this preoccupation with increase. The layout of villages of the DOGON of Mali symbolizes the human body, complete with male and female sexual organs in its centre. A pillar of earth serves as the male shrine, over which millet beer is poured during rituals. The female shrine consists of simple stones that are used to crush the *lannea acida* seed to produce oil (see Griaule, 1965, pp. 95–7). For the Batammaliba of Benin, the village plan represents the body of the goddess of the earth and underworld. At planting time, the villagers conduct a ritual procession around the village, tracing the outline of her body and identifying their reproductive capacities with hers (see Blier, pp. 90–96). The Batammaliba house, as the seat of reproduction, is a temple to the Creator, and its construction by men and women in concert is likened to the creation of a baby. Each part of the house is given an anatomical name (Blier, pp. 118–26, 199).

African ritual has a communal character. A male initiation, for example, functions not only to advance young men to an adult rank but serves to renew the society as a whole, promoting the entire participating community to a higher plane. Each initiation is, in turn, a re-creation of other markers of time such as original divine creation, birth and death and moments of cosmological significance. Through ritual, each member of the community internalizes cosmological forces to produce an atmosphere of fertilization; among the Temne of Sierra Leone, for example, women begin their initiation for girls by singing of a return to the mythical home of their ancestors (Futha), which is the place of primordial birth where the spiritual body politic meets.

It is often said that Africans think of time, at least symbolically, as cyclical (though some may pursue a linear path in mundane matters), and this is in itself a fertile view. Among the KONGO of Zaïre, the cycle is represented as a diamond or circle on which four cardinal points are indicated, symbolizing the four moments of the sun: rising, zenith, setting and nadir. This symbol relates to the life of man and is basic to motifs and gestures in sculpture, especially funerary sculpture (see 1981 exh. cat., p. 43). For the Temne, the four moments are related to four quadrants of space, indicated not only in the location of ritual sites and in dance movement but also in a small white quartered circle stamped all over the exterior walls of the sacred houses of the men's Pörö society (see fig. 30). As a central symbol of the men's initiation, its full meaning is known only to the elders. They will say only that it is the 'nucleus of the world', but it probably signifies, among other things, semen (see Lamp, in preparation). For the Malinke of Guinea, the fonio seed distributed in the pod of the okra—in cross-section a segmented circle—represents semen (see Dieterlen, p. 126). Among the Temne, okra is certainly a euphemism for semen.

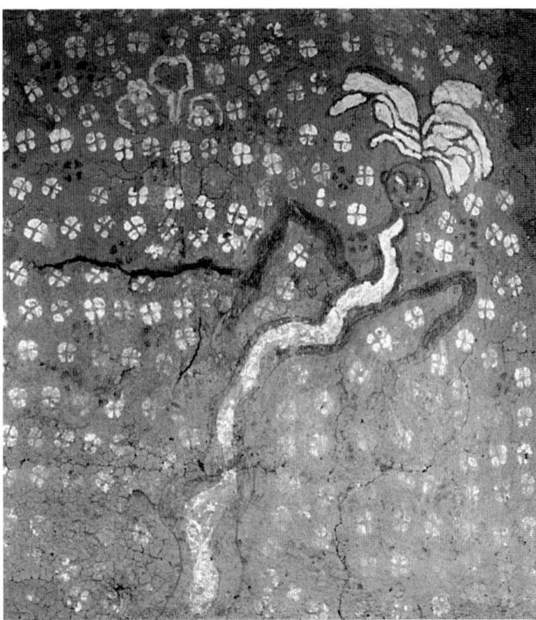

30. Wall painting on a house of the men's Pörö society among the Temne, Sierra Leone, h. *c.* 1 m, featuring serpent image and symbols of the 'nucleus'; from a photograph by Frederick Lamp, 1979

(ii) Human increase. African art and ritual contain many explicit references to sexuality. The monolithic columns of the Nta Ejagham of Nigeria are clear phallic representations of the ancestral power to procreate (*see* EJAGHAM, fig. 2). These are generally *c.* 1.5 m high and are said to represent 30 or 40 generations of deceased chiefs and elders (see Allison, pp. 25–35). Masks used by boys in initiation among the YAKA of Zaïre are replete with images of the phallus, sexual intercourse and birth (see Bourgeois), intended to have an instructive effect on the initiates. Similarly, in the Chizungu initiation of girls among the Bemba of Zambia, the initiates are given clay figures; these often include pregnant or nursing females, nude males and phallic serpents (Richards, pp. 87, 209–11). Women of the Bamana of Mali maintain a nursing maternity figure called Daughter of the Gwan Society (Gwandusu). She is often surrounded by other figures, including one called 'the little pregnant one', and infertile women make sacrifices at the door of her shrine, promising to dedicate future children to her (see 1981 exh. cat., pp. 26–7). An object's function as a fertility figure, however, can only be ascertained when the ethnographic data confirm it. Geometric forms, especially vertical columns, are universal and clearly not always primarily phallic. Even explicit sexual images may have many subtle references peripheral to the goal of increase. For example, well-endowed male and female figures may simply be comic, or they may stress spiritual power, youthfulness or the importance of an ancestor. Public performances of sexually suggestive movement and form may express rebellion or chaos or a reversal of roles. Maternity images (*see* §5 below) have been shown to refer to the mother as progenitor, nurturer and punisher among the IGBO of Nigeria (see 1985 exh. cat., p. 9); as an instrument of divination among the Yombe of Zaïre (see 1978–9 exh. cat. fig. 21); and as the symbol of social prohibition, depicting a woman in sexual abstinence during the two years after a birth, among the YORUBA of Nigeria (see 1977 exh. cat., p. 5). Copulating images embellishing the chairs of Chokwe (*see* CHOKWE AND RELATED PEOPLES) and PENDE royalty in Zaïre are said to refer simply to the chief's dominion over even the most private aspects of community life (Vansina, p. 110).

In contrast, a sexual meaning is often conveyed by imagery that may seem non-sexual to the outside observer. Dogon women who wish to conceive keep a female figure in a shrine (see fig. 31), on which the only direct sexual gesture is the pointing of her hands to her abdomen.

31. Dogon female figure, wood, h. 730 mm, from Mali (New York, Paul and Ruth Tishman Collection)

G. Dieterlen has revealed deeper levels of meaning (see 1981 exh. cat.). The figure's long hair-braid represents the sheat-fish, which in turn symbolizes a foetus in uterine waters; a lip labret represents the fish's barbules. Four rows of beads around the head and four bracelets connect her with the female principle and indicate that she carries in her head the image of the child she wishes to conceive. Her pierced ear lobe suggests sexual penetration. The woman's ornaments denote original creation, the gift of speech. The weaving of words in turn indicates the symbolically rich act of weaving cloth with a shuttle, which has its own sexual connotations in the intersection of warp and weft (see Griaule, 1965, pp. 24–9, 69–74, 138–43). Another instance of such complexity of interpretation is to be found among both the BAGA of Guinea and the Yaka of Zaïre (Bourgeois, p. 48), for whom the house was an erotic image, often included on their masks and headdresses. For the young male still under sexual prohibition before initiation, the house evoked his future right to take a new bride, build his own home and engage there in previously unobtainable pleasures. The Asante of Ghana are well-known for a female figure called *akuaba* (*see* ASANTE AND RELATED PEOPLES, fig. 4), which is worn on a woman's back, tucked into her skirt, much as an infant would be carried. Although its purpose is to effect the birth of a beautiful child, and it is worn by both barren and expectant women (McLeod, pp. 162–6), its form is a simple disc or cylinder with only the slightest suggestion of sexual features or capacities.

Euphemism in sexual imagery relies on the power of the cosmological paradigm. Thus in the ritual of the girls' Chizungu initiation of the Bemba the penis is represented by the farmer's hoe, connecting the penetration of earth and women (see Richards, pp. 102–206). Proverbs of the Bondo (Bundu) association for Temne women refer to the opening and closing of a butterfly's fluttering wings as a symbol of a woman's legs, open in sexual receptivity (see Lamp, 1985, p. 33). A small head or a simple topknot carved on the top of the black helmet masks of the Bondo refers to conception, and the primordial child was said to have been born through a woman's head, both images suggesting that procreation begins in the mind (Lamp, 1985, p. 37). For the Temne, wearing a mask is a metaphor for bearing a child. Women say, 'I have carried the mask on my head' (Sayers, p. 111). Such containers as pots, spoons or gourds often symbolize the female as bearer of the seed or giver of sustenance (see Griaule, 1935; Turner, 1975, pp. 225–6). Among the Batammaliba, the word for gourd means 'multiplication', and when a woman marries she offers her gourd to her husband, who in turn presents it to the ancestors (Blier, pp. 39, 111, 186, 239).

Throughout Africa, the frog refers to birth and rebirth, as a creature of primordial water who emerges on land and heralds transitions in the daily and seasonal cycles (see Lamp, 1978; 1984 exh. cat., p. 50). The python is another powerful symbol of fertility and transition. Among the Baga it appeared to initiates in the form of a tall wooden headdress. As 'author of earthquakes, master of river sources', the python is the spirit of ends and beginnings, or the cycle of death and life (see Appia, p. 161). Among the Batammaliba also, it is a patron of male initiates, who trace its winding path through the village, enter its bedroom shrine and climb out one by one from a circular portal to be reborn (Blier, pp. 101–5).

Among the NDEBELE of South Africa, the progress and propriety of a family are celebrated and measured by the accumulation of elaborate beadwork worn on a woman's body (Schneider, pp. 62–4). She chronicles her own life and the life of the family by wearing, for example, a different type of beaded apron upon marriage or a long strand of beads from the head when her son goes into initiation. Her image, furthermore, becomes transfigured into the beaded doll in the form of a cylinder enveloped in heavy rings given to girls expressly to engender maternal instincts. Here the image of the woman bears a heavy load of generative import.

Royal display is frequently concerned with community increase. On state occasions the king of the Kuba of Zaïre (*see* KUBA (iii)) is surrounded by his scores of wives. This expresses the fecund nature of his own household and, by extension, the fertility of the Kuba community. In the Cameroon Grasslands, an annual ceremony is held to honour the ancestors in which the royal and noble families display their material wealth with maskers (see 1984 exh. cat.). Greater prestige is assumed by families with greater displays of masks. The display itself is a tribute to the achievement of the ancestors, but it could also be said that it perpetuates the well-being and productivity of the family.

(iii) Agricultural increase. The earth is considered to be female in much of African thought, and its working by man is often likened in ritual to coitus (see Blier, p. 39; 1981 exh. cat., p. 22). Dogon female images display on their abdomens a chequerboard pattern that symbolizes the ploughed field. In female initiation ceremonies among the Temne, the men sing of their betrothal: 'I've secured my own plot of ground; when I get there, I'll sow the seed' (see Lamp, 1988, 'Heavenly Bodies'). Champion cultivators among the SENUFO of the Côte d'Ivoire are given a trophy staff with a voluptuous female figure as its finial that had earlier been displayed in the field to encourage the young men. It promises the champion 'a beautiful fiancée, increase for the kinship unit, abundant harvests and many children' (see 1981 exh. cat., p. 48). For the Baga, the image of a beautiful mother with long pendant breasts, called D'mba or Nimba, was danced at both agricultural rituals and marriages. This honouring of the mother for her nurturing of many children served metaphorically to commemorate a bountiful harvest and celebrate the spirits that made it possible. Granary buildings in Africa are, by their very form, often clear symbols of female fecundity and nurturing (see Prussin, pp. 144–69), most notably among the Bororo of Niger. Among the Dogon, the thatched roof of the granary is tied with a cord spiralling down from the peak in reference to the descending acts of original creation, and its door locks are constructed of movable intersecting forms, suggesting sexual intercourse (see Griaule, 1965, pp. 30–34, 41–2, 71–2, 138–41; Laude, p. 60).

The Bamana celebrate agricultural success through the dance of the Chi Wara, whose headdress takes the form of a composite of the antelope, anteater and hornbill. The antelope, whose pawing movements are imitated in dance, suggests male prowess and potency. The anteater is celebrated as a burrowing animal that resembles the farmer tilling the soil and also the penis in penetration. The hornbill is frequently associated with fertility, combining a long, phallic beak with a pot-bellied body. Dancing the Chi Wara in male and female pairs, the male represents the sun and the female the earth. This confluence of the male and female principles links human sexual intercourse, the fertility of the earth, the movements of heavenly bodies and the activities of the natural world (see 1981 exh. cat., pp. 22, 25; Imperato, p. 72; Zahan).

(iv) Transition. Concern for the fate of the dead is based on more than nostalgia and a feeling of personal loss. They enter another world of former and future beings, a world in which the germination of new life takes place. From the Sapi culture of the 15th century in what is now Sierra Leone, small stone figures survive that were probably used in shrines dedicated to ancestors. Two sub-groups of their descendants, the Temne and KISSI, continue a version of the tradition (see Lamp, 1983; Paulme, pp. 141–9). Among the Temne, a stone is taken from the deceased's grave and placed in a shrine that contains many stones representing noble ancestors. To the west of the stones are anthills, representing the entry of the dead into the underworld. The anthills are 'hot' and the stones are 'cool', bathed in cool water during a ritual intended to reincarnate the dead, in concert with the birth of the sun in the cool eastern dawn. This 'House of Stones' is visited at every rite of passage in order to align all phenomena of birth and rebirth. The ancient stones of the Sapi, on the other hand, are revered today as representations of the primordial owners of the land by the immigrant MENDE, who now occupy most of the land where the stone figures are discovered in the fields. The Mende keep them in their fields to encourage the growth of crops, rewarding them for a bountiful harvest and punishing them with a flogging if the crop is poor.

Among the Kongo, death and the continuity of the lineage coincided in the placing of stone images on the graves of the noble dead. Although not actual portraits, they represented the deceased in his or her aspects of highest moral and physical authority. Numerous examples depict nursing mothers. On the chest of such female figures, three keloids are often indicated, representing the three stages of life (child, leader and elder) and by extension the qualities of vitality, leadership and wisdom.

Initiation into adulthood is the quintessential ritual devoted to increase, as children are considered asexual and initiation is thus crucial to their metamorphosis into sexual beings. Among the Loma and Gbande of Liberia, visitors (see Harley; Schwab and Harley) have described an institution called Bön or Pölö that is responsible for the transformation of young men into adults. Although procedure varies greatly from area to area, similar events characterize men's initiation throughout the region. Every four years, boys between the ages of about 8 and 20 are taken into the forest to be guided by their elders for a period ranging from a few days to a full four-year term. In an act symbolizing their death as boys and their rebirth as men, they were formerly thrown over a fence in the darkened forest, believing that they would be impaled on spears or disappear into the open jaws of the ancestral spirit, Landa or Dandai. Landa, the founder of Bön/Pölö, was said to ingest the boys of the village in his belly and, at the end of the initiation, to regurgitate them, fully metamorphosed into adult men, as if giving birth. He appeared in a mask resembling a crocodile head, and the scarification marks given to the boys during initiation were advertised as his tooth-marks.

For the Temne, the organization known as Bondo transforms girls into marriageable young women. Motifs found throughout the initiation are the butterfly and its chrysalis, the serpent that sheds its skin and devours whole living beings, the planted and germinating seed, and the moon that waxes and wanes, dies and is reborn. The final ceremonies of Bondo are a microcosm of fertile processes that turn the girls, through their ritual immersion in universal flow, into reproductive women. These 'graduation' ceremonies are probably scheduled to coincide with the girls' period of most likely fertilization, when they are released to their new husbands (see Lamp, 1988, 'An Opera...').

Their graduation (the 'pouring out' or 'birth-giving') involves four distinct acts. In the first (the 'transferring') the girls, still painted white (symbolizing spiritual invisibility) from their year in initiation, 'sweep the way' through the village in a probable reference to the cleansing action of menstruation. Nurturing and death are then contrasted in a dance involving a black cooking pot and a mysterious white bundle. A chaotic rampage follows, in which the villagers perform a symbolic 'uprooting' and 'transplanting'. Finally the villagers come together in a circle of cooperation to re-enact the cultivation of their fields and allude through song to the 'sowing of the seed', that is, the impregnation of the new brides. In the second act (the 'uprooting by the serpent') the ancestral serpent spirit returns in the night in the medium of a woman whining eerily through the village. Shut inside the initiation house, the initiates are said to have been devoured by the serpent. In the darkness of the early morning, the house is demolished as a metaphor for the opening of the serpent's belly, and the girls are rushed to the river to re-enact primordial birth, emerging through water.

The third act is the dance of the mask in the form of a butterfly chrysalis (Nöwo or Sowo). Beginning in the dimness of pre-dawn and ending at the rising of the sun, she symbolizes not only metamorphosis but also an enlightening of the mind that is essential to productivity. In the final act, all 'birth-givers' are saluted, a symbolic womb is created in the central village meeting-house, and the women 'descend' from the river through the village in a serpentine spiral to deposit the initiates, concealed under a canopy, in the meeting-house. Here they are described in song as 'germinating greens'. Thus, through the metaphorical association of the ritual acts of the girls and their community with productive forces throughout the cosmos, the increase of that community is ensured for another year.

BIBLIOGRAPHY

E. Sayers: 'A Few Temne Songs', *Sierra Leone Stud.*, x (1927), pp. 109–11
M. Griaule: 'Calebasses', *A. & Métiers Graph.*, 45 (1935), pp. 45–8
G. W. Harley: *Notes on the Poro in Liberia*, Pap. Peabody Mus. Archaeol. & Ethnol., xix/2 (Cambridge, MA, 1941)
B. Appia: 'Masques de Guinée française et de Casamance', *J. Africanistes*, xiii (1943), pp. 153–82
G. Schwab and G. Harley: *Tribes of the Liberian Hinterland*, Pap. Peabody Mus. Archaeol. & Ethnol., xxxi (Cambridge, MA, 1947)
M. Griaule: *Dieu d'eau: Entretiens avec Ogotemmêli* (Paris, 1948; Eng. trans. as *Conversations with Ogotemmêli: An Introduction to Dogon Religious Ideas*, London, 1965)
D. Paulme: *Les Gens du riz* (Paris, 1954)
A. I. Richards: *Chisungu: A Girls' Initiation Ceremony among the Bemba of Northern Rhodesia* (London, 1956/*R* as *Chisungu: A Girls' Initiation Ceremony among the Bemba of Zambia*, 1982)
G. Dieterlen: 'The Mande Creation Myth', *Africa*, xxvii/2 (1957), pp. 124–38
V. Turner: *The Forest of Symbols: Aspects of Ndembu Ritual* (Ithaca, NY, 1967/*R* 1970)
P. Allison: *African Stone Sculpture* (London, 1968)
P. J. Imperato: 'The Dance of the Tyi Wara', *Afr. A.*, iv/1 (1970), pp. 8–13
L. Prussin: 'West African Mud Granaries', *Paideuma*, xviii (1972), pp. 144–69
J. Laude: *African Art of the Dogon* (New York, 1973)
V. Turner: *Revelation and Divination in Ndembu Ritual*, Symbol, Myth and Ritual (Ithaca, NY, 1975)
Traditional Art of the Nigerian Peoples: The Milton D. Ratner Family Collection (exh. cat. by H. J. Drewal, Washington, DC, Mus. Afr. A., 1977)
F. Lamp: 'Frogs into Princes: The Temne Rabai Initiation', *Afr. A.*, xi/2 (1978), pp. 34–49, 94–5
A Survey of Zairian Art: The Bronson Collection (exh. cat. by J. Cornet; Raleigh, NC Mus. A.; Washington, DC, Mus. Afr. A.; Los Angeles, CA, Nat. Hist. Mus.; 1978–9)
D. Zahan: *Antilopes du soleil: Arts et rites agraires d'Afrique noire* (Vienna, 1980)
M. McLeod: *The Asante* (London, 1981)
For Spirits and Kings: African Art from the Paul and Ruth Tishman Collection (exh. cat., ed. S. M. Vogel; New York, Met., 1981)
The Four Moments of the Sun: Kongo Art in Two Worlds (exh. cat. by R. F. Thompson and J. A. Cornet, Washington, DC, N.G.A., 1981–2)
A. P. Bourgeois: 'Yaka Masks and Sexual Imagery', *Afr. A.*, xv/2 (1982), pp. 47–50, 87
F. Lamp: 'House of Stones: Memorial Art of Fifteenth-century Sierra Leone', *A. Bull.*, lxv/2 (1983), pp. 219–37
J. Vansina: *Art History in Africa: An Introduction to Method* (New York, 1984)
The Art of Cameroon (exh. cat. by T. Northern, Washington, DC, Smithsonian Inst. Traveling Exh. Serv., 1984)
F. Lamp: 'Cosmos, Cosmetics, and the Spirit of Bondo', *Afr. A.*, xviii/3 (1985), pp. 28–43, 98–9
E. A. Schneider: 'Ndebele Mural Art', *Afr. A.*, xviii/3 (1985), pp. 60–67
Mother and Child in African Sculpture (exh. cat. by H. Cole, Los Angeles, CA, Co. Mus. A., 1985)
S. P. Blier: *The Anatomy of Architecture: Ontology and Metaphor in Batammaliba Architectural Expression*, Res Monographs in Anthropology and Aesthetics (Cambridge, 1987)
F. Lamp: 'An Opera of the West African Bondo: The Act, Ideas and the Word', *Drama Rev.*, xxxii/2 (1988), pp. 83–101
——: 'Heavenly Bodies: Menses, Moon and Rituals of License among the Temne of Sierra Leone', *Blood Magic: The Anthropology of Menstruation*, ed. T. Buckley and A. Gottlieb (Berkeley, 1988), pp. 210–31
——: *The Art of Balancing Spatial and Temporal Valuation among the Temne* (in preparation)

FREDERICK LAMP

2. GESTURE. In African art, as in other contexts, gestures can both express an emotional condition or use established conventions to convey meaning (*see* GESTURE). In other words they define unspoken aspects of a work's meaning and significance. Some gestures have symbolic meanings; others provide visual cues expressive of emotions. Aesthetic concerns also influence gesture. Among the YORUBA of Nigeria, for whom the predominating aesthetic is one of symmetry, sculptures often emphasize the balanced placement of hands on parts of the body or on objects that are held (see fig. 32), while among the BAULE of Côte d'Ivoire, where asymmetry is a widespread feature, slight shifts from a strictly symmetrical portrayal are often introduced. Material and medium may affect the gestures portrayed in African art. DOGON works in iron (Mali) show a distinctive resistant bend in their gestures, a feature imparted by the material itself. The gestural expressions of LOBI wood sculptures in Burkina

32. Yoruba *edan* Ogboni staffs, brass, h. 195 mm (Amsterdam, private collection)

Faso and Côte d'Ivoire often intentionally draw on the natural curves, bends and texture of the wood (see fig. 38 below), with artists using the twisting form of a branch to reinforce the angling of an arm. Among the Batammaliba (Tamberma), the living branch is considered an essential component of the vitality of the sculpture. A group of artists, gazing up at the branches of a tree, will discuss the virtues of a particular section as they mentally superimpose a figure on it, noting the placement of the head, hands, torso and legs. After reaching a decision, one of them will climb up to cut the chosen branch for carving. Sometimes gestures are incorporated or omitted for functional reasons. The outstretched arms of Fanti and Asante *akuaba* figures, for example (*see* ASANTE AND RELATED PEOPLES, fig. 4), serve as a means of support when such figures are worn tucked into a woman's wrapper against her back. In FON, TEKE and some KONGO power figures the torso is sometimes bound, wrapped or otherwise covered, and one frequently finds a minimalization or outright elimination of gestures that would be hidden from view. Some of the most interesting figural representations in African art are those associated with body alterations and deformities, the one-legged, no-headed, no-armed images and similar forms that deviate from nature (*see* §4 below). For the Lobi, figures with more than two arms (see fig. 38 below) denote enhanced protective power.

(i) Religious themes. (ii) Social roles. (iii) Emotional expression.

(i) Religious themes. With no single gestural language employed throughout African art, gestures must be understood according to their cultural context. This is perhaps best illustrated by the examples of gestures for prayer. In Kongo art, prayer is defined by the gesture of palms drawn to the stomach. Among the Kaka, prayer to the deity Nwie, creator of earth and sky, is defined by the gesture of the right hand outstretched, palm up. In contrast, Mambila sculptures depict a person praying with arms held tightly to the chest. Among the Baule the right hand clasped in the palm of the left is identified with ceremonies to supplicate the earth, particularly after a crime against the earth has been committed. For the Dogon, raised arms are identified with prayers to the deity Amma.

Gestures in African art also convey other religious themes. In Yoruba sculptures, the diversity of such gestures is particularly striking and is used to identify affiliation to a religious association. Sculptures of the Ogboni society, dedicated to the deity of the earth, are recognized by the gesture of left hand fisted over right hand to hide an extended right thumb (see fig. 32). The sculptures of Ogun, god of iron and war, are characterized both by actions related to smithing and by the holding aloft of fanlike Ogun insignia. Sculptures dedicated to Eshu, the trickster–messenger deity (*see* §8 below), are often associated with thumb-sucking or whistle-blowing gestures. Shango, the god of lightning and thunder, is represented both by the action of balancing two celts on top of the head and by gestures in which Shango staffs and rattles are displayed. Memorial twin figures (*ibeji*) are recognized by their characteristic frontal pose, the hands held rigidly to the side.

(ii) Social roles. Gestures can be used to convey social roles and identities. This is particularly well defined in the Cameroon Grassfields, where gestures identify works as representing ruler, court servant, criminal or slave (*see* BAMILEKE AND RELATED PEOPLES; *see also* BAMUM). Kings are frequently seated, one hand supporting the chin, the other resting on the knee. This is a gesture assumed by judges when reflecting on legal matters, and it underscores the king's important subsidiary role as adjudicator. Royal retainers are most frequently identified by a gesture in which one hand is placed in front of the mouth, a pose traditionally assumed by servants when approaching the king. In other examples, servants are shown presenting objects of state (as would be done at prescribed times during ceremonies). Criminals and prisoners are often shown with anguished, angled and uncomfortable gestures and postures, in marked contrast to the more formally composed gestures of royalty.

Further examples of gestures being used to identify social position are found in Zaïre among the Chokwe, where powerful men and elders are frequently portrayed in the seated 'hocker' position, with elbows resting on upraised knees (*see* CHOKWE AND RELATED PEOPLES). Teke sculptures representing diviner-healers (*nganga*) are defined by a modified version of this same gesture. Baule elders, in contrast, are often identified by gestures in which the hand touches their carefully braided beards, and Lega sculptures of Zaïre representing elderly *bwami* initiates are recognized through gestural caricature, with rounded back and stooped body suggesting the weight of their years and responsibilities (*see* LEGA AND RELATED PEOPLES).

Gestural reference may be used to identify gender and social role. In Yoruba art, female sculptures with hands on the solar plexus are said to represent expectant women. Among the Dogon, pregnancy is suggested by the gesture of forearms resting against the abdomen (see fig. 31 above); sculptures with this gesture are found on altars dedicated to women who died while pregnant. In Kongo art the female gesture of palms against the stomach represents a woman communicating with the child she carries. Another important female gesture shows the placement of hands on the breast. For the Yoruba this gesture suggests the nursing mother and, by extension, the general idea of motherhood and generosity (see fig. 32). Among the Baule and Asante, hands supporting the breasts allude to the importance of maternal nurturing.

(iii) Emotional expression. Other gestures are used to convey emotion. For the Lobi the arms drawn behind the back imply anguish, while among the BANGWA and other Cameroon Grassfield groups the placement of the arms behind the head represents a brooding person or a child who is contemplating. Gestures used to portray sadness, sorrow, hardship and distress vary between peoples. The standard image of mourning and sorrow in such Zaïre cultures as the Kongo, Chokwe, LUBA and Ndembu is the hand drawn upwards to clasp or support the head, neck, cheek or chest while weeping or pondering in grief. Variations on this basic form include the Chokwe gesture of the hand on the mouth, which signifies someone with no chance in life. In Kongo sculptures sadness is conveyed in a number of ways. Both arms drawn upwards towards the mouth connote enormous grief; arms held aloft indicate crying or lamentation; touching the chin or cupping it with one's hand suggests the state of pondering and sadness; wrapping one arm about the body portrays loneliness and self-comfort; an outstretched arm indicates hunger; the arm crossed in front of the chest communicates coldness and silence; hands placed on the stomach or in an akimbo position express idleness; and a hand hanging loosely by the side suggests shame.

Gestures may be used in place of verbal messages, as an extension of speech. One of the most frequently seen has the hand being brought up towards the chin or mouth. This gesture is common in sculptures of the Bafo and Bakundu of southern Cameroon, where it suggests the action of swearing an oath. A single finger drawn up to the mouth represents the same idea among Kongo and Cameroon Grassfields groups. Pende sculptures that incorporate a hand gesturing towards the mouth define instead the moment of surprise when hearing some shocking news. Similarly, the hand-to-the-mouth gesture in Chokwe art is used to portray one who is startled on receiving secret information. Among the Luba, figures with this gesture are worn by women during childbirth, suggesting the newsworthiness and heightened excitement of the occasion.

Gesture may be used to elicit specific responses in the onlooker. Thus the Mambila gesture of arms outstretched to the side, frequently seen in sculptures of this society, is identified as a pose of protection or guardianship and may be intended to effect in the Mambila viewer a response of either security or fear depending on the person's role and relationship to the sculpture. The gestures of certain Lobi sculptures, believed to have a protective role in the house, can also be best understood in this way. Some figures turn their heads to the side as a signal of attentiveness; others raise one or both arms above the head defensively. Still others are depicted stretching out their arms horizontally to bar enemies from entering the house. Seeing such figures may invoke a response of restraint on the part of those intending harm to the house or its occupants. Gestural forms also play a significant part in helping to channel the viewer's emotional response to a work. A sculpture of an exuberant mother presenting her child in public invites an emotional response with the enthusiastic, forward-thrusting movement of her arms and the child she holds within them. A shrine figure may similarly draw an onlooker to the image through the gesture of outstretched hands, an action that for the IGBO of Nigeria conveys both the idea of a deity's request for recognition and devotion and the wish on the part of his or her faithful worshippers for generous aid.

As the eye will generally follow the dominant line of a work, attention may be directed by gesture to important details. A mother portrayed with hands reaching towards her child, for example, directs attention to the child's face, reinforcing the maternal theme. A hand raised to stroke a beard draws the eye to the beard, underscoring both the masculinity of the figure and his status as elder. In seated or kneeling figures, the depiction of hands resting on the knees reinforces the stability of persons portrayed in these works.

BIBLIOGRAPHY

R. Lecoq: *Les Bamileke* (Paris, 1953)
K. E. Laman: *The Kongo*, 3 vols, Studia Ethnographica Upsaliensia, iv, viii, xii (Uppsala, 1953–68)
L. de Sousberghe: *L'Art Pende* (Brussels, 1958)
P. Gebauer: *Spider Divination in the Cameroons*, Milwaukee, WI, Pub. Mus. Publications in Anthropology, x (Milwaukee, 1964)
W. Fagg: *Tribes and Forms in African Art* (New York, 1965)
M. Griaule and G. Dieterlen: *Le Renard pâle: Le Mythe cosmogonique*, Trav. & Mém. Inst. Ethnol., lxxii (Paris, 1965; Eng. trans., 1986)
K. Krieger: *Westafrikanische Plastik*, 3 vols, Veröff. Mus. Vlkerknd., Berlin, n. s. 7, Abt. Afrika, ii (Berlin, 1965–9) [col. cat.]
M.-L. Bastin: 'L'Art d'un peuple d'Angola, I: Chokwe'/'Arts of the Angolan Peoples, I: Chokwe', *Afr. A.*, ii/1 (1968), pp. 40–47, 60–64
W. Fagg: *African Tribal Images: The Katherine White Reswick Collection* (Cleveland, 1968)
R. Brain and A. Pollock: *Bangwa Funerary Sculpture*, A. & Soc. Ser. (London, 1971)
M. Lima: *Fonctions sociologiques des figurines de culte Hamba dans la société et dans la culture Tshokwe (Angola)* (Luanda, 1971)
C. Odugbesan: 'Femininity in Yoruba Religious Art', *Man in Africa*, ed. M. Douglas and P. M. Kaberry (London, 1971), pp. 199–211
R. F. Thompson: *Black Gods and Kings: Yoruba Art at UCLA* (Los Angeles, 1971/*R* Bloomington and London, 1976)
D. P. Biebuyck: 'The *Kindi* Aristocrats and their Art among the Lega', *African Art and Leadership*, ed. D. Fraser and H. M. Cole (Madison, 1972), pp. 7–20

N. B. Schwartz: *Mambila: Art and Material Culture*, Milwaukee, WI, Pub. Mus. Publications, iv (Milwaukee, 1972)
D. P. Biebuyck: *Lega Culture: Art, Initiation, and Moral Philosophy among a Central African People* (Berkeley, 1973)
R. Lehuard: *Statuaire du Stanley-Pool* (Villiers-le-Bel, 1974)
African Art in Motion: Icon and Act (exh. cat. by R. F. Thompson, Washington, DC, N.G.A.; Los Angeles, UCLA, Wight A.G.; 1974)
V. Guerry: *Life with the Baule* (New York, 1975)
The Arts of Ghana (exh. cat. by H. M. Cole and D. H. Ross, Los Angeles, UCLA, Wight A.G.; Minneapolis, MN, Walker A. Cent.; Dallas, TX, Mus. F.A.; 1977–8)
Traditional Art of the Nigerian Peoples: The Milton D. Ratner Family Collection (exh. cat. by H. J. Drewal, Washington, DC, Mus. Afr. A., 1977)
A. P. Bourgeois: 'Mbwoolo Sculpture of the Yaka', *Afr. A.*, xii/3 (1979), pp. 58–61
P. Gebauer: *Art of Cameroon* (Portland, OR, 1979)
P. Ben-Amos: *The Art of Benin*, Tribal A. (London, 1980)
P. L. Ravenhill: *Baule Statuary Art: Meaning and Modernization*, Working Pap. Trad. A., v (Philadelphia, 1980)
S. M. Vogel: *Beauty in the Eyes of the Baule: Aesthetics and Cultural Values*, Working Pap. Trad. A., vi (Philadelphia, 1980)
G. Dieterlen: 'Female Figure', *For Spirits and Kings: African Art from the Paul and Ruth Tishman Collection* (exh. cat., ed. S. M. Vogel; New York, Met., 1981), pp. 16–17
C. Geary: 'Bamum Thrones and Stools', *Afr. A.*, xiv/4 (1981), pp. 32–43
R. Kauenhoven-Janzen: 'Chokwe Thrones', *Afr. A.*, xiv/3 (1981), pp. 69–74
Kunst und Religion der Lobi (exh. cat. by P. Meyer, Zurich, Mus. Rietberg, 1981)
The Four Moments of the Sun: Kongo Art in Two Worlds (exh. cat. by R. F. Thompson and J. A. Cornet, Washington, DC, N.G.A., 1981–2)
Gestures in African Art (exh. cat. by S. P. Blier, New York, Kahan Gal. Afr. A., 1982)
Igbo Arts: Community and Cosmos (exh. cat. by H. M. Cole and C. C. Aniakor, Los Angeles, UCLA, Mus. Cult. Hist., 1984–6)

SUSAN PRESTON BLIER

3. PORTRAITURE. African portraits are simultaneously personal, because recognition of the subject's identity depends upon knowledge of the community and person portrayed, and impersonal, in that they stress social identity rather than individual likeness. Characteristically, name and context particularize the image, and representation of the subject is correct rather than idiosyncratic. Such is the economy of African sculpture that portraits embody individual and social identities simultaneously: the image of a king may represent a particular king and all kings; a woman's commemorative mask may stand for a particular woman and all similarly entitled women.

(i) Introduction. (ii) Anthropomorphic images. (iii) Representational and idealized images. (iv) Emblematic portraits.

(i) Introduction. African portraits identify important individuals within the often overlapping frameworks of ancestor cult, political organization and ritual activity. Most African portraits serve as memorials and so represent specific ancestors whose responsibility it is to aid the living by solving vital problems, by shielding them from harm and by contributing to their material success. Individuals who have demonstrated their capabilities during a lifetime of success are selected as most likely to be efficacious ancestral forces. Thus, African memorial portraits recognize, for example, heads of household, heads of state, women of strength and courage, priests and ritual actors, presenting them in terms of social identity rather than idiosyncratic personality and holding them up as embodying ideals of society and exemplifying correct behaviour. While portraiture is the successful person's privilege and honour, and remembrance his or her reward, a portrait's generalized nature shows that he or she is not differentiated for individual qualities but for being an admired example of the ideal. Nigerian Ijo funerary screens (*see* IJO, fig. 2) show the subject of the portrait as a member of a group but distinguish him by centrality and size rather than by physiognomic characteristics. The Oron of south-eastern Nigeria show their respect for successful individuals by the relative articulation of the memorial image: ordinary individuals are represented by uncarved sticks or staffs, leaders by stylized but highly differentiated and elaborately rendered figural sculpture (see Nicklin).

Any account of portraiture in African art is complicated by lack of recognition of images as portraits by cultural outsiders. Factors contributing to this failure include stylized ideals of comportment, an aesthetic of generalization and conventions of identification and record-keeping that differ from Western conventions. The specific identities of many African portrait subjects are unknown, because the works have been separated from their cultural context. Thus many images labelled by scholars 'ancestor figures' are actually unidentified portraits.

The general problem of recognition is demonstrated by FON commemorative tableaux (see 1985 exh. cat.; *see also* §(ii) below). In these tableaux the links between object and individual identity are extra-aesthetic and often ephemeral, dependent on cultural knowledge not readily accessible to an outsider. Tableau messages originate in discussions between donor and artist on the sentiments to be conveyed and on the selection of appropriate symbols. No-one is responsible for preserving a narrative explanation of the cryptic visual allusions and metaphoric references in the tableau; so, unless it contains a particularly striking or cleverly conceived message, the meaning will be lost with the passage of time.

The identity of African portraits is established or confirmed by association with the subject through siting, biographical references, use of actual clothing, relics or—most importantly—name rather than by literal physical description. Because name and context particularize the African image rather than physical likeness, dramatically disparate visual configurations work as portraits. The Kurumba of Burkina Faso, for example, represent high-ranking elders by masquerades depicting the protective antelope (*Hippotragus koba*), the totem of most Kurumba clans. Headdresses are carved at the death of an individual to enhance his prestige, and, when danced at funerals and public performances following the funeral, the masquerades serve as physical re-embodiments of the deceased and are addressed with his name (see Roy, pp. 198–202; *see also* §VI, 3 below). In Benin, Battamaliba families honour recently deceased elders by giving them the attribute of youth, portraying them in the form of houses wearing the garments of initiation (see Blier, 1987; *see also* §1(ii) above).

In contrast, the YORUBA of southern Nigeria use generalized human figures to commemorate deceased twins. These diminutive figures are linked to their subjects by being gender-specific and having appropriate lineage and scarification marks. The family addresses the image by name and makes gifts appropriate to the deceased child's place in the lineage (see Drewal). The DAN of Liberia and Côte d'Ivoire commission portraits of favourite wives from skilled carvers. These images, made after a meeting between artist and subject, are unusually specific, reflecting individual physiognomies, and, like most African portraits, they also bear the name of the subject (see 1976 exh. cat.).

Even the most representational African portrait, however, tends to be idealized, since the African aesthetic is a generalizing one. A realistic depiction of age or peculiarity implies a lack of respect for the subject (see Brain and Pollock; Ben-Amos, 1980). Completeness rather than verisimilitude may be the representational ideal, as it is for the exceptionally naturalistic commemorative portraits used by the Owo Yoruba (Abiodun, 1976).

An overview of African portrait images produces three broad and slightly overlapping categories. The largest category is that of generalized anthropomorphic images; the others are representational and idealized images and emblematic portraits.

(ii) Anthropomorphic images. Portraits taking this form are individuated by means of such specific references to the subject as naming. The Okpella of southern Nigeria recognize a woman's commemorative masquerade by personal and praise names. Although such a masquerade may dance in public during the lifetime of its subject, it assumes her name only after her death. It is not obviously distinguishable as a likeness, with its stylized features and elaborate coiffure. Instead, identity is established by its name and its location within the kin group that accompanies the masquerade when it appears in public during the annual ancestral festival (see fig. 33; Borgatti, 1979).

Images may be further identified through specific sculptural references to the subject's coiffure and personal decoration, a method used by AKAN artists to personalize commemorative terracotta portraits (see 1977–8 exh. cat.; Preston; Sieber; Soppelsa; Visona). Iconographic devices may also 'name' subjects: for example, portraits of Kuba kings (*see* KUBA (iii)) in Zaïre reflect ideals of body image and comportment, individuated only by an emblem shown at the base of the figure (see Vansina; Rosenwald). The 17th-century King Shyaam A-Mbul A-Ngoong is recognized by his game-board, while the 18th-century King Misha Mi-Shyaang A-Mbul (formerly Bom Bosh) is identified by a carved cup with its handle carved in the form of a human hand (see fig. 34).

The EDO of Benin depict kings in relief sculpture by associating a generalized figure with specific attributes or images linked to events occurring during his reign. The 16th-century Oba Ozolua, known as 'the conqueror', wears full battledress and carries a shield on his left arm; he brandishes a sword in his right hand and holds the severed head of an enemy in his left. His son, Esigie (1515–20), is portrayed wearing the red parrot-feather regalia of a senior priest of the Ovia cult, which he introduced to the palace during his rule (see Blackmun, 'Remembering...'). More complex biographical references are incorporated into the images of 17th- and 18th-century kings. The early 17th-century ruler Oba Ewuakpe's idiosyncratic headgear and staff and pair of emaciated attendants are explained by oral traditions of the period and the known problems he faced in acceding to the throne (see Ben-Amos, 1983).

33. Okpella memorial portrait mask of Olimi Elewo (made 1935) sitting with her mask herald and family members at the Olimi festival, New Iddo, Nigeria; from a photograph by Jean M. Borgatti

Fon memorial tableaux commemorate the honoured dead by depicting them in positions of authority through the idiom of royal dress, stance or regalia or by showing an individual at work. The subject of the sculpture holds a central position in the composition, with the donor's figure often occupying a more peripheral zone. Although the figures are generic in form, specific names may be directly represented in rebus form within the composition, as in an example where images of fish (*hue*) and a grinding stone (*li*) created the proper syllabic references to the subject's name (see 1985 exh. cat., p. 20). Alternatively, visual puns on the family or given name may establish identification, or the name may be spelt out in letters on a small metal plate.

The IBIBIO living in the area of Ikot Ekpene in Nigeria celebrate men of distinction with banners of cloth appliqué and patchwork. In the past, the banner-maker would be invited to stay at the compound of the deceased for several months in order to learn his life history, especially his acts of bravery, so that the shrine cloth would portray his achievements in full (see Salmons). A more recent practice is for the artist to absorb information about his subject during funeral ceremonies, where the exploits of the deceased are praised in song and mime.

34. Figure of the Kuba king Misha Mi-Shyaang A-Mbul, wood, h. 495 mm, from Zaïre, *c.* 1750 (New York, The Brooklyn Museum)

In southern MADAGASCAR, the Antanosy, Bara, Sihanaka, Antaimoro and Mahafaly remember individuals with sculptures that present them in the context of their actual possessions or in terms of their life history. One memorial sculpture by the Antanosy sculptor Fesira depicts the subject seated at the side of a large monument comprising two images that recall important aspects of his life: his service with the French authorities as a mounted policeman and his purchase of the first motor-car in the village (see Mack).

Such groups as the KONGO, BEMBE and Bwende of Zaïre identify a portrait by incorporating relics from the body of the deceased into the memorial figure. The Bwende artist Makoza of Kingoyi (*fl c.* 1900) also studied the face and body of the deceased whose mummy he was making in order accurately to represent such features as filed teeth and scarification (see 1981–2 exh. cat., pp. 60–61).

Contextual association of image and subject is stressed by the BAULE, whose portrait masks publicly express the admiration evoked by some exceptional quality associated with the subject (see Vogel). In such examples, identification is completed by the subject's partnering the portrait mask in performance. The masks also bear the names of their subjects and often wear clothing or accessories owned by them.

(iii) Representational and idealized images. Representational images are physiognomic likenesses, the subject (or an appropriate relative) having sat for the artist. Such portraits are found among the Bamileke (*see* BAMILEKE AND RELATED PEOPLES) and BANGWA of Cameroon (see Brain and Pollock; Lecoq; Rudy; Harter) and the Hemba of Zaïre (see Neyt and de Stryker). In other cases, the artist may simply familiarize himself with the individual, executing the work without further visual reference to the subject (see Himmelheber; 1981–2 exh. cat.).

Even the most representational African portraits idealize and generalize their subjects, demonstrating what Rowland Abiodun (1976) has called a 'controlled naturalism' in contrast to the idiosyncratic or literal naturalism of much Western portraiture. An Ijebu Yoruba artist's rendering of Queen Victoria based on her 1887 Jubilee portrait clearly illustrates this bias in African portraiture (see fig. 35). In keeping with Yoruba principles of representation, the artist has depicted the Queen as a respected and powerful member of society, treating her fan as the equivalent of the Yoruba royal fly-whisk and dramatizing her head and hand to signal their importance. (In Yoruba thought the head is the seat of an individual's luck, wisdom and destiny and consequently is emphasized, comprising up to a quarter of the total composition.) Additionally, the artist has honoured the Queen with youth, smoothing her wrinkles, firming up her chin and regularizing her features to reveal the strength and beauty within.

(iv) Emblematic portraits. Just as the most representational images may be seen to draw upon the generalizing aesthetic that informs all African portraits, the emblematic portrait takes the cultural and historic markers present in all the images and raises them to a further degree of abstraction. Emblematic portraits use symbolic devices to evoke an image of the subject in the mind's eye of the viewer. They are often non-anthropomorphic and may include an assemblage of goods or visual referents that recall the individual to the spectator. Generally, they may be said to represent an intellectualized vision of the subject and his personality or the spiritual side of the individual not normally visible. The imagery may be either personal and subtle, and therefore dependent upon the viewer's specialized knowledge, or public and dramatic, to impress more firmly on the audience the particular characteristics or achievements of the individual portrayed.

Many Nigerian groups remember male ancestors with non-anthropomorphic characterizations based on shrouds, a classic 'ghost form' (see fig. 36). The distribution of this commemorative masquerade follows the path of the Niger and the Benue rivers with a clustering in the

35. Ijebu Yoruba figure of Queen Victoria, wood, h. 622 mm, from Nigeria, after 1887 (Los Angeles, CA, University of California, Fowler Museum of Cultural History)

confluence area. Among the Edo-speaking Okpella, these Dead Fathers return for an annual celebration with their living kin during a festival of ancestors. The masquerade takes the form of a cloth sack constructed of expensive, handwoven cloth, some of it with ritual significance, held together at the top around a stick that may be used to extend its height. A Dead Father may be simultaneously general and specific: the commemorative masquerade with the greatest seniority represents simultaneously all deceased heads of household in the congregation as well as the specific individual whose name it bears. The masquerade's vigorous performance asserts masculinity in the dynamic expression of energy, and visual references to men's title status may be included to indicate a social ideal of achievement. Relics from the body of the deceased may be sewn into the costume to personalize the representation in an incontrovertible way. Attendants related to the deceased accompany the masquerade, thus placing the apparition in a lineage group, and members of the community salute it by name, using the greetings for welcoming someone who has come back from a long journey and thus offering further evidence of its identity. Comparable commemorative masks for men occur among the Yoruba, the IDOMA, the Igbira, the IGALU, the IGBO and other northern Edo groups besides the Okpella. The nuancing of the imagery varies from group to group.

The Fon of Benin (see Blier, 1990) make masterful emblematic portraits in both sculpture and cloth appliqué, relying for identification upon literary reference (proverbs

36. Okpella commemorative masks of the deceased chiefs Ikor and Sado, Afokpella, Imaiamune Quarter, Nigeria; from a photograph by Jean M. Borgatti, 1972

and history) and indirection (using images in a rebus fashion to spell the name of the subject). Fon royal portraits range from such large-scale wooden sculptures as the allegorical portrait of *King Glele* (Paris, Mus. Homme), depicting a man with the head of a lion, to such two-dimensional works as the wall hanging dedicated to him and featuring the lion image, used because his name-sentence states, 'I am the lion's whelp who sows terror as soon as his teeth have sprouted'. Glele's mission as king was to avenge his father's defeat at the hands of the neighbouring Yoruba at Abeokuta: the name he chose upon ascending the throne clearly states this goal.

BIBLIOGRAPHY

GENERAL

K. Nicklin: *Guide to the National Museum, Oron* (Lagos, n.d.)
R. Lecoq: *Les Bamileke* (Paris, 1953)
R. Horton: *Kalabari Sculpture* (Lagos, 1965)
R. Brain and A. Pollock: *Bangwa Funerary Sculpture*, A. & Soc. Ser. (London, 1971)
R. F. Thompson: *Black Gods and Kings: Yoruba Art at UCLA* (Los Angeles, 1971/*R* Bloomington and London, 1976)
G. Dieterlen, ed.: *La Nation de personne en Afrique Noire* (Paris, 1973)
R. Lehuard: *Statuaire du Stanley-Pool* (Villiers-le-Bel, 1974)
J. Rosenwald: 'Kuba King Figures', *Afr. A.*, vii/2 (1974), pp. 26–31, 92
F. Neyt and L. de Stryker: *Approche des arts Hemba*, Col. A. Afrique Noire, xi, suppl. (Villiers-le-Bel, 1975)
P. Ben-Amos: *The Art of Benin*, Tribal A. (London, 1980)
P. Harter: *Arts anciens du Cameroun* (Arnouville, 1986)
J. Mack: *Madagascar: Island of the Ancestors* (London, 1986)
C. Roy: *Art of the Upper Volta Rivers* (Meudon, 1987)
J. Borgatti and R. Brilliant: *Likeness and Beyond: Portraits from Africa and the World* (New York, 1990)

SPECIALIST STUDIES

B. Holas: 'Remarques sur la valeur sociologique du nom dans les sociétés traditionelles de l'ouest africain', *J. Soc. Africanistes*, xxiii/1–2 (1953), pp. 77–86
——: 'Nom, invocation, prière: Transposition du problème général sur le terrain des recherches negro africain', *Bull. Inst. Fr. Afrique Noire*, ser. B, xvii/1–2 (1956), pp. 109–28
H. Himmelheber and W. Tame-Tabmen: 'Wunkirle: Die gastichste Frau', *Festschrift Alfred Buhler*, ed. C. M. Schmitz (Basle, 1965), pp. 171–81
H. Himmelheber: 'Das Porträt in der Negerkunst', *Baessler-Archv*, xx (1972), pp. 261–311
S. Rudy: 'Royal Sculpture in the Cameroon Grasslands', *African Art and Leadership*, ed. D. Fraser and H. M. Cole (Madison, 1972), pp. 123–36
R. Sieber: 'Kwahu Terracottas, Oral Traditions, and Ghanaian History', *African Art and Leadership*, ed. D. Fraser and H. M. Cole (Madison, 1972), pp. 173–84
J. Vansina: 'Ndop: Royal Statues among the Kuba', *African Art and Leadership*, ed. D. Fraser and H. M. Cole (Madison, 1972), pp. 41–56
B. Söderberg: 'Les Figures d'ancêtres chez les Bambémbé', *A. Afrique Noire*, 13 (1975), pp. 21–33; 14 (1975), pp. 14–37
R. Abiodun: 'A Reconsideration of the Function of Ako, Second Burial Effigy in Owo', *Africa*, xlvi/1 (1976), pp. 4–20
S. M. Vogel: *Baule Art as the Expression of a World View* (diss., New York U., Inst. F.A., 1977)
J. M. Borgatti: 'Dead Mothers of Okpella', *Afr. A.*, xii/4 (1979), pp. 48–57
M. J. Adams: 'Fon Appliqued Cloths', *Afr. A.*, xiii/2 (1980), pp. 28–41, 87–8
J. R. Salmons: 'Funerary Shrine Cloths of the Annang-Ibibio, South East Nigeria', *Textiles of Africa*, ed. D. Idiens and K. Ponting (Bath, 1980), pp. 99–141
P. Ben-Amos: 'Who is the Man in the Bowler Hat? Emblems of Identity in Benin Royal Art', *Baessler-Archv*, n. s., xxxi (1983), pp. 161–83
B. W. Blackmun: 'Remembering the Warrior Kings', *The Art of Power, the Power of Art: Studies in Benin Iconography*, ed. P. Ben-Amos and A. Rubin, Museum of Cultural History Monograph, xix (Los Angeles, 1983), pp. 49–50
——: 'Reading a Royal Altar Tusk', *The Art of Power, the Power of Art: Studies in Benin Iconography*, ed. P. Ben-Amos and A. Rubin, Museum of Cultural History Monograph, xix (Los Angeles, 1983), pp. 59–70
H. J. Drewal: 'Art History and the Individual: A New Perspective for the Study of African Visual Traditions', *IA Stud. Afr. A.*, i (1984), pp. 87–114
E. Fischer: 'Self-portraits, and Copies among the Dan: The Creative Process of Traditional African Mask Carvers', *IA Stud. Afr. A.*, i (1984), pp. 5–28
S. P. Blier: *The Anatomy of Architecture: Ontology and Metaphor in Batammaliba Architectural Expression*, Res Monographs in Anthropology and Aesthetics (Cambridge, 1987)
R. Poynor: 'Ako Figures of Owo and Second Burials in Southern Nigeria', *Afr. A.*, xxi/1 (1987), pp. 62–4, 81–3, 86
N. Barley: *Foreheads of the Dead: An Anthropological View of Kalabari Ancestral Screens* (Washington, DC, 1988)
R. T. Soppelsa, J. Hellman and C. Keim: 'Western Art-historical Methodology and African Art: Panofsky's Paradigm and Ivorian Mma', *A. J.* [New York], xlvii/2 (1988), pp. 147–53
W. E. A. Van Beek: 'Functions of Sculpture in Dogon Religion', *Afr. A.*, xxi/4 (1988), pp. 58–65, 91
Afr. A., xxiii/3 (1990) and xxiii/4 (1990) [special issues on 'Portraiture in Africa']
S. P. Blier: 'King Glele of Danhome—Part One: Divination Portraits of Lion King and Man of Iron', *Afr. A.*, xxiii/4 (1990), pp. 42–53
G. N. Preston: 'People Making Portraits Making People: Living Icons of the Akan', *Afr. A.*, xxiii/3 (1990), pp. 70–76
R. T. Soppelsa: 'A Mna in the Metropolitan Museum of Art', *Afr. A.*, xxiii/3 (1990), pp. 77–8
M. B. Visona: 'Portraiture among the Lagoon Peoples of Côte d'Ivoire', *Afr. A.*, xxiii/4 (1990), pp. 54–61
S. P. Blier: 'King Glele of Danhome—Part Two: Dynasty and Destiny', *Afr. A.*, xxiv/1 (1991), pp. 44–55, 101–03

EXHIBITION CATALOGUES

Die Kunst der Dan (exh. cat. by E. Fischer and H. Himmelheber, Zurich, Mus. Rietberg, 1976; Eng. trans., rev., Zurich, 1984)
The Arts of Ghana (exh. cat. by H. M. Cole and D. H. Ross; Los Angeles, UCLA, Wight A.G.; Minneapolis, MN, Walker A. Cent.; Dallas, TX, Mus. F.A.; 1977–8)
The Four Moments of the Sun: Kongo Art in Two Worlds (exh. cat. by R. F. Thompson and J. A. Cornet, Washington, DC, N.G.A., 1981–2)
Asen: Iron Altars of the Fon People of Benin (exh. cat., ed. E. G. Bay; Atlanta, Emory U. Mus. A. & Archaeol., 1985)

JEAN M. BORGATTI

4. PHYSICAL ANOMALIES. Among the most visually powerful African works of art are those associated with physical anomalies. Although not every African society seeks to portray deformity in its arts, many do. The function of such works is quite varied, and artistic examples of physical anomaly, deformity and deficiency have important cultural associations. Some, including many of the two-faced figures that show a surfeit of bodily features, use their excess powers to convey greater than normal strength, force and status. Other works suggest, through the absence or distortion of body parts, ideas of stigmatized behaviour or social incompleteness. Spiritual and physiological sickness is suggested through body deformity as well. Still other sculptures through their inclusion of monstrous attributes are associated with antisocial qualities and those persons who depart from tradition and the interests of the group.

(i) Figures and dolls. Among the FON of Benin, certain genres of *bocio* power figures show body deformation in provocative ways. Known as *bocio-bigble* ('corrupted *bocio*'), such works display striking visual and emotional power (see Blier, 1995). While some such figures have missing legs or arms (see fig. 37), by far the most common forms incorporate two heads, faces or bodies. In these works faces may be carved on two sides of the head, or two or more heads set on a single pair of shoulders, or a single pair of legs and hips may support two torsos. Questions

37. Fon deformed figure sculpture (*bocio-bigble*), wood, h. 584 mm, from Benin (Indianapolis, IN, Museum of Art)

of psychological power and social difference are often addressed in Fon *bocio* through aberrant visual imagery of this sort. These works are identified with individual danger, sorcery and empowerment. Accordingly they are often employed as guardian figures to protect the house, compound, temple or city. The perceived ability of multi-headed works to observe activity both inside and outside the compound is of considerable importance. Fon deformity imagery of this sort carries with it important associations not only with protection (and a wish to see in front and behind at the same time) but also with the desire to control one's personal and social landscape through the fragmentation and replication of key body parts. Such works also convey provocative ideas of gender conflation, with many incorporating the sexual attributes of both sexes. Most of these *bocio* draw their potency from tiny invisible *aziza* spirits who are believed to inhabit the forests. These spirits are generally described as having a single foot and arm. Also important to *bocio* figural empowerment are various *vodun* forces such as the *hoho* (twins) or Mawu (the solar god), both of whom are said to have clairvoyant, four-eyed vision. Sorcerers and kings are also believed to have this power. Fon deformity figures in this and other ways reinforce the vital interconnections between religion, power, psychology and art.

Deformity sculptures produced by LOBI artists in northern Ghana are also of interest. Lobi sculptures show a range of physical anomalies, including a head surmounting a single leg, a person missing an arm or leg, a figure with three or more arms, a person with two or more heads and a person with three or more legs supporting a single torso. These figures, which represent *ti bala* ('extraordinary persons'), are said to protect the house by frightening away all who would do it harm (see fig. 38). Because of their body incompleteness and/or deformities, they are viewed as especially dangerous (see 1981 exh. cat., p. 95).

Deformity figures that show missing or distorted body attributes suggest similarly important sociological concerns in other African cultures (see 1982 exh. cat.). Many are

38. Lobi deformity sculpture (*ti bala*), wood, h. 350 mm (Paris, private collection)

associated with antisocial attributes. Among the PENDE of Zaïre, sculptures with a single arm and leg are identified with loneliness, with persons who have neither close relatives nor friends (de Sousberghe, p. 109). It has been suggested that deformity figures of the Lega, another Zaïrean group (*see* LEGA AND RELATED PEOPLES), are identified with antisocial individuals as well (see Biebuyck, 1972, p. 17). Thus Lega figures displaying a single arm are described as representing an individual given to quarrelling, the deformity deriving from his aggressive character. A Lega work missing both arms is associated with adultery (see Biebuyck, 1973, pl. 69).

Physiological and mental illness is also suggested through features of physical anomaly. In the Cameroon Grasslands sufferers of disease, witchcraft ills and spiritual trauma are depicted in figural form through distortions of the abdomen (see Brain and Pollock). With the Nguu of Tanzania illness-causing sorcerers are shown turned on their heads (Cory, pp. 48–9). Illness-causing bush spirits among the SENUFO of the Côte d'Ivoire are represented in turn by figures with feet turned backwards or transformed into fins (Glaze, p. 65). A Rotse work with body attributes articulated on only half the figure represents a madness-causing, half-human creature called Mwenda-Njangula or Mwenda Lutaka (Reynolds, pp. 50, 65). Physiological or spiritual anomaly and figural distortion are in this way conjoined.

Carved doll forms that display deliberately underdeveloped limbs also are of interest in the context of physical anomaly. It has been suggested (see McLeod, p. 174) that Asante doll forms known as *akuaba* (*see* ASANTE AND RELATED PEOPLES, §4(i)) lack essential human attributes because of their identity as potential rather than fully realized beings. As McLeod explains, children cannot assume their own characters and roles until much later in life. Robert Farris Thompson notes similarly (see 1974 exh. cat., p. 53) that the lack of feet on many of these figures reinforces their association with social dependency. Doll-form figures that lack full body development or attributes are also employed by the MOSSI (Burkina Faso) and ZULU (South Africa) among other groups. These works too may suggest ideas of dependency, disempowerment and immaturity.

African sculptures that are characterized by a surfeit of features through their incorporation of multiple heads and/or members also form an important corpus of anomaly works. As with the Fon multi-headed figures discussed above, what unites this group is the increased power and presence that is identified with bodily surplus or abundance. Among the Bini of Nigeria, four-legged figures are identified with Ofoe, a death-associated deity who is said to be able to travel readily between the earth and sky (see Ben-Amos, p. 149). With the DOGON of Mali, figures with multiple arms or legs are said to be identified with the increased power of two sky *nommo* (see Griaule and Dieterlen, pl. 18). A seven-legged figure that is believed to be able to outrun thieves with ease is used by the Mburi of northern Cameroon to protect palm-wine stocks (Gebauer, p. 185). Added power is also attributed to two-faced sculptures because they have increased sensory properties. The TEKE of Zaïre employ such figures as a special prerogative of great chiefs (Lehuard, p. 37).

(ii) Masks and masquerades. Among the IGBO, IBIBIO and neighbouring Cross River peoples in Nigeria, masquerades displaying physical anomalies also have important power associations. With the EJAGHAM some such masks portray humans with distorted features including huge noses or off-centre mouths. These 'beast' personifiers often wear dirty or torn costumes and display aggressive dance steps and fierce actions (see Jones, 1945, pp. 194, 196). M. Ruel states that the Ejagham 'beast' masker Emanyankpe 'presents the more "fearsome" aspect of the association and when it appears non-members are expected to flee and hide' (p. 266).

Among the nearby Ibibio, Ekpo members wearing masks with various physical anomalies represent ancestors of bad character such as murderers, sorcerers, poisoners, paupers without kin and stealers of sacred objects. These ancestors are said to be responsible for the sickness and accidents of their descendants and townsmen (Messenger, pp. 120–21). Maskers of this sort, which are known as *idiok ekpo* ('evil Ekpo'), often have exaggerated features that jut out from the mask surface at irregular angles (see fig. 39). Many such works combine human and animalistic elements in terrifying compositions. Others portray horrible deforming diseases such as lupus, yaws (gangosa is an indicator of religious impurity), syphilis and leprosy (see Jones, 1984, p. 77; Messenger, p. 122). These diseases are represented in such features as sores, split tongues, twisted or eaten-away lips or noses, protruding teeth and tongues, mouths out of line and flapped eyes (symbolizing blindness). Skulls, snakes, lizards (witch familiars) and tortoises are often incorporated into these masks as well. Reinforcing the dangerous identity of these masks,

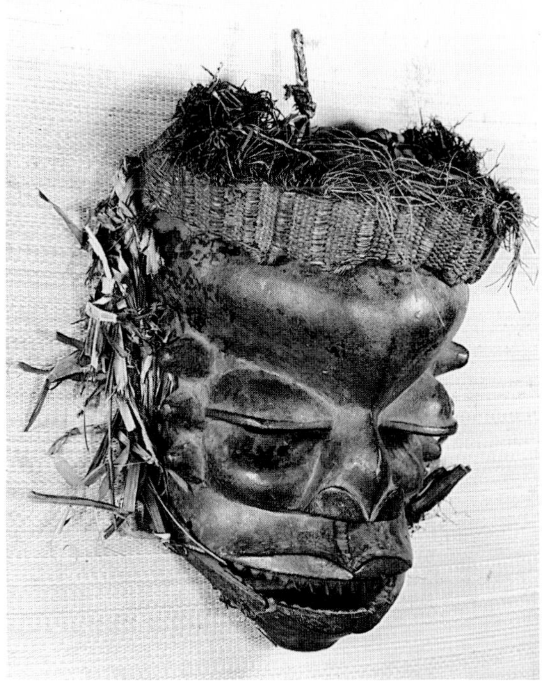

39. Ibibio *idiok ekpo* mask, wood, h. 355 mm (Stuttgart, Linden-Museum)

associated performers carry weapons such as machetes or bows and arrows. Their choreographed actions are frequently wayward and violent, with related maskers often shaking their bodies furiously, running through the village, climbing trees or houses, destroying property or harming people.

Okoroshi and Mwo 'beast' masquerades of the nearby Igbo also display various body anomalies. Southern Igbo Okoroshi masks often have ugly, diseased and animalistic features, which are either carved into the mask surface or glued on to it with a thick gum. These features include bloody fangs, thrust-forward mouths, furrowed foreheads and eyebrows, protruding, bent and tubular tongues, broken noses and twisted mouths (see Deji, p. 177; Cole, p. 38). Northern Igbo Mwo masks display complementary forms. Some of the latter masks are carved to represent terrifying animalistic monsters with a mixture of leonine, elephant and buffalo features. As with the Okoroshi 'beasts', the Mwo works draw analogies between human aggressiveness and the fierceness and violence of wild animals (Boston, p. 58).

BIBLIOGRAPHY

Deji: 'Okorosia', *Niger. Field*, iii/4 (1934), pp. 175–7
G. T. Basden: *Niger Ibos* (London and New York, 1938)
G. I. Jones: 'Masked Plays of South Eastern Nigeria', *Geog. Mag.*, xviii/5 (1945), pp. 190–200
H. Cory: *African Figurines: Their Ceremonial Use in Puberty Rites in Tanganyika* (London, 1956)
L. de Sousberghe: *L'Art Pende* (Brussels, 1959)
J. Boston: 'Some Northern Ibo Masquerades', *J. Royal Anthropol. Inst. GB & Ireland*, xc (1960), pp. 54–65
B. Reynolds: *Magic, Divination and Witchcraft among the Barotse of Northern Rhodesia* (Berkeley, 1963)
M. Griaule and G. Dieterlen: *Le Renard pâle: Le Mythe cosmogonique*, Trav. & Mém. Inst. Ethnol., lxxii (Paris, 1965; Eng. trans., 1986)
H. M. Cole: 'Art as a Verb in Iboland', *Afr. A.*, iii/1 (1969), pp. 34–41
M. Ruel: *Leopards and Leaders: Constitutional Politics among a Cross River People* (Cambridge and New York, 1969)
R. Brain and A. Pollock: *Bangwa Funerary Sculpture*, A. & Soc. Ser. (London, 1971)
D. P. Biebuyck: 'The *Kindi* Aristocrats and their Art among the Lega', *African Art and Leadership*, ed. D. Fraser and H. M. Cole (Madison, 1972), pp. 7–20
——: *Lega Culture: Art, Initiation and Moral Philosophy among a Central African People* (Berkeley, 1973)
J. C. Messenger: 'The Carver in Anang Society', *The Traditional Artist in African Societies*, ed. W. L. d'Azevedo (Bloomington and London, 1973), pp. 101–27
R. Lehuard: *Statuaire de Stanley-Pool* (Villiers-le-Bel, 1974)
African Art in Motion: Icon and Act (exh. cat. by R. F. Thompson; Washington, DC, N.G.A.; Los Angeles, UCLA, Wight A.G.; 1974)
S. P. Blier: *Masking Traditions of Southeastern Nigeria* (diss., New York, Columbia U., 1976)
A. J. Glaze: 'Senufu Ornament and Decorative Arts', *Afr. A.*, xii/1 (1978), pp. 63–71
P. Gebauer: *Art of Cameroon* (Portland, OR, and New York, 1979)
P. Ben-Amos: *The Art of Benin*, Tribal A. (London, 1980)
M. D. McLeod: *The Asante* (London, 1981)
Kunst und Religion der Lobi (exh. cat. by P. Meyer, Zurich, Mus. Rietberg, 1981)
Gestures in African Art (exh. cat. by S. P. Blier, New York, Kahan Gal. Afr. A., 1982)
G. I. Jones: *The Art of Eastern Nigeria* (Cambridge, 1984)
Igbo Arts: Community and Cosmos (exh. cat. by H. M. Cole and C. C. Aniakor, Los Angeles, UCLA, Mus. Cult. Hist., 1984)
S. P. Blier: *African Vodun: Art, Psychology and Power* (Chicago, 1995)

SUZANNE PRESTON BLIER

5. Mother-and-child imagery.

(i) Introduction. (ii) Formal interpretation. (iii) Religious context.

(i) Introduction. The mother-and-child group is for many the most affecting and compelling theme in African art. Partly owing to the biological model of a mother with her baby and partly to the Christian icon of the Virgin and Child, the subject is easily related to art elsewhere in the world, even if information is lacking on its values in specific cultures. The varied uses and meanings of African versions of this representation both illuminate the universal character of the icon and reveal aspects of the richness of African thought.

Renderings of the mother and child have a long history on the continent: paintings on the rock surfaces of Tassili and nearby sites in the Sahara date from *c.* 3000–2000 BC. The earliest known sculptural versions are pottery figures ascribed to the NOK cultures of northern Nigeria (*c.* 500 BC–AD 200). The most important prehistoric cluster of maternities is the corpus of pottery sculptures (*c.* AD 1000–1500) from the inland delta of the Niger River in Mali. Some of these are quite naturalistic renderings in lifelike poses, but others, showing a mother with one or two diminutive 'adult' children, are conventionalized and clearly symbolic, although their precise meanings are unknown. The majority of surviving examples of this form, however, come from the vast ethnographic corpus of 19th- and 20th-century artefacts, which, unlike many works from archaeological contexts, are informed by quantities of anthropological and art-historical data. While most maternities of this period are wood-carvings, fine pottery figures such as those of the AKAN peoples are also known, as are examples in sun-dried clay or mud, brass or bronze, and occasional examples in iron, stone, fibre and appliqué beadwork. Virtually all were made by well-trained professional artists, usually male, although there are pottery examples produced by Akan and IGBO female potters.

(ii) Form and interpretation. Most mother-and-child images are free-standing wood sculptures destined for shrines, but such representations, including birth scenes, may also be found on masks, chairs, stools, doors, house-posts, wooden gongs, combs, bowls and other utilitarian artefacts. In rare instances, too, the mother-and-child form may appear in wholly secular contexts, for example on Akan goldweights. Generally, however, the image has a spiritual connotation and use. The prevalence and recurrence of the maternity group attests to its importance in African life and thought (for discussion of the theme of 'increase' *see* §1 above), although its uneven distribution among various peoples is difficult to explain. The sculptors and patrons of the KONGO (e.g. Yombe, Vili) and YORUBA peoples, for example, are prolific in their use of the theme (see fig. 40), producing many variations in pose, size, shape, object type and even style. Neighbouring and other Central and West African cultures, for whom the biological imperative of motherhood is no less important, however, have exploited the theme far less fully, and occasionally not at all (e.g. Benin, Lega, Kalabari Ijo). There is no apparent correlation between matrilineal or patrilineal descent in a society and its preoccupation with the mother-and-child image, for the theme occurs unevenly in each. Pluralism in cultural preferences and local tradition seem to be better (although unsatisfying) explanations for distribution patterns. Clearly biological and demographic reality are not the same as artistic and spiritual reality, since

40. Mother and child, wood, glass beads, glass inlay and metal, h. 258 mm, from the Yombe group, Kongo people, Congo or Zaïre, collected before 1914 (Washington, DC, National Museum of African Art)

productive women are highly valued among all African peoples.

Basic to the elucidation of the theme are the identities of the mothers and children represented. It is easiest to say who they are not, since they are rarely portraits of real people. Even if ancestral images, they are usually not specifically named; rather, they are symbols of lineage or clan forebears, the generalized, idealized, 'incarnate dead'. In other cases the woman may be the primordial mother, the legendary founder of the people. Most DOGON maternities can probably be so identified, and it is certainly true of some large SENUFO examples, known as 'Ancient Mother'. Research indicates that the latter refer primarily to a complex of ideas about culture and social relationships rather than to the biological unit of a mother with her baby. Suckling here does refer to nurture, but the emphasis is not so much on a mother's nutritional provision for her infant as on the Ancient Mother's protection and guidance of all Senufo males during the 21-year cycle of initiation and education, which imparts the 'milk of knowledge' and results in the development of 'complete human beings' (see 1981 exh. cat., pp. 45–6). In the dualistic opposition between nature and culture so characteristic of African thought, the mother-and-child image refers more often to culture than to nature, while also acknowledging their interdependence.

A well-known 'maternity' among the Owerri Igbo of Nigeria is Ala, the earth goddess, who is portrayed larger than (presumed) life-size as the honoured recipient of elaborate temple-like structures (*mbari*), which are filled with dozens of human images in sun-dried clay. All of these, including the two who sit on her lap or beside her, are her 'children'. Ala also has the pendulous breasts and title regalia of an older woman. As a major tutelary deity, she presides over village morality and health, and, as the greatest of mothers, she yields or withholds children, crops and animals. She nurtures, but she also kills swiftly when offended. She incarnates cyclical regeneration, life, death and rebirth. She is revered and feared. All villagers and many deities are her children, and she demands their respect and honour.

It is notable that an intimate, emotional bond between the mother and her child is rarely expressed, even when the baby is suckling. Equally, the sculptor seldom gives the child any real personality. This can be partly accounted for by Africa's high rates of infant mortality. Moreover, children, however much desired by parents, were often regarded as useful property rather than as individual personalities, especially during infancy. Children were not always raised by their biological parents and might be pawned or sold into slavery. High infant mortality also accounts for the tradition of the changeling, the child who, it was believed, was born to die, often just as its parents began to cherish it. Believed to appear on earth several times, dying and being born again, a changeling plagued its parents with its mysterious actions and caused them not only anguish but also expense in the form of sacrifices to avert its death. In such circumstances, an emotional and psychological distance between mother and baby in a work of art and the child's lack of personality or character are understandable.

Mother-and-child sculptures are often called 'fertility figures'. Human productivity, of course, is crucial to the continuity of the race, and it is certainly true that many shrines and cults emphasize the fertility of women, their health during pregnancy and the infant's survival. Rather than being celebrated in and for itself, however, the biology of maternity serves the more important social states of motherhood and fatherhood, the creation of a family. An African female normally is not recognized as a real woman unless and until she is a mother, and her ideal status is as the mother of a large family. Children are social and economic assets, and they are also expected to honour parents and, at death, to organize a proper burial, which is often in fact a delayed funerary festival (*see* §III, 5(ii) above) that in turn ensures their beneficence as ancestors.

That there is ancestral intervention in daily life is widely believed, and this helps to maintain the institution of ancestor veneration. It is thought that dead parents, as ancestors, will stimulate and promote the fertility of their children and the productivity of farmlands. Ancestral cults are therefore difficult to separate from fertility cults, and the mother-and-child icon serves both (*see* §1 above).

Several such images from the Cameroon Grassland kingdoms (*see* e.g. BAMILEKE AND RELATED PEOPLES) commemorate royal ancestors, who may occasionally be named; they are placed in ensembles of statuary, housed in kings' treasuries (see fig. 41). Royal ancestors and retainer figures are not themselves the focus of the ancestral cult. They are, however, honoured and attended as memorials to the wealth and dignity of the court and the strength of the dynasty. In addition, they are occasionally brought out as display pieces and backdrops for kingship rituals. Female figures in this genre represent a chief's favourite wives or his queen mother (who is in fact his sister), and they celebrate womanhood, fertility and maternity. Most, though not all, of these sculptures of women are dressed with ivory bracelets and anklets, which are male attributes of royal status. They embody the frequent coalescing of socio-political and spiritual meanings.

(iii) Religious context. Elsewhere mother-and-child images were, and still are, housed in shrines of tutelary deities responsible for general protection and well-being. Statuary is more common in such contexts and in diviners' shrines than it is in ancestral cults. Tutelary deities (e.g. Ala) are accorded broad positive and negative powers. In return for blood sacrifices they offer guidance and succour and they regulate human behaviour. Their images are generic, and they may be named after the deity or considered to be his or her children, messengers, servants or worshippers. Placed beside other shrine images, they refer especially to the protection, nurture and productivity expected of wives and mothers while also representing the mysterious power of woman as child-bearer and the critical role of wife and mother. Ensembles of family members are common in shrines as projections of idealized domestic life, for the gods in their realm, it is believed, lead lives parallel to those of real people.

Specialist practitioners of the Yoruba, Baule, Igbo, Senufo, Kongo and other peoples interact with spirits, ascertaining their desires through divining practices (*see* §VI, 7 below) and passing them on to the clients who consult them. The greatest variety of mother-and-child images is found in the shrines and workplaces of Yoruba diviners and doctors, where they often embellish bowls, tappers and divining trays. The complexity and the value of such iconography on these implements has been noted by H. J. Drewal (see 1977 exh. cat., p. 5): 'Images of women in ritual contexts and mother and child figures represent much more than symbols of fertility. They communicate sexual abstinence [of a nursing mother], inner cleanliness [because her menses are suppressed, and therefore], ritual purity, female force, and spirituality'. Many Yoruba maternities show the woman kneeling in a position of respect, devotion and even submission to the gods: an appropriate posture when it is recalled that most women in Yoruba sculpture represent worshippers, not the gods themselves.

Sculptures of mother-and-child groups embellish various types of shrines, where they serve as display pieces, as evidence of the spiritual and material success of the ritualist and as an advertisement for his or her expertise. Accomplished, and therefore wealthy, diviners and cult priests are more likely to have statuary than mediocre ones, so such images can, to some extent, be considered an index of wealth and prosperity, although this also suggests that the presence of sculpture in a shrine may have an arbitrary element.

Mother-and-child imagery is metaphorical and value-laden far beyond its limited biological reference. To see such imagery merely as a collection of fertility figures or specific mothers with their babies is to undervalue the richness of African thought. This prevalent, recurrent icon is an archetype: Great Mother as earth and water, childbirth and initiation as repetitions of cosmogony, the mother as symbol of a compound or village, her children its inhabitants, the genetrix as the source of social institutions. African thought and symbolism accord with those of the rest of the world in creating from this icon a universe far greater than the sum of its parts. Dynamic and regenerative, the mother-and-child symbol reflects the verities and complexities of African spiritual thought and the continuity of culture.

BIBLIOGRAPHY

D. Zahan: *The Religion, Spirituality and Thought of Traditional Africa* (Chicago and London, 1970)

R. Brain and A. Pollock: *Bangwa Funerary Sculpture*, A. & Soc. Ser. (London, 1971)

Traditional Art of the Nigerian Peoples: The Milton D. Ratner Family Collection (exh. cat. by H. J. Drewal, Washington, DC, N. Mus. Afr. A., 1977)

The Arts of Ghana (exh. cat. by H. M. Cole and D. H. Ross; Los Angeles, UCLA, Mus. Cult. Hist.; Minneapolis, MN, Walker A. Cent.; Dallas, TX, Mus. F.A.; 1977–8)

A. J. Glaze: *Art and Death in a Senufo Village*, Trad. A. Africa (Bloomington, 1981)

For Spirits and Kings: African Art from the Paul and Ruth Tishman Collection (exh. cat., ed. S. M. Vogel; New York, Met., 1981)

Icons: Ideals and Power in the Art of Africa (exh. cat. by H. M. Cole, Washington, DC, N. Mus. Afr. A., 1989)

6. ANIMAL IMAGERY. Images of animals are found in Africa wherever the visual arts exist. Animals are depicted in such contexts as rock art, shrines, masquerades, regalia and jewellery, body decoration (tattoo and scarification) and household settings, forming a major subset within the larger corpus of arts.

(i) Introduction. (ii) Types. (iii) Perceived functions.

(i) Introduction. In most sub-Saharan cultures, even today, people contend with both wild and domestic animals. These are hunted and herded, chased from fields and sacrificed in rituals, while their spirit counterparts are consulted in divination and evoked in song, story and dance. Men are believed to transform themselves into animals, and animal spirits are called upon or avoided because of their mystical powers. Animals killed ritually are divided, each meaningful part being given to a certain person or group according to time-honoured rules.

Animal behaviour is closely observed and well understood, but it is also mythic and imagined. Hence animals

41. Queen Nana and child, wood with ochre pigment, h. 1.01 m, by Mbeudjang, Batufam Kingdom, Bamileke, Cameroon, *c.* 1912 (Toronto, Murray and Barbara Frum Collection)

figure in many creation myths and arts not as they exist in the forest or plain but as proto-humans, indeed metahumans, furnished with such specifically human traits as language.

They also appear as legendary heroes in proverbs and folktales, as spirits, ancestors and oracles, often with extraordinary powers. Beliefs about animals are possibly more important to an understanding of this imagery than are empirical facts, since animal images are seldom merely decorative but usually also convey metaphorical and symbolic meanings, even if they are naturalistically rendered in their own environment, as in rock art (*see* §VI, 15 below). Animal representation is therefore selective and depends on the purpose served by the art object and/or its messages.

(ii) Types. Although some animal imagery is cross-cultural, the variety of forms employed and the diversity of local significances mean that much interpretation is culture-specific. For example, while leopards and elephants are everywhere associated with leadership and authority, unrelated qualities may be locally ascribed to their representations. Thus an AKAN proverb—'rain will not wash the spots off a leopard'—associates the animal not with chiefs or authority but with the idea that people's essential nature is not easily changed.

Animal imagery includes representations of most of the important classes of animals. They fall into two basic groups: the arthropods (crustacea, insects, arachnids) and the vertebrates (fish, amphibians, reptiles, birds and mammals). Over a hundred identifiable species are found in the corpus of cast-brass goldweights of Akan peoples in Ghana and Côte d'Ivoire (*see* ASANTE AND RELATED PEOPLES). These entirely secular counterbalances of known weight, used in commercial transactions from the 16th century to the late 19th, include miniatures of most animals found in West African forest and savannah zones, supplemented by fanciful creatures.

Many of these creatures, including those fashioned in such other media as ceramics, wood-carving and textiles, are associated with Akan proverbs, folktales and aphorisms. It is notable that the owl and the cat are never seen as goldweights, the former because it is a bird of ill omen, the latter because the word for cat, *okra*, is also the word for soul. In contrast, the rarity of goldweights fashioned into spiders, which are otherwise common in Akan arts and folklore, may be more practical, caused by the difficulty of casting such delicate creatures. Akan goldweights, gold-leaf linguist staffs and Asante cast-gold sword ornaments bear animal motifs the meanings of which are logical to us as well as to their makers and users (see fig. 42): the spider is seen as clever, the hen represents a mother or a chief, the porcupine is a warrior, the goat stupid, the chameleon changeable and the crocodile dangerous.

In addition to such universal symbols, a number of Akan objects bear single or multiple animal imagery with associations that are more arbitrary, involved and cryptic to outsiders. For example, if an object bore images of a monkey, an anthill and an antelope, a correct interpretation would depend upon knowledge of a proverb that refers to wishful thinking: when the monkey rubs an anthill, it does not become an antelope (see 1977–8 exh. cat., p. 152). Sword ornaments showing a viper catching a hornbill refer to patience, a meaning understood only in the light of a

42. Fante linguists with staffs surmounted by images of a leopard (right) and perhaps a porcupine (centre), Enyan Abassa, Ghana; from a photograph by Herbert M. Cole, 1975

folktale about a debt, a drought and the viper's long wait at the world's last waterhole, where the debtor hornbill had to come to drink (see 1977–8 exh. cat., p. 16).

Such examples are selected from thousands. It should be remembered that, within and across ethnic groups, variations of meaning arise out of local interpretations that are repeated and then harden into convention. In addition, of course, both the images used and their meanings are subject to temporal change. A further level of complication is introduced by the range of images produced, from highly schematic, compressed symbols to more elaborate representational images.

(iii) Perceived functions. Leaders throughout Africa have long used animal imagery to consolidate, symbolize and broadcast their powers. In the kingdom of Benin (*see* BENIN), for example, the divine king, court and chiefs have used brass, ivory and some wooden animal sculptures for about 500 years to express values, contrasts and hierarchies seen as parallel in human and natural realms. As P. Ben-Amos puts it (1976, p. 244): 'The ontological distinction between human and animal is expressed symbolically in art, myth, and ritual in the contrast between their respective spheres of activity—the home (the social world of the village) versus the bush (the wild forest areas)'. Within each sphere, relationships are hierarchical and orderly: the king dominates home and bush, day and night, as the leopard, elephant, crocodile and eagle dominate their species and habitats. The more accessible, docile or domestic animals—cow, mudfish, fowl, goat, ram—are associated with home and commoners and may be freely sacrificed, while only the king may sacrifice his mythological and metaphorical counterpart, the leopard, a frequent symbol of royal strength. Images of animals abound in Benin as free-standing brass shrine sculpture, on high-relief plaques used as architectural decoration and on such ritual implements as diviners' staffs. Depictions on the latter include animals considered dangerous and liminal—snakes, chameleon, frogs and the night heron—because they violate boundaries and order. Their magical powers come from the bush, and they, or their unseen spirits, are invoked firstly by leaders to help them govern, secondly by diviners to read omens, heal, and fight witches and thirdly by witches themselves to hurt or kill.

Leopard, buffalo, elephant and eagle sculptures are common in the kingdoms of West Africa (Akan, FON, Yoruba, Cameroon Grassfields) and in other less famous chiefdoms (see 1992 exh. cat.). Such emblems occur frequently in regalia and are supplemented by such tangible parts of the animals as skins, horns, tusks and feathers. Depictions of these animals and their parts relate to leadership in many cultures. Also, although less frequently, the lion, shark, python, crocodile, pangolin, scorpion and other creatures serve as leadership and power symbols. Given that leaders are overwhelmingly the major patrons of African artists, it is not surprising that much animal imagery, directly or indirectly, refers to leaders' putative qualities.

A general distinction can be made between the uses of animal symbols by paramount leaders in large, hierarchical polities and the animal imagery seen among more egalitarian societies. In the former, many of the animals are emblematic, conveying fairly simple political messages to the people. In smaller-scale cultures, on the other hand, animal imagery has stronger spiritual orientations and concerns itself with the complexities of social relationships in daily life, with fertility, the food supply and threats to the socio-spiritual order. Animal emblems in Fon or Akan kingdoms refer mostly to the varied powers of different kings, while for the BAMANA and SENUFO animal motifs are constellations of spirit forces, many from the bush (savannah or forest) rather than the village.

The physical, mystical and metaphorical powers of animals are especially evident in masquerades (*see* §VI, 3 below). In general, masquerades are more important in non-hierarchical societies than they are in large, centralized kingdoms, although there are exceptions to this tendency (e.g. the Yoruba and Cameroon kingdoms). Masks act as embodiments of unseen spiritual forces and are used to initiate, instruct, regulate and entertain. All masking cultures have animal masks that use dance and music, mime, free interpretation and even satire to amplify the character of the animal spirits: antelopes are majestically acrobatic, goats are lewd and stupid, buffaloes are marauding bullies. The danced character sometimes alludes only to the animal, but more often it also refers to human traits, for it is playing in an arena of belief and social force that it seeks to emulate, mock, idealize or otherwise influence.

Although masks may refer to single animals, artists often interpret these creatures freely, using a kind of structural shorthand. This stylized, symbolic nature is exemplified by the elephant masks danced by Bamileke (Cameroon) and Kuba peoples (Zaïre). Bamileke examples are made of beaded appliqué over cloth, the trunk is a long rectangular panel, and the ears are large circular discs (*see* fig. 43; *see also* BAMILEKE AND RELATED PEOPLES). These are worn with sumptuous royal cloths by noble, wealthy members of Elephant societies. They are deputized by kings, and in former times the maskers had powerful regulatory and executive roles. Mukyeem masks, used by leaders among Kuba-related peoples (*see* KUBA (iii)), are humanoid helmets made of such prestigious materials as leopard-skin, with a schematic bead and

43. Elephant masks worn by Kuosi society members, Bandjoun, Cameroon; from a photograph by Father Christol, 1930

cowrie-covered elephant trunk springing from the crown of the head. In both instances rich costume materials and abbreviated elephant references project the wealth, dignity, grandeur and authority of chiefs.

Composite animal masks are common in West Africa, if less prevalent than those referring to specific species. Several cultures (Baga, Toma, Senufo, Baule, Bamana, Bobo and others) have variations on horizontally or diagonally worn three-part (horns, head, snout) masks, which are often a metre or more in length. Because both the artistic structure and the symbolism of such masks are similar, they may all have developed from a single form. Various aspects of crocodile, antelope, buffalo and wart-hog are imaginatively combined in these composite masks, often with human eyes and noses and sometimes with added eagle feathers and porcupine quills. Most represent aggressive bush spirits, who operate as messengers and mediators in a zone between the gods and mankind, between wild nature and ordered civilization. These bristling, ferocious, magic-laden power-images, often considered ugly and dangerous, are invoked for social benefit by elders and others in authority and are danced in rituals to combat witchcraft, disease and other forms of evil and disorder.

Numerous animal images decorate the instruments used by diviners and other ritual specialists. Acting as mediators, oracles and doctors, they tap the esoteric, charged realms of nature and its sources of spiritual energy and arcane knowledge and bring their wisdom to the service of mankind. Pythons, turtles, chameleons and certain birds serve these specialists and figure in their shrines and equipment because their zone-crossing (i.e. land to water) qualities and their consequent intermediary existence suit the role of messenger between the spirit and human realms. Senufo diviners use images of pythons in mud reliefs, as portable props in shrines and in amuletic jewellery worn by ritual specialists and some of their clients. Small brass castings of simplified python, chameleon, tortoise, lizard, mudfish and other animal motifs are worn as protective and redemptive charms by Senufo, Lobi and other peoples. These symbols of zoomorphic spirits, often mentioned in creation myths, are accorded a variety of special traits. Common among them is their ability to transform themselves into human beings and to cause and cure physical and mental disorders. The mysteries and energies of the animal kingdom are repeatedly brought to bear in the uncertain realm of human affairs in man's ceaseless effort to rebalance the cosmos and maintain health in the specific human body and in the body politic.

BIBLIOGRAPHY

F. Willett: *Ife in the History of West African Sculpture* (London and New York, 1967)

D. P. Biebuyck: *Lega Culture: Art, Initiation, and Moral Philosophy among a Central African People* (Berkeley, 1973)

P. Ben-Amos: 'Men and Animals in Benin Art', *Man*, n. s., ii/2 (1976), pp. 243–52

D. H. Ross: 'The Iconography of Asante Sword Ornaments', *Afr. A.*, x/1 (1977), pp. 16–25, 90
The Arts of Ghana (exh. cat. by H. M. Cole and D. H. Ross, Los Angeles, CA, UCLA, Wight A.G.; Minneapolis, MN, Walker A. Cent.; Dallas, TX, Mus. F.A.; 1977–8)
P. Ben-Amos: *The Art of Benin*, Tribal A. (London, 1980)
B. de Grunne: *Terres cuites anciennes de l'ouest africain*, Pubns Hist. A. & Archéol. U. Cath. Louvain, xxii (Leuven, 1980)
A. J. Glaze: *Art and Death in a Senufo Village* (Bloomington, 1981)
J. Mack: 'Animal Representations in Kuba Art: An Anthropological Interpretation of Sculpture', *Oxford A.J.*, iv/2 (1981), pp. 5–56
Elephant: The Animal and its Ivory in African Culture (exh. cat., ed. D. H. Ross; Los Angeles, UCLA, Mus. Cult. Hist., 1992)

7. EQUESTRIAN IMAGERY. Ownership of a horse in tropical Africa indicates affluence. The wealth, elevation and speed represented by the rider and his mount derive not only from the power and swiftness of a warrior on horseback but also from the symbolic power of a leader or spirit personage. Riders are literally and figuratively superior beings, higher than their animal mounts and dominant over the common people. Such dominance is more important than mobility alone, and African equestrian sculpture thus expresses ideology and belief more than it depicts daily life. The identity of the rider depicted in sculptures varies. In many cases he may be a spirit, a deity or a legendary ancestor. Some are actual ancestors, while others are feared and respected alien leaders from the 'north', whence horses originally came. Rider sculptures may also commemorate élite hunters, warriors and chiefs. Equestrians appear on rulers' staffs and sceptres and on a number of YORUBA and SENUFO doors that were the property of kings and chiefs and symbolized their prestige, wealth and patronage. Most, however, were housed in shrines, where they reflected the powers and leadership traits attributed to spirits and deities, not to mention the authoritative positions of patron priests and priestesses. Sometimes shrine sculptures represented deities, but just as often they depicted worshippers.

The materials, styles and forms of these works vary considerably. The most common sculptural medium is wood, followed by bronze, then wrought iron, terracotta and unfired clay. In such exceptional cases as the large bronze castings from Benin (e.g. London, BM), both rider and beast are rendered in naturalistic detail. Simplification and generalization, however, are more usual, especially in the representation of the animal. Indeed these images were frequently conceived as metaphors; horses may thus look more like crocodiles or dogs or unidentifiable quadrupeds with tails and elongated heads. The fact that horse and rider symbolize spirits may help to account for their nonspecific character. Other renderings often appear schematic and highly distorted anatomically. The rider is frequently rendered on a larger scale, overwhelming the animal and manifesting what may be called ideological scale, since the human is more significant than the beast.

Among the earliest equestrian sculptures are large ceramic images from Djenné and other sites in the inland delta of the Niger River, dating perhaps to AD 1000. Although these have little firm cultural data accompanying them, it is probable that their riders were prominent leaders. Such peoples of the Western Sudan as the BAMANA, DOGON and Senufo and the Yoruba of Nigeria were Africa's most prolific producers of equestrian statuary. In the areas occupied by these peoples horses were able to survive, whereas in most forested regions they fell prey to diseases borne by the tsetse fly. Despite the hostile environment, however, some leaders of forest peoples imported horses to ride in occasional ceremonies for heightened prestige, for example the Oba of Benin, divine king of the EDO people of southern Nigeria.

Mythology and the legendary ancestors that populate their creation stories 'explain' equestrian imagery among the Dogon, the Bamana and the nearby Senufo of Mali and Burkina Faso. Dogon equestrians in the form of small, cast-brass finger-rings, as well as larger wooden images of horsemen, probably depict the mythic, primordial *hogon*, called Lebe, whose priestly, human counterpart is a ritual and temporal leader of great importance. Probably employed as display pieces in shrines, these equestrian images have a wealth of associations set forth in myth, including fertility and the origin of death, as well as referring to wealth, chiefship and leadership in warfare. Bamana art from Mali includes numerous wrought-iron shrine sculptures of equestrians (e.g. New York, Met.; Paris, Mus. N.A. Afr. & Océan.), which were manufactured by the powerful blacksmith group who act as prominent priests, educators, diviners and doctors and thus hold critical leadership positions. Iron horsemen represent the smiths and their mythical forebears in their roles as ritual specialists responsible for harnessing and directing spiritual energy for the benefit of society.

In common with other African peoples, the Senufo associate horses with leadership, wealth, status, hunting and militarism. Riders sculpted by Senufo artists are often armed with spears or hold guns at the ready. They represent the multi-dimensional powers of forest or bush spirits (see fig. 44). In equestrian statuary a bush spirit is appropriately shown as a forceful, well-armed leader, since these spirits are capricious, fast-travelling, nocturnal, mysterious and aggressive. Senufo equestrian figures are executed in many sizes, using wood, brass and sometimes iron, and they appear on the clay façades of shrines and carved in relief on doors and locks. Such figures are optional display pieces in a diviner's or priest's shrine, where, like much display sculpture in African shrines, they connote luxury, good taste and prestige (see Glaze, p. 72). Although the equestrian theme is not found in all leadership contexts, wherever the rider occurs the power of leadership is being evoked.

Yoruba equestrians provide the most varied and numerous examples of the rider theme. The forms they take are diverse—small, schematic renderings, sculptures elaborated far beyond observable realities, monumental figures—and they appear as shrine statuary, mask superstructures, divination objects and house-posts and doors for palaces and shrines. Although meanings vary, the power of leaders, whether divine or temporal, is always implicit. Updated versions of the theme, for example cyclists, are also found, especially on doors. Equestrian figures are favoured subjects in the large Yoruba Epa and Elefon helmet masks that are danced in the Ekiti region. The rider here is often identified as the culture hero and warrior Jagunjagun and is depicted as a chief equipped for battle, sometimes with retainers at his side, ideologically scaled down. Ironically perhaps, these massive headdresses

44. Senufo equestrian figure representing a bush spirit, wood, h. 320 mm, from Côte d'Ivoire or Mali, 19th–20th centuries (London, British Museum)

themselves 'ride' on the heads of agile young men as they dance a masquerade that, as one of its meanings, identifies them as bearers of their culture, extolling heroes and upholding, as it were, its ancient values. Equestrian figures also support Yoruba divination bowls, which themselves support and contain the sacred palm kernels used by diviners. Such diviners' bowls are understood to be temples of Orunmila (see Fagg and Pemberton, p. 64), and the equestrian theme implies the elevated status of this crucial god of divination, who imparts balance, control and order to a world beset by chaos and mystery. As the divination bowl supports the diviner's implements, so equestrian house-posts in the palaces of Yoruba kings support the edifice of kingship: ancestral heroes uphold the powers and privileges of divine rulers, who are thereby elevated and idealized in the eyes of their people.

Socio-spiritual aggrandizement and propaganda are no doubt factors among the Yoruba and others in the production of equestrian figures. Yet much more is involved, reaching deeply into the values and psychology of the people. The exercise of power by leaders and the response of those led are complex and critical factors in African life: equestrian statuary has had important, multi-dimensional roles in projecting and reinforcing these values.

BIBLIOGRAPHY

African Art in Motion: Icon and Act (exh. cat. by R. F. Thompson; Washington, DC, N.G.A.; Los Angeles, UCLA, Wight A.G.; 1974)

Iron Art of the Blacksmith in the Western Sudan (exh. cat., ed. P. R. McNaughton; West Lafayette, IN, Purdue U., 1975)

A. J. Glaze: *Art and Death in a Senufo Village*, Trad. A. Africa (Bloomington, 1981)

W. Fagg and J. Pemberton III: *Yoruba Sculpture of West Africa* (New York, 1982)

Icons, Ideals and Power in the Art of Africa (exh. cat. by H. M. Cole, Washington, DC, N. Mus. Afr. A., 1989)

HERBERT M. COLE

8. TRICKSTERS. In Africa tricksters figure prominently, not only in oral narrative and in such visual representations as those of the Yoruba deity Eshu/Elegba but also in philosophic and aesthetic concepts expressed through iconographic and morphological elements.

(i) Concepts. (ii) Eshu/Elegba complex.

(i) Concepts. A character in universal folklore, the trickster personifies apparent disorder. He is the enemy of fixed hierarchies and boundaries, ordered social and sexual roles and categorical separations. In psychological terms, he is the undifferentiated energy of the unconscious. In whatever form and medium he is made manifest, the trickster expands the terms of discourse by introducing what is selfishly desired within the fixed boundaries of what is socially permitted (see Kerenyi, p. 185). In African folklore and mythology, the trickster is realized diversely in trickster deities, in such characters as *enfants terribles* and, most elementally and pervasively, in tales about such morphologically ambiguous animals as Ananse the spider of the Akan, Hlakanyana the mongoose of the Southern Nguni, the mantis of the Khoisan, the hare of the Wolof and the Kagura or the tortoise of the Guinea Coast. The list could be extended to all African groups, since trickster tales are quantitatively the most numerous in African oral narrative traditions. Nevertheless, physical representations of these animal tricksters are surprisingly scarce: the Tiv of central Nigeria fabricate a copy of the hare trickster for their Kwagh Hir puppet tradition, the Nupe of the lower Niger valley of Nigeria create aluminium tortoises for the tourist markets, and wax printed cloths throughout West Africa are now adorned with images of the spider. Contemporary versions of the animal trickster are likely to be borrowed from universal mass-media imagery, which has spread depictions of Mickey Mouse and Donald Duck almost

45. Mende Gonde and Suwi masks, wood and raffia, 305×203 mm, from Sewa Mende area, Sierra Leone, before 1970 (New York, private collection)

everywhere, from the walls of ice-cream shops in Mogadishu, Somalia, to commemorative stamps in Sierra Leone.

Implicit in the dualistic concept of order and disorder that generates the trickster character is the 'principle of opposition', which operates at the core of many African cultures. The animal trickster is most representative of this principle in oral tradition, but African artists have also expressed the principle in diverse material forms. Thus in their construction of Eyima, the FANG of Gabon incorporate into wooden ancestral figures such infantile features as large head and torso, disproportionately small legs, a protruding stomach and a ruptured umbilicus. These contradictory qualities of infantile physical features in an ancestral figure give the Eyima a vitality it would not have if it were simply a figure of an aged person or an infant (see Fernandez, pp. 365–6). In African mythology, the same disproportion between the physical and the spiritual is realized in such diminutive or crippled heroes as Mwindo of the Nyanga of Zaïre and Sundiata of the Mande. Like the Eyima and all trickster figures, these epic heroes achieve power by disregarding the categorical separation between youthful energy and the cunning of age.

The TABWA of Zaïre and northern Zambia use a generic term (*mulalambo*) to express this principle of opposition, which they perceive in all phenomena, from the Milky Way's division of the sky to the fine line (*linea nigra*) that splits the human belly from navel to genitals. Tabwa artists give physical expression to this dualistic principle in the two-faced figures they carve on staffs, whisks, headrests and medicine containers (see Roberts, p. 31). Defying categorical separation by incorporating double-faced motifs, these diverse objects are used ritually to effect transitions from one state to another, and such expressions of transition as gates, doorways and the advent of a new year are the special province of the African trickster.

Since tricksters respect no boundaries or social conventions, their spirit is manifested in satiric and derisive images. The MENDE of Sierra Leone and Liberia mock the Suwi masker, their most sacred image of female beauty, by sometimes making her dance with Gonde, a grotesque parody often constructed from a discarded Suwi mask embellished with junk (Cosentino; see fig. 45). For similarly satirical reasons, the Egungun cult of ancestral power and entertainment among the YORUBA of south-western Nigeria brings out a mask called Big Nose. In sunlight its eyes become opaque, its mouth a lipless gash over stumps of teeth. All organic detail is obliterated down to the bone structure. Yoruba audiences laugh at this misshapen horror, and thus Big Nose satirizes the pompous and vain, mirroring their spiritual distortions with physical ones (see Thompson, 1971, p. 379). Both of these 'anti-masquerade' figures highlight the artificiality of categorical divisions, the trickster's special target.

(ii) Eshu/Elegba complex. Yoruba culture provides the most complete realization of the trickster in African art. In folktales, the Yoruba celebrate the misadventures of the tortoise Ijapa (or Obarun), whose motif analogues may be found throughout Congo–Kordofonian oral narrative traditions. But the Yoruba go on to attribute cosmic dimensions to the trickster. In a complex of myths, festival performance and ritual art, they celebrate the apotheosis of the trickster deity, who is known as either Eshu or Elegba, interchangeably. The trickster traits already described—animal cunning, the contrarieties of Gonde or Eyima, the perversity of Big Nose, the liminality of the Tabwa double-faced figure—all reach full development in Eshu/Elegba. His cult has spread from its Nigerian homeland westward to the Fon kingdom of Dahomey, to the Ewe of Togo and Ghana and across the Atlantic to the diaspora African American communities in Cuba, Brazil and Haiti (*see* §VIII below).

In Yorubaland, Eshu takes his place within a vast pantheon; many of these deities are grouped into a dozen or so cults for which the profusion of Yoruba ritual art has been created. Eshu's place within these cults varies. Worshippers of the hot/hard gods (Ogun of iron, Shango of lightning, Shapona of smallpox) say Eshu is their brother and is vain, handsome and sexually prolific. Icons of him, in mud or terracotta, are sometimes included in Shango's shrines. In Oshogbo, centre of the cult to Oshun, the cool mother of terrestrial waters, Oshun herself is held to be Eshu's wife and possessed of his cunning. For devotees of the Funfun cult, who worship the beneficent 'white gods', Eshu is totally evil and very ugly, with no wife and children, while to Muslims and Christians Eshu is simply Satan, the devil. The mythological Eshu is consistent with these contradictory interpretations: one myth tells of him wearing a two-sided hat so that farmers who were the best of friends would quarrel over his appearance and cause dissension in the world. Another myth tells how he enticed the sun and moon to change places, thereby reversing the primal order of things (see Wescott, p. 340). Despite their other cult affiliations, all Yoruba recognize Eshu and respect his control of the market-place and the crossroads. They also generally recognize him as an instigator who tricks men into offending each other and the gods (*orisha*). At the same time, however, Eshu is the mediating force who makes men turn to the gods in both expiation and propitiation and without whom they would starve for lack of sacrifice. His double role of instigator and mediator commands Eshu's presence wherever there is trouble or a state of transition.

Originally, Eshu may have been worshipped using 'stones of atonement', which commemorate a myth about the origin of his eyes (see Thompson, 1983, p. 21). However, more common Eshu representations are laterite pillars or mounds of mud called *yangi*. These are 0.3–1.2 m tall and are found at crossroads and in market-places and shrines. Daily offerings of palm oil are made on behalf of the town by cult officials. Smaller chunks of laterite (diam. 250–300 mm) protrude from the right side of passageways at the entrance of domestic compounds and serve as entrance shrines (see Pemberton, p. 20). According to myth, all *yangi* are part of Eshu's mystical body.

Eshu is also worshipped in household shrines. In some compounds a large chamber is reserved for him; this contains a raised altar, elaborately decorated with pieces of broken pottery inset in a blackened mud base. Other shrine rooms might contain sacred calabashes, painted with three black concentric circles (*igba eshu*), which are placed on large, open-mouthed terracotta pots (*ikoko*). These are framed by ritual cloth, wands and vestments, just as a dossal frames the cross on a Christian altar (Pemberton, p. 22).

The representations of Eshu most familiar to scholars are wood sculptures, although these are regarded by cult members as less ancient and less essential than the *yangi*. Such carvings may be divided into three categories: paired male and female supplicant figures united by cowrie strands; figural dance hooks that rest on the shoulders of ritual performers; and large votive images for decorating shrines and gates.

The sculptures are invariably painted black and are decorated with cowrie-shell dresses that may contain combs, pieces of calabash, spoons, knives and strings of coins. Some hold whistles, flutes, clubs, pipes or calabashes in their hands, while others suck their thumb. The most distinctive feature shared by these sculptures is a long, curved headdress, which may be overtly or suggestively phallic (see fig. 46). The priests of Eshu sometimes wear their hair in this manner, as do the possession priests of the lightning god, Shango. The figures are worn over the shoulder of a male worshipper, or a pair may be worn, one over each shoulder. When not in use, they are put back in the shrine. Female worshippers normally hang the images over their breasts or wear wrist sculptures of Eshu. The latter have a small head and limbless torso but retain the characteristic headdress and cowries; repeated arrowhead motifs may be used, possibly to represent stylized phalluses (see Wescott, p. 339). There are also more elaborate representations, some on horseback or wearing the two-coloured hat of dissension, which are used to decorate house and palace roof-posts and are also carved in low relief on doors.

46. Yoruba figure of Eshu/Elegba, wood with fluted coiffure and leather collar with cowrie shells, h. 395 mm, before 1960 (Los Angeles, CA, University of California, Fowler Museum of Cultural History)

Scholars concur on the symbolic significance of cowrie costumes that connect the Eshu of the market-place to this ancient form of currency (*see* §VI, 10 below). They also associate the knife and club with aggression, the comb and mirror with vanity, and the pipe and whistle with offensive, assertive behaviour or, like the thumb-sucking and the long-tailed phallic headdress, with libidinous behaviour. The precise nature of Eshu's sexuality, however, is debated. J. Wescott argues that the pubic apron Eshu usually wears indicates that his concern is with erotic energy, not procreation. J. Pemberton (p. 68) argues, from the iconography of a very old drum depicting Eshu with a snake above his head and juxtaposed (*inter alia*) with two couples copulating, that he gains vitality from sexual oppositions and from his mediating power, which overcomes such oppositions.

One of the oldest known pieces of Yoruba wood sculpture, the Ifa divination tray (Ulm, Ulm. Mus.), carved before 1659, includes images of Eshu with tailed headdress sucking his thumb and one of him smoking a pipe (see Thompson, 1983, p. 32). The association of Eshu with Ifa divination is of supreme philosophic importance to the Yoruba: the god Ifa is the master of the world's order, while Eshu is the personification of its chance. The Yoruba say, with profound simplicity, that Eshu and Ifa eat together. Eshu's bowl must be present at each divination, and a part of every sacrifice commanded by Ifa must be offered to Eshu, hence the spoon that adorns his statues. This is the greatest source of Eshu's power (*ashe*), for sacrifice is at the heart of Yoruba religious life and Eshu is at the heart of sacrifice.

The mythology of Eshu/Elegba was borrowed by the FON of Dahomey (now Benin Republic). They transformed him into their deity (*vodun*) Legba, maintaining his relationship with divination, while increasing his procreative sexuality and his intimacy with their highest god (Mawu) and reinventing his iconography. Travelling through Dahomey at the end of the 19th century, Sir Richard Burton observed (see Herskovits, p. 222):

> Legba himself is a horrid spectacle. A mass of red clay is roughly moulded by the clumsy, barbarous artist into an imitation man, who is evidently like Jupiter, 'a devil of a god for following the girls'. The figure is at squat, crouched, as it were, before its own attributes, with arms longer than a gorilla's, huge feet, and no legs to speak of. The head is of mud or wood, rising canonically to an almost pointed poll; a dab of clay represents the nose; the mouth is a gash from ear to ear, and the eyes and teeth are of cowries, or painted ghastly white.

These mud-sculpture representations of Legba spread further west to the Ewe, where they still decorate town gateways (see Gilbert), and also, via the forced migrations of the slave trade, to Cuba and Brazil, where local artists continue to create clay forms of the deity and to honour him in ritual services (see Thompson, 1983, pp. 18–33). In Haiti, Papa Legba is the first of the deities (*loa*) to be invoked at *vodun* services, at which his devotees remember his authority over crossroads by imploring him to 'open the barriers' for the other spirits from 'Guinee' (Africa).

Eshu/Elegba, Lord of Unpredictability, is the most manifold and generative personification of the trickster, conceived in a continent that has devoted much of its mythology, religion and art to the expression of this shadowy aspect of the human condition.

BIBLIOGRAPHY

L. Frobenius: *Und Afrika sprach* (Berlin, 1912; Eng. trans. in 2 vols, London and New York, 1913)
M. K. Herskovits: *Dahomey: An Ancient West African Kingdom*, ii (New York, 1938/*R* Evanston, IL, 1967)
J. Wescott: 'The Sculpture of Eshu-Elegba', *Africa*, xxxii/4 (1962), pp. 336–53
J. W. Fernandez: 'Principles of Opposition and Vitality in Fang Aesthetics', *J. Aesth. & A. Crit.*, xxv/1 (1966), pp. 53–64; repr. in *Art and Aesthetics in Primitive Societies: A Critical Anthology*, ed. C. F. Jopling (New York, 1971), pp. 356–73
R. F. Thompson: 'Aesthetics in Traditional Africa', *ARTnews*, lxvi/9 (1968), pp. 44–5, 63–6; repr. in *Art and Aesthetics in Primitive Societies: A Critical Anthology*, ed. C. F. Jopling (New York, 1971), pp. 374–81
K. Kerenyi: 'The Trickster in Relation to Greek Mythology', *The Trickster*, ed. P. Radin (New York, 1969), pp. 173–91
J. Pemberton III: 'Eshu-Elegba: The Yoruba Trickster God', *Afr. A.*, ix/1 (1975), pp. 20–27, 66–70, 90–92
R. D. Pelton: *The Trickster in West Africa* (Berkeley, 1980)
D. Cosentino: *Defiant Maids and Stubborn Farmers* (Cambridge, 1982)
M. V. Gilbert: 'Mystical Protection among the Anlo Ewe', *Afr. A.*, xv/4 (1982), pp. 60–66, 90
R. F. Thompson: *Flash of the Spirit: African and Afro-American Art and Philosophy* (New York, 1983)
A. F. Roberts: 'Duality in Tabwa Art', *Afr. A.*, xix/4 (1986), pp. 26–35, 86–7, 91–2

DONALD J. COSENTINO

V. Materials and techniques.

1. Earth. 2. Metal. 3. Paint. 4. Wood. 5. Stone. 6. Ivory. 7. Fibre. 8. Beads. 9. Leather. 10. Mixed media. 11. Gourds.

1. EARTH. In its raw state as soil, earth is the basic component of mud and ceramics, two of the commonest materials in African art and architecture, as well as being an ingredient in the manufacture of bricks and paints. Earth is both the simplest of materials and the most malleable. Its uses range from the simple smeared designs of some traditions of body decoration to complex sculptural and architectural forms.

(i) Mud. Depending on the amount of water present mud can be a liquid, paste or solid. Technically mud is a very wet soil or clay, forming a sub-aqueous sediment, with a particle size of not less than 0.004 mm. Any mineral substance can be made into mud with sufficient liquid, and the liquid is the medium by which the substance is applied. While the term 'mud' is used here, it should be noted that some scholars have preferred the term earth, since 'mud' is said to have pejorative connotations (e.g. see Cranstone). With clay and water mud can be fashioned into almost any shape or form. It can be used to make sculptures and items of personal adornment, to make dwellings or to decorate buildings.

There is no reliable method for dating works in mud. Some African buildings of mud and mud brick, however, notably the mud mosques of the Western Sudan, are possibly 1000 years old, and the technique of building with mud is probably much older. Sculpting in mud is also probably ancient in Africa; it is certainly widespread. Building in mud is practised over a more limited area, as it is impractical in areas of heavy rainfall.

Mud is an efficient insulator against the heat of the sun and can thus significantly reduce indoor temperatures during the summer months. This makes it a highly suitable building material for houses and compounds. Another advantage of using mud for dwellings is that it is not a permanent form, and buildings made out of it can be easily adapted to fit the changing requirements of the inhabitants (see Tobert, 1989). Mud buildings are also themselves used as a medium for art, the mud providing a kind of canvas. Painting of mud walls is done in many parts of Africa. Among the NDEBELE of Southern Africa women paint the exterior walls of their dwellings with bold, highly coloured designs. Ornate mud reliefs are also found, for example, on the royal palaces of Abomey and Benin and on the palaces and houses of the Hausa. Among the Gurens of north-eastern Ghana women use coloured mud to decorate the walls of their houses with figurative and geometrical designs, and some walls are so well burnished they shine. Mud walls of royal houses in Kano, Nigeria, are inset with small pieces of mica that glint in the light, while in southern Nigeria cowrie shells may be inset into the mud walls of Igbo houses.

While building in mud has received a lot of scholarly attention, its use within a dwelling has been sadly neglected. Mud can be used in many functional and yet artistic ways, for example to make a hearth, a pot stand or a granary. Among the Zaghawa of Northern Darfur, Sudan, mud has been used in the construction of beds and to construct modesty walls that protect the interior of a dwelling from view. Such walls, built for the houses of brides, are often decorated with raised and coloured patterns (see Tobert, 1989).

Mud has also been used as a paint and in body arts. Paintings in rock shelters in Southern Africa were produced using earth colours mixed to a paste and may have been applied with brushes made of animal hair attached to a stick (see Woodhouse). In some parts of Africa, mud is believed to have curative properties and may be applied to the body. In Zaïre, widows mourning the death of their husbands covered their bodies in a white clay (see Cannizzo). Among the Ndebele of Southern Africa young men paint their bodies with white clay during the three-month seclusion of their initiation rites. Among the Hamar of southern Ethiopia and other pastoral peoples of eastern Africa men construct elaborate coiffures out of clay smoothed over the head (see Ebin, pp. 74–9). Among the Bamana of Mali solutions of mud are applied with a bamboo stick to make designs on cotton textiles, known as *bogolanfini* or 'mud cloth' (see Imperato and Shamir; *see* MALI, fig. 1).

BIBLIOGRAPHY

H. C. Woodhouse: 'Rock Paintings of Southern Africa', *Afr. A.*, ii/3 (1969), pp. 44–9
P. J. Imperato and M. Shamir: 'Bokolanfini: Mud Cloth of the Bamana of Mali', *Afr. A.*, iii/4 (1970), pp. 32–41, 80
F. T. Smith: 'Gurensi Wall Painting', *Afr. A.*, xi/4 (1978), pp. 36–41
V. Ebin: *The Body Decorated*, Tribal A. (London, 1979)
N. Tobert: *The Ethnoarchaeology of the Zaghawa of Darfur (Sudan): Settlement and Transience*, Brit. Archaeol. Rep., 445/Cambridge Monographs in African Archaeology, 30 (Cambridge, 1988)
J. Cannizzo: *Into the Heart of Africa* (Toronto, 1989)
N. Tobert: 'Domestic Architecture and the Occupant's Life Cycle', *Traditional Dwellings & Settlements Rev.*, i/1 (1989), pp. 18–37
B. A. L. Cranstone: 'Earth as a Building Material', *J. Mus. Ethnog.*, 2 (1991), pp. 3–14

NATALIE TOBERT

(ii) Ceramics. Fired clay objects have been called variously, and with generally little scientific distinction, ceramics, pottery, earthenware and terracotta. 'Ceramics' is the umbrella term, with 'terracotta' frequently used to distinguish figurative ceramic sculpture from ceramic vessels and what is taken to be 'art' from 'craft'. Generally it is women who produce African ceramics, although it is often men who are responsible for figurative sculpture. Ceramics are among the earliest and most ubiquitous forms of art produced in Africa. Archaeological evidence indicates that Africans have been making pottery and sculptures of fired clay since Neolithic times. Although the evidence is fragmentary, it appears that domestic pottery was introduced into northern Africa shortly after its discovery in the Levant in the 6th millennium BC. Objects made of fired clay from sites in the Sahara Desert have been dated to the 8th millennium BC, a fact that might indicate independent invention of pottery in Africa. Pottery was produced in the area that is now Kenya as early as the Upper Paleolithic and was probably being produced throughout the continent by the 2nd millennium BC. Controlled excavations in Ghana and Mali have indicated dates in the 1st and 2nd millennia BC for terracotta sculptures, while radiocarbon dating of the Nok finds in northern Nigeria shows that the terracottas are from the early 1st millennium BC, and there is evidence that indicates a date of the mid-1st millennium AD for terracottas in Southern Africa. Despite the availability of mass-produced metal containers in Africa in the late 20th century, the production of ceramics has persisted, often quite vigorously.

(a) Manufacture. The clays used for making pottery in Africa vary from region to region but are generally coarse, and crushed potsherds are often mixed into the clay. The resulting material fires very rapidly and at low temperatures to a remarkably lightweight terracotta that is highly tolerant of thermal shock and functions well for both cooking pots and water vessels. Before the introduction of the potter's wheel from Europe all African pottery was hand-built, except in Egypt, where the potter's wheel was in use from at least the 2nd millennium BC. Even in the late 20th century almost all African pottery was still being built by hand, using one of several methods. The techniques vary from place to place and usually combine moulding, that is punching and pulling, and building with coils and slabs. Depending on the size of the desired pot, the potter either sits on the ground or on a low stool, turning the work between her legs, or moves around the pot as she works. Generally she begins either by coiling and modelling a long rope of clay on to itself using no support or, more frequently, by punching and pulling a mass of clay with her hands or a hammer over or within a mould, usually a fragment of an older pot, a gourd or a rounded stone. For spherical pots, top and bottom are built separately, left to stiffen until leather-like, then finally luted together.

The techniques for modelling and firing sculptures are similar to those used for pots, and the same clays and tools are used. Most small sculptures are solid, consisting of an interior of coarse clay, which establishes the basic shape of the object, and a surface of much finer clay, which is used for the detailing. Solid pieces up to 500 mm high are known; however, large pieces are more often hollow and sometimes very thin. Armatures of wood or palm fibre are sometimes used to support the clay during the modelling of larger objects.

Firing is done after the pots or sculptures have been preheated in one of two ways. They are either inverted over small fires or filled with grass that is burnt before the firing. This preheating dries out the clay so that only a brief firing at rather low temperatures is required. For the firing itself, which is most often done in the open, the preheated items are stacked in a pyramid that includes straw, wood and often dung. This is then covered with wood and potsherds. The whole is set afire and burns for an hour or two. The pots are removed from the stack immediately after firing and left to cool.

(b) Decoration. The greatest variation in African utilitarian ceramics lies in their decoration. Surfaces may be modified by burnishing, by applying slips before firing or pigments after firing (generally red, white and black), by blackening the entire vessel in a reduction atmosphere and by dipping or splashing the pots immediately after firing in a vegetal solution. Most distinctive to African pottery is

47. Ga'anda woman decorating a clay pot with a gourd chip, north-eastern Nigeria; from a photograph by Marla C. Berns, 1981

its range of impressed ornamentation (see fig. 47), done by means of rouletting, grooving, incising and comb stamping. Less typical is the application of clay pellets, spikes or bands.The amount and type of decoration is partly determined by function. Cooking pots have minimal ornamentation, for they are quickly blackened by the soot from open fires.

BIBLIOGRAPHY

D. Drost: *Topferei in Afrika: Ökonomie und Soziologie* (Berlin, 1968)

M. Cardew: *Pioneer Pottery* (London, 1969)

R. Thompson: 'Abatan: A Master Potter of the Egbado Yoruba', *Tradition and Creativity in Tribal Art*, ed. D. P. Biebuyck (Berkeley, 1969/*R* 1973), pp. 120–82

B. Fagg and J. Picton: *The Potter's Art in Africa* (London, 1970/*R* 1978)

R. Guardi: *African Crafts and Craftsmen* (New York, 1970)

S. Leith-Ross: *Nigerian Pottery* (Lagos, 1970)

C. Roy: *West African Pottery Forming and Firing Techniques* (diss., Bloomington, IN U., 1975)

J. Picton, ed.: *Earthenware in Asia and Africa* (London, 1984)

A. Stossel: *Afrikanische Keramik: Traditionelle Handwerkskunst südlich der Sahara* (Munich, 1984) [excellent plates and geographical coverage]

N. David, J. Sterner and K. Gavua: 'Why Pots are Decorated', *Current Anthropol.*, xxix/3 (1988), pp. 365–89

M. C. Berns: 'Ceramic Arts in Africa', *Afr. A.*, xxii/2 (1989), pp. 32–6, 101–02

N. Barley: *Smashing Pots: Feats of Clay from Africa* (London, 1994)

MARLA C. BERNS, ROBERT T. SOPPELSA

2. Metal. Historically, the main metals worked in Sub-Saharan Africa were iron, copper (including alloys) and gold. In addition, there was some localized use of lead, tin and, to a minor extent, silver. Africa is particularly well endowed with deposits of alluvial and reef gold and with iron ores, especially oxides in the form of haematite, magnetite and limonite, which are found in the laterite crust of the continent and in river sands. Copper is sparse in West Africa but plentiful in parts of Central and Southern Africa.

(i) Introduction. The earliest evidence for the smelting of metallic ores (as opposed to the working of native metals) comes from the southern Sahara, where copper was being worked by the early 1st millennium BC in the Aïr region of Niger and, shortly thereafter, to the west at Akjoujt in Mauritania. Even earlier dates for both copper and iron smelting have been claimed, but the evidence remains problematical. Although archaeological research is still too fragmentary to plot the course of diffusion, metal technology gradually spread through the subcontinent, albeit somewhat discontinuously, until by *c.* AD 1000 virtually all the peoples of the African mainland, with the exception of the Pygmy and Khoisan groups, used and probably also worked iron to some degree.

The ultimate source of this technology is uncertain. Some have contended that metalworking techniques were independently invented in Sub-Saharan Africa, but present evidence argues against this. It is now generally assumed that metalworking spread southward from North Africa and the Mediterranean, a view bolstered by the early dates of Saharan metallurgy. There seems to have been no chronological sequence from copper to copper alloys to iron, that is from simpler to more complex metallurgies, as happened in the ancient Near East and Europe. Rather, the introduction of iron and copper seems to have been roughly contemporaneous throughout the continent, except in the southern Sahara. There were few peoples of colonial Africa who did not themselves work metals, but some were far more skilled than others. In some cases metalworkers were itinerant craftsmen, for example the Awka of south-eastern Nigeria; in others they were hereditary occupational groups, sometimes referred to as 'castes', as among the Mande of Western Sudan; in still others they were people recognized as ethnically distinct, for example the smiths associated with the pastoral Tuareg and those associated with the Maasai.

In many areas the smith is socially marginalized and despised but also feared and respected, a set of attitudes reinforced by the smith's frequent role as circumciser, burier of the dead and maker of magical charms. In West Africa smiths are often also sculptors, creating works in both iron and wood, and their wives are potters. The separateness of smiths is commonly perpetuated by endogamy among metalworkers. In contrast, in Western Equatorial Africa and the interlacustrine region there is a strong association between the smith and the kingship and political authority. Here, oral traditions attribute the introduction of metalworking to culture heroes or even known kings. The smith's peculiar power, like that of the chief or the hunter, derives only in part from his technical skills; more especially it derives from his ability to invoke supernatural forces through his command of medicinal and ritual knowledge. His long apprenticeship teaches him not only to make the constant adjustments that variable ores, fuels and weather conditions demand but also to perform ritual sacrifices and offerings to the ancestors and other spirits without whom his work cannot prosper. He also learns how to protect the enterprise from malevolent forces or spiteful competitors through the use of medicines and prescribed behaviour. Indeed, medicines are often built into the structure of a smelting furnace or placed in its base to strengthen and protect it, or the furnace may be decorated with materials for the same purpose.

Metallurgy is often highly sexualized. It is very common for smelters to observe sexual abstinence during the construction of furnaces and during the smelting process and for menstruating women or women of childbearing age to be forbidden from going near the operation. Moreover, in regions as widely scattered as the Ader (Niger), Bassar (Togo), southern Tanzania, Zambia and Zimbabwe the furnace is said to be a woman gestating iron in a 'womb' and delivering a bloom as a mother delivers a child.

In areas where rich ores and sufficient fuels sustained intensive production, different villages specialized in smelting, refining, forging or charcoal-making. Such was the case among the Bassari of western Togo, where smelting dates back at least to the 12th century AD, reaching a quasi-industrial scale by the 19th. Similar levels of iron production were probably reached on the Ndop Plain of north-western Cameroon about the same time. By the late 20th century metal smelting had almost entirely died out in Africa owing to the availability of cheap imported scrap metal and the dwindling supplies of fuel. While smithing has continued to thrive, its practitioners are more often called on to repair objects than to create them.

(ii) Iron. African ironworking presents a bewildering variety of technological adaptations expressed in an almost infinite array of furnace types, bellows and tool kits. The primary distinctions relate to size and to the use or absence of bellows. Some furnaces are scarcely more than pits or shallow bowls, capable of smelting only small quantities of ore at a time; they are difficult to distinguish from forges in the archaeological record. The largest (3–4 m in height) tend to be those relying on a natural draught rather than forced air (see fig. 48). Some furnaces must be broken down after smelting to extract the bloom; others may be used repeatedly over many years. Wide variations in type are found even within a limited area, as they are adapted to local ores, fuels and other constraints.

The induced-draught furnace seems to have been an independent African innovation, since there is no record of it anywhere else except Burma. This type of furnace has a number of holes around the base that draw in air, which then rises as it heats, setting up a natural draught and achieving the desired temperatures without the need for bellows and someone to work them. Such furnaces have been documented in parts of West and Central Africa but have not been found south of the Zambezi River nor in the equatorial forest. While some scholars regard them as more sophisticated and therefore later than either the bowl furnace or the low shaft furnace, both of which rely on forced air, their introduction may be a response to social rather than technological factors. For example, in areas of heavy and sustained production, there may not have been adequate manpower to keep bellows operating for long periods.

An unusual feature of African ironworking was the ability, in some areas at least, to produce steel through the smelting process itself, rather than in subsequent forging. This carburization could be accomplished in the natural-draught furnace, if it was tall enough, or in an ordinary-sized furnace, if the twyers were inserted deep inside with the other end close to but not attached to the bellow's mouth, allowing more air to be drawn in. Cast iron, on the other hand, was rarely if ever produced by African smelters. In many cases the raw iron contained too many impurities

48. Iron-smelting furnace under construction, Banjeli, Togo; from a photograph by Carlyn Saltman, 1985

to be worked directly and needed to go through a refining process. This customarily involved breaking up the bloom and reheating it, sometimes in crucibles, in a small refining furnace or fire. It could then be forged by a smith through repeated heating and hammering.

The two main types of bellows used in Africa are bag and bowl, but the materials and forms vary almost as much as the furnaces and probably for the same reasons. Because bellows are more perishable than furnaces, the archaeological record is too incomplete to allow a reconstruction of their geographical diffusion. A cylindrical form, with pistons operated by sticks, is found only in Madagascar, bearing witness to the island's connections with Indonesian metalworking traditions. Bellows were always used in refining operations and in forging the metal.

While smiths produced a range of metal tools, weapons, jewellery and sculpture, they themselves often worked with stone anvils and hammers and with wooden tongs. Their dexterity was such that with unhafted stones they could pound red-hot metal into the various shapes required. Where iron anvils were used, they frequently took the form of large spikes or wedges, with the pointed end implanted in the ground.

(iii) Other metals. The main indigenous sources of copper in Sub-Saharan Africa are carbonates, such as malachite. Copper smelting requires lower temperatures than iron, and it was carried out in smaller-bellows furnaces. The copper was refined in crucibles and then worked or alloyed with other metals, principally lead. In the eastern Transvaal and possibly in the Aïr region and south-eastern Nigeria it was alloyed with local tins to produce bronze. Brass, the copper alloy found most commonly in Sub-Saharan Africa, was an imported metal, transported across the desert from the Muslim world or by sea from Europe.

Copper and its alloys were frequently worked by hammering and ornamented by heightening the colour of the metal or by the addition of chiselled, stippled or encrusted designs. A large number of West African peoples, from

Senegal to Lake Chad and south to the Cameroon Grassfields, perfected the art of lost-wax casting. The delicately detailed bronze corpus from Igbo-Ukwu in south-eastern Nigeria is dated to the late 1st millennium AD. It is very different in style and in metal content from the better-known, later works of Ife, which depict much larger human figures and life-size heads cast in either pure copper or brass. The enormous repertory of Benin castings, created over a period of perhaps 500 years, reveals the virtuosity of casters, who were able to produce complex free-standing figures, plaques in high relief and an array of ceremonial objects, using an elaborate system of armatures and runners in the casting process. Akan casters excelled in miniature work, producing thousands of brass gold-weights, which illustrated with refined detail proverbs and activities of daily life. Akan casters used not only conventional wax models but also direct casting of such items as beetles, seeds and crustaceans.

While lost-wax casting was limited to West Africa, peoples in Equatorial and Central Africa used open-mould casting, especially in the production of massive collars and bracelets. In areas of Southern and Eastern Africa wire-drawing of both iron and copper was practised. Wiredrawing equipment dated to *c.* AD 1400 has been found in the archaeological site of Ingombe Ilede on the middle Zambezi River, and coils of wire are a common feature of graves in south-western Zaïre. While an abundance of coiled wire was found at Igbo-Ukwu, it seems to have been made by hammering rather than drawing.

Working gold is simpler than working either iron or copper, because it does not need to be smelted but can be simply separated from its rocky or alluvial matrix by crushing, washing and winnowing. The gold is then melted at low temperatures and cast into ingots in open moulds or into objects by means of the lost-wax method. Among the Asante of Ghana it was also pounded into leaf to cover items of regalia (*see* ASANTE AND RELATED PEOPLES, §3(i)). Goldsmiths in the Senegambian region produced gold jewellery, finely worked in spirals and filigree, that was undoubtedly influenced by North African conventions.

BIBLIOGRAPHY

W. B. Cline: *Mining and Metallurgy in Negro Africa* (Menasha, 1937)
M. Eliade: *Forgerons et alchimistes* (Paris, 1956); Eng. trans. by S. Corrin as *The Forge and the Crucible* (New York, 1972)
N. Echard: 'Notes sur les forgerons de l'Ader (Pays Hausa, République du Niger)', *J. Africanistes*, xxxv/2 (1965), pp. 353–72
G. Dieterlen: 'Contribution à l'étude des forgerons en Afrique occidentale', *Annu.: Ecole Pratique Hautes Etud.*, lxxiii (1965–6), pp. 5–28
J. A. R. Wembah-Rashid: *Iron Working in Ufipa* (Dar es Salaam, 1973)
P. McNaughton: *Iron Art of the Blacksmith in Western Sudan* (West Lafayette, IN, 1975)
G. Célis and E. Nzikobanyanka: *La Métallurgie traditionnelle au Burundi* (Tervuren, 1976)
N. Neaher: 'Awka Who Travel', *Africa*, xlix/4 (1979), pp. 352–66
J. P. Warnier and I. Fowler: 'A Nineteenth-century Rhur in Central Africa', *Africa*, xlix/4 (1979), pp. 329–51
P. de Maret: 'Ceux qui jouent avec le feu: La Place du forgeron en Afrique centrale', *Africa*, i/3 (1980), pp. 263–79
C. Goucher: '"Iron is Iron 'Til it is Rust": Trade and Ecology in the Decline of West African Iron Smelting', *J. Afr. Hist.*, xxii/3 (1981), pp. 179–89
B. Martinelli: *Métallurgistes bassari: Techniques et formation sociale* (Lome, 1982)
The Art of Metal in Africa (exh. cat. by M.-T. Brincard, New York, Afr.–Amer. Inst., 1982)
N. Echard, ed.: *Métallurgies africaines* (Paris, 1983)
F. J. Kense: *Traditional African Iron Working* (Calgary, 1983)
E. W. Herbert: *Red Gold of Africa: Copper in Precolonial History and Culture* (Madison, 1984)
R. Haaland and P. Shinnie, eds: *African Iron Working: Ancient and Traditional* (Oslo, 1985)
P. R. McNaughton: *The Mande Blacksmiths: Knowledge, Power, and Art in West Africa*, Trad. A. Africa (Bloomington, 1988)
T. Childs: 'Style, Technology, and Iron Smelting Furnaces in Bantu-speaking Africa', *J. Anthropol. Archeol.*, x (1991), pp. 332–59
E. W. Herbert: *Iron, Gender and Power: Rituals of Transformation in African Societies* (Bloomington, 1993) [extensive bibliog.]
Iron Master of Them All (exh. cat. by W. J. Dewey and A. F. Roberts, Iowa City, U. IA Mus. A., 1993)

FILM AND VIDEO RECORDINGS

N. Echard: *Noces de feu* (Paris, 1968) [film, 16 mm]
E. W. Herbert, C. Goucher and C. Saltman: *The Blooms of Banjeli: Technology and Gender in West African Ironmaking* (Bloomington, 1986) [videotape; study guide, 1987]

EUGENIA HERBERT

3. PAINT. By the late 20th century, African artists had access to the full range of local 'natural' and commercial 'manufactured' paints. Local pigments include those derived from natural earth or mineral elements, ground in a stone mortar and mixed with animal fat, tree sap or a similar substance to produce a type of oil paint. Such pigments were used in rock art, which has a long history in Africa (*see* §VI, 15 below). They were probably applied with the hand or an implement made from fibre, animal hair or bone. The use of ochres was especially widespread. This article provides an overview of the other uses to which paint has been put in African art.

(i) Body and shrine art. Throughout Africa people embellish their bodies with paint (*see also* §VI, 4(ii) below). This is an ancient practice. In the Sudan, for example, the use of ochre as a cosmetic dates back to at least 4000 BC. Among the Kuba and related groups in Zaïre, camwood mixed with palm oil is rubbed on the skin to increase its beauty; the mixture is also applied to a corpse before burial. Among the Nuba of the Sudan, men paint the body in order to enhance its form (see fig. 89 below). Among the Turkana of Kenya, men cake their hair with clay and red colour to celebrate a successful hunt or the end of planting (see fig. 141 below). Among the Igbo of Nigeria, women paint curvilinear designs, derived from plant and animal forms, on their faces and torsos (see fig. 49). The designs, called *uli*, demonstrate the wearer's status and beauty. The pigment used is a stain extracted from the fruit or pods of plants, for the application of which the body is prepared by covering the appropriate areas with a mixture of camwood and palm oil. The pigment is then applied with a quill feather or thin stick of palm frond.

The use of white clay or kaolin chalk is widespread in West Africa and is often used as a marker of spirituality. In Benin, kaolin is used for both body and shrine decoration and symbolizes the essence of ritual purity. Among the Asante and other Akan-speaking groups in Ghana and Côte d'Ivoire, white on the face, arms, shoulders and torso is the mark of a priest or priestess. Among the Fulani, or Peul, in Niger and Burkina Faso women paint white and black designs on their faces for protective purposes. During puberty ceremonies among the Dan of Côte d'Ivoire young women decorate themselves, especially their faces, with bold geometric patterns. Body painting is also practised during men's initiation among a number of

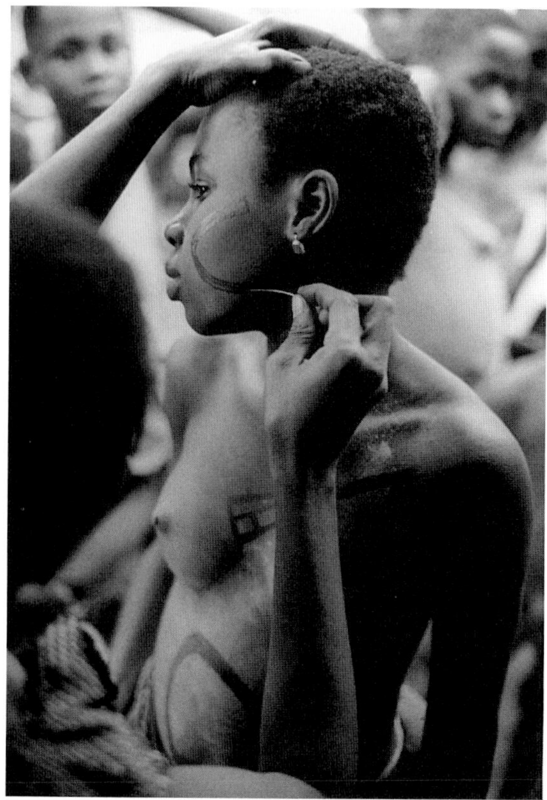

49. Igbo girl being painted with *uli* designs, Nigeria; from a photograph by H. M. Cole, 1983

groups in Liberia and Côte d'Ivoire. In the Tikar area of Cameroon, a red camwood paste is worn by women to mark the death of a chief or other important individual.

The appearance of shrines and religious structures is frequently enhanced by painting. This ranges from simple geometric decoration on ancestor shrines in northern Ghana and southern Burkina Faso, through the more elaborate shrines associated with various Yoruba and Benin deities in Nigeria, to the painted walls of women's initiation huts among the Bemba of Zambia. The *mbari* houses of the southern Igbo are particularly striking, as are the *asafo* shrines of the traditional warrior organizations of the Fante of Ghana (see fig. 79 below). The *mbari* house is a shrine, usually dedicated to Ala, the earth goddess, and has an exterior niche filled with figures representing a range of human and animal forms. These, as well as the walls themselves, are painted with complex representational and non-representational motifs that are both symbolic and decorative. The traditional pigments used provide white, red-brown, yellow, green and pink colours, while black is made from charcoal and red from camwood; blue is obtained from European washing blue. More recently, commercial paints have been used as well (*see also* IGBO, §3).

(ii) Decoration of domestic structures. In many parts of the continent, both the interior and exterior walls of domestic structures are painted. This is usually done by women (see fig. 50). Among the Frafra of northern Ghana, for example, wall decoration consists of a limited number of painted geometric motifs from which the artist chooses. Before a wall is painted, it is plastered with a mixture of cow-dung, clay and water. Compound walls usually need replastering every four or five years, but whether or not they are decorated, or redecorated, depends on the women's initiative. Three colours are used: red-brown, made from a clay of limited availability; black, from a soft, pulverized stone; and white, from a soft, chalklike stone. The wall is initially painted red-brown with a small wicker broom. Black is then applied with a feather or fibre brush. Usually black lines define the specific motifs. Next, the white is added, also with a fibre brush. After the wall has been painted and allowed to dry, it is burnished with a stone. Finally, it is sprayed with a varnish-like fixative made from the seed pods of the African locust-bean tree. The use of these three colours is characteristic of painting traditions from Mali to northern Ghana. Among the Frafra, walls are painted in order to embellish the compound and as a statement of female unity and support for the entire family.

The painted walls that traditionally frame the entrance of Igbo compounds are also executed by women and may be said to symbolize the status of the family head. The motifs used in Igbo wall painting have been strongly influenced by *uli* designs (*see* §(i) above). In fact, wall painting is called *uli aja* or 'wall *uli*' in Igbo. The walls are embellished with various plant and mineral pigments. In addition charcoal, soot, indigo and kaolin are used. In parts of Sudan, especially in the Nubian area near the Egyptian border, both men and women decorate compound walls. Many of the men are professional artists who use commercial paints bought in the market. Women, in contrast, use earth colours and lime from nearby hills. The women also sometimes use washing blue. Much of this art disappeared as a result of the construction of the Aswan dam.

Probably the most polychromic walls on the continent are those decorated by the southern NDEBELE and other peoples of Southern Africa. Here compound walls are decorated by women in a basically geometric style. Among regional variations are differences in colour, consequent upon the type of clay available in any particular area. Other Southern African groups, such as the Swazi and Pedi, are also noted for their painted compound walls. Throughout Africa, by the late 20th century commercial establishments (especially small businesses) advertised their products and services by having images or slogans painted on their walls. Various kinds of shop signs have also been popular; the barber's sign illustrating different hairstyles is probably the best-known type. These are done with commercial paints, usually by self-taught artists.

(iii) Decorations of vehicles, textiles, masks and other objects. Many types of secular objects are painted. Boats, donkey carts, vans and lorries are frequently decorated with proverbs, prayers, statements of status or affiliation, advertisements, and figurative and non-figurative motifs, often combined. Vans and lorries, for example, may carry such sayings as 'No condition is permanent' or 'God's word' along with a figure of a reclining lion or intertwined floral patterns. Most commonly, however, painted decoration is applied to pottery. The majority of painted pottery

50. Group of Gurensi women (co-wives) painting a hut wall, Zuarungu, Frafra region, northern Ghana; from a photograph by Fred T. Smith

designs are geometric, and with only a few exceptions they are executed by women, who are also the potters. The motifs may be symbolic for ritual vessels or purely aesthetic for utilitarian ware. Most unpainted African pottery is either red or black. Paint made from charcoal, earth pigments or white kaolin may be used for decoration.

Gourd bowls and spoons, drums, stools, staffs, shields and textiles may also be decorated with colour. Although pyro-engraving and carving are the most important techniques of gourd decoration, painting and dyeing also occur. Again, earth or vegetable pigments, charcoal, soot and chalk are commonly used, although imported enamel paints were in use throughout the continent by the late 20th century. In East Africa wooden and hide shields are painted with earth pigments and chalk. Among the Senufo of Côte d'Ivoire, black or dark brown human and animal forms are painted on a coarsely woven white cloth with a small brush or knife, the dye being made from a mud solution. In decorating Asante *adinkra* cloth, bamboo or wooden combs are used to outline square or rectangular areas in black. These areas are then filled in with a geometric stamped motif. A thick, black paint produced from tree bark and iron slag serves as the dye.

Masks and figures are also decorated with paint. Traditionally, various earth colours (especially ochres), charcoal, soot, indigo, ground eggshell, kaolin and chalk were employed, the pigments usually being mixed with water or egg white before application. By the late 20th century, the use of enamel paint was common in many areas. The Yoruba of Nigeria have decorated masks and some figures with enamel paint since the mid-19th century. Elaborate designs embellish the surfaces of masks and figures among the Dogon, Mossi, Bwa, Kuba, Teke, Pende and Yaka, among others. Among these groups, colour minimizes form while emphasizing the surface. Complex and elaborate decoration, especially the combination of triangles and parallel lines, is particularly characteristic of the aristocratic art of the Kuba. Moreover, paint is an important component of almost all masking styles. White-faced masks, for instance, usually with a heart-shaped face, are found over a wide area from eastern Nigeria to eastern Zaïre. Among some Igbo groups, white-faced masks are associated with beauty and harmony, while darker examples are associated with bravery and aggression. A similar dichotomy is also found among the Okpella, a northern Edo group. Among some peoples, for example the Yoruba of Nigeria, masks may be repainted if they begin to show signs of wear or if they are to appear at a particularly significant event (see fig. 16 above).

Increasingly throughout the 20th century, easel painting and other originally Western art forms have been taken up by African artists. For an overview of the use of paint by such artists *see* §IX below and entries on modern developments in individual countries; *see also* COLOUR, colour pl. I, fig. 2.

BIBLIOGRAPHY

H. Lhote: *The Search for the Tassili Frescoes* (London and New York, 1959)

D. Mazonowicz: 'Prehistoric Rock Painting at Tassili', *Afr. A.*, ii/1 (1968), pp. 24–5, 74–5

African Arts of Transformation (exh. cat. by H. M. Cole, Santa Barbara, U. CA, A. Gals, 1970)
F. Willett: *African Art: An Introduction*, World A. (London, 1971, rev. 1993)
M. Wenzel: *House Decoration in Nubia*, A. & Soc. Ser. (London, 1972)
African Textiles and Decorative Arts (exh. cat., ed. R. Sieber; New York, MOMA, 1972)
M. W. Mount: *African Art: The Years since 1920* (Bloomington, IN, and London, 1973, rev. New York, 1989)
The Arts of Ghana (exh. cat., ed. H. M. Cole and D. H. Ross; Los Angeles, UCLA, Wight A.G.; Minneapolis, MN, Walker A. Cent.; Dallas, TX, Mus. F.A.; 1977–8)
F. T. Smith: 'Gurensi Wall Painting', *Afr. A.*, xi/4 (1978), pp. 36–41
R. Brain: *Art and Society in Africa* (London, 1980)
R. Sieber: *African Furniture and Household Objects* (Bloomington, IN, 1980)
African Artistry: Technique and Aesthetics in Yoruba Sculpture (exh. cat. by H. J. Drewal, Atlanta, GA, High Mus. A., 1980)
H. M. Cole: *Mbari: Art and Life among the Owerri Igbo* (Bloomington, IN, 1982)
J. Vansina: *Art History in Africa: An Introduction to Method* (London and New York, 1984)
P. Ben-Amos: 'Artistic Creativity in Benin Kingdom', *Afr. A.*, xix/3 (1986), pp. 60–63
F. T. Smith: 'Compound Entryway Decoration: Male Space, Female Creativity', *Afr. A.*, xix/3 (1986), pp. 52–9

FRED T. SMITH

4. WOOD. The techniques and tools for carving wood are remarkably consistent throughout Sub-Saharan Africa. Almost invariably carved items are monoxylous or carved from one piece of wood. The few exceptions include such items as Chokwe and Akan chairs and Kalabari Ijo funerary screens. In these cases, however, the artists were influenced by European prototypes and/or European carpentry techniques. The type of wood used depends upon the object's intended use. Stools and doorposts are usually carved of heavy woods, while masks are carved of woods that are light but sturdy. There have been few studies of the species used in African wood-carving (but see Dechamps). Similarly, little work has been done to determine whether there are correlations between the symbolic attributes of species and the types of carvings for which they are used.

Traditionally the main tools used for carving were adzes and knives. Adzes are axelike tools with the blade set at a right angle to the handle. The most common type of adze in Africa has the narrow shaft of the metal blade set into or through a slot in the wooden handle. Another, rarer type has the rear section of the blade flattened and curved to form a socket into which the handle is inserted. Each carver uses a variety of sizes of adze. Often the blades can be removed from their handles to be employed as chisels. Knives are primarily used in the finishing stages for carving fine details, for incising surface decorations or for scraping down rough spots. Final smoothing was often done with a rough leaf or sand. Such tools as saws, files, drills and sandpaper had become quite common throughout Africa by the late 20th century, but adzes and knives were still the main tools used.

Usually the wood is carved while it is still moist. As it dries it is very carefully monitored, so that, if necessary, action can be taken to prevent cracking. The Mossi, for example, periodically bury carvings in moist earth during the carving process to slow down the drying. In the initial stages of carving the carver uses the adze blade almost perpendicularly and cuts deeply into the wood. The basic shapes are quickly roughed out. When more detailed work begins, smaller, sharper adzes are used, the angle at which the blade strikes the wood decreases and the shavings being cut away become progressively thinner (see fig. 51). An account of carving among the Jukun describes a process seen throughout Africa (see Rubin):

> The easy virtuosity of the carvers must be acknowledged. With the left hand, the work was braced on the ground against each adze stroke but kept almost constantly in motion. Whether the carver worked with or across the grain, whether he took off large chunks of wood in the early stages of the work or shavings as fine as any plane would make as the mask neared completion, adze strokes were unerringly accurate.

Distinct stages of the carving may be recognized explicitly. For example, the Yoruba distinguish blocking out, dividing up the masses, smoothing the forms and cutting the details (see Carroll). In a study in which a Yoruba carver was filmed at work it was found that, while the early stages were shorter than the later ones, and more

51. Large wooden spoon being carved with an adze by Si, a Dan sculptor, Nyor Diaple, north-east Liberia; from a photograph by Eberhard Fischer, 1960

wood was removed in them, a greater amount of time was spent in the early stages on 'thinking' (see Willett). Indeed, African sculptors frequently characterize the 'thinking' part of carving as the most difficult aspect of their work. As they do not use models or sketch out what they are going to carve beforehand, all the details must be conceived mentally. The early stages are, of course, the most important, and master carvers will often do these themselves, leaving the final stages to their apprentices. In many parts of Africa rituals must be carried out to ensure the success of the 'technical' processes. This is especially so for carvings that will have a ritual usage. Among the Mijikenda of Kenya, for example, elaborate rites are performed and offerings made before a tree can be cut down in order to be carved into a commemorative sculpture for a deceased elder. Often ritual prohibitions are placed on the behaviour of the carver throughout the carving process, and magical incantations are pronounced to ensure the efficacy of the mask or sculpture. Carvers frequently work in private, especially if the product of their work is to have a restricted audience.

Generally, wood-carvers are part-time specialists who are also subsistence farmers. They learn their skills growing up in a carving family or by undergoing a period of apprenticeship. In many cases all males are expected to be able to carve such simple utilitarian items as spoons and handles, while specialists are commissioned to carve more complex items. In most parts of Africa wood-carving is a male activity. Among the pastoral Turkana of Kenya, however, women carve elegantly shaped containers (see Donovan).

See also WOOD, colour pl. III, fig. 2.

BIBLIOGRAPHY

K. Carroll: *Yoruba Religious Carving: Pagan and Christian Sculpture in Nigeria and Dahomey* (London, 1967)
R. Dechamps: 'L'Identification anatomique des bois utilisés pour des sculptures en Afrique' [series of articles in *Africa-Tervuren*, beginning with xiv (1970)]
W. Bascom: 'A Yoruba Master Carver: Duga of Meko', *The Traditional Artist in African Societies*, ed. W. L. d'Azevedo (Bloomington, 1973), pp. 62–78
J. C. Messenger: 'The Role of the Carver in Anang Society', *The Traditional Artist in African Societies*, ed. W. L. d'Azevedo (Bloomington, 1973), pp. 101–27
F. Willett: 'An African Sculptor at Work', *Afr. A.*, xi/2 (1978), pp. 28–33, 96
C. Roy: 'Mossi Zazaido', *Afr. A.*, xiii/3 (1980), pp. 42–7, 92
A. Rubin: 'Akuma: Carving the Masks at Takum', *Afr. A.*, xviii/2 (1985), pp. 60–62, 103
D. Hersak: *Songye Masks and Figure Sculpture* (London, 1986), pp. 56–68
Vigango: Commemorative Sculpture of the Mijikenda of Kenya (exh. cat., ed. E. Wolfe, III; Williamstown, MA, Williams Coll. Mus. A., 1986)
A. Donovan: 'Turkana Functional Art', *Afr. A.*, xxi/3 (1988), pp. 44–7

5. STONE. Stone-carving traditions are comparatively rare in Sub-Saharan Africa. Moreover no traditional stone-carving practices have survived, so the techniques used can only be surmised from the extant carvings themselves. Soft-stone carvings are much more common than hard-stone ones and are mainly of steatites or talcs (commonly referred to as soapstone). The best-known examples are the bird pillars of Great Zimbabwe (for illustration *see* GREAT ZIMBABWE), the statues of Esie, memorial figures found among the Kissi and other peoples of Sierra Leone and Guinea, which are commonly known as *nomoli* or *pomdo*, and the funerary sculptures of the Kongo kingdom. From an unfinished stone in a quarry in the Kongo area, it has been deduced that the carvers of these figures made an initial blocking out before the stone was moved and so the method of stone-carvers is thought to be similar to that of wood-carvers. The carving tools used seem to have been essentially the same as those used by Kongo wood-carvers.

African hard-stone carvings are commonly of granite gneiss or basalt. The best-known examples include the *akwanshi* memorial carvings of the Cross River area of Nigeria, the archaic monoliths of Ife and the rock engravings of the San of Southern Africa. In both cases shallow surface decoration appears to have been scratched, pitted or ground away with stone tools.

BIBLIOGRAPHY

P. Allison: *African Stone Sculpture* (London, 1968)
P. Stevens: *The Stone Images of Esie, Nigeria* (Ibadan, 1978)
The Four Moments of the Sun: Kongo Art in Two Worlds (exh. cat. by R. F. Thompson and J. A. Cornet, Washington, DC, N.G.A., 1981–2)
F. Lamp: 'House of Stones: Memorial Art of Fifteenth-century Sierra Leone', *A. Bull.*, lxv/2 (1983), pp. 219–37
T. A. Dowson: *Rock Engravings of Southern Africa* (Johannesburg, 1992)

WILLIAM J. DEWEY

6. IVORY. Elephant tusks are the source of most African ivory, although hippopotamus and warthog teeth are also used. In general, the tools used to carve wood (i.e. adzes and knives) are also used in carving ivory, and ivoryworkers are usually also woodworkers. Ivory's hard, fine grain allows for very delicate, detailed carving as well as for undercutting and extensive openwork. The form of the tusk itself is often followed in the carving process, artists thus incorporating its natural curvature. This can be seen in such works as the divination tappers of the Yoruba (see fig. 98 below), the royal ancestral tusks of Benin, and across the continent in trumpets with side-blown embouchures used to announce the beginning of funerals, wars and initiations and the arrival of rulers. Cross-cut sections of tusk are frequently carved as bracelets or anklets. Some, such as those worn by titled Igbo women, are left unadorned, while in Benin, Owo and elsewhere specialist artists have created *tour de force* pieces, splitting one tusk section to form two interlocking, openwork cylinders. For example, a pair of interlocked armlets from Benin depict kings in their coral-bead regalia, carved in high relief, surrounded by royal emblems such as elephant and crocodile heads, leopards and mudfish (London, BM; see fig. 52).

The colour of African ivory objects is highly varied. In some areas the natural white of the ivory is associated with purity and so retained through bleaching with citrus juice or scrubbing with sand. In other areas the ivory is reddened or browned with palm oil or camwood and given a glossy surface.

In Africa elephant ivory has been a precious commodity since ancient times and generally signifies wealth. Throughout much of Africa the medium is associated with royalty. At Benin one tusk from each slain elephant belonged to the ruler, and he had the right to purchase the second. Such ivory objects of authority as sceptres, fly-whisks, staffs and snuff containers are features of Yoruba, Benin, Kongo, Mangbetu and other courts. In non-royal contexts,

52. Ivory armlet with bronze inlay, h. 150 mm, diam. 100 mm, from Benin City, 16th century (London, British Museum)

ivory is still usually associated with high status. Among the Igbo of Nigeria, titled men own tusks and on personal wooden shrines are often depicted holding them. Similarly, among the Lega of Zaïre only the highest-ranking members of the Bwami society are entitled to own ivory masks and objects.

The prestige of ivory is partially symbolic, for in Africa the power of a leader is often metaphorically likened to that of an elephant. Like antelope horns, porcupine quills, leopard's teeth and other media (*see* §10 below), tusks have both protective and aggressive functions, as do leaders who are empowered by the possession and/or representation of these material symbols. Indications of this empowerment can be seen in the ivory-hung costumes (*orufanran*) of Owo Yoruba chiefs and in the encircling of the body of the ruler of Benin with ivory bracelets and waist pendants.

While many African peoples carve ivory, a few areas stand out as important centres of ivory production. These include the peoples of Sierra Leone and Benin who produced the so-called Afro-Portuguese ivories (*see* §VI, 2(ii) below), the Yoruba and Benin kingdoms of Nigeria, and several regions of Zaïre (*see* LEGA AND RELATED PEOPLES, §2; KONGO, §4; PENDE, §3).

BIBLIOGRAPHY

African Textiles and Decorative Arts (exh. cat. by R. Sieber, New York, MOMA; Los Angeles, CA, Co. Mus. A.; San Francisco, CA, de Young Mem. Mus.; Cleveland, OH, Mus. A.; 1972–3)

R. Poynor: 'Edo Influence on the Art of Owo', *Afr. A.*, ix/4 (1976), pp. 40–45, 90

A Survey of Zaïrian Art: The Bronson Collection (exh. cat. by J. Cornet, Raleigh, NC Mus. A., 1978)

P. Gebauer: *Art of Cameroon with a Catalog of the Gebauer Collection of Cameroon Art at the Portland Art Museum and the Metropolitan Museum of Art* (Portland, 1979)

Treasures of Ancient Nigeria (exh. cat. by E. Eyo and F. Willett, Detroit, MI, Inst. A.; Oslo, N.G.; London, RA; and elsewhere; 1980–83)

J. Henggeler: 'Ivory Trumpets of the Mende', *Afr. A.*, xiv/2 (1981), pp. 59–63

F. Neyt: *Traditional Arts and History of Zaïre* (Brussels, 1981)

For Spirits and Kings: African Art from the Paul and Ruth Tishman Collection (exh. cat. by S. M. Vogel, New York, Met., 1981)

M.-L. Bastin: *La Sculpture Tshokwe* (Meudon, 1982)

African Ivories (exh. cat., ed. K. Ezra; New York, Met., 1984)

Igbo Arts: Community and Cosmos (exh. cat. by H. M. Cole and C. C. Aniakor, Los Angeles, UCLA, Mus. Cult. Hist., 1984–6)

African Masterpieces from Munich (exh. cat. by M. Kecskesi, New York, Cent. Afr. A., 1986)

N. Barley: 'Africa', *Ivory: An International History and Illustrated Survey* (London, 1987), pp. 170–87

Sounding Forms: African Musical Instruments (exh. cat., ed. M.-T. Brincard; Washington, DC, N. Mus. Afr. A.; Richmond, VA Mus. F.A.; Kansas City, MO, Nelson–Atkins Mus. A.; Paris, Mus. A. Afr. & Océan.; 1989)

Yoruba: Nine Centuries of African Art and Thought (exh. cat. by H. J. Drewal and J. Pemberton III, with R. Abiodun, New York, Cent. Afr. A., 1989)

H.-J. Koloss: *A Survey of Zaïrean Art* (New York, 1990)

African Reflections: Art from Northeastern Zaïre (exh. cat. by E. Echildkrout and C. A. Keim, New York, Amer. Mus. Nat. Hist., 1990)

Elephant: The Animal and its Ivory in African Culture (exh. cat., ed. D. Ross; Los Angeles, UCLA, Fowler Mus. Cult. Hist., 1992–3)

KATHY CURNOW

7. FIBRE.

(i) Weaving. (ii) Basketry.

(i) Weaving.

(a) Raw materials. In North Africa and in limited areas immediately south of the Sahara, sheep's wool is used in weaving, while goat's wool is most fully exploited in southern Madagascar. Silk, the other animal-derived fibre used traditionally in Africa, has a more restricted distribution. The main traditional production is in West Africa, especially in Nigeria, although waste silk from Europe was imported in the 19th century, and in Ghana European silk textiles were once unravelled and rewoven by local weavers. Silk is also produced in Madagascar.

Cotton, raffia and bark are the principal vegetable fibres used. Cotton is widely cultivated in West and North-East Africa and was exploited into the 20th century by weavers in the east and south of the continent. Raffia is woven in West Central Africa and Madagascar. Bark has been used mainly to produce a beaten and felted fabric rather than a woven textile. It can, however, be prepared for weaving and has been so used in parts of West Africa and Madagascar.

(b) Preparation. Wool, silk and cotton are all prepared for mounting on the loom by spinning. Each type of material is subjected to different procedures. Wool is soaked and then combed or carded (drawn across a series of spikes to yield a sheet of fibre); it may then be rolled and mounted on a distaff ready to be spun. Silk is prepared by boiling up the silk cocoons in an alkaline solution to release the fibres of which they are constructed. Cotton is

ginned to squeeze out its seeds and then bowed (fluffed out by flicking a bowstring against it). All three are spun in an essentially similar manner. A length of fibre is drawn from the distaff and twisted by hand. This is attached to the spindle, which is allowed to spin in mid-air, drawing out further lengths. These are wound on to the spindle giving a continuous yarn.

Raffia is the most easily prepared fibre. Derived from the upper epidermis of the cut leaves of the raffia palm, it is simply peeled off and then split lengthways. The bark of appropriate trees is retted to yield bast fibre. It is immersed in water, and the longitudinal fibres are separated out. As with raffia fibres, bark fibres may be tied together neatly or twisted to give longer lengths.

(c) Manufacture. While both men and women weave in Africa, in most areas the occupation is exclusive to one or the other gender. Thus in Berber North Africa and in Madagascar it is reserved to women, and in many parts of West Africa, Zaïre and East Africa it is a male activity. In Nigeria and Arab North Africa, however, both men and women weave, but they use different types of loom. Furthermore, while in some areas men weave professionally, for women weaving is generally a domestic activity.

African looms vary in the angle at which they are mounted, the means of creating tension in the warp system and how they are addressed in weaving. Perhaps the most basic distinction, however, is in the nature of the shedding device, the means of creating the shed and countershed whose alternation with each pick of the weft is the essential act performed by the loom. Two main possibilities are exploited in Africa. The loom may be furnished with a shed stick and a single heddle tied to one group of warp elements (see fig. 53). The shed stick creates the shed, and the weft may be passed through; pulling the heddle forward brings the warp elements from behind to the front and forms the countershed ready for the next pick of the weft. Varieties of this simple mechanism are widely distributed throughout the continent and are used by women in North Africa, Nigeria and Cameroon and in Madagascar; men weave on equivalent looms in West Central Africa and in the east and south of the continent. All such looms are fixed horizontal structures, with the exception of a foot-pedal loom in some isolated parts of Zaïre and a rare backstrap loom in Madagascar.

Alternatively, paired heddles are used, each attached to a group of warp elements. The heddles are connected by a cord that passes over a pulley and that is worked by pedals beneath. Pressing one pedal pulls one of the heddles down and simultaneously raises the other, enabling shed and countershed to be formed rapidly. This type of double-heddle loom is used exclusively by men in West and North-East Africa and by women in isolated parts of Madagascar. In Madagascar only one end of the warp is attached to the loom; the other is held either by a weight or tied to a pole. In West Africa the cloth woven on such looms is characteristically in the form of narrow strips that are sewn together selvage to selvage to give greater width.

(d) Decoration. The weaving process itself, dyeing, printing, appliqué and embroidery are the main techniques used in decorating African textiles. In weaving, variations

53. Raffia fibre being woven on an upright loom, Ndundu region, Zaïre

of texture and colour are widely exploited as a means of introducing design, as are most of the structural possibilities familiar in other weaving traditions. Both warp- and weft-faced textiles (*see* TEXTILE, colour pl. IV, fig. 1) are widely distributed, and the Asante of Ghana incorporate both in a single cloth. Tapestry weaves are characteristic of some Berber textiles. Perhaps the most common method of introducing pattern, however, is the use of float weaves. In an unusual subtractive technique the Kalabari Ijo of Nigeria cut and remove threads from manufactured cloth to create new patterns.

A wide variety of vegetable dyes is used. Indigo is the most common, yielding either a blue or a red colour. Ikat techniques, though rare in Africa, are found among the Baule of Côte d'Ivoire and were formerly used by the Sakalava in Madagascar. Resist-dyeing of woven cloth is widespread, and the techniques of tying, stitching and applying starch are used. The Bamana of Mali use a unique method of discharge-dyeing in the manufacture of their *bogolanfini* or 'mud cloth'.

The techniques of printing, drawing and stencilling cloth are all rare in Africa. In one of the few historic traditions, among the Asante of Ghana, a black dye produced from tree bark is applied with stamps cut from gourds. In many parts of the continent the technique of applying both cloth and other materials, including beads, shells, animal fur and medicine bundles, to a textile base is common. Prominent examples of applying cloth to other textiles are the banners and flags of the Sudanese Mahdists in the 19th century, those of the Akan peoples of Ghana and those of the Fon of the Republic of Benin. The Kuba of Zaïre make raffia appliquéd skirts. Embroidery techniques are applied in many parts of West and North-East Africa to gowns, trousers and cloaks. Those from West Africa are associated with Islamic fashions. The Kuba of Zaïre are noted for their production of pile cloth using techniques known in Europe as Richelieu embroidery.

BIBLIOGRAPHY

H. Loire: 'Le Tissage du raffia au Congo Belge', *An. Mus. Congo Belge, Anthropol. & Ethnog.*, iii/3 (1935) [whole issue]
R. Boser-Sarivaxevanis: *Textilhandwerk in Westafrika* (Basle, 1972)
K. P. Kent: 'West African Decorative Weaving', *Afr. A.*, vi/1 (1972), pp. 22–7, 67–70, 88
B. Menzel: *Textilien aus Westafrika*, 3 vols (Berlin, 1972)
R. Boser-Sarivaxevanis: *Recherche sur l'histoire des textiles traditionnels tissés et teints de l'Afrique occidentale* (Basle, 1975)
V. Lamb: *West African Weaving* (London, 1975)
J. Picton and J. Mack: *African Textiles* (London, 1979, rev. 1989)
D. Idiens and K. Ponting, eds: *Textiles in Africa* (Bath, 1980)
V. Lamb and J. Holmes: *Nigerian Weaving* (Lagos, 1980)
C. Polakoff: *Into Indigo: African Textiles and Dyeing Techniques* (Garden City, 1980)
Pelete Bite: Kalabari Cut-thread Cloth (exh. cat. by J. Eicher and T. Erekosima, Saint Paul, U. MN, Goldstein Gal., 1982)

JOHN MACK

(ii) Basketry.

(a) Raw materials. Nearly all the materials used in African basketry are vegetable. Stems such as grasses, reeds, sedges and creepers are used, as are the split leaves from various palm trees and irises. Wood is widely used in the form of withies, roots and timber in wattle-and-daub. Bark, both the outer bark of trees and the fibrous inner bast, is used as a twining material or for oversewing. Fibres are obtained from the scraped and soaked leaves of various sanseverias and from the leaves of the raffia palm. Animal materials such as rawhide, leather and sinew are also used in basketry. In the 20th century plastic fibres from grain sacks and telephone wire have been added to the range of African basketry materials.

(b) Preparation and manufacture. Preparation of these materials varies but often involves cutting and splitting or sometimes flattening with a mallet. Fibre cords are rolled on the leg and twisted and are often used two-ply. Basketry materials are commonly soaked in water to make them pliable.

The tools used are minimal. A small knife may be used for trimming off raw ends or for preparing the material for use. An awl, of iron, pointed wood or thorn, is used to pierce holes in coil-sewn baskets, to allow threading of the sewn element or the passage of a needle. An iron needle is used in mat-making, to join lengths of split cane and plaited strips or in making coiled baskets. By the late 20th century African basketry and its techniques had not yet been studied in depth, except for Southern Africa, where almost 300 different techniques have been identified (see Shaw). These vary according to the fabric, whether chequered, twilled, wrapped, twined, wickerwork, wattlework or plaited, and according to form, whether sewn, flat, straight, circular or cylindrical. Other variations concern the starting foundations, shaping, edging and finishing off; the combinations of materials; and different weaves and stitches. Such functional additions as leather-reinforced rims and bases or carrying slings (which may also be decorative), basal feet and lids, with or without hinges, also require their own techniques.

(c) Decoration. A great variety of decorative interlacing techniques are used in African basketry. Some materials, such as split reeds, are used so that the glossy outside contrasts with the matt inner surface. Similarly, different materials may be used in the same piece of basketry to provide variety in texture and hue. The use of dyed elements, to contrast with the natural pale creamy yellow or pale brown of the undyed material, is widespread. Black is usually obtained from immersion in swamp mud; shades of red, yellow or brown are obtained from vegetable dyes; while red, green, violet and yellow synthetic dyes are also used. Further decoration is achieved through the addition of animal skin, leather, cowries, beads, brass buttons and animal fur. Bentwood rims may be ornamented with pyrogravure or stained black.

For royal use, ceremonial presentations and special occasions such as weddings, baskets with extra fine stitching (see fig. 54) are made; they may also be patterned and embellished with beads. In Ethiopia they take the form of hanging inverted cones covered in beadwork, in Kenya baskets with beads and metal dangles; women of the Ganda royal households in Uganda make minutely stitched baskets with conical lids, coloured in black and pale straw.

(d) Uses. Domestic containers are the most common form of basketry. A great variety of baskets for storing food, spoons and trinkets and for serving food are made almost everywhere in Africa. In some areas, for example among the Shilluk of Sudan and the Somali, baskets are so tightly sewn that they become waterproof as the fibres swell. In these areas, therefore, baskets can be used for storing milk, water and other liquids. Winnowing baskets are often made from square mats, their corners trimmed off before they are pressed and stitched into a circular hoop. Another specialist basket is bottle-shaped, for sifting cassava flour. In Southern Africa traditional beer-making involves the use of long strainer baskets and openwork basketry spoons. Around Lake Victoria basketry drinking straws with fine sieves at the ends are used. Some large gourds and earthenware pots are reinforced with a twined basketry casing; other vessels may be encased in a basketry sling; and some have a basketry rim added for strength and decoration. Pottery and gourd vessels often have a decorative basketry lid.

Basketry techniques are used in some traditional house-building where the roof framework is of wattles, trimmed branches or stems twined with bast ties and the walls are of wattle-and-daub. Basketry is also used in making various forms of granaries, pigeon houses and chicken coops. Some houses in the Zaïre basin area and around Lake Victoria may be walled with large, screenlike mats, often patterned in black. Elsewhere others are roofed with

54. Basket with lid, split palm-leaf, l. 760 mm, from Lower Zaïre or northern Angola, early 19th century (London, British Museum)

decoratively plaited mats. In many parts of Africa, house doors are made of reeds twined together. Basketry mats are used as tent roofs among nomadic peoples in Somalia. Almost everywhere in Africa mats are used for sleeping or sitting on. In north-eastern Zaïre, beds traditionally were made of mats tied on to a wooden frame. The headrests of the Turkana of Kenya have twined thongs between the legs to prevent splitting.

In some areas basketry is used to make conical fish traps, sometimes of great size; where fish poison is employed oval floating baskets are used to gather the catch. Finger-stall-shaped traps that contract and grip cane rats and other small animals have a wide distribution. In the Sahel, a special basket is used to harvest grain knocked off the plant. Large, open-mesh baskets of various forms are made for carrying tubers and other crops. Crudely made baskets are used for carrying chickens to market, while twined nets are used for stacks of pottery. Among the Lozi of Zambia and the Ndebele of Zimbabwe, basketry sleds made of wattlework on wooden runners are used for transporting bulk. In north-eastern Zaïre strong basketry shields made of split cane of palm leaf patterned in black on natural straw colour were used.

Basketry hats come in a great variety of forms, often embellished with fur, feathers, beads and tufts of raffia. In Zaïre basketry visors were used to protect the wearer's face from being cut by long, sharp grass. In Uganda basketry hoods protect a baby on its mother's back from the sun, and baby-carriers of wickerwork and wood were used in Liberia. Long ear-plugs covered with finely plaited, colourful grass were made in Uganda and Rwanda; in Mali fine straw is plaited in imitation of filigree gold; plaited bracelets of split palm leaves are made in Southern Africa. Basketry masks, though uncommon, do exist. The Chewa of Zambia make vast basketry masks, while in north-western Zambia and eastern Angola masks are made of painted barkcloth on a basketry frame.

By the late 20th century baskets were also being made for the export market. Bowl-shaped carrying bags made of twined sisal fibre have been exported in large numbers from Kenya, while coiled baskets from Nigeria and Botswana and shallow baskets of varicoloured telephone wire from South Africa have also been successful export items.

BIBLIOGRAPHY

M. Trowell and K. P. Wachsmann: *Tribal Crafts of Uganda* (London, 1953)

African Furniture and Household Objects (exh. cat., ed. R. Sieber; Indianapolis, IN, Mus. A., 1980)

R. Levinsohn: *Art and Craft of Southern Africa* (Craighall, 1984)

M. Shaw: 'The Basketwork of Southern Africa: Part I. Technology', *An. S. Afr. Mus.*, c/2 (1992), pp. 53–248

T. Katzenellenbogen: 'Imbenge', *J. Mus. Ethnog.*, 4 (1993), pp. 49–72

M. E. Terry and A. Cunningham: 'The Impact of Commercial Marketing on the Basketry of Southern Africa', *J. Mus. Ethnog.*, 4 (1993), pp. 25–48

N. Tobert: 'Rizekat Wedding Baskets', *J. Mus. Ethnog.*, 4 (1993), pp. 73–82

MARGRET CAREY

8. Beads. In Africa beads are fashioned from natural objects, such as seeds and seed pods, shells, nuts, teeth and bones, as well as from clay, stone, glass and metals, including gold, iron and copper alloys. Beads are worn as simple strings or attached to cloth, leather or other material. Beads are also fashioned into bead embroidery, while in some areas bead strings are wrapped around a central coil of cloth or fibre and the coils fashioned into necklaces, belts and other articles. Beads are found among African peoples inhabiting all geographic regions and ecological zones, among hunter-gatherers, herders and subsistence farmers as well as among peoples living in large, politically centralized chiefdoms and kingdoms. In centralized societies, beadwork is traditionally the domain of professional artisans, while elsewhere it is women who are generally responsible for making the beaded ornaments worn by themselves and members of their families.

(i) History. There is substantial evidence of early beaded ornamentation in archaeological remains. A Nok terracotta figurine (*c.* 500 BC–AD 200) shows a male wearing what appears to be a stone bead necklace. Cast-copper alloy figures and heads from Ife (*c.* 11th–15th centuries) portray kings wearing beaded necklaces, anklets, bracelets and crowns. Elaborate beaded ornamentation is also depicted on Benin art objects from the 14th century to the 19th. Life-size cast-copper alloy heads depict kings wearing high, beaded collars and crowns of coral or stone beads. Commemorative queen mother heads are similarly embellished with beaded collars and netlike hair coverings representing coral or stone beads.

There have been a number of bead-making centres in Africa. Stone beads were worked in Ilorin, Nigeria, while quantities of stone and coral beads were crafted in Benin. The manufacture of glass beads in Africa has never been widespread, although glass beads recovered from Mapungubwe in southern Africa are believed to have been locally crafted. The glass industry of Bida, Nigeria, has continued to flourish into the late 20th century. The Krobo of Ghana also have continued to produce powder-glass beads, made with scrap glass ground to a fine powder, then poured into moulds and fired in a furnace. Powder-glass beads are also produced in Kiffa and neighbouring centres in Mauritania.

Historically, however, most of the glass beads and stone beads found in Africa are either of Indian or European origin. From early times glass beads of Indian manufacture were brought by Arabs, Persians, Indians and Chinese traders through Egypt, Zanzibar and other Muslim trading centres along the East African coast. From there they were dispersed through much of East and Central Africa. The earliest European traders continued the trade in Indian beads, gradually introducing beads of European manufacture into eastern and southern Africa. In West Africa, Europeans imported enormous quantities of glass beads manufactured in such European beadmaking centres as Amsterdam, Venice, Idar-Oberstein, Bohemia and Moravia.

(ii) Uses. In subsistence-level economies, generally characterized by a dearth of material wealth, artistic expression frequently focuses on body ornamentation, and glass beads are among the materials used. In Kenya and the Sudan, among the Pokot, Turkana, Samburu, Maasai, Kikuyu, Dinka and other peoples, the colours of beads, as well as the specific types and quantity of ornaments worn, reflect different stages and statuses in life. The degree of elaboration increases with the age and status of the wearer. Children's ornamentation tends to be minimal, such as single or multiple bead strings worn round the waist or neck. Through adolescence and into adulthood, the amount of beaded ornamentation worn increases. Examples are the massive assemblages of beaded necklaces worn by adolescent girls and married women among the Samburu, the beaded corsets of young Dinka men and women and the richly beaded leather garments worn by Turkana married women (see fig. 55).

55. Turkana woman's beaded skin apron, glass beads and iron beads, from Kenya (Cambridge University, Museum of Archaeology and Anthropology)

The San of Botswana and Namibia make beads from ostrich eggshells to fashion decorative ornaments and decorate leather garments. Elsewhere in southern Africa the Nguni-speaking peoples, for example the Zulu, Swazi, Ndebele, Xhosa and Thembu, use glass beads in elaborate beaded ornamentation. Following the emergence of the Zulu and Swazi kingdoms in the late 18th and early 19th centuries, kings strictly controlled the distribution and use of beads among their subjects. Ornaments fashioned from beads and such other prestige materials as brass, prized animal skins and feathers, were an important means of visually enhancing the power and prestige of the king and other high-ranking individuals. The smaller chiefdoms of the Xhosa, Thembu and others had similar restrictions on the use of beads. With the increased availability of beads in the second half of the 19th century, these restrictions became increasingly difficult to enforce, and the fabrication of beaded ornaments gradually proliferated among the general population. Specific styles of beaded ornaments and garments visually signify a girl's progression from childhood to womanhood, and on special occasions young men may also wear beadwork provided by their girlfriends and sisters. Nguni beadwork is often characterized by sharp contrasts of brightly coloured beads against a white background. This is especially evident among the Ndebele, where the designs in traditional beadwork can also be seen in the painted murals for which they have become particularly well known.

Beads are frequently used in the production of objects of prestige. Stone and glass beads are relatively durable and long-lasting in contrast to much traditional African material culture and may thus convey a sense of permanence and immortality. The relative scarcity of beads also serves to enhance their importance. When first introduced into Africa, imported beads were extremely rare, difficult to obtain and relatively costly. Only the wealthier members of society had the means to obtain them. In centralized chiefdoms and kingdoms the right to possess and display beads, as personal adornment or symbols of status, often continues to be restricted to higher-ranking members.

Among the Yoruba of Nigeria, the use of beads is reserved for those individuals who possess the power to communicate between the world of the living and the world of the gods. Thus beads are prominent in the regalia of kings and in the ceremonial or ritual objects used by priests and devotees of important sacred cults (*see* BEADWORK, colour pl. I, fig. 3). The most important element of the king's regalia is the veiled, beaded crown (see fig. 56). The veil conceals the wearer's identity, focusing the spectator's attention on the spiritual power of the king as the embodiment of the dynasty. Besides crowns, beaded regalia of the king include ceremonial staffs and sceptres, hats and other elements of clothing. Yoruba diviners are also permitted to use ceremonial or ritual objects featuring elaborate bead embroidery. Beaded sheaths 'clothe' or cover the metal staff of Oku, deity of the farm, when it is not in ritual use, and beautifully beaded dance panels are worn in pairs by devotees at the annual festivals for a number of Yoruba deities. Yoruba twin figures, *ibeji*, carved on the advice of a diviner as memorials to deceased twins, may also be clothed in elaborate, bead-embroidered garments.

Beads and beadwork are also important indicators of wealth and status in the stratified and hierarchically organized kingdoms of the Cameroon Grassfields. Formerly used as a medium of exchange, beads literally represent wealth and denote affluence and high status within the community. Beads and other prestige materials, including ivory and brass, embellish articles of personal adornment worn by high-ranking individuals on important occasions. The accoutrements range from beaded staffs and dance-whisks to necklaces, bracelets and earplugs, as well as beaded caps, loincloths, belts and bags. Thrones or stools, used by men of rank and carved in the form of human or animal caryatids, are sometimes lavishly decorated with beads and other valued materials; the degree of elaboration indicates the owner's status (*see* BAMUM, fig. 2). Ancestor figures may also be richly adorned with beaded ornamentation.

56. Yoruba beaded crown with veil, raffia, cloth and beads, h. without veil 254 mm (Los Angeles, CA, University of California, Fowler Museum of Cultural History)

Elephant masks, found throughout the Bamileke area of the Cameroon Grassfields, are among the most striking examples of bead-embellished art works (see fig. 43 above). Typically the mask consists of a tightly fitting cloth hood with long front and back panels representing the animal's trunk. The facial area and panels of the mask are elaborately decorated with beads, which when the mask dances become a whirling kaleidoscope of colour.

Beads, like cowrie shells, are important symbols of status among the Kuba of Zaïre. Wooden masks and masks of raffia fibre are richly decorated with glass beads, cowrie shells, fur, seeds and copper. The royal regalia of the Kuba king and his court likewise incorporate vast quantities of glass beads and cowrie shells, as well as raffia-embroidered cloth.

BIBLIOGRAPHY

R. F. Thompson: 'The Sign of the Divine King: An Essay on Yoruba

Bead-embroidered Crowns with Veil and Bird Decorations', *Afr. A.*, iii/3 (1970), pp. 8–17, 74–80
H. M. Cole: 'Artistic and Communicative Values of Beads in Kenya and Ghana', *Bead J.*, i/3 (1975), pp. 29–37
The Sign of the Leopard: Beaded Art of Cameroon (exh. cat. by T. Northern, Storrs, U. CT, Benton Mus. A., 1975)
S. Priebatsch and N. Knight: 'Traditional Ndebele Beadwork', *Afr. A.*, xi/2 (1978), pp. 24–7
W. Fagg: *Yoruba Beadwork* (New York, 1980)
U. Beier: *Yoruba Beaded Crowns: Sacred Regalia of the Olokuku* (London, 1982)
M. Carey: *Beads and Beadwork of East and South Africa*, Shire Ethnography, 3 (Princes Risborough, 1986)
L. S. Dubin: *The History of Beads from 30,000 BC to the Present* (New York, 1987)
M. Carey: *Beads and Beadwork of West and Central Africa*, Shire Ethnography (Princes Risborough, 1991)

CAROLEE G. KENNEDY

9. LEATHER. The ability to work animal hides and skins is known throughout Sub-Saharan Africa and has been employed since prehistoric times to serve a variety of utilitarian, social and aesthetic needs. With the introduction of the loom and cotton to Africa, textiles began to replace leather and skin products as the primary form of dress. The protective qualities of leather and hide and their durability and pliability, however, have continued to make them ideal for a wide variety of objects.

The best-known hide products of eastern and southern Africa are perhaps the elaborate rawhide shields of warriors and hunters, made from the thick skins of domestic cattle and buffalo. The skins are not dressed but are usually pegged a few inches from the ground, allowed to dry and cut to shape. Sometimes they are beaten with a stone to toughen and shape them. Among the Luo of Tanzania, the raw skins are stretched on to a basketry framework that gives shape and additional strength to the finished product. A variety of methods are used to decorate these shields. Most commonly the surfaces are rubbed or painted with red and yellow ochres or other natural pigments. Less commonly the short hairs left on the hide are shaved into a decorative pattern, or the hard surface is carved, and white kaolin is rubbed into the recessed areas to produce a stark design.

To produce the pliable leather required for items of dress, the peoples of eastern and southern Africa treat the skins of calves, goats and other small animals with fats and oils in a process that stabilizes the skin without actually tanning it. This process is generally a collaborative effort between men and women. The raw skins are moistened and either stretched on a frame or pegged on the ground. The flesh side is scraped to clean, compress and level the surface. If desired, the hairs are also scraped off; fresh dung is sometimes spread on the hairy side to facilitate this part of the process. The skins are then softened by rubbing with grease, fat or oils until they are quite supple. Among the Xhosa, women raise a rough nap on the surface with the thorny leaves of the aloe plant or a rough stone before working the fat into the skin. Aside from the surfaces being coloured with ochre or charcoal, these skins may be left undecorated or may serve as a backing for elaborate beadwork designs.

The Sudanic region of West Africa has long been known for its fine leatherwork. Among the Tuareg and Moor peoples in the north, women are the principal tanners and leatherworkers. Elsewhere, these crafts are a monopoly of men, although wives often assist their husbands. Cow hides, as well as those of other large animals such as giraffes and camels, are used untanned for shields and the soles of sandals and slippers. Although the skins of wild animals, including those of snakes, crocodiles and lizards, are sometimes tanned, goats and sheep are the primary source of skins in West Africa. The hair is usually removed prior to tanning by soaking in a caustic alkaline or lye solution and scraping the surface with a blunt knife or wooden implement. The skins are immersed and rubbed in a container of chicken manure and water and allowed to steep for several hours or overnight. The skins are then cleansed with a solution of fermented millet bran and water and scraped. These processes prepare the skin to accept and absorb the tannin. Throughout West Africa, acacia pods are the most common source of tannin. The skins are allowed to soak in a solution of macerated acacia pods and water of varying degrees of strength and frequently rubbed and kneaded. When the skins are sufficiently tanned, after between one and four days, they are washed and allowed to dry, then scraped, stretched and beaten to make them smooth and pliable.

Throughout West Africa, there are many ways by which leather is manipulated for decorative effect. The most widespread technique is perhaps that of dyeing or painting the surface of the leather. Although a variety of European chemical pigments and dyes have been available in the region since the beginning of the 20th century, leatherworkers tend to prefer the colours previously obtained exclusively with vegetable and mineral dyes. Traditionally, a deep maroon red was produced from the sheaths and kernels of specially cultivated millet or sorghum, while yellow was obtained from a variety of roots and leaves. Before the introduction of commercial pigments, green leather was highly prized and difficult to produce. Hausa and Tuareg leatherworkers had several ways of obtaining it, including a complex process using copper or brass filings and a mineral salt on untanned skin. Despite the availability of imported inks, leatherworkers have continued to mix their own black dye in the traditional manner using an acidic liquid such as lemon juice, iron residue and sugar or honey. Mande and Fula leatherworkers of the Western Sudan paint the surface of the leather with these same colours as part of the creation of the object. Geometric designs are the most common, either painted on in broad swathes or delicately applied with a reed pen or, more recently, with felt-tip and ball-point pens. Circular designs are sometimes made with the aid of a pair of compasses.

Appliqué is also quite widespread in West Africa, particularly in Northern Nigeria where the whole skins are dyed before being sold to leatherworkers. Shapes cut out of leather and cloth are secured to the surface with commercial or homemade paste and carefully stitched to the foundation piece with leather or cotton threads. Reverse appliqué, in which a pattern is cut into a piece of cloth or leather of one colour and layered over that of another colour, is especially common in Nigeria. Embroidery techniques are employed with a variety of materials, including leather, cotton, wool and occasionally silk or rayon. The technique of embroidery with palm fibres is

57. Leatherworker Sulemani Kouyaté incising patterns before embroidering them on a knife sheath; from a photograph by Malim Kangata, 1988

particularly characteristic of Mande leatherwork in the Western Sudan.

One technique takes particular advantage of the special properties of leather. In this, the smooth surface is incised with geometric patterns and selected portions are peeled off, revealing the soft suede underneath and providing a contrast in both texture and colour (see fig. 57). Designs impressed or stamped into a dampened surface become permanent when the leather dries. Leather may also be stretched and shaped around various objects, and craftsmen often build up the surface in patterns or ridges over which the leather is moulded.

Finally, one of the most visible features of leatherwork throughout much of West Africa is the fringe. Leather is cut into thin strips by hand to adorn objects to be suspended and, in the case of some trappings, to serve the useful purpose of keeping flies away. In addition, there are a variety of twisting and plaiting techniques used to create durable straps, cords, loops and ties.

For further illustration see fig. 142 below.

BIBLIOGRAPHY

J. M. Dalziel: 'African Leather Dyes', *Kew Bull.*, vi (1926), pp. 225–38
S. Ben Sai: 'Plantes à tannins, tannage et teinture indigène au Soudan', *Notes Afr.*, xxiii (1944), pp. 20–22
J. Gabus: *Arts et symboles* (1958), ii of *Au Sahara*, 3 vols (Neuchâtel, 1955–8)
J. Nicolaisen: *Ecology and Culture of the Pastoral Tuareg*, Nationalmuseets Skrifter, Ethonografisk Roekke, ix (Copenhagen, 1963)
M. Trowell: *African Design* (London, 1965)
V. Z. Gitywa: 'The Arts and Crafts of the Xhosa in the Ciskei: Past and Present', *Fort Hare Pap.*, v/2 (1971), pp. 111–16
D. Heathcote: 'A Leatherworker of Zaria City', *Niger. Field*, xxxix/1 (1974), pp. 12–26; xxxix/3 (1974), pp. 99–117
E. M. Shaw and N. J. Van Warmelo: 'The Material Culture of the Cape Nguni', *An. S. Afr. Mus.*, lviii/2 (1974), pp. 178–83
F. L. Lambrecht and D. J. Lambrecht: 'Leather and Beads in N'gamiland', *Afr. A.*, x/2 (1977), pp. 34–5
M. Lamb: 'The Hausa Tanners of Northern Nigeria (and the Production of Sokoto Tanned Goatskins)', *New Bkbinder*, i (1981), pp. 58–62
A. Hodge: *Nigeria's Traditional Crafts* (London, 1982)
P. J. Imperato: 'Luo Shields from Tanzania', *Afr. A.*, xvi/1 (1982), pp. 73–7, 96
I. Anagbogu: *The History of the Indigenous Leather Industry in Sokoto and Kano, Northern Nigeria, 1903–1960* (diss., U. Birmingham, 1986)
B. E. Frank: *Mande Leatherworking: A Study of Style, Technology and Identity* (diss., Bloomington, IN U., 1988)
L. Hooper, P. Davison and G. Klinghardt: 'Some Nguni Crafts Part 4: Skin-working Techniques', *An. S. Afr. Mus.*, lxx/4 (1989), pp. 313–404 [published as self-contained monography]

BARBARA E. FRANK

10. MIXED MEDIA. Virtually every traditional art form in Africa incorporates mixed media. An examination of any artistic endeavour, including those discussed below as well as, for example, the construction of shrines and performance arts, reveals a combination of materials embodying sophisticated aesthetic criteria and a rich and complex artistic symbolism. The range of materials and techniques used is vast. This entry can only hint at this range through a discussion of some of the main arenas for mixed-media arts in the traditional African context.

Much African sculpture may be characterized as mixed media or accumulative in nature, incorporating a variety of natural and manmade materials with the predominant sculptural medium of wood. The sculptural surface may be painted with natural and commercial pigments, embedded with seeds, shells, beads and metal, rubbed with vegetable oils or camwood, wrapped with cloth, skin or fibre, and encrusted with earth and the libations of millet beer, palm wine, water mixed with flour, and the blood of animal offerings. Both local and imported objects and materials may be attached to embellish sculptural forms. A partial inventory of such materials in African art would include: wooden and metal objects; locally made and imported cloth; natural fibres; animal skulls, horns, skins, claws, bones and teeth; bird beaks and feathers; beads and shells; and a variety of imported items such as mirrors, shotgun shells and European Christmas decorations.

In a discussion of the accumulative nature of African sculpture a distinction is made between display materials that 'are primarily oriented toward enhancement of the splendor of the objects to which they are attached' and materials 'connected with the organization and exploitation of power' (see Rubin, p. 8). These broad categories provide a useful approach to understanding the layers of meaning and intention in the variety of forms and materials of mixed-media African sculpture. Thus, Kalabari Ijo water-spirit masquerades include inventive combinations of local and imported materials, such as cloth, mirrors and Christmas ornaments, that heighten the visual splendour of the masquerade performances, provide information on the kinds of materials appropriate for the depiction of water spirits and point to the important position of the Kalabari Ijo in long-standing trade networks with their neighbours and with Europeans.

58. Mixed-media Kuba mask, Mwaash aMbooy, wood, fabric, feathers, cowries, beads and metal, h. 446 mm, from Zaïre (Washington, DC, National Museum of African Art)

In some African societies the capacities associated with the wilderness and nature are drawn on to imbue art objects with power. Thus, porcupine quills, leopard's teeth, tusks, horns, feathers, hides and other materials are used to suggest the powers of the wilderness and the abilities of certain individuals to manage that domain. The use of these materials refers both visually and symbolically to the distinctive capacities for survival that characterize animals of the wilderness and, by association, provides a commentary on the powerful capacities of those individuals and organizations that utilize such materials and motifs in their arts and regalia. Indeed, there are specific categories of African art that tend towards the use of mixed media derived from the wild. Many initiation, age grade and secret societies draw on powers associated with the wilderness in the construction of their masquerades and cult paraphernalia and in the spatial orientations of their rituals. Some of the masks made by the Bamana, Senufo, Igbo and Kuba, for example, are accumulative sculptures that embody both opposing and complementary categories of knowledge and experience and contrast concepts and powers of the wilderness with the civilized, orderly realm of village and community life.

Arts associated with hunters, healers and diviners often use materials derived from the wild. They emphasize the ritual specialists' mediating qualities and spiritual powers within their communities and validate their assertions to control, to some extent, aspects of nature and the wild. Medicines are used to imbue with power both individuals and the objects they use or make. Earth, bark, stones, leaves and other natural materials, as well as metals (themselves the product of a process of transformation), are used as medicines in many parts of Africa and are incorporated into sculptural forms to enhance their effectiveness. Although these medicines are often derived from the natural world, manmade objects are also used, including glass, mirrors and manufactured nails, as in the power figures of the Chokwe, Kongo, Yaka and Suku of Zaïre. The physical appearance of these sculptural forms changes over time as more and more materials are accumulated.

The arts associated with leadership often employ a variety of materials derived from both nature and culture, including animal skins and teeth, feathers and elaborate gold, ivory and beaded ornaments, that visually display royal wealth and prestige and state the king's capacity to control the disruptive, unpredictable and aggressive forces that threaten orderly domestic society. Masquerades associated with royalty embody many of these same characteristics. The full costumes of two Kuba royal masks,

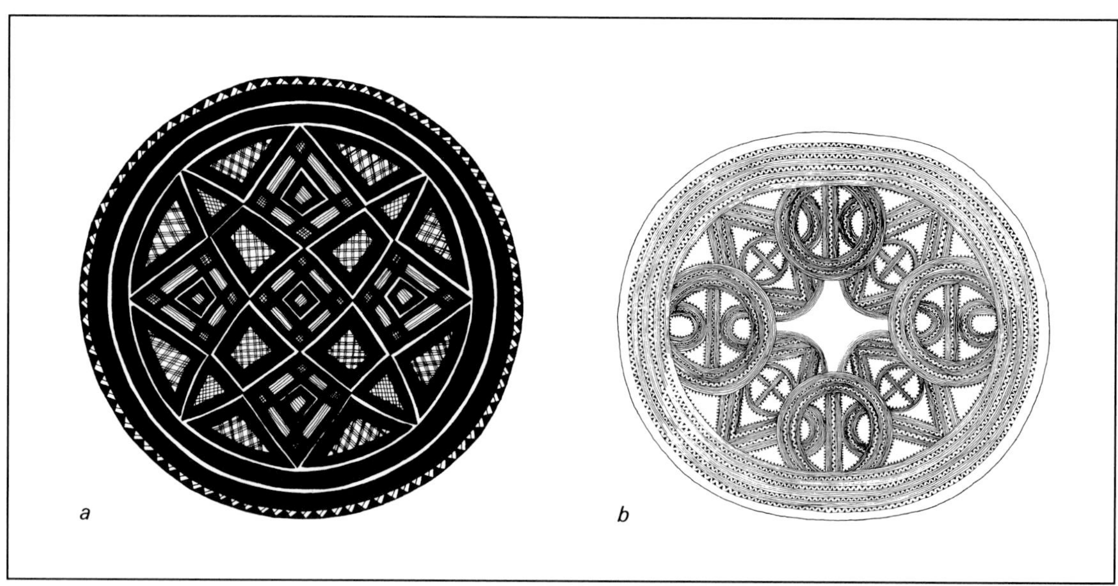

59. Gourd designs: (a) pyro-engraved gourd design, diam. 322 mm, settled Fulani, Song, Song District, Adamawa State, Nigeria, *c.* 1965; (b) pressure-engraved gourd design, diam. 305 mm, Yungur, Suktu, Yungur District, Adamawa State, Nigeria, *c.* 1959 (Lagos, National Museum)

Mwaash aMbooy, for example, include feather headdresses, animal skins, leaves, textiles, cowries and beads; even the mask headpieces are mixed-media objects (see fig. 58).

BIBLIOGRAPHY

A. Rubin: *African Accumulative Sculpture: Power and Display* (New York, 1974)

Wild Spirits, Strong Medicine: African Art and the Wilderness (exh. cat., ed. M. G. Anderson and C. M. Kreamer; New York, Cent. Afr. A., 1989)

CHRISTINE MULLEN KREAMER

11. GOURDS. The decoration of these African hard-shelled fruit (*Lagenaria siceraria*) in some parts of Africa has been developed into an art form. The term 'calabash' is often used to refer to the African gourd, although strictly speaking it should be used only for the South American equivalent. The African gourd was one of the continent's earliest cultivated plants and remains a staple commodity, especially in rural areas. There are four main shapes—globular, flattened, bottle-shaped and tubular—rendering it suitable for numerous practical uses, whether preserved whole or cut into pieces. Its primary function, however, is as a domestic utensil, since the hollowed-out shell of the predominantly symmetrical gourd provides an inexpensive, durable, light and portable receptacle for transporting, storing and serving foodstuffs and liquids. In many parts of Africa a woman's collection of gourds, which enables her to fulfil her domestic and economic roles in the community, is reckoned among her most prized possessions. Its intimate association with female attributes and activities also ensures the gourd's wide association with femininity and motherhood, and in some areas it may even serve as a symbol of a bride's integration into her husband's family (*see* FULANI, §2).

Gourds are also used as protective bonnets for children, as fishing floats, seed-drills, henna baths, smoking pipes, drinking canteens, toys and small tools, and as personal containers for snuff, medicines and cosmetics. Gourds figure prominently in many social and ritual contexts, ranging from communal beer-drinking to agricultural and marriage ceremonies, burial rites and divination. They are also used in a wide range of musical contexts, both as percussive and wind instruments and as resonators on drums, harps and xylophones. Gourds used in ceremonial and ritual contexts often remain undecorated, a restriction that probably serves to emphasize the non-secular aspects of the occasion. Moreover, in such areas as north-eastern Nigeria, where gourd decoration is practised mainly by women (elsewhere this is a predominantly male art form), the use of undecorated gourds in ceremonial and ritual contexts probably reflects the exclusion of women from these areas of activity. Conversely, in many domestic and social contexts a decorated gourd is more highly valued than its undecorated counterpart, and not only for aesthetic reasons.

(i) Decorative techniques. The multiplicity of uses to which the African gourd is put is matched by the diverse methods employed, singly or in combination, in its decoration. Among the most common of these is pyro-engraving (see fig. 59a) or poker-work, including scorching, which involves the use of a heated metal engraving tool, usually consisting of a leaf-shaped blade with elongated shaft hafted into a circular wooden handle. Working with a succession of knives, carvers often facilitate the passage of the heated instrument across the work surface by simultaneously rotating the gourd with the non-carving hand (see fig. 60). Different colour and texture effects may be achieved by, for instance, a 'rocking' technique with a partially cooled blade, which produces a bronze or reddish-brown tone, or by scorching with the flat of the blade to produce a contrasting matt finish, as in the leaf pattern designs typical of south-eastern Nigeria.

The two other most common techniques are pressure-engraving (including scraping) and carving. In the former

60. Waja woman pyro-engraving a gourd bowl, Dela Waja, Nigeria; from a photograph by Marla C. Berns, 1982

a metal point is dragged, dagger-like, across the work surface towards the carver's body in a laborious and painstaking technique that in many areas pre-dates the introduction of pyro-engraving. First an outline of the design is made, and then, in the scraping or filling-in stage, the surface shell is wholly or partially removed, often between alternate pairs of engraved lines (as among some pastoral Fulani groups in West Africa), either by scraping or some form of hatching. The design is then reversed by filling in the engraved areas with a blackening agent. Among some groups, such as the Kamba of Kenya and a number of groups in north-eastern Nigeria, including the Longuda, the scraping stage is unnecessary, the whole design being composed of finely engraved lines that are then reversed (see fig. 59b). Carving is the reverse of pressure-engraving: after the design has been outlined with a sharp knife, the background is cut or scraped away, leaving the unmarked shell as a relief pattern (e.g. among the Hausa of northern Nigeria or the Bariba and Fon of Benin). To increase the contrast between white background and yellow relief, chalk or clay may be applied to the engraved areas and the shell stained or engraved with a texture pattern. Deep carving with an angled blade (e.g. among the Yoruba of south-western Nigeria) produces shadows that give an additional three-dimensional effect.

Less common techniques include painting, which only rarely serves as a group's primary technique (for example in the Potiskum area of north-eastern Nigeria). For practical reasons, such designs tend to be confined to the interior of the gourd, which is likely also to have an exterior decoration (e.g. among the settled Fulani of north-eastern Nigeria and Cameroon). Traditionally, locally produced pigments are used, often mixed with various oils in order to improve adhesion. Uniform interior coatings, polished to an enamel-like finish, help to make gourds watertight, to render them impervious to termite attacks and to improve their insulating properties. A recent innovation in north-eastern Nigeria, one of the richest areas of gourd decoration in Africa, is the use since *c.* 1960 of imported enamel paints and stamped designs. Among some peoples (such as the Ga'anda and settled Fulani of north-eastern Nigeria) gourds are dyed, although this is a subsidiary technique, invariably used as an adjunct to an engraved design. The favoured colour is red, produced from a mixture of guinea corn stalks and indigo leaves. A further refinement is the introduction of a resist-dye pattern through the application of an oily paste to those areas that are to remain undyed, producing an intricate polychrome effect (e.g. among the settled Fulani of north-eastern Nigeria and Cameroon). Gourds may also be decorated by adding extraneous materials, ranging from leather, basketry and elaborate coverings of patterned beadwork (as in the Cameroon Grassfields) to stitched 'embroidery' patterns using such prestigious materials as glass beads, cowrie shells and metal wire, including gold thread (as among the Asante of Ghana).

(ii) Designs. The designs used are partly determined by the gourd's curved surface and partly by the technique employed. For instance, in the case of the most commonly decorated receptacle, the hemispherical bowl, the whole surface is usually treated as a single compositional field, delimited by an outer rim band of decoration. The technique of pyro-engraving favours a broad, rapid treatment, in which the division and subdivision of the design field by a process of reduction tends to establish a rather formal, geometric framework, where the individual design units are filled in with incised lines and texture patterning (see fig. 59a). The relationship of figure to ground is sometimes ambiguous, but in most designs the engraved area serves as the background, while the untreated shell emerges as the relief pattern. Although pyro-engraving and especially pressure-engraving (which encourages the use of small design units) do not obviously favour free-flowing, curvilinear forms, these are nevertheless common among some groups, such as the Hausa, Tiv, Igbo and Ibibio of Nigeria and the Kiga of Uganda.

Design motifs tend to be non-figurative in most parts of Africa, even where there are no religious restrictions on figurative representations. Invariably, they have acquired conventional pattern names based on perceived associations either with objects in the environment or technical processes, but generally gourd designs seem to have no dominant subject-content, consisting instead of a composite arrangement of heterogeneous elements inspired largely by abstract aesthetic considerations. The Hausa, Kanuri and some pastoral Fulani groups (in northern Nigeria), the Kamba (in Kenya) and the Bariba and Fon (in Benin), among others, do, however, include representational imagery in their designs, and in the latter case these carved pictographs, alluding to well-known stories and proverbs, may be used to convey messages of love.

BIBLIOGRAPHY

G. Lindblom: *The Akamba in British East Africa: An Ethnological Monograph*, Archvs Etud. Orient., 17 (Uppsala, 1920)

M. Griaule and G. Dieterlen: 'Calebasses dahoméennes (Documents de la Mission Dakar-Djibouti)', *J. Africanistes*, v/2 (1935), pp. 203–46, pls xxvi–xxvii

M. J. Herskovits: *Dahomey: An Ancient West African Kingdom*, 2 vols (New York, 1938)

K. C. Murray: 'The Decoration of Calabashes by Tiv (Benue Province)', *Nigeria*, 36 (1951), pp. 469–74

C. Jest: 'Décoration des calebasses foulbées', *Notes Afr.*, 72 (1956), pp. 113–16

P. Malzy: 'Les Calebasses', *Notes Afr.*, 73 (1957), pp. 10–12

D. J. Stenning: *Savannah Nomads: A Study of the Wodaabe Pastoral Fulani of Western Bornu Province, Northern Region, Nigeria* (London, 1959)

M. Trowell: *African Design* (London, 1960, rev. 1965)

M. Dupire: *Peuls nomades: Etude descriptive des Wodaabe du Sahel Nigérien*, Trav. & Mém. Inst. Ethnol., lxiv (Paris, 1962)

B. Rubin: 'Calabash Decoration in North East State, Nigeria', *Afr. A.*, iv/1 (1970), pp. 20–25

L. E. Jefferson: *The Decorative Arts of Africa* (New York, 1973/*R* London, 1974)

T. J. H. Chappel: *Decorated Gourds in North-eastern Nigeria* (Lagos, 1977)

The Arts of the Hausa (exh. cat. by D. Heathcote, London, Commonwealth Inst., 1977)

S. Kay: 'Peter Nzuki: Calabash Carver of Kenya', *Afr. A.*, xii/1 (1978), pp. 40–41, 108

R. Sieber: *African Furniture and Household Objects* (Bloomington, 1980)

The Art of Cameroon (exh. cat. by T. Northern, Washington, DC, Smithsonian Inst. Traveling Exh. Serv., 1984)

J. Perani: 'Hausa Calabash Decoration', *Afr. A.*, xix/3 (1986), pp. 45–7, 82–3

The Essential Gourd: Art and History in Northeastern Nigeria (exh. cat. by M. C. Berns and B. R. Hudson, Los Angeles, UCLA, Wight A.G.; Honolulu, HI, Acad. A.; New York, Cent. Afr. A.; Washington, DC, N. Mus. Afr. A.; 1986–8)

T. J. H. CHAPPEL

VI. *Art forms.*

1. Architecture. 2. Sculpture. 3. Mask and masquerade. 4. Body arts. 5. Dress. 6. Regalia. 7. Divination instruments. 8. Musical instruments. 9. Arms and shields. 10. Currency, weights and measures. 11. Tools and implements. 12. Furniture. 13. Tobacco containers and pipes. 14. Household utensils. 15. Rock art.

1. ARCHITECTURE.

(i) Introduction. (ii) Materials. (iii) Vernacular architecture. (iv) Christian architecture. (v) Islamic architecture. (vi) Western architecture. (vii) Further developments.

(i) Introduction. Discussion of African architecture is beset with problems of definition, scope, timespan and identity. North Africa may be seen as part of the Middle East, coastal East Africa as part of Arabian culture and South African cities as part of a Western cultural tradition. Much of the eastern and southern parts of the continent were only settled by Bantu-speaking peoples comparatively recently; Trans-Saharan trade, Islamic jihads and Fulani migrations in the western Sudan have all influenced architecture; while European colonization and subsequent national independence have also affected building types, methods of construction and settlement patterns.

This survey is concerned principally with the architecture of Sub-Saharan Africa, although reference is also made to northern, eastern and Saharan regions. Archaeological study of all but the largest sites in Africa is in its infancy, and information on the architecture of African cultures is often fragmented and unsystematic where it exists at all. Future studies may well change substantially the picture presented here.

Although by the late 20th century a third of Africans were living in cities, the majority were still rural, and their buildings may be loosely classified as 'vernacular architecture', i.e. indigenous buildings of community origin, not designed by specialist architects. Environmental factors influence the economies of different regions, which in turn affect population densities, settlement types and hence architecture. About 95% of the continental land mass has less than 80 people per sq. km, with densities conditioned by access to water. Such rivers as the Nile in Egypt and Sudan and the Niger in Mali have made a broad band of cultivation possible. In contrast, such desert regions as the Sahara in the northern half of the continent support fewer than eight persons to the sq. km. Here, water reserves are tapped through tunnelled water courses, cultivated depressions in the *erg* (sand desert) or by such oases as Touggourt and El Oued (both Algeria). Many desert inhabitants are camel- and goat-herding nomads, who live in tents or collapsible and transportable frame-and-mat structures. Other inhabitants of desert regions live in small concentrations in the mountains. The Matmata Berber, for example, excavate deep shafts off which are burrowed rooms, stables and an access ramp. At the bottom of the shaft a well, cistern and latrine may be sunk. This modifies the climate by means of the slow transmission of radiated heat through the rock, which warms interior spaces at night and, after re-radiation, keeps them cool during the day.

In the grassland steppes and savannah regions, permanent settlements are to be found, with dispersed farms worked by family units growing maize, sorghum and millet. Houses in these regions must afford protection from both solar radiation and seasonal rains. Those in open areas must also be able to resist high winds, while in areas of higher humidity, through-ventilation is important. In the tropical forests of West and Equatorial Africa, where farming of copra and plantains is year-round, protection from heavy rains is necessary. Permanent settlements are more clustered in these areas, and indigenous towns and cities are concentrated there. Trading complexes and market centres, sometimes with specialized functions, are widely distributed. Such centres have developed as cities and grew either indigenously or under colonial and post-colonial administrations.

(ii) Materials. The earliest forms of human shelter include cave dwellings. In Southern Africa artefacts and midden heaps provide evidence of continuous cave occupation over hundreds, even thousands, of years. In the Erongo Mountains, Namibia, rock shelters with collapsed screens still *in situ* have been uncovered. Caves were still in use in Nakapapula, northern Zambia, in the 1960s, and nomadic Hadza on the borders of Lake Eyasi, northern Tanzania, were using rock shelters into the 1990s. For peoples living in areas with no caves and for those requiring more adaptable shelters, however, vernacular architecture was dependent on available resources. Although such materials as mangrove poles from the swamps off the Kenyan coast were sent by dhow to the Gulf states, there is limited

evidence of any other extensive trading of building materials before the colonial period.

(a) Stone. (b) Soil. (c) Brick. (d) Wood and palm. (e) Grass. (f) Hair and hide.

(a) Stone. Historically, there were few tools appropriate for excavating, cutting and trimming stone. Where schists and other limestones cleaved naturally into suitable blocks, these were used. The best-known use of stone for indigenous building is in Zimbabwe, where, as well as GREAT ZIMBABWE, many other stone ruins survive, including Naletale, Dhlo Dhlo and the complex of walls and passages of the Khani Ruins. There are also numerous domestic rock sites, suggesting widespread knowledge of dry-stone building. Some of these sites are characterized by skilled and sophisticated use of decorative chevron patterning. In other parts of Southern Africa a number of corbelled, stone-domed dwellings have been found. In the 1990s stone was still being used by the Tigre and other Ethiopian peoples for domestic building, the rubble being bonded with mud. In West Africa stone plinths have been constructed to support earthen buildings, and some settled Tuareg build stone houses. Further west in Mauritania such ancient trading cities as Tegdaoust and Tichitt were constructed of coursed sandstone blocks. Stone is widely used in Morocco and Algeria, where it is often bonded with earth or used in association with sun-dried earth blocks. The settled Berber of northern Algeria employ stone for the construction of their one- and two-storey farm buildings. The techniques for building with stone may have spread to these areas with the advance of Islam, as was the case with the use of local coral ragstone in the building of the trading cities on the East African coast.

(b) Soil. The local soils are complex in the eastern and central parts of the continent and simpler in the northern and southern regions. Desert soils of broken rock, sand and pebbles are spread across the north, where pockets of calcareous crusts provide gypsum, used for making a building plaster. Gypsum-plastered barrel vaults and domes displaying a high level of craftsmanship are to be found in Tunisia and Algeria, in such towns as Takrouna and El Oued. South of the desert, in the semi-arid savannah steppe, a transcontinental band of brown soils gives way to ferralitic tropical red soils or laterites, which cover a third of Africa. Red in colour and friable in the well-drained and leached areas, the soils become black clays in poorly drained, humid areas. Low in fertility, the laterites make a good building material, being malleable, yet hardening to a stonelike surface. They are laid spirally in a technique (known as *banco*) closely related to that of coil pottery to form the cylindrical huts and linking-walls of compounds. These are often built by the compound head with his family participating in the preparation of the material. Women mould clay to make interior sleeping platforms, cooking areas and storage spaces for gourds and pottery vessels, all of which may be finished with ornamented edges.

In some parts of tropical West Africa the use of a wooden framework for building has been replaced by the use of mass walling of laterite mud. The earth is compressed in large balls, and the walls are laid in 'lifts', or layers, of *c.* 500 mm, each of which is allowed to dry before the next lift is raised. This technique, known as 'swish', was used in the historic city of Benin and has become widespread. Many savannah and Sahelian peoples build with excavated earth, mixed with water and straw and allowed to cure. The mixture is then formed into egg-shaped balls (*tabale*), which are laid in rows with the narrow ends uppermost and interlocking with the next row. Such peoples as the Sanga of Togo use pronounced, inclined lifts to produce a series of overhangs, off which the water runs in the seasonal rains. Erosion, however, remains a problem: the rapid passage of water over the walls causes considerable surface damage, while splash-back and run-off water deeply undercut the walls at ground-level. In addition, severe cracks may form as the walls dry out after the rains. Repairs are made to these cracks and may be painted over with a water-repelling preparation of locust-beans.

See also §2(iii) and (iv) below; §V, 1(i) above.

(c) Brick. In areas where there is considerable influence from the north, adobes or earth blocks have been used for building. Shaped by hand or cast in a wooden mould, the bricks are sun-dried before use. In the Nigerian centres of Katsina and Kanuri two- and three-storey houses have been built by this method. Their cubic forms, flat roofs and common walls all reduce the surface area on to which sunlight falls, helping to lower the level of solar radiation. Thick walls slow the transmission of heat from the outside to the inside of the building: by night, when the heat has passed through the walls, the rooms are warmed; during the day, rooms remain cool and comfortable.

Fired brick is not widely used in Sub-Saharan Africa, although evidence of early use has been found in Chad. In areas of European influence such bricks have been used for prestigious buildings. In Sudan the 'clamp' type of kiln is used, in which bricks are stacked so that the lower ones make a furnace and the flames pass around those above. The whole structure is covered with clay during the firing. There is, however, high consumption of palm for fuel and high wastage of bricks broken in the kiln. Although firing makes bricks more durable and less prone to erosion, their use is still limited. Successful experiments have been conducted in Sudan in producing bricks bonded with waste engine oil. These have proved to be considerably more durable than sun-dried bricks and less wasteful of resources.

See also BRICK, §V, 5.

(d) Wood and palm. More than a third of Africa has little or no vegetation suitable for building use, but the savannah and steppe regions produce baobab, dom palm and, in the more vegetated regions, acacia. Palm is not a structurally strong building material, but it is used for beams by the Hausa and Bornu and for the reinforcement of the parabolic arches by which the shallow domes of their houses are supported. Shorter lengths of palm are also employed, in a corbelling technique, to span the corners of a square room to produce a dome. Palm leaves are used extensively as a roof cover, either in layers alternating with brushwood and earth, as in the Sudan, or

61. Agar Dinka raising grass-thatched roof on to a house on wood posts, near Pacong, Agar Dinka, Southern Sudan; from a photograph by Jeremy Coote, 1981

as a thatching material. The splines are an effective tensile material for light spans, while the leaves may be woven to form mat walls. The gnarled lengths of acacia are not suitable for structural use. Slender poles from local trees are used by the Maasai and other East African peoples in the construction of huts, cattle kraals and so on. Young stands of pole wood are generally preferred to heavier timber. Here, as elsewhere in Africa, however, trees may be valued more for the shade they provide than as a source of building material.

Among nomadic peoples thin poles, often preformed into arcs to facilitate rapid erection, are used as armatures for their movable huts. These are usually domed structures with curved ridges. The north-east African Borana, Somali and Danakil, among others, use this form of structure, which may have been introduced southwards by the nomadic Beja. It is also used by southern Tuareg and by those other Tuareg who are becoming more settled. Here the roof frame may be supported on short poles to give more headroom. Some frame-and-mat structures, such as those used by the Baggara of Sudan, reach 10 m across. Covering mats may be of woven grass, palm leaves or similar material, which can be rolled up and packed on donkeys or camels as the group seeks new pasture.

Light wood and pole frames are also used by hunter-gatherer peoples in Africa's desert and scrub regions. In the Kalahari Desert the San built temporary camps of shelters erected from a few branches and a grass cover. When a longer stay was anticipated, these were more carefully made, with horizontal wands interwoven with the vertical members and covered with bunched grass, sometimes with its roots. In regions with plentiful wood such hunters as the Hadza of Tanzania used wands and branches to make thatched temporary shelters, while the Mbuti and other pygmy bands of the Ituri Forest in Zaïre constructed domical shelters of branches interwoven with lighter wands and covered with large leaves. Such light, temporary shelters may be built in a few hours and then used for two to three months, until the area's game has been hunted out and the group moves on.

In forested regions where timber is readily available, houses with a square or rectangular plan are commonly found. While these are often referred to as examples of 'carpentered' or trabeated architecture, most are not made of sawn and squared timber, even those built after European tools became generally available. African timber-framed buildings generally have no sill, the houseposts being driven directly into the ground. Many do not have roof trusses, but the ridges are supported by central poles and the wall plates by end- and side-poles. Such structures are often framed with a ring-beam of poles or intertwined, pliable branches, and further lateral poles or branches may be used to strengthen the side walls. The roof structure may have true purlins, but common rafters, with horizontal rafters laid to take thatching, are customary.

In such timber buildings most joints are secured by bark-strip lashing. Mortice-and-tenon, and even lap joints, were known but were often used only for doorways and door sills. Such skills in working timber with an adze, as are evident in sculpture throughout West and Central Africa, indicate that it was not for the lack of ability or tools that such methods were not employed. Although triangulation is sometimes employed to stabilize a structure, bracing tends to be horizontal unless considerable live loads from wind pressure are to be withstood. In very tall buildings, such as those of the Bafut of Cameroon, diagonal bracing is used both functionally and decoratively.

Although some peoples (e.g. the Kikuyu) use such termite-resistant woods as cedar, most timber buildings are constructed from soft woods that are subject to both termite infestation and wood rot. The damage these cause frequently necessitates rebuilding after a few years. In both forest and savannah woodland regions wood may be used in association with mud daub. A double layer of poles may be used, as among the Lamba of Zimbabwe, to produce a thicker wall section that may be strengthened both inside and out with horizontal woven branches and withies. Mud is used to pack the intervening space and for plastering the whole wall surface, both internally and externally. When smoothed and polished the building may appear to be constructed totally of earth.

(e) Grass. Bamboo is employed widely as a structural material. This is especially so in the lusher grassland areas, where it is most ambitiously used in the high structures of the Bamileke of the Cameroon Highlands. Here the main living space is constructed as a cube out of vertical bamboo poles with stout, timber corner posts. A platform of thin bamboos is raised on top of the dwelling space and the pyramidal roof erected above. A second stabilizing platform may be inserted in the roof structure, which frequently reaches 6 m in height. Roof structures are prefabricated from triangles of bamboo, lashed and braced, and the whole roof is thickly thatched by specialists.

Although a few nomadic groups (e.g. some pastoral Fulani) use unsupported grass as a temporary shelter, it is most often used for roof thatching or as a cladding material, for which purpose some South African peoples have developed intricate grass-weaving techniques. In some areas where grass is abundant it may be pulled in bunches with the roots still attached, these being used to secure the grass to the roof frame. Grass is usually layered from the eaves to the ridge, sometimes over a hipped roof among rain-forest peoples. Circular-plan houses have conical roofs that are thatched in layers from the eaves. Among the Dinka of Sudan the grass roof is made separately on the ground and then lifted onto the hut walls (see fig. 61). The peak of the roof is capped with a woven and bound grass finial or a pad of packed earth. Sometimes, for example among the Kipsigis of Kenya, the last bundles of grass are attached to a pole inserted at the crest, and an upturned broken pot is slid over the pole. In each case the purpose is to make the roof watertight at its weakest point. Where reeds or elephant grass are available these are used, tightly secured with bound straw. Forked sticks inserted through the wall structure at the eaves take the weight of the thatch.

(f) Hair and hide. Cattle nomads and camel nomads commonly use tents relating to the intercontinental tent culture. Bedouin and Berber tribes of the northern Sahara construct tents from strips of woven goat-hair, made on ground looms and sewn together to form a membrane. This membrane is held in tension by guy-ropes affixed with wooden stay fasteners. Strong, supporting webbing-bands take the lateral strains that would otherwise separate the strips. The centre of the tent is supported by a curved length of wood raised on two poles, its length varying from tribe to tribe, thus giving the tent a characteristic profile. The edge of the membrane is held up with poles. The Kababish of the Sudan often have boxlike tents, while among the Tuareg and the Fulani a Berber tent type is used, differing in that the membrane is made of goatskins sewn together (see fig. 62). Usually 40 such skins are used, but as many as 200 may be used in the membrane of a chief's tent. The trailing ends of the hides are cut and plaited by the women to provide internal decoration, and dyed patterns are also used. Among many tent cultures decorative hangings are used as side walls, to cover openings and to divide the internal spaces of the tent.

62. Fulani goatskin tent, Niger; from a photograph by Sarah Errington

(iii) Vernacular architecture.

(a) Building types. (b) Scale. (c) Spatial organization. (d) Symbolism. (e) Decoration.

(a) Building types. Most African buildings are domestic. Among these a distinction may be made between a 'hut', which is single-celled and conceived as one unit of space, and a 'house', which has not been divided but rather conceived and built as a number of separate units, or to accommodate a variety of discrete functions. Huts with a more temporary function are related to the dwelling and are often virtually identical in form. These include 'menstrual' huts, where pubertal girls may be confined prior to a celebration to mark their transition to womanhood, and circumcision huts, constructed for young boys awaiting initiation rites.

Movements of peoples and the persistence of building types in areas settled in modern times have meant that differing systems may be found in proximity to each other. Nevertheless, it is broadly possible to identify major areas where specific building forms occur. The cylindrical hut is the most widely dispersed, occurring in Southern and East Africa and through the savannah belts of West Africa. In Southern Africa it is commonly known as the rondavel.

In the tropical rain-forest and savannah woodlands rectangular- and square-plan buildings are common, while the so-called 'beehive' style of dome was built by many peoples.

Vernacular buildings that are similar in form may vary considerably in construction: a cylindrical, single-dwelling unit may be built wholly of mud, or it may be constructed of poles driven into the soil, bound with creepers or bark, mud daubed and mud plastered over; or it may be built of sun-dried blocks or bricks, which, when plastered, display similar formal characteristics. Rectangular-plan buildings, though constructed by different techniques, may also be rendered, and thus the structural differences between the building systems employed are obscured.

Basic forms. The dome is the simplest form, being an undifferentiated structure with no separation of roof from walls. Structural members are inserted in the ground and bent over to join at the apex to form a peaked, ribbed dome, held in tension. Such buildings are found as far west as among the Conagui of Guinea, as far east as among the Chencha of Ethiopia and as far south as among the Zulu of South Africa. Frequently the domes are thatched in layers of bundled grass. An alternative form of dome, developed by the Zulu and Nguni, consists of semicircular hoops, inserted into the ground concentrically to form a tight mesh, over which layers of grass thatch and woven grass mats are placed. Generally the grass dome receives a final thatch layer that is secured with a net of weighted grass ropes.

Though structurally more complex, the cylindrical hut with a differentiated, conical roof has a number of advantages, allowing not only additional headroom but also space for smoke from internal fires. In addition, the eaves can protect the exterior from both sun and rain. A low verandah with an outer ring of poles may take some of the roof's weight. Traditionally such houses were rarely subdivided, as the introduction of ceilings or walls reduces air circulation.

Centrally located on a line drawn from the Bight of Benin to the Horn of Africa, the territory of the Zande may be seen as a fulcrum of African shelter forms, a nodal region through which the main currents of influence appear to have passed. Zande house types include the *buguru* with mud walls and a timber door lintel for the senior wife; the *dondoma* with low eaves and no walls for other wives; and the *basura*, or temporary sleeping hut. They have also adopted such other forms as the *naderugi* hut, built on a platform of beaten clay; the *kata*, a type constructed of blocks of termite hill earth; the *basa*, formed in the shape of a tunnel; and a square hut, the *gbiliki*, influenced by European 'rest-houses'. Even 'traditional' Zande huts built at the end of the 20th century differ somewhat from 19th-century forms, which had high, pointed, conical roofs and verandahs offering protection from the rain. Although not all societies are as eclectic in their architectural tastes as the Zande, the diversity of forms adopted and built by them indicates the problem of ascribing a single type to any people or of assuming that types existing today are those of the past. In areas of West Africa with relatively low rainfall, cylindrical huts may have crossbeams supporting a flat roof and layers of brush and earth as well as, perhaps, a low parapet. Roofs of this type are used to dry and store grains and fruits and as outdoor sleeping areas that catch any available breeze. Flat-roofed cylindrical huts are not found in East Africa.

Houses with a square or rectangular plan occur most frequently in forested regions, where the availability of timber and bamboo permits a frame construction. Regular-square plans are comparatively unusual: most buildings with right-angled corners tend to be rectangular, with the entrance often on one of the shorter sides. As the ridge is usually supported by poles rather than by a roof truss, and the roofs take a burden of thatch, pitches of *c.* 45° are common. In some rain-forest regions there are thatched, hipped roofs. An extended eaves structure may permit a covered verandah, and, more rarely, thatched porches may be added. Wall openings other than doorways are rare, enhancing security but reducing light and cross-ventilation. Interiors can be subdivided relatively easily with a rectangular plan, and the simplest form of this—the erection of a cross-wall to create two rooms—is most common.

Stone, earth and mud-brick buildings of rectangular plan are also found throughout North Africa. Here more complex internal subdivision is common, both horizontally and vertically. Islamic requirements for the segregation of women also necessitated the further partitioning of rooms, which usually had small window openings.

Under Islamic influence, indigenous, circular forms south of the Sahara were replaced by houses of earth construction and rectangular plan, although both types existed in such areas as the northern Nigerian Hausa emirates. Flat roofs also superseded conical roofs, although arches and domes were used by the Hausa and Fulani to span larger spaces.

Palaces. Although the architecture of chiefs' compounds is closely based on that of ordinary dwellings, many African rulers expressed their power and influence architecturally. They did so by using the finest craftmen and by developing spatially elaborate complexes to accommodate not only themselves, their kinsmen, wives and children but also other retainers, courtiers, visitors and supplicants. At the time of early European contact, West African domestic architecture was in many ways comparable with that of Europe, with wattle-and-daub and timber-framed houses with thatched roofs. As a result, early Western observers were impressed not so much by essentially similar African building types and techniques as by the formal sophistication and decorative embellishment of the 'palaces'. As early as the 16th century, for example, accounts of the palace of the Oba of Benin reached Europe, with details of its sanctuaries, shrines and ceremonials (*see* BENIN).

Of all such palaces, the citadel of the Mambo Mutota (King Monomotapa) of Zimbabwe, with its impressive scale, skilful building in stone and evidence of a sophisticated culture has attracted most attention from archaeologists and historians (*see* GREAT ZIMBABWE). The lavish palace of the Shaykh of Mogadishu, further north, was described by the Moroccan traveller Ibn Battuta as early as 1332; all the east-coast shaykhdoms may have had similar palaces. Many Bantu chiefdoms and kingdoms had large compounds for their principal lineages, and these were also identified as 'palaces' by Europeans. King Mutesa of the Baganda built his capital, Kasubi Nabulagala, by covering a hillside with immense, domed houses, finely thatched in reed, laid out so that his regional chiefs lived in the part closest to their lands. The royal enclosure included a house for the keeper of the sacred fire, the house of the King's wives, the royal drum-room, the royal smithy, a waiting-room, court rooms and an Ivory Court, where the King discussed matters of state. Such neighbouring peoples as the Bunyoro and the Banyankole also had large palace complexes.

In the Bamenda highlands of Cameroon a number of Tikar tribes built notable palace compounds. That of the chief of Batoufam featured a cluster of tall, conically thatched buildings of bamboo construction of the traditional Bamileke form. Its arrangement was similar to the palace of the Fon of Bafut, which was approached through a courtyard flanked by enclosures for the older and the younger wives and their respective children. In the 1950s the Fon's enclosure included a reception hall, medicine huts, the storage and assembly halls of secret societies, dormitories and burial houses, but only two traditional buildings remained, the others having been replaced by earth-block houses with tiled roofs. The King of Bamum also had an impressive palace (*see* BAMUM).

Peoples inhabiting the rain-forests built large and complex palaces, although few survive. Such palaces include the *afins* of the Yoruba. These were the seats of the Obas of each city and comprised large complexes of courtyards surrounded by rectangular thatched buildings. Such palaces normally faced the city market, from which access was gained by a portico and gate to the main courtyard, overlooked by the Oba's verandah (*kobi*). The portico and arcade of the Oni at Ife was of immense dimensions with a frontage more than 100 m long.

See also PALACE, §VIII.

Shrines and other religious buildings. Palace complexes are often also spiritual centres, containing temples and shrines, a reflection of the concept of divine kingship that prevails in many African kingdoms. Among those peoples who build sanctuaries and cult houses are the Asante of Ghana. Their 'fetish-house' (*abosomfie*) is in the form of the customary dwelling, with four rectangular buildings around a court (*paito*). One open-fronted unit houses a drum orchestra: a shrine-room, the domain of the village priest, is opposite. The Yoruba of Nigeria, who follow a complex religion with many gods, build large temples, shrines and cult houses, among the most significant of which are a temple to Ogun Igbo at Isheda Benin, the cult houses to Sango the god of thunder and the river god Oshun at Oshogbo, and a number in various places to Omolu, the god of smallpox. Yoruba shrine-rooms have painted and sculptured pillars, and they and the cult objects they contain are guarded by a priest or priestess.

Among the peoples of eastern Nigeria members of Ekpe and other secret societies build houses for the performance of fertility rites. The Igbo construct open-fronted mud temples, from which are hung the skulls of

63. Dogon men's meeting-house (*togu na*), Ireli, Mali; from a photograph by Angela Fisher, 1981

sacrificial animals, fenced with a sacred shrub. The Ibibio build commemorative funerary shrines (*see* IBIBIO, §4). Often, however, a village priest works magic or invokes spirits in a sacred place that may be marked only by a ring of stones or protective charms. Ancestral hunters' shrines among the Ndembu of Zambia are encircled with animal horns, and each shrine contains a forked stick, a square of termite earth and a grass braid, all of which have symbolic connotations. Among many savannah peoples ancestral shrines may be built within the domestic hut or compound. They may take the form of cones or phallic columns and may sometimes contain the ancestor's remains.

Meeting-houses. In some societies, large communal meeting-houses served as council chambers. The most impressive include those of the MANGBETU of Zaïre, often being nearly 100 m long, 50 m wide and some 15 m high at the ridge. Rows of internal posts supported the interior roof framework, which was constructed of bamboo and palm fronds. Others, open at one end and of considerable size, were built by the Igbo of eastern Nigeria and used by masking societies. These and the meeting-houses of the Yakö (also of eastern Nigeria) were substantial constructions built of logs.

Special houses were often built for use by male clan members or by members of societies. These are often open-sided shelters with flat roofs supported on piers, on which may be stored reeds and firewood that act as insulation during the day. Such shelters are made by the Senufo and other peoples of Côte d'Ivoire and Mali, but the best-known type is the *togu na* of the Dogon, with its supporting forked pillars carved with female breasts and symbolically rich motifs (see fig. 63; *see also* DOGON).

Granaries and stores. The grain stores of the West African savannah generally take the form of large clay pots resting on short piers of rock or timber. Those of East and Southern Africa, in contrast, generally take the form of large baskets raised off the ground on stilts. Some attain great size; those of the Songhai of Mali, for example, being 3 or 4 m high. Among such savannah peoples as the Lobi of Burkina Faso and the Mofou of Cameroon, however, granaries are built inside an ordinary hut. Within, the grain stores may be built to roof-height and shaped like immense pottery vessels with internal subdivisions. Access to granaries is usually through the top of the container, which may have a removable lid or thatch roof (see fig. 64). When the level of the grain is low, a door in the side may be used. Such doors are hung on hinges, or on projections that turn in recesses, and have wooden locks. Other kinds of storage baskets and jars, often free-standing, at times rivalling in size associated sleeping huts, are found throughout Africa. They need to be constructed well to resist the thrusts of their loads and will often last without maintenance for long periods.

The stores of the Kiga of Uganda are as much as 3 m high and 1.5 m in diameter. Woven of pliable papyrus or bamboo lengths, they are highly resilient and fill out their shape as the container is filled. The *ngula* baskets of the Tonga of Zambia were built only after the size of the

64. Kirdi granary being filled, Mandara Mountains, Cameroon; from a photograph by Angela Fisher, 1980

65. Zulu settlement with central cattle *kraal*, South Africa

harvest had been ascertained. Many cylindrical grain stores are made of reeds or canes, the structure supported by strong poles, sometimes daubed with mud, and topped with a conical thatched roof. These are to be found in many eastern and southern regions, reflecting the southward movement of former migrant peoples. There is evidence that the basket-weave, cylindrical wattle or wattle-and-daub granary and the pottery grain store are all traceable historically to the inter-lacustrine region. Among some peoples, such as the Zulu, storage pits are also used for keeping root crops.

(b) Scale. In parts of Morocco and Algeria, fortified towns often had look-out towers and houses that were several storeys high. These were built around central shafts or light-giving wells and were accessed via stairways of timber and stone. In Sub-Saharan Africa the buildings of Islamicized societies are generally lower than those in the north, although two-storey houses are not uncommon, and some defensive towers are higher. Non-Islamic Sub-Saharan buildings are rarely more than one storey, although there are exceptions, including the two-storey, cylindrical houses of the rural Tigre in Ethiopia and the two- and sometimes three-storey dwellings of the Somolo of Burkina Faso and the Fante of Ghana. Platform dwellings on stilts are used by the Dinka of Sudan (see fig. 61 above) as well as by such riverain and lacustrine fishing peoples as the Nyasa of Tanzania and the Tofinou of Lake Nokwé, Togo.

The prevalence of single-storey, low-profile buildings may be accounted for by a variety of factors. There was no lack of space, they were considered relatively inconspicuous, and their low level was also seen as a defensive measure. Height is often associated with prestige, however, and many peoples, while still building single-storey dwellings, construct accentuated, high roofs. The narrow, pyramid-shaped huts of the Ngelima of Zaïre (more than 8 m high, though little more than 3 m sq. at the base) are examples.

(c) Spatial organization. It is in the disposition of structures and their lateral arrangement that African building is spatially most varied. Quadrangular-plan houses are often grouped around a courtyard either with individual units making contact only at the corners, as among the Asante, or with a continuous articulated roof, as in the traditional compound of the Yoruba or of the Fon of the Republic of Benin. Low dwellings arranged in lines facing each other or around a courtyard may be extended by adding further courts, some of which may function as impluvia, collecting rain-water from the roofs in large pottery vessels or a central circular tank. Another building arrangement based around a rectangular courtyard is the *tembe* of the Iraqw and Barangi of Tanzania. This is a continuous structure, which can be 100 m long, with a backward-sloping roof. The largest could provide refuge for, perhaps, a hundred people at times of attack. Some were made less conspicuous by being built in a deep trench or even totally below ground-level, with trench or tunnel access.

Kraal arrangements are common in Southern and East Africa and often take a circular or oblate form. Among, for example, the Ila Tonga, they may be of considerable size, as much as 0.5 km in diameter. Circular-plan huts may be unconnected but arranged in an approximate arc, circle or horseshoe-shape and surrounded by a defensive thicket or hedge of euphorbia (see fig. 65; *see also* MILITARY ARCHITECTURE AND FORTIFICATION, §IX). Among the Bahima of Uganda a number of clusters may be contained within one enclosure, while in Lesotho, where there is little danger from predators or from attack and population densities are low, dwellings may be widely dispersed and without any significant arrangement. Where there is considerable pressure on land, however, as among the Tswana and Ndebele of Botswana, fences may define family territory. Within the boundary a number of huts may be grouped around a cleared and carefully maintained area, often encircled by a low, sculptured wall. The area is used, in effect, as an outdoor room. Storehouses, latrines and screened washplaces may also be constructed within the larger area.

The greatest variety of settlement types occurs in the savannah regions of West Africa, in an arc from Sudan to Senegal. Among those peoples using circular dwelling units the customary settlement is the compound. For example, in the mountains of Southern Kordofan, Sudan,

Nuba often locate their houses on defensive positions on rocky edges overlooking their fields and cattle. Constructed as small cylinders, houses remain discrete units while being built close together, with narrow passages and gaps closed with stones and brush. A Nuba family compound comprises a hut for the wife, additional sleeping huts and granaries and an open communal space that is sometimes partially shaded. Among the Moro sub-group there are separate huts for the daughters, huts containing storage pots, a cooking space and an 'access' hut (*khodo*), divided by low walls and with sleeping ledges for the sons.

The dwellings of such craftsmen as smiths and metalworkers, who often belonged to a separate caste and were considered to be magically dangerous by virtue of the transformative nature of their work, were often set apart. This separation also had the advantage of keeping the forge and bellows ventilated and away from inflammable thatch. Other craft buildings such as workshops, dye-pits, potteries, tanneries, weaving sheds and furnaces (see fig. 48 above) were often located in specific areas within the community. In smaller settlements a local market may be held under a light, monopitch structure, under awnings or with little cover at all. In the towns, long rows of market stalls occupy designated spaces under monopitch or pitched roofs. Village shops, often comprising a single dwelling with an open side or room adapted for the sale of mixed commodities and imported goods, may be found in rain-forest areas. In the towns, of course, the mix of building types is correspondingly greater, including a variety of shops, schools and urban housing.

Although individual circular-plan huts are not easily extensible, the compound settlement form is extremely adaptable, and many examples of great beauty and complexity have been recorded in Burkina Faso, Togo, Mali, Guinea and elsewhere. Although in general such compounds are limited to the dwellings of extended families, each under a household head who may have more than one wife, in some areas several may be grouped together to form a village.

Throughout the Sahel, compounds have been adapted to meet cultural requirements for domestic privacy and the seclusion of women. In rural areas the curvilinear plans of traditional West African compounds persisted into the late 20th century, dwelling-units being usually circular with conical or flat roofs and linked by encircling and dividing walls. However, Mande influence has led in some areas to more regular, square-plan units sharing common side walls and clustered in rectilinear groupings. Many compounds have internal walls to distinguish the domain of the male household head from those of the women and children. Among the Hausa an entrance room (*zaure*) opens on to the head's area, which may include a stable and bachelor hut. The female section is situated beyond the vestibule (*sigife*). While seldom strict in their geometry, such compound plans are found in peri-urban areas of Mali, Burkina Faso and northern Côte d'Ivoire, but they are most characteristic of the towns. Even in the Hausa emirates of the western Sudan rural settlements may consist largely of circular-plan huts or a mixture of these with rectilinear forms; in the cities, however, round huts have become increasingly rare in the 20th century.

(d) Symbolism. Although some vernacular African architectural forms may have arisen out of functional considerations, it is rare for any to be without symbolic associations. The partly subterranean houses of the western Kassena of Burkina Faso, for example, display great formal originality in the use of sculpted platforms, tiers of steps, partitioning walls, dwelling spaces, tunnels and openings and in such functional structures as fish-drying kilns, hearths and storage shelves for gourds and pottery vessels. Similar moulded structures are also used by the Tallensi of Ghana and other peoples of the region. These forms have anthropomorphic associations, with parts identified with the mouth, the head or the 'face of the deceased'. The Dogon of Mali have a complex symbolic system that encompasses within it the settlement and compound architecture. Thus the smithy and the men's meeting-house (*togu na*; see fig. 63 above) were conceptualized as the head; individual families' houses as the chest; the women's house as the hands; the oil-crushing stones and village altar as the male and female genitalia; and other altars as the feet. In the individual dwelling, units are similarly conceptualized, and the whole compound is perceived as a man lying on his side in the act of procreation.

The architectural symbolism of the Fali of Cameroon is no less complex. They similarly associate parts of the village and the dwelling with human form and with procreation. The principal groups associate themselves with cardinal points within the settlement. Modelled and painted surfaces enrich Fali compounds, which are virtually autonomous, although communality is reinforced by the shared meeting-house. Fali cosmology is bipartite and related to a creation myth involving an ancestral toad and turtle. Each house represents this, with the cylindrical shape representing the female toad, in union with the conical roof-shell of the male turtle. There are, however, other layers of meaning: the settlement at the nodal centre is male, the encircling ring of cultivation is female, while the structure of the dwelling and the space it contains reflect the symbolic duality of earth and sky. The Batammaliba of northern Togo and the Republic of Benin regard their houses and settlements as icons of their cosmology. Concepts of the individual in society are expressed not only in the buildings' forms but also in the construction processes and in their subsequent use.

(e) Decoration. Much of the appeal of African architecture is due to its sculptural quality. Among many peoples the use of earths in pottery-related techniques has resulted in forms of great aesthetic beauty. Moreover, the use of curvilinear walls and details, door openings and mouldings in shell-like structures of considerable resilience gives a feeling of movement to the constructions.

Painted decoration is frequently executed by women, as among the Frafra of Ghana, using either their fingers or frayed sticks as brushes (see fig. 50 above). Traditionally, such earth colours as white, red and black were used, often with no fixing medium. Certain colours often have specific connotations: white is frequently linked with purity, power and health, red with blood and power and black with disease and death. (The traditional range of colours was extended in the second half of the 20th century with the

66. Ndebele decorated mud house inside enclosing wall, built and decorated by Christina Skosana and family, near Devon, Transvaal, South Africa; from a photograph by Elizabeth A. Schneider, 1980

adoption of washing 'blue' and commercial paints.) It should not be concluded, however, that the use of a colour always carried such connotations. Nor do all motifs convey meaning: the extensive use of triangles and simple geometric shapes on Shona houses may be purely decorative.

The townships in South Africa have been the location for the emergence of a 20th-century development in painted decoration. Highly abstract, simplified but forceful designs serve the dual purpose of visually increasing space and enriching the environment. Such decoration often comprises large shapes painted in bold colours, sometimes differentiated by textures in the plaster. Razor-blades and other objects have been the inspiration for some motifs.

Figurative wall painting, common in both ancient and modern Egyptian vernacular architecture, is not unknown in other African societies but normally appears only in such conventionalized and two-dimensional forms as the hunting scenes and totemic birds and animals painted in 'stick-figures' and silhouette on the external walls of some Lunda (Angola) and Ngere (Côte d'Ivoire) houses. With the growth in 'Chop Bars' and shops a lively and popular form of wall art has evolved featuring highly modelled figures, vignetted in decorative borders, often captioned with epigrams and representing images of affluence and sophistication.

Decorative wall painting may be used in conjunction with modelled decoration. Such Southern African peoples as the southern Sotho and Taung use finger-furrows on wall surfaces, with mosaics of pebbles and broken china to increase the textural contrast and curvilinear designs to define shapes. Among the Tswana the apron-court (*lolwapa*) is often decorated with a painted and sculpted defining wall. It is, however, among the Ndebele that the richest forms of wall painting are to be found (see fig. 66; *see also* NDEBELE). The walls of their cylindrical dwellings are decorated with strong abstract motifs, which became more geometric and rectilinear as rectangular plans were adopted. Exteriors of houses have continued to be lavishly painted with marked symmetry in patterning, the entrances to the compounds defined by high gateways or ziggurat-form gate-posts. Motifs were originally derived from blanket and beadwork patterns, but car number plates and the Victorian buildings of Pretoria later became design sources. The Ndebele also decorate the interiors of their homes: a painted sideboard of moulded clay, with clay fittings, is a typical feature.

Some West African peoples also use a combination of paint and high-relief modelling to decorate their dwellings. Asante houses were formerly decorated with abstract symbolic motifs painted in white and red, some of which were modelled as open-fret screens, with interlaced strapwork, spirals and volutes. These motifs had similar meanings to those of designs found on goldweights and *adinkra* cloth and may be Islamic in origin. After the sacking of Kumasi by the British in 1874, this art declined on houses, but it was retained for many years in shrines (*abosomfie*), where moulded walls, pillars, pilasters, plinths and openwork screen walls survived. Open screens, more heavily moulded and less formal, were also used elsewhere. Perhaps the most structurally daring are the arcades of the earth houses of the Fouta Djallon, Senegal, where abacus-like columns support massive loads and openings are pierced in a variety of audacious shapes, symmetrically disposed.

A combination of moulded and painted decoration also adorned the walls of the former palace of King Gozo of

Abomey in the Republic of Benin. Here deeply recessed, moulded panels once contrasted with the surface painting. Heavily weathered, many of these panels are now only distinguishable by their polychrome paintwork. Yoruba palaces in western Nigeria were often similarly decorated, and, by the 1990s, concrete was regularly used for the sculpting of three-dimensional figures and heraldic animals, notably lions, often derived from motifs imported from Brazil. Such heraldic animals are moulded on parapets and positions of prominence on the houses of the wealthy.

Other types of sculpted relief include carved doors, an important feature of many palace buildings, shrines and houses of important people (*see also* DOOR, §VII). Among the Dogon, granary doors had sculptured protective figures and elaborately carved locks. The Senufo and the Baule carve high-relief fertility devices, closely related in form to their buffalo and ram masks, on door panels. Under Baule influence the Senufo have developed door panels with spatially inventive arrangements of fish, bird and water motifs. Although some were polychromatically painted, Baule doors were often wholly in red and those of the Senufo in black. The palaces of the Yoruba also had elaborately carved doors, though their design was more constrained than that of the Senufo, being arranged in horizontal bands of figures with supporting panels of interlaced designs. Apart from the door, the entrance frame itself has sometimes been the focus of sculptural detail: Bamileke bamboo houses have heavy, wood surrounds carved with heads and figures symbolic of increase.

Three-dimensional architectural sculpture reached a high level in the *mbari* houses built by the Owerri Igbo to honour Ala, the earth goddess and guardian of morality. Square in plan and open-sided, they frequently have tiers or steps on which figures are moulded in mud. Other sculptures, often life-size, may include both traditional and modern totemic animals and ribald or witty representations of figures of authority (*see also* IGBO).

Larger, although perhaps not as inventive, are the so-called 'monuments' of the Asafo military companies of the Fante of Ghana. Each company has a polychrome, concrete command post (*posuban*), whose form is thought to derive ultimately from European trading forts (see fig. 79 below). Monumental in form, they may have verandahs, flights of stairs, arcades and life-size figures of men and lions and may terminate in a metal palm tree. They are used to store the company's drums and act as a focus for its ceremonial life.

(iv) Christian architecture. African architectural interpretation of Christian forms dates to at least the 4th century AD when Christianity was first established in Nubia. In Adulis and Aksum in Ethiopia, monasteries and churches existed in large numbers by the 6th century, although their numbers later declined as Islam was adopted in the region. The 13th-century Zagwe dynasty in the Lasta region of Ethiopia left 11 churches, carved from solid rock under

67. Christian church, Debre Libonos, Eritrea, probably before 1500; from a photograph by David Buxton, 1930s

the direction of King Lalibela (*see* ETHIOPIA, fig. 1). The church of St George was formed by digging a trench to create its cruciform plan. Aksumite influences include such exterior architectural features as simulated 'monkey-head' beam ends (see fig. 67). Links with more distant traditions are evident in the interior details of some of the churches. Although the churches of Lalibela are the most celebrated, many other churches, adapted from caves or carved into rock faces, have been documented in the Tigre region. These include the great churches at Cherkos, Wkro, Abreha Atsbehj and Medhane Alem, as well as the extraordinary plateau stronghold of Debra Damo with its almost inaccessible monastery.

Many of the churches and monasteries of the Ethiopian Christian enclave were destroyed by the non-Christian Galla in the 16th century. The establishment of the kingdom of Gondar under Fasiladas led to the building of a splendid palace–fortress, over 40 churches and the monastery of Kusquam with the now ruinous round church of Debra-Tsahay. It is possible that this circular church was based on wooden, thatched prototypes: a church of this form still stands at Manz and is locally attributed to Nagassi, a prince of Shoa at the time of Gondar's flourishing. Fasiladas was also responsible for rebuilding the cathedral at Aksum, the holiest place in Christian Africa, but Gondar was levelled by Theodore II in the mid-19th century. At the end of the 19th century Menelik II, the founder of Addis Ababa, built the three-tiered and domed octagonal church of Debra Raguel at his first capital of Entotto. With colonial partition of the continent a new ecclesiastical architecture appeared, but this had little effect on the development of indigenous forms.

See also COPTIC ART, §II, 3; ETHIOPIA, §I; NUBIA, §VI. For information on colonial and post-colonial Christian architecture in Africa see individual country entries.

(v) Islamic architecture. The impact of Islam on architecture in Africa has been profound. It has been felt through the influence of Islamic calligraphy, patterns and decorative forms, as well as through domestic house forms and the larger forms of religious architecture. Islam brought to Africa a taste for the monumental, with tombs, mosques and minarets introducing a vertical dimension that was new to African architecture south of the Sahara. Islam also brought with it some technological changes, including the occasional use of kiln-dried bricks. More importantly, it led to the concentration of dwellings in trading centres and entrepôts, where mosques, palaces, markets and people's homes were clustered together. Islam's impact has been felt throughout the continent, especially in urban areas, but has been at its strongest in the Muslim areas of the western Sudan, in the towns and cities of the East African coast and, of course, in North Africa and the Maghrib. Seen as the near and distant west by their Arab colonizers, North Africa and the Maghrib may be considered stylistically part of the Middle East.

(a) Building types. (b) Decoration.

(a) Building types.

Secular. From Cairo in Egypt to Salé in Morocco characteristically Islamic house and settlement forms are seen. There are medinas, souqs and kasbas; there are courtyard houses, linked by interconnecting lanes and passages, with their shared walls and flat roofs; and there is also the segregation of the women's quarters. At the coastal town of Sousse in Tunisia, an Islamic city was built next to the pre-existing medieval city, leaving the latter largely intact. In contrast, such towns as Ghadames, El Oued and those, such as Ghardaia, in the valleys of the Mzab, as well as Constantine, MARRAKESH and FEZ, developed environments that were responsive to the urban economies and social mores of Islam.

In such towns as Djenné in Mali a more syncretic response to Islam resulted in the development of regional styles. In the Dambougalsoria quarter, for example, there is a cluster of houses said to date from the Moroccan invasion of 1591. Their marked portals, known locally as *potigé*, flanking the entrances and the reception chamber above are topped with a row of pre-Islamic-style pinnacles. The Djenné masons, mostly of Songhay or Bamana origin, were renowned in the region into the late 20th century.

By the 10th century AD Muslims were established on the east coast of Africa. Indeed, the town of Manda may have been settled in the 9th century, while Mogadishu, Malindi, Zanzibar and other ports are of later date. Many of these Islamic towns were highly developed. Excavations at Gedi, a former sultan's palace on the Kenyan coast abandoned in the 14th century, revealed coral ragstone walls and portals, reception-rooms and audience courts, apartments, ablution chambers and lavatories. Extensive archaeological evidence of sophisticated spatial organization has been uncovered at the Husuni Kubwa palace, Kilwa, which, in the 13th century, was the largest building south of the Sahara.

Early in the 16th century many Swahili towns were sacked by the Portuguese. Lamu, an island town off the Kenyan coast, largely escaped destruction, and later a treaty of protection with Oman helped to preserve it. While none of its buildings dates from before the 18th century, their form may well reflect earlier domestic architecture. Two-storey merchants' houses made of stone have servants' quarters on the ground-floor and the main living spaces above. Flat roofs made of mangrove poles covered in lime span the walls. A succession of narrow, shallow rooms with plastered walls and rows of moulded display niches, though elegant, are climatically more appropriate to the Persian Gulf than to the Kenyan coast. While these town houses reveal a taste for sophisticated urban living, the central complex of stone houses was surrounded by smaller houses, with walls of wattle-and-daub and deep, open-gabled thatched roofs, which were more suitable climatically.

Palaces were built for the emirs of Muslim societies in West Africa as expressions of their religious authority and secular power and as the focus of the community. They include the elaborately decorated palaces of Zaria and KANO. Other Hausa palaces such as that of the Emir of Daura are less decorated, and the strength of the structural detail is clearer. The arches that provide structural support are typically made with stepped mud corbels, reinforced with lengths of termite-resistant *azara* wood from the dom palm and plastered with mud to produce a simulated continuous curved arch. Although the construction differs, the form may derive from the armatures of the frame-and-mat structures of the local nomads (*see* §(ii)(d) above). Arches may intersect at a central apex, often marked by an inset brass plate, or may form a grid of crossed parabolas. Although this technique can be seen in palaces and other important buildings, the normal method of spanning roofs in domestic houses is with lengths of *azara*. Spans are increased by crossing the corners and making a shallow, corbelled-roof platform, which may be further supported by piers or a central pillar to take the weight of the covering of sticks and earth.

Sacred. The earliest Sub-Saharan mosques to have been discovered are those at Koumbi Saleh, the capital of the former empire of Ghana. Trade links had been established with this area as early as the 9th century AD through the trans-Saharan camel caravans. The Koumbi Saleh mosque type comprised a court, a sanctuary and a square minaret. Elements of this mosque type were common in other parts of the Sudanic region and may be regarded as comprising a distinct Sudanic tradition, which nevertheless had many variants owing to the different currents of influence over many centuries. For example, although the square tower minaret of the Great Mosque at KAIROUAN in Tunisia may have been the source for the Sudanic square-based minaret-towers (*ṣawma'a*), such examples as the tower at Chinguetti, Mauritania, where the mosque may date from the 14th century, differ by having a tapering form, with reinforcements and projecting beams.

The rulers of the successive empires of Ghana, Songhai and Mali embraced a vast territory, which became progressively Islamicized. Cities on the trans-Saharan routes adopted elements of Berber culture, and, under Songhai influence, pyramidal minaret structures on three levels were built. The mosque–tomb of Askia-al-Hajj Muhammed at Gao (Mali) is characteristic, with its bristling, stepped tower that reaches only half the height it was in the mid-19th century. The Sankoré Mosque at TIMBUKTU, a seat of Islamic scholarship in the 15th century, had a buttressed, tapering minaret and arcaded sanctuary. Contacts with the Mzab are evident at Gao and even more marked at Agades in Niger where the pyramid tower of the great mosque is related stylistically to that at Ghardaia in Algeria.

As Islam penetrated further south, building styles were developed that incorporated traditional non-Islamic forms. The mosques built under the influence of Dyula mullah-traders, for instance those in Kong, a Dyula centre of learning and commerce in present-day Mali, though changing through time, were notable for such features reminiscent of traditional Dogon forms as slender, tapering pyramidal minarets and walls buttressed with tall pinnacles. Sculptural in form, these are reinforced by horizontal cross-poles between, or projecting from, the buttresses. The mosques of Bobo-Dioulasso in Burkina Faso, Kawara in Côte d'Ivoire and Banda Nkwanta in Ghana show a lively variety of forms that are, nonetheless, clearly related.

Such Hausa mosques as the Shehu Mosque at Sokoto and the Friday Mosque at Bauchi (both Nigeria) had different forms. Made of reinforced earth, they had pillared prayer-halls supporting flat roofs of palm and mud. Regarded as the finest of the Hausa type, the Friday Mosque at Zaria (also Nigeria) had an undulating roof of shallow domes supported by internal parabolic arches of mud, reinforced with palm and sculpted in high relief.

68. Djenné, Mali, Great Mosque, eastern façade and qibla wall, with the market-place in the foreground; from a photograph by Mick Csaky, *c.* 1980

This remarkable building was substantially altered during restoration in 1975. Other types of mosque also exist in Africa. In the Futa Jallon and Guinea highlands an indigenous savannah building type has accommodated the formal requirements of Islam without sacrificing regional identity: thatched mosques, including those at Manou Degala and Fougoumba, were built by Fulani in the form of vast, ribbed domes. Entirely covered with layered grass thatch, each has a large cap or crest to deflect the rains. Within, a cubic earth sanctuary surrounded by the posts of the supporting structure is oriented to Mecca. Other hybrids are to be found, as in Lagos, where slaves repatriated to Nigeria from Brazil built a number of mosques in a style that derived from the Latin American ecclesiastical Baroque, with classical pilasters and broken pediments, but that bore in their polychrome façades such Islamic motifs as the star and crescent.

An external influence with even greater impact was that of the French engineers who, in 1935, remodelled the great mosque at Mopti in Mali, giving it a greater symmetry and tall, tapering external pilasters. Similarly, although the original structure of the mosque at Djenné dated from the 14th century, it was largely demolished in the early 19th century and then reconstructed in similar form under French colonial direction in 1907 (see fig. 68). Although both are hybrids, their much-photographed images established a popularized form of Sahelian architecture that is evident, for example, in the substantial rebuilding and considerable enlargement of the Great Mosque of Niono, Mali, by the designer, contractor and mason Lassine Minta (*b c.* 1920). The original building was finished in 1948; Minta's rebuilding and extension of it was completed in 1973.

Elsewhere the reconstruction of mosques was less happily resolved. Earlier mud mosques were replaced by new ones, often in stone with conventional minarets and prayer-halls on the Egyptian pattern. Among these was the four-minaret Friday Mosque in Kano, Nigeria, and the somewhat heavily proportioned mosque at Bouake, Côte d'Ivoire, which, nevertheless, has finely cut screens and balustrades and ogee domes of almost Mughal character. Mosques built towards the end of the 20th century tended to be similar, if smaller, and generally undistinguished. The Niliem Mosque at Omdurman, Sudan, designed by Jamal Abdullah, is a radical departure from this, being in the form of a tetrahedral dome standing on tapering pillars over an open prayer-hall.

(b) Decoration. Islamic influence is clearly seen in the decorative details of much African architecture. These may be drawn from ideograms and calligraphy and from such geometric patterns as the subdivided rectangular magic squares known as *hatumere*. Other motifs have been derived from textile patterns, wood-carving and so on. Decorations found among the settled Kabyle Berber in Algeria include cursive patterns created in white plaster on internal, red earth walls, the rugged stone exteriors of such houses preventing external ornamentation. These patterns are used to frame windows and doorways and recall the decorated bed-frames of the nomadic Berber peoples. They are widespread, being found on the other side of the Sahara in Oualata, Mauritania. Strongly associated with the privacy of the women's domain, they were created by members of the lower castes (*harratin*) for wives of aristocrats as symbols of fertility and maternity. Other decorative elements include sculptures, water vessels and moulded sideboards.

Abstract forms are sculpted on the façades of the houses of important men in central Mali. More impressive are the age-set houses (*saho*) of the Sorko of the Niger River in Mali in such centres as Kolenze and Aore. These structures, built by youths in preparation for marriage, are deeply moulded with phallic motifs, verandahs and crenellated roof terraces. The use of clay bricks in this region also permits high-relief framing and structural expression, with geometric openings and recessed patterns achieved by omitting bricks from the outer wall layers. More dramatically moulded, houses in the Djenné style with tall, flanking *potigé* piers beside the entrances and phallic pinnacles are the apogee of Malian architectural decoration (see fig. 65 above).

The *zanen gida* decorations on the façades of the houses of Hausa merchants are notable for their complexity and richness. They are based on the surface enrichment of the walls, ceilings, arch ribs and coffers of Hausa palaces and mosques. Moulded over the mud-plastered surfaces of walls and coated with a locally made cement (*laso*), the motifs are in deep relief, emphasizing doorways or window openings and sometimes extending over the entire façade (see fig. 69). The endless knot (*dagi*) is a common motif, and others are rifles, bicycles, cars and even aeroplanes. The *zanen gida* technique is probably of 18th-century origin and may be derived from the tent hangings of the nomadic Fulani. It was popularized in the 20th century but was in decline by the 1990s.

In contrast to the internal relief plasterwork of Swahili houses (*see* §(a) above) external surfaces were simply treated, emphasis being mainly on the massive doors, with iron studs, spikes and bosses: a style as common in Bahrain as in Lamu, Kenya. Direct decorative influence from Arabia was evident in the now deserted coral stone city of Sawakin, Sudan, once an island trading port on the Red Sea coast and the focus for African pilgrims on their way to Mecca. It was built by Hijazis and had a number of Ottoman-style houses of a considerable size and three storeys in height. Richly decorated internally with banded walls infilled with geometric designs etched in plaster, these houses had doorways with carved stone hoods and cusped stone heads embellishing the wall niches. Windows were fitted with carved, boxed shade screens (*rowshan*s or *mashribiyya*s), some of which have ornately carved grilles and opening panels. After 1866 an Egyptian style emerged in Sawakin, sometimes including European details.

Indeed, Egyptian domestic architectural styles permeated northern Sudan during the 19th century, especially along the Nile. A further development in African Islamic decoration occurred in Nubia, where the internal walls of houses were painted and sometimes sculpted and external decorations painted or applied around the entrance. In Wadi Halfa an elaborate and prestigious style was developed by Ahmad Batoul, who began to make mud reliefs and incised patterns in the early 1930s. Craftsmen competed to invent new motifs, borrowing from contemporary Art Deco sources in Egypt and using saucers and ceramics

69. Hausa decorated house, Tudun Wada, Zaria, Nigeria; from a photograph of 1962

inset in the plaster. Local people also decorated their own houses, men favouring scenes of pilgrimages to Mecca and women painting banded abstract wall friezes. This style of Nubian wall paintings ended with the flooding of the valley by the Aswan Dam in 1970.

(vi) Western architecture. European architecture was first introduced to Africa through the building of trading posts and forts, the first probably being built by the Portuguese on Arguin Island, Cape Blanco, in 1445. Over the centuries others were built along the western seaboard, from Goree to the Kongo, with the greatest concentration on what were known as the Ivory, Slave and Gold coasts. The great Portuguese citadel of Fort Jesus was begun in 1593 at Mombasa. A number of forts were founded by one European power and taken over by another, with the Portuguese-built slave court and dungeons of Elmina in Ghana being taken over by the Dutch in 1637, while the British built a fort on Swedish foundations at Cape Coast. These forts, which often included barracks, chapels, slave quarters, stores and armouries, were frequently quadrangular in plan and had typically Renaissance defensive fortifications at the corners, designed to deflect missiles and to give good artillery command over the approaches. Traders' and merchants' houses were often built near by, either of stone, as at Dixcove, Ghana, or of timber with shaded balconies, as at Calabar, Nigeria (*see also* MILITARY ARCHITECTURE AND FORTIFICATION, §III, 2(v)).

(a) Colonial influences. Away from the coasts, mission churches, built in local materials with thatched roofs or with imported stone in neo-Gothic form, and the houses of the missionaries were among the few European buildings to be seen. The exception was the Cape Colony, settled in the mid-17th century by the Dutch. Their simple, linear farmhouses had stoeps along the front and evolved into both a T-plan, with the kitchen set back from the front, and a larger H-plan. These larger farmhouses were notable for their fine 17th–18th-century CAPE DUTCH STYLE and Cape Flemish gables, with double curved outlines and decoration. Such villages as Philippolis and Graaff-Reinet, the 'gem of the Karoo', retained their 19th-century charm and quality into the 1990s. Later settlements in Southern Africa included the fortified farmsteads of the eastern frontier and the homes of the first Voortreker settlers and were simple and sturdy, some being built of rammed earth or stone with thatched roofs.

Extensive European settlement did not occur until after the partition of Africa was completed at the turn of the 20th century, when small towns were established in the colonies. Although indigenous techniques were sometimes used by early settlers, stone structures were built where possible to replace the pole-and-daub. In addition, prefabricated houses were brought from England, and, from the mid-19th century, corrugated iron was imported in large quantities. The bungalow, originally developed in India, became the ubiquitous colonial house type. Raised on piers, these mostly one-storey buildings had verandahs, spacious interiors and high roofs that permitted air circulation. Their light, corrugated-iron roofs could make the interiors uncomfortably hot, but, despite this, bungalows fitted with mosquito screens were popular with settlers. With Europeanization the bungalow became a desirable urban house type among Africans, gradually replacing traditional compounds. Europeans in West Africa also favoured an alternative type of dwelling—the Basle Mission house. This was raised on piles to a high level and had a projecting upper storey fitted with louvred screens. Immigrant Malays may have had some effect on house types in Cape Town, while Indians influenced architecture in Kenya and Uganda, where Indian-styled rows of shop-houses developed between the World Wars, often with modest Art Deco details in the rendered façades.

In the mid-19th century, ex-slaves returning from the Americas introduced a number of architectural elements: those resettled in Liberia built wooden houses, entirely clad in shingles, applying a roofing technique developed in the USA. More significant and lasting was the *Pètési* (upstairs) house that was developed by repatriated slaves from Brazil, which appeared in Lagos, Abeokuta and, later, Ibadan (*see* NIGERIA, §IV). Such buildings had grand façades comprising elaborately detailed balconies, window mouldings, pillars and porticos. Each consisted of some three floors, perhaps eleven rooms and a rear courtyard. One family would occupy each room of such houses, which continued to be built until the mid-1950s.

(b) Modernism. Until World War II, many towns developed by Europeans were modest in scale, with low-rise architecture dominated only by government buildings of conventional European form. Such colonial cities as Dakar, Senegal, were well planned, its superb peninsula site having government buildings arranged about a star-plan crossing of main thoroughfares. Such others as JOHANNESBURG, DURBAN and Salisbury (now Harare, Zimbabwe) were laid out in a conventional grid plan, and their rigid formalism contrasted with the relaxed disposition of traditional African settlements.

Modernism was introduced with the direct involvement of such European architects as Ernst May, who worked in Kenya. In the early 1930s the Transvaal Group led by Rex Martienssen and including W. Gordon McIntosh and Norman Hanson enthusiastically followed the works of Le Corbusier and Walter Gropius. High-rise building with reinforced concrete or steel framing was not extensively developed until after the 1950s, when the growth of such towns as Lusaka, Zambia, and Blantyre, Malawi, was rapid. At this time the central business and administrative districts of cities throughout the continent assumed an increasingly uniform appearance. In Nigeria, annual concrete imports multiplied elevenfold in 20 years, branches of West African Portland Cement were opened, and the impact on the African urban environment was considerable.

Post-war modern architecture in Africa has been the work of both expatriates and African architects trained in European schools of architecture or at such African universities as Khartoum, Kumasi, Nairobi, Addis Ababa and the Witwatersrand, Johannesburg (*see also* SOUTH AFRICA, §III). University buildings in themselves presented challenging opportunities to architects: James Cubitt built a number at the Kumasi University of Science and Technology (1952–4) as well as the Teachers Training College (1951–4) at Sekondi, Ghana. Julian Elliott undertook the building of the University of Zambia, Lusaka, and Alan Vaughan-Richards designed houses at the University of Lagos, Nigeria. Cubitt's firm designed over 70 projects for African clients, many in Ghana and Nigeria, while Maxwell Fry and Jane Drew were responsible for more than 80, including the University College, Ibadan. Attempts were made to make these buildings suitable for the climate, with deep relief, cross-ventilation and *brises-soleil.* At the same time their strongly rectilinear forms, flat roofs and contrasting masses, designed to cast strong shadows, show their indebtedness to Le Corbusier. The influence of these Modernist forms was pervasive and had few challengers.

Among the most original architects working in Africa was AMANCIO GUEDES, whose sculptural houses, designed in Mozambique, combined spatial innovation and surrealist imagery. A more controlled but still eclectic approach to design is evident in the prolific output of the French-trained Moroccan architect Jean-François Zevaco. His fertile inventiveness is well illustrated by such works of the 1960s as the low-lined Groupe Scolaire in Agadir, the strong forms and contrasting textures of the Palace of Justice (1962–3) at Mohammedia, the exposed concrete of the Post Office (1966) at Agadir and the hopper-like Pavilion (1970) that he and E. J. Duhon created for the International Fair at Casablanca. His compatriot Elie Azagury designed many houses in the De Stijl idiom, of which the Civic Centre (1967), Rabat, is a dramatic example (*see* RABAT).

A new generation of African architects, mainly Nigerian, came to prominence in the 1960s. Of these the best known is OLUWOLE OLUMUYIWA, whose long, unobtrusive school buildings, housing for the United Africa Company, and other projects in Lagos are obviously Modernist but not ostentatious. Fellow Nigerian architects include ALEX EKWEME, architect of the hospital at Ebutametta for the Nigerian Railway Corporation, ISOLA KOLA-BANKOLE and DAVID MUTISO. Ekweme's laboratory building at St Gregory's College, Lagos, has an upper-storey *brise-soleil* and is essentially within a Corbusian idiom. Although admired for their clean lines and white, primary forms broken by projecting frames, such Modernist buildings have not always been responsive to the prevailing climate conditions. Many concrete structures are now green with algae and leak in heavy rains. Nor are they always fully appropriate to local environments. They may exploit the light and shade of tropical sunlight, but they seldom reflect local architectural genres.

(vii) Further developments. Traditional forms are occasionally re-interpreted, an example being the cone-and-cylinder concrete housing units built early in the 20th century for African railway workers in the Sudan. A lead in this field was given by the Egyptian architect HASSAN FATHY who used local methods of passive cooling and employed Sudanese Nubian masons to build barrel vaults by traditional techniques without formwork for his town of New Gourna near Luxor in 1946. Local forms, materials and cooling systems were also used by ANDRÉ RAVÉREAU and his partners in their designs for houses and the post office

in Ghardaia, in the Mzab, Algeria. The same architect's work with the Historical Monuments Service of Algeria led to his invitation to design the Medical Centre (completed 1976; see fig. 70) at Mopti, Mali. It was sited near the Friday Mosque and executed in reinforced soil–cement and Cinva–Ram adobes to harmonize with its context.

Although such experiments have seldom been wholly successful, culturally or environmentally, African forms have provided architectural inspiration in, for example, the design of tourist hotels. Typical is the El Kalas complex (1971) by Faraoui and de Mazieres, which derives its style from a Moroccan *ksar*. Simpler, low-rise hotel complexes such as Olivier-Clement Cacoub's Tourist Centre (1966) at Skanes, Tunisia, were also based on local vernacular architecture, but it is evident that this was more to satisfy European perceptions of Africa than to meet indigenous requirements. While the work of such architects as the Islamic-influenced André Ravéreau and the French-trained CHARLES BOCCARA responded to traditional building cultures and contributed towards the development of a modern indigenous architecture, Western influences more frequently had an impoverishing effect. The West African deep-pitch roof, which arose in response to the tropical rainfall of the area and was widespread in Nigeria, virtually disappeared under the influence of international styles, being replaced by the concrete deck and long-span, shallow-pitch aluminium roofs, often hidden behind a fascia, which give the impression of being flat.

In the 1970s wars and economic problems in many countries reduced the numbers of new buildings erected, permitting a pause in development. Subsequent attempts to solve housing needs were made, but J. C. Laederach's experimental house type in 1969 was one of the few to attempt to respond to local traditions.

Although prestigious, European-style parliamentary, commercial, transport and hotel buildings have been extensively developed throughout Africa, their social and environmental impact was probably less than that of such dam-building projects as the Volta Dam (1961–8) at Akosombo, Ghana, the Kariba Dam (begun 1959), the Aswan (High) Dam (begun 1969) and the Limpopo Valley Irrigation and Settlement Scheme. The successes and failures of resulting resettlement projects such as that of the Volta River Authority have been carefully monitored (see Chambers). In the 1980s a number of low-cost housing schemes tackled the problems of increasing African urbanization, and extensive self-help projects are being supported by non-governmental organizations in Kenya, Angola, Ghana, Malawi, Mozambique, Zimbabwe, Botswana and elsewhere, with innovations in, for example, servicing and soil–cement block manufacture. As confidence in the evolving technologies grows and develop-

70. Medical Centre, Mopti, Mali, by André Ravéreau, 1976; from a photograph by Emmanuelle Roche, 1979

ments in the design and building of dwellings become evident, new vernacular forms may emerge with values and meanings related to the changing nature of African societies of the future.

BIBLIOGRAPHY

GENERAL

P. Oliver, ed.: *Shelter and Society* (London, 1969/*R* 1978)
A. Rapoport: *House Form and Culture*, Foundations of Cultural Geography (Englewood Cliffs, 1969)
C. Duly: *The Houses of Mankind* (London, 1979)
E. Guidoni: *Primitive Architecture* (London, 1979)
P. Oliver: *Dwellings: The House across the World* (Oxford, 1987)

MATERIALS

C. G. Feilberg: *La Tente noire: Contribution ethnographique à l'histoire culturelle des nomades*, Nationalmuseets Skrifter, Ethnografisk Roekke, ii (Copenhagen, 1944)
J. Walton: *African Village* (Pretoria, 1956)
J. Nicolaisen: *Ecology and Culture of the Pastoral Tuareg with Particular Reference to the Tuareg of Ahaggar and Ayr*, Nationalmuseets Skrifter, Ethnografisk Roekke, xii (Copenhagen, 1963)
R. Gardi: *Indigenous African Architecture* (New York, 1974)
P. Oliver: *African Shelter* (London, 1975)

VERNACULAR ARCHITECTURE

J. Poujade: *Les Cases décorées d'un chef du Fouta-Djallon* (Paris, 1948)
J.-P. Béguin and others: *L'Habitat au Cameroun* (Paris, 1954)
J. F. Glück: 'Afrikanische Architektur', *Tribus*, n. s., vi (1956), pp. 65–82; Eng. trans. in *The Many Faces of Primitive Art: A Critical Anthology*, ed. D. Fraser (Englewood Cliffs, 1966), pp. 224–43
J.-P. Lebeuf: *L'Habitation des Fali: Montagnards du Cameroun septentrional—technologie, sociologie, mythologie, symbolisme* (Paris, 1961)
R. Ritzenthaler and P. Ritzenthaler: *Cameroons Village: An Ethnography of the Bafut* (Milwaukee, 1964)
G. J. A. Ojo: *Yoruba Palaces: A Study of Afins of Yorubaland* (London, 1966)
L. Prussin: *Architecture in Northern Ghana: A Study of Forms and Functions* (Berkeley, 1969)
M. Swithenbank: *Ashanti Fetish Houses* (Accra, 1969)
P. Oliver, ed.: *Shelter in Africa* (London, 1971)
W. E. Knuffel: *The Construction of the Bantu Grass Hut* (Graz, 1973)
A.-P. Lagopoulos: 'Semiological Urbanism: An Analysis of the Traditional Western Sudanese Settlement', *Shelter, Sign and Symbol*, ed. P. Oliver (London, 1975), pp. 206–18
G. N. Preston: 'Perseus and Medusa in Africa: Military Art in Fanteland, 1834–1972', *Afr. A.*, viii/3 (1975), pp. 36–41, 68–71
J. Walton: 'Art and Magic in the Southern Bantu Vernacular Architecture', *Shelter, Sign and Symbol*, ed. P. Oliver (London, 1975), pp. 117–34
R. W. Hill: *African Cities and Towns before the European Conquest* (New York, 1976)
K. B. Andersen: *African Traditional Architecture: A Study of the Housing and Settlement Patterns of Rural Kenya* (Nairobi, 1978)
S. Denyer: *African Traditional Architecture: An Historical and Geographical Perspective* (London, 1978)
J.-L. Bourgeois and C. Pelos: *Spectacular Vernacular: A New Appreciation of Traditional Desert Architecture* (Salt Lake City, 1983)
G. Philippart de Foy: *Les Pygmées d'Afrique centrale* (Marseille, 1984)
J.-P. Bourdier and T. H. Minn-ha: *African Spaces: Designs for Living in Upper Volta* (New York, 1985)
R. Plant: *Architecture of the Tigre* (Worcester, 1985)
S. P. Blier: *The Anatomy of Architecture: Ontology and Metaphor in Batammaliba Architectural Expression*, Res Monographs in Anthropology and Aesthetics (Cambridge, 1987)

ISLAMIC ARCHITECTURE

H. Labouret: 'Afrique occidentale et équatoriale', *L'Habitation indigène dans les possessions françaises*, ed. A. Bernard and others (Paris, 1931)
C. Monteil: *Une Cité soudanaise: Djenné—métropole du delta central du Niger* (Paris, 1932)
J. Kirkman: *Gedi: The Palace*, Studies in African History (The Hague, 1963)
M. Wenzel: *House Decoration in Nubia*, A. & Soc. Ser. (London, 1972)
N. Chittick: *Kilwa: An Islamic Trading City on the East African Coast*, 2 vols (Nairobi, 1974)
D. Dalby: 'The Concept of Settlement in the West African Savannah', *Shelter, Sign and Symbol*, ed. P. Oliver (London, 1975), pp. 197–205
J.-P. Greenlaw: *The Coral Buildings of Suakin* (Stocksfield, 1976)
F. Ago: *Moschee in adobe: Storia e tipologia nell'Africa occidentale* (Rome, 1982)
F. W. Schwerdtfeger: *Traditional Housing in African Cities: A Comparative Study of Houses in Zaria, Ibadan, and Marrakesh* (Chichester, 1982)
J. C. Moughtin: *Hausa Architecture* (London, 1985)
L. Prussin: *Hatumere: Islamic Design in West Africa* (Berkeley, 1986)

FURTHER DEVELOPMENTS

J. Walton: *Homesteads and Villages of South Africa* (Pretoria, 1952)
U. Kultermann: *New Architecture in Africa* (New York, 1963)
——: *New Directions in African Architecture*, New Directions in Architecture (London, 1969)
A. W. Lawrence: *Trade Castles and Forts of West Africa* (London, 1963); rev. as *Fortified Trade-posts: The English in West Africa, 1645–1822* (London, 1969)
R. Chambers, ed.: *The Volta Resettlement Experience* (London, 1970)
J. Beinart: 'Patterns of Change in an African Housing Environment', *Shelter, Sign and Symbol*, ed. P. Oliver (London, 1975), pp. 160–82
A. Ravéreau: *Le M'Zab: Une Leçon d'architecture*, preface by H. Fathy (Paris, 1981)
A. D. King: *The Bungalow: The Production of a Global Culture* (London, 1984)

PAUL OLIVER

2. SCULPTURE. Without doubt, figure sculpture (especially in wood) has received more attention than any other African art form. This applies not only to scholars but also to Western artists and the lay public. The only rival to figure sculpture's perceived position as the African art form *par excellence* is mask and masquerade, and many African masks could themselves be classified as figure sculptures. This article provides a general introduction to this huge subject; further information on materials, forms, production and use will be found in other entries on African art, and discussion of particular traditions will be found in the entries elsewhere in this dictionary on individual peoples.

(i) Wood. (ii) Ivory. (iii) Ceramic. (iv) Mud. (v) Cement.

(i) Wood.

(a) Introduction. (b) Formal analysis.

(a) Introduction. Wood is the most commonly used material for sculpture throughout Sub-Saharan Africa. No doubt there are good practical and environmental reasons for this, but another point has been emphasized (see Schmalenbach): wood, with its strength and its sap, must be seen as a fragment of nature that artistic intervention has not completely subdued and that, as such, counts for a great deal in the expressive capacity of African sculpture, whether this strength is seen as a natural or as a supernatural phenomenon. Thus wood is seen more as the 'substance' of the work than as a material pure and simple. Moreover, the choice of wood is important, as are the ritual ways in which the tree is felled. The shape of the statue often reveals traces of the original form of the trunk. Not all surfaces are treated with the same care, as if the raw material were part of the finished sculpture. African figure sculpture in wood favours the representation of human beings. Usually modest in size, African sculptures are portable, even if the way the forms are structured sometimes fulfils criteria of monumentality. Most figures are between 200 and 800 mm high, and only occasionally do they measure less or more. They are made to be handled rather than looked at. The techniques of carving reinforce this impression, as the sculptor, with his adze or knife, turns the piece or wood again and again to give it its shape (*see* §V, 3 above).

The male or female figure is either a representation of the ancestor, the father or mother of the line, with an individual identity (as among the Bamileke of the Cameroon Grassfields, where every district houses a series of royal ancestor figures), or seen as a generic and symbolic ancestor (as among the Fang of Western Equatorial Africa, where the figure watches over the precious relics). Usually nude, ancestral figures are strongly sexuate. Combined male and female figures are not necessarily man and wife but may be twins or representations of humanity's two components. Sculpted scenes are less common than single figures, but, in addition to the primordial couple, figures of a mother, or occasionally a father, and child, as well as equestrian figures (*see* §IV, 5 and 6 above) and even groups of warriors, servants, women and concubines are also known.

Figures are often represented standing tensed, with half-bent knees, or seated (most often on a circular stool), stiffly immobile but apparently serene. Few African sculptures show people in movement, while the depiction of asymmetrical gesture is limited to a few rare schools of sculpture usually linked to such powerful societies as Benin, Asante, Bamileke, Yoruba and Kuba (*see* §IV, 2 above). Animals are also represented, though much less frequently than in masquerade. Among the better-known examples are great Senufo birds, Kurumba antelopes, Baule monkeys, Kongo dogs, Baga snakes and Benin leopards (*see* §IV, 3(vi) above).

BIBLIOGRAPHY

M. Leiris and J. Delange: *Afrique noire: La Création plastique* (Paris, 1967); Eng. trans. as *African Art* (London, 1968)

W. Schmalenbach: 'Force et mesure', *A. Afrique Noire* (1988)

LOUIS PERROIS

(b) Formal analysis. African sculpture in wood is very plastic and is characterized by many unique formal inventions. The following discussion focuses on some of those that are most characteristically and distinctively African.

Volume. African artists frequently switch from a full round, three-dimensional treatment of some parts of a sculpture to a flat, relief carving in others without any transition. For example, a Dogon mother-and-child figure may be rendered in sculptural rods and knobs except for the hands and feet, which are simply deep grooves cut in the surface (see fig. 71). Similarly, among the Chokwe a neckrest may switch without warning from the bulky, rounded presentation of the body to a shallowly engraved face, while among the Mambila the airy, billowing forms of a figure may suddenly stop at the face, which has no volume at all. African sculptors also freely mix an organic treatment of the body with a completely geometric, inorganic one, again without transitions. In Fang reliquaries the full round, muscular arms and softly curving stomach flow directly into a metal-capped, cylindrical peg representing the navel. There are many other examples of a shockingly abrupt change in the sculptural language used by African artists.

71. Dogon figure sculpture of a mother and child, wood, metal and leather, h. 665 mm (USA, private collection)

African sculpture also shows an extraordinary sense of mass, of weight and density occupying space, one of its fundamental qualities. Much African sculpture suggests, not an inert shell, but an inner mass pressing towards the viewer. Swelling, bulging forms are the clearest manifestation of this, but there are subtler ones. To sense the density of African sculptures, they should be experienced as displacing air, containing volume; their surfaces should be felt not as enclosing a hollow core but as full, as the edge of thickness, in order to sense the active interior. The alternative conception of sculpture that sees it not as volume, but as flat or curved surfaces and lines, as for example in Cycladic or Cubist sculpture, is rare in African art, though some Kota figures are examples of this approach. This quality of dense mass in African art partly accounts for what is often experienced as an aggressiveness, described as a projection of energy. Though the outward projection of mass is probably the real source, energy may be perceived as coming from such non-formal attributes as posture and gesture or such features as horns, teeth or puffed cheeks—frequent concentrations where the inner volume thrusts towards the viewer. The same aggressive energy can be seen in body parts not normally thought of as aggressive, such as foreheads, breasts or buttocks, when they are rendered as masses pushing outward.

This active inner volume is so pervasive, it can be seen even in unaggressive, naturalistic sculptures, for example many Fang heads, where the domed forehead expresses the tense containment of volume, suggesting the power of intellect and numinous presence within (*see* FANG, fig. 3). More obvious thrusting forms are often found in Fang figures, in Luba figures (*see* LUBA, fig. 3) and in Bangwa masks. Even slender, linear sculptures have this same quality—an active interior. They may barely show outward volumes but suggest instead a wild current running through tubular limbs, as with the Bamana female figure whose dangerously pointed breasts and smoothly rounded posterior thrust against the skin of the surface, while the strong movement of the sculpture as a whole courses down the coiffure, down the widening torso and legs (see fig. 72). By contrast, the masses of the Senufo figures called rhythm pounders generally move upwards in a slower, more majestic pulse, rising from the ankles, swelling (throbbing) at the hips, then rising again to the beat of the shoulders and breasts, and finally rising once more in the slender neck (*see* SENUFO, §2(ii) and fig. 1).

Active voids ingeniously used are another fundamental quality of African sculpture. African works do not passively occupy space; they interact with and interpenetrate space, most obviously through the use of pierced forms and open compositions. The most extreme and evident pieces capture space, which becomes a positive element, not a negative zone against which the sculpted parts are read. Voids contained in a sculpture often repeat the shapes of the volumes and become part of the composition, not empty air. The triangular spaces under the arms of a Shankadi neckrest, which are the same size and shape as the flaring coiffure, become parts of the design. The space between the legs of a Southern African figure of a young girl duplicates exactly the shape of the torso, creating a negative echo of the positive form above. Even sculptures that seem densely compact engage the surrounding space. The air in front of a Zulu meat dish becomes the face and stomach of the figure, shaped by the artist into two visible voids, as surely as he shaped the wood.

The volumes of African sculpture are usually articulated as segments rather than continuous form. In fact, African artists rarely compose a fluidly unified whole (though this is less rare in sculptures from East and Southern Africa). They may isolate parts of a work with deep grooves or treat them as completely discrete units; thus an eye or knee may become a clean cylinder quite separate from the flat surface of the face. The arm and breast are often rendered as a single unified segment, sharply demarcated from the neck and torso, as in a Baule figure of a mother

72. Bamana figure sculpture, wood, h. 595 mm, late 19th century to mid-20th (USA, Horstmann private collection)

and child (see fig. 73). The segments are organized into patterns that transform the face and body into designs.

The organization of African sculptures, like that of all art works, proceeds from the repetition and variation of a limited number of elements. A common device is to render the different parts of the body with the same shape: for example the calves, thighs and buttocks of a figure may be rendered as similar swelling ovals, while the knees are completely suppressed in the interests of design. Designs can also be created out of similar positive and negative shapes, as seen in Bangwa night masks. More interesting (and sometimes disconcerting) are sculptures in which dissimilar features are given equivalent shapes. African sculptures are often so tightly organized that the works acquire a quality of inevitability. The rigorous construction sometimes means that no single part could be changed without altering everything else.

73. Baule figure sculpture of a mother and child, wood, h. 495 mm, late 19th century to mid-20th (USA, private collection)

Symmetry. It is often said that African sculpture is symmetrical. While its overall design is usually balanced and symmetrical compared to some sculptural traditions, it is almost never literally symmetrical. Overtly asymmetrical compositions, however, are rare. In fact, traditional African artists tend to create symmetrical designs but deliberately avoid symmetry in the execution; their works mock symmetry to create interest. A close look at an apparently regular figure such as a Fang reliquary guardian, for example, may reveal that the left arm is much fuller than the right, creating a small imbalance and different spaces under the arms. Like the living face and body, African sculptures are animated by subtle irregularities. In a Baule mask the coiffure may tilt faintly to the right, the left ear be lower than the right, the eyes slightly uneven and the nostrils not the same size. African artists set the viewer up to expect the paired sides of a composition to match, then leave him to enjoy the interplay between what is expected and what is seen. Moreover, variations may be played, not just on the horizontal axis but through space, forming a spiral movement. The body of a small Luba figure rotates so that the elbows are not aligned with the knees, creating a disjunction at waist level (see fig. 74). A spiral stance is central to the Bangwa conception of figure sculpture, so that in many figures, in relation to the head, the shoulders rotate to the left.

Continuous view. African figure sculpture often has no principal view; in fact it often does not seem to have any privileged vantage points. An African work may be best understood from the continuous view obtained by walking around it or by holding it in the hand and turning it. As the viewer circles the object, the sculptural shapes move in relation to each other; the viewer can gain a complete sense of its three-dimensionality and watch the order of the piece unfold. African works may be so complicated formally that without circling the piece it may be impossible to understand how the different masses interact in the parts of the sculpture that are momentarily out of sight. As part of their exceptional plasticity, African sculptures have what may be termed a continuous view. Many sculptures in other traditions have a principal view; they were designed to be seen from a particular angle (examples of this are the pedimental sculptures on ancient Greek temples). This is sometimes related to the artist's preliminary sketch on paper or on the uncarved block and is especially true of sculpture made to stand in a niche. A principal view is akin to a low relief in that it appears as an arrangement of masses in front of a picture plane. Sculptures conceived more fully in the round may never-

74. Luba figure sculpture (neckrest) by the Master of the Cascading Coiffure, wood and beads, h. 160 mm, late 19th century to mid-20th (USA, Horstmann private collection)

theless have numerous points of view. These, however, are only a succession of single views.

African artists often say they see the sculpture inside the raw wood and cut away material to free it. Its exceptional plasticity may come from that approach—from the fact that African art is unrelated to two-dimensional images. Non-African artists of all eras often began work by drawing the outline of the future sculpture on the front and sides of the block of wood or stone, or they might sketch studies of sculptures before executing them. African artists conceive their works directly as three-dimensional, envisioning them as they would exist in space, not on paper.

African sculpture is often mistakenly described as frontal, probably because its conventional pose—arms to the sides, eyes forward, weight on both feet equally—corresponds to frontal figures from other traditions (such as Egyptian statues). African sculpture, however, is not frontal in a purely sculptural sense, because it is developed fully in the round and can be viewed from all sides. Moreover, African sculpture is not conceived for a predetermined kind of display. Most will not stand on a flat surface. Many were meant to be carried, to lean against something or to be sunk partially into the ground; in any case they were not meant to stand in a particular way and be viewed from a single point. African artists did not usually create their works mainly to be displayed and were not primarily concerned with the reactions of a human viewer.

Conclusion. In the context of Western art history, a striking feature of African art in general, and wooden figure sculpture in particular, is that it is not normally narrative, does not depict movement or groups of figures interacting and is not pictorial; it does not seek to create any illusion of motion, perspective or verisimilitude. If an artist wants hair on his figure that exactly resembles hair, he will not hesitate to attach some of the real thing. If movement is wanted, the figure is worn or carried in dance.

Since African art is not an illusion of reality and does not depict the visible world, we must recognize that it creates a new kind of reality. In carving, African artists introduce new beings into the world. Field research confirms the independent reality created in sculptures. A new figure is almost always given a personal name like a new child; the sculpture of a nature spirit makes newly visible a being that was not accessible before the carving was made.

African sculptures are generally single figures unframed by any space boundary that would set them in their own small stage. They are unaccompanied by any reference for scale (such as a carved shrub or rock). Perspective, frontality and a principal view all imply a viewer positioned in a particular place. African sculpture has none of these qualities. African artists created movable objects that were not destined to be seen in a single setting; almost all might have different settings according to phases of their use (in a cluttered shrine, wrapped in cloth or carried in the sun in an annual procession, for example). Consequently, such objects inhabit human space; they are small or large in relation to the human body and not in relation to an architectural background or setting conceived for them. This quality is fundamental, for it means that African sculptures intrude upon inhabited space, not separate, artistically created space, and they interact directly with the viewer. Further, it implies their existence as independent entities, as newly created beings with an existence as palpable as our own.

BIBLIOGRAPHY

A. Maesen: *Umbangu: Art du Congo au Musée royal du Congo Belge* (Brussels, 1960)

J. Laude: *Art de l'Afrique noire* (Paris, 1968); Eng. trans. by J. Decock (Berkeley, 1971/*R* 1973)

African Aesthetics: The Carlo Monzino Collection (exh. cat. by S. Vogel, New York, Cent. Afr. A., 1986)

Perspectives: Angles on African Art (exh. cat. by J. Baldwin and others, New York, Cent. Afr. A., 1986)

J. Kerchache, J.-L. Paudrat and L. Stéphan: *L'Art africain* (Paris, 1988); Eng. trans. by M. de Jager (New York, 1993)

Art of Central Africa: Masterpieces from the Berlin Museum für Völkerkunde (exh. cat. by H.-J. Koloss, New York, Met., 1990)

Closeup: Lessons in the Art of Seeing African Sculpture (exh. cat. by J. L. Thompson and S. Vogel, New York, Cent. Afr. A., 1990)

SUSAN VOGEL

(ii) Ivory. Among the best-known African ivory sculptures are those produced in West Africa for export to Europe in the late 15th and 16th centuries. These ivories incorporate a number of European forms and motifs and have commonly been dubbed 'Afro-Portuguese'. Generally, however, even the most heavily influenced works strongly retain local style and iconography and might therefore be better called 'Luso-African', reflecting their production under African rather than European control. These ivory

sculptures have been studied in detail, and this entry focuses on them. It should be noted, however, that African sculpture in ivory is not limited to these objects. For information on other uses of ivory in African art, *see* §V, 5 above.

(a) Introduction. Nearly 200 of these early export ivories are extant, although contemporary customs records suggest that hundreds more were imported. Spoons seem to have been the most popular items; the fragility of their openwork stems probably resulted in frequent breakage and disposal. The Portuguese were the first Europeans to sail to Sub-Saharan Africa, and they brought back a number of art objects, as well as raw materials. For the most part, these early artworks had been made for local consumption and obtained at public markets or through gift exchanges. From the late 15th century to the mid-16th, however, ivory sculptures were also created specifically for the Portuguese.

The ivories were produced in only two areas, coastal Sierra Leone and Benin, both of which had established ivoryworking traditions. Although the Portuguese recognized the craftsmanship of the traditional sculptures, they did not appreciate the objects themselves. Their styles were very dissimilar to those of Europe, and the forms and motifs were associated, in Portuguese minds, with paganism. The Portuguese thus began to commission works directly from the artists themselves, to their own tastes and drawing from European iconography. The types of object commissioned were those valued by the European aristocracy, namely salt-cellars, pyxides, hunting horns and cutlery. Produced in the valuable medium of ivory, and with an exotic origin, the works had great prestige value in Europe. Although these works took European forms and used European motifs, aspects of local style and iconography were also maintained. The ivories are thus visual and conceptual hybrids.

(b) Sierra Leonean production. More than half the extant works are Sierra Leonean. When first contacted by the Portuguese in 1462, coastal Sierra Leone was occupied by the Temne and Bullom, or Sherbro, peoples; population shifts occurred later in the 16th century. Speaking distinct but related languages, these peoples were organized into village clusters, each with its own leader, while powerful men's and women's associations exerted substantial social and political influence. Ivoryworkers and other artists worked for these societies, as well as for other traditional patrons, before and during the time of Portuguese contact.

The ivories from Sierra Leone share some general characteristics. They frequently include spectacular openwork sections and display a contrast of smooth, unadorned surface sections with clusters of beaded or zigzagged banding. Many include human figures in high relief, usually representing Portuguese men and African women. Stylistically, these figures are very close to the region's soapstone heads and figures, which seem to be contemporary with the ivories (*see* KISSI and MENDE). In general, the heads are prognathous, with a strong horizontal thrust, and are often one-third to one-quarter of the figures' total height. Eyes dominate the face, noses are curved and prominent, and lips are often lifted slightly at the corners. Despite these general similarities, however, the works formally and iconographically fall into two distinct groups, apparently due to different geographic origins.

75. Ivory salt-cellar, h. 430 mm, from Sierra Leone, late 15th century to early 16th (Rome, Museo Nazionale Preistorico ed Etnografico Luigi Pigorini)

The first, and larger, set of Sierra Leonean ivories is the product of at least four workshops. It also shows the greatest evidence of European involvement. The decoration, for example, often includes the European surface treatment of spiralled gadrooning, producing undulations common on European metalwork of the period. In form, these objects also follow European patterns. Salt-cellars (average height 290 mm) have the sphere-on-cone structure of European covered metal cups. Circular pyxides are decorated with Christian scenes and derive from Portuguese metal models. Hunting horns are endblown in the European fashion, instead of employing the characteristic African side embouchure. Long-stemmed spoons (*c.* 230 mm long) are ribbed at the back in imitation of European metal prototypes. Their shallow, pointed bowls rise into virtuoso stems, often openworked in knotlike forms. Several two-tined forks are also known. These were not used in Africa and were still rare in 15th century Europe, so their occurrence confirms the patronage of upper-class Europeans.

The iconography of these works is a fascinating composite. Local motifs of pythons, crocodiles and parrots are frequently accompanied by images drawn from European heraldry and mythology, from Christian sources and from such aristocratic activities as stag hunting. The artists were supplied by their European patrons with drawings, printed materials, coins, textiles and religious articles as motif sources.

A second group of Sierra Leonean export ivories, fewer in number, includes salt-cellars, spoons and knife handles that show little evidence of direct contact with Portuguese patrons. Salt-cellars of this type have a sphere-on-cylinder structure, which is not European-derived. The imagery on these works is indigenous and includes anthropomorphized quadrupeds, double-faced heads and crocodiles. Only one extant example actually includes Western-derived motifs, although representations of long-haired Europeans accompanying Sierra Leonean women do occur on many pieces. Even these Portuguese are sometimes Africanized by their placement within local metaphors of leadership—astride an elephant or amidst captives. On the base of one example are figures of two seated Portuguese surrounded by African women and crocodiles, while the finial shows the figure of another Portuguese in a traditional Sierra Leonean leadership pose, surrounded by trophy heads (Rome, Mus. N. Preist. & Etnog.; see fig. 75). This non-European emphasis on form and symbolism suggests that these pieces had a non-coastal origin. They may have been carved upcountry along the Upper Scarcies River. This region, which an early account noted was a production centre of ivories for export, was the site of considerable trade between Cape Verdean smugglers and illegal Portuguese settlers. Living under African control, the settlers learnt the language, married local women and became initiates of the men's society; many of the Portuguese depicted on the 'upcountry' ivories bear initiation scarifications.

(c) Benin production. In contrast to the Sierra Leonean pieces, the export ivories from Benin are consistent in form and style. The Portuguese first reached the kingdom of Benin in the early 1470s, at which time it was a powerful centralized state. Its arts were centred on the royal court, with palace guilds producing elaborate brass, ivory and wooden objects for the ruler. Although Benin court ivories included ancestral tusks, jewellery and boxes, the objects made for export again followed foreign preferences. The salt-cellars (see fig. 76), hunting horns and spoons made at Benin, however, differ from Sierra Leonean examples in both form and decoration. The salt-cellars (h. *c.* 280 mm) are tripartite, as some contemporary Portuguese metal examples are, and have an unusual form, consisting of two globular, lidded compartments separated by a short stem. The exteriors are carved with high-relief figures of mounted or standing Portuguese dignitaries and

76. Ivory salt-cellar, from Benin, late 15th century to early 16th, (London, British Museum)

their attendants. The hunting horns are not endblown in the European style but sideblown, like traditional Benin court oliphants. Benin spoons (*c.* 250 mm long) have longer, deeper bowls than their Sierra Leonean counterparts, curving around at the front in a three-lobed 'duck-foot' formation, and have stems carved with animal figures.

The objects from Benin were created by at least eight artists within the royal carvers' guild. As in traditional Benin art, social hierarchy is stressed through detailed, rank-linked costumes and the use of hieratic scale. The figures of the most important people are static and frontal; figures shown in three-quarters view or with intimations of movement are of people of lower status, and, as in objects from Sierra Leone, are adaptations of European models. The figures conform to local style in proportion, the head being as much as one-quarter the length of the whole body. Surfaces are heavily decorated with crowded, small-scale designs from the Benin guild repertory, including guilloche, basketweave and scale patterns. Other than representations of Portuguese people, Portuguese motifs are minimal; although the horns contain a few European heraldic elements, the spoons are carved with animals of African, not European, origin, including crocodiles, snakes, snails and birds. They are often combined in relationships that suggest proverbial or metaphorical references of local significance, and some seem to share themes with art works of the neighbouring Yoruba peoples.

BIBLIOGRAPHY

F. Heger: 'Alte Elfenbeinarbeiten aus Afrika in den Wiener Sammlungen', *Mitt. Anthropol. Ges. Wien*, xxix (1899), pp. 101–09
C. H. Read and O. M. Dalton: *Antiquities from the City of Benin and from Other Parts of West Africa in the British Museum* (London, 1899)
W. Foy: 'Zur Frage der Herkunft einiger alter Jagdhörner: Portugal oder Benin?', *Abh. & Ber. Kön. Zool. & Anthropol.–Ethnog. Mus. Dresden*, ix (1900–01), pp. 20–22
R. Andrée: 'Alte westafrikanische Elfenbeinschnitzwerke im Herzoglichen Museum zu Braunschweig', *Globus*, lxxix (1901), pp. 156–9
R. Pettazoni: 'Avori scolpiti africani in collezioni italiane: Contributo allo studio dell'arte del "Benin"', *Boll. A.*, v (1911), pp. 388–98; vi (1912), pp. 56–74, 147–60; repr. as book (Rome, 1912)
R. Andrée: 'Seltene Ethnographica des Städtischen Gewerbe-Museums zu Ulm', *Baessler-Archv*, iv/1 (1913), pp. 29–38
J. Marquart: *Die Benin-Sammlung des Reichsmuseums für Völkerkunde im Leiden*, Veröffentlichungen des Reichsmuseums für Völkerkunde in Leiden, ser. 2, vii (Leiden, 1913)
F. von Luschan: *Die Altertümer von Benin*, 3 vols (Berlin, 1919)
K. Degen: 'Das Köllesche Elfenbeinhorn', *Heimatkundliche Bl. Kreis Tübingen* (1952), no. 4, pp. 14–15; (1953), no. 1, pp. 18–19
W. Fagg: *Afro-Portuguese Ivories* (London, 1959)
J. A. de Lasarte: 'La cope afro-portuguesa del Emperador', *Colóquio*, vii (1960), pp. 33–6
S. Wolf: 'Afrikanische Elfenbeinlöffel des 16. Jahrhunderts im Museum für Völkerkunde, Dresden', *Ethnologica*, n. s., ii (1960), pp. 410–25
C. Fyfe: *Sierra Leone Inheritance* (Oxford, 1964)
A. F. C. Ryder: 'A Note on the Afro-Portuguese Ivories', *J. Afr. Hist.*, v (1964), pp. 363–5
M. de Sampayo Ribeiro: 'O olifante de Drummond Castle', *Panorama*, ser. 4, ix (1964)
F. R. Cortez: 'O hostiário luso-africano de Museu de Grao Vasco', *Panorama*, ser. 4, xxi (1967), pp. 69–72
K. Dittmer: 'Bedeutung, Datierung und kulturhistorische Zusammenhänge der "prähistorischen" Steinfiguren aus Sierra Leone und Guinée', *Baessler-Archv*, n. s., xv (1967), pp. 183–238
P. Allison: *African Stone Sculpture* (London, 1968)
J. Atherton and M. Kalous: 'Nomoli', *J. Afr. Hist.*, xi/1 (1970), pp. 39–74
E. Bassani: 'Antichi avori africani nelle collezioni medicee', *Crit. A.*, cxliii (1975), pp. 69–80; cxliv (1975), pp. 8–23
V. L. Grottanelli: 'Discovery of a Masterpiece: A 16th Century Ivory Bowl from Sierra Leone', *Afr. A.*, viii/4 (1975), pp. 14–23
A. Teixeira da Mota: 'Gli avori africani nella documentazione portoghese dei secoli XV–XVII', *Africa* [Rome], iii (1975), pp. 580–89
P. Ben-Amos: *The Art of Benin*, Tribal A. (London, 1980)
G. Brooks: *Kola Trade and State-building: Upper Guinea Coast and Senegambia, 15th–17th Centuries*, Afr. Stud. Cent. Working Pap. (Boston, 1980)
E. Bassani: 'Trompes en ivoire du XVI siècle de la Sierra Leone', *Ethnographie*, lxxxv (1981–2), pp. 151–68
——: 'Antichi manufatti dell'Africa Nera nelle collezioni europee del rinascimento e dell'età barocca', *Quad. Poro*, iii (1982), pp. 9–34
K. Curnow: *The Afro-Portuguese Ivories: Classification and Stylistic Analysis of a Hybrid Art Form*, 2 vols (diss., Bloomington, IN U., 1983)
Africa and the Renaissance: Art in Ivory (exh. cat. by E. Bassani and W. Fagg, New York, Cent. Afr. A., 1988)
K. Curnow: 'Alien or Accepted: African Perspectives on the Western "Other" in 15th/16th Century Art', *Visual Anthropol. Rev.*, vi/1 (1990), pp. 38–44
——: 'Oberlin's Sierra Leonean Saltcellar: Documenting a Bicultural Dialogue', *Allen Mem. A. Mus. Bull.*, xliv (1991), pp. 12–23
W. A. Hart: 'A Rediscovered Afro-Portuguese Horn in the British Museum', *Afr. A.*, xxvi (1993), pp. 70–71
E. Bassani: 'Additional Notes on the Afro-Portuguese Ivories', *Afr. A.*, xxvii (1994), pp. 34–45
W. A. Hart: 'A Reconsideration of the Rediscovered "Afro-Portuguese" Horn', *Afr. A.*, xxvii (1994), pp. 92–3
A. Jones: 'A Collection of African Art in Seventeenth-century Germany: Christopher Weickmann's Kunst- und Naturkammer', *Afr. A.*, xxvii (1994), pp. 28–43

KATHY CURNOW

(iii) Ceramic. Fired clay is one of the earliest materials to be used for producing art objects in Africa (*see* §V, 1(ii) above). Ceramic sculpture is produced by either women or men depending on the practices maintained by particular African peoples. Examples of functional ceramic sculpture in Africa include finials used to secure the thatch of roofs and to prevent rain entering at the apex; these often designate the houses of important persons or structures serving as shrines. In the Mandara Mountains of the Nigeria–Cameroon border, finials made by women may be quite elaborate and may include clusters of human or animal figures. Throughout Africa functional vessels may be embellished with sculptural decoration.

Ceramic vessels modelled with a human head (sometimes referred to as cephalomorphic), which surmounts the neck, date mainly to the late 19th and 20th centuries, although some examples have been found in archaeological contexts. Cephalomorphic pots have been made by the Akye of southern Côte d'Ivoire; the Yoruba of south-western Nigeria; the Yungur, Jen, Tula, Longuda, Cham/Mwona, Bata and Mambila of north-eastern Nigeria; the Matakam, Koma and Mafa of northern Cameroon; the Mangbetu, Zande and related groups of the Uele region of north-eastern Zaïre; the Lunda, Lwena and Chokwe of the southern savannah of Zaïre, Angola and Zambia; and the Woyo of the Cabinda–Zaïre borderlands. Modelling of heads and bodies varies considerably from group to group. Some, such as those made by Lwena men, are very finely sculptured and have precisely incised linear decoration closely resembling the same group's style of wood-carving. Among the Yungur of north-eastern Nigeria, women produce animated and stylized images of deceased male leaders. Some of the best-known anthropomorphic pots from Africa are those made by men among the Mangbetu of Zaïre as prestige objects for local chiefs and for colonial officials and missionaries. The heads are idealized portraits of Mangbetu women, featuring elongated foreheads and elaborate fanlike coiffures (see fig. 77). Mangbetu ceramic sculpture flourished from the end of the 19th century to the early 1930s, after which production virtually ceased.

Detachable lids or stoppers for pots may also be conceived as heads. Among the Yoruba of south-western Nigeria, pots with figurative ceramic lids are made by women for cults honouring the river deity Erinle. One Egbado Yoruba woman, Abatan Odefunke Ayinke Ija (*b* ?1885), became well known in several Yoruba provinces for her lids, which are dominated by the half-figure of a woman (see Thompson). Voania Muba, an innovative male Woyo potter and chief (*d* ?1928), produced a unique group of pots with full-length figures and sometimes figurative groupings modelled on top of vessels with low, globular bases. His work was influenced by the Europeans who became his clientele, and each of Voania's pots bears his name in large capital letters.

It is common in West Africa to use figurative elements, in high or low relief, to adorn the walls of vessels generally used in ritual contexts. The best-known examples are from Nigeria and include bowls for worshipping the thunder god, Sango, among the Yoruba; pots used in shrines dedicated to the god of the seas and rivers, Olokun, in Benin; and vessels made for the cult of the yam spirit, Ifijioku, among the Igbo. The Fon and Gun peoples of the neighbouring Republic of Benin also make vessels with projecting human figures. Among other groups, decoration on ceramics includes a range of zoomorphic as well as anthropomorphic imagery. Several pots excavated from a disposal pit at Igbo-Ukwu, in south-eastern Nigeria, are remarkable for the combination of deep grooving, protruding bosses, multiple handles and relief images of coiled snakes, chameleons and rams' heads (*see* IGBO-UKWU). Dated to the 9th–10th centuries, these ceramics show the same elaborate surface decoration as Igbo-Ukwu artefacts cast in bronze. Although not as ornate, several pots unearthed at Ife, in south-western Nigeria, are modelled with arrangements of human figures and animals. Complex representational imagery is found on ritual vessels made by specialists among the Akan of Ghana and kept at grave sites and in shrine rooms. On these pots whole human figures or heads, snakes, lizards, frogs and crocodiles are worked in relief, often with reference to proverbs. Vessels made by the Bamana of Mali and by peoples of the Cameroon Grassfields have relief images of lizards, spiders, snakes, turtles and other animals.

Most early figurative ceramic sculpture is from West Africa, although a group of seven ceramic heads, dated to *c.* AD 500, have been found at Lydenburg in the Transvaal region of South Africa (now Cape Town, S. Afr. Cult. Hist. Mus.). The earliest known sculpture is associated with the Nok culture of northern Nigeria (500 BC–AD 200). These highly celebrated ceramic sculptures include nearly life-size hollow-built heads, which were probably once attached to full figures up to 1.2 m high, and small, solid figurines (h. 130 mm). Their function remains a mystery. NOK terracottas are remarkable for their technical sophistication and for their formal variation, despite such stylistic conventions as 'D'-shaped eyes and perforations in the pupils, nostrils, mouths and ears (features that aided their successful firing).

77. Ceramic double pot, h. 235 mm, from Mangbetu, Zaïre, collected 1913 (New York, American Museum of Natural History)

Also from Nigeria are the relatively naturalistic, though distinctively stylized, figurative ceramics associated with Ife, Benin and Owo royalty. The terracottas from Ife (12th–15th centuries) include free-standing heads, complete figures (and heads that have broken away from them) and such animals as rams and leopards (*see* IFE). The delicately modelled heads (h. 160–320 mm) often have faces bearing fine vertical lines and elaborately sculptured coiffures, crests or crowns. In Benin ceramic commemorative heads have continued to be associated with altars set up by members of bronze-casters' guilds. The ceramic heads and figures unearthed from sites in Owo have stylistic features typical of Ife and Benin, between which Owo lies. These ceramics date to the 15th century, and they are distinguished by the variety of subject-matter represented, including sacrificial offerings and severed heads.

Figurative ceramics associated with an ancient, and probably largely mythical, people called the Sao have been recovered from mound sites south of Lake Chad. Produced between the 11th and 13th centuries, the Sao corpus includes small, solid heads (h. 80–120 mm), human figurines (200–350 mm) and zoomorphic figurines (60–120 mm). Most have been described as grave goods, discovered in or near large, clay burial urns. The human figurines, most of which came from the site of Tago, have faces with thick, rather swollen features and bodies with such dress details as crossed baldrics and epaulets (see fig. 78).

Another major centre of sculptural ceramic production was the Middle Niger region of Mali. Hand-built figures (80–500 mm) have been recovered from a series of mound sites around the modern town of Jenne. Their complex postures and iconographical details have raised tantalizing questions about who produced them and how they were

78. Ceramic figure, h. 200 mm, Sao, Chad, 11th–13th centuries (Paris, Musée de l'Homme)

used (*see* MIDDLE NIGER CULTURES). Based on excavations made at Jenne-jenno, R. J. McIntosh and S. K. McIntosh have dated terracotta production in this area to AD 1000–1200, coinciding with the town's progressive urbanization.

In northern Ghana, Koma ceramics provide evidence of trade links with Jenne and other towns in the Middle Niger. Koma material in the form of animals and human heads and figures (70–300 mm) has been discovered, mostly in burial contexts. The treatment of the eye with its raised elliptical socket and bulging eyeball is distinctive of these rather schematically sculpted images. Koma involvement in the trans-Saharan trade network (*c.* 8th–16th centuries) is reflected in representations of riders on camels in the Koma corpus.

Also involved in this network were the Akan peoples of southern Ghana who, in addition to their ritual vessels discussed above, also produced commemorative ceramic heads used in post-burial funerary rites. They were mostly portraits of state chiefs, and they were displayed in groups on grave sites. Although there are certain stylistic consistencies in the sculpting of the faces, such as high, arching eyebrows and coffee-bean eyes and lips, it is in fact possible to identify from which specific Akan city-state each head comes. This funerary tradition dates to at least the 17th century, and among certain Akan groups women have continued to make portrait heads for funerary and shrine purposes.

Many African peoples have continued to use ceramic sculpture in ritual contexts into the late 20th century. For example, distinctive figurative shrine sculpture has continued to be made by Igbo women in Nigeria. Although it has generally been assumed that such ceramic archaeological treasures of Africa as those of Nok, Sao and the Middle Niger were made by men, the Igbo example, among others, raises the distinct possibility that some of them may have been made by women.

BIBLIOGRAPHY

R. Thompson: 'Abatan: A Master Potter of the Egbado Yoruba', *Tradition and Creativity in Tribal Art*, ed. D. Biebuyck (Berkeley, 1969/*R* 1973), pp. 120–82

B. Fagg and J. Picton: *The Potter's Art in Africa* (London, 1970/*R* 1978)

S. Leith-Ross: *Nigerian Pottery* (Lagos, 1970)

B. E. B. Fagg: *Nok Terracottas* (Lagos and London, 1977)

J.-P. Lebeuf and A. Lebeuf: *Les Arts des Sao* (Paris, 1977)

B. de Grunne: *Terres cuites anciennes de l'ouest africain/Ancient Terracottas from West Africa* (Louvain-la-Neuve, 1980) [bilingual text]

Treasures of Ancient Nigeria (exh. cat. by E. Eyo and F. Willett, Detroit, MI, Inst. A.; London, RA; 1980–82)

T. Maggs and P. Davidson: 'The Lydenburg Heads and the Earliest African Sculpture South of the Equator', *Afr. A.*, xiv/2 (1981), pp. 28–33, 88

J. Picton, ed.: *Earthenware in Asia and Africa* (London, 1984)

A. Stossel: *Afrikanische Keramik: Traditionelle Handwerkskunst südlich der Sahara* (Munich, 1984) [excellent pls and geog. coverage]

J. Anquandah and L. van Ham: *Discovering the Forgotten 'Civilization' of Komaland, Northern Ghana* (Rotterdam, 1985)

N. David, J. Sterner and K. Gavua: 'Why Pots Are Decorated', *Current Anthropol.*, xxix/3 (1988), pp. 365–89

M. C. Berns: 'Ceramic Arts in Africa', *Afr. A.*, xxii/2 (1989), pp. 32–6, 101–2

E. Schildkrout, J. Hellman and C. Keim: 'Mangbetu Pottery: Tradition and Innovation in Northeast Zaïre', *Afr. A.*, xxii/2 (1989), pp. 38–47

M. C. Berns: 'Pots as People: Yungur Ancestral Portraits', *Afr. A.*, xxiii/3 (1990), pp. 50–60, 102

——: 'Art, History and Gender: Women and Clay in West Africa', *Afr. Archaeol. Rev.*, xi (1993), pp. 129–48

MARLA C. BERNS

(iv) Mud. Sculpture in mud or non-baked clay is widespread in Africa, unsurprisingly, perhaps, given its easy availability and great malleability (*see* §V, 1(i) above). Most mud sculpture in Africa is associated with shrines and their related ritual activities. Indeed, shrine sculptures are most often made by priests rather than professional artists. In regions where there is heavy rainfall, mud sculptures have often been sheltered by fragile palm-thatch roofs; even when so protected, however, they have seldom lasted longer than a year. Given that mud sculptures anyway usually deteriorate and disappear after their ritual purpose has been fulfilled, the techniques used to produce them are difficult to document. Most African mud sculptures are massive with few or abbreviated details. In most cases their ritual efficacy is apparently more important than their aesthetic appearance or permanence. As a result, mud sculpture as an art form has been generally ignored by scholars, despite its wide distribution. In Benin, Nigeria, one of the most popular deities, Olukun, bringer of life-changes, wealth and children, is often represented by a mud figure. The material out of which these figures are made is brought from the river bank, a zone of transition

between land and water, and is itself considered a sacred substance that mediates between the world of the living and the world of the dead.

An exception to the general account given above, however, is provided by the *mbari* houses of the Igbo of Nigeria (*see also* IGBO). These often complex works are village projects, built by specialist sculptors with the help of the community at large, and are great sources of civic pride. Moreover, they have often been maintained long after their execution. In the later 20th century *mbari* made of mud and cement or just cement have become permanent (*see* §(v) below). The structure itself is built of heavily packed mud walls with painted, geometric designs on the surfaces. The *mbari* are alive with mud animals, people and 'monsters', all built on frameworks of bamboo. Some *mbari* have up to a hundred modelled images representing scenes from life; the iconography changes with the times and in the late 20th century commonly included radios, telephones and cars.

BIBLIOGRAPHY

U. Beier: *African Mud Sculpture* (Cambridge, 1963)

H. M. Cole: *Mbari: Art and Life among the Owerri Igbo* (Bloomington, 1982)

ROBERT T. SOPPELSA, NATALIE TOBERT

(v) Cement. This material first became available in Sub-Saharan Africa at the beginning of the 20th century, and by the 1980s it was the preferred material for monumental sculpture. More readily available than carvable stone and less expensive than bronze, cement is also easier to work and more durable than wood. Typically cement is modelled over iron rods or wire.

Generally it has replaced mud as a material in African art. The initial development of cement sculpture was concentrated within the coastal regions of what are now Nigeria and Ghana during the period just before World War I, although it quickly spread to neighbouring countries and probably developed independently in a number of areas at the same time. Its earliest manifestations followed European, and especially British colonial, practices of erecting cement headstones and crosses on the graves of their dead. In a merging of European and African belief systems, African funerary sculpture in cement developed first in those areas where there were similar but indigenous traditions of memorials to the dead.

The earliest documented cement sculptures are the grave markers in the Cross River area of south-east Nigeria (see Rosevear). Most are inscribed with dates in the 1920s, but one (in a graveyard at Okuni near Ikom) appears to be from 1911. Although several of these memorials are in the shape of an embellished Celtic cross, the predominant form is a schematic human figure with its right arm raised (*see also* EJAGHAM, §3).

One of the best-documented transitions from non-cement monuments to those made of cement is provided by the funerary memorials of the Ibibio peoples of south-east Nigeria. Traditionally, a bamboo and raffia-palm hut was constructed in the forest some years after the actual burial. Mud sculptures representing the deceased and selected relatives were often erected in front of the structure. The whole ensemble was subsequently allowed to deteriorate. During the 1920s, under the influence of Christianity and with a desire for more enduring forms, the Ibibio began to site memorials at the grave and began making the monuments in cement, eventually including angels and biblical figures, usually brightly painted, in the sculptural programme (*see also* IBIBIO, §4).

Among the Fante and neighbouring Akan-speaking peoples in southern Ghana a tradition of terracotta sculpture dates back at least 400 years. Images, occasionally life-size, were placed in groups near the burial ground; they represented the deceased and his family or, in the case of a chief, the court officials who served him. With the increased availability of cement in the 1920s, and again under the influence of British Christian practices, a tradition of polychrome-cement grave-site monuments was developed, with many of the same sculptural themes as found among the Ibibio.

Even outside the British sphere of influence, a similar pattern of development occurred in some places. Among the Kongo peoples of western Zaïre a rich and varied tradition of stone funerary sculpture was the foundation for a tradition of memorials in cement. On occasion, and perhaps initially, the stone figures were embedded in a concrete monument, but this gave way to figures fully realized in cement. One elaborate structure, dated 1926, features representations of cacti, lizards, spoked wheels, large bells and nesting hens (see 1981 exh. cat.). Another complex tomb, erected before 1949, includes two women with infants, an armed policeman, a blacksmith with bellows, a tailor with his sewing-machine and a man in Western dress with his right hand raised. By the 1970s some form of cement funerary monument had developed in most non-Muslim African countries, with elaborate examples proliferating in Kenya, Madagascar and Côte d'Ivoire, as well as in Nigeria, Ghana and Zaïre.

Cement has also been used to build shrines, with peoples in Ghana and Nigeria again leading the way. With the introduction of cement to the area in the 1920s, the shrines of the *asafo*, traditional warrior groups of the Fante, expanded, both in size and conceptually, into structures of up to three storeys, adorned by as many as twenty brightly painted, three-dimensional sculptures (see fig. 79). Images featured have included group leaders and respected elders, as well as motifs representing traditional proverbs, which incorporate lions, leopards, elephants and other animals. By 1981 there were at least 65 cement shrines in Fanteland.

From the early 1960s cement also became an increasingly common material in the construction of the *mbari* houses of the Owerri Igbo of south-east Nigeria, which typically displayed a complex array of mud sculptures of gods and village scenes. Originally designed as community-wide sacrifices to specific deities in the face of such problems as drought or disease, *mbari* were allowed to decay. As in other cases in Africa, the use of cement turned a deliberately ephemeral structure into a more permanent and, perhaps, more secular one, since religiously prescribed materials were ignored in favour of the modern.

The most famous and best-documented series of cement sculptures in Africa are those of the Yoruba shrines of Oshogbo in south-west Nigeria. Under the patronage and tutelage of the Austrian painter Susanne Wenger, a number of sculptors were employed during the 1960s to refurbish and embellish the town's shrines. The flowing

79. Cement shrine of a Fante *asafo* by Kwamina Amoaku, Gomoa Mankesim, Ghana, 1979; from a photograph by Doran H. Ross, 1980

forms of the shrine to Oshun (the riverain goddess of love and fertility) demonstrate a clear departure from the more rigidly posed and symmetrical tendency in traditional Yoruba art. The cement shrines of Oshogbo became a major tourist attraction, and the Sacred Grove of Oshun was designated a national monument.

Having become a substitute material for wood, stone, terracotta and mud in traditional religious sculpture, cement has also become the chosen material for secular sculpture bought by a growing population of middle- and upper-class African patrons to adorn homes and business premises. As early as the 1930s wealthy Yoruba were decorating the balustrades of their houses with cement lions and elephants. With the advent of national independence for most countries in Sub-Saharan Africa programmes of public sculpture were developed, honouring politicians, war heroes and other celebrated individuals, further increasing the number of commissions for cement sculptors. The technical and aesthetic aspects of cement sculpture became established components of the fine arts courses of many universities throughout Africa.

As the medium's popularity increased, individual artists achieved both national and, increasingly, international reputations. For example, the work of Koffi Mouroufié of Côte d'Ivoire was shown at the Centre Georges Pompidou, Paris, in 1977, while a number of life-size figures by the Ibibio artist Sunday Jack Akpan (*b c.* 1940) are owned by museums throughout the world (see fig. 80). Of the Oshogbo artists, Adebisi Akanji has received the most acclaim. The cement openwork screens he sculpted at the Esso petrol station opposite the Mbari Mbayo club, Oshogbo, comprise one of the most frequently published works of modern African art. The screens are composed of three tiers of stylized human and animal figures drawn from Yoruba myth and cosmology as well as from contemporary life (see, e.g., Kennedy, p. 62). Ovia Idah (1903–68) of Benin City, Nigeria, and Massinguitana (*b* 1926) of Mozambique have also gained international followings. (For further information on these cement artists see the works listed in the bibliography.)

80. Sunday Jack Akpan: *Portrait of a Man in Coat and Tie*, cement and acrylic paint, h. 1.92 m, 1989 (Lyon, Musée Saint Pierre Art Contemporain)

BIBLIOGRAPHY

U. Beier: 'Yoruba Cement Sculpture', *Nigeria Mag.*, 46 (1955), pp. 144–53

——: 'Ibibio Monuments', *Nigeria Mag.*, 51 (1956), pp. 318–36

——: 'Idah: An Original Bini Artist', *Nigeria Mag.*, 80 (1964), pp. 4–16

——: *Contemporary Art in Africa* (London, 1968)

——: *The Return of the Gods: The Sacred Art of Susanne Wenger* (Cambridge, 1975)

G. Preston: 'Perseus and Medusa in Africa: Military Art in Fanteland, 1834–1972', *Afr. A.*, viii/3 (1975), pp. 36–41, 68–71, 91–2

B. Schneider: 'Massinguitana of Mozambique', *Afr. A.*, x/1 (1976), pp. 24–9

K. Nicklin and J. Salmons: 'S. J. Akpan of Nigeria', *Afr. A.*, vii/1 (1977), pp. 30–34

Atelier aujourd'hui: Koffi Moroufié (exh. cat. by N. Beauthéac, Paris, Pompidou, 1977)

P. Breidenbach and D. Ross: 'The Holy Place: Twelve Apostles Healing Gardens', *Afr. A.*, xi/4 (1978), pp. 28–35

D. Ross: 'Cement Lions and Cloth Elephants: Popular Arts of the Fante Asafo', *Five Thousand Years of Popular Culture: Popular Culture before Printing*, ed. F. E. H. Schroeder (Bowling Green, 1980), pp. 287–317

The Four Moments of the Sun: Kongo Art in Two Worlds (exh. cat. by R. F. Thompson and J. A. Cornet, Washington, DC, N.G.A., 1981)

S. Domowitz and R. Mandirola: 'Grave Monuments in Ivory Coast', *Afr. A.*, xvii/4 (1984), pp. 46–52, 96

D. Rosevear: 'Cross River Tombstones', *Afr. A.*, xviii/1 (1984), pp. 44–7

Sculptures en ciment du Nigéria de S. J. Akpan and A. O. Akpan (exh. cat. by J. Soulillou, Calais, Mus. B.-A., 1985)

J. Kennedy: *New Currents, Ancient Rivers: Contemporary African Artists in a Generation of Change* (Washington and London, 1992) [discusses and illustrates the work of a number of Afr. cement artists]

DORAN H. ROSS

3. MASK AND MASQUERADE. The term 'mask' refers primarily to the object that is worn to hide the face of the masker. The term 'masquerade', however, refers to the multimedia activity of transforming a human being into a powerfully animated characterization. While much art-historical research has focused on the mask object itself, the African art form of masquerade comprises an entire ensemble of costume, dance, music and song. Indeed, masquerade is one of Africa's major contributions to world art; it is certainly the most spectacular. Further information on African mask and masquerade will be found in the entries on the arts of individual peoples, cross-references to several of which appear in the article below.

Mask forms have often been reproduced in other media. They have sometimes been adapted as architectural ornamentation or reproduced in miniature for personal adornment, as for example among the Pende of Zaïre (*see* PENDE, §2). There are several traditions of miniature masks, which are not worn over the face or head but simply displayed as symbols of status and achievement. Among the Lega of Zaïre, for example, small wooden and ivory masks are status objects that are displayed during the rituals of the multi-graded initiation societies (*see* LEGA AND RELATED PEOPLES, §2). Among the Dan and neighbouring peoples of Côte d'Ivoire and Liberia miniature masks are the personal property of young men and women whose families own full-size masks. The miniature masks represent the spiritual power embodied in the full-size mask and serve a variety of protective functions for their owners (*see* DAN, §2).

(i) Introduction. (ii) Forms and styles. (iii) Manufacture, preparation and performance. (iv) Contexts. (v) Women and masquerade. (vi) Boys' masquerades.

(i) Introduction. From a conventional Western perspective the aesthetic dynamism of an African mask emerges from analysis of the formal qualities of the static sculptural form, the wooden, facial portion of the mask, devoid of all costume and accompanying dance and music. Indeed, it was the startling sculptural inventiveness of African masks that first attracted the attention of European ethnographers, museum curators, painters and sculptors to African art in the early 20th century. In line with prevailing Western sensibilities and taste, the surfaces of masks in Western collections were cleaned and polished to accentuate their sculptural form; this practice further removed them from their original African context. The distortion of the true nature of African masks as elements of the performance of masked dancers in masquerade leaves the museum viewer devoid of the rich sights and sounds that are the essential aesthetic components of this art form.

Ethnographic reports on a variety of African cultures reveal dramatic differences in the elaboration of masking traditions. Some cultures have paid little attention to the creative potential of masking, while others have developed elaborate masquerades that appear throughout the year. The origins of masking on the African continent will probably never be known, for the perishable organic materials out of which masks are made (i.e. wood, fibre, cloth and so on) are highly susceptible to insect and environmental damage, and neither masks nor their accompanying costumes survive in the archaeological record. While it is thus impossible to trace the origins of mask-making in Africa, there is some evidence to suggest that it is very ancient. Rock paintings and engravings at the site at Tassili N' Ajjer and adjacent sites in southern Algeria have been interpreted as evidence that masquerade was already a fully established and vital form of artistic expression in the 5th and 4th millennia BC (see Cole, 1985, p. 15). In modern times the distribution of cultures that make and dance masks relates directly to the distribution of Bantu-speaking peoples throughout the area south of the Sahara Desert from the Atlantic to the Indian Ocean. It is within this vast area of West, Central and East Africa that the major masking traditions are found.

The origins of each mask are recorded in oral tradition for the peoples who make and perform them. Thus a mask may have come from the supreme god or from a tutelary deity, such as an ancestral or nature spirit. In a number of African cultures oral traditions state that women first made masks and that it was only later that mask-making was assumed by men. Masquerade continues to be predominantly a male activity. Throughout the continent, even in cultures where women may wear masks on occasion, only men ever carve masks. This is explained by men's exclusive role as wood-carvers and by the general dominance of men's secret societies, which ultimately control the manufacture and appearance of masks. Indeed, in many African cultures masquerade is a public assertion of male secular and spiritual dominance. Moreover, masking is often used to define gender and status differences in the community, separating men from women and the initiated from the uninitiated. Most African masking traditions are highly secret, and novices are taught the importance of retaining these powerful traditions within the male sphere. Women are nevertheless vital to the success of many masquerades, even if they appear to have only a passive role as observers (*see also* §(v) below).

In general, then, masked figures and the knowledge to make and dance them are associated with centres of political and/or spiritual authority in the community. These are often secret or semi-secret associations or societies whose members have passed through a period of initiation and instruction. In other cases masks 'belong' to the entire village, although they are often owned by aristocratic families, lineages or clans who control their appearance in the community and, when they are not in use, safeguard the masks and their costumes.

The disguise of the human face and body by the use of a mask creates powerful images. Masks suppress identity and transform the masked into powerful entities. In some African cultures the wearing of masks is likened to disappearance or even death. These are appropriate metaphors for masks that often appear at funerary rituals or during initiation rituals, when people 'die' from one status or identity to be 'reborn' in another.

In general masks represent two types of spirit forces: first, ancestral spirits who return to the land of the living in the form of masks to instruct, counsel, heal, aid and protect the living members of the secret cult or society; and, secondly, generalized nature spirits who, like ancestral spirits, demand respect through proper ritual observances but reward society members with good health, bountiful harvests and many children. The names given to masks suggest collective spirit forces rather than the names of actual people who once lived. Among the Mossi of Burkina Faso, masks are said to be the 'eyes' of clan ancestors (*see* MOSSI, §2), while among the Kuba of Zaïre masks are named *ngesh* or *mungici* after the names of nature spirits (see Binkley). Thus, when masks enter the community they do so as spirit forces. Masks are the visual embodiment of the power of the secret society that has brought them into being. Indeed, among the Yoruba there are some masks that still form part of the sacred paraphernalia placed on household shrines dedicated to tutelary deities even though they are damaged and no longer danced (see H. J. Drewal and M. T. Drewal, p. 250). Spirit forces in the form of masks provide the means by which the masking association or society conducts initiation rituals, buries its dead, promotes agricultural, animal and human fertility and passes judgement on those who have broken the society's rules.

During masquerade, other powers and values are expressed. These include the powers of elders over juniors and the power of men over women, as well as the power of the society's secret knowledge over the community's secular knowledge. Pride of membership in the secret society is also expressed, as is the self-respect and pride of the community as a whole in its masks and masquerades.

(ii) Forms and styles. African masks and mask costumes are stylistically varied. In general, masks can be grouped into three basic types. The first is the face mask, which is attached to or held in front of the face. The second is the helmet mask, which covers the entire head like a helmet or casque. The third and final category is the headdress or cap mask, which consists of a more or less elaborate superstructure worn on top of the head like a cap; in this case cloth or fibre attached to the base of the cap covers the face and sometimes the body of the performer, thus obscuring his identity. Within these three basic categories an immense variety of styles is found, ranging from a simple wooden or cloth face-covering to huge and complex sculptural forms that cover the entire body and may rise 5 m or more above the head of the masker. Such masks are immense mobile sculptures, especially when the masker wears stilts or incorporates other devices to increase overall height.

The form and style of African masks relate directly to the characters they embody in masquerade. These characters range from founders of the community, famous warriors and hunters to wild forest creatures. Even clowns, fools, drunkards and prostitutes may be subjects for characterization. The full style of a mask emerges during its performance. Masks may be male or female, young or old, wealthy or destitute. Masks may be benign and restrained or uncontrolled and dangerous. The characterization is completed by the adoption of appropriate gestures and sounds.

Often masks are made using the forms and materials symbolically associated with the realms of the hereafter and the wild: the savannah, forest, rivers and lakes. During masquerade these realms are contrasted with the civilized world of the community. These associations are reinforced by naming masks after ancestors and culture heroes and such, or after such forest creatures as birds, crocodiles and antelopes, or nature spirits. The forms and styles of masks visually evoke these other worlds and characters.

Physically, masks may represent everything from idealized beauty to grotesques or the results of disfiguring disease. In many African cultures, there is a direct link between outward physical beauty and inner moral and spiritual purity. Masks of good character and moral fortitude usually display marks of social status, wealth and achievement. For example, among the Mende of Sierra Leone and Liberia, a Sowei mask depicts a high-ranking member of the women's Sande society. The elaborate multi-crested hair arrangement, for instance, is carved in great detail. Carved scarification patterns on the face of this and other masks mark ethnic identity and social status but are also protective and decorative (*see* MENDE).

Other masks appear to glorify physical disease and deformity with an apparent disdain for aesthetic principles and artistic finesse. Often, these masks directly incorporate various natural materials, including dark, sticky resins and waxes, unworked raffia fibre and bark, as well as quills, bird beaks, animal horns and teeth (see fig. 81). Such masks represent unrestrained power and malevolent force and often serve as warnings to those in the community who are tempted to indulge in antisocial behaviour.

Colour plays an important role in the characterization of masks. While it is used to add decorative interest, it also often has important symbolic connotations. For example, black is generally associated with decay, death, ugliness and malevolent spirits, while white often symbolizes peace, purity, beauty and benevolent spirits. Red is more ambiguous: in some cultures it is associated with healing and well-being, while in others it is symbolic of blood, danger, power and death. In addition, the formal qualities of masks may convey quite specific meanings. Among the Igbo of

81. Mask representing Idu, a mythical bush monster, at the Otsa festival, Ekperi, Ugbekpe, northern Edo, southern Nigeria; from a photograph by Jean M. Borgatti, 1972

82. Mask representing Banda, Nalu, Guinea; from a photograph by Michael Huet, 1970s

Nigeria, for example, light-coloured masks with refined features often represent female characters, while dark-coloured masks with distorted features represent male characters from the forest or bush (*see* IGBO).

Many masks combine human and animal imagery, which may be enlarged, reduced or adjusted for both decorative and expressive purposes. Many mask-carvers use their understanding of human and animal facial anatomy and of the underlying skeletal structure to produce imaginative reinterpretations in a highly sophisticated abstract language while also taking into account the fact that the complete mask figure will be seen moving, rather than still, during masquerade. The deeply cut geometric planes and elaborate superstructure found on many masks are aesthetically powerful components.

Masks also frequently represent specific birds and animals. The heads may be realistic, or certain details may be exaggerated for added sculptural interest and visual impact. The jaws of forest animals are often enlarged in scale and carved open, with emphasis given to sharp teeth. Beaks, tusks and horns are often exaggerated in scale and multiplied in number for added dramatic impact. Masks may also represent such fantastic creatures as nature spirits or other potent forces, which have no single prototype in the visible world. Mask-makers thus often combine elements from a number of different animals to create powerful sculptural statements. For example, the Banda mask of the Nalu of Guinea does not represent just one animal but the collective danger, mystery and uncertainty of the forest world (see fig. 82).

Added visual and symbolic impact is obtained from using material directly appropriated from the bush and forest. Unworked raffia and other fibres, which often make up the voluminous costumes of masks, not only disguise the body of the dancer but also evoke the organic forms seen in the bush. Beaks, feathers, quills and animal skins are often integral parts of costumes. Masks may also carry paraphernalia associated with the forest, such as bows and arrows, spears, hunting nets and bells.

The costume accessories worn or carried by masks are often chosen for their symbolic power relating to an elevated station in life or supernatural power. The coiffure of the Sowei mask of the Mende, for example, is often carved with amulets and other protective charms. These power-related objects add to the efficacy, wealth and prestige of the mask. Among the Southern Kuba of Zaïre masks wear ornaments associated with wealth and high status, such as shell and beaded necklaces, bracelets and anklets (see fig. 83), and may also carry objects made of iron, copper or ivory. Among the Yoruba of Nigeria, Gelede and Egungun masks display expensive cloth. The display of such cloth and other objects of status on masks adds immeasurably to their aesthetic impact and also reflects favourably on the masking society that brought the mask into being and controls its appearance. Furthermore, the lavish display honours the spirit forces evoked by the masked performance.

Regardless of how dynamic the carving is, or how suggestive the various costume elements are, the mask is

83. Mask representing Inuba, an important titleholder, at a funerary masquerade, Northern Kete village, Southern Kuba area, Zaïre; from a photograph by David A. Binkley, 1981

still a static form that is only fully animated and defined by the movements and sounds of the masker. It is through such animation that the true nature of the forest and spirit world emerges. If the mask represents an animal or nature spirit its performance may be threatening or unpredictable. The mask may crawl on the ground, appear to fly in the air, breathe fire, run in all directions or be led into the village tethered on the end of a cord. Among the Mende of Sierra Leone and Liberia, the mask called Goboi is beaten by its attendants and then doused with cold water to 'cool' its rage. Among the Yoruba and other peoples, maskers representing females often wear false breasts and women's clothing and also dance and mime the behaviour traditionally associated with such women's roles as working in the fields, preparing food or nursing a child (see fig. 84). A female mask widely distributed among masking societies in Sierra Leone and Liberia even 'gives birth' to small costumed figures that have previously been hidden under its voluminous costume during the course of the performance. Unrefined and foolish masks may talk nonsensically and awkwardly meander through the village. In contrast, an important titleholder, such as the Kuba mask Inuba, struts its way through the village accompanied by an entourage of village titleholders, as is appropriate for a respected and influential visitor to the community (see fig. 83 above).

The voices of masks are as varied as their physical appearance. In some cultures maskers use voice disguisers to imitate swarming insects, screeching birds or the growl of a forest predator. A mask may also speak in a special language that has to be deciphered by an interpreter. Other sounds are also important components of masquerade. The sounds of gun shots, war trumpets and drums accompany the entrance into the village of certain Kuba masks in re-enactments of mythic battles in which the mask was originally captured. Among the northern Edo of Nigeria, complex instrumental and choral arrangements accompany masked performances, and music is considered essential to the success of a performance. Although musicians are not the centre of attention when masks perform, they may actually control the tempo and duration of the dances. Virtuosity and improvisation are essential ingredients of the ensemble presentation. The songs that are sung at masquerades often evoke the spirit under whose sanction the event is taking place. For example, for a funeral the qualities of the deceased and his family may be lauded. Songs also praise the power and authority of the masks and of the society under whose auspices the masquerade is being performed.

(iii) Manufacture, preparation and performance. Most masks, especially complex ones, are commissioned from a specialist in the particular type or style of mask required. Although mask-carvers are often specialists, they are not always full-time artists but often practise their skill as a part-time activity. The carving of a mask is by no means an everyday occurrence. The process of making a mask, whether carved from wood or made from some other materials, is often governed by strict rules of segregation and ritual observance. In many African cultures the artist is regarded as being in a state of ritual impurity during the carving process, and he will therefore segregate himself

84. Mask of the Gelede society, representing a nursing mother, Yoruba, Benin; from a photograph by Michael Huet, 1970s

from the rest of the community. If a mask is to be carved from wood, the spiritual forces that inhabit the tree or surrounding forest may have to be contained or appeased before the tree is cut and the carving begun. Once the carving is completed, further sacrifices and prayers may be required to ensure that the spirit whom the mask represents will find favour with it and with the masquerade in which it will perform.

In addition to being carved from wood, masks may be made from a variety of other materials, including cloth, plaited fibre, leather, gourd, metal, hide and feathers. To prepare a single mask and its costume may require the skills of many individuals, including those of a woodcarver, a costume-maker, a blacksmith and a weaver. For example, if feathers, animal skins or other materials are required, these must be obtained from a hunter or trapper; if a sword, bow and arrows, iron gong, bells or mirrors are to be part of the mask's paraphernalia, then these must be made or purchased.

Mask-making may also be a part of the training novices undergo during initiation rituals (see fig. 85). While generally it is the elders who actually make the mask, by observation and participation the novices learn the techniques necessary both to make and to dance masks. This experience will be the novices' first sanctioned foray into the creative world of adult masquerade, although, in the spirit of imitation and play, they may have already made 'unofficial' examples of masks they have seen dance (*see* §(vi) below).

The presentation of the completed mask in performance requires the cooperation and skills of many individuals. Meetings are held to select the dancers and to plan the masquerade, which may consist of several distinct performances over a number of days. Since a mask rarely

85. Mask being made by initiation novices, Northern Kete village, Southern Kuba area, Zaïre; from a photograph by David A. Binkley, 1981

appears alone, other masks must be made or refurbished. In addition, musicians, singers and other specialists must be organized before the masquerade can take place. Generally each mask has one or more retainers who accompany it throughout its performance. One retainer may act as spokesman for the mask, interpreting its speech; others adjust its costume when necessary, clear the dance area and ensure that the performance is completed without incident.

Ritual precautions are also taken during the preparations for a masquerade performance. Among the Kuba of Zaïre, the Dan of Côte d'Ivoire and the Igbo of Nigeria, for example, maskers often believe themselves to be especially vulnerable during a performance. Through witchcraft, sorcery or the actions of a malevolent spirit they may injure themselves or find themselves weak and dance poorly. To ensure success, maskers may rub medicines on their joints and back or carry an efficacious charm in the mouth or hand during the performance. The behaviour of the community as a whole is also strictly regulated during the time of mask performances. Stealing, adultery, active disputes and other antisocial acts disruptive to community harmony are strictly forbidden during masquerade performances.

To keep the identity of the dancers secret from the uninitiated, maskers dress in a secluded location. The refurbishment of an older mask with a coat of paint may be augmented with additional sacrifices to the spirit forces, which 'call' it into being just before the performance begins. Through repeated sacrifice and application of pigment before each dance, a mask may be thought to gain in power. For example, among the Dan of Liberia and Côte d'Ivoire, masks that are first used purely for entertainment may become, after many years of dancing, powerful masks used as judges or hunters of witches and sorcerers. At the conclusion of the performance, before the mask is put away, it may be ritually 'cooled', thus dissipating the 'heat' generated in the performance.

Once the maskers are dressed, the masks enter the village as spirit forces, the maskers remaining 'in costume' throughout the performance, only returning to the forest or a designated enclosure at its conclusion. Often the audience and performers mingle and on occasion even change roles. For example, a musician may leave the dance area and be replaced by a member of the audience, or an elderly man, inspired by the performance, may walk to the centre of the dancing ground and imitate the dance of the mask. African masquerade is thus fluid and dynamic, following a loosely choreographed programme with its own rules of presentational style and decorum.

Some masks may only appear during the day, others only at night, or the masquerade cycle may last for several days including day and night performances. Generally masquerades take place in a prescribed area. This may be a central dancing area set aside for the purpose, although performances may also take place in specific locations, such as at the deceased's compound during a funeral. The masks may appear before the entire population of the village or only a select group of individuals, such as senior members of the masking society. Sometimes the masks may appear not in the village at all but deep in a forest enclosure.

Masks rarely perform alone. Although the appearance of dozens of masks on a single occasion has been documented, usually a much smaller number appear together. When several masks perform, they generally do so in the order of their relative importance. For example, among the Kuba of Zaïre, several lower-ranked masks perform on the day preceding the appearance of the senior mask. The hierarchy of masks corresponds to a similar hierarchy of membership in the masking society. Among the Senufo of Côte d'Ivoire, Mali and Burkina Faso, for example, lower-ranking masks are danced for entertainment by the junior members of the society, while the more powerful, senior masks appear under the aegis of the society's elders on more serious occasions. The senior masks, representing the highest political authority in the community, command great attention and respect (*see* SENUFO). The maskers, as well as the singers and musicians, are judged on their competence, aesthetic ability and, in the case of the maskers, athleticism. Competition between individual maskers, between masking societies and between families who own masks is a vital part of the dynamics of African masquerade.

(iv) Contexts. Masquerades are rarely held solely for entertainment. Masks most often appear during events

that mark periods of stress or transition in the life of the community. Such events include initiation and funeral rituals as well as such cyclical occasions as the onset of the planting season or harvest time. Masks also appear in response to such events as a long drought, a severe epidemic or a crop failure.

The most frequent occasions for masquerade in West and Central Africa are funerary rituals, especially those held for elders and other members of the masking society. Masks perform singly or in groups for several days at the funeral itself. Alternatively the masquerade may take place a year or more after the death; the masks then dance for all those who have died in the interim. Among the Dogon of Mali, for example, dozens of masks may appear at a second funeral to honour deceased members of the masking society (*see* DOGON). Among the Southern Kuba of Zaïre the powerful mask Inuba (see fig. 83 above) appears only at funerals of senior titleholders (see Binkley). During such funeral performances, masks are regarded as intermediaries between the living and the recently deceased. The masks dance to honour the latter and to dispel any ill feelings of the spirit of the deceased or members of his family because of his death. The memory of the deceased is honoured, and his spirit is conducted safely to the land of the dead.

Another frequent occasion for the appearance of masks is initiation rituals, in which young men (and sometimes young women) learn the secret knowledge that allows them to become full participating members of adult society. In many masking societies membership is mandatory for all who have reached the appropriate age. Masks play a major role throughout the initiation cycle, and they are often employed to 'steal' the uninitiated youths from the village and install them in a bush or forest camp. Among several groups in Liberia a large masked figure with exaggerated jaws and teeth stained red symbolically 'kills and eats' the novices at the onset of the rite before they are 'reborn' as adults through the initiation process. In the initiation enclosure, masks serve as guardians of the novices and, together with the elders, discipline and educate the novices. Masks also safeguard the novices' physical and spiritual well-being. In some cultures, masks are given the names of important deceased family members who are called upon to protect the novices from harm. This is especially important when circumcision is involved as the ancestral spirits, in the guise of masks, are thought to help the novices' wounds heal quickly. Masks also monitor the activities of the initiation camp and make certain that non-members keep their distance. Masks may also be used to obtain food and other materials for the camp. The making of masks is part of the secret knowledge imparted to the novices during initiation rituals. Indeed, masks are thought to be among the most secret of initiation-related lore; they are visible symbols of the secret nature of the institution. Depending on the stage of initiation, the masks dance for society members in the forest or enter the village to dance for the women and children. On these occasions masks express pride of membership in the society and the prestige of those who are undergoing the initiation rite.

In some societies masks form part of the regalia of aristocratic rulers and their families and appear at festivals and rituals, adding to the splendour of the royal court. For example, among the Kuba of Zaïre several masks are reported to form part of the ruler's patrimony. Maskers also appeared at the royal court of Bamum in the Cameroon Grassfields at festivals associated with the payment of tribute and at lavish feasts held to consolidate ties between the king and his subjects (see fig. 86; *see also* BAMUM).

Among the Dan, We and related groups in Côte d'Ivoire and Liberia masks play a multitude of roles. For example, some masks play a significant role in the judicial affairs of the community, while another is worn during competitive footraces, and another enters the village to control cooking

86. Mask representing a crocodile, at the Nja festival, Foumban, Bamum, Cameroon; from a photograph by Marie-Pauline Thorbecke, 1912

fires that, if left unattended, could burn the entire village. Historically, a very powerful Dan mask prepared and then led warriors into battle, while another was considered a judgement mask of great power and influence that sanctioned proceedings of various kinds, settled disputes and allocated fines (*see* DAN, §2).

The Bamana of southern Mali also have elaborate masking traditions. The Chi Wara society and its masks are primarily concerned with the fertility of the fields and proper farming practices. Members of the society dance in crest masks during agricultural rituals in honour of a mythic half-man/half-animal who was instrumental in bringing agriculture to the Bamana (*see* BAMANA, fig. 4). The powerful Komo society uses masks composed of an accumulation of symbolically charged material to identify and eliminate such destructive forces as thieves and sorcerers (*see* BAMANA, §3).

In parts of West Africa a number of elaborate regional initiation and masking societies developed. The masks of one of these, the Poro society, danced at the initiations and funerals of society members but also served important functions as agents of social control in protecting the community against antisocial behaviour. Some of these masks were sacred and had great power and authority. Acting in consort with a council of elders, the masks pronounced sentence on murderers, thieves and other deviants and then supervised the carrying out of the sentence.

Masks also appear in dramatic presentations of mythic or historical tales relating to village or clan histories. On these occasions masks represent important chiefs, warriors or culture heroes, while drunkards and fools may also appear. Masks also sometimes play important roles as social commentators. For example, masks may dance to comment on the antisocial behaviour of a specific community member, even if he or she is an elder. The mask may directly name the individual, or a skit may be enacted that graphically presents the immoral behaviour, such as drunkenness or adultery. In this role the mask stands in a privileged position as a third party protected by anonymity that can break the normal rules of decorum and comment on social behaviour without fear of reprisal.

In addition to all the above, masks in Africa are highly entertaining. Even on the most sombre of occasions a comical mask may appear to relieve the mood of seriousness or sadness. With increasing cultural influences from both the West and the Islamic world, however, many African masking traditions have lost or altered their ritual and ceremonial importance. By the late 20th century in some areas masks performed only for entertainment, often at such non-traditional occasions as Christmas or New Year festivals or in performances for tourists.

(v) Women and masquerade. Generally in Africa masquerade is regarded as a potentially dangerous occasion for people who are not members of the masking society, and this is especially the case for women. Masks are often regarded as dangerous to the health and fertility of women. If a woman touches a mask or even walks across the ground on which masks dance, infertility, still-births or illness may result. Precautions are taken, therefore, to ensure that women keep their distance and do not touch the masks during performance. These sanctions may also be explained by men's concern that the secrets possessed by their masking society are kept from the uninitiated. Thus, for the most part, women are excluded from direct participation in mask-making and dancing.

There are, however, several exceptions to this prohibition. Among the Mende and related peoples of Sierra Leone and Liberia, for example, women belong to a powerful initiation society called Sande. The society commissions the making of masks and organizes performances during initiation rites for society members (*see* MENDE; see also fig. 13 above). In some cultures the participation of elder women, usually those past the menopause, is crucial to the setting up of the men's initiation camp, and sometimes women are instrumental in the manufacture of some masks, even making a part of the costume worn by masked dancers. Among the southern Kuba of Zaïre, some masks cannot dance without a gift first being given to the women of the community, while among the Yoruba of Nigeria women actively participate in both Gelede and Egungun masquerades by contributing the expensive cloth for the mask costume. In a number of cultures women play the essential role of choral accompaniment at mask performances.

BIBLIOGRAPHY

The works listed below are only a very few of those devoted to mask and masquerade in Africa. For additional references see the bibliographies of the various entries on individual peoples, especially those cross-referred to above. Articles on African mask and masquerade appear regularly in such journals as *African Arts*.

G. Kubik: 'Masks of the Mbwela', *Geographica*, Revisita da Sociedade de Geografia de Lisboa, xx (1969)

S. Ottenberg: 'Humorous Masks and Serious Politics among Afikpo Ibo', *African Art and Leadership*, ed. D. Fraser and H. M. Cole (Madison, 1972), pp. 99–121

D. Biebuyck: *Lega Culture: Art, Initiation, and Moral Philosophy among a Central African People* (Berkeley, 1973)

S. Ottenberg: 'Afikpo Masquerades: Audience and Performers', *Afr. A.*, vi (1973), pp. 32–5, 94–5

R. A. Bravmann: *Islam and Tribal Art in West Africa* (Cambridge, 1974)

K. Nicklin: 'Nigeria Skin-covered Masks', *Afr. A.*, vii (1974), pp. 8–15, 67–8, 92

S. Ottenberg: *Masked Rituals of the Afikpo: The Context of an African Art* (Seattle, 1975)

A. Vrydagh: 'Makisi of Zambia', *Afr. A.*, x (1976), pp. 12–19, 88

H. J. Drewal: 'The Arts of Egungun among the Yoruba Peoples', *Afr. A.*, xi (1978), pp. 18–19, 97–8

B. DeMott: *Dogon Masks: A Structural Study of Form and Meaning*, Studies in the Fine Arts, 4 (Ann Arbor, 1979)

E. Tonkin: 'Masks and Power', *Man*, xiv (1979), pp. 237–48

From the Hands of Lawrence Ajanaku (exh. cat. by J. M. Borgatti, Los Angeles, UCLA, Mus. Cult. Hist., 1979)

Ethnol. Z. Zürich, i (1980) [special issue on masking and initiation societies in Sierra Leone, Liberia and Côte d'Ivoire]

A. J. Glaze: *Art and Death in a Senufo Village* (Bloomington, IN, 1981)

A. P. Bourgeois: 'Yaka Masks and Sexual Imagery', *Afr. A.*, xv (1982), pp. 47–50, 87

M. T. Drewal and H. J. Drewal: *Gelede: Art and Female Power among the Yoruba* (Bloomington, IN, 1983)

M.-L. Bastin: 'Ritual Masks of the Chokwe', *Afr. A.*, xvii (1984), pp. 40–45, 92–3, 95

A. P. Bourgeois: *Art of the Yaka and Suku* (Meudon, 1984)

E. Fischer and H. Himmelheber: *The Arts of the Dan in West Africa* (Zurich, 1984)

G. I. Jones: *The Art of Eastern Nigeria* (Cambridge, 1984)

The Art of Cameroon (exh. cat. by T. Northern, Washington, DC, Smithsonian Inst., 1984)

Igbo Arts: Community and Cosmos (exh. cat. by H. M. Cole and C. C. Aniakor, Los Angeles, UCLA, Mus. Cult. Hist., 1984–6)

H. M. Cole, ed.: *I Am Not myself: The Art of African Masquerade*, Los Angeles, Mus. Cult. Hist. UCLA, Monograph Ser., 26 (Los Angeles, 1985)
F. Lamp: 'Cosmos, Cosmetics and the Spirit of Bondo', *Afr. A.*, xviii (1985), pp. 28–43, 98–9
D. Biebuyck: *The Arts of Zaire*, 2 vols (Berkeley, 1985–6)
M. J. Arnoldi: 'Puppet Theatre: Form and Ideology in Bamana Performances', *Emp. Stud. A.*, iv (1986), pp. 131–50
D. Hersak: *Songye Masks and Figure Sculpture* (London, 1986)
D. A. Binkley: 'Avatar of Power: Southern Kuba Masquerade Figures in a Funerary Context', *Afr. A.*, lvii/1 (1987), pp. 75–97
J. W. Nunley: *Moving with the Face of the Devil: Art and Politics in Urban West Africa* (Urbana, 1987)
C. D. Roy: *Art of the Upper Volta Rivers* (Paris, 1987)
S. L. Kasfir, ed.: *West African Masks and Cultural Systems* (Tervuren, 1988)
D. A. Binkley: 'Masks, Space and Gender in Southern Kuba Initiation Ritual', *IA Stud. Afr. A.*, iii (1990), pp. 157–76
K. Yoshida: *Masks and Transformation among the Chewa of Eastern Zambia*, Osaka, N. Mus. Ethnol., Senri Ethnological Studies, xxxi (1992), pp. 203–73
Masks and the Art of Expression (exh. cat., ed. J. Mack; London, BM, 1994)

DAVID A. BINKLEY

(vi) Boys' masquerades. Children's masquerades are widespread in Africa, particularly in those areas where adult masking is found, that is, mainly in West and Central Africa. They are almost never performed by girls, however, even in Liberia and Sierra Leone where women's masquerades are as common as men's. A growing tendency to initiate boys into adult masquerade societies at a younger age means that boys have become less likely to have their own traditional masquerades. Even in the late 20th century, however, there was a great deal of boys' masquerading in Africa. Boys' masquerading can be usefully presented according to three categories: where its organization is linked to adult forms; where adult forms are emulated, but there is a great deal of autonomy; and where, if adult forms exist at all, they are not closely related. It should be noted that mask size alone is not a good criterion for identifying children's masks; adult forms are sometimes just as small, and boys' may be large.

Boys' masquerade among the Bamana of Mali can be taken to exemplify the first category (see Zahan). Each Bamana village has a number of masquerade associations based on residence, the boys' being the youngest association of six (*see also* BAMANA, §3). Each boys' group is highly organized, with established leadership positions, its own shrine and spirit and its characteristic wooden mask, which, though made by adult blacksmiths, is unique to boys. The mask has an elongated human face with a number of horns, the body being covered with a cloth shirt and long trousers. The masquerader is accompanied by other boys who drum and sing. He performs at festivals, receiving gifts from adults, and has important duties at the millet harvest, when the mask's spirit blesses the new crop of each farmer.

Among the Yoruba of Nigeria boys of all ages, though not yet really members, perform in the adult masquerades of Gelede, Egungun and other Orisa societies. They are individually integrated, joining the society of their father, unless advised by a diviner because of illness to join a different one. Boys as young as five years old often perform at the beginning of adult performances, guided by their fathers or other senior men. In Gelede the boys wear adult-style headpieces, usually representing human

87. Boy masqueraders prepared for Dodo, Bobo Dioulasso, Burkina Faso; from a photograph by René A. Bravmann, 1972

faces or animal forms, with cloth masks and body costumes. In Egungun they may wear a cloth hood and face piece and a variety of textile costumes. The close integration of uninitiated boys into adult masquerade societies also occurs among the Bobo of Burkina Faso (*see* BOBO, §2; see also Le Moal) and the Senufo of Côte d'Ivoire (*see* SENUFO).

Where boys' masking groups are separate from adult forms but emulate them, the religious aspect is less important. At Afikpo, among the Igbo of Nigeria, boys organize themselves into masking groups and perform masquerades in direct emulation of adult versions (see Ottenberg, 1975, 1982, 1989). Wood and gourd masks are reserved for adults, but masks of cloth, coconut or leaves are used with a raffia costume. During the festival season many boys perform together before an audience of children and some adults (*see* IGBO). Copying of adult forms also occurs in towns and cities, as has been described for Bo in Sierra Leone (see Cannizzo, 1978, 1979). Here, groups of boys perform as Alikali Devils in their local neighbourhoods and in the main streets, in imitation of the adult forms that derive from the capital, Freetown. Each boys' group performs a single masquerade with one of four different mask types, consisting of either a wood or cloth mask, various attachments and a variety of cloth body costumes. Despite their emulation of adult forms, these ethnically, religiously and socially mixed groups draw much of the imagery of their masquerades from popular Sierra Leone culture. Such emulating forms of boys' masquerades also exist among various other Igbo groups, among the Dogon of Mali, among the Gola of Liberia and among groups in Zaïre.

Boys' masquerades unrelated to prevalent adult forms are exemplified by the Dodo of Ouagadougou and other parts of Burkina Faso (see Hinckley, 1985, 1986). This secular form apparently originated among adults in northern Nigeria and was brought to Burkina Faso by Hausa traders in the 19th century, after which it became widespread in the country. By the late 20th century it had become a predominantly children's form. The outfit comprises a horned, white gourd mask with a costume of shorts, wristlets and anklets and sometimes body paint (see fig. 87). The boys' groups perform in their residential areas and in other parts of the town, and since the 1970s some of them have performed in a popular government-sponsored competition each year at Ramadan. The groups are often of mixed religious and ethnic background. One of their aims is to gain funds through performance, often the boys' major source of income. Other autonomous, non-emulating boys' masquerades are found in Ghana, where adult masking is uncommon (see Bravmann, 1979, 1983), and among the Igede in Nigeria. In various parts of Africa boys perform in a variety of costumes at Christmas, sometimes dressing as Father Christmas but also using traditional masks; some masquerading takes place during Ramadan.

Boys are only rarely directly taught the skills of masquerade by men, often learning from other boys of their own age or slightly older. Original praising, satiric and abusive songs are commonly composed by the boys, even when the mask and costume are conventional copies of adult types. Dance movements tend to be erratic, unlike in many adult masquerades, and the dress simpler, sometimes produced from odds and ends of materials. Receiving gifts for performances is generally very important. Musical instruments are often made out of tin cans, bits of metal and wood, although sometimes ordinary drums are used. The boys strive for autonomy and creativity, but parental encouragement, advice and assistance are common.

In the late 20th century changes in African life were leading to a decline in boys' masquerading in rural areas but to a growth in urban areas in forms that draw on the imagery of popular culture as seen in the media. These forms in turn were being adopted in rural areas.

BIBLIOGRAPHY

M. Griaule: *Jeux dogons*, Trav. & Mém. Inst. Ethnol., xxxii (Paris, 1938)
C. Béart: 'Jeux et jouets de l'ouest africain', *Mém. Inst. Fr. d'Afrique Noire: Mél. Ethnol.*, xlii (Dakar, 1955)
D. Zahan: *Sociétés d'initiation bambara: Le n'Domo, le kore, le monde d'outre-mer, passé et présent* (Paris, 1960)
U. Beier: 'The Agbegijo Masquerades', *Nigeria Mag.*, 82 (1964), pp. 189–99
H. Kreutzinger: *The Eri Devils in Freetown, Sierra Leone*, Ethnologische Gesellschaft Acta Ethnologica et Linguistica, ix (Vienna, 1966)
O. Balogun: 'Christmas at Aba in the Early 1950s', *Nigeria Mag.*, 101 (1969), pp. 436–41
E. Dahlschem: *Children in Zambia* (Ndola, 1972)
S. Ottenberg: *The Masked Rituals of Afikpo: The Context of an African Art* (Seattle, 1975)
M. Vander Heyden: 'The Epa Mask and Ceremony', *Afr. A.*, x/2 (1977), pp. 14–21, 91
C. Aniakor: 'Omabe Festival', *Nigeria Mag.*, 126–7 (1978), pp. 3–12
J. Cannizzo: *Alikali Devils: Children's Masquerading in a West African Town* (diss., Seattle, U. Washington, 1978)
R. Bravmann: 'Gur and Manding Masquerades in Ghana', *Afr. A.*, xii/4 (1979), pp. 44–51, 98–9
J. Cannizzo: 'The Alikali Devils of Sierra Leone', *Afr. A.*, xii/4 (1979), pp. 64–7, 90
M. Fellous: 'Socialisation de l'enfant bambara', *J. Africanistes*, v/1 (1981), pp. 201–15
G. Le Moal: 'Les Activités religieuses des jeunes enfants chez les Bobo', *J. Africanistes*, v/1–2 (1981), pp. 235–50
S. Ottenberg: 'Boys' Secret Societies at Afikpo', *African Religious Groups and Beliefs*, ed. S. Ottenberg (Meerut, 1982), pp. 170–84
R. Bravmann: *African Islam* (Washington, DC, 1983)
P. B. Hinckley: *'Let Them Dance before You': The Educative Role of Performance in a West African Children's Masquerade* (diss., U. Boston, MA, 1985)
——: 'The Dodo Masquerade of Burkina Faso', *Afr. A.*, xix/2 (1986), pp. 74–7, 91
S. Ottenberg: *Boyhood Rituals in an African Society: An Interpretation* (Seattle, 1989)

SIMON OTTENBERG

4. BODY ARTS. In Africa body arts, an integral part of dressing the body, are widely varied and include both permanent and temporary modifications of the body's contours and surface (*see also* §5 below). The head, neck, hair, teeth, nose, ears, lips, trunk and limbs may all be decorated or in some way altered for aesthetic or ritual purposes. Evidence of the antiquity of some of these body arts can be seen in Saharan rock art of *c.* 5000 BC, in Egyptian and Nubian mummies dating from *c.* 1800 BC, and in Nok terracotta sculpture (*c.* 500 BC–AD 200) and Igbo–Ukwu metalwork (*c.* AD 900) from Nigeria. The sculptural traditions of the more recent past often provide rich documentation of body arts practices. Although Euro-American practices and cosmetics are now employed in Africa, local customs of dressing the hair and painting, scenting, oiling, tattooing or cutting the skin continue to be performed in many areas and contexts.

The most extreme forms of body arts in Africa are those in which body shapes are transformed for aesthetic enhancement. Among the Ibibio and Ejagham of Nigeria and the Mende of Sierra Leone, girls are fattened before betrothal (*see* IBIBIO, §5; EJAGHAM, §6). In contrast, among the Kalabari Ijo of Nigeria, fattening occurs after childbirth. After being sequestered and pampered the new Kalabari mother displays her ample contours to the community in a series of outfits of cloth, cosmetics and jewellery. Alterations to the natural form of babies' heads are made by the Akan in Ghana and by the Mangbetu in north-eastern Zaïre. Among the Yoruba, mothers make two depressions with the thumb and a finger on the lower back of a newborn child to emphasize the separation of the back from the buttocks. Among such peoples as the Ovimbundu, Chokwe, Lwena and Songo in Angola, teeth are filed to a point, while among many peoples lips and ears are stretched and may be punctured to hold many types of ornament.

(i) Coiffure. (ii) Painting. (iii) Marking.

(i) Coiffure. Hairdressing is a widespread form of body art found in both rural and urban areas. Throughout the continent both men and women are expected to dress their hair, for being unkempt is considered a sign of mental

illness or grief. Though the wearing of veils, particularly in North Africa, often makes study of coiffure difficult, in Sub-Saharan Africa women are well known for fashioning a wide variety of intricate designs, both for themselves and for other women, and men also display and create elaborate coiffures, especially in East Africa. Hairdressing is often a domestic activity but may be a specialist occupation. The pliable nature of hair allows its transformation into an endless variety of sculptural designs through parting, packing, tying, weaving or plaiting (braiding and cornrowing) and coating with pomade, oils, mud or grease (see fig. 141 below). Early evidence of African hairdressing is found in rock paintings of Tassili N'Ajjer in southern Algeria. At Jabbaren a female figure is depicted with a hanging braid, and there are numerous figures with crested styles resembling those worn by Fulani women in Nigeria. Hair tied into buns is also found on Nok terracotta heads, as in an example from Rafin Kura (Lagos, N. Mus.).

Many techniques are used for shaping hair. Plaiting hair in many small braids, sometimes tied with decorative objects such as beads or shells, is common. Hair can be fluffed out by teasing and backcombing or clipped closely to the head. Shaved patterns on the scalp provide a contrast between textured hair and smooth scalp. Special thread, either glossy or dull, gives different textural effects when wound around bunches of hair separated to create a design on the scalp and a patterned effect for the hair. Adding pastes made from clay, ochre and various oils, for example, preserves the hair design and allows it to be moulded into a wide variety of sculptural forms. Such items as buttons, beads, pins and metal clippings are sometimes tied or woven into the hair to add colour and textural contrast. In order to increase the volume of their hair old Igbo women in Nigeria sometimes wear wigs made of fibres to imitate elaborate hair designs, while among the Mangbetu of Zaïre hair is interwoven with straw to create a halo-like form projecting from the crown of the head (see fig. 88). In contrast Maasai women shave their heads and smear them with red ochre and animal fat. Hair colour can be changed by bleaching or dyeing, for instance among the Mende, who admire deep black hair and enhance their hair colour with an indigo dye.

Some designs relate to a particular occupation. Fulani milk-hawkers, for example, wear elaborately worked sections of their coiffure on the sides of the head for greater comfort and visibility. Male priests of Sango, the Yoruba god of thunder, wear an elaborate hairstyle to show their devotion to the deity and to his authority. The attendants in Yoruba courts are distinguished by their partially shaved heads. Tonsure may be an indication of different phases of life or special status, or it may be a sign of mourning. The heads of Nuba women in the Sudan are shaved upon the consummation of marriage; this practice is abandoned during pregnancy and by those who are barren until the onset of the menopause. Among the pastoral Fulani, teenage boys grow long hair to display what is known as the 'courting style', but after undergoing their puberty ritual their heads must remain clean-shaven. In Kenya tonsure not only marks coming of age among many peoples but also indicates the esteemed status of an elder among the Mbeere. In contrast, young Afar males in Ethiopia have shaved heads, but upon reaching manhood

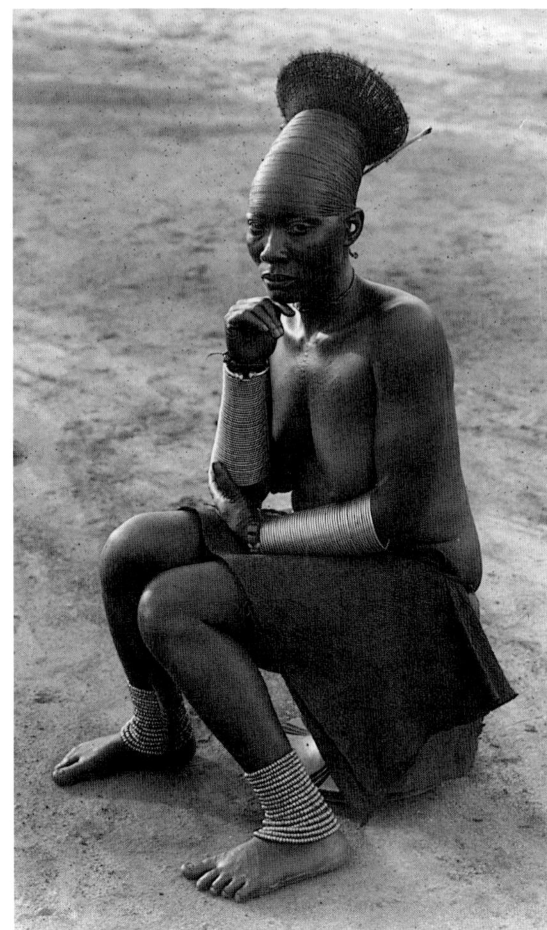

88. Mangbetu woman with artificially elongated head and coiffure, Okondo's village, north-eastern Zaïre; from a photograph by Herbert Lang, 1910

they grow their hair in a distinctive shape. Hair styles have even been given names relating to significant events, such as the Yoruba women's style called 'the war is over', which refers to the end of the Nigerian civil war in 1970. They may also be expressions of aesthetic preference and, as among the Mende of Sierra Leone, of ideals of female beauty, epitomized in the elaborate, plaited designs represented on Mende Sowei helmet-masks (*see* MENDE, fig. 1).

(ii) Painting. Temporary changes in status are frequently marked by temporary body modifications, especially of the skin. Skin colour and texture may be changed daily or occasionally with the application of cosmetics that wash or wear off. Camwood and henna are used for red hues, and white kaolin provides a stark contrast to dark skin. In many societies of North Africa, where skin colour is generally lighter, intricate henna designs are painted on the hands of brides. The colour of the design can range from red to a blue-black, depending on how long the henna is allowed to remain on the skin during the coloration process. Igbo women use the juice of a berry that temporarily stains the skin an indigo colour. Kalabari

Ijo women apply a similar dye to the legs, upper body, arms and face in patterns called *buruma*. To make the skin glisten and shine, the Baganda of Uganda apply an ointment, particularly to the face, producing a smooth, glossy, light-reflecting finish that is considered beautiful. Some Asante have been reported to grease the skin and sprinkle it with gold-dust twice daily. Kohl is used widely, especially by women, to darken the rims of the eyes. The lips and cheeks, however, are generally not stained or coloured.

The Baluyia of Kenya use body paint in funereal, martial and social contexts. Both men and women paint themselves in the first and last cases; in martial contexts men paint lines or dots in several colours across the forehead, cheeks and upper torso. Among the Maasai elaborate body painting is an important aspect of male initiation into warriorhood. Among the Nuba of Sudan men use red and yellow ochres, black ash, grey-white chalky limestone and even commercial blueing to produce a wide variety of representational and non-representational designs, many of which are zoomorphic (see fig. 89; *see also* NUBA, §1). These designs become progressively more elaborate and intense in colour as a man passes from one age-grade to another. The Baule have various uses for kaolin, using it to adorn and protect newborn babies and to paint the eyes and mouths of spirit mediums to aid in clairvoyance and ensure speaking and hearing the truth. Among the Dan in Liberia, the Mangbetu in Zaïre and the Mende in Sierra Leone body painting is also done for the initiation of girls. While the Dan do not keep to specific patterns, the Mangbetu produce an enormous variety of patterns, including stars, Maltese crosses, flowers, lines, zigzags, chequered patterns, ribbons, knots, bees, zebra stripes and leopard spots. Mende girls' bodies are smeared entirely with white clay for their initiation to show that they are under the control and protection of the Sande society. The Igbo, particularly women, decorate their bodies with continuous, asymmetrical and curvilinear motifs similar to those with which they decorate doors and walls. The patterns in Ibibio body painting are also curvilinear but are contained within small, independent units. Their body-painting designs are redolent of an ideographic writing system (*nsibidi*) that encoded messages of power and wisdom.

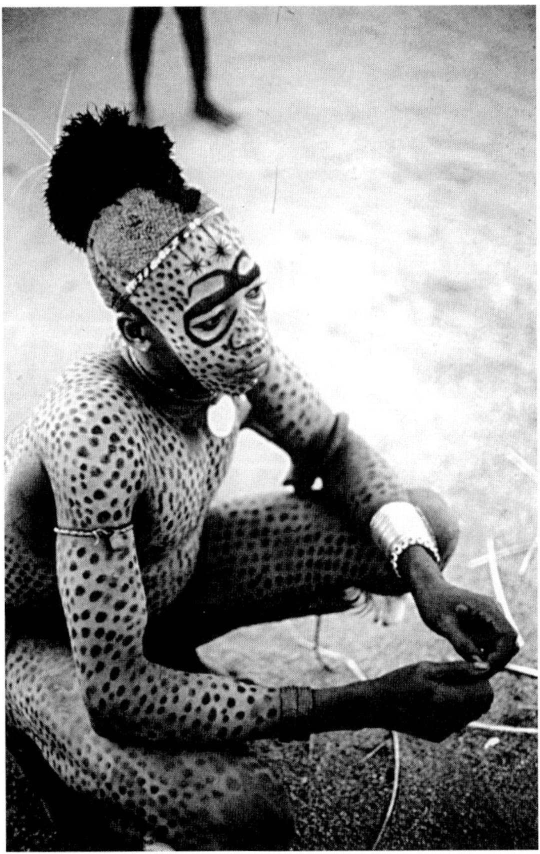

89. Nuba youth with body-paint design representing a species of leopard, south-east Nuba Mountains, Sudan; from a photograph by James C. Faris, 1969

(iii) Marking. Scarification, cicatrization and tattoo are three forms of permanent modification of the skin used in Africa. Markings made by simply cutting the skin are called scarification. Raised weals or keloids made by introducing foreign matter into the cuts are called cicatrizations. The term tattoo (from the Tahitian *tatau*), used incorrectly in the past to refer to all forms of body marking, is created by tapping and pricking the skin with colour. In Africa such designs are usually green and mostly figurative. Permanent body markings in Africa are generally combinations of bold or thin linear cuts variously arranged.

Although many African peoples, such as the Baule and the Tabwa, claim the permanent marking of the body to be a beautifying act that separates human beings from animals, reports have often related African body markings to the slave trade. Markings have been said to have been used as a device to identify and thus redeem members of one's group sold as slaves or as disfigurement to make the members of a group unattractive to slave-buyers. Both explanations are unsatisfactory, the former being based on the assumption that the captured member would be found, while there seems to be no factual evidence for the latter. Although records indicate that 19th-century slave-traders did not usually buy Igbo with *ichi*-type facial scarifications, this was not because the slave-buyers saw marking as disfigurement. Instead the marked Igbo were members of the Ozo title society and were respected by other Igbo, who usually followed their orders to mutiny or to commit suicide rather than submit to slavery. Indeed *ichi* markings have not been popularly adopted; they remain the exclusive preserve of Ozo title-holders and are seen mainly in northern Igboland.

Markings on some archaeological finds have designs that continue to be worn in the vicinity. A cylindrical Nok head from Katsina Ala (Jos, N. Mus.) displays bold lines from the corners of the mouth and diagonals by the side of the nose; such markings are still the characteristic facial scars worn by various peoples around the Niger–Benue confluence at the southern edge of the Nok area. The same components are also present among peoples on the same latitude west of the Niger–Benue confluence as far as the northern part of Côte d'Ivoire.

Items from Igbo Isaiah, such as a 9th–10th-century AD pendant with a human face (Lagos, N. Mus.; *see* IGBO-UKWU, fig. 1) and the male figure on an 'altar stand' (Lagos, N. Mus.), have their faces covered with raised, diagonal lines, which are probably an earlier version of present-day Igbo *ichi* scarifications. The female figure on the 'altar stand' has concentric, raised patterns on the forehead and a radiating sunflower pattern on the stomach that resembles the abdominal markings (*nbumbu* or *egbugbu*) displayed by Igbo women as a prerequisite for marriage and is also found among neighbouring peoples.

Facial scarifications are not found throughout Africa but were probably introduced in three independent regions (the Upper Nile Valley, West and Central Africa), gradually spreading and mixing with increased inter-cultural relations. Archaeological data from before the slave trade provide evidence for a long history of body marking, probably for decorative purposes. Patterns may derive from elements found in any of the three original areas or combinations of elements from any two. In northern Nigeria, for example, between the area of Kanuri influence near Lake Chad and the Niger–Benue confluence, face markings mainly comprise vertical elements, markings at the corner of the mouth or diagonals on the sides of the nose, typical of types in the Nuo–Chadean area and the Niger–Benue confluence. A mixture of simple scars (from the Niger–Benue confluence) and keloids (from south-east Nigeria) are also found among some peoples living south and east of the confluence. The face markings of south-west Nigeria and elsewhere in West Africa north of the Niger–Benue latitude are similar to those found in northern Nigeria outside the region of Kanuri influence.

90. Adamawa woman with facial scarification, Benue-Gongola Valley, north-east Nigeria; from a photograph by Marla C. Berns, 1982

(a) Scarification. Marking, particularly of the face, is sometimes associated with specific ethnic groups or with permanent and progressive status changes, especially among women (see fig. 90). Many such marks, however, are not made primarily for group identification but for aesthetic satisfaction, rituals, medicinal purposes or erotic sensation. Whatever the reason, the markings are usually made with aesthetic sensitivity and definite patterning. In most societies scarifications are executed by specialists: among the Oyo Yoruba, for example, these may be from particular lineages, while Hausa experts in scarification (*yan jarfa*) service various neighbouring ethnic groups.

According to the Yoruba, specific facial patterns, such as those called *keke* or *abaja*, are worn for beauty's sake. Their adoption as aspects of personal beauty is suggested in a traditional account of the origin of Yoruba scarification, which says that they are derived from the scars of bruises meted out to a slave for neglecting to carry out the orders of Sango, the first ruler of Oyo. The scars were found to be so attractive that they were adopted by members of the royal household. No single pattern is common to all sub-groups of the Yoruba. Even one of their most common patterns, *pele* (three thick, vertical lines on each cheek), is not seen among the Owo, Ondo, Ilaje and Ikale. Only the Oyo and related groups such as the Egba, Egbado, Ibolo and Igbomia have standard patterns, but these are reserved for lineages or extended families rather than being markings of ethnic identity. In many Yoruba areas in the late 20th century permanent markings were frowned upon, leading to a decline in public or easily visible marking, but the practice of marking other parts of the body has continued, for example the incision on the stomachs of young children of their parents' (particularly their father's) names.

Some scarifications are employed as part of healing practices while still displaying a definite sense of composition. The Hausa create scarifications by using horns to draw 'impure' blood from ailing parts of the body. The practice of cupping mainly consists of making small, irregular cuts clustered around and over the ailing spots; after healing these are hardly noticeable. The same thing happens to *gbere*, the Yoruba method of inserting medicines under the skin. *Akara*, the marking used by the Igbo to ward off spirits believed to be causing frequent ailments in children, is made up of a distinctive pattern of parallel, vertical cuts (l. *c.* 10 mm) on both temples, close to the eyes. Between Igala country in the Niger–Benue confluence in Nigeria and the Dogoma area of northern Ghana, diagonal marks 20 mm long are made beside the nose to ensure that children believed to have been reborn after previous death in infancy live to adulthood. However, since half the Igala population has such markings it is likely that they were also popularly adopted. Participation in ritual may also involve scarification, particularly of the face. Among the Bamana of Mali men undergo scarification as part of agricultural rites, receiving two vertical marks at the base of the nose and three under each eye. This is in imitation of Chi Wara, the mythical being who taught them agriculture, and in the belief that through it Chi Wara will impart his agricultural zeal to the wearers: the more the marks are multiplied, the more plentiful the harvest will be.

(*b*) *Cicatrization.* Keloid marking is characteristic of body arts in the area from south-east Nigeria to Zaïre (see fig. 91). The common components are concentric shapes, dots and combinations of short, hatched lines. Raised weals are obtained through retarded healing. The Tabwa of Zaïre practised extensive cicatrization (*see* TABWA), sometimes covering their bodies with intricate, symmetrical designs that are said to signify the Tabwa world-view and its moral, social and cosmological order. Tabwa cicatrizations were executed by a skilled woman on young girls in preparation for marriage. Similarly, older women are responsible for the complex scarification programme (*bleeta*) that Ga'anda females of north-east Nigeria begin when aged five or six and that continues through six stages until the conclusion of the marriage contract. These markings are both a form of socialization and visible proof of positive spirit intervention (*see* §III, 5(i) above).

The Higis of Baza clan in Nigeria link the origin of their geometric keloid patterns to the scaly back of a crocodile. This association derives from the story of a man who had two wives, one of whom he confined to her room with a crocodile. The wife so admired the patterns on its back that the husband had these markings made on her body, and other women copied the patterns. Evidence of scarring females for erotic purposes has also been documented among groups including the Tiv of Nigeria and the Baluyia of Kenya. Among the Tabwa it is reported that the design and textural quality of scars on the stomach and buttocks make them intriguing for an intimate partner; moreover, the individual whose skin has been cut and scarred is said to be stimulated when touched.

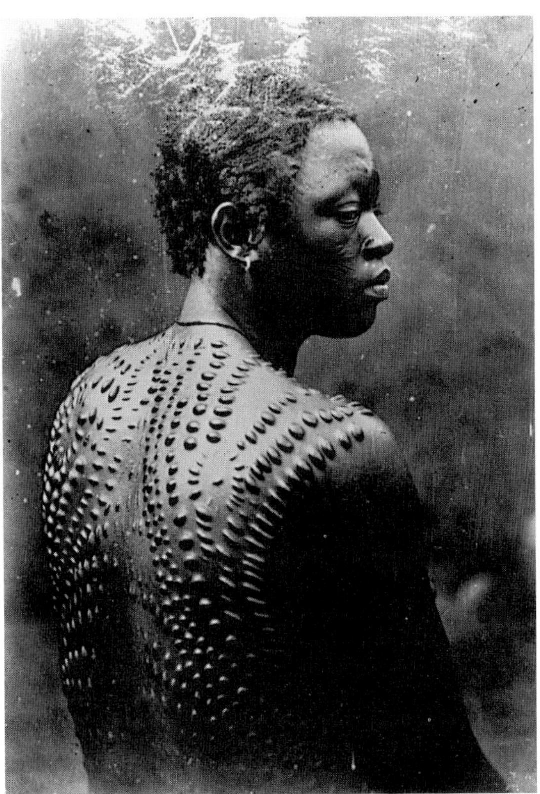

91. Tabwa woman with keloid markings, Kirungu, Zaïre; print by Allen F. Roberts, from a glassplate negative, early 1900s (Rome, Central Archives of the Missionaries of Our Lady of Africa)

(*c*) *Tattoo.* Generally in Africa tattoo is purely ornamental, and, despite its pictorial character and use of colour, it is more closely related to scarification than to body painting. African tattoos are made either by razor cuts or by tapping and pricking the skin with needles. Berber women in North Africa tattoo their chins, and in some parts of North Africa both men and women wear tattoos. In Sub-Saharan Africa razor designs are normally hatched, resembling some scarifications, and the same specialists are responsible for both. On the occasion of marking a baby, people sometimes request pictorial designs from the specialist markers. Among the Yoruba these are described as 'sympathy' marks, and they caution people on how to take care of the marked baby.

The art of tattoo was probably practised in Africa long before it was noticed on the coast by European travellers. The marks on a dessicated human skin from a Middle Nubian cemetery (*c.* 1800 BC), described as puncture tattoos, are actually scarified hatches like razor tattoos. The subsequent history of African tattoo is difficult to reconstruct owing to the scarcity of evidence. However, some early European travellers to the west coast of Africa mentioned pictorial decorations. Until the 18th century references were made to the practice of pictorial incisions or razor tattoos away from the coast. Needle tattoos, used alongside razor tattoos, are coastal phenomena. It would appear that the razor type was adopted first, followed by the needle type, which was perhaps introduced to coastal peoples by European sailors. Tattoos seem most prevalent in the area of Hausa influence across West Africa, and the practice may have been popularized by itinerant Hausa specialists. As the markings appear most clearly on light complexions, however, the presence of the light-skinned Fulani, who are very interested in tattoos, may also have contributed to its popularity.

The parts of the body covered with tattoos are usually the face, neck, chest, back, arms, legs and especially the calves. The thighs, although rarely exposed, may also be tattooed. Sometimes tattoo patterns are displayed alongside scarifications. The nature and quantity of the patterns generally reflect individual preferences and local fashions: in the area of Kontagora, Nigeria, for example, especially around Rijau and Zuru on the way to Sokoto, some people have their bodies almost entirely covered with tattoos. Both abstract and figural designs are employed. The former generally comprise individual or combined rectilinear shapes, such as squares, triangles, lozenges and simple straight lines. Sometimes these patterns are given names, often related to imagery suggested by the design; the Tiv, for example, describe two triangles set together at an angle as a sparrow, for each triangle suggests an outspread wing.

The graphic precision of tattooing and the pain involved in its execution demand that tattooers select motifs that can be easily recognized and executed without error. Such crawling animals as crocodiles, lizards, snakes, crabs and scorpions are invariably depicted as seen from above. Sometimes only the vital parts that enable identification are shown. Large animals or any creatures that walk rather than crawl are depicted in profile. In Nigeria those most commonly represented are elephants, cows, camels and such birds as the egret and duck. The chameleon, although a small creature, is also depicted in profile with its accentuated ridge back. Human figures are rarely represented. Plant motifs range from simple leaf shapes, attached on the sides to represent creepers or climbing plants, to big trees, especially distinctively shaped palms. Floral motifs were also noticed along the West African coast by early European travellers. In more recent times other commonly depicted objects with easily recognizable shapes include swords, daggers, umbrellas and aeroplanes. Graphic representations from printed sources and industrial goods are also sometimes adopted. In 1975 a design of two native hoes intersecting each other, derived from the symbol of a defunct Nigerian political party, was seen on a Hausa woman. Such insignia as the Nigerian coat of arms have also been recorded.

BIBLIOGRAPHY

J. Decorse: 'Le Tatouage: Les Mutilations ethniques et la parure chez les populations du Soudan', *L'Anthropologie*, xvi (1905), pp. 129–47

H. L. Roth: 'Tatu in Tunis', *Man*, v/72 (1905), pp. 129–31

P. Noel: 'Tatouages et leur technique au Cameroun Central', *Rev. Ethnog. & Trad. Pop.*, iii/11 (1922), pp. 241–4

C. H. Armitage: *The Tribal Markings and Marks of Adornment of the Natives of the Northern Territories of the Gold Coast Colony* (London, 1924)

W. D. Hambly: *The History of Tattooing and its Significance with Some Accounts of Other Forms of Corporal Marking* (London, 1925)

S. de Ganay: 'On a Form of Cicatrization among the Bambara', *Man*, xlix/5 (1949), pp. 53–5

M. D. W. Jeffreys: 'The Winged Solar Disk or Ibo Itzi Facial Scarifications', *Africa*, xxi/2 (1951), pp. 93–111

J. C. Froelich: 'Catalogues des scarifications en usage chez certaines populations du Dahomey et du Nord Togo', *Mém. Inst. Fr. Afrique Noire: Mél. Ethnol.*, xxiii (1953), pp. 253–64

R. Baker and M. Z. Yola: 'The Higis of Bazza Clan', *Nigeria*, 47 (1955), pp. 213–22

P. Bohannan: 'Beauty and Scarification amongst the Tiv', *Man*, 129 (1956), pp. 117–21

M. D. W. Jeffreys: 'Negro Abstract Art or Ibo Body Patterns', *S. Afr. Mus. Assoc. Bull.*, vi/9 (1957), pp. 218–29

E. de Negri: 'Hairstyling of Southern Nigeria', *Nigeria Mag.*, 65 (1960), pp. 191–8

M. Trowell: *African Design* (London, 1960, rev. 1965)

G. Neher: 'Chibuk Face Marks', *Niger. Field*, 29 (1963), pp. 16–27

B. de Rachewiltz: *Eros nero* (Milan, 1963); Eng. trans. by P. Whigham as *Black Eros: Sexual Customs of Africa from Prehistory to the Present Day* (London, 1964)

E. de Negri: 'Tribal Marks, Decorative and Painted Patterns', *Nigeria*, 81 (1964), pp. 106–16

J. B. Eicher: *African Dress: A Select and Annotated Bibliography of Subsaharan Countries* (East Lansing, 1969)

H. Cole: *African Arts of Transformation* (Santa Barbara, 1970)

J. C. Faris: *Nuba Personal Art* (London, 1972)

African Textiles and Decorative Arts (exh. cat. by R. Sieber, New York, MOMA; Los Angeles, CA, Co. Mus. A.; San Francisco, CA, de Young Mem. Mus.; Cleveland, OH, Mus. A.; 1972–3)

C. O. Adepegba: *A Survey of Nigerian Body Markings and their Relationship to other Nigerian Arts* (diss., Bloomington, IN U., 1976)

The Arts of Ghana (exh. cat. by H. M. Cole and D. H. Ross, Los Angeles, UCLA, Wight A.G.; Minneapolis, MN, Walker A. Cent.; Dallas, TX, Mus. F.A.; 1977–8)

C. O. Adepegba: 'Ife Art: An Enquiry into the Surface Patterns, and the Continuity of the Art Tradition among the Northern Yoruba', *W. Afr. J. Archaeol.*, xii (1982), pp. 95–109

E. C. Burt: 'Eroticism in Baluyia Body Arts', *Afr. A.*, xv/2 (1982), pp. 68–9, 88

E. Sagay: *African Hairstyles: Styles of Yesterday and Today* (London, 1983)

S. Searight: *The Use and Function of Tattooing on Moroccan Women*, 3 vols (New Haven, 1984)

Igbo Arts: Community and Cosmos (exh. cat. by H. M. Cole and C. C. Aniakor, Los Angeles, UCLA, Mus. Cult. Hist., 1984–6)

S. A. Boone: *Radiance from the Waters: Ideals of Feminine Beauty in Mende Art* (New Haven, 1986)

A. Rubin: *Marks of Civilization: Artistic Transformations of the Human Body* (Los Angeles, 1988), pp. 19–105

CORNELIUS ADEPEGBA, JOANNE BUBOLZ EICHER

5. DRESS. In the broadest sense the art of African dress involves totally or partially covering the body with garments, accessories, paint and jewellery and/or modifying the body itself (*see* §4 above). Both body modifications and body supplements involve manipulating colour, texture, shape, volume, scent and sound. For many Africans, to dress well involves proper decorum and elegant style. Display of appropriate apparel, cosmetics and coiffure is often accompanied by magnificent carriage, graceful movement, fastidious toilette and immaculate garments.

(i) Introduction. (ii) Dressing the torso. (iii) Headdress. (iv) Footwear. (v) Jewellery.

(i) Introduction. The understanding of African dress as an art form requires a consideration of both single items and total ensembles. Occasionally, only a single item is used to adorn the body of an individual, for example a string of beads around the waist. In such a case the texture, colour and shape of the beads, whether of seeds, pods, shells or glass, are judged in the context of the texture and colour of the skin and the body shape. African dress ensembles range from simple to complex. A simple ensemble may consist of a wrapper, body paint and uncomplicated hairdo; a complex one may combine several richly decorated garments, an intricate coiffure, opulent jewellery and other accessories. Both single items and total ensembles may have an additive, cumulative character; examples include clusters of beads, layers of cloth or layers of jewellery. Such clusters and layers are often necessary components, adding the sounds of rustling fabrics and jingling jewellery to the ensemble's visual impact. Layering of garments also provides the effect of bulk, as does the use of heavy fabric. The importance of an individual's social position may be visually reinforced by the size of his or her ensemble. The robes of a ruler are often massive, as is the wrapper set of a powerful and successful trader. Moreover, such accessories as canes, walking-sticks, horsehair switches, umbrellas, fans, purses, handbags, handkerchiefs, linguist staffs and tusks are often needed to complete an ensemble.

In the late 20th century dress in Africa included items fashioned from local resources and tools (such as wrappers from Sierra Leone made of 'country cloth', handwoven from handspun cotton threads) and imported items made by complex machines and techniques (such as British top hats, French *haute couture* gowns, Italian shoes and handbags and Swiss laces). Purely indigenous ensembles were becoming increasingly rare. Borrowed items, however, are no less African for being borrowed when used creatively and juxtaposed with other items resulting in a readily identifiable ethnic style such as that of the dress of Kalabari Ijo men and women (see fig. 92). The term 'cultural

92. Characteristic dress of the Kalabari Ijo, Nigeria, *c.* 1980

authentication' may be used to designate adopted items that are selected, characterized by indigenous nomenclature, incorporated and transformed into a costume item or ensemble. The shape of the Nigerian Kalabari Ijo man's ceremonial hat, the *ajibulu*, for example, is adopted from the bicorne hat of military and naval officers of later 18th- and early 19th-century Europe. Decoration for the hat includes hair from the beard of a ram and such ornamentation as tiny mirrors, shiny balls, multicoloured feathers and hair ornaments. The total configuration is distinctively Kalabari. In contrast individuals of European and Asian descent ordinarily refrain from incorporating African items into their dress repertory and maintain forms of dress current in the lands from which their ancestors emigrated.

(ii) Dressing the torso. In general, dress may be classified as enclosing or attached. Enclosing dress may be further subdivided into categories of wrap-around, preshaped and suspended, all of which are found throughout Africa. Most attached and many suspended enclosing items of dress come into the category of jewellery, which is discussed separately (*see* §(v) below). To form a wrap-around garment, rectangular textile pieces are usually folded, crushed or twisted around the body. Throughout Africa variations of the wrapper (also called *lappa* or *pagne*) predominate for both men and women. The prevalent high temperatures (whether dry or humid), plus the availability of such materials as skins, bark (for barkcloth), or wool, cotton and raffia for handwoven cloth, make the loose fit of wrap-around apparel particularly appropriate. Preshaped garments in general, and trousered garments in particular for males, did not gain widespread use until contact with Europeans and Middle Eastern men and their clothing styles became frequent. Trousers or other bifurcated garments are not usually worn by Sub-Saharan African women.

The wrapper is ubiquitous in Sub-Saharan Africa. Women wear the cloth wrapped from the waist to the knees, calves or feet, with or without the upper body being covered, though sometimes wrapping the cloth under the armpits to cover the breasts. Men wrap a small length of cloth from their waist to their feet, with the chest bare or covered, or have a larger rectangle wrapped round their whole body with one shoulder covered, toga fashion. Wrap-around examples include the striped, handwoven silk *kente* of the Asante of Ghana; the handwoven shawls of sheer, white cotton of the Amharic women in Ethiopia; the hand-dyed indigo batik wrappers of Yoruba women in Nigeria; the raffia skirts of the Kuba in Zaïre; commercially woven blankets worn by Ndebele and Xhosa women in Southern Africa; the skin aprons of Zulu men; and the barkcloth garments worn by both sexes among the Baganda in Uganda.

With preshaped dress, lengths of cloth are cut and sewn before being worn. Examples include shirts, blouses, robes and trousers, or, for example, the *baba riga* (big gown) of the Hausa. Many preshaped garments show the influence of cross-cultural contacts. The long gown (*boubou*) of Wolof women in Senegal, for example, has a probable Muslim and Middle-Eastern origin. The gowns of Herero women in Namibia and of Efik women in Nigeria, and the 'granny' gown of women in Egypt, show 19th-century European influences. Trouser shapes vary from enormously large drawstring breeches worn by Hausa men in the north of Nigeria to some narrow ones worn by Yoruba men. With trousers or wrappers, men wear shirts and other preshaped, hip-length garments like tunics over the upper torso with a variety of details. Among the Fon of the Republic of Benin men wear an ensemble with a heavily embroidered, sleeveless tunic pleated at the neckline and flared at the hipline, embroidered trousers and embroidered cap. In Côte d'Ivoire and Ghana other male tunic-type garments include the war shirts and hunters' shirts of the Maninka and Akan. These are decorated with amulets comprising animal horns, claws, teeth or packets containing pieces of paper on which have been written magical words (see fig. 93). Yoruba men wear a three-piece outfit consisting of a robe (*agbada*) and shirt (*dansiki*), with either closely fitting or wide, loose trousers. The same style is regarded as less formal if tailored from a colourful, wax-printed cotton, and more formal if made from damask, lace, eyelet, brocade, or the handwoven textile of native silk known as *sanyan* or *alari*.

Suspended items of dress are generally of circular form with an opening to slip over a body part, for example necklaces and loose bangles. Two or more subtypes of enclosing garments may be used to produce a combination form, such as the royal cape worn by a Fulani emir in Nigeria that is preshaped and stitched but loose enough to be suspended from the shoulders.

The dress of different peoples is often distinguished by colour, texture and/or fabric motif. The textiles used in African dress range from handcrafted fabrics to commercially produced, both imported and domestic, textiles made of cotton, wool or synthetic fibres. Designs include prints of many kinds, plus woven patterns of plaids and checks (*see* DYE, colour pl. III, fig. 2, and TEXTILE, colour pl. IV, fig. 1). Fabric types range from plain broadcloth to laces,

93. Asante war shirt and shoulder-bag, cloth and leather, h. 1.09 m, before 1850 (Copenhagen, Nationalmuseum)

eyelets, damasks, brocades and velvets. Manufacturers in the UK, the Netherlands, Switzerland, India and Africa have been responsive to the specific textile motif and colour preferences of consumers in Africa. For example, printed cottons in brilliant pink and purple have been favoured in Zaïre; clear yellow, orange and green in eastern areas of Nigeria; burgundy and indigo in western Nigeria; and subdued purple, khaki and muted blue in Togo and the Republic of Benin. Sombre plaid designs are favoured by Ijo and Igbo groups in Nigeria. Some groups prefer monochrome textiles in soft pastels and dazzling white.

In parts of West Africa groups of people buy identical textiles to wear for special events. Frequently, the textile is commercially manufactured with a screenprinted portrait of a significant person (usually political) who is being honoured. This custom of wearing identical cloth is known as *aso ebi* (family dress) and *aso egbi* (association dress) among the Yoruba, where it began. It has also been adopted by some other groups, among the Igbo, for example, who call identical dress 'uniform'.

Decoration of garments includes the techniques of embroidery, beading (see fig. 142 below) and appliqué, the latter used particularly in ceremonial and masquerade gowns. Various male robes throughout West Africa are heavily embroidered, as among the Hausa (*see* HAUSA, fig. 1). Simpler embroidery is seen on some of the contemporary kaftans worn by women, especially those being made for the tourist market in the later 20th century. Beading is found on robes of some royalty; sequins and beads decorate women's blouses, for example among the Yoruba and Kalabari Ijo.

(iii) Headdress. Ensembles are often completed by modifications of the hair and face (*see* §4 above) and headdresses that reinforce information about gender, age, political position or community standing. Men's headwear includes caps, hats, veils and turbans and exhibits greater variety of type than the headties and veils of women. The wider range for men may be related to the wider range of statuses and political and religious positions, such as chieftaincy ranks and priesthood categories, available to them. The headties of women are often responsive to fashion change and are expressions of the fanciful imagination and flair of individuals.

Materials used for men's hats and caps include textiles, skins, feathers, straw, raffia and beads. Some hats, encrusted with precious metals or jewels or heavily embroidered with gold and silver threads, designate high (sometimes royal) status. Imported top hats, Derbys and fedoras are also worn by men in some areas as part of a dress ensemble, again indicating high status, if not that of chieftaincy, then achieved local honour or age grade. Veils and turbans may also be part of male dress. The wrapped veil of a Hausa male shows that he has been to Mecca. The shiny, deep indigo-dyed cotton veils of Tuareg males make them easily identifiable. Headties of cloth wrapped in numerous shapes and styles are most often worn by adult females, in particular by the Yoruba of Nigeria and the Ndebele of Southern Africa. In the 1800s Herero women of Southern Africa used skins. Some Muslim women wear a preshaped or suspended veil, revealing only the eyes.

(iv) Footwear. Much African footwear is preshaped and completes many ensembles, especially those of men and women of special ranks. Many types of sandal, boot and shoe are worn, made either by hand or commercially, locally or abroad. Decoration includes flamboyant and rare feathers, beads, precious metals or incised leather. The footwear of Hausa emirs, worn with ceremonial gowns and capes, has ostrich feathers over the insteps. Horsemen of the Hausa royal household wear leather boots. In his full ceremonial dress the Oba of Benin wears slippers covered with coral beads, whereas the Alake of Abeokuta, in his royal regalia, wears slippers covered with tiny imported glass beads.

BIBLIOGRAPHY

R. Murphy: 'Social Distance and the Veil', *Amer. Anthropologist*, lxvi/6 (1965), pp. 1257–74

J. B. Eicher: *African Dress: A Select and Annotated Bibliography of Subsaharan Countries* (East Lansing, 1969)

H. Cole: *African Arts of Transformation* (Santa Barbara, 1970)

A. A. Mazrui: 'The Robes of Rebellion: Sex, Dress, and Politics in Africa', *Encounter*, xxxiv/2 (1970), pp. 19–30

R. Boser-Sarivaxévanis: *Textilhandwerk in West-Afrika: Weberei und Farberei* (Basle, 1972; Eng. trans. as *West African Textiles and Garments from the Museum für Völkerkunde, Basel* (Minnesota, 1980))

J. B. Eicher: 'African Dress as an Art Form', *A Current Bibliography on African Affairs*, 5/5–6, n.s., ii (1972), pp. 516–20

African Textiles and Decorative Arts (exh. cat. by R. Sieber, New York, MOMA; Los Angeles, CA, Co. Mus. A.; San Francisco, CA, de Young Mem. Mus.; Cleveland, OH, Mus. A.; 1972–3)

A. Mertens and J. Broster: *African Elegance* (Cape Town, 1973/*R* London, 1974)

E. de Negri: *Nigerian Body Adornment* (Lagos, 1976)

The Arts of the Hausa (exh. cat. by D. Heathcote, London, Commonwealth Inst., 1977)
A. Elliott: *Sons of Zulu* (London, 1978)
J. M. Cordwell and R. A. Schwarz, eds: *The Fabrics of Culture* (New York, 1979), pp. 87–102, 103–17, 331–48, 349–97
Afr. A., xv/3 (1982) and xxv/3 (1992) [issues on Afr. dress and textiles]
J. M. Cordwell: 'The Art and Aesthetics of the Yoruba', *Afr. A.*, xvi/2 (1983), pp. 56–9, 93–4, 100
D. P. Biebuyck and N. Van den Abbeele: *The Power of Headdresses: A Cross-cultural Study of Forms and Functions* (Brussels, 1984)
A. Fisher: *Africa Adorned* (London, 1984/*R* 1989)
I. Pokornowski and others, eds: *African Dress II: A Select and Annotated Bibliography* (East Lansing, 1985)
M. C. Daly, J. B. Eicher and T. V. Erekosima: 'Male and Female Artistry in Kalabari Dress', *Afr. A.*, xix/3 (1986), pp. 48–51, 83
A. Rugh: *Reveal and Conceal: Dress in Contemporary Egypt* (New York, 1986)
O. C. Thieme and J. B. Eicher: 'African Dress: Form, Action, Meaning', *Afr. J.*, xiv/2–3 (1987), pp. 115–38
'History, Design and Crafts in West African Strip-woven Cloth', *Proceedings of the Symposium Organized by the National Museum of African Art, Smithsonian Institution, Feb 18–19, 1988* (Washington, DC, 1992), pp. 53–81, 95–112, 133–68
K. T. Hanson: 'Dealing with Used Clothing: Salaula and the Construction of Identity in Zambia's Third Republic', *Public Culture* (1994), pp. 503–22
J. Morris with E. Preston-Whyte: *Speaking with Beads* (New York, 1994)
Crowning Achievements: African Art of Dressing the Head (exh. cat. by M. J. Arnoldi and C. M. Kreamer, Los Angeles, UCLA, Fowler Mus. Cult. Hist., 1995)

JOANNE BUBOLZ EICHER

(v) Jewellery. The adornment of the body with jewellery is one of the most characteristic forms of African dress for both men and women, at least traditionally. The earliest evidence of African jewellery is in the form of the bead necklets, bracelets and anklets shown on the late 1st-millennium BC terracottas from Nok in Nigeria. Bronzes and terracottas of the 12th to 14th centuries AD from Ife, Nigeria, and terracottas of similar date from Jenne-Jeno in Mali add to this record. Much African jewellery was and has continued to be made of natural, often perishable materials, such as grasses, split palm leaves, wood, dried and scented clay, roots and furs. As a rule African jewellery uses no precious stones. Ivory arm-rings, usually left plain, are used as status symbols in many areas. Those of Benin City are finely carved and rate high in African art (see fig. 52 above). The pendants of elephant or hippopotamus ivory found among the Pende, Luba and Hungana of Zaïre are also of high quality. Amber, coral and low-grade silver are used where there has been Arab cultural influence, mainly in northern Africa, the Sahara and its southern fringe, the Horn of Africa and down the east coast. Coral, imported from the Mediterranean since the late 15th century, is essential to the regalia of the Oba of Benin City, Nigeria, and is highly valued by the Kalabari Ijo of southern Nigeria. Gold jewellery is virtually confined to Western Africa, where the Wolof of Senegambia make large earrings of beaten gold. Baule and Asante aristocrats of Côte d'Ivoire and Ghana have hollow gold pendants, rings and beads, cast by the lost-wax process. Bronze is widely used. The metal is either imported or derived from smelted ores and is worked by the lost-wax technique or by hammering and chasing. Copper, brass and iron wire are used in coiled neck, arm and leg ornaments. Thick wire may be drawn to make fine wire, which can be coiled around a fibre core to make flexible armlets; plaited vegetable fibre is used in a similar way. Stone beads, mostly of cornelian and including those from Cambay (Khambhat), in western India, are made or traded over much of Sub-Saharan Africa. Stone bracelets are found in parts of the Sahel.

94. Samburu girl wearing characteristic beaded jewellery, Kenya; from a photograph by George Zaloumis

Beadwork is perhaps the best-known form of African jewellery; many beads are of African make, of brass, iron, wood, shell, stone or terracotta. Disc beads made of ostrich eggshell or snail shell are well known; by the late 20th century similar beads in red and black plastic had become popular. Glass beads have entered Africa since perhaps the early first millennium AD (*see* §V, 7(i) above). The most common bead is the small round 'seed' bead, used to make bead ornaments in great variety and number, especially among the Bantu peoples of Southern Africa. The larger and more elaborate beads were worn as status symbols or regalia by dignitaries or wealthy people in western and central Africa; they were usually worn singly or as a single string.

The types of jewellery found in Africa include necklaces and broad collars, armlets and anklets of different sorts, finger rings, earrings and earplugs, lip ornaments and head ornaments, as well as jewellery worn on the body. In general, women wear more jewellery than men.

African necklaces and neck ornaments range from heavy collars of cast or beaten brass, often with chased decoration, to single strings of beads or broad beadwork collars, sometimes strung on fine wire. The effect may be reinforced by wearing many strings of beads, as among the Samburu of Kenya, so that the breasts are partly covered (see fig. 94). The Ndebele women of Transvaal wear numerous massive ring collars of grass coils covered with beads and similar beaded rings on their arms, legs and body. Anklets similarly range from the heavy and unwieldy brass discs worn by Igbo women in Nigeria to numerous fine wire, beaded or plaited-fibre rings, sometimes covering the leg from knee to ankle. The heavy, iron-bead leg ornaments of the Herero of Namibia and Angola weigh up to 5 kg each. Several garters, usually beaded, form part of the festive dress of both sexes among the Bantu of Southern Africa.

Arm ornaments include ivory bracelets, some of which are very heavy. The royal burial at Igbo Richard (*c*. AD 850) in Nigeria contained cuff-shaped bead armlets; others occur among the Zulu of southern Africa. Among the Xhosa of South Africa, on special occasions women wear numerous bracelets covering the upper and lower arms. These may be bead strings, flexible rings wrapped with a bead string, plastic bangles or vegetable fibre rings, often finely plaited. Finger-rings are not much worn, apart from the elaborate gold rings cast by the lost-wax process among the Asante of Ghana. Silver rings are found in the areas of Arab culture contact.

Ear ornaments include earrings and earplugs. These range from the heavy gold earrings of the Wolof, through wooden discs to the cane cylinders used as snuff-boxes in eastern and southern Africa. Earplugs are often ornamented with pyrogravure, paint, beads or applied plastic. In Kenya and Tanzania, women wear a variety of beaded leather and wire ear pendants and earrings, sometimes combined with beaded headbands. Lip jewellery includes the large lip-discs formerly worn in both lips by women in Chad; smaller lip plugs, lip pegs and lip pendants were worn by both sexes among various peoples in eastern Africa, partly for adornment but also symbolically to protect the mouth.

African head jewellery includes headbands and types of headdresses. Detachable headdresses in a variety of styles and ornamented with beads were worn among the Fang of Gabon, the Ngbaka of Zaïre and the Lango of Sudan, among many others. In the late 20th century Zulu women wore headdresses ornamented with sundry beadwork ornaments. African body jewellery includes many sorts of waist- and hip-bands, pubic aprons, pendants, bandoliers and other ornaments found especially among the Bantu peoples of Southern Africa. The bead 'corsets' of the Dinka of Sudan, the ostrich eggshell 'corsets' of the Kwanyama of southern Angola, the bead 'waistcoats' of the Tembu and other Xhosa peoples of South Africa may also be better regarded as jewellery rather than clothing. The beaded waist-bands worn under their clothing by women in many parts of Africa constitute a private but important form of personal jewellery.

BIBLIOGRAPHY

A. Fisher: *Africa Adorned* (London, 1984/*R* 1989)

M. Carey: *Beads and Beadwork of East and South Africa*, Shire Ethnography, 3 (Princes Risborough, 1986)

J. Mack, ed.: *Ethnic Jewellery* (London, 1988)

T. F. Garrard: *Gold of Africa: Jewellery and Ornaments from Ghana, Côte d'Ivoire, Mali and Senegal in the Collection of the Barbier-Mueller Museum* (Munich, 1989)

M. Carey: *Beads and Beadwork from West and Central Africa*, Shire Ethnography, 21 (Princes Risborough, 1991)

MARGRET CAREY

6. REGALIA. In Africa regalia include the raiment that adorns a ruler, the insignia carried by a ruler and the emblematic devices that support or shelter the ruler as symbols of royal power. The interaction between ruler and emblems glorifies both the royal personage and the reign itself. Art objects commissioned by a king or queen, together with royal vestments, headgear, jewellery, thrones, stools, special weapons or other implements, constitute the regalia that embody the strength and spirit of each monarch's rule, and they are intimately involved in the exercise of leadership. The regalia of the Asante king, for example, are symbols of the kingly office, chronicles of royal history and evidence of traditional religion, cosmology and social organization (see Kyerematen, p. 1).

(i) Introduction. (ii) Elevation. (iii) Protection. (iv) Magnification.

(i) Introduction. In many African kingdoms a concept of divine right exists, wherein a ruler is chosen by virtue of his or her special relationship with the deities. There are, however, other modes of succession to office relating to the political position of a candidate, clan membership, consequences of gift exchange or victory in warfare. Whether considered divine or semi-divine, all rulers in Africa are perceived as larger than life and, as such, are vested at their coronations with material symbols expressing their rank and claim to power. Certain possessions are intended to reinforce this image both physically and metaphorically, thus legitimizing and validating the ruler's authority and right to rule.

There is often a degree of detachment and isolation inherent in the role of king or leader, and one of the functions of regalia is to distinguish the ruler from the ruled. Ownership of the regalia, a royal palace and special furnishings not only render the leader conspicuous but also emphasize his or her ability to control wealth and bestow privileges, often in the form of art objects or items of regalia that serve as documents of service or emblems of acquired rank. Regalia are not always conspicuously treated, however, but may be hidden from sight, creating an aura of secrecy. In addition to the regalia that cover or veil a ruler, there are those that are hidden by the ruler, as when a royal stool is occupied by an enrobed monarch sitting in state.

African rulers, whatever the size of their kingdoms or the extent of their power, tended to share certain common themes in the exercise of their rule. They claimed ownership of the land with rights to tribute, but at the same time they were responsible for the well-being of their people and carried out ceremonies on their subjects' behalf. The king, set apart from the people, lived in an elaborate establishment, attended by servants, wives and notables. These features, reflected in regalia, enhanced the ruler's image as an awe-inspiring figure. The degree of elaboration of the regalia was generally in direct proportion to the size, wealth, influence and political complexity of each kingdom.

The characteristic properties of African regalia include the use of rare or precious materials, usually durable and often lustrous or refractory, for example copper, bronze,

95. King Njoya of Bamum (*reg c.* 1887–1924) on his royal throne; from a photograph by Marie-Pauline Thorbecke, 1912

silver, gold, ivory, shells and beads. Cast-copper alloys, such as bronze and brass, were fashioned into royal jewellery, crowns, ceremonial weapons, implements, vessels and even stools and memorial royal portraits, especially among the ancient kingdoms of Ife and Benin in what is now Nigeria. In the Asante kingdom of Ghana a similar purpose has been served by worked gold, which was customarily reserved for the exclusive use of the ruling hierarchy. Cast or hammered, it was fabricated as embellishment for most items of regalia and sometimes for royal portrait masks. Ivory, a royal prerogative and favoured material in Benin, was fashioned into kingly portrait masks, worn at the hip by the monarch, or into royal zoomorphic aquamaniles, used for the ritual washing of the king's hands. In the Yoruba kingdoms of south-west Nigeria, elaborately carved ivory bracelets and ceremonial swords were signs of kingship. For centuries shells and beads have adorned the intricately worked and richly embellished state vestments and royal drums of the king of the Kuba peoples of Zaïre. Elaborate beaded decoration of royal garments, thrones and hand-held regalia is characteristic of other African kingdoms as well, especially those of the Cameroon Grassfields. Special textiles, animal skins or woven mats may also comprise part of a king's regalia. Several iconographic themes are prominently incorporated into African regalia design, particularly depictions of the elephant and leopard, whose formidable strength and courage make them suitable visual metaphors for the monarch. As such, they may be represented interchangeably with images of the king. In regalia their tusks, pelts, teeth, claws and other characteristic features are used to symbolize the king's power. Certain stylistic devices were commonly employed in the design of regalia to enhance the powerful image of the leader and were based on the principles of physical elevation, protection and extension.

The quantity, quality and elegance of all royal artistic expressions, used to glorify the ruler and sanction his reign, reflected the power of the king and the extent of his kingdom. African items of regalia function on several different levels. Aesthetically they are superbly crafted, dramatic and dazzling, but they can also be chronicles of historical events serving to recall and validate a king's right to rule. They may embody the meaning of religion, the history of statehood and the interpretation of cosmology and ethics. Items of regalia form part of a totality, and it is through the presentation of the panoply as a whole, in its intimate association with the person of the ruler, that its full impact can be perceived.

(ii) Elevation. The elevation of the ruler was intended to emphasize his or her exalted status and to proclaim his or

her royal power and grandeur. Thrones and stools dominate this category, but such other items of regalia as palanquins, cushions, sandals or even animal skins spread upon the ground also heighten and validate the ruler's position of leadership by separating him or her from the ground.

Among the most celebrated objects of regalia in Africa is the Golden Stool of the Asante (*see* ASANTE AND RELATED PEOPLES, fig. 1). A sacred symbol of kingship surrounded by myth and legend, it is considered to embody the soul of the Asante nation. The Golden Stool, with its elaborately curved seat and central supporting pedestal, is made of solid gold. Attached to the stool are other items of regalia, which include gold effigies of defeated enemies cast in the form of bells, along with two brass bells, a gold bell and precious beads. The stool rests on its own specially decorated throne, which in turn is placed on an elephant skin. On great public occasions the stool is carried in procession or is displayed resting on its side on its special chair under a splendid umbrella that shelters both the stool and the Asantehene as he sits in state beside it.

An elaborate type of beaded throne was the most significant item of regalia among the Bamum of the Cameroon Grassfields during the reign of King Njoya (*c.* 1887–1924). The complex anthropomorphic and zoomorphic iconography of the Bamum thrones expresses the essence of Bamum kingship, as they figuratively as well as literally elevate the monarch (see fig. 95). Two important beaded thrones from Njoya's reign survive today; one remains in the Bamum capital of Foumbam, the other is in the Museum für Völkerkunde, Berlin (*see* BAMUM, fig. 2). Their design, size, structure, materials and iconography are similar, although the former example is the older of the two, having been part of the regalia of Njoya's father and predecessor, King Nsangu. Both these large wooden thrones are intricately carved with multiple images and are covered by a solid overlay of beads arranged in complex polychrome designs. Their structure combines a cylindrical stool with carved base, two human figures that form the backrest, and a raised rectangular footrest surmounted by two figures with flintlock guns, one at each end. A dense mosaic of cowrie shells covers the tops of the stool and the footrest. Carved in openwork on the stool base are intertwined double-headed serpents, emblems of Bamum kingship reserved for the king's exclusive use. Carved in openwork on the footrest are five dancing figures. The male and female figures on the back and the warriors and dancers on the footrest represent the retainers and guardians of the king.

(iii) Protection. Items of regalia that enhance the image of a ruler and dazzle the populace may at the same time disguise, veil, shelter and protect the royal personage. These include garments that enshroud or envelop the wearer in massive folds or heavy and rigid materials, as well as veiled crowns, headdresses, umbrellas, canopies and even palace architecture. Beaded and veiled crowns, worn by all the Yoruba kings for example, exalt the ruler by their splendour while simultaneously shielding the king's face from public view (*see also* YORUBA). They serve as supreme royal attributes and are a symbol of the highest aspirations of Yoruba traditional civilization. Claiming

96. Ademuwagun Adesida II (*reg* 1957–76), Yoruba ruler of Akure, Nigeria, in his state robes and beaded crown; from a photograph by Eliot Elisofon, 1959

descent from Oduduwa, the mythic father of the Yoruba who initiated the wearing of the beaded crown, rulers of each of the Yoruba states have continued to wear them. The crowns are generally high and cone-shaped and are fully covered with beads of many colours in designs that represent a human face, birds, flowers, crosses and abstract interlace patterns (see fig. 96; see also fig. 55 above). The face on the front of the crown represents Oduduwa. Small representations of birds fashioned in the round and completely covered with beads are sewn on to the sides or sometimes attached to the crown's summit. For the Yoruba, bird imagery refers to the vital force held and controlled by women, living or dead, who are collectively known as 'our mothers'. The birds on the crown signify that the king rules only with the protection and cooperation of the mothers. From every crown falls a veil made of strands of beads that cover the face of the wearer rendering him more awesome because he is unseen. The only face visible to a viewer looking upon the crowned king is the face of Oduduwa that is depicted on the crown. By masking the face of the king, the veiled crown removes him from the world of mortals and places him in a sacred realm.

Beaded apparel also figures prominently as regalia in other African kingdoms. In Benin, for example, the ceremonial costume of coral beads is the emblem and the essence of the Oba's office. Only he can own the royal coral beads, and he alone can wear the full beaded regalia consisting of mantle, headgear and jewellery. Strands of the tubular beads, of a rich orange-red colour, are woven into a full gown of reticulated mesh that envelops the Oba's body; a fully beaded crown with winged projections covers his head; and masses of beaded necklaces, as well as baldrics, belt and pendants, create a virtual armour of coral. The royal beads are not merely ornamental but confer upon their possessor the power of *ase*, the ability to bring to pass proclamations or prophecies. Similarly, the full state costume of the king of the Kuba people of Zaïre provides both a physical and metaphorical shield of protection around him. The royal costume is so heavily embellished with beads, cowrie shells and other precious materials that it weighs 84 kg (see Cornet, p. 246).

Other regalia that shelter a ruler are exemplified by state umbrellas or canopies, which are used at important ceremonial events, for great processions or when the king sits in state. For example, the enormous fringed and decorated umbrellas of the Asante kingdom are made locally of richly woven and beautifully coloured textiles, including silk, brocade, damask and *kente*, elegantly patterned strip-woven cloth. Each umbrella may be surmounted by a gold- or silver-leafed symbol representing a person, an animal, an object or a scene, which usually refers to a proverb. The Asantehene owns at least 23 state umbrellas, each of which is used for a particular occasion as a symbol of his office. The use of canopies as sheltering devices was also a feature of royal protocol in the kingdom of Toro in Uganda. Ceremonies of royal burial and coronation were marked by the lavish use of regalia, which included drums, animal skins, bracelets, anklets and barkcloth. Worn at his coronation, the king's crown and royal shoes, his robes of barkcloth decorated with fringes of beads and elephant hair, the beads around his ankles and his necklace of lions' claws were all symbolic of wealth, power and courage. For the coronation ceremony, royal musicians played gourd trumpets, drums and flutes, and under a sheltering canopy of barkcloths the chiefs lined up on either side to signify their loyalty to the king.

(iv) Magnification. Regalia sometimes serve to extend or magnify a ruler's aura of authority, both literally and figuratively. The literal extension of the royal dimensions can be accomplished through the use of hand-held implements that physically enlarge the holder by extending his range. More abstractly, regalia that represent or allude to the ruler, such as royal portrait figures, serve also to magnify the royal personage.

Among the regalia that literally and metaphorically extend the ruler's reach are sceptres, swords, spears, axes, fly-whisks and knives. Though derived from purely utilitarian forms, their elaboration and iconography transform these otherwise functional tools and weapons into symbolic emblems of prestige. Of crucial importance to the kings of Benin were hand-held regalia, such as the ceremonial sword called *ada*. Fashioned with a long, curved and decorated iron blade with an elaborate hilt of bronze or brass, the *ada* symbolized the Oba's right to take human life. By presenting the sword to a subordinate chief, the Oba could thus delegate to the recipient his power of life and death over his subjects.

In the Asante kingdom of Ghana, swords were second only to stools as the most important items of ceremonial regalia (*see* ASANTE, §3(iii)). There are six different types of swords among the regalia of the Asantehene, each used for a different ceremonial purpose. The typical state sword consists of a wide curved blade of iron with a hilt of carved wood encased in gold leaf. The handle of the hilt is flanked by two globular spheres that strengthen the wielder's grip. A cast-gold ornament, usually depicting an animal and often representing a proverb, adorns the scabbard of the sword and symbolizes the power of the king. The importance of the sword is shown by the fact that at the coronation or enstoolment of the Asantehene it is held by the ruler-elect as he takes the oath of office. Swords are also used by subordinate chiefs to swear allegiance to the king, and they are carried by messengers of the king on official errands. Staffs and fly-whisks serve similar functions among the Asante. Cast or plated with gold, they convey messages through their rich decoration and iconography. Staffs are carried by royal messengers to identify themselves as spokesmen for the king, and fly-whisks, their handles carved with symbols alluding to proverbs, are carried by rulers as objects of prestige.

Staffs of office are among the most important items of regalia among many other hierarchical societies in Africa, for example among the Luba of south-eastern Zaïre. From about the 17th century and up to the 19th Luba rulers affirmed their positions of power through the use of regalia consisting of ceremonial stools, staffs, spears, bowstands, axes, bowls, cups and other items, of which staffs were among the most important. At his investiture the king, seated on a carved and decorated caryatid stool, held a staff in his right hand while taking the oath of office. Besides that of the ruler, passed down the royal line from king to successor, staffs could also be owned by chiefs, counsellors and noblemen, but the degree of the staff's sculptural elaboration depended on the rank, financial means or aesthetic taste of its owner.

The elegantly carved female figure that often surmounts Luba staffs refers to the founding female ancestor who represents the spirit of all Luba kings and the extent of their power (see fig. 97). Further down the staff, flaring oval or lozenge-shaped sections punctuate the lines of the slender shaft. These sections are engraved with geometric designs representing women's scarification patterns, which encrypt mythical and lineage information and map ancient centres of political organization. Oral history and tradition are thus recorded on these emblems, while affirming the owner's ties to the Luba dynasty.

In addition to the physical extension of the ruler, figurative extension can be achieved by portrait figures that replicate and thus magnify the ruler's person. The great commemorative royal heads of bronze commissioned by Benin rulers to grace their ancestral altars served to glorify the ruling dynasty. Among the Kuba peoples of

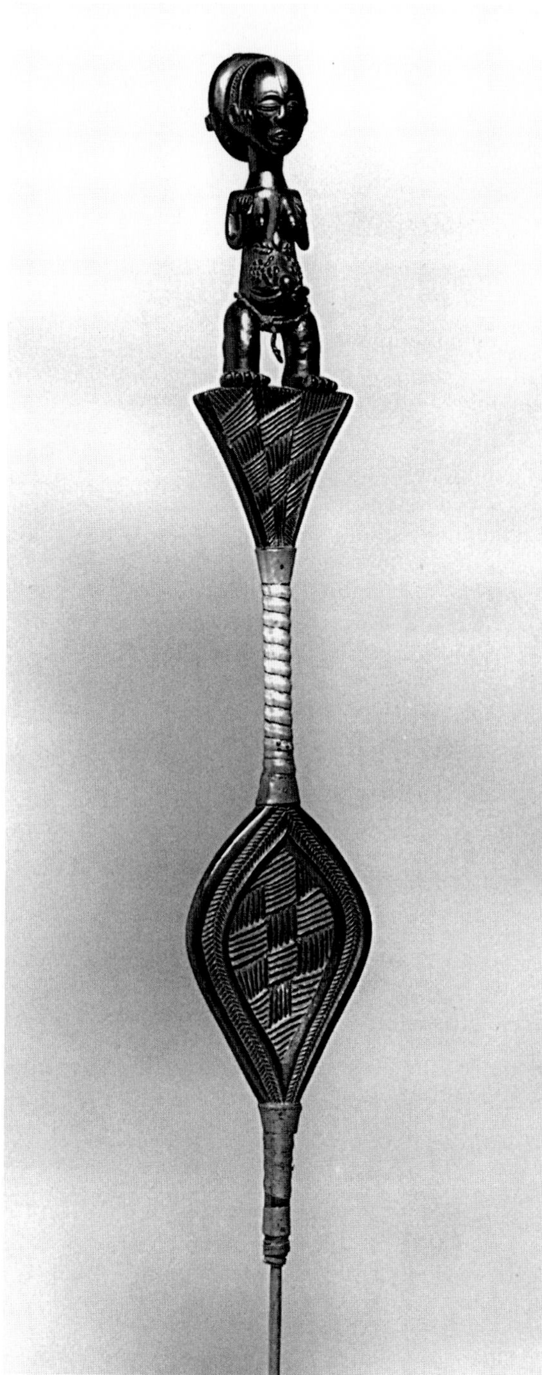

97. Luba staff of office, wood, metal, fibre and leather, h. 1.42 m (Toronto, private collection)

Zaïre the king maintained one of the most sumptuous of all African courts. Kuba regalia, consisting of portrait sculptures, drums, metalwork and textiles created by professional craftsmen, brilliantly expressed the wealth and power of the king and his court at Mushenge. Most important among the items of regalia were the *ndop* figures, or portrait statues of each reigning king, each carved with an identifying symbol associated with the ruler (*see also* KUBA (iii), §3). These figures functioned as effigies of past and existing rulers but also served as the vehicle for transferring the essence of kingship to the new king by means of a special ceremony of succession. Each king is portrayed seated cross-legged on a pedestal, resplendent in royal dress and regalia including bracelets, necklaces, belts and anklets, with a royal knife in his left hand. His form is symmetrical and contained, his expression calm and serene with an air of gravity. Before him is placed his personal emblem, or *ibol*, which distinguishes him from all others. Upon his enthronement, each king had a drum of office carved and elaborately decorated with copper, beads and cowrie shells. At the king's death, his drum and *ndop* figure were secreted in a storage room, to be brought out only for display on important occasions.

BIBLIOGRAPHY

A. Maesen: *Umbangu: Art du Congo au Musée royal du Congo belge* (Brussels, 1960)

A. A. Y. Kyerematen: *Panoply of Ghana* (London and Accra, 1964)

R. F. Thompson: 'The Sign of the Divine King: An Essay on Bead-embroidered Crowns with Veil and Bird Decorations', *Afr. A.*, iii/3 (1970), pp. 8–17, 74–80

D. Fraser and H. M. Cole, eds: *African Art and Leadership* (Madison, 1972)

Traditional Art of the Nigerian Peoples: The Milton D. Ratner Family Collection (exh. cat. by H. J. Drewal, Washington, DC, Mus. Afr. A., 1977)

The Arts of Ghana (exh. cat. by H. M. Cole and D. H. Ross, Los Angeles, UCLA, Wight A.G.; Minneapolis, MN, Walker A. Cent.; Dallas, TX, Mus. F.A.; 1977–8)

P. Ben-Amos: *The Art of Benin*, Tribal A. (London, 1980)

C. Geary: 'Bamum Thrones and Stools', *Afr. A.*, xiv/4 (1981), pp. 32–43

J. Cornet: *Art royal kuba* (Milan, 1982)

P. Ben-Amos and A. Rubin, eds: *The Art of Power, the Power of Art: Studies in Benin Iconography*, Mus. Cult. Hist. UCLA, Monograph Ser., xix (Los Angeles, 1983)

Princess Elizabeth of Toro: *African Princess: The Story of Princess Elizabeth of Toro* (London, 1983)

M. H. Nooter: *Luba Leadership Arts and the Politics of Prestige* (MA thesis, New York, Columbia U., 1984)

The Art of Cameroon (exh. cat. by T. Northern, Washington, DC, Smithsonian Inst. Traveling Exh. Serv., 1984)

T. F. Garrard: *Gold of Africa: Jewellery and Ornaments from Ghana, Côte d'Ivoire, Mali and Senegal in the Collection of the Barbier-Mueller Museum* (Munich, 1989)

M. H. Nooter: 'Secret Signs in Luba Sculptural Narrative: A Discourse on Power', *IA Stud. Afr. A.*, iii (1990), pp. 35–60

NANCY INGRAM NOOTER

7. DIVINATION INSTRUMENTS. The arts of divination are practised in a wide variety of African societies with a wide range of objects. An account of the divinatory process must be given before the objects themselves can be understood.

(i) Introduction. In most African societies where divination is practised it is a decision-making and problem-solving process rather than a fixed system of prediction. The future is not predetermined but can be influenced by human actions. Individuals or communities use divination to resolve problems ranging from the trivial to the cataclysmic: from finding a lost or stolen possession, deciding whom to marry, discovering how to cure an illness, to determining when and where to move a whole village during a drought. Moreover, in many African societies disease, otherwise unexplained deaths and other

98. Divination instruments of the Yoruba of south-west Nigeria, from left: Ifa tapper, ivory, h. 320 mm, 19th century (private collection); Ifa tray, wood, diam. 338 mm, *c.* 1920 (Los Angeles, University of California, Fowler Museum of Cultural History); Ifa bowl, wood, h. 273 mm, *c.* 1920 (private collection)

misfortunes are often attributed to neglected deities, offended ancestors or malevolent witches and sorcerers; a common goal of divination is therefore to identify the perpetrator and to divine a remedy. Solutions to the problem may range from a prescribed ritual sacrifice to execution of the identified guilty party.

The divination process is rarely straightforward and clearcut: interpretation by the diviner, or sometimes by his client, is generally required. Diviners typically undergo long periods of apprenticeship to religious specialists, since their role is to facilitate communication between the gods and the human world. Most African cultures practise some form of divination, and many practise several. Some diviners interpret the tracks of animals or the flights of birds, and others 'read' the entrails of animals. Poison oracles are employed by some societies to determine guilt, especially in instances of suspected murder: the suspect is administered the poison, and death or survival establishes the verdict. Spirit possession and dream analysis are also common means of gaining knowledge from the gods. In a few African cultures the divining process is embodied in a masquerade. Among the Bamana peoples of southern Mali, horizontal helmet masks of the Komo society feature an assemblage of such organic elements as antelope horns, porcupine quills and vulture feathers (*see* BAMANA, §2). These, along with an encrusted surface of sacrificial materials, bring power to the mask. Wearing a costume laden with amulets, and possessed by the powers of the mask, the dancer responds through song to questions posed prior to the performance. These songs are interpreted by the diviner.

Divination arts may be taken to include not only the manipulated objects discussed here but also the special ornaments and dress worn by the diviner, the containers for storing divining equipment and the charms and sculptures that are prescribed as remedies for various problems. Indeed, figurative sculpture representing ancestors, nature spirits and deities plays an important role in divination among many African peoples. These spirit forces and their corresponding sculptures are generally consulted by a diviner through possession trances or through dreams. In some cases only a limited range of problems is dealt with, but others are more far-ranging in their divinatory powers. Among the Yaka, Kongo and Songye of Zaïre, for example, figures with medicine bundles and charms are associated with divination. Among other objects that have been documented performing as oracles or otherwise involved in divination are Igbo terracottas, Ibibio shrine sculptures, Baga *elek* altars, Mende female figures, Kissi stone-carvings and Baule monkey and nature spirit images. The critical importance of divination is highlighted, however, by the large number of cultures that employ crafted instruments specifically for this purpose. These enhance the process aesthetically and bring prestige to the spirits and to the diviner.

(ii) Instruments. The best-studied and most artistically elaborate system of divination in Africa is that practised by the Yoruba of south-west Nigeria and known as Ifa. The focal object in the divination ensemble is a wooden tray with a smooth central surface framed by a band of relief carving (see fig. 98). The relief typically includes one or more faces of Eshu, the Yoruba trickster and messenger god (*see* §IV, 8 above). Other motifs depict a variety of sacrificial animals sacred to Ifa, equestrian figures, copulating couples and sometimes divination scenes. Simpler boards have geometric decoration, an interlace motif being common.

The Ifa divining process is begun by hitting the point of a wood, brass or ivory tapper against the tray to attract the attention of the gods. The tapper often features an image of a kneeling woman grasping her bare breasts in a gesture of supplication (see fig. 97 above). The tray is dusted with powdered wood and the diviner then repeatedly manipulates palm nuts to determine which one of sixteen set patterns to trace in the dust. Each pattern refers to a specific body of oral literature called *odu*. A repetition of this process determines another pattern that identifies one of sixteen sub-sections of the previously selected *odu*. These verses are then recited by the diviner. Usually the verses suggest rituals or sacrifices as solutions to the client's problem. The sacred palm nuts are stored in a cup with elaborately carved support figures such as female devotees, maternity figures, animals (especially roosters), and equestrian figures (see fig. 99). Larger containers and bowls, with many of the same motifs, may be used to store the entire assortment of divination instruments. Diviners also employ elaborately beaded bags displaying the face of Eshu to carry their equipment. All of these artefacts may be housed, possibly with additional sculpture, in an Ifa diviner's shrine.

A highly specific form of divination is found among the Guro, Yaure and Baule peoples of central Côte d'Ivoire. It employs field mice, whose proximity to the earth makes them ideal messengers of the ancestors and other spirits. A mouse is placed in the upper chamber of a two-tier wooden vessel (a hole connects the vessel's two chambers). This top chamber contains a small metal plate with ten thin, sticklike forms attached along one edge so they can pivot freely. The movements of the mouse in the chamber manipulate the sticks, and their resulting position is then interpreted by the diviner. The exterior surface of such vessels is sometimes embellished with representations of miniature masks or with figures carved in relief (*see* BAULE). These images are thought to be purely decorative, with no symbolic meaning.

Among the Kuba and related groups in central Zaïre friction oracles are commonly used to communicate with nature spirits; they are considered especially effective in identifying thieves, witches and adulterers. Generally the oracle is carved in the shape of a quadruped with a flat, polished area on its back. After dipping a wooden knob in oil, the diviner rubs it back and forth along the polished surface while reciting questions and possible answers. When the knob sticks firmly to the oracle, the correct answer has been reached. Warthogs and crocodiles are favoured decorative motifs, because they are closely associated with nature spirits and are respected for their ability to communicate with them. Dogs and elephants are also common and are thought to have special clairvoyant powers. Some friction oracles have a human head facing upwards on one or both ends, possibly referring to a revered ancestor or diviner.

Among the Luba, Hemba and Tabwa in south-eastern Zaïre carved figures attached to gourds were employed in divination. These figures were associated with the Buhabo secret society and were especially useful in determining cures for illness. The images are typically female, truncated at the waist and grasping their breasts. In some instances an ensemble of snail shells and animal skins, rather than a gourd, was tied to the base of the figures. In either case, a hole was drilled through the full length of the carving, which was either filled with medicines or left open so that small objects could be dropped through the head of the figure during the divination process. The Luba also use a rectangular block of wood with a hole in the centre and surmounted by a carving of a human head. Both the diviner and his client insert the first finger of their right hand into the hole and move the oracle back and forth on the ground or occasionally on a neckrest, which may also be carved with one or two caryatid figures. In order to identify an ancestor who has brought illness or misfortune to his client, the diviner interrogates the oracle, and when the pattern of movement changes abruptly the answer has been given.

The principal art form involved in divination among the Yaka of western Zaïre is a wooden slit-drum with a handle carved in the shape of a human head, sometimes two-faced. The drum serves multiple functions: it is used to announce the diviner's visits to other villages and as a stool; medicines prescribed by the divination process are prepared within it, and the client may subsequently drink from it. In some areas a male and female pair of slit-drums are played by the client and the diviner respectively as part of the consultation. Elaborately embellished slit-drums are also employed in divination by many neighbours of the Yaka, including the Suku, Mbala, Kongo, Holo and Pende. The Pende also use an unusual divination instrument called *galukoshi* (*see* PENDE, fig. 2).

Among the Chokwe peoples of northern Angola and adjacent parts of Zaïre, baskets containing an elaborate complex of up to 60 objects, including carved figures, are employed in divination. After shaking a pair of double rattles to remove evil forces, the diviner chants to enlist the participation of ancestral spirits. The basket is then shaken firmly, and the diviner interprets the specific meaning of each object in relation to its position in the basket. Carved images in such ensembles may include a headless figure representing a warrior killed in battle and a copulating couple. If the headless figure comes to rest on the edge of the basket, it indicates that the patient is troubled by the spirit of someone who has suffered a violent death. If the copulating-couple figure falls on the edge of the basket it could mean that the mother of one of the client's wives is causing trouble. Other small carvings, each with its own significance, include a woman carrying a load, a crying girl, a strong man, four people on a road, a gourd, a phallus, a neckrest and miniature masks. Elsewhere in Zaïre, the Songye and Holo have their own systems of divination involving various natural and carved objects that are tossed and read by the diviner.

The Senufo of northern Côte d'Ivoire and southern Mali also employ a combination of manmade and natural objects, which are thrown on the ground in front of the diviner and interpreted. The divination instruments include an assortment of human and animal images made of iron, brass and wood as well as non-figurative symbolic objects in various materials and such organic items as seeds, shells, and the teeth and horns of animals. Particularly important in Senufo divination are large forged iron and cast-brass bracelets in the form of a python, a primordial creature and principal messenger of the spirits.

Although these bracelets are particularly emblematic of the diviner's role, they are rarely worn but decorate the diviner's shrine or are kept beside him during consultations with clients. Also critical to the process is a pair of male and female figures representing bush spirits. These are placed facing the diviner, and an assortment of divining objects is tossed between them. The figures are thought to relate messages from the spirits to the diviner. These small carvings (h. 150–200 mm) include some of the most accomplished of all Senufo wood sculpture. Senufo divination sculpture also frequently includes a small equestrian figure that further evokes the power of the spirits and embellishes the visual display.

BIBLIOGRAPHY

L. Tucker: 'Divining Baskets of the Ovimbundu', *J. Royal Anthropol. Inst. GB & Ireland*, lxx (1940), pp. 171–201

T. Thomas: 'Les Itombwa: Objets divinatoires sculptés conservés au Musée royal du Congo belge', *Congo-Tervuren*, vi/3 (1960), pp. 78–83

G. Park: 'Divination and its Social Context', *J. Royal Anthropol. Inst. GB & Ireland*, xciii/2 (1963), pp. 195–209

W. Bascom: *Ifa Divination: Communication between Gods and Men in West Africa* (Bloomington, 1969)

R. F. Thompson: *Black Gods and Kings: Yoruba Art at UCLA* (Los Angeles, 1971/*R* Bloomington, 1976)

A. Hauenstein: 'L'Oracle à souris des Baoule de la Côte d'Ivoire', *Bull. Annu., Mus. Ethnog.* [Geneva], xv (1972), pp. 9–34

M. de Areia: 'Le Panier divinatoire de Tskokwe', *A. Afrique Noire*, xxvi (1978), pp. 30–44

P. McNaughton: *Secret Sculptures of Komo: Art and Power in Bamana (Bambara) Initiation Associations*, Working Pap. Trad. A., 4 (Philadelphia, 1979)

D. Biebuyck: '*Buhabo* Statues from the Benembaho (Bahoma)', *Africa-Tervuren*, xxvii/1 (1981), pp. 18–31

A. J. Glaze: *Art and Death in a Senufo Village*, Trad. A. Africa (Bloomington, 1981), pp. 54–72

J. Mack: 'Animal Representations in Kuba Art: An Anthropological Interpretation', *Oxford A. J.*, iv (1981), pp. 50–60

A. Bourgeois: 'Mukoku Ngoombu: Yaka Divination Paraphernalia', *Afr. A.*, xvi/3 (1983), pp. 56–9, 80

M. T. Drewal and H. J. Drewal: 'An Ifa Diviner's Shrine in Ijebuland', *Afr. A.*, xvi/2 (1983), pp. 60–67, 99–100

Igbo Arts: Community and Cosmos (exh. cat. by H. M. Cole and C. C. Aniakor, Los Angeles, UCLA, Mus. Cult. Hist., 1984–6), pp. 72–4

DORAN H. ROSS

8. Musical instruments.

(i) Introduction. (ii) Types.

(i) Introduction. Music forms an integral part of African life-cycle celebrations, festivals and rituals, as well as providing entertainment. Instruments are played solo, with vocal accompaniment or in ensembles. Four categories are represented: chordophones (instruments such as harps and zithers, in which a vibrating string produces the sound), membranophones (in which a vibrating membrane produces the sound, as with various kinds of drum), aerophones (in which the sound is produced by the passage of air, as with flutes, trumpets or reed instruments) and idiophones (a less precisely defined category that includes rattles, gongs, cymbals and *mbira*, a sub-category of instruments made of wooden or metal strips arranged flat on a soundboard and often mounted on a resonator). A variety of materials are used, including ivory and metal, but wooden instruments are by far the most numerous. Although both women and men may play, some instruments, such as the harp and the *mbira*, are the exclusive domain of men. While music has a central role in many African cultures, it is not only the sounds produced by the instrument that are important. A musician may be admired, for example, for the dexterity with which his fingers move on the keyboard of the *mbira*, creating a pattern that is itself perceived as a decorative motif. The aesthetic qualities of the instruments as objects are also important and are believed to reinforce the power of the player, both in enhancing his communication with the worlds of the spirits and of the ancestors and in signifying his status and prestige.

Instruments are commonly made by their players, who may also be responsible for their ornamentation, although if highly wrought decoration is required the player may enlist the help of a professional carver or blacksmith. The importance and extent of visual considerations in the design of instruments vary greatly; some are decorated with simple designs and abstract ornament, while others are elaborate sculptural objects in themselves. Generally, the immediately Sub-Saharan and Central African regions are particularly rich in such highly sculpted instruments, as are areas in Tanzania and Zambia, but examples of finely sculpted instruments may also be found in other areas, where two-dimensional abstract ornamentation is more usual. These sculptural objects are sometimes held in particularly high esteem for their value within a far-reaching system of symbolism, in which, for example, the instrument can also be designated as male or female (according to its pitch) or in which parts of the instrument may represent some aspect of social structure or illustrate some belief. Among the Dogon, according to one disputed interpretation (see Griaule and Dieterlen), for example, different parts of an instrument, such as the concave portion of a *gingiru*'s resonator, may symbolize the vault of the sky as opposed to the resonator itself, symbolizing the earth, and the inside of the trough, symbolizing the atmosphere. The four strings may refer to the four cardinal points. In the *ngombi* (harp) of the Bwiti (a religious cult found among the Fang of Gabon), the complementarity of male and female is translated into the parts of the harp: the resonator symbolizes the womb and the neck male virility, so that the junction of the two signifies sexual union. In this it repeats both the structure of a Bwiti chapel, which is divided into male and female halves, and the equal participation of men and women in the Bwiti cult (see 1989 exh. cat.). Furthermore, the harp can be seen to unite the microcosmic world of the living and the macrocosmic world of the gods and ancestors.

(ii) Types. Those instruments that can be claimed to be three-dimensional sculptural works fall readily into two principal categories—zoomorphic and anthropomorphic—with a third, minor category that comprises object-forms. The present discussion will limit itself to anthropomorphization only. The instruments that bear anthropomorphic representations show variations on the human theme ranging from the exquisite naturalism of a figure surmounting an instrument to the humanization of the instrument's abstract form (see figs 99 and 100). In some instances, the sculptor has sought with extravagant ingenuity to bend and subordinate (or integrate) the entire instrument to a recognizable human shape. The importance of this humanization probably derives from the symbolism these objects may bear: some Africans view

99. Kissi slit-gong, wood, h. 515 mm, from Guinea (Paris, Musée de l'Homme)

them as amplifications or extensions of the performer's soul and body and use terms of human anatomy to describe parts of the instruments; the sounds themselves are also characterized in terms of the human voice (see Laurenty).

(a) Chordophones. Examples of the total anthropomorphization of an instrument are remarkable but rare, even among peoples with strong traditions of figurative sculpture such as the Fang of Gabon and the Chokwe of Angola. There seems to be a concentration of fully anthropomorphized harps among the Mangbetu and the Nbaka in north-eastern Zaïre, an area also noted for incorporating the human figure in *mbira*, vessels and bark storage boxes for honey. In such harps, either the elongated neck of the harp ends in a finely carved head, with two flexed legs supporting the torso, which serves as the resonator, or the neck of the harp is carved as a complete human figure; one rare example (Zurich, Mus. Rietberg) presents a neck carved as a hermaphrodite figure with two

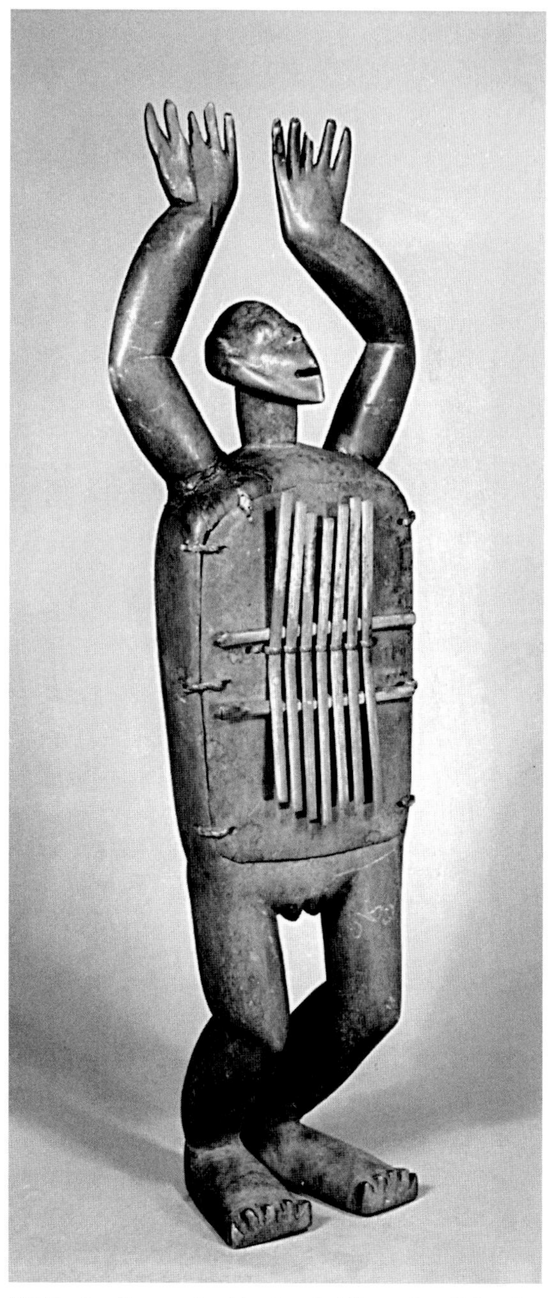

100. Zande *mbira*, wood and bamboo, h. 660 mm, from Uele region, Zaïre, collected 1908 (Tervuren, Koninklijk Museum voor Midden-Afrika)

finely modelled heads. Among the Nbaka three styles of harp stand out: the first is characterized by a prominent head, clearly defined facial features and flexed legs (see 1989 exh. cat., p. 86); the second is defined by a small head at the end of an elongated neck, and with straight legs (see 1989 exh. cat., p. 87); and the third style is characterized by a heart-shaped face on which the nose is only suggested by line, an enlarged rectangular cavity for the torso and short legs. The stylistic characteristics of this third group are shared by the Mongo, Ngombe and Ngbandi of Zaïre.

(b) Membranophones and aerophones. Examples of fully anthropomorphized membranophones include two monumental Luba-Kasai drums from Zaïre (Berlin, Mus. Vlkerknd.). Among the Bete of Côte d'Ivoire, some drums assume the form of a human torso. Stylistically, these are recognizable by linear bands around the waist, a prominent navel, scarification and stout legs, or by the navel only, with legs that have been reduced to an openwork support (see 1989 exh. cat., fig. 45).

Trumpets and horns are not commonly carved into a human figure, but such representations are found on megaphones or voice disguisers from Congo, Zaïre and Sudan. A few such examples have also been found in Sierra Leone, where such instruments belonged to the men's secret society known as Ghbandi. These instruments could not be seen by women or non-members and were only occasionally brought out for performance before members (see Hart, pp. 49–51). Some fully anthropomorphized examples of such instruments present the human figure in striking and significant poses. The hands, for example, may appear clasped against the back of the head, raised straight along the sides of the head, extended down along the sides of the torso or placed against the abdomen. Such positions recall for some Congolese peoples the classic poses of mourning, bewilderment or prayer (see 1981–2 exh. cat., pp. 74, 225). Among the Bembe of the Congo some of these instruments are carved in groups as a 'family' (father, mother, daughter and son), among the Dondo of Zaïre as female figures; among the Bongo of the Sudan at least one splendid human figure has been found with a face conveying an expression of awe (Rome, Mus. N. Preist. & Etnog., no. 29604). Whistles are particularly well suited to the human figure, many examples being found in Western Sudan and Central Africa, two regions particularly rich in sculpture where realism and abstraction are found side by side.

(c) Idiophones. Among idiophones, anthropomorphization of wooden slit-gongs (slit-drums) is prevalent among the Bamana of Mali, the Kissi of Guinea, the Dan of Côte d'Ivoire and the peoples of the Cameroon Grassfields. They range in size from small to monumental: the small slit-gongs are hand-held and serve as emblems for members of secret societies or associations, while the monumental slit-gongs often provide a focal point in community events. In style, the slit-gongs range from stylization of the human form to naturalistic representations. Indeed, in the case of one Dan instrument it has been argued that not merely naturalism but even portraiture is involved (see 1976 exh. cat., pp. 117, 120). Conversely, the slit-gongs of the Kissi are highly stylized: a long cylinder forming the bust terminates at the bottom in a cylindrical-conical base and is topped by a crescent coiffure. The figures, arms and hands are simply indicated by engraved lines (see fig. 99). In the Cameroon Grassfields, monumental slit-gongs carved with human-like figures at their top are kept in or near the palace. None of the older Bamum slit-gongs has survived, but smaller examples embodying the same theme are commonly found in the Grassfields region and span a broad spectrum of human forms, from the bold forms of the Mambila (e.g. Paris, Mus. Homme) to the stark, angular and expressive forms of the Bamileke (Berlin, Mus. Vlkerknd.). Monumental slit-gongs are found also among the Baule of Côte d'Ivoire and among the M'Bembe of Nigeria, who are noted for adorning either one or both ends of their slit-gongs with large figures called *idoro.* While only two such M'Bembe slit-gongs are known (Berlin, Mus. Vlkerknd.), several of the end-figurative sculptures survive (e.g. Paris, Mus. N.A. Afr. & Océan.). Both the fragments and the complete slit-gongs attest to a wide stylistic range, from naturalistic facial features, including scarification patterns, to abstraction and minimalization of features. Human figures can also be found adorning miniature slit-gongs among the Kongo groups (Vili, Yombe, Sundi). Not only do they have the fluid lines, attention to detail and fine execution of facial features characteristic of Kongo art but they also demonstrate unusual dynamism in the poses of the figures: kneeling with hands tied behind the back, standing in a group of four figures with knees bent and hand to abdomen, and seated with right knee raised and left leg stretched out (e.g. Rotterdam, Mus. Vlkenknd.).

Mbira and wooden bells from north-eastern Zaïre reflect the sculptural ideas familiar from the chordophones of the same region. In the case of examples of *mbira* of the Zande an entire woman's torso becomes the sounding chamber. A unique Zande bell is carved with swelling forms that might allude to a skirt, with semicircular handles as stylized arms and with two clappers suggesting the figure's legs (Antwerp, Etnog. Mus.). In the Lower Congo region there is an impressive diversity of very fine bells topped by figures in various positions: standing, kneeling, crouching and sitting. These are part of the paraphernalia of the *nganga* (healer).

Anthropomorphism may also be expressed in three other ways besides the above examples of full figurative representation. First, a full human figure may crown or support the instrument and may be depicted in high or low relief on its surface. As in African sculpture generally, these figures may assume a number of positions to which significance is often attached. Such sculptures are said 'to symbolize life and spirit in patterned sound' (see 1989 exh. cat., p. 39). Second, but less commonly, a pair of figures may appear facing each other on either side of the instrument. Finally, a single part of the human body, such as head, nose, mouth or phallus, may be incorporated into the instrument's design (this treatment tends to be restricted to drums, whistles and slit-gongs). The most frequently depicted feature is not surprisingly the head, the apparent seat of speech and sound. In some exceptional instances, such as bells from the Lower Niger and among the Kuba, as well as Senufo *mbira*, the instrument as a whole assumes the form of a human head.

BIBLIOGRAPHY

Grove Instr.
E. M. von Hornbostel and C. Sachs: 'Systematik der Musikinstrumente: Ein Versuch', *Z. Ethnol.* xlvi (1914), pp. 553–90
S. Chauvet: *Musique nègre* (Paris, 1929)
M. Griaule and G. Dieterlen: 'La Harpe-luth des Dogon', *J. Soc. Africanistes*, xx (1950), pp. 209–28
J. Laurenty: *Les Cordophones du Congo Belge et du Ruanda-Urundi*, 2 vols (Tervuren, 1960)
K. Krieger: *Westafrikanische Plastik*, 3 vols, Veröff. Mus. Vlkerknd., Berlin, n. s. 7, Abt. Afrika (Berlin, 1965–9) [col. cat.]
Sculptures africaines dans les collections publiques françaises (exh. cat., Paris, Mus. Orangerie, 1972)
H. Kamer: *Ancêtre Bembe* (Paris, 1974)
Die Kunst der Dan (exh. cat. by E. Fischer and H. Himmelheber, Zurich, Mus. Rietberg, 1976; Eng. trans. and rev., Zurich, 1984)
P. Berliner: *The Soul of Mbira* (Berkeley, 1978)
Oggetti e riti: Strumenti dell' Africa (exh. cat., Rome, Mus. N. Preist. & Etnog., 1980)
The Four Moments of the Sun: Kongo Art in Two Worlds (exh. cat. by R. F. Thompson and J. A. Cornet, Washington, DC, N.G.A., 1981–2)
Praise Poems: The Katherine White Collection (exh. cat., Seattle, WA, A. Mus., 1984)
W. A. Hart: 'Wood Carving of the Limba of Sierra Leone', *Afr. A.*, xxiii/1 (1989), pp. 44–53
Sounding Forms: African Musical Instruments (exh. cat., ed. M.-T. Brincard; New York, Amer. Fed. A., 1989)
African Reflections: Art from Northeastern Zaire (exh. cat. by E. Schildkrout and C. Keim, New York, Amer. Mus. Nat. Hist., 1990)
E. de Dampierre: *Harpes Zande*, Domaine Musicologique (Paris, 1991)

MARIE-THÉRÈSE BRINCARD

9. ARMS AND SHIELDS. African craftsmen have made many types of refined and elaborate weapons, including bows and arrows, knives, swords, spears, axes, clubs and firearms as well as a peculiarly African weapon, the throwing knife. Many of these are notable for their fine proportions, shapes and workmanship but still remain functional, while others may be elaborated or embellished to the extent that they can no longer serve the original purpose of their type, becoming instead identifying emblems and often serving as symbols of leadership and prestige. This is increasingly the case as weapons incorporating Western technology become more prevalent. Particularly in Central Africa, knives and other weapons were traded extensively, sometimes serving as forms of currency. This has made it difficult, if not impossible, in many instances to identify a specific form with a single ethnic group. One example is the throwing knife, designed to be thrown at human or animal targets and with an effective range of 20–30 m. This consists of a stem, which serves as the handle and is usually covered with fibre or skin, and two or more branching blades (see fig. 101). This multi-bladed design is unique and has allowed for an astonishing variety of shapes. Throwing knives are common over a wide area from Sudan to Gabon and the Zaïre River basin and are the African weapon most likely to be collected by Westerners.

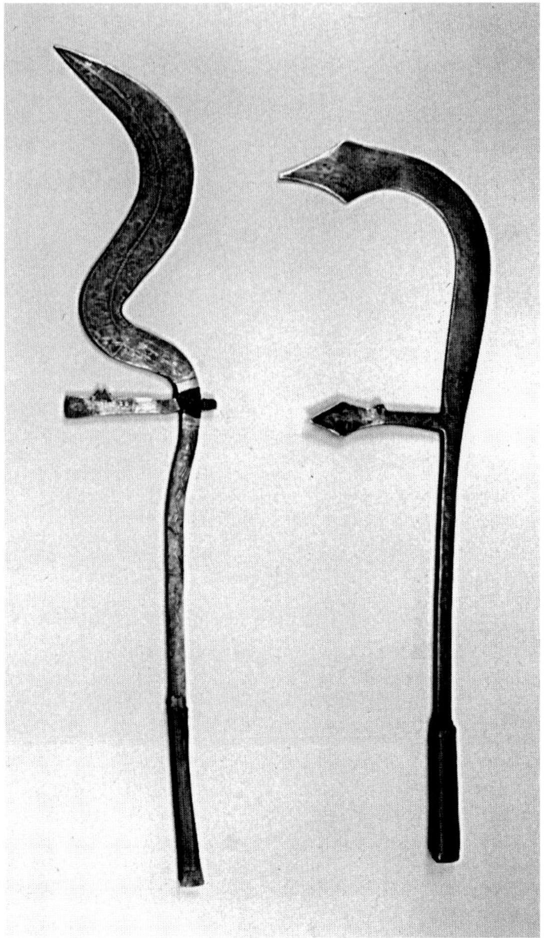

101. Ingessana throwing knives, metal, max. l. 830 mm, from Blue Nile Province, Sudan (London, British Museum)

Knife and sword blades are also found in a seemingly endless variety of shapes and sizes. Blades may be punctuated with openwork or, more commonly, incised, usually with linear and frequently asymmetric patterns. Among several Central African peoples, blades are divided into dark and light areas: the dark side is carbonized steel, a result of the forging process, while the light area is cleaned by abrasion after forging. In other cases, blades may be inlaid with, or may be made entirely from, precious metal such as copper. In some areas brass tacks, wire or thin strips of metal, gold ornaments, fur, reptile or animal skin often decorate wooden hilts, adding to a knife's prestige value. Handles may also be carved in figural forms or made from precious materials such as ivory or copper. In some areas knives and swords have assumed purely ceremonial functions. In the Nigerian kingdom of Benin, for example, a royal sword formerly used by the king's executioner is now carried in front of the king as a symbol of his right to take a human life, while in Ghana's Asante confederacy, swords, often with openwork patterns on the blades, were carried by envoys of the paramount chief as a symbol of their authority (*see* ASANTE AND RELATED PEOPLES, fig. 2). Among the Kuba of Zaïre, decorated wooden versions of the *ikula*, a knife with a leaf-shaped blade, serve as insignia of royalty or as indications of rank within the hierarchy of Kuba society. Axes too may serve several functions within a single culture. Among the Shona of Zimbabwe, for example, axes are not only weapons and tools but also part of the paraphernalia of spirit mediums and healers, as well as a symbol of resistance to colonial rule.

The shapes of blades vary with the area of origin: those from south-eastern Africa, for example, are shaped like half-moons with single tangs, while those of northern Nigeria are crescent-shaped with two places at which the blades fit into the shafts. Spears, either the light, throwing type or the heavier, longer, stabbing variety, are perhaps the most common traditional weapon in Africa. In some areas they are among the accoutrements of traditional dress for some social groups. When young Maasai men become warriors, for example, they are expected to carry their hunting spears at all times. Elsewhere spears may become exclusively display items through the intricate wrapping or decoration of the shaft, usually with metal strips or wire, or by elaboration of the spearhead. Among the Tutsi of Rwanda, for instance, such usually non-functional spears were carried as part of ordinary male attire. The spearheads of the Tutsi are known for their intricacy, often consisting of multiple points or multiple twists in the metal, a sign of skilled craftsmanship, adding to the spear's value.

Most bows and arrows, clubs and throwing sticks are in standard shapes and are undecorated. Exceptions include the arrows used by the Mangbetu in Zaïre, which have geometric relief patterns on the shafts; the fighting sticks made by the Turkana of Kenya, which are studded with nails or inlaid with wire; and Zulu clubs from South Africa, called knobkerries by Westerners, which are made from wood or rhinoceros horn and wrapped with elephant hair or wire in decorative patterns. Certain types of bracelets and rings with sharpened edges found among the pastoralist peoples of southern Sudan and northern Kenya and Uganda are also notable. These 'fighting' or 'razor' bracelets and rings are generally not meant for warfare but rather for spontaneous fights among men within the community. Although not indigenous to Africa, rifles and pistols are made by blacksmith specialists using both imported and locally made parts. Like simpler weapons, these too are sometimes embellished with such decorations as metal tacks or inlay.

Shields offer effective protection from all of these weapons except firearms and may be large enough to cover and protect the body or much smaller, affording greater visibility and mobility for the shield holder but necessitating quick reflexes and agility. A variety of shapes and materials can be found. The round hide shields of some peoples in Ethiopia, Somalia and Sudan have elaborate decoration, which includes not only patterns embossed into the hide but also additions of velvet and metal bosses and strips. Many of the latter are apparently made for display rather than serving as functional defensive weapons. Further south, the Maasai and the Zulu traditionally used colour and pattern both to decorate their elliptical hide shields and to identify the age grades or regiments of their owners, their ranks and their deeds of bravery. Maasai shields are painted in white, black and red, while those of the Zulu are fur-covered skins in particular colours and patterns. In the forest areas of Central Africa finely and tightly worked basketry shields, sometimes with painted decoration or coloured fibres, or wooden shields, sometimes covered with cane or other fibres, are more typical.

BIBLIOGRAPHY

P. R. McNaughton: 'The Throwing Knife in African History', *Afr. A.*, iii/2 (1970), pp. 54–60, 89
W. Fischer and M. A. Zirngibl: *African Weapons: Knives, Daggers, Swords, Axes, Throwing Knives* (Passau, 1978) [Ger. & Eng. text]
T. Northern: *The Ornate Implement* (Hanover, NH, 1981)
M. A. Zirngibl: *Seltene afrikanische Kurzwaffen/Rare African Short Weapons* (Grafenau, 1983)
P. Westerdijk: *African Metal Implements: Weapons, Tools and Regalia* (Greenvale, 1984)
——: *The African Throwing Knife: A Style Analysis* (Utrecht, 1988)
C. Spring: *African Arms and Armour* (London and Washington, DC, 1993)

DIANE M. PELRINE

10. Currency, weights and measures. There is considerable documentary information regarding the means of exchange used by traders in Africa. The caravans of the Egyptian Cosmas Indicopleustes, for example, trading in the early 6th century AD, bought gold on the Upper Nile with iron and salt, which were used in commercial transactions until the 20th century. Other commercial arrangements included *troc muet* (Fr.: 'silent barter'), in which the two parties did not meet, but each in turn left his merchandise in a prearranged spot, although no description of the rules governing such arrangements has survived.

Local currencies, including red cloth and pieces of iron, are mentioned in medieval documents (including Arabic, Jewish and Italian). These sources more usually refer, however, to their authors' own monetary systems, even where these had no validity in the place where the transaction occurred. The Arabs introduced not only the dinar but also the mitkal, which was the equivalent of the dinar in weight, and they must also have introduced the use of cowries, which came from the Maldives *c.* AD 1000. During the 14th century, shells were used as coins of small value in the area within the great curve of the River Niger.

During the 15th century, as they gradually advanced along the Atlantic coast, the Portuguese took up the trading customs of the Arab world, which were well known to the indigenous peoples they encountered. The Portuguese effectively devoted themselves to cabotage (coastal trade), ferrying local products from one region to another, but, after trying to introduce their own currency, they resorted to using cloth and metals (in the form of bars and bracelets) and often replaced local forms of currency with others that they controlled, such as glass beads or cheap trading goods. Metal rods, for example, were replaced by copper or iron bars (*barriferi*), and the squares of raffia used and made in the Congo had to compete first with others made in regions controlled by the Portuguese, then with pieces of cotton fabric introduced mainly by Portuguese soldiers, who received their pay in this form. In the late 18th century, thalers issued under the Austrian sovereign Maria-Theresa began to appear in Ethiopia. These silver coins came to be used across Northern Africa and even as far as Ubangi, Zaïre. During the 19th century, the coins were transported by caravan from Tripoli to the lands of the Hausa. One of the great Nigerian traders, Malan Yavoh, intercepted one such caravan at the end of the 19th century and, by virtue of the trading routes he controlled, introduced the coin into commercial circulation. As with the other silver pieces in use, the thaler was often considered as a piece of jewellery and was evaluated purely on the basis of the quality of the metal it contained.

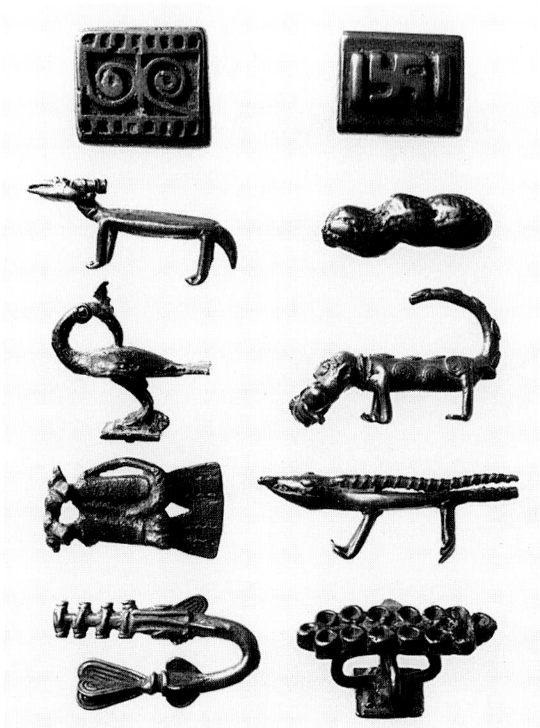

102. Brass weights for gold, Asante, Ghana, collected before 1930: (left, top to bottom) rectangular weight, 26×30 mm; antelope, l. 50 mm; Sankofa bird, l.35 mm; two men with heads placed side by side, l. 40 mm; sawfish, l.47 mm; (right, top to bottom) rectangular weight, 23×28 mm; peanut, l. 38 mm; leopard with porcupine in its jaws, l. 48 mm; crocodile swallowing mudfish, l. 75 mm; mancala game-board, l. 44 mm (Washington, DC, National Museum of Natural History)

Many other currencies have been used in Africa besides those adopted for trading purposes, but most of them have remained less well known. The oldest must have been the pierced shells of the Mauritania region, which may have been in use as early as the Neolithic age. Small copper crosses from *c.* 900 AD have been found in south-eastern Zaïre, and similar crosses of various sizes up to 250 mm in length continued to be used as currency from the Zambezi to the Kasai as late as the 20th century; trading caravans even disseminated them to the coast of Kenya to the east and that of Angola to the west. In this region, again *c.* 1000 BC, there were also strings of mollusc shell, which are still worked by older men among the Sakata. These currencies could include seeds, honey and drinks just as well as shells, stone or metal and were not constrained by any concern for durability, convenience or standardization: for example, although the strings of the Lega of Zaïre are all the same length, each varies slightly from every other. The same can be said of the metal rods used as currency, such as the *sompê* from central Côte d'Ivoire (which were very thin with flattened edges, varying from 180 mm to 250 mm in length), used by the Guro and the Malinke, and the *guinzé* of Guinea and Sierra Leone, with a twisted shaft, flattened edges and thickness varying from 250 mm to 800 mm, used by the Toma, the Kissi and the Mande.

Sometimes different currencies were used by a given people at the same time and for different types of payments. The function of these currencies was primarily ritual and social, with trading activities holding little importance for the societies concerned. Those using them often explained the value of such currencies in terms of their having been chosen by a founding ancestor, and indeed some of these coinages look similar to items of regalia, such as the *kul* of the Sara of Chad, which take the form of a miniature jet knife with two arms, 2 mm thick and 600 mm in length. In certain groups, the *kul* was the reference unit of value before the introduction of modern currency and was used alongside various iron ploughing tools (the crescent shaped *seme*), balls (*mbal*) or bars 200 mm to 500 mm in length and *c.* 2 mm in thickness. It was generally the village chief, the spokesperson for the founding ancestor, accompanied by the council of elders in whose keeping such items were stored, who took charge of the most important payments. These included marriage payments and the purchase of millet in case of food shortages. Payments were also made to the initiation priest or to the ancestors to help infertile women to conceive. This function of reinforcing social cohesion was also evident with the Kissi and the Toma: the *guinzé* were placed at the entrance to the village as a form of protection, or at the head of the tombs of heads of families; when one of their children left the village, they would take some *guinzé* with them and then replace them on their return.

There were fewer recognized currencies in the monarchies. Examples included the gold dust of the Asante kingdom, the *olivancillaria nana* or *n'zimbu* shells of the Kongo kingdom and the raffia squares and cowries of the Fon kingdom of Abomey. The entire range of a given kingdom's monetary usage is known only in a few cases, but the sovereigns exercised direct control over the production, entry into the kingdom and distribution of each currency. Each new dynasty may well have found the existing currency problematic, however, and for this reason it may have proved convenient to adopt means of exchange imported from abroad. A number of ancient currencies, impossible to dissociate from their ritual functions, can also be found decorating sculptures or masks in the form of jewellery, and all of these had a symbolic value. Imported products such as cowries or glass beads might be substituted for other, older local elements and could take on their names: thus cowries are still known as *n'zimbu* among the Kongo.

Weights and measures remained relative concepts in such societies. Some measures of length and volume served to evaluate certain types of currency, such as the cubit for valuing lengths of cotton, the string for beads or shellfish tests, the basket for *n'zimbu* and the gourd for grain. Weights appear to have been associated primarily with long-distance trade and could be made from stone, glass or seeds. They were used all along the trans-Saharan caravan routes and were all apparently calibrated in relation to the Arab unit of the mitkal. The other area to have produced a large number of weights, especially in brass, was the Akan in the forest regions of Ghana and Côte d'Ivoire. Here the weights were calibrated on the Arabic

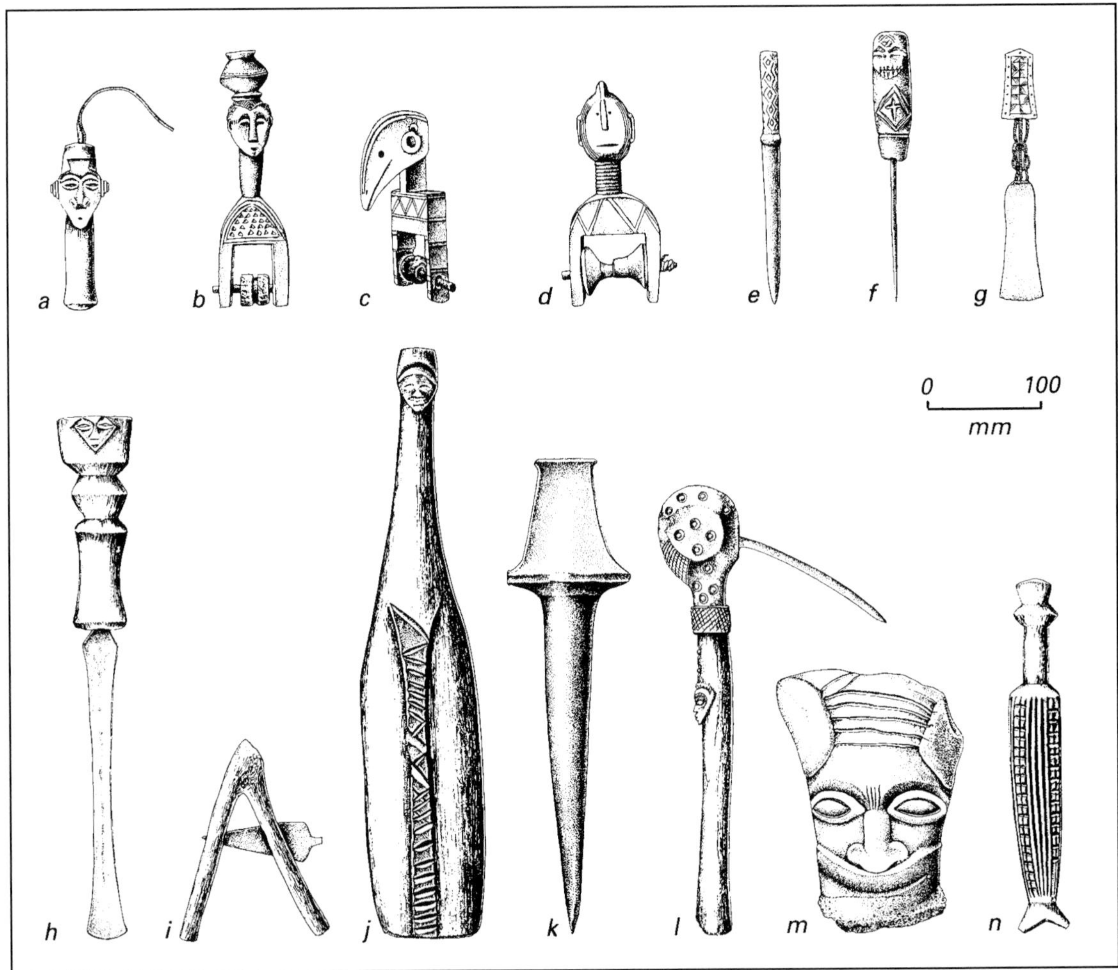

103. African tools and implements, 20th century unless otherwise stated: (a) Kuba bark scraper, wood and iron, h. 174 mm, from Zaïre; (b) Baule heddle pulley, wood, h. 210 mm, from Côte d'Ivoire; (c) Tura heddle pulley, wood, h. 155 mm, from Côte d'Ivoire; (d) Mossi heddle pulley, wood, h. 182 mm, from Burkina Faso; (e) Yombe weaving peg, wood, h. 201 mm, from Zaïre; (f) Kuba chasing chisel, wood and iron, h. 215 mm, from Zaïre; (g) Bushong (Kuba) razor, iron, h. 198 mm, from Zaïre; (h) Lulua chisel for palm-tree tapping, wood and iron, h. 414 mm, from Zaïre; (i) Lobo drawing knife, wood and iron, h. 163 mm, from Zaïre; (j) Gonge (Zande) clay paddle, wood, h. 470 mm, from Zaïre; (k) Mongo blacksmith's hammer, iron, h. 382 mm, from Zaïre; (l) Luba adze, wood and iron, h. 357 mm, from Zaïre; (m) Kissi twyer, soapstone, h. 210 mm, from Guinea, 19th century; (n) mallet, wood, h. 281 mm, from north-east Zaïre (Tervuren, Koninklijk Museum voor Midden-Afrika)

system in the northern regions and according to various European standards in the southern regions. They were closely linked with the trade in gold dust and played an important role in the families of the various kingdoms, where it appears that weight itself was of only relative importance. The decorations on these weights, using symbols associated with the different societies, were often considered to carry a coded message that guaranteed the value of the transaction (see fig. 102).

BIBLIOGRAPHY

M. M. Fischel: *Le Thaler de Marie-Thérèse: Etude de sociologie et d'histoire économique* (Paris, 1912)
P. Einzig: *Primitive Money in its Ethnological, Historical and Economic Aspects* (London, 1948)
E. Dartevelle: 'Les N'zimbu: Monnaie du royaume du Congo', *Bull. Soc. Royale Belge Anthropol. Préhist.*, n. s., 1, xliv (1953)
A. H. Quiggin: *A Survey of Primitive Money* (London, 1963)
M. Johnson: 'The Cowrie Currencies of West Africa', *J. Afr. Hist.*, xi/1 (1970), pp. 17–49; xi/2 (1970), pp. 331–53
A. Salifou: 'Malan Yavoh: Grand négociant du Soudan Central à la fin du XIXème siècle', *J. Soc. Africanistes*, xlii (1972), pp. 7–27
T. F. Garrard: *Akan Weights and the Gold Trade* (London, 1980)
R. Antoine: *L'Histoire curieuse des monnaies coloniales* (Nantes, 1986)
J. Cribb: *Money: From Cowrie Shells to Credit Cards* (London, 1986)
J. Hogendorn and M. Johnson: *The Shell Money of the Slave Trade*, Afr. Stud. Ser., xlix (Cambridge, 1986)
J. Rivallain: *Paléomonnaies africaines* (Paris, 1986)
F. A. Iroko: *Les Cauris en Afrique Occidentale du Xème au XXème siècle* (diss., U. Paris I, 1987)
M. Servet: 'La Monnaie contre l'Etat ou la fable du troc', *Droit et monnaie: Etats et espace monétaire transnational* (Lyon, 1988), pp. 49–62
J. Rivallain: *Poids akans à peser la poudre d'or: Collection Abel* (Paris, 1989)

JOSETTE RIVALLAIN

11. TOOLS AND IMPLEMENTS. The oldest known tools in the world are the African flaked cobbles and stone

flakes from *c.* 2.5 million years BC. From this time stone artefacts gradually became more elaborate. Acheulian tools, mainly hand axes, from *c.* 1.5 million years BC represent a remarkable intellectual achievement: the equilibrium of the shapes, the fine workmanship and the choice of the raw materials combine a functional approach with some concern for aesthetics. Later, polished tools, such as one made of haematite from Uele in Zaïre (see Van Noten), showed outstanding craftsmanship. Such materials as wood, vegetable and animal fibres, ivory, leaves, bones, horns, leather, eggshells, snail shells, seashells, gourds, clay and metal have also all been in use for millennia. In some places specific tools were developed to work these materials, which were used in turn to create numerous other implements, mainly for cultivating, hunting, fishing, animal husbandry, cooking and drinking. The number of tools owned by any given family, however, was quite small, with basic objects such as a knife, hoe or axe serving several purposes.

In African languages, usually one specific term is used to designate what in European languages is a rather vague category of objects. Often there is confusion, however, between the technical and symbolic use of an object, so that a ceremonial object may be in the same category as a simple knife; a very simple tool may have a more important symbolic role than highly decorated objects. This is the case with the hammer-anvil of the blacksmith (see fig. 103k), a sort of iron nail that is often used in enthronement rituals throughout Central Africa, where the king is often symbolically assimilated to the blacksmith. Like the blacksmith's other tools—pliers, wire drawing plate, cutter—it is not decorated unless it is used as regalia, as among the Kuba of Zaïre or in the interlacustrine zone. In some cases, as with the Kongo, the bellows can be carved, while the Kissi of Guinea carve cephalomorphic twyers in soapstone (103m).

As in other parts of the world, the simplest objects, those used for the most basic physical tasks, are rarely decorated, except with a few small designs as a sort of signature of the artisan or mark of the owner. The most widespread tool is the adze, which is highly versatile and can be used to carve with great precision (103l). Adzes and axes are usually associated with men's work, such as clearing the woods and war, and they are often decorated and used as objects of prestige. Knives and razors are usually not highly decorated but sometimes display remarkable craftsmanship; among the Kuba they are also used to cut velvet fabric (103g). Unusual and very characteristic drawing knives found in Central Africa and used to smooth wood of cylindrical objects, such as spear shafts or paddle handles, are composed of an arrowhead fixed across a forked branch (103i). The Kuba of Zaïre, well known for their careful decoration of many unusual objects, have chasing chisels (103f) and cephalomorphic bark scrapers (103a), used to collect the red powder used in many rituals.

Also relatively unusual are the large wooden paddles, sometimes decorated (103j), that are used to pack the clay floors and walls among the Zande of north-eastern Zaïre. Among fishermen, the very large paddles used in canoeing are often decorated with elaborate designs. Wooden or ivory mallets used to beat bark in order to make bark cloth are known in several parts of the forest area of West and Central Africa. Their grooving can be made in an elaborate and decorative pattern, as in some fine examples from north-east Zaïre (103n).

Weaving implements can also be decorated, the heddle pulleys in West Africa, for instance, being unusually beautifully carved (103b–d) in the shape of a man, an animal or even an inanimate object such as a headrest. In other areas, for weaving, wooden pegs (103e) are planted in the ground, and the warp is looped around them. Specialized tools are also employed in agriculture, the iron hoe being the most characteristic, often with the machete. Another tool characteristic of forest peoples is a big chisel used to cut the palm tree in order to collect the sap for palm wine (103h).

BIBLIOGRAPHY

F. Van Noten: *The Uelian* (Tervuren, 1968)

F. N'Diaye: 'Iconologie des poulies de métier à tisser Dogon', *Obj. & Mondes*, xi/4 (1971), pp. 355–70

African Furniture and Household Objects (exh. cat. by R. Sieber, New York, Amer. Fed. A., 1980–81)

'Les Instruments aratoires en Afrique tropicale', *Cah. ORSTOM Sci. Humaines*, xx/3–4 (1984)

R. Haaland and P. Shinnie, eds: *African Iron Working: Ancient and Traditional* (Oslo, 1985)

F. N'Diaye: *Poulies de métier à tisser: Masques et sculptures d'Afrique et d'Océanie* (Paris, 1986)

V. Bounoure: 'A propos des poulies de tisserance de la collection Liotard', *A. Afrique Noire*, 64 (1987), pp. 11–19

PIERRE DE MARET

12. FURNITURE. Some African peoples have rich traditions of furniture, almost all of which is made of wood and in the main out of single pieces. While no African household completely lacks furniture of some sort, large wooden objects are, for obvious reasons, scarce among nomadic peoples and in communities where villages are relocated at intervals.

In Africa the stool is the most basic item of furniture. A man's stool is extremely personal to him, as well as being a status symbol. There are some examples, for example from Liberia, of stools of composite construction made from palm-rib pieces. Generally, however, African stools are made from a section of tree trunk (see fig. 104). There is considerable stylistic variation in African stools, both between peoples and between those used by chiefs or elders and those used by commoners. That of an important person may be distinguished by the number of legs, by the elaboration of its carving or by its ornamentation with beadwork, metal plate or brass studs. For example, in northern Zambia, an ordinary man's stool has up to three legs, that of a headman five or more, while a chief's stool is also elaborately carved. Women, on the other hand, sit on a short piece of wood or a mat. In the Cameroon Grasslands the basic carved stool has a seat supported by a caryatid figure or by a hollow cylinder of openwork carving of such figures as stylized frogs and spiders. A chief's stool is larger and more elaborate, while a state stool is enhanced by an additional figure or figures carved to form a back- or armrest and beadwork covering. The Hemba of Zaïre also have caryatid stools (*see* HEMBA, fig. 2). Such stools are indeed not domestic furniture but form part of the regalia without which the chiefly succession is invalid. Footstools or footrests are also found in such contexts, since a chief, when sitting in state, may not

104. Tabwa high-backed stool with a human head, possibly of a tribal ancestor, wood, h. 858 mm, from south-eastern Zaïre (London, British Museum)

have his feet touching the ground. Some stools have backs formed from carved figures and are virtually chairs. In some cases, however, the seat is too shallow to sit on and the carved figure may then symbolize the presence of an ancestor (see fig. 104).

European chairs were brought as gifts for African kings and chiefs from at least the 16th century. In some areas European styles and forms were readily adopted. Among the Asante of Ghana there are two types of European-style chairs, both ornamented with brass studs. Among the Pende of Zaïre and the Chokwe of Angola, chiefs' chairs in European form occur, with the backs and cross-pieces carved with small figures in the local style, and are among the few pieces of African furniture carpentered from several pieces of wood. Another form of European seating is the small folding deckchair, with a skin or mat in place of canvas, used by village headmen in many areas. This form was copied from the travelling equipment of district commissioners.

Backrests are particularly common in Zaïre. They usually take a tripod form and are made from a tree trunk with its branches cut to shape. Those used by commoners may be quite basic, while those of Kuba chiefs, for example, are elaborately carved. Tip stools, found among the Bole of Zaïre, combine the functions of stool and backrest, having a central upright and a long surface to act as seat or backrest.

Headrests, which are almost always monoxylous, may be grouped with stools and backrests. The simplest headrests comprise a branch of which the surface has been smoothed, having perhaps three or four branchlet supports. Larger headrests double as stools. Among nomads headrests may be simple monopods or bipods with a neckpiece and carrying loop. Most African headrests are purely functional in form, although those of the Somali combine a graceful, basic shape with chip-carved decoration. Headrests with zoomorphic or other figural decoration are relatively uncommon and, when not carved for the Western market, may have been made for important people. The Zulu of Southern Africa have produced double headrests. The Bwaka of Zaïre make headrests comprising a lidded box, perhaps for holding trinkets.

Among such nomadic peoples as the San, beds are made on the ground, with a skin for both over- and underlay. Many traditional houses have an earth platform with sleeping-mats. Bedsteads, whether made by the local blacksmith-carpenter or constructed out of a framework of bamboo, palm ribs or long straight sticks with overlaid mats or mattress, have tended to replace the earth platform, since they give some protection against vermin and ants. Chiefs usually have more elaborate beds as befits their status; in the 1870s the king of the Mangbetu had a fine composite bed of bamboo and raffia matting. In the Cameroon Grasslands, a chief's bed was carved from one piece of wood, with supporting sides in the form of rows of carved figures.

Tables are hardly found outside Northern Africa and the Swahili coast, where Arab influence is strong. Swahili tables are small, like Western occasional tables, and often consist of a tray on a stand. In Ethiopia, food baskets were made with a circular tray top. Chests are only found where Arab influence is strong and are often ornamented with brass overlay. Wall niches, shelves and outdoor platform stands are otherwise common. Boxes made of wood or bark, lidded baskets and gourds, hanging nets and pots are also used for storage. Other belongings may be hung from a wooden hook in the wall or stuck into the thatch, which is a good place to keep small valuables safe or an axe or knife out of harm's way. Mats are an important item of African furnishing. Since many beds are 'built-in', mats serve as bedding. Where houses are built on a raised platform foundation, mats laid on the platform under the overhanging thatch provide sheltered built-in seating. Other pieces of African furniture are simple and multi-purpose, such as stout forked sticks that may serve as stands for waterpots.

See also BAMUM and SWAHILI, §3; for illustration *see* WOOD, colour pl. III, fig. 2.

BIBLIOGRAPHY

R. Sieber: *African Furniture and Household Objects* (Bloomington, 1980) [pubd in conjunction with an exh. organized by the Amer. Fed. A., New York, 1980–81]

C. Geary: 'Bamum Thrones and Stools', *Afr. A.*, xiv/4 (1981), pp. 32–43, 87–8

J. de V. Allen: 'The *kita cha enzi* and Other Swahili Chairs', *Afr. A.*, xxii/3 (1989), pp. 54–63, 88

The Art of the Personal Object (exh. cat. by P. Ravenhill, Washington, DC, N. Mus. Afr. A., 1991)

13. TOBACCO CONTAINERS AND PIPES. Tobacco was introduced into Africa from America by Europeans in the 15th century, while hemp, often called *dagga*, may have entered Africa from the east and north, via Arab contacts. In much of Sub-Saharan Africa, especially in the east and south, the preferred form of tobacco was snuff, made from dried, ground tobacco leaves, which in the late 20th century continued to be taken by both sexes. Snuff-boxes belonging to chiefs or important men might be distinguished by their size, superior workmanship or use of some exclusive material, such as elephant ivory. The great majority of snuff-boxes, however, are quite small and are portable as neck or waist pendants or, if they are made from a length of reed or wood, worn as an ear-plug. Small gourds are often used, either left plain or decorated in a variety of ways, such as pyrogravure, impressed beads or wire and beaded covers; and short lengths of cane or bamboo used to keep snuff may also be decorated by pyrogravure, shallow carving and beaded covers. In Malawi, for example, cane snuff-boxes have carved, wooden, mushroom-like stoppers. Among the Bantu of Southern Africa, ovoid snuff-boxes made from wood or ox-horn have a loop at the end for wearing as a pendant or are attached by a wooden link to the end of a headrest. A horn snuff-box of this shape might also be carved at the end of a long horn hairpin to wear in the hair, perhaps along with a carved bone snuff-spoon. Other horn snuff-boxes are carved as small conical flasks surmounted by the figure of an antelope or human head or torso. In Southern and South-eastern Africa, typically among the Shona, wooden chip-carved snuff-boxes are shaped like flasks or thistle-heads, with circular gourd stoppers. In Southern Africa containers in the shape of a flask or a miniature ox are made from a mixture of inner-skin scrapings and earth, shaped over a clay core. The surface is then lifted into numerous tiny spikes, and, after this has set, the clay core is removed through the neck of the flask or a hole cut in the ox's head. This method is known as 'blood and clay' (*tandu* in northern Nigeria).

Water-pipes occur in Central, South-eastern and Southern Africa but do not seem to exist in West Africa. They are the most common implement for smoking hemp (except in Northern Africa) and are also often used for smoking tobacco. The water container through which the smoke is inhaled and filtered is very often a gourd, but antelope horns, hollowed-out wood and bamboo stems also occur, again often decorated with pyrogravure, brass studs or twisted wire. The mouthpiece may be just a hole at one end of the water container, while the bowl for the tobacco or hemp is usually mounted on a short length of reed and can be made of stone (often soapstone), pottery or wood lined with sheet tin. The shapes vary but are basically like vases or funnels, often with a lug for securing to the water container and ornamented with grooved lines or chip-carving. In North-eastern Africa, notably the Nilotic Sudan, a small spherical gourd stuffed with bast is secured to the top of the long wooden stem by tight-fitting dried rawhide and acts as a filter.

Other forms of pipe include the earth pipes of Southern Africa, in which a short tube is connected to a small, hollow mound containing the hemp, and short pieces of stone or bone. Others again may be similar to European-style pipes but with the bowl carved to represent a human head, animal or other fancy shape. The bowls of these European-style pipes are made from such materials as metal, wood or clay, while the stems are made of reed, wood or a long gourd. In Northern Africa, for example,

105. Shilluk pipe, clay, bamboo, metal, beads and pigment, l. 740 mm, from Malakal area, Sudan (London, British Museum)

hemp is smoked from a straight reed stem attached to a small red clay bowl, decorated with incised Islamic ornamentation. Clay pipe-bowls are made, usually by men, using a technique somewhat akin to wood-carving. A rough clay form is made, with a smoke-hole pierced in it, and this is allowed to dry until 'leather-hard'. It is then carved to shape, and when the drying process is almost complete, the pipe-bowl is finished off with ornament in the local style and fired. Among the Asante of Ghana, pipe-bowls are made of red clay, with white kaolin in the grooves and in a variety of shapes, such as leopards, shells or human heads. In Uganda, traditional pipe-bowls were conical, burnished black, with fine red-and-white incised lines. The Tonga and Ila of southern Zambia make pipe-bowls of red or black clay carved with supports and representing antelope or buffalo forequarters. Pipe-bowls in the Nilotic Sudan are mostly vase-shaped, with a small foot, while among the Shilluk, ornamental pipe-bowls, representing a hyena's head, are carved from clay and burnished black, with white incised hatchings (see fig. 105). In the Cameroon Grasslands, while pipes for ordinary people or women are functional and plain, elaborate ceremonial pipes are owned by chiefs, with large bowls made of either carved clay or brass cast by the lost-wax process, perhaps in the shape of a mask or an elephant's head. These pipes have a long stem, often covered with beadwork in polychrome geometric patterns.

In Central Africa the favourite material is wood, with chiefs' pipes often being ornamented either with copper or brass wire strip wound around the stem or with brass domed nails, while the bowls are sometimes finely carved. Among the Bantu of Southern Africa, wooden pipes are usually carved from one piece of wood, with the bowl inlaid with zinc in a pattern or even carved with the bowl as a pot on a woman's head. The bowls are normally lined with sheet tin-plate; a separate short length of cane or wood is stuck in the end of the stem as a mouthpiece. Each smoker uses only his own mouthpiece, to prevent his spiritual essence falling into the hands of an enemy. Conversely, pipes with multiple wooden bowls are found among the Pondo of Southern Africa, and in Nigeria multiple vase-shaped pipe-bowls are made in carved clay.

BIBLIOGRAPHY

A. Dunhill: *The Pipe Book* (London, 1924)

M. Shaw: 'Some Native Snuff-boxes in the South African Museum', *An. S. Afr. Mus.*, xxiv/3 (1935), pp. 141–62

——: 'Native Pipes and Smoking in South Africa', *An. S. Afr. Mus.*, xxiv/5 (1938), pp. 277–302

——: 'South African Native Snuff-boxes', *An. S. Afr. Mus.*, xxiv/5 (1938), pp. 221–52

MARGRET CAREY

14. HOUSEHOLD UTENSILS. One of the most essential domestic items is the knife, which may be used for such diverse tasks as skinning animals, cutting meat or fish, peeling root vegetables, splitting reeds or cutting bark tie when making baskets, shaping wood, trimming fingernails or shaving the head. Generally, knives belong to the individual rather than the task. Forks feature little in African culture, other than as tourist commodities, but spoons are significant and are made in a wide range of forms and materials. The most important are those used for serving food, which have large bowls and are sometimes elaborate. The Dan people of Liberia, for example, have special rice spoons with a large bowl, sometimes decoratively carved at the back, and with the handle often carved in human or animal form (see fig.106 and fig. 51 above; *see also* DAN, fig. 4). Such spoons are used by women in lavish hospitality at times of festival and help celebrate women's social role. They are often the work of a master carver and are inherited. Many have decoratively carved handles or bowls, as they may be used for ritual feeding of respected elders, for making offerings to the

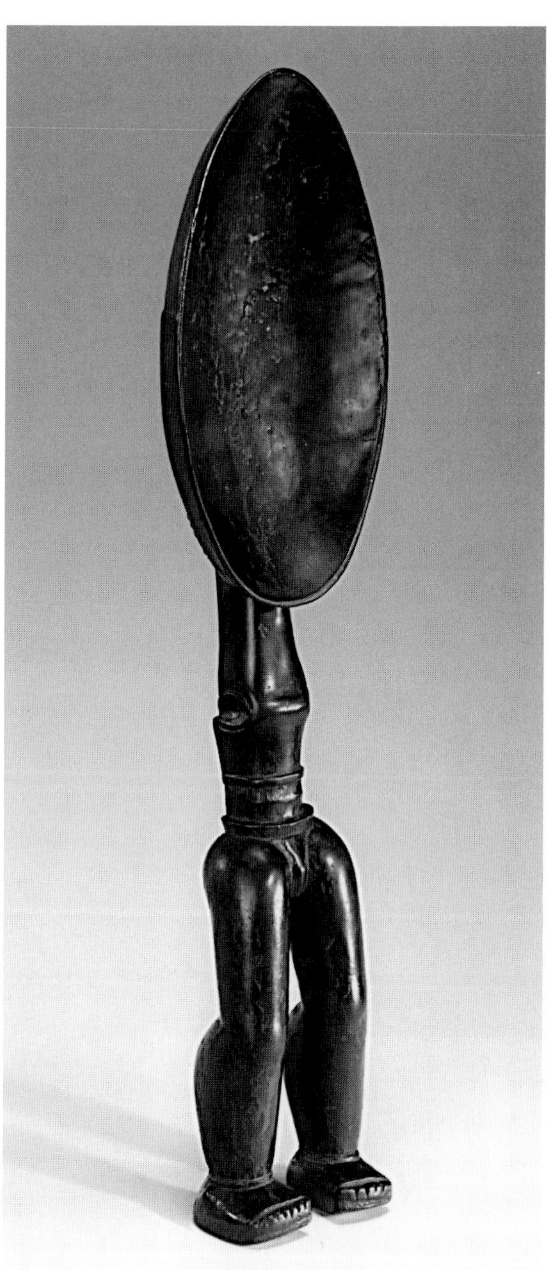

106. Dan spoon, wood, h. 465 mm, late 19th century–early 20th (Norwich, University of East Anglia, Sainsbury Centre for Visual Arts)

spirits or for serving food on special occasions. The Asante of Ghana have a unique form of spoon with a flat pestle-like end to the handle; this is used in levelling mashed yam (*fufu*). A paddle-shaped spoon is widely used to stir and serve the stiff porridge that provides the staple diet of much of Sub-Saharan Africa. In Northern and Eastern Africa, where the influence of Arabic culture is evident, spoons may be decorated with elaborate chip-carving (as among the Somali) or made of pearl-shell bowls mounted in a lacquered handle (as in Northern Africa).

Dippers, for ladling water out of a pot or for use as a drinking cup, are made from suitably shaped long-stemmed gourds or from coconut shells mounted on sticks, or carved from wood. Another special form is the strainer spoon, common among the Bantu-speaking peoples of Southern Africa, used to skim the floating mash from local beer. In general, spoons used for eating are rare but are made of wood, although brass alloys, iron and white metal are also used. In Central Africa the oval shell of the river-mussel is used as a spoon, while among the Zulu each person has his or her own spoon, often with an ornamented handle; these are kept in individual basketry wallets.

Water containers are often among the most highly decorated ceramic wares, and the variations in impressed decoration are striking. The water-carrying pots of the Makonde of Mozambique, for example, have all-over incised designs filled with kaolin, while the water-carrying jars of the Nupe of Nigeria have fine linear incisions and registers of rouletting (see fig. 107). The Nupe jars have elegantly clinched necks and hour-glass contours, reminiscent of the shape of some bottle gourds. In some cases (e.g. among the Bole of northern Nigeria and the Gbaya of the Central African Republic), highly ornamented pots are stacked around the interior of a woman's sleeping room and reflect her, or her household's, economic and social standing. Other ceramic vessels may be used for storing or transporting such items as beer, palm wine, grains, oils, butter, cosmetics, medicines, ink or dye solutions. Pots with perforations are used as sieves or as drying chambers for meat or fish; bowls with heavily incised interiors are used as grinders, and shallow dishes raised on stands can function as serving dishes or oil lamps. Pots for storing and cooling water are large, with little or no neck, for easy access and to allow the maximum surface area for evaporation. Vessels for transporting water, on the other hand, often have an elongated neck and sometimes a rim to minimize spillage. Other water containers can be made from gourds and, among nomadic peoples, of an entire animal skin, wood or closely sewn coiled basketry. The fibres of such baskets swell with the moisture to become virtually watertight, and the insides are coated with dried milk and are then smoked to increase impermeability. The San use ostrich eggshells as water containers. Such pots are not necessarily watertight, since seepage is a means of cooling the water inside. In Central Africa, especially large gourds or pots are also used in brewing beer, which is very important in social life.

107. Nupe water pot, ceramic and metal (?tin), h. 400 mm, from Bida, Nigeria (Washington, DC, National Museum of African Art)

Cooking vessels are usually either of earthenware or in the form of iron three-legged pots. The traditional earthenware pots are usually not elaborately decorated and generally have a round base, since they are designed to stand in a forked stick, on a ring-stand or on a traditional cooking hearth. Such hearths are made of a group of three stones, inverted pots (as among the Asante of Ghana), small shaped termitaries or moulded potter's clay, which hardens during use. Small charcoal stoves made from recycled oil drums have also become popular, especially in the less rural areas. The use of enamel basins as serving dishes has become common, although food is also served in bowls, dishes or trays made of earthenware, basketry, wood or gourd. For example, the Zulu have large, elaborately carved wooden meat dishes, while in eastern Africa a bride's trousseau may include decorated baskets and gourds made for serving her husband with his first meal in the new home and for subsequent special occasions.

Other culinary utensils include drinking straws covered with fine grass plaiting and ending in a fine bulbous strainer. These are used for drinking beer by the Interlacustrine peoples around Lake Victoria such as the Ganda. The pestle and mortar are almost ubiquitous, and sieves are used wherever yams or cassava are eaten, to sift the flour free of fibres; they are made of basketry with spaced elements or of perforated zinc or fine wire mesh on a wooden frame. Cleaning equipment generally comprises a hand broom, made of grass stems (with or without the feather heads), split palm leaves, a bunch of twigs or a bunch of stems with the leaves attached. Those made of grass or palm leaves are often carefully made and have a handle secured with ornamental plaiting. One unusual piece of cleaning equipment is the wash-table found among the Senufo of Côte d'Ivoire. It is shaped like an oblong-seated stool with four legs and made of hard, heavy wood so that it will not float in shallow water, and the women bang wet clothing on it.

BIBLIOGRAPHY

African Furniture and Household Objects (exh. cat. by R. Sieber, New York, Amer. Fed. A., 1980–81)

MARLA C. BERNS, MARGRET CAREY

15. Rock art.

(i) Introduction. (ii) Regional survey.

(i) Introduction. Rock art is widely distributed throughout the African continent in a number of independent traditions; some Southern African examples are among man's oldest artistic endeavour. Two principal techniques were employed: rock paintings, sometimes called pictographs, are almost exclusively found in shallow overhangs and rock shelters rather than in deep, underground caverns, as is Upper Palaeolithic art in Western Europe (*see* PREHISTORIC EUROPE, §II, 2); by contrast, rock engravings, or petroglyphs, made by incising and pecking, are found in open sites and in rock shelters. Incised engravings were cut through the patina, or outer skin, of rocks with a sharp stone implement. Pecked engravings were made by hammering the patina to remove it. Sometimes the engravers left part of the patina to represent features such as folds of skin or an eye and in some regions they polished the entire configuration.

African rock art research evinces two principal tendencies: interpretation of 'meaning', and formal chronological and geographical classification. At different times and for different regions of the continent one or other has predominated, although the desire to move beyond catalogues, counts and chronologies has seldom been fulfilled. Furthermore, since the 1980s there has been a shift away from various issues that were central to earlier rock art research. Formerly, much attention was accorded rock art as evidence for migrations, diffusions and cultural contacts. Often this evidence consisted merely of visual comparisons between arts from different cultures. Many students are now dubious about comparing superficial traits and prefer to seek the nature and social circumstances of any diffusions and contacts that may have taken place; the mere fact of contact tells us little. Another issue that has diminished in importance is that of artistic and cultural evolution. It was thought that art and society both evolved from simple, 'primitive' beginnings to more complex and sophisticated heights. Undoubtedly, art does change through time, but the technical simplicity of a work tells us little about the evolutionary status or the role of that work in its living social context. It follows from this that little can be gained from using Western notions and canons of art history to address prehistoric works.

(ii) Regional survey. Rock art regions are difficult to define, but the following are generally recognized (see fig. 108).

(a) North Africa. (b) Horn of Africa. (c) East Africa. (d) Southern Africa.

(a) North Africa. Most North African rock art is concentrated in the Saharan massifs of Adrar des Iforas, Tadrart Acacus, Tibesti, Ennedi, Hoggar and Tassili N' Ajjer. Further north, there is a considerable concentration in the Atlas Mountains. The proximity to the Iberian Peninsula of these northernmost depictions has raised questions of diffusion from Europe (*see* SPANISH LEVANTINE ROCK ART). Although there are some superficial points of similarity, most researchers now accept the African art as an independent tradition. Dating this tradition, or indeed any rock art, is notoriously difficult, however, and few reliable North African dates are available. Unlike organic archaeological finds, neither paintings nor engravings can be dated by radiometric methods. Most work is therefore based on the analysis of styles by superpositions. Despite these limitations and the debatable nature of some postulated stylistic sequences, four broad periods of Saharan rock art can be recognized: the *Bubalus antiquus* period; the 'Round Head' (or Bovidian) period; the Pastoral period; and the Post-Neolithic period.

Bubalus antiquus and Round Head periods. The earliest identified period of African rock art, termed *Bubalus antiquus*, comprises engravings of large game animals, including the eponymous extinct giant buffalo. These engravings are executed with remarkable élan. They are on rock walls outside shelters, where there is little hope of finding a connection between them and datable layers. However, F. Mori's work with an unusually indicative panel in the Acacus suggests that the engravings of this period belong to the Upper Pleistocene, more than 10,000 BP.

More is known about the Round Head period, a name bestowed by Abbé Breuil on account of the distinctive heads of many human figures. Rock art of this period mainly comprises paintings. Mori obtained a radiocarbon date of 8072±110 BP from samples of charcoal in a deposit that also contained fragments of a grindstone with traces of red and yellow pigment. Other excavations by B. Barich suggest an earlier date of 9080±70 BP (see Roset, 1984). It is, of course, difficult to link these dates to the paintings, but they do show the great length of occupation by hunter-gatherers. At this time the Sahara was experiencing a period of heavy rain; large lakes formed, and a Mediterranean type of vegetation prevailed.

The first human and animal depictions of this period are simple silhouettes, frequently with a darker outline. The later polychrome paintings are larger and have heavy, powerful shapes. Human figures often carry weapons such as spears, bows and other objects and have various body patterns (see fig. 109). They are usually drawn frontally, and their large heads merge with their bodies. The figures are frequently covered with networks of lines, chevrons, grids and rows of dots. Sometimes the heads are marked with semicircles and are crowned by lunate forms (see fig. 110). In the Tassili massif, one of the most remarkable of these is a painting of a striding woman in yellow ochre and white. The head has two large horns surrounded by dots. Beneath her is another, incomplete, female figure under a set of curving lines (see fig. 111). The animal depictions of this period, like those of the *Bubalus*, are of big game, sometimes very large and portrayed in awkward postures. Like the human figures, they are executed as outlined silhouettes. Among them are fantasy animals, bodiless hoofs and horns.

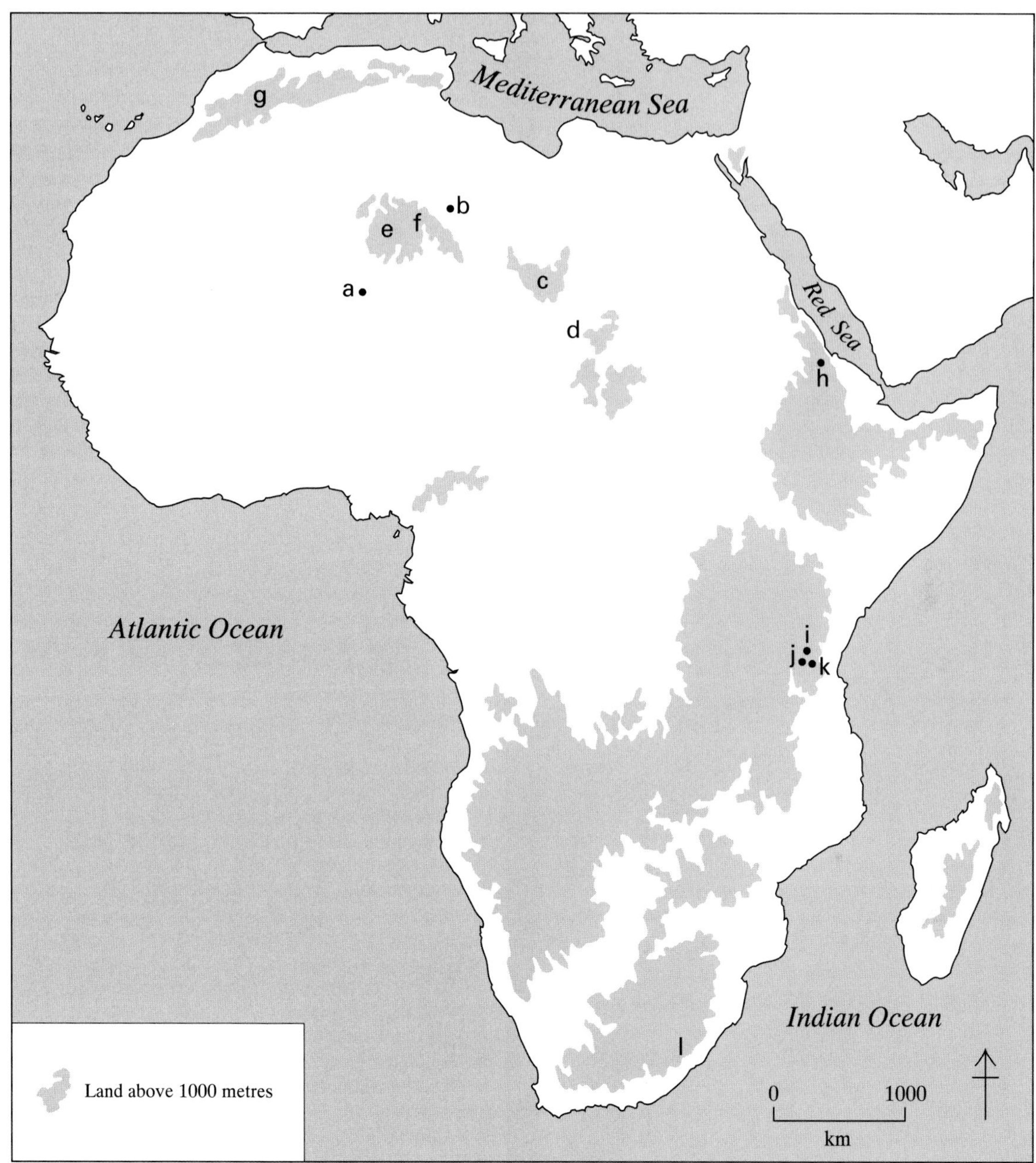

108. Map of Africa showing rock art sites: (a) Adrar des Iforas; (b) Tadrart Acacus; (c) Tibesti; (d) Ennedi; (e) Hoggar; (f) Tassili N' Ajjer; (g) Atlas Mountains; (h) Zeban Ona Libanos; (i) Kisese 2; (j) Fenga Hill; (k) Chungal 3; (l) Drakensberg

Because the paintings of both the *Bubalus* and the Round Head periods are ascribable to hunter-gatherers, and because the distinction between them is not clear, they may, for our purposes, be considered together. Recent research has developed a model of graphic depiction that appears to be applicable to both periods.

A widespread, perhaps universal, feature of hunter-gatherer religion is SHAMANISM: the exploitation of altered states of consciousness to gain access to the spirit world, to control animals and the weather and to cure the sick. Because the human nervous system is, of course, common to all people and has probably not changed much since the beginning of the Upper Palaeolithic, *c.* 30,000 BP, we can construct a generalized model of the experience of the altered state of consciousness known as trance. This model, derived from neuropsychological laboratory research, has been tested and found to fit known shamanistic arts. It can therefore be used to assess the content of arts not known *a priori* to be shamanistic.

Broadly speaking, the neuropsychological model identifies two stages through which people experience trance. In the first stage all people, irrespective of their cultural

109. North African rock painting of the Round Head period representing an archer, Sefar, Tassili N' Ajjer, Algeria

hearth in a layer overlying a piece of fallen rock from the wall of the shelter; on it were painted two oxen (see Roset, 1984).

The pollen record suggests a comparatively humid climate at this time with conditions suitable for the keeping of large herds. This climatic condition and also, according to some writers, the Pastoral art, reached a turning point *c.* 6000 BP. Thereafter the climate became gradually drier and, although livestock keeping was still viable, xerophilous plants (i.e. plants adapted to extremely dry conditions) began to appear.

The herdsmen drawn into the Sahara during this climatically favourable period left behind them a wealth of striking art. Cattle are depicted singly and in large herds of up to a hundred. Mostly in profile and remarkably naturalistic, the creatures seem to move gracefully over the rock walls. There is also greater mastery of colour than in the Round Head period, the hide patterns of the cattle being faithfully reproduced. The presence of some fine

background, 'see' a range of luminous, geometric forms that pulsate, rotate, fragment and multiply in the visual field. These entoptic phenomena include grids, zigzags, sets of parallel lines, lunate forms and dots both in scintillating lines and in scatters. As the trance deepens, the culturally determined aspect increases. Entoptic phenomena persist but are now combined with true hallucinations, mainly of people, animals and emotionally charged objects. Accompanying these visual experiences are physical and aural hallucinations. People feel dissociated from their bodies; their bodies feel elongated and seem to have more digits and limbs than normal. They also hear sounds that they interpret as their culture directs them, for example rushing winds, waterfalls, crickets and bees.

If we apply this model to the art of the *Bubalus* and Round Head periods, we find not just one but a set of correspondences. Some of the body patterns may represent cicatrization, but others are more probably entoptic forms combined with human figures. Placed above the heads of some of these figures are lunate shapes and chevrons. Some are also surrounded by lines of dots, as are hallucinatory paintings in other cultures. These features lead us to believe that, like much hunter-gatherer rock art elsewhere, the art of these two periods contains a strong shamanistic element. However, the depictions were not necessarily executed by people actually in a trance. Rather, they were done subsequently upon recollection of such experiences. The rocks thus proclaim the reality of the other world and thereby underscore the status of the shamans, or medicine men, who were responsible for the well-being of the community and the renewal of nature.

Pastoral period. After the Round Head period there appears to have been a temporal hiatus during which new people settled in the Sahara. No transitional paintings have been found linking the Round Head period with the subsequent Pastoral period. The oldest date obtained by Mori for the Pastoral period is 7438±226 BP. A more recently obtained date for this period, 4730±310 BP, is particularly interesting because it was obtained from a

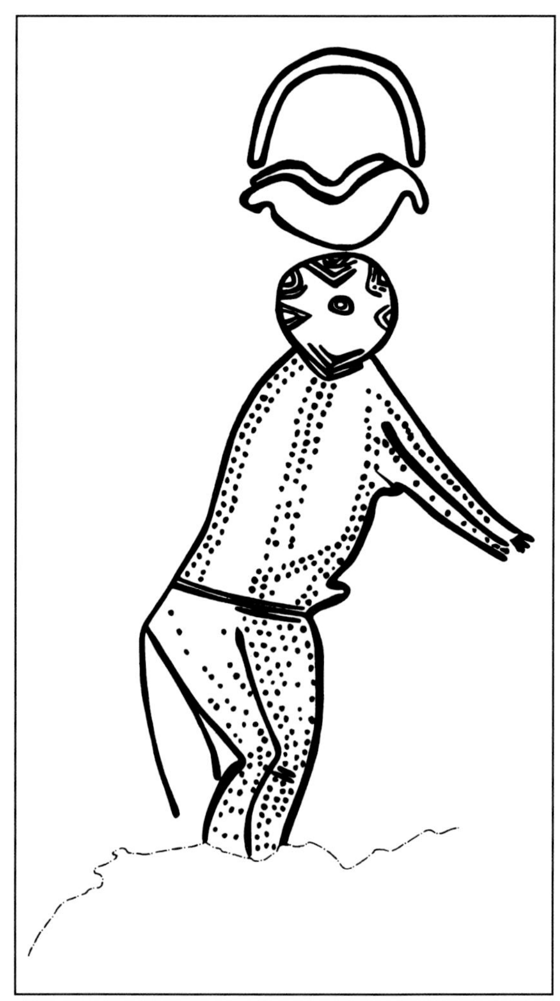

110. North African rock painting representing 'an ornate figure', Jabbanen, Tassili N' Ajjer, Algeria, Round Head period; redrawn from J. D. Lajoux, 1963, p. 57

111. North African rock painting representing 'a horned goddess', Aouanrhet, Tassili N' Ajjer, Algeria, Round Head period; redrawn from H. Lhote, 1959, fig. 35

engravings possibly indicates that the artists first scratched the outlines of the cattle before they coloured them.

Composed scenes also first appeared in the Pastoral period. What seem to be scenes of daily life abound. Figures are seated or recumbent, apparently dancing, hunting, herding cattle and fighting with bows and arrows. The basic shamanistic elements of Round Head-period rock art seem to be absent in the Pastoral phase, or at any rate far less prominent, but mundane interpretations cannot account for all images. For instance, the remarkable two-headed cows of Tassili would fit a hallucinatory context, as confirmed by both San and North American Shoshone shamanistic rock art. Similarly, some of the 'camp scenes' may depict rituals, as do many of the scenes in San rock art.

A ritual interpretation for the Pastoral period paintings has been strengthened by a Fulani man, Amadou Hampaté Ba, who interpreted copies of the paintings as pre-Islamic depictions of initiation rituals (see A. Hampaté Ba and Dieterlen). The Fulani have been thought to be the descendants of Saharan pastoralists who moved south as the desert dried out. Today they live nomadic lives in the basins of the Senegal and Niger rivers. One of the details on which Ba commented was the calf-rope that features so prominently in the art. He explained that this rope is used during the initiation of herdsmen and is considered sacred as it symbolizes the lifeline of the herd. Similarly, the herdsman's staff, also depicted in the art, is presented to initiates as part of the rituals and is used in oath swearing. A ceremony possibly associated with the paintings of two-headed animals is the ritual purification of cattle. Ba explained that on the rare occasion when a calf is born with two heads it is kept alive and then sacrificed during this ritual. If such an animal is not available, an effigy is made out of two cattle skins. Although there are, of course, objections to using modern informants to explain prehistoric art, Ba's interpretations suggest that we may at the very least be dealing with two similar, or cognate, belief systems.

Post-Neolithic period. The Pastoral period was followed by the Post-Neolithic period. Although there were moister times between 3500 and 3000 BP and again between 2500 and 2000 BP, the Sahara was becoming increasingly desiccated. In the Post-Neolithic period cattle are absent from the art, but there are depictions of camels, horses, chariots and shields as well as simple inscriptions. These paintings are generally less animated than those of the Pastoral period. Some depictions have been used in plotting migration and trail routes, but subsequent finds cast doubt on the conclusions.

The creators of this final phase of North African rock art have not been clearly identified. It is possible that the paintings were made not by the newcomers represented in the art but by small pastoral groups who remained in the Sahara. Certainly, the continued depiction of giraffe, elephant and lion (and the vegetation with which these species are associated) suggests that some pastoralism was still possible.

(b) Horn of Africa. Connections between the Saharan rock art and that found in the Horn of Africa (Somalia, Ethiopia and Eritrea) have been suggested (see Willcox, 1984), but the exact nature of these connections has not been established. In this area, it seems that pre-pastoral, hunter–gatherer art is absent for unknown reasons. The earliest art depicts cattle and people relatively naturalistically but to a much lesser degree than in the Saharan massifs. Clark (1954) tentatively dates the earliest art to *c.* 2000 BP; certainly, it must post-date the first appearance of cattle in the area during the preceding millennium. Like the Saharan cattle, those depicted in the Horn are long-horned and humpless, although the only cattle now in the area are humped zebu.

The Abbé Breuil attempted to define a series of eight successive styles, but subsequent writers have been unable to discern his groupings. Others have discovered what they believe to be affinities with San rock art. At Zeban Ona Libanos, for example, there are simplified human figures with spears and shields and a milking scene.

In addition to the paintings there are a number of petroglyph sites. The engravings depict human beings with shields and spears, cattle, camels and some geometric motifs. Many of these are thought to be no older than the 4th century AD.

The principal interest in the rock art of the Horn of Africa has been from a diffusionist perspective. Citing comparable stone industries from North Africa to the Cape and the fact that human figures tend to be less naturalistic than animals, some writers have postulated a diffusion route from Spain through the Sahara to the Cape with the Horn of Africa as an intermediate region. This view, however, has been seriously questioned by evidence considered below.

(c) East Africa. The rock art of Tanzania, Uganda, Kenya and Malawi, the next stage south on the supposed diffusion route, may be divided into two broad phases or groups: hunter–gatherer art and Iron Age art. As elsewhere, the dating of East African rock art is questionable and vague. At Kisese 2, in Tanzania, Inskeep (1962) uncovered 6 m of deposit. Red ochre, some pieces of which were faceted by wear, and 'palettes' on which ochre had been ground were found above the 29,000 BP level. In addition, rock spalls with paint were found in a layer said to be earlier than 8000 BP. A larger piece of rock with red and white paintings has been dated to *c.* 1500 BP. On the other hand, E. ten Raa shows that the Sandawe-speaking hunter-gatherers of this region were painting as late as the 20th century. The largely red hunter-gatherer paintings show closer affinities with San art to the south than with that of either the Sahara or the Horn of Africa. Mary Leakey, who remarks on this point, has recorded much Tanzanian rock art.

The neuropsychological model that suggested shamanistic elements in the Sahara can also be applied to the art of East Africa. In this area there are painted forms, some of which have been interpreted as traps, that conform to entoptic phenomena. These include dots, undulating lines, sets of short dashes and 'sun' images. The blending of entoptic shapes with human and animal forms, characteristic of a deep stage of trance, is also found (see fig. 112). Moreover, human and animal features are combined in therianthropic depictions, and there are distortions of the human form that can be explained as somatic hallucinations. These include elongations and 'hairiness'. Even more interesting are distortions of the human head that resemble the Round Head figures of the Sahara. (Persons in trance speak of the head appearing to swell and of marked tingling sensations in the scalp.)

The hallucinatory interpretation of these forms is greatly strengthened by other features. The art depicts dancers bending forward. San shamans speak of their stomach muscles contracting and so causing them to adopt this posture as their potency 'boils' in their stomachs. Tanzanian paintings also show short dashes falling from the noses of some figures (see fig. 113). For the rock art of Southern Africa this has been identified as the nasal haemorrhage experienced by San shamans as they enter trance. Some San shamans enter trance so violently that they execute a complete somersault. This probably accounts for the inverted figures in both San and Tanzanian rock art that appear to be cavorting around animals.

This shamanistic interpretation of East African hunter–gatherer art may well be correct, for there is evidence of an ecstatic 'spirit possession' cult among the Sandawe-speaking people that may have fulfilled a role comparable to the trance dance in San society.

Post-dating the hunter–gatherer art is a distinct series of thick white paintings that appear to have been done with a finger. They include zoomorphic figures, sometimes spreadeagled, birds and geometric forms such as dots, crosses and circles containing an inverted Y-shape. It is now known that many of these 'late whites', as they are often known, were connected with the Nyau societies. The Nyau are a society of male masked dancers who perform at funeral rites and female initiation ceremonies.

112. East African rock painting representing elephants, human figures and entoptic phenomena, Fenga Hill, Tanzania, hunter–gatherer phase; redrawn from H. A. Fosbrooke, 1950, pl. IIIB

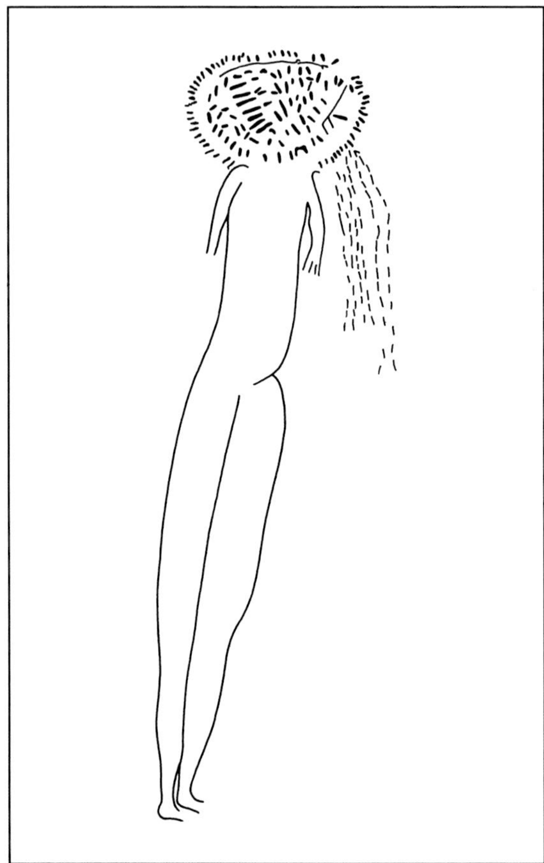

113. East African rock painting representing 'a shaman in trance bleeding from the nose', Chungal 3, Tanzania, hunter–gatherer phase; redrawn from M. Leakey, 1983, pl. 44

Some Nyau paintings mark the hiding places of masks and animal effigies used in the dance, and they also indicate meeting places for initiates. The paintings depict dancers and creatures associated with the ritual. The spreadeagled forms, for instance, probably depict crocodiles and mythical reptiles. Most Nyau paintings are associated with the Chewa and are found in Malawi. Similar paintings are known in Zambia. In Kenya, white geometric designs have been interpreted as depictions of cattle brands. These are associated with the Maasai warriors' practice of meat-feasting at sites distant from open-air settlements.

(d) Southern Africa. South of the Zambezi lies one of the richest areas of rock art in Africa, not only in the number of sites and depictions but also in the detail and elegance of the works. Although a fundamental distinction exists elsewhere in Africa between the art of hunter-gatherers and that of pastoralists or agriculturalists, in Southern Africa most depictions can be confidently ascribed to San hunter-gatherers. Some may have been made by the pastoral Khoi (Hottentots) and, in restricted areas, by mixed-farming Bantu-speaking groups.

SAN art is among the best understood hunter-gatherer rock art in the world because there is a considerable body of relevant ethnography—a vital component lacking for all the regions so far discussed. Some of the ethnography was collected in the 19th century and is thus contemporary with the last painters. The rest comes from the modern San of the Kalahari Desert. Striking correspondences between these two bodies of ethnography show that the San over a vast geographical area and probably for many millennia shared a fundamental cognitive system irrespective of local variations.

This system of belief derives from a shamanistic view of the world. The principal ritual, the trance or medicine dance, affords shamans access to the spirit world. Clapping, singing, hyperventilation and intense concentration induce trance. In this state the shamans cure the sick, drive off evil spirits and malign shamans in feline form, make rain and control antelope herds. San art depicts these activities as well as symbols of the supernatural potency harnessed by the shamans and the bizarre hallucinations they experience (*see* SAN, fig. 2). Trance imagery includes geometric entoptic forms, rain-animals, feline shamans and shamans blended with animal power in therianthropic figures. Apart from these 'non-realistic' elements, much San rock art is noteworthy for its remarkable portrayals of animals. In Zimbabwe graceful giraffes and kudu with finely drawn horns abound. Further south the eland predominates. This, the largest antelope, is, in the south-eastern mountains, depicted in the shaded polychrome technique many writers consider the apogee of all African rock art (*see* SAN, fig. 1). The red and white paint is delicately shaded to suggest the contours of the animal's body, and details, such as ears, mouth and cloven hoofs, are immaculately drawn. Some of the Saharan paintings show animals looking round; in the south, however, eland are drawn in every conceivable posture with an exceptional mastery of technique.

Also in the San area, there are complex scenes involving many individual depictions. They portray dances, fights, hunts (though much less frequently than often supposed) and rows of figures with their hunting equipment. The late 19th-century paintings sometimes show the conflict with the White colonists that effected the demise of the southern San. These apparently narrative scenes seem to argue for a literal component; however, on closer inspection, details can be found relating to religion and trance.

Unlike the Saharan and East African art, distinct periods are difficult to discern in any of the Southern African regions. None of the elaborate stylistic sequences that have been proposed stands up to scrutiny, although it appears that the shaded polychromes of the south-eastern mountains date from *c.* 1750.

BIBLIOGRAPHY

H. A. Winkler: *The Rock-drawings of Southern Upper Egypt* (London, 1938–9)

H. A. Fosbrooke: 'Tanganyika Rock Paintings', *Tanganyika Notes & Rec.*, xix (1950), pp. 1–61

J. D. Clark: *The Prehistoric Cultures of the Horn of Africa* (Cambridge, 1954)

H. Lhote: *The Search for the Tassili Frescoes* (London, 1959)

R. Summers, ed.: *Prehistoric Rock Art of the Federation of Rhodesia and Nyasaland* (Salisbury, 1959)

R. R. Inskego: 'The Age of the Kondoa Rock Paintings in the Light of Recent Excavations at Kiese II Rock Shelter', *Proceedings of the Fourth Panafrican Congress on Prehistory* (Tervuren, 1962), pp. 249–56

J. D. Lajoux: *The Rock Paintings of Tassili* (London, 1963)

F. Mori: *Tadrart Acacus* (Turin, 1965)

A. Hampaté Ba and G. Dieterlen: 'Les Fresques d'époque bovidienne du Tassili N'Ajjer et les traditions des Peul: Hypothèses d'interprétation', *J. Soc. Africanistes*, xxxci (1966), pp. 141–57
P. Hellstrom: *The Rock Drawings*, i of *Scandinavian Joint Expedition to Sudanese Nubia* (Odense, 1970)
H. Pager: *Ndedema* (Graz, 1971)
E. ten Raa: 'Dead Art and Living Society: A Study of Rock Paintings in a Social Context', *Mankind*, viii (1971), pp. 42–58
P. Cervicek: *Felsbilder des Nord-Etbai, Oberägyptens und Unternubiens* (Wiesbaden, 1974)
J. H. Chaplin: 'The Prehistoric Rock Art of the Lake Victoria Region', *Azania*, ix (1974), pp. 1–50
F. Mori: 'The Earliest Saharan Rock-engravings', *Antiquity*, xlviii (1974), pp. 87–92
R. M. Gramly: 'Meat-feasting Sites and Cattle Brands: Patterns of Rock-shelter Utilisation in East Africa', *Azania*, x (1975), pp. 107–21
H. Nowak, S. Ortner and D. Ortner: *Felsbilder der spanischen Sahara* (Graz, 1975)
D. W. Phillipson: *The Prehistory of Eastern Zambia* (Nairobi, 1976)
P. Vinnicombe: *People of the Eland* (Pietermaritzburg, 1976)
W. E. Wendt: ' "Art Mobilier" from Apollo 11 Cave, South West Africa: Africa's Oldest Dated Works of Art', *S. Afr. Archaeol. Bull.*, xxxi (1976), pp. 5–11
D. W. Phillipson: *The Later Prehistory of Eastern and Southern Africa* (London, 1977)
N. E. Lindgren and J. M. Schoffeleers: *Rock Art and Nyau Symbolism in Malawi* (Limbe, 1978)
J. D. Lewis-Williams: *Believing and Seeing: Symbolic Meanings in Southern San Rock Paintings* (London, 1981)
M. Leakey: *Africa's Vanishing Art: The Rock Paintings of Tanzania* (London, 1983)
W. Davis: 'Representation and Knowledge in the Prehistoric Rock Art of Africa', *Afr. Archaeol. Rev.*, ii (1984), pp. 7–35
J.-P. Roset: 'The Prehistoric Rock Paintings of the Sahara', *Endeavour*, viii (1984), pp. 75–84
A. R. Willcox: *The Rock Art of Africa* (Johannesburg, 1984)
P. Garlake: *The Painted Caves: An Introduction to the Prehistoric Art of Zimbabwe* (Harare, 1987)
J. D. Lewis-Williams: 'Beyond Style and Portrait: A Comparison of Tanzanian and Southern African Rock Art', *Contemp. Stud. Khoisan*, ii (1987), pp. 93–139
J. D. Lewis-Williams and T. A. Dowson: *Images of Power: Understanding Bushman Rock Art* (Johannesburg, 1989)
T. A. Dowson: *Rock Engravings of Southern Africa* (Johannesburg, 1992)

J. D. LEWIS-WILLIAMS

VII. Regions.

1. Northern Africa. 2. North-east Africa. 3. Western Sudan. 4. Guinea Coast. 5. Western Equatoria. 6. Central Africa. 7. East Africa. 8. Southern Africa.

1. NORTHERN AFRICA. Region to the north of the Sahara desert comprising the modern states of EGYPT, LIBYA, TUNISIA, ALGERIA, MOROCCO, WESTERN SAHARA and MAURITANIA (see fig. 114). Northern Africa shares the geography, climate, flora and fauna of the Mediterranean basin. Moreover, the sea was traditionally less of a barrier to the movement of men, materials and ideas than was the Sahara, although from early times important routes across the desert were established along the Nile Valley in the east and from Morocco to the Niger in the west. The southern border of the Mediterranean zone has been defined (see Braudel) as the limit of cultivation of wheat, grapes and olives; this line coincides with the northernmost limit of the compact palm grove. The close cultural ties between Northern Africa and southern Europe cannot be overemphasized: the straight-line distance between Tunis (anc. Carthage) and Rome, for example, is only 600 km.

(i) History. The history of Northern Africa over at least the last two millennia is known with remarkable precision, although most of the documents and all the histories were written by foreigners. The record of the arts in Northern Africa is equally rich and continuous, but it is normally studied in the discrete disciplines of prehistoric archaeology, ancient and Classical archaeology (*see* EGYPT, ANCIENT; GREECE, ANCIENT; and ROME, ANCIENT), EARLY CHRISTIAN AND BYZANTINE ART, ISLAMIC ART and archaeology and anthropology.

People later known as the Capsians or Proto-Mediterraneans appeared in the Maghrib (Maghreb, Magreb; a

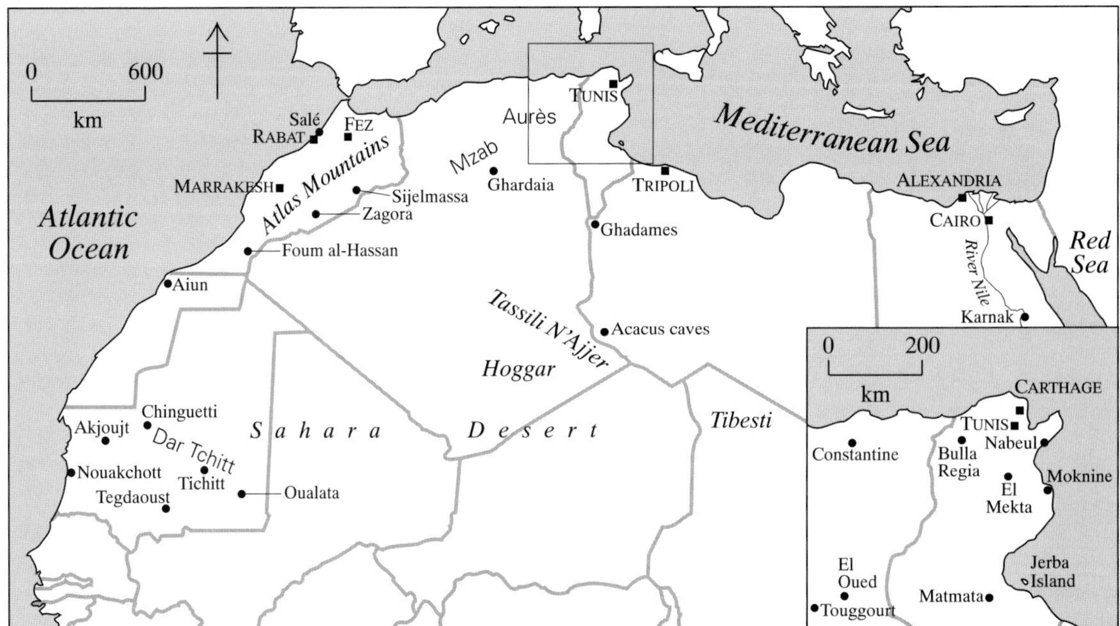

114. Map of Africa, northern regions; those sites with separate entries in this dictionary are distinguished by CROSS-REFERENCE TYPE

115. Mosaic pavement depicting *Ulysses and the Sirens*, 1.30×3.44 m, from Dougga, Tunisia, 3rd century AD (Tunis, Musée National du Bardo)

collective term often applied to Tunisia, Algeria and Morocco; from the Arabic word for 'west') in the 9th or 8th millennium BC. Rock engravings and sculptures with representations of elephants, rhinoceroses, giraffes and buffaloes have been found at sites such as El Mekta (near Gafsa, Tunisia); they date from the 7th millennium BC. The artefacts of settled agriculturalists and pastoralists (5th millennium BC) show evidence of stone-polishing, pottery-making and the use of grains. Megalithic cemeteries have been found with dolmens and sepulchral chambers carved into the rock. An inscription from Karnak, Egypt (*c.* 1220 BC), mentions the Libyans, one of the names for this indigenous population, later also known as Berber.

In the 9th century BC Phoenician traders from Tyre founded Carthage, which by the 6th century BC was the largest and richest city in the western Mediterranean, trading in tin from Cornwall, gold from West Africa, ivory from Central Africa and textiles (*see* PUNIC ART). In 146 BC the Romans invaded Northern Africa, destroyed Carthage, and made nearby Utica the capital of a new Roman province, which supplied Italy with wheat, wine and olive oil. The large estates of absentee landlords contrasted with the smaller holdings of settlers, who pressed further south and came increasingly in conflict with the semi-nomadic Berbers in their mountain retreats. In the 2nd and 3rd centuries AD Roman civilization spread from the cities, and great public monuments and baths were erected. In 439 AD, the Germanic Vandals seized Carthage and introduced Aryan Christianity. The first Muslim invasions took place in the 640s, and KAIROUAN, the first Muslim settlement west of the Nile, was established in the 670s. Carthage fell definitively in 698 (*see also* CARTHAGE, §§1, 2 and 3). After a century of direct control by caliphs, the region became increasingly self-governing from the late 8th century until about the mid-13th, when it again came under external rule. In the late 16th century Libya, Tunisia and much of Algeria became provinces of the Ottoman empire, while Morocco remained independent under the Sharifs. France, Germany, Italy and Spain gained colonies in the region and maintained them until independence was won in the 20th century.

(ii) Architecture, arts and crafts. Architecture has always been the most important art form in Northern Africa in the historical period. Public buildings were normally built of stone, which was easily quarried throughout the region, although unbaked and baked brick has also been used since Punic times (*c.* 3rd century BC) when stone was unavailable or impracticable. The building techniques and types generally belong to the Mediterranean traditions of trabeated stone construction roofed with wood, although vaulting was occasionally used, as in the early Islamic buildings from Sousse, Tunisia, or the more recent ones of the 10th century AD up to the 20th in the Mzab district of Algeria. The variety of religions followed in Northern Africa gave rise to a corresponding diversity of religious architecture, but congregational buildings, whether basilicas or mosques, were often hypostyle structures. Houses, as throughout the Mediterranean region, are single- or multi-storey, with rooms grouped around an open court. Variants include the houses of Bulla Regia, Tunisia (2nd–3rd centuries AD), with a subterranean level for relief from the summer heat; the troglodyte houses of Matmata, Tunisia, which have a circular pit serving as a court with chambers excavated in its walls; and the *ksour* of the north-western Sahara, which are Berber fortified farming villages with dwellings of rammed earth or unbaked brick.

Rock paintings at sites such as Tassili, Algeria (6th–2nd millennia BC), are the earliest examples of the visual arts in the region, while the most important and extensive are the thousands of mosaic pavements of Roman North Africa (*in situ* and in collections, e.g. Algiers, Mus. N. Ant.; Tunis, Mus. N. Bardo; see fig. 115). The earliest mosaic pavements at Carthage (?5th century BC) suggest that the mosaic technique may have been derived from *pavimenta punica*, in which mortar pavements were inlaid with bits of stone or glass. Black-and-white mosaics, based on Italian models, appeared in the 1st century AD, but the finest and most elaborate, which illustrate scenes of mythology and everyday life in many colours of marble, stone and glass tesserae, date from between the 3rd century and the 5th. The mosaic technique continued to be used under Christian patronage for tombs and church pavements but seems to have been abandoned soon after the coming of Islam.

Punic terracotta figurines (4th or 3rd century BC; Tunis, Bardo Mus.) show modes of representation based on the Greek or Egyptian models that had been imported into the region. Representational sculptures in terracotta, marble, limestone and other materials were produced throughout the Roman period; a few unusual figural sculptures were produced in Tunisia in the 10th and 11th centuries. These include a marble relief of a seated prince holding a cup (Tunis, Bardo Mus.). In the Islamic period tombstones and stucco revetments were decorated with geometric, plant and epigraphic sculptural designs. Some of the finest ceramics of antiquity, red wares with moulded decoration known as *terra sigillata*, were made over a long period in Tunisia and exported widely. Islam brought with it new ceramic techniques, including glazing and overglaze painting with metallic oxides to create a lustre effect. Lustre tiles were used in the mid-9th-century surround of the mihrab in the Great Mosque of Kairouan, but pavements and dados of glazed ceramic tile, one of the most characteristic features of western Islamic architecture, did not appear until the 11th century.

The Phoenicians may have introduced the eastern vertical loom to North Africa, and the Romans may also have introduced textile techniques, but the earliest fine weaving in the region is a textile inscribed with the name of the Umayyad caliph Marwan II (*reg* AD 744–50). Fine woollens were made from early Islamic times in many of the coastal cities (*see* ISLAMIC ART, §VI, 2(i)(c)), and, during the reign of al-Ma'mun (*reg* 813–33), 120 large carpets were sent from Tunisia to Baghdad in part-payment of taxes. North African woven and decorated textiles were eventually surpassed by those from Turkey and Iran, but the traditional textiles of Tunisia and Morocco, ranging from the exquisite silk embroideries of Fez to the sturdy carpets of Kairouan, have come to be highly appreciated. The traditional floor coverings in mosques are reed mats, and basketry is widely practised, particularly, for example, at Nabeul in Tunisia.

The arts of the book, including binding, calligraphy and illumination, became extraordinarily important in the Islamic period (*see* ISLAMIC ART, §III), as is clear from the exquisitely tooled leather bindings and fine parchment of a large collection of Koran manuscripts (*c*. 9th and 10th centuries; Kairouan, Great Mosque, Library). Glassmaking, probably also introduced by the Phoenicians, continued into the Islamic period, although Northern Africa was never a major centre of glass manufacture. Metals, including gold, copper alloys and lead, were used to make a wide range of tools, boxes, mirrors and jewellery and to mint coins from Punic times. Wood-carving and joinery, for which ample supplies of timber were to hand from the forests of North African mountains, were important throughout the Islamic period. The major congregational mosques have wooden minbars (pulpits) and *maqṣūra*s (enclosed area reserved for the sovereign, often marked by a screen). The earliest, among them that of Kairouan (mid-9th century), relied entirely on the effects of carving and turning, while later examples introduced colour effects through the use of marquetry in other woods and ivory.

The art of the region in colonial and post-colonial times is discussed in entries on individual countries.

BIBLIOGRAPHY

F. Braudel: *La Méditerranée et le monde méditerranéen à l'époque de Philippe II* (Paris, 1966); Eng. trans. by S. Reynolds as *The Mediterranean and the Mediterranean World in the Age of Philip II* (New York, 1972)

A. Laroui: *L'Histoire du Maghreb: Un Essai de synthèse* (Paris, 1970); Eng. trans. as *The History of the Maghrib: An Interpretive Essay* (Princeton, 1977)

D. Hill and L. Golvin: *Islamic Architecture in North Africa* (London, 1976)

From the Far West: Carpets and Textiles of Morocco (exh. cat. by P. L. Fiske, W. R. Pickering and R. S. Yohe, Washington, DC, Textile Mus., 1980)

De Carthage à Kairouan: 2000 ans d'art et d'histoire en Tunisie (exh. cat., Paris, Petit Pal., 1982–3)

I. Reswick: *Traditional Textiles of Tunisia and Related North African Weavings* (Los Angeles, 1985)

Carthage: A Mosaic of Ancient Tunisia (exh. cat., ed. A. B. A. Ben Khader and D. Soren; New York, Amer. Mus. Nat. Hist., 1987)

De l'empire romain aux villes impériales: 6000 ans d'art au Maroc (exh. cat., Paris, Petit Pal., 1990)

JONATHAN M. BLOOM

2. NORTH-EAST AFRICA. Region comprising the modern states of SUDAN, ETHIOPIA, Eritrea, DJIBUTI and SOMALIA (see fig. 116). Prehistoric art includes cave paintings depicting animals and figures (e.g. in Somalia), but the later dominant cultural and artistic traditions in the region are associated with two world religions: Islam in much of Sudan, in parts of Ethiopia and in Djibuti and Somalia; and Christianity in highland Ethiopia and, in vestigial forms, as late as the 15th century in NUBIA in the Sudan. In ancient times, Egyptian culture (*see* EGYPT, ANCIENT) impacted strongly on Nubia, as did the pre-Islamic civilization of South Arabia on Ethiopian or Aksumite culture (named after the city of AKSUM). Imported traditions were gradually assimilated to indigenous models, giving rise to quite independent and distinctive cultures. Sudan and Ethiopia, however, exhibit a wide degree of ethnic diversity, and some of their peoples, such as the NUBA in the Sudan and many of the Oromo in Ethiopia, have maintained their own artistic traditions.

Archaeology provides the sole evidence for the art of ancient Nubia and ancient Ethiopia. Monumental architecture and, to a lesser degree, pottery and metalwork have survived, but painting or sculpture in more perishable materials have not. The art and architecture of ancient Nubia or MEROË are clearly derived from those of ancient Egypt, but are sufficiently different to be considered as more than a mere provincial aberration. Distinctively Meroitic art dates from the 3rd century BC to around the beginning of the 4th century AD and is mostly known from monumental sculpture, both in the round and in relief, representing either royal persons and their activities or divine figures. In Ethiopia, too, the earliest examples of monumental architecture, such as the temple at Yeha, date from the last centuries BC and exhibit a South Arabian style, with a massive rectangular construction of fine ashlar masonry on a stepped plinth. The architecture of Aksum, dating from the first centuries AD, is somewhat different and probably represents an indigenous development from the older South Arabian tradition. Typical of Aksumite monuments are the famous obelisks or stelae, which faithfully copy in a single block of stone multi-storey

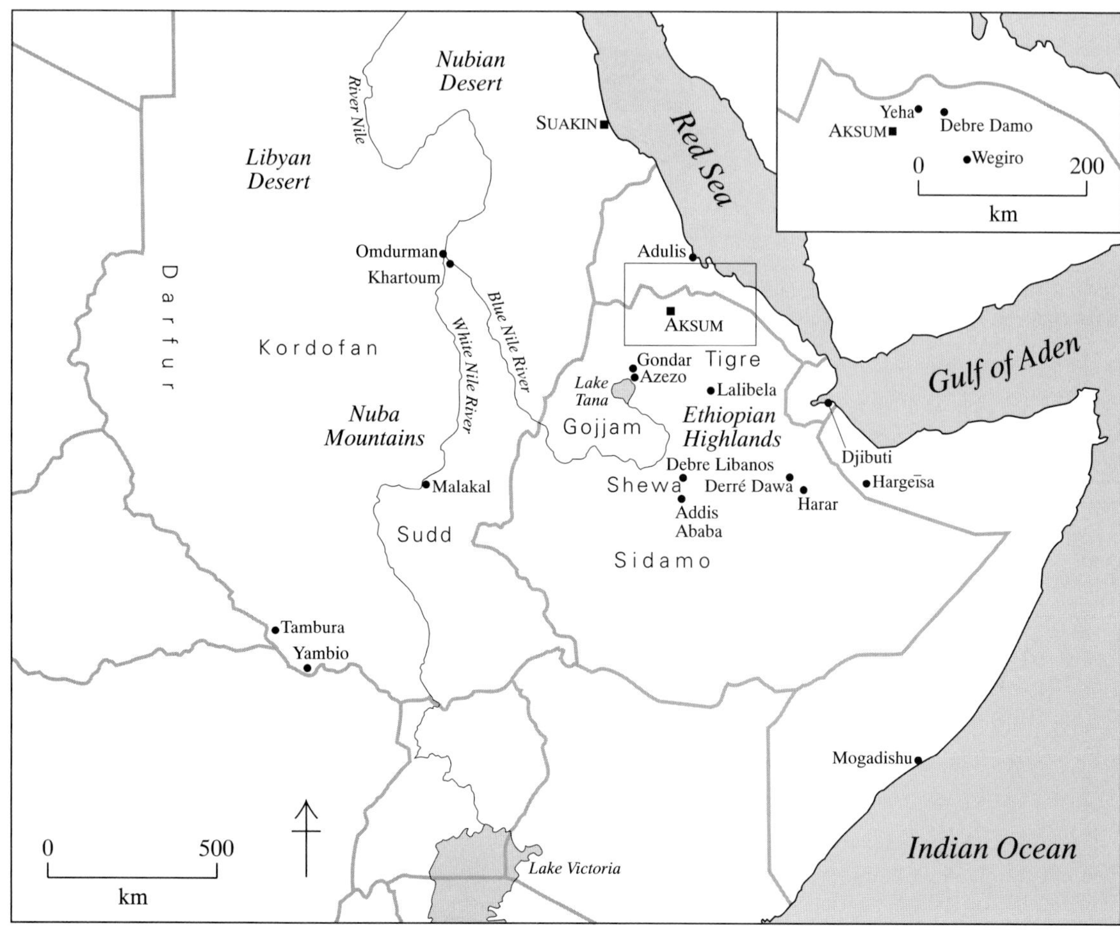

116. Map of North-east Africa; those sites with separate entries in this dictionary are distinguished by CROSS-REFERENCE TYPE

constructions with features such as door- and window-frames, protruding beams and corner joists (*see also* ETHIOPIA, §III). This architectural style was still in use in Ethiopia many centuries later, for example in the monastic church at Debre Damo (*c.* 11th century).

Christianity, adopted in both Ethiopia (mid-4th century) and Nubia, brought with it new artistic styles and genres. Paintings, on walls, on panels or as manuscript illuminations, were from then on all purely religious in content. Only wall paintings, such as those at the ruined cathedral at FARAS, survive from Christian Nubia (*see also* NUBIA, §VI). From Ethiopia, where Christianity still flourishes, examples of manuscript painting in illustrated Gospels and lives of saints, painted panels and murals are extant. The earliest Ethiopian Christian painting (13th and 14th centuries), though clearly derived from Syria and Armenia, as well as from Coptic Egypt, exhibits characteristics of its own, such as a marked tendency towards geometric design (for a 17th-century example see fig. 117). Like other Eastern Christian art, Ethiopian religious painting was highly conservative, developing markedly only in response to contacts with Western Europe, notably from the late 15th century to the early 17th, which gave rise to the Gondarene style, adopted in and around the old capital and cultural centre of GONDAR (*see also* ETHIOPIA, §II). In early Ethiopian church architecture (*see* ETHIOPIA, §I) a simplified basilican plan along the lines of Eastern Christian models became the standard form and persisted until the 19th century, when a circular plan became the norm in all but the north of the country. A remarkable development was the rock-cut church, the most famous examples being at Lalibela. Like the Aksumite obelisks, these faithfully imitate in stone constructions built of other materials. Also typical of Ethiopian Christian art is fine, pierced metalwork in the form of crosses, both hand-held and processional, and other church furniture and appurtenances such as thuribles and chalices.

In regions where Islam became the dominant religion different influences are detectable. For example, in the coastal towns of Somalia, such as Mogadishu, and in Harar, the centre of Ethiopian Islam, a tradition exists of complex and intricate geometrical carving in wood and stone belonging to the Azanian complex that extends down the East African coast as far as Mozambique. The Arab quarters of Mogadishu, which were once walled, contain mostly one- and two-storey stone houses. In north-western Somalia are the ruins of stone-built towns that flourished in the 15th and 16th centuries: porcelain,

117. Ethiopian illumination depicting *St Mark*, 268×249 mm, from a Gospel book, Lasta, 17th century (London, British Library, BM Or. 516, fol. 64*v*)

pottery, glass, metal and stone remains attest to their prosperity and to trading links with Egypt and western, Central and East Asia.

Much traditional or folk art in North-east Africa is concentrated in essentially portable personal and domestic objects, such as fabrics, weaving, bead- and needlework, leatherwork, basketwork, copper, silver and gold jewellery and metalwork, wood-carving and wood-engraving. Ivory-carving is widespread in Sudan. Dwellings among pastoral and agricultural communities may be made of clay, sun-dried mud, brick, branches, cow-dung plaster, mats and skins; conical thatched roofs are found among the sedentary agriculturalists of Somalia. Often, however, the artistic impulse, in settled as well as in semi-nomadic and pastoral societies, finds freer expression in language and oral literature than in visual art.

A notable form of artistic expression in North-east Africa is popular secular painting in Ethiopia, increasingly important since the beginning of the 20th century. These paintings, usually on canvas, often either illustrate events in recent history such as battles, splendid official ceremonies or scenes of everyday life or portray in strip-cartoon form the story of the Ethiopian national epic of King Solomon and the Queen of Sheba.

The art of the region in colonial and post-colonial times is discussed in entries on individual countries.

BIBLIOGRAPHY

P. L. Shinnie: *Meroe: A Civilization of the Sudan*, Ancient Peoples and Places (London, 1967)

G. Gerster: *Kirchen im Fels* (Stuttgart, 1968; Eng. trans., London, 1970; Ger. rev. Zurich and Freiburg im Breisgau, 1972)

D. Buxton: *The Abyssinians*, Ancient Peoples and Places (London, 1970)

S. Chojnacki: *Major Themes in Ethiopian Painting: Indigenous Developments, the Influence of Foreign Models and their Adaptation (from the 13th to the 19th Century)*, Äthiopische Forschungen (Stuttgart, 1983)

Somalia in Word and Image (exh. cat. by K. S. Loughran, J. L. Loughran, J. W. Johnson and S. S. Samatar, Washington, DC, Found. Cross Cult. Understanding, 1986)

Pittura etiopica tradizionale (exh. cat., Rome, Ist. It.–Afr., 1989)

DAVID APPLEYARD

3. WESTERN SUDAN. Region between Lake Chad and the mouths of the Senegal and Gambia rivers, comprising NIGER, NIGERIA, MALI, BURKINA FASO, northern GHANA, SENEGAL and GAMBIA (see fig. 118). It is characterized by savannah grasslands, with patches of forest, and large river systems, including the Niger, Bani and Benue. The region has been subject to alternating wet and dry periods and consequently to tremendous changes in vegetation and desertification.

(i) Introduction. (ii) Regions.

(i) Introduction. In terms of cultural history, the Western Sudan includes, in the east, the NOK culture, which began in northern Nigeria in the latter half of the 1st millennium BC with the flourishing of complex societies based on metal technology and sophisticated ceramic sculpture, and, in the west, the early communities around a now extinct lake in the Dar Tchitt area of southern Mauritania, from which stemmed an era of great savannah state- and empire-building. Among these entities were the empires of Ghana, Mali and Songhai, the BAMANA states of Segou and Kaarta, the Fula state of Macina, the MOSSI states in southern Burkina Faso and the Kororofa and Hausa states in northern Nigeria. The northern Yoruba states such as Old Oyo may also have contributed to the character of Western Sudan.

In addition to sophisticated statecraft, the region has been typified by phenomenal commercial enterprise, dramatic religious developments and dynamic art traditions. Short- and long-distance trade have apparently long been a part of the area's economy, and many cultural groups have taken full advantage of ecological and technological developments to maximize the commercial potential in their human and natural environments. Western Sudan was one of the first African regions to be reached by Islam, which became both implanted and transformed as a powerful spiritual institution. Local religions, with their emphasis on special relations with ancestors and the earth, have also responded to new situations and changing conditions. Cult groups, which constitute a basic element of spiritual organization, are especially sensitive to their environments, moving in and out of regions and adjusting their tenets readily, thereby constantly reinvigorating the arts.

Although there is tremendous cultural variation across this area, as reflected in the proliferation of language and ethnic groups, artistic styles, while also encompassing great variety, nevertheless show a striking continuity. This is especially noteworthy in the 'Pole style' of maskmaking and figure sculpture, so called because of its abstract attenuation and elongation. Further characteristics are minimization of features and an orientation towards geometric interpretations of people and animals. This is obvious among the Voltaic peoples in Burkina Faso, whose masks are often decorated with basic geometric shapes in vivid colours, and in northern Nigeria, where many mask and figure types are reduced to geometric

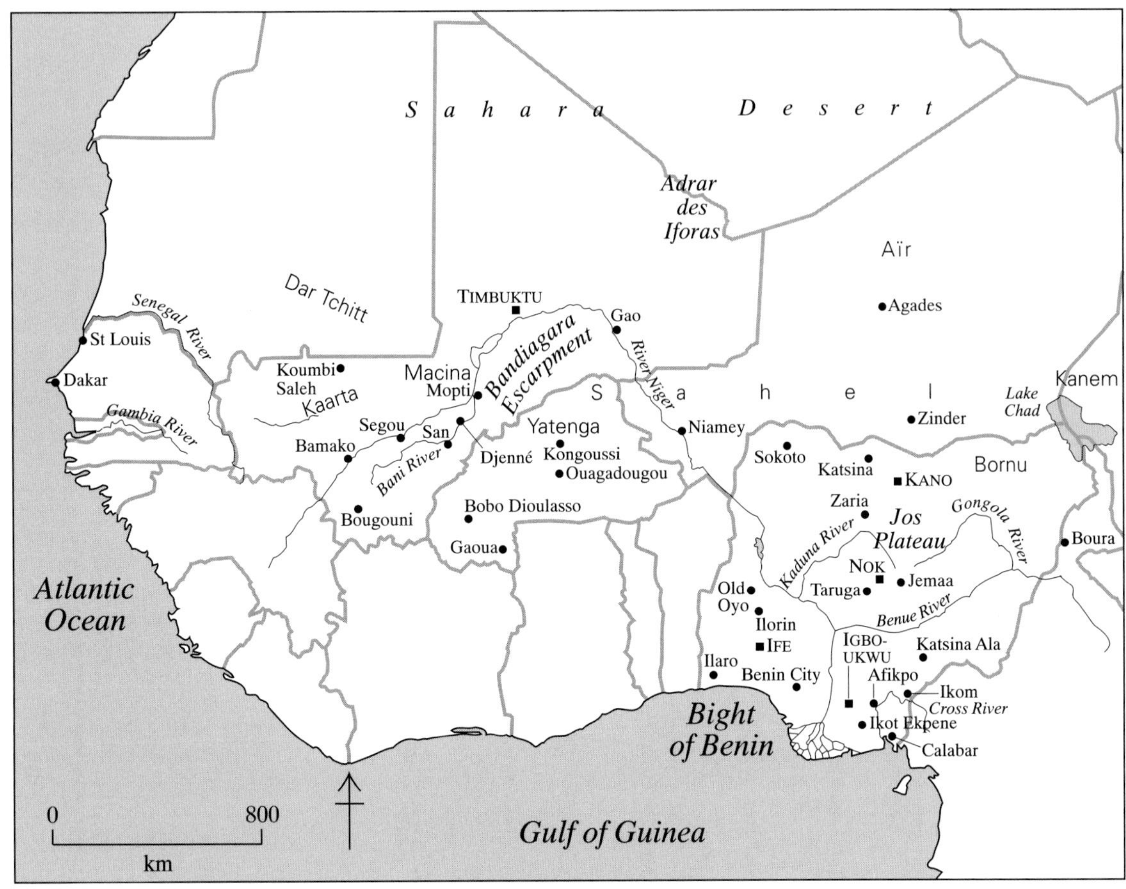

118. Map of Western Sudan; those sites with separate entries in this dictionary are distinguished by CROSS-REFERENCE TYPE

volumes, becoming almost the conceptual counterparts of 'primary form' sculptures of the West.

Knowledge of the history of Western Sudanic art is minimal. In the 1st millennium BC subtle ceramic sculpture was being manufactured extensively on and around the Jos Plateau in northern Nigeria; it portrayed humans, animals and, to a lesser extent, insects and vegetables. Many scholars associate this repertory with political and spiritual leadership complexes and the existence of an ancient and widespread social and economic unity. To the east, near Lake Chad, a slightly later ceramic sculpture tradition flourished. Later still, in the 1st millennium AD, clay sculpture was made to the west of the Niger–Benue confluence.

In the great bend of the River Niger another constellation existed of complex societies, active several centuries before and after the time of Christ and producing also terracotta sculpture, of which, unfortunately, very few pieces have been found in archaeological contexts, the rest having been illicitly removed to serve demand from Western collectors. Along the Bandiagara escarpment in Mali, art works of iron and wood have been found in burial caves. They date from the early 2nd millennium AD and are ascribed to people known to modern scholars as Tellem. Further west, in Senegal, large stone monuments have been found, built, apparently, over long periods during the 1st millennium AD.

Art, especially in the form of ornate precious-metal regalia, was associated with the courts of the Ghana and Mali empires. Arab sources indicate that Ghana's capital included a sacred forest housing secret sculpture. The Arab traveller Ibn Battuta (1304–68) observed carved wooden birds' heads worn with elaborate bird costumes by 'poets' who commented at court on the qualities of past and present leaders. Oral traditions suggest that sculpture associated with *komo* (initiation) may have existed early in the 2nd millennium AD. In the Mande expansion regions of the Gambia, occult iron staffs with figural tops may have been used as symbols of leadership by about the 15th century AD.

(ii) Regions.

(a) Eastern. (b) Central. (c) Western.

(a) Eastern. The eastern region is centred in northern Nigeria. In the Gongola River area clay and cultivated gourds are favoured media (see 1986–8 exh. cat.). Several ethnic groups, including the Bena, Cham, Ga'anda, Longuda, Tula and Yungur, create clay vessels of highly sacred character that can be found in shrines and are used in local medical practices and to honour ancestor and guardian

119. Kebere headdress, fibre and pigment, h. 1.13 m, Koro, Western Sudan (Bloomington, IN, Indiana University Art Museum)

spirits. They are elaborately embellished and, though anthropomorphic, often highly abstracted and stylized, sometimes to the extent that individual pots cannot be identified as portrayals without knowledge of important cultural practices such as scarification. Such is the importance of clay vessels that, for example, the culture hero among the Ga'anda is identified as a spirit pot.

In this area decorated gourds are a highly prized art form used by many ethnic groups, including the HAUSA and the Fulani (*see* FULANI, fig. 1). They often serve utilitarian purposes and include containers for storing and serving food and drink, head-balanced carriers, measuring devices, spoons and ladles, pipes and snuff bottles, and even sun bonnets for children. Others are used as musical instruments, such as drums, xylophones and horns, perhaps with sacred or occult associations. Gourds may constitute part of a bride's dowry or be given to her by husband or friends, and they are often central elements in carefully created displays indicating the married status of a woman. Gourds are often carried or worn at initiations, funerals and agricultural ceremonies. They may also symbolize membership of secret initiation associations, and several groups use them in soothsaying.

Like the ceramic pieces, gourds are embellished with carefully conceived and executed, sometimes three-dimensional, patterns that are extremely imaginative and greatly appreciated. Individual motifs have names and refer to the natural and social environments. The interpretations of both established and new designs respond to changing cultural situations, offering ways of contemplating and manipulating local experience.

To the west, in the Benue River area, among groups such as the Chamba (for illustration *see* CHAMBA (ii)), Jukun and MUMUYE, wooden masks and figures are the dominant art form. Great diversity in figure and especially mask forms have been recorded (especially by R. Sieber and A. Rubin; see 1961, 1974 and 1978 exh. cats, and Rubin, 1969), associated with a flexible approach to meaning and function. Among the mask and headdress types are some fantastic monumental raffia constructions (see fig. 119). The most widely known category of mask, which crosses at least ten ethnic boundaries, takes a variety of formal and conceptual configurations, emphasizing the horizontal plane. It apparently takes its inspiration from the awesome bush buffalo that formerly populated the entire savannah. Mama versions of the mask often display carved horns in the shape of an exaggerated crescent moon, attached to an abbreviated snout construction. The masks represent ancestor spirits and, providing access to occult power, are used in a cult called mangam which is involved in agricultural and funeral rites and the general well-being of the community.

Jukun versions are much more abstract, with a concave dish with cut-away designs serving as the horns, and other parts of the head attenuated in a creative fashion. Town chiefs claim that these masks, which also represent both bush cows and ancestors, are their own divine doubles, and wear them when performing at the funerals of leaders and other important persons. Goemai versions are similar formally, but, in addition to appearing at chiefs' funerals, are worn for dances at chiefs' installations and annual agricultural ceremonies. They are also employed in local medical practices. Chamba masks, worn at important funerals, embody the paramount female ancestors of the royal lineages. Mumuye versions are used in initiation rituals held every seven years. Each generation of neophytes commissions a new mask, which symbolizes that group at all subsequent performances.

Sculpted figures from this area are as reductionistically abstract as the masks. Jukun figures (for illustration *see* JUKUN) are used by chiefs to represent and communicate with ancestors; they are also used in a cult called Mam during propitiation ceremonies at planting and harvest seasons, and at times of duress. Mumuye figures are used in similar ways, bringing the spirits of ancestors into tangible focus, to be used by rainmakers greeting visitors, to help ascertain guilt at trials, to identify thieves by divination and as spiritual prophylactics to protect households. They are also linked to initiations, military activities and ironworking. Wurkun figures, used in male–female pairs, are believed to protect families as well as crops. Tiv figures, generally female, emerge from the tops of posts and are used in hunting, circumcision and prenuptial ceremonies. All these Benue figures, including those made by Chamba and other groups, have elongated torsos, arms, legs and necks and emphasize angularity and the lively, rhythmic interplay of shapes. Tiv figures are perhaps the least stylized. Brassworking in many areas of the Western Sudan was an important means of artistic expression, although it has gone undocumented (for illustration *see* BURKINA FASO). The Jukun are believed to have made brass pieces in various geometric configurations, such as cylinders and cones, with sonorific attachments, and openwork figures with fish-shaped legs, probably also as emblems of leadership.

Slightly to the west, in the Niger–Benue confluence area, the Idoma and the Igalu make art with strong stylistic affinities to Igbo groups to the south; indeed, the Igalu have imported mask types from their Igbo neighbours. These masks (for illustration *see* IDOMA and IGALU) are meant to call forth the spirits of ancestors of clan groups and thus help enhance the authority of community elders. Royal masquerades, also involving ancestors, reflect the ebb and flow of Igalu history. Idoma masks are associated not only with initiation into societies oriented towards military aggression but also with agricultural ceremonies and funerals. A formal eclecticism characterizes masks of both ethnic groups. Some take the helmet form, others are dance crests, and still others have horizontal configurations, some Idoma examples being of monumental size (l. *c.* 2 m). Both groups use figures in connection with health care, human fertility and general well-being and in particular with the protection of children.

The Igalu and the NUPE, the westernmost group in this region, used to carve doors for the entrances to family compounds. Elaborate collections of motifs asserted the wealth and prestige of the family heads who owned them. Made of several wood panels joined along vertical seams, Nupe doors (see fig. 120) were particularly large and were composed of many and elaborate motifs, from birds and Islamic writing-tablets to aeroplanes.

120. Nupe door, wood, from Western Sudan (Bloomington, IN, Indiana University Art Museum)

Several masquerades have been documented among the Nupe, who use cloth and cowrie compositions adapted from Yoruba Egungun masquerades (*see* YORUBA, §5 (i)) and, in an apotropaic practice called *ndako gboya*, tubes of cloth up to 3.5 m tall representing spirits and performing in twos or threes. A tradition of delicate face masks, surmounted by oval shapes and animals and figures aligned along a vertical shaft, is said to have reached the Nupe from sources to the south on the River Niger; these are brought into play in an entertainment masquerade performed on Muhammad's birthday.

The Hausa, commonly thought of primarily as craftsmen, in fact create arts that are sometimes subtle, sometimes flamboyant examples of rich expressive traditions. Their clay buildings and wall decoration (*see* HAUSA, fig. 2) constitute a vivid example, as seen in such structures as the 19th-century Friday Mosque in Zaria and the emir's palace in Kano (*see also* NIGERIA, §III). Exteriors are striking for their massive but elegant balustrades; interiors flow with arches and ribbing. Grand, geometric motifs, painted or in high relief, decorate the interiors and, since the 1930s, many exteriors too. Similar patterns are used in gourd decoration and in the embroidery that makes Hausa gowns (*see* HAUSA, fig. 1) among the most spectacular in West Africa. Modified, they are used also in leatherwork, such as sandals, cushion covers, bags, riding-boots and saddles. Hausa metalworking skill is evident in lovely jewellery and more practical items such as stirrups.

(b) Central. Dominant in this area are peoples who speak the Voltaic or Gur languages. Little scholarship has been devoted to their arts. Exceptions are Suzanne Blier's work on Tamberma iron jewellery, with its rich relationship to spirituality, myth and lore, and Fred Smith's studies on the sophisticated and aesthetically striking traditions of house-painting among certain groups in northern Ghana. Many of these groups also construct fantastic, two-storey, walled, clay family residences, using a coiling technique rather like that employed in making pottery; these buildings are sometimes referred to as castles.

Many Voltaic language-speaking ethnic groups, including the Mossi and LOBI, have become well known for their figure and, especially, their masking traditions, thanks largely to the work of Chris Roy (see 1979 exh. cat., and Roy). The Lobi make three-legged stools for men and four-legged stools for women; these artefacts are elegantly shaped, with highly imaginative leg shapes and angles, sweeping concave seats and often little sculpted human heads at the side. Lobi figures, which range in height from a few centimetres to *c.* 600–900 mm, frequently have minimally articulated torsos and limbs, the arms sometimes projecting in strange gestures, although the faces may be extremely sensitively carved. Research indicates (see 1981 exh. cat. by P. Meyer) that most are the embodiment of *thila* (spiritual beings), whom the creator god designed to assist and protect humankind. The Mossi produce chiefs' figures and dolls that are among the most refined, minimal abstractions created in Africa (*see* MOSSI, fig. 2). Figures made in this region are generally used in soothsaying

121. Bwa leaf mask for the cult of Do, worn at a funeral, Boni village, Western Sudan; from a photograph by Christopher D. Roy, 1985

and sorcery, both of which are practised in socially beneficial ways.

The masking traditions of these people are among the richest in Africa (see fig. 121). They are of major importance because they link individuals, clans and entire communities with the positive forces of the spirit world and serve in many capacities, including the regulation of commerce, the cleansing of communities, the practice of farming and the imparting of valuable cultural knowledge. Most groups have a mask society, admission to which may require extensive educational and socializing processes. The societies are linked, through the masks, to wilderness spirits, ancestor spirits or both, believed to be capable of bestowing blessings and benefits. The masks portray wild animals, such as antelopes (see fig. 122), buffalo, wild boar, hornbills, hyenas and snakes, as well as human characters, domestic animals, such as the cock, and unidentifiable, abstract conceptualizations. Even those that obviously depict animals are based on a central helmet form, with horns or other parts protruding up from it and snouts descending (*see*, for example, SENUFO, fig. 4). This format, though minimal, supports tremendous variation. Most masks are embellished with bold geometric patterns in black, white and red.

Masks appear, often in large groups, at funerals and burial ceremonies and agricultural cycle celebrations and in market-day entertainments, as well as in community problem-solving and initiation procedures. In the 20th century many young men have left Burkina Faso for employment and adventure elsewhere in West Africa, but they return for the farming season, a custom that is essential for the survival of their home communities. Mask performances are considered to have the power to draw the youth back home.

The DOGON are an intermediate group between the Voltaic language-speaking peoples of the central region

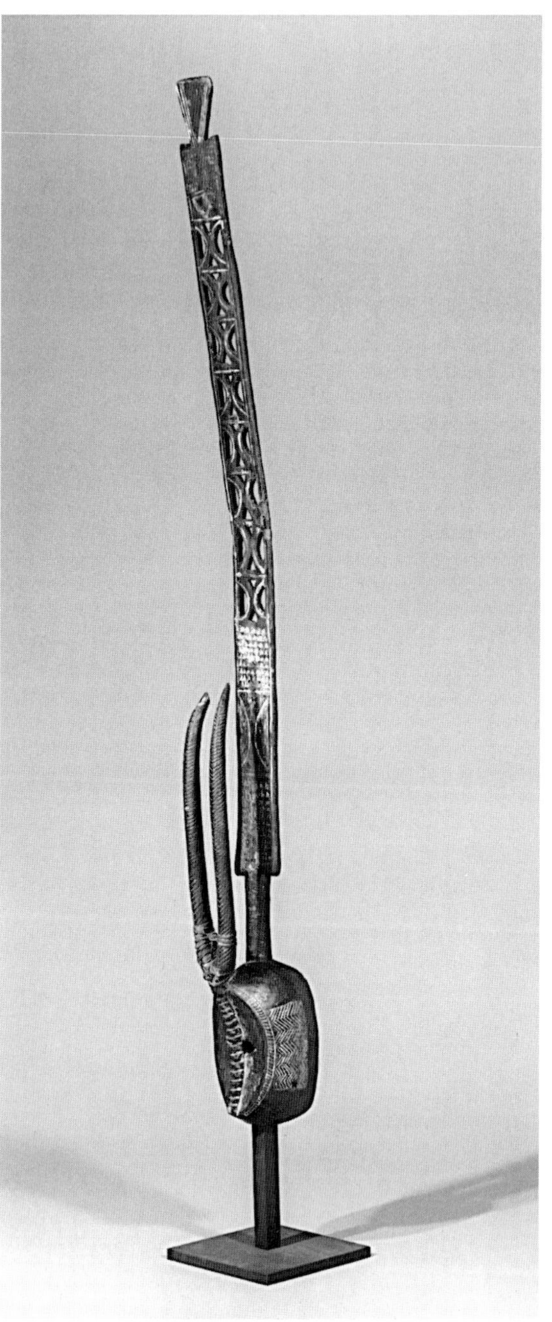

122. Mossi mask of Karanga type, wood, from Western Sudan (Bloomington, IN, Indiana University Art Museum)

and the Mande-speaking peoples of the western region. They speak a Voltaic language and, like many other Voltaic groups, have for many centuries interacted with the Mande, but with a greater intensity than most. Indeed, Mande oral traditions assert that the Dogon were of Mande origin, and the Dogon keep an earth shrine that allegedly contains soil brought during migrations from the Mande heartland in the mid-2nd millennium AD.

The Dogon are famous for their architecture, much of which graces the steep slopes of the Bandiagara escarpment. It features minimal, geometric house shapes, richly decorated shrines and spiritual residences, and elder men's public meeting-places (*togo na*) composed of massive, sculpted posts supporting thick straw roofs. Their figure sculpture is poorly documented, but in general it seems to serve as a means of warding off ill fortune and encouraging the intervention of benevolent spirits (*see* DOGON, fig. 1). Fine wrought-iron sculpture apparently functions as insignia for important priests (*hogan*): staffs are graced with extending arms that support small bells and are often topped with abstract, minimally articulated figures. In some examples iron strands on top are forged into cages that contain smooth stones.

Like other Voltaic peoples, the Dogon have a mask association. There are 78 recorded types of mask, which depict various characters, including humans and predators such as hyenas and crocodiles. The masks are often embellished with highly abstract, bold geometric patterns. Some extend a metre or more above the dancer's head. The masks are donned at funerals, at ceremonies to mark the end of formal periods of mourning and at *sigui*, dramatic ceremonies held every 60 years to mark the passing of the generations.

The SENUFO live to the south and the west of the Dogon, in southern Burkina Faso and Côte d'Ivoire. They too speak a Voltaic language, but their history includes a great deal of interaction with the Mande, and in many communities they live side by side with Mande Bamana. The Senufo make a vast array of sculpture, which exhibits many features of the savannah 'Pole style' but is sleeker and more curvilinear. Dramatic horizontal masks are used in their male initiation association (Poro) to help counteract negative spiritual forces. Almost antithetical are the face masks that depict great feminine beauty; these are used in initiation and funerary ceremonies by the Poro association and by the women's counterpart association (Sandogo). Tiny figures, along with miniature brass sculptures, are used in divination procedures by these women, while large, seated mother-and-child figures (*see* §IV, 5 above) represent a protective and nourishing female spirit force who plays a central role in Poro initiation. Large standing male and female figures also play important symbolic roles in Poro. Staffs topped by seated females or soaring birds with smaller birds balanced on their wings serve as prizes for young men who win annual cultivation contests (*see* SENUFO, figs 1–3).

(c) Western. The western region is dominated by Mande language-speaking groups such as the Bamana (Bambara), Maninka (Malinke) and Marka. Little art-historical research has been carried out on most Mande groups; the most dependable information relates to the Bamana, although the Maninka seem to have similar art forms.

The Bozo, who live in the western reaches of the Niger bend, share much with their Mande neighbours except language. They belong to a complex of peoples that includes the Bamana and the Marka, who are noted for marvellous and richly symbolic puppet performances staged by young people's volunteer work associations (*ton*). Boldly carved heads, masks and puppets, richly decorated with striking colours and perhaps dyed and woven cloth sewn into miniature clothing, are made to represent a cast of characters that includes not only people and animals but even objects such as jet aeroplanes. They are brought into play for skits and masquerades performed during the agricultural season.

The Bamana (*see* BAMANA, figs 3 and 4) also use masks in their secret initiation associations, which serve two principal types of function: soothsaying, healing and protection from evil; and education, individual contemplation and the opportunity for personal adjustment to the social and natural environment. The sculptures of one association, Chi Wara, which holds agricultural ceremonies and promotes good farming practice, take the form of an antelope headdress. Another society, N'tomo, which initiates young men into adulthood, has sculptures in the form of often delicate face masks presenting accepted ideas about intelligent, successful behaviour. Another association, Komo, stresses self-sufficiency, fulfilment and law and order: its major sculptures are dramatic, ambiguously carved horizontal masks, said to represent power and secrecy. Yet another association, Kore, reserved for mature male members of the community, also makes ambiguous masks, but these combine clearly recognizable human and animal features in highly imaginative compositions.

All these sculptures typify the geometric reductiveness that characterizes styles in the Western Sudan. One monumental form of Bamana sculpture is made for Gwan and Jo association activities and to celebrate the values of Mande society. These figures are much more curvilinear than the others and in many ways resemble the large Senufo sculptures mentioned above. Not surprisingly, these sculptures occur only in the southern portions of Bamana territory, where the Bamana live in close contact with the Senufo. Sadly, like other art objects in the Western Sudan, these figures have been subject to illicit collecting on a large scale.

Iron sculpture takes the form of lamps and figures on top of staffs and is often highly sophisticated, both aesthetically and technically. It too seems largely in decline. The staffs were used to grace the altars of the religious associations and of powerful individuals. In spite of the difficulties of working red-hot iron, the facial details often received delicate treatment. The staff portions were usually constructed of several pieces of metal, forge-welded together, with graceful hooks emerging from the joints to end in small conical knobs. The lamps consisted of a cup or cups of iron mounted on armatures attached to a central shaft. A lamp in the city of San is said to have had over 50 cups and was used to illuminate the popular night-time wrestling matches. Such iron lamps are still used in San for this purpose, although by and large iron lamps have been replaced by kerosene lanterns. Among the Mande small carved wooden figures are made, as playthings for children, as memorials in honour of the souls of deceased twins or for members of the male initiation association to enhance their public performances and emphasize their eligibility to young ladies.

See also articles on individual countries and §§II–VI above.

BIBLIOGRAPHY

Sculpture of Northern Nigeria (exh. cat. by R. Sieber, New York, Mus. Primitive A., 1961)
A. G. Rubin: *The Arts of the Jukun-speaking Peoples of Northern Nigeria* (diss., Bloomington, IN U., 1969)
R. A. Bravmann: *Islam and Tribal Art in West Africa*, African Studies Series (London and New York, 1974)
Interactions: The Art Styles of the Benue River Valley and East Nigeria (exh. cat., ed. R. Sieber and T. Vevers; West Lafayette, IN, Purdue U., 1974)
D. Heathcote: *The Arts of the Hausa: An Aspect of Islamic Culture in Northern Nigeria* (Chicago, 1977)
Bamana and Bozo Puppetry of the Segou Region Youth Societies (exh. cat. by M. J. Arnoldi, West Lafayette, IN, Purdue U., 1977)
Tellem: Een bijdrage tot de geschiedenis van de Republiek Mali (exh. cat. by R. M. A. Bedaux, Berg en Dal, Afrika Mus., 1977)
A. R[ubin]: '3: Masque-buffle/Buffalo Mask', *Vingt-cinq sculptures africaines/Twenty-five African Sculptures* (exh. cat., ed. J. Fry; Ottawa, N.G., 1978), pp. 54–7
T. Shaw: *Nigeria: Its Archaeology and Early History*, Ancient Peoples and Places, lxxxviii (London, 1978)
Three Rivers of Nigeria (exh. cat. by M. K. Wittmer and W. Arnett, Atlanta, GA, High Mus. A., 1978)
African Sculpture: The Stanley Collection (exh. cat. by C. D. Roy, Iowa City, U. IA Mus. A., 1979)
A. J. Glaze: *Art and Death in a Senufo Village*, Trad. A. Africa (Bloomington, 1981)
D. Idiens: *The Hausa of Northern Nigeria: A Catalogue of the R. E. Miller Collection and others in the Royal Scottish Museum*, Royal Scottish Museum Studies (Edinburgh, 1981)
F. T. Smith: 'Architectural Decoration of Northeastern Ghana', *Ba Shiru*, xi/1 (1981), pp. 24–32
For Spirits and Kings: African Art from the Paul and Ruth Tishman Collection (exh. cat. by S. M. Vogel, New York, Met., 1981)
Kunst und Religion der Lobi (exh. cat. by P. Meyer, Zurich, Mus. Rietberg, 1981)
T. Celenko: *A Treasury of African Art from the Harrison Eiteljorg Collection* (Bloomington, 1983)
S. P. Blier: 'Antelopes and Anvils: Tamberma Works of Iron', *Afr. A.*, xvii/3 (1984), pp. 58–63, 91
The Human Ideal in African Art: Bamana Figurative Sculpture (exh. cat. by K. Ezra, Washington, DC, N. Mus. Afr. A., 1986)
The Essential Gourd: Art and History in Northeastern Nigeria (exh. cat. by M. C. Berns and B. R. Hudson, Los Angeles, UCLA, Wight A.G.; Honolulu, HI, Acad. A.; New York, Cent. Afr. A.; Washington, DC, N. Mus. Afr. A.; 1986–8)
C. D. Roy: *Art of the Upper Volta Rivers* (Meudon, 1987)
S. K. McIntosh and R. J. McIntosh: 'From Stone to Metal: New Perspectives on the Later Prehistory of West Africa', *J. World Prehist.*, ii/1 (1988), pp. 89–133
P. R. McNaughton: *The Mande Blacksmiths: Knowledge, Power, and Art in West Africa*, Trad. A. Africa (Bloomington, 1988)
R. A. Sargent: 'Igala Masks: Dynastic History and the Face of the Nation', *West African Masks and Cultural Systems*, ed. S. L. Kasfir (Tervuren, 1988), pp. 17–44
African Art from the Rita and John Grunwald Collection (exh. cat. by D. M. Pelrine, Bloomington, IN U. A. Mus., 1988)
M. C. Berns: 'Ceramic Clues: Art History in the Gongola Valley', *Afr. A.*, xxii/2 (1989), pp. 48–59, 102–03

PATRICK R. MCNAUGHTON

4. GUINEA COAST. Region of Africa comprising the countries of the Atlantic coast from GUINEA-BISSAU in the north-west to the BENIN REPUBLIC and including GUINEA, SIERRA LEONE, LIBERIA, the CÔTE D'IVOIRE, GHANA and TOGO (see fig. 123). Specifically, the region may be defined in cultural terms as the narrower strip of coast, generally 100–150 km wide, loosely delimited by the extent of tropical rain-forest and its adjoining areas of diffuse vegetation and high grassland. The topographical

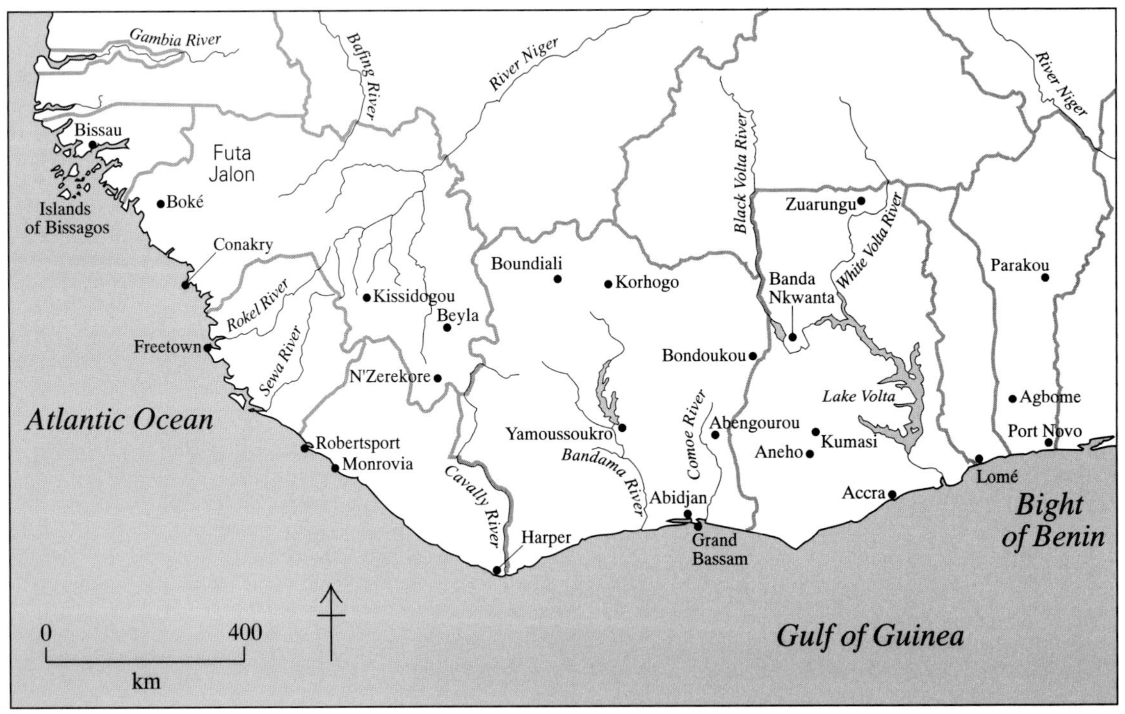

123. Map of the Guinea Coast

and climatic features of the land are factors in the formation of art styles. For example, the density of the forest in such places as Liberia and the Côte d'Ivoire has limited the mobility of peoples and thus insulated the indigenous groups from each other. Swampy, tidal lowlands along the coast, as in Guinea, often inaccessible for the annual six-month rainy season, compound this isolation. In most of the area, the rainy season extends fairly predictably from June to November and the dry from December to May.

(i) Historical introduction. (ii) Cultural traditions. (iii) Ritual organizations. (iv) Regional style clusters.

(i) Historical introduction. European contact with Africa has wrought a series of monumental transitions along this coast, where it penetrated early, from the 15th century, and has maintained a strong foothold. Before then, the coastal areas remained largely outside the reach of the centralized political movements of the Western Sudan and the trans-Saharan trade that so greatly affected the savannah. When commercial contact and, later, Christian missionary involvement began along the coast, West Africa turned its face towards the sea. This resulted in a scramble for the control of access, with an influx of northern immigrants, the creation of new lines of communication criss-crossing the forest zone, the realignment of power structures throughout the region and the creation of centralized kingdoms. The extant corpus of art derives from a period marked by fluidity in the movement of peoples and ideas and the consciousness of a cosmopolitan presence, resulting in immense cultural diversity. Urbanization has been a major factor throughout the 20th century, which has also been marked by familiarity with Western concepts and artistic forms and the introduction of many West African traditions.

During the period of the slave trade and the repatriation of slaves (*see* §VIII below), colonies of Afro-Americans were transplanted to the Guinea Coast; and in colonial times paid labourers migrated across international boundaries. In the two world wars, African subjects served their respective European colonial powers, which exposed them to each other's cultures and gave rise to new settlement patterns. By the end of the 19th century, Christian missionary activity involved cross-boundary exchanges, particularly between Nigeria and Sierra Leone. In the early 20th century coastal West African cities received an influx of immigrants from North Africa and the Middle East, attracted by the commercial possibilities. Further ethnic mixing, with the assignment of local administrators and the movement of labour forces, paved the road to political independence.

Cultural conventions continue to exhibit considerable dissemination. The power of the Yoruba (Nigerian) ancestral society for men continues to grow among the Temne in Sierra Leone. The cult of the water spirit, derived partly from the image of a female serpent-handler on Indian chromolithographs, has spread all along the coast. A Brazilian colonial style of architecture is often found in the Yoruba towns in Benin and Nigeria. Aeroplanes, motorcycles and European royal insignia have been used commonly in the 20th century on traditional forms of art. Ceremonial societies that were once unique have become unified and standardized, the most striking example being the Poro (more accurately Pörö) Society of Sierra Leone, Liberia, the Côte d'Ivoire and Guinea, reflecting political expediency in both its name and its international format. Trade in masks and linguist staffs exists between groups.

Nevertheless, in the rural areas of the interior and in many modern cities, the integrity of many ceremonial organizations and their artistic forms has remained relatively intact, as many examples attest. Masked ceremonies of the BAGA of Guinea survived until the 1950s much as described in the late 19th century. Both the Biri (Poro; men's society) and the Sande (women's society) of the Vai of Liberia were described by Olfert Dapper (?1635–89) in 1668 (Poro was mentioned as early as 1615 by Manuel Álvares (1573–?1617)) with many striking similarities to current conventions, and the present masks and costumes were illustrated as early as 1890 by J. Büttikofer. The description by de Faro (1664) of the shrines of the Temne of Sierra Leone, containing stones representing the ancestors, remained accurate in the 20th century. In Ghana, Krobo girls emerging from their period of initiation wear the same elaborate gold jewellery and long loincloths as they did in 1853, when described by Cruickshank (see 1977–8 exh. cat., p. 22).

(ii) Cultural traditions.

(a) Introduction. The length of the coast is dominated by six central language groups, divided into many subgroups and amalgamations. The largest is the Mande group, which is centred among the Malinke in the interior of Guinea but has spread with variants throughout the region. To a large extent, Mande has replaced Mel, which is now confined to small pockets along the littoral, in Guinea, Sierra Leone and Liberia. The Peul (or Fula, Fulani), speakers of the Pular languages, are believed to have subsumed and displaced Mande and Mel groups in parts of Guinea between the 14th and 18th centuries and are now prominent throughout coastal Guinea, Sierra Leone, Liberia and other parts of West Africa. A large area of southern Liberia and the Côte d'Ivoire is dominated by the Kru language group, also considered aboriginal. The Kwa group of languages includes Twi, which embraces nearly every ethnic group from the Côte d'Ivoire to Togo. Of these peoples, known as the AKAN, the best known are the Asante (*see* ASANTE AND RELATED PEOPLES). Ewe-related languages dominate in Togo and Benin.

Around the time of the first European contacts, several major kingdoms and larger alliances were developing, among them the Sapi of Sierra Leone and Guinea. Europeans described them as civil and prosperous, and they suffered invasions of Mande-speakers, who coveted their wealth. Before their conquest *c.* 1550 by the Mande groups known to Europeans as Mani, and perhaps from the 12th century onwards, the Sapi were known to carve miniature stone figures (*nomoli*; see fig. 124) and almost life-size stone heads now known as *mahen yafe* ('spirit of kings'). The figures probably represented royalty and nobility. For the European trade were also carved ivory trumpets and salt-cellars with intricate figural ornament.

By the mid-16th century, the interior of Sierra Leone was heavily infiltrated by Mande-speakers, who were

124. Sapi male figure sculpture, with two smaller figures and infant on back, steatite, h. 324 mm, 15th century (Oxford, Oxford University, Pitt Rivers Museum, 1934.24.2)

responsible for the formation of new kingdoms throughout the area and probably brought with them many continuing cultural conventions, including ironworking, strip-weaving, the ritual motif of the python and the bases of several ceremonial societies including the Poro.

(b) Kingdom of Asante. Further along the coast to the east, many smaller kingdoms rose and fell, but the most important political movement was the development of the great kingdom of the Asante on the Gold Coast (now Ghana). Having gained control of central Ghana in the 16th century, the Asante began a programme of expansion, beginning dramatically with the establishment of their capital at Kumasi under the leadership of the legendary Osei Tutu (*reg* 1697–1731). In the 17th century Tutu became the first Asantehene (king), when, it was said, the magnificent Golden Stool miraculously descended from heaven to rest on his knees (*see* ASANTE AND RELATED PEOPLES, fig. 1). The stool had long been an Akan symbol for the *sunsum* (spirit) of its owner, and the Golden Stool represented the divine right of the line of the Asantehene and the spirit of the whole nation, the prosperity of which depended on its ritual 'feeding' and care. It was exhibited at coronations, exclusive receptions and certain national festivals. Each Asantehene had his own personal, gold-plated stool, which occupied a chair at his side on state occasions. The queen mother and the chief also owned a gold- or silver-plated stool, and the more important officials had stools carved with supports in the form of a leopard or elephant, expressing the king's power, with abstract, openwork designs. When an important person died, his stool was blackened and placed in a shrine to be the focus of ancestral ritual.

The regalia of the Asante court, and, to a varying extent, the Akan court in general, included carved sceptres and sword hilts, plated in gold and carried by the royal staff on state occasions to indicate their official positions (see fig. 125). The most elaborate of the sceptres was held by the king's spokesman. The tradition may owe something to the silver- and gold-headed canes distributed by Europeans in the late 17th century and the 18th but is most likely to be a syncretization of foreign and indigenous sources. By the mid-20th century sceptres became elaborately ornamented with images of roosters and hens, elephants and leopards and with motifs derived from traditional Akan proverbs. Other important royal regalia included huge umbrellas topped with finials resembling the sceptres, caps with gold and silver ornament, intricately designed containers for gold dust and brilliantly coloured cloths made from strip-woven cotton and silk.

125. Asantehene Otumfuo Nana Opuko Ware II with sword-bearers and other attendants; from a photograph by Eliot Elisofon, 1971

The wealth of the Asante kingdom was based almost exclusively on gold and slaves, and its expansion was the result of an insatiable desire to control the markets of these commodities. The gold market existed before the coming of the Europeans, its trade directed northwards to the Western Sudan, but with the establishment of European trading forts along the Gold Coast, the Asante turned their attention to the elimination of the role of middleman occupied by surrounding states. By 1814 they controlled all access to the coast as well as most of modern Ghana and bordering areas. In 1874 the British sacked Kumasi, and in 1896 the Asantehene was exiled. On his return in 1924, however, the Asante confederacy was reconstituted, and in 1933 it was formally established, with Prempe II (*reg* 1892–1970) at its head, under British colonial rule. From this period date many of the most astounding forms of art.

(c) Kingdom of Dahomey. The coast of modern Togo and Benin, having no gold or safe harbours, experienced little early European contact. By the 19th century the powerful kingdom of Dahomey had emerged as a result of westward migrations of the Ewe and Aja peoples centuries earlier (*see* FON). The kingdom was famous principally for its role in the slave trade. While it never produced the volume of art of kingdoms to the east or west, its corpus includes some outstanding carved-wood memorials to the kings, monumental metal figure sculpture, decorative wooden figures and large, appliquéd textiles, originally made only for the king and his dignitaries and illustrating, in brilliant colours, the royal exploits. For the most part, the art of the kingdom of Dahomey served the royal court and was displayed in annual royal ceremonies. Its style reflects ethnic origins in, and continued connections with, the Yoruba kingdoms of Nigeria.

Much art production was instigated and inspired by King Glele of Dahomey. He came to the throne in 1858 and was the last great ruler of that kingdom, which fell only five years after his death. The son of a usurper, Glele was regarded by many of his subjects with ambivalence. During his reign he seems to have triumphed over many economic and military problems, but fires set by his antagonists destroyed the objects in the palace treasure houses, after which King Glele set about having new images produced that would reflect his reign and the reigns of his predecessors. His attributes and thus the predicted character of his rule were characterized by images derived from symbols in verse and narrative. An outstanding work from his reign, a lion-headed human figure in wood (Paris, Mus. Homme), refers symbolically to one of his titles, Lion of Lions. Huge figures in brass and iron refer to Gu, the god of iron and of war, decorative iron swords were used for display on state occasions, and iron and copper staffs with figurative scenes on a platform at the top refer to Glele's heritage, his right to rule and his numerous abilities. Common images were horses, dogs, umbrellas, pots and the right hand; the dog and the antelope symbolizing the spiritual sponsorship of the ancestors; a representation of a swirling storm symbolizing his immovability in the face of conflict; and the hornbill, with its heavy protrusion from the head symbolizing the bearer of burdens, much used in sculpture, architectural ornament and in appliqué textiles. Iron and brass memorial staffs (*asen*) continued to be used as ritual items in the 20th century, and the large, appliquéd cloths with symbols of royalty are still obtainable in markets.

The contribution to art made by the spirit-life of the region may be further exemplified in Vodun, the ritual employed to pay tribute to Dahomey spiritual beings, which has played an important part in African-American tradition in Haiti and later in the United States. The important trickster god, Legba, shown in wooden shrine figures in Dahomey, has a counterpart in both Cuba and Brazil in some physical representation and, more so, in ritual narrative and verse (*see* §VIII below). The diffusion of YORUBA imagery in the New World may be attributed to Dahomey's role in the traffic in slaves drawn during warfare largely from the neighbouring Yoruba groups to the east and especially from the sub-group Anago.

(iii) Ritual organizations. During the period of European contact, the western Guinea Coast has been noted not for its vast indigenous empires but for its powerful ritual organizations, which are mostly lacking in the eastern region. These organizations, usually restricted by gender, are spiritually and socially dominant throughout Guinea, Sierra Leone, Liberia and the Côte d'Ivoire. They usually serve as the major patrons of artistic activities that include the making of magnificent masks and figures, costumes and religious regalia and the performances at festivals that form the setting for much sculptural art. Their membership, often universal within any given ethnic group, is divided into distinct ranks, with separate initiation procedures and an elaborate structure of official titles and duties; the proceedings of ritual organizations are held in strict secrecy from outsiders. Such organizations often serve as a political counterbalance to the local, indigenous chiefs and their courts.

The most powerful and extensive ritual organization for men is the Poro, now generally thought to be a loose amalgamation of similar traditions generated from certain common origins but exhibiting some unique structures. Individual regional organizations of the Poro type go by different names but share a similar legend of origin and have many common titles, procedures and roles. Members of these organizations are responsible to a complex array of spiritual beings, and their rituals are designed to involve and channel some of the powers of the spirits into the world of mankind. Shrines, masks and figures are employed chiefly in the context of such ritual.

One important mask represents a founding spirit of Poro among peoples of the Sierra Leone–Guinea–Liberia border area. The monumental Landai (or Dandai) mask consists of a long, horizontal wooden head with open snout; a panache of plantain-eater feathers crowns its head, and black fur fringes its snout. The mask is worn with a costume of bleached raffia fibre. The masked dancer, who represents the founding spirit of the organization, appears during the boys' initiation, announcing their induction at the beginning, by figuratively devouring them, and their triumphal return to the village at the end, when he 'regurgitates' them (*see also* MENDE, fig. 2).

Among the Mende of Sierre Leone, dance costumes of cloth and yarn are worn over a substructure of rattan. The most important of the character costumes represent Gbini and Goboi, aspects of the great founding spirit of the Pö; they dance in sequence, with sudden occasional thrusts towards the audience. An essential feature of the dance is the frenetic movement of the masked dancer, which the guardians attempt to control. The dancers are magnificent in their colourful, pillbox-shaped headdresses, leopard-skin or antelope-skin capes and huge, billowing, bleached-raffia costumes.

The masks used among the ethnic groups of northern Liberia and adjacent areas of Guinea and Sierra Leone, such as the Dan, Kpalla, Mano and Loma (see fig. 126), are highly varied, not only in appearance but also in significance: in the north-western area they form part of the ritual regalia of the Poro organization, while in the south-east they do not. Sometimes identified in the literature as Poro masks, they are in fact an overlapping tradition. Although most studied by Western scholars among the DAN outside of the Poro area, the masks form the central core of Poro ritual among other groups. Among the Dan, 11 major mask types have been distinguished (see 1984 exh. cat., pp. 8–105; *see also* DAN, §2 and figs 1–3). Each mask incarnates a type of *du*, an ethereal force that makes itself known to a man and permits itself to be carved in wood. Its wearer speaks in unintelligible 'croaks, growls or twitters', which are interpreted by an accompanying savant. Masks are ascribed gender: the female masks are regarded as 'gentle', with smooth, oval faces; the male masks are angular, with a beard and tubular eyes, or in the form of an animal face or exceptionally large. Characters, given their own personal names as well as generic titles, include a female mask used in initiation, male or female 'miming' masks, a racing mask, a war-related mask with tubular eyes and ferocious mouth, and a mask with a bird's beak. A great variety of masking traditions exist throughout the Poro area that do not belong to the Dan complex. Some are local; others are distributed widely but differ greatly from each other in style of characterization and in role.

126. Loma female Nyangbai mask, wood, string and cowrie shells, h. 480 mm, early 20th century (Baltimore, MD, Baltimore Museum of Art)

In most of these societies membership is universal. Initiation into the organization is thought of as a metamorphosis of both body and spirit, without which a young man cannot marry, bear children or participate in the cultural life of the community. Procedures are quite similar from one area to the next, involving stages of initiation and an official hierarchy with a series of ritual roles.

The female counterpart to the Poro throughout most of the same area of Sierra Leone and Liberia is a group of related organizations best known by the names Sande or Bondo. In any area of Bondo/Sande, several types of spiritual beings, both masked and otherwise take part in the proceedings. The most powerful and feared are never revealed to outsiders and often take the form of a bundle carried on the head or an eerie voice heard in the night. The mask of one lesser spirit is well known, and examples exist in many collections: this is a helmet mask, painted or dyed black, consisting of a face, a heavily ringed neck, an elaborately carved coiffure and additional carved ornament (see Lamp, 1985). The masked dancer, called Nowo, Sowo or Zogba according to region, represents an idealized female type among all Sierra Leone groups but a male type among some Liberian groups. Best known among the former, she appears during initiation, in order to instruct the girls in moral comportment, and afterwards, when the female initiates return to the village. Her antithesis is Gonde, characterized by an anti-aesthetic, disorderly, dishevelled, masked dancer wearing a deteriorated or disfigured Nowo mask. The Bondo/Sande is a unique case in African art in that a wooden female mask is worn by women, although costuming and other forms of masking for women are common and distinctive in the upper Guinea Coast, from Guinea-Bissau to the border of Liberia and the Côte d'Ivoire.

(iv) Regional style clusters. Early studies of African art tended to group styles according to ethnic boundaries, assigning to each 'tribe' a definitive style, from which all departures were viewed as sub-styles. At the time, this was a valuable way of classifying objects in museums, but most modern scholars agree that such classification is somewhat misleading and that styles tend rather to develop around particular artists and their workshops, of whom some attract a large regional following, others not. Often this following adheres to ethnic boundaries, but in other cases it is cross-ethnic and not universal within any one ethnic

group. The style clusters described in this article are identified by their dominant ethnic designation, with the caveat mentioned.

(a) Bijogo. The northernmost cluster of importance is found off the shores of Guinea-Bissau, on the islands of Bissagos, inhabited by the BIJOGO. They are best known for their *iran*, highly schematized figures, often in the form of a head and torso, with reasonably naturalistic, concave face, and attached to a stool, on which the figure's legs may or may not be indicated. The figure often wears a flat hat with a narrow brim. Such figures were placed in community or personal shrines. Unlike most figural sculpture along the Guinea Coast, Bijogo sculpture is usually of unstained, natural, light wood. The Bijogo are also known for their varied masks and headdresses worn by neophytes and their masters in initiation proceedings. The best known is a bovine mask (Dugn'be) worn before initiation by a young boy, who crawls on the ground and imitates the movements of a village ox (see Galhano; Gallois Duquette).

(b) Nalu, Landuma, Baga and Mmani. From the southern border of Guinea-Bissau to the coastal border of Guinea and Sierra Leone, a number of different peoples carve monumental works in wood that are related in style and function. The peoples include the Nalu in the north, the Landuma somewhat inland, seven isolated groups calling themselves Baga (although all are not related linguistically) and the Mmani in the south. Common to all is a form of naturalistic figure sculpture characterized by large, bulging eyes and a long, aquiline nose, traits that recur in other of their art forms. Regional forms also exist. The Nalu and Baga are famous for an immense, horizontal mask (Banda) resembling a crocodile with long antelope horns and an anthropomorphic face (see fig. 127). The best-known Baga work is the huge wooden headdress commonly called Nimba (or D'mba; *see* BAGA, fig. 2), representing a female bust with an enormous nose, crested coiffure and long, pendant breasts. A tall, undulating wooden serpent carried on the head in ritual among the Nalu and the Baga is also an important work.

(c) Temne, Mende and Bullom of Sierra Leone. Many wooden female figures unconnected with the ritual organizations are used in private shrines dedicated to mental and physical health among the Temne, Mende and Bullom (Sherbro) of Sierra Leone. These are generally the property of women and are characterized by a naturalism that lacks, however, the consistent schema of the Bijogo or Baga. They have a blackened, highly polished surface, generally without a socle or base, with prominent buttocks and breasts and a ringed neck. Among these peoples many staffs of office are carved in similar manner, as well as many kinds of wooden and cloth masks used in ceremonial contexts both within Poro/Bondo/Sande and outside. A magnificently understated pattern of narrow-strip weaving is found especially among the Mende and their Mande neighbours.

(d) We, Kru, Grebo and Bete. Throughout the area of the We and also extending to the Kru and Grebo of south-eastern Liberia and the Bete in south-western Côte d'I-

127. Nalu/Baga dance headdress (Banda), wood and paint, h. 1.42 m, early 20th century (Zurich, Museum Rietberg)

voire, masks with horrific features occur, attached to elaborate costumes composed of frightful ensembles of objects. The Gela masks are best known. Female masks have a large, oval face studded with designs in carpet tacks, with bulging, oval eyes, a broad, flat nose and heavy, protruding lips. The entire mask is often fringed with metal bells. The male mask has tubular projections often described as warts, bulging bumps on the cheeks, an open jaw with teeth bared and wart-hog tusks carved on the forehead or cheeks. To the mask are attached wooden spikes, human and animal hair, shotgun cartridges, feathers and piles of overlapping fabric, producing an effect of chaos. The male masks appear to represent wild, uncontrollable forces of the forest. Like the Dan-complex masks, these are incarnations of the image of a spirit that has revealed itself to man (see Tiabas).

(e) Baule, Yaure and Guro. During the past few centuries the central Côte d'Ivoire has become a crossroads for the meeting of traditions and languages. The art style of the Baule, Yaure and Guro is characterized by a pleasing, serene refinement in figural sculpture and masking, and a schema that includes a concavity of the face sometimes recalling the sculpture of the Senufo to the north, gentle volumes resembling those of their neighbours to the west, the Dan, extensive carving of detailed body scarification patterns and a deep, dark, polished patina. Zoomorphic masks are in widespread use, their gentle, diminutive style contrasting sharply with the grotesque masks of their northern and western neighbours. The Baule bring an Akan influence from the east (whence they claim to have migrated in the early 18th century), while the Guro and Yaure derive from Mande origins (for illustration *see* BAULE, fig. 1, AKAN and GURO).

The best-known Baule objects are exquisite, small, human figures in wood, long prized by Western collectors. A standard aesthetic is followed in any one workshop, but the figures fall into two types serving different ritual functions. One type is the *blolo bla* ('other-world woman') or *blolo bian* ('other-world man'). These are commissioned by persons to whom it has been revealed that they are romantically involved with a being from a former spiritual existence. The figures are carved to represent the spiritual mate, kept in shrines and cared for lovingly, to appease the jealous intentions of the spiritual being. The figures are recognized by their highly polished patina. Masks of the other type represent *asie usu* ('nature spirits'), cantankerous beings who attempt to disrupt personal and community life. Though they are ugly, their representation is made pleasing in order to induce them to occupy the wooden body, so that they can be placated through ritual attention (see Vogel). These figures are usually encrusted on the surface from ritual applications.

Artists and craftsmen of the Baule–Guro area are among the most prolific in Africa, producing an enormous range of masks, including gentle, female face masks, often bearing petite, decorative images above the head, and masks incorporating certain characteristics of the antelope, leopard, buffalo and monkey (see 1985 exh. cat., pp. 108–20). Narrow-strip weaving has reached a peak of refinement in this area and is the context for small heddle pulleys carved with delicate figures, human and animal heads, and miniature representations of the masks. The Baule, especially, have retained the Akan fascination with gold, producing ornaments in intricate detail.

(f) Akan peoples. The Akan peoples have almost no masking tradition, but their other art forms are highly developed. Akan art is primarily court art, dedicated to the functions of prestige, the display of wealth and the veneration of nobility. This is an aspect of Baule art, found also among the Ebrie, Attie and Anyi in the Côte d'Ivoire, the Asante and Fanti in Ghana, and the Ewe on the coast of Togo and the Benin Republic.

Figural sculpture of the Akan is generally simpler and more direct than the polished work of the Baule and Guro, and in some cases highly abstract. The face tends to be round and flat, the neck bears the ringed creases that are found also in Sierra Leone figures, and limbs are often attenuated. Outside a royal context, the best-known figures of the Asante and Fanti are the schematized, wooden female figures known as *akua'ba* ('child of Akua'; *see* ASANTE AND RELATED PEOPLES, fig. 4). The form consists of a large, flat disc representing the head, a long, ringed neck, a simple cylinder representing the torso, brief indications of the breasts and two short, horizontal pegs for the arms. The *akua'ba*, symbolizing the epitome of female beauty, may be carried tucked into the back of a woman's wrapped skirt in the hope that it will help her conceive or that it will ensure a healthy pregnancy and the safe delivery of an attractive child. Once this is accomplished, the figure is returned to a private shrine, where it honours the woman's spiritual benefactors.

Gold weights are literally the trademark of the Asante, who use them as counterbalances in the weighing of gold-dust. Among other cast-brass items employed in this trade are containers, spoons, sieves and plates. Gold weights usually take the form of small, geometric abstractions, anthropomorphic and zoomorphic figures or miniaturizations of Asante material and agricultural elements. In addition to their function, they are designed as objects of delight, with proverbs and popular symbolic references (*see also* §VI, 10 above).

The Akan seem to have been less interested in the ethereal and more conscious of the real world including that of the departed ancestors. A group of important ceramics is found throughout the Akan area, especially among the Anyi, consisting of full or truncated figures or heads, which were used to commemorate the deaths of important elders in a period extending probably from 1875 to 1935. They were sculpted by women, like most clay artefacts throughout the Guinea Coast, and placed in a forest grove near the village but apart from the cemetery. The image was formed after the likeness of the deceased and served as the repository for his soul. The tradition of funerary sculpture continues in the Akan area in the form of monumental cement sculpture.

(g) Other styles. Throughout the Guinea Coast pockets of unique styles appear that do not conform to any of the above clusters: these include isolated ritual conventions and associated works of art, and examples of innovative brilliance by single artists and workshops, works that are highlighted rather than diminished by their exclusivity. The category includes the a-Rong-e-Thoma horned and snouted mask of the Temne, the flat Nyangbai mask of the Loma (see fig. 126 above), the disc-shaped Kplekple mask used by the Baule Goli association, the flat masks with tubular eyes used by the Grebo, and the fibre masks and costumes of the Djola and Tenda of Senegal, Guinea

and Guinea-Bissau. Certain peoples of the Guinea Coast, for example the Peul and Susu of Guinea, produce little in the way of plastic arts but are noted for their magnificent architecture, dance and music.

For further discussion of the art of the Guinea Coast region, *see* AKAN, AKYE, ASANTE AND RELATED PEOPLES, BAGA, BAULE, BIJOGO, DAN, FON, GURO, KISSI, MENDE and YORUBA. Art produced since colonial times is discussed in the relevant country entries.

BIBLIOGRAPHY

O. Dapper: *Nauwkeurige beschrijvinge der Africaensche gewesten* (Amsterdam, 1668; Eng. trans., London, 1670)

J. Büttikofer: *Reisebilder aus Liberia: Resultate geographischer, naturwissenschaftlicher und ethnographischer Untersuchungen, während der Jahre 1879–1882 und 1886–1887*, 2 vols (Leiden, 1890)

R. S. Rattray: *Religion and Art in Ashanti* (London, 1927/*R* 1954)

H. U. Hall: *Sherbro of Sierra Leone: A Preliminary Report on the Work of the University Museum's Expedition to West Africa* (Philadelphia, 1938)

G. W. Harley: *Notes on the Poro in Liberia*, Pap. Peabody Mus. Archaeol. & Ethnol., xix/2 (Cambridge, MA, 1941/*R* New York, 1968)

G. Schwab: *Tribes of the Liberian Hinterland*, Pap. Peabody Mus. Archaeol. & Ethnol., xxxii (Cambridge, MA, 1947)

G. W. Harley: *Masks as Agents of Social Control in Northeast Liberia*, Pap. Peabody Mus. Archaeol. & Ethnol., xxxii/2 (Cambridge, MA, 1950/*R* New York, 1975)

A. A. Y. Kyerematen: *Panoply of Ghana* (London and Accra, 1964)

F. Galhano: *Esculturas e objectos decorados da Guiné Portuguesa no Museo de Etnologia do Ultramar* (Lisbon, 1971)

D. Fraser and H. M. Cole, eds: *African Art and Leadership* (Madison, 1972)

R. Sieber: 'Art and History in Ghana', *Primitive Art and Society*, ed. A. Forge (London and New York, 1973), pp. 70–96

S. Vogel: 'People of Wood: Baule Figure Sculpture', *A.J.* [New York], xxiii/7 (1973), pp. 23–6

Die Kunst der Dan (exh. cat. by E. Fischer and H. Himmelheber, Zurich, Mus. Rietberg, 1976; Eng. trans., rev. Zurich, 1984)

M. Crowder: *West Africa: An Introduction to its History* (London, 1977)

The Arts of Ghana (exh. cat. by H. M. Cole and D. H. Ross, Los Angeles, UCLA, Wight A.G.; Minneapolis, MN, Walker A. Cent.; Dallas, TX, Mus. F.A.; 1977–8)

F. Lamp: 'Frogs into Princes: The Temne Rabai Initiation', *Afr. A.*, xi/2 (1978), pp. 34–49, 94

H. B. Tiabas: 'Masques en pays Guéré', *An. U. Abidjan*, ser. F, vii (1978), pp. 85–90

T. F. Garrard: 'Akan Metal Arts', *Afr. A.*, xiii/1 (1979), pp. 36–43

D. Gallois Duquette: 'Les Masques bovins des Iles Bissagos (Guinée-Bissau)', *Bull. Mus. Barbier-Müller*, xii (1981), pp. 3–4

M. V. Gilbert: 'Ewe Funerary Sculpture', *Afr. A.*, xiv/4 (1981), pp. 44–6

M. D. McLeod: *The Asante* (London, 1981)

For Spirits and Kings: African Art from the Paul and Ruth Tishman Collection (exh. cat. by S. M. Vogel, New York, Met., 1981)

D. H. Ross: 'The Verbal Art of Akan Linguist Staffs', *Afr. A.*, xvi/1 (1982), pp. 56–67

F. Lamp: 'House of Stones: Memorial Art of Fifteenth-century Sierra Leone', *A. Bull.*, lxv/2 (1983), pp. 219–37

B. Paxson: 'Mammy Water: New World Origins?', *Baessler-Archv*, n. s., xxxi (1983), pp. 407–46

S. F. Patton: 'The Asante Umbrella', *Afr. A.*, xvii/4 (1984), pp. 64–73

F. Lamp: 'Cosmos, Cosmetics, and the Spirit of Bondo', *Afr. A.*, xviii/3 (1985), pp. 28–43, 98–9

Die Kunst der Guro: Elfenbeinküste (exh. cat. by E. Fischer and L. Homberger, Zurich, Mus. Rietberg, 1985)

M. Adams: 'Women and Masks among the Western We of Ivory Coast', *Afr. A.*, xix/2 (1986), pp. 46–55

J. W. Nunley: *Moving with the Face of the Devil: Art and Politics in Urban West Africa* (Bloomington, 1987)

T. F. Garrard: *Gold of Africa: Jewellery and Ornaments from Ghana, Côte d'Ivoire, Mali and Senegal in the Collection of the Barbier-Mueller Museum* (Munich, 1989)

S. P. Blier: 'King Glele of Danhomé—Part One: Divination Portraits of a Lion King and a Man of Iron', *Afr. A.*, xxiii/4 (1990), pp. 42–53, 93–4

F. Lamp: 'Ancient Wood Figures from Sierra Leone: Implications for Historical Reconstruction', *Afr. A.*, xxiii/2 (1990), pp. 48–59, 103

S. P. Blier: 'King Glele of Danhomé—Part Two: Dynasty and Destiny', *Afr. A.*, xxiv/1 (1991), pp. 44–55, 101–3

——: *La Guinée et ses héritages culturels* (Conakry, 1992)

FREDERICK LAMP

5. WESTERN EQUATORIA. Region extending from the Central Cameroon Highlands in the north to the Ndogo Lagoon in the south, from Rio del Rey in the north-west to Bangui in the north-east, and from Setta Cama in the south-west to Kwamouth in the south-east. The west bank of the Zaïre River defines its eastern limit. It thus includes all or parts of the modern states of CAMEROON, CENTRAL AFRICAN REPUBLIC, CONGO, GABON and EQUATORIAL GUINEA (see fig. 128). For coverage of the colonial and post-colonial art and architecture of the region, refer to the entries on individual countries. *See also* BAMILEKE AND RELATED PEOPLES, BAMUM, BANGWA, FANG, KOTA and TEKE.

(i) Geography and cultural history. (ii) Contexts of production. (iii) Figure sculpture. (iv) Mask and masquerade. (v) Painting. (vi) Metalwork. (vii) Other arts.

(i) Geography and cultural history. Geographically the region varies greatly, from the forest–savannah mosaic pattern of the Cameroon Highlands to the central Sudanese parkland, with the equatorial rain-forest below this extending south until riven and then halted by the large forest–savannah mosaic west of the middle Zaïre River. With the exception of the central Cameroon Highlands and the north-eastern region, Western Equatorial Africa is peopled entirely by Bantu-speakers (including the bilingual pygmy groups associated with them). Bantu-speaking peoples form the core of the area. They have common origins and may generally be said to share a common culture. Over the last few centuries, however, previously related groups have become separated and their culture subject to fragmentation and recombination, leading to the development of different artistic styles.

To the north of this core area, in the central Cameroon Highlands, societies are characterized by strongly centralized and elaborated government, relatively stable settlements and extensively developed material cultures. Indeed, the distinctiveness of the area could justify its treatment as a separate region in its own right. There are only slight connections between its art forms and those of the core area; its art shows the influence of peoples to the north and west much more than of those to the south. To the south of the core area are the Kongo-speaking peoples, whose culture has affected that of the southernmost people of the region, the Shira-Punu, Nzabi and Teke-speakers. The southern Teke, moreover, share the pattern of divine kingship and centralized government long associated with the western Kongo states. Indeed, the intense development and sophisticated imagery of the arts of the Kongo kingdom seem to have been influential throughout a part of Western Equatorial Africa.

It is assumed that the Bantu-speaking cultivators, whose descendants now occupy the area, migrated from north to south. The earliest migrations seem to have bypassed the forest by following the large rivers and the Atlantic littoral. Later migrations, harder-pressed, also went southward, but in diverse directions. The oral histories of the region do not record the previous presence of any autochthonous

128. Map of the Western Equatorial region of Africa

(and conceivably non-Bantu-speaking) cultivators and hunters other than the pygmies who still live in the area. Either the pygmies were the only previous occupants of the core area or any non-pygmy autochthons were assimilated by the incoming Bantu-speakers. This latter possibility might be significant for the study of the distinctive features of the iconographies and rituals characteristic of the forest-dwelling peoples of the area.

The history of scattered and loosely cohesive groups of cultivators entering and adapting to the forest region with differing degrees of sophistication strongly affected the development of their arts. Each group that entered the forest had to follow a similar pioneering strategy involving the adoption of shifting residence, diffuse and ephemeral political authority, and competition for wealth and power based largely on trade for European goods. Moreover, the cultural and ideological climate created by the need to adapt to a dramatically new environment led to the development of religious beliefs based on enlisting supernatural aid through the interaction of familial spirits with autochthonous ones controlling fecundity, food, trade and power. These societies were essentially anarchic, lacking strong authority above the level of the minimal family lineage. This allowed for, if not encouraged, an extensive concern with competitive display, both in personal adornment and in the embellishment of religious objects. Similar principles sustained the development of art among societies outside the forest, but their longer intervals of fixed settlement and their elaboration of cults and chieftainship often led to the development of iconographic themes and contexts into more consistent, more widely observed and, generally, more secular institutions.

While these differences between forest pioneer and parkland sedentary societies, and the forms and contexts of their visual arts, may be partly due to ecological factors, any analysis must take into account both the particular historical circumstances of individual societies and the persistence of their pre-separation and pre-migration traditions. Unfortunately, there is little promise that archaeology might help in the reconstruction of the material culture of the core area before European contact, although the peripheral parklands may eventually yield more archaeological information. In the core area wood, other plant-derived materials and forged iron are for the most part quickly perishable. The advent of brass was relatively recent. It seems that most of the art traditions originated outside the region and that subsequent innovations from them did not precede the mid-18th century.

A firm chronology for the visual arts of the area has yet to be established. It seems, however, that such a chronology would rest upon five bases. The first and most substantial of these is provided by the records of Portuguese contact, from the late 15th century onwards, with the long-established kingdoms of the Kongo to the south of the region. This contact involved mainly Kongo-speakers along the Atlantic coast and along the Zaïre River from its mouth to the town of Matadi and the basin of the Lelunda River in northern Angola. The extensive presence of this group at the edge of the Western Equatorial region suggests that its southern part at least was well settled by Bantu-speakers when the Portuguese arrived. The second basis is provided by early 16th-century reports of settlements established on the coast from southern Cameroon to southern Gabon; the third by late 15th-century reports of the kingdom of the Tio in the south-east of the region; the fourth by early 19th-century accounts of peoples (presumably Bantu-speakers) in the forest country inland from the Atlantic coast; and the fifth by later 19th-century accounts of southward and westward population movements from northern parkland and forest margins into and through the forest. In addition, inferences from language distribution and shared elements of material culture support the idea of the established presence of Bantu-speaking groups along the Atlantic coast and quite possibly the middle bank of the Zaïre River. Moreover, a few of these material culture items indicate a persistence of sculptural style—stressing a distinctive mode of conventionalization—since at least the 17th century.

Early European accounts of the Kongo kingdoms record the existence of a plethora of images used for religious purposes. Few such figures have survived, making it difficult to substantiate these accounts, but the records of the Museo Nazionale Preistorico ed Etnografico Luigi Pigorini in Rome attest to the arrival in Italy in 1695 of two wooden female half-figures that had previously come to Portugal from West Africa. These seem to be in the same style and by the same hand, and authorities now attribute them to Kina, a district in the south-west of the Kongo kingdom, on the north bank of the Dande River and due south of the state of Bamba. Despite the obscurity of their origins, the existence of these two figures helps to make two points: first, that a conventionalizing tradition of sculpture probably flourished among the Kongo well before the great southward Bantu movements of the 19th century; and second, that the tradition relates significantly to much of the sculpture made in the 19th and early 20th centuries in Western Equatoria. Indeed, although the particular style of the Kina figures seems to be no longer extant, its elements are discernible in more recent styles, from central Angola to the western part of the Ogowe Basin.

(ii) Contexts of production. The contexts of art production in the region have developed out of religious beliefs and political institutions that are widespread in Sub-Saharan Africa. Most societies in the area attempted to deal with the supernatural world through men's cults. These associations were organized either on familial or local (i.e. supra-familial) principles, and their officiants were either individual family heads or important religious specialists. (The observance of individual or personal cults does not seem to have developed to the extent that it did in the societies of the Guinea Coast.) Village cults are concerned with autochthonous protective spirits, either directly or through the spirits of deceased cult members. In the latter case, the power of deceased men and women is thought to remain transitorily in such relics of their living form as bones, hair and nails. In the cults that depended on relics to influence the unseen world, apotropaic iconography was developed in which anthropomorphic images guarded and personified the power residing in the reliquaries. Many cults, whether or not they were based on a belief in the power of relics, personified their protective spirits in the form of statues and/or mask disguises worn by unidentified cult members. Again, these statues or masks symbolized either family groups or local groups made up of unrelated families. The institution of cult houses seems not to have been strongly developed through most of the area. Special buildings with large-scale architectural and liturgical elements representing mythic or supernatural figures are recorded only from central Gabon and the Lundu-Mbo complex near the northern Cameroon coast. Unfortunately, early European travellers recorded little about this practice.

The absence of stable political organization and centralized government over most of the area provided a context in which both individuals and families sought to emphasize their status through the enhancement of their appearance and that of the objects indicative of their position in society. Wealth and leadership often found expression in prestigious styles of personal attire and adornment and luxurious elaborations of such personal and professional effects as staffs, display weapons, musical instruments, bellows and eating-spoons. The representational imagery with which such objects were embellished may have been primarily secular, or it may invoke protective spirits. The ownership and performance of masks and masquerades were also matters of wealth and prestige, and their striking iconography may be seen as a product of this context of their production and use. The quest for prestige also extended to the decoration of house-doors and such parts of house interiors as room-screens, supporting pillars and beds.

The artistic skill required to produce these goods was generally diffused throughout society. In most of the region there were neither castelike groups nor family guilds of artisans. Otherwise family relationships or voluntary apprenticeships were the means by which individuals became practising artists. The status of the artist seems to have varied greatly over the region. Artists working in the kingdoms of Central Cameroon enjoyed the protection and support of rulers, but this relationship greatly limited their role in leadership and, in turn, their social prestige. Much less is known about the status of artists in the less fixed and centralized societies to the south and east, but the evidence suggests that outstanding carvers occupied an ambivalent position. While their work might gain them wealth, their status in the society as a whole depended, as it did for non-artists, on such other attributes as supernatural endowments and/or personality. While a connection between technical skill and supernatural power was recognized in most societies, that alone need not have led to wide renown. In the core area, the carver and the religious specialist who prescribed the carving could be the same man. Less frequently, that man could also be a political leader. The roles played by artist, religious specialist and political leader in the innovation of a form, the creation of a theme and the fixing of a tradition, whether formal or iconographic, remain unknown, although the ethnographic data strongly suggest that formal creativity and conformity did not always rest entirely with the artist. Such complex circumstances of production do not seem, however, to have especially complicated the meaning of the images themselves. Iconographic themes tend to be simple and religious imagery 'multivocal', although this quality has not been adequately investigated.

(iii) Figure sculpture. Most representational art of the region was carved in wood. The main tools were, in order of use, axe, occasionally a hewing knife, adze and fine knives, with finishing generally being done by smoothing with rough leaves and sometimes sealing and darkening with a glowing iron blade. A greater variety of materials and tools was used in the Central Cameroon area and in the areas immediately to the north and south of the region. Most figure sculptures take human form; representations of animals are less frequent. Male figures seem to predominate in the core area, while female figures prevail in the imagery of the south-western corner. Many of the numerous small magical figures made in the Lundo–Mbo area seem to be of inderterminate sex. Throughout most of the region, twins are credited with great supernatural power and held in great respect, so it is likely that some sculptures are surrogate figures representing dead twins.

So far, there is little evidence to suggest that statues in this region generally embodied deceased family members. In the core area, ancestors were represented more by relics than by images. Instead, statues served mainly to embody the protective spirits who watched over reliquaries, assemblages of magical materials, cult houses and homes. Some figures, kept carefully concealed, were made to be sent out at night by magicians in order to enthrall their rivals or punish their enemies. In the Central Cameroon area some groups used statues to commemorate deceased rulers and their first wives. Paired figures of men and women found standing in cult houses in the south of the region, for example among the Tsogho and probably other groups, are said to represent primal couples.

In the south-west corner of the region genre figures of women carrying bottles and gourds suggest the use of statuary to attain, and then flaunt, wealth and prosperity; the bottles probably symbolized European spirits and the gourds palm wine. Otherwise, such secular figures seem traditionally to have been more or less insignificant. There are no reports of carved figures being used primarily as dolls, and although statues seem to have been used in cult initiations there is little evidence of their having played primarily didactic roles. Compared with many other areas of west and central Africa, the formal themes of the statuary of the region tend to be simple and austere. Sculptural groups occur in the initiation tableaux of the northern Yaunde–Fang and the Sanaga regions, in the multiple figures of the Lundu–Mbo in the north-west corner and in the miniature figures of the Shira–Punu group. Otherwise, statues are usually single figures, representing people standing or crouching. Figures of women holding children are rare and of scattered distribution in the core area. Half-figures and heads on protracted necks are known. They are found mainly through a central belt. Integral compositions of a head or half-figure on a prestigious type of stool are quite distinctive of the core area but are also found in north-eastern Zaïre. In the west there are several traditions of openwork statuary in which the arms extend well away from the body, either holding an object (see fig. 129) or brought up to the chin or beard. In general, integral sculptural decoration, such as the representation in relief of elaborate scarification patterns (see fig. 130) and items of regalia, yields to incised surface effects, polychromy and metal appliqué.

Wooden statuary ranges in height from *c.* 150 to 900 mm. Early travellers noted life-size and even larger figures, apparently regarded as highly important, but their reports do not describe these figures. The importance of such images and the difficulty of transporting them probably precluded their coming into Western collections in any quantity. Such large figures came to the attention of Europeans mainly along the coast. They were later found to exist among relatively long-settled peoples in the south-western part of the Ogowe Basin, an occurrence that indicates a connection between a sedentary tradition

129. Ngumba-style figure sculpture, wood, mirror glass and brass, h. 566 mm, from Western Equatoria, before 1929 (Frankfurt am Main, Museum für Völkerkunde)

and an increase in the size of imagery. By the same token, the sculpture produced by nomadic societies tends to be of modest size. The colonial policy of fixing such groups in permanent villages may also have led, in certain instances, to an increase in the size of traditional statuary. The scale of representation in architectural sculpture, both structural and decorative, and in ritual tableaux exceeded the general limits observed in the production of free-standing figures. The lack of early accounts of the embellishment of traditional architecture with representational imagery between the western Cameroon Highlands and the Kongo states is striking. One would certainly have expected more from the south-western area, if only as a development out of a presumably long history of sculptural exuberance.

Traditions of miniaturism in three-dimensional representation are widely scattered. The finest miniature carving

130. Kuyu/Mboshi figure sculpture from Western Equatoria (Paris, Musée d'Art Moderne de la Ville de Paris)

131. Mbete reliquary figure, wood, pigment, cowrie shell and brass, h. 736 mm, from Congo, Western Equatoria, late 19th century–early 20th (San Francisco, CA, private collection)

seems to come from the south-western corner and probably reflects the influence of the north-western Kongo states.

It may be argued that, along with bold polychromy (*see* §(v) below), the distinctiveness of the art of this region, at least at its core, lies in its characteristically dramatic reduction of the human form (the northern and south-western areas encompass more naturalistic styles). Both the faces of masks and the composition of statues share an almost complete lack of naturalistic modelling of anatomical detail. This striking tendency to simplify expresses itself in highly contrasting modes. The intent to depart from nature is evident in all of them, but the nature of the stylization may vary greatly, ranging from a prevailing curvilinearity and roundness at one pole to a prevailing angularity and the use of flat, often steeply banked contours at the other (see fig. 131). Broadly speaking, the first type centres in the west and the second in the east. These contrasting stylistic canons frame a richly diversified continuum in which the distinctive features of both are combined in quite individual ethnic or local traditions. The intermingling of styles prevails to the extent that it is often impossible to infer the provenance of an image through the features generally thought to be the most salient and significant. In many cases insufficient background information prevents the assignment of an object to an ethnic style. Indeed, lack of secure evidence as to where objects were found might undermine many of the aesthetic conclusions on which current stylistic groupings are based.

For the moment, precision of attribution is at the level of geographical–cultural area rather than language family or ethnic group. The turbulent history of most of the area's peoples has encompassed migrations, dispersals, interactions, changes of group identity and, in some cases, extinction. In many, if not most cases, this precludes any assurance in the existence of precisely defined styles of sculpture.

(iv) Mask and masquerade. Masks of this region generally represent autochthonous spirits enlisted in the aid of a lineage group, village, religious specialist or dance association (see figs 132 and 133). There are reports that link masks with the shades of the dead, but these seem tenuous. Unlike other regions where masking is intensive, such genre themes as old dotards, easy women, village buffoons and overbearing warriors, brought forth to comment on antisocial behaviour, seem to be absent here. Instead, the didactic roles played by masks in this region tend to be direct rather than allegorical. References to masquerades involving different masks acting together or sequentially in a narrative performance are infrequent, and the extent of any such traditions is unknown. One early 20th-century report tells of Mboshi-speakers in the far east of the region acting out regional myths by means of disguised dancers (see Poupon). This might in fact be attributable to the western Mongo peoples on the other side of the Congo River. In some cases a cult owned a series of masks materializing different spirits, often in considerable numbers. In others, only one or two masks would embody paramount protective spirits. Although masks were employed mainly in religious contexts, a strong element of play can be identified in their forms and characteristic behaviour. Often masks appeared mainly as entertainers, although they doubtless always retained some supernatural

qualities. Except in the Cameroon Highlands, and perhaps in a few instances in central Gabon, masks do not seem to have participated significantly in funerary or 'second-burial' ceremonies. Their field of public, or quasi-public, activity was centred in rites of passage for the living and rites that dealt with general crises.

Some groups conceived of mask spirits as being predominantly animal in nature, while others visualize them in human form. These conceptions are not mutually exclusive but may be combined in many ways, especially in societies that use a variety of masks in their major cults, as in western Cameroon and central Gabon. The differences in conceptualization may nevertheless be important in tracing the cultural history of different groups. The question is, however, complicated by the tendency to give human faces to masks with salient animal attributes; and the reverse can also occur, especially in the case of monkey-associated spirits. Furthermore, some mask themes cross ethnic boundaries, while others do not.

The masks of the region represent a far wider sculptural range than that of its figure sculptures. This is especially so when the total configuration of form, colour and texture is taken into account; even just the part that covers the wearer's face or head is characterized by a wide range of forms. In the Cameroon Highlands, for example, the mask can sit atop or aslant the wearer's head, the wearer looking out through a cloth hood. To the south of the region an imposing and characteristic theme extends through the forest societies. Here, a large helmet- or bell-shaped wooden form covers the whole of the wearer's head. This disguise is usually embellished with great crests and/or multiple faces. The type coexists with a wide range of masks that are worn more or less over the face. These frontal masks are remarkably diverse in form, size and style. Their presence extends well beyond the central part of the region and reaches to the southern limit in the west. With a few exceptions, the main groups in the south-eastern area seem not to have had an important tradition of frontal masks. In southern Cameroon the Lundu–Mbo and Saa (Basa) peoples had distinctive dance-headdresses consisting of featureless helmets and caps surmounted by human figures.

133. Kwele mask, wood and pigments, h. 265 mm, from north-western People's Republic of the Congo, probably 1930s or 1940s (London, British Museum)

132. Shira–Punu mask, wood decorated with red and white paint, h. 280 mm, from Gabon, Western Equatoria, before 1904 (London, British Museum)

Many of the peoples who seem not to have employed such wooden masks devised other ways of representing fantasic personages. These included the use of more or less featureless garments and carapaces of plant bark, plant fibre and branchwork. Some Mboshi-speaking peoples invented a singular dance in which the performer, enveloped in a great cone of raffia cloth, held up a solid wooden head at arm's length as he whirled about.

(v) Painting. There is little evidence that two-dimensional graphic representation was important in this region, though this may be partly due to its generally ephemeral nature. The outer faces of the bark walls of traditional

houses were sometimes decorated with free-hand drawings, mainly of simplified human and animal figures, and silhouettes of weapons. These appear to have been done purely for diversion, and to have no symbolic, magical or even display purpose. On the other hand, colour was applied to many objects throughout the area, though again it was generally ephemeral. The range of pigments was generally limited to white, black, and shades of red and brown, which were applied to masks, statues, house-parts, drums and the bodies of those taking part in ritual events. Boldly contrasting and diversely shaped geometric fields were often further embellished by small motifs applied by improvised brushes and stamps. The intensive use of contrasting colours—most of them ephemeral—characterizes the use of paint on the sculpture of most of the area.

(vi) Metalwork. In Sub-Saharan Africa, techniques of applying copper alloy sheet and wire over shaped wooden forms probably reached their highpoint in this region. Iron was worked and brass cast with a high degree of skill and imagination. Bronze does not seem to occur. The secondary decorative treatment of metal forms, for example engraving, punchwork and repoussé, is also highly accomplished. Not all groups smelted iron, however, and some peoples enjoyed reputations as specialized ironworkers, supplying their neighbours with smelted metal, as well as implements and other objects. A few iron weapons have, or at least suggest, representational form, while many have quite distinctive abstract outlines. Many ironworkers embellished blades with graceful ridges and finely engraved geometric designs. For weapons, however, the main field of decoration was the wooden handle and the bark or hide scabbard, both of which were often covered with brass sheet or wire worked in various ways. The working of brass, mostly of European origin, is especially characteristic of the area. For example, massive, boldly contoured and often richly engraved penannuli were cast for personal adornment. The technique of brass-casting was limited to the use of moulds that were either open or partially closed. The lost-wax method appears to have been used only in the Central Cameroon area and possibly in the extreme south-west of the region.

(vii) Other arts. The other arts of the region included the making of the ivory side-blown horns and delicate hairpins used in some areas. Pipe bowls of soft stone are known from the south-west, otherwise stone was hardly used, except to a small extent in Central Cameroon. In most areas pottery was utilitarian and non-representational, though of some aesthetic quality. Surface decoration consists mainly of a few bands of incised or low-relief motifs. The ceramic art of the region reached its highest points in the furthest north and south. Some groups in the centre made earthen figures of men and animals, prone or supine, in varying degrees of relief. These ranged from life-size to immense and were limited to use by cults in their initiations and other ordeals. Textile techniques were more developed outside the core area. Traditionally, cotton cloth was woven in Central Cameroon, but its decorative effects are limited mainly to embroidery, which is likely to have been introduced from the north. Through much of the remaining area weaving is confined to raffia-strip cloth made on a vertical loom. Most of the material produced is monochrome and austere. Embroidery and resist-dyeing seem not to have been practised. In the core area ornamental mats were made with geometric patterns, both representational and 'abstract', produced through plaiting and twilling.

BIBLIOGRAPHY

EARLY TRAVEL WRITINGS

P. B. Du Chaillu: *Explorations and Adventures in Equatorial Africa* (London and New York, 1861)
——: *A Journey to Ashango-land* (London, 1867)

GENERAL WORKS

K. Krieger and G. Kutscher: *Westafrikanische Masken*, Veröff. Mus. Vlkerknd. Berlin, n. s. 1, Abt. Afrika, i (Berlin, 1960) [col. cat.]
A. R. Walker and R. Sillans: *Rites et croyances des peuples du Gabon* (Paris, 1962)
K. Krieger: *Westafrikanische Plastik*, 3 vols, Veröff. Mus. Vlkerknd. Berlin, n. s. 7, Abt. Afrika, ii; n. s. 17, Abt. Afrika, iv; n. s. 18, Abt. Afrika, v (Berlin, 1965–9) [col. cats]
I. Bolz: 'Zur Kunst in Gabon', *Ethnologica*, n. s., iii (1966), pp. 85–221, pls 38–62
L. Perrois: 'Gabon gestern und heute', *Z. Mus. Hildesheim*, n. s., xxiv (1973), pp. 1–72
M. Huet: *The Dance, Art and Ritual of Africa* (New York, 1978)
L. Perrois: *Arts du Gabon: Les Arts plastiques du Bassin de l'Ogooué* (Arnouville and Paris, 1979)
Masterpieces of the People's Republic of the Congo (exh. cat., New York, Afr.-Amer. Inst., 1980)
L. Perrois: *Ancestral Art of Gabon from the Collections of the Barbier-Mueller Museum* (Geneva, 1985)

SPECIALIST STUDIES

M. A. Poupon: 'Etude ethnographique de la tribu Kouyou', *L'Anthropologie*, xxix (1919), pp. 53–88, 297–335
G. Tessmann: *Die Bafia* (Stuttgart, 1934)
——: *Die Baja*, 2 vols (Stuttgart, 1934–7)
T. Thomas: 'Variation on a Theme: Analysis of Small Carved Figures from Bali, Cameroons, Africa', *Man*, xxxviii (1938), pp. 33–7, pl. C
M. Guthrie: *The Bantu Language of Western Equatorial Africa* (London, 1953)
J. Millot: 'De Pointe-noire au pays Tsogo', *Obj. & Mondes*, i/3–4 (1961), pp. 65–80
P. Harter: 'Les Courses de pirogues costumières chez les Doualas', *Bull. Assoc. Fr. Rech. & Etud.*, ii (1966), pp. 33–47
L. Perrois: *Gabon: Culture et technique, catalogue du Musée des Arts et Traditions de Libreville* (Paris, 1969)
L. Siroto: 'Gon: A Mask Used in Competition for Leadership among the BaKwele', *African Art and Leadership*, ed. D. Fraser and H. M. Cole (Madison, 1972), pp. 57–77
O. Gollnhofer, P. Sallée and R. Sillans: *Art et artisanat tsogho* (Paris, 1975)
L. Siroto: '*Njom*: The Magic Bridge of the Beti and Bulu of Southern Cameroon', *Afr. A.*, x/2 (1977), pp. 38–51, 90–91
E. Bassani: 'Les Sculptures Vallisnieri', *Africa-Tervuren*, xxiv/1 (1978), pp. 15–22
F. Bontinck: 'La Provenance des sculptures Vallisnieri', *Africa-Tervuren*, xxv/4 (1979), pp. 88–90
L. Siroto: 'Witchcraft Belief in the Explanation of Traditional African Iconography', *The Visual Arts: Plastic and Graphic*, ed. J. Cordwell, World. A. (The Hague, 1979), pp. 241–91
A. Fourquet: 'Chefs d'oeuvre de l'Afrique: Les Masques Pounou', *L'Oeil*, 321 (1982), pp. 52–7
T. Northern: *The Art of Cameroon* (Washington, DC, 1984)
A-M. Bénèzech: 'So-called Kuyu Carvings', *Afr. A.*, xxii (1988), pp. 52–9

LEON SIROTO

6. CENTRAL AFRICA. The area between the Atlantic coast and the Western Rift Valley, which corresponds to the modern nations of ZAÏRE, CONGO, Cabinda, ANGOLA and ZAMBIA (see fig. 134), is divided into several climatic zones, including high-altitude tropical forests, savannah-woodlands and semi-arid plains. The many rich and diverse categories of Central African art can be associated with three distinct spheres: politics, ritual and the home. Figure sculpture, masks, ceremonial stools, staffs (see fig. 135)

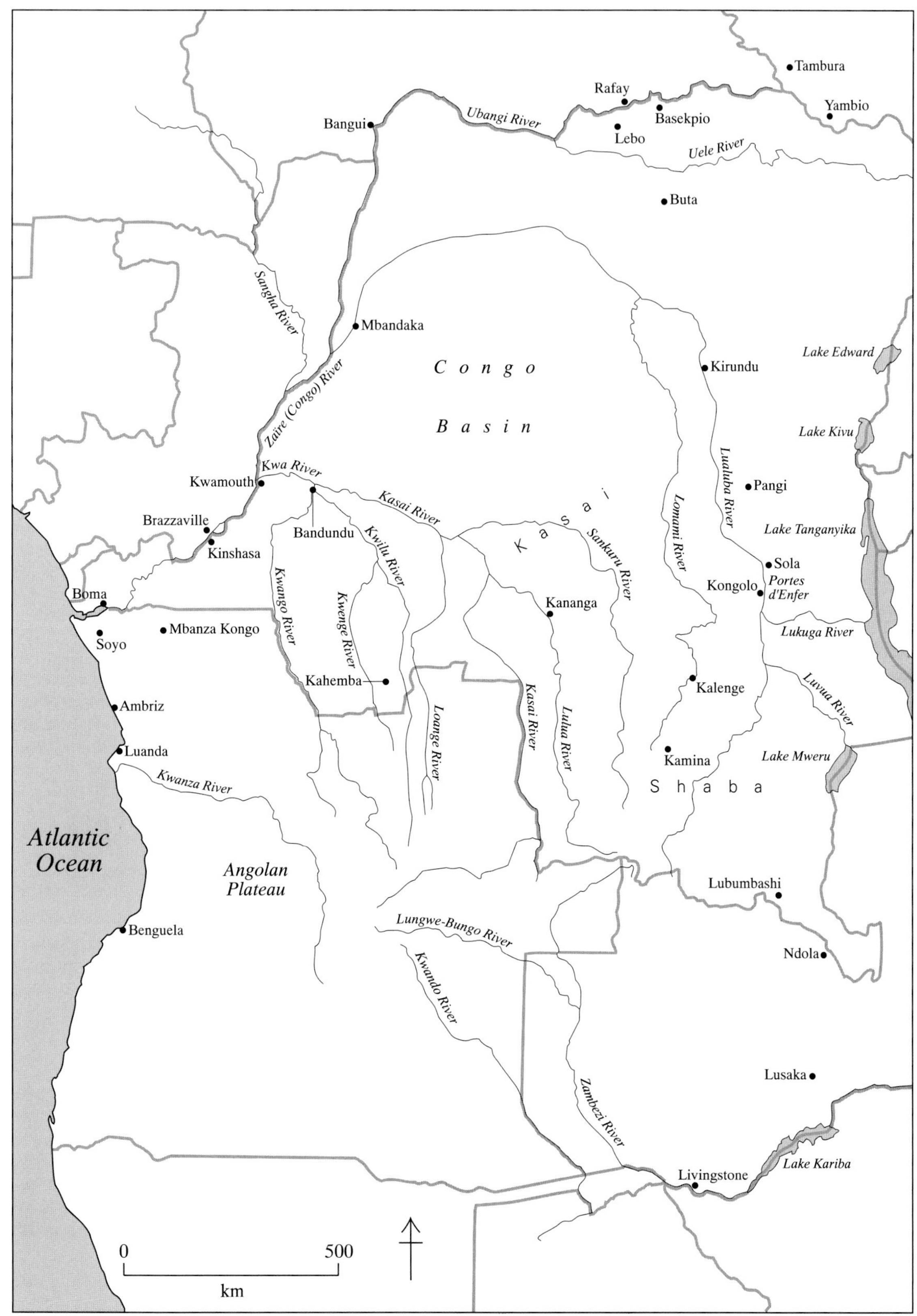

134. Map of Central Africa

135. Luba-Hemba (?or Eastern Luba) staff, wood, h. 250 mm (figures), 1.34 m (overall), from Zaïre (Prague, Náprstek Museum of Asian, African and American Culture)

and weapons symbolize political power and are used by ritual specialists, diviners and healers, while the domestic environment is the context for decorated utilitarian artefacts.

(i) Introduction. (ii) Sculpture. (iii) Masks. (iv) Textiles and ceramics. (v) Architecture. (vi) European influence.

(i) Introduction. The earliest human artefacts from Upper Acheulian and Post-Acheulian archaeological contexts are handaxes, cleavers, picks and leaf-shaped points made from polymorphic sandstones. Later artefacts—tanged arrowheads and polished axes—were made with greater care. Proto-Bushmen and early proto-Bantu-speaking peoples were probably the carriers of this Neolithic culture. Early Iron Age culture becomes apparent in the interlacustrian region by *c.* AD 200, and in the extreme south-east hemispherical pottery with the slight dimple base and rather short neck is commonly found in graves containing hoes, knives and iron spearheads. The oldest example of wood sculpture (Tervuren, Kon. Mus. Mid.-Afrika), attributed to the 8th century AD, was found in gravel banks along the Liavela River in Central Angola and represents an animal image. To the south-east around Lake Kisale, from the end of the 1st millennium AD, social stratification is evident with the presence of grave goods including ceremonial axes studded with nails, cylindrical iron anvils, copper bangles, anklets, belts, necklaces, bracelets, rings and copper cross-ingots.

Compared to other regions of Africa, rock art is poorly represented due to the limited number of exposed surfaces suitable for decoration. In the south-west, silhouettes of wild animals and a few human representations are found in rock painting regarded as the work of Final Neolithic hunter-gatherers, while schematic petroglyphs by Early Iron Age peoples consist of concentric and linked circles, chevrons, grids or ladder-like designs. In the lower Zaïre area, rock shelters present only zigzag engravings and black-and-ochre paintings thought to date from the 16th century. The general types of traditional ethnic art—so-called 'tribal' art—include both anthropomorphic and zoomorphic figures and masks, sculptured decoration of sceptres, staffs, ceremonial spears, adzes, knives, hairpins, pipes, cups, neckrests, ladles, caryatid stools, ritual implements, musical instruments and various items for building decoration. The principal medium is wood, although metal, stone and clay are occasionally used in three-dimensional work. Abstract designs are found in textiles, pottery and basketwork. Styles of art work are generally categorized by ethnic names, although recent field studies assert that a given style is not necessarily uniform within a given ethnic unit: borrowings of art objects between different groups appear, as well as unexpected forms of stylistic synthesis. Moreover, a style can be linked with ritual institutions that overlap ethnic groupings and thus are effectively 'trans-tribal'. Much of the literature on Central African art centres on broad regional and local stylistic classifications based upon the morphological study of carved statuettes. The classic work by Frans Olbrechts (1946) established the framework of classification for subsequent researchers. It recognizes five stylistic regions, each with several styles and substyles: the Lower Congo or South-west; Kuba or South Centre; Luba or South-east; the North-west; and the North-east.

(ii) Sculpture. The Lower Congo stylistic region, the western limit of which is the Atlantic Ocean, is subdivided into the

Coastal style area, the TEKE style to the north and the Kwango style to the east: the Coastal style includes sculptures of the Kongo (*see* KONGO, figs 1 and 3), Kakongo, Solongo, Yombe, Woyo, Sundi, Bwende and Vili peoples. Free-standing sculpture is noted for asymmetry and diversity in posture, with the head rendered in a naturalistic manner. Eyes are commonly picked out in kaolin or mirror fragments. Examples of the mother-and-child theme, together with the varied imagery of magical assemblages on the head or torso, are distinctive. Items attached to figures include metal rings and seed pods, inserted blades, nails and wrapped screws, tied packets, suspended containers and tufts of various materials, all of which offer sculptural qualities in an accumulative aesthetic mode. Research has identified independent style groups of the Bwende, BEMBE, Mboma and Sundi or simply designates given objects by the various Kongo ethnic components.

The Pool Malebo or Teke-style subdivision includes sculpture of the Lari, Mfinu and Wuum. Figures are shown in stiff standing postures, with striated faces, square beards, and on the head either a sagital crest or bunlike hairstyle. Back-to-back double statuettes among the Teke and Teke-related populations are known. Usually the magical load—diverse substances of metonymic and metaphorical reference—surrounds the torso enclosed in a resin adhesive, occasionally reinforced by cloth or skin. Thus arms are often omitted and sexual organs rarely shown. Related imagery appears among the Northern Mbala (see fig. 136), Yansi, Buma, Sakata and Npepe.

The Kwango-style subgroup includes sculpture of the YAKA, Mbala and PENDE, consisting of figures shown in a standing or squatting posture, with hands held up to chest or chin. Highly expressive eyes, noses, eyebrows, facial framing and elaboration of headgear are richly developed, with the spectrum of creativity ranging from simplified naturalism to grotesque caricature. The applied materials and textures that alter the sculptural form include antelope horns, packets, sticks, skins, bones, encrustations of camwood and other ingredients suspended, wrapped or otherwise attached to the statuettes. Further breakdown designates styles of the Suku, Nkanu, Hungaan, Holo, Southern Yaka, Tsotso, Kwese, Soonde, Lula, Dikidiki and Mbeko.

The South Centre or Kasai stylistic group centres on Bushoong court statues of the Kuba, in which sovereigns are depicted seated cross-legged with symbolic attributes carved on the plinth (*see* KUBA (ii), fig. 1). Rounded treatment of face and forehead, angled hairline and annulated neck are shared to varying degrees with the Ndengese, Biombo, Northern Kete, Mbagani and Salampasu, although figure sculpture may include a diversity of polychrome patterns painted on to the human face.

The South-east or LUBA stylistic cluster, stretching from Katanga to the Eastern Kasai, presents a smooth naturalism in human forms, with domed forehead, lowered eyes and pursed lips highlighted by an elaborate tiered hairdress that may cascade or end in a cross configuration. Hands and feet may be elongated and simplified, but more attention is given to body scarification. Characteristic are depictions of the young female with hands to breast or holding a bowl, or as a caryatid supporting a seat. Males

136. Northern Mbala headrest, wood, h. 175 mm (London, British Museum)

appear either holding regalia or standing with arms flanking a protruding stomach. Substyles of Luba Shankadi, Luba Upemba, Luba Kasai, Hemba, Eastern Luba, Zela, Kanyok, TABWA, Tumbwe, Holoholo, Bangubangu, Bemba, Sikasingo, Bembe and Boyo have been distinguished. The SONGYE substyle is differentiated by geometric treatment of the human face and body forms, which are segmented into distinct volumes. Apart from the figure-of-eight-shaped mouth, prominent chin and large flat hands and feet, there is the characteristic collage aspect, with attachments of copper sheeting, blades, tacks, feathers and cowrie shell together with the power packet enclosed in a protruding abdomen or inserted into a horn projecting vertically from the figure's head.

The Angolan Plateau stylistic group, formerly regarded as a Luba substyle tending to the baroque, centres on the Chokwe (*see* CHOKWE AND RELATED PEOPLES; see fig. 137). Distinct are the broad shoulders and slender torsos with arms thrown back in a dynamic stance. Attention is given to the flaring headgear and body detail down to fingernails and toes. Almond-shaped eyes can be recessed in deep sockets, and the beard projects laterally or is formed of fibre or human hair. Other attachments are usually limited to a proliferation of brass tacks. As with the Kuba and Luba, Chokwe styles overflow into many forms of minor arts with the decoration of pipes, combs, staffs, musical instruments and furniture. Mbunda, Lwena, Songo, Ovimbundu and Ngangela substyles present variations on scarification designs and headdresses but add new subjects, for example a figure mounted on an ox and both cruciform and framed figures of types shared on the Kwango River with the Holo.

In the North-eastern Equatorial stylistic region, various rudimentary human forms are produced in bone, ivory and wood. Diagnostic are the half figures, double-faced, double-headed or fully double figures with superimposed faces, heads or bodies placed in opposition or linked together, many without arms, with one arm or short stumps for arms. Relatively small, heart-shaped faces are distinctive, with arched eyebrows forming a single unit with a narrow ridge or flat triangular nose. Best-known is

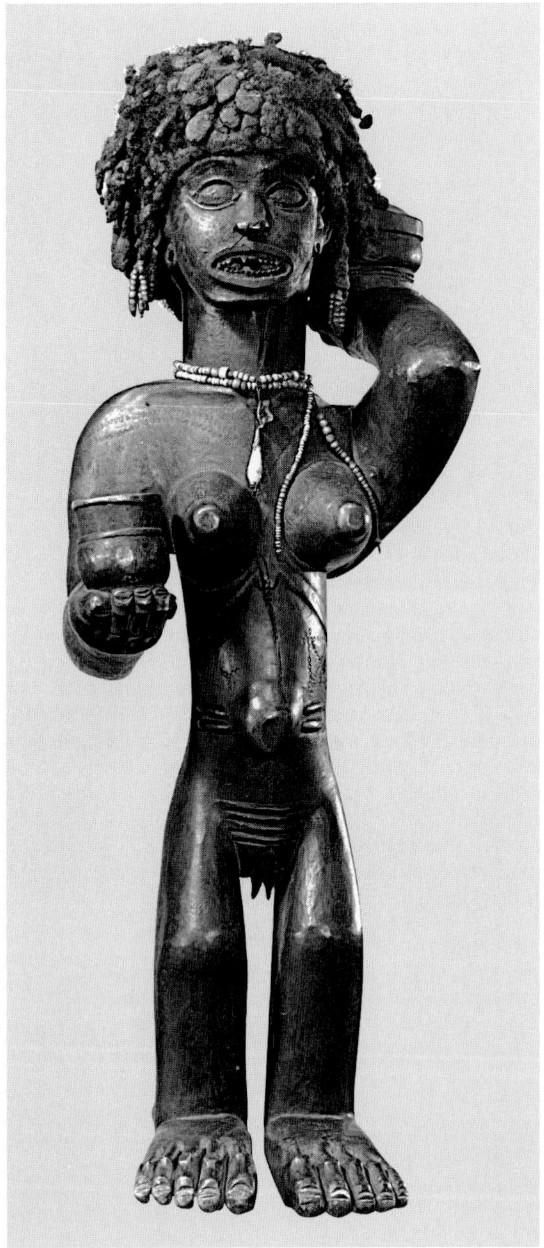

137. Chokwe figure sculpture, wood, human hair, glass beads, camwood powder, iron and traces of copper sheeting, h. 590 mm, collected 1883 (Berlin, Museum für Völkerkunde)

the imagery of the Lega (*see* LEGA AND RELATED PEOPLES), although similar anthropomorphic figurines are found among the Yela, Lengola, Mitoko, Bembe, Pere, Komo, Nyanga, Kwami, Nyindu, Songola and Zimba.

North-central and North-western stylistic groups are less uniform categories that include the MANGBETU (see fig. 138), ZANDE and Boa on the one hand and Ngbaka and Ngbandi further to the west. Figurative sculpture for the Mangbetu and Zande more commonly consisted of decoration on everyday objects rather than a prolific tradition in statuary. Delicate female figures decorate the bridges of harps covered with reptile skin. Their highly embellished realism shows distinct cranial deformation and expanding cylindrical headdresses. Zande styles of free-standing sculpture range from rounded forms to greatly abstracted figures with zigzag or stumplike legs

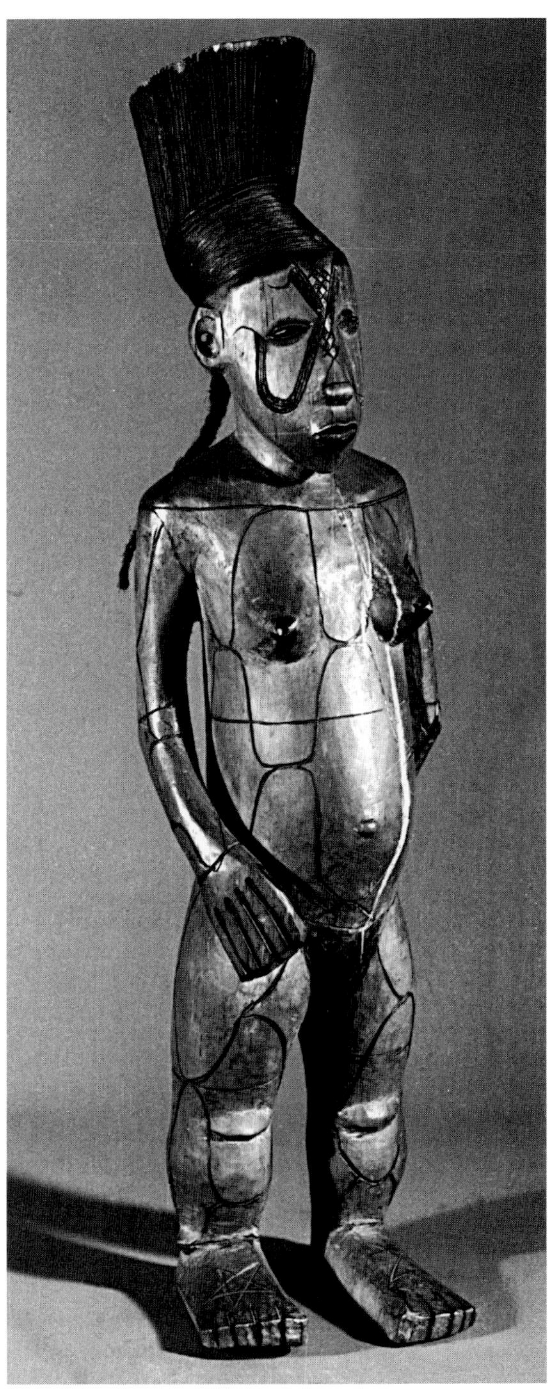

138. Mangbetu female figure sculpture, wood and hair, h. 485 mm, probably early 20th century, from Uele, Zaïre (Tervuren, Koninklijk Museum voor Midden-Afrika)

and underdeveloped arms, a characteristic shared with Ngbaka and Ngbande. Additives to such figures include multiple metal rings and strings of beads embedded in resin. Ngbandi and Ngbaka sculpture is equally rare; it is characterized by large spherical heads, often with heart-shaped faces and brows lined with ridges of scars that also bisect the forehead vertically. Flipper-like arms commonly hang freely at the side, and in highly abstract varieties human features are barely recognizable.

(iii) Masks. Central African masks range from miniatures to face coverings, from cap and helmet varieties that surround the wearer's head to massive creations that completely engulf the person beneath. Although the facial portion may be formed of woven materials, bark cloth or carefully carved and painted wood, masks are found decorated with strips of metal, tacks, shells, calabash segments, beads, feathers, fur, animal horns or constructed headgear and commonly include either a knitted hood or a free-flowing fibre fringe (see fig. 139). Representation includes humans, animals and composite creatures made up of elements of both. The system for classifying masks, like that of free-standing figures, is by ethnic unit or tribe, stressing the uniqueness of a chosen mask type. Resemblances in size or form are apparent both in contiguous ethnic groups and in isolated pockets within Central Africa. Miniature masks, small enough to be held in the palm of the hand, appear in the north-east among the Lega, Nyindu and Kwami, where they are carved of bone and ivory. In the south-west, amid the Pende, Southern Suku, Holo and Chokwe, such masks are made of wood, ivory, seed-pit, lead and other materials. In the south-west among the Songye, Luba-Hemba and northernmost Luba they appear in wood as miniature white-faced masks with striated markings.

Giant masks are defined as masks measuring 900 mm or more in any direction. They are reported across the southern savannah and the Angolan Plateau made of woven materials, bark cloth or carved from wood, often featuring a face with bloated cheeks or a horned animal. The massive fibre masks of the western or Kwilu Pende called *gikuku mingangi* are the largest recorded in Central Africa: during the dance five or six other masked personages emerge from the mask's flowing fringe skirt.

The white, heart-shaped face is characteristic of mask imagery across the equatorial forest region among Bantu-speaking peoples, including the Mbole, Komo, Tembo, Lega, Bembe, Jonga and Ngbaka, and into Gabon, where the form dominates. The heart-shaped face can also be found in isolated contexts on the southern savannah amid the Kwese and easternmost Kasai Pende, and indeed whiteness in faces and white areas around eyes of masks are prevalent throughout Central Africa. Contrasts between the schematization or abstract reductions in mask imagery of the equatorial forest and examples of naturalism among the Vili, Suku, Pende, Chokwe and Luba are readily apparent. Yet within the savannah belt alone fantastic exaggerations distantly removed from human facial physiognomy occur in masks of the Yaka, Pende, Kete, Luluwa, Lwalwa, Songye, Chokwe and HEMBA.

South of the Zaïre Basin two macrostyles encompass the diverse ethnic expressions in masking: an upper zone

139. Salampasu mask, fibres and feathers, h. 914 mm, from Zaïre (Los Angeles, CA, University of California, Fowler Museum of Cultural History)

of predominantly wooden helmet-shaped masks, found among populations living near the northern edge of the savannah and nearby forests (e.g. Suku, Kasai Pende, Kwese, Kete, Kuba, Binji, Kanyok and Luba), and a secondary tier of predominantly resin-and-fabric masks made by peoples across the savannah to the south (e.g. the Chokwe, Lwena, Lunda, Soonde, Yaka and Nkanu). Moreover, the towering projections, mitre-like elements, discs and painted decoration imply transtribal interaction of styles. The principal context for both resin-and-fabric masks and wooden helmet-shaped masks across southern Central Africa is that of *mukanda*, an institution involving collective circumcision and initiation to manhood with widespread similarities in terminology, sequence of events and use of masks at crucial moments of initiation and coming-out festivities. In north-eastern Zaïre, use of the white, heart-shaped face in masking of the Lega and their neighbours is associated with an age-graded association known variously as Bwami, Bukota, Lilwa and Nsubi.

Masks in these contexts serve as mnemonic devices that aid in learning an enormous number of proverbs and ritual actions, secrets reserved to members alone. Other trans-tribal examples in masking styles may be observed in the oblong or oval masks with patterns of incised facial striations among the Songye, Kalebwe and Luba-Hemba, which are associated with a secret organization known as Kifwebe. A still broader view might include diverse peoples using fibre masks and body coverings made of palm leaves and occasionally decorated with other materials. They generally signify bush monsters that terrorize the uninitiated; they are widespread and are the likely source from which more elaborate mask-making derives.

(iv) Textiles and ceramics. In the artistic production of textiles, Central African cut-pile embroidery, called 'Kasai velvets', has been admired by outsiders since first discovery. The oldest examples came to Europe between 1666 and 1674 from the mouth of the Zaïre River and Angola. Since the late 19th century production has been limited to Kuba-related peoples of the Kasai region, and it continues in the 20th century among the Shoowa and Ngombe of the Sankuru. The wide range of various rectilinear and abstract patterns are assigned individual names by their makers, although patterns bearing the same name are not necessarily identical. The classification of patterns is paralleled by distinctive social meanings of its use. Some were worn by women, others by men; some appeared on ceremonial occasions only, others were in everyday use and distinguished the social position of the wearer. Early accounts further describe a variety of uses: as blankets, in adornment of stools, as shrouds and as currency.

Pottery exists primarily as domestic ware. Forms range from jars with long, bottle-shaped necks made in the coastal region to the spherical forms made in the east, which bear short necks and a small mouth. Decoration of surfaces with bands of incised crosshatching and zigzag is common, as are impressions made with cords and other objects. Painting with mineral or vegetable pigments, as well as use of glazes, often enhances vessels. Noteworthy is the marbled or mottled effect achieved by splashing oil on the newly fired surface in Kongo and Teke wares. Although rare, figurative decoration on lids takes the form of birds, dogs or humans among the Kongo, while a few ceramic heads and busts used as containers appear among certain groups of the Kwango and Kasai rivers and the Mangbetu to the north. The influence of woven design is reflected in ceramic decoration, particularly in the Kasai region.

(v) Architecture. The most common traditional structure has a square or rectangular plan with walls of palm fronds and a hipped roof of thatch or palm leaf. Distinctive variations appear among Kuba-related peoples, who embellish this basic framework with interwoven materials and mats. The Mangbetu in the 19th century amplified it into a vast rectangular assembly hall some 15 m high. Roof structure and thatching could achieve a convex profile, found in structures from the Holo and Southern Suku to the Luba, or the pyramidal roof of leaves in the north among the Ngelima and Nalya. Granaries could be elevated versions of the pitched roof structure or miniature versions of cylindrical buildings with conical roofs, as found among the Chokwe and related peoples in Angola. Carved posts, panels or figures embellished the domestic dwellings of dignitaries, especially among the Kongo, Chokwe and Pende, while dressed wooden doorframes were made by the Southern Suku and Holo, and the Mangbetu elaborately painted pillars and walls.

(vi) European influence. Both stylistic diversity and traditional conservatism, apparent in the early 20th-century art of the region, were products of past isolation as well as of steady intergroup contacts, intermixing and political emulation or domination. Since then, the disruption of traditional structures of authority, religious proselytizing, the establishment of mission and government schools and rural projects and the external economic pressures of a cash economy have dramatically changed the traditional setting of art. In some areas a wholesale rejection of traditional ritual and accompanying paraphernalia has resulted. In others, masking in the context of initiations survived or has been revived, both in a quest for cultural authenticity and as a source of local revenue. Retention of the original significance or regulation of art works by traditional leadership is rare in the late 20th century.

The earliest influence of European imagery in Central Africa, however, dates from the beginning of the 16th century, following the arrival of Catholic missionaries. The Kongo king Alfonso I (*reg* 1509–41) gave the crucifix to clan chiefs and judges presiding over tribunals both in the Mbanza capital and outlying provinces. Later the crucifix became a standard item for the investiture of Kongo chiefs and was incorporated into a syncretic belief system. Cast by the lost-wax or open-mould methods, all brass *nkangi kiditu* ('attached Christ') are based on 14th–16th-century European examples, although African-like features illustrate indigenous adaptation. Wooden crucifixes and free-standing statuary of the Virgin and St Anthony were also produced. Within the south-western region, Christian religious influence into the 20th century is equally apparent in the *ntadi* stone funerary monuments of the Mboma, Holo framed figures and some Chokwe woodcarving.

For more information on continuing traditions, on colonial and post-colonial arts and on art patronage, museums and art education, *see* the individual country entries.

BIBLIOGRAPHY

F. M. Olbrechts: *Plastiek van Kongo* (Antwerp, 1946)
A. Maesen: 'Un Art traditionnel au Congo Belge: La Sculpture', *Les Arts au Congo Belge et au Ruanda-Urundi* (Brussels, 1950), pp. 9–33
L. de Sousberghe: *L'Art Pende* (Brussels, 1958)
J. Cornet: *Art d'Afrique noire au pays du fleuve Zaïre* (Brussels, 1971); Eng. trans. as *Art of Africa: Treasures from the Congo* (London, 1971)
D. Biebuyck: *The Arts of Zaire*, 5 vols (Berkeley, 1985–)
——: *The Arts of Central Africa: An Annotated Bibliography*, Ref. Pubns A. Hist. (Boston, MA, 1987)
M. L. Felix: *100 Peoples of Zaire and their Neighbors: The Handbook* (Brussels, 1987)
H.-J. Koloss: *Art of Central Africa: Masterpieces from the Berlin Museum für Völkerkunde* (New York, 1990)

A. P. BOURGEOIS

7. EAST AFRICA. For present purposes East Africa is taken to be the vast area occupied by the modern states of KENYA, UGANDA, RWANDA, BURUNDI, TANZANIA, ZAMBIA and MALAWI (see fig. 140). It thus includes what is often referred to as East Central Africa. Reference will

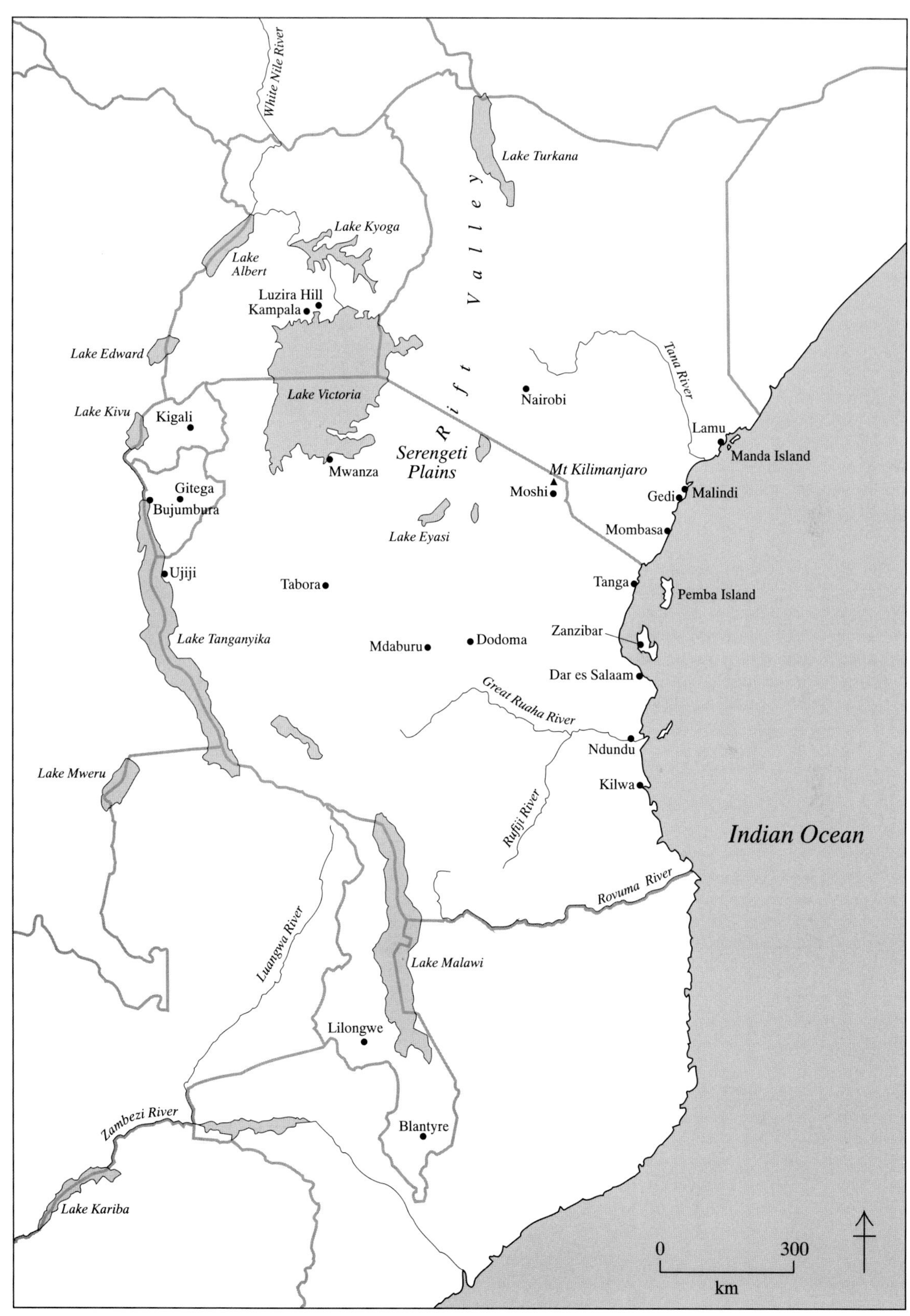

140. Map of East Africa

also be made to peoples living within the southern parts of Sudan whose cultural traditions link them with other East Africans rather than with the predominantly Islamic populations to their north, as well as to peoples living in adjacent areas of other neighbouring countries. The island of MADAGASCAR is often treated as part of East Africa, but it is dealt with separately in this dictionary.

(i) Introduction. (ii) Body arts. (iii) Mask and masquerade. (iv) Figure sculpture. (v) Architecture. (vi) Domestic and other arts.

(i) Introduction. The region whose art is discussed here straddles the Equator and lies well within the tropics, yet it does not experience a typical Equatorial climate, nor is it characterized by the dense lowland rain-forests found at similar latitudes on the west of the continent. The Ruwenzori Mountains, which constitute part of the western boundary of the area, are also the limit of the forests of the Zaïre River Basin. Generally, East Africa is high plateau country whose altitude ensures temperate conditions and a vegetation cover that, except in more mountainous parts, is typically that of dry woodland. In lower-lying areas, notably in the Rift Valley and the Serengeti Plains of northern Tanzania, there are vast areas of dry grassland. The north has the most arid climate, such that the area around Lake Turkana in northern Kenya includes large expanses of desert. The southern Sudan, through which flows the White Nile, includes both dry woodland and the vast swamps of the Sudd. With the Ethiopian Highlands this provides the northern limits of the region.

Most East and East Central Africans speak one of the innumerable Bantu languages and are descended from peoples who moved into the area from the west from *c.* AD 100. Today they live south of a line running through southern Uganda, including much of Tanzania and taking in eastern Kenya. The populations of Zambia and Malawi are almost entirely Bantu-speaking. Characteristically, such peoples practise mixed farming with an emphasis on cultivation, particularly in areas where cattle-keeping is made impossible by the presence of the tsetse fly.

Along the eastern coast and on such off-shore islands as Lamu, Pemba and Zanzibar, the SWAHILI established a series of Arab-style town states or sultanates. Their language, also Bantu though with many Arabic loan-words, and their political systems developed in parallel with their evolving cosmopolitan culture. Regular trading networks linked the East African coast to the Arabian Sea and beyond from the end of the 1st millennium AD, and Islam became the dominant faith of this maritime corridor. Swahili-speaking traders set up links with the interior, and forms of Swahili became the lingua franca throughout much of the region and into eastern Zaïre. Both Islam and the tradition of town states, however, have remained essentially coastal phenomena. Throughout the rest of the region, traditional political authority tends to be invested in local chiefs or village headmen. Only exceptionally did more elaborate kingdoms develop, for example those of the Ganda of Uganda, the Lozi or Rotse in Zambia, and among some of the peoples of Tanzania. None, however, attained the opulence that was achieved by some kingdoms in West and Central Africa.

In the north of the region the dominant languages are those of the Nilotic family, spoken by, for example, the Dinka in southern Sudan, the Karamojong in Uganda, the Turkana in Kenya and the Maasai in Kenya and Tanzania. Most of these peoples are noted for the attention they devote to their herds of cattle. These are of both economic and social importance and are sometimes in themselves vehicles for artistic expression and aesthetic contemplation, their hides being decorated and their horns twisted into pleasing shapes (see fig. 14 above; see also Coote). Pure pastoralism, however, is rare, and most East African cattle-keepers also grow crops. Among the peoples of the Kenya Highlands, known collectively as the Kalenjin, agricultural production is intensive and replaces cattle-keeping as the mainstay of the traditional economy. In general, political authority extending beyond the local level is rare among Nilotic peoples, although in Rwanda the Tutsi have established themselves as a local aristocracy. Despite being conquerors, however, they have adopted the language of the conquered and speak a Bantu dialect.

The Hadza of southern Tanzania are, along with Pygmy groups in Uganda, the last to maintain a hunter–gatherer economy in East Africa. Their material culture has been well documented (see Woodburn).

The region as a whole has often been described as being 'without art'. Such a statement, however, seriously misrepresents the situation. First, the assumption that art is limited to certain types of sculptural or graphic traditions can be challenged; and second, even on such a limited definition art is far from absent in the region. Since the 1950s more and more examples of East African sculptural traditions have come to light, both through the publication of previously unknown examples in museum collections and through fieldwork. Unfortunately, however, many pieces are only vaguely provenanced, and further information about context and use is often lacking. More importantly, until the early 1990s the art history of East Africa was still in its infancy. It is this fact and the restrictive definitions often applied, rather than any lack of materials, that has led to the perception of East Africa as being without art.

Indeed, there is evidence that artistic traditions are of considerable antiquity in the region. Among archaeological finds a striking head (and probably separate torso) found at Luzira Hill near Lake Victoria in Uganda remains undated and so far without parallel in the region (for illustration see *The Potter's Art in Africa* by W. Fagg and J. Pictor (London, 1970), p. 32). There are, however, paintings and petroglyphs on rock surfaces and in caves throughout most of the area, the largest concentrations being in central Tanzania (see figs 110 and 112 above). These works range from schematic designs to representations of both wild and domesticated animals, often in naturalistic styles, as well as human figures. Dating these works is difficult, and the overall timespan probably extensive. The depictions of wild animals are generally assumed to be among the oldest, though at Mt Elgon in Kenya depictions of long-horned cattle, which are not found anywhere in the area today, may date to the 1st millennium BC. To judge by its subject-matter, much of the rock art, except the very earliest, might most readily be associated with pastoralists. Certainly, pastoralists in the north have continued to make their own contributions to the rock art of the region late into the 20th century.

The principal and most visible subject of decoration among these peoples, however, is the human body.

(ii) Body arts. Among the Nilotic peoples of East Africa both men and women decorate their bodies using a wide variety of materials. For the Karamojong of Uganda and their Kenyan neighbours the Turkana and Pokot, mud is a major component in male decoration. This is applied particularly to the back of the head, where clay is pressed into the hair, building up successive layers. These dry to form a hard and smooth surface that can then be painted. Zips, pins and other small items may be incorporated, together with holders into which feathers are implanted (see fig. 141). Bead ornaments and other jewellery, often made of aluminium or brass from spent cartridge cases, are also worn. Again it is the head or parts of it that are emphasized. Ornaments may thus be attached to the ears, nose and lower lip, while beads and beaded discs are strung over the forehead. In addition, most of the men among these peoples carry with them a small headrest (*see* §(vi) below). This is used when lying down to prevent decorated areas from being crushed and destroyed.

Female decoration also frequently serves to focus attention on the head rather than the body. Here, however, it is not principally by altering or emphasizing the natural features of the head and face that the effect is achieved but by separating them visually from the rest of the body. Thus, typically, the neck is encircled by numerous strings of beads, often richly coloured and so massed as sometimes to give the illusion that the neck itself has been elongated (see figs 27 and 94 above; *see also* MAASAI). In the hot, dry regions clothing for both men and women is often minimal. Yet, where women clothe the body, it is normally in leather skins that are little embellished other than with small areas of beadwork usually applied to the back or skirts or small pubic aprons. Sometimes, however, as among the Turkana, the beadwork can be quite elaborate (see fig. 55 above). Otherwise, the most elaborate of such beaded skirts are those made not by Nilotic pastoralists but further south among the Cushitic-speaking Iraqw of Tanzania. Here red, blue, yellow and black beads may be applied in lazy stitch in bands and symbolic designs to a skirt consisting of three or four hides, thus producing a heavy and richly decorated garment (see fig. 142).

Understanding of these Nilotic styles of decoration would be advanced by greater knowledge of each people's conception of the body. For some of the Bantu peoples of the region there is more information. For them scarification is the most important form of body decoration, especially in western Tanzania and northern Zambia, where the elaborate traditions of cicatrization found in Zaïre also occur. Among Nilotic peoples, and most dramatically among the Dinka, Nuer and Shilluk of southern Sudan, such scarification is concentrated on the forehead. By contrast, the tendency among Bantu peoples around Lake Tanganyika is to embellish the natural symmetry of the body as a whole rather than to alter or emphasize specific parts of it. Thus, many systems of scarification are articulated around a central axis of the body running down the forehead to the tip of the nose and from the neck via the navel to the genitalia. The most

141. Turkana man with characteristically decorated head, northern Kenya; from a photograph by Fabby K. J. Nielsen

completely analysed case is that of the TABWA of Zaïre and adjacent parts of Zambia.

The patterns and designs thus created are also reproduced on figure sculpture in the area and are to be found in works associated with the Bemba and Bisa of Zambia as well as up the western coast of Lake Tanganyika to the cosmopolitan centre of Ujiji in Tanzania. The interpretation of such patterns is complex, but it is clear that particular motifs applied to particular parts of the body have specific significance. There are, however, a number of points where patterns of scarification concentrate or intersect. One is the navel, a reminder perhaps of birth and a place of transitions; another is the forehead, the seat of wisdom and the source of dreams and visions. In all such cases patterns of scarification are likely to take account of the symbolic topography of the body particular to different cultures. Our further understanding of such traditions of body arts thus depends on more studies of the symbolic systems of which they form a part.

Unsurprisingly, among the Muslim Swahili traditions of body art are very different from those discussed above. The focus here is on dress and elaborate jewellery (*see* SWAHILI, §4).

(iii) Mask and masquerade. Elaborate traditions of masking are found only among Bantu-speaking peoples of the region and then only in certain areas. Probably the best-known masking traditions are those of the two Makonde peoples of southern Tanzania and northern Mozambique. The wooden helmet masks of the Mozambican Makonde are often vividly realistic caricatures, though, with their characteristic scarification patterns applied with beeswax or carved into the wood, they are unmistakably Makonde (*see also* MAKONDE, §2). The best-studied masking tradition of the region, however, is probably that of the Chewa of adjacent parts of Zambia, Malawi and Mozambique (see Yoshida, 1992, 1993). Generally speaking, the Chewa

142. Iraqw hide skirt with beadwork decoration, l. 635 mm, from Tanzania (London, Commonwealth Institute)

tradition is similar to that of Central and West Africa (*see* §VI, 3 above). All the men are initiated into a secret masking association that performs at funerary rituals and other events including, at least in the later 20th century, some purely for entertainment. There are three types of mask among the Chewa. The first two, a feathered spirit mask and a wooden face mask, are used to represent spirits of the dead. The third, known collectively as *nyau yolemba*, are large zoomorphic basketwork structures, most of which represent wild animals, though cars, cattle, sorcerers and Europeans are also represented.

Masks, mostly in wood but also in hide and fibre, are known from a number of other East African peoples, especially in Tanzania. They are, however, mostly known from museum collections, and further details concerning their imagery and use are generally lacking (see Holy; Krieger).

(iv) Figure sculpture. In much of the region the dominant sculptural form is the pole, variously decorated and more or less anthropomorphized. Such pole sculptures have been recorded from the Bongo and Bari in the north of the region in the southern Sudan, from the Konso in southern Ethiopia and from numerous other peoples down to the Zaramo in Tanzania. Such sculptures are often associated with graves, or at least with the dead, or with entrances to villages. Among the best-known sculptures of this sort are the memorial posts (*vigango*, sing. *kigango*) of the Giriama and other Mijikenda-speaking peoples of Kenya. Among the Giriama the posts range in height from 1 to 3 m and are made of durable hardwoods. The dominant motif used in their decoration is the triangle—used to represent ribs, perhaps, or ropes or snakes entwined around the body or the snuff container and chain worn by elders around the neck. The carved triangles are painted in red, white and black, and this simple motif is combined and arranged in a vast variety of patterns (*see also* §III, 5(ii)(b) above). The top is either flat and disc-shaped or a three-dimensional head; some of the latter were given silver dollars for eyes.

Traditions of figure sculpture are known from many other areas of the region. The figures of the MAKONDE are well known, while many other traditions are represented in museum collections (see Holy; Krieger). Among the more spectacular examples are the zoomorphic iron figures of the Karagwe (e.g. Stuttgart, Linden-Mus.) and a particularly naturalistic male figure carved by a Nyamwezi artist among the Kerewe (Berlin, Mus. Vlkerknd.).

In the south of the region, in Tanzania and Zambia, there is a widespread tradition of using pottery figurines in initiation ceremonies and other rituals (see Cory, 1956; Corbeil).

(v) Architecture. East Africa's best-known architectural tradition is that of the Swahili towns of the coast and islands. The tradition can be traced from the ruins of Gedi and Kilwa to the bustling towns of Lamu and Zanzibar. The dominant features are the use of coral blocks and mangrove poles, decorative plasterwork and intricate wood-carving especially of doors and windows (*see* SWAHILI, §2).

In rural areas, traditional East African architecture is characterized by the use of wood, grass and mud. These deceptively simple materials have been combined in a vast variety of ways to produce a range of temporary and semi-permanent buildings for humans, animals and the storage of foodstuffs. The forms these structures take are often referred to as 'beehives' or 'cone-and-cylinder', but there are in fact a vast range of forms, architectural details, methods of construction and materials. The arrangement of buildings in compounds or villages also shows great variety. One of the most distinctive of such arrangements is that of the Maasai *manyatta*, constructed by women for their sons' circumcision and initiation ceremonies, in which 100 or more low, oblong cowdung-plastered huts are arranged in a circle with their doorways opening on to a large open area. Most grass, wood and mud buildings in East Africa are single-storey, but huts on stilts are found among some Dinka in southern Sudan (see fig. 61 above).

Many houses are decorated. Among the Kipsigis of Kenya houses may be topped with a carved finial, while generally throughout the area the arrangement of grass thatching on the roof and walls and the shapes and surfaces of mud walls and floors are the focus of much aesthetic attention. Both external and internal walls may be painted. Among the Hima of south-western Uganda the entrances and interior walls of houses are painted with bold geometric black-and-white designs. Among the Sukuma of Tanzania the interior walls of the lodges of the secret charmers' society are painted with images of humans, snakes and mythological figures.

(vi) Domestic and other arts. There are rich traditions of furniture, personal objects, weapons and other items throughout East Africa. Indeed, because of the perceived paucity of sculpture and masks, such objects have received proportionately greater attention from scholars and publishers anxious to fill the East African 'gap' in surveys of African art. For example, though not restricted to East Africa, the carved headrest has often served as the stereotypical example of East African art. The vast range of style and forms of this typically personal object makes it difficult to provide a generalized account. It is perhaps, however, useful to distinguish between headrests that are the product of opportunist carving, as among the Dinka, Nuer and their neighbours in Southern Sudan, and the more formal, geometric headrests produced by the Pokot and other peoples in Kenya. The simple forms produced by the Dinka and Nuer are often little more than the result of some judicious pruning of a found branch to produce a three- or four-legged stool-cum-headrest, a technique that also characterizes their production of poles and shrine posts (for illustration see Coote). Zoomorphic features, such as a tail, are sometimes 'brought out', or spots or stripes may be incised or scratched on the surface. The more formal carvings of the Pokot are sometimes elaborately decorated with the addition of metal, beads, hide and so on, though this could not be said to be typical (see fig. 143). The most elaborate type of East African furniture is probably the Indian-influenced chair produced by the Swahili, but high-backed chairs with sculptured figures are also produced by the Nyamwezi and neighbouring peoples in Tanzania (for illustrations see Krieger, pls 102–3). The range of other East African domestic arts includes pots, decorated gourds, snuff-containers, tobacco pipe-bowls, staffs, tools, implements and utensils.

Among the best-known of East African objects are the shields of the Maasai of Kenya and Tanzania. These are made of an oval of buffalo hide attached to a wooden 'backbone' and are painted with geometric designs whose complexity and significance have only rarely been appreciated (Winter). The 'shields' worn on the upper arm during initiation dances by young men among the Kikuyu of Kenya are also well known (see fig. 144). Carved from a single piece of wood (like the vast majority of East African carved objects), they are made by specialist craftsmen. The shield were painted with soot, a red paint and a white earth pigment. The shields were passed from older to younger brothers and the designs retained or scraped off and replaced with newly fashionable ones. As with most East African art forms, the art-historical study of Maasai shields and Kikuyu dance shields has hardly begun. The superficial simplicity of many of the forms has meant that they have only recently begun to receive the attention that they deserve from scholars.

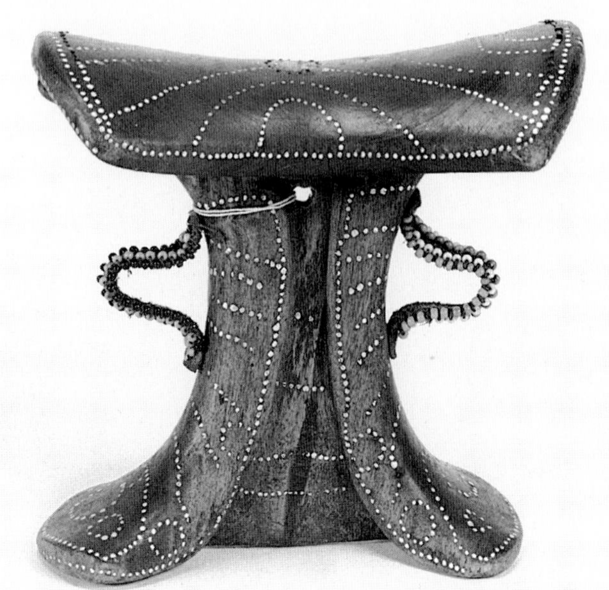

143. Tiati Pokot headrest (*ngachar*), wood, aluminium, copper, beads and hide, h. 170 mm, collected 1960s, from northern Kenya (Oxford, University of Oxford, Pitt Rivers Museum, 1978.20.35)

For more information on continuing traditions, on colonial and post-colonial arts and on art patronage, museums and art education, *see* the individual country entries. *See also* MAASAI, MAKONDE, SWAHILI and TABWA.

BIBLIOGRAPHY

H. Cory: *Wall-painting by Snake Charmers in Tanganyika* (London, 1953)
M. Trowell and K. P. Wachsmann: *Arts and Crafts in Uganda* (London, 1953)
H. Cory: *African Figurines: Their Ceremonial Use in Puberty Rites in Tanganyika* (London, 1956)
C. M. Sekintu and K. P. Wachsmann: *Wall Patterns on Hima Huts*, Uganda Museum Occasional Papers (Kampala, 1956)
L. Holy: *The Arts of Africa: Masks and Figures from East and South Africa* (London, 1967)
G. W. Hartwig: 'East African Plastic Art Tradition: A Discussion of the Literature', *Genève Afrique*, vii/1 (1968), pp. 31–52
——: 'An Historical Perspective of Kerebe Sculpturing, Tanzania', *Tribus*, xviii (1969), pp. 85–102
——: 'The Role of Plastic Art Traditions in Tanzania: The Northeastern Region', *Baessler-Archv*, n.s., xvii (1969), pp. 25–31

144. Kikuyu dance arm-shield (front and back views), wood, soot, paint and earth, l. 640 mm, from Embu, Kenya, *c.* 1930 (Oxford, University of Oxford, Pitt Rivers Museum, 1933.26.4)

A. M. Lugira: *Ganda Art* (Kampala, 1970); review by D. Banabakintu in *J. Afr. Relig. & Philos.*, i/2 (1990), pp. 137–40

J. M. Woodburn: *Hunters and Gatherers: The Material Culture of the Nomadic Hadza* (London, 1970)

H. M. Cole: 'Vital Arts in Northern Kenya', *Afr. A.*, vii/2 (1974), pp. 12–23, 82

J. A. R. Wembah-Rashid: *Introducing Tanzania through the National Museum* (Dar es Salaam, 1974)

D. W. Phillipson: *The Later Prehistory of Eastern and Southern Africa* (London, 1977)

J. C. Winter: 'Maasai Shield Patterns: A Documentary Source for Political History', *Zur Sprachgeschichte und Ethnohistorie in Afrika: Neue Beiträge afrikanistischer Forschungen*, ed. W. J. G. Möhlig, F. Rottland and B. Heine (Berlin, 1977), pp. 324–47

K. B. Andersen: *African Traditional Architecture: A Study of the Housing and Settlement Patterns of Rural Kenya* (Nairobi, Oxford and New York, 1978)

G. W. Hartwig: 'Sculptures in East Africa', *Afr. A.*, xi/4 (1978), pp. 62–5, 96

N. E. Lindgren and J. M. Schoffeleers: *Rock Art and Nyau Symbolism in Malawi* (Limbe, 1978)

H. M. Cole: 'Living Art among the Samburu', *The Fabrics of Culture: The Anthropology of Clothing and Adornment*, ed. J. M. Cordwell and R. A. Schwarz, World Anthropol. (The Hague, 1979), pp. 87–102

E. Burt: *An Annotated Bibliography of the Visual Arts of East Africa*, Trad. A. Africa (Bloomington, 1980); see also 'Bibliography of the Visual Arts in East Africa: Supplement', *Afr. J.*, xix/2–3 (1983), pp. 205–52

A. B. C. Ocholla-Ayayo: *The Luo Culture: A Reconstruction of the Material Culture Patterns of a Traditional African Society*, Stud. Kultknd., liv (Wiesbaden, 1980)

J. E. Arensen: *Sticks and Straw: Comparative House Forms in Southern Sudan and Northern Kenya*, International Museum of Cultures Publication, xiii (Dallas, 1982)

J. J. Corbeil: *Mbusa: Sacred Emblems of the Bemba* (Mbala, Zambia and London, 1982)

J. Mack: 'Material Culture and Ethnic Identity in Southeastern Sudan', *Culture History in the Southern Sudan: Archaeology, Linguistics and Ethnohistory*, ed. J. Mack and P. Robertshaw, British Institute in Eastern Africa Memoir, viii (Nairobi, 1982), pp. 111–30

M. Leakey: *Africa's Vanishing Past: The Rock Paintings of Tanzania* (London, 1983)

A. Fisher: *Africa Adorned* (London, 1984/*R* 1989) [excellent photographs of body adornment]

M. Carey: *Beads and Beadwork of East and South Africa*, Shire Ethnography, iii (Princes Risborough, 1986)

Vigango: The Commemorative Sculpture of the Mijikenda of Kenya (exh. cat., ed. E. Wolfe, III; Williamstown, MA, Williams Coll., Mus. A., 1986)

J. Barbour and S. Wadibba, eds: *Kenyan Pots and Potters* (Nairobi, 1989)

A Tanzanian Tradition: Doei, Iraku, Kerewe, Makonde, Nyamwezi, Pare, Zaramo, Zigua and Other Groups (exh. cat. by C. Bordogna and L. Kahan, Tenafly, NJ, Afr. A. Mus., 1989)

K. Krieger: *Ostafrikanische Plastik*, Veröff. Mus. Vlkerknd., Berlin, n.s. 50, Abt. Afrika, x (Berlin, 1990) [coll. cat.]

J. Coote: '"Marvels of Everyday Vision": The Anthropology of Aesthetics and the Cattle-keeping Nilotes', *Anthropology, Art, and Aesthetics*, ed. J. Coote and A. Shelton, Oxford Studies in the Anthropology of Cultural Forms (Oxford, 1992), pp. 245–73

K. Yoshida: 'Masks and Transformation among the Chewa of Eastern Zambia', *Africa 4*, ed. S. Wada and P. K. Eguchi, Senri Ethnological Studies, xxxi (Osaka, 1992), pp. 203–73

E. C. Burt, ed.: *Preliminary Study of the Distribution of Art and Material Culture in East Africa: Kenya, Tanzania, and Uganda* (Seattle, 1993)

W. J. Dewey: *Sleeping Beauties: The Jerome L. Joss Collection of African Headrests at UCLA* (Los Angeles, 1993)

S. Somjee: *Material Culture of Kenya* (Nairobi, 1993)

K. Yoshida: 'Masks and Secrecy among the Chewa', *Afr. A.*, xxvi/2 (1993), pp. 34–45, 92

C. A. Kratz: *Affecting Performance: Meaning, Movement, and Experience in Okiek Women's Initiation*, Smithsonian Series in Ethnographic Enquiry (Washington, DC, and London, 1994)

Tanzania: Meisterwerke afrikanischer Skulptur (exh. cat. by M. Felix and others; Berlin, Haus Kult. Welt; Munich, Lenbachhaus; 1994)

JEREMY COOTE, JOHN MACK

8. SOUTHERN AFRICA. Region comprising the area south of the Zambesi River Basin, the Okavango Delta and the Caprivi, including the modern states of ZIMBABWE, MOZAMBIQUE, NAMIBIA, BOTSWANA, SOUTH AFRICA, LESOTHO and SWAZILAND (see fig. 145). The people who inhabit this region speak different Bantu and Khoisan languages and display many different cultural traits. Among the larger language groups are the Ila-Tonga (Zambia–Zimbabwe), the SHONA (Zimbabwe; western Botswana), the NDEBELE (Zimbabwe), the Ovambo and Herero (Namibia), the Hambukushu (Botswana), the Tswana (Botswana; Northwest Province and western Transvaal, South Africa), the North-Sotho, VENDA and Ndebele (Northern Transvaal and Gauteng), the South Sotho (Lesotho; Orange Free State, South Africa), the Swazi (Swaziland), the ZULU (Kwazulu-Natal, South Africa), the Xhosa (eastern Cape, South Africa) and the Tsonga and Chopi of Mozambique. Many of these groups including the Shona, Tswana, North Sotho, Zulu, Xhosa and Tsonga can be subdivided further, both linguistically and culturally. The linguistic and cultural shifts reflect historical and political allegiances and splits among the peoples concerned. Khoisan peoples previously inhabited the whole region. Today they are largely confined to the Kalahari and Okavango areas of Namibia and Botswana.

(i) Introduction. (ii) Architecture. (iii) Wood-carving. (iv) Pottery. (v) Clay sculpture. (vi) Beadwork and costume.

(i) Introduction. Within the region as a whole, there are a number of shared and derived cultural and political institutions, such as initiations and forms of kingship, which cut across traditional linguistic and ethnic classifications. In some instances this is a direct result of impositions by expanding powers, as with the Zulu generals who carried Shaka-style military organizations and insignia to the far corners of the subcontinent. In other cases it reflects adoptions of institutions by neighbouring groups, as when the Lovedu, of Shona origins, adopted Pedi-style male initiations in two stages. Associated with these initiation institutions and following the same distribution in the Transvaal area are types of objects, such as carved figures or drums. However, there are also object-types with a wide distribution that are not linked directly to institutions; these include divining instruments and headrests. Where there is a wide distribution of the same object-type, similar stylistic and compositional features may obtain, but iconographic nuances may differ. There are some groups within the region whose cultural traits are closer to those of peoples in Central Africa (*see* §6 above). This is so in the case of the Ovambo, who are

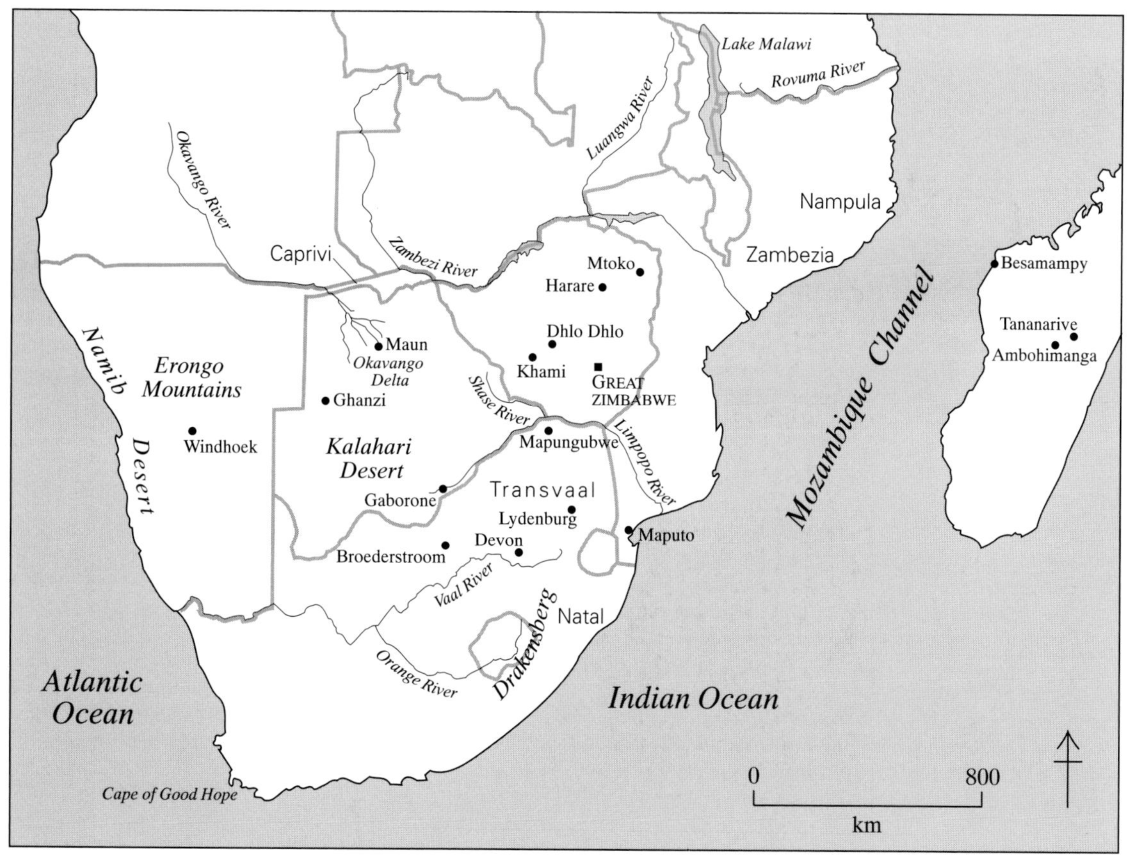

145. Map of Southern Africa; the site GREAT ZIMBABWE has a separate entry in this dictionary

clearly related to the Ovimbundu and Lunda-Chokwe of Angola.

Historically, a number of important states have risen and fallen within the region. The culture of Mapungubwe at the confluence of the Limpopo and Shase rivers flourished on trade in gold with the east coast as early as the 11th century. It was succeeded by the cultures of the Monomotapa empire at GREAT ZIMBABWE (*c.* 1250–*c.* 1450) and by that of Khami under the Changamire dynasty (*c.* 1450–*c.* 1640) in Zimbabwe itself. These cultures all shared the use of monumental stone architecture, clay figurines and, in Zimbabwe, soapstone sculptures (Masvingo, Great Zimbabwe N. Mnmt; Groote Schuur Zoo, Cape Town). In the Transvaal large empires were established by the Venda (*c.* 1700–1894), by the Pedi (*c.* 1750–1880) and the Ndebele (1820–92). The rise of the famous Zulu kingdom *c.* 1800 was thus part of a larger tendency to centralization in the region; it had many offshoots, such as the Swazi kingdom and the Zimbabwean Ndebele kingdom between 1820 and 1830. Other offshoots reached Mozambique (Matshangane) and Malawi (Ngoni). In all these states there was a tendency to produce prestige objects for a nobility who controlled trade and thus the sources of production. No large political conformations arose in the western part of the region, although in the areas of the northern Cape and Botswana there were some fairly centralized states before the invasions of the Ndebele under Mzilikaze (1820).

Trade links were established with the east coast as early as the 11th century and continued to the 19th century, first through the Arabs and later the Portuguese. White settlement in Southern Africa from the 17th century saw increasing encroachment on the lands of the indigenous populations and extensive culture contact. During the 19th century white rule expanded throughout the region, and acculturation among black peoples began. This brought with it the destruction and neglect of traditional institutions and many of the arts associated with them.

(ii) Architecture. Architectural structures and planning show great variation from one area to another but can be seen as falling into distinct settlement patterns. On the one hand are the highly concentrated settlements associated with the peoples of the plateau regions, from the Shona in the north to the Pedi and Ndebele and including the Tswana in the east. Stone-walled construction is a feature in many of the historical settlements of this type. The better known of these are those at Great Zimbabwe, Khami and Dhlo-Dhlo (Zimbabwe), but there are many others in the Transvaal and the northern Cape, including Mapungubwe, Dzata and Machemma's Kop. The Zimbabwean and northern Transvaal ruins all show the same architectural features, including decorative coursing in the walls of flat stones, whereas the Tswana and early Sotho stone constructions in the Magaliesberg area (e.g. Broederstroom, ?*c.* AD 600) used a much rougher stone construction. Stone walling was used only for the capitals of chiefs; it is still used by Venda chiefs. Within these walls homesteads of mud and thatch constructions were erected, often with mud or reed fences between the houses. The typical form of conical hut roofs on a circular base was found throughout the Zimbabwean, Botswanan and South African highveld area, with minor variations from one culture to the next.

Among some peoples in the western swamplands around the Okavango and in the Gwembe Valley, construction was predominantly wood or wattle-and-daub. Houses were built either on the ground or on stilts of wood, and little decoration occurs here on their walls. Wooden doors were used for ground-level houses. The Herero and Ovambo of Namibia use both mud construction and thatch, as well as some wooden construction. Little is known of traditional decoration in these areas.

In the coastal areas, particularly among the Nguni of Natal and the eastern Cape, beehive constructions of woven grass mats over wood and wicker framework were the norm in the past. Homesteads were widely spaced, lacking the degree of urban concentration more common in other regions. Perhaps as a result, boundary fences are less in evidence. Today most Zulu architecture follows the rondavel type and, as in most other areas, zinc sheeting is replacing the traditional thatch. In the construction of the homesteads and capitals men and women were responsible for different aspects of the labour. Men did all the work connected with the erection of stone walling, and all the wooden elements were prepared by them. In most cases men did the thatching, except among the Zulu, and men were responsible for the grass technology. Women were responsible for plastering the walls and the floors and for decorating the walls.

While finger-traced patterns on floor surfaces may be of some antiquity, the painting of walls with earth pigments or purchased paints developed much later. Walls in the ancient Zimbabwean cultures were decorated with patterns in the stone coursing. Wall decoration is found today throughout the Orange Free State, South Africa, in South Sotho homesteads, where designs of a predominantly organic nature are executed with textural elements, such as pebbles set into the plaster. In the Transvaal, Ndebele mural art with its predominantly geometric designs arose after 1945, and from this other forms have developed among the Pedi, Ntwane, Lobedu and Venda. While the patterns used in these later mural expressions are also mostly geometric, they are less flamboyant than Ndebele examples and show a tendency to divide walls into differing design fields rather than to treat a single wall as a compositional whole.

(iii) Wood-carving. Wood-carving was the sole province of men in this region. The traditional craftsman could produce many different kinds of items, and the degree of specialization varied from one group to another. In some areas, for example among the Venda and Tsonga, some carvers would specialize in carving figures and drums, while others would make bowls, mortars or milk-pails. In other instances, as among the Khakha (North Sotho), Zulu and Tonga, a carver might be called upon to carve the full range of items used within his society, from yokes and hoe handles to elaborately decorated headrests, stools and doors or free-standing figures. It was common, however, for only a few carvers to be involved in the manufacture of the more exclusive items such as figures, drums and doors, partly as a response to market forces and partly as a result of differing degrees of ability among

the carvers. Most carvers would have undergone some form of training, although formal apprenticeship outside of the patriline was uncommon. Styles thus tend to be identifiable in terms of areas and villages, i.e. in fairly localized distributions.

Evidence of the use of carved wooden prestige objects can be traced back to the use of wooden doors at Broederstroom (6th century AD) and the carved wooden rhinoceros figures from Mapungubwe that were plated with gold leaf (Pretoria, U. South Africa, Anthropol. Mus.). There is evidence of gold-plated headrests having been used at Khami (16th–17th centuries), and the carved soapstone birds, pillars and bowls from Great Zimbabwe are well known. There is no particular stylistic or cultural coherence among the objects from these successive cultures, but they bear witness to a long-standing artistic tradition within the area.

(a) Free-standing figures. (b) Decoration.

(a) Free-standing figures. Free-standing figurative carving was, in fact, produced only by a few groups within the region, the Venda, Tsonga-Shangane, Sotho and Tswana. It was made for use, generally in one of three contexts: as teaching aids in initiation lodges; for housing spiritual powers during healing or divination procedures; or as sentinels in homesteads or around fields.

Wooden sculpture was traditionally used in male initiation lodges by the Tswana, North Sotho, Tsonga-Shangane and Venda. It was only ever used in female initiation by the Venda and Valenge-Chopi. The main aim of the use of these figures was to instil in the initiates an understanding of and respect for sexual and social mores as well as some sense of group identity. Most of these initiations were held in two stages, at puberty and on a person's acceptance into full adult society. The sculptures of these different groups display some differences in style and iconography.

In the initiation lodges of Tswana and some North Sotho groups, wooden figures of animals representing group totems were used in various ways. Among the Gonanwa of the Blaauwberg, the initiates were required to eat their corn porridge from the hollowed underside of a large carved crocodile. Other groups required initiates to mime a killing of their own totem in order to reinforce the prohibitions. The style of the smaller animal figures used in this way is ubiquitous, as the figures were often produced by the fathers of initiates, not by specialist carvers. Some Tswana styles are identifiable, for example that of the Shatsi, but such particularity is not possible elsewhere in this region.

Other North Sotho groups, such as the Pedi and Khakha, made figures for teaching the initiates about sex and marriage. The fully rounded, naturalistic figures of the Pedi, with the head between one quarter and one third the size of the body in typical 'African proportion', are detailed in such a way that they clearly represent different ages and statuses—old man, young man, old woman and young woman. Other figures include representations of initiates and other functionaries. Among the Khakha, figures of humans and animals were carved by the initiates' fathers in a rather rough style and placed on the stockades erected around the initiation lodge. These figures were burnt with the rest of the lodge at the end of the initiation. Pedi figures, however, appear to have been kept from one initiation to another.

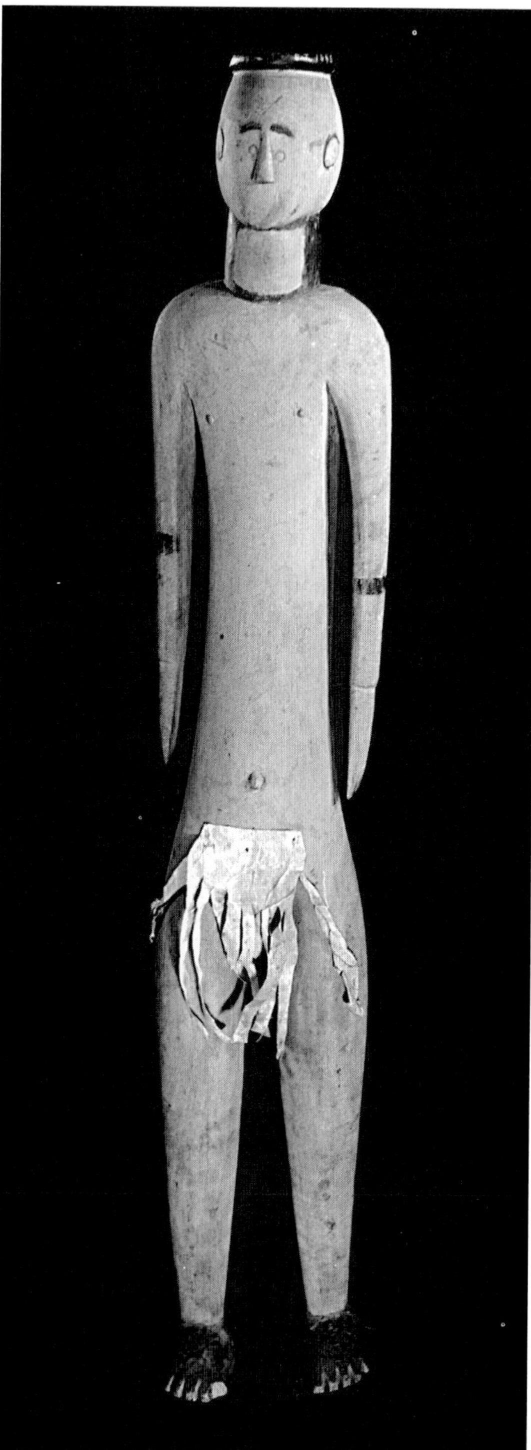

146. Tsonga figure sculpture, wood, h. 1.03 m, *c.* 1850–1900 (Tervuren, Koninklijk Museum voor Midden-Afrika)

147. Shona headrest, wood, h. 115 mm, 19th century (Johannesburg, University of the Witwatersrand, University Art Galleries)

Similar usages can be postulated for figures made both in the Transvaal and Mozambique by the Tsonga-Shangane, who were in contact with Sotho, whose initiation lodges the Tsonga often attended. Tsonga-Shangane figures are, however, distinctive in style and may have been used in other contexts as well.

Tsonga-Shangane figures tend to be much larger than those of the other groups in the area. They are elongated, with smallish heads, spatulate hands and domed feet. Most of them have clearly demarcated genitals and protruding buttocks, as well as clearly demarcated chests or breasts. In some the hair is rendered in Nguni fashion, a headring for the male (see fig. 146) and peaked hairstyles for the female: in others it is rendered as a raised chequered pattern. Details were often heightened by the burning and burnishing of the surface to render it black. In the past many of these figures were erroneously attributed to the Zulu. Figures of this type were used by the Tsonga-Shangane in initiations and as honorific markers outside the homes of important leaders or chiefs. The larger figures, some up to 1.75 m high, probably acted only in the capacity of markers. The figures with headrings may also have been displayed at the ceremonies where Tsonga-Shangane warriors were given their headrings. The figures always appear to have been used in pairs, one male and one female. The presence of the female figures at the headring ceremony may be explained by the fact that it was at this point that men were allowed to take wives.

The Venda also make and use wooden figure sculpture in their initiations, particularly in the Domba, the final stage of female initiation. These figures are executed in a style that combines some of the rounded naturalistic forms of Pedi sculpture and its small scale with the spatulate hands and domed feet of Tsonga sculpture. Venda carvers do not, however, appear to have used much burnt detail in their figures. Unlike the other groups the VENDA still make and use these figures. The Chopi also use a pair of wooden figures in their female initiation as didactic tools in explaining sexual matters. These figures are close in style to the Tsonga figures but are much smaller in scale and have rather stockier proportions, possibly as a result of the reduced scale. There are other figures that stylistically fall between the Chopi ones and the fully elongated Tsonga-Shangane type; these have been recorded as Nyai in origin but may be considered as part of the Tsonga complex.

Other forms of figure sculpture made by the peoples in the region include those used in divinatory or healing contexts. Among these are the articulated puppets used by many different groups, possibly originating in Mozambique among the Tsonga or Nyai. These puppets have been collected as far afield as Lesotho, Swaziland, Natal and the Transvaal as well as in Mozambique. They have a lesser degree of stylistic variation; although some idiosyncratic examples are known, they generally follow the same rather simplified forms. Their distribution may have followed the routes of famous itinerant Tsonga diviner-healers throughout the region. The Tsonga-Shangane healers also use other figures as containers for medicines: sometimes the whole figure may be carved of wood, or the head and shoulders may be carved, but the body formed by a calabash. There is evidence to suggest that in the past Shona diviners and spirit mediums used figures to represent their tutelary spirits. These figures are close in style to the Tsonga-Nyai style, although they are known only from photographs.

(b) Decoration. Objects carved for both daily and ceremonial use by most of the peoples in this region were decorated in some way. Often this took the form of sculptural embellishment with fully rounded figurative forms or relief designs. In this way useful objects were often given symbolic or figurative content. Thus the wooden doors carved by the Tonga, some Shona and the Venda were often decorated with compositions made up of chevrons and concentric circle motifs and were in some cases painted (Tonga). These designs may well have carried symbolic meaning. Stools and headrests made by the Tonga, Shona and Tsonga often had their caryatid sections carved as animal or human figures, but more often these sections were composed of geometric forms in apparently abstract conformations. Tonga stools had an open fretwork support composed of triangles and diamonds for the circular seat. Ovambo stools also used a fretwork support, in this case cylindrical, between the seat and base of the stool. Often a set of four mask forms typical of the Chokwe style were carved integrally with this support.

Headrests are ubiquitous throughout the Southern African region. They can be divided into two main groups: the Shona–Tsonga complex and the Zulu–Swazi complex. The headrest form of the Shona–Tonga complex is generally quite small and has a bilobed oval base with the thin horizontal and upward curving cross-piece supported by a caryatid of some decorative embellishment. In Northern and Central Shona headrests, the caryatid is composed of flat cut-out triangles with circles between them so that the whole has a form reminiscent of the female figure. The flat cut-out shapes are further embellished with relief patterns recalling the keloid scars used to decorate the human body, and on some headrests the circle elements bear three-dimensional 'breasts'. This type of Shona headrest is mostly stained black. In Tsonga and Southern and Eastern Shona headrests the supports vary more widely. Some use segmental arcs with cylindrical rods above them to support the cross-piece, while others have rectangular slabs in varying number and at varying angles between the base and the cross-piece. The slab-type caryatid is more common among the Tsonga and often has further relief embellishment. These latter headrest types have also spread far afield among Tswana and North Sotho groups such as the Ntwane. When animal figures are used by the Shona and Tsonga as caryatids (see fig. 147), the base may be dispensed with, but the cross-piece is always supported on rods or slabs above the back of the animal. These animals are most often horned and may represent cattle, goats or antelope, the last two being the most likely among the Tsonga.

The classic Zulu–Swazi headrest type rarely uses animal figures as caryatids. The classic form consists of two, three or four, but often more, generally square-shaped legs supporting a heavy rectangular cross-piece, which curves downwards towards the centre. At this point a cylindrical lug may be carved to project downwards, while at either end of the cross-piece other embellishments such as scrolls may indicate a 'head' or 'tail'. It is possible that in many of these headrests there is some reference to the bovine form, cattle being especially important in Zulu and Swazi society. On the legs themselves there is often geometric decoration in raised relief. There are many other variations on the basic form, but most follow the same scale and composition. Zulu headrests can be used as stools as well as pillows. Following a similar basic form, the headrests of some Pedi and Tau groups nevertheless show some differences. They are smaller in scale, the legs are generally cylindrical, and the cross-piece takes the form of an inverted triangle with its point replacing the lug of the Zulu type. The entire surface of the sides of these headrests is covered with engraved curvilinear, interlace patterns. A few headrests of similar type are known from Xhosa, Fingo and Bhaca sources, but there are not enough to outline any specific styles.

Among virtually all these groups, headrests could become associated with deceased members of a society and would then pass into use in ancestor veneration. Headrests were portable objects and were closely associated with their users. Among the Tsonga a man would make his first offering to his father as ancestor by rubbing tobacco on the cross-piece. Many of the headrests were further embellished with beads, and some had staffs or tobacco containers carved integrally with them.

Many other objects are embellished with carved decoration. These include snuff-containers, knives, milk-pails, mortars, drums, xylophones, plates, staffs and divining instruments. Among the Zulu, Swazi and Pedi four-legged plates are used to serve meat. The undersides of these plates are often given a composition of triangular designs or of interlace and may again recall animal forms, in that they are given handles at their 'heads' and 'tails'. Among the Shona, Swazi and Southern Sotho, knife-sheaths and

148. Zulu staffs, max. h. 675 mm, 19th century (Johannesburg, University of the Witwatersrand, University Art Galleries)

knife-handles were carved with abstract and figurative designs in both bone and wood, and among the Korana and the Tswana spoons were often elaborated with figures for handles and abstract designs under the bowl of the spoon. Venda and Tsonga carvers placed carved breasts as decoration on mortars, a motif also used on lintels over granary doors by the Tsonga. Many of these objects functioned as indices of status and prestige for their owners. Staffs probably also fall into this category. Staffs were used by both men and women among many groups. However, the longer and more elaborately carved (or beaded) examples were generally used by men or by women of extraordinary status, such as diviners or healers. The carving on such staffs varied from group to group. Shona staffs often used engraved designs along the entire stem of the staff; Zulu, Swazi and Tsonga staffs often had their tops carved with human heads or figures, animal figures or elaborate knobs (see fig. 148). They also, along with Southern Nguni and Zimbabwean Ndebele groups, produced staffs with snakes curling up around the stem. Among both Venda and Tonga a favourite staff motif was the hand-claw enclosing an egg. For the most part, these staffs were finely finished and given a shiny patina.

(iv) Pottery. Fired clay vessels were made by virtually every Southern African group. Some Khoi and Khoisan peoples, such as the San and the Hottentots, do not appear to have made any pottery, unless under direct external influence. Both fired and unfired pottery sculptures have a wide

distribution throughout the region. All pottery vessels were traditionally made by women using locally available clays. The pots were built up on a coiling method and fired in open fires. Pots were often burnished and decorated with graphite and incised designs. Patterns were generally engraved into the surface of the clay before firing and coloured after. Some women became specialists in the craft, selling their vessels to others within the group.

Fired pottery is one of the main tools used in dating the successive ancient cultures in the region. In many cases a stylistic range can be traced in historical depth for different Southern African Bantu-speaking cultures. Stylistic variation can also be traced synchronically across different cultures within the region. However, it is not always possible to do the same with clay sculpture (*see* §(v) below), as it does not always follow the same historical distribution as clay vessels. Both the shapes of the vessels and their decorations can be used as indices of stylistic affiliation. The decorative elements of style include the placing of the motifs on the vessel, the types of motifs and the technique of execution.

The pottery vessels made by the peoples of the Gwembe Valley, particularly the Tonga, are generally spherical with short necks that often flare towards the rim. The decoration is generally placed in two separate bands, one around the neck, the other around the shoulder of the pot. This decoration is composed largely of triangles or semicircles in a dark colour against the red of the pot. Shona domestic pots typically follow a similar form but do not have flaring necks. The decoration is largely engraved in a band around the shoulder of the pot, and the whole pot is burnished and blackened. Shona potters also make zoomorphic vessels for ceremonial use in ancestor veneration. These generally take the form of a headless 'zebra', the stripes being engraved into the surface of the pot and coloured red and black after firing.

North Sotho pottery, such as that made by the Pedi, Ntwane and Khakha, tends to follow a hemispherical shape with no neck on the vessel. The decoration is found in a wide band on the shoulder of the pot set away from the rim. The patterns are largely composed of arcs and triangles incised and coloured red or black. Venda pottery is similar today to Pedi pottery but in the past favoured the Shona style. Tsonga pottery is generally blackened and burnished with incised decoration around the shoulder of the pot, which has a slightly flattened profile. Here the designs are also geometric, using a combination of chevrons and triangles.

Zulu pots are also spherical in their basic shape, most pots traditionally having no necks. Their designs are placed largely lower down around the belly of the pot, rather than on the shoulder, and are rendered as raised geometric patterns and, often today, as engraved leaf- or shieldlike motifs. These pots are entirely blackened and do not use colour decoratively. Similar forms are found in some Southern Nguni groups, such as the Bhaca. There was generally a smaller range of types of vessels used among these peoples, as they used woven grass vessels rather than pots as containers for beer and milk.

(v) Clay sculpture. Clay sculpture is known throughout the Southern African region in two contexts. On the one hand there is the almost universal manufacture of generally unfired clay figurines for use as toys; usually given animal forms, most commonly cattle, these can be made by the women or by the children who play with them. On the other hand, fired clay figurines are known from archaeological sites dating back to the 6th century AD. Fired clay heads excavated in Lydenburg, Transvaal (Cape Town, S. Afr. Mus.), may well have been used in initiation contexts. They are made on the same coiling principle as the North Sotho pots in the area and bear similar decorative elements. Fired clay sculptures are also known from the Limpopo sites of Schroda (9th century AD; Pretoria, N. Cult. Hist. Mus.), Mapungubwe (11th–13th centuries; Pretoria, U. South Africa, Anthropol. Mus.), Great Zimbabwe (14th–16th centuries) and Dhlo-Dhlo (16th–17th centuries; Harare, Zimbabwe Mus. Human Sci.), all having similar stylistic characteristics. They have small heads, basically cylindrical bodies, often truncated limbs or no limbs, and emphasized genital areas. These figures were probably used in initiations, as are similar figures today among the Venda (Transvaal), the Bembe (Malawi) and the Nguu (Tanzania). Among the Tonga, fine pipe-bowls of zoomorphic form are made of a hard-fired clay. These pipe-bowls are modelled in the form of antelope cattle and occasionally bush-pigs.

(vi) Beadwork and costume. Throughout the Southern African region the making of beaded objects and fine costume is one of the major areas of artistic expression. The use of brightly coloured glass beads dates from the mid-19th century, and possibly the early 19th century in the south-east, with the expansion of European trade. Within the development of beadwork traditions, however, not only did different styles emerge but also different approaches to colour. The vast majority of early beaded items throughout the region was limited, by choice, to the use of white, red and blue or black; only occasionally were yellow and green used. Since the 1920s, however, the number of colours used has increased, particularly among the Ndebele, Xhosa, Tembu, Fingo, Zulu and Swazi. The beads were always strung by women.

In the past skin was the support on to which beaded finery was sewn. Generally cattle or goat skins were cured, decorated and sewn by men and then passed to women if they were to add any beaded motifs. Skins were decorated by patterns cut into the surface, by the retention of fur or hair in parts and by their shape. They could be used for short front aprons, long back aprons, capes and full skirts. Today beaded skin aprons, and occasionally some of the other forms, are still made, but are generally worn only on ceremonial occasions. In some areas, particularly on the south-east coast, decorated cloth with embroidered or appliquéd elements has largely replaced the older skin garments. In many areas even cloth was sewn by the men, but the effects of migrant labour have turned this into a female craft.

Possibly the best-known beadwork is that of the NDEBELE, but many other, as highly developed if not as flamboyant, traditions are known in the area. Among the Tonga, beaded front and back apron was worn by the women. The front aprons were short and completely beaded in patterns of triangles in red, white and black (see fig. 149). The back apron was long and had beaded triangular elements sewn on it in rows. Together with this, women wore fibre skirts, beaded headbands, necklaces and waist-bands as well as bands of beaded decoration around the upper arms. Beaded ropes were worn around the waist by women in many of the cultures in the region, including the Tswana, Venda, Shona, Pedi, Swazi, Zulu and Ndebele.

Beaded aprons vary in the amount of beaded elements used. Generally the short front aprons of women were more fully beaded than the back aprons. This is the pattern found among the Tswana, North Sotho, Venda, Tsonga-Shangane and Ndebele. Zulu and Swazi beaded aprons do not have leather backing. Longer skirts in use among some Nguni seem to have been preferred to short aprons.

The largest and most elaborate development of beaded costumes is found among the Nguni-speakers of the south-east coast, the Swazi, Zulu, Xhosa, Fingo, Bhaca, Tembu, Galeka, Pondo and Pondomise, and also the Southern Ndebele. In most of these groups, beaded items included headbands, neck-bands, necklaces, flaring collars, neck ropes, baldrics, waistbands, bracelets, armbands, anklets and today even sunglasses and handbags. Also beaded were staffs and clubs used in ceremonial dances; modern versions often feature cars or aeroplanes as finials. In many of the earlier examples the beadwork is predominantly white with coloured motifs woven in, but in the 20th century both colour and pattern have developed to a greater complexity. Generally patterns are geometric, based on triangles and chevrons. Stylistic differentiation between the groups concerned has not been definitely determined to date. In virtually all cases, however, one would find the most elaborate costumes reserved for certain occasions or for particular persons. Marriages were ceremonies where the bride and groom would be decked out with a great deal of finery not worn on other occasions. Diviners and healers engaged in any form of ceremony would also wear a great deal of very distinctive beadwork, this also being the case among non-coastal peoples.

In some areas the influence of missionary civilizing practices had led to the burgeoning of different dress arts. Among the Herero of Namibia, 19th-century Victorian dress is still worn today, and among the Pedi a similar kind of dress was adapted in cotton cloths and now forms an entirely distinctive style, with colourful patterns largely in the working of embroidery and appliqué.

Traditional Herero dress is reflected in the 'dolls' made by Herero women for their daughters or daughters-in-law. These 'dolls', made of stuffed cloth, have leather clothing of a short front apron and long back apron, a cloak and three-peaked cap with leather trains. Similarly, aspects of traditional dress are found in other dolls made within the region. Among the South Sotho and Southern Nguni, conical-shaped dolls were made, originally with clay or wicker cores, more recently with sand-filled bottles or stuffed cloth. These dolls were covered with cloth and some beaded elements and were carried by young wives who had difficulty conceiving or by those who had been given them by their husband's female relatives. Similar dolls were found among elements of the Zulu, among the Southern Ndebele and the North Sotho groups such as the Ntwane and the Pedi. The degree of beaded finery on these dolls varies, the Ndebele and Ntwane (see fig. 150) probably having most. Today these dolls are made for sale on the Western market, and many idiosyncratic elements have crept into their forms.

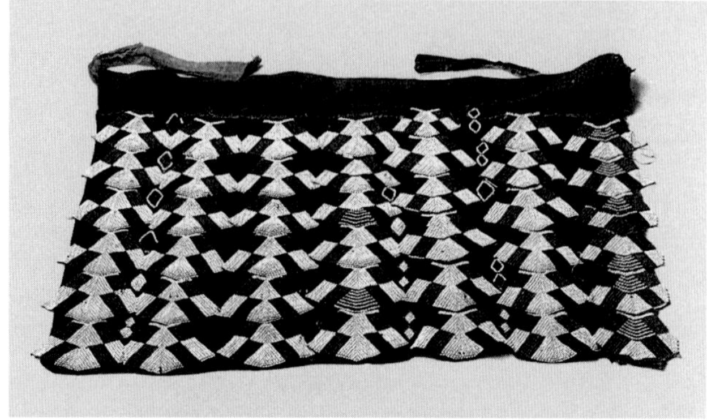

149. Tonga apron, beads and cloth, w. 600 mm, 20th century (Johannesburg, University of the Witwatersrand, University Art Galleries)

See also entries on individual countries.

BIBLIOGRAPHY

G. F. Angas: *The Kafirs Illustrated in a Series of Drawings Taken among the Amazulu, Amaponda and Amakosa Tribes etc.* (London, 1849)

J. T. Bent: *The Ruined Cities of Mashonaland* (London, 1893)

S. Schonland: 'Arts and Crafts of the Natives of South Africa', *Rep. Brit. Assoc. Adv. Sci., S. Africa*, iii/2 (1905), pp. 130–46

N. Roberts and C. A. T. Winter: 'The *Kgoma* or Initiation Rites of the Bupedi of Sekukuniland', *S. Afr. J. Sci.*, xii (1915), pp. 561–78

W. Blohm: 'Schöpferische Kräfte in der Gesellschaft der Xosa Gruppe', *Archv Anthropol.*, n. s., xiii (1916), pp. 159–95

R. McLaren: 'Arts and Crafts of the Xosas: A Study Based on Philology', *S. Afr. J. Sci.*, xv (1918), pp. 441–9

A. Muller: 'Zur materiellen Kultur der Kaffern', *Anthropos*, xxxi (1918), pp. 852–8

S. S. Dornan: 'Divination and Divining Bones', *S. Afr. J. Sci.*, xx (1923), pp. 504–611

E. A. T. Dutton: *The Basutos of Basutoland* (London, 1926)

P. Davidson and J. Hosford: 'Lobedu Pottery', *An. S. Afr. Mus.*, lxxv (1928), pp. 8–291

H. A. Junod: 'La Seconde Ecole de circoncision chez les Bakhakha du Nord Transvaal', *J. Royal Anthropol. Inst. GB & Ireland*, lix (1929), pp. 131–47

L. Fouché and G. A. Gardner: *Mapungupwe: Ancient African Civilization on the Limpopo*, 2 vols (Cambridge and Pretoria, 1937–63)

I. D. Krige and E. J. Krige: *The Realm of a Rain Queen* (London, 1943)

E. Goodall: 'Rhodesian Pots with Moulded Decorations', *Native Affairs Dept Annu.*, xxiii/1 (1946), pp. 36–49

J. Schofield: *Primitive Pottery* (Cape Town, 1948)

M. Shaw: 'Fertility Dolls in South Africa', *Native Affairs Dept Annu.*, xxv (1948), pp. 63–8

——: 'The Art of the Bantu', *The Studio*, cxxxvi/2 (1948), pp. 256–9

P. R. Kirby: *The Musical Instruments of the Native Races of South Africa* (Johannesburg, 1956)

R. Summers: 'Human Figures in Clay and Stone from Southern Rhodesia and Adjoining Territories', *Occas. Pap.: N. Mus. S. Rhodesia*, iii/21a (1957), pp. 61–75

K. R. Robinson: *Khami Ruins* (1959)

M. De Lange: 'Dolls for the Promotion of Fertility as Used by Some of the Nguni Tribes and Basotho', *An. Cape Prov. Mus.*, i (1961), pp. 86–101

L. Holy: *The Arts of Africa: Masks and Figures from East and South Africa* (London, 1967)

A. C. Lawton: 'Bantu Pottery of Southern Africa', *An. S. Afr. Mus.*, xlix (1967), pp. 1–440

P. Allison: *African Stone Sculpture* (London, 1968)

H. O. Mönnig: *The Pedi* (Pretoria, 1968)

B. Reynolds: *The Material Culture of the Peoples of the Gwembe Valley*, Kariba Studies, ii (1968)

150. Ntwane fertility 'doll', grass, beads, wool and plastics, h. 280 mm, 20th century (Johannesburg, University of the Witwatersrand, University Art Galleries)

J. Broster: *The Tembu: Their Beadwork, Songs and Dances* (Cape Town, 1976)
T. H. Matthews: 'Mural Painting in South Africa', *Afr. A.*, x/2 (1977), pp. 28–33
A. Kuper: 'Symbolic Dimensions of the Southern African Bantu Homestead', *Africa*, 1/1 (1980), pp. 7–23
A. Nettleton and W. D. Hammond-Tooke, eds: *African Art from Southern Africa: From Tradition to Township* (Johannesburg, 1989)
Art and Ambiguity: Perspectives on the Brenthurst Collection (exh. cat. by J. Lowen, Johannesburg A.G., 1992)
Ezakwantu: Beadwork from the Eastern Cape (exh. cat., ed. E. Bedford; Capetown, N.G., 1993)

ANITRA NETTLETON

VIII. Diaspora.

The African diaspora is principally a result of the slave trade, in the course of which millions of Africans were deported to the Americas and elsewhere. On a smaller scale, many other factors have contributed to the presence of active African cultural traditions outside Africa itself. This article discusses African art as retained, modified or blended with local traditions world-wide.

1. Historical introduction. Because African cultures have been misrepresented, many people, including many African Americans, believe that the slaves came from cultures so 'primitive' that they had nothing worth bringing to the New World and even welcomed Western technology as superior. Scholars have attempted to remedy this situation by showing the strength, beauty and complexity of African cultures so long denigrated in order to justify slavery. Anthropological and historical research has brought to light ample evidence of just how much of their intellectual and aesthetic traditions the enslaved Africans were able to preserve and transport intact and to re-establish in the New World. With little privacy and less power, the Africans managed to retain both those aspects of their cultures that their masters did not know or care about (i.e. religious beliefs, medical practices and folklore) and those which their masters needed or enjoyed (i.e. tool- and weapon-making, woodworking, weaving and other textile arts, narrative, music, dance and cuisine). Furthermore, it has become apparent that some of the slaves knew more about tropical agriculture than did their masters, while others possessed technical and artistic skills comparable to or surpassing those of their European counterparts.

This article is not primarily concerned with the myriad arts produced throughout the world by peoples of African descent but rather with African art itself as it developed and adapted in its many new milieux overseas. In evaluating the evidence, M. J. Herskovits (1941) suggested that the Africans were able to retain fully some African traits, while many other traits were reinterpreted or modified, and a few were blended or syncretized with local practices. All cultures, even the most conservative, are open to innovation, and the enslaved Africans, facing up to one of the cruellest displacements in human history, were certainly eager to grasp any appropriate practice, object or opportunity, from whatever source, that might alleviate their predicament. Thus while preserving the best, most beloved and most useful from Africa, they were far from conservative and adapted more or less willingly not only many Western culture traits, notably in language and religion, but also a considerable number from the Native Americans.

Sub-Saharan African slaves were known in ancient Egypt, Classical Greece (Aesop the fable-teller is thought to have been an African slave) and Rome. With the rise of Islam in the 8th century AD they spread across North Africa and the Near East and from there were taken with the Mughals into India, where some, such as the Siddis of Janjira and the Habshis of Gujarat, became mercenaries and established states (Harris, 1982). Domestic slavery through debt, crime or capture was widespread within African societies, and after the arrival of the Europeans in the mid-15th century Africans were again brought in significant numbers to Europe; this explains the presence of African faces in Spanish and other European paintings. The Atlantic slave trade began early in the 17th century, transporting Africans first to the Atlantic and Indian Ocean islands and then widely throughout the Americas until as late as 1888, when slavery was finally outlawed in Brazil.

The extensive documents of the slave trade analysed by P. D. Curtin demonstrate that virtually all Africans in the New World came either from West Africa (from Senegal to Nigeria) or from west Central Africa (present-day Congo, Zaïre and Angola), nearly always from within 300 km of the coast; only a few were brought from Southern or East Africa. For Europeans, slavery was a means of servicing a huge new market. The burgeoning plantations of the New World required cheap labour to produce sugar, cotton and other valuable crops. Although Europeans sometimes raided the coast for slaves themselves, it was easier and cheaper for them to encourage the local African states, some (such as Asante, Dahomey and Benin) built on slavery, to war among themselves in order to capture prisoners to be traded for guns, ammunition, liquor, cloth and other European trade goods. Thus most of the New World Africans came from those parts of Africa with the heaviest populations and the most developed technology. They can claim kinship with the Asante, Fanti, Baule and other Akan-speaking peoples, with the Ewe of Togo, the Fon, the Manding, Serer and Wolof of the western Sahel, the Kongo of Zaïre and especially the Yoruba and Igbo of Nigeria. An estimated one-quarter of the ancestors of African Americans were Igbo from south-eastern Nigeria, an independent-minded agricultural and trading people that resisted incorporation into a unified state, which might have been more effective in resisting enslavement than disunity proved to be. That is not to say, however, that the Igbos accepted slavery lightly: a warning proverb known throughout the plantation world was *Ibo pend li* ('the Igbos hang themselves').

By the time slavery ended in the New World in the late 19th century an estimated 12 million Africans had been transported (42% to the Caribbean, 38% to Brazil and a mere 6.8% to the USA), and they and their descendants, already much mixed with both European and Native American ancestry, could be found in every nation from Argentina to Canada. Today, by their own choice, Africans and their Caribbean cousins are again migrating, to the USA, Canada, Britain, France, Portugal, Scandinavia, even Australia, intermarrying everywhere.

Herskovits's system of retention, reinterpretation and syncretism works well for the arts, especially when they are combined with equally beloved religious and secular ritual. Indeed, the most African characteristic of the diasporic aesthetic is that all the arts combine in vibrant public displays, both religious and secular, which are quite different from the contemplative 'shrine' art central to much European and Asian religious artistic expression.

The widespread and increasingly popular New World religion that syncretizes Yoruba *orisa* and Fon *loa* (gods or spirits) with Catholic saints, termed Candomblé or Macumba in Brazil, Shango in Trinidad, Vodoun in Haiti and Santeria in Cuba and the USA (where it is spreading rapidly), is a leading vehicle bringing African arts to the New World. Sculptures, costumes, ritual objects (rarely masks) and finely embellished musical instruments, as well as songs, chants, prayers and incantations sometimes sung in the Yoruba language, are coming directly out of Africa. With the increasing ease in intercontinental travel, Yoruba priests can be found teaching their language and faith in Brazil, London and Miami, while prosperous West Indian faithful visit the shrines in Nigeria. There has been intermittent contact via Brazilian sailors between West Africa and Brazil for the past several centuries at least, and sizeable communities still exist in Cotonou, Accra and elsewhere that are descended from freed Brazilian slaves who returned to Africa, paralleling the Sierra Leone creoles from Britain and the Americo-Liberians from the USA.

2. Architecture. As Stuckey and other revisionist historians have pointed out, some slaves arrived from Africa possessing advanced skills in such areas as tropical agriculture, metalwork and woodwork. In building construction they shared a knowledge of the two-room gabled house, thatching and wattle-and-daub. These skills were immediately employed in every kind of building, both Europeans and Africans needing to adapt the buildings they knew to the new climates, materials, techniques and requirements of the New World plantation societies.

While African artisans undoubtedly quickly learnt the architectural methods and styles of the transplanted Europeans, they also constructed truly African-inspired buildings, such as the circular house on the Keswick Plantation

151. 'Shotgun house', Port-au-Prince, Haiti; from a photograph by John Michael Vlach, 1973

in Virginia and the two-storey hip-roof structure at Natchitoches, Louisiana. On the Costa Chica on the Pacific coast of Mexico, circular houses with conical thatched roofs introduced by the Mande of Mali and Senegal were still being built in the 1990s. More important, the Africans discovered that their oblong 'shotgun house' (see fig. 151), which derived from the basic unit of the common traditional compound architecture, served well in both rural and urban settings. Unlike European-derived folk buildings, such as the classic American log cabin with its long side facing the street and gables at right angles to the street, the shotgun house has one gable-side facing the street, with the rooms of the house extending one behind the other and opening one into the next, so that a shotgun could be fired through the successive doorways without hitting anything. (The Yoruba word *to-gun*, 'place of assembly', is another possible derivation.) These houses, sometimes double or with a second floor at the back, can be found throughout the USA's southern states and the Caribbean, often with porches and/or Georgian or Victorian façades. The relatively small size of the rooms, rarely more than 4×4 m, and the widespread use of the front porch reflect African practice. CHARLESTON's I-shaped two-storey houses, with narrow façades and long side-porches, can be seen as adaptations of Caribbean–African origin to suit South Carolina's notoriously humid climate. The small, square, simple buildings of Africa became the models for the slave cabins 'behind the Big House', not only in the USA but throughout the plantation societies.

Porches, balconies, elegant wrought-iron fences, gates and window-grilles were all made by African ironworkers and their descendants, often working under European blacksmith-designers, throughout the southern USA. For instance a German artisan, Christopher Werner (*fl* 1828–70), employed five slave blacksmiths to produce much of the finest monumental ironwork in Charleston, and this tradition was continued and strengthened in the 20th century by the improvisational work of Philip Simmons, the son and grandson of slave-ironworkers.

African artisans and their descendants left their mark also on churches, theatres and public buildings throughout the New World. Perhaps the most famous of these was Antônio Francisco Lisboa (*see* LISBOA, (2)), a physically disabled mulatto freedman in late 18th-century Brazil, better known as Aleijadinho ('little cripple'). His spectacular Late Baroque churches and the monumental sculptures in wood and stone that surround them have made the old mining towns around Ouro Preto world-famous. His astonishing originality and unique ability to manipulate an otherwise drab and worked-out provincial style bear witness to his African roots.

3. SCULPTURE. In contrast to architectural ironwork, wood sculpture of African inspiration is richly preserved throughout the Americas, the most spectacular examples being the religious figures of Yoruba *orishas* (spirits or gods) found in north-eastern Brazil (see Verger). A sculpture of the popular goddess of the sea—Yemoja in Yoruba, Yemanja in Brazil—has been found in use in Afro-Brazilian Candomblé ceremonies in the old slaving port of Salvador da Bahia, so completely in Yoruba style that it is uncertain whether it was carved in Nigeria or in Brazil. Other sculptures of Candomblé divinities in wood, clay and wrought-iron with obvious African antecedents abound wherever the cult is found.

An example of secular sculpture from the USA is an early 19th-century near-life-size cigar-store Indian figure (Cooperstown, Mus. NY State Hist. Assoc.; see fig. 152), a common signpost type indicating a tobacco shop but in this case carved by an African named Job. The sculptor

152. Job: cigar-store Indian figure, painted wood, h. 1.5 m, early 19th century (Cooperstown, NY, Museum of New York State Historical Association)

recalls traditional African forms in the masklike head, which, however, is set atop a typical 19th-century American body made up of seven other pieces of wood. More common are finely carved canes decorated with human heads, snakes and reptiles, strikingly reminiscent in both subject and technique of the *bweji* canes produced by the Chokwe of Angola and Zaïre. In this west Central African area, such animals as lizards and frogs are associated with water and hence with divinity.

The African maroons who escaped from coastal plantations into the interior of Surinam (former Dutch Guiana) and French Guiana in northern South America from the late 16th century onwards set up what many consider to be the most 'African' societies in the Americas, having developed religious and political institutions. A complex pierced style of wood-carving, which may have carried arcane, multi-level, possibly erotic symbolism, was used to decorate superb combs (see fig. 153), stools, clothes-beaters, peanut-pounding boards, paddles and doorframes that suggest but do not duplicate the finest Asante and Fon sculpture. (*See* SURINAM, §III; FRENCH GUIANA, §III.)

153. Comb, wood, h. 336 mm, from a village of the Djuka maroons on the Tapanahoni River, Surinam, collected late 1920s (New York, American Museum of Natural History)

4. MASK AND MASQUERADE. As the most popular sculptural expression in Africa, masks have managed to retain their central position in the secular carnival complex of theatrical arts throughout the New World, although they occur only rarely in religious art. Carnivals or carnival-like street parades exist widely, from cities in the USA such as New Orleans, Mobile and Philadelphia to virtually every Caribbean island and every Latin American city. They have recently spread, via Caribbean immigrants, to Miami, Brooklyn, Toronto and even London and Copenhagen.

In the mid-19th century, particularly in Brazil, Cuba and Trinidad, freed Africans recognized the possibilities of the European colonial carnival for their own individual and group self-expression and gradually took over the street parades previously dominated by the planter class (at which time they had been allowed to provide only music). With their brilliant masks and costumes, controversial and often witty themes, throbbing drum *baterías*, ecstatic dancing and huge, extravagant floats pulled by horses, humans and nowadays giant trucks, New World carnivals are quite distinct from their European antecedents. The choosing and development of an often historical or topical theme and the designing of the costumes and floats require the full- or part-time work of theme researchers, designers, sketch-artists, seamstresses, embroiderers, wire-workers, styrofoam-carvers, shoe- and bootmakers, tinsmiths (for armour and chain-mail), electricians and welders (for the immense floats and decorated double-decker trucks carrying maskers, musicians and literally earth-shaking sound equipment). Artistic innovation and creativity are expected and indeed required in all these crafts, some of them otherwise rarely considered as art forms.

Masks and masquerades are not associated, however, with secular ritual alone. A remarkable example of full retention of an African art form in the New World is in the cloth masks and richly embroidered costumes representing female ancestors of the Yoruba Egungun cult, still made near Salvador da Bahia in north-eastern Brazil. Their panels of cloth swinging around the dancing wearer and symbolic objects decorated with cowrie shells and glass beads are indistinguishable from their African antecedents. Some of the Candomblé divinities today wear nylon and spandex held on by velcro and carry chromium-plated staffs, while finely detailed oil paintings on canvas delineate the ritual details of their costumes.

5. TEXTILES. West African weavers long ago invented a distinctive horizontal loom, between 50 and 100 mm wide but with a warp that can extend many metres, producing with considerable speed and minimum effort a long, narrow strip of cloth, plain or intricately designed, which can be cut and stitched together to produce superbly complex textiles. Once slavery began, male and female

slave weavers were brought to the previously unpopulated Cape Verde Islands some 500 km off the coast of Senegal in West Africa and put to work producing the finest possible narrow-strip-weave textiles. Their products were then used to trade for more slaves with the African élites who gloried in the rich clothing made from these intricately designed textiles. Modern Caboverdianas and the Manjaco in nearby coastal GUINEA-BISSAU still make these superb weavings, among the finest in Africa, and some are displayed as part of the carnival costumes of the urban creoles in Guinea-Bissau. Somewhat similar *kente* cloth made by the Asante of Ghana, using imported Italian silk yarn, as well as cotton-print copies of it have become a popular symbol among African Americans to signify pride in their African heritage.

The maroons of Surinam and French Guiana have probably managed the cleverest variant on the African narrow-strip-weave aesthetic. More than a century ago, in their South American jungle homes, they cut European trade cloth of several contrasting designs into narrow strips and sewed them combined together in the African manner to make capes and covers of surprisingly traditional beauty and style (see fig. 154). Today similar print-cloth strip-design clothing can be found in West African markets.

Quilting is an ancient sewing technique known throughout Asia, Muslim Africa and Europe, where since the 14th century quilted bedcovers have been a powerful form of art expression for women. In the 19th century Polynesian, Native American and African American women also became adept, but whereas European American quiltmakers are famous for the precision and complexity of their designs and the fineness of their stitchery, African Americans have long defied the Western concept of symmetry with their wildly asymmetrical 'crazy quilts'. For example, on an otherwise neatly chequered quilt of alternating black and floral squares, the squares towards the right top corner are placed diagonally at uneven angles. In another quilt with three kinds of oblongs, most of the darker ones alternate with the paler oblongs, but the rest are grouped together along one edge. Although these quilts do indeed suggest lunacy to a 'straight' quilter, scholars of the African American tradition see in them the visual embodiment of 'offbeat' phrasing in music, as well as a form of magical protection, since 'the Devil can only go in straight lines'.

Closer and more specific parallels exist, however, between African and African American textile arts. Two appliqué 'Bible Quilts', made in the late 19th century by Harriet Powers (1837–1911) of Athens, Georgia, using brightly coloured trade cloth and associated with the Royal Court of Dahomey, so closely follow the style of Fon appliqué hangings that the similarity can hardly have been accidental, despite their Christian subject-matter (see fig. 155). Somehow, through at least a generation or two, the appliqué technique had been preserved and reinterpreted.

154. Shoulder-cape, cotton, l. 1 m, Saramaka maroons, Surinam, collected 1960s (Los Angeles, CA, University of California, Fowler Museum of Cultural History)

6. OTHER ARTS. Traditionally, African pottery is made by the built-up method of attaching one flattened piece of clay to another to form the desired shape rather than by coiling or by the potter's wheel. Women usually make pottery for their own use, but in areas where good clay produces superior pots, valuable for sale or barter, men are also potters. No built-up pottery has been found in the Americas, but, as in the other arts, African potters quickly adapted their traditional skills to the new methods, materials and forms needed in the plantation societies. Although African potters are known to have produced fine pottery in Brazil and the Caribbean, they are best known for elegantly turned bowls, urns and curiously animated 'face vessels' in the southern USA. With their inlaid eyes and teeth in contrasting colours, some of these face vessels, also known as devil jugs or monkey jugs, suggest African masks, particularly those of the Kongo peoples from the mouth of the great Congo (Zaïre) River. Some may have been made as grave ornaments in the manner of ceramic heads so used in coastal Ghana and Côte d'Ivoire.

Coiled grass baskets made in the creolized Gullah culture of the rice-growing Sea Islands off South Carolina are virtually interchangeable with baskets from Senegambia and Angola in technique, form and function (see fig. 156). Similar baskets are made, however, by Europeans and Native North Americans. As with other African arts, their New World exponents have felt free to modify and change their traditional ancestral designs to suit new uses and new markets, producing hats, table-mats and flower baskets with handles.

155. Harriet Powers: Bible Quilt, pieced and appliquéd cotton, embroidered with plain and metallic yarn, 1.75×2.67 m, *c.* 1895–8 (Boston, MA, Museum of Fine Arts)

The existence of other long-hidden or misunderstood African religious expression from the Mande, Fon, Yoruba, Ejagham and Kongo peoples, among others, has been revealed by the research of Robert Farris Thompson (1983) and his students. African form and colour symbols or cosmograms, somewhat modified or creolized, still exist throughout the New World, examples being the Haitian *vèvè* ground designs (*see* HAITI, fig. 3); protective charms made of cloth, leather and other materials; grave ornaments featuring shells, crosses and arrow-forms; and even one or more writing 'scripts', such as the *nsibidi* of the Ejagham (Ekoi) of south-central Nigeria (*see* EJAGHAM, §1). These different expressions suggest that many more persisting African beliefs and practices remain to be discovered in the New World.

Possibly the most 'African' people in the New World after the maroons, the Haitians have developed a strong painting tradition initiated in 1944 by an American teacher, De Witt Peters (1902–66), who exposed a number of young uneducated men to a wide range of foreign arts and then encouraged them to experiment, using their own local folklore and history as subject-matter. Besides the colourful street life, the rituals of Vodoun, the local religion syncretizing Catholicism with Fon cosmology, became the subject of many paintings and the source of national pride and much-needed income from avid tourist-collectors. Later, wood-carving and pierced sheet-iron panels (made from flattened steel oil drums) on the same subjects continued the tradition in sculpture as well. Although some painted wall decoration is known in Africa among the Mangbetu of Zaïre and the Ndebele of South Africa, Haitian mural and easel paintings on canvas or board using acrylic or oil paints have a Western form and a content paralleling that of other 'naive' (i.e. not academically trained) genre painters, including modern African sign-painters, whose work is now similarly appreciated abroad.

In virtually every other country of the New World, painters, sculptors and other artists of African or part-African ancestry, and with some knowledge and pride in their ancestral traditions, have made major contributions. They include WIFREDO LAM in Cuba, Agnaldo Manuel dos Santos and Rubem Valentim (*b* 1922) in Brazil, and in the USA Lois Mailou Jones (see fig. 157) and John Biggers (*b* 1925).

See also AFRICAN AMERICAN ART.

BIBLIOGRAPHY

M. J. Herskovits and F. S. Herskovits: *Rebel Destiny: Among the Bush Negroes of Dutch Guiana* (New York and London, 1934)

M. J. Herskovits: *The Myth of the Negro Past* (Boston, MA, 1941)

P. Dark: *Bush Negro Art: An African Art in the Americas* (London and New York, 1954)

P. Verger: *Dieux d'Afrique: Culte des Orishas et Vodouns à l'ancienne Côte des Esclaves en Afrique et à Bahia, la Baie de tous les Saints au Brésil* (Paris, 1954)

J. H. Rodrigues: *Brazil and Africa* (Berkeley, 1965)

P. D. Curtin: *The Atlantic Slave Trade: A Census* (Madison, 1969)

S. Lewis: *Art African American* (New York, 1969)

R. F. Thompson: *Black Gods and Kings: Yoruba Art at UCLA* (Los Angeles, 1971/*R* Bloomington and London, 1976)

156. Sewing basket, sweet grass, h. 380 mm, from Sea Islands, off South Carolina, 1975 (Washington, DC, National Museum of American History)

African Art in Motion: Icon and Act (exh. cat. by R. F. Thompson; Washington, DC, N.G.A.; Los Angeles, UCLA, Wight A.G.; 1974/*R* 1979)

J. Drachler: *Black Homeland, Black Diaspora: Cross-Currents in the African Relationship* (Port Washington, 1975)

G.-M. Fry: 'Harriet Powers: Portrait of a Black Quilter', *Missing Pieces: Georgia Folk Art* (Atlanta, 1976)

J. M. Vlach: 'The Shotgun House: An African Architectural Legacy', *Pioneer America*, viii (1976), pp. 47–80; also in *Afro-American Folk Art and Crafts*, ed. W. Ferris (Boston, MA, 1983) and *By the Work of their Hands: Studies in Afro-American Folklife*, by J. M. Vlach (Charlottesville and London, 1991), pp. 185–213

A. M. Pescatello: *Old Roots in New Lands: Historical and Anthropological Perspectives on Black Experiences in the Americas* (Westport, 1977)

S. Rodman: *Genius in the Backlands: Popular Artists of Brazil* (Old Greenwich, CT, 1977)

Haitian Art (exh. cat. by J. Stebich; New York, Brooklyn Mus.; Milwaukee, WI, A. Cent.; New Orleans, LA, Mus. A.; 1978–9)

The Afro-American Tradition in Decorative Arts (exh. cat. by J. M. Vlach; Cleveland, OH, Mus. A.; Milwaukee, WI, A. Cent.; Birmingham, AL, Mus. A.; and elsewhere; 1978–9)

Carybe: *Iconografia dos Deuses Africanos no Candomble da Bahia* (São Paulo, 1980)

Afro-American Arts in the Surinam Rain-Forest (exh. cat. by S. Price and R. Price; Los Angeles, UCLA, Wight A.G.; Dallas, TX, Mus. F.A.; Baltimore, MD, Walters A.G.; New York, Amer. Mus. Nat. Hist.; 1980–82)

The Four Moments of the Sun: Kongo Art in Two Worlds (exh. cat. by R. F. Thompson and J. A. Cornet, Washington, DC, N.G.A., 1981–2)

J. H. Harris: *Global Dimensions of the African Diaspora* (Washington, DC, 1982)

R. A. Perry: *What Is It? Black American Folk Art from the Collection of Regenia Perry* (Richmond, 1982)

W. Ferris, ed.: *Afro-American Folk Art and Crafts* (Boston, MA, 1983)

R. F. Thompson: *Flash of the Spirit: African and Afro-American Art and Philosophy* (New York, 1983)

D. J. Crowley: *African Myth and Black Reality in Bahian Carnival* (Los Angeles, 1984)

J. O. Horton: 'Double Consciousness: Afro-American Identity in the Nineteenth Century', *Sharing Traditions: Five Black Artists in Nineteenth Century America*, ed. L. R. Hartigan (Washington, DC, 1985)

D. E. Reno: *Collecting Black Americana* (New York, 1986)

S. Stuckey: *Slave Culture: Nationalist Theory and the Foundations of Black America* (New York, 1987)

Visionary Images from the South (exh. cat. by M. Wahlmann, Lafayette, U. SW LA, A. Mus., 1987–8)

J. Wilson: 'The Myth of the Black Aesthetic', *Next Generation: Southern Black Aesthetic* (Winston-Salem, 1990)

Free within Ourselves: African-American Artists in the Collection of the National Museum of American Art (exh. cat. by R. A. Perry; Hartford, CT, Wadsworth Atheneum; New York, IBM Gal. Sci. & A.; Sacramento, CA, Crocker A. Mus.; Memphis, TN, Brooks Mus. A.; Columbus, GA, Mus.; 1992–4)

R. F. Thompson: *Divine Inspiration from Benin to Bahia* (Albuquerque, 1993)

J. M. Vlach: *Back of the Big House: The Architecture of Plantation Slavery* (Chapel Hill, 1993)

——: *By the Work of their Hands: Studies in Afro-American Folklife* (Charlottesville and London, 1993)

Face of the Gods: Art and Altars of Africa and the African Americas (exh. cat. by R. F. Thompson, New York, Mus. Afr. A., 1993)

M. D. Harris: 'From Double Consciousness to Double Vision: The Africentric Artist', *Afr. A.*, xxvii (1994), pp. 44–53

DANIEL J. CROWLEY

IX. Contemporary developments.

Modern African art has largely developed since the mid-20th century. It is marked by the exploration of new media and engendered by aesthetic intentions very different from those that informed works from earlier times (*see* §II, 2 above). Any consideration of modernity in African art has

157. Lois Mailou Jones: *Les Fetiches*, oil on linen (Washington, DC, Museum of American Art)

to begin by examining its relationship to the ancient and continuing tradition. In each country, it is possible to determine whether a continuous development may be traced, within which the essential African culture is merely presented using different technical modes, or whether modern African art has to be considered a novel invention based upon foreign borrowings that, by their origins, distort the presentation of indigenous experience and reflect little of African antecedents.

1. Continuity and change. 2. Types of artist. 3. Art training and guidance.

1. CONTINUITY AND CHANGE. The power of art from Africa has been more appreciated since the earlier belief that it was pagan and primitive gave way in the 1930s to the respect of European artists such as Picasso, whose response moved beyond admiration into emulation. Their perception of the originality of the African aesthetic modified the formal qualities of Western art. It may be that in the 1990s the direction of influence was reversed, as African artists borrowed from those contemporary European styles that still showed residual evidence of prior influence from the African continent.

(i) Religious context. (ii) Adaptation to contemporary markets. (iii) Craft skills. (iv) New forms.

(i) Religious context. It has often been observed that traditional African art is closely linked to the religion it was designed to celebrate, although this thesis may have been over-emphasized by anthropologists, who tended to explain all cultural phenomena in terms of social function, and by missionaries who disapproved on theological grounds of representation of the animist beliefs they had arrived to supplant. The unwillingness to discriminate between form and purpose is based on the justification that sculpture is assessed by its efficacy rather than its appearance. In such a context beauty might have little relevance. However, experiment has shown that aesthetic evaluation can exist separately from any required function. Nevertheless, the concept of function remains predominant, and this assumption introduces a difficulty for the modern African artist. To a large extent he shares the secular principles of the West and therefore exists in a contextual framework that is no longer defined by the system of patronage, status and purpose established in the past. Recognition of this change requires deliberate artistic choices.

Many artists simply continue to carve in the traditional mode, for the demand and context for such work have not totally disappeared. African belief systems, though challenged by changing standards, have a remarkable resilience and adaptability. The Yoruba *ibeji* cult, for example, has survived generations of Christian conversion (*see* YORUBA, §4(i)). The production of personal twin figures requires artistic expression, and the designs have become increasingly transitional. Some are stylized as if to minimize their association with the orthodox forms. In other cases the wooden figures are replaced with manufactured dolls or photographs. Similarly, masking enactments remain popular, though the performances may be less closely connected to their religious origins. Even when such events lose some of their reverent intention and are subsumed into something approaching carnival, they still demand elaborate and familiar artefacts from established craftsmen.

(ii) Adaptation to contemporary markets. There are also established sculptors who continue to produce formally conventional figures but seek a market outside the local culture. Such works may be absorbed by the tourist trade. These carvers are not necessarily participants in the wholesale production of crude replicas, such as the *chiwawa* antelopes that line the pavements of Dakar, Senegal. The production of formal sculpture is a diversified wholesale industry ranging in quality from the excellent reproductions carved in the workshops of major museums, such as those in Abidjan or Bamako, to the crudest 'Senoufu' conveyor-belt factories. Experienced carvers may still exhibit great skill, regardless of the destination of their product and the intentions of its buyers. Strictly speaking, aesthetic excellence should be embodied in the work itself rather than dependent on the intention of either artist or patron, but that logic does not prevail in the assessment of collectable African art. Works are required to have been used in formal ritual. Fine carvings without that functional antecedent (or at least the intent of contextual use) have

158. Lamidi Fakeye: church doors, wood, Oke-Padi, Nigeria, 1956–7

a limited market regardless of any abstract evaluation of their technical calibre. Inevitably, many modern sculptures, sometimes with visible demerits, are given false patina and deliberate termite damage to provide evidence of antiquity and usage, so allowing them to be more convincingly but fraudulently presented as 'genuine'. Their contrived appearance is sustained by spurious assurances that they have been actively 'danced' in the correct manner. This will enhance their collectability and value by means that have little connection with any purely aesthetic quality (*see* §X below).

A different kind of development allows modern carvers to incorporate tradition into an alternative product. This option, which sometimes offends purists, is exemplified by the Nigerian artist Lamidi Fakeye (see fig. 158), who was born into a family of Benin carvers. As well as absorbing traditional skills within this renowned artistic environment, he underwent an eclectic education, attending both Muslim and Catholic schools in his youth and the Paris Ecole des Beaux-Arts at maturity. He has achieved a considerable reputation for his ability to merge conventional styles with modern utility. For example, he works with the local adze to create the basic form but uses imported German chisels for the completion of fine detail. He adapts the characteristic design of Yoruba house-posts to local commercial architecture, and Yoruba figure-carving is the basis for his production of genre figures such as musicians in regional costume. His style has been widely copied by younger carvers. To meet demand he has established a workshop in which apprentices undertake the primary shaping. This arrangement, though common enough in the studios of European Renaissance painters, has been criticized as undermining individual authenticity. Most early carvers remain anonymous, but expectations have changed, and the name of the individual artist has become synonymous with value, as it is in Western galleries. (*See also* §III, 4 above.)

(iii) Craft skills. Traditional craft skills have continued into the later 20th century, although it must be recognized that the Western art–craft distinction is far less clear in Africa. The essential and active manufacture of pottery, vessels and textiles has had to be modified to cope with changing conditions and to maintain sales in the face of competition with manufactured goods. For common usage, cheap and sturdy imports have largely replaced many of the indigenous products: enamel bowls are preferred to breakable clay pots, while factory-made cloth is far cheaper and more uniform than the handwoven product, though sometimes these manufactured bales are printed to emulate the designs of the indigenous hand-dyed fabrics. Faced with the loss of trade the traditional craft-workers modify their products and survive by serving new ends, but some indigenous quality is lost. Etched gourds achieve a new market as bowls for cocktail peanuts; the skilful plaiting of raffia produces coasters and glass holders; the important Yoruba practice of indigo-dyeing is extended into the making of tablecloths, wall hangings and place-mats; clothing lengths are defined by shirt, not skirt, lengths. In these ways, traditional techniques survive, but at the expense of their original purpose.

The most intriguing examples of this adaptation are the familiar goldweights of Ghana. The early castings dating back into the 18th century were made specifically to measure gold dust but were superseded by more efficient measuring devices (*see also* §VI, 10 above). The residual pieces were very popular among visitors, who regarded them as unusual local novelties. Figurines and complex geometric shapes were so energetically exported that few genuine ones remained, yet demand remained unsatisfied, so the complex lost-wax technique was resumed for the new buyers. Some were merely replicas of original designs and thus could be described as fakes, but as market needs became more specific, Western-influenced designs such as cowboy figures were developed. Forming a substyle deemed to appeal to inhibited Europeans were the mildly pornographic figures called *bêtises* (Fr. 'naughty things'), which have no African antecedent at all. In this case it is arguable that the influence of tourism, generally condemned as meretricious, may be sustaining a traditional skill that would otherwise have died out.

(iv) New forms. In the examples of continuity and adaptation outlined above there is a direct if sometimes tenuous connection with the creative past. There is another kind of modern African art that develops where a similar form had once existed, but its association with the more recent expression is too remote to be demonstrable. The new variations are so different in style and purpose that it is hard to see them as other than a spontaneous creativity that occurred in a country where the indigenous inheritance has largely vanished. Modern art of the MAKONDE in Tanzania and the SHONA of Zimbabwe exemplify this renewed application of earlier techniques to modern demand. The Yoruba artists who work at Oshogbo certainly call upon a more resilient and continuing history, but their actual works indicate a similar gulf between production and tradition.

The Makonde people are divided by the Tanzania and Mozambique border. They have a well-known carving tradition, but this has little connection with the tourist phenomena of contemporary Makonde art. Its origin in the late 1950s has occasioned much controversy. Some have asserted that it was invented and commissioned by the Indian owner of a souvenir shop in Dar es Salaam; others look for some more mystic causation. Regardless of its precise beginnings, the idea took root, and Makonde carving has become an industry geared entirely to tourists. The works are a mix of unthinking repetition and real ingenuity, of sloppy chopping and polished refinement. Some types such as the tree of life—relief figures climbing around a heavy tree stump—are so recognizable that the design can be ordered by name (see fig. 25 above), while others are highly abstract. Pieces such as the *shetani* figures of bush spirits display a strikingly wild, surrealist imagination and, unusually for Africa, are sometimes grotesquely pornographic, a characteristic that confirms their export destination. Here one finds a vigorous community art style, for as yet only a few of the artists are identified by name, and whole families seem to be involved in the making and sale. It is hard to say whether this carving will develop into a more serious individualistic art or degenerate into the repeated production of cheap souvenirs.

The stone-carving of the Shona of Zimbabwe, although sustained by a more sophisticated critical acclaim, derives from a somewhat similar historical background (*see* ZIMBABWE, §3). There is an antecedent, most commonly observed in the carved birds that decorate the top of the walls of the Great Temple of Zimbabwe, yet no one has yet convincingly demonstrated a continuance of this medieval competence into modern times. There is little evidence of any interim production during the last 500 years. It took European intervention to reactivate the tradition. Frank McEwen, himself an artist, was appointed director of the Rhodesian National Art Museum in 1954. He urged his attendants to experiment with art. After some sporadic attempts at painting, they turned instinctively to the carving of the beautiful coloured stones found in the countryside. Their huge success, carefully nurtured by McEwen with exhibitions in Paris, engendered a recognizable regional style, and there are now many artists, some of whom have achieved acclaim for their individuality and have held one-man shows. The work of others is less distinctive, and generally there is a sense of a group functioning within a single medium. The artists often work in groups: Vukutu was founded as one such cooperative base, and a farmer, Tom Bloomfield of Tengenenge, also supported numerous carvers. All the sculptors choose to work in hard stone. The works are regularly explained as making reference to the old Shona creation myths, but their visual attraction derives rather from purely artistic elements, a sensitive exploitation of the colour and structure of the stone. Carefully introduced to the European market, these works have attracted critical respect and the highest prices, which have multiplied the number of producers. Demand, inspired by the better-known artists such as John Takawira and Bernard Takawira, has spawned a host of inferior imitators, though the difficulty of working in the hard material enforces some restriction on expansion. Each piece is individually worked, and there are as yet no production-line workshops equivalent to those of the Kamba people in Kenya.

Both these groups of artists reflect an external impetus that may have resuscitated a lost historical competence. McEwen has denied that he offered any training or guidance to his sculptors, but the presence of a sympathetic and responsible outsider who offers even general critical appreciation must have some effect on the direction of an artist's development. Since few work in isolation, emulation of the successful is an inevitable threat to personal style. The question of external influence takes on more complicated form in the venture established in the Nigerian town of Oshogbo, where a more complex involvement between tradition and foreign assistance became the basis of an important artistic enterprise established in IBADAN in 1961. This was a meeting-place and club that was known as Mbari, the Igbo word for a ritual building (*see* IGBO, §3). It was initially organized in Ibadan by Ulli Beier, a professor at the university. Subsequently other 'Mbaris' were set up to function as artists' cooperatives in Oshogbo (1962) and Enugu (1963). Later a similar venture was exported to Nairobi as Chemchemi, directed by the South African author Ezekial Mpahehlele.

In Nigeria, tradition is by no means as moribund as it seems to be in Zimbabwe. The extraordinary artistic

159. Twins Seven Seven: *Baptist Church of Bush of Ghost*, etching, 375×305 mm, *c*. 1969 (Oxford, private collection)

imagination of the Yoruba people remains a virile and active presence after unbroken centuries of achievement. Nevertheless, Beier helped to focus this creativity into more modern modes of expression, with the international magazine *Black Orpheus* as its literary focus. He invited the attendance of young people who had artistic potential, requiring only that they had had no destructive formal art education. He did, however, arrange workshops to demonstrate techniques such as printmaking that would make efforts more profitable. Under Beier's encouragement the content remained identifiably Yoruba in both subject and design, but the materials were imported and the product contemporary. Oshogbo, which propelled several artists to considerable fame, must be considered one of the most imaginative programmes in Africa. An unemployed blacksmith named Ashiru was encouraged to experiment with repoussé designs that had something in common with the classical plaques from Benin but were beaten on to sheets of imported aluminium. Another artist, Fabunwe, stitched coloured thread pictures of Yoruba deities on black cloth using a Singer sewing-machine. Jimoh Buraimoh produced a new effect by gumming cheap imported beads on to hardboard to create designs that may make a passing satiric comment on the whole bead-trade culture in African history. All the artists take their subjects and patterns from their Yoruba inheritance. Because of their deliberate decision to use Western media, the manner in which they

160. Tshibumba Kanda-Matulu: *Colonie Belge 1885–1959*, paint on flour sack, 360×450 mm, 1970s (private collection)

explore these indigenous themes cannot be seen as a precise continuance.

One consistent feature of this work reveals the resilience of the tradition even in these circumstances. Perhaps because the local artistic antecedent is carving rather than painting, many artists seek to construct a three-dimensional effect by superimposing a raised level of material upon the flat surface characteristic of the usual pictorial format. One of the most famous Oshogbo artists is Twins Seven Seven (see fig. 159). His work embraces music and dance as well as design, demonstrating his attachment to Yoruba lore. His ink drawings are applied to cloth as well as paper, while his major paintings achieve the three-dimensional effect with fret-sawed plywood figures glued to the base. Other artists fix cut metal, cloth and strips of knitting wool to their surfaces to escape from the flat finish anticipated in much Western art. These efforts to maintain depth are philosophically more suggestive than collage, which might be considered the European equivalent. The formulation derives from an aesthetic conflict that arises whenever the African artist seeks to create a painted picture, which is primarily a Western form. There are many examples of depiction on wall surfaces, going back to the ancient Saharan petroglyphs (*see* §VI, 15 above), and textiles are displayed in a similar way. Nevertheless the concept of a separate illustration to be hung on a wall has little African antecedent except in Ethiopian ecclesiastical art (*see* ETHIOPIA, §II).

2. TYPES OF ARTIST. Within the field of contemporary art in Africa, there are two types of artists. Broadly, they can be described either as self-taught or as academic, depending on their educational background. The self-taught can in turn be subdivided according to their patron support as much as by style. Some predominantly cater to European buyers and are naive only in the technical sense. Others, local craftsmen, may be judged as more authentically connected to an African audience, because their efforts are available at a price that permits local purchase. They thus avoid the expectation of expatriate preference that sometimes compromises the integrity of artists when they become aware of another more lucrative, if foreign, market.

At the most functional level the craftsman artist creates murals on the walls of bars, perpetrates the elaborate decoration of mammy-wagon lorries and advertises hairstyles for barbers. There are also narrative shop-signs, showing a woman pounding *fou-fou* for a chop bar or humorously depicting the prosperous happiness of an owner who allows no credit and the misery of one so foolish as to do so. In this genre the artist has a clear function and fulfils a local service. Paintings at this level, constructed by using enamel house paint on sacking or denim, are touted in the streets, particularly in Zaïre. Their subjects are highly conventionalized. Forest fires and villages by the river are popular and repetitive themes—the 'canoe and palm tree' school. The ubiquitous water spirit Mamy Wata is sometimes drawn, by order, with a recognizable female face. The expectation is that Zaïrois may buy them to display on the walls of their urban quarters, even while multicoloured Indian chromo prints of Hindi mythology remain inexplicably popular. Curiosities that indicate the absorption of another dimension of neo-colonial influence are scenes using only black and white paint, which are claimed to reflect the images observed on local television screens.

A more political subject of paintings for this local audience in Zaïre is a sequence of popular history. The Belgian mismanagement of the Congo colony is illustrated by a judicially mandated public beating supervised by an arrogant colonial officer (see fig. 160). The series culminates with depictions of the battles fought during the period of UN intervention in the Congo after independence in 1960. Deposed premier Patrice Lumumba (1925–61) is invariably portrayed, in a version of his capture and murder entitled *La Calvaire*, as a cruelly treated martyr. The experiments of such artists when they become aware of alternative materials can produce fascinating works. An example of this process is to be seen in the work of Tito Zungu (*b* 1946), a South African Zulu who uses felt marking pens of various colours to depict such examples of modern progress as aeroplanes, trains and ocean liners (see fig. 161), with rigorous lines determined by the constant use of a ruler's edge. Originally these designs decorated envelopes for sale to goldminers for their letters home. Later his efforts, assisted by the Durban Art Institute, engendered a cult audience in South Africa and a nationally distributed calendar, which opened up another means by which patronage brings an unknown artist to prominence. Yet, like many African artists, Zungu has not subsequently chosen to explore any technique other than the one that brought him success. This adherence to a single idiosyncratic style may be explained by the need to maintain profitable commissions.

There is a considerable difference between such craftsmen artists, with their roots in the commerce of their community, and artists who though technically untaught are nonetheless patronized by predominantly non-African collectors. Two such painters who have achieved renown are Edward Saidi Tingatinga (1937–72) from Dar es Salaam (*see* TANZANIA, §3) and Jak Katarikawe of Kampala.

161. Tito Zungu: *Untitled*, ball-point pen ink on paper, 330×220 mm, *c*. 1972 (Durban, African Art Centre)

Tingatinga's works are highly distinctive. He depicts stylized animals in the boldest colours, controlled by cartoon-like black outlines. His pictures became so popular that at his death many borrowed his strikingly dramatic and sellable technique. Jak Katarikawe (see fig. 162) is naive in the conventional sense, as the word might be applied to Henri Rousseau. He uses both oil paints and crayon to present genre scenes of local myth, often enhanced by amusing anecdotal explanation. His style exhibits considerable wit and an extravagant design that has appealed to European collectors.

Much contemporary art derives from some measure of European intervention. Almost all of the more distinguished artists have had the opportunity of study and training abroad. An exception is Malangatana Valente Ngwenya (*b* 1936), detained in Mozambique during the period of political upheaval and an artist who has achieved international recognition without formal instruction (*see* MOZAMBIQUE, §3). It is clear that there must be some measure of alienation for an artist influenced by new techniques and exotic materials. Especially challenging to the modern African artist is the priority given in modern Western art to unfettered individuality and experiment, which contradicts his inherited expectation of modified replication of form. Despite assertions of aesthetic neutrality, European involvement cannot avoid becoming to some degree manipulative. Even teaching at the purely technical level imposes expectations in subsequent performance.

3. ART TRAINING AND GUIDANCE. The missionary schools sponsored several early schemes. Typical was the programme at the Cyrene Mission, Matopo Hills, near Bulawayo in Zimbabwe, which in 1939 was used as an educational centre offering little more than the teaching of manual skills to the handicapped. Under a period of direction by the Revd Edward Patterson up to 1953, a lively arts centre developed that, in spite of modest intentions, took on the Christian ambience around the resident artists. A similar influential programme was initiated in Nigeria by Father Kevin Carroll in 1947. He was commissioned by African Missions to set up a workshop in Oye-Ekiti to nurture local carving skills. With these ventures, there was a genuine desire to sustain local artists, but too often such projects encouraged the carving of wooden madonnas.

(i) Francophone Africa. In Francophone Africa the colonial artistic instruction was more deliberate and formal, so its consequences were more intrusive. One important institution was the Congolese Académie des Arts, which was established in Elisabethville in 1944 under the direction of a French artist from Brest, Pierre Romain-Defosse. Another, L'Académie des Beaux-Arts, was established somewhat later by Laurent Moonens (*see also* ZAÏRE). They were both organized on the same principles as similar art schools in Europe. The directors publicly announced that they would encourage indigenous expression and not suggest themes, propose models or impose styles and insisted that their students were free to explore their own inspiration, but in practice they failed to recognize how inevitably both overt and covert influences would affect any African attending an institution based on so European a pattern.

162. Jak Katarikawe: *Football Match*, oil on paper, 730×610 mm, *c.* 1986 (Frankfurt am Main, Museum für Völkerkunde)

Two artists of high reputation learnt their distinctive techniques from Romain-Defosse's academy: Pili-Pili Mulongoya, with his evocative pictures contrived out of spaced dots (see fig. 163), and Mwenze Kibwanga, who exploited short, separated brushstrokes. Both gained a profitable reputation among Belgian residents. How genuinely African their results are is debatable.

A similar art school, named after the Brazzaville suburb Poto-Poto, was founded under the direction of Pierre Lods in 1951 (*see also* CONGO). The enterprise inspired pottery, enamelling and weaving. The most familiar result appears to have been the origination of those now ubiquitous pictures of sticklike dancers drawn against a black background, which may have some antecedents in cave paintings. They are now touted throughout Africa. Lods moved on to Dakar, where the Académie Africaine des Arts Plastiques and, from 1961, the School of Arts and Letters were important centres of modern art, though the French influence remained paramount. Iba N'Diaye and Papa Ibre Taal were the most prominent artists; both were African but, after years of study and residence in Paris, steeped in French culture. Christian Lattier, from Côte d'Ivoire, chose to devise sculptural designs made of elaborately coiled ropes. Such are the complexities of transitional aesthetics, he announced that he had deliberately selected this unusual medium because it had no conceivable African antecedent that might impose upon him the expectation of some inherited style.

(ii) Nigeria. In Nigeria modern art teaching began in 1922 under the direction of Chief Aina Onabolu (1882–1963). In 1927 he arranged the appointment of Kenneth Murray, whose decades of work for Nigerian culture became legend. He taught Ben Enwonwu, who after achieving success as a sculptor became Federal Art Adviser. The best-known artists were trained in formal art departments attached to the major universities, first Zaria, then Ibadan and Lagos. As these were all staffed by expatriates, their curriculum did not vary greatly from the courses found in British art schools. Zaria was the most influential centre during the 1950s, producing an entire generation of modern Nigerian artists. Yusuf Grillo, Jimo Akolo, Uche Okeke and Bruce Onobrakpeya became the senior professionals; several in turn joined the faculty of other university art departments and thus passed on the principles they had learnt. Their work showed varied styles, but in each case a combination of international technique and African subject-matter was apparent, signalling the continuing dualism that remains so noticeable in modern African art. (*See also* NIGERIA, §VII.)

(iii) East Africa. In East Africa, formal art was substantially engendered by Margaret Trowell, who went to Kampala, Uganda, in 1929 and offered classes in her home. When Makerere became a college associated with London University, a School of Fine Art was founded under her direction and given her name after her retirement in 1958 (*see also* UGANDA). In 1964 Barbara Brown founded the prominent and influential Nommo Gallery, but it did not survive the Amin presidency (1971–9), and many artists, such as Eli Kyeyune, regrouped in Nairobi. This city offers a vigorous and sustaining market of residents and travellers; European cultural centres such as the German Goethe

163. Pili-Pili Mulongoya: *Termites and Birds*, acrylic on hardboard, 1970s (Bremen, Übersee-Museum)

Institute were generous with exhibitions, and white boutique entrepreneurs encouraged sales. Elimo Njau, a Makerere graduate, was a key figure in the fostering of new artists, at first through Paa-ya-paa Gallery, then from 1965 through an art colony that he set up with his author wife at Kibo across the border in Tanzania. Chemchemi also contributed support. Artists during the 1960s included a wide range, from university academics such as Francis Nnagenda to the brilliant untutored Herzbon Owiti. Foundation sponsorship released artists from total dependence on the tourist market, and the result was an exciting period of vigorous creativity. Work in Tanzania centred on the National Gallery. Another Makerere artist, Sam Ntiro (*b* 1923), combined support for art with important political appointments, while Francis Msangi (*b* 1937) achieved a reputation that led to teaching connections abroad. Generally economic conditions attracted Tanzanian artists to Nairobi rather than Dar es Salaam.

(iv) Other regions. There are comparable similarities in the growth of an African modern art in much of Africa. Three countries, because of their special histories, have acquired recognizably unique styles: Sudan, Ethiopia and South Africa. Art from the Sudan is primarily from the northern Muslim region and thus relates to the Middle East rather than Europe. Yet, unlike work from the Mediterranean coastal countries, it is usually considered African. Formal art training began in 1945 with the founding of the School of Design at the Gordon Memorial College in Khartoum by a young Englishman, Jean Greenlaw. He was succeeded in 1951 by J. Cottrell. After independence in 1956 Sudanese staff replaced the expatriates, and the name changed to the School of Fine Art. The school's most distinguished figure is IBRAHIM EL SALAHI, who employs characteristic Arabic calligraphic forms in his work. A major artist of the next generation is Mohamed Omer Bushara (*b* 1946), whose training in London did not seem to interfere with his highly idiosyncratic style and choice of media (inked cartoon-like outlines were drawn on a ground prepared with various pigments including coffee). Amir I. M. Nour (*b* 1936) moved to Chicago and experimented with sculpture. Many Sudanese artists seem inhibited from experimentation by the expectations of the formal teaching they receive and the Muslim environment the regime imposes. (*See also* SUDAN, §§4 and 5.)

The powerful Christian Orthodox Church has a profound influence in Ethiopia, where religious themes have dominated most art. In the late 20th century the senior artist was Afewerk Tekle, most renowned for his remarkable work in stained glass, a technique he studied in Paris in 1954. A major achievement is the window adorning the Organization of African Unity Hall in Addis Ababa. The black outlines of the patterning required by the medium recall the controlled boundaries of an icon and later became a personal characteristic when the style was transposed to his painting. The awareness of an extensive Church tradition may have originally been a stimulus to Ethiopian artists, but it also made for a confining obstacle to imaginative invention. Perhaps for this reason the two major young artists, Skunder Boghossian and Gebre Kristos Desta, chose to work abroad, the former training in Britain, the latter in Germany. Both have deliberately selected the technical freedom of non-representational forms. This is rare in Africa because, as is evident in traditional pieces, even the most extreme symbolic modification of naturalism does not totally divorce the residual design from the underlying realism of the object.

The peoples of South Africa, though they are supreme in the verbal art of poetry, have a more limited inheritance in the plastic arts compared with West Africans. Modern artists have less visual antecedent on which to draw. Even before the apartheid system was dismantled in the early 1990s, many worked quite closely with white artists and received both encouragement from galleries and a sympathetic, though perhaps too directive, audience for their work. The most important project was the Polly Street Art Centre established in 1952 and supervised by the renowned artist CECIL SKOTNES. This provided a place for work and an outlet for sales. An early associate was the sculptor SYDNEY KUMALO, who achieved the greatest reputation. But generally painting was the preferred medium. When Polly became the Jubilee Art Centre and moved to Soweto in 1960, there was a dramatic flowering of local art, presenting the black experience of life in Johannesburg. One characteristic style, rather casually called 'township art', portrayed urban existence in Soweto. Because of the anticipated audience the pictures tended to depict the cheerful vitality of the street scenes rather than signs of hardship and deprivation. As political antagonisms intensified, the emphasis changed and the art began to reflect the brutality of the system. A major figure who reacted with visceral anger was FENI DUMILE. His powerfully contorted lines were a direct challenge to the regime, and he was forced into exile in New York. In South Africa, however, his style continues to have a profound influence. His painting in Fort Hare, *African Guernica*, is a masterpiece linking the international theme with purely African imagery. Although Dumile himself now concentrates on clay sculpture, the characteristics of his early drawings have been repeatedly borrowed, as a shorthand expression of resistance. His preference for ink drawing, necessitated initially by limited equipment, prompted emulation from artists such as CYPRIAN SHILAKOE, who extended the technique to present poignant and ferocious displays of his environment.

One of the major preoccupations of South African artists during the apartheid years was to give artistic structure to the overwhelming oppression of their society, which tended to impose restrictions of content. In the search for a physical distancing, LOUIS KHELA MAQHUBELA, a Polly Centre artist, escaped to London, where he chose to experiment with brilliant, painterly colours and a semi-abstract style. Such modernist works would find few buyers in South Africa, where expectations of the familiar circumscribe style. (*See also* SOUTH AFRICA, §IV.)

(v) Economic context. In every African country the contemporary artist still finds it necessary to follow the dictates of the market. The problem is not only the too familiar international choice of teaching or starvation for all but a successful few. The additional dilemma derives from the predominantly non-African nationality of patrons and buyers, though exceptions are to be found. Educated Nigerians are beginning to acquire the work of local artists

for their homes, but the bulk of the art described has been bought by outsiders. Public galleries of modern art are few, and they are only just beginning to collect. Most nations have enough problems in financing the secure display of traditional works, which have achieved a higher degree of recognition and value, and governments are no more eager than many formal scholars to enter the uncharted sea of contemporary production. The exact effect of the primarily foreign source of available financial support by purchase is not easy to determine. Artists may resist direct pressures, but the nature of the audience must remain a factor. The development of modern African art often begins with a European impetus, initiated either by local programmes of assistance or by overseas scholarships. It regularly leads to European purchase. This may be judged as supportive or intrusive, and its power may be diminishing, but it nonetheless exists. Given this pattern, the variety and originality of so much of the work produced are remarkable and its authenticity convincing.

JOHN POVEY

BIBLIOGRAPHY

E. S. Brown: *Africa's Contemporary Art and Artists* (New York, 1966)
K. Carroll: *Yoruba Religious Carving: Pagan and Christian Sculpture in Nigeria and Dahomey* (London and New York, 1967)
U. Beier: *Contemporary Art in Africa* (London and New York, 1968)
R. B. Armstrong: *The Affecting Presence: An Essay in Humanistic Anthropology* (Urbana, IL, 1971)
J. DeJager: *Contemporary African Art in South Africa* (Cape Town, 1973)
M. W. Mount: *African Art: The Years Since 1920* (Bloomington and London, 1973, rev. New York, 1989)
M. Wahlman: *Contemporary African Arts* (Chicago, 1974)
Tradition and Change in Yoruba Art (exh. cat. by J. J. Arneson; Sacramento, CA, Crocker A. Mus., 1974)
J. von D. Miller: *Art in East Africa: A Guide to Contemporary Art* (London and Nairobi, 1975)
R. Jeffreys: *African Art Today* (New York, 1979)
K. Fosu: *20th Century Art of Africa* (Zaria, 1986)
G. Younge: *Art of the South African Townships* (London and New York, 1988)
H. M. Cole: 'Change and Continuity: The Icons in Twentieth-Century Art', *Icons: Ideals and Power in the Art of Africa* (exh. cat. by H. M. Cole, Washington, DC, N. Mus. Afr. A., 1989–90), pp. 160–74
J. Agthe: *Wegzeichen: Kunst aus Ostafrika, 1974–89/ Signs: Art from East Africa, 1974–89*, Frankfurt am Main, Mus. Vlkerknd. (Frankfurt am Main, 1990)
Art from the Frontline: Contemporary Art from Southern Africa (exh. cat.; Glasgow, A.G. & Mus.; Salford, Mus. & A.G.; Dublin, City Cent.; London, Commonwealth Inst.; 1990)
Africa Explores: 20th Century African Art (exh. cat. by S. Vogel, New York, Cent. Afr. A., 1991)
Africa Now (exh. cat.; Las Palmas de Gran Canaria, Cent. Atlantic. A. Mod.; Groningen, Groninger Mus.; Mexico City, Cent. Cult. A. Contemp.; 1991–2)
N. Guez: *L'Art africain contemporain/Contemporary African Art: Guide Edition 92–94* (Paris, 1992)
J. Kennedy: *New Currents, Ancient Rivers: Contemporary African Artists in a Generation of Change* (Washington, DC, and London, 1992)
C. B. Steiner: *African Art in Transit* (Cambridge, 1993)

For further bibliography *see* §III, 4 above. *See also* bibliographies for individual country entries and MAKONDE.

JEREMY COOTE

X. Forgery.

1. INTRODUCTION. In the traditional art of Sub-Saharan Africa, forgery almost always involves sculpture, primarily carvings of wood and ivory, and castings of cuprous alloys. The development of contemporary African art, such as printmaking, oil painting and other non-traditional work, is not considered in this article (*see* §§III, 4 and IX above). The market for this artwork is limited, and there is little reason for deception. Central to an understanding of forgery in African art is the issue of authenticity. In its purest sense, an authentic object is one of traditional form that was made by an African artist and used in a traditional context within the artist's own ethnic group. However, there are exceptions to this rule that make it difficult to establish a universally accepted definition for authenticity. For instance, a mask may be commissioned and carved for traditional use but, before it is worn, sold to a foreigner. This example should not be considered a forgery, unless it was misrepresented.

A forgery is a work intentionally made in the likeness of, or in imitation of, an original work of art; it is created to deceive and is always a fake. A fake, however, is not always a forgery. A fake is an inauthentic object that is presented as genuine. For example, in West Africa, tourist or airport carvings, mass-produced for sale to foreigners as well as to local élites, are frequently presented as old traditional artefacts by art dealers and other middlemen. They are only 'fakes' when presented in this way, and museum shops and other institutions sometimes sell them in a 'genuine' context at inexpensive prices. Three broad categories may thus be established: intentional forgeries, middlemen fakes and authentic objects.

Forgeries include newly created objects made to look old and presented as genuine. They may be copied from an original, constitute a pastiche or imitate a particular style and subject. They may be made by Africans or non-Africans. In some instances the same Africans who carve forgeries also carve objects for traditional use. A category of fraud that may be considered forgery of a special kind is misrepresented authentic objects that have been altered or falsified; for example an authentic figure with a newly made head, or a head from an authentic figure that is attached to another genuine figure that has lost its head.

Middlemen fakes are not necessarily made to deceive. Most are made by Africans in Africa. When attempting to present these artefacts as genuine traditional art works, traders, art dealers, collectors and other intermediaries use some of the same techniques as forgers in the falsification of surfaces and artificial ageing of objects by, for example, staining, scorching, burying and weathering. They also invent provenances and early dates of manufacture. Such fakes include handcarved but mass-produced contemporary tourist or airport pieces; early examples of tourist art, examples of which survive from as early as the 16th century; and copies made for visitors, researchers and museums.

Authentic objects are made by an African and used within his own ethnic group. However, there can be some flexibility to this definition (see above); for example, it may include an object made by a carver of one ethnic group but used by a neighbouring ethnic group, or an object of non-traditional form made by an African from imported material (e.g. plastic, aluminium) and used in a traditional context.

2. HISTORY. European interest in African objects as art was first shown during the first decade of the 20th century by such artists as Pablo Picasso and André Derain.

African sculptures could be viewed in ethnological museums and were accessible in curio shops. Despite this interest in African sculpture by some avant-garde artists of the day, the market demand was almost non-existent compared to that for European and Asian art. Indeed, before World War II the supply of African art was ample relative to the limited demand. Perhaps the best-known and earliest African fake is the 'Olokun' bronze head, collected by the German ethnologist Leo Frobenius in 1910 at the Yoruba town of Ife in south-western Nigeria. The following year British authorities forced Frobenius to return the head to its owners, and in 1934 it was placed in the Ife palace for safe-keeping. In the 1940s when the head was being cleaned at the British Museum, it was discovered to be a modern copy made by sand-casting rather than by the traditional lost-wax casting. Evidently, some time between 1910 and 1934 the original head, which probably dates to the 12th to 15th century, had been replaced with a forgery (see *Afr. A.*, 1976).

Since the 1950s and 1960s the demand for African art has grown steadily, as have prices; and only since this period has fraud become a serious matter. There are hundreds of collectors around the world, and many museums acquire African art. In a London auction at Christie's on 4 July 1989, a Benin bronze head (lot 86) realized more than £1 million; in a New York auction at Sotheby's on 21 April 1990, a Bangwa wooden figure (lot 127) was sold for over £3 million. There are reports of private sales with even higher prices. With escalating monetary values it is not surprising that fraud in African art has become a paramount concern to collectors, curators, dealers and appraisers. No one is exempt from making mistakes. For example, on 14 May 1981 Sotheby's, New York, had to withdraw an Ibibio-style wooden mask (lot 105), which was illustrated on the front cover of an auction catalogue, because it was discovered that the piece was a fake. Again, on 9 April 1984 Sotheby's, London, withdrew a metal-sheathed wooden reliquary figure in the Bwiti (Mahongwe) style and a Kwele-style wooden mask (lots 128, 133), apparently for the same reason.

Workshops both in and out of Africa have produced and still are producing forgeries. There is published documentation of forgers and forgery workshops in Africa (see Kamer; Cornet; Barbier), although their counterparts in Europe and America are not so well publicized. Particularly well documented are two groups of Asante woodcarvers in Kumasi, Ghana, who have been active since the 1970s (see Ross and Reichert). These carvers produce handsome sculptures of the highest quality with styles and iconographic elements drawn from authentic carvings as well as from their own imaginations. They then artificially age the surfaces. A number of their works have been published as authentic, and some can be found in museum and private collections.

3. Methods of detection. Despite the increasing number of scientific tools available, the most effective means for determining authenticity is a knowledgeable individual with an experienced eye who has seen and handled many objects. It is essential to have a full understanding of the use of objects in an African context. This understanding is critical when dealing with African and other 'ethnographic' art since, unlike much European art, which was intended to hang on a wall or sit on a table, authentic African sculptures were used during rituals, political ceremonies and other occasions.

In some instances, as with some types of Dogon or Bamana figures, wood-carvings are kept in shrines and, as part of rituals, are subjected to repeated applications of blood, beer or other substances. The surface of these objects can become heavily encrusted. In those instances where forgers have simulated an incrustation, this can usually be detected by the nature of the coating. A fraudulent incrustation is usually added in one application, whereas a traditional incrustation is applied in thin layers over a period of years. A microscopic or chemical analysis of the incrustation or pigmentation may also reveal forgery. Alernatively, some wooden figures, such as Yoruba twin figures, are not subject to ritual applications but rather are frequently handled, fondled and rubbed. This treatment results in a smooth surface associated with the traditional use of this type of object. Yet another class of African objects, such as some Ebrie cast goldwork, is simply displayed on rare occasions and stored away at other times. These castings have the traditional function of displaying an important man's wealth and may date from before the 20th century, but their physical condition may appear pristine. Thus every authentic object carries an expectation—based on traditional use patterns of a specific ethnic group and object type—of a particular patination and other physical features.

Among the most convenient, inexpensive and non-destructive tools available for determining authenticity is radiography (see Sieber and Celenko). Radiography can reveal a non-traditional means of manufacture, for example iron nails used to assemble a wooden figure that should be a monoxylous carving (i.e. from a single block). It can also expose hidden restoration that, if concealed, would increase the value of an object. Other visual analyses that do not require samples to be removed from objects include examination with high-powered microscopes and viewing under ultraviolet or 'black' light. Examination under infra-red light is also useful but requires an expensive camera and monitor. These techniques can readily reveal repairs and restorations not seen by the unaided eye.

Some analyses are destructive to a minor extent, since they usually require a small sample from the object in question. Among these methods are pigment or accretion analysis by means of microchemical testing to determine non-traditional or inappropriate substances, microscopic wood cross-section analysis to determine tree species, and microscopic analysis and identification of plant fibre and animal hair to ascertain their nature and origin. X-ray fluorescence (no sample required), X-ray diffraction and atomic absorption spectrometry provide an elemental analysis of an object. With African art these techniques are especially useful when dealing with copper-alloy castings.

There are scientific dating methods that may be used to detect fakes. Thermoluminescence, which can determine the date when clay was last fired, has become an important technique in authenticating ceramic sculptures that may have been made centuries ago. The radiocarbon method can be applied to organic materials, either charcoal or other material from an archaeological context, or to actual art works of wood or other organic material. In some cases the size of the sample required precludes the use of this technique on small wooden and ivory objects. However, a recently developed radiocarbon procedure using an accelerator mass spectrometer requires a minimal sample.

A troublesome aspect of the radiocarbon method is that the technique dates only the wood of the object in question without necessarily giving a date of manufacture of the artwork. In other words, a fraudulent object could be carved from a much older piece of wood. This question most often arises with pieces from dry climates, where wood may survive for centuries, for example in Dogon country at the edge of the Sahara Desert. The base of a Dogon figure with a restored arm yielded a 16th- to 18th-century date. That the radiocarbon method provides an approximate date when the organic matter died, rather than when an artefact was created, demonstrates that a scientific test does not necessarily provide the definitive information sought.

BIBLIOGRAPHY

H. Kamer: 'De l'authenticité des sculptures africaines', *A. Afrique Noire*, 12 (1974), pp. 17–40

J. Cornet: 'African Art and Authenticity', *Afr. A.*, ix/1 (1975), pp. 52–5

Afr. A., x/3 (1976) [special issue on authenticity]

R. Sieber and T. Celenko: 'Rayons x et art africain: De l'utilisation des rayons x dans l'étude de l'art africain', *A. Afrique Noire*, 21 (1977), pp. 16–28

'This Matter of Fakes', *Primitive A. Newslett.*, i/4 (1978), pp. 1, 4–5

W. Gillon: *Collecting African Art* (London, 1979)

C. K. Provost: 'The Valuation of Traditional Art: Special Problems in Connoisseurship', *Valuation*, xxvi (1980), pp. 137–48

D. H. Ross and R. X. Reichert: 'Modern Antiquities: A Study of a Kumase Workshop', *Akan Transformations: Problems in Ghanaian Art History*, Museum of Cultural History, UCLA, Monographs Series, xxi (exh. cat., ed. D. H. Ross and T. F. Garrard; Los Angeles, UCLA, Mus. Cult. Hist., 1983), pp. 82–91

Is This for Real? Problems of Authenticity in Art (exh. cat., Bloomington, IN U.A. Mus., 1985)

E. M. Mauer: 'Art and Imitation: Original Works and Forgeries of Tribal Art', *Ant. & F.A.*, vii/1 (1989), pp. 45–52

W. M. Robbins: 'What African Art Is and What It Is Not', *African Art in American Collections: Survey 1989*, by W. M. Robbins and N. I. Nooter (Washington, DC, 1989), pp. 11–18

J. P. Barbier: 'Concluding Remarks', *Text*, i of *Art of Côte d'Ivoire: From the Collections of the Barbier-Mueller Museum*, 2 vols, ed. J. P. Barbier (Geneva, 1993), pp. 402–11

THEODORE CELENKO

XI. Historiography.

Despite the dramatic increase in the number of art historians specializing in Sub-Saharan Africa since 1960, the notion that African art has a history—and one that can be partially reconstructed—has yet to become firmly established (*see also* §II, 1 above). This is partly due to the nature of the source materials: the study of rock art is difficult, and only a fraction of the plastic art from Africa known today dates from before 1850. Moreover, early written sources are scarce, uneven in their coverage and mostly composed by outsiders.

A more fundamental reason is the preconceptions of scholars. African artefacts were collected by Europeans from *c.* 1500 onwards but were perceived as curiosities, fetishes or simply material culture. Only after relatively naturalistic works in bronze and ivory from Benin reached European collections in 1897 did scholars and artists begin to realize that Africa possessed something that could be called art. Since then writing on African art has been tied to aesthetics, including stylistic studies, and anthropology—at first evolutionist or diffusionist, then structural–functionalist, and today mainly fieldwork-orientated. Consequently, most art historians have implicitly adopted ahistorical models, such as the 'culture area' and 'one tribe, one style'.

Against this sombre background may be noted several efforts to place African art in a diachronic context. The key issues are spatial (provenance and distribution) and temporal (chronology). Where documentation is absent or unreliable, museum curators constantly face the question of provenance. Art historians, however, are frequently confronted by the wider problem of origin. Several 19th-century scholars speculated about the 'migration' of culture from North-east to West or Central Africa, and in the early 20th century European ethnologists pursued more sophisticated diffusionist approaches, trying to explain the present-day distribution of cultural traits—including art—in terms of historical movement. Although the early diffusionist hypotheses have been abandoned, the relationship between spatial distribution and time remains a historical issue.

Absolute chronology is often impossible, but relative chronology is essential if art is to have a historical meaning. F. M. Olbrechts demonstrated this weakness in African art studies and outlined some of the remedies, including the systematic documentation of objects, use of all printed and archival sources, and technical analysis of the materials used. In recent historical work the following four types of source have been used: an analysis of the art objects themselves; archaeological excavations; European writings and pictorial representations; and oral traditions.

A major impetus towards diachronic thinking came in the 1950s and 1960s from archaeologists working in southern Nigeria. The discovery of ceramic art from NOK, terracottas from Yelwa and metalwork from IGBO-UKWU, combined with more refined analysis of objects already known from the Kingdom of BENIN, IFE and elsewhere, prompted art historians to propose historical sequences linking various cultures. While the sequences remain controversial, they helped to stimulate historical thinking with reference to art. Subsequently attempts were made to refine the chronology with the help of oral tradition and written documents. Archaeological research in Mali and northern Ghana has transformed what is known about the art history of West Sudan, and progress has also been made with regard to other parts of Africa. Meanwhile, the study of changing art forms in the 20th century has gradually become accepted as a legitimate undertaking, thanks partly to the pioneering work of anthropologists. Most took as their starting-point the ahistorical notion of a 'traditional' tribal society. Nevertheless, important research has been conducted since 1960 on artistic change in the colonial and post-colonial periods, notably with reference to the effects of shifts in patronage. The journal *African Arts* has often provided a forum for such studies. For coastal regions with a long history of European contact it has been possible to document artistic change and continuity over a period of several centuries.

BIBLIOGRAPHY

F. M. Olbrechts: *Plastiek van Kongo* (Antwerp, 1946)

W. Gillon: *A Short History of African Art* (Harmondsworth, 1984)

S. L. Kasfir: 'One Tribe, One Style: Paradigms in the Historiography of African Art', *Hist. Afr.*, xi (1984), pp. 163–93

J. Vansina: *Art History in Africa: An Introduction to Method* (London and New York, 1984)

ADAM JONES

XII. Museums.

In the context of museum collections, Africa usually refers to Sub-Saharan Africa and excludes Ancient Egypt and the Islamic lands of North Africa. The way African material has been exhibited (*see also* §XIII below) indicates the evolution of Western attitudes to the continent. The first African artefacts to reach Europe in the early 16th century were treated as curiosities whose exact origins were often not acknowledged. A small group of West African pieces came to the museum at Ulm in the 17th century, and in the 18th century Sir Hans Sloane, whose collection became the nucleus of the British Museum collections, acquired several artefacts of African origin.

The colonial period saw the establishment of museums celebrating European empires in Africa, such as the Koninklijk Museum voor Midden-Afrika, Tervuren, which houses one of the most extensive collections of Central African art and material culture in the world. Increasing quantities of African material found their way into European collections as a by-product of missionary activity and trade, but the stimulus given to the study of ethnography by the imposition of colonial rule led to the establishment of ethnographic museums with strong colonial connections in the late 19th century, for example the Museum für Völkerkunde, Berlin, the British Museum, London, the Pitt Rivers Museum, Oxford, and the Musée des Arts Africains et Océaniens and the Musée de l'Homme, Paris. In the United States the colonial connection was absent, but the ethnological impulse was equally strong, as in the Peabody Museum of Archeology and Ethnology at the University of Harvard, Cambridge, MA, the American Museum of Natural History, New York, and the Field Museum of Natural History, Chicago. In the post-colonial period ethnography has made way for archaeology and anthropology. In 1970 the Ethnography Department of the British Museum was given an independent building in London as the Museum of Mankind. Other important anthropological collections are to be found at the Fowler Museum of Cultural History of the University of California in Los Angeles and the Barbier-Mueller Museum in Geneva. Apart from the Koninklijk Museum in Tervuren, the only other museum dedicated to Africa and maintained by public funds is the National Museum of African Art, opened in 1987 as part of the Smithsonian Institution, Washington, DC. The museums of the nation states of Africa, established either during or after the colonial period, are largely concerned with the exhibition of national material. The one exception is the National Museum of Accra, where an attempt has been made to situate Ghana in the Pan-African context. Art museums in the United States, notably the Metropolitan Museum, New York, and the Art Institute of Chicago, have led the way in collecting and exhibiting African art. Their only rival in Europe is the Rietberg Museum in Zurich. The Museum for African Art in New York, while hosting innovative exhibitions and maintaining an educational programme, does not yet have its own collection and depends entirely on grants and private donations; the same is true of the privately funded Fondation Olfert Dapper in Paris.

BIBLIOGRAPHY

H. J. Braunholtz: *Sir Hans Sloane and Ethnography*, ed. W. Fagg (London, 1970)

J.-L. Paudrat: 'From Africa', *'Primitivism' in 20th Century Art: Affinity of the Tribal and the Modern*, ed. W. Rubin, i (New York, 1984), pp. 125–75

Africa and the Renaissance: Art in Ivory (exh. cat. by E. Bassani and W. Fagg, New York, Cent. Afr. A., 1988)

E. Bassani and M. D. McLeod: *Jacob Epstein: Collector* (Milan, 1989)

S. Peters and others, eds: *Directory of Museums in Africa/Répertoire des musées en Afrique* (London and New York, 1990)

Africa Explores: 20th Century African Art (exh. cat. by S. Vogel, New York, Cent. Afr. A., 1991)

M. D. McLeod: 'Collecting for the British Museum', *Quad. Poro*, 8 (1993)

XIII. Exhibitions.

Long before the largely post-independence development of museums and galleries in the countries of Sub-Saharan Africa, the idea of display was an integral part of individual works of African art, many of which were intended to be seen in the performative context of the masquerade or royal procession. Works of art from Sub-Saharan Africa have been present in European collections since the 16th century. When these origins were acknowledged, the works themselves were accorded the status of curiosities. This changed with the arrival of works of art from the kingdom of BENIN (1897), and later the collection of works from colonized territories and the attention drawn to them by European artists (*see* §XIV below). The manner of display could be described as ethnographic, according to the perceptions of the time, with works of art placed on exhibition ordered according to tribal origins within a particular region, and with ritual artefacts representing particular communities and their ritual life. The notable exception was the Pitt Rivers Museum, Oxford, which displayed a typology of artefacts with the intention of illustrating a now untenable view of the temporally progressive development of human skill.

In more recent years in some museums, such as the Museum of Mankind, London, three modes of exhibition have emerged in contrast to ethnography or typology: concentrating on the work of art, the artefacts in context, and the 'cabinet of curiosities'. Each is problematic in its own way, and none is capable of resolving the problems contingent upon the circumstances in which the pieces were acquired or the previous mode of display. In the first mode, the artefact is carefully placed and lit, perhaps within a glass case. Although this enables the perception of form, it is also an appropriation to a 'fine art' conception that may have little to do with original context of the object. The second mode seeks to replicate the original context by recreating the environment with available materials. One of the finest of these exhibitions was the 'Yoruba Religious Cult' exhibition (London, Mus. Mankind, 1974). The problem here is not simply that of creating an ethnographic illusion but that the exhibition environment itself becomes the focus of the exhibition at the expense of the artefacts within it. The third mode (e.g.

'Lost Magic Kingdoms'; London, Mus. Mankind, 1985) is perhaps the most satisfactory because it makes apparent curatorial mediation without pretending to objectivity. In the late 1970s the Museum of Mankind had examples simultaneously of all three modes of exhibition.

Museums are now faced with the dilemma of how best to exhibit their African collections. The solution that is generally adopted (e.g. New York, Met.) is the tasteful display, in which objects are placed in uncluttered cases, suitably lit with brief descriptive labels, and ordered according to an ethnographic model. In the 1980s travelling or temporary exhibitions were used to explore inherent problems. Examples of problem-solving exhibitions are the 'Torday Exhibition' (London, Mus. Mankind), which placed an example of an early-20th-century collection in the context of anthropology and British Modernism; 'Art/Artefact' (1988), which considered different modes of display and representation; 'Africa and the Renaissance' (1988), which explored the ivory sculptures that reached European collections in the 16th century; 'Close-up' (1990), which focused on the artefact as form; 'Africa Explores' (1991), which concentrated on 20th century developments (all New York, Cent. Afr. A.); 'Echoes of the Kalabari' (1988–9), which featured the work of Kalabari sculptor Sokari Douglas-Camp; 'Astonishment and Power' (1993–4), which paired a deconstruction of Kongo sculpture with the work of African-American artist Renée Stout (both Washington, DC, N. Mus. Afr. A.); and 'Elephant' (Los Angeles, UCLA, Fowler Mus. Cult. Hist., 1992–3). European exhibitions, with the exception of those held at the Tropenmuseum, Amsterdam, tend to concentrate on the display of national masterpieces, adding little to the debate on how to display African material. The one other recent European exception was 'Lotte or the Transformation of the Object' (Graz, 1988), which explored the ethnographic mode of exhibition.

BIBLIOGRAPHY

C. H. Read and O. M. Dalton: *Antiquities of the City of Benin and from other Parts of West Africa in the British Museum* (London, 1899)

Lost Magic Kingdoms and Six Paper Moons from Nauhuatl: An Exhibition at the Museum of Mankind (exh. cat. by E. Paolozzi, London, Mus. Mankind, 1985)

N. Barley: *Foreheads of the Dead: An Anthropological View of Kalabari Ancestral Screens* (Washington, DC, 1988) [pubd on occasion of exh., Washington, DC, N. Mus. Afr. A., 1988–9]

Africa and the Renaissance: Art in Ivory (exh. cat. by E. Bassani and M. D. McLeod, New York, Cent. Afr. A., 1988)

Art/Artefact: African Art in Anthropology Collection (exh. cat. by A. Danto and others, New York, Cent. Afr. A., 1988)

Echoes of the Kalabari: Sculpture by Sokari Douglas Camp (exh. cat., Washington, DC, N. Mus. Afr. A., 1988–9)

Close-up: Lessons in the Art of Seeing African Sculpture (exh. cat. by J. L. Thompson and S. Vogel, New York, Cent. Afr. A., 1990)

J. Mack: *Emil Torday and the Art of the Congo* (London, 1991)

Africa Explores: 20th Century African Art (exh. cat. by S. Vogel, New York, Cent. Afr. A., 1991)

Elephant: The Animal and its Ivory in Africa Culture (exh. cat., ed. D. H. Ross; Los Angeles, UCLA, Fowler Mus. Cult. Hist., 1992–3)

Astonishment and Power (exh. cat., Washington, DC, N. Mus. Afr. A., 1993–4)

Africa: The Art of a Continent (exh. cat., London, RA, 1995–6)

JOHN PICTON

XIV. Collectors and dealers.

The earliest private collections of African art were those of European royalty and nobility, whose cabinets of curiosities preserved exotica brought back from overseas travels. The 19th century was marked by the acquisition of ethnographic objects either as scientific specimens, war trophies or curiosities, which found their way into museum collections. Early dealers in ethnographic objects and curios, such as W. D. Webster in Oxford or William O. Oldman in London, sold what would today be called art.

African art as a category of *objets d'art* has been defined largely by collectors, dealers, critics and artists, whose tastes and preferences restricted it almost exclusively to figural sculpture and masks. Modern collecting began in Paris in the early 20th century, with sculptures from the French colonies. Dan/Wobé masks, Baule and Fang figures, Mpongwe white-faced masks and Kota reliquaries began turning up in studios of artists and other Left Bank *cognoscenti* and in the few art galleries that catered for collectors. Negrophilism in Paris in the 1920s fuelled this passion for *art nègre.*

Among these early artist-collectors were Eduard von der Heydt (*b* 1882), Félix Fénéon, Tristan Tzara, Guillaume Apollinaire, Maurice de Vlaminck, Jacob Epstein, Modigliani, Matisse, Braque and Picasso, while some of the prominent dealers were PAUL GUILLAUME, Joseph and Ernest Brummer, Louis Carré, Charles Ratton (1895–1986) and ANDRÉ LEFÈVRE. The German Expressionists, too, developed a fascination with *art nègre.* Carl Kjersmeier (1889–1961), unique among these early collectors for his systematic approach to collecting and studying African art, travelled to West Africa in the 1930s to collect sculptures and subsequently published the landmark four-volume work, *Centres de style de l'art africain* (1935–9).

Although Parisian-based artists were the first serious collectors of African art, it was the American photographer and dealer ALFRED STIEGLITZ who mounted the first exhibition of African sculpture in the United States in 1914. The eccentric ALBERT C. BARNES acquired African sculptures in the 1920s, as did a few other Americans, including Frank Crowninshield (1872–1947), John Graham, John Quinn (1870–1924), Walter Arensberg (1878–1954) and Agnes Meyer (1887–1970). Authenticity was not an issue with these early collectors, who were attracted by the visual power of the works and were not concerned with origin, function and meaning. The influence of French ethnology in the 1930s and 1940s led dealers, such as PIERRE LOEB, systematically to mine new fields. Dogon, Senufo and Bamana works, for example, appeared in quantity for the first time in the 1950s and 1960s, and Africans themselves began dealing. The popularity of African art inspired the production of copies and forgeries (*see* §X above), and collectors and dealers were among the victims of fraud. Not surprisingly, authenticity became a major concern. But the motivations for collecting also became less pure, tainted by prestige, fashion and art as investment. The leading auction houses in Paris, London, Brussels and New York catered for the increasing demand for tribal art by private collectors, and the handful of commercial galleries devoted to African art gathered followers. Paris remains the centre of buying and selling, followed by Brussels, New York and London. The estimated number of serious collectors of African art worldwide in the period 1970–90 was around 500.

Decolonization, modern wars in Africa and archaeological discoveries since the 1960s have brought new objects to the art market. Prices have escalated as the supply of quality sculptures has diminished, due in part to the Unesco Treaty on Cultural Property (1970), which discouraged international trafficking in antiquities, and to increasing calls for the repatriation of art works. Some private collections have had high visibility, because they have been exhibited, published, donated to a museum or sold at auction. By the 1930s some of the first great early collections were going to auction, such as those of André Breton and Paul Eluard or Georges de Miré. These were followed by the sale of collections owned by Frank Crowninshield (1941), Jacob Epstein (1961), Helena Rubinstein (1966), James Hooper (1976) and Harry Franklin (1990). American private collections are often donated to museums. Nelson Rockefeller's collection led to the establishment of the Museum of Primitive Art and ultimately to the Rockefeller Wing of the Metropolitan Museum of Art (*see* ROCKEFELLER, (4)), and other donations include those of Clark Stillman (*b* 1907) to Dallas, Katherine White to Seattle, Max Stanley to the University of Iowa Museum of Art, and Lester Wunderman to the Metropolitan Museum of Art in New York. The visibility of African art in public art museums has in turn stimulated collectors' interest. Modern African art has yet to attract much critical attention and serious collectors. Ulli Beier's tireless devotion since the 1950s to African modern art and his collection (now at the University of Bayreuth, Iwalewa-Haus) are an exception.

BIBLIOGRAPHY

Arts primitifs dans les ateliers d'artistes (exh. cat., Paris, Mus. Homme, 1967)

W. Raymonde: 'Quelques Grands Amateurs et collectionneurs' and 'Les Grandes Ventes publiques', *Le Guidargus de l'art primitif: 1965–1985, 20 ans d'art primitif en ventes publiques* (Paris, 1985), pp. 19–21, 35–63

R. Lehuard: 'Charles Ratton et l'aventure de l'art nègre', *A. Afrique Noire*, lx (1986), pp. 11–33

P. Amrouche: 'Objets et collections d'art primitif: Réflexion sur les variations du goût de 1890 à nos jours', *Anthropologie de l'art: Formes et significations: Arts de l'Afrique, de l'Amérique et du Pacifique* (Paris, 1988), pp. 44–9

J. MacClancy: 'A Natural Curiosity: The British Market in Primitive Art', *Res*, 15 (Spring 1988), pp. 163–76

W. H. Robbins and N. Ingram Nooter: *African Art in American Collections: 1989 Survey* (Washington, DC, 1989)

L'Art d'Afrique noire dans les collections d'artistes (exh. cat. by F. N'Diaye, Arles, 1991)

XV. Art libraries and photographic collections.

The study of African art history has roots in the older field of cultural anthropology, which is primarily concerned with material culture rather than art. Most of the literature before 1960 falls into this category, and even today African art research still draws extensively on ethnography, history and archaeology (*see also* §§II, 1 and XI above). Serious study of the subject, therefore, remains dependent on libraries with strong collections in these fields.

Museums of ethnography, which were concerned with material culture and had colonial connections, sprang up in Europe during the late 19th century (*see* §XII above). They built library collections to support curatorial research and often also served as repositories for photographs, manuscripts and other official records. These institutions, such as the Museum für Völkerkunde, Berlin, the British Museum, London, the Pitt Rivers Museum, Oxford, the Koninklijk Museum voor Midden-Afrika, Tervuren, and the Musée de l'Homme, Paris, grew into significant research collections that remain only partially tapped. Although many are underfunded and their libraries are not being actively developed, their historical material makes them a critical group of repositories. In the United States libraries and photo-archives with extensive African material were developed by such institutions as the Peabody Museum of Archaeology and Ethnology at Harvard University, Cambridge, MA, the American Museum of Natural History, New York, and the Field Museum of Natural History, Chicago.

Colonial libraries with collections on African history, geography, law, economics, sociology and ethnology, with regional emphasis on colonial territories, are also essential sources. Although the development of the collections and financial support may have dwindled in the post-colonial era, these institutions, such as the libraries of the Royal Commonwealth Society and the Royal Geographical Society, both London, the Académie des Sciences d'Outre-Mer, Paris, and the Bibliothèque Africaine, Brussels, remain historically important. The Biblioteca Apostolica Vaticana in Rome holds even older material dating back to the earliest Catholic contacts with Africa. Missionary societies, such as the Baseler Mission, also retained photographs taken in the course of their work, although similarly they were not intended to document material culture. In addition, some of the European national and state libraries have surprisingly rich collections of African materials.

As the discipline of African art history emerged in universities, and African art was increasingly collected and exhibited (*see* §§XII and XIII above), libraries and photo-archives became more important. Important library collections of Africana were developed in the United States with the establishment of major graduate programmes from the 1960s at Indiana University, the University of California at Los Angeles, Yale University, the University of Iowa and Columbia University. Seminars in African art held at the Sorbonne, Paris, the School of Oriental and African Studies, London, and at many other universities, including Ghent, Brussels and Florence, created further demands for library collections. There were similar developments at contemporary German research centres, such as the Frobenius-Institut in Frankfurt am Main and Mainz University, although their emphasis is on ethnography and material culture rather than art history. The Frobenius-Institut is fortunate in having much early library and archival material while maintaining an active research programme that involves contemporary documentation.

Art museums in the United States (and to a lesser extent in Europe) have led the way in collecting and exhibiting African art, but their supporting libraries lack the earlier resources of their European ethnological counterparts. These newer centres, however, are developing true African art libraries with the acquisition of exhibition and auction catalogues, books, journals and dissertations documenting late 20th-century African art, including the work of contemporary artists who exhibit in galleries and museums. This shifting emphasis from ethnography to art history can be seen in Paris at the Musée National des Arts Africains et Océaniens and the Olfert Dapper Foundation; in Norwich, England, at the Sainsbury Centre for the Visual Arts, University of East Anglia; in New York at the Robert Goldwater Library of the Metropolitan Museum of Art and the Center of African Art; and at the Smithsonian Institution's National Museum of African Art, Washington, DC. The library at the last-named institution seeks to combine the historical and ethnographical with the artistic and art-historical streams of research materials within its collection policy. Although the newer repositories may lack the wealth of historical photographs found in those of the colonial era, their contemporary pictorial collections are focused directly on African art and contain many more studio photographs of individual objects and contextual field photographs taken by recent researchers.

Much older material has become available to newer collections through reprints and micro-publishing, and the increasing use of electronic technologies allows the sharing and transmission of images between institutions. The application of these technologies to the documentation and dissemination of African art has been pioneered by the Museum of Cultural History at the University of California in Los Angeles and by the University of Iowa.

Libraries and photo-archives in Africa remain sadly underdeveloped. The few isolated collections of note, such as those in Guinea-Bissau, Senegal and Nigeria, mostly date from the colonial period and are not being actively developed or preserved. The museums and archives in Zimbabwe and South Africa, however, have been more fortunate and are collecting printed and visual documentation on their material culture collections. They alone have been able to collect both historical and contemporary material at close range, but with an ethnographical rather than an art-historical emphasis.

BIBLIOGRAPHY

H. Hannam, ed.: *The SCOLMA Directory of Libraries and Special Collections on Africa in the United Kingdom and Western Europe* (Oxford, rev. 4/1983)

J. E. M. Gosebrink: *African Studies Information Resources Directory* (Oxford, 1986)

JANET L. STANLEY

African American [Afro-American; Black American] **art.** Term used to describe art made by Americans of African descent. While the crafts of African Americans in the 18th and 19th centuries continued largely to reflect African artistic traditions (*see* AFRICA, §VIII), the earliest fine art made by professional African American artists was in an academic western style.

1. Before *c.* 1920. 2. *c.* 1920–*c.* 1960. 3. *c.* 1960 and after.

1. BEFORE *c.* 1920. The first African American artist to be documented was JOSHUA JOHNSON, a portrait painter who practised in and around Baltimore, MD. Possibly a former slave in the West Indies, he executed plain, linear portraits for middle-class families (e.g. *Sarah Ogden Gustin*, *c.* 1798–1802; Washington, DC, N.G.A.). Only one of the *c.* 83 portraits attributed to Johnson is signed, and none is dated. There are only two African American sitters among Johnson's attributions. Among the second generation of prominent 19th-century African American artists were the portrait-painter William E. Simpson (1818–72) of Buffalo, NY, Robert Douglass jr (1809–87) and Douglass's cousin and pupil David Bowser (1820–1900) of Philadelphia. Douglass, none of whose works survives, started as a sign-painter and then painted portraits as a disciple of Thomas Sully. Engravings and lithographs were produced by Patrick Reason (*b* 1817) of New York, whose parents were from Haiti. His engravings included illustrations for publications supporting the abolition of slavery and also portraits (e.g. *Granville Sharp*, 1835; Washington, DC, Gal. A., Howard U.).

Julian Hudson (*fl c.* 1831–44) was the earliest documented African American painter in the South. Having studied in Paris, he returned to his home town, New Orleans, where he taught art and painted portraits. Although his quarter-length figures were rigidly conventional, Hudson was a skilful painter of faces. His *Self-portrait* (1839; New Orleans, LA State Mus.) is the earliest surviving self-portrait by an African American artist. Jules Lion (1810–66) also studied and practised in Paris prior to returning to New Orleans, where he produced paintings and lithographs. He was also credited with introducing the daguerreotype to the city, where he was one of the earliest professional photographers.

Throughout the 19th century African American artists in Louisiana apparently did not experience as much professional discrimination as their peers in other areas of the USA. However, even in Louisiana there are few examples of work commissioned by African Americans at this time. The Melrose Plantation House, built *c.* 1833 for the mulatto Metoyer family in Melrose, near Natchitoches, LA, is the only surviving plantation manor house built by an African American family in the southern states. It contained portraits of members of the family, probably executed by an unknown mulatto painter before 1830. The brick and timber African House, an out-house used in part as a prison for the control of slaves in the plantation at Melrose, was remarkable for the width and height of its roof: it was probably constructed during the early 19th century by African-born slaves owned by the Metoyer family.

Another artist from New Orleans, Eugene Warbourg (1826–59), was among the leading black sculptors of the 19th century. He worked in Rome, developing a Neo-classical style, as did Mary Edmonia Lewis, who trained in Boston before becoming the first professional African American sculptor, producing such works as *Hagar* (see fig. 1).

The most important African American landscape painters of the 19th century were ROBERT S. DUNCANSON, Edward Mitchell Bannister and Grafton Tyler Brown (1841–1918). Duncanson, who worked in Cincinnati and Detroit, was the earliest professional African American landscape painter. He studied in Glasgow and travelled extensively in Italy, France and England, as well as in Minnesota, Vermont and Canada. He was the first African American artist to receive international recognition. Although Duncanson painted portraits and still-lifes, he is best known as a Romantic realist landscape painter in the Hudson River school tradition. His largest commission came in 1848, when he painted eight large landscape panels and four over-door compositions in the main entrance hall of Nicholas Longworth's mansion 'Belmont' (now the Taft Museum) in Cincinnati.

1. Mary Edmonia Lewis: *Hagar*, marble, h. 1337mm, 1875 (Washington, DC, National Museum of American Art)

Bannister was the leading painter in Providence, RI, during the 1870s and 1880s. Born in Nova Scotia, he started by making solar prints and attended an evening drawing class in Boston. He is reported to have taken up painting in reaction to a newspaper statement in 1867 that blacks could appreciate art but not produce it. He was a moderately talented painter of poetic landscapes (e.g. *Landscape*, *c.* 1870–75; Providence, RI Sch. Des., Mus. A.), influenced by Alexander Helwig Wyant and the Hudson River school. He was the earliest African American artist to receive a national award when he received a gold medal for *Under the Oaks* (untraced) at the Philadelphia Centennial Exposition in 1876. He was also one of the seven founder-members in 1873 of the Providence Art Club, which became the nucleus of the Rhode Island School of Design. He was the only prominent African American artist of the 19th century not to travel or study in Europe.

Brown was the earliest documented professional African American artist in California. He was first employed in San Francisco as a draughtsman and lithographer, also printing street maps and stock certificates, before turning to landscape painting. His most productive years were during the 1880s, when he painted many Canadian landscapes and scenes of the American north-west. He also lived in Portland, OR, and Washington. After 1891 Brown apparently ceased painting and in 1892 moved to St Paul, MN, where he worked as a draughtsman.

The most distinguished African American artist who worked in the 19th century was HENRY OSSAWA TANNER. His early paintings of the 1890s included African American genre subjects and reflect the realist tradition of Thomas Eakins under whom Tanner studied at the Pennsylvania Academy of Fine Arts in Philadelphia. From 1903 he painted religious subjects, portraits and landscapes, primarily in subdued blues and greens. Like the majority of prominent 19th-century African American artists, Tanner went to Europe for further training and to escape racial and professional discrimination: he lived in Paris during most of his career and developed a painterly style influenced by Symbolism. He held his first one-man exhibition of religious paintings, however, at the American Art Galleries in New York in 1908, and in 1909 he became the first African American to be elected to the National Academy of Design.

In 1907 the Tercentennial Exposition in Jamestown, VA, included among the pavilions a 'Negro Building': its exhibits focused primarily on African American crafts, carpentry and inventions. Although there were 484 paintings and drawings, no works by prominent African American painters were included. The most important African American artist to be included in the Jamestown exhibition was the sculptor Meta Vaux Fuller, who had studied in Paris, where she had gained the approval of Rodin: she exhibited a series of dioramas depicting various aspects of black life in America. Other contemporary exhibitions, however, such as that of the Eight (*see* EIGHT, THE (ii)) in 1908 and the Armory Show in 1913, both held in New York, had little initial stylistic impact on African American art.

2. *c.* 1920–*c.* 1960. The most significant African American stylistic and aesthetic movement of the early 20th century was the Harlem Renaissance or 'New Negro' movement of the 1920s. The Harlem district of New York became, during the decade, the 'cultural capital of black America'. The ensuing Harlem Renaissance drew upon the community's African heritage and was the earliest race-conscious cultural movement by African Americans. Primarily political and literary, the spirit of the Harlem Renaissance was most eloquently expressed by Alain

Locke in his book *The New Negro* (New York, 1925). The earliest African American painter consciously to incorporate African imagery in his work was Aaron Douglas, a prominent figure in the Harlem Renaissance and later. Other significant artists who contributed to the movement included Meta Vaux Fuller, Palmer Hayden (1890–1964), who painted satirical images of life in Harlem, William E. Scott (1884–1964) and Malvin Gray Johnson (1896–1934). The most important African American photographer of that period was James Van Der Zee, who photographed people and scenes in Harlem for more than 50 years and also served as the official photographer for the Pan-Africanist Marcus Garvey during his frequent parades and rallies in Harlem.

The artists of the Harlem Renaissance received a great stimulus from the exhibitions of the Harmon Foundation. This was founded in New York in 1922 by William E. Harmon, a white Ohio-born philanthropist and real estate developer, and in 1926 it began promoting African American artistic talents and offering awards in the fine arts. The foundation's first *Exhibit of Fine Arts Productions of American Negro Artists* opened at International House in New York in January 1928. Following the success of the pilot exhibition, the foundation mounted additional shows at International House in 1929 and 1930. In 1931 it moved the location of its exhibitions to the galleries of the Art Center in E. 56th Street in New York. During the early years of the foundation's operation, annual travelling exhibitions were organized that introduced African American art to broad audiences for the first time. The exhibitions included artists working in traditional western, naive and modernist styles. Although some critics felt that the foundation's jurors were not critical enough in their selection procedures, the Harmon Foundation's awards, exhibitions and exhibition catalogues continued to promote African American art until 1966, when it closed. Its files, which formed the most comprehensive single body of materials relating specifically to African American art during the first half of the 20th century, were placed in the Library of Congress and the National Archives in Washington, DC. The large art collection that the foundation amassed was divided between the National Collection of Fine Arts (now the National Museum of American Art of the Smithsonian Institution) in Washington, DC, Fisk University in Nashville, TN, and the Hampton Institute (now Hampton University) in Hampton, VA.

The Stock Market crash of 1929 brought the golden era of the Harlem Renaissance to an end and plunged the USA into the Great Depression of the 1930s. The Depression paralysed the nation's economy, and President Franklin D. Roosevelt established the Federal Art Project (1935–43), a division of the Works Progress Administration (*see* UNITED STATES OF AMERICA, §VI), which provided employment for many African American artists. The early school of African American muralists reached its apogee during the 1930s, and numerous murals by African American artists were commissioned to decorate schools, hospitals, banks, post offices and other public buildings.

These murals ranged greatly in style: such artists as Charles White (1918–79) and Hale Woodruff executed historical murals that showed the influence of Mexican social realism, for example the *Amistad* murals (1939) by Woodruff in the Slavery Library in Tallageda College, Tallageda, AL, which depicted a slave mutiny in 1839. Other artists produced mural work in a primitivist style, for example Aaron Douglas, whose murals of African life included elongated, angular figures with stylized features, and Charles Alston (?1907–78), a painter and sculptor. Alston painted mural panels (1937) in the Harlem Hospital, New York, depicting tribal African and modern scientific medicine in a style also characterized by expressively distorted figures. Some murals had themes that were not specific to African Americans, for example the mural panel by Archibald J. Motley (1891–1980) entitled *United States Mail* (1936) in the post office in Wood River, IL. Motley also made easel paintings of scenes from African, American and even Parisian life, employing both a naive and a highly naturalistic style. Murals were also produced by such artists as the painter William E. Scott (1884–1964) and the sculptors Sargent Johnson (1887–1967) and Richmond Barthe (1901–89), who carved reliefs with highly formalized figures. Barthe was also an accomplished painter and figure-sculptor of black subjects (e.g. *Blackberry Woman*, 1932; New York, Whitney), as well as executing portraits of theatrical characters. The sculpture of Sargent Johnson was characterized by ingenuous figure studies in various materials such as porcelain, terracotta and lacquered wood (e.g. *Forever Free*, 1936; San Francisco, CA, MOMA).

The most important national commission received by an African American artist during the 1930s went to the sculptor Augusta Savage, who created a large sculpture, *The Harp* (later called *Lift Every Voice and Sing*; painted plaster, h. 4.87 m) for the Negro Pavilion of the New York World's Fair of 1939. It was intended to represent African American music and consisted of a receding line of singing figures arranged in the shape of a harp. The sculpture, cast in plaster and gilded to resemble bronze, never received permanent casting and was destroyed following the fair's closing (see Dover, pl. 72). Selma Burke was another important African American female sculptor whose career blossomed during the 1930s and 1940s. In 1935 she received a Roosevelt Foundation Fellowship, and in 1943 she participated in a competition sponsored by the Fine Arts Commission of the District of Columbia to depict a bust of President Roosevelt. The bust, which was completed and unveiled in 1945, was adapted in 1946 for use on the American dime coin.

During and immediately after World War II, there arose to prominence a new school of African American artists, many of whom were the so-called 'children of the Harlem Renaissance'. Such artists as Selma Burke, Charles White and William H. Johnson, who had attracted attention before the war, continued their achievements, for example in the social realism of the *Contribution of the Negro to American Democracy* (1953) in the Hampton Institute in Virginia. Johnson, who was influenced by Chaïm Soutine, worked in France, Denmark and Norway before returning to the USA in 1938. He painted Expressionist works and naive images of black life in the USA (e.g. *Going to Church*, *c.* 1940–44; see fig. 2). Over 1000 of his works were in the collection of the Harmon Foundation when it closed. The art of African Americans was encouraged by the exhibition of the *Art of the American Negro, 1851–1940*, assembled

2. William H. Johnson: *Going to Church*, oil on burlap, 968×1121 mm, *c.* 1940–44 (Washington, DC, National Museum of American Art)

by Alonso Aden with assistance from the Harmon Foundation and the Works Progress Administration, at the *American Negro Exposition* in Chicago in 1940. Among the artists exhibited was Jacob Lawrence (*b* 1917), who painted highly coloured naive images of black life and history, eschewing perspective (e.g. the 60 gouache panels of the *Migration of the Negro Northwards*, 1941; Washington, DC, Phillips Col. and New York, MOMA). Other prominent African American artists of this time were Elmer Simms Campbell, who contributed illustrations for such periodicals as *Esquire*, and the painters Romare Bearden (1912–88), Eldzier Cortor (*b* 1915), Frederick Flemister and Horace Pippin (1888–1947), whose paintings included depictions of figures from the history of black emancipation. Significant figure-sculpture was made by Elizabeth Catlett (*b* 1915) and William Artis (1914–77); the latter was a pupil of Augusta Savage and produced highly naturalistic portrait busts.

During the 1950s African American art was dominated by two stylistic trends: Abstract Expressionism and realism. Some artists developed an abstract style that was related to contemporary Abstract Expressionism but also was motivated by a belated interest in Cubism, most noticeable in the works of Charles Alston, Romare Bearden, Hale Woodruff and James Wells (*b* 1902). This contrasted with the realistic styles championed by Sargent Johnson and William Artis and heralded a new direction in African American art.

3. *c.* 1960 AND AFTER. In the 1960s and 1970s new classifications appeared in African American art based on continuing developments in abstract art and the rise of the figurative style known as Black Expressionism. A new generation of artists came to prominence, influenced by such developments as Abstract Expressionism, colour field painting and hard-edge painting. These artists produced large, colourful, non-representational art that was not racially identifiable: such work was more successful commercially and more likely to be included in museums, exhibitions and galleries than that of the Black Expressionists. The most prominent African American abstract painter was Sam Gilliam, based in Washington, DC, whose colour field painting employed folded, draped and hanging canvases as well as other forms of support (e.g. *Abstraction*, acrylic on aluminium-treated paper, 1969; Washington, DC, Evans-Tibbs Col., see 1989 exh. cat., p. 94).

3. Barbara Jones-Hogu: *Unite*, screenprint, 711×345 mm, 1969 (R. A. Perry private collection)

The leading African American abstract sculptor was Richard Hunt from Chicago: in his youth he worked under Julio González, after which he went on to produce elegant welded and cast metal sculpture that included figurative and organic elements. A variety of other abstract styles also appeared in the work of such sculptors as Barbara Chase-Riboud (*b* 1936), Martin Puryear (*b* 1941), Daniel Johnson (*b* 1938), Juan Logan (*b* 1946) and Fred Eversley (*b* 1941). Chase-Riboud produced expressive, distorted sculptures, using various media (e.g. *Monument III*, bronze and silk, 2134×914×152 mm, 1970; New York, Betty Parsons Gal.). Logan's sculpture, however, was concerned with the formal qualities of geometric shapes and the use of industrial materials (e.g. *Traditional Trap*, galvanized steel, 2.16×1.02×2.35 m, 1972; artist's col., see 1974 exh. cat., fig. 57), while Eversley's work aimed at producing complex optical effects (e.g. *Untitled*, polyester, 1970; New York, Whitney).

The 1960s and 1970s were also marked by fertile associations between the older and younger generations of abstract painters, such as the Spiral group, founded in New York in 1963 by Hale Woodruff, Romare Bearden and Norman Lewis (*b* 1909), which attracted such younger artists as Richard Mayhew (*b* 1934). Mayhew, who was also a jazz singer, expressed his love of music in lyrical, colourful abstractions (e.g. *Vibrato*, 1974; Washington, DC, Evans-Tibbs Col., see 1989 exh. cat., p. 86). Varying degrees of abstraction characterized the paintings of such artists as Norma Morgan (*b* 1928), Alvin Loving (*b* 1935), Bill Hutson (*b* 1936), William T. Williams (*b* 1942) and Robert Reid (*b* 1924). The development of innovative effects of colour and space also affected Robert Thompson (1937–66), who reinterpreted Renaissance themes with flat figures, colours influenced by Fauvism and rich impasto painting techniques (e.g. *Music Lesson*, 1962; Washington, DC, Evans-Tibbs Col., see 1989 exh. cat., p. 92).

Black Expressionism was a movement that grew out of the political unrest of the 1960s, in particular the struggle for civil rights. It also grew from the outrage of African American artists at the professional discrimination that they faced. As a result, many black artists began producing political art directed primarily towards black audiences. Black Expressionist art was always figurative and often employed bright colours, such as the black, red and green of the Black Nationalists' flag: the works frequently bore slogans and extolled the virtues of black Africa. The racial pride and political radicalism of this art led to regular depictions of such subjects as Angela Davis, the Black Panther Party (e.g. Eliot Knight's mural *Panther Tribute*, 10.97×7.32 m, early 1970s; Roxbury, MA, Warren Street, destr., see 1980 exh. cat., p. 10), Muhammad Ali and anti-Vietnam War slogans. The American flag was a constantly recurring motif and often appeared blood-spattered as a noose around the neck of a lynched black male or with yellow instead of white stripes to indicate the cowardice of the white American political structure.

Among the artists associated with Black Expressionism there was, however, a multiplicity of subjects, styles and techniques, ranging from the threatening images created by Dona Chandler (*b* 1941) even from such subjects as a domestic still-life, to the work of Faith Ringold (*b* 1934), who depicted ritualistic African subjects in so-called 'soft sculpture', while a preoccupation with unorthodox media is apparent in the collage paintings of Benny Andrews (*b* 1930), which contain real pieces of clothing. Other artists representative of the diversity of Black Expressionism included Charles Searles (*b* 1937), Murry DePillars (*b* 1939), David Hammonds (*b* 1943), Joe Overstreet (*b* 1934), Melvin Edwards (*b* 1939), John Riddle (*b* 1933), Malcolm Bailey (*b* 1947), Gary Rickson (*b* 1942), Phillip Mason (*b* 1942) and Vincent Smith (*b* 1929). Black Expressionism also influenced older artists such as Romare Bearden, Charles White, Elizabeth Catlett, Jacob Lawrence and John Biggers (*b* 1925).

One of the most important movements to develop out of Black Expressionism was the Black Neighborhood Mural Movement, which originated in Chicago during the early 1960s. Motivated partly by the fact that African Americans were not primarily museum-oriented and by the belief that American museums had few relevant programmes for African Americans, numerous artists transformed drab walls in run-down, predominantly black neighbourhoods with brilliant, glowing murals incorporating subject-matter with which almost every African American could identify. These served to instil black pride and a sense of heritage and racial identity. Chicago produced the largest number of murals, followed by Detroit; Boston; San Francisco; Washington, DC; Atlanta and New Orleans. The most famous were the *Wall of Respect and Community as One* in Chicago (1967; see 1989–91 exh. cat., p. 28) and the *Wall of Dignity* in Detroit, completed during the early 1960s: both were lost when the buildings on which they were painted were demolished.

The *Wall of Respect and Community as One*, which took as its general theme black heroes, was executed by the Visual Arts Workshop of the Organization of Black American Culture (OBAC). This included Barbara Jones-Hogu (*b* 1938) and Jeff Donaldson (*b* 1932). They were among a splinter group in Chicago which, after the mural was completed, formed the African Commune of Bad Relevant Artists (AfriCobra), 'bad' meaning 'good' in African American slang. AfriCobra artists employed fluorescent colours such as strawberry pink, 'hot' orange, lime green and grape purple in their highly rhythmic message-emblazoned art, which, they declared, was produced exclusively for African American audiences. They produced a series of high-quality screenprints that were originally sold very inexpensively to promote the doctrine of 'black art for every black home in America' (e.g. *Unite* by Barbara Jones-Hogu, 1969; see fig. 3).

Another important group that developed in the 1960s was Weusi Nyumba Ya Sanaa (Swahili: Black House of Art) in Harlem. Founded in 1965, it established an academy and a gallery (1967–78). The Weusi artists incorporated some aspects of African iconography in all of their art: many members abandoned their former 'slave' names, officially adopting African names and converting to African religions. Weusi's spokesman was Ademola Olugebefola (*b* 1941), who used traditional African materials such as cowrie shells to create ritualistic images.

4. Sam Gilliam: *Bluesette*, acrylic on canvas, 2.03×2.29 m, 1980 (Washington, DC, Corcoran Gallery of Art); from the series *Chasers*

Following such reforms as the Public Accommodations Act of 1964, which made racial discrimination in public places illegal, and the Voting Rights Act of 1965, which enforced African Americans' right to vote, there was an increasingly heavy reliance on West African and sometimes Egyptian themes as the militancy of Black Expressionism gradually diminished. The Weusi and AfriCobra collaborations continued, however, to produce colourful, message-bearing art for African American audiences. In 1987 AfriCobra experienced its first cross-cultural exposure when it was invited to exhibit with Groupe Fromagé in Martinique at the 16th annual Sermac festival of the arts and culture. AfriCobra and Groupe Fromagé shared a similar philosophy and an aesthetic based on African, African American and Caribbean forms.

Such artists as Sam Gilliam and Richard Hunt continued meanwhile to explore abstract art, both completing a number of large-scale public commissions. Gilliam's paintings of the 1980s and early 1990s frequently employed metal, fabric and paint in dramatic impasto techniques, as well as using more conventional techniques such as acrylic (e.g. *Bluesette*, 1980; see fig. 4). Martin Puryear emerged during the 1980s as a leading African American abstract sculptor, working primarily in wood in a post-Minimalist style and frequently incorporating such materials as rope, leather and hide. During the late 1970s and early 1980s Puryear created a number of public projects and wall pieces that were ring-shaped or reflected biomorphic forms and organic materials.

In the 1980s African American art was the subject of a number of pioneering exhibitions. In particular, in 1982 the Corcoran Gallery of Art in Washington, DC, mounted the first major travelling exhibition of African American folk or self-taught artists. The artists, the majority of whom were born and still lived in the southern states of the USA, were frequently elderly when their careers began, following retirement or a work-related injury. Many were self-styled religious ministers, prophets and missionaries. As well as referring to childhood experiences they frequently used bird, animal and reptilian imagery: they also often represented figures associated with emancipation and civil rights, such as George Washington, Abraham Lincoln, John F. Kennedy and Martin Luther King. Such artists displayed an amazing ingenuity for converting *objets trouvés* and discarded materials, including costume jewellery, bones, bottle caps, chewing gum, foam packing, sawdust, mud, tree trunks, branches and Mardi Gras beads, into unique artefacts. The influence of traditional African culture on African American art was explored in an exhibition organized in 1989 by the Dallas Museum of Art. *Black Art—Ancestral Legacy: The African Impulse in African American Art* was the first major exhibition to bring together the works of African, Caribbean and African American academic and folk artists.

BIBLIOGRAPHY

J. A. Porter: *Modern Negro Art* (New York, 1943)

The Negro in American Art: One Hundred and Fifty Years of Afro-American Art (exh. cat. by J. A. Porter, Los Angeles, CA, Davis U. CA; San Diego, CA, State U., A. Gal.; Oakland, CA, Mus.; 1966–7)

The Evolution of Afro-American Artists, 1800–1950 (exh. cat., intro. C. Greene jr; New York, City Coll. City U., 1967)

M. J. Butcher: *The Negro in American Culture* (New York, 1969)

C. Dover: *American Negro Art* (London, 1969)

Harlem Artists 69 (exh. cat., intro. T. Gunn; New York, Stud. Mus. Harlem, 1969)

S. Lewis and R. Waddy, eds: *Black Artists on Art*, 2 vols (Los Angeles, 1969–71)

Afro-American Artists, 1800–1969 (exh. cat. by R. J. Craig, F. Bacon and B. Harmon, Philadelphia, PA, Mus. Civ. Cent., 1970)

Dimensions of Black (exh. cat., ed. J. Teihet; La Jolla, CA, A. Cent., 1970)

J. W. Chase: *Afro-American Art and Craft* (New York, 1971)

E. Fax: *Seventeen Black Artists* (New York, 1971)

Contemporary Black Artists in America (exh. cat. by R. Doty, New York, Whitney, 1971)

R. Bearden and H. Henderson: *Six Black Masters of American Art* (New York, 1972)

A New Vitality in Art: The Black Woman (exh. cat. by G. Garrison and P. Long, South Hadley, MA, Mount Holyoke Coll. A. Mus., 1972)

E. H. Fine: *The Afro-American Artist: A Search for Identity* (New York, 1973)

Blacks: USA: 1973 (exh. cat., intro. B. Andrews; New York, Cult. Cent., 1973)

Directions in Afro-American Art (exh. cat., intro. R. R. Jeffries; Ithaca, NY, Cornell U., Johnson Mus. A., 1974)

E. Fax: *Black Artists of the New Generation* (New York, 1977)

S. Lewis: *Art: African American* (New York, 1978)

Spirals: Afro-American Art of the '70s (exh. cat. by E. B. Gaither, Roxbury, MA, Mus. Afro-Amer. Hist., 1980)

L. M. Igoe: *Two Hundred and Fifty Years of Afro-American Art: An Annotated Bibliography* (New York, 1981)

J. Anderson: *This Was Harlem* (New York, 1982)

D. L. Lewis: *When Harlem Was in Vogue* (New York, 1982)

W. Ferris, ed.: *Afro-American Folk Arts and Crafts* (Jackson, MS, 1983)

R. F. Thompson: *Flash of the Spirit: African and Afro-American Art and Philosophy* (New York, 1984)

M. S. Campbell and others: *Harlem Renaissance: Art of Black America* (New York, 1987)

C. D. Wintz: *Black Culture and the Harlem Renaissance* (Houston, 1988)

African-American Artists, 1880–1987: Selections from the Evans-Tibbs Collection (exh. cat. by G. C. McElroy, R. J. Powell, S. F. Patton and D. C. Driskell, Washington, DC, Smithsonian Inst. Travelling Exh. Serv., 1989)

Black Art—Ancestral Legacy: The African Impulse in African–American Art (exh. cat., ed. R. V. Rozelle, A. J. Wardlaw and M. A. McKenna; Dallas, TX, Mus. A.; Atlanta, GA, High Mus. A.; Milwaukee, WI, A. Mus.; Richmond, VA Mus. F.A.; 1989–91)

REGENIA A. PERRY

Afro (Basaldella) (*b* Udine, 4 March 1912; *d* Zurich, 24 July 1976). Italian painter. He was the brother of MIRKO. He learnt to paint in the workshop belonging to his father and uncle, both of whom were painter–decorators. From 1926 to 1931 he studied at the Accademia di Belle Arti in Florence, with his brother Dino Basaldella (*b* 1909) and then in Venice. In 1932 he was in Milan, where he met Renato Birolli and Ennio Morlotti, and where an exhibition of his work was held the following year at the Galleria Il Milione. From 1933 he was in Rome working with such artists of the Scuola Romana as Corrado Cagli, whose influence is apparent in Afro's early figure-paintings and still-lifes, Fausto Pirandello, Giuseppe Capogrossi and Mirko. The artists were based in the Galleria della Cometa, where Afro exhibited in 1937. They opposed the classicism of Novecento Italiano, combining instead primitivism and metaphysical naturalism with expressionistic brushwork. During World War II Afro taught mosaic design at the Accademia di Belle Arti in Venice. After the war, between his participation in the Fronte Nuovo delle Arti (1946) and in the group of Otto Pittori Italiani (1952–4) his work was characterized by a tonal post-Cubist style. He held exhibitions in Rome at the Galleria Lo Zodiaco in 1946, at the Galleria dell'Obelisco in 1948 and at the Studio d'Arte Palma in 1951. Gradually he developed a style of lyrical abstraction that delicately balanced the expression of subconscious impulses with an objective vision, for example in *Still-life* (1948) and *Burnt Shadow* (1956; both Rome, G.N.A. Mod.). From 1949 he made numerous visits to the USA: he exhibited in New York and taught at Mills College in Oakland, CA. He also became acquainted with the Abstract Expressionism of Franz Kline, Willem de Kooning and especially Arshile Gorky, whose work he introduced in Rome in 1957 at the Galleria dell'Obelisco. He had one-man shows at the Venice Biennale in 1954, 1956 and 1960, and also participated in the *New Decade* exhibition (1955) at MOMA, New York, and the *Documenta* exhibition at Kassel. During the 1950s he received numerous public commissions for murals in Udine and, in 1958, in the UNESCO building in Paris (the *Garden of Hope*). During the 1960s his painting became more gestural and highly coloured, and he also employed collage. In the 1970s, however, he used crisper geometric forms.

BIBLIOGRAPHY

L. Venturi: *Afro*, Commentari (1954)

C. Brandi: *Afro* (Rome, 1977)

Afro (exh. cat., ed. B. Mantura; Rome, G.N.A. Mod., 1978)

ANTONELLO NEGRI

Afshar, Muhammad Hasan. *See* MUHAMMAD HASAN AFSHAR.

Afzal [Mir Afżal al-Ḥusaynī al-Tūnī] (*fl* Isfahan, 1640–51). Persian illustrator. Active during the reign of the

Safavid shah 'Abbas II (*reg* 1642–66), Afzal produced manuscript illustrations and single pages for albums in different styles. Most of the 62 paintings he made for the voluminous copy (St Petersburg, Saltykov-Shchedrin Pub. Lib., Dorn 333) of Firdawi's *Shāhnāma* ('Book of kings') presented to the monarch by the head of the royal guard, Murtiza Quli Khan, are scenes of battles and combats in the metropolitan style that was transferred from Herat to Bukhara (*see* ISLAMIC ART, §III, 4(vi)(c)). Unlike the tinted drawings of his contemporaries, Afzal's single-page compositions use a rich, sombre palette highlighted with gold. Most depict the standard repertory of languid youths and lovers in the style of RIZA, but are more erotic. *Bishop with a Crosier* (Los Angeles, CA, Co. Mus. A., M.73.5.456) is the only known Persian portrait of an Armenian religious figure; it shows a broad-faced, sensitively modelled figure similar in style to those in the *Shāhnāma* illustrations.

BIBLIOGRAPHY

Enc. Iran.: 'Afżal al-Ḥosaynī'

M. M. Ashrafi: *Persian-Tajik Poetry in XIV–XVII Centuries Miniatures* (Dushanbe, 1974), no. 94

P. Pal, ed.: *Islamic Art: The Nasli M. Heeramaneck Collection* (Los Angeles, 1974), no. 248

M. Farhad: *Safavid Single Page Painting, 1628–1666* (diss., Cambridge, MA., Harvard U., 1987), pp. 85–101 and catalogue nos 1–11

□

Agabiti [Agapiti], **Pietro Paolo** (*b* Sassoferrato, *c*. 1470; *d* Cupramontana, *c*. 1540). Italian painter and possible woodcutter. He spent his early years in Sassoferrato, where his family owned a ceramics workshop. Around 1497 he probably visited the Veneto region, since his *Virgin and Child with Saints* (Padua, Mus. Civ.) painted that year shows the strong influence of painters active there such as Cima da Conegliano. The painting also reflects the Bolognese style of Francesco Francia and that of the Romagnian Marco Palmezzano. In Venice, Agabiti may have made woodcuts after the illustrations for Francesco Colonna's *Hypnerotomachia Poliphili* (Venice, 1499). By 1502 he had returned to the Marches, where he executed a painting (untraced) for S Rocco, Jesi, the town where in 1507 he is documented as residing. After 1510 he was again in Sassoferrato, where in 1511 he signed and dated both the *Virgin and Child Enthroned with Saints* (Sassoferrato, Gal. A. Mod. & Contemp.) and the *Nativity* in S Maria del Piano. In 1518, for the same church, he signed and dated an altarpiece depicting the *Virgin and Child with SS Catherine and John the Baptist* (*in situ*). In S Fortunato, Sassoferrato, he executed the *Virgin and Child with Saints* (1521; *in situ*), in which the influence of Marco Palmezzano is even more evident.

Between 1522 and 1524, in collaboration with Andrea da Jesi the younger, Agabiti executed a series of frescoes in the Palazzo di Città, Jesi. In 1524, for Santa Croce, Sassoferrato, he painted a panel with *SS Benedict, Maurus and Placid* on the front and *SS Peter Damian and Scholastica* on the rear (Fonte Avellama, Abbazia; Urbino, Pal. Ducale). In 1528 he painted the *Virgin and Child Enthroned with SS John the Baptist and Anthony* (Jesi, Pin. Civ.). The lunette depicts *St Francis Receiving the Stigmata* and the predella shows the *Nativity*, the *Adoration of the Magi* and various *Saints*. Here the links with Cima da Conegliano and Marco Palmezzano are again in evidence, and there are also references to Carlo Crivelli's use of colour. In 1530 Agabiti painted the *Virgin and Child with Saints* for the Badia, San Lorenzo in Campo. The following year he retired to the Convento dell'Eremita, Cupramontana, where he remained until his death. Agabiti's work is retardataire; he did not adapt his style to suit 16th-century taste and remained instead nostalgically attached to the formal language of the 15th century.

BIBLIOGRAPHY

DBI; Thieme–Becker

R. Pallucchini: 'La pala dell'Agabiti per S Francesco di Corinaldo', *Festschrift Ulrich Middeldorf*, ed. O. Kosegarten and P. Tigler (Berlin, 1968), pp. 213–17

S. Salvadori: 'Pietro Paolo Agabiti', *Lorenzo Lotto nelle Marche* (exh. cat., ed. P. dal Poggetto and P. Zampetti; Ancona, Chiesa del Gesù, S Francesco alle Scale and Loggia Mercanti; 1981), pp. 132–4

A. Parronchi: 'Lo xilografo della *Hypnerotomachia Poliphili*: Pietro Paolo Agabiti', *Prospettiva*, 33–6 (1983–4), pp. 101–11 [Luigi Grassi *Festschrift*]

GENNARO TOSCANO

Agache, Donat-Alfred (*b* Tours, 1875; *d* 1934). French architect, urban planner and writer. He graduated in 1905 from the Ecole des Beaux-Arts, Paris, where he was a student in the atelier of Victor Laloux. In 1902 he came into contact with the Musée Social, a non-profit organization of bourgeois reformers, which sent him to visit the Louisiana Purchase International Exposition (1904) in St Louis, MO. Like a number of French architects of his generation such as Léon Jaussely and Marcel Auburtin (1872–1926), with whom he founded the Société Française des Architectes Urbanistes in 1913, he established a practice focused on urban design, achieving an international reputation in this field. Agache claimed to have coined the word 'urbanisme' and in 1914 he organized the first courses ever taught on the subject in France at the Collège Libre des Sciences Sociales et Economiques in Paris. His professional work included a prizewinning entry (1912; unexecuted) to the international competition for the design of Canberra, the new capital city of Australia, and master plans for Dunkerque (1912), Creil (1924) and Poitiers (1928). In 1927 he was invited to prepare a masterplan for Rio de Janeiro, then the capital city of Brazil. His proposals were based on traffic analysis; they stressed comprehensive zoning, with the establishment of a strong hierarchy between economic sectors and the creation of neighbourhood units separated by open space, as well as an architectural gradation from high-rise office buildings to small suburban houses. The plan was completed and published in 1930, but a change in government prevented its implementation. Agache produced several books on urban planning, including *La Remodélation d'une capitale* (1932), a comprehensive city planning manual based on his plan for Rio. His architectural work was limited but it is notable that in his Maison de Tous, a model communal house built in the precincts of the Village Français at the Exposition Internationale des Arts Décoratifs et Industriels Modernes (1925), Paris, this former advocate of a picturesque reconstruction of rural architecture was influenced by Tony Garnier's modernist architectural style.

WRITINGS

with J. M. Auburtin and E. Redont: *Comment reconstruire nos cités détruites* (Paris, 1915)

Nos Agglomérations rurales (Paris, 1918)

Où est l'urbanisme en France et à l'étranger? (Paris, 1923)
Cidade del Rio de Janeiro: Extensão, Remodelação, Embelezamento (Paris, 1930)
La Remodélation d'une capitale: Aménagement, extension, embellissement (Paris, 1932)

BIBLIOGRAPHY

J.-C. Tougeron: 'Donat-Alfred Agache: Un Architecte urbaniste', *Cah. Rech. Archit.*, 8 (1981), pp. 31–49

ISABELLE GOURNAY

Agalma. Term used for an ancient cult statue.

□

Agam, Yaacov (*b* Rishon-le-Zion, Palestine [now Israel], 11 May 1928). Israeli painter and sculptor. He studied at the Bezalel Academy in Jerusalem under Mordecai Ardon in 1946, and from 1951 in Paris at the Atelier d'Art Abstrait and at the Académie de la Grande Chaumière. The major influences on his early work were Kandinsky's *Über das Geistige in der Kunst* (1912), the Bauhaus ideas disseminated by Johannes Itten and Siegfried Giedion, with whom he came into contact in Zurich in 1949, and the work of Max Bill. Between 1951 and 1953 his work consisted of a series of *Contrapuntal* and *Transformable Pictures*, such as *Transformable Relief* (1953; Paris, R. N. Lebel priv. col., see Metken, p. 6). In 1953 he held his first one-man exhibition at the Galerie Craven in Paris. Although his claims that this was the first exhibition of kinetic art, and that he was the first optical-kinetic artist, have been disputed, he was certainly among the first artists to encourage spectator participation in such a direct way.

In the *Transformable Pictures* Agam allowed the spectator to arrange the elements either by plugging them into holes or by activating them manually or even by means of sound, as in *Sonore* (1961; Krefeld, Mus. Haus Lange), which he described as a tactile painting with acoustic effects; such works came to be called 'aleatoric' art. Agam's *Contrapuntal* and related later works, such as *Double Metamorphosis II* (oil on metal, 0.29×4.35 m, 1965; New York, MOMA), are as much optical as kinetic in their effects. They consist of a grid of painted strips that incorporate contrasting designs on opposite sides so that when viewed from the left or right a more or less distinct pattern takes form. These patterns merge, change and dissolve as the spectator passes from one side of the picture to another, conveying the impression of movement and changing colour. The transience of forms, and the power of light to dissolve them, could be said to have been Agam's real subject.

BIBLIOGRAPHY

J. Reichardt: *Yaacov Agam* (London, 1966)
Agam (exh. cat. by H. Gambu, New York, Marlborough-Gerson Gal., 1966)
Yaacov Agam: Pictures-sculptures (exh. cat. by H. Gambu, Tel Aviv, Tel Aviv Mus., 1973)
F. Popper: *Agam* (New York, 1976)
G. Metken: *Yaacov Agam* (London, 1977)

D. C. BARRETT

Agano. Japanese region in Buzen Province (now part of Fukuoka Prefect.), northern Kyushu, where stonewares were manufactured at various sites from *c.* 1600 (*see also* JAPAN, §VIII, 6(ii)).

The first potter to make Agano ware was the Korean master Chon'gye (Jap. Sonkai; 1576–1654). Deported to Kyushu during one of the Japanese invasions of Korea in 1592 and 1597, he entered the service of Hosokawa Tadaoki (1563–1645), the newly appointed governor of Buzen. On the completion of Tadaoki's fortress at Kokura (now Kitakyushu), Chon'gye built the Saienba kiln, probably within the castle precincts. A site thought to be Saienba was found beneath Myōkōji, the temple that replaced the castle in 1679, and excavations took place between 1979 and 1983. Sherds of both tea ceremony and everyday wares have been found there; they have transparent glazes made with a wood-ash flux, opaque glazes made with a straw-ash flux or brown-black glazes pigmented with iron oxide. Inscriptions on surviving pieces and entries in contemporary diaries indicate that these early products were also called Buzen or Kokura ware. After a few years the Saienba kiln closed, and Chon'gye, apparently still in Tadaoki's service, moved to the much larger Kamanokuchi kiln in the town of Akaike. Excavations there in 1955 uncovered thin-walled, finely finished wares mainly with transparent glazes; similar characteristics are found in early examples of Karatsu, Takatori and Hagi wares. Roughly coeval with the Kamanokuchi kiln was the Iwaya Kōrai kiln, a private enterprise that operated in nearby Hōjō. It made thick-walled vessels coated with an opaque glaze that is suggestive of north Korean origins. Both kilns produced wares for the tea ceremony and for utilitarian purposes.

A new phase began *c.* 1624, when the Saruyama Hongama kiln was opened, also in Akaike. It is believed to have been founded by Chon'gye and his assistants, who abandoned the Kamanokuchi kiln to a group of potters from the recently closed Takatori-ware kiln at Uchigaiso in the next valley. Initially the Saruyama Hongama kiln maintained the elegant standards of Kamanokuchi, but it ceased to make fine tea wares after 1632, when Hosokawa Tadaoki was made governor of the adjacent province of Higo (now part of Kumamoto Prefecture), and Chon'gye followed him there. Production of Agano wares continued for 250 years under the Ogasawara family, who succeeded the Hosokawa as lords of Buzen. In response to intense competition from the porcelain kilns at Arita, the Agano potters sought greater diversity and technical finesse. In the late 18th century Totoki Hoshō, a descendant of Chon'gye who worked at the Saruyama kiln, was sent to Kyoto and Edo to study the latest techniques, and the use of polychrome glazes and virtuoso textural effects dates from that time. Agano declined after the dissolution of the feudal domains in 1868, but production of wares in the Old Agano style was revived in the 20th century.

BIBLIOGRAPHY

G. Kōzuru: *Agano. Takatori* [Agano and Takatori] (1975), ii of *Nihon no yakimono* [Famous ceramics of Japan] (Tokyo, 1975–6, Eng. trans., 1981–4)
Nihon no tōji [Japanese ceramics] (exh. cat., ed. Y. Yoshiaki; Tokyo, N. Mus., 1985)

RICHARD L. WILSON

Agar, Eileen (*b* Buenos Aires, 1 Dec 1904; *d* London, 17 November 1991). English painter of Argentine birth. She arrived in England in 1906; in 1924 she studied with Leon Underwood (1890–1975), and she attended the Slade School of Fine Art, London, from 1925 to 1926; she also studied art in Paris from 1928 to 1930. She was a member of the LONDON GROUP from 1933, and her work was selected by Roland Penrose and Herbert Read for the International Surrealist Exhibition at the New Burlington Galleries, London, in 1936. Agar exhibited with the Surrealists both in England and abroad. From 1936 she experimented with automatic techniques and new materials, taking photographs and making collages and objects, for example *The Angel of Anarchy* (fabric over plaster and mixed media, 1936–40; London, Tate). By the 1960s she was producing Tachist paintings with Surrealist elements.

BIBLIOGRAPHY

Eileen Agar: Retrospective Exhibition (exh. cat., London, Commonwealth Inst., 1971)
W. Chadwick: *Women Artists and the Surrealist Movement* (London, 1985)

WHITNEY CHADWICK

Agar, Jacques d' (*b* Paris, 1640; *d* Copenhagen, 16 Nov 1715). French painter, also active in Denmark and England. He was probably a pupil of Jacob Ferdinand Voet (1639–?1700) and practised chiefly as a portrait painter. Having failed with his first submission to the Académie Royale in 1672, he was received (*reçu*) as a member in 1675 on submission of portraits of the sculptors *François Girardon* (untraced) and *Michel Anguier* (Versailles, Château). As a Protestant, he fled to London (where he became a denizen in October 1681) and as a result was expelled from the Académie Royale in 1682. He may also have travelled to the Netherlands but by 1685 had settled in Copenhagen, where he became chief court painter to Christian V (*reg* 1670–99) and then to Frederick IV (*reg* 1699–1730). Most of his portraits for the Danish court were destroyed in 1794, in the fire at Christianborg Castle. In 1699 he provided painted decorations for the funeral of Christian V, and between 1701 and 1706 he contributed several history paintings (destr.) to the decoration of Frederiksborg Castle. Among his authenticated surviving works are the portraits of *Jean-Baptiste Tavernier* (Copenhagen, Stat. Mus. Kst), *Christian V* (Copenhagen, Rosenborg Slot) and a *Self-portrait* (1693; Florence, Uffizi). His son Charles d'Agar (1669–1723) accompanied him to both London and Copenhagen; he settled in London in 1691, becoming a fashionable portrait painter. His few certain works, such as the full-length portrait of *Lord George Douglas as a Child* (1709; Duke of Buccleuch, priv. col.), are in the style of Michael Dahl. The works of father and son are often confused.

BIBLIOGRAPHY

Waterhouse: *16th & 17th C., 18th C.*
P. Lespinasse: 'Jacques d'Agar, portraitiste des rois de Danemark', *Gaz. B.-A.*, n. s. 5, xv (1927), pp. 241–9

D. BRÊME

Agar-Ellis, George James Welbore, 1st Baron Dover. *See* ELLIS, (2).

Agasse, Jacques-Laurent (*b* Geneva, 24 March 1767; *d* London, 27 Dec 1849). English painter of Swiss birth. Born into a wealthy and politically influential Huguenot family, Agasse spent his early childhood at the country estate of Crévin, where he may have developed the interest in animals and natural history that was to guide his later career as an artist in England. Agasse trained first at the Ecole du Colibri in Geneva and subsequently in Paris under Jacques-Louis David (beginning in 1787) and possibly under Horace Vernet. His early artistic output consisted chiefly of unpretentious silhouette 'cut-outs' in the style of Jean-Daniel Huber. At this time he also undertook a serious study of dissection and veterinary science.

Jacques-Laurent Agasse: *Nubian Giraffe*, oil on canvas, 1.27×1.01 m, *c.* 1827 (Windsor Castle, Berks, Royal Collection.)

Agasse first visited England in his early 20s, at the invitation of the Hon. George Pitt, 1st Baron Rivers (?1722–1803), whom he had met in either Geneva or Paris *c.* 1790. He stayed briefly at Rivers's home, Stratfield Saye, Hants, before returning to Europe for another decade, then emigrated permanently to England in 1800. He painted several animal and hunting scenes, for example *Lord Rivers's Stud-farm at Stratfield Saye* (1807; New Haven, CT, Yale Cent. Brit. A.), for Rivers and his sporting colleagues, who became his only steady source of patronage. A group of racing subjects was engraved from 1803 to 1807 by arrangement with Charles Turner, but Agasse's commercial contacts were generally few, and his business acumen was notably poor.

Despite exhibiting occasionally at the Royal Academy and British Institution, Agasse played little part in London's artistic society, preferring the company of, and sometimes collaborating with, fellow émigrés such as Adam-Wolfgang Töpffer. In his early years in London he stayed at the house of John James and Alfred Edward Chalon. Between 1810 and 1835 he was the permanent guest of George Booth, whose children modelled for some of his rural genre scenes. Although he produced several coaching, market and London street scenes (as well as a group of Thames views), and even designs for illuminations in Hyde Park, his strongest personal interest was in natural history. He frequented London's menageries, especially Polito's in the Strand, where he seems to have formed a tentative friendship with its owner, Edward Cross. In *Nubian Giraffe* (*c.* 1827; Brit. Royal Col.; see fig.), one of two pictures of exotic animals commissioned by George IV, Cross is thought to be portrayed in the group of figures standing prominently in the right foreground. Agasse's style, based on a detailed study of nature, bears some affinity to the work of George Stubbs. The combination of committed naturalism and an overall artificiality in the compositions of both artists received neither critical acclaim nor lucrative patronage.

A commission *c.* 1821 from the Royal College of Surgeons for a series of portrayals of wild animals suggests that there was some market for Agasse's art, but for these he was paid at the rate of little more than £10 per picture. Many of his studies of flowers, birds and animals were painted without particular buyers in mind, and they did not sell easily. His reputedly haughty demeanour and intransigent personality cannot have helped relations with patrons; he died poor and unrecognized. Most of his paintings can be closely dated from the record book that he maintained throughout his career in England.

UNPUBLISHED SOURCES

Geneva, Mus. A. & Hist. [*Le Livre de raison*; MS. record book]

BIBLIOGRAPHY

D. Baud-Bovy: *Peintres genevois du XVIII et du XIXe siècle* (Geneva, 1903–4)

C. Hardy: *La Vie et l'oeuvre de Jacques-Laurent Agasse* (Geneva, 1921)

Jacques-Laurent Agasse, 1767–1849, ou la séduction de l'Angleterre (exh. cat., Geneva, Mus. A. & Hist.; London, Tate; 1988–9)

STEPHEN DEUCHAR

Agatharchos (*fl* late 5th century BC). Greek painter. He was the son of Eudemos and came originally from Samos, but worked in Athens; none of his work survives. He was said to be self-taught. Vitruvius (*On Architecture* VII.praef.11) claimed that Agatharchos was the first artist to paint a stage set on wooden panels. This was for a tragedy by Aeschylus (525/4–456 BC), although it may have been a revival presented later in the 5th century BC. Vitruvius added that he wrote a commentary discussing the theoretical basis of his painted scenery and that the philosophers Demokritos (late 5th century BC) and Anaxagoras (*c.* 500–428 BC) followed him in exploring theories of perspective. It is unlikely that Agatharchos organized his compositions around a single vanishing point. More probably, individual objects and buildings or groups of buildings were depicted receding towards separate vanishing points. If Agatharchos' experiments in perspective were confined to stage scenery, they would have been limited to architectural backgrounds, before which the actor moved. Aristotle (384–322 BC), however, credited the tragedian Sophocles (*c.* 496–406 BC) with the introduction of painted scenery (*Poetics* 1449a.18–19), which creates some uncertainty about the accuracy of Vitruvius' account.

Two anecdotes about Agatharchos place him in the late 5th century BC. One, recounted by Plutarch (*Pericles* xiii.2), tells how Agatharchos boasted to his great contemporary Zeuxis of the speed and facility with which he painted, to which Zeuxis retorted that his own work both took, and lasted, a long time. Two versions exist of the other (Plutarch: *Alkibiades* xvi.4, and Pseudo-Andokides: *Against Alkibiades* xvii). Plutarch alleges that the brilliant and audacious Athenian Alkibiades (*c.* 450–404 BC) imprisoned Agatharchos in his house until he had decorated it with paintings. Alkibiades then dismissed the artist with a generous gift. Pseudo-Andokides writes that Agatharchos was confined despite his plea to finish other commissions. In the fourth month of his imprisonment, he fled. This story is the earliest extant evidence of wall paintings in private houses in Greece. The only contemporary wall paintings known to have been executed in a similar context were those by Zeuxis in the palace of Archelaos, King of Macedon (*c.* 413–399 BC), and the inference in the speech of Pseudo-Andokides was that Alkibiades had behaved in a manner more appropriate to a foreign monarch than to a citizen of democratic Athens. No ancient writer lists Agatharchos' works or describes his style.

BIBLIOGRAPHY

J. Overbeck: *Die antiken Schriftquellen zur Geschichte der bildenden Künste bei den Griechen* (Leipzig, 1868/*R* Hildesheim, 1959), nos 1118–25

C. HOBEY-HAMSHER

Ageladas [Hageladas] (*fl c.* 520–*c.* 450 BC). Greek sculptor. Said to be the teacher of Polykleitos, Myron and Pheidias, he was a bronze sculptor from Argos, active in the Late Archaic and Early Classical periods. His early works were statues at Olympia for victors of 520 BC, 516 BC and 507 BC. His monument at Delphi depicting captive Massapian women and horses may belong to the second quarter of the 5th century BC. The *Zeus Ithomatas* for the Messenians at Naupaktos was probably made in the 450s BC. Problematic is the date of his *Herakles Alexikakos* in Athens, said to be a dedication after the plague in the 420s BC. That has led to speculation on the existence of a second Ageladas. Unknown are the dates of his *Zeus Pais* and *Youthful Herakles* at Aigion. The statues for the Messenians and at Aigion seem to have been under life-size since they were easily transportable. A sense of their appearance is given by coins that show statues with stances like that of the *Zeus/Poseidon* from Cape Artemision (*see* GREECE, ANCIENT, fig. 43), which is sometimes connected with Ageladas. The Ludovisi *Herakles* herm has been proposed as a copy of the *Herakles Alexikakos*, but that is unlikely.

BIBLIOGRAPHY

Pauly–Wissowa: 'Hageladas'

A. Frickenhaus: 'Hageladas', *Jb. Dt. Archäol. Inst.*, xxvi (1911), pp. 24–34

C. A. Robinson jr: 'The Zeus Ithomatas of Ageladas', *Amer. J. Archaeol.*, xlix (1945), pp. 121–7

W. H. Gross: 'Kultbilder, Blitzschwinger und Hageladas', *Mitt. Dt. Archäol. Inst.: Röm. Abt.*, lxx (1963), pp. 13–19

H. von Heintze: 'Herakles Alexikakos', *Mitt. Dt. Archäol. Inst.: Röm. Abt.*, lxxii (1965), pp. 14–40

S. Woodford: 'Herakles Alexikakos Reviewed', *Amer. J. Archaeol.*, lxxx (1976), pp. 291–4

CHARLES M. EDWARDS

Agelii, John Gustaf. *See* AGUÉLI, IVAN.

Agha, Zubeida (*b* Faisalabad, 1922). Pakistani painter. She introduced non-traditional pictorial imagery in Pakistan and initiated a new era in painting. She completed a degree in political science at Kinnaird College, Lahore. Her introverted disposition and concentrated study of philosophy formed the background against which her abstract 'idea' paintings emerged. At the Lahore School of Fine Art (1945), Agha began a study of Western art. In addition to copying Old Masters, she came into contact with contemporary Indian painting and folk art.

Mario Perlinglieri, an Italian painter who had studied with Picasso, introduced Agha to abstraction in 1946. Unlike the majority of Pakistani artists in the 1950s and 1960s, who emulated Cubism (*see* CUBISM, §1), Agha evolved a personal style synthesizing East and West. Four years in London and Paris (1950–53) brought her face to face with modern European art. Agha's predilection for discordant shapes, tension, and mysterious and irrational juxtapositions link her art to that of Marc Chagall and Edvard Munch. Her work is in the collections of the Karachi Arts Council and the Pakistan National Council of Arts (both Islamabad), as well as in numerous private collections. An intensely private and cerebral individual, she was awarded the President's Medal for Pride of Performance in 1965.

See also PAKISTAN, §III.

BIBLIOGRAPHY

A. A. Hamid: 'Zubeida Agha', *Arts and the Islamic World*, ii/4 (Winter 1984–5), pp. 59–64

S. Hashmi: 'Beyond the Canvas', *The Star* (21 Feb 1985), p. iv

Paintings from Pakistan (Islamabad, 1988)

A. ul-Hasan: *Painting in Pakistan* (Lahore, 1991)

M. Nesom-Sirhandi: *Contemporary Painting in Pakistan* (Lahore, 1992)

MARCELLA NESOM-SIRHANDI

Aghlabid. Islamic dynasty that governed Tunisia, Algeria and Sicily from AD 800 to 909. The province of Ifriqiya, roughly corresponding to modern Tunisia, had been administered from KAIROUAN since the Islamic conquest in the 7th century by governors named by the Umayyad and Abbasid caliphs. The caliph authorized one of these governors, Ibrahim ibn al-Aghlab (*reg* 800–12), to appoint his own successor, thereby engendering a dynasty that maintained its position by paying the caliph an annual tribute. Ibrahim immediately built a satellite city, which he named al-ʿAbbasiyya, with a palace, known as the Qasr al-Abyad, and a congregational mosque. His sons ʿAbdallah I (*reg* 812–17) and Ziyadat Allah I (*reg* 817–38) continued to put down insurrections, and Tunis was temporarily outside the authority of the Aghlabid amir in Kairouan. The conquest of Sicily (827) was conducted like a holy war against the Byzantines, and the troops, encouraged by indoctrination in fortified convents (Arab. *ribāṭ*), were led by a wise man (*faqih*) of proverbial piety. The Great Mosque of Kairouan, founded *c.* 670 and rebuilt many times, was demolished in 836 and rebuilt in its present form (*see* ISLAMIC ART, §II, 4(iii)). The next rulers, Abu ʿIqal (*reg* 838–41) and Muhammad I (*reg* 841–56), had relatively peaceful reigns. The small mosque of Bu Fatata (838–41) was built at SOUSSE, and the congregational mosques of Sfax (*c.* 849) and Sousse (850–51) were erected.

The dynasty reached its apogee under Abu Ibrahim Ahmad (*reg* AD 856–63) when the Great Mosque of Kairouan was embellished: galleries were added around the court, the prayer-hall was given a splendid MINBAR of small carved panels of teak (*see* ISLAMIC ART, §VII, 1(iii)) and the mihrab received a magnificent covering of lustre-painted tiles imported from Iraq (*see* ISLAMIC ART, §V, 2(v)). Hydraulic improvements included an aqueduct feeding two enormous polygonal cisterns outside the walls of Kairouan. The Zaytuna Mosque in Tunis, a building that rivalled the Great Mosque of Kairouan, was restored in a campaign that was completed in 864–5. Kairouan became an important religious and cultural centre, attracting scholars and artisans who developed local variants of the ABBASID metropolitan styles. A group of manuscripts of the Koran found in the library of the Great Mosque of Kairouan, of which the earliest are traditionally attributed to the Aghlabid period, include some of the finest examples of early Islamic calligraphy and bookbinding (*see* ISLAMIC ART, §III, 7). Muhammad II (*reg* 863–75), known as Abu'l-Gharaniq, had a passion for hunting, pleasure and drink. Although Ibrahim II (*reg* 875–902) began his reign as an excellent prince, he soon slid into limitless absolutism, unleashing his bloodiest passions even on his own children. Nevertheless this strange ruler had the city of Raqqada built several kilometres from Kairouan, and Arab authors praised this splendid city for the beauty of its palaces, orchards and pools. Ibrahim's successors could not contain the growing strength of the FATIMID troops, and their taking of Kairouan in 909 put an end to the Aghlabid dynasty.

BIBLIOGRAPHY

Enc. Islam/2

K. A. C. Creswell: *Early Muslim Architecture*, 2 vols (Oxford, 1932–40; 2nd edn of vol. i in 2 parts, Oxford, 1969)

G. Marçais and L. Poinssot: *Objets kairouanais: IXe au XIIIe siècle: Relieures, verreries, cuivres et bronzes, bijoux*, 2 vols (Tunis, 1948–52)

M. Solignac: 'Recherches sur les installations hydrauliques de Kairouan et des steppes tunisiennes du VIIe au XIe siècle (J. C.)', *An. Inst. Etud. Orient. U. Alger*, x (1952), pp. 5–273 and xi (1953), pp. 60–170

G. Marçais: *L'Architecture musulmane d'occident* (Paris, 1954), pp. 1–54

A. Lézine: *Le Ribat de Sousse* (Tunis, 1956)

G. Marçais and L. Golvin: *La Grande Mosquée de Sfax* (Tunis, 1960)

A. Lézine: *Architecture de l'Ifriqiya: Recherches sur les monuments aghlabides* (Paris, 1966)

M. Talbi: *L'Emirat aghlabide, 184–296/800–909* (Paris, 1966)

L. Golvin: 'Le Mihrab de Kairouan', *Kst Orients*, v (1968), pp. 1–38

G. Kircher: 'Die Moschee des Muhammad b. Hairun ("Drei-Tore-Moschee") in Qairawân, Tunesien', *Mitt. Dt. Archäol. Inst.: Abt. Kairo*, xxvi (1970), pp. 141–68

L. Golvin: *Essai sur l'architecture religieuse musulmane*, iii (Paris, 1974), pp. 123–276

J. Bloom: *Minaret: Symbol of Islam* (Oxford, 1989), pp. 86–98

LUCIEN GOLVIN

Aght'amar. Island on Lake Van in south-eastern Turkey. It is the site of the church of the Holy Cross (Sourb Khatch), which was built in AD 915–21 as the palatine church of the Ardsruni king Gagik (*reg* 908–*c.* 943) of the Armenian kingdom of Vaspurakan. The church is of singular importance for the history of medieval art because of the form, content and iconography of its sculptural reliefs and wall paintings. It is the oldest surviving church almost entirely covered on the exterior with figural relief in stone (*see* ARMENIA, fig. 7).

According to information in a text of the late 18th century or early 19th and an inscription on the building's façade now hidden by a *gavit'* or assembly hall (1793; *see* ARMENIA, §II), the church was built by the King's

Armenian architect Manuel (Lalayan, 1910). An anonymous continuator of the 10th-century *History of the House of the Ardsrunik* described Gagik's other building activities on the island as including a harbour, citadel, towered walls, gardens and a palace (all destr.). He also reports that Manuel entrusted the sculptural programme to a monk.

In plan and construction, the church follows the classic 4th–7th-century Armenian tradition of building domed churches entirely in stone. Its plan (interior 14.8×11.5 m) is a variant of that of the Armenian churches of Avan (6th century) and of St Hrip'sime (618; *see* ĒDJMIADZIN), since it has four vaulted, axial niches and four smaller, diagonal niches and lacks only the four corner chambers of the earlier churches. The dome rests on a 16-sided drum and is covered by a conical roof (rest. 1292–6) that gives it the characteristic silhouette of Armenian churches; it rises 20.4 m above the ground. An unusual feature was the south façade's stone staircase (destr.), richly carved with figural reliefs, which once led to the royal gallery on the interior.

The encyclopedic sculptural programme includes themes and motifs drawn from the classic period of Armenian art and architectural sculpture as well as from Early Christian, Byzantine, Iranian, Sasanian and Islamic art. It consists essentially of four horizontal bands encircling the building at different levels. The three upper zones include an Evangelist carved under each gable, animals (real and mythical), hunting, harvesting and feasting scenes within a vine scroll, the bust of *Adam* and (on the east wall) a *Feasting Prince.* The main band includes Old Testament kings and prophets and *Adam and Eve*; deliverance scenes such as *David and Goliath* and *Jonah and the Whale* (south façade); *Daniel and the Three Hebrews* (north façade); *Christ*, the *Virgin and Child*, *St John the Baptist*, three cavalier saints and Armenian personages such as *St Grigor the Illuminator* (239–325/6), *King Gagik Presenting a Model of the Church to Christ* and two Ardsruni ancestors who were martyred in 786.

The church of the Holy Cross is also the oldest church in the Christian East (aside from 10th-century Cappadocian churches) in which the interior wall paintings have survived almost in their entirety. Its *Genesis* cycle, on the upper portion of the drum, is unique in a church of this period in either East or West, with certain features attributed by Mathews to Armenian traditions and non-scriptural sources. The lower walls have three horizontal zones of painting, with twenty-five scenes from the *Life of Christ* that incorporate modifications in accordance with Armenian church ritual; the eastern apse shows *Christ and the Apostles.*

BIBLIOGRAPHY

H. F. B. Lynch: *Armenia: Travels and Studies*, ii (London, 1901/*R* Beirut, 1967)

E. Lalayan: 'The Famous Monasteries of Vaspurakan: The Monastery of the Holy Cross at Aght'amar', *Azgagrakan Handes*, xii (1910), p. 208 [in Armen.]

J. Strzygowski: *Die Baukunst der Armenier und Europa*, i (Vienna, 1918)

A. Sakisian: 'Notes on the Sculpture of the Church of Akhthamar', *A. Bull.*, xv (1943), pp. 346–57

T'. T'ōramanyan: *Nyut er haykakan Tjartarapetut'yan patmut'yan* [Materials for the history of Armenian architecture], ii (Yerevan, 1948)

K. Otto-Dorn: 'Turkisch-Islamisches Bildgut in den Figurenreliefs von Achtamar', *Anatolia*, vi (1961), pp. 99–167

M. Ipsiroglu: *Die Kirche von Achtamar: Bauplastik im Leben des Lichtes* (Berlin, 1963)

S. Der Nersessian: *Aght'amar, Church of the Holy Cross* (Cambridge, 1965)

S. Der Nersessian and H. Vahramian: *Aght'amar* (Milan, 1974)

K. Maksoudian, ed.: *Armenian Architecture* (Zug, 1981–), i [in microfiche; incl. text by L. Der Manuelian and photographs of Aght'amar]

T. F. Mathews: 'The Genesis Frescoes of Alt'amar', *Rev. Etud. Armén.*, n. s., xvi (1982), pp. 245–57, 260–61

S. Mnac'akanyan: *Aght'amar Church of the Holy Cross, 915–921* (Finland, 1986)

C. L. Waltz: *Sources and Iconography of the Figural Sculpture of the Church of the Holy Cross at Aght'amar* (diss., Columbus, OH State U., 1986)

J.-M. Thierry and P. Donabedian: *Les Arts arméniens* (Paris, 1987; Eng. trans., New York, 1989)

P. Cuneo: *Architettura armena dal quarto al diciannovesimo secolo* (Rome, 1988)

LUCY DER MANUELIAN

Aghurmi. *See under* SIWA OASIS.

Agighiol. Iron Age burial mound in Dobrogea, Romania. It is important for a collection of figurally decorated, partly gilded silver objects that accompanied a Getic chieftain in death. The Getae had affinities to both Thracians and Scythians (*see* THRACIAN AND DACIAN ART and SCYTHIAN AND SARMATIAN ART). Imported Greek Red-figure pottery dates the burial to *c.* 350 BC, but the precious metalwork shows traces of wear and repair and was probably manufactured in the early 4th century BC.

The body armour recovered includes two sheet-silver greaves with knees in the form of human faces. Although their design is clearly adopted from Greek models with Medusa-head knees, the treatment is distinctively Thracian; one of the faces is covered with bands of gilding, probably representing the tattoos that both Thracians and Scythians are known to have had. One greave depicts a mounted huntsman holding aloft his bow and a seated huntsman drinking from a horn, with a hawk perched on his wrist, a motif clearly derived from representations of Zeus on Greek coinage. Hunting scenes also adorn the neck and cheek guards of an elaborate partly gilded silver helmet—one of only five known—which is remarkable for the dramatic representation of a pair of eyes, bordered by feathers, directly above the eyes of the wearer (*see* THRACIAN AND DACIAN ART, fig. 2). This device is based on apotropaic Greek models, in which the eyes served to avert evil or harm, especially in battle, but the local meaning also appears to relate to 'seeing twice' or having eyes like a hawk.

Two biconical silver drinking cups are decorated with animals of the chase, including wild goats, roe deer and a hawk-like bird grasping a fish in its beak and a hare in its talons; an image of a stag with eight legs is reminiscent of the confusion of paired horses' legs in Greek pottery painting and probably indicated extreme swiftness (*see* THRACIAN AND DACIAN ART, fig. 3).

BIBLIOGRAPHY

D. Berciu: *Arta traco-getica* (Bucharest, 1969)

——: 'Das thraco-getische Fürstengrab von Agighiol in Rumänien', *Ber. Röm.-Ger. Komm.*, l (1969), pp. 209–65

B. Goldman: 'Late Scythian Art in the West: The Detroit Helmet', *Jb. Prähist. Ethnog. Kst*, xxii (1969), pp. 67–75

TIMOTHY TAYLOR

Agitprop [Rus. *agitatsionnaya propaganda*: 'agitational propaganda']. Russian acronym in use shortly after the

Bolshevik Revolution of 1917 for art applied to political and agitational ends. The prefix *agit-* was also applied to objects decorated or designed for this purpose, hence *agitpoyezd* ('agit-train') and *agitparokhod* ('agit-boat'), decorated transport carrying propaganda to the war-front. Agitprop was not a stylistic term; it applied to various forms as many poets, painters and theatre designers became interested in agitational art. They derived new styles and techniques for it from Futurism, Suprematism and Constructivism.

The characteristics of the new art forms were defined as public, political and communal in purpose and execution. The poet Mayakovsky called for artists to abandon their studios and make the streets their brushes and the squares their palettes. Mass spectacular theatre provided vigorous examples of agitprop either by re-enacting recent events or by providing pageants of the progress of Communism. In 1920, for example, the theatre director Nikolay Yevreinov (1879–1953) re-enacted the *Storming of the Winter Palace* in Petrograd with a cast of 10,000 and an audience of 100,000. Concerts of factory sirens were performed in Petrograd (1918) and Moscow (1923). Trams were decorated with geometric designs, as were banners and posters, and, in response to Lenin's call in 1918 for monumental propaganda, temporary monuments to the Revolution and its heroes appeared in city streets. Tatlin's utopian design for his *Monument to the Third International* (1919–20; unexecuted) was a Constructivist response to this call. Printed works too played a role in agitprop, from the hand-stencilled posters of Mayakovsky's 'ROSTA-windows' (posters published by ROSTA, the Russian Telegraphy Agency, and displayed in shop windows; for illustration *see* MAYAKOVSKY, VLADIMIR) to Rodchenko's advertisements for state produce (*see* RODCHENKO, ALEKSANDR, fig. 2). Even sweet wrappers and tableware reflected the aims of agitprop. The state porcelain factory produced a dish elegantly bearing the word *Golod* ('Famine'), Sergey Chekhonin decorated a plate with the slogan *Kto ne s nami, tot protiv nas* ('Who is not with us is against us'), while another by Maria Lebedeva (1895–1942) declared *Kto ne rabotayet, tot ne yest* ('Who does not work does not eat'). Agitational vehicles included the trains *V. I. Lenin No. 1* (1918), *Oktyabr'skaya Revolyutsiya* ('October Revolution', 1919), *Krasnyy Vostok* ('Red East', 1920) and the boat *Krasnaya Zvezda* ('Red Star', 1920).

BIBLIOGRAPHY

I. I. Nikonova and K. G. Glont: *Agitatsionno-massovoye iskusstvo pervykh let Oktyabrya* [Agitational mass art of the first years of the October Revolution] (Moscow, 1971)

S. Bojko: *New Graphic Design in Revolutionary Russia*, trans. R. Strybel and L. Zembrzuski (New York, 1972)

The Avant-Garde in Russia, 1910–1930: New Perspectives (exh. cat., ed. S. Barron and M. Tuchman; Los Angeles, CA, Co. Mus. A., 1980)

JOHN MILNER

Ağlasun. *See* SAGALASSOS.

Aglio. *See* ALLIO.

Agneesens, Edouard(-Joseph-Alexandre) (*b* Brussels, 24 Aug 1842; *d* Uccle, Brabant, 20 Aug 1885). Belgian painter. He initially studied at the Académie Royale des Beaux-Arts in Brussels before entering Jean-François Portaels's studio in the same city, where he was one of Portaels's most important pupils. By the age of 18 he had already painted the mature work *Torso of an Adolescent* (1860; Brussels, Mus. A. Anc.). In 1863 he competed unsuccessfully in the Prix de Rome but he soon established himself with his exhibition of portraits at the Salon of 1866 in Brussels. In 1869 Agneesens went to St Petersburg, where he painted the portraits of various notable figures, including the actor *Vasily Vasil'evich Samoilov*. He returned to Brussels in 1870, where he settled.

In 1872 Agneesens exhibited his portrait of the sculptor *Gaston Marchant* (1868; Brussels, Mus. A. Anc.) in Vienna. The period between 1872 and 1875 was the most productive of his short life, during which time he painted such works as *Mother and Child* (1875; Brussels, Mus. A. Anc.). In 1875 he began to suffer from a nervous illness; during brief periods of lucidity he continued to paint, although there are no works dated after 1880. Most of his paintings consist of isolated figure and portrait works, such as the portrait of *Diane Vernon* (1876; Ghent, Mus. S. Kst.), executed in warm, harmonious colours. His painting marked an important step in the increasing freedom of Belgian art from traditional, academic styles.

BIBLIOGRAPHY

BNB [suppl. ii]

P. Colin: *La Peinture belge depuis 1830* (Brussels, 1930)

E. de Seyn: *Dictionnaire biographique des sciences, des lettres et des arts en Belgique* (Brussels, 1935)

□

Agnew, Tho(ma)s, & Sons, Ltd. English firm of art dealers and print publishers. Thomas Agnew (*b* Liverpool, 16 Dec 1794; *d* Fair Hope, Eccles, Greater Manchester, 24 March 1871) became a partner in the Manchester firm of Vittore Zanetti, framemaker, dealer in works of art and scientific instruments, and print publisher, in 1817. He took sole control of the business in 1835, opening a branch in London in 1860. His greatest achievement was to develop the market for contemporary English pictures among the newly wealthy class of northern businessman. He specialized in genre and modern-life subjects by such artists as William Mulready, William Collins, William Powell Frith, Edwin Landseer and John Phillip, which he sold for high prices. He was motivated by the utilitarian principles of Swedenborgianism, which encouraged him to help found the Salford Museum in 1850 and bequeath pictures to it. He retired in 1861 in favour of his sons, Sir William Agnew (*b* Salford, 20 Oct 1825; *d* London, 31 Oct 1910) and Thomas Agnew (1827–83). William was the most influential art dealer of the Victorian era, a figure of indefatigible energy and self-confidence. His deep purse and unrivalled eye for a profitable picture helped to keep the market for contemporary art buoyant. He paid William Holman Hunt £10,500 for the *Shadow of Death* (1873; Manchester, C.A.G.) and Edward Burne-Jones £15,000 for the *Briar Rose* cycle (1890; Buscot Park, Oxon, NT); these works were successfully exhibited and engraved by Agnew's. He did much to establish the career of Fred Walker.

The firm became a leading and highly successful print publisher, producing portrait mezzotints, commemorative engravings of such events as the Indian Mutiny, chromolithographs of John Leech's humorous sporting scenes, and reproductions of popular Royal Academy pictures;

the most lucrative was the photogravure issued in 1892 after Luke Fildes's *The Doctor* (exh. RA 1891; London, Tate). In a similar vein Agnew's commissioned Roger Fenton to photograph the Crimean War in 1855.

From the 1850s William Agnew was an increasingly dominant presence in the Christie's salerooms. He was one of the first to appreciate the change in fashion in the 1870s among rich collectors towards Old Masters and 18th-century English portraits, forming the collections of Sir Charles Tennant and E. C. Guinness along these lines. He also encouraged the growing internationalization of the art market in the late 19th century. He was a strong supporter of Gladstone and a Liberal MP from 1880 to 1886, and his political opinions were reflected in *Punch*, of which he was a director from 1872. He retired in 1895.

The London branch of the firm was taken over by William's son, Morland (1855–1931), and nephew, Lockett (1858–1918), who, in collaboration with Duveen and Knoedler's in New York, fostered the boom in the prices of Old Masters, particularly in America, which continued until 1931. The firm opened a branch in New York in 1925. Among their most important clients were J. Pierpont Morgan and George Salting. The economic slump of the 1930s almost destroyed the business and it did not regain relative prosperity until the Joseph Neeld sale in 1944. In the 1930s Agnew's began selling contemporary paintings by the London Group and the London Artists' Association, and it continued thereafter to show work by established living artists.

In the post-war years the business, primarily in top quality Old Master and 19th-century British paintings, grew with the revival of the international art market. Agnew's sold outstanding works to most of the major American museums, for example Murillo's *Return of the Prodigal Son* in 1948 to the National Gallery of Art, Washington, DC. The firm developed a particular expertise in Turner, an artist well represented in their watercolour exhibitions held annually since 1867. The firm handled many of Turner's greatest works, including *Dort or Dordrecht: The Dort Packet-boat from Rotterdam Becalmed* (New Haven, CT, Yale Cent. Brit. A.), sold to Paul Mellon in 1966. Evelyn Joll, who joined the firm in 1949, was the co-author of *The Paintings of J. M. W. Turner* (New Haven and London, 1977).

BIBLIOGRAPHY

DNB
A. J. [London], vii (1 Oct 1861), p. 319
G. Agnew: *Agnew's, 1817–1967* (London, 1967)
Great Victorian Pictures (exh. cat. by R. Treble, ACGB, 1978), p. 44
Presents from the Past: Gifts to Greater Manchester Galleries (exh. cat.; Bolton, Mus. & A.G.; Oldham, A.G.; Stockport, War Mem. Bldg A.G.; 1978), pp. 32–5
A Dealer's Record: Agnew's, 1967–81 (London, 1981)
E. Conran: 'Art Collections', *Art and Architecture in Victorian Manchester* (Manchester, 1985), pp. 71–2
Sir Geoffrey Agnew, 1908–1986: Dealer and Connoisseur (exh. cat., London, Thos Agnew & Sons, Ltd, 1988)

OLIVER GARNETT

Agniolo di Cosimo di Mariano Tori Bronzino. *See* BRONZINO, AGNOLO.

Agnolo, Andrea d'. *See* SARTO, ANDREA DEL.

Agnolo, Baccio d'. *See* BACCIO D'AGNOLO.

Agnolo del Moro. *See* ANGOLO DEL MORO, DELL'.

Agnolo di Polo (*b* Florence, 1470; *d* after 1498). Italian sculptor. He belonged to a family of well-known artisans; his grandfather Agnolo di Lippo di Polo had worked as an assistant on the stained glass for the cupola of Florence Cathedral and took the name de' Vetri, sometimes also used by his descendants. Agnolo's father, Polo di Agnolo, made masks and had his workshop on the Ponte Vecchio, Florence, and his brother Domenico engraved precious stones and medals. Vasari said that Agnolo was a pupil of Verrocchio, adding that 'he worked very well in clay and has filled the city with works from his hands'. Given the artist's birth date and that Verrocchio left Florence forever in 1483, Agnolo's apprenticeship would have been very brief; it is probable that he stayed on in the workshop when it was directed by Lorenzo di Credi.

Two of Agnolo's works are documented. On 16 August 1495 the Ufficiali della Sapienza commissioned a statue of *St Mary Magdalene* for the oratory of the Spedale della Morte at Pistoia, restored three years later by the artist himself because it was broken. This has been identified as the *Female Saint* (New York, Met.), which has many stylistic similarities with his only other known documented work, the terracotta bust of the *Redeemer* (Pistoia, Mus. Civ.), commissioned from him in 1498 by the same Ufficiali for their audience-chamber in Pistoia. Several versions of the bust of the *Redeemer* seem to derive either from the Pistoia bust or from a lost prototype by Verrocchio. Not all can be attributed to Agnolo, but a polychrome terracotta bust (Florence, Loggia del Bigallo) is of comparable size to another example (San Miniato, Mus. Dioc. A. Sacra) and perhaps even comes from the same mould; two other terracotta busts of the *Redeemer* (London, V&A; Florence, Mus. Horne) are very close. They are all derived ultimately from the head of Christ in the *Doubting Thomas* group (Florence, Orsanmichele).

Agnolo's documented works are stylistically very close to the work of Lorenzo di Credi, Pietro Torrigiani and of later members of the della Robbia family. He may have had contacts with the Dominicans of S Marco, Florence, where Savonarola was Prior. This might account for the profusion of small terracotta sculptures; the use of this malleable material enabled large numbers of comparatively inexpensive sacred images to be produced for private devotional use. The realistic representation of traditional subjects was designed to inspire intense spiritual fervour. Further works by Agnolo di Polo may yet be recognized among sculpture attributed to the della Robbia workshop.

BIBLIOGRAPHY

Thieme–Becker
G. Vasari: *Vite* (1550, rev. 2/1568); ed. G. Milanesi (1878–85), iii, pp. 371–2
P. Bacci: 'Agnolo di Polo, allievo del Verrocchio', *Riv. A.*, iii (1905), pp. 159–71
J. Mesnil: 'Polo del Maestro Agnolo dei Vetri', *Riv. A.*, iii (1905), pp. 256–8
J. Pope-Hennessy: *Catalogue of Italian Sculpture in the Victoria and Albert Museum*, i (London, 1964), p. 209
F. Rossi: *Il Museo Horne a Firenze* (Milan, 1967), p. 152
J. Goldsmith Phillips: 'A Sculpture by Agnolo di Polo', *Met. Mus. A. Bull.*, xxx/1 (1971), pp. 81–9
H. Kiel: *Il Museo del Bigallo a Firenze* (Milan, 1977), p. 127

La civiltà del cotto: Arte della terracotta nell'area fiorentina dal XV al XX secolo (exh. cat., Impruneta, Mus. Santuario, 1980), p. 102

FRANCESCA PETRUCCI

Agocchi, Giovanni Battista. *See* AGUCCHI, GIOVANNI BATTISTA.

Agocchiari, Barnaba. *See* BARNABA DA MODENA.

Agora. Place of public meeting or market place in an ancient Greek polis or city, the equivalent of a Roman forum (*see* GREECE, ANCIENT, §II, 1(i)(b))

□

Agorakritos (*b* Paros, *fl c.* 450–*c.* 420 BC). Greek sculptor. He was a prominent member of the group of artists led by Pheidias that executed the Periclean building programme on the Athenian Acropolis. Ancient literary sources provide little information on his career, and even this takes the form of later anecdotes, such as the story of his rivalry with Alkamenes in a competition to produce a statue of Aphrodite (Pliny: *Natural History*, XXXVI.iv.17), or has been distorted by the legends surrounding Pheidias, to whom two of his works were wrongly attributed: his statue of the *Enthroned Mother of the Gods* in the metroon in the Athenian Agora (Pausanias: *Guide to Greece*, I.iii.5) and his cult statue of *Nemesis* (*c.* 420 BC; Pausanias: I.xxxiii.3) for the temple at RHAMNOUS. The *Nemesis* was allegedly carved out of a colossal block of Parian marble brought to Marathon in 490 BC by the Persians, who intended to use it for a trophy after defeating the Athenians (Pausanias: I.xxxiii.2). Agorakritos was also credited with bronze statues of *Athena* and *Zeus-Hades* in the Boiotian Temple of Athena Itonia (Pausanias: IX.xxxiv.1).

A single fragment of the *Nemesis* head was discovered at Rhamnous in the late 18th century, and for a long time this formed the only basis for analysis of Agorakritos' style. However, Despinis's investigations in the storerooms of the Athens National Archaeological Museum have revealed a great number of other fragments from later excavations, which show that the statue of *Nemesis* was reproduced in several Roman copies (the best in Copenhagen, Ny Carlsberg Glyp.). Further investigation of the site by Petrakos has produced many fragments from the base of the statue, allowing its reliefs to be reconstructed (Athens, N. Archaeol. Mus.).

The identification of copies of the statue of *Nemesis* has also confirmed earlier theories that a Roman statue from Levadhia (Chaironeia, Archaeol. Mus.) reproduced Agorakritos' *Mother of the Gods.* However, attempts to identify copies of the cult statues in the Temple of Athena Itonia and to attribute to Agorakritos sculptures from the Parthenon have been less successful. Although some of the finest pedimental figures from the Parthenon, such as the group with the reclining *Aphrodite*, have been ascribed to Agorakritos, more research and perhaps other discoveries are needed to confirm this. Agorakritos' style is characterized by close adherence to the Classical ethos, structure and iconography. In his rendering of drapery, however, and his working of the marble he seems to look forward to the Rich Style of the last quarter of the century (*see* GREECE, ANCIENT, §IV, 2(iii)(b)).

BIBLIOGRAPHY

J. Overbeck: *Die antiken Schriftquellen zur Geschichte der bildenden Künste bei den Griechen* (Leipzig, 1868/*R* Hildesheim, 1959), nos 829–43

G. I. Despinis: *Symbole ste melete tou ergou tou Agorakritou* [Contribution to the study of the work of Agorakritos] (Athens, 1971)

V. Petrakos: 'Problemata tes bases tou agalmatos tes Nemeseos' [Problems of the base of the statue of Nemesis], *Archaische und klassische griechische Plastik: Akten des internationalen Kolloquiums: Athen, 1985*, pp. 89–107

A. DELIVORRIAS

Agostini, Angelo (*b* Vercelli, Italy, 1843; *d* Rio de Janeiro, 1910). Brazilian caricaturist and painter. He came to Brazil in 1859, having already acquired some knowledge of painting in Paris. He settled initially in São Paulo, where he at once started to publish caricatures attacking black slavery. There, in 1864, he was one of the founders of the comic newspaper *O Diabo Coxo*. His abolitionist spirit continued after he moved to Rio de Janeiro, through his frequent collaboration in periodicals such as *A Vida Fluminense*, *O Mosquito*, *Don Quixote* and *O Malho*. In the *Revista Ilustrada* he began to publish in 1884 the first long-running strip cartoon in Brazil, the adventures of Zé Caipora, a sertão (hinterland) character, depicting a lesser-known side of Brazil. As a painter he specialized in landscapes but also produced portraits with the same fervour that fired his enjoyable and impassioned satirical drawings, for example *Portrait of the Writer Joaquin Augusto Ribeiro de Sousa* (*c.* 1890; Rio de Janeiro, Mus. Hist. N.).

BIBLIOGRAPHY

L. Gonzaga Duque: *A arte brasileira* (Rio de Janeiro, 1888)

H. Lima: *História da caricatura no Brasil* (Rio de Janeiro, 1963)

Art of Latin America since Independence (exh. cat. by S. L. Catlin and T. Grieder, New Haven, CT, Yale U. A.G.; Austin, U. TX, A. Mus.; San Francisco, CA, Mus. A.; La Jolla, CA, A. Cent.; 1966)

J. L. Werneck da Silva: 'Angelo Agostini: 80 anos depois', *Cadernos Brasileiros*, 47 (1968)

ROBERTO PONTUAL

Agostino dei Musi. *See* MUSI, AGOSTINO DEI.

Agostino (di Antonio) di Duccio (*b* Florence, 1418; *d* ?Perugia, after 1481). Italian sculptor and architect. His father, Antonio di Duccio, a weaver, reported in his *catasto* (land registry declaration) of 1427 that Agostino was eight years old. On his father's death, the young Agostino enrolled in the company of the mercenary Giovanni da Tolentino, with whom he was serving in 1433. He may be the apprentice named Agostino who was working on the external pulpit for Prato Cathedral on 14 May 1437; this would suggest that he trained in the circle of Michelozzo and Donatello. What may be his earliest known work, datable *c.* 1440 (Rosenauer, 1977), is a marble statue of the *Virgin and Child* (Florence, S Maria del Carmine), influenced by Michelozzo.

Agostino's first certain work, commissioned by Ludovico Forni for Modena Cathedral, was an antependium that included four relief scenes from the *Life of St Geminian* (1442; dismembered, statue of *St Geminian* in Modena Cathedral sacristy, reliefs built into the cathedral's outer wall). The scenes are carved in high relief, the figures arranged in a stiff frieze formation. In 1446 he was in Venice, having apparently fled there after he and his brothers Costantino and Cosimo were accused in 1441 of stealing silver from the Compagnia dell'Osservanza in SS

Annunziata, Florence. Agostino may have worked in the Venice studio of Bartolomeo Bon (*d* 1529), whose influence is apparent in the statue attributed to him (Brunetti, 1950) of *St Louis of Toulouse* (Venice, S Alvise).

From 1449 to 1456 Agostino was in Rimini, employed by Sigismondo Pandolfo Malatesta on the decoration of the interior of the church of S Francesco (transformed and remodelled by Leon Battista Alberti and Matteo de' Pasti; *see* RIMINI, §1(ii)). There Agostino supervised a large group of sculptors working on the most richly sculptured Renaissance building in Italy. He was probably personally responsible for all the major figural carving in the six chapels that were built in the church (*see* RIMINI, fig. 4). In these he developed an individual, gothicizing linear style of great intensity, revealing a knowledge of Donatello's work and perhaps reflecting the use of line in paintings by Andrea del Castagno and Filippo Lippi. In 1454 Agostino also worked in Cesena, carving the elephant relief over the entrance to the Biblioteca Malatestiana, and at Forlì, making a tabernacle with a relief of the *Trinity* and a statue of the *Virgin and Child* on the façade for the sanctuary of the Madonna at Fornò. In 1456 his brother, Ottaviano di Antonio di Duccio (*b* 1422; *d* after 1478), a sculptor and goldsmith, joined him as an assistant at S Francesco, Rimini. (Ottaviano's only certain work is the tomb of *Antonio Malatesta* (1467) in Cesena Cathedral.)

Between 1457 and 1461 Agostino was working on the façade of the oratory of S Bernardino, Perugia. Although the architectural framework of the façade recalls Alberti's design for S Francesco, the sculpture, originally highly polychromed, is rich and intricate, emphasizing line and movement. Above a double door framed by reliefs of angels, a high tympanum contains a relief of *St Bernardino in Glory. God the Father* appears in the upper pediment, and four aedicules contain statues. Agostino also carved a large stone and terracotta dossal (dismantled and reconstituted in 1484) for the altar of S Lorenzo, in the church of S Domenico, Perugia, for the heirs of Lorenzo di Ser Giovanni. Between December 1462 and February 1463 Agostino was in Bologna, where he presented a wooden model (untraced) for the façade of S Petronio.

In 1463 Agostino returned to Florence and enrolled in the Arte dei Maestri di Pietra e Legname (the sculptors' guild). In 1463–4, for the Opere del Duomo, he made a colossal figure (untraced) to be placed in the cathedral tribune; they commissioned a second colossal statue from him in 1464, but this was abandoned, the marble block later being used by Michelangelo for his *David* (Florence, Accad.). For SS Annunziata he made a terracotta *Resurrection* (1470; untraced). Also belonging to this Florentine period are the marble relief of the *Virgin and Child with Angels* (Florence, Bargello), originally in the Carmine, Florence, and a tabernacle with *Two Angels Holding Back a Curtain* (Florence, Bargello) from the church of the Ognissanti, Florence; both works are carved in an intricate, linear style. The highly wrought marble relief of the *Virgin and Child*, known as the d'Aubervilliers *Madonna* (Paris, Louvre), and the terracotta statue of the *Angel of the Annunciation* (Budapest, Mus. F.A.) would seem to be of the same date.

In 1473 Agostino returned to Perugia as architect in charge of the design and execution of the Porta S Pietro, left unfinished at the time of his death. He also executed the altar of the *Pietà* (1473; destr. 1625; fragments Perugia, G. N. Umbria) for Perugia Cathedral, commissioned by the hospital of the Misericordia, and the marble low reliefs of *Christ Taking Leave of his Mother* (New York, Met.) and the *Virgin and Child* (*c.* 1473; Washington, DC, N.G.A.; see fig.). Among his other contemporary commissions, from small towns in Umbria and Lazio, are two *Archangels* for Acquapendente Cathedral (Viterbo) and two wall tombs, both originally in S Francesco, Amelia (Terni), those of *Giovanni Geraldini, Bishop of Catanzaro* (1476; Amelia Cathedral) and of *Matteo and Elisabetta Geraldini* (1477; *in situ*). Brunetti (1965) attributed the tomb slab of *Bishop Ruggero Mandosi* (Amelia Cathedral) to Agostino, which would imply that he was still alive in 1484, the year of the Bishop's death; however Agostino was last documented in 1481 working on the Porta S Pietro. He died before 1498, when his wife remarried.

BIBLIOGRAPHY

DBI; Thieme–Becker

A. Rossi: 'Prospetto cronologico della vita e delle opere di Agostino d'Antonio, scultore fiorentino, con la storia e documenti di quelle da lui fatte in Perugia', *G. Erud. A.*, iv (1875), pp. 3–25, 33–50, 76–83, 117–22, 141–52, 179–84, 202–11, 241–9, 263–75

A. Venturi: *Storia* (1901–40), vi, pp. 388–406, 1024

A. Pointner: *Agostino d'Antonio di Duccio* (Strasbourg, 1909)

A. Colasanti: 'La tomba di *Giovanni Geraldini*, opera di Agostino di Duccio', *Rass. A.*, iii (1916), pp. 38–42

C. Ricci: *Il tempio Malatestiano* (Milan, [1924]), pp. 103–37

C. L. Ragghianti: 'La mostra della scultura italiana antica a Detroit', *Crit. A.*, iii (1938), pp. 178–9

H. W. Janson: 'The Beginnings of Agostino di Duccio', *A. Bull.*, xxix (1942), pp. 330–34

Agostino di Duccio: *Virgin and Child*, marble relief, 720×573 mm, *c.* 1473 (Washington, DC, National Gallery of Art)

R. Mather: 'Documents, Mostly New, Relating to Florentine Painters and Sculptors of the Fifteenth Century', *A. Bull.*, xxx (1948), pp. 20–22
G. Brunetti: 'Il soggiorno veneziano di Agostino di Duccio', *Commentari*, i (1950), pp. 82–4
C. Ravaioli: 'Agostino di Duccio a Rimini', *Stud. Romagn.*, ii (1951), pp. 113–20
C. L. Ragghianti: 'Problemi di Agostino di Duccio', *Crit. A.*, vii (1955), pp. 2–21
C. Brandi: *Il tempio Malatestiano* (Turin, 1956), pp. 29–47
F. Santi: 'L'altare di Agostino di Duccio in S Domenico a Perugia', *Boll. A.*, i–ii (1961), pp. 162–73
A. Zanoli: 'Il tabernacolo di Fornò di Agostino di Duccio', *A. Ant. & Mod.*, no. 13 (1961), pp. 148–50
G. Marchini: *Il tesoro del duomo di Prato* (Milan, 1963), pp. 73–5
J. Pope-Hennessy: *Italian Renaissance Sculpture* (London, 1963, rev. 3/1985), pp. 83–9, 324–8
A. Zanoli: *Perugia: Oratorio di San Bernardino*, Tesori d'Arte Cristiana (Bologna, 1963)
G. Brunetti: 'Sul periodo "Amerino" di Agostino di Duccio', *Commentari*, xvi (1965), pp. 47–55
M. Bacci: *Agostino di Duccio*, I Maestri della Scultura (Milan, 1966)
Sigismondo Pandolfo Malatesta e il suo tempo (exh. cat., ed. F. Arduini and others; Rimini, Pal. Arengo, 1970), pp. 75–95, 125–64
M. Kühlenthal: 'Studien zum Stil und zur Stilentwicklung Agostino di Duccios', *Wien. Jb. Kstgesch.*, xxiv (1971), p. 60
A. Rosenauer: 'Bemerkungen zu einem frühen Werk Agostino di Duccios', *Munchn. Jb. Bild. Kst*, xxviii (1977), pp. 133–52
P. Meldini and P. G. Pasini: *La cappella dei pianeti nel tempio Malatestiano* (Milan, 1983)
P. G. Pasini: *I Malatesti e l'arte* (Milan, 1983)
——: 'Una *Madonna* di Agostino di Duccio a Fornò', *Culture figurative e materiali tra Emilia e Marche: Studi in onore di Mario Zuffa*, ii (Rimini, 1984), pp. 533–5
P. Santi: *Galleria Nazionale dell'Umbria: Dipinti, sculture e oggetti dei secoli XV e XVI*, Perugia, G.N. Umbria cat. (Rome, 1985), pp. 227–34
G. Cuccini: *Agostino di Duccio: Itinerari di un esilio* (Perugia, 1990)
La basilica cattedrale del S Sepolcro di Acquapendente (exh. cat. by P. M. Fossati, Bolsena, 1990)

PIER GIORGIO PASINI

Agostino di Giovanni (*fl* Siena, 1310; *d* before 27 June 1347). Italian sculptor and architect. He is first documented in 1310 in Siena, when he married Lagina di Nese, who was possibly a sister of the sculptor Cellino di Nese of Pistoia. Their two sons Giovanni d'Agostino (*b* Siena, 1311; *d* ?1348) and Domenico both became sculptors and master builders, but Agostino seems to have been the most significant artist in the family.

In his relief sculpture Agostino di Giovanni explored the possibilities opened up by the illusion of depth created in Sienese paintings of the period; Simone Martini appears to have been his main source of inspiration. In 1321 he signed a wooden statue of the *Virgin Annunciate* (Pisa, Mus. N. Civ. S Matteo) with the painter Stefano Acolti, and he may also have made the Arca di S Vittore (*c.* 1325; fragments in Volterra, Mus. Dioc. A. Sacra). In 1330 he and the sculptor–architect Agnolo di Ventura signed the monumental tomb of *Bishop Guido Tarlati* in Arezzo Cathedral, the design of which was based on Tino di Camaino's tomb for *Emperor Henry VII* in Pisa Cathedral; his son Giovanni was also involved in its execution. The second row of reliefs in the cycle of scenes of Tarlati's life, the effigy and the right-hand side of the funeral relief can be regarded as Agostino's work.

In 1331 Agostino di Giovanni and his son Giovanni worked on the chapel of the presbyter Goro (destr.) in the Pieve, Arezzo, and on the Palazzo Pubblico, Siena; in 1332, again with Giovanni, he obtained the commission to build the Ghini Chapel in the Pieve, Arezzo, but only a few fragments survive (London, V&A; Paris, Louvre; Budapest, Mus. F.A.). From 1334 Agostino may also have contributed to the sculptural decoration of the south side of Grosseto Cathedral, again with Giovanni. He was paid by the Sienese civic authorities for work on the citadel of Massa Marittima in 1336. His commission for the tomb of the jurist *Gino de' Sigibuldi* in Pistoia Cathedral was almost certainly obtained with Cellino di Nese's support, and the work was carried out *c.* 1337–9. Between 1339 and 1343 he was working as an architect in Siena, on the Torre del Mangia at the Palazzo Pubblico, on the rear street elevation of the Palazzo Sansedoni and on a water-conduit system for the Fonte Gaia on the Piazza del Campo. It is uncertain whether he was also involved in the execution of the sculptural decoration for the extension to Siena Cathedral, begun in 1340.

The career of Giovanni d'Agostino was closely linked to that of his father, with whom he may have been apprenticed. He made a font for the Pieve, Arezzo, while he was working with Agostino on the chapels in the church (1331–2). Its reliefs, representing scenes from the *Life of St John the Baptist*, are typical examples of his style, in which illusionistic devices like those of painting are employed, and the marble is worked with smooth, slurring strokes. His figures resemble those of Agostino, but they are less elegant. During the following years Giovanni d'Agostino may have sculpted a shrine in Volterra Cathedral, of which only fragments survive (Volterra, Mus. Dioc. A. Sacra). He worked on the Tarlati Chapel in Arezzo Cathedral (1334–5) and carved the font in Montepulciano Cathedral (*c.* 1339). The signed relief of the *Virgin and Child* in S Bernardino, Siena, and the figure of *Christ* in the parish church at Serre di Rapolano were made *c.* 1340. On 23 March 1340, with the express approval of his father, he took over the post of Master of the Works of Siena Cathedral for five years. During this period the huge extension to the Cathedral was begun, and he contributed to its sculptural decoration. His younger brother Domenico is mentioned in documents from 1343, but nothing can be attributed to him with certainty. He succeeded Giovanni as Master of the Works of Siena Cathedral and held this position until the end of the 1360s.

BIBLIOGRAPHY

G. Milanesi: *Documenti per la storia dell'arte senese*, i (Siena, 1854), pp. 132, 200–204, 209, 231–42, 246–7, 251–3
S. Borghesi and L. Banchi: *Nuovi documenti per la storia dell'arte senese* (Siena, 1898), pp. 17–21
A. Venturi: *Storia* (1906), iv, pp. 367–86
W. R. Valentiner: 'Studies in Italian Gothic Plastic Art: ii, Agostino di Giovanni and Agnolo di Ventura', *A. America*, xiii (1924), pp. 3–18
W. Cohn-Goerke: 'Giovanni d'Agostino', *Burl. Mag.*, lxxv (1939), pp. 180–94
E. Carli: 'Sculture inedite di Giovanni d'Agostino', *Boll. A.*, xxxiii (1948), pp. 129–42
J. Pope-Hennessy: *Italian Gothic Sculpture* (London, 1955), pp. 189–90
J. White: *Art and Architecture in Italy, 1250–1400*, Pelican Hist. A. (Harmondsworth, 1966, rev. 2/1987), pp. 287–9
A. Garzelli: *Sculture toscane nel dugento e nel trecento* (Florence, 1969), pp. 77–201
E. Carli: *Scultori senesi* (Milan, 1980), pp. 18–20
A. Bagnoli: 'Giovanni d'Agostino', *Il gotico a Siena* (exh. cat., Siena, Pal. Pubblico, 1982), pp. 209–12
R. Bartalini: *Una bottega di scultori senesi del trecento: Agostino di Giovanni e i figli Giovanni e Domenico* (diss., U. Siena, 1985/6)

——: 'Spazio scolpito: Novità del rilieva "pittorico" di Giovanni d'Agostino', *Prospettiva*, 45 (1986), pp. 19–34
G. Kreytenberg: 'Drei gotische Grabmonumente von Heiligen in Volterra', *Mitt. Ksthist. Inst. Florenz*, xxxiv (1988), pp. 69–100
R. Bartalini: 'La facciata del Battistero di Siena e Giovanni d'Agostino', *Ant. Viva*, xxxviii/2–3 (1989), pp. 57–65
G. Kreytenberg: 'Drei gotische Grabmonumente von Heiligen in Voltera', *Mitt. Ksthist. Inst. Florenz*, xxxiv (1990), pp. 69–100
R. Bartalini: 'Agostino di Giovanni e compagni, I: Una traccia per Agnolo di Ventura', *Prospettiva*, 61 (1991), pp. 21–8
——: 'Agostino di Giovanni e compagni, II: Il possibile Domenico d'Agostino', *Prospettiva*, 61 (1991), pp. 29–37
G. Kreytenberg: 'Der heilige Galganus und der Bildhauer Agostino di Giovanni', *Pantheon*, li (1993), pp. 4–17

G. KREYTENBERG

Agostino Veneziano. *See* MUSI, AGOSTINO DEI.

Agra. City and administrative seat of the district of the same name, in Uttar Pradesh, India. Situated on the Yamuna River in the fertile north Indian heartland, it is 200 km south of Delhi and 55 km south of the ancient city of Mathura. A centre of Mughal culture and government in the 16th and 17th centuries, Agra has numerous monuments of that period, including the famed Taj Mahal (*see* §II, 1 below and fig. 1).

I. History and urban development. II. Buildings.

I. HISTORY AND URBAN DEVELOPMENT. Agra's antiquity is indicated both by a living literary and religious tradition and by occasional archaeological discoveries of ancient pottery, bricks, pillars and sculpture in and around the city. Pilgrimage centres upstream on the Yamuna are associated with the great epic the *Mahābhārata*, and nearby Mathura is one of the ancient sites identified with the worship of Vasudeva Krishna. The name Agra may derive from the ancient Hindu sage Angira. The area was ruled by Rajput chiefs prior to the Muslim conquest (*c.* 1200).

The first known occurrence of the name Agra is in the work of the Persian poet Khwaja Ma'sud ibn Sa'd ibn Salman, who served the Ghaznavid rulers of Afghanistan. He wrote that Mahmud Shah captured the strong fort of Agra after a fierce battle in 1080–81. In the chronicles of the Delhi Sultanate (1206–1526), Agra is first referred to in the reign of 'Ala al-Din (*reg* 1446–51) of the Sayyid dynasty, when it is described as a dependency of Bayana (*see* INDIAN SUBCONTINENT, §III, 6(ii)(b)). Turbulent political conditions in the area led Sultan Sikandar Lodi (*reg* 1489–1517) to establish a strategic presence in Agra. Although Delhi remained a ceremonial centre, for practical purposes Agra became the seat of his government and thus rose to prominence. Ruined Lodi-period mosques and tombs are reputedly scattered around SIKANDRA, a suburb 8 km west of Agra. The Lodi fortress was probably a brick structure located on the site where Akbar built his red sandstone fort (*see* §II, 3 below and fig. 2). Little trace of Lodi-period urban planning is discernible: Agra apparently grew haphazardly like most medieval Indian cities. The river was its lifeline, and principal roads seem to have led to it. Besides its important role in navigation, the Yamuna was the main source of water for residents, as well-water is brackish.

Agra became the centre of Mughal government in 1526 on the victory of Babar (*reg* 1526–30) over Ibrahim Lodi (*reg c.* 1517–26). Babar occupied the Lodi fortress and recorded in his diary that he laid out gardens graced by channels of running water in the city. The gardens known as Ram Bagh on the eastern bank of the Yamuna may have been established by Babar (but were rebuilt by later Mughal rulers). Agra remained the seat of government during the reigns of Humayun (1530–40, 1555–6) and Sher Shah Sur (1540–45), who wrested the throne from him. Both spent much of their time elsewhere, although Sher Shah made Agra the base for his campaign in Malwa, Rajasthan and Punjab. The first city wall was probably built during his reign.

The Mughal emperor Akbar (*reg* 1556–1605), who ruled first from Delhi, made Agra his capital from 1558. It was renamed Akbarabad ('City of Akbar') and became the grandest city of the empire. Many fine structures were erected, including Agra Fort (*see* §II, 3 below) and a new city wall with impressive gateways. Akbar provided the city with a drainage system to control the flow of rainwater (but not intended for sewage). All main roads were paved with red sandstone slabs sloping outward and lined with open drains, also of stone. Water flowed from the open drains to large, underground stone-lined drains, which emptied into two great canals running on the northern and southern perimeters of the city. These carried the water to the river. Residences of nobles were built on both sides of the river, although the main city was on its western bank. The city was extolled by Mughal chroniclers of the period of Akbar and his successors and praised by foreign travellers, who compared it to London, Paris and Constantinople.

While remaining an important political centre, Agra occasionally ceased to be the centre of Mughal government. From 1572 to 1585 Akbar's capital was the new city of FATEHPUR SIKRI. He went from there to LAHORE, returning to reside in Agra only in 1598. Akbar died at Agra in 1605; his tomb is located in the suburb of Sikandra. Jahangir (*reg* 1605–27) resided mainly in Agra until 1613; he spent 1618 there but passed most of the remaining years before his death in 1627 in Lahore and Kashmir. Agra's most outstanding Jahangir-period monument is the tomb of I'timad al-Daula (*see* §II, 2 below and INDIAN SUBCONTINENT, fig. 99), built by Jahangir's queen, Nur Jahan, for her parents. The emperor Shah Jahan (*reg* 1628–58) retained Agra as the capital for the first ten years of his reign. He renovated the fort, demolishing many of Akbar's red sandstone buildings and replacing them with elegant white marble structures (*see* §II, 3 below). He also gave the city its most famous monument, the Taj Mahal. Although in 1638 Shah Jahan transferred the Mughal capital to Delhi, which continued to be the seat of Mughal government throughout the reign of Aurangzeb (*reg* 1658–1707) and the declining decades of Mughal rule, Agra remained strategically important. In the 18th century it was held intermittently by the Jat rulers of Dig and Bharatpur (1761–74) and the Marathas (1784–1803), until it was captured from them by the forces of the British East India Company.

Agra remains a centre of production for many of the specialities encouraged by Mughal patronage, including *darīs* (flat-woven floor coverings), carpets, marble-inlay work, carved red sandstone screens, ivory work, gold jewellery, embroidery and shoes.

II. Buildings.

1. Taj Mahal. 2. Tomb of I'timad al-Daula. 3. Agra Fort.

1. Taj Mahal. Built by the emperor Shah Jahan (*reg* 1628–58) as the tomb for his favourite wife, Arjumand Banu Begum (*d* 1631), the Taj Mahal (1631–48; see fig. 1) is situated on the south bank of the Yamuna River some distance from the city centre. The building's name (literally 'Crown Palace') is a corruption of the queen's title, Mumtaz-i Mahal ('Chosen of the Palace'). She died in Khandesh giving birth to her 14th child, while accompanying the emperor on a military campaign. First entombed at Burhanpur, her body was brought to Agra in 1632, when the Taj Mahal was under construction. The tomb, often described as a monument to love and grief, and its garden setting mark the high point in the evolution of Mughal tomb architecture.

The land selected for the tomb site was in possession of the Rajput rulers of Amer, who served as nobles at the Mughal court. Records show that four mansions (Hindi *havelīs*) were given in exchange for the land to Mirza Raja Jai Singh (*reg* 1622–67). Masons, stonecutters, inlayers and other craftsmen were assembled for the project from various parts of the empire. The tomb was completed at a cost, according to later traditions, of 30 million rupees, when the price of gold was 15 rupees per tola (11.66 g).

The tomb is set within a walled garden designed on the conventional *chār-bāgh* (four-plot) plan with a monumental entrance gateway on the south. The plan is symmetrical; a broad water channel with marble fountains on the north–south axis serves as a reflecting pool for the tomb itself; stone-paved pathways divide and subdivide the quarters. The *chār-bāgh* plan has been significantly modified, however, in the placement of the tomb. While earlier Mughal tombs such as those of Humayun (*see* Delhi, §III, 4), Akbar (*see* Sikandra) and I'timad al-Daula (*see* §2 below) occupy the centre of the garden, in the Taj Mahal complex a raised pond of white marble reached by stairs on all sides is placed at the central point. The tomb is situated at the northern extreme of the complex, overlooking the Yamuna River, with neither tree nor building behind to detract from its outline and with the ever-changing tones of the sky reflected on its white marble surface. On the west of the tomb is a mosque and on the east an identical building often called the *javāb* (Pers.: 'answer'), which was built for symmetry and which served as an assembly hall (*jam'āt khāna*). These structures and the walls and gateways are constructed of red sandstone, which serves as a foil for the whiteness of the tomb. All three structures stand on a red sandstone platform (l. 295.83, w. 111.2, h. 01.22 m (height above garden)).

The tomb is square in plan (57 m on each side), with its angles chamfered, and stands on a white marble plinth (l. 100.05, w. 100.05, h. 5.79 m). The truncated angles are counterbalanced by four minarets at the corners of the plinth. Each of the building's façades is composed of a grand recessed arch (*īwān*) (h. 27.13 m) set within a rectangular frame and flanked by alcoves in two storeys. Double alcoves are also provided at the angles. Each section of the façade is outlined with pilasters inlaid with a chevron pattern in black and yellow marble. Rising above the building line, they form slender pinnacles that are crowned by lotus buds. The spandrels of the arches are inlaid with graceful arabesques in hardstones and the rectangular frame outlined in fine black inlaid calligraphy.

1. Agra, Taj Mahal, 1631–48

The alcoves of the four great recessed arches are decorated with delicate flowers carved in the white marble.

The superstructure is dominated by a grand bulbous dome set on a high drum and culminating in a lotus motif and metal finial. The domes of four open pavilions (*chatrīs*) are of a more traditional hemispherical form. The total height of the tomb is 74.22 m; the height of the dome (including the drum) is 44.4 m. The four minarets (h. 40.2 m), which lead the eye upward, rise higher than the domed pavilions but not the full height of the dome. The minarets are round (with a circumference of 19.51 m at the base) and tapering. They are built in three storeys, separated by balconies supported on brackets, and crowned by domed pavilions (*chatrīs*). The white blocks of marble from which they are constructed are outlined in inlaid black stone.

The tomb's lofty exterior has been translated into a pleasing interior space by the use of a double dome. The octagonal central hall (17.68 m on the diagonal) has a height of 24.38 m. The panels on the dados have beautiful vase and foliage compositions, carved in somewhat higher relief than the flowers of the exterior alcoves. Borders have stylized designs inlaid with hardstones. The cenotaph of Arjumand Banu Begum is placed at the centre with that of Shah Jahan at her side, the only asymmetrical feature of the complex. It would appear that the Emperor (who spent his last years imprisoned by his son) intended to build a separate tomb for himself, although stories of a proposed black Taj on the other side of the Yamuna are dubious. The most delicate and detailed inlay work is that on the borders of a finely carved marble screen surrounding the cenotaphs and on the cenotaphs themselves. The graves are in a chamber below. The hall has rectangular rooms on the sides and octagonal rooms at the corners, all interconnected by passages. The same arrangement is repeated in an upper storey. All sides except the entrance are closed by marble meshlike screens filled with glass admitting a subdued light.

The impressiveness of the Taj Mahal results in part from the quality and texture of the materials used. The fine white marble was quarried at Makrana in Rajasthan, the inlay work includes lapis lazuli, jasper, agate, chalcedony, cornelian, jade, onyx, coral, amethyst and turquoise. One of the building's surprises is the numerous colour contrasts that emerge from a distant impression of whiteness. The precision of the detail in the decoration is exceptionally fine, but there is an abundance of plain surface. The Taj Mahal exemplifies the Mughal development of line and colour to complement the use of space and mass creating a harmonious whole.

See also INDIAN SUBCONTINENT, §III, 7(i)(a).

2. TOMB OF I'TIMAD AL-DAULA. Situated on the eastern bank of the Yamuna River, this tomb (*see* INDIAN SUBCONTINENT, fig. 99) was constructed over a six-year period (1622–8) by Jahangir's queen, Nur Jahan, for her parents. Her father, Mirza Ghiyath Beg, was an Iranian courtier and able administrator who served as Jahangir's minister, and he was given the title I'timad al-Daula ('Pillar of the State'). Buried with him are his wife, Asmat Begum, and other family members.

The tomb occupies the middle of a walled garden laid out on a *chār-bāgh* ('four-plot') plan. Raised stone pathways with shallow water channels in the middle connect the tomb with the entrance gateway on the east and ornamental false gateways on the north, south and west. All of the gateways are constructed of red sandstone; that on the west is an elegant and beautifully decorated two-storey structure overlooking the river. The garden setting is enhanced by such water effects as cascades, lotus ponds and fountains (including ponds and fountains set in the plinth of the tomb).

Relatively small in scale, the tomb is admired most for the delicacy of its decoration. Intricate inlay work in shades of yellow, brown, grey and black contrasts with the smooth whiteness of the marble from which the tomb is constructed. Stones include yellow porphyry, agate, jasper and black marble. Geometrical designs and arabesques are combined with motifs featuring wine cups, vases with flowers and cypress trees.

The form of the building is similar to that used for the tomb of Akbar. Square in plan (measuring 21 m on each side), the tomb has engaged octagonal towers at the corners. These become circular above the roof line and are crowned by domed *chatrīs* (open pavilions). The second storey consists of a square pavilion set in the middle of a roof terrace, which is lined by low screenwork balustrades. The pavilion has an elongated, canopy-like roof culminating in a lotus petal motif topped by two pinnacles. The line of a broad *chajjā* (stone projection), casting a deep shadow, is paralleled on the lower level and towers by a cornice supported by brackets. Each façade of the lower and upper level is composed of three arches, the centre arch sometimes serving as an entrance, while the others are closed by delicately carved marble screens (Ind.-Pers. *jālī*). The soffits of the lower-level arches are incised with intricate lace-like arabesques.

The interior of the lower level consists of a central, square tomb chamber with cenotaphs of I'timad al-Daula and Asmat Begum. (The graves are in a chamber below.) Four oblong rooms on the sides and four square chambers at the corners are all interconnected. The whole is embellished with stucco and painted decoration in designs shared with fine embroidery, carpets and wall hangings. Birds and animals appear in some compositions. The interior of the upper pavilion is decorated with inlay work and has a fine patterned floor. It contains two more cenotaphs.

3. AGRA FORT. Built by the Emperor Akbar over a period of 14 years (1565–79), the fort (see fig. 2) has an irregular semicircular plan, with its base along the west bank of the Yamuna River. Access to the river was possible through the Khidri Darvaza ('Water Gate'). Fortifications on the city side include a double wall: the lower outer defence backed at some 12 m distance by a more massive rampart (h. 21.34 m). Both are faced with red sandstone ashlar. The lower wall has a battlemented parapet with oblong stone merlons sloping outward to prevent scaling. Embrasures and machicolations are positioned at regular intervals. Massive circular bastions project from the higher wall, which is lined by pointed merlons, provided with embrasures and machicolations and embellished with several string courses. The result is a strong military

structure that is also a work of great architectural beauty. A broad deep moat runs along the city side of the outer wall. Two drawbridges provided access to the Delhi Gate, on the west, which served as the main entrance, and the Akbar Gate (known later as the Amar Singh Gate) on the south.

The buildings within the fort are arranged so that those that the public was permitted to enter are nearer the Delhi Gate, while the more private apartments are situated along the eastern wall overlooking the river. Among the few surviving structures that probably date from the reign of Emperor Akbar are the Akbari Mahal and the Jahangiri Mahal in the south-eastern corner of the fort. Both are trabeated structures of red sandstone. Each has a large courtyard approached through a bent entrance, for security and the seclusion of women. The lower portion of the outer wall of these apartments on the river side is composed of thick stone masonry, while the upper part has ashlar headers and stretchers in typical Mughal fashion, indicating that Akbar may have built on older foundations. Much of the Akbari Mahal, the simpler and probably the earlier of the two, has been destroyed, although the range of apartments on the east of the courtyard survives. The Jahangiri Mahal, still in a fine state of preservation, has a variety of rooms and galleries in two storeys arranged round the central courtyard. A roof terrace with delicate carved railings overhangs the upper level and is supported by carved brackets. Paralleling it, a broad eave carried by heavier and more ornately carved brackets projects from the top of the lower level. Richly carved piers surround the courtyard. A few halls have vaulted ceilings, but most ceilings are flat, composed of beams and slabs. Among the most interesting apartments is the northern hall, which has an upper-level gallery. Stone struts, extending from the base of the gallery to the ceiling beams, are carved with crocodile-like creatures emitting scrolls of foliage from their mouths in the fashion of a *makara toraṇa* (Skt: a gateway, usually in a temple complex, employing a mythical crocodile motif). Rooms within the complex probably served a variety of purposes, both residential and ceremonial.

Situated just north of the Jahangiri Mahal is the Shah Jahan-period Khas Mahal ('Private Palace'; 1631–40). On the east it overlooks the river and on the west the Anguri Bagh (a four-plot garden), with water channels, fountains and cascades. The main building, of pure white marble, was profusely painted with floral patterns, which are now faded. It is situated on a terrace flanked by red sandstone pavilions that were plastered white. Each of these has a curved cornice, derived from Indian, probably Bengali, prototypes.

Two chambers on the north-east corner of the Anguri Bagh form the Shish Mahal ('Glass Palace'; *c*. 1631–40). All the wall surfaces except the painted marble dados had small convex mirrors embedded in the plaster in floral and other patterns. At night, with candles lit, the interior glittered. Water channels ran through the room; fountains and cascades, with niches behind for candles that made the water sparkle, added to the ethereal atmosphere. Court historian ʿAbd al-Hamid Lahauri described the glass used in these apartments as 'glass from Aleppo' (Pers. *shīsha-yi ḥalabī*), and some or all of the glass may have been imported from there.

2. Agra Fort, 1565–79

Just north of the Shish Mahal is the Muthamman Burj ('Octagonal Tower'; 1628–30), a spacious white marble pavilion on a massive bastion. Pillars line the exterior; a *chajjā* is supported on beautifully carved marble brackets. The decoration of the chamber features inlay work in hardstones, similar to that of the Taj Mahal. Dados have graceful flowers carved in relief with borders of inlaid arabesques; even the white marble pillars are decorated with inlay work. On the west is a spacious portico with a sunken marble fountain.

Further north is a section of the complex known as the Machchi Bhavan ('Fish Palace'), so named, it is said, because its courtyard consisted of a large pond with fish. A colonnade in two storeys runs around three sides of the now empty courtyard. An extensive terrace forms the upper level of the fourth side. Facing on to it is the Divan-i Khas ('Hall of Private Audience'; 1635), which consists of an open colonnade leading to a hall closed on three sides. The façade is composed of five cusped arches with a *chajjā* (stone projection) above. The whole is constructed of white marble with lavish inlay work in hardstones as well as carved relief work.

On the north-eastern corner of the Machchi Bhavan is a little white mosque, the Nagina Masjid ('Jewel Mosque'; 1631–40), built for the private use of the palace. The prayer chamber is two aisles deep, its façade composed of three cusped arches supported on slender piers. The larger central arch is emphasized by a curved cornice. The superstructure consists of three bulbous domes, of which the central one is the largest. All are crowned by a lotus petal motif topped by finials.

Away from the river front and on a lower level, the Divan-i ʿAm ('Hall of Public Audience'; *c*. 1631–40) occupies one side of a vast courtyard. Measuring 63.3×22.8 m, it is open on three sides. Three aisles of cusped arches form the interior, which is nine bays across and which has nine cusped arches forming the western façade. The repeated line of the arches receding down the vast aisles creates a sense of harmony as well as splendour. The throne chamber, recessed in the eastern wall, is of white marble embellished with inlay work in hardstones. The rest of the structure is built of red sandstone covered over with white shell-plaster creating the impression of white marble. The exterior arches are supported on double pillars of a type used frequently in Shah Jahan-period architecture and consisting of a squarish base, octagonal or 12-sided shaft and a *muqarnas* or stalactite capital. ʿAbd al-Hamid Lahauri noted in his history that the Divan-i ʿAm replaced a wooden hall in which the emperor previously received the public sitting beneath a rich cloth canopy.

One of the most impressive buildings within the fort is the Moti Masjid ('Pearl Mosque'; completed 1654), situated north of the Divan-i ʿAm. It is entered through a red sandstone gateway, but the interior is of pure white marble. The courtyard (48.16×48.16 m) has arcades on three sides and the prayer hall (49.94×17.07 m) on the west. The prayer hall is three aisles deep and seven bays wide, with seven cusped arches forming the façade. The superstructure consists of three bulbous domes; there are octagonal *chatrīs* at the corners of the prayer hall and seven square *chatrīs* above the parapet (one over each arch), creating a varied and pleasing composition. A Persian inscription inlaid in black marble running along the eastern arcade praises Shah Jahan and the building, comparing it to the heavenly tabernacle.

See also INDIAN SUBCONTINENT, §III, 7(i)(a).

BIBLIOGRAPHY

Enc. Islam/2
E. W. Smith: *Mogul Colour Decoration at Agra*, pt 1, Archaeol. Surv. India, New Imp. Ser., xxx (Allahabad, 1901)
P. Brown: *Indian Architecture, Islamic Period* (?Bombay, [1942], rev. Bombay, 1956) [rev. edn with additional photographs]
J. Burton-Page: 'Taj Mahal', *Splendours of the East*, ed. M. Wheeler (London, 1965)
G. Hambly: *Cities of Mughal India: Delhi, Agra and Fatehpur Sikri* (London, 1968)
R. Nath: *Colour Decoration in Mughal Architecture* (Bombay, 1970)
D. Carroll: *The Taj Mahal* (New York, 1972)
Marg, xxvi (Dec 1972) [issue on Mughal gdns]
R. Nath: *The Immortal Taj Mahal* (Bombay, 1972)
——: *Agra and its Monumental Glory* (Bombay, 1976)
——: *Some Aspects of Mughal Architecture* (New Delhi, 1976), pp. 102–11 [on the tomb of Iʿtimad al-Daula]; pp. 150–61 [on the Taj Mahal]
W. Begley: 'Amanat Khan and the Calligraphy on the Taj Mahal', *Kst Orients*, xii, 1/2 (1978–9), pp. 5–39, 40–60
——: 'The Myth of the Taj Mahal and a New Theory of its Symbolic Meaning', *A. Bull.*, lxi/1 (1979), pp. 7–37
R. Nath: *Calligraphic Art in Mughal Architecture* (Calcutta, 1979)
——: *History of Mughal Architecture*, 2 vols (New Delhi, 1982–5)
——: *The Taj and its Incarnation* (Jaipur, 1985) [trans. of Pers. mat. on bldrs, mat., costs etc]

R. NATH

Agrab, Tell. *See under* DIYALA REGION.

Agrate, Marco d' [Marco Ferreri; Ferrari d'Antonio d'Agrate] (*b* Agrate, *c.* 1504; *d* Milan, *c.* 1574). Italian sculptor. He came from a Lombard family of sculptors, collaborating with his brother Gianfrancesco on a funerary monument to *Sforzino Sforza* (1524–31) in S Maria della Steccata, Parma. Records show that Marco was in the service of Milan Cathedral from 1522. From 1541 to 1571 he worked for the Cathedral Works and may have contributed reliefs for the façade of the Certosa di Pavia. This suggests that his style was formed by the classicizing environment of Agostino Busti, Andrea Fusina and Cristoforo Lombardo. In 1547 d'Agrate was contracted to complete the four remaining sarcophagi, with reclining figures above, for the Trivulzio Chapel in S Nazaro Maggiore, Milan. The chapel had been left incomplete by Bramantino and was continued by Lombardo. The austere funerary monument of *Giovanni del Conte* (Milan, S Lorenzo) dates from 1556 to 1558. The architectural structure is the work of Vincenzo Seregni, but the recumbent effigy of the deceased is by d'Agrate.

Only two works for Milan Cathedral survive: the marble relief of the *Marriage at Cana* (1562; *in situ*), mentioned by Vasari, and the celebrated marble *St Bartholomew* (*c.* 1562; *in situ*), on the base of which is the self-glorifying inscription *Non me Praxiteles sed Marc' finxit Agrat.* This is a life-size *écorché* statue: the skin is draped around the flayed body of the saint, who carries a knife and an open book. The inscription may date from 1664, when the statue was removed from its original location to its present position in the right transept. Much praised in the past and admired by Grand Tourists and literary travellers, the statue is an essay in academic skill, indebted in many ways to Leonardo's anatomical drawings.

BIBLIOGRAPHY

G. Vasari: *Vite* (1550, rev. 2/1568); ed. G. Milanesi (1878–85), vi, p. 517
C. Baroni: 'Intorno a tre disegni milanesi per sculture cinquecentesche', *Riv. A.*, xx (1938), pp. 392–410
L. Price Amerson: 'Marco d'Agrate's *San Bartolomeo*: An Introduction to Some Problems', *Il Duomo di Milano: Atti del congresso internazionale* (Milan, 1969), i, pp. 189–206 [with bibliog. and crit. hist.]
M. T. Franco Fiorio and A. P. Valerio: 'La scultura a Milano tra il 1535 e il 1565: Alcuni problemi', *Omaggio a Tiziano: La cultura artistica milanese nell'età di Carlo V* (exh. cat., Milan, Pal. Reale, 1977), p. 126

MARIA TERESA FIORIO

Agreda, Esteban de (*b* Logroño, 26 Dec 1759; *d* Madrid, 1842). Spanish sculptor and ceramicist. He moved to Madrid at an early age and was apprenticed to the French sculptor Robert Michel (i), who was employed at the court. He won first prize in a competition at the Real Academia de Bellas Artes, and organized the royal workshop for the carving of precious stones, where he executed two magnificent cameo portraits of *Charles IV* and *Queen Maria Luisa* (*c.* 1796; Madrid, Pal. Real). He was a leading sculptor in the Buen Retiro porcelain factory, for which he produced a large amount of work. In 1797 he entered the Real Academia de Bellas Artes and was promoted until he was finally appointed Director-general in 1821. He was also appointed Honorary Chamber Sculptor to Charles IV. His successful career made him an influential figure in Spanish art. He was one of the leading exponents of Neo-classical sculpture, producing works that were technically accomplished although stylistically rather cold. He executed a large amount of work between 1792 and 1804 for the gardens of the Palacio Real at Aranjuez, including the fountain and statues of *Neptune*, the *Ceres* fountain and the children on the *Apollo* fountain. He produced such notable religious works as the two *Angels* (*c.* 1802) in the chapel of the Palacio Real de Madrid. He also made the models for the allegorical sculptures of the *Second of May* obelisk (1823; Madrid, Paseo del Prado), commemorating the heroes who died in the uprising against Napoleon in 1808.

BIBLIOGRAPHY

E. Pardo Canalís: *Escultores de cámara del siglo XIX* (Madrid, 1951)

P. Navascués, C. Pérez and A. M. de Cossío: *Historia del arte hispánico*, v (Madrid, 1978)

CARLOS CID PRIEGO

Agrest, Diana (*b* Buenos Aires, 1945). American architect and theorist of Argentine birth. She received her Diploma of Architecture at the University of Buenos Aires in 1967 and studied further in Paris at the Ecole Pratique des Hautes Etudes and the Centre du Recherche d'Urbanisme (1967–9). She moved to New York in 1971. From 1976 Agrest taught at Cooper Union, New York, and at Columbia, Princeton and Yale universities. In 1980 she went into partnership with her husband, Mario Gandelsonas (*b* 1938), in the firm A & G Development Consultants Inc., in New York. She also formed her own firm, Diana Agrest, Architect, in New York. Agrest was deeply involved in theoretical research, and was a Fellow at the Institute for Architecture and Urban Studies, New York, from 1972 to 1984. She was strongly influenced by semiotics and developed the idea that architecture can refer beyond itself, discussed particularly in her essay on architecture and film (1991). She also argued for a contextual and integrative approach to architecture, as seen in her master plan (1986) for Deep Ellum, Dallas, which proposes a development for a section of downtown Dallas, integrating retail, office and residential spaces. The visual concerns of the plan are classically orientated towards symmetry and clarity. Surfaces are characterized by unornamented planarity. This severity also appeared in Agrest's designs for 'Shingle–Schinkel holiday house' (1981–2). The shingle siding and roof refer to the traditions of the projected East Hampton location, and they enliven the surfaces of the otherwise severe cubic forms, which include two towers. Agrest and Gandelsonas also designed office and apartment interiors and furniture. These interiors (e.g. Park Avenue apartment, *c.* 1990) can be somewhat playful, combining materials such as pink marble, granite and exotic woods, yet they are still geometrically severe.

WRITINGS

with M. Gandelsonas: 'Two Pavilion House' and 'Shingle Schinkel', *Lotus Int.*, 44 (1984), pp. 51–4; 55–7
Architecture From Without: Theoretical Framings for a Critical Practice (Cambridge, MA, 1991); review by R. Moore in *Archit. Rev.* [London], cxc/1143 (1992), p. 13

BIBLIOGRAPHY

'Deep Ellum, Dallas, Texas', *Lotus Int.*, 50 (1986), pp. 47–57
C. Lorenz: *Women in Architecture: A Contemporary Perspective* (New York, 1990), pp. 10–11
'Agrest and Gandelsonas', *Archit. Dig.* (1991), pp. 20–21

WALTER SMITH

Agricola, Christoph Ludwig (*b* Regensburg, 1667; *d* Regensburg, 1719). German painter. He travelled to England, the Netherlands, France and Italy, working for longer periods in Rome, Naples and Augsburg. He was strongly influenced by French landscape painters active in Italy, such as Gaspard Dughet and Claude Lorrain. In Agricola's paintings the balanced arrangement of the picturesque landscape elements creates a lucid pictorial structure, and unusual light effects, such as twilight or the darkness before a storm, are used to convey a particular mood. The small scale of his figures expresses the contrast between human frailty and the forces of nature. He painted with lively local colours, especially ochres and deep greens for the rich tones of earth and vegetation. The multicoloured costumes of his figural staffage provide pictorial accents and reveal the romantic orientation of his paintings. Scenes of country people at work, for example *Landscape with a Millstone* (Dresden, Gemäldegal. Alte Meister), express his yearning for a return to nature. Paintings representing the life of nomadic Orientals, such as *Evening Landscape with Praying Turks* (Brunswick, Herzog Anton Ulrich-Mus.), show an increasing interest in exotic motifs that may have been a consequence of the Turkish invasions of Central Europe. Agricola's concept of landscape is an early expression of Baroque Romanticism in German painting. His pupils and followers included Christian Hilfgott Brand, Fabio Ceruti (*d* 1761) and Johann Alexander Thiele (1685–1752).

BIBLIOGRAPHY

R. Eisen: *Die deutsche Landschaftsmalerei des Spätbarock* (Leipzig, 1936), pp. 42–4
Deutsche Kunst des Barock (exh. cat., ed. R. Klessmann, B. Hedergott, C. von Heusinger and S. Jacob; Brunswick, Herzog Anton Ulrich-Mus., 1975), p. 16
G. Adriani: *Deutsche Malerei im 17. Jahrhundert* (Cologne, 1977), pp. 108–77
L. Salerno: *Pittori di paesaggio del seicento a Roma*, ii (Rome, 1977), p. 897
Die deutschen Gemälde des 17. und 18. Jahrhunderts (exh. cat. by J. Jacoby and A. Michels, Brunswick, Herzog Anton Ulrich-Mus., 1989)

HANA SEIFERTOVÁ

Agrigento. *See* AKRAGAS.

Agrippa(, Marcus Vipsanius) (*b* 64 or 63 BC; *d* Campania, March 12 BC). Roman general and patron. He was a faithful friend and supporter of AUGUSTUS (*reg* 27 BC–AD 14). As aedile in 33 BC he began a programme of grandiose and sensible public works for Rome, of which little survives. Leaving the ancient centre intact, he built a monumental quarter in the Campus Martius, following a plan originally conceived by Julius Caesar. Reserving an area for military exercises (the Campus Agrippae), he completely reclaimed the area with an extensive network of sewers, created a vast bathing pool (the Stagnum Agrippae), and in 26 BC completed the Saepta Julia, an enclosure with marble porticos (1.6 km long) along the first part of the Via Flaminia. He also built a *diribitorium* (a series of buildings in which ballots were sorted), and added the Portico of the Argonauts and the Basilica of Neptune, the arches of the Aqua Virgo aqueduct, the Pons Agrippae over the Tiber (just above the present Ponte Sisto), the Porticus Vipsania (finished after his death by his sister) and the magnificent complex of the Pantheon (27–25 BC; destr.; existing structure built by Hadrian *c.* AD 118–25). The Baths of Agrippa were begun in 25 BC just south of the Pantheon and in line with it, and completed *c.* 19 BC with the Aqua Virgo and the addition of gardens along the west side, traversed by the Euripus Canal. They were among the first great Imperial baths in Rome and the first to be given the name of *thermae* (as opposed to the traditional *balneae*; *see* BATH (ii), §1). The baths were almost entirely rebuilt by Hadrian between AD 120 and 125.

BIBLIOGRAPHY

C. Hülsen: *Die Thermen des Agrippa* (Rome, 1910)
G. Gatti: 'I Saepta Iulia nel Campo Marzio', *Urbe*, ii/9 (1937), pp. 8–24

——: 'Il Portico degli Argonauti e la Basilica di Nettuno', *Atti del III congresso nazionale di storia dell'architettura: Firenze, 1938*, pp. 61–76

LUCA LEONCINI

Agua Blanca [anc. Salangome]. Pre-Columbian site in Manabí Province, Ecuador, 8 km inland in the Buenavista River Valley. It was a principal town, controlled by a lord, of the powerful indigenous polity of Salangome, recorded in 1528 by the navigator of the Spanish explorer and conquistador Francisco Pizarro. Human occupation at Agua Blanca spanned at least 5000 years and included components of all the principal ceramic-using cultures identified along Ecuador's coasts. The ceramic sequence began with VALDIVIA wares in the early 3rd millennium BC, and continued uninterrupted during the MANTEÑO culture (*c*. AD 800–*c*. 1500) encountered by the Europeans in the 16th century.

The visible archaeological remains at Agua Blanca are of Manteño date. They comprise the wall foundations of several hundred domestic structures, storehouses, temples and other public buildings, which together make the site the largest and best-preserved of all surviving Manteño towns. The orientations of some buildings were clearly governed by astronomical considerations. The long axis of the principal temple, for example, is directed towards the point of sunrise on the December solstice, and this alignment determined the east–west axis of many buildings at the site. A secondary or derived axis, at right angles to the first, determined the layout of other structures. In still other areas, buildings were arranged radially around a central mound, a practice resembling the principles of spatial organization expressed in the earlier dated NAZCA lines on the south coast of Peru, and incorporated into certain, partly contemporary, settlement plans. Marked regularities are also evident in the disposition of public buildings, these being found frequently in pairs and groups of four. This patterning represents an architectural expression of the moiety (two-part) divisions underpinning Andean social organization. Similar regularities are observed in the distribution of monolithic carved stone seats or thrones found in association with large structures at this and other major Manteño centres. At Agua Blanca eight such seats were found aligned along the inside wall of one building.

As the capital of an important Pre-Columbian trading alliance, Agua Blanca channelled many coastal products and goods toward the highlands. Among these was the warm-water marine shell *Spondylus princeps*, highly valued in the Andean world for its vivid red colour, which embodied notions of femininity and fertility. Mother-of-pearl workshops have also been reported from the nearby satellite settlement of Los Frailes. Although the Incas failed in their attempts to subjugate the populous Manteño polities, sporadic finds of imperial Cuzco pottery at Agua Blanca indicate at least a transitory Inca presence on the coast.

For further discussion of the Pre-Columbian art of the Northern and Central Andes *see* SOUTH AMERICA, PRE-COLUMBIAN, §§II and III.

BIBLIOGRAPHY

M. H. Saville: *Antiquities of Manabí*, 2 vols (New York, 1907–10)
E. Estrada: *Prehistoria de Manabí*, Museo Victor Emilio Estrada, iv (Guayaquil, 1957)
——: *Arqueología del Manabí Central*, Museo Victor Emilio Estrada, vii (Guayaquil, 1962)
B. J. Meggers: *Ecuador* (London, 1965)
M.-I. Silva: *Pescadores y agricultores de la costa central del Ecuador: Un modelo socio-economico de asentamientos precolombinos* (MA diss., Urbana, U. IL, 1984)
A. M. Mester: *The Pearl Divers of Los Frailes: Archaeological and Ethnohistorical Explorations of Sumptuary Good Trade and Cosmology in the North and Central Andes* (diss., Urbana, U. IL, 1990; microfilm, Ann Arbor, 1990)
C. McEwan: 'Sillas de Poder', *5000 años de ocupación—Parque Nacional Machalilla*, ed. P. Norton (Quito, 1992)

COLIN McEWAN

Aguado, Alejandro María. *See* LAS MARISMAS DEL GUADALQUIVIR, Marqués de.

Aguado de la Sierra, Miguel (*b* Madrid, 1842; *d* Madrid, 6 March 1896). Spanish architect and teacher. He trained as a painter under Luis Ferrant (1806–68) and graduated as an architect in 1866. He began his career in the office of Jerónimo de la Gándara (*b* 1825; *d* after 1870), an architect working in a historical Neo-classical style. A scholarship to study in Rome determined Aguado de la Sierra's choice of specialization. He taught Theory of Art and Projects at the Escuela de Arquitectura, Madrid, which he later directed (1888–96). He also had a private academy, where followers such as Pascual Herráiz y Silo (1859–1903) were trained and helped him with projects.

Aguado de la Sierra's work belongs to a period of eclecticism that characterized the period after the restoration of Alfonso XII in 1874. He combined rationalist concepts—evident in his use of readily available materials such as iron and undressed brick—and volumes that are precise and cubic in form, thus demonstrating his fidelity to the precepts of the Academia de Bellas Artes de S Fernando, Madrid. His training in Rome provided him with a particularly elegant method of applying classical solutions. The best example of these characteristics is the Real Academia Española (1891–4), near S Jerónimo el Real, Madrid. He also constructed the pedestal of the monument to *Queen María Christina* (1893) behind the Academia, and certain carefully finished palaces such as that of the Marqués del Pazo in the Paseo de Recoletos, Madrid. He was elected as an academician of the Academia in 1883.

WRITINGS

Plan de un curso de teoría general de la arquitectura (Madrid, 1870)

BIBLIOGRAPHY

J. A. Gaya: *Arte del siglo XIX*, A. Hisp. xix (Madrid, 1966)
P. Navascués: *Arquitectura y arquitectos madrileños del siglo XIX* (Madrid, 1973)
Guía de arquitectura y urbanismo de Madrid, Colegio Oficial de Arquitectos de Madrid, 2 vols (Madrid, 1982–3)

ALBERTO VILLAR MOVELLÁN

Agucchi [Agocchi; Agucchia; dalle Agocchie]**, Giovanni Battista** [Machati, Gratiadio] (*b* Bologna, 20 Nov 1570; *d* San Salvatore, 1 Jan 1632). Italian prelate, diplomat and theorist. He had a successful career as a papal diplomat, serving his uncle Filippo Sega, the Apostolic nuncio to France, in 1591, and later the Secretary of State, Cardinal Pietro Aldobrandini; from 1621 he was private secretary to Pope Gregory XV, and in 1623 he was appointed Bishop of Amasea by Urban VIII and Apostolic nuncio to the Republic of Venice, where he remained until 1630. He then left Venice to escape the plague, moving first to Oderzo and then, in 1631, to San Salvatore.

A man of letters and a member of Bologna's Accademia dei Gelati, Agucchi was also a lover of mathematics and astronomy: he conducted a lengthy correspondence with Galileo Galilei in 1611–13. His importance for art history is considerable, even though his reputation rests mainly on the surviving fragment of his *Trattato della pittura* (Bologna, Bib. U., MS. 245). This was published in the preface by G. A. Mosini, the pseudonym of Giovanni Antonio Massani, to *Diverse figure al numero di ottanta* (Rome, 1646), a collection of prints by Simon Guillain after Annibale Carracci (also known as the *Arti di Bologna*). Mosini attributed the *Trattato* to Gratiadio Machati, the pseudonym used elsewhere by Agucchi. It is a lively document on official Roman art circles during the years 1607–15 and concentrates specifically on exalting the *'idea della bellezza'*, which Agucchi identifies particularly in ancient sculpture and in the painting of Raphael, the Carracci (on whom he provides particularly important biographical information) and DOMENICHINO (who was a part of his household). This conception of ideal beauty as superior to natural beauty, and attainable only by judicious selection from the various forms scattered through nature's different aspects, is in stark contrast to the imitative and naturalistic style of painting pursued by Caravaggio and others. In proposing the art of Annibale Carracci as an exemplar, Agucchi singled out Carracci's Roman period, when he achieved a happy union of 'design' and 'colouring'. The concept of ideal beauty had already been formulated in the 16th century, and it seems likely that Agucchi was also partially indebted to his friends Domenichino and Annibale Carracci for his ideas on the subject. He should nevertheless be regarded as the first writer to assert the influential classicist theory of the 17th century, anticipating the better-known discourse by Giovanni Pietro Bellori on the *'Idea della pittura, scultura e architettura'*, which introduces his *Vite de' pittori, scultori et architetti moderni* (Rome, 1672).

In the *Trattato* Agucchi also deals with the distinction to be made between the different schools of painting: as well as the Bolognese, such as Carracci, he considered the Roman (e.g. Raphael), the Venetian (e.g. Titian), the Tuscan (subdivided into Florentine and Sienese), the Lombard (e.g. Correggio) and those of Flanders, Germany and France. These ideas were undoubtedly developed in collaboration with Domenichino who, in a letter to Francesco Angeloni, took credit for dividing art and artists in this fashion.

Another of Agucchi's writings is the *Descrizione della Venere dormiente di Annibale Carrazzi*, an elaborate literary description of Carracci's *Sleeping Venus* (Chantilly, Mus. Condé), which Carlo Cesare Malvasia incorporated into his *Felsina pittrice* (Bologna, 1678).

According to Bellori, one of the figures in Domenichino's fresco of the *Meeting of St Nilus and Emperor Otto III* (*c.* 1609–10; Grottaferrata Abbey, Cappella dei SS Fondatori) represents Agucchi. In 1608–9 Agucchi collaborated with Domenichino on a monument to his brother, *Cardinal Girolamo Agucchi* (*d* 1605), for S Giacomo Maggiore, Bologna (drawings in Windsor Castle, Royal Lib., MS. 1742; Spear).

UNPUBLISHED SOURCES

Bologna, Bib. U., MS. 75, I [G. B. Agucchi: *Vita Hieronymi Agucchi*]

WRITINGS

Trattato della pittura (*c.* 1607–15); fragment, ed. G. A. Mosini [Massani] as part of A. Carracci and S. Guillain: *Diverse figure al numero di ottanta* (Rome, 1646); Eng. trans. and ed. D. Mahon, *Studies in Seicento Art and Theory* (London, 1947); ed. A. Marabottini, *Le arti di Bologna di Annibale Carracci* (Rome, 1966)

D. Dolcini, ed.: *L'antica fondatione, e dominio della città di Bologna* (Bologna, 1638)

Descrizione della Venere dormiente di Annibale Carrazzi; ed. C. C. Malvasia, *Felsina pittrice* (1678); ed. M. Brascaglia (1971)

BIBLIOGRAPHY

DBI; Meissner; Portoghesi

G. P. Bellori: *Vite* (1672); ed. E. Borea (1976), pp. 84, 88, 309–11, 329

G. M. Mazzuchelli: *Gli scrittori d'Italia*, i (Brescia, 1753), pp. 202–5

G. Lenzi: 'Vita di monsignor G. Agucchi', *L'Album*, xvii (1850), pp. 41–5

A. Favaro: 'Amici e corrispondenti di Galileo Galilei: x: G.B.A.', *Atti Reale Ist. Ven. Sci., Lett. & A.*, lxiii (1904), pp. 167–87

J. Schlosser: *Die Kunstliteratur* (Vienna, 1924), pp. 534, 543

D. Mahon: *Studies in Seicento Art and Theory* (London, 1947), pp. 111–54, 231–75

G. Natali: 'Monsignor G. B. Agucchi e le scuole pittoriche italiane', *Siculorum Gym.*, n. s., iv (1951), pp. 117–19

D. Mahon: 'Eclecticism and the Carracci: Further Reflections on the Validity of a Label', *J. Warb. & Court. Inst.*, xvi (1953), pp. 313, 322, 326–30, 332

E. Panofsky: *Galilei as a Critic of the Arts* (The Hague, 1954)

L. Grassi: *Teorici e storia della critica d'arte*, 2 vols (Rome, 1970–73), i, pp. 44, 184; ii, pp. 27, 30–32, 43–4, 61

R. Spear: *Domenichino*, i (New Haven and London, 1982), pp. 88–90, 143–4, 151–3

G. C. Sciolla, ed.: *Letteratura artistica dell'età barocca: Antologia di testi* (Turin, 1983), pp. 7–8

PETER BOUTOURLINE YOUNG

Agudo, José de Madrazo y. *See* MADRAZO, (1).

Aguéli, Ivan (Gustave) [Agelii, John Gustaf] (*b* Sala, Västmanland, 24 May 1869; *d* Barcelona, 1 Oct 1917). Swedish painter. He started to paint of his own initiative on Gotland at the age of 20. In the spring of 1890 he went to Paris, where he studied under Emile Bernard, through whom he became familiar with the work of Paul Cézanne and Vincent van Gogh. He became involved in theosophical circles, with Jacques Tasset, M. E. J. Coulomb and other members of the theosophical group Ananta. During the summers of 1891 and 1892 he went back to Gotland to paint. On returning to Paris he painted only sporadically, while studying oriental languages and religions. In the autumn of 1894 he went to Egypt and began painting intensively, producing such works as *Egyptian Landscape* (1894/5; Stockholm, Nmus.). In 1895 he was again in Paris where he was an enthusiastic student of Islam, to which he converted in 1898. In 1900 he shot and wounded a banderillero at a bullfight in Paris in protest against the cruelty to the animals: this led to the abolition of bullfights in France.

From 1902 to 1909 he lived in Egypt, working, among other things, as a newspaper editor and for the most part neglecting art. In Paris in 1910 he became interested in Cubism and met Pablo Picasso and Fernand Léger; he took up painting again in Stockholm the following year, concentrating on figure painting with such works as *Standing Female Model* (1911; Stockholm, Nmus.). He became an art critic on his return to Paris in 1912. He was deported from Egypt in 1916 and, now completely deaf, was run over by a train outside Barcelona while awaiting a ship's passage to Sweden the following year.

Aguéli was the first Swedish painter to be influenced by Synthetism in his landscapes, figure paintings and portraits. He was aware, well before his Swedish contemporaries, of the art of Paul Cézanne and van Gogh. The concise simplification at which he aimed was further emphasized after his confrontation with Cubism. The constructive, cerebral features of his exactly proportioned paintings are balanced by his exceptional sensitivity to colour. His paintings often attain greater intensity through their small format. The best collections of Aguéli's works are in the Aguéli Museum at Sala, the Moderna Museum and Prins Eugens Waldemarsudde, Stockholm, and the Göteborg Konstmuseum.

BIBLIOGRAPHY

A. Gauffin: *Ivan Aguéli: Människan, mystikern, målaren* [Ivan Aguéli: the man, the mystic, the painter], 2 vols (Stockholm, 1940–41)
G. Ekelöf: *Ivan Aguéli* (Göteborg, 1944)
V. Wessel: *Ivan Aguéli: Porträtt av en rymd* [Ivan Aguéli: portrait of a space] (Stockholm, 1988)

HANS-OLOF BOSTRÖM

Aguesca. Spanish family of printmakers. Jerónimo Aguesca (*fl* Huesca, 1638–44), an etcher, was commissioned to illustrate the *Conclusiones* (scholarly theses) produced by the Universidad Sertoriana in Huesca with numerous handsomely decorated coats of arms. He executed various religious engravings and made the plates of archaeological remains for Juan Francisco Andrés's *Monumento de los Santos Mártires Justo y Pastor* (Huesca, 1644). He signed his works *Jerónimo Aguesca Oscae*, *Aguesca F.* or simply *Oscae.* His brother, Lorenzo Aguesca, engraved the vignettes for Vicencio Juan de Lastanosa's *Museo de las medallas desconocidas de España* (Huesca, 1645). Jerónimo's daughter, the engraver Teresa Aguesca (*b* Huesca, 1654) became famous for producing, at the age of nine, an engraving of *St Anthony and the Christ Child* (1663). She also collaborated with her father on a large number of coats of arms and armorial bearings.

BIBLIOGRAPHY

A. Gallego: *Historia del grabado en España* (Madrid, 1979), p. 193
E. Páez Ríos: *Repertorio* (Madrid, 1981–3)
B. García Vega: *El grabado del libro español: Siglos XV–XVI–XVII* (Valladolid, 1984), p. 275

BLANCA GARCÍA VEGA

Aguiar, João José de (*b* Belas, 1769; *d* Lisbon, 1841). Portuguese sculptor. He was probably trained by his father, a stone mason employed at the Palacio Nacional de Queluz, near Lisbon. In 1784 João Aguiar went to the drawing school of the Casa Pia do Castelo, Lisbon, and in 1785 to Rome on a scholarship from the Intendência with the support of D. I. de Pina Manique (1735–1805). There he studied drawing with Tomaso Labruzzi, modelling with Giuseppe Angellini (1735–1811) and then moved to the workshop of Antonio Canova. Aguiar's first recorded works made in Rome were *Cippus*, *Aeneas* and *Creusa* (1792–3; Lisbon, Pal. Belém Gdns) and a portrait medallion of *Giovanni Antinori* (1792; untraced), Professor of Architecture at the Academia de Portugal in Rome, which is known from an engraving (1792) by João Caetano Rivara (studying in Rome, 1788–99).

In 1794 Pina Manique was engaged on a project to erect a monument to Queen Mary I that would also celebrate the achievements of Portuguese artists who had received scholarships to study in Rome. After finding that Canova and the Genoese Nicolò Stefano Traverso would be too expensive, he turned to Aguiar for the statues and bas-reliefs and to G. G. de Rossi, Director of the Academia de Portugal in Rome, to design the pedestal. A preliminary maquette in bronze and marble inscribed *Dominicus Pieri fecit* (Queluz, Pal. N.) has thrown doubts on the authorship of the monument, and after its completion in 1802 there were rumours that the hand of Canova was detectable. The marble memorial to *Queen Mary I* (installed 1942, Queluz, Pal. N.) represents the first important work of Neo-classicism in Portugal (*see* BRAGANZA, (9)). The Queen, a dignified and hieratic royal image, dressed in Classical robes, is represented as Minerva; she points to the statues of four Greco-Roman female figures symbolizing the four continents in which Portugal possessed dominions. The sides of the severe rectilinear base are decorated with reliefs depicting the principal events of the reign. The four allegorical figures can be compared with the statuettes of the Wellington Silver (1813–16; London, Apsley House), designed by Domingos António Sequeira.

Aguiar returned to Lisbon in 1798 and worked at the foundry of the Arsenal do Exército, where he executed some fine altar plate for the basilica at Mafra as well as reliefs of the *Last Supper*, the *Holy Family* and a *St Anthony* (*in situ*), which are eloquent expressions of Neo-classicism. One of his finest works is the full-length marble statue of *John VI* (*c.* 1801–23), made after the lost original, that was installed in the Hospital da Marinha, Lisbon, in 1823. The principal exponent of Neo-classicism in Portugal, Aguiar here shows an elegant and harmonious treatment of his subject. Aguiar's ability at academic modelling of the nude is apparent in the face, with its noble features, and the body clad in Classical costume, all highly idealized.

Aguiar succeeded Joaquim Machado de Castro in 1801 as director of sculpture at the royal palace of Ajuda, and from 1805 he executed 10 allegorical statues for niches in the circular vestibule of the palace, including *Loyalty*, *Justice*, *Prudence* and *Providence* (*in situ*), as well as the sculptural group on the pediment, but these are merely decorative and of a cold and banal classicism. He was unable for health reasons to teach at the Academia de Belas Artes, founded in Lisbon in 1836, and died in poverty.

BIBLIOGRAPHY

L. Xavier da Costa: *As belas-artes plásticas em Portugal durante o século XVIII* (Lisbon, 1935)
D. de Macedo: *João José de Aguiar: Vida de um malogrado escultor português* (Lisbon, 1944)
A. de Carvalho: *A escultura em Mafra* (Mafra, 1950), pp. 32, 37
J. A. França: *A arte em Portugal no século XIX* (Lisbon, 1966), pp. 36, 67, 70, 72, 74, 90, 100, 107–11, 140, 198, 210, 217, 220–22
R. C. Smith: *The Art of Portugal, 1500–1800* (London, 1968), p. 193
V. Ernesto Soares: *História da gravura artistica em Portugal*, ii (Lisbon, 1971), p. 516
R. Anacleto: 'O neoclassicismo', *Hist. A. Portugal*, x (1986), pp. 46–51
J. A. França: 'Art et vie artistique au Portugal au XIXe siècle', *Soleil et ombres: L'Art portuguais du XIXe siècle* (exh. cat. by J. A. França, Paris, Petit Pal., 1987), pp. 118–20

JOSÉ FERNANDES PEREIRA,
ANTÓNIO FILIPE PIMENTEL

Aguilar, Pablo. *See* SERRANO, PABLO.

Aguilar Ponce, Luis (*b* Panama City, 6 Nov 1943). Panamanian painter. He studied painting from 1960 to 1962 at the Escuela Nacional de Artes Plásticas in Panama City and from 1964 to 1970 at the Universidad Autónoma, Mexico. From 1971 he taught at the Escuela Nacional de Artes Plásticas, Panama City, of which he was director from 1980 to 1982. Under the influence of Pop art he produced semi-abstract paintings that combined geometric shapes and lines with sensuous parts of human anatomy painted with an airbrush and set in vaporous spaces of flowing colours. A typical example is *Profiles of Attraction* (1976; Panama City, Mus. A. Contemp.). In later works such as *Attack II* (1987; Panama City, Mus. A. Contemp.) he added expressionist brushstrokes for visual contrast.

BIBLIOGRAPHY

M. Gasteazoro: *Homenaje* (exh. cat., Panama City, Gal. Etcétera, 1982)
R. Oviero: 'Luis Aguilar Ponce: Ahora mi pintura se une a la humanidad', *La Prensa* [Panama City] (19 Oct 1984), p. 1B
B. Ramón: *Aguilar Ponce: Otro contexto, otros criterios* (exh. cat., Panama City, Mus. A. Contemp.)

MONICA E. KUPFER

Aguilera Silva, Gerardo (*b* Barcelona, Venezuela, 22 April 1907; *d* 13 Oct 1976). Venezuelan painter. He was self-taught and painted his first portraits and self-portraits *c.* 1930. In 1965 his first exhibition was held at the Museo de Bellas Artes, Caracas. His paintings, which later included nudes, possess a very particular atmosphere, developing from a small focal point, to which successive layers of paper or card are added, creating the effect of a collage; heavily and energetically worked, the works are small scale, which lends a further intensity to their expressiveness. Aguilera Silva had exhibitions throughout Venezuela, and examples of his work are held in the Galería de Arte Nacional, Caracas.

BIBLIOGRAPHY

Gerardo Aguilera Silva (exh. cat. by L. Luksic and J. Jordán, Caracas, Mus. B.A., 1965)
Gerardo Aguilera Silva (exh. cat. by J. Calzadilla, L. Luksic and J. Jordán, Caracas, Gal. A. N., 1978)

Based on information supplied by LELIA DELGADO

Aguilonius [de Aguilón; Aguillon], **Franciscus** [François] (*b* Brussels, ?4 Jan 1567; *d* Antwerp, 20 March 1617). Flemish scientist and architect. His father was a Spaniard, Pedro de Aguilón; his mother, Anna Pels, was of Flemish origin. Aguilonius studied at the Jesuit Collège de Clermont in Paris and at Douai. He entered the novitiate of the Jesuits in Tournai. After a brief visit to Salamanca in 1596 he was ordained. He taught philosophy at Douai for five years, and in 1598 moved to Antwerp, where he became confessor to the Spaniards and Italians and a teacher at the city's Jesuit college. In 1614 he was appointed rector of the college.

Aguilonius's reputation rests on his book on optics, illustrated by Rubens, and on the part he played in building the Jesuit church in Antwerp (S Carlo Borromeo), which contributed to the popularity of Italian Baroque architecture with Flemish Jesuits. By December 1611 Aguilonius had written *Opticorum libri sex*, which was published by the Plantin press in 1613. The title-page and six vignettes were engraved after designs by Rubens. According to Parkhurst, Rubens's *Death of Argus* (Cologne, Wallraf-Richartz-Mus.) is strongly influenced by the book in its use of colouring. Held has drawn attention to an inscription on a landscape drawing by Rubens which bears a close affinity to passages in the same book. Under Aguilonius's direction projects for the Jesuit church in Antwerp were sent to the Jesuits in Rome for approval, and the foundation stone was laid on 15 April 1615. The first designs (Paris, Bib. N.) were drawn by Aguilonius himself. Two show a central dome surrounded by chapels; a third is close to the ground-plan of the Gesù, the Jesuit church in Rome. The style of these drawings is similar to that of a ground-plan known to be by Aguilonius for the chapel of the novitiate in Tournai, built under his direction in 1608. It is possible that the final design of the Antwerp church owes something to Aguilonius, although the completed building was designed by Peter Huyssens in collaboration with Rubens.

BIBLIOGRAPHY

S. Brigode: 'Les Projets de construction de l'église des jésuites à Anvers d'après les plans conservés à la Bibliothèque Nationale de Paris', *Bull. Inst. Hist. Belge Rome*, xiv (1934), pp. 157–74
C. Parkhurst: 'Aguilonius' Optics and Rubens' Color', *Ned. Ksthis. Jb.*, xii (1961), pp. 35–49
M. Jaffé: 'Rubens and Optics: Some Fresh Evidence', *J. Warb. & Court. Inst.*, xxxiv (1971), pp. 362–6
J. R. Judson and C. Van de Velde: *Book Illustrations and Title-Pages* (1975), XXI/i of *Corpus Rubenianum Ludwig Burchard* (Brussels, 1971), pp. 101–15
W. Jaeger: *Die Illustrationen von Peter Paul Rubens zum Lehrbuch der Optik des Franciscus Aguilonius* (Heidelberg, 1976)
J. S. Held: 'Rubens and Aguilonius: New Points of Contact', *A. Bull.*, lxi (1979), pp. 257–64
O. Batschmann: 'Farbengenese und Farbentrias in N. Poussin *Die Heilung der Blinden*', *Von Farbe und Farben: Albert Knoepfli zum 70. Geburtstag* (Zurich, 1980), pp. 329–36
F. Baudouin: 'De toren van de Sint-Carolus-Borromeuskerk te Antwerpen', *Acad. Anlct.: Kl. S. Kst.*, xliv/3 (1983), pp. 15–56

FRANS BAUDOUIN

Aguirre, Andrés Ginés de. *See* GINÉS DE AGUIRRE, ANDRÉS.

Aguirre, Miguel. *See under* OTERO & AGUIRRE.

Agustín, Don **Antonio** (*b* Saragossa, 1517; *d* Tarragona, 1586). Spanish ecclesiastic and antiquarian. He studied law at the University of Alcalá, then received his doctorate in civil law at Salamanca in 1534. In 1536 Agustín entered the Collegio di Spagna in Bologna, where he was exposed to the revolutionary method of the *nova jurisprudentia* being propounded by Andrea Alciati. Agustín's reputation as a philologist was established with his critical collation of the Florentine codex of the *Digest*, published as the *Emendationum et opinionum libri* (Venice, 1543). In Rome, where he was appointed in 1544 as an Auditor of the Rota, Agustín's interests turned to numismatics and epigraphy, fostered by his friendship with such antiquarians as Pirro Ligorio, Onofrio Panvinio and Fulvio Orsini. Following a period of diplomatic missions as papal nunciate, Agustín devoted his time to redactions of Varro's *De lingua latina* (1557) and the 2nd-century Sextus Pompeius Festus' *De verborum significatu* (1559). Between 1561 and 1563 he took a vital role in the closing deliberations at the Council of Trent. In 1564 he retired permanently to Spain, serving until 1576 as Bishop of Lérida and from then until his death in 1586 as Archbishop of Tarragona. Agustín was consulted first by Paul V and then Gregory XIII for a corrected text of the *Decretum* by Gratian. Although this project was never realized, Agustín completed two other works on Roman law: *De diversis regulis antiqui iuris explanationes* (1581) and *De legibus et senatusconsultis Romanorum* (1583). The *Familiae Romanae* (Rome, 1577), on which he collaborated with Orsini, was illustrated with ancient coins. This volume led to further researches in numismatics, culminating in two posthumous publications: *Dialogos de medallas inscriciones y otras antiquedades* (Tarragona, 1587) and *Antiquitatum Romanarum Hispanarumque in Nummis Veterum Dialogi XI* (Antwerp, 1617). At his death, Agustín was preparing an edition of Isidore of Seville's *Etymologiarum*.

Concerning Agustín's character, Paulus Manutius referred to him as an 'arca universae antiquitatis'; and he was often approached by fellow antiquarians to judge the authenticity of an ancient coin or inscription. Agustín's position was unequivocal when it came to archaeological sources: 'io do più fede alle medaglie, alle tavole e alle pietre che a tutto quello che dicono gli scrittori'. Although Ligorio's penchant for forgeries hardly passed unnoticed among his contemporaries, Agustín considered him a 'grande antiquario' with a prodigious knowledge of antiquity for someone who did not know Latin.

BIBLIOGRAPHY

A. Schott S. I.: 'Laudatio funebris . . . Antonii Augustini', *De veteribus canonum collectionibus dissertationum sylloge*, ed. A. Gallandi (Mainz, 1750)

J. Andresio, ed.: *Antonii Augustini Archiepiscopi Tarraconensis, Epistolae Latinae, et Italicae* (Parma, 1804)

C. L. Neuber: *Anton Augustin und sein zivilisticher Nachlass* (Berlin, 1832)

R. del Arco: *El Arzobispo D. Antonio Agustín: Nuevos datos para su biografía* (Tarragona, 1910)

J. P. Wickersham Crawford: 'Unedited Letters of Fulvio Orsini to Antonio Agustín', *Pubns Mod. Lang. Assoc.*, 28 (1913), pp. 577–93

F. de Zulueta: *Don Antonio Agustín* (Glasgow, 1939)

C. Mitchell: 'Archaeology and Romance in Renaissance Italy', *Italian Renaissance Studies*, ed. E. F. Jacob (London, 1969), pp. 455–85

PHILIP J. JACKS

Ágústsson, Hörður (*b* Reykjavík, 4 Feb 1922). Icelandic painter, writer and designer. He studied engineering in 1941–2 at the University of Iceland, Reykjavík, and architecture privately. He then studied at the Icelandic School of Arts and Crafts (Myndlista-og handíðaskóli Íslands), Reykjavík (until 1943), the Kongelige Kunstakademi in Copenhagen (1945–6), the Académie de la Grande Chaumière in Paris (1947–8) and with Marcel Gromaire in Paris (1949–50). He promoted the movement towards abstract art in Iceland in 1948–52, particularly in its theoretical aspects.

Ágústsson came to geometric abstraction through an interest in Renaissance compositional theory and the theories of the Bauhaus. His meeting with Victor Vasarely in Paris in 1953 encouraged him to continue with a highly reductive series of paintings on which he had embarked shortly before. Later that year Ágústsson was one of the organizers of the Autumn Exhibition (Haustsýningin), the first group show of geometric abstraction in Iceland. At its opening he gave a lecture that became a kind of manifesto for the movement. He followed it up with a series of articles in the cultural review *Birtingur*, which he edited along with other artists and writers for over a decade; these include an interview with Denise René (*Birtingur*, i-ii, 1957, pp. 39–43) and one with Herbin (*Birtingur*, iv, 1957, pp. 10–17). During the second half of the 1950s and well into the 1960s Ágústsson's art slowly evolved from geometric abstraction to a kind of minimalism, which reached its apogee in the compositions executed with coloured tape and exhibited in 1976 (e.g. *Windows*, 1975; Reykjavík, N.G.). During the 1960s Ágústsson became increasingly active as a teacher and as a scholar of Icelandic architecture, on which he wrote pioneering studies.

WRITINGS

Skálholtskirkjur [The churches at Skálholt] (1990)

BIBLIOGRAPHY

A. Ingólfsson: 'Efnið og andinn' [The spirit and the flesh], *Dagblaðið* (9 Oct 1976) [interview]

A. Bergmann: 'Tveir menn í einum' [Two men in one], *Þjóðviljinn* (5–6 Nov 1983) [interview]

Hörður Ágústsson (exh. cat., Reykjavík, N.G., 1983) [incl. essay by B. Nordal]

Norren konkretlist [Nordic concrete art] (exh. cat., Helsinki, Nord. A. Cent., 1987) [also pubd in Eng.]

AÐALSTEINN INGÓLFSSON

Agylla. *See* CERVETERI.

Ahenny. Site of an obscure Early Christian settlement formerly known as Kilclispeen (St Crispin's Church) in Co. Tipperary, Ireland. The only remains are two outstanding stone crosses and the base of a third (*c.* 750–900), which are situated in a graveyard below the village. The crosses belong to a well-defined regional group and were constructed of three characteristic elements: a square base with sloping sides, a shaft with an unusually wide ring and a peculiar, rather ill-fitting, conical cap (the latter missing on the south cross). With its capstone, the north cross measures 3.7 m in height. The form of the Ahenny crosses is emphasized by a bold cable ornament along the outer contours. Projecting from the main faces are sculpted bosses, the most prominent feature of the 'Ahenny school'. The ring and shaft of the crosses are covered with dense patterns of carved ornament, including interlace, spirals, frets, entangled beasts and interlocking men. Much of this decoration can be compared with the metalwork and manuscript illumination of the period, and it appears that the sculptors were in effect transposing altar or processional crosses into stone. With the addition of pigment, the analogy with metalwork would have been complete. In contrast to the shafts and rings, the bases bear figure sculpture in low relief. That on the north cross is best preserved and represents Adam and Eve with the animals in the Garden of Eden (*see* CROSS, fig. 1), a chariot procession (a theme repeated on other Irish crosses), seven ecclesiastics (possibly symbolizing Christ's mission to the Apostles) and an enigmatic funeral procession with a headless corpse.

For further discussion *see* INSULAR ART, §4.

BIBLIOGRAPHY

H. M. Roe: *High Crosses of Western Ossory* (Kilkenny, 1958, 2/1962), pp. 13–25

F. Henry: *Irish Art in the Early Christian Period (to 800 AD)* (London, 1965), pp. 139–54

N. Edwards: 'An Early Group of Crosses from the Kingdom of Ossory', *J. Royal Soc. Antiqua. Ireland*, cxiii (1983), pp. 5–46
P. Harbison: *The High Crosses of Ireland* (Bonn, 1992)

ROGER STALLEY

Ahhotpe (*d c.* 1550–1530 BC). Egyptian queen and patron. Perhaps the wife of King Kamose, she should be distinguished from the later Ahhotpe, mother of King Ahmose (*reg c.* 1540–*c.*1514 BC). Her intact burial was discovered at Thebes in 1859. The massive anthropoid coffin with gilded lid (Cairo, Egyp. Mus., CG 28501) was of the *rishi* type, characteristic of the 17th and early 18th dynasties (*see* EGYPT, ANCIENT, §XII, 2(i)(c)). Four lidless alabaster vases, which probably served as canopic jars, were also found, but most important was the large collection of gold and silver jewellery and ceremonial weapons discovered inside the coffin. These pieces, all of which are in the Egyptian Museum, Cairo, constitute the prime evidence for goldsmiths' and jewellers' techniques at the beginning of the New Kingdom (*see* EGYPT, ANCIENT, §XV, 4).

The principal pieces included an inlaid golden pectoral, two collars, a massive golden armlet (possibly belonging to King Ahmose) and a variety of bracelets of gold, precious stones and beadwork. There were three daggers, including a particularly fine specimen of gold (CG 52658), with ornamental handle and inlaid blade. Of the three axes, the finest (CG 52645) has a gilded blade, richly inlaid with figured scenes and royal names; it is secured to the cedar-wood handle by a lashing of golden thongs. There were also three large golden fly pendants on a chain (*see* EGYPT, ANCIENT, fig. 92) and two model boats, one of gold and the other of silver. The silver model boat is mounted on a four-wheeled carriage of wood and bronze. Perhaps the finest piece, technically, is an inlaid scarab on an elaborately constructed gold chain of very small links.

Many of the pieces bear the names of Kamose and Ahmose and are decorated with religious scenes or symbolic devices. They represent a transitional phase in the crafts of jewellery and goldworking. Middle Kingdom traditions are still apparent in form such as the shrine-shaped pectoral and the collar with falcon-head terminals. The workmanship of most of the pieces, however, is much inferior to that of jewellery from the tombs of 12th Dynasty (*c.* 1938–*c.* 1756 BC) princesses at Dahshur and el-Lahun. This deterioration was probably caused by the limited availability of fine craftsmen in Upper Egypt before Ahmose defeated the foreign Hyksos rulers. Stylistic and technical innovations are, however, evident in the appearance of rigid bracelets opening on a hinge and in the methods of stringing and fastening the bead bracelets.

BIBLIOGRAPHY

E. Desjardins: 'Découvertes de M. Mariette en Egypte', *Rev. Gén. Archit.*, xviii (1860), cols 98–112, pls 1–6
F. W. von Bissing: *Ein thebanischer Grabfund aus dem Anfang des neuen Reichs* (Berlin, 1900)
E. Vernier: *Bijoux et orfèvreries*, 2 vols (Cairo, 1907–27), pp. 202–48
H. E. Winlock: 'The Tombs of the Kings of the Seventeenth Dynasty at Thebes', *J. Egyp. Archaeol.*, x (1924), pp. 251–5, pls XVI–XVII
A. M. Roth: 'Ahhotep I and Ahhotep II', *Serapis*, iv (1977–8), pp. 31–40
For further bibliography *see* EGYPT, ANCIENT, §XV.

J. H. TAYLOR

Ahichchhatra [Ahicchatra; Adhicchatrā]. Fortified site in Bareilly District, Uttar Pradesh, India. It flourished from *c.* 500 BC to AD 1100, and it was identified by Alexander Cunningham as the capital of North Panchala, an early kingdom mentioned in the *Mahābhārata* epic of the 1st millennium BC. The fortifications of the site measure 5.6 km in circuit, and the mounds within stand 23 m above the surrounding plain. Early visitors such as the 7th-century Chinese pilgrim Xuanzang noted a number of Buddhist stupas; although these can no longer be located, Cunningham's excavations of 1862–5 produced a reliquary casket at one stupa site. Some years later A. Führer undertook the excavation of a temple without much result. However, the principal excavation of Ahichchhatra was carried out between 1940 and 1944 by the Archaeological Survey of India under the direction of Rao Bahadur K. N. Dikshit, assisted by Amalananda Ghosh. This yielded evidence of nine successive periods of occupation in the western sector of the city dating from 500 BC to AD 1100.

These periods have been defined chiefly on the evidence of coins, pottery, terracottas and beads (see Panigrahi, Agrawala and Dikshit): the important ceramics known as Northern Black Polished ware and Painted Grey ware (*see* INDIAN SUBCONTINENT, §VIII, 5(i)) were first defined at this site (Deva and Wheeler). Rather crudely executed grey terracotta figurines of the mother goddess found in Stratum VII (3rd–2nd centuries BC) can be related to similar figurines from Mathura, and moulded plaques of Shunga and Panchala affinity were recovered from Strata VII and VIII (4th–2nd centuries BC). Distinctive figurines of dwarfs and grotesques occurred in Stratum IV (2nd–4th centuries AD).

A Shiva temple of the 5th–6th century AD yielded some remarkable terracotta figures of river deities (New Delhi, N. Mus.). Etched cornelian beads of the early historical type were recovered from Stratum VIII and faience beads from Stratum III (*c.* AD 350–750). Glass beads overlaid with gold foil were found in Strata III and I (*c.* AD 850–1100). Further excavations carried out by the Archaeological Survey of India between 1963 and 1965 yielded evidence of a Bronze Age habitation with Ochre Coloured pottery dating from the 1st half of the 1st millennium BC. Finds from the site are currently held by by Archaeological Survey of India and in the National Museum, both in New Delhi.

BIBLIOGRAPHY

A. Cunningham: 'Ramnagar and Ahichchhatra', *Archaeol. Surv. India Rep. 1862–5*, i (1871), pp. 255–65
A. Führer: *Monumental Antiquities and Inscriptions of the N.W. Provinces and Oudh* (Allahabad, 1891)
K. Deva and R. E. M. Wheeler: 'Appendix A: Northern Black Polished Ware, the Pottery of Ahichchhatra', *Anc. India*, i (1946), pp. 55–8
——: 'Appendix B: Note on the Painted Grey Wares at Ahichchhatra', *Anc. India*, i (1946), pp. 58–9
A. Ghosh: 'Introduction: The Pottery of Ahichchhatra, District Bareilly, U.P.', *Anc. India*, i (1946), pp. 37–40
K. C. Panigrahi: 'The Pottery of Ahichchhatra, District Bareilly, U.P.', *Anc. India*, i (1946), pp. 40–55
V. S. Agrawala: 'Terracotta Figurines of Ahichchhatra, District Bareilly, U.P.', *Anc. India*, iv (1947–8), pp. 104–79
M. G. Dikshit: 'Beads from Ahichchhatra, U.P.', *Anc. India*, viii (1952), pp. 33–63
Archaeol. Surv. India (1963–4), pp. 43–4 [excavation report from Ahichchhatra]
Archaeol. Surv. India (1964–5), pp. 39–42 [excavation report from Ahichchhatra]

GREGORY L. POSSEHL

Ahlberg, Hakon (*b* Harplinge, Halland, 10 June 1891; *d* Stockholm, 12 March 1984). Swedish architect and writer. He graduated from the Kungliga Tekniska Högskolan (1914) and from the Kungliga Akademien för de fria Konsterna in Stockholm (1918), before working in the office of Ivar Tengbom. From 1921 to 1924 Ahlberg was a writer for and editor of *Byggmästaren*, the Swedish journal of building and architecture. His architectural production encompassed the traditionalism and neo-classicism of the early 20th century, as well as the International Style, characterized by rational, pragmatic design. His Arts and Crafts Stand at the Göteborg Jubilee Exposition (1923), with its mannered, slender pavilions, was an early contribution to the neo-classical revival of the 1920s. The Freemasons' Orphanage (1928–31) at Blackeberg outside Stockholm showed his development of this classicism into austere geometrical simplicity, while the buildings of the Trade Union High School (1928–50) at Brünnsvik, Dalecarlia, are based on the national timber-building tradition, with red panelling, white-framed windows and tiled, hipped roofs. The same combination of rational simplicity and romantic traditionalism occurs in Ahlberg's ecclesiastical buildings, such as Mälarhöjden Chapel (1928), Stockholm, and Malmberget Church (1945), Lapponia. Ahlberg was the founder and president of the Svenska Arkitekters Riksförbund (1936–45). As architect to the National Board of Health and Welfare (from 1935) he planned a number of hospitals throughout Sweden and abroad. Sidsjön Mental Hospital (1939–44) near Sundsvall is a complex of pavilions in yellow brick. The concrete and glass University Hospital (1946–54) in Maricaibo, Venezuela, is typical of modern, large-scale hospital planning. In hospital planning and housing in particular Ahlberg adopted functionalist ideals, and his contributions to the Stockholm Exhibition of 1930 were on these lines. Hjorthagen housing estate (1934–40) in Stockholm is an extreme example: a series of very slim, parallel three-storey concrete 'slabs' and plain plaster façades. In later projects, with his young associates Sven Backström and Leif Reinius, he followed a softer line with richer and more traditional use of materials. In public and civic buildings, for example the Court of Appeal in Göteborg (1945) and the Civic Centre (1955) and Dalarnas Museum (1960) in Falun, he preferred traditional brickwork, while his industrial and office buildings such as those for the LKAB Mining Co. at Malmberget and Kiruna in the 1950s and 1960s are examples of the International Style in concrete, glass and sheet metal.

WRITINGS

with F. Yerbury: *Modern Swedish Architecture* (London and Paris, 1925)
intro. *Gunnar Asplund, Architect, 1885–1940* (Stockholm, 1950); *R* with subtitle *Plans, Sketches and Photographs* (Stockholm, 1987)

BIBLIOGRAPHY

60 års jobb: Hakon Ahlberg (exh. cat., Stockholm, Arkitmus., 1971)
Nordisk klassicism/Nordic Classicism, 1910–1930 (exh. cat., ed. S. Paavilainen; Helsinki, Mus. Fin. Archit., 1982)
H. O. Andersson and F. Bedoire: *Swedish Architecture Drawings, 1640–1970/Svensk arkitektur ritningar* (Stockholm, 1986) [dual-lang. text]

□

Ahlers-Hestermann, Friedrich (*b* Hamburg, 17 July 1883; *d* W. Berlin, 11 Dec 1973). German painter. He studied in Hamburg under the German painter Arthur Siebelist (1870–1946) in 1900. In 1907 he went to Paris, where he sought contact with French modernism and its protagonists in the Café du Dôme and as a student at the Académie Matisse. His works completed before World War I reflect the colour of Matisse and the fragmented planes of Cézanne (e.g. *Girl in Kimono*, oil, 1910; priv. col., see exh. cat., pl. 5). In the inter-war years his depictions of landscapes, portraits and still-lifes are characterized by the harmony of the abstract rhythm of their planes and forms and by the use of silhouettes indebted to Cubism (e.g. *From Old Letters*, 1933; priv. col., see exh. cat., pl. 10). From 1928 until his dismissal by the Nazis in 1933 Ahlers-Hestermann taught at art colleges in Hamburg and Cologne. From 1946 to 1949 he was head of the Landeskunstschule in Hamburg.

BIBLIOGRAPHY

F. Ahlers-Hestermann: Ölbilder und Pastelle (exh. cat. by E. Streiff, Cologne, Baukst-Gal., 1973–4)
A. Manigold: *Der Hamburger Maler Friedrich Ahlers-Hestermann, 1883–1973* (diss., U. Hamburg, 1986)

CLAUDIA BÜTTNER

Ahlsén. Swedish family of architects. Erik Ahlsén (*b* Stockholm, 12 Oct 1901) and his younger brother Tore Ahlsén (*b* Stockholm, 29 July 1906) trained as engineers at the Vocational College and then studied architecture at the Royal Institute of Technology in Stockholm (1933 and 1934). They both worked for the Swedish Cooperative Union under Eskil Sundahl, where Erik Ahlsén was an associate (1926–46) and head of department (1936–46). Tore Ahlsén also worked with Erik Lallerstedt and Erik Gunnar Asplund. In 1937 their winning entry for the extension to Kristianstad Town Hall allowed them to establish their own practice.

During their 30-year partnership the Ahlséns combined rational planning with a great sympathy for volumes and materials, continuing the tradition established in Asplund's late works. Aesthetic considerations, such as the integration of artistic decoration in buildings, were important in all their work; design of the interior and furniture was a vital part of projects, particularly for their civic buildings. Their community centre (1943–53) for the Årsta Housing Estate, Stockholm, comprises a group of concrete buildings decorated with brick patterning and murals on the façades. The soft forms of the curved walls and roofs became standard features of their designs, in the style known as New Empiricism.

Among their commercial buildings, the PUB Department Store Annexe (1955–9) in Stockholm is an all-glass building, which reflects light down into a narrow city street. Their interest in volumetric and sculptural effects was also expressed in housing schemes such as Södra Biskopsgården Housing Estate (1956) in Göteborg, a series of curved volumes with projecting cylindrical stairwells with glass façades, and Henriksdalsberget (1964–9) near Stockholm. The Medborgarhuset Civic Centre (1965), Örebro, is a block-like structure containing a theatre, meeting rooms, restaurant and hotel, with façades in glass, red sandstone and teak, terminated by a corbelled upper storey and a convex copper roof. The Krämaren commercial complex (1953–60) opposite acts as a base for a pair of high-rise blocks of flats with enamelled sheet-metal façades. Both buildings made a prominent contribution to the modernization of Örebro city centre.

BIBLIOGRAPHY

G. Lundahl, ed.: *Recent Developments in Swedish Architecture* (Stockholm, 1983)

F. Bedoire and H. O. Andersson: *Swedish Architecture* (Stockholm, 1986), pp. 39, 162, 248–9

Ahmad [Aḥmad] (*fl* 1815–50). Persian painter. He specialized in oil portraits of the Qajar rulers Fath ʿAli Shah (*reg* 1797–1834) and Muhammad (*reg* 1834–48). To judge from Ahmad's style, he was a pupil of MIHR ʿALI (*see* ISLAMIC ART, §VIII, 11(i)). His early works include two portraits of Fath ʿAli Shah. One dated 1818–19 (untraced) shows the Shah, whose face has been repainted, in full armour seated on the chair-like throne known as the *takht-i nādirī* and part of the Iranian Crown Jewels. A second portrait dated 1822–3 (Tehran, Brit. Embassy) shows the ruler seated on a jewelled carpet with a hooka at his side. Ahmad's later work is more Europeanized in style. A large painting dated 1844 (Tehran, Gulistan Pal. Lib.) depicts Muhammad reviewing his troops, and another oil dated 1846 (Tehran, Firuz priv. col.) is a fine bust portrait of the monarch.

BIBLIOGRAPHY

B. W. Robinson: 'The Court Painters of Fatḥ ʿAlī Shāh', *Eretz-Israel*, vii (1964), pp. 94–105

——: 'Persian Painting in the Qajar Period', *Highlights of Persian Art*, ed. R. Ettinghausen and E. Yarshater (Boulder, 1979), pp. 331–62

——: 'Persian Royal Portraiture', *Qajar Iran: Political, Social and Cultural Change 1800–1925*, ed. E. Bosworth and C. Hillenbrand (Edinburgh, 1983), pp. 219–310

M. A. Karimzada Tabrizi: *Aḥvāl u āthār-i naqqāshān-i qadīm-i īrān* [The lives and art of old painters of Iran] (London, 1985), no. 84

B. W. Robinson: 'Painting in the Post-Safavid Period', *The Arts of Persia*, ed. R. W. Ferrier (New Haven and London, 1989), pp. 225–31

——: 'Persian Painting under the Zand and Qājār Dynasties', *From Nadir Shah to the Islamic Republic*, vii of *The Cambridge History of Iran* (Cambridge, 1991), pp. 870–90

□

Ahmadabad [Ahmedabad]. City in western India, until 1970 the state capital of Gujarat.

1. HISTORY. Remains of bones and tools indicate occupation in the area around Ahmadabad during the second millennium BC. The earliest permanent settlement, called Ashaval after its founder Asha Bhil, was established on the eastern bank of the Sabarmati River in the 8th century AD and prospered in subsequent centuries. In 1391 Zafar Khan was appointed Governor of Gujarat by the Sultanate rulers in Delhi. In 1403 his rebellious son, Tatar Khan, proclaimed himself Sultan of Gujarat at Ashaval but died a few months later, possibly from poisoning. His father regained power and, assuming the title Muzaffar Shah I, proclaimed himself Sultan of Gujarat. On his death he was succeeded by his grandson, Ahmad Shah I (*reg* 1411–42), who built a capital at Ashaval, naming it Ahmadabad. Ahmad's reign chiefly involved the expansion of his realm and the propagation of Islam.

From Ahmad's death until 1572, when Gujarat came under Timurid rule, Ahmadabad prospered. While intermittent wars with surrounding Rajput clans occurred, the court at Ahmadabad was a centre for artistic and literary patronage. The reign of Sultan Mahmud Bigara (*reg* 1458–1511) was particularly noteworthy in this respect, and his military campaigns increased Gujarat's status and power. From 1526 the Gujarat sultanate was marked by a series of very short reigns, revolts and the growing aggression of the Mughals. In 1572 the Mughal emperor Akbar (*reg* 1556–1605) peacefully entered Ahmadabad and subsequently conquered the surrounding area. Gujarat's commercial prosperity increased, with Ahmadabad becoming an important centre for textile production, particularly silks and velvets.

A period of decline began around the 1630s, a decade marked by severe famine followed by heavy flooding. The decline was aggravated by the military campaigns of the emperor Aurangzeb (*reg* 1658–1707). During the late Mughal period in Gujarat there were conflicts between the Mughals and the Marathas. Various negotiations between the two powers resulted in joint rule (1739–44). In 1758, after a decade of the Marathas struggle, the Mughals surrendered to them at Ahmadabad. In 1817 the city came under British protection, ending a period of disorder and insecurity under the Marathas. There was a revival of industry and trade, particularly with Europe. The first textile mills were established in 1861, leading to Ahmadabad's reputation by the end of the 19th century as the 'Manchester of India'.

Since India gained independence in 1947 Ahmadabad has become a leading industrial centre and a major producer of textiles. The state capital of Gujarat was moved in 1970 to the newly constructed city of Gandhinagar, but loss of its role as a political centre has hardly diminished Ahmadabad's importance. Material prosperity has led to the establishment of several cultural and educational institutions. The major museums are the Calico Museum of Textiles, the Museum of Tribal Research and Training Institute and the History Museum at Gujarat Vidyapith, the Museum of Gujarat Vidya Sabha at the B. J. Institute of Learning and Research, the Sanskar Kendra Museum and the Shreyas Folk Art Museum.

2. URBAN DEVELOPMENT. Although none of the urban fabric of Ashaval survives, sculptural remains from the 10th–12th centuries indicate the existence of temples at this time. Local traditions supported by 14th-century writings refer to a town called Karnavati, built by the Solanki ruler Karnadeva in the 11th century. Its exact location is not clear, but inscriptions and architectural fragments suggest an area to the south of the present city, near the eastern bank of the Sabarmati River.

Ahmadabad proper, founded by Ahmad Shah I in 1411, was built on an elevated plain called the Bhadra on the eastern bank of the Sabarmati. It comprised an open area to the east, with a palace and royal mosque to the west; parts of the fortification wall along the river survive. To the east of the fort are a triple gateway, the Tin Darvaza, and the Jamiʿ Masjid (*see* §3 below). The area around the mosque, known as Manek Chowk, was a major nucleus of mercantile activity. Ahmadabad burgeoned over the next 400 years. During the 15th and 16th centuries, noblemen developed 'suburban' settlements called by the Sanskrit word *puras*, which were more or less independent units organized around the urban centre. By *c.* 1525 the area within the fortifications was a fully developed urban

Ahmadabad, Jamiʿ Masjid, entrance to prayer-hall, completed 1424

network. An early city wall (now destr.) built around the Bhadra, probably begun by Ahmad Shah, was followed by a second wall enclosing the city, developed after 1582. These walls precluded further outward expansion, forming a semicircular boundary about 10 km in circumference and punctuated by numerous gates leading to the roads that criss-crossed the city.

Ahmadabad's prosperity under the Mughals is indicated by the various repairs and renovations to the Bhadra, the fortifications and the city gates; numerous mosques, tombs, palaces, gardens and baths (*hammāms*) were also built. However, in the 18th century, the conflicts between the Mughals and Marathas led to somewhat of a decline: levels of general maintenance of the city diminished, and many of the *puras* were abandoned. This period also marked the burgeoning of tightly knit residential areas or *pols* (Gujarati from Skt. *pratolī*: 'gate', 'road', 'street'), compact housing clusters that had begun to form in the 16th century and that answered the perceived need for greater security after communal riots in 1714. A typical example has an entry gate with houses grouped around a single street.

With the advent of the British in the early 19th century, Ahmadabad experienced phenomenal regeneration. In 1830 a cantonment was built to the north-east. In the 1860s railway lines were established, and areas of the city wall were torn down to make way for new roads leading towards the railway station. The area around the station, to the city's east, became an industrial zone, supporting textile mills and other factories. Growth—primarily in residential buildings with various educational institutions—also occurred on the western side of the Sabarmati. After 1922 most of the city walls were demolished, eventually leading to uncontrolled urban sprawl. After Independence, industry and population greatly increased. High-rise buildings have modernized the skyline, but impoverished labourers dwell in slums.

3. BUILDINGS. No structure from the early period survives, despite the fact that local belief ascribes the intact STEPWELL known as Mata Bhavani Vav, even if much altered, to the 11th century. The earliest mosques, from the period of Ahmad Shah I (*reg* 1410–42), are trabeate constructions built of masonry from demolished temples. Local artisans incorporated indigenous decorative forms from the earlier temple tradition. The Ahmad Shahi Masjid (1414) is a long hall with a series of Gujarati-style domes supported on pillars (*see* INDIAN SUBCONTINENT, fig. 91). Its arched central entry is flanked by massive piers, a feature that continued in later mosques. The Jamiʿ Masjid (see fig.), a vast, pillared prayer-hall set in a huge courtyard, was completed in 1424. Subtle architectural rhythms pervade the building, from the elevation of the façade to the precise detailing of the pillars, domes and pierced stone screens (*jālīs*) carved with geometric and floral motifs. The massive piers flanking the central entrance were originally tall minarets; the upper portions fell in an earthquake in 1819. A seraglio complex in the Bhadra, built during the 17th century, is much altered and in the late 20th century houses administrative offices. Opening from the palace on to a vast processional way is the Tin Darvaza (Triple Gate), while to the east of the Jamiʿ Masjid are the tombs of Ahmad Shah and his queens.

During the second half of the 15th century, architecture acquired a greater maturity and more comprehensive synthesis of Gujarati and Islamic elements. This can be seen in such buildings as the Sayyid Usman mosque (1460) in Usmanpur, north-west of Ahmadabad, and the mosque of Miyan Khan Chishti (1465) 2 km north of the city, where flamboyantly rendered Gujarati motifs are integral with, rather than simply attached to, the architectural elements. This robustness gave way in the early 16th century to the exquisite delicacy seen in the mosque and tomb of Rani Sipari (*c.* 1515) and the mosque of Sidi Said (1572). Rani Sipari's domed pavilion-tomb is wrapped in a mesh of pierced square stone window screens. The semicircular windows of Sidi Said's mosque have similar designs, as well as more open, flowing renditions of trees and foliage. In the Mughal period, the architects of mosques and tombs largely rejected indigenous Gujarati forms in favour of a strongly imperial style. The Shahi Bagh, a palace complex built by Prince Khurram (later Shah Jahan) in 1621–2, was typically Mughal in design and layout, although it has since been greatly altered (until 1970 it was the residence of the governor of Gujarat). More 'alien' in style are the 17th-century classicizing tombs built by Dutch and Armenian merchants near the Kankaria Tank on the eastern outskirts of the city.

From the late 16th century Jaina temples were built resembling wooden residential dwellings (an example is the Ajitnath), and the *wada* house form introduced by the Marathas (*see also* INDIAN SUBCONTINENT, §III, 7(ii)(c)) became established in the area of the Bhadra. The Jaina temple of Sheth Hathsingh (1848) revived the style of medieval Gujarati architecture. The 20th-century Hindu Swaminarayan Temple combines concrete and brightly painted wood with temple superstructures derived from central Indian styles. Works by celebrated contemporary Western architects include the Millowners' Association Headquarters (1951–4), the Sanskar Kendra Museum and Cultural Centre (1951–8), Sarabhai House (1955) and Shodham House (1956), all by LE CORBUSIER, and the Indian Institute of Management (1962–74) by LOUIS KAHN.

See also INDIAN SUBCONTINENT, §III, 6(ii)(c) and INDIA, fig. 1.

BIBLIOGRAPHY

T. C. Hope and J. Fergusson: *Architecture at Ahmedbad, the Capital of Goozerat*, ii (London, 1866)
J. Burgess: *The Muhammadan Architecture of Ahmadabad* (London, 1900–05)
M. A. Chaghatai: *Muslim Monuments of Ahmadabad through their Inscriptions* (Poona, 1934)
M. S. Commissariat: *History of Gujarat*, ii (Bombay, 1957)
K. V. Soundara Rajan: *Ahmadabad* (New Delhi, 1980)
S. B. Rajyagor, S. Tripathy and U. M. Chokshi, eds: *Ahmadabad District Gazetteer*, Gujarat State Gazetteers (Ahmadabad, 1984)
G. Michell and S. Shah, eds: *Ahmadabad* (Bombay, 1988)

R. N. MEHTA

Ahmad al-Suhrawardi [Aḥmad ibn al-Shaykh al-Suhrawardī al-Bakrī] (*b* Baghdad; *fl* 1302–28). Calligrapher. He came from a well-known family of mystics and was probably the grandson of the Sufi master Shihab al-Din Abu Hafs 'Umar al-Suhrawardi (1145–1234). He was often called Shaykhzada ('Son of the shaykh'). Ahmad was one of the six disciples of YAQUT AL-MUSTA'SIMI (*see also* ISLAMIC ART, §III, 2(iii)) and is said to have transcribed the Koran 33 times. He penned several small, single-volume copies (e.g. 1301–2, Dublin, Chester Beatty Lib., MS. 1467; 1318, Istanbul, Mus. Turk. & Islam. A., MS. 486), but the most famous is a large 30-volume manuscript (dispersed, Tehran, Archaeol. Mus.; Istanbul, Topkapı Pal. Lib.; Dublin, Chester Beatty Lib.; New York, Met.) copied at Baghdad between 1302 and 1308 and illuminated by Muhammad ibn Aybak ibn 'Abdallah. Although no patron is mentioned, the stunning size of the manuscript (500×350 mm) suggests that it was probably produced under royal auspices. Each folio has five lines of majestic *muḥaqqaq* script, penned in black. Ahmad al-Suhrawardi may also have calligraphed the finest Koran manuscript produced for the Ilkhanids, another 30-volume manuscript (dispersed, Leipzig, Karl-Marx-U.; Istanbul, Topkapı Pal. Lib.; Copenhagen, Kon. Bib.) made for Uljaytu between 1306 and 1313 and bequeathed to his mausoleum at Sultaniyya. Even larger than the earlier copy (720×500 mm), this manuscript has the same fine script and is also illuminated by Muhammad ibn Aybak. Ahmad also designed many architectural inscriptions in Baghdad. According to the Safavid chronicler Qazi Ahmad, he wrote the entire *Sūrat al-kahf* ('The cave') xviii for the congregational mosque there (destr.); masons reproduced the inscription in baked brick in relief.

BIBLIOGRAPHY

Qāżī Aḥmad ibn Mīr Munshī: *Gulistān-i hunar* [Rose-garden of art] (*c.* 1606); Eng. trans. by V. Minorsky as *Calligraphers and Painters* (Washington, DC, 1959), p. 60
M. Lings: *The Quranic Art of Calligraphy and Illumination* (London, 1976), pl. 48
D. James: *Qu'rāns of the Mamlūks* (London and New York, 1988), pp. 76–100; nos 37, 39–40, 48

Ahmad Jalayir. *See* JALAYIRID, (1).

Ahmad Karahisari [Aḥmad Qarāḥiṣārī] (*b* Afyonkarahisar, 1469; *d* Istanbul, 1556). Ottoman calligrapher. A pupil of ŞEYH HAMDULLAH, he studied with Asadullah al-Kirmani and became the most famous calligrapher during the reign of the Ottoman sultan Süleyman, when he was given the title Shams al-Din ('Sun of religion'). Ahmad took the six scripts canonized by YAQUT AL-MUSTA'SIMI as models, and perfected *thuluth* and *tawqī'* (*see* ISLAMIC ART, §III, 2(iii)(c)). Ahmad is known for his use of chain script (Arab. *musalsal*), in which the letters are joined as though the pen had never been lifted from the page. The frontispiece to a collection of religious texts (Istanbul, Mus. Turk. & Islam. A., 1443, fols 1*r*–2*v*) shows how he combined decorative and bold elements to produce a unique and attractive style. In addition to manuscripts of the Koran and albums of calligraphic exercises (e.g. 1552–3; Istanbul, Topkapı Pal. Lib., A. 3654), Ahmad designed architectural inscriptions, such as the circular panels around the mihrab and the frieze around the dome of the Süleymaniye Mosque. Unlike Hamdullah, Ahmad had few pupils. The most famous was his adopted son, Hasan Çelebi (*d* 1594), who finished transcribing a monumental manuscript of the Koran begun by his master (620×410 mm; Istanbul, Topkapı Pal. Lib., H.S. 5).

BIBLIOGRAPHY

H. Lowry: 'Calligraphy: Hüsn-i hat', *Tulips, Arabesques & Turbans:*

Decorative Arts from the Ottoman Empire, ed. Y. Petsopoulos (London and New York, 1982), p. 173, no. 183
The Age of Sultan Süleyman the Magnificent (exh. cat. by E. Atıl, Washington, DC, N.G.A.; Chicago, IL, A. Inst.; New York, Met.; 1987–8), pp. 47–50, nos 9a, 10, 11
D. James: *After Timur: Qur'ans of the 15th and 16th Centuries* (1992), iii of *The Nasser D. Khalili Collection of Islamic Art*, ed. J. Raby (London, 1992–)

NABIL SAIDI

Ahmad Musa [Aḥmad Mūsā] (*fl c.* 1330–50). Persian illustrator. In the preface to an album he compiled for the Safavid prince Bahram Mirza in 1544 (Istanbul, Topkapı Pal. Lib., H. 2154), the Safavid librarian DUST MUHAMMAD wrote that during the reign of the Ilkhanid Abu Sa'id (*reg* 1317–35) the master Ahmad Musa 'lifted the veil from the face of depiction, and the [style of] depiction that is now current was invented by him'. Dust Muhammad credited Ahmad Musa with illustrating an *Abūsa'īdnāma* ('Book of Abu Sa'id'), a *Kalila and Dimna*, a *Mi'rājnāma* ('Book of the ascension') and a *Tārīkh-i Chingīzī* ('History of Genghis Khan'); ten illustrations from a 14th-century *Mi'rājnāma*, four of them attributed to Ahmad Musa, are included in Dust Muhammad's album. He presented Ahmad Musa as a major link in the development of Persian book painting in the 14th century (*see* ISLAMIC ART, §III, 4(v)(b) and (c)): having learnt the art from his father, Ahmad Musa in turn trained Amir Dawlatyar and Shams al-Din, who worked under the Jalayirid sultan Uways I (*reg* 1356–74). Attempts have been made to connect Ahmad Musa with paintings in the great Mongol copy (ex-Demotte priv. col., dispersed) of the *Shāhnāma* ('Book of kings'), and with paintings from a fragmentary manuscript of *Kalila and Dimna* included in an album (Istanbul, U. Lib., F. 1422) prepared for the Safavid shah Tahmasp.

BIBLIOGRAPHY

Enc. Iran.
Dūst Muḥammad: 'Preface to the Bahram Mirza Album' (1544); Eng. trans., ed. W. M. Thackston, in *A Century of Princes: Sources on Timurid History and Art* (Cambridge, MA, 1989), p. 345
L. Binyon, J. V. S. Wilkinson and B. Gray: *Persian Miniature Painting* (Oxford, 1933/*R* New York, 1971), pp. 183–8
M. A. Chaghtai, ed.: *A Treatise on Calligraphists and Miniaturists by Dust Muhammad, the Librarian of Bahram Mirza, d. 1550* (Lahore, 1936) [copy of Pers. text of original doc. as written in Istanbul, Topkapı Pal. Lib., H. 2154]
E. Schroeder: 'Ahmad Musa and Shams al-Din: A Review of Fourteenth-century Painting', *A. Islam.*, vi (1939), pp. 113–42
R. Ettinghausen: 'Persian Ascension Miniatures of the Fourteenth Century', *Accademia nazionale dei Lincei, atti del XII convegno 'volta' promossa dalla classe di scienze morali, storiche e filologiche. Tema: Oriente e occidente nel medioevo: Roma, 1957*, pp. 360–83

ERNST J. GRUBE

Ahmar, Tell. *See* TIL BARSIP.

Ahmed Dalgıç [Dalgıç, Ahmet Ağa] (*d* Ulubad, Bandırma, Jan 1608). Ottoman architect and worker in mother-of-pearl. He followed the typical career path of an artist at the Ottoman court: recruited as a janissary, he was trained in the imperial palace in Istanbul and studied mother-of-pearl inlay under Ahmed Usta and architecture under Sinan (*see* SINAN (ii)), whom he assisted in the construction of the Selimiye Mosque (1567–75) in EDIRNE. Ahmed was appointed superintendent of the water supply for the capital in 1595–6 and assisted DAVUD AĞA with building the Yeni Valide Mosque on a waterlogged site at Eminönü in Istanbul. The difficulty of building foundations with constant seepage from the sea earned Ahmed the honorific *dalgıç*, or diver. He succeeded Davud Ağa as Chief Court Architect in September 1598 and carried out repairs to several buildings in Istanbul such as the Eski Saray, Yeni Saray, Galata Saray, Fetiye Mosque, Kağıdhane arsenal and janissary barracks. He continued Davud Ağa's work on the Yeni Valide Mosque and on the tomb for Mehmed III (*reg* 1574–95) beside Hagia Sophia in Istanbul, for which he fashioned the mother-of-pearl inlaid doors. Ahmed is also responsible for the adjacent tomb of Mehmed III (*reg* 1595–1603), for which he made an elegant Koran box of walnut inlaid with mother-of-pearl and tortoise-shell (Istanbul, Mus. Turk. & Islam. A., 19; *see* ISLAMIC ART, §VII, 2(iv)). Promoted to pasha, probably in 1606, he was appointed governor of Silistra in the Balkans and was killed suppressing the Kalenderoğlu rebellion in Anatolia.

BIBLIOGRAPHY

Z. Orgun: 'Mimar Dalgıç Ahmet' [The architect Ahmed Dalgıç], *Arkitekt*, xi (1941), pp. 59–62
L. A. Mayer: *Islamic Architects and their Works* (Geneva, 1956), pp. 58–9
S. Akalin: 'Mi'mar Dalgıç Ahmed Paşa' [The architect Ahmed Dalgıç Pasha], *Tarih Derg.*, ix (1958), pp. 71–80
The Anatolian Civilization III: Seljuk/Ottoman (exh. cat., 18th Council of Europe exh.; Istanbul, 1983), p. 198

HOWARD CRANE

Ahmed Nakşi (*fl* 1619–22). Ottoman painter and astrologer. Employed as the official timekeeper at the Süleymaniye Mosque in Istanbul, he was also the foremost illustrator of historical manuscripts under Sultan Osman II (*reg* 1618–22). His earliest known work is the series of 49 illustrations he provided for a copy of the *Shaqā'iq al-nu 'māniyya*, a biographical dictionary of Ottoman scholars by Taşköprülüzade Ahmed Efendi (Istanbul, Topkapı Pal. Lib., H. 1263). The manuscript was commissioned in 1619 by the grand vizier Öküz Mehmed Pasha as a gift for the Sultan, and the last scene shows the Grand Vizier presenting the book to the Sultan in the presence of the artist. The illustrations in the *divan* (collected poems) of the court epic-writer Nadiri (Istanbul, Topkapı Pal. Lib., H. 899), made in *c.* 1620, can be attributed to Ahmed Nakşi on stylistic grounds, as can those in the same author's *Şâhnâme*, an account of Osman II's campaign against Poland in 1621 (Istanbul, Topkapı Pal. Lib., H. 1124), and at least three copies of the Turkish translation of the Persian epic, the *Shāhnāma* ('Book of Kings') of Firdawsi, two dated 1620 (Uppsala, U. Lib., MS. Celsing I, and New York, Pub. Lib., Spencer col. Turkish MS. 1) and one dated *c.* 1622 (Paris, BN, MS. suppl. turc 326). Other paintings were incorporated into albums.

Ahmed Nakşi combined the traditional compositions of Ottoman painting of the 16th and early 17th centuries (*see* ISLAMIC ART, §III, 4 (vi)(e)) with conventions drawn from European prints, particularly perspective. He attempted to produce depth by giving a back view of some of the figures in the foreground, incorporating other figures into the background and having doors, windows and arches opening on to distant vistas. The source for these borrowings may be the Dutch and Italian engravings of the second half of the 16th century bound together in three albums in the Palace Library (Istanbul, Topkapı Pal.

Lib., H. 2135, 2148, 2153). His work is marked by a sarcastic sense of humour, notable in his caricatured figures and whimsical vignettes, as well as by impeccable draughtsmanship, superb use of colour and dramatic compositions.

BIBLIOGRAPHY

A. S. Ünver: *Ressam Nakşi: Hayatı ve eserleri* [The painter Nakşi: his life and works] (Istanbul, 1949)

E. Atıl: 'Ahmed Nakşi: An Eclectic Painter of the Early 17th Century', *Fifth International Congress on Turkish Art: Budapest, 1978*, pp. 103–21

ESIN ATIL

Ahmet Ali [Şeker Ahmet Pasha] (*b* Üsküdar, Istanbul, 1841; *d* Istanbul, 1907). Turkish painter. In 1859 he became an assistant teacher of painting at the Military Medical High School in Istanbul. In 1864 Sultan Abdülaziz (*reg* 1861–76) sent him to Paris where, after a preparatory education at a special Ottoman school, he studied painting in the studio of Gustave Boulanger and then under Jean-Léon Gérôme at the Ecole des Beaux-Arts. Ahmet Ali was also instrumental in the acquisition of paintings from France for the Ottoman court. After nearly eight years of studies in Paris, he stayed in Rome for a year before returning to Istanbul, where he resumed his work at the Military Medical High School. In 1873 he organized in Istanbul the first group exhibition of paintings by Turkish and foreign artists to be held in Turkey. He was later appointed master of ceremonies at the Ottoman court and by the time of his death had risen to the office of intendant of the palace. His paintings were influenced by European art. They include landscapes, such as *Pastoral Scenery* (1895; Ankara, Mimar Sinan U., Mus. Ptg & Sculp.), and still-lifes such as *Quinces* (1904; Ankara, Işbank priv. col.). He also painted a notable *Self-portrait* in the 1880s (Istanbul, Mimar Sinan U., Mus. Ptg & Sculp.) and *Military Practice on the Hills of Kâğıthane-Istanbul* (1897; Istanbul, Mus. F.A.).

BIBLIOGRAPHY

Z. Güvemli: *The Sabancı Collection of Paintings* (Istanbul, 1984) [Eng. and Turk. texts]

S. Tansuğ: *Çağdaş Türk sanatı* [Contemporary Turkish art] (Istanbul, 1986), pp. 54–9, 64, 85, 90, 92–4, 97, 107, 110–11, 119, 132, 177, 194, 365–7, 370

G. Renda and others: *A History of Turkish Painting* (Geneva, Seattle and London, 1988), pp. 88, 93–4, 97, 99–101, 105, 111, 113, 115, 119, 134, 138, 143, 236

S. J. VERNOIT

Ahnas. *See* HERAKLEOPOLIS MAGNA.

Ahrbom, Nils (*b* Hudiksvall, 25 May 1905). Swedish architect and writer. He graduated from the Kungliga Tekniska Högskola in Stockholm in 1927 and entered the office of Ivar Tengbom to work on office and commercial buildings. In 1931 he formed a partnership with Helge Zimdal, who had studied with him at the Kungliga Tekniska Högskola. The partnership lasted until 1950. Their winning entry in the competition for Sveaplan Girls High School (1931), Stockholm, was a functionalistic design based on a rational plan that divides classrooms from special facilities by placing them in architecturally separate areas. A series of school buildings, including Skanstull High School (1943), Eriksdal Schools and Gubbängen Public School (1947), High School and Gymnasium (1954), all in Stockholm, develop this method of rational planning but with a less ostentatiously modern vocabulary of red or yellow brickwork. The Östergötlands Länsmuseum (1938) in Linköping with its carefully designed gallery lighting is of a similar type. Ahrbom was appointed professor at the Kungliga Tekniska Högskola in 1942 and undertook the extension of its campus with a series of brick buildings of simple layout and carefully detailed, economical design. As a teacher he pursued a rationalist and empiricist line, which stressed the social and economic aspects of architecture: this attitude is also evident in his writings. After his retirement (1963), he worked as a consultant for the National Board of Building and contributed to a structuralist design philosophy that made its imprint on state institutional building during the 1960s and 1970s. He also designed several embassy buildings.

WRITINGS

Ny svensk arkitektur (Stockholm, 1939)

'Strukturalismen i arkitekturen', *Utvecklingen mot strukturalism i arkitekturen* [Developments towards structuralism in architecture], ed. A. Ekholm (Stockholm, 1980)

Arkitektur och samhälle [Architecture and society] (Stockholm, 1983)

BIBLIOGRAPHY

H. O. Andersson and F. Bedoire: *Swedish Architecture Drawings, 1640–1970/Svensk arkitektur ritningar* (Stockholm, 1986) [dual-lang. text]

Åhrén, Uno (*b* Stockholm, 6 Aug 1897; *d* Arvika, 8 Oct 1977). Swedish architect and writer. While a student at the Kungliga Tekniska Högskola in Stockholm (1915–19), he participated in the *Home Exhibition of the Swedish Society of Arts and Crafts* at Liljevalchs Konsthall in Stockholm. He worked in the office of Gunnar Asplund (1921–3), and his early works are in the then-prevalent Neo-classical style. However, he soon adopted the Modernism of Le Corbusier's Pavillon de l'Esprit Nouveau (1925) and the Weissenhofsiedlung at Stuttgart (1927), and he became a protagonist of rational and socially directed planning and architecture. His Students' Union building at the Kungliga Tekniska Högskola (1928; with Sven Markelius), the Flamman Cinema (1929) and the Ford Motor Co. warehouse (1930), all in Stockholm, represent this new aesthetic. Furniture and industrial design were also an important part of his work during the 1920s and 1930s. As a prolific writer for the press and professional journals, he was an effective propagandist of Modernism, contributing to the Stockholm Exhibition of 1930 with a project for the housing section, using up-to-date statistics and economic calculations and a prototype for terraced housing. He was also one of the authors of *acceptera* (1931), the manifesto of Swedish functionalism. From 1932 he devoted himself to housing and urban planning as an initiator and active member of the government Committee on Social Housing (1933–47) and City Planning Officer in Göteborg (1932–43). In 1943 he became manager of Svenska Riksbyggen, one of the first housing associations in Stockholm, and in 1947 he was appointed Professor of Urban Planning at the Kungliga Tekniska Högskola. He was influential in the formulation of the new planning legislation of 1947 and contributed to the development of comprehensive planning both as a teacher and as a planning consultant until 1963.

WRITINGS

Arkitektur och demokrati (Stockholm, 1942)

BIBLIOGRAPHY

E. Rudberg: *Uno Åhrén: En föregångsman inom 1900-talets arkitektur och samhällsplanering* [U. Åhrén: a pioneer in 20th-century architecture and planning] (diss., Stockholm U., 1981)

H. O. Andersson and F. Bedoire: *Swedish Architecture Drawings, 1640–1970/Svensk arkitektur ritningar* (Stockholm, 1986) [dual-lang. text]

☐

Ahrends, Burton & Koralek. British architectural partnership formed in 1961 by Peter Ahrends (*b* Berlin, 30 April 1933), Richard Burton (*b* London, 3 Nov 1933) and Paul Koralek (*b* Vienna, 7 April 1933). All three partners had studied at the Architectural Association School, London, between 1951 and 1956. The partnership was set up as a result of an initial collaboration in the competition (1960) for Trinity College Library, Dublin, which won first prize. Subsequent educational projects included a residential building (1965) for the Technological College, Chichester; new buildings (1976), including residential accommodation, a library and bursary for Keble College, Oxford; and the new Arts Faculty Building (1978) for Trinity College, Dublin. Major public buildings by the partnership include Redcar Central Library (1971), the Roman Catholic Chaplaincy (1971), Oxford, the Public Library (1972), Maidenhead, and St Mary's Hospital (1982), Newport, Isle of Wight. A series of commercial projects, including the Habitat Warehouse and Showrooms (1974), Wallingford, Berks, the Cummings Engine Factory (1975–83) at Shotts, Lanarks, and offices (1982–4) for W. H. Smith plc, Swindon, reflected the partnership's versatility. The firm received numerous awards, including the Structural Steel Design Award (three times). The award of first prize for their entry in the competition for the Hampton site extension (1982) to the National Gallery, London, aroused controversy, and the commission failed to materialize. As a result of this and other equally bold and radical designs, however, the firm retained a prominent reputation for relating new building technology to very specific urban contexts of a historic nature.

BIBLIOGRAPHY

J. Donat and R. Einzig: 'Ahrends, Burton & Koralek', *A + U* (Dec 1974), pp. 102–11

M. Vance: *Ahrends, Burton & Koralek, Architects: A Bibliography* (Montecello, 1985)

MICHAEL SPENS

Ai ['Ay; now Khirbet al-Tall; et-Tell, Arab.: 'The Ruin']. Site of a walled Early Bronze Age city of 11.1 ha, 24 km north of Jerusalem. It was built *c.* 3100 BC by outsiders from north Syria over a village of *c.* 3200 BC. It survived through four major phases until *c.* 2350 BC, when an unknown enemy sacked and burnt the entire city and drove away its inhabitants; even its ancient name was lost. In about 1200 BC, pioneer settlers from the coastal region moved inland and established a village of 1.2 ha on the acropolis ruins of the ancient site, which was occupied until *c.* 1050 BC. The site was excavated from 1933 to 1935 by Judith Marquet-Krause and from 1964 to 1972 by Joseph Callaway. Finds are in the Rockefeller Museum and the Hebrew University, both in Jerusalem. The site has been identified as the biblical city of Ai, captured by Joshua (Joshua 7:2–5 and 8:1–29), although there is, in fact, no evidence of occupation then.

A temple-palace complex dominated the city at its highest point, and it was surrounded by an enclosure wall 2 m wide. This basic plan was kept throughout the Early Bronze Age urban phases. The original temple was founded upon unworked cyclopean stones, and its roof was supported by five piers resting on flat stone bases in a straight line across a long rectangular central room. In about 2650 BC the temple-palace complex was reconstructed using fine Egyptian-style workmanship. Four stone bases replaced the five original ones; they were shaped by sawing deep grooves outlining a rectangle on the top, after which the stone outside the grooves was chipped away, leaving a clean raised surface upon which piers of stacked stone could rest. Some trimming on top of the rectangle indicates that the edges of the piers were set in about 40 mm on top of the base, leaving a sharply defined projection around the base of the pier. This provided a pleasing detail between the smoothly plastered surface of the floor and the pier, and added a unique and significant element to the building.

The walls of the temple were constructed of hammer-dressed stones shaped and laid like large bricks. The interior walls preserve fragments of a thick layer of red clay and straw plaster on the face of the brick-like walls, covered with a thin layer of fine white plaster, which apparently extended to the ceiling and joined the plastered floor surrounding the piers. It is probable that the piers of stacked stones were also plastered to the ceiling, giving the interior an elegant off-white décor. One patch of wall plaster preserved traces of black paint, suggesting a possible cultic design, although this cannot be reconstructed.

Two large alabaster bowls, probably imported from Egypt, were recovered in the excavation of the temple. Several other bowls and objects were found in a nearby structure designated a 'sanctuary' by the excavator, including a segmented alabaster jar and fragments of an alabaster zoomorphic vessel shaped like a waterskin.

Callaway (1972) argued that all the alabaster and stone vessels from the sanctuary belonged originally in the temple building, and that they were moved when the acropolis area was taken over by a non-Egyptian-orientated régime in the last phase of the city and used as an administrative centre. This associates the Egyptianizing phase, in which the highest cultural achievements at Ai took place, with the beginning of the 3rd Dynasty (*c.* 2650–*c.* 2575 BC). The technique of mud-brick construction faced with plaster is evident in the TOMB OF HESYRE, and the pyramid complex of Djoser (*see* SAQQARA, §1) has a temenos wall of coursed rubble masonry of local limestone set in clay like bricks. A transitional period in Egypt between the 2nd and 3rd Dynasties paralleled that at Ai from Early Bronze II to Early Bronze III (*c.* 2650 BC). It is possible that the new temple was completed by the time of Djoser's reign (*c.* 2630–*c.* 2611 BC), early in the 3rd Dynasty. At the same time, also with Egyptian influence, a unique stone-paved water reservoir was constructed in the south-east corner of the city walls to collect up to half a million gallons of water for use by the estimated 2000 inhabitants.

BIBLIOGRAPHY

J. Marquet-Krause: *Les Fouilles de 'Ay (et Tell) 1933–1935*, 2 vols (Paris, 1949)

R. Amiran: 'The Egyptian Alabaster Vessels from Ai', *Israel Explor. J.*, xx (1970), pp. 170–79
J. Callaway: *The Early Bronze Age Sanctuary at Ai (et-Tell)* (London, 1972)
——: 'New Perspectives on Early Bronze III in Canaan', *Archaeology in the Levant: Essays for Kathleen Kenyon* (Warminster, 1977), pp. 46–58
——: *The Early Bronze Age Citadel and Lower City at Ai (et-Tell)*, The American Schools of Oriental Research (Cambridge, MA, 1980)

JOSEPH A. CALLAWAY

Aiala, Josefa de. *See* AYALA, JOSEFA DE.

Aida, Takefumi (*b* Tokyo, 5 June 1937). Japanese architect, teacher and writer. He graduated from Waseda University, Tokyo, in 1960 and obtained his MArch in 1966 and DEng in 1971. He began teaching architecture at Shibaura Institute of Technology in 1962, becoming a lecturer in engineering there in 1966 and subsequently assistant professor (1973) and professor (1976). In 1967 he opened his own office in Tokyo. A founding member of the counter-Metabolist group ARCHITEXT (1971), Aida was one of the New Wave of avant-garde Japanese architects, expressing his theories in both buildings and writings. His journal articles clearly state his desire to question—if not overthrow—orthodox Modernist ideas of rationality, order and suitability of form to function. He likened architectural design to an intellectual game, and he was one of the first to equate deconstruction with the art of construction, for example in his Artist's House (1967), Kunitachi, Tokyo, in which all the elements have arbitrary relationships with each other. In other buildings he focused on the creation of architectural experiences that reflect immediate events. In the Nirvana House (1972), Fujisawa, Annihilation House (1972), Mutsuura, House Like a Die (1974), Tokyo, and PL Institute Kindergarten (1974), Osaka, for example, he placed considerable emphasis on the act of 'encounter' between different elements, forms and textures, linking conscious and unconscious responses in such a way as to afford pleasure to the user. He is perhaps best known for a series of ten designs for 'Toy Block' houses built at seven sites near Tokyo between 1978 and 1984; Toy Block House III (1981), Nakano, for example, is composed of simple, abstract elements similar to children's building blocks. A later work, Kazama House (1987), Kawaguchi, is a beautiful composition of white and pale-grey parallel wall planes orientated east–west to focus views on to a group of trees; sandwiched between the planes are 'spatial layers' of rooms and aluminium shoji screens, with additional layering provided by 'house-shaped' screen walls on the exterior.

WRITINGS

Theory of Architectural Forms (Tokyo, 1975)
Toy Block House: Works by Takefumi Aida (Tokyo, 1984)
Regular contributions to *A + U, Japan Architect, Kenchiku Bunka/Archit. Cult., Shinkenchiku, Space Des., Toshijutaku*

BIBLIOGRAPHY

C. Jencks: *Modern Movements in Architecture* (London, 1973)
A New Wave of Japanese Architecture (exh. cat., ed. K. Frampton; New York, Inst. Archit. & Urb. Stud., 1978)
B. Bognar: *The New Japanese Architecture* (New York, 1990)

MICHAEL SPENS

Aigai (i). Site of Greek settlement in north-west Turkey at Nemrud Kalesi, 35 km south of Pergamum. It is situated on a steep-sided hill easily accessible only from the north, about three hours walk inland from the modern coast road. Its foundation date is uncertain: although Herodotus (*Histories*, I.cxlix.1) listed it among the 12 Aeolian Greek cities in the region, there are few traces of it in either the historical or the archaeological record until the 3rd century BC, when Attalos I Soter of Pergamum (*reg* 241–197 BC) incorporated it into his kingdom. Its substantial fortifications make clear its function as a defensive position. The earliest walls, of crude, irregular masonry, are on the north side and presumably belong to the Aeolian city. Much more substantial walls on the other sides show Pergamene characteristics and must date to the later redevelopment. Several buildings of this period are well preserved, the most important being the agora, built in the Pergamene manner on a terrace against the eastern hillside supported by a massive retaining wall. This wall is incorporated into a three-storey stoa (the 'Market Building') with a lower floor containing shops facing down the slope, an enclosed floor acting as a storeroom above this, divided by a central arcade, and an upper floor at the level of the terrace with a conventional Doric stoa facing on to the agora. Other important buildings are a temple with a two-storey stoa enclosing its precinct and a theatre with vaulted substructures. About 45 minutes walk to the east of the city is the Ionic Temple of Apollo Chresterios, which bears a Roman dedication but is Hellenistic in form and perhaps in date.

BIBLIOGRAPHY

R. Bohn and C. Schuchhardt: *Altertümer von Aegae* (Berlin, 1889)

R. A. TOMLINSON

Aigai (ii). *See* VERGINA.

Aigina [Aegina]. Greek island in the Saronic Gulf of the Aegean Sea, mid-way between Athens to the north and Argos to the west. It is almost triangular, occupying *c.* 85 sq. km. The interior is mountainous, rising to a peak of 531 m, and the soil is largely infertile. Aigina is conspicuously visible from the Athenian port of Peiraeus, although Pericles' description of it as 'the eyesore of the Peiraeus' (Plutarch: *Pericles*, viii) stemmed from political rivalry rather than its actual appearance. The main modern settlement is in the north-west of the island, occupying part of the site of the ancient town of Aigina, which it has entirely obliterated, apart from the remains of some tombs. Outside the town there are two important sanctuaries, that of Zeus and that of Aphaia, a local goddess. The city state of Aigina was important in the 7th and 6th centuries BC, when it took part in many Greek trading ventures and developed the largest navy in Greece. Aigina was for a long time a rival of Athens and was finally defeated in a naval battle in 458 BC. In 431 BC the entire population was banished. In antiquity the island was renowned as a centre for sculpture and was also famous for its coins, which showed sea-turtles on the obverse.

MARGARET LYTTELTON

1. Bronze Age. 2. Greek period. 3. Byzantine and after.

1. BRONZE AGE. An important factor in the prehistory of Aigina was its central position between the Greek mainland and the numerous islands of the Aegean Sea. Research on the island has been concentrated mainly on Kolonna, an easily defensible peninsula on the west coast.

A prehistoric settlement was founded there, at latest, in the Final Neolithic period (*c.* 4500–*c.* 3600/3000 BC). Two Neolithic idols of marble were discovered near the Archaic Temple of Aphaia, but prehistoric habitation seems to have been centred around Kolonna.

Excavations by V. Stais (late 19th century), G. Welter (1930s) and the Archaeological Institute of the University of Salzburg (after 1966) have distinguished a sequence of ten architectural stages, called 'towns'. Phase I falls into the final Neolithic period; Towns II and III into Early Helladic II (EHII; *c.* 2900/2600–*c.* 2400 BC); Towns IV–VI into EH III (*c.* 2400–*c.* 2050 BC); and the rest into the Middle Helladic (MH) period (*c.* 2050–*c.* 1600 BC). Towns II and III are notable for their houses, among them the monumental White House, which is a 'corridor house'. The marked mainland character of both architecture and pottery during this phase shows that Aigina was an integral part of the Helladic (as distinct from the Cycladic) cultural sphere (*see* HELLADIC, §§II and III). Of great interest is Town V. It consisted of a fortification wall with protruding half-circular towers that protected several groups of houses arranged in blocks; these houses each had two rooms and an open porch. The pottery of this phase again corresponds closely to pottery wares known from EH III mainland centres. Together with the architecture, they represent a new cultural epoch.

When Town V had been destroyed, the remains of its houses were included in the strongly reinforced new fortifications of Town VI. It is mainly the repeated reinforcements of this wall, plus some minor changes, that are counted as Towns VI–VIII. A new layout is seen in Town IX: the older outside fortification wall was covered with fill, and a new one was built. During this phase the settlement was considerably enlarged by the addition of a further fortified sector, the Lower Town. This so far singular series of massive fortifications indicates that Aigina held an extraordinary, perhaps unique, position among MH settlements. This prominence is supported by the pottery dating from this phase, both locally produced and foreign. Apart from importing Minoan and Cycladic pottery wares in remarkable quantities, MH Aigina was clearly an outstanding centre for the production of both Red-burnished and Matt-painted pottery (*see* HELLADIC, fig. 7; the latter is also called Aigina ware). A richly furnished warrior's grave, found immediately outside the Lower Town and probably contemporary with Town IX or Town X, heralds the shaft-grave period. Moreover it supports the reported provenance and authenticity of the famous Aigina Treasure, a rich collection of late Middle Bronze Age jewellery (London, BM). Less is known about Late Helladic (LH, *c.* 1600–*c.* 1050 BC) Aigina, although its independence and importance during these centuries seem to have diminished.

A small colony of immigrant Minoans may have lived at Kolonna, continuing to produce pottery in Minoan style in the Mycenaean period (*c.* 1600–*c.* 1375 BC), and an increased population in later years is indicated by some new settlements from LH III (*c.* 1390–*c.* 1050 BC). The general recession of *c.* 1200 BC, however, also affected Aigina: extremely few pottery items dating from LH IIIC (*c.* 1180–*c.* 1050 BC) have been found at Kolonna, although burials were carried out there in the Protogeometric period (*c.* 1000–*c.* 900 BC).

BIBLIOGRAPHY

G. Welter: *Aigina* (Berlin, 1938, rev. 1956)
S. Hiller: *Mykenische Keramik* (1975), iv of *Alt-Ägina* (Mainz, 1974–)
R. Wünsche: *Studien zur äginetischen Keramik der frühen und mittleren Bronzezeit* (Munich, 1977)
R. Higgins: *The Aegina Treasure* (London, 1979)
H. Walter and F. Felten: *Die vorgeschichtliche Stadt* (1981), III/i of *Alt-Ägina* (Mainz, 1974–)
H. B. Siedentopf: *Mattbemalte Keramik der mittleren Bronzezeit* (1991), IV/ii of *Alt-Ägina* (Mainz, 1974–)

STEFAN HILLER

2. GREEK PERIOD.

(i) Architecture. (ii) Sculpture.

(i) Architecture. Aigina benefited from the development of trade links with the east Mediterranean and Egypt in the 7th century BC and particularly in the 6th, and its architectural importance stems from the buildings put up as a result of this prosperity. The ancient Greek town has been largely destroyed by the construction of the modern town, in particular the 19th-century harbour wall.

The principal temple, dedicated to Apollo, was built towards the end of the 6th century BC over the remains of a prehistoric settlement. Only the stump of one column is still standing. The foundations of the Temple of Apollo had to be cut deep into the decayed mud-brick of the prehistoric settlement, and the large numbers of square stone blocks required provided a ready source of building material for the modern harbour. The temple was Doric, peripteral (only 6×11 columns), with a width–length ratio of approximately 1 : 2, distinctly short for its date. There are fragments of pedimental sculpture (*see* §(ii) below), and a single carved metope (Aigina, Archaeol. Mus.) may be from this temple: if so, its good state of preservation suggests that it belonged to a porch entablature, rather than the exterior colonnade. The surviving details of this temple are not in themselves sufficient for an accurate reconstruction of its original form. They are, however, directly comparable with those of its near contemporary, the Temple of Aphaia.

This temple is much better preserved, providing important evidence for the form of Doric temples at the time of transition from the Archaic (*c.* 700–525/480 BC) to Early Classical (*c.* 525/480–*c.* 450 BC) periods, as well as being important for its outstanding pedimental sculpture. Aphaia was a goddess of local significance, and the site of her sanctuary is a hilltop at the north-east corner of the island, commanding extensive views of Attica and the Saronic Gulf. A non-peripteral Doric temple to her was built about 570 BC, and, although it was demolished, many fragments have been discovered. Its main features were a heavy entablature and an internal entablature behind the front entablature. This was destroyed by fire about 510 BC, and work seems to have begun almost immediately to replace it with a larger, peripteral temple, which, though on a slightly different alignment, was built over the remains of the earlier building.

The new temple (see fig. 1) measures 13.77×28.12 m and has 6×12 columns. The proportions are almost certainly identical to those of the slightly earlier Temple of Apollo. The cella is conventional, with pronaos and

1. Aigina, second Temple of Aphaia, east end, early 5th century BC

opisthodomos, although the latter was closed by a grille, with an access door cut later in the rear wall of the cella. Despite the relatively modest dimensions, the cella ceiling and the roof timbers were supported by internal colonnades, arranged in two storeys (*see* GREECE, ANCIENT, fig. 21). Some of the upper columns are now restored to their original position. The architraves between the lower and upper colonnades later supported a floor over the space between them and the cella walls. Most of the columns are monolithic, reflecting the older, Archaic method of construction, although three at the east end of the north side are built from drums, as was normal for mainland Doric temples of the 5th century BC. The Temple of Aphaia was made from local poros limestone and stuccoed, with pedimental sculptures of marble. No trace survives of the metopes, which may also have been of marble and deliberately removed. Other well-preserved and distinctive features are the U-shaped grooves for lifting-ropes, visible, for example, in the ends of the entablature blocks; a central ramp at the east end; and a wide altar placed directly in front of the temple. The chronology of the temple is confused by the existence of remains of a third group of pedimental statues and by the difference in style between the pedimental groups at the east and west ends. The earlier, west pediment is still distinctly Archaic, while the east is in the initial stage of transition to the Early Classical style. The stratigraphy of the terrace on which the temple stands includes fragments of the predecessor as well as construction debris of the replacement. Work had probably started by the late 6th century BC, but there seems to have been a delay before the temple was completed, perhaps caused by the Persian Wars and a resulting decline in Aigina's resources. Around the temple are 6th-century BC buildings belonging to the sanctuary, including a small propylon and a feasting building.

Also on the island are some Hellenistic (323–27 BC) buildings, notably a terraced Sanctuary of Zeus. Constructed on a saddle just below the summit of the highest mountain at the centre of the island, this has a broad approach staircase. Pergamene influence can be detected here, following the acquisition of Aigina by Attalos I (*reg* 241–197 BC).

BIBLIOGRAPHY

A. Furtwängler: *Aegina: Das Heiligtum der Aphaia* (Munich, 1906)
G. Welter: *Aigina* (Berlin, 1938, rev. 1956)
W. W. Wurster: *Der Apollontempel* (1974), I/i of *Alt-Ägina* (Mainz, 1974–)
E.-L. Schwandner: *Der altere Porostempel der Aphaia auf Aigina* (Berlin, 1985)

R. A. TOMLINSON

(ii) Sculpture. From the references in ancient sources to works from Aigina, the existence of an Aiginetan school of sculpture and its chronology have long been debated. As implied by Pausanias (e.g. II.xxx.1, VII.v.5, X.xvii.12), the style of Archaic Aiginetan sculpture was clearly recognizable, regardless of the material. The sources indicate that Aigina was a major centre for sculpture during the Late Archaic period (*c.* 550–*c.* 500/480 BC) and especially for bronze sculpture of the Early Classical period (*c.* 500/480–*c.* 450 BC). Finds from Aigina itself bear witness to the importance of local Archaic stone sculpture and the primary role of marble sculpture production in

the economic flourishing of the island in the late 6th century and early 5th BC, although the specifically local contribution here is difficult to define precisely. Strong artistic influences and trade in sculpture operated both ways between Aigina and the Aegean islands, Attica and Corinth, as confirmed by both the surviving stone sculpture and the literary sources.

(a) Early works. Apart from a few Archaic statues on the island, such as the cult image of *Apollo*, Pausanias mentioned Aiginetan statues at Megara (an ebony *Apollo*), at Antikyra (an *Artemis* in black stone), near Tegea (an ebony *Artemis*) and at Olympia (a wooden statue of a victor). Wood was the main material for early works, apparently continuing a still more ancient tradition. For example, the type of the standing figure seems to belong to such a tradition, in contrast to the striding pose of later stone kouroi. On the evidence of documented works now lost (e.g. the wooden cult statue of *Hera*; Pausanias, VII.iv.4), Aigina produced at least one sculptor of more than local importance as early as the 6th century BC, named as Smilis, son of Eukleides. From his recorded collaboration with Rhoikos and Theodoros on Samos, it is possible that he brought the new technique of bronze-casting back to Aigina. However, the earliest securely documented bronze sculptor from Aigina was KALLON, who made a wooden *Athena* for Troizen and a bronze one for the Acropolis at Athens, as well as a bronze tripod in Amyklai, at the end of the Archaic period (Pausanias, II.xxxii.5, VII.xviii.10). He was not a pupil of Smilis but of Tektaios and Angelion, who made the cult images in the Sanctuary of Apollo on Delos.

2. Aigina, *Herakles*, marble, h. 790 mm, from the east pediment of the Temple of Aphaia, first quarter of the 5th century BC (Munich, Glyptothek)

The earliest surviving sculpture from Aigina dates from the mid-7th century BC, although it exists only in severely damaged fragments. Architectural and votive sculpture has been found primarily in the Sanctuary of Apollo in the city and in the Sanctuary of Aphaia on the other side of the island. In the first half of the 6th century BC the front of the Temple of Apollo received pedimental sculpture representing battle scenes, including the figure of a kneeling *Herakles* (Aegina, Museum, 731). The stone used was local poros, and a further series of sculptures in poros was made at this time, some being exported to Athens. In addition, there is a series of kouroi and korai in Naxian and Parian marble and two votive columns with sphinxes, also from Naxos. It is uncertain to what extent poor quality marble sculptures can be connected to local workshops on Aigina. Towards the end of the 6th century BC, the renovated Temple of Apollo was provided with metopes, pedimental sculpture and acroteria. The east pediment may have shown a gathering of the gods with a chariot; the west, an *Amazonomachy*, possibly with Athena in the middle. The acroteria were of Parian marble and have been ascribed to Athenian sculptors. The provenance of an over-life-size relief fragment depicting two chariots passing one another (Aegina, Museum, 752), which has been attributed (Walter-Karydi) to the Heroon of Aiakos (Pausanias II. xxix, 6), is unclear.

(b) Temple of Aphaia. The most famous sculptures from Aigina are those from the pediments of the Temple of Aphaia. Most of these were discovered in 1811 and finally arrived, via the antiquities market, in Munich (now in Munich, Glyp.). The original pedimental figures, dating from the early 5th century BC, still exemplify the full-blown Late Archaic style. The east pediment, however, was destroyed and then replaced immediately after the Persian Wars. The new sculptures were in the Early Classical style of the period (for example the kneeling figure of *Herakles*; see fig. 2). The remains of the earlier pedimental sculptures were also preserved in the sacred area. Both pediments show mythical battles, in which the victors press out from either side of a calm central standing figure of Athena. In this way the fighting groups, passing from standing figures to kneeling, falling and ultimately reclining bodies in the corners (*see* GREECE, ANCIENT, fig. 91), adapt to the triangular space. Both groups show developments in pedimental composition, and the way the composition is united in the west pediment anticipates the Classical solution. The new east pediment presented a more compact composition of the same conception. The acroteria, which comprised korai in the middle and sphinxes at the sides, display the same style. The figures had numerous metal attachments, including weapons, locks of hair and the snakes of Athena's aegis. Although they are of Parian marble, this does not necessarily indicate Parian workmanship, since this material was already widely exported. On the contrary, many shared motifs and stylistic affinities with contemporary and slightly older votive sculpture from Aigina suggest a connection with a local workshop. An ivory eye from the cult image of the Temple of Aphaia may also point to a native sculptor. At the same

time it has not been possible to attribute these works securely to particular sculptors known from ancient sources.

(c) Bronze sculpture. According to Pausanias, Aigina had its own school of bronzeworking, although most of its possible productions are now known only through literary references. Colossal bronze statues in a special Aiginetan alloy were apparently made by Myron of Eleutherai at Athens and Kanachos of Sikyon at Didyma, and by many Early Classical sculptors from Aigina. Only a few small bronzes have been found on the island, including a Late Archaic figure of *Zeus Hurling a Thunderbolt* (Princeton U., NJ, Mus.) in the Early Classical style. A Late Archaic life-size bronze head with a stylized, jutting beard (Athens, N. Archaeol. Mus., 6446), found on the Athenian Acropolis near the Propylaia, has often been attributed to the Aiginetan school on the basis of its resemblance to the pedimental sculpture of the Temple of Aphaia. The colossal *Bull* at Delphi, donated by the inhabitants of Kerkyra (Corfu), was the work of Theopropos (Pausanias, X.ix.3–4), who supposedly signed another, donated by the Plataians. ANAXAGORAS OF AIGINA is ascribed a colossal *Zeus Hurling a Thunderbolt* at Olympia, commissioned by the victor of Plataia (Pausanias, V.xxiii.1). Three early 5th-century BC bronze victory statues of famous boxers by GLAUKIAS OF AIGINA stood in Olympia, as did his statue of the tyrant *Gelon of Syracuse* in a chariot (Pausanias, VI.ix.4–9, x.1, xi.9). Simon of Aigina collaborated with Dionysios of Argos on a bronze group of fighters and horses in Olympia (Pausanias, V.xxvii.2, VI.xxi.1). Other Early Classical works included bronze victor statues by Serambos and by Ptolichos at Olympia (Pausanias, VI.ix. 1, x.9), and one by Philotimos from the mid-5th century BC (Pausanias, VI.xiv.12).

ONATAS was Aigina's most famous sculptor. Pausanias' comments, together with signed bases, point to an extensive oeuvre through the first half of the 5th century BC. Onatas seems to have specialized in statues of gods and groups of heroes, with works in Athens (equestrian statuette on the Acropolis), Delphi (large group of *Fighting Tarentines*), Olympia (colossal statues of *Herakles*, *Hermes with the Ram of Pheneos*, a group of *Achaians Drawing Lots before Nestor*, the *Chariot of Hieron of Syracuse*), Phigalia (*Demeter*) and Pergamon (colossal statue of *Apollo*). Although Pausanias singled Onatas out as having been unexcelled (V.xxv.13), the reconstruction of his oeuvre and the definition of his style have nevertheless proved elusive. A late Early Classical marble votive sphinx from the Sanctuary of Apollo on Aigina, which has been associated with Onatas' *Apollo* at Olympia, in fact recalls Parian workmanship and may be an import. Finally, the attempt to attribute a seated goddess from Taranto to an Aiginetean sculptor is inconclusive.

(d) Grave reliefs. Although only a few tiny fragments of Archaic marble stelai have been found, the few Early Classical grave stelai include some masterpieces. The handshake motif, which dominated Attic grave reliefs from the end of the 6th century BC, occurs for the first time on a stele depicting an enthroned woman with a man standing in front of her (Aigina, Archaeol. Mus., 729), and there is a fine late Early Classical stele depicting a man with a boy and a dog (Aegina, Museum, 733). Sculpture production ceased with the dissolution of the city state of Aigina by Athens in 458 BC and the final expulsion of the population in 431 BC. Two grave reliefs, one depicting a man with a horse (*c.* 430 BC) and the slightly later 'Cat Stele' (both Athens, Nat. Archaeol. Mus.), belong to the period of Attic settlement of the island and clearly relate to the Parthenon sculptures, and all later finds essentially belong to the categories of Attic sculpture.

BIBLIOGRAPHY

Pausanias: *Guide to Greece*
A. Furtwängler: *Aegina: Das Heiligtum der Aphaia*, 2 vols (Munich, 1906)
K. Lehmann-Hartleben: *Drei Entwicklungsphasen griechischer Erzplastik* (1937/*R* 1981), pp. 7–14
G. Welter: *Aigina* (Berlin, 1938, rev. 1956)
G. Lippold: *Die griechische Plastik* (Munich, 1950), pp. 33–4, 97–103
L. Guerini: 'Sculture di Egina', *Archeol. Class.*, xiv (1962), pp. 135–47
H. Herderjürgen: *Untersuchungen zur Thronenden Göttin aus Tarant in Berlin und zur archaischen und archaistischen Schrägmanteltracht* (Waldsassen, 1968)
D. Ohly: *Die Ostgiebelgruppe* (1976), i of *Die Agineten* (Munich, 1976)
J. Dörig: *Onatas of Aegina, Monumenta Graeca et Romana* (Leiden, 1977)
J. Floren: *Die geometrische und archaische Plastik* (1987), i of *Die griechische Plastik* (Munich, 1987–), pp. 309–11
E. Walter-Karydi: *Die äginetische Bildhauer-Schule: Werke und schriftliche Quellen* (Mainz, 1987), II/ii of *Alt-Ägina* (1974–)
U. Sinn: 'Aphaia und die "Aegineten"', *Mitt. Dt. Archäol. Inst.: Athen. Abt.*, cii (1987), pp. 131–67
C. C. Mattusch: *Greek Bronze Statuary from the Beginnings through the Fifth Century B.C.* (Ithaca, NJ, and London, 1988), pp. 89–94, 142–3

REINHARD STUPPERICH

3. BYZANTINE AND AFTER. During the Byzantine period Aigina was repeatedly plundered by the Saracens, forcing its inhabitants to move their capital inland during the 9th and 10th centuries on to a naturally fortified hill, known as Palaiochora, where it remained until 1826. There they built houses, some 35 small churches and a castle. From 1204 to 1451 Aigina was the fief of Venetian and Catalan families. It then passed to Venice, was captured by the Turks in 1537 and recaptured by the Venetians in 1654, and ceded to Turkey in 1718. In 1826–8 the town was the temporary capital of newly liberated Greece.

The only Early Christian remains are at a basilica behind the modern church of St Nicholas in the town. Numerous ruined later Byzantine churches include those of St Nicholas of Mavrika (12th century) and St Theodore (1284), known as the 'Beautiful Church'. The former is a domed Greek cross in plan and contains the remains of three phases of fresco decoration. The earliest programme depicts a full-length figure of *Christ* and a mounted *St George and the Dragon*. The modelling of Christ's figure and face, and the use of green shadows in the skin tones, suggest a date in the second half of the 12th century. Although little of the second-phase frescoes survives, they are dated by inscription to 1330.

The interior of the small, single-nave church of St Theodore also has fresco decoration. The iconographic programme is exclusively concerned with the *Life of Christ*, particularly scenes of the *Passion*. In general the iconography follows Middle Byzantine models, as characterized by the limited number of figures in the scenes and the depiction of certain themes, such as the *Preparation of the Throne* in the sanctuary. The *Suckling Virgin* and the eyes on the cave of the *Nativity*, representing celestial glory,

Aigues-Mortes, aerial view from the east

are much older and rarer iconographic motifs. Stylistically the linear, flat and decorative qualities of these frescoes suggest that they were executed by a provincial painter still working within the Komnenian tradition, although certain scenes are similar in style to Romanesque frescoes.

The post-Byzantine churches of Aigina, most of which are in Palaiochora, belong to four architectural types: the single nave, the single nave with a transverse sanctuary, the double-aisled and the domed Greek cross. Wall paintings from the period have survived in a number of churches, such as the third-phase frescoes in the church of St Nicholas of Mavrika, which are dated by an inscription to 1522. Most of the extant frescoes in Palaiochora have been attributed to a local 17th-century school. The best-preserved churches are Episkopi (St Dionysius), with frescoes of the *Life of Christ* (dated 1610) in the nave, and St Kyriaki, with painted scenes of the Akathistos Hymn and the *Second Coming* (dated to 1680). The monastery of Panagia Chryssoleontissa (1600) houses two 17th-century Cretan icons: the *Virgin 'the Joy of the World'* by Theodoros Poulakis (first half of the 17th century) and the *Virgin Platytera* (1651–80) by Emmanouil Skordilis.

BIBLIOGRAPHY

RBK

G. A. Sotiriou: 'E Omorfi Ekklesia Aigines' [The Beautiful Church of Aigina], *Epeteris Hetaireias Byz. Spoudon*, ii (1925), pp. 243–76

N. K. Moutsopoulos: *E Paleachora tes Aigines: Istorike kai morfologike exetasis ton mnemeion* [Palaiochora of Aigina: an examination of the history and morphology of the monuments] (Athens, 1962)

A. Lentakis: 'Oi iereis kai agiografoi Emmanouel kai Antonios Skordiles' [The sanctuaries and icons of Emmanouil and Antonios Skordilis], *Kimoliaka*, vii (1977), pp. 352–3

S. Lauffer, ed.: *Griechenland: Lexikon der historischen Stätten: Von den Anfängen bis zur Gegenwart* (Munich, 1989), pp. 83–6

MELITA EMMANUEL

Aigner, Chrystian Piotr (*b* Puławy, June 1756; *d* Florence, 8 Feb 1841). Polish architect and writer, also active in Italy. He probably studied in Rome in the late 1770s and returned to Italy in 1785–6 under the aegis of Stanisław Kostka Potocki, a collector and amateur architect with whom he collaborated throughout his life. In 1786 Aigner and Potocki refronted the church of St Anna, Warsaw, using a giant composite order on high pedestals. The political turmoil of the 1790s disrupted Aigner's career, but during his second phase of creativity (1797–1816) he won fame through his work on the great estate of the Czartoryski family at Puławy, on the Vistula west of Lublin, the most important centre of cultural life in Poland during the Enlightenment. Aigner had already erected the Marynka Palace there in 1790, a variation on the Petit Trianon at Versailles, France, and from 1798 he began to add ornamental buildings to go with the new Picturesque layout of the Puławy gardens: a Chinese pavilion, a Gothick house and a peripheral Temple of the Sibyl with a shallow dome. In 1800 Aigner worked for Izabella Lubomirska. He designed the orangery and neo-Gothic elevation of the castle at Łańcut and the decoration of the Ball Room, as well as a semi-circular colonnade in the grounds, where he also built a little castle with a corner tower in the Picturesque taste. For Potocki, at his old Baroque palace at Wilanów, just outside Warsaw, Aigner landscaped the grounds and added the mandatory Gothick gallery and the Morysinek Rotunda (1802–12). Together with Potocki, he carried out alterations (1806–8) to the house at Natolin, south of Warsaw, designed for the Czartoryski family by Simon Bogumil Zug, converting it from a summer retreat to a year-round residence and incidentally changing the order at the entrance from Ionic to Roman Doric.

In 1812 Aigner left Poland for Italy, becoming a member of the Accademia di S Luca in Rome. He returned to Poland in 1816, where he was appointed Professor of Architecture at Warsaw University and Inspector General of Works for the Kingdom of Poland.

Aigner's third phase of activity (1812–25) was centred mainly in Warsaw, where the Radziwiłł Palace was rebuilt in accordance with his plans (1818–19). His church of St Aleksander is an amphiprostyle hexastyle domed cylinder (destr. 1944, rebuilt 1949), recalling the features of his church at Puławy. Aigner left Poland for good in 1827, living first in Rome and moving to Florence in 1837. He was one of the leading architects of Polish Neo-classicism, strongly influenced by Andrea Palladio in his first phase and later deviating into Gothick and other styles in response to the demands of Picturesque revivalism.

WRITINGS

Budownictwo wiejskie z cegły glino-suszonej [Rural buildings in dried brick] (Warsaw, 1791)

O świltyniach u starożytnych i o słowiańskich [On the temples of the ancients and of the Slavs] (Warsaw, 1811)

Rozprawa o guście w ogólności, a w szczególności o architekturze [On taste in general and especially on architecture] (Warsaw, 1812)

Budowa kościołów cz.I [The building of churches, part 1] (Warsaw, 1825)

BIBLIOGRAPHY

T. S. Jaroszewski: *Chrystian Piotr Aigner, architekt warszawskiego klasycyzmu* [Chrystian Piotr Aigner, architect of Varsovian classicism] (Warsaw, 1970)

ANDRZEJ ROTTERMUND

Aigues-Mortes [Lat. *aquae mortuae*: 'dead waters']. Town in Gard, southern France, in the north-western section of the Rhône Delta or Camargue. It is one of the largest surviving medieval fortified towns (see fig.). Although documents show that there was a port on the site of

Aigues-Mortes in the late 12th century and first third of the 13th, the town was officially not founded until the Charter of 1246, which exempted inhabitants from taxes. Louis IX (*reg* 1226–70) conceived of the walled city. He wanted a port to establish a royal presence in, and access to, the Mediterranean, and he needed a fortified town to protect crusaders, pilgrims and merchants, providing a safe haven from which to launch crusades, as well as a commercial centre for trade between the Levant and northern France. The only land available for this purpose lay between that owned by the bishop of Maguelonne and king of Aragon (which included the region around Montpellier) on the west, and Provence controlled by Emperor Frederick II on the east. Negotiations with the Benedictine monks of Psalmodi for the acquisition of land for the walled city began in 1240 and ended in 1248. The astute monks kept the fishing rights and the salt beds.

Soon after 1240 Louis IX began the construction of the Tour de Constance, the isolated tower on the north-western corner of the site ; it was finished in 1249, the year after he launched the Seventh Crusade. Construction of the walled town did not, however, begin until 1272 during the reign of Louis's son Philip III (*reg* 1270–85), and work continued into the early years of the 14th century. Funds for the huge project were raised by taxes on the Genoese, Venetian, Catalan and other merchants who made Aigues-Mortes one of the richest ports in the Mediterranean. The town became the major commercial link between the Mediterranean trade and the fairs of Champagne, via Lattes, the port of Montpellier. During the years 1309–77, when the popes were in Avignon, much of the food, especially fish and spices, was supplied to the papal city by the merchants of Aigues-Mortes. The demise of Aigues-Mortes occurred in 1481, when Provence became part of France and Marseille emerged as the major port of southern France.

The limestone blocks of Aigues-Mortes have been replaced here and there, but most of the masonry is original. Unlike most medieval towns, which grew by accretion around a monastery, castle, chapel or cathedral, Aigues-Mortes was planned as a whole. In shape it is a slightly irregular rectangle, with streets laid out to a grid plan, derived from the Roman *castrum*. The northern wall is 520 m long, while the southern one is 510 m; the western wall measures 285 m in length and the eastern 325 m. The disposition of streets seems to be related to the routes converging on Aigues-Mortes as well as to the two structures built before the walls were erected: Notre-Dame-des-Sablons and the convent of the Cordeliers. An axis runs from the main road from the north-east via the main north gate to a street leading to the main square, the Place St Louis, after passing Notre-Dame-des-Sablons. Roads on the east are linked by two other gates and lead to streets framing the convent of the Cordeliers. The rest of the streets more or less conform to the rectangular plan.

There are six main gates, each with two towers and two portcullises, and four other secondary gates. On three of the corners are large circular towers, while the north-west corner is protected by the Tour de Constance with its moat. These towers are all connected to the curtain walls but can be isolated in time of attack. Distances between the mural towers are close enough for bowmen to protect the curtain walls with their arrows and thus prevent sapping and breaching. Originally no houses were built against the walls so that soldiers had easy access to all the defences. The construction of the gates and towers, with crenellations and slits for archers and allowing free circulation, represents the high point in military architecture before the invention of artillery in the 14th century. Architecture similar to Aigues-Mortes can be seen in the later 13th-century fortress of Saint-André in Villeneuve-les-Avignon.

Notre-Dame-des-Sablons, erected in the mid-13th century, is a handsome if simple unvaulted structure of nave and two aisles with a flat east end. It was restored between 1964 and 1967. The most impressive building in Aigues-Mortes is Louis IX's Tour de Constance. This huge circular tower with its moat and crowning lighthouse was designed as the fortress and symbol of the developing port. It is 47 m high and has 3 storeys, with a diameter of 23 m and walls 7 m thick. The three chambers with their radiating ribbed vaults and ingeniously placed fireplaces and spiral staircases are very impressive. The carving of the ornamental capitals is of the highest quality and stylistically reminiscent of Ile-de-France sculpture.

Two other structures, not attached to Aigues-Mortes, were integral to its planning. The deep water docks, called La Payradé, with quays of large limestone blocks, are 2.7 km south of Aigues-Mortes and were connected to the original canal to Maguelonne. The Tour Carbonnière, 3.5 km north of Aigues-Mortes, guarded the land route to the town, as well as the water route by the River Vistre.

BIBLIOGRAPHY

A. Fliche: *Aigues-Mortes et Saint-Gilles*, Petites Monographies Grands Edifices France (Paris, 1961), pp. 6–27

J. Nougaret and others: *Inventaire général des monuments et des richesses artistiques de la France: Gard, Canton Aigues-Mortes*, 2 vols (Paris, 1973), vol. i, pp. 34–85; vol. ii, figs 1–629

C. Landes and others: *Les Etangs à l'époque médiévale d'Aigues-Mortes à Maguelonne* (Lattes, 1986), pp. 144–5

WHITNEY S. STODDARD

Aihole [Aihoḷe, Aivalli; anc. Āryapura, Ayyāvoḷe]. Temple site and city in Karnataka, India, that flourished *c.* AD 525–1200.

1. HISTORY. An important centre of the early Chalukya dynasty (*see* CHALUKYA, §1), Aihole is situated, like the nearby sites of PATTADAKAL and BADAMI, near the Malaprabha River. Little is known of the ancient urban complex, but there are remains of a massive city wall with bastions and fragmentary crenellations. Inscriptions indicate that Aihole was a prominent commercial centre and the home of the 'Ayyavole Five Hundred', a corporation of traders and craftsmen. The remains of about 150 temples (in diverse styles) are preserved at the site. The oldest date to the mid-6th century and later examples to the time of the RASHTRAKUTA dynasty (*c.* 752–973) and Chalukyas of Kalyana (973–1189; *see* CHALUKYA, §2).

The temples at Aihole were first photographed and published in the mid-19th century by Col. Thomas Biggs, Bhau Daji and James Fergusson. Further work was subsequently carried out by James Burgess and Henry Cousens. Cousens's numbering system, with some addition and alteration, is that still used. Since India's independence

1. Aihole, India, Ravana Phadi cave, interior, mid-6th century AD

Aihole has received substantial attention and re-evaluation, including extensive clearing and restoration by the Archaeological Survey. The numerous later monuments have, however, received little systematic study.

2. ROCK-CUT SHRINES. Four rock-cut temples at Aihole, dating to the early Chalukya period, are the earliest shrines to survive in the Karnataka region. The first excavation is the Shaiva Ravana Phadi, which faces the ancient town from a low rocky hill to the north. The sculpture and profuse decoration (see fig. 1) show some affiliation with the late 5th-century and early 6th-century caves of Maharashtra, as does the plan, with its central hall and flanking subsidiary shrines.

The Jaina Meena Basti (no. 70), near the centre of the site, is also rock-cut. It had an open verandah (later filled in) similar to those at Badami, while the decoration is much like that of the Ravana Phadi. To its north is an unusual two-storey Buddhist temple, the only such dedication to survive from early Chalukya times. A few metres to the west is a Jaina or Buddhist shrine hollowed out of a single boulder.

3. STRUCTURAL TEMPLES. Aihole exhibits the full range of architectural forms used during the early Chalukya period. The south temple of the Ravana Phadi complex (see fig. 2), with its unarticulated square cupola, appears to be the simplest and earliest example in the southern (Skt *drāviḍa*) idiom to have survived to the late 20th century. The only other building in the southern style is the Jaina Meguti, dedicated in AD 634–5 (Shaka era 556), which dominates the town from a small hill. The plan, with its square hall enclosing the sanctum, is a general type appearing often in early Chalukya architecture. The original superstructure has disappeared, but the wall articulation is typically southern. The pilasters, brackets and scrollwork are executed with precision and clarity.

In the second half of the 6th century a number of elements of the *latina* form of the northern (*nāgara*) style were introduced at Aihole, as well as some anomalous temples that defy conventional definition; these buildings show that the tendency toward creative hybrids in Karnataka started at an early date. Many of these temples carry inscriptions, but none gives an unarguable date; dedications tend to favour the god Shiva. The idiosyncratic Lad Khan, long considered to be one of the earliest temples in India, is best dated to the late 7th century or the early 8th on the basis of the similarity of its interior to that of the Jambulinga temple (dated 699) at Badami. The Lad Khan is a stoutly proportioned building, square in plan with a closed pillared hall lit by pierced screens. The roof, built of sloping slabs, carries a miniature temple over the centre.

More standard are the temples in the northern style erected from the late 7th century to the mid-8th. (The Kannada word for temple, *gudi*, often forms part of the name.) The Huchchimalli Gudi and Tarappa Gudi, to the north of the town, have fully developed but austere superstructures of the curvilinear northern (*nāgara*) kind. The halls are closed, like those of the Lad Khan, and built of massive blocks of masonry. The Mallikarjuna and Temple 10, in the Galagnath complex, present a distinct variation, with interior details northern in style and the spires composed of rows of cornice mouldings (*kapota*). This simplified northern form of superstructure has sometimes been called 'kadamba' on the mistaken assumption that it is traceable to the Kadamba dynasty that preceded the early Chalukyas in the Deccan. Other examples are found at Bhadranayika Jalihal and Mahakuta near Badami.

Three temples at Aihole show influence from the architecture of the Andhra or Telingana region. The Chekki Gudi (no. 15) shares interior features with the Huchchimalli Gudi, but the outer walls are closely related to the Kumara Brahma at ALAMPUR. Elements traceable to the Andhra region are also evident in the Durga temple, the most elaborate and ornately sculpted building at the site. Standing on a richly moulded base (*adhiṣṭhāna*), the Durga temple is apsidal-ended and has an open ambulatory (*pradakṣiṇapatha*) running around the whole structure. The porch and ambulatory are decorated with southern-style niches, while the sanctum carries an elegant superstructure of the northern type. There are splendid images in the niches in the outer wall of the hall (*maṇḍapa*), and remains of a gateway beside the temple. After a long controversy, this building is now recognized as a Sun (Aditya) temple from the end of Vijayaditya II's reign (*reg c*. 696–733).

The most impressive of Aihole's sculpture is generally found on temple doorways, lintels and ceiling panels, the last usually depicting Brahma, Vishnu and Shiva. Fine ceiling panels from the time of Vikramaditya II (*reg c*. 734–46) remain in the north-western temple of the Konti Gudi group (no. 5). The set from the Huchchappayya Gudi, designed by the craftsmen Narasobba and Ganasobba, have been removed to the Prince of Wales Museum, Bombay. Some fragmentary sets and individual ceiling panels remain in the Galagnath and Ravana Phadi complexes; an example from the latter group depicting Vishnu is now in the National Museum, New Delhi.

Quality varied towards the end of the early Chalukya period: richly carved fragments in the Jyotirlinga group indicate continued patronage, while the Chakra Gudi, begun with care, was finished in a patchwork of anomalous pieces. Finally there are entirely haphazard works, such as Temple 47 and the eastern structures of the Ambiger group (no. 21). Temples from the Rashtrakuta period—the south-western and north-eastern temples of the Konti Gudi group (nos 4 and 6), Temple 11, Temple 39, the Ambiger Gudi and Santa Gavunda's temple in the Huchchimalli Gudi group—have little figurative sculpture, and what there is is small in scale. Buildings from the time of the Chalukyas of Kalyana include the Charanti Matha (no. 40) and the Virupaksha, both 12th century.

Remains of other early Chalukya-period structures are located within a few kilometres of Aihole: at Siddhanakola, to the south, a Lakulisha temple, a panel depicting the seven mother goddesses (*saptamātṛkā*) and a rock-cut Lajja Gauri; across the Malaprabha River at Damoa a southern-style temple; and at Sulibhavi, to the east, a ritual tank and gateway with workmanship stylistically similar to that of the Durga temple.

See also INDIAN SUBCONTINENT, §§III, 5(i)(g) and 6(i)(f); IV, 7(vi)(c).

2. Aihole, India, south temple of the Ravana Phadi complex, mid-6th century AD

BIBLIOGRAPHY

M. Taylor and J. Fergusson: *Architecture in Dharwar and Mysore* (London, 1866)
J. Burgess: *Report on the First Season's Operations in Belgām and Kaladgi Districts*, Archaeol. Surv. India, New Imp. Ser., i (London, 1874)
J. F. Fleet: 'Sanskrit and Old Canarese Inscriptions', *Ind. Antiqua.*, viii (1879), pp. 237–46
H. Cousens: *Chālukyan Architecture of the Kanarese Districts*, Archaeol. Surv. India, New Imp. Ser., xlii (Calcutta, 1926)
M. Rama Rao: 'Early Chalukyan Architecture: A Review', *J. Ind. Hist.*, xli (1963), pp. 431–59
R. S. Gupte: *The Art and Architecture of Aihole: A Study of the Early Chalukyan Art through Temple Architecture and Sculpture* (Bombay, 1967)
S. Settar: 'A Buddhist Vihara at Aihole', *E. & W.*, xix (1969), pp. 126–38
G. Tarr: *The Architecture of the Early Western Chalukyas* (diss., Los Angeles, UCLA, 1969; microfilm, Ann Arbor, 1970)
——: 'Chronology and Development of the Chalukya Cave Temples', *A. Orient.*, viii (1970), pp. 155–84
M. S. Mate and S. Gokale: 'Aihole: An Interpretation', *Studies in Indian History and Culture*, ed. S. Ritti and B. R. Gopal (Dharwar, 1971), pp. 501–4
A. Lippe: 'Early Chālukya Icons', *Artibus Asiae*, xxxiv (1972), pp. 273–330
G. Michell: *An Architectural Description and Analysis of the Early Western Chalukyan Temples*, 2 vols (London, 1975) [fine measured drgs]
S. Padigar: 'The Durga Temple at Aihoḷe, an Āditya Temple', *Archaeol. Stud.*, ii (1977), pp. 59–64
G. M. Tartakov: 'The Beginning of Dravidian Temple Architecture in Stone', *Artibus Asiae*, xlii (1980), pp. 39–99
C. E. Radcliffe (Bolon): *Early Chalukya Sculpture* (diss., New York, Inst. F.A., 1981)
S. Rajasekhara: *Early Chalukya Art at Aihole* (New Delhi, 1985)
K. V. Soundara Rajan: *Cave Temples of the Deccan*, Archaeological Survey of Temples, iii of Archaeol. Surv. India, New Imp. Ser. (New Delhi, 1986)
G. M. Tartakov: *The Durga Temple and the History of Indian Art* (New Delhi, 1994)

GARY MICHAEL TARTAKOV

Ai Khanum [Aï Khanoum; Ay-Khanum]. Site of a Hellenistic town of the Greco-Bactrian kingdom, located at the confluence of the Kokcha and Pyandzh rivers (tributaries of the Amu River), northern Afghanistan. The site was excavated by the Délégation Archéologique Française en Afghanistan under Paul Bernard, from 1965 until the outbreak of the Afghan civil war in 1978. The town was founded on the eastern border of the *oikoumene* (inhabited territory) in the late 4th century BC or early 3rd, after the conquest of this region by Alexander the Great and, Bernard suggested, was first called Alexandria Oxiana. The name was changed to Eukratidea (after the Greco-

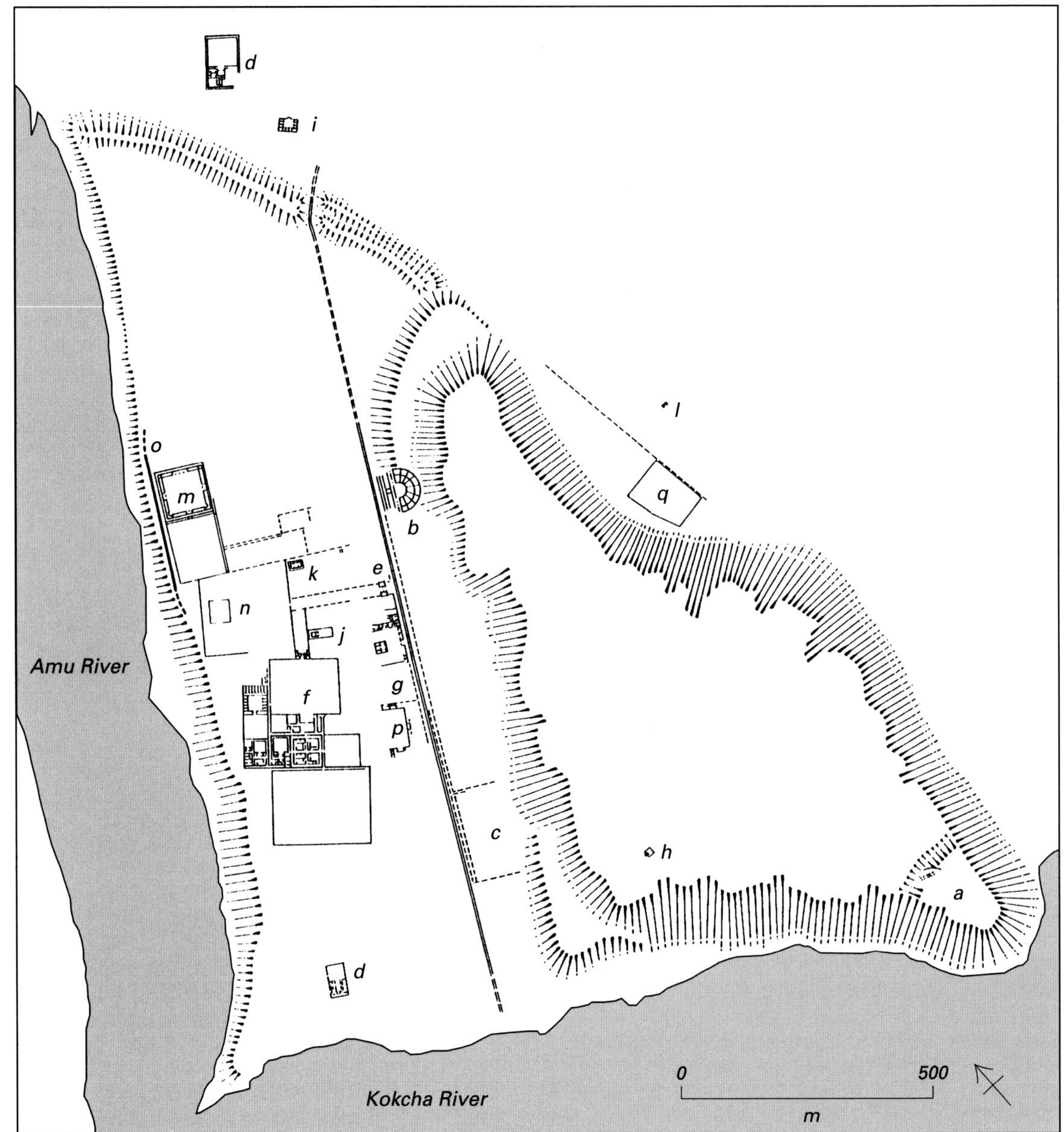

1. Ai Khanum, late 4th century BC/early 3rd–*c.* 140 BC, plan: (a) citadel; (b) theatre; (c) arsenal; (d) house; (e) propylaeum; (f) palace enclosure; (g) temple 'à redans' or 'à niches indentées'; (h) podium temple; (i) temple; (j) heroon or temple of Kineas; (k) mausoleum; (l) necropolis; (m) gymnasium; (n) swimming pool; (o) fountain; (p) public building; (q) vineyard

Bactrian king Eukratides), *c.* 170–*c.* 150 BC, when an extensive programme of construction was carried out. After the town was attacked and destroyed *c.* 140 BC, it was abandoned by its inhabitants. Later, during the Yueh-chih and Kushana periods (*c.* 1st century BC–3rd century AD), the ruined buildings were occupied by 'post-Greek' peoples who did not undertake any significant repair work. Little has yet been published concerning this later period at the site. Finds from the site were placed in Kabul Museum, although they appear to have been looted after the museum was bombed in 1993.

The principal building material was the traditional mudbrick of the region (square bricks, 390–450 mm in size), but this was widely combined with stone, both for construction and for decorative purposes. Over 800 stone fragments were found in the area of the Propylaeum alone. The town thus had the appearance of having been built of stone, despite the combination of this material with, for instance, wooden architraves or clay roofs. Construction elements include stone bases, column shafts and capitals. At Ai Khanum not only a wide range of styles based on the Greek Doric, Ionic and Corinthian orders are found in various combinations, but torus-shaped (with an integral torus) and bell-shaped bases that relate both to the Achaemenid architectural tradition and to late Attic bases also occur. Any oriental influence is more apparent in the use of construction devices, rather than architectural principles, and did not become the norm. Bernard suggested that a combination of a tendency towards the grandiose and an infallible sense for the selection of the most rational devices was characteristic of Greco-Bactrian architecture. The most important determining principle was, however, to reproduce, as fully and perfectly as possible, the essential elements of a Greek way of life (not only in everyday terms but also in the philosophical sense), even if this meant building a theatre or gymnasium that far exceeded the needs of the population.

The site is triangular in plan (2400×1800×1600 m; see fig. 1). The upper town or citadel (1a) was located on a natural acropolis that rises to a height of 60 m. On the lower terraced slope of this hill was a theatre (1b) with a seating capacity of 6000, which comprised an orchestra (h. 15 m, diam. *c.* 42 m), 35 semicircular stepped rows (h. 450–500 mm; w. 600–700 mm) of mud-brick (not stone, as was usual for Greek theatres), and three paired boxes in the centre of the amphitheatre. On the same terrace was an 'arsenal' (1c), consisting of a series of long, narrow storerooms with traces of racks along the walls and a central courtyard. The main street (l. *c.* 1700 m) extends the length of the site and separates these buildings and the acropolis from the lower town. The residential quarter with its luxurious houses (1d) in the south-western part of the site and the administrative centre were reached from the main street via the propylaeum (1e). When first built (*c.* 280–*c.* 250 BC), the propylaeum had a staircase and four-columned portico that were replaced, following reconstruction in the third quarter of the 2nd century BC, by a ramp and an eight-columned portico (10.5×28.5 m).

The most important administrative buildings were located in the palace enclosure (1f). A large formal northern courtyard with a columned portico around the perimeter and a columned vestibule gave access to offices and reception areas in the centre, a treasury with numerous storerooms on the north-western side and private apartments to the south-west. Finds in a storeroom of the treasury, possibly a library, included papyrus imprints, one comprising 28 lines of a philosophical treatise in the form of a dialogue resembling those of Plato or Aristotle's *Metaphysics*, the other the text of a dramatic work. Two large squares adjoined the complex to the east and south.

A primary religious building was the temple 'à redans' or 'à niches indentées' (1g), comprising a pronaos and a cella or naos with two lateral chapels, set on a podium (20×20×1.5 m). In front of a niche in the cella was the stone foundation for the pedestal of a statue, possibly of Zeus, for large stucco locks of hair covered with gold leaf and fragments of an ivory throne were found. The niche contained the remains of painting, gilding and other traces of the former glory of the building before it was robbed and burnt down *c.* 140 BC. The two other temples at Ai Khanum were located on a podium on the acropolis (1h) and outside the northern gate of the city (1i).

Another sacred site was a heroon within a temenos (1j), 40 m to the north of the palace. The building, a replica of a temple with a sloped roof, was erected on a three-stepped stylobate of mud-brick, and comprised a pronaos with two wooden columns and a naos. Under the floor of the naos were two stone and two fired-brick sarcophagi. An inscription identified the edifice as the tomb of Kineas, founder of the city. To the north was another rectangular mausoleum (29.5×20.0 m; 1k), with a row of stone columns along each side and containing a vestibule and two rooms, which functioned as a family burial vault for a member of the aristocracy. According to Greek custom, most of the dead were buried in mausolea outside the city (1l).

2. Ai Khanum, head of a bearded man, detail of a stone herm, h. 770 mm, from the gymnasium, *c.* 150 BC (Kabul, Kabul Museum)

The gymnasium (1m) covered an area of over 2 ha, and comprised a courtyard (*c.* 100×100 m) surrounded on four sides by rooms, exhedras and peripheral corridors used for classes and various kinds of physical exercise. The sundial was an obligatory part of such buildings. There was also a yard containing a small square swimming pool (40×40×2 m; 1n). Later, a rotunda (diam. 9.5 m) enclosing a circular reservoir faced with unbaked brick was adapted for swimming. According to an inscription, the gymnasium was protected by Hermes and Herakles. A stone herm with the head of a bearded man (see fig. 2) from the site may represent an actual person connected with the gymnasium (*see also* AFGHANISTAN, §II, 1(ii)(b)). The complex differs from most other Greek gymnasia in the absence of a peristyle around the central courtyard, although the function of a gallery for walks may have been fulfilled instead by a peripheral corridor (385×2.85 m). On the river bank, 50 m north of the gymnasium, was a fountain (1o) set in a niche (5.8×4.0 m) of stone blocks, which, according to Pausanias (*Guide to Greece* X.iv.1), was as much a vital element of a true *polis* as a theatre or a gymnasium.

Sculpture is best represented among the works of art discovered at Ai Khanum. The temple 'à redans' contained the remains of two statues, both made by building up layers of clay on a wooden armature. Some imported marble pieces of a left foot (l. 270 mm), part of a right hand and fragments of a left hand holding some object obviously came from a single statue that has been justifiably identified by Bernard as an acrolithic figure of Zeus, that is with the head, hands and feet made of stone and the remaining parts of unfired clay on a wooden carcass. Zeus seems to have been seated on a throne, as in depictions of the god on the coins of Alexander the Great and other Hellenistic rulers. Pieces entirely of stone include limestone statuettes, the herm from the gymnasium, an unfinished statuette of an athlete with a wreath, 29 fragments of a relief with the image of a young man (h. 570 mm) from the temple outside the north gate, and spouts for a fountain in the form of a lion head, a dolphin head and a grotesque mask of an old man. Other finds include a bronze statuette of a young Herakles, a plaster cast depicting a galloping horse and a terracotta form for a half-length image of a woman in a *chiton* and *himation*. Ivory marionettes of naked female figures in 'hieratic' pose have attached arms and a thread for operating them that passed down a canal drilled through the body to the centre of a small pedestal (*see also* CENTRAL ASIA, §I, 8(iv)). Small items included a medallion with Ajax and Cassandra and a gilded silver disc with a Hellenistic scene depicting the goddess Cybele accompanied by Nike in a chariot pulled by lions. Two priests, one standing on a three-stepped altar in front of the chariot and the other behind the chariot, holding a canopy over the goddess, are elements that owe their origins to Mesopotamia or Syria. Generally however, the finds of Ai Khanum, even those clearly of local origin, are all dominated by Greek prototypes and traditions, albeit occasionally exhibiting evidence of slight influence from Asia Minor.

The epigraphical finds are of great significance. Inscriptions of the 3rd century BC, such as the gymnasium inscription, the dedication of Klearchos and Delphic maxims, contain no names of non-Greek type, while later financial documents from the treasury (mid-2nd century BC) already record high-ranking officials, including the chief treasurer, who bear local names with a clear Iranian etymology, such as Aytat, Arvand, Ksatran, Oxeboakes and Oxubazes. The evidence suggests the hellenization of the upper levels of Bactrian society, in a climate where the mastery of Greek language, habits and culture undoubtedly led to increased social status, rather than the barbarization of the Greek population, culture and art of Ai Khanum.

See also AFGHANISTAN, §§I, 4 and II, 1(i)(b), (ii)(b), (iii), (iv)(c), and CENTRAL ASIA, §I, 2(i)(a) and (iii).

BIBLIOGRAPHY

P. Bernard: 'Fouilles d'Aï Khanoum', *Acad. Inscr. & B.-Lett.: C. R. Séances* (1966), pp. 127–33, 554–5; (1967), pp. 306–24; (1968), pp. 263–79; (1969), pp. 313–55; (1970), pp. 301–49; (1971), pp. 385–453; (1972), pp. 605–32; (1974), pp. 280–306; (1975), pp. 167–97; (1976), pp. 287–322; (1978), pp. 421–63

——: 'Aï Khanum on the Oxus: A Hellenistic City in Central Asia', *Proc. Brit. Acad.*, liii (1967), pp. 71–95

——: 'Chapiteaux corinthiens découverts à Aï Khanoum', *Syria: Revue d'art oriental et d'archéologie*, xlv (1968), pp. 111–51

P. Bernard and others: *Fouilles d'Aï Khanoum*, 9 vols, Mém. Dél. Archéol. Fr. Afghanistan, xxi, xxvi–xxxi, xxxiii (Paris, 1973–92)

P. Leriche: 'Un Rempart hellénistique en Asie Centrale', *Rev. Archéol.* (1974), pp. 231–70

P. Bernard: 'Fouilles à Aï Khanoum (Afghanistan): Campagne de 1974', *Bull. Ecole Fr. Extrême-Orient*, lxiii (1976), pp. 5–58

——'Les Traditions orientales dans l'architecture gréco-bactrienne', *J. Asiat.*, cclxiv (1976), pp. 245–75

P. Leriche and J. Thoraval: 'La Fontaine du rempart de l'Oxus à Aï Khanoum', *Syria: Revue d'art oriental et d'archéologie*, lvi (1979), pp. 170–205

P. Bernard and others: 'Campagne de fouilles 1978 à Aï Khanoum (Afghanistan)', *Bull. Ecole Fr. Extrême-Orient*, lxviii (1980), pp. 1–104

P. Bernard: 'Gimnasiy v Aykhanum' [The gymnasium in Ay-Khanum], *Gorodskaya kul'ture Baktrii, Tokharistana i Sogda. Antichnost', ranneye srednevekov'ye: Materialy sovetsko-frantsuzskogo kollokviuma (Samarkand, 1986)* [The urban culture of Bactria, Tokharistan and Sogdian antiquity, early medieval period: materials of the Soviet–French colloquium (Samarkand, 1986)] (Tashkent, 1987), pp. 22–31

YE. V. ZEYMAL'

Aikman, William (*b* Cairnie, Forfar, Tayside, 24 Oct 1682; *d* London, 4 June 1731). Scottish painter. He came from a professional background, and his maternal uncle, Sir John Clerk of Penicuik, may have provided Aikman with an introduction to Sir John Baptist Medina, under whom he studied painting in London from 1704. In 1707 Aikman set out on travels to Italy, Constantinople (now Istanbul) and Smyrna, on the proceeds made from the sale of his estate at Cairnie. When he returned to Edinburgh in 1711, he adopted a heavy Baroque style for his portraits: *Sir William Carstares* (*c*. 1712–15; U. Edinburgh, Old Coll., Upper Lib.) shows bravura, although the handling is coarse. The three-quarter-length portraits of *Patrick, 1st Earl of Marchmont* (1720; Mellerstain, Borders) and *Sir Hew Dalrymple, Lord North Berwick* (1722; Edinburgh, Parliament House) show a greater sophistication, which he may have acquired during a further trip to London in 1720.

Aikman was widely patronized, especially by the Duke of Argyll and his circle; after the Act of Union in 1707 (which transferred Scotland's seat of government to London), however, the art market in Edinburgh inevitably declined. After the death of Sir Godfrey Kneller in 1723, Aikman left for London; apart from a brief visit to Edinburgh in 1730, he remained there for the rest of his life. This astute business move resulted in patronage from Richard Boyle, 3rd Earl of Burlington, Sir Robert Walpole, the prime minister, and Queen Caroline, through Argyll. By 1728 he commanded 40 guineas for a full-length portrait. While retaining the acute observation of the *Carstares* portrait he also adopted the decorative approach of Jonathan Richardson (i) and Charles Jervas, as in the double portrait of his nieces *Anne and Elizabeth Clerk* (1730; Penicuik House, Lothian). Aikman was a close friend of the poet Allan Ramsay, and his consequent influence on his eldest son, the painter Allan Ramsay, establishes his significance in the history of Scottish art.

UNPUBLISHED SOURCES

Edinburgh, Register House [Penicuik Papers]

BIBLIOGRAPHY

D. Irwin and F. Irwin: *Scottish Painters at Home and Abroad, 1700–1900* (London, 1975)

Painting in Scotland: The Golden Age (exh. cat. by D. Macmillan, U. Edinburgh, Talbot Rice Gal.; London, Tate; 1986)

J. Holloway: *William Aikman* (Edinburgh, 1988)
——: *Patrons and Painters: Art in Scotland, 1650–1760* (Edinburgh, 1989)

HUGH BELSEY

Aila. *See under* NAXOS, §1.

Aillaud, Emile (*b* Mexico City, 18 Jan 1902; *d* Paris, 29 Dec 1988). French architect. He graduated from the Ecole des Beaux-Arts, Paris, and worked for a time in the office of André Ventre (1874–1951). In the late 1930s, when he was unable to obtain larger commissions in Depression-stricken France, his activity was limited to ceremonial decorations and exhibition displays such as the Pavillon de l'Elégance at the Exposition Internationale des Arts et Techniques dans la Vie Moderne, Paris (1937), and the Salle de la Haute Couture in the French pavilion at the World's Fair, New York (1939), which gave him a taste for theatrical settings. In 1945 he was appointed Chief Architect of the Houillères de Lorraine, a coal-mining conglomerate in a drab area where reconstruction and industrial modernization was urgently needed; as well as industrial structures, he also designed some single-family workers' housing such as the Cité Bellevue (1945–7) in Creutzwald, and this marked the beginning of his dedication to the improvement of low-cost housing.

From the mid-1950s Aillaud's activity was centred mostly on the Paris region and upon the improvement of suburban *grands ensembles*, dormitory cities of several thousand housing units that were considered by French authorities as the only possible remedy to the housing crisis caused by the exodus from rural areas. Aillaud was alone among Beaux-Arts-trained architects of his generation in fighting the dehumanizing uniformity of such large-scale residential development. Early examples of his work, based on Scandinavian models, include the 1500-unit Cité de l'Abreuvoir (1956–60), Bobigny; the 1700-unit Les Courtillères (1958–64), Pantin; and Le Wiesberg (1959–63), Forbach, in the Moselle. In each case the spine of the composition was a long, winding four- or six-storey building consciously reminiscent of the terraced crescents in Bath, with a few oddly shaped 15-storey towers. Softer sculptural forms were also used: for example the child-care centre at Pantin echoed Oscar Niemeyer's chapel (1942) in Pampulha and the church at Forbach, with its egg-shaped sanctuary, recalled work by Alvar Aalto. The façades, clad with prefabricated concrete panels using the Camus process implemented by Bernard Zehrfuss, were enhanced with colour, and Aillaud also attempted to create secondary rhythms in the placement of windows.

At La Grande Borne (1964–71; *see* PARIS, fig. 13), Grigny, near the new town of Evry, Aillaud achieved a greater degree of sophistication in the general composition and in the design of pedestrian spaces where he relied on his close contacts with artists including his son, Gilles, and Fabio Rieti (*b* 1927) to produce baroque, theatrical effects. He created a city with different neighbourhoods of contrasting densities and landscaping; instead of 'green spaces', he emphasized Mediterranean-style enclosed and secluded spaces, incorporating perspective and visual surprise by the use of familiar elements, such as a foot, at a surrealistic scale. Grigny was widely publicized by the media and by Aillaud himself and brought him considerable public attention. It was followed by La Noë (1971–5), Chanteloup-les-Vignes, and the Quartier Picasso (1974–8), Nanterre, where he used small, clover-leaf windows as a feature. In 1970 he was appointed a juror in the international competition for the Centre Georges Pompidou, Paris. He was also entrusted with the design of a structure to terminate the 'triumphal way' from the Place de l'Etoile, Paris, and from 1972 to 1983 he proposed several designs, the best known being two low curvilinear 'mirror' buildings (unexecuted).

Aillaud achieved considerable public stature in France and abroad but he deliberately cultivated an image as a misunderstood architect–artist and remained a marginal figure, uninterested in peer recognition. His work in low-cost housing, despite its remarkable originality and consistency, was criticized as being based more on plastic preoccupations than on social awareness; for example his efforts to provide a rich environment at Grigny did not address the problems of teenage leisure, and his use of cultural references was sometimes inappropriate. The curvilinear shapes he used in order to avoid uniformity did not always lend themselves to practical planning, especially in slender, high-rise towers, and the concrete panels and coloured wall surfaces weathered very badly due to poor quality execution, a general phenomenon of French architecture at the time. Restriction of traffic to the periphery of the development at Grigny also increased its geographic and stylistic isolation from the surrounding suburban context. In spite of these problems, his work should be regarded as an outstanding attempt at restoring humanity and dignity to low-cost housing, a lesson that was reflected in the work of a younger generation of French architects in the 1980s, especially in the new towns of Paris.

WRITINGS

Désordre apparent, ordre caché (Paris, 1975)
Chanteloup-les-Vignes: Quartier La Noë (Paris, 1978)

BIBLIOGRAPHY

G. Gassiot-Talabot and A. Devy: *La Grande Borne à Grigny: Ville d'Emile Aillaud* (Paris, 1972)
J.-F. Dhuys: *L'Architecture selon Emile Aillaud* (Paris, 1983)

ISABELLE GOURNAY

Ai Mitsu [Nichirō Aikawa; Nichirō Ishimura] (*b* Hiroshima Prefecture, 24 June 1907; *d* Shanghai, 19 Jan 1946). Japanese painter. On leaving school he became an apprentice in a print-shop in Hiroshima, where he learnt design and plate-making. In 1923 he entered Tensai Gajuku, a private school of painting in Osaka, intending to become a painter, and in the following year he went to Tokyo to study at the Taiheiyō Painting Study Centre. Like many other young painters of the time he was influenced by modern European painting, including the work of van Gogh. After submitting work to the 13th exhibition of the Nikakai (Second Division Society) in 1926 he began a career in which he showed works in various group exhibitions.

From the depression of the late 1920s and up to and during World War II Japanese society became increasingly militarized; in spite of the hardships experienced by Ai Mitsu during this period, his work entered one of its most significant stages in the latter part of the 1930s. In *Lion* (1936; Saitama Prefecture, priv. col., see Miyagawa and

Asahi, pl. 12) there is a feeling of emotional oppression, which is also represented by the image of an apparently starving dog in *Horse* (1936; Tokyo, N. Mus. Mod. A.). In *Horse* Ai Mitsu's interest in the paintings of the Chinese Song (960–1279) and Yuan (1279–1368) periods is clear. It was perhaps this interest in Chinese painting and in *Nihonga*, the traditional Japanese-style painting, that made Ai Mitsu's work so individual.

In the 1930s Ai Mitsu was influenced by Surrealism, evidence of which can be seen in works such as *Landscape with an Eye* (1938; Tokyo, N. Mus. Mod. A.; *see* JAPAN, fig. 114) and *Bird* (Sendai, Myagi Prefect. Mus. A.). In these paintings he also succeeded in giving form to thoughts and feelings that were generally suppressed in Japan at that time. Towards the end of World War II he returned to objective figurative painting, for example *Self-portrait* (1944; Tokyo, N. Mus. Mod. A.), but after being drafted into the army, he was sent to the Chinese front; afflicted by amoebic dysentery, complicated by malaria, he died in hospital in Shanghai.

BIBLIOGRAPHY

Y. Kikuchi, ed.: *Ai Mitsu* (Tokyo, 1965, rev. 1975)

T. Miyagawa and A. Asahi: *Gashū Ai Mitsu* [The collected paintings of Ai Mitsu] (Tokyo, 1980)

TORU ASANO

Aimo [Amio; de Amis; de Jami; Lamia; da Varignana], **Domenico** [il Bologna; il Varignana; il Vecchio Bolognese] (*b* Varignana, *c.* 1460–70; *d* Bologna, 12 May 1539). Italian sculptor and architect. He was the son of Giovanni da Varignana and is mentioned in a contemporary poem as a pupil of Andrea Sansovino. According to Vasari, after the discovery in 1506 of the *Laokoon* (1st century AD; Rome, Vatican, Mus. Pio-Clementino), Aimo participated in a contest arranged by Bramante to make the best copy in wax of the ancient marble statue for later casting in bronze. His fellow competitors were Zaccaria Zacchi, Alonso Berruguete and Jacopo Sansovino. Raphael, who had been appointed as judge, decided in favour of Sansovino.

A payment to Aimo of 21 January 1511 documents two sculptures for the lunette of the Porta Magna of S Petronio, Bologna: an archivolt relief depicting a half-length figure of *Moses*, and a statue of *St Ambrose.* The latter was commissioned to provide a symmetrical counterpart to Jacopo della Quercia's *St Petronius*, which is also in the lunette. St Ambrose's robe, held together by a clasp, is gathered up to hip level by the right hand; below this is rich drapery with numerous dish-shaped folds. The figure as a whole is stockier than della Quercia's and stands upright in contrast to the Gothic swing of *St Petronius.* The theory that the statue was constructed by della Quercia and merely reworked by Aimo is unacceptable. The figure of a sibyl, in S Petronio, may also be by Aimo (Brugnoli).

In 1514 Aimo received a commission from the Roman senate to execute a statue of *Pope Leo X* in the Palazzo dei Conservatori, Rome. The statue (now Rome, S Maria in Aracoeli), resting on a plinth that bears three inscriptions, was installed in the Palazzo dei Conservatori in 1521. The Pope is shown seated, and his face is rendered realistically. The figure as a whole does not have an imposing effect, and even if this were intentional, Aimo's lack of artistic force can still be felt.

Probably in 1518 Aimo produced a design for the façade of S Petronio (Bologna, Mus. S Petronio, n. 1a, *see* BOLOGNA, §IV, 2), incorporating the existing plinth and the vertical divisions determined by the original architect. At portal level Aimo planned a row of niches, freeing the lower area for sculptures. Horizontal bands divide the façade above the portal. Large quantities of obtrusive plaques surmount the cusps over the whole area. Aimo's sculptural talents are revealed in the decoration of the gable ends and the wall sections, which end in tabernacles. The ornamentation of these sections is lavish: especially striking are the half-leaping, half-flying angels sounding trumpets on the abundant, foliated finials. In terms of architectonic detail, the central window complex and the corner sections are particularly striking. Altogether the design presents a mixture of styles and creates the impression of an oversized stage set. Owing only to conflicts within the building committee, the façade decoration was undertaken following Aimo's drawing and was completed to the present level by the end of the 1550s. Around 1520, Aimo undertook to execute a relief of the *Death of the Virgin* for the Santa Casa, Loreto Cathedral. He worked on the sculpture in Ancona from the end of 1523 until 5 August 1525. Aimo, Niccolò Tribolo and Francesco da Sangallo received payment on 31 December 1536 on completion of the work. In the meantime Aimo had again taken up residence in Bologna.

BIBLIOGRAPHY

DBI; Meissner

G. Vasari: *Vite* (1550, rev. 2/1568); ed. G. Milanesi (1878–85)

R. Bernheimer: 'Gothic Survival and Revival in Bologna', *A. Bull.*, xxxvi (1954), pp. 263–84

J. Pope-Hennessy: *Italian High Renaissance and Baroque Sculpture* (London, 1963, 2/1970)

J. H. Beck: 'A Document Regarding Domenico da Varignana', *Mitt. Ksthist. Inst. Florenz*, xi (1963–5), pp. 193–4

M. G. Ciardi Duprè: 'La scultura di Amico Aspertini', *Paragone*, xvi/189 (1965), pp. 3–25

A. M. Mateucci: *La porta magna di S Petronio* (Bologna, 1966)

H. H. Brummer and T. Janson: 'Art, Literature and Politics: An Episode in the Roman Renaissance', *Ksthist. Tidskr.*, xlv (1976), pp. 79–93

M. V. Brugnoli: 'Problemi di scultura cinquecentesca', *La basilica di San Petronio in Bologna*, 2 vols (Bologna, 1983), ii, pp. 103-16

ANDREW JOHN MARTIN

Ain, Gregory (*b* Pittsburgh, PA, 28 March 1908). American architect. He received his architectural training at the School of Architecture (1927–8), University of Southern California, Los Angeles. He worked with Rudolph Schindler (1932) and Richard Neutra (1932–5) who both influenced his development greatly. In 1936 he opened his own office in Los Angeles. His principal early work consisted of private houses in the Los Angeles area, but like both Schindler and Neutra, Ain had a marked interest in low-cost housing. One example is his Dunsmuir Flats (1937–9), 1281 South Dunsmuir Avenue, Los Angeles. In 1940 Ain received a Guggenheim Fellowship to explore a system of panel design for such housing. In collaboration with landscape architect Garrett Eckbo (*b* 1910) Ain produced setback housing units in garden settings for various locations in the Los Angeles area; most notable were Park Planned Homes (1946), Altadena, CA, and two groups in Los Angeles, the Mar Vista Housing complex and the Avenel Housing complex, 2839–45 Arenel Street, Silver Lake (both 1948). In 1950, with Joseph Johnson and Alfred Day, Ain designed an exhibition house for the garden of MOMA, New York. Ain served as Dean of the School of Architecture, Pennsylvania State University, from 1963 to 1967.

BIBLIOGRAPHY

Contemp. Architects
Built in the USA since 1932 (exh. cat., ed. E. Mock; New York, MOMA, 1945)
E. McCoy: *The Second Generation* (Salt Lake City, 1984)

LELAND M. ROTH

Ainai, Geoffroi d'. *See* GEOFFROI D'AINAI.

Ain Dara [Ayin-Dara]. Site on the west bank of the River Afrin in Syria, about 5 km south of the town Afrin. Attention was drawn to the ancient site by surface finds of sculpture, and a large Neo-Hittite temple of the early 10th century BC was located below five levels of later occupation. Excavations here by the Syrian General Directorate of Antiquities in 1956, 1962 and 1964 have been reported, but more recent work has not been published. Finds are *in situ* or in the National Museum in Aleppo.

Parts of the north-west and south-west sides, with a fragment of a south-east façade, have been excavated and published. The remains suggest a structure of regular rectangular plan measuring in total not less than 38×32 m. An exterior terrace wall seems originally to have been faced with continuous slabs of fine black basalt on a dressed plinth; some of these were found *in situ*. They were carved with lions (north-west wall) and winged sphinxes (south-west wall), but unfortunately the stone has suffered damage, and most slabs are badly flaked and splintered from the top. Within the terrace wall the outline of the inner shrine is visible, and the remains of three carved orthostats serving as pilasters on its outer wall remain *in situ*, showing the lower parts of a hero with bull, a throned figure and a palmette. On the fragment of south-east façade the slabs with lions and sphinxes are surmounted by badly damaged lion protomes. The only well-preserved sculpture comes from the interior of the shrine, apparently *in situ*, and consists of two sets of three small blocks, each with a central mountain-man flanked by pairs of bull-men, winged lion-men or winged griffin-men, all the figures being in caryatid posture, as if supporting a divine throne or something similar. Elsewhere on the site a well-preserved basalt portal lion was found out of context. The sculpture is rendered in the heavy, robust style recognized as the earliest Neo-Hittite, found elsewhere only at CARCHEMISH in the Water-Gate sculpture, dating from the early 10th century BC. The profusion of this style at Ain Dara, and the promise of more, give the site its importance. Unreported discoveries are known to have been made, including the first inscribed fragments from the site.

It is probable that Ain Dara belonged to the kingdom of Unqi in the 10th century BC. It has even been suggested as the site of Kinalua, the capital city, but this seems more likely to have been TELL TAYINAT. In the absence of an elucidatory inscription, the status of Ain Dara will remain uncertain.

BIBLIOGRAPHY

F. Seirafi: 'The Excavations of Ayin-Dara, First Campaign 1956', *An. Archéol. Syrie*, x (1960), pp. 87–102 [in Arab.]
F. Seirafi and A. Kirichian: 'Recherches archéologiques à Ayin-Dara', *An. Archéol. Syrie*, xv/2 (1965), pp. 3–20
W. Orthmann: *Untersuchungen zur späthethitischen Kunst* (Bonn, 1971)
A. Abou Assaf and W. Khayata: 'Les Fouilles archéologiques à Ain Dara', *An. Archéol. Arabes, Syr.*, xxxiii/1 (1983) [in Arab.]
A. Abou Assaf: 'Septième Campagne de fouilles à Ain Dara', *An. Archéol. Arabes, Syr.*, xxxiii/2 (1983) [in Arab.]
E. de Crombrugghe: 'Un Huitième Relief de Ain Dara au Musée d'Alep', *Mélanges Paul Naste* (Louvain-la-Neuve, 1984), pp. 13–20

J. D. HAWKINS

Ain Ghazal [Arab. ʿAyn Ghazāl]. Neolithic site in Marka, north-eastern Amman, Jordan. Excavations have yielded impressive lime-plaster statues and clay figurines dating to the Pre-pottery Neolithic B period (*c.* 7200–6000 BC). The site covers 11 ha, but less than 1% has been excavated. Houses have been found with walls constructed of undressed stones bonded with a mud mortar. Sometimes they were built on previously levelled ground and often had no foundation trenches. By the late 20th century no complete house plan had been recovered, but a two-room dwelling was probably typical. The main walls were rectilinear. Houses were much modified in design detail and by renovation, indicating long periods of use. The interior walls were covered with a mud plaster to which a finer lime plaster was applied. The floors, incorporating shallow, basin-like hearths, were covered with a thick bed of coarse lime plaster, which levelled the ground and provided a base for a fine, thin lime plaster. Both floor and walls were frequently painted with red iron oxide and burnished, with pigment applied either as solid colour or in splotches and biomorphic patterns.

Decoration was also applied to personal adornment, such as stone, shell and bone beads and pendants. Cicatrix, tattooing, body paint and cosmetics may also have been used, as suggested by figurines and statues found at Ain Ghazal and Nahal Hemar. The Ain Ghazal figurines are representations of animals and human figures, usually composed of a yellow clay with poor drying properties or a finer reddish-brown clay. Most were unbaked, and the firing of some baked examples seems to have been accidental. There was clearly experimentation with materials and techniques. Most of the animal figurines are easily identifiable as cattle, while others may be equids, sheep or goats, a fox and a wild boar. They were usually made in one piece. Two of the cattle have flint blades embedded in their forequarters possibly relating to hunt ritual. The human figurines, chiefly female, seem to have been assembled from separately modelled parts. Of these, the 'Venus' or 'mother-goddess' figurines, naked, broad-hipped, full-bellied, globular-breasted, either standing or squatting and with impressed decoration, symbolize fecundity.

The larger lime-plaster statues are the most impressive artistic contribution of the Pre-pottery Neolithic B period. Similar objects have been discovered at JERICO, RAMAD and Nahal Hemar, but the remarkable preservation and large numbers of the Ain Ghazal collection make it unique. These statues are among the earliest large-scale statuary of the human form. The smaller ones (h. *c.* 350 mm) can be interpreted either as busts or as schematic representations of the body with arms, hips, legs and feet not portrayed.

The larger ones (h. *c*. 900 mm) are stylized but full portrayals of the human form, with rounded torsos, disproportionately small arms and hands and divided legs with the weight evenly distributed (see fig.). They were constructed by applying slaked lime to an armature of reeds or rushes tied with coarse twine. This organic core survives only as impressions on the inside of the plaster. Knees and ankles are defined in the plaster.

The faces were sculpted with care, particularly the eyes, which have a haunting quality. A bituminous mastic was pressed into grooves around the eyeballs to delineate them, and discs of mastic were used to represent irises and pupils. The eyeliner sometimes retains traces of a green pigment (dioptase) dusted on to it. The noses are retroussé with vertical slits representing the nostrils, and the mouths are simple horizontal slits with modelling confined to the upper lip. The ears are represented by small protuberances on the sides of the heads with roughly circular depressions lending detail. The tops of the heads, recessed from the brows, sometimes bear traces of black pigment, suggestive of hair. Most of the figures do not exhibit sexual attributes, but some have pendulous breasts and, in one case, female pudenda are prominently displayed. At least two are polydactyl: one figure has a six-fingered hand, and a six-toed foot fragment has also survived. It has been suggested, in view of similar finds at Jerico, that there may be a direct genetic link between the inhabitants of Jerico and those of Ain Ghazal. The statues were embellished occasionally with shallow impressions and frequently with paint. The painted decoration included solid washes of white, comet-shaped strokes on cheeks and legs in a range of orange to red iron oxide colours, and stripes of red on a cape modelled in plaster.

The statues have been recovered from pits, none of which has been linked archaeologically to any structure that might suggest their use. They were designed to stand, the smaller pieces having solid, broad bases and the larger being anchored by projections of the reed bundles through the feet. This indicates that they were not made only to be buried. Further evidence supporting this conclusion is derived from the damage the pieces had sustained before burial (fragmentary heads not associated with bodies, bodies without heads or with severely damaged heads, missing toes and fronts of feet). The disposition of the statues in the pits suggests that these objects had been revered and buried with care, despite their deteriorated condition.

The inhabitants of Ain Ghazal sometimes venerated skulls. One plastered skull was found in a cluster of four buried in a pit outside a house. Its decoration is much more rudimentary than the examples from Jerico, Beisamun and Ramad. A small area of thin plaster remains on the parietals, and the sockets of the eyes are roughly packed with plaster, poorly finished around the edges. A bituminous mastic has been used to give definition to the eyes. A further plastered skull of much finer quality, but damaged, was found in 1988 (now Yarmuk U., Mus. Jord. Her.). The architectural and artistic use of large quantities of lime plaster constitutes a major investment of time and resources and could only have been possible in a diversified, complex and sophisticated society.

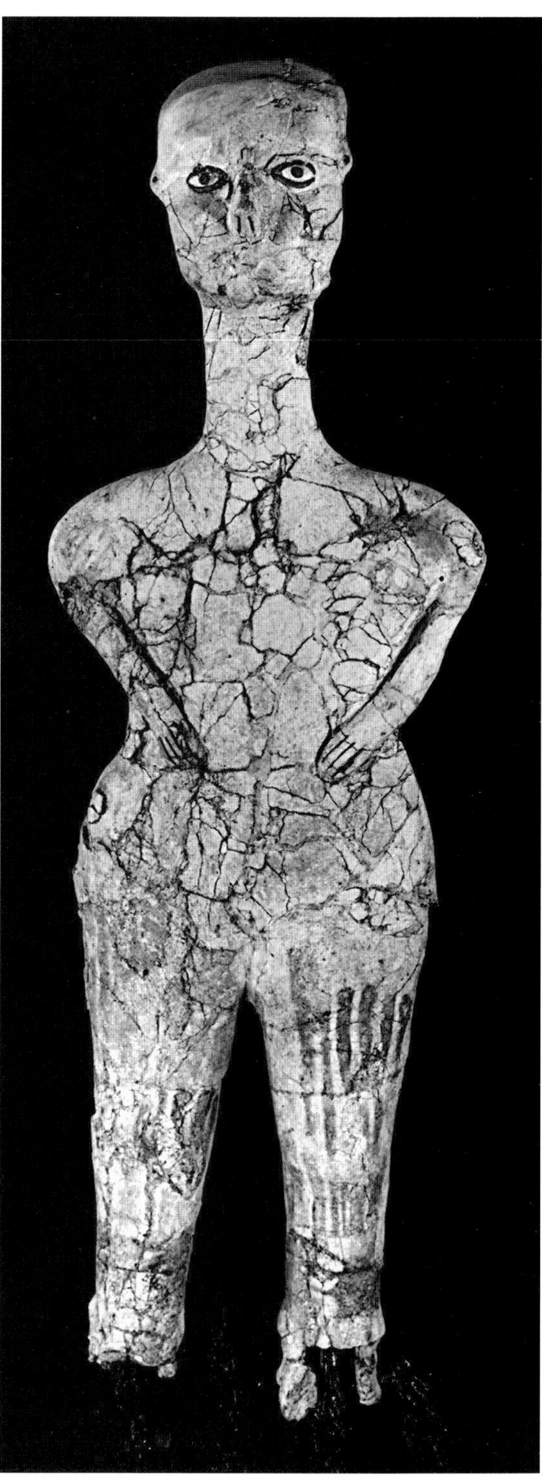

Ain Ghazal, lime-plaster statue (after conservation), h. *c*. 950 mm, 7th millennium BC (Amman, Jordan Archaeological Museum)

BIBLIOGRAPHY

G. O. Rollefson: 'Ritual and Ceremony at Neolithic Ain Ghazal (Jordan)', *Paléorient*, ix (1983), pp. 29–38

E. B. Banning and B. F. Byrd: 'The Architecture of PPNB Ain Ghazal, Jordan', *Bull. Amer. Sch. Orient. Res.*, 225 (1984), pp. 15–20
G. O. Rollefson: 'Early Neolithic Statuary from Ain Ghazal (Jordan)', *Mitt. Dt. Orient-Ges. Berlin*, cxvi (1984), pp. 185–92
G. O. Rollefson and others: 'The Pre-Pottery Neolithic B Village of Ain Ghazal (Jordan): Preliminary Report of the 1982 Excavation Season', *Mitt. Dt. Orient-Ges. Berlin*, cxvi (1984), pp. 139–83
A. H. Simmons and G. O. Rollefson: 'Neolithic Ain Ghazal (Jordan): Interim Report on the First Two Seasons, 1982–1983', *J. Field Archaeol.*, xi (1984), pp. 387–95
O. Bar-Yosef: *A Cave in the Desert: Nahal Hemar* (Jerusalem, 1985)
G. O. Rollefson and others: 'Excavation at the Pre-Pottery Neolithic B Village of Ain Ghazal (Jordan), 1983', *Mitt. Dt. Orient-Ges. Berlin*, cxvii (1985), pp. 69–116
K. W. Tubb: 'Preliminary Report on the Ain Ghazal Statues', *Mitt. Dt. Orient-Ges. Berlin*, cxvii (1985), pp. 117–34
A. H. Simmons and others: 'A Plastered Skull from Neolithic 'Ain Ghazal, Jordan', *J. Field Archaeol.*, xvii (1990), pp. 107–10

For further bibliography *see* JERICO and RAMAD.

KATHRYN WALKER TUBB

Ainu [Emishi; Ezo; Mishihase]. Peoples who once lived in northern Japan and are now restricted to the islands of Hokkaido (Japan), southern Sakhalin and the Kuril chain. The Ainu live in an area that has been influenced by Chinese, Siberian and especially Japanese culture. Until the 17th century, when the Ainu began to practise small-scale agriculture in south-western Hokkaido, they subsisted by fishing and hunter–gathering. Although the gradual Japanese colonization of Hokkaido had almost eradicated Ainu culture by the early 20th century, the post-war period has witnessed a revival of Ainu culture and language.

Ainu art is characterized by the preponderance of geometric designs. Some have parallels in Japan proper, while others show similarities with motifs found in the art of the Gilyaks, their northern neighbours on Sakhalin, of the Ostyaks and Samoyeds of northern Siberia and even of the peoples of the north-west coast of North America. Human and animal motifs are extremely rare and restricted to the decoration of libation wands (*iku pasuy*). Also known as moustache lifters, these wooden wands (*c.* 300×20–40 mm) are used during the ceremonial drinking of rice wine. They are dipped into the cup and a few drops of wine sprinkled on the ground as an offering to the gods. The decorations of the upper surface of the wand range from a few parallel lines, indicating ownership, to intricate depictions of animals, boats, weapons and geometric patterns. The animals depicted include bears, seals, foxes, birds, snakes, grampuses and fish, which all played an important role in Ainu life and religion. Another wand-like ritual object is the *inau* (l. *c.* 1 m; shaving-tufted prayer stick). Traditional Ainu dwellings were rectangular pole-framed houses thatched with bamboo-leaf roofs, and fenced with sticks with wood shavings attached and stick-mounted animal skulls.

Ainu men were accomplished woodcarvers and decorated most utilitarian objects. Round, square and oval plates, bowls and trays were ornamented with engraved geometric designs. The same designs could be found on wooden tobacco boxes with attached pipe holders, the handles of knives, forks and spoons, weaving equipment and ceremonial weapons. Women produced clothing, mats and smaller items such as purses. Winter clothing was made from animal skins and summer clothing from *attush*-cloth woven from the inner bark of the elm (*Ulmus laciniata*) in Hokkaido or of the linden (*Tilia japonica*) and nettles (*Laportea bulbiflora*) in Sakhalin. Ainu dress consisted of robes worn by both sexes, with belts, aprons and hoods. Formal robes were richly ornamented with geometrical designs unique to each village. The *appliqué* ornaments on robes, aprons and hoods—often made of dark cotton cloth—were sewn to the *attush*-cloth with additional embroidery in lighter thread (see fig.). Belts in a stripe pattern were woven on small looms (*see* JAPAN, §XV, 4(v)). The growth of tourism in the post-war period has promoted a revival of traditional Ainu crafts, including wood-carving and *attush*-cloth weaving, to meet the demand for souvenirs.

Ainu man's *attush*-cloth robe, decorated with strips of black cotton cloth embroidered with white thread, l. 210 mm, w. 120 mm, ?*c.* 1900 (Hamburg, Museum für Völkerkunde)

BIBLIOGRAPHY

H. Schurtz: 'Zur Ornamentik der Aino', *Int. Archv Vlkerknd.*, ix (1896), pp. 233–51
J. Batchelor: *The Ainu and their Folklore* (London, 1901)
F. Maraini: 'Gli iku-bashui degli Ainu', *Pubn. Ist. Cult. Tokio*, i (1942)
S. M. Low: 'Contemporary Ainu Wood and Stone Carving', *Ethnic and Tourist Arts*, ed. N. H. H. Graburn (Berkeley, 1976), pp. 211–25
J. Kreiner and H. D. Ölschleger: 'Ainu: Jäger, Fischer und Sammler in Japans Norden', *Ethnologica*, xii (1987)

HANS DIETER ÖLSCHLEGER

Aiolic order. *See under* ORDERS, ARCHITECTURAL.

Airbrush. Hand-held painting instrument, of about the same size as or slightly larger than a pen, that delivers paint in a controlled spray. It is connected to a supply of compressed air by a flexible hose and draws paint from an integral reservoir or attached cup. Depending on the sophistication of the model, the user may control the supply of air and paint and the spray pattern in varying degrees. Additional effects are achieved by a form of stencilling, using special masking film or other means of temporary protection of the artwork. An airbrush may be used with any paint if it is sufficiently thinned and contains pigment particles that are suitably fine. Dyes are also employed. Versions of several media exist that are specifically intended for airbrush application.

The first airbrush was patented in 1893 by Charles L. Burdick, an American living in Britain. It was manufactured by the Fountain Brush Co. and was called an 'aerograph'. Burdick eventually became friends with Dr Alan De Vilbiss, who *c.* 1890 had invented a system for applying medicines without using a swab; in 1931 the two men combined their inventions to create the airbrush as it is now known. Several designs have since developed, offering different technical features.

The airbrush is mainly a designers' and illustrators' tool, used to enhance photographic images by retouching and for realistic illustrations where photography would be unsuitable or impracticable. It has also been adopted for other purposes, for example for hand-painting textiles and for custom-car decoration. Typically, airbrush art features smooth, sharp images and exceptionally subtle gradations of tone and colour. It is therefore well-suited to Photorealism. The airbrush need not be used exclusively and may be employed just for particular effects. The illustrations of George Petty and Alberto Vargas (or Varga), both of whom worked in the USA in the 1930s and 1940s (on *Esquire* magazine), provide early examples of airbrush art.

BIBLIOGRAPHY

P. Owen and J. Sutcliffe: *The Manual of Airbrushing* (London, 1986)

J. Stephenson: *Graphic Design, Materials and Equipment* (London, 1987), pp. 41–9

JONATHAN STEPHENSON

Aire Libre, Escuelas de Pintura al. *See* ESCUELAS DE PINTURA AL AIRE LIBRE.

Aires de Sá e Meneses, Rodrigo. *See* FONTES E ABRANTES, Marquês de.

Airikiṇa. *See* ERAN.

Airport. Complex of buildings, runways and service facilities for handling the arrival and departure of aircraft and their passengers and freight. In the early days of aviation at the beginning of the 20th century, almost any space suffcently level to take off and land an aircraft was used as a landing-field, with sheds serving as workshops and stores. As the air transport industry began to develop after World War I, landing-fields were developed into small airports on the fringes of urban areas, with simple buildings and grass or lightly hardened runways often laid out in the form of a wind rose. By the late 1920s passengers had begun to expect more sophisticated facilities, although designers often failed to appreciate the technical requirements of airports and their growth potential. An airport design competition (1927) held by Lehigh Portland Cement Co. of Allentown, PA, for example, produced schemes in which public buildings were sited at the ends of runways, while visionary ideas included an airport designed as a huge wheel supported on the flat roofs of city skyscrapers (Pisano). Observation platforms were common, reflecting public interest in aviation that increased enormously after the pioneering transatlantic flight of Charles Lindbergh in 1927. Long-distance airline schedules in the USA, inaugurated in the early 1930s, were often operated in conjunction with existing railway networks, with passengers travelling by rail at night; at this time railway terminals provided the predominant model for airport terminal design, with an emphasis on comfortable waiting rooms and restaurants.

In Europe, where the world's first international air service (London–Paris) was inaugurated in 1919, air transport was embraced as a prestigious form of travel, and the design of airports for capital cities was considered an expression of national pride. By the late 1920s most European cities had adequate airports, which subsequently underwent continual improvement and renewal as air transport expanded. London's first airport, for example, built at Croydon in 1915 as part of London's air-defence system, was rebuilt in 1928 and then superseded by Heathrow Airport in 1946; and Le Bourget, Paris, where Lindbergh landed after his flight in 1927, was rebuilt in 1937 for the Exposition Internationale des Arts et Techniques dans la Vie Moderne. One of the best-equipped airports was considered to be Tempelhof, Berlin, built in 1925. One of the most interesting was Gatwick Airport (1936; by Frank Hoar), which had a small circular terminal with telescopic canvas-covered gangways to the aircraft; the plan was intended to provide increased access and unimpeded movement for individual aircraft, although it subsequently proved unsuitable for larger aircraft and airports—few airports of this period still serve present needs. The principle was nevertheless reflected in later satellite airport designs.

After World War II, as air travel became the world's principal means of long-distance mass transport, airports began to grow rapidly. Heathrow Airport, for example, handled a total of 3 million passengers in 1955 and over 51 million in 1994, requiring the successive construction of four terminals and a proposal for a fifth. Modern international airports are shaped by exacting requirements: sufficient space to accommodate the runway needs (up to 4 km) of the largest commercial jet aircraft, together with sophisticated passenger terminals, hangars, cargo and other buildings required for efficient operation and future expansion; easy access from highways and public transport; and proximity to large cities while minimizing noise pollution for encroaching suburban and industrial areas. Terminal design involves planning for the efficient movement of passengers and aircraft, different aircraft sizes, security and immigration controls, and the needs of commerce: since the first duty-free shop opened at Shannon Airport, Ireland, in 1951, many modern airports have come to incorporate large-scale shopping centres as well as public entertainment and catering facilities and associated office and hotel buildings. Hub terminals such as Baltimore/Washington International (1979), which serve large numbers of transit and transfer passengers who do not leave the airport, have simpler requirements, and their design is often based on domestic terminals.

Principal types of airport layout include traditional design, with a separate terminal building remote from the aircraft; pier design, where aircraft dock against double-sided piers extending out from the terminal (e.g. O'Hare

Haj Terminal, 1981–2, by Skidmore, Owings & Merrill, King Abdul Aziz International Airport, Jiddah, Saudi Arabia

International Airport, Chicago, 1959–63; by C. F. Murphy Associates); satellite design, where aircraft dock against island buildings connected to a central terminal (e.g. Aérogare 1, Charles de Gaulle Airport, Roissy, Paris, 1974; by Aéroports de Paris); and linear design, where aircraft dock against the terminal building or its arms (e.g. Terminal 4, Heathrow Airport, London, 1986; by Scott Brownrigg & Turner). Pier design offers easy potential for expansion but increases passenger walking distances; at O'Hare, for example, the furthest gates are 1.6 km apart. Satellite design allows passenger traffic and services to be decentralized, as at Cologne/Bonn Airport (1962–70; by Paul Schneider-Esleben), where star-shaped satellites surround an angular horseshoe-shaped main terminal. Expansion may be difficult, however, as at Aérogare 1, Roissy, with seven trapezoidal island terminals in a tightly circular overall plan. Newark International Airport (1973; by Port Authority of New York and New Jersey), NJ, has multiple satellites, conceived as three for each of three curved terminals (third terminal later designed with piers). Linear design offers more direct landside–airside access, and expansion can be achieved by constructing terminals in series on either side of a central access spine. Examples include Dallas/Fort Worth Airport (1968–73; by Hellmuth Obata & Kassabaum and Brodsky Hopf & Adler), with several pairs of giant semicircular terminals, and Aérogare 2 (1982, 1989; by Aéroports de Paris), Roissy, with a series of curved terminals. Hybrid types include multiple island pier design, where aircraft dock against isolated linear buildings linked to the main terminal by a subway (e.g. London Stansted New Terminal, 1991; by Foster Associates). A combination of linear and satellite systems was designed (1967) for San Francisco International Airport (by John Carl Warnecke & Associates and Dreyfuss & Blackford), handling commuter flights at the main building and long-distance flights at the satellites.

The increasingly sophisticated planning and technical design of airports was often accompanied by highly imaginative architectural responses. Notable examples include Eero Saarinen's TWA Terminal (1956–62; *see* ROOF, fig. 3) at Idlewild (now John F. Kennedy) Airport, Queens, New York—an airport that has a total of ten individual airline terminals around a central parking and traffic circulation area; and Dulles International Airport Terminal (1958–62; for illustration *see* SAARINEN, (2)), Chantilly, VA, which operates with mobile lounges. Both terminals have expressive roof forms, the former being a sculptural, reinforced-concrete shell echoing the wings of a bird. Stansted New Terminal (*see* ENGLAND, fig. 13) was designed by Norman Foster as a sophisticated, two-storey, square shed, with high-tech cantilevered steel 'tree' structural elements and modular roof shells incorporating skylights. The expressive structure and streamlined planning—with all passenger functions on the upper level and supporting facilities below—were intended to mark a return to the simplicity of the early days of flying: glazed lounges in the island pier buildings overlook the runways like observation platforms.

Other notable designs have responded to individual site conditions. The unique design of the Haj Terminal at King

Abdul Aziz International Airport, for example, was a direct response to its desert site (*c.* 64 km north-west of Jiddah) and its function: to serve more than a million pilgrims travelling to Mecca during six weeks in the year, with extended waiting periods at the terminal. This led to the concept of the terminal as a huge rectangular tent, with an interior largely open to air circulation but covered by 210 translucent fibreglass tent units (45 m square) supported by steel radial cables and suspended from steel pylons (see fig.), together comprising the world's largest fabric roof. The informal design of the terminal thus fulfils its functional requirements while conforming to the spirit of the desert pilgrimage. Kansai International Airport (1987–94; by Renzo Piano), Osaka Bay, is the world's first purpose-built offshore airport, designed to permit 24-hour operation while minimizing noise pollution in a densely populated urban area. Built on a 500 ha manmade island 5 km from the coast, to which it is linked by a road and rail bridge, Kansai comprises a linear terminal more than a mile long, filled with mature trees over which a huge, wave-like curved roof appears to float, supported on trusses spanning 60 m. Offshore airports, which offer potential integration with sea transport but limit associated commercial development, were first proposed in 1961; they offer a solution for continuing growth in air transport and its conflict with spreading urban populations, as well as an echo of the great translantic flying boats of the 1930s, then thought to be the logical future for aviation.

See also IRELAND, fig. 6 (Dublin Airport).

BIBLIOGRAPHY

D. A. Pisano: *American Airport Designs* (Allentown, PA, 1930/*R* Washington, DC, 1990)

'Inside Eero Saarinen's TWA Building', *Interiors* (July 1962), pp. 86–93

E. G. Blankenship: *The Airport: Architecture, Urban Integration, Ecological Problems* (London, 1974)

M. Greif: *The Airport Book: From Landing Field to Modern Terminal* (New York, 1979)

S. Cantacuzino, ed.: *Architecture in Continuity: Building in the Islamic World Today* (New York, 1985), pp. 122–7 [Haj Terminal]

W. Hart: *The Airport Passenger Terminal* (New York, 1985)

C. J. Blow: *Airport Terminals* (Oxford, 1991)

K. Powell: *Stansted: Norman Foster and the Architecture of Flight* (London, 1992)

P. Buchanan: 'Kansai', *Archit. Rev.* [London], cxcvi/1173 (1994), pp. 31–81

VALERIE A. CLACK

Aïrtam. *See* AYRTAM.

Aisle. Longitudinal passage between seats in a church, auditorium or similar building. In a church, the term refers more commonly to the space flanking and parallel to the nave, usually separated from it by columns or piers (*see* CHURCH, fig. 2).

Aison. *See* VASE PAINTERS, §II.

Aitken, William Maxwell, 1st Baron Beaverbrook (*b* Maple, Ont., 25 May 1879; *d* Cherkley, nr Leatherhead, 9 June 1964). British publisher, financier, politician, collector and patron, of Canadian birth. As Minister of Information during World War I, he was responsible for the War Records Office in London, through which Wyndham Lewis, Muirhead Bone, William Orpen, Christopher Nevinson, Augustus John and six Canadian artists, J. W. Beatty (1869–1941), Maurice Cullen, C. W. Simpson (1878–1942), Fred Varley, David Milne and A. Y. Jackson, received commissions to record Canada's military contribution to the war effort. The Canadian War Memorials were deposited at the National Gallery of Canada, Ottawa, in 1921, and since then all but the major canvases have been transferred to the Canadian War Museum, also in Ottawa.

Beaverbrook was instrumental in developing the National Gallery of Canada's collection of historical pictures; he was directly responsible for the gift of Benjamin West's *The Death of Wolfe* by the Duke of Westminster in 1918, and the acquisition of George Romney's portrait of the Chief of the Six Nations Native Americans, *Joseph Brant*; also Reynolds's portrait of *Lord Amherst*, and a portrait of *Sir Alexander Mackenzie*, the first white man to cross the Canadian Rockies and reach the Pacific, attributed to Lawrence. His friendship with Walter Richard Sickert and Graham Sutherland was based on his interest in talented people, as he was not an art connoisseur. His most sustained patronage was directed towards Graham Sutherland. He ensured that Sutherland remained in the vanguard of the art world in the 1950s through the considerable press coverage that his newspapers afforded the artist. In addition to providing residences for Sutherland and his wife and then arranging for the financing of La Villa Blanche in Menton, Beaverbrook sat to Sutherland immediately after the artist's acclaimed portrait of Somerset Maugham was exhibited. During the sittings he convinced Sutherland that he must paint Winston Churchill, and later directed the wife of the Canadian department store magnate, Signy Eaton, to the artist for a portrait commission. When Beaverbrook embarked upon his plan to build an art gallery in Fredericton, NB, he told Sutherland in 1957 that it was to be 'the great Sutherland Gallery'; to this end he bought up 40 paintings and drawings by the artist, mostly preparatory drawings and oil sketches for the portraits of Churchill, Rubinstein, Maugham and Sackville-West.

Beaverbrook also assisted less established artists through the Daily Express Young Artists' Exhibitions, from which he bought heavily for the gallery in Fredericton, the most perspicacious acquisition being Lucian Freud's painting *Hotel Bedroom* (1954). Not having a cultivated eye for pictures, he sought advice from everyone from his secretaries to directors of major international museums in acquiring works for Fredericton. The significant collection of British and Canadian pictures he put together reflects in a sense his 'dual' citizenship. He also secured numerous pictures for his gallery from friends and business associates, including part of the collection of James Boylen (founder of Brunswick Mines), which comprised the Cornelius Krieghoff collection, and several important paintings from the estate of Sir James Dunn, as well as Dalí's imposing *Santiago El Grande*, purchased by the Sir James Dunn Foundation in 1959 and presented to Beaverbrook's gallery. On 18 September 1959 the Lord Beaverbrook Art Gallery was officially opened, the only public collection in Canada that is the creation and gift of one man.

BIBLIOGRAPHY

T. Driberg: *Beaverbrook: A Study in Power and Frustration* (London, 1956)

D. Farrer: *G-For God Almighty: A Personal Memoir of Lord Beaverbrook* (New York, 1969)
A. J. P. Taylor: *Beaverbrook* (New York, 1972)

IAN G. LUMSDEN

Aivalli. *See* AIHOLE.

Aiwan. *See* IWAN.

Aix-en-Provence [Lat. Aquae Sextiae]. French spa and university city, capital of Provence from the 14th to the 19th centuries. It is situated in the Arc Valley *c.* 30 km north of Marseille and has a population of *c.* 125,000. The capital of the Celtic Salluvians, Entremont, was destroyed in 123 BC by Gaius Sextius Calvinus, who set up a fortified camp close to some thermal springs nearby in 124 BC. This became the prosperous colony of Aquae Sextiae, capital of Gallia Narbonensis Secunda from *c.* AD 375. The city became a bishopric under St Maximinus (*fl* 1st century AD) and an archbishopric in the 5th century, when the baptistery of St Sauveur Cathedral was built on the Roman forum. In 574 the city was sacked by the Lombards and abandoned.

Situated at what was once a major crossroads of the ancient town, Aix Cathedral is a composite monument, its various parts dating from different ages. Three churches are identifiable—Roman, Gothic and Baroque. The cathedral's baptistery dating back to the 5th century was transformed in the 10th/11th century, when it was crowned by a cupola, and it was revised again during the Renaissance. In effect the cathedral has grown and changed with the town of Aix itself.

By the 12th century Aix was the main residence of the counts of Provence, and a period of expansion began. A cloister with foliate and historiated capitals and a Romanesque south aisle (incorporated into the present Gothic nave in the late 13th century) were added to the cathedral; the façade and bell-tower (rest.) were built over the following two centuries. St Jean de Malte (13th century), with its bell-tower (h. 67 m), was once the priory church of the Knights of Malta and necropolis of the counts of Provence. The university was founded in 1409. The patronage of René I, Duke of Anjou, attracted many artists to Aix, including Nicolas Froment, whose triptych of the *Virgin in the Burning Bush* (completed 1479; *see* FROMENT, NICOLAS and fig.) is in the cathedral.

Provence passed to the French crown in the 1480s, and in 1501 a parliament was established in Aix; a new class of patrons arose who were interested in the arts and eager to use them to affirm their social status. Aix was repeatedly under threat during the religious and civil strife of the 16th century, and was captured by Emperor Charles V in 1536; major expansion subsequently began. A dome supported by eight pillars, six of them antique, was added to the baptistery during restoration in 1579. New *quartiers* were created (Villeneuve (1583); Villeverte (1608)); and the Hôtel de Carcès (1593) was the first of the new aristocracy's town mansions. New church façades, statues, fountains, municipal towers and bourgeois houses were built, and existing buildings were enlarged or renovated. Most of the artists involved were foreigners from Paris, Italy, Flanders or Burgundy, although *gypserie* (modelled or carved plasterwork) was a local innovation used widely and lavishly, especially on staircases. Unlike stucco, *gypserie* is not intended to look like marble.

From 1646 the Quartier Mazarin was built by Archbishop Michel Mazarin (1607–48) and his architect, Jean Lombard (1580–1656), with a new emphasis on perspective and right-angled ground-plans, as in the Cours à Carrosses (1650; now Cours Mirabeau; see fig.). Baroque developments, characterized by a taste for monumentality and *trompe l'oeil*, gave Aix its present appearance. Giant orders were used, for example, on the Hôtel d'Estienne de St Jean (17th century; now Musée du Vieil-Aix), and large workshops developed in which architects, painters and sculptors worked closely together. The Parisian architect Pierre Pavillon (1612–70), with the sculptor–architect Jean-Claude Rambot (1621–94) and the sculptor Jacques Fossé (1613–1703), rebuilt the Hôtel de Ville (1655–70), notable for its striking staircase consisting of twin interlocking spirals, as well as the Pavillon Vendôme (1667; enlarged 18th century), later owned by Jean-Baptiste van Loo. Pavillon also built the Hôtel de Châteaurenard (1660), which was decorated by JEAN DARET and which includes a remarkable *trompe l'oeil* staircase. In the 18th century new building declined (although Robert de Cotte built the Hôtel de Caumont in 1720) in favour of the restoration and interior decoration of existing buildings. In 1765 the Musée des Beaux-Arts was founded, and in 1774 the Ecole Municipale de Dessin was established, directed (1786–95) by JEAN-ANTOINE CONSTANTIN, who taught FRANÇOIS-MARIUS GRANET and Auguste, Conte de Forbin, among others. After Granet bequeathed the bulk of his collection (1849), including many of his own works, to the Musée

Aix-en-Provence, Cours à Carrosses (now Cours Mirabeau), 1650, showing the Roi René Fountain (1823) by David d'Angers

des Beaux-Arts, it was renamed the Musée Granet. It has particularly good holdings of 18th- and 19th-century French art.

Under local-government reforms following the Revolution, Aix ceased to be a provincial capital. Marseille assumed political and economic dominance, and Aix became nostalgic instead of forward-looking; 19th-century development, which included the Roi René Fountain (1823) by David d'Angers (see fig.), the Rotonde Fountain (1860) and the Palais de Justice (1832), was sparse, so preserving the 17th- and 18th-century city. Aix became somewhat like a museum, although still a lively cultural centre—the Académie was founded in 1829 and the Société des Amis des Arts in 1894. Paul Cézanne painted the Montagne Sainte Victoire and the landscape around the city (*see* CÉZANNE, PAUL and fig. 6). The Fondation Vasarely (1975), consisting of eight hexagonal cells of glass, metal and marble, contains a collection of the work of Victor Vasarely.

BIBLIOGRAPHY

P.-J. Haitze: *Curiosités les plus remarquables de la ville d'Aix* (Aix-en-Provence, 1679)

J. Boyer: 'La Peinture et la gravure à Aix-en-Provence aux XVIe, XVIIe, et XVIIIe siècles', *Gaz. B.-A.*, 78 (1971), pp. 3–188

M. Berrios and N. Coulet: *Histoire d'Aix-en-Provence* (Aix-en-Provence, 1977)

J.-J. Gloton: *Renaissance et Baroque à Aix-en-Provence*, 2 vols (Rome, 1979)

J.-P. Coste: *Aix-en-Provence et le pays d'Aix* (Aix-en-Provence, 1981)

NICOLE MARTIN-VIGNES

Aix-la-Chapelle. *See* AACHEN.

Aizanoi [Lat. Aizani]. Site of Hellenistic and Roman city, 54 km south-west of Kütahya in Turkey. Its remains comprise a Temple of Zeus, two agoras, a heroon, a macellum (market), a round structure with the *Edict on Prices* of Diocletian (AD 301) carved on its exterior walls, a stadium and theatre complex, a bath–gymnasium, bridges and quays. Most date to the 2nd century AD, the period of the city's greatest prosperity. The theatre–stadium group and the Temple of Zeus were both built during the reign of Hadrian (*reg* AD 118–37).

The temple is particularly significant because of its excellent state of preservation and its combination of Greco-Anatolian and Roman architectural forms. Inscriptions on the exterior walls of the cella attest to the date of construction. They also record a gift of land to Zeus made by the Hellenistic rulers Attalos I Soter (*reg* 241–197 BC) and either Prusias I (*reg* 230/227–182 BC) or his son Prusias II (*reg* 182–149 BC). However, there are no traces of an earlier temple on the site. It is a pseudo-dipteral, marble structure with eight Ionic columns on its ends and fifteen on its sides, all standing on Ephesian-style bases, each of which consists of two members. The lower is formed from three sets of double roundels, divided by two concave mouldings (the scotiae). The lowest pair of roundels projects the most, the central pair the least. The second member is the torus, which is horizontally fluted and sits on top of the lower member (see J. D. Beazley and D. S. Robertson: *Greek and Roman Architecture*, Cambridge, 1927, 2/1977, p. 46, fig. 42). The many-stepped podium (36.92×32.96 m) gives the building extra height. The pronaos is fronted by four prostyle columns of the Composite order; the opisthodomos has two columns *in antis*. A wooden staircase led down from the opisthodomos into a barrel-vaulted chamber under the cella that was probably used for the worship of the Anatolian mother goddess Kybele, since she is represented by small terracottas found in the chamber. There is epigraphic evidence for her cult at Aizanoi, and the chamber has a west-facing entrance, a standard feature of western Anatolian temples dedicated to mother goddesses.

Older, Hellenistic Greek stylistic elements dominate the temple's design: the pseudo-dipteral plan, the external Ionic order, the Ephesian bases, the inclusion of an opisthodomos and the use of a high podium. The presence of the cult room for Kybele's worship points to pre-Greek Anatolian concerns. However, the barrel-vaulted chamber under the cella, the use of the Composite order for some columns and the dry rendering of the ornament are all Roman features. The temple may have been one of several that Hadrian commissioned during his promotion of a pan-Hellenic confederation. This was to have been centred in Athens on the rebuilt Temple of Olympian Zeus and to have included cities in Macedonia, Asia Minor and North Africa. In any case, Hadrian's philhellene leanings may have encouraged the architects at Aizanoi to resurrect Greek architectural forms. After the 4th century AD Aizanoi became the seat of a Christian bishop, and the Temple of Zeus was transformed into a church.

BIBLIOGRAPHY

E. Akurgal: *Ancient Civilizations and Ruins of Turkey* (Istanbul, 1969, rev. 8/1985), pp. 267–70

H. Weber: 'Der Zeus-Tempel von Aezani: Ein panhellenisches Heiligtum der Kaiserzeit', *Mitt. Dt. Archäol. Inst.: Athen. Abt.*, lxxxiv (1969), pp. 182–201

U. Laffi: 'I terreni del tempio di Zeus ad Aizanoi', *The Athenaeum*, xlix (1971), pp. 3–53

R. Naumann: *Der Zeustempel zu Aizanoi* (Berlin, 1979)

WILLIAM E. MIERSE

Aizelin, Eugène-Antoine (*b* Paris, 8 July 1821; *d* Paris, 4 March 1902). French sculptor. A pupil of Etienne-Jules Ramey and Augustin-Alexandre Dumont at the Ecole des Beaux-Arts, Paris, he made several unsuccessful attempts to win the Prix de Rome. He nevertheless pursued a successful career and produced sculpture as markedly classical in style as that of his contemporaries who had studied at the Académie de France in Rome. He received numerous commissions from the State and from the City of Paris for the decoration of public buildings, working on the three great Parisian building projects of the Second Empire (1851–70), the new Louvre, the Opéra and the Hôtel de Ville, as well as on theatres, churches and other institutions. Apart from decorative sculpture, his output consists of classicizing statues on mythological, biblical and allegorical subjects, which were exhibited at the Salon and were sometimes reproduced in bronze editions. Among these works are *Psyche* (marble, 1863; Quimper, Mus. B.-A.), *Judith* (bronze, 1890; Le Mans, Mus. Tessé) and *Hagar and Ishmael* (marble, 1889; Belleville-sur-Bar, Sanatorium). He also exhibited genre sculpture, widely circulated in bronze editions (many cast by Ferdinand Barbedienne, 1810–92), including *Marguerite in Church*, *Mignon* and *The Youth of Raphael*. A collection of his

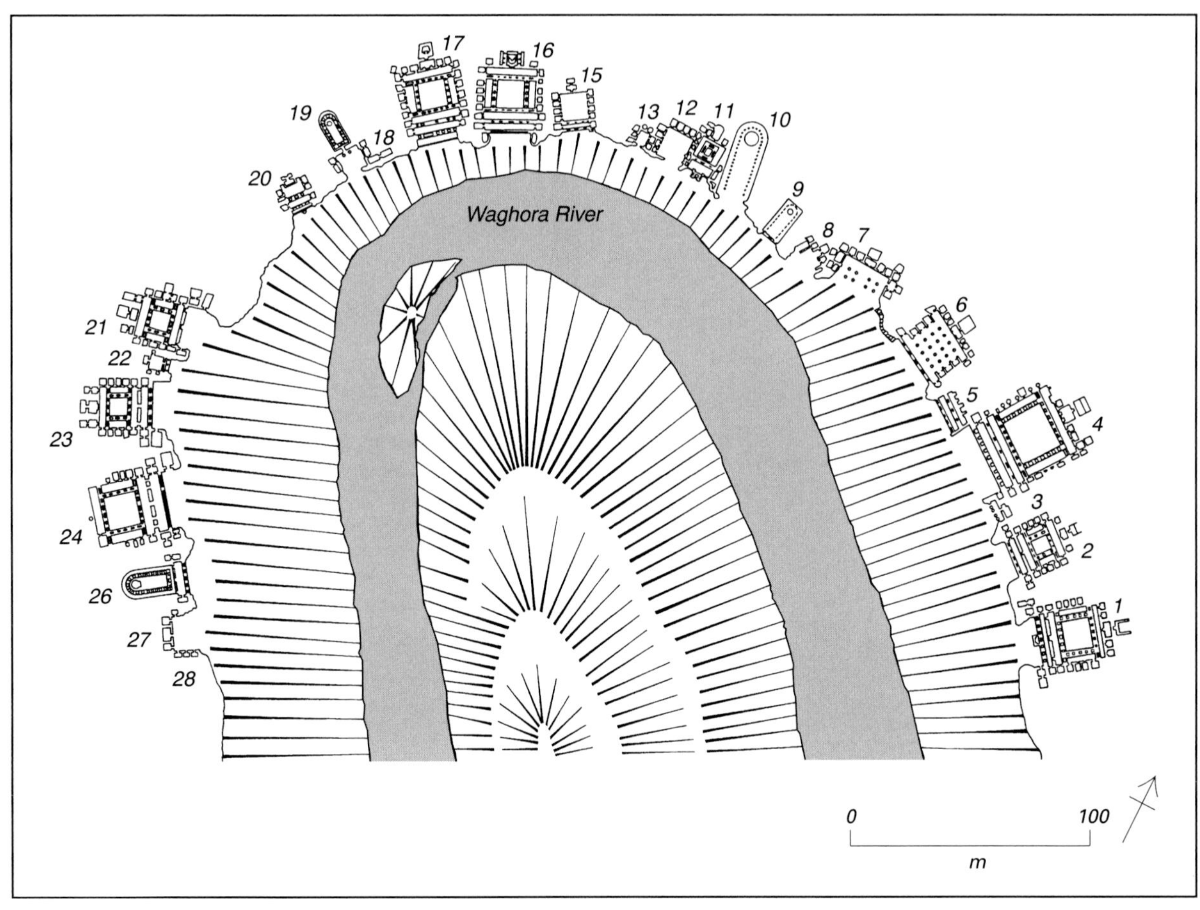

1. Ajanta, plan of site

works was given to the Musée Départemental de l'Oise, Beauvais, in 1975.

BIBLIOGRAPHY

Lami

LAURE DE MARGERIE

Aizenberg, Roberto (*b* Federal, Entre Ríos, 22 Aug 1928). Argentine painter, draughtsman and collagist. He studied under Juan Batlle Planas from 1950 to 1953 and quickly established the terms of his work, rooted ideologically in Surrealism and indebted in particular to the work of René Magritte and Giorgio de Chirico. All the elements of his mature art are evident in an early painting, *Burning of the Hasidic School in Minsk in 1713* (1954; artist's col.): architecture, space, light and ordered series. He developed an essentially intellectual approach, working in a variety of media (paintings, drawings, gouaches and collages) in rigorous sequences and picturing objects in cold impersonal light that confers on them a sense of distant majesty. The most common motif is that of a geometric, almost abstract structure, often in the form of a tower pierced by rows of large plain windows. Aizenberg's work, while far removed from the Surrealist presumption of achieving a synthesis of wakefulness and dream, acquires its strength through the ordering of the unreal and the strange in the search for a transcendent essence capable of perturbing and jolting the viewer by bringing into play the archetypes of silence and solitude.

BIBLIOGRAPHY

Aizenberg: Obras, 1947/1968 (exh. cat. by A. Pellegrini, Buenos Aires, Inst. Torcuato Tella, 1969)

H. Safons: 'Los poderes de lo imaginario', *Periscopio*, 47 (1970), pp. 57–8

HORACIO SAFONS

Ajanta [Ajaṇṭā]. Ancient Buddhist monastic and pilgrimage site (*c.* 200 BC–AD 500) located 100 km north of Aurangabad in the Sahyadri range of western India.

1. INTRODUCTION. Ajanta is India's richest surviving Buddhist complex. Far from any city, but close to the trade routes linking northern India with the western coast and the Deccan plateau, the monastery (*saṅghārāma*) and pilgrimage centre are composed of some 30 halls cut into the coarse, volcanic rock of a horseshoe-shaped gorge of the Waghora River (see fig. 1). The 'caves' were excavated along a 550 m-long stretch of a single path 10–30 m above the river bed. Five halls are in an early aniconic style, lacking images of the Buddha, and 24 are in the later image-filled style conventionally associated with Mahayana Buddhism of the Gupta age (*c.* 4th–5th centuries AD). The aniconic series, created between *c.* 200 BC and AD 100, is made up of two *caitya* halls (temples), Caves 9 and 10,

flanked by four *vihāras* (monasteries or dormitories), Caves 8, 12, 13 and 5A. These are relatively austere, echoing the motifs and architectural elements of the contemporary wood, brick and plaster structures they reproduce.

The chronology of the later caves has been the subject of continuing speculation since the first published study of the site in 1819. Burgess and Fergusson considered the second phase as extending from *c.* AD 500 to 650. Over the years this span has been stretched and squeezed from both sides. Late 20th-century studies tend to see relatively less difference between the earliest and latest architectural styles, with agreement growing around Walter Spink's contention that the entire second phase can be associated with the rule of the Vakataka dynasty in the second half of the 5th century, mostly with the reign of Harisena (*c.* AD 460–77). The second phase of work began with the modest Cave 11, at the centre of the earlier group. From there it spread to either side. Unlike the brief inscriptions of the first series, the lengthy dedications in several later caves indicate noble patronage. Whereas the first phase is severely plain, the second phase is profusely ornamented and dominated by images of Buddhas and *bodhisattvas* (future Buddhas). Previous distinctions between *caityas* and *vihāras* were dropped, as residence halls were elaborated to include worship shrines.

In the unique survival of its magnificent sculpture and painting, Ajanta offers an eloquent expression of the impact of lay patronage on the Buddhist monastic community. The amazing display of wealth and beauty clearly transcends the expressed purposes of meditation, worship and world renunciation. The visual impact of the site on the lay visitors who financed it has taken priority over the meditation needs of the *bhiksu* (literally, 'beggars') intended to occupy it. The separate monasteries and temples are packed side by side in a single, unified composition. Except for a break at a seasonal waterfall, they fill every space along the sweep of the gorge with more or less complete façades, although most of the interiors, including the residential cells, were left incomplete. How many monks ever inhabited this palatial world of conspicuous display is an open question.

2. Buildings.

(i) Caityas. Ajanta's vaulted *caitya* halls (*see also* INDIAN SUBCONTINENT, §III, 1(b)) provide an evolutionary record of this genre. Cave 10 (*c.* 200 BC), the earliest of the series, has no façade, although an inscription on the outer arch mentions that a donor, Vasishthipurta, provided for one. As at BHAJA, it appears that a no-longer-extant façade in perishable materials was added after excavation. The hall's inward-leaning, octagonal pillars and half-arched side aisle are also characteristic of the earliest *caitya* remains. The murals illustrating the previous lives of the Buddha (*jātakas*) running in a shoulder-high band around the aisle are the oldest surviving wall paintings in India.

The much smaller Cave 9 is probably a few decades later. Its façade is cut from the rock and decorated with intricately carved railings, lattices and *candraśālās* (horseshoe-shaped arches). Like Cave 10 the plain, geometric stupa that is the focus of the interior was designed to hold a wooden parasol, and the smooth vault of the roof was intended to be fitted with wooden rafters. Cave 9's pillars are vertical (like those of later halls), and its ambulatory is flat-roofed. Some 1st-century paintings survive, but the original aniconic state of the decoration is obscured by images of the Buddha added at the end of the 5th century.

Two more *caitya* halls (Caves 19 and 26) were excavated in the second phase of work; their numerous Buddha images illustrate the high achievement of 5th-century sculpture. Cave 19 is generally believed to be the 'perfumed hall' (*gandhakuṭi*) referred to in the Vakataka minister Varahadeva's inscription in Cave 17 and a creation of the third quarter of the 5th century. About the same size as Cave 9, it has a façade articulated to suggest several storeys (*see* INDIAN SUBCONTINENT, fig. 31). Enlightenment-promising Buddhas flank its doorway. The Buddha figure on the immediate right accompanied by a child has been identified as Shakyamuni Buddha offering the promise of enlightenment to his son, Rahula; other figures seem to extend the promise to all who enter. Giant *yakśas* (nature spirits associated with wealth) flank the façade's great horseshoe-shaped arch. Buddhas sit side by side above in ranks of Southern-style pavilions, symbolizing an infinity of Buddha worlds. Inside, in a major change from previous practice, a standing Buddha image is carved in the front of the stupa (see fig. 2): the personification of enlightenment equated with, or raised above, the *nirvāna* of the

2. Ajanta, *caitya* hall, Cave 19, interior showing the front of the stupa holding the Buddha's image, third quarter of the 5th century AD

relic mound. Other Buddhas surround it, carved on the pillar capitals and the entablature and painted on the walls of the cave. Every element of the design is richly ornamented; the rafters and parasols are cut in stone.

Cave 26, dedicated by the monk Buddhabhadra to the Ashmaka minister Bhavviraja, is larger, more elaborate and probably finished a little later than Cave 19. Its façade included a porch (now damaged) and three entrances. In keeping with a progressive diminution begun with Cave 9, the façade's great horseshoe-shaped arch is proportionately smaller. Cave 26's decoration, however, is even more elaborate. The Buddha on the stupa within sits on a towered throne surrounded by other Buddhas. Painting applied to the chamber's carved decoration shows how most, if not all, the architecture of Ajanta's last phase was finished.

(ii) Vihāras. The oldest Buddhist architectural form, the *vihāra*, a monastic enclosure edged by monks' cells, underwent a significant transformation at Ajanta. Those of the first phase have rectangular courts lined by square cells on three sides. The cells have stone benches within and railing and arch ornamentation around the walls. The best preserved of these is Cave 12, which seems to have had an added structural façade. In the second phase a Buddha image was placed in a central cell at the back of the hall as, for example, in Cave 11, dating from the beginning of this phase. It is not yet clear whether such halls were intended as *vihāras* with attached worship shrines or symbolic representations of paradises where the monks were living *bodhisattvas* surrounding the stone Buddha.

Three clusters of *vihāra* quarters were added to the original core: Caves 1 to 7 on the east, Caves 15 to 20 grouped around *caitya* hall 19 and Caves 21 to 28 grouped around *caitya* hall 26 on the west. Their relative chronological development has been debated on the basis of the elaboration of their layouts and the progressive refinement of their decorative and symbolic forms. Recent studies conclude that most were worked on sporadically, accruing complex combinations of advanced and retarded elements.

In Cave 11 the axial rear cell was expanded into a shrine. In Caves Lower 6 and 17 a pillared forechamber was added to the shrine. Cave 1 adds double-celled, pillar-framed chapels to the outer porch. Cave 2 has chapels flanking the central sanctum, and in Caves 21 and Upper 6 chapels were added on the transverse axis of the hall. Other elements such as pillars grow in complexity and differentiation. The most complete examples, such as Caves 1 and 2, were painted magnificently inside and out. Carved Buddha images and their retinue in the sanctum were painted in the same way as the decorative motifs and figurative murals of the surrounding walls and ceilings (*see* INDIAN SUBCONTINENT, fig. 239). Paintings of *bodhisattvas* cover the walls flanking the sanctum, intended as heavenly counterparts of the identically dressed live *bodhisattva* monks who inhabited the surrounding cells (*see* INDIAN SUBCONTINENT, figs 240 and 241).

See also INDIAN SUBCONTINENT, §III, 4(ii).

BIBLIOGRAPHY

J. Burgess: *Notes on the Bauddha Rock-temples of Ajunta, their Paintings and Sculptures and on the Paintings of Bagh Caves, Modern Bauddha Mythology, Etc.*, Archaeol. Surv. W. India, ix (Bombay, 1879)
J. Fergusson and J. Burgess: *The Cave Temples of India* (London, 1880), pp. 280–349
J. Burgess: *Report on the Buddhist Cave Temples and their Inscriptions*, Archaeol. Surv. W. India, iv (London, 1883)
G. Yazdani: *Ajanta*, 4 vols (Oxford, 1930–55)
R. S. Gupte and B. D. Mahajan: *Ajanta, Ellora and Aurangabad Caves* (Bombay, 1962)
V. V. Mirashi: *Inscriptions of the Vākāṭakas*, Corp. Inscr. Indicarum, v (Ootacamund, 1963)
W. Spink: 'History from Art History', *Proceedings of the International Congress of Orientalists* (New Delhi, 1964)
W. Begley: *The Chronology of Mahāyāna Buddhist Architecture and Painting at Ajaṇṭā* (diss., Philadelphia U. PA, 1966; microfilm, Ann Arbor, 1967)
A. Ghosh, ed.: *Ajanta Murals: An Album of Eighty-five Reproductions in Colour* (New Delhi, 1967)
W. Spink: 'Ajantā and Ghatotkacha: A Preliminary Analysis', *A. Orient.*, vi (1967), pp. 135–55
——: *Ajanta to Ellora* (Bombay, 1967)
——: 'Ajantā's Chronology: The Problem of Cave Eleven', *A. Orient.*, vii (1968), pp. 155–68
V. Dehejia: *Early Buddhist Rock Temples* (Ithaca, 1972)
W. Spink: 'Ajanta: A Brief History', *Aspects of Indian Art*, ed. P. Pal (Leiden, 1972), pp. 49–58
P. Stern: *Colonnes indiennes d'Ajantâ et d'Ellora* (Paris, 1972)
W. Spink: 'Ajanta's Chronology: The Crucial Cave', *A. Orient.*, xi (1975), pp. 143–69
S. Weiner: *Ajanta: Its Place in Buddhist Art* (Berkeley, 1977)
S. Nagaraju: *Buddhist Architecture of Western India (c. 250 BC–AD 300)* (New Delhi, 1981)
W. Spink: 'Ajanta's Chronology: Cave I's Patronage', *Chhavi*, ii (Varanasi, 1981), pp. 144–57
——: 'Ajanta's Chronology: Politics and Patronage', *Kalādarśana*, ed. J. Williams (New Delhi, 1981), pp. 109–26
J. Williams: *The Art of Gupta India: Empire and Province* (Princeton, 1982), pp. 181–7
W. Spink: 'The Great Cave at Elephanta: A Study of Sources', *Essays on Gupta Culture*, ed. B. L. Smith (New Delhi, 1983), pp. 235–82
J. Williams: 'Vakataka Art and the Gupta Mainstream', *Essays on Gupta Culture*, ed. B. L. Smith (New Delhi, 1983), pp. 215–33
D. Schlingoff: *Studies in Ajanta Painting* (New Delhi, 1987) [detailed explanations of narrative paintings]
R. Parimoo and others, eds: *The Art of Ajanta: New Perspectives* (New Delhi, 1991)

GARY MICHAEL TARTAKOV

Ajjul, Tell el- [Tell el-ʿAjjul; anc. Sharuḥen]. Site of a Bronze Age city in Israel that flourished in the 2nd millennium BC. It consists in a large mound 6 km south-west of Gaza, which was excavated by Sir Flinders Petrie in the early 1930s. Petrie presumed that he was excavating ancient Gaza, the Egyptian administrative capital of the southern province of Canaan during the Late Bronze Age (*c.* 1500–*c.* 1200 BC). Re-evaluation of the historical and archaeological evidence has confirmed the identification of the site with Sharuḥen, the Hyksos stronghold besieged and plundered by Ahmose (*reg c.* 1539–*c.* 1514 BC), the founder of the New Kingdom, at the close of the Middle Bronze Age (the Hyksos were Semitic rulers of Egypt in the 17th and 16th centuries BC). Finds are widely spread, with important collections in the Rockefeller Museum, Jerusalem, the British Museum, London, and the Petrie Museum at University College, London.

The Hyksos stronghold was founded in the 17th century BC. It succeeded a smaller settlement and consisted of a large fortified enclosure surrounded by a deep fosse. The city lying within it, covering about 11 ha, was well planned. Blocks of spacious buildings were erected along two of the main streets leading from the residential areas to the palace. This was a large building, situated at the highest part of the mound and distinguished by solid stone foundations and a typical layout of rooms around a vast courtyard.

The city was destroyed by fire in the mid-16th century BC and partly rebuilt on the old plan. However, the palace was replaced by a smaller structure, presumably the residency of the new governor stationed in the conquered city, built entirely of bricks in the Egyptian fashion. The people occupying the site in this period were still wealthy enough to acquire luxury pottery vessels from Cyprus and to possess a considerable amount of locally made jewellery. Four goldsmiths' hoardings, which were concealed under the floors of their houses *c.* 1450 BC, consist mainly of pendants worked in repoussé. A series of elaborate earrings from the hoardings indicates that sophisticated techniques of cloisonné and granulation were fully mastered by the goldsmiths of Tell el Ajjul in the initial phase of the Late Bronze Age (e.g. London, BM).

BIBLIOGRAPHY

F. Petrie: *Ancient Gaza*, 4 vols (London, 1931–4)
E. J. H. Mackay and M. Murray: *Ancient Gaza*, v (London, 1952)
F. Petrie: *City of Shepherd Kings* (London, 1952)
H. W. Kassis, ed.: *Tell el Ajjul*, Stud. Medit. Archaeol. 37 (Göteborg, 1974)
O. Tufnell: 'El-'Ajjul, Tell', *Encyclopaedia of Archaeological Excavations in the Holy Land*, i, ed. M. Avi-Yonah (London, 1975), pp. 52–61
W. H. Shea: 'The Conquests of Sharuhen and Megiddo Reconsidered', *Israel Explor. J.*, xxix (1979), pp. 1–5
R. Gonen: 'Tell el-'Ajjul in the Late Bronze Age—City or Cemetery?', *Eretz-Israel*, xv (1981), pp. 69–78 [in Hebrew; Eng. summary, p. 80]

ORA NEGBI

'Ajman. *See under* UNITED ARAB EMIRATES.

Ajmer [anc. Ajayameru]. City in Rajasthan, India, that flourished from *c.* 12th century. Ajmer was an important centre of Jainism in the 8th century, but it was not until *c.* 10th century that the area came into prominence under the Chahamanas (Chauhans) of Shakambhari. King Ajayapala is said to have founded the city in the 12th century, naming it Ajayameru after himself. He is also credited with building the now ruined hilltop fort called Taragarh. His son and successor Arnoraja (also called Anaka) constructed the massive embankment that created Ana Sagar Lake. The Chahamanas, especially Prithviraja (1178–92), constructed numerous temples and other buildings at Ajmer, as well as bathing ghats at Pushkar Lake some 11 km west. None of these are preserved in their original state.

Ajmer, Arha'i Din ka Jhompra, façade of prayer hall, *c.* 1200

Ajmer was sacked by Mu'in al-Din Muhammad of Ghur in 1192 and again by Qutb al-Din Aybak in 1193, the latter incorporating it into the Delhi sultanate. The Sanskrit college complex of Visaladeva and numerous temples were destroyed, and the building materials were reused to raise an impressive mosque in *c.* 1200. Its name, Arha'i Din ka Jhompra (Hindi: 'Two-and-a-half-day mosque'), may refer to the short time in which it was built or to a fair previously held for two and a half days at the site. The mosque consists of a large cloistered quadrangle with the remains of minarets on each outer corner. Inside, the prayer hall has a handsome central portal, originally crowned by small towers matching the outer minarets. The prayer hall façade (see fig.) is boldly carved with Arabic inscriptions and geometric ornaments borrowed from the temple repertory; some of the arches of the façade are cusped. The hypostyle interior was made of reused temple pillars. The ceiling panels and domes are likewise reused (*see also* INDIAN SUBCONTINENT, §III, 6(ii)(c) and fig. 21).

The Persian Sufi saint Mu'in al-Din Chisti (1142–1256) taught at Ajmer, and after his death a modest tomb was raised over his remains. In the late 14th century, Ajmer suffered from the chaos that followed Timur's invasion, and the city was successively occupied by Rana Kumbha (or Kumbhakarna) of Mewar, the Sultans of Malwa and the Rathor king Maladeo of Marwar. Finally in 1556 the city was annexed by the Mughals and made an administrative centre of their empire. Humayun (*reg* 1530–40; 1555–6), who briefly held the city during his troubled reign, enlarged the tomb of Mu'in al-Din Chisti, and further renovations and additions were made by Akbar (*reg* 1556–1605), Jahangir (*reg* 1605–27) and Shah Jahan (*reg* 1628–58; *see also* INDIAN SUBCONTINENT, §III, 7(i)(c)). Akbar reconstructed Ajmer fort in 1570–71 (AH 976). With the decline of Mughal power, Ajmer was occupied by the Rathors of Jodhpur and the Scindias of Gwalior. The British annexed Ajmer in 1818, and the Agent-General for Rajputana had his office there. The Rajputana Museum was opened in one of Akbar's palace buildings in 1908. It contains a superb collection of sculpture, architectural fragments, inscriptions, coins and other objects from all parts of Rajasthan.

BIBLIOGRAPHY

Har Bilas Sarda: *Ajmer, Historical and Descriptive* (Ajmer, 1911)
H. Cousens: *Architectural Antiquities of Western India* (London, 1926)
H. C. Ray: *Dynastic History of Northern India*, 2 vols (Calcutta, 1931)
P. Brown: *Indian Architecture, Islamic Period* (?Bombay [1942], rev. Bombay, 1956 with add. phot.)
S. A. I. Tirmigi: *Ajmer through Inscriptions (1582–1852)* (New Delhi, 1966)
K. C. Jain: *Ancient Cities and Towns of Rajasthan* (Delhi, 1972)

ASOK KUMAR DAS

Akan. Group of separate but related peoples living in the forest and coastal areas of south-western Ghana, West Africa. Sub-groups include the Asante (*see* ASANTE AND RELATED PEOPLES), Fante, Brong, Wassa, Aowin and Akuapem. The term 'Akan' is also sometimes used to refer to peoples in Côte d'Ivoire speaking closely related languages, for example the BAULE, Anyi and Nzima. In addition, Akan-derived arts are found among many unrelated but adjacent groups such as the Lagoon peoples, AKYE, Attie and Ebrie, for example, of south-eastern Côte d'Ivoire and the Ewe of south-eastern Ghana. Traditionally, all the Akan peoples were organized into a series of states each headed by a paramount chief who ruled with the aid of a council of elders and a hierarchy of divisional, town and village chiefs. The Asante are the largest and best known of these kingdoms, and much art from other Akan areas has been misidentified as Asante.

Most types of objects found among the Asante are also produced by, or are found among, other Akan peoples. These include such items of regalia as royal stools, a variety of chair types, swords with ornamented hilts and sheaths, linguist (or chief's counsellor's) staffs with figurative finials, state umbrellas with carved finials, and decorated crowns, sandals and jewellery. Many of the above feature cast-gold or gold-leaf ornamentation. Other examples of art forms found among Asante and Akan in general include cast-brass gold weights, cast- and sheet-brass containers, assorted shrine sculptures, and carved combs and drums. Documentation of the historical, formal, stylistic and iconographic variations in Akan arts is only beginning, but some basic distinctions for *akua'ba* fertility figures have been made. The typical Asante *akua'ba* has rudimentary arms, a disc-shaped head, and is painted black (for illustration *see* ASANTE AND RELATED PEOPLES, fig. 4). Among the Fante, the *akua'ba* is usually unpainted and armless, with an elongated rectangular head. In Brong areas the armless torso is proportionately thicker and the head is shaped like a short cylinder divided diagonally front to back. Painted and unpainted forms seem equally common.

Probably the single most important Akan art form not found among the Asante (although commonly labelled as such) is free-standing, figurative funerary terracottas (see fig.). Created as memorials to chiefs or other important individuals, the terracottas often represented not only the deceased but also surviving members of the court or family of the person being honoured. Generally, these figures were not grave-markers, but rather were situated at sacred spaces near the cemetery or, less commonly, in shrine or ancestral-stool rooms. Typically, they were given offerings of food and libations from time to time. In a few Akan areas, figurative terracottas, or in some cases terracotta heads, represent local deities rather than ancestors.

The other major non-Asante Akan arts centre on those produced by the traditional military groups, or *asafo*, of the Fante peoples. The focus of *asafo* activities are large multicoloured shrines adorned with numerous cement sculptures. Each sculpture or sculptural grouping depicts traditional proverbs, boasts or insults, as found in much Asante art. These same conventionalized verbal forms are depicted on appliqué flags, which are danced, flown from a pole on the shrine, or strung in large numbers between poles. In addition, appliqué banners up to 100 m in length, and featuring as many as 30 different motifs, are paraded through the streets during annual festivals and are also occasionally hung from poles. The *asafo* companies are often highly competitive. Each group claims ownership of particular colours, cloth patterns and motifs. Violations of the artistic prerogatives of one company by another may lead to open hostilities.

Akan funerary female figure with twins, terracotta, h. 463 mm, Fante, 19th century (Seattle, WA, Seattle Art Museum)

BIBLIOGRAPHY

A. A. Y. Kyerematen: *Panoply of Ghana* (London and Accra, 1964)

The Arts of Ghana (exh. cat. by H. M. Cole and D. H. Ross, Los Angeles, UCLA, Wight A.G.; Minneapolis, MN, Walker A. Cent.; Dallas, TX, Mus. F.A.; 1977–8)
P. C. Coronel: 'Aowin Terracotta Sculpture', *Afr. A.*, xiii/1 (1979), pp. 28–35
D. H. Ross: *Fighting with Art: Appliqué Flags of the Fante Asafo*, Museum of Cultural History Monograph Series, iv (Los Angeles, 1979)
M. D. McLeod: *The Asante* (London, 1981)
M. Gilbert: 'Akan Terracotta Heads: Gods or Ancestors?', *Afr. A.*, xxii/4 (1989), pp. 34–43

DORAN H. ROSS

Akasegawa, Genpei. *See under* HI-RED CENTER.

Akbar. *See under* MUGHAL.

Ak-Beshim [Ak-Peshin]. Site in the eastern Chu River Valley, near Tokmak, northern Kirgizstan. It has been identified as the Silk Route merchant city on the Su-ye River visited by Xuanzang (AD 600–64) in 629, and as Suyab (Sughati), capital of the western Turkish khanate of the Türgesh (*c.* 700–39) and subsequently of the Qarluq dynasty (8th–10th century). The site has been investigated by M. Ye. Masson (1927), A. Terenozhkin (1929), A. Bernshtam (1938–40), P. Kozhemyako (1953–4) and L. Zyablin (1955). Finds are in Bishkek (Kirgizstan Hist. Mus.) and St Petersburg (Hermitage). The site (96 ha) comprised two town centres and a citadel, surrounded by buildings varying in density and plan, and encircled by a fortified wall 16 km in length. Following the Islamization of the country in the 10th century, the Qarakhanid Turks founded a new neighbouring capital, known as Kuz-Ordu (also Balasaghun; *see* BURANA). The two towns coexisted as a single political entity during the 10th–12th centuries.

A Buddhist monastery and clock-tower were discovered at Ak-Beshim in 1940. Outside the town walls two Buddhist temples have been excavated, dating from the 6th to the 7th century and from the 7th to the mid-8th century respectively. They differ in plan, but both have central stupas, ambulatories, spacious courtyards, domestic quarters and monastic cells. The arched and domed sanctuaries of mud-brick and beaten clay were decorated with wall paintings, vast clay, stucco and stone statues placed on pedestals or in niches, and stone stelae and reliefs of Buddhist subjects. In the north-west part of the eastern town centre was a Nestorian Christian church of the 8th century. The plan is cruciform, with an open courtyard in place of a nave, and a baptistry. The courtyard contained Christian burials. Other excavated buildings include houses of the 10th-11th century, and the remains of a Zoroastrian burial complex, containing riveted ossuaries; it had been built on the ruins of a 5th–6th century castle. Analysis of 8th-century coins from the site allowed G. Clauson to identify Ak-Beshim with Suyab.

BIBLIOGRAPHY

Xuanzang: *Da-Tang-Xi-yu-ji* [Records of western lands of the great T'ang period]; trans. by T. Watters as *On Yuan Chwang's Travels in India*, ed. T. W. Rhys Davids and S. W. Bushell, i (London, 1905), pp. 68–81
Hudūd al-'Ālam [The regions of the world] (AD 629); ed. and trans. by V. Minorsky as *Hudūd al-'Ālam, 'The Regions of the World': A Persian Geography, 372 AH-982 AD* (London, 1937, rev. 1970), pp. 99, 286–9, 291, 294–5
L. R. Kyzlasov: 'Arkheologicheskiye issledovaniya na gorodishche Ak-Beshim v 1953–1954 gg.' [Archaeological research in the Ak-Beshim settlement, 1953–4], *Trudy Kirgiz. Arkeol.-Etnog. Eksped.*, ii (1960), pp. 160–227
G. Clauson: 'Ak-Beshim–Suyab', *J. Royal Asiat. Soc. GB & Ireland*, 1 (1961), pp. 1–13
L. P. Zyablin: *Vtoroy buddiiskiy khram Ak-Beshimskogo gorodishcha* [The second Buddhist temple of the Ak-Beshim settlement] (Frunze, 1961)
Istoriya Kirgizskoy SSR, s drevneyshikh vremyon do nashikh dney [The history of the Kirgiz SSR, from earliest times to the present], i (Frunze, 1984), pp. 267–71, 350–55

V. D. GORYACHEVA

Aken [Haecken], **Joseph van** [Vanacken, Vanaken, Joseph] (*b* ?Antwerp, *c.* 1699; *d* London, 4 July 1749). Flemish painter, active in England. In Antwerp he began painting genre scenes in the Flemish tradition, such as *The Washerwomen* (*c.* 1715; priv. col., see Edwards, fig. VI). He arrived in London with his family *c.* 1720 and continued to produce genre paintings as well as conversation pieces. His *Interior of an Alehouse* (sold London, Christie's, 31 July 1953, lot 106; see Waterhouse, p. 377) reveals his Flemish training, although the figures are wooden and stilted and the work devoid of moralizing intent. His *Covent Garden Market* (*c.* 1726–30; version, London, Mus. London) and *The Old Stocks Market* (*c.* 1740; version, London, Bank of England) show his adaptation of this genre tradition to contemporary London scenes, and the several versions of these works attest to their popularity. Van Aken also painted portraits, such as *Lady with a Fan* (untraced; mezzotint, 1735). His conversation pieces include *A Musical Party on a Terrace* (*c.* 1725; Eastbourne, Towner A.G. & Local Hist. Mus.), which betrays a French influence in its lively brushwork and informal composition.

In the 1730s and 1740s van Aken abandoned independent work, taking up employment as a drapery painter for other artists. He worked for Joseph Highmore, Thomas Hudson, George Knapton, Henry Winstanley, Arthur Pond, Allan Ramsay, Bartholomew Dandridge and others. Usually, these artists painted only the face, leaving van Aken to fill in the rest. Some of them relied heavily on his judgement: Winstanley painted his faces on a piece of cloth, which van Aken would then paste on to a larger canvas, arranging the composition himself; others, such as Ramsay, sent him drawings and instructions suggesting postures and draperies. Van Aken was especially known for his costumes inspired by those in Anthony van Dyck's paintings, as well as that derived from Rubens's portrait of *Hélène Fourment* (Vienna, Ksthist. Mus.); he used the latter, for example, in Ramsay's *Mrs Madan* (1746; priv. col., see Edwards, colour pl.).

Horace Walpole's quip 'Almost every painter's works were painted by van Aken' suggests van Aken's prolific output has led to problems of attribution. In addition, artists to an extent made their reputations on his ability, and his elegant poses and sumptuous draperies attracted patronage for them. In 1745 his services were solicited by John Robinson (*c.* 1715–45), a portrait painter from Bath; but van Aken's other employers were so jealous of his ability that they threatened to withdraw offers of employment if he agreed to work for Robinson. He received a similar threat when he was offered work by the popular portrait painter Jean-Baptiste van Loo. Such extreme reaction is a gauge of van Aken's popularity at the time, as well as a reflection of his discreet input into the works of important artists. In 1748 he travelled to Paris with

Hogarth and Hayman, and then by himself to the Netherlands.

Ramsay and Hudson were joint executors of van Aken's will. His younger brother, Alexander van Aken (*d* 1757), was also a drapery painter and was employed by Hudson after Joseph's death. Another brother, Arnold (*d* 1736), was also an artist, but his output was limited to small conversation pieces and a series of engravings of fish, entitled *The Wonders of the Deep* (1736).

BIBLIOGRAPHY

Waterhouse: *18th C.*

'The Note-books of George Vertue', *Walpole Soc.*, xxii (1934) [indexed in xxix (1947)]

R. Edwards: 'The Conversation Pictures of Joseph van Aken', *Apollo*, xxii (1936), pp. 79–85

J. Steegman: 'A Drapery Painter of the 18th Century', *Connoisseur*, xcvii (1936), pp. 309–15

Manners and Morals: Hogarth and British Painting, 1700–1760 (exh. cat. by E. Einberg, London, Tate, 1987)

SHEARER WEST

Akersloot, Willem. *See* ACKERSLOOT, WILLEM.

Akhalgori Hoard. Pieces of jewellery dating to the 6th–4th centuries BC from a ruined burial site, discovered in 1908, at Sadzeguri, a ravine on the River Ksani in eastern Georgia. It includes numerous gold items: huge neck pendants, bracelets, necklaces, signet-rings, belts, earrings; silver and bronze vessels; and gold, silver and bronze items from horses' harnesses. In its manufacture, its forging, chasing and filigree, and its ornament (e.g. rosettes and palmettes), the jewellery displays a combination of local, Ionic and Achaemenid traditions. Of particular note are the filigree or chased gold pendants in the form of teams of horses and the gold rosettes on which stamp decoration is soldered.

BIBLIOGRAPHY

Ya. I. Smirnov: *Akhalgoriyskiy klad* [The Akhalgori Hoard] (Tbilisi, 1934)

V. YA. PETRUKHIN

Akhenaten [Amenophis IV, Neferkheperurewaenre] (*reg c.* 1353–*c.* 1336 BC). King of Egypt in the late 18th Dynasty, son of AMENOPHIS III and husband of NEFERTITI. His reign was characterized by revolutionary changes in religion and art. Soon after his accession, Amenophis IV, as Akhenaten was at first known, began to build a temple complex at Thebes for the Aten, the disc-shaped manifestation of the traditional sun-god Re. In the fifth year of his reign, he founded a new capital in Middle Egypt at the site now known as EL-AMARNA: the period roughly encompassed by Akhenaten's reign is therefore usually known as the Amarna period. Thereafter the King changed his name to Akhenaten ('Beneficial to the Aten'), and throughout Egypt the worship of traditional gods was neglected, while the cult of the previously pre-eminent god Amun was actively persecuted.

Akhenaten's name is inextricably associated with the AMARNA STYLE created during his reign, according to which the King, his family and their relationship to the sun-god were the only proper subjects for art. Reliefs in the earlier Amarna style are known from reused fragments (the so-called *talatat*-blocks) of the temple to the Aten built by Akhenaten at eastern Karnak (Thebes) and from a few private tombs at Thebes (such as the TOMB OF RAMOSE). At the city of Akhetaten (el-Amarna) the early style is documented by various architectural elements (such as fragments of balustrades; Cairo, Egyp. Mus., 30/10/26/12 and New York, Brooklyn Mus., 41.82). Depictions of a *sed*-festival (royal jubilee) occur only in the early reliefs at Thebes, whereas other early themes are elaborated in the later style at el-Amarna, such as the royal couple's chariot drive between palace and temple, the royal family in intimate 'domestic' contexts, scenes showing officials receiving awards and, above all, the offering ritual for the Aten. At el-Amarna the later relief style is documented on the walls of private tombs, stelae and altarpieces serving the cult of the royal family (e.g. Berlin, Ägyp. Mus., 14145, and Paris, Louvre, E.11624), as well as blocks from official buildings.

The unusual rendering of Akhenaten's physiognomy and anatomy—which typically included an elongated face (with slanted eyes, hanging chin and thick lips), fleshy, almost female breasts, swollen thighs and a pendulous belly—in the earlier expressionistic style was once believed to be a realistic depiction of his pathologically affected physique, but it is correctly to be understood as resulting from new stylistic conventions. Representations of the King in the later Amarna style show the same physiognomic structure, but they are depicted in another, non-expressionistic, idealizing manner. Among the surviving colossal statues of Akhenaten in the earlier style, created for the Aten Temple at Karnak, is a nude figure without male genitalia that may represent Akhenaten's wife, Nefertiti. At el-Amarna, statuary in the earlier style derives from the Great Aten Temple, the palace complex and some of the boundary stelae (rock-cut reliefs defining the boundaries of the site).

Comparatively well-preserved works depicting Akhenaten in the later Amarna style include two heads in plaster (Berlin, Bodemus., 21348 and 21351), two life-size busts (Berlin, Ägyp. Mus., 21360, and Paris, Louvre, E.11076), a standing statuette (Cairo, Egyp. Mus., 43580), a dyad representing both Akhenaten and Nefertiti (Paris, Louvre, E.15593) and a seated statue (Paris, Louvre, N.831). Two iconographically significant pieces are a fragmentary head from a statue depicting Akhenaten as the child of the Aten (Berlin, Ägyp. Mus., 21290) and an unfinished, seated statuette with a woman on his lap (Cairo, Egyp. Mus., 44866).

BIBLIOGRAPHY

N. de G. Davies: *The Rock Tombs of El-Amarna*, 6 vols (London, 1903–8)

G. Roeder: *Amarna Reliefs aus Hermopolis* (Hildesheim, 1969)

Akhenaten and Nefertiti (exh. cat. by. C. Aldred, New York, Brooklyn Mus., 1973)

R. W. Smith and D. B. Redford: *Initial Discoveries* (Warminster, 1976), i of *The Akhenaten Temple Project* (1976–88)

M. Eaton-Krauss: 'Miscellanea Amarnensia', *Chron. Egypte*, lvi (1981), pp. 245–64

——: 'Eine rundplastische Darstellung Achenatens als Kind', *Z. Ägyp. Sprache & Altertknd.*, cx (1983), pp. 127–32

D. B. Redford: *Akhenaten: The Heretic King* (Princeton, 1984)

C. Aldred: *Akhenaten: King of Egypt* (London, 1988)

M. Muller: *Die Kunst Amenophis' III und Echnatons* (Basle, 1988)

D. B. Redford: *Rwd-Mnw and Inscriptions* (Toronto, 1988), ii of *The Akhenaten Temple Project* (1976–88)

R. KRAUSS

Akhetaten. *See* AMARNA, EL-.

Akhlaq, Zahoor ul- (*b* 1941). Pakistani painter, sculptor and printmaker. Educated in Pakistan and abroad, he has consciously and successfully synthesized Eastern and Western aesthetic traditions. In 1963, a year after graduating from the National College of Arts, Lahore, he joined the faculty as a lecturer in art, later becoming a professor and head of the Department of Fine Arts. His studies abroad have included post-graduate work in London (1966–7, 1968–9) and the United States (1987–9).

Like many of his colleagues, Zahoor was influenced by his mentor, SHAKIR 'ALI, principal of the National College of Art from 1961 to 1975. Both artists were motivated by art history, philosophy and aesthetics. Zahoor's non-figurative paintings of the 1960s evolved into tangible—though not always realistic—images addressing the dualities of space and time, East and West. Most of his triptychs and single canvases were conceived within a grid that provides a stabilizing structure for their compositions. This grid refers to Zahoor's admiration for the American artist Jasper Johns and, in a more abstract way, to the Islamic obsession with geometry. Clouds, originally derived from a series commemorating the bombing of Hiroshima and Nagasaki and later changing colour, shape and texture according to the subject, and motifs from Zahoor's personal experiences are also important in his work.

Zahoor was an enthusiastic participant in the modern calligraphy movement. His abstract compositions feature *farmān*s as well as elements from Koranic manuscripts and Indian miniature painting. He also has been influenced by Japanese prints, Zen philosophy, Hindu and Sufi literature and the work of various philosophers. His work is in the Bibliothèque Nationale, Paris, the Bibliothèque Nationale, Belgium, and the collection of the Pakistan National Council of Arts, Islamabad.

See also PAKISTAN, §§III and IV.

BIBLIOGRAPHY

A. Mirza: 'Humanism Pervades Zahoor's Paintings', *Dawn* (13 May 1985)
N. Mir: 'Art In a Grid', *The Herald* (March 1986), pp. 120–21
M. Nesom: 'Zahoor ul-Akhlaq', *The Nation* (25 March 1987), pp. 1–2
I. ul-Hasan: *Painting in Pakistan* (Lahore, 1991)
G. Minissale: 'Keeping an Open Mind', *Dawn* (3 May 1991)
M. Husain: 'In Search of Aesthetics', *Tues. Rev.* (24 Dec 1991), pp. 18–19
H. Zaman: 'Zahoor's Latest Are Not Painterly Paintings', *Muslim Mag.* (27 Dec 1991), p. 8
M. Nesom-Sirhandi: *Contemporary Painting in Pakistan* (Lahore, 1992)

MARCELLA NESOM-SIRHANDI

Akhmedov, Abdulla (Ramazanovich) (*b* Kurakr, Dagestan, 15 Sept 1929). Turkmenian architect. He studied from 1948 to 1953 at the Azerbaijan Polytechnical Institute, Baku, with Mikael' Useynov. His first buildings, in Turkmenia (now Turkmenistan), such as the district Waterworks Building (1954) above an artesian well in Archman and the building of the Ashkhabadstroy Trust (1956) in Ashkhabad, followed the neo-classical trend. In subsequent years he adopted a Rationalist approach, which combined adaptations to the extreme climatic conditions and cultural traditions of the republic. His first significant building, the Hotel Ashkhabad (1969), Ashkhabad, is distinguished by its bulk, which is emphasized by the deep chiaroscuro of its loggias and the powerful sculpting of the non-figurative reliefs on the terrace parapet. In the 1960s Akhmedov directed the planning of the centre of Ashkhabad, the focal point of which is a main square with irrigated flowerbeds. Its sides are defined by the isolated masses of the principal buildings designed by Akhmedov: the headquarters (1967) of the Karakumstroy Trust, the Library of the Republic of Turkmenia (1969–74) and the memorial to Revolution (1970s). The character of the buildings is unified by the use of complex forms and powerful, expressive sculpting of the surfaces of monolithic reinforced concrete. Particular originality can be seen in the architecture of the Library of the Republic of Turkmenia, where the interiors of the reading rooms are arranged around small courtyards with 'aquatic joke' fountains. The façade has prominent concrete ribs, which are turned at an angle to its plane and its horizontal framings, and its sculpted surface is raised on huge pillars over a stone garden of geometrical design. In the plans he drew up in the second half of the 1970s, such as those for a new building for the Academy of Arts, Moscow, and for a library in Makhachkala, Dagestan, experiments with complex curvilinear forms, in the tradition of Expressionism, conflict with an interpretation of Rationalist orthogonal forms. He was Chief Architect of Ashkhabad from 1965 to 1987. From 1989 he worked in Moscow.

BIBLIOGRAPHY

N. B. Sokolov: 'Arkhitekt Akhmedov' [The architect Akhmedov], *Arkhit. SSSR*, 6 (1971), pp. 44–7

A. V. IKONNIKOV

Akhmim [anc. Egyp. Khent-Min; Gr. Chemmis; Lat. Panopolis]. Site of the capital of the 9th Upper Egyptian nome, 200 km north of Luxor, which flourished from Early Dynastic times to the Roman period (*c.* 2925 BC–AD 395). Apart from a few excavations during the 20th century, the ruins of the town, as well as temples and extensive cemeteries, have never been completely surveyed or excavated.

Only one of the temples—a rock-cut chapel with relief decoration, dedicated to Min, the principal local god—has survived even partially intact. It was built by a local priest of Min during the reign of the 18th Dynasty king Ay (*reg* *c.* 1323–*c.* 1319 BC) and restored by another priest of Min during the reign of Ptolemy II Philadelphos (*reg* 285–246 BC). Within the main city there were two large temples with pylons (ceremonial gateways), one in the north-west area built by Tuthmosis III (*reg c.* 1479–*c.* 1426 BC) and restored several times in the Greco-Roman period, and the other built during the Roman period (30 BC–AD 395) in the south-west sector. Both of these survived until the 14th century AD, when the masonry was dismantled for use in Islamic buildings. Descriptions written by visitors during the Islamic period suggest that the temple dating to the Roman period was comparable in scale and decoration to those at Edfu, Dendara and Philae.

Traces of an Old Kingdom (*c.* 2575–*c.* 2150 BC) temple were discovered in excavations at el-Hawawish, which is also the site of the largest and best excavated of the cemeteries at Akhmim. The tombs, dating from the early pharaonic period to Roman times, contained wall paintings and painted wooden coffins. The paintings in the Greco-Roman tombs are very unusual in that they reflect a variety of Classical and Egyptian religious practices and artistic styles. The numerous carved offering tables and funerary stelae (Cairo, Egyp. Mus.; London, BM; Paris, Louvre) are also unusual in their choice of inscriptions and decoration—the offering tables, for instance, are the only Egyptian examples to incorporate human figures in the imagery. It is possible that this unusual decoration on the funerary equipment reflects Akhmim's importance as an independent religious centre during the Greco-Roman period.

BIBLIOGRAPHY

LÄ: 'Achmim'

P. E. Newberry: 'The Inscribed Tombs of Ekhmim', *Liverpool An. Archaeol. & Anthropol.*, iv (1912), pp. 101–20

F. W. von Bissing: 'Tombeaux d'époque romaine à Akhmîm', *An. Service Ant. Egypte*, i (1950), pp. 547–76

S. Sauneron: 'Le Temple d'Akhmîm décrit par Ibn Jobair', *Bull. Inst. Fr. Archéol. Orient.*, li (1951), pp. 123–35

N. Kanawati: *Rock Tombs of El-Hawawish: The Cemetery of Akhmim*, 6 vols (Sydney, 1980)

JANICE W. YELLIN

AKhRR. *See* ASSOCIATION OF ARTISTS OF REVOLUTIONARY RUSSIA.

Akhvlediani, Yelena (*b* Telavi, 18 April 1898; *d* Tbilisi, 28 Dec 1975). Georgian painter. From 1922 she studied at the Tiflis (now Tbilisi) Academy of Arts, where her talent was noted by the patriarch of Georgian realist painting, Georgy Gabashvili. She visited Italy and France, attending Colarossi's academy in Paris. She painted both Tiflis and Paris in similar style using brown, red and grey half-tones, somewhat reminiscent of the work of Albert Marquet, as in *Paris: Working Class Area* (1926; Tbilisi, Yelena Akhvlediani Mem. Mus.). After several successful exhibitions in Paris, where she mixed with the small Georgian community and was close to Lado Gudiashvili, in 1927 she returned to Georgia, holding several exhibitions there to mark her progress. For some time she was unable to find an application for her art, and from 1930 she worked as chief artist for the Detskaya Literatura (children's literature) publishing house, producing pen and ink and watercolour illustrations to the works of Mark Twain, Victor Hugo, Il'ya Chavchavadze and other writers. In 1928 she started working at the theatre of the director Kito Marjinashvili, and she also designed numerous theatre productions and films in Russia and the Ukraine as well as Georgia. In each work she sought to vary the means of building up the scenic space, using both traditional and avant-garde forms, in particular those of Constructivism. She gained the highest praise from the critics for her designs for Z. Antonov's play *Zatmeniye solntsa v Gruzii* ('Solar eclipse in Georgia'; 1932–3; production by Marjinashvili). For it she created mock-up buildings that fused with the painted backdrop as they got further away from the viewer. From the end of the 1950s she again took Tbilisi as her theme, creating a series in watercolour, pencil and ink called *Old and New Tbilisi* (1961–7).

BIBLIOGRAPHY

N. A. Urushadze: *Yelena Akhvlediani* (Tbilisi, 1979)

N. Sh. Janberidze: *Yelena Akhvlediani* (Tbilisi, 1980)

M. Karbelashvili: *Yelena Akhvlediani* (Tbilisi, 1980)

SERGEY KUZNETSOV

Akimov, Nikolay (Pavlovich) (*b* Kharkiv, 16 April 1901; *d* Moscow, 6 Sept 1968). Russian stage designer, director, painter and graphic artist of Ukranian birth. He studied in Petrograd (now St Petersburg) from 1915 to 1919 in an artists' workshop under Mstislav Dobuzhinsky, Aleksandr Yakovlev and Vasily Shukhayev. From 1920 to 1922 he worked as a stage designer in Khar'kov (now Kharkiv). In 1923 he returned to Petrograd, where he worked as a book illustrator and stage designer at the Theatre of Musical Comedy, the Theatre of Drama and the Gor'ky Bol'shoy Theatre of Drama; he also worked in Moscow, at the Theatre of the Revolution, the Vakhtangov Theatre and the Moscow Art Theatre (MKhAT). From 1929 he worked as a director, designing his own productions. He was the Art Director of the Leningrad Theatre of Comedy (1935–49), where the most notable productions he directed and designed were Shakespeare's *Twelfth Night* (1938), Lope de Vega's *Dog in the Manger* and *Widow of Valencia* (1939) and Yevgeny Shvarts's *The Shadow* (1946), among others. From 1951 to 1955 Akimov was the artistic director of the Leningrad Soviet Theatre; *Shadows* (by Saltykov-Shchedrin) and *The Case* (by Sukhovo-Kobylin) stand out among the productions he directed and designed there. From 1955 to the end of his life he was at the Leningrad Theatre of Comedy as Artistic Director; among his best productions there were Shvarts's *An Ordinary Miracle* (1956) and *The Dragon* (1962), and *Motley Stories* (1960) after Chekhov.

Akimov's productions were characterized by their liveliness, subtle wit, sharp characterization and rich fantasy. The style of his painting and graphic art, which was similar to the grotesqueness of German Neue Sachlichkeit and daringly sarcastic in relation to other art, played a significant role in their success. He also designed film sets (e.g. *The Immortal Kashchey*, 1945, and *Cinderella*, 1947) and he was responsible for a large number of original posters for his productions. He also executed easel paintings and drawings, among them a range of portraits of renowned artistic figures such as the composer *Dmitri Shostakovich* (1931; untraced) and the ballerina *Galina Ulanova* (1940; untraced). His portraits are distinguished by their keen feeling for the model's personality, their finish and their draughtsmanlike precision. Akimov wrote a number of articles and books on theatre arts.

WRITINGS

O teatre [About theatre] (Leningrad, 1962)

Ne tol'ko o teatre [Not only about theatre] (Leningrad, 1966)

Teatral'noye nalsediya [Theatrical heritage], 2 vols (Leningrad, 1978)

BIBLIOGRAPHY

M. G. Etkind: *N. P. Akimov: Khudozhnik* [N. P. Akimov: Artist] (Leningrad, 1960)

F. Syrkina, ed.: *Teatral'nyy plakat N. Akimova* [Theatre posters by N. Akimov] (Moscow, 1963)

V. V. VANSLOV

Akkadian. Name given to the people responsible for the first Mesopotamian empire, established in the later 3rd millennium BC. The period is noted for a high degree of artistic and technical achievement in statues, carved stelae, cylinder seals and cast metalwork.

1. Introduction. 2. Sargon (*reg* 2334–2279 BC). 3. Manishtushu (*reg* 2269–2255 BC). 4. Naram-Sin (*reg* 2254–2218 BC).

1. INTRODUCTION. During the first two-thirds of the 3rd millennium BC, southern and central MESOPOTAMIA

(bibl. Chaldaea) were divided into a number of independent Sumerian city states. The Sumerians had established the first urban civilization and had developed a script into which they transcribed their language. They co-existed peacefully with the Semitic-speaking population of nomads or settled descendants of nomads who formed the majority in the north. The Semitic capital was the city of Kish (close to the future site of Babylon), which exercised a theoretical sovereignty over the country as a whole; in fact each state was governed by an independent ruler. Various ill-fated attempts were made to unite the country until, towards the middle of the 24th century BC, a Semite, Sargon, ousted the king of Kish, subdued all the other states and imposed a centralized organization on them for the first time. Sargon campaigned to the north, in Syria and even perhaps in Anatolia, and to the east where he annexed Susa. When his title, King of Kish, could be extended to the 'King of the Universe', he founded a new capital. The name of this capital, which probably lay near Kish, has always been transcribed as Agade, after the surrounding Semiticized country which was known from then on as Akkad. The Sumerian script was adapted to this country's language and is known as Akkadian; the script became more stylized, allowing inscriptions to be inserted into designs.

Sargon became, in a semi-legendary tradition, the archetype of the conquering king on whom fortune smiles, although, like his successors, he had to put down revolt. His two sons Rimush (*reg* 2278–2270 BC) and Manishtushu succeeded him and campaigned mainly in Iran and (by sea) on the route to India, where the Indus Valley (Harrapan) civilization had recently emerged. They must have reached at least as far as the Oman peninsula, the land of Magan or Makkan, which was rich in metals and stone suitable for sculpture. The dynasty's apogee was under Naram-Sin, who was deified in his lifetime in a logical extension of the old tradition whereby the king played the part of patron god of the state in religious ceremonies. He also took the new, specifically imperial title of King of the Four Regions (of the world). Some finely engraved seals can be dated to the reign of his successor, Shar-Kali-sharri (*reg* 2217–2193), but thereafter the empire collapsed under the onslaught of the Gutians from the east.

Agade, the capital city of Akkad, has not been found, and nothing is known of its temples and palace. Curiously, the kings of Akkad (who were great administrators) appear to have built little in the cities of their empire. It is not known whether they patronized a particular style of architecture. Only a fortress-warehouse built by Naram-Sin to cover his northern frontier at TELL BRAK in north-east Syria has been found. Agade must have been practically abandoned when the dynasty fell and it was pillaged a millennium later by the Elamites. They transported its works of art to their capital of Susa and added their own inscriptions to some of them. These monuments were brought to light when Susa was explored by a French expedition from 1897, along with others that came from Akkadian cities such as Sippar and Eshnunna. Some stelae and fragments of statues were found elsewhere, particularly at Girsu (Telloh) and at Nineveh. These reveal that art had been almost entirely taken over by the monarchy, which used it as an instrument of its imperial ideology. While previously both the rich and those of modest resources had commissioned statues of themselves to perpetuate their prayers in the temples, Akkadian statuary, such as bas-relief, was monopolized by royalty. Royal victories became the constant and almost the only theme, imposed on artists who were grouped together in official workshops and given the task of producing series of monuments that were sent to the various towns of the empire.

2. SARGON (*reg* 2334–2279 BC). Three fragments of probably similar diorite stelae dedicated to Sargon were found at Susa. The King's image is identified on the largest stele (Paris, Louvre) by the inscription 'Sargon the King', which is engraved in front of a figure on the lower register. The various episodes of a victory are divided between different registers; below, the victorious King marches at the head of a group of dignitaries, while above, soldiers are pressing on the vanquished prisoners and starting to massacre them. The reverse of the stele shows the massacre itself, with birds of prey and dogs tearing at the corpses. Damage to the stele makes it impossible to appreciate fully the quality of the relief and of the design, but this is apparent in the last scene. It is considerably superior to the scene on the same theme that decorates the famous Stele of the Vultures (Paris, Louvre; for illustration *see* MESOPOTAMIA, fig. 3) erected at Girsu (Telloh) some two centuries earlier. The King may be recognized by his long beard and particularly by his hair, which is dressed in the specifically royal style with a headband and a large chignon. He appears to be slaughtering a vanquished enemy. He is followed by a parasol-bearer and by beardless dignitaries who carry a kind of scimitar over their shoulders. Their hair was cut pudding-bowl style, perhaps so that they might more easily wear helmets. The qualities of the Akkadian artist can be better appreciated in a less damaged fragment (Paris, Louvre), where the naked figures have a sculptural realism far superior to that of earlier Sumerian pieces. The Akkadian soldiers wear a wide sash crossed over the chest. This sash must have been made of leather and served as a breastplate. The sculptor was careful to show ethnic variations and represented the defeated figures with a different hairstyle, reduced to a few curly locks on the crown of the head. One of these figures, in what remains of an upper register, is shown with remarkable realism, falling to the ground.

On a third fragment (Paris, Louvre) it is possible to reconstruct an extremely interesting scene. All that is left of the King is his arm, bearing a mace and wearing part of a garment of soft woolly tufts. His enemies are piled up in a large net and he is clubbing their chief and sacrificing him to a seated goddess. Little remains of her, but her emblematic weapons show that she is a goddess of war. The same subject had been depicted on the Stele of the Vultures, whose inscription explains that the King of Lagash has thrown the 'great net of the god Enlil' over his enemies. The Bible, too, takes up this image (e.g. Ezekiel 12:13). This scene, furthermore, corresponds to an episode in Sargon's history that was handed down by soothsayers until Neo-Assyrian times:

> It is the omen of Sargon against whom, upon this sign, in his old age, the whole of the land having risen and having besieged him in Akkad, Sargon in a sortie beat their forces, consummated their defeat, laid low their great army (then) bound their goods upon them and cried: This is yours, Ishtar!

The correspondence between text and image is such that the goddess, whose figure has almost entirely disappeared, may be supposed to be the warrior Ishtar, patroness of Akkad.

Sargon's daughter Enheduanna was made priestess of the moon god Nanna at Ur. Leonard Woolley found a calcite disc there, suggesting the moon, which bears a carving of the only known scene of worship from this period (Philadelphia, U. PA, Mus.). The princess, who played the role of consort to the god, is preceded by a libator and appears in prayer before a monumental stepped altar (an inscription tells the story of its construction). This altar is therefore not a ziggurat, which it resembles, but a sacrificial table that orientated human prayer towards the heavens.

3. MANISHTUSHU (*reg* 2269–2255 BC). No monument to Rimush, Sargon's successor, has survived. However, Manishtushu, the third king of Akkad, brought back large blocks of gabbroic olivine (a type of diorite) from his maritime expeditions to the Oman peninsula. This allowed his sculptors to execute works that reveal their perfect mastery of this extremely hard stone. The lower half of a standing figure (Paris, Louvre) has been subsequently re-engraved with an Elamite inscription indicating that it comes from Akkatu (i.e. Akkad) and that the figure represents Manishtushu. The King is dressed in a fine robe fringed with tassels, draped about his legs with sober folds falling in a spiral. This is the only example in Mesopotamian art in which the sculptor accurately represented such folds. The finely detailed hands are placed together at the waist with the left folded over the right with greater suppleness than in the slightly later hands on the statues of Gudea of Lagash. Another statue (Paris, Louvre), without an epigraph, probably represents the same king. Its base survives, decorated with the bodies of enemies which he tramples underfoot. The statue would thus seem to be the equivalent of a victory stele. Another, found at Assur, is more complete; a garment covers only the left shoulder of the torso, thus revealing its heroic proportions (Berlin, Pergamonmus.). Manishtushu also had himself represented, with equal mastery, as a seated figure. Fragments of a victory stele (Paris, Louvre) from Girsu (Telloh) can be dated to the same period. On both sides of the stele, scenes of massacre unfold in the six registers that partially survive. The technique may be good, but the inspiration shows undeniable impoverishment and monotony. Such decline is obscured by the purity of the work on apparently contemporary stelae in green alabaster found near Ur and at Susa.

4. NARAM-SIN (*reg* 2254–2218 BC). Both Akkad's power and its art reached their apogee under the fourth king, Naram-Sin. Two of his stelae have survived. One, erected at Pir Husein in the empire's northern marches, shows only the figure of the King, apparently in isolation (Istanbul, Mus. Anc. Orient). The other, first erected at Sippar and later taken to Susa, is a masterpiece (Paris, Louvre; see fig. 1). The sculptor appears to have been inspired by a relief carved into the side of a mountain, which led him to abandon the customary use of registers and to concentrate all the different episodes into a single scene, rich in detail, set in a sparingly suggested mountain landscape. The King, shown in giant proportions, has climbed the slopes of the Zagros mountains at the head of his troops, who are disposed in columns climbing behind him. Wearing a helmet decorated with horns symbolizing divine power, he tramples underfoot the bodies of two enemies; one of his arrows has pierced the throat of a third and two others are begging for mercy. Here again, the sculptor recorded different ethnic types by showing the barbarians dressed in animal skins, like Assyria's tributary Medes 1500 years later. A copper head found at Nineveh (Baghdad, Iraq Mus.; see fig. 2) may also be attributed to the reign of Naram-Sin (although it is frequently attributed to Sargon's). Its hair is dressed in the royal style already seen on Sargon's stele but is treated

1. Akkadian stele of Naram-Sin, limestone, h. 2 m, from Susa, *c.* 2250 BC (Paris, Musée du Louvre)

2. Head of an Akkadian ruler, copper, h. 366 mm, from Nineveh, *c.* 2300–2200 BC (Baghdad, Iraq Museum)

with greater skill. The beard is more elaborate than it would have been in reality, and the head thus appears to be, despite its splendid realism, a theoretical portrait in accordance with the imperial ideal of the King of the Four Regions. The stele found at Susa illustrates another version of this ideal. Metalworking skills are further illustrated by a statue in copper, securely dated by an inscription to the time of Naram-Sin, found at Bassetki in Assyria. The lower half of this statue survives, a crouching mythical hero who would have held a gate-post beside a temple gate (Baghdad, Iraq Mus.). This character, who was once wrongly identified as Gilgamesh, is familiar from the designs on seals where he appears as a 'master of the animals' and as guardian of the domain of the god of fresh water.

Cylinder seals continued to depict combats between heroes and animals, but the seal cutters also developed a repertory in which the principal gods were given a specific iconography. The Water god is shown with gushing springs; the Sun god appears with flames, like the god of fire who also carries a torch; the god of storms is borne on a dragon; vegetation deities have branches growing out of their bodies; the goddess Ishtar has weapons growing out of her shoulders and is sometimes winged (in her aspect as the planet Venus; *see* MESOPOTAMIA, fig. 5). These deities take part in actions designed to explain the order of the world from the viewpoint of a farming people. The young Sun god is therefore shown, together with vegetation growing out of the earth, in the presence of his 'father', the Water god, and of the winged goddess. This peaceful scene represents the events of the new year at the spring equinox, when all the powers of nature join forces in a general rebirth. Combats between the gods are more often shown, however; a young warrior resembling the King, accompanied by the god of fire, strikes down other gods (who sometimes have branches as their attributes). One of the few texts of this period reports that Erra (one of the aspects of the warrior god Nergal, the destructive power of the sun in summer) fights with Naram-Sin and triumphs, while waiting for his temple to be inaugurated. A military monarchy must have favoured a mythological theme presenting the destruction of plant life as the destruction of the enemy and conceiving of it as an indispensable element in the yearly cycle of nature. In fact, the warrior Nergal was always honoured with devotion. During the Akkadian period (in scenes of great interest to the religious historian) he was represented as the model for the king.

BIBLIOGRAPHY

A. Moortgat: *The Art of Ancient Mesopotamia* (London, 1969), pp. 45–54

P. Amiet: *L'Art d'Agadé au Musée du Louvre* (Paris, 1976)

PIERRE AMIET

Akkerman, Ben [Bernardus] **(Everhardus)** (*b* Enschede, 29 Feb 1920). Dutch painter and draughtsman. Between 1936 and 1982 he worked as a bookkeeper for Enschede town council. As an artist he was self-taught. During World War II he came into contact with the art of Cézanne, Matisse, Braque and others, mainly through art journals, which influenced his work considerably. From 1946 until 1953 he was a member of the Nieuwe Groep, which brought together painters to promote contemporary art through exhibitions, mainly locally in Twente, such as Johann Haanstra (*b* 1914). Initially he painted stylized cityscapes and landscapes with objects, representing primarily their spatial structure and colour (e.g. *Landscape with Tree*, oil on canvas, 1966–7; Chicago, IL, Mus. Contemp. A.), although from 1972 the landscape as such was no longer recognizable. After 1970 he began to emphasize the nature of a painting as an object rather than a means of representing nature, applying parallel horizontal and diagonal lines, later grids, to the surface, which was often painted in shades of grey, green, ochre and blue (e.g. *Untitled*, oil on canvas, 1981–2; Amsterdam, Stedel. Mus.). Akkerman continued the paint along the edges of the canvas, meticulously rounding off the borders. His work shows an affinity with that of Brice Marden and Robert Ryman.

BIBLIOGRAPHY

G. van Tuyl: 'Ben Akkerman', *Dut. A. & Archit. Today*, xii (Dec 1982), pp. 2–7

M. M. M. Vos: *Ben Akkerman* (Amsterdam, 1988)

JOHN STEEN

Akkoyunlu. *See* AQQOYUNLU.

Ak-Peshim. *See* AK-BESHIM.

Akragas [Lat. Agrigentum; now Agrigento]. Greek colony on the southern coast of Sicily. Believed to have been founded *c.* 580 BC from Gela, a city further down the coast, it flourished as an independent state until 406 BC, when it was sacked by the Carthaginians. It maintained some degree of independence until the Roman conquest of Sicily in 210 BC. The extensive town, lying some 2 km from the sea, was enclosed by walls following natural precipices and includes a steep acropolis now occupied by the modern settlement. Only a small part of the residential area has been excavated, dating to the Hellenistic and Roman periods; it was organized in regular, rectangular blocks after the Hippodamian system (*see* HIPPODAMOS).

An early column capital, probably made immediately after the foundation of Akragas, is the only remaining example of Doric architecture from the site before *c.* 500 BC. Small temple buildings without columns were constructed in several locations later occupied by monumental temples. A cluster of such buildings of different shapes, some of them probably unroofed, occupied a sanctuary to the fertility gods in the south-west corner of the town, with round and rectangular monumental altars. Near the east gate, on the edge of the acropolis, a small fountain sanctuary with sacred caves precedes and is associated with a large Temple of Demeter (*c.* 480 BC) with two Doric columns in the porch.

The so-called Temple of Herakles, at the south-west edge of the city, was the earliest example of Doric monumental architecture from after 500 BC and was perhaps founded by the tyrant Theron (*reg* 488–472 BC). Its plan reflects that of late Archaic temples in mainland Greece, such as the Temple of Apollo at Delphi: both have a colonnade of 6 by 15 columns arranged symmetrically around a cella with pronaos and opisthodomos. There are also local Archaic features, including the shape of the capitals and almost no angle contraction. The cella is wide and lacks inner columns; the overall dimensions (stylobate 25.28×67.04 m) are slightly greater than those of the earlier Temple C at Selinus, which also has wide stairs in front of the temple.

The Temple of Olympian Zeus (Olympieion; see fig.) in the south-west of the town is the largest ever built in the Doric style (stylobate 52.74×110.10 m). It was inspired by gigantic Ionian temples, such as the third Temple of Hera at Samos, and by the earlier Temple G at Selinus, and probably commemorated Theron's victory over the Carthaginians at Himera in 480 BC. The exterior has the unique form of a closed wall with engaged columns (7 by 15) rendered as pilasters on the inside of the wall and a normal Doric entablature with pediments; giant male figures (telamones) standing on ledges between the engaged columns of the exterior (the precise arrangement is disputed) helped to support the architrave. The interior consists of three long, narrow spaces of equal width, separated by two rows of square pillars connected by walls; the central space was open to the sky. Relief sculpture in the pediments (only insignificant fragments remain) showed the *Fall of Troy* and the *Battle of the Gods and Giants.*

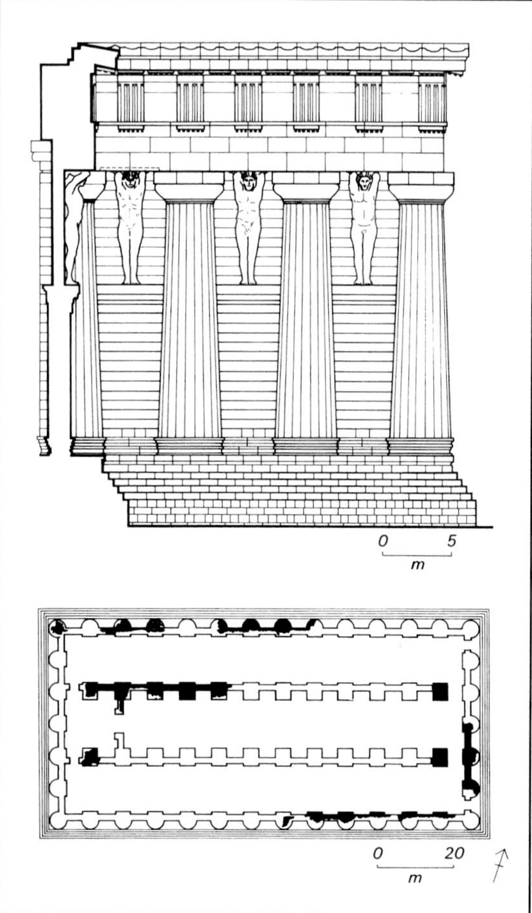

Akragas, Temple of Olympian Zeus (Olympieion), plan and elevation, *c.* 480 BC

The temples of the later 5th century BC are of a size similar to that of mainland temples, with stylobates measuring 16–17×38–40 m, and have a standard colonnade of 6 by 13 columns (although elsewhere in Sicily 6 by 14 was more frequent) and a cella with pronaos and opisthodomos; Sicilian characteristics include high foundations with four steps, closely spaced colonnades with heavy columns and frequent use of double angle contraction, wide steps in the front and omission of columns in the cella. An imperfectly known Doric temple under the church of S Maria dei Greci, on the acropolis in the modern city, may have been the first of this group (?*c.* 470 BC). The temples D (to Hera Lakinia) and F (Concord) in the south-east of the town (*c.* 450 BC and 425 BC respectively) differ only in minor details and a more accurate execution in the later building. Both have double angle contraction (Temple D only at the eastern front). Temple F is one of the best-preserved ancient temples in the world. Temples D and F, together with the Temple of Zeus and the so-called Temple of Herakles, are arranged scenographically on a ridge at the southern boundary of the town (Valle dei Templi; see GREECE, ANCIENT, fig. 35). A smaller Doric temple dedicated to Asklepios (late 5th century BC), with two columns in the porch and two engaged columns at the rear, lies south of the town.

Monumental building during the Hellenistic and Roman periods includes two impressive mausolea, the Tomb of Phalaris (2nd century BC) and the Tomb of Theron (*c.* 75 BC), both Ionic structures with Doric decoration; the latter had a pyramidal roof comparable to North African funerary buildings of the 1st century BC. A circular ekklesiasterion (open-air structure for political meetings) of Hellenistic date resembles those found at Paestum and Metapontion (Metaponto) in southern Italy.

As elsewhere in Sicily, Archaic sculpture was mostly of terracotta and included some fine, ambitious, almost life-size heads, as well as ordinary votive figurines and small reliefs. Large female busts (perhaps of Persephone) and decorative reliefs on the rims of large jars were local specialities. Two important sculptures of imported marble, made after 480 BC and similar in style, were also probably local products: a kouros with raised forearms in a slightly contrapposto pose (akin to the *Kritias Boy*, Athens, Acropolis Mus.; *see* GREECE, ANCIENT, §IV, 2(ii)(c) and fig. 55), and a helmeted head connected with a torso (no proper joins) of a falling warrior, which was probably part of an independent sculptural dedication (perhaps depicting Athena and a giant) rather than pedimental sculpture. Related to this stylistic group are the badly worn giants from the Temple of Zeus, carved in a 'lingering Archaic' style similar to the later relief metopes from Temple E at SELINUS. Architectural sculpture was otherwise limited to water spouts in the shape of lion heads, preserved in several fine examples from the 5th century BC. The principal sculpture from a later period is the fine Roman sarcophagus of Attic type (*c.* AD 200), carved with scenes from the myth of Hippolytus, housed in the 13th-century church of S Nicola. All the other works mentioned above are in the Museo Archeologico Regionale, Agrigento.

BIBLIOGRAPHY

R. Koldewey and O. Puchstein: *Die griechischen Tempel in Unteritalien und Sicilien* (Berlin, 1899), pp. 138–84
P. Marconi: *Agrigento* (Florence, 1929)
——: *Studi agrigentini* (Rome, 1930)
——: *Agrigento arcaica* (Rome, 1933)
E. Langlotz: 'Die Ephebenstatue in Agrigent', *Mitt. Dt. Archäol. Inst.: Röm. Abt.*, lviii (1943), pp. 202–12
V. Tusa: *I sarcofagi romani in Sicilia* (Palermo, 1957), pp. 21–36
D. Ahrens: 'Stufen der Verbildlichung in der Terrakottenkunst von Selinus, Akragas und Gela', *Jhft. Österreich. Archaöl. Inst. Wien*, xlvi (1961–3), suppl., pp. 95–144
G. Gruben: *Die Tempel der Griechen* (Munich, 1966, rev. 4/1986), pp. 269–315
E. De Miro: 'Il "guerriero" di Agrigento e la scultura di stile severo in Sicilia', *Cron. Archeol. & Stor. A.*, vii (1968), pp. 143–56
M. Bell: 'Stylobate and Roof in the Olympieion at Akragas', *Amer. J. Archaeol.*, lxxxiv (1980), pp. 359–72
J. A. De Waele: 'Der Entwurf der dorischen Tempel von Akragas', *Archaeol. Anz.* (1980), pp. 180–241
——: 'I frontoni dell'Olympieion agrigentino', *Aparchai in onore di P. E. Arias* (Pisa, 1982), pp. 271–8
B. A. Barletta: *Ionic Influences in Archaic Sicily* (Göteborg, 1983), pp. 265–88
I. Ceretto Castigliano and C. Savio: 'Considerazioni sulla metrologia e sulla genesi concettuale del tempio di Giunone ad Agrigento', *Boll. A.*, lxviii (1983), pp. 35–48
A. Siracusano: *Il santuario rupestre di Agrigento* (Rome, 1983)
D. Mertens: *Der Tempel von Segesta und die dorische Tempelbaukunst des griechischen Westens in klassischer Zeit* (Mainz, 1984), pp. 92–130
G. Pugliese Carratelli and others: *Sikanie* (Milan, 1985), pp. 208–40, 398–408, 474–83
Veder greco—Le necropoli di Agrigento (Rome, 1988)
G. Pugliese Carratelli and G. Fiorentini: *Agrigento, Museo Archeologico* (Palermo, 1992)

ERIK ØSTBY

Akrotiri. *See under* THERA.

Aksum [Axoum; Axum]. Capital of the ancient kingdom of Aksum, in the modern Tigray Province of Ethiopia, *c.* 600 km north of Addis Ababa. It flourished between the 1st and 8th centuries AD. The modern town occupies part of the site, which faces south over a fertile plain at the foot of a flat-topped hill, Mt Beta Giyorgis. The ancient city's importance is attested by the many monuments scattered throughout the modern town, including huge stelae and throne bases, broken pillars, inscriptions and royal hypogea. The first extensive investigations were undertaken in 1906 by a German team under E. Littmann. During the 1960s and 1970s French, British and Italian teams carried out further excavations, led by Francis Anfray, Neville Chittick and Lanfranco Ricci, respectively.

From the 5th century BC the surrounding region was ruled by a local monarchy with a major centre of Yeha, less than 50 km north-east of Aksum, with close ties to the kingdom of Saba in southern Arabia. Elements of this strong southern Arabic influence survived in the culture of Aksum and its kingdom, which was founded in the 1st century AD and underwent remarkable development between the 3rd and 6th centuries. By the 8th century, however, it was already in decline. The most important factor affecting the economic and cultural development of Aksum was its close relations with the eastern Mediterranean. Under Roman impetus, during the 1st century AD commercial traffic on the Red Sea increased and navigational standards improved. The earliest known reference to Aksum appears in the *Periplus of the Erythrean Sea*, a maritime and commercial guide dated *c.* AD 95–130; it is not mentioned in Ethiopian sources until the early 3rd century. The development of the kingdom's main port at Adulis encouraged the creation of cities in the hinterland and trading in ivory, metals, fabrics, implements, precious stones, jewellery, aromatics, spices and other commodities. Most of the inland trade passed through the capital, which lay at the crossroads of the caravan routes between the Nile basin and the Red Sea.

Some 200 stelae of the 3rd and 4th centuries have survived. Six of these bear representations of buildings with multiple storeys. Only one (h. 21 m) stands *in situ*: four lie broken, including one originally more than 33 m high; one (h. 24 m) stands in the Piazza di Porta Capena in Rome. Their function and symbolism are uncertain, although it has been suggested that they were funerary cippi, memorials or representations of royal residences in the next world. Near the giant stele is the Nefas Mawcha, a vast granite slab (17.5×6.5×1.3 m), which is set on a masonry structure to form the roof of what was probably a royal funerary chamber and surrounded by a double gallery. The whole must have been covered with soil. Chittick excavated a number of monumental tombs near by.

Another group of monolithic monuments consists of 26 stone platforms, of which 12 lie near the stelae. Some of these measure more than 2.5 m square. They probably served as the bases for thrones, which, according to an important body of inscriptions carved on large stone slabs, occupied a notable place in the ritual practices of the kings of Aksum. These inscriptions, written in Ethiopian, pseudo-south-Arabic and Greek, relate the military expeditions undertaken by the kings Ezana (4th century), Kaleb and Waazeb (both 6th century) and reveal the extent of their rule. Eight of the ten texts at Aksum refer to the reign of Ezana, who was converted to Christianity in AD 340. There is little evidence of monumental sculpture in the ancient city, except for a reference in one of the inscriptions to the gold, silver and bronze statues erected by Ezana in honour of the god 'Ares the Invincible'. None of these has been recovered, although bronze, stone and terracotta animal figurines have been discovered, and pottery includes jars with spouts in the form of female heads.

Aksumite architecture is characterized by the use of basalt and nepheline-syenite in a masonry bonded together and to the ground by wooden joists and wall plates. Wood was also used for door- and window-frames, for piers and for transverse joists, the butt-ends of which protruded beyond the walls in parallel rows. The square and massive buildings were set on stepped bases, and their façades were decorated with projections and recesses. Evidence for this structural method recurs regularly throughout the kingdom's territory, such as at Matara and Kohayto on the Eritrean plateau, and it was perpetuated in the walls of churches long after Aksum's decline.

One of the best examples of Aksumite architecture is the ruined structure at Dungur (6th–7th centuries; see fig.), *c.* 500 m south-west of the modern town. Its foundations were excavated by Anfray in the 1960s. The quadrangular building covers an area of *c.* 3000 sq. m and comprises a central block of apartments (18 m square) on a high, stepped base with a monumental stairway and several small courtyards bordered by a series of outbuildings, including three brick ovens and a hypocaust. Other excavated structures include three large buildings surveyed in 1906 and known locally as Ta'akha Maryam, Enda Mika'el and Enda Semon; little has survived. In the hills to the north-east are what were probably the royal hypogea. Ricci excavated the churches on Mt Beta Giyorgis. Certain aspects of Aksumite architecture, such as the quadrangular plan, the stepped base and the combined use of stone and wood, are clearly derived from building methods employed at Yeha. With the rise of Aksum, however, the buildings underwent a change of layout that undoubtedly resulted from growing cultural contact with the Roman East.

BIBLIOGRAPHY

The Periplus of the Erythrean Sea (AD *c.* 95–130); Eng. trans., ed. G. W. B. Huntingford (London, 1980), pp. 20, 90
E. Littmann, T. von Lupke and D. Krencker: *Deutsche Aksum-Expedition* (Berlin, 1913)
U. Monneret de Villard: *Aksum* (Rome, 1938)
Y. Kobischanov: *Aksum* (Moscow, 1966)
F. Anfray: 'Aspects de l'archéologie éthiopienne', *J. Afr. Hist.*, ix/3 (1968), pp. 345–66
F. Anfray, A. Caquot and P. Nautin: 'Une Nouvelle Inscription grecque d'Ezana, roi d'Axoum', *J. Sav.* (Oct–Dec 1970), pp. 260–74
F. Anfray: 'L'Archéologie d'Axoum en 1972', *Paideuma*, xviii (1972), pp. 60–78
N. Chittick: 'Excavations at Aksum, 1973–4: A Preliminary Report', *Azania*, ix (1974), pp. 159–205
L. Ricci: 'Excavations at Aksum in 1974: Short Report', *An. Ethiopie*, x (1976), pp. 327–8

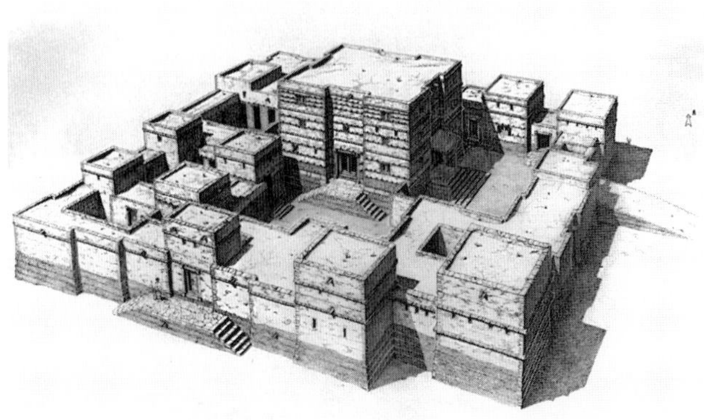

Aksum, Dungur building, 6th–7th centuries AD; reconstruction (only the foundations remain)

F. Anfray: 'La Civilisation d'Axoum du 1er au 7e siècle', *Afrique ancienne*, ed. G. Mokhtar (1980), ii of *Histoire générale de l'Afrique* (Paris, 1980–), pp. 385–405
R. Plant: *Architecture of the Tigre, Ethiopia* (Worcester, 1985)

FRANCIS ANFRAY

Aktionen. *See* PERFORMANCE ART.

Aktionismus. Austrian group of performance artists, active in the 1960s. Its principal members were Günter Brus, Otto Muehl and Hermann Nitsch, who first collaborated informally in 1961, and Rudolf Schwarzkogler, who was introduced to the group in 1963. Others associated with the group included Anni Brus, the film maker Kurt Kren, the composer Anetis Logosthetis and the actor Heinz Cibulka. The group were influenced by the work of Adolf Frohner (*b* 1934), Arnulf Rainer and Alfons Schilling (*b* 1934), who were all in turn influenced by American action painting and by the gestural painting associated with Tachism. The members of Aktionismus attached significance, however, not so much to the paintings produced by the artist as to the artist as a participant in the process of production, as a witness to creation rather than as a creator. Muehl, Brus and Nitsch all felt drawn to public performances celebrating and investigating artistic creativity by a natural progression from their earlier sculptural or painterly activities. In 1962 Muehl and Nitsch staged their first *Aktion* or performance, *Blood Organ*, in the Perinetgasse in Vienna. In 1965 Brus produced the booklet *Le Marais* to accompany an exhibition of his work at the Galerie Junge Generation, Vienna. Muehl, Nitsch and Schwarzkogler all contributed, referring to themselves as the Wiener Aktionsgruppe.

The group's interest in exploring sexuality and ritual, and their rejection of convention, aesthetics and morality often led to controversy. Although the participation of Nitsch, Brus and Muehl (as the recently formed Institut für Direkte Kunst) in the Destruction in Art Symposium in London in September 1966 was followed by international acclaim, the *Aktion* organized by Nitsch (*Abreactionplay*) led to the prosecution of Gustav Metzger and John Sharkey, the organizers of the symposium, for an 'indecent exhibition contrary to common law', images of male genitalia having been projected on a lamb's carcass as it was dismembered. Brus's *Art and Revolution* (1968) led to further scandal and the artist's imprisonment. With Brus's departure to Berlin in 1969 and Schwarzkogler's death, the group disbanded.

Each of the four members of Aktionismus approached the realization of his actions from a different perspective, although the basic aims of bringing about a state of cathartic awareness, an unburdening of repressed desires and the recognition and flouting of taboos (including those that reflected Austrian cultural isolation as well as sexual repression) were held by them all, and they often collaborated. However, it was Nitsch alone who continued to work with *Aktionen* after 1970, as part of his work on the *Orgies–Mysteries Theatre*.

For illustration *see* BRUS, GÜNTER.

WRITINGS

O. Muehl and others: *Die Blutorgel* (Vienna, 1962)
G. Brus and others: *Le Marais* (Vienna, 1965)

BIBLIOGRAPHY

P. Weibel and V. Export: *Wien: Bildkompendium Wiener Aktionismus und Film* (Frankfurt am Main, 1970)
L. Vergine: *Il corpo come linguaggio* (Milan, 1974), pp. 9, 21–7, *passim*
R. Fleck: *Avantgarde in Wien: Die Geschichte der Galerie Nächst St Stephan, 1954–1982* (Vienna, 1982), pp. 194–6, 199–202, 226, 240, 304, *passim*
Von der Aktionsmalerei zum Aktionismus: Wien, 1960–1965 (exh. cat., ed. D. Schwarz and V. Loers; Kassel, Mus. Fridericianum; Winterthur, Kstmus.; Edinburgh, N.G. Mod. A.; Vienna, Mus. Angewandte Kst; 1988–9)
Wiener Aktionismus, 1960–71 (exh. cat., ed. H. Klocker; Vienna, Albertina; Cologne, Mus. Ludwig; 1989)

ANDREW WILSON

Akye. Largest of the 12 Akan-speaking groups, known as the Lagoon Peoples (*lagunaires*), of south-eastern Côte d'Ivoire. Their eastern boundary is formed by the Comoe River, and they live south of the Moronu Anyi and east of the Abe (Abbey), another Lagoon group. Their southernmost villages are close to communities of such other *lagunaires* as the Gwa (M'batto), Kyaman (Ebrie), Abure (Abouré), Aladyan (Alladian) and Adjukru (Adioukrou), and some have been absorbed within the area of Abidjan, the major city of Côte d'Ivoire. The Akye are composed of three different groups, located in the préfecture of Adzopé and the sous-préfectures of Alépé and Anyama. Each population speaks a distinct dialect.

The proximity of most Akye villages to other Lagoon and Akan populations has had important ramifications for their art, with regular interchange between clients and carvers of the various ethnic groups. As a result, it is inaccurate to speak of an 'Akye style'. The art created by the Akye and their Lagoon neighbours would be better described as a 'Lagoon style'. In addition to the art forms discussed below, portrait vases for display during funerals were once made, and Lagoon and Anyi artists continue to make elaborate cement grave monuments for wealthy families. Much traditional statuary was destroyed by followers of the Liberian missionary William Wade Harris, who arrived in the Lagoon area *c.* World War II. In contrast, the Harrists have also been the patrons of ambitious architectural programmes. The art of the Akye and their neighbours has been relatively understudied, and the scholarly literature is sparse (see bibliography below). The Musée Barbier–Mueller, Geneva, and the Museum Rietberg, Zurich, hold fine examples of Lagoon art. The majority of other museum holdings are in French collections.

1. FIGURE SCULPTURE. Akye or Lagoon-style figures usually have bulbous, segmented limbs, a cylindrical or slightly tapered torso, large feet and cupped hands. The heads of older statues are adorned with elaborate conical and hemispherical forms representing traditional hairstyles. Scarification patterns of the 19th century may be indicated by tiny wooden pegs. Separate pieces of wood may be used for arms, attached to the shoulders in an extended position. Lagoon sculptors work alone, without mentors or apprentices, so stylistic diversity and artistic innovation within these general parameters are quite common.

Although nominally Christian, many Akye still conceive of the universe as filled with spirits that may persuade men and women to become diviners (*kösen/köshi*). Such individuals may own a wooden statue known as a 'person of wood' (*zakwebi*) or 'wooden woman' (*nkpasopi*). Some of these figures are said to have been able to speak or walk; the extended arms of some Akye figures may have helped to create these impressions of movement and vitality. Sometimes the statues are portraits of their owners or of members of their families and are named accordingly. Others are an idealized personification of a spirit, after which they are named. A wooden image is, therefore, a visible reminder to clients of the links between the diviner and the supernatural realm.

Figures used in secular dances are identical to these sacred images (*see* §3 below). Larger statues, which are central to the dance performance and represent its guardians, are idealized portraits of the female dance groups' leaders. Smaller figures are carried by the best dancers as both their portrait and their prize (see fig.), while others are used as props by women playing the part of diviners in theatrical dances. The original use of each statue cannot be ascertained unless its individual history is known, for a figure used in a satirical dance and a sculpture for a tutelary spirit may have the same visual features, dimensions and patina. Thus, if a figure is removed from its original setting, its former role is almost impossible to reconstruct.

2. REGALIA AND RELATED ARTS. As Akye communities are quite egalitarian, and the head of each village maintains his position only as long as his age-grade retains control of village affairs, the iconography of Lagoon regalia refers to a leader's personal influence and resources rather than to any established rules or sacred powers. At formal public gatherings the elders carry staffs with carved finials of wood or ivory. Alternatively, wooden finials may be covered with gold leaf or embellished with brass studs. These finials frequently display a carved fist, which metaphorically proclaims the leader's ability to hold all his people in his hand, as well as illustrating a proud and defiant gesture. Some finials depict a rich man riding upon the shoulders of an attendant, or a leader's young, female stool-bearer. Rectangular or cylindrical stools (some of which also served as containers for packets of gold nuggets) were formerly passed from generation to generation to be used as seating on ceremonial occasions, but

Akye dance figures, wood, h. 282 mm and h. 295 mm, by Mambo Besho, *c.* 1950 (Denver, CO, Blackmun Visonà private collection)

their value as regalia has been diminished by the widespread adoption of more grandiose chairs.

Wealthy men are considered natural leaders, and the Akye terms for 'rich person' (*biabi/shiabi* or *hobi/shobi*) have been extended to mean 'kings'. In the southern Akye region, this title is conferred upon the ceremonial sponsors of formal displays of solid gold ornaments. These large abstracted works covered with fine striations are no longer cast by Akye goldsmiths but only by Kyaman workshops. The motifs employed may refer to the hard work that produced the wealth and its resulting benefits, or to the discretion with which the owner amassed his riches. Faces of ancestors are often depicted, while simple gold discs are believed to deflect jealousy and witchcraft.

Ivory trumpets and horns are also the prerogative of the wealthy. Long, side-blown ivory trumpets are made of whole tusks, the tips of which are carved in abstract forms. These are played in groups or pairs. Smaller, two-note horns are played singly. Miniature ivory combs were once worn on special occasions as hair ornaments by men and women.

3. Ceremonial and festival arts. Both regalia and figural sculptures appear during age-grade ceremonies (*fokwe*), at which leaders and members of the age-grade wear family heirlooms and carry ornamented staffs, and to which other participants may bring statuary and other sacred objects. Art works specifically commissioned for age-grade ceremonies include wooden objects hung around the necks of war captains and other officers. From the 1960s or so, large, brilliantly coloured sculptures arranged upon planks were carried upon the heads of the dancers. The traditional focus of an age-grade initiation is the great *fokwe* drum, which is beaten to inspire the age-grade, to call it to (spiritual) battle and to announce the death of one of its members. The large drum, carved with rows of figures or male heads, is accompanied by smaller ones that lead the age-grade in war cries and dance rhythms. Masks sometimes appear in Lagoon age-grade festivals. Except for the zoomorphic helmet masks imported by the northern Akye from their Anyi and Baule neighbours during the early 20th century, Lagoon masks are not supernaturally charged, and they do not seek out sorcery. Their purpose is only to scare children and amuse spectators. Overall, these age-grade festivals provide visual juxtapositions that are both dramatic and loaded with symbolic meaning. The dress of the officials and dancers makes complex aesthetic statements about the nature of the age-grade's strength.

BIBLIOGRAPHY

H. Hecquard: *Voyage sur la côte et dans l'intérieur de l'Afrique occidentale* (Paris, 1855)

M. B. Visonà: *Art and Authority among the Akye of the Ivory Coast* (diss., Santa Barbara, U. CA, 1983)

——: 'Carved Posts of the Lagoon Region, Ivory Coast', *Afr. A.*, xx/2 (1987), pp. 60–64, 83–4

——: 'Divinely Inspired Artists from the Lagoon Cultures of the Ivory Coast', *IA Stud. Afr. A.*, iii (1987)

T. F. Garrard: *Gold of Africa: Jewellery and Ornaments from Ghana, Côte d'Ivoire, Mali and Senegal in the Collection of the Barbier-Mueller Museum* (Munich, New York and London, 1989)

Corps sculptés, corps parés, corps masqués: Chefs-d'oeuvre de Côte d'Ivoire (exh. cat., Paris, Gal. N. Grand Pal., 1989)

M. B. Visonà: 'Portraiture among the Lagoon Peoples of Côte d'Ivoire', *Afr. A.*, xxiii/4 (1990), pp. 54–61, 94–5

——: 'The Lagoon Peoples', *Text*, i of *Art of Côte d'Ivoire from the Collections of the Musée Barbier-Mueller*, ed. J. P. Barbier (Geneva and New York, 1993), pp. 368–83

MONICA BLACKMUN BISONA

al-. For proper names containing this Arabic definite article, *see under* the part of the name preceding the article if there is one; otherwise *see under* the part following the article.

□

'Ala' al-Din 'Ali ibn 'Abd al-Karim. *See* Ali Acemi.

Alabaster. Term used to describe two types of stone, one of gypsum and one of limestone.

1. Types and properties. 2. History and uses.

1. Types and properties. 'True' alabaster is hydrated calcium sulphate, a finely fibrous form of gypsum. It occurs as nodular masses with a felted, fibrous microstructure, variably intermixed with streaks of red or green clay. Deposits of economic size accumulate as precipitated salts in evaporating saline lakes in arid areas. The variety satin spar occurs in vein-like form with the fibres in regular parallel arrangement, giving the mass a silk-like lustre. Alabaster is slightly soluble in water and therefore not suitable for outdoor works; it is very soft and readily cut and polished with the simplest tools. It provides an excellent surface for painting and gilding, without priming being necessary. Geologically ancient deposits provided

material for sculptors, although gypsum continues to form in suitable environments in the Middle East, the USA and elsewhere. European sources exploited for decoration since the Middle Ages are present in England (S. Derbys and Staffs), France (Paris), Spain (e.g. nr Mérida) and Italy (nr Volterra and Castellina), while German deposits have given material since the 18th century. More recently alabaster from the USA and the former USSR has been used.

The second type is the stone that was referred to as alabaster by Theophrastus and Herodotus and that is now known as calcite alabaster, onyx-marble, Egyptian alabaster or Oriental alabaster (although alabaster is still used as a synonym in the eastern Mediterranean area). Onyx-marble is a stalagmitic limestone marked with patterns of swirling bands of cream and brown. It was an admired decorative stone in the Ancient Near East and the Mediterranean region (see §2 (i) below). The early authors named stone types from their outward appearance, rather than their chemical or mineralogical composition, and 'alabaster' was used for stone of any composition that showed large-scale banding similar to that of the Egyptian alabaster or onyx-marble. During the Middle Ages in Western Europe, where useful deposits of stalagmitic limestone are rare, other material of similar appearance was named as, and used in place of, the rare stone, then available only as salvage from Roman ruins. At this time, English alabaster, a massive, fine-grained, translucent form of gypsum, became famous as a material for finely carved tomb figures and altar furnishings (see §2(ii) below). Later mineralogists retained this use of the term, and it is in this sense that it is currently generally understood. In addition to its use as a sculptural medium, true alabaster is used crushed for mineral white or terra alba and as a filler in paint and paper. Plaster of Paris, Keene's cement and Parian cement are prepared from calcined gypsum (*see* STUCCO AND PLASTERWORK, §II).

BIBLIOGRAPHY

R. Webster: *Gems: Their Sources, Descriptions and Identification*, 2 vols (London, 1962, rev. 4/1983)

W. A. Deer, R. A. Howie and J. Zussman: *Non-silicates*, v of *The Rock-forming Minerals*, 5 vols (London, 1962–3, 2/1978)

R. Gnoli: *Marmora Romana* (Rome, 1971)

R. W. SANDERSON

2. HISTORY AND USES.

(i) Ancient world. (ii) Europe.

(i) Ancient world. Calcite alabaster was used in the Ancient Near East, Egypt, Greece and Italy mostly for vessels, small boxes and caskets and for small-scale sculpture (*see* STONE, colour pl. X, fig. 1). The ancient Egyptians were particularly fond of the stone, and some of the best-known alabaster objects come from there, discovered in the tomb of Tutankhamun. They include some 50 vases (e.g. chalices carved in the form of lotus flowers), painted boxes, portrait stoppers for the alabaster canopic jars in which the internal organs of the king were preserved, and unguent vases carved in animal shapes (all Cairo Mus.). In addition, sarcophagi were sometimes created from great slabs of the stone (e.g. sarcophagus of Sethos I, *c.* 1279 BC; London, Soane Mus.; see fig. 1).

Alabaster finds from Mesopotamia include busts from Sumer (Paris, Louvre) that date to as early as the 3rd millennium BC, the same period as some carved alabaster heads from Tell Brak in Iran (London, BM, and Aleppo, N. Mus.; *see* MESOPOTAMIA, §III, 2). Even earlier (6th millennium BC) are alabaster vases and figurines from TELL ES SAWWAN (Baghdad, Iraq Mus.). Later, alabaster was used for wall reliefs in the Assyrian palace at Nineveh

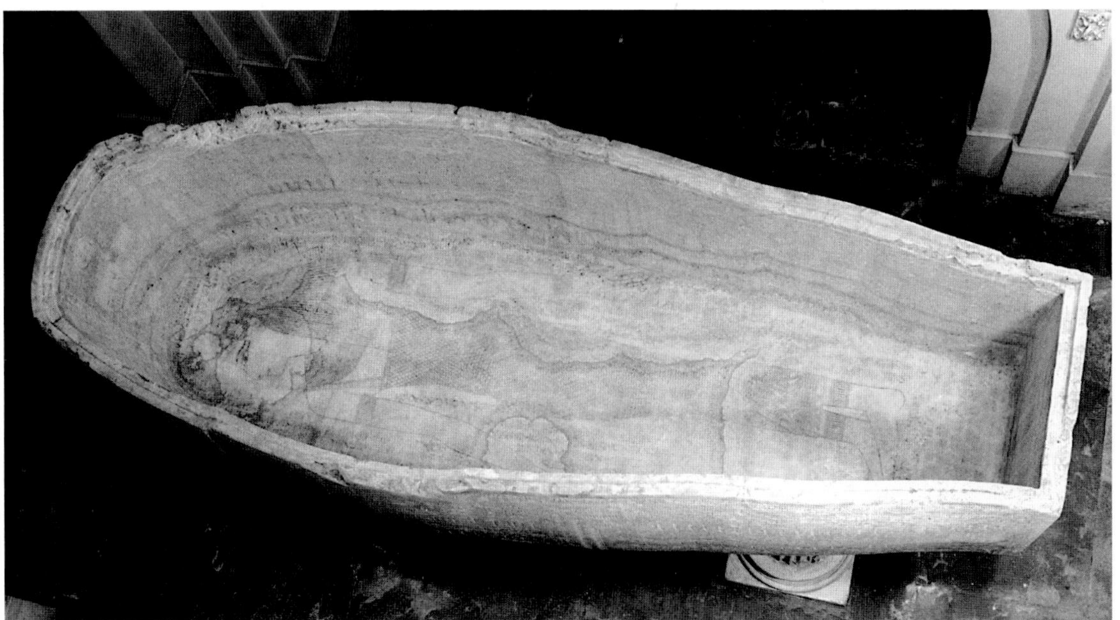

1. Alabaster sarcophagus of Sethos I, Egyptian, *c.* 1279 BC (London, Sir John Soane's Museum)

(*c.* 640 BC; for illustration *see* ASSYRIAN) and at the Neo-Assyrian North-west Palace of Assurnasirpal II at Nimrud (*c.* 865 BC; *see* MESOPOTAMIA, fig. 15).

The Bronze Age Minoans on Crete used calcite alabaster for carved vases—some 40 are known, including a vase in the form of a triton shell from Knossos (*c.* 1450 BC; Herakleion, Archaeol. Mus.)—but they also employed 'true' alabaster (the soft, gypseous form of the stone) as a thin veneer for facing walls, floors and benches. Using long bronze saws they cut the stone into sheets over 2 m square and often less than 30 mm thick. Alabaster continued to be used by the Greeks, Etruscans and Romans for fine carved vessels and statuettes; the Etruscans even used the stone for carved cinerary urns such as one found at Volterra. □

(ii) Europe. During the later Middle Ages and afterwards, especially in the 16th and 17th centuries, alabaster was much used by sculptors for small panels and figures and for tombs both on the Continent and in England. Marks on the backs of some 15th-century English panels indicate that medieval carvers initially shaped the alabaster by saw. Thenceforward, because of the soft and easily bruised quality of the stone, the carving would have been done more in the nature of wood-carving, using a gouging motion with a chisel or knife. Deep undercutting was probably effected by a small drill. Once the carving had been completed and before the application of paint and gilding on parts of the panel or figure, the surface would doubtless have been smoothed by fine abrasives such as sand or pumice powder and given a final polish with a piece of rough leather.

Alabaster was a popular material in Germany during the 15th century. Spanish alabaster can be seen in a particularly fine tomb, made in 1512, of Prince John, only son of Ferdinand II and Isabella, in the royal monastery of St Thomas in Ávila. In the Low Countries, from the middle of the 16th century to the first quarter of the 17th, the town of Mechelen was an important centre for the carving of small alabaster panels, mainly of religious subjects. In England tomb-carvers used alabaster increasingly from the beginning of the 14th century until the end of the 17th, and carvers of images, panels and altarpieces used it from the mid-14th century until towards the end of Henry VIII's reign in 1547. The English alabaster industry, with its lively export trade, was important in Europe, and it is on this subject that the following survey concentrates.

(a) Before *c.* 1540. (b) After *c.* 1540.

(a) Before c. *1540.*

Forms and sculptors. The earliest use of alabaster in England occurs in an architectural context, on one of the inner mouldings of the west door (*c.* 1160) of St Mary's priory church at Tutbury, Staffs, but this appears to have been an isolated use of a local stone. The first alabaster quarries seem to have been at Tutbury, for the earliest surviving alabaster effigy, probably representing *Sir John de Hanbury* (*d* 1303; see fig. 2), lies in the nearby parish church of St Werburgh, Hanbury, Staffs. Tutbury was a possession of the Duchy of Lancaster and royal interest in alabaster is attested by a document of 1362, which refers to six cartloads to be taken from Tutbury to London on the instructions of Queen Philippa (*d* 1369). By the mid-14th century the quarries of Chellaston, between Derby and Nottingham, became more prominent. Documentary evidence for other alabaster quarries, which may well have existed, has not survived, although alabaster carvings were also produced at Burton-on-Trent, York and London. The sculptors were not foreign immigrants:

2. Alabaster tomb of *?Sir John de Hanbury*, English, soon after 1303 (Hanbury, Staffs, St Werburgh)

in the 15th century such names as Roper, Hill, Hilton and Walker are mentioned in the Nottingham borough records.

The first sculptors to exploit alabaster as a medium were makers of tomb effigies; it became popular for this purpose, especially during the 15th and 16th centuries, doubtless owing to its suitability for the detailed rendering of dress and ornament. By the mid-14th century, however, there is material and documentary evidence for the production of religious figures and panels. Workshops seem to have specialized: in Nottingham they concentrated on altarpieces, figures, panels and small shrines, especially plaques of the head of St John the Baptist. In 1367–9 Peter the Mason of Nottingham was paid £200 for an alabaster altarpiece for St George's Chapel, Windsor, which suggests that Nottingham was now the most important centre in England for carving alabaster images, a pre-eminence that apparently continued until the Reformation. Tombs were apparently the speciality of Burton and Chellaston, and the only reference to tomb-carving in Nottingham is an order dated 1495 from Henry VII for a tomb (destr.) to be made for Richard III (*reg* 1483–5) in the Greyfriars' church, Leicester, through the alabasterman Walter Hilton. Although surviving alabaster images and altarpieces are anonymous, the work of some of the documented tomb-carvers is known: the tomb of *Sir Ralph Greene* (*d* 1417) and his wife in St Peter's, Lowick, is by THOMAS PRENTYS and Robert Sutton of Chellaston, who contracted to carve it for £40 in 1418–19. The earliest examples of non-sepulchral alabaster work are the mid-14th-century horizontal panels that combine the *Nativity* and *Adoration of the Magi* (e.g. that in Holy Trinity, Long Melford, Suffolk; 385×655 mm). Slightly later are such figures as *God the Father with the Crucified Christ Holding the Souls of the Righteous* (h. 875 mm; *c.* 1375–80; Glasgow, Burrell Col.) and those of the *Virgin and Child* (h. 813 mm), *St Peter* and a *Bishop* from St Peter's, Flawford, of about the same date (all Nottingham, Castle Mus.).

The present appearance of many alabaster-carvings is misleading, owing to the loss of the painted colour that was integral to their production. The surviving paint is often discoloured with dirt or even chemical change, the latter often affecting green copper resinate, which usually turns dark. The stone itself provided an excellent smooth and non-absorbent surface, so that paint was often applied without a ground. The lower part of the panels was usually painted green with a characteristic 'daisy' pattern of white dots surrounding a red dot. In contrast, the background of the upper part was often gilded, the surface being first frequently decorated with applied dots of gesso. In painting the carvings, the craftsmen were usually sensitive to the attractive, translucent quality of alabaster, and unpainted areas were usually left to contrast with the rich colours. The draperies and armour of figures were often left unpainted, with the edges of the robes picked out in gilding and the interior folds coloured in reds and blues. The faces of figures were almost always left unpainted, except for such evil characters as torturers and executioners, whose faces were blackened, a practice that may reflect the influence of the medieval stage.

By the late 14th century the horizontal format had given way to a vertical arrangement that continued more or less unchanged until the Reformation and was designed to display thematic series. Many late 14th-century panels have decorative battlements along the top edge. The panels and figures were attached to their wooden frameworks by latten wires, which were secured to the backs of alabasters by placing the wires into a drilled hole, which was then filled with molten lead. This was a simple and effective way of securing the carvings, avoiding the need for strips or clips that would have covered part of the front.

Iconography. Alabaster carvings were almost entirely religious in content. Late 14th-century themes included series of the Joys of the Virgin and the Passion, but by the mid-15th century the themes were more diverse, and the designs of the panels became increasingly crowded, for example the seven-panel altarpiece of the *Passion* in the Palazzo Schifanoia, Ferrara, which also shows lively and sensitive carving. The subjects were ultimately derived from two main sources: the New Testament and the Golden Legend compiled by Jacobus da Voragine. The designs and iconography used by the alabaster-carvers reflect contemporary developments in other media both in England and on the Continent. Graphic influence on alabaster panels was important even in 14th-century examples, where a number of similar carvings have the design in reverse, showing that a tracing was made from a drawing. As the 15th century progressed, the circulation of woodcuts and other prints in England, usually of German, Netherlandish or French origin, became an important iconographic source (e.g. the *Christ before Herod*, London, V&A, which is derived from a print of 1500 produced in Antwerp; Brussels, Bib. Royale Albert).

The two most common themes for alabaster, like those in other media, were the Passion of Christ and the Life of the Virgin. Usually they were made up of five panels—the centre panel being slightly taller than the rest—flanked by two standing figures of saints. A number of virtually complete examples survive. Notable in Britain is the *Passion* altarpiece (Nottingham, Castle Mus.) and the Swansea Altarpiece of the *Joys of the Virgin* (1450–1500; London, V&A; see fig. 3); examples outside Britain include *Passion* altarpieces in Iceland (Reykjavík, N. Mus.), France (the church of Issac-la-Tourette, Puy-de-Dome) and Italy (Naples, Capodimonte). Altarpieces of the *Life of the Virgin* are to be seen in Gdańsk, Poland (Gdańsk, N. Mus.), in the church of Montréal (Yonne) and in S Maria in Majori, Salerno (Campania).

During the 15th century other themes were developed, in particular the lives of individual saints, such as *St George* in the church at Borbjerg, Denmark, and *St John the Baptist* in the church of Issac-la-Tourette (Puy-de-Dome). At least two surviving 15th-century altarpieces were probably special orders: *St James the Great* in Santiago de Compostela Cathedral and *St Catherine* (Venice, Ca' d'Oro) from S Caterina, Venice. Occasionally more general themes were employed, such as the *Apostles' Creed* (London, V&A), the *Martyrdom of Saints* (Norwich, Castle Mus.) and the *Te Deum* (Genoa, Gal. Pal. Bianco). A late 15th-century development was the production of large, two-tiered altarpieces, for example the altarpiece of *St George and the Joys of the Virgin* in the church of La Celle (Normandy) and an altarpiece of the *Passion* in the Hôtel de Ville, Compiègne, which until the Revolution was in St

3. Alabaster Altarpiece of the *Joys of the Virgin* (the Swansea Altarpiece), 838×2134 mm, English, 1450–1500 (London, Victoria and Albert Museum)

Germain-l'Auxerrois, Paris. The latter contains no fewer than 10 large panels of scenes from the *Passion*, 4 large panels of saints, 14 canopies and 16 small figures with an additional 16 small canopies, all in a richly carved and painted wooden framework.

Individual devotional images were also produced, for example the panels dating from the second half of the 15th century of the *Virgin and Child* (h. 240 mm), now in Worcester Cathedral, and the *Trinity* (Reykjavík, N. Mus.), both in their painted wooden housings. Heads of St John the Baptist were particularly popular and were a speciality of the Nottingham alabaster-carvers. There is a reference in 1491 in one court action in Nottingham to money owing on 'fifty-eight heads of St John the Baptist, part of them in tabernacles and in niches'. At least ninety examples still survive, including five in their original housings. These were in the form of a small cupboard with two hinged doors painted on the inside, which could be opened to reveal the carving (e.g. Glasgow, Burrell Col.; 255 mm×478 mm). Such housings were placed in the private homes of the wealthy as well as in churches. In the 15th century and the early 16th tomb-makers also carved panels of individual saints for the sides of tombs. Examples are to be seen in All Saints, Harewood (W. Yorks), on the tomb of *Edward Redman* (*d* 1510) and his wife *Elizabeth Huddlestone* (*d* 1529); in All Saints, Ashover (Derbys), on the tomb of *Thomas Babyngton* (*d* 1518); and in St Mary's, Ross-on-Wye (Heref. & Worcs), on the tomb of *Judge William Rudhall* (*d* 1529).

Export trade. An export trade in English carved alabaster appears to have been established in northern Europe by about the middle of the 14th century, for the combined *Nativity* and *Adoration of the Magi* horizontal panels dating from that period are still to be found in Paderborn Cathedral, Zukau Church (nr Gdańsk), St Mary's, Gdańsk, and at Kaliningrad (formerly Königsberg) and the Catholic church at Grefrath (formerly Bottenbroich, nr Cologne). The earliest document specifically relating to the alabaster export trade is a permit of 1382 granted by Richard II to Cosmato Gentilis, the Pope's representative in England, to export four alabaster images from Southampton. Most of the English altarpieces surviving in Europe date from the second half of the 15th century, however, and range from Iceland to the Dalmatian coast of Croatia, with the most examples in France, but with a scattering in Spain and Italy. Many 15th-century documentary references support this material evidence of a lively export trade from the 1450s onwards. There is also a record of the export of an alabaster tomb. In 1408 a safe conduct was granted by Henry IV for such a tomb to be exported to Nantes, to be placed over the grave of Jean, Duke of Brittany (*d* 1399); it was destroyed during the Revolution. That unworked stone was also exported is evident from an agreement drawn up in 1414 between Thomas Prentys and Alexandre de Berneval, mason, on behalf of the Abbot of Fécamp in Normandy.

Some 2000 medieval English alabaster-carvings can be seen all over Europe, most of which were exported during the second half of the 15th century and the beginning of the 16th. In addition some 69 more or less complete altarpieces survive in Iceland, Norway, Denmark, Poland, Germany, France, Spain, Portugal, Italy and Yugoslavia. Some of these carvings were certainly exported to the Continent when the Reformers began to despoil the furnishings of English churches. Most of the altarpieces appear to be still in or near the churches that housed them in the Middle Ages, and they are therefore important material evidence of the widespread nature of English trade in alabaster-carvings.

(b) After c. *1540.* The alabaster-carving industry was doubtless immediately affected by the suppression of the monasteries (1536–9), for much monastic spoil was released on to the market and at the same time the number of possible patrons was reduced. The accession of the strongly Protestant government of Edward VI in 1547 signalled the end of the industry, for all images were ordered to be systematically destroyed, and the Act of January 1550 specifically mentions images in alabaster. The carving of tombs continued, however, for memorial effigies were not officially regarded as 'images'. After such

systematic destruction, it is unlikely that the carving of alabaster altarpieces and images became re-established during the brief restoration of Roman Catholicism under Queen Mary (*reg* 1553–8).

The production of alabaster tombs continued steadily in the 16th century in the workshops of the Midlands, especially Burton-on-Trent, and in a traditional style and manner. Characteristic examples lack canopies, and the recumbent effigies have their hands joined in prayer, often with images of their children on the sides of the tomb chests. The continuation of Gothic traditions is seen in the effigies, but Renaissance motifs were occasionally introduced, as in the work of RICHARD PARKER and RICHARD ROYLEY and in the appearance of putti holding shields on the sides of some tombs, such as that of *Sir John Salusbury* (*d* 1578) in Whitchurch (Dyfed). Cheaper variants of the sculptured effigy, ranging in date from the 15th century to the 17th, were incised alabaster slabs, usually about 2 m in length, which were occasionally raised on tomb chests. A good example is in St Peter's, Ipsley (Heref. & Worcs), of *Nicholas Huband* and his wife *Dorothy Danvers* (1553).

This provincial traditionalism was, however, affected by an influx of craftsmen from the Netherlands during the reign of Elizabeth I. Garat Johnson from Amsterdam established a workshop in Southwark in London in 1567 and was commissioned by Roger Manners, 5th Earl of Rutland (*d* 1612), to make tombs of the 3rd and 4th Earls to be erected in St Mary's, Bottesford (Leics), less than 23 km from Nottingham, an area previously much under the influence of the Midland alabaster-carvers. These two wall tombs have recumbent effigies, their hands together in prayer. One Dutchman, Jasper Hollemans, actually set up business in Burton-on-Trent and carved tombs for the Spencer family for St Mary's, Great Brington (Northants), in 1599. The leading London sculptor in the 1620s and 1630s, Nicholas Stone I, also used alabaster in some of his work, noticeably on the canopied tomb of *Sir Charles Morison* (1619) in St Mary's, Watford (Herts), and on the tomb of *Lord Knyvett* and his wife (1623) in St Mary's, Stanwell (Middx), where two white marble figures kneel on an alabaster sarcophagus. By the end of the 17th century, however, alabaster ceased to be a popular stone for carving, imported marble being preferred. Alabaster was thereafter used only occasionally with other materials, and its long period of dominance effectively ended. English alabaster has, however, occasionally been used in more recent times by sculptors, notably Jacob Epstein, for example his *Jacob and the Angel* (h. 2.13 m; 1940; U. Liverpool), and Henry Moore, who in the late 1920s and early 1930s was attracted by the particular qualities of alabaster (e.g. *Seated Figure*, h. 470 mm; 1930; Toronto, A.G. Ont.).

RDK

BIBLIOGRAPHY

Abbé Bouillet: 'La Fabrication industrielle des retables en albâtre', *Bull. Mnmtl.*, lxv (1901), pp. 45–62
R. Papini: 'Polittici d'alabastro', *L'Arte*, xiii/3 (1910), pp. 2–13
Illustrated Catalogue of the Exhibition of English Medieval Alabaster Work held in the Rooms of the Society of Antiquaries, 26th May–30th June, 1910 (London, 1913)
P. Nelson: 'English Medieval Alabaster Carvings in Iceland and Denmark', *Archaeol. J.*, lxxvii (1920), pp. 192–206
G. Swarzenski: 'Deutsche Alabasterplastik des 15. Jahrhunderts', *Städel-Jb.*, i (1921), pp. 167 ff
P. Chatwin: 'Monumental Effigies in the County of Warwick', *Trans. & Proc. Birmingham Archaeol. Soc.*, xlvii (1921); xlviii (1922); xlix (1923)
W. L. Hildburgh: 'A Datable English Alabaster Altarpiece at Santiago de Compostela', *Antiqua. J.*, vi (1926), pp. 304–7
A. Rostand: 'Les Albâtres anglais du XVe siècle en Basse Normandie', *Bull. Mnmtl.*, lxxxvii (1928), pp. 257–309
A. Gardner: *Alabaster Tombs of the Pre-Reformation Period in England* (Cambridge, 1940)
S. B. Feyo: 'A collecção de esculturas de Nottingham do Museu Nacional de Arte Antiga', *Bol. Mus. N. A. Ant.*, i/2 (1947), pp. 75–9
A. Gardner: *English Medieval Sculpture* (Cambridge, 1951)
W. L. Hildburgh: 'Some English Medieval Alabaster Carvings in Italy', *Antiqua. J.*, xxxv (1955), pp. 182–6
L. Stone: *Sculpture in Britain: The Middle Ages*, Pelican Hist. A. (Harmondsworth, 1955, rev. 1972)
A. S. Tavender: 'Medieval English Alabasters in American Museums', *Speculum*, xxx (1955), pp. 64–71; xxxiv (1959), pp. 437–9
W. Paatz: 'Stammbaum der gotischen Alabasterskulptur, 1316–1442', *Kunstgeschichtliche Studien für Hans Kauffmann* (Berlin, 1956), pp. 127–35
J. H. Perera: 'Alabastros ingleses en España', *Goya*, 22 (1958), pp. 214–22
F. W. Cheetham: *Medieval English Alabaster Carvings in the Castle Museum, Nottingham* (Nottingham, 1962, rev. 1973)
M. Whinney: *Sculpture in Britain, 1530 to 1830*, Pelican Hist. A. (Harmondsworth, 1964); rev. by J. Physick (Harmondsworth, 1988)
Exposition de sculptures anglaises et malinoises d'albâtre (exh. cat. by G. Dervaux-van Ussel, Brussels, Musées Royaux A. & Hist., 1967)
M. B. Fiorin: 'Due serie di bassorilievi alabastrini al Museo Civico di Storia ed Arte di Trieste', *Atti Civ. Mus. Stor. & A. Trieste*, vi (1969–70), pp. 137–65
S. Alcolea: 'Relieves ingleses de alabastro en España: Ensayo de catalogación', *Archv Esp. A.*, xliv (1971), pp. 137–53
C. Fisković: 'English Monuments in Dalmatia', *Dubrovnik's Relations With England: Zagreb, 1976*, pp. 157–85
S. Guimarães de Andrade: *Alabastros medievais ingleses: Colecção do Museu Nacional de Arte Antiga* (Lisbon, 1977)
M. K. Wustrack: *Die Mechelner Alabaster-Manufaktur des 16. und frühen 17. Jahrhunderts* (Frankfurt-am-Main and Berne, 1982)
F. W. Cheetham: *English Medieval Alabasters with a Catalogue of the Collection in the Victoria and Albert Museum* (Oxford, 1984)

FRANCIS CHEETHAM

Alabastron. Ancient form of vessel, used to contain cosmetics, oils and perfumes (*see* GREECE, ANCIENT, figs 71 and 146 and HELLADIC, fig. 8d).

□

Alaca Höyük [Alaca Hüyük; Alaja Hüyük]. Site in north-central Turkey, *c.* 40 km south-west of Çorum and 160 km east of Ankara. It was occupied in the Bronze Age (from *c.* 3400 BC) and later. Of greatest artistic interest are 14 Early Bronze Age (EB) royal tombs and the sculptures from the Hittite city gate. The ruin mound is on a natural hillock; it measured *c.* 250×320 m and had *c.* 14 m of deposit. A lower town has not been identified. Early investigations of the site were conducted by Ernest Chantre (1863), Georges Perrot (1865), Henry John Van Lennep (1869), Sir William Mitchell Ramsay (1881) and Théodor Macridy (1906). The Turkish Historical Society began systematic excavations in 1935 under Remzi Oğuz Arık, and these continued under Hamit Zubeyr Koşay, assisted by Mahmut Akok, in 1936–49 and 1963–79. In the excavations up to at least 1967 the stratigraphic discipline seems to have been weak and the recording poor, with the result that many objects and some features are of uncertain date and association. The excavators distinguished 14 phases: in current terminology the deepest levels, 14–9, are EB I (*c.* 3400–*c.* 2700 BC); levels 8–5 are

EB II (*c.* 2700–*c.* 2460 BC); level 4 appears to include EB III and the Middle Bronze Age (*c.* 2460–*c.* 1700 BC); levels 3–2 are Late Bronze Age (*c.* 1700–1200 BC); and level 1, the topmost, covers the period from the Iron Age onwards. A modern village near the site has been the subject of an ethnographic study. The pottery sequence lacks both clarity and interest. Published architectural remains are meagre except in level 2, to which belong a glacis, a casemate fortification wall, two city gates, a postern gate with subterranean corbelled stone passage and, inside the citadel, houses and streets with stone-built underground drains, two massive buildings on the summit and a possible palace complex covering *c.* 5000 sq. m. The material from the excavations is housed in a small site museum and in the Museum of Anatolian Civilizations, Ankara.

1. Royal tombs. 2. Hittite sculpture.

1. ROYAL TOMBS. Fourteen tombs with rich contents lay on the south side of the mound. Their precise dates are uncertain, but probably none is later than level 4 or earlier than level 6. A chronological range within late EB II–early EB III (*c.* 2600–*c.* 2300 BC) seems likely. The material is very homogeneous. The tombs were rectangular (up to 9.0×5.2 m) and 5.0–7.5 m deep. Floors were of clay or stone, and sides were faced with stones. Typically the single occupant, fully dressed when buried, lay crouched in a corner with head to the west and facing south. The tomb was roofed with timbers and clay, covered in turn by the skins of cattle, sheep, goats or pigs, with skulls and leg-bones left intact. Probably it was then covered with earth and marked with stones.

There are few weapons among the grave goods: two types of sword, two iron daggers (one with crescentic gold-plated handle), one silver dagger, a stone battle-axe with gold-plated haft, and a number of flat axes and spikes (possibly arrowheads). Jewellery is more plentiful. Thin gold sheet was used to make brooches with repoussé work, openwork diadems, disc-pendants and a tubular spiral hair-ring with chased decoration. More substantial are a chased gold bracelet, gold earplugs, and combs of gold and copper. There are many gold and electrum pins, the best having, for example, a head set with five rock-crystal beads. Winged disc, cruciform, double-spiral and tubular beads are common; beads of cornelian and faience also occur. Other items of adornment include a gold sceptre-head with 14 projecting knobs, a stone mace with wooden handle covered in gold leaf, and many examples of tubular silver or gold plating for staves or sceptres, sometimes corrugated or chased. Many small swastikas, twin female figurines and rows of three conical sequins (all of thin gold sheet) were pierced with holes, perhaps for sewing on to cloth. Also attested are a gold scaraboid buckle and silver toggles.

Metal vessels (of copper, silver and gold) include bowls, cups, chalices, jugs, jars and a teapot. Some are plain, but chased, grooved and fluted decoration is common. The body and handle of a gold jug from Tomb B are covered with chased chevrons. Fluting can be horizontal or vertical. Grooving of curves or chevrons may be arranged in horizontal registers. The body of one silver jug from Tomb H is grooved with a multiple running-spiral design, and a

Alaca Höyük, ritual standard consisting of a stag and two bulls passing through a ring, bronze, h. 220 mm, *c.* 2600–2300 BC (Ankara, Museum of Anatolian Civilizations)

silver-and-gold jar from the same tomb has a grooved decoration of concentric, pendent loops. Grooving on the stem of a chalice from Tomb B resembles interwoven bandaging. A gold jar is set with four cornelian beads at the carination. The body of a silver teapot from Tomb K is covered with snakes in relief. Some of the material resembles the local pottery or recalls that of the Pontic region. A series of metal 'goads', hooks and discs with hollow stems projecting from the centre are of uncertain purpose. Four copper boots (Tomb K) may derive from the legs of a wooden stool.

Most striking are the objects of probable religious significance. A series of flat bronze discs (h. *c.* 200–350 mm) with two short tangs at the base includes a variety of forms. Usually there is a circular frame surrounding an openwork design, which may be simple latticework or cast as interconnected swastikas (Tomb B) or as a star (Tomb E). Two curving horns usually project sideways from the base of the disc. The circular frame may carry one or three miniature pendent discs and even model buds and birds. In some examples from Tombs A', D and K, a stag (*see* ANATOLIA, ANCIENT, fig. 8) or a bull is shown passing through the centre of the disc. A second series of latticework frames is semicircular in shape. Examples from Alaca do not have the two curving horns, model buds or emerging stags or bulls found on those from Horoztepe (now in Ankara). Instead the frame always carries up to seven rigid miniature discs and usually up to four pendent miniatures. Quadrangular latticework frames and solid circular discs with central holes also occur.

Related to the bronze discs is a series of bronze rings of similar size. These may be plain or twisted and can be ornamented with buds, curving horns set at the base, and animals passing through the centre. One from Tomb B shows a stag flanked by two bulls, all going in the same direction (see fig.); another (also Tomb B) shows a stag flanked by two animals, perhaps panthers, going in the opposite direction. Tombs may contain two to six discs or rings.

Figures of stags and bulls (h. 360–570 mm), mounted on short staves, occur in all but three tombs. In Tomb B a bronze stag is inlaid with concentric circles, crosses and chevrons of silver. In Tomb E a bronze bull is inlaid with electrum stripes and another with electrum studs. In Tomb H a copper bull is plated with electrum on its neck, saddle and tips of horns, and inlaid with concentric circles. Usually there is only one such 'standard' per tomb. Human figurines, which are rare, are either flat and stylized (Tombs L, A') or are three-dimensional and fairly naturalistic (Tomb H).

Interpretation of all this ritual material is uncertain. The discs with rigid miniatures on the frame recall flat stone female figurines from Kültepe: the rigid miniatures may thus represent heads, and the pendants may represent infants. The rays, latticework and swastikas suggest an identity with the sun; yet the addition of buds and birds looks terrestrial. A goddess associated with both sun and earth would seem most appropriate, such as the sun goddess of Arinna, equated in later Hittite and Hattian texts with the mother goddess of the earth, the underworld and death. In Hattian mythology the destruction of mankind followed the entrance of the storm god Nerik into her domain; his return from the underworld brought fertility and life. As she was his mother, his return was a rebirth. The discs and rings with transient animals may depict some such story and, with the projecting horns at the base, may recall the plaster female figures of ÇATAL HÜYÜK with outstretched legs giving birth to bulls and rams. The deceased at Alaca Höyük was thus perhaps accompanied by reminders of the mother of all things, to whom he was returning, and perhaps of the possibility of rebirth. What practical purpose was served by the standards and sun-discs is unknown, although it is possible that before burial they were attached to some wooden item, such as a bed or burial-cart, since decayed.

The wealth of the tombs is striking but not out of scale with the period. While much of the jewellery is poor by comparison with that from west Anatolia, the vessels are of good quality, and the discs and standards are sophisticated, many having been cast in one by the lost-wax technique. Sweating, soldering and bi-mould casting were used, and some bronzes were given a silver appearance by the application of a thin coating of arsenical copper. Metalworking equipment is not known from the site, so manufacture may have taken place in the Pontic region, where comparable vessels, standards and sun-discs are known from Horoztepe, Mahmatlar and other sites (all now in Ankara).

2. HITTITE SCULPTURE. The south-east gate and flanking towers of level 2 bore an impressive series of reliefs carved *in situ* on the Cyclopean masonry and left incomplete. The placing of some blocks is uncertain, but the overall conception is clear. A frieze in three registers decorated the south façades of both gate-towers, depicting two religious processions converging on the gateway and, at the inner corners of the towers, honouring a bull on a pedestal (west) and a goddess in a niche (east). Above these were two lion protomes holding in their forepaws a bull (west) and a human figure (east). On each side the protomes formed the head of a lion's body carved in relief. Here a ramp rose to the level of the gate-chamber, and a frieze below each lion showed the processions continuing up the slope. From the jambs of the outer gate-chamber two sphinx protomes gazed down the ramp, but the processions continued along the faces of the inner gateway without the sphinxes' bodies being depicted. It is possible that the procession on each side culminated in a relief of a seated god receiving libations or worship from the king, queen and other dignitaries. Two more sphinx protomes on the jambs of the inner gate faced into the city.

The reliefs on the west tower are the best preserved. The procession on the bottom register includes the king, queen, four priests and four rams. The same register contains a separate scene showing an acrobat climbing a ladder, a juggler, a sword-swallower, a lutenist, a man with what may be a performing monkey and (unfinished) a huge bull rhyton on wheels. The second register shows a kneeling archer poised to shoot as a stag, lured by a tethered decoy, approaches unawares while three others take flight. The top register, least complete, shows a kneeling archer about to shoot at a charging boar. The east tower may have carried reliefs of a charging bull, an archer with dog and rampant lion, and a hunter with two dogs, spearing a leaping lion. On the east side of the gate-chamber is a relief of a double-headed eagle holding a hare in each talon and supporting a long-robed figure.

Apart from the gate-guardians (the lions and sphinxes) the entire composition may depict a religious festival and associated celebrations. The use of multiple registers in narrative depiction is known from Old Hittite relief vases (especially from Bitik and Inandıktepe, now in Ankara), but its application to architecture may reflect the influence of north Syrian fashions. The converging processions are paralleled in the reliefs of Yazılıkaya (*see* YAZILIKAYA (i)). All the figures are shown in profile, except for the gate-guardians and the leaping lion. The protomes are rather schematic, but the sculptor has turned the corner from the lion's face to the relief of the lion's body quite adroitly; the leaping lion, shown in unconvincing full-face, has parallels in Minoan glyptic art. The carving is clear and confident, and the animals are modelled with vivacity, although the humans are stiff. The rendering is most closely comparable to Old Hittite material, but the surfaces are flat, as in north Syria, rather than rounded as at the Hittite capital at BOĞAZKÖY. Apart from the leaping lion (perhaps Minoan), the charging bull (Mesopotamian) and the sphinxes (ultimately Egyptian), the content is distinctively Anatolian and has analogies in pottery, ivory-carving, seals, metalwork and other Hittite rock reliefs.

For further discussion of Hittite sculpture *see* ANATOLIA, ANCIENT, §III.

BIBLIOGRAPHY

T. Macridy-Bey: *La Porte des sphinx à Euyuk: Fouilles du Musée Impérial Ottoman*, Mitteilungen des Vorderasiatische Geschichte (Berlin, 1908) [Fr. summary]

R. O. Arik: *Alaca Hoyuk hafriyatının ilk neticeleri* [First results of the excavations at Alaca Höyük] (Ankara, 1937)

H. Z. Koşay: *Ausgrabungen von Alaca Höyük, 1936* (Ankara, 1944)

K. Bittel: 'Nur hethitische oder hurritische Kunst?', *Z. Assyriol.*, xlix (1950), pp. 256–90

H. Z. Koşay: *Alaca-Höyük: Anadolu'nun etnografya ve folklorina dair malzeme/Das Dorf Alaca Höyük: Materialien zur Ethnographie und Volkskunde von Anatolien* (Ankara, 1951) [bilingual text]

——: *Türk Tarih Kurumu tarafından yapılan Alaca Höyük kazısı: 1937–1939 daki çalışmalara ve keşiflere ait ilk rapor/Les Fouilles d'Alaca Höyük entreprises par la Société d'histoire turque: Rapport préliminaire sur les travaux en 1937–1939* (Ankara, 1951) [bilingual text]
H. G. Güterbock: 'The Sphinx Gate of Höyük, near Alaca', *Anatol. Stud.*, vi (1956), pp. 54–6
H. Z. Koşay and M. Akok: *Ausgrabungen von Alaca Höyük, 1940–1948* (Ankara, 1966)
Anatol. Stud., xix–xxx (1969–80) [brief annual excav. rep.]
M. J. Mellink: 'Observations on the Sculptures of Alaca Höyük', *Anadolu*, xiv (1970), pp. 15–27
H. Z. Koşay and M. Akok: *Alaca Höyük Excavations, 1963–1967* (Ankara, 1973)
M. Korfmann: 'Die "grosse Göttin" in Alaca Höyük', *IX Türk Tarih kongresi* (Ankara, 1986), pp. 153–63 [with bibliog.]

DONALD F. EASTON

Alaçatı. *See* CAN HASAN.

Aladrén y Mendívil, Luis (*fl* 1882–97). Spanish architect. His work is representative of the eclecticism of late 19th-century Spanish architecture, which is especially marked by classical values. His idiom was derived from Mannerist architecture and has a strong Baroque element. The influence of French art is also evident, especially the ostentatious style of Charles Garnier. Aladrén y Mendívil's early works are more restrained in style and show a mastery of plan and façade design. This is apparent in the Diputación de Guipúzcoa (1885), San Sebastián, which he executed in collaboration with Adolfo Morales de los Ríos. With this same architect he designed his most renowned work, the Casino (now Ayuntamiento; 1882–7) at San Sebastián, which was promoted by the city council to take advantage of wealthy visitors, as San Sebastián was the court summer residence. The upper part of the building was set aside for gaming and the lower for relaxation and recreation, with banqueting-rooms, a café and restaurant. It is French in style and incorporates medieval, Renaissance and Baroque influences, combining these with the use of iron technology. These official works recommended him to industrial magnates in the Basque region, who made important commissions. These he executed with an academic respect for symmetry and following French models, as in the elegant country house (1890) of the Conde and Condesa de Lersundi. The Diputación de Vizcaya (1897) in Bilbao marks the culmination of his style.

BIBLIOGRAPHY

J. A. Gaya: *Arte del siglo XIX*, A. Hisp., xix (Madrid, 1966)
P. Navascués: *Del Neoclasicismo al Modernismo* (Madrid, 1979)
M. Gómez-Morán Cima: *Arquitectura del siglo XIX* (1987), v of *Historia de la arquitectura española* (Saragossa, 1985–7)

ALBERTO VILLAR MOVELLÁN

Alahan Monastery [Koca Kalesi]. Early Christian monastery on the southern slopes of the Taurus Mountains in Isauria, part of the Roman province of Cilicia in south-western Turkey. It is some 300 m above the main road between Silifke (anc. Seleucia) and Konya (anc. Iconium), 21 km north of Mut (anc. Claudiopolis). From two funerary inscriptions, pottery and coins, the monastery may be securely dated to the reigns of two Isaurian emperors, Leo (*reg* AD 457–74) and Zeno (*reg* 474–91).

The monastery was originally founded in a series of caves in a limestone outcrop at the west end of a narrow mountain ledge. The largest of these caves contained two rock-cut churches. The ledge was later enlarged by quarrying to the north and by the construction of a retaining wall to the south. The earliest building, immediately to the east of the caves, was the three-aisled Basilica. It was originally lavishly decorated, both inside and out, with architectural sculpture in a flowing naturalistic style, including plant forms, birds and fishes; figures occur only on the jambs and lintel of the main doorway between the narthex and the central aisle. On the west side of the lintel is a head of Christ set in a circle supported by angels, and at each end of the lintel and on the doorposts are four busts in high relief, possibly of the Evangelists. On the inner faces of the jambs are full-length figures of the archangels Michael and Gabriel in flat relief, while on the underside of the lintel is a remarkable relief of the four *Beasts of the Apocalypse* carved in the form of a tetramorph, a rare and early representation of high artistic quality (see fig.). There is evidence that part of the main aisle of the Basilica was plastered and painted, as was the south *pastophoria*, which is painted to resemble marble. The apse and bema walls were embellished with mosaic, and the floor of the bema, and almost certainly that of the apse, consisted of *opus sectile*. The next building along the ledge formerly had two storeys and was probably a hospice for pilgrims. Then follows a twin-aisled baptistery with a

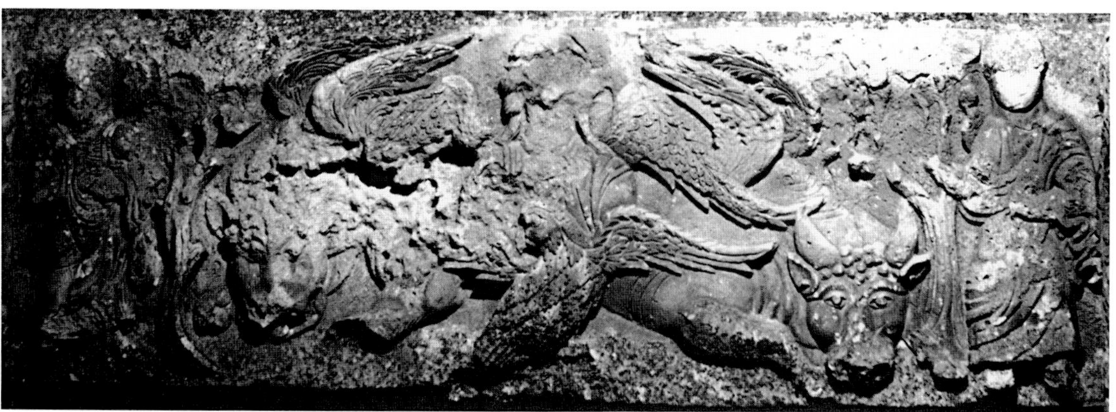

Alahan Monastery, Basilica, underside of lintel of the so-called Evangelists' door showing the *Beasts of the Apocalypse*, second half of the 5th century AD

cruciform font sunk into the west floor of the north aisle; both aisles terminate in an apse, the northern one plastered and again painted to resemble marble. Beyond comes the necropolis area.

At the extreme eastern end of the ledge is the three-aisled East Church, which is built directly against the cliff that forms its north wall. Both the main structure and its centralized tower survive to roof height. Although the technique of setting a round dome on a square bay was known, the tower roof was probably pyramidal and built of timber and tile. The exterior is undecorated except for the west façade, where the three doorways reflect the luxuriant sculptural style of the Basilica. The sculpture of the interior, however, is more formal and localized, and shows use of the drill. While the Basilica recalls the Acheiropoietos church at Thessaloniki, the East Church may be compared with the domed basilica at Meryemlık and the domed church at Dağpazarı, both Turkey. The difference in architectural style between the Basilica and the East Church is particularly noteworthy, since the archaeological evidence points to the monastery's rapid construction and to the work on the East Church beginning soon after or even before the Basilica's completion.

The East Church and the Basilica were linked by a covered colonnade set on the retaining wall; it was never completed but a highly decorated shrine is incorporated in it, exactly opposite the earlier of the two funerary inscriptions. This would seem to indicate that the grave had become a place of pilgrimage. Alahan had a sophisticated water supply, drainage system and ample domestic quarters, which included a small bath building. Workshops were identified below the retaining wall. It is possible that the funding of ecclesiastical foundations in Isauria ceased with the death of Zeno, thus accounting for the unfinished state of some of Alahan's monuments. It is thought that the monastery was abandoned in the face of the Arab invasions of the 7th century, although there is no evidence of sacking. There was a secondary occupation, however, probably as late as the 13th century, when a small church was built inside the Basilica and the baptistery was rehabilitated.

BIBLIOGRAPHY

P. Verzone: *Alahan Manastır mimarisi üzurinde bir inceleme* [A study on the architecture of the Alahan Monastery] (Istanbul, 1955)

C. Mango: 'Isaurian Builders', *Polychronion: Festschrift Franz Dolger zum 75. Geburtstag* (Heidelberg, 1966), pp. 358–65

M. Gough: 'The Emperor Zeno and some Cilician Churches', *Anatol. Stud.*, xxii (1972), pp. 199–212

M. Gough, ed.: *Alahan: An Early Christian Monastery in Southern Turkey* (Toronto, 1985)

MARY GOUGH

Alain [Chartier, Emile-Auguste] (*b* Mortagne, Orne, 3 March 1868; *d* Le Vésinet, nr Paris, 2 June 1951). French philosopher and writer. He studied philosophy under Jules Lagneau (1851–94) at the Lycée de Vanves, near Paris, and from 1889 to 1892 studied at the Ecole Normale Supérieure in Paris, where he read avidly the works of Plato, Aristotle and Immanuel Kant. He then became a professor at the Collège de Pontivy, moving in 1893 to the Lycée de Lorient, where he developed a strong interest in politics. In 1900 he was appointed a professor at Rouen and in 1902 became a professor at the Lycée Michelet in Paris.

In 1906 Alain published the first of his *propos* or brief articles, in *La Dépêche de Rouen*; these were entitled 'Propos d'un Normand' and signed Alain, after the medieval poet Alain Chartier, whose work he admired. Between 1906 and 1914 over 3000 of these appeared, each covering no more than 2 pages in manuscript and written without correction. They covered a diverse range of subjects, including literature, education, aesthetics and politics. Most of them reappeared in collections, such as *Propos sur l'esthétique* (1923), which discussed Proust, Shakespeare, matter and form, music and the Romanesque. An additional 1800 *propos* were published in the weekly *Les Libres-propos (journal d'Alain)*, which appeared from 1921 to 1924 and from 1927 to 1935. In 1909 Alain was appointed Professeur de Première Supérieure at the Lycée Henri IV in Paris, teaching philosophy there until his retirement in 1933. Through his teaching and writing he exercised a powerful influence over French thought, especially in the inter-war period.

At the outbreak of World War I Alain joined the artillery, despite being forcefully opposed to the war. During this time he wrote his *Système des beaux-arts* (1920). It is divided into 10 books: Book 6 deals with architecture, Book 7 with sculpture and Book 8 with painting; poetry, dance and music also receive discussion. In Book 1, 'De l'Imagination creatice', he expounded his ideas regarding the development of the arts from the communal to the private realms. The book is structured according to this, and consequently it starts with dance and costume, the most public of arts, and ends with drawing, the most abstract and solitary. Alain saw public ceremonies, religious or otherwise, as the source of the arts. From these dance and theatre evolved and later sculpture, painting and drawing, all of them bound by the common purpose of ordering the passions and enabling human expression. It was also this initial, purely communal, aspect of the arts that contributed to the eventual development of private thought and reflection. In the section on painting Alain explained the structure whereby a two-dimensional image is viewed as if three-dimensional. The use of colour, he believed, is the key to all true painting and the painter must therefore learn to see colours apart from their accepted signification, such as blue for sky, in order to capture the true appearance of objects. *Vingt leçons sur les beaux-arts* (1931) is an extended treatment of the ideas in *Système des beaux-arts. Préliminaire à l'esthétique* (1939) is a collection of *propos* on various aspects of art, ranging in date from 1907 to 1936, published in support of the aesthetic theories propounded in *Système des beaux-arts.* His numerous other books included several monographs on writers. Though primarily a philosopher, Alain brought no major innovations to the subject. His importance rested rather on his ability to communicate his understanding to an unusually wide audience, in a succinct and elegant literary style.

WRITINGS

Système des beaux-arts (Paris, 1920)

Propos sur l'esthétique (Paris, 1923)

Vingt leçons sur les beaux-arts (Paris, 1931)

Préliminaire à l'esthétique (Paris, 1939)

BIBLIOGRAPHY

A. Maurois: *Alain* (Paris, 1950)

G. Bénézé and others: *Hommage à Alain, 1868–1951* (Paris, 1952)
G. Pascal: *Pour connaître la pensée d'Alain* (Paris, 1957)

□

Alalakh. *See* ATCHANA, TELL.

Alalya. *See* THOMAS RESERVOIR.

Alamanno, Pietro. *See* ALEMANNO, PIETRO.

Alampur [anc. Alampūra, Hatampura]. Temple site in Karnataka, India. It flourished *c.* AD 650–1140 and is notable for its well-preserved 7th- and 8th-century temples. Alampur is located on the west bank of the Tungabhadra River, near its confluence with the Krishna, in the western part of the Andhra region of southern India. A number of copperplate grants show that Alampur was a centre of the early Chalukya dynasty known as the Chalukyas of Badami (*reg* mid-6th to mid-8th century; *see* CHALUKYA, §1).

The main group of temples, known as the Nava Brahma, was begun sometime before AD 713, the date inscribed on an enclosing wall (Skt *prakara*) once surrounding a part of the complex. All the temples are dedicated to the god Shiva. They exhibit a local variation of the north Indian style of architecture and are especially important as contemporary versions of forms that have not survived elsewhere. The earliest is the modest Kumara Brahma, probably begun in the later 7th century. It was followed by the Bala Brahma, now encrusted in later accretions, though particularly notable for its magnificent sculpture of the seven mother goddesses (*saptamātṛkā*). The four succeeding temples at the site are the Arka Brahma and Vira Brahma, added toward the end of the 7th century, and the later Svarga Brahma and Garuda Brahma. The series displays representative early examples of the north Indian curvilinear superstructure. The last of the series were the Padma and Vishva Brahma, built well into the 8th century. The typical south Indian imagery of the Svarga and Vishva Brahma (such as Lingobhava and Bhiksatana Shiva; *see* INDIAN SUBCONTINENT, figs 13 and 62) shows a substantial connection with the sculptural traditions of southern India.

The Tarka Brahma is the one early Chalukya temple at Alampur constructed in the southern style. Its domed superstructure shows a very close likeness to the Malegitti temple at BADAMI, suggesting that craftsmen were brought from that site. Temple building continued at Alampur during the reign of the Rashtrakutas (*c.* 752–973) and the Chalukyas of Kalyana (973–1189); notable structures of these later periods include the inscribed gateway to the west of the site and the Suryanarayana and Papavinashani Tirtha temples. The nearby Kudaveli Sangamesvara Temple has been moved to Alampur.

See also INDIAN SUBCONTINENT, §IV, 7(vi)(c).

BIBLIOGRAPHY

G. Yazdani: *Annu. Rep. Archaeol. Dept Nizam's Dominions* (1926–7), pp. 7–12
M. Rama Rao: 'Early Chalukyan Architecture: A Review', *J. Ind. Hist.*, xli (1963), pp. 431–59
G. S. Gai: 'Alampur Inscription of Chalukya Vijayāditya of Śaka 635 and 636', *Epig. Ind.*, xxxv (1963–4), pp. 121–4
M. Rama Rao: *Early Chalukyan Temples of Āndhra Dēśa* (Hyderabad, 1965)
G. Tarr: *The Architecture of the Early Western Chalukyas* (diss., Los Angeles, UCLA, 1969; microfilm Ann Arbor, 1970)
O. Divakaran: 'Les Temples d'Alampur et de ses environs au temps des Calukyas de Badami', *A. Asiatiques*, xxiv (1971), pp. 51–101
M. R. Sarma: *Temples of Telingāṇa: The Architecture, Iconography and Sculpture of the Cāḷukya and Kākatīya* (Hyderabad, 1972)
B. R. Prasad: 'Temples of the Latina Form at Alampur', *J. Ind. Soc. Orient. A.*, v (1972–3), pp. 53–75
P. R. Ramachandra Rao: *Alampur* (Hyderabad, 1977)
G. M. Tartakov: 'The Significance of the Early Chalukya Art of Andhradesa', *J. Archaeol. Stud.*, v (1980), pp. 49–62
B. R. Prasad: *Chalukyan Temples of Andhradesa* (New Delhi, 1983)
Encyclopedia of Indian Temple Architecture, South India, Upper Dravidesa, Early Phase, AD 550–1075 (1986)
Encyclopedia of Indian Temple Architecture, North India, Foundations of North Indian Style, c. 250 BC–AD 1100 (1988)

GARY MICHAEL TARTAKOV

Alamut [Alamūt]. Mountainous valley in Iran, 35 km north-east of Qazvin, and the name of one of the fortresses that defended the valley. From 1090 to 1261 it was the main headquarters of the Nizari branch of the Isma'ili Shi'ites, a religious community organized on a military basis. Their rigid hierarchy, esoteric practices and use of terrorism encouraged the development of romantic tales about them. Reputed to use hashish, they became known in the West as 'Assassins' (Arab. *hashhīshiyyīn*). Like all Isma'ili fortresses, Alamut is strategically located on rocky heights and has an elaborate storage system for water and provisions so that the fortress was never taken by force. It consists of two parts: a higher and larger western fort and an eastern one.

BIBLIOGRAPHY

Enc. Iran.; *Enc. Islam/2*
F. Stark: *The Valley of the Assassins* (London, 1934)
W. Ivanow: *Alamut and Lamasar* (Tehran, 1950)
P. Willey: *The Castles of the Assassins* (London, 1963)
W. Kleiss: 'Berichte über Erkundungsfahrten in Iran im Jahre 1970', *Archäol. Mitt. Iran*, iv (1971), pp. 88–96
F. Daftary: *The Ismā'īlīs: Their History and Doctrines* (Cambridge, 1990), p. 326 [extensive bibliog.]

ABBAS DANESHVARI

à la poupée. *See* POUPÉE, À LA.

Alarcón, Rodrigo de Tapia y. *See* TAPIA Y ALARCÓN, RODRIGO DE.

Alari-Bonacolsi, Pier Jacopo di Antonio. *See* ANTICO.

Alart [Allart] **du Hameel** [de Hameel; de Hamel; Duhameel; Duhamel; du Hamel; Duhamiel; Dumeel; van Hameel] (*b c.* 1449; *d* Antwerp, before 27 Jan 1507). South Netherlandish architect and engraver. He is first mentioned in a contract drawn up on 19 October 1478 between the church-wardens of the St Janskerk, 's Hertogenbosch, and Jan Quaywante, a stone supplier, which was witnessed by *Loetsmeester* (stone dresser) de Hameel. In the same year he joined the Brotherhood of Our Lady. His first wife, Margriet van Auweningen (*d* 1484), is commemorated on a gravestone possibly made by du Hameel in the St Janskerk. In late 1494 or early 1495 he moved to Leuven, where he was appointed 'the town's workman stone mason' and master of the works of the St Pieterskerk. In 1496 he was imprisoned in Mechelen as a hostage for debts owed there by the city of Leuven. In 1500 he became an external citizen of Antwerp. On 12 December 1505 he made his will, and on 27 January 1507 masses were arranged in memory of the late (*quondam*) master Alart.

Du Hameel's contribution to the building of the St Janskerk (*see* 'S HERTOGENBOSCH, §2) can be inferred from the sources and the building history. The contract of 1478 reveals that he was working on the nave, but it is uncertain whether he was responsible for such characteristic details as the clustered piers and the integral altars, as the first piers were already in place when he arrived. His hand is possibly detectable on such exterior decoration as the gable traceries and the numerous little figures perched on the extradoses of the flying buttresses. These may have been inspired by the ideas of Hieronymus Bosch, who was then also working on the St Janskerk and on other projects in 's Hertogenbosch.

Du Hameel's part in the building of the Brotherhood Chapel (now the chapel of the Sacrament) off the north transept dates from before 1478. He received regular payments, but from 1488 the project was officially led by his former assistant Jan Heyns (*d* 1516). At the completion of the chapel in 1494, du Hameel was described as 'consulting craftsman' (*Raetsgesel*) and Heyns (now his brother-in-law) as 'master of the work'. The Brotherhood Chapel is lavishly flamboyant both inside and out, with a finish characteristic of du Hameel's style. Interior buttresses supporting elaborate net vaults are themselves hollowed to form complicated canopies. Intersecting ogee arches forming a cross motif, which seems to be his invention, connect the decoration of the chapel both with the portico of the south transept porch and with the curvilinear canopy on the north-east crossing pier.

Du Hameel's departure to Leuven was probably prompted by the stagnation of the building activities on the west front of the St Janskerk. It is noteworthy that in Leuven he began preparations for building a new towered façade for the St Pieterskerk. He also restored the town hall. In 1499 he decorated the Kamerijk Hof for the reception of Emperor Maximilian I and his son Philip, Duke of Burgundy (later King of Spain, *reg* 1504–6). He enlarged the refugees' home (1502; destr. 1865) and built an archive building for Park Abbey. His cross motif recurs in his design for a monstrance (1484–5; Vienna, Albertina). This monstrance, executed by the Cologne goldsmith Hendrick de Borchgrave (*fl* 1484), survives only in the form of a copy (Oss, church of the Immaculate Conception). In 1492 du Hameel made wooden models (destr.) for copper railings (destr.) later cast by Aert van Tricht for the Brotherhood Chapel of the St Janskerk, 's Hertogenbosch. The style of the font made by van Tricht in the same year suggests that it was made in close collaboration with du Hameel. Eleven engravings by du Hameel survive, scattered among various collections. Besides the design for a monstrance mentioned above, these include a design for a canopy (Vienna, Albertina) and a few scenes inspired by the work of Hieronymus Bosch.

BIBLIOGRAPHY

NBW; 'Duhameel, Alart'

M. Lehrs: 'Verzeichnis der Kupferstiche des Alart du Hameel', *Oud-Holland*, xii (1894), pp. 15–25

C. C. Verreyt: 'Allart du Hamel of du Hameel, bouwmeester en plaatsnijder', *Oud-Holland*, xii (1894), pp. 7–14

C. J. A. C. Peeters: 'Nederlandse bouwmeesters uit vroeger eeuwen, Alart du Hamel, *c.* 1440–*c.* 1506', *Bouw: Cent. Wkbld Bouwvzn Nederland & België*, xvii (1962), pp. 1307–11

Meesterwerken van de Europees prentkunst, 1410–1914 (exh. cat., ed. M. D. de Hoop Schieffer and J. Verbeet; Amsterdam, Rijksmus., 1966), p. 39

J. A. J. van der Vaart: 'De westtoren van de Bossche Sint Janskerk', *Brabantia*, xvii (1968), pp. 405–8

P. Gerlach: 'Bossche architecten ten tijde van Jeroen Bosch', *Brabants Heem*, xxii (1970), pp. 154–62

——: 'Het huismerk van Alart du Hamel', *Brabants Heem*, xxii (1970), p. 124

——: 'Het testament van de Bossche bouwmeester Alart Duhameel en Jan Heyns', *Bos. Bijdr.*, xxx (1970–71), pp. 206–14

G. de Werd: 'Alart Duhameels monstrans-ontwerp voor de Sint-Jan te 's-Hertogenbosch', *Brabantia*, xx (1971), pp. 102–3

F. J. van der Vaart: 'Alart du Hamel (midde vijftiende eeuw–voör 1507), bouwmeester' *Brabanste biografieën*, i, ed. J van Oudheusden (Meppel, 1992), pp. 79–82

FRANS JOZEF VAN DER VAART

Alava [Ibarra]**, Juan de** (*b* Alava, *c.* 1480; *d* Salamanca, 3 Sept 1537). Spanish architect. After an initial training in Burgos, an important centre of Gothic architecture towards the end of the 15th century, he moved to Salamanca, where his patrons included Alonso de Fonseca, Archbishop of Santiago de Compostela and Patriarch of Alexandria, and subsequently his son, Alonso de Fonseca y Acevedo, Archbishop of Santiago de Compostela and then of Toledo. Alava worked during a period of transition from the Gothic to the Renaissance style and made a synthesis of the two that was not entirely successful. Even his late churches have a Gothic structure, with rib vaults and buttresses terminating in pinnacles. His façades are embellished with early Renaissance motifs, such as friezes, grotesques and medallion busts. In his use of the orders, he was notably uninhibited by conventional forms and proportions. In 1505 Alava built the sacristy for the chapel of Salamanca University, and he may have contributed to the university façade (1510–20), a masterpiece of the Plateresque style. From 1514 he was involved with the new cathedral at Plasencia, building the transept and north façade (*see* GOTHIC, §II, 2). In 1515, together with Enrique Engas, he produced designs for the new Royal Chapel of Seville Cathedral. In Santiago de Compostela he designed and began the Gothic cathedral cloister (from 1521), commissioned by Archbishop de Fonseca. He built the Archbishop's funerary chapel (begun 1522) in the church of the convent of S Ursula, Salamanca, and also took part in the construction of the new cathedral of Salamanca, executing the north chapels and part of the façade. In 1524 he began the church of the Dominican monastery of S Esteban in Salamanca, which was financed by Juan Alvárez de Toledo, son of the Duque de Alba. Although he was replaced after ten years by Fray Martín de Santiago, the church is Alava's masterpiece. The interior, with a single nave flanked by side chapels, is Late Gothic in style, but its façade consists of an enormous triumphal arch conceived in the manner of a gigantic altarpiece. Alava's secular works include the Colegio de Santiago Alfeo in Santiago de Compostela, founded by Archbishop Alonso de Fonseca y Acevedo. He also built the Colegio de Cuenca in Salamanca (1510; destr.) and the house known as the Casa de las Muertes, also in Salamanca, which has an elegant proto-Renaissance façade.

BIBLIOGRAPHY

F. Chueca: *La catedral nueva de Salamanca* (Salamanca, 1951)

J. M. Pita Andrade: 'La huella de los Fonseca en Salamanca', *Cuad. Estud. Gallegos*, xiv (1958), pp. 173–93

M. Sendín: *El colegio mayor del Arzobispo Fonseca en Salamanca* (Salamanca, 1977)

J. M. López Martín: *La arquitectura del renacimiento placentino* (Cáceres, 1986)

A. R. Ceballos: *La iglesia y el convento de San Esteban de Salamanca* (Salamanca, 1987)

ALFONSO RODRÍQUEZ CEBALLOS

Alavoine, Jean-Antoine (*b* Paris, 1778; *d* Paris, 13 Nov 1834). French architect. He was the son of a sculptor and worked in his father's studio from an early age. He studied at the Ecole des Beaux-Arts, Paris, from 1797 until 1808, apart from the years 1798–1801, when he was on military service in Italy. Initially a pupil of Jean-Thomas Thibaut (1757–1826) and drawn to classical art, he came into contact with Jean-Nicolas-Louis Durand, who taught architecture at the Ecole Polytechnique, and he thus profited from the twofold influence of the Ecole des Beaux-Arts and of engineers involved in building, the results of which were later seen in his work at Rouen Cathedral.

In 1807 he was appointed inspector by the Conseil Général des Bâtiments Civils, under Jacques Cellerier, and in 1811 he became site architect for a monument to *Napoleon* on the Place de la Bastille, Paris, commissioned from Cellerier. He replaced Cellerier as architect when the latter turned to other projects. Alavoine had completed only the foundations of a fountain and the plaster model of an elephant to be cast in bronze when the Empire fell in 1814. He collaborated with the sculptor Pierre Charles Bridan on a scheme (1817; unexecuted) for a fountain enclosed by a colonnade for the same site, but not until 1830 did the government commission him to complete the monument, amended to commemorate instead those killed in the revolutions of 1789 and 1830. He designed a simple, bronze Doric column but died before it was executed and his design was so altered by his successor, Louis Duc, that the *Colonne de juillet* (inaugurated 1840) is now considered to be Duc's work.

Alavoine was keen to experiment with new materials and in his restoration (1817–23) of the cathedral at Sées he replaced stone colonnettes with cast-iron ones. It was at Rouen, however, that he embarked on his most ambitious experiment in this field, presenting a project (1824) for a spire in cast iron to replace the medieval one that had been destroyed by lightning in 1822. Apart from the difficulties connected with its manufacture and assemblage, Alavoine had to face the declared hostility of the entire Gothic Revival school, led by Jean-Baptiste-Antoine Lassus and Eugène-Emmanuel Viollet-le-Duc, who thought that the reproduction in cast iron of forms intended for stone was irrational. Consequently work, begun in 1829, proceeded slowly until 1848, when it stopped, and the spire was not completed until 1875. Despite his success and his official positions, Alavoine left no works of importance after the spire of Rouen Cathedral. All his works were of secondary importance, have been destroyed or remained unexecuted.

WRITINGS

Notes sur l'emploi du fer comme tirans ou entraits en fer forgé (Paris, 1826)

BIBLIOGRAPHY

A. Lance: *Dictionnaire des architectes français* (Paris, 1872), pp. 3–7

P. Chirol: *Jean-Antoine Alavoine* (Rouen, 1920)

J.-P. Desportes: 'Alavoine et la flèche de la cathédrale de Rouen', *Rev. A.* [Paris], xiii (1971), pp. 48–62

JEAN-MICHEL LENIAUD

ʿAlawi [ʿAlawī; Filālī]. Islamic dynasty and rulers of Morocco since 1631. Like their predecessors the Saʿdis, the ʿAlawis are *sharīfs* (descendants of the Prophet Muhammad), and both dynasties are sometimes classed together as the 'Sharifs of Morocco'. From a base in the Tafilalt region of south-east Morocco, the ʿAlawi family was able to overcome the centrifugal forces exerted by the Berber tribes who had destroyed the Saʿdi state in the first half of the 17th century. To restore political authority and territorial integrity, Mawlay Ismaʿil (*reg* 1672–1727) added a new black slave corps to the traditional tribal army. Although royal power was weak during the 19th century and the early 20th, when the French and Spanish established protectorates, the ʿAlawis' power was fully restored after independence from the French in 1956.

ʿAlawi building activities (*see* ISLAMIC ART, §II, 7(v)) were concentrated in the four cities that have served as their capitals: Fez and Marrakesh at various times from 1666 to 1912, Meknes under Mawlay Ismaʿil, and Rabat from 1912. The two greatest patrons were Mawlay Ismaʿil and his grandson Sidi Muhammad (*reg* 1757–90). Mawlay Ismaʿil transformed Meknes by the addition of an immense royal city (the Kasba) to the old town. It preserves conventional Hispano-Moresque features, but it is marked by the rational organization of its layout and the huge volumes of its individual elements. Sidi Muhammad built the splendid Dār al-Makhzen in Marrakesh. Even at the end of the 19th century court dignitaries were building sumptuous residences in the traditional manner, such as the Palais Jamaï at Fez and the Palais Bahia at Marrakesh. Interiors were typically decorated with carved stucco and tile mosaic (*zallīj*). Members of the dynasty also commissioned beautifully illuminated Koran manuscripts copied boldly in the Maghribi form of Arabic script (e.g. Cairo, N. Lib., Koran MS. 25; *see also* ISLAMIC ART, §III, 2(iv–v) and 3(i)). In other arts the Moroccan vernacular tradition continued uninfluenced by dynastic changes.

Before 1912, when Rabat became the capital, the art produced under the ʿAlawis was as conservative as the society that produced it, reproducing formulae established as early as the 14th century. Occasional attempts were made to introduce foreign ideas and techniques, as when Sidi Muhammad had a captive French architect plan the city of Essaouira; the new sense of volume and rational organization seen in secular architecture may also reflect European ideas. Under Hasan II, who became King in 1962, traditional Moroccan crafts have been revived. The mausoleum in Rabat for his father, Muhammad V (completed 1971), was designed by the Vietnamese architect Vo Toan, who kept to traditional Moroccan techniques and motifs.

BIBLIOGRAPHY

Enc. Islam/2: "Alawis'

E. Lévi-Provençal: *Les Historiens des Chorfa: Essai sur la littérature historique et biographique au Maroc du XVIe au XXe siècle* (Paris, 1922)

M. Barrucand: *L'Architecture de la Qasba de Moulay Ismaïl à Meknès*, 2 vols, Etudes et Travaux d'Archéologie Marocaine, vi (Rabat, 1976)

A. Paccard: *Le Maroc et l'artisanat traditionnel islamique dans l'architecture*, 2 vols (St-Jorioz, 1979)
M. Barrucand: *Urbanisme princier en Islam: Meknès et les villes royales islamiques post-médiévales* (Paris, 1985)

MARIANNE BARRUCAND

Alb. *See under* VESTMENTS, ECCLESIASTICAL, §1(i).

Alb, Mihu de la Crișul. *See* MIHU DE LA CRIȘUL ALB.

Alba [now Berwick y Alba], Duques de [Alvárez de Toledo]. Spanish family of politicians and collectors. The prominent role of the Alvárez de Toledo family in the history of Spain and the dynastic marriages that have joined many other titles into the house of Berwick y Alba have placed the Alba collection among the finest in Europe. Don Fernando Alvárez de Toledo (1507–82), the 'Gran-Duque' de Alba, Governor of the Netherlands (from 1567), commissioned paintings from Anthonis Mor and Titian (*General Pardon Conceded to Flanders by the Duque de Alba*; *Christ in the House of Martha*; portrait of *Don Fernando Alvárez de Toledo, Duque de Alba, in Armour*; all Madrid, Pal. Liria, Col. Duke of Alba). His namesake, Don Fernando Alvárez de Toledo, the 6th duke, returned to Spain in 1653 from an embassy in Italy with a large shipment of works of art. The family collection, which included an impressive holding of tapestries, was housed in the palace of La Abadia in Extremadura and at the former ducal seat in Alba de Tormes.

The marriage in 1688 of Catalina Méndez de Haro y Guzmán (*b* 1672), heir to the conjoint houses of Olivares, Carpio and Monterrey, to Francisco Alvárez de Toledo, who became the 10th Duque de Alba, led to the incorporation of the CARPIO and MONTERREY collections, as well as the famous library of the Conde-Duque de Olivares (*see* OLIVARES), into the Alba collection. Included were works such as the Alba *Madonna* by RAPHAEL (*c.* 1509; Washington, DC, N.G.A.), the Rokeby *Venus* (*c.* 1648–50) by Diego de Velázquez and *Mercury Instructing Cupid before Venus ('School of Love')* by CORREGGIO (*c.* 1525, both London, N.G.). The collection was subsequently enriched by paintings commissioned from FRANCISCO DE GOYA (e.g. the *Marques de Villafranca y Duque de Alba*; 1795; Madrid, Prado) by the Duke consort, Don José Alvárez de Toledo y Gonzaga (1756–96), and his wife, Doña Maria Teresa Cayetana Silva y Alvarez y Toledo, the 13th Duquesa de Alba (1762–1802; married 1775). Doña Cayetana played a further role in Goya's career, developing an intimate relationship with the much older artist soon after her husband's death in June 1796. In that year, or early in 1797, Goya apparently accompanied the Duquesa to her estate at Sanlúcar de la Barrameda, producing one of the first great modern portraits, the *Duquesa de Alba* (1797; New York, Hisp. Soc. America; see fig.). From this period also date the so-called Sanlúcar album of drawings depicting the Duquesa and her female companions in surprisingly intimate poses, as well as the charming portrait of the *Duquesa de Alba and her Dueña* (1796; Madrid, Prado). The inscription on the portrait of 1797 suggests that the affair, if there were one, quickly subsided.

Unfortunately fires and a plundering of the Alba holdings upon the death of Doña Cayetana without issue in 1802 left only fragments of the collection intact by 1815 (*see also* GODOY, MANUEL). Many of the works of art to be seen today in the ducal seat, the Palacio de Liria, Madrid, are the result of the collecting activities of the later Duques de Berwick y Alba, such as (1) the 14th Duque de Alba, Carlos Miguel Fitz-James Stuart, who acquired many fine pieces in Italy in the wake of the Napoleonic Wars (1816–22), and (2) the 17th Duque de Alba, James Fitz-James Stuart, to whom fell the task of reconstructing the Palacio de Liria after it was reduced to a shell in the fighting in Madrid during the Spanish Civil War (1939). The picture collection and many of the documents relating to the history of art survived and are now displayed at the Palace. In the late 20th century members of the Alba family continued to play important roles in the patronage of music, architectural restoration and fine arts publishing.

Duquesa de Alba by Francisco de Goya, oil on canvas, 2.10×1.49 m, 1797 (New York, Hispanic Society of America)

BIBLIOGRAPHY

A. M. de Barcia: *Catálogo de la colección de pinturas del Exmo. Sr Duque de Berwick y Alba* (Madrid, 1911)
M. Burke: *Private Collections of Italian Art in 17th-century Spain* (diss., New York U., 1984; microfilm, Ann Arbor, 1986), ii, docs 2.22a–f [further bibliog.]

MARCUS BURKE

(1) 14th Duque de **Alba** [Carlos Miguel Fitz-James Stuart y Silva; 7th Duque de Berwick] (*b* 19 May 1794; *d* Switzerland, 7 Oct 1835). Following the death (1802) of María Teresa Cayetana de Silva y Alvarez de Toledo, 13th Duquesa de Alba, without heir, he received the dukedom of Alba (he was the 7th Duque de Berwick as a descendant of James II, King of England). He was the most important

Alba collector since the 17th century and among the greatest collectors and patrons of the arts in 19th-century Spain. In 1814 he began travelling through France, Italy and Germany, during which time he began acquiring large quantities of paintings and sculptures. In Rome he was in contact with the Nazarenes, especially Friedrich Overbeck, and also commissioned works from Spanish artists pensioned there, such as the Neo-classical sculptor José Alvarez Cubero. In addition, he awarded numerous stipends between 1818 and 1821 to Spaniards coming to Rome to study and also commissioned works from contemporary French artists, including Ingres (e.g. the *Duque de Alba at Ste Gudule, Brussels*, 1816–17; Montauban, Mus. Ingres; *see* INGRES, JEAN-AUGUSTE-DOMINIQUE, §I, 4). Carlos Miguel imported approximately 70 crates of works of art into Spain and in 1824 tried, but failed, to open a public gallery. Many works were later sold to recover losses.

(2) 17th Duque de **Alba** [Jacobo Fitz-James Stuart y Falcó; 10th Duque de Berwick] (*b* Madrid, 17 Oct 1878; *d* Madrid, 24 Sept 1953). Historian, great-great-grandson of (1) 14th Duque de Alba. He was the Spanish ambassador to London and revived the family tradition of collecting, which had declined with his immediate predecessors. He added numerous works to improve the variety of paintings in the Alba collection, including portraits by Joshua Reynolds (*Mrs Porter*; 1765), Thomas Gainsborough, Henry Raeburn and George Romney (*Richard Palmer*; 1787), while his interest in family history led him to acquire various portraits (all Madrid, Pal. Liria) of his ancestor the Gran-Duque de Alba by Rubens (thought to be a copy after Titian), Titian and Alonso Sánchez Coello. He was also an active supporter of such contemporary artists as Mariano Benlliure (1862–1947), Joaquín Sorolla y Bastida, Ignacio Zuloaga, Fernando Alvarez de Sotomayor (1875–1960), and José María Sert (1874–1945), who, in 1932, decorated the chapel of the Palacio de Liria, Madrid, with murals (*in situ*). In 1919 Jacobo was admitted to the Real Academia de la Historia, Madrid, of which he later became Director, and in 1924 he became a member of the Real Academia de Bellas Artes de S Fernando in Madrid. He published numerous works on family history, such as *El Mariscal de Berwick: Bosquejo biográfico* (1925). In his *Discurso leído* (1943) he expressed his attitude towards collecting and patronage, stating that the aristocracy 'are the ones who have known how to conserve . . . the most noteworthy of paintings, sculptures, sepulchral monuments and other artistic treasures' (pp. 25–7).

WRITINGS

El Mariscal de Berwick: Bosquejo biográfico (Madrid, 1925)

Discurso leído en el acto de su recepción por el excelentísimo Duque de Alba (Madrid, 1943)

OSCAR E. VÁZQUEZ

BIBLIOGRAPHY

A. M. de Barcia: *Catálogo de la colección de pinturas del Exmo. Sr Duque de Berwick y Alba* (Madrid, 1911)

Guía de las colecciones artísticas de la Casa de Alba (Madrid, 1947)

J. M. Pita Andrade: 'El Palacio de Liria reconstruído: La colección de cuadros de la Casa de Alba', *Goya*, 12 (1956)

M. Burke: *Private Collections of Italian Art in 17th-century Spain* (diss., New York U., 1984; microfilm, Ann Arbor, 1986), ii, docs 2.22a–f [incl. bibliog.]

El arte en las colecciones de la Casa de Alba (exh. cat., Madrid, Pal. Liria, 1987)

P. Diener: 'Die Albas—eine Familie und ihre Sammlungen', *Du*, 6 (1988), pp. 32–73

L. A. Buñuel Salcedo: 'Der XVII. Herzog von Alba (1878–1953) und die Residencia de Estudiantes', *Du*, 6 (1988), pp. 25, 32–73

MARCUS BURKE, OSCAR E. VÁZQUEZ

Alba, Macrino d' [Alladio, Gian Giacomo d'] (*b* Alba; *fl* 1495–1515; *d* before 1528). Italian painter. Inscriptions on his altarpieces indicate he was born in Alba. He probably trained elsewhere; his early works, with the exception of the portrait of *Andrea Novelli, Bishop of Alba* (Isola Bella, Mus. Borromeo), cannot be traced to a precise location. His patrons were mainly from the Paleologo court at Casale Monferrato, where he was the official painter. His earliest signed and dated work is the triptych of the *Virgin Enthroned between SS John the Evangelist, James the Greater, John the Baptist and Thomas Aquinas and Two Donors* (1495; Turin, Mus. Civ. A. Ant.), and it and the *Virgin and Child between SS Nicholas and Martin* (Rome, Pin. Capitolina) show the influence of Lombard painters, particularly Ambrogio Bergognone; some writers have suggested that this may indicate a journey through central Italy, perhaps to Rome.

By 1496 Alba's *Virgin Enthroned between SS Hugh and Anselm* had been placed in the Certosa di Pavia (*in situ*). This painting (see fig.), now incorporated in a polyptych of which the upper section (1488; destr.) was by Bergognone, contains the first appearance in his work of antique ruins, which later became so typical. In the same year Alba was at Asti working in the Certosa on frescoes (destr.). There in 1498 he completed the *Virgin in Glory between SS John, James the Greater, Hugo and Jerome* (Turin, Gal. Sabauda). His style in this period is dry and metallic, with strong, cold colours and a sense of abstraction. The face of the Virgin was used again in his triptych of the *Virgin and Child between SS Augustine and John the Baptist with a Donor* (1499; Tortona, Pal. Vescovile) for the abbey of Lucedio, commissioned by Annibale Paleologo, the natural son of Marchese Guglielmo Paleologo, and then repeated in the *Virgin and Child with SS Francis and Thomas and Two Female Donors* (1501; Alba, Pal. Com.).

Alba's style reached a high-point in the altarpiece of the *Virgin Enthroned between SS John the Baptist and James, a Bishop Saint and St Jerome* (1503; Casale Monferrato, Santuario Crea) commissioned by Giovanni Giacomo Biandrate of San Giorgio Monferrato. It is a sober and dignified composition, flooded with light and colour. Also in this period he executed the wings of the altarpiece of the *Virgin and Child* (Frankfurt am Main, Städel. Kstinst. & Städt. Gal.), depicting *St Joachim* and the *Meeting of SS Joachim and Anne*. These suggest a new influence from northern European art. He also executed numerous paintings of the *Nativity* (e.g. 1505; New York, NY Hist. Soc.; Kansas City, MO, Nelson–Atkins Mus. A.; signed and dated 150(?8), Alba, S Giovanni Battista). The polyptych with *SS Paul and Luigi* (Turin, Gal. Sabauda) dates from 1506. Late works, such as the *Mystic Marriage of St Catherine* (Neviglie, S Giorgio), are characterized by increased simplicity and elegance. His last known dated work is the *Virgin Enthroned* (21 Oct 1513; priv. col., see Romano, 1970, fig. 3). In 1515 Alba was replaced by Gian Francesco Caroto as court painter at Casale Monferrato.

Macrino d'Alba: *Virgin Enthroned between SS Hugh and Anselm*, before 1496 (Pavia, Certosa)

He died before 1528, the year he was commemorated by the Alban poet Paolo Cerrato (*c.* 1485–*c.* 1540) in *De Virginitate* (Paris, 1528).

BIBLIOGRAPHY

Thieme–Becker

A. M. Brizio: *La pittura in Piemonte dall'età romanica al cinquecento* (Turin, 1942), pp. 65–73, 237–42

G. O. Della Piana: *Macrino d'Alba* (Como, 1962)

B. Berenson: *Central and North Italian Schools*, i (1968), pp. 236–7

G. Romano: *Casalesi del cinquecento: L'avvento del manierismo in una città padana* (Turin, 1970), pp. 4–6

——: 'Schede Vesme', *L'arte in Piemonte*, iv (Turin, 1982), pp. 1450–67

RICCARDO PASSONI

Alba Iulia [Hung. Gyulafehérvár]. Romanian city in Transylvania. It was founded on the site of the Roman fort and settlement of Apulum, the ruins of which include a palace with mosaics. The nucleus of the medieval city is the fortress situated on a terrace of the River Mureş. In the south-east of the fortress four churches were built. The first, a rotunda partially preserved in the present Roman Catholic cathedral, is thought to date from *c.* 950 and was probably dedicated to St John the Baptist. It comprises a circular Roman tower, reused as the nave of the church with the addition of a semicircular apse. The second building, a single-aisled church with a semicircular apse, dates from the first half of the 11th century. This church, probably the first Roman Catholic cathedral, appears to have been founded by Stephen I, King of Hungary (*reg* 1000–38). It was probably used until the construction in the late 11th century of the first basilica at Alba Iulia. Architectural and sculptural fragments from the basilica survive in the present cathedral above the south door.

The existing Roman Catholic cathedral (l.82 m) was begun under King Andrew II (*reg* 1205–35). This edifice is also a basilica but adopts the *Gebundenes System* (each bay of the nave corresponds to two in the aisles). It had a choir with a semicircular central apse (replaced in the 14th century by an elongated choir and polygonal apse), a transept with small apses, and also two towers enclosing an atrium at the west end. The cathedral was largely completed by 1277, when it was set on fire during an uprising of the Saxon population, after which it was restored. The disastrous Tatar invasion of 1294 interrupted building after the erection of the apses, the transept and possibly the south aisle wall. In the following stage, with the replacement of the semicircular arches by pointed ones, the plan of the basilica was modified to incorporate a nave and four aisles. In the third phase building continued with three aisles. The cathedral is adorned with highly important examples of Late Romanesque sculpture, including reliefs linked with the studio of Benedetto Antelami. To the north-east of the cathedral, near the city centre, were constructed the monastery of the Augustine Hermits, dedicated to St Stephen (1295), and the Dominican convent of St Mary (1295; destr. 1890); to the east of the basilica is the Benedictine convent of the Holy Spirit (1299). In the south-west of the city, the seat of the bishopric, mentioned in 1291 and still existing in 1711, comprised an episcopal palace, as well as the cathedral.

The medieval fortifications were strengthened by order of King Vladislav II Jagiellon (*reg* 1490–1516). In this period, when Alba Iulia was an important Renaissance centre in Transylvania, a chapel was built on the north side of the cathedral, named after its founder, Canon János Lázói. Finished in 1512, this important construction has varied decoration, mainly showing Lombard and Tuscan characteristics. The importance of the city was connected with the presence there of the princely court (1541–1691). In the mid-16th century fortification works directed by General Giovanni Castaldo are associated with such Italian architects as Antonio da Bufalo, Andrea da Treviso and Francesco da Pozzo. In the second half of the 16th century the construction of the splendid princely palace was begun to the south of the cathedral, together with the transformation of the episcopal palace and that of the canons. Work continued for *c.* 150 years, in particular under Prince Gabriel Bethlen (*reg* 1613–29). Under Michael the Brave, Voivode of Wallachia (*reg* 1593–1601), who conquered the city in 1599–1600, the Orthodox Metropolitan church was built south-east of the curtain wall. It was the centre of a monastic complex, which was demolished after Transylvania came under Austrian rule (1699), and was replaced by fortifications of the type developed by SÉBASTIEN LEPRESTRE DE VAUBAN. These were begun (1714) at the order of Emperor Charles VI (*reg* 1711–40) according to the plans of G. M. Visconti and were largely completed before 1738. The rich Baroque decoration of the city gates, designed as triumphal arches, glorified the Emperor. In 1719 the Trinitarian monastery was built in the south-west of the city. Its church was modified at the same time as the establishment (1794) of the Batthyaneum Library by Bishop Ignatius of Transylvania, Count of Batthyáni.

BIBLIOGRAPHY

V. Vătăşianu: *Istoria artei feudale în ţările române* [History of feudal art in Romanian countries], i (Bucharest, 1959), pp. 42–57, 154–9, 736–9

A. Popa and I. Berciu: *Cetatea Alba Iulia* [The fortress of Alba Iulia] (Bucharest, 1962)

G. Sebestyèn and V. Sebestyèn: *Arhitectura renaşterei în Transylvania* [Renaissance architecture in Transylvania] (Bucharest, 1963), pp. 34–5, 42–3, 108–9, 110–11, *passim*

G. Arion: 'Date noi referitoare la prima catedrală catolică de la Alba Iulia' [New data regarding the first Catholic cathedral at Alba Iulia], *Stud. & Cerc. Istor. A.* [from xi (1964), pubd as: *Seria Artě plastică*], xiv/2 (1967), pp. 155–9

I. Serban: 'Un monument de arhitectura gotică ă in cetatea Alba Iulia: Biserica Báthory' [A monument of Gothic architecture in the fortress of Alba Iulia: the Bathory church], *Apulum*, xv (1977), pp. 313–33

G. Anghel: 'Noi date în legătură cu vechea cetate medievală de la Alba Iulia' [New data concerning the old medieval fortress of Alba Iulia], *Apulum*, xxii (1985), pp. 113–22

——: 'Cetăţile medievale de la Alba Iulia [The Medieval fortresses at Alba Iulia], *Apulum*, xiii (1987)

V. Moga: *De la Apulum la Alba Iulia: Fortificaţiile oraşului* [From Apulum to Alba Iulia: the town's fortifications] (Bucharest, 1987)

SUZANA MORE HEITEL

Albanese. Italian family of sculptors and architects. (1) Francesco Albanese, who was active in Vicenza, established the family workshop in which his two sons (2) Giovanni Battista Albanese and (3) Girolamo Albanese worked.

(1) Francesco Albanese (*b* ?Asolo, 1535-40; *d* after 1611). He worked mainly on architectural sculpture, particularly altars and funerary monuments, continuing in the style of Danese Cattaneo; the local stone, *pietra dei Berici*, soft and white, is able to show subtle modulations of light and shade. The keystone heads (1564) of the lower gallery of the loggia of Palladio's basilica facing the Piazza dei Signori, Vicenza, marked the beginning of a long association of the Albanese workshop with the buildings of Palladio. Francesco's main works were the funerary monument of *Gaetano Thiene* (1583) in the cathedral at Vicenza, an austere architectonic work of Palladian derivation; and the Trissino Altar (1587) in S Maria dei Servi, Vicenza. Works executed by the workshop in Vicenza that are attributed to Francesco include the Conti Altar (1592) in S Chiara; the funerary monument of *Giuliano Rutilio* (1593) in the cathedral, a rich and decorative work; the low relief of the *Virgin* (1596) on the Torre di Piazza, with figures in heavy drapery and conventional poses; and the *S Antonio* altar (1598) in S Corona.

(2) Giovanni Battista Albanese (*b* Vicenza, 1573; *d* Vicenza, 1630). Son of (1) Francesco Albanese. He was the most prominent member of the family and was involved mainly in the architectural sculpture for buildings by Palladio. From 1593 he collaborated with his father on the keystone heads of the loggia of the basilica. The statues (1595) surmounting the Arco delle Scalette, for which he was Master of Works, already show signs of a distinctive style: they are almost Mannerist in their elongated bodies and sinuous lines. He went on to execute (*c.* 1614) the polygonal stairs that run from the loggia of the basilica to the Piazza delle Erbe and the statues above the balustrade on the façade of the basilica facing the Piazza dei Signori. He also executed the twelve acroteria (1606) of the Villa Rotonda, Vicenza, and the five acroteria (1619) of S Giorgio Maggiore, Venice. Other works in Vicenza attributed to him include the statues (1596) on the high altar of the modest church of S Pietro; the façade (1596) of the oratory of the Gonfalone, a severe temple front; and the Capra Altar (*c.* 1605) in S Lorenzo, notably the *Adam and Eve*. His masterpiece was the *Pietà* (1617), a low relief in the tympanum of S Vicenzo (1614–16), for which he also designed the acroteria; these figures have dynamic poses and flowing drapery. Soon after, he began work on the chapel of the Rosary in S Corona, completed in 1642 by his brother Girolamo. From 1621 to 1623 he was Master of Works on the bridge of S Michele, to an earlier design by Tommaso Contini (*fl* 1600–18) and Francesco Contini (*fl* 1618–49).

(3) Girolamo Albanese (*b* Vicenza, 1584; *d* Vicenza, before 1663). Son of (1) Francesco Albanese. He trained in the family workshop. His masterpiece is the statue of the *Redentore* (*c.* 1640) in the Piazza dei Signori, Vicenza. The statue of *St John the Baptist* in the baptistery and the four statues in the chapel of S Giuseppe (now Sacra Famiglia), dating from 1650, in Vicenza Cathedral, exhibit a Baroque theatricality with their exaggerated poses and heavily modelled drapery. The rather weak and mannered group on the south-west corner of the balustrade of Palladio's basilica in Vicenza is attributed to Girolamo, as are the statues on the entrance staircase of Palladio's Villa Poiana at Poiana Maggiore, near Vicenza.

BIBLIOGRAPHY

DBI
A. Venturi: *Storia*, x (1933), pp. 333–48
F. Barbieri, R. Cevese and L. Magagnato: *Guida di Vicenza* (Vicenza, 1953)
B. T. Forlati and F. Barbieri: *Il Duomo di Vicenza* (Vicenza, 1956)
F. Barbieri: *The Basilica of Andrea Palladio*, Corpus Palladianum, ii (Vicenza, 1970)

□

Albani. Italian family of ecclesiastics, patrons and collectors.

(1) Pope **Clement XI** [Giovanni Francesco Albani] (*b* Urbino, 22 July 1649; elected 23 Nov 1700; *d* Rome, 19 March 1721). He became a cleric at the age of 28 after pursuing studies in law, literature, philosophy and theology in Rome. When working within the curia he acted in succession as governor of Rieti, Spoleto and Orvieto. In this same period he was involved in the academic activities of the intellectual circle around Christina, Queen of Sweden. He was created a cardinal in 1690, receiving the title first of S Maria in Aquiro, then of S Adriano and finally of S Silvestro in Capite. As cardinal he initiated the restoration of S Brigida, Rome, where the ceiling fresco by Biagio Puccini of *St Bridget in Glory* (late 1690s) incorporates his papal coat of arms. His pontificate as Clement XI was disturbed by the War of the Spanish Succession (1701–14), while the fight against Jansenism in France reached its apogee with his publication of the bull *Unigenitus* in 1713; in East Asia he had a dispute with the Jesuits over church ritual.

Clement XI's patronage was characterized by his intellectual training and interests in archaeology. He built up an oriental collection in the Biblioteca Apostolica, Rome, and was a patron to Mgr Francesco Bianchini (1662–1729), who, as archaeologist, became Presidente delle Antichità (1703), supervising excavations and overseeing exports of antique works of art, as regulated by the edicts of 1701 and 1704. Clement XI accepted the idea of the Galleria Lapidaria in the Vatican and also planned a museum of Christian antiquity, the Museo Ecclesiastico (1703–16); he applied extensive knowledge of antique art to the collections in the Capitoline palaces (now Rome, Mus. Capitolino); antique statues were installed and collections of coins and inscriptions, among other antiquities, were added. He patronized the new Accademia of Bologna, which took the name 'Clementina' in his honour, and he created the Concorso Clementino at the Accademia di S Luca (first awarded 1702). His favourite painter was Carlo Maratti, who restored the frescoes by Raphael in the Vatican Palace, painted the large canvases for the baptismal chapel in St Peter's (*in situ*) and executed the cartoons for mosaics and lunettes intended for the choir of the canons and the Cappella della Presentazione, also in St Peter's.

Pope Clement's incessant activity transformed the urban environment of Rome (*see* ROME, §II, 3). Under him the series of statues on Gianlorenzo Bernini's colonnade at St Peter's was completed. Within the basilica the monument by Carlo Fontana to Christina, Queen of Sweden, was finished, several altarpieces were made into mosaics and the equestrian statue of *Charlemagne* (1720–25) by Agostino Cornacchini was executed. At the basilica of S Giovanni in Laterano the nave was decorated with statues of the *Twelve Apostles* (by Camillo Rusconi, Giuseppe Mazzuoli and others), each with a corresponding painting (by Benedetto Luti, Andrea Procaccini and others) showing one of the prophets. He had the Pantheon restored, along with SS Apostoli (by Francesco Antonio Fontana), and the church of the Stimmate di S Francesco rebuilt, by Giovanni Battista Contini and Antonio Canevari. He initiated the redecoration of S Clemente, and the wooden ceiling over the nave incorporates his coat of arms and a painting of the *Glory of St Clement* by Giuseppe Chiari. Other churches redecorated included S Maria in Monticelli, S Sisto Vecchio, and the addition of new façades to S Maria in Cosmedin by Giuseppe Sardi; S Maria in Trastevere by Carlo Fontana; and S Anna dei Palafrenieri by Alessandro Specchi. Outside Rome, he took an interest in Nocera Umbra Cathedral, and in Urbino he embellished the Cappella di S Crescenzio in the cathedral and the church of the Scolopi, S Domenico.

As an administrator Clement supported works in the public interest. These include several fountains in Rome, among them the Fontana del Tritone by Carlo Bizzaccheri, the port of Ripetta by Specchi and the granary (1703–5) near the Baths of Diocletian by Carlo Fontana (not completed; drawings Windsor Castle, Berks, Royal Lib.). He was also responsible for the enlarging of the port of Ancona, the aqueduct of Civitavecchia and the public baths in Nocera Umbra. The most important constructions under his patronage were recorded in medals and in 16 paintings by Giuseppe Nicola Nasini (1657–1736) and Andreas Spägl (*in situ*), hung in the Gran Sala of the Palazzo della Cancelleria (decorated 1718).

BIBLIOGRAPHY

DBI
R. Venuti: *Numismata romanorum pontificium praestantiora a Martino V ad Benedictum XIV* (Rome, 1744), pp. 327–42
L. von Pastor: *Geschichte der Päpste (1886–9)*, xv
S. Pressouyre: *Rome au fil du temps: Atlas historique d'urbanisme et d'architecture* (Boulogne sur Seine, 1973)
R. Enggass: *Early Eighteenth-century Sculpture in Rome* (London and University Park, PA, 1976)
S. Rudolph: 'The "Gran Sala" in the Cancelleria Apostolica: A Homage to the Artistic Patronage of Clement XI', *Burl. Mag.*, cxx (1978), pp. 592–601

OLIVIER MICHEL

(2) Cardinal **Alessandro Albani** (*b* Urbino, 15 Oct 1692; *d* Rome, 11 Dec 1779). Nephew of (1) Clement XI. Having studied law in Rome, in 1708, at just 16 years of age, he became a colonel in the papal cavalry; but he soon abandoned his military career for an ecclesiastical one. In 1718 Pope Clement XI appointed him secretary of memorials. The following year he became Clerk of the Apostolic Chamber. In 1720 he was an extraordinary nuncio in Vienna. After he returned to Rome, on 24 September 1721 Pope Innocent XIII made him a cardinal, assigning him the church of S Adriano. Later he was Cardinal of S Maria in Cosmedin (1722), S Agata (1740), S Maria ad Martyres (1743) and S Maria in Via Lata (1747). He took an active part in the diplomatic initiatives that in 1726 led to the concordat between the Holy See and the

Kingdom of Sardinia. In recognition of this he was appointed by Victor Amedeus III, Duke of Savoy, as Protector of the Realm. As a politician he was impartial and ambitious, at times motivated by personal financial interest. In the conclaves he often played a dominant role, thanks to his diplomatic ability. During the pontificates of Clement XIII (*reg* 1758–69) and Clement XIV (*reg* 1769–75) he was among the cardinals who opposed the bull on the suppression of the Company of Jesus. In 1743 he was appointed protector of the hereditary estates of the House of Austria and in 1745 of the Empire. He also had important diplomatic relations with England, the interests of which he looked after in Rome in the absence of an ambassador accredited by the Holy See. He often collaborated with his friend PHILIPP STOSCH, who was a secret agent of the British government as well as a famous scholar.

Albani was much more famous for his antiquarian interests and his important collection of statues than for his political and diplomatic activities. As a youth he was a pupil of Francesco Bianchini (1662–1729), an eclectic scholar, scientist and archaeologist, who was appointed by Pope Clement XI in 1703 as Presidente delle Antichità of Rome. Bianchini inspired in Albani a passion for ancient art, and was responsible, among other things, for the first systematic excavations on the Palatine Hill. In his mature years Albani followed in his footsteps, promoting vast excavations from which he obtained some of the most important pieces for the museum he was setting up in the Palazzo Albani del Drago at the Quattro Fontane, under the direction of Bianchini. In 1728, 30 of the finest statues of the collection were sold to Augustus II, King of Poland. This episode, which caused a great outcry in Rome, was followed in 1733–4 by the purchase of the whole Albani collection by Clement XII (*reg* 1730–40), who feared the dispersal of the Roman archaeological patrimony. The great collection of busts, together with such famous statues as the two della Valle *Satyrs*, the Cesi *Juno* (both Rome, Mus. Capitolino) and the *Antinous* that had recently been found in Hadrian's Villa at Tivoli (Rome, Villa Torlonia), came to form the nucleus of a new museum on the Campidoglio. From the excavations at Tivoli, Albani later obtained numerous antique pieces (including a great number of bronzes, as well as the famous relief of *Antinous*, Rome, Mus. Torlonia). With these he formed a new collection for his new villa by CARLO MARCHIONNI in the Via Salaria. This villa, with frescoes by ANTON RAPHAEL MENGS including the famous *Parnassus*, and its Gran Salone for the display of sculpture, was perhaps the most demanding project undertaken by Cardinal Albani. It was conceived as a villa-museum, to provide a worthy setting for the famous collection. The Cardinal also had important collections of epigraphs and coins.

JOHANN JOACHIM WINCKELMANN was taken under Albani's protection. He stayed in the Cardinal's home and was his librarian as well as his friend. It was thanks to the support and encouragement of his patron that Winckelmann completed *I monumenti antichi inediti* (Rome, 1767). Albani also assisted the Italian architect Bernardo Antonio Vittone and acquired paintings for Eugene, Prince of Savoy. He furthermore sponsored many English artists in Rome (Richard Wilson, Joseph Wilton, William Chambers, Thomas Jenkins, Robert Adam, Robert Strange, James Berry). These were recommended to him by his friend Horace Mann, a British diplomat in Florence, with whom he maintained a constant correspondence. Albani also helped to enrich numerous British antique collections. In 1749 he collaborated with Matthew Brettingham the younger (*see* BRETTINGHAM, (2)) in searching Rome for antique statues for Thomas Coke, 1st Earl of Leicester. The following year Bubb Dodington also asked him to acquire some antique pieces. Between 1753 and 1755 the Cardinal followed the work of Pompeo Girolamo Batoni, Mengs, Agostino Masucci and Placido Costanzi as they carried out a commission to copy Italian paintings for Hugh Smithson, later 1st Duke of Northumberland. In 1761 Albani became an honorary member of the Society of Antiquaries in London. The next year King George III of England bought his collections of drawings by Carlo Maratti and those gathered by Cassiano dal Pozzo (*see* POZZO, (1)), all of which he had been given by his uncle, Pope Clement XI.

BIBLIOGRAPHY

DBI

Antiqua numismata maximi moduli, aurea, argentea, aerea, ex museo Alexandri S. R. E. Card. Albani in Vaticanam Bibliothecam a Clemente XII . . . translata et a Radulphino Venuto . . . notis illustrata (Rome, 1739–44)

G. Marini: *Iscrizioni antiche delle ville e de' palazzi Albani* (Rome, 1785)

D. Strocchi: *De vita A.A. cardinalis* (Rome, 1790)

S. Morcelli, C. Fea and E. Q. Visconti: *La villa Albani ora Torlonia descritta* (Rome, 1869)

C. Justi, ed.: *Antiquarische Briefe des Baron Philipp von Stosch* (Marburg, 1871), p. 20

L. von Pastor: *Geschichte der Päpste* (1886–9), xv–xvi

N. Blakiston: 'Relazioni italo-inglesi nel settecento secondo i documenti del Record Office', *Rass. Stor. Tosc.*, i (1955), pp. 56–7

F. Haskell and N. Penny: *Taste and the Antique: The Lure of Classical Sculpture, 1500–1900* (New Haven and London, 1981), pp. 62–73

LUCA LEONCINI

Albani, Francesco (*b* Bologna, 17 March 1578; *d* Bologna, 4 Oct 1660). Italian painter and draughtsman. He was a distinguished artist of the Bolognese school, deeply influenced by Annibale Carracci's classicism, who worked in Rome as well as Bologna, painting altarpieces, frescoes and and cabinet pictures. His fame rests on his idyllic landscapes and small mythological pictures, the lyrical qualities of which earned him the soubriquet 'the Anacreon of painters'.

1. Life and work. 2. Influence and critical reputation.

1. Life and work.

(i) Bologna, to 1600. The 12-year-old Albani began his studies in the Bolognese studio of the Flemish-born painter Denys Calvaert, after which he transferred (*c.* 1595) to the Carracci Accademia degli Incamminati, also in Bologna, where life drawing and theoretical discussion predominated. For the next four years he studied with Ludovico Carracci and through him obtained his first public commissions. These were for Bolognese palazzi and churches, such as the oratory of S Colombano, where his fresco of the *Repentance of St Peter* (*c.* 1597–8) closely imitates the dramatic and emotional qualities of Ludovico's manner, particularly in the expressive figure of the apostle and in the nocturnal lighting. The oratory's altarpiece, painted in the same period, showing the *Risen Christ Appearing to*

the Virgin, is, however, more indebted to Annibale Carracci for its general composition and individual motifs. This change of mentor signalled a decisive shift in Albani's approach, which increasingly inclined towards Annibale's idealizing and classicizing style. According to Malvasia, Albani's work in S Colombano stood out from that of the other Carracci pupils for its invention and expression. An altarpiece painted in 1599, the *Virgin and Child Enthroned with SS Catherine of Alexandria and Mary Magdalene* in SS Fabiano e Sebastiano, Bologna, marks the start of Albani's career as an independent master. This, his first dated work, exemplifies the elements of his initial style. Its composition is indebted to Annibale's altarpiece of the *Virgin and Child Enthroned* (1593; Bologna, Pin. N.), while the intimate mood, slight figural proportions, graceful attitudes, *sfumato* and sweet facial expressions reflect Albani's study of Correggio.

(ii) Rome, 1601–17. Albani moved to Rome in 1601 with his close friend Guido Reni, working there until 1617, when he returned to Bologna to take charge of his family's interests. During these 16 years he established a successful career, first in Annibale Carracci's studio, then independently. He was Annibale's chief assistant on work for the frescoes illustrating the *Life of St James of Alcalà* (*c*. 1605–6; Rome, S Giacomo degli Spagnoli). Elaborating Annibale's sketches, Albani learnt to design classicizing compositions in which monumental figures enact the narrative through expressive gesture. He also supervised the completion of the Aldobrandini lunettes (*c*. 1604–5/1610–13; Rome, Gal. Doria-Pamphili), left unfinished on Annibale's death in 1609. The lunette of the *Landscape with the Assumption* shows Albani's assimilation of his mentor's landscape style: small figures move against a grand landscape, the idealized forms of which complement the sacred narrative.

The success of Albani's work for Annibale led to five major Roman fresco commissions—for the Palazzo Mattei (1606–7), the Palazzo Giustiniani at Bassano di Sutri (1609–10), the chapel of the Annunciation of the Palazzo Quirinale (1610), the Palazzo Verospi (*c*. 1611–12) and for S Maria della Pace (1612–14). The largest and most challenging of these was the series showing the myth of *Phaeton* painted on the walls and ceiling of the gallery at Bassano di Sutri, the country residence of Marchese Vincenzo Giustiniani. The ceiling's design surprisingly rejects the architectonic structure of Annibale's ceiling in the Farnese Gallery (1597–1608; Rome, Pal. Farnese) and instead turns to the tradition of illusionistic ceilings with a unified expanse of open sky. The figural composition retains, however, classical equilibrium and legibility. A preparatory nude study of *Phaeton* (Windsor Castle, Berks, Royal Lib.), in black chalk heightened with white, clearly reveals Annibale's influence and is a good example of Albani's draughtsmanship. According to Sandrart, the work for Giustiniani established Albani's fame in Rome.

Unlike his contemporaries and compatriots, Reni, Domenichino and Giovanni Lanfranco, Albani received no major commissions for altarpieces in Rome, but his reputation grew nonetheless through his frescoes and his numerous cabinet pictures illustrating devotional or mythological subjects. In such small paintings on copper as *Diana and Actaeon* (*c*. 1614–16; Paris, Louvre; see fig. 1) he created a personal manner, characterized by graceful and delicate, usually female, figures with softened contours set against gentle landscapes.

(iii) Bologna, after 1617.

By the end of 1617 Albani was back in Bologna, and he celebrated his marriage shortly afterwards. He established a large studio that rivalled Reni's for the most important public commissions. His main work became the painting of large-scale altarpieces for Bolognese and provincial churches and easel pictures for an international clientele. Cupids and cherubs increasingly populate both his secular and sacred paintings, perhaps reflecting his growing family, which by 1643 numbered 12 children. His biographers ascribed the vivacity of his highly praised putti to their being modelled on his own babies, supposedly suspended from the ceiling with ropes! In the 1630s Albani also began a treatise on painting, the general content of which is known from the excerpts of his notes published in Malvasia's biography. Albani's theories for the most part reflect the current classic–idealist stance, emphasizing the importance of invention and the artist's education and sharply criticizing the naturalism of Caravaggio and his followers. As is evident from a later exchange of letters (1651) with his pupil Andrea Sacchi, Albani had little regard for the northern Bamboccianti in Rome, although his comments show an unexpected appreciation of their paintings' satirical and humorous content.

Albani's mature Bolognese altarpieces differ, in their classicizing compositions and monumental figures, from his early altarpieces, reflecting the artist's intervening Roman experience. In the two most significant, the *Allegory of the Passion* (1627–32; Bologna, Madonna di Galliera, Cappella Cagnoli) and the *Annunciation 'dal bell'angelo'* (1632; Bologna, S Bartolomeo), he responded to contemporary piety with novel imagery. In the *Allegory of the Passion* the traditional themes of redemption and penitence are accompanied by allusions, typical of Counter-Reformation thought, to the Double Trinity and to the Christ Child's foreknowledge of his fate. In the *Annunciation* the standing Virgin and God the Father's presence are in the tradition of 16th-century Bolognese painting, but the figure of Gabriel, dubbed the 'bell'angelo' by Malvasia, was, though idealized, conceived in the most modern idiom, full and vibrant in form. Both compositions are deliberately simple and legible but mitigate a formal severity reminiscent of Reni's and Domenichino's later Bolognese altarpieces with charming individual details, such as Gabriel's soft ringlets and swirling garments or the delightful cherubs in the *Annunciation.* Albani's last important altarpiece, the *Noli me tangere* (1644; Bologna, S Maria dei Servi), illustrates his final stylistic phase, in which he employed a more slender figure type with stylized poses and gestures. This heightened refinement reflects his imitation of Reni's second manner of the 1630s and finds echoes in Guercino's works after 1640. Albani's mature Bolognese altarpieces bequeathed the principles of the Carracci reform of painting to his pupils and to younger Bolognese artists. Extensive workshop assistance and the execution of many replicas account, however, for the decline in quality of works datable after 1645.

1. Francesco Albani: *Diana and Actaeon*, oil on copper, 520×615 mm, *c*. 1614–16 (Paris, Musée du Louvre)

Albani's idyllic landscapes assumed an important place in his mature artistic activity. His mythological fables set in landscapes evoking the Bolognese countryside were seen as the visual equivalent of the classically inspired idylls by the poet Giambattista Marino (1569–1625) and can also be likened to the lyric verse of the Bolognese poet Claudio Achillini (1574–1625). The most important examples of this genre are the four cycles that Albani painted between 1617 and 1634. The first was the *Loves of Venus and Diana* (*c*. 1617; Rome, Gal. Borghese) for Cardinal Scipione Borghese. Albani invented a narrative that unfolds across the cycle's four roundels (see fig. 2), loosely following Ovid's fable of Venus and Adonis and also borrowing from Marino's *L'Adone* (Paris and Turin, 1623). Small in scale, the figures move with consummate grace and are set in front of deep vistas punctuated by meadows, lakes and hazy mountains. The cycle's novel imagery, charming motifs and allegorical allusions earned Albani a reputation for inventiveness and elicited further commissions. His early critics judged this to be one of his finest works, along with his other three cycles on related poetic themes: that begun in 1621 for Ferdinando Gonzaga, 6th Duke of Mantua, and finished in 1633 for Prince Giovanni Carlo de' Medici (Paris, Louvre); the *Four Elements* (1625–8; Turin, Gal. Sabauda) for Cardinal Prince Maurice of Savoy; and the cycle (1634; Fontainebleau, Château) for Jacques Le Veneur, Comte de Carrouges. In subject-matter, composition and mood, these works help define the ideal landscape tradition, but their looser structure and softer handling, which reveal study of Titian's *Bacchanals* (London, N.G.; Madrid, Prado), contrast with Annibale Carracci's or Domenichino's landscapes. They most closely parallel, with their luminous skies, towering trees and deep panoramas, Claude Lorrain's contemporaneous landscapes.

2. Influence and critical reputation. Albani's studio, which he opened in Bologna about 1618, served as both a school for artists and a workshop to execute the master's designs. His most famous pupils included Andrea Sacchi, Pier Francesco Mola and Carlo Cignani, who developed independent artistic personalities. Albani's importance as a transmitter of the classical ideal was recognized by Giovanni Pietro Bellori, who traced a line of descent from the Carracci through Albani to Sacchi and to Sacchi's pupil Carlo Maratti. A similar chain links Albani

2. Francesco Albani: *Venus and Adonis*, oil on canvas, tondo, diam. 1.54 m, *c.* 1617 (Rome, Galleria Borghese)

to Cignani and his pupil Marcantonio Franceschini, the protagonists of the pastoral mode in Bologna. Less well-known artists, such as Giovanni Battista Mola, assisted in the studio's large production of cabinet pictures and closely imitated Albani's style.

Albani's reputation was high in his own lifetime and throughout most of the 18th century. His biographers and critics ranked him among the leading painters and especially singled out his cabinet pictures for praise, remarking on their high prices. The small-scale, exquisitely finished panels appealed especially to French collectors, as André Félibien and the inventories of French estates attest. At the end of the 17th century Louis XIV had a large collection of cabinet pictures by Albani, more than by any other Bolognese painter. The sensuous elegance of Albani's nymphs, the appealing putti and idyllic landscapes inspired French court painters, such as the Boullogne brothers, and anticipated François Boucher's pastorals. In the 19th century a general change in taste resulted in the disparagement of the Bolognese school and a negative appraisal of Albani's works, which were judged frivolous and repetitive. Modern scholarship has generally ignored the importance of Albani's large-scale works but recognized to some extent his contribution to landscape painting.

BIBLIOGRAPHY

F. Scannelli: *Il microcosmo della pittura* (Cesena, 1657); ed. R. Lepore (Bologna, 1989), pp. 345, 364–5, 368

A. Félibien: *Entretiens sur les vies et sur les ouvrages des plus excellens peintres, anciens et modernes* (Paris, 1666–88; rev. Trévoux, 1725), iii, pp. 521–9

G. P. Bellori: *Vite* (1672); ed. E. Borea (1976)

L. Scaramuccia: *Le finezze de' pennelli italiani* (Pavia, 1674); ed. G. Giubbini (Milan, 1965), pp. 14, 34, 36–7, 54, 56, 62–3, 159–60, 177

J. von Sandrart: *Teutsche Academie* (1675–9); ed. A. R. Peltzer (1925)
C. C. Malvasia: *Felsina pittrice* (1678); ed. M. Brascaglia (1971), ii, pp. 149–99 [most detailed early biography]
G. Passeri: *Vite* (1679); ed. J. Hess (1934), pp. 260–78 [important early biography]
F. Baldinucci: *Notizie* (1681–1728); ed. F. Ranalli (1845–7), esp. iv, pp. 51–8
A. Boschetto: 'Per la conoscenza di Francesco Albani pittore', *Proporzione*, ii (1948), pp. 109–66 [important for Roman period and illustrations]
M. V. Brugnoli: 'Gli affreschi dell'Albani e del Domenichino nel Palazzo di Bassano di Sutri', *Boll. A.*, xlii (1957), pp. 266–77 [Phaeton cycle at the Palazzo Giustiniani; documents]
F. Arcangeli: 'Una gloriosa gara', *A. Ant. & Mod.*, iii–iv (1958), pp. 236–54, 354–72 [work at oratory of S Colombano]
D. Posner: 'Annibale Carracci and his School: The Paintings of the Herrera Chapel', *A. Ant. & Mod.*, xii (1960), pp. 397–412
E. van Schaack: 'An Unpublished Letter by Francesco Albani', *A. Bull.*, li (1961), pp. 72–4
M. Mahoney: 'Some Graphic Links between the Young Albani and Annibale Carracci', *Burl. Mag.*, civ (1962), pp. 386–9
G. Panofsky-Soergel: 'Zur Geschichte des Palazzo Mattei di Giove', *Röm. Jb. Kstgesch.*, xi (1967–8), pp. 109–88 [incl. documents for frescoes in Palazzo Mattei, Rome]
A. Sutherland Harris: 'Some Chalk Drawings by Francesco Albani', *Master Drgs*, vii (1969), pp. 152–5
E. van Schaack: *Francesco Albani* (diss., New York, Columbia U., 1969) [incl. cat. rais.]
L. Salerno: *Pittori del paesaggio del seicento a Roma*, 3 vols (Rome, 1977–80)
D. Benati: 'Qualche osservazione sull'attività giovanile di Francesco Albani', *Paragone*, xxxii/381 (1981), pp. 48–58
C. R. Puglisi: 'Early Works by Francesco Albani', *Paragone*, xxxii/381 (1981), pp. 26–47
N. Turner: 'Some Thoughts on Francesco Albani as a Draughtsman', *Renaissance Studies in Honor of Craig Hugh Smyth*, ed. A. Morrogh and others, 2 vols (Florence, 1985), i, pp. 493–500 [new attributions]
A. Brejon de Lavergnée: *L'Inventaire Le Brun de 1683: La Collection des tableaux de Louis XIV* (Paris, 1987) [Albani's reputation in France]
A. Brejon de Lavergnée and N. Volle: *Musées de France, répertoire des peintures italiennes du XVIII siècle* (Paris, 1988) [Albani in French public collections outside Paris]
C. R. Puglisi: *Francesco Albani* (Bologna, in preparation) [with cat. rais.]

CATHERINE R. PUGLISI

Albania [Shqipëri]. Country in south-eastern Europe, bordering the Adriatic Sea and adjacent to northern Greece. The country covers *c.* 28,500 sq. km and has a population of *c.* 3 million. The capital is Tiranë. Albania is predominantly mountainous, with a narrow zone of fertile land along the coast (see fig. 1). The coastal climate is Mediterranean, and that of the mountainous interior is more generally continental.

1. Map of Albania; those sites with separate individual entries in this dictionary are distinguished by CROSS-REFERENCE TYPE

I. Introduction. II. Architecture. III. Painting and graphic arts. IV. Sculpture. V. Interior decoration and furniture. VI. Ceramics. VII. Glass. VIII. Metalwork. IX. Textiles. X. Institutions and collections. XI. Art education.

I. Introduction.

The earliest traces of art on Albanian territory date from the beginning of the Neolithic period (6th millennium BC). During the Bronze Age (2nd millennium BC) the emergence took place of the Illyrians, whose art later flourished at the time of their independent states (5th–2nd centuries BC). The Roman occupation (167 BC–AD 395) and the Byzantine occupation were characterized by the development of Roman culture, the Hellenistic tradition and Early Christian art. At the beginning of the Middle Ages Albania remained outside the sphere of Byzantine domination. This was the period of the evolution of the Illyrian race into the Albanian people, a process that was hindered by neither the restoration of Byzantine rule (820–52) nor the long Bulgarian occupation (852–1018). In the period between the 11th and 14th centuries Albania was occupied by various powers from the West (Normans, Angevins and Venetians) as well as the East (Byzantines, Serbs and Bulgarians). After the second half of the 14th century, when these occupations came to an end, there emerged a number of Albanian feudal states, but their coalescence into a single Albanian state was impeded by the Ottoman invaders, who first penetrated Albania in 1384. The Albanians adopted Christianity as early as the 1st century AD, and at the time of the Ottoman invasion they were divided into the Orthodox Church in the south and the Roman Catholic Church in the north. Irrespective of their religious allegiances, however, Albanians of both churches united around the nationalist leader Gjergj Kastrioti (1404–68), known as Scanderbeg, and under his leadership they liberated the country and established the Albanian national state, which they defended through a 25-year struggle (1443–68). After the country fell completely under Ottoman rule (1479), many Albanians became Islamic converts in the Ottoman empire. A National Renaissance Movement, however, which began in the third quarter of the 19th century, ended with the liberation of the country and the establishment of the national state in November 1912.

Albania remained independent for less than three decades (1912–39). It lost its independence with the Italian Fascist occupation in April 1939, which was followed by the German occupation from September 1943 to November 1944. It then regained national independence but in January 1946 was proclaimed a People's Socialist Republic. Increasingly isolated in Western Europe, Albania pursued a Stalinist line under the First Secretary of the Communist Party, Enver Hoxha (1908–85), and this eventually led to a rift with the USSR. All cultural activities from 1945 were subject to strict ideological control. In 1992, however, in line with the general liberalization within the Communist bloc, Albania held free elections, and a non-Communist government gained power.

This article discusses predominantly the art and architecture of Albania from the medieval period onwards. For a discussion of the arts in earlier times *see* ROME, ANCIENT; EARLY CHRISTIAN AND BYZANTINE ART; and ISLAMIC ART.

BIBLIOGRAPHY

S. Islami and K. Frashëri: *Historia e shqipërisë* [History of Albania], 2 vols (Tiranë, 1959–65; rev. as 4 vols, 1984)

S. Anamali and others: *The History of Albania: From its Origins to the Present Day* (London and Boston, 1981)

KRISTO FRASHËRI

II. Architecture.

The barbarian migrations resulted in the destruction of many Illyrian cities, including Apollonia (now Pojan), in the first centuries of the early Middle Ages. While other cities such as Lezhë, Butrint and Durrës were rebuilt with powerful fortifications, other new cities sprang up alongside them between the 7th and 11th centuries, such as Krujë and Sardë. The castle of Petrelë, the architecture of which was typically medieval, was also built around this time. This period was also a time of construction of many small single-nave churches, such as the chapel of the amphitheatre at Durrës with its wall mosaics (10th century); some of the earlier churches were also reconstructed.

An important stage in the development of Albanian architecture was the period between the 11th and 15th centuries, when the state of Arbër, with Krujë as its capital, emerged (11th–12th centuries) and the Albanian principalities flourished (13th–14th centuries) with centres in Berat, Shkodër, Gjirokastër, Lezhë, Durrës, Kaninë and elsewhere. The technology of building fortifications was improved further, and new defensive architectural elements were introduced, such as fortified courtyards, loopholes for missiles, machicolations and complicated gates with many doors and long galleries. The cities and large castles had internal walls dividing the acropolis (the residence of the family of the feudal lord) from the rest of the buildings. With the invention of firearms, architectural innovations were introduced, possibly earlier than in some other European countries, in Albanian castles such as Krujë, Petrelë, Kep i Rodonit and Stelush, where important battles were fought against Ottoman armies during the 15th century. The churches of this period were also noted for their sophisticated architecture. They were basically Byzantine in style (*see* EARLY CHRISTIAN AND BYZANTINE ART, §II, 2(iii)), with some examples, such as St Mary in Pojan, distinguished as variants on the design of the basilica with a single dome on a tall drum, while St Nicholas in Mesopotam is notable for its apses. New types of Byzantine architecture, based on the domed cross-in-square plan, were introduced in southern Albania, and elements of Romanesque and Gothic architecture appeared in northern Albania, for example the Good Friday Church in Kavajë. The extent of architectural activity in the 13th and 14th centuries is reflected in the large number of churches, represented by examples from the Komnenian and Palaeologan dynasties or in the Romanesque and Gothic styles. In central Albania, however, these churches appear with special local features, forming a synthesis of the two styles of architecture. The Albanian schools of architecture of the time, such as those on the northern coast at Durrës and Berat, were apparently trying to fulfil the demands of the Albanian princes for the creation of a church with an Albanian religious outlook that would help to unite the population.

After Ottoman occupation (1384–1479) and the introduction of Islam, such new cities as Tiranë (1614) were established, and new quarters were built outside the fortified centres of medieval towns. These new town centres, found throughout Albania, contained new building types, of which the most important was the congregational mosque (e.g. the King Mosque, Berat, 1492; the Mirahori Mosque, Korçë, 1496; and the Market Mosque, Krujë, 1533), which often formed the centrepiece of a complex of buildings (Alb. *kullie*; *see* KÜLLIYE). These included such charitable and commercial institutions as schools and markets and often became the architectural symbol of the new city centres. As elsewhere in the Ottoman empire, mosques were of two types: those covered with a wooden roof and tiles, where priority was given to wooden decoration on the interior, and domed mosques, where the monumental character of the exterior was emphasized. Although the plans might have been sent from the Ottoman capital at Constantinople (now Istanbul), the projects were realized by local masters with local systems of construction and decoration. Some of these projects may have been designed by Ottoman architects of Albanian origin, such as MEHMED AĞA or KASIM AĞA, who had been reunited as children in the Ottoman janissary corps and who trained in engineering and design. There is evidence beginning in the 16th century that practitioners from the imperial corps of architects (*see* ISLAMIC ART, §II, 7(i)(a)) worked in the main cities.

Many Islamic and Christian religious buildings were erected between the 17th and 19th centuries. Local architecture reflected the Baroque and Neo-classical spirit popular in the Ottoman capital. The most monumental type of mosque had a hemispheric dome covered with lead sheets, a deep hypostyle porch and elegant, slender minarets. Among the classic examples are the Helveti sufi hospice (Turk. *tekke*) in Berat, built in 1782, and the mosque of Ethem Bey (1821) in Tiranë. Efforts were also made to create a representative type of Christian architecture, with single-nave, cross-shaped churches with a cupola, and with basilicas with a cupola and arches. Albanian Christian architecture flourished in the 18th century, with the introduction of new structural solutions and Baroque and Neo-classical decorations. Among the finest examples are the church of St Nicholas (1721) in Voskopojë and the church of the monastery of Ardenicë (1731). From the period of the National Renaissance in the late 19th century, the construction of religious buildings declined. Seeking autonomy, the Albanian pashas of the 18th and 19th centuries concentrated on the construction of fortifications, bridges and aqueducts. Built by such Albanian architects as PETRO KORÇARI, these fortifications reflect a thorough knowledge of the technology of construction and of the military architecture of the time.

The seraglios of the pashas, for example at Shkodër, Krujë, Vlorë and Berat, were a synthesis of a rich and powerful architectural tradition. There were also various types of two- and three-storey urban houses for the middle classes. Among the most notable variants are the houses, with a central porch and balcony, as found in parts of Berat (see fig. 2), and the tall, thick-walled houses associated with Gjirokastër. One of the most characteristic types is the fortified house from northern Albania known as the 'Albanian tower', with a closed, hermetic structure.

By the end of the 19th century and the first decades of the 20th, Albanian architecture had changed radically with the introduction of new building materials. In the 1920s and 1940s public buildings were greatly influenced by Western architecture, and the lyrical, functional aspect of the interior was often accompanied by excessive Rococo-inspired decoration on the exterior. After World War II Albanian architecture assumed a new character, largely determined by the dictates of the State. Until the 1960s, such architects as ANTON LUFI and SKËNDER LUARASI, and after them Eqerem Dobi, Besim Daja and others, who founded the basic concepts of modern Albanian urban planning in some reconstructed cities, made possible the design of uniform housing complexes and harmonized their modern buildings with the inherited urban surroundings. They also sought a functional–aesthetic compositional unity in individual public buildings that had been lacking in the architecture of the past, and a modern national style (e.g. Lufi's Migjeni Theatre, Shkodër, 1957). In the period from 1960 to 1980 other architects such as Valentina Pistoli, SOKRAT MOSKO, Petraq Kolevica and Enver Faja were distinguished for their further experiments with a rationalist Functionalism and the creation of a traditional plasticity, characterized by the emphasis of volumes on the façade, geometrical decorations and a contrast of light and shade (for example the Great Palace of Culture, Tiranë, 1965). In the 1980s young architects of the Albanian school designed such monumental social buildings as the Palace of Congresses (1986; designed by Dobi, Mosko and others) and the International Centre of Culture (1988; formerly the Enver Hoxha Museum), both in Tiranë.

2. Berat, Albania, the Mangalem city quarter

UNPUBLISHED SOURCES

Tiranë, U., Archvs Chair Archit., MS. [*Historia e arkitekturës shqiptare* ('History of Albanian architecture')]

BIBLIOGRAPHY

Shqipëria arkeologjike [Archaeological Albania], Tiranë, N. Mus. Archaeol. cat. (Tiranë, 1971)

Monumente të arkitekturës në Shqipëri [Architectural monuments in Albania], Institute of Cultural Monuments (Tiranë, 1973)

S. Anamali: 'Antikiteti i vonë dhe mesjeta e hershme në kërkimet shqiptare' [Late antiquity and the early Middle Ages in Albanian research], *Iliria* (1979–80), nos 9–10, pp. 5–21

E. Riza: 'Arkitektura popullore në qytetet tona gjatë shek. XVIII–XIX' [Folk urban architecture in the 18th–19th centuries], *Kult. Pop.* (1980), no. 2, pp. 13–27

G. Karaiskaj: *5000 vjet fortifikime në Shqipëri* [5000 years of fortifications in Albania] (Tiranë, 1981)

G. Frashëri: 'Y a-t-il une architecture albanaise au moyen-âge?: Entretien avec le couple Buschauzen', *Lett. Alb.* (1983), no. 4, pp. 154–81

A. Meksi: *Arkitektura mesjetare në Shqipëri* [Medieval architecture in Albania] (Tiranë, 1983)

G. Frashëri and S. Dashi: 'Zhvillimi i arkitekturës islamike shqiptare të xhamive: Probleme të periudhizimit' [The development of Albanian mosque architecture: problems of division into periods], *Monumentet* (1986), no. 2, pp. 51–76

GJERGJ FRASHËRI

III. Painting and graphic arts.

Few traces remain of Albanian painting of the early Middle Ages. However, the fact that anthropomorphic miniatures had already been introduced in the illustrations of such sacred books as the 9th–10th-century Codices of Berat (Tiranë, Cent. Archvs) points to a general development in post-iconoclastic painting. Between the 11th and 14th centuries Albanian monumental religious painting was transformed in both the Orthodox south and the Roman Catholic north. The broad development of the art of painting, especially that in the style associated with the PALAEOLOGAN dynasty, is illustrated by, for example, the paintings of the ensemble of the monastery of the church of St Mary in Apollonia (now Pojan). The wall painting of the monastery's refectory (late 13th century) points to close links with such major centres as Durrës, as well as using local features. Most icon and wall painters of the period remain anonymous, although documents mention a painter called Gjon from Durrës (14th century), and the name Stano is preserved beside the 14th-century painting in the cave of Kosharisht, Librazhd. The names of some

3. Abdurrahim Buza: *Azem Galica Breaking through the Encirclement*, oil on canvas, 450×540 mm, 1976 (Tiranë, Art Gallery)

calligraphers are also known, such as Minaj of the 14th-century Codex 10 of Vlorë and those of the 12th–15th-century Codices of Berat written on parchment (both Tiranë, State Archvs).

In the first period after the Ottoman occupation the walls and iconostases of the few small churches built in remote zones were decorated with paintings reflecting the resistance of the population to Islamicization and assimilation. Several talented painters emerged at this period, who produced remarkable works based on Byzantine tradition. One of these was Master Onufri of Berat, whose creative activity reached its peak by the middle of the 16th century in the Good Friday Church (1554) in Valësh, near Elbasan, and his son Nikolla, who worked in the church of St Mary of Vllaherna (1576) in Berat.

The nationalist movement of the 18th century in Albania gave Albanian painting a new direction. Religious paintings lost their hieratic character and mysticism and tended towards a more direct depiction of nature. The figure of the merchant *Haxhi Jorgji* (1726) in the church of St Nicholas in Voskopojë, near Korçë, as well as many other subjects of the paintings of David Selenica of Vlorë (*fl* 1715–27) and his assistant Kristo Kostandini, are depicted in a more earthly manner, with a more realistic sense of light and colour. The influence of the European Baroque style is seen in the 18th century in the works of such church painters as Kostandin Jeromonaku, Kostandin Shpataraku, the brothers Kostandin Zografi and Athanas Zografi (both *fl* 1744–83) from Korçë, and, in the early 19th century, in that of the painters of the Kadro family. Islamic decorative painting also developed greatly in the 17th to 19th centuries, with mosques and other Islamic religious buildings decorated with arabesques and floral and architectural motifs combined with landscapes. The same painters often worked in both churches and mosques, judging by the similarity of the palette and the structure of the compositions (e.g. the painting, 1822–3, of the mosque of Ethem Bey in Tiranë; see fig. 5 below). The interiors and façades of town houses were also often painted.

The National Renaissance Movement, after the middle of the 19th century, introduced secular subjects. Characteristic of the painting of this period is the treatment both of national historical subjects, depicted in a Romantic, patriotic spirit, and of topical themes. The medieval national hero Scanderbeg, who was depicted by SPIRO XEGA and others as a symbol of the struggle for independence, was a source of inspiration for history painters, while other artists concentrated on the daily life, social activity and psychological make-up of ordinary people, as in *Sister Tone* (1883; Tiranë, A.G.) by KOL IDROMENO, a landmark in Albanian Realist portraiture. Graphic arts also developed in the period of the National Renaissance Movement. Interest in the psychology and social life of the Albanian people became increasingly important for the painters of the National Renaissance in the early 20th century, including Idromeno, Xega, NDOC MARTINI and later SIMON RROTA, VANGJUSH MIO, ZEF KOLOMBI and others. Their works were notable for their identification with the suffering of the poor, and for their critical sense of Realism. Their Impressionist style, occasionally with formalist or folk tendencies, represented a transitional period in their development as Realists. Their view of daily life and customs was increasingly optimistic, as in Idromeno's *Shkodër Wedding* (1924; Tiranë, A.G.). Their landscapes, too, reflected their sensitivity to natural surroundings allied to a critical attitude. In the 1930s Albanian painting further consolidated its Realist style, and it was at this period that such painters as ABDURRAHIM BUZA, SADIK KACELI and the sisters Sofia Zengo and Androniqi Zengo (*b* 1913), the first Albanian women Realist painters, began their careers.

After World War II, when Albania became a People's Socialist Republic, Albanian painters began to treat a much wider range of subjects, generally in a Socialist Realist style. Although all genres appear, special importance was devoted to figure compositions and graphic art. The painters of the pre-war period continued their activity (e.g. Abdurrahim Buza: *Azem Galica Breaking through the Encirclement*; see fig. 3), and new painters emerged in the 1960s, including Bukurosh Sejdini (*b* 1916), Kel Kodheli (*b* 1918) and Guri Madhi (1921–88), who produced dramatic treatments of Albanian heroism in war and optimistic depictions of reconstruction. From 1960 to 1980 the work of such painters as SALI SHIJAKU, FATMIR HAXHIU and PANDI MELE was characterized by its realist and dynamic draughtsmanship, poetic treatment and rich colours, exploiting strong light and graphic contrast. Graphic art, too, was distinguished for its expressive lines, balance of tone and modest, laconic temperament. In the 1980s Albanian painting assumed monumental dimensions, especially in such wall frescoes as *Partisan Attack* (1981; Tiranë, N. Hist. Mus.) by Sali Shijaku (*b* 1933) and Myrteza Fushekati (*b* 1942) and in such works as *Confrontation* (1982; Krujë, Nat. Mus. Scanderbeg) and the *Assembly of Dukagjin* (1986; Burrel, Hist. Mus.) by NAXHI BAKALLI. With political liberalization, Socialist Realism lost its State-sponsored primacy, with the result that Albanian painting began to develop more freely, some artists seeking to assimilate modern European artistic developments and others endeavouring to re-create links with the earlier tradition of Albanian Realist art.

BIBLIOGRAPHY

V. Puzanova: 'Piktori shqiptar i shek. XVI Onufri nga Neokastra (Elbasan)' [The Albanian painter of the 16th century, Onufri of Neokastra (Elbasan)], *Bul. Shkencat Shoqërore* (1953), no. 3, pp. 8–25

——: 'Shënime mbi artin shqiptar në shek. XVIII' [Notes on Albanian art of the 18th century], *Bul. Shkencat Shoqërore* (1957), no. 1, pp. 44–62

D. Dhamo: 'Mbi karakterin kombëtar dhe realist të arteve tona figurative' [On the national and Realist character of our figurative art], *Stud. Hist.* (1971), no. 2, pp. 23–41

——: *La Peinture murale du moyen âge en Albanie* (Tiranë, 1974)

Artet figurative shqiptare [Albanian figurative arts] (Tiranë, 1978)

K. Buza: 'Artet figurative në rrugën e zhvillimit' [Figurative arts in development], *Nëntori* (1984), no. 6, pp. 67–73

D. Dhamo: 'Vepra dhe tipare të pikturës në Shqipëri në shek. X–XV' [Works and features of Albanian painting of the 10th–15th centuries], *Stud. Hist.* (1984), no. 1

A. Kuqali: 'Thellimi i frymës popullore dhe i tipareve të reja kombëtare forcon militantizmin e arteve figurative' [A more powerful national spirit and new national features consolidate the militant spirit of figurative arts], *Nëntori* (1984), no. 6, pp. 141–6

DHORKA DHAMO, ANDON KUQALI

IV. Sculpture.

During the Middle Ages and the period of the Ottoman occupation the human figure scarcely appeared in sculpture, although there are traces in the religious scenes found in wooden decorative sculpture of the 17th to the 19th centuries in the iconostases and pulpits of churches and in the ceilings and latticed lofts of houses, the latter amid a wealth of floral decorations and bird and animal motifs. It was not until the National Renaissance Movement, associated with the struggle for independence, that the human figure was reintroduced into sculpture, as in the two Romantically inspired busts of *Scanderbeg* by MURAD TOPTANI (1899 and 1917; Tiranë, A.G.). Modern Albanian Realist sculpture was developed in the 1920s and 1930s by ODHISE PASKALI and such sculptors as JANAQ PAÇO and LLAZAR NIKOLLA, whose careers began around this time. Such works as Paskali's statue of the *National Fighter* (1932; Vlorë, central square) and his bust of *Scanderbeg* (1939; Tiranë, A.G.) represent the first efforts to emphasize the patriotism and other virtues of the Albanian national character.

After World War II and the establishment of the People's Socialist Republic, sculpture flourished. Up to the 1960s it was characterized by the treatment of historical subjects, depicting outstanding Albanian personalities who fought for national liberation in the Middle Ages and World War II. The sculptors of this period were noted for their monumental works, such as Paço's bust of *Qemal Stafa* (1949) in Qemal Stafa Square, Tiranë, and his equestrian statue of *Scanderbeg* in the central square of Krujë (see fig. 4). From 1960 to 1980 the Socialist Realist style of modern Albanian sculpture was consolidated by such sculptors as SHABAN HADËRI, KRISTAQ RAMA, MUNTAZ DHRAMI and others. Works such as Dhrami's *Keep High the Revolutionary Spirit* (1966; Tiranë, A.G.) were noted for an expressive realism, popular characterization, dynamic movements of large forms and inspired revolutionary pathos. There were also many successful memorial reliefs and many Realist portraits. The 1980s were characterized by a growth of monumental sculpture used in architecture, and by many statues and sculptural groups erected in the parks and squares of Albanian cities.

4. Janaq Paço: *Scanderbeg*, bronze, h. 6 m, 1949–55, central square, Krujë

BIBLIOGRAPHY

Shqipëria arkeologjike [Archaeological Albania], Tiranë, N. Mus. Archaeol. cat. (Tiranë, 1971)

Monumente të arkitekturës në Shqipëri [Architectural monuments in Albania], Institute of Cultural Monuments (Tiranë, 1973)

Përmendore të heroizmit shqiptar [Monuments of Albanian heroism] (Tiranë, 1973)

G. Frashëri: 'Enigma e tre relievëve' [The enigma of three reliefs], *Drita* (20 Nov 1983), pp. 11–12

L. Blido: *Shënime për pikturën dhe skulpturën* [Notes on painting and sculpture] (Tiranë, 1987)

Albanien: Schätze aus dem Land der Skipetaren (Mainz, 1988)

V. Interior decoration and furniture.

Interior decoration from the 11th to the 15th century can be studied through church architecture. Churches were usually in Romanesque or Gothic style in the north, Byzantine style in the south and a synthesis of the two in central Albania. Parallel influences of the West and the East are visible in carved reliefs in religious institutions and in the houses of feudal landowners; these show a marked stylization of such heraldic motifs as eagles, lions, wolves and such mythological beasts as the griffin, illustrated for example in the emblems of the Arbër Principality (marble, 12th century) and the Topia Family (stone, 14th century; both Tiranë, N. Mus. Archaeol.). Mosaics, used since the 1st century AD, continued to be employed to decorate church floors. Icons were encased in ornamental wood iconostases (e.g. 14th century; Maligrad, St Mary). The interiors of churches and some palaces were decorated with wall paintings. The majority of these works were Byzantine in character, even in Roman Catholic churches in the north and on the coast, as illustrated by the murals in Vau i Dejës church (12th century) and in the church of the Saviour Monastery in Rubik (1272).

From 14th- and 15th-century paintings it is possible to glean information about the furniture of the period. Among many storage devices are remarkable folding shelves, richly carved with classical motifs and painted with angels, ornamental crosses, eagles and floral patterns. Paintings of church and house interiors depict glazed ceramics and decorative metal objects. Chronicles of the period describe elaborate decoration in the halls of feudal lords, which included tapestries, embroideries and other costly fabrics.

Following the Ottoman occupation of Albania, in the 15th century interior decoration and furniture-making came under the enriching influence of Islamic culture. Mural and icon painting, however, continued in the Byzantine tradition, albeit with refinements. Concurrently with Christian church building there was an extensive programme of building mosques, the interiors of which were decorated with arabesque and landscape paintings (see fig. 5).

The richest interior in Albanian homes from the 17th to the 19th century was in the guest room, which sported painted doors, ceilings with rosettes and elaborate built-in cupboards. In pashas' palaces and the homes of rich citizens it was usual for the ceiling and the chimneys to be ornamented with plaster reliefs, while the floors were covered with carpets and animal skins. Windows were decorated with multicoloured fragments of glass. Pillows, tablecloths and curtains were elaborately embroidered. Guns and musical instruments adorned the walls. The finest objects were crafted from gold, silver and copper and were displayed on shelves and dressers around the room.

It was not until the period of the independent pashaliks in the late 18th century that Neo-classicism influenced interior decoration in Albania. This was most vividly expressed in the stonework of columns, capitals, window-frames and door-frames. The tradition of highly skilled craftsmanship in wood continued, particularly in the districts of Dibër, Shpirag (near Berat) and Konica (near Korçë). The masters of Dibër were distinguished for their pine and oak ceilings, verandahs, porches, halls, shelves and doors; their work is recognizable by the predominance of botanical (especially oak-leaf) and geometric motifs and stylized figures. The masters from Shpirag worked mainly in elm, preferring foliate motifs, trees and half-opened rosebuds for decorative effects. Most of their work was produced for houses in the towns of Berat, Tiranë and Gjirokastër. In Konica master craftsmen produced fine walnut furniture and iconostases, characterized by deep carving and attention to detail, both for use in Albania (e.g. iconostasis, early 19th century; Sopik, St Mary) and for export to Greece.

During the 19th century and in the first decades of the 20th such influences as the Baroque and later the Rococo were evident in Albanian interior decoration. In the 1920s the first machinery for mass producing furniture was imported into Albania; the vast majority of furniture,

5. Wall painting, Ethem Bey Mosque, Tiranë, 1822–3

however, continued to be handmade. After World War II there was a marked growth in the production of furniture and interior-design goods; one of the most notable furniture makers was BURHAN ISHMAKU. Demands for better living standards from a growing urban population made it necessary to create specialized departments for the production of furniture and interior architectural elements. The two largest industrial centres were the Misto Mame Woodwork Combine (est. 1947) in Tiranë, producing various types of furniture and tiles, and the Woodwork Combine in Elbasan (est. 1952), making decorative veneers, chairs and tables etc.

BIBLIOGRAPHY

Mosaïques de l'Albanie, Institute of Cultural Monuments (Tiranë, 1973)

Monumente të arkitekturës në Shqipëri [Architectural monuments in Albania] (Tiranë, 1974)

F. Shkupi: 'Tipari popullor i zbukurimores së banesës shkodrane' [Folk characteristics in the decoration of houses in Shkodër], *Monumentet* (1980), no. 20, pp. 105–26

G. Frashëri: 'Y a-t-il une architecture albanaise au moyen-âge?: Entretien avec le couple Buschauzen', *Lett. Alb.* (1983), no. 4, pp. 154–81

Z. Shkodra: *Qyteti shqiptar gjatë Rilindjes Kombëtare* [The Albanian town during the National Renaissance Movement] (Tiranë, 1984), pp. 89–162, 351–427

F. Shkupi: 'Zbukurimorja e disa banesave gjirokastrite' [Decoration in houses of Gjirokastër], *Monumentet* (1986), no. 2, pp. 99–116

Albanien: Schätze aus dem Land der Skipetaren (Mainz, 1988)

VI. Ceramics.

In the 15th century, during the Ottoman occupation of Albania, ceramic manufacture suffered an artistic decline. Pottery survived as a peasant craft with the production of such utilitarian wares as earthenware dishes, cups, cooking pots and dairy and oil jars mainly made by women; these wares resemble early Illyrian and Arbër pottery. From the 16th century there was a considerable development in ceramics especially in Shkodër, Prizren (now in Kosovo, Serbia), Elbasan, Berat, Kavajë, Gjakevë, Pejë, Dibër, Korçë, Tiranë, Gjirokastër and Vlorë. Terracotta tobacco pipes with a variety of low-relief decoration and multicoloured glazes, faience candleholders, cult objects, glazed plates and small, children's cups with natural motifs were produced. In the village of German in the Mat Valley ceramics were hand-moulded up to the early 20th century; in Gojan (near Pukë) and Farkë (near Tiranë) potters used hand-turned wheels; and in Bradvicë and Kavajë kick-wheels and multicoloured glazes were used. The elegant shapes of the pottery of Kavajë, the decoration of the jugs of Bradvicë and the pleasing proportions of the Farkë pottery wares are typical of Albanian ceramics produced between the 19th century and 1939.

After World War II, State pottery enterprises were established in Kavajë (1948) and Tiranë (1950), followed in the 1950s by the ceramic factory in Kavajë and the Porcelain Factory in Tiranë (both 1959). Traditional ceramics with an emphasis on function rather than decoration were produced in Kavajë. Special workshops opened in the 1960s and 1970s in Tiranë, Korçë, Vlorë, Krujë and Shkodër. The products of Tiranë include vases, flower pots, dinner services and decorative plates. In Vlorë traditional, simply shaped terracotta vases are made in biscuit or colourfully decorated with animals and figures in folk costumes in multicoloured glazes. Production in Korçë specializes in decorative ceramics for interiors with motifs from folklore and contemporary life. Examples of the use of architectural ceramics include the unglazed terracotta panelling on the exterior of the Partizani Sports Palace in Tiranë (1963), the grey-glazed, mosaic-like ceramic panelling on the exterior of the Art Gallery (1976) in Tiranë by Dhimo Gogollari (1931–87) and the *Maize Harvest* (1982), by Fatmira Kuçuku, with glazed multicoloured ceramic tiles, in the interior of the restaurant of the Youth Park in Tiranë.

BIBLIOGRAPHY

D. Komata: 'Disa tipare të qeramikës mesjetare në Shqipëri' [Some features of medieval ceramics in Albania], *Ilirët dhe gjeneza e Shqiptarëve: Tirane, 1968* [The Illyrians and the genesis of the Albanians: Tiranë, 1968], pp. 221–43

K. Krisiko: 'Qeramika artistike në arkitekturë' [Artistic ceramics in architecture], *Drita* (23 Nov 1980)

M. Turkeshi: 'Qeramika dhe jeta' [Ceramics and life], *Nëntori* (1984), no. 6, pp. 292–5

VII. Glass.

The first glass production in Albania dates from the early Middle Ages, with glass-bead necklaces made in the Arbër glassworks (6th–8th century). Stained glass was used in the windows of religious buildings and in dormer windows of urban houses. Multicoloured glass panes and partitions decorated with vegetable or geometric motifs and arabesques were used from the 16th century in the interiors of religious buildings (mosques, churches, *tekkes*) and in the palaces of feudal lords. After World War II the first state glassworks were set up: glassware was produced in the specialized workshops of the Tiranë Glass Factory (1957), the Kavajë Glassworks (1970) and the Korçë Glass and Ceramics Factory, which were all managed by their own design departments, composed of state-trained painters and sculptors. In the late 20th century glass partitions, which often feature compositions of folk motifs combined with elements of contemporary life, became popular in the interiors of public buildings.

GJERGJ FRASHËRI

VIII. Metalwork.

Decorative metalwork developed in Albania from the 15th century following the Ottoman occupation. From the 16th century such cities as Shkodër, Prizren (now in Kosovo, Serbia), Elbasan, Berat, Gjakevë, Pejë, Dibër, Tiranë, Korçë, Krujë and Gjirokastër were important centres for the production of religious objects, weapons and functional and decorative pieces; these were made in copper, silver and gold, inlaid with precious stones. From the 17th century silversmithing in particular flourished in these centres, with the production of jewellery, weapons, household utensils, religious objects, toiletry boxes, trays, cup holders and cigarette boxes. Albanian silversmiths were skilled in such techniques as chasing, beating, casting and filigree. In the 18th and 19th centuries Albanian silversmiths were recognized as specialists in openwork filigree. In some cities silversmiths set up communities: in the 18th century in Shkodër there were about 100 silversmiths, and in Elbasan there were 60.

Traditional weaponry assumed new features with the production of rifles, pistols, scimitars, daggers, cartouches and cartridge belts. The Albanian flintlock rifle (17–19 mm calibre), known as either the *karaifilja* or the *arnautka*, was inlaid with beaten or cast gold plates decorated with national emblems. In northern Albania the plates were filigreed and gilt, while in southern Albania they were cast by the 'savat' technique, seen for example on an 18th-century *karaifilja* (Tiranë, N. Hist. Mus.) decorated with zoomorphic, vegetable and anthropomorphic motifs. The hilts of scimitars were of ivory inlaid with coral and silver. Silver pistols produced in Shkodër in the 17th century were cast and engraved with stylized vegetal reliefs. The handles were shaped like serpent heads, inlaid with gilt silver plates. The gunsmiths of Elbasan and Berat were noted for their original decorations on iron, brass and silver cartouches and cartridge belts. Gunsmiths who became well known in the Balkans and in the Middle East were Hasan Tetova (*fl* 17th century), Osman Ali Dibra (*fl* 17th century), Ali Harkova from Grabova in Gramsh (*fl* 17th century), Tush Mirdita (*fl* 18th century), Ali Tetova (*fl* late 18th–early 19th century) and JAKUP DIBRA. Weapons were an integral part of Albanian costume until the beginning of the 20th century, when production gradually declined as a result of European competition.

After World War II metalworking was organized into a state-run system. Production was initially concentrated in Handicraft Cooperatives, followed by the establishment of the first artistic products enterprise in Tiranë in 1966 (*see* TIRANË). Further enterprises were opened in other cities for the production of articles for interior decoration, furniture and jewellery, made from designs by artists trained in the applied arts. Late 20th-century Albanian metalwork was characterized by its reliance on tradition, although there was an increased range of art forms, techniques and media (iron, copper, aluminium and bronze, inlaid with wood, glass, ceramics etc), and Socialist Realist decorative motifs were introduced.

BIBLIOGRAPHY

R. Drishti: *Armët dhe armëtarët shqiptarë* [Albanian weapons and gunsmiths] (Tiranë, 1976)

L. Mitrushi: 'Punimi i argjendarisë' [Silverwork], *Konferenca Kombëtare e Studimeve Etnografike: Tiranë, 1976* [National conference of ethnographic studies: Tiranë, 1976]

Z. Shkodra: *Qyteti shqiptar gjatë Rilindjes Kombëtare* [The Albanian town during the National Renaissance Movement] (Tiranë, 1984), pp. 139–57

SULEJMAN DASHI

IX. Textiles.

The oldest surviving textile fragment from Albania is the 'Glavinica Epitaph', a linen shroud embroidered with silk, gold and silver thread (1373; Tiranë, N. Hist. Mus.). The image on the cloth is possibly a Pietà, with Christ recumbent and the Virgin Mary, St John the Baptist, the Evangelists, prophets and angels in attendance; it is accompanied by an inscription. The shroud was presented to the Orthodox monastery in Ballsh by two Albanian princes, Gjergj I Balsha (*reg* 1372–9) and Balsha II Balsha (*reg* 1379–85), who in the 14th century attempted to create a unified Albanian state. From the 14th to the 16th century imported red, violet and green velvet, embroidered with gold, silver and silk thread, was made into luxury garments for noble families. The master tailors who produced these garments also embroidered imported undyed cotton cloth. The locally produced type of hat worn by Albanian soldiers later came to be used as part of the military uniform of other Western European armies.

During the Ottoman occupation of the 15th century many Oriental textiles were introduced, but by the middle of the 16th century indigenous textile production had accelerated markedly and was able to compete with imports. Most of the textiles were woven on horizontal looms with two or four reeds. The simpler form of loom was used to make cloth for aprons, carpets, blankets and rugs. The more advanced form made possible the weaving of twills and double warps for heavier cloths and more complex patterns for jackets, waistcoats, trousers, tunics, pouches and saddle-bags. The majority of master weavers were women. The textiles produced in the 16th to 19th centuries featured a variety of designs. In rural areas decorative geometric patterns were prevalent, while in the towns and cities plant and animal motifs predominated. The most common colour was red, contrasted with black or violet. The most popular motifs were the sun (the source of life); the snake (loyalty to ancestors); the dragon and the hydra (symbols of good and evil); a head of wheat (fertility); a pitcher, tray and coffee-cup (hospitality); and the Cross, grapes, doves and the moon (religious symbols).

Differences in dress helped to identify the region from which the wearer came, and by the 19th century there were no less than 140 different types of embroidered folk costume. Women's costumes were the most elaborately decorated, particularly the blouses, embroidered with silk and cotton around the neck, breasts and sleeves, the headdresses and the aprons. Outer garments (*zhupja* or *cibun*), for both men and women, were noted for their elaborate embroidery and red and multicoloured braids. The embroidery was worked domestically and also in town workshops. Silk fabrics were in great demand in the first half of the 19th century in Austria and Lombardy for their delicate designs and rich colours. They were produced in Shkodër, then the most important centre for silk production and trade in the Balkans, and were used for women's blouses and baggy trousers, and for coats that were often embroidered with gold and silver thread. Coarse felt was an important traditional textile product used for peasants' and shepherds' coats, and also for lighter garments. It was sold in the markets of Turkey and in the Mediterranean countries. At the end of the 19th century the towns of Korçë, Prizren (now in Kosovo, Serbia) and Monastir (now Bitola, Former Yugoslav Republic of Macedonia) produced over one million metres of felt a year, and Prizren alone had seventy felt workshops. Felt was still being produced in Korçë at the end of the 20th century.

Carpets, rugs and blankets were other main exports—fringed blankets from southern Albania were exhibited at the Exposition Universelle of 1855 in Paris. There were seven basic carpet designs: the 'Korçë', with a red or blue background decorated with wheels, discs, coffee-cups and mosques; the 'Luma', which usually had a pink background decorated with stylized plant motifs (these carpets had a long, dense pile like a clothes-brush); the 'Dibër', with a red background, stylized figures and geometric patterns; the 'Labëria', with animal motifs on different-coloured backgrounds (made in two halves stitched together); the 'Tiranë Highland', which was predominantly red with primitive designs; the 'Krasniqa', which had an unusual asymmetric, dense decoration that tended to obscure the background colour; and the 'Vallach', with a light blue or brown background and elegant designs. Most of the rugs produced in Albania were used for covering the floors of mosques, and many bore the image of the mihrab. In 1946 eight women master weavers in Korçë established what was later (1967) named the '8 March' Carpet Enterprise, which produced rugs and carpets in traditional styles, mainly for export.

In the first decades of the 20th century industrial machinery was introduced. After World War II, state textile handicraft cooperatives were set up in many Albanian towns, notably the textile combines in Tiranë and Berat, the 'Hammer and Sickle' knitwear combine in Korçë and the fabrics factory in Shkodër. At the end of the 20th century handmade textiles were still being produced alongside industrial textiles in Tiranë, Krujë, Shkodër, Korçë and Kavajë (see fig. 6).

BIBLIOGRAPHY

A. Viquesnel: *Voyage dans la Turquie d'Europe* (Paris, 1868), i, pp. 302–7
Popular Art in Albania (Tiranë, 1959)
Qilimat Shqiptarë [Albanian carpets] (Tiranë, 1959)
A. Gjergji: 'Données sur l'habillement des siècles XIV–XV en Albanie', *Stud. Alb.*, ii (1967), pp. 127–34
——: 'Mbi disa analogji shqiptaro-rumane në veshjet popullore' [Comparisons of Albanian and Romanian folk costume], *Stud. Hist.*, ii (1967), pp. 115–26
——: 'Elemente të përbashkëta të veshjes së fiseve të ndryshme ilire dhe vazhdimësia e tyre në veshjet tona popullore' [Common elements in the garments of Illyrian tribes and their survival in Albanian folk costume], *Stud. Hist.*, ii (1969), pp. 145–54
I. Bihiku: 'Për një shfrytëzim më të drejtë të motiveve tona popullore në tekstilet e artizanatit' [For a better use of folk motifs in craft textiles], *Etnog. Shqiptarë*, iv (1972), pp. 75–81
A. Dojaku and A. Gjergji: 'Rezultatet e punës në fushën e etnografisë gjatë 25 vjetëve' [Results of work in ethnography over 25 years], *Etnog. Shqiptarë*, iv (1972), pp. 3–18
Qilima shqiptarë të bëra me dorë [Albanian handmade carpets], Chamber of Foreign Trade of PSR of Albania (Tiranë, 1978)
Sixhade shqiptarë të bëra me dorë [Albanian handmade rugs], Chamber of Foreign Trade of PSR of Albania (Tiranë, 1978)
Z. Shkodra: *Qyteti shqiptar gjatë Rilindjes Kombëtare* [The Albanian town during the National Renaissance Movement] (Tiranë, 1984), pp. 113 38

GJERGJ FRASHËRI

X. Institutions and collections.

The first known collectors of art were the rulers of the Albanian pashaliks of the Ottoman empire in the last quarter of the 18th century and the first quarter of the 19th, such as Kurt Pasha (*d* 1787) in Berat, Ali Pasha Tepelenë (1740–1822) in Ioánnina (now in Greece) and Kara Mehmed Bushatli (1796–1860) in Shkodër, who collected mainly works of decorative and applied arts. The first known collector of antique figurative art was Mustafa Pasha Vlora (*d* 1894) in Vlorë, who was followed by Shtjefën Gjeçovi (1873–1929) in Gomsiqe and Kol Idromeno in Shkodër, the first collecting Illyrian artefacts and the second contemporary Albanian paintings. Since in Albania art collecting was sporadic and late in development, the public display of works of art was largely dependent on state initiatives in periods of independence. The first state-organized effort to open a museum of

6. Carpet (wall hanging) by Z. Erzeni: *Our Children*, 1.65×2.40 m, 1980 (Tiranë, Art Gallery)

works of art was made in Tiranë in 1922 but was short-lived for lack of funds. The earliest national exhibition of figurative art in Albania, however, was held in Tiranë in 1931 on the initiative of the sculptor Odhise Paskali and the painters Andrea Kushi and Abdurrahim Buza. The first museum to be opened after World War II, when Albania became a People's Socialist Republic, was the Archaeological–Ethnographic Museum (founded 1948) in Tiranë, on the basis of which the National Museum of Archaeology in Tiranë was set up, as well as three local archaeological museums, in Durrës, Pojan and Butrint, displaying objects of antique and medieval figurative, decorative and applied arts. By this time the state had taken possession of all works in private collections. In 1952 the Pinakoteka was opened in Tiranë, where hundreds of paintings of the 19th and 20th centuries inherited from previous public or private collections and paintings by contemporary Albanian artists were deposited. Two years later it was replaced by the Gallery of Figurative Art, also in Tiranë, which became the main institution for the collection, exhibition, promotion and study of figurative and decorative works by Albanian painters and sculptors, with *c.* 3500 works in its collection. Galleries of figurative art were later opened in other cities, while permanent sales exhibitions made it possible for citizens to create personal collections of works by Albanian artists, and works of applied art were sold in art and craft shops. Various state cultural institutions periodically opened thematic or individual exhibitions of works of art.

The Museum of Medieval Art (1980) in Korçë has a rich collection of religious paintings and icons from the 12th to the 18th centuries, as well as religious objects in stone, wood and silver. The main centres for the display of modern and contemporary fine and applied arts are the Art Gallery in Tiranë and those in the main cities. A limited number of works of art of all periods and genres are displayed in the National Historical Museum in Tiranë (1981), the Gjergj Kastrioti Scanderbeg National Museum (1982), Krujë, and the local museums set up in the centres of the country's 26 districts. There are also sculptures and paintings by contemporary Albanian artists in the Museum of the National Liberation War (1947) in Tiranë, Gjirokastër (1966) and Berat (1960), the Museum of National Independence (1982), Vlorë, the National Renaissance Museum (1969), Gjirokastër, the Museum of National Education (1967), Korçë, and the Museum of the People's Army (1962), Tiranë. Works of art can also be seen in memorial museums devoted to outstanding historical figures and events and in local museums. The National Exhibition of Folk Culture (1981), Shkodër, is the main museum of folk handicrafts and applied arts. There is a Museum of Weapons (1971) in Gjirokastër.

Before the end of World War II no public institution existed in Albania for the protection of works of art or for their restoration. The first step in this direction was taken with the ruling of the Anti-Fascist National Liberation Congress of Përmet in May 1944, prohibiting the plunder and export of archaeological objects. A law was passed in 1948, placing monuments under the protection of the Institute of Sciences in Tiranë on behalf of the state. In 1955 the Council of Ministers made the Institute of Sciences responsible for scientific preservation and in 1959 also for scientific restoration. The department for preservation and restoration of the monuments of culture at Tiranë University was established in the same year. The Institute of Cultural Monuments, attached to the Ministry of Culture and Education, was set up in Tiranë in 1964 and has numerous branches in main cities. Other specialized institutions, such as the Committee of Art and Culture, the Higher Institute of Art, the Centre of Archaeological Research, the League of Writers and Artists and cultural departments of local authorities, were made responsible for the protection of works of art. Legislation continued with the charter of 1985 on the 'Criteria and Principles for the Restoration of Works of Art and Other Monuments of Culture and Architecture in Albania'. By 1992 over 1200 architectural monuments had been placed under the protection of the state (in 1948 there had been 92), including houses, castles, churches, mosques, bridges, theatres and such urban areas as the old quarters of Gjirokastër and Berat, each with hundreds of buildings.

BIBLIOGRAPHY

S. Adhami: 'Muzeumet shqiptare' [Albanian museums], *Stud. Hist.* (1971), no. 2, pp. 77–192

Shqipëria arkeologjike [Archaeological Albania], Tiranë, N. Mus. Archaeol. cat. (Tiranë, 1971)

Mbrojtja e monumenteve [The protection of monuments] (Tiranë, 1972)

A. Meksi: 'Probleme dhe aspekte të restaurimit të kishave bizantine' [Problems and aspects of the restoration of Byzantine churches], *Monumentet* (1976), no. 12, pp. 75–85

H. Nallbani: 'Probleme dhe aspekte të restaurimit të ikonave' [Problems and aspects of the restoration of icons], *Monumentet* (1976), no. 12, pp. 86–100

K. Zheku: 'Probleme të restaurimit në sistemet e fortifikimit të qyteteve ilire' [Problems of restoration in the fortification systems of Illyrian cities], *Monumentet* (1976), no. 12, pp. 17–25

P. Leka and K. Naslazi: 'Le Musée national de l'art médiéval albanais', *Stud. Alb.* (1980), no. 2, pp. 212–15

G. Frashëri: 'Restaurimi i monumenteve të arkitekturës: Çështje të metodës dhe të metodologjisë' [Restoration of monuments of architecture: questions of method and methodology], *Pasuri e trashëguar në shekujt* [Wealth inherited through the centuries] (Tiranë, 1981), pp. 18–28

'Ekspozita kombëtare e kulturës popullore' [The national exhibition of folk culture], *Drita* (4 Feb 1982)

E. Riza: 'Historia e arkitekturës dhe restaurimi: Dy disiplina plotësuese' [History of architecture and restoration: two complementary disciplines], *Monumentet*, xxvii/1 (1984), pp. 5–15

XI. Art education.

The masters who trained painters, sculptors, mosaicists, architects and master builders in the Middle Ages remain anonymous, and it is only in more recent centuries that they began to be identified in connection with traditional regional schools such as the Dibër school of building, an artisanal school (16th–20th century) for monumental constructions such as churches, mosques and baths, and for town and country houses. There were also several traditional regional schools of religious painting such as the school of Tivar and the school of Durrës (12th–15th century), the school of Berat and the school of Voskopojë (16th–18th century), the representatives of which painted the frescoes and icons of numerous churches in Albania and elsewhere. In the 19th and 20th centuries there were schools of applied arts in Shkodër, Korçë and other towns. The first formal art school in Albania was the Drawing School (1932–9) in Tiranë, a secondary school offering training in painting. After World War II, when the provision of art education became the sole responsibility of the State, the training of artists was tied to the sanctioned style of Socialist Realism. Immediately after the educational reform of 1946, the Jordan Misja Lyceum of Art was opened in Tiranë, a secondary art school with four departments giving tuition in the fine arts, singing, instrumental playing and dance. It was followed by similar schools in Durrës, Shkodër, Korçë, Elbasan, Vlorë and Gjirokastër. The first higher school was the Institute of Figurative Arts (founded 1960) in Tiranë, which was later merged with the Higher School of Drama (1959) and the Conservatory (1962) to form the Higher Institute of Art (1966) in Tiranë, one of whose three branches gives tuition in sculpture, painting and graphic, applied and decorative arts. Architects and builders are trained at the Faculty of Engineering at Tiranë University. The history of art is discussed in secondary school textbooks on general culture and history, while Albanian art is covered in textbooks on Albanian history. Mass art education is also carried out in extracurricular ways through illustrated publications, temporary art exhibitions, special conferences and radio and television programmes, while Albanian cultural organs, particularly the magazine *Nëntori* and the newspaper *Drita*, regularly discuss Albanian and non-Albanian works of art.

BIBLIOGRAPHY

A. Uçi: *Estetika, jeta, arti* [Aesthetics, life, art] (Tiranë, 1973)
——: *Edukimi estetik në shkollë* [Aesthetic education in schools] (Tiranë, 1974)
M. Dhrami: 'Shkolla që rrit dhe edukon piktorët dhe skulptorët e ardhëshëm' [The school that raises and trains the future painters and sculptors], *Zëri Pop.* (25 Jan 1975), p. 3
A. Uçi: 'Vëndi i artit popullor në kulturën artistike socialiste' [The place of folk art in Socialist artistic culture], *Konferenca kombëtare e studimeve etnografike: Tiranë, 1976* [National conference of ethnographic studies: Tiranë, 1976]

KRISTO FRASHËRI

Albenga [Lat. Albingaunum; Albium Ingaunum; Album Ingaunum]. Italian town and bishopric, 72 km south-west of Genoa. It was a port in the Roman period, and its street grid-plan has partly survived, but, with the silting of the River Centa, it is now 1 km inland. Pottery and sections of the hull of a merchant ship that sank offshore *c.* 80–60 BC are preserved in the Museo Navale Romano in the Palazzo Peloso-Cepolla (13th century). The Civico Museo Inguano is housed in the Palazzo Vecchio del Comune (1387 and 1421). The cathedral, which was built in the 11th century and enlarged in the early 14th century, has a galleried apse and a campanile built in 1391.

The most important monument, however, is the 5th-century baptistery. Its ground-plan is decagonal without and octagonal within, the alternating rectangular and semicircular niches being flanked by columns. The original cupola was destroyed in the 19th century. The edge of the octagonal font at the centre of the hall has starlike points and was surmounted by a baldacchino. The only mosaics that survive are on the front wall of the building and on the vaulting of the presbytery niche. Although the latter has been heavily restored, it can be dated to the 5th century. At the centre of the vault is a christogram comprising the letters A and ω in three shades of blue, which may refer to the Trinity. The representation of 12 doves in the surrounding area, facing a cruciform medallion at the upper edge, may symbolize the Apostles, as Paulinus of Nola (353/4–431) specified for the apse decoration of his church at CIMITILE-NOLA. On the front wall two lambs flank a gem-studded cross in a meadow landscape. Both mosaics are framed by a foliage border.

Two 4th-century Christian basilicas, S Vittore and the cemetery church of S Calocero, which are situated outside the town, remained in use until the 11th and 8th centuries respectively.

BIBLIOGRAPHY

N. Lamboglia: 'Albenga', *Enc. A. A.*, ed. D. Bartolini, i (Rome, 1958), p. 196
G. Radtke: 'Album Ingaunum', *Das kleine Pauly Lexikon der Antike*, ed. K. Ziegler and W. Sontheimer, i (Stuttgart, 1964), p. 236
V. Sciaretta: *Il battistero di Albenga* (Ravenna, 1966)
J. Wilpert and W. N. Schumacher: *Die römischen Mosaiken der kirchlichen Bauten vom 4.–13. Jahrhundert* (Freiburg im Breisgau, Basle and Vienna, 1976), p. 323
P.-A. Février: 'Baptistères, martyrs et reliques', *Studien zur spätantiken und byzantinischen Kunst: F. W. Deichmann gewidmet*, ii (Bonn, 1986), pp. 1–10

FRANZ RICKERT

Alberdingk Thijm, Josephus Albertus (*b* Amsterdam, 13 Aug 1820; *d* Amsterdam, 17 March 1889). Dutch writer, critic and collector. He was raised in a cultivated and artistic merchant family but preferred writing to commerce. In addition to serving as an editor of the *Volksalmanak voor Nederlandsche Katholieken*, he published the *Dietsche Warande*. His lifelong advocacy of Roman Catholic emancipation is reflected in many of his short stories (written under the pseudonym Pauwels Foreestier) concerning Catholic life in 17th-century Holland. In 1876 he was appointed professor of aesthetics and the history of art at the Rijksacademie voor Beeldenden Kunsten, Amsterdam. An architectural preservationist and an important critic of the art and architecture of his time, he asserted that art should serve a religious function, as it had during the Middle Ages. It should be social, idealistic and transcendental. In his ideal society the arts would form a harmonious unit under the heading of architecture. His brother-in-law P. J. H. Cuypers was the leading Dutch architect of the day, whose career was assisted by Alberdingk Thijm's advocacy of Gothic Revivalism in architecture. Alberdingk Thijm was particularly opposed to the painters of the Barbizon and Hague schools, whose work he considered to have no underlying purpose. Rather, he preferred the Düsseldorf school, which displayed a knowledge of history and literature. His large collections reflected his philosophical orientation. His numerous 17th and 18th-century Dutch paintings, mostly by minor masters, represented all the genres. He also owned a large collection of drawings and prints, as well as books, manuscripts and religious art from the Middle Ages and Renaissance, which included a Gothic ciborium, a Byzantine crucifix and embroideries on silk, which were dispersed at auction after his death (Amsterdam, Muller, 10–12 Dec 1889; 10–14 April, 21–5 April, 5–8 May 1890).

WRITINGS

J. F. M. Sterck, ed.: *Verzamelde werken*, 6 vols (Amsterdam, 1909)

BIBLIOGRAPHY

A. J. [L. van Deyssel]: *J. A. Alberdingk Thijm* (Amsterdam, 1893)
W. Bennink: *Alberdingk Thijm, kunst en karacter* (Utrecht, 1952)
G. Brom: *Alberdingk Thijm* (Utrecht, 1956)
C. Blotkamp: 'Art Criticism in De Nieuwe Gids', *Simiolus*, v (1971), pp. 119–20

W. van Leeuwen: 'Alberdingk Thijm: Bouwkunst en symboliek', *Sluitsteen*, v (1989), pp. 1–43
P. A. M. Geurts and others, eds: *J. A. Alberdingk Thijm (1820–1889): Erflater van de negentiende eeuw* (Nijmegen, 1992)

Albermann, Wilhelm (*b* Werden, Essen, 28 May 1835; *d* Cologne, 9 Aug 1913). German sculptor and teacher. He trained (1851–4) as a wood-carver in Elberfeld, and from 1855 he studied at the Akademie der Künste, Berlin, also working in the studios of August Fischer (1805–66) and Hugo Hagen (?1818–1871). In 1865 Albermann moved to Cologne and established his own workshop. From 1871 to 1896 he taught the modelling class at the Gewerbliche Zeichenschule, and from the 1890s onwards he was active in the Verein zur Förderung der Bildhauerkunst in Rheinland und Westfalen, which was established in reaction to Berlin's dominance in commissions for monumental sculpture.

Albermann's early work consists mostly of figurative and ornamental decoration for private houses in Cologne. From the late 1870s, however, he produced many war memorials and statues, of *Emperor William I*, *Frederick III*, *Bismarck* and *Moltke*, often combined in groups as founders of the German Reich. These works were erected further afield, although still all within the Rhineland, for example at Bielefeld; Werden, Essen, and Kettwig, Essen; Kempen; Neuss and Zweibrücken.

Albermann also produced seated statues of the museum founders *Franz Ferdinand Wallraf* and *Johann Heinrich Richartz* (1900; Cologne, Rechtschule). Other official commissions included monumental fountains, notably those of *Jan van Werth* (1884; Cologne, Alter Markt) and *Hermann Joseph* (1894; Cologne) and more light-hearted decorative installations, such as the Fairytale Fountain (*c*. 1900; Wuppertal-Elberfeld, Zooviertel). Albermann also made portraits and tombstones (Cologne, Melatenfriedhof) and numerous statues and reliefs for public and private buildings, for example the town hall in Wuppertal-Barmen, and the playhouse (destr.) in Cologne.

Albermann sought to show the historical and atmospheric context of his subjects. In the fountains he combined stylistic elements from Romanesque to Baroque with realistic detail and the muted emotional pathos of his monumental figures. These are in the tradition of later 19th-century Berlin sculpture, whereas works such as the Tortoise Fountain (erected 1914; Cologne-Mülheim) barely rise above crass Naturalism. Only Albermann's religious sculpture, which is oriented towards Gothic models, is close to the work of other Rhineland sculptors, in its element of local colour. As a whole, Albermann's work shows little independent development; his eclecticism corresponds to the stylistic pluralism of the last years of Wilhelmine sculpture at a time when it had already been overtaken by new forms.

BIBLIOGRAPHY

Meissner; Thieme–Becker
P. Bloch: *Skulpturen des 19. Jahrhunderts im Rheinland* (Düsseldorf, 1975), pp. 42–5
J. Abt and W. Vomm: *Der Kölner Friedhof Melaten* (Cologne, 1980)
Rheinland-Westfalen und die Berliner Bildhauerschule des 19. Jahrhunderts (exh. cat., ed. P. Bloch; W. Berlin, Skulpgal., 1984), pp. 46–7

M. PULS

Albers. American artists of German birth.

(1) Josef Albers (*b* Bottrop, Ruhr, 19 March 1888; *d* New Haven, CT, 25 March 1976). Painter, printmaker, sculptor, designer, writer and teacher. He worked from 1908 to 1913 as a schoolteacher in Bottrop and from 1913 to 1915 trained as an art teacher at the Königliche Kunstschule in Berlin, where he was exposed to many current art movements and to the work of such Old Masters as Dürer and Holbein. His figurative drawings of the next few years, which he kept hidden and which were discovered only after his death (many now in Orange, CT, Albers Found.), show that he applied these influences to his consistent concern with the simplest and most effective means of communicating his subject; he drew rabbits, schoolgirls and the local landscape in as dispassionate and impersonal a manner as possible. After his studies in Berlin he returned to Bottrop and from 1916 to 1919 began his work as a printmaker at the Kunstgewerbeschule in nearby Essen. In 1919 he went to Munich to study at the Königliche Bayerische Akademie der Bildenden Kunst, where he produced a number of nude drawings and Bavarian landscapes (Orange, CT, Albers Found.).

In 1920 Albers attended the preliminary course (*Vorkurs*) at the recently formed Bauhaus in Weimar, where he designed stained glass, furniture, metalwork and typography (see Alviani, pp. 18–21) as well as architecture. He was among the first students to be appointed a master (in 1925) and was one of the most influential teachers of this renowned course. He was deeply involved with technical mastery and with abstract form, particularly in his glass assemblages; the first of these, such as *Untitled (Window Picture)* (589×553×213 mm, 1921; Washington, DC, Hirshhorn), were made from broken bottle fragments found in the city dump in Weimar, while later works were made from sand-blasted multi-layered glass in precise, right-angled, abstract forms and pure, radiant colours in careful arrangements, for example *Factory* (*c*. 1925; New Haven, CT, Yale U., A.G.).

Albers was the longest-serving member of the Bauhaus when it was closed under pressure from the Nazis in 1933, and he was among the faculty members who agreed with its Director at the time, Mies van der Rohe, that the school be shut down. Albers and his wife (2) Anni Albers, whom he had married in 1925, were asked in the same year to teach art at the newly formed BLACK MOUNTAIN COLLEGE in North Carolina on the recommendation of Philip Johnson at MOMA in New York; they remained there until 1949, and Albers became one of the best-known and most influential art teachers in the USA. He also continued his foray into printmaking, notably in a series of woodcuts and linoleum cuts of 1933–44 (see Alviani, pp. 30–46), and pursued abstract painting in a highly innovative way. During this period he first developed the idea of producing series of paintings in standard formats but different colours, for example *Bent Black (B)* (1940; Washington, DC, Hirshhorn) and *Bent Dark Grey* (1943; New York, Guggenheim). In 1947 he began a large series of rectangular abstractions entitled *Adobes*, for example *Variant: Inside and out* (1948–53; Hartford, CT, Wadsworth Atheneum) and *Variant* (1948–52; Bottrop, Albers Mus.), in which he often used equal quantities of five different colours in a precisely calculated geometric arrangement. It was in these and related works that he first developed a rather mechanical, emotionless technique to achieve highly poetic results.

In 1950 Albers was appointed chairman of the Department of Design at Yale University, New Haven, CT, a post he retained until 1958, although he remained there as visiting professor until 1960. His students there and previously at Black Mountain College included Eva Hesse, Robert Rauschenberg, Kenneth Noland and Richard Anuszkiewicz. His teaching of colour at Yale led to the publication of his renowned treatise *Interaction of Color* (1963), a book that was later translated into eight languages as one of the major tools of art teaching throughout the world. In it Albers investigated the properties of colour (for illustration *see* COLOUR INTERACTION and colour pls VII, fig. 1 and VIII, fig. 2), including the illusory ability of opaque colours to appear translucent and overlapping, which he had begun to explore in 1950 in his best-known series of works, *Homage to the Square*, on which he was occupied until his death. These were exhibited all over the world and were the basis of the first one-person show given to a living artist at the Metropolitan Museum of Art in New York (1971). Works from this series, of which Albers did over 1000, are in the Josef Albers Museum (opened 1983) in Bottrop, Germany, as well as numerous public collections (e.g. New Haven, CT, Yale U., A.G.; New York, Guggenheim; Berlin, N.G.; Paris, Pompidou; see fig.). Each consists of either three or four squares of solid planes of colour nested within one another, in one of four different arrangements and in square formats ranging from 406×406 mm to 1.22×1.22 m. In these paintings, and in related prints and tapestries, Albers explored effects of perception, such as the apparent oscillation between the flat surface design and an illusion of movement across or into space and the interaction of adjacent colours to produce effects of modulation and tonal variation.

Albers painted the *Homages* in a precise arrangement and under laboratory-like conditions, always working on the rough side of Masonite (wood fibreboard) panels, primed with at least six coats of white liquitex. Under a careful arrangement of fluorescent lights (bulbs arranged warm/cool/warm/cool over one work table, warm/warm/cool/cool over another), he worked on each painting in alternate light conditions, applying unmixed paints straight out of the tube with a palette knife, often starting with the centre square and working outwards. However systematic and even mechanical their execution, these paintings remain mysterious and enormously varied in mood and colour.

On his retirement from Yale, Albers continued to live near New Haven and to paint, monitor his own exhibitions and publications, write, lecture and work on large commissioned sculptures for architectural settings, many of which were based on a series of drawings and engravings entitled *Structural Constellations* (see Alviani, pp. 72–84). Such works as *Repeat and Reverse* (stainless steel, 1.98×0.91 m, 1963; New Haven, CT, Yale U., A. & Archit. Bldg) dominate major open spaces in cities as far afield as Sydney and Münster and the insides of such important New York skyscrapers as the Pan Am and Time-Life buildings. Whatever their basis, all of Albers's work points

Josef Albers: *Homage to the Square*, oil on hardboard, 609×609 mm, 1965 (Bottrop, Josef Albers Museum)

to the beauty of simple geometry and technical proficiency and to 'the discrepancy between physical fact and psychic effect', which the artist regarded as one of the major goals of his art.

WRITINGS

'Concerning Art Instruction', *Black Mountain Coll. Bull.*, 2 (1934), pp. 2–7
Zeichnungen: Drawings (New York, 1956)
Interaction of Color (New Haven, 1963, rev. 1975)
'Op Art and/or Perceptual Effects', *Yale Sci. Mag.*, xl/2 (1965), pp. 8–15
Josef Albers: Formulation, Articulation (New York, 1972)

BIBLIOGRAPHY

F. Bucher: *Josef Albers: Despite Straight Lines: An Analysis of his Graphic Constructions* (New York, 1961)
Josef Albers: Homage to the Square (exh. cat. by J. Albers and K. McShine, New York, MOMA, 1964)
Josef Albers: White Line Squares (exh. cat., essays by K. E. Tyler, H. Hopkins and J. Albers, Los Angeles, Co. Mus. A., 1966)
E. Gomringer: *Josef Albers* (New York, 1968)
W. Spies: *Albers* (New York, 1970)
Josef Albers (exh. cat., essays by W. Hofman, K. Alsleben, D. Helms and J. Wissmann, Hamburg, Ksthalle, 1970)
Josef Albers (exh. cat., essays by W. Spies and others, Düsseldorf, Städt. Ksthalle, 1970)
J. Miller: *Joseph Albers: Prints, 1915–1970* (New York, 1973)
N. F. Weber: *The Drawings of Josef Albers* (New Haven, 1984)
N. D. Benezra: *The Murals and Sculpture of Josef Albers* (New York, 1985)
G. Alviani: *Josef Albers* (Milan, 1988) [English, German and Italian]
Josef Albers: A Retrospective (exh. cat. by N. F. Weber, M. E. Harris, C. E. Rickart and N. D. Benezra, New York, Guggenheim, 1988)

(2) Anni [Anneliese] **Albers** [née Fleischmann] (*b* Berlin, 12 June 1899; *d* Orange, CT, 10 May 1994). Textile designer, draughtsman and printmaker, wife of (1) Josef Albers. She studied art under Martin Brandenburg (*b* 1870) in Berlin from 1916 to 1919, at the Kunstgewerbeschule in Hamburg (1919–20) and at the Bauhaus in Weimar (1922–5) and Dessau (1925–9). In 1925 she married (1) Josef Albers, with whom she settled in the USA in 1933 after the closure of the Bauhaus, and from 1933 to 1949 she taught at Black Mountain College in

North Carolina; she became a US citizen in 1937. Her Bauhaus training led her as early as the 1920s to produce rectilinear abstract designs based on colour relationships, such as *Design for Rug for Child's Room* (gouache on paper, 1928; New York, MOMA), but it was during her period at Black Mountain College that she began producing her most original work, including fabrics made of unusual materials such as a mixture of jute and cellophane (1945–50; New York, MOMA) or of mixed warp and heavy linen weft with jute, cotton and aluminium (1949; New York, MOMA). She began producing prints in 1963, using lithography, screenprinting, etching and aquatint and inkless intaglio (see exh. cat., pp. 106–30).

PUBLISHED WRITINGS

Anni Albers: On Designing (New York, 1959/*R* Middletown, CT, 1961)
Anni Albers: On Weaving (Middletown, CT, 1965/*R* 1972)

BIBLIOGRAPHY

The Woven and Graphic Art of Anni Albers (exh. cat. by N. F. Weber, M. J. Jacob and R. S. Field, Washington, DC, N. Mus. Amer. A., 1985)

NICHOLAS FOX WEBER

Albert, Archduke of Austria. *See* HABSBURG, §I(14).

Albert [Albrecht], Duke of Saxe-Teschen. *See* WETTIN, (9).

Albert [Albrecht], Duke of Saxony. *See* WETTIN, (2).

Albert (of Saxe-Coburg-Gotha), Prince. *See* HANOVER, (7).

Albert [Albrecht] **V**, Duke of Bavaria. *See* WITTELSBACH, §I(3).

Albert, Brat [Brother]. *See* CHMIELOWSKI, ADAM.

Albert, Tótila (*b* 1892; *d* 1967). Chilean sculptor. From 1902 to 1939 he lived in Germany; he studied under Franz Metzner in Berlin. On his return to Chile, he taught at a private school and then taught sculpture in the Academia Particular of the Universidad de Chile in Santiago, also executing important works such as the tomb of President Pedro Aguirre Cerda (1941; Cementerio General de Santiago) and a large relief, *La naturaleza*, in Parque Cousiño (1945; Santiago, Escuela Jard. Parque Cousiño).

Albert's training in Germany, when Expressionism was at its height, led him to use distortion of form as the sign of vehement emotion. In his *Ariel and Caliban* (bronze, h. 8 m, 1960; Santiago, Parque Forestal) limbs are lengthened, muscles swell, tendons are visible beneath the skin, and one body yields and droops while the other rises imposingly into space. These traits are found in all his other sculptures, with the stress on subjectivity impelling him towards the metaphysical notion that the 'real' materials with which he works are his own feelings. Yet there is also a meditative depth in his work and a calming effect arising from an idealized geometry of forms. Albert's concern with mass, which brought out the sensual qualities of his materials, was part of a profound examination of the specific problems of sculptural language: rhythm, movement and tension of surfaces.

BIBLIOGRAPHY

M. Ivelič: *La escultura chilena* (Santiago, 1979)
V. Carvacho: *Historia de la escultura chilena* (Santiago, 1983)

CARLOS LASTARRIA HERMOSILLA

Alberthal [Albertal; Albertalli; Alberthaler], **Hans** [Johann] (*b* ?Roveredo, nr Bellinzona, *c.* 1575–80; *d* Pressburg, Hungary [now Bratislava, Slovakia], *c.* 1657). Italian architect. He was probably the most important member of a large family group of masons originating from the Swiss canton of Grisons and resident from *c.* 1600 at Dillingen on the River Danube; Alberthal's presence there is recorded until 1623. The Protestant parish church at Haunsheim (Swabia, Germany) was built by Alberthal (from 1603) to a design by Joseph Heintz (i). From *c.* 1610 he was Master Builder to the bishops of Augsburg and Eichstätt, while continuing to accept commissions from other patrons and erecting a series of buildings over a wide area. For example, at Eichstätt he erected a bishop's palace, the Willibaldsburg (from 1609), to another architect's plan, and the Jesuit church (1617–20), also following another architect's plan. At Dillingen itself he built the Jesuit church of the Ascension (from 1610) to a design by another architect, as well as a hall church, the parish church of St Peter (1619–29), probably to his own design. He also built the tower of the former court church of St Maria (*c.* 1630) at Neuburg an der Donau to a design attributed to Johann Serro (*fl* 1630–70). In 1639 Alberthal is referred to in a Dillingen source as 'Imperial Master Builder at Pressburg'. His presence there was probably due to his Augsburg patron, who may have had contacts there and who secured commissions for Alberthal in Hungary.

Alberthal was one of the numerous Swiss–Italian artists who worked north of the Alps after the beginning of the 16th century and who were responsible for introducing Italian styles into the German lands and beyond. In his buildings he followed the late Renaissance architectural style created in Augsburg by Heintz, Elias Holl (i) and Johann Matthias Kager, although his own designs (e.g. St Peter, Dillingen) lack any reference to Classical architectural theory and were occasionally subject to technical problems.

BIBLIOGRAPHY

Meissner; *SKL*
A. von Reitzenstein and H. Brunner: *Reclams Kunstführer Deutschland*, I/i (Stuttgart, 1956/*R* 1983)

JÜRGEN ZIMMER

Alberti. Italian family of artists. They came from Borgo San Sepolcro (now Sansepolcro, Tuscany), a town set on one of the crossroads between Tuscany, the Marches and Umbria, and flourished primarily in the 16th century, when the family workshop grew in size and several members achieved prominence in the visual arts. Alberto [Berto III] Alberti (*b* 2 June 1525; *d* 1598) worked in Borgo San Sepolcro and Rome primarily as a wood-carver but also as a painter, military engineer and cartographer, and left detailed diaries and account books covering 50 years of his family's activities.

The diaries of Alberto, Durante and Andrea Alberti form part of the Alberti archive in the Biblioteca delle Gallerie degli Uffizi, Florence. By the 1990s none of the diaries had been published in its entirety. They were published (Florence, 1914) in 'Inventario degli Archivi di S Sepolocro', *Gli archivi della storia d'Italia*, IV, i, pp. 123ff, and in 1915 in volume IV, ii, pp. 195–255. The contents of a now-lost diary by Alberto Alberti were published in 1845 by Michelangelo Gualandi as 'Memorie intorno la celebre famiglia degli Alberti di S Sepolcro', in Gualandi's *Memorie originale italiane risguardanti le belle arti*, II, 6 (Bologna, 1845), pp. 50–91. The same 'diary' was published again (more or less the same as in Gualandi's edition) by Francesco Corazzini as *Appunti storici e filologici su la Valle Tiberinan Superiore* (Sansepolcro, 1875).

Three of Alberto's children became artists of some distinction: (1) Alessandro Alberti, (2) Cherubino Alberti and (3) Giovanni Alberti. Durante Alberti (*b* Borgo San Sepolcro, 1538; *d* Rome, 1613), a painter who moved to Rome before 1560, was the best-known member of another branch of the family. He produced paintings for numerous churches in Rome, including S Maria in Vallicella, Il Gesù and several Capuchin churches outside the city. His only son, Pier Francesco Alberti (*b* Borgo San Sepolcro, 1584; *d* Rome, 1638), worked as a painter, engraver and book illustrator. Among his works are the engraving *Accademia de' pittori*, illustrations for Antonio Bosio's *Roma sotteranea* (1632–4) and for the edition of Leonardo da Vinci's *Trattato della pittura* (Paris, 1651) prepared by Cassiano dal Pozzo and Galeazzo Maria Arconati, a documented painting in the Palazzo Mattei di Giove, Rome, and several paintings in Borgo San Sepolcro (in S Bartolomeo, S Giovanni and the Cathedral). Durante's two daughters Maria Ancilla Alberti and Chiara Alberti (*b* 1560) are also documented as painters; Chiara did a *Pietà* for the high altar of the Buon Gesù in Borgo San Sepolcro. Durante's nephew Romano Alberti was involved in the Roman Accademia di S Luca, and co-authored with Federico Zuccaro the treatise *Origine e progresso dell'Accademia del disegno di Roma* (Pavia, 1604).

(1) Alessandro Alberti (*b* Borgo San Sepolcro, 9 March 1551; *d* Rome, 10 July 1596). Painter. He was the oldest son of Alberto Alberti, whose diary documents his activities. Alessandro was the first member of the family to study painting, perhaps with Raffaello dal Colle. He first visited Rome in 1566 and travelled frequently between Rome, Borgo San Sepolcro and Naples. In Città di Castello he decorated the Bufalini Chapel in S Francesco (1576–7; *in situ*); in Rome he painted an altarpiece of *St Susanna* for S Susanna (untraced), known through an engraving of 1578 by his brother (2) Cherubino Alberti. After some years in Naples and Borgo San Sepolcro, he was commissioned in 1586 by Vespasiano Gonzaga, Duke of Sabbioneta, to decorate the Galleria degli Antichi (*in situ*) in the Palazzo Ducale, Sabbioneta (nr Mantua). He painted the long walls with a fictive architectural scheme supporting decorative motifs derived from his Roman experience. His brother (3) Giovanni Alberti later joined him to paint the end walls. In 1588 Alessandro was back in Borgo San Sepolcro working with his brothers on the decoration of the Palazzo Tornabuoni and of the refectory (now the oratory) of the Compagnia del SS Crocifisso. Later in that year he was in Naples decorating the palace of Don Luigi di Toledo. In 1596, already terminally ill, he was summoned to Rome to assist his brothers in the decoration of the Sala Clementina (*in situ*) in the Vatican. Most of his documented works are untraced, and only a few drawings have been attributed to him in the Alberti family sketchbook (Rome, Gab. N. Stampe).

(2) Cherubino Alberti (*b* Borgo San Sepolcro, 24 Feb 1553; *d* Rome, 18 Oct 1615). Painter and printmaker, brother of (1) Alessandro Alberti. The best known of the three sons of Alberto Alberti, he distinguished himself as a printmaker at an early age. One of his earliest prints, an etching of the *Virgin and Child* (1568; B. 149) shows his interest in Raphael as well as in contemporary Mannerist art. In Rome he studied with Cornelius Cort, whose swelling burin line he adopted to create pictorial effects of strong chiaroscuro. Between 1571 and 1575 he made several prints after Federico Zuccari and Taddeo Zuccari (B. 131, 136, 140, 159, 171, 176). During the next ten years he reached the height of his fame as a printmaker, producing engravings after Raphael, Michelangelo, Polidoro da Caravaggio and of ancient statues. His prints of Polidoro are particularly valued as documents of lost works. He also made prints from paintings by Andrea del Sarto, Rosso Fiorentino, Marco Pino, Pellegrino Tibaldi and Cristofano Gherardi. He made numerous original engravings, among them an *Angel Supporting the Body of Christ* (B. 139), which exemplifies his concern with graceful postures and ornamental draperies. In his later years he designed elaborate presentation prints, such as a portrait of *Henry IV of France* in an ornamental cartouche (B. 248) and a large *Adoration of the Shepherds* (B. 129) for Pope Clement VIII. His oeuvre includes over 180 prints.

From the late 1580s Cherubino collaborated on fresco decorations with his brothers (1) Alessandro Alberti and (3) Giovanni Alberti, executing most of the narrative scenes and figures. In 1587 he decorated the façade of the Palazzo Rigi, Borgo San Sepolcro, with a *sgraffito* scheme in which allegorical figures surrounded by frolicking putti rest upon an imaginary architecture of broken pediments. In 1588, also in Borgo San Sepolcro, he painted a *Flagellation* for the Palazzo del Comune (now in the Cassa di Risparmio, Florence), and designed and painted narrative scenes of the *Life of Christ* for the Oratory of the Compagnia del SS Crocifisso. Returning to Rome in 1589, he worked with Giovanni on vault decorations in the Vatican (chapel of S Silvestro and the Sala Clementina; *see* FRESCO, figs 2 and 3) and in the Canons' Sacristy at S Giovanni in Laterano, where they painted scenes from the *Life of St Clement* (*c.* 1602–5). For the Palazzo Ruggieri, Rome, he prepared designs for allegorical figures and narratives of the *Life of Pompey*, working with his brother Giovanni and Cristoforo Roncalli. His compositions and figure style show the impact of his eclectic study of 16th-century and antique art: like the Zuccaro brothers, he designed monumental figures with swelling draperies, often posed in elegant contrapposto and arranged in frieze-like, symmetrical compositions. He joined Federico Zuccaro's Accademia di S Luca at its inception in 1593 and lectured the following year on decorum, explaining the importance of gesture and costume as well as setting and ornaments.

After Giovanni's death in 1601, Cherubino finished several projects for Clement VIII: frescoes in the lunettes of the Canons' Sacristy in S Giovanni in Laterano, and others on the side walls of the Sala Clementina in the Vatican (in collaboration with Baldassare Croce; see fig.) and in the adjoining Sala del Concistoro. For the same patron he also undertook vault decorations in the Vatican apartment of the papal Secretary of State, and in the Aldobrandini Chapel in S Maria sopra Minerva, Rome. These independent works show little interest in architectural perspective but reveal a great mastery in foreshortening figures and objects, as well as in creating colour and chiaroscuro effects. In his later years Cherubino fell into a state of melancholy and diverted himself by collecting crossbows (*baglione*). He became a Roman citizen in 1612 and was elected Principe of the Accademia di S Luca in 1613. He frescoed the façade of his house on Via Ripetta (destr.) with an *Allegory of Rome*. His last commission was for the decoration (1612–14) of the lunettes and spandrels in the Casino dell'Aurora in the Palazzo Pallavicino-Rospiglioso, Rome. His sketchbooks (Rome, Gab. N. Stampe) include preliminary designs for his engravings and frescoes, copies of antique art and 16th-century masters, and also show him to have been an avid student of ancient architecture.

Alberti's drawings (mostly in Rome, Gab. N. Stampe, and Florence, Uffizi) include preliminary designs for his engravings and frescoes, copies of antiquities and Cinquecento masters, and reveal that he was an avid student of ancient architecture. He was responsible for many drawings after Polidoro da Caravaggio in the Lugt collection album.

(3) Giovanni Alberti (*b* Borgo San Sepolcro, 19 Oct 1558; *d* Rome, 10 Aug 1601). Painter, brother of (1) Alessandro Alberti. He distinguished himself as an expert in perspective design, for which he was praised by Ignazio Danti (in his commentary on Vignola, 1583), Federico Zuccaro and Giovanni Baglione. He is thus usually credited with the design of the architectural perspectives in the fresco decorations he painted in collaboration with his brothers. He also painted putti and ornamental figures. He assisted Danti in the Sala dei Palafrenieri and Sala Vecchia degli Svizzeri in the Vatican (after Feb 1582) and was influenced by Danti's belief that perspective decorations should be oriented for the most typical viewing point of the spectactor. In 1586 he went to Sabbioneta (nr Mantua) to assist his brother Alessandro at the Palazzo Ducale and painted the fictive colonnades on the end walls of the Galleria degli Antichi. This trip gave him the opportunity to study the illusionistic frescoes of Andrea Mantegna in Mantua and of Correggio in Parma.

When Giovanni returned to Rome, a series of papal commissions for ceiling decorations allowed him to synthesize his knowledge of architectural perspective with his interest in foreshortened airborne figures. For Sixtus V he decorated the vault of the chapel of S Silvestro in the

Vault fresco by Cherubino Alberti and Giovanni Alberti, and wall frescoes by Cherubino Alberti and Baldassare Croce, Sala Clementina, Vatican Palace, Rome

Vatican (1589–90; *in situ*) with an illusionistic oval opening to the sky, revealing a vision of flying putti holding the Peretti family insignia and papal attributes. Clement VIII employed him and his brother (2) Cherubino Alberti on several important projects: the vault of the Canons' Sacristy in S Giovanni Laterano and the vault of the Sala Clementina in the Vatican palace. For the former Giovanni designed illusionistic oculi in each of the six lunettes and a large rectangular opening in the centre; through these openings appear colonnaded loggias with flying putti and angels seated on clouds holding the Aldobrandini insignia and papal attributes. The perspective is angled for the viewer entering the room from the old sacristy. Gradations of clarity, colour saturation and contrast, as well as a gradual lightening of hues from base to top, create a convincing illusion of distance as forms seem to become enveloped in a luminous atmosphere. Angels holding banderoles fill the corners, while festoons of fruit and flowers ornament the ribs of the vault. Cavaliere d'Arpino's decoration of the Cappella Olgiati in S Prassede, Rome, is closely related. A further development of these ideas took place in Giovanni's decoration of the choir vault of S Silvestro al Quirinale, Rome, where the lunettes and a large circular opening in the centre reveal visions of putti cavorting in the sky. Here the perspective was designed to be viewed from the crossing.

By contrast, Giovanni decorated the vault of the Sala Clementina in the Vatican (begun 1595) with a single illusionistic opening to the sky, a solution that inspired later ceiling painters such as Pietro da Cortona. Fictive balustrades rise from the walls, supporting fictive statues and six allegorical figures of papal virtues; behind are colonnades and loggias, creating an imaginary extension of space in all directions. In the centre a cloud-filled sky is dominated by a ring of winged putti surrounding a vision of the kneeling *St Clement Witnessing the Trinity*. At either end, putti holding Aldobrandini and papal emblems transform the scene into a glorification of Clement VIII. Aerial perspective is again integrated with linear perspective to produce a convincing illusion of distance and height (*see* FRESCO, figs 2 and 3). This integration was recorded by Cesare Ripa (1603) in his description of perspective, which he based directly upon Giovanni's *Allegory* on the east wall of the Sala, showing the artist kneeling before a female figure who stands beside two enormous astrolabes.

Giovanni also decorated the *salone* of the Palazzo Ruggieri, Rome, with frescoes of the *Life of Pompey* and worked in several churches and oratories in Borgo San Sepolcro. Many of his drawings of foreshortened putti and copies of High Renaissance works survive (Rome, Gab. N. Stampe).

BIBLIOGRAPHY

Bolaffi; *DBI*

J. Vignola: *Le due regole della prospettiva pratica*, ed. I. Danti (Rome, 1583), p. 73 [Giovanni]

C. Ripa: *Iconologia* (Rome, 1593; 2/1602; rev. Rome, 1603) [Giovanni]

F. Zuccaro: *Idea* (Turin, 1607); ed. D. Heikamp in *Scritti d'arte di Federico Zuccaro* (Florence, 1961), p. 239 [Giovanni]

G. Baglione: *Vite* (1642); ed. V. Mariani (1935) [Cherubino, pp. 131–3; Giovanni, pp. 70–71]

G. degli Azzi: *Inventario degli archivi di Sansepolcro* (Rocca S Casciano, 1914)

H. Posse: 'Das Deckenfresko des Pietro da Cortona im Palazzo Barberini und die Deckenmalerei in Rom', *Jb. Ksthist. Samml. Wien*, xl (1919), pp. 93–118, 126–73 [Giovanni]

L. Servolini: 'Cherubino Alberti: Italian Engraver of the Sixteenth Century', *Prt Colr. Q.*, xxvii (1940), pp. 216–37

F. Würtenberger: 'Die manieristisches Deckenmalerei in Mittelitalien', *Röm. Jb. Kstgesch.*, iv (1940), pp. 59–141

M. Brugnoli: 'Un palazzo romano del tardo '500 e l'opera di Giovanni e Cherubino Alberti a Roma', *Boll. A.*, 4th ser., xlv (1960), pp. 223–46

G. Gaeta Bertelà, S. Ferrara, R. d'Amico and P. Bellini: *Incisori toscani dal XV al XVII secolo*, iv of *Catalogo generale della raccolta di stampe antiche della Pinacoteca Nazionale di Bologna*, 26 vols (Bologna, 1973–80)

M. Abromson: 'Clement VIII's Patronage of the Brothers Alberti', *A. Bull.*, lx (1978), pp. 531–47

K. Hermann-Fiore: 'Giovanni Albertis Kunst und Wissenschaft der Quadratur: Eine Allegorie in der Sala Clementina des Vatikan', *Mitt. Ksthist. Inst. Florenz*, xxii (1978), pp. 61–84

——: 'Studi sui disegni di figure di Giovanni e Cherubino Alberti', *Boll. A.*, v (1980), pp. 39–64

C. Witcombe: *Giovanni and Cherubino Alberti* (diss., Bryn Mawr Coll., PA, 1981) [for diaries, see Appendix I]

S. Buffa: *Italian Artists of the Sixteenth Century (1982)*, 34 [XVII/i] of *The Illustrated Bartsch*, ed. W. Strauss (New York, 1978–) [B.]

K. Hermann-Fiore: 'Disegno e giudizio: Allegorical Drawings by Federico Zuccaro and Cherubino Alberti', *Master Drgs*, xx (1982), pp. 247–56

J. Gere, P. Pouncey and R. Wood: *Artists Working in Rome, 1550–1640*, viii and ix of *Italian Drawings in the Department of Prints and Drawings in the British Museum* (London, 1983)

Disegni degli Alberti: Il volume 2503 del Gabinetto Nazionale delle Stampe (exh. cat. by K. Hermann-Fiore, Rome, Villa Farnesina alla Lungara, 1983)

C. Witcombe: 'A New Fresco by Cherubino Alberti in the Vatican', *Source: Notes Hist. A.*, iv (1984), pp. 12–16

JANIS CALLEN BELL

Alberti (da Ferrara), Antonio (di Guido) (*b* ?Ferrara, ?1390s; *d* before 1449). Italian painter. His early career is hard to determine; Vasari improbably described him as a pupil of Agnolo Gaddi. He must have been well known in Ferrara before working for the condottiere Braccio Fortebraccio at Montone in Umbria, where he is documented in either 1420 or 1423. Frescoes at S Francesco in Montone depicting the *Life of St Francis* are almost certainly by him. In the same year he was in Urbino, where Vasari reported that he was working on frescoes (destr.) at S Francesco. The frescoes in the chapel of S Martino in S Maria, Carpi (the Sagra di Carpi; see fig.), are of a similar date. They show a style in which formal elements deriving from Serafino Serafini are put into a Late Gothic context, under the influence of work by Gentile da Fabriano seen in central Italy. Other work by Alberti from between 1419 and 1431 includes the triptych of the *Virgin and Child between SS Bartholomew and Benedict* (Città di Castello, Pin. Com.), on the basis of which the votive panel of *Pietro de' Lardi* (Paris, Trotti priv. col.) should probably be assigned to him; the fresco of scenes from the *Life of St Anthony* (Città di Castello, S Domenico) and the scenes from the *Life of St John the Evangelist* (Ferrara, Pin. N.) have also been assigned to his earlier phase (Longhi).

There are records of payments to Alberti in Urbino in 1435, 1437 and 1438. Some are probably connected to the frescoes in the Cella at Talamello signed *Antonio de Ferraria habitator Urbini Pixit* and dated 1437. On 10 July 1438 he was paid for a standard (Urbino, Pal. Ducale), which also contains a polyptych signed and dated 1439. A *St Agatha*, stylistically related to the polyptych, has been assigned to Alberti's later work, as have the *Virgin and Child with Four Saints*, *Crucifixion* and an *Annunciation* dated 1436 (all Urbino, Pal. Ducale). It has been suggested that he returned to Ferrara *c.* 1438 to paint frescoes of the *Council of Ferrara* (destr.) in the Palazzo del Paradiso for

Antonio Alberti: *Adoration of the Magi* (early 1420s), fresco, chapel of S Martino, S Maria, Carpi

Niccolò III d'Este, but this would have been only a brief visit, as Alberti is documented in Urbino shortly thereafter and until 1442. Renewed contact with Emilian painting would help to account for a new robustness entering his Late Gothic manner in the later works, probably stemming from the rough and forceful rhythms of Giovanni da Modena and the Bolognese painters of the earlier 15th century.

BIBLIOGRAPHY

Bolaffi

R. Longhi: *Officina ferrarese* (Rome, 1934, rev. Florence, 1940, rev. 2/1955, rev. 3/1975)

F. Zeri: 'Arcangelo di Cola da Camerino: Due tempere', *Paragone*, i (1950), no. 7, pp. 33–8

M. T. Zanchi: 'Antonio Alberti da Ferrara e il suo itinerario umbromarchigiano', *Commentari*, n. s., xv/3–4 (1964), pp. 173–85

P. Zampetti: *La pittura marchigiana da Gentile a Raffaello* (Venice, 1969)

S. Padovani: 'Materiale per la storia della pittura ferrarese nel primo quattrocento', *Ant. Viva*, xiii/5 (1974), pp. 3–21

——: 'Nuove personalità della pittura emiliana nel primo quattrocento', *Paragone*, xxvii (1976), nos 317–19, pp. 40–59

——: 'La decorazione pittorica della cappella del Castello di Vignola', *Il tempo di Nicolò III: Gli affreschi del Castello di Vignola e la pittura tardogotica nei domini estensi* (exh. cat., Vignola, Rocca, 1988), pp. 61–77

MARIA CRISTINA CHIUSA

Alberti, Leandro (*b* 12 Dec 1479; *d* ?Bologna, *c.* April 1552). Italian historian, topographer, writer and patron. He was a friar and first entered the Dominican Order at Forlì but was in Bologna from 1495 and was officially transferred to the monastery there in 1500. Alberti received an extensive grounding in humanist studies under the Bolognese rhetorician Giovanni Garzoni. After acting as companion to the head of the order, Tomaso de Vio Cajetan, Alberti was made Provinciale di Terra Santa in Rome in 1520. This included the role of travelling companion to Tomaso's successor, Fra Silvestri da Ferrara ('il Ferrariense'). His travels with Silvestri throughout Italy, including the islands, laid the foundations for his most important work, the *Descrittione di tutta l'Italia* (1550), modelled on the *Italia illustrata* of Flavio Biondo. It was reprinted many times: the Venice edition of 1561 was the first to include Alberti's sections on the islands of Italy, which were not covered by Biondo; the Venice edition of 1568 includes seven maps. Alberti acted as the patron and initiator of two great works of art in the church of S Domenico in Bologna. The earliest of these comprised 16 magnificent intarsia panels depicting scenes from the *Life of St Dominic* and from the Old Testament, executed by Fra Damiano Zambelli (*c.* 1490–1549) of Bergamo between 1530 and 1532; they were known as the *spalliera* (headboard) *di St Domenico* and formed the wooden panelling of the west wall of the chapel of St Dominic. The second work was the marble base (begun 1532) with three fine low reliefs by Alfonso Lombardi depicting scenes from the *Life of St Dominic*, which was added to Nicola Pisano's tomb of the saint to mark the tercentenary of his canonization (*see* DOMINICAN ORDER, §1).

WRITINGS

Historie di Bologna (Bologna, 1541)

Descrittione di tutta l'Italia (Bologna, 1550, rev. Venice, 1561, rev. 2/1568)

BIBLIOGRAPHY

DBI; Michaud

R. Renzi: *Il coro di San Domenico in Bologna* (Parma, 1969), pp. 134–46, 311–16, 334

D. H. Farmer: *The Oxford Dictionary of Saints* (Oxford, 1990), pp. 119–20

CLAIRE BAINES

Alberti, Leon Battista (*b* Genoa, 14 Feb 1404; *d* Rome, April 1472). Italian architect, sculptor, painter, theorist and writer. The arts of painting, sculpture and architecture were, for Alberti, only three of an exceptionally broad range of interests, for he made his mark in fields as diverse as family ethics, philology and cryptography. It is for his contribution to the visual arts, however, that he is chiefly remembered. Alberti single-handedly established a theoretical foundation for the whole of Renaissance art with three revolutionary treatises, on painting, sculpture and architecture, which were the first works of their kind since Classical antiquity. Moreover, as a practitioner of the arts he was no less innovative. In sculpture he seems to have been instrumental in popularizing, if not inventing, the portrait medal, but it was in architecture that he found his métier. Building on the achievements of his immediate predecessors, Filippo Brunelleschi and Michelozzo di Bartolomeo, he reinterpreted anew the architecture of antiquity and introduced compositional formulae that have remained central to classical design ever since.

I. Life and commissions. II. Theory. III. Works. IV. Influence and posthumous reputation.

I. Life and commissions.

Alberti was the illegitimate second son of Lorenzo di Benedetto Alberti, a member of a prominent Florentine banking family. Although born in Genoa during a period of his family's exile from their native city, Alberti quickly removed with them to Venice and from there in 1416 to Padua, where he perhaps attended the school of Gasparino Barzizza. There he may have met other pupils who later became leading humanists and thinkers, including Vittorino da Feltre. From 1421 to 1428 Alberti studied canon law at Bologna University and was thus the only artist of the period to receive a university education and a thorough grounding in the classics. It was during this period that his illegitimacy dealt him a severe blow: soon after he had embarked upon his university education his father died and grasping relatives claimed his inheritance. Nevertheless, despite financial worries and illness, Alberti, in addition to pursuing his course of study, became particularly interested in geometry and mathematics, and he gave free rein to his emerging literary bent by writing a Latin comedy, *Philodoxeus* (1424). This work marked the start of his career as a prolific author that continued until the end of his life. Nothing is known of his activities between 1428 and 1432, although unsupported claims have been made that he served as a secretary to Cardinal Albergati. In 1432, through Bishop Biagio Molin, he went to Rome and entered papal service as a secretary (*abbreviatore apostolico*) to Eugenius IV (*reg* 1431–47). The security of his new job enabled him to pursue his researches, which resulted in a series of literary works beginning with his *Della famiglia* (*c.* 1433–4), a treatise on family ethics.

Shortly afterwards Alberti's interests turned towards the visual arts. In 1434 Eugenius IV took refuge in Florence from republican rioting in Rome, and Alberti, as a member of the papal *curia*, followed him there. The ban exiling the Alberti family from Florence had been lifted in 1428, but this may well have been his first visit to his family's native city and his first full contact with the revolutionary renascence in the arts led by Brunelleschi, Donatello, Lorenzo Ghiberti and Masaccio. His enthusiasm for this movement and his acquaintance with three of these artists had an immediate impact and led him to produce in 1435 the first Renaissance treatise on the arts, *De pictura*, which was a truly theoretical analysis of its subject rather than a practitioner's handbook (*see* §II, 1 below); for the benefit of practising artists, he translated the work the following year from Latin into Italian. After moving with the papal court to Bologna later in 1436, Alberti went to Ferrara in January 1438 to attend the ultimately fruitless congress (transferred to Florence in 1439) convened to consider the reunification of the Roman and Orthodox churches; while there he forged a close friendship with Lionello d'Este (i), 13th Marchese of Ferrara, to whom he dedicated a treatise on horses (*De equo animante*). In 1441–2 he was invited by Lionello to judge a competition for an equestrian monument to *Niccolò III d'Este* (destr.). Alberti's involvement in this scheme has led to speculation that he designed the monument's surviving pedestal, which stands outside the Palazzo del Comune, and the campanile of the nearby cathedral (begun 1451), but there is no documentary foundation for such claims. He was, however, urged by Lionello to set about the study of Vitruvius with a view to publishing a work on architecture to set beside his earlier volume on painting.

In 1443, after nine years' residence in Florence and northern Italy, Eugenius IV returned with his court to Rome, where Alberti was based for the rest of his life. During the remaining years of the 1440s he seems to have written his monumental study of architecture, *De re aedificatoria* (brought to final completion in 1452; *see* §II, 2 below), his treatise on sculpture, *De statua* (*see* §II, 1 below), and also his *Descriptio urbis Romae*, in which he proposed a means of accurately surveying the city of Rome by using an instrument of his own design. It was in the same period that Alberti's practical skills as an archaeologist were sought by Cardinal Prospero Colonna in an unsuccessful attempt (1446) to raise a Roman ship from the bed of the Lago di Nemi, a project that led Alberti to compose a treatise on the ships of antiquity (*Navis*). At the end of the decade he may even have played an active part, perhaps as an architectural adviser, in the vigorous programme of urban renewal for Rome that was conceived by Pope Nicholas V as the manifestation of a revitalized papacy.

In the early 1450s Alberti became a practising architect (*see* §III below). The constraints of his employment at the Vatican, however, meant that, unlike other architects, he

1. *Leon Battista Alberti* and his *impresa*; obverse and reverse of a bronze commemorative medal by Matteo de' Pasti, 1454–6 (Washington, DC, National Gallery of Art)

could never supervise construction; he consequently conducted operations from afar and sent designs and instructions by post to local executants, including Matteo de' Pasti and Luca Fancelli. Alberti's first major commission was the renovation (*c.* 1450) of S Francesco in Rimini for Sigismondo Pandolfo Malatesta, Lord of Rimini. He subsequently began to act as architect for the Florentine banker Giovanni Rucellai, who was most likely a personal friend, providing him with designs for a façade (begun *c.* 1453) to his new palace in Florence, for the façade (*c.* 1458) of S Maria Novella, the city's principal Dominican church, and for a funerary chapel (*c.* 1458) in S Pancrazio. Alberti may also have designed the new apse of the Florentine priory church of S Martino a Gangalandi at Lastra a Signa. In this case he himself seems to have been the patron, since the apse bears the family arms and he had been granted the benefice in 1432. No date for the structure is known, but even though it is mentioned as being unfinished in Alberti's will it would appear for stylistic reasons to be an early work.

The late 1450s and early 1460s was a particularly busy time for Alberti in his capacity as an architect. In 1459 he accompanied the papal court to Mantua, where the recently elected pope, Pius II, was staging a congress to promote a crusade against Ottoman expansionism. While there, Alberti produced several designs for their host, Ludovico II Gonzaga, 2nd Marchese of Mantua, whose father, Gianfrancesco Gonzaga, had been the dedicatee of the revised Latin version of Alberti's treatise on painting; one design was for the votive church of S Sebastiano and another was for the redevelopment of the Piazza dell'Erbe and the nearby Romanesque rotunda of S Lorenzo (unexecuted). There is no documentary evidence that Alberti ever worked for Pius II as an architect, although he seems to have been valued highly by the Pope, who, in his *Commentarii* (1462), recorded walking around the aqueducts of Rome in his company. Yet it is conceivable that he acted for him as an architectural adviser, especially as many of the buildings erected by Pius display Albertian features, most of all his palace in Pienza, the Palazzo Piccolomini by Bernardo Rossellino, which is closely modelled upon the Palazzo Rucellai in Florence.

Following Pius' death (1464), Alberti's career as papal secretary came to an abrupt end when the new pope, Paul II, disbanded the college of *abbreviatori apostolici.* With less reason to be tied to Rome, Alberti was increasingly drawn towards other artistic centres. He became closely associated with the intellectual circle in Florence centred around the young Lorenzo de' Medici, to whom he dedicated his treatise on oratory, *Trivia* (1460s), and he may have played a direct part in the reformulation of architectural ideas in Florence at around this time. Lorenzo certainly maintained his acquaintance with Alberti and was guided around Rome's antiquities by him on a visit to the city in 1471. Moreover, a design for a villa sent in 1474 by Bernardo Rucellai (Giovanni Rucellai's son and a friend of Alberti's) to Lorenzo, his brother-in-law, who was then planning his own villa at Poggio a Caiano, may very possibly have been one prepared earlier by Alberti himself. Alberti was also in the custom of spending some time each year with his friend Federigo II da Montefeltro, Count (later Duke) of Urbino and himself an enlightened patron of the arts and expert in matters architectural. These visits occurred at precisely the time that Federigo was rebuilding the Palazzo Ducale at Urbino to designs prepared by Luciano Laurana, about which Alberti was presumably consulted at some considerable length. A drawing by Alberti for a bath complex (Florence, Bib. Medicea-Laurenziana, Cod. Ash. 1828 App., fols 56*v*–57*r*; *see* ARCHITECTURAL DRAWING, fig. 4) may have been one of his own proposals for the palace. Alberti's last works were commissioned by Ludovico Gonzaga, for whom in 1470 he set about the completion of SS Annunziata in Florence, a building begun by Michelozzo in 1444 (*see* FLORENCE, §IV, 3); also in 1470 Alberti sent Ludovico designs for his masterpiece, S Andrea in Mantua. Little of S Andrea had been realized at the time of his death; indeed none of his major projects had been completed.

Alberti's insatiable passion for knowledge, which embraced not only the visual arts but also ethics, mathematics, philology and even cryptography, is epitomized by his *impresa* (see fig. 1): an eye carried on speeding wings alludes to his perceptiveness; its shape with flaming corners, perhaps based on Jupiter's thunderbolt, refers to his incisiveness; the surrounding laurel suggests his confidence in success; and the accompanying motto, '*quid tum*' (what next?), points to a willingness to embrace new fields of endeavour and indicates that the modern understanding of Alberti as a 'universal man' is essentially one he cultivated himself.

II. Theory.

1. *De pictura* and *De Statua*. 2. *De re aedificatoria*.

1. 'De pictura' and 'De statua'. Alberti was inspired to write his treatise on painting, *De pictura*, soon after he arrived in Florence (*c*. 1434), where he encountered for the first time and with evident enthusiasm the recent innovations in the visual arts. The original Latin text was written in 1435, and it was soon followed by an Italian version (*Della pittura*), produced before July of the following year and dedicated to Brunelleschi, who had presumably become a personal acquaintance. Alberti's aim in writing the treatise was to give the art of painting, the 'mistress' of the three visual arts, a theoretical model based upon antique precept and precedent. Indeed, *De pictura* was the first truly theoretical work on the visual arts, and Alberti was quite clear about its importance when he declared that he was 'the first to write about this most subtle art' (Bk III). The truth of this remarkable claim is borne out when the work is compared with previous treatments of the subject. First, the treatise is quite different in conception from antique accounts of painting, as Alberti himself emphasized when remarking that he was 'not writing a history of painting like Pliny [the elder] but treating art in an entirely new way' (Bk II). Alberti's was a work of theory, not history, even though many of the principles he elicited and all the examples he drew upon, except for a lone reference to Giotto, were derived from Pliny the elder's *Natural History* and other ancient sources. Second, the treatise marks an abrupt departure from more recent treatments of the subject, such as Cennino Cennini's early 15th-century handbook on painting, *Il libro dell'arte*, a departure that in its intention could not have been much greater. Cennini's book deals with the practicalities of the artist's profession, providing such sundry information as how to prepare panels for tempera painting, or how to mix the *intonaco* for fresco, and it is based on the implicit notion that the painter is a craftsman. Alberti's treatise, on the other hand, presents a coherent analysis of the forms and aims of painting, and its underlying argument is founded on the new or renewed conviction that the art of painting is primarily the product of the intellect.

In the first of the three books of *De pictura* Alberti set out a scientifically accurate method for the illusionistic representation of three-dimensional objects on a two-dimensional surface, the method now usually known as one-point linear perspective. Although Brunelleschi has been accredited with the original formulation of the method, or one very much like it, and although Masaccio followed a similar procedure in his *Trinity* fresco (*c*. 1425–7; Florence, S Maria Novella; *see* Masaccio, fig. 5), Alberti's analysis is the first as well as one of the fullest and clearest written expositions of the subject. The stated aim of his account is to construct an image that would resemble a 'view through a window', the 'view' corresponding with the pictorial image and the 'window' to the picture surface. Alberti conceived his method in terms of lines of sight (later known collectively as the 'visual pyramid') that radiate from the eye of the artist, linking it with the various objects in the 'view', and which, when intersected by the plane of the 'window', produce the pictorial composition. The illusion of the 'view through a window' described by Alberti is achieved by making all orthogonal lines in the image (i.e. all those at right angles to the picture plane) converge at a single point on the horizon (later known as the 'vanishing point'), and hence the name 'one point' perspective. Alberti's method also enables the artist to establish with precision the relative sizes of objects in the picture, however close or far they may be from the position of the viewer. Alberti gave as an example the problem of how to create an illusion of a chequerboard floor so that the gradual diminution of the tiles is believable. The key difficulty resides in how to establish the precise position of the horizontals as the floor recedes into the distance. To do so, the artist must mark their position upon the 'window' while keeping his eye at a constant distance from it. As Alberti himself recognized, the effectiveness of the perspective illusion depends to a great extent on the picture being seen from a single, ideal viewing point at exactly the same distance and height as the artist was in relation to the supposed 'window'. Indeed, it was the concept of the chequerboard floor as a means of creating space as much as the method itself that influenced subsequent artists (*see* Perspective, §II, 2, and fig. 1).

In the second book Alberti dealt primarily with what later became known in Florentine art theory as 'design' (*disegno*), a concept that embraces both drawing outlines and pictorial composition. He began by dividing painting itself conceptually into three constituent elements: *circumscriptio*, *compositio* and *receptio luminum*. The first of these, *circumscriptio*, refers to the definition of all objects, or parts of objects, by means of very fine outlines, in supposed imitation of the Greek painter Apelles. The second element, *compositio*, is broader in meaning than the modern term 'composition', which usually refers to the disposition of the principal elements within an image. Alberti's term refers instead to a more elaborate notion of *compositio* borrowed directly from rhetoric; it embraces a four-tier hierarchy in which 'parts of the *historia* [i.e. the subject-matter] are bodies, a part of the body is a member, and a part of a member is a surface', a system in which the whole of the image is thus related to what are conceived as its smallest delineated constituents. The third element, *receptio luminum*, concerns the supplementary applications of tone and hue to the delineated image, of which the former is regarded as demanding from the artist much the greater skill and is consequently the more important. Alberti particularly censured the customary use of gold leaf as opposed to the skilful imitation of the appearance of gold achieved through tone and hue. He then examined at length the notion of the *historia*, which for him was the highest form that the art of the painter could take. Although the term can be broadly understood as meaning 'narrative painting', it is not used to mean only the depiction of stories, since it also encompasses purely allegorical imagery. Crucial to an understanding of Alberti's concept of the *historia* are his attitudes towards decorum and variety, which ultimately proved to be enormously influential. Alberti conceived of such paintings primarily as idealized figure compositions that are limited, for the sake of clarity, to around ten appropriately conceived individuals who, through their actions, gestures and expressions, contribute as fully as possible to the meaning of the work while at the same time, for the sake of interest, being differentiated from one another as much as possible (for further discussion *see* ISTORIA; *see also* EXPRESSION, §1).

In the third and final book Alberti dealt primarily with the education of the artist. He placed an unprecedented emphasis on the artist's innate character and broader learning, stating that he should be 'a good man, well versed in the liberal arts' and arguing that only by being equipped in this way would he be able to fulfil his potential and achieve fame. Such a view underlies Alberti's primary objective of raising the status of the artist to that of an intellectual, an objective that was further supported by his reference to ancient custom, when painting was not considered merely a craft and 'was given the highest honour by our ancestors'. Alberti enjoined artists to imitate nature. For example he stressed the value of practice through drawing, an exercise that, so as not to foster bad habits, should be conducted whenever possible directly from nature or, failing this, from sculpture, but never from the paintings of other artists. For Alberti, however, copying from nature would not by itself result in beauty, a quality he regarded as essential to art. Nature had to be improved if beauty was to be attained. In support of this principle he cited the example of Demetrios, who failed to obtain the highest praise because he was devoted more to likeness than to beauty. The method Alberti advocated was that of Zeuxis, who created an idealized image of Helen of Troy by selecting the most perfect features of several models and combining them, a composite procedure modelled on Aristotle's notion of the ideal. A basic ingredient of beauty for Alberti was decorum: for example when devising compositions, beauty could be attained only if measure and harmony were observed and when the 'members' of figures accorded with one another in size, function, kind and colour.

Alberti's treatise, although responding to recent developments in the visual arts such as those in the work of Masaccio, in effect amounted to a manifesto by offering painters a new and compelling vision of their art. This vision, founded upon references to painting in ancient texts, suggested alternatives not only for the treatment of form in a picture but also for its possible subject-matter. Indeed, the Italian version of Alberti's treatise, with its detailed accounts of such long-lost masterpieces as Apelles' *Calumny*, became a prime source of information for painters who could not read the Latin or Greek of the original ancient texts. In this respect, therefore, Alberti succeeded in laying the foundations for the mythological and allegorical genres that were soon afterwards revived.

The later and much shorter treatise on sculpture, *De statua*, is of much narrower scope than that on painting, although it is again highly innovative. Alberti's aim here was not to present a full and methodical examination of the art, which would have duplicated much of what he had already written about painting, but instead to outline a technical method for designing a statue that might potentially be realized at any scale from the less than life-size to the colossal. The discussion hinges on two main concepts, that of *dimensio*, which concerns the main dimensions and proportions of the ideal human figure, and that of *finitio*, which concerns the disposition of the ideal figure in a particular pose. Under *dimensio* Alberti described an apparatus of his own invention with which to measure the component parts of the body, consisting of a vertical rod and a device for gauging widths. Reaffirming that beauty is dependent on proportion, he then supplied a detailed list of the measurements based on his own researches for an ideal man, which, presumably inspired by the lost 'canon' of Polykleitos, was the earliest such list of the Renaissance (*see also* HUMAN PROPORTION, §2). Under *finitio* Alberti also described another apparatus of his own invention, a *finitorium*, with a rotating arm and plumb line, which enabled the relative position of key points on the surface of any figure or statue to be recorded. As he observed, the *finitorium* made it possible to cut into a solid substance by a precise amount and consequently to replicate a particular pose in stone, a process thereby anticipating that of 'pointing' employed in subsequent times by such sculptors as Canova.

2. 'DE RE AEDIFICATORIA'. By far the most extensive of Alberti's three works on the visual arts, this treatise was the first comprehensive treatment of architecture of the Renaissance and the first fully to address Classical architecture since Vitruvius' *On Architecture*, the sole surviving architectural treatise from antiquity. Although *De re aedificatoria* was the last of Alberti's three works to be completed, he may have been considering it as early as the 1430s. In its final form it must certainly post-date 1445, as it mentions Filarete's doors of St Peter's, Rome, which were unveiled in that year; it was presumably completed by 1452 when, according to the diary (Florence; Bib. N. Cent. and Bib. Medicea–Laurenziana) of Mattia Palmieri (1406–75), it was presented to Pope Nicholas V. On its eventual publication in 1485 it was in fact the very first book on architecture to leave the printing presses, anticipating the publication of Vitruvius' text by a year. In its conception Alberti's treatise is in many respects modelled on that of Vitruvius (*see* VITRUVIUS, §2). Both are written in Latin, both are divided into ten books and both cover much the same material, including even the discussion of such ancient building types as amphitheatres, which by Alberti's day were of academic interest only. Indeed, Alberti may originally have set out to produce a critical edition of Vitruvius' work, but through increasing dissatisfaction with the obscurities of the text he may have felt forced to abandon this idea and to compose an alternative

treatise instead. Criticisms of Vitruvius appear throughout the work, most explicitly at the beginning of Book VI, where Alberti commented that Vitruvius' language was such 'that the Latins might think that he wanted to appear a Greek, while the Greeks would think that he babbled Latin', adding that 'his very text is evidence that he wrote neither Latin nor Greek, so that as far as we are concerned he might just as well not have written at all since we cannot understand him'. By contrast, Alberti declared his own intention of writing 'in proper Latin and in comprehensible form'. For this reason, he deliberately avoided almost all Greek terminology, so that, for example, when referring to a temple with a frontal portico, he abandoned Vitruvius' Greek-derived term 'prostyle' in favour of the more literal and Latin '*porticus pro fronte*'. The same approach was even embodied in his actual title for the work *De re aedificatoria*, which is little other than a pointed latinization of Vitruvius' (*De architectura*).

Alberti also set out to give his work a much more systematic and coherent structure than Vitruvius had done. Although basing his discussion on the Vitruvian concepts of strength, utility and beauty, unlike Vitruvius he used the same concepts as the basis for organizing the work, devoting the first half (Bks I–V) to the practical considerations of strength and utility and Bks VI–IX of the second half to the aesthetic considerations of beauty. In its scope the treatise is comprehensive, combining a discussion of sometimes recondite literary and archaeological material with sound practical advice of value to a contemporary builder. In the first half of the treatise, following a discussion of basic definitions and concepts, including that of architectural drawing (BR II), Alberti ran through the various building materials (II) and discussed matters of construction (III) before considering the form and disposition of the city and its public buildings (IV) and analysing the arrangements of private dwellings (V), including villas (*see* VILLA, §II, 3). In the second half of the treatise Alberti introduced the concept of beauty in architecture (VI) before examining its applicability to religious buildings (VII), to public buildings (VIII) and to domestic buildings (IX). He concluded with some discussion of faults and abuses in architecture, appending miscellaneous information about such matters as restoration and water supply (X).

In his quest to make better sense of Classical architecture, Alberti adopted many of the typical methods of humanist scholarship. Sometimes he resorted to etymology as a means of elucidating Vitruvian terminology; for example, he interpreted the term 'amphitheatre' to mean two theatres joined together as one, on the basis that *amphi-* can mean 'both' or 'around'. More frequently he adopted the philological method of comparing the information given by Vitruvius with examples drawn from his own observations of ancient buildings. In some instances he was even prepared to discount Vitruvius where archaeological confirmation was lacking, as in the notable case of his discussion of the Ionic base. Being unable to find a base with precisely the same sequence of mouldings specified by Vitruvius (*On Architecture* III.v.3; from bottom upwards: plinth, scotia, astragal, astragal, scotia, torus), he described instead the one used for the Corinthian columns of the portico of the Pantheon (from bottom upwards: plinth, torus, scotia, astragal, astragal, scotia, torus). Alberti's readiness to amend Vitruvius' treatment of a subject is also evident in his discussion of the orders. Unlike Vitruvius, he conceived of them as a hierarchy in which the various kinds of column are differentiated from one another much more systematically. Moreover, he made a further significant departure from Vitruvius with his observation that ancient Roman architects had commonly used a type of capital not mentioned by Vitruvius at all, a type Alberti termed 'Italic', thus conceiving it as a specifically Roman rather than Greek variety; this later became known as Composite. By adding a fifth specific column type to those mentioned by Vitruvius (i.e. Tuscan, Doric, Ionic and Corinthian), Alberti played an important role in the eventual formulation of the canon of five orders that was to remain at the very heart of subsequent theory (*see* ORDERS, ARCHITECTURAL, §I, 2(iii)(a)).

In *De re aedificatoria* Alberti set out a conception of beauty much more fully than in his earlier treatises, and with customary clarity of thought he developed a consistent and cogent theory. His central premise is that beauty in architecture can only be achieved if the design is founded in nature, or in other words upon natural laws and universal principles. This view accords with the Platonic notion that beauty is intrinsic to an object and does not depend upon individual taste, the latter being an attitude that Alberti explicitly condemned when he declared (VI.ii): 'Some . . . maintain that beauty . . . is judged by variable criteria, and that the forms of buildings should vary according to individual taste and must not be bound by any rules of art. This is a common fault among the ignorant, to deny the existence of anything they do not understand.' On the other hand, Alberti also took account of the Aristotelian notion that beauty is in part dependent upon fitness of purpose. For this reason he linked beauty itself inextricably with the two other elements of the Vitruvian triad, strength and utility, on the grounds that 'they have such a mutual agreement with one another that, where any one of them is wanting, the others also lose their commendation' (VII.i). As an example he cited how beauty might contribute to strength (VII.ii): 'The Ancients, especially the Etruscans, preferred to use vast, squared stone for their walls. . . . I approve of this form of construction very much: it has a certain air of antique severity, which is an ornament to the city. This is how I would build the city walls, that the enemy might be terrified by their appearance and retreat, his confidence destroyed.' For Alberti, fitness of purpose or decorum had moral overtones not evident in Vitruvius' interpretation of the concept. His text frequently includes such comments as: 'we decorate our property as much to distinguish family and country as for any personal display (and who would deny this to be the responsibility of a good citizen?)' (IX.i). This moralizing notion of decorum probably derives from Cicero's *De officiis*.

In his analysis of how beauty can be attained in architecture, Alberti subdivided beauty into a number of constituent elements, chief among which is *concinnitas* (harmony). The term *concinnitas* is the precise equivalent of the Vitruvian term *symmetria* and concerns the harmonious proportional relationship between a building's constituent parts: beauty thus arises when there is a '*concinnitas* of all the parts such that nothing can be added or taken away except for the worse' (VI.ii). It was defined by Alberti as the product of the correct application, according to natural principle, of *numerus* (number), *finitio* (dimensional proportion) and *collocatio* (placement). In designs for buildings, *numerus* and *collocatio* should follow natural principle, for example by adopting an even number of supporting members like humans and animals and by arranging them in accordance with such principles as symmetry. *Finitio* is described as a 'certain correspondence between the lines that define the dimensions, one dimension being length, another width and the third height'; in concerning the disposition of proportionate dimensions, it is thus a development of the similar concept he had previously employed in *De statua.* Through this idea of *concinnitas* as the harmonious composition of proportionally related parts, Alberti conceived beauty as residing not so much in the physical fabric of a structure but in the metaphysical disposition of its design (*see also* ARCHITECTURAL PROPORTION, §§I, 2, and II, 3). In this sense, his conception of beauty in architecture mirrors precisely his earlier conception of beauty in painting, where it was considered to reside in the *disegno* rather than in the materials. Even though he commended material richness and variety, he thus firmly rejected the medieval notion that allied beauty in architecture with its material worth.

Alberti also made a critical distinction between a building's intrinsic beauty and its 'ornament', which he defined as an 'auxiliary brightness and complement to beauty'. As used by Alberti, the term 'ornament' has a much broader meaning than the modern one of applied decoration; although it embraces the latter, it refers rather to a component of any larger entity. Thus while a console may indeed be an 'ornament' to a window, or a capital an 'ornament' to a column, by the same token a watchtower may be an 'ornament' to a road and a building or even a park an 'ornament' to a city. The mistaken interpretation of this term to mean only 'applied decoration' has given rise to the false impression that the treatise is in certain passages inconsistent, particularly in its conception of the column. Having first established that a row of columns 'is nothing else but a wall open and discontinued in several places' (I.x), and hence that a column is a structural element, he later referred to the column as 'the principal ornament of architecture' (VI.xiii). In Alberti's terms the two passages are not contradictory, since 'ornament' can refer to both supporting members and elements of applied decoration. A further key distinction between 'beauty' and 'ornament' in Alberti's theory is that beauty lies in the building's design, whereas ornament lies in the building's fabric.

See also TREATISE, esp. §I.

III. Works.

1. Painting and sculpture. 2. Architecture.

1. PAINTING AND SCULPTURE. Not only did Alberti write about painting and sculpture, but he also apparently practised both arts, at least to a limited extent. He is recorded in the 15th century as having produced a number of portraits, some painted and others modelled in wax (*Vita di Leon Battista Alberti*, ed. A. Bonucci), and he is credited by Vasari with several other works of painting, including a small triptych with perspectives and a 'picture of Venice in perspective'. A number of surviving works of sculpture are also commonly attributed to Alberti. These include two bronze portrait medals (Paris, Louvre; Washington, DC, N.G.A.) with depictions of Alberti himself (the Washington example bearing the inscription L.BAP). Since they appear to represent a man in his early thirties, they have been assigned to the mid- to late 1430s and so may well precede the earliest portrait medal by Pisanello, that of *John VIII Palaeologus, Emperor of Byzantium* (1439–40). Even if they do not, they are still very early examples of their type and consequently hold an important position in the emergence of a new genre. Unlike Pisanello's medals, which are circular and two-sided, Alberti's are oval and one-sided and are thus conceived more as plaquettes than as medals. Other sculptures in bronze that are attributed to Alberti include a bust of *Ludovico Gonzaga* (*c.* 1460; versions Berlin, Skulpgal.; Paris, Mus. Jacquemart-André). The naturalistic style of all these works, with their controlled roughness and rawness of surface, suggests a considerable debt to Donatello.

2. ARCHITECTURE. Although it is not clear precisely when Alberti made the transition from architectural theorist to practitioner, it presumably began while he was writing *De re aedificatoria* in the late 1440s. He certainly refers to himself in the treatise as, for example, having 'not inconsiderable experience' in the construction of roofs (II.i), which may suggest that he had acquired practical expertise by this time, although he still could have gained his 'experience' as an interested observer rather than as a working architect, for example on Nicholas V's projects for Rome. All that can be said for sure is that he was sufficiently equipped in the skills of his profession by the mid-point of the century and the time of his first certain design, S Francesco in Rimini (see below).

(i) Rome and Rimini. (ii) Florence. (iii) Mantua. (iv) Style and development.

(i) Rome and Rimini. The building programme inaugurated in Rome by Pope Nicholas V in the late 1440s included the partial reconstruction of St Peter's, which was at least supervised by Bernardo Rossellino; the redevelopment of the Vatican Palace; the fortification and replanning of the surrounding district, the Borgo, together with the refurbishment of the nearby Ponte S Angelo; and other works throughout the city. While Alberti is often considered to have played a central role in this programme, it is difficult to establish the nature of his contribution or indeed to substantiate these claims at all. There is no mention of his involvement in any early account of Nicholas V's improvements, and Alberti makes no mention of his involvement himself in *De re aedificatoria*, where, for example in his several references to St Peter's, he would have had ample opportunity to do so. The only written evidence specifically linking Alberti with any of these schemes is a comment by Vasari, who claims to have had in his possession a drawing by Alberti of a colonnade for the Ponte S Angelo. This evidence is very unreliable, however: it was written a century after the event, and it is based on an attribution

by a man whose connoisseurship of 15th-century drawings has proved to be notoriously untrustworthy. Persuasive evidence suggesting that Alberti had little to do directly with these schemes is provided by a contemporaneous note in Mattia Palmieri's diary, which records that Alberti actually advised the Pope to halt the work on St Peter's. Nevertheless Alberti may still have been involved in some indirect way, perhaps as a general adviser, as Vasari claims. The radical *all'antica* classicism espoused in *De re aedificatoria* has much more in common with some of these schemes than it does with mid-15th-century architecture in Florence. It underlies, for example, the new transept of St Peter's, which was closely modelled on the Basilica of Maxentius, and the stonework design of the Vatican Tower of Nicholas V, which is derived from that of the Round Temple by the Tiber. The same ethos underlies a number of other projects from this time or a little later, such as the courtyard of the Palazzo Venezia, the façade of S Marco and the Benediction Loggia (destr.) commissioned by Pius II for St Peter's; the latter, with arches supported not on columns but on piers in the manner of the Colosseum, accorded with one of the key principles in Alberti's treatise (VII.xv).

Alberti's first certain work as an architect was the external casing of S Francesco in Rimini, more commonly known as the Tempio Malatestiano (*see* RIMINI, §1(i); *see also* MALATESTA, (1)). It was designed for Sigismondo Malatesta in 1450, the date recorded on the façade and on the commemorative foundation medal, or perhaps a little earlier. Sigismondo had already begun (1447) to refashion the interior of the 14th-century building, founding new chapels there for himself and his mistress (later his wife), Isotta degli Atti. Alberti, who can have played no part in devising the internal decoration, with its Classical detailing uncertainly superimposed on Gothic forms, was responsible for encasing the building in a virtually free-standing white limestone shell of resolutely Classical design, and he also proposed the addition of a vast domed rotunda to the east end (unexecuted). The effect of his scheme was to transform the building from a Franciscan church that happened to house Malatesta tombs into a Malatesta monument that commemorated not just members of the immediate family but the whole court. The tombs of Sigismondo and Isotta were apparently in the first instance to be located on the façade (ultimately erected inside the church), while those of the *letterati* who made up the court were to be accommodated in a less prestigious location along the sides, as indeed many eventually were. Construction, supervised by Matteo de' Pasti, who also designed the foundation medal (1450), seems to have begun around 1453, the stone in part being pilfered from Early Christian churches in Ravenna, most notably S Apollinare in Classe. The work ground to a halt in 1461 when Sigismondo fell from power, leaving the upper façade and much of the north side incomplete.

By the conventions of the period, the façade of the Tempio Malatestiano is innovative and highly uncompromising. Its design, known from the foundation medal (*see* RIMINI, figs 1 and 3), holds an important position in Renaissance architecture, as it is the first attempt, partially realized, to apply Classical architecture to the standard medieval format produced by a tall nave and lower aisles or (as in this case) side chapels. It is composed in a two-tier arrangement, with a one-bay upper storey linked to a three-bay lower storey by flanking quadrants (replaced in 1454 by triangular elements) and intended to be crowned by a richly embellished semicircular cornice. In its curvilinear silhouette the façade has no parallel in either Florence or Rome and in this respect is sometimes regarded as an innovation. However, medieval façades of similar shape are in fact relatively common in northern Italy, where Alberti had spent his youth, with examples in Mantua (cathedral; refaced), Milan (cathedral; refaced) and especially in Venice (S Aponal and the Frari). In the precise arrangement of the lower storey, with arches on piers, applied half-columns and roundels in the spandrels, the design is directly dependent on the nearby ancient Arch of Augustus (*see* ROME, ANCIENT, fig. 25), thus establishing a parallel between antiquity in Rimini and its revival there under Sigismondo. Its triumphal associations are presumably deliberate and would refer both to the Christian idea of life triumphant over death and to the Classical idea of fame triumphant over oblivion. The arcaded system of the façade is continued along the sides of the building, although without the half-column articulation. This difference establishes an appropriate architectural distinction between façade and side elevation, which, given the probable arrangement of the sarcophagi, matches neatly the social distinction between Sigismondo and his courtiers.

Alberti's ideas for the completion of the building are known only in outline. The frontal part of the church, according to a letter of his of 1454, would have been vaulted in wood, an idea probably again inspired by ecclesiastical architecture in northern Italy, and particularly that of the Veneto region. The domed rotunda intended for the east end was presumably inspired, like Michelozzo's for SS Annunziata in Florence, by such ancient prototypes as the Mausoleum of St Helena, which is joined to the rear of the church of SS Pietro e Marcellino outside Rome. Its diameter, as indicated by the image on the foundation medal—which presumably follows the orthogonal method of representation Alberti recommended in *De re aedificatoria* and may even be based on a drawing by Alberti himself—would have been the same as the façade's. Its height, as again indicated by the medal, would have been only a little more than the diameter, presumably on the model of the Pantheon, a building Alberti specifically cited in his 1454 letter when objecting to the taller proportions for domes preferred by his Florentine contemporary Antonio di Ciaccheri Manetti.

(ii) Florence. Alberti's works in Florence for Giovanni Rucellai are all likely to post-date his design for the Tempio Malatestiano. Rucellai, a wealthy banker closely allied to the anti-Medicean faction led by the Strozzi family, initiated four major projects in the city: a new palace, a free-standing loggia opposite, a funerary chapel in the nearby church of S Pancrazio and a façade for S Maria Novella, the principal church in his quarter of the city. Alberti's involvement, which is not documented, must have resulted from his presumed personal friendship with Rucellai (who certainly owned one of Alberti's self-portrait medals), a friendship that was subsequently continued with his son

Bernardo Rucellai. Alberti was probably responsible not for all the works, as Vasari claims, but for the façade of the Palazzo Rucellai, the funerary chapel in S Pancrazio and the scheme for S Maria Novella, the designs that accord best with Alberti's approach and with the ideas propounded in *De re aedificatoria.*

(a) Palazzo Rucellai. The earliest of the designs, the innovative façade of the Palazzo Rucellai, was probably begun around 1453 under the supervision of Bernardo Rossellino. As was customary in Florentine practice, the façade was grafted on to a number of pre-existing houses. It is three storeys high and was constructed out of the local *pietra forte* sandstone. The design was originally conceived with five bays, soon afterwards extended to eight bays when the palace was enlarged, the final bay remaining uncompleted. The key innovation of the Palazzo Rucellai façade lies in the application to the three storeys of superimposed orders of pilasters (see fig. 2). Although Brunelleschi had used pilasters for the façade of the Palazzo di Parte Guelfa (begun 1420s) and the Ospedale degli Innocenti (begun 1419), Florence, where superimposed orders may originally have been intended, he did so simply to frame the design rather than to articulate it as a grid. Alberti may have had in mind the elevations of the Colosseum or the Theatre of Marcellus, Rome, which are articulated with superimposed orders of half-columns (*see* ROME, ANCIENT, figs 10 and 28), but he may have also been aware of such ancient domestic buildings as the Praetorium at Hadrian's Villa in Tivoli or, most notably, the Roman villa at Anguillara, which have façades articulated with pilasters.

2. Leon Battista Alberti: façade of the Palazzo Rucellai, Florence, begun *c.* 1453

Alberti's grid of pilasters imposes on the design a more rigorous organization than had been customary in Florentine palaces of the period. Unlike earlier buildings, such as the Palazzo Medici (for illustration *see* PALAZZO), where there are large arches on the ground storey that do not correspond with the window openings above, the ground-floor openings of the Palazzo Rucellai are precisely aligned with the windows above. The only departure from the regularity of the grid is in the slightly greater width given to the two portal bays, a variation sanctioned by Vitruvius in his discussion of temples and by ancient temples themselves. In the choice of order used for each of the three storeys, Alberti was guided by customary differences in their relative status, although he did not follow the sequence used in the Roman buildings: for the lower storey of the Palazzo Rucellai, used primarily for storage, the pilasters are of a plain Doric type; for the *piano nobile*, the principal floor, they are of a lavish Corinthian type; and for the top storey, the subsidiary living floor, they are of a rather less lavish Corinthian type. The greater height of the lower storey, which little befits its lowly status, is ingeniously concealed by raising the Doric pilasters upon pedestals.

The detailing of the façade is typically resourceful. The most innovative of the three types of pilaster is the Doric, the capital of which has a fluted neck with an echinus of egg-and-dart. Although in design not unlike the colonnettes of Donatello's Cantoria (1433–9; Florence, Mus. Opera Duomo), it is the first such appearance of the order in the Renaissance. The Corinthian type used for the *piano nobile*, the capitals of which are embellished with both acanthus and egg-and-dart, is similar to that once decorating the base of the Mausoleum of Hadrian. Further allusions to Classical antiquity are provided by the square-topped portals in place of the arched entrance traditional for Florentine palaces, their design closely following Vitruvius' description of an Ionic doorway, and by the imitation *opus reticulatum* that decorates the pedestal level of the lower storey. Despite its novelty, the façade is in many respects dependent upon local Florentine example. Several features have precedents in Michelozzo's Palazzo Medici (begun 1444), such as the continuous bench and the large crowning cornice, and the way in which the three storeys are successively of diminishing height. Even the ashlar work of the Palazzo Rucellai, with its horizontal bands of varying height and haphazardly arranged vertical joints, has a close parallel in the *piano nobile* of the Palazzo Medici.

(b) S Maria Novella. The second design commissioned by Giovanni Rucellia, the spectacular green-and-white patterned stone façade of S Maria Novella (*see* FLORENCE, fig. 20), was begun in or soon after 1458, the year in which Rucellai obtained rights of patronage, and was probably completed in 1470. For this project, Alberti was not only faced with the problem of devising a classical scheme for a church with a tall nave and lower side aisles, but he was also required to incorporate the beginnings of an earlier façade. This had been begun in the previous century under the patronage of the Baldesi family, and when the rights

of patronage were transferred to Rucellai it was agreed that those parts already built should be retained. Precisely how much of the lower part of the existing façade was built before Alberti's time is still not clear, but the earlier work must have included the tomb-filled niches (*avelli*) with their pointed arches as well as the side portals with their pointed arches and crocketed gables. Alterations were, however, made even to this lower level with the insertion of a new main portal, its pilasters supporting a coffered arch inspired by the portal of the Pantheon in Rome, a pair of framing Corinthian half-columns and a further pair coupled with wider pilasters to mark the façade's corners, a motif derived from the Baptistery in Florence.

As with the Tempio Malatestiano, Alberti again conceived the façade in two storeys, a wider one at the bottom and a narrower one at the top. In this instance the lower one, articulated by the inserted half-columns and corner pilasters, carries an attic, and the upper one, articulated by four pilasters, carries a pediment. To provide a visual transition from the wider lower storey to the narrower upper one, Alberti installed a pair of giant S-shaped scrolls, inspired by those of Brunelleschi's lantern (designed 1436) at Florence Cathedral (*see* BRUNELLESCHI, FILIPPO, fig. 7), and these became the façade's most imitated feature. There are again medieval precedents for the format of the façade, especially in the local church of S Miniato al Monte, but not for the classical rigour of its decoration. In this respect, Alberti was not prepared to compromise, let alone continue the façade in the Gothic style in which it was begun. For him, the only beautiful style was that based on Classical principle and example. It seems that Alberti made every effort to conceive the façade in conformity with his notion of beauty and to base the design upon strict proportional relationships. The façade is thus arranged so that its total width is equal to its total height, its two storeys are of the same height and its lower storey is twice the width of its upper storey. The design can also be imagined as fitting neatly into a square, with the lower storey occupying the bottom half and the upper storey occupying one half of the top half, a conceptualization that may have been intentional.

The need to tailor the façade to the pre-existing medieval structure imposed severe difficulties, which Alberti obviated with consummate skill. One particular problem resulted from the edges of the upper part of the façade being situated directly above the side-portals, an arrangement contrary to the Classical principle of solid above solid and void above void. To distract attention from this unfortunate alignment, Alberti decorated the attic of the lower storey with a bold pattern of squares that corresponds neither with the architectural articulation above nor with that below. Another problem resulted from the presumably pre-existing rose window's being situated in an ungainly manner right at the bottom of the upper level. To make the window less conspicuous, Alberti incorporated other roundels (modelled on a Romanesque floor design in S Miniato) into the design of the giant scrolls at either side, which he centred at a slightly lower level.

(c) Rucellai Chapel, S Pancrazio. This was the third design for Giovanni Rucellai and was finalized a little after the two earlier projects. Rucellai had initially thought about building himself a funerary chapel, to be dedicated to the Holy Sepulchre, as early as 1448, around the time he first conceived his extensive building programme. He was then undecided whether he should attach it to S Maria Novella, where in the right transept his family already had patronage rights, or to the church of S Pancrazio, which stood immediately to the rear of his palace. He finally decided upon S Pancrazio when he resolved to build the façade of S Maria Novella in 1458. Construction of the chapel was certainly under way by 1464–5 and was probably completed in 1467, the date appearing in an inscription.

Although much altered, the chapel's original appearance can be reconstructed confidently. It takes the form of a rectangular structure, with one of its longer sides abutting the left wall of the church. Access was originally gained via a wide trabeated columnar screen in the nave wall, which was subsequently removed when the opening into the chapel was blocked and then inserted into the church's façade. The chapel is covered with a magnificent barrel vault, a form of ceiling revived in fact by Michelozzo in his projects for the library at S Marco and the Palazzo Medici, and one much favoured by Alberti. At the chapel's centre stands a small, richly decorated marble-faced structure, articulated with pilasters and crowned with a lantern (see fig. 3), and designed in imitation of the structure in Jerusalem that marks the supposed site of Christ's burial. Derivatives, or 'copies', of the Holy Sepulchre were fairly

3. Leon Battista Alberti: interior of Rucellai Chapel, S Pancrazio, Florence, *c.* 1464–7

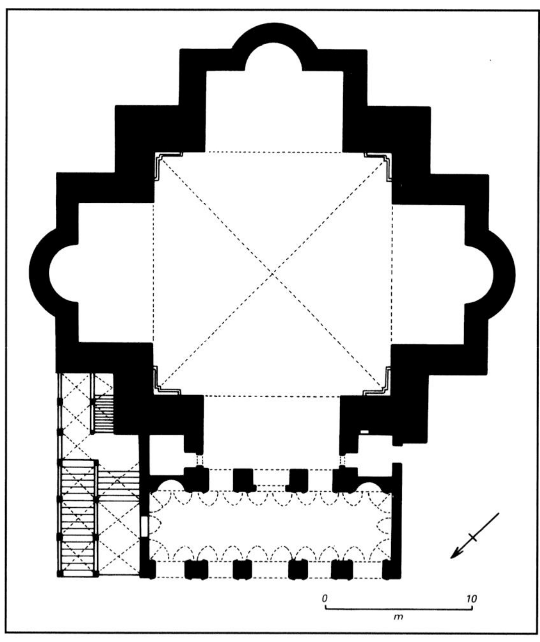

4. Leon Battista Alberti: plan of S Sebastiano, Mantua, designed 1459–60

5. Leon Battista Alberti: façade of S Sebastiano, Mantua, begun 1460

common in funerary contexts throughout the Middle Ages, and the tradition persisted into the Renaissance, one well-known 'copy' being Brunelleschi's Old Sacristy at S Lorenzo (begun 1421). This is crowned with a lantern supporting a spirally fluted, ogee-shaped dome, a motif derived from the prototype in Jerusalem and one that Alberti himself used for the S Pancrazio structure. Compared with the Old Sacristy, however, the S Pancrazio Holy Sepulchre is a far more literal derivative in its shape and arrangement, perhaps indicating that Alberti adopted a more scholarly approach towards 'copying'.

(iii) Mantua. The designs commissioned by Ludovico Gonzaga *c.*1460 came at a very busy time for Alberti, who had three projects in hand in Florence, but the opportunity they presented was considerable. In 1459, following the arrival in Mantua of Pope Pius II and the delegates he had invited to attend his congress (*see* §I above), the city suddenly became the focus of national and international attention. Ludovico hastily set about refurbishing it and asked Alberti, who had accompanied the Pope to Mantua, to put some ideas on paper. As well as supplying outline designs (1460) for the central Piazza dell'Erbe, which involved providing it with a tower and a 'loggia' (realized soon afterwards), Alberti may also have provided outline proposals at this time for rebuilding the nearby church of S Andrea, a project he eventually developed a decade later. In addition, he provided detailed plans for a new church dedicated to S Sebastiano, work on which was begun straight away.

(a) S Sebastiano. With the commission for S Sebastiano (1459), Alberti for the first time had the opportunity to design a building for a virgin site unencumbered by pre-existing structures. The result was a revolutionary design planned as a Greek cross, the first such layout of the Renaissance (see fig. 4). So novel was the plan that Ludovico's son, Cardinal Francesco Gonzaga, said in bewilderment that he did not know whether the building was 'a church, a mosque or a synagogue'. The church as it stands reflects Alberti's original scheme, if only in outline. The main body of the church is raised on to an extremely tall undercroft and has a central, square groin-vaulted crossing (10×10 m) with four short barrel-vaulted arms (3.6×6 m), three terminating in a small apse and the fourth connected with a frontal block that accommodates an entrance portico. The brick-built façade (see fig. 5) rises from an arched basement and is articulated with four pilasters, two flanking the main portal and two at the corners; the latter support a tall entablature, broken in the middle by a window with an arch above, and a crowning pediment. There are five portals in all, a large rectangular one at the centre, two smaller rectangular ones at either side, and two arched ones at either end, to which rise two modern (1925) flights of steps. A further flight of steps, installed late in the 15th century, joins the portico at its northern end.

Alberti's drawings were sent to Ludovico Gonzaga on 27 February 1460 and work must have begun soon after. Construction at first proceeded quickly and the undercroft appears to have been vaulted by 1462; but it slowed down considerably afterwards and the vault in the crossing was only begun *c.* 1499. During the course of construction, supervised in Alberti's absence by Luca Fancelli, a number of changes appear to have been made to the design. At least one of them was made by Alberti himself who, in a letter of 1470, sought permission to 'reduce the piers (*pilastri*) of the portico'. Although obscure in its precise meaning, which has been the subject of much debate, the instruction probably refers to a reduction in the size of the piers of the arched basement rather than to the reduction in the number of pilasters on the façade from a presumed six to the existing four.

More radical changes were made after Alberti's death in 1472, as can be established from a list of measurements on a drawing of the church (Florence, Uffizi, inv.

no. 1779A) made by Antonio Labacco in the 16th century, which records Alberti's original scheme with some precision. It appears that originally the building would have been much taller than at present and that the crossing would have been covered by a dome (*cupola*) rather than a groin vault. What presumably happened is that work on the building was eventually discontinued, perhaps at Alberti's death in 1472. At this stage the walls would have been rather lower than their present height but higher than the top of the apses, since the dimension given by Labacco for the height of the apses is the same as in the actual building. Indeed, this is the only height dimension that corresponds with those recorded by Labacco. The walls would then have been vaulted over as the building was being left in its present truncated state. A small elevational sketch by Labacco for the exterior is often used as the basis for a reconstruction of the original project, but it is much less reliable as evidence. Indeed, considering its size and sketchiness and its placement on the sheet, it may be little other than Labacco's own attempt at a reconstruction based on his list of measurements. The portico façade may well have been altered in its upper reaches, at least in detail, as the uncanonical frieze with dentils and open oculi is typical of Fancelli's style and untypical of Alberti's. For access, Alberti may have originally proposed flights of steps at either end of the portico, an arrangement implied in Labacco's ground-plan drawing and one that is similar to those in marginal illustrations from Filarete's treatise (Florence, Bib. N. Cent., Cod. Magliabechianus II, IV, 140, fols 108*r* and 119*v*).

The measurements given in Labacco's list suggest that Alberti used a method of designing the interior elevation that was new to Renaissance architecture. The method is essentially different from the one employed earlier by Brunelleschi, as at Santo Spirito (begun 1436), Florence, in which one element is related to another visually rather than proportionally, so that a smaller arch might support an entablature, which becomes the impost of a larger arch and so on. In Alberti's scheme at S Sebastiano, however, it is proportion that organizes and unites the design, and a standard width-to-height ratio of 3:5 governs the main portal, the apses, the arms and the crossing. In the design of S Sebastiano, Alberti also drew more heavily than before on ancient prototypes, a dependency that is evident not just in the detailing but in the building's whole conception. The Greek-cross plan appears to have been inspired by ancient mausolea, such as the one subsequently illustrated in Book IV (Venice, 1537) of Serlio's treatise *Regole generali*. The arrangement of the raised portico and perhaps its steps may have been derived from the Tempietto of Clitumnus, near Spoleto, which may well be 'the ancient Umbrian shrine' Alberti mentions (*De re aedificatoria* I.viii) as being partly buried by the build-up of soil at the foot of the mountains. The arrangement of the façade, with the break in the entablature capped by an arch, recalls the side elevation of the Arch of Tiberius at Orange, southern France, Alberti again adapting Roman triumphal architecture to the needs of the Christian Church. On the other hand, Alberti again drew on medieval precedents as well, the general layout of the undercroft and the arrangement of the niches in the apses there being apparently derived from the plan of St Mark's in Venice.

(*b*) *S Andrea.* Alberti's design for rebuilding S Andrea (1470) was a particularly prestigious commission as the church housed a much-venerated relic of Christ's blood and was Mantua's foremost pilgrimage shrine. An initial proposal to rebuild the church seems to have been made around 1460, and it may have formed part of an ambitious scheme to redevelop not only the Piazza dell'Erbe but the surrounding area as well. At this stage Alberti may have been consulted, and one of the leading Florentine architects of the day, Antonio di Ciaccheri Manetti, is known to have sent in a detailed design; but the project was blocked for a decade by the intransigence of the incumbent abbot. In 1470, when it finally became possible to proceed with the project, Alberti sent his own unsolicited design to Ludovico Gonzaga, together with a letter (Mantua, Archv Stato) comparing his scheme with Manetti's and arguing that his was both more suitable and cheaper. Manetti's scheme may have had a basilican layout like Brunelleschi's S Lorenzo, Florence, with a nave and two aisles separated by arches on columns. Alberti considered it inconveniently cluttered and needlessly costly, since the

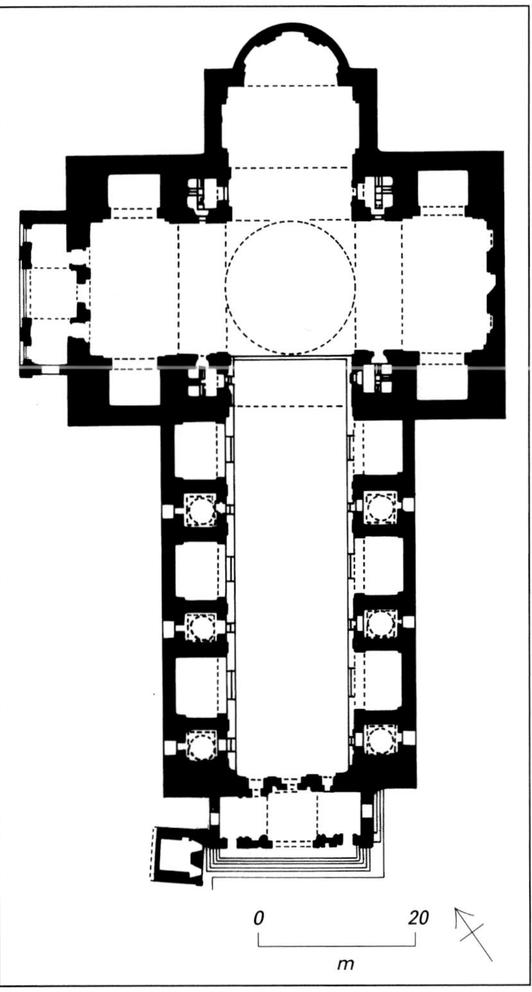

6. Leon Battista Alberti: plan of S Andrea, Mantua, designed 1470

7. Leon Battista Alberti: interior of S Andrea, Mantua, begun 1472

stone for the columns could have been imported into Mantua only at enormous expense. His own scheme, with a wider nave and no aisles, he considered more practical, as it would enable a greater number of people to see the precious relic, and also more economical, since it could be built entirely from brick. With Alberti's design duly approved, construction began at the west end in 1472, and the nave and principal façade were both largely complete by 1488. Subsequent work progressed at a greatly reduced rate; the north portico was built in the years around 1550, the south transept was still unbuilt in 1629, and the dome was eventually added by Filippo Juvarra in 1733.

The church has a Latin-cross plan with a broad nave and a domed crossing (see fig. 6). To either side of the nave, which is covered by a vast, longitudinal barrel vault, are three smaller domed chapels alternating with three larger chapels with transverse barrel vaults. The nave walls are articulated with tall pilasters to form a sequence of alternating bays, with low portals in the small bays giving access to the smaller chapels and broad open arches in the wide bays giving access to the larger ones. The dome at the crossing rests upon pendentives, and the three other arms of the church, which are around the same size, continue the pilaster articulation of the nave.

Few Renaissance church interiors can match S Andrea in sheer drama and monumentality (see fig. 7). In conceiving of his vast barrel-vaulted nave, Alberti rejected the aesthetic preference for trabeated ceilings that Brunelleschi had established, but he may have been influenced by the newly built choir of St Peter's in Rome or the Badia (after 1456) in Fiesole, both projects having barrel vaults of a comparable scale. Alberti drew his inspiration principally from antique example, however, as he makes clear in his letter to Ludovico Gonzaga, where he referred to the design as a *templum etruscum* (a temple of Etruscan type). As a specific model he may have had in mind the Basilica of Maxentius, an enormous vaulted structure with three exedrae on either side: in *De re aedificatoria* he describes the *templum etruscum* as a building of a very similar shape and arrangement to the Basilica of Maxentius, prescribing the overall proportions of 5:6 (breadth:length) that were eventually used for the nave of S Andrea. Regarding the building as a whole, it is not clear from Alberti's letter whether the original design was just for a nave and chapels, an inference that has been drawn, or whether it was for the complete Latin-cross layout eventually constructed. That he did in fact intend a Latin cross is suggested by the design of the crossing piers (later refaced), which originally had roundels facing both the nave and the transept. If so, this would imply, not unreasonably, that Alberti had adapted his notion of the *templum etruscum* to Christian uses and traditions. (For an illustration of Etruscan temple proportions according to Alberti *see* ARCHITECTURAL PROPORTION, fig. 6.)

For the first time in Alberti's architecture the internal arrangement of the building is mirrored in the façade. This is attached not directly to the main body of the church but, as in S Sebastiano, to a frontal block accommodating a portico. The portico has a tall central passageway with a longitudinal barrel vault and two lower lateral passageways with transverse barrel vaults. The façade (see fig. 8) is articulated with four giant pilasters, arranged so as to give a wider bay at the centre for the main passageway and narrower bays at each side punctuated vertically by niches set above the side portals, the latter giving access into the lateral passageways. The arrangement of the façade and portico is thus strikingly similar to the internal elevation of the nave walls and to the internal disposition of spaces, though it may also have been partly inspired by the internal transept ends of Brunelleschi's S Lorenzo. The fact that the façade is unusually much less wide than the nave and chapels combined was determined by the need to retain the medieval campanile to the left. In addition, as with S Sebastiano, the façade carries associations with ancient triumphal arches and, being crowned by a pediment, with ancient temples. Above the pediment is the façade's most puzzling feature, that of an arched canopy known as the *ombrellone.* Although its precise purpose remains unclear, it certainly serves to reduce the amount of direct light entering the nave, which, being otherwise lit only from individual roundels at the back of each chapel, is particularly dark. This darkness accords with Alberti's expressed preference in *De re aedificatoria* (VII.xii) that churches should be dimly lit in order to concentrate the mind upon the holy.

(iv) Style and development. In the preface to the Italian version (1436) of his treatise on painting Alberti had expressed a profound admiration for Brunelleschi's architecture, but in his own designs he gradually began to distance himself from Brunelleschi's principles. Whereas Brunelleschi, in applying his rigorously systematic classicism, had relied on plan types that were essentially medieval—Santo Spirito, for example, depends on such medieval prototypes as Santi Apostoli in Florence and Pisa Cathedral—Alberti introduced plan types, as in S Sebastiano and S Andrea, that were largely based on antique models. In architectural detailing there is a broadly similar difference. Whereas Brunelleschi relied for his details largely on such Florentine Romanesque buildings as the Baptistery, which he may have believed to have had an ancient pedigree, and only later turned on occasion to genuine antiquities, Alberti always used a much broader range of models, which included the Baptistery (for the corner pilasters at S Maria Novella) and other Florentine Romanesque buildings but much more frequently included actual Roman buildings, such as the Pantheon (for the portal of S Maria Novella) and the Mausoleum of Hadrian (for the *piano nobile* pilasters of the Palazzo Rucellai).

Moreover, Alberti was always much more concerned than Brunelleschi with principles derived from antique buildings. Brunelleschi, for example, often marked an axis with a supporting element, as in the plan of Santo Spirito, where there is a column, or in the main domes of the Old Sacristy at S Lorenzo and the Pazzi Chapel at Santa Croce, where there is a rib (*see* BRUNELLESCHI, FILIPPO, figs 3 and 4); Alberti, by contrast, almost always followed antique models in placing openings or niches rather than supports

8. Leon Battista Alberti: façade of S Andrea, Mantua, begun 1472

on the axes of his plans and coffers rather than ribs on the axes of his vaults.

More vexing is the question of whether Alberti's style developed during his career. Certainly his buildings in Rimini, Florence and Mantua are very different, and their differences might suggest a development in style. Equally, however, they might reflect differences in patronage, local styles, site and physical context, availability of building materials and a host of other factors. Indeed, it is probable that the appearance of the earlier Florentine buildings is due to their being commissioned by a Florentine banker, realized in a city with strong local traditions, constructed in very restrictive urban contexts and built of stone; and that the appearance of the later Mantuan buildings is due to their being commissioned by an imperial marchese, realized in a city with comparatively ephemeral local traditions, constructed on free sites and built of brick.

IV. Influence and posthumous reputation.

Alberti's influence is difficult to overestimate and it affected patrons and artists alike. Although not noble, the Alberti family had great status in Florentine society, a status that placed Leon Battista Alberti on almost equal terms socially with many of his patrons and that may have allowed him to persuade them of the virtue of his ideas more easily than would otherwise have been possible. His ideas and theories, before the advent of printing, were initially disseminated as much by his peripatetic lifestyle as papal secretary, which took him from his base in Rome to Ferrara, Florence, Mantua and Urbino, as they were by the manuscript writings themselves. In fact only six manuscript copies of *De re aedificatoria* survive, all of which can be dated to the period 1480–85.

By the end of the 15th century, most Italian painters and sculptors would have been inspired directly or indirectly by his treatises. His revolutionary formulation of the principles of linear perspective in particular marks a turning point in the development of naturalistic representation, and his method was subsequently exploited in the works of many mid-century painters, above all Uccello, Domenico Veneziano and Piero della Francesca. His more general concept of the *historia* underlies many of the great 15th-century cycles of narrative painting, especially those of Fra Angelico in the Nicholas V Chapel in the Vatican (*c.* 1448–9) and Filippo Lippi in Prato Cathedral (begun 1452), as it does subsequently the history paintings of Raphael and Titian. His concept of ideal beauty in nature remained central to aesthetic appreciation until it was rivalled by that of Michelangelo; and his belief in the pre-eminence of drawing as the basis of art remained a fundamental feature of subsequent painting despite the challenge of Giorgione and Titian, who advocated the practice of applying paint directly to the canvas without making a series of drawings. Other suggestive ideas may have also borne fruit in the fertile minds of younger artists—his recommendation that artists might copy sculpture, for example, perhaps influencing Mantegna in his partiality for ancient statuary, while his view of painting as the 'mistress' of the three arts may well have fuelled the later debate between painters and sculptors concerning the primacy of their respective arts (*see* PARAGONE; *see also* UT PICTURA POESIS).

Patrons, too, may have been influenced by the treatises on painting and sculpture, thereby themselves contributing to a change in taste. As the 15th century progressed, they increasingly came to value the kind of art commended by Alberti, demanding works that exhibited skill in *disegno* rather than costliness of material. They also increasingly demanded the kinds of picture described in *De pictura*, especially works of mythological or allegorical subject-matter, and the kind of sculpture envisaged in *De statua*, most particularly the large-scale, male nude statue. Alberti's treatises thus contributed in no small part to a shift in taste and custom that eventually resulted in the commissioning of Botticelli's *Calumny of Apelles* (1490s; Florence, Uffizi) and Michelangelo's *David* (1501–4; Florence, Accad.).

Directly or indirectly, *De re aedificatoria* had a considerable impact on subsequent architecture. Initially its direct influence may have been limited because, being written in Latin, it was accessible to few architects until published in Italian (Florence, 1550) by Cosimo Bartoli. Through verbal dissemination, however, Alberti's ideas may have had much greater impact. For example, in the trabeated colonnades at S Maria Maddalena de' Pazzi (early 1490s), Cestello, or the transverse barrel-vaulted *salone* and pedimented portico at the Villa Medici (1480s), Poggio a Caiano, Giuliano da Sangallo may well have followed Alberti's recommendations, but he most likely knew of them though Lorenzo de' Medici, who was familiar with *De re aedificatoria* in the original Latin.

De re aedificatoria had little immediate influence on subsequent 15th-century theorists, who apparently did not read or fully understand it. Neither Filarete, writing in the early 1460s, nor Francesco di Giorgio Martini, at least during the 1470s, can have been aware of the extent to which Alberti had understood the terminology, forms and uses of the orders of architecture; and their own attempts to make sense of Vitruvius and to relate his text to ancient buildings are dismal by comparison. It was only at the beginning of the 16th century that architects seem to have read Alberti's treatise themselves. Raphael may have known it, for in his famous letter (1519; Vatican; see V. Golzio: *Raffaelo nei documenti*, Vatican City, 1936) to Pope Leo X he reiterated Alberti's contention that good architecture depends on the use of rich and varied materials and his list is remarkably similar to that in *De re aedificatoria* (VI.v). Giulio Romano, Raphael's pupil, certainly owned a copy. Later in the century, Serlio and Palladio both freely acknowledged their debt to Alberti, a debt that lay not only in the elucidation of Vitruvius and the language of Classical architecture but also in the establishment of an aesthetic based upon natural law and reason.

It is, however, through his buildings, which have exerted so powerful and enduring a hold over the imagination of subsequent periods, that Alberti's influence has been greatest. The Palazzo Rucellai, with its applied architectural orders, established a norm for palazzo façade design for centuries thereafter; the S Maria Novella façade, with its two-storey format linked with S-shaped scrolls, established the standard elevational formula for subsequent churches; S Sebastiano, with its centrally planned Greek-cross layout, established a new plan-type in Renaissance ecclesiastical architecture; and S Andrea, with its wide, barrel-vaulted nave and side chapels, supplied one of the key models for future Latin-cross churches. These were truly visionary buildings.

WRITINGS

De pictura (MS., 1435; Basle, 1540); It. trans. as *Della pittura* (MS., 1436); ed. in H. Janitschek: *L. B. Albertis kleinere kunsttheoretische Schriften* (Vienna, 1877); ed. L. Mallè (Florence, 1950)

De statua (MS., *c.* 1440s); ed. in H. Janitschek: *L. B. Albertis kleinere kunsttheoretische Schriften* (Vienna, 1877)

De re aedificatoria (Florence, 1485); It. trans. and ed. G. Orlandi and P. Portoghesi (Milan, 1966); Eng. trans. by J. Rykwert, N. Leach and R. Tavernor as *On the Art of Building in Ten Books* (Cambridge, MA, and London, 1988)

G. Mancini, ed.: *Opera inedita et pauca separatim impressa* (Florence, 1890)

C. Grayson, ed. and trans: *An Autographed Letter from Leon Battista Alberti to Matteo de' Pasti, November 18, 1454* (New York, 1957)

C. Grayson, ed.: *Opere volgari*, 3 vols (Bari, 1960–73)

G. Orlandi, ed.: 'Descriptio urbis Romae', *Ist. Elem. Archit. & Rilievo Mnmt. Quad. [Genova]: Quad.*, 1 (1968), pp. 60–88

C. Grayson, ed. and trans.: *On Painting and Sculpture: The Latin Texts of 'De pictura' and 'De sculptura'* (London, 1972)

H.-K. Lücke, ed.: *Index verborum to L. B. Alberti's 'De re aedificatoria'*, 4 vols (Munich, 1975–9) [with facs. of original edn]

BIBLIOGRAPHY

DBI

EARLY SOURCES

G. Vasari: *Vite* (1550, rev. 2/1558); ed. G. Milanesi (1878–85)

M. Palmieri: 'De temporibus suis, Rerum italicum scriptores', ed. J. Tartinius, i (Florence, 1748), col. 241

'Vita di Leon Battista Alberti', *Opere volgari di Leon Battista Alberti*, ed. A. Bonucci (Florence, 1843)

GENERAL

R. Wittkower: *Architectural Principles in the Age of Humanism* (London, 1949, rev. 4/1973)

M. Baxandall: *Giotto and the Orators: Humanist Observers of Painting in Italy and the Discovery of Pictorial Composition, 1350–1450* (Oxford, 1971)
L. H. Heydenreich and W. Lotz: *Architecture in Italy, 1400–1600*, Pelican Hist. A. (Harmondsworth, 1974), pp. 27–38
M. Kemp: *The Science of Art: Optical Themes in Western Art from Brunelleschi to Seurat* (New Haven and London, 1992)

MONOGRAPHS

G. Mancini: *Vita di Leon Battista Alberti* (Florence, 1882, rev. 2/1911)
J. Gadol: *Leon Battista Alberti: Universal Man of the Early Renaissance* (Chicago, 1969)
F. Borsi: *Leon Battista Alberti: L'opera completa* (Milan, 1975; Eng. trans., London, 1977, 2/New York, 1986)

THEORY

P. H. Michel: *La Pensée de L. B. Alberti* (Paris, 1930)
M. Gosebruch: '"Varietà" bei Leon Battista Alberti und der wissenschaftliche Renaissancebegriff', *Z. Kstgesch.*, xx (1957), pp. 229–38
C. Grayson: 'The Humanism of Alberti', *It. Stud.*, xii (1957), pp. 37–56
——: 'The Composition of Alberti's *Decem libri De re aedificatoria*', *Münchn. Jb. Bild. Kst.*, xi (1960), pp. 152–61
R. Krautheimer: 'Alberti and Vitruvius', *Studies of Western Art: The Renaissance and Mannerism. Acts of the XXth International Congress of the History of Art: Princeton, 1963*, pp. 42–52; repr. in *Studies in Early Christian, Medieval and Renaissance Art* (New York, 1969), pp. 323–32
J. Białostocki: 'The Power of Beauty: An Utopian Idea of Leon Battista Alberti', *Studien zur toskanischen Kunst: Festschrift für Ludwig Heinrich Heydenreich* (Munich, 1964), pp. 13–19
S. Lang: '*De lineamentis*: L. B .Alberti's Use of a Technical Term', *J. Warb. & Court. Inst.*, xxviii (1965), pp. 331–5
R. Krautheimer: 'Alberti's *Templum Etruscum*', *Studies in Early Christian, Medieval and Renaissance Art* (New York, 1969), pp. 65–72
H. Lorenz: *Studien zum architektonischen und architekturtheorischen Werk L. B. Albertis* (diss., U. Vienna, 1971)
J. Onians: 'Alberti and Filarete: A Study in their Sources', *J. Warb. & Court. Inst.*, xxxiv (1971), pp. 96–114
L. Vagnetti: '*Concinnitas*: Riflessioni sul significato di un termine albertiano', *Stud. & Doc. Archit.*, ii (1973), pp. 139–61
E. Battisti: 'Il metodo progettuale secondo il *De re aedificatoria* di L. B. Alberti', *Il Sant' Andrea di Mantova* (Mantua, 1974), pp. 131–3
P. Naredi-Rainer: 'Bemerkungen zur Säule bei L. B. Alberti', *Jb. Ksthist. Inst. Graz*, xi (1976), pp. 51–61
——: 'Musikalische Proportionen, Zahlenästhetik und Zahlensymbolik in architektonischen Werk L. B. Albertis', *Jb. Ksthist. Inst. Graz*, xii (1977), pp. 81–213
R. Feuer-Toth: 'The *"apertionum ornamenta"* of Alberti and the Architecture of Brunelleschi', *Acta Hist. A. Acad. Sci. Hung.*, xxiv (1978), pp. 147–52
L. Vagnetti: 'Lo studio di Roma negli scritti albertiani', *Accademia Nazionale dei Lincei. Convegno internazionale indetto nel V centenario di Leon Battista Alberti: Rome, 1979*, pp. 73–144
J. Andrews Aiken: 'L. B. Alberti's System of Human Proportions', *J. Warb. & Court. Inst.*, xlii (1980), pp. 68–96
H. Mühlmann: *Aesthetische Theorie der Renaissance: Leon Battista Alberti* (Bonn, 1981)
R. Tavernor: *Concinnitas in the Architectural Theory and Practice of L. B. Alberti* (diss., U. Cambridge, 1985)
H. Biermann: 'Die Aufbauprinzipien von L. B. Albertis *De re aedificatoria*', *Z. Kstgesch.*, liii/4 (1990), pp. 443–85

ARCHITECTURE

C. Ricci: *Il Tempio Malatestiano* (Milan, 1925)
C. Mitchell: 'The Imagery of the Tempio Malatestiano', *Stud. Romagn.*, ii (1951), pp. 77–90
L. H. Heydenreich: 'Die Cappella Rucellai', *De artibus opuscola: Essays in Honour of Erwin Panofsky* (New York, 1961), p. 219
E. Hubala: 'L. B. Albertis Langhaus von Sant' Andrea in Mantua', *Festschrift Kurt Behrend* (Berlin, 1961), p. 83
G. Kiesow: 'Die gotische Südfassade von S Maria Novella in Florenz', *Z. Kstgesch.*, xxv (1962), pp. 10ff
C. Perina: *La basilica di Sant' Andrea in Mantova* (Mantua, 1965) [very full bibliog.]
P. Portoghesi: *Il Tempio Malatestiano* (Florence, 1965)
M. Dezzi Bardeschi: 'Il complesso monumentale di S Pancrazio a Firenze e il suo restauro', *Quad. Ist. Stor. Archit.*, xiii (1966), pp. 1–66
——: *La facciata di S Maria Novella* (Florence, 1970)
G. Guidetti: 'L. B. Alberti direttore della fabbrica di S Sebastiano', *Il Sant' Andrea in Mantova* (Mantua, 1974), pp. 237–41
C. W. Westfall: 'Alberti and the Vatican Palace Type', *J. Soc. Archit. Historians*, xxxiii (1974), pp. 101–21
E. Johnson: *Alberti's Church of S Andrea in Mantua* (London and University Park, 1975)
M. Spallanzani: 'L'abside dell'Alberti a San Martino a Gangalandi', *Mitt. Ksthist. Inst. Florenz*, xix (1975), pp. 241–50
K. Forster: 'The Palazzo Rucellai and Questions of Typology in the Development of Renaissance Buildings', *A. Bull.*, lviii (1976), pp. 109–13
H. Lorenz: 'Zur Architektur L. B. Albertis: Die Kirchenfassaden', *Röm. Jb. Kstgesch.*, xxix (1976), pp. 65–100
D. S. Chambers: 'Sant' Andrea at Mantua and Gonzaga Patronage, 1460–1472', *J. Warb. & Court. Inst.*, xl (1977), pp. 99–127
B. Preyer: 'The Rucellai Loggia', *Mitt. Ksthist. Inst. Florenz*, xxi (1977), pp. 183–98
B. L. Brown: *The Tribuna of SS Annunziata in Florence* (diss., Evanston, IL, Northwestern U., 1978)
A. Calzona: *Mantova città dell'Alberti* (Parma, 1979)
R. Lamoureux: *Alberti's Church of S Sebastiano in Mantua* (London and New York, 1979)
H. Burns: 'The Church of San Sebastiano', *Splendours of the Gonzaga*, ed. D. Chambers and J. Martineau (London, 1981), pp. 125–6
B. Preyer: 'The Rucellai Palace', *Giovanni Rucellai ed il suo Zibaldone*, ii (London, 1981), pp. 155–224
J. Rykwert and R. Tavernor: 'Sant' Andrea in Mantua', *Architects' J.*, clxxxiii/21 (1986), pp. 36–57
M. Naldini and D. Taddei: *La piazza, la loggia, il Palazzo Rucellai* (Florence, 1989)
H. S. Ettlinger: 'The Sepulchre on the Façade: A Re-evaluation of Sigismondo Malatesta's Rebuilding of S Francesco in Rimini', *J. Warb. & Court. Inst.*, liii (1990), pp. 133–43
C. Hope: 'The Early History of the Tempio Malatestiano', *J. Warb. & Court. Inst.*, lv (1992), pp. 51–155

SPECIALIST STUDIES

K. Badt: 'Drei plastische Arbeiten von Leon Battista Alberti', *Mitt. Ksthist. Inst. Florenz*, vii (1958), p. 81
R. N. Watkins: 'L. B. Alberti's Emblem, the Winged Eye, and his Name Leo', *Mitt. Ksthist. Inst. Florenz*, ix (1960), pp. 256–8
A. Parronchi: 'Leon Battista Alberti as a Painter', *Burl. Mag.*, liv/712 (1962), pp. 280–88
G. Morolli: 'Saggio di bibliografia albertiana', *Stud. & Doc. Archit.*, i (1972), pp. 11–56
F. W. Kent: 'The Letters Genuine and Spurious of Giovanni Rucellai', *J. Warb. & Court. Inst.*, xxxvii (1974), pp. 342–9
H. Burns: 'A Drawing by L. B. Alberti', *Archit. Des.*, xlix/5–6 (1979), pp. 45–56
K. Andersen: 'The Problem of Scaling and of Choosing Parameters in Perspective Construction, Particularly in the One by Alberti', *Anlct. Romana Inst. Dan.*, xvi (1987), pp. 107–28
P. W. Lehmann: 'Alberti and Antiquity: Additional Observations', *A. Bull.*, lxx/3 (1988), pp. 388–400
M. Tafuri: 'Cives esse non licere: Niccolò V e Leon Battista Alberti', *Ricerca del rinascimento*, ed. M. Tafuri (Turin, 1992), pp. 33–88

PAUL DAVIES, DAVID HEMSOLL

Albertinelli, Mariotto (di Biagio di Bindo) (*b* Florence, 13 Oct 1474; *d* Florence, 5 Nov 1515). Italian painter. Albertinelli's contribution to the Florentine High Renaissance was inspired by the work of FRA BARTOLOMMEO, and the two artists worked together in a partnership, their paintings appearing to be the product of a single hand. Albertinelli, however, always retained artistic independence, as is revealed in certain paintings that are eccentrically archaic and in others that show a preference for conventions more typical of the early Renaissance.

1. LIFE AND WORK.

(i) Before 1503. According to Vasari, Albertinelli and Fra Bartolommeo were both apprenticed to Cosimo Rosselli. The two young painters became friends and after their emancipation operated a joint workshop in the 1490s. Vasari also stated that in an interlude before 1494 Alber-

tinelli worked exclusively for Alfonsina Orsini, the wife of Piero II de' Medici (*reg* 1492–4), but the works made for her cannot be identified. Albertinelli initially specialized in small, elegantly framed paintings destined for the homes of sophisticated patrons. These works were produced independently of Fra Bartolommeo and are stylistically distinguishable. From Piero di Cosimo, the most creative personality in Cosimo Rosselli's workshop, Albertinelli absorbed Flemish techniques, a spirited versatility in imitation and a tendency towards eccentricity. For example, the *Virgin and Child* depicted in the central panel of a portable triptych (1500; Milan, Mus. Poldi-Pezzoli) refers to Filippino Lippi, the right shutter of *St Barbara* to Flemish painting, and the architecture on the left shutter showing *St Catherine of Alexandria* derives from Perugino. Another portable triptych (Chartres, Mus. B.-A.) recalls, in a bizarre fashion, works of the 14th century.

Albertinelli and Fra Bartolommeo collaborated on larger paintings; the *Annunciation* (1497; Volterra Cathedral), a medium-sized altarpiece, has been attributed to both painters, but their collaboration is proved by Albertinelli's drawing for the grotesque on the left pilaster (Florence, Uffizi), while a study for the angel (Florence, Uffizi) is by Fra Bartolommeo. In March 1501 Albertinelli completed the fresco of the *Last Judgement* (Florence, Mus. S Marco) that Fra Bartolommeo had left unfinished in July 1500, when he entered the Dominican Order and renounced painting for four years. The artists' collaboration had allowed Albertinelli to master Fra Bartolommeo's technique sufficiently to paint in a style that blended with that of his partner (Vasari). Fra Bartolommeo had painted the upper tier with the *Apostles*; Albertinelli started on the three angels below *Christ*, for which he made new drawings despite the pre-existing ones by his partner. He also made new studies for the *St Michael* and included portraits of monks at S Maria Nuova, one of Giuliano Bugiardini and his own self-portrait (Vasari). He managed to make these changes to the composition without distorting the original concept.

(ii) 1503–9. In 1503 Albertinelli completed the high altarpiece for S Martino, Florence; the main panel shows the *Visitation* (see fig. 1), and the predella illustrates the *Circumcision*, the *Adoration of the Child* and the *Annunciation* (all Florence, Uffizi). Although the figural composition of the *Visitation* was based on drawings by Fra Bartolommeo, a black chalk study for the *Virgin* (Berlin, Kupferstichkab.) by Albertinelli shows that he replaced Fra Bartolommeo's strong contrasts in light and dark with smoother gradations of tone. In the painting, too, he made minimal use of monochrome and worked in soft highlights and colours in imitation of Perugino, who was also the source for the background arcade. For the next two years Albertinelli was guided more by Perugino and Piero di Cosimo than by Fra Bartolommeo, and his works were conceived in stylistic frameworks typical of the early Renaissance. Dating from these years are the large fresco of the *Crucifixion* (1505; Florence, Certosa dell Galluzzo (also known as di Val d'Ema), chapter house) and the *Virgin and Child with SS Jerome and Zenobius* (1506; Paris, Louvre), painted for the chapel of Zanobi del Maestro in Santa Trìnita, Florence. The undated altarpiece of the

1. Mariotto Albertinelli: *Visitation*, oil on canvas, 2.32×1.46 m, 1503 (Florence, Galleria degli Uffizi)

Annunciation with SS Sebastian and Lucy (Munich, Alte Pin.) appears, stylistically, to belong to the same period.

In 1506 Albertinelli was commissioned to paint the *Annunciation with God the Father* (Florence, Accad.; see fig. 2) for the altar of the chapel of the Canons in Florence Cathedral. He received payments in 1507 and 1508 and completed it in 1510. A dispute arose over its value, and Perugino, Francesco Granacci and Ridolfo Ghirlandaio were called in to mediate. It is the first altarpiece of the period to show a glory of life-sized figures suspended in an architectural interior that acts as a dramatic component of the representation, rather than being projected as a symbol of harmony. Its novelty in the interplay of colours with light and dark was Albertinelli's own interpretation of the synthesis achieved by Fra Bartolommeo, after his visit to Venice in 1508, between Venetian luminosity and Leonardo da Vinci's monochromatic underpainting.

(iii) 1509–13. In 1509 Albertinelli and Fra Bartolommeo, who had resumed painting, entered into a partnership under the auspices of the convent of S Marco, Florence. The partners were on an equal footing, each entitled to half the profit of a shared commission. The partnership was dissolved in January 1513, as is evidenced by the survival of the relevant document. Fragmentary records of payment also survive for some works, though Vasari

2. Mariotto Albertinelli: *Annunciation with God the Father*, oil on panel, 3.35×2.30 m, 1506–10 (Florence, Galleria dell'Accademia)

did not mention the partnership in Albertinelli's *Vita.* In July 1509 Albertinelli's name appears in the records of S Marco in connection with *God the Father with SS Magdalene and Catherine of Siena* (Lucca, Villa Guinigi), originally commissioned from Fra Bartolommeo by the Dominican convent of S Pietro Martire in Murano. The same year he collaborated with his partner on the *Virgin and Child with SS Catherine, Mary Magdalene, John the Baptist, Nicholas, Peter Martyr and Benedict* (Florence, S Marco), and through this experience he adopted the process by which Fra Bartolommeo gave instability to colours, but altered it by dividing them sharply on the forms. He also received almost half the profit for the *Virgin and Child with SS Stephen and John the Baptist* (Lucca Cathedral) and was named in the document concerning the Great Council Altarpiece (Florence, Mus. S Marco), although the commission was Fra Bartolommeo's alone. In January 1513 Albertinelli relinquished his rights to the Great Council Altarpiece, but in compensation he was given, among others, two paintings begun by Fra Bartolommeo, the *Pietà* (Florence, Pitti) and *Adam and Eve* (Philadelphia, PA, Mus. A.).

The collaboration between the partners on individual panels must have been selective: there is no evidence that Albertinelli participated in Fra Bartolommeo's two paintings of the *Mystic Marriage of St Catherine of Siena* (Paris, Louvre; Florence, Accad.), but he obviously worked on the Pitti *Pietà* and on the altarpiece for Ferry Carondelet comprising the *Coronation of the Virgin* (fragments Stuttgart, Staatsgal.) and the *Virgin and Child in Glory with SS Sebastian, John the Baptist, Stephen, Anthony Abbot and Bernard and the Donor Ferry Carondelet* (Besançon Cathedral). The Carondelet Altarpiece is the supreme accomplishment of both artists. A sketch for the composition in black chalk (Rotterdam, Mus. Boymans–van Beuningen) proves that Albertinelli contributed to the invention of the central panel; in addition, the *Coronation*, originally in the arched top of the panel, was entirely painted by him. In the *Annunciation* (1511; Geneva, Mus. A. & Hist.), though signed by both artists, Albertinelli's style is dominant.

Meanwhile Albertinelli continued to work independently. The *Virgin and Child with the Infant St John the Baptist* (1509; Harewood House, W. Yorks) is signed only by him. Also his are two paintings for the convent of S Giuliano, Florence: the *Virgin and Child with SS Julian, Dominic, Nicholas and Jerome* and the *Trinity* (both Florence, Accad.). Why the partnership was abruptly terminated in January 1513 is not known. For Albertinelli it had unquestionably been a financial success, reflected in his acquisitions of property in Florence and vineyards in the countryside.

(iv) 1513–15. Vasari claimed that Albertinelli's career ended in 1512. More accurately he reported that Albertinelli stopped painting for some months and ran two public houses in Florence: documents show that at the time of his death Albertinelli received an income from a tavern near the Ponte Vecchio. The interruption was brief and occurred immediately after the dissolution of the partnership. Proof that he returned to painting is the existence of an altarpiece that is signed and dated 1514 (Volognano, Pontassieve, S Michele) and Vasari's report that Albertinelli painted a *Faith, Hope and Charity* (untraced) for Leo X on his elevation to the papacy on 11 March 1513. Also true is Vasari's account of Albertinelli's visit to Viterbo and Rome in the summer of 1513, because his hand is recognizable in the upper part of the *Coronation of the Virgin* (Viterbo, S Maria della Quercia), which he left unfinished and which was later completed by Fra Paolino. Several small panels of 1513–15 done in Albertinelli's late style also prove that he remained active to the end of his life; their style is either wilfully archaistic or eccentric. Typical examples include the *Creation* (U. London, Courtauld Inst. Gals), the *Expulsion from the Garden* (Zagreb, Slika Gal.) and *Cain and Abel* (Bergamo, Gal. Accad. Carrara), which recall 15th-century Flemish paintings. In his *Virgin and Child* (Venice, Semin. Patriarcale), the figures, drastically out of scale with the framing architecture, represent a rejection of the ideals of the High Renaissance.

Vasari pictured Albertinelli as a libertine, excessively fond of good living and politically opposed to the faction of Savonarola. Records for two loans he contracted and failed to make good confirm his disorderly life style: he was excommunicated posthumously in 1516 for not having repaid a loan granted to him by the prioress of the convent of S Giuliano, and in 1517 Raphael sued his estate for a loan made many years earlier, which again had remained unpaid. Antonia, Albertinelli's wife since 1506, agreed to repay both loans.

2. Working methods and technique. On account of Vasari's statement that Albertinelli knew he was a less gifted draughtsman than Fra Bartolommeo (as a remedy he took to drawing after the ancient statues in the Medici collection), later historians found it difficult to attribute drawings to Albertinelli. From the few of them known in 1903, Berenson concluded that Albertinelli could not draw and that he relied entirely on his partner's draughtsmanship. However, later attributions of drawings to Albertinelli show him to be quite proficient, capable of either following or modifying Fra Bartolommeo's drawings, and of making his own original contributions. He abandoned metalpoint as early as Fra Bartolommeo, adopting the pen and black chalk as his favourite media for studies, either for compositions or for single figures; he also achieved good effects with red chalk.

As a painter engaged in large productions, Albertinelli needed assistants. Giuliano Bugiardini, who rented quarters next to his in 1503, certainly became one. In 1506 Fra Bartolommeo's younger brother, Piero, entered the workshop under terms of a guardianship that called for Albertinelli to instruct him in painting. According to Vasari, Franciabigio, Pontormo and Innocenzo da Imola also worked under Albertinelli, but the dates of their apprenticeships are problematic. Vasari also spoke of a certain Visino who supposedly went to Hungary after making his name in Florence, but he has not been identified.

BIBLIOGRAPHY

DBI; Meissner; Thieme–Becker

G. Vasari: *Vite* (1550, rev. 2/1568); ed. G. Milanesi (1878–85), iv, pp. 217–31

V. Marchese: *Memorie dei più insigni pittori, scultori e architetti domenicani*, 2 vols (Florence, 1854, rev. Bologna, 2/1879)

J. A. Crowe and G. B. Cavalcaselle: *A History of Painting in Italy* (London, 1865–6, rev. 2/1903–14), iii, p. 484

G. Gruyer: *Fra Bartolommeo della Porta et Mariotto Albertinelli* (Paris, 1886)

A. Castan: *La Physionomie primitive du retable de Fra Bartolommeo à la cathédrale de Besançon* (Besançon, 1889)

A. Venturi: *Storia* (1901–40), IX/i, p. 348

B. Berenson: *The Drawings of the Florentine Painters* (London, 1903, rev. Chicago, 2/1938)

F. Knapp: *Fra Bartolommeo della Porta und die Schule von San Marco* (Halle, 1903)

P. Bagnesi-Bellincini: 'Due documenti sul *Giudizio universale* di Fra Bartolommeo', *Riv. A.*, vi (1909), pp. 245–50

H. von der Gabelentz: *Fra Bartolommeo und die Florentiner Renaissance* (Leipzig, 1922)

H. Bodmer: 'Opere giovanili e tarde di Mariotto Albertinelli', *Dedalo*, ix (1928), pp. 598–620

Mostra del cinquecento italiano (exh. cat., Florence, Pal. Strozzi, 1940), p. 24

S. J. Freedberg: *Painting of the High Renaissance in Rome and Florence* (Cambridge, MA, 1961, rev. New York, 2/1972)

B. Berenson: *Florentine School*, i (London, 1963), pp. 1–2

L. Borgo: 'Albertinelli, Fra Bartolommeo and the *Pietà* for the Certosa di Pavia', *Burl. Mag.*, cviii (1966), pp. 463–8

M. Winner: 'Zwei unbekannte Zeichnungen von Fra Bartolommeo und Albertinelli', *Festschrift H. Mühle* (Berlin, 1967)

L. Borgo: 'The Problem of the Ferry Carondelet Altarpiece', *Burl. Mag.*, cxiii (1971), pp. 362–71

S. J. Freedberg: *Painting in Italy, 1500–1600*, Pelican Hist. A. (Harmondsworth, 1971), p. 52

C. von Holst: 'Florentiner Gemälde und Zeichnungen aus der Zeit von 1480 bis 1580', *Mitt. Ksthist. Inst. Florenz*, xv (1971), pp. 1–64

L. Borgo: 'Mariotto Albertinelli's Smaller Paintings after 1512', *Burl. Mag.*, cxvi (1974), pp. 245–50

C. von Holst: 'Fra Bartolommeo und Albertinelli', *Mitt. Ksthist. Inst. Florenz*, xviii (1974), pp. 273–318

S. R. McKillop: *Franciabigio* (Berkeley, 1974), p. 253

L. Borgo: *The Works of Mariotto Albertinelli* (New York, 1976)

M. Natale: *Peintures italiennes du XIVe au XVIIIe siècle*, Geneva, Mus. A. & Hist. cat. (Geneva, 1979), p. 2

Il primato del disegno (exh. cat., Florence, Pal. Strozzi, 1980), p. 49

Le XVIe Siècle florentin au Louvre (exh. cat. by S. Béguin, Paris, Louvre, 1982)

Disegni di Fra Bartolommeo e della sua scuola (exh. cat. by C. Fischer, Florence, Uffizi, 1986)

A. M. Petrioli Tofani: *Gabinetto disegni e stampe degli Uffizi, Inventario, 1: Disegni esposti*, Florence, Uffizi cat. (Florence, 1986)

LUDOVICO BORGO, MARGOT BORGO

Albertini, Francesco (*b* Florence; *d* Rome, 1517–21). Italian antiquary. He was appointed chaplain of S Lorenzo in Florence in 1493 and canon of the basilica six years later. In Florence he learnt painting from Domenico Ghirlandaio and poetry from the Medici courtier Naldo Naldi. In 1502 he went to Rome, where from 1505 he served as chaplain to the cardinal of S Sabina, Fazio Santori. Only one copy of Albertini's *Memoriale di molte statue e pitture della città di Firenze* (Florence, Bib. N. Cent.), published by Antonio Tubini in Florence on 2 October 1510, survives; there is also a revised and corrected manuscript copy of the printed text (Rome, Bib. Angelica, MS. 2053). Dedicated to the Florentine sculptor Baccio da Montelupo, it was written as a brief guide to the city by *quartieri*, beginning with the Baptistery. Albertini is better known for his *Opusculum de mirabilibus novae et veteris urbis Romae*, published in Rome by Giacomo Mazzochio on 4 February 1510. This was composed at the behest of Cardinal Galeotto della Rovere, to fill the need for an updated version of the medieval *Mirabilia*. The frontispiece bears an epigram by the antiquary Andrea Fulvio, who had trained in the Roman academy of Pomponio Leto. In the prefatory epistle Albertini mentioned Giovanni Tortelli and Flavio Biondo, along with Leto, as his precursors; unlike Leto, whose guidebook to ancient Rome, the *Fragmenta*, is organized in the form of an itinerary, Albertini divided his material topically, following the tradition of Biondo's *Roma instaurata* (1446). The first book is devoted to the ancient city, with chapters on the walls, portals, roads and so on. The second book deals with such topics as temples, basilicas, triumphal arches and sepulchres. Albertini was not particularly discriminating in his use of historical sources (glosses to Classical authors are interspersed with quotations from the forgeries of the Dominican friar Annio da Viterbo), yet his citation of numerous inscriptions, including the *cippus* recording the Claudian extension of the *pomerium*, suggests that his epigraphic knowledge was extensive. The third book, on current building activity, is of particular interest, dealing, for example, with Adriano Castellesi da Corneto's palace in the Borgo, and with Donato Bramante's additions to the Vatican apartments and the Cortile del Belvedere under Pope Julius II.

WRITINGS

Memoriale di molte statue e pitture della città di Firenze (Florence, 1510)

Opusculum de mirabilibus novae et veteris urbis Romae (Rome, 1510/*R* 1515, 1523; Basle, 1519; Lyon, 1523); ed. A. Schmarsow (Heilbronn, 1886)

Both repr. in *Five Early Guides to Rome and Florence*, intro. by P. Murray (Farnborough, 1972)

DBI

BIBLIOGRAPHY

R. Weiss: *The Renaissance Discovery of Classical Antiquity* (London, 1969), pp. 84–6

E. Bentivoglio: 'Un manoscritto inedito connesso al *Memoriale di molte statue et pitture* di Francesco Albertini', *Mitt. Ksthist. Inst. Florenz*, xxiv/3 (1980), pp. 345–56

D. E. Rhodes, ed.: *La stampa a Firenze, 1471–1550: Omaggio a Roberto Ridolfi* (Florence, 1984)

PHILIP J. JACKS

Alberto [Sánchez, Alberto] (*b* Toledo, 8 April 1895; *d* Moscow, 12 Oct 1962). Spanish sculptor. Of humble origins, he worked as an apprentice blacksmith, baker and shoemaker before dedicating himself to sculpture. From 1912 he served as an apprentice in the studio. Of the sculptor José Estanys, learning how to cast in plaster. While performing his military service from 1917 (beginning in Melilla on the North African coast) he made busts and figures of Arabs in plaster. On his return to Madrid in 1920 he worked as a baker but also visited museums and produced posters for public meetings, and through Rafael Barradas, whom he knew casually, he began to inform himself about avant-garde artistic trends.

Until 1922 Alberto worked in a neo-Cubist style. His successful participation in 1925 in the first Exposición de Artistas Ibéricas in Madrid helped him obtain a grant from the Diputación Provincial de Toledo, which permitted him to dedicate himself exclusively to art. By this time he had begun to sign and exhibit his works with just his first name. In 1925 he helped found the Primera Escuela de Vallecas, through which students met for discussions and for outings into the countryside. Alberto's own observations of nature during this period inspired some essentially abstract sculptures full of vitality, such as *Untitled* (*c*. 1925–30; see 1970 exh. cat., p. 31), one of several works presumed destroyed during the Spanish Civil War (1936–9).

In the 1930s Alberto participated in the *Primera Exposición de arte revolucionario* organized by the magazine *Octubre* and in another exhibition organized by the Constructivist Group led by Joaquín Torres García. When the Spanish Civil War broke out he joined the 'Cultural Brigades' and the Fifth Regiment. In 1937 he produced a colossal symbolic piece, representing Spain and its people in conflict, entitled *The Spanish People Have a Path which Leads to a Star* (h. 12.5 m; destr.; see Martin, fig. VI), which was placed outside the Spanish Pavilion at the Exposition Internationale in Paris.

In 1938 Alberto settled in Moscow, where at first he taught art to evacuated children. He dedicated himself until 1956 to teaching and to producing graphic work, wooden toys, mural paintings and stage sets; he designed a production of Federico García Lorca's play *Bodas de Sangre* for the Gypsy Theatre and served as artistic adviser to Grigory Kozintsev for his film version of *Don Quixote* (1957). Changes in official Soviet policy from 1956 encouraged Alberto to return to sculpture abstracted from the figure or from animals, in a manner reminiscent of work by Picasso and Miró. He used materials such as wood, metal sheeting, metal wire, fabrics and paint to fashion geometric and organic shapes as separate components that he joined together. Conceptually the themes of these works, such as *Castilian Woman* (sheet iron, h. 820 mm, 1958–62; Moscow, Pushkin Mus. F.A.), were reminiscent of those he had made in Spain. He began work in 1961 on a *Monument to Peace* (wood, h. 1.5 m; priv. col., see 1970 exh. cat., p. 58), with ascending lance-like shapes whose points resemble doves; this was left unfinished on his death in 1962 from gall-bladder failure. The Fundación Alberto, established in Madrid in 1974, contains a wealth of documentary and graphic material.

WRITINGS

A. Sánchez: *Palabras de un escultor* (Valencia, 1975)

BIBLIOGRAPHY

P. Martin: *Alberto* (Budapest, 1964)

Alberto (1895–1962) (exh. cat., texts P. Picasso, P. Neruda and R. Alberti; Madrid, Mus. A. Contemp., 1970)

Escultura española, 1900–1936 (exh. cat., Madrid, Min. Cult., 1985)

INMACULADA JULIÁN

Albert of Brandenburg, Cardinal and Duke of Prussia. *See* HOHENZOLLERN, (1).

Albertolli. Swiss family of artists and teachers. They were active in northern Italy in the 18th century and the first half of the 19th and were particularly influential in the field of art teaching, since the chair in design at the Accademia di Belle Arti di Brera in Milan was held by a member of the family from 1776 to 1844. The head of the family was the architect and engineer Francesco Saverio Albertolli (*b* Bedano, nr Lugano, 1701), who worked with his sons Michele Albertolli (*b* Bedano, 29 Sept 1732) and later (1) Giocondo Albertolli at Aosta, where Michele's son Alberto Albertolli (*fl* 18th century) was active as a stuccoist. Both Francesco Saverio's brother and his third son, Grato Albertolli (*fl* 1744–5; *d* 1812), were also stuccoists. The most distinguished member of the family was (1) Giocondo, who documented the history of the family. His son (3) Raffaele Albertolli and Michele's other sons, (2) Giacomo Albertolli, (4) Ferdinando Albertolli and Fedele Albertolli (*b* Bedano, 1789; *d* Monza, Feb 1832), also worked in the arts. According to Giocondo, who championed the unity of architecture, applied decoration and furnishings, the family inspired the French architects Charles Percier, Pierre-François Fontaine and Moreau, who themselves reawakened artistic interest in the applied arts in France.

Meissner

BIBLIOGRAPHY

C. Cantù: Obituary [of Fedele Albertolli], *Gaz. Privileg. Milano*, cxli (20 May 1832), pp. 555–6

M. Caffi: 'Di alcuni architetti e scultori della Svizzera italiana', *Archv Stor. Lombardo*, xii/1 (1885), pp. 65–85

G. B. Intra: 'La reggia mantovana sotto la prima dominazione austriaca', *Archv Stor. Lombardo*, xv/2 (1888), pp. 473–90

L. Brentani: *Antichi maestri d'arte e di scuola delle terre ticinesi*, 5 vols (Como, 1937–44), ii, pp. 61–4, 67–70, 73–5, 100–01, 105, 174, 216–21; iv, pp. 24–56, 115–20; v, pp. 90–92

M. Guidi: 'Gli Albertolli', *Z. Schweiz. Archäol. & Kstgesch.*, viii (1946), pp. 243–51

C. L. V. Meeks: *Italian Architecture, 1750–1914* (New Haven, 1966), pp. 78, 101

S. Franscini: *La Svizzera italiana* (Lugano, 1973), pp. 256, 266–9

Mostra dei maestri di Brera, 1776–1859 (exh. cat., ed. A. M. Brizio and M. Rosci; Milan, Pal. Permanente, 1975), pp. 46–51, 77–9, 84–6, 133–6

A. Finocchi: 'Desegni: degli Albertolli nella raccolta Maggiolini di Milano e all'Archivio Cantonale di Bellinzona', *Dis. Archit.* (Sept 1990), pp. 17–20

(1) (Giuseppe) Giocondo Albertolli (*b* Bedano, 24 July 1742; *d* Milan, 15 Nov 1839). Architect, decorator and teacher. He was educated in Aosta and was then sent by his father to Parma to stay with his uncle, a stuccoist. He finished his training in the local Accademia di Belle Arti where he was awarded prizes in 1766 and 1768. He worked first in Parma, executing decorations in S Brigida (1765), decorations from a design by Ennemond-Alexandre Petitot for a triumphal arch (1768, destr. 1859) for the wedding celebrations of Ferdinand, Duke of Parma, and Maria Amalia of Austria and ceiling decorations in the palace of the Duca di Grillo (begun 1769). From 1770 to 1775 Giocondo carried out the stuccowork in the Gran Salone of the villa of Poggio Imperiale, outside Florence, for Leopold, Grand Duke of Tuscany. French designs were sent from Vienna, and the resulting room, later painted white, recalls the Petit Trianon, Versailles, though the scale is very large, with a Corinthian order of pilasters along the walls. These serve to mark off the garlands, trophies and low reliefs in frames that are applied in decoration. During his time in Florence he became familiar with Tuscan stuccowork of the 15th and 16th centuries, which was fundamental for his future career. Giocondo's personal style was also influenced by a visit he made to Rome, Naples, Pompeii and Herculaneum. On that occasion he executed models of Corinthian capitals for the church of the Annunciation in Naples for the architect Carlo Vanvitelli, son of Luigi Vanvitelli. These professional contacts may have brought his work to the appreciative attention of Giuseppe Piermarini, imperial and royal architect in Milan, who in 1774 invited him to leave Bedano, where he had returned in 1773, to decorate the Palazzo Reale. In 1774 and 1775 he divided his time between Milan and Florence, having been summoned again to Florence by the architect Gaspero Maria Paoletti to decorate the ceilings of the Sala degli Stucchi and the Palazzina della Meridiana in the Palazzo Pitti. He also began the decoration of the Sala delle Niobi in the Uffizi Gallery. All his Tuscan projects were completed by his brother Grato. In Milan he took two years to complete the room of the caryatids in the Palazzo Reale.

When the Accademia di Belle Arti di Brera was founded, he held the post of Professor of Design and continued teaching until 1812, when an eye complaint and his grief at the death of his son (3) Raffaele forced him to retire. His publications, widely circulated in Italy and Europe, also had a didactic purpose. Containing engravings of his completed works and designs, they laid the foundations for a style based on a mixture of ancient Greek and Roman details with others derived from 16th-century Lombard and Florentine art. In his last volume, published in 1805, the range of motifs is the outcome of endless combinations, governed by the dictates of the underlying architectural form. The book's teaching method is based on the student copying the designs until perfect before coming to terms with greater difficulties.

The intervention of Carl Joseph von Firmian and an increase in his stipend prevented him from accepting an invitation in 1782 to teach at the Accademia di Belle Arti in Parma. In addition to decorating many rooms in the Palazzo Reale to designs by Piermarini, he undertook commissions for the Teatro alla Scala (1778), for the Galleria Vecchia in the Palazzo Ducale in Mantua (to his own design, 1779) and for various rooms in the Villa Reale, Monza (to his own design, 1780–83; see fig.). Piermarini supplied him with designs for the decoration of the Palazzo Casnedi (*c.* 1775), Milan, the Palazzo Greppi (*c.* 1776), Milan, and the Palazzo Belgiojoso (late 1770s), Milan, while he himself devised decorative schemes for the Palazzo Serbelloni (*c.* 1793), Milan, and the Palazzo Busca Arconati, Milan. Piermarini and Giocondo Albertolli had an identical approach to design: they interpreted the Classical canons liberally, adopted the example set by Raphael and his followers (reproductions of the Vatican Loggie formed part of the teaching aids in the school of design) and derived their architectural mouldings from the observation of nature.

Giocondo's architectural works include the rebuilding of his house at Bedano (1797–9); a monument (1808–9; destr.) in the marketplace at Lodi commemorating Napoleon's victory over the Austrians in 1796; the Villa Melzi (1808–9) for the Duca di Lodi at Bellagio, near Como, with a chapel added later (1814–16); the external and internal restructuring of Palazzo Melzi (1805; destr.) in Milan; and the exterior of the 16th-century tempietto in the form of a Greek cross that was dismantled at Lugano and rebuilt at Moncucco near Monza in the park

Giocondo Albertolli: carved wood door decoration (1780–83) for the Villa Reale, Monza; from G. Albertolli: *Alcune decorazioni di nobili sale ed altri ornamenti* (Milan, 1787), pl. V

of the Villa Andreani. He also designed altars, for example the main altar (1816) in S Marco, Milan, furnishings and funeral decorations.

A severe critic of 'reforms that served to corrupt good taste', he was firmly opposed to the innovation of the Gothic Revival, especially while serving as a member of the committees that judged architectural competitions and on the Milan Planning Applications Board. He was a member of the commission that drew up the new decorative scheme for the Teatro alla Scala (1806–7) and helped to judge the competition to design the Porta Orientale in 1826.

WRITINGS

Ornamenti diversi (Milan, 1782)

Alcune decorazioni di nobili sale ed altri ornamenti (Milan, 1787)

Miscellanea per i giovani studiosi del disegno (Milan, 1796)

Corso elementare di ornamenti architettonici ideato e disegnato ad uso de' principianti (Milan, 1805)

C. Cantù: *Storia della città e della diocesi di Como*, ii/10 (Como, 1832), pp. 526–36 [Giocondo contributed biographical entries for members of his family]

Cenni storici sovra una cappella antica ricostruita in oratorio a Moncucco (Milan, 1833)

S. Samek Ludovici: *Storia di Milano*, xiii (Milan, 1959), p. 545 [transcription of Giocondo's autobiographical work]

BIBLIOGRAPHY

C. Cantù: Obituary, *Bib. It. G. Lett. Sci. & A.*, xcvi (Oct–Dec 1839), pp. 416–18

A. Annoni: 'Dal Rococò all'Impero: Giocondo Albertolli', *A. It. Dec. & Indust.*, xvi (1907), no. 9, pp. 69–72, no. 10, pp. 77–80

A. Kauffmann: *G. A. der Ornamentiker des italienischen Klassizismus* (Strasburg, 1911) [with bibliog. and sources]

G. Marangoni: 'L'artista neoclassico dell'arredamento: Giocondo Albertolli', *Cult. Mod.*, xxxviii/12 (1929), pp. 705–13

G. Nicodemi: 'Giocondo Albertolli', *Milano*, liii/4 (1937), pp.177–85

L. Grassi: 'La Villa Melzi a Bellagio', *A. Figurative*, vii/5 (1959), pp. 30–37

G. Mezzanotte: 'Giocondo Albertolli', *Architettura neoclassica in Lombardia* (Naples, 1966), pp. 140–70

A. Gonzales-Palacios: 'Disegni di G. Albertolli', *A. Illus.*, iv/41–2 (1971), pp. 24–33

M. Candia: 'G. A. e Michele Canzio: Contributi ed indirizzi in rapporto alla formazione e all'elaborazione di un linguaggio decorativo neoclassico', *A. Lombarda* (1980), pp. 265–72

S. Della Torre: 'Villa Melzi a Bellagio', *Civiltà neoclassica nell'attuale provincia di Como* (exh. cat. by B. Fasola, Como, S Francesco, 1980), pp. 63–7

A. Gonzalez-Palacios: 'Disegni di Giocondo Albertolli', *A. Illus.* (May–June 1981), pp. 24ff

G. Ricci: 'La formazione degli architetti nell'Accademia di Belle Arti di Brera: 1776–1815', *Costruire in Lombardia* (Milan, 1983), pp. 161–76

T. Casari: *Cronaca di una vita al servizio dell'arte* (Chiasso, 1991)

(2) Giacomo Albertolli (*b* Mugena, nr Lugano, 1761; *d* Milan, 6 Jan 1805). Teacher and architect, nephew of (1) Giocondo Albertolli. He studied at the Accademia di Brera and finished his training at the Accademia di Belle Arti in Parma. Of his collaboration with Piermarini, of which he boasted, only his contribution to decorations for the Festa della Federazione (1797) is documented. From 1783 he was in Parma, in 1793 in Verona and in 1797 in Padua, where he taught at the seminary as an instructor in civil architecture. He was subsequently employed as public works architect and as inspector and director of the school of architecture in the university in Padua. Dismissed as a francophile by the Austrian government after the Treaty of Campoformio (1797), he went to Milan where he was appointed to the chair of architecture in 1798. In 1799 he was suspended from his post on the return of the Austrians and was reappointed on the return of the French. In his teaching, he introduced the study of Greek antiquities, as illustrated in the publications of Le Roy, James Stuart and Nicholas Revett. From 1803, together with his uncle (1) Giocondo, Giacomo was part of various commissions set up to control the city's building trade.

(3) (Stefano) Raffaele Albertolli (*b* Bedano, 21 Sept 1770; *d* Milan, 7 Jan 1812). Printmaker and painter, son of (1) Giocondo Albertolli. He suffered from ill-health from infancy. After having attended the Accademia di Belle Arti di Brera in Milan, he assisted his father in his teaching. He executed designs for architectural ornament and furniture (in collaboration with Giuseppe Maggiolini) and painted portraits and landscapes (e.g. *Garden and Villa Reale at Monza*, 1803; De Giacomi priv. col.). He made prints after drawings by his father and by the architect Luigi Cagnola, using engraving, etching and aquatint; this last technique he introduced to Milan. In 1803 he was elected an Academician of the Brera.

(4) Ferdinando Albertolli (*b* Bedano, 11 Nov 1780; *d* Milan, 24 April 1844). Architect, printmaker, designer and teacher, nephew of (1) Giocondo Albertolli. He married Giocondo's daughter Maria. He studied at the Accademia di Belle Arti di Brera in Milan and won the first prize for design in 1806. From 1804 he taught design and architecture at the high school in Verona and in 1807 became professor of design at the Accademia di Belle Arti in Venice. In 1812 he succeeded his uncle as professor of design at the Brera, where he taught almost until his death. His publications drew on his stay in Verona and in Venice; he also travelled to Tuscany, Rome, Greece and London (where he went to gather material on some Greek friezes for publication) and, according to his uncle's account, to Naples and Paris.

In 1838 he became an Honorary Fellow of the Royal Institute of British Architects and in 1843 was nominated a member of the Akademie der Bildenden Künste in Vienna. He constructed some buildings in Genoa (from 1824), planned the Palazzo Taverna (1835) in Via Monte Napoleone, Milan, and designed the sepulchre for the Duca di Lodi at Villa Melzi, in Bellagio, near Como. He was noted for his decorative designs for interiors, furnishings (he won a gold medal for his design of a clockcase), altars and funerals, for which he adopted the Empire style. His fame also rests on his work as a printmaker, above all for his skill in aquatint. He provided illustrations for his uncle's publications; some plates for Giovanni Antonio Antolini's *Il Tempio di Minerva in Assisi confrontato con le tavole di Andrea Palladio* (Milan, 1803) and the *Descrizione del Foro Bonaparte* (Parma, 1806); some for Cagnola's *Le solenni esequie di monsignor Filippo Visconti* (Milan, 1802) as well as views of the Arco del Sempione; and some plates for Cosimo Morelli's *Descrizione delle feste celebrate in Venezia per la venuta di S.M.I.R. Napoleone* (Venice, 1808).

WRITINGS

Porte di città e di fortezze, depositi sepolcrali ed altre principali fabbriche pubbliche e private di Michele Sammicheli (Milan, 1815)

Fregi trovati negli scavi del Foro Traiano con altri esistenti in Roma, in diverse città d'Italia e in Atene, disegnati e misurati sul luogo da Ferdinando Albertolli (Milan, 1824)

GIULIANA RICCI

Albert the painter [Albertus pictor] (*fl c.* 1460; *d* after 1509). Painter and textile designer, active in Sweden. He was probably of German origin. He married in 1473 and was a burgher of Stockholm, where he ran a workshop for liturgical embroidery. Apparently well-to-do, during the years 1501–7 he paid a higher tax than any other painter in Stockholm. About this time he also seems to have delivered an altarpiece to the Brigittine convent of Naantali (Swed. Nådendal) in Finland. He is last mentioned in 1509, when he played an instrument, probably the organ, at the Corpus Christi Guild of Stockholm.

Albert thus had many talents, but his main field must have been wall painting. His earliest works are in Södermanland and include the signed wall paintings in the church at Lid, where he also painted his self-portrait. It has been conjectured that Albert may have been an apprentice of a Master Peter, whose existence is deduced from a presumed signature in the church at Ösmo, but this theory is very tenuous. About 35 churches with paintings by Albert or his workshop are known in the provinces of Södermanland, Västmanland and Uppland. Some of the best-preserved paintings are in the churches at Floda (Södermanland), Kumla (Västmanland), Härkeberga, Härnevi, Almunge and Odensala (Uppland).

Albert's style is comparatively realistic, and he could depict with equal competence the sublime and the burlesque, which are often contrasted in his work. Although his paintings are characterized by a sculptural figure style and some knowledge of perspective, the elongated figures, broken drapery folds and the ornamental backgrounds are still Gothic in style. The ornamental motifs on piers, arches and vault ribs are also in the Gothic tradition. All the spaces are filled with ornamentation, and the proportion of narrative scenes is greater than in the work of his forerunners. For some pictures Albert sought inspiration in woodcuts and copperplate engravings by German masters, such as Master E.S., the Housebook Master and Martin Schongauer, and he must also have owned a copy of a Biblia pauperum (*see* BIBLE, §I, 3(ii)), although he never followed these models slavishly. Albert also introduced the typological programme into late medieval religious art in Sweden; earlier, there had been only occasional attempts at typological compositions. He was the most prolific Swedish mural painter of his time and perhaps also the most successful, exercising strong influence on both his contemporaries and successors in Middle Sweden.

Albert was also a successful textile designer, and a large number of his works in this field have survived. His figure embroideries show a similar style to his paintings and are made of gold, silver, pearls and coloured silks. One of his most renowned works in this field is a chasuble (Uppsala, Cathedral). On its back is depicted the *Virgin and Child*. The Statens Historiska Museum in Stockholm has a representative collection of Albert's works in textile.

BIBLIOGRAPHY

A. Geijer: 'Albertus Pictor som pärlstickare' [Albertus Pictor as an embroiderer], *Upplands Fornminnesfören. Åb.* (1940), pp. 37–50

——: *Albertus Pictor, målare och pärlstickare* [Albertus Pictor, painter and embroiderer] (exh. cat. by A. Geijer, Stockholm, Nmus., 1949)

B. G. Söderberg: *Svenska kyrkomålningar från medeltiden* [Swedish church paintings from the Middle Ages] (Stockholm, 1951), pp. 216–24

E. Lundberg: *Albertus Pictor* (Stockholm, 1961)

H. Cornell and S. Wallin: *Zwischen Meister E. S. und dem Meister des Hausbuchs: Der Stockholmer Maler Albertus Pictor etwa 1440–1509* (Stockholm, 1972)

A. Nilsén: *Program och funktion i senmedeltida kalkmåleri: Kyrkmålningar i Mälarlandskapen och Finland, 1400–1534* [Programme and function in late medieval painting: mural painting of churches in the Mälar provinces and Finland, 1400–1534] (Stockholm, 1986)

Å. Nisbeth: *Bildernas predikan* [The pictorial sermon] (Stockholm, 1986), pp. 187–96

ANNA NILSÉN

Albert van Ouwater. *See* OUWATER, ALBERT VAN.

Albi. French city and capital of the south-eastern département of Tarn. The wedge-shaped quarter known as Castelviel, on the south bank of the River Tarn and directly west of the cathedral (*see* §1 below), constitutes the oldest part of the city, originally a Celtic settlement. Although important during Gallo-Roman times as a distribution centre for local agricultural goods, Albi developed formal urban institutions only in the 6th century AD when the city was under Frankish rule. Christianity was probably introduced into the Albigeois shortly after AD 250, and an episcopal see was established at Albi a century and a half later. Until 1678, when it was elevated to an archdiocese, the bishopric of Albi was suffragan to the metropolitan see at Bourges. Despite the upheavals resulting from the Albigensian Crusade, the Inquisition and conflicts between the townspeople and their rulers, the 13th century was a prosperous one for Albi. During this period a number of important religious and civic buildings were initiated, and they still largely define the city's architectural character. The earliest is the fortified episcopal palace, La Berbie, begun *c.* 1228, which, like most Gothic and later monuments in Albi, is built almost entirely of brick. The palace now houses the city's museum, and included in its collections are works by Henri de Toulouse-Lautrec, who was born in Albi in 1864. Beside the cathedral, other notable Gothic monuments are the fortified walls and towers guarding the southern bank of the Tarn and the collegiate church of St Salvi, which still preserves a portion of its original Romanesque fabric. St Salvi is unusual among Gothic churches in south-central France in possessing a basilican plan and flying buttresses. During the Renaissance and later periods Albi's architectural landscape was enriched by numerous large, urban residences (hôtels), many of which still stand.

1. CATHEDRAL. Constructed in the region's local Gothic style, the fortified cathedral of Ste Cécile ranks as one of the most accomplished and imposing monuments erected in southern France during the later Middle Ages (see fig.). Building began shortly after 1277, but it was only when the foundations started emerging from the ground that the corner-stone was laid, on 15 August 1282, by Bishop Bernard de Castanet (*reg* 1276–1308). The polygonal apse and its radiating chapels, as well as the two adjoining straight bays of the choir and their corresponding chapels, were vaulted by 1322; the remaining nine bays to the west were built and vaulted in successive campaigns by 1390. Work on the cathedral's massive western tower (h. 78 m) began *c.* 1355. Its first three stages, with rounded buttresses at the corners, similar to those lining the nave and apse, were completed *c.* 1365; the final three stages,

Albi Cathedral, view from the east, begun after 1277

less austere in appearance, were constructed between *c.* 1485 and 1493 at the behest of Bishop Louis d'Amboise (*reg* 1474–1503; *see* AMBOISE, D').

Since the church does not have side aisles, the choir and nave vaults are supported directly by tall buttress walls set perpendicular to the building's longitudinal axis. Until their division in the late 15th century, the chapels in the spaces between these supports rose uninterrupted to the full height of the main vaults (30 m). Their external walls are pierced high above ground- level by long, narrow traceried windows that provide most of the illumination for the broad and spacious interior; the width of the nave alone measures 19.2 m.

Albi Cathedral shares with other Gothic churches in the region such typical southern traits as a nave without aisles, no transepts, lateral chapels and narrow windows, but its full range of tall chapels around the periphery is unique. This scheme is aesthetically and physically quite distinct from the one employed in most other southern churches, where the chapels normally rise to about half the height of the nave, leaving only the upper portions of the buttresses exposed on the exterior. In such churches the low chapels and narrow windows allow the wall surfaces to dominate the interior space, but with the completely internalized buttressing system at Albi the nave is surrounded by deep, vertical trenches of space that expand the nave space laterally, and also, by pushing out the enclosing wall of the nave to the external edges of the buttresses, render the skeletal framework of Gothic construction completely visible from within.

The choice of such an unusual elevation was dictated by Bernard de Castanet, who intended from the beginning to build a fortified church, partly as a bulwark against the Albigensian heretics but more importantly as a defence against the local citizenry and the representatives of the French king who sought both violently and peacefully to reduce the considerable temporal power of the bishops of Albi.

In the Middle Ages a good defensive system required that walls be high and sheer in order to make them less vulnerable to scaling by the enemy, and the tall chapels served this purpose. A smooth, precipitous elevation also allowed defenders to repel attackers by dropping missiles without damaging the structure. A number of other defensive measures were also employed at the cathedral: a robust, sloping base to protect the building from sapping and ramming, as well as providing it with a surface for bouncing projectiles towards the enemy; windows placed high above ground-level (the lower rank of windows piercing the choir belong to a late 15th-century remodelling), and finally an upper zone, which, had it been finished, would probably have been crenellated. The present parapet above the chapel windows was added by César-Denis Daly, who restored the cathedral between 1846 and 1876. It is easily distinguished from the medieval fabric by the lighter tone of the brickwork. All the elements of the cathedral's outer face, except for the fenestration, clearly derive from contemporary military architecture. The exterior of the building and the defensive walls built along the north and east sides of the episcopal complex in Castanet's time are so similar that they may be the work of the same architect.

The severe, formidable exterior of the cathedral is relieved on the south side by an opulent porch of monumental proportions, which incorporates both Flamboyant and Renaissance motifs. It was begun by Bishop Adrien de Gouffier (*reg* 1519–23) and was probably not finished until the mid-16th century. The magnificent rood screen and accompanying choir enclosure that together occupy the cathedral's eastern half were probably executed between 1474 and 1483. These exquisite furnishings are each composed of linked panels of openwork tracery; at their junctures they are punctuated by intricate canopied niches mostly bearing figures from the Old and New Testaments. Most of the rood screen statuary was destroyed shortly after the French Revolution (1789–95), but the figures corresponding to the inner and outer sides of the choir enclosure are well preserved. The Albi carvings show closest affinity stylistically with the Late Gothic art of the south Netherlands and Burgundy, as well as with local sculpture.

The cathedral still possesses most of its painted decoration. The oldest portion is found along the western wall of the nave, where there is a vast tempera painting of the *Last Judgement* (15×18 m), executed by an artist working in a late 15th-century Franco-Flemish style. The central scene was destroyed in 1693 when the wall was pierced in order to create a chapel at the base of the tower. The cathedral is also ornamented with wall and ceiling frescoes painted in a Renaissance style by a team of Italian artists from Lombardy and Emilia, headed by Giovanni Francesco Donella (*fl* 1508/9–1514) of Carpi (near Modena). The entire programme, which includes many biblical and hagiographic narrative scenes, was executed between 1509 and 1514.

BIBLIOGRAPHY

J. Laran: *La Cathédrale d'Albi*, Petites Monographies Grands Edifices France (Paris, [1911], 5/1965)
C. Auriol: 'Albi: La Cathédrale', *Congr. Archéol. France*, xcii (1929), pp. 362–91
E. Lambert: 'La Berbie, cité épiscopale d'Albi', *Rev. Tarn* (1944), pp. 383–400, 428–38, 468–76; (1945), pp. 45–57; repr. in *Etud. Méd.*, ii (1956–7), pp. 189–229
E. Mâle: *La Cathédrale d'Albi* (Paris, 1950, 2/1974)
Congr. Archéol. France, cxl (1982) [issue dedicated to Albi and its region]
J.-L. Biget: *Histoire d'Albi* (Toulouse, 1983)
R. A. Sundt: 'La Cathédrale d'Albi et les églises gothiques à chapelles hautes: Style, fonction et diffusion', *Actes du 3e colloque d'histoire de l'art méridional au moyen-âge: Narbonne, 1992*

RICHARD A. SUNDT

Albiker, Karl (*b* Ühlingen, 16 Sept 1878; *d* Ettlingen, 26 Feb 1961). German sculptor. He studied in Karlsruhe, Munich and Paris (partly with Auguste Rodin); from 1903 to 1905 he worked in Rome. By 1910 he had developed his style: he modelled figures of young people, which appear restrained and introverted in spite of poses that convey considerable movement (e.g. *Woman in Mourning*, 1909–11; Hagen, Osthaus Mus.; *Youth*, 1911; Essen, Mus. Flkwang). At the same time he created sculptures for buildings in decoratively stylized forms such as those for the Konzerthaus in Karlsruhe.

In 1919 Albiker was appointed to the Akademie der Bildenden Künste in Dresden and worked there as a teacher until 1945. By this time his works were heavier and more compact, and they included nudes, portraits and several important war memorials (e.g. *Pallas Athene*, 1925; Karlsruhe, U. Fridericiana). He created two monumental groups of *Sportsmen* (h. *c*. 6 m, incl. base) for the Olympic stadium in Berlin in 1936.

WRITINGS

Das Problem des Raums in den bildenden Künsten (Frankfurt am Main, 1962)

BIBLIOGRAPHY

L. Ziegler: 'Die Bewegung in der Plastik', *Die Plastik*, iii/6 (1913), pp. 46–56
Karl Albiker: Das gesammelte Werk (exh. cat., Mannheim, Städt. Ksthalle, 1939)
C. Albiker: *Karl Albiker Werkbuch* (Karlsruhe, 1978)

URSEL BERGER

Albini, Alfred (*b* Zagreb, 15 July 1886; *d* Zagreb, 4 Nov 1978). Croatian architect and teacher. He studied in Vienna and completed studies at the Technical High School in Zagreb in 1923. He then worked in the studios of Viktor Kovačić and Hugo Ehrlich and started his own practice in 1927. At the same time he was a lecturer and, later, professor in the Faculty of Architecture at the University of Zagreb until his retirement. His outstanding early work is the cultural centre (1936–40), in the suburb of Sušak, Rijeka. This building, a skyscraper wedged in a very tight corner between two steep streets, with an articulated horizontal mass containing office space and an auditorium, was ahead of its time and was of seminal importance in the development of a refined functionalism in Croatia. Among his other few but carefully designed buildings are the Villa Meixner (1934), Malinov Street, the residential block Arko (1938), Basariček Street, and the Technological Faculty (1959), all in Zagreb; the Savings Bank and Croatian Cultural Centre (both 1930) in Osijek; and a small but very fine residential block (1954) in Zadar. Although he was a participant in the Modern Movement, Albini often included restrained decorative elements in his work in order to fit his buildings into the existing traditional context. As a professor he was responsible for educating several generations of Croatian architects, who practised in various countries.

BIBLIOGRAPHY

Z. Vrkljan: 'In Memoriam: Alfred Albini', *Covjek & Prostor*, xxv/308 (1978), p. 4

PAUL TVRTKOVIĆ

Albini, Franco (*b* Robbiate, Como, 17 Oct 1905; *d* Milan, 1 Nov 1977). Italian architect, urban planner and designer. After graduating from the Polytechnic of Milan (1929), he set up individual practice in Milan. One of the group of Rationalist architects who formed around the magazine *Casabella*, his work in the 1930s ranged from workers' housing in Milan (1936, 1938; with Renato Camus and Giancarlo Palanti) to an ideal flat and furniture, exhibited at the Triennale in Milan in 1936. Immediately after World War II a series of masterplanning projects included schemes for the City of Milan (1946; with BBPR, Piero Bottoni, Luigi Figini and Gino Pollini) and for Reggio Emilia (1947–8; with Giancarlo De Carlo). Albini's post-war architecture has a Rationalist clarity combined with sensitivity to context, tradition and history. Expressed first in the Rifugio Pirovano (1949–51) at Cervinia, Aosta, it was the office building for the Istituto Nazionale delle Assicurazioni (INA; 1950), Parma, with its simply stated concrete frame that set the pattern developed later in La Rinascente department store (1957–61), Rome. In this a steel frame forms Renaissance cornices at each floor level, and vertically folded red masonry panels pick up the immediate urban context. The post-war schemes for INA workers' housing (1950–51; with BBPR and Gianni Abricci) at Cesate and Mangiagalli workers' housing (1950–51; with Ignazio Gardella), both in Milan, are equally sensitive in their use of local materials: the theme was developed throughout the 1960s and 1970s in such housing schemes as those in Aosta (1965–70), Parma (1968–71) and Genoa (1969–74). Albini's international reputation was also based on his exhibition and museum design, including the conversion of the Palazzo Bianco (1950–51), Genoa, into a museum; its functional abstraction prefigured the work in the Palazzo Rosso (1952–61), Genoa, and in the Museo del Tesoro di San Lorenzo (1952–6), Genoa.

BIBLIOGRAPHY

G. C. Argan: *Franco Albini* (Milan, 1962)
F. Helg, C. De Seta and M. Fagiolo: *Franco Albini, 1930–1970* (Florence, 1979; Eng. trans., London, 1981)
Franco Albini, architettura e design, 1930–1970 (exh. cat., Milan, Rotonda Besana, 1979)
M. Tafuri: *Storia dell'architettura italiana, 1944–1985* (Turin, 1986)

ANDREA NULLI

Albisola. Italian centre of ceramic production. The town, situated near Savona in Liguria, was a flourishing centre of maiolica production during the Renaissance. It was, however, only during the 17th and 18th centuries that a distinctive style developed. Important families in the pottery business included the Grosso, Chiodo, Corrado,

Salomone, Pescio, Seitone, Seirullo, Levantino and Siccardi, all of whom produced large quantities of polychrome plates (e.g. by the Corrado, mid-17th century; Nino Ferrari priv. col., see Morazzoni, pl. 43), albarelli and vases, which were sometimes inspired by silverware and contemporary Delftware. In some cases, yellow and an olive green were used on a turquoise ground. Wares were decorated in a calligraphic style with an emphasis on naturalistic motifs including such animals as leverets; this style later evolved into Baroque forms painted with soft, loose brushstrokes.

BIBLIOGRAPHY

G. Morazzoni: *La maiolica antica ligure* (Milan, 1951)

C. Barile: *Antiche ceramiche liguri: Maioliche di Albisola* (Milan, 1965)

H. Blake: 'Pottery Exported from Northwest Italy between 1450 and 1830: Savona, Albisola, Genoa, Pisa and Montelupo', *Archaeol. & It. Soc.* (1981), pp. 99–124

Maioliche liguri dal XVII al XVIII secolo (exh. cat., ed. C. G. Bernardi; Albisola Superiore, Oratory of S Maria Maggiore, 1985)

LUCIANA ARBACE

Albrecht, Balthasar Augustin (*b* Berg, nr Starnberg, Bavaria, 3 Jan 1687; *d* Munich, 15 Aug 1765). German painter and administrator. He was the son of Augustin Albrecht, a carpenter, and he was probably taught in Munich by his uncle, the painter Benedikt Albrecht (*d* 1730), before he went to Italy, where he is thought to have stayed in Rome and Venice. Albrecht returned to Munich in 1719 and executed his first works (all 1723–4) for the former Hofmarkkirche (now Katholische Pfarrkirche; *in situ*) in Schönbrunn, near Dachau. These were a ceiling fresco, *Celebration of the Cross*, and three altar panels, *Mourning Angel* (high altar), *Martyrdom of St Catherine* (left altar) and *St Anne* (right altar). He also painted two altar panels, *St John of Nepomuk* and *St Leonard* (both 1724–5; untraced), for the Katholische Pfarrkirche Mariahilf in der Au in Munich. Unlike Cosmas Damian Asam, Matthäus Günther and Johann Baptist Bergmüller, he was influenced by 16th-century Venetian and Roman models, and both in these works and in later ones he continued to look to the past for inspiration. Between 1727 and 1732 he was nominated court painter to the Elector Charles of Bavaria (*reg* 1726–45), although he had only a small workshop and few apprentices, the best-known being Franz Ignaz Öfele (1721–97). In 1738 Albrecht painted one of his principal works, the *Assumption of the Virgin* for the Augustiner-Chorherrenstift in Diessen (*in situ*). This was a kind of 'curtain' for the *theatrum sacrum* and seems to be influenced by the stage-altar (1719–22) of the same subject by Egid Quirin Asam in the Klosterkirche Mariae Himmelfahrt in Rohr. In 1746 Albrecht was put in charge of gallery inspection and restoration for the Bavarian castles and drew up inventories of the paintings. As a result of these activities he produced few works of his own between 1746 and 1759, one being the important *Assumption of the Virgin* (1755–6; *in situ*) for the Klosterkirche SS Dionys und Juliana in Schäftlarn, again influenced by 16th-century Italian art. Albrecht's religious paintings often have a dramatic diagonal composition, and they are far removed from any feeling of playful Rococo brilliance. His few secular pieces (e.g. *Children Playing Dice*, 1731–2; Munich, Alte Pin.) show a link with French academic painting, and the few surviving drawings relate mainly to preliminary work for his altar panels. His stairwell fresco of 1724–5 at Schloss Dachau has been destroyed, as have his frescoes of 1732–4 in the chapel and on the ceiling of the Green Gallery at the Residenz in Munich; the *Miracle* frescoes in the Pfarr- und Wallfahrtskirche Mariae Himmelfahrt in Aufkirchen were painted over in 1900.

BIBLIOGRAPHY

Thieme–Becker

F. Bachter: *Balthasar Augustin Albrecht, 1687–1765: Ein bayerischer Hofmaler des Barock* (Mittenwald, 1981)

RÜDIGER AN DER HEIDEN

Albrecht, Gretchen (*b* Auckland, 7 May 1943). New Zealand painter. She studied at the Elam School of Fine Arts, Auckland, from 1960 to 1963 and subsequently travelled extensively in the USA and Europe. Her paintings are abstractions with a basis in nature, to which she alludes in her titles. An early and enduring influence on her work were the colour paintings of Helen Frankenthaler. Albrecht's painting is distinguished by its strong colouring and feeling. Among her most important works are her *Hemisphere* paintings from a series begun in 1981, in which the canvases are semi-circular. An example is the *Fire and the Rose* (1984; Wanganui, Sarjeant A.G.). Since 1989 Albrecht has been working on an oval format and has introduced a deeper, more reflective tone to her paintings. Her work is represented in public art galleries in Auckland, Wellington, Christchurch and Dunedin and in private collections worldwide.

BIBLIOGRAPHY

After Nature: Gretchen Albrecht. A Survey: 23 Years (exh. cat., ed. J. Ross; Wanganui, Sarjeant A.G., 1986)

A. Kirker: *New Zealand Women Painters* (Wellington, 1986), pp. 145–51

L. Gill: *Gretchen Albrecht* (Auckland, 1991)

MICHAEL DUNN

Albright, Ivan (le Lorraine) (*b* North Harvey, nr Chicago, 20 Feb 1897; *d* Woodstock, VT, 18 Nov 1983). American painter, sculptor, printmaker and film maker. He was brought up in the suburbs of Chicago and was exposed to art at an early age by his father, Adam Emory Albright (*b* 1862), a portrait painter. He passed on to his son the interest in careful draughtsmanship that he had developed from tuition with Thomas Eakins. Ivan's initial field of interest was architecture, which he studied at Northwestern University, Evanston (1915–16), and at the University of Illinois, Urbana (1916–17). During World War I he served with an Army medical unit, making surgical drawings with great precision. He subsequently decided to become a painter and attended the Art Institute of Chicago (1920–23), the Pennsylvania Academy of Fine Arts, Chicago (1923), and the National Academy of Design, New York (1924). Around this time he began to exhibit regularly.

Albright settled in Chicago in 1927, and, isolated from New York circles, he developed his personal, mature style. From 1929 to 1930 he painted his first monumental work, *Into the World There Came a Soul Named Ida* (Chicago, IL, A. Inst.); in this modern *vanitas* painting, Albright transformed an attractive 21-year-old sitter into a withered old woman who looks sorrowfully into a mirror. Agitated light effects, deadened purple tones and microscopic detail emphasize the transitory nature of beauty, as do the burnt paper, wilting flowers and other debris.

In the 1930s Albright fully developed his meticulous technique, which included creating numerous detailed drawings, grinding his own colours and painting with hundreds of tiny brushes, often covering only a tiny area of canvas per day. He devised inconsistencies in perspective by moving objects on rotating stands as he painted. He generated flickering illumination by varying the light in his studio and introducing arbitrary shadows, a technique he used in one of his most renowned paintings, *That which I Should Have Done I Did Not Do (The Door)* (1931–41; Chicago, IL, A. Inst.). A haunting assemblage of memorabilia, including a weathered Victorian door, a cheap funeral wreath and a woman's hand, is depicted with cold, metallic lighting, a scarred paint surface and a warped perspective that makes the door appear coffin-shaped.

Albright continued to work in this same mode for six decades, examining the concept of mortality through portraits and still-lifes, including the powerful *Poor Room—There Is No Time, No End, No Today, No Yesterday, No Tomorrow, Only the Forever, and Forever, and Forever, Without End* (1941–62) and *If Life Were Life, There Would Be No Death* (1966–77, both Chicago, IL, A. Inst.). He experimented, however, with a variety of media besides painting. His sculptures similarly explore tactile values, as evident in the jagged, asymmetrical features of *Adam Emory Albright* (1935; New York, MOMA). His lithographs, for example *Self-portrait at 55 East Division Street* (1947; see Croyden, p. 212), were often inspired by his paintings; their strong tonal patterns, created without the use of colour, intensify their expression. Albright also experimented with film, culminating in *Unfinished Portrait of an Artist* (1963). He wrote prolifically and left a series of 31 notebooks in which he investigated the relationship between word and image, reality and illusion.

BIBLIOGRAPHY

Ivan Albright (exh. cat. by F. Sweet and J. Dubuffet, Chicago, A. Inst., 1964)
J. van der Marck: 'Ivan Albright: More than Meets the Eye', *A. America*, lxv/6 (1977), pp. 92–9
M. Croyden: *Ivan Albright* (New York, 1978)
Graven Image: The Prints of Ivan Albright, 1931–1977 (exh. cat. by M. Croyden, Lake Forest, Coll., 1978)

JANET MARSTINE

Album. Bound edition of paintings, drawings, calligraphy, writings or a combination of these, by a single or several artists. This article deals with its existence in the East, where it was a common format for illustration; a special case in the West was the ALBUM AMICORUM. (*See also* MOUNTING.)

1. East Asia. 2. Indian subcontinent. 3. Islamic world.

1. EAST ASIA. The album originated in China and spread from there to Korea and Japan. In China it was the last of the major painting formats to be developed, preceded by the wall painting, standing screen, handscroll, fan and hanging scroll (*see* CHINA, §V, 1). Since early Chinese texts on the subject of the album are limited and lack adequate terminology, and since in the remounting of early works of art formats were frequently changed, the detailed history of the album remains obscure. However, it seems that calligraphy and book printing, rather than painting, were important in establishing the early use of the album, both for the remounting of antique pieces and as a format for contemporary works.

Two major types of album mounting (Chin. *ce ye*) for painting developed, both of them related to the evolution of book writing and printing forms (*see* CHINA, §XIII, 3). The first albums were probably in the accordion-folded form (see fig. 1) in which stiff paper leaves, when closed, create a protective envelope. Such albums were first introduced by the 9th century AD, for use in writing, most popularly for handwritten Buddhist texts, hence their alternative name of 'sutra folded binding' (*jing zhe zhuang*). The use of albums for paintings is said to have begun in the early part of the Song period (960–1279) with the remounting of silk handscrolls, which were sliced into sheets and applied to a long, stiff, accordion-folded backing strip. The advantage of the form was that any part of a long painting could be turned to at once, without the tedious rolling required for a scroll. The second popular album form, called 'butterfly binding' (*hudie zhuang*) in early Chinese bookbinding, was more like the modern book, consisting of multiple leaves that were folded inwards and bound together at the fold, leaf by leaf, with paste. Attached to both ends of albums, whether of accordion or butterfly form, were rigid covers made of carved wood or paper packets wrapped with decorative fabric.

By the late 10th century the album was used for remounting and preserving damaged and often fragmentary works of calligraphy and painting that had originally been mounted as handscrolls, screens or hanging scrolls.

1. Album of Nanjing masters, accordion-folded paper leaves between wooden covers, each leaf 247×321 mm, 17th century (London, British Museum)

The first use of albums by Chinese artists, as opposed to collectors, seems to have occurred in the early 12th century at the court of the emperor Huizong. Huizong probably found the small, intimate album well suited to his artistic preference for focused themes, lyric moods, poetic derivation and subtle articulation, usually executed on silk. Court painters, competing to render themes prepared by the Emperor, predominantly produced large numbers of small leaves, both rectangular and fan-shaped, apparently all single works that were mounted individually. In addition, however, even before multiple-leaved albums by single artists had become common, Huizong (presumably with his court artists) began routinely to fill albums with depictions of newly arrived foreign tributes, rare birds and rocks, flowers and fruit. More than a thousand such albums, each consisting of fifteen leaves with paintings on both sides, were produced, none of which survives. Perhaps the earliest extant multiple-leaved album paintings in China are 12th- to early 13th-century water scenes by Ma Yuan (Beijing, Pal. Mus.), which have titles inscribed by Empress Yang (1162–1232). However, the mounting of these may not be original; indeed, it is not certain that any original Song album mounting has survived. Typical Song paintings intended for album mounting, whether rectangular or fan-shaped, were between 220 and 280 mm in height; rectangular leaves were either single-width sheets (*c.* 180–210 mm wide), which occupied a single page, or, like the Ma Yuan leaves, double-width sheets folded vertically and spread over two successive pages.

In the Song period early literati artists such as Wen Tong, Su Shi and Mi Fu may also have used the album format, though the evidence is scant. Not until the later part of the Yuan period (1279–1368) did the album begin to gain widespread appeal among the literati, who were attracted by its intimate scale. A more sequential approach to the multiple-leaved album soon emerged, occasionally pedagogical in intent. Among those to adopt the format were WU ZHEN, who produced 20 leaves depicting bamboo (1350; Taipei, N. Pal. Mus.), and Ni Zan, who is said to have painted 10 leaves each related to the theme of *Wan* ('myriad'). Ming-period (1368–1644) artists often based their album sequences either on distant travel or on well-known local views, such as Wang Li's (1332–after 1383) 40 or more scenes of Mt Hua (some in Shanghai Mus. and Beijing, Pal. Mus.) or Shen Zhou's *Twelve Views of Tiger Hill* set in Suzhou (Cleveland, OH, Mus. A.). SHEN ZHOU and his follower Wen Zhengming firmly established the album among China's literati artists, fully realizing the form's potential for creating extended works with separate scenes, changing subjects and different styles, and for matching painting with calligraphic inscriptions. Unlike single works in other formats, the multiple-leaved album could display a whole range of themes and styles and illustrate consistency (or inconsistency) in artistic quality. The intention was often to communicate concepts rather than achieve polished results, so album paintings were frequently both more sketchy and more imaginative than work in other formats. Albums produced by Shen Zhou and others typically had 8, 10, 12, 16, 20 or 24 leaves.

From the 17th century the album was frequently used by scholar-painters to express themselves through the varied styles of early painting masters. This was probably also the time when Chinese artists such as DONG QICHANG first began to paint directly on prepared albums, as calligraphers had long been doing. One major development of the Qing period (1644–1911) was the emergence of collective albums, in which works by various contemporary artists were grouped together, commissioned or gathered by a single patron and emphasizing his taste and role as much as that of the artists themselves. A well-known collective album is Zhou Lianggong's 18-leaf album with facing inscriptions (Taipei, N. Pal. Mus.).

Korean artists seem not to have modified the album format or its usage in any significant way, though the Korean album was important for the transmission of the form from China to Japan. In Japan the major forms of album mounting, the accordion binding or 'folded book' (Jap. *orihon*) and the 'butterfly' binding (*detchōsō*), were introduced from the mainland probably in the early 9th century, primarily in the context of Buddhist scriptures and literary manuscripts (both forms are designated generally as *sasshibon*). Unlike the Chinese album, the Japanese album never achieved sufficient status to rival the scroll and screen formats in popularity. However, album paintings assumed a distinctively Japanese character in association with native literature and pictorial and calligraphic styles. They were important for the illustration of poetic texts and literary narratives such as the Genji and Ise tales (*Oenji Monogatari* and *Ise Monogatari*); representation of famous locales, landscapes and activities depicted according to the various seasons and months; and portraiture of the Thirty-six Immortal Poets.

The relationship of the album with certain themes and styles was first established in the Heian period (AD 794–1185; *see also* JAPAN, §VI, 3(iii)(d)). Although no narrative album survives from this period, the depiction of a picture book with a separate text occurs in the 12th-century *Genji Monogatari* scroll (*Azumaya* chapter; Nagoya, Tokugawa A. Mus.). The refined taste of Heian court art is epitomized by the oldest preserved version of the *Anthology of Thirty-six Poets* (Kyoto, Nishi Honganji, *c.* 1112), consisting of 32 unaltered butterfly-bound volumes with *waka* verses inscribed on double-leaves of sumptuously decorated, multicoloured papers. A unique set of folding fans, painted and printed in *Yamatoe* style during the 12th century, some possibly illustrating Genji and Ise tales and inscribed with the unrelated text of the *Lotus sūtra* (Osaka, Shitennōji and Tokyo, N. Mus.), is thought originally to have been mounted in albums, with each fan folded in half across two album pages.

The album seems to have declined in popularity during the Kamakura (1185–1333) and Muromachi (1333–1568) periods; only a few Muromachi-period ink paintings were created for album mounting. Whereas albums dating from before the Muromachi period indicate a preference for the butterfly style of binding, Muromachi and later examples suggest a reversion to the accordion form. The album came into vogue again in the Azuchi–Momoyama (1568–1600) and Edo (1600–1868) periods, with the revitalization of native styles, particularly by artists of the Tosa lineage (*see* TOSA SCHOOL), who preserved the court traditions of the Heian period, as exemplified by illustrations of Genji by Tosa Mitsuyoshi (1539–1613) and Tosa Mitsunori

(1583–1638) (Kyoto, N. Mus. and Nagoya, Tokugawa A. Mus.). Early Edo-period paintings in the *Yamatoe* manner by artists of the Rinpa school, executed on decorated papers backed by stiff cardboard (called *shikishi* when square or nearly square and *tanzaku* when long and narrow), are in modern times typically mounted in albums, although many may have originally appeared on screens.

The increasing popularity of album mounting in this period was probably related to the use, from the later 16th century, of albums of collected calligraphy (*te kagami*), filled with fragments from dismembered books and scrolls dating back to the Nara period (AD 710–94). Edo-period album painting was furthered by artists of the Nanga school, who took Chinese literati artists of the Ming and Qing periods as their models, often matching paintings with Chinese-style poems, as for example the famous pair of albums on the hermit's life, *Jūbenjō* and *Jūgijō* (1711; Kamakura, Kawabata Yasunari Mem. Mus.), contrasting the personalities and talent of Ike Taiga and Yosa Buson.

Painting or calligraphy was rarely executed directly on albums; sketchbooks by artists of the Nanga school and painters of the realistic Maruyama–Shijō schools were exceptions. *Ukiyoe* artists from the late 17th century to the 19th, such as OKUMURA MASANOBU, Katsukawa Shunshō (*see* KATSUKAWA, (1)) and KITAGAWA UTAMARO, also produced paintings and woodblock prints in bound format, usually 12 thematically related leaves, often explicitly erotic. These represented de luxe editions at a time when stitched-bound books with pictures were beginning to reach an increasingly wide audience.

BIBLIOGRAPHY

H. Yamamoto: *Hyogu no shiori* [Guidebook to mounting] (Kyoto, 1930)
Song ren huace [Album leaves by Song-period artists] (Beijing, 1957)
R. H. van Gulik: *Chinese Pictorial Art as Viewed by the Connoisseur* (Rome, 1958)
J. Cahill: *Chinese Album Leaves in the Freer Gallery of Art* (Washington, DC, 1961)
T. H. Tsien: *Written on Bamboo and Silk: The Beginnings of Chinese Books and Inscriptions* (Chicago, 1962)
C. C. Wang: *Album Leaves from the Sung and Yuan Dynasties* (New York, 1970)
Masterpieces of Chinese Album Painting in the National Palace Museum (Taipei, 1971)
M. Kinoshita: *Te kagami* [Writing models], Nihon no bijutsu [The arts of Japan], 84 (Tokyo, 1973)
D. Chibbett: The History of Japanese Printing and Book Illustration (Tokyo, 1977)
S. Fu: *Traces of the Brush: Studies in Chinese Calligraphy* (New Haven, 1977)
M. Murase: *Iconography of the Tale of Genji* (New York, 1983)
Y. Shimizu and J. Rosenfield: *Masters of Japanese Calligraphy, 8th–19th Century* (New York, 1984)
N. Yamamoto, ed.: *Kokuhō daijiten* [Comprehensive dictionary of national treasures], iii (Tokyo, 1986)

JEROME SILBERGELD, DAVID SHRENSEL

2. INDIAN SUBCONTINENT. Albums occupy a significant place in the history of Indian painting. Following well-established Persianate models, Mughal emperors had splendid examples of painting and calligraphy gathered together and sumptuously bound. Though the practice had certainly begun by the time of Akbar (*reg* 1556–1605), very little from his (or any) period survives in anything like its original form. For example, it is well known from Abu'l Fazl's history of the reign—the *Akbarnāma*—that a large album of portraits of grandees of the realm was assembled on the Emperor's order, but only a few stray pages mounted in later borders survive from this important document. Better known are the albums associated primarily with Akbar's son Jahangir (*reg* 1605–27), though the earliest that survives was in fact begun in the reign of Akbar. Only two significant examples remain in some semblance of their original form. Of these, the larger and better preserved is the *Muraqqaʿ-i gulshan* (Pers.: 'Album of a rose garden') with dates from 1599 to 1609 (Tehran, Gulistan Pal. Lib.). There is also a smaller and more fragmentary album section bearing dates from 1608 to 1618 (Berlin, Staatsbib., Orientabt., Libr. pict. A.117). Single pages are in various public and private collections.

It is impossible to describe exactly the great lost albums, but their general outlines can be reconstructed with some accuracy. The practice was to alternate calligraphy and miniatures. The range of pictures is considerable, encompassing portraits, genre scenes, allegorical subjects, literary and historical subjects, natural history studies and European prints that had entered the imperial collection. Either miniatures were commissioned especially for an album or earlier pictures were incorporated into assemblages. Many leaves are masterpieces of Mughal, Deccani or Persian miniature painting and calligraphy. The works are on paper pasted on to thin board. A special feature that the albums share with some imperial manuscripts of the late 16th century is richly decorated margins, sometimes coloured (*see* INDIAN SUBCONTINENT, fig. 236). The covers were of leather or lacquer boards.

It is perhaps partly through accident of survival that the painting workshop of the Akbar period is associated primarily with manuscript production and the workshops of later reigns primarily with albums, but this does apparently indicate a general direction of development. The making of albums predominated in the Jahangir period (*see also* INDIAN SUBCONTINENT, §V, 4(i)(c)) and seems to have encouraged the production of miniatures by individual artists rather than as collaborative efforts, as was common in late Akbar-period manuscript production. Albums also dominated production in the reign of Shah Jahan (*reg* 1628–58) almost to the exclusion of manuscript illustration. Exhibiting continuity with earlier examples in format and technique, the albums are undeniably splendid, and individual leaves are sometimes great works, but overall the albums are more homogeneous and less vivacious than their predecessors (*see also* INDIAN SUBCONTINENT, §V, 4(i)(d)). Most of them are dispersed or altered, though the Minto Album, probably acquired between 1807 and 1813, when the Earl of Minto was Governor-General of India, is divided into only two parts (Dublin, Chester Beatty Lib., MS. 7; and London, V&A, I.M. 8 to 28-1925). An album presented by Prince Dara Shikoh to his wife in 1642 also survives (London, BL, Orient. & India Office Col., Add. Or. 3129).

As Mughal taste permeated the courtly life of India, the album format became generally popular. From at least the first half of the 16th century a traditional Indian method of assembling paintings without running texts was in unbound series tied in cloth-wrapped portfolios (as had long been done with both illustrated and unillustrated manuscripts). It was but a short step from this to binding leaves in the manner of an album, and, although the

2. Album page (211×121 mm; 18th century) of paintings from the early 17th century, including (top left) Bishan Das (attrib.): *Riza Khudebanda Mirza* and (bottom left) Muhammad Nadir of Samarkand (attrib.): *Hawk*, all opaque watercolours on paper (London, British Museum)

traditional method was never abandoned, in later times many series were bound in album form. Typical examples of this include numerous sets of *Rāgamālā* paintings produced commercially in the 18th and 19th centuries in such centres as Jaipur (*see* INDIAN SUBCONTINENT, §VI, 4(iii)(e)).

European patrons assembled albums as foreigners entered Indian cultural life, often following exactly the Indian examples in their collections. An extensive set of albums survives from the collection of the French–Swiss adventurer Antoine Louis Henri Polier (1741–95). After his murder in France they passed into the collection of William Beckford and then mostly to his daughter Susan Euphemia, Duchess of Hamilton. At the dispersal of the Hamilton collection they were purchased by the Prussian state and are today in the Islamisches Museum and the Museum für Indische Kunst, Berlin. Other of Polier's albums are in the British Library, London, and the Achenbach Foundation for Graphic Arts, San Francisco (see *The Art of the Book in India*, p.150; Ehnbom, p. 84). Indian in everything but patron, they contain major examples of Mughal, Deccani and Lucknow painting and calligraphy of the 16th–18th century. A collection of 67 albums assembled by RICHARD JOHNSON, active in India from 1770 to 1790, was sold in 1807 to the India Office Library and forms the largest portion of its Indian painting collection.

The making of albums continued into the 19th century, often under less agreeable circumstances. The dispersal of the imperial Mughal library began in the 18th century, feeding the collections of Indians, Persians and Europeans alike, and the process accelerated as the power of the empire declined (see fig. 2). By about 1800 workshops in Delhi were copying imperial album pages and mixing early originals with late work. Such hybrid productions have caused much confusion among scholars and dealers. After the fall of Lucknow to the British in 1858, the royal library, which contained a significant portion of the imperial Mughal library, was systematically looted. Some manuscripts were taken away intact, but many were destroyed. Some of their abraded and dirtied pages were retrieved, assembled into albums and preserved by the nawabs of Rampur. Thus illustrated pages of Jahangir's personal account of his reign, intended to grace a manuscript of the highest quality, now repose in a modest album in the Raza Library, Rampur.

BIBLIOGRAPHY

P. Brown: *Indian Painting under the Mughals* (Oxford, 1924)

E. Kühnel and H. Goetz: *Indian Bookpainting from Jahangir's Time in the State Library in Berlin* (London, 1926)

J. V. S. Wilkinson and B. Gray: 'Indian Paintings in a Persian Museum', *Burl. Mag.*, lxvi (1935), pp. 168–71

T. W. Arnold: *The Library of A. Chester Beatty: A Catalogue of the Indian Miniatures*, 3 vols, rev. and ed. J. V. S. Wilkinson (London, 1936)

Y. Godard: 'Les Marges du Murakka' Gulshan', *Athar-é Iran*, i (1936), pp. 11–33

B. Gray and A. Godard: *Iran: Persian Miniatures–Imperial Library* (Greenwich, CT, 1956)

The Grand Mughal: Imperial Painting in India, 1600–1660 (exh. cat. by M. C. Beach, Williamstown, MA, Clark A. Inst.; Baltimore, MD, Walters A.G.; Boston, MA, Mus. F.A.; New York, Asia House Gals; 1978–9)

R. Hickmann and V. Enderlein: *Indische Albumblätter: Miniaturen und Kalligraphien aus der Zeit der Moghul-Kaiser* (Leipzig, 1979)

T. Falk and M. Archer: *Indian Miniatures in the India Office Library* (London, 1981)

The Art of the Book in India (exh. cat. by J. P. Losty, London, BL, 1982)

D. Ehnbom: *Indian Miniatures: The Ehrenfeld Collection* (New York, 1986)

DANIEL EHNBOM

3. ISLAMIC WORLD. The album (Arab. *muraqqa'*, literally 'patchwork'; Pers. *jung*, literally 'ship') appears to be a 15th-century phenomenon in the Islamic world. The earliest surviving example (*c.* 1430; Istanbul, Topkapı Pal. Lib., H. 2310) contains specimens by 14th-century master calligraphers collected for the Timurid prince and bibliophile Baysunghur (*see* TIMURID, §II, (7)) at Herat. Dust Muhammad, the 16th-century historian of painting and calligraphy, referred to a *jung* made in Baghdad for Sultan Ahmad Jalayir (*reg* 1382–1410) for which paintings were produced, but it is not clear that *jung* refers to what was later understood as an album, and 'miscellany' may be a better translation. Generally albums were made to preserve and display older pieces of calligraphy and book illustration, as MIR SAYYID AHMAD wrote in the preface to the album (Istanbul, Topkapı Pal. Lib., H. 2161) he prepared in 1564–5 for the Safavid military commander Ghayb Beg: 'It was deemed necessary. . . to review and inspect. . .tomes

and specimens [of calligraphy]. Since they had not been arranged or organized, it was difficult, nay impossible to locate any particular thing one wanted, and therefore it was seen as fitting to organize this album so that the confusion would be righted.'

There are two types of album prevalent in the Islamic world, the 'scrapbook' album, in which dissimilar pieces (e.g. calligraphy, painting, pounces, designs) are pasted at random, and the planned album, consisting generally of facing pages of painting and calligraphy. Several examples of the 'scrapbook' type (Istanbul, Topkapı Pal. Lib., H. 2152, H. 2153 and H. 2160 and Berlin, Staatsbib., Diez A 70–73) contain specimens of 14th- and 15th-century Persian calligraphy and manuscript painting and were probably assembled at Tabriz in the early 16th century. Planned albums typically contain elaborately illuminated borders and rulings. In the albums prepared for the Safavid amirs Husayn Beg (1560; Istanbul, Topkapı Pal. Lib., H. 2151) and Ghayb Beg, pieces of majuscule exhibition calligraphy face paintings on a two-page spread. Elaborate illumination and margins were made, and often pieces of minuscule manuscript calligraphy were cut from particularly fine calligraphed poetic works and pasted around the principal centrepiece. This arrangement was also adopted under the Mughals in India (*see* §2 above). Safavid albums are typically prefaced with a short history of calligraphy and painting and a list of the artists whose works are included.

Albums were bound both as normal books on the long side and with edge-to-edge accordion bindings. The latter type of binding was particularly favoured for Ottoman calligraphic albums, which typically contain only calligraphy and no paintings, with texts generally selected from the Hadith and executed in *thuluth* and *naskh* scripts (e.g. a *muraqqa*ʿ by HAFIZ OSMAN; Berlin, Mus. Islam. Kst).

BIBLIOGRAPHY

M. S. Ipşiroğlu: *Saray-Alben: Diez'sche Klebebande aus der Berliner Sammlungen* (Wiesbaden, 1964)

F. Çağman: 'On the Contents of the Four Istanbul Albums H. 2152, 2153, 2154 and 2160', *Islam. A.*, i (1982), pp. 31–6

F. Çağman and Zeren Tanındı: *The Topkapı Saray Museum: The Albums and Illustrated Manuscripts*, trans. J. M. Rogers (London, 1986)

E. Niewöhner-Eberhard: 'Die Berliner Murakka von Hafiz Osman', *Jb. Berlin. Mus.*, xxxi (1989), pp. 41–59

W. Thackston: *A Century of Princes* (Cambridge, MA, 1989), pp. 335–56 [Eng. trans. of Dust Muhammad's preface (1544) to the Bahram Mirza Album (Istanbul, Topkapı Pal. Lib. H. 2154), Malik Daylami's preface (1560–61) to the Amir Husayn Beg Album (H. 2151) and Mir Sayyid Ahmad's preface (1564–5) to the Amir Ghayb Beg Album (H. 2161)]

WHEELER M. THACKSTON

Album amicorum [Lat.: 'book of friendship'; Ger. *Stammbuch*]. Bound collection of autographs, writings, paintings and drawings collected by the owner from his friends and acquaintances. The earliest detailed study of the *album amicorum* (Michael Lilienthal's Königsberg dissertation, 1712) traced its origins to peerages with genealogical information, which is believed to have played some role in tournaments. Lilienthal added, however, that no examples of such peerages were known to exist at the time of writing; he also noted that the emergence of the *album amicorum* seemed to be closely connected with the beginning of the Reformation. The Keil brothers (1893) adopted Lilienthal's theory, according to which the albums originated from lost peerages, but they disregarded the rest of his observations. Many scholars followed this view uncritically, but in 1910 the theory was challenged by Rosenheim, who rightly pointed out that the earliest known albums did not, in fact, include coats of arms and that they came from academic circles in Germany, in particular Wittenberg. After Nickson (1970) had supported Rosenheim, it was Klose (1982) who provided the final arguments that show that the album actually came into being in Wittenberg in the time of Luther and Philipp Melanchthon. The oldest known album, that of Claude de Senarclens (1545–59; Geneva, Bib. Pub. & U., MS. lat. 328), as well as the oldest album known to have belonged to someone outside German-speaking territory—that of the Dutchman Stephanus van Rhemen (1556–61; Arnhem, Rijksarchf Gelderland, fam. arch. van Rhemen, Hs. 134)—both open with contributions from Wittenberg. Students who went from one university to another rapidly spread the custom throughout Germany and Switzerland, and soon albums were also circulating among students in Leuven, Douai, Paris and Orléans. The cult flourished particularly in Leiden after 1575, and thereafter the northern Netherlands became, with Germany, the most important area of circulation for the album, which elsewhere in Europe (with the exception of Scandinavia) never developed beyond its simplest form.

Despite the university connection, albums were soon compiled by people other than students, mainly members of the bourgeoisie, including women. Several albums exist from noblewomen who resided at the court of William the Silent (e.g. the album of Marie de Marnix, 1579–83; London, BL, Sloane MS. 851). Often these albums have the character of a songbook. In German- and Dutch-speaking regions the album remained in fashion until the beginning of the 19th century, when it gradually developed into the sort of album of verses commonly exchanged by young girls at school.

At first album inscriptions were made on the spare pages within printed books, such as Melanchthon's *Loci communes theologici* (Leipzig, 1548), for example Christophe von Teuffenbach's album (1548–68; Nuremberg, Ger. Nmus.); sometimes on sheets bound in for the purpose. Soon, however, there developed a liking for well-worn copies of emblem books (e.g. Andrea Alciato, Johannes Sambucus, Hadr. Junius) and for books comprising devices and moral sayings (e.g. Claude Paradin's *Devises héroïques*; *see* EMBLEM BOOK). By *c.* 1558 Jean de Tournes in Lyon was printing his *Thesaurus amicorum*, a book specially intended for album use: the pages were decorated with borders and left partly blank so that inscriptions could be added between proverbs or portrait medallions of famous people, chiefly Classical and humanist scholars from the past (e.g. Erasmus and Melanchthon). Many similar publications, some published in German, followed. In addition there were completely blank copy books, often lavishly bound and with gold tooling, which in the course of the 17th century came to replace the printed album book altogether. During the 18th century these were increasingly oblong in format, although unusually shaped albums, such as oval, did occur, and in the 19th century people would also use loose-leaf, boxed albums.

Albums that belonged to members of the nobility usually contain many drawings of arms, with or without some heraldic device, a date and the contributor's name. Date and place, a motto or quotation and a name, usually embedded in some flowery dedication, formed the standard elements of a contribution. There were also album owners who loved to travel and had an eye for cultural curiosities. Some collected rare paper types, but above all these travellers were interested in drawings of local costumes. Album owners who knew draughtsmen or painters would ask for an inscription in the form of, or decorated with, an illustration by the artist (e.g. the album of PETRUS SCRIVERIUS, 1601–38; The Hague, Kon. Bib., MS. 133 M 5; see fig.). There are several albums, for example, that contain drawings by Rembrandt. Other albums include drawings of cultural or historical interest because of their particular subject-matter (e.g. scenes from student life, sports, games, allegorical and symbolical subjects). Most of the albums, however, are literary in character, and in the earliest period the main language used was Latin. Sometimes the owner himself would open with a poem or poems dwelling upon the value of his album as a lasting token of his friendships. Such owners certainly expected their literary friends to contribute an appropriate poem for their inscription. The number of inscriptions in an album indicates not only the network of contacts maintained by its owner but also his mobility during a particular phase of his life. Many albums thus provide useful biographical and prosopographical information and shed light on the relationships that existed among members of the literary community. The albums also contain important material on the history of universities.

Systematic study of the albums has long been advocated, but so far very little has actually been undertaken. Since Lilienthal, virtually no general study of substantial length has been published. The most extensive works are the catalogues and inventories of the (sadly) few large public collections. In addition there are a few descriptions of albums in private collections, mostly to be found in sale catalogues. Such catalogues have become important sources of information about lost albums. The number of detailed studies of one or more albums, however, is impressive and rapidly growing. The ideal form for these studies is the annotated facsimile edition, but so far only a few albums have appeared in this form. The phenomenon of the album was discussed in broader terms during two international conferences held in Wolfenbüttel (1978, 1986). A computerized project, the *Corpus Alborum Amicorum*, has been initiated by W. Klose in order to draw up an inventory of all albums compiled before 1600 and to give a detailed analysis of every inscription written before 1573. The *Nederlandse alba tot 1800* ('Dutch albums up to 1800') project (Heesakkers and Thomassen) aims to make an annotated inventory of all albums that were compiled either partly or completely in the Netherlands.

BIBLIOGRAPHY

M. Lilienthal: *Schediasma critico-literarium de philiothecis varioque earundum usu et abusu, vulgo von Stamm-Buchern* (Königsberg, 1712, rev. Wittenberg, 1740; repr. in Fechner, 1981, pp. 237–98)

Illustration from the *album amicorum* of Petrus Scriverius: Pieter Saenredam: *View of Haarlem*, 127×194 mm, 1629 (The Hague, Koninklijk Bibliotheek, MS. 133 M 5, fol. 153*r*)

F. W. Hölbe: *Geschichte der Stammbücher* (Camburg an der Saale, 1798)
A. M. Hildebrandt: *Stammbuch-blätter des norddeutschen Adels* (Berlin, 1874)
R. Keil and R. Keil: *Die deutschen Stammbücher des sechzehnten bis neunzehnten Jahrhunderts* (Berlin, 1893/*R* Hildesheim, 1975)
K. Bogen: 'Die Stammbuchsammlung in der Stadtbibliothek zu Königsberg', *Vjschr. Wap.-, Siegel- & Famknd.*, xxix (1901), pp. 1–62
K. Masner: 'Die schlesischen Stammbücher und ihre künstlerische Ausschmückung', *Schlesiens Vorzeit Bild & Schr.*, 2nd ser., iv (1907), pp. 137–61
G. van Obernitz: 'Verzeichnis hervorragender Namen von Gelehrten, Schriftsteller, hohem und niederem Adel aus einem grozsen Theil der Stammbücher, welche auf der Grossherzoglichen Bibliothek zu Weimar sich befinden', *Vjschr. Wap.-, Siegel- & Famknd.*, xxix (1910), pp. 285–399
M. Rosenheim: 'The Album Amicorum', *Archaeologia*, vxii (1910), pp. 251–308
A. W. Kiesling: 'Die Stammbücher der Bibliothek des Königlichen Kunstgewerbemuseums in Berlin', *Vjschr. Wap.-, Siegel- & Famknd.*, xxxix (1911), pp. 160–223
J. Hoffmann: *Ein Stammbuch aus vier Jahrhunderten* (Leipzig, 1926)
E. Herold-Zollikofer: *Libri amicorum (Stammbücher) der Zentralbibliothek und des schweiz Landesmuseums in Zürich* (Neuchâtel, 1939)
A. Fiedler: *Vom Stammbuch zum Poesiealbum: Eine volkskundliche Studie* (Weimar, 1960)
M. A. E. Nickson: *Early Autograph Albums in the British Museum* (London, 1970)
V. Helk: 'Stambøger in det kongelige Bibliotek', *Fund & Forsk.*, xxi (1974), pp. 7–46
J.-U. Fechner, ed.: *Stammbücher als kulturhistorische Quellen*, Wolfenbütteler Forschungen, xi (Munich, 1981)
K. Goldmann: *Nürnberger und Altdorfer Stammbücher aus vier Jahrhunderten: Ein Katalog* (Nuremberg, 1981)
W. Klose: 'Stammbücher: Eine kulturhistorische Betrachtung', *Bib. & Wiss.*, xvi (1982), pp. 41–67
C. L. Heesakkers and K. Thomassen: *Voorlopige lijst van alba amicorum uit de Nederlanden voor 1800* (The Hague, 1986)
L. Kurras: *Zu gutem Gedenken: Kulturhistorische Miniaturen aus Stammbüchern des Germanischen Nationalmuseums, 1570–1770* (Munich, 1987)
W. Klose: *Corpus alborum amicorum—CAAC: Beschreibendes Verzeichnis der Stammbücher des 16. Jahrhunderts* (Stuttgart, 1988)
L. Kurras: *Die Stammbücher des Germanischen Nationalmuseums Nürnberg*, i (Wiesbaden, 1988)
W. Klose, ed.: *Stammbücher des 16. Jahrhunderts*, Wolfenbütteler Forschungen, 42 (Wiesbaden, 1989)
K. Thomassen, ed.: *Alba amicorum: Vijf eeuwen vriendschap op papier gezet: Het album amicorum en het poëziealbum in de Nederlanden* (Maarssen and The Hague, 1990)

CHRIS L. HEESAKKERS

Albumen print. *See under* PHOTOGRAPHY, §I.

Albuquerque, Brás [Afonso] **de** (*b* Alhandra, nr Lisbon, 1500; *d* Lisbon, 1580.) Portuguese statesman, patron and writer. He was the natural son of Afonso d'Albuquerque (1453–1515), who was involved in the Portuguese conquest of India. In 1506 he was legitimized by Manuel I, who ordered that he take the name of Afonso in honour of his father. Marriage to Dona Maria de Noronha, daughter of the Conde de Linhares, a minister of the King, together with royal favours, brought him a substantial fortune; he later became the Inspector of Finances to John III and President of the Senate of Lisbon. His *Commentarios de Affonso d'Albuquerque* (1557), based on his father's memoirs, became a standard history of the Portuguese in India. In 1521 Albuquerque travelled to Italy in the suite of the Infanta Dona Beatriz and developed an interest in Italian Renaissance architecture. This is apparent in the work carried out to the late 15th-century Quinta da Bacalhoa, Azeitão, which he purchased in 1528. While the regular plan and Tuscan loggia, overlooking a formal garden, show Italian influence, the cylindrical corner towers of the house are firmly Manueline in style. The Quinta contains important *azulejos*, including a panel of *Susanna and the Elders* (1565) attributed to Marçal de Matos. The palace of the Albuquerque family in Lisbon, the Casa dos Bicos (damaged 1755, rest. 1983), is faced with diamond-shaped bosses similar to those on the Palazzo dei Diamanti, Ferrara.

BIBLIOGRAPHY

I. F. da Silva: *Diccionario bibliographico portuguez*, i (Lisbon, 1858)
J. Serrão, ed.: *Dicionário de história de Portugal*, i (Lisbon, 1963)
C. de Azevedo: *Solares portugueses: Introdução ao estudo da casa nobre* (Lisbon, 1969)

ZILAH QUEZADO DECKKER

Alcalá, Duques de. *See* RIBERA (i).

Alcalá de Henares. Spanish city in Castile, 30 km east of Madrid. It lies on the site of the Roman city of Complutum and a subsequent Moorish fortification, the castle (Arab. al-Kalá) of Qal'at 'Abd al-Salám. A small Mozarabic settlement developed here at the supposed site of the martyrdom of SS Justus and Pastor. From the 13th century Alcalá was the country retreat of the archbishops of Toledo; its considerable growth during the Middle Ages was due partly to Archbishop Carrillo's extension of the city walls in 1454, but most of all to the founding of the Complutensian University there in 1498 (transferred to Madrid, 1836) by Cardinal FRANCISCO JIMÉNEZ DE CISNEROS. The university occupied more than a third of Alcalá within the walls. Two radial streets were extended with a rectilinear layout of parallel side-streets, and this regular plan dominates the university area and links it with the medieval part of the city, from which it is separated by the Plaza Mayor.

Dating from the Middle Ages are the Calle Mayor (see fig.)—the main street and business centre of the Jewish community—the Hospital de Antezana (15th century) and the Magistral church (1479–1509), which is dedicated to SS Justus and Pastor and was extended and completed by Cardinal Cisneros. It was designed by Antón and Enrique Egas and built by Pedro Gumiel, and it resembles Toledo Cathedral but on a smaller scale. The nave is in five oblong bays, with aisles and an ambulatory. The plain, flat-topped west front between buttresses is relieved by an ornamental overdoor. The tomb of the saints lies beneath the high altar; their relics are preserved in an ornate 18th-century silver sarcophagus. A small museum contains liturgical and other religious objects, as well as a collection of paintings, including *St Louis with Donor* by Bartolomé Carducho.

Many new buildings were erected in Alcalá de Henares during the Renaissance, especially within the university complex. The magnificent Colegio Mayor de S Ildefonso, the main seat of the university, is by Rodrigo Gil de Hontañon, who also created its striking plateresque façade (1537–53). The Colegio is a rebuilding in stone (1543–83) of the original modest brick structure begun 1501 by Pedro Gumiel. Its assembly hall, the Paraninfo (1518–19; attrib. Gumiel) is two storeys high with an upper-level tribune on three sides, allowing the public to observe through segmental arched openings. Another important building from the same period is the Archbishop's Palace abutting the Magistral church. Originally begun in 1209, it

Alcalá de Henares, Calle Mayor

was transformed by Alonso de Covarrubias from *c.* 1530 to *c.* 1540 into a Renaissance palace for Cardinal Juan Pardo de Tavera (for illustration *see* ARTESONADO). The palace was damaged by fire in 1940 and subsequently restored. Other plateresque residences built for the nobility include the palaces of Doña Juana Mendoza and the Marqués de Lonzarote, which became the convents of S Catalina and the Carmelitas de la Imagen respectively and are variations on the Toledo plateresque style of Covarrubias.

In the 17th century a new series of foundations introduced the austere Madrid forms of Baroque. Colleges were constructed within the university precinct to harmonize with the conventual buildings. The Colegios del Rey, de Málaga, de S Basilio Magno, de los Irlandeses and de Caracciolos are interesting examples of the adaptation of conventual models to the needs of a university community. A large number of ecclesiastical buildings also date from the Baroque period, notably the oratory of the Filipenses, the convents of the Carmelitas de Afuera, Trinitarios Descalzos and Agostinos Recoletos, and the Jesuit college and church. The convent of Las Bernardas was founded in 1617 by Cardinal Bernardo de Sandoval y Rojas. Its oval church (1618), designed by Juan Gómez de Mora (i), contains a fine altar with a baldacchino by Francisco Bautista and an interesting series of paintings (1620) by Angelo Nardi. These include the *Coronation of the Virgin* and the *Martyrdom of St Lawrence*, and scenes from the *Childhood of Christ*. The complex of buildings for the Jesuits is also interesting. The façade was designed by de Mora after Il Gesú in Rome, with rounded niches containing sculptures of *St Ignatius* and *St Francis Xavier* by Manuel Pereira. The chapel of the Holy Forms was painted in 1699 by Juan Vicente Ribera (*fl* 1699–1725) with Baroque *trompe-l'oeil* effects.

Secular building suffered during this period of mainly ecclesiastical construction; only in the mid-19th century was there a revival of civic architecture, with the Príncipe barracks (1863), the town hall, the municipal abattoir and the Teatro Cervantes. The use of brick as a building material has continued with the Círculo de Contribuyentes and the unusual Hotel Laredo, both built in the early 20th century in the *Mudéjar* revival style. Although 20th-century development extends well beyond the city walls, Alcalá de Henares, with its many historic buildings, retains something of its appearance during the Spanish Golden Age.

BIBLIOGRAPHY

E. Tormo: *Alcalá de Henares* (Madrid, n.d.)
A. de Morales: *La vida, el martyrio, la invención, las grandezas y las traslaciones de los gloriosos niños Martyres San Iusto y Pastor y el solemne triunfo con que fueron recibidas sus santas reliquias en Alcalá de Henares en su postrera traslación: Sus antigüedades* (Alcalá de Henares, 1568)
M. de la Portilla y Esquivel: *Historia de la ciudad de Compluto, vulgarmente Alcalá de Santiuste y ahora Henares*, 2 vols (Alcalá de Henares, 1725–8)
E. Azaña y Catarineu: *Historia de la ciudad de Alcalá de Henares (antigua Compluto)*, 2 vols (Alcalá de Henares, 1882–3)
M. A. Castillo Oreja: *Ciudad, funciones y símbolos: Alcalá de Henares, un modelo urbano de la España moderna* (Alcalá de Henares, 1982)

MIGUEL A. CASTILLO

Alcantara Téllez Girón y Pacheco, Pedro de, Duque di Osuna. *See* OSUNA, (2).

Alcanyis [Alcañiz]**, Miguel** [Gil Master] (*b* ?Mallorca; *fl* 1408–47). Spanish painter. First documented in Valencia in 1408, he was active as a painter in Barcelona in 1415, in Mallorca in 1420 (described as 'painter of Majorca'), in Valencia between 1421 and 1432 and in Mallorca from 1433; he is last recorded in Mallorca in 1447. Of his documented commissions, only two fragmentary works can be identified: the wings of an altarpiece of *St Michael* (Lyon, Mus. B.-A.), painted in 1421 for the town of Jérica (Valencia), and two predella panels of the *Death of the Virgin* and *St Thomas Receiving the Virgin's Girdle* from an altarpiece of the *Virgin* executed in 1442 in Mallorca (Alcudia, Mus. Parroq.). Other works have been attributed to Alcanyis on the basis of stylistic comparisons with these panels, and he has been identified as the Gil Master, an artist named after the fragmentary altarpiece—consisting of an *Ascension* and *St Vincent* (both New York, Hisp. Soc. America) and a *St Giles* (New York, Met.)—commissioned by Vicente Gil for a chapel in S Juan del Hospital, Valencia. A few scholars have also attempted to identify Alcanyis with the MASTER OF THE BAMBINO VISPO (*see* MASTERS, ANONYMOUS, AND MONOGRAMMISTS, §I).

Alcanyis's *Virgin and Child* (*c.* 1400; ex-Fontana priv. col., Barcelona) reveals close connections with the Florentine Starnina, who is documented in Valencia between 1395 and 1401, and it also shows signs of Franco-Flemish influence. The altarpiece of the *Virgin and St Mark* (*c.* 1405; Valencia, Serra de Alzaga priv. col.) is a typically Florentine composition, in which the figures are of prime importance. The undulating line of their contours is skilfully used to descriptive ends. This use of line becomes progressively accentuated in Alcanyis's work, taking on an expressionist character that culminated *c.* 1425–30 in the altarpiece of the *Ascension* and *St Vincent*, especially in the *Entombment* panel (New York, Hisp. Soc. America) from its predella, in which the line serves an acutely dramatic purpose. This expressionism has disappeared in the *Death of the Virgin* panel of 1442 in Alcudia.

Miguel's finest work is the altarpiece of the *Holy Cross* from S Domingo, Valencia (*c.* 1410; Valencia, Mus. B.A.). The central *Crucifixion*, which combines elements characteristic of Valencian Gothic painting, is distinguished, however, by its rare intensity. Alcanyis's skill in the use of colour is seen particularly in the panels at Lyon. He was also a fine draughtsman and a master of composition.

BIBLIOGRAPHY

L. de Saralegui: 'Miguel Alcanyis', *Archv A. Valenc.*, xxvii (1956), pp. 3–41

C. R. Post: *A History of Spanish Painting*, xiii (Cambridge, MA, 1966), pp. 310–15

G. Llompart: *La pintura medieval mallorquina*, 4 vols (Palma de Mallorca, 1977–80), i, pp. 83–5; iv, pp. 141–7

M. Hériard Dubreuil: 'Du Nouveau sur un primitif espagnol', *L'Oeil*, 270–71 (Jan–Feb 1978), pp. 52–9, 94–5

——: 'Gótico internacional', *Historia del arte valenciano*, ii (Valencia, 1988), pp. 182–235

MATHIEU HÉRIARD DUBREUIL

Alcaraz, Francisco Salzillo y. *See* SALZILLO Y ALCARAZ, FRANCISCO.

Alcázar, Luis Paret y. *See* PARET, LUIS.

Alcherius [Alcerius; Alchiero; Archerius]**, Johannes** [Jehan; Giovanni] (*fl* 1382–1411). Writer, active in Paris. Between 1382 and 1410 he travelled to Italy on a number of occasions, where he collected recipes for the manufacture of pigments and other techniques from the artists that he met. He also borrowed manuals or handbooks on the washing, purifying and grinding of colours to assist him in his research. In 1431 his collection of recipes was obtained by Jehan Le Bègue (1368–after 1431), a licentiate in the law and notary to the Master of the Mint in Paris. Le Bègue copied out the recipes in his own hand and incorporated them in two sections (*De coloribus diversis modis tractatur* and *De diversis coloribus*) into a collection of texts discussing the practice of painting, entitled *Experimenta de coloribus* (Paris, Bib. N. MS. 6741), first published in 1849 (Merrifield). Le Bègue's compilation begins with a glossary of terms, mostly taken from Alcherius and the *Catholicon*, a Latin dictionary written in 1286 (pubd Mainz, 1460). Alcherius's account relates almost entirely to the art of manuscript illumination.

Alcherius's profession is unknown; although he does not appear to have practised as a painter or illuminator himself, his treatise states that he tried out many of the formulae described. It records that he left Milan for Paris in March 1382 after having obtained a recipe for ink from Alberto Porzello, a calligrapher who also taught his art. The next date for his activities is given in the preface to *De coloribus diversis modis tractatur*, which was written in Paris on 28 July 1398. In the preface Jacques Coene is cited as the source for his information. The treatise begins with a description of methods for laying gold to be burnished, and continues with recipes for making the pigments for the colours pink, blue and green, as well as describing how to prepare parchment, paper, primed panels and linen to be drawn on with a pencil or stylus. Also described is the method for laying gold on parchment, paper, cloth and *sindone* (It.: 'very fine linen'). His second brief treatise, *De diversis coloribus*, follows on and is dated 8 August 1398. It comprises information obtained from the illuminator Antoine de Compiègne. Alcherius was still in Paris in October 1398. The only external document relating to him dates from 1399, when he recommended three artists to be employed at Milan Cathedral. In March 1409 he was again in Milan and there wrote down further recipes from Fra Dionisio, a Servite. Included is a recipe for a Brazil lake made with a base of powdered eggshell, a 14th-century innovation. On 2 February 1410 Alcherius obtained a recipe for the preparation of ultramarine from a Master Johannes, then residing in the Paris house of Pietro Sacchi da Verona (*fl* 1397–1421), who was an illuminator, and, by 1415, librarian to Jean, Duc de Berry. Alcherius was in Bologna on 11 February 1410 where he met a Netherlandish embroiderer, Theodore, who had worked at Pavia for Gian Galeazzo Visconti. Theodore gave Alcherius certain recipes for preparing transparent colours (lakes) for use in painting and to dye and decorate cloth. According to Theodore these recipes originated from London. On 13 February 1410 a further 17 recipes were obtained from a book lent to him by Johannes de Modena, a painter living in Bologna. These included a recipe for ultramarine, mordants for laying down gold and one for gesso sottile. Alcherius was in Venice on 4 May 1410 where he met the illuminator Michelino da Besozzo, who had worked in Pavia and who gave him another formula for the preparation of ultramarine. Alcherius returned to Paris during 1410 and in December 1411 he revised and corrected his work.

BIBLIOGRAPHY

M. P. Merrifield: *Original Treatises Dating from the XIIth to XVIIIth Centuries on the Arts of Painting*, i (London, 1849/*R* New York and London, 1967), pp. 3–14, 258–91

G. Loumyer: *Les Traditions techniques de la peinture médiévale* (Brussels and Paris, 1914), pp. 55–9

L. Dimier: *L'Art d'enluminure* (Paris, 1927)

□

Alchi. Buddhist monastery in a small valley on the left bank of the River Indus, *c.* 64 km west of Leh in Ladakh, India. Tradition attributes the monastery's origin to the Tibetan scholar and temple-builder Rinchen Sangpo (AD 958–1055), the 'great translator', and although its buildings mostly date from the 11th century, the site is replete with his memory, from the ancient tree he planted to his portraits and images in the temples. A treasure-house of art, Alchi has been preserved because of its isolation from trade routes and the decline of its community, the monks of the Dromtön sect of the Kadampa order.

Ringed by a wall and votive chortens (stupas), the religious enclave (Tib. *chökhor*) comprises three entrance chortens, a number of shrines and temples, the Dukhang (assembly hall) with its courtyard and monastic dwellings (*see* TIBET, §II, and INDIAN SUBCONTINENT, §III, 6(i)(a)). The Sumtsek Lhakhang, or Three-tiered Temple (11th–

12th century), is remarkable for its life-size clay sculptures and its paintings; repairs undertaken in the 16th century largely followed the original works. The Lhakhang Soma (New Temple), the Manjushri Lhakhang (Temple of Manjushri, the *bodhisattva* of Wisdom) and the Lotsawa Lhakhang (Temple of the Great Translator) perhaps date to the 12th–13th centuries; all three are small, square shrines. The stone and mud-brick buildings of the complex are in a purely Tibetan style, but the woodwork is in the Kashmiri Buddhist tradition (*see also* TIBET, §V, 11). The paintings that profusely adorn the interior walls exhibit early Kashmiri, Sasanian and Central Asian styles; some Tibetan and later Kashmiri–Mughal influence is also in evidence (*see* TIBET, §IV, and INDIAN SUBCONTINENT, §VI, 3(i)(c)).

BIBLIOGRAPHY

S. Khosa: *Art History of Kashmir and Ladakh (Medieval Period)* (New Delhi, 1977)
D. L. Snellgrove and T. Skorupski: *Central Ladakh* (1977), i of *The Cultural Heritage of Ladakh* (London and New Delhi, 1977–80)
P. Pal and L. Fournier: *A Buddhist Paradise: The Murals of Alchi, Western Himalayas* (Hong Kong, 1982)
G. Michell: *The Penguin Guide to the Monuments of India*, i (London, 1989)
R. Goepper: 'The "Great Stūpa" at Alchi', *Artibus Asiae*, liii (1993), pp. 111–43
R. Linrothe: 'The Murals of Mangyu: A Distillation of Mature Esoteric Buddhist Iconography', *Orientations*, xxv/11 (1994), pp. 92–102

W. A. P. MARR

Alciati, Andrea (*b* Milan, 8 May 1492; *d* Pavia, 12 Jan 1550). Italian lawyer, writer and scholar. A distinguished jurist, who applied humanist philological methods to legal studies, he enjoyed immense fame throughout Europe. He taught at the universities of Avignon (1518–22; 1522–7) and Bourges (1529–33); he worked at Milan, Pavia and Bologna and was patronized by Ercole II d'Este (ii) at Ferrara. His phenomenally successful *Emblematum liber* was composed in his spare time in 1520–21. In its original form this was a collection of Latin epigrams, almost a third of which were based on the *Anthologia Graeca* (Florence, 1494). Alciati had intended them for a circle of friends and acquaintances but the first edition appeared in Augsburg in 1531 without his consent. Commercial reasons inspired the printer, Heinrich Steiner (*fl* 1522–48), to add images illustrating each epigram, so creating the first emblem book (*see* EMBLEM BOOK, esp. §2). An emblem consists of a vignette, a proverb or title and an epigram which explains the whole. In contrast to imprese (*see* IMPRESA), which never include human figures, emblems deal with Classical gods and heroes, personifications, as well as animals, trees and artefacts. A general lesson is drawn from some aspect of their nature or behaviour. It was thanks to Steiner's initiative, followed by all later editors, that the emblem, whose origins can be found in heraldry, was established as a genre based on the association of text and image.

WRITINGS

Emblematum liber (Augsburg, 1531) [numerous further edns followed]

BIBLIOGRAPHY

DBI
A. Henkel and A. Schöne: *Emblemata, Handbuch zur Sinnbildkunst des XVI. und XVII. Jahrhunderts* (Stuttgart, 1967)
H. Miedema: 'The Term *Emblema* in Alciati', *J. Warb. & Court. Inst.*, xxxi (1968), pp. 234–50
C. Balavoine: 'Les Emblèmes d'Alciati: Sens et contresens', *L'Emblème à la Renaissance*, ed. Y. Giraud (Paris, 1982), pp. 49–59
P. Daly and V. W. Callahan, eds: *The Latin Emblems* (Toronto, 1985)
P. Daly and S. Cutler, eds: *Emblems in Translation* (Toronto, 1985)
A. Saunders: *The Sixteenth Century French Emblem Book* (Geneva, 1988)
P. Daly, ed.: *Andrea Alciati and the Emblem Tradition: Essays in Honor of Virginia Woods Callahan* (New York, 1989)

FRANCOIS QUIVIGER

Alciati, Enrique (*b* Marseille; *d* after 1912). Italian sculptor and teacher, active in France and Mexico. He began his career in Marseille as a sculptor of the French school, and in 1888 he received an honourable mention at the Salon des Artistes Français, where he exhibited regularly until 1913. He probably moved to Mexico at the end of 1889. He won critical acclaim for his first works there, marble and bronze busts of important Mexican figures. In 1891 the government commissioned him to create statues of national heroes and dignitaries for the Paseo de la Reforma, Mexico City; the statue of *Col. Miguel López* was exhibited at the World's Columbian Exposition in Chicago, IL, in 1893 and at the World's Fair in Atlanta, GA, in 1895, winning prizes on both occasions. This was Alciati's most dramatic and realist work, and the influence of Rodin is clear. In 1895 he was appointed professor of sculpture, decoration and modelling at the Escuela Nacional de Bellas Artes, Mexico City. At the turn of the century he was commissioned to create, under the direction of Antonio Rivas Mercado, all the sculptures for the Independence Column in Mexico City. He sculpted the marbles in Mexico and Florence, and the bronzes were also cast in Florence. The monument was inaugurated in September 1910. In all Alciati's work his fine technique and his adherence to the classical tradition are evident.

BIBLIOGRAPHY

J. Fernández: *Arte moderno y contemporáneo de México* (Mexico City, 1952/*R* 1983), pp. 172–4
E. García Barragán: 'El escultor Enrique Alciati', *An. Inst. Invest. Estét.*, xxxix (1970), pp. 51–66

ELISA GARCÍA BARRAGÁN

Alcobaça Abbey. Cistercian abbey in Portugal. The abbey, dedicated to S Maria, was founded as part of the policy of repopulation and territorial improvement of the first king of Portugal, Alfonso I (*reg* 1139–85), who in 1152 granted a large area of land to St Bernard of Clairvaux by a charter known as the *Carta dos Coutos* (Lisbon, Arquiv. N.). Work on the monastery started in 1158 and adhered to the rigid precepts of the Order. Although the exterior was extended and altered in the 17th and 18th centuries, especially the Baroque façade of the church, the interior essentially preserves its original Early Gothic appearance.

BIBLIOGRAPHY

W. Beckford: *Recollections of an Excursion to the Monasteries of Alcobaça and Batalha* (London, 1835/*R* 1972)
M. V. Natividade: *Ignez de Castro e Pedro o Cru perante a iconografia dos seus túmulos* (Lisbon, 1910)
E. Korrodi: *Alcobaça: Estudo histórico, arqueológico e artístico da Real Abadia de Alcobaça* (Oporto, 1929)
B. Feio: *A escultura de Alcobaça* (Lisbon, 1940)
A. N. de Gusmão: *A Real Abadia de Alcobaça: Estudo histórico arqueológico* (Lisbon, 1948)
——: *A expansão da arquitectura borgonhesa e os mosteiros de Cister em Portugal* (Lisbon, 1953)
——: 'Vitrais de Santa Maria de Alcobaça, Lisboa', *Separata de Belas Artes*, xv (1960)
L. Verdelho da Costa: 'Morte e espaço funerário na arquitectura religiosa do século XV', *J. Portugal Med.* (1983), pp. 223–73
D. M. Cocheril: *Alcobaça—Abadia cisterciense de Portugal* (Lisbon, 1989)

C. A. Ferreira de Almeida: 'A roda da fortuna/Roda de vida da túmulo de D. Pedro em Alcobaça', *Homenagem ao Prof Doutor Artur Nobre de Gusmão* (Oporto, 1991), pp. 255–63

1. MEDIEVAL. The interior of the church is exactly 100 m long. The aisled nave has 13 bays with quadripartite rib vaults, leading via an unmarked crossing to the sanctuary, which has nine radiating chapels contained within the perimeter wall, as at the mother house of Clairvaux III. The two-bay transepts have western aisles and square eastern chapels. The impression of austerity is intensified by the height of the main nave (20.1 m) and the aisles (19.4 m), and by their comparatively narrow width (8–9 m in the nave, 2.5–2.8 m in the aisles). These proportions are exceptional in Cistercian buildings and explain the buttressing of the aisle walls and the treatment of the main arcade. Massive cruciform piers support chamfered corbels, from which the vault supports rise. In the absence of the original choir-screens, this arrangement creates a space in which the present austerity of bare stone is powerfully asserted. The rib vaulting of the aisles and transepts creates an impression of great lightness in relation to the thickness of the walls. The building is lit from the aisles and transepts, and from the large circular window and other openings in the original façade, which were retained in the 18th-century rebuilding. The chevet consists of a two-storey apse with two levels of narrow windows and a vault of nine segments. The radiating chapels have barrel vaults.

The tombs of King Peter I and Inês de Castro, now respectively in the south and north transepts, were originally in one of the transept chapels. Commissioned by the future Peter I in 1355 in homage to his beloved Inês, whose death was ordered by his father, Alfonso IV (*reg* 1325–57) in the same year, they are masterpieces of Portuguese monumental sculpture of the second half of the 14th century. Apart from the effigies and their canopies, there are sculptured scenes of the *Passion* and the *Life of St Bartholomew* on the sides of the tombs, the *Last Judgement* at the foot of the King's tomb, and a 'wheel' in the form of a blind rose window containing a series of scenes arranged in concentric circles at the head (*see* GOTHIC, fig. 45). These are supposed to represent episodes in the story of the royal lovers, but considering the original disposition of the tombs as described by the chronicler Fernão Lopes in the *Chronicle of Peter I*, it is more likely that they represent *Purgatory*, associated with the *Passion* and *Redemption* themes on the tomb of Inês (*see* PORTUGAL, fig. 10).

The conventual buildings are on the north side of the church. The Cloister of Dom Diniz, also known as the Cloister of Silence, was built in 1308 by Domingos Domingues and Mestre Diogo on the orders of King Diniz (*reg* 1279–1325). It is 50 m square and follows the usual arrangement of Cistercian cloisters, with a large arcade of double and triple bays separated by twin columns. In the 16th century another storey was added, with Manueline openings of triple arcades on columns with thick shaftrings following the rhythm of those below. The chapter house is 18 m square, divided into three aisles by piers of bundled shafts, which support the quadripartite vaults. The capitals have projecting stylized foliage. The first-floor dormitory (66.5×21.5 m), which formerly communicated with the north transept, is divided into three aisles of eleven bays, with rib vaults of square profile borne on dumpy columns in the central aisle; they are corbelled into the walls. Next to the staircase leading to the dormitory, in the corner of the cloister, is the former novices' dormitory, later used as the scriptorium. Beyond the huge kitchen, built in 1752, and opposite the cloister *lavatorium*, is the monks' refectory (29.98×21.43 m; see fig.). This is two floors high, and the stairway leading to the lector's pulpit is cut into the thickness of the wall and opens to the refectory through five arches with delicate foliage capitals. This is another example of the importance of walls as material support in Cistercian building.

LUCILIA VERDELHO DA COSTA

Alcobaça Abbey, begun 1158, view of the monks' refectory from the east, showing the flight of steps to the lector's pulpit

2. 17TH CENTURY AND AFTER. In the 17th and 18th centuries the monastery was enlarged by the addition of a hostel; three more cloisters (of Alfonso VI (*reg* 1656–83), of the Cardinal, and of the library); a sacristy; the chapel of Relics and the chapel of Nosso Senhor do Desterro; the Royal Pantheon (containing the tombs from the former galilee); a college; and a library. Between 1660 and 1690 the chancel and the altars of both transept and ambulatory were embellished, and the Hall of Kings (Sala dos Reis) was built, as well as a new sanctuary and the circular reliquary chapel at the east end of the sacristy. Statues of stone, wood or clay, groups of sculpture and carved reliefs were placed in the apse and throughout the building; the workshop of sculptors responsible for this work was headed by FREI PEDRO. Between 1675 and 1678, during the priorate of Frei Sebastião Sotomaior, changes were made to the high altar: a terracotta group of the *Annunciation* was placed on either side, with the figures of the *Archangel Gabriel* to the right and the *Virgin* to the left standing between the small Gothic columns supporting the triumphal arch. At the same height, but within the semicircle of the apse, were placed eight large statues, including those of *St Benedict*, *St Bernard*, *St Gregory the*

Great and *St Thomas Becket*. Above them and between the apertures were eight music-making angels playing different instruments, gracefully and realistically portrayed. All these statues were subsequently removed and place in the chapter house and other subsidiary buildings at Alcobaça during restoration at the beginning of the 20th century. The circular reliquary chapel, lit from and oculus above, was built between 1669 and 1672 during the period when Frei Constantino Sampaio was prior of the abbey. Around the walls is a series of niches of differing sizes containing statues, including the *Virgin*, *St Bernard* and *St Augustine*, and reliquary busts of Cistercian saints as well as those from other orders; almost all are life-size, made of gilded and polychromed wood, and carved with great realism. The glowing, glittering chapel is crowned with a ring of graceful, agitated cherubs that surround the main cornice. The *Apostolate* (dismantled), formerly in the chapel of St Peter, shows the figure of Christ entrusting the keys to the first pontiff (Alcobaça, chapter house).

The west front of the church was rebuilt in 1726 to the design of Frei João Turriano. In the centre of a façade 221 m wide, the result of successive additions to the monastery, he provided a striking contrast to the interior of the first abbey, which, with its monumental, sober and harmonious proportions and lines, is exceptional both in Portuguese architecture and among the foundations of the Cistercian Order.

LUCÍLIA VERDELHO DA COSTA, PEDRO DIAS

Alcoverro y Amorós, José (*b* Tivenys, Tarragona, 1835; *d* Madrid, Dec 1908). Spanish sculptor. He studied at the Escuela Superior de Pintura, Escultura y Grabado, Madrid, where he later taught, and also under the sculptor José Piquer y Duart. His oeuvre is diverse in subject-matter—including religious compositions, portrait busts and monumental sculpture—and also in material—he worked in clay, plaster, marble and stone, as well as producing polychrome statues. Alcoverro y Amorós was a regular exhibitor at the Exposiciones Nacionales de Bellas Artes, and it was largely through them that his work became known; in 1867 he exhibited *Ishmael Fainting with Thirst in the Desert of Beer-Sheba* (Valencia, Real Acad. B.A. S Carlos). In 1870 he carved a *St John the Baptist* (1870; untraced) for Bermeo, Vizcaya, and at the following year's Exposición he showed *Lazarus at the Gate of Dives* and *Christ and Mary Magdalene* as well as two portrait busts (one, in clay, of Rossini). In 1876 he exhibited a statue of *Hernán Cortés* (untraced), and in 1881 he won a 3rd-class medal with *Love's First Knot*, followed by 2nd-class medals for the *Lamentations of Jeremiah* (1884) and *Mars* (1890).

By this time Alcoverro y Amorós was devoting more attention to monumental sculpture, and in 1889, the year he exhibited at the Exposition Universelle in Paris, he executed the bronze statue of *Father Francisco Piquer* (Madrid, Plaza de las Descalzas Reales), notable for its realistic depiction both of the subject's features and of his ecclesiastical vestments. He also completed statues in marble of *Alfonso X, the Wise* (of Castile and León, *reg* 1252–84), and of the sculptor *Alonso Berruguete* (1892) for the exteriors of the Biblioteca Nacional and the Museo Arqueológico Nacional, respectively, in Madrid. In 1893 Alcoverro y Amorós won a medal at the World's Columbian Exposition in Chicago, and in 1895 he won a 1st-class medal at the Exposición Nacional with his majestic stone statue of the seated *St Isidore of Seville* (Madrid, Bib. N.). He executed a clay bust of *Jaime Balmes* (1899), for a sculpture commissioned by the Ministry of Public Works, and a 19th-century-style marble statue of the politician *Agustín Arqüelles* (1902; Madrid, Parque Oeste). Other statues include the seated figure of *Courage* (Madrid, Cuartel Gen. Ejército), personified as a naked warrior and worked in limestone, and the figure of *Agriculture* (1904) on the monument dedicated to *Alfonso XII* in the Parque del Retiro, Madrid; the former was later reworked by Lorenzo Coullaut Valera (1876–1932). Alcoverro y Amorós also collaborated on the decoration of a number of buildings, among them the Banco Hispano-Americano in Madrid for the façade of which he executed the figures of *Calculation* and *Economy* (1904) with their Classical Roman features and robes.

BIBLIOGRAPHY

M. Ossorio y Bernard: *Galería biográfica de artistas españoles del siglo XIX* (Madrid, 1869, 2/1883–4/*R* 1975)

E. Serrano Fatigati: 'Escultura en Madrid desde mediados del siglo XVI hasta nuestros días', *Bol. Soc. Esp. Excurs.*, xix (1911), pp. 142–3

C. Pérez Reyes: *Escultura: Neoclasicismo al modernismo*, v of *Historia del arte hispánico*, ed. R. Buendía (Madrid, 1979), pp. 195–6

FRANCISCO PORTELA SANDOVAL

Aldegrever [Trippenmeker]**, Heinrich** (*b* Paderborn, 1502; *d* Soest, Westphalia, 1555–61). German engraver, painter and designer. He was the most important graphic artist in Westphalia in the 16th century. His reputation rests largely on his ornamental designs, which make up about one third of his *c.* 300 engravings. They were principally intended as models for metalworkers but were also adapted by other craftsmen for such decorative arts as enamel, intarsia and book illustration. Aldegrever followed Dürer and the Nuremberg LITTLE MASTERS, deriving models for his paintings and subject prints as well as a full repertory of Renaissance ornamental motifs: fig and acanthus foliage, vases and cornucopia, combined with putti and satyrs, tritons, mermaids and dolphins, sphinxes, masks and medallions. From the beginning of his career Aldegrever was aware of the artistic trends of the time: the Dürer influence was strongest at its outset yielding somewhat in work of the 1530s to Mannerist tendencies under Netherlandish influence, though never waning entirely.

1. Early work, 1527–30. 2. Mature work, 1531–41. 3. Final work, 1541–55.

1. EARLY WORK, 1527–30. Aldegrever was the son of Hermann Trippenmeker (*d* 1545) from Paderborn. The year of his birth is calculated from two dated engraved self-portraits (B. 188–9) of 1530 and 1537 giving his age as 28 and 35 respectively. He was married and had two children, a daughter and a son, Christoph (*fl* 1553–61), who became a goldsmith. After an initial apprenticeship as a goldsmith, Heinrich Aldegrever trained as a painter, probably in Soest, judging by the typically Westphalian Late Gothic traits of his early work. He probably spent some of his time as a journeyman in the Netherlands, rather than in Nuremberg as has been proposed. He settled in Soest *c.* 1525, became a master and guild member soon after and a citizen in 1530.

For the church of St Peter, Soest, Aldegrever painted the wings and predella of an altarpiece (1526–7; Soest, S Maria zur Wiese) with a *Virgin in Glory* and *SS Agatha and Anthony* on the outside and a *Nativity* and *Adoration of the Magi* on the inside, based on Dürer's *Life of the Virgin* (B. 77). The inside scenes are repeated on the outer predella with an added *Annunciation,* while its inside features six *Apostles.* This panel bears the signature HT for Heinrich Trippenmeker (Ger.: 'maker of clogs'), while the *Nativity* shows a clog as signature above a shepherd (Aldegrever's self-portrait), who looks out at the viewer. From 1527 Heinrich used the name Aldegrever consistently and signed his works AG, shaped like Dürer's famous monogram. The altarpiece was one of the last large church commissions in Westphalia before the Reformation spread to northern Germany.

One quarter of Aldegrever's ornamental prints bear monograms but no dates. Some vignettes of simple symmetrical design predate four lively engravings (1527) that are technically and structurally more advanced. In 1528 Aldegrever first employed the vertical format, employing pilaster decorations, and he produced his first paired dagger-sheath designs, with a *Standard-bearer* (B. 225) and the *Whore of Babylon* (B. 226) atop rising foliage patterns. He used the same principle of horizontal division for two sheaths (1529) representing *David with the Head of Goliath* (B. 234) and an *Executioner with the Head of John the Baptist* (B. 235).

The models for a set of five very small engravings of the *Virgin and Child* (1527; B. 51, 53–56) are those that Dürer (B. 32, 37–9) engraved between 1516–20, and a *St Christopher* (1527; B. 61) closely follows Dürer's print (B. 52) in composition and in minor details. In a half-length *Judith with the Head of Holofernes* (1528; B. 34) Aldegrever employed the profile view, popular in Italian Renaissance portraiture. Two small representations of *Samson and Delilah* (1528; B. 35–6), *The Lovers* (1529; B. 73) and a few other early prints were designed in tondo form. These themes and *Lot and his Daughters* (B. 13–17), inspired by Dürer's *St Anthony Reading,* allude to the Power of Women, a favourite conceit of the time and often addressed by Lucas van Leyden. Subjects from Greek and Roman antiquity were also introduced early (1529) with *Medea and Jason* (B. 65), *Hercules and Antaeus* (B. 96) and *Mutius Scaevola before Porsena* (1530; B. 69). In these prints Aldegrever demonstrated familiarity with Renaissance décor and contemporary proportion studies. Technically and compositionally the most accomplished work of this period is a *Landsknecht with Brazier and Bucket* (1529; B. 174); the *Self-portrait* (B. 188) is relatively tentative in its perspective and hatching. Aldegrever tried the new medium of etching, not very successfully, in 1528 with an *Orpheus and Eurydice* (B. 100), a *Standard-bearer* (B. 176) and a *Portrait of a Man Crowned with Vine Leaves* (B. 187). A good woodcut of *Pyramus and Thisbe* (Hollstein, v. 1, no. 143) dates to the same year.

2. MATURE WORK, 1531–41. Soest became a Protestant community in 1531, and Aldegrever embraced the new faith wholeheartedly. This is evident from the subjects he engraved, including the *Monk* and *Nun* (1530; B. 178), which is a reverse copy after Georg Pencz. With diminishing demand for sacred art, Aldegrever concentrated on engraving such secular subject-matter as landsknechts, dancing couples and genre scenes, portraits, allegories, mythological scenes and Old Testament stories, in the wake of Luther's translation of the Bible. Given his Lutheranism, it is surprising that, in 1536, he executed major engravings of the imprisoned Münster Anabaptist leaders *Jan van Leyden* (B. 182; see fig. 1) and *Bernard Knipperdolling* (B. 183) for the Bishop of Münster. He represented van Leyden, the leader of the group, not as an ignominious figure but as a dignified and forceful man. All the ennobling trappings of a Renaissance portrait are present; his insignia are carefully rendered, and an explanatory Latin inscription on a plaque fastened to a parapet includes the artist's name and home town. The engraved portraits of *Martin Luther* and *Philip Melanchthon* (both 1540; B. 184–5) are rather eclectic, while those of the Anabaptists, the *Self-portrait* (B. 189) and that of *Duke William V of Jülich-Kleve-Berg* (1540) are of high quality. The vivid portrait of *Graf Philip III Zu Waldeck* (1537; Arolsen, Residenzschloss) is the only correctly attributed painting of this period.

The change to a Mannerist style during the middle period of Aldegrever's career is evident in the engraved series of the *Story of Joseph.* Whereas three scenes, *Joseph Explaining his Dreams to Jacob* (B. 18), *Joseph and Potiphar's Wife* (B. 19) and *Potiphar's Wife Accusing Joseph* (B. 20), were executed in 1532, the last scene, *Joseph Selling Wheat to his Brothers* (B. 21), is earlier and is dated 1528.

1. Heinrich Aldegrever: *Jan van Leyden*, engraving, 272×253 mm, 1536 (Münster, Westfälisches Landesmuseum für Kunst und Kulturgeschichte)

In the later prints the figures are elongated and their heads have become appreciably smaller, an impression emphasized by the replacement of Joseph's broad-rimmed hat in the print of 1528 by a small cap in the others. There is also a notable change in tonality from a more even lighting to greater contrasts between dark and light. In *Bathsheba in her Bath* (B. 37), *Rhea Silvia* (B. 66) and *Marcus Curtius* (B. 68; all 1532) Aldegrever depicted muscular nudes in various twisted, Mannerist poses. The elongation is more pronounced in the series of *Gods who Preside over the Seven Planets* (1533; B. 76–82), as the figures fill the frames from top to bottom; in the case of *Luna* (*Diana*; B. 81), *Jupiter* (B. 78) and *Saturn* (B. 80) the crowns of the heads are cropped.

From 1534 to 1536 Aldegrever concentrated on ornamental designs, returning to the nude in 1538 with the minute frieze of *Hannibal Fighting Scipio* (48×215 mm; B. 71), which contains no fewer than 26 men, and a *Judgement of Paris* (B. 98). In the same year he produced two sets of *Wedding Dancers*, one comprising eight engravings (B. 144–51) in postage stamp size (54×36 mm), the other with twelve (B. 160–71) twice as large (117×56 mm). Their main importance rests in their technical excellence and their documentary value for the history of costume and dance. A set of *Four Evangelists* (1539; B. 57–60) follows Pencz once more. Aldegrever reached the climax of his Mannerist style in two series dated 1540, the *Story of Adam and Eve* (B. 1–12) and the *Story of Amnon and Tamar* (B. 22–7). The figures no longer fill the entire picture space but are embedded in landscapes and interiors. The *Power of Death* suite (1541; B. 135–42) includes scenes with a pope, cardinal, bishop and abbot as Death's victims.

The ornamental works include horizontal designs for three single scabbards (1532) with a pair of *Dancers* (B. 247), a *Nude Couple* (B. 248) and a *Soldier Embracing a Nude Woman* (B. 249). Four more undated sheaths (B. 213–16) with single figures, with Mannerist, elongated figures and drapery style, were made later. Particularly rich and sophisticated are three designs (1536; B. 259, 1537; B. 265, 1539; B. 270; see fig. 2) for daggers with scabbards that are proportionally partitioned by swellings. The spiral and fluted column motifs at their points, the decoration with profile heads in medallions as well as the unity of patterns and the articulated, symmetrical composition are clearly inspired by Italian ornament engravers. The same full-blown Renaissance style is evident in engraved models for three brooches (1536; B. 258), a buckle (1537; B. 263) and two crossed folding spoons that could also be used as whistles (1539; B. 268). At this time Aldegrever also executed a number of fashionable putti friezes (B. 252, 257, 262).

2. Heinrich Aldegrever: design for a dagger with scenes of *Cain Slaying Abel* and a *Satyr Couple*, engraving, 326×89 mm, 1539 (Coburg, Kupferstichkabinett der Kunstsammlungen der Veste Coburg)

3. Final work, 1541–55. After an unexplained lacuna in his oeuvre from 1541 to 1549, Aldegrever produced relatively few single engravings. A series of 14 *Allegorical Figures* (1549–50; B. 103–16) displays a new affection for fancily creased, billowing draperies that tend to move independently of the bodies they cover. But in two related sets of *Virtues* (B. 117–23) and *Vices* (B. 124–30) dated 1552 these features are exaggerated, and the prints are inferior in composition and technique. Another group of small *Wedding Dancers* (1551; B. 152–9) suffers from the same weaknesses, hiding bodies under masses of crumpled garments and rendering movements incomprehensible. Of much better quality are the *Twelve Labours of Hercules* (1550; B. 83–95): the bodies of the hero and his antagonists are well proportioned and solid, movements are articulated and tonal values balanced. The designs may have an Italian model.

Aldegrever's last works employ biblical subject-matter. The *Lazarus* (B. 44–8) and *Good Samaritan* (B. 40–43) series (both 1554) use horizontal format to accommodate the large number of figures that are successfully integrated within complex surroundings; the more solid types in the *Good Samaritan* series emerge with greater clarity, while those in the *Lazarus* prints dissolve in a glitter of light and dark spots. This scintillating effect of rumpled garments and hair is a hallmark of Aldegrever's late works. In the *Story of Susanna* (B. 30–33) and the *Story of Lot* (B. 14–17), both dated 1555, he displayed for the last time his technical virtuosity and excellent craftsmanship, his expert treatment of even the smallest detail.

A small panel of *Lot and his Daughters* (1555; Budapest, N. Mus.) is the only authentic late painting. The late ornamental prints depict grotesques and attempt the compact organization of forms into cohesive relief strata, but Aldegrever overloaded the designs with excessive detail and patterns, resulting in a loss of clarity and vitality. His late pieces were old-fashioned, in that they did not include the newly popular elements of scrollwork and arabesque. His main influences at this time were Zoan Andrea, Marcantonio Raimondi and Raimondi's assistants, Agostino dei Musi and Marco Dente. The influence of Dürer was still present, however. Aldegrever's *Fortune*, dated 1555 (B. 143), retains the essential elements of Dürer's *Large Fortune* (B. 77).

BIBLIOGRAPHY

Hollstein: *Ger.*; Meissner

M. Geisberg: *Die Münsterischen Wiedertäufer und Aldegrever*, Stud. Dt. Kstgesch., lxxvi (Strasbourg, 1907)

H. Zschelletzschky: *Das graphische Werk Heinrich Aldegrevers*, Stud. Dt. Kstgesch., ccxcii (Strasbourg, 1933, rev. Baden-Baden, 1974)

R. Fritz: *Heinrich Aldegrever als Maler* (Dortmund, 1959)

——: 'Ein Selbstbildnis Heinrich Aldegrevers', *Berlin. Mus.*, n. s. x (1961), pp. 15ff

E. Meyer-Wurmbach: 'Heinrich Aldegrever als Siegelschneider Herzog Wilhelms von Kleve', *Wallraf-Richartz-Jb.*, xxii (1962), pp. 393–400

A. Shestack: 'Some Preliminary Drawings by Heinrich Aldegrever', *Master Drgs*, viii (1970), pp. 141–8

R. A. Koch: *Early German Masters*, 16 [VIII/iii] of *The Illustrated Bartsch*, ed. W. L. Strauss (New York, 1980) [B.]

G. Luther: *Heinrich Aldegrever: Ein westfälischer Kupferstecher des 16. Jahrhunderts*, Bildhefte des Westfälischen Landesmuseums für Kunst- und Kulturgeschichte, xv (Münster, 1982)

The Prints of Altdorfer and Aldegrever (exh. cat., Cambridge, Fitzwilliam, 1983)

Heinrich Aldegrever: Die Kleinmeister und das Kunsthandwerk der Renaissance (exh. cat., ed. K. B. Heppe; Unna, Hellweg-Mus., 1986)

A. Somers Cocks: 'Aldegrever and the Decorative Arts', *Pr. Q.*, iv (1987), pp. 177–80

The World in Miniature: Engravings by the German Little Masters, 1500–1550 (exh. cat., ed. S. H. Goddard; Lawrence, U. KS, Spencer Mus. A.; New Haven, CT, Yale U. A.G.; Minneapolis, MN, Inst. A.; Los Angeles, UCLA, Grunwald Cent. Graph. Art; 1988–9)

ROSEMARIE BERGMANN

Aldenham, 1st Baron. *See* GIBBS, HENRY HUCKS.

Aldobrandini. Italian family of lawyers, ecclesiastics and patrons. The family was Florentine, of ancient origin but modest distinction. Silvestro Aldobrandini (1499–1558) was a lawyer whose republican leanings forced him into exile after the restoration of the Medici in Florence in 1527. In 1548 he secured the protection of Cardinal Alessandro Farnese, under whose aegis his career and family flourished in Rome in the service of successive popes. Silvestro's son, Ippolito, who became (1) Pope Clement VIII, elevated the family to the pinnacle of its fortune. He created his nephews (2) Pietro Aldobrandini and Cinzio Passeri (1551–1610) cardinals in 1593 and made them his principal secretaries of state. Cinzio was the son of Clement VIII's sister; he took the name Aldobrandini on his uncle's election, but was generally known as the Cardinal di S Giorgio in Velabro. He is chiefly distinguished as the last patron and protector of the poet Torquato Tasso and was also an avid collector of antiquities, including the then recently discovered ancient Roman fresco known as the *Aldobrandini Wedding* (Rome, Vatican, Mus. Sacro Crist.), and of Renaissance art, including works by Albrecht Dürer.

Clement VIII's lay nephew, Gian Francesco Aldobrandini (*d* 1601), was also honoured, becoming Governor of the Borgo (1592) and General of the Church (1594). It was in Gian Francesco's children that the apparently brilliant future of the family was vested. Ambitious marriages were arranged for his daughters, Margherita marrying Ranuccio Farnese, 4th Duke of Parma, in 1600, and Elena marrying Antonio Carafa, Duke of Mondragone, in 1602. Gian Francesco's eldest son, Silvestro Aldobrandini (1589–1612), became cardinal as early as 1603 (so far was Clement VIII prepared to compromise his principles over nepotism), and his posthumous son, Ippolito Aldobrandini (*d* 1638), was made cardinal by Gregory XV in 1621. Gregory's niece Ippolita Ludovisi was married to Gian Francesco's secular son, Giorgio Aldobrandini (*d* 1637), Prince of Meldola, Sarsina and Rossano, who inherited (2) Cardinal Pietro's villa at Frascati and his palace in Rome. Giorgio's only child, Olimpia (*d* 1681), married firstly Paolo Borghese and secondly Prince Camillo Pamphili; her vast inheritance was divided between the two families, the former acquiring the Villa Aldobrandini, the latter the Palazzo Aldobrandini al Corso (now Palazzo Doria-Pamphili). By the year of Olimpia's first marriage (1638), the male line of the Aldobrandini was extinct.

(1) Pope **Clement VIII** [Ippolito Aldobrandini] (*b* Fano, the Marches, 24 Feb 1536; elected 30 Jan 1592; *d* Rome, 5 March 1605). He was the son of Silvestro Aldobrandini and a protégé of Cardinal Alessandro Farnese and was appointed a cardinal in 1585. As Pope he supported literary and intellectual endeavour, although his tastes in the visual arts reflected a prudent conservatism. Official commissions were given to the most traditional artists, and Tuscan painters were particularly favoured. Giuseppe d'Arpino, who received his title Cavaliere di Cristo from Clement, became the Pope's principal painter, while the revolutionary developments of Caravaggio and the Carracci were ignored. Clement was concerned to convey the triumph of the restored Roman Catholic church, and many Roman churches, ancient and modern, were restored, built or completed in preparation for the Jubilee Year (1600); this activity, encouraged by the Pope, was, however, chiefly under the patronage of individual cardinals.

Clement was responsible for two extensive decorative programmes at S Giovanni Laterano and St Peter's, both of which stressed the legitimacy and the power of the papacy. In St Peter's he completed the unfinished projects of Sixtus V. The dome was crowned with its huge gilt-bronze ball and cross (1593); in the interior the inscription at the foot of the lantern justly attributes the achievement to Sixtus. The mosaic decoration of the interior was entrusted to the Cavaliere d'Arpino, that of the pendentives to Cesare Nebbia. Beneath the dome Giacomo della Porta erected a new high altar, encrusted with ancient marbles (1592–4); the pavement of the church was also raised to create the subterranean Grotte Vaticane. Della Porta also constructed the lateral chapel, the Cappella Clementina, opposite the Cappella Gregoriana, where the vault was decorated with mosaics of Clement's coat of arms and of figures by Cristoforo Roncalli (1601). Roncalli and a team of artists that included Lodovico Cigoli, Francesco Vanni, Giovanni Baglione, Domenico Passignano and Bernardo Castello painted a cycle of six altars for the Cappella Clementina and for the four main piers of the church; the theme of the cycle, which stressed the supremacy of the papacy, was derived from the life of St Peter (later replaced by mosaic copies; originals in Rome, S Maria degli Angeli; Rome, St Peter's, subterranean deposit).

The decoration of S Giovanni in Laterano, newly restored by Giacomo della Porta, was under the direction of the Cavaliere d'Arpino, who painted scenes (1597–8) in the Baptistery and contributed, with Cristoforo Roncalli, Giovanni Baglione, Cesare Nebbia and Paris Nogari (1536–1601), to the frescoes of the transepts (1599–1601) showing scenes from the *Life of Constantine*. In the left transept, above the grandiose and sumptuous Altar of the Holy Sacrament (1600) designed by Padre Paolo Olivieri, d'Arpino frescoed a large *Ascension* (1599–1601). The Canon's sacristy was decorated by Giovanni and Cherubino Alberti (*c*. 1600) and Agostino Ciampelli, with scenes from the *Life of St Clement* (*c*. 1602–5).

In S Maria sopra Minerva, Clement had the funerary chapel of his parents enlarged by della Porta and Carlo Maderno and decorated with paintings by Federico Barocci and Cherubino Alberti and sculptures by Guglielmo della Porta, Camillo Mariani, Nicolas Cordier and Stefano Maderno.

In the Vatican Palace (roofed 1595–6), Clement was chiefly concerned with completing the vast additions of Sixtus V. He was responsible for the decoration of the Sala del Concistoro (1600–02) with landscapes by Paul Bril, depicting celebrated Italian hermitages, and *quadratura* by Giovanni Alberti, and of the magnificent, two-storey Sala Clementina on which the Alberti brothers worked between 1596 and 1600. Here the elaborate illusionistic vault by Giovanni Alberti is a grandiose glorification of the papal family; the walls were decorated by Cherubino Alberti and also include Bril's monumental *Martyrdom of St Clement* (*c*. 1600–02/3).

From 1594 Clement regularly spent the hottest months of the year at the Palazzo del Quirinale, Rome, where he employed the Alberti brothers and added extensively to the gardens, contributing the water organ that bears his arms, set in a grotto of shellwork (the *Ninfeo Aldobrandini*; *in situ*) decorated with Old Testament scenes and aquatic mythologies in painted stucco. On the Campidoglio he ordered the continuation of Michelangelo's plans for the Capitoline palazzi; Girolamo Rainaldi built the façade of the Palazzo del Senatore (1592–8). Outside Rome, Clement ordered the completion and restoration of bridges, forts and harbours. Clement's pontificate was a period of transition between the Counter-Reformation triumphalism of Sixtus V and the more worldly era of Paul V, symbolized by the position of Clement's tomb in the latter's Cappella Paolina, opposite the former's Cappella Sistina (Rome, S Maria Maggiore). Clement VIII is also known to have owned a set of twelve tazze (ten untraced, one London, V&A; one New York, Met.), decorated with figures of Roman emperors, that became known as the Aldobrandini Tazze.

(2) Cardinal **Pietro Aldobrandini** (*b* 1572; *d* Rome, 1621). Nephew of (1) Pope Clement VIII. Clement appointed him as the Keeper of Castel Sant'Angelo (1592). In 1593 both Pietro and his older cousin Cinzio were made cardinals, and from then effectively controlled the running of the government, ostensibly as equals. Pietro's greater diplomacy, subtlety of mind and tenacity of character, however, quickly distinguished him as the more influential. Clement VIII sent him on the two most important diplomatic missions of the pontificate: the annexation of Ferrara in 1598 and the cementing of Henry IV of France's conversion to Catholicism by his marriage to Marie de' Medici (1600). Pietro's mission to Ferrara was also of great artistic consequence to Rome, as he brought back treasures from the Este collection, including Titian's *Bacchanals*—the *Andrians* and *Worship of Venus* (both Madrid, Prado) and *Bacchus and Ariadne* (London, N.G.). He even commissioned his favoured painter, the Cavaliere d'Arpino, to make copies of them (untraced).

In his office of Camerlengo, Pietro Aldobrandini oversaw construction work on the Campidoglio, where (1) Clement VIII had ordered the completion of Michelangelo's plans for the buildings. Pietro also commissioned the fresco decoration of the Palazzo dei Conservatori with *Histories of Ancient Rome* from Arpino (for illustration *see* ARPINO, CAVALIERE D') and Tommaso Laureti (from 1595). Pietro employed Arpino to provide the altarpiece of *St Barbara* (unveiled 1597) for the chapel of the Compagnia dei Bombardieri, of which he was patron, in S Maria in Traspontina. Arpino also decorated the funerary chapel (completed 1596) of Pietro's uncle, Pietro Aldobrandini the elder (*d* 1587), in S Maria in Via, Rome. Cardinal Pietro's other ecclesiastical works in Rome included the restoration of his titular church, S Niccolò in Carcere, where he employed Orazio Gentileschi and Giovanni Baglione, and the continuation of his abbey of Tre Fontane. There he commissioned Giacomo della Porta to erect the small porticoed church of S Paolo alle Tre Fontane (1599–1601) and to complete the domed rotunda of S Maria Scala Coeli (begun by Cardinal Farnese in 1584) and ordered an altarpiece, the *Crucifixion of St Peter*, from Guido Reni (Rome, Pin. Vaticana).

Arpino was among the artists who embellished the masterpiece of Pietro's patronage, the Villa Aldobrandini (begun 1598) at Frascati, near Rome. In 1598 a small villa had been bequeathed to Clement VIII, who intended it as a holiday residence in the town. He handed the inheritance, with other revenues, to his nephew with the encouragement to complete the work quickly; it was largely finished by 1603. The result was the most grandiose, symmetrical and homogeneous of the villas of Frascati, in which the example of Mannerist forerunners was transformed into a prototype of the great Baroque villas of the 17th century. The design, by Giacomo della Porta, included such influential details as the oval ramps below the entrance façade, the pediments dominating the latter's skyline and, especially, the superimposed columned loggias of the garden front. Other elements, for example the richly decorated water theatre and long cascade (*see* FRASCATI and fig. 1), were elaborate versions of the then customary villa features. All the numerous waterworks of the gardens were supplied by an aqueduct presented to Cardinal Pietro by Duca Giovanni Angelo Altemps of the Villa Mondragone, who was eventually ruined by the cost. The interior of the main casino was decorated by the artists officially favoured by Clement VIII: the ceiling of the Gran Salone by Federico Zuccaro, other rooms with Old Testament subjects by Arpino and the chapel, dedicated to St Sebastian, by Domenico Passignano. In later years Cardinal Pietro showed his appreciation of more progressive trends by commissioning Domenichino to fresco a room adjacent to the water theatre with ten scenes from the *Life of Apollo* (1616–18; four panels *in situ*; six London, N.G.).

Clement VIII had also granted Pietro the old palazzo of the Dukes of Urbino on the Via del Corso (now Palazzo Doria-Pamphili). Improvements included the decoration of the chapel with six lunettes of biblical scenes, begun by Annibale Carracci and completed by various pupils, notably Francesco Albani and Sisto Badalocchio (*c*. 1604–13; Rome, Gal. Doria-Pamphili). Annibale's lunette of the *Flight into Egypt* was the first truly classical landscape of the Roman Baroque.

After Clement VIII's death (1605), Pietro remained an influential figure in the College of Cardinals and had a decisive effect on the following three conclaves. He also continued his interest in Roman churches, completing his grandparents' chapel (1610) in S Maria sopra Minerva and rebuilding the Barnabites' S Paolo alla Colonna (1617–18; destr.) after a fire. The new limits of his power were revealed by the actions of the nephew of Pope Paul V, Cardinal Scipione Borghese, who took a liking to Domenichino's *Diana and Nymphs at Play* (Rome, Gal. Borghese), which Pietro had commissioned. Domenichino, foolishly attempting to honour his contract, was imprisoned (albeit briefly), and Pietro Aldobrandini sharply reminded of the realities of politics and patronage in Baroque Rome.

BIBLIOGRAPHY

G. Baglione: *Vite* (1642); ed. V. Mariani (1935)

D. Barriere: *Villa Aldobrandini Tuscolana sive varii illius hortorum et fontium prospectus* (Rome, 1647)

Ludwig, Freiherr von Pastor: *Geschichte der Päpste* (1886–9), Eng. trans. xxiii and xxiv (1933)

K. Schwager: 'Kardinal Pietro Aldobrandinis Villa di Belvedere in Frascati', *Röm J. Kstgesch.*, ix/x (1961–2)

G. Briganti: *Il Palazzo del Quirinale* (Rome, 1962)

F. Haskell: *Patrons and Painters* (London, 1963, rev. New Haven and London, 1980)

C. d'Onofrio: 'Inventario dei dipinti del cardinal Pietro Aldobrandini compilato da G. B. Agucchi nel 1603', *Palatino*, viii (1964), pp. 15–20, 158–62, 202–11

M. L. Chappell and W. Chandler Kirwin: 'A Petrine Triumph: The Decoration of the Navi Piccole in San Pietro under Clement VIII', *Stor. A.*, 21 (1974), pp. 119–70

M. C. Abromson: 'Clement VIII's Patronage of the Brothers Alberti', *A. Bull.*, lx (1978), pp. 531–47

——: *Painting in Rome during the Papacy of Clement VIII* (New York, 1981)

A. Zuccari: *Arte e committenza nella Roma di Caravaggio* (Turin, 1984)

B. Mitchell: *1598: A Year of Pageantry in Late Renaissance Ferrara* (New York, 1990)

□

Aldrich, Henry (*b* Westminster, London, Jan 1647 or 1648; *d* Oxford, 14 Dec 1710). English architect and scholar. The son of Henry Aldrich, later auditor to James, Duke of York, he was educated at Westminster School, London, and at Christ Church, Oxford, where he graduated as a BA in 1666 and an MA in 1669. He remained in Oxford for the rest of his life, becoming in 1682 a canon of Christ Church and in 1689 Dean of the College and Cathedral. From 1692 to 1695 he served as Vice-Chancellor of Oxford University.

Aldrich was a highly accomplished man who was well known for his learning in many fields. He edited Greek and Latin texts, wrote a standard book on logic, and also published works on mathematics, music and architecture. He had a large library that included books on antiquities and many architectural and other engravings. He left his library to Christ Church, where it remains, but directed that all his personal papers were to be destroyed. As a result, relatively little is known about his architectural interests and activities. However, there is reason to think that he had visited France and Italy, and he was certainly regarded by contemporaries as an authority on architectural matters. He was himself an excellent draughtsman and made the drawings for the allegorical engravings that decorate the Oxford almanacks for 1676 and 1689. Towards the end of his life he began to write a systematic treatise on architecture, 'intended to have been divided into two parts treating respectively of Civil and Military Architecture'. Only part of the civil section was completed; apart from a few proof copies of the first 44 pages, the first edition was not published until 1789, when it was issued in English and Latin under the title *Elementa architecturae civilis*. It is a scholarly rather than a practical work and contains many quotations from Vitruvius and Palladio, the authors whom he accepted as his chief authorities.

Only two or three buildings are known to have been designed by Aldrich: the Peckwater Quadrangle at his own college of Christ Church, built in 1706–14, the parish church of All Saints, Oxford (1701–10), and perhaps the Fellows' Building at Corpus Christi College (1706–12). The Peckwater Quadrangle is remarkable for its orthodox classicism at a time when English architecture was at its most Baroque. Its three pilastered and pedimented façades are almost Palladian in character, and indeed anticipate the English Palladian Revival by twenty years. The Fellows' Building at Corpus Christi College is similar in character, but All Saints, with its pairs of giant pilasters, has affinities with buildings by Wren and John Webb. Its steeple was not completed until some time after Aldrich's death and appears to represent a compromise between his original proposal and an alternative one submitted later by Hawksmoor. There is no evidence for the attribution to Aldrich either of Trinity College Chapel (1691–4) or the library of

Queen's College (1693–4), both in Oxford. Indeed, the survival of awkwardly ungrammatical designs for both buildings makes it highly unlikely that he was responsible for either: but it is possible that he played some part in correcting the infelicities of both designs.

Despite his small architectural output Aldrich is notable as an academic forerunner of the Palladianism that was to dominate English architecture from the 1720s onwards. As he was a genial and much-respected don with many friends and pupils, his influence may have been more pervasive than the written record suggests. He was buried in Christ Church Cathedral, where a monument with a portrait in relief was later erected by his friend and colleague Dr George Clarke. Several other portraits of him are preserved at Christ Church and in the Bodleian Library, Oxford.

WRITINGS

Elementa architecturae civilis (Oxford, 1789, 2/1818)

BIBLIOGRAPHY

Colvin
W. G. Hiscock: *Henry Aldrich* (Oxford, 1960)
H. M. Petter: *The Oxford Almanacks* (Oxford, 1974)

HOWARD COLVIN

Aldrovandi [Aldovrandi]. Italian family of patrons. The Aldrovandi were one of the oldest patrician families in Bologna and were prominent in the city's civic life from at least the 12th century. Giovanni Francesco Aldrovandi (*d* 1512) was ambassador to Rome and Ferrara, a poet and patron of literature. According to Vasari, Michelangelo stayed in Aldrovandi's palazzo in 1494–5 (*see* MICHELANGELO, §I, 1(i)). The most renowned family member was (1) Ulisse Aldrovandi, the naturalist and antiquarian. Conte Filippo Aldrovandi commissioned paintings from Guercino, such as the *Portrait of a Dog* (*c.* 1625; Pasadena, CA, Norton Simon Mus.), and fresco decorations in the Villa Giovannina, near Cento. The earliest inventory of the family collection (1644) lists 72 items; by *c.* 1690 this had grown to 293. Pompeo Aldrovandi (1668–1752), who was made a cardinal in 1734, began rebuilding the family palazzo (now the Palazzo Montanari) in 1725 to a design by Francesco Maria Angelini (1680–1731), with a façade (1744–52) by ALFONSO TORREGGIANI and frescoes by Stefano Orlandi (1681–1760) and VITTORIO BIGARI. The tomb of *Cardinal Pompeo Aldrovandi* (begun before 1728; Bologna, S Petronio) was made by Camillo Rusconi and Angelo Gabriello Piö. Pompeo's brother, Filippo Aldrovandi, changed the family name to Aldrovandi-Marescotti. The art collection gathered in the family palazzo, especially the Classical sculpture, was noted by Marcello Oretti (*c.* 1760–80; Bologna, Bib. Com., B. 104); by 1782 there were 617 canvases. Carlo Filippo Aldrovandi-Marescotti (1763–1823) was president of the Accademia di Belle Arti (1807–22; *see also* PALAGI, PELAGIO). Many works were sold in the first half of the 19th century, until by 1868 there were only 208 paintings remaining. The changing composition of the collection towards a wider reflection of European art may be traced through the detailed inventories.

BIBLIOGRAPHY

DBI
G. Vasari: *Vite* (1550, rev. 2/1568); ed. G. Milanesi (1878–85), vii, pp. 146–7
K. Lankheit: 'Das "Sposalizio d'Amore e Psiche" von Palagi', *Pantheon*, xxxvii (1979), pp. 391–9
E. Calbi and D. Scaglietti Kelescian, eds: *Marcello Oretti e il patrimonio artistico privato bolognese* (Bologna, 1984), pp. 216–18, 230
F. Montefusco Bignozzi: '"Vari pensieri da dipignersi": Programmi iconografici per affreschi di Vittorio Bigari nei palazzi Ranuzzi e Aldrovandi di Bologna', *Il Carrobbio*, xi (1985), pp. 159–80 [Pompeo Aldrovandi]
O. Bonfait: 'Le collezioni Aldrovandi a Bologna in età moderna', *Il Carrobbio*, xiii (1987), pp. 25–50 [with full references to the inventories]
L. Salerno: *I dipinti del Guercino* (Rome, 1988)

OLIVIER BONFAIT

(1) Ulisse Aldrovandi (*b* Bologna, 11 Sept 1522; *d* Bologna, 4 May 1605). Naturalist and antiquarian. In 1550 he wrote *Le statue antiche di Roma*, a catalogue of the most celebrated collections of ancient sculpture in 16th-century Rome. This early work, published in 1556 and reprinted several times, is one of the most precise accounts of antique art known from the Renaissance. In 1554 he was appointed to the chair of natural sciences at the University of Bologna. He formed a celebrated private museum and engaged artists to draw the minerals, plants and animals that he studied, collected and classified. The most famous of his collaborators was Jacopo Ligozzi. Celebrated artists, such as Prospero Fontana and Lavinia Fontana, visited the museum. Almost 7000 drawings and engravings resulted from this project, constituting a colossal encyclopedia of natural history. Between 1559 and 1664 but mainly after Aldrovandi's death (1605), this work was published in Bologna, where the manuscripts and their illustrations are held in the university library.

Aldrovandi read and made comments on several chapters of the *Discorso intorno alle immasini sacre e profane* by Cardinal Gabriele Paleotti, a long-standing friend of his to whom he addressed his ideas on art in two letters. In these he reiterated the definition of painting as the imitation of nature, requiring of it the exactitude of scientific illustration. This ideal of precision and truth to nature finds a parallel in the historical realism recommended by Counter-Reformation theorists of art.

WRITINGS

Le statue antiche di Roma (MS.; *c.* 1550); as an appendix to L. Mauro: *Le antichità della città di Roma brevissimamente raccolte* (Venice, 1556)
Modo di esprimere per la pittura tutte le cose dell'universo mondo (1582; Bologna, Bib. Com. Archiginnasio, MS. B 244); ed. P. Barocchi in *Scritti d'arte del cinquecento* (Milan and Naples, 1971), i, pp. 923–30
Avvertimenti del dottore Aldrovandi all'illmo e rmo cardinale Paleotti sopra alcuni capitoli della pittura (*c.* 1582; Bologna, Bib. Com. Archiginnasio, MS. B 244); ed. P. Barocchi in *Trattati d'arte del cinquecento* (Bari, 1961), ii, pp. 511–17

BIBLIOGRAPHY

DBI [incl. bibliog. to 1962]
L. Frati: *Catalogo dei manoscritti di Ulisse Aldrovandi* (Bologna, 1907)
P. P. Bober: 'Francesco Cioca's Collection of Antiquities: Footnote to a New Edition of Aldrovandi', *Essays in the History of Art Presented to Rudolf Wittkower on his Sixty-fifth Birthday*, ed. D. Fraser, H. Hibbard and M. J. Levine (London, 1967), ii, pp. 119–22
G. Olmi: 'Osservazione della natura e raffigurazione scientifica in Ulisse Aldrovandi, 1522–1605', *An. Ist. It.-Ger. Trento*, iii (1977), pp. 105–81
S. de Rosa: 'La bottega artistica di Ulisse Aldrovandi in una lettera inedita di Cristoforo Coriolano da Norimberga', *Mitt. Ksthist. Inst. Florenz*, xxv (1981), pp. 391–8
G. Olmi: 'Ulisse Aldrovandi and the Bolognese Painters in the Second Half of the 16th Century', *Emilian Painting of the 16th and 17th Centuries: A Symposium: Bologna, 1987*, pp. 63–7

FRANÇOIS QUIVIGER

Alechinsky, Pierre (*b* Brussels, 19 Oct 1927). Belgian painter, draughtsman, printmaker and film maker. He studied book illustration and typography at the Ecole Nationale Supérieure d'Architecture et des Arts Décoratifs from 1944 to 1946. In 1947 he became a member of the Jeune Peinture Belge group and had his first one-man exhibition in the Galerie Lou Cosyn in Brussels. In 1949 he became a founder-member of the COBRA movement after meeting Christian Dotremont. With a number of artist friends he set up a type of research centre and meeting-place in Brussels, the Ateliers du Marais. Towards the end of 1951 he went to Paris, moving to Japan in 1955 to study the art of calligraphy, also making a film called *Calligraphie japonaise* (1956). He adopted the Oriental manner of painting, whereby the paper is spread on the floor and the artist leans over the work holding the bottle of ink, allowing a greater freedom of movement. In 1957 he made his first large works on paper in Indian ink and afterwards mounted the paper on canvas.

Alechinsky's monumental oil painting the *Last Day* (1964; Antwerp, Kon. Mus. S. Kst.) forms the climax of his membership of Cobra and is also a homage to James Ensor; the figures in the picture are scattered over the surface like pieces of thread, colourful and fresh. A work characteristic of his narratives is *Central Park* (artist's col.; see Hannover exh. cat., p. 43), a painting begun in New York in 1965; it is painted in acrylics, and the colourful centre is surrounded by a border containing black-and-white drawings in Indian ink. From 1972 Alechinsky began to use ink in the centre, reserving colour for the edges. The use of paper, brushes and ink or quick-drying acrylic paint enabled him to render his images spontaneously one next to the other, almost at random. His pictures contain volcanic eruptions flowing into one another, monsters, deep rifts, grotesque snakes, waterfalls, lively clouds and birds. He often used pieces of paper that had previously served some other purpose, such as legal documents, invoices and bonds, on which he left his marks. Alechinsky was fascinated by anything related to printmaking and continually experimented with new ideas; in *Seismographic Armful* (lithograph with logogram, 1972; New York, Guggenheim) he collaborated with Dotremont, who created the logogram which Alechinsky surrounded with a characteristic border.

WRITINGS

Alechinsky: Paintings and Writings, foreword E. Ionesco (New York, 1977)

BIBLIOGRAPHY

Pierre Alechinsky: Margins and Centers (exh. cat., New York, Guggenheim; Hannover, Kstver.; Brussels, Mus. A. Mod.; 1987) [different versions for each venue]
Alechinsky: L'Autre Main (Montpellier, 1988)

ELS MARÉCHAL

Alee, John. *See* LEE, JOHN.

Aleijadinho, O. *See* LISBOA, (2).

Alekseyev, Fyodor (Yakovlevich) (*b* St Petersburg, 1753/4; *d* St Petersburg, 23 Nov 1824). Russian painter. The son of a retired soldier, he studied from 1766 at the Academy of Arts, St Petersburg, from 1767 in the class of bird, animal, fruit and flower painting. In 1772 the rector of the Academy, the history painter Anton Losenko, drew attention to Alekseyev's skill in rendering perspective, and Alekseyev joined the landscape class, studying under Gavriil Kozlov (?1738–91) and Antonio Peresinotti (1708–78). He graduated in 1773, and he was sent to Venice for three years to study scenery painting. There he worked under the direction of Giuseppe Moretti and Pietro Gaspari (*c*. 1720–85). He was not disposed to working in the traditions of the late Baroque, and he soon gave up the idea of becoming a scenery painter, deciding instead to paint landscapes and to move to Rome, where there were skilled classicist painters. He did not, however, receive the Academy's permission, and in 1777 he was recalled to St Petersburg. During his years of study abroad he completed a copy (1776; St Petersburg, Rus. Mus.) of Canaletto's the *Staircase of the Accademia, Venice* and two original works: *Venice: View of the Schiavoni Embankment* (1775; Minsk, Belorus A. Mus.) and *Seascape* (1777; untraced), both of which show the traits of a student artist.

Back in St Petersburg, Alekseyev was appointed to the Management of the Imperial Theatres, where he worked in the studio of Francesco Aloisii Gradizzi (1729–93) from 1779 to 1786. From 1787 he made numerous copies, commissioned by Catherine II, of paintings by Canaletto, Bernardo Bellotto and Hubert Robert, and he was thus able to abandon scenery painting. The copies were a success and gained Akekseyev the nickname 'the Russian Canaletto'. Having perfected his copying skills, he decided to be the first in Russian art to turn to creating original townscapes. In 1793–4 he became the first to paint St Petersburg with his *View of the Peter and Paul Fortress and the Palace Embankment* (1793; Arkhangel'skoye, Mus.-Estate; second version, 1799; St Petersburg, Rus. Mus.) and *View of the Palace Embankment from the Peter and Paul Fortress* (1794; Moscow, Tret'yakov Gal.), for which he was made an academician. With his compositional and technical skills, Alekseyev presented a harmonious and intriguing picture of the glittering new capital as well as of its solemn and lyrical qualities.

In Alekseyev's later pictures of St Petersburg, painted from 1800 to 1810 in watercolour and in oil, the depiction is more profound and tangible, less poetic and reserved. Architectural details are more prominent and more faithfully rendered, and everyday details such as small street scenes and ships on the River Neva appear, as in the *View of the Mikhail Palace from the Fontanka Side* (*c*. 1800), *View of the English Embankment from the Vasil'yevsky Island Side* (1810s), *View of the Admiralty and the Palace Embankment from the First Cadet Corps Academy* (1810s; all St Petersburg, Rus. Mus.); *View of the Exchange and the Admiralty from the Peter and Paul Fortress* (1810; Moscow, Tret'yakov Gal.) and *View of Kazan Cathedral* (1810s; St Petersburg, Rus. Mus. and Pavlovsk Pal.). In the latter, the most successful, Alekseyev achieved a particularly logical, natural and harmonious composition. The tempered colour range and subdued lighting effects soften the harshness of the outline and give the painting a restrained tone.

Alekseyev also became the first Russian artist to paint Moscow. In September 1800 he was dispatched to Moscow with two students by the Academy of Arts, and his main task was to record the distinctive features of Moscow's ancient architecture and monuments. This conflicted with his classical ideals, and Alekseyev did not find it easy to paint the city. Nonetheless, he was able to produce views that were typical of Moscow and retain the usual compositional structure of his paintings. He managed to capture Moscow's distinctive features, its crowded state and its concentration of architectural structures in the town centre, and he organized his paintings in such a way as to give these views the characteristics of an interior, a possible link with his scenery painting experience. For this reason in his Moscow works there are technical errors in the grouping and proportions of the buildings and in the perspective, but at the same time the real Moscow first sprang to life in them as a picturesque, elegant and bustling city. On his return from Moscow in June 1802, besides several works in oils he brought with him a portfolio of watercolours by him and by his students. He continued to paint views of Moscow throughout his life, and this succession of compositions brought him great fame. In December 1802 he became an adviser to the Academy, and in 1803 he became the head of perspectival painting. His work was greatly admired by Russian writers and critics, and he became universally recognized. Certain views, several of which he painted more than once, evoked particular admiration, for example *Red Square in Moscow* (1801), *Cathedral Square in the Kremlin* (1800s; see fig.), *Parade into the Kremlin: Cathedral Square* (1800s), *View of the Voskresenskye and Nikol'skye Gates from Tver Street* (1811; all Moscow, Tret'yakov Gal.) and *View of the Kremlin from the Stone Bridge* (1800s; St Petersburg, Rus. Mus.).

BIBLIOGRAPHY

A. Fyodorov-Davydov: *F. Ya. Alekseyev* (Moscow, 1955)
M. Androsova: *F. Ya. Alekseyev* (Leningrad, 1979)
A. Fyodorov-Davydov: *Russkiy peyzazh* [Russian landscape painting] (Moscow, 1984)

G. A. PRINTSEVA

Alemán, Juan (*b c.* 1398; *d c.* 1468). Sculptor, possibly of Netherlandish or German origin (Sp. *alemán*: 'German'), active in Spain. He worked on the Puerta de los Leones on the south transept of Toledo Cathedral, which was begun in 1452 under the direction of the Master of the Works, Hanequin de Bruselas. The portal is important because it establishes Netherlandish influence in Toledo from the middle of the 15th century. Juan Alemán collaborated on the portal with Egas Cueman and Francisco de la Cuevas, but he was given the commission for the most important sculptures: the statues of four Apostles, the three Marys and Nicodemus (for the embrasures) and twenty-four angel groups (for the archivolts). His style shows strong German influence, seen in the accentuated, metallic drapery folds, which impart strong chiaroscuro effects and add to the nobility of the stylized figures. The tympanum of the inner portal, depicting the *Tree of Jesse*, must also be by Juan Alemán; it includes the original

Fyodor Alekseyev: *Cathedral Square in the Kremlin*, oil on canvas, 817×1120 mm, 1800s (Moscow, Tret'yakov Gallery)

iconographic motif of the tree sprouting from Jesse's cheek. He probably carved the *Risen Christ* on the trumeau as well.

Juan Alemán was no relation to the sculptor of the same name who collaborated on the reredos of the Hospital de la Sangre, Jerez de la Frontera (Cadiz), in 1506 and the choir-stalls of Seville Cathedral (1512–13).

BIBLIOGRAPHY

M. R. Zarco del Valle: *Datos documentales para la historia del arte español*, ii: *Documentos de la catedral de Toledo*, 2 vols (Madrid, 1916)

B. Gilman Proske: *Castilian Sculpture: Gothic to Renaissance* (New York, 1951)

A. Duran Sanpere and A. J. Ainaud de Lasarte: *Escultura gótica*, A. Hisp., v (Madrid, 1956)

Alemán [Duque]**, Rodrigo** (*fl* 1485; *d* before 1512). Spanish wood-carver. He was the most important wood-carver in Toledo in the last decade of the 15th century. His family name was probably Duque, because he is named Rodrigo Duque in a document of Sigüenza Cathedral (Guadalajara). He is first recorded in 1485 in connection with the lower choir-stalls of Toledo Cathedral, which were completed in 1495. The ornamental detail is carefully executed and shows Lower Rhenish stylistic characteristics. The unusual iconography of the 52 stalls represents events in the reconquest of Granada from the Moors, according to accounts of contemporary chroniclers (notably Fernando del Pulgar). The narrative is brisk and lively and enriched by the inclusion of realistic incidents. Alemán was next commissioned to execute the central section of the base of the high altar retable in Toledo Cathedral, which bears fine ornamental carving.

From 1497 Alemán worked simultaneously on the magnificent choir-stalls in the cathedrals of Plasencia (Cáceres) and Ciudad Rodrigo (Salamanca). The former include portraits of King Ferdinand and Queen Isabella and animated biblical scenes, while the latter are dominated by tracery. Alemán probably also provided designs or contributed to the initial stages of work on the choir-stalls of Zamora Cathedral. In 1496 he is mentioned at Sigüenza Cathedral in connection with a commission for the pulpit (finally given to another sculptor to execute in alabaster), but the carving of the episcopal throne there is attributed to him. He stands out as an extremely meticulous and exquisite wood-carver, using both religious and fantastic subject-matter, and including profane and anecdotal scenes largely inspired by popular proverbs and sayings. According to a tradition, he died in Plasencia when flying a machine of his own invention, which, after crossing the city, crashed in a neighbouring field.

BIBLIOGRAPHY

M. Perez-Villamil: *La catedral de Sigüenza* (Madrid, 1899)

B. Gilman Proske: *Castilian Sculpture: Gothic to Renaissance* (New York, 1951)

A. Duran Sanpere and A. J. Ainaud de Lasarte: *Escultura gótica*, A. Hisp., v (Madrid, 1956)

H. L. Arena: *Die Chorgestühle des Meister Rodrigo Alemán* (Heidelberg, 1965)

——: 'La silleria de coro del maestro Rodrigo Alemán', *Bol. Semin. Estud. A. & Arqueol.*, xxxii (1966), p. 89

I. Mateo Gomez: *Temas profanos en la escultura gótica española: La silleria de coro* (Madrid, 1979)

J. Carriazo: *Los relieves de la guerra de Granada en la silleria del coro de la catedral de Toledo* (Granada, 1985)

JOSÉ MARIA AZCÁRTE RISTORI

Alemanno [Alamanno]**, Pietro** (*b* Göttweich, Austria, *c.* 1430; *d* Ascoli Piceno, the Marches, between 18 Sept 1497 and 22 Nov 1498). Italian painter of Austrian birth. He is first documented in 1477 in his adopted home of Ascoli Piceno. A badly preserved fresco of the *Virgin and Child with Saints* in the church of the Madonna delle Rose in Torre San Patrizio, near Ascoli, has been attributed to him; it is dated 1466, providing possible evidence of his presence in the area two years before his master, Carlo Crivelli, was first documented there. Alemanno's style was based on Crivelli's work of the 1470s and hardly evolved at all throughout his career. His expressionistic, anatomical distortion may be derived from Giorgio Schiavone. The *Virgin and Child Enthroned* and the *St Lucy* (both Montefortino, Pin. Com.), which formed part of a dismembered polyptych dating from *c.* 1470, are typical of his work, with their dark outlines and strong hatching in both shadows and highlights.

Alemanno produced mostly polyptychs with the Virgin and Child enthroned, framed by standing saints on separate panels, or small-scale, half-length Virgin and Child pictures, ultimately deriving in form from similar compositions by Donatello. An exception is the *Annunciation* (Ascoli Piceno, Pin. Civ.), painted in 1484 for the city government of Ascoli: it is Alemanno's only surviving unified altarpiece with an architectural setting. Alemanno worked in or near Ascoli, where most of his works can still be found, until his death.

BIBLIOGRAPHY

L. Serra: *L'arte nelle Marche*, ii (Pesaro, 1934), pp. 395–405

P. Zampetti: *La pittura marchigiana del quattrocento* (Milan, 1969; Eng. trans., 1971), pp. 188–93

JEANNETTE TOWEY

Alen, William van. *See* VAN ALEN, WILLIAM.

Alenza y Nieto, Leonardo (*b* Madrid, 6 Nov 1807; *d* Madrid, 30 June 1845). Spanish painter and illustrator. He studied at the Real Academia de S Fernando, Madrid, under Juan Antonio Ribera y Fernández and José de Madrazo y Agudo. He worked independently of court circles and achieved some fame but nevertheless died in such poverty that his burial was paid for by friends. He is often described as the last of the followers of Goya, in whose *Caprichos* and drawings he found inspiration for the genre scenes for which he became best known. Of these scenes of everyday life and customs the more interesting include *The Beating* (Madrid, Casón Buen Retiro) and *Galician with Puppets* (*c.* 1835; Madrid, Casón Buen Retiro; *see* SPAIN, fig. 17). Alenza y Nieto's numerous drawings include the illustrations for Alain-René Lesage's *Gil Blas* (Madrid, 1840), for an edition of the poems of Francisco de Quevedo published by Castello and for the reviews *Semanario pintoresco* and *El Reflejo.* The painting *Triumph of David* (1842; Madrid, Real Acad. S Fernando, Mus.) led to his election as an *Académico de mérito* at the Real Academia de S Fernando in 1842, and he produced such portraits as that of *Alejandro de la Peña* (Madrid, Real Acad. S Fernando, Mus.) and a *Self-portrait* (Madrid, Casón Buen Retiro). His two canvases entitled *Satire on Romantic Suicide* (Madrid, Mus. Romántico) are perhaps the most characteristic of his works.

BIBLIOGRAPHY
R. Mesonero Romanos: *Nuevo manual histórico-topográfico de Madrid* (Madrid, 1854), pp. 135–6
M. Ossorio y Bernard: *Galería biográfica de artistas españoles del siglo XIX* (Madrid, 1869, 2/1883–4/*R* 1975), pp. 19–22
J. M. Arnaiz: *Eugenio Lucas: Su vida y su obra* (Madrid, 1981), pp. 175–8

JOSÉ MANUEL ARNAIZ

Aleotti, Giovanni Battista [l'Argenta] (*b* Argenta, nr Ferrara, 1546; *d* Ferrara, 9 Dec 1636). Italian architect, engineer and designer. He was the son of Vincenzo Aleotti (not Francesco Aleotti, as is sometimes erroneously stated), from whom Giovanni Battista claimed he 'learnt the art . . . as much as from all the other teachers I had' (letter, 1583; see Coffin, p. 121). In 1575 he succeeded Galasso Alghisi as architect to Alfonso II d'Este (ii), Duke of Ferrara and Modena, who nicknamed him l'Argenta after the town of his birth. When, on the death of the Duke, the Este duchy devolved to the Papal States (1598), Aleotti was confirmed as official architect, with a stipend of 20 scudi per month. His activity extended to various parts of the Po plain, embracing different architectural genres and including some important urban projects.

Among Aleotti's religious buildings were several churches in Ferrara, including S Barbara (1586–8), S Maria della Rotonda at Castel Tedaldo (1597; destr. 1608), the oratory of S Margherita delle Zitelle (1604), the oval church of S Carlo (1612) and that of S Francesca Romana (1618–22). He also designed the church of S Maria del Quartiere (1604) in Parma, with an external profile that is built up like a pagoda, and the porticos (1607) of the Capuchin church at Comachio, and he directed the building of the church of the Celletta in Argenta. In addition Aleotti is credited with an initial scheme (two drawings, 1621; Paris, Bib. N.) for the church of S Lucia for the Jesuit college in Bologna, which was finally built to a design by Girolamo Rainaldi in 1623.

As a civic architect, Aleotti was responsible for remodelling the Rocca Gualtieri, Ferrara, into the Palazzo Bentivoglio, a task he is thought to have taken over in 1583 following the death of Pirro Ligorio; his collaboration with the Bentivoglio family continued all his life, probably even after their fief had been transferred to Scandiano. He took part in the restoration of Ferrarese buildings damaged by the earthquakes of 1570, including the castle, the towers which he completed, and the Palazzo della Ragione, to which he added an upper storey (1603). He also designed the tower (1610) of the Palazzo del Paradiso, Ferrara, which became the seat of the university from 1586 to 1962, and the gate of S Paolo (1612). The early 17th-century extension of the Rocca di Scandiano, with a monumental circular staircase commissioned by Giulio Thiene, has also been attributed to Aleotti (Cuoghi). His versatility is revealed also in his work as a military and hydraulic engineer: he built several bastions, worked on the ports of Magnavacca (now Porto Garibaldi) and the Mésola and created fountains and other water displays in the gardens of the Castellina. His most important military work was the fortress at Ferrara. As a hydraulic engineer he made numerous contributions to the reclamation of the land in the Po delta around Ferrara.

Aleotti's most original work was that for the theatre. He was not only a builder of theatres but a talented creator

Giovanni Battista Aleotti: interior of the Teatro Farnese, Parma, 1618–19; restored 1960–62

of complex stage designs. An early example of this was the setting for the *Sacrificio* by Agostino Beccari (with intermezzos by Giovanni Battista Guarini), for which he also built the theatre and the temporary decorations that added drama to the town of Sassuolo (1587). In 1592 he was engaged in Mantua for the staging of Guarini's *Il pastor fido*, although it was not performed on that occasion. On the initiative of Marchese Enzo Bentivoglio, he converted an old granary at Ferrara into the Teatro di S Lorenzo (1606; destr. 1679) for the Accademia degli Intrepidi (*see* THEATRE, §III, 3(i)(a)), with an elongated, semicircular auditorium and a raised stage. In 1612 he completed the reconstruction of the so-called Teatro della Sala Grande, which was also run by the Intrepidi. His masterpiece was the Teatro Farnese in Parma (rest. 1960–62; see fig.), commissioned by Ranuccio I Farnese, 4th Duke of Parma and Piacenza, in 1617 and built in 1618–19; with its rectangular proscenium arch and elongated, semicircular auditorium, it was the prototype of the modern theatre.

UNPUBLISHED SOURCES

Modena, Archv Stor. [MS. of *La idrologia ovvero vaso della scienza et arte delle acque*]

WRITINGS

Gli artifitiosi et curiosi moti spiritali di Herrone, tradotti etc. Aggiuntovi Quattro Theoremi non meno belli et curiosi. Et il modo con che si fa salire un canal d'acqua viva in cima ogn'alta torre con grandissima facilità (Ferrara, 1589)

Difese di Giovanni Battista Aleotti per riparare alla sommersione del Polesine di S Giorgio, et alla rovina dello stato di Ferrara etc. (Ferrara, 1601)

Relazione intorno alla Bonifazione Bentivoglio (Ferrara, 1612)

L. N. Cittadella, ed.: *Dell'interrimento del Po di Ferrara e divergenze delle sue acque nel ramo di Ficarolo: Discorso inedito di Giambattista Aleotti Argentano premesse le memorie per servire alla biografia dell'autore* (Ferrara, 1847)

BIBLIOGRAPHY
D. R. Coffin: 'Some Architectural Drawings of Giovan Battista Aleotti', *J. Soc. Archit. Hist.*, xxi/3 (1962), pp. 116–28
S. M. Bondoni, ed.: *Teatri storici in Emilia Romagna* (Bologna, 1982)
A. Frabetti: 'Il teatro della Sala Grande a Ferrara e i tornei aleottiani', *Mus. Ferrar: Boll. Annu.*, xii (1982), pp. 183–208
——: 'L'Aleotti e i Bentivoglio', *Il Carrobbio*, ix (1983), pp. 197–208
——: 'L'Aleotti urbanista: La fortezza di Ferrara', *Il Carrobbio*, xi (1985), pp. 114–21
J. Bentini and L. Spezzaferro, eds: *L'impresa di Alfonso II* (Bologna, 1987)
G. P. Brizzi and A. M. Matteucci, eds: *Dall'isola alla città: I Gesuiti a Bologna* (Bologna, 1988)

D. Cuoghi: 'La rocca di Scandiano nei progetti di Giovanni Battista Aleotti', *Atti e memorie della deputazione di storia patria per le antiche province modenesi*, XI/xvi (Modena, 1994)

ALESSANDRA FRABETTI

Aleppo [Arab. Ḥalab; Fr. Alep]. Chief city of northern Syria. The major feature of the city is a truncated conical tell, which made it one of the strongest and most easily defensible positions in the north of Syria since the 20th century BC. After the Turkish conquest of Anatolia in the late 11th century, Aleppo became increasingly important as a regional capital, and, under the Zangid (*reg* 1127–1222) and Ayyubid (*reg* 1183–1260) dynasties, the city played a fundamental role as a centre for the reconquest of Crusader territories in the Levant. Under the Mamluk (*reg* 1250–1517) and Ottoman (*reg* 1281–1924) dynasties, Aleppo was the second city of the Arab world after Cairo, a focus of Middle Eastern trade and a meeting point between East and West.

The prehistoric village on the site seems to have gained ascendancy over others in this fertile agricultural area due to the presence of the rocky eminence on which the citadel stands (*see* MILITARY ARCHITECTURE AND FORTIFICATION, fig. 25). At the end of the 19th century BC, Aleppo was conquered by the Hittites, and a few low reliefs and inscriptions survive from the period of Hittite domination. The urban character of the city was revived when Seleucus Nicator founded a colony of Macedonians there between 301 and 281 BC. It had square ramparts enclosing a regular grid of streets, and it was supplied by spring water brought by canals. In 64 BC the city was incorporated into the Roman province of Syria, and a period of peace ensued: magnificent buildings including an agora and a colonnaded street were constructed. In the Persian campaign of AD 540, the town but not the citadel was burnt; the Byzantine emperor Justinian (*reg* 527–65) rebuilt the walls and the cathedral, which had been erected on the site of the principal pagan temple. The cathedral, a tetraconch around a central dome nearly 10 m in diameter, remained the principal sanctuary of the Christian community until the early 12th century, when it became the Halawiyya Madrasa.

The city surrendered to a Muslim army in 636; the first congregational mosque was made by walling the bays of a monumental arch on the colonnaded street. The present congregational mosque was founded *c.* 715 on the site of the ancient agora. Only its general outline dates from the Umayyad period, but it is known to have had mosaic decoration like that of the contemporary mosque in Damascus. The lavish decoration of the tall square minaret (1090) continues the antique tradition of fine stone-carving. The court, paved in geometric patterns of black basalt and white limestone, was renovated under the Ottomans. Following the transfer of power from Syria to Iraq under the Abbasids (*reg* 749–1258), Aleppo became a provincial centre, although it enjoyed a revival under Hamdanid and Mirdasid rulers in the 10th and 11th centuries.

The city reached its apogee in the 12th and 13th centuries. The Zangid Nur al-Din (*reg* 1146–74) ruled from Aleppo and he rebuilt the walls, citadel, congregational mosque, souks and canals. He founded a hospital, six madrasas and the little shrine (Arab. *maqām*) of Abraham in the citadel. It had fine marble panelling and decoration in carved and inlaid wood, including a beautiful wooden mihrab (destr.). Saladin, the founder of the Ayyubid dynasty, gave the town to his son al-Malik al-Zahir Ghazi (*reg* 1186–1216), who made it the capital of a strong and prosperous city state. The presence of the court stimulated trade, and Venice maintained permanent factories there. New suburbs were established for the Turkish cavalry, and the citadel was rebuilt to become one of the most splendid examples of medieval military architecture. A fosse was dug and a glacis of bonded stone, which still covers part of the talus, erected. The monumental entrance block has three handsome gateways with iron doors; the passage has five right-angled bends. Al-Zahir Ghazi also erected a second mosque in the citadel (*c.* 1214); it has been heavily restored, but it still retains a handsome square minaret. The royal palace in the citadel, probably the main palace of al-Zahir Ghazi, was built on earlier foundations and was restored several times. It is remarkable for its handsome portal, constructed in alternating courses of black and yellow stone, with a *muqarnas* semi-dome. A long entrance corridor with several bends leads to service areas and an open square court with an ornamental pond in the centre and a large iwan. Five other doors lead to a bath, two small reception rooms, a staircase to the second storey (destr.) or the roof and a service corridor. Al-Zahir Ghazi also repaired the city walls, three gates and several towers and renovated two Shiʿite martyria, the Mashhad al-Muhassin (founded 1142) and the Mashhad al-Husain (founded 1173–4). The jewel of Ayyubid architecture is the Firdaws Madrasa (1235–7), built in a south-west suburb by Princess Dayfa Khatun, widow of al-Zahir Ghazi and regent for her grandson. It is the largest (44×55 m) and most developed of the madrasas erected by the Ayyubids and combines classrooms, a mausoleum, hospice and mosque in a structure with longitudinal rooms and an iwan arranged around an arcaded court (*see* ISLAMIC ART, fig. 41). An unusual second iwan opening to the exterior is flanked by small apartments. The mihrab surrounded by inlaid multicoloured marbles is a fine example of Aleppan stonework and displays the 'Syrian knot' motif typical of the period (see fig.). Aleppo was a lively intellectual centre with many madrasas and Sufi convents, including the Khanaqah al-Farafira (1237–8). Remains of secular architecture include the Matbakh al-ʿAjami ('Kitchen of the ʿAjamis'), the main room of a Zangid palace. Ayyubid architecture in Aleppo is remarkable as much for the quality of its stonework as for the variety of spaces created and the structural solutions employed.

Architectural activity continued under the Mamluks, as seen in the Maristan Arghuni (1354), a large hospital built by the governor Arghun al-Kamili with six units disposed around a rectangular court. At the citadel a throne-room was constructed over the entrance (restored with questionable accuracy in the 1960s) and the northern and southern towers below the plateau erected. The city walls and gates (e.g. Bab Antakiya, 1420) were again restored. The flourishing economy is attested by the many new markets, caravanserais, baths (e.g. Hammam al-Jawhari, 1384) and mosques (e.g. the ʿUtrush Mosque, 1399).

Aleppo, Firdaws Madrasa, 1235–7; mihrab in prayer-hall

The picturesque residential quarters, which are one of the city's most attractive features, are largely a product of the Ottoman period and are an excellent setting for the ancient monuments in them. The stone structures lend an austerity and precision that characterize the city's urban fabric. The residential buildings include many large houses and palaces, normally comprising an iwan and a massive reception room (Arab. *qāʿa*) overlooking an open court. Clusters of monumental caravanserais and markets vaulted in stone survive in the city centre around the congregational mosque. The Khan al-Wazir (mid-17th century), for example, has a massive entrance block and offices arranged around an open court. These commercial structures, constructed when trade was expanding in the 16th and 17th centuries, remain an integral part of the modern city. Other large mosques and madrasas were built in the style of Istanbul, such as the mosque complex of Khusraw Paşa (1546), attributed to the Ottoman court architect Sinan (*see* SINAN (ii)). Many minor structures, such as baths, cafés, fountains and groups of workshops for textile weavers, were also constructed. The development of the city makes it one of the key monuments in the urban history of the Arab world (*see* ISLAMIC ART, §II, 10(i) and fig. 84).

The old city, which covers nearly 370 ha, remains the major component of modern Aleppo. Certain ancient areas, in particular the north-west corner of the inner city, have been subject to the pressures of town planning and were partly destroyed by redevelopment undertaken in the 1960s. Badly damaged remnants of the city's past mingle with inferior modern buildings, but the historic district has been protected and new restoration projects launched. Archaeological excavations at the citadel have been concerned more with uncovering elements for touristic purposes than with science. An ersatz theatre in the ancient style, for example, was built at the expense of some hastily uncovered archaeological layers.

Aleppo was famous for its manufactures, which formed an important part of its trade. During the 12th and 13th centuries, for example, fine metalwares (e.g. a ewer made in 1232 for the Ayyubid ruler; Washington, DC, Freer; *see* ISLAMIC ART, §IV, 3(ii)), glass, silks and leather were produced. The most important craft was woodworking, and several Aleppan masters and their sons signed works. The finest example was the minbar (destr.) that Nur al-Din commissioned in 1168–9 for the Aqsa Mosque in Jerusalem; it was signed by four artisans and extensively decorated with marquetry and ivory inlay (*see* ISLAMIC ART, §VII, 1(i)(b)).

Under the Mamluks and Ottomans the city became an important centre of textile manufacture and trade, and Aleppo became one of the chief textile centres of the Ottoman empire, producing cheap cotton fabrics as well as luxury silk cloths woven with gold and silver. Aleppo supplied local markets and exported to the Ottoman empire and Europe. Certain aspects of traditional culture, such as architecture, decoration, crafts and music, have attracted renewed interest, and they inspire modern artists, who exhibit in several galleries. The National Museum in Aleppo, founded in 1960, houses antiquities from such local sites as TELL HALAF, MARI, EBLA, UGARIT and Hama (*see* HAMA, §1).

BIBLIOGRAPHY

Enc. Islam/2: 'Ḥalab'

K. al-Ghazzī: *Kitāb Nahr al-dhahab fī ta'rīkh Ḥalab* [The river of gold in the history of Aleppo], 3 vols (Aleppo, AH 1342/1926)

J. Sauvaget: 'Inventaire des monuments musulmans de la ville d'Alep', *Rev. Etud. Islam.* (1931), pp. 59–114

——: *Alep: Essai sur le développement d'une grande ville syrienne des origines au milieu du XIXème siècle*, 2 vols (Paris, 1941)

E. Herzfeld: *Matériaux pour un corpus inscriptionum Arabicarum, Pt 2: Syrie du Nord: Inscriptions et monuments d'Alep*, 2 vols (Cairo, 1954–6)

J.-C. David: 'Alep, dégradation et tentatives actuelles de réadaptation des structures urbaines traditionnelles', *Bull. Etud. Orient.*, xxviii (1975), pp. 19–50

A. Raymond: 'Les Grands Waqfs et l'organisation de l'espace urbain à Alep et au Caire à l'époque ottomane (XVIe–XVIIe s.)', *Bull. Etud. Orient.*, xxxi (1979), pp. 113–28

J.-C. David: *Le Waqf d'Ipshīr Pāshā à Alep (1063/1653)* (Damascus, 1982)

H. Gaube and E. Wirth: *Aleppo: Historische und geographische Beiträge zur baulichen Gestaltung*, 2 vols (Wiesbaden, 1984)

A. Raymond: *Grandes Villes arabes à l'époque ottomane* (Paris, 1985)

A. Marcus: *Aleppo in the Eighteenth Century* (New York, 1989)

Y. Tabaa: 'Circles of Power: Palace, Citadel and City in Ayyubid Aleppo', *A. Orient.*, xxiii (1993), pp. 181–200

JEAN-CLAUDE DAVID

Aleš, Mikoláš (*b* Mirotice, nr Písek, 18 Nov 1852; *d* Prague, 10 July 1913). Czech painter, illustrator and designer. He studied at the Academy of Fine Arts in Prague under Josef Mathias von Trenkwald (1824–97) and Jan Swerts (1820–79), and he rarely travelled, except to Vienna in 1873 and Italy in 1877. He was one of the leading Bohemian artists of the so-called Generation of the National Theatre. The décor of this theatre, opened in 1881 and again after a fire in 1883, marked a national artistic rebirth. Aleš, together with František Ženíšek, had won the competition in 1877 to decorate the walls, lunettes and ceilings of the theatre foyer. Aleš's cycle *My Country*, designed for the lunettes, is one of the most famous Czech works of art.

In the late 1870s Aleš emerged as a draughtsman and painter with a rich imagination. He outlined many cycles to be finished later and he studied heraldry, which contributed to the development of his original ornamental style. He applied this style for the first time on painted furniture, as in *Elements, Spanish Wall* (1878; Prague, N.G., Convent of S Agnes). His paintings date mainly to this period, under the stimulus of late Romanticism. He produced small-scale sketches with themes from Bohemian history, often of a personal nature, for example *May Triptych* (1878; Prague, Alois Jirásek & Mikoláš Aleš Mus.), and also large paintings, such as *Meeting of King George of Poděbrady and Matthias Korvinus* (1878; Prague, N.G., Convent of S Agnes). Unprecedentedly, Aleš was left out of the Prague anniversary exhibition, which may have contributed to his decision to abandon oil painting.

Conflicts with academic authorities impeded an official career, but Aleš was greatly admired by the younger generation who, in 1886 and 1887, elected him honorary president of two influential groups of young Bohemian artists, the Škréta group and the Mánes Union of Artists respectively. In the 1880s he became a leading illustrator in Czech magazines, both humorous and satirical, and he was a founder of modern Czech book illustration. Among his most skilful illustrations are those for *Rukopis královédvorský* (Králův Dvůr manuscript), a Romantic forgery of an early medieval fragment (1886; Prague, N.G., Kinský Pal.). His popularity grew from the 1890s, owing to his illustrations of Czech folk-songs and children's books (e.g. *Alšův Špalíček*). His wall paintings and *sgrafitti*, which depicted mythological and historical national subjects with folklore elements and plant ornament, were also well regarded. His style of decorating the façades of buildings, executed mainly in Prague (e.g. the house of the architect Antonín Wiehl, Wenceslas Sq.) and in Pilsen, incorporates late historicism and elements of Secessionist style.

BIBLIOGRAPHY

M. Míčko and others: *Dílo Mikoláš Aleš* [The work of Mikoláš Aleš], 10 vols (Prague, 1951–7)

H. Volavková: *Mikoláš Aleš* (Prague, 1982)

M. Nováková: 'M. Aleš', *Die tschechische Malerei des XIX. Jahrhunderts* (exh. cat. by J. Kotalík, Vienna, Belvedere, 1984), pp. 25-7

J. Brabcová and M. Nováková: 'M. Aleš', *Tschechische Kunst, 1878–1914: Auf dem Weg in die Moderne* (exh. cat. by J. Kotalík, Darmstadt, Ausstellhallen Mathildenhöhe, 1985), ii, pp. 1–5

ROMAN PRAHL

Alesio, Mateo Pérez de. *See* PÉREZ DE ALESIO, MATEO.

Alessandro da Padova. *See* PADOVANO, ALESSANDRO.

Alessi, Andrea [Aleši, Andrija; Alexii, Andreas; Andrea di Niccolò da Durazzo] (*b* Dürres, *c.* 1425; *d* Split, 1504). Dalmatian sculptor and architect of Albanian birth. Although he is recorded in 1435 at Zadar as a pupil of Marco di Pietro da Troia, his most important artistic influence was the Late Gothic style of Giorgio da Sebenico, with whom he worked in 1445 on Šibenik Cathedral and in 1452 at Ancona on the Loggia dei Mercanti. Between 1448 and 1460 Alessi also controlled his own workshop at Split and Rab. In 1466 he began work on his masterpiece, the baptistery at Trogir, which was finished in 1467. The chapel is rectangular in plan, covered with a barrel vault with acute angled coffers; its richly decorated interior is an eclectic blend of Late Gothic and Renaissance elements. The sculpture shares these characteristics: the *Baptism of Christ* over the entrance, with its elongated figures and complex drapery patterns, derives from Giorgio da Sebenico's mannered style, while *St Jerome in the Desert* and the putti bearing garlands in the interior show the influence of Niccolò di Giovanni Fiorentino, with whom Alessi collaborated on the chapel of the Blessed Giovanni Orsini (1468–*c.* 1497) at Trogir Cathedral, where Alessi's contribution was limited to a statue of *St Jerome* and several reliefs of putti carrying torches. In 1472, again with Niccolò, he restored the campanile of Split Cathedral, and a year later they collaborated on the façade and doorway of S Maria al Mare on the island of St Nicholas in the Tremiti. From 1474 Alessi lived in Split, where he executed some minor works, including the altar in St Jerome at Mt Marjan (signed and dated 1480) and several small reliefs of *St Jerome in the Desert* (Florence, Fond. Longhi; Liverpool, Walker A.G.). In 1488 he gave his services free of charge to reinforce fortifications against the Turks. Alessi was an eclectic artist, capable of absorbing stylistic elements from other masters, but never able to match their creative force.

BIBLIOGRAPHY

DBI; Thieme–Becker

A. Venturi: *Storia* (1901–40), vi, pp. 1012–22

D. Frey: 'Der Dom von Sebenico und sein Baumeister Giorgio Orsini', *Jb. Ksthist. Inst. Ksr.-Kön. Zent.-Komm. Dkmlpf.*, vii (1913), pp. 1–169

H. Folnesics: 'Studien zur Entwicklungsgeschichte der Architektur und Plastik des XV. Jahrhunderts in Dalmatien', *Jb. Ksthist. Inst. Ksr.-Kön. Zent.-Komm. Dkmlpf.*, viii (1914), pp. 27–196

P. Kolendić: 'Dokumenti o Andriji Alešiju u Trogiru' [Documents about Andrea Alessi in Trogir], *Arhv Arbanasku Starinu, Jezik & Etnol.*, ii (1924), pp. 70–78

——: 'Aleši i Firentinac na Tremitima' [Alessi and Fiorentino at Tremiti Islands], *Glasnik Skopskog Naučnog Društva*, i/1–2 (1926), pp. 207–14

G. Praga: 'Documenti intorno ad Andrea Alessi', *Rass. March.*, viii (1929–30), pp. 1–26

C. Fisković and K. Prijatelj: *Albanski umjetnik Andrija Aleši u Splitu i Rabu* [The Albanian artist Andrea Alessi in Split and Rab] (Split, 1948)

C. Fisković: 'Aleši, Firentinac i Duknović u Trogiru' [Alessi, Fiorentino and Dalmata in Trogir], *Bull. Inst. Likovne Umjetnosti JAZU*, vii/1 (1959), pp. 20–43

Walker Art Gallery, Liverpool: Foreign Catalogue (Liverpool, 1977), p. 285

A. Markham Schulz: *Niccolò di Giovanni Fiorentino and Venetian Sculpture of the Early Renaissance*, i (New York, 1978)

I. Petricioli: 'Alešijev relief *sv. Jeronima* u Zadru' [*St Jerome* relief by Alessi in Zadar], *Tragom srednjevjekovnih umjetnika* [Studies in medieval art] (Zagreb, 1983), pp. 139–51

J. Höfler: *Die Kunst Dalmatiens vom Mittelalter bis zur Renaissance (800–1520)* (Graz, 1989)

SAMO ŠTEFANAC

Alessi, Galeazzo (*b* Perugia, 1512; *d* Perugia, 30 Dec 1572). Italian architect and writer. He was the leading High Renaissance architect in both Genoa and Milan, his villas and town palazzi establishing a definitive pattern for the genre. His greatest sacred building was S Maria Assunta in Carignano, the central planning of which shows the influence of Donato Bramante and Michelangelo.

1. TRAINING AND EARLY CAREER, *c.* 1530–48. The Perugia of Alessi's youth was an important centre of the Papal States, with a lively humanist and philosophical cultural life. Alessi received his early training in the school of the architect and painter Giovan Battista Caporali, whose edition of Vitruvius is notable for its tendency to rationalize the Antique and for its reference to music as a means of further perfecting the study of harmonic proportion in the visual arts. Alessi was also friendly with the architect Giulio Danti (1500–75), who was equally well versed in rhetoric and philosophy.

Alessi's diverse cultural experience recommended him to the papal court in Rome, where he moved in 1536. There he worked for Cardinal Lorenzo Campeggia and Cardinal Girolamo Glinucci and, most notably, for Cardinal Agostino Parisani, Bishop of Rimini. He became familiar with the architectural projects carried out in Rome for the papal court under Paul III, and particularly with the work of Antonio da Sangallo (ii) at St Peter's (1520–46), at the Vatican Palace (Sala Regia and Pauline Chapel, 1540) and at the Palazzo Farnese (1514–46). When Parisani was appointed papal legate for Perugia, Alessi returned with him and worked on a scheme drawn up by Sangallo for the fortress known as the Rocca Paolina (1543–8). According to Vasari, Alessi was responsible for the principal apartments (destr.; the loggia is recorded in a 19th-century drawing, see *Genova, 1975*, fig. 108).

Alessi assumed an even more important role in 1545, when Cardinal Parisani was replaced as papal legate by Cardinal Tiberio Crispo, who became the driving force behind the architectural renewal of the city (*see* PERUGIA). Alessi probably designed for Crispo the loggia on the upper floor of the Corso façade of the Palazzo dei Priori, which, like that of the Rocca, is built in the Doric order and which focuses the eye on the legate's apartment, formed from the existing rooms of the Priori. Alessi was probably responsible also for the construction for Crispo of the public loggia (1545–8), with pillars emphasized by Doric pilaster strips and simply profiled framing arches; the loggia was subsequently transformed into the oratory of S Angelo della Pace. Stylistically, Alessi's work on the loggia recalls such Roman models as the Loggia of Paul III at the Castel Sant'Angelo, built by Raffaello da Montelupo.

Further works by Alessi in Perugia include the church of S Maria del Popolo (1547), which recalls Sangallo's design for the Pauline Chapel in the Vatican Palace, Rome, both in the entrance and in the plan of the interior, with its aisleless nave roofed by a coved vault intersected by four segments of barrel vaulting. In 1548 he received payment for the design and model for the convent of S Giuliana (now S Caterina), where, despite later modifications, it is still possible to identify traces of his work. Although the opening up of the Via Nuova between the Corso and the Sopramuro at Perugia has sometimes been attributed to Alessi, it is now clear that this was carried out by Sangallo.

Alessi's work in Perugia reveals his early competence in various specialized fields of architecture, employing a vocabulary, based on the classicizing Roman style of Sangallo and on the works of other early 16th-century Italian architects, which he continued to recall even in his later years. He articulated internal space by robust yet simple pilasters, emphasized by an order (generally Doric) and covered by vaults that are frequently coffered. Already it is possible to see his cultivated and intelligent understanding of his classicizing sources.

2. GENOA, 1548–57.

(i) Patrons and urban development schemes. From early on Alessi was capable of maintaining relationships of mutual trust and respect with his patrons. His employment with the papal legates in Perugia enabled him to meet members of the rich Genoese families that provided the administrators of the Papal States. Among them were members of the Sauli family, who were responsible for many of Alessi's commissions: Stefano Sauli, apostolic protonotary, who as early as 1543 is recorded as having made a loan to Alessi, and Gerolamo Sauli and Bartolomeo Sauli, treasurers of the papal administration in Perugia in the 1540s. These contacts opened the way for Alessi's transfer to Genoa in 1548 and then brought him his first commissions there—for the basilica of S Maria Assunta in Carignano, the family church of the Sauli, and for the villa (see fig. 1) in Albaro of Luca Giustiniani, who was married to a Sauli (*see* §(iii) below). Further commissions came from other noble families of Genoa, such as the Grimaldi and the Pallavicini, while Gerolamo Sauli, who was appointed Archbishop of Genoa in 1550, was associated with Alessi's work in Genoa Cathedral and in the Palazzo Comunale, Bologna, during his time as papal vice-legate (1550–55); Alessi's contribution to the palazzo included the main entrance, another doorway off the courtyard and part of the chapel.

In contrast to other architects in the city, Alessi was treated as an equal by his patrons, participating at all levels in the transformation of Genoa throughout one of the most important periods of architectural innovation in the later 16th century. His buildings provided the central points of reference for the transformation of the city. He also drew up plans for the reorganization of the hill of Carignano involving the development of Sauli properties in the area, but they remained unexecuted, while the development of the Strada Nuova in Genoa, formerly attributed to Alessi, has been shown to be the work of other hands (*see* GENOA, §1).

(ii) S Maria Assunta in Carignano. The contract between Alessi and the Sauli for the construction of S Maria Assunta in Carignano (see fig. 2) dates from September 1549, but the foundation stone was laid only in 1552, the wooden model was constructed between 1552 and 1554, and by 1567 it had reached the stage of vaulting; only then was thought given to the dome, with probable variations

1. Galeazzo Alessi: Villa Giustiniani (now Villa Cambiaso), Albaro, Genoa, 1548

made to the original model. The church was completed in 1603.

The model for the Sauli church was clearly derived from Bramante's work in Rome—not just from St Peter's, but also, and more precisely, from the church of SS Celso e Giuliano (destr. 1733), which was built under Sangallo's direction. The plan of the building is centralized, consisting of a Greek cross set within a square, with a central dome and smaller domes over the arms of the cross and four bell-towers emphasizing the corners of the square. Deriving from the same Roman background are the powerful, solid pillars and the coffered vaults, where the contrast of light and shade is brought out by the white plaster walls. The façade, with its alternating areas of white and pink, achieves a remarkable clarity of composition, both defining and emphasizing the structural elements without detracting from the ample, interlinking areas of wall surface that surround the dome. The high podium planned for the church was partly built only in the 19th century, and the completion of the altar and the entrance date from the Baroque period. Despite the church's centralized plan, a sense of orientation, towards the sea and the heart of the old city, was stressed during construction by eliminating two of the four planned bell-towers; it is possible this axiality may have been envisaged in the original plans. The link with the landscape and the surrounding natural environment must have been strongly felt by Alessi, and during the construction of the church he changed the design of the dome, providing it with a drum in the form of a covered arcade opening on to four high terraces on each of the sides, access to which is gained by four convenient spiral stairways.

Between 1550 and 1557 Alessi provided his services free for the rebuilding of Genoa Cathedral and probably drew up an overall plan. This was never carried out in its entirety, but his hallmark can be seen in the dome resting on a polygonal drum, elegantly coffered within and articulated on the exterior by Ionic columns and pilaster strips on high bases decorated with panels.

(iii) Villas. Alessi's first project in Genoa was the Villa Giustiniani at Albaro (1548; renamed Villa Cambiaso and now the headquarters of the Faculty of Engineering, Università di Genova). It was planned as a solid block without a central courtyard, but its hilltop location made it a focal point for the surrounding countryside. The elevation is composed of two floors, and the seaward side is decorated with a superimposed order of Doric half columns on the ground floor and fluted composite pilasters in the upper floor, paired at the ends of the wall in order to balance the opening on the ground floor created by the central triple-arched portico (see fig. 1). The layout is

2. Galeazzo Alessi: S Maria Assunta in Carignano, Genoa, 1552–1603

based on the two loggias between the two slightly projecting wings: the loggia of the entrance front is on the ground floor, while that at the rear is on the upper floor, giving access to a salon situated over the lower portico. The loggias are rectangular in plan, with an apse at each end, and while the stylistic solutions once again derive from Roman models and from Sangallo, the treatment of the façade walls is more decorative, with details suggesting the influence of Michelangelo. Inside, the solid architectural orders and coffered ceilings are complemented by decorative elements, such as herms, caryatids and tablets, recalling Perino del Vaga and the pupils of Raphael. These characteristics—a compact plan with variety provided by the decoration—were subsequently developed by Alessi in other villas.

The Villa Pallavicino (*c.* 1555; also known as the Villa delle Peschiere; *see* VILLA, fig. 5) is a looser reworking of the plan for the Villa Giustiniani. The central block, opening out on to the garden, has two entrances of equal importance, one at the centre of the U-shaped layout, the other dominating the garden-front terrace above the nymphaeum. The latter, reached through a portico divided in three by Doric pilasters, is elliptical in plan; it is a fine example of grotesque decoration executed in multicoloured pebbles, imitated later in other Genoese buildings.

Between 1552 and 1554 Alessi also designed a villa for Giovanni Battista Grimaldi (renamed Villa Sauli). Here great play was made of the relationship of the building with the space surrounding it, the courtyard in front being articulated by a series of *serliane*, which were repeated, in two superimposed orders, on the façade of the villa itself. The villa has been transformed into apartments, and only the original cornice remains, with its emphatic carved decoration of vegetation and masks. Alessi's solutions are found echoed in many villa buildings that were once attributed to him but are in fact the work of others: the Villa Grimaldi (called La Fortezza), the Villa Lercari and the villa built for Vincenzo Imperiali have now been attributed respectively to Bernardo a Spazio, Bernardino da Cantone, and Domenico and Giovanni Ponzello.

(iv) The Porta del Molo. Alessi's early experience on the Rocca Paolina site at Perugia had given him a certain knowledge of military architecture, in terms not only of defensive techniques of fortification, and in particular of the Rocca Paolina *tenaille*, but also of the influence of the military style on the city itself. He used this experience at Genoa in 1553 when he built the Porta del Molo (or Porta Siberia) and also, once again, referred back to Sangallo, in particular to the Porta di S Spirito in Rome (from 1540). He resolved the problem of the seaward fortifications by borrowing from the *caudate*, or tail-shaped, designs described in Classical treatises, creating between the two lateral ramparts a curved, semi-elliptical space with a central gateway in a Doric order. The columns and walls of the gateway are covered by bands of rustication, recalling the work of Giulio Romano and designs represented in Sebastiano Serlio's treatise *Regole generali* (Venice, 1537). By contrast, the city side, with its portico articulated by pairs of pilasters supported by piers and framing arches, has an elegant linear rhythm. Alessi did not undertake this type of fortification again, but it forms the probable basis of the attribution to him by Baldini of a manual of military architecture now in the Biblioteca Estense, Modena. The manual provides a systematic illustration of systems of fortification, but the analogy with Alessi's designs is not very persuasive, and the attribution remains somewhat uncertain.

3. LATER WORKS, 1557–72.

(i) Lombardy.

(a) Palazzo Marino. Tommaso Marino, a banker from a family of Genoese origin, summoned Alessi to Milan in 1557 and commissioned a design for a mansion, which developed in an urban context several ideas already used in the Genoese villas. The closed and compact external block of the building is in fact made up of three separate elements: courtyard, salon and garden. The exterior of the mansion is unified by a solid wall of breccia articulated by three orders: Doric half columns on the ground floor embrace window aedicules that sport a rusticated minor order; Ionic pilaster strips on the *piano nobile* frame tapered window surrounds that support pediments, broken to enclose grotesque heads, and prop the mezzanine window surrounds. The top-floor pilasters have flutings that converge downwards, while their capitals take the form of female heads linked by a richly decorated frieze. The façade on to the present Piazza della Scala is a 19th-century addition; originally the house was only roughly finished on this side, which overlooked a passageway separating it from other buildings.

The courtyard (see fig. 3), with direct access to the street, has a two-storey elevation with a portico and loggia

3. Galeazzo Alessi: Palazzo Marino, Milan, view of courtyard, begun 1558

articulated by *serliane*; on the ground floor these are relatively plain, but the upper floor is enriched with an exuberant decoration of caryatids bearing baskets and garlands of flowers and fruit, as well as ornamental tablets. The decorative programme of the courtyard is for the most part inspired by themes from Ovid's *Metamorphoses*; the same source was employed for the stucco and fresco decoration of the salon, where the legends of Perseus and Psyche are depicted following a programme (reconstructed in Scotti) derived from engravings and medals associated with the school of Raphael. The Grand Salon has, in addition to its access from the courtyard, a second entrance directly from the road; this served to connect, and at the same time separate, Marino's own apartments and those of his two sons, which extended around the garden lying behind the house.

The many alterations made to the house over the centuries have left intact only the courtyard and part of the salon, where the vaults were destroyed by bombing in 1943. The design of the courtyard at the Palazzo Marino, however, influenced other Milanese buildings, such as Vincenzo Seregni's Palazzo dei Giureconsulti (begun 1561), for which Alessi provided the design of a door.

(b) Church designs. Probably at the request of the Sauli family, Alessi also collaborated on the rebuilding of SS Barnaba e Paolo, Milan, a church belonging to the BARNABITES, who were supported by Alessandro Sauli. Alessi's contribution to the reconstruction, which began as early as 1547, is documented in 1561 in connection with the rebuilding of the choir. His involvement, however, extended to the redesigning of the entire church, which has an aisleless nave flanked by chapels and covered with a barrel vault decorated with delicate stucco ornament. The rebuilt church of S Barnaba comprised a succession of three communicating but distinct spaces: the nave, presbytery and choir, each with a different vaulting system and with the presbytery raised three steps above the nave (now transformed by the 19th-century opening of the crypt below). It was one of the earliest churches in Milan to fulfil the requirements of the Counter-Reformation, in which the Barnabite Order was deeply involved. The solutions adopted by Alessi, enhanced by the vaults and their delicate and subtle stuccowork, accentuate his perception of space as a matter of proportion, harmony and intellectual order.

Around 1560 Alessi must also have prepared a design for the rebuilding of the Olivetan church of S Vittore, Milan, following his earlier intervention to provide the design for a tripartite Doric window for the monastery there. The church was planned with a nave and two aisles, chapels, a high dome and an elongated presbytery with a monks' choir ending in an apse.

Through his contacts with Marino, Alessi came to the attention of other Lombard patrons, including the d'Adda family. Giacomo d'Adda turned to him for the designs required to complete the façade and the interior decoration (the inside wall of the façade and the choir) of the church of S Maria presso S Celso, of which he was the administrator. In the mid-1560s Alessi drew up an extensive corpus of designs (now Milan, Bib. Ambrosiana), arranging above the Doric ground floor a further four storeys articulated not by Classical rules but by a free association of tablets and frames, pilaster-strips and half columns, creating through continuous, vibrant chiaroscuro an architecture that is both directed and affirmed by the values of the wall surface. This harmony of surface and decoration is a lively feature of the designs for the inside wall of the façade and the choir but is less evident in the actual construction of the building, which was carried out after 1570 under the direction of Martino Bassi.

(c) Design of the Sacro Monte, Varallo. Also under the patronage of Giacomo d'Adda, Alessi produced designs for the restructuring of the Sacro Monte in Varallo, the home town of d'Adda's wife. These form a complete corpus of designs in a volume entitled *Il libro dei misteri* (Varallo Sésia, Bib. Civ.), which Perrone has dated to 1565–9 and reattributed, in its entirety, to Alessi. The Sacro Monte was the work of the Franciscan Bernardino Caimi (*d* 1499), who returned from Jerusalem *c.* 1486 with the aim of reproducing the form and layout of the holy sites there in a series of chapels (*see* VARALLO, SACRO MONTE). In his *Libro dei misteri* Alessi worked out a complex new overall design, which considerably extended the scope of the Sacro Monte, subdividing it into three distinct zones, dedicated respectively to the Life of Christ (but with an antecedent in the form of a chapel dedicated to Adam and Eve), to the Passion, and to representations of Limbo, Purgatory and Hell. The first zone was to be located on the side of the hill, the densely covered and uneven slopes of which were to form a backcloth for the clear-cut outlines of the chapels, distributed over a winding course. The second zone was to be situated on the level summit of the hill. Around an octagonal piazza (the true centre of the plan) were to have been laid out the buildings most representative of the city of Jerusalem (the Courthouse and the Temple). Finally the third zone, situated in a large valley, was to have housed chapels intended to be seen from above in a complex scenic plan. Alessi thus devised a sacred hill based on works of architecture and designed to take best advantage of the surrounding space. Even the sacred scenes and the mysteries depicted inside each chapel became subordinated to the architecture: in

many chapels the scenes were contained in shrines, as precious objects to be contemplated on a separate, intellectual, level.

Between 1565 and 1568 the main gate and the chapel of Adam and Eve were erected according to Alessi's designs, and the entire route on the hillside was cleared. The chapels and structures built after 1569, however, were based on a new plan dictated by Cardinal Carlo Borromeo's insistence that there should be a greater concentration on the emotional involvement of the faithful, rather than on the intellectual contemplation of a sacred theme.

(ii) Umbria. Alessi returned to his native Umbria four times in the 1560s, both for family reasons and to act as a consultant. In 1567, for example, he supplied designs for a tabernacle (destr.) for the basilica of S Pietro at Perugia and for the south door of the cathedral there. In 1569, however, he returned for good and took on such demanding projects as the restructuring of the convent of S Pietro, where he added the Chiostro delle Stelle (1571), and the reorganization of the Palazzo dei Priori.

Work started on construction of the basilica of S Maria degli Angeli, below Assisi, to Alessi's designs in 1569. This was intended as a tangible reminder to the pilgrims, who arrived in great numbers, particularly during the local feast of Pardon (1–2 August), of the birth of the Franciscan movement: the church enclosed, as in a shrine, the venerated chapels associated with the movement, the Porziuncola (the original little oratory of St Francis) and the chapel of the Transito. The basilica was planned with a nave, two aisles with side chapels, a transept contained within the main block and a deep presbytery, all decorated in the Doric order. Following Alessi's designs, the nave and aisles with their chapels were built fairly rapidly; in this part of the church a severe architectural style prevailed, based on solid, robust piers and with alternating barrel and groin vaults. The transept, dome and presbytery, however, were built only during the 17th century, to a partial modification of the original plans. The interior of the nave and aisles and the external walls of the chapels reflect Alessi's designs with some accuracy, despite the reconstruction of the vaults following the earthquake of 1832. The façade, on the other hand, rebuilt in a totally different style in 1924–30, destroys the original scheme's characteristic linking of elements.

During the same period Alessi was also working on designs for the internal rebuilding of the cathedral of S Rufino at Assisi; work began in 1571, although once again he never returned to the site once he had submitted his designs. The old Romanesque building was transformed into a modern church with a nave and two aisles in the Doric order and plastered surfaces, while both the barrel vaults of the nave and the groin vaults of the aisles are lower than in the original building. Finally, Alessi eliminated the original rise to the presbytery and organized the space at the end of the church as a tribune on an octagonal plan, with four of its sides pierced to form a cross with the apsidal chapel longer than the others. Access to the tribune was to have been from the nave (the present additional entrances from the aisles were opened up at a later date), while the dome was to have been lit only indirectly, from the wings and the central oculus. Again Alessi appears to have intended an extremely purist architecture, based on the exclusive use of a single order, in all its severity, emphasized further by the simplicity of the wall surfaces. The only departure from this eminently rational and intellectual perception of space is the presence of single elements of refined ornamentation. Alessi also designed the precious tabernacle made by Vincenzio Danti for the church of S Francesco (Assisi, Tesoro Mus. Basilica S Francesco), applying these same principles of rationality.

Alessi's approach to design was reflected in his working practices, and throughout his career he concentrated above all on the intellectual aspects and hence the purely planning side of his work, progressively distancing himself from any direct contact with the actual construction of his buildings. Once he had provided the model, the design of the complete building and the decorative elements, he ceased to intervene, leaving the work to well-trained site managers with whom he often communicated in writing.

WRITINGS

Il libro dei misteri (MS.; 1565–9; Varallo Sésia, Bib. Civ.); ed. A. M. Brizio and S. Perrone as *Galeazzo Alessi: Il libro dei misteri: Progetto di pianificazione urbanistica, architettonica e figurativa del Sacro Monte di Varallo in Valsesia* (Bologna, 1974)

BIBLIOGRAPHY

DBI

G. Vasari: *Vite* (1550, rev. 2/1568); ed. G. Milanesi (1878–85), vii, pp. 552–5

F. Alberti: *Elogio di Galeazzo Alessi da Perugia* (MS.; *c.* 1573; Perugia, Bib. Augusta); ed. L. Beltrami (Milan, 1913)

L. Pascoli: *Vite de' pittori, scultori ed architetti moderni*, 2 vols (Rome, 1730–36/*R* 1933), i, pp. 279–87

S. Varni: *Spigolature artistiche nell'archivio della Basilica di Carignano* (Genoa, 1877)

E. de Negri: *Galeazzo Alessi, architetto a Genova* (Genoa, 1957)

M. Tafuri: *L'architettura del manierismo nel cinquecento europeo* (Rome, 1966)

A. Peroni: 'Architetti manieristi nell'Italia settentrionale: Pellegrino Tibaldi e Galeazzo Alessi', *Boll. Cent. Int. Stud. Archit. Andrea Palladio*, ix (1967), pp. 272–92

L. Vagnetti, ed.: *Genova: Strada Nuova* (Genoa, 1967)

E. Poleggi: *Strada Nuova: Una lottizzazione del cinquecento a Genova* (Genoa, 1968, 2/1972)

——: 'Genova e l'architettura di villa nel secolo XVI', *Boll. Cent. Int. Stud. Archit. Andrea Palladio*, xi (1969), pp. 231–42

E. Robbiani: 'Un'opera milanese di Galeazzo Alessi: Palazzo Marino', *Ist. Elem. Archit. & Rilievo Mnmt. [Genova]: Quad.*, 2 (1969), pp. 151–82

M. Labò: 'G. Alessi, architetto perugino', *I palazzi di Genova di P. P. Rubens ed altri scritti d'architettura* (Genoa, 1970), pp. 56–73

Galeazzo Alessi e l'architettura del cinquecento: Atti del Convegno internazionale di studi: Genova, 1975 [extensive bibliographies]

G. Fusconi: 'Perino del Vaga e Galeazzo Alessi: Influssi della seconda attività romana di Perino sul formarsi della decorazione alessiana', *Commentari*, xxvii (1976), pp. 69–81

N. Carboneri: 'Le chiese dell'Alessi', *Boll. Cent. Int. Stud. Archit. Andrea Palladio*, xix (1977), pp. 191–8

P. Carpeggiani: 'Per una bibliografia sistematica su Galeazzo Alessi', *Riv. Semest. Stor. A.*, vi/2 (1977), pp. 38–49

A. Scotti: 'Per un profilo dell'architettura milanese (1535–1560)', *Omaggio a Tiziano: La cultura artistica milanese nell'età di Carlo V* (exh. cat., ed. M. Garberi; Milan, Pal. Reale, 1977), pp. 103–5, 114–17

G. Baldini: 'Un ignoto manoscritto d'architettura militare autografo di Galeazzo Alessi', *Mitt. Ksthist. Inst. Florenz*, xxv (1981), pp. 253–78

N. Houghton Brown: *The Milanese Architecture of Galeazzo Alessi*, 2 vols (New York and London, 1982)

E. Poleggi and F. Caraceni: 'Genova e Strada Nuova', *Stor. A. It.*, ed. P. Fossati, xii (Turin, 1983), pp. 301–61

F. Vignoli: 'L'Alessi in Assisi', *Atti Accad. Properz. Subasio-Assisi*, vi/13 (1986), pp. 197–243

F. F. Mancini and A. Scotti, eds: *Storia e architettura* (1989), i of *La Basilica di S Maria degli Angeli* (Perugia, 1989–)

K. Zeitler: *Galeazzo Alessis Villen Giustiniani-Cambiaso und Grimaldi Sauli: Ein Genueser Beitrag zur Villenarchitektur im Cinquecento* (Munich, 1993)

AURORA SCOTTI TOSINI

Aleu y Teixidor, Andrés (*b* Tarragona, 1832; *d* Barcelona, 1901). Spanish sculptor. He entered the Escuela de Bellas Artes de la Lonja, Barcelona, when still very young and was a student of the Neo-classical artist Damián Campeny y Estrany, who was also influenced by Romanticism and naturalism. In 1855 Aleu y Teixidor applied for the Chair in Modelling at the Escuela, a position to which he was eventually appointed after the committee had been involved in intrigues and disputes. He taught Catalan sculptors for half a century and wielded an enormous, though not entirely positive, influence. He became Deputy Director of the Escuela de Bellas Artes, belonged to the Academia de Ciencias y Artes of Barcelona and won first prize at the Exposición Nacional de Madrid in 1871.

Almost all the work of Aleu y Teixidor is in Barcelona. The best is the over life-size stone sculpture of *St George* (1871) for the façade of the Palau de la Diputació General de Catalunya; it is heraldic, lively and appropriate to its location, although lacking in originality. Also important is the large equestrian statue of the *Marqués del Duero* (1883), the central bronze monument in the Paseo de la Castellana in Madrid. The work stimulated the revival, led by Catalan sculptors, of the equestrian statue in 19th-century Spain, although the results are often stiff and puppet-like. Stylistically Aleu y Teixidor's work belongs to the painstaking, academic realism of his time.

BIBLIOGRAPHY

P. Navascués Palacio, C. Pérez Reyes and A. M. Arias de Cossío: *Del Neoclasicismo al Modernismo*, Historia del Arte Hispánico, v (Madrid, 1978), p. 195

CARLOS CID PRIEGO

Alexanco, José Luis (*b* Madrid, 1942). Spanish painter, sculptor and printmaker. After studying at the Escuela Superior de Bellas Artes in Madrid he came under the influence of Pop art during a stay in London in 1965. On settling again in Madrid in that year he began to concentrate on images of movement, as in the screenprint *Story of the Man Who Falls I*, for which he was awarded a prize at the Kraków Biennale in 1966. He continued to explore movement through serial forms and stereotyped images in plexiglass constructions such as the *Changeable Movement* series (1967) and from 1968 used computers as part of this process. These interests led to sculptures and paintings titled *Transformable Movements*, which he presented in association with aleatoric music.

Alexanco became increasingly involved with performance and collaborated with the Spanish composer Luis de Pablo (*b* 1930) on *Soledad interrumpida* (1971) and *Historia natural* (1972), which combined de Pablo's tapes of electronic music with plastic objects provided by Alexanco; in 1972 he organized and coordinated *Encuentros de Pamplona*, an exhibition at the Ciudadela in Pamplona that proved to be an interdisciplinary event of great importance to the development of the avant-garde in Spain. Alexanco returned to painting between 1977 and 1979, notably in an exhibition, *Alfabeto para una constitución* (1978; Madrid, Gal. Vandrés), that was clearly political in its intentions.

BIBLIOGRAPHY

F. Calvo Serraller: *Alexanco: Lectura en imágenes, proceso y movimiento* (Madrid, 1983)

M. DOLORES JIMÉNEZ-BLANCO

Alexander VI, Pope. *See* BORGIA, (2).

Alexander VII, Pope. *See* CHIGI, (3).

Alexander, Christopher (*b* Vienna, 4 Oct 1936). British architect, theorist and writer. He studied architecture and mathematics at Cambridge University, England (1956–9), and at Harvard University, Cambridge, MA (1960–63). While at Harvard he was the joint author with Serge Chermayeff of *Community and Privacy* (1963), which was a discussion of urban courtyard house-plans by others of the time but which already contained the beginnings of a view of architecture as involving interactive processes rather than finished forms. In 1963 he took up his first faculty position at the University of California at Berkeley, later becoming professor of architecture there. In 1964 he published *Notes on a Synthesis of Form*, discussing the use of information theory in planning, with examples from his consulting work in India; in April and May 1965 he applied similar observations from mathematics to the current debate on lack of complexity in urban planning in the article 'A City is not a Tree'. In 1967 he was one of the founders of the Center for Environmental Structure in Berkeley, a cooperatively organized research group and practice.

The group's work was mainly devoted to competition entries and planning studies, and although this did not produce a large number of built examples, the publication of each project gave their ideas a wide audience and influence. One of the best known was an entry for a community housing competition (1969) for Lima, Peru, which proposed the use of unconventional technologies to build houses based on existing social patterns (published in 1968 as *Houses Generated by Patterns*). By the mid-1970s the group's theoretical ideas had begun to take the form exemplified in the project for a user-designed residential complex (1974) in St-Quentin-en-Yvelines, France, a three- to five-storey assembly of highly individualized dwelling units around courtyards, with exterior stairs and access decks.

At the core of Alexander's later work was his belief that there are universal principles of form and space based in the fundamental nature of human cognition and that these principles can be objectively determined by analysis and reproduced. In the aggregate these principles produce a quality that he referred to as 'timeless', which is found in the best buildings of all periods and cultures. In this search for unchanging universals of good design, he belonged to a long tradition of architectural thought; to this he added 20th-century science and philosophy, and in particular the idea that recent discoveries about the nature of information processing could be used to identify and codify individual criteria to which good buildings must adhere and which he called 'patterns'. For Alexander the actual substance of which the human environment is made consists of these patterns, rather than materials or buildings *per se*, and for an environment to be successful these patterns must be present in it. To arrive at such a condition requires large numbers of people.

The procedural consequences of these conclusions include substantial practical changes in the present relationship between the designer and society; in the relationship between the designer and the building contractor; in the processes of construction; in the flow of money through the environment; and finally in the politics of land ownership and control. Taken as a whole Alexander's work formed a new paradigm for architecture because it led directly to a fundamentally different way of perceiving and making buildings and towns, entailing the recognition that to produce the quality of timelessness the building itself needs to be constantly adapting or changing to meet its changing demands and inhabitants, and thus it is in a constant state of creation. To achieve this an amalgamation of designer, builder and user must occur. The codified summary of these ideas was published as *A Pattern Language* (1977); its companion volume, *The Timeless Way of Building* (1979), dealt with the basic philosophy behind the patterns and a history of how they were applied. The buildings of the new Eishin School Campus near Tokyo, completed between 1982 and 1985, represent the first mature demonstration of the Alexander group's ideas.

WRITINGS

with S. Chermayeff: *Community and Privacy: Towards a New Architecture of Humanism* (New York, 1963)
Notes on a Synthesis of Form (Cambridge, MA, 1964)
'A City Is not a Tree', *Archit. Forum*, cxxii (1965), no. 1, pp. 58–62; no. 2, pp. 58–61
'Thick Wall Pattern', *Archit. Des.*, xxxviii (July 1968), pp. 324–6
with others: *Houses Generated by Patterns* (Berkeley, 1968)
with others: *The Oregon Experiment* (London, 1975)
with others: *A Pattern Language* (London, 1977)
with others: *The Timeless Way of Building* (London, 1979)

BIBLIOGRAPHY

S. Grabow: *Christopher Alexander: The Search for a New Paradigm in Architecture* (Boston, 1983)
J. Shipskey: 'Christopher Alexander, Theory and Practice', *Architecture* [USA], lxxiii/7 (1984), pp. 54–63
'Construction of the New Eishin Campus', *Japan Architect*, lx/8 (1985), pp. 15–35
P. Valadis and T. Fisher: 'P/A Profile: Harmony and Wholeness', *Prog. Archit.*, lxvii/6 (1986), pp. 92–103

STEPHEN GRABOW

Alexander, Francis (*b* Killingly, CT, 3 Feb 1800; *d* Florence, 27 March 1880). American painter and lithographer. He studied briefly with Alexander Robertson (1768–1841) in New York and copied portraits by John Trumbull and Samuel Waldo. From 1821 to 1825 he painted portraits in Killingly, CT, and Providence, RI. He received encouraging advice from Gilbert Stuart in Boston, probably in 1825, and by 1828 was a prominent portrait painter and lithographer there. Portraits such as *Mrs Jared Sparks* (1830; Cambridge, MA, Harvard U.) demonstrate a well-developed sense of pattern and design but display some deficiency in draughtsmanship, with conventional shapes used to determine the sitter's features.

From 1831 to 1833 Alexander travelled and painted in Italy. After returning to Boston he exhibited 39 paintings in 1834 at Harding's Gallery, many of which were derived from the Italian trip. His unusually theatrical portrait of *Senator Daniel Webster* (1835; Hanover, NH, Dartmouth Coll., Hood Mus. A.) shows the effect of his exposure to Romanticism; Webster is presented with fiery eyes and wild hair, silhouetted against a dramatic sky. When Dickens visited America in 1842, Alexander aggressively sought him out and depicted him as a slight youth (Dickens was 30) seated casually behind a large table (Boston, MA, Mus. F.A.).

Alexander was made an honorary member of the National Academy of Design in New York in 1840. He returned to Italy in 1853, settling in Florence, where he collected early Renaissance art, gave up painting and became a friend of Hiram Powers, the leader of the city's American art colony. He revisited America only once, in 1868–9. Most of the paintings in his collection, which included works attributed to Perugino, Orcagna and Ghirlandaio, were destroyed while in storage in Boston during the great fire of 1873; the remainder were sold at auction at Leonard & Co., Boston, in 1874. His daughter Esther Frances (1837–1917), known as Francesca, became a painter, illustrator and poet.

UNPUBLISHED SOURCES

Cole papers, New York, Hist. Soc. [copies of Alexander's corr. etc, comp. E. Parker Lesley (1938–48)]

BIBLIOGRAPHY

C. G. Alexander: *Francesca Alexander* (Cambridge, MA, 1927)
W. Dunlap: *History of the Rise and Progress of the Arts of Design in the United States*, iii (New York, 1934, rev. 3/1965), pp. 232–40
C. W. Pierce: 'Francis Alexander', *Old-Time New England*, xliv (1953), pp. 29–46

LEAH LIPTON

Alexander, John White (*b* Allegheny, PA, 7 Oct 1856; *d* New York, 31 May 1915). American painter and illustrator. He began his career in New York in 1875 as a political cartoonist and illustrator for *Harper's Weekly*. In 1877 he went to Paris for his first formal art training, and then to Munich, where he enrolled at the Kunstakademie under Gyuala Benczur. In 1878 he joined a colony of American painters established by Frank Duveneck in Polling, Bavaria. In 1879 they travelled to Italy, where Alexander formed friendships with James McNeill Whistler and Henry James. In 1881 he returned to New York, working as an illustrator for *Harper's*, as a drawing instructor at Princeton and as a highly successful society portrait painter. He also exhibited at the National Academy of Design. By 1893 his reputation in both Europe and America had soared, and in 1895 he was awarded a prestigious commission for a series of murals entitled the *Evolution of the Book* in the newly established Library of Congress in Washington, DC. After 1901 Alexander became deeply involved with the promotion of the arts in America. He won numerous mural commissions (e.g. Pittsburgh, PA, Carnegie Inst.; from 1905, unfinished) and continued to paint portraits.

Alexander's stylistic development falls into several distinct stages. His early landscapes and genre scenes of the 1870s bear the stamp of Wilhelm Leibl's Munich realism as espoused by Duveneck and William Merritt Chase. His fluid brushwork resembled that of Frans Hals and Diego Velázquez, painters he deeply admired. After his return to the USA in 1881 and under the influence of Whistler, he favoured a more limited palette and experimented with the evocation of mood through shadow and gesture. His portrait of *Walt Whitman* (1886–9; New York, Met.) is one of his finest works of the 1880s. Many of his later portraits, notably of women, were psychological studies rather than specific likenesses: e.g. *The Ring* (1911; New York, Met.). His brushwork became less painterly and more concerned with suggesting abstracted shapes. He also adopted a very coarse-weave canvas, the texture of which became an important element in his mature work. By applying thinned-down paint to the absorbent surface, his pictures appear to have been dyed in muted tones, in marked contrast to the glossy, impasted surfaces of his earlier work. Throughout his career Alexander favoured compositions with a single figure placed against a sharply contrasting background. The sinuous curvilinear outline of the heroine standing full-length in *Isabella, or the Pot of Basil* (1897; Boston, MA, Mus. F.A.) evokes contemporary Art Nouveau forms. Like the Symbolists, he sought by gesture and strong lighting to intensify the viewer's response to his sensuous treatment of the subject.

UNPUBLISHED SOURCES

Washington DC, Smithsonian Inst., Archv Amer. A. [John White Alexander papers]

BIBLIOGRAPHY

G. Monrey: 'An American Painter in Paris: John W. Alexander', *Int. Studio*, xi (1900), pp. 71–7

Amer. Mag. A., vii (1916) [whole issue]

Catalogue of Paintings: John White Alexander Memorial Exhibition (Pittsburgh, PA, Carnegie Mus. A., 1916)

John White Alexander (1856–1915) (exh. cat. by M. Goley, Washington, DC, N. Col. F. A., 1976)

John White Alexander (1856–1915): Fin-de-siècle American (exh. cat. by S. Leff, New York, Graham Gal., 1980)

ELEANOR JONES HARVEY

Alexander, William (*b* Maidstone, Kent, 10 April 1767; *d* Maidstone, 23 July 1816). English painter, engraver, draughtsman and museum official. The son of a coach-builder, he was apprenticed to Julius Caesar Ibbetson before enrolling in 1784 at the Royal Academy Schools, London. In 1792 he accepted the post (previously declined by Ibbetson) of draughtsman to George, 1st Earl Macartney, on his embassy to China. As the embassy returned by inland waterway from Beijing to Canton, Alexander made detailed sketches of the Chinese hinterland—something achieved by no British artist previously and by very few subsequently. These sketches formed the basis for finished watercolours (e.g. *Ping-tze Muen, the Western Gate of Peking*, 1799; London, BM) and for numerous engravings by both himself and others. For over fifty years his images of China were widely borrowed by book illustrators and by interior decorators in search of exotic themes.

Alexander was also a keen student of British medieval antiquities, undertaking several tours in order to make drawings of churches and monuments; many of these were reproduced in the antiquarian publications of John Britton and others. In 1802 he became the first Master of Landscape Drawing at the Royal Military College, Great Marlow, Bucks. During his vacations he made drawings (engraved and published in 1805–7) of Egyptian antiquities in the British Museum, London, where he was appointed Assistant Keeper of Prints and Drawings in 1808. He suffered from rheumatism, contracted (he believed) from the damp in the walls of the newly built British Museum.

BIBLIOGRAPHY

S. Legouix: *Image of China: William Alexander* (London, 1980)

William Alexander: An English Artist in Imperial China (exh. cat. by S. Legouix and P. Conner, Brighton, A.G. & Mus., 1981)

PATRICK CONNER

Alexander of Abingdon (*fl* 1291–1317). English sculptor. His first recorded works are in connection with the funerary monuments for Queen Eleanor of Castile (*d* 1290), the first wife of King Edward I. Alexander of Abingdon supplied wax models for three small images cast by William of Suffolk for the heart tomb in the Dominican church of the Blackfriars, London, as well as a painted cloth and ironwork to stand round the tomb (all destr.). From 1291 to 1294 he was also employed with Dymenge de Legeris on carving the Purbeck marble tomb-chest for the bronze effigy (both destr.) of Eleanor in Lincoln Cathedral. From William Sedgwick's drawing of *c.* 1641, which is included in Sir William Dugdale's *Book of Monuments* (London, BL, Loan MS. 38, fol. 98*v*), it appears to have been very similar to that still surviving at Westminster Abbey, London. Alexander supplied seven images at a cost of 5 marks each for the Charing Mews Eleanor Cross (destr.; *see* CROSS, §II, 3).

Alexander's only surviving documented works are the three statues from the Waltham Eleanor Cross (on loan to London, V&A). All are very weathered, and one has lost its original head, but they still reveal the restrained poses, elegant draperies and idealization that can also be seen in the imagery on the tombs of *Edmund Crouchback, Earl of Lancaster* (*d* 1296) in Westminster Abbey and of *Bishop de Luda* (*d* 1298) at Ely Cathedral. In 1312 Alexander entered into a bond to complete his contract (presumably for figure sculpture) with the parson of Stanwell Church, Middx (now Surrey). Alexander was perhaps the most influential English sculptor of his day and worked alongside the greatest craftsmen of his generation: in 1316–17, when he is last documented, he was associated with Michael of Canterbury and William de Hoo.

BIBLIOGRAPHY

Harvey

B. Botfield: *Manners and Household Expenses of England in the Thirteenth and Fifteenth Centuries*, ed. T. Hudson Turner, Roxburghe Club (London, 1841)

E. S. Prior and A. Gardner: *An Account of Medieval Figure-sculpture in England* (Cambridge, 1912)

L. Stone: *Sculpture in Britain: The Middle Ages*, Pelican Hist. A. (Harmondsworth, 1972)

P. G. Lindley: 'The Tomb of Bishop William de Luda: An Architectural Model at Ely Cathedral', *Proc. Cambridge Antiqua. Soc.*, lxxiii (1984), pp. 75–87

The Age of Chivalry: Art in Plantagenet England (exh. cat., ed. J. J. G. Alexander and P. Binski; London, RA, 1987)

M. J. H. Liverside: 'Alexander of Abingdon', *Abingdon Essays: Studies in Local History* (Abingdon, 1989), pp. 89–111

PHILLIP LINDLEY

Alexander the Great [Alexander III], King of Macedon (*b* Pella, Macedonia, 356 BC; *reg* 336–323 BC; *d* Babylon, 10 June 323 BC). Macedonian monarch and patron. Having inherited the kingdom from his assassinated father, Philip of Macedon (*reg* 359–336 BC), he invaded Asia in 334 BC and twice defeated the Persians. After invading Egypt, he founded ALEXANDRIA in 331 BC and was hailed by the oracle of Amun at Siwah as 'Son of Zeus'. He then moved into Persia, crushed the main Persian army at Gaugamela, occupied Persepolis, Susa and Pasargadae and declared himself Great King. Advancing via Afghanistan into India, he founded *en route* several other Alexandrias. However, after his defeat of the Indian king Porus in 326 BC, his army mutinied, compelling his return to Babylon. Increasingly alcoholic and devastated by the death of his lover Hephaistion but still planning further conquests, he died of a fever in 323 BC. Alexander's patronage of major artists and his conquest of the Near East were major catalysts for change in Greek art, so that within a generation of his death the parochial artistic styles of the Classical city states had given way to the cosmopolitan art of the Hellenistic world.

Though an edict (Pliny: *Natural History* VII.xxxvii.125) whereby no-one but the bronze sculptor LYSIPPOS, the painter APELLES and the gemcutter Pyrgoteles could make Alexander's portrait is certainly fictitious, and no original portraits have survived, those three artists virtually created the iconography of royal portraiture that became central to the Western artistic tradition. Lysippos established the heroic ruler portrait as a distinct genre, while Apelles painted Alexander with the attributes of the gods, though Pyrgoteles' particular contribution remains obscure. Moreover, both sculptor and painter represented the King in narrative scenes: the battles, hunts and processions that became the staples of later royal iconography. All three artists were technical virtuosos: though Pyrgoteles' skills are unspecified, Lysippos blended subtle idealization of the King's features with realistic detail, while Apelles introduced new technical devices, such as lustre, and painted with exceptional grace.

Deinokrates of Rhodes was also associated with Alexander (e.g. by Vitruvius: *On Architecture* II. Preface). Though the King rejected his proposal to turn Mt Athos into a gigantic royal portrait, he employed him to plan Alexandria and to build Hephaistion's memorial in Babylon. Both schemes influenced later works: Alexandria's wide, straight streets and rectangular blocks organized on the Hippodamian pattern (*see* HIPPODAMOS) provided the prototype for hundreds of new foundations in the Hellenistic East, while the memorial, which apparently had a profusion of gilded statues, costly tapestries and other embellishments, heralded the extravagances of the Hellenistic monarchs.

The new cities founded in the wake of Alexander's conquests created an immense demand for buildings and works of art, met by the pupils of Lysippos and Apelles as well as by many independent artists. Looted Persian treasure provided the financial base for this unprecedented expansion of Greek culture and engendered a taste for luxury among the colonial élites. Fourth-century BC Macedonian court art had been largely inspired by Attic models: the gold, silver and bronze vessels in Macedonian tombs reproduced Attic shapes and were embellished with updated versions of the elaborate figures and florals of later 5th-century BC Attic pottery. Thanks to Alexander, this Macedonian decorative art came to dominate Hellenistic culture from Egypt to Afghanistan.

BIBLIOGRAPHY

Plutarch: *Life of Alexander*
——: *On the Fortune or Virtue of Alexander*
Diodorus Siculus: *Universal History XVII*
Arrian: *Anabasis of Alexander*
Quintus Curtius Rufus: *History of Alexander*
W. W. Tarn: *Alexander the Great* (Cambridge, 1948/*R* 1979)
J. R. Hamilton: *Alexander the Great* (London, 1973/*R* Pittsburgh, 1979)
M. Andronikos and others: *The Search for Alexander: An Exhibition* (Boston, 1980)
R. Lane Fox: *The Search for Alexander* (Boston, 1980)
B. Barr-Sharrarr and E. N. Borza, eds: *Macedonia and Greece in Late Classical and Early Hellenistic Times* (Washington, DC, 1982)
J. J. Pollitt: *Art in the Hellenistic Age* (Cambridge, 1986)
A. Stewart: *Faces of Power: Alexander's Image and Hellenistic Politics* (Berkeley and Los Angeles, 1993)

ANDREW F. STEWART

Alexander von Buren. *See under* PASQUALINI, (1).

Alexandre, Arsène [Pierre Urbain] (*b* Paris, 1859; *d* Paris, 1937). French writer and collector. He wrote for a number of journals including *Le Figaro*, *Le Voltaire* and *L'Evénement*. He was the first to use the term Neo-Impressionism in a French publication (*L'Evénement*, 10 Dec 1886) after its use by Félix Fénéon in September in *Art moderne* in Brussels. His attitude to the emerging Neo-Impressionist movement was somewhat equivocal. In *Paris* (13 Aug 1888) he wrote of Seurat as 'the man of great achievements who is in some danger of having the paternity of his own theory wrested from him by ill-informed critics or unscrupulous colleagues'. Although he admired Seurat, he had grave doubts about the effect of his theories on other artists, claiming (in the same article) that they had 'spoilt some great talents, painters like Angrand and Signac'. His comments particularly infuriated Paul Signac and caused tension within the group. He also wrote on the work of the Impressionists and showed more wholehearted support for the older movement than for Neo-Impressionism. He wrote the catalogue preface for the large retrospective exhibition of his friend Renoir's work at the Durand-Ruel Galerie in Paris in 1892. Later he wrote a review of the first Cézanne exhibition at Ambroise Vollard's gallery in Paris in November 1895, stating that many young artists, consciously or otherwise, had been influenced by Cézanne. He also wrote catalogue prefaces for other exhibitions and sales of Impressionist painting: on Pissarro in 1896, on Sisley in 1899 and on Monet in 1919 for his exhibition at the Bernheim Gallery, Paris. The monograph *Claude Monet* (1921) included many of his more general opinions on Impressionism. He claimed that the label Impressionist was misleading as a description of the works usually denoted by it: while some paintings could be so described, many others could not. He suggested *harmoniste* as a more appropriate term that reflected what he felt to be the primary aim of the Impressionists: an attempt to achieve a harmony of colour and line.

In *Histoire de la peinture militaire en France* (1890), Alexandre surveyed French military painting from the 17th century onwards, including such artists as Jacques Callot, Joseph Parrocel, Anne-Louis Girodet, François Gérard, Carle Vernet, Antoine-Jean Gros, Théodore Géricault and Eugène Lami. He hoped the book would rebut the criticism that military painting was superficial, unrefined and only depicted subjects that were better forgotten. In *Histoire de l'art décoratif du XVIe siècle à nos jours* (1891) he surveyed all aspects of the applied arts, including furniture, jewellery, porcelain, textiles and armour. In 1892 he founded and then directed the humorous journal *Le Rire* and, confirming this interest in comic art, wrote *L'Art de rire et de la caricature* (1893), in which he described the history of European caricature from the classical period to his own day. He commissioned many works for *Le Rire* from Henri de Toulouse-Lautrec and wrote several staunch defences of Toulouse-Lautrec's work in *Le Figaro.* He was also an avid collector. A number of his Impressionist paintings were sold in 1919, including Seurat's *Seine at Courbevoie* (*c.* 1887; U. London, Courtauld Inst. Gals), Toulouse-Lautrec's *Yvette Guilbert Singing 'Linger Longer Loo'* (1894; Moscow, Pushkin Mus. F.A.) and works by Cézanne, Renoir, Pissarro, Henri Fantin-Latour, Albert-Charles Lebourg and Jean-François Raffaëlli.

WRITINGS

Honoré Daumier: L'Homme et l'oeuvre (Paris, 1888)
Histoire de la peinture militaire en France (Paris, 1890)
Histoire de l'art décoratif du XVIe siècle à nos jours (Paris, 1891)
L'Art de rire et de la caricature (Paris, 1893)
Donatello (Paris, 1905)
Jean-François Raffaëlli: Peintre, graveur et sculpteur (Paris, 1909)
Claude Monet (Paris, 1921)
Maxime Maufra: Peintre marin et rustique, 1861–1918 (Paris, 1926)
Paul Gauguin: Sa vie et le sens de son oeuvre (Paris, 1930)

BIBLIOGRAPHY

J. Sutter, ed.: *The Neo-Impressionists* (London, 1970)
S. Monneret: *Impressionisme et son époque*, i (Paris, 1978), p. 37

□

Alexandria. Egyptian city situated on the Mediterranean coast west of the delta of the River Nile, capital of Egypt from *c.* 320 BC to AD 642, seaport and centre of ancient Greek culture.

1. Early history. 2. Hellenistic and Roman. 3. Christian. 4. Islamic.

1. EARLY HISTORY. Alexandria was founded in 331 BC by ALEXANDER THE GREAT, on the site of the small Egyptian settlement of Rhakotis. Its location, with access by canal to the River Nile, enabled it to become an important and highly prosperous trading centre, and by *c.* 320 BC Alexandria was the capital of Ptolemaic Egypt. During Ptolemaic times (304–30 BC) it became a major centre of learning, with famous scholars of literature, mathematics, astronomy, medicine and geography, and it played a major role in the transmission of Greek culture to the East.

With the defeat of the last Ptolemaic monarch, Cleopatra VII (51–30 BC), by Octavian (later called Augustus) at the Battle of Actium in 30 BC, Egypt became a Roman province, though enjoying certain privileges. In AD 116 under Trajan conflict erupted between the Greek and Jewish sections of the population. In AD 215 Caracalla (AD 211–17) visited Alexandria and ordered the massacre of the city's youth. Following a short period of rule by Zenobia, Queen of Palmyra (*reg* AD 260–70), Roman reassertion of control by Aurelian (AD 215–75) reportedly resulted in the destruction of the royal quarter in AD 272. The revolt of the city from Rome in AD 297/8 initiated further destruction by Diocletian, who four years later began the 'Great Persecution' of the Christians. Under Theodosius I, however, pagan cults were formally abolished and their sacred buildings razed (AD 391).

Alexandria remained the administrative centre of Egypt throughout Byzantine times and during the Persian occupation of AD 618–28. After the Arab conquest in AD 642, however, the capital of Egypt was moved to Cairo, and Alexandria declined. Even so, despite extensive earthquake damage in the 14th century, it remained Egypt's main port, although by the beginning of the 19th century the former city was no more than a small village. Its redevelopment began under Muhammad 'Ali, Viceroy of Egypt 1805–48.

2. HELLENISTIC AND ROMAN.

(i) Architecture. (ii) Sculpture. (iii) Mosaics. (iv) Pottery. (v) Painting.

(i) Architecture. Virtually none of Alexandria's ancient buildings remains visible, and the only famous buildings whose sites are known are Pharos (the lighthouse), the Serapeion and the Caesareum (Temple of Augustus). Thus knowledge of the city's plans and buildings is based almost entirely on literary references. Aristeas' *Letter to Philokrates* (IV.g.109) describes it in the mid-2nd century BC as 'a city surpassing all others in size and prosperity', and around 59 BC Diodorus Siculus (*Historical Library* XVII.lii.5) described it as the first city of the civilized world. Strabo (*Geography* XVII.i.6–10) described the city layout and certain specific buildings as they appeared *c.* 24–20 BC, and, although many of these were doubtless altered by Byzantine times, the main structures are recognizable in descriptions of the city by early Arab historians, who marvelled at its architecture. The earthquakes of the 14th century obliterated the remaining buildings of ancient Alexandria, although the subsidence that caused at least part of the royal quarter to sink under water means that some remains are visible on the harbour bed. With this exception, the ancient city is covered by the buildings of modern Alexandria, constructed during the 19th and 20th centuries. Digging foundations for these has resulted in the discovery of Ptolemaic and Roman rock-cut tombs at Shatby, Moustapha Pasha, Wardian, Gabbari, Anfoushy and Kom el Shogafa and also in the discovery of architectural fragments that suggest that many features of Baroque architecture were originally invented in Ptolemaic Alexandria. Since 1960, formal excavations by Polish archaeologists have uncovered some Roman and Byzantine buildings, including houses, a small theatre and baths.

Alexander the Great is said to have designated the main areas of the city: the walls, the agora and the sanctuaries of the Greek gods and Isis (see Arrian: *Anabasis* III.i.5). He was helped by the Macedonian architect and city planner Denokrates (Vitruvius: *On Architecture* II. Preface. 1–4). It is generally assumed that Alexandria was laid out on a grid pattern, but the only detailed description of its plan occurs in Strabo (XVII.i.6–10). The first landmark for those arriving by sea was the Island of Pharos, with its famous lighthouse and Sanctuary of Isis. This was connected to the mainland by a causeway seven stades (*c.* 1400 m) long, the Heptastadion, built by Cleomenes or Ptolemy I (*reg c.* 323–282 BC), which formed two harbours: the Great Harbour to the east and the harbour of Eunostos to the west. South of this, the city centre was marked by the intersection of two avenues, one running east–west, the other north–south. According to Strabo, immediately to the east of the Heptastadion were the ship-sheds, warehouses, emporion (market) and Caesareum. Further east, along the shore of the eastern harbour, was the royal quarter including the Mouseion, the Sema (or Soma), an inner palace, and the theatre overlooking the sea. Along the principal east–west road were some temples, the gymnasium and the law court. To the south-west was the Serapeion, and the necropoleis were outside the city on the east and west.

The lighthouse of Pharos (begun *c.* 297–270 BC) stood *c.* 100 m high and was one of the Seven Wonders of the ancient world. It is known mainly from literary sources and representations on coins, and it consisted of four storeys: the lowest was square, the second octagonal, the third cylindrical, with a fourth supporting the lantern and its reflector. It continued in use until the Arab conquest in AD 642, but around AD 700 the top two storeys fell down. They were restored, but *c.* 1100 the octagonal section again collapsed, and the rest was destroyed by an earthquake in the 14th century. The modern site is marked by the 15th-century Fort Qa'itbay.

The Mouseion (Sanctuary of the Muses) was founded by Ptolemy I (or Ptolemy II) and was an enlarged version of that at Athens. It was the workplace of Alexandrian scholars and included a promenade, an 'exedra', a large dining-room and the largest library in the ancient world. The history of the latter is controversial (*see* §4 below). Some of its books were possibly burnt by Julius Caesar in 48 BC, others possibly by Aurelian *c.* AD 272, but the reports of the Arab historians, which claimed that even after the Arab invasion there remained sufficient books to fuel the furnaces of Alexandria's baths for six months, have caused much argument. There were also private libraries, as well as libraries in temples, churches and monasteries. Both Severus (in AD 200) and Diocletian (in *c.* AD 300) attempted to ban or burn some books.

The tomb of Alexander was built by Ptolemy I. It possibly survived the reported destruction of the royal quarter in AD 272: there are 5th-century AD reports of the Sema being near the city crossroads.

The site of the Serapeion, marked by 'Pompey's Pillar', was determined by the discovery in 1944 of foundation plaques recording its construction (or rebuilding) by Ptolemy III (*reg* 246–222 BC). It was surrounded by a colonnade enclosing shrines of Serapis, Isis and Harpocrates. It was burnt down in AD 181 and rebuilt by the early 4th century. In AD 391 it was damaged by the Christians, who later erected a monastery and church on its ruins. 'Pompey's Pillar' is a red granite Corinthian column, which seems to have been erected *c.* AD 296–7 or 302 and may have carried a statue of Diocletian. Its popular misnomer may have originated with the crusaders.

The site of the Caesareum was marked by Cleopatra's Needles (two red granite obelisks, now in London, on the Thames Embankment, and New York, Central Park; moved in 1887 and 1889 respectively). The temple was begun by Cleopatra VII in honour of Mark Antony, but after her death it was completed by Augustus, who consecrated it to himself. The obelisks came originally from the temple at Heliopolis and were erected in 13 BC. The Caesareum was described by Philon of Alexandria (*Legation to Gaius*, 151) as decorated on an unparalleled scale and housing various structures in an enormous precinct. It was converted in AD 324–8 to a church of St Michael, which became the seat of the Patriarch of Alexandria but was finally destroyed in AD 912.

Visits to Alexandria by Roman emperors sometimes prompted construction or renovation projects. Thus around 31 BC Augustus built the suburb of Nikopolis to the east of the city, while in AD 130 Hadrian restored the monuments damaged during the conflicts with the Jews during Trajan's reign. Antoninus Pius (AD 138–61) constructed the Gate of the Sun in the east of the city and the Gate of the Moon in the west.

The Graeco-Roman Museum in Alexandria contains numerous Ptolemaic architectural fragments (see fig. 1). These show that the earliest examples of many features later associated with Baroque architecture survive from Ptolemaic Alexandria, including broken pediments, segmental pediments, pediments with recessed centres, broken out entablatures and vertically and horizontally curved entablatures. Ptolemaic cornices and Corinthian capitals have distinctive forms, which influenced the architecture of other regions. In this way, depictions of architecture in Pompeian wall paintings of the Second Style (*c.* 60–30 BC; such as those in the House of the Labyrinth; *see* POMPEII, §IV) and such monuments at Petra as the Khasneh both reflect Alexandrian models and lend credence to descriptions of the pavilion of Ptolemy II (*reg* 285–246 BC) and the riverboat of Ptolemy IV (Athenaeus: *Deipnosophists* V.196a–197c and 204d–206d).

BIBLIOGRAPHY

E. Breccia: *Alexandrea ad Aegyptum* (Bergamo, 1922)

E. M. Forster: *Alexandria: A History and a Guide* (Alexandria, 1922, 2/1938, rev. 3/1986, London)

A. Adriani: *Annuaire du musée gréco-romain, 1933–50* (Alexandria, 1934–52)

——: *Repertorio d'arte dell'Egitto greco-romano*, C (Palermo, 1963–6)

1. Ptolemaic architectural fragments from Alexandria, *c.* 323–*c.* 30 BC (Alexandria, Graeco-Roman Museum)

S. K. Hamarneh: 'The Ancient Monuments of Alexandria according to Accounts by Medieval Arab Authors (IX–XV Century)', *Fol. Orient.*, xiii (1971), pp. 77–110
P. M. Fraser: *Ptolemaic Alexandria*, 3 vols (Oxford, 1972)
M. Lyttelton: *Baroque Architecture in Classical Antiquity* (London, 1974)
N. Hinske, ed.: *Alexandrien* (1981), i of *Aegyptiaca Treverensia* (Mainz, 1981–)
J. McKenzie: *The Architecture of Petra* (Oxford, 1990), pp. 61–104
P. Pensabene: *Elementi architettonici di Alessandria e di altri siti Egiziani* (Rome, 1993)

JUDITH MCKENZIE

(ii) Sculpture. A substantial body of sculpture survives from Alexandria. While scholars no longer look for an all-embracing Alexandrian style, the sculptures do have a number of distinctive features, most clearly in marble technique and in royal portraiture. Alexandria had to import all its marble, and various stone-saving techniques can lend its sculpture a characteristic appearance. 'Piecing' different parts of marble statues was common practice in the Hellenistic period, but at Alexandria a single head could be made up of several pieces. Stucco was also used frequently to complete hair, beards and the backs of heads, making a virtue of economy by its light, impressionistic effect. The best marble pieces also have a distinctive surface treatment: the marble is brought to a near polish that exposes its crystal structure. This technique is often combined in the heads of gods and kings with a rather formless or simplified treatment of the face and features.

Royal heads, in a strikingly consistent and homogeneous style, make up the largest single category of sculpture surviving from Hellenistic Alexandria. The portraits tend to have short hair, round, bulging eyes (greatly exaggerated on the coinage) and placid, often plump features. This stiffer, more subdued royal style makes a clear contrast with the longer-haired, more heroic-looking image of the contemporary Seleukids. The unusual prominence of Ptolemaic queens is also well reflected in the sculptural record. The great 3rd-century BC queens, Arsinoe II and Berenike II, were represented in striking images of refined, sometimes mannered, beauty, seen both on coins and in sculpture. *Arsinoe* is fine-featured, *Berenike* full-faced. Their idealized portraits provided influential models for images of queens elsewhere and for Hellenistic women in general. In the 2nd century BC a more vigorous and 'masculine' royal style appeared in some of the portraits of the first Cleopatras (I–III), often combined with the long cork-screw hairstyle of Isis (e.g. a fine head in Paris, Louvre).

Sculptured representations of Isis and Serapis, the two major deities promoted by the Ptolemies, survive in great numbers from Alexandria, both being portrayed in a purely Hellenistic style. BRYAXIS produced a famous seated cult statue of Serapis in the 4th century BC. The great range of more ordinary small-scale sculpture in marble, bronze and terracotta is also typical of other Hellenistic centres and includes grave reliefs, marble statuettes of *Aphrodite* and refined 'Tanagra' ladies in terracotta. Hellenistic genre realism was clearly part of the Alexandrian repertory. One of the rare life-size statues in this manner, the *Drunken Old Woman*, a remarkable, harshly observed figure known in two Roman copies (2nd century BC; Munich, Glyp., and Rome, Mus. Capitolino; *see* GREECE, ANCIENT, fig. 68), was probably from an Alexandrian context: the old woman clutches a *lagynos*, a type of wine jar associated with a festival of Dionysos at Alexandria founded in the later 3rd century BC.

In the Roman period several important changes occurred. The imperial image replaced the Ptolemaic; mixing of Egyptian and Hellenistic forms became much more pronounced (best seen in the Kom al-Shawqafah necropolis); and imported marble became much more abundant, especially from the 2nd century AD. Much of the imported marble is marked by heavy grey veins that can discolour a whole head; it came probably from the imperial quarries on Prokonnesos. The many Alexandrian garland sarcophagi of the 1st and 2nd centuries AD are now recognized to have been carved locally from imported Prokonnesian 'blanks'. In the 1st century AD imperial portrait sculptors continued to employ the old Hellenistic marble-saving techniques. They also tended to adjust the metropolitan portrait models with a variety of expressive Hellenistic traits more in keeping with local perceptions of the emperor. This can be seen in major surviving heads of *Augustus*, *Tiberius*, *Claudius*, *Agrippina the Younger* and *Vespasian* (Alexandria, Gr.–Roman Mus.). In the 2nd century AD both imperial and private portraits depended much more closely on Roman models and styles, carved in the larger blocks of marble now available. As everywhere in the 2nd century AD and early 3rd, there is increased quantity and uniformity. Alexandria's latest Roman sculpture includes some slender togate statues of the later 4th century AD or the 5th.

BIBLIOGRAPHY

A. W. Lawrence: 'Greek Sculpture in Ptolemaic Egypt', *J. Egyp. Archaeol.*, xi (1925), pp. 179–90
A. Adriani: *Testimonianze e monumenti di scultura alessandrina* (Rome, 1948)
——: *Repertorio d'arte dell'Egitto greco-romano*, A/ii (Palermo, 1961)
H. Kyrieleis: *Bildnisse der Ptolemäer* (Berlin, 1975)
H. Jucker: 'Römische Herrscherbildnisse aus Ägypten', *Aufstieg und Niedergang der römischen Welt*, II/xii/2 (Berlin, 1981), pp. 667–725
Z. Kiss: *Etudes sur le portrait impérial romain en Egypte* (Warsaw, 1984)
R. R. R. Smith: *Hellenistic Sculpture* (London, 1991), chap. 11

R. R. R. SMITH

(iii) Mosaics. Mosaic floors were introduced to Egypt by the Greeks after the conquest of the country by Alexander the Great, although they were popular only in Alexandria where the specialized workshops were apparently concentrated. Twenty-four Hellenistic mosaics have been found in the city: eight with figural decoration and sixteen (complete or fragmentary) either plain or with geometric decoration consisting of simple coloured bands or three-dimensional depictions of wave-crests and meanders. The number of mosaics increased greatly in the Roman period, with over 100 examples uncovered in Alexandria and its vicinity (at Canopos and the Mareotis region), although many of them have since been destroyed.

The three earliest mosaics were found within the royal quarters of the town, and, significantly, the Zenon Papyrus (Cairo, Egyp. Mus., P. Zenon 59665) implies the existence of a royal mosaic workshop in Alexandria around the mid-3rd century BC. The earliest specimen (probably end of the 4th century BC; Alexandria, Gr.–Roman Mus., 11125) was made of pebbles and a few tesserae (cut stones) and represents a warrior surrounded by a frieze of real and mythological animals. The second one (Alexandria, Gr.–

Roman Mus., 21643), superbly executed in tesserae and pebbles, may be dated to the first half of the 3rd century BC. It depicts *Three Erotes Hunting a Stag* and a frieze of animals (*see* GREECE, ANCIENT, fig. 144). The third mosaic (second half of the 3rd century BC; Alexandria, Gr.–Roman Mus., 25659, 25660), made of tesserae and only a few pebbles, represents a running centaur and a stag. The three examples demonstrate the transition from pebble mosaics to those made of tesserae. All are largely black and white, although some red, yellow and blue tesserae or pebbles were used for details, particularly in the second pavement. Lead strips were used for contours and anatomical details. Iconographically and stylistically, these works continued the tradition of early Hellenistic pebble mosaics in Macedonia and Greece, and, although some scholars have regarded them as examples of a Neo-classical style of the late 1st century BC, this has now been discredited.

By the late 3rd century BC or early 2nd, mosaics in *opus vermiculatum* (made of extremely small multicoloured tesserae) appeared for the first time. The best examples, apparently by Alexandrian artists, were found in Thmuis (Tell Timai), to the south of the city. Of particular interest is a mosaic emblema signed by Sophilos depicting a woman in military attire (see fig. 2). Long considered a personification of Alexandria or some maritime city, it has now been identified as a copy of a painting most likely of Queen Berenike II (*reg* 246–221 BC). Datable to *c.* 200 BC, it is the earliest emblema in *opus vermiculatum* known from antiquity. Two excellent mosaics with figural decoration, probably of the same workshop, were accidentally found in 1993 in the royal quarters of the town. In the late 2nd and 1st century BC Alexandrian artists continued the *vermiculatum* and fine *tesselatum* techniques. Small mosaic pictures on terracotta or stone trays made for local use or export depicted subjects such as domestic and wild birds, mythological themes and realistic Nilotic scenes.

In Roman Imperial times the Alexandrian mosaics developed in the same general way as their counterparts elsewhere, though with closer links to Italy and the West than to the eastern provinces or North Africa. Their decoration was mostly geometric, often in black and white only. Several interesting compositions feature a shield of scales within a square frame; mythological subjects and pictures of birds are rare. Notable complexes of mosaics of the late 1st and the 2nd and 3rd centuries AD were found at Kom el-Dikka in Alexandria and in Canopos, while the latest specimens, geometric and rather crude, dating to the 6th century AD, were also found at Kom el-Dikka.

2. Alexandrian mosaic by Sophilos: *Queen Berenike II*, 1.44 m. sq., from Thmuis, *c.* 200 BC (Alexandria, Graeco–Roman Museum)

BIBLIOGRAPHY

B. R. Brown: *Ptolemaic Paintings and Mosaics and the Alexandrian Style* (Cambridge, MA, 1957)

K. Parlasca: 'Hellenistische und römische Mosaiken aus Ägypten', *La Mosaique gréco-romaine ii: Colloque international: Vienne, 1971*, pp. 363–9

W. A. Daszewski: 'Some Problems of Early Mosaics from Egypt', *Das Ptolemaischen Ägypten: Akten des internationalen Symposiums: Berlin, 1976*, pp. 123–36

D. Salzmann: *Untersuchungen zu den antiken Kieselmosaiken* (Berlin, 1982), nos 133, 134, 143, 147, 152

M. Rodziewicz: *Alexandrie III: Les Habitations romaines tardives d'Alexandrie* (Warsaw, 1984)

W. A. Daszewski: *Corpus of Mosaics from Egypt I: Hellenistic and Early Roman Period* (Mainz, 1985)

WIKTOR A. DASZEWSKI

(iv) Pottery. The excavations at Alexandria have yielded a mass of pottery that by the late 1990s had been studied only superficially. Formerly much of this was attributed to Alexandria, but now it has become clear that most of the fine pottery was imported. Imports include examples of late Red-figure ware, Gnathia ware, glossy black-glazed ware, West Slope ware and moulded bowls, the last especially from Asia Minor. The Hadra vases, a class of clay-ground vases with a decoration in black clay paint, were once held to be Alexandrian, but they were in fact made in Crete, mainly in the second half of the 3rd century BC. They were exported in great numbers to Alexandria to serve as cinerary urns and later imitated by a native Egyptian workshop. The Alexandrian white-ground hydriai, sometimes also called Hadra vases, are, however, genuinely Alexandrian, as their clay shows. On the white surface they bear polychrome painting, sometimes very well done. These hydriai too were meant to serve as cinerary urns. The Plakettenvasen, a class of black-glazed ribbed ware with reliefs, seem to have originated in south Italy, but there is some evidence that production was continued later on at Alexandria, where a number have been unearthed. At any rate there seems to have been production of black-glazed pottery of lower quality. No doubt some of the Greco-Egyptian faience vessels were made in Alexandria, especially those with a marked Greek character, for example the oinochoai depicting Ptolemaic queens, nearly all of which have been found at Alexandria.

Most of the undecorated and coarse pottery found at Alexandria was also made there. The suggestion that good clays were not available in the Delta seems to be incorrect. Several different clays were used there, the most characteristic being the marly clays, which contain a lot of mica and white particles. Both Greek and Egyptian potters worked at Alexandria. The latter used simple marly clays and apparently did not know the techniques of levigation and turning. There are, however, examples of good Greek pottery made of fine local clay. In late Hellenistic times, when wine factories around the nearby Lake Mareotis started to flourish, a great number of transport amphorae were needed, and many pottery workshops were established near the lake. The big mounds of wasters they left can still be seen, and many amphorae from the Mareotis region have been found at Alexandria. During the Roman period fine ware such as *terra sigillata* and North African *sigillata* was imported.

BIBLIOGRAPHY

D. Burr Thompson: *Ptolemaic Oinochoai and Portraits in Faience: Aspects of the Ruler-cult* (Oxford, 1973)

M. Rodziewicz: *La Céramique romaine tardive d'Alexandrie* (1976), i of *Alexandrie* (Warsaw, 1976–)

P. J. Callaghan and R. E. Jones: 'Hadra Hydriai and Central Crete: A Fabric Analysis', *Annu. Brit. Sch. Athens*, lxxx (1985), pp. 1–17

T. Dohrn: 'Schwarzgefirnisste Plakettenvasen', *Mitt. Dt. Archäol. Inst.: Röm. Abt.*, xcii (1985), pp. 77–106

A. H. Enklaar: 'Chronologie et peintres des hydries de Hadra', *Bull. Ant. Besch.*, lx (1985), pp. 106–51

J.-Y. Empereur: *Recherches sur les amphores grecques* (Paris, 1986), pp. 103–9

A. H. Enklaar: 'Les Hydries de Hadra II: Formes et ateliers', *Bull. Ant. Besch.*, lxi (1986), pp. 41–65

——: *Etudes alexandrines* (in preparation)

A. H. ENKLAAR

(v) Painting. Virtually all the extant examples of Ptolemaic and Roman painting from Alexandria come from funerary contexts. Because the site has been continuously occupied since the foundation of the city, few frescoes from houses or public buildings have survived, and consequently we have a distorted view of the techniques, style and subject-matter of Greco-Roman painting in the metropolis. In addition, scholars dispute questions of dating, the possible influence of Alexandrian art on painting styles elsewhere, and the extent to which contemporary mosaics can provide reliable evidence for the style and subject-matter of paintings now lost.

3. Painting from the Wardian tomb, Alexandria, with an ox-drawn water-wheel and a boy playing the panpipes, probably mid-2nd century AD (Alexandria, Graeco-Roman Museum)

The earliest examples of Alexandrian paintings are on the so-called *loculus* slabs excavated in the cemeteries of Ibrahimiya and Hadra. These grave stelai, carved in the form of a temple façade, have a central panel, flanked by columns and surmounted by a pediment, bearing a painted representation of the deceased executed in a naturalistic style comparable with contemporary funerary art from elsewhere in the Hellenistic world, particularly Athenian grave monuments: there is no discernible Egyptian influence. The *loculus* slabs have a narrow range of subjects, with soldiers usually depicted 'heroically' on horseback or standing frontally holding their weapons; females are seated, often with an attendant or child, as in the Attic precursors of these stelai. The Mustafa Pasha tomb, probably mid-3rd century BC, is decorated with figures, in a lively post-Praxitelean style, which recall frescoes of the same period from Delos. Later rock-cut tombs, however, such as those in the Anfushi cemetery and the Tegran tomb, show an interesting blend of Hellenistic and Egyptian iconography. A niche in the Tegran tomb (probably 2nd century BC) has a typically Egyptian funerary scene, with the mummified deceased on a bier flanked by two mourning goddesses and the necropolis god Anubis. However, the smilax garlands and the draperies on the bier are executed in a Hellenistic idiom and are not elements of the same scene when it appears in purely Egyptian contexts. Some paintings in the Anfushi tombs, such as the scenes of ritual corpse lustration in Tomb II, are grounded firmly in indigenous traditions of wall painting, while other tombs in the same necropolis have a mixture of styles. A burial chamber in Tomb V, for instance, has a decorative scheme of an entablature supported by 15 ornamental pilasters, with date and palm trees between the pilasters painted in Egyptian style; the ceiling, however, has a typical Hellenistic coffered intarsia pattern in light colours on a dark ground, and the cornice is painted to imitate alabaster.

Some contemporary papyri give a good idea of the geometric decorative schemes that wealthy Alexandrians chose for their houses, none of which has survived. Around 255 BC one Diotimos arranged to have the portico of his house 'painted with a purple border, the upper part of the wall variegated like marble . . . and the pediment with circular veining. For the seven-couched dining-room . . . do the vault according to the pattern that you saw, and paint the wall below the dado an agreeable shade, and also paint the Lesbian-style cornice.'

There is surprisingly little evidence among the extant paintings for the so-called 'Alexandrian style' of naturalistic landscape and genre painting, supposedly created during the reign of Ptolemy VI Philometor (180–145 BC) by DEMETRIOS OF ALEXANDRIA. The Nilotic landscapes found on the Nile mosaic from Palestrina (*see* PRAENESTE, §3) and in the border of the Alexander mosaic from Pompeii have often been presumed to represent lost Alexandrian paintings, since the scenes represented on them are specifically Egyptian, but these are now thought to be a form of conscious exoticism, rather like the chinoiserie decorative schemes of the 18th century, and there is no evidence for them originating in Egypt. The superb paintings of rural scenes from the Wardian tomb (probably mid-2nd century AD; see fig. 3) show affinities with landscapes from the Pompeian Second Style (*see* POMPEII, §IV) and may reflect the bucolic interests of Alexandrian poetry.

In the absence of many extant paintings from Roman Alexandria, it is necessary to examine the literary evidence. According to Pliny (*Natural History* XXXV.114, 138), Roman-period Alexandrian genre painting centred on special light effects and utilized scenes from low life: to illustrate this he describes two paintings by ANTIPHILOS, one showing a boy blowing on the embers of a fire that illuminates his face and the room behind him, and the second a workshop of women weavers. Another painting ascribed by Pliny to Antiphilos showed a character from a comedy in full costume, and parallels have been drawn between this interest in caricature and the mosaics from Pompeii showing grotesque theatrical performers. Pliny also mentioned eight other works by Antiphilos, however, which seem to have had such standard mythological subjects as Dionysiac scenes, the death of Hippolytos, and Europa. Also interesting are the *compendiariae* from Alexandria mentioned by Petronius (*Satyricon* II.ix), which he said were ruining the purity of Roman painting. This term has often been interpreted as referring to some sort of small-scale impressionistic painting showing an interest in colourism and perspective, such as the Pompeian sacro-idyllic landscapes, but in the absence of any examples this must remain in doubt.

BIBLIOGRAPHY

G. Botti: *Fouilles à la Colonne théodosienne* (Cairo, 1897)
A. Schiff: *Alexandrinische Dipinti* (Leipzig, 1905)
E. Breccia: *La necropoli di Sciatbi* (Cairo, 1911)
——: *Alexandrea ad Aegyptum: Guide de la ville ancienne et moderne et du Musée gréco-romain* (Alexandria, 1914; Eng. trans., Bergamo, 1922)
R. Pagenstecher: *Nekropolis: Untersuchungen über Gestalt und Entwicklung der alexandrinischen Grabanlagen und ihrer Malereien* (Leipzig, 1919)
I. Noshy: *The Arts in Ptolemaic Egypt* (Oxford, 1937)
B. R. Brown: *Ptolemaic Paintings and Mosaics and the Alexandrian Style* (Cambridge, MA, 1957)
W. Dorigo: *Pittura tardoromana* (Rome, 1970); Eng. trans. by J. Cleugh and J. Warrington as *Late Roman Painting: A Study of Pictorial Records, 30 BC–AD 500* (London, 1971)
D. E. Johnston: 'Some Mosaics and Murals in Roman Tripolitania', *Roman Provincial Wallpainting of the Eastern Empire*, ed. J. Liversedge, Brit. Archaeol. Rep., Int. Ser. (Oxford, 1982), pp. 193–200

DOMINIC MONTSERRAT

3. CHRISTIAN. The assertion by Eusebios of Caesarea that Christianity was introduced into Egypt at Alexandria by St Mark in AD 62 (*Ecclesiastical History*, II, 24) is not supported by independent evidence, but during the first two centuries of the Christian era the city exercised considerable influence in the affairs of the Church. Its importance was further enhanced in the 2nd century AD by the foundation of the Catechetical school, which rose to its greatest prominence under the leadership of Clement of Alexandria (*c.* 190–202) and Origen (*c.* 202–31).

During the early Christian period Alexandria was a flourishing and cosmopolitan city, essentially Greek in character but with large Egyptian and Jewish communities. The latter was severely reduced in the revolt of AD 116. The doctrinal controversies of the 4th and 5th centuries resulted in the virtual isolation of the Egyptian Church, but the decline of Alexandria had already been signalled by the creation of Constantinople (now Istanbul) as the eastern capital in 330. Although the locations of a number of early churches are known, structural remains survive only where they have been converted into mosques (e.g. the church of St Athanasius, now the al-Juyushi or al-ʿAttarīn mosque). Similarly, the Christian catacombs, which were situated near the ancient city of Rhakotis, to the west of the Serapeum and not far from the pagan burial site of Kom al-Shawgāfah, have long since been lost. Only one, usually referred to as Catacomb Wescher, has been studied in any detail. Its paintings have been attributed to the 3rd–5th centuries, and they include a representation of Christ subduing an assortment of dangerous creatures, which has close links with earlier portrayals of the child-god Horus. There is also a frieze that seems to depict the *Wedding at Cana*, the *Miracle of the Loaves and Fishes* and three figures engaged in the Eucharistic act (Alexandria, Gr.–Roman Mus.). Excavations since 1960 in the Kom el-Dikka district, undertaken by the Polish Institute in Cairo, have yielded valuable information on the late Roman and Byzantine periods. Among the material discovered has been a collection of clay ampullae associated with the cult of St Menas, whose tomb and pilgrimage centre lay *c.* 45 km south-west at ABU MINA.

BIBLIOGRAPHY

F. Cabrol and H. Leclercq: *Dictionnaire d'archéologie chrétienne et de liturgie*, i (Paris, 1907–53), col. 203–51
E. Breccia: *Alexandrea ad Aegyptum* (Bergamo, 1922)

C. WALTERS

4. ISLAMIC. For centuries after the Islamic conquest in AD 642 Alexandria was the second city of Egypt and perhaps second only to Constantinople in the Mediterranean basin. In the later medieval period the city fell behind more vigorous maritime centres in Europe, but it retained some of its ancient glory when international commerce revived in the 12th century after the First Crusade (1099). On the ruins of the city's most notable monument, the Pharos (*see* §2(i) above), the Mamluk sultan Qa'itbay (*reg* 1468–96) built a fortress to defend the harbour. Alexandria regained importance in the 19th century, when the viceroy Muhammad ʿAli began construction of the Mahmudiyya canal that reconnected the city to the Nile and once again transformed Alexandria into a centre of international commerce.

For two centuries following the Arab conquest the Christian population, led by the patriarch and clergy, remained rich and influential. The extent of Arab destruction has perhaps been exaggerated, for General ʿAmr b. al-ʿAs would not have left Egypt's maritime gateway vulnerable to Byzantine attack. The antique and Byzantine defences, street plan, facilities and buildings remained in service, but the city declined slowly as Fustat (old Cairo) grew in importance. The population and urban area probably shrank by two-thirds. The city walls, too large and difficult to defend, were rebuilt in the second half of the 9th century, and a second line was soon added; these walls were studied during Napoleon's expedition to Egypt (1798) and largely survived until the early 20th century.

Within the walls the town retained its ancient east–west axis, but some transverse streets disappeared. New buildings were built of materials salvaged from ruins, and antique marble columns and capitals were used for wave-breakers to protect walls or exported to Cairo. The urban area was never as densely built up as it had been in ancient times: ruins abounded and barren areas were used as temporary cemeteries. The cemetery at Kom al-Dikka, for example, was used from the 7th century to the early 8th, in the 9th and from the 11th century to the early 12th; the names and locations of other burial-grounds can be deduced from written sources. In the later medieval period on their emplacements two high earthen hills were raised up, becoming topographical landmarks shown on all the engravings.

Although some churches were confiscated and transformed into mosques (*see* §3 above), many new buildings, such as large and finely decorated mosques, a government house (Arab. *dār al-ʿimāra*), fortresses, an arsenal, covered markets (*qaisariyya*), residences for foreign consuls and even churches and a few monasteries, were erected under Muslim rule, but few have survived. The mosque of Ibrahim Terbana (1684) was built with reused Greco-Roman capitals and columns, and the mosque of Sidi Abu'l-ʿAbbas al-Mursi was reconstructed in 1767 over the tomb of a 13th-century saint. In the medieval period Alexandria was famous for linen, woollen, silk and cotton textiles, which were exported as far as India, and its public brocade workshop (*dār al-tirāz*) produced luxury textiles for the court. The city was also a centre of glass-making and metal-casting.

The Graeco-Roman Museum was founded in 1892 by Giuseppe Botti (1853–1903) and transferred in 1895 into the west wing of the present building, which has been expanded several times. The Museum of Fine Arts (1954) exhibits the work of contemporary Egyptian and foreign artists and organizes a biennial exhibition.

BIBLIOGRAPHY

Enc. Islam/1: 'al-Iskandariyya'
G. Le Père: 'Mémoire sur la ville d'Alexandrie', *Description de l'Egypte, état moderne*, ii (Paris, 1822), pp. 269–324
G. Jondet: *Atlas historique de la ville et des ports d'Alexandrie* (Cairo, 1921)
E. Combe: *Alexandrie musulmane: Notes de topographie et d'histoire de la ville depuis la conquête arabe jusqu'à nos jours* (Cairo, 1933)
ʿA. Salem: *Ta'rīkh al-iskandariyya wa-ḥadāratihā fī ʿaṣr al-islāmī* [The history and culture of Alexandria in the Islamic period] (Cairo, 1962)
J. al-Shayyāl: *Ta'rīkh madīnat al-iskandariyya fī ʿaṣr al-islāmī* [The history of the city of Alexandria in the Islamic period] (Alexandria, 1967)
W. Kubiak: 'Stèles funéraires arabes de Kom el Dick', *Bull. Soc. Archéol., Alexandrie* (1967), xlii, pp. 17–26; xliii (1975), pp. 133–42; xlvii (1975)
E. Promińska: *Investigations on the Population of Muslim Alexandria* (Warsaw, 1972)
W. B. Kubiak: 'Pre-Muslim Network of Streets in Medieval Alexandria', *Afryka, Azja, Ameryka Łacinska*, lxxi (1993), pp. 21–32

WLADYSŁAW B. KUBIAK

Alexandria Eschate. *See* KHODZHENT.

Alexandrino, Pedro. *See* CARVALHO, PEDRO ALEXANDRINO.

Alfani, Domenico (di Paride) (*b* Perugia, 1479–80; *d* 1549–57). Italian painter. The son of a goldsmith, he was a pupil of Perugino and a friend of Raphael, whose style influenced him strongly. An undated letter (Lille, Mus. B.-A.) from Raphael to Alfani, which includes a drawing of the *Holy Family*, asks Alfani to intervene with Atlanta Baglioni, for whom Raphael had painted the *Entombment* (1507; Rome, Gal. Borghese), to ask her to settle a fee. In 1510 Alfani became a member of the Perugian painters' guild. Alfani's earliest surviving work, painted in 1518 for S Gregorio della Sapienza, Perugia, depicts the *Virgin and Child Enthroned with SS Gregory and Nicholas* (Perugia, G.N. Umbria) and is based on Raphael's *Virgin and Child* (the Orléans *Madonna*, *c*. 1506–7; Chantilly, Mus. Condé). Alfani based the design of an altarpiece executed with Pompeo d'Anselmo in 1520 for S Simone del Carmine, Perugia (Perugia, G.N. Umbria), on the drawing sent to him by Raphael. In the mid-1520s Alfani came under the influence of the Florentine Mannerists, particularly Rosso Fiorentino, to whom he gave shelter in 1527 when the artist was fleeing the Sack of Rome. According to Vasari, Rosso gave Alfani a drawing of the *Three Magi* (destr.), on which he based his altarpiece for S Maria dei Miracoli, Castel Rigone (ex-Rinuccini priv. col., Florence). In 1553 Alfani was commissioned to paint a *Crucifixion* for S Francesco, Perugia. He was assisted by his son Orazio Alfani (*c*. 1510–83), who continued his father's business. In 1556 Orazio received payment for work he had executed for the choir of S Pietro, a commission his father had undertaken in 1547.

BIBLIOGRAPHY

G. Vasari: *Vite* (1550, rev. 2/1568); ed. G. Milanesi (1878–85)
W. Bombe: *Geschichte der Peruginer Malerei*, Italienische Forschungen, v (Berlin, 1912), pp. 13, 127, 335, 346
E. Jacobsen: *Umbrische Malerei* (Strasbourg, 1914), pp. 139–41 [illus.]
E. A. Caroll: 'Lappoli, Alfani, Vasari and Rosso Fiorentino', *A. Bull.*, xlix (1967), pp. 297–304
J.-R. Gaborit: '*L'Adoration du Christ mort*: Terre cuite ferraraise du Musée du Louvre', *Mnmts Piot*, lix (1975), pp. 209–30

SUSANNE KIEFHABER

Alfaro, Andreu (*b* Valencia, 5 Aug 1927). Spanish sculptor. In 1932 he entered the Institución Libre de Enseñanza, Valencia, directed by José de Navarro (*b* 1931) who had a great influence on his early education. He later studied at the Instituto Escuela in Valencia and in 1942 joined the Bachillerato Studios at the Colegio de S Tomás de Villanueva. The exhibition in Valencia in 1953 of work by the sculptor Rafael Alvarez Ortega greatly impressed Alfaro, encouraging his enthusiasm for experimental work. In 1955 he established contact with the artists José Solar Vidal Monjalés, Vicent Ventura, Pepe Iborra and Joan Fuster. In 1958 he visited Paris and Brussels, where he saw the major exhibition *Les Années cinquante de l'art moderne*. In the later 1950s he was associated with Aguliera Cerni, Eusebio Sempere and José Maria de Labra (*b* 1925), who were among the members of the Parpalló group of Valencian artists formed in Valencia in 1957 and led by Alfaro. The group was inspired by the new American abstract group of artists such as Elsworth Kelly, exhibited in the Hispano-American biennale in Barcelona in 1955. After several group exhibitions in Valencia and Barcelona the Parpalló group went their separate ways. At this time also Alfaro encountered the sculpture of JORGE OTEIZA, which became a key factor in his development.

Alfaro participated in Parpalló group exhibitions in Madrid and held solo exhibitions of his work at the Sala Mateu, Valencia, Galeria Dayo, Madrid, and later at international art fairs and exhibitions in Cologne, Mainz, Düsseldorf and Basle. In 1964 he was awarded the Gold Medal at the seventh international salon of Valencia.

The central elements of Alfaro's work are rhythm and movement, executed with a distinctive lightness of touch and elegance of design. The early sculptures, in bent and moulded metal, recall the work of the Valencian Impressionist Joaquín Sorolla y Bastida, painter of the sea. It was this subject that inspired Andreu's earliest works (e.g. the *Lady of the Sea* and *Life*), in which gently billowing shapes echo the sensuous curves of sails in the wind. In the 1960s the artist moved towards Minimalism, evoking forms in their most concentrated states. He became attracted to the colder aspects of industrial materials, and he began to use steel and iron, while maintaining the liberated quality of his style. Alfaro explored linear structure using metallic tubing to create open-weave structures of musical resonance, culminating in such noted works as the *Olympus of Weimar* and the *Lady from the Sea* (1982). In the later 1980s Alfaro returned to traditional methods and materials, using pink and Carrara marble as in, for example, the softly turned forms of the *Three Graces* (1989, exh. Paris, Gal. de France). Works such as *Aphrodite* (1989) incorporate the motif of an open leaf, repeated upwards in columns of painted iron, reminiscent of Constantin Brancusi's monumental work but realized with Alfaro's graceful style.

BIBLIOGRAPHY

W. Dyckes: *Contemporary Spanish Art* (New York, 1975), pp. 82, 83, 126
Alfaro: De Goethe y nuestro tiempo (New York, 1975)
Alfaro (exh. cat., Paris, Gal. de France, 1989)

□

Alfaro, Brooke (*b* Panama City, 5 Sept 1949). Panamanian painter and printmaker. After completing a degree in architecture, he held his first exhibition in Panama in 1979. From 1980 to 1983 he studied at the Art Students League in New York, his only formal training as an artist. His admiration for Sandro Botticelli and Diego Velázquez led him to specialize in human figures painted from life; he favoured oil paints but also worked in pastel and produced pencil drawings and screenprints. His first works were portraits of young women surrounded by surreal elements or in dream settings. From 1983 he painted humorous images of traditional or religious subjects such as church processions, as well as portraits of imaginary ecclesiastical figures and war heroes; capitalizing on Panama's strong Catholic tradition, Alfaro even invented his own saints, including the *Virgin of All Secrets* (1986; Washington, DC, A. Mus. Americas).

BIBLIOGRAPHY

V. Gould Stoddart: 'The Magical Realism of Brooke Alfaro', *Américas*, xxxviii/4 (1986), p. 59
P. Heilbron: 'Brooke Alfaro: Profile of an Artist', *Cordialidad*, iii (May–June 1988), pp. 30–32

MONICA E. KUPFER

Alfaro, Matías de Arteaga y. *See* ARTEAGA Y ALFARO, MATÍAS DE.

Alfaro y Gómez, Juan de (*b* Córdoba, 1643; *d* Madrid, 1680). Spanish painter. He served his apprenticeship in Córdoba, where he was a pupil of Antonio del Castillo, and completed his training in Madrid in the workshop of Velázquez. He wrote a biography of Velázquez, now lost, which was used by Palomino de Castro y Velasco. Apart from brief visits to Córdoba, Alfaro spent his life in Madrid, and he was associated with the court. He painted religious scenes, but his principal activity was portraiture (both large-scale and miniature), in which he was particularly successful, developing a style influenced by Velázquez. Although he was a prolific artist, few of his paintings have survived. While young he painted a series of works depicting the life of St Francis for the cloister of the convent of S Francisco in Córdoba and also an *Assumption of the Virgin* for the convent of the Discalced Carmelites. For the episcopal palace at Córdoba he painted a portrait of *Bishop Francisco de Alarcón* and portraits of other earlier bishops (*in situ*). In Madrid he painted a portrait of *Don Pedro de Arce* (untraced) and the *Portrait of a Jesuit* (Madrid, Bib. S Isidoro Labrador), in which the influence of van Dyck is evident; Alfaro y Gómez had access, for purposes of study, to the royal collections, and, according to Palomino, he made copies there of paintings by van Dyck. In 1986 the portrait of *Doña María Josefa Díaz de Morales y Córdoba* (1675; Madrid, priv. col., see exh. cat., p. 279), painted in Córdoba, was attributed to Alfaro. An *Assumption of the Virgin* (1668; Madrid, S Jerónimo Real), signed by Alfaro, is of excellent quality; its composition is inspired by Rubens, and the technique and brushwork derive from Velázquez.

BIBLIOGRAPHY

A. A. Palomino de Castro y Velasco: *Museo pictórico* (1715–24/*R* 1947), p. 999
D. Angulo Iñiguez: *Pintura del siglo XVII*, A. Hisp. (Madrid, 1971), p. 302
Carreño, Rizi, Herrera y la pintura madrileña de su tiempo (exh. cat. by A. Pérez Sánchez, Madrid, Prado, 1986), pp. 278–9, pls 115–16
A. Pérez Sánchez: *Pintura barroca en España, 1600–1750* (Madrid, 1992), pp. 389–90

ENRIQUE VALDIVIESO

Alfei, Francesco di Bartolomeo (*b* ?Montalcino, 1421; *d* Siena, after 1491). Italian painter. In 1453 he was living in Siena in the district called the Chompagnia di Realto et Chartagine, where he had a painter's studio (*'buttiba de l'arte de dipentori'*; Siena, Pal. Piccolomini, Archv Stato, *Lira*, MS. 139.c.50). He was chiefly employed by the Sienese Republic but also worked for Pope Pius II in 1460 (see Müntz), for the diplomat Leonardo Benvoglienti, for the Ottieri della Ciaia family and for Sinolfo di Castellottieri. In 1455 Alfei was paid by the magistrates of Siena for his painting of Monte Argentario near Orbetello (Siena, Pal. Piccolomini, Archv Stato, *Balia*, MS. 1.c.215), work that Alessi suggests may be recognized in the *Town by the Sea* and the *Castle by the Sea* (both Siena, Pin. N.), previously attributed to Ambrogio Lorenzetti and to Sassetta. In 1473 the Sienese Republic recommended Alfei to the papal legate, Cardinal Roverella, on the occasion of the artist's visit to the Marches; the Cardinal's reply confirms that Alfei executed works there. Alessi and Scapecchi have proposed that the anonymous MASTER OF THE OSSERVANZA (*see* MASTERS, ANONYMOUS, AND MONOGRAMMISTS, §I) can be identified with Francesco di Bartolomeo Alfei. They demonstrated that the works attributed to the Master were produced between 1440 and 1470, not in the 1430s and 1440s as previously believed. The dated inscription of 1436 on the *Virgin and Child with SS Jerome and Ambrose*, which was thought to refer to the date of execution, is in fact the date of the foundation of the chapel in S Maurizio, Siena. Given the revised dating, the Master cannot be identified with Sano di Pietro, as has also been proposed, but Alfei had many connections with Sano, which would account for the two painters' stylistic similarities.

It is likely that the scenes from the *Life of St Anthony Abbot* from a dispersed altarpiece (panels in Washington, DC, N.G.A.; New York, Met.; Wiesbaden, Mus. Wiesbaden; and elsewhere), attributed first to Sassetta and later to the Master of the Osservanza, originally came from the region of the Marches and the Abruzzi, an area in which Alfei was active. The *Charity of St Anthony Abbot* (Washington, DC, N.G.A.) bears the coat of arms of the Martinozzi family, and the connection between Alfei and that family is documented by Sano di Pietro's assessment in 1475 of paintings made by Alfei for Ludovico Martinozzi. Pope-Hennessy, however, does not accept the identification of Alfei with the Master of the Osservanza.

BIBLIOGRAPHY

E. Romagnoli: *Biografia cronologica de bellartisti senesi* (*c.* 1835, Bib. Com. di Siena, MS.L.II.3); facs. iv (Florence, 1976), pp. 139–48

G. Milanesi: *Documenti per la storia dell'arte senese*, ii (Siena, 1854), pp. 299–300, 327, 329–30, 355–6, 396–7, 421

E. Müntz: *Les Arts à la cour des papes*, i (Paris, 1878), pp. 264, 309

S. Borghesi and L. Banchi: *Nuovi documenti per la storia dell'arte senese* (Siena, 1898), pp. 238–9, 260–61, 277–8, 350

C. Alessi and P. Scapecchi: 'Il maestro dell'Osservanza: Sano di Pietro o Francesco di Bartolomeo', *Prospettiva*, 42 (1985), pp. 13–37

J. Pope-Hennessy: *Italian Paintings in the Robert Lehman Collection*, New York, Met. cat. (Princeton, 1987), pp. 105–11

CECILIA ALESSI

Alfieri, Benedetto Innocente (*b* Rome, 1699; *d* Turin, 9 Dec 1767). Italian architect. Descended from an impoverished ducal family of Asti, Piedmont, Alfieri spent his first 16 years in Rome. A papal stipend enabled him to study law at the Collegio dei Nobili in Turin, after which he settled as a lawyer in Asti. Even as a successful architect in public office, he continued to make use of his legal knowledge, and in Asti and later Turin he served as mayor intermittently. Alfieri was extraordinarily versatile, with no single personal style. He worked simultaneously in three separate styles: Roman high and late Baroque; French Rococo (for decoration); and early classicism. His attitude to these styles was functional rather than historical, and his choice of which one to use usually depended on the nature of the project and the wishes of his client. Thus Alfieri built Catholic churches in Roman Baroque and Protestant churches in a puristic classicism. Piedmontese State commissions were executed in the severe manner of the Turin State style as practised by Amadeo di Castellamonte and Filippo Juvarra before him. For the royal court and the aristocracy French Rococo was appropriate. Façades of palaces were decorated in the idiom of a restrained Baroque classicism, like that which Gianlorenzo Bernini and Carlo Fontana had developed in Rome. Whatever the style, Alfieri worked with facility and elegance, blending disparate elements into ingenious, harmonious creations. He was not a great innovator, but his work anticipates in certain respects the purpose-built functional architecture of the 20th century. With his flexible use of existing architectural vocabulary, he was a first-class architect of the second rank.

Benedetto Innocente Alfieri: Palazzo Ghilini (now Palazzo del Governo), Alessandria, 1732

1. SECULAR WORKS. The mathematical training, famous in its day, that Alfieri had received at the Collegio dei Nobili, and his knowledge of architectural theory, probably acquired at the same college, enabled him to carry out small building projects for relatives. In 1730 his uncle, the Marchese Ghilini, entrusted him with the construction of a large family palace at Alessandria (see fig.). This demanding task was made easier for him by the availability of a design by Filippo Juvarra, who was apparently not concerned with the implementation of his schemes. Alfieri took advantage of Juvarra's absence to revise the plans, showing an ability to combine motifs from different sources into a harmonious whole. The two-storey palace (1732), built around a square court, has 13 bays on the main façade. The corners are accentuated with narrow projections, whereas the three middle bays with a main entrance and a central ceremonial window are only slightly offset. To ensure a unified contour Alfieri omitted the broken pediment as well as the mezzanine over the ground-floor windows envisaged by Juvarra. The ground-floor was thus made one-third lower than the *piano nobile*, which now seems to rest rather heavily on its substructure. As in Andrea Palladio's Palazzo Thiene at Vicenza, the *piano nobile* was increased in height by one-third with a solid wall over the windows. The windows of the mezzanine, which is located behind it, look on to the inner courtyard, a layout also encountered in the 15th-century palaces of Ferrara. Roman motifs embellish the niche of the balconied window, modelled on the main window of Francesco Borromini's façade of the oratory of S Filippo Neri in Rome. The rounded corners of the palace, common in the 17th century, are another Roman borrowing. Although it is an early work, the Palazzo Ghilini remains Alfieri's most outstanding palace. The rich and robust plasticity of the whole and the sparse but confidently positioned individual motifs show greater spontaneity and more individual style than most of his later private palaces, which display an undynamic flatness and a cool, impersonal décor.

Alfieri was commissioned to build the Teatro Regio (1738–40) in Turin, which brought him international fame and succession to Juvarra's post as First Architect to the King. The growing prosperity of the rising bourgeoisie and their avid cultural interests began to displace the exclusive court theatres that formed part of the royal palaces in favour of independent public theatres. Alfieri's Teatro Regio straddled these two positions. Although it was the first public theatre in Turin, it was set in a remote side wing of the Palazzo Reale, which also contained the rooms of the Segreteria di Stato. King Carlo Emanuele III had no need to leave his suite of rooms to get to his theatre box. Paradoxically, therefore, Alfieri was able to develop his ideas on the theatre as a public building only in the internal layout of the Teatro Regio. The auditorium provided a clear view and comfort for all spectators, not just for the King. The excellent acoustics, which became famous all over Europe, were achieved by building a hollow sound-board under the orchestra pit. The best possible sightlines were gained by arranging the tiers of boxes in the form of a horseshoe. This ground-plan had been developed by Carlo Fontana in 1671 for the Teatro Tor di Nona in Rome. French treatises spread the fame of the Teatro Regio, and the horseshoe plan became mandatory for many later European theatres (*see also* THEATRE, §III, 3(i)(a)).

Alfieri's adaptation to urban requirements of the tucked-away theatre, hemmed in by other structures, was highly successful. He transformed the lower level under the tiers of boxes into a spacious multi-aisled hall with columns. It served as a vestibule, allowing numerous carriages to draw up to the wide flight of steps protected from the weather. Once the passengers had alighted, the carriages had no need to execute complicated turning manoeuvres because they could drive through, under the boxes, to an adjoining courtyard to park. The Teatro Regio became a centre of the city's social life—outside the exclusive royal court—with its grand and spacious stair-hall, serving as a promenade, the various elegant public side-rooms and the wide comfortable corridors to the boxes. The most modern stage mechanism and the scene-changing apparatus by Francesco Bibiena contributed further to make the Teatro Regio a key work of theatre construction in the 18th century. A fire in 1939 shortly before World War II destroyed this major architectural work; it was replaced in the 1960s with a modern building.

While building the Teatro Regio, Alfieri extended and refurbished the Segretaria di Stato (1739–67). The result was a piece of severe, impersonal administration architecture that exalted efficiency and sobriety above artistic originality. The building rises from an arcaded ground-level. Above are three rows of unadorned windows with alternating triangular and segmental pediments in the two lower storeys, extending for 120 m in a monotonous succession along one side of the Piazza di Castello. Other Turin squares such as the Piazza d'Erbe by Alfieri are characterized by the same cold rationalism. It is unusual in Italy for a piazza to have a levelled-off, uniform façade of a type known in France since the 17th century even if of a more elegant design. These works reflect the anonymous, almost Prussian absolutism of the State in Piedmont (*see* TURIN, §I, 1).

Alfieri created his most severe interpretation of Piedmontese functionalist architecture in the design for a prison, the Carceri Senatoriali. Devoid of all decoration, the layout of a central circular pavilion and long side wings presents a clear, logical plan, reduced to absolute functionality. The aggressively rusticated façades and quoins make the building's purpose clear. A measure of humanity was added by the provision of a sick bay and the good ventilation and lighting of the prisoners' cells.

As decorator of interiors for royal and aristocratic patrons, Alfieri drew inspiration from French rather than Roman prototypes. His royal apartments in the Palazzo Reale and the Palazzo Isnardi di Caraglio (from 1739) in Turin, among others, are adorned with elegant French Rococo ornaments on the walls and ceilings that do not distract from the rational clarity of the structures. His personal touch is especially evident in the mirrors, framed in ornaments that make them appear to float freely and weightlessly in space, but all the forms, such as cartouches and ribands, are nonetheless subject to the rules of symmetry. For all its lightness and playfulness, Alfieri's Rococo strikes a rational note.

2. ECCLESIASTICAL WORKS. Alfieri's rationalism is given classical expression in the entrance portico of Geneva's main Calvinist church, the Gothic cathedral of St Pierre (1752). His adaptation of the vestibule of the Pantheon in Rome is of crystalline purity, precisely articulated. The depressed false cupola over the pediment of the portico, which masks the end wall of the Gothic nave, harks back to Baroque illusionism. St Pierre's façade was acclaimed as exemplary by French architects such as Jacques-Germain Soufflot.

Alfieri's most famous and unconventional spatial creation in church architecture was SS Remigio e Giovanni (1757–67) at Carignano. Its most outstanding feature is the semicircular ground-plan, while the chancel and side chapels are conventionally disposed. The entrance is placed at the centre point of the base line. Facing it, fanned out on the periphery of the half-circle, the seven chapels are placed in a row, the chancel at the vertex with an opening twice the normal width. On entering, however, this string of chapels is not perceived as a uniform panorama, because the view into the church is divided into seven separate fields of vision by the columns of the entrance vestibule, which is itself semicircular. The priest's station at the altar of the centrally placed chancel directly opposite the entrance affords a panoramic view of intense plastic movement. Here it is not the segmentation of the field of vision that counts, but a dynamic whole, made up of three semicircular features: the curve of the entrance vestibule, which from this point reads like a tempietto, thrusting powerfully into the space, and, to the left and right, the semicircular walls with their side portals falling back with a complementary motion. This concept of the entrance wall imbued with forces and counter-forces recalls High Baroque façades, such as those of Guarino Guarini's Palazzo Carignano in Turin and Gianlorenzo Bernini's first design for the Louvre, Paris. The coloured marble decorations point to another Bernini building, S Andrea al Quirinale in Rome. The inspiration for this unique spatial creation can be found in Juvarra's stage design for the Teatro Ottoboni in Rome, where the stage is seen through the openings of a semicircular tempietto. The counterview from the priest's station at the main altar of Alfieri's church is the reverse of this perspective.

The cathedral façade (1763–7) at Vercelli presents an interesting example of the architect looking back to the early 18th century in Italy and the architecture of Carlo Maderno. It is a reduced version of the façade of St Peter's in Rome. Alfieri left out the upper storey with the papal loggia, while taking over from the lower storey the central aedicula with half columns and the side openings with the straight architrave over free-standing columns. In its academic sobriety and austerity Alfieri's adaptation is not comparable to Maderno's original. It is hard to believe that the sober façade of the cathedral at Vercelli was created at the same time as the brilliant and inspired parish church (1757–64) of Carignano.

The characteristics peculiar to Piedmontese State architecture (*see* §1 above) can be detected even in monastery buildings. Alfieri's seminary (1764–7) in Asti has the functional severity of a barracks. The windows are devoid of decorative detailing, and the courtyard has the same monotonous arcades as the squares of Turin. In the seminary's oval dining-room, with its bare, whitewashed walls and dark furniture, Alfieri struck a note of ascetic restraint. Doors and windows are cut into the walls with sharp edges, without any framing. The only articulation is the heavy moulding at the base of the vault. The shape of the room was copied from Borromini's refectory at the oratory of S Filippo Neri in Rome.

WRITINGS

Il nuovo teatro regio di Torino apertosi nel anno 1740 (Turin, 1761)

BIBLIOGRAPHY

G. della Valle: *Prefazione al tomo xi delle 'Vite' del Vasari* (Siena, 1794)
M. Paroletti: *Vita e ritratti di settanta piemontesi illustri* (Turin, 1824)
G. Chevalley: *Un avvocato architetto: Il conte Benedetto Alfieri* (Turin, 1916)
M. Rosci: 'Benedetto Alfieri e l'architettura del '700 in Piemonte', *Palladio*, iii (1953), pp. 91–100
N. Carboneri: *Catalogo della mostra del barocco piemontese: Architettura* (Turin, 1963)
C. G. Argan: 'Lo zio di Vittorio', *Il Messagero* (8 Feb 1964)
R. Pommer: *Eighteenth-century Architecture in Piedmont* (New York, 1967)
A. Cavallari Murat: 'Attualità e inattualità di Benedetto Alfieri a duecent' anni dalla morte', *Boll. Soc. Piemont. Archeol. & B.A.*, xxii (1968), pp. 8–43
A. Bellini: *Benedetto Alfieri* (Milan, 1978)
——: *Palazzo Ghilini di Alessandria* (Alessandria, 1983)

PETER STEIN

Alfonso. Spanish photographic firm. It was founded by Alfonso Sánchez García (*b* Ciudad Real, 21 Feb 1880; *d* Madrid, 13 Feb 1953) and later run with his son Alfonso [Alfonsito] Sánchez Portela (*b* Madrid, 16 Nov 1902). After apprenticeship to a number of important Madrid-based studio photographers, Alfonso Sánchez García alternated studio photography and photojournalism. In 1909 he covered the calamitous campaign in Spanish Morocco. A year later he opened the successful Madrid Alfonso studio and photographic agency, where his son Alfonsito was apprenticed. Alfonsito, known as Alfonso after 1930, published press photographs while still in his mid-teens, and in 1921 he accompanied his father on a trip to document the continuing hostilities in North Africa. A year later Alfonsito photographed the Moroccan chieftain Abd al-Karim, but it was during the dictatorship of Primo de Rivera (1923–30), the Spanish Republic (1931–6) and the Spanish Civil War (1936–9) that he made the memorable portraits and the press photographs for which he is best known. During the war he documented the first hours of rebellion, the defence of Madrid, the siege of the Alcázar, Madrid, the battles of Guadalajara and Teruel and the entry of the victorious Nationalist troops into Madrid. Rejecting an offer to flee before Franco's advancing forces, both father and son chose to remain in Madrid. Their studio was destroyed during the Civil War, but, having been denied press credentials by Franco's authorities, in 1939 they opened a new studio on the Gran Via in Madrid, where the father devoted himself entirely to studio photography. The son's photographic archive is now regarded as a national treasure.

BIBLIOGRAPHY

J. Altabella: 'Los grandes de la fotografía española: Alfonso', *ABC* (13 July 1976), pp. 12–17
Idas y caos: Aspectos de las vanguardias fotográficas en España (exh. cat., ed. J. Foncuberta; Madrid, Min. Cult., 1984), pp. 138–72, 181
Memoria de Madrid: Fotografías de Alfonso (exh. cat., ed. P. López Mondéjar; Madrid, Min. Cult., 1984)
J. Green: 'Alfonso: Spain's Premier Photojournalist', *History of Photography*, ii/3 (1987), pp. 189–211

JERALD R. GREEN

Alfonso I, King of Naples. *See* ARAGON, (2).

Alfonso II, King of Asturias. *See* ASTURIAS, (1).

Alfonso II, King of Naples. *See* ARAGON, (4).

Alfonso III, King of Asturias. *See* ASTURIAS, (3).

Alfonso V, King of Aragon and Sicily. *See* ARAGON, (2).

Alfonso V, King of Portugal. *See* AVIZ, (3).

Alfonso X [the Wise; the Learned], King of Castile and León [Alfonso, King of Germany] (*b* Toledo, 23 Nov 1221; *reg* 1252–84; *d* Seville, 4 April 1284). Spanish ruler and patron. He was a man of wide learning, a legislator and a poet. Although moderately successful in the Reconquest, following the tradition of his father Ferdinand III, King of Castile and León (*reg* 1217–52), he provoked opposition by raising taxes and seeking election as Holy Roman Emperor (1256).

Alfonso sponsored translations of Arab writings on astronomy and astrology. He himself composed works of history, poetry and law. His *Cantigas de St María*, a collection of over 400 poems, which survive in four manuscripts (Madrid, Escorial, Real Bib. Monasterio S Lorenzo, MSS B.I.2 and T.I.1; Madrid, Bib. N., MS. 10069; Florence, Bib. N. Cent., MS. B.R.20), were written in Galician over a period of 25 years ending in 1279. The songs of the Virgin are accompanied by an important and extensive series of over 1000 small genre scenes 'structured like a modern comic-strip to tell the song's narrative visually' (Burns). Bullfights and street scenes are shown; battles depict both Christians and Muslims, and several pictures reveal Alfonso himself (he considered himself to be a troubadour of the Virgin Mary). Burns has described the *Cantigas* as 'that unique *summa* of medieval painting-cum-music-cum-poetry'.

WRITINGS

Las cantigas de Santa María (MS.; completed 1279); ed. W. Mettmann, 4 vols (Coimbra, 1959–72)

Las cantigas de Santa María, 2 vols (Madrid, 1989) [with stud. by M. López Serrano and others]

BIBLIOGRAPHY

E. S. Proctor: *Alfonso X of Castile: Patron of Literature and Learning* (Oxford, 1951)

J. Keller: *Alfonso X el Sabio* (New York, 1967)

——: 'Iconography and Literature: Alfonso himself in *Cantiga* 209', *Hispania*, lxvi (1983), pp. 348–52

R. I. Burns: *The Worlds of Alfonso the Wise and James the Conqueror* (Princeton, 1985)

J. R. L. HIGHFIELD

Alfonso, Luís (*b* Palma de Mallorca, 1845; *d* Madrid, 17 Jan 1892). Spanish writer. He began writing art criticism in Valencia, where he appears to have lived for a time, and after moving to Madrid he contributed articles to such periodicals as *La Ilustración española y americana*. Important among these are the various studies he published on the Catalan painter José Bernardo Mariano Fortuny y Marsal in 1874, the year of the artist's death. In 1876 he was invited by the Minister of Public Works, Conde de Toreno, to attend the Centennial International Exhibition in Philadelphia, PA, as the official correspondent of the Spanish government. His articles on the exhibition adversely criticized the Spanish pavilion, both for the choice of works displayed and because the most interesting artists, such as Eduardo Rosales Martines and Fortuny, were not included. Two years later he was appointed Spanish representative at the International Literary Congress in Paris. In 1886 he published his first book, *Murillo: El hombre, el artista, las obras* in the 'Arte y Letras' series, published in Barcelona under the direction of José Ixart. As a critic Alfonso always gave due consideration to such history painters as Rosales and Federico de Madrazo y Küntz, whose work formed a prominent genre in 19th-century Spanish art.

WRITINGS

La Exposición del centenario: Noticia del Certamen Universal de Filadelfia en 1876 (Madrid, 1878)

Murillo: El hombre, el artista, las obras (Barcelona, 1886)

Regular contributions to *Ilus. Esp. & Amer.*

BIBLIOGRAPHY

J. A. Gaya Nuño: *Historia de la crítica de arte en España* (Madrid, 1975)

PILAR BENITO

Alfred, King of Wessex. *See* WESSEX, (1).

Algardi, Alessandro (*b* Bologna, 31 July 1598; *d* Rome, 10 June 1654). Italian sculptor, architect and draughtsman. He was, with Gianlorenzo Bernini, the most important sculptor active in Rome in the middle years of the 17th century. After the early death of François Duquesnoy in 1643, Algardi's work came to represent the classicizing stylistic antithesis to the High Baroque sculpture of Bernini, and the two artists were perceived by their contemporaries as equals and rivals. During Algardi's first years in Rome, Bernini was the principal sculptor in demand at the court of Urban VIII, and Algardi had to be content with relatively modest commissions given to him by patrons with connections to his native Bologna. It was only during the papacy of Innocent X (1644–55) that he came to true artistic prominence, revealing himself to be one of his century's greatest relief and portrait sculptors. At a time when few sculptors drew with any skill, Algardi was an accomplished draughtsman, making drawings for his sculptural projects and also original works for engravers. In addition he worked as an architect, though the exact extent of his involvement with the design of many of the buildings with which his name has been associated is unclear.

1. Life and work. 2. Working methods and studio organization. 3. Posthumous influence and reputation.

1. LIFE AND WORK.

(i) Subject sculpture. (ii) Portrait sculpture.

(i) Subject sculpture.

(a) Training and early works in Bologna and Mantua, to 1625. (b) First years in Rome, 1625 to mid-1630s. (c) Monumental works, mid-1630s to 1644. (d) The patronage of Innocent X, the Pamphili family and others, 1644–54.

(a) Training and early works in Bologna and Mantua, to 1625. Algardi was the son of a Bolognese silk merchant and received his first artistic training at Ludovico Carracci's Accademia degli Incaminati in Bologna, a decisive factor in the formation of his style. He is said to have been taught sculpture by Giulio Cesare Conventi (1577–1640), a minor Emilian sculptor in terracotta and stucco. Algardi's earliest known work is a life-size stucco group of *St Filippo Neri Embracing St Carlo Borromeo* (*c.* 1613–16; ex-S Barbara, Bologna). Surviving early works are all made of stucco or terracotta (Bologna having no natural sculptural stone). They are not outstanding: *Two Cherubs Holding Lamps* (stucco, 1619; Bologna, S Domenico, Cappella del Santo) is the only fully documented sculpture of these years, while two over life-size stucco statues of *St Petronius* and *St Proculus* (*c.* 1615; Bologna, S Maria della Vita, Oratory) show the influence of local, provincial modellers such as Gabriele Fiorini (*fl* 1571–1605) but, still more, reveal the powerful stylistic influence of contemporary Bolognese painters, in particular Guido Reni.

Around 1622 Algardi left Bologna for Mantua, where the Bolognese architect Gabriele Bertazzoli (1570–1626) had recommended him to Ferdinando Gonzaga, 6th Duke of Mantua. According to Bellori, Algardi made small ivory *objets d'art* and produced small models to be cast in bronze and silver for the Gonzaga court. None of these is known to survive. In Mantua he was able to study the works of Giulio Romano and above all the famous ducal collection, which included antique sculpture and Annibale Fontana's carved gemstones.

(b) First years in Rome, 1625 to mid-1630s. In 1625, after a period spent in Venice, Algardi went to Rome with a recommendation from Ferdinando Gonzaga. He was to remain there for the rest of his life, and from the start Bolognese artists and patrons played a decisive role in his career: he presented two ivory Crucifixes (untraced) to Cardinal Ludovico Ludovisi, a prominent collector and nephew of the deceased Pope Gregory XV. As a result the Cardinal offered him employment as a restorer of antique sculpture. This relatively modest employment as a restorer, proof that he must already have worked as a sculptor in marble before going to Rome, was to be Algardi's main activity for the next ten years. His earliest

known restoration is a reworking for Ludovisi in 1626 of an antique torso into a statue of *Prometheus the Torchbearer*, a work followed by the statues known as the *Athena Ludovisi* and, in 1631, the *Hermes Logios* (all Rome, Mus. N. Romano), as well as the *Child with a Mask* (untraced). Bellori recorded that Algardi also restored antiques for Mario Frangipane (*d* 1654); these works were later bought by Cardinal de Richelieu. He was, in addition, responsible for the restoration in 1628 of the well-known sarcophagus front representing the *Four Seasons* (Rome, Mus. Conserv.).

Algardi's first known independent work in marble was a small sculpture for Ludovisi of a *Putto Playing the Pipes Seated on a Tortoise* (untraced), intended as a pendant to Bernini's *Putto Bitten by a Viper* (untraced); they represented Security and Deceit respectively. It may have been Ludovisi who introduced Algardi to Domenichino, a Bolognese painter and former Carracci pupil, to whose design he executed *c.* 1628 one of the stucco telamones in the Cappella di Strada Cupis at S Maria in Trastevere (*in situ*). It was also through Domenichino that he obtained his first commission for a monumental public work: two over life-size stucco statues of *St John the Evangelist* and *St Mary Magdalene* (see fig. 1) for wall niches in the chapel of Cardinal Ottavio Bandini (*d* 1629) in S Silvestro al Quirinale (before July 1629; *in situ*), where Domenichino was executing the fresco decoration. While the *St John* is in the heroic style favoured by Domenichino, the *St Mary Magdalene* is clearly based on careful study of Bernini's statue of *St Bibiana* (1626; Rome, S Bibiana), the most stylistically advanced female embodiment of passion to be seen in Rome at that time. In his statue, however, Algardi moderated the full-blooded Baroque drama of his model with references to antique representations of *Niobe* and to the idealized female figures of Reni. In doing so, and in choosing a path between the opposing trends of Bernini's Baroque and François Duquesnoy's classicism, he created his first fully individual and successful work.

The first documented work of a long series of bronzes by Algardi belongs to the same period: the overall design of the urn of *St Ignatius Loyola* (1629; Rome, Pal. Gesù) was by the Jesuit Father Orazio Grassi, while Algardi was responsible for the detailed design and superb modelling of the decorative details, in particular the relief of *St Ignatius and the Early Saints of the Jesuit Order* (drawing, St Petersburg, Hermitage). He continued to be active as a restorer of antiques, receiving a commission in 1630 from the Roman Conservatori to rework and complete the torso of an armoured figure for a memorial statue of Urban VIII's brother, *Carlo Barberini* (Rome, Mus. Conserv.). Bernini was responsible for the design and the execution of the head. Algardi again played a subordinate role to Bernini in his contribution to the lavish catafalque (destr.) designed by the latter for Barberini's funeral in S Maria in Aracoeli. A bronze statuette of *Charity* known in several versions (e.g. Ferrara, Mus. Civ. A. Ant. Pal. Schifanoia) perhaps represents on a reduced scale one of Algardi's four statues of *Virtues* for this project.

Algardi's friendship with Pietro da Cortona, a connection that was to exert a strong effect on his style, and his relationship with the Roman Accademia di S Luca, of which Cortona was Principe, go back to his early years in Rome. The earliest recorded artistic association between the two men was in 1634, when during Cortona's restoration of S Martina, the Accademia's church, the relics of the early Christian martyrs St Martina, St Concordio, St Epifanio and an anonymous companion were discovered in the foundations. In the consequent rebuilding of the church, a chapel was created dedicated to St Martina's companions, and for this Algardi created the near life-size terracotta group of *Three Martyr Saints* (Rome, SS Luca e Martina). As in the religious paintings of Cortona and Domenichino, the object was to create an evocation of Christian antiquity that gives an appearance of historical truth through archaeological accuracy. In the foremost figure of the group, Algardi succeeded in creating a model for a young warrior saint that was to be imitated frequently. Also in 1634 he began his connection with Marcantonio Borghese, Prince of Sulmona, who commissioned models for the six bronze herms that bear the jasper slab forming what is known as the Borghese Table (Rome, priv. col., see Montagu, 1985, pl. 23). Algardi was later commis-

1. Alessandro Algardi: *St Mary Magdalene*, stucco, over life-size, *c.* 1629 (Rome, S Silvestro al Quirinale)

sioned by the same patron to design or make models for a whole range of smaller objects, for instance silver room fountains and bronze braziers. The only surviving objects that can be associated with these commissions are a black marble urn, resting on the Borghese dragons, executed by Silvio Calci, and two black marble vases with serpent and eagle handles (all Rome, Gal. Borghese). The vases originally accompanied the small, black marble statue of a child with butterfly's wings symbolizing *Sleep* (1635–6; Rome, Gal. Borghese). Algardi had already collaborated with Calci in 1634 when Nicolò Ridolfi, the General of the Dominican Order, commissioned the urn of *St Mary Magdalene* (Saint-Maximin-la-Sainte-Baume, Var, St Madeleine) to contain the saint's relics. It consists of a porphyry urn, executed by Calci, standing on two gilt-bronze dogs (symbols of the Dominican Order) modelled by Algardi and surmounted by a superb gilt-bronze statuette of *St Mary Magdalene* in a kneeling pose. Algardi's small relief of the *Ecstasy of St Mary Magdalene* (1635; Saint-Maximin-la-Sainte-Baume, St Madeleine; full-size terracotta model, Rome, SS Luca e Martina) is his first marble relief. Its relatively low-relief composition shows the influence of Domenichino, while technically the quality is modest.

(c) Monumental works, mid-1630s to 1644. Algardi had no major commissions for monumental works until the mid-1630s, when he received three. In July 1634 he signed the contract for the tomb of *Pope Leo XI* (marble, completed 1644, erected 1652; Rome, St Peter's; see fig. 2). Leo XI, who belonged to a collateral branch of the Medici family, had died in 1605 after a reign of only 27 days, and his great-nephew, Cardinal Roberto Ubaldini (*d* 1635), gave Algardi the commission. The tomb, which is fitted skilfully into a narrow passageway in the north aisle of St Peter's and is composed to be seen at an angle from both sides, is similar in type to Bernini's tomb of *Pope Urban VIII* (1628), also in St Peter's. The statue of Leo XI enthroned is set into a niche above the sarcophagus, which is flanked by standing allegorical figures of *Magnanimity* and *Liberality*. Above the niche Leo XI's coat of arms is held by hovering putti. The sarcophagus is ornamented with a relief representing *Cardinal de' Medici's Legation to France*. The monument is, however, considerably smaller than Bernini's and is striking in that Algardi abandoned the combination of white and coloured marbles with bronze used by Bernini, preferring instead white marble throughout to underline the compositional simplicity of the work.

2. Alessandro Algardi: tomb of *Pope Leo XI*, marble, completed 1644 (Rome, St Peter's)

In October 1634 Algardi signed the contract for the over life-size, free-standing group, the *Beheading of St Paul* (marble, completed 1644; Bologna, S Paolo Maggiore; *see* ALTARPIECE, fig. 5; terracotta models, St Petersburg, Hermitage; Riggisberg, Abegg-Stift.). This important commission came from the Spada family and was intended to form part of the unusually lavish high altar designed by Bernini as a memorial to Paolo Spada (*d* 1631). It is unclear which of the two artists was responsible for the composition of the group, which is full of tension, though it has limited dramatic impact. Nevertheless, with its visual embodiment of the opposite moral states of executioner and martyr it perfectly illustrates contemporary notions of artistic decorum and is one of Algardi's masterpieces. Its echo of the classicizing and idealizing style of Guido Reni's paintings is not accidental. A low-relief, gilt-bronze tondo also representing the *Beheading of St Paul* (1648) is affixed to the altar as an antependium below the group and continues the narrative: it depicts the miracle of the three fountains in Rome, showing how, as the severed head of the apostle touched the ground three times, three springs welled up from it. Unlike the iconically conceived monumental group, it is a dramatically narrated *istoria*; the miracle is reflected in the momentary stupefaction of the participants, particularly of two figures in the foreground who face each other in contrapposto pose, and in the exaggerated gesticulation of the terrified executioner and the corresponding noble gesture of surprise from the kneeling Christian woman. The relief, which must have been conceived as well as executed considerably later than the main group, is particularly beautiful in its linear rhythmicality.

Algardi's third major monumental commission of the 1630s is the over life-size marble group of *St Filippo Neri with an Angel* (1635–8; Rome, S Maria in Vallicella), carved for Pietro Buoncompagni, a descendant of a Roman Jewish family who possibly had Bolognese connections. It stands above the sacristy altar and was intended to provide the focal-point of a vista from a side entrance to the church in the right transept. Like the four gigantic statues by Bernini, Duquesnoy, Francesco Mochi and Andrea Bolgi under the dome of St Peter's, which had been in existence since 1629, Algardi's work demonstrates the conflict typical of the period between iconical *statua* and *istoria*, as well as the resolution of that conflict in a measured, comparatively conservative formulation that was widely imitated: the figure of Neri is frontally posed but at the same time it conveys an action, looking and gesturing towards heaven, moved by his love of God. This message is clarified by an inscription on the open book held by the angel, *Viam mandatarum tuarum cucurri, nam dilatasti cor meum* ('I have followed the path of your commandments, for you have swelled my heart'; Psalm 119), a reference to the mystical experience in which the saint's heart physically swelled with the love of God.

At this time, during his second decade in Rome, Algardi was also still active as a restorer of antique statuary. The restoration of *Hercules and the Hydra* (Rome, Mus. Capitolino) is the most important example of this work. He worked together with the Bolognese painter, stuccoist and architect Giovanni Francesco Grimaldi on the decoration of the Cappella Gessi in S Maria della Vittoria, Rome. Their respective roles in the design of the architectural setting are unclear, however. On the death of Marchese Ludovico Facchinetti in 1644, Algardi collaborated again with Grimaldi to create the catafalque (destr.) and temporary decoration for his obsequies at the church of SS Giovanni e Petronio dei Bolognesi in Rome. The high altar was adorned temporarily with the life-size bronze Crucifix (untraced; painted clay model, Rome, Vatican, Pal. Governatorato, chapel), which Algardi had just made for Ercole Alamandini. The stucco bas-relief of the *Trinity* (Rome, SS Luca e Martina) also belongs to this period; it is a typical example of Algardi's early style of relief, with its flat, two-dimensional quality and linear rhythm.

(d) The patronage of Innocent X, the Pamphili family and others, 1644–54. Algardi produced his greatest works during the papacy of Innocent X Pamphili (*reg* 1644–55). Bernini was ousted from his supreme artistic position in Rome because of his close personal connections with the Barberini, the family of the deceased Pope Urban VIII, and a circle well disposed towards Algardi dominated the papal court. This included the Oratorian Virgilio Spada, the new pope's artistic adviser, his major-domo Cristoforo Segni, who came from Bologna, and also Giacomo Franzone, whose family were notable patrons of Algardi (*see* FRANZONE). Algardi presented himself to Innocent X with a silver Crucifix (untraced; bronze version, Rome, S Maria del Popolo) and a silver group depicting the *Baptism of Christ* (untraced; terracotta model, Rome, Vatican, Bib. Apostolica; bronze version, Cleveland, OH, Mus. A.).

As a project for a monumental baptismal font for St Peter's came to nothing, commissions to Algardi from the new pope were at first small, the largest being for the Fountain of St Damasus (1645–8; Rome, Vatican, Cortile de Damaso), one of the few architectural structures that Algardi certainly designed. It consists of a monumental aedicular structure with Ionic columns modelled on those by Michelangelo for the Capitol. This structure, supporting a balcony, is applied to the arcade of the cortile and dwarfs the marble basin beneath. The whole is, however, redeemed from failure by the insistently plastic quality of the marble relief on the front of the basin, *St Liberius Baptizing Neophytes* (terracotta model, Minneapolis, MN, Inst. A.). Algardi contributed two designs (Paris, Louvre; Venice, Accad.) for a fountain for the centre of the Piazza Navona in the heart of Rome, which Innocent X wanted to turn into a vast forecourt to his family palace, the Palazzo Pamphili. Algardi's old-fashioned project for a small fountain with figures, still stylistically close to Giambologna, was, however, rejected in favour of Francesco Borromini's proposal for a fountain in the form of an obelisk dominating the whole square. Bernini subsequently developed his spectacular Fountain of the Four Rivers (1648–51) from this.

Algardi's chief patron during his last decade, and the channel through which papal patronage came, was the pope's nephew, Camillo Pamphili. The first important building put up during the new pontificate, the Villa Belrespiro (now Villa Doria-Pamphili; Rome, Porta S Pancrazio), was erected for him. It was at one time the most magnificent of all the villas for a papal nephew in Rome, designed *all'antica* inside and out and lavishly decorated with antique sculpture. Algardi's precise role in the architectural design, for which he seems to have been given responsibility, has long been debated. The design of the stucco decoration on the ground floor on the garden side is certainly by him. A rotunda, its vestibule and two side galleries, the Gallery of Roman Customs and the Gallery of Hercules are covered with figural reliefs surrounded by classicizing motifs. The design is derived from antique stuccowork, such as that at Hadrian's Villa at Tivoli, from Renaissance stucco by Raphael and Giovanni da Udine Nanni, as well as from Annibale Fontana's engraved crystal work. Both the antique appearance of the scheme and its iconographic programme were designed to emphasize the *Romanitas* and ancient origin of the Pamphili family, which traced its descent back to Numa Pompilius (=Pamphilius) and Hercules in a pseudo-historical family tree. The stuccoes in the villa were executed by professional stuccoists, but Algardi himself executed those in the Grotto of Venus in the gardens. A stucco garden fountain no longer exists and a large wall fountain depicting a personification of the *Aqua Vergine* against a brightly coloured landscape background, once in the courtyard of the Palazzo Pamphili al Corso, Rome, has also disappeared.

Algardi has also been suggested as the architect of the second large Jesuit church in Rome, S Ignazio, a building paid for by Cardinal Ludovico Ludovisi and dedicated in 1650. His contribution was, however, limited to the stucco high-relief figures of *Religion* and *Magnificence* that support an inscription tablet on the inside wall of the vestibule. In these he resolved the problem of the robed female figure in an unusually rich and animated form. He also designed the frieze of putti holding the arms of Ludovisi above the tablet. It is not clear what part he played in the biggest artistic undertaking of Innocent X's papacy, the renovation of the basilica of S Giovanni in Laterano, Rome. With Bernini, Mochi and others, he was supposed to execute the 12 colossal statues for niches in the nave, a project that was not carried out until the early 18th century. It is probable, but not certain, that Algardi provided the designs for at least some of the 12 stucco reliefs on the walls of the nave, in which scenes from the New Testament were placed opposite equivalent scenes from the Old Testament in accordance with a programme worked out by the Vatican librarian Annibale Albani.

Around 1646 Algardi received from the Conservatori of the city of Rome the prestigious commission for a bronze, seated statue of *Innocent X* (1646–50; Rome, Mus. Conserv.; terracotta model, Vienna, Ksthist. Mus.). It was procured by Algardi by means of intrigue, having originally been assigned to the older sculptor Mochi. Despite the fact that the first cast was flawed, Algardi was awarded the cross of the Cavaliere di Cristo. In the Holy Year of 1650 the statue of *Innocent X Giving his Blessing*, one of the finest in the long series of commemorative statues of the popes, was installed opposite Bernini's *Urban VIII.* It forms a contrast to this because of the calmer dignity of the Pope's appearance and gestures and the different approach to modelling. Also for Holy Year, 1650, Algardi designed for the Roman Archiconfraternità del Gonfalone a processional float representing the *Lamentation over the Dead Christ* (untraced; drawing, Zurich, Graph. Samml. Eidgenöss. Tech. Hochsch.), which was executed by his pupil Michel Anguier in wood or papier-mâché. According to Bellori, it was Diego Velázquez who, on his embassy to Rome in 1649–50, ordered four bronze groups symbolizing the four elements for the court of Spain. *Jupiter*, the symbol of fire, and *Juno*, symbolizing air (both ex-Aranjuez, Pal. Real, see Montagu, 1985, pls 124–5), were vertical compositions, originally serving as firedogs. *Neptune*, representing water, and *Cybele*, earth (both Aranjuez, Pal. Real), were intended from the start to stand on top of fountains and are more statuesque in conception. They were not completed until after Algardi's death. He continued to make models for smaller works to be cast in metal right to the end of his career. Among them are a *Flagellation of Christ* (bronze; Vienna, Ksthist. Mus.), which has been ascribed variously to Algardi and François Duquesnoy, *Venus and Adonis* (bronze; Paris, Marquis de Lastic priv. col., see Montagu, 1985, pl. 187), a *Pietà* (ex-Victor Spark priv. col., New York, see Montagu, 1985, pl. 188) and a *Rest on the Flight into Egypt* (bronze; Cambridge, Fitzwilliam). Outstanding in Algardi's late period are the *Virgin and Child* (bronze; Norfolk, VA, Chrysler Mus.) and the group *St Michael Overcoming the Devil* (bronze; Bologna, Mus. Civ.), made for a Bolognese patron and cast by Domenico Guidi. Twelve bronze busts of saints (Genoa, SS Vittore e Carlo) made for the Franzone family were not cast until after Algardi's death, using a variety of models.

It was also during Innocent X's papacy that Algardi became a truly accomplished relief artist. His main work in this genre, the *Encounter of Leo the Great and Attila* (1646–53; Rome, St Peter's; see fig. 3; terracotta maquette, Florence, Bargello; full-scale stucco model, Rome, oratory of the Filippini), is one of the greatest marble reliefs of the 17th century. The event depicted took place on the banks of the Mincio in AD 453 when Pope Leo the Great, supported by a threatening apparition of SS Peter and Paul in the clouds, successfully forced the king of the Huns to retreat. It had been perceived ever since as a triumph of the papacy in conflict with temporal power. In Algardi's relief there is a skilfully built-up drama of emotions: only the Pope and his barbarian adversary are aware of the apparition. While the army of Huns is still surging forward,

3. Alessandro Algardi: *Encounter of Leo the Great and Attila*, marble relief, 8.58×4.94 m, 1646–53 (Rome, St Peter's)

Attila, equally struck by the appearance of the Pope and that of the two apostle princes, is already reeling back in consternation, prepared for flight and retreat. The clarity and conviction of the composition have meant that the relief has become a much admired example of an *istoria.* The foremost figures are modelled almost fully in the round, with the result that the event portrayed thrusts into the viewer's space as if on a stage. The same tendency to overstep the traditional boundaries separating different genres is evident in the design for the altar of St Nicholas (marble; 1651–5) in S Nicola da Tolentino, Rome, which was commissioned by Camillo Pamphili and completed after Algardi's death by Guidi, Ercole Ferrata and Francesco Baratta. Algardi gave the conservatively designed aedicule-style altar a revolutionary centrepiece. Like the contemporaneous *Ecstasy of St Teresa* (1651; Rome, S Maria della Vittoria) by Bernini (*see* BAROQUE, fig. 1), *St Nicholas of Tolentino's Vision of the Madonna, St Augustine and St Monica* is a relief that is conceived almost as a group in the round. It has no relief background but emerges straight out of the curved wall of its niche.

Algardi's small bas-relief of *St Constantia's Vision of St Agnes* (bronze; Genoa, SS Vittore e Carlo; plaster version,

Rome, Pal. Venezia) is connected with the foundation dearest to Innocent X's heart, the new church of S Agnese in the Piazza Navona (the foundation stone was laid on 15 August 1652), which he added to the family palace to house his tomb and serve as a huge palace chapel. Its special feature was that all altars were to be decorated not with paintings but with reliefs. Algardi himself designed the relief for the high altar, the *Miracle of St Agnes* (drawing, Copenhagen, Stat. Mus. Kst; maquette cast in bronze, Vienna, Ksthist. Mus.). The youthful saint is depicted iconically, raised above the flow of action with her eyes turned upwards towards her heavenly bridegroom, kneeling on the spot where she was martyred under the arches of Domitian's stadium, which form the crypt of S Agnese. Although Algardi's pupils Guidi and Ferrata prepared a full-size stucco model (Rome, oratory of the Filippini) after his death, the project was never carried out because the decorative scheme for the church was changed. Algardi's project for a tomb for *Innocent X*, to be situated in the right transept of the church, met the same fate. It is unclear whether he had completed designs for the reliefs for the side altars, which finally were started in 1660 by his pupils Francesco Peroni and Ercole Ferrata, Ferrata's pupil Melchiorre Caffa, and Francesco de' Rossi (*fl* 1640–77).

(ii) Portrait sculpture. How and why Algardi came to work as a sculptor of portraits remains unclear. His earliest work, a bust of *Costanzo Patrizi* (marble; Rome, S Maria Maggiore), dates from the late 1620s or early 1630s, its subject having died in 1623; it fits into an oval niche in an epitaph, hence the old-fashioned smallness of scale. The marble busts of *Lelio Frangipane*, *Muzio Frangipane* and *Roberto Frangipane* (before 1638; Rome, S Marcello al Corso), executed in the mid-1630s, represent an early peak of achievement. Algardi, restricted by the 16th-century series of busts already in existence and the round shape of the niches in the family chapel, modelled ideal portraits of the mature and youthful warrior in the busts of *Muzio* (*d* 1588) and of *Lelio* (*d* 1606). The spectacular portrait achievement of these years, however, is the marble bust of *Cardinal Giovanni Garzia Mellini* (1637–8; Rome, S Maria del Popolo; see fig. 4), also a posthumous image, in which the Cardinal, represented down to the waist, is shown leaning forward slightly from the niche in his tomb and turned towards the altar with an expression of dignified devotion. The expressive realism of the work suggests that a death mask was used. Another closely related piece is the grandiose bust of *Cardinal Laudivio Zacchia* (Berlin, Bodemus.), similarly based on a death mask. It too is characterized by the generous size of the bust in outline, created by the broad folds of the Cardinal's cape, and by the same balance between sharply observed detail and an overall effect of dignity.

The monumental bronze bust of *Gregory XV* (Rome, S Maria in Vallicella, Sacristy) was completed in 1640; illusionistically leaning forward from an oval niche, with hands clasped, the Pope seems to pay homage across the width of the room to the statue of St Filippo Neri whom he had canonized. The marble bust of *Cardinal Carlo Emanuele Pio* (Imbersago, Villa Mombello) was made shortly after 1641, the year of his death. The angle of the head, the facial expression and the displaced edge of the bishop's cape, suggesting arm movement, combine to convey a moment full of life, a concept of the bust reminiscent of such animated portraits by Bernini as the bust of *Cardinal Scipione Borghese* (Rome, Gal. Borghese). Other portraits made around this time include the marble bust of *Prospero Santacroce* (after 1643; Rome, S Maria della Scala), which is the centrepiece of a memorial of coloured marbles designed by Algardi himself.

4. Alessandro Algardi: *Cardinal Giovanni Garzia Mellini*, marble, 1637–8 (Rome, S Maria del Popolo)

Algardi executed several likenesses of Innocent X and his family. The bronze version of his bust of the Pope (probably after 1647; Rome, Pal. Doria-Pamphili, private apartments; drawing, Madrid, Real Acad. S Fernando) was cast by Guidi, while the marble version (Rome, Pal. Doria Pamphili) would have been carved by studio assistants. The white-painted terracotta bust of *Innocent X* (Rome, Pal. Odeschalchi) is characteristic of Algardi's concept of a papal bust: a calm composition, with an expression of dignity and thoughtful mildness. Marble busts of the family include the Pope's brother *Benedetto Pamphili* (Rome, Pal. Doria-Pamphili) and his influential sister-in-law *Olimpia Maidalchini* (*c.* 1646–7; Rome, Pal. Doria-Pamphili). The subtly modelled terracotta bust of *Gaspare Mola* (St Petersburg, Hermitage), with the unusual motif of the sitter's hand caught up in the drapery, was intended as a model for an unexecuted marble version for Mola's tomb.

Among portraits made in the final phase of Algardi's career are the marble busts of *Giovanni Savenier* (Rome, S Maria dell'Anima), *Antonio Cerri* (Manchester, C.A.G.), *Elisabetta Contucci Coli* (Perugia, S Domenico) and *Odoardo Santarelli* (Rome, S Maria Maggiore); the last of these is inside a frame designed by Algardi himself. For the bust of *Giacinta Sanvitale Conti* (*d* 1652) Algardi made only the terracotta model (1652–4; Rome, Pal. Venezia), while the marble version (Parma, S Rocco) was carved by Guidi, as was the bust of *Cardinal Paolo Emilio Zacchia*

(Florence, Bargello), incomplete when Algardi died. The terracotta model (London, V&A) is, however, entirely by Algardi; in the simulated naturalness of the pose—the Cardinal is shown in the act of turning the pages of a book—and the simplicity of the forms achieved by masterly differentiation in the modelling, this is a late masterpiece, contributing to Algardi's reputation as one of the most important portrait sculptors of the 17th century.

2. WORKING METHODS AND STUDIO ORGANIZATION. Algardi was by training a modeller in stucco and terracotta in the Bolognese tradition. His earliest works were in these materials, and, though his skill as a restorer of antique sculpture makes it clear that he must have learnt to carve marble before he arrived in Rome, there was a pervasive rumour during his first years in the city that he was unable to carve. It is possible that the small black marble statue of *Sleep* in the Borghese collection was made by Algardi to disprove these rumours. However, the works produced during his second decade in Rome demonstrate the superb skills he acquired in working marble. Nevertheless, like all his major contemporaries, he was reliant on a workshop of assistants to help him fulfil the many large-scale commissions that came his way, particularly during the papacy of Innocent X. Equally, no sculptor of the period would have expected to have the technical skills necessary for the casting of works in bronze or silver, and here he would have relied on professional mould makers, founders and chasers. Much of the stucco decoration designed by him, as at the Villa Belrespiro, would have been executed by specialist stuccoists.

The names of only some of Algardi's collaborators are known, and details of the scope and organization of his workshop are difficult to establish. Algardi's main pupil and the closest to him personally was Domenico Guidi. He went to Algardi in 1648 from the workshop of his uncle, Giuliano Finelli, in Naples; he was also valuable to Algardi because of his experience in bronze-casting and was involved, sometimes recognizably, in the execution of the large-scale marble works of Algardi's late period, such as the reliefs of the *Encounter of Leo the Great and Attila* and *St Nicholas of Tolentino's Vision*. Working with Algardi as his second main pupil was the artistically more talented Ercole Ferrata, an older man who left Naples in the late 1640s and worked first for Bernini. Paolo Carnieri's share in the output of the workshop is almost impossible to assess. Girolamo Lucenti must have been employed mainly as an expert in metal-casting. In 1654 Algardi's artistic estate, consisting of the works that were in the papal foundry near St Peter's, which served him as a studio, was inherited equally by Guidi, Ferrata, Carnieri and Lucenti, his principal collaborators in his late period. Before their time there is evidence that Francesco Maria Ricci from Genoa, hardly known except in this context, and Giuseppe Peroni (*c.* 1626–63), a Roman, were Algardi's assistants, while Antonio Raggi, an important figure, worked both for him and for Bernini. Pupils from Algardi's late period whose names are known are Giovanni Battista Morelli (*d c.* 1665), the three Frenchmen Michel Anguier, Simon Guillain and Alexandre Jacquet (called Grenoble), probably the Belgian Jean Delcour, and three sculptors from Emilia, Camillo Mazza (1602–72), Gabriele Brunelli (1615–82) and Francesco Agnesini (1616–after 1661).

3. POSTHUMOUS INFLUENCE AND REPUTATION. Algardi's influence on the contemporary artistic scene and on his successors was considerable, even if in the 17th century it was at first overshadowed by that of Bernini. Long after Algardi's death, large numbers of casts were made from his models. In addition, copies of his works and models were in widespread use throughout Europe as teaching and demonstration material. His principal successor and the man who took over his workshop was Domenico Guidi, and Algardi's style lived on in a less disciplined form in Guidi's extensive sculptural output to the end of the century; but the true, uninterrupted continuation of Algardi's style is to be found in the work of the more important Ercole Ferrata, and as a component in the style of Ferrata's extremely talented pupil Melchiorre Caffa. As Ferrata was entrusted by the Grand Duke of Tuscany with the training of young sculptors from his duchy in Rome, there was a whole generation of Tuscan students of sculpture, headed by Giovanni Battista Foggini and Massimiliano Soldani, who were taught in that academy in the style of Algardi.

Especially as a relief artist and portrait sculptor, Algardi exercised a long-lasting influence on European sculpture. As Bernini's prestige waned, Algardi's importance increased with the general change in style and taste towards classicism in the early 18th century, and he was a formative influence on Camillo Rusconi and such French sculptors as Edme Bouchardon. Algardi was portrayed by Bellori, the principal 17th-century advocate of classicism, as the main representative with François Duquesnoy (who died young) of a classicizing current in sculpture equivalent to that in painting represented by Annibale Carracci and the Bolognese school. This literary portrait, which by implication opposed Algardi's style to the High Baroque of Bernini, was remarkably successful. The idea of Algardi as a 'Baroque classical' artist was accepted largely uncritically until the 1980s, when more probing research into his work, most notably that of Montagu, produced a more complex picture of an artist whose works contain Baroque and Mannerist as well as classicizing elements, often dependent on medium and scale.

BIBLIOGRAPHY

EARLY SOURCES

S. della Staffa, ed.: *Poesie dedicate alle glorie del sig. Alessandro Algardi, ottimo degli scultori* (Perugia, 1643)

G. P. Bellori: *Vite* (1672); ed. E. Borea (1976), pp. 387–402

C. C. Malvasia: *Felsina pittrice* (1678); ed. M. Brascaglia (1971), i, pp. 88, 331, 347, 351, 359; ii, pp. 26, 90, 153, 212, 225, 407

G. Passeri: *Vite* (1679); ed. J. Hess (1934), pp. 195–211

GENERAL

Thieme–Becker

O. Pollak: *Die Kunsttätigkeit unter Urban VIII*, 2 vols (Vienna, 1928–31)

M. Hager: *Die Ehrenstatuen der Päpste*, Römische Forschungen der Bibliotheca Hertziana, vii (Leipzig, 1929)

A. Riccoboni: *Roma nell'arte: La scultura nell'evo moderno dal quattrocento ad oggi* (Rome, 1942)

J. Pope-Hennessy: *Italian High Renaissance and Baroque Sculpture* (1963), iii of *An Introduction to Italian Sculpture* (London, 1958–63)

J. Garms, ed.: *Quellen aus dem Archiv Doria-Pamphili: Zur Kunsttätigkeit in Rom unter Innocenz X* (Rome and Vienna, 1972)

MONOGRAPHS

W. Vitzthum: *Alessandro Algardi* (Milan, 1966)

M. Heimbürger Ravalli: *Alessandro Algardi: Scultore* (Rome, 1973)
J. Montagu: *Alessandro Algardi*, 2 vols (New Haven and London, 1985)
E. Neumann: *Mehrfigurige Reliefs von Alessandro Algardi: Genese, Analyse, Ikonographie*, Bochumer Schriften zur Kunstgeschichte, vii (Frankfurt, 1985)

SPECIALIST STUDIES

Specific sculptures

C. Galassi Paluzzi: 'Un bozzetto di Alessandro Algardi per l'urna di S Ignazio al Gesù', *Roma*, iii (1925), pp. 17–18
R. Wittkower: 'Un bronzo dell'Algardi a Urbino', *Rass. March.*, vii (1928), pp. 41–4
J. Hess: 'Ein Spätwerk des Bildhauers Alessandro Algardi', *Münchn. Jb. Bild. Kst.*, n. s., viii (1931), pp. 292–303
A. Riccoboni: 'Un'opera dimenticato di Alessandro Algardi', *Capitolium*, xviii (1943), pp. 313–16
O. Raggio: 'A Rediscovered Portrait: Alessandro Algardi's Bust of *Cardinal Scipione Borghese*', *Connoisseur*, cxxxviii (1956), pp. 203–8
A. Nava Cellini: 'Per un busto dell'Algardi a Spoleto', *Paragone*, viii/87 (1957), pp. 21–9
N. Wibiral: 'Die Agnesreliefs für S Agnese in Piazza Navona', *Röm. Hist. Mitt.*, iii (1958–60), pp. 255–78
R. Enggass: 'Algardi's Portrait Bust of *St Philip Neri*', *A. Ant. & Mod.*, 9 (1960), pp. 296–9
R. Wittkower: 'Algardi's Relief of *Pope Liberius Baptizing Neophytes*', *Bull. Minneapolis Inst. A.*, xlix (1960), pp. 29–42
A. Marti Bomboi: 'Due terracotte dell'Algardi', *Capitolium*, xxxvii (1962), p. 479
E. Eglinski: 'A *Flagellation* Group by Algardi', *Register [Lawrence, U. KS]*, iii (Dec 1963), pp. 18–23
J. Montagu: 'A *Flagellation* Group: Algardi or du Quesnoy?', *Bull. Mus. Royaux. A. & Hist.*, 4th ser., xxxviii–xxxix (1966–7), pp. 153–93
R. S. Spear: 'Algardi's *St Proculus*', *Burl. Mag.*, cxi (1969), pp. 220–23
J. Montagu: 'Alessandro Algardi's Altar of S Nicola da Tolentino and some Related Models', *Burl. Mag.*, cxii (1970), pp. 282–91
——: '*Le Baptême du Christ* d'Alessandro Algardi', *Rev. A.*, xv (1971), pp. 64–78
O. Raggio: 'Alessandro Algardi e gli stucchi di Villa Pamphili', *Paragone*, xxii/251 (1971), pp. 3–38
F. Negri Arnoldi: 'Un busto algardiano di *Innocenzo X* a ricordo di una pace in famiglia', *Commentari*, xxiv (1973), pp. 323–7
J. Pope-Hennessy: 'Some Newly Acquired Italian Sculptures: A Portrait Sketch by Algardi', *V&A Mus. Yb.*, iv (1974), pp. 38–46
M. Heimbürger Ravalli: 'Postilla su Algardi scultore', *Stud. Romani*, xxiii (1975), pp. 190–91
J. Montagu: 'Alessandro Algardi and the "Borghese Table"', *Antol. B. A.*, iv (1977), pp. 311–28
——: 'Alessandro Algardi and the Statue of *St Philip Neri*', *Jb. Hamburg. Kstsamml.*, xxii (1977), pp. 75–100
E. Neumann: 'Das Figurenrelief auf der Urne des Hl. Ignazio im römischen "Gesù": Vergleich mit einer bisher unbeachteten Algardi-Zeichnung in der Leningrader Ermitage', *Pantheon*, xxxv (1977), pp. 318–28
H. F. Senie: 'The Tomb of *Leo XI* by Alessandro Algardi', *A. Bull.*, lx (1978), pp. 90–95
E. Neumann: 'Algardis Figurenreliefs am Grabmal *Leos XI.* in St Peter im Vatikan', *Pantheon*, xxxix (1981), pp. 172–5
U. Schlegel: 'I Crocifissi degli altari in San Pietro in Vaticano', *Ant. Viva*, xx (1981), pp. 37–42
S. Androsov: 'Some Works of Algardi from the Farsetti Collection in the Hermitage', *Burl. Mag.*, cxxv (1983), pp. 77–83

Architecture and drawing

O. Pollak: 'Alessandro Algardi (1602–1654) als Architekt', *Z. Gesch. Archit.*, iv (1910–11), pp. 49–79
W. Vitzthum: 'Disegni di Alessandro Algardi', *Boll. A.*, n. s. 3, xlviii (1963), pp. 75–98
C. Johnston: 'Drawings for Algardi's *Cristo vivo*', *Burl. Mag.*, cx (1968), pp. 459–60
M. Heimbürger: 'Un disegno certo dell'Algardi e alcuni probabili di Gregorio Spada', *Paragone*, xx/237 (1969), pp. 59–98
——: 'Un disegno di Alessandro Algardi per la pala di *S Agnese in Agone*', *Stud. Romani*, xviii (1970), pp. 216–19
——: 'Alessandro Algardi architetto?', *Anlct. Romana Inst. Dan.*, iv (1971), pp. 197–224

Other

H. Posse: 'Alessandro Algardi', *Jb. Kön.-Preuss. Kstsamml.*, xxvi (1905), pp. 169–201
M. Neusser: 'Alessandro Algardi als Antikenrestaurator', *Belvedere*, xiii (1928), pp. 3–9
M. Labò: 'La Cappella del'Algardi nei SS Vittore e Carlo a Genova', *Dedalo*, xi (1930–31), pp. 1392–1405
A. Nava Cellini: 'Aggiunte alla ritrattistica berniniana e dell'Algardi', *Paragone*, vi/65 (1955), pp. 23–31
A. Arfelli: 'Tre note intorno ad Alessandro Algardi', *A. Ant. & Mod.*, 8 (1959), pp. 461–6
A. Nava Cellini: 'Per Alessandro Algardi e Domenico Guidi', *Paragone*, xi/121 (1960), pp. 61–8
I. Toesca: 'Un ritratto dell'Algardi', *Boll. A.*, n. s. 3, xlv (1960), pp. 336–8
A. Mezzetti: 'Alessandro Algardi', *L'ideale classico del seicento in Italia e la pittura di paesaggio* (exh. cat., Bologna, Pal. Archiginnasio, 1962), pp. 345–60
A. Nava Cellini: 'Il Borromini, l'Algardi e il Grimaldi per Villa Pamphili', *Paragone*, xiv/159 (1963), pp. 25–37
——: 'Per l'integrazione e lo svolgimento della ritrattistica di Alessandro Algardi', *Paragone*, xv/177 (1964)
G. Gallo Colonni: 'Note sur Alessandro Algardi', *A. Lombarda*, x (1965), pp. 161–8
A. Nava Cellini: 'Note per l'Algardi, il Bernini e il Reni', *Paragone*, xviii/207 (1967), pp. 35–52
D. Batorska: 'Additional Comments on the Iconography of the Sala di Ercole at Villa Doria-Pamphili in Rome', *Paragone*, xxvi/303 (1975), pp. 22–54
M. Heimbürger Ravalli: *Architettura, scultura e arti minori nel barocco italiano: Ricerche nell'archivio Spada* (Florence, 1977)
J. Gash and J. Montagu: 'Algardi, Gentile and Innocent X: A Rediscovered Painting and its Frame', *Burl. Mag.*, cxxii (1980), pp. 55–60, 63
J. Montagu: 'Alessandro Algardi's *Saint Peter* and *Saint Paul* and the Patronage of the Franzoni Family', *Bull. Detroit Inst. A.*, lxi (1983), pp. 19–29

RUDOLF PREIMSBERGER

Algarotti, Francesco (*b* Venice, 11 Dec 1712; *d* Pisa, 12 May 1764). Italian patron, collector and writer. The second son of a wealthy Venetian merchant, he was educated in Bologna, where he studied under the eminent scientists Eustachio Manfredi and the Zanotti brothers. Afterwards he travelled in the Veneto and developed a particular admiration for the works of Veronese, Guido Reni and Andrea Palladio. In Florence in 1733 he was impressed by the art of Titian and Fra Bartolommeo. He then spent a year in Rome, where the ancient monuments and paintings by the Caracci and Domenichino had a considerable impact on him. There, too, he made the acquaintance of the scholar and antiquarian Giovanni Gaetano Bottari. A period in Paris led to contacts with Pierre-Louis Moreau de Maupertuis, an early champion of Newton's principles, and with Voltaire and the collectors Pierre Crozat and Pierre-Jean Mariette. Then in England in 1736 he was a social success; during this visit Jonathan Richardson made two portrait drawings of him (London, V&A). After a further stay in Paris, with Voltaire, he spent a year in Milan and Venice and published a popular exposition on Newton's discoveries in optics, *Il Newtonianismo per le dame* (1739). In the form of a humorous dialogue, it was the first of many writings in which he presented new, complex theories in an accessible form. Algarotti then resumed his European travel: to France, England, Russia and Germany, where he met Frederick the Great, King of Prussia, with whom he struck an immediate rapport, and who made him a count. A pastel portrait of Algarotti at around this time by Jean-Étienne Liotard (1741; Amsterdam, Rijksmus.) is extant.

In 1742 Algarotti was invited to Dresden by Frederick-Augustus II, Elector of Saxony, and the following year was given the task of acquiring paintings for the royal collection, which the King was rapidly enlarging. In his capacity as agent, Algarotti travelled to Venice in May 1743 where he remained until 1745. His talent as a patron and critic became evident in this period. With great foresight, he set about restructuring the collection according to school so as to form a chronological survey rather than an arbitrary collection based on personal taste. He also felt that it should include the works of living artists, a sentiment not held by the King, who was more anxious to acquire Old Masters. Among the paintings Algarotti purchased for the King were works by Palma Vecchio, Veronese, Bernardo Strozzi, Sebastiano Ricci, Rosalba Carriera and Hans Holbein. He also commissioned paintings (untraced), mostly historical pictures of classical subjects, from Giovanni Battista Piazzetta, Giambattista Pittoni and Francesco Zuccarelli. Algarotti was particularly sensitive to the individual strengths of the artists and attempted to choose subjects accordingly. During this period he also developed a friendship with Giambattista Tiepolo; Algarotti sought Tiepolo's advice on acquisitions and purchased a number of his paintings for the Dresden galleries, including the *Banquet of Cleopatra* (1743–4; Melbourne, N.G. Victoria). In order to justify the inclusion of Tiepolo's work in the collection, the classical and traditional qualities of his paintings were emphasized to the King. Algarotti also added substantially to his own family art collection, which had been established by his father and brother Bonomo Algarotti. He gradually acquired 200 paintings, 13 of which were by Tiepolo, including a modello (Paris, Mus. Cognacq-Jay) for the *Banquet of Cleopatra* and a reduced version of the *Finding of Moses* by Veronese, which Algarotti had acquired for Frederick-Augustus. Algarotti's collection of drawings included numerous works by Tiepolo, Canaletto, Ferdinando Galli-Bibiena, Sebastiano Ricci, Carlo Maratti and Hogarth.

From 1745 to 1753 Algarotti lived mostly in Prussia, where he acted as adviser to Frederick the Great and was instrumental in introducing the work of Palladio to the country. On the death of his friend the opera singer Felice Salimbeni (1712–51), Algarotti commissioned George Friedrich Schmidt (1712–75) to engrave a portrait of him; in 1752 Schmidt also engraved a profile portrait of *Algarotti* (Berlin, Kupferstichkab.), an image that was subsequently used as the model for a number of portraits, including that of his funerary monument.

Algarotti was in Venice again from 1753 to 1756. From this visit possibly dates the commission to Canaletto to paint a capriccio of Palladio's *Design for the Rialto Bridge* (sometimes identified as the painting in Milan, Conti priv. col.; see Constable, 2/1976, pl. 86, illus. 458). Algarotti spent the remaining years of his life in Italy, first in Bologna (from 1756), where he met Gasparo Prospero Pesci (*d* 1784) and Mauro Antonio Tesi, forming a particularly close relationship with the latter. Both Pesci and Tesi executed many paintings for him, mostly of architectural fantasies, sometimes from his own sketches. He received a visit in 1757 from the architect Robert Adam. He then moved to Florence and finally to Pisa.

In his last years Algarotti prepared a complete edition of his writings. This collection of theoretical treatises reflected his wide-ranging interests and included essays on opera, the Académie de France in Rome and architecture; the last discusses the practical approach to architecture of Carlo Lodoli. In his essay on painting (1762), a text intended as a manual for artists and dedicated to the Society of Arts (founded 1754), Algarotti discussed perspective, composition and anatomy and described the workings of the camera obscura. He also advocated the study of antique models and emphasized the importance of drawing. During this period he also corresponded extensively with patrons and collectors including Mariette and Anton Maria Zanetti (i), and with Tiepolo and Canaletto. Algarotti died of consumption and was buried in a tomb in the Camposanto, Pisa. Frederick the Great provided the funds for his funerary monument, which was designed by Tesi and completed (1768) under the supervision of the sculptor Carlo Bianconi (1732–1802).

WRITINGS

Il Newtonianismo per le dame ovvero dialoghi sopra la luce e i colori (Milan, 1739)

Saggio sopra l'architettura (1756)

Saggio sopra la pittura (Bologna, 1762; Eng. trans., London, 1764)

Opere, 17 vols (Venice, 1791–4)

BIBLIOGRAPHY

DBI

M. Levey: 'Two Paintings by Tiepolo from the Algarotti Collection', *Burl. Mag.*, cii (1960), pp. 250–57

W. G. Constable: *Canaletto* (Oxford, 1962, 2/1976)

F. Haskell: *Patrons and Painters* (London, 1962, rev. New Haven and London, 2/1980), pp. 347–60

R. W. Holland: *Critical Observations of Francesco Algarotti as Expressed in Three of his Essays on the Fine Arts* (PhD thesis, Ohio U., 1975)

An Album of Eighteenth-century Venetian Operatic Caricatures Formerly in the Collection of Count Algarotti (exh. cat. by E. Croft-Murray, Toronto, A.G., 1980)

R. P. Ciardi: '"Non omnis": Il monumento Algarotti nel Camposanto pisano e la tipologia illuminista della tomba', *Artista*, i (1989), pp. 52–63

□

Algeria, Democratic and Popular Republic of [Arab. Al-Jumhūriyyah al-Jazā'iriyyah al-Dimuqrāṭiyyah al-Sha'biyya; Al-Jazā'ir]. Country in North Africa with its capital at Algiers.

1. Geography and history. 2. Architecture. 3. Painting, graphic arts and sculpture. 4. Other arts. 5. Museums.

1. GEOGRAPHY AND HISTORY. Algeria is the second largest country in Africa, with an area of *c.* 2,400,000 sq. km. Extending south from the Mediterranean Sea to the Sahara, it is bordered to the west by Morocco, Western Sahara and Mauritania, to the south by Mali and Niger and to the east by Libya and Tunisia. Geographically Algeria can be divided into three regions: the most populated region of the coastal Atlas range (including the Kabylie Mountains) and small plains in the north; the salt flats and high plateau of the Saharan Atlas range; and the desert (including the Hoggar Mountains), which comprises four-fifths of the country. Most of the population (22,600,000, 1986 est.) is Arab or Arabized, although about 20% have retained their Berber identity and language. Nearly all are Sunni Muslim. Many people from the old-established Jewish and more recent European communities left when independence from France was won in 1962; about a million Algerians live in Europe, most of them in France. In the 1970s oil deposits and huge gas reserves financed rapid industrialization, while

agriculture was neglected, and there was a massive rural exodus.

The earliest inhabitants of the area were the BERBER, and the earliest examples of artistic activity are the innumerable rock carvings and paintings in the Sahara region, especially in the caves of the Tassili National Park near Djanet, the oldest dating to *c.* 6000 BC. Punic Cirta (now Constantine) was the ancient capital of the Numidian kings and grew in importance from the 4th–3rd century BC. Roman control was extended along the coast into Algeria after Carthage was destroyed in 146 BC; Cirta was renamed after the Roman emperor in AD 311. The best-preserved Roman ruins are at CHERCHEL (anc. Caesarea), Annaba (anc. HIPPO REGIUS), DJEMILA (anc. Cuicul) and Timgad (anc. THAMUGADI). There are Phoenician tombs, Berber mausolea, Byzantine forts and basilicas (e.g. at Tebessa, anc. THEVESTIS) and fine medieval Islamic buildings, particularly those at TLEMCEN and the site of QAL'AT BANI HAMMAD.

From the early 16th century northern Algeria was under Ottoman rule, although it was in effect autonomous. In 1830 Algiers was seized by French troops; there was resistance in various parts of the country until the early 1870s. Algeria became part of France, and European settlers were encouraged until eventually one-third of all cultivable land was farmed by the French. Modern anti-colonialism began during World War I and was strengthened after the occupation of France by Nazi Germany in 1940. The armed struggle in Algeria began in 1954, led by the Front de Libération Nationale (FLN), and continued until 1962 when, despite a campaign of terror by some French settlers, independence was finally won and most Europeans left the country. Ahmed ben Bella of the FLN was elected president of a one-party state in 1963, but, after conflict within FLN ranks, he was deposed by Houari Boumedienne in 1965. Until Boumedienne's death in 1978, policies were increasingly socialist; under his successors the Arabization movement, which had begun immediately after independence, was intensified, government centralization was relaxed and relations with the West improved, although opposition came from Berberists and radical Muslims. After the cancellation of the first elections since independence, held in 1992, there was growing tension between the government and its Islamic fundamentalist opponents.

This article discusses the art produced in Algeria from *c.* 1830. For discussion of the art of earlier periods *see* AFRICA, §VII, 1; ROME, ANCIENT; NUMIDIA; EARLY CHRISTIAN AND BYZANTINE ART; ISLAMIC ART; ALMORAVID; ALMOHAD; and HAFSID.

2. ARCHITECTURE. From 1830 the Neo-classical style of the French building programme was soon accompanied by an official neo-Moorish style that was used for such buildings as schools, administrative and military headquarters, barracks and post offices (e.g. the main post office in Algiers). French arcaded buildings are plentiful in Annaba and Oran, and there is typical colonial building in Tlemcen, Sétif and Tiaret, which was destroyed in 1841 and supplied with buildings in the standard French style.

Between 1830 and 1870 the medina in Algiers was partly destroyed by the French, and the souk expanded into an arcaded boulevard. In the 1950s large-scale housing estates were built, designed by FERNAND POUILLON, the Chief Architect of Algiers. After independence, merchants and craftsmen moved out of the medina for modern quarters and were replaced by low-income workers. In the 1980s UNESCO assisted the Government in surveying the urgent conservation needs of the kasba, an outstanding example of an Islamic city centre.

The traditional architecture of Algeria influenced such Western architects as Antoni Gaudí, and Le Corbusier and ANDRÉ RAVÉREAU, who were impressed by the BERBER architecture of the Mzab Valley (*c.* 450 km south of Algiers). The five towns of the Mzab (Ghardaia is the largest) were founded in the 11th century; the unadorned buildings have a pronounced functionalism that is adapted to the life of the people and belongs to the landscape. Ravéreau's buildings in the Mzab in the 1960s and 1970s show his understanding of the local style. However, traditional buildings were not immune from modernist schemes. Le Corbusier devised various plans for the development of Algiers between 1931 and 1942, but none was accepted. Since independence, apartment blocks have been built in most Algerian towns, and industrialization has damaged some areas.

3. PAINTING, GRAPHIC ARTS AND SCULPTURE. In the period ofter independence two strands of Algerian painting evolved: a Western Neo-classical style as implemented by the Orientalist painters (*see* ORIENTALISM) and an Islamic one based on miniature painting, classical calligraphy and arabesque decoration. Eugène Delacroix, in 1832, was the first French painter to visit Algeria. He was followed by many French Orientalists, who introduced European easel painting into the country. In 1851 the Société des Beaux-Arts was founded in Algeria; membership was restricted to artists of French origin. By 1894, the Orientalist painters of Algeria were numerous enough to organize an annual salon in Paris, and in 1897 the Société des Peintres Algériens et Orientalistes was founded in Algiers. There was even an Ecole d'Alger in Orientalist painting that depicted Algerian subjects with compassion. The most important Orientalist artist in Algeria was Alphonse-Etienne Dinet (1861–1929). A Parisian-born French painter, he studied at the Ecole des Beaux-Arts and made several visits to the new province between 1884 and 1888. He became so interested in North Africa that on his return to Paris in 1887 he founded the Société des Peintres Orientalistes Français, with Léonce Bénédite as its president. He then studied Arabic and eventually converted to Islam. From 1904 Dinet divided his time between Algeria and France, introducing Western academic teaching into Algeria through the Société des Beaux-Arts.

Early in the 20th century, native Algerian artists who had preferred traditional Islamic art to imported Western painting began to follow a style initiated by Mohammed Racim (1896–1974). This was a style of miniature painting, arising out of Racim's respect for Western three-dimensional painting, that combined Western and Islamic aesthetics. These Islamic artists also reverted to calligraphy. Meanwhile, Western art in Algeria was most often practised by the descendants of French settlers, whose works were regarded as superior to those of Algerian artists. In 1920, the French authorities established the Ecole Nationale des Beaux-Arts in Algiers and staffed it with French teachers who prepared the students for the Ecole des Beaux-Arts in Paris. Similar schools of fine arts were also opened in Oran and Constantine. Most trained native artists who evolved in the 1930s and 1940s either followed in the footsteps of artists of French origin and their Orientalist and neo-classical styles or developed a naive style, as did their self-taught counterparts. One such painter was the self-taught, illiterate orphan named BAYA (*b* 1931), who began painting and working with clay in 1943. Her style was based on infantile dreams and imagination expressed in naive–surrealistic forms, for example *Untitled* (1980; Amman, N.G.F.A.; see fig. 1).

A few native Algerian painters of the 1950s shifted from the neo-classical style towards modernism. Ali Khodja (*b* 1923) began his artistic career as a miniaturist depicting traditional Algerian interiors. He later took up easel painting and experimented with the distribution of coloured masses in a style that wavered between Fauvist and abstract. Bachir Yelles (*b* 1921) and Muhammad Bouzid (*b* 1929) explored Cubism, Fauvism and Expressionism while maintaining local themes. During the same decade, a number of Algerian artists went to Paris. The most prominent was M'hammad Issiakhem, who in 1953 enrolled at the Ecole Nationale Supérieure des Beaux-Arts in Paris, graduating in 1958.

Like most Algerian artists who appeared in the 1950s and 1960s, MUHAMMAD KHADDA was a self-taught painter. In his abstract compositions, which display a sophisticated study of colour, he used Arabic characters and signs taken from Berber tattoos. Issiakhem and Khadda, along with Abdulkader Geurmaz (*b* 1919), Arezki Zerarti (*b* 1938) and Abdullah Benanteur (*b* 1931), are regarded as the pioneers of Algerian modern art. Most Algerian artists who matured in the 1950s and 1960s were self-taught. With no formal training and having suffered deculturalization through colonialism, they wanted their work to portray a national trait by using local signs and motifs in abstract formations. During the years of resistance against the French, a number of artists fought with the National Liberation Army. Fares Boukhatim (*b* 1941), who was well known as the artist of the revolution, began painting when he was in the army. After independence, most Algerian artists living abroad returned to their country to contribute to the development of the modern art movement in Algeria.

The Union Nationale des Arts Plastiques, founded in 1964, is the only body to which most plastic artists in Algeria belong. Overseen and supported by the Ministry of Culture and Information and the Algerian National Liberation Front, it has chapters in Constantine and Oran

1. Baya: *Untitled*, watercolour, 0.75×1.0 m, 1980 (Amman, National Gallery of Fine Art)

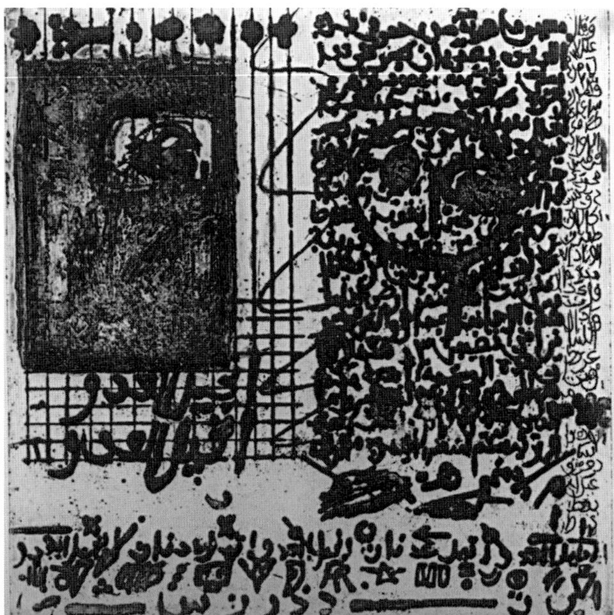

2. Rachid Koraïchi: *Testament of the Enemy*, engraving, 325×300 mm, 1981 (Paris, Institut du Monde Arabe)

and has opened an exhibition hall in Algiers. Several artistic groups have been formed within the union, such as the Tattoo Group (*aouchem*), which draws on folk art, the First Group, the 54 Group and the Young Painting Group.

Artists of the generation that appeared after independence were able, unlike their predecessors, to acquire a formal art education and were usually trained at art schools in Algeria, with fewer trained abroad. Thus their Arab–Islamic cultural identity was reinstated. In general, the works of post-independence artists of the 1970s and 1980s are mostly abstract and Abstract Expressionist in style. They either feature an attempt to depict local subject-matter through the manipulation of Arab and Berber signs, or simply ignore them and hold on to the concepts of international art. Among the first group are two artists: Mahjoub ben Bella (*b* 1946) and RACHID KORAÏCHI. Ben Bella uses Arabic calligraphy for its pictorial value, not for its literal meaning (e.g. *Painted Writing*, 1983; Paris, Inst. Monde Arab.). Colour has an important role in his work. In contrast, Koraïchi focuses on black with white, though he also uses calligraphy for its powerful abstract quality (see fig. 2).

4. OTHER ARTS. The Société Nationale de l'Artisanat Traditionnel promotes traditional art forms, and there is some training for apprentices (e.g. in weaving, embroidery and pottery at Nédroma, north-west Algeria), but many of the old techniques are being lost. The Kabylie region east of Algiers, a predominantly Berber area, produces pottery with geometric designs and silver jewellery, which is also found in Tamanrasset. The silver is sometimes worked with coral or enamel, although at the beginning of the 20th century corals were often replaced by red bakelite. Knotted carpets and rugs are a speciality in Ghardaia and El Oued, which hosts a carpet festival in the spring; designs vary from region to region. In the Gourara oases in the Great Western Erg a handwoven material is made with Berber and Malian geometric designs; in the Aurès (north-east Algeria), wool and goat-hair rugs have simple striped patterns and colourful lozenge designs. Traditional Algiers embroideries are influenced by those of Turkey, but the standard has declined.

5. MUSEUMS. In Algiers in 1896 there was an exhibition of Islamic art and antiquities in a purpose-built building, and in 1897 the collection was inaugurated, by President Faure, as the Musée National des Antiquités Algeriennes et d'Art Musulman. In 1901 there was an extension to the Islamic section, and additions were made by the archaeologist Stéphane Gsell. After the Algiers Exhibition of 1905 the museum was enriched with the acquisition of the Islamic collection of Ben Aben, and a more methodical classification of Islamic art was introduced. Other museums in Algiers include the Bardo Museum of Ethnography and Prehistory (founded 1928), which also has handicrafts, costumes and coral-studded jewellery; the Museum of Fine Arts (founded 1930) with paintings, sculpture, graphic arts and a specialized art library; the Museum of Popular Arts and Traditions in a fine, 16th-century Ottoman palace with good displays of rugs, jewellery, pottery and costumes. Outside Algiers the Cirta Museum (founded 1853), Constantine, has archaeological exhibits, particularly coins; the Demaeght Museum, Oran, has archaeology and ethnography; the Museum of Antiquities at Tlemcen, in a 13th-century mosque, has Islamic pieces; the Museum of Sétif has some fine mosaics; and the Museum of Skikda has Punic and Roman antiquities and modern art. There are also museums at various archaeological sites, particularly at Djemila, which has superb mosaics.

BIBLIOGRAPHY

P. Eudel: *L'Orfèvrerie algérienne et tunisienne* (Algiers, 1902)
G. Marçais: *Le Costume musulman d'Alger* (Paris, 1930)
A. Giacobetti: *Les Tapis et tissages du Djebel-Amour* (Paris, 1932)
J. Alazard: *Catalogue des peintures et sculptures exposées dans les galeries du Musée national des beaux-arts d'Alger* (Paris, 1936, rev. 1939)
M. A. Bel: *Les Arts indigènes féminins en Algérie* (Algiers, 1939)
G. Marçais: *Le Musée Stéphane Gsell: Musée des antiquités et d'art musulman d'Alger: L'Art musulman* (Algiers, 1950)
L Golvin: *Les Arts populaires en Algérie*, 2 vols (Algiers, 1950–53)
G. Marçais: *L'Art des Berbères* (Algiers, 1956)
——: *La Vie musulmane d'hier: Vue par Mohammed Racim* (Paris, 1960)
H. Camps-Fabrer: *Les Bijoux de Grande Kabylie* (Paris, 1970)
A. Marok: *La Casbah d'Alger* (Algiers, 1976)
L. S. Tesdell: *Cities in Algeria* (Monticello, IL, 1977)
S.-A. Baghli: *Aspects of Algerian Cultural Policy* (Paris, 1978)
F. Benatia: *L'Appropriation de l'espace à Alger après 1962* (Algiers, 1978)
F. Béguin: *Arabisances: Décor architectural et tracé urbain en Afrique du Nord, 1830–1950* (Paris, 1983)
D. Lesbet: *La Casbah d'Alger: Gestion urbaine et vide sociale* (Algiers, 1985)
M. Sgroï-Dufresne: *Alger, 1830–1984: Stratégie et enjeux urbains* (Paris, 1986)
Art contemporain arabe, Paris, Inst. Monde Arab. (Paris, [1988])
W. Ali, ed.: *Contemporary Art from the Islamic World* (London, 1989)

Alghisi, Galasso (*b* Carpi, nr Modena, *c.* 1523; *d* Ferrara, 1573). Italian architect and writer. He worked intermittently in Rome from 1549 to 1558, probably on the Palazzo Farnese under Michelangelo and on the city fortifications decreed by Pope Paul III. He was in Loreto in 1549, working on the basilica of S Maria, and in 1550, outside Macerata, began the church of S Maria delle Vergini, on which work continued for the rest of his life. The plan is a Greek cross, with a tall, octagonal drum over the crossing, in which are set large rectangular windows that transmit a bright but diffused light to the centre of the church. The interior is impressive in its refined simplicity, with almost all architectural elements reduced to their most essential forms. The great square nave piers, for example, are devoid of decoration other than their simple plinths and cornice-like capitals. The church is built throughout in brick, which is left exposed, with decorative inlaid panels, in the cross-vaulting to the right-hand eastern chapel. The façade (1581) is attributed to Lattanzio Ventura da Urbino (*fl* 1575–87).

In 1558 Alghisi submitted a design for a municipal tower at Macerata, but most of his subsequent career was spent at Ferrara in the service of Duke Alfonso II d'Este, for whose palace he built a theatre and the Loggiata dei Camerini. An unexecuted scheme by Alghisi for a new palace in Ferrara was engraved (1566) at Bologna by Domenico Tibaldi; from the same year a contract survives for the construction of a campanile to Alghisi's design for the Carthusian monastery of S Cristoforo in Ferrara. Alghisi published a three-volume work on military architecture (1570) that invoked the traditional apparatus of Renaissance scholarship to produce such geometrical *tours de force* as 18 versions of a star polygon with bastions at the points. The treatise had some influence on Dutch fortification theory in the 17th century.

WRITINGS

Delle fortificationi di M. Galasso Alghisi da Carpi, architetto dell'ecc. Signor Duca di Ferrara libri tre, all'invittissimo Imperatore Massimiliano Secondo, Cesare Augusto, 3 vols (Venice, 1570/*R* 1575)

BIBLIOGRAPHY

DBI; Thieme–Becker
G. Vasari: *Vite* (1550, rev. 2/1568); ed. G. Milanesi (1878–85)
A. Venturi: *Storia* (1901–40)
G. Natale: 'Un tempio bramantesco poco noto (S Maria delle Vergini a Macerata)', *Raccolta di scritti in onore del Prof. Giacinto Romano* (Pavia, 1907)
A. Colasanti: *Loreto* (Bergamo, 1910)
L. Serra: *L'arte nelle Marche*, 2 vols (Pesaro, 1929)

□

Alguacil Blázquez, Casiano (*b* Mazarambroz, Toledo, 14 Aug 1832; *d* Toledo, 3 Dec 1914). Spanish photographer. He moved to Toledo *c.* 1862, and he and Fernando González Pedroso were the first two professional photographers to set up a permanent establishment there. His suite of *12 vistas de Toledo* (Toledo, 1871) consisted of 14 photographs mounted on decorated passe-partouts. Alguacil is known for this format, which he enlarged for certain views contained in the 1870s series of publications of *Monumentos artísticos do España* (Toledo; R. Amador de los Ríos, ed.). Alguacil is usually identified with this series, in which the views were not limited to Toledo. He also maintained a 'Museo fotográfico', produced a series of photographs on San Juan de los Reyes (1895) and in 1906 won the photographic competition in La Mancha for photographing monuments and art objects. The Alguacil archives are located in the town hall in Toledo.

BIBLIOGRAPHY

M. Carrero de Dios and others: *Toledo en la fotografía de Alguacil, 1832–1914* (Toledo, 1983)

LEE FONTANELLA

ʿAli [ʿAlī; Ḥusayn ʿAlī] (*fl c.* 1800–20). Persian enamel painter. All of his work is associated with the patronage of the Qajar monarch Fath ʿAli Shah (*reg* 1797–1834). ʿAli signed his work with the title *ghulām khānazād* ('slave born in the household') signifying 'artist in the royal service'. A jewelled nephrite dish (Vienna, Ksthist. Mus., Samml. Plastik & Kstgew., M3223) presented in 1819 by the Persian ambassador Abu'l-Hassan Khan to the Austrian emperor Francis I (*reg* 1792–1835) has a central gold plaque enamelled with a full-length portrait of Fath ʿAli Shah (dated 1817–18), inspired by MIHR ʿALI's life-size oil portrait (Tehran, Nigaristan Mus.). Other objects enamelled by ʿAli include an oval mirror with a carved jade handle (Tehran, Bank Markazi, Crown Jewels Col.); on the back is an enamel portrait of Fath ʿAli Shah seated within a floral frame, probably the finest painted enamel in the collection (*see* ISLAMIC ART, §VIII, 3). ʿAli may also have enamelled a set (Tehran, Bank Markazi, Crown Jewels Col.) comprising a decanter, stemcup with saucer, and domed cover decorated with portraits of the Shah and his sons, dancing women and musicians, for the cup is signed Husayn ʿAli. ʿAli's style is similar to that of BAQIR and is notable for its delicate execution and brilliant colours.

BIBLIOGRAPHY

V. B. Meen and A. D. Tushingham: *Crown Jewels of Iran* (Toronto, 1968)
B. W. Robinson: 'Qājār Painted Enamels', *Paintings from Islamic Lands*, ed. R. Pinder-Wilson (Oxford, 1969), pp. 187–204
M. A. Karimzada Tabrizi: *Aḥvāl u āthār-i naqqāshān-i qadīm-i īrān* [The lives and art of old painters from Iran] (London, 1985), no. 632
B. W. Robinson: 'Persian Painting under the Zand and Qājār Dynasties', *From Nadir Shah to the Islamic Republic* (1991), vii of *The Cambridge History of Iran* (Cambridge, 1968–91), pp. 870–90

S. J. VERNOIT

Ali, Ahmet. *See* AHMET ALI.

ʿAli, Shakir (*b* Rampur, 1916; *d* Lahore, 1975). Pakistani painter. A seminal figure, Shakir ʿAli introduced CUBISM to Lahore in 1952. His style quickly became fashionable there, was adopted in Karachi and dominated the art scene for more than a decade (*see* PAKISTAN, §III).

Shakir ʿAli first studied painting at the Ukil Brothers Studio in Delhi. In 1938, after a year in that city, he joined the J. J. School of Art, Bombay, which promoted the British system of art education—drawing from cast and copying Old Masters. From the school's director, Charles Gerrard, Shakir learned mural painting and was introduced to IMPRESSIONISM. He also learned about indigenous art such as that at Ajanta (*see* AJANTA, §2(i) and (ii)) and the modern work of JAMINI ROY and AMRITA SHER-GIL.

After receiving a diploma in fine art from the Slade School of Art, London, Shakir ʿAli studied with ANDRÉ LHOTE in France. Moving to Prague, he joined the School of Industrial Design and studied textile design. From Prague, Shakir went to Lahore, where he was appointed Professor and head of the art department at the Mayo School of Arts. In 1961 he was appointed Principal of the National College of Arts (former Mayo School of Arts). In the 1960s his personal style matured. Moving away from the Cubist idiom, his painting began to reflect local culture as well as the Indian tradition. Shakir ʿAli's work has been preserved by the Shakir ʿAli Museum, in his personal residence in Lahore.

BIBLIOGRAPHY

S. Mir: 'Shakir Ali: Painter's Painter', *Contemp. A. Pakistan*, i/6 (June 1960), pp. 2–9
A. Gauhar: 'Shakir Ali: Urge to Belong', *Art Asia*, i/2 (Spring 1966), pp. 9–28
J. Marek: 'Shakir Ali', *New Orient*, vi (Aug 1967), pp. 112–14
H. Zaman: 'Shakir Ali: Passion for Purity', *Morning News* (30 Jan 1975)
Asmi: 'The Shakir Museum: Homage to an Artist', *The Herald*, vi/6 (June 1976), pp. 6–10
S. A. Imam: 'Shakir Ali', *Douaness*, iii/5 (Dec 1981), pp. 47–50
I. ul-Hasan: 'The City on a Canvas', *The Star* (Aug 1982), pp. 27–31
M. Nesom-Sirhandi: *Contemporary Painting in Pakistan* (Lahore, 1992)

MARCELLA NESOM-SIRHANDI

Ali, Wijdan, Princess [ʿAlī Wijdān; Wijdan] (*b* Baghdad, 29 Aug 1939). Jordanian painter and art patron. She studied history at Beirut University College (formerly Beirut College for Women), receiving a BA in 1961. In 1993 she took a PhD in Islamic Art at the School of Oriental and African Studies, University of London. After serving in the Jordanian Ministry of Foreign Affairs and representing her country at United Nations meetings in Geneva and New York, she became a full-time painter in 1966. In her early works she created textures with layers of colour worked with a palette-knife (e.g. *Harana Castle*; oil on canvas, 1981; Amman, N.G. F.A.). In 1979 Ali founded the Royal Society of Fine Arts in Jordan and in 1980 the Jordan National Gallery of Fine Arts (*see* JORDAN). Since 1979 she has experimented with Arabic calligraphy in her work. In her 'Karbala Series' she incorporated signs, letters and Arabic poetry with strong primary colours (e.g. *Karbala*; mixed media on paper, 1993; London, BM). In 1988 she organized in Amman the Third International Seminar on Islamic Art, entitled 'Problems of Art Education in the Islamic World', and in 1989 she organized the exhibition *Contemporary Art from the Islamic World* at the Barbican Centre, London. She has received numerous awards in recognition of her work in the arts.

WRITINGS

ed.: *Contemporary Art from the Islamic World* (London, 1989)
A Survey of Modern Painting in the Islamic World and the Development of the Contemporary Calligraphic School (diss., U. London, SOAS, 1993)

□

Ali Acemi [Esir; ʿAlā' al-Dīn ʿAlī ibn ʿAbd al-Karīm] (*b* ?Tabriz; *d* Istanbul, *c*. 1537). Ottoman architect. His epithets, *acemi* (Persian) and *esir* (prisoner), suggest that he was captured in the 1514 campaign against the Safavids of Iran by the Ottoman sultan Selim I (*reg* 1512–20). He served as chief imperial architect from at least September 1525 until March 1537. Works attributed to him include the mosque of Çoban Mustafa Pasha (1515) in Eskişehir, the complex of Çoban Mustafa Pasha in Gebze (1519–25) and the mosque and tomb of Selim I in Istanbul (1523). He also founded the Mimar Mosque and dervish hostel (Turk. *zaviye*), near the Mevlevihane Yeni Kapı in Şehremini, Istanbul, where he is buried. His style is marked by sound engineering and extreme eclecticism. The complex in Gebze, for example, was decorated with marble panelling in the style of Mamluk buildings in Egypt, while the mosque of Selim is a direct quotation of the mosque of Bayezid II in EDIRNE (1484–8).

BIBLIOGRAPHY

Hafiz Hüseyin al-Ayvansarayi: *Hadīkat al-cevāmiʿ* [The garden of mosques], i (Istanbul, 1281/1864–5), pp. 206–7
K. Altan: 'Klâsik Türk mimarlarindan Esir Ali' [Esir Ali, one of the classical Turkish architects], *Arkitekt*, v (1937), pp. 81–3
H. B. Kunter: 'Mimar Ali Bey'in bilinmeyen iki vakfiyesi' [Two unknown vakfiyes of Mimar Ali Bey], *Teblígler V. Türk Tarih Kongresi: Ankara, 1956*
L. A. Mayer: *Islamic Architects and their Works* (Geneva, 1956)
G. Goodwin: *A History of Ottoman Architecture* (Baltimore, MD, 1971), pp. 184–7

HOWARD CRANE

ʿAli Ashraf [Ashraf; ʿAlī Ashraf] (*fl* *c*. 1735–80). Persian painter. Known for a large number of painted and varnished ('lacquered') bookbindings, penboxes and mirror-cases (*see* ISLAMIC ART, §VIII, 10), ʿAli Ashraf worked in a small floral style with a characteristic motif of pansies or African violets on a black ground. His style, notable for its richness and delicacy, is derived directly from that of his teacher MUHAMMAD ZAMAN but is standardized and simplified. His debt to his teacher can be seen in his signature, *az baʿd-i muḥammad ʿalī ashraf ast*, which can be read as either "Ali [the Prophet's son-in-law] is the noblest after Muhammad [the Prophet]' or "Ali Ashraf is a follower of Muhammad [Zaman]'. This is the way he signed four mirror-cases with fine bird-and-flower designs (1740–1, Edinburgh, Royal Mus. Scotland, 1921–43; 1747, London, V&A, 758–1876; 1751–2, New York, Brooklyn Mus., 88.92; and 1755–6, London, J. Pope-Hennessy priv. col.) and a similar but undated penbox (Berne, Hist. Mus., 21–1912). ʿAli Ashraf worked for several provincial patrons, such as Ahmad Khan Dunbuli, a powerful Kurdish overlord in north-west Iran, and for members of the Afsharid dynasty (*reg* 1736–95). Together with Muhammad Hadi, another painter who specialized in floral designs, ʿAli Ashraf signed the varnished covers on a sumptuous album (St Petersburg, Hermitage), which are dated 1738 and depict flowers and birds in a framework of medallions and borders.

ʿAli Ashraf's style was perpetuated by his family, students and imitators. His brother painted one of the finest portraits of the early 19th century (see Karpova, no. 7), and his son Riza continued his father's style, as on a varnished penbox (London, BL, ex-Godman priv. col.) dated 1802–3. His pupils included Muhammad Baqir (*see* MUHAMMAD BAQIR (i)), MUHAMMAD SADIQ and Najaf ʿAli Isfahani (*see* ISFAHANI, (1)). ʿAli Ashraf's designs continued to be popular well into the 19th century, for the inscription on a penbox (Tehran, Nigaristan Mus.) states that it was done in 1849 by Ahmad ibn Muhammad-Mahdi following a design taken from the late-lamented ʿAli Ashraf.

BIBLIOGRAPHY

B. W. Robinson: 'Persian Lacquer in the Bern Historical Museum', *Iran*, viii (1970), pp. 47–50
N. K. Karpova: *Stankovaya zhivopis Irana XVIII–XIX vekov* [Easel painting in Iran in the 18th and 19th centuries] (Moscow, 1973)
M. A. Karimzada Tabrizi: *Aḥvāl u āthār-i naqqāshān-i qadīm-i īrān* [The lives and art of old painters of Iran] (London, 1985), no. 648
Eastern Lacquers: An Exhibition of 50 Pieces of Persian, Indian and Turkish Lacquer (exh. cat. by B. W. Robinson, London, Bernheimer F.A. Ltd, 1986)

L. S. Diba: 'Lacquerwork', *The Arts of Persia*, ed. R. W. Ferrier (New Haven and London, 1989), pp. 243–54
——: 'Persian Painting in the Eighteenth Century: Tradition and Transmission', *Muqarnas*, vi (1989), pp. 147–60
B. W. Robinson: 'Persian Painting under the Zand and Qājār Dynasties', *From Nadir Shah to the Islamic Republic*, vii of *The Cambridge History of Iran* (Cambridge, 1991), pp. 870–90

□

Aliense. *See* VASSILACCHI, ANTONIO.

Aligarh [anc. Koil]. City in Uttar Pradesh, India, 135 km south-east of Delhi. A Rajput stronghold, Koil fell to Muslim invaders in AD 1194. Several later monuments were built on the foundations of its Hindu temples, no early examples of which survive. During the first half of the 15th century Koil figured in the confrontations between the Sharqis of JAUNPUR and the armies of the Delhi Sultanate. The fort, built in 1524 during the reign of Ibrahim Lodi, was rebuilt by Sabit Khan in 1717 and extensively redesigned by the French in the early 19th century. Several monuments attributed to the period of the Mughal emperor Akbar (*reg* 1556–1605) in the Bagh-i-Gesu Khan (now a public cemetery) include a pillared pavilion with a low dome and the remains of another double-storey pavilion; the supposed tomb of Gesu Khan, an official of Akbar, is a red sandstone structure set on a plinth with lattice screens and crowned by a low dome. The Jamiʿ Masjid, at the summit of a long, steep slope called the Bala Qila, was begun in the 17th century but almost completely reworked in 1728 by Sabit Khan. The smaller Moti Masjid to its south-east dates to the 17th century. A focal point of the city is the Achal, a large reservoir or tank, which is surrounded by temples and attractively landscaped spaces. The most impressive temple, the Achaleshwar, was built during the 18th century; the others are of the same period or later.

During the 1850s a cantonment was built by the British to the north-east of the old city. This enclave, constructed on a grid plan, has several notable buildings, including the court, jail and district school, as well as the Anglican cemetery. Other distinctive structures are Crosthwaite Hall and the Harrison Clock Tower of the late 19th century, the latter built in a Gothic Revival style. The Lyall Library (1899) was constructed in the eclectic manner often described as Indo-Saracenic, while the architecture of the Aligarh Muslim University, founded in 1875 by Sir Sayyid Ahmad Khan, is reminiscent of the colleges of Oxford and Cambridge in England.

BIBLIOGRAPHY

E. A. H. Blunt: *Christian Tombs and Tablets of Historical Interest in the United Provinces of Agra and Oudh* (Allahabad, 1911)
J. M. Sidiqi: *Aligarh District: A Historical Survey* (New Delhi, 1981)
P. Davies: *Islamic, Rajput, European*, ii of *The Penguin Guide to the Monuments of India* (London, 1989)

WALTER SMITH

Alighieri, Dante (*b* Florence, May 1265; *d* Ravenna, ?14 ?Sept 1321). Italian writer. He is universally recognized as the greatest poet of the Middle Ages. His masterpiece, the *Divine Comedy* (begun 1307 or 1314), contains many passages in which Dante expressed his appreciation of painting and sculpture, and the themes in the poem have challenged artists from the 14th century to the present day.

1. Life and work. 2. Influence of the *Divine Comedy*.

1. LIFE AND WORK. Dante was the only child of a notary, Alighiero II, son of Bellicione degli Alighieri and his first wife Bella. The Alighieris were descendants of the Elisei, an ancient and noble Florentine family. Dante may have studied at Bologna University, but he admitted to having taught himself the art of versifying. About 1283 he married Gemma di Manetto Donati, who bore him four children. His sons Pietro and Jacopo wrote commentaries on the *Divine Comedy*.

Dante met Bice Portinari, whom he called Beatrice, in 1274. He recorded his love for her in *La vita nuova*, *c*. 1293, and later immortalized her in the *Divine Comedy*. After her death in 1290, he sought consolation in the study of philosophy and theology. Between 1296 and 1302 he was prominent in the government of Florence and was drawn into the strife between the Guelphs and the Ghibellines. As a White Guelph, he was banished from Florence in 1302. The remainder of his life was spent travelling through Italy, and it was during his exile that most of his literary work was produced. He was buried in the convent of the Friars Minor in Ravenna; later efforts to return his remains to Florence have proved futile.

Dante wrote in both Latin and Italian. He composed the *Divine Comedy* in the vernacular in order to promote the beauty of the Italian language and ensure the poem's accessibility to all his countrymen. It is divided into three parts, or *cantiche*, corresponding to the three kingdoms of the afterlife, Hell, Purgatory and Paradise, and contains 100 cantos. Analogies between the interlocking, architectonic structure of the poem, written in terza rima, and the constructive principles of the Gothic cathedrals have been suggested, the proposed parallels between the structure and symbolism of the rose window and the Celestial Rose of *Paradiso* xxx and xxxi being particularly cogent.

There has been much speculation concerning Dante's interest in the visual arts. Nowhere is his appreciation of painting and sculpture more apparent than in his description of the three sculptural reliefs representing acts of humility in *Purgatorio* x, 28–93. Artists lavished special care on their interpretation of this canto. An outstanding example is found in a Dante manuscript in London (London, BL, Add. MS. 19587; see fig.), the illustrations of which rank among the major works of 14th-century Neapolitan illumination. Two representations are traditional symbols of humility, the *Virgin of the Annunciation* and *King David Dancing before the Ark of the Covenant*, with Mical observing him with disdain from a tower. The third act of humility represents a legendary event in the life of the Roman emperor Trajan, who encountered a poor widow demanding redress for the death of her son. This event has been treated as a medieval pageant, with mounted soldiers, gaily caparisoned horses and fluttering banners. Meanwhile, on the extreme right, Dante and Virgil observe three of the proud, so burdened by huge boulders they are likened to corbels (*Purgatorio* x, 130–38).

Examples of Humility by a follower of Cristoforo Orimina, from Dante Alighieri's *Divine Comedy*, *Purgatorio* x, 28–93, 1362–70 (London, British Library, Add. MS. 19587, fol. 77*r*)

Dante evidently held the art of illumination in high regard, equating it with monumental painting and poetry (*Purgatorio* xi, 79–99). Such commendation was exceptional during a period when the craft of painting was designated one of the lowly mechanical arts. The famous passage extolling Giotto (*Purgatorio* xi, 95) has provided the basis for a supposed friendship between the poet and the artist that is entirely without substance. Equally suspect is the attribution to Giotto of a dubious portrait of Dante in the fresco of *Paradise* in the Bargello, Florence, dated in the 1330s. The most authentic likeness of the poet, and one that agrees closely with the description given by Giovanni Boccaccio in his biography of Dante of *c*. 1351, appears in the mid-14th-century fresco of the *Last Judgement* by Nardo di Cione in the Strozzi Chapel, S Maria Novella, Florence (*see* CIONE, (2)).

2. INFLUENCE OF THE 'DIVINE COMEDY'. Those sections of the *Divine Comedy* that can be read as an adventure story or a *chronique scandaleuse* offer lively subject-matter for artistic representation. Its greatest appeal, however, lies in its striking verbal imagery. In the *Inferno* and the *Purgatorio*, both figures and objects are described with startling vividness. Artists who choose to concentrate on the literal or moral aspects of the poem can work within the sphere of narrative and didactic art, but the allegorical concepts pose greater difficulties and are frequently omitted. Illustrating the *Paradiso* presents problems of another kind: the system of spiritual relationships with which it deals defies the capabilities of many artists. Consequently, illustrators often rely on traditional religious imagery that has no direct relationship to the text of the third *cantica*.

An iconographic canon for the compositional arrangements and the appearance of the main protagonists was established during the 14th century and continued to influence the illustrations to the poem well beyond the 15th; indeed, vestiges of this iconography have persisted into the 20th century (e.g. Incerti's powerful, machine-age Lucifer; see *La Divina Commedia dipinta da Achille Incerti*, Milan, 1988). Monochromatic pen-and-ink drawings or engravings have proved the most popular medium for those who undertake a canto-by-canto illustration of the poem. Artists who prefer to depict individual cantos or themes, however, have worked in a variety of media and are generally attracted by the pathos and tragedy of a story such as that of Paolo and Francesca (*Inferno* v), or the drama and violence surrounding the fate of Ugolino (*Inferno* xxxiii). The *Inferno* remains the most frequently illustrated of the three *cantiche*.

Artists of exceptional ability and reputation have contributed to the vast body of illustrations that exist in manuscript illumination, woodcuts, engravings, monumental paintings and sculpture. Outstanding examples by Luca Signorelli, SANDRO BOTTICELLI, WILLIAM BLAKE, EUGÈNE DELACROIX, Gustave Doré, Dante Gabriel Rosetti (*see* ROSSETTI, (1)) and Auguste Rodin all testify to the enduring appeal of Dante's poem as a vehicle for artistic expression. Some of the finest examples are by MICHELANGELO, who is known to have revered Dante, his compatriot, and who wrote two sonnets to his memory. The figures of Charon and Minos in the Sistine Chapel frescoes of the *Last Judgement* are modelled on their counterparts in the first *cantica* of the *Divine Comedy* (*Inferno* iii, 83 and v, 4), and the figures of Rachel and Leah, designed to flank the monumental figure of Moses in S Pietro in Vincoli, Rome, were inspired by their descriptions given in *Purgatorio* xxvii, 94–108.

WRITINGS

F. Chiapelli, ed.: *Opere di Dante Alighieri* (Milan, 1967)

C. S. Singleton, ed. and trans.: *The Divine Comedy*, 6 vols (London, 1971–5)

BIBLIOGRAPHY

DBI

Dante Soc. America: Annu. Rep. (Cambridge, MA, 1882–1965)

G. Locella: *Dante in der deutschen Kunst* (Dresden, 1890)

F. X. Kraus: *Luca Signorelli's Illustrationen zu Dante's Divina Commedia* (Freiburg, 1892)

——: *Dante, sein Leben und sein Werk, sein Verhältnis zur Kunst und zur Politik* (Berlin, 1897)

L. Volkman: *Iconografia Dantesca: The Pictorial Representations to Dante's Divine Comedy* (Leipzig, 1897; Eng. trans., rev. London, 1899)

G. Boccaccio: *De origine vita studiis et moribus viri clarissimi Danti Aligerii Florentini poete illustris et de operibus compositis ab eodem*; Eng. trans. by G. R. Carpenter as *Life of Dante* (New York, 1900), p. 84

Studi danteschi (Florence, 1920–) [var. articles]

I. de Vasconcellos: *L'Inspiration dantesque dans l'art romantique français* (Paris, 1925)

P. Schubring: *Illustrationen zu Dantes Göttlicher Komödie, Italien 14. bis 16. Jahrhundert* (Vienna, 1931) [important for iconog. stud.]

W. O. Hassall: *Dante, Divina Commedia, Holkham Hall MS. 514* (London, 1960)

L. Donati: *Il Botticelli e le prime illustrazioni della Divina Commedia* (Florence, 1962)

Dante Studies (Cambridge, MA, 1966–) [ed. 1966–87 by A. L. Pellegrini, ed. 1988 by A. L. Pellegrini and C. Kleinhenz, ed. 1989– by C. Kleinhenz]

P. Breiger, M. Meiss and C. S. Singleton: *Illuminated Manuscripts of the Divine Comedy*, 2 vols (Princeton, NJ, 1969)

D. Ronte: *Die Nazarener und Dante* (diss., Münster, Westfäl. Wilhelms-U., 1970)

Enciclopedia dantesca, 6 vols (Rome, 1970–78) [var. articles, with a comprehensive bibliog. in vol. vi]

G. Fallini: *Dante e la cultura figurativa medievale* (Bergamo, 1971)

M. Rotili: *I codici danteschi miniati a Napoli* (Naples, 1972)

J. Leyerle: 'The Rose-Wheel Design and Dante's Paradiso', *U. Toronto Q.*, xlvi (1977), pp. 280–308

M. Klonsky: *Blake's Dante: The Complete Illustrations to the Divine Comedy* (New York, 1980)

E. A. Maser: 'Dante and the History of Art: Reflections Inspired by Dante Gabriel Rossetti's Painting, "La Pia de' Tolomei"', *Shape of the Past:*

Studies in Honour of Franklin D. Murphy (Los Angeles, 1981), pp. 181–94
D. Gillerman: 'Dante's Early Readers: The Evidence of Illustrated Manuscripts', *The Divine Comedy and the Encyclopedia of Arts and Sciences: Acts of the International Dante Symposium, New York, 1983*, pp. 65–80
G. C. Di Scipio: *The Symbolic Rose in Dante's Paradiso* (Ravenna, 1984), pp. 137–59
J. I. Friedman: 'Il paradiso terrestre di Dante: Simbolo e visione nella miniatura napoletana del trecento', *Letteratura italiana e arti figurativi: Atti del XII convegno dell'associazione internazionale per gli studi di lingua e letteratura italiana, Toronto, Hamilton and Montreal, 1985*, i, pp. 245–52
——: 'La processione mistica di Dante: Allegoria ed iconografia nel canto xxix del *Purgatorio*', *Dante e le forme dell'allegoresi*, ed. M. Picone (Ravenna, 1987), pp. 125–48

JOAN ISOBEL FRIEDMAN

Alighiero e Boetti. *See* BOETTI, ALIGHIERO.

Aligny, Théodore Caruelle d' (*b* Chaume, Nevers, 24 Jan 1798; *d* Lyon, 24 Feb 1871). French painter. His father was the artist Jean-Baptiste Caruelle (*d* 1801). About 1859 he added to his name that of his stepfather, Claude Meure-Aligny. He spent his early life in Paris, leaving the Ecole Polytechnique in 1808 to frequent the studios of Jean-Baptiste Regnault and the landscape artist Louis-Etienne Watelet (1780–1866). He exhibited at the Salon for the first time in 1822 with *Daphnis and Chloe* (untraced), which went unremarked. He finished his apprenticeship with the customary journey to Italy, staying in Rome from 1822 to 1827. During 1826 and 1827 he became friendly with Corot, whom he acknowledged as his master, although Aligny preceded Corot in his repeated studies of the Roman countryside and even appears to have led the way for the group of landscape artists who stayed there at the same time as himself, such as Edouard Bertin and Prosper Barbot. The sketches from this period (Rennes, Mus. B.-A. & Archéol., and Rome, Gab. Stampe) already bear witness to his conception of landscape as an organization of form and mass. He established himself in Paris in 1827 and that year exhibited at the Salon with *Saul Consulting the Witch of Endor*, which went unnoticed. From 1828 he spent much time in the Forest of Fontainebleau, one of the first of several generations of landscape artists who frequented the place.

In 1831, Aligny exhibited six landscapes and a historical landscape, *Massacre of the Druids under the Emperor Claudius* (Nîmes, Mus. B.-A.), which won him a second-class medal. He made trips to Normandy (1831) and Switzerland (1832). From 1833 he exhibited regularly at the Salon. The same year, he presented three landscapes that surprised his contemporaries with their naturalism. In 1834–5 he made a second journey to Italy, where he made large numbers of studies and sketches, especially in the environs of Rome and Naples. He returned to Fontainebleau, once more keeping company with Corot, Diaz and Rousseau. At the Salon of 1837 his *Prometheus on the Caucasus* (Paris, Louvre) was bought by the state and won

Théodore Caruelle d'Aligny: *Infant Bacchus Reared by the Nymphs on the Island of Naxos*, oil on canvas, 1.63×2.28 m, 1848 (Bordeaux, Musée des Beaux-Arts)

him a first-class medal; his studio became much visited, and numerous landscape artists studied there, including Eugène Desjobert (1817–63), Charles Lecointe (1824–86), Jean-Joseph Bellel (1816–98), Théophile Chauvel, François-Louis Français and Auguste Ravier. Aligny spent the summer of 1838 in the Auvergne, where he executed an important series of drawings. He exhibited regularly at the Salon and drew attention in 1842 with his *Hercules Fighting the Hydra* (Carcassone, Mus. B.-A.), for which he was awarded the Légion d'honneur. The same year, he was given a state commission to paint a *Baptism* (*in situ*) for the church of St-Paul-Saint-Louis in Paris. Two years later, Corot was to paint the same subject in the chapel of St Nicolas du Chardonnet in Paris. Aligny's next commission followed in 1850 with two decorative paintings for the church of St-Etienne-du-Mont in Paris: *Baptism* and *St John Preaching in the Desert* (both *in situ*).

With all the advantages of an official career, Aligny was commissioned to draw the sites of ancient Greece. The year after his return in 1844 he published a series of engravings entitled *Views of the Most Famous Sites of Ancient Greece*; these were admired by Baudelaire who paid homage to his 'serious and idealistic talent' (Salon, 1846). His Salon exhibits bore witness to his travels, for example the *Infant Bacchus Reared by the Nymphs on the Island of Naxos* (Salon of 1848; Bordeaux, Mus. B.-A.; see fig.) and *Solitude of a Monk at Prayer in a Landscape* (Salon of 1850; Rennes, Mus. B.-A. & Archéol.). These large compositions were accompanied by more modest landscapes, all attesting to a profound knowledge of nature founded on the constant practice of sketching from life. In 1861 he reached the height of his career as Director of the Ecole des Beaux-Arts in Lyon, a position he occupied until his death, but he continued to produce studies from nature, in Haute-Saône and around Lyon and Grenoble, and to take part in the Salon until 1869. Two sales of his studio were held in Paris (Hôtel Drouot) in 1874 and 1878.

Aligny belonged to a generation of landscape artists for whom landscape painting was first and foremost a study of nature. His large paintings seem marked by a concern for strict and rigorous composition, dominated by the search for arabesques and the harmonies of large masses: rocks, foliage and depressions. This aesthetic, which became less rigid after 1860, was nevertheless considered cold when Realism triumphed. His art continued to be founded on careful study of, and meditation on, nature as his numerous drawings and sketches in oil demonstrate. His contemporaries saw him as the true leader of landscape reform.

BIBLIOGRAPHY

M. M. Aubrun: *Théodore Caruelle d'Aligny et ses compagnons* (exh. cat., Orléans, Mus. B.-A.; Dunkirk, Mus. B.-A.; Rennes, Mus. B.-A. & Archéol.; 1979)

P. Ramade: 'Théodore Caruelle d'Aligny: Dessins du premier séjour italien (1822–7)', *Rev. Louvre*, ii (1986), pp. 121–30

M. M. Aubrun: *Théodore Caruelle d'Aligny, 1798–1871: Catalogue raisonné de l'oeuvre peint, dessiné, gravé* (Paris, 1988)

PATRICK RAMADE

Alimpy (*fl* second half of 11th century; *d* Kiev). Russian painter and monk. He learnt the art of painting in the Pecherskaya Lavra (cave monastery) in Kiev, working alongside Greek artists who were decorating the cathedral of the Dormition (1073–89; destr. 1941) with mosaics and wall paintings: 'Alimpy himself helped them and studied under them' (Kievo-Pechersky *Paterikon*). The *Paterikon*, the source of all information about Alimpy, relates that the monk produced icons for the monastery itself and on commission, and the numerous references to the use of silver and gold suggest that he also practised as a jeweller. A wealthy citizen of Kiev ordered seven icons from Alimpy to form a *Deësis* made up of images of *Christ*, the *Virgin*, *John the Baptist*, Archangels *Michael* and *Gabriel* and two Apostles. The *Paterikon* also states that Alimpy's icon of the *Virgin* was sent by Vladimir Monomakh (*reg* 1076–8; 1094–1125) to Rostov, where it is mentioned in early 13th-century sources. No surviving Old Russian icon, however, can be definitively attributed to Alimpy. He is buried in the caves of the Pecherskaya Lavra, alongside other 'venerable Fathers'.

BIBLIOGRAPHY

M. I. Uspensky and V. I. Uspensky: *Zametki o drevnerusskom ikonopisanii. Izvestnyye ikonopistsy i ikh proizvedeniya. I Sv. Alimpy* [Notes on Old Russian icon painting: famous icon painters and their works, I St Alimpy] (St Petersburg, 1901)

V. Putsko: 'Kiyevsky khudozhnik XI veka Alimpy Pechersky (po skazaniyu Polikarpa i dannym arkheologicheskikh issledovaniy)' [The 11th-century Kievan artist Alimpy Pechersky (according to the tale of Polikarp and the results of archaeological investigations)], *Wien. Slav. Jb.*, xxv (1979), pp. 63–88

'Kiyevo-Pecherskiy Paterik' [The Kievo-Pechersky *Paterikon*], *Pamyatniki literatury drevney rusi: XII vek* [Literary monuments of Old Russia: 12th century], ed. L. A. Dmitriev and D. S. Likhachev (Moscow, 1980), pp. 586–99

G. I. VZDORNOV

'Ali Muhammad Isfahani ['Alī Muḥammad Iṣfahānī ibn Ustād Mahdī] (*fl* 1870s–1888). Persian potter and tile-maker. Trained as a mason in Isfahan, he probably followed his father's trade and chose to specialize in making pottery and tiles. His experiments making tiles that imitated the fine work produced under the Safavids (*reg* 1501–1732), when Isfahan was the capital of Iran, caught the attention of Major-General Robert Murdoch Smith, director of the Persian Telegraph Department and collector of Persian art, and in 1884 Murdoch Smith ordered wall tiles from 'Ali Muhammad. The potter soon moved to Tehran, seat of the Qajar court (*reg* 1779–1924), where he established a workshop at the gate of the Shahzada 'Abd al-'Azim. Several large tiles made for the royal music master in 1884–5 (540×427 mm; London, V&A, 511.1889, 512.1889) depicting young men reading poetry in an orchard imitate Safavid work of the 17th century. Seven smaller tiles datable 1884–7 (470×340 mm; Edinburgh, R. Harvey-Jamieson priv. col.) show a more evolved style in which black is used as an incised slip and figures are moulded in relief. The tiles depict scenes from Persian literature such as Shirin and Farhad at Mt Bisitun, and royal receptions, but the faces and dress are in typical Qajar style. 'Ali Muhammad's mature style is seen in 12 tiles (1887) in a broad palette, which incorporate such European conventions as shading and perspective. Two (Edinburgh, R. Harvey-Jamieson priv. col.) are portraits of Murdoch Smith made from a photograph. Others (Edinburgh, Royal Mus. Scotland, 1888.105, and London, V&A, 565.1888) show scenes from Persian literature but include details of modern life such as binoculars and an umbrella. A large circular table top (diam. 1.36 m; London, V&A, 559.1888) shows the potter's technical proficiency. Most of ʿAli Muhammad's 21 signed pieces are painted in polychrome under a transparent alkaline glaze on a hard white composite paste, but he occasionally worked in lustre. A border tile with a kufic inscription in cobalt blue reserved against a golden ground (London, V&A, 567.1889) imitates 14th-century work and may have been made to replace a damaged panel. In 1888, at the request of Murdoch Smith, ʿAli Muhammad composed a technical treatise describing the organization of the tile industry and the underglaze technique.

WRITINGS

On the Manufacture of Modern Kashi Earthenware Tiles and Vases, Eng. trans. by J. Fargues (Edinburgh, 1888); also printed in W. J. Furnival, *Leadless Decorative Tiles, Faience and Mosaic* (Stone, 1904)

BIBLIOGRAPHY

J. M. Scarce: ''Ali Mohammed Isfahani, Tilemaker of Tehran', *Orient. A.*, xxii/3 (1976), pp. 78–88

□

ʿAli Naqi. *See under* SHAYKH ʿABBASI.

Alinari. Italian family of photographers. From 1845 to 1850 Leopoldo Alinari worked in Florence for a wealthy lithographer, Giuseppe Bardi. With him he organized Fratelli Alinari, Presso Bardi, a small photographic laboratory in the Via Cornina, Florence. In a city that took a keen interest in the thriving photographic industry, their venture was soon successful. By 1854 Leopoldo was able to purchase the business from Bardi, and with his brothers Romualdo Alinari (1830–91) and Giuseppe Alinari (1836–92) he founded Fratelli Alinari, Editori Fotografichi. They specialized in art reproductions, as well as portraits and landscapes (e.g. photographs of Tuscany and of the buildings and monuments in Florence, Pisa, Siena, Rome and Naples). In 1861 they moved the studio to new premises at 8, Via Nazionale. After Leopoldo's death his brothers carried on the business. Giuseppe experimented with such new photographic processes as wet collodion, and the firm published numerous catalogues, concentrating on photographs of buildings and works of art. In 1887, as a jury-member, Giuseppe took part in the first Italian photographic exhibition, held in Florence. This led to the establishment of the Società Fotografica Italiana (1889) and the publication of the *Bolletino della Società fotografica italiana*, to which the Alinari brothers actively contributed. In 1890, after the deaths of Romualdo and Giuseppe, Leopoldo's son Vittorio Alinari (1859–1932) took over the business. He strengthened their catalogue publishing, organized important campaigns to promote architectural and documentary photography and continued to experiment with photographic materials. In 1892 the firm was renamed Fratelli Alinari IDEA (Istituto di Edizioni Artistiche). Although Vittorio sold it in 1920 it is still in business, and the new owners maintained its success by producing over 70,000 items, which represent a valuable source of information about Italy's cultural heritage.

BIBLIOGRAPHY

F. Alinari, 1978 Agenda Alinari, centoquattro ritratti femminili dagli Archivio Alinari (Florence, *c.* 1977)

Gli Alinari: Fotografi a Firenze, 1852–1920 (exh. cat. by W. Settimelli and F. Zevi, Florence, Forte Belvedere, 1977)

Firenze: Un sogno nell'obbiettivo (Florence, *c.* 1988)

ERIKA BILLETER

Alinari, Mélida y. *See* MÉLIDA Y ALINARI.

Alipheira. *See under* MEGALOPOLIS.

ʿAliquli Jabbadar [ʿAlīqulī Jabbadār; ʿAlīqulī Jubbadār; ʿAlīqulī Beg; ʿAlīqulī Farangī] (*fl* 1666–94). Persian painter. He was one of a small group of artists working in Iran in the second half of the 17th century who painted in an eclectic manner (*see* ISLAMIC ART, §III, 4(vi)(a)). His name appears on a number of miniatures, including four in the St Petersburg Album (St Petersburg, Hermitage, E-14; fol. 93 dated AH 1085/1674) and four in the Davis Album (New York, Met., 30.95.174.2), as well as on painted papier mâché objects (*see* ISLAMIC ART, §VIII, 10). Although the wording of these signatures varies, they all seem to be in the same hand. In one variant he referred to himself as *farangī* ('the Frank'); this led Welch to suggest that ʿAliquli was a European who arrived in Persia in the mid-17th century, was converted to Islam and was then taken into the service of the Shah. A more convincing explanation is that he came from Georgia, as had other soldiers and artists attached to the Safavid court. The epithet *farangī* is suitable for a Georgian, and two paintings in the St Petersburg Album (fols 98–9) bear Georgian inscriptions. He also referred to himself as *ghulāmzāda-i qadīmī* ('former slave'), *beg* ('lord') and *jabbadār* ('keeper of the armoury'), from which it seems that he was born a bondsman and then had a successful career within the Shah's household. Although the subject-matter of the miniatures in the St Petersburg and Davis albums is typical of their period, ʿAliquli also incorporated European images of the 16th and 17th centuries, developing a distinctive style that is not as homogeneous as that of his contemporaries Muhammad Zaman and Shaykh ʿAbbasi. In his scenes of Safavid courtly life, he was especially careful in his rendition of the physical setting and of details of dress, accoutrements of war and the hunt, while he portrayed men with a rather wicked veracity.

BIBLIOGRAPHY

A. A. Ivanov: 'Persidskiye miniatyury' [The Persian miniatures], *Al'bom indiyskikh i persidskikh miniatyur XVI–XVIII vv.* [An album of Indian and Persian miniatures of the 16th–18th centuries], ed. L. T. Guzal'yan (Moscow, 1962), pp. 55–9

A. Welch: *Shah ʿAbbas and the Arts of Isfahan* (Greenwich, 1973), pp. 148–9

E. G. Sims: 'Late Safavid Paintings: The Chehel Sutun, the Armenian Houses, the Oil Paintings', *Akten des VII. Internationalen Kongresses für iranische Kunst und Archäologie: München, 1976*, pp. 408–18

T. Falk, ed.: *Treasures of Islam/Tresors d'Islam* (Geneva, 1985), p. 126 [bilingual text]

A. Soudavar: *Art of the Persian Courts* (New York, 1992), pp. 369–73 and figs 148–50

O. Akimuškin and others: *Il Murakka' di San Pietroburgo: Album di miniature indiane e persiane del XVI–XVIII secolo* (St Petersburg, Lugano and Milan, 1994), pp. 20–21, 64, 80, 89–90, 108–9, 113, 115–16

ELEANOR SIMS

Alisal, José María Casado del. *See* CASADO DEL ALISAL, JOSÉ MARÍA.

Alişar [Alishar] **Hüyük.** Site in north-central Turkey, *c.* 45 km south-east of Yozgat, once occupied by a town of considerable importance in the development of ANCIENT ANATOLIA. It flourished from the Early Bronze Age (EB), before *c.* 3000 BC, and reached its apogee in the Middle Bronze Age (MB), *c.* 2000–*c.* 1500 BC, when it boasted an Assyrian trading colony and was probably the seat of an Anatolian king. It comprises a mound (245×145 m), which rises 32 m beside a tributary of the Konak Su, and a lower terrace (520×350 m). The site was excavated by the University of Chicago from 1927 to 1932, clearing the mound to Post-Hittite levels and then trenching down to ground-water level; virgin soil was reached only on the terrace. Nineteen occupation phases were distinguished on the mound and fourteen on the terrace. Finds from the excavations are housed in the Museum of Anatolian Civilizations, Ankara.

A full, if imprecise, pottery sequence began in the Late Chalcolithic and EB I (mound levels 19–12; *c.* 4000–*c.* 2700 BC) with the use of predominantly black-slipped wares, characteristic shapes including tall-stemmed 'fruit-stands'. In EB II (mound levels 11–8, terrace levels 14–13; *c.* 2700–*c.* 2400 BC) there were red-slipped wares and cups and bowls with red-on-yellow painted designs. During EB III (mound levels 7–5, terrace level 12; *c.* 2400–*c.* 2000 BC) the strong but simple zigzagging geometric designs of the brown-on-buff Intermediate ware from mound level 7 were replaced in level 6 by the complex polychrome Cappadocian ware also found at KÜLTEPE. From at least EB II both the mound and the terrace were fortified, the south side of the mound having a gateway with two towers in level 5. EB human figurines in clay or stone are violin-shaped, discoid or have stumpy legs and a long neck; clothes are indicated by criss-cross incisions. Perforated stone amulets are flat and animal-shaped.

Cappadocian ware continued in use during the Middle Bronze Age (terrace levels 11–10; *c.* 2000–*c.* 1500 BC), together with red-polished, wheelmade 'Old Hittite' ware. No structures were excavated on the mound, but the lower town on the terrace was fortified with an earth-filled casemate wall with regular offsets. Gates to the north and south had two sets of double doors positioned between towers with internal chambers; a third, internal gate-house led through a corbelled subterranean passage to an external postern gate built into the glacis. The interior was filled with angular alleys and irregular mud-brick houses, one with orthostats. A fine collection of moulded lead figurines depicting cultic and mythological subjects was found in these levels.

After a gap of 400–500 years the site was reoccupied in the Iron Age (mound level 4, terrace levels 9–8). The dark-on-light ware from these strata features stags and small concentric circles in panels framed by geometric designs; this was followed by the densely decorated Phrygian pottery known from GORDION. The oval citadel (65×55 m) was enclosed by a heavy, three-towered wall with an L-shaped gate; inside were two complexes of rectangular buildings, which were probably entered by steps to second-storey balconies. At this time the lower town consisted of a triangular enclosure (110×120 m) to the west. A broken basalt relief sculpture depicts a 'ceremonial feast'.

Stamp seals were found in all periods: those of the Early Bronze Age use filled-cross and simple animal designs, while during the Middle Bronze Age more complex designs were introduced as at Kültepe, apparently including Luwian hieroglyphs, which also appear on EB discoid seals. MB cylinder seals reflect the Old Assyrian presence, which is also responsible for a collection of cuneiform tablets recording business transactions and private letters. The surviving metalwork (pins, needles, blades and projectile-points) is undistinguished. Iron Age levels produced the first fibulae and a long iron sword with its bronze-coated wooden scabbard. Stone and bone were used throughout. Fragments of a plain twill-woven textile from EB I have been uncertainly identified as linen.

Hellenistic remains (mound levels 3–2, terrace levels 7–4) are meagre, although the pottery included an attractive 'Galatian' ware with human, animal and floral motifs on cream panels. During the Roman and Byzantine periods (mound level 1, terrace levels 3–1), however, the site was densely occupied. Buildings included a Roman basilica, with a tiled nave and adjoining rectory, and cement baths with steps and funnel-shaped bottoms. Byzantine buildings were later cut into and reused during the Ottoman period, finds from which included two carved pipe-bowls.

BIBLIOGRAPHY

H. H. von der Osten and E. F. Schmidt: *The Alishar Hüyük: Season of 1927*, 2 vols (Chicago, 1930–32)

E. F. Schmidt: *The Alishar Hüyük: Seasons of 1928 and 1929*, 2 vols (Chicago, 1932–3)

H. H. von der Osten: *The Alishar Hüyük: Seasons of 1930–32*, 3 vols (Chicago, 1937)

DONALD F. EASTON

ʿAlishir Nava'i [ʿAlīshīr Navāʾī; Mīr ʿAlī Shīr; Alisher Navoi] (*b* Herat, 9 Feb 1441; *d* Herat, 3 Jan 1501). Poet and patron. He was active at the court of the Timurid ruler Husayn Bayqara (*see* TIMURID, §II, (8)). Born into a cultured family of Uyghur chancellery scribes that had long been in service to the Timurids, ʿAlishir joined his foster brother Husayn Bayqara at HERAT after studying in Mashhad and Samarkand. Briefly governor of Herat in the Sultan's absence, ʿAlishir established himself as an intimate of the Sultan without specific duties. As one of the wealthiest men of his time, he joined the Sultan as a major patron of the arts. Together they supported the poet and mystic ʿAbd al-Rahman Jami (*d* 1492), who initiated ʿAlishir to membership in the Naqshbandi order of mystics. He was a patron of the lutenist Husayn and the flautist Shaykhi, as well as many historians, poets and littérateurs. Under the pen-name Nava'i, which referred to his musical interests, ʿAlishir himself composed nearly 30 literary works in all the major contemporary genres, and he is universally recognized as the greatest practitioner of Chaghatay (eastern) Turkish literature. A standing portrait of ʿAlishir in old age signed by MAHMUD MUZAHHIB (Mashhad, Imam Riza Shrine Mus.) may be a posthumous copy of an original by BIHZAD, the greatest master of the age.

ʿAlishir and the Sultan together raised the arts in Herat to an unprecedented level of excellence. ʿAlishir maintained a library-workshop (Pers. *kitābkhāna*), which was directed by Hajji Muhammad *naqqāsh*, himself a ceramicist experimenting in Chinese wares. ʿAlishir joined Husayn

Bayqara in patronage of the leading calligrapher SULTAN ʿALI MASHHADI, and his pupil Sultan-Muhammad Nur also worked for ʿAlishir. He was also a major patron of painters, including Bihzad, QASIM ʿALI and Shah-Muzaffar ibn Ustad Mansur (*d* 1485). Manuscripts of ʿAlishir's literary works were favourites for sumptuous decoration in his own time and remained so until the 19th century. For example, a copy of ʿAlishir's *Dīvān* (collected poetry; 1500, Istanbul, U. Lib., MS. 5470) has a splendid leather binding on which gold thread and blue were embroidered. As a patron of architecture, ʿAlishir is reported to have restored or endowed 370 public works, buildings and architectural ensembles, where many of his protégés also found support. His major commission in Herat was the large Ikhlasiyya complex (1476–7; destr.) to the north of the city, which contained a mosque, madrasa, *khānaqāh*, hospital, bath and his principal residence. He also had the main iwan of the congregational mosque in the city restored (1498–1500) and decorated with calligraphy by MIRAK, laid out three gardens in the suburbs and built a covered market and several *ribāṭ*s (?hospices) and caravanserais on the roads from the city. He joined the Sultan in adorning the shrine of ʿAbdallah Ansari at Gazur Gah with a garden and buildings. At the shrine of the imam ʿAli Riza at MASHHAD, ʿAlishir added an avenue with water-course and the Golden Iwan (1467), which served as the north entrance to the shrine.

BIBLIOGRAPHY

Enc. Islam/2: 'Mīr ʿAlī Shīr Nawāʾī'
Ghiyāth al-Dīn Khwāndamīr: *Makārim al-akhlāq* [panegyric biography of ʿAlishir] (1501), ed. T. Ganjei (Cambridge, 1979)
V. V. Barthold: *Mīr ʿAlī Shīr* (1962), iii of *Four Studies in the History of Central Asia*, trans. V. and T. Minorsky (Leiden, 1962)
B. Gray, ed.: *The Arts of the Book in Central Asia, 14th–16th Centuries* (London, 1979)
T. Allen: *A Catalogue of the Toponyms and Monuments of Timurid Herat* (Cambridge, MA, 1981)
K. Sulaymon and F. Sulaymonova: *Miniature Paintings Illustrating the Works of ʿAli Shir Nawaʾi, XV–XIX Centuries* (Tashkent, 1982) [text in Uzbek, Russian and English]
T. Allen: *Timurid Herat* (Wiesbaden, 1983)
B. O'Kane: *Timurid Architecture in Khurasan* (Costa Mesa, CA, 1987)
L. Golombek and D. Wilber: *The Timurid Architecture of Iran and Turan*, 2 vols (Princeton, 1988)
T. W. Lentz and G. D. Lowry: *Timur and the Princely Vision* (Los Angeles, 1989)

BASIL GRAY

Alix, Pierre-Michel (*b* 1762; *d* Paris, 27 Dec 1817). French printmaker. During the last two decades of the 18th century he followed Jean-François Janinet and Louis-Marin Bonnet in popularizing the technique of multiple-plate colour printing for the progressive tonal intaglio processes of mezzotint, aquatint, stipple and crayon manner. Alix produced many illustrations of contemporary Parisian life and fashion but was best known for his colour aquatint portraits of celebrated figures of the French Revolution and the Napoleonic period. In 1789 he provided 18 sheets for an engraved portrait collection published by Levacher de Charnois, which documented members of the French National Assembly. Alix also produced colour prints of such Revolutionary heroes as *Jean-Paul Marat*, *Marie-Joseph Chalier* and *Antoine-Laurent de Lavoisier*, after pastel drawings by Jacques-Louis David and other artists. Chief among such prints, which were widely distributed to promote patriotic zeal, were Alix's portraits of the boy heroes *Joseph Barra* and *Agricola Viala*. One of his best works of the period is a portrait of *Queen Marie-Antoinette*, after Elisabeth Vigée-Lebrun. During the late 1790s, with the establishment of the Directory and the Consulate, Alix destroyed many of his best copperplates, fearing that his depiction of Revolutionary subjects might invite persecution. He then took up historical subjects and styles derived from Classical antiquity. Important works of his late career include *Napoleon as General of the Army of Italy* (1798), *Napoleon as First Consul* (1803) and *Napoleon with Cambacérès and Lebrun*. (Copies of all works cited in this article Paris, Bib. N., Cab. Est.; see also Laran and Roux).

BIBLIOGRAPHY

Portalis–Beraldi; Thieme–Becker
J. Laran: *Inventaire du fonds français: Après 1800*, Paris, Bib. N., Cab. Est. cat., i (1930), pp. 84–8
M. Roux: *Inventaire du fonds français: Graveurs du dix-huitième siècle*, Paris, Bib. N., Cab. Est. cat., i (1931), pp. 77–117

VIVIAN ATWATER

Alix, Yves (*b* Fontainebleau, 19 Aug 1890; *d* Paris, 22 April 1969). French painter. The first art to impress him was that of Cézanne on show at a memorial exhibition in 1908. That same year he enrolled at the Académie Julian in Paris, although he moved almost immediately to the Académie Ranson, where Pierre Bonnard, Edouard Vuillard, Ker-Xavier Roussel, Maurice Denis and Paul Sérusier all taught. He first exhibited at the Salon des Indépendants in Paris in 1912. Like many artists of his generation, he was at first influenced by Cubism, in particular by that mild version of it espoused by Roger de La Fresnaye. Although traces of Cubism remained in his pictures after World War I, like the work of other artists involved in the 'retour à l'ordre' it became more conservative. In the *Master of the Harvest* (1921; Paris, Pompidou), for example, this trend is evident in the solid, geometrical construction of the aggressive figures. Soon afterwards however he settled into a neo-classical style, aligning himself with the French tradition, and produced landscapes and figure paintings in restrained colour such as *Young Woman Asleep* (1924; priv. col., see Allard, p. 51).

Alix's style showed little development during the 1930s in works such as *The Coliseum* (1931) and *Surrender (Scene from the Spanish Revolution)* (1933; both Paris, Pompidou), the latter reflecting recent events. He was also commissioned to produce the decorations for the Pavilion of the Ile de France at the Exposition Internationale des Arts et Techniques dans la Vie Moderne held in Paris in 1937. During and after World War II his palette brightened and his paintings became more joyful, though in the period of transition his output also included a number of austere religious works in an Expressionist style, such as *Descent from the Cross* (1945; see Cassou). He came to concentrate particularly on the landscape around Brittany and St Tropez, as in *Hills above St Tropez* (1947; Paris, Pompidou). His public commissions included decorations for the Mairie of Puteaux and for the Lycée Camille-Sée (1937) in Paris. He also produced tapestry cartoons for Beauvais, Aubusson and Gobelins and illustrated books such as *Antigone* by Sophocles and Pierre Benoît's *Mademoiselle de la Ferté* (Paris, 1926).

BIBLIOGRAPHY

R. Allard: *Yves Alix* (Paris, 1925)
J. Cassou: *Yves Alix* (Paris, 1946)

□

Alkamenes (*fl* second half of the 5th century BC). Greek sculptor. His date of birth and origins are uncertain; later sources mention both Athens and Lemnos as his birthplace. After the departure of Pheidias to Olympia, Alkamenes became the most eminent exponent of Athenian art. Sources that regard him as a student of Pheidias are not reliable, and the workshop in which he trained and developed his stylistic idiom is unknown. The number of his works in Athenian public buildings and the fact that Thrasybulus entrusted him with the production of a commemorative monument for his Theban allies after the fall of the Tyranny in 403 BC implies that Alkamenes was a supporter of the democratic party.

This monument, the form of which is difficult to visualize, is Alkamenes' last attested work. His earliest work remains unknown, despite increasing acceptance of the assertion by Pausanias (V.x.8) that Alkamenes helped to execute the architectural sculptures of the temple of Zeus at Olympia. Two 'archaistic' works for the Athenian Acropolis indicate that he must already have been active before the mid-5th century BC: the *Hermes* herm set up in the Propylaea of the Acropolis (Pausanias, I.xxii.8)—the best preserved copy of which survives in the inscribed herm from Ephesos Selçuk (Selçuk, Ephesos Archaeol. Mus.)—and the *Hecate Epipyrgidia* set up on the bastion of the temple of Athena Nike (Pausanias, II.xxx.2), recently identified in a single copy from Hadrian's Villa at Tivoli (Tivoli, Mus. N. Archaeol., Villa Adriana).

Alkamenes certainly collaborated with Pheidias in the Periclean building programme on the Acropolis, and his hand can be recognized in the Parthenon sculptures, especially in the east frieze plaque depicting *Poseidon, Apollo and Artemis.* At the same time, *c.* 435 BC, he executed the marble statue of *Aphrodite in the Gardens* for her temple in the vicinity of the River Illisos (Pausanias, I.xix.2). Roman copies of this statue showing the goddess leaning on a pillar (e.g. Paris, Louvre, MA 414) were identified by reference to a fragment of the cult statue (Athens, N. Archaeol. Mus.) from the Temple of Aphrodite at Dafni. This fragment, which reproduces, with slight variations, the iconographical type of the *Aphrodite in the Gardens,* helps to define the development of Alkamenes' style *c.* 420 BC. Among attested work by Alkamenes, the chryselephantine statue of *Dionysos* (Pausanias, I.xx.3), dating from before 431 BC, has been recognized in a single Roman copy (Rome, Vatican, Mus. Gregoriano Profano). The *Prokne and Itys* group (Athens, Acropolis Mus.), seen by Pausanias on the Acropolis, dates to about the same period, although there is disagreement over whether it is attributable to the master himself or to one of his assistants.

The cult statue of *Ares*—recorded by Pausanias (I.viii.4) in the Temple of Ares in the Athenian Agora as part of a group with the statue of *Athena Areia* that he assigns to the otherwise unknown sculptor Lokros—has been identified with the type of the Borghese *Ares* (Paris, Louvre). A colossal torso of Athena found in the Athenian Agora and dated to 430–420 BC (Athens, Agora Mus., S 654) has been attributed to this group; the discovery of a copy of the same Athena type in Palmyra (see Starkey, pp. 566–7, no. 28) seems to reinforce its interpretation.

Epigraphical evidence dates Alkamenes' bronze group of *Hephaestos and Athena* in the Hephaesteion at Athens to the following decade. It has been suggested that the relief decoration of its base consisted of an assembly of deities surrounding a central scene, the *Birth of Erichthonios,* which may be recognizable in a copy (Rome, Vatican, Mus. Chiaramonti). Part of a copy of the figure of *Hephaestos* (Athens, N. Archaeol. Mus.) has been identified, and the numerous Roman copies of the Athena Ince type (e.g. Liverpool Mus.) may be reproductions of the statue of *Athena.*

There is no clear evidence about Alkamenes' other works, such as the statue of *Asclepios* in Mantineia (Pausanias, VIII.ix.1) or that of *Hera* in her temple on the road from Athens to Phaleron (Pausanias, I.i.5), although the latter is probably reflected in late 5th-century BC reliefs. Many architectural sculptures, however, as well as votive or funerary monuments, have been attributed to his workshop, particularly the so-called 'three-figured' reliefs (e.g. Paris, Louvre; Berlin, Pergamonmus.; Rome, Villa Albani).

The works of Alkamenes that have been recognized with some certainty in Roman copies follow closely the Classical ideal and spirit of Attic tradition embodied in the Parthenon sculptures, in the principles that govern the structure, the pose and rhythm of the figures, the innovative elegance of composition and the inspired execution. Alkamenes' apparent invention of the leaning figure exercised an important influence on later sculptors from KEPHISODOTOS and Praxiteles to those of the Hellenistic age.

BIBLIOGRAPHY

Pausanias: *Guide to Greece*
J. Overbeck: *Die antiken Schriftquellen zur Geschichte der bildenden Künste bei den Griechen* (Leipzig, 1868/*R* Hildesheim, 1959), nos 808–28
E. B. Harrison: 'Alkamenes' Sculptures for the Hephaisteion', *Amer. J. Archaeol.*, lxxxi (1977), pp. 137–78, 265–87, 411–25
W. H. Schuchhardt: *Alkamenes* (Berlin, 1977)
W. Fuchs: 'Zur Hekate des Alkamenes', *Boreas*, i (1978), pp. 32–5
G. Neumann: 'Dionysos en Limnais', *Stele: Tomos eis mnemen N. Kontoleontos* [The stele: a volume in memory of N. Kontoleon] (Athens, 1980), pp. 615–17
J. Starkey: 'Allath', *Lexicon Iconographicum Mythologiae Classicae*, i (Zurich, 1981), pp. 564–70
P. Bruneau: 'L'Arès Borghèse et l'Arès d'Alcamène, ou de l'opinion et du raisonnement', *Rayonnement grec: Hommages à Ch. Delvoye* (Brussels, 1982), pp. 177–99
G. Donnay: 'A propos d'Alcamène', *Rayonnement grec: Hommages à Ch. Delvoye* (Brussels, 1982), pp. 167–76
J. P. Barron: 'Alkamenes at Olympia', *Bull. Inst. Class. Stud. U. London*, xxxi (1984), pp. 199–211
A. Delivorrias: 'Aphrodite', *Lexicon Iconographicum Mythologiae Classicae*, ii (Zurich, 1984), pp. 3–33, nos 193–221
——: 'Sparagmata: Aus der klassischen Ikonographie der Athena', *Archaische und klassische griechische Plastik: Akten des internationalen Kolloquiums von 22.-25. April 1985 in Athen, II*, ed. H. Kyrieleis (Mainz, 1986), pp. 149–54
A. Linfert: 'Quellenprobleme: Zu Alkamenes und Kolotes', *Riv. Archaeol.*, xii (1988), pp. 33–41

A. DELIVORRIAS

Alkema, Wobbe (Hendrik) (*b* Borger, 11 Feb 1900; *d* Drachten, 30 Jan 1984). Dutch painter and printmaker.

He trained between 1919 and 1923 as a cabinetmaker, taking evening classes in furniture drawing and design at the Academie Minerva in Groningen. He also took private drawing lessons with the Dutch sculptor Willem Valk (1898–1977). Around 1920 he started to make drawings and paintings in an abstracted, geometric style, similar to that of Bart van der Leck (e.g. *En passant*, 1921–2; priv. col., see 1984 exh. cat., p. 17). From 1924 he worked in the architectural firm of Van Lingen in Groningen, and he continued to design furniture until the 1930s. He joined De Ploeg and started to mix with Dutch artists such as Jan Wiegers, Jan Altink (1885–1971) and Hendrik Nicolaas Werkman. He produced geometric abstract works such as *Composition with Yellow Circles* (1924; Groningen, Groninger Mus.). From *c*. 1924 he began to associate with the Belgian Constructivists involved in the magazine *Het Overzicht* and later *De Driehoek*, including Jozef Peeters and Paul van Ostaijen (1896–1928). In 1926 some of his prints were published in the magazines *The Next Call* and *De Driehoek*. During this period his style was a form of geometric abstraction, and his prints of the 1930s show the influence of Kandinsky (e.g. *With Trapezium*, 1931; see 1984 exh. cat., p. 37). In addition to paintings and drawings he also produced watercolours, woodcuts and linocuts and worked on the restoration of medieval churches. After a visit to Germany in 1935 Alkema felt unable to continue painting until 1947, but when he resumed he adopted some surrealist elements (e.g. *Four Sounds*, 1950; priv. col., see 1984 exh. cat., p. 41); in the late 1950s he returned to geometric compositions determined by grids, as in *Composition 19* (1959; priv. col., see 1984 exh. cat., p. 45). He continued to experiment with graphic and printmaking techniques, combining them with delicate photographs of plants and insects for his series *149 Slides* (1973–8; see 1984 exh. cat., pp. 50–53).

BIBLIOGRAPHY

H. W. van Os: *Wobbe Alkema en de Groninger Schilderkunst* (Groningen, 1978)

Het vroege werk van Wobbe Alkema (exh. cat. by A. Petersen; Amsterdam, Stedel. Mus.; The Hague, Gemeentemus.; 1978)

Wobbe Alkema (exh. cat. by H. W. van Os, A. Taverne and J. Falize, Groningen, Groninger Mus., 1984)

JOHN STEEN

Alken. English family of artists of Danish descent. The earliest member active in England was Sefferien Alken (1717–82), who was a wood-carver, gilder and stone-carver employed by William Chambers. His son (1) Samuel Alken was an engraver. Four of Samuel Alken's sons, Samuel Alken (1784–*c*. 1825), (2) Henry (Thomas) Alken, George Alken (*c*. 1794–?1837) and Sefferien John Alken (1796–1857), were sporting artists. In the next generation Henry Alken's sons Samuel Henry (Gordon) Alken (1810–94), known as Henry Alken junior, and Sefferien Alken (1821–73) were also artists.

BIBLIOGRAPHY

Gunnis

F. Siltzer: *The Story of British Sporting Prints* (London, 1928, rev. 1979)

S. Mitchell: *The Dictionary of Equestrian Artists* (Woodbridge, 1985)

(1) Samuel Alken (*b* London, 22 Oct 1756; *bur* London, 9 Nov 1815). Engraver. He entered the Royal Academy Schools, London, as a sculptor in 1772. In 1779 he published *A New Book of Ornaments Designed and Etched by Samuel Alken*, afterwards establishing himself as one of the most competent engravers in the new technique of aquatint. His varied output of singly issued prints after designs by other artists from 1784 to 1793 includes such satirical works as *An Italian Family* (1785; see George, no. 9670) and *A French Family* (1792; see George, no. 9686), both after Thomas Rowlandson. His many sporting prints include the sensitive print of the racehorse *Soldier* after George Garrard (1793). From *c*. 1788 he was much in demand reproducing topographical watercolours as illustrations for travel books. There are some sporting paintings signed *S. Alken*, but they may be the work of his eldest son, Samuel.

BIBLIOGRAPHY

S. T. Prideaux: *Aquatint Engraving* (London, 1909, rev. 1968)

M. D. George: *A Catalogue of Political and Personal Satires*, London, B.M. cat., vii (London, 1942)

DAVID ALEXANDER

(2) Henry (Thomas) Alken (*b* London, 12 Oct 1785; *d* London, 7 April 1851). Painter and engraver, son of (1) Samuel Alken. He worked in London and the provinces and was prolific in a variety of media while unadventurous in his range of subject-matter. Early instruction by the miniature painter J. T. Beaumont (1774–1851) helped to give a certain graphic precision—lacking in most of the work of his many relatives—to his often flippant and always anecdotal early paintings, etchings and watercolours of hunting, coaching, racing and other animal subjects. He was also employed by sporting periodicals as an illustrator and provided plates for the *National Sports of Great Britain* (London, 1821), strengthening the market for his work in sporting circles, in particular the notorious clique of wealthy and reckless huntsmen who gathered at Melton Mowbray, Leics. Characteristic of his prints is the set of six humorous engravings *How to Qualify for a Meltonian*, which was published in 1819. After *c*. 1820 his artistic competence declined, rendering his later works barely distinguishable from those of his son Samuel Henry Alken and firmly reminiscent of those of his father.

BIBLIOGRAPHY

W. Shaw Sparrow: *Henry Alken* (London, 1927)

STEPHEN DEUCHAR

Alladio, Gian Giacomo d'. *See* ALBA, MACRINO D'.

Allahabad [anc. Prayaga]. City of religious, strategic and administrative importance in Uttar Pradesh, India. Located at the confluence of the sacred rivers Ganga, Yamuna and mystical Saraswati, Allahabad has drawn Hindu pilgrims for centuries. The earliest monument is a stone pillar, inscribed with edicts of Ashoka (*reg c*. 269–*c*. 232 BC), a panegyric of the Gupta king Samudragupta (*reg c*. AD 335–76) and a record of its re-erection in 1605 by the Mughal emperor Jahangir (*reg* 1605–27). Brooding over the Sangam (sacred bathing area) is the massive sandstone fort of Akbar (*reg* 1556–1605), built in 1584 to guard the river-route to Bengal. As at Agra, Delhi and Lahore, the fort enclosed residential quarters and palace buildings, but these were substantially altered during British tenure in the 19th and 20th centuries. Some indication of their former splendour is given in aquatints by Thomas and William DANIELL.

Mughal residences and gardens straggled along the Yamuna from the fort to the city. Prince Salim, the future emperor Jahangir, while Governor of Allahabad from 1600 to 1603, here laid out the Khusrau Bagh. This garden, which has parterres and water-channels, also contains the tombs of Prince Khusrau (*d* 1622), his sister Sultan al-Nisa (*d* ?1624) and his Rajput mother, Shah Begum (*d* 1604). Shah Begum's tomb consists of an open trabeate pavilion standing on two platforms above a masonry plinth. Elaborate pierced stone parapets shown in a print by Thomas Daniell are now missing. Prince Khusrau's mausoleum is an arcaded, two-storey structure surmounted by a dome on an octagonal drum. The interior contains faded paintings of Persian couplets and flower designs.

In 1801 Allahabad came under British control. A leading monument of the early 19th century is Holy Trinity Church (1839), modelled on the church of St Martin-in-the-Fields, London. During the 1857 rebellion, Allahabad became the base for re-establishing British control of the middle-Gangetic plain and consequently superseded Agra as capital of the North-western Provinces and Oudh (Avadh). In the 1860s a new town known as Canning Town, built north of the East Indian Railway line, represented the largest town-planning exercise carried out in India before the establishment of New Delhi. Major Richard Strachey prepared the plan (1857–8), and Commissioner Cuthbert Bensey Thornhill supervised its execution from 1858. Broad, tree-lined roads laid out in a formal grid provided space for a rail complex, a garrison, residences, provincial administration buildings and later a university. An exceptionally well-preserved city, Allahabad is a key site for the study of British India in the 19th century. The civil lines contain an interesting variety of bungalows, a notable example being that of the speculative builder Robert Carr (1819–84). Many prosperous Indians moved into the European enclave, while for others mini-civil lines were planned: these included George Town (1901), Lukerganj (1906, for Government Press employees), Tagore Town (1909) and Mumfordganj (begun late 1930s). Although architectural styles were modified to suit local tastes, the overall plans remained strikingly unchanged. The main exception to this rule is the railway colony, which has small brick huts with courtyards for workers and Calcutta-style classical houses for senior staff.

Queen's Road, Allahabad's processional way, runs north from the railway station. The road is lined with such public buildings as the hospital, cathedral, Telegraph Office and General Post Office, Government Press and Secretariat. The Anglican All Saints' Cathedral (1871–1929) by WILLIAM EMERSON is a successful exercise in the Gothic Revival style, but its west end lacks the twin towers and spires originally planned. The Secretariat buildings (1870) by General Peile of the Royal Engineers are handsomely severe, with an open verandah of paired Ionic columns set above a rusticated arcade. Queen's Road was intended to end triumphantly at an Italianate Government House, but, instead, economy dictated the purchase of the 107th Regiment Mess east of Alfred Park in 1869; this was enlarged by the addition of two wings connected by curved corridors at the front. The Lieutenant-Governor's Council met at the Mayo Memorial Hall (1879), built by subscription for public functions. Designed by R. Roskell Bayne, an engineer with the East Indian Railway, the hall has a semicircular concrete roof and a 55 m-high tower. The interior has a superb dance floor, and it was decorated to designs sent out from England by Professor Gamble of the South Kensington Museum (now the Victoria and Albert Museum), London. The last major government building was the High Court (1911–16) by Frank Lishman; a further wing was opened in 1954.

With the development of new areas after 1857, the old cantonments were redeveloped as Alfred Park (1870), which contained a bandstand, tennis-courts and a statue of Queen Victoria under a marble canopy (now removed to the Collector's compound). Government House occupied the park's eastern flank, while the Thornhill–Mayne Memorial Library (1878) lay to the west. The library, by Bayne, is in a Scottish Baronial style with an elaborate hammerbeam roof. To the north is Muir Central College (1872–86) by William Emerson, which is dominated by its 73 m-high Cairene-style minaret-tower and blue-tiled domes. Further north still is the campus of Allahabad University (1887). The library, Senate House and Law College were designed by SAMUEL SWINTON JACOB in an enjoyable Indo-Saracenic style. West of the park is the Italianate St Joseph's Roman Catholic Cathedral (1871–9) and the United Provinces Club, the work respectively of the firms of J. Frizzoni and of Bruno Vassal. More recent additions to the park are the Music Academy and Allahabad Museum, noted for its outstanding collections of central and eastern Indian sculptures of the 2nd century BC–12th century AD.

The old Indian portions of the city stand completely apart from those areas laid out by the British. Centred around a square (*chowk*), the old city is a tangle of narrow lanes and residential areas (*mohallas*) once closed off at night by gates. The principal mosque, built over shops, has an elaborate engrailed doorway and melon domes. Adjacent are the traditional residences (*kothis*) of the leading local families.

BIBLIOGRAPHY

U. Singh: *Allahabad: A Study in Urban Geography* (Varanasi, 1961)
M. Bence-Jones: *Palaces of the Raj: Magnificence and Misery of the Lord Sahibs* (London, 1973)
R. Thapar: *Asoka and the Decline of the Mauryas* (Delhi, 2/1973) [trans. of the edicts]
C. A. Bayly: *The Local Roots of Indian Politics, Allahabad, 1880–1920* (Oxford, 1975)
A. D. King: *Colonial Urban Development: Culture, Social Power and Environment* (London, 1976)
M. Archer: *Early Views of India: Picturesque Journeys of Thomas and William Daniell, 1786–94* (London, 1980)
J. B. Harrison: 'Will and Deed, or Secrets of a Sub-registrar', *S. Asia Res.*, ii/1 (May 1982)
——: 'Four Gridirons (Philadelphia, Singapore, Rangoon, Allahabad)', *East India Company Studies*, ed. K. Ballhatchet and J. Harrison (Hong Kong, 1986)

J. B. HARRISON

Allan, David (*b* Alloa, 13 Feb 1744; *d* Edinburgh, 6 Aug 1796). Scottish painter and illustrator. In 1755 he was apprenticed to Robert Foulis, a printer who, with his brother Andrew Foulis, founded the Foulis Academy, Glasgow, at which Allan was a student until 1764. Allan's association with the Foulis brothers was long and fruitful; several of his sets of illustrations in the 1780s were for books published by the brothers. In the mid-1760s Charles, 9th Baron Cathcart (1721–76), and several families, including the Erskines of Mar, provided Allan with funds that enabled him to study in Italy, considered essential at that time for any aspiring artist. He probably reached Rome by 1767 and remained there until 1777. During this period he studied with Gavin Hamilton, the leading Scottish artist resident there, and Hamilton encouraged Allan's ambitions to become a history painter.

In 1771 Allan sent two history pictures to the Royal Academy exhibition in London: *Pompey the Great after his Defeat* and *Cleopatra Weeping Over the Ashes of Mark Antony* (both untraced). In 1773 he won the Accademia di S Luca's gold medal for *Hector's Farewell from Andromache* (Rome, Accad. N. S Luca). The *Continence of Scipio* (1774; Edinburgh, N.G.) is typical of Allan's history pictures executed in Rome: the figures are stiff and wooden, the architecture forms a rigidly geometric stage, the archaeological details are pedantically spread out for inspection, and the colouring is harsh. That he later abandoned this genre is often put down to the paucity of British clients for modern pictures other than portraits; his history paintings, however, were simply not sufficiently original to attract even favourably disposed patrons. While in Rome, Allan also produced numerous genre drawings and paintings, the best known of which are pen and wash drawings of the Roman Carnival (*c.* 1775; Brit. Royal Col.), etched by Paul Sandby in 1780. Allan may have realized that his true talents and future prospects lay in this direction: in 1777 he sent *Italian Shepherd Boy* and *Neapolitan Girl* (both untraced) to the Royal Academy's exhibition.

In 1777 Allan moved to London, where he mostly worked as a portrait painter. In 1780 he settled in Edinburgh, earning his living as a painter and (from 1786) as Master at the Trustees' Academy. For some time he reconciled his lingering ambitions to be a history painter with his greater talents for genre, by producing various drawings and illustrations for books on themes from Scottish history. Notable examples include his scenes of rural Scotland for Allan Ramsay's *Gentle Shepherd* (Glasgow, 1788), the first fully illustrated edition of James Macpherson's *Ossian* (Perth, 1795) and an extensive series of drawings depicting the life of Mary Queen of Scots (examples, Edinburgh, N.G.). Allan's final years were largely taken up with drawings, watercolours, etchings and oil paintings in which he recorded the people and customs of Scotland, for example his pen-and-watercolour *Penny Wedding* (1795; Edinburgh, N.G.). He was not 'the Scots Hogarth' he was once made out to be (there is little of the satirist or moralist to be found in his work), but Allan's anecdotal and sentimental realism established a new direction for art in Scotland and inspired the next generation of Scottish painters, most notably David Wilkie.

BIBLIOGRAPHY

DNB; Waterhouse: *18th C.*

D. Irwin and F. Irwin: *Scottish Painters at Home and Abroad, 1700–1900* (London, 1975)

Painting in Scotland: The Golden Age (exh. cat. by D. Macmillan, U. Edinburgh, Talbot Rice Gal.; London, Tate; 1986–7)

PETER WALCH

Allan, William (*b* Edinburgh, 1782; *d* Edinburgh, 23 Feb 1850). Scottish painter. He served an apprenticeship as a coach painter before studying under John Graham (1754–1817) at the Trustees' Academy, Edinburgh. Graham inspired in his pupils the urge to travel and to gain a broad knowledge of the world, an approach that strongly influenced Allan's early career. Allan formed a lasting friendship with his fellow student David Wilkie and followed him to London, where he continued his studies, possibly at the Royal Academy Schools although there is no documentation to support this. In 1805 he exhibited *Gypsy Boy and Ass* (untraced) at the Royal Academy and that year left England for St Petersburg, carrying letters of introduction from a Scottish patron to the court of Tsar Alexander I (*reg* 1801–25). He was well regarded there and learnt Russian, spending many years touring the hinterland, Tartary, Circassia and Turkey. He made extensive studies of these areas, recording the appearance, habits and character of villagers, townspeople and princes (e.g. *Circassian Prince on Horseback Selling Two Boys*, 1814; St Petersburg, Hermitage). He collected costumes, armoury and other artefacts to use as studio props and himself adopted Circassian dress.

In 1814 Allan returned to Edinburgh, where his exotic, Oriental pictures introduced new subject-matter to Scottish painting. At the time his work was described as reflecting a style midway between the severity of classicism and the 'burlesque feeling' of the Dutch masters (Irwin and Irwin). Over several years he continued to exhibit paintings of this sort, but with the encouragement of his friends Wilkie and Walter Scott he eventually turned to Scottish history for inspiration. He was commissioned by Constable & Co., Edinburgh, to provide illustrations for an edition of Scott's *Waverley* novels, which were engraved and published as a set in 1820. His choice of Scottish themes was moulded by Wilkie's own essays into history painting, and like Wilkie he concentrated on the narrative content. In 1821 he showed the first of his Scottish pictures, the *Murder of Archbishop Sharpe* (untraced), at the Royal Academy, London, and the following year painted *Knox Admonishing Mary Queen of Scots* (John Holloway priv. col., see Caw, p. 109). He began these major compositions by making oil sketches of clay models arranged on a miniature stage and by doing chalk studies from life of hands, heads and facial expressions. He was celebrated for his painstaking accuracy with details of period costume and setting, although his sense of form was not always as sure. He also painted biblical and genre scenes (e.g. *Christmas Eve*, Aberdeen, A.G.), sea battles and portraits.

Allan was a popular figure in art circles in Edinburgh and in 1826 was appointed Master of the Trustees' Academy, where his culture and worldly erudition influenced a generation of students. He was elected ARA in 1825 and RA in 1835. He spent some time in the late 1820s travelling in Italy, Greece and Turkey, and in 1830 he returned to Scotland. In 1832, the year of Scott's death, he executed a series of watercolours (Edinburgh, N.G.)

of the interiors of Abbotsford, Scott's home near Melrose. In 1834 he again went abroad, this time to Spain and Morocco. The trip prompted his return to exotic subject-matter, as seen in such works as the *Slave Market, Constantinople* (1838; Edinburgh, N.G.). Historical romance continued to preoccupy him, however, and *Heroism and Humanity* (1840; Glasgow, A.G. & Mus.) recreated an incident from the reign of Robert the Bruce (*reg* 1306–29). In 1838 he became President of the Royal Scottish Academy, and in 1842 he was knighted. In 1844 he revisited Russia, where he produced several paintings for Tsar Nicholas I (*reg* 1825–55), for example *Peter the Great Teaching his Subjects the Art of Shipbuilding* (St Petersburg, Hermitage), after which he returned to Edinburgh.

BIBLIOGRAPHY

J. L. Caw: *Scottish Painting: Past and Present, 1620–1908* (Edinburgh, 1908), pp. 108–10

S. Cursiter: *Scottish Art to the Close of the Nineteenth Century* (London, 1949), pp. 68–9

D. Irwin and F. Irwin: *Scottish Painters at Home and Abroad, 1700–1900* (London, 1975), pp. 204–13

D. Macmillan: *Scottish Art, 1460–1990* (Edinburgh, 1990), p. 182

all'antica [It.: 'after the Antique']. Style of decoration in a work of art that mimics, quotes or derives from a Classical model (*see* ANTIQUE, THE, fig. 1).

□

Allard, Roger (Charles Félix) (*b* Paris, 22 Jan 1885; *d* 1961). French critic and poet. His poetry was influenced by Joachim du Bellay (1522–60), Charles Baudelaire and Auguste Angellier (1848–1911), and the many volumes he published include *La Féerie des heures* (Paris and Lille, 1902) and *L'Appartement des jeunes filles* (Paris, 1919). He was briefly associated with the Abbaye de Créteil in 1907–08, and he moved to Paris from Lille in spring 1910, soon coming into contact with the Cubists. He was one of their earliest and most perceptive defenders. In his first article on art, a review of the Salon d'Automne of 1910, he wrote approvingly of the work of Jean Metzinger, Albert Gleizes and Henri Le Fauconnier as marking the final rout of Impressionism. Allard played a leading role in bringing these and other Cubists together for the first group exhibition at the Salon des Indépendants of 1911 and largely remained a supporter of Salon Cubism. He maintained a broad attitude towards Cubism, seeing it as a return to the balance and composure of classicism, blended with the more modern ideas of Henri Bergson. Initially unaware of the pioneering work of Picasso and Braque, he reacted with hostility in his article 'Sur quelques peintres' (1911), professing himself especially dismayed at the 'foreign' influence of Picasso. Increasingly he accused them of leading painting away from nature and towards hermeticism. As their prominence grew, through the efforts of Guillaume Apollinaire and others, he became marginalized as an avant-garde critic. After World War I, while editing his own periodical *Le Nouveau spectateur* (1–20, May 1919 to Feb 1921), his antipathy continued, and he began to support naturalistic artists.

WRITINGS

'Au Salon d'Automne de Paris', *A. Libre* (Nov 1910)

'Sur quelques peintres', *Marches Sud-Ouest* (June 1911)

BIBLIOGRAPHY

D. Cottington: *Cubism and the Politics of Culture in France, 1905–14* (PhD diss., U. London, 1985)

C. Green: *Cubism and its Enemies* (London, 1987)

For further bibliography *see* CUBISM.

PHILIP COOPER

Allart du Hameel. *See* ALART DU HAMEEL.

Allebé, August [Augustus] (*b* Amsterdam, 19 April 1838; *d* Amsterdam, 10 Jan 1927). Dutch painter and lithographer. He attended evening classes in drawing at the Felix Meritis School in Amsterdam and on 27 May 1854 sat the entrance exam at the city's Koninklijke Academie. Lodewijk Royer, the director, gave him lessons in figure drawing and taught him about Greek art. As a student at the Academie he won several prizes. In 1855 he took up lithography under the influence of the French lithographer Adolphe Mouilleron (1820–81), whom he had seen at work in Amsterdam in 1854. He wanted to become a professional lithographer, and from 1858 to 1859 he was in Paris in order to learn the art at the Ecole des Beaux-Arts under Mouilleron's direction. He made copies after paintings in the Louvre and the Musée du Luxembourg and visited Barbizon. In Paris he met Fantin-Latour and Courbet, but his special admiration was reserved for Ingres, Delacroix and Decamps. In the 1850s and 1860s Allebé frequently sought inspiration in the countryside, staying at Laren in the Gooi area, Oosterbeek and the Brabant village of Dongen. In 1860 he returned to the Felix Meritis School to study painting and also worked in the studio of P. F. Greive (1811–72).

Allebé's reputation rests primarily on the position he held as professor (from 1870) and director (from 1880) of the Rijksacademie van Beeldende Kunsten in Amsterdam. During his 37 years there—he retired in 1907—he was responsible for training several generations of artists, almost all of whom were later to claim that Allebé's influence had been of crucial importance for their artistic formation. His pupils included W. A. Witsen, J. P. Veth, Jacobus van Looy and G. H. Breitner.

Allebé's own oeuvre is fairly modest. His small cabinet paintings were genre pieces characterized by pure, accurate drawing, a balanced use of colour and a captivating manner of painting even the smallest details: for example, *Old Woman by the Fireplace* (Amsterdam, Rijksmus.). His use of colour and rendering of materials are particularly distinguishing features of his work (e.g. *Young Woman*, 1863; Amsterdam, Rijksmus.). He chose his subjects from everyday life (see fig.), but seldom depicted a scene or object for its own sake: there was always a carefully thought-out story or anecdote underlying the image, and he often added a humorous touch. As a lithographer Allebé was a genuine innovator, although this was hardly realized by his contemporaries. His detailed watercolours have become, perhaps, more famous than the rest of his work, but he seems to have felt most at ease in his numerous quick sketches. From the beginning his work was favourably received by critics. Before his appointment as professor in 1870 he was invariably described as 'talented' and seemed to have great promise, but, because he devoted his later career almost entirely to the Rijksacademie, he was felt never fully to have developed as an artist. Insecurity and a

August Allebé: *Two Children at Mierlo*, 1.07×1.37 m (Rotterdam, Museum Boymans–van Beuningen)

tendency to follow the advice of others also prevented Allebé from fully exploiting his potential.

BIBLIOGRAPHY

C. H. de Stuers: *Het lithographisch werk van August Allebé: Beschrijvende catalogus met inleiding* [The lithographic work of August Allebé: descriptive catalogue with index] (Utrecht, 1929)

F. J. Dubiez: 'August Allebé', *Ons Amsterdam*, xxii/11–12 (1970), pp. 329–35, 354–9

M. B. Lohmann-de Roever: 'August Allebé', *Ons Amsterdam*, xxx/10–11 (1978), pp. 302–6, 325–9

W. Loos and C. van Tuyll, eds: *'Waarde heer Allebé': Leven en werk van August Allebé (1838–1927)* ['Dear Mr Allebé': the life and work of August Allebé (1838–1927)] (Zwolle, 1988)

The Age of Van Gogh: Dutch Painting, 1880–1895 (exh. cat., ed. R. Bionda and C. Blotkamp; Glasgow, Burrell Col., 1990)

CHR. WILL

Allegory [Gr. *allegoria*, description of something under the guise of something else]. Term used to describe a method of expressing complex abstract ideas or a work of art composed according to this. An allegory is principally constructed from personifications and symbols (*see* SYMBOL), and, though overlapping in function, it is thus more sophisticated in both meaning and operation than either of these. It is found primarily in Western art and constitutes an important area of study in ICONOGRAPHY AND ICONOLOGY.

I. Introduction. II. Classical. III. Medieval. IV. Renaissance. V. Baroque. VI. Romanticism, Realism and decline.

I. Introduction.

Allegory, a means of making the 'invisible' visible, is a product of the philosophical thought of Classical antiquity and was used by the ancients not only in the fine arts but also in literature and rhetoric (Cicero: *On the Orator*, xxvii.94; Quintilian: *Principles of Oratory*, VIII.vi.44; IX.ii.92; Plutarch: *Moralia*, 19, E-F). In contrast with the symbol, which is a phenomenon of nearly all cultures and religions, allegory is thus essentially a feature primarily of Western art.

The mechanism of allegory further distinguishes it from both symbolism and personification. Symbolism, in ordinary parlance, occurs when an object is used by convention to refer to a general idea, while personification occurs when abstract terms are expressed by human figures, generally with significant attributes. An allegory, however, includes combinations of personifications and/or symbols, which, on the basis of a conventionally agreed relation between concept and representation, refer to an idea outside the work of art.

Allegories themselves can be subdivided into the categories of dynamic and static. In dynamic allegories the personifications perform an active role, as, for example, in Prudentius' *Psychomachia* (beginning of the 5th century AD), the strife between Vice and Virtue. In a static allegory the different elements of the picture illustrate different elements of an intellectual concept—taken as a whole, they may be the pictorial formula expressing, for example, the universality and inner connection of knowledge, faith etc. Furthermore, an allegorical significance may be attached to subjects with a prior sense of their own, such as mythology, genre or historical events, and the resulting ambiguity is sometimes pursued as an end in itself. The generation of allegorical meaning takes place without the need for aesthetic appreciation, although Renaissance (and later) art theories stipulated rules for DECORUM, so that, for example, a noble subject must be expressed in noble forms. Allegory, whether or not in conscious imitation of the ancients, continued to be employed until the 19th century, when it fell into disfavour because it was considered to be 'intellectualistic' and a hindrance to visual communication.

II. Classical.

Two related developments of great importance characterized the Greek attitude towards religion and distinguished it from that of other ancient peoples. These were the ability to reflect rationally on the preternatural forces by which life is governed and the gift of transposing religious experience into anthropomorphic metaphors. Gradually, in the 6th and 5th centuries BC, myth became transformed into poetry, ritual action into drama, and cult objects with a fetish character into allegorical ones, thus creating a distinction between outer appearance and significance. In place of the old homogeneous mythology, there arose, within the same external forms, a 'paramythology', a new mythic idiom that was allegorical: 'The image came to be interpreted allegorically when it had lost its self-evident character' (Hinks, 1939, p. 11). This made it possible, for example, to see the war of the Greeks against the Amazons as an allusion to the war against the Persians. A further step in this direction led to purely allegorical representations without a mythological pretext, such as Apelles' lost painting incorporating personifications of Calumny and

1. Allegorical theme on the *Great Cameo of France*, sardonyx cameo, 310×265 mm, AD 17 (Paris, Bibliothèque Nationale, Cabinet des Médailles)

others or the *Kairos* (Opportunity) of Lysippos (Roman relief copy, Turin, Mus. Ant.; *see* ICONOGRAPHY AND ICONOLOGY, fig. 3), and depictions of *Psychomachia*, especially as literary themes (e.g. *Hercules at the Crossroads*; *Tabula Cebetis*).

At a very early stage, personifications came into use to represent abstractions of ideas comprising almost the whole world picture of ancient times: seasons, towns, continents, Fortune, Conquest, Peace and so on. These personifications, especially in Roman art, were used in symbolic terms (e.g. as references to triumph or apotheosis) in relation to particular historical events, as in the *Great Cameo of France* (AD 17; Paris, Bib. N., Cab. Médailles; see fig. 1), which possibly commemorates the departure of Germanicus to the east. Personifications of the seasons, depicted on sarcophagi, allude to the revolutions of time and may thus symbolize the cycle of birth, death and rebirth (life after death, reincarnation, transmigration of the soul and so on); in this way, besides being an allegory of eternity, they can also be an allegory of the harmony between macrocosm and microcosm. The use of allegorical personifications on coins and medals is of great importance on account of their dissemination throughout the Greco-Roman world and their continuance in post-Classical times.

III. Medieval.

1. UNTIL THE 12TH CENTURY. Late Antique personifications retained their validity in early medieval art. Also important was the adoption of the antique theory of allegory by St Augustine (AD 354–430) and by St Isidore of Seville (*c.* AD 560–636), who wrote, 'An allegory is a manner of speaking figuratively; it sounds like one thing but means another' (*Etymologiae*, I.xxxvii.22). This refers to literature, but in relation to the fine arts it became an argument with regard to iconoclasm, as reflected in the comment of Pope Adrian I (*reg* AD 772–95), who supported the use of allegory as a means 'to show the invisible through the visible'. More generally, such ideas provided a theoretical basis for the use of symbolism and allegory in art.

Of great importance in the thinking about allegory was the development of biblical exegesis. A distinction was drawn between *sensus litteralis*, the literal narration of a biblical story, and *sensus spiritualis*; the latter was again divided into *sensus allegoricus* (the true meaning hidden behind the literal sense), *sensus tropologicus* (the moral significance) and *sensus anagogicus* (the meaning in the light of eschatology), although those distinctions were not always used strictly in practice. Typology, developed from the *sensus spiritualis*, had far-reaching effects on the visual arts, linking Old Testament scenes (the Type) with New Testament ones (the Antitype). In Carolingian times the contrast between *Ecclesia* and *Synagoge* developed from this line of thought.

The continuance of the Classical literary tradition of allegory, and the development both of multiple interpretations of the Bible and of typology, helped to form the basic medieval attitude that everything in the visible world may have a symbolic meaning. Moreover, the Neo-Platonist Pseudo-Dionysius the Areopagite (*fl* early 6th century AD) had expressly associated allegory with beauty: visible things are images of the beauty of the invisible. This view influenced Suger, Abbot of Saint-Denis, in the 12th century.

As an inheritance from antiquity, the four cardinal virtues had a firm place in Christian iconography: Prudence, Temperance, Fortitude and Justice, which Cicero and Ambrosius Macrobius (*fl c.* AD 400) subdivided into various aspects and facets. These were combined with the three 'theological virtues', Faith, Hope and Charity, mentioned by St Paul (1 Corinthians 13:13), to constitute the seven principal virtues. Three main types of iconography of the virtues developed in the early Middle Ages: that derived from the Classical idea of an author, with Virtue as inspiration; the conflict between Virtues and Vices, elaborated in Prudentius' *Psychomachia*; and that derived from the latter and from the image of the triumphant Christ, with Virtue crushing Vice underfoot. Another important Classical heritage was the tradition of the liberal arts: the Trivium of grammar, rhetoric and dialectic and the Quadrivium of arithmetic, geometry, music and astronomy. The pictorial tradition related to these begins with the exhaustively described personifications in *De nuptiis philologiae et Mercurii* by Martianus Mineus Felix Capella (*fl c.* 480). As regards both form and content, the iconography of the liberal arts derived from that of the Muses.

2. 12TH AND 13TH CENTURIES. Visual unity began to be achieved thanks to the great 12th- and 13th-century encyclopedias, such as the *Glossa ordinaria*, attributed to

Anselmus of Laon (*c.* 1050–1117), and the *Speculum majus* of Vincent of Beauvais (*c.* 1190–1264). The two main trends of medieval thought (the irrational and mystical, influenced by Neo-Platonism, and the rational and didactic, influenced by Aristotle) were reflected in these encyclopedias and in the visual arts. Vincent of Beauvais regarded the liberal arts as the foundation of all knowledge required by the philosopher (*Speculum doctrinale*, II. 31), and this was reflected in the monumental decoration of cathedrals. The point of departure for the fine arts continued to be the allegorical interpretation of reality as, in Thomas Aquinas's words, 'spiritual meanings expressed in material metaphors'.

At the beginning of the 12th century the first truly Christian illustrations of comprehensive encyclopedic knowledge appeared and also two important forms for the allegorical expression of hierarchical relations: the rosette (e.g. in the *Mystical Paradise* in the *Speculum virginum*, *c.* 1135–53; London, BM, Arundel MS. 44, fol. 13*r*); and the allegorical tree (e.g. *Tree of the Virtues and Vices* in *Liber Floridus Lamberti*, *c.* 1120; Ghent, Bib. Rijksuniv., cod. 1125, fols 231*v*–232*r*). From the allegory of the tree there developed that of the cross, as a systematic aid to mystical contemplation.

The principle that human wisdom is dependent on divine wisdom and must be directed towards it is equally expressed in the rational–didactic programmes of the portal decorations of Chartres Cathedral (1145–55; *see* CHARTRES, §I, 2) and Notre-Dame (1210–20; *see* PARIS, §V, 1(ii)) in Paris and in the decoration of, for example, the Trivulzio candelabrum (*c.* 1210; Milan Cathedral), attributed to Nicholas of Verdun, the whole structure of which expresses the metaphor of Christ as the 'True Light'. Each of these programmes in itself forms an allegorical representation of the structure of Church and faith. The rational–didactic and the irrational–mystical ways of thought found a happy synthesis in the *Hortus deliciarum* (*c.* 1180; Strasbourg, Bib. Mun., destr.; copy, Paris, 1870; London, BL, 1703. d. 7, fol. 32*r*) by Herrad von Landsberg, one of the earliest documented women artists. This serves mystical ends thanks to a stoutly built systematic 'edifice': the representation of Philosophy (see fig. 2) reflects the system of the work as a whole. Roughly contemporaneous with the *Hortus deliciarum* is the allegorical poem *Anticlaudianus* (1181–4) by Alanus de Insulis (Alain de Lille; *c.* 1116–1202/3), a Christian transcription of Martianus Mineus Felix Capella's *De nuptiis philologiae et Mercurii*. Apart from psychomachy, this poem is chiefly of interest for its allegorical cosmology, which foreshadows Dante's *Divine Comedy*.

The *Bible moralisée* (*c.* 1220–30) is not a typological Bible like the later *Biblia pauperum* (*c.* 1300) or the *Speculum humanae salvationis* (*c.* 1310–24) but an allegorical commentary on the Bible. In some of the illustrations, genre scenes are given an allegorical significance influenced by the iconography of virtues and vices in the portal decorations of Notre-Dame in Paris, which were created somewhat earlier, though in the same cultural climate, and in which the vices are symbolized by instances from everyday life. This method rapidly became popular through miscellanies containing model sermons and through the many translations and adaptations of the ethico-theological treatise *La Somme le Roy* (1279) by Frère Laurent (*c.* 1228–*c.* 1300/02).

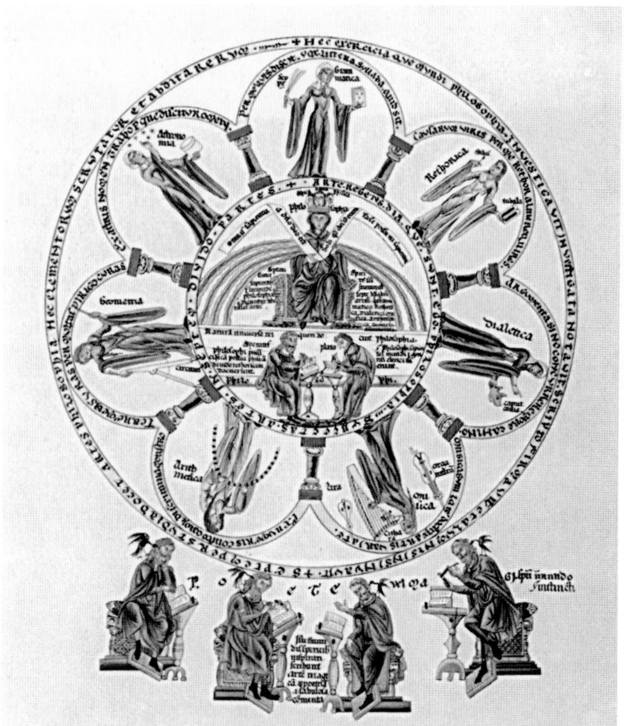

2. Allegory of *Philosophy with the Seven Liberal Arts*, from Herrad von Landsberg: *Hortus deliciarum*, *c.* 1180 (destr.; copy, Paris, 1870) (London, British Library, 1703. d. 7, fol. 32*r*)

3. 14TH AND 15TH CENTURIES. In the late Middle Ages there was a predominant taste for allegories calculated to arouse an emotional response. These included exhortations to poverty and chastity, for example in the *Mystic Marriage of St Francis and Poverty* (early 14th century; Assisi, S Francesco, Lower Church) by the Master of the Assisi Vault (Maestro delle Vele), and allegories of the vicissitudes of life and the triumph of death, for example the Camposanto (*c.* 1350), Pisa, and the *Ars moriendi* treatises. The idea of the *Imitatio Christi*, expressed in affective devotion, formed the leitmotif of late medieval ethics. Also from this period is the theme of the vices crucifying Christ, emphasis being laid on Christ's willing sacrifice as the supreme example of divine love (e.g. the south German Psalter of Bonmont, *c.* 1260; Besançon, Bib. Mun., MS. 54, fol. 15*v*). There was also an attempt to arouse emotion in depicting the conflict between virtues and vices, as in the *Etymachia* (*c.* 1330) or the *Pèlerinage* (1331) by Guillaume de Deguilleville (*b* 1295; *fl* 1358). With help from the technique of the *Ars memorandi*, there appeared in the late Middle Ages personifications combining in themselves all virtues or all vices (e.g. *c.* 1425–50; Rome, Bib. Casanatense, MS. 1404, fol. 2*v*). The female personification embodying all vices here takes on the form of '*Frau Welt*'.

Secular or political allegories, such as Ambrogio Lorenzetti's *Good and Bad Government* frescoes (1337–40;

3. Allegory with personifications of the Cardinal Virtues: *Prudence* (above left); *Justice* (above right); *Fortitude* (below left); *Temperance* (below right); from Martin of Braga [pseudo-Seneca]: *De quattuor virtutibus*, translated by Jean de Courtecuisse, *c.* 1470 (Paris, Bibliothèque Nationale, MS. Fr. 9186, fol. 304*r*)

Siena, Pal. Pub.), depict the opposition of Justice and Injustice on various levels of abstraction. At the end of the 13th century and the beginning of the 14th the encyclopedic work of Vincent of Beauvais and Thomas Aquinas was continued by Bruno Latini in *Tesoretto* (before 1267), by Dante in his *Divine Comedy* (after 1314) and further by Dante's son Jacopo di Dante Alighieri (1299–1349) in *Dotrinale.* Against this background some monumental cycles of an allegorical–encyclopedic character were created in Italy, such as the reliefs (1337–41) of the Campanile in Florence by Andrea Pisano, completed by Luca della Robbia, and the decorations of the Spanish Chapel (1366–8; Florence, S Maria Novella) by Andrea da Firenze (i), a *summa* of church doctrine and an allegory of the overthrow of heresy.

In line with the allegorical way of thought in religious matters, the medieval attitude to Classical antiquity was characterized by a search for Christian values that were present in the classics in an imperfect form. The *Ovidius moralizatus* (*c.* 1330) by Petrus Berchorius (*c.* 1285/1300–1362), *Fulgentius metaphoralis* (*c.* 1330) by John Ridewall and Christine de Pisan's *Epître d'Othéa* (*c.* 1400), in continuation of fragmentary attempts in earlier centuries, present a moralized exposition of mythology and ancient history, using, among other things, the method of multiple biblical exegesis.

In the first half of the 15th century the representation of the virtues in northern Europe went through a phase known as 'the new iconography'. The various medieval treatises on the virtues had so differentiated these personifications that the traditional attributes were no longer adequate. The tradition of Cicero and Ambrosius Macrobius, plus the differentiation of virtues into new aspects and facets, called for new attributes that were duly devised: for example the sieve and coffin for Prudence and the clock, spectacles and windmill for Temperance, as in the illustrations to *De quattuor virtutibus* (*c.* 1470; Paris, Bib. N., MS. Fr. 9186, fol. 304*r*; see fig. 3). A full century later these attributes were still being used by Pieter Bruegel the elder in a cycle of engravings of the *Virtues* (1559–60).

Secular allegory in the late Middle Ages was dominated by the related themes of love, folly and death. The allegory of courtly love (*Roman de la rose*; *see* GARDEN, fig. 36) was blended in the 15th century with aspects of social irony, for example by Master E. S. and the Housebook Master. Partly owing to the *Narrenschiff* (Strasbourg, 1493/4) by Sebastian Brant (1458–1521), folly and vanity became leitmotifs of Dutch art in the 16th and 17th centuries.

At the end of the Middle Ages a type of allegory was developed in the Netherlands that did not make use of personifications but consisted of the allegorical interpretation of landscape. The iconography of the two paths of life, expressed in landscape terms, for example by Joachim Patinir, developed on the one hand from Classical themes such as *Hercules at the Crossroads* and *Tabula Cebetis* and on the other from St Augustine's distinction between the *Civitas Dei* (city of God) and the *Civitas terrena* (earthly city); these were connected with the theme of the pilgrimage of mankind, which developed later and which was depicted by, for example, Hieronymus Bosch.

IV. Renaissance.

1. Italy. 2. Northern Europe.

1. ITALY. In the Renaissance the almost exclusive orientation of allegory towards the Christian doctrine of salvation gave way to a broader application of philosophical systems and social phenomena. It became an expression of Neo-Platonism and of the self-aggrandizement of princes, city states and burghers, a witness to the cultural link with antiquity and the expression of a new sense of history. The transition to the Renaissance was accompanied by iconographic and conceptual developments. Classical personifications that had taken on unclassical appearances during the Middle Ages were now restored to their Classical forms, but they retained aspects belonging to the medieval interlude. Consciously or otherwise, in some cases (e.g. Cupid blindfolded, or Father Time; *see* ICONOGRAPHY AND ICONOLOGY, figs 1–3) these were aspects that expressed the development of these personifications in the Middle Ages (something described as 'pseudomorphosis', Panofsky, 1939).

The medieval use of differentiated virtues (*virtutes*) was replaced by that of Virtue in general (with a recollection of the antique *virtus*), personified first by Hercules, later (*c.* 1510) as a female figure sitting or standing on a

4. Allegory by Andrea Mantegna: *Pallas Expelling the Vices from the Garden of Virtue*, tempera on canvas, 1.59×1.92 m, 1499–1502 (Paris, Musée du Louvre)

rectangular block to emphasize her stability as compared with Fortune, who is poised on a sphere. Virtue and Fortune are two forces, differing in degree, which govern human fate and together express the Ciceronian maxim *Duce Virtute, comite Fortuna* ('With Virtue as leader and Fortune as companion'), as depicted, for example, on the medal produced in honour of Giuliano II de' Medici (1513; Florence, Bargello). In the iconographic tradition, Virtue wars with Fortune and is victorious. Virtue in general also takes on the aspect of Minerva in her various functions as bringer of peace, protectress of the arts and sciences, defender of chastity and so on. Antique Roman coins were an important iconographical source for this development.

Among the medieval themes that were continued in the Renaissance were cosmological cycles (e.g. the cycle of the months, with *Aries*, *Taurus* and *Gemini* (1469–70, by Francesco del Cossa; Ferrara, Pal. Schifanoia; *see* FERRARA, fig. 3), cycles of *Virtues* (e.g. Piero Pollaiuolo and Botticelli's series of *Virtues*, 1469–71; Florence, Uffizi) and cycles of the *Liberal Arts* (e.g. Bernardino Pinturicchio's *Liberal Arts*, *c.* 1495; Rome, Vatican, Appartamento Borgia). Raphael's Stanza della Segnatura (1509–11) in the Vatican in Rome represents a continuation of the monumental late-medieval encyclopedic cycles.

In Neo-Platonist philosophy, personifications and allegories are the manner in which the supernatural, the Idea, manifests itself, being otherwise inaccessible to mortal senses. By intuition and in moments of ecstasy (*'furor poeticus'*) the artist, thanks to love and to his desire for divine beauty and for the good, is able to depict the beauty of the Idea. Everything material is to be conceived as a symbol of perfection in the divine world (*icones symbolicae*). Christian and non-Christian sources of knowledge are both of divine origin and of equal value. This explains the particular respect paid to the hieroglyphs of Horapollo (early 5th century AD), which were thought to reflect divine wisdom. Horapollo's *Hieroglyphica* (1419; printed in Venice, 1505) and the allegorical romance *Hypnerotomachia Poliphili* (Venice, 1499) by Francesco Colonna (*fl* 1490–1527), which was influenced by it, constitute the Neo-Platonic foundations of the science of emblems. The Neo-Platonic world picture, in which Reason plays a mediating role in the conflict between body and spirit, forms the background to many allegorical representations, such as Botticelli's *Minerva and a Centaur* (*c.* 1482–3;

5. Allegory by Raphael: *Dream of the Young Scipio Africanus Major*, egg tempera with oil on panel, 1.71×1.71 m, *c.* 1504 (London, National Gallery)

6. *Allegory of Marriage* by Titian, oil on canvas, 1.07×1.21 m, *c.* 1530–35 (Paris, Musée du Louvre)

Florence, Uffizi) and Giorgione's *Three Philosophers* (1525; Vienna, Ksthist. Mus.).

Increased knowledge of Classical antiquity did not lead to a simplification of the allegorical interpretation of mythology, but rather the contrary. Marsilio Ficino developed the concept of the '*duae Veneres*', the heavenly and the natural Venus, corresponding respectively to *Amor divinus* (divine love) and *Amor humanus* (human love): different in rank but both of heavenly origin, the two forms of love are honourable in themselves and are opposed to *Amor ferinus* (sensual passion). These ideas of love were reflected in Botticelli's *Primavera* (the natural Venus; 1478) and the *Birth of Venus* (the heavenly Venus, 1480–85; both Florence, Uffizi). In a complementary interpretation these paintings also represent an allegory of spring, a pictorial reflection of the poetry of Angelo Poliziano. Titian's *Sacred and Profane Love* (*c.* 1514–15; Rome, Gal. Borghese) depicts the same Neo-Platonic pair of Venuses, but this time in the mythological disguise of a marriage portrait. The concept of the '*duae Veneres*' developed in the direction of the older opposition between sensual love and love of virtue, along with a second pair of concepts, that of Eros and Anteros (*Amor virtutis*), and it was applied in the more general context of *psychomachia.* This is exemplified in the paintings for the *studiolo* of Isabella d'Este, Marchioness of Mantua, in Mantua, such as Mantegna's *Pallas Expelling the Vices from the Garden of Virtue* (1499–1502; Paris, Louvre; see fig. 4).

The allegorical motif of a triumphal procession offered opportunities of presenting a hierarchical order of precedence. Use could be made of examples from biblical, antique and contemporary history, and (an important difference from the Middle Ages) there was room for the historically based reconstruction of processions from Classical antiquity. Petrarch's *Trionfi* (1351–3) are a Christian counterpart of antique triumphal processions. The motif was as suitable for allegorical triumphs of princes (as in Piero della Francesca's *Triumph of Federigo da Montefeltro*, *c.* 1465; Florence, Uffizi) as for Christian themes (as in Titian's *Triumph of Christ*, woodcut, *c.* 1510), as well as for processions of gods, seasons and so on. An interest in antiquity is clearly felt in Mantegna's *Triumphs of Caesar* (*c.* 1486–1505; London, Hampton Court, Royal Col.), which contains elements from Horapollo and the *Hypnerotomachia Poliphili*, some of which were used by Dürer in his engraving of the *Allegorical Triumph of Maximilian I* (1512; e.g. Vienna, Albertina).

Fresh allegorical themes were borrowed from EKPHRASIS literature (antique descriptions of statues or pictures), such as *Hercules at the Crossroads* (as in Sebastian Brant's *Narrenschiff*, Latin edn, Lübeck, 1497; or Raphael's *Dream of the Young Scipio Africanus Major*, *c.* 1504; London, N.G.; see fig. 5), the *Tabula Cebetis* (as in Hans Holbein the younger's woodcut for the title page of Desiderius Erasmus's *Annotationes in Novum Testamentum*; Basle, 1522) and the *Calumny of Apelles* (as in Botticelli's painting of that name, 1490s; Florence, Uffizi). About the middle of the 16th century a spate of emblem books, based on Horapollo and the *Hypnerotomachia Poliphili*, explained by means of examples the symbols of the ancient world, for example Andrea Alciati's *Emblematum liber* (Augsburg, 1531) and works by Lylius Gyraldus (Lilio Giraldi; 1479–1552) in 1548, Natale Conti (Natalis Comes; *c.* 1520–82) in 1551, Achille Bocchi (1488–1562) in 1555, Piero Valeriano (Bolzani; 1477–1558) in 1556 and Vincenzo Cartari in 1556 (*see* EMBLEM BOOK). All these were used as sources by Cesare Ripa in his highly influential *Iconologia* (Rome, 1593; first illus. edn, Rome, 1603). Before the appearance of the handbooks, this scholarly knowledge had already been put to use in some allegorical cycles: in Correggio's Camera di S Paolo (1518–19; Parma, monastery of S Paolo) and Giulio Romano's decorations for the Palazzo del Tè (*c.* 1525–35) in Mantua. Titian's allegorical themes also owe much to the science of emblems and antique symbolism, as shown, for example, in his *Allegory of Marriage*, altered to an *In memoriam*, incorrectly known as the *Allegory of Alfonso d'Avalos, Marchese del Vasto* (*c.* 1530–35; Paris, Louvre; see fig. 6), and his *Allegory of Prudence* (*c.* 1570; London, N.G.).

The intellectualizing and complicating tendencies of Mannerist allegory entailed a loss of clarity. Vasari in his *Ragionamenti* (Florence, 1588) described his own mythological decorations (1570) in the Palazzo Vecchio in Florence but accompanied the allegorical interpretations with alternatives. Bronzino's *Allegory of Venus and Cupid* (*c.* 1545; London, N.G.) is a confusion of different themes (disarming of Cupid, unmasking of deceit), which makes interpretation difficult (Triumph of Venus, or warning against illicit love). Allusions to the patron's own exploits and circumstances form the key to the allegorical interpretation of such mythological cycles as the decoration of the Palazzo Doria (1528–35) in Genoa by Perino del Vaga with the *Glorification of Andrea Doria* and that of the Galerie François I (1534–7) at Fontainebleau by Rosso Fiorentino with the *Glorification of Francis I* 'under the cloak of fables' (Panofsky, 1958).

2. NORTHERN EUROPE. In Dürer's time Nuremberg was a centre of Neo-Platonism, and its influence can be seen in his allegorical themes. Dürer was acquainted with humanists such as Hartmann Schedel (1440–1514), Sebastian Brant, Konrad Celtis and Willibald Pirckheimer, and his theory of proportion was based on Neo-Platonic foundations. Neo-Platonic circles evolved the doctrine of the 'golden mean' (*aurea mediocritas*), according to which the highest good could be achieved by combining virtue (*virtus*) with pleasure (*voluptas*, in the Epicurean sense). This is probably the theme of Dürer's engraving *Hercules* (*c.* 1498; B.73). The Neo-Platonic philosophy is expressed most eloquently in the engraving *Melancolia I* (1514; B.74; *see* DÜRER, (1), fig. 9). The pose and attributes of the figure are a combination of the personifications of Geometry and creative Melancholy, and it may be regarded as a spiritual self-portrait.

Other allegorical representations bear witness to Dürer's familiarity with philosophical or literary sources of a humanistic kind, for instance Angelo Poliziano's *Manto* (Bologna, 1492) as a source for the *Large Nemesis* (1501–2; B.77). The melancholic temperament was also depicted by Lucas Cranach the elder (e.g. *Allegory of Melancholy*, 1532; Copenhagen, Stat. Mus. Kst).

In northern Europe the allegorical language of the Renaissance harmonized well with the late-medieval tradition of ceremonial processions, pageants and plays by Chambers of Rhetoric. German and Dutch humanism, flavoured as it was with a touch of irony, guaranteed the continuation of allegories of folly and satire at the expense

7. *Allegory of War and Peace* by Peter Paul Rubens, oil on canvas, 2.04×2.98 m, 1629–30 (London, National Gallery)

of wealth, ambition and so on. Moreover, the Reformation, openly or otherwise, gave its endorsement to allegorical imagery, as shown in the works of Lucas Cranach the elder, Hans Baldung, Hans Weiditz the elder, Cornelis Anthonisz. and Jan Swart.

Several series of engravings by Maarten van Heemskerck, such as the *Allegory of the Unbridled World* (1550; Hollstein, nos 200–03), *Jacob's Ladder* (1550; Hollstein, nos 187–200) and the *Triumph of Patientia* (1559; Hollstein, nos 151–8) express the doctrine of perfectibility developed by the philosopher and engraver Dirck Volkertsz. Coornhert. According to this, mankind could achieve salvation by the use of reason and by placing love of God above all things; folly, on the other hand, was culpable ignorance. Both in Coornhert's 'rhetorician' plays and in Heemskerck's engravings, biblical figures play an allegorical role; sacred and secular characters are on the same footing and are inseparably connected.

The existing preoccupation with the VANITAS idea was reinforced by humanistic and theological literature. The theme of the Prodigal Son gave rise to allegories of the vanity of earthly pleasure (e.g. in the work of Cornelis Anthonisz.). The kitchen scenes of Pieter Aertsen and Joachim Beuckelaer combine the Vanitas motif with the contrast between *vita activa* and *vita contemplativa.* Alongside the motif of a putto with a death's head, there arose, as a visual rendering of one of Erasmus's *Adagia*, the figure of a putto blowing bubbles, as in Hendrick Goltzius's engraving *Quis evadet?: Homo bulla* (1594; *see* ICONOGRAPHY AND ICONOLOGY, fig. 10).

8. Allegorical *portrait historié* by Paulus Moreelse: *Sophia Hedwig, Countess of Nassau Dietz, as Charity, with her Children*, oil on canvas, 1.40×1.22 m, 1621 (Apeldoorn, Rijksmuseum Paleis Het Loo)

V. Baroque.

In Baroque allegory the emotions (*'affetti'*) are depicted in a naturalistic manner: the gods and personifications behave in a human and dramatic way, thus increasing the spectator's interest in the idea expressed. The gods and personifications are no longer mere 'invisible' inspirers or companions belonging to a supernatural reality but may take part in the action alongside historical personages, who are thereby endowed with a touch of heroic status. The illusionism of *quadratura* ceiling painting also helped to obscure the difference between symbol and reality.

The Counter-Reformation doctrine that salvation was to be found only in the Church gave rise to allegorico-didactic programmes in which clarity was the first requirement, for example Theodor Galle's illustration for the *Occasio arrepta, neglecta* (Antwerp, 1605) of Jan David (*fl* 1601–17), and emblems in which visual metaphors became a vehicle for Church dogmas (e.g. Otto van Veen's *Amoris divini emblemata*, Antwerp, 1615), as well as to more disguised representations (e.g. Nicolas Poussin's allegorico-typological cycle of the *Seasons*, 1660–64; Paris, Louvre).

The development of the glorification theme received a decisive impulse from the decorations of the Palazzo Ducale in Venice by Tintoretto, Veronese and Giacomo Palma Giovane, which had its effect on Rubens's panegyric cycles and on those of Pietro da Cortona, such as the *Glorification of Urban VIII* (1633–9; Rome, Pal. Barberini). The allegorical triumph was the formula *par excellence* not only for glorifying princes but also for portraying the victory of the Counter-Reformation Church, as in Rubens's tapestry cycle *Triumph of the Eucharist* (1625–8; Madrid, convent of the Descalzas Reales). It thus satisfied the humanistic preference for antique forms as a means of depicting abstract ideas.

The creators of programmes with visual metaphors were ideally served by the increasing profusion of emblem literature and ICONOGRAPHIC HANDBOOKS (the many translations of Cesare Ripa's *Iconologia* indicate its widespread use), and encyclopedias of symbols, such as the *Mondo simbolico* (Milan, 1653) by Filippo Picinelli (*c.* 1604–67) and *Il cannocchiale Aristotelico* (Turin, 1654) by Emmanuele Tesauro (1592–1675). The theme of secular glorification, in which the prince was lauded as *'exemplum virtutis'* with the help of allegorico-mythological personifications and emblematic allusions, as well as references to the Golden Age, was deployed on a grand scale in Rubens's work, such as the cycle (1622–5; Paris, Louvre) for the Medici Gallery in the Palais du Luxembourg in Paris and the decoration of the Banqueting Hall (1630–35) in London (*in situ*). In many respects Rubens's great cycles formed a model for the decoration of the Huis ten Bosch (1647–52) at The Hague by, among others, Théodore van Thulden, Jacob Jordaens and Gerrit van Honthorst, although it differs from them in structure and intention.

For his frequent allegories of peace and war Rubens used the whole repertory of iconographic means developed for this purpose since the Renaissance, as in *Mars Defeated by Minerva* (e.g. sketch, *c.* 1635–7; Paris, Louvre). This theme forms the background of the *Allegory of War and*

9. *Allegory of the Marriage of Virtue and Science, Effected by Religion*, by Bartolomeo Altomonte, 1747, ceiling fresco after the design by Daniel Gran, library of St Florian Abbey

Peace (1629–30; London, N.G.; see fig. 7) in which the central figure, Venus Pacifera rather than Pax, embodies love, fertility, abundance and prosperity, which is the precondition and also the effect of peace. In Rubens's sombre *Allegory of War* (1637; Florence, Pitti), Mars, the personification of fury, tramples on the arts and sciences.

Allegory was an approved way of expressing a political viewpoint, either in satire or in official commissions, as in Théodore van Thulden's allegories of the political aspirations of Brabant (e.g. *c.* 1650; 's Hertogenbosch, Stadhuis) and Abraham van den Tempel's allegories of the cloth industry (e.g. 1650–51; Leiden, Stedel. Mus. Lakenhal). The *portrait historié*, a combination of portrait and allegory, was an internationally familiar genre. Practised since the Renaissance, it identified the subject with a biblical or mythological figure regarded as an '*exemplum virtutis*' or with a Virtue, as in Paulus Moreelse's *Sophia Hedwig, Countess of Nassau Dietz, as Charity, with her Children* (1621; Apeldoorn, Pal. Het Loo; see fig. 8).

Along with overt allegories, in 17th-century Dutch and Flemish painting there developed the genre of 'concealed allegory': an everyday scene, or what appeared to be such, containing a moral exhortation or warning, often indicated by an emblematic motif, taken perhaps from *Sinnepoppen* (Emblematic poetry; Amsterdam, 1614) by Roemer Visscher (*fl* 1586/7–1652), *Sinne- en minnebeelden* (Symbols and love emblems; Middelburg, 1618) by Jacob Cats (i) or some other visual metaphor such as a proverb. Many 'instructive series', composed in the 16th century with the aid of personifications, appeared in the 17th century in a naturalistic form, for example in the work of Willem Buytewech, Adriaen van de Venne, Jan Miense Molenaer, Gerrit Dou, Gerard ter Borch the elder and Jan Steen. These included such subjects as the five senses (with a warning against earthly vanity); the four temperaments (with a warning against depravity), the four times of life (warning against the rashness of youth and the folly of age); and many other themes connected with love, folly and vanity. An essential feature is the combination of 'instruction and delight' and the principle that the ideas expressed can be interpreted in either a good or a bad sense. Later in the century, under the influence of classicism and because the hidden implications were often no longer understood, there was a return to the Classical pictorial vocabulary for the representation of abstract ideas, as in the works of Gérard de Lairesse.

Artists in Italy continued the tradition of concealing or revealing several layers of meaning by the use of mythological forms. The Ovidian love scenes in Annibale Carracci's decorations for the Farnese Gallery (1597–1600) in the Palazzo Farnese in Rome (*in situ*) form a Neo-Platonic allegory of love and at the same time allude to the famous deeds of Cardinal Alessandro Farnese. In Pietro da Cortona's decorative cycle (1640–46) in the Palazzo Pitti in Florence (*in situ*), the astrological and mythological elements are also a glorification of Cosimo I de' Medici, Grand Duke of Tuscany. Such allusions are also found, though less prominently, in religious allegory, for example in Andrea Sacchi's *Allegory of the Divine Wisdom* (1629–33; Rome, Pal. Barberini), with its symbolic references to Pope Urban VIII.

In the mid-17th century, as an intimate counterpart to the great fresco cycles, the work of Pietro Testa, Giovanni Benedetto Castiglione and Salvator Rosa evinced a romantic–philosophical approach to such traditional themes as vanity and melancholy. Around 1670 religious allegory on a monumental scale was revived by Neo-classical academicians with Giovanni Pietro Bellori as their spokesman, as shown, for example, by Carlo Maratti's *Triumph of Clemency* (after 1673; Rome, Pal. Altieri). The tradition of monumental allegorical decoration was continued by Giambattista Tiepolo (e.g. *Allegory of the Four Continents*, 1752–3; Würzburg, Residenz) and by the masters of south German Baroque, as in the ceiling fresco (1747; St Florian

Abbey, library; see fig. 9) executed by Bartolomeo Altomonte after a scheme by Daniel Gran.

VI. Romanticism, Realism and decline.

Allegory fell into a crisis in the second half of the 18th century. The routine application of Ripa's rules showed that it had lost its inner strength. Theorists of art such as Moses Mendelssohn and Gotthold Ephraim Lessing raised the question of the aesthetic value of allegory and soon began to criticize and reject it as a system of 'arbitrary' signs. Johann Joachim Winckelmann attempted in *Versuch einer Allegorie, besonders für die Kunst* (Dresden, 1766) to breathe new life into allegory, for instance by introducing models from antiquity in place of what he considered to be Ripa's absurdities. However, this attempt was doomed to failure, as it completely failed to meet the need for a type of image that possessed an inner unity with that which it signified. As opposed to the purely rational transference of ideas, art was required to produce an emotional effect. After the way had been prepared by Karl Philipp Moritz and Johann Gottfried Herder, Goethe (1797) and Schelling (1802) formulated this problem in terms of an opposition between allegory and symbol: allegory being the significant indication of an idea outside the work of art, while the symbol does not indicate but actually *is* the idea, thanks to the organic and indivisible unity of image, expression and significance.

At about the same time, symbolism was enhanced in value from a different angle. Romantic philosophers such as Friedrich Schlegel, August Wilhelm Schlegel and Johann Joseph von Görres took up the old religious–mystical idea of the symbol as the bearer of a hidden, deeper meaning. There thus arose the conception of art as the medium and the artist as interpreter, of the mystical truth contained in symbolic language (hieroglyphs), and the irrational element was made one of the basic principles of art and art theory. It was this conception of symbols that found expression in Romantic art, especially in Germany (*see* ROMANTICISM). In addition, 19th-century artists became aware of the tension between reality and allegorical figures. If, for instance, one wished to raise a historical event to a higher, more general plane, it was necessary to combine time-conditioned and timeless elements in a viable synthesis. Artists wrestled with this problem almost throughout the century.

This synthesis was achieved for the last time in Eugène Delacroix's *Liberty Leading the People* (1830; Paris, Louvre; see fig. 10), in which Liberty embodies the abstract notions of freedom and victory, making use of an older pictorial tradition, but at the same time forms an integrated part of

10. Allegory by Eugène Delacroix: *Liberty Leading the People*, oil on canvas, 2.60×3.25 m, 1830 (Paris, Musée du Louvre)

the action, in a 'naturalized' allegorical personification. Attempts to bridge the gap between tradition and the present day by means of a compromise (combining traditional allegorical personification with 'modern' elements such as steam-engines) aroused little response, as witnessed in Horace Vernet's ceiling painting of the Salle de la Paix (1838–47) in the Palais Bourbon in Paris and the entries submitted for the prize of 1848 for an allegorical personification of La République.

In 1855 Gustave Courbet introduced the conception of '*allégorie réelle*' in connection with his *Painter's Studio* (1854–5; Paris, Mus. d'Orsay; *see* COURBET, GUSTAVE, fig. 3), an allegory in terms of contemporary activity. As in the concealed allegories in 17th-century Dutch painting, Courbet also completely discarded the traditional language of allegory in favour of a realistic presentation, while retaining the allegorical significance. Given the artistic development of the second half of the 19th century, his '*allégorie réelle*' was rather a terminus than the beginning of a new stage. With the emergence of SYMBOLISM, allegory as opposed to symbol was no longer regarded as an adequate means of expressing transcendental truth. At the end of the 19th century and the beginning of the 20th, allegorical personification still enjoyed some application in the field of nationalist propaganda (e.g. in Wilhelmine Germany), with its counterpart of caricature and political satire; nevertheless, in these fields also the traditional pictorial language must finally be regarded as having been superseded.

BIBLIOGRAPHY

GENERAL

EWA; Kindler; *LCI*; *RDK*

H. Blümner: *Über den Gebrauch der Allegorie in den bildenden Künsten*, i of *Laokoon-Studien* (Freiburg im Breisgau, 1881)

J. Burckhardt: 'Die Allegorie in den Künsten', *Vorträge, 1844–1887*, ed. E. Dürr (Basle, 1918), pp. 374–94

E. Panofsky: *Studies in Iconology: Humanistic Themes in the Art of the Renaissance* (Oxford, 1939/*R* New York, 1972)

——: *Meaning in the Visual Arts* (Garden City, NY, 1955)

R. Klibansky, E. Panofsky and F. Saxl: *Saturn and Melancholy: Studies in the History of Natural Philosophy, Religion and Art* (London, 1964)

G. Hermerén: *Representation and Meaning in the Visual Arts: A Study in the Methodology of Iconography and Iconology* (Lund, 1969)

W. Kemp: *Natura: Ikonographische Studien zur Geschichte und Verbreitung einer Allegorie* (diss., U. Tübingen, 1970)

E. H. Gombrich: *Symbolic Images: Studies in the Art of the Renaissance* (London, 1972)

H. van de Waal: *Iconclass: An Iconographic Classification System*, 17 vols (Amsterdam, 1973–85) [extensive bibliog.]

R. Wittkower: *Allegory and the Migration of Symbols* (London, 1977)

Formen und Funktionen der Allegorie, Symposium: Wolfenbüttel, 1978

SPECIALIST STUDIES

Classical

R. Hinks: *Myth and Allegory in Ancient Art*, Stud. Warb. Inst., vi (London, 1939)

K. Reinhardt: 'Personifikation und Allegorie', *Vermächtnis der Antike: Gesammelte Essays zur Philosophie und Geschichtsschreibung* (Göttingen, 1960; rev. 2/1966), pp. 7–40

O. Seel: 'Antike und frühchristliche Allegorik', *Festschrift für Peter Metz*, ed. U. Schlegel and C. Zoege von Manteuffel (Berlin, 1965), pp. 11–45

Medieval

A. Katzenellenbogen: *Allegories of the Virtues and Vices in Medieval Art*, Stud. Warb. Inst., x (London, 1939)

W. Stammler: 'Allegorische Studien', *Dt. Vjschr. Litwiss. & Geistesgesch.*, xvii (1939), pp. 1–25

F. Saxl: 'A Spiritual Encyclopaedia of the Later Middle Ages', *J. Warb. & Court. Inst.*, v (1942), pp. 82–142

A. Katzenellenbogen: 'The Representation of the Seven Liberal Arts', *Twelfth-century Europe and the Foundations of Modern Society: Proceedings of a Symposium: Madison, 1957*, pp. 39–55

R. Tuve: 'Notes on the Virtues and Vices', *J. Warb. & Court. Inst.*, xxvi (1963), pp. 264–303; xxvii (1964), pp. 42–72

——: *Allegorical Imagery: Some Mediaeval Books and their Posterity* (Princeton, 1966)

W. Harms: *Homo viator in bivio: Studien zur Bildlichkeit des Weges*, Medium Aevum, Philologische Studien, xxi (Munich, 1970)

Simboli e simbologia nell'alto medioevo, xxiii of *Settimane di studio del centro italiano di studi sull'alto medioevo: Spoleto, 1975*

C. Meier: 'Überlegungen zum gegenwärtigen Stand der Allegorie-Forschung: Mit besonderer Berücksichtigung der Mischformen', *Frühmittelalt. Stud.*, x (1976), pp. 1–69

Renaissance

Hollstein: *Dut. & Flem.*

A. von Bartsch: *Le Peintre-graveur* (1803–21) [B.]

K. Giehlow: 'Die Hieroglyphenkunde des Humanismus in der Allegorie der Renaissance, besonders der Ehrenpforte Kaisers Maximilian I', *Jb. Ksthist. Samml. Allhöch. Ksrhaus.*, xxxii (1915), pp. 1–232

L. Volkmann: *Bilderschriften der Renaissance: Hieroglyphik und Emblematik in ihren Beziehungen und Fortwirkungen* (Leipzig, 1923/*R* Nieuwkoop, 1962)

E. Panofsky: *Hercules am Scheidewege und andere antike Bildstoffe in der neueren Kunst*, Stud. Bib. Warb., xviii (Leipzig, 1930)

D. Panofsky and E. Panofsky: 'The Iconography of the Galerie François Ière at Fontainebleau', *Gaz. B.-A.*, n. s. 6, lii (1958), pp. 113–90

S. C. Chew: *The Pilgrimage of Life* (New Haven, 1962)

J. A. Emmens: '"Eins aber ist nötig": Zu Inhalt und Bedeutung von Markt- und Küchenstücken des 16. Jahrhunderts', *Album Amicorum J. G. van Gelder*, ed. J. Bruyn and others (The Hague, 1973), pp. 93–101

R. Schleier: *Tabula Cebetis oder 'Spiegel des menschlichen Lebens darin tugent und untugent abgemalet ist': Studien zur Rezeption einer antiken Bildbeschreibung im 16. und 17. Jahrhundert* (Berlin, 1973)

B. Walbe: *Studien zur Entwicklung des allegorischen Porträts in Frankreich von seinen Anfängen bis zur Regierungszeit König Heinrichs II* (Frankfurt am Main, 1975)

I. M. Veldman: *Maarten van Heemskerck and Dutch Humanism in the Sixteenth Century* (Amsterdam, 1977)

D. Cast: *The Calumny of Apelles: A Study in the Humanist Tradition* (New Haven, 1981)

K. G. Boon: '"Patientia" dans les gravures de la Réforme aux Pays-Bas', *Rev. A.* [Paris], lvi (1982), pp. 7–24

Baroque

E. Mâle: *L'Art religieux de la fin du 16ième siècle, du 17ième siècle et du 18ième siècle* (Paris, 1932, 2/1951)

K. L. Schwartz: 'Zum ästhetischen Problem des "Programms" und der Symbolik und Allegorik in der barocken Malerei', *Wien. Jb. Kstgesch.*, xi (1937), pp. 79–88

W. Mrazek: *Ikonologie der barocken Deckenmalerei*, ccxxviii/3 of *Sitzungsberichte österreichische Akademie der Wissenschaften, Philosophisch-historische Klasse* (Vienna, 1953)

K. Garas: 'Allegorie und Geschichte in der venezianischen Malerei des 18. Jahrhunderts', *Acta Hist. A. Acad. Sci. Hung.*, xi (1965), pp. 275–302

E. Panofsky: '"Good Government" or Fortune? The Iconography of a Newly-discovered Composition by Rubens', *Gaz. B.-A.*, n. s. 5, lxviii (1966), pp. 305–26

E. de Jongh: *Zinne- en minnebeelden in de schilderkunst van de zeventiende eeuw* [Symbols and love emblems in 17th-century painting] (Amsterdam and Antwerp, 1967)

R. Wishnevsky: *Studien zum 'portrait historié' in den Niederlanden* (diss., U. Munich, 1967)

J. Montagu: 'The Painted Enigma and French Seventeenth-century Art', *J. Warb. & Court. Inst.*, xxxi (1968), pp. 307–35

F. Bardon: *Le Portrait mythologique à la cour de France sous Henri IV et Louis XIII: Mythologie et politique* (Paris, 1974)

R. Baumstark: 'Ikonographische Studien zu Rubens Kriegs- und Friedensallegorien', *Aachen. Kstbl.*, xlv (1974), pp. 125–234

F.-W. Wentzlaff-Eggebert: *Der triumphierende und der besiegte Tod in der Wort- und Bildkunst des Barock* (Berlin, 1975)

Tot lering en vermaak [For instruction and delight] (exh. cat., ed. E. de Jongh; Amsterdam, Rijksmus., 1976)

J. Bruyn: 'Mittelalterliche "doctrina exemplaris" und Allegorie als Komponente des sog. Genrebildes', *Holländische Genremalerei im 17. Jahrhundert: Symposium: Berlin, 1984*, pp. 33–59

Romanticism, Realism and decline

B. A. Sørensen: *Symbol und Symbolismus in den ästhetischen Theorien des 18. Jahrhunderts und der deutschen Romantik* (Copenhagen, 1963)

L. D. Couprie: 'De allegorie in de negentiende-eeuwse realistische kunst' [Allegory in 19th-century realistic art], *Opstellen voor H. van de Waal* [Essays for H. van de Waal] (Amsterdam and Leiden, 1970), pp. 28–44

B. A. Sørensen: *Allegorie und Symbol: Texte zur Theorie des dichterischen Bildes im 18. und frühen 19. Jahrhundert* (Frankfurt am Main, 1972)

G. Hess: 'Allegorie und Historismus: Zum Bildgedächtnis des späten 19. Jahrhunderts', *Verbum und Signum, Festschrift Friedrich Ohly*, i (Munich, 1975), pp. 555–91

H. Rüdiger: 'Eine vergessene Kunstlehre: Winckelmanns "Versuch einer Allegorie"', *Kaleidoskop, Festschrift Fritz Baumgart* (Berlin, 1977), pp. 126–43

H. T. Wappenschmidt: *Allegorie, Symbol und Historienbild im späten 19. Jahrhundert: Zum Problem von Schein und Sein* (Munich, 1984)

J. Benoît: 'La Peinture allégorique sous le consulat: Structure et politique', *Gaz. B.-A.*, n. s. 5, cxxi (1993), pp. 77–92

Allegory of art. Type of allegorical representation of the artist's conception of himself and his work. Many allegories of art owe their origin to attempts, in the 16th and 17th centuries, to classify the fine arts, especially painting, as *artes liberales.* An improvement in the status of art was to bring with it an improvement in the social standing of the artist. The allegory of art took many forms, which often appeared in combination with one another, including: personifications of *Pictura* or *Disegno*, sometimes in the role of inspirer in portraits of the artist; the conquest of *Ignorantia* and *Invidia*; and pictures of private galleries. The decoration of the artist's own house—such as Vasari's at Arezzo and Florence and Federico Zuccaro's in Rome—provided an obvious opportunity to develop the theme (*see* ARTIST'S HOUSE and figs 1 and 2).

1. Inspiration. 2. Enhancing the status of painting. 3. *Kunstkammern.* 4. Portrait of the artist with, or as, *Pictura.* 5. Academy representations.

1. INSPIRATION. The theme of the artist's inspiration originates in Classical art: the inspiration of the poet by the muse, which is frequently depicted on sarcophagi. It was continued in Late Antique portraits of authors and in early Christian portraits of the Evangelists. A miniature in the Vienna *Dioscurides* (5th century; Vienna, Österreich. Nbib., MS. med.gr. 1, fol. 5*v*) is the earliest representation of the inspiration of a painter. According to Leonardo da Vinci, the belief that the artist's creative power was due to divine inspiration entitled painting to be ranked among the *artes liberales.* This idea was reflected in, for example, works by Vasari such as *Minerva and Vulcan as Ingenium and Ars* (1563; Florence, Uffizi), Federico Zuccaro's *Lament of Painting*, engraved by Cornelis Cort (1579; BdH 221) and Hendrick Goltzius's *Ars and Usus* (engraving, 1582; B. 111).

2. ENHANCING THE STATUS OF PAINTING. The first allegorical personifications of the arts, modelled on the pattern of the *artes liberales*, were designed by Vasari for the encyclopedic decoration of the Camera della Fama (1542) in his house at Arezzo. These were a breach with the medieval tradition whereby the fine arts, as *artes mechanicae*, were depicted in the form of craftsmen at work. More important to the development of the allegory of art, however, were Vasari's later designs (partly the invention of Vincenzo Borghini) for the Porta al Prato, erected for the entry of Francesco I de' Medici into Florence in 1565, and for the decoration of the Sala delle Arti (1569–73) of Vasari's house in that city. The innovations here were connected with the gradual merging of the concepts of *disegno* and *idea. Disegno*, the art of drawing or draughtsmanship, was regarded as the parent of architecture, sculpture and painting—an umbrella notion of art in general such as was considered necessary for their elevation to the status of *artes liberales.* This conception of the threefold character of *disegno* did not attract much following, but that of the three sister arts as the three Graces became popular, for example through the engraving (1597; B. 76) by Jan Muller after Bartholomeus Spranger. In Vasari's Sala delle Arti, *Disegno Triciput* dominates the entrance to a depiction of the studio of Apelles, the model Classical painter, in which studio Vasari places a portrait of himself. This was the forerunner of numerous works in which artists represented themselves in the character of Apelles at his easel; in the northern countries, especially, this was linked with the theme of St Luke painting the Virgin, as in the *Apelles and Campaspe* of Joos van Winghe, painted *c.* 1585 (Vienna, Ksthist. Mus.). The Sala delle Arti as a whole is to be understood as an allegory of art in which the dominant theme, together with *disegno*, is *giudizio*: nature perfected by design and judgement, the artist's mind and hand, the starting-point of the '*bella maniera*'.

The theory of *disegno* was developed further by Federico Zuccaro, who distinguished *disegno interno*, coinciding with *idea*, from *disegno esterno*, its material realization. *Disegno interno*, described by Zuccaro as the light of the understanding, is the divine spark that works in man as a creative force. In a ceiling painting (1593–1600) in his house in Rome (Pal. Zuccari, Sala del Disegno) he expressed the deification of *Disegno* by depicting it in the style of God the Father, thus likewise symbolizing the role of design as parent of the three fine arts. *Disegno*'s triple halo is an allusion to the Trinity and also to the emblem expressing Michelangelo's mastery of the three arts. In another room of his house, the Sala Terrena, Zuccaro depicted the *Apotheosis of the Artist*, whose virtue is emphasized by a representation of *Hercules at the Crossroads* in the corridor that forms a unit with the Sala Terrena.

An important theme in allegories of art is the conquest of *Ignorantia* and *Invidia* by *Virtus* or Minerva (Wisdom). Vasari gave the lead in his house at Arezzo (Camera di Fortuna): *Virtus Conquering Fortuna and Invidia* (1548). Zuccaro combined the theme with elements of the *Calumny of Apelles* in his *Lament of Painting*, engraved by Cornelis Cort (1579; BdH 221), and in the satire *Porta Virtutis* (drawing, 1581; Oxford, Christ Church Pict. Gal.; see fig.), in which Minerva bars the way to Ignorance and Calumny, while *Invidia* lies prostrate. The *Porta Virtutis* is the first work to show Minerva expressly concerned with the painter, personifications of whose good qualities—*Fatica* (Painstaking), *Diligentia* (Industry), *Studium* (Excercitation), *Intelligentia* and so on—decorate Minerva's bastion. Elements of the *Porta Virtutis* are also present in the above-mentioned *Apotheosis of the Artist.*

The defeat of *Ignorantia* and *Invidia*, the protection of the arts by Minerva (later also by Mercury) and the artist's self-portrait as Apelles were constant elements in allegories of art from the time of their invention by Vasari and

Allegory of art by Federico Zuccaro: *Porta Virtutis: Art Triumphant over Ignorance and Calumny*, pen and brown wash, squared in red chalk, 378×276 mm, 1581 (Oxford, Christ Church Picture Gallery)

Zuccaro. They were frequently placed in the general context of the victory of Virtue over Vice, for example in Hendrick Goltzius's *Hercules and Cacus, Painting Mercury and Minerva with Midas* (1611–13; Haarlem, Frans Halsmus.). The endeavour to raise the status of painting found expression at the Prague court of Emperor Rudolf II in 1595: by imperial decree, *Pictura* was ranked among the *artes liberales.* This may be seen in Hans von Aachen's *Minerva Introducing Pictura into the Company of Artes Liberales*, engraved by Aegidius Sadeler I in 1596. The *Hermathena* motif of Minerva and Mercury as patrons of the arts originated in the same circle. Some allegories of art not only express the victory of Virtue over Vice, but even the triumph of Painting over Death and Oblivion. In this notion it is Painting (and art in general) that is capable of keeping the memory and fame, for example, of a portrayed person, alive even after death (e.g. Gesina ter Borch, *Allegory of Painting*, watercolour, title page of a studio album, *c.* 1660, Amsterdam, Rijksmus.).

3. *Kunstkammern.* There arose in Antwerp *c.* 1612–15 a new type of allegory of art, 'gallery pictures', paintings representing a picture gallery (either real or imaginary), generally with allegorical additions symbolizing the liberal arts, *Pictura*, *Disegno*, *Virtus*, *Ignorantia* and so on. These appeared in *Kunstkammern* (Ger.: private art collections; *see* KUNSTKAMMER). The encyclopedic learning displayed in these galleries and the frequent portrayal of distinguished visitors to the collection helped to enhance the status of painting and of the collectors and artists depicted. Whereas in Italy only allegorical personification was used, in Flanders the art of painting was represented by its tangible products. The subjects of the depicted paintings also contributed to the emblematic character of the *Kunstkammern.* Specialists in this type of picture were Frans Francken II, Adriaen van Stalbemt, David Teniers (ii) and Willem van Haecht II, whose *Picture Gallery of Cornelis van der Geest Visited by Archduke Albert and Archduchess Isabella* (1628; Antwerp, Rubenshuis; *see* COLLECTING, fig. 1) represents the genre well. Velázquez's *Las Meninas* (1656; Madrid, Prado) can also be classified as a painting of this type.

4. PORTRAIT OF THE ARTIST WITH, OR AS, *Pictura.* In view of the emphasis on painting as a liberal art, it was not thought suitable for portraits of artists, including self-portraits, to contain references to physical labour. The tendency thus to keep theory and practice apart began in the 16th century and continued in the 17th, especially in academy circles, although a tendency towards integration gradually became more evident.

In Poussin's *Self-portrait* of 1650 (Paris, Louvre) the connection between idea and reality is established by the harmony between the eye-diadem of *Pictura/Prospettiva*, the diamond ring and the painter's own eyes, gazing intently at the spectator: in Poussin's theory of art, painting was synonymous with perspective and optics. In Vermeer's *Art of Painting* (1666–7; Vienna, Ksthist. Mus.) theory and practice are directly related; the art of painting is inspired by Clio, the Muse of History, who was regarded as 'the first impulse to learning' (Francis Junius) and who thus expressly symbolized the learned character of the art of painting. The complete integration of theory and practice, idea and reality was achieved in Artemisia Gentileschi's *Self-portrait as Pictura Painting* (*c.* 1630; London, Kensington Pal., Royal Col.) in which allegorical personification, the model and the artist coincide in a single image. A frequent 17th-century theme with *Pictura* implications is that of a visit to the studio, depicting a learned conversation between artists and/or critics and art-lovers (e.g. Pieter Codde: Paris, Fond. Custodia, Inst. Néer.).

5. ACADEMY REPRESENTATIONS. Leonardo da Vinci's dictum that the painter must also be a philosopher met with response especially in academic circles. Pietro Testa's etching of the *Classical School of Painting* (*c.* 1640–44; B. 34), following the concept of Raphael's *School of Athens* (1500/1504; Rome, Vatican, Stanza della Segnatura), is a pictorial philosophy of painting based on the Aristotelian opposition of natural and moral philosophy. The isolated figures, on the left and right, of fettered Theory and blind Practice, depicted according to Cesare Ripa's *Iconologia* (Rome, 1593), are an emblematic allusion to the helplessness of the ignorant apprentice painter. *Giudizio*, the figure in the centre, forms a pivot from the compositional and also the conceptual point of view, pointing the way to *Mathematica* and representing the unification of theory and practice. Other *Pictura* allegories by Testa, such as the *Triumph of Painting* (etching, before 1644; B. 35), have the same theoretical background.

The identification of art with Virtue is already found in Zuccaro's *Porta Virtutis*. In academic theories of art, the concepts of Truth and Labour were developed into foundations of Virtue. In Bernini's eyes sculpture was the highest form of art, because it was the truest; this is expressed in his figure of *Truth* (1646–52; Rome, Gal. Borghese). *Labour* figures in *Pictura* allegories as an allegorical personification and in the pseudo-realistic form of a painter's apprentice engaged in drawing, as in Adriaen van der Werff's *Children Playing in Front of a Hercules Group* (1687; Munich, Alte Pin.). Besides artists' houses, academy buildings were also suitable for decoration with allegories of art. There was in academic circles an almost obsessive preoccupation with the theme of the defeat of *Ignorantia* and *Invidia*, connected with the opposition between academies and guilds. When the guilds were finally abolished at the end of the 18th century, the theme lost its attraction almost immediately. In the 19th century the attitude towards allegory was radically altered by the emergence of realism and naturalism. The '*allégorie réelle*' of Courbet's *Painter's Studio* (1855; Paris, Mus. d'Orsay) is, in form, a continuation of the studio-visiting theme but abandons the pictorial language in which reflection on art was formerly expressed.

BIBLIOGRAPHY

E. Panofsky: *Idea: A Concept in Art Theory* (Leipzig, 1924; 2/Berlin, 1960; Eng. trans., New York, 1968)
J. C. J. Bierens de Haan: *L'Oeuvre gravé de Cornelis Cort, graveur hollandais, 1533–78* (The Hague, 1948) [BdH]
A. Pigler: 'Neid und Unwissenheit als Widersacher der Kunst', *Acta Hist. A. Acad. Sci. Hung.*, i (1954), pp. 215–35
M. Winner: *Die Quellen der Pictura-Allegorien in gemalten Bildergalerien des 17. Jahrhunderts zu Antwerpen* (diss., U. Cologne, 1957)
J. G. van Gelder: *De Schilderkunst van Jan Vermeer*, commentary J. A. Emmens (Utrecht, 1958)
M. Winner: 'Gemalte Kunsttheorie: Zu Gustave Courbets "Allégorie réelle" und der Tradition', *Jb. Berlin. Mus.*, iv (1962), pp. 151–85
G. Kubler: 'Vincente Carducho's Allegories of Painting', *A. Bull.*, xlvii (1965), pp. 439–45
L. D. Ettlinger: 'Muses and Liberal Arts: Two Miniatures from Herrad of Landsberg's *Hortus Deliciarum*', *Essays Presented to R. Wittkower*, ii (London, 1967), pp. 29–35
M. Winner: 'Bernini's "*Verità*" (Bausteine zur Vorgeschichte einer "*Invenzione*")', *Munuscula Discipulorum, kunsthistorische Studien [für] Hans Kauffmann* (Berlin, 1968), pp. 393–413
E. Cropper: 'Bound Theory and Blind Practice: Pietro Testa's Notes on Painting and the *Liceo della pittura*', *J. Warb. & Court. Inst.*, xxxiv (1971), pp. 262–96
J. Gaus: 'Ingenium und Ars: Das Ehepaarbildnis Lavoisier von David und die Ikonographie der Museninspiration', *Wallraf-Richartz-Jb.*, xxxvi (1974), pp. 199–228
W. Kemp: 'Disegno: Beiträge zur Geschichte des Begriffs zwischen 1547 und 1607', *Marburg. Jb. Kstwiss.*, xix (1974), pp. 219–40
M. M. Kahr: 'Velázquez and *Las Meninas*', *A. Bull.*, lvii (1975), pp. 225–46
W. Prinz: 'Das Motiv "Pallas Athena führt die Pictura in den Kreis der septem artes liberales ein" und die sogenannte Cellini-Schale', *Festschrift für P. W. Meister* (Hamburg, 1975), pp. 165–73
J. Becker: '"Dieses emblematische Stück stellet die Erziehung der Jugend vor": Zu Adriaen van der Werff, München, Alte Pinakothek, Inv. Nr. 250', *Oud-Holland*, xc (1976), pp. 77–107
E. McGrath: 'The Painted Decoration of Rubens's House', *J. Warb. & Court. Inst.*, xli (1978), pp. 245–77
K. Herrmann-Fiore: 'Die Fresken Federico Zuccaros in seinem römischen Künstlerhaus', *Röm. Jb. Kstgesch.*, xviii (1979), pp. 35–112
M. D. Garrard: 'Artemisia Gentileschi's Self-portrait as the Allegory of Painting', *A. Bull.*, lxii (1980), pp. 97–112
W. L. Strauss: *Netherlandish Artists (1980)*, 3 (III/i) and 4 (III/ii) of *The Illustrated Bartsch*, ed. W. L. Strauss (New York, 1978–) [B.]
T. DaCosta Kaufmann: 'The Eloquent Artist: Towards an Understanding of the Stylistics of Painting at the Court of Rudolf II', *Leids Ksthist. Jb.*, i (1982), pp. 119–48
I. Gerards-Nelissen: 'Federigo Zuccaro and the "Lament of painting"', *Simiolus*, xiii (1983), pp. 44–53
M. Winner: 'Poussins Selbstbildnis im Louvre als kunsttheoretische Allegorie', *Röm. Jb. Kstgesch.*, xx (1983), pp. 417–49
E. Cropper: *The Ideal of Painting: Pietro Testa's Düsseldorf Notebook* (Princeton, 1984)
F. H. Jacobs: 'Vasari's Vision of the History of Painting: Frescoes in the Casa Vasari, Florence', *A. Bull.*, lxvi (1984), pp. 399–416
H.-J. Raupp: *Untersuchungen zu Künstlerbildnis und Künstlerdarstellung in den Niederlanden im 17. Jahrhundert* (Hildesheim, 1984)
L. Cheney: *The Paintings of the Casa Vasari* (New York, 1985)
H. P. Chapman: 'A *Hollandse Pictura*: Observations on the Title Page of Philips Angel's *Lof der schilder-konst*', *Simiolus*, xvi (1986), pp. 233–48
C. Schuckman: 'Allegorieën op de beeldhouwkunst door Pierre Biard de Jonge (1592–1661)', *Bull. Rijksmus.*, xxxiv (1986), pp. 93–105
G. Luijten: 'De Triomf van de Schilderkunst: Een titeltekening van Gesina ter Borch en een toneelstuk', *Bull. Rijksmus.*, xxxvi (1988), pp. 282–314
G. J. M. Weber: *Der Lobtopos des 'lebenden' Bildes: Jan Vos und sein 'Zeege der Schilderkunst' von 1654* (Hildesheim, 1991)

WILLEM F. LASH

Allegrain. French family of artists. (1) Etienne Allegrain was a landscape painter who worked predominantly in the tradition of classical scenes established in the mid-17th century by Nicolas Poussin and Claude Lorrain. His brother Jean-Baptiste Allegrain (1644–before 1714) was a sculptor, while his son Gabriel Allegrain (i) (1679–1748) was also a landscape painter, whose works (e.g. *Landscape with Apollo and the Sibyl*, Tours, Mus. B.-A.) can be distinguished from those of his father only with difficulty. Gabriel's son (2) Christophe-Gabriel Allegrain was a sculptor who was much influenced by his more illustrious contemporary and brother-in-law Jean-Baptiste Pigalle. Christophe-Gabriel's own son Gabriel Allegrain (ii) (1733–after 1779) was a sculptor who worked in the naval dockyard at Rochefort.

(1) Etienne Allegrain (*b* Paris, 1644; *d* Paris, 2 April 1736). Painter and draughtsman. He was possibly the pupil of Henri Mauperché and in 1676 was admitted (*agréé*) by the Académie Royale, becoming a full member in 1677 on presentation of his painting *The Flight into Egypt* (untraced). In 1691 he completed part of a series of paintings of views of the château and park of Versailles still *in situ* at the Grand Trianon (Trianon de Marbre). Jean Cotelle II and Jean-Baptiste Martin I also contributed to this project. Among Allegrain's pictures is the somewhat stiff and mannered *La Salle de Conseil*, with elegantly elongated figures in a formal garden.

Between 1690 and 1695 Allegrain's work came to rely more on the recent tradition of French classical landscape painting, in particular Poussin's mythological landscapes of 1647–8. His later landscape work at the Trianon (1694–5) shows a clear contrast with his earlier productions for that building. In 1700 he produced a pair of landscape paintings for the ante-chamber of the summer apartment of the Ménagerie at Versailles, *Landscape with Flocks* and *Landscape with a River* (both Paris, Louvre). In the latter, a composition of lucid clarity and symmetry, with three figures presenting an idyllic vision of antiquity, the sombre note introduced by a fourth figure, a weeping woman, is given added resonance by the skeletal wreck of a boat, an idea apparently borrowed from Poussin. In the *Landscape with Flocks* there is a clear step-by-step recession through the picture, but also a more decorative prettification of the flowers and foliage than one would find in either Claude or Poussin. Allegrain renders all the elements with a meticulous care that in some ways foreshadows the works of such later Neo-classical landscape painters as Pierre-Henri de Valenciennes.

At this time in France two distinct categories of landscape painting were recognized: the rustic and the heroic. Allegrain produced works of both types. The themes explored in the *Landscape with a River* and *Landscape with Flocks* may be considered as rustic, but other works that include antique temples and ruins, such as *Landscape with a Lake* (Kingston, Ont., Queen's U., Agnes Etherington A. Cent.), are in the heroic mode.

For the most part Allegrain's landscapes are imaginary, and although he does include specific Roman features it is unlikely that he ever visited Rome, instead taking his details from engravings by other artists. He occasionally ventured into topographical painting, for example with the early works for the Trianon mentioned above and with *View of the Invalides* (Troyes, Mus. B.-A.).

A precise chronology of Allegrain's work remains to be established. The only signed and dated work known is a drawing of 1697 (priv. col.), and his work has often been confused with that of such artists as Francisque Millet, Gaspard Dughet, Jan Frans van Bloemen and his son Gabriel Allegrain, although the last's canvases tend to be both brighter and less formal than those of his father.

BIBLIOGRAPHY

A. Schnapper: *Tableaux pour le Trianon de Marbre, 1688–1714* (Paris, 1967)

The Age of Louis XV: French Painting, 1710–1774 (exh. cat. by P. Rosenberg; Toledo, OH, Mus. A.; Chicago, IL, A. Inst.; Ottawa, N.G.; 1975), p. 19

Le Classicisme français: Masterpieces of Seventeenth Century Painting (exh. cat. by S. Laveissière, Dublin, N.G., 1985), p. 1

A. Lossel-Guillien: *Etienne et Gabriel Allegrain* (diss., U. Paris), 1985

C. and Y. Marander: *Etienne et Gabriel Allegrain* (diss., U. Lille), 1985

A. Lossel-Guillien: 'A la recherche de l'oeuvre d'Etienne Allegrain, paysagiste à la fin du règne de Louis XIV', *Bull. Inf. Inst. N. Hist. A.*, iv (1988), pp. 69–79

SIMON LEE

(2) Christophe-Gabriel Allegrain (*b* Paris, 8 Oct 1710; *d* Paris, 17 April 1795). Sculptor, the grandson of (1) Etienne Allegrain. He was a pupil of one Martin, an ornamental sculptor, and by his first marriage, in 1733, became brother-in-law to Jean-Baptiste Pigalle. He was accepted (*agréé*) by the Académie Royale in 1748 and received (*reçu*) as a full member in 1751 on presentation of the statuette *Narcissus Gazing at his Reflection in the Water* (plaster, exh. Salon 1747; marble, exh. Salon 1753; probably destr. 1871 but known in particular from a drawing by Joseph Nollekens, Oxford, Ashmolean). His earlier career was dominated by the relationship with Pigalle, with whom he seems to have collaborated, probably in a subordinate capacity, on monuments including the mausoleum of the *Maréchal de Saxe* (marble, designed 1753; Strasbourg, St Thomas) and the monument to *Louis XV* for the Place Royale, Reims (bronze, completed 1765; partially destr.). Other works were executed to the designs of others, such as the stone female statue, the *Butter-churner* (untraced; a Sèvres statuette modelled by Jean-Baptiste Defernex in 1754 may represent this work; Sèvres, Mus. N. Cér.), commissioned in 1753 by Mme de Pompadour for her dairy at the château of Crécy and based on a drawing by François Boucher. His own talents and limitations in the field of portrait sculpture and funerary art can be appreciated in the monument to *Charles-Joseph de Pollinchove* (marble, set up 1763) in the church of St Pierre, Douai.

It was not till 1767, however, that Allegrain emerged from Pigalle's shadow with the success of his statue of a *Young Woman Bathing* (marble; Paris, Louvre). The work had been originally commissioned in 1755 by the Marquis de Marigny, then director of the Bâtiments du Roi. Diderot's enthusiastic description of this imposing female nude, which combines a classical form with acute observation of the living model, is justly famous. *Young Woman Bathing* was given by Louis XV to Mme Du Barry, who installed it at the château of Louveciennes, Yvelines, and in 1776 requested a companion piece showing *Diana Surprised while Bathing* (marble; Paris, Louvre), a work in which Allegrain failed to repeat his earlier success. Much of his documented output remains work of a relatively modest, decorative nature, such as the pair of allegorical bas-reliefs representing *Sleep* and *Morning* for the bedroom of the Comte de Brancas (exh. Salon 1769; untraced). He rose to the rank of Recteur of the Académie in 1783.

For portrait of Allegrain *see* DUPLESSIS, JOSEPH-SIFFRED.

BIBLIOGRAPHY

Lami

D. Diderot: *Salons* (1759–81); 4 vols, ed. J. Adhémar and J. Seznec (Oxford, 1957–67, rev. 1983)

M. Furcy-Raynaud: *Inventaire des sculptures exécutées au XVIIIème siècle pour la direction des Bâtiments du Roi* (Paris, 1927), pp. 30–37

Diderot et l'art de Boucher à David (exh. cat., Paris, Hôtel de la Monnaie, 1985), pp. 436–9

G. Scherf: 'Un Monument méconnu: Le Mausolée de Charles-Joseph de Pollinchove par Christophe-Gabriel Allegrain (1710–1795)', *Bull. Soc. Hist. A. Fr.* (1989), pp. 117–30

GUILHEM SCHERF

Allegri, Antonio. *See* CORREGGIO.

Allegrini, Francesco (*b* ?Cantiano, 1615–20; *d* ?Gubbio, after 1679). Italian painter. A pupil of Cavaliere d'Arpino, he was attracted early on by the art of Pietro da Cortona, although the full Baroque remained alien to him. He has often been confused with his father, Flaminio Allegrini (?1587–?1663), who was also a painter. The early sources state that Francesco worked in Savona Cathedral and in the Durazzi and Gavotti palaces in Genoa, yet it remains unclear whether these commissions should be attributed to him or to his father. Francesco worked mostly in Rome, where many of his canvases and frescoes are preserved in churches and palaces. Around 1650 he executed the *St Catherine* altarpiece in the church of SS Domenico e Sisto, Rome (*in situ*). Between 1652 and 1654 he was working on frescoes in the Speralli Chapel in the cathedral at Gubbio. In 1653 he took part in an important project to decorate the church of S Marco, Rome, under the supervision of Cortona. The two canvases he painted there, *SS Abdon and Sennen Yoked to the Cart of Emperor Decius* and the *Consecration of the Basilica of St Mark* (both *in situ*), reveal the influence of Andrea Sacchi's and Pier Francesco Mola's neo-Venetian art. At about the same time he painted the *Scenes from the Old Testament* in the

Palazzo Pamphili in Piazza Navona, Rome. Allegrini also painted battle scenes, and his works in this genre include frescoes in the Palazzo Rospigliosi (*c.* 1655) and the Palazzo Altemps. Between 1659 and 1660 he produced what is perhaps his most important work, a cycle of three frescoes—the *Battle of Muret*, the *Martyrdom of St Peter of Verona* and the *Triumph of St Thomas Aquinas*—in the Palazzo del Sant'Uffizio, Rome. His last Roman commission was the series of frescoes depicting scenes from the *Life of St Alexander* in the church of SS Cosmo e Damiano. He left Rome *c.* 1661 and settled in Gubbio, where he painted numerous altarpieces in a style that pallidly echoes Cortona, for example the *Virgin and Child with Saints* in Santa Croce della Foce (1668; *in situ*). His last works include the frescoes painted between 1674 and 1678 in the church of the Madonna del Prato.

BIBLIOGRAPHY

DBI

R. Lefevre: 'Appunti sugli Allegrini da Gubbio, pittori del seicento', *Stud. Seicent.*, ix (1968), pp. 127–55

P. Ciuferri: 'Una scheda su Francesco Allegrini', *Ric. Stor. A.*, 6 (1977), pp. 121–5

F. Zeri: 'Francesco Allegrini: Gli affreschi del Sant'Ufficio', *Ant. B. A.*, i/3 (1977), pp. 266–70

M. Gregori and E. Schleier, eds: *La pittura in Italia: Il seicento*, 2 vols (Milan, 1988, rev. 1989), ii, p. 612 [with bibliog.]

ELEONORA VILLA

Allélit. *See under* HÉBERT (i).

Alleman. *See* DEUTSCH.

Allianz. Swiss group of painters and sculptors founded in 1937 from various avant-garde elements, with Max Bill, Walter Bodmer, Richard Paul Lohse, Robert S. Gessner (*b* 1908), Camille Graeser, Fritz Glarner, Max Huber (*b* 1919) and Verena Loewensberg (*b* 1912) among its original members; its president was the painter Leo Leuppi (*b* 1893). The group had no official aesthetic but was not as heterogeneous or politically motivated as the roughly contemporary Gruppe 33, instead displaying a notable bias towards Constructivism and geometric abstraction. The first group exhibition, *Neue Kunst in der Schweiz* (Basle, Ksthalle, 1938), was followed by a second at the Kunsthaus in Zurich in 1942 and by further group shows at the Galerie des Eaux Vives in Zurich, starting with two in 1944. The *Almanach Neuer Kunst in der Schweiz*, published by the group in 1940, brought together reproductions of their works with those of artists such as Paul Klee, Le Corbusier and Kurt Seligmann. The publication also included texts by Bill, Leuppi, Le Corbusier, Seligmann, Siegfried Giedion and others. Allianz exhibitions continued to be held into the 1950s.

BIBLIOGRAPHY

Almanach Neuer Kunst in der Schweiz (Zurich, 1940)

Walter Bodmer im Kunstmuseum Basel (exh. cat. by L. Klotz, C. Geelhaar and D. Koepplin, Basle, Kstmus., 1978)

Dreissiger Jahre Schweiz: Konstruktive Kunst, 1915–45 (exh. cat. by R. Koella and others, Winterthur, Kstmus., 1981)

H. J. Albrecht and others: *Richard Paul Lohse: Modulare und serielle Ordnungen, 1943–1984* (Zurich, 1984)

□

Allied Artists' Association [A.A.A.]. Organization established in London in 1908, dedicated to non-juried exhibitions of international artists' work. The main impetus for the A.A.A. came from Frank Rutter (1876–1937), art critic of the *Sunday Times*, and the first exhibition was held at the Albert Hall, London. Inspired by the Salon des Indépendants in Paris, Rutter wanted to set up an exhibiting platform for the work of progressive artists. On payment of a subscription, artists were entitled to exhibit five works (subsequently reduced to three) and over 3000 items were included in the first show. Rutter also wanted the A.A.A. to have a foreign section and for the first exhibition collaborated with Jan de Holewinski (1871–1927), who had been sent to London to organize an exhibition of Russian arts and crafts.

Among those involved in the organization of the A.A.A. was Walter Sickert, who urged complete impartiality and insisted that the catalogue should not be alphabetical but decided by ballot. When it was suggested that work by the better artists should be more prominently displayed, Sickert replied: 'In this society there are no good works or bad works: there are only works by shareholders'. By the second exhibition it had been decided that all members should be eligible to serve on the hanging committee and invitations to do so were issued on an alphabetical basis. In this way Charles Ginner met Harold Gilman and Spencer Gore in 1910. Although A.A.A. shows suffered from a lack of quality control, they were refreshingly democratic and allowed Kandinsky's abstract work to be shown for the first time in Britain.

BIBLIOGRAPHY

F. Rutter: *Since I was Twenty-five* (London, 1927)

FRANCES SPALDING

Allingham [née Paterson], **Helen** (*b* Burton on Trent, Staffs, 26 Sept 1848; *d* Haslemere, Surrey, 28 Sept 1926). English illustrator and painter. The daughter of a physician, she was brought up in Altrincham, Ches, and, after her father's death in 1862, in Birmingham. She studied at the Birmingham School of Design and, from 1867, at the Royal Academy Schools, London. From 1869 she provided illustrations for Joseph Swain and subsequently for the *Graphic* and *Cornhill* magazines. She exhibited watercolours at the Dudley Gallery. In 1874 she married the Irish poet William Allingham, and her consequent financial independence allowed her to abandon black-and-white illustration. Her new circle of friends included Tennyson, Ruskin and Thomas Carlyle, whose portrait she drew (version of 1879; Edinburgh, N.P.G.). In 1875 she was elected an associate of the Old Water-Colour Society (she became a full member in 1890 after the prohibition on lady members was withdrawn); she was a regular exhibitor there.

After 1881, when the family moved to Witley, Surrey, Allingham developed a characteristic style and subject-matter in her watercolours: views of the vernacular architecture of southern England, garden scenes (such as *Feeding the Fowls, Pinner*, 1890; London, Bankside Gal.), pure and figurative landscapes, and interior views depicting her own house and family. In each case she sought the informal and intimate character of a subject; her closeness of observation was the result of careful study from nature. She was impressed by the rural subjects of Frederick Walker and learnt from his watercolour technique. She also admired the work of her friend and neighbour Myles

Birket Foster. While most of her work depicts the English countryside, she did paint some scenes of Venice. Her contemporary reputation was considerable, her work well known from exhibitions and reproductions.

BIBLIOGRAPHY

M. B. Huish: *Happy England* (London, 1903) [illus. with 81 colour pls after Allingham's watercolours; contains much biog. information]

S. Dick: *The Cottage Homes of England* (London, 1909) [illus. with 64 colour pls after Allingham's watercolours]

A. Lester: *The Exhibited Works of Helen Allingham* (Wallingford, 1979)

CHRISTOPHER NEWALL

Allio [Aglio; Allio de Löwenthal; Garovaglio; Laio; Lalio]. Italian family of artists. Originally from Scaria, Intelvi, in the 16th and 17th centuries many members of the family moved to Austria, Bavaria, Bohemia and Hungary, where they worked in a variety of fields associated with the building industry. The complex relationships of the members of the various branches of the Allio family to each other are sometimes problematic in view of their many intermarriages. The most important representatives of the four branches of the Allio family are dealt with below.

BIBLIOGRAPHY

Meissner; Thieme–Becker

F. Rogatsch: *Die Schule der Lalios* (diss., U. Graz, 1933)

1. ALLIO (i). The first branch of the family active in the Habsburg lands was descended from Martino Allio I (*fl* 1520), a master mason from Scaria, recorded as working on the fortifications of Radkersburg, on the border between Austria and the Ottoman Empire. He had three sons, the architect and engineer (1) Domenico Allio, who was the most important member of the family, Gianmaria Allio (*d* 1593) and Andrea Allio I (*fl* 1551–8).

(1) Domenico Allio (*b* ?Lugano, 1505, or ?Scaria, 1515; *d* Graz, 1563). Architect and engineer. He trained in northern Italy, and he is recorded in Styria from 1530. Together with a fairly large team of builders, Domenico renewed and modernized the fortifications against the Turks in Styria (Graz; after 1543), Carinthia (Klagenfurt, plan of the town fortifications; 1535) and Slovenia (Varaždin, Maribor; 1554) and Croatia (Zagreb). He sometimes worked on non-military projects, including the castle at Neuhaus an der Donau (1554–63), the grand staircase (destr. 19th century) at Graz Castle, the royal oratory and a chapel (1554) in Graz Cathedral and the Landhaus (1556–63) at Graz. Not only is the Landhaus Allio's most important work, it is also one of the most architecturally interesting 16th-century monuments north of the Alps. The north and east sides of the courtyard are articulated with three superimposed ranges of arcaded loggias in High Renaissance style. Allio enjoyed the confidence of his patron Ferdinand I, King of Bohemia and Hungary (later Holy Roman Emperor), and in 1553 he was appointed royal master builder and in 1555 chief master builder of the Croatian and Slovene frontier area; in 1558 he was ennobled.

BIBLIOGRAPHY

Meissner

A. Hajdecki: 'Die Dynastenfamilien der italienischen Bau- und Maurermeister der Barocke in Wien', *Ber. & Mitt. Altert.-Ver. Wien*, xxxix (1906), pp. 9–30

E. Morpurgo: *Gli artisti italiani in Austria*, i (Rome, 1937)

F. Cavarocchi: 'Artisti delle Valle Intelvi e delle diocesi comense attivi in Baviera alla luce di carte d'archivio del Ducato di Milano', *A. Lombarda*, x/2 (1965), pp. 135–48

E. Kraigher: 'Domenico dell'Allio: Familie, Leben und Werk', *Bericht über den 13. Historikertag in Klagenfurt*, Veröffentlichungen des Verbandes der österreichischen Geschichte-Verein (1977), pp. 263–77

PETER FIDLER

2. ALLIO (ii). Active in Austria and Germany and working as stuccoists, architects and masons, the members of this branch were related to the Carlone family (*see* CARLONE (ii)), who also came from northern Italy and worked in Germany and Austria. The most important members of the branch were (1) Paolo Allio I, (2) Donato Felice Allio, and Paolo's son (3) Giovanni Battista Allio III.

(1) Paolo [Johann Paul] **Allio I** (*b* Scaria, Intelvi, 1655; *d* Scaria, 6 Feb 1729). Stuccoist. Paolo trained with his uncle Giovanni Battista Carlone II, who had been running a stucco business in Passau since 1675, working on the Jesuit church (now St Michaelkirche) and Passau Cathedral. Paolo Allio is named from July 1681 as mandatary ('Gevollmächtiger') and 'consort' of Carlone in the Passau Cathedral papers and he remained the impresario of his uncle until 1704. He then worked in the same capacity for Carlone's son, Diego Francesco Carlone, until 1715. The stucco decoration in the Kuenburg Theological College in Passau is Paolo's first authenticated independent work. Although he worked in Austria and Germany, he spent the winters in Scaria. From 1705 Paolo Allio and Diego Francesco Carlone were employed as stuccoists at the Collegiate Church in Salzburg, where the works were supervised by Johann Bernhard Fischer von Erlach. They also worked at Schloss Klessheim. In 1715 Paolo set up his own workshop, in which his two sons, (3) Giovanni Battista Allio III and Sebastiano Domenico Allio (1697–1782), were also employed.

Paolo Allio's style is characterized by an emphasis on modelling and motifs from plants of the *Allium* genus; he was also renowned for his stucco marble altars. His work in Germany includes the choir vaulting and high altar (1688–90) of the pilgrimage church at Gartlberg, near Pfarrkirchen, and interior decoration and altars (1701–05) of the Carmelite church in Straubing. Important works in Austria by Paolo Allio include the choir vaulting, pulpit and altars (1707) of the Servite church at Rattenburg and the winter sacristy (1721) of the abbey church at Kremsmünster. After completing his last large commission—stuccowork (1721) for the church of the Teutonic Order in Linz, under Johann Lukas von Hildebrandt—Paolo returned to Scaria.

BIBLIOGRAPHY

Meissner

I. Dalchow: *Italienische Stukkatoren und ihre Ornamentik in der bayrischen Architektur um 1700* (diss., U. Cologne, 1926)

S. Einbeck: *Stuck an Bauten Fischer von Erlachs in Salzburg* (diss., U. Salzburg, 1970)

H. SCHMIDHUBER

(2) Donato Felice [Donat Felix, Donatus Felix] **Allio** (*b* Scaria, 24 Oct 1677; *d* Vienna, 6 May 1761). Architect, builder and engineer, brother of (1) Paolo Allio I. He arrived in Vienna before 1698 and, after taking his craftsman's qualifying examination in May 1704, worked there as a master mason on civic projects. From 1711 to

1747 he held an appointment with the Army Works Department, where his main function was to submit reports, give specialist advice and modify plans. Donato Felice Allio's two principal creations were the convent and church (1717–28) of the Salesian nuns in Vienna and Klosterneuburg Abbey (1730–55) near Vienna. The designs of both were based on the concept of two symmetrical courtyards, arranged one behind the other and divided by the main axis, which was determined by the central location of the church. Links with monastery building in Lombardy and in neighbouring Switzerland are evident in these schemes, as is a connection with the layouts of hospitals and homes for old soldiers. In Allio's first plans for the abbey buildings at Klosterneuburg, which involved the construction of five courtyards, the east section featured a hall and an axial staircase placed opposite the existing church. At the end of 1730 Gundacker Ludwig Joseph, Graf von Althann, Surveyor of the Imperial Works, announced that an imperial residence should be built within the monastery (then already under construction). This did not result in any fundamental departure from the concept but in modifications, some by Allio and some by the Imperial Office of Works under Joseph Emanuel Fischer von Erlach, that augmented the grandeur of the building and gave greater emphasis to its secular aspect. These were reflected on the exterior in a reordering of the storeys and projecting bays, the introduction of cupolas and a more imposing façade. Fischer von Erlach's innovations were implemented by Allio in his own personal style.

Donato Felice's church buildings are centrally based and mainly cruciform or, in the case of the Salesian church, exhibit the longitudinal oval shape then popular in Vienna. By giving the porch and the presbytery the same form, the main space is defined at each end. Externally, the main elevation of the Salesian church features two superimposed orders of pilasters with flanking volutes, in the Italian manner. Allio's concept of architecture was in fact rooted in the artistic tradition of northern Italy and consequently in that of 17th-century Austrian as well. Around 1730 he began to experiment with stylistic innovations from France, a move prompted by the intervention of Fischer von Erlach in the plans for the abbey at Klosterneuburg. The building of the Salesian church brought Allio into contact with the decorative art of Antonio Beduzzi, who was responsible for the interior furnishings. A great number of Beduzzi's motifs were subsequently adopted by Allio for his own repertory. Allio's substantial collection of drawings by gifted decorative artists working in his studio is kept at Klosterneuburg (Stiftarchv). Donato Felice Allio is also credited with the design of castles at Gerasdorf, Steinfeld, and Ladendorf (1722–3) in Lower Austria, and with the Palais Kayserstein (1728) in Vienna. His churches include those at Gross-Siegharts (1720–27) and Wilhelmsdorf (Maria Bründl, 1740–50) in Lower Austria, and that of St Mary (1741–6) at Janovicky/Kosumberka in eastern Bohemia.

BIBLIOGRAPHY

Meissner; Thieme–Becker

A. Ilg: 'Die Allio', *Ber. & Mitt. Altert.-Ver. Wien*, xxiii (1886), pp. 115–20

A. Hajdecki: 'Die Dynastenfamilien der italienischen Bau- und Maurermeister der Barocke in Wien', *Ber. & Mitt. Altert.-Ver. Wien*, xxxix (1906), pp. 17–30

W. Pauker: 'Donato Felice von Allio und seine Tätigkeit im Stifte Klosterneuburg', *Beiträge zur Baugeschichte des Stiftes Klosterneuburg*, ed. W. Pauker, i (Vienna and Leipzig, 1907), pp. 1–95

T. Zacharias: *Joseph Emanuel Fischer von Erlach* (Vienna and Munich, 1960), pp. 49–60

E. Mahl: *Donato Felice d'Allio: Beiträge zu einer Monographie* (diss., U. Vienna, 1961)

S. Mojzer: 'Werke Deutscher Künstler in Ungarn, Teil 1: Architektur', *Stud. Dt. Kstgesch.*, cccxxix (Baden-Baden and Strasbourg, 1962), p. 35

E. Mahl: 'Donato Felice d'Allio und die Planungsgeschichte des Stiftes Klosterneuburg', *Jb. Stift. Klosterneuburg*, n. s., v (1965), pp. 161–83

G. Hajós: 'Beiträge zur Geschichte des Salesianerinnenklosters in Wien', *Wien. Jb. Kstgesch.*, xxi (1968), pp. 216–31

——: 'Kloster und Kirche der Salesianerinnen', *Österreich. Ksttop.*, xli (1974), pp. 201–52

W. G. Rizzi: 'Donato Felice d'Allio: Der Architekt der Pfarrkirche in Gross-Siegharts', *Jb. Stift. Klosterneuburg*, n. s., xi (1979), pp. 87–98

——: 'Zur Architektenfrage des Palais Geymann-Windischgraetz und der Projekte für den ehemaligen Klosterneuburger Stiftshof in der Renn gasse in Wien', *Jb. Stift. Klosterneuburg*, n. s., xii (1983), pp. 63–93

W. GEORG RIZZI

(3) Giovanni Battista [Johann Baptisto] **Allio III** (*b* Scaria, Intelvi, 1690; *d* ?Scaria, ?1753). Stuccoist and sculptor, son of (1) Paolo Allio I. Giovanni Battista was trained in his father's workshop in Passau, where he worked from 1716 to 1720. From 1720 Giovanni Battista ran his own workshop, where his younger brother, Sebastiano Domenico Allio (1697–1782), worked until 1733 and where Franz Ignatius Holzinger and Giovanni Martino Luraghi were also active. His was the leading group of stuccoists in the Passau region. Giovanni Battista Allio's works include several houses and churches in Passau, most notably St Nikola Abbey Church (1716–17), and the decoration of the nave (1720–22) of the Benedictine monastery of Niederaltach, together with his brother Sebastiano and Holzinger. Allio also worked on the summer sacristy (1724) for the abbey church at Kremsmünster, and he carried out an extensive decorative scheme (1732) at Schloss Schwarzenau in Lower Austria. His repertory of forms was largely taken over from his father's workshop, displaying interlacing, vine scroll and latticework, volute cartouches, palmettes, rosettes, leaf garlands and ragged ornamentation. In his late works coffering appears frequently, and symmetry of decoration is retained. Giovanni Battista Allio's works are hardly distinguishable from those of his brother Sebastiano; however Giovanni Battista's *oeuvre* also includes free-standing sculptures, stuccolustro and scagliola altars.

BIBLIOGRAPHY

Meissner

I. Schemper-Sparholz: *Stuckdekorationen des 17.Jh. im Wiener Raum* (diss., U. Vienna, 1978), p. 15

F. Cavarocchi: *Der Passauer Dom, Festschrift* (Passau, 1980), p. 135

I. Schemper-Sparholz: 'Die Stuckdekorationen im Schloss Schwarzenau', *Kamptal-Stud.*, iii (1982–3), pp. 79–96

H. SCHMIDHUBER

3. ALLIO (iii). Of this branch the most important were the sculptors and architects Matteo di Guaro Allio (*b* Scaria, Intelvi, *c.* 1605; *d* Padua, 25 Feb 1670) and Tommaso Allio (*b* Scaria, Intelvi, *c.* 1620; *d* Padua, 18 Sept 1667), who were brothers and worked in Padua. Their first recorded work was the monument to *Giandomenico Sala* (1644–8) in the basilica of Il Santo, Padua. The two

brothers executed a number of works together in Il Santo, including the altar of St Francis (1648; to a design by Matteo Carnero), the *De Lazara* monument (1651–2) and the right-hand pilaster (1652) of the altar of the tomb of *St Anthony*, the three outer sides of which they decorated. In 1662 they were still working on the high altar of the basilica. In 1660 they were commissioned to execute the high altar of the church of S Benedetto in Padua, and payments for this are recorded until 1664. To Tommaso are attributed the statues of the two *Archangels* and the marble figures of *St Benedict* and *St Gregory*, while Matteo probably carved the stone figures of the *Virgin and Child*, *St Anthony* and *St Scholastica*. Tommaso was probably also responsible for the marble statues of *Faith* and *Hope*, originally in the church of S Agostino (destr.) in Padua and now in the church of S Lorenzo, Abano. Between 1661 and 1662 the two brothers executed the monument to *Lucrezia Dondi Degli Obizzi* (Padua, Pal. Ragione). In 1664 they worked on the doorway of the sanctuary of Monteortone in the Euganean Hills. The only architectural work known to be by either brother is the relocation by Matteo (1668) of the high altar in the choir of Il Santo. The Allio brothers were far removed from the flourishes of the Baroque. Their Lombard training is evident in the late Mannerist elements in their work, which are combined with a somewhat conventional study of form.

BIBLIOGRAPHY
F. Cessi: 'Gli scultori Allio', *Padova* (1961), nos 4, 6–7, 9–12
C. Semenzato: 'I fratelli Allio', *La Scultura veneta del seicento e del settecento* (Venice, 1966)

CAMILLO SEMENZATO

4. ALLIO (iv). Many members of this branch of architects, masons, sculptors and stuccoists worked north of the Alps, especially in Vienna and Bohemia. The Bohemian line includes the two brothers Andrea Allio III (*d* 1645) and Francesco Allio (*d* 1653), and Andrea's sons, Pietro Allio (*fl* 1643–6) and Giovanni Battista Allio I 'de Löwenthal' (*bapt* 1644; *bur* 1716). Traceable in Vienna from 1641, Andrea Allio III ran a business as a master builder with 21 assistants and worked on the inner courtyard of the Loreto Chapel in Prague. His brother Francesco was a master mason and died in Vienna. The mason Giovanni Battista I concluded his apprenticeship with the master mason Giovanni Battista Spineta in Prague in 1663. In 1694 Giovanni Battista I was granted the noble title 'de Löwenthal'. The masonry in the Barnabite monastery in Prague is the only work securely attributed to him. Pietro Allio was enrolled in the masons' guild in Prague in 1675. Other members of the Allio family active in Prague included Andrea Allio V, who is traceable in Bohemia between 1671 and 1678. Andrea was a member of the Prague guild and in 1678 he became a citizen of that city, together with Martino Allio II (*b* Scaria, 1654; *d* Prague, 1701). In 1694 Martino was also granted the title 'de Löwenthal'. Martino, with his supposed brother, the head mason Giovanni Battista Allio II, worked for the Benedictines in Broumov and for Count Černin. Giovanni Battista II is documented in Bohemia between 1685 and 1694 and in 1689 also became a citizen of Prague. The mason Benedikt (Benedetto) Allio II is mentioned in Prague in 1705 and 1709. In Bohemia, the importance of the Allios lay more in mediating the Italian idiom than in their individual artistic achievements.

BIBLIOGRAPHY
Meissner
A. Hajdecki: 'Die Dynastenfamilien der italienischen Bau- und Maurermeister der Barocke in Wien', *Ber. & Mitt. Altert.-Ver. Wien*, xxxix (1906)
H. G. Franz: *Bauten und Baumeister der Barockzeit in Böhmen* (Leipzig, 1962)
H. Rokyta: *Die böhmischen Länder* (Salzburg, 1970)

H. SCHMIDHUBER

Alliprandi, Giovanni Battista (*b* ?Laino d'Intelvi, *c.* 1665; *d* Litomyšl, Bohemia, ?13 March 1720). Italian architect, active in Bohemia. The son of Lorenzo Alliprandi (*d* *c.* 1712), a stucco artist who worked in Vienna, he served his apprenticeship with the master builder Francesco Martinelli (1651–1708) in Vienna from 1685 to 1688 and is recorded as working in Bohemia in 1690 as a foreman. From 1696 to 1702 Alliprandi was in the service of Count Heřman Jakub Černín (1659–1710) as an architect. At the same time, and also later, he worked for the Counts Pachta, Přehořovský, Kaiserstein, Špork and others. In 1706 he was appointed military engineer in Prague, where he acquired citizenship of the Malá Strana quarter in 1709, from which year he was in the service of Count František Václav Trautmansdorf (1676–1753). In 1712 he also served as a military engineer in Cheb.

Alliprandi brought to Bohemia an interesting personal reinterpretation of the achievements and inspirations of such Viennese masters as Johann Bernhard Fischer von Erlach, Domenico Martinelli and Johann Lukas von Hildebrandt. His designs for such buildings as the country house at Liblice (1699–1706) and the Přehořovský Palace (1702–7) in Prague, featuring an oval central block with swept-back curves that link on to rectangular side wings, represented something entirely new in Bohemia's Baroque architecture, though deriving from Guarino Guarini's Palazzo Carignano (1679–83) in Turin, as mediated through the published schemes of Fischer von Erlach. Alliprandi's harmonious and elegant façade for the Kaiserštejn Palace in Prague (1700–07) constitutes a new type of prestige architecture for Prague, with an attic storey displaying statues of the Four Seasons, delicately moulded profiles around the windows and a gently undulating parapet. Other palaces in Prague of the period around 1700 have been attributed to Alliprandi, such as the Šternberk Palace (*c.* 1698–1708) on the Hradčany and the Hrzán Palace (1702) in the Old Town. There is documentary evidence for his authorship of the design for Hartig Palace; its main portal is related to the portal of the former Orsini-Rosenberg Palace in Vienna.

Alliprandi's ecclesiastical architecture also shows an avant-garde conception of the Baroque. One of his major achievements is the church at Kuks (begun 1707). Its ground-plan consists of an octagon interpenetrating a Greek cross. The bevelled-off piers exhibit a diagonal articulation via large niches that frame the columns standing in front of them. This gives the impression of an oval foundation to the main space, one that is reinforced by the vaulting with a pendentive dome. The dynamic façade of the church with its bevelled corners and deep concave hollows is further proof of his talent. Alliprandi's Piarist

Church at Litomyšl (begun 1714) also has a noteworthy façade. Diagonally set towers flank a convex central bay, a solution that shows the inspiration of Fischer von Erlach and Hildebrandt.

BIBLIOGRAPHY

V. Naňková: 'Die Architektur Böhmens und die Tätigkeit des Architekten Giovanni Battista Alliprandi', *Akten des XXV. internationalen Kongresses für Kunstgeschichte: Vienna, 1983*, vii, *Wien und der europäische Barock*, pp. 71–5

Z. Kudělka: 'Zur Barockarchitektur in Böhmen und Mähren in den Jahren 1683–1740', *Prinz Eugen und das barocke Österreich* (Salzburg and Vienna, 1985)

P. Preiss: *Italští umělci v Praze* [Italian artists in Prague] (Prague, 1986), pp. 296–310

Dějiny českého výtvarného umění [History of Czech plastic art], II/1 (Prague, 1989), pp. 392, 394, 406–11

VĚRA NAŇKOVÁ

Allori. Italian family of painters and draughtsmen. They were active in Florence from the second half of the 16th century to the first quarter of the 17th. (1) Alessandro Allori enjoyed a career in the mainstream of the Florentine Mannerist tradition. Essentially an imitator, he produced work that was most characteristically influenced by Bronzino, Vasari and Michelangelo. His son (2) Cristofano Allori broke with the traditions kept alive by his father to become one of the foremost exponents of the Florentine Baroque.

(1) Alessandro (di Cristofano di Lorenzo del Bronzino) Allori (*b* Florence, 31 May 1535; *d* Florence, 22 Sept 1607). After the death of his father in 1540, he was adopted by Bronzino, a friend of his father, and he trained in Bronzino's workshop. From 1554 to 1560 Allori was in Rome, where he studied antique statuary and the works of Michelangelo and became known as a portrait painter. His first documented work on his return to Florence was an altarpiece, heavily influenced by Michelangelo, depicting the *Last Judgement*, painted in 1560 for the Montauti Chapel, SS Annunziata. Allori became involved in a number of projects relating to Florence's recently formed (1563) Accademia del Disegno. These included preparation of the decorations for the funeral of Michelangelo in 1564 and for the marriage the following year of Duke Cosimo I de' Medici's son, Francesco (later Francesco I de' Medici, Grand Duke of Tuscany) to Joanna of Austria.

Between 1570 and 1571 Allori executed the *Pearl Fishers* (see fig.) as part of the prestigious commission given to Vasari and his followers to decorate Francesco's *studiolo* in the Palazzo Vecchio, Florence. It is located on the western wall of the *studiolo*, which is devoted to scenes connected with water. Its elegant artificiality reveals Allori's careful study of Vasari's decorative paintings in the Palazzo Vecchio (Vasari's *Perseus* for the *studiolo* heavily inspired Allori's panel). The smooth bodies of the divers have a marmoreal quality like that found in Bronzino's work, and Allori quoted directly from Michelangelo for certain poses. Thematically a seascape, the idyllic scene conveys a sense of unnatural, arrested energy that is reinforced by the use of soft colours. The *Pearl Fishers* has become perhaps the most familiar painting from the second half of the 16th century in Florence, almost a symbol of the late Florentine *maniera*.

In 1571 Allori executed a fresco of the *Trinity* for the seat of the Florentine painters' guild, the chapel of St Luke

Alessandro Allori: *Pearl Fishers*, oil on slate, 1.27×1.04 m, 1570–71 (Florence, Palazzo Vecchio)

in SS Annunziata. Two related projects in the 1570s were executed for members of the Salviati family, who were cousins of the Medici. From 1570 to 1572 Allori painted three large mythological panels for Alamanno Salviati's villa at Ponte alla Badia near Florence, depicting the *Rape of Proserpina* (Malibu, CA, Getty Mus.), *Aeneas and Anchises* and *Narcissus* (both Washington, DC, Turk. Embassy). Between 1574 and 1580 he painted a series of frescoes depicting scenes from the *Odyssey* for the Florentine palazzo of Jacopo Salviati.

In 1575 Allori painted an altarpiece depicting *Christ and the Samaritan Woman* (Florence, S Maria Novella). The panel is typical of a number of his religious paintings that adopt Santi di Tito's Counter-Reformation revival of pre-Mannerist aesthetic values. Rejecting Bronzino's often cluttered and confused religious compositions, Allori concentrated on the previously unfashionable didactic and inspirational role of sacred art and produced an easily legible and devout altarpiece. The narrative theme is emphasized by the placing of Christ, seated, on the well and the prominent display of the Samaritan woman's vessel. Christ and the Samaritan woman are depicted in natural poses and are simply dressed. Facing one another in the foreground, they serve as a frame for the apostles, who are seen returning from the village in the background. In the 1570s Allori also painted the frescoes of the cupola of the Gaddi Chapel in S Maria Novella, designed by Giovanni Antonio Dosio (1575–6). During the 1580s Allori closely followed Andrea del Sarto, another model for Counter-Reformation values, in three versions of the *Last Supper* (1582, Bergamo, Accad. Carrara B.A.; 1582, fresco, Florence, S Maria del Carmine; 1584, Florence, S Maria Novella) and a *Virgin and Child with Saints* (1583; Cardiff, N. Mus.).

Allori's most significant secular decorative commission was a series of frescoes (1578–82) for the Salone Grande of the Medici villa at Poggio a Caiano, near Florence. The two central scenes, *Scipio Entertained by Syphax* and the *Oration of Titus Flaminius*, function iconographically as historical allegories for the Medici family's diplomatic successes. The design of the frescoes is clearly dependent on Veronese's banqueting scenes, for example the *Feast in the House of Levi* (Venice, Accad.; *see* VERONESE, PAOLO, fig. 4), both in the architectural perspectives of their backgrounds and in the lavish staffage compositions. Allori's Florentine Mannerist style remains evident, however, in the almost comical overposturing of his Michelangelesque cast and the general lack of clarity in the figural arrangement. In 1581 Allori supervised the execution, by assistants, of the extensive series of *Grotesques* in the corridors on the top floor of the Uffizi, Florence, and from *c.* 1583–8 he again undertook work for the Salviati family: a commission to decorate the family chapel dedicated to S Antonino in S Marco, Florence. In addition to a series of frescoes in the upper zone of the chapel depicting scenes from the *Life of St Anthony*, Allori executed the central altarpiece, depicting the *Descent into Limbo*. This work ranks among his most important religious paintings and, like the *Samaritan Woman*, continues Allori's imitation of Santi di Tito, which is also apparent in his work as a draughtsman (see 1970 exh. cat.), which includes drawings that are primarily figural sketches in charcoal, with the occasional compositional sketch in pen and ink.

During the 1590s Allori's painting style fluctuated between such strikingly devout works as *St Fiacre Healing the Sick* (1596; Florence, S Spirito), again based on Santi di Tito's style, and the highly mannered *Vision of St Hyacinth* (1596; Florence, S Maria Novella), an anachronistic revival of the mid-16th-century Mannerist compositions of Bronzino and Vasari. Towards the end of his career, Allori produced one of his most atypical works, the *Sacrifice of Isaac* (1601; Florence, Uffizi). The painting is unusual in that the predominant element is landscape instead of figural composition. Allori had painted the same theme during the 1580s (Florence, S Niccolò sopr'Arno), adhering to the compositional focus on Abraham and Isaac that had typified versions of the subject since Ghiberti's bronze competition relief panel of 1402. The most probable source of inspiration for the 1601 composition, with its small figures scattered throughout an extensive landscape, was northern European painting. Paul Bril and Adam Elsheimer were among the many landscape artists in Italy during this period, and Jacopo Pontormo had set a precedent by borrowing from Dürer's prints for his *Joseph in Egypt* (1515–18; London, N.G.).

Allori's influence on 17th-century Florentine painting was limited. His oeuvre shows little stylistic evolution: the dominant impression that emerges from a career that spanned half a century is of imitation rather than innovation. He remained open throughout his life to a variety of stylistic influences, among which Michelangelo's perhaps remains the most constant.

BIBLIOGRAPHY

G. Vasari: *Vite* (1550, rev. 2/1568); ed. G. Milanesi (1878–85)
R. Borghini: *Il riposo* (Florence, 1584); ed. M. Rosci (Milan, 1967)
F. Baldinucci: *Notizie* (1681–1728); ed. F. Ranalli (1845–7)
A. Venturi: *Storia* (1901–40)
I. B. Supino: *I ricordi di Alessandro Allori* (Florence, 1908)
H. Voss: *Die Malerei der Spätrenaissance in Rom und Florenz*, ii (Berlin, 1920), pp. 338–49
W. Paatz and E. Paatz: *Die Kirchen von Florenz: Ein kunstgeschichtliches Handbuch*, 6 vols (Frankfurt am Main, 1940–55)
Mostra di disegni di Alessandro Allori (exh. cat., ed. S. Lecchini Giovannoni; Florence, Uffizi; 1970)
M. Hall: *Renovation and Counter-Reformation: Vasari and Duke Cosimo in Sta Maria Novella and Sta Croce, 1565–1577* (Oxford, 1979)
J. Spalding: 'Observations on Alessandro Allori's Historical Frescoes at Poggio a Caiano', *Stor. A.*, lix (1987), pp. 11–14
A. Cecchi: 'A Design for a Tapestry by Alessandro Allori', *Master Drgs*, xxv (1987), pp. 146–9
E. Pilliod: 'Alessandro Allori's *The Penitent St Jerome*', *Rec. A. Mus., Princeton U.*, xlvii/1 (1988), pp. 2–29
S. Lecchini Giovannoni: 'Osservazioni sull'attività giovanile di Alessandro Allori', *Ant. Viva*, xxvii/1 (1988), pp. 10–31
J. Cox-Rearick: 'Pontormo, Bronzino, Allori and the Lost *Deluge* at S Lorenzo', *Burl. Mag.*, v/134 (1992), pp. 239–48

JACK J. SPALDING IV

(2) Cristofano Allori (*b* Florence, 17 Oct 1577; *d* Florence, 1 April 1621). Son of (1) Alessandro Allori. He became one of the foremost Florentine artists of the early Baroque period, also winning renown as a courtier, poet, musician and lover. Baldinucci's biography suggests a complex character, ardent, devoutly religious and obsessively perfectionist.

1. DEVELOPMENT AND EARLY WORKS, 1590–1605. His earliest known works are commissions from the Medici family and include the portrait of *Count Hugo of Tuscany* (1590; Florence, Uffizi) and the double portrait of *Francesco and Catherine de' Medici as Children* (*c.* 1596; Florence, Pitti), which in its clear drawing, sculptural forms and highly polished naturalistic detail recalls portraits by Bronzino and by Cristofano's father, Alessandro, with whom he initially studied. Cristofano made copies (untraced) of the venerated 14th-century fresco of the *Annunciation* (Florence, SS Annunziata) and of compositions of the Virgin and Child by Raphael and other artists. He also made a cartoon for the Medici tapestry works after Raphael's *Madonna della Sedia* (*c.* 1516–17; Florence, Pitti).

Between 1600 and 1605, under the influence of Florentine artists such as Lodovico Cigoli, Jacopo da Empoli, Domenico Passignano and Gregorio Pagani, Cristofano developed a more naturalistic and individual style. These masters had been inspired by the Counter-Reformation and by critical writings such as Raffaello Borghini's *Il riposo* (Florence, 1584), which castigated the extreme Mannerism of Bronzino and praised Santi de Tito's restrained compositions and Federico Barocci's use of colour. Cristofano's new mentors reacted against the Michelangelesque Mannerism exemplified by much of his father's work, hoping to create a clearer, more direct and naturalistic art, taking as their models Fra Bartolommeo, Andrea del Sarto and the earlier classical style of Michelangelo. After intense arguments about art, Cristofano broke with his father and moved to the studio of Gregorio Pagani. This may have been around 1600, when he assisted Cigoli in the fresco decorations of rooms in the Palazzo Pitti, Florence (unidentified). Cigoli's influence may be seen in the new simplicity of Cristofano's *Adoration of the Shepherds* (*c.* 1600; Florence, Pitti) and in his several copies of *St Mary Magdalene Reading* (destr.) by Correggio, whom Cigoli admired as a supreme colourist. The *Blessed Manetto dell'Antella Curing a Crippled, Deaf and Mute Youth* (1602; Florence, SS Annunziata) is the first major work displaying the descriptive naturalism, rich colours, creamy textures and introspective mood that became characteristic of Cristofano's art. By portraying himself as the youth and including powerfully realistic portraits of his father, Cigoli and Pagani, he gave the painting another level of meaning, making it a declaration of his new artistic beliefs. Several preparatory drawings define the poses of the figures; a study in red chalk and white heightening on blue paper for the two clerics (Rome, Gab. N. Stampe) has a vividness and freshness that recalls Cigoli, whose influence is likewise apparent in many of Cristofano's studies for individual figures (examples in Florence, Uffizi; Paris, Louvre).

In this period Cristofano also painted landscapes (untraced) that were greatly praised by Baldinucci, who recorded that the artist went into the countryside around Florence to sketch. He may have used such drawings as the *Landscape* (Florence, Uffizi; 869P) and the *Study of Trees and Mountain* (Florence, Uffizi; 870P) as studies for the background of religious pictures. His approach was influenced by Adriano Fiammingo, who is documented in Cigoli's studio *c.* 1600. The *Landscape with Scenes of Tobias and the Angel* (1618–21; Florence, priv. col.; see 1986–7 exh. cat., p. 180) suggests that through Fiammingo he absorbed the northern landscape style of Paul Bril and that, like contemporary landscape artists in Florence such as Remigio Cantagallina and Jacques Callot, he was moving towards a fresher, more natural style. He was also celebrated for his portraits, among which are the vivid and penetrating *Bernardo Davanzati* (*c.* 1605; Oxford, Ashmolean), the *Portrait of a Young Man in Black* (*c.* 1605; Florence, Pitti) and a *Portrait of a Youth* (Brunswick, ME, Bowdoin Coll. Mus. A.).

2. MATURE WORKS, 1605–21. In the period *c.* 1605–18 Cristofano, whose principal patrons were Grand Duke Cosimo II de' Medici, Maria Maddalena of Austria, the Archduchess Christine of Lorraine and the poet Michelangelo Buonarroti the younger, emerged as one of the most individual painters in Florence, and certainly the most patronized. His commission in 1605 for the ceiling painting of the *Embarkation of Marie de' Medici for Marseille*, for the church of the Cavalieri di Stefano, Pisa (*in situ*), is evidence of his growing reputation. Yet he was the least productive of the leading painters of this period and from 1606 delayed or failed to finish a number of the important commissions he received. These included the vast *Resurrection*, commissioned for the cathedral in Pistoia in 1601, on which he worked in 1602 and again in 1606–10 (h. *c.* 19 m, *in situ*); the *Virgin Giving the Rosary to St Dominic* (*c.* 1609; Pistoia, S Domenico); the large, unfinished *Adoration of the Magi* (1611; Florence, Pitti); the *Virgin and Saints in Glory* (1606–10; Pisa Cathedral), finished in 1625 by Zanobi Rosi (1580/90–1633); and *Michelangelo and the Muse of Poetry* (started 1615, finished 1622 by Rosi; Florence, Casa Buonarroti).

In these years Cristofano also painted the works that established his reputation: *St Francis Receiving the Stigmata* (1612–18; version, Rome, Mus. Francescano), *St Francis in Prayer* (1618–21; Florence, Pitti), both known in many replicas and copies, and *St Catherine of Siena in Prayer* (1612–18; version, Dallas, TX, S. Methodist U., Meadows Mus. & Gal.)—all marked by the intense emotionalism of the Florentine Baroque. The *Hospitality of St Julian* (1612–18; Florence, Pitti; see fig. 1) is distinguished by graceful movement, lyrical mood and psychological delicacy. There are many preparatory studies (Florence, Uffizi), most in black and red chalk on blue paper, rehearsing the poses of individual figures and details of arms and legs. The *Judith with the Head of Holofernes* (*c.* 1615; version, Florence, Pitti; see fig. 2) was celebrated in poetry by Giambattista Marino (1619), copied numerous times and remained the most famous Florentine Baroque painting throughout the 18th and 19th centuries. Cristofano's mistress, La Mazzafirra, coolly beautiful and clad in boldly coloured and courtly dress, was the model for Judith, and her mother for Abra (Baldinucci). The severed head of Holofernes is a self-portrait.

Cristofano was also celebrated for a distinctive type of painting: small, multi-figured scenes, monumental in composition and energetically painted *alla prima*, using a loaded brush and bold handling. The 15 known paintings of this type raise questions of dating and purpose. Some, such as the *Resurrection* (Florence, Uffizi) and the *Virgin and Child with Saints* (Lawrence, U. KS, Spencer Mus. A.), are preparatory studies for known paintings. Others may have been made as independent oil sketches at different times in Cristofano's career (see Pizzorusso in 1986–7 exh. cat.; Chappell, 1987). From 1619 to 1621 Cristofano, confined

1. Cristofano Allori: *Hospitality of St Julian*, oil on canvas, 2.59×2.02 m, 1612–18 (Florence, Palazzo Pitti)

2. Cristofano Allori: *Judith with the Head of Holofernes*, oil on canvas, 1.39×1.16 m, *c.* 1615 (Florence, Palazzo Pitti)

to bed with a fatal illness, could paint only with the use of a specially designed table (Baldinucci). Many of the oil sketches, particularly those whose abbreviated execution shows marked similarities, such as the three versions of the *Martyrdom of St Stephen*, the *David and Goliath* and the *Susanna and the Elders* (1619–21; all Florence, Uffizi), and those sketches that repeat specific themes, may date from this period.

Cristofano Allori had many pupils and followers, including Lorenzo Cerrini, Monanno Monanni, Lorenzo dal Borgo and, briefly, Cesare Dandini and Francesco Furini. His most devoted were Zanobi Rosi and Giovanni Battisti Vanni (1600–60), whose draughtsmanship and painting were greatly indebted to him (see Baldassari in 1986–7 exh. cat.). Allori's chief legacy to Florentine art was the lyricism of his style, comparable to the development in contemporary Florentine music of the *stile recitativo*, with its emphasis on clarity and beauty of melodic line (Bigongiari), a direction pursued in painting by such artists as Jacopo Vignali and Carlo Dolci.

BIBLIOGRAPHY

DBI; Thieme–Becker

F. Baldinucci: *Notizie* (1681–1728); ed. F. Ranalli (1845–7), iii, pp. 717–38

L. Berti: *Bozzetti delle gallerie di Firenze* (Florence, 1952)

M. Gregori: 'Cristofano Allori', *Mostra del Cigoli e del suo ambiente* (exh. cat., ed. M. Bucci and others; S Miniato, Accad. Buteleti, 1959), pp. 220–23

E. K. Waterhouse: *Italian Baroque Painting* (London, 1962), pp. 156–7

C. del Bravo: 'Su Cristofano Allori', *Paragone*, xviii/205 (1967), pp. 68–83

C. Thiem: 'Zum Frühwerk des Cristofano Allori', *Pantheon*, xxxi (1973), pp. 131–7

Disegni italiani del paesaggio (exh. cat. by M. Chiarini, Florence, Uffizi, 1973), p. 28, no. 27

Disegni e bozzetti di Cristofano Allori (exh. cat. by G. Cantelli and G. Chelazzi Dini, Florence, Pal. Strozzi, 1974)

M. L. Chappell: 'Portraits and Pedagogy in a Painting by Cristofano Allori', *Ant. Viva*, xvi/5 (1977), pp. 20–34

M. Gregori: 'Note su Cristofano Allori', *Scritti di storia dell'arte in onore di Ugo Procacci*, ed. M. G. C. D. dal Poggetto and P. dal Poggetto (Milan, 1977), pp. 520–26

C. Thiem: *Florentiner Zeichner des Frühbarock* (Munich, 1977), pp. 330–34, nos 91–6

Painting in Florence, 1600–1700 (exh. cat. by C. McCorquodale, London, RA, 1979), pp. 17–21, nos 1–3

P. Bigongiari: *Il caso e il caos: Il seicento fiorentino tra Galileo e il 'recitar cantando'* (Milan, 1974/*R* Florence, 1982)

C. Pizzorusso: *Ricerche su Cristofano Allori* (Florence, 1982)

G. Cantelli: *Repertorio della pittura fiorentina del seicento* (Fiesole, 1983), pp. 14–17

Cristofano Allori (exh. cat. by M. L. Chappell, Florence, Pitti, 1984)

Il seicento fiorentino (exh. cat., Florence, Pal. Strozzi, 1986–7), i, pp. 180, 181–91, nos 163–72; ii, pp. 131, 170–75, nos 77, 116–23; iii, pp. 31–3 [biog.]

M. L. Chappell: 'Cristofano Allori's *Madonna and Saints in Glory*', *Register* [Lawrence, U. KS, Spencer Mus. A.], vi/4 (1987), pp. 45–63

P. Bigongiari: 'Alcune riflessioni sul barocco fiorentino e un'ipotesi per il *San Pietro che cammina sulle acque*', *Studi di Storia dell'arte in onore di Mina Gregori* (Milan, 1994), pp. 238–44

MILES L. CHAPPELL

All-over painting. Term usually applied to abstract painting that has no traditional compositional structure, no dominant point of interest or any indication of which way is up. Examples include Jackson Pollock's Abstract Expressionist drip paintings (for illustration *see* POLLOCK, JACKSON).

□

Allston, Washington (*b* Waccamaw, SC, 5 Nov 1779; *d* Cambridgeport, MA, 9 July 1843). American painter. The son of a prominent South Carolina plantation owner of English descent, he began to draw around the age of six, and he moved to his uncle's home in Newport, RI, at the age of eight. While there he came into contact with the portrait painter Samuel King, but it was the exhibited portraits of Robert Edge Pine that offered him inspiring models of glazing and colouring. Dubbed 'the Count' by his Harvard College classmates for his way with fashion, Allston explored alternatives to the portrait tradition with landscapes, as well as with depictions of irrational figures, for example *Man in Chains* (1800; Andover, MA, Phillips Acad., Addison Gal.). After graduating in 1800 he sold his patrimony to fund study abroad.

In 1801 Allston went with Edward Greene Malbone to London, where he frequented the circle of Benjamin West and studied drawing at the Royal Academy. In late 1803 he departed with John Vanderlyn for Paris, where an enthusiasm for heroic landscape temporarily usurped the ideals that he had attached to history painting. Allston exhibited at the Royal Academy in 1802 and 1803, and at the Paris Salon of 1804, but he achieved his first critical success with *Diana and her Nymphs in the Chase* (1805; Cambridge, MA, Fogg; see fig.), which he painted in Rome soon after his arrival there in 1805. The monumental canvas presents Classical figures, a chasm rupturing the shore of a crystalline lake and a jagged, gleaming mountain beyond. Allston achieved his brilliant sunlight and strikingly transparent colour with a Venetian method of glazing readily learnt in London but little known in Paris or Rome; it cast him into the role of an international conduit for

Washington Allston: *Diana and her Nymphs in the Chase*, oil on canvas, 1.66×2.48 m, 1805 (Cambridge, MA, Fogg Art Museum)

ideas about painting technique and consolidated his reputation. While in Rome he painted several portraits including his *Self-portrait* (1805; Boston, MA, Mus. F.A.) and one of his friend *Samuel Taylor Coleridge* (1806; Cambridge, MA, Fogg).

Allston returned to Boston in 1808 and married the next year; during this stay he composed much of the verse that he published as a collection in 1813 and painted a few comic pieces, such as *The Poor Author and the Rich Bookseller* (1811; Boston, MA, Mus. F.A.). In 1811 he departed for London with his wife and his pupil, Samuel F. B. Morse. At this time he began to depict biblical themes, emphasizing in particular figural and facial expression. Participating in the current English vogue for resurrection imagery, Allston chose a rarely treated Old Testament subject, the *Dead Man Restored to Life by Touching the Bones of the Prophet Elisha* (1811–14; Philadelphia, PA Acad. F.A.). The prostrate protagonist, inspired by Louis-François Roubiliac's monument to *Gen. William Hargrave* (London, Westminster Abbey), unfurls his shroud and thereby illustrates the divine process of reanimation. The other figures' dramatic responses to this miracle exemplify Allston's Romantic historical style (*see also* UNITED STATES OF AMERICA, fig. 13). The prize awarded by the British Institution to the *Dead Man* in 1814 and purchases made by English aristocrats and Americans in London provided Allston with a decided degree of success. Yet around the time of the sudden death of his wife in 1815, he first met the financial pressures that would plague him for the balance of his career. Despite a first prize at the British Institution in 1818 for *Uriel in the Sun* (1817; U. Boston, MA, Mugar Mem. Lib.), Allston sailed for Boston that year.

Allston thought he had but several months' work remaining on a 3.6×4.8 m canvas that he had begun in London of *Belshazzar's Feast* (1817–18, 1820–28, 1839–43; Detroit, MI, Inst. A.), which, like West's treatment of the subject, emphasizes Daniel's act of interpretation. Allston intended from the outset to exhibit the canvas in America; the subject, a type of both the advent of the millennium and the Last Judgement, was especially potent for American audiences, given the formative role of Jeremiads in American thought. Before his recommencement of the project in 1820, Allston elaborated on the imagery of prophecy and divine vengeance in canvases featuring the Old Testament figures Miriam, Saul and Jeremiah (e.g. *Jeremiah Dictating his Prophecy of the Destruction of Jerusalem to Baruch the Scribe*, 1820; New Haven, CT, Yale U. A.G.), yet it was *Belshazzar's Feast* that he planned as his homecoming masterpiece, hoping it to be worthy of comparison with the great works of the past.

The ceaseless revisions that characterized Allston's work on the composition began with an overhaul of its spatial organization. Among the fruits of the protracted labours of 'Belshazzar's slave', as he referred to himself in 1825, were expressive chalk drawings (Cambridge, MA, Fogg) of the King's fear-stricken hands. In the winter of 1825–6 illness interrupted Allston's progress, just as it had in 1813 when work on the *Dead Man* undermined his health. Given Allston's European successes, technical sophistication and intellectualism, such exertions only enhanced for many Americans his identification with the Romantic ideal of the fine arts. By 1827 twelve patrons had created a fund of £10,000 to free Allston from financial pressures; this increased his sense of obligation to complete the canvas, although the original idea must have been long lost to him. Moving to a smaller studio in 1828, Allston stored the canvas until 1839, when he began a final and unsuccessful period of work on it. Insecurity about his fitness for the task had progressively overwhelmed his aspirations, and he never completed the canvas.

In 1830 Allston married his late wife's cousin and moved to Cambridgeport, MA. While he had painted solitary, idealized women from the time of his first marriage, in his later years he was persistently concerned with depicting the single figure. The shimmering, mist-filled setting of his richly coloured and heavily glazed *Spanish Girl in Reverie* (1831; New York, Met.) creates a mood conducive to peaceful reflection, although the figure's poised right hand and the towering peaks beyond contribute dramatic counterpoints. Such cabinet pictures and his late landscapes (e.g. *Italian Landscape*, *c.* 1828–30; Detroit, MI, Inst. A.), exhibited in the major retrospective of his works in Boston in 1839, set the tone for his posthumous reputation as a refined and poetic Romantic genius. Allston inspired numerous American artists including William Page and the sculptor Horatio Greenough.

WRITINGS

R. H. Dana jr, ed.: *Lectures on Art and Poems* (New York, 1850) [essays composed in the 1830s; the first art treatise by an American]

BIBLIOGRAPHY

J. B. Flagg: *The Life and Letters of Washington Allston* (New York, 1892)
E. P. Richardson: *Washington Allston: A Study of the Romantic Artist in America* (Chicago, 1948, rev. New York, 1967)
E. Johns: 'Washington Allston's *Dead Man Revived*', *A. Bull.*, lxi (1979), pp. 79–99
'A Man of Genius': The Art of Washington Allston (1779–1843) (exh. cat. by W. H. Gerdts and T. E. Stebbins jr, Boston, Mus. F.A., 1979)
B. J. Wolf: 'Romanticism and Self-consciousness: Washington Allston', *Romantic Re-vision: Culture and Consciousness in Nineteenth-century American Painting and Literature* (Chicago and London, 1982), pp. 3–77
D. Bjelajac: *Millennial Desire and the Apocalyptic Vision of Washington Allston* (Washington, DC, 1988)

DAVID STEINBERG

Alma, Petrus (*b* Medan, Sumatra, 18 Jan 1886; *d* Amsterdam, 23 May 1969). Dutch painter and printmaker. He trained at the Academie voor Beeldende Kunsten in The Hague (1904–6). From 1907 until 1914 he stayed in Paris, where he worked at Studio Humbert. Initially he used an impressionistic style, but after contact with Dutch artists in Paris, including Conrad Kikkert (1882–1965), Piet Mondrian and Lodewijk Schelfhout (1881–1943), *c.* 1914 he became influenced by Cubism. In 1912 he took part in the Sonderbund exhibition in Cologne and in 1915 he exhibited at the Kunstkring in Rotterdam with Henri Le Fauconnier and Mondrian. In 1921 he travelled to the USSR, where he met Vasily Kandinsky, El Lissitzky, Vladimir Tatlin and Kazimir Malevich. In 1923 Alma organized the exhibition of contemporary Russian art at the Stedelijk Museum in Amsterdam, which had been shown as the Erste russische Kunstausstellung in the Galerie van Diemen in Berlin in 1922. His first one-man show was held at the Stedelijk Museum in 1924. From 1929 until 1931 he worked at the Institut für Bildstatistik (Pictogram Institute, originally part of the Gesellschafts- und Wirtschaftsmuseum) in Vienna. During this period he made a series of eight woodcut *Social Portraits* (Amsterdam, Stedel. Mus.), showing a priest, dancer, diplomat, jailer, etc. In 1932–3 he introduced the pictogram into the USSR. From the 1930s he received many monumental commissions, especially in Amsterdam. In 1966–7 a retrospective exhibition of his work was organized at the Stedelijk Museum in Amsterdam.

BIBLIOGRAPHY

Petrus Alma 80 jaar (exh. cat., Amsterdam, Stedel. Mus., 1966)
Petrus Alma 1886–1969 (exh. cat., Amsterdam, Ksthandel M. L. de Boer, 1975)

JOHN STEEN

Almada. Portuguese family of administrators and patrons.

(1) João de Almada e Melo (*b* Troviscoso, Monção, 15 Aug 1703; *d* Oporto, 3 Oct 1786). He was a cousin of Sebastian Carvalho e Melo, 1st Marquês de Pombal, and held influential posts in the city of Oporto until his death: Governador das Armas do Porto (from 1757), Governador das Justiças da Relação (from 1764) and first President of the Junta das Obras Públicas. In this last position he was responsible for extensive urban alterations to Oporto from 1763 onwards, including Rua de Almada, Rua de S João, Praça de S Ana with the chapel of S Roque, Rua de S António and improvements made to Praça da Ribeira. John Whitehead, architect and British Consul (1756–1802), has been attributed with the project of the Casa da Feitoria. Two notable buildings in Oporto from the second half of the 18th century are the hospital of S Auronio by the English architect John Carr and the Relação Prison and Court by the engineer-architect Eugenio dos Santos e Carvalho (1711–60), who was also responsible for the majority of the reconstruction work done in Lisbon after the earthquake of 1755.

(2) Francisco de Almada e Mendonça (*b* Olivais, *bapt* 28 Feb 1757; *d* Oporto, 19 Aug 1804). Son of (1) João de Almada e Melo. He studied law at the Universidade de Coimbra and from 1784 held important posts in Oporto and northern Portugal, including Corregidor e Provedor da Comarca, Intendente da Marinha and Inspector das Obras Públicas. The buildings constructed in Oporto under his supervision include the barracks of S Ovídio (1790), the Alameda das Fontainhas (1790) and the Teatro de S João (1796; destr. 1908) by the Italian designer Vicente Mazzoneschi. Almada e Mendonça is also associated with various building projects (all 1784–1804) in northern Portugal, including the council building at Póvoa de Varzim, the bridges of Vila do Conde and S Tirso across the River Ave, and the main church at Valongo.

BIBLIOGRAPHY

J. Gandra: 'Apontamentos biográficos do Dr Francisco d'Almada e Mendonça', *Bol. Amigos Porto*, i (1951), pp. 23–35
C. de Passos: 'Os Almadas: Reformadores do Porto', *Bol. Amigos Porto*, iii (1960), pp. 3–39
B. J. Ferrão: *Projecto e transformação urbana do Porto na época dos Almadas, 1758–1813: Uma contribuição para o estudo da cidade pombalina* (Oporto, 1985)

J. J. B. Ferreira Alves: *O Porto na época dos Almadas, 1757–1804: Arquitectura: Obras públicas*, 2 vols (Oporto, 1987–8)

JOAQUIM JAIME B. FERREIRA ALVES

Almada Negreiros(, José Sobral de) (*b* Cape Verde, 7 April 1893; *d* Lisbon, 15 June 1970). Portuguese painter, draughtsman and writer. His early caricatures attracted the attention of the poet Fernando Pessoa whose posthumous portrait he painted in 1954 (Lisbon, Câmara Mun.; replica, 1964, Lisbon, Mus. Gulbenkian). He choreographed, designed and danced in a number of ballets (1915–19), before spending a year (1919–20) in Paris. In 1925 two of his paintings were among those chosen to hang in the Lisbon café A Brasileira. After returning to Lisbon from a sojourn in Madrid (1927–32), he married in 1934 the painter Sara Affonso with whom he portrayed himself in a double portrait (1934–6; Lisbon, Mus. Gulbenkian). He retained the sinuous, elegant quality of his line which in the 1930s and 1940s owed a great deal to Picasso.

Almada's most important pictorial projects were frescoes (*see* PORTUGAL, fig. 9) for the two principal quays of the port of Lisbon: the Gare Marítima de Alcântara (1943–5) and the Gare Marítima da Rocha (1946–8). He also designed stained-glass windows, ceramic tile-panels and tapestry cartoons. His last major project was the intaglio mural *Beginning* (1969; Lisbon, lobby of Gulbenkian), a vast geometrical abstraction based on complex geometrical and metaphysical precepts.

Almada's career as a polemicist began in 1915, with the *Manifesto anti-Dantas e por extenso* ('Complete anti-Dantas manifesto'). He also wrote numerous novels (e.g. *Nome de guerra*, 1925, pubd 1938), plays and poems. In 1917 he organized a Futurist evening at the Teatro Republicano, in which Santa-Rita also took part. He contributed texts and drawings to numerous periodicals, including *Orpheu* in 1915 and *A contemporânea* in 1922, founding and editing his own, *Sudoeste*, which was published in three issues in 1935.

WRITINGS

Obras completas, 2 vols (Lisbon, 1985–6)

BIBLIOGRAPHY

Almada Negreiros (exh. cat., ed. J. Sommer Ribeiro; Lisbon, Mus. Gulbenkian, 1984)

J.-A. França: *Amadeo de Souza-Cardoso: O Português à força. Almada Negreiros: O Português sem mestre* (Lisbon, 1986)

RUTH ROSENGARTEN

Almain, Steven [Alman, the]. *See* HASCHENPERG, STEFAN VON.

Almăşanu, Virgil (*b* Baccealia, Bessarabia [now Bakchaliya, Moldova], 28 Feb 1926). Romanian painter. He studied at the Academy of Fine Art in Bucharest (1945–52), and from 1954 undertook several study tours in Italy and France. He established his reputation between 1954 and 1959 with landscapes and portraits that were subtle in colour and showed the influence of Ion Andreescu, Camil Ressu and Dumitru Ghiaţă (e.g. *Landscape at Grozăvesti*, 1954; Suceava, Distr. Mus.). From 1965 he concentrated on large-scale official commissions, which he painted in a style unaffected by the accepted academic views of the time, and that were contemporary while still having thematic and stylistic elements from earlier periods in Romanian art (e.g. *Epitaph*, 1967; Bucharest, Mus. A.). The constructive synthesis of his forms and volumes is based on a continuous dynamism of planes and linear rhythms, originating from the Cubist decomposition of forms, and from the Neo-classical mode between the two World Wars, especially that practised by Picasso and Jacques Villon. In his large historical compositions, which in their rhythm and use of colour show the influence of *Art informel*, he evoked the Revolution of 1848, the peasants' uprising of 1907, and the representation of Michael the Brave, a great symbolical figure of Romanian national history. He used a wide range of greys, with scattered lagoons of fading opaque yellow or of sombre or matt reds. In a series of still-lifes (*Fruit Dishes*) painted between 1970 and 1972 the subject is absorbed in the lyrical metaphor of the lines and colour nuances, recalling the visual subtlety of Ben Nicholson. Between 1959 and 1978 Almăşanu worked on a number of monumental decorative compositions, such as a fresco for a Youth Cultural Centre in Bucharest (1959) and a project for murals at the National Theatre in Bucharest (unaccomplished). From 1986 to 1990 he lived in California, concentrating on landscapes and still-lifes, often containing flowers.

BIBLIOGRAPHY

L. Lambertini: 'V. Almăşanu la bienala de la Veneţia', *Arta* (1968), no. 8, p. 27

T. Enescu: *Virgil Almăşanu* (Bucharest, 1979)

THEODOR ENESCU

Alma-Tadema. English artists.

(1) Sir **Lawrence** [Laurens, Lorenz, Lourens] **Alma-Tadema** [Alma Tadema] (*b* Dronrijp, Friesland, 8 Jan 1836; *d* Wiesbaden, 28 June 1912). Painter and designer of Dutch birth. The son of a notary, Alma-Tadema demonstrated an early artistic ability. In 1852 he entered the Antwerp Academy, where he studied under Gustaf, Baron Wappers, and Nicaise de Keyser. An important influence at this time was Louis De Taye, Professor of Archaeology at the academy and a practising artist. Alma-Tadema lived and worked with De Taye from 1857 to 1859 and was encouraged by him to depict subjects from the early history of France and Belgium. This taste for historical themes increased when Alma-Tadema entered Baron Henri Leys's studio in 1859 and began assisting him with his monumental frescoes for the Antwerp Town Hall. While in Leys's studio, Alma-Tadema produced several major paintings, for example the *Education of the Children of Clovis* (1861; ex-Sir John Pender priv. col., see Zimmern, p. 3) and *Venantius Fortunatus Reading his Poems to Radagonda* (1862; Dordrecht, Dordrechts Mus.), which are characterized by their obscure Merovingian subject-matter, rather sombre colouring and close attention to detail.

In 1863 Alma-Tadema travelled to Italy, where his enthusiastic exploration of Pompeii turned his attention from the Dark Ages to the Ancient World. His interest in this period was further strengthened both by his friendship with the Egyptologist Georg Ebers (1837–98) and by the success of his painting *Pastimes in Ancient Egypt: 3000 Years Ago* (1863; Preston, Harris Mus. & A.G.), which won a gold medal at the Paris Salon of 1864. During a visit to Paris in that year Alma-Tadema was introduced to Jean-Léon Gérôme, one of the Néo-Grec school whose classical genre painting had much in common with Alma-Tadema's work. During this period he also came to the notice of Ernest Gambart, an influential Victorian dealer, who commissioned a series of paintings from the artist. Most of these were Classical subjects, such as *Tibullus at Delia's* (1866; Boston, MA, Mus. F.A.), whose detailed interior and rich 'Pompeian' colouring were typical of his style during the late 1860s.

Alma-Tadema had moved to Brussels in 1865, but when his first wife died and Gambart successfully promoted his work in England, he settled permanently in London in 1870. His reputation in England was based on such major paintings as *Phidias and the Parthenon* (1868; Birmingham, Mus. & A.G.), *Pyrrhic Dance* (1869; London, Guildhall A.G.) and *Vintage Festival* (1870; Hamburg, Ksthalle). *Vintage Festival* is a good example of the illusionistic portrayal of marble at which Alma-Tadema excelled. In these pictures, he sought to emphasize the material reality and human interest of the past. This combination of archaeology and genre had little in common with the detached idealism of English classical painters such as Frederic Leighton, although Alma-Tadema's pictures of ancient Egypt, notably *Death of the First Born* (1872; Amsterdam, Rijksmus.), can be compared to similar works by Edward Poynter and Edwin Long.

After Alma-Tadema's move to England, a gradual change in his style became apparent. A progressive lightening of his palette softened the darker colours of his earlier work and introduced a new luminosity to paintings such as *Sculpture Gallery* (1874; Hanover, NH, Dartmouth Coll., Hood Mus. A.). This was also apparent in his watercolours, which were frequently used as replicas or as preliminary studies for his oil paintings, for example *Balneatrix* (1876; Paris, Setton priv. col., see Swanson, pl. 10).

During the 1870s and 1880s Alma-Tadema rose to professional and social prominence in the Victorian art world. In 1871 he married the artist Laura Epps (*see* (2) below), and two years later he became a naturalized British citizen. By 1873 he was a member of the Old Water-Colour Society. The continuing success of his work at the Royal Academy exhibitions in London, in particular his large-scale paintings such as *Picture Gallery* (1874; Burnley, Towneley Hall A.G. & Mus.) and *Audience at Agrippa's* (1876; Kilmarnock, Dick Inst.), ensured his election as ARA (1876) and RA (1879). His position as a leading artist was reaffirmed by the major exhibition of his work held at the Grosvenor Gallery in 1882. The following year he moved to his residence in Grove End Road, which he had magnificently decorated in a variety of historical styles. Here the Alma-Tademas lavishly entertained the musical and artistic circles of London.

The latter part of Alma-Tadema's career was marked by a decline in the number of his pictures. Although the subject-matter remained relatively unchanged, there was less concern with illustrating actual historical events and more interest in scenes of a domestic and sentimental nature. A mild eroticism also became more apparent in his later work, such as *In the Tepidarium* (1881; Port Sunlight, Lady Lever A.G.). This move towards pure genre was paralleled by simpler compositions, as specific architecture was replaced by more generalized surroundings, for example in *Silver Favourites* (1903; Manchester, C.A.G.; see fig.). A notable exception to this trend was the *Finding of Moses* (1904; priv. col., see Gaunt, pl. 16), painted after his visit to Egypt in 1902 and one of his most spectacular works.

One aspect of Alma-Tadema's art that gained in prominence during this period was his portraiture. He had always produced portraits, but his public reputation as a portrait painter dated only from the second half of his career, when he painted a large number of leading figures, for instance the *Rt Hon. Arthur James Balfour* (1891; London, N.P.G.).

In the 1880s and 1890s Alma-Tadema was also involved in stage design. Originally commissioned to design the sets for Henry Irving's *Coriolanus* in 1880, he went on to produce designs for Charles Kingsley's *Hypatia* (1896) and *Cymbeline* (1897) and Beerbohm Tree's *Julius Caesar* (1898). The historical accuracy of his designs, including furniture and costumes, was remarkable by 19th-century standards and was based on his huge collection of archaeological drawings and photographs. In 1906 the RIBA awarded him their gold medal for the consummate depiction of ancient architecture in his paintings. His paintings

Lawrence Alma-Tadema: *Silver Favourites*, oil on panel, 691×422 mm, 1903 (Manchester, City Art Gallery)

were later a strong influence on D. W. Griffith and the early cinema. Alma-Tadema was a prolific artist, who carefully inscribed each of his works with an opus number (I–CCCCVIII). Knighted in 1899, he was awarded the OM in 1907.

BIBLIOGRAPHY

G. Ebers: 'Lorenz Alma-Tadema', *Westermann's Mhft.* (Nov–Dec 1885); Eng. trans. as *Lorenz Alma-Tadema: His Life and Works* (New York, 1886)
H. Zimmern: 'L. Alma-Tadema, RA', *A. J.* [London] (1886) [special suppl.], pp. 1–29
F. Dolman: 'Illustrated Interviews, LXVIII: Sir Lawrence Alma-Tadema, RA', *Strand Mag.*, xviii (1899), pp. 603–14
R. P. Spiers: *The Architecture of 'Coriolanus' at the Lyceum Theatre* (London, 1901)
P. Standing: *Sir Lawrence Alma-Tadema, OM, RA* (London, 1905)
R. Dircks: 'The Later Works of Sir Lawrence Alma-Tadema OM, RA', *A. J.* [London] (1910) [Christmas issue], pp. 1–26
W. Gaunt: *Victorian Olympus* (London, 1952)
M. Amaya: 'The Roman World of Alma-Tadema', *Apollo*, lxxvii (1962), pp. 771–8
J. Maas: *Gambert: Prince of the Victorian Art World* (London, 1975)
Victorian Olympians (exh. cat., ed. R. Free; Sydney, A.G. NSW, 1975), pp. 12–16
Sir Lawrence Alma-Tadema, 1836–1912 (exh. cat., ed. A. Goodchild; Sheffield, Mappin A.G., 1976)
V. Swanson: *Sir Lawrence Alma-Tadema: The Painter of the Victorian Vision of the Ancient World* (London, 1977)
M. Raven: 'Alma-Tadema als amateur-egyptoloog', *Bull. Rijksmus.*, iii (1980), pp. 103–18
R. Ash: *Sir Lawrence Alma-Tadema* (London, 1989)
L. Lippincot: *Lawrence Alma-Tadema: 'Spring'* (Malibu, CA, 1990)
V. G. Swanson: *The Biography and Catalogue Raisonné of the Paintings of Sir Lawrence Alma-Tadema* (London, 1990)
R. Tomlinson: *The Athens of Alma-Tadema* (Stroud, 1991)

ALISON INGLIS

(2) Lady **Laura (Theresa) Alma-Tadema** [née Epps] (*b* London, 17 April 1852; *d* London, 15 Aug 1909). Painter and illustrator, wife of (1) Lawrence Alma-Tadema. At an early age she made copies from the Antique in the British Museum, London, and later studied at the British Museum School under William Cave Thomas (1820–*c.* 1884) and William Bell Scott. In 1870 she began her studies with Lawrence Alma-Tadema, whose second wife she became in 1871. The principal subjects of her paintings are children at play, often placed in 17th-century Dutch settings, among Dutch furniture and accessories modelled on those in her husband's collection. She emphasized everyday scenes in domestic interiors, as seen in *Airs and Graces* (Amsterdam, Rijksmus.). Although the costumes and setting of this painting, as well as the general composition with the light coming from a window on the right, are characteristic of 17th-century Dutch works, the anecdotal sentiment conveyed by the pretty, graceful girls dancing vainly is thoroughly Victorian in feeling. She also painted children in contemporary settings, portraits of children (mainly in pastel), still-lifes (e.g. *Still-life with a Self-portrait*, The Hague, Rijksmus. Mesdag) and some Classical subjects. From 1873 she exhibited at the Royal Academy of Arts and in other galleries in London and elsewhere in Great Britain. She also showed in Berlin and Paris and in 1878 was one of only two women to be invited to participate in the Exposition Universelle in Paris, where she was awarded a silver medal. She also produced illustrations for the *English Illustrated Magazine*. She travelled frequently with her husband to Italy, where she executed a number of small landscape studies, and to France, Belgium and the Netherlands. As she also signed her canvases *L. Alma-Tadema*, her paintings are sometimes confused with those of her husband. Her sister Ellen [Nellie] Gosse (*fl* 1879–90) and her stepdaughter Anna Alma-Tadema (1865–1943) were also painters.

BIBLIOGRAPHY

Meissner [with bibliog.]
A. Meynell: 'Laura Alma-Tadema', *A. J.* [London], n.s., iii (1883), pp. 345–7

□

Almaty [formerly Alma-Ata; Verny]. Capital of KAZAKHSTAN. Situated at the foot of the northern Zailiyskoye Alatau mountain range, the modern settlement was established in 1854 as a Russian fortification, initially called Zailiyskoye but soon renamed Verny, on the site of medieval Almata. Archaeological finds in the locality bear witness to the assimilation of various cultures in this region from the middle of the 1st millennium AD. Its statute was granted in 1867, and it became the capital of the Semirechensky region. The city suffered greatly during earthquakes in 1887 and 1910 and also endured several landslides. In 1921 it was renamed Alma-Ata (now Almaty). In 1929 it became the capital of the Kazakh SSR and developed rapidly, especially with the construction of the Turkestan–Siberian railway. Most of its streets were reconstructed and the city was replanned as a network of avenues and boulevards. Prominent architects of the USSR participated in the construction of major buildings. A second stage of intensive construction took place after World War II. The outstanding cathedral (1907; architect A. P. Zenkov) is one of the largest wood constructions in the world. The Central Museum of Kazakhstan houses comprehensive collections of archaeological relics found throughout the republic. Archaeological discoveries are also well represented in the museum affiliated to the Institute of History, Archaeology and Ethnography at the Academy of Sciences. Collections of Kazakh and Russian art are on display at the Kasteyev Museum of the Art of Kazakhstan, formerly the T. G. Shevchenko Art Gallery.

BIBLIOGRAPHY

A. A. Goryacheva: *Osnovaniye i razvitiye goroda Vernogo* [The founding and development of Verny] (Moscow, 1952)
M. M. Mendikulov: *Arkhitektura goroda Alma-Ata* [The architecture of Alma-Ata] (Alma-Ata, 1953)

A. V. IVANOV

Almeida, Belmiro (Barbosa) de (*b* Cerro, 1858; *d* Paris, 1935). Brazilian painter and caricaturist. Brought as a child from the interior of the state of Minas Gerais to Rio de Janeiro, he graduated in 1877 from the Academia Imperial das Belas Artes. By then he had already published his first caricatures in the Rio press, and he continued to be a frequent contributor to such humorous periodicals as *O Binóculo*, *O Rataplan* (which he founded in 1886), *O Mercúrio*, *A Bruxa*, *O Malho*, *Fon-Fon!* and *Don Quixote*. He first went to Europe in 1888, where he finished his studies with Jules Lefebvre in Paris and travelled to Italy. On his return to Brazil at the beginning of the 1890s, he taught drawing at the Escola Nacional de Belas Artes in Rio de Janeiro, but he spent most of the latter part of his life in Paris. There, despite the underlying academicism from which his work was never entirely free and unlike the majority of Brazilian artists of the time, he showed genuine interest in the avant-garde developments of modernist art.

Essentially Almeida was a realist who, with a healthy dose of mordacity and humour, tried to capture the life that went on around him in pictures such as *Lovers' Tiffs* (1887), *Chatterbox* (1893) and *Fine Weather* (1893; all Rio de Janeiro, Mus. N. B.A.). His *Landscape at Dampierre* (1912; Rio de Janeiro, priv. col., see Pontual, p. 66) makes slightly dated use of Georges Seurat's pointillism but blends it with the angular and geometrically precise composition characteristic of Cubism. Similarly, *Woman in Circles* (1921; Rio de Janeiro, priv. col., see Pontual, p. 67) illustrates his cautious assimilation of Futurist energy, fusing it with a basically Art Nouveau atmosphere. Such a synthesis of progressive styles places him among the precursors of modernism in Brazil.

BIBLIOGRAPHY

Pontual

L. Gonzaga Duque: *A arte brasileira* (Rio de Janeiro, 1888)

J. M. dos Reis Júnior: *História de pintura no Brasil* (São Paulo, 1944)

A. Galvão: *Subsídios para a história da Academia Imperial e da Escola Nacional de Belas Artes* (Rio de Janeiro, 1954)

H. Lima: *História da caricatura no Brasil* (Rio de Janeiro, 1963)

ROBERTO PONTUAL

Almeida, Feliciano de (*b* Lisbon, 1634; *d* Lisbon, 1695). Portuguese painter. He was a member of the Irmandade de S Lucas, the guild of painters in Lisbon. An able portrait painter, Almeida won the praise of Felix da Costa. He painted the portrait of *Edward Montagu, 1st Earl of Sandwich* (Hinchingbrooke House, Cambs) in 1663, when the English admiral and diplomat visited Lisbon for the wedding of Catherine of Braganza; the Earl described the portrait in his diary as 'an extraordinary like Picture'. Almeida was a knight of the royal household and was in contact with such painters as António de Sousa (*fl* 1658–87), court painter to Peter II. He also assessed private collections, notably that of the Bishop of the Algarve, José de Menezes, about which he wrote a report in 1680. He is also known to have painted religious subject-matter, but these works are untraced.

BIBLIOGRAPHY

F. da Costa Meesen: *Antiguidade da arte da pintura* (MS.; 1696); ed. G. Kubler (New Haven and London, 1967), p. 272

C. Ferreira: 'Documentos da Biblioteca da Ajuda referentes a pintores e pinturas antigas', *A. & Arqueol.* [Coimbra], i/3 (1930), p. 183

C. de Azevedo: 'Um retrato português em Inglaterra', *Rev. Fac. Let.*, xxii, n.s. 2, i (1956), pp. 263–70

VITOR SERRÃO

Almeida, Jorge de, Bishop of Coimbra (*b* Lisbon, 1458; *d* Coimbra, 1543). Portuguese bishop and patron. He was the son of Lopo de Almeida, the 1st Conde de Abrantes (*d* 1508), and brother of Francisco de Almeida (1450–1510), the first viceroy of India. Jorge de Almeida was closely connected with the royal court of Portugal and in 1490 accompanied John II to the border of Spain to meet the King's future daughter-in-law, Isabella of Castile (1470–98). As Bishop of Coimbra, he instituted a systematic revival of art at a particularly fortunate period of history, facilitated by the length of his episcopal rule (1481–1543). He was the principal benefactor of the Sé Velha (Old Cathedral, *c.* 1150–1200) in Coimbra, which he began to modernize in 1498 by giving it suitable surroundings and widening its broad façade. At the same time, with the permission of the chapter, he commissioned from the Flemish wood-carvers Jean d'Ypres (*fl* 1498–1510) and Olivier of Ghent a magnificent Gothic retable of gilt and polychromed wood, completed in 1502. In 1503, continuing his policy of enriching the cathedral, he had the interior walls lined with 10,000 *azulejos* (Port.: 'glazed tiles') that he had purchased in Seville. His most important contribution to the cathedral was the commissioning from João de Ruão of the Porta Especiosa (*c.* 1535) on the north front. Perhaps replacing a temporary structure connected with the ceremonial entries of John III into Coimbra in 1526–7, the portal shows the influence of a new style encouraged by the presence of João de Ruão in the city and also reflects Italian models, particularly the west front (before 1474) of the Palazzo Ducale in Urbino. The rich collection of liturgical objects and vestments Jorge de Almeida left to the cathedral exemplifies the refined taste of his patronage. Above all, the collection is representative of the succession of styles favoured by 16th-century Portuguese society. Among significant pieces are a silver gilt monstrance (1527), Gothic in form and decoration but with some Renaissance elements, and a holy water vase (1551), made posthumously (both Coimbra, Mus. N. Machado de Castro). The decorative vocabulary of the latter consists of cartouches, garlands and atlantids that derive from Flemish Mannerist works, especially the engravings of Cornelis Bos.

See also COIMBRA.

BIBLIOGRAPHY

R. Moreira: 'Arquitectura', *Os descobrimentos portugueses e a Europa do renascimento* [Portuguese discoveries and Europe during the Renaissance] (exh. cat., Lisbon, Mus. N. A. Ant., 1983), pp. 307–52

Feitorias [Trading posts] (exh. cat., ed. P. Dias; Brussels, Europalia, 1991)

Portugal et Flandre (exh. cat., ed. R. Moreira; Brussels, Europalia, 1991)

MIGUEL SOROMENHO

Almeida, José de (*b* Lisbon, 1700; *d* Lisbon, 1769). Portuguese sculptor. He was the leading Portuguese sculptor of the mid-18th century, although only a small part of his work can be identified. He was sent to Rome by John V to study under Carlo Monaldi. Traces of his apprenticeship with Monaldi can be seen in his treatment of crumpled drapery. Almeida is known to have won a prize in a papal contest in competition with Italian sculptors. He returned to Lisbon about 1728 and formed a workshop that became very successful; it was renowned at the time, although almost all the production has been lost. He was the first Portuguese sculptor to carve well in stone at a time when most work in that medium was executed by foreigners and when other Portuguese sculptors generally preferred to work in clay or wood. Almeida's work in marble includes the statue of *St Paul* on the façade of the chapel of the Palácio das Necessidades, Lisbon. His marble statues of *St Elizabeth* and of *St John the Baptist* (begun in 1735), inside the portico of the chapel of Bemposta, later completed by Joaquim José de Barros Laborão, show the lightly agitated treatment of fabric that is characteristic of Almeida. These statues are hard and angular in character, and the presentation of the human body is rather lifeless, despite the accuracy of draughtsmanship.

Almeida's role in the important programme of decoration of the church and palace at Mafra is unclear. Also unknown is his relationship with the Italian sculptor Alessandro Giusti, who was said to have been his rival earlier in Rome. In Lisbon Giusti was commissioned by the King to replace the painted altarpieces at Mafra with relief sculpture. It is documented that Almeida carved the group of wood figures representing *Christ on the Cross between Two Kneeling Angels* (1730), intended to be installed provisionally above the high altar of the church at Mafra and replaced in 1731 by a group of the same subject in marble, sent by the Genoese sculptor Francesco Maria Schiaffino. In 1751 Almeida's group was placed in the apse of the church of S Estevão, Lisbon. These figures show how Almeida had absorbed the gestures of Roman Baroque, especially in the angels, one with hands clasped in prayer, the other with arms extended in a theatrical gesture; however, the undulating drapery, with the soft flowing quality also seen in the faces and manner of Almeida's statues, is more Rococo in style. Almeida inaugurated this phase in Portuguese figure sculpture, and he may also have created the prototype Rococo Virgin carved in gilt and polychromed wood, a type of image that is seen in many altarpieces of the period. Two of these statues of *Our Lady of the Immaculate Conception*, one in the church of Nossa Senhora da Conceição Velha, Lisbon, the other in the church of S Mamede, Lisbon (both *c.* 1750), have been attributed to him on the basis of an engraving of such a statue by Almeida, published in 1754, that shows the same delicately agitated garments seen in the angels at S Estevão (de Carvalho, 1963).

BIBLIOGRAPHY

Machado

D. de Macedo: *A escultura portuguesa nos séculos XVII e XVIII* (Lisbon, 1945)

A. de Carvalho: *A escultura de Mafra* (Mafra, 1950)

——: 'Os escultores José de Almeida e A. Giusti', *Belas A.*, 19 (1963), pp. 27–38

JOSÉ FERNANDES PEREIRA

Almeida, José Simões de. *See* SIMÕES DE ALMEIDA, JOSÉ.

Almeida, Sebastião Inácio de (*d* Lisbon, 1779). Portuguese potter and painter. He became director and painting master of the REAL FÁBRICA DO RATO in Lisbon after the expulsion in 1771 of the first director TOMÁS BRUNETTO. With his predecessor, Almeida is associated with the factory's most successful and distinctive period. Initially he collaborated with the potter and painter Severino José da Silva (*d* 1797) who was also vice-director and head of the potters' workshop. Almeida planned to reform the factory, but his ideas were thwarted in 1772 when the board of directors instructed him to dismiss many employees including da Silva and the painters João and Antonio Berardi. However, in 1777 Almeida was granted a ten-year monopoly, the conditions being that he was obliged to have six well-trained artisans at hand, and he was to be given all the materials he needed, provided that he reimbursed the board of directors within the ten-year period. There was a marked change in style in the wares produced at the factory under Almeida's direction. In particular, the large pieces enamelled with polychrome decoration were abandoned in favour of smaller and more delicately executed items of blue-and-white tableware that were influenced by wares from the Rouen faience factories (*see* ROUEN, §III). Almeida's brother José Baptista de Almeida became submaster of the potters' workshop in 1783.

BIBLIOGRAPHY

J. Queirós: *Cerâmica portuguesa* (Lisbon, 1907, rev. in 2 vols, 1948/*R* 1987)

G. de Matos Sequeira: *Depois do terremoto: Subsídios para a história dos bairros ocidentais de Lisboa*, iv (Lisbon, 1922–34)

R. dos Santos: *Oito séculos de arte portuguesa: História e espírito*, iii (Lisbon, 1970)

A. de Sandão: *Faiança portuguesa, séculos XVIII, XIX*, 2 vols (Oporto, 1976–85)

BERNADETTE NELSON

Almeida, Dom **Tomás de**, Patriarch of Lisbon (*b* Lisbon, 1670; *d* Lisbon, 1754). Portuguese ecclesiastic and patron. He was a member of the aristocratic Avintes family. He received a university education, and in the reign of Peter II held office from 1705 as Secretary of State and High Chancellor of the kingdom. He was appointed Bishop of Lamego in 1707 and of Oporto in 1709. In Oporto he revived an earlier plan of 1691 to construct a square, 120×120 m, which was intended to rival the Plaza Mayor in Madrid. However, with the end of the conflict between Spain and Portugal (the War of Succession) and his nomination as the first Patriarch of Lisbon in 1717, this ambitious project was abandoned. In his new appointment, which was created at the personal request of John V, Dom Tomás built a summer residence at Santo Antão do Tojal, Loures, near Lisbon, whose architect from 1727 to 1732 was the Italian Antonio Canevari. The scheme is a remarkable urban complex, which is both theatrical and rhetorical in style. An earlier church attached to the palace was restored and the façade redesigned, with statues of Carrara marble, reflecting Roman Baroque architecture. An aqueduct, also designed by Canevari, leads to an elaborate fountain, topped by a typical Joanine arch, set in the middle of one of the palace façades, which contains a suite of apartments for the King. This wing, together with another belonging to an earlier 16th-century palace that was then enlarged, surrounds a public square of irregular shape.

From 1740 Dom Tomás built the church of Senhor da Pedra (unfinished) at Obidos, designed by Rodrigo Franco. The centralized plan, consisting of a regular hexagon, constitutes an important innovation in Portuguese Baroque architecture.

BIBLIOGRAPHY

J. Fernandes Pereira: *A acção artística do primeiro Patriarca de Lisboa* (Lisbon, 1984)

M.-T. Mandroux França: 'Quatro fases da urbanização do Porto no século XVIII', *Bol. Cult. Camãra Mun. Porto*, 2nd ser., ii (1984), pp. 1–23

JOSÉ FERNANDES PEREIRA

Almeida, Valentim de (*fl* Lisbon, *c.* 1720–60). Portuguese decorative artist. His apprenticeship was probably undertaken with Master PMP, the painter of glazed tiles. His most important commission between 1729 and 1731 was for the panels of blue and white tiles, made in Lisbon, that cover the lower storey of the cloister of Oporto Cathedral, which represent scenes from the Song of Solomon. These panels are characteristic of the High Baroque phase of tile-making and show an appreciation of theatre and stage design in the deepening landscape backgrounds of the figurative panels, in the bold outlines and in the enlarged ornamental framing. The spectacular arched frames of the Oporto panels were influenced by Roman Baroque architectural ornament.

The attractive blue and white panels (*c.* 1735–45) in the cloister of the monastery of S Vicente de Fora, Lisbon, are attributable to Almeida. They contain landscapes, buildings, gardens, Baroque fountains, hunting scenes and other secular subjects, some after the engravings of Jean Le Pautre. The flying cherubs and figures that act as atlantids in the frames derive from contemporary Portuguese wood-carved retables. Almeida's panels in the church of S Pedro, Sintra, contain scenes from the life of St Peter (*c.* 1740), in which the *Miracle of the Fishes* is based on Raphael's tapestry cartoon of the same subject (London, V&A).

BIBLIOGRAPHY

F. Gonçalves: 'A data e a origem dos azulejos do claustro da Sé do Porto', *O comércio do Porto* (8 Feb, 14 March, 11 April, 11 July 1972)

J. Meco: *Azulejaria portuguesa* (Lisbon, 1985)

——: *O azulejo em Portugal* (Lisbon, 1986)

JOSÉ MECO

Almeida Júnior, José Ferraz de (*b* Itu, 1850; *d* Piracicaba, 1899). Brazilian painter. Deeply attached to the interior of the state of São Paulo, where he was born, Almeida Júnior returned there as soon as he had finished his studies with, among others, Victor Meirelles de Lima at the Academia Imperial das Belas Artes in Rio de Janeiro. Under the patronage of the Emperor Peter II he travelled to Europe in 1876 to complete his studies with Alexandre Cabanel in Paris. There from 1879 to 1882 he took part in the annual Salon of French Artists. The influence of Courbet's realism on works produced during his stay in France, such as *Brazilian Woodchopper* (1879; Rio de Janeiro, Mus. N. B.A.), remained in evidence on his return to Brazil in 1882, especially in his more picturesque paintings.

Although Almeida Júnior worked in many different genres, his most original paintings were those done late in life on rural themes vividly capturing the types and customs of life in the interior of the state of São Paulo. Such pictures as *São Paulo Woodsman Chopping Tobacco* (1893), *Knife-sharpening Interrupted* (1893) and *The Viol-player* (1899; all São Paulo, Pin. Estado), in spite of their relatively conventional technique, capture the essence of daily life in Brazil. His nationalism led him also to paint historical works such as the large canvas *Leaving Monção* (U. São Paulo, Mus. Paulista). Although he remained faithful to European styles, his genuine enthusiasm for rural everyday life in Brazil was untainted by academic pretentions and linked him to the Brazilianist tendency, which from the middle of the 1910s emerged in its maturity with the modernist revolution.

BIBLIOGRAPHY

S. Millet: *Pintores e pinturas* (São Paulo, 1940)

F. Acquarone: *Primores da pintura no Brasil* (Rio de Janeiro, 1941)

Art of Latin America since Independence (exh. cat. by S. L. Catlin and T. Grieder, New Haven, CT, Yale U. A.G.; Austin, U. TX, A. Mus.; San Francisco, CA, Mus. A.; La Jolla, CA, A. Cent.; 1966)

A. Amaral: *Pinacoteca do Estado de São Paulo* (São Paulo, 1982)

Q. Campofiorito: *História da pintura brasileira no século XIX* (Rio de Janeiro, 1983)

ROBERTO PONTUAL

Almeloveen, Jan van (*b* Mijdrecht, *c.* 1652; *d* after 1683). Dutch etcher and draughtsman. His birthplace and date are inscribed on his mezzotint portrait of his father, *Johannes ab Almeloveen* (1678; Hollstein, no. 38), who was a preacher in Mijdrecht. Jan's other 37 prints are all etchings, mainly landscapes. In his topographical views of Dutch rivers and occasionally the Rhine, van Almeloveen followed the tradition of established masters. Twenty of these landscapes are based on designs by Herman Saftleven, including a series of twelve depictions of Dutch villages such as *Langerack* and an unusual diamond-shaped series of the *Four Seasons*. The remaining, less lively compositions were made after his own designs. An annotation on one of his landscape drawings (Leiden, Rijksuniv., Prentenkab., AW #1008) indicates that on 8 August 1680 he was working at Frankfurt an der Oder, but he was presumably in Utrecht for most of the period from 1678 to 1683, when he dated his last known print, one in a series of six landscapes (Hollstein, 21–6).

BIBLIOGRAPHY

Hollstein: *Dut. & Flem.*

I. de Groot: *Landscape Etchings by the Dutch Masters of the Seventeenth Century* (Maarssen, 1979), nos 242–4

D. Freedberg: *Dutch Landscape Prints*, London, BM, cat. (London, 1980), pp. 66–7

I. de Groot and R. Vorstman: *Maritime Prints by the Dutch Masters* (London, 1980), p. 13, nos. 121–32

CHRISTIAAN SCHUCKMAN

Almohad [al-Muwaḥḥidūn]. Islamic dynasty that ruled parts of north-west Africa and Spain from 1130 to 1269. Muhammad ibn Tumart (*d* 1130), a Masmuda Berber, preached a faith based on the Koran and the Sunna, stressing above all the oneness of God (Arab. *tawḥīd*), a doctrine from which the movement took the name al-Muwaḥḥidūn ('believers in the oneness of God'). Ibn Tumart, who declared himself also as the infallible Mahdí, was able to unite disparate groups of Berbers and in 1121 began an insurrection against the ALMORAVID rulers with the help of the Berbers of the Atlas Mountains. After the conquest of the Anti-Atlas and Sus region, he emigrated to Tinmal (Tinmallal), south of Marrakesh in the High Atlas, an event likened to the Prophet's Hegira from Mecca to Medina in AD 622. A defeat near Marrakesh temporarily stopped the rise of the Almohads, and even Ibn Tumart's lieutenant and successor, ʿAbd al-Mu'min (*reg* 1130–63), could not conquer his arch-enemy, ʿAli ibn Yusuf (*reg* 1106–42). After the Almoravid's death, however, ʿAbd al-Mu'min conquered all of Morocco and Islamic Spain and made Marrakesh his capital. In 1152 he annexed the Hammadid state in Algeria and in 1160 put an end to ZIRID rule in Tunisia. For the first time the whole Maghrib was united under one dynasty, although some keepers of pure Almohad dogma opposed Ibn Tumart's Mu'minid successors.

Abu Yaʿqub Yusuf I (*reg* 1163–84) was killed in battle against the Christians near Santarém (Portugal), but his successor Abu Yusuf Yaʿqub (*reg* 1184–99) routed the Castilians near Alarcos in 1195 and took the epithet al-Mansur ('the Victorious'). Muhammad al-Nasir (*reg* 1199–1214) also fought the Christian kings of the peninsula, but he was decisively defeated at Las Navas de Tolosa (1212), and the decline of the Almohad empire began. After Abu Yusuf Yaʿqub II (*reg* 1214–24), Almohad shaykhs began to appoint the ruler, but a Spanish pretender, Idris I al-Ma'mun (*reg* 1229–32), supported by 500 Christian knights, conquered Marrakesh, massacred the shaykhs and condemned the Almohad dogma of the infallibility of the Mahdí and the memory of Ibn Tumart. In 1228 the HAFSID governor of Tunisia threw off the authority of the Almohad caliphs, and in 1269 the MARINID dynasty destroyed the remnants of the Almohad–Mu'minid empire in the west.

The Almohad courts at Marrakesh and Seville were centres of Islamic learning, especially philosophy, and art. Typical Almohad fortresses (*see* MILITARY ARCHITECTURE AND FORTIFICATION, §IV, 2), such as the walls of Fez, Rabat and Marrakesh, have brick or rammed earth curtains with rectangular towers and cut stone gates with splendid decoration. Perhaps the finest is the Udayas Gate, Rabat (after 1191), which has a richly carved horseshoe arch flanked by projecting salients. The Almohads replaced the Almoravid mosque in Marrakesh with the first Kutubiyya Mosque (1147–58; fell into ruin at an unknown date; *see* ISLAMIC ART, §II, 5(iv)(d)). The second Kutubiyya (begun 1158), an identical extension of the first slightly skewed to the south, has a large prayer-hall with 17 naves perpendicular to the qibla. An aisle along the qibla wall has five cupolas, soberly decorated with *muqarnas*. The minaret, a square tower standing more than 60 m high at the juncture of the two mosques, is decorated with network panels of foliate arches, and it served as a model for virtually all the later minarets in the region. The first Kutubiyya Mosque was equipped with an extraordinary wooden MAQṢŪRA (destr.), a screened enclosure that apparently rose from the floor when the ruler entered it, and other mosques (e.g. Fez, Andalusiyyin) have preserved contemporary minbars. The mosque in Tinmal (1153–4; *see* ISLAMIC ART, fig. 47) is notable for its careful geometric planning, fine lambrequin arches and *muqarnas* cupolas along the qibla wall and short minaret unusually placed over the mihrab. Of the new congregational mosque (1172–6) in Seville (*see* SEVILLE, §I, 1), only the courtyard, the stately minaret (La Giralda; *see* BRICK, fig. 13) and a portal survive in the present cathedral. After the victory at Alarcos, Ya'qub al-Mansur transformed a Moroccan coastal fortress into a city which he called *ribāṭ al-fatḥ* ('the fortress of victory'; *see* RABAT). The huge but unfinished congregational mosque, known as the mosque of Hasan, preserves the stump of a minaret planned to be 90 m high. Other important Almohad mosques include the mosque at Taza (1142) and the Qasba Mosque (1195) in Marrakesh.

Several copies of the Koran, attributable to the period, show that paper began to replace parchment during this period. Bookbindings with strapwork designs include an engraved, gilded and coloured binding for a copy of the Koran dated 1178 (Rabat, Bib. Gén. & Archvs, 12609) and a magnificent multi-volume copy of the Koran (London, BL, Or. 13192) penned in Marrakesh in 1256 by the penultimate Almohad sultan Abu Hafs 'Umar al-Murtada (*reg* 1248–66); this binding is the earliest dated example of gold tooling. The only illustrated manuscript attributable to the period is a copy (Rome, Vatican, Bib. Apostolica, MS. arab. 368) of the romance *Bayad and Riyad* (*see* ISLAMIC ART, fig. 106 and ISLAMIC ART, §III, 4(iv)(b)), probably produced *c.* 1200 in Morocco or Spain. The cast-bronze chandelier in the Andalusiyyin Mosque in Fez is the earliest surviving from North Africa; it probably dates from the reign of Ya'qub al-Nasir (1199–1214); a contemporary one in the Qarawiyyin Mosque was made from a Spanish church bell taken as booty. A cast-bronze fountain spout in the form of a lion (Paris, Louvre, 7883) engraved with textile-like patterns is also attributed to the period. Luxury silk textiles (*see* ISLAMIC ART, §VI, 2(i)(c)), most preserved in Christian contexts, were used for clothing and furnishing and, like bindings, show a trend towards geometricization. Perhaps the most famous is the splendid banner (3.3×2.2 m; Burgos, Real Monasterio de las Huelgas, Mus. Telas & Preseas) thought to have been an Almohad trophy won at the battle of Las Navas de Tolosa by Ferdinand III (*d* 1252; *see* ISLAMIC ART, §VI, 2(ii)(a)).

BIBLIOGRAPHY

Enc. Islam/2: 'Muwaḥḥidūn', 'Abū Ya'ḳūb Yūsūf', 'Abū Yūsūf Ya'ḳūb', 'Ibn Tūmart', 'Marrākūsh' [Marrakesh]
H. Basset and H. Terrasse: 'Sanctuaires et forteresses almohades', *Hespéris*, iv (1924), pp. 9–91, 181–203; v (1925), pp. 311–76; vi (1926), pp. 102–270; vii (1927), pp. 117–71, 287–345; also as *Sanctuaires et forteresses almohades* (Paris, 1932)
H. Terrasse: 'La Grande Mosquée almohade de Séville', *Mémorial Henri Basset*, ii (Paris, 1928), pp. 249–66
——: *La Mosquée des Andalous à Fès* (Paris, 1942)
——: *La Grande Mosquée de Taza* (Paris, 1943)
——: *Histoire du Maroc des origines à l'établissement du Protectorat français*, i (Casablanca, 1949)
L. Torres Balbás: *Arte almohade, arte nazarí, arte mudéjar* (1949), iv of A. Hisp. (Madrid, 1947–81)
J. Meunié and H. Terrasse: *Recherches archéologiques à Marrakech* (Paris, 1952)
J. Caillé: *La Mosquée de Hasan à Rabat* (Paris, 1954)
A. Huici Miranda: *Historia política del Imperio Almohade* (Tetouan, 1956–7)
J. Meunié and H. Terrasse: *Nouvelles recherches archéologiques à Marrakech* (Paris, 1957)
G. Deverdun: *Marrakech: Des origines à 1912*, 2 vols (Rabat, 1959–66)
R. Le Tourneau: *The Almohad Movement in North Africa in the Twelfth and Thirteenth Centuries* (Princeton, NJ, 1969)
C. Ewert and J.-P. Wisshak: *Forschungen zur almohadischen Moschee*, 2 vols (Mainz, 1981–4)
M. Attahiri: Kriegsgedichte zur Zeit der Almohaden (Frankfurt am Main, Berne, New York and Paris, 1990)
Al-Andalus: The Art of Islamic Spain (exh. cat., ed. J. D. Dodds; Granada, Alhambra; New York, Met.; 1992)

KARL-HEINZ GOLZIO

Almonacid, Sebastián de. *See* SEBASTIÁN DE TOLEDO.

Almoravid [al-Murābiṭūn]. Islamic dynasty that ruled parts of the Sahara, Morocco, Algeria and Spain from 1056 to 1147. The Sanhaja Berber chief Yahya ibn Ibrahim, on returning from a pilgrimage to Mecca, founded a reform movement intended to strengthen orthodoxy among the Saharan Berbers, who were only superficially Islamisized, but according to many Arab historiographers they adhered to Kharijite doctrine. With the support of the Malikite jurist Ibn Yasin and the Lamtuna Berber chiefs Yahya ibn 'Umar and his brother Abu Bakr, a fortress for a Muslim brotherhood (Arab. *ribāṭ*) was established on an island at the mouth of the Senegal River. The fortress soon became a centre for the tribes living near by, and the increasing power of those who lived there (*al-murābiṭūn*) led to the submission of all the Sanhaja tribes. Their renewal of Islam showed strong ascetic trends along with a simple piety that resulted in a holy war against the corrupt culture and errant Muslims of the Maghrib. In 1054 Yahya conquered Sijilmasa, the entrepôt for Saharan trade in Morocco, and by 1059 Abu Bakr controlled the Sus region. Quarrels among the desert tribes forced Abu Bakr to yield supreme command to Yusuf ibn Tashufin (*reg* 1070–1106), the real founder of the Almoravid empire. In 1069 he conquered FEZ, in 1070 he established MARRAKESH and made it capital of his realm, and by 1081 all of northern Morocco and parts of Algeria were under his control. As Abu Bakr had occupied the Sudanese empire of Ghana in 1076, the Almoravids controlled important North African ports as well as the trans-Saharan trade. After the Castilians conquered the Muslim kingdom of Toledo (1085), the Muslim kings of Spain asked Yusuf for help, and in 1086 he routed the Castilian forces at the Battle of al-Zallaqa (Sagrajas) near Badajoz. In 1090–94 the Almoravids annexed all the Muslim kingdoms in the Iberian peninsula and renewed the holy war against the Christian forces that culminated in the conquest of Valencia in 1102. Yusuf's son and successor ʿAli (*reg* 1106–43) was a powerful ruler who personally went to war four times against the Christians in Spain, but the growing strength of the ALMOHAD dynasty destroyed the Almoravid empire between 1144 and 1147.

The early Almoravids promulgated an extremely simple life in the areas they controlled, and the simplicity is reflected in their architecture (*see* ISLAMIC ART, §II, 5(iv)(c)). Their mosques, for example, have no contemporary minarets because they were considered impious innovations (*see* MINARET). Shortly before conquering Spain, Yusuf built a small and simple mosque at Nédroma in Algeria. The prayer-hall has nine naves and three bays, extended on each side of the court by a triple gallery of horseshoe-shaped arches. The Great Mosque of Algiers (*c.* 1097) has a prayer-hall of eleven naves perpendicular to the qibla and five bays deep. Each nave is covered with a tiled roof. The interior decoration is extremely sober, the monotony broken only by two lines of transverse arches, some of them cusped, and a finely carved wooden MINBAR (1087; Algiers, Mus. N. Ant.). Yusuf brought Andalusian artisans to North Africa, and they introduced new ideas to the arts of Fez and Marrakesh. In Fez, the Qarawiyyin and Andalusiyyin quarters were united by the erection of the Qasba Bu Julud on top of the highest point of the city.

ʿAli did not continue his father's strong asceticism and was in the thrall of Andalusian traditions. The congregational mosque built by the Almoravids in Marrakesh has been destroyed except for a small domed structure, the Qubbat al-Barudiyyin, which formed part of the ablution complex. The rectangular base is pierced with many openings and arched windows and supports an octagonal zone of transition and a ribbed dome. The stucco interior is beautifully decorated with *muqarnas* and stylized floral and shell motifs. Another surviving element from this mosque is a spectacular inlaid wooden minbar (Marrakesh, Badiʿ Pal. Mus.) made in Córdoba *c.* 1125–30 and later transferred to the Kutubiyya Mosque in Marrakesh (*see* ISLAMIC ART, fig. 216). ʿAli was also responsible for enlarging the Great Mosque of TLEMCEN in Algeria, including the exquisite pierced and ribbed stucco cupola (1136). Between 1135 and 1142 ʿAli also extended the Qarawiyyin Mosque in Fez, adding three naves to the existing seven. The cupolas and upper parts of the walls were decorated with *muqarnas* embellished with fine polychromatic floral ornament, later whitewashed by the Almohads and only uncovered in the 20th century. ʿAli also appreciated fine textiles, for the Chasuble of San Juan de Ortega at Quintanaortuña (Burgos) is made from a splendid Spanish silk decorated with roundels enclosing paired animals and inscribed with the name of the Almoravid ruler (*see* ISLAMIC ART, §VI, 2(i)(c)).

BIBLIOGRAPHY

Enc. Islam/2: 'Murābiṭūn', 'Marrākūsh' [Marrakesh]

H. Terrasse: *Histoire du Maroc des origines à l'établissement du Protectorat français*, i (Casablanca, 1949)

J. Bosch Vilá: *Los Almorávides* (Tetouan, 1956/*R* Granada, 1990)

P. F. de Moraes Farias: 'The Almoravids: Some Questions concerning the Character of the Movement during its Periods of Closest Contact with the Western Sudan', *Bull. Inst. Fond. Afrique Noire*, xxix (1967), pp. 794–878

H. Terrasse: *La Mosquée al-Qaraouiyin à Fès* (Paris, 1968)

R. Bourouiba: *L'Art religieux musulman en Algérie* (Algiers, 1973)

D. Hill and L. Golvin: *Islamic Architecture in North Africa* (London, 1976)

C. Ewert and J.-P. Wisshak: *Forschungen zur almohadischen Moschee*, i (Mainz, 1981)

K.-H. Golzio: 'Berber, Araber und Islam in Morokko vom 7. bis 13. Jahrhundert', *Madrid. Mitt.*, xxx (1989), pp. 432–97

Al-Andalus: The Art of Islamic Spain (exh. cat., ed. J. D. Dodds; Granada, Alhambra; New York, Met.; 1992), no. 115 [Kutubiyya minbar]

KARL-HEINZ GOLZIO

Almqvist, Osvald (*b* Trankil, Värmland, 2 Oct 1884; *d* Stockholm, 6 April 1950). Swedish architect. After graduating from the Kungliga Tekniska Högskola in Stockholm (1909), with Gunnar Asplund, Sigurd Lewerentz and others he joined the Klara School, a free studio for drawing established in opposition to the classical academy education. He began by training in industrial planning and workers' housing: both Forshuvudfors hydro-electric power station (1917) and Bergslagsby housing estate (1915) at Borlänge have traditionalist architectural elements, although their planning is rational and economical. In collaboration with Vattenbyggnadsbyrån Consulting Engineers he developed the planning of hydro-electric plants into a process of constructional simplicity, where the design is derived from the machinery and functional requirements. The exteriors make expressive use of plain, sharply defined elements such as thin sheet-metal roofs and ribbon windows: characteristic examples include the stations at Hammarfors and Krångfors (1925–8; later extended) in northern Sweden, and the Chenderoh Plant (1926–30; with Palmer & Tritton Consulting Engineers) on the Perak River in Malaysia. A series of school buildings, including Domnarvet Training School (1932), Borlänge and Luleå Vocational School (1936), employs the same vocabulary of plain, smooth-cast façades and thin, low-pitched roofs. Almqvist contributed to the development of modern housing in work for a committee for the design of workers' housing (1920), in his studies of kitchen standardization (1922–34) and in a series of flats and homes at the Stockholm Exhibition of 1930. He also worked in industrial design (e.g. lampposts and a standard spiral staircase in cast iron). As a pioneer of modern urban planning he made development plans for Arsta (1939), a suburb of Stockholm, and for smaller communities. From 1936 to 1938 he was head of the Stockholm City Park

Department and from 1940 to 1948 urban-planning officer in Södertälje.

WRITINGS

Köket och ekonomiavdelningen i mindre bostäder [Kitchen and utility space in smaller dwellings] (Stockholm, 1934)

BIBLIOGRAPHY

B. Linn: *Osvald Almqvist: En arkitekt och hans arbete* (Stockholm, 1967)

H. O. Andersson and F. Bedoire: *Swedish Architecture Drawings, 1640–1970/Svensk arkitektur ritningar, 1640–1970* (Stockholm, 1986) [bilingual text]

□

Almuce. *See under* VESTMENTS, ECCLESIASTICAL, §1(iii).

Alois I, Prince of Liechtenstein. *See* LIECHTENSTEIN, House of, (6).

Alois II, Prince of Liechtenstein. *See* LIECHTENSTEIN, House of, (8).

Alonso, Raúl (*b* Buenos Aires, 25 Jan 1923). Argentine draughtsman, painter and printmaker. He was self-taught and in 1943 began to illustrate publications throughout Latin America, continuing to do so for more than 20 years. His early work consisted of highly emotive ink drawings marked by an intricacy of design and lack of idealization, for example *The Vacuum Cleaner* (1975; New York, Bronx Mus. A.). He later worked in both pastels and oils to create spectral images of love, death, eroticism and the obscure world of nightmares, fears and terrors. Critics sometimes spoke of these in terms of Magic Realism, although he did not subscribe to any specific stylistic tendency. He often treated human heads and figures in fragmentary form, as if they were the victims of violent torture, and with a veiled but sarcastic humour.

With time Alonso gradually simplified his drawings and replaced his invented characters with fictional objects and childhood memories, moving towards more intimate and abstract work, for example in the pastel *The Sideboard* (1983; Rio de Janeiro, Mus. A. Mod.). His other series included *The Seven Deadly Sins*, *Martín Fierro*, *The Circus* and *Childhood Toys*, and he collaborated with the Argentinian poet Alberto Girri on three illustrated books, published in Buenos Aires: *Los 10 mandamientos* (1981), *Borradores* (1982) and *Amatoria* (1985).

BIBLIOGRAPHY

Arte argentino actual (Buenos Aires, 1979)

R. Squirru: *Arte argentino hoy* (Buenos Aires, 1983), p. 10

NELLY PERAZZO

Alonso de Cartagena (*b* Burgos, *c.* 1385; *d* Burgos, 1455). Spanish bishop, patron and builder. He was the son of an eminent Jewish banker, who converted to Christianity and became a bishop. Alonso, as Dean of Compostela, led Castile's delegation to the Council of Basle, and he travelled in France, Switzerland, Austria, Germany and Bohemia from 1434 to 1439. On his return he became Bishop of Burgos. He worked on a funerary chapel (Capilla de la Visitación; 1440–44) in Burgos Cathedral and on spires of openwork tracery (1442–58) on the cathedral's 13th-century western towers. Both are the work of Juan de Colonia, who was very probably brought to Castile by Alonso for this express purpose. The spires are based closely on German models, in particular the early 15th-century design for the spires at Cologne Cathedral. Don Alonso was a key figure in the introduction of Late Gothic architecture into Castile, for Juan de Colonia founded an energetic school of Late Gothic design based at the Burgos Cathedral workshops.

BIBLIOGRAPHY

M. Martinez Sanz: *Historia del Templo Catedral de Burgos* (Burgos, 1866)

L. Serrano: *Los conversos don Pablo de Santamaria y don Alonso de Cartagena* (Madrid, 1952)

T. Lopez Mata: *La Catedral de Burgos* (Burgos, 1957)

STEVEN BRINDLE

Alonso de Sedano (*fl* 1486–1530). Spanish painter. He has been identified as the author of works in Burgos and Palma de Mallorca showing the influence of Netherlandish and Italian Renaissance painting. He worked in Mallorca, first in the workshop of Joan Desi (*fl* 1481–1515) and then in that of Pere Terrenchs (*fl* 1488–96), the most important on the island during the reign of the Catholic kings. His name appears as a member of the painters' guild of St Luke at its foundation in April 1486. In February of that year Alonso received the commission for an altarpiece of *St Sebastian* for the chapel of the Sureda family in Palma de Mallorca Cathedral. This may correspond to the *Martyrdom of St Sebastian* (oil on panel; 2.44×1.77 m; Palma de Mallorca, Mus. Catedrálicio), his earliest known work. It shows the influence of Antonello da Messina, although the forms are more angular than in Antonello's work. A *Crucifixion* (oil on panel; 1.60×0.93 m; Palma de Mallorca, Mus. Dioc.) can also be attributed to him. In October 1488 Alonso was commissioned with Pere Terrenchs to paint panels of *St Sebastian* and *St Praxedes* for the altarpiece of the Guardian Angels' Chapel in Palma de Mallorca Cathedral, but there is some evidence to suggest that these may not have been completed. Alonso's influence on Mallorcan painting is seen in such works as the *Holy Cross* in the convent of S Jerónimo, Palma de Mallorca, which is closely related to works in Logroño, for example a *Crucifixion* (Logroño, Mus. Rioja). Alonso de Sedano is documented in Burgos from 1490, and possibly from 1489. The panels from an altarpiece depicting scenes of the *Infancy of Christ*, with the *Passion of Christ* on the reverses (Burgos, Mus. Dioc.–Catedrálicio), have been identified as his work.

BIBLIOGRAPHY

C. R. Post: *History of Spanish Painting* (1930–66), iv, pp. 202–19; v, pp. 326–30; ix, pp. 800–05; x, pp. 342–6; xii, pp. 457–9

G. Llompart: *La pintura medieval mallorquina* (Palma de Mallorca, 1977–80), i, pp. 91–2; iii, pp. 149–52; iv, pp. 27, 220–22

GABRIEL LLOMPART

Alonso Pimental, María Josefa de la Soledad. *See* OSUNA, (3).

Alpatov, Mikhail (Vladimirovich) (*b* Moscow, 10 Dec 1902; *d* Moscow, 9 May 1986). Russian art historian. He graduated from Moscow University in 1921. Much of his time was devoted to teaching, at the Higher State Artistic and Technical Institute (Vkhutein), the Theatre and Architecture institutes, Moscow University and the institute attached to the Academy of Arts. His main areas of interest were Old Russian art, the art of the Renaissance, and

Russian art of the 18th and 19th centuries. He was particularly concerned with the links between the art of different regions, trying to combine iconographical method with a stylistic analysis. His premise was that 'art is a metaphor for life'. In his descriptions of works of art he aimed to provide a written equivalent of visual images, using his skills as a poet and artist. He was internationally respected and his work was published in the journals *Iskusstvo*, *Slavia*, *Commentari*, *Belvedere*, *Revue des études grecques*, among others. He became known in 1924 after the publication of a series of works in German written with Oskar Wulff, Viktor Lazarev and N. I. Brunov. These works dealt with the history of Byzantine and Old Russian architecture and painting. In the West, historiographical surveys often mistakenly describe Alpatov's work as Structuralist; in fact his method was to create an 'essay' bringing together art, culture and history.

WRITINGS

Geschichte der altrussischen Kunst (Baden-Baden, 1932)
Andrey Rublyov (Moscow, 1939)
Etyudy o zapadnoyevropeyskom iskusstve [Studies in Western European art] (Moscow, 1939)
Ital'yanskoye iskusstvo epokhi Dante i Dzhotto [Italian art of the era of Dante and Giotto] (Moscow, 1939)
Vseobshchaya istoriya iskusstva [General history of art], 3 vols (Moscow, 1948–55)
Russkiy vklad v mirovoye iskusstvo [The Russian contribution to world art] (New York, 1950)
Geschichte der Kunst (Dresden, 1964)
Drevnerusskaya ikonopis' [Old Russian icon painting] (Moscow, 1974)
Le icone russe (Turin, 1976)
Feofan Grek [Theophanes the Greek] (Moscow, 1979; rev. 1983)
I. Y. Danilova, ed.: *Alpatov M. V. Vospominaniya* [M. V. Alpatov: reminiscences] (Moscow, 1994)

V. S. TURCHIN

Al'pert, Maks (Vladimirovich) [Alpert, Max] (*b* Simferopol' [now in Ukraine], 18 March 1899; *d* Moscow, 30 Nov 1980). Russian photographer. He was the son of an artisan. In 1914 Al'pert moved to Odessa and entered a photographic studio as an apprentice. After serving in the Red Army, he worked from 1924 as a photojournalist, taking news photographs for *Rabochaya gazeta*. He was already distinguished by his energy and his ability to capture events in a highly professional manner. Many of his photographs (e.g. *Maxim Gorky's Return from Italy*, 1928; see Shudakov, p. 21) were widely published. In 1928 he moved to the newspaper *Pravda*, where he began to work systematically on serial photography (e.g. *The Construction of the Magnitogorsk Metallurgical Factory*, 1929; see Morozov and Lloyd, pp. 130–31). The photoseries *24 Hours in the Life of the Filippov Family* (1931; see Shudakov, pp. 22–3) became widely known; it was executed by a collective of photographers in which Al'pert and Arkady Shaykhet played an active role. A consummate example of photonarrative, it reveals in detail the life of a simple Moscow worker's family.

From 1931 Al'pert was employed on the periodical *SSSR na stroyke*, for which he photographed the most important new constructions of the first Five-Year Plan (e.g. the *Great Fergana Canal*, 1939; see Shudakov, pls 210, 212–18) and the collectivization of agriculture. In the 1930s he became one of the foremost Russian photojournalists working with the series. During World War II Al'pert was a war correspondent for the Soviet news agency TASS, producing memorable action shots (e.g. *Combat*, 1941; see Morozov, no. 242). After the war he photographed further new constructions and heroic figures of the USSR. His psychological study of the work of the cardiologist, *Mind and Heart (N. M. Amosov Operating)* (1973; see Morozov, pls 295–300), stands out among his works from the 1970s.

WRITINGS

Bespokoynaya professiya [Restless profession] (Moscow, 1962)

BIBLIOGRAPHY

G. Shudakov: *Pioneers of Soviet Photography* (London and New York, 1983)
S. Morozov and V. Lloyd, eds: *Soviet Photography, 1917–1940: The New Photojournalism* (London, 1984)
S. Morozov: *Tvorcheskaya fotografiya* [Creative photography] (Moscow, 1986)
Antologiya sovetskoy fotografii [Anthology of Soviet photography], i, *1917–1940* (Moscow, 1986); ii, *1941–1945* (Moscow, 1987)

A. N. LAVRENTIEV

Alphand, (Jean-Charles-)Adolphe (*b* Grenoble, 26 Oct 1817; *d* Paris, 6 Dec 1891). French landscape architect and civil engineer. A graduate of the Ecole Polytechnique (1835) and Ecole Nationale des Ponts et Chaussées (1838), Paris, he was sent to Bordeaux to reorganize the harbour's access and the forest of the Landes. In 1851 Georges Eugène Haussmann, the newly appointed Préfet de la Gironde, asked Alphand to prepare the festivities in honour of the official visit of the French President, Prince Louis Napoleon. After the Prince became emperor, as Napoleon III, in 1852, he ordered Haussmann to transform Paris into a modern metropolis (*see* FRANCE, fig. 13). In 1854 Haussmann summoned Alphand to redesign the Bois de Boulogne. Alphand arrived from Bordeaux with the horticulturist and landscape architect Jean-Pierre Barillet-Deschamps (1824–75), and together they carried out a vast number of projects, cutting straight avenues through historic, often picturesque, districts. Alphand also designed airy public gardens and parks, in accord with Haussmann's overall scheme. He laid out the Bois de Vincennes (1860) and created many *squares*, smaller public gardens, such as the Square des Batignolles (1866). Among Alphand's finest works are the parks of Monceau (1862), Buttes-Chaumont (1867) and Montsouris (1869) and a whole network of tree-lined thoroughfares, including those of l'Observatoire, Breteuil and Daumesnil and the boulevards Voltaire, Richard-Lenoir and Montparnasse.

Under Alphand's direction, Barillet-Deschamps and Edouard André (1840-1911) created Paris's horticultural gardens at La Muette (1860; moved, 1895, to Boulogne), in which a large variety of plants were grown to decorate public ways and gardens. For the first time, city streets were adorned with evergreens. In 1867 Alphand was made supervisor of the public ways of Paris, and, after the Franco-Prussian War (1870–71), he was put in charge of all public works. These included the suburban Parisian cemeteries, such as the Cimetière de Bagneux (1886), each avenue of which was lined with a different species of tree, alongside square plots bordered with mixed hedges. Alphand improved upon the ideas of Denis Bühler (1811-90), who, following the lead of Gabriel Thouin (1747-1829), had made parks with wide, circular walks and broad and smaller paths, the last crossing vast, flat, clump-dotted lawns. Alphand laid out large walks with broad intersections and junctions. These, forming elegant curves, ovals and rounds, encircled finely proportioned lawns slightly sunk at the centre, while the removed earth was piled up into neat mounds, raised at intervals along the margins, and thickly planted with shrubs, trees or flowers. Through the wider gaps between them, long views were kept open, visually connecting the separate lawns and giving depth to the overall composition. Examples of this rather repetitive formula, saved from monotony through rich vegetation, survive at the gardens of the Champs Elysées, the *jardin anglais* of the Palais du Luxembourg and in the Avenue de l'Impératrice (1855; now the Avenue Foch), which has a monument to Alphand near l'Etoile. Alphand was also responsible for the International Exhibitions of 1867, 1878 and 1889 (with the newly erected Eiffel Tower astride the Champ de Mars), and in 1891 he succeeded Haussmann at the Académie des Beaux-Arts. His reputation rests on his efforts to introduce garden art into the fabric of an old city that he helped to restructure.

WRITINGS

Les Promenades de Paris, histoire, description des embellissements, dépenses de création et d'entretien des Bois de Boulogne et de Vincennes, Champs Elysées, parcs, squares, boulevards, places plantées: Etude de l'art des jardins et arboretum (Paris, 1867/*R* Princeton, 1984)

BIBLIOGRAPHY

A. A. Ernouf: *L'Art des jardins: Parcs, jardins, promenades, étude historique, principe de la composition des parcs et jardins, plantations, décoration pittoresque et artistique des parcs et jardins publics, traité pratique et didactique* (Paris, 1868, rev. 3/1886)

W. Robinson: *Gleanings from French Gardens* (London, 1868)

——: *The Parks, Promenades and Gardens of Paris* (London, 1869)

E. André: *L'Art des jardins: Traité général de la composition des parcs et jardins* (Paris, 1879)

DENIS A. LAMBIN

Als, Peder (*bapt* Copenhagen, 16 May 1726; *d* Copenhagen, 8 July 1776). Danish painter. Although he was mentioned in the court account-books as early as 1743, his first known painting dates from 1750. From then until 1756 he was active as one of the most important portrait painters of the Danish Rococo. His colouristic style and impasto technique were strongly influenced by the Swedish painter Carl Gustaf Pilo. The double portrait of the *Court Jeweller C. F. Fabritius and his Wife* (1752; Copenhagen, Stat. Mus. Kst) and the full-length *Frederik V* (1756; priv. col., see A. Russell, ed.: *Danske slotte og herregårde* [Danish palaces and manor houses] (Copenhagen, 2/1963–8), iv, p. 385) are among his masterpieces. An important collection of portraits by Als from this period is housed in the Nationalhistoriske Museum på Frederiksborg, Hillerød.

In 1755 Als was the first major gold medal winner at the newly founded Kongelige Danske Kunstakademi in Copenhagen, and the next year he began a six-year study trip to Italy and France. In Rome (1756–61) he met the theorist J. J. Winckelmann; and his experience working in Anton Raphael Mengs's studio led to a fundamental alteration in his style, which was also influenced by Pompeo Batoni. Als adopted a classicizing mode in his portraits, marked by monumentality, gravity and deeper colours. Both the profile portrait of the sculptor *Johannes Wiedewelt* (1766; Copenhagen, Kon. Kstakad.) and the portrait of *Sophie Hedvig Moltke* (1766; priv. col., see Holck Colding, p.82) were clearly inspired by his studies in Rome. Appointed court painter in 1763, Als executed a number of studies and portraits of Queen Caroline Mathilde, as well as the coronation portrait of *Christian VII* (St Petersburg, Hermitage). In 1766 Als was appointed professor at the Kongelige Danske Kunstakademi in Copenhagen.

BIBLIOGRAPHY

DBL

T. Holck Colding: 'Kongen og kunsten' [The king and art], *Akademiet og guldalderen* (Copenhagen, 1972), iii of *Dansk kunsthistorie*, pp. 78–85

M. Saabye: '*Augustus og Cleopatra*: Dokumentation omkring et maleri af Anton Raphael Mengs', *Kstmus. Arssk.* (1976), pp. 12–38 [with Ger. summary]

MARIANNE SAABYE

Alsloot [Alslot], **Denijs** [Denis] **van** (*b* Brussels, before 1573; *d* Brussels, between 15 Jan 1625 and 11 Dec 1626). Flemish painter. The earliest document referring to him is a receipt dated 26 May 1593 for the gilding and decoration of the Garnier family monument in Notre-Dame-du-Sablon in Brussels. The records of the Brussels painters' guild, which survive only from 1599 onwards, do not mention his admission as a master but show that he took on four apprentices between 1599 and 1625, the last being Pieter van der Borcht. In 1599–1600 he entered the service of Archduke Albert and Archduchess Isabella, who entrusted him with many important commissions. In 1603 and 1604 van Alsloot received two payments from them for the design and weaving of two-and-a-half laps of tapestry with grotesques. This has often been taken, erroneously, to indicate that he held a prominent place in the development of Brussels tapestry manufacturing.

Like Jacques d'Arthois, Lucas Achtschellinck (1626–99) and Lodewyk de Vadder, van Alsloot belonged to the school of Brussels landscape artists who drew much of their inspiration from the Forêt de Soignes. In several of van Alsloot's works, which are generally topographically accurate, it is possible to identify places that still survive, especially near the abbeys of Groenendael and Ter Kameren. Some paintings, for example *Rest on the Flight into Egypt* (1606; sold London, Christie's, 16 Nov 1973, lot 130) and *Landscape with Tobias and the Angel* (1610; Antwerp, Kon. Mus. S. Kst.), are obviously inspired by a late 16th-century style of landscape painting. Both have a pronounced, old-fashioned three-colour scheme (brown, green and blue for the foreground, middle ground and background respectively) and a composition clearly divided into two by a central clump of trees, to the left of which is a path surrounded by trees and to the right a panoramic view with a river meandering through rocks and mountains. *Landscape with Cephalus and Procris* (1608; Vienna, Ksthist. Mus.) reveals compositional affinities with the wooded landscapes that Gillis van Coninxloo painted around the turn of the century. As in many of van Alsloot's paintings, the figures, whose vividly coloured clothing clashes with the brown-green tonality of the landscape, were painted by Hendrik de Clerck. There are undoubted affinities between the paintings of van Alsloot and van Coninxloo, although the latter's influence has generally been overstated. Van Alsloot's style is calmer and more static, his colours softer, his touch more precise and his compositions generally more realistic. His work can best be seen as a synthesis of the styles of van Coninxloo and Jan Breughel I.

Landscape also featured among the works commissioned from van Alsloot by Albert and Isabella, for example, views of their estates at Mariemont (Brussels, Mus. A. Anc.) and Tervuren and of the Abbey of Groenendael. His most valuable commission, worth 10,000 guilders, was a series of paintings commemorating the *Ommegang* procession held in Brussels on 31 May 1615. That particular procession was especially splendid, because two weeks earlier, at the jay-shooting ceremony of the Crossbowmen's guild, Isabella had attached the jay to the spire of Notre-Dame-du-Sablon, successfully shot it and been crowned Queen of the guild. Ten scenes from the series survive (e.g. two in Madrid, Prado, and two in London, V&A). Artistically they are rather undistinguished, probably because their function was primarily documentary. After van Alsloot's death two paintings he had bequeathed to his niece Leonore Cousins were bought by Albert and Isabella.

BIBLIOGRAPHY

E. Larsen: 'Denis van Alsloot, peintre de la forêt de Soignes', *Gaz. B.-A.*, n.s. 5, xxxiv (1948), pp. 331–54

M. De Maeyer: 'Denijs van Alsloot (voor *ca.* 1573–1625/6) en de tapijtkunst', *A. Textiles*, i (1953), pp. 3–11

Y. Thiéry: *Le Paysage flamand au XVIIe siècle* (Paris and Brussels, 1953), pp. 130–33

M. De Maeyer: *Albrecht en Isabella en de schilderkunst* (Brussels, 1955), pp. 162–8

Y. Thiéry and M. Kervyn de Meerendré: *Les Peintres flamands de paysage au XVIIe siècle: Le Baroque anversois et l'école bruxelloise* (Brussels, 1987), pp. 99–107, 229

HANS DEVISSCHER

Alt, Rudolf (von) (*b* Vienna, 28 Aug 1812; *d* Vienna, 12 March 1905). Austrian painter, draughtsman and printmaker. He was perhaps the most productive and accomplished watercolour painter in German-speaking Europe in the 19th century. On his frequent travels he produced local views, landscapes and interiors, often commissioned by aristocratic patrons. He studied with his father, Jakob Alt (1789–1872), a landscape and watercolour painter and one of the first to use the new technique of lithography. From the age of six Rudolf accompanied him on study trips, and, together with Alt's other children, he coloured his father's drawings. During his student days at the Akademie der Bildenden Künste in Vienna (1825–32), Rudolf joined his father on further journeys and collaborated in his studio. In 1832 he won a prize, which simultaneously freed him from military service and marked the beginning of his independent artistic activity. In the same year he produced his first oil painting, after his own watercolour, of the *Stephansdom, Vienna* (Vienna, Belvedere), a subject that he treated on many occasions until 1898. In 1833 he and his father travelled to northern Italy; Venice, in particular, made a lasting impression on him. Two years later he went to Rome and Naples. In the brilliant southern light Alt adopted a far wider range for his radiant and transparent colour. Many of his views of Italy, and also those of locations throughout the Austro-Hungarian Empire, were intended for use in a peep-show, commissioned by the Austrian Archduke (later Emperor) Ferdinand. Alt continued to receive such official commissions until 1848.

A change in Alt's artistic outlook occurred in the second half of the 1830s. He no longer concentrated on *vedute* (landscape views with figures or animals) but rather on scenes of rural or urban life, synthesizing nature, architecture, people and animals (e.g. *Harbour of Como*, 1837; Vienna, Albertina). The high points of this period are his drawings of Prague and various parts of Galicia. The latter were reproduced in 1840 by the recently developed process of chromolithography and published by H. F. Müller in *Pittoreskes Österreich* (Vienna, 1840–43). The 1840s were the most creative and strongest phase of Alt's career. He extended his range of subjects, producing animal, costume and portrait studies in addition to landscapes, townscapes and interiors. His style and outlook began to change. His brushwork took on a sketchy simplicity, and his colour an almost crystalline clarity. He combined the suggestion of prevailing atmosphere with exceptional truth to detail, achieving a remarkable synthesis. Alt heightened the impression of light, representing the brightest areas of the subject with the blank paper, particularly when using Whatman paper (a particularly dense, white type). From *c.* 1850 he also used industrially manufactured wood-pulp paper heightened with white. The reputation Alt had established by this point led to numerous commissions; in 1844 the Russian Count Baryatinsky ordered ten miniature *Views of Vienna* (Munich, Staatl. Graph. Samml. and elsewhere). Alt also worked for Alois II, Prince of Liechtenstein. For the Viennese publisher Neumann he provided original drawings for 48 lithographs, which appeared in 1845 as *Malerische Ansichten von Pesth und Ofen.*

Following the political unrest of 1848 Alt fled from Vienna. After his return he found himself in financial difficulties. His light painting style changed. He now used gouache with added highlighting, as in *Stephansdom, Vienna* (1855; Munich, Staatl. Graph. Samml.; see fig.). The commissions Alt received in 1863 from the court of the Russian tsar Alexander II for views of imperial residences in the Crimea helped the artist regain a fresh approach to nature. Subsequently, in a looser painting style, Alt completed a further series of views of Austria and Italy, made during a journey in 1865–6, such as *Roman Forum with a View of the Capitol* (1866; Schweinfurt, Samml. Schäfer). Alt received an almost uninterrupted series of official commissions during the 1870s. For the Weltausstellung in Vienna (1873) he was asked to record the more monumental constructions of the Wiener Wasserversorgung. Every year subsequently he painted three or four outstanding structures owned by the Danubian monarchy, for example the *Old Fortress at Cheb* (1876; Vienna, Gemäldegal. Akad. Bild. Kst.). As well as depicting architecture in landscape, or interiors, Alt also focused attention on subjects from everyday life, as in the *Promenade at the Spa of Teplitz* (1876; Munich, Staatl. Graph. Samml.) and *Kitchen Garden in Liezen* (1879; Vienna, Albertina).

During the last 25 years of his long life Alt had to restrict his travels because of ill-health. He made journeys only within Austria, and for Italian subjects he went back to earlier sketches. In Gastein, where he often stayed to take the cure, he produced magnificent sheets such as the *Great Pine Tree near Gastein* (1892; Vienna, Albertina). In his later works Alt often enlarged his drawing surface by adding strips of paper to his sheets, in order to do justice to his subjects. In 1897 Alt was visited by Adolph Menzel, who became a friend. In atmosphere and painting style,

Rudolf Alt: *Stephansdom, Vienna*, watercolour and gouache, 310×230 mm, 1855 (Munich, Staatliche Graphische Sammlung)

Alt's last works recall those from Menzel's earlier period. *Ironworks in Skodagasse* (1903; Vienna, Albertina), a view from the artist's apartment, and the unfinished *Workroom* (1905; Munich, Staatl. Graph. Samml.), his last watercolour, are comparable to Menzel's industrial pictures and interiors. Since Alt recorded virtually all the architectural changes in Vienna during the 19th century, his work has documentary as well as artistic importance. In his lifetime, Alt accepted numerous distinctions and honours. He became a professor and an honorary citizen of Vienna, and he was ennobled. The young generation around Gustav Klimt elected him honorary president of the Vienna Secession, in whose exhibitions he participated.

BIBLIOGRAPHY

Meissner; Thieme-Becker

W. Koschatzky: *Rudolf von Alt* (Salzburg, 1975)

Rudolf von Alt: Aquarelle (exh. cat. by W. Koschatzky, Vienna, Albertina, 1984)

SEPP KERN

Altamira. Cave site near the coast of northern Spain, 2 km south of Santillana del Mar, Santander. It is important for its cave art of the Late Upper Palaeolithic period (*c*. 20,000–*c*. 10,000 BP; *see also* PREHISTORIC EUROPE, §II, 1 and 2). The cave of Altamira, nicknamed the 'Sistine Chapel of Rock Art', was decorated at various times *c*. 16,000–14,000 BP (see fig.). Material from excavations in the cave, including the engraved shoulder-blades of deer, is housed in the Museo Arqueológico Nacional, Madrid, and in the Museo de las Cuevas de Altamira at the site.

First discovered by a hunter in 1868, the cave was visited in 1876 by a local landowner, Don Marcelino Sanz de Sautuola, who noticed some black painted signs on a wall. He returned to excavate in 1879, and it was on this occasion that his daughter spotted a cluster of polychrome paintings of bison on the ceiling. The figures seemed to have been executed with a fatty paste, and de Sautuola noticed a close similarity in style between these huge figures and the small examples of portable prehistoric art that he had seen at an exhibition in Paris. He therefore deduced that the cave art was of a similar age, but his attempts to present this discovery to the academic establishment met with widespread rejection. The validity of de Sautuola's claim was not established until the early 20th century, years after his premature death in 1888.

The Altamira cave measures 296 m in length and is divided into different chambers and passages, ending in a long, narrow section. Although the site is famous for the great painted bison, it would be classed as a major decorated cave even without them, since its galleries are filled with an abundance of engravings, including some particularly fine deer heads identical to those found carved on shoulder-blades. There are also some meandering finger tracings, some of which form a bovine head. A remarkable feature is a series of 'masks'—natural rock formations that were changed into humanoid faces by the addition of eyes and other details. The 'Great Hall', with its high vault, has engravings and painted red compartmentalized quadrilateral signs akin to those of EL CASTILLO. There are also black paintings—often occurring in different zones from the red figures—some stencilled hand outlines, and a few rare positive painted hand prints. Inside the cave entrance to the left is the 'Great Hall of Paintings', measuring *c*. 20×10 m. The floor has been lowered to allow easier access and viewing of the low ceiling on which the large painted animals are distributed. Eighteen bison are shown, together with a horse and a hind, the last measuring *c*. 2.5 m in length. They are polychrome paintings, executed in ochre and manganese. Most of the animals are standing, but a few natural bosses in the ceiling are painted with curled-up bison, which thus appear three-dimensional. Two or three of the painted figures on the ceiling have been described as boars, animals that rarely feature in Palaeolithic art, but, as one has horns, they probably also represent bison. The curled-up bison on the bosses have been variously described as sleeping, wounded, dying or falling, as females giving birth, or as males rolling in the urine-impregnated dust used to mark their territory. In fact, they may simply have been drawn to fit the bosses, as they are rendered with the same volume, form and dorsal line as the bison standing around them, differing only in that their legs are bent and their heads lowered. Some scholars see this chamber as a symbolic pound, with a bison drive depicted on the ceiling—the curled-up animals at the centre are seen as dead, while those around them stand and face the 'hunters', the figures of human males engraved at the edge of the scene. Another interpretation is that the ceiling is a depiction of a bison herd in rutting season.

Although the Altamira ceiling has sometimes been regarded as a single composition, it actually comprises a series of superimpositions. Scholars have distinguished five separate phases of decoration, beginning with some

Altamira cave, painted deer, Late Upper Palaeolithic period, *c.* 16,000–14,000 BP

continuous-line engravings and followed in sequence by figures in a flat, red wash, multiple-line engravings, black figures, and finally the famous polychrome paintings. As at El Castillo, the multiple-line figures are identical to some portable artefacts dated to *c.* 15,550 BP, found in the cave. It is therefore clear that the two earlier phases predate these, while the black figures and polychrome paintings are later. Charcoal used in three polychrome bison paintings at the centre of the ceiling (for illustration *see* CHARCOAL) has produced a mean radiocarbon date of 14,000±400 BP. The cave may have been blocked shortly after this period. De Sautuola saw the Altamira ceiling as a unified work, and the French scholar Abbé HENRI BREUIL insisted that one artist of genius could have executed all the polychrome paintings in the cave. Subsequent detailed observation has confirmed that a single expert artist was probably responsible for all the bison on the ceiling.

BIBLIOGRAPHY

E. Cartailhac and H. Breuil: *La Caverne d'Altamira à Santillane, près de Santander (Espagne)* (Monaco, 1906)

H. Breuil and H. Obermaier: *The Cave of Altamira at Santillana del Mar* (Madrid, 1935)

F. Jordá Cerdá: 'Las superposiciones en el gran techo de Altamira', *Santander symposium: Actas del symposium internacial de arte rupestre: Santander, 1970*, pp. 423–56

M. A. García Guinea: *Altamira y otras cuevas de Cantabria* (Madrid, 1979)

F. Jordá Cerdá: 'El gran techo de Altamira y sus santuarios superpuestos', *Altamira symposium: Actas del symposium internacial sobre arte prehistórico: Madrid, 1980*, pp. 277–87

J.-M. Apellániz: 'El autor de los bisontes tumbados del techo de los polícromos de Altamira', *Homenaje al Prof. M. Almagro Basch*, i (Madrid, 1983), pp. 273–80

L. G. Freeman and others: *Altamira Revisited* (Chicago and Santander, 1987)

H. Valladas and others: 'Direct Radiocarbon Dates for Prehistoric Paintings at the Altamira, El Castillo and Niaux Caves', *Nature*, ccclvii (1992), pp. 68–70

PAUL G. BAHN

Altamira, Condes de [Osorio Moscoso y Guzmán; Astorga, Marqueses de]. Spanish family of patrons. The 10th Conde de Altamira, Joaquín Ventura Osorio de Moscoso y Guzmán (*bapt* Madrid, 4 Feb 1724; *d* Madrid, 28 Aug 1783), inherited the title of Marqués de Astorga from his mother, and on his father's side his ancestors were the Conde-Duque de Olivares and the Marqués de Leganés, both notable collectors. The 10th Conde served as Councillor of the Real Academia de Bellas Artes de S Fernando in Madrid and was an honorary academician of the Academia de S Carlos in Valencia. His wealth was fabled, and he commissioned Ventura Rodríguez to design an opulent new palace (1772) in the Calle de S Bernardo, Madrid. It was feared that the building might outshine the Palacio Real, and the single surviving façade gives some measure of its earlier glory. The same architect also designed special decorations for the palace of the Conde in 1789 on the occasion of the proclamation of Charles IV as king.

Joaquín's son, Vicente Joaquín Osorio Moscoso y Guzmán (*b* Madrid, 16 Jan 1756; *d* 26 Aug 1816), 11th Conde de Altamira, was 'smaller than many dwarfs exhibited for money', according to Henry Richard Fox, 3rd Baron Holland. Some of the artists he patronized, such as Augustín Esteve y Marques, seem to have disguised his small stature in their portraits of him. A portrait by Goya for the Banco Nacional de S Carlos (1787; Madrid, Banco de España), of which the Conde was a director, however, depicts him seated, showing that the table reached his shoulder rather than his elbow. Goya was also commissioned to paint other members of the 11th Conde's family: his eldest surviving son, *Vicente Isabel with a Pet Dog* (*c.* 1786–7; New York, Ch. S. Payson priv. col.); and one of his younger sons, *Manuel María with Magpie, Finches and Cats* (1788; New York, Met.). Esteve y Marques painted another of the sons, *Juan María Osorio* (*c.* 1785; Cleveland, OH, Mus. A.), perhaps posthumously. The Conde's wife, María Ignacia Alvarez de Toledo, was the sister of José Alvarez de Toledo y Gonzaga, 17th Duque de Alba (1756–96). Goya portrayed her with her daughter on her lap in *Condesa de Altamira with her Daughter María Augustina* (1787–8; New York, Met.).

During the Peninsular War (1808–14) an inventory and valuation of the Altamira Collection were made by the French. Some 470 pictures and 68 prints were listed. Religious subjects comprised nearly a quarter of the collection; portraits, mythological or allegorical subjects, animals or hunting scenes and landscapes made up the remainder. By 1808 the 11th Conde had added Goya's portrait of the architect *Ventura Rodríguez* (1784; Stockholm, Nmus.) to the collection. There was also a set of eight large pictures by Frans Snyders and Paul de Vos depicting animals and fruit, two pendant pictures of *Land* and *Sea* by Vos, an *Allegory of the Five Senses* by Daniel Seghers (Madrid, Prado); a set of twelve paintings of the *Life of Tobias* by Andrea Vaccaro, two portraits of the *Marqués de Leganés* by van Dyck and an *Annunciation* by Rubens (Brussels, Dulière priv. col., on dep. Antwerp, Rubenshuis). Spanish pictures included religious paintings by Luis Morales, copies of portraits by Velázquez, two portraits by El Greco, one of which may have been the *Self-portrait* (*c.* 1590–1600; New York, Met.), saints by Ribera and a set of six pictures of the *Life of the Virgin* by Francisco Antolínez.

The fortunes of the Condes de Altamira declined in the 1820s, when the family lost its Mexican properties on independence. They were forced to sell estates in Spain to help pay off the debts that Vicente Joaquín had left to his heir, and pictures and books owned by the family were sold abroad in the same decade. A considerable number of paintings from the family's gallery was auctioned in London in 1827. The Museo del Prado, Madrid, acquired an *Allegory on the Birth of Don Fernando, Son of Philip II* by Michele Parrasio, formerly attributed to Veronese.

UNPUBLISHED SOURCES

Paris, Archv Louvre [*Evaluation des tableaux et estampes qui se trouvent à l'Hôtel du Comte d'Altamira*]

Madrid, Archv Hist. N., MS. Carlos III, Expediente 70 [*Pruebas de Vicente Joaquín Osorio*]

Madrid, Archv Hist. N., MS. Orden de San Juan, Expediente 23509 [*Pruebas de Manuel Maria Osorio*]

BIBLIOGRAPHY

C. B. Curtis: *Velázquez and Murillo: A Descriptive and Historical Catalogue of the Works* (London, 1883/*R* 1973)

E. du Gué Trapier: *Goya and his Sitters* (New York, 1964), pp. 5–6

N. Glendinning: 'Goya's Patrons', *Apollo*, cxiv/236 (1981), p. 239, notes 10, 11

NIGEL GLENDINNING

Altamouras, Ioannis (*b* Florence, 1852; *d* Spetses, 1878). Greek painter. In early life he studied in Athens under Nikiforos Lytras and subsequently in Copenhagen (1873–6) with Carl Frederik Soerensen. He travelled in Scandinavia and spent the last two years of his life on the Greek island of Spetses, where he died of consumption. He produced marine scenes almost exclusively, mostly small-scale, which show the influence of 17th-century Dutch seascapes and French *plein-air* painting. Nevertheless he developed a style of his own, frequently discarding academicism in favour of Impressionism, and created atmosphere by the predominant use of blues, greens, yellows and greys. Most of his works are in Athens (e.g. *Sailing Ship at Spetses*, 1877; Athens, N.G.).

BIBLIOGRAPHY

S. Lydakes: *E historia tes neoellenikes zographikes* [History of modern Greek painting] (Athens, 1976), p. 335–7, iii of *Oi ellenes zographoi* [The Greek painters], ed. S. Lydakes and A. Karakatsane (Athens, 1974–6)

C. Christou: *Greek Painting, 1832–1922* (Athens, 1981), pp. 37–8

N. Missirli: *Ellenike zographike* (Athens, 1993), pp. 152–7, 194 [18th–19th century]

ALKIS CHARALAMPIDIS

Altar. Table or similar raised structure used in many cultures and throughout history for sacrificial, eucharistic or other religious purposes. (African and Afro-American altars began to receive serious scholarly attention only in the late 1980s and early 1990s (see, e.g., R. F. Thompson: *Face of the Gods: Art and Altars of Africa and the African Americas*, New York and Munich, 1993).)

□

I. Ancient world. II. Europe. III. Americas. IV. Asia.

I. Ancient world.

1. Near East. 2. Egypt. 3. Greece. 4. Etruria. 5. Roman Empire.

1. NEAR EAST. Structures built of bricks have been found in the cella of temples throughout the Ancient Near East and are generally cited as a reason for identifying the building as a temple. They were sometimes plastered and one early example from the late 4th millennium BC, at Tell 'Uqair in southern Mesopotamia (now Iraq), had miniature steps leading up it and was painted to resemble a temple decorated with mosaics, with guardian leopards in red and black paint. Another example of much the same date, from the Eye Temple at Tell Brak in Syria, was decorated with a frieze of blue and white limestone and gold and supported a symbol with an enormous pair of 'eyes'. Monolithic stone altars from Assur (Berlin, Pergamonmus.; Istanbul, Archaeol. Mus.), dating to the reign of the Assyrian king Tukulti-Ninurta I (*reg* 1243–1207 BC), are both rectangular, on stepped bases, with semicircular projections at the top. The relief on one of these altars shows the King standing and kneeling before an identically shaped altar that supports a cult symbol. Similar altars have also been found in Neo-Assyrian contexts of the 9th–7th century BC (e.g. London, BM). The reliefs and seals of the Achaemenid Persians of the 6th–4th century BC (e.g. from their royal city PERSEPOLIS) show stepped altars that supported a fire. Actual fire altars have been found in the hills of south-western Iran.

BIBLIOGRAPHY

R. Ghirshman: *The Art of Ancient Iran from its Origins to the Time of Alexander the Great* (London, 1964)

A. Moortgat: *Die Kunst Vorderasiens* (Cologne, 1967); Eng. trans. as *The Art of Ancient Mesopotamia: The Classical Art of the Near East* (London and New York, 1969)

DOMINIQUE COLLON

2. EGYPT. In the tombs and temples of ancient Egypt, altars were used to carry offerings brought to propitiate deities or the deceased. Since the earliest offerings tended to comprise a loaf of bread placed on a woven mat, this image came to be used in the hieroglyphic writing system to represent the act of offering itself (*hetep*). Thus the *hetep* symbol, a rectangle surmounted by a small conical loaf shape, eventually became one of the most common shapes adopted for stone offering tables or altars, particularly in tomb chapels. The surfaces of such funerary altars were often carved with reliefs of libation vessels and items of food and drink, enabling the altar itself magically to supply the tomb owner with eternal nourishment.

An altar in the court of the sun temple of Neuserre (*reg c.* 2416–*c.* 2392 BC) at ABU GHURAB is one of the most impressive surviving examples of an early temple altar. It consists of a huge circular monolithic slab of travertine surrounded by four separate pieces of travertine, each carved in the form of a *hetep* sign. In the Temple of Amun at Karnak (*see* THEBES (i), §II) a pink granite offering table in the form of a *hetep* sign (Cairo, Egyp. Mus., JE 88803) was erected by Tuthmosis III (*reg c.* 1479–*c.* 1426 BC); relief scenes carved on the front show two kneeling figures of the King presenting offerings to Amun-Re. In the New Kingdom (*c.* 1540–*c.* 1075 BC) many large-scale stone temple altars were constructed with ramps or sets of steps: a massive limestone altar dedicated to Re-Harakhty on the upper terrace of the temple of Hatshepsut (*reg c.* 1479–*c.* 1458 BC) at Deir el-Bahri (*in situ*; *see* THEBES (i), §IV) had a flight of ten steps on its western side, while the mid-14th-century BC Great Temple of the Aten at Akhetaten (destr.; *see* AMARNA, EL-) is known to have included a large central altar approached by a ramp, as well as courtyards filled with hundreds of stone offering tables. From the Late Period (*c.* 750–332 BC) onwards, Egypt began to be more influenced by Hellenistic and Syrian forms of worship, and the 'horned altar', consisting of a stone or brick-built block with raised corners, was introduced from Syria-Palestine; an altar of this type was erected in front of the TOMB OF PETOSIRIS (*c.* 320 BC), a priest of Thoth, at Tuna el-Gebel.

See also EGYPT, ANCIENT, §VIII, 2.

BIBLIOGRAPHY

LÄ

G. Jéquier: 'Autel', *Bull. Inst. Fr. Archéol. Orient.*, xix (1922), pp. 236–49

IAN M. E. SHAW

3. GREECE.

(i) Bronze Age. Forms and materials of Bronze Age altars vary widely, and small portable altars (notably the 'tables of offering') can be distinguished from more substantial structures of ashlar masonry or rubble with a plastered surface. Mud-brick and wood were also employed on occasion: some altars consisted simply of accumulated sacrificial debris. In the Early Bronze Age stone-built altars are sometimes associated with Minoan tombs and funerary rites. The temple at Ayia Irini on Kea had stone bench altars in the Late Bronze Age at least, which were mainly occupied by large terracotta votive figures. In Minoan and Mycenaean religion the 'tables of offering' were sometimes set on or near larger altars. Altars occur in the courts of Minoan palaces and villas and in Minoan peak sanctuaries (e.g. Mt Iouktas), where they are accompanied by sacrificial debris and offerings. Altars were frequently equipped with 'horns of consecration'. In the Middle Minoan II shrine at Anemospilia, near Archanes, a low altar was apparently used for human sacrifice. The Late Bronze Age cult centre at Mycenae seems to have had an altar with a sacrificial stone beside it. Late Minoan and Mycenaean shrines were regularly equipped with stone bench or platform altars (e.g. the Shrine of the Double Axes at Knossos, Mycenae cult centre, Phylakopi sanctuary etc) on which were placed small offerings, some perhaps perishable. Cult statues may have stood on them but none is identified with certainty. Some sanctuaries (e.g. Apollo Maleatas at Epidauros, Artemis and Apollo at Kalapodhi) seem to have had a continuous series of altars from Mycenaean times into the Iron Age.

BIBLIOGRAPHY

M. P. Nilsson: *The Minoan–Mycenaean Religion and its Survival in Greek Religion* (Lund, 1927, 2/1950)

C. G. Yavis: *Greek Altars* (St Louis, MS, 1949)

G. E. Mylonas: *Mycenaean Religion: Temples, Altars and Temenea* (Athens, 1977)

Sanctuaries and Cults of the Aegean Bronze Age: Proceedings of the First International Symposium at the Swedish Institute in Athens: Athens, 1980

N. Marinatos: *Minoan Religion* (Columbia, SC, 1993)

R. L. N. BARBER

(ii) Later periods. Sacrifice at an altar—normally a burnt offering—was the central act of ritual worship at Greek religious festivals, and the altar was therefore a focus of cult. Its form varied considerably. It was usually situated in the open air, outside the temple, if one existed, where it was visible to the full throng of worshippers. References exist to altars inside temples, but archaeological evidence for them is lacking, with the dubious exception of the early 'hearth altars' (8th and 7th centuries BC), low-edged fireplaces inside religious buildings that might better be interpreted as the area where the meat consumed by human worshippers, rather than the gods, was cooked.

Some altars were very simple. That of Zeus at Olympia was nothing more than the accumulated pile of ash from sacrificial fires. More generally, the altar formed a table or block of stone, on top of which the burnt offering was made. This could be small, square or circular in plan and of no great height, perhaps with carved embellishment on its side (a form often used for subsidiary altars, or in minor sanctuaries, particularly in Hellenistic times).

Altars in major sanctuaries were often larger, and frequently more elaborate, the table being extended to form a rectangular block. The width varied, but it was by no means unusual for the altar to extend for the full width of the temple in front of which it stood, as with the altars of Hera at Perachora (5th century BC) and Poseidon (also 5th century BC) at Isthmia. Architectural embellishment might be restricted to the table, with moulded decoration around the foot and the top edge, and the whole structure was sometimes raised on a low platform approached by steps. Examples in the Argolid and Corinthia may be

1. Great Altar, Pergamon, detail of the Great Frieze showing a *Gigantomachy*, h. 2.3 m, *c.* 180–*c.* 160 BC (Berlin, Pergamonmuseum)

further adorned with a Doric triglyph and metope frieze, here clearly betraying a decorative rather than a structural origin (the Perachora altar is a good example of this type).

In the Hellenistic period cylindrical altars are often found in funerary complexes. These are particularly common in the Greek East and there is a good collection of them in Rhodes town. They are decorated with bulls' heads, garlands and snakes, but are sometimes left plain.

Most elaborate of all are those where the altar slab is given a heightened architectural treatment, perhaps situated on a platform, as with 'Cape Monodendri' (late 6th century BC), Miletos, and the altar of Artemis (6th century BC) in front of her temple at Ephesos, and approached by steps or a ramp; or those surrounded by a screen, generally a wall with architectural treatment, including attached colonnades and sculptured decoration. Such altars are more typical of the East Greek area, and there are some splendid Hellenistic examples, culminating in the biggest of them all, that of Zeus at PERGAMON (2nd century BC), with its high stepped approach, through an open Ionic screen, flanked by walls with Ionic colonnades over a massively carved frieze showing a *Gigantomachy* (see fig. 1). There is another at the Sanctuary of Artemis (2nd century BC) at Magnesia, where the screen wall formed, it seems, a series of niches each containing a life-size statue. Examples also exist in mainland Greece (where the less ornate types are more frequent), an especially elaborate one, not properly understood despite the survival of much material from it, being the 'Throne' of Apollo at Amyklai outside Sparta, embellished, if not necessarily designed, by Bathykles of Magnesia in the 6th century BC. The 4th-century BC altar of Athena Alea at Tegea is another example.

BIBLIOGRAPHY

A. von Gerkan: *Der Altar des Artemistempels in Magnesia am Mäander* (Berlin, 1929)
C. G. Yavis: *Greek Altars* (St Louis, 1949)
K. Lehmann and D. Spittle: *The Altar Court* (1964), iv/2 of *Samothrace* (Princeton, 1958–)
E. Schmidt: *The Great Altar of Pergamon* (London, 1965)
H. Plommer and F. Salviat: 'The Altar of Hera Akraia at Perachora', *Annu. Brit. Sch. Athens*, lxi (1966), pp. 207–15
O. Broneer: *The Temple of Poseidon* (1971), i of *Isthmia* (Princeton, 1971–)
R. Martin: 'Bathycles de Magnésie et le "trône" d'Apollo à Amyklae', *Rev. Archéol.* (1976), p. 205
P. M. Fraser: *Rhodian Funerary Monuments* (Oxford, 1977)
W. Hoepfner: 'Altar des Artemision in Magnesia', *Hermogenes und die hochhellenistische Architektur* (Mainz, 1990), pp. 16–17

R. A. TOMLINSON

4. ETRURIA. Altars have been found in the sanctuaries of Etruria and territories elsewhere in Italy under Etruscan control within an urban context, for example at Marzabotto, Faesulae (two altars in front of the temple, dated *c.* 300 BC), outside the walls of Veii (at the Portonaccio temple, *c.* 6th century BC) and several sites at Cività Castellana, the oldest *c.* 500 BC or earlier. They also occur at sanctuaries associated with cemeteries, as in the Cannicella Necropolis outside Orvieto. They are characterized by simple but heavy convex mouldings, often rising from an ashlar plinth, which may be stepped. Symmetrical about the central waisted section is a further series of mouldings similar to those on the base. A square or rectangular plan is most common, although circular examples are known. A rectangular block-shaped altar was found in the mid-2nd-century BC Tomb of the Typhon at Tarquinia.

BIBLIOGRAPHY

G. C. Giglioli: *L'arte etrusca* (Milan, 1935)
A. Boëthius: *Etruscan and Early Roman Architecture*, Pelican Hist. A. (Harmondsworth, 1970, rev. 2, 1978)
Santuari d'Etruria (exh. cat. by G. Collonna, Arezzo, Mus. Archeol. Mecenate, 1985)

5. ROMAN EMPIRE. The most famous Roman altar is the Ara Pacis Augustae, originally built near the Campus Martius, Rome, between 13 and 9 BC to commemorate Augustus' return from the provinces, and reconstructed on a nearby site in 1938 (*see* ROME, §V, 4). The altar is on a platform of steps within a square enclosure, elaborately decorated with panels recording the formal dedication, mythological and allegorical scenes, and ornamental friezes. The related Ara Pietatis Augustae in honour of Livia, Augustus' wife, was sited on the Capitol and was not completed until AD 43. These were both political in expression as compared to most other examples found throughout the Empire. The latter take the form of an upright rectangular block with slightly larger base and moulded details. The altar capital has mouldings or panels of ornament surmounted by cylindrical bolsters, and in the centre a dish-shaped section for offerings. The front panel may be incised with a dedicatory inscription; a blank face may represent a painted one now lost. The sides may have reliefs related to the iconography of the deity, or the sacrificial ritual. Circular altars are known, and folding tripods were used, as witnessed by a relief panel of Marcus Aurelius, reused on the Arch of Constantine in Rome, and on coinage issued from the late 1st century AD into the Tetrarchy (early 4th century). Altars were placed outside temples in direct line of view of the main doors and the cult image; Vitruvius, writing in the 1st century BC, suggested that they should face east (*On Architecture*, IV.ix). Most examples were made of stone, although a temporary altar could be made of turves. Some small examples may be votive, or used in domestic shrines.

BIBLIOGRAPHY

H. Mattingley and E. A. Sydenham: *Roman Imperial Coinage*, ii–vi (London, 1926–67)

E. Nash: *Pictorial Dictionary of Ancient Rome*, 2 vols (London, 1961–2, 2/1968)

J. B. Ward Perkins: *Roman Imperial Architecture*, Pelican Hist. A. (Harmondsworth, 1981)

N. Hannestad: *Roman Art and Imperial Policy*, Jutland Archaeological Society Publications, xix (Århus, 1986)

G. LLOYD-MORGAN

II. Europe.

The Christian altar originated as a symbol of the table of the Last Supper, and, as one of the earliest elements of church furniture, it came to be used for the celebration of the Eucharist. Altars can be fixed or portable, examples of the latter being more common in the Western Church, and can vary in form, decoration and setting. The most important altar in a church is usually located at the east end in the apse; secondary altars may be located in side apses, chapels or crypts.

BIBLIOGRAPHY

J. Braun: *Der christliche Altar in seiner geschichtlichen Entwicklung*, 2 vols (Munich, 1924)

K. Heimann: *Der christliche Altar: Übersicht über seinem Werdegang im Laufe der Zeiten* (Abendsberg, 1955)

□

1. Early Christian. 2. Eastern. 3. Western to *c.* 1550. 4. Roman Catholic after *c.* 1550. 5. Protestant.

1. EARLY CHRISTIAN. The eucharistic meal instituted by Christ became for the Apostolic Church a sign of shared faith. It was distinguished from other meals by being celebrated on Sunday. The bread and wine were placed on a table and the Lord's Supper was re-enacted using the liturgical form recorded by St Paul (1 Corinthians 11:23–7). Before the end of the 1st century AD the Eucharist took on the sacrificial nature of the crucifixion. As the elements became identified with Christ's flesh and blood, communion became imbued with a sense of awe and mystery. A single celebrant, representing all the faithful, stood in front of a plain table, now also an altar. The early Church Fathers used the term *thysiastirion* ('place of sacrifice'), derived from *thysia*, which was used to mean the sacrifice of the Eucharist in the 2nd-century *Didache* (Christian manual on morals and Church practice). The altar was still moved to the centre of the room for the Eucharist, but its place had become the province of the clergy, and its sacred nature was emphasized. The shift in emphasis from spiritual to real sacrifice was made by such writers as Irenaeus, Bishop of Lyon (*c.* 177–200), in his *Adversus haereses* in response to heretical denials of Christ's humanity.

Table fragments surviving from the 2nd and 3rd centuries AD suggest that wooden altars had round or U-shaped tops, probably with a raised rim decorated with scalloping. A 3rd-century wall painting in the catacomb of St Calixtus in Rome depicts a priest standing at a small, round three-legged table, a style of altar in common use at the time.

In AD 313 Christianity was officially recognized by the Roman State. This inspired an extensive programme of church-building, and altars—still in the form of wooden tables, though now also made of stone—became a standard item of church furniture (*see* CHURCH, §IV, 1). The absence of floor-fixings in the sanctuary, even in Old St Peter's basilica, Rome, indicates that the altar was movable and could be placed in front of the bishop's chair for mass. Simple table altars, supported on one, four or five legs, were small (*c.* 1 sq. m) but just adequate for chalice and paten, gospels and mass books. Four stone altars of this type survive from 4th- and 5th-century France. Of these, the Auriol altar (see fig. 2) is supported by a single pedestal, while the altars from Saint-Quénin (Vaison-la-Romaine

2. Stone altar from Auriol, France, 4th–5th centuries AD (Aix-en-Provence, Musée Granet)

Cathedral) and Saint Marcel (St Germain-en-Laye, Mus. Ant. N.) and the Minerve altar (Marseille, Mus. Borély), thought to have belonged to Bishop Rusticus of Marseille (*c.* 456), rest on four legs. The table-tops are edged with iconographic motifs, including the chi-rho, vines that refer both to the Eucharist and to Chapter 15 in St John's Gospel, and doves that, in this context, may symbolize the souls of the Apostles or the martyred faithful (Revelation 6:9). Mosaics in the dome of the Orthodox baptistery (*c.* 400) and in S Vitale (consecrated 547), Ravenna, also depict table altars with raised decorated edges resting on four columns.

As early as the 2nd century AD, Christians began holding eucharistic meals at the tombs of the martyrs (*see* MARTYRIUM). Especially during times of persecution, this form of honouring the dead on the day of their death confirmed the sacrificial nature of their deaths and strengthened a sense of the communion of saints, living and dead. A stone *mensa* was placed over the grave or tomb to create an altar. The invocation of the Holy Spirit during the liturgy served as a dedication. The growing cult of the martyrs led, after 313, to churches being built as close to the grave as possible, and grave and altar were connected by means of a vertical shaft. This was boxed in below the altar, and objects lowered through an opening or fenestella took on the status of relics. The burgeoning cult of relics brought about the transition from table to box altars in which relics could be housed. The 5th-century altar of S Alessandro in Rome has panels pierced with a pattern of small arches and a fenestella. Some fenestellae were closed with elaborate doors of gold or silver, and the *Liber pontificalis* mentions numerous gifts of this type from popes to Roman churches. A reliquary could also be displayed through the fenestella. When churches came to be built far from the tomb of the patron saint, a relic or an object that had touched the body was enclosed in the altarstone. A third type of altar was a monumental structure carved from a single block of stone. In 532 Bishop Eufrasius presented the cathedral at Poreč, Croatia, with a block altar (*in situ*) that is decorated with reliefs and that has a niche in the front, probably for a reliquary.

Once Christianity became associated with the authority of the emperor, an imperial language was increasingly adopted in the Church, and the altar came to be called the heavenly throne. In conjunction with the bishop's cathedra it symbolized the divine authority of the Church. The altar presented to Old St Peter's by Constantine, however, was made of silver-gilt inlaid with jewels and surmounted by a pyramidal ciborium (*see* CIBORIUM (ii), §1) on four columns. Altars of gold and precious gemstones were presented by Empress Pulcheria (*reg* 414–53) and Justinian I (*reg* 527–65) to Hagia Sophia in Constantinople (now Istanbul; see Mango, pp. 51, 88–9). In general, however, altars were made of less precious materials, and by the 6th century wooden altars had been replaced by stone, although the design remained simple.

BIBLIOGRAPHY

Irenaeus: *Adversus haereses* (AD 185–9); Eng. trans. by A. Roberts and J. Donaldson as 'Against Heresies', in *The Ante-Nicene Fathers*, i (1867/*R* Grand Rapids, MI, 1975)
L. Duchesne, ed.: *Le Liber pontificalis*, 2 vols (Paris, 1886–92/*R* 1955–7); vol. 3, ed. C. Vogel (Paris, 1957)
H. Leclerq: 'Autel', *Dictionnaire d'archéologie chrétienne et de liturgie*, ed. F. Cabrol, I/11 (Paris, 1907), pp. 3155–89
J. G. Davies: *The Origin and Development of Early Christian Church Architecture* (London, 1952)
J. N. D. Kelly: *Early Christian Doctrines* (New York and London, 1958, rev. 1960)
J. A. Jungmann: *The Early Liturgy to the Time of Gregory the Great* (Notre Dame, IN, 1960)
C. Mango: *The Art of the Byzantine Empire, 312–1453: Sources and Documents* (Englewood Cliffs, NJ, 1972/*R* Toronto, Buffalo and London, 1986)
A. Grabar: 'Une Forme essentielle du culte des reliques et ses reflets dans l'iconographie paléochrétienne', *J. Sav.* (July–Sept 1978); repr. in *L'Art du moyen âge en Occident: Influences byzantines et orientales* (London, 1980)
G. Müller, ed.: *Theologische Realenzyklopedie*, ii (Berlin and New York, 1978), pp. 305–27

2. EASTERN. Altars used in Eastern churches are primarily made of stone, although the remains of wooden altars have been found at archaeological sites, especially in Ethiopia; altars in Syrian and Maronite churches are made of either stone or wood. Most churches have table altars, although the Coptic Church continues the Early Christian tradition of using block altars made of stone or brick. Churches are usually furnished with a single altar, but Armenian, Maronite and Coptic churches can have as many as three to five altars, while Nestorian churches of the 11th century had two.

A particular type of portable altar, known as an *antimension*, is first recorded in the 8th century AD. It is mentioned more frequently from the 12th century onwards when it refers to a consecrated piece of silk or linen cloth with a small pocket for relics. Although its usage was common in the Late Byzantine and Post-Byzantine periods, surviving examples apparently date no earlier than the 18th century (e.g. Athens, Byz. Mus.). Their decoration varies but may include a central scene of the *Entombment* surrounded by the Virgin and other holy figures, with an inscription around the border (e.g. Valkenburg, Ignatius Koll.; see Braun, i, p. 520). In the Ethiopian church, portable altars are made of wood and may be inscribed in Geëz (e.g. Valkenburg, Ignatius Koll.; see Braun, i, pl. 100).

See also CHURCH, §IV, 2.

BIBLIOGRAPHY

J. Braun: *Der christliche Altar in seiner geschichtlichen Entwicklung*, 2 vols (Munich, 1924)
J. Izzo: *The Antimension in the Liturgical and Canonical Tradition of the Byzantine and Latin Churches* (Rome, 1975), pp. 23–144
Age of Spirituality: Late Antique and Early Christian Art, Third to Seventh Century (exh. cat., ed. K. Weitzmann; New York, Met., 1977–8)

3. WESTERN TO *c.* 1550. Following its development in the Early Christian period the altar became central to the Christian liturgy. Two basic types evolved in the Western Church: the fixed (or monumental) altar, which was the most important element in a church, and the portable altar, used for the celebration of the Eucharist outside the confines of a church.

(i) Monumental.

(a) Types. Stone altars (as opposed to the earlier wooden ones) became a permanent feature within Christian churches by the 6th century AD, especially following the

Council of Epaone (Burgundy) in 517, as well as subsequent councils, which forbade the use of wooden altars. Breaches of this ruling were fairly rare, although fixed altars of wood or of precious metal were in some cases still being built in the 12th century. The great majority of altars followed one of the three basic types (table altar, block altar and box altar) that had developed in the Early Christian period (*see* §1 above). In each case the altar consisted of the top surface (the *mensa*) resting on a support (the *stipes*). The third essential element of an altar was the *sepulchrum*, a sealed compartment for the storing of relics. This could either be located in the *stipes* or in the *mensa* itself. The *mensa* always had to be of a single slab of natural stone, preferably marble, and firmly attached to the *stipes*, which was also required to be of natural stone. The only new type of altar to develop in this period was the sarcophagus altar, which consists of a *mensa* resting on a sarcophagus, reflecting the Early Christian practice of celebrating the Eucharist on a slab placed directly on, or above, the tomb of a saint. The sarcophagus altar was introduced in the early 16th century, but it flourished particularly in the Baroque period (*see* §4(i) below).

Table altars vary primarily in the design of the *stipes*, which can be a single column or, more commonly, can comprise several supports. The altar in Barcelona Cathedral crypt and that in S Matteo, Perugia, are typical examples of a single, columnar *stipes*, whereas the *mensa* at S Manno, near Perugia, rests on a single central support that is square in section. A variety of solutions were adopted for table altars with more than one supporting element. The most common arrangement was with four supports, one at each corner of the *mensa*, but occasionally a fifth, central column would be added, as for example at S Luigi dei Francesi, Rome. The box altar, with the *stipes* constructed in the form of a hollow chamber, developed from the Early Christian type of altar that was connected by a shaft with the saint's tomb below. After the 9th century, when the distribution of relics became an accepted practice, the box altar was usually constructed with a compartment in which the relics were stored (e.g. at S Ambrogio, Genoa). The block altar, with its *stipes* constructed as a solid masonry block, usually with marble veneer, frequently also had built-in compartments for storing relics (e.g. at S Pietro della Pieve, Bagnacavallo, near Ravenna).

(b) Settings. The most important altar in a church, the high altar, is usually raised on several steps and located at the east end of the church, often in the apse. In the Middle Ages the high altar was free-standing, allowing the celebrant to walk around it. It was also commonly protected (both physically and symbolically) by a ciborium, usually a domed or pyramidal roof structure supported by four columns (e.g. in S Giovanni in Zoccoli, Viterbo; see fig. 3).

From the 6th century AD it became customary for a church to have several side altars in addition to the high altar. This was associated particularly with the introduction of private masses, which could be celebrated simultaneously in various parts of the church. The requirement for the celebrant to be able to walk around the altar and to face the congregation was lifted, and it became common for side altars to be placed against a wall. These developments influenced ecclesiastical architecture, and by the 12th century many churches were built with absidiole chapels, each with their own altar. Separate altars were also installed in the various chapels that were built in churches by private patrons, guilds and confraternities.

3. High altar with ciborium, S Giovanni in Zoccoli, Viterbo

A secondary altar placed against a wall could also be surmounted by a ciborium (as in the crypt at S Susanna, Rome), or, more frequently, by a half-ciborium (e.g. in Orvieto Cathedral), or a niche-ciborium (e.g. in Verona Cathedral). In some cases (e.g. Ravello Cathedral) the altar was constructed (1272) under the pulpit, which thus took on the additional function of the ciborium. By the late 12th century the forms of ciboria built over altars became much more varied; at the Johanniskirche, Lüneburg, for example, the altar is surmounted by a half-barrel-shaped canopy projecting from the wall. Other liturgical developments that took place by the 12th century led to the separation of the celebrants from the congregation, resulting in the development of screens, which frequently incorporated an altar (e.g. in Magdeburg Cathedral).

(c) Decoration. On account of its liturgical importance and focal position the altar consistently attracted the attention of artists, providing much scope for decoration both of the actual altar and of the various objects associated with it. The *mensa* itself is usually a rectangular slab, although other forms have also been used; for example, the medieval *mensa* at Besançon Cathedral is circular. The top surface of the *mensa* often has a carved border that projects slightly above the central area. The carvings

4. High altar, S Francesco, Sansepolcro, 1304

usually include five crosses (one at each corner and one in the middle) and may additionally comprise simple geometric designs based on such motifs as the circle and semicircle (e.g. the late 11th-century *mensa* at St Sernin, Toulouse), sometimes with the addition of bead-and-reel designs (e.g. *mensa* of 1068; Elne Cathedral). In many cases the top surface of the *mensa* has an inscription, which might mention the bishop of the diocese, the date of the consecration and the names of saints whose relics were placed in the altar. The vertical edges of the *mensa* are also frequently carved, typically with one design repeated on the short sides, another on one or both of the long sides. For example, the 5th-century *mensa* from Auriol (*see* §1 and fig. 2 above) has a chi-rho with an alpha and omega inscribed in a circle, flanked on each side by six doves carved in profile; on the sides is a vine motif with bunches of grapes. Variations on this type of decoration continued through the medieval period. The underside of the *mensa* is usually flat and undecorated, but in some cases (e.g. at S Matteo, Perugia) it rests on a single central support and takes the form of an upside-down truncated pyramid.

The altar's supporting structure, the *stipes*, is usually its most decorated part. Entire Roman altars were in some cases reused as the support for a Christian altar (e.g. in S Galla, Rome); in other instances such spolia as a Roman tub have fulfilled the same role (e.g. in S Bartolomeo, Rome). Block altars were frequently decorated with Cosmatesque mosaic decoration (e.g. the altar in S Scholastica, Subiaco), or faced with stone panels carved with figural reliefs; for example, the front of the high altar (1383) in S Michele, Pavia, comprises three panels showing St Michael, a kneeling donor and two bishop saints. Architectural elements were also widely used as decorative features; for example, the high altar at S Domenico, Arezzo, has a block support faced with panels with blind Gothic arches separated by pilasters and surmounted by an elaborate cornice. Various combinations of such elements are common. The altar in S Francesco, Sansepolcro, for example, has a central block with relief panels surrounded by a separate Gothic arcade (see fig. 4). In some cases, as in the high altar of S Ambrogio, Genoa, a Gothic arcade extends across the width of the altar and is enriched by the addition of a sculptural group showing the *Nativity* under the larger, central arch. In table altars the supporting structure frequently consists of one, four or five plain columns. More decorative forms were also employed, especially in the 15th century and later, for instance baluster columns (e.g. at S Nicola, Pisa), amphora-shaped supports (e.g. at S Annunziata, Florence), consoles and even putti or angels.

The altar was also decorated with various external elements that were usually dictated by the liturgy. Unless the front of the altar was made of marble, had reliefs or other forms of decoration or contained a reliquary, it was commonly covered with an antependium of cloth, precious metal or wood. Cloth antependia were frequently of silk richly embroidered with gold thread; a common subject was *Christ Enthroned Flanked by Saints*, as in a 13th-century example (Brussels, Pal. Cinquantenaire) from Rupertsberg Abbey at Bingebruck near Mainz. In the Renaissance period various embroidery techniques were used, including stumpwork and *or nué* (for the latter *see* SPAIN, fig. 61), allowing such naturalistic effects as shading. Metalwork examples include a splendid Ottonian antependium of repoussé gold with *Christ between the Three Archangels and St Benedict* (Paris, Mus. Cluny; *see* OTTONIAN ART, fig. 7), a 12th-century silver-gilt antependium with *Christ Blessing* and scenes from the *Life of Christ* (Città di Castello, Mus. Capitolare) and a silver-gilt antependium in Monza Cathedral with scenes from the

Life of St John the Baptist, made by the Milanese goldsmith Borgino dal Pozzo (*fl* 1350–57). Three altarcloths of pure white linen or hemp were required to be placed on the altar for the celebration of mass; the topmost was required to cover the sides of the altar and the front also, if the latter was not specially decorated. Although it was usually prescribed that the altarcloths should have little or no decoration, in some cases they were embroidered with such eucharistic symbols as the cross, the chi-rho, the agnus dei, sheaves of wheat or grape vines. The few objects allowed on the altar include a crucifix (which had to be placed on the altar for the celebration of mass unless the Crucifixion was the main subject of the altarpiece), a tabernacle for storing the Host, a CHALICE and PATEN, a monstrance, a Sacramentary (*see under* MISSAL), a book rest (sometimes in the form of an embroidered silk-covered cushion), candlesticks (*see* CANDLESTICK) and an ALTARPIECE; these objects were often richly ornamented and offered much scope for artistic expression.

BIBLIOGRAPHY

J. Braun: *Der christliche Altar in seiner geschichtlichen Entwicklung*, 2 vols (Munich, 1924)

O. v. Falke and E. Meyer: *Bronzegeräte des Mittelalters* (Berlin, 1935)

K. Heimann: *Der christliche Altar: Übersicht über seinem Werdegang im Laufe der Zeiten* (Abendsberg, 1955)

J. B. O'Connell: *Church Building and Furnishing: The Church's Way* (Notre Dame, IN, 1955)

L. Perpeet-Frech: *Die gotischen Monstranzen im Rheinland* (diss., U. Bonn, 1956)

H. Hagen: *Die Anfänge des italienischen Altarbildes* (Munich, 1962)

R. Huber and R. Reith: *Liturgische Geräte, Kreuze und Reliquiare der christlichen Kirchen* (Tübingen, 1972)

JOHN N. LUPIA

(ii) Portable. The portable altar is a consecrated surface, usually of stone, on which mass is celebrated outside the confines of a church (for the sick, in time of war, during travel or missionary work) or in the absence of a more substantial altar. While councils at Paris (AD 509) and Epaone (517) required that an altar table be made of stone, the oldest surviving portable altar consists of an oak plaque found in the tomb of St Cuthbert (*d* 687) at Durham Cathedral.

In 857, as part of the Carolingian standardization of church practice, Archbishop Hincmar of Reims prohibited celebration of mass without a consecrated altar, or without a tablet of marble, black stone or slate consecrated by a bishop. A footed portable altar of porphyry and gold containing relics of SS James, Stephen and Vincent was among the recorded gifts of Charles the Bald to Saint-Denis Abbey (*see* CAROLINGIAN ART, §V, 2). The gold ciborium (Munich, Residenz) given by King Arnulf (*reg* 887–99) to St Emmeram, Regensburg, and probably from the court workshop of Charles the Bald, is a unique form of portable altar. The *mensa* is surmounted by a miniature architectural canopy of gold, studded with gems. The Uta Evangelary (*c.* 1020; Munich, Bayer. Staatsbib., Clm. 13601, fol. 4*r*) records a miniature votive crown (untraced) that was suspended from the canopy.

While portable altars in France are known largely through documentary evidence, two important early examples are preserved in the treasury at Ste Foy, Conques. One, with a porphyry slab and engraved and nielloed silverwork, bears an inscription recording its consecration in 1100, under Abbot Bégon III (*reg* 1087–1107), by Pons, Bishop of Barbastre. The second, also of the 11th century, has an alabaster slab surrounded by cloisonné-enamel medallions, the disposition of which recalls bookcover decoration. Most surviving portable altars were produced in the Rhine, Meuse and Lower Saxon regions in the 12th century. Generally, they take the form of a rectangular wooden box, encased in metal (or occasionally ivory) and decorated with gems, enamels, niello or *email brun*. The stone slab set in the top is most often of porphyry, jasper, alabaster or rock crystal (the last allowing the relics to be seen). Less precious stone was used if it was associated with a holy place, such as the birthplace of Christ, the tomb of the Virgin, or the site of a saint's martyrdom.

The dimensions of portable altars range from *c.* 170 to *c.* 400 mm, with the depth of the box largely dependent on the size of the stone and the presence of relics. In 1310 a synod at Trier dictated that portable altars should be large enough to accommodate a chalice and paten; minimum dimensions were specified only in 1501–2. The decoration usually includes images of Christ, the Apostles, the cardinal virtues and Old Testament prefigurations of the Eucharist (e.g. the Sacrifice of Isaac or the Meeting of Abraham and Melchisedech). Donors are also often shown; a portable altar (*c.* 1120; Paderborn, Diözmus. & Domschatzkam.) by ROGER OF HELMARSHAUSEN shows the patron Heinrich of Werl, Bishop of Paderborn (*reg* 1084–1127), censing a cloth-covered altar upon which stands a portable altar with a chalice, paten and Host.

The placement of relics in a portable altar was only standardized in the 13th century, but it never became an absolute requirement. In two celebrated examples, the portable altar and reliquary of St Andrew's sandal (977–93; Trier, Domschatz) and the head reliquary of Pope Alexander (1145; Brussels, Musées Royaux A. & Hist.; *see* RELIQUARY, fig. 3) from Stavelot Abbey, the distinction between portable altar and reliquary is obscured. The rectangular form of portable altars remained standard, however, as seen in the porphyry and silver example (1273) in the treasury of St Just, Narbonne, signed by Gui de Pileo. Regulations of the 13th and 14th centuries insisted upon episcopal authorization for the use of portable altars, which could be extended to services in royal households. A portable chapel was made for St Louis to use on crusade, and one is registered in the inventories of the Sainte-Chapelle, Paris. In 1306 Pope Clement V gave permission to Philip the Fair for his two eldest sons' chaplains to have portable altars. Increased regulation concerning the use and form of portable altars seems to have coincided with decreased usage. For the Gothic period, as with the pre-Romanesque period, documentary evidence about portable altars is more abundant than surviving examples.

BIBLIOGRAPHY

A. Darcel: 'Trésor de Conques: Les Autels portatifs', *An. Archéol.*, xvi (1856), pp. 77–89

J. Corblet: 'L'Autel chrétien: Etude archéologique et liturgique', *Rev. A. Chrét.* (1883), pp. 531–6

——: *Histoire dogmatique, liturgique et archéologique du sacrement de l'Eucharistie*, ii (1886), pp. 209–320

R. de Fleury: 'Autels portatifs', *La Messe*, v (Paris, 1887), pp. 1–56

A. Vidier: 'Le Trésor de la Sainte-Chapelle', *Mém. Soc. Hist. Paris & Ile-de-France*, xxiv (1907), p. 218 [Sainte-Chapelle inventory of 1341]

J. Braun: *Der christliche Altar in seiner geschichtlichen Entwicklung*, i (Munich, 1924), pp. 71–91, 419–517

J. Taralon: *Treasures of the Churches of France* (Paris, 1967), pp. 296–7 [Conques altars]

Treasures from Medieval France (exh. cat. by W. D. Wixom, Cleveland, OH, Mus. A., 1967), pp. 164–5, 364, no. IV-25

H. Westermann-Angerhausen: 'Die Goldschmiedearbeiten der Trierer Egbertwerkstatt', *Trier. Z. Gesch. & Kst Landes & Nachbargebiete*, xxxvi (1973), pp. 21–32

P. E. Schramm and F. Mütherich: *Denkmale der deutschen Könige und Kaiser I: Ein Beitrag zur Herrschergeschichte von Karl dem Grossen bis Friedrich II, 768–1250* (Munich, 1981), p. 738, no. 61 [Arnulf ciborium]

J. Squilbeck: 'Le Chef-reliquaire du pape Alexandre aux Musées royaux d'art et d'histoire: Critique historique et examen des formes', *Rev. Belge Archéol. & Hist. A./Belge Tijdschr. Oudhdknde & Kstgesch.*, cxi (1984), pp. 3–18

Ornamenta ecclesiae: Kunst und Künstler der Romanik (exh. cat., ed. A. Legner; Cologne, Schnütgen-Mus., 1985), i, C34, p. 454 [Paderborn altar]

The Making of England: Anglo-Saxon Art and Culture, A.D. 600–900 (exh. cat., ed. L. Webster and J. Backhouse; London, BM, 1991), pp. 134–5, no. 99 [St Cuthbert altar]

BARBARA DRAKE BOEHM

4. Roman Catholic after *c.* 1550.

(i) Monumental. At the Council of Trent (1545–9), Carlo Borromeo assigned the Eucharist a central place in the order of the liturgy, with important consequences for church furnishings, especially altars. The Host was kept in the altar itself, and not in a separate tabernacle as before, and the placement of a protective ciborium above the altar became a requirement. The number of altars in each church increased sharply: in addition to the high altar, side altars were established in the chapels around the choir and in the aisles. As the altars grew in importance, they became increasingly monumental and more heavily ornamented. As before, the high altar was built of expensive and durable materials. Natural stone (particularly marble) or artificial stone (e.g. brick) was preferred for the structure, but the *mensa* itself still had to be of natural stone. If costly materials were unavailable or too expensive the altar could be built of marbled wood. Wood was used primarily for side altars or for the altars of poorer churches, but in the second half of the 17th century it was used for altars with important paintings, as it was feared that cold stone would cause condensation on the paintings.

The four basic types of altar (the table altar, the box altar, the block altar and the sarcophagus altar; *see* §1 and 3(i)(a) above) continued to be used with some modifications. The table altar was especially popular in Italy in the 17th and 18th centuries and changed comparatively little. The box altar, though forbidden by the Council of Milan (1583), remained popular for centuries, especially in Spain, Italy and France, and was used primarily for side altars. Block altars also changed little, beyond a reshaping of the *stipes* in the Baroque and Rococo periods, when curved lines were introduced on the corners, accentuated by sculptures, and colour was also used. The sarcophagus altar, however, evolved the most, as it was a fairly new type that first appeared in the early 16th century in Italy. It subsequently flourished, primarily during the Baroque and Rococo periods, when the flowing curves that characterized sarcophagi were particularly popular, although it is interesting that this type of altar became far more widespread in Austria, Germany, the southern Netherlands, France and north-western Spain than in Italy. Throughout the 17th century the *stipes* increased in height, although the basic, somewhat swollen form remained otherwise unchanged.

During the 16th century the altar increasingly came to be fused with the ALTARPIECE and also with the Ciborium (*see* CIBORIUM (ii)). Many such structures were given architectural forms, frequently in a tripartite arrangement resembling a triumphal arch or a Serlian opening. They became increasingly massive, eventually extending across the entire east wall of a church and usually also comprising painting or sculpture, which fulfilled the role of an altarpiece. Giovanni Marigliano's altar at S Anna dei Lombardi, Naples, with its tripartite architectural structure richly decorated with festoons and putti, is a typical example of this type. A *Virgin and Child* forms the central sculptural group, enclosed in a niche surmounted by a shell-shaped round arch, while life-size figures of saints stand between Corinthian columns that separate the lateral compartments. In the High Baroque period the architecture of altars became heavier, with columns being grouped in pairs and given higher bases, while pediments were made more substantial. As a result the altar projected more emphatically from the wall, and increasingly sculpture took the place of painting in the central section.

In 1583 the Council of Milan decreed that every altar should be covered by a ciborium or baldacchino of stone, wood or cloth. This stipulation clearly was not always followed, as it was repeated continuously until as late as 1697. Of the many ciboria that were built a certain number were modelled on earlier forms. For example, the ciborium (1652) above the high altar at Taranto Cathedral was based on that of 1285 at S Paolo fuori le Mura, Rome (*see* ARNOLFO DI CAMBIO, fig. 2). Most 17th-century ciboria followed new, often innovative designs, as at S Crisogono, Rome, where the domed ciborium of 1627 is supported on four Corinthian columns surmounted by pediments and decorated with putti and garlands. The development reached a high point with Gianlorenzo Bernini's baldacchino (1623–34) above the high altar in St Peter's, Rome. The ciborium subsequently lost its crowning character, frequently being reduced to a group of columns supporting volutes and surrounded by apparently floating putti. Such was the arrangement chosen by Bernini for the *Cathedra Petri* (1657–66; Rome, St Peter's; *see* BERNINI, (2), fig. 2), where the easternmost altar is surmounted by the throne of St Peter. Ornamental volutes are supported on columns and rise towards the centre, but the space between them is free.

By the late 17th century the highly theatrical and richly decorated type of altar had been adopted throughout Italy and most of Europe. A good Italian example is the altar of Il Gesù, Lecce, which extends across the entire east wall of the church and is characteristically overstated (see fig. 5). A tall, heavily ornamented base is surmounted by a two-tier structure that combines twisted columns, niches and other features all densely covered in stuccowork, as well as statues and paintings. In the same period in the southern Netherlands, Germany and Austria, altars were also designed with numerous columns, usually twisted or ornamented with foliage and often fluted. Typically, the height of the superstructure was reduced, and its upper border was given a richly ornamented profile. It would

5. High altar, Il Gesù, Lecce, *c.* 1696

often be surmounted by a triangular or semicircular pediment containing sculpture or painting and ornamented with garlands, foliage and cherubs' heads. By the end of the century the sides of the pediment took on the form of volutes, often with allegorical figures, angels or saints placed either side. The flanking wings of the altar structure gradually became detached from the back wall, curving forwards following an oval plan. Henricus-Franciscus Verbrugghen was the principal innovator in the development of the altar in the southern Netherlands, where examples were comparatively restrained. Despite the fact that Verbrugghen's high altar (1699–1709) in St Augustine, Antwerp, featured painting rather than sculpture in the centre, it was given great depth, and it became the model for other elliptical altars in that region. Sculpture was chosen for the central section with increasing frequency, as for example in the high altar (1713–19) at St Bavo, Ghent, and in most subsequent designs. In Germany the earlier tradition of wood-carving was displaced by a preference for stuccowork by the late 17th century. By the 18th century there was a characteristic merging of the various constituent elements of an altar and its surroundings, successfully expressed by such works as Egid Quirin Asam's high altar (1733–46) in St Johannes Nepomuk, Munich (*see* ASAM, (3), fig. 2). Bernini's structures in St Peter's, Rome, must have served as the prototype for this work, which is characterized by twisted, extravagantly ornamented columns arranged on a trapezoidal plan. The altar merges completely with the wall behind it; the only elements suggesting the separation are the altar's balustrade and elaborate crowning cornice. While the development of altar designs and settings in other parts of Europe was on the whole closely related to that in Italy, Germany and the Netherlands, a distinctive tradition evolved in Spain (for discussion and illustration *see* RETABLE, §1).

BIBLIOGRAPHY

J. Braun: *Der christliche Altar in seiner geschichtlichen Entwicklung*, 2 vols (Munich, 1924)

A. Jansen: 'Het 17de eeuwse kerkelijk meubilair', *Hand. Kon. Kring Oudhdknd., Lett. & Kst Mechelen/Bull. Cerc. Archéol., Litt. & A. Malines* (1965), p. 69

A. Merck: *Altarkunst des Barock* (exh. cat., Frankfurt am Main, 1980)

R. Laun: *Studien zur Altarbaukunst in Süddeutschland, 1560–1650* (Munich, 1982)

C. Claes, M.-F. Jacobs and N. Perrin: 'L'Autel et le tabernacle de la fin du XVIe siècle au milieu du XIXe siècle', *Rev. A.* (1986), no. 71, pp. 47–70

U. Becker: *Studien zum flämischen Altarbau im 17. und 18. Jahrhundert* (Brussels, 1990)

IRIS KOCKELBERGH

(ii) Portable. The privilege of using portable altars granted by Pope Clement VII in 1527 was renewed by Pope Paul III in 1537 and 1540, and in 1549 he extended its use to religious orders (including the Jesuits, Trinitarians, Carmelites and Servites). Pope Clement VIII published the *Roman Pontifical* in which he defined the form, composition and consecration rite of portable altars. They were to be constructed of wood or precious metal, with a consecrated stone *mensa* on which the chalice and paten could stand during mass. Most were of the box altar type, with a compartment for relics inside. These altars were usually built with feet and were placed on table tops so that missionaries, travelling bishops and any authorized priest could celebrate mass when no consecrated fixed altar was available. The Cathedral Museum of Trier and that of Augsburg have several 16th–19th-century examples of portable altars. A typical 16th-century portable altar would have had a wood or metal frame with a stone of white, red or green marble or jasper set in the centre. In one example (1561; Trier, Bischöf. Dom- & Diözsmus.; see Braun, i, pl. 84) a cross is inscribed in each corner of the frame, and there is a fifth cross on the latch that seals in the stone. Baroque portable altars were often given unusual forms and very rich decoration. One interesting example (Augsburg, Dom S Maria.; see Braun, i, pl. 94) resembles a contemporary silver tray, with scrolling floral engravings; its concave and convex sides form a band filled with reliefs depicting Passion symbols, as well as Veronica's veil.

Restrictions regulating the use of portable altars began in 1579, during the pontificate of Pope Gregory XIII. In 1703 Pope Clement XI increased the restrictions, so that a bishop travelling outside his diocese was required to obtain authorization from the local bishop to use a portable altar; he was permitted to use it only in the bishop's home, and not in that of a layman. In his Apostolic Constitutions of 1723, Pope Innocent III reversed this ruling, allowing a visiting bishop to use a portable altar in the home of a layman. The form of portable altars changed after the 19th century and especially following the resolutions of the Second Vatican Council (1962–5), which revised the canons and statutes regulating the materials, form and construction of altars. In the late 20th century portable altars were simple lightweight tables, usually made of wood and somewhat smaller than fixed altars within the church.

BIBLIOGRAPHY

J. Braun: *Der christliche Altar in seiner geschichtlichen Entwicklung*, 2 vols (Munich, 1924)

JOHN N. LUPIA

5. PROTESTANT. During the Reformation in the 16th century there was great opposition to the abundance of altars in churches. In 1522 Martin Luther declared that altars, no longer associated with sacrifice in theological terms, were completely inessential for the confession of faith, and he wanted them to be removed from churches. Somewhat later he realized that altars could have a certain pedagogical function through association with the Last Supper, and in 1533 he ruled that the altar, consisting of a single stone, could remain, with the proviso that the priest or celebrant should always stand behind it and face the congregation. Thus the altar came to be used in Protestant churches only as a place from which to conduct the service. This led to a loss of liturgical significance for the east end of the church, although in the northern Netherlands (in contrast to German-speaking areas) the altar remained in the choir.

Altars in Protestant churches continued to follow one of the four basic types of Christian altar (i.e. table altar, box altar, block altar and sarcophagus altar), although the simple and severe forms of table and block altars were best suited to the new ideology. A low, unornamented altar was preferred, without a predella, altarpiece or antependium. In practice, however, not much changed in the conception of the altar during the first years of the Reformation. Use was made of medieval examples, and richly ornamented carved or painted altarpieces, often winged and with predellas, were placed on altars. In some cases the service was simply conducted from the old, pre-Reformation altar. The main change that took place in the 16th and 17th centuries was in the iconography of altarpieces; the Last Supper, Baptism and Confession became the most frequently represented themes.

Two new types of altar developed in the German Reformed and Protestant churches from the 17th century: the pulpit altar and the organ altar. The architectural connection between altar and pulpit was very popular in the Lutheran Church, and many variants of the type exist. The pulpit altar (1717) in the parish church at Dorndorf near Jena is an interesting example. It has three horizontal sections: the altar with an antependium is surmounted by the pulpit, which in turn is crowned by a sculpture with a representation of Christ. Either side of the altar there are two small doors which give access to the pulpit. In 1721 Johann Philip Göbel built a pulpit altar in the church of the Trinity in Erlangen, and the structure combines elements of Gothic and Baroque. The altar itself is framed by four heavy columns supporting the pulpit, with statues of saints on the extreme left and right, and is crowned by a classical cornice. The organ altar, a type that was particularly widespread in the northern Netherlands, is similar in construction to the pulpit altar. A simple table altar, often with an altarpiece, is usually flanked by columns supporting an organ that crowns the whole structure. Such, for example, is the organ altar of *c.* 1700 in the parish church at Kunreuth near Erlangen. This type was also popular in the southern Netherlands and even appeared occasionally in Catholic churches. The plain type of altar with restrained decoration increasingly became the norm; a basic style, with columns and a flat altarpiece, was retained into the 19th century, but block altars were predominant in the 20th.

6. Altar 4, basalt, La Venta, Mexico

BIBLIOGRAPHY

A. Beeckman: *Het altaar* (Oosterhout, 1933)

H. Mai: *Der evangelische Kanzelaltar: Geschichte und Bedeutung* (Halle, 1969)

P. Posharsky: 'Der Altar in den protestantischen Kirchen der Pfalz', *Der Turnhahn*, xvi (1972), pp. 1–16

——: 'Altar', *Theologische Realenzyklopedie*, ed. G. Krause and G. Muller, ii (Berlin and New York, 1986), pp. 321–7

IRIS KOCKELBERGH

III. Americas.

1. PRE-COLUMBIAN. The term 'altar' is applied to particular small-scale stone structures such as carved blocks and slabs associated with ceremonial centres, although their true purpose is often uncertain. Architectural structures comprising pyramids, terraces and platforms built around plazas may also be defined as altars, since religious ceremonies were performed on and around them and sacrifices made. Most platforms supported a temple, in which there were separate altars or benches along the interior walls. Others, such as Cuicuilco (Valley of Mexico; *fl c.* 500 BC–AD 1), had open altars on top.

Carved basalt blocks from Olmec sites, often with a seated human figure carved on one side, are also called altars. Altar 4 at La Venta, for example, has a figure holding a rope attached to a bound captive on the other side (see fig. 6), and Altar 5 has humans depicted carrying infant were-jaguars (see Kubler, fig. 78). Stone slabs supported by atlantids, such as Monument 5 (*c.* 500 BC) at Potrero Nuevo, may also have been altars (see Kubler, fig. 81).

The Maya carved stone blocks, drums and boulders in low relief; these are called altars, although their function is commemorative, and are often placed in prominent positions (accompanied by stelae) in plazas and at the bases of stairways leading to the tops of platforms (see Porter Weaver, fig. 6.34), although at Altar de Sacrificios they line the stairway. At Izapa (Late Pre-Classic period, *c.* 300 BC–*c.* AD 250) mythical scenes and gods are portrayed on these altars, at Classic period Copán (*c.* AD 250–*c.* 900) they are carved in high relief with zoomorphic deities, and at Classic period Quiriguá mythical monsters are depicted. Altars O and P (both late 8th century AD) at Quiriguá are sandstone boulders with dancers surrounded by ornamentation on one side and glyphs on the other (see Kubler, figs 201 and 202).

The Toltecs also carved atlantid altars, as well as stone *chacmools*, reclining human figures holding dishes believed to be altars for receiving the viscera of human sacrifices (see Coe, Snow and Benson, p. 135). *Tzompantli*, stone skull-rack platforms, carved with human skulls, upon which sacrificial skulls were placed, also served as altars.

The Aztecs (Late Post-Classic, *c.* AD 1200–1521) used atlantid altars, *chacmools* and *tzompantli*, as well as *cuauhxicalli* (Náhuatl: 'eagle house'), carved stone boxes with representations of eagles on them in which sacrificial human hearts may have been burnt. Some altars were used for human sacrifice; the stone of Tizoc (late 15th century; Mexico City, Mus. N. Antropol.; see Kubler, fig. 48), a huge carved cylindrical stone (diam. 2.65 m) may have been used for this purpose.

Andean cultures also built monuments incorporating ceremonial platforms, but there are few structures that may be called altars. At the Temple of the Crossed Hands (*c.* 1500 BC), Kotosh, Peru, stone niches in which offerings were found may have been altars. Numerous Chavín sites, such as Chavín de Huántar, Punkurí and Moxeke (Early Horizon, *c.* 900 BC–*c.* 200 BC), have temple platforms where human and animal sacrifice took place, but no altars have been found.

The Early Intermediate period (*c.* 200 BC–*c.* AD 600) Nazca (southern coastal Peru) and Moche (northern coastal Peru) cultures, and the Late Intermediate period (*c.* AD 1000–1476) Chumú (northern coastal Peru) and other Andean cultures all practised sacrifice and built temple platforms, but no altars have been identified. The Incas, however, also sacrificed victims over stone altars. A rock carved into seats of platforms in the Semicircular Temple at Machu Picchu (16th century) was probably an altar for burnt offerings. Many rocks were also considered sacred and may have served as altar-shrines, for example the Intihuatana ('hitching post of the sun') at Machu Picchu (16th century), or the Throne of the Inca, the carved platform that stands above Cuzco.

BIBLIOGRAPHY

G. Kubler: *The Art and Architecture of Ancient America*, Pelican Hist. A. (Harmondsworth, 1962, rev. 3/1984)

M. Porter Weaver: *The Aztecs, Maya, and their Predecessors: Archaeology of Mesoamerica* (New York, 1972, rev. 3/1993)

M. Coe, D. Snow and E. Benson: *Atlas of Ancient America* (Oxford, 1986)

SIAN E. JAY

2. NATIVE NORTH AMERICAN. Among Native North American peoples there is almost nothing that can truly be called an altar. This is because much Native American religious practice is on a personal basis, even when within a communal ceremony: individuals seek communion with spirits through such personal acts as fasting, tobacco smoking and other methods of inducing vision quests.

Among the Ohio mounds studied by E. G. Squier in the 19th century, one type, labelled 'altar mounds', was described as containing 'symmetrical altars of burned clay or stone'. Similarly, the 'temple mounds' of the Mississippian culture of the Southeast (*see* CAHOKIA) apparently supported temple structures, but few details of these structures and of the ceremonies that took place in and around them are known.

In the prehistoric cultures of the Southwest, the KIVA was a chamber specially constructed for ceremonial purposes (*see* AWATOVI, CANYON DE CHELLY and CHACO CANYON). They are usually round, although rectangular *kivas* were also occasionally built. Some, known as Great Kivas, were apparently built to serve a whole community as opposed to small sets of clansmen. However, although Great Kivas typically contain such internal features as an encircling wall bench, niches, a central, square, raised firebox and paired rectangular masonry 'vaults', none can be called an altar in functional terms. Sand (more accurately, 'dry') paintings among the Pueblo are usually connected with wooden 'slat altars'; the origins of these are uncertain and may have been in the 19th century.

BIBLIOGRAPHY

E. G. Squier and E. H. Davis: *Ancient Monuments of the Mississippi Valley* (Washington, DC, 1848)

J. D. Jennings, ed.: *Ancient Native Americans* (San Francisco, 1978), pp. 221–79, 281–325 and 327–401

C. F. Feest: *Native Arts of North America* (London, 1980, rev. 1992)

L. S. Cordell: *Prehistory of the Southwest* (New York, 1984)

M. Coe, D. Snow and E. Benson: *Atlas of Ancient America* (Oxford, 1986)

DAVID M. JONES

IV. Asia.

Many of the region's religions—Buddhism, Hinduism, Daoism, Confucianism, shamanism and animism—have produced a variety of altars to serve both spiritual and practical purposes. In imperial China vast platforms, often open to the air, permitted ritual sacrifices to be performed on the altar. In Hindu temples the altar holds the sacrificial fire. In many Buddhist temples altars receive offerings as well as accommodating censers and candlesticks and often statuettes and elaborate superstructures. In nomadic societies such as those of Mongolia, the altar must be small and portable. Although many altars are made in rectangular shape from wood and placed within a hall of worship, some take the form of an area, often open to the elements, in front of a shrine; others take the form of a stone terrace or terraces supporting a smaller altar at the summit. Instead of a boxlike shape, an altar may take that of a linga or of a human figure; or a pillar-stupa may function as an altar. In South-east Asia the pedestal of a statue may serve the purpose. Among Buddhists a connection is made between the altar and Mt Meru, the cosmological mountain of Buddhist belief. In temples with fixed altars, furnishings and banners often flank the altar, which may itself be elaborately carved and painted. Simpler makeshift altars are used for special ceremonies or domestic use.

1. CHINA. Altars have played an important part in ceremony and ritual at all levels in China. In annual rites of fertility and prosperity the emperor offered sacrifices at or on large altars, often in the open air. Smaller altars abounded in Buddhist, Daoist and Confucian temples. Domestic altars allowed worship of household gods.

(i) Architectural. The earliest known Chinese altars date from the Shang period (*c.* 1600–*c.* 1050 BC). At Zhengzhou

7. Altar of Heaven, Beijing, white marble, top platform diam. 33.3 m, 1530; enlarged 1749

and Anyang, both in modern Henan Province, the latter the site of the last Shang capital, large square platforms of stamped earth (Chin. *hangtu*) are believed to have served as ceremonial altars. A three-tiered ceremonial platform excavated at Yangzishan in modern Sichuan Province is contemporary with the Shang examples. These ceremonial platforms continued to be constructed in the Zhou period (*c.* 1050–256 BC).

The standard histories of the Han (*Han shu*), compiled in the 1st century AD, describe the use of earth mounds or altars. The *Book of Rites* (*Liji*), versions of which were compiled during the Han period (206 BC–AD 220), specifies that the altars dedicated to the soil and to grain were always placed to the east and west respectively of the capital city. Ritual structures called *lingtai* (spirit altars) are also recorded as being located to the south of the Western Han (206 BC–AD 9) capital of Chang'an, now Xian in modern Shaanxi Province. The ritual hall excavated there comprises a raised circular earth platform surrounded by a moat, with another platform at the centre, on which stood the ritual hall, including the *lingtai*, which was used as an observatory. At Mt Tai on the Shandong Peninsula, the most sacred of the Five Holy Mountains of China, is an altar at which the emperors made their offerings to heaven. There the oldest altar is the Ancient Altar for the Sacrifice to Heaven (Gu fengshan tai), a square stone platform said to date back to the Han period. A further large altar of similar shape is dedicated to the worship of the Great Dipper (*Beitou tan*).

The use of raised platforms serving as altars continued into the Tang (AD 618–907) and up to the Qing (AD 1644–1911) periods. The hall of the temple of Nanchan si at Wutai in Shanxi Province, used throughout these periods, has a U-shaped tiled altar or platform (*Xumi tai*), modelled on Mt Sumeru or Mt Meru, the cosmic mountain, which became identified with the altar for Buddhist images.

The Chinese imperial cities, from the Tang period onwards, had increasing numbers of altars built around them. The first emperor of the Ming period (AD 1368–1644) built a circular mound for sacrifices to heaven and a square mound for sacrifices to the earth at his capital at Nanjing. These, and the altars to the soil and to grain, were located to the south-east of the city, and they followed the Han system of double altar mounds. They were enclosed by a square balustrade, surrounded in turn by auxiliary halls. A spirit star gate (*lingxing*) in each of the four sides of the balustrade allowed access to the complex. The southern gate had a triple entrance. In 1371 upper and lower mounds were added (see Shatzman Steinhardt, pl. 10.4), and in 1377 the whole mound was covered over by a building called the Great Sacrifice Hall (Dasi dian; see Shatzman Steinhardt, pl. 10.5).

By the time the Ming moved their capital to BEIJING in 1421, a large number of altars were located at various places in and around the city. The altar to the ancestors and the single altar to soil and grain were located within the Imperial City, immediately to the south of the Forbidden City (which was surrounded by the Imperial City). The altars to heaven and to agriculture were further south in the outer city. The altars to the sun and moon were to the east and west respectively of the city walls, and the altar to the earth was placed to the north-east of the city. All these altars were merely low, plain terraces without embellishment. The most important was the altar to heaven, where the emperor made his annual offerings to heaven at the winter solstice.

The group of buildings known popularly as the Temple of Heaven (Tian tan) was built in 1420 and restored in 1530 and 1757. The original structure consisted of a circular mound (Huan qiu) with a sacrificial hall in the middle, following the original model at Nanjing. In 1530 a square altar was built to the north of the Great Sacrifice Hall (Daxiang dian) and a round altar to the south. The hall was renamed Altar for Prayer for Harvest (Gigu tan), but that name was changed back to Great Sacrifice Hall 12 years later. Today it is referred to as the Hall for Prayer for a Prosperous Year (Qinian dian; *see* BEIJING, fig. 2)

The altar to the south, consisting of a huge circular mound (*tai*) open to the sky, was enlarged in 1749 to its present form (see fig. 7). It consists of three tiered marble terraces, the flagstones on each terrace being carefully arranged in multiples of nine. Three and nine have important symbolic and cosmological associations in China. Each terrace is surrounded by a carved marble balustrade, the pillars of each balustrade forming multiples of three (for illustration see Juliano, p. 99). The whole structure is enclosed by a low circular wall topped with glazed tiles. At each of the cardinal points a marble stairway leads up to the altar. At the foot of each stairway is a triple gate. The whole structure is enclosed by a second, square wall.

BIBLIOGRAPHY

L. C. Arlington and W. Lewisohn: *In Search of Old Peking* (Beijing, 1935/*R* Hong Kong, Oxford and New York, 1987)

Chang Kwang-chih: *The Archaeology of Ancient China* (London, 1971)

M. Pirazzoli-t'Serstevens: *Living Architecture: Chinese* (London, 1972)

J. Rawson: *Ancient China: Art and Archaeology* (London, 1980)

A. Juliano: *Treasures of China* (London, 1981)

Liang Ssu-ch'eng: *A Pictorial History of Chinese Architecture* (Cambridge, MA, 1984)

N. Shatzman Steinhardt: *Chinese Traditional Architecture* (New York, 1984)

SIAN E. JAY

(ii) Other. The ancestral cult is one of the oldest religious expressions of the Chinese. Altars for the worship of forebears are recorded in the earliest literature. The usual ancestral altar consists of an oblong table with a memorial tablet placed in the centre. Accessories are an incense burner, vases for flowers and candlesticks. Wealthy families may have a detached shrine to house the ancestral altar, but usually a separate room in the dwelling is used. Traditionally all houses had at least one, but often several, small altars dedicated to various divinities and spirits, often no more than a painted shelf holding the image or name of the god in question, as well as offerings and incense. Larger household altars in the form of miniature houses are also known.

Celebration of the birthday of Confucius was marked annually at the altars of the Confucian temples once found in most cities and towns in China. The most important of such altars are found in the Temple of Confucius in his birthplace, Qufu in Shandong Province, dating to the early 16th century. There the images of the founder and his disciples are placed in niches in large closet-like altar structures made of carved and lacquered wood. Altars made during the Qing dynasty were usually in the form of an elaborately carved temple building of painted and gilded wood with a tablet bearing Confucius's name inside.

Altars are found in all places of Buddhist worship. The Dunhuang caves of the 5th–6th century AD contain several pillar-stupas that served as altars (*see* STUPA, §6). More generally a main altar consists of a large platform, made of stone or wood, raised *c*. 1–2 m above the floor, with a lower table for offerings and ritual paraphernalia in front. Often the altars are tiered to accommodate Buddhas, *bodhisattvas* and *luohans* on their respective 'levels'. Buddhist altars are normally decorated with streamers and embroidered banners made of silk. During the Yuan (1279–1368) and Ming (1368–1644) periods Buddhist altars became increasingly uniform with standardized design and decoration. The use of wooden superstructures on the altars became popular, often painted in bright red and gold, and the organization of the images on the altars more regular. Lamaist altars, introduced during the Mongol domination of China, generally retain their early Tibetan features.

Daoist altars are generally similar in design to Buddhist ones: tiered and sometimes placed in niches with superstructures that include pillars and imitation roofs. Several altars to various divinities are commonly found within the same hall, although important groups of major gods, such as the Three Pure Ones (Chin. *Sanqing*) normally share the same altar. Makeshift altars are frequently used in Daoist rituals to house 'visiting gods' as well as in ceremonies held out of doors. Basic altar adornments are the same as for Confucian and Buddhist altars: a pair of candlesticks, an incense burner and a pair of vases for flowers.

BIBLIOGRAPHY

D. C. Baker: *T'ai Shan: An Account of the Sacred Eastern Peak of China* (Shanghai, 1925/*R* Taipei, 1972)

J. Prip-Møller: *Chinese Buddhist Monasteries* (Copenhagen and London, 1937/*R* Hong Kong, 1968)

H. Welch: *The Practice of Chinese Buddhism, 1900–1950*, Harvard East Asian Series (Cambridge, MA, 1967)

K. M. Schipper: *Le Fen-teng: Rituel taoïste* (Paris, 1975)

Zhongguo fojiao yishu [Buddhist art in China] (Taipei, 1978)

Guangji si [Guanji temple], Buddhist Association of China (Beijing, 1981)

E. Boerschmann: *Old China in Historic Photographs* (New York, 1982)

J. Largerwey: *Taoist Ritual in Chinese Society and History* (New York and London, 1987)

C. Müller and Wu Shun-chi: *Wege der Götter und Menschen: Religionen im traditionellen China*, Veröffentlichungen des Museum für Völkerkunde, Berlin (Berlin, 1989)

HENRIK H. SØRENSEN

2. JAPAN. The Japanese altar has two basic forms, Shinto and Buddhist. Lay worship groups and religious healers often use altars that combine elements from both types. Much variation occurs with sect and over time. Originally, Shinto deities (*kami*) were not worshipped in buildings but were called down into a temporary rock- or tree altar (*iwasaka*, *himorogi*). Shrine buildings probably became permanent between the 6th and 8th centuries AD, influenced by the Buddhist temples erected then. The Shinto altar is the area in front of the doors of the closed sanctuary (*naijin*) in the building in which the deity is enshrined (*honden*), and may be open to the elements (see fig. 8). It may be an elaborate series of steps and platforms from the elevated doors to the ritual and seating area, enclosed within a building (*heiden*), or it may be only a few rickety steps outside a small shrine building. Ritual furnishings include a mirror at the centre of the doors, which symbolizes purity of heart. An upright stick (*gohei*) in the centre of the area with a symmetrical set of zigzag papers (like lightning bolts) symbolically represents the deity, which is rarely depicted anthropomorphically. Brightly coloured brocade banners with the shrine's crest hang on both sides of the altar. A pair of statues protect the sacred area; these may be warriors or guardian animals such as 'lion-dogs' (*koma inu*) or foxes. Behind the area where worshippers sit is an offering box and large bell with pull-cord, rung to announce the worshipper's presence.

The Buddhist altar is usually at the back of a large room floored with straw mats (*tatami*). The altar itself (*shumidan*) is the central dais on which the main Buddhist statue rests. It is modelled on Mt Sumeru, the mountain at the centre of the Indian, and later Buddhist, cosmologies. The mountain is shaped like an hour-glass and is surrounded

8. Altar dedicated to Inari, Fushimi Inari shrine, Kyoto

by nine rings of mountains and eight oceans; like the mountain, the altar narrows at the middle. The Buddha statue, usually with attendants, may be either free-standing or inside a house-like enclosure (*kyūden*; *zushi*). In front of this is a table with incense, candles and flowers. Facing both is a cushion for the priest surrounded by low tables with ritual implements and *sūtra* books, bells, a drum and a list of the parish deceased (*kakochō*). Flanking the main altar are subsidiary altars to other Buddhist figures and the founder of the temple. Gold canopies (*tengai*) hang from the ceiling over the Buddha and the priest's seat, and rich brocades add red, purple, yellow and green accents. Furnishings are glossy red or black lacquer, and most metal surfaces are gold-coloured, producing an overall effect of stately otherworldliness.

Most homes have a miniature version of both these altars. The small altar known as the *kamidana* enshrines a number of Shinto deities that protect the home. It is placed on a high shelf and a sacred rope (*shimenawa*) is stretched across to protect it from defilement. In the miniature Buddhist altar (*butsudan*) in a black lacquered box with folding doors are sectarian images and the family's ancestral tablets.

BIBLIOGRAPHY

J. Herbert: *Shinto: The Fountainhead of Japan* (New York, 1967)
R. J. Smith: *Ancestor Worship in Contemporary Japan* (Stanford, 1974)
'Jinja kenchiku' [Shrine architecture], *Shinto jiten* [Dictionary of Shinto] (Tokyo, 1978)
N. Koike: *Jinja bukkaku monoshiri gaido* [Connoisseur's guide to shrines and temples] (Tokyo, 1981)
'Shumidan' [Altar], *Butsugu daijiten* [Dictionary of Buddhist objects] (Tokyo, 1982)
D. Buisson: *L'Architecture sacrée au Japon* (Paris, 1989)

KAREN A. SMYERS

3. KOREA. Altars have an important function in all forms of worship in Korea (for a discussion of religions in Korea *see* KOREA, §I, 4). Most Buddhist main halls have at least two: a main altar with one or more Buddhas, and a smaller, secondary altar for the protective deities of the temple. Most main altars consist of a raised platform, placed at the back of the hall and facing the entrance. The front of an altar is often elaborately decorated with carvings or brightly coloured paintings, sometimes both. In some temples the altar is set against the back wall, but often there is a passage behind it to allow circumambulation. Different kinds of main altar are found: in some instances the image of the Buddha is merely seated on the altar (*see* KOREA, fig. 23); in others the main image is placed inside a wooden superstructure that emulates a temple building, complete with beams and roof construction. Minor altars often consist of little more than a shelf with a painting of the deity in question on the wall behind it, an incense burner and a pair of candlesticks. Altars for rituals performed in the open are made by placing an oblong altar table with the offerings in front of a large banner painting of a Buddha.

Ancestral altars are used in Confucianism. These are generally unadorned tables with a spirit-tablet and nothing more. On the prescribed memorial days offerings of food and wine are placed on the table. In the shrine dedicated to Confucius in Seoul, the founder's birthday is celebrated with large-scale rituals each year, when offerings are placed on tables in front of the image of Confucius.

As in Buddhism, altars play a central role in the practice of shamanism, the native religion of Korea. The *kut* or shaman ritual is performed for various reasons, but normally in order to heal a sick person or secure for the soul of a deceased a happy rebirth in heaven. It may be held in the house of the *mudang* (shaman) or in the homes of those who request the ritual. Depending on the kind of *kut* to be performed or its length, appropriate makeshift altars, usually in the form of low tables, are set up according to a predefined rule and offerings arranged on them. Large folding screens are normally used as backdrop for the tables. Most of the items placed on the altar tables consist of varied and elaborate food offerings.

BIBLIOGRAPHY

S. J. Palmer: *Confucian Rituals in Korea*, Religions of Asia Series, iii (Berkeley, n.d.)
Halla Pai Huhm: *Kut: Korean Shamanist Rituals* (Seoul, 1980)
Cho Hung-youn [Cho Hŭng-yun]: *Koreanischer Schamanismus: Eine Einführung*, Wegweiser zur Völkerkunde, 27 (Hamburg, 1982)
Sin Yŏng-hŭn: *Sawŏn kŏnch'ŭk* [Architecture of Buddhist temples] (1983), ix of *Kukbo* [The national treasures of Korea] (Seoul, 1983–5)
Hanguk-ŭi myŏngch'al: T'ongdosa [Famous temples of Korea: T'ongdo temple] (T'ongdosa, 1987)
Korean Buddhism, Korean Buddhist Chogye Order (Seoul, 1988)
Yŏngsan chae [The Yŏngsanjae ritual] (Seoul, 1989)

4. TIBET. Tibetan Buddhism, or Lamaism, is a local development of Indian Tantric Buddhism (*see also* BUDDHISM, §III, 6). Rituals play a significant and persuasive role in the general structure of the religion, so altars constitute the material focus of most religious activity. The pantheon of Tibetan Buddhism is extensive and complex, consisting of a large number of standard Buddhas, *bodhisattvas* and protectors. In addition each school has its distinct pantheon and lineage of masters. A large monastery usually features several halls dedicated to one particular deity or group of related deities; each individual

shrine-hall may have several altars. A standard altar may consist of a raised platform of painted wood-bricks and/or clay with its back placed against the wall. It holds an image of a central Buddha, deity or major lama flanked by attending *bodhisattvas* or protectors. In some cases the main deities are placed within elaborately carved and gilded superstructures resembling heavenly palaces. Tibetan altars are generally so piled with offerings and ritual paraphernalia that the deities are almost hidden from view. Large banners of silk and brocade trail from the ceiling. It is not unusual for large altars to consist of a narrow shelf on which are placed ritual vessels and offerings. The backdrop is in some cases made into a cupboard (usually of carved or painted wood) with several nichelike shelves holding images, holy scriptures and relics. Behind most altars are displayed scrolls (Tib. *tangkas*) with images of the Buddha or deity to whom the altar is dedicated. Special types of altar include the *maṇḍala*-altar (from Skt *maṇḍala*: a cosmic diagram) set up in connection with a particular elaborate ritual, an open, three-dimensional structure placed in the middle of the shrine-hall, and the stupa-altar, consisting of a reliquary (*sarīrā*-stupa) in bronze or other material placed on the altar. Other rituals require the use of makeshift altar tables on which offerings and implements are arranged in accordance with a detailed plan. The standard altar implements are vases for ambrosia, water bowls and incense burners of brass or precious metals, butter-lamps and stylized offerings of moulded and painted butter or clay.

The altars of Bon, the native Tibetan religion, are generally identical to those used by Buddhism in terms of structure and form. Naturally iconography, symbolism and the rituals practised differ in accordance with the beliefs (*see also* TIBET, §I, 6(i)). Many ritual implements, however, such as sacrificial vessels and offerings, are the same.

BIBLIOGRAPHY

R. B. Ekvall: *Religious Observances in Tibet: Patterns and Functions* (Chicago, 1964)
D. White: 'Homa (The Solemn Rite of Burnt Offering to Heaven)', *Gugong Jikan*, iii/2 (1968), pp. 13–20
S. Beyer: *The Cult of Tārā, Magic and Ritual in Tibet* (Berkeley, 1973)
D. I. Lauf: *Tibetan Sacred Art* (Berkeley and London, 1976)
Zhongguo fojiao yishu/Buddhist Art in China (Taipei, 1978), pls 74–84 and 127
P. Rawson: *Sacred Tibet* (London, 1991)

5. MONGOLIA. The Mongols were first exposed to Buddhism under Genghis Khan (*reg* 1206–27). After the establishment of the Yuan dynasty (1279–1368) in China as their centre of power, Tibetan Buddhism—also known as Lamaism—was eventually adopted as their main creed (*see also* BUDDHISM, §III, 7). Hence the temple architecture, altars, iconography and ritual paraphernalia were copied more or less directly from Tibetan Buddhism. In the early phase of Mongolian Buddhism, altars were made in accordance with the ritual procedures of the dominant Sakya sect. After the world power of the Mongols collapsed, the Gelugpa School became most influential. Being a mainly nomad culture, the Mongols devised small, boxlike, wooden altar tables that could easily be packed for travel. Large ceremonies, held in a tent, required several such altar tables to hold the ritual implements, holy scriptures, food offerings, butter-lamps etc.

Knowledge about the use and construction of shamanist altars dates from the 18th century, when the indigenous beliefs known as SHAMANISM and Lamaism had already been practised side by side since the 13th century. Small portable altar tables of the type used by the lamas are also common to shamanism. Indeed, most shamanist altars feature Buddhist deities and often share the same ritual objects. Ancestral worship involving shrines and altars is known to have been practised by the Mongols during the Yuan period. These rites, however, were adopted from the Chinese ancestral cult as practised by the emperors. In 1263 Kublai Khan (*reg* 1260–94) had a great ancestral temple built in Dadu (the site of modern Beijing), where sacrifices were made for his forefathers, including Genghis Khan.

BIBLIOGRAPHY

Hashimoto Koho: *Mokō no ramakyō* [Lamaism in Mongolia] (Tokyo, 1942)
R. J. Miller: *Monasteries and Culture Change in Inner Mongolia* (Wiesbaden, 1959)
L. Jisl: *Mongolei: Kunst und Tradition* (Praha, 1960)
L. Chandra and R. Vira: *A New Tibeto-Mongol Pantheon*, 20 vols (New Delhi, 1961–72)
W. Heissig: *The Religions of Mongolia* (Berkeley, 1979)
E. Taube and M. Taube: *Schamanen und Rhapsoden* (Vienna, 1983)
J.-P. Roux: *La Religion des Turcs et des Mongols* (Paris, 1984), pp. 59–154
M. Rossabi: *Khubilai Khan* (London, 1988), pp. 133–4

HENRIK H. SØRENSEN

6. INDIA. The Indo-European peoples that settled in the Gangetic plain of India from *c.* 1500 BC developed elaborate ritual practices in which altars figured prominently; almost a third of the *satapatha Brāhmaṇa*, written *c.* 1200–*c.* 800 BC, is devoted to the construction of hawk-shaped altars used in the Soma sacrifice. Altars of various shapes and sizes were set with sacrificial fires for making offerings that were regarded as serving both to provide nourishment for the gods and to maintain order in creation. The building of altars was consequently identified with the ritual reconstruction of the universe, which was envisaged as the body of a primal man (Skt *puruṣa*). The sacrificer became, by extension, a microcosm of creation; altars were thus sites of both individual and universal regeneration. This concept of the altar entered the subsequent tradition of temple architecture, and many of the Sanskrit terms used to describe temples allude to the sacrificial precinct and to the temple building as a divine body; the sanctum containing the altar and divine image is known as the 'womb-chamber' (*garbha-gṛha*), emphasizing the idea of the altar as the locus of divine manifestation and spiritual rebirth.

See also INDIAN SUBCONTINENT, §III, 1(ii)(b).

BIBLIOGRAPHY

S. Kramrisch: *The Hindu Temple*, 2 vols (Calcutta, 1947)
L. Renou: *Religions of Ancient India* (London, 1953)
A. K. Coomaraswamy: 'An Indian Temple: The Kandarya Mahadeo', *Coomaraswamy*, i, ed. R. Lipsey (Princeton, 1977), pp. 3–10

MICHAEL D. WILLIS

7. SOUTH-EAST ASIA. In South-east Asian Hindu and Buddhist temples the altar is generally a simple table upon which offerings are placed, although the term is also sometimes applied to other structures that may or may not have formerly served this function. Pre-Hindu megalithic monuments in South-east Asia that are thought to

have served as altars for sacrificial and other offerings include a structure at the megalithic sanctuary of uncertain date on the Yang Plateau in the Argapura mountains, East Java, which consists of a series of stone terraces culminating in a stone altar. Similar megalithic altars have been found at Tan An village in Quang Tri Province, Vietnam. The Badui people of West Java, who practise a debased form of Hinduism, still make offerings to their ancestors on stone altars placed on top of terraced mountain sanctuaries.

Most early Shaivite temples in South-east Asia originally contained a centrally placed Shiva *liṅga* (Shiva's phallic symbol), usually associated with a *yoni*, representing the female principle and serving as a plinth over which libations were poured. It may be that in later Khmer and Cham temples offerings were laid on the edge of the plinth, which were sometimes elaborately carved with floral motifs, animal and human figures. Some of the Hindu terraced sanctuaries built in Central and East Java in the late Majapahit period (15th century), such as Candi Sukuh and Candi Ceto, on the slopes of Mt Lawu in Central Java, consist of stone terraces with up to three altars placed on the summit. Among the structures at Candi Sukuh that may have served as an altar is a terrace decorated with relief carvings illustrating Hindu legends of Garuda, Durga and Tamprapetra. At the base are figures of the cosmic turtle, which have sometimes erroneously been described as altars. In Vietnamese Buddhist temples elaborately carved wooden altar tables are placed in front of images, and altar boxes consisting of wooden panels latticed with Buddhist symbols, floral, bird and animal motifs, have figures placed inside them.

Many of the peoples of Indonesia use altars for their ancestor cults. In the Tanimbar Islands domestic altars (*tavu*) are carved in human form with outstretched arms and are associated with the ancestors. In Leti they are also carved in the form of a human being, usually portrayed squatting on a platform above a crescent of openwork scrolls representing a boat. They are sometimes decorated with beads, and the eyes may be inlaid with shell. In Nias ancestral altar seats (*daro-daro*) consist of chair- or boat-shaped structures carved into side panels, and they are often decorated with elaborate carvings.

BIBLIOGRAPHY

H. G. Quaritch Wales: *The Making of Greater India* (London, 1951, rev. 1961)

——: *The Mountain of God: A Study in Early Religion and Kingship* (London, 1953)

Nias Tribal Treasures: Cosmic Reflections in Stone, Wood and Gold (exh. cat., ed. J. A. Feldman and others; Delft, Vlkenknd. Mus. Nusantara, 1990)

P. M. Taylor and L. V. Aragon: *Beyond the Java Sea: Art of Indonesia's Outer Islands* (New York, 1991)

SIAN E. JAY

Altar de Sacrificios. Site of Pre-Columbian MAYA ceremonial centre in the Río Pasión drainage, near the source of the Usumacinta River, El Petén, Guatemala. It was occupied nearly continuously from the Middle Pre-Classic period (*c.* 1000–*c.* 300 BC) into the Early Post-Classic period (*c.* AD 900–*c.* 1200). Known since 1883, the site was explored early in the 20th century and excavated by Harvard University of Cambridge, MA, during 1958–63, particularly because it was hoped that it would shed some light on problems of the Classic 'Maya collapse' of *c.* AD 900. The site is strategically located on a major river system, between highlands and low country on the southernmost edge of the Lowland Maya region, and the ceremonial centre consists of three architecturally independent groups. The North Plaza has the largest mounds and most of the stelae.

The corpus of stone sculpture includes: 26 circular altars, most of them plain, although 7 are carved with hieroglyphs; 21 stelae carved with glyphic panels and rulers holding symbols of office; 3 'censer' altars (basins behind deity masks); and various panels and obelisks. The earliest known monument is Stele 10, with a date of AD 455 in the Maya Long Count calendar (*see* MESOAMERICA, PRE-COLUMBIAN, §II). Monuments erected before AD 633 are made of local red sandstone, and the site is named after one of these. Later monuments are of limestone and are less finely carved. Some stelae were found in fragmented condition and may have been used in construction fill. Earlier architectural block masonry was also of red sandstone, then of limestone. The earliest masonry found is dated *c.* 500 BC, when lime-encrusted shells set in mud mortar were used for platform facings. Superstructures were made of wood and thatch.

The ceramic sequence begins earlier in the Middle Pre-Classic period, *c.* 900 BC. There are solid, hand-modelled figurines, depicting human beings and animals, as well as vessels. During the Classic period (*c.* AD 250–*c.* 900) Altar de Sacrificios potters produced fine polychrome and low-relief vessels, and mould-made, hollow figurine-whistles representing humans (often warriors) and animals of various kinds. The best-known ceramic piece is a polychrome cylinder vessel of Long Count date AD 754 called the 'Altar Vase' (Guatemala City, Mus. N. Arqueol. & Etnol.), discovered in Harvard excavations. It has a complex scene of supernatural figures, dancing humans (one in jaguar-skin garments), a drummer, a singer and possibly an autosacrifice. The jaguar figure is named by hieroglyphs and may portray Bird-Jaguar, the contemporary ruler of YAXCHILÁN. Worked obsidian, flint and some jade were also found at the site.

The last dated monument is AD 771, and after this the site declined for several reasons. It was a time of disorganization throughout the area, and the final ceramic phase (after *c.* AD 900) seems to represent an instrusive, non-Maya group towards the end of the Late Classic period (*c.* AD 600–*c.* 900). Construction of major monuments ceased *c.* AD 909, but the site was not abandoned until the mid-10th century.

BIBLIOGRAPHY

G. R. Willey and A. L. Smith: *The Ruins of Altar de Sacrificios: An Introduction*, Pap. Peabody Mus. Amer. Archaeol. & Ethnol., lxii/1 (Cambridge, MA, 1969)

R. E. W. Adams: *The Ceramics of Altar de Sacrificios*, Pap. Peabody Mus. Amer. Archaeol. & Ethnol., lxiii/1 (Cambridge, MA, 1971)

J. A. Graham: *The Hieroglyphic Inscriptions and Monumental Art of Altar de Sacrificios*, Pap. Peabody Mus. Amer. Archaeol. & Ethnol., lxiv/2 (Cambridge, MA, 1972)

A. L. Smith: *Excavations at Altar de Sacrificios*, Pap. Peabody Mus. Amer. Archaeol. & Ethnol., lxiv/2 (Cambridge, MA, 1972)

G. R. Willey: *The Artifacts of Altar de Sacrificios*, Pap. Peabody Mus. Amer. Archaeol. & Ethnol., lxiv/1 (Cambridge, MA, 1972)

G. R. Willey: *The Altar de Sacrificios Excavations: General Summary and Conclusions*, Pap. Peabody Mus. Amer. Archaeol. & Ethnol., lxvi/3 (Cambridge, MA, 1973)

ELIZABETH P. BENSON

Altarpiece [Fr. *postautel, retable*; Ger. *Altar, Altaraufsatz, Altarbild, Altarretabel, Altarrückwand, Retabel*; It. *ancona, dossale, pala (d'altare)*; Sp. *retablo*]. An image-bearing structure set on the rear part of the altar (*see* ALTAR, §II), abutting the back of the altarblock, or set behind the altar in such a way as to be visually joined with the altar when viewed from a distance. It is also sometimes called a retable, following the medieval term *retrotabulum* [*retabulum, retrotabularium*].

1. Definition. 2. Historical overview.

1. DEFINITION. The altarpiece was never officially prescribed by the Church, but it did perform a prescribed function alternatively carried out by a simple inscription on the altarblock: to declare to which saint or mystery the altar was dedicated. In fact, the altarpiece did more than merely identify the altar; its form and content evoked the mystery or personage whose cult was celebrated at the altar. This original and lasting function influenced the many forms taken by the altarpiece throughout its history. Since the altarpiece was not prescribed by the Church, its form varied enormously. For this reason, it is often impossible, and historically inaccurate, to draw neat distinctions between the altarpiece and other elements occasionally associated with the altar apparatus. For example, movable statues, often of the Virgin and Child, were occasionally placed on altars according to ritual needs, and at those times fulfilled the function of the altarpiece. Altarpieces also often contained relics, and in those instances served both as altarpiece and reliquary. Sacrament tabernacles, although often placed on a wall to the side of the altar, were occasionally placed on or above the altar and effectively assumed the role of the altarpiece. The reredos, originally a decorated hanging or screen behind the altar, was so often associated with the function of the altarpiece that the term has become an antiquated alternative to that of altarpiece. Finally, the original association of the Christian altar with the tomb of a saint, and theologically with the tomb of Christ, sometimes resulted in the amalgamation of a decorated tomb structure (traditionally that of a saint but eventually also of important lay figures) with the altarpiece.

Altarpieces adorned both high altars and side altars. High altars, which sustained the dedication of the entire church and served the purposes of High Mass, often carried large altarpieces with elaborate programmes. Side altars served a more private piety and their altarpieces were often endowed by private individuals. Such altars could be used by the faithful for extra-liturgical, private prayer more easily than the altarpiece on high altars, which were often concealed behind screens separating the choir from the nave of the church. Private devotional images often took the form of altarpieces and are frequently described as such, but they do not strictly belong to that category except in the relatively rare cases when they served on consecrated altars.

Altarpieces were produced in various materials; wood, stone and metal were all used in the Middle Ages. Metal altarpieces, of gold or silver, were rarer due to the preciousness of the materials. Stone was more commonly used in England and France, although wooden altarpieces, either carved or painted, eventually predominated all over Europe. In the large architectural altarpieces of the Baroque period, stone re-emerged as an important material, sometimes replaced by stucco. Sculpted altarpieces of ivory and of terracotta were made in Italy (the latter coming into conspicuous use in the 15th century), while alabaster altarpiece production was a speciality of England (*RDK*).

2. HISTORICAL OVERVIEW.

(i) Origins. (ii) Forms and development.

(i) Origins. The altar, a square block free on all sides, traditionally stood alone as the primary focus of the church. In the Early Christian Church nothing was allowed on the sacred table, or *mensa*, except for the sacred books and the instruments (pyx, chalice and paten) necessary for celebrating the Eucharist. A free-standing ciborium was one means devised to adorn the simple altar without violating this rule. By AD 1000, the altar had evolved into a rectangular form with a more defined front and back (Bishop, 1918). This development prepared the way for the appearance, on the rear edge of the altar table, of a panel decorated with sacred figures: the altarpiece.

There is no agreement among scholars as to the conditions and factors that led to the appearance of the altarpiece; sources for its development have been located in the various kinds of images traditionally associated with the altar. The most important images in Early Christian art were placed in the central cupola or apse, and bore an evident relation to the altar positioned beneath them (Hager, 1962). Already in the Early Christian period mural decorations were designed to be seen in direct relation to altars affixed to the painted walls or to the niche-like openings in the wall known as arcosolia (Rohault de Fleury, 1983; Barbier, 1968). Indeed, the development of the altarpiece has often been seen in relation to the contemporary proliferation of side altars set against the wall in this manner. Most scholars, however, would agree that the later medieval form now known as the altarpiece evolved not from fixed wall images but from the first image-bearing objects allowed on to the surface of the altar.

A crucial development in this history was the practice of setting relics, traditionally embedded within or underneath the altar, in decorated reliquaries on top of the altar (*see* RELIQUARY, §II, 2). This practice is documented as early as the 9th century in a homily of Pope Leo IV (*reg* 847–55). Reliquaries in this period served on the one hand to protect and preserve the relic from exposure and, on the other, to proclaim in figures, ornament and rich materials the sacred presence that they hid from view. Smaller reliquary shrines were placed towards the rear of the altar. Large ones containing the entire body of a saint were set either lengthwise on a block behind the altar or transversely, with one end resting on the back edge of the altar and the other on a support set up behind (Bishop).

1. *Pentecost*, gilt copper, 0.57×2.17 m, 12th century (Paris, Musée de Cluny)

Another type of reliquary took the form of a statue and was placed on the altar or on a support behind it. The appearance of this new source of imagery on the altar was a precedent for the later development of the altarpiece as a permanent feature of the altar apparatus. Another source of imagery on the altar was provided by the decoration, either textile or sculpted, covering the front of the altar-block and known as the antependium or altar frontal. The early format and composition of the altarpiece, a rectangular field containing a row of frontal figures usually arranged under an arcade, strongly resembles the earlier antependium type (*see* §(ii) (a) below).

The advent of the altarpiece marks a significant development not only in the history of the altar, but also in the nature and function of the Christian image. The autonomous image now assumed a legitimate position at the centre of Christian worship. Rather than adorning the outer surface of another sacred object, whether reliquary, altar frontal or church wall, it now stood in a structure made for no purpose other than to hold the image up to view. As a part of the altar apparatus, the image was now an important element of church architecture in its own right. The appearance of this new element on or behind the altar accompanied changes in the positions assumed by priest, deacon and subdeacon while celebrating mass. Until the 10th century, it was common for the celebrant to stand on the far side of the altar, facing the congregation, but later he came to stand before the altar, with his back to the congregation. As long as the celebrant stood on the far side of the altar, it can be assumed that an altarpiece would have constituted an impermissible obstruction. The records, however, are scattered so sparsely over the period between the 9th and the 11th centuries that it cannot be determined whether the changes they document are causes or consequences of the appearance of the altarpiece.

(ii) Forms and development.

(a) Before c. *1400.* Although claims have been made to document or to date altarpieces to the 8th century or 9th, significant numbers of records of their existence appear only in the 11th century, and the earliest surviving group of any size dates from the 12th century. The basic form of the earliest known altarpieces is an antependium-like rectangular panel, usually showing a series of saints flanking a central figure of Christ or the Virgin (e.g. Pala d'Oro, gold and silver, 1105, with later additions; Venice, S Marco; *see* VENICE, fig. 20; *Virgin and Child with Saints*, stone, 12th century; Brauweiler, St Nikolaus und Medardus). This basic form was also sometimes given extensions on the upper border of the frame (e.g. *Pentecost*, gilt copper, 12th century; Paris, Mus. Cluny; see fig. 1).

In Italy, the altar became a primary setting for painting on panel, a format developed in the West from the example of Byzantine icons, which were imported in increasing numbers after the conquest of Constantinople in 1204. Under the influence of the cults of the Virgin and of the Cross, propagated by the mendicant orders, icons with the Virgin and monumental crucifixes, besides being used as processional images, or hung on church walls or rood screens, were also adapted for use on altars. Gabled panels in a vertical format representing a full-length saint flanked by scenes of his or her life (sometimes called *vita* retables) were also popular in 13th-century Italy, especially in mendicant settings (e.g. Bonaventura Berlinghieri's *St Francis*, 1235; Pescia, S Francesco; for illustration *see* BERLINGHIERI, (2); *St Catherine*, 1250s; Pisa, Mus. N. S Matteo). Marian images grew larger and higher (e.g. *Madonna degli Occhi Grossi*, before 1260; Siena, Mus. Opera Duomo; Coppo di Marcovaldo's *Madonna del Bordone*, 1261; Siena, S Maria dei Servi; *see* COPPO DI MARCOVALDO, fig. 1), and eventually also took on the large, vertical, gabled format (e.g. Cimabue's Santa Trinità *Madonna*, 1280–85; Florence, Uffizi; Duccio's Rucellai *Madonna*, 1285; Florence, Uffizi; *see* DUCCIO, fig. 1; Giotto's Ognissanti *Madonna*, *c.* 1310; Florence, Uffizi).

Although the early history of the painted altarpiece in Italy is marked by experiments with these various formats, the most important source for its later development was the horizontal painted panel, often known as a dossal. It followed from the antependium tradition, with a central figure of Christ or the Virgin flanked by figures of saints (e.g. Margarito d'Arezzo's *Virgin and Child with New*

Testament Scenes, *c.* 1285; Monte San Savino, S Maria di Vertighe). These soon developed single-gabled forms and painted or carved arcades above the figures (e.g. *Christ with Saints*, *c.* 1265; Pisa, Mus. N. S Matteo; Meliore's *Christ with the Virgin and Saints*, 1271; Florence, Uffizi). By the 1280s, this type had evolved a many-gabled tier above the arcade (e.g. Vigoroso da Siena's *Virgin and Child with Saints*, 1280s; Perugia, G.N. Umbria). The development of an elaborate gabled outer structure enframing several vertically conceived individual compartments, in contrast to the earlier, horizontally unified single panel, paved the way for the development of the POLYPTYCH in the 14th century. The new several-tiered format was probably related to the simultaneous appearance of the PREDELLA, the decorated step-like block that developed to support this enlarged structure and to ensure the entire altarpiece's visibility.

Duccio's colossal double-sided *Maestà* (1308–11; for locations *see* DUCCIO, §1 and fig. 2), painted for the high altar of Siena Cathedral, was a grandiose resolution of the various strains of altarpiece design produced up to that time in Italy. It combined the full-length gabled Virgin type with the horizontal composition comprising a row of saints into one, vast, integrated vision of the celestial court. On the predella and on the back were smaller panels with scenes from the *Life of the Virgin* and the *Life of Christ*. The sheer grandeur and complexity of the altarpiece made it a virtually autonomous structure, and it has been argued that the *Maestà* was the first in a long series of Italian altarpieces to be buttressed by an independent structure (Gardner von Teuffel, 1979).

Duccio's *Maestà* remained something of an exception, and the many-tiered polyptych became the most characteristic form of the period. Polyptychs were increasingly elaborate, their frames often featuring piers, colonettes, cusped arches, tracery, pinnacles, crockets and finials, eventually transforming the altarpiece into an architectonic structure resembling in detail and spatial principles the façades of contemporary full-scale Gothic architecture. In Italy such altarpieces were usually made of wood and painted (e.g. Simone Martini's S Caterina Altarpiece, 1320; Pisa, Mus. N. S Matteo; *Virgin and Child with Saints* by Pietro Nelli (*fl* 1375–1419) and Tommaso del Mazza (*fl* 1375–91), 1375; Impruneta, S Maria; see fig. 2). In northern Europe they were commonly executed in stone, as in the high altar (1290) of the Elisabethkirche in Marburg, or the 14th-century *Passion* altarpiece (Paris, Mus. Cluny). Stone altarpieces were less common in Italy, and they usually show the influence either of Italian painted works or of north European stone altarpieces (e.g. Tommaso Pisano's *Virgin and Child with Angels*, 13(?60s); Pisa, S Francesco; *Virgin and Child with Saints*, *c.* 1370; Arezzo Cathedral; Pierpaolo and Jacobello dalle Masegne's *Coronation of the Virgin*, 1388–92; Bologna, S Francesco).

The winged altarpiece, or *Flügelaltar*, developed in Germany and the Netherlands in the early 14th century. The movable wings made it possible to vary the altarpiece imagery in accordance with the changing requirements of the liturgical calendar. Even in its earliest examples this form achieved grand proportions (e.g. high altar, *c.* 1320; Cismar, Benedictine Abbey Church, see fig. 3; high altar, 1331; Oberwesel, Unsere Liebe Frau). Most typically, it

2. Pietro Nelli and Tommaso del Mazza: *Virgin and Child with Saints*, 1375 (tempera on panel, Impruneta, S Maria)

3. Altarpiece, stone, 6.50×6.37 m, *c.* 1320, former Benedictine abbey church, Cismar

was sculpted on the inside and painted on the outside (e.g. Master Bertram's Grabow Altarpiece, 1383; Hamburg, Ksthalle; Jacques de Baerze's and Melchior Broederlam's altarpiece for the Charterhouse of Champmol, 1390–99; Dijon, Mus. B.-A.).

(b) c. *1400–* c. *1600.* In the 15th century there was a proliferation of altarpieces, largely the result of the growing initiative of non-ecclesiastical and non-aristocratic patrons. The endowment of altars and chapels was often the concern of individual families or confraternities, and by the end of the 15th century churches north and south of the Alps were filled with privately endowed altars, each with its own altarpiece. The prevalence of private sources of patronage is reflected in the frequent appearance of donor portraits in altarpieces of this period.

In the Netherlands in the 15th century panel painting flourished and entirely superseded sculpture on the winged altarpiece. Hubert and Jan van Eyck's Ghent Altarpiece (*c.* 1423–32; Ghent, St Bavo) was the first and the greatest monument in this tradition. Its apocalyptic *Adoration of the Lamb* is set into an all-encompassing pictorial illusion including a sweeping landscape, crowds of saints, architectural interiors and even marble sculpture. This altarpiece represented a world of such illusionistic and iconographic complexity as to assume the scope and symbolic allusions of the High Gothic cathedral (Brand Philip, 1971), and it set the precedent for many ambitious painted winged altarpieces in the Netherlands, including Rogier van der Weyden's *Last Judgement* (1443–51; Beaune, Hôtel-Dieu), and Hugo van der Goes's Portinari Altarpiece (*c.* 1473–8; Florence, Uffizi; *see* GOES, HUGO VAN DER, fig. 1).

In Germany, by contrast, the wood-carving tradition remained predominant in winged altarpiece production and reached its climax in the later 15th-century SCHNITZALTAR, which consisted of a box-like central shrine (*Corpus*) carrying the main figures, wings (*Flügel*), sometimes double, either painted or carved in relief, a predella (*Sarg*), usually carved, and a richly carved architectural superstructure (*Auszug*) above the shrine (e.g. Michael Pacher's St Wolfgang Altarpiece, 1471–81; St Wolfgangsee, St Wolfgang; *see* PACHER, MICHAEL, fig. 1; Veit Stoss's altarpiece, 1477–89; Kraków, St Mary; Michel Erhart's *Virgin and Child with Saints*, *c.* 1493–4; Blaubeuren, Benedictine Klosterkirche; for illustration *see* SCHNITZALTAR). The status and quality of wood-carving achieved such high levels in this tradition that eventually altarpieces were made to be displayed without painting or gilding. Tilman Riemenschneider's dismembered altarpiece (1490–92) for St Maria Magdalena, Münnerstadt, is the first known uncoloured altarpiece of this type. Painting, however, was not neglected in Germany; Matthias Grünewald's Isenheim Altarpiece (1515; Colmar, Mus. Unterlinden; *see* GRÜNEWALD, MATTHIAS, fig. 2), although it has a sculpted centre, is known primarily for its dramatically painted double wings.

In Spain the architectonic altarpiece, usually made of polychrome wood, was the dominant form from the 15th century and throughout the 16th (*see* RETABLE, §1). It eventually reached enormous proportions, virtually replacing the church architecture of the apse (e.g. Nicolò Delli's high altar, *c.* 1445; Salamanca, Old Cathedral; high altar by Pedro Berruguete, Diego de la Santa Cruz and Juan de Borgoña, 1506; Ávila Cathedral; high altar, 1504; Toledo Cathedral).

4. Titian: *Assumption of the Virgin*, oil on panel, 6.9×3.6 m, 1518 (Venice, S Maria Gloriosa dei Frari)

In 15th-century Italy the polyptych was largely outmoded by the unified, framed panel. This development involved changes both in altarpiece construction and pictorial convention. If the traditional polyptych was a painted and gilded piece of ecclesiastical furniture, the new type of altarpiece, known as the *pala*, was closer to a framed picture. The single, large panel was now made and painted independently of its frame, which, supported by the predella, was now designed in the style of classical architecture, with flanking pilasters mounted by an entablature. Within the frame, the painting was treated as a window giving on to a natural or architectural space and was thus differentiated pictorially as well as structurally from the frame. This pictorial realm was typically inhabited by saintly figures arranged around the Virgin and Child in a *sacra conversazione* (e.g. Domenico Veneziano's *St Lucy* altarpiece, *c.* 1445–7; main panel Florence, Uffizi; *see* DOMENICO VENEZIANO, fig. 2; Fra Angelico's S Marco Altarpiece, *c.* 1438–40; Florence, Mus. S Marco; Piero della Francesca's Brera Altarpiece, *c.* 1475; Milan, Brera). In several Venetian altarpieces of this period the frame stands as the architectural entrance into a fictive chapel, conceived as an extension of the church space (e.g. Giovanni Bellini's S Zaccaria Altarpiece, 1505; Venice, S Zaccaria; for illustration *see* SACRA CONVERSAZIONE). The strong interest in natural setting and figural expression gave new dramatic force to narrative subjects (e.g. Leonardo da Vinci's *Adoration of the Magi*, 1481–3; Florence, Uffizi; Raphael's *Entombment*, 1507; Rome, Gal. Borghese; Titian's *Assumption of the Virgin*, 1518; Venice, S Maria Gloriosa dei Frari; see fig. 4), and prompted an increased use of narrative scenes as the main subjects of the altarpiece, which had hitherto more often consisted of a simple grouping of saintly figures.

The rise of the single painted panel as the predominant format for altarpieces was of great consequence for the history of European art. It encouraged the rise of the art of panel painting and paved the way for the predominance of the easel picture in the following centuries. A single picture commanding ceremonious attention at the focus of Christian worship, the Italian *pala* set a powerful structural and functional precedent for the easel pictures which, despite any religious context, were later appreciated as works of art in museums (Belting, 1987). The histories of several Renaissance altarpieces themselves document this transition; for example Raphael's *Entombment* (1507; Rome, Gal. Borghese) was taken from its church within a century and hung in a private gallery where it has remained to this day.

Italian sculpture and sculpted altarpieces also underwent important changes in this period. Donatello's high altar with the *Virgin and Child with Saints* (1443–50; Padua, Santo) and Niccolò Baroncelli's *Crucifixion and Saints* (1450; Ferrara Cathedral) were early examples of the transposition of the *sacra conversazione* into bronze sculpture and played an important role in disseminating the type in northern Italy, both for painted and sculpted altarpieces. Relief sculpture, in both terracotta and marble, was also commonly used on Italian altarpieces, for example Antonio Rossellino's *Nativity* (1470–75; *see* NAPLES, fig. 6) and Benedetto da Maiano's *Annunciation* (1489; both Naples, S Anna dei Lombardi) and Luca della Robbia's *Virgin and Child with SS Blaise and James* (*c.* 1465–70; Pescia, Palazzo Vescovile). Large statuary, free of an altarpiece structure, made a dramatic appearance on the altar at the turn of the 16th century with Michelangelo's *Pietà* (*c.* 1498–9; Rome, St Peter's) and his Bruges *Madonna* (1503; Bruges, Onze Lieve Vrouwe) and Andrea Sansovino's *Virgin and Child with St Anne* (1511–12; Rome, S Agostino).

The religious reforms of the 16th century brought new attention and some important changes to the form and function of the altarpiece. In northern Europe, the effect of the Protestant Reformation was to reduce sharply the number of altarpieces produced and to change the nature of those in existence. Private endowments conceived as 'good works' were all but eliminated. Rather than as instruments of intercession, altarpieces made under Protestant auspices were conceived as a means of returning to the Word of God. Reformers preferred that altarpiece iconography be restricted to subjects well-suited to the sacrament celebrated at the altar, such as the Last Supper (e.g. Lucas Cranach II's Dessau Altarpiece, 1565; Dessau-Mildensee, Parish Church). In their most extreme form, Protestant altarpieces displayed the actual text from the Bible instead of images (e.g. altarpiece of 1537; Dinkelsbühl, Spitalkirche). Eventually the Protestant conception of the altarpiece found expression in the *Kanzelaltar*, or pulpit altar, in which the altarpiece literally became the place from where the word was preached (e.g. Thomas Maler's *Passion* altarpiece, *c.* 1500, altered, overpainted and attached to pulpit *c.* 1605; Berneuchen, nr Landsberg, Parish Church).

The Counter-Reformation in Italy also stimulated the reform of altars. In the interest of clarity and unity, numerous medieval screens separating the choir and high altar from the nave were removed. The reforming authorities also worked to regain control over the endowment

5. Alessandro Algardi: *Beheading of St Paul*, marble, 1644, (Bologna, S Paolo Maggiore)

6. Egid Quirin Asam: *Assumption of the Virgin*, marble, 1719–23 (Rohr, abbey church of Mariae Himmelfahrt)

and the dedication of side altars, and thereby also to regulate the form and iconography of their altarpieces. The late medieval profusion of private altars and chapels gave way to systematically conceived schemes in which all chapels of the same church were given the same design, with their altarpieces planned as a cycle through the entire church. Such were the schemes conceived in 1565 by Duke Cosimo I de' Medici for the Florentine churches of Santa Croce and S Maria Novella, which were adorned with altarpieces by Giorgio Vasari and his school. A similar, even more regular scheme was conceived by Andrea Palladio and the Capuchin friars at the Venetian church, Il Redentore, in the late 1570s.

(c) After c. *1600.* The dynamic qualities that characterize Baroque art brought important changes to altarpiece design. Figures in motion entirely superseded static devotional images and statues, and designs more often transgressed the traditional restriction to a two-dimensional panel format. Important altarpieces consisting of a single painting or relief continued to be made (e.g. Caravaggio's *Virgin of Loreto*, 1603; Rome, S Agostino; Alessandro Algardi's *Encounter of Pope Leo the Great and Attila*, 1646; Rome, St Peter's; *see* ALGARDI, ALESSANDRO, fig. 3), but increasingly architecture was used as the theatrical setting for the three-dimensional display of the altarpiece's subject in sculpture, as in Algardi's *Beheading of St Paul* (1644; Bologna, S Paolo Maggiore; see fig. 5). The conception could expand to include painting, as in the high altar of S Andrea al Quirinale, Rome, conceived by Gianlorenzo Bernini *c.* 1660, in which Guglielmo Cortese's painting of the *Martyrdom of St Andrew* is carried aloft by a host of sculpted angels rising up through the architecture.

In such works, the fictitious architecture of the altarpiece and the architecture of the church intermingle. In Rococo churches, particularly in northern Europe, such integration became so complete as to transform the entire church into a fanciful confection, and in such otherworldly surroundings the miracle revealed at the altar acquires an unexpected believability (e.g. *Assumption of the Virgin*, 1719–23; Rohr, abbey church of Mariae Himmelfahrt; see fig. 6).

These works fully realize a development already discernible in the Gothic altarpiece. If the altar began as a free block set in the middle of the church architecture, it was now again a free block, set into the middle of an all-encompassing altarpiece architecture. The altar, once the setting for the altarpiece, was now one element in the machinery of the altarpiece.

Although altarpiece commissions continued to be made and fulfilled in the 19th century, the altarpiece was no longer an evolving form but had become a relic, a symbol of a former integration of art in religious life: for example Ingres's famous altarpiece, the *Vow of Louis XIII* (1824; Montauban Cathedral; *see* INGRES, JEAN-AUGUSTE-DOMINIQUE, fig. 3), is itself a depiction of an altar surmounted by a Virgin modelled on the Virgins of Raphael's altarpieces. For Ingres, the painting of an altarpiece was primarily an occasion to pay homage to the great Renaissance painter, and to the idea of artistic perfection in the service of religion that Raphael represented.

For the Romantics, who found in the Christian faith a model for a new cult of nature and of art, the symbolic charge of the altarpiece format was particularly powerful. When Caspar David Friedrich, in his *Cross in the Mountain* (1807–8; Dresden, Gemäldegal. Neue Meister), gave to the landscape painting the form and status of the altarpiece, he did so in order to induce a sacral attitude towards the subject of his art: it was a devotional image of a new kind. The altarpiece format lent an aura of holiness to various kinds of aesthetic experience throughout the 19th century, and at the end of the century became a favourite device of the Pre-Raphaelites, who used it in various secular genres (e.g. Dante Gabriel Rossetti's *Blessed Damozel*, 1875; Cambridge, MA, Fogg).

The design of 20th-century churches has espoused values of simplicity and has not contributed significantly to the history of the altarpiece. By reinstating a single, free-standing altar as the focus of the church, modern churches have in a sense returned to Early Christian ideals. Indeed, the Second Vatican Council's decree (1962) that a priest should celebrate *ad populum*, or towards the congregation, is a return to Early Christian practice and has again precluded the use of altarpieces. The 1000-year history of their making is now a closed episode in the history of art.

BIBLIOGRAPHY

RDK: 'Altarretabel'

G. Rohault de Fleury: *La Messe: Etudes archéologiques sur ses monuments*, i (Paris, 1883)
J. Burckhardt: 'Das Altarbild', *Beiträge zur Kunstgeschichte von Italien* (Basle, 1898), pp. 3–161; Eng. trans. and ed. by P. Humfrey as *The Altarpiece in Renaissance Italy* (New York, 1988)
F. Bishop: 'On the History of the Christian Altar', *Liturgica historica: Papers on the Liturgy and Religious Life of the Western Church* (Oxford, 1918/*R* 1962), pp. 20–38
J. Braun: *Der christliche Altar in seiner geschichtlichen Entwicklung*, 2 vols (Munich, 1924)
M. Hasse: *Der Flügelaltar* (Dresden, 1941)
H. Hager: *Die Anfänge des italienischen Altarbildes: Untersuchungen der Entstehungsgeschichte des toskanischen Hochaltarretabels* (Munich, 1962)
M. Cämmerer-George: *Die Rahmung der toskanischen Altarbilder im Trecento* (Strasbourg, 1966)
E. Barbier: 'Les Images, les reliques et la face supérieure de l'autel avant le XIe siècle', *Synthronon: Art et archéologie de la fin de l'antiquité et du moyen âge* (Paris, 1968), pp. 199–207
L. Brand Philip: *The Ghent Altarpiece and the Art of Jan van Eyck* (Princeton, 1971)
C. Gardner von Teuffel: 'The Buttressed Altarpiece: A Forgotten Aspect of Tuscan Fourteenth-century Altarpiece Design', *Jb. Berlin. Mus.*, xxi (1979), pp. 21–65
M. Baxandall: *The Limewood Sculptors of Renaissance Germany* (New Haven, CT, 1980)
D. L. Ehresmann: 'Some Observations on the Role of the Liturgy in the Early Winged Altarpiece', *A. Bull.*, lxiv (1982), pp. 359–69
C. Gardner von Teuffel: 'Lorenzo Monaco, Filippo Lippi, Filippo Brunelleschi: Die Erfindung der Renaissance Pala', *Z. Kstgesch.*, xxxxv (1982), pp. 1–30
B. C. Lane: *The Altar and the Altarpiece: Sacramental Themes in Early Netherlandish Painting* (New York, 1984)
H. van Os: *Sienese Altarpieces, 1215–1460*, i (Groningen, 1984)
H. Belting: 'Vom Altarbild zur autonomen Tafelmalerei', *Kunst: Die Geschichte ihrer Funktionen*, ed. W. Busch and P. Schmook (Weinheim and Berlin, 1987), pp. 128–49
J. Berg Sobré: *Behind the Altar Table: The Development of the Painted Retable in Spain, 1350–1500* (Columbia, MO, 1989)
P. Humfrey and M. Kemp, eds: *The Altarpiece in the Renaissance* (Cambridge, 1991)
E. Borsook and F. S. Gioffredi, eds: *Italian Altarpieces, 1250–1550: Function and Design* (Oxford, 1994)
P. Humfrey: *The Altarpiece in Renaissance Venice* (New Haven and London, 1995)

ALEXANDER NAGEL

Alta Vista. Site of Pre-Columbian culture near Chalchihuites, Zacatecas, northern Mexico. It was explored by Gamio in 1910 and by Kelly in 1971 and 1976. Its chronology is still uncertain, but the most important occupation was during the Classic period (*c*. AD 250–*c*. 900). Alta Vista was a small, highly developed ceremonial centre that exploited a massive mining complex for malachite, azurite, hematite, limonite, coloured chert, galena, cinnabar, rock crystal and other semi-precious materials. More than 800 mines, some of them over 1 km in extent, have been surveyed (Weigand); they are made up of chambers, adits, shafts, tunnels, internal spoil heaps and external spoil heaps comprised of millions of tons of residue. Because far more material was produced than could possibly have been used regionally, there is a strong argument for central Mexican sponsorship, possibly even control, of the mines by TEOTIHUACÁN.

The ceremonial centre comprises a complex series of interrelated buildings whose overall effect is monumental. The main compound is a square plaza surrounded by a banquette topped by platforms. On the north side there is a small pyramid covering a crypt, which contained three high-status burials. Adjacent to the plaza is a structure, once roofed, known as the Hall of Columns, which also contained prestige burials. At an angle to the Hall of Columns is an 'observatory' structure, which, because of its placement on the Tropic of Cancer, clearly had special meaning for Mesoamericans. It may have been coordinated with the pecked, double calendar circle at Cerro de Chapín, a nearby site to the south. Other architectural features include a colonnaded entrance fronting a road to the mines, a palace-like court with a skull rack (*see* TZOMPANTLI), and a habitation area, damaged by modern ploughing, in the surrounding fields. The mining complex, observatory and pecked stone circle all point to a sophisticated society that was well-integrated with central Mesoamerican civilization. Human sacrifice also occurred on a large scale at Alta Vista. In addition to the trade in mined materials with central Mesoamerica, long-distance contacts were made with the south-west of the USA to import turquoise in large quantity. Pottery from Alta Vista includes elaborate 'pseudo-cloisonné'; incised, polished black tripods; finely painted red-on-brown wares; and small carved lapidary items. Only one large stone sculpture, of a skeletized fire-god (Mexico City, Mus. N. Antropol.), has been found, at Cerro de Motecuhzuma.

In adjacent valleys other sites related to Alta Vista include Cerro de Motecuhzuma, which may also have had a columned hall; Gualterio, with a ballcourt; and numerous agricultural hamlets and villages.

The major finds from Alta Vista are in the Museo Nacional de Antropología, Mexico City, and at the Instituto Nacional de Antropología e Historia, Guadalupe, Zacatecas.

For further discussion of Pre-Columbian Mexico *see* MESOAMERICA, PRE-COLUMBIAN.

BIBLIOGRAPHY

M. Gamio: 'Los monumentos arqueológicos de las inmediaciones de Chalchuites, Zacatecas', *An. Mus. N. Arqueol., Hist. & Etnog.*, ii (1910), pp. 469–92
J. C. Kelly: 'Archaeology of the Northern Frontier: Zacatecas and Durango', *Hb. Mid. Amer. Ind.*, xi (1971), pp. 768–801
——: 'Alta Vista: Outpost of Mesoamerican Empire on the Tropic of Cancer', *Las Fronteras de Mesoamérica, XIV Mesa Redonda de la Sociedad Mexicana de Antropología: 1976*, pp. 21–40
P. Weigand: 'Mining and Mineral Trade in Prehispanic Zacatecas', *Anthropology*, vi (1982), pp. 87–134

PHIL C. WEIGAND

Altdeutsch style. German 19th-century historicist revival style, which imitated in architecture, furniture and other arts the characteristics of works from earlier periods, especially the 15th and 16th centuries.

Altdorfer [Altdorffer; Altorfer]. German family of painters, draughtsmen, printmakers and architects. The painter Ulrich Altdorfer (*fl* 1468–91), who became a Regensburg citizen in 1478, may have been the father of (1) Albrecht Altdorfer and (2) Erhard Altdorfer. The family name undoubtedly derives from one of several towns named Altdorf in Switzerland and Bavaria, though Albrecht Altdorfer's Regensburg citizenship record (1505) refers to him as a 'painter from Amberg'.

BIBLIOGRAPHY

Hollstein: *Ger.*
Albrecht Altdorfer und sein Kreis (exh. cat. by E. Buchner, Munich, 1938), pp. 147–9
F. Winziger: 'Neue Zeichnungen Albrecht und Erhard Altdorfers', *Wien. Jb. Kstgesch.*, xviii (1960), pp. 7–27

——: 'Unbekannte Zeichnungen der Brüder Albrecht und Erhard Altdorfer und des "Meisters der Historia"', *Pantheon*, xxiv (1966), pp. 24–7
Prints and Drawings of the Danube School (exh. cat., ed. C. Talbot and A.Shestaek; New Haven, CT, Yale U.A.G., 1969)
R. A. Koch: *Early German Masters*, 14 [VIII/ii] of *The Illustrated Bartsch*, ed. W. L. Strauss (New York, 1978–) [B.]
Altdorfer and Fantastic Realism in German Art (exh. cat., ed. J. and M. Guillaud; Paris, Cent. Cult. Marais, 1984)

(1) Albrecht Altdorfer (*b c.* 1480; *d* Regensburg, 12 Feb 1538). He was one of Germany's most innovative artists in an era spanning late medieval piety, the Renaissance and the Reformation, and his work reveals many facets of a changing society. It is especially noteworthy for an expressive use of nature and for introducing landscape as a theme of its own in art. In this respect Altdorfer is the central figure of the DANUBE SCHOOL.

1. Life. 2. Work. 3. Format

1. LIFE. Altdorfer became a citizen of Regensburg in 1505 and bought a house there in 1513, another in 1518 and a third in 1532; he also owned several vineyards. From 1517 he held seats on the outer and inner councils of Regensburg and represented the city on important official business. In 1526 he was appointed city architect and constructed a municipal slaughterhouse and a building for wine storage. In 1529–30 he was also charged with reinforcing certain city fortifications in response to the Turkish threat. Except for the will he dictated on the day of his death, there are no surviving papers or letters by him; nor are there contemporary writings about him. The closest thing to a portrait of Altdorfer is found in an illumination in the *Freiheitenbuch* (1536; Regensburg, Stadtmus.) by Hans Müelich, which represents him in minute profile among Regensburg's city councillors.

The corpus of Altdorfer's surviving work comprises *c.* 55 panels, 120 drawings, 125 woodcuts, 78 engravings, 36 etchings, 24 paintings on parchment and fragments from a mural for the bathhouse of the Kaiserhof in Regensburg. This production extends at least over the period 1504–37. Most of the early works are dated: engravings 1506–11, woodcuts 1511–13; and although after 1513 Altdorfer ceased dating his prints, most, it would seem, and most of the surviving drawings, were executed by 1522. Therefore, with the notable exception of the *Battle of Alexander at Issos* (1529; Munich, Alte Pin.), the works on which his reputation rests derive predominantly from a concentrated period of activity, 1506–22.

2. WORK.

(i) Early work, 1504– *c.* 1510. (ii) Mature work, *c.* 1510 and after.

(i) Early work, 1504– c. 1510. There are drawings and engravings with Altdorfer's signature and a date from 1506, and small panels from 1507. The signature takes the form of a double-A monogram, one majuscule nested over the other in the manner of Dürer's familiar precedent; it is found on two of 13 tiny, inexpertly executed woodcuts of saints (Vienna, Albertina), which came from the abbey of Mondsee in the Salzkammergut, not far from the pilgrimage church at St Wolfgang containing Michael Pacher's influential altarpiece of 1471–81. It has been suggested (Winziger, 1963) that the woodcuts date as early as 1500, but this remains questionable. One attribution prior to 1506 has gained wide acceptance: that of the *Seated Couple in a Landscape* (1504; Berlin, Kupferstichkab.), a large pen drawing that owes much to graphic sources by Dürer and Cranach; it was long attributed to Cranach, whose name, written by someone else, appears along the bottom of the sheet, but the amorous theme, the dominant landscape, certain anatomical idiosyncrasies and the vigorous pen lines are consistent with Altdorfer's other early drawings.

Many of Altdorfer's drawings were made on paper prepared with a dark coloured ground. By and large these are not studies or preparatory designs for paintings but rather independent works of art, for which one must assume the existence of clients. Using a pen trimmed to a fine point, he worked with black and white ink, the latter producing flickering highlights that stand out against grounds with hues of either brown, blue or green. He applied his chiaroscuro technique mainly to outdoor scenes, in such a manner that it yields a mysterious, nocturnal ambience rather than systematic modelling in light and shade. In *Samson and Delilah* (1506; New York, Met.) the coloured ground, in this case a yellowish-brown hue, unifies the figures with the landscape; in fact the figures are represented as if they would have no existence independent of their natural setting, so pliable and devoid of skeletal structure do they appear.

Curiously such beings are the norm in Altdorfer's early figural repertory, and they betray his indifference to individual likenesses and anatomical accuracy, as do the faces composed of the merest indication of features with little circles for a mouth or eyes. Unlike most German artists of the time, Altdorfer seems to have made few portraits: apart from donors, who appear as part of larger scenes, there are only two independent portraits (Winzinger, 1975, nos 42, 52). The forest was the outdoor setting most favoured by Altdorfer, and it sets the tone of many subjects both secular and religious, as can be seen in such drawings as the *Witches' Sabbath* (1506; Berlin, Kupferstichkab.), on brownish prepared paper, the *Agony in the Garden* (1509; Berlin, Kupferstichkab.), on a rust-brown ground, and the *Forest People* (Vienna, Albertina), on a grey-brown ground. The forest rises over the figures and envelops them; it imbues each of these subjects with a sense of the unfathomable power that nature wields over human events.

Early drawings by Altdorfer on ungrounded white paper exist in only a few undisputed examples. Example such as the *Loving Couple in a Wheatfield* (1508; Basle, Kstmus.) reveal the fine, swiftly drawn pen lines and curving parallel hatching familiar from the chiaroscuro drawings; but in the absence of the coloured ground and highlights Altdorfer's lines command attention for their calligraphic vitality, apart from their capacity to describe appearances. There is also a strong resemblance between the style of these drawings and that of 46 pen-drawn illustrations in the manuscript made for Emperor Maximilian entitled *Historia Friderici et Maximiliani* (Vienna, Haus-, Hof- & Staatsarchv), attributed by Mielke (1988) to Altdorfer rather than to an anonymous follower known as the MASTER OF THE HISTORIA FRIDERICI ET MAXIMILIANI (*see* MASTERS, ANONYMOUS, AND MONOGRAMMISTS, §I).

Like the drawings on coloured paper, Altdorfer's seven known early paintings were made small for private viewing. Also like the drawings, they emphasize nature as a pervasive, animated presence. Although the figural subjects occupy the foregrounds, as was usual at the time, they are shown as part of the larger world and do not dominate it. The landscape is more likely to have the upper hand, as in *St George and the Dragon* (1510; Munich, Alte Pin.), where thick forest foliage fills the picture space almost entirely but for a glimpse of distant horizon and the diminutive foreground figures. The artist's fascination with the domain of wilderness is also played out in the enigmatic so-called *Landscape with a Family of Satyrs* (1507; Berlin, Gemäldegal.). It is in fact a human mother and child, living in the forest with a satyr, who together anxiously watch the approach of two figures, one a nude male who apparently forces a clothed woman into the woods. The forest, it seems, is a place at once innocent and wild. It is also where saints retreat from human society, as in a pair of small panels, the *Stigmatization of St Francis* and the *Penitence of St Jerome* (both 1507; Berlin, Gemäldegal.). Nature can also contribute intimacy and enchantment, as in the *Nativity* (1507; Bremen, Ksthalle), where the design of Dürer's *Nativity* engraving (1504; B. 2 [31]) has been transformed into a fantasy of Altdorfer's own making.

As a printmaker Altdorfer started *c.* 1506 with engraving. He appears to have executed no woodcuts until 1511, excluding the 13 modest examples of uncertain date from Mondsee. Landscape made only a limited appearance in the early engravings, except in the *Temptation of the Hermits* (1506; Winzinger, 1963, no. 96), with its nocturnal forest setting. Most of Altdorfer's engravings are very small, which accounts for his reputation as a founder of the small-format German engraving as practised by the LITTLE MASTERS. Characteristically in Altdorfer's early engravings the small area of the plate is occupied by one or two figures, with only a minimal suggestion of place. On one plate (only 30×25 mm) he engraved a single head of a youth (W 103). Other engravings represent saints, soldiers, mythological and allegorical figures. Dürer inevitably influenced Altdorfer's thinking about the medium, but Italian intaglio prints provided him with the greater inspiration in both technique and image. For example, in the engraving *Allegorical Figure* (1506; W 99) the woman holding a mirror and the dragon on which she sits bear similarities to the Babylonian Whore and certain beasts in Dürer's *Apocalypse* (B. 61 [127]–75 [129]), but the image derives mainly from a niello print of *Prudence* (A. M. Hind: *Nielli* [London, 1936], no. 187) by Peregrino da Cesena. The intensely black background of Altdorfer's engraving also resembles the enamel-like substance from which niello plaques take their name. Unlike Dürer's precise burin lines, Altdorfer's are sketchy and fleeting, as if giving the appearance of shadowy forms viewed in an uncertain light.

(ii) Mature work, c. *1510 and after.*

(a) Landscape subjects. (b) Religious and history subjects.

(a) Landscape subjects. Altdorfer is associated in particular with the emergence of landscape as an independent subject in the 16th century (*see* LANDSCAPE PAINTING, §5). His contributions to this development include, firstly, some of the earliest drawings made from identifiable sites; secondly, the first landscape prints that do not depend on the presence of a figural subject; and thirdly, what seem to be the first autonomous landscape paintings in Europe.

The pen drawing of the *Danube at Sarmingstein* (1511; Budapest, Mus. F.A.; for illustration *see* DANUBE SCHOOL) documents Altdorfer's presence in Upper Austria and the fact that he sketched from a specific site. The main precedent for this type of work, Dürer's landscape watercolours of 1494–9, did not circulate during Dürer's lifetime. Altdorfer was also influenced by woodcuts, especially those in *Peregrinatio in terram sanctam* (Mainz, 1486), written by Bernhard von Breydenbach (*c.* 1440–97) and *Das Buch der Chroniken* (Nuremberg, 1493) by Hartmann Schedel (*fl* 1493–1514), commonly known as the *Nuremberg Chronicle*, which set precedents both for the representation of landscape views and for the graphic means of realizing them. Erhard Reuwich's illustrations for the *Peregrinatio*, involving systems of long and short parallel hatchings, seem to have informed Altdorfer's *Danube at Sarmingstein* and the *Alpine Landscape with Two Trees* (Vienna, Akad. Bild. Kst.), though they exhibit too much personal expression in line and image to be considered objectively as being topographical views. The forms of nature seem shaped or misshapen by the energy of pen strokes, and the surface of the land vibrates in patterns of light and shade.

When Altdorfer extended his interest in landscape to etching, he became the first European artist to produce prints (apart from topographical book illustrations) in which landscape was the subject rather than the setting for a subject with figures. Since prints were made to be circulated, his etchings also indicate the existence of an audience for landscape in art. None of the nine etchings is dated, but evidence indicates that they fall within the years 1518–22, in the first phase of etching's use as a printmaking technique. Whereas Dürer, who was working in the medium by 1515, executed his etchings from carefully prepared drawings, Altdorfer worked the stylus much more freely on the plate, as the medium allowed, to convey the irregularity and complexity of forms in nature. In the *Landscape with a Double Pine* (*c.* 1520; see fig. 1) he produced an image not only of the various components of landscape but also of its unifying matrix of light, space and weather. Transparent coloured washes have been added to some impressions (Coburg, Veste Coburg; Vienna, Albertina) without obscuring the etched lines themselves; the colourist worked with a light touch and with much understanding for the suggestiveness of the underlying image. Possibly this was Altdorfer's doing: during this period he was making watercolour drawings of landscapes, of which three examples are known (e.g. 1522; Erlangen, Graph. Samml. Ubib.); these are not primarily wash drawings but were executed with much gouache, which gives them a finished appearance like that of the miniature paintings for the *Triumphal Procession of Maximilian* (*see* §(b) below). Exaggerations of scale and heightened effects of light, as in the sunset, indicate that these are imaginary landscapes or at least a combination of observation and fantasy.

The same is likely true of two small paintings, the *Landscape with a Footbridge* (?1516–20s; London, N.G.)

1. Albrecht Altdorfer: *Landscape with Double Pine*, etching, 110×160 mm, *c.* 1520 (Cambridge, Fitzwilliam Museum)

and the *Landscape with Castle* (?1520–*c.* 1532; Munich, Alte Pin.). Both have been claimed as the earliest surviving representatives of autonomous landscape painting in the Western world. This assessment is complicated by the fact that their dates are uncertain and that they are not strictly panel paintings, being executed like miniatures on parchment, albeit parchment laid down on wood. The departure of human protagonists, leaving nature to play the leading role, implied a new kind of picture, in which the continuum of the land and sky into the distance was as significant as any particular thing located front and centre on the pictorial stage. The *Landscape with Castle* is indeed an example of a new pictorial concept—autonomous landscape—since the central foreground is devoid not only of figures but of any dominant object whatsoever.

(b) Religious and history subjects. Altdorfer's art was an important instrument in the propagation of the cult of the *Schöne Maria* in Regensburg *c.* 1520, which entailed finding a visual language befitting the devotional image and enlivening to the contemporary mind. His interpretations of religious themes were indeed enlivening and often startling in their originality, while retaining authority and meaning by reference to religious and artistic precedent. He worked on his most important religious commissions in the period 1510–*c.* 1520, when he also seems most often to have produced religious art, for reasons of his own.

In the small paintings of the *Rest on the Flight into Egypt* (1510; see fig. 2) and the *Nativity* (*c.* 1512; both Berlin, Gemäldegal.) the scenes are mysterious yet playful—with frolicsome angels—and the landscapes awe-inspiring. The sky of the *Nativity* is pitch dark, except for the celestial light, while everything on the ground is aglow as if ordinary matter had suddenly become luminous. In the *Rest on the Flight* Mary is seated at a huge fountain adorned with pagan figures, the spectacular coastal landscape and town being probably inspired by one or more of Dürer's engravings, such as the *Sea Monster* (B. 71) or *St Eustace* (B. 57). The exaggerated proportions and perspective show Altdorfer's imagination as uninhibited by the limits of earthly reality. He painted the picture for himself and for the Virgin Mary, to whom he dedicated it in an inscription.

In 1511 Altdorfer started making woodcuts. His sudden interest in the medium may have been stimulated by the rash of Dürer's woodcut publications in that year, including the *Large Passion* (B. 4 [117]–15 [118]). Dürer's *Resurrection* (B. 15 [118]) from this series served Altdorfer as the basis for his own (1512; W 20). He also adopted Dürer's technique of using crosshatching to establish a grey middle value across a broad area of the woodcut, in order to make area of exposed white paper, as around the head of Christ, appear more radiant and to establish a measured scale of values from brightest light to darkest shadow. But in contrast to Dürer's rational system of lighting, Altdorfer shattered the uniform fabric of hatching into countless fragments of light and shadow, as if the Resurrection itself had occurred by explosion, causing the night to flicker and tremble. Understandably Dürer's engraving of the *Virgin with a Pear* (1511; B. 41 [59]) also appealed to him,

2. Albrecht Altdorfer: *Rest on the Flight into Egypt*, oil on panel, 570×380 mm, 1510 (Berlin, Gemäldegalerie)

given the light-filled landscape in front of which the figures are sitting, but this landscape seems controlled and static compared with Altdorfer's less elegant variant, the *Virgin and Child in a Landscape* (*c.* 1515; W 122), in which unruly clouds throw a shadow over the faces of mother and child.

Two of Altdorfer's most successful projects, which display his sense for dramatic interpretation, were narrative cycles involving the Passion, namely 16 panels from the now dismembered altarpiece for St Florian Abbey, Austria (probably commissioned 1509 and completed by 1518; 14 *in situ*; the *Burial of Christ* and the *Resurrection*, Vienna, Ksthist. Mus.), and a series of 40 woodcuts known as the *Fall and Redemption of Mankind* (*c.* 1513; Hollstein, nos 1–40). The two projects have much in common in their design and expression, despite the disparities of medium and size. The altarpiece was originally a double-winged polyptych. The exterior presented four scenes from the *Life of St Sebastian* (see fig. 3) and then, at the first opening, eight scenes from the *Passion*, concluding with two more on the predella. Sculpture that once occupied the interior of the altarpiece is lost. Architecture plays an important part in the design of both the *St Sebastian* and the *Passion* cycles. Its scale and depth are like those of Michael Pacher's architectural settings, but the Renaissance motifs derive principally from Italian engravings. The *Passion* scenes have all the complexity and exaggerated movement that contemporaries would have expected from Late Gothic treatments of the theme. Altdorfer's painterly execution, on the other hand, moved into a new expressive realm, where colours leap like flames from the darkness or where paint, as if by its own viscosity, suggests the blood running from Christ's wounds. The new expression is combined with traditional symbols, for example in the *Resurrection* where glazed red (a colour denoting the Passion) and gold leaf (the traditional ground for sacred paintings) achieve the appearance of a spectacular sunrise that proclaims Christ's triumph over darkness and death. Alongside the paintings, the small prints of the *Redemption and Fall* are masterfully concise, imparting action, drama and even monumentality within their restricted formats.

The cult of the *Schöne Maria* in Regensburg had a large impact on Altdorfer's work *c.* 1519. The cult's basis, a 13th-century version of the originally Byzantine *Virgin of St Luke* or *Hodegetria* (Regensburg, Alte Kapelle), appears in Altdorfer's drawing, the *Beautiful Virgin on a Crescent* (1518; Berlin, Kupferstichkab.), recognizable by the stars and fringe on her shawl. But unlike the static Byzantine prototype, this figure has a stance and drapery reminiscent of the *Schöne Maria* statues of *c.* 1400, characterized by a youthful figure of curvilinear posture. Thus this like other Virgins by Altdorfer embodies two Marian traditions: one of St Luke's 'authentic portrait' and another from the German 'Soft' style.

In 1519 the cult of the *Schöne Maria* turned ugly. The Regensburg city council, of which Altdorfer was a member, expelled the Jews and razed the synagogue. Before the

3. Albrecht Altdorfer: *Martyrdom of St Sebastian*, panel from the *Life of St Sebastian* altarpiece, *c.* 1509–18 (St Florian Abbey)

4. Albrecht Altdorfer: *Birth of the Virgin*, oil on panel, 1.4×1.3 m, *c.* 1520 (Munich, Alte Pinakothek)

building was destroyed, Altdorfer made two etchings of its interior (W 173, 174). Subsequently a temporary wooden chapel dedicated to the *Schöne Maria* was erected on the site, and almost immediately throngs of pilgrims seeking indulgences and miracles made their way there, as shown in Michael Ostendorfer's woodcut (for illustration *see* OSTENDORFER, MICHAEL). Among the images of the *Schöne Maria* that Altdorfer made on this occasion was a painting (Regensburg, Kollegiatstift St Johann) that freely replicates the local prototype and that was presumably used on the altar of the new chapel. He also produced two woodcuts (W 89, 90) of Renaissance-style altarpieces with the *Schöne Maria* as the central image. One of these was printed in colours from as many as six blocks, depending on the edition; with a separate block used for each colour, it stands as an important early example of colour printing.

Out of the charged and disturbing circumstances of the cult of the *Schöne Maria* came one of Altdorfer's most spirited and imaginative paintings, the *Birth of the Virgin* (Munich, Alte Pin.; see fig. 4). Unnoticed by St Joachim, who trudges home with a loaf under arm, St Anne's bedchamber has been transformed into a church interior ringed by angels. The innovatorily oblique view of the interior imparts a forest-like mystery to imagery related to Jan van Eyck's *Virgin in a Church* (Berlin, Gemäldegal.; *see* EYCK, VAN, (2), fig. 5); the vaulted space and distinctive mixture of Gothic and Renaissance architectural forms (comparable to architectural settings by Altdorfer's contemporary Wolf Huber) seem to derive from Hans Hieber's wooden model (Regensburg, Stadtmus.), from which the permanent pilgrimage church of the *Schöne Maria*, today the Neupfarrkirche, would be partially built.

The imperial and ducal commissions that Altdorfer received from Emperor Maximilian I and the Duke William IV of Bavaria signal the artist's status and that of art in Germany at the time. In 1528, the year before Altdorfer finished the *Battle of Alexander at Issos* for the Duke, he was chosen to be burgomaster of Regensburg, but declined because the painting took precedence. For the Emperor's *Triumphal Arch*, a billboard-sized print made from 192 woodblocks, Altdorfer designed five out of six scenes on each corner tower. He was more involved with two other graphic projects of the Emperor's, the *Triumphal Procession* and the *Prayerbook* (*see* HABSBURG, §I(3)). All three were conceived *c.* 1512 and carried out over the following two to five years. The *Prayerbook* gave the best opportunities for Altdorfer's fantasy and keen observation of nature. The 28 pages containing his pen drawings in coloured ink are in the Bibliothèque Municipale, Besançon. Perplexingly, only seldom do the illustrations correspond recognizably to the text. Nevertheless, Altdorfer found the margins of the manuscript a happy format in which to give free rein to his calligraphic line. It leaps from floral to Renaissance ornaments to the portrayal of a beguiling array of life—peasants, angels, animals and mythological creatures.

For the frieze-like *Triumphal Procession* Altdorfer, taking the second largest share after Hans Burgkmair, delivered designs for some 39 blocks (e.g. 1984 exh. cat., nos 151–61), including work by assistants. The final six in the series, by his own hand, portray the baggage train passing through a forested, alpine landscape. The presentation copy of the *Triumphal Procession*, of which 57 out of 109 original parchment leaves survive (Vienna, Albertina), is now recognized (Winzinger, 1966, 1972/73 and 1975) as the work of Altdorfer and assistants. These leaves are executed on parchment with pen and brown ink, watercolour washes, gouache and gold highlights. There is little correspondence between the scenes of this version and the one in woodcut.

The *Battle of Alexander at Issos* (1529; Munich, Alte Pin.; *see* GERMANY, fig. 19) was Altdorfer's contribution to a cycle of at least 16 history paintings involving biblical and ancient heroes and heroines, commissioned for the ducal residence in Munich (*see* WITTELSBACH, §I(2)). The multifigured architectural extravaganza *Susanna and the Elders* (1526; Munich, Alte Pin.) may be an earlier ducal commission. Like the other paintings in the cycle representing heroes, Altdorfer's *Battle of Alexander* has a vertical format (it was originally *c.* 100 mm taller) and offers a bird's-eye view of the scene. But it overwhelms conventional topographical views and battle scenes, not to mention the other pictures from the same series. The historical subject of the painting, identified by the plaque suspended in the sky and inscriptions on banners within the battle, is Alexander's victory in 333 BC over the Persian king Darius at Issos. The two protagonists are, however, nearly lost among waves of cavalry and foot-soldiers. Each of the countless small figures holds up remarkably to individual inspection, making the picture a *tour de force* of miniature painting. Yet the most astonishing thing is not the myriad details but rather the far-reaching view of the earth. Altdorfer took a schematic map of the world surrounding the Mediterranean, published in 1493 in the *Nuremberg Chronicle*, and transformed it into a cosmic landscape that extends as far as the Nile Valley and the Red Sea and shows the sky stretching between the moon and the sinking sun. Ostensibly the point is to suggest the global magnitude of Alexander's victory, but, compared to the immensity of nature, even heroic human actions pale into insignificance.

3. FORMAT. An astonishing contrast also exists in the sizes of Altdorfer's works. After *c.* 1515 nearly all his engravings were made on plates that, at their longest, are shorter than a little finger: some are the size of small postage stamps (e.g. *Putto Holding an Escutcheon with Altdorfer's Monogram*, W 149). The majority, representing Classical subjects, were probably made for humanists who collected medals and antique coins. Among the later intaglio prints (the production of woodcuts ceased *c.* 1520, with the possible exception of four or five blocks), only the etchings were made on plates as large as a handbreadth. Apart from the landscapes, there are 23 designs for silver or gold cups and two details of Classical columns. Yet this engraver of miniatures was able to paint on an architectural scale. What would have been one of his most arresting paintings now exists only in the form of 22 mural fragments (21, Regensburg, Stadtmus.; one, Budapest, Mus. F.A.) and a compositional drawing squared for transfer (*c.* 1535; Florence, Uffizi). The fragments were discovered in 1887 on the walls of the now destroyed bathhouse in the Bischofshof at Regensburg. The section of the mural at the entrance, *c.* 3.4×4.8 m, presented an illusionistic view of a vaulted Renaissance interior with a grand staircase, where some couples bathed or caressed and others in elegant dress looked on.

On the whole Altdorfer's single paintings, throughout his career, are of the size known as cabinet pictures. His later works, such as *Christ on the Cross between Two Thieves* (*c.* 1526) and *Beggary Sits on the Train of Pride* (1531; both Berlin, Gemäldegal.), are painted in a fine manner that represents a developing taste among many collectors throughout the rest of the century. The latter painting, according to the Berlin *Catalogue of Paintings* (1975, no. 638C), provided the imagery for the German proverb 'Der Hoffart sitzt der Bettel auf der Schleppe', which is not known in contemporary or earlier sources. Altdorfer's latest-known work, *Lot and his Daughters* (1537; Vienna, Ksthist. Mus.), is strikingly profane, with imagery akin to that of several small engravings but uncommon among Altdorfer's paintings, except for the bathhouse murals. It seems that Altdorfer left the stage playing the part of painters like Cranach and Baldung whose clientele had grown fond of large, smooth-skinned nudes.

BIBLIOGRAPHY

EARLY SOURCES

J. von Sandrart: *Teutsche Academie* (1675–9); ed. A. R. Peltzer (1925)

GENERAL

L. Baldass: *Der Künstlerkreis Kaiser Maximilians* (Vienna, 1923)

A. Stange: *Malerei der Donauschule* (Munich, 1964)
The World in Miniature: Engravings by the German Little Masters, 1500–1550 (exh. cat., ed. S. H. Goddard; Lawrence, U. KS, Spencer Mus. A., 1988)

MONOGRAPHS

M. J. Friedländer: *Albrecht Altdorfer: Der Maler von Regensburg* (Leipzig, 1891)
——: *Albrecht Altdorfer* (Berlin, [1923])
H. Tietze: *Albrecht Altdorfer* (Leipzig, 1923)
O. Benesch: *Der Maler Albrecht Altdorfer* (Vienna, 1938, 4/1943)
L. von Baldass: *Albrecht Altdorfer* (Vienna, 1941)
K. Oettinger: *Altdorfer-Studien*, iii of Erlanger Beiträge zur Sprach- und Kunstwissenschaft (Nuremberg, 1959)
E. Ruhmer: *Albrecht Altdorfer* (Munich, 1965)
F. Ficker: *Altdorfer* (Milan, 1977)
J. Krichbaum: *Albrecht Altdorfer: Meister der Alexanderschlacht* (Cologne, 1978)
R. Janzen: *Albrecht Altdorfer: Four Centuries of Criticism*, ix of Studies F.A.: Crit. (Ann Arbor, 1980)
F. Winzinger: 'Albrecht Altdorfer', *Allgemeines Künstler-Lexikon*, ii (Leipzig, 1986/*R* Munich, 1992), pp. 671–5
G. Goldberg: *Albrecht Altdorfer: Meister von Landschaft, Raum, Licht* (Munich, 1988)

CATALOGUES

Hollstein: *Ger.*
H. Voss: *Albrecht Altdorfer und Wolf Huber*, iii of Meister der Graphik (Leipzig, 1910)
C. Dodgson: *Catalogue of Early German and Flemish Woodcuts Preserved in the Department of Prints and Drawings in the British Museum*, ii, London, BM cat. (London, 1911/*R* 1980), pp. 221–38
E. Waldmann: *The Masters of Engraving and Etching: Albrecht Altdorfer* (London, 1923)
M. Geisberg: *Der deutsche Einblatt-Holzschnitt in der 1. Hälfte des 16. Jahrhunderts* (Munich, 1923–30); Eng. trans. as *The German Single-leaf Woodcut, 1500–1550*, i, ed. W. L. Strauss (New York, 1974), pp. 11–32
H. L. Becker: *Die Handzeichnungen Albrecht Altdorfers*, i of Münchner Beiträge zur Kunstgeschichte (Munich, 1938)
E. Buchner: *Albrecht Altdorfer und sein Kreis* (exh. cat., Munich, Neue Staatsgal. 1938), pp. 147–9
F. Winzinger: *Albrecht Altdorfer: Zeichnungen* (Munich, 1952)
F. W. H. Hollstein, ed.: *German Engravings, Etchings, and Woodcuts*, i (Amsterdam, 1954)
F. Winzinger: *Albrecht Altdorfer: Graphik* (Munich, 1963) [W]
C. A. zu Salm and G. Goldberg: *Altdeutsche Malerei*, Munich, Alte Pin. cat., ii (1963)
F. Winzinger: *Die Miniaturen zum Triumphzug Kaiser Maximilians I.*, v of Veröffentlichungen der Albertina, 2 vols (Graz, 1972–3)
——: *Albrecht Altdorfer: Die Gemälde* (Munich, 1975)
Catalogue of Paintings, Picture Gallery, Staatliche Museen, Preussischer Kulturbesitz, Berlin (rev. 2/1978, trans. by L. B. Parshall)
A. Smith: *Early Netherlandish and German Paintings*, London, N.G. cat. (London, 1986)
H. Mielke: *Albrecht Altdorfer: Zeichnungen, Deckfarbenmalerei, Druckgraphik* (exh. cat., Berlin, Kupferstichkab., 1988)

SPECIALIST STUDIES

H. Hildebrandt: *Die Architektur bei Altdorfer* (Strasbourg, 1908)
L. Réau: 'Albrecht Altdorfer et les origines du paysage allemand', *Gaz. B.-A.*, 4th ser., v (1911), pp. 113–35
O. Benesch: 'Altdorfers Badstubenfresken und das Wiener Lothbild', *Jb. Preuss. Kstsamml.*, li (1930), pp. 179–88; *R* in *Collected Writings*, iii, ed. E. Benesch (London, 1972), pp. 307–13
F. Winzinger: 'Die Architekturbilder in Altdorfers Altar von St. Florian', *Z. Kstwiss.*, iv (1950), pp. 159–63
E. Buchner: *Altdorfer: Die Alexanderschlacht* (Stuttgart, 1956)
K. Oettinger: 'Datum und Signatur bei Wolf Huber und Albrecht Altdorfer', *Erlang. Forsch.*, viii (Erlangen, 1957)
F. Winzinger: 'Der Altdorfer-Brunnen', *Ber. Ehem. Preusz. Kstsamml.*, n. s., xiii (1963), pp. 27–32
S. Appelbaum, ed.: *The Triumph of Maximilian I* (New York, 1964)
A. Stange: 'Albrecht Altdorfer, Hans Leinberger und die bayerische Kunst ihrer Zeit', *Alte & Mod. Kst*, x/80 (1965), pp. 14–19
D. Koepplin: 'Altdorfer und die Schweizer', *Alte & Mod. Kst*, xi/84 (1966), pp. 6–14
F. Winzinger: 'Albrecht Altdorfer und die Miniaturen des Triumphzuges Kaiser Maximilians I.', *Jb.Ksthist. Samml. Wien*, lxiii (1966), pp. 157–72
D. Koepplin: 'Das Sonnengestirn der Donaumeister: Zur Herkunft und Bedeutung eines Leitmotivs', *Werden und Wandlung: Studien zur Kunst der Donauschule* (Linz, 1967), pp. 78–114
A. Stange: 'Das Bildnis im Werke Albrecht Altdorfers', *Pantheon*, xxv (1967), pp. 91–6
C. Meckseper: 'Zur Ikonographie von Altdorfers Alexanderschlacht', *Z. Dt. Ver. Kstwiss.*, xxii, 3/4 (1968), pp. 179–85
K. Martin: *Die Alexanderschlacht von Albrecht Altdorfer* (Munich, 1969)
A. Burkhard: *The St Florian Altar of Albrecht Altdorfer* (Munich, 1970)
C. Talbot: 'Landscapes from Incunabula to Altdorfer', *Gesta*, xv (1976), pp. 321–6
J. Harnest: 'Zur Perspektive in Albrecht Altdorfers Alexanderschlacht', *Anz. Ger. Nmus.* (1977), pp. 67–77
G. Brucher: *Farbe und Licht in Albrecht Altdorfers Sebastiansaltar in St. Florian* (Graz, 1978)
H. Appuhn, ed.: *Der Triumphzug Kaiser Maximilians I, 1516–1518* (Dortmund, 1979)
B. Eschenburg: 'Altdorfers *Alexanderschlacht* und ihr Verhältnis zum Historienzyklus Wilhelms IV.', *Z. Dt. Ver. Kstwiss.*, xxxiii (1979), pp. 36–67
D. Heinrich, ed.: *Albrecht Altdorfer und seine Zeit*, v of Schriftenreihe der Universität Regensburg (Regensburg, 1981)
W. Hütt: 'Albrecht Altdorfer und die Reformation', *Bild. Kst*, xxix (1981), pp. 83–6
H. Schindler: 'Albrecht Altdorfer und die Anfänge des Donaustils', *Ostbair. Grenzmarken*, xxiii (1981), pp. 66–73
G. Goldberg: *Die Alexanderschlacht und die Historienbilder des bayerischen Herzogs Wilhelm IV. und seiner Gemahlin Jacobea für die Münchner Residenz*, v of Bayerische Staatsgemäldesammlungen Künstler und Werke (Munich, 1983)
W. Mersmann: 'Altdorfer und der ältere Holbein', *Von österreichischer Kunst, Franz Fuhrmann gewidmet* (Klagenfurt, 1983), pp. 55–63
M. Seidel and E. M. Landau: *Altdorfer: Leidensweg, Heilsweg. Der Passionsaltar von St. Florian* (Stuttgart, 1983)
L. Silver: 'Forest Primeval: Albrecht Altdorfer and the German Wilderness Landscape', *Simiolus*, xiii (1983), pp. 4–43
Albrecht Altdorfer: Christ Taking Leave of his Mother (exh. cat. by A. Smith, London, N.G., 1984)
K. Möseneder: 'Gestaltungsmittel Albrecht Altdorfers und ihre ikonologischen Entsprechungen', *Aufsätze zur Kunstgeschichte: Festschrift für Hermann Bauer zum 60. Geburtstag*, ed. K. Mösenender and A. Prater (Hildesheim, 1991), pp. 137–49
A. Prater: 'Zur Bedeutung der Landschaft beim frühen Altdorfer', *Aufsätze zur Kunstgeschichte: Festschrift für Hermann Bauer zum 60. Geburtstag*, ed. K. Mösenender and A. Prater (Hildesheim, 1991), pp. 150–68
C. S. Wood: *Albrecht Altdorfer and the Origins of Landscape* (London, 1993)

(2) Erhard Altdorfer (*b c.* 1480/85; *d* Schwerin, 1561/2). Brother of (1) Albrecht Altdorfer. He probably occupied a place in his brother's Regensburg workshop *c.* 1506, the year in which he signed and dated an engraving of a *Lady with a Peacock Coat of Arms* (B. 416, 1). In 1512 Erhard was documented as ducal court painter in Schwerin, a post that he held until his death. His signed and dated three-part woodcut of a *Tournament* (?1512–13; unique copy, Schwerin, Mecklenburg. Landesbib.; Hollstein, no. 91) was modelled on woodcuts (1506, 1509; B. 124 [293], 126 [294]) by Lucas Cranach the elder. Cranach's Bible illustrations (Wittenberg, 1523) were the basis for Erhard's most extensive surviving work, 82 woodcut illustrations for the Low German Bible (Lübeck, 1531–4; e.g. Hollstein, no. 75) published by Ludwig Dietz (*c.* 1504–59), in which he also included mountainous and forested landscape settings similar to those he knew and probably painted in Regensburg or in other regions of the Danube.

On the basis of the *Lady with a Peacock Coat of Arms*, Erhard is attributed with two small engravings, *Vanitas* (Mielke, no. 178) and *Man with Two Courtesans* (Hollstein, no. 3), and at least four pen drawings, including the

Baptism of St John (Regensburg, Stadtmus.) and the more elaborate *Social Gathering in a Room with a Large Fountain* (Berlin, Kupferstichkab.), which date from 1506 to *c.* 1508–10. They are closely related by theme, technique and amorphous rendering of the body to contemporary works by Albrecht Altdorfer, but Erhard's pen and burin lines are even wispier and his shading more finely striated than his brother's; thin drapery with fine pleats and the nude figure of Vanitas suggest that the engravings of Jacopo de' Barbari were also a factor in these designs. Such delicacy soon gave way to more robust figures and heavier drapery, as in the woodcuts for the Lübeck Bible, the basis for most of the later attributions. For example *St John on Patmos* (see fig.), which shows the saint seated in a forest landscape with notably fluffy foliage, makes reasonable the attribution to Erhard of a chiaroscuro drawing of the same subject on reddish-brown paper (Frankfurt am Main, Städel. Kstinst. & Städt. Gal.). This in turn has led to the proposal that a panel painting of *St John on Patmos* (Kansas City, KS, Nelson–Atkins Mus. A.) and two other altarpiece panels (ex-Stift Lambach, Upper Austria; Regensburg, Stadtmus.) are also by him. But in the absence of a single signed or documented example, attributions of paintings are uncertain. *St Leopold Finding the Virgin's Veil* (Klosterneuburg, Mus. Chorherrenstiftes) has been associated with his early style and with altarpiece panels depicting scenes from the *Life of St John the Baptist* (?before 1512; Gutenstetten, Parish Church). Presumably later are panels depicting the *Life of St Mary Magdalene* and *SS Michael and Christopher* (Lübeck, St Annen-Mus.), though here too the evidence for the attributions is circumstantial and stylistically general.

Erhard Altdorfer: *St John on Patmos*, woodcut, 216×145 mm, from the Lübeck Bible, 1531–4 (Lübeck, St Annen-Kloster)

Erhard's only known etching establishes him as one of the first artists to treat landscape as a subject of interest on its own: this is a monogrammed, undated alpine landscape (Hollstein, no. 2; B. 71), in the manner of his brother, presumably inspired by Albrecht's examples rather than being the forerunner of its type. It shows that he had a practised hand with such compositions. On the basis of this etching, several drawings of landscapes (Erlangen, Graph. Samml. Ubib.; Paris, Louvre) are considered with good reason to be his. The *Mountainous and Sea Landscape* (Vienna, Albertina) compares closely with the etching in its controlled execution and sense of freshness in light and atmosphere. Quite different in expression is the dense, explosive *Landscape with a Large Spruce* (Copenhagen, Stat. Must. Kst), a chiaroscuro drawing on grey-green prepared paper, the attribution of which derives from similarities to the landscape settings of the Lübeck Bible and the chiaroscuro drawing of *St John on Patmos.*

BIBLIOGRAPHY

Hollstein: *Ger.*

C. Dodgson: 'Erhard Altdorfer als Kupferstecher und Zeichner', *Mitt. Ges. Vervielfält. Kst*, ii (1911), pp. 21–3

W. Jürgens: *Erhard Altdorfer* (Lübeck, 1931)

O. Benesch: 'Erhard Altdorfer als Maler', *Jb. Preuss. Kstsamml.*, lvii (1936), pp. 157–68; repr. in *Collected Writings*, iii, ed. E. Benesch (London, 1972), pp. 326–35

K. Oettinger: *Altdorfer-Studien*, iii of Erlanger Beiträge zur Sprach- und Kunstwissenschaft (Nuremberg, 1959)

K. Packpfeiffer: *Studien zu Erhard Altdorfer* (Vienna, 1978)

F. Ficker: 'Erhard Altdorfer', *Allgemeines Künstler-Lexikon*, ii (Leipzig, 1986/*R* Munich, 1992), pp. 675–6

H. Mielke: *Albrecht Altdorfer: Zeichnungen, Deckfarbenmalerei, Druckgraphik* (exh. cat., Berlin, Kupferstichkab., 1988)

CHARLES TALBOT

Altemps [Alta Emps, Hohenems]. Italian family of patrons, of German origin. The Hohenems family from Salzburg Italianized their name when Cardinal Marcus Sitticus Altemps (1533–95) brought the dynasty to Rome. A soldier by training, he pursued an ecclesiastical career under the patronage of his uncle, Pope Pius IV (*reg* 1559–65). Marcus was made Bishop of Konstanz in 1561 and legate to the Council of Trent. He began the development of the massive Villa Mondragone (*see* FRASCATI and fig. 2), to the designs of his house architect Martino I Longhi (i); Pope Gregory XIII (*reg* 1572–85) often visited it. Through papal favour he accumulated enormous wealth, which he used to rebuild the Palazzo Riario near Piazza Navona, Rome, into a magnificent family palace (known thereafter as the Palazzo Altemps) and to build the Altemps Chapel in S Maria in Trastevere; both of these designs were by Longhi. Effects of the Cardinal's patronage or his generosity survive in the many estates that he purchased or received as gifts, at Loreto, Gallese and in the area around Frascati (e.g. at Mondragone, Monte Compatri and Monte Porzio). Giovanni Angelo Altemps, son of Roberto Altemps (himself the illegitimate son of Cardinal Marco Sittico Altemps), inherited the family estates but in 1613 sold the Villa Mondragone to the Borghese family. In

1602 he built a sumptuous chapel in the Palazzo Altemps to house the newly discovered relics of Pope Anicetus (*reg c.* AD 154–*c.* 166). He was also a scholar and bibliophile who assembled one of the most famous libraries of Early Baroque Rome, the Biblioteca Altempsiana. This was enlarged in 1611 by the purchase of the library of Pope Marcellus II (*reg* 1555). The Biblioteca Altempsiana survived intact until its dispersal by auction in 1907–8.

BIBLIOGRAPHY

DBI

H. Friedel: 'Die Cappella Altemps in S Maria in Trastevere', *Röm. Jb. Kstgesch.*, xvii (1978), pp. 89–123

D. R. Coffin: *The Villa in the Life of Renaissance Rome* (Princeton, 1979), pp. 174–8

JOSEPH CONNORS

Altena, J(ohan) Q(uirijn) van Regteren (*b* Amsterdam, 16 May 1899; *d* Amsterdam, 18 Oct 1980). Dutch museum curator and art historian. After a short stay at the Koninklijk Academie voor Kunsten, Amsterdam, he studied in Paris (with Frits Lugt), Rome and Utrecht (with W. Vogelsang), gaining his doctorate at Utrecht in 1935 with a study of the drawings of Jacques de Gheyn. After an interlude in the art trade, Altena became curator of three small municipal museums in Amsterdam (1932–7) and then a professor in the history of art at the University of Amsterdam (1937–69). Concurrently he served as director of the Rijksprentenkabinet of the Rijksmuseum, Amsterdam (1948–62), keeper of the art collections of the Teyler Foundation, Haarlem (1952–73), and co-editor of the journal *Oud-Holland* (1946–73). Altena's professional writings include numerous articles, mostly concerning Netherlandish painting of the 15th–17th centuries, but his main interest lay in drawings, of which he was recognized as an outstanding connoisseur and collector. He enriched the Rijksprentenkabinet with choice examples of French, Italian, English and German drawings from his own collection. His major achievement, a three-volume catalogue of the paintings and drawings of the three members of the de Gheyn family, was published posthumously.

WRITINGS

The Drawings of Jacques de Gheyn (Utrecht, 1936)

Miscellanea I. Q. van Regteren Altena (Amsterdam, 1969), pp. 236–40 [complete list of writings]

Jacques de Gheyn: Three Generations (Amsterdam, 1983)

BIBLIOGRAPHY

K. G. Boon: 'Bij het afschied van J. Q. van Regteren Altena' [On parting from J. Q. van Regteren Altena], *Bull. Rijksmus.*, x (1962), pp. 52–5

Obituary, *Oud-Holland*, xcv (1981), pp. 1–2

ROBERT W. SCHELLER

Altenbourg [Ströch], **Gerhard** (*b* Rödichen-Schnepfenthal, Thuringia, 22 Nov 1926; *d* Dresden, 30 Dec 1989). German painter, printmaker and sculptor. He studied at the Hochschule für Baukunst and Bildende Kunst in Weimar under H. Hoffmann-Lederer (*b* 1899). From the start his interest was directed towards modernism, especially by its literary aspects, which inspired him to produce lyrical works of his own. Even in his first drawings, for example *Ecce homo I* (1949; priv. col., see 1969 exh. cat., no. 142), in which he addressed the painful experience of war, he achieved a marked individual style. His determined preoccupation with modern art and the vocabulary of form set him at odds with the prevailing artistic ideology until late in his life. In the 1940s and 1950s, although his plants and figures were depicted objectively, he produced tight-woven but reduced abstract shapes that anticipated the meticulously applied successive layers of non-objectivism. His work was always closely influenced by the area in which he was born and lived, particularly his landscapes, for example *Garden at the Spinnbahn* (1951; priv. col., see 1969 exh. cat., no. 23). The large-format work *These Artists* (1957; see 1969 exh. cat., no. 54) shows the abstract developing from the figurative. Examples of his later work are *Over to Byzantium* (1971/2; Berlin, Kupferstichkab.) and the *Splendour of the Abyss* (1981; Dresden, Kupferstichkab.)

BIBLIOGRAPHY

Werkverzeichnis 1947–1969 (exh. cat., ed. D. Brusberg; Hannover, 1969) [rev. edn in preparation]

G. Altenbourg. Arbeiten 1947–1987 (exh. cat., ed. S. Salzmann; Bremen, Ksthalle; Tübingen, Ksthalle; Hannover, Sprengel Mus.; W. Berlin, Akad. Kst.; 1988)

EUGEN BLUME

Altenburg. *See under* CLUJ-NAPOCA.

Alternating system [alternation]. Term applied to medieval ecclesiastical architecture and referring to the deliberate use of differing pier forms in an arcade. Alternation is found in aisled churches throughout western Europe from the 11th to the 14th century. Its purpose is to articulate internal elevations through the subdivision of the main arcades and in some instances to emphasize certain liturgically important areas. In its simplest form the alternating system consists of the use of both the column (cylindrical) and the pier (square or rectangular in section). In antiquity these two types of support had specific functions that were almost always observed: the column supported the horizontal entablature and the pier supported the arch. By the Middle Ages this rule had been abandoned, and both types of support were used for arcades.

The earliest examples of alternation occur in the eastern Roman Empire during the 5th and 6th centuries AD. In most instances its use may be attributed to structural function, as at the church of St John, Ephesos, or Hagia Eirene in Constantinople (now Istanbul), where the massive piers interrupting the colonnades support the domes that form the nave roofs. Nevertheless, the aesthetic advantages of varied supports were also exploited. In Syria at Rusafa, for example, the church of St Sergius (518) had a column/projecting pier alternating system that would not have looked amiss in 12th-century Europe. The building that makes the link with Europe, however, is Hagios Demetrios (late 5th century) in Thessaloniki, where the arcades are supported on columns interrupted occasionally by rectangular piers (*see* THESSALONIKI, §III, 3(i)). If A is taken to represent the pier and B the column, the rhythm created for both of the main arcades is A B B B A B B B B A B B B A. Alternation first appeared in western Europe in Saxony at the nuns' church of St Cyriakus (founded 959) at Gernrode, where the same type of supports alternate in a simple A B A B A fashion. It is possible that direct influence from Byzantium explains the occurrence of alternation at Gernrode, through the patronage of the Empress Theophanu (*d* 991), the Greek bride of Emperor Otto II (*see* ROMANESQUE, §II, 2(i)), even though the marriage did not take place until 972. The next appearance of this column/pier alternation is at St Michael (1010–33), Hildesheim (see fig.), a key building for the development of the Romanesque style (*see* HILDESHEIM, §2(i)). The nave elevation is divided into three compartments with the rhythm A B B A B B A B B A (only the north-east bay retains its original columns). This type of alternation became common in northern Europe during the late 11th century and the 12th.

The next or parallel stage in the development of alternation is linked to the introduction of the compound pier. This type of support occurs in many different combinations, but the important distinction is that one element of the pier projects from the wall plane and is carried up the full height of the nave elevation, thereby increasing the definition into bays. The basic type is the cross-shaped pier. An early use of this pier in an arcade may be seen at Saint-Martin-du-Canigou Abbey (1001–20s), where simple six-bay arcades on columns are interrupted midway by a cruciform pier that supports a transverse arch across the barrel-vaulted nave. This is an example of alternation between column and compound pier in its simplest form.

During the 11th century the application of the half column to each face of a square pier was used to great effect in alternating designs. At Notre-Dame (*c.* 1040–67; ruined) at Jumièges Abbey, for example, this type of pier alternates with columns in a regular A B A B rhythm (*see* JUMIÈGES ABBEY, fig. 1). There the compound piers probably supported diaphragm arches, which accentuated the

Alternating system, St Michael, Hildesheim, 1010–33; interior looking east

rhythm. A similar design was employed at S Miniato al Monte (1062–90), Florence, where the diaphragm arches survive (*see* FLORENCE, §IV, 7). The effect is further complemented by each pair of compound piers forming a square (in plan) with the next pair. Therefore each single bay is a rectangle, and a double bay forms a square. This method of planning is frequently reflected in alternating systems. The column/compound pier type of alternation to the A B A rhythm is the commonest in Romanesque architecture, and it is found in all regions of western Europe. Early Gothic architecture in northern France also adopted the system because the square double bay related admirably to early sexpartite rib vaults, as is illustrated by the cathedrals of Sens (*see* SENS, §1(i)), Noyon (begun *c.* 1150) and Senlis (begun *c.* 1151–6).

The column/pier system exists in a vestigial state in a number of Romanesque buildings. At the cathedrals of Ely (*see* ELY CATHEDRAL, §1(i)) and Norwich (1096–1130), for example, the columnar piers are disguised by shafts so that only segments of circles are revealed. At Santiago de Compostela the square core of every other pier is rounded to create an alternating effect (*see* ROMANESQUE, fig. 11). The same technique was used at Holy Trinity (*c.* 1050), Great Paxton (Cambs), where the device is so subtle as to be barely noticeable, yet is clearly deliberate.

The alternating system was not confined to the column/pier type. Many examples of alternation consist of very slight variations to pier plans, such as that at St Etienne (begun 1060s) in Caen, where the only variation is created by the existence of a thin pilaster behind the half column on every other pier (*see* CAEN, fig. 1; ROMANESQUE, §II, 5(vii)). Similarly at Wymondham Abbey (begun 1107; Norfolk) the alternation consists simply of single and double half shafts on the nave elevation.

More important is the use of polygonal piers in alternating systems, which was particularly common in medieval Britain. The abbey (now cathedral) of Peterborough (begun 1117) is one of the earliest buildings to use polygonal piers. The system of alternation used in the three-bay eastern arm (*see* ROMANESQUE, fig. 17) consists of a pair of twelve-sided piers at the east, circular columns further west and octagonal piers to the bay before the crossing. This variety of pier forms is further accentuated by the two octagonal piers being orientated in different directions; the angles of the octagon on the north side reflect the principal axis, while to the south the sides of the octagon correspond to the principal axis. This eccentric attitude and delight in experimentation with alternation is characteristic of English high Romanesque and Early Gothic architecture. At Castle Acre Priory (early 12th century; Norfolk), for example, every pair of nave piers is different in an arcade of seven bays. The variety was produced by using differing numbers of half columns, segmental forms and also, undoubtedly, polygonal forms. Homogeneity was achieved by matching opposing pier faces across the nave, beneath each arch of the main arcades and across the aisles. Similarly, at Rochester Cathedral (early 12th century) each pair of nave piers is different, in this case with matching pier faces occurring only across the nave. As regards the Gothic period, the rebuilt choir of Canterbury Cathedral (1175–7) employs alternating octagonal and circular piers (*see* CANTERBURY, fig. 9), and this type of alternation became common in parish churches throughout Britain.

Alternation in Early Gothic architecture in England took an astonishing variety of forms. At Lincoln Cathedral, for example, seven different pier forms are used in the nave and western transept (*c.* 1215–*c.* 1235). The three different pier forms defining the eastern aisles follow the same sequence in each transept arm. Thus the pattern can be fully appreciated only by looking at both transept arms at once, which is, of course, impossible in the building itself. A similar device is used in the transepts of Salisbury Cathedral (1220–66); six different pier forms are used in the whole church by varying the number of free-standing shafts clustered around a pier and varying the shape of the pier core. There is a degree of symmetry, if not logic, at Salisbury, but apparently neither quality was considered necessary by medieval masons, and it is not unusual to find an odd pier in an arcade. At Lincoln, for example, there is a markedly different odd pier in the middle of the north nave arcade, while in lesser buildings single odd piers, always more elaborate, are sometimes found. By the middle of the 13th century interest in pier alternation had waned, perhaps in favour of the newly invented window tracery.

Different pier forms were sometimes used to mark or accentuate specific areas of liturgical importance such as the position of an altar or screen. In the Romanesque Marienkirche, Bad Segeberg (Schleswig-Holstein), the former abbey church (begun 1099) at Alpirsbach (Baden-Württemberg) and Romsey Abbey (Hants), for example, the pairs of piers between the first and second bays of the nave are different from the others. Their presence is a response to the division that originally existed between the choir reserved for the clergy and the nave open to the laity. At the cathedrals of Norwich and Laon four odd piers, marking a two-bay square immediately west of the screen, emphasized the position of the nave altar.

BIBLIOGRAPHY

E. Lambert: 'L'Ancienne Eglise du prieuré de Lay-Saint-Christophe et l'alternance des supports dans les églises de plan basilical', *Bull. Mnmtl*, ci (1942), pp. 225–53

L. Grodecki: *L'Architecture ottonienne* (Paris, 1958)

B. Cherry: 'Romanesque Architecture in Eastern England', *J. Brit. Archaeol. Assoc.*, cxxxi (1978), pp. 1–30

E. C. Fernie: 'The Use of Varied Nave Supports in Romanesque and Early Gothic Architecture', *Gesta*, xxiii/2 (1984), pp. 107–17

L. Hoey: 'Pier Alternation in Early English Gothic Architecture', *J. Brit. Archaeol. Assoc.*, cxxxix (1986), pp. 45–67

STEPHEN HEYWOOD

Althann [Althan]**, Gundacker Ludwig Joseph**, Graf von (*b* Zwentendorf, 15 May 1665; *d* Vienna, 28 Dec 1747). Austrian administrator and patron. In 1716, after a military career under Prince Eugene of Savoy, he was appointed Director General of Works by the Holy Roman Emperor Charles VI. Responsible for all court construction projects, he was authorized to issue directives in the Emperor's name. In 1726, in his capacity as Imperial Director of Artistic Affairs, he was appointed Honorary President of the Akademie der Bildenden Künste in Vienna. In the face of resistance from an administration still clinging to its traditional rights, he attempted to reorganize the court's inefficient building industry, in order to execute the Emperor's ambitious construction schemes and to make the Court Surveyor's office a central authority administering buildings in all the Habsburg territories, although he was unsuccessful in the latter. The Hofbibliothek (1716–21, 1724–6), the concept of which is attributed to Althann in a building decree issued by the Emperor, the Winterreitschule and the Josephssäule, all in Vienna, carry inscriptions paying tribute to his services. He was responsible for the completion (1716–37) of the Karlskirche in Vienna (*see* VIENNA, §V, 2). He is also credited with the creation of the imperial art gallery (1721) in the Stallburg in Vienna, the reorganization (1722–6) of the Treasury in the Hofburg and the conversion (1730–55) of Klosterneuburg Abbey into an imperial residence. As an architectural expert, Althann was consulted by the Schönborn family on the planning of the Residenz in Würzburg and the palace in Pommersfelden. He is also named on the medals of honour awarded by the Akademie from 1731 to competition winners in its various artistic disciplines.

BIBLIOGRAPHY

W. Hauser: *Das Geschlecht derer von Althan* (diss., U. Vienna, 1949), pp. 39, 108–28

B. Pohl: *Das Hofbauamt: Seine Tätigkeit zur Zeit Karls VI. und Maria Theresias* (diss., U. Vienna, 1968)

C. Diemer: 'B. F. Moll und G. R. Donner: Die Portraitreliefs im Österreichischen Barockmuseum und ihre Vorbilder', *Mitt. Österreich. Gal.*, xxi (1977), no. 65, pp. 67–133, figs 67–71

F. Matsche: *Die Kunst im Dienst der Staatsidee Kaiser Karls VI.: Ikonographie, Ikonologie und Programmatik des 'Kaiserstils'*, i (Berlin and New York, 1981), pp. 35–43

FRANZ MATSCHE

Altherr, Heinrich (*b* Basle, 11 April 1878; *d* Zurich, 27 April 1947). Swiss painter. He studied in Basle, in Munich under Heinrich Knirr, and in Rome. He worked from 1913 to 1939 as a teacher of composition at the Staatliche Akademie der Bildenden Künste, Stuttgart, gaining international recognition as one of the few Swiss Expressionists. In his panel paintings and murals, he tried to achieve a synthesis of Expressionism, Symbolism and Classicism, using startling contrasts of light and dark tones. He also produced mosaics and stained-glass windows. His brother Paul Altherr (1870–1928) was also a painter.

BIBLIOGRAPHY

W. Überwasser and W. Braun: *Der Maler Heinrich Altherr: Sein Weg und Werk* (Zurich, 1938)

HANS-PETER WITTWER

Altichiero (di Domenico da Zevio) (*fl* 1369; *d* before 10 April 1393). Italian painter. He was one of the most important northern Italian painters of the 14th century. His style is characterized by an interest in the depiction of space and volume and by a preference for soft colours bathed in suffused light. His narrative paintings have a solemnity and grandeur that is mitigated by the lively realism and animation of the figures, convincingly integrated into settings of architectural complexity.

1. Early work in Verona, before *c.* 1377. 2. Padua, *c.* 1377–*c.* 1384. 3. Late work in Verona, *c.* 1384 and after. 4. Critical reception and posthumous reputation.

1. EARLY WORK IN VERONA, BEFORE *c.* 1377. He is first recorded in Verona, where he witnessed a contract

on 2 March 1369. Vasari stated that he was a most trusted member of the household (*famigliarissimo*) of the della Scala, the rulers of Verona, and his *Vita* of Carpaccio contains an appreciative, first-hand description of Altichiero's frescoes in the Sala del Podestà, originally the Sala Grande, of the della Scala palace (*c.* 1364) in Verona. The subject of the frescoes was taken from Flavius Josephus's *Jewish Wars*. Their appearance can be partially reconstructed from two anonymous north Italian drawings, one of which, *Mounted Soldiers at the Entrance to a Castle* (sold Monaco, Sotheby's, 20 June 1987), is inscribed *di maestro altichiero qual dipinse la sala del podestà* ('by master Altichiero who painted the Sala del Podestà'). Vasari described rich borders surrounding the scenes, in the upper parts of which were a series of portrait medallions. Quatrefoils with profile portraits of eminent Romans were rediscovered on soffits of a loggia of the Palazzo del Governo in Verona and were attributed by Mellini (1959) to Altichiero as part of his decoration of the Sala Grande. Some of these seem to be derived from Roman coins and are an indication of the interest in Classical antiquity which was a feature of cultural life in north Italian courts at the time.

2. PADUA, *c.* 1377–*c.* 1384. Knowledge of Altichiero's painting style depends on the documented fresco cycles that have survived in Padua. The date of his arrival in the city is unknown but his earliest commission there was probably a series of frescoed portraits in the Sala Virorum Illustrium (Hall of Famous Men, now Sala dei Giganti) in the Palazzo Carrara, which owed its inspiration to Petrarch's *De viris illustribus*, a celebration of ancient and modern heroes. The decoration of the room was completed by 1379. The sole surviving section is a portrait of FRANCESCO PETRARCH in his study, the background of which was repainted in the mid-16th century. A more complete idea of the original scheme may be given by an illustrated translation of Petrarch's text (Darmstadt, Hess. Landes- & Hochschbib., MS. 101). Petrarch died in 1374, and Altichiero's portrait may have been commissioned as a memorial by the poet's patrons.

The first document relating to Altichiero's frescoes in the Santo in Padua is dated 12 February 1372, when the Venetian sculptor and architect Andriolo de' Santi was contracted to build the Cappella di S Giacomo (now S Felice). The blind arcade of the south wall echoes the five Gothic arches through which the chapel is entered: the three central bays of this south wall are painted with a continuous scene of the *Crucifixion*. The arch to each side contains a marble tomb: that on the left has a *Pietà* painted above it and that on the right a *Risen Christ with Two Angels*. The spandrels at each end of the arcaded wall have an *Annunciation*, but all the other spandrels in the chapel are painted with roundels with half-length saints. On the west wall above the stalls is a fresco showing the donors Bonifacio Lupi di Soragno and his wife Caterina dei Franceschi presented by their patron saints to the Virgin and Child enthroned. The scenes painted above the stalls on the east wall and all the lunettes into the vault illustrate the *Legend of St James*, to whom the chapel was dedicated.

Throughout the cycle figures are conceived on a monumental scale and endowed with a narrative force and gravity of expression worthy of Giotto. The convincing integration of figures and setting is remarkable. The treatment of architecture and its use in organizing compositions and describing space show an accomplishment not seen in earlier Italian painting. Buildings not only place the drama and set the scale but suggest space in several remarkable ways: in the *Dream of King Ramiro* on the east wall, the painted architecture relates to the architectural form of the chapel itself, easing the transition from representation to reality. Altichiero's naturalism is also apparent in portraiture: likenesses of contemporary figures including Petrarch, King Louis I of Hungary and the donors have been identified in the *Council of King Ramiro*, alluding to the cultural and political affiliations of the da Carrara, lords of Padua (Plant, 1981).

By the 16th century a tradition had grown up that Jacopo Avanzi had collaborated with Altichiero. No documentary sources can substantiate these claims but there are stylistic reasons to attribute some of the lunettes of the Cappella di S Giacomo to another hand. This would have been one of the first areas to be painted, either before March 1377, when a large section of scaffolding in the chapel was dismantled, or in early 1378, when payments were made for the erection of more scaffolding. Altichiero may have been delayed by his earlier assignment in the Sala Virorum Illustrium and, in order to keep to his schedule, called in another painter to execute the first few lunettes. The large sum of 792 ducats paid to Altichiero in 1379, when the decoration was probably completed, suggests that he played the primary role in its planning and execution.

During the same period Altichiero probably also painted the tomb of the Dotto family in the church of the Eremitani in Padua (destr.). This consisted of a *Coronation of the Virgin* in which the two donors were shown with their patron saints George and James. Diamante Dotto, shown on the left of the fresco, died in 1381. The spandrels above were painted with an *Annunciation*, while the roundels on the inner surface of the arch contained half-length saints.

While Altichiero was frescoing the Cappella di S Giacomo for Bonifacio, another member of the family, Raimondino de' Lupi, founded the oratory of S Giorgio (near the Santo), which bears an inscription of 1377. Like the Arena Chapel, which it recalls, it seems to have been planned specifically for an elaborate fresco cycle. The frescoes are in two registers: on the west wall are eight scenes from the legends of St Catherine and St Lucy; on the east are scenes from the life of St George and a votive fresco showing Raimondino de' Lupi's parents followed by all the Lupi knights, before the Virgin and Child enthroned. The north entrance wall contains an *Annunciation* and four scenes from the infancy of Christ, while the altar wall is decorated with a *Crucifixion* surmounted by a *Coronation of the Virgin*. The tomb of Raimondino de' Lupi originally stood in the centre of the chapel, and the painting was probably partly completed by the time masses were said following his death on 30 November 1379. Only on 30 May 1384 did Altichiero and Bonifacio Lupi (now acting as executor) record their mutual satisfaction with the contract's fulfilment. A layer of whitewash covered

1. Altichiero: *Crucifixion* (*c.* 1379–84), fresco, oratory of S Giorgio, Padua

the frescoes until 1837, and the paint surface has lost the *a secco* additions and in places some of the *intonaco* as well.

Unlike the Cappella di S Giacomo frescoes, those in the oratory of S Giorgio are painted in a more or less homogeneous style, and with the exception of certain details they are attributable to Altichiero alone. The critical history of the cycle has been confused, however, and Jacopo Avanzi named as a possible collaborator, although the earliest local guide, by Michele Savonarola (*c.* 1445–7), does not mention his working there. Altichiero's inventive and varied architectural settings clarify and complement an often complicated narrative and are frequently illusionistic, especially where they intersect framing elements. In the vast *Crucifixion* (see fig. 1) the treatment and disposition of the figures owe much to Giotto, but Altichiero enriched this source with figure grouping on a grand scale and included lively, genre-like subordinate scenes. His preference for middle-range colours, such as purple and blue-green, and his sparing use of primaries were original and attractive. Local colour predominates, especially in architectural and landscape settings. To ascribe Altichiero's exquisite sense of colour to contact with Sienese sources, as some critics have done, seems mistaken. (For further illustration *see* DRESS, fig. 19.)

3. LATE WORK IN VERONA, *c.* 1384 AND AFTER. On 29 September 1384 Altichiero was appointed with four others to act on behalf of Gianpaolo Pantagliati da Arzignano, who was then in Padua, in accepting benefices pertaining to Verona Cathedral. By then the painter may have returned to Verona, where Vasari described him 'at a later period' working in the palace of the Counts Serenghi (this decoration since lost). The votive fresco of the Cavalli family in their chapel in S Anastasia in Verona probably dates from the late 1380s (Kruft suggested it was completed by autumn 1390). In this, the family members kneel in a Gothic audience chamber before the Virgin and Child, who are enshrined in a tabernacle at the left (*see* fig. 2). Their patron saints, George, Martin and James, complete this chivalric scene whose mood and format recall the earlier dedication scene in the oratorio of S Giorgio.

On 10 April 1393, when two goldsmiths were commissioned to make a cross after his design for a convent of Poor Clare nuns at S Francesco, Mantua, Altichiero was described as *bonae memoriae*, implying that he had died by then. Other works attributed to Altichiero include a panel of *Christ on the Cross between the Virgin and St John* (Richmond, VA, Mus. F.A.) and two drawings, both depicting the *Triumph of Fame*, one in ink and wash and the other coloured (in copies of Petrarch's *De viris illustribus*, Paris, Bib. N., MS. Lat. 6069F and 6069I).

4. CRITICAL RECEPTION AND POSTHUMOUS REPUTATION. Altichiero's style has been linked to that of the early Veronese painter Turone. Other northern Italian artists such as Tomaso da Modena and especially Guariento have been cited as major inspirations. Altichiero's involved architectural scenes are surely indebted to those of the latter. However, Giotto was certainly the most profound influence.

Nothing is known of the work of Altichiero's nephew Antonio, who was probably an assistant, nor of Marco di Giovanni, for whom Altichiero witnessed an agreement in 1383. Jacopo da Verona, who worked in Padua, and Martino da Verona may also have trained with him. Altichiero's art was crucial to the succeeding generation of painters in northern Italy. Pisanello made drawings after his work, and his spatial settings inspired Jacopo Bellini among others. Donatello and Mantegna, the founding figures of Renaissance art in Padua, were reported by Vasari to have praised Altichiero's work, and Fra Filippo Lippi learnt lessons in spatial design from Altichiero's Paduan works that profoundly influenced his compositions of the late 1430s and 1440s as well as his frescoes in Prato Cathedral.

BIBLIOGRAPHY

M. Savonarola: *Libellus de magnificis ornamentis regiae civitatis Padue* (*c.* 1445–7); ed. A. Segarizzi (Città di Castello, 1902)

M. Michiel: *Notizia d'opere di disegno* (*c.* 1520–40); ed. G. Frizzoni (Bologna, 1884)

G. Vasari: *Vite* (1550, rev. 2/1568); ed. G. Milanesi (1878–85), vol. iii, pp. 628, 633–4, 656, 658

G. L. Mellini: 'La "Sala Grande" di Altichiero e Jacopo d'Avanzo ed i palazzi scaligeri di Verona', *Crit. A.*, vi (1959), pp. 313–34

P. Pettenella: *Altichiero e la pittura veronese del trecento* (Verona, 1961)

A. Sartori: 'Nota su Altichiero', *Il Santo*, iii/3 (1963), pp. 291–326 [valuable doc. and bibliog.]

G. L. Mellini: *Altichiero e Jacopo Avanzi* (Milan, 1965) [good illus.]

H.-W. Kruft: *Altichiero und Avanzo: Untersuchungen zur oberitalienischen Malerei des ausgehenden Trecento* (diss., Bonn, Friedrich-Wilhelms U., 1966)

A. Sartori: 'La Cappella di S Giacomo al Santo di Padova', *Il Santo*, vi/2–3 (1966), pp. 267–359

——: *Documenti per la storia dell'arte a Padova*, ed. C. Fillarini (Verona, 1976), pp. 3–4

R. Simon: 'Altichiero versus Avanzo', *Pap. Brit. Sch. Rome*, n.s. 32, xlv (1977), pp. 252–71 [interpretation of doc. evidence for Padua frescoes]

2. Altichiero: *Cavalli Family Adoring the Virgin and Child* (late 1380s), fresco, Cavalli Chapel, S Anastasia, Verona

F. Sforza Vattovani: 'Tomaso e Altichiero', *Tomaso da Modena e il suo tempo: Atti del convegno internazionale di studi per il 6° centenario della morte: Treviso, 1979*, pp. 271–6

M. Plant: 'Portraits and Politics in Late Trecento Padua: Altichiero's Frescoes in the S Felice Chapel, S Antonio', *A. Bull.*, lxiii (1981), pp. 406–25

F. D'Arcais: 'La decorazione della Cappella di San Giacomo', 'La decorazione della Cappella di San Giorgio', *Le pitture del Santo di Padova*, ed. C. Semenzato (Vicenza, 1984), pp. 15–42, 43–62

ELIOT W. ROWLANDS

Altieri. Italian family of patrons. Of noble rank, the Altieri, who claimed ancient Roman ancestry, enjoyed a recognized place in Roman society from the 14th century. The tombs of the 15th-century Altieri, including Marc Antonio Altieri (1450–1532), holder of various public offices, stand in the family chapel of the south transept of S Maria sopra Minerva, Rome. The most important member of the family was Cardinal Emilio Altieri (*b* Rome, 12 July 1590; *d* Rome, 22 July 1676) on whose election to the papacy in 1670, as Clement X, the Altieri became the first family in Rome. When the male line of the Altieri failed in the 1660s, Emilio adopted the Roman nobleman, Gasparo Paluzzo degli Albertoni (1646–1720) as his heir, on condition that the issue of Gasparo's marriage (1667) to Altieri's niece and sole heir, Laura Caterina, would bear the Altieri name. Gasparo was given the rank of prince and inherited the Altieri palace. On his election as Pope, Emilio also bestowed the Altieri name on Gasparo's father, Angelo Paluzzi degli Albertoni, Marchese di Rosina (1624–1706), and on his uncle, Paluzzo Paluzzi degli Albertoni (1623–98), who had been raised to the cardinalate by Alexander VII in 1666 and who now became the all powerful Cardinal Padrone, controlling access to the elderly Pope.

Although the Altieri's opportunities as patrons of art were limited by severe economic depression, and the austere Clement X was anxious to curb the excesses of nepotism, they nonetheless recognized the power of art to enhance the Altieri name. Angelo and his son, Gasparo, commissioned from Claude Lorrain two of his largest and most celebrated pictures, whose subjects reflect the splendour of their ancient lineage, and which became known as the Altieri Claudes. The *Landscape with the Father of Psyche Sacrificing at the Milesian Temple of Apollo* (1663; Anglesey Abbey, Cambs, NT), commissioned by Angelo in 1663, shows a father negotiating an advantageous marriage for his daughter. Its pendant, *Landscape with the Arrival of Aeneas at Pallanteum* (1675; Anglesey Abbey, Cambs, NT; *see* CLAUDE LORRAIN, fig. 6), was commissioned a little later (*c.* 1673) by Gasparo; the Altieri proudly traced their origins back to Aeneas, and here the Altieri flag flies from the masts of Aeneas' ship. A preparatory drawing (Cantalupo Sabina, Camuccini priv. col.; RD 1077) makes it clear that Gasparo himself chose the subject.

Clement X continued to patronize Gianlorenzo Bernini and his school; under him Bernini's decoration of the

Ponte Sant'Angelo was completed, and his gilt bronze tabernacle (1673–4) for the chapel of the Sacrament in St Peter's was finally realized. Cardinal Padrone also revealed a keen interest in grand artistic undertakings. In 1671 Clement X beatified Lodovica Albertoni (1473–1533), the family's venerated ancestor, and a little later Cardinal Padrone further glorified the family name by commissioning her statue from Bernini for the Altieri chapel in S Francesco a Ripa, Rome, where she was buried. Also for this chapel, Giovanni Battista Gaulli executed a new altarpiece, *Virgin and Child with St Anne* (*c*. 1675; *in situ*). It was at Padrone's urging that the Altieri palace in the Piazza del Gesù was enlarged to the design of Giovanni Antonio de Rossi and sumptuously decorated by a team of artists, led in 1673 by Carlo Maratti and directed by Cardinal Camillo Massimo. The decoration, devised by Giovanni Pietro Bellori, was never completed, but Maratti's frescoed ceiling in the great hall, the *Allegory of Clemency* (1673) celebrates the Altieri family; to the right of the fresco Gasparo, in ancient armour, stands beside Justice and Abundance. The mounting costs of the work, and the speed with which they were implemented, lest the Pope should die too soon and the family lose its position, gave rise to scandal, and the Pope dissociated himself from the project. The Altieri favoured classicizing artists, and their picture collection, dominated by Maratti, also included works by Nicolas Poussin, Pietro Testa and Guido Reni. Padrone commissioned from Mattia de Rossi a tomb for Clement in St Peter's, and was himself buried in S Maria in Campitelli, Rome, where he had rebuilt the chapel of S Giovanni Battista.

BIBLIOGRAPHY

DBI [with good bibliog.]

Ludwig, Freiherr von Pastor: *Geschichte der Päpste* (1886–9), xxxi, pp. 438–53

T. Amayden: *Storie delle famiglie romane, con note ed aggiunte del Comm. Carlo Augusto Bertini* (Rome, 1910–17/*R* 1987), pp. 41–5

A. Schiavo: *Palazzo Altieri* (Rome, 1962)

F. Haskell: *Patrons and Painters: Art and Society in Baroque Italy* (London, 1963; rev. New Haven and London, 1980), pp. 118, 156, 161–2

M. Röthlisberger: *Claude Lorrain: The Drawings* (Berkeley and Los Angeles, 1968)

□

Altini, Eustatie (*b* Zagora, Greece, *c*. 1772; *d* Iaşi, 1815). Romanian painter. He studied from 1789 at the Akademie der Bildenden Künste in Vienna under Heinrich Füger, Johann Baptist Lampi (i) and Hubert Maurer (1738–1818). The classicism of his academic studies was tempered by the influence of the complex Viennese pictorial culture. His first known achievement in the field of religious painting was the iconostasis (1802) of the Banu Church in Iaşi, commissioned by Metropolitan Iacov Stamati (1748–1803), a prelate with illuminist cultural views. He also painted the iconostasis (1805) of the episcopal church in Roman and that of St Spiridon Church (1813) in Iaşi, where his talent reached full maturity. Altini sometimes individualized the faces of the sacred personages, especially the prophets, to whom he gave portrait features, while in his compositions he utilized Western engravings. The figures in some of his royal icons are sensitively represented against a landscape background. Through his pupils and imitators Altini propagated classicism in religious painting in Moldavia. Long after his death church painters were obliged by their contracts to reproduce his icons. His portrait painting is less well known, but it included portraits of *Scarlat Callimachi* (*c*. 1812–15; Iaşi, Metropolitan Palace), the prince of Moldavia between 1812 and 1818, and of women in elegant court costumes (e.g. *Safta Costachi Talpan* and a second portrait of an anonymous sitter, Bucharest, Mus. A.). He also painted the *Admission of Metropolitan Veniamin Costachi into Monachism* (1813; Neamţ Monastery, Mus.) in a Romantic spirit.

BIBLIOGRAPHY

R. Niculescu: 'Eustatie Altini', *Stud. & Cerc. Istor. A.: Ser. A. Plast.*, xii/1 (1965), pp. 3–64

REMUS NICULESCU

Altıntepe. Citadel and temple complex of the URARTIANS, 20 km east of Erzincan, Turkey, which flourished in the 8th and 7th centuries BC. Altıntepe is in the eastern half of the fertile Erzincan plain, on the main Erzincan–Erzurum highway, an east–west trade route of great historical and strategic importance. Systematic excavations began there in 1959 on behalf of the Turkish Historical Society and the Directorate General of Ancient Monuments, under the direction of Tahsin Özgüç, and continued until 1968. The finds are in the Museum of Anatolian Civilizations in Ankara.

Altıntepe is a very steep and rocky natural hill 60 m high and 200 m across, surrounded by two sets of defensive walls. The outer wall, the older of the two, is 12 m thick. These citadel walls are built of huge blocks of stone with square towers placed at regular intervals. Urartian

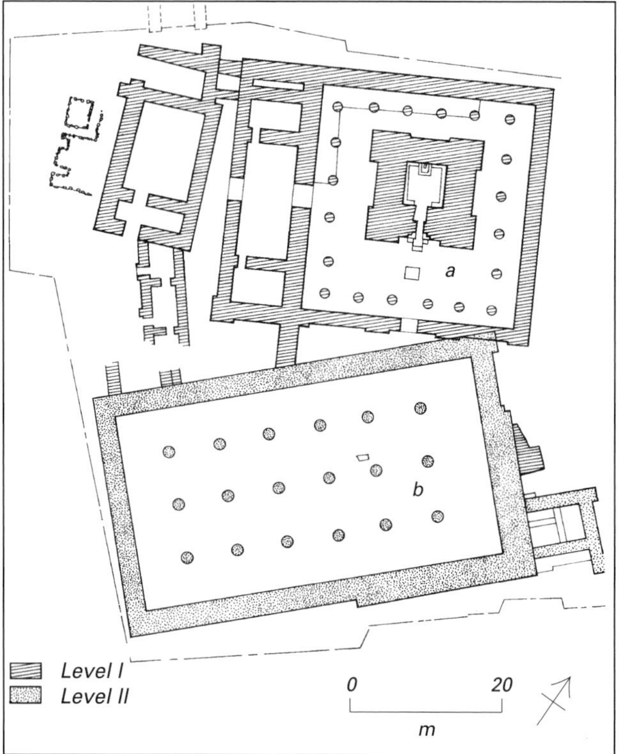

1. Altıntepe, plan, 8th–7th centuries BC: (a) temple; (b) reception hall

2. Altıntepe, lion formerly decorating a bronze tripod from the temple, ivory, l. 295 mm, last quarter of the 8th century BC–first quarter of the 7th (Ankara, Museum of Anatolian Civilizations)

buildings excavated on the hill include a temple, tombs, an open-air shrine, storerooms and living-quarters, as well as a reception hall (see fig. 1). There are two building levels at Altıntepe: the reception hall represents the second, which lasted for not more than two generations. The other buildings belong to an earlier level (level I) that can be dated by inscriptions in the cuneiform script to the reigns of Argishti II (*reg* 714–*c.* 680 BC) and Rusa II (*reg c.* 680–640 BC); it was Altıntepe's most brilliant period.

The temple is the best-preserved example of an Urartian place of worship and provides a complete plan of such a structure. It was laid out on a specially prepared area of the hill and consists of living-quarters, service areas and a cella in an open courtyard. This courtyard is 27 m square and is surrounded by colonnades where people gathered, religious ceremonies were conducted and the statues of deities and altars were situated. The colonnades were composed of wooden pillars 4.5 m high that rested on beautifully worked round stone bases found *in situ*. The walls of the cella, to a height of 13.8 m, are in the best tradition of Urartian ashlar masonry. Upon them rested a tower with thick mud-brick walls. The stone base for the statue of a god has survived *in situ*. The cella and some of the side rooms were decorated with attractive wall paintings rendered in blue, red, black and beige, featuring palmettes, rosettes, intertwining pomegranates, supernatural beings, lions, stags and geometrical motifs executed in the Assyrian style. The interior of the temple must have given as great an impression of colour and refinement as the exterior did of mass.

Cult objects found in the cella included bronze and iron spearheads (symbols of the god Haldi), sceptre heads, vessels and carved wooden plaques. The site's richest collection of votive offerings was discovered under the colonnade beside the courtyard gate: bronze shields, which had been hung on the doorposts, helmets of the god, ivory figurines of lions (see fig. 2), which decorated the god's thrones, tables and tripods, ivory griffin-demons, gold repoussé stags, winged sun-discs and palmettes, and unworked ivory. The bronze doorchain of the temple, consisting of a large number of decorated links, was found in the entrance. These objects, though strongly influenced by the Assyrian style, are among the finest examples of Urartian art.

As at most Urartian sites, a storehouse was built at Altıntepe against the long winters and in case of siege. Huge pithoi were placed in orderly rows in two large halls. Neo-Hittite hieroglyphic inscriptions on the jars give the names of two measures that were previously known only from inscriptions in the cuneiform script from other sites.

The princes of Altıntepe were buried in chamber tombs built into the south-eastern slopes of the hill. These three tombs occupy an important place among the funerary monuments of ancient Anatolia because of the stone-working techniques used, their design and the grave goods found in them. The tombs were carefully built of fine ashlar and covered with either a flat roof or a false vault made of huge blocks of stone. The area above them was filled in with earth and rubble. Each tomb is the replica of a house. Two of the tombs have three chambers: in one case the main chamber measures 4×2 m, while in the other the three chambers are set side by side and each is 3.05×2 m; the third tomb consists of a single room 4×2.75 m, approached by a dromos. All three tombs have niches in the walls. The internal doorways were blocked with flat stone slabs and the external doorway was closed with heavy blocks of stone. The dead were either buried alone or a man and a woman were buried together in the same chamber. The corpses were dressed in decorated clothing and placed in stone or wooden sarcophagi. Luxury goods made of gold, silver and semi-precious stones were placed with the women, while iron and bronze weapons were placed with the men. Grave goods included various objects of gold, silver, bronze, iron, ivory and faience, as well as wooden footstools and tripods. A chariot, chariot and horse trappings, bronze cauldrons and wooden chairs with legs sheathed in silver or bronze were also discovered. In one small chamber there were silver and bronze sections of a large table and small tripods. Some of this furniture, the product of an exquisite woodworking tradition, had legs that were sheathed in bronze bulls' and lions' feet. Other examples of Urartian art found at Altıntepe include bronze and silver plaques for horse trappings, and decorated bronze belts, originally backed with leather, decorated with the figures of deities, galloping horsemen, threatening lions and bulls, and winged horses. Immediately next to the tombs stands an open-air shrine that may have been connected with a cult for the dead. It is surrounded by stone walls and contains four stelae in front of which is a stone altar. This kind of open-air shrine, which was also depicted on seals, is peculiar to the Urartians.

Level I was destroyed and the buildings of level II were immediately constructed in great haste on top of the ruins, re-using stone from the earlier structures. A reception hall 44 m long and 25.3 m wide is the main building of this later level. Its mud-brick walls were erected on stone foundations 3 m thick, and mud-brick pillars, arranged in three rows of six and resting on broad, round, stone bases, supported a flat roof. Rooms that opened onto the courtyard in front of the hall formed the living-quarters and service areas of the complex. The most important feature of the hall is the series of lively paintings which cover the length of its long brick walls. The light blue and light brown field is decorated with rich motifs in black and white, arranged in friezes, and the beauty and liveliness of the images was obtained by this contrast of light and dark colours. One of the friezes is situated at a height of 2.5 m and is ornamented with pomegranates, rosettes, winged genii on either side of a sacred tree, bulls on either side of concave squares, sphinxes and palmettes, in a typically Assyrian style. The images in the topmost frieze, which shows lions watching deer from behind leafy trees and lions that have caught deer, are distinctively Urartian.

BIBLIOGRAPHY

H. H. von der Osten: 'Neue urartäische Bronzen aus Erzincan', *Bericht über den 6. internationalen Kongress für Archäologie: Berlin, 1939*, pp. 225–9

R. D. Barnett and N. Gökçe: 'The Find of Urartian Bronzes at Altıntepe, near Erzincan', *Anatol. Stud.*, iii (1953), pp. 21ff

T. Özgüç: 'Altıntepe kazılari' [Excavations at Altıntepe], *Belleten*, xxv/98 (1961), pp. 253–67

——: 'Altıntepe'de Urartu mimarlık eserleri' [Urartian architecture on the summit of Altıntepe], *Anatolia*, vii (1963), pp. 43–57

——: *Altıntepe*, 2 vols (Ankara, 1966–9)

K. Emre: 'Altıntepe'de Urartu seramiği' [The Urartian pottery at Altıntepe], *Belleten*, xxxiii/131 (1969), pp. 279–301

N. Özgüç: 'The Decorated Bronze Strip and Plaques from Altıntepe', *Mansel'e Armağan/Mélanges Mansel*, ed. E. Akurgal and U. B. Alkım (Ankara, 1974), pp. 847–60

T. Özgüç: 'Horsebits from Altıntepe', *Archaeologia Iranica et Orientalis, Miscellanea in Honorem Louis Vanden Berghe*, ed. L. de Meyer and E. Haerink (Ghent, 1989), pp. 409–19

TAHSIN ÖZGÜÇ

Altissimo, Cristofano (di Papi) dell' (*fl* 1552; *d* Florence, 21 Sept 1605). Italian painter. He was a pupil of Pontormo and Bronzino. In July 1552 he was sent to Como by Cosimo I de' Medici to copy the portraits of famous men in Paolo Giovio's museum. By the end of May 1553, Cristofano had sent 24 finished portraits to Florence, followed by 26 more by September 1554 and another 25 by October 1556. The following month Cristofano received 100 scudi from Cosimo. By 1591 the works had been transferred to the corridors of the Uffizi, where they form part of the museum's large collection of portraits. During his stay in Como, Cristofano travelled to Milan to execute two portraits of the *Duchess Ippolita Gonzaga* in competition with Bernardino Campi, who was declared the winner. (One of the portraits went eventually to her father, Giuliano Groselino.) In November 1562 Cristofano was noted as treasurer of the Accademia del Disegno in Florence, which received its official recognition in January 1563. On 18 January 1564 Vasari wrote to Angelo Riffoli, the ducal treasurer, requesting payment for ten portraits executed by Cristofano for Cosimo. On 5 April 1565 Vincenzo Borghini recommended Cristofano to Cosimo for employment in connection with the preparations for the marriage of Cosimo's son Francesco (later Francesco I de' Medici, Grand Duke of Tuscany) to Joanna of Austria. On 22 February 1567 Cristofano enrolled in the Arte dei Medici e Speziali. Between 1587 and 1589 he sent another group of works to Florence from the Giovio museum. The following year he was back in Florence, and in 1596 his lawsuit against Donato Bandinelli, concerning a portrait and drawing depicting *Francesco Ferrucci*, was submitted to a tribunal of the Accademia.

BIBLIOGRAPHY

Colnaghi; Thieme–Becker

G. Vasari: *Vite* (1550, rev. 2/1568); ed. G. Milanesi (1878–85)

F. Baldinucci: *Notizie* (1681–1728); ed. F. Ranalli (1845–7)

A. Venturi: *Storia* (1901–40)

Gli Uffizi: Catalogo generale (Florence, 1979) [entries by S. Meloni Trkulja and W. Prinz], pp. 601–2

CARMEN FRACCHIA

Altman, Benjamin (*b* New York, 12 July 1840; *d* New York, 7 Oct 1913). American merchant and collector. He was the son of Bavarian Jewish immigrants who ran a small dry goods business in New York before the Civil War. About 1863 he entered into a business partnership with his brother; after Morris Altman's death in 1876, Benjamin re-established the business and quickly developed it into a highly profitable enterprise. Altman's aesthetic interests extended from European and Oriental decorative arts to Old Master paintings. A self-educated connoisseur, Altman depended a great deal on the advice of dealers such as Duveen, Agnew, Gimpel and Wildenstein, but also developed a fine discrimination as a result of a few short trips to Europe and the accumulation of a valuable art library. As he became more deeply involved in art, he began to devote his entire time to its study. Although never a recluse, he did not participate actively in New York society, never married and insisted on privacy.

During the 1880s and 1890s Altman collected mainly American and Barbizon paintings. From 1905, when he moved to a new Fifth Avenue home, he turned to Old Masters, particularly of the Dutch and Flemish schools, expensive porcelain, Oriental rugs and 18th-century furniture. From the Rodolphe and Maurice Kann collections he acquired Vermeer's *Girl Asleep*, three Rembrandts and paintings by Nicolaes Maes, Pieter de Hooch, Meindert Hobbema and Aelbert Cuyp. Later he acquired Jacob van Ruisdael's *Wheatfields*, Rembrandt's *Toilet of Bathsheba*, Velázquez's *Christ and the Pilgrims of Emmaus*, Fra Angelico's *Crucifixion*, Francesco Francia's *Federigo Gonzaga*, Titian's *Portrait of a Man* and Botticelli's *Last Communion of St Jerome*. (All works mentioned are in New York, Met.) His collection of simple but dignified portraits of bankers and merchants from the Low Countries and Germany are among the finest examples of Flemish and German painting of their period: for example, Hans Memling's *Tommaso Portinari* and Hans Maler (i) zu Schwaz's *Ulrich Fugger of Augsburg*. Haskell has concluded that Altman's collection constituted his 'gallery of ancestors' (1970, p. 261).

By bequeathing his 51 pictures, Chinese porcelain, works in gold, crystal and enamel, tapestries, sculptures, Japanese lacquer and rugs to the Metropolitan Museum, New York, Altman paid homage to the city responsible for his success, but he also hoped his collection would benefit mankind.

BIBLIOGRAPHY

'The Benjamin Altman Bequest', *Bull. Met.*, viii (1913), pp. 226–41
F. Monod: 'La Galerie Altman au Metropolitan Museum de New York', *Gaz. B.-A.*, n.s. 5, viii (1923), pp. 179–98, 297–312, 367–77
Handbook of the Altman Collection (New York, 1928)
F. Haskell: 'The Benjamin Altman Bequest', *Met. Mus. J.*, iii (1970), pp. 259–80; repr. in *Past and Present in Art and Taste* (New Haven, 1987), pp. 186–206

LILLIAN B. MILLER

Al'tman [Altman]**, Natan (Isayevich)** (*b* Vinnitsa, Ukraine, 22 Dec 1889; *d* Leningrad [now St Petersburg], 12 Dec 1970). Russian painter, graphic artist, sculptor and designer of Ukrainian birth. He studied painting at the School of Art in Odessa (1901–7) under Kiriak Kostandi (1852–1921), at the same time attending classes in sculpture. In 1908–9 he made a series of pointillist paintings. He visited Vienna and Munich in 1910 before going to Paris, where he worked at Vasil'yeva's Free Russian Academy until 1912, producing paintings on Jewish themes and studying Cubism. In 1912 he went to St Petersburg, where he painted a number of Cubist portraits, for example of the poet *Anna Akhmatova* (1914; St Petersburg, Rus. Mus.; *see* ST PETERSBURG, fig. 8). His Cubist work makes much use of faceting and transparent planes. From 1918 to 1921 he taught at the Department of Visual Arts (IZO) of Narkompros in Petrograd, but he was criticized for his attempts to identify Futurism with the art of the proletariat. Al'tman became well known as the designer of post-Revolutionary mass parades and monuments, for example the celebration of the first anniversary of the Revolution on 7 Nov 1918 on Uritskaya (now Dvortsovaya) Square, which employed abstract geometric forms on huge panels (copies, 1957, in St Petersburg, Mus. Hist. St Petersburg). He also published an album of sketches of Lenin in the Kremlin (*Lenin*, Petrograd, 1920).

Al'tman's drawings combine elements of Cubo-Futurism and Suprematism, while his paintings bring together elements of abstraction, poster and panel design, often including words (e.g. *Petrokommuna*, 1919–21; St Petersburg, Rus. Mus.). He also executed a number of reliefs and abstract constructions, experimenting with combinations of different materials. In 1921–2 he was involved in Jewish artistic life in Moscow, designing sets for the Jewish Kamerny Theatre and exhibiting at the Jewish Cultural League with Marc Chagall and David Shterenberg. He lived in Berlin in 1922–4 and took part in the *Erste Russische Ausstellung*. Between 1925 and 1927 he was again in Moscow, designing for the Jewish Kamerny Theatre and the cinema and painting lyrical landscapes and portraits. In 1928 he went to Paris, returning in 1935 to live in Leningrad, where he illustrated books (e.g. Maksim Gor'ky's *Peterburgskiye povesti*, 'Petersburg stories', 1937) and continued designing for the cinema and theatre (e.g. *Hamlet*, Pushkin Theatre, 1954).

BIBLIOGRAPHY

A. Efros: *Portret Natana Al'tmana* [A portrait of Nathan Al'tman] (Moscow, 1922)
B. Arvatov: *Natan Al'tman* (Berlin and Petrograd, 1924)
M. Osborn: *Yevreyskaya grafika Natana Al'tmana* [The Jewish graphics of Nathan Al'tman] (Berlin and Petrograd, 1924)
M. Etkind: *N. Altman* (Dresden, 1984)
Natan Al'tman: Katalog vystavki k 100-letiyu so dnya rozhdeniya [Nathan Al'tman: Catalogue of the Exhibition on the Centenary of his Birth] (exh. cat., Leningrad, Rus. Mus., 1988)

V. RAKITIN

Altobello, Francesco Antonio (*b* Barletta, 1637; *d* after 1695). Italian painter. He received his first artistic training in the workshop of Carlo Rosa in Apulia, although his earliest known works, the *Holy Family* (1675; Barletta, S Maria della Vittoria) and a painting of the same subject attributed to him (Barletta, Pal. Monte di Pietà), reveal the influence of Cesare Fracanzano and Francesco Cozza. Altobello probably went to Naples during the 1670s and was certainly living there in 1687. Works attributed to him from this period are the *Vision of St Ignatius* (Naples, S Ferdinando) and a *Visitation* and *Vision of St Francis* (*c*. 1680; both Naples, S Maria la Nuova). They show his full acclimatization to the Neapolitan Baroque, clearly reflecting the monumentality of Giovanni Lanfranco, the tonal contrasts of Luca Giordano and the chiaroscuro of Mattia Preti; they represent the height of Altobello's artistic development. Also attributed to his Neapolitan period is *St Jerome* (Naples, Pin. Pio Monte della Misericordia). Numerous canvases, listed in the inventory of Stefano Carrillo y Salsedo, Regent of the Royal Chancellery, are untraced, as is *Danaë and the Shower of Gold*, which once belonged to the Orsini, Dukes of Gravina in Puglia.

Altobello's last known works are the *Vision of St Roch* (1684; Montella, S Maria la Libera) and a *Virgin and Child* (1692; Bitonto, Pal. Vescovile). Both seem to indicate a stylistic regression, conditioned perhaps by the backwardness of the provincial climate in which he was then working.

BIBLIOGRAPHY

Bolaffi

B. de Dominici: *Vite* (1742–5), iii, p. 113

R. Ruotolo: 'Collezioni e mecenati napoletani del XVII secolo', *Napoli Nob.*, 3rd ser., xii (1973), pp. 145–53

S. Milillo: 'Note per la biografia di V. Giordano, N. Gliro, F. A. Altobello, C. Rosa ed altri', *Stud. Bitontini*, xxx–xxxi (1980), pp. 129–30

L. Mortari: 'Appunti sulla pittura del sei e settecento in Puglia', *Ricerche sul sei-settecento in Puglia*, 2 vols (Fasano di Puglia, 1980), i, pp. 24–5

M. D'Elia: 'La pittura barocca', *La Puglia fra barocco e rococò* (Milan, 1982), pp. 258–60

Civiltà del seicento a Napoli, 2 vols (exh. cat., ed. S. Cassani; Naples, Capodimonte, 1984–5), pp. 115, 185

MARGHERITA PALATUCCI

Altomonte. Austrian family of artists. (1) Martino Altomonte was the son of Michael Hohenberg, a baker who had emigrated from the Tyrol to Naples, and it was Martino who changed the family name to its Italian form in 1684. Martino and his son (2) Bartolomeo Altomonte both became celebrated for their decorative paintings in Austria, which continued the traditions of the Viennese school of late Baroque fresco. Of Martino's other sons, Franz Lorenz Altomonte (*b* Poland, after 1693 or Vienna, 1698; *d* Prague, May 1765), an engraver, studied under Antonio Maria Gennaro (1679–1744) in Vienna. From 1727 he worked as an engraver at the Mint in Prague. Examples of his work can be found in the Kunsthistorisches Museum, Vienna. Andreas [Andrea] Altomonte (*b* Warsaw or Vienna, 1699; *d* Vienna, 12 June 1780), an architect, studied at the Akademie der Bildenden Künste in Vienna from 1726 to 1728. His projects included designing the high altar and probably the interior for the abbey church at Wilhering (1738); the indoor riding arena (1744–7), Mask Room (1748), water display (1749–62), chapel (1750–53) and pleasure pavilion (1755–7) at the castle at Krumau (now Český Krumlov, Czech Republic); the front porch of the Peterskirche in Vienna (1751–3); and the redesign of the gardens at Schwarzenberg Palace in Vienna (1751). He served as administrator of the Porzellanmanufaktur in Vienna from 1755. Another possible family member, Giacomo Altomonte (*b* Cagliari, Sardinia, first half of the 18th century), was presumably related to Martino Altomonte as there is a painting by him at St Florian Abbey. He also produced frescoes and paintings for the churches of S Antonio (1721) and S Domenico (1722), both in Cagliari.

(1) Martino Altomonte [Johann Martin Hohenberg] (*b* Naples, 8 May 1657; *d* Vienna, 14 Sept 1745). Painter. At the age of 15 he was apprenticed to Giovanni Battista Gaulli in Rome, where he next studied with Carlo Maratti. In 1684 he was offered an appointment at the court of King John III of Poland and altered his name to Martino Altomonte. He travelled to Warsaw, where he produced paintings of royal battles and portraits (untraced) for the royal castle of Zólkiew (now Nesterov) near Lwów (now L'viv, Ukraine). It appears that he also painted a fair number of altarpieces. Of these, only the *Sacrifice of Abraham* (now Tarnów, Dioc. Mus.) survives, a work that reveals Altomonte as a follower of Neapolitan chiaroscuro painting. Between 1699 and 1702 Altomonte moved to Vienna, where he became a teaching member of the Akademie der Bildenden Künste in 1707. It was probably in connection with his admission to the Akademie that he was commissioned to decorate the Neue Favorita, an annexe of Schloss Augarten. The few surviving oil paintings from this period, for example *Susanna and the Elders* (1709; Vienna, Belvedere; see fig.), show the strong impact of the Neapolitan painting of Luca Giordano and suggest Venetian influence as well. Altomonte developed a mixed Neapolitan–Venetian style that incorporated the illusionistic architecture of Andrea Pozzo and created a style that set the standard for Viennese Baroque painting. In his oil paintings he scattered Venetian pastel tones among dramatic elements of Neapolitan chiaroscuro. In 1709–10 he worked on ceiling paintings for the archbishop's Residenz at Salzburg, and about 1710 he became imperial court painter. He also produced altar paintings in Vienna for the Dorotheerkirche (1713; now in Rheindorfer Parish Church), the Peterskirche and the Stephansdom (both 1714) and for the parish church in Krems and the Deutschordenskirche in Laibach (now Ljubljana, Slovenia; both 1715). In 1716 he painted the ceiling frescoes in the Lower Belvedere in Vienna.

Altomonte moved to Linz in 1719 and worked for the nearby St Florian Abbey. He provided ceiling paintings for the prelate's rooms (red drawing-room, 1719–20; *saletta* and private chapel, 1720). In 1721 he worked at Kremsmünster Abbey, providing 15 portraits of the Habsburgs for the Kaisersaal. From this point he devoted his

Martino Altomonte: *Susanna and the Elders*, oil on canvas, 1.31×1.07 m, 1709 (Vienna, Belvedere, Österreichische Galerie)

time mainly to painting altarpieces, leaving ceiling painting, which he obviously found onerous, to his son Bartolomeo. His altarpieces of the 1720s include those for the Wallfahrtskirche at Stadl-Paura (1722), the Deutschordenskirche (Priesterseminarkirche) in Linz (1724), the abbey church in Pöllau (1725), the abbey church in Admont (1726) and the parish church in Kefermarkt (1728; all *in situ*).

From about 1729 Altomonte had a studio in Vienna in the Heiligenkreuzerhof, and it is probable that he had established close links with Heiligenkreuz Abbey, where he painted side altar pictures in 1729 and 1731 (*in situ*). In 1730 he provided paintings for the Heiligenkreuzerhof chapel in Vienna (*in situ*). During the 1730s there was a distinct shift of emphasis in Altomonte's work, with the picture being increasingly subordinated to the overall decorative scheme. Compositions were divided by pictorial means and the figures became more slender and delicate. This change may be seen in many works from this period, including his altarpieces (all *in situ*) for the Karlskirche and Peterskirche in Vienna (1731); the parish church in Timelkam (1733); the abbey church in Zwettl (1734, 1736 and 1737); the chapel of the Gartenpalais Harrach in Vienna (1735); the Neuklosterkirche in Wiener Neustadt and the abbey church at Lilienfeld (both 1737); the Ursulienkirche in Linz (1738); and the abbey church at Wilhering and the parish church in Retz (both 1739).

The breaking down and distortion of forms by pictorial means became still more marked in Altomonte's work in the following years, and there is evidence of the influence of the Venetian painting of Giovanni Battista Pittoni and Sebastiano Ricci. Among Altomonte's last works were more altarpieces for the Neuklosterkirche in Wiener Neustadt and the abbey church at Lilienfeld (both 1740), the abbey church at Wilhering (1741) and the choir chapel at Herzogenburg Abbey (1744; all *in situ*). Between 1742 and 1745 he mainly painted small-scale gallery pictures, including still-lifes, which did not overtax his strength.

(2) Bartolomeo Altomonte (*b* Warsaw, 24 Feb 1694; *d* Markt St Florian, 9 Nov 1783). Painter, son of (1) Martino Altomonte. He was first taught by his father and from 1717 studied in Bologna with Marco Antonio Franceschini, then in Rome with Benedetto Luti and finally in Naples with Francesco Solimena. The sketchbook dated 1718 (Vienna, Albertina) contains only copies after Italian drawings from Luti's collection (now mostly Windsor Castle, Royal Lib.). Other surviving early studies (Melk, Stiftsmus., and Markt St Florian, Stiftssamml.) have a nervous energy that shows the influence of Ricci (also represented in the Luti collection). In 1722 Altomonte returned to Austria to work with his father at St Florian Abbey. As Bartolomeo's work here reveals, it was largely technical expertise that he obtained in Italy, his greater debt being to his father, a representative of the Vienna school of late Baroque fresco painting, closely allied to Roman decorative painting. Bartolomeo's work at St Florian follows in this tradition in that the atmosphere and the elements of colour and light are of crucial importance, while narrative is abjured. Forms are depicted as if viewed from above and not with a vertical perspective. At St Florian, Bartolomeo painted ceiling frescoes in the Dechantzimmer (1722), the Marmorsaal (1722–4), the antechamber (1725), the Kunstkammer (1727), the Sommerrefektorium (1727) and the Tafelzimmer (1732).

In 1730 Altomonte married and moved to Vienna, where he was appointed a court painter. He thus came into contact with the decorative style being practised in Venetian painting, in particular that of Giovanni Battista Pittoni, known in Vienna through paintings and etchings. Altomonte abandoned the late Baroque ideal of the weighty figure in favour of more delicate, elongated forms, in line with the mannered tendency of the time. He was probably influenced by Solimena as well, as the alternation of light and dark areas of colour later became important in Altomonte's work. In Vienna he provided ceiling paintings for the lower sacristy at the Stephansdom (1732) and an altar picture, *St John Nepomuk in Glory*, for the Schwarzspanierkirche (now Minoritenkirche) in Vienna.

In 1737 Altomonte returned to Upper Austria where he painted ceiling frescoes at the abbey church in Spital am Pyhrn (1737–9), the sacristy at St Florian Abbey (1739) and the abbey church in Wilhering (1739–41). He later provided ceiling frescoes for the stairwell at Seitenstetten Abbey (1744), the library (1747; e.g. *Allegory of the Marriage of Virtue and Science, Effected by Religion*; for illustration of preparatory sketch *see* ALLEGORY, fig. 9) and oratory of the abbey church (1748) and the chapter-house (1749–50) at St Florian Abbey. From 1753 to 1755 he worked on the ceiling frescoes of the abbey church at Herzogenburg and about 1760 on those for the abbey church and library of Engelszell Abbey.

Of Altomonte's altar paintings, the most notable are the side altar pictures for the abbey church at Herzogenburg (1761–3; *in situ*). From about 1768 a new calmness and sense of space appeared in his work, possibly attributable to the influence of Roman Neo-classicism. Smaller figures emphasize even more clearly the peaceful expanse surrounding them. He took his inspiration from Daniel Gran, an artist of the Viennese school who had never abandoned the late Baroque ideal. Work from Altomonte's late period includes ceiling frescoes for the Klosterkirche der Elisabethinen in Linz (*c.* 1768) and the Klosterkirche der Englischen Fräulein in St Pölten (1769) and hall frescoes at Fürstenzell Abbey in Bavaria (1773). His last commission was for frescoes in the Admont Abbey library (1774–6). Altomonte became a member of the Akademie der Bildenden Künste in Vienna in 1770. Between 1776 and his death his output was limited to a few oil paintings.

BIBLIOGRAPHY

Meissner; Thieme–Becker

L. Koller: 'Die beiden Altomonte', *Christ. Kstbl.*, lvi (1915)

J. Klaus: *Martin Altomonte Leben und Werk in Österreich* (Vienna, 1916)

W. Mrazek: *Die barocke Deckenmalerei in der 1. Hälfte des 18. Jahrhunderts in Wien* (diss., U. Vienna, 1947)

B. Heinzl: *Bartolomeo Altomonte* (Vienna and Munich, 1964)

H. Aurenhammer: *Martino Altomonte* (Vienna and Munich, 1965)

T. Korth: 'Stift St Florian', *Erlang. Beitr. zur Sprach- und Kstwiss.*, xlix (1975)

BRIGITTE HEINZL

Alton Towers. English house and garden in Staffordshire. The garden was first laid out between 1814 and 1827 by the owner, Charles Talbot, 15th Earl of Shrewsbury, with assistance from the landscape gardener John Buonarotti Papworth and the architect Robert Abraham (1774–1850);

it was further improved by John Talbot, 16th Earl of Shrewsbury (*see* TALBOT, (3)). The major landscape feature at Alton Towers is the valley in the grounds, which Shrewsbury, Papworth and Abraham filled with an astonishing 'labyrinth of terraces, curious architectural walls, trellis-work arbours, vases, statues, stairs, pavements ... ornamental buildings, bridges, porticoes, temples, pagodas, gates, iron railings, parterres, jets, ponds, streams, seats, fountains, caves, flower baskets, waterfalls, rocks, cottages ... rock-work, shell-work, root-work, moss houses, old trunks of trees [and] entire dead trees' (*Gdnrs Magazine*, vii, 1831); in addition a fashionable Swiss-style cottage was built. Some of these works, in particular Abraham's three-storey, cast-iron Pagoda Fountain, survive intact. In 1827 John Talbot, the 16th Earl, inherited the Alton Towers estate; he provided for the construction of a copy of the Choragic Monument of Lysikrates (4th century BC), Athens, which he dedicated to the 15th Earl and inscribed 'He made the desert smile'. He also commissioned Abraham to build a conservatory in the classical style. Shrewsbury then came under the influence of the architect A. W. N. Pugin, who made alterations to the house in a Gothic Revival style (from 1837; mostly gutted in the 1950s) and, with assistance from the garden designer William Andrews Nesfield, added more formal gardens to the layout. Shrewsbury's head-gardener, Alexander Forsyth (*c.* 1809–85), was responsible for softening the disparities with a massive tree-planting programme. In 1924 the property was acquired by Alton Towers Ltd, which kept the gardens open as a commercial attraction; from the 1970s a large portion of the grounds was turned into a popular amusement park.

BIBLIOGRAPHY

D. Jacques: *Georgian Gardens: The Reign of Nature* (London, 1983), pp. 175, 187–8

B. Elliott: *Victorian Gardens* (London, 1986), pp. 37–9

BRENT ELLIOTT

Altorf, Johan Coenraad (*b* The Hague, 6 Jan 1876; *d* The Hague, 11 Dec 1955). Dutch sculptor and ceramicist. He trained at the Academie van Beeldende Kunsten in The Hague (1894–7) and in various sculpture studios. In 1898 he decorated the shop-front of the gallery Arts and Crafts in The Hague after a design by Johan Thorn Prikker, who advised him to set up on his own. From 1901 Altorf exhibited regularly and successfully; he was represented at the Prima Esposizione Internazionale d'Arte Decorativa Moderna in Turin in 1902, where he won a silver medal, and at the Exposition Internationale des Arts Décoratifs et Industriels Modernes in Paris in 1925.

Altorf was a leading exponent of Dutch Art Nouveau. His work is characterized by a strong simplification of form. It is often compared with that of Joseph Mendes da Costa but is somewhat more angular and austere. At first Altorf made mainly animal forms from various types of wood, ivory, bronze and ceramic. In firing his modelled figures, he worked with the ceramicist C. J. Lanooy (1881–1948) between 1911 and 1913. After 1910 he made human figures as well as animals, including biblical characters. One of his well-known works is his portrait of *Jan Toorop* (bronze, h. *c.* 510 mm; Otterlo, Kröller-Müller Sticht.).

Altorf also made many monumental works, including sculptures on and in buildings, chiefly in The Hague. He also collaborated on several free-standing sculptures including the lions of the Juliana fountain in The Hague (1910), the *3 October* monument in Leiden and the monument for the statesman *Hendrik Goeman Borgesius* in The Hague (both from 1924). In addition he designed furniture and wall panelling and small utensils manufactured in wood and ivory. His work is mainly in Dutch collections (Otterlo, Kröller-Müller Sticht.; Rotterdam, Mus. Boymans–van Beuningen; The Hague, Gemeentemus.; Heino, Hannema–De Stuers Fund.).

BIBLIOGRAPHY

Scheen; Thieme–Becker

F. M. Huebner: *Niederländische Plastik der Gegenwart* (Dresden, n.d.), pp. 25–7

A. Hallema: 'J. C. Altorf, de beeldhouwer' [J. C. Altorf, the sculptor], *Elsevier's Geïllus. Mdschr.*, xxviii/55 (1918), pp. 77–91

MIEKE VAN DER WAL

Altoviti, Bindo (*b* Rome, 26 Nov 1491; *d* Rome, 22 Jan 1557). Italian banker and patron. He was born of a noble Florentine family. At the age of 16 he inherited the family bank in Rome and, after the closure in 1528 of the rival bank founded by Agostino Chigi, became the most important papal financier in the city. Despite his position as Florentine consul in Rome, he was vigorously opposed to the Medici regime and his residence near the Ponte Sant'Angelo became the gathering place of many Florentine exiles. This palazzo (dem. 1888) was restored by Altoviti in 1514 and housed a rich collection of antiquities from Hadrian's Villa (*see* TIVOLI, §2(ii)) and many commissioned works. Raphael painted for Altoviti the *Madonna dell'Impannata* (1511–16; Florence, Pitti) and his portrait, which is generally agreed to be the one (*c.* 1518) that is now in the National Gallery of Art, Washington, DC. In 1534 Francesco Salviati also executed a portrait of Altoviti (untraced) and frescoed the arms of Pope Paul III on the façade of the palazzo. BENVENUTO CELLINI made a magnificent bronze portrait bust of the banker (*c.* 1552; Boston, MA, Isabella Stewart Gardner Mus.), which was greatly admired by Michelangelo. Unfortunately, a disagreement over his fee caused Cellini to fall out with his patron.

Altoviti was a close friend and supporter of Giorgio Vasari. He commissioned from Vasari a painting for his chapel in SS Apostoli, Florence, an *Immaculate Conception* (1540; *in situ*), together with a miniature replica (Florence, Uffizi) for his private collection. Other commissions included a *Pietà* (1542), now known from a drawing (Paris, Louvre), with a small replica (Siena, Col. Chigi–Saracini), also a *Venus and Cupid*, based on a cartoon by Michelangelo and a *Virgin and Child* (untraced). In 1553 Vasari decorated two loggias for Altoviti, both based on programmes by Annibal Caro: one was at his palazzo, with frescoes of the *Worship of Ceres* and personifications of the months (Rome, Pal. Venezia), the other was at Altoviti's villa (destr.) in the Prati near Castel Sant'Angelo, Rome, where the decoration followed a similar scheme of planetary gods, the seasons and the zodiac, but is known only from engravings by Tommaso Piroli (1752–1824). It was Altoviti who, together with Paolo Giovio, introduced Vasari to a future patron, Cardinal Alessandro Farnese.

Altoviti had a taste, precocious for his time, for collecting preparatory drawings and modelli as well as finished works of art. He was given by Michelangelo the cartoon for the *Drunkenness of Noah* on the Sistine Chapel ceiling, and he acquired a modello for the marble figure of *St James the Greater* (Florence Cathedral) from Jacopo Sansovino. The latter also designed a fireplace for Altoviti's Florentine palace, a residence that was subsequently confiscated by the Medici. Altoviti is buried in his chapel in S Trinità dei Monti, Rome.

BIBLIOGRAPHY

DBI

L. Passerini: *Genealogia e storia della famiglia Altoviti* (Florence, 1871)

D. Gnoli: 'Il Palazzo Altoviti', *Archv Stor. A.*, i (1888), pp. 202–11

C. Belloni: *Un banchiere del Rinascimento* (Rome, 1935)

C. Avery: 'Benvenuto Cellini's Bronze Bust of Bindo Altoviti', *Connoisseur*, cxcviii (1978), pp. 62–72

C. Davis: 'Per l'attività romana del Vasari nel 1553', *Mitt. Ksthist. Inst. Florenz*, xxiii (1979), pp. 197–223

Giorgio Vasari (exh. cat., ed. L. Corti and M. D. Davis; Arezzo, Mus. Casa Vasari, 1981), pp. 86–8

CLARE ROBERTSON

Altun Ha. Site of Pre-Columbian MAYA culture in the southern lowland Maya region of Belize, *c.* 56 km north of Belize City. The site flourished *c.* 200 BC–*c.* AD 900, although it was occupied both before and after these dates. Large-scale, intensive excavations carried out between the 1960s and the 1980s under the direction of David Pendergast and his associates from the Royal Ontario Museum, Toronto, Canada, have revealed much important information about Altun Ha. Finds are in Belize Government collections and in the Royal Ontario Museum.

The central part of the site is organized around two plazas. Plaza A, the earlier, is bordered by four temples and several platforms. Two of these structures investigated by Pendergast are known as A-1 and A-6. Structure A-1, the 'Temple of the Green Tomb', is named after the tomb found inside it, dated AD 550–600, which contained several hundred pieces of jade and numerous other burial goods, including large ceremonial flints, pottery bowls, shell necklaces and pearls. It also yielded the vestiges of an ancient Maya manuscript or codex, the pages of which had disintegrated. Structure A-6, the largest structure in terms of mass, underwent three building stages. During the second phase, the building had 13 doorways in the front and an elaborate stucco frieze on the upper wall. Plaza B consists of six structures, including several residences and the tallest ceremonial building at Altun Ha, Structure B-4, the 'Temple of the Masonry Altars'. This temple, which was rebuilt several times, contained seven tombs, the best known of which is the 'Tomb of the Sun God', dated AD 600–650. A huge jade head carved in the likeness of the Maya sun god was found among the burial furniture. This head is the biggest known piece of Pre-Columbian Maya carved jade, measuring 149 mm in height and weighing 4.42 kg. Other remains, including a number of house mounds and the 'Temple of the Reservoir', a multi-tiered structure *c.* 16 m high, were found beyond the ceremonial heart of Altun Ha.

BIBLIOGRAPHY

D. M. Pendergast: *Altun Ha: A Guidebook to the Ancient Maya Ruins* (Belize City, 1969)

——: *Excavations at Altun Ha, Belize, 1964–1970*, 3 vols (Toronto, 1979–90)

JEREMY A. SABLOFF

Altyn Tepe [Altyn-Depe]. Site of Neolithic and Bronze Age activity near Mian, 150 km south-east of Ashkhabad, in southern Turkmenistan. The site of 25 ha, surrounded by a further tract (w. 30 m) of cultivated land, was extensively excavated in 1965–6 by the Academy of Sciences, southern Turkmenistan, and the Institute of Archaeology, Academy of Sciences, St Petersburg. Altyn Tepe exemplifies the gradual development from a farming culture to an urban centre. The earliest layers, dating from the 5th millennium BC, contained bronze objects and ceramics with large geometric designs, similar to those from Namazga I (a comparable settlement also in southern Turkmenistan). From the end of the 4th millennium BC, the greatly expanded settlement was fortified with a mud-brick wall and rectangular towers. Typical finds of this period include polychrome ceramics of the Geoksyur type, limestone vessels, flat seals, and statuettes of women with ornate hairstyles. During the 3rd millennium BC, specialized trades developed: pottery was made on the wheel, while copper and bronze mirrors, pins, daggers and other items were widely produced. Sanctuaries had oval altars, and mass burials were placed in mud-brick tombs. By the end of this millennium, monumental gates with two turreted pylons, and an artisans' quarter had been built. In the separate quarter for the nobility, lavish burials were found containing ornaments and seals of bronze, silver and gold. In the centre of the city was a religious complex that had a monumental stepped tower similar to the ziggurats of Sumer. A tomb in this complex appears to have been dedicated to a lunar god resembling the Mesopotamian Nanna and contained numerous gold, silver, azurite and turquoise ornaments and gold heads of wolves and bulls, the latter with inset azurite crescents on their foreheads. Finds of inscribed Harappan seals and ivory objects provide evidence of close links with the Indian site of HARAPPA in this period. Altyn Tepe belonged to a group of highly developed cultures of the 3rd millennium BC and early 2nd, which stretched from Mesopotamia to India. By the middle of the 2nd millennium BC Altyn Tepe had been completely abandoned, but its cultural traditions can be traced at sites in the delta of the Murgh River and the central Amu River valley (later Bactria), where part of the population seems to have resettled.

BIBLIOGRAPHY

V. M. Masson and V. I. Sarianidi: *Sredneaziatskaya terrakota epokhi bronzy* [Central Asian terracottas of the Bronze Age] (Moscow, 1973)

V. M. Masson: 'Altyn-Depe and the Bull Cult', *Antiquity*, l/1 (1976), pp. 14–19

——: *Altyn-Depe* (Leningrad, 1981); Eng. trans. by H. N. Michael (Philadelphia, 1988)

——: 'The Proto-Bactrian Group of Civilisations in the Ancient East', *Antiquity*, lxii/238 (1988), pp. 536–41

V. M. MASSON

Aluminium. Silvery white metal. The third most abundant element in the earth's crust (after oxygen and silicon), aluminium is found only in the form of its compounds, such as alumina or aluminium oxide. Its name is derived from *alumen*, the Latin name for alum, and in the 18th century the French word *alumine* was proposed for the oxide of the metal, then undiscovered. The name aluminium was adopted in the early 19th century and is used world-wide except in the USA, where the spelling is aluminum, and in Italy where *alluminio* is used. Following the discovery of processes for separating the metal from the oxide, at first experimentally in 1825, then commercially in 1854 and industrially in 1886–8, aluminium rapidly came to be valued as an adaptable material with both functional and decorative properties. Thus in addition to being used in engineering, transport, industrial design and household products, it was also widely adopted in architecture, sculpture and the decorative arts.

1. Properties. 2. History and uses.

1. PROPERTIES. Aluminium is produced by smelting after the extraction of alumina from bauxite, a reddish-brown ore first mined in 1816 at Les Baux in France. The metal is ductile, non-magnetic and can be shaped by stamping, drawing, spinning, forging and extrusion, and it can be rolled into sheets and foil. It can be cast by all known foundry methods and joined by soldering, brazing, welding, adhesive bonding and by such mechanical methods as riveting and bolting. In the late 20th century a 'superplastic aluminium' was developed, which, when heated, acts like plastic and can be blown into a mould with compressed air to produce intricate shapes. The particular advantages of aluminium are its light weight, workability and versatility; its strength when alloyed with other metals; its heat reflectivity and electrical conductivity; and its resistance to corrosion. Aluminium can be mechanically buffed and textured, chemically cleaned, etched and brightened, with finishes ranging from dull to mirror. The main method of finishing is anodizing, an electrolytic process by which the metal is coated with a hard, protective layer of oxide, enhancing its corrosion resistance. Colour can be introduced into this layer by means of dyes, producing a characteristic effect quite unlike paint or lacquer finishes. Typical colours of anodized aluminium include silver, gold, bronze, grey and dead black, which is highly resistant to fading. Other applied finishes include organic coatings, the most durable being porcelain enamel. In the early 1970s powder colour coatings were introduced and proved to be highly resistant to impact and corrosion. The attraction of aluminium as an alternative casting material lies in its natural silvery white colour, which is one of the only finishes not obtainable through the patination of bronze.

See also METAL.

BIBLIOGRAPHY

E. Dorre and others: *Alumina: Processing, Properties and Applications* (Berlin and New York, 1984)

F. King: *Aluminum and its Alloys* (Chichester, NY, 1987)

R. G. King: *Surface Treatment and Finishing of Aluminium* (Oxford, 1988)

MARK FIRTH, LOUIS SKOLER

2. HISTORY AND USES.

(i) Architecture. (ii) Sculpture. (iii) Decorative arts.

(i) Architecture. From its first recorded architectural use (1884) as a cast pyramidal cap for the Washington Monument, aluminium was initially employed mainly for such utilitarian elements as doors, windows and roofing components, and for elements of constructional and mechanical systems that were often concealed. It also served as an economical substitute for other metals. The key to the history of its use in architecture lies in the development of the MODERN MOVEMENT and its adoption of such technologies as industrial production, skeletal frame construction and the non-load-bearing curtain wall (*see* CURTAIN WALL (ii)): aluminium is eminently suited to the mass-production of lightweight rigid composite panels incorporating insulation. Aluminium began to receive greater recognition as an important visual element in architectural expression after World War II, when the demands of reconstruction led to the widespread adoption of new technologies in structure, construction and materials. Its aesthetic potential lay in the many finishes, textures and patterns inherent in its forms (*see* §1 above).

Early examples of the use of aluminium as a structural and visual element include the experimental Modernist house on Long Island, NY, built as early as 1931 by the partnership of Frey & Kocher, with an aluminium skeletal structure and corrugated aluminium walls. In the late 1940s Albert Frey and John Clark designed houses in Palm Springs, CA, in which, anticipating industrial production, they used aluminium both for its practical advantages and for its aesthetic qualities. The machine-produced metal contrasts brilliantly with the surrounding desert foothills. In 1945–8 Pietro Belluschi designed gleaming aluminium cover plates for the 12-storey reinforced-concrete frame structure of his Equitable Building, Portland, OR.

This new role for aluminium was acknowledged in 1947 by the R. S. Reynolds Memorial Award, which was subsequently offered each year by the American Institute of Architects to the architect or architects who 'made the most significant contribution to the use of aluminum, aesthetically or structurally, in the building field'. Increasingly wide-ranging and innovative use was made of the material. The Dome of Discovery, designed for the Festival of Britain (1951) by Ralph Tubbs with Powell & Moya, was constructed of aluminium trusses; it had a clear span of 110 m and was the largest structure built of aluminium at that time. The 30-storey Alcoa Building (1953, Pittsburgh), designed by Harrison & Abramovitz, was the first building to have curtain walls of aluminium, one of the most advanced construction ideas of the period. In 1954 G. A. Bernasconi, A. Fiocchi, and Marcello Nizzoli employed aluminium for exterior surfaces, interior movable partitions and, most expressively, for an exterior eight-storey curtain of mechanically operated vertical louvres for sun control in the Olivetti Building in Milan. Frank Lloyd Wright's Beth Sholom Synagogue (1956), Elkins Park, Philadelphia, incorporates aluminium in the form of patterned castings, sculpture and furnishings, reflecting his conception of the temple as 'a great symbol of Mt Sinai, a mountain of light'. In the same period the Commonwealth Promenade Apartments and the 900 Esplanade Apartments, both twin-tower 29-storey frame structures in Chicago by Mies van der Rohe, were designed with all-aluminium, prefabricated curtain walls, one in natural finish and the other anodized black.

Extensive research was undertaken in the 1960s into composite metal-faced panel construction for exterior screen walls and this culminated in 1970–76 with Richard Meier's Bronx Developmental Center, New York, in which the architect used only aluminium and glass for the building's exterior walls, in an integrated system of panels, windows and frame covers. The American architect Frank O. Gehry made highly original and unorthodox use of various materials, including aluminium. For example, his own house (1979) in Santa Monica, CA, 'reflects the disorder of Los Angeles' in its use of chain-link fencing as canopy and unfinished plywood and corrugated aluminium as walls (*see* ARTIST'S HOUSE, fig. 7). Gehry pursued similar ideas and used aluminium extensively in his Law School Building (1981) for Loyola University and in his Aerospace Museum (1982; for illustration *see* GEHRY, FRANK O.), both in Los Angeles.

Aluminium played an important role in the concept of the 'machine aesthetic' that inspired HIGH TECH architecture, which developed in England in the 1970s and is seen particularly in the work of Norman Foster, Richard Rogers, Nicholas Grimshaw and Michael Hopkins. Among the best-known examples are Foster's Sainsbury Centre for Visual Arts (1977), University of East Anglia, Norwich, the walls and roof of which are clad with ribbed, insulated aluminium panels (for illustration *see* SPACE FRAME); and his Hongkong & Shanghai Bank (1985), Hong Kong (for illustration *see* FOSTER, NORMAN), with exterior sun screens and floor panels of aluminium in various shades of grey. Rogers' Lloyds Building, London (1979–87) has aluminium wind-bracing fins, mullions and panels, and spun aluminium is used extensively for interior lighting shields; for his Channel 4 headquarters building, London (1994), grey powder-coated aluminium was used as a major exterior cladding material. The Dutch architect Rem Koolhaas used corrugated aluminium for multilevel flat and undulating surfaces in the Eurolille Grand Palais, Lille (1994).

Japanese architects also made considerable use of aluminium in architecture. Arata Isozaki pursued ideas similar to those of Richard Meier in his concept of cubes represented by square-gridded aluminium and glass surfaces, utilizing metal panel construction: this can be seen in his Prefectural Museum of Modern Art (1971–4), Gunma, and the Tsukuba Center (1979–83), Tsukuba (for illustration *see* ISOZAKI, ARATA); artificial stone was also used. In the Museum of Contemporary Art (1981–6), Los Angeles, Isozaki further experimented with materials, introduced green aluminium panels in gridded flat and undulating surfaces. Another notable Japanese architect in whose work aluminium plays a major role is Hiroshi Hara, whose design for Yamato International Office Building (1987), Tokyo, was intended to represent an urban scene, with gleaming cloud-shaped aluminium-clad structures placed above the roof of the main block, which is situated at the end of an adjoining park. Fumihiko Maki's Wacoal Art Centre (1985) in Tokyo is one of the most expressive aluminium designs in contemporary architecture. Its street façade was conceived in part as a composition of quotations from the works of Modern masters, and it incorporates flat square-gridded surfaces, undulating walls, conical forms, and covers for columns and beams, all made of aluminium (see fig. 1). The Rise Cinema (1986), Tokyo, by Atsushi Kitagawara, also shows very expressive use of aluminium. The building takes the form of a hemisphere sheathed in die-cast aluminium, which looks like a gigantic fabric curtain that has just been pulled aside to reveal the entrance, anticipating a stage curtain and screen.

1. Aluminium and glass street elevation of the Wacoal Art Centre (1985), Tokyo, by Fumihiko Maki

BIBLIOGRAPHY

J. Peter, ed.: *Aluminum in Modern Architecture*, 2 vols (Louisville, KY, 1956)
——: *An International Review of Aluminum in Modern Architecture*, 2 vols (Louisville, KY, 1958–60)
C. Davies: *High Tech Architecture* (New York, 1988)
B. Bognar: *The New Japanese Architecture* (New York, 1990)

LOUIS SKOLER

(ii) Sculpture. The use of aluminium in sculpture has, in common with all modern materials, evolved in parallel with the availability of different forms of the material as dictated by the demands of industry, particularly the construction industry. As a result the immense variety of sheets, plates, tubes, rods, structural sections, extruded shapes and different alloys that developed for mundane purposes have all been used in some way to make sculpture. The first use of aluminium in sculpture was in the Shaftesbury Monument, a statue of *Eros* cast in 1892 and erected in Piccadilly Circus, London (*see* GILBERT, ALFRED, fig. 1). As aluminium became more widely available in such forms as wire, rod and sheet, it became a part of the material vocabulary of the new sculpture developing in Russia at the beginning of the 20th century. Vladimir Tatlin, for example, used aluminium with iron and zinc in his seminal Constructivist piece, *Corner Relief* (1915;

destr.). Artists working in constructed sculpture subsequently relied heavily on steel due to its ease of use, ready availability and comparative cheapness. Aluminium was more often used in its cast form wherever light weight was required, as in Jacob Epstein's large *Christ in Majesty* (1954) in Llandaff Cathedral and Barbara Hepworth's wall sculpture (1962) for John Lewis, London. The particular colour and nature of aluminium were emphasized in the *Head as a Still Life* (1942; estate of the artist) by David Smith and in *Towards a New Laocoon* (1963; London, Brit. Council) by Eduardo Paolozzi, who was also the first artist to use paint on cast aluminium.

Aluminium was often used by the Minimalists in the late 1960s and early 1970s, as it was ideally suited to the manufactured perfection required by their large, simple forms. Donald Judd used the precision of flat sheet in *Untitled, Aluminium and Glass* (1965; London, Saatchi Col.) and Sol LeWitt used it as a substrate for impeccable white stove enamel in *Serial Project 1 (A,B,C,D)* (1966; London, Saatchi Col.). Exploiting the strength and lightness of structural sections, Kenneth Snelson used anodized aluminium tubes for *Needle Tower* (1968; Washington, DC, Hirschhorn and version in Otterlo, Rijksmus. Kröller-Müller) and in England Nigel Hall (*b* 1943) used very thin, internally wired tubes for his delicate wall pieces. In the mid-1970s American artists produced kinetic sculptures using brightly polished aluminium in conjunction with neon tubes, glass, lasers, television screens and computers. Notable in this field were Takis, Otto Piene and Julio Le Parc. The first artists to explore the use of aluminium for its specific material qualities as finished surface rather than as a substrate for paintwork were Donald Judd, Carl André, who used 25 one-metre squares of bare aluminium plates for *Aluminium Square* (1968; New York, MOMA), and Frank Stella, whose aluminium honeycomb panel constructions were etched and inscribed, abraded and partially painted. In Japan in the 1970s Morio Shinoda (*b* 1931) perfected the treatment of unpainted aluminium in his exquisite machine-like constructions, notably *Tension and Compression* (1972; Humlebæk, Louisiana Mus.; see fig. 2).

The use of anodizing as a colouring method rather than just an added corrosion protection was first used as early as 1969 by Judd and was still being explored in the late 20th century by various sculptors, notably Karl Schantz (*b* 1944) and Barbara Brown (*b* 1958). Unlike steel, aluminium became readily available in plate form of considerable thickness, enabling sculptors to carve directly into large blocks of the material using machine-shop techniques, as with *Relic* (1989; London, Eagle Star priv. col.) by Mark Firth (*b* 1952). Cast aluminium became popular once again in the 1980s and 1990s and was used for example by Jürgen Goertz (*b* 1939) in his surreal figurations and in a spectacular installation by Arnaldo Pomodoro at the 1988 Venice Biennale. Contemporary uses of aluminium in art were explored in 1989 in *Artluminium*, an international exhibition held in Montreal, Canada. It showed that whereas the metal had traditionally been considered by sculptors merely as an alternative to steel, to be employed where corrosion or weight was a factor, its own particular expressive characteristics were still being explored.

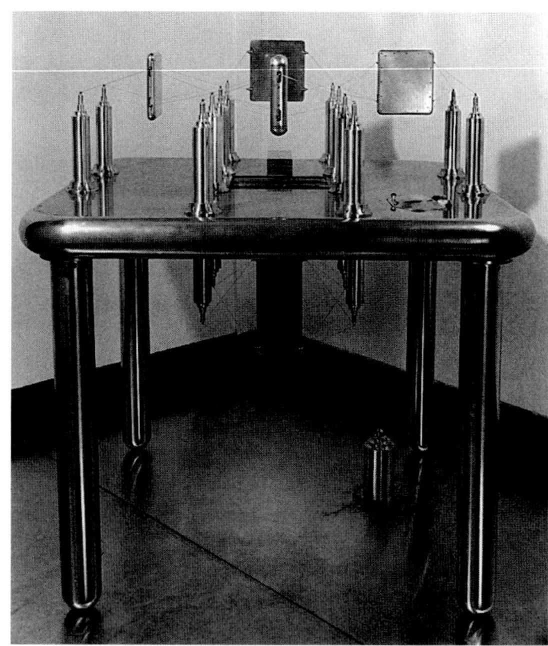

2. Aluminium sculpture by Morio Shinoda: *Tension and Compression 414, 415*, 1.0×1.0×1.12 m, 1972 (Humlebæk, Denmark, Louisiana Museum)

BIBLIOGRAPHY

D. Davis: *Art and the Future* (London, 1973)

W. Rotzler: *Constructive Concepts* (Zurich, 1977)

P. Schjeldahl, ed.: *Art of our Time*, London, Saatchi Col. cat. (London, 1984)

K. W. Jensen, ed.: *Louisiana: The Collection*, Humlebæk, Louisiana Mus. cat. (Copenhagen, 1986)

E. Lucie-Smith: *Sculpture since 1945* (London, 1987)

A. M. Hammacher: *Modern Sculpture: Tradition and Innovation* (New York, 1988)

M. G. Gervasoni, ed.: *43rd Venice Biennale* (exh. cat., Venice, 1988)

D. Wheeler: *Art since Mid Century* (New York, 1991)

MARK FIRTH

(iii) Decorative arts. From the 1920s and 1930s aluminium was widely used for industrial design, household products and interior features, due to its lightness and durability. At the Bauhaus in the 1920s aluminium was used experimentally in fabrics, and Marianne Brandt and others incorporated it into lighting fixtures. Aluminium staircase railings and light fixtures were used in the De La Warr Pavilion, Bexhill-on-Sea (1936), by Serge Chermayeff and Erich Mendelsohn. During this period it was particularly favoured by American designers, for example DONALD DESKEY (e.g. furniture and lamps in the Radio City Music Hall, New York, 1932) and RUSSEL WRIGHT. It was cast and wrought for ornamental gates, lift and radiator grilles and has been used for jewellery making. The stacking chair (1938) by Hans Coray (*b* 1907) was mass-produced for parks and gardens, the seat and back being formed of a single piece of aluminium. After World War II such designers as ERNEST RACE used aluminium for furniture, due to timber shortages. Eero Saarinen used aluminium as the base of his fibre-glass tulip chair (1956–7) produced by Knoll. Aluminium has enjoyed a continuous and widespread popularity for the production of kitchen utensils, although

it was slowly superseded in the late 20th century by stainless steel and plastics (*see* PLASTIC, §2(iv)).

BIBLIOGRAPHY

L. Aitchison: *A History of Metals* (London, 1960)

□

Alunno, l'. *See* NICCOLÒ DA FOLIGNO.

Alunno di Domenico. *See* BARTOLOMEO DI GIOVANNI.

Alva de la Canal, Ramón (*b* Mexico City, 29 Aug 1892; *d* Mexico City, 4 April 1985). Mexican painter and draughtsman. He studied at the Academia de San Carlos in Mexico City from 1910. In 1917 he was employed as a draughtsman by the Ministry of Agriculture and began to attend the Escuela de Pintura al Aire Libre de Santa Anita under Alfredo Ramos Martínez, his palette gradually lightening. In 1920 he was appointed assistant draughtsman in the Ministry of Education and then tutor at the Academia de San Carlos. In 1922 he was commissioned by the Ministry of Education to paint a mural, the *Landing of the Cross* (fresco, 7×8 m; Mexico City, Escuela N. Prep.), an allegorical depiction of the implantation of Catholicism in New Spain in the 16th century, with large classical figures set in a steeply inclined composition. Over the next 40 years, Alva de la Canal painted six public murals with allegorical and historical themes, such as the *Life of Morelos* (encaustic and fresco, 1937; Janitzio, nr Pátzcuaro). This is a sculptural monument to Morelos, into which the painting is inserted, and which depicts scenes from the life of the Independence figure arranged in an ascending spiral form around the interior of the monument.

During the 1920s Alva de la Canal was associated with ESTRIDENTISMO. He lived in Jalapa, near Villahermosa, in 1925–6, when the movement was patronized by the governor of the state of Veracruz, and he provided illustrations for Estridentista books and reviews such as *Horizonte*. During this period he depicted scenes of contemporary working life in bold black-and-white pencil and ink drawings, using geometric forms and rounded outlines. In 1928 he helped found the ¡30–30! group in Mexico City, which advocated the use of open-air teaching methods instead of academic ones; his drawings were used as illustrations in the *¡30–30!* magazine, and he participated in exhibitions mounted by the group in cafés and theatre-halls in Mexico City.

Between 1928 and 1932, Alva de la Canal worked on the 'cultural missions' organized by the Ministry of Education, travelling to states in the north and south of Mexico, painting murals and teaching in primary schools. On his return to Mexico City in 1932 he became involved with the Teatro Guiñol sponsored by the Instituto Nacional de Bellas Artes, providing puppets, costumes and scenery, an activity that he continued throughout his life. He painted portraits, numerous local landscapes and scenes with Indian figures, using soft contours and large areas of single colours. From 1953 to 1977 he taught painting at the Centro Universitario de Artes Plásticas in Jalapa, of which he became the director on its inauguration in 1953. On his return to Mexico City he became involved with the Taller de Gráfica Popular, and in 1981 he was named a member of the Academia Mexicana de Artes.

BIBLIOGRAPHY

Homenaje: Ramón Alva de la Canal, 1892–1985 (exh. cat., Jalapa, U. Veracruzana, Gal. Ramón Alva de la Canal, 1986)

NICOLA COLEBY

Alvarado, Antonio (*b* Le Havre, France, 19 Oct 1938). Panamanian painter and printmaker of French birth. He first studied with the figurative painter Alberto Dutary but established himself in the 1960s as one of the few abstract artists in Panama with paintings such as *Green Force* (Panama City, Mus. A. Contemp.), which attest to the influence of American Abstract Expressionism; in other works he was also influenced by Post-painterly Abstraction. During a visit to Japan in 1969 he came into contact with Japanese art and Zen Buddhism, after which he sought to achieve the maximum impact of form and colour through reduction to essentials. The techniques used in his acrylic paintings and drawings were well suited also to screenprints such as the series *Form and Space* (1975; Panama City, Gal. Etcétera). Alvarado was also active in organizing exhibitions for others and promoting the arts in Panama as director from 1970 to 1975 of the Departmento de Artes Plásticas of the Instituto Nacional de Cultura y Deportes.

BIBLIOGRAPHY

R. de Henestrosa: 'Antonio Alvarado', *Vanidades México*, xvi/18 (1976)

R. Ros: 'La pintura de Antonio Alvarado', *Rev. N. Cult.* 7–8 (1977), pp. 151–60

MONICA E. KUPFER

Alvarado Lang, Carlos (*b* La Piedad Cabadas, Michoacán, 1905; *d* Mexico City, 1981). Mexican printmaker. His skill as a printmaker became apparent at an early age when he was employed as an assistant metal-engraver by Francisco Díaz de Léon at the Academia de San Carlos in Mexico City. In 1929 he succeeded his teacher Emilio Valadés as professor of printmaking and subsequently became Director of the Escuela Nacional de Artes Plásticas and of the Escuela Nacional de Pintura y Escultura La Esmeralda, both in Mexico City. He was influential both as a teacher and for his virtuoso handling of traditional printmaking techniques including line-engraving, drypoint, aquatint, mezzotint, wood-engraving and linocut. His prints, mainly of Mexican landscapes, combine technical skill with affective expressiveness. He experimented constantly with methods of improving procedures, especially with mezzotint, with the modification of printing presses and with the introduction of new acids.

Alvarado Lang also did much to popularize 19th-century Mexican prints as a collector and writer.

WRITINGS

El grabado a la manera negra (Mexico City, 1938)

39 estampas populares (Mexico City, 1947)

'La obra de José Guadalupe Posada', *El Centavo* (1988), no. 136, pp. 30–31

BIBLIOGRAPHY

A. Rodríguez: *Carlos Alvarado Lang, baluarte del grabado mexicano* (Mexico City, 1990)

JULIETA ORTIZ GAITÁN

Alvares. Portuguese family of architects and military engineers.

(1) Afonso Alvares (*fl* 1550–75; *d* 15 Feb 1575). He became Master of the Royal Works (Mestre das Obras) in 1550, Master of the Works of the Cano do Prato of the city of Évora and Master of the Works in Alentejo, and in 1570 he succeeded Manuel Pires as Master of the Fortifications of the Kingdom (Mestre das Fortificações do Reino). He is closely associated with two types of church: the hall church (*igrejas-salão*), and the influential form used for the first Jesuit buildings in Portugal, and subsequently in Brazil.

The cathedrals at Leiria (1559–74) and Portalegre (begun 1556) are attributed to Alvares. Both are of the hall-type plan and have unified interior spaces, already explored during the Manueline period, and the continued use of Gothic elements (ribbed vaulting and strongly vertical windows). Although there is some use of a classical vocabulary, they do not represent the most erudite form of Italian classicism. Alvares collaborated with Pires on the Jesuit church of Espírito Santo (1567–74), Évora, which has a broad undivided nave with lateral chapels joined by passages. This crypto-collateral plan was adopted by Alvares for the contemporary Jesuit church of S Roque (1567), Lisbon. The plan has been seen as deriving from the aisleless Late Gothic church of S Francisco (1480–1500), Évora. Other works by Afonso Alvares are: the convent of S Helena do Monte Calvário (1569–74), the Jesuit Colégio do Espírito Santo (1567–74), where he collaborated with Pires, and S Antão (reconstruction in 1568), all in Évora; the churches of S Sebastião (1569) and S Catarina dos Livreiros (1572) in Lisbon (both destr.); the enlargement of the Torre Velha, opposite the Torre de Belém in Lisbon; and other fortifications along the coast of the Algarve from 1571.

Alvares's work is related to the utilitarian style of military architecture and engineering associated with his father-in-law, Miguel de Arruda, which centres on the qualities of simplicity, austerity, neatness, clarity and functionality. This constitutes the so-called Plain style, which heralded the Spanish *estilo desornamentado* but preceded it by some ten years.

(2) Baltazar Alvares (*fl* 1570–1624; *d* 1624). Nephew of (1) Afonso Alvares. He trained with his uncle, with whom he collaborated until 1575, and he was sent to Italy by King Sebastian, where he remained until 1578 to complete his education. In 1580 he succeeded his uncle as Master of the Works in Alentejo; he was appointed Master of the Works in the palaces of Santarém, Almeirim and Salvaterra (1581), Master of the Works of the Orders of S Tiago and S Bento de Avis (2 Oct 1597), and architect of the church and convent of S Vicente de Fora, Lisbon, from 1597 to 1624, succeeding Filippo Terzi in these positions. He also worked for the Jesuits.

Alvares is most closely associated with S Vicente de Fora (begun 1582; for illustration *see* TERZI, FILIPPO), commissioned by Philip II of Spain following the union of the Spanish and Portuguese crowns in 1580. The design of the building has been variously attributed to Terzi or Juan de Herrera, but Alvares played an important part in its realization and worked on it from 1590 (taking over from Terzi in 1597) until his death. Several Italian features are evident at S Vicente de Fora, such as the plan that derives from that of S Andrea, Mantua (design, 1470), and from that of Il Gesù, Rome (begun 1568), by Jacopo Vignola, the alternating curved and straight pediments for the doors and windows, the system of lighting, the retro-choir and the general use of classical elements. Spanish influence is also apparent in the plan, which is similar to that of Valladolid Cathedral (design 1578–86) by Herrera, and the narthex and ciborium derive from the Escorial (1563–84). The paired towers are characteristically Portuguese, and they were used by Afonso Alvares. The façade (see fig.) was almost certainly designed by Baltazar in 1615, and it combines many of these influences. Baltazar was responsible for stimulating the widespread use of the type of façade seen at S Vicente de Fora, which incorporates the narthex and has three arches framed by giant pilasters. Such a design is associated more with palaces than with religious architecture, and it derived from both Spanish and Portuguese sources. Alvares also developed the concept of the façade being in the form of a great retable of stone with rectangular panels and pedimented niches.

Alvares's most important works for the Jesuits are S Antão, Lisbon (destr.), built from 1613 after revising over-elaborate designs made in 1579, and the plan of which followed that of S Vicente de Fora; the completion of S Roque, begun by his uncle, in which he introduced polychrome mosaic (1619); the Onze Mil Virgens Church (begun 1598), now the Sé Nova, in Coimbra, in which the concept of the façade as retable is again evident; and S Lourenço (dos Grilos; begun 1614) in Oporto, which has formal similarities to Sé Nova, particularly through its fine Mannerist façade. For the Benedictines he designed the convent of S Bento (begun 1598) in Lisbon and a church of the same dedication in Coimbra (1576; destr.). Other works attributed to Alvares are the church of the Desterro, of which only part of the façade remains; the Mosteiro

Baltazar Alvares: façade of S Vicente de Fora, Lisbon, designed 1615

das Trinitárias and Mosteiro da Encarnação das Comendadeiras de Avis (both begun 1618); the convent of S Bento de Avis, all in Lisbon; and the completion of the convent of S Tiago at Palmela (begun by Terzi), whose two large cloisters in Plain style are particularly fine.

Alvares's work combined various traditions and influences: Portuguese, because of his uncle; Italian, due to his training, his contact with Terzi and the influence of Serlio and Vignola; and Spanish, because of his knowledge of Spanish art and artists such as Herrera. Essentially a classicist, he broke with the most orthodox principles of the Plain style, which had then been dominant in Portugal.

BIBLIOGRAPHY

Viterbo

P. F. Santos: 'Contribuição ao estudo da arquitectura da Companhia de Jesus em Portugal e no Brasil', *Actas do V colóquio internacional de estudos luso-brasileiros: Coimbra, 1966*, iv, pp. 515–40

R. Smith: *The Art of Portugal, 1500–1800* (New York, 1968)

G. Kubler: *Portuguese Plain Architecture between Spices and Diamonds, 1521–1706* (Harmondsworth, 1972)

J. Segurado: *Da obra filipina de São Vicente de Fora* (Lisbon, 1976)

J. H. Pais da Silva: *Estudos sobre o maneirismo* (Lisbon, 1982, rev. 1986)

A. Haupt: *A arquitectura do renascimento em Portugal* (Lisbon, 1986)

J. E. Horta Correia: 'A arquitectura—Maneirismo e estilo chão', *História da arte em Portugal*, vii (Lisbon, 1986)

A. Medina Mouzinho: *Afonso Alvares, arquitecto funcionalista: A tradicão e a modernidade na arquitectura portuguesa do século XVI, os eixos das invariantes funcionais* (diss., Lisbon, U. Nova, 1986)

A. Bustamante and F. Marías: 'Francisco de Mora y la arquitectura portuguesa', *As relacões artísticas entre Portugal e Espanha na época dos descobrimentos, II simpósio luso-espanhol de história da arte: Coimbra, 1987*, pp. 277–318

R. Moreira: 'A escola de arquitectura do Paço da Ribeira e a Academia de matemáticas de Madrid', *As relacões artísticas entre Portugal e Espanha na época dos descobrimentos, II simpósio luso-espanhol de história da arte: Coimbra, 1987*, pp. 65–77

V. Serrão: 'Documentos dos protocolos notariais de Lisboa referentes a artes e artistas portugueses (1563–1650)', *Bol. Cult. Assembl. Distr. Lisboa*, xc/1–2 (1988), pp. 55–105

J. E. Horta Correia: *Arquitectura portuguesa—Renascimento, maneirismo, estilo chão* (Lisbon, 1991)

EDUARDO DUARTE

Alvarez. Spanish family of sculptors and architects.

(1) José Alvarez Cubero (*b* Priego, Córdoba, 23 April 1768; *d* Madrid, 26 Nov 1827). Sculptor, also active in Italy. He was the most important and the most rigorous of the Spanish Neo-classical sculptors and the only one to achieve European renown in his lifetime. The many institutions of which he was a member included the Real Academia de Bellas Artes de S Fernando, Madrid, the academies of Carrara, Naples and Antwerp, the Accademia di S Luca, Rome, and the Institut de France, Paris. He created a coherent oeuvre that owed a debt both to Greek models and to the works of Antonio Canova, Pietro Tenerani and Bertel Thorvaldsen.

1. Early training and first works, 1784–99. 2. Years of maturity: Paris, Rome, Madrid, 1799–1827.

1. Early training and first works, 1784–99. José Alvarez Cubero was the son of the stonemason Domingo Alvarez, who had a decisive influence on his education. Alvarez Cubero completed his training with his godfather, the sculptor of retables Francisco Javier Pedrajas, and collaborated with him in 1784 on the decoration of the chapel of the Sagrario in the parish church of the Asunción, Priego, and probably on that of the Cartuja de El Paular in Rascafria, Madrid, where panels in the choir are attributed to him. He also worked with Pedrajas on the stalls in S Barbara, Efija, some time before 1790–91, when, again in collaboration with Pedrajas, he carved 34 panels for the choir in S María, Cabra. While still in Priego he also executed a Baroque stone sculpture of *Flora*, for the garden of Doña María de la Salud Madrid Alcalá-Zamora, and a *Lion Fighting a Snake*, for the King's fountain.

1. José Alvarez Cubero: *Winter*, stone figure from the Fountain of Apollo, Paseo del Prado, Madrid, 1795–1800

After 1791 Alvarez Cubera left his home town for Córdoba, with the support of the Bishop of Córdoba, Don Antonio Caballero y Góngora. The Bishop, who also came from Priego, had founded the Escuela de Bellas Artes in Córdoba in 1791 to promote the teaching of art along Neo-classical lines. Alvarez Cubero lodged in the episcopal palace and received a grant to study at the school, first under the Aragonese sculptor Joaquín Arali, with whom he came into conflict, and then under a French sculptor, Jean Michel Verdiguier (1706–96). Shortly afterwards Alvarez Cubero also worked in Granada under the Catalan artist Jaime Folch (1760–1816), who was much influenced by Neo-classical trends and particularly by Antonio Canova, then director of the Escuela de Nobles Artes in Granada. In 1794, again supported by the Bishop of Córdoba, Alvarez Cubero travelled to Madrid, to study at the Real Academia de Bellas Artes de S Fernando. There

Manuel Francisco Alvarez de la Peña of Salamanca commissioned from him stone figures of the *Four Seasons* (1795–1800) including *Winter* (see fig. 1) for the Fountain of Apollo (Madrid, Paseo del Prado). While at the Academia he executed a copy of Camillo Rusconi's *Memorial to Gregory XIII* (1715; Rome, St Peter's), and a statue after the *Flora* in the Capitoline, Rome.

On the death in 1796 of his protector, Alvarez Cubero endured some hardship until he won the Academia's first prize in 1799 with his reliefs, the *Removal of St Isidore's Mortal Remains to León* and the *Wrath of Manasseh against Isaiah*. This entitled him to a grant of 12,000 reales from Charles IV (*reg* 1788–1808) to study in Paris and Rome.

2. Years of maturity: Paris, Rome, Madrid, 1799–1827. In Paris Alvarez Cubero worked with Claude Dejoux and attended the dissection theatres of the College of Medicine. In 1804 his statue of *Ganymede* won him a gold medal and 500 francs, and in the same year he married Isabel de Bouquel. He executed busts of *Charles IV* and his wife, *María Luisa of Parma*, and these adorned the façade of the Ayuntamiento in Salamanca from 1806 to 1868.

In 1805 Alvarez Cubero and his wife left for Rome. There he met Bertel Thorvaldsen and Antonio Canova. In 1808, following the Spanish uprising against the occupying French government, he refused to recognize the rights of the Bonapartes in Spain, and he was imprisoned in the Castel Sant' Angelo in Rome and deprived of his Spanish grant. Canova intervened to have him freed, and Alvarez Cubero was commanded to make four reliefs on Classical themes for the Emperor's bedroom in the Quirinal, but these were never installed. At this time he also began work on a statue of a *Youth with a Swan* (Madrid, Prado), and on four statues commissioned by Charles IV for the Casa del Labrador at Aranjuez. Of these the *Apolino* (Madrid, Prado) is very delicate; the others were *Eros*, the running figure of *Diana the Huntress* and *Morpheus*, now known as *Amor dormido* (San Sebastián, Mus. Mun. S Telmo). The four were acquired by Ferdinand VII in 1827.

In 1816 Alvarez Cubero joined the ranks of Spanish court artists, and he was made Escultor de Cámara. Around the same time he executed several important works, including three seated figures that recall Canova's statue of Napoleon's mother, Letitia Bonaparte, known as *Mme Mère* (1804–7; Chatsworth, Derbys). The statues depict Napoleon's queen, *Marie Louise* (1816; Madrid, Cason Buen Retiro), *Queen María Isabel of Braganza* (*c.* 1816; Madrid, Prado; see fig. 2), which is unfinished, and the *Marquesa de Ariza* (1817). All the sitters were depicted in Empire-style costumes that closely resemble Classical Roman robes. The third statue was one of several works commissioned from Alvarez Cubero by Carlos Miguel Fitz-James Stuart, 14th Duque de Alba; others included the tomb of the Marquesa in the archpriest's church of Liria (finished by Antonio Sola after 1827) and the colossal statue of the Duque's relative, the *Duke of Berwick* (untraced), which was never cast in bronze.

Around 1817–18 Alvarez Cubero began work on his most popular piece, the *Defence of Saragossa* (Madrid, Prado; *see* Spain, fig. 23). This group was first shown in plaster in October 1818, and it became the most famous of all Spanish Neo-classical works. Its subject-matter was heroic and contemporary, yet in formal terms it related to Classical antiquity. While working on the piece, Alvarez Cubero visited Spain in 1819, but he returned to Rome, and the group was executed in marble in 1823 with the support of Ferdinand VII; it was moved to Madrid in 1826 after Alvarez Cubero rejected offers made by Francis II, the Emperor of Austria, and his minister Metternich to take it to Vienna. The artist himself wrote a dramatic description of the episode depicted, in which a Saragossan warrior dies defending his wounded father. The Duque de Frías dedicated a poem to the work in his famous *Oda a las bellas artes* (1842), and it was also the subject of a poem by José Felix Reinoso (1772–1841).

2. José Alvarez Cubero: *Queen María Isabel of Braganza*, white marble, *c.* 1816 (Madrid, Museo del Prado)

In 1823 Alvarez Cubero was made Primer Escultor de Cámara at the Spanish court, but he continued to live in Rome for a while and executed a masterly bust of *Don Antonio de Vargas y Laguna* (Rome, church of Monserrat) shortly before his eventual return to Spain late in 1825 or early in 1826. On his way to Madrid he stopped in Saragossa, where he met the 13-year-old Ponciano Ponzano y Gascon at the Academia de Bellas Artes de S Luis, of which he was a member, and offered him protection. Alvarez Cubero then settled permanently in Madrid, but he died soon after. His likeness and manner are vividly depicted in his portrait by Juan Antonio Ribera y Fernández. He left a daughter and two sons, the sculptor José Alvarez Bouquel (1805–30) and (2) Aníbal Alvarez Bouquel.

BIBLIOGRAPHY

'José Alvarez de Pereira y Cubero, escultor', *Mus. Univl* (30 July 1857)
M. Ossorio y Bernard: *Galería biográfica de artistas españoles del siglo XIX* (Madrid, 1883–4), pp. 29–32
E. Pardo Canalís: *Escultores del siglo XIX* (Madrid, 1951), pp. 61–78
J. A. Gaya Nuño: *Arte del siglo XIX*, A. Hisp., xix (Madrid, 1966), pp. 71–5
J. Marín Medina: *La escultura española contemporánea, 1800–1978: Historia y evolución crítica* (Madrid, 1978), pp. 18–20
F. Zueras Torrens: *José Alvarez Cubero* (Priego, 1986)

WIFREDO RINCÓN GARCÍA

(2) Aníbal Alvarez Bouquel (*b* Madrid, 1806; *d* Madrid, 5 April, 1870). Architect and son of (1) José Alvarez Cubero. He received a sound education and academic training under Isidro González Velázquez (1765–1840), of whose pupils he is considered the best. In 1832 Alvarez Bouquel won the national prize in architecture and a bursary to go to Rome and travel in France. His time in Italy had a decisive influence on his style. Designated Arquitecto de Mérito in 1839, he belongs, with Matías Laviña Blasco (1796–1868) and Narciso Pascual y Colomer, to the generation of the last academicians who inaugurated the Escuela de Arquitectura, Madrid. He was a professor there from 1844.

The Italianate flavour of Alvarez Bouquel's work before the 1850s can be seen in the elegant country houses he built for the upper bourgeoisie of Madrid; these had stone foundations, two floors articulated with the Ionic order, and each was surmounted with a balustrade. The finest is that of Manuel Gaviria on Calle Arenal. Alvarez Bouquel also remodelled the convent of María de Aragón for the Senate palace, retaining the original elegant assembly room, the Sala de Sesiones. In 1846 he built between the Calle Victoria and the Calle Espoz y Mina, Madrid, one of the first arcades constructed of metal. He eventually became director of the Escuela de Arquitectura (1857–64) and collaborated in the publication of *Monumentos arquitectónicos* (Madrid, 1859–86). He was also chief architect at the Palacio Real in Madrid and in 1857 became a member of the Real Academia de Bellas Artes de S Fernando, Madrid.

BIBLIOGRAPHY

M. Lopez: 'Don Aníbal Alvarez Bouquel', *Rev. de Arquit.*, lxxxiii (1948), p. 465
J. A. Gaya: *Arte del siglo XIX* (Madrid, 1966)
P. Nevascués: *Del neoclasicismo al modernismo* (Madrid, 1979)

ALBERTO VILLAR MOVELLÁN

Alvarez, Augusto H. (*b* Mérida, 24 Dec 1914). Mexican architect. He graduated from the Universidad Nacional de México, Mexico City, in 1939. In his early works he was influenced by the theories of José Villagrán García and later by those of Le Corbusier, Mies van der Rohe and Gropius. He is notable in Mexican architecture for his adherence to Rationalism throughout his long career. In construction he used steel and concrete, prefabricated units and glass, and there is an evident unity in his works, especially in the high quality of his finishes. A notable example of his buildings is a small bank branch (1958; destr.), Mexico City, in which the International Style is clearly visible in the cleverly composed structure and in the neon illumination of the exterior, recalling Mondrian. The Jaysour Building (1961), Mexico City, is the clearest example of his assimilation of the International Style, evident in the ground-plan, structure and even the glass cladding. Also in Mexico City are the IBM Building (1971–2), an innovative and flexible design adapted to different functions on each of its six levels, and the La Mitra offices (1972–3), in which he managed to blend the exposed concrete structure with a system of metal mezzanines, the use of space being fundamental.

BIBLIOGRAPHY

T. G. Salgado: *Augusto H. Alvarez* (Mexico City, 1984)
L. Noelle: *Arquitectos contemporáneos de México* (Mexico City, 1988)

XAVIER MOYSSÉN

Alvarez, Mario Roberto (*b* Buenos Aires, 14 Nov 1913). Argentine architect. He studied architecture at the University of Buenos Aires, graduating in 1937 with two gold medals and the Ader Scholarship, which enabled him to spend a year studying architecture in Europe. He joined the Ministry of Public Works and then became Municipal Architect at Avellaneda (1942–7); he established his own office in Buenos Aires in 1947. Alvarez became one of the most prolific and successful architects in Latin America, winning first prize in a large number of competitions and building a great number of works. His designs were based on a rationalist approach, developing consciously simple structural form in the manner of Mies van der Rohe; his goal was to produce functional buildings utilizing modern technology and efficient workmanship, allowing for flexibility and change and contributing to the quality of the environment. Important works include the Medical Centre (1936–7) at San Martín; the Roncatti Restaurant (1938), Pergamino; the San Martin Cultural Centre (1953–60), Corrientes; the IBM building (1979–83), Catalinas Norte; the Alto Palermo flats and shopping centre (1983–6), Buenos Aires; and many other health centres, stadiums, multi-storey blocks of flats and office buildings. His persistent hard work over several years resulted in the extension of the Municipal Theatre (1953) at San Martín into the most important cultural centre of Buenos Aires. His interest in technology was revealed in his work on the Santa Fé–Paraná River Tunnel (1965), Entre Rios Province, which experiments with prefabricated construction techniques, and his design for the Somisa Headquarters (1966), Buenos Aires, was the first building in Argentina to be built entirely of steel and the first in the world to be entirely welded.

BIBLIOGRAPHY

M. A. Trabucco: *Mario Roberto Alvarez* (Buenos Aires, 1965)
'Mario Roberto Alvarez: 50 años de arquitectura', *Summa*, 233–4 (1987) [issue dedicated to Alvarez], pp. 35–100

LUDOVICO C. KOPPMANN

Alvarez Bravo, Manuel (*b* Mexico City, 4 Feb 1902). Mexican photographer. He studied painting and music at the Academia Nacional de Bellas Artes in Mexico City in 1918. In 1922, after training as an office worker, he began to take an interest in photography, and in 1923 he met Hugo Brehme shortly before buying his first camera. In 1929, through his friendship with Tina Modotti, he got to know Diego Rivera. In 1930, when Modotti left Mexico, he provided illustrations for Francis Toor's book *Mexican Folkways*. From 1930 to 1931 he was cameraman for Eisenstein's film *Viva Mexico*. Subsequently he met Paul Strand and Cartier-Bresson, and became friendly with Mexico's leading painters and writers. In 1938 he met André Breton, who was visiting Mexico and who was deeply impressed by the mysterious and suggestive nature of his photographs. Breton was keen to enlist him for the Surrealist cause, and published some of his photographs in *Minotaure*.

In his photographs Alvarez Bravo captured the essential spirit of Mexico by a process of reconstruction, not reproduction. As a young man he encountered the revolutionary Muralist movement, the first embodiment of an individual and indigenous artistic movement in Mexico, and this, together with childhood experience of the Mexican Revolution, was to have a considerable influence on his development. Though he travelled for short periods to Europe and the USA, and was in contact with photographers such as Strand and Edward Weston, his images were drawn almost exclusively from Mexico, capturing unnoticed details that encapsulated the mysterious in the everyday. When not derived from his personal domestic life, his subjects were drawn from those of the indigenous Indian peoples, whether urban or rural, whose roots in deeper non-European culture and tradition are suggested by unexpected juxtapositions of objects and activities. Often his photographs give a vivid impression of the political and social problems faced by Mexico in the 20th century, for example in *Striking Worker, Assassinated* (1934; see 1978 exh. cat., fig. 45), in which the worker's sprawling corpse is seen in close-up, its head lying in a pool of blood. A less dark side of Mexican life is featured in *Daydreaming* (1931; *see* PHOTOGRAPHY, fig. 24), which shows a contemplative young girl leaning on a balustrade in the half-light of a city courtyard.

Alvarez Bravo rarely strove for dramatic effect; like Walker Evans and Dorothea Lange he never monumentalized his subjects. He depicted human beings reduced to their existential presence. His influence on the younger generation of photographers in Latin America has been decisive, not only because of his subject-matter, but also because in his work he combined awareness of current trends in international photography with an appreciation of his own country's traditions.

WRITINGS

Mucho sol fondo de cultura económica (Mexico, 1989)

PHOTOGRAPHIC PUBLICATIONS

Manuel Alvarez Bravo: Fotografías (Mexico City, 1945)
Photographs by Manuel Alvarez Bravo (Geneva, 1977)

BIBLIOGRAPHY

F. Toor: *Mexican Folkways* (Mexico, 1930)
D. Rivera: *Manuel Alvarez Bravo* (Mexico, 1945)
Manuel Alvarez Bravo (exh. cat. by F. Parker, Pasadena, A. Mus., 1971)
C. Beaton and G. Buckland: 'Manuel Alvarez Bravo', *The Magic Image* (Boston and London, 1975)
Manuel Alvarez Bravo (exh. cat. by J. Livingston, Washington, DC, Corcoran Gal. A., 1978)
E. C. Garcia: 'Manuel Alvarez Bravo', *Photo-Vision* (April–June 1982)

ERIKA BILLETER

Alvarez de la Peña, Manuel Francisco (*b* Salamanca, 1727; *d* Madrid, 1797). Spanish sculptor. He was a member of the first generation of sculptors trained at the Real Academia de Bellas Artes de S Fernando, Madrid. He won a scholarship to Rome, which he was unable to take up for health reasons. His knowledge of Classical sculpture won him the nickname of 'el Griego', although the influence of the Rococo is also evident in his work. In the Spanish tradition he carved in wood as much as in stone.

Alvarez de la Peña took part in the programme of decoration for the Palacio Real, Madrid, to which he contributed statues of kings (*c*. 1750) and a relief, *Council of War* (*c*. 1760). In 1762–5 he carved three medallions with scenes from the *Life of the Virgin* and a series of saints and angels, all for the chapel of the Virgin in the church of Nuestra Señora del Pilar, Saragossa. The elegant Fountain of Apollo (1777–80) in the Paseo del Prado, Madrid, is his most successful and celebrated work. His fine relief of the *Virgin with St Ildefonso* (1780–82) for the chapel of S Ildefonso in Toledo Cathedral (*in situ*) shows Rococo influences. His finest works carved in wood are the two graceful interpretations of the *Immaculate Conception* made for the Palacio Real between 1771 and 1776 and, slightly later, for the Archbishop's Palace in Toledo (both *in situ*), which demonstrate the elegance of some of the best sculpture of the period.

BIBLIOGRAPHY

F. J. Sánchez Cantón: *Escultura y pintura del siglo XVIII*, A. Hisp., xvii (Madrid, 1958)
C. Pérez: *Historia del arte hispanico*, v (Madrid, 1979), p. 156

JUAN NICOLAU

Alvárez de Toledo. *See* ALBA.

Alvarez Ijjasz Murcia. Architectural partnership in Bogotá, Colombia, established in 1972 by Cecilia Alvarez Pereira (*b* Manizales, 23 July 1934) and Emese Ijjasz de Murcia (*b* Budapest, 18 May 1936). Alvarez studied at the University of Javeriana School of Architecture in Colombia from 1953 to 1958. Before establishing her own firm she worked with the firms Guillermo Gonzalez Zueleta and Pizano Pradilla & Caro between 1957 and 1964. Between 1964 and 1979 she worked in the Department of Works, Special Projects and Urban Politics at the Instituto Credito Territorial. De Murcia studied at the National University of Argentina from 1956 to 1958, Catholic University, Santiago, Chile, from 1958 to 1961, and the National University of Colombia at Medellín in 1962. De Murcia also worked for the Instituto Credito Territorial from 1964 to 1971 and designed more than 17,000 dwellings during this time. From 1970 she taught at the University of the Andes, Bogotá, becoming Vice-Dean in 1978. While they have built or renovated offices, medical centres and private housing, Alvarez and de Murcia have been primarily involved with large-scale, high-density social housing. One of their largest such projects is NIZA VIII (won in competition in 1979; built 1982–3), a housing estate of 684 apartments in the Niza area, on the outskirts of Bogotá. While the housing units are only six storeys high, their modernist-inspired geometry is uninviting. The architects have been concerned, however, with softening the buildings' impact on the environment. Extensive landscaping has been incorporated, and water for the apartments is heated with solar energy. Both Alvarez and de Murcia worked on projects with other organizations in addition to their joint work.

BIBLIOGRAPHY

Proa, 287 (1979), pp. 9–53 [competition for residential area in the north of Bogotá]

C. Lorenz: *Women in Architecture: A Contemporary Perspective* (New York, 1990)

□

Alvaro de Castro, Fernando. *See* CASTRO, FERNANDO DE.

Alvaro di Pietro. *See* PIREZ, ALVARO.

Alviani, Getulio (*b* Udine, 5 Sept 1939). Italian painter. He began his experiments in visual perception and psychology in the late 1950s. In this economic boom period there was considerable collaboration between artistic research and industrial production, to which Alviani contributed. In 1959–60 he created his *Surfaces with Vibratory Texture*, metallic planes with modular incisions that create an illusion of constantly changing distances, depending on the angle from which they are viewed and the way in which the light strikes them. In 1961 he collaborated in serial production of plastic objects, and between 1962 and 1964 he participated in the exhibitions of *arte programmata* promoted by Olivetti in Venice, Rome, Trieste, Düsseldorf and London. In the 1960s he also took part in the *Nouvelle tendance* movement. In 1965 Alviani's work began to display a greater interest in spatial articulation (e.g. *Surface with Vibratory Texture*; Wuppertal, von der Heydt-Mus.). In a kindergarten in Pregelstrasse in Leverkusen he created a reflective aluminium wall (two *Aluminium Plates*, each 1×1 m, 1965) to convey a feeling of optical vibration, and in 1967 he repeated the experiment in the hall of the palace housing the Festival del Cinema in Venice. Comparisons with architecture gradually became increasingly important, not only through the multiplication of standard modular elements, but with the creation of mirrored structures, which were curved or rotated to create particular perceptual and environmental effects.

In the 1970s, after producing Minimalist works made from steel sheets, he became more interested in the role of colour in his experiments.

BIBLIOGRAPHY

Getulio Alviani (exh. cat. by U. Apollonio, Ferrara, Padiglione A. Contemp., 1980)

L. Vergine: *Arte programmata e cinetica, 1953–1963. L'ultima avanguardia* (Milan, 1983)

DANIELA DE DOMINICIS

Alvino, Enrico (*b* Milan, 29 March 1809; *d* Rome, 7 June 1876). Italian architect, urban planner and teacher. He trained in Naples at the Istituto di Belle Arti, where he later taught (from 1835) and became a professor of civic architecture (1859). In 1830 he went to Rome on a scholarship to study architecture and a few years later he was appointed municipal architect in Naples, where he worked for the rest of his life. In his prolific and eclectic oeuvre he showed a broadly classicist tendency that ranged from Renaissance Revival to Neo-classical styles. His early work, such as the Palazzo Benucci (1843) at Castellammare di Stabia on the Bay of Naples, recalled the High Renaissance. For his restoration (1853) of the church of S Maria di Piedigrotta, which King Ferdinand II (*reg* 1830–59) wished to have decorated with mosaic in Byzantine style, Alvino chose to combine the Lombard-Romanesque and Renaissance styles, thus anticipating a tendency towards the mixing of forms from different historical styles that in the 1860s was manifested all over Europe. In 1863 he began work on the conversion of the monastery of S Giovanni Battista into the Istituto di Belle Arti. This building was a synthesis of Neapolitan Renaissance Revival elements. Its particular character lies in the coexistence of Renaissance taste and the new articulation of the building. The new centre of the institute is built around a large rectangular courtyard. The internal façade is the part that most reflects its previous monastic function, especially in the wide gallery surrounding the court. The three external façades are based on a single architectural module consisting of three orders of arched windows, one above the other, of which the middle order is the widest. Built in Campanian tufa, the ground floor is rusticated, and on the upper two floors are Tuscan and Corinthian pilasters.

Alongside his building works of this period Alvino also became a prolific urban planner during an economic revival in the reign of Ferdinand II, when numerous public works were carried out by the royal administration, including programmes for the expansion of the city of Naples. The idea was to connect the modern developments to the north-east and south-west with the historic city centre. From 1852 to 1860 he worked on the Corso Maria Teresa (now Corso Vittorio-Emanuele), a new street following a wide curve halfway up the southern slopes of the Vomero hill and connecting the two peripheral nuclei. Urban development on the hill began with the opening of the Corso, which favoured the expansion of the quarter to the west of Chiaia. In 1853, Alvino laid out and built the Via della Pace connecting the Chiaia quarter to the coastal zone of S Lucia and to S Fernando; he then constructed the royal cavalry barracks and the first tunnel under Mount Echia, which linked the Piazza Reale with Chiatamone, following a suggestion of Antonio Niccolini. In the same street, Alvino built the Palazzo Nunziante (1855), which was conceived on classical lines and occupies the whole block, representing the Neapolitan prototype of the modern middle-class residential building.

From the 1860s Alvino was constantly involved in public works. In the Chiaia quarter he widened the beach as far as Chiatamone and restored the grotto of Posillipo, bringing a considerable expansion of the street network between Naples and the Flegrea area. He sat on the commission (1871–6) considering a long-term city plan, and he designed the Piazza Municipio (1871) and the nucleus of the Stazione Centrale (1875; destr. 1950s), later developed by Nicola Breglia. He still maintained an interest in the restoration of ancient buildings, among other commissions designing and building the new cathedral (1868) at Cerignola, near Foggia, in Tuscan style. He produced a competition entry for the façade of Florence Cathedral (unexecuted) and a Gothic Revival design for the façade of Naples Cathedral, the latter executed in a modified form (1877–1905) by Breglia and Giuseppe Pisanti (1826–1913). He also rebuilt the façade of Amalfi Cathedral (with Luigi Della Corte and Guglielmo Raimondi) but this work collapsed in 1961. His last work, completed posthumously in 1877, was the Casa Armonica in the Villa Comunale of Naples. Constructed of cast iron and glass, it shows Alvino's interest in new materials and construction techniques.

BIBLIOGRAPHY

C. N. Sasso: *Storia dei monumenti di Napoli* (Naples, 1856)

R. De Fusco: *La scuola napoletana nei concorsi per la facciata di S Maria del Fiore* (Naples, 1930)

C. Lorenzetti: *L'Accademia di Belle Arti di Napoli* (Florence, [1952])

R. De Fusco: 'L'attività edilizia dal 1860 al 1915', *Napoli dopo un secolo*, ed. G. Ciccone and R. De Fusco (Naples, 1961), pp. 178–241

G. Bruno and R. De Fusco: *Enrico Alvino: Architetto e urbanista napoletano dell'Ottocento* (Naples, 1962)

M. L. Scalvini: 'La facciata neogotica in Europa nel XIX e XX secolo', *Il neogotico nel XIX e XX secolo*, ed. R. Bossaglia and V. Terraroli (Milan, 1990)

ANTONELLA D'AUTILIA

Amadas, Robert (*b* ?London, *c.* 1470; *d* ?London, 1532). English goldsmith. He was the son of a London goldsmith and was the most successful goldsmith working at the Tudor court; his work bridged the transition between the Gothic and the Renaissance styles. He was an official at the Mint from 1504 to almost the end of his life, his appointment possibly facilitated by his marriage to Elizabeth, granddaughter of Sir Hugh Bryce (*d* 1496), Court Goldsmith to Henry VIII. In 1524 Amadas became the first working goldsmith to become Master of the Jewel House to Henry VIII, an office he retained until 1532, supplying spangles, wire and ribbons to the court. In the 1520s his orders included a large amount of plate for gifts to foreign ambassadors; he also supplied a number of New Year's gifts for the court. Cardinal Thomas Wolsey was one of Amadas' most important clients, and Amadas supplied him with a number of lavish objects. Other clients included Edward Stafford, 3rd Duke of Buckingham (1478–1521), and Charles Brandon, Duke of Suffolk (*d* 1545). At his death Amadas was the wealthiest goldsmith in London, owning a large house in the city and a country estate.

BIBLIOGRAPHY

P. Glanville: 'Robert Amadas: Goldsmith', *Proc. Silver Soc.*, iii/5 (1986), pp. 106–13

——: *Silver in Tudor and Early Stuart England* (London, 1990)

EMMA PACKER

Amadei, Giuliano. *See* AMEDEI, GIULIANO.

Amadeo (de Souza-Cardoso) (*b* Manhufe, 14 Nov 1887; *d* Espinho, 6 July 1918). Portuguese painter and draughtsman. In Paris from 1906, he frequented the *académies libres*. After producing caricature drawings, he began painting small landscapes. In 1911–12 his style approached that of Modigliani, whom he knew and with whom he exhibited in 1911. He was also impressed by the luxuriant orientalism of the Ballets Russes. His drawings at the time were linear and decorative, with medieval and heraldic references.

In 1912–13 these early influences gave way to that of Cubism, which henceforth provided the structure of Amadeo's works. In 1913 his works were included in the Armory Show and the Sturm Gallery in Berlin.

In 1912 he met the Delaunays and under their influence colour became increasingly important, for example in *Study B* (1913; Lisbon, Mus. Gulbenkian). In *Horsemen* (1913; Paris, Pompidou) the figures are a pretext for the interplay of coloured arcs. His exploration of abstraction, however, was shortlived. The landscapes painted in the summer of 1914 in Brittany show a leaning towards Expressionism in their use of violent colours and gestural handling.

Like Eduardo Viana, Santa-Rita and his other compatriots, Amadeo left Paris at the outbreak of World War I, returning to his family home in Manhufe. He worked in isolation, maintaining only occasional contact with Viana and the Futurists, as well as with the Delaunays during their stay in Portugal (1915–17). His exhibition in 1916 in Oporto and then Lisbon was dubbed 'orphic' and 'futurist'. 'Futurist' was inappropriate, as speed and movement do not characterize his carefully constructed works. He saw in himself someone who participated a little in all the modern movements. His last paintings, dated 1917, are bright, complex compositions incorporating letters, numbers, *trompe l'oeil*, sand and collage. The death of Amadeo and Santa-Rita closed the first phase of Portuguese modernism.

BIBLIOGRAPHY

J.-A. França: *Amadeo de Souza-Cardoso* (Lisbon, 1957, 1972)

——: *A arte em Portugal no século XX* [Art in Portugal in the 20th century] (Lisbon, 1974, 1986)

RUTH ROSENGARTEN

Amadeo, Giovanni Antonio (*b* Pavia, *c.* 1447; *d* Milan, 28 Aug 1522). Italian sculptor and architect. He was principally active in Bergamo, Cremona, Milan and Pavia. His professional success, in terms of the architectural and sculptural commissions and official appointments that he received, was far greater than that of any of his contemporaries in Lombardy in the late 15th century, including Bramante. Amadeo's influence in both fields, for example in his use of *all'antica* ornament of local origin, was considerable.

1. Before 1490. 2. From 1490.

1. BEFORE 1490. He was trained as a sculptor and evidently apprenticed to Francesco Solari (*fl* 1464–71) in Milan and at the Certosa di Pavia (*see* PAVIA, §2(i)(b)). In 1466 Amadeo assisted in the decoration of the large cloister of the Certosa and was apparently responsible for the terracotta lavabo in the small cloister. His first signed work, directly influenced by the Late Gothic style of Solari, is the carved portal in the small cloister with a lunette of the *Virgin and Child with SS John the Baptist and Bruno with Carthusians.* In 1469 Amadeo and Martino Benzoni agreed to carve a *Lamentation* (untraced) for Monza Cathedral consisting of eight wooden figures. During the first half of the 1470s Amadeo executed the tomb of *Medea Colleoni* (*d* 1470; not completed until after Bartolomeo Colleoni's death in 1475) for the Dominican sanctuary of S Maria at Basella (near Urgnano, Bergamo). Simultaneously he supervised the construction of the Colleoni Chapel in S Maria Maggiore at Bergamo (where the tomb of *Medea Colleoni* was moved in 1842; *see* BERGAMO, fig. 1) and carved the tomb of the condottiere *Bartolomeo Colleoni* (see fig. 1). Amadeo's style by this time had changed radically from that manifested in his earliest works at the Certosa di Pavia. Although in terms of its

1. Giovanni Antonio Amadeo: tomb of *Bartolomeo Colleoni*, marble, *c.* 1470–75 (Bergamo, S Maria Maggiore, Colleoni Chapel)

organization the Colleoni tomb can be related to earlier Lombard monumental sculpture, Amadeo made considerable use of *all'antica* ornament. The narrative reliefs for which he is presumed to have been responsible (the two reliefs on the ends of the sarcophagus are generally assigned to the so-called Flagellation Master) retain some similarity to the style of the Certosa lunette, but they are infinitely more sophisticated in composition and execution. The design of the Colleoni Chapel is dependent both on the Portinari Chapel in S Eustorgio, Milan, and, more particularly, on Antonio Filarete's design for Bergamo Cathedral, from which Amadeo took the form of the cupola and the delight in using multicoloured stone surfaces. The chequer-board pattern of the façade is antique in origin, and Amadeo included for the first time on a large scale in Lombardy numerous quotations from antique coins to provide the decoration for the tondi and lozenges, a technique he used again on a grand scale at the Certosa di Pavia. This mode of decoration, involving the use, wherever possible, of locally available *all'antica* sources, dominated the work of Lombard architects and tomb sculptors for the next 30 years and was the most important single element in Amadeo's legacy.

Amadeo left Bergamo in 1475, without completing the work on the Colleoni Chapel and tomb. He moved temporarily to Milan, where he was immediately employed at the cathedral to execute figures, including a free-standing statue of *St Elizabeth*, and decorative sculpture for the altar of S Giuseppe, a project begun for Galeazzo Maria Sforza, Duke of Milan, in 1472. The extent of Amadeo's contribution is not precisely known. A large number of other sculptors were involved and the altar itself was dismantled in the late 16th century (untraced). In 1478 he produced a design for the *Edicula Tarchetta* commissioned by Alesso Tarchetta and installed in the left aisle of the cathedral. In its present restored state, it reveals nothing of Amadeo's original intentions. Some decorative relief fragments (Milan, Mus. Civ. Milano) from the cathedral have been associated with it. In 1473 Amadeo, his brother-in-law Lazzaro Palazzi (*fl* 1473–1508), Giovanni Giacomo Dolcebuono, Giovanni Antonio Piatti (*d* 1479) and Angelo da Lecco agreed to share the profits and losses should any of them be commissioned to execute the façade of the Certosa di Pavia. Shortly afterwards, Amadeo was engaged in this capacity by the Certosa authorities (see fig. 2). In the same year, the Carthusians stipulated another contract for work on the façade, this time with Antonio Mantegazza and his brother Cristoforo Mantegazza. Difficulties arose over the division of labour, and in 1474 Amadeo and the Mantegazza brothers agreed that each would take responsibility for half of the façade.

In 1481 the reigning Duke of Milan proposed that Amadeo should succeed his father-in-law Boniforte (or Guiniforte) Solari as chief architect of Milan Cathedral. The cathedral's deputies did not approve his nomination at this stage, however, and the position eventually went to the Austrian architect Hans Niesenberger. During the 1480s Amadeo continued working at the Certosa as well as on a number of other sculptural projects, usually collaborative. In 1480 he was engaged to complete the tomb of the *Persian Martyrs* (dispersed in the 19th century: Cremona Cathedral; Milan, Castello Sforzesco; Paris, Louvre) for Cremona Cathedral, originally commissioned from Piatti a year before his death by Antonio Meli, Abbot of S Lorenzo, Cremona. In view of the fragmentary condition of the work, Amadeo's contribution is difficult to assess. From 1482 to 1484 Amadeo worked on another project for Cremona, the tomb of *St Arealdo* (non-autograph fragments, Cremona Cathedral). During the same period he was paid by the cathedral works authorities for a relief, the marble *St Imerio Giving Alms* (now mounted in a pier to the right of the presbytery) for the front of the tomb of *St Imerio.* Amadeo's works of the early 1480s are characterized by complex compositions filled with rather thin, angular figures clad in chartaceous—that is paper-like—draperies. These qualities, particularly the drapery type, represent a departure from the style of the Colleoni tomb reliefs and have been seen as evidence of the influence on Amadeo of the Mantegazza brothers. While their importance is undeniable, they were by no means the only practitioners of this style, and it is more likely that

2. Giovanni Antonio Amadeo: detail of a window in the façade of the Certosa di Pavia, *c.* 1473

Amadeo's adaptation of it may be attributed to his extensive collaboration with Piatti.

2. From 1490. In the late 1480s and early 1490s Amadeo was employed by officials of the Duchy of Milan on a number of civil engineering projects in the Valtellina region. On 27 June 1490 Amadeo and Dolcebuono were entrusted with building the *tiburio* (completed 1500) of Milan Cathedral. Amadeo was responsible for the first of the exterior pinnacles and also performed the normal supervisory tasks of chief architect, a post he held from 1490 until his death. His solution to the problem of constructing the *tiburio* rejected the proposals of some of the most celebrated architects of the day, including Bramante, Leonardo, Francesco di Giorgio Martini, Giovanni Battagio and Luca Fancelli, returning to a modified form of the system of triangulation suggested, and in part carried out, by the mathematician Gabriele Stornaloco at the end of the 14th century. The resulting structure conforms stylistically and geometrically with the rest of the cathedral and with local construction techniques. In 1492 Amadeo's work on the altar of S Giuseppe in the cathedral, suspended since 1480, was resumed, and between 1493 and 1499 he executed a large number of sculptures for it, including a history relief; an *Adoration of the Child* that included twelve figures of children; a number of decorative relief panels, some with ducal arms; a relief panel depicting *Hercules and Antaeus*; two nymphs; a kneeling *St Joseph*; a kneeling shepherd; a kneeling child and four angels (all untraced).

During the 1490s and the first decade of the 16th century Amadeo undertook several other sculptural and architectural projects. These included work for: S Maria di Canepanuova, Pavia (from 1492); the Casa Bottigella, Pavia (from 1492); the Ospedale Maggiore, Milan (1493–4), where he was appointed general architect in 1495, although he never actually served in this capacity; the cupola of S Maria presso S Celso, Milan (from 1494); S Maurizio, Ponte in Valtellina (1495–8, completed by Tomaso Rodari and his brother Giacomo Rodari (*fl* 1487–1526)); Pavia Cathedral (from 1497); S Maria delle Grazie, Milan, and the church of the Incoronata at Lodi (from 1498); the cupola of the sanctuary at Saronno (1505); the castle in San Colombano al Lambro (1506) and S Maria alla Fontana, Milan (from 1508). Amadeo was involved in the first discussions relating to the vast cathedral of Pavia (1488) and was later appointed its engineer (1497). The design appears to be essentially that of Bramante, who initially planned a centralized structure that was altered, probably by Amadeo after 1497, by the addition of a nave and a great increase in the height of the structure.

Between 1492 and 1499 Amadeo and Antonio Mantegazza directed the decoration of the façade of the Certosa di Pavia. Among those engaged to work on this project were Benedetto Briosco, Antonio della Porta and Cristoforo Solari. Before August 1501 Amadeo completed the reliefs of the *Life of St Bruno* for the socle of the main portal, undertaken with Briosco. The ornamentation of the portal was later completed under Briosco's supervision. Probably in 1498 Amadeo received the commission to execute the tomb of *St Lanfranco* for S Lanfranco, outside Pavia. In 1508, pressed by his patron, Pietro Pallavacino da Scipione, he promised to finish it as soon as possible. In 1507 he made a model for two tombs for the funerary chapel of the family of Filippo Bottigella, and in the same year he carved a relief sculpture intended for S Fedele, Milan, commissioned by Francesco Corio.

Both the (collaborative) tomb of *St Lanfranco* and the reliefs from the portal of the Certosa are calmer and more classical than the Cremonese reliefs. The *St Lanfranco* monument may be to some extent old-fashioned, but Amadeo had, nonetheless, by this date clearly been influenced by the younger generation of sculptors he had helped to train. Some of the narrative reliefs are carved in extremely high relief, a technique later carried to its practical limits by Agostino Busti. In 1503 Amadeo, as chief architect of Milan Cathedral, presided over discussions about the design of the Porta versus Compedum, an issue never definitively settled. In 1505 he executed his last marble sculptures for the cathedral: the *Virgin and*

Child and the *Four Evangelists* for the baldacchino over the high altar (untraced). After 1512 he cut back on his routine work at the cathedral, although he oversaw the construction of a wooden model of it. In 1514 he arranged for a sum of money to be left to the cathedral on his death to be used to create dowries for the daughters of indigent stonecutters and minor sculptors and to found a school of design in the Camposanto. Amadeo's architectural career has never been studied seriously despite its vast local influence. His stature in Lombardy is indicated by the fact that he seems to have been the executive architect of the new tribune of S Maria delle Grazie, the mausoleum of Ludovico Sforza, Duke of Milan. Although the design of the interior clearly owes much to Bramante's ideas, both the interior and especially the exterior exhibit many indications of Amadeo's architectural presence and reliance on local sources, particularly S Lorenzo. Thereafter Amadeo's work as an architect is difficult to understand: the designs of the Palazzo Bottigella in Pavia and the cupola at Saronno are comprehensible in relation to the Colleoni Chapel, the façade of the Certosa and S Maria delle Grazie, but the architecture of S Maria alla Fontana (1508) contains elements, particularly the Doric arcade below, that are difficult to reconcile with what is known of his work.

BIBLIOGRAPHY

Macmillan Enc. Architects
C. Magenta: *La certosa di Pavia* (Milan, 1897)
R. Maiocchi: 'Giovanni Antonio Amadeo: Secondo i documenti negli archivi pavesi', *Boll. Soc. Pavese Stor. Patria*, iii (1903), pp. 39–80
F. Malaguzzi-Valeri: *Gio. Antonio Amadeo: Scultore e architetto lombardo (1447–1522)* (Bergamo, 1904)
U. Middeldorf: 'Ein Jungendwerk des Amadeo', *Kunstgeschichtliche Studien für Hans Kauffmann* (Berlin, 1956)
J. A. G. Bernstein: 'A Reconsideration of Amadeo's Style in the 1470s and 1480s and Two New Attributions', *A. Lombarda*, 13 (1968), pp. 33–42
——: *The Architectural Sculpture of the Cloisters of the Certosa of Pavia* (diss., New York U., 1972)
R. V. Schofield: 'Amadeo, Bramante and Leonardo and the *tiburio* of Milan Cathedral', *Achad. Leonardi Vinci: J. Leonardo Stud. & Bibliog. Vinciana*, ii (1989), pp. 68–100
R. V. Schofield, J. Shell and G. Sironi, eds: *Giovanni Antonio Amadeo: Documents/I documenti* (Como, 1989) [docs and bibliog.]
J. G. Bernstein: 'Milanese and Antique Aspects of the Colleoni Chapel: Site and Symbolism', *A. Lombarda*, 100 (1992), pp. 45–52
R. V. Schofield: 'Avoiding Rome: An Introduction to Lombard Sculptors and the Antique', *A. Lombarda*, 100 (1992), pp. 29–44
J. Shell: 'The Mantegazza Brothers, Martino Benzoni and the Colleoni Tomb', *A. Lombarda*, 100 (1992), pp. 53–60
L. Chiappa Mauri and others: *Giovanni Antonio Amadeo: Scultura e architettura del suo tempo* (Milan, 1993)

RICHARD SCHOFIELD, JANICE SHELL

Amadeus I, Duke of Savoy. *See* SAVOY §II, (1).

Amadeus VI, the 'Green Count'. *See under* SAVOY, §I(1).

Amador, Manuel E(ncarnación) (*b* Santiago de Veraguas, Panama, 25 March 1869; *d* Panama City, 12 Nov 1952). Panamanian painter and printmaker. He is known chiefly as the designer of the national flag (1903) of Panama. He studied business administration and had a long career in public office. When Panama became independent in 1903, he became Secretario de Hacienda and in 1904 Consul-General *ad-honorem* to Hamburg. In 1908 he moved to New York, where he studied with Robert Henri, who strongly influenced his style of vigorous drawing, loose brushwork, distorted expressionist images and sombre colours, as in *Head Study* (1910; Panama City, R. Miró priv. col.; see Miró). He produced most of his work between 1910 and 1914 and again after the late 1930s; his main subject was the human figure, but he also painted portraits, landscapes and still-lifes. On his return to Panama in the 1930s he worked as an auditor in the Contraloría General. After his retirement he resumed painting and produced some of his most passionate works, such as *Flowers* (*c.* 1939; Panama City, R. Ozores priv. col.; see E. Wolfschoon: *Las manifestaciones artísticas en Panamá*, Panama City, 1983, p. 447), receiving recognition as an artist only late in life. Nine days after his death, his first one-man show opened at the Universidad de Panamá, which holds the largest collection of his drawings, watercolours and etchings.

BIBLIOGRAPHY

R. Miró: *Manuel E. Amador: Un espíritu sin fronteras* (Panama City, 1966) [unpaginated]
Maestros de la plástica panameña: Manuel E. Amador (exh. cat., essay A. Herrerabarría; Panama City, U. Panama and Inst. N. Cult., 1979)

MONICA E. KUPFER

Amador de los Ríos, José (*b* Baena, Córdoba, 1 May 1818; *d* Seville, 17 Feb 1878). Spanish art historian, writer, poet and playwright. He studied the arts and humanities in Córdoba and Seville and graduated in philosophy from the Universidad Complutense de Madrid. He worked firstly as a painter but, lacking success, became a poet, publishing his verses in the journals *La Floresta andaluza* (Madrid) and *El Cisne* (Madrid), as well as in a book, *Poesías recogidas* (Seville, 1839). He later moved to Madrid, where he was given support by his friends, the distinguished Romantic writers the Duque de Ribas and Alberto Lista (1775–1848). Amador de los Ríos wrote several historical plays: *Felipe el atrevido*, *Empeño de amor y de honra* and *Don Juan de Luna*. He then entered politics and was, for a short time, a Conservative *diputado* in the Spanish parliament.

Amador de los Ríos's fame comes from his work as a historian and writer on literature and art. In his *Estudios históricos, políticos y literarios sobre los judíos en España* (Madrid, 1848) he included writings by Jews and converts (*conversos*) from the 11th to the 15th centuries, and discussed the culture of the Spanish Jews expelled in 1492. He also wrote a *Historia crítica de la literatura española* and worked on the definitive editions of the works of the historian Gonzalo de Oviedo (1478–1557) and of the poet the Marqués de Santillana (1398–1458). His first and most important contribution to Spanish art history was *Monumentos arquitectónicos de España*, written by numerous authors, whose work he supervised, and to which he also contributed texts. This huge project, begun in 1856, was interrupted in 1882, after the death of Amador de los Ríos, due to high costs. Despite the title, sculpture and gold- and silverwork are discussed, as well as architecture, from Early Christian times to the Renaissance, with particular emphasis on the Middle Ages. In 1861 he published *El arte latino-bizantino*, illustrated with beautiful plates; 'Latin-Byzantine' was the term used at the time for Early Christian and Romanesque art. These texts by Amador de los Ríos were not surpassed until the mid-20th century and continue to constitute a primary reference source.

WRITINGS

Estudios históricos, políticos y literarios sobre los judíos en España (Madrid, 1848)

El arte latino-bizantino (Madrid, 1861)

Historia crítica de la literatura española (Madrid, 1861–65)

ed.: *Monumentos arquitectónicos de España* (Madrid, 1856–82); 'Principado de Asturias', ed. J. Blas, L. Romero de Tejada Dorado and E. Urrutia de Hajos (Oviedo, 1988)

BIBLIOGRAPHY

J. Sainz Rodríguez: *Biografía de Amador de los Ríos* (Madrid, 1907)

CARLOS CID PRIEGO

Amalia von Solms, Princess of Orange. *See* ORANGE NASSAU, (4).

Amalteo, Pomponio (*b* Motta di Livenza, 1505; *d* San Vito al Tagliamento, 9 March 1588). Italian painter and draughtsman. His father's name was Leonardo, his mother was Natalia Amalteo, sister of the humanist poet Paolo Amalteo and the Latin scholar Francesco Amalteo. Probably in 1515 Pomponio entered Pordenone's workshop and is thought to have collaborated in the numerous works executed by Pordenone in Friuli between 1524 and 1529. Amalteo's first independent works were frescoes of *Virtues* inspired by Roman historical subjects for the Palazzo del Consiglio dei Nobili, Belluno (1529, destr. 1838; fragments Belluno, Mus. Civ.; Treviso, Mus. Civ. Bailo; Venice, Correr). Although the influence of Pordenone is strong, the fragments reveal an original artistic personality capable of producing compositions of classical dignity, less bold perhaps than his master but employing a more spirited and luminous range of colours.

In 1534, with his career as a panel painter well established, Amalteo married Pordenone's daughter. His earliest surviving altarpieces and panels date from around this time. After Pordenone's departure from Friuli in 1535 and his death four years later in Ferrara, Amalteo became the leading artist in Friuli, taking over his father-in-law's commissions. These included fresco decorations at the Loggia in Ceneda (1535–6), Santa Croce in Casarsa (1536–8), near Pordenone, S Maria Assunta in Lestans (1548), near Spilimbergo, the organ shutters for Valvasone Cathedral (1549) and the design for the façade of the Palazzo Comunale in Pordenone (after 1542).

Because of their close relationship, the work of Amalteo and Pordenone has often been confused. A prolific artist, Amalteo produced high-quality works until his last years. He was highly regarded by his contemporaries and received prestigious commissions, for example the frescoes for the hall of the castello at Udine (1568) and the corona over the main altar in Aquileia Cathedral (1569, destr.). Drawing was an essential stage in the production of his works, and there is a close interdependence between the paintings and the surviving drawings (e.g. Paris, Louvre; Vienna, Albertina). Notwithstanding Pordenone's influence, Amalteo absorbed new developments in both Venetian painting and central Italian Mannerism and was able to exercise a decisive influence on Friulian painting throughout the 16th century.

BIBLIOGRAPHY

Meissner; Thieme–Becker

G. Vasari: *Vite* (1550, rev. 2/1568); ed. G. Milanesi (1878–85)

F. di Maniago: *Storia delle belle arti friulane* (Udine, 1819, rev. 2/1823), pp. 65–73, 152–64

R. Zotti: *Pomponio Amalteo: Pittore del sec. XVI* (Udine, 1905)

P. Goi and F. Metz: 'Alla riscoperta del Pordenone: Ricerche sull'attività di Giovanni Antonio Pordenone in Friuli', *Noncello*, 33 (1971), pp. 119–24; 34 (1972), pp. 7–20

C. E. Cohen: 'Drawings by Pomponio Amalteo', *Master Drgs*, xi (1973), pp. 239–67

——: *I disegni di Pomponio Amalteo* (Pordenone, 1975)

P. Goi and F. Metz: 'Amalteiana', *Noncello*, 45 (1977), pp. 195–218; 48 (1979), pp. 25–60; 50 (1980), pp. 5–46; 51 (1981), pp. 173–90

Amalteo (exh. cat., ed. L. Menegazzi; Pordenone, Mus. Civ. Pal. Ricchieri and Cent. Odorico, 1980)

C. Furlan: 'Novità sull'Amalteo decoratore: Gli affreschi nel castello di Zoppola', *A. Ven.*, xxxvi (1982), pp. 204–10

PAOLO CASADIO

Aman, Theodor (*b* Cîmpulung-Muscel, 20 March 1831; *d* Bucharest, 19 Aug 1891). Romanian painter, sculptor and printmaker. After mastering the principles of painting in Craiova and Bucharest, where he studied under Constantin Lecca (1807–87) and Carol Valştein (1795–1857), he left for Paris around 1850. There he attended the studio of Michel-Martin Drolling and, after Drolling's death, that of François-Edouard Picot. In 1853 he made his public début at the Paris Salon with a *Self-portrait* (Bucharest, Mus. A. Col.). A year later he travelled to Constantinople (now Istanbul), where the Sultan bought his painting the *Battle of Olteniţa* (1854; Istanbul, Dolmabahce Pal.). Aman then went to the Crimea, where he documented the *Battle of Alma* (Bucharest, N. Mus. A.) in a painting shown at the Exposition Internationale in Paris (1855). The autumn of the same year and the spring of the following year were spent in Wallachia, where the prince, Barbu Ştirbei, honoured Aman with a minor nobiliary title and a grant to enable him to continue his studies in France. In September 1856, after an interval in Italy, he finally returned to Romania, thereafter leaving only sporadically.

In addition to his historical paintings, such as the *Chasing of the Turks at Călugareni* (1872; Bucharest, Mus. A. Col.), the majority of Aman's subjects were dedicated to the Romanian people's aspiration for independence, while more freely executed, more spontaneous and partially unfinished works, such as the *Servants of Matei-Basarab Revolting against Some Landowners* (*c*. 1872; Bucharest, Theodor Aman Mus.) and the *Landlords Taken by Surprise at a Banquet by the Emissaries of Vlad Ţepeş* (*c*. 1886; Bucharest, Mus. A.), represent aspects of the old conflicts between the prince and the landlords. Aman was also the first Romanian painter to present contemporary scenes and contemporary political events, in such canvases as the *Union Hora Dance in Craiova* (1857; Bucharest, Mus. A. Col.). He was also the first Romanian artist to dedicate himself on a large scale to genre painting, representing either interiors or *plein-air* scenes, sometimes inspired by peasant life but based mainly on observations made in his own studio and on family life. Among these is *On the Terrace at Sinaia* (1888; Bucharest, Mus. A. Col.). Other, similar paintings, especially those depicting scenes from the life of his own society, show the influence of Mariano José Bernardo Fortuny y Marsal, Mihály Munkácsy, Giuseppe De Nittis and Giovanni Boldini. Aman was also a gifted painter of portraits, painting leading national personalities, such as *Tudor Vladimirescu* (Bucharest, N. Mus. A.), the leader of the revolution of 1821, and

Princess Zoe Brancoveanu (1859; Bucharest, Mus. A.), as well as friends and relatives, such as his wife, *Ana Aman* (1863; Bucharest, Mus. A.). His portraits of women, in particular, convey tenderness, expressiveness and grace as well as sensitive colouring and tonal harmony.

Aman also insistently manifested himself as a landscape artist, especially after 1870, although his landscapes rarely succeeded in avoiding the conventional academic treatment and were often painted in the studio rather than in the *plein-air* manner favoured by the Barbizon school and the Impressionists, and, in Romania, by Nicolae Grigorescu and Ion Andreescu. Those landscapes that he did paint in the country, or in his own garden, brought with them a note of freshness and, when people appear, a picturesqueness that gives an accurate flavour of the period. *A View with Country Houses* (*c.* 1880; ex-Bucharest, Zambaccian Mus.; priv. col.), is, by the vibration of the colouring and the atmospheric effect, probably the best of Aman's landscapes. In addition to still-lifes and flower paintings, he was an active watercolourist and printmaker (particularly in 1872–81), and he was one of the first Romanian artists to execute etchings. Around 1870 Aman made some wax and plaster sculptures, at the same time occasionally creating stained glass, furniture and decorative mural paintings for the house he built in Bucharest in 1869, which is now the Theodor Aman Museum.

From 1864 until the end of his life Aman dedicated much time to governing and teaching at the Fine Arts School in Bucharest, which was founded by the government on his initiative. He was also the founder of the Museum of Art in Bucharest (inaugurated 1908), and he co-founded the first official exhibitions, forerunners of the Official Salons.

BIBLIOGRAPHY

O. W. Cisek: *Aman* (Craiova, 1931)
G. Oprescu: *Romanian Painting in the 19th Century* (Bucharest, 1937), pp. 123–36
R. Bogdan: *Theodor Aman* (Bucharest, 1955)
V. Florea: *Theodor Aman* (Bucharest, 1965)
C. Dan: *Theodor Aman* (Bucharest, 1984)

RADU BOGDAN

Aman-Jean, Edmond(-François) (*b* Chevry-Cossigny, Seine-et-Marne, 13 Nov 1858; *d* ?Paris, 1935–6). French painter, pastellist and printmaker. He studied from 1880 under the academic painter Henri Lehmann at the Ecole des Beaux-Arts in Paris; there he befriended Georges Seurat with whom he shared a studio for several years. He also studied under Pierre Puvis de Chavannes, working as his assistant on the *Sacred Grove* (1884; Lyon, Mus. B.-A.). In 1886 he obtained a travel scholarship to Rome and on his return befriended Symbolist poets such as Stéphane Mallarmé, Paul Verlaine and Philippe-Auguste Villiers de l'Isle Adam. While the poets sought to subvert language in order to express new sensations, Aman-Jean relied on pictorial and iconographic traditions. He specialized in pictures of languid young women turned in profile to the left or gazing into space, as in *Girl with Peacock* (1895; Paris, Mus. A. Déc.), using broken brushstrokes and colour contrasts that by then had largely shed their avant-garde connotations. Typical works such as the colour lithograph *Beneath the Flowers* (1897; Paris, Bib. N.) and the portrait of *Mlle Thadée C. Jacquet* (1892; Paris. Mus. d'Orsay) led the critic Camille Mauclair to identify him as an heir to the English Pre-Raphaelite Brotherhood.

Similar images were favoured by Aman-Jean in pastels such as *Woman in Pink* (*c.* 1898; Dijon, Mus. B.-A.), often in pinks, reds and violets and with a technique of thick undulating strokes. His decorative commissions included eight panels for the Musée des Arts Décoratifs in Paris (1910) and the four *Elements* for the chemistry amphitheatre at the Sorbonne (1912). He exhibited regularly at the Salon de la Société Nationale des Beaux-Arts, on whose jury he served, and in the Salons de la Rose+Croix in 1892 and 1893, designing the poster for the second show. His later work revealed the influence of Pierre Bonnard.

BIBLIOGRAPHY

'Aman-Jean graveur et lithographe: Conversation', *Rev. A.* (1926), Jan, pp. 42–6
Souvenir d'Aman-Jean (1859–1936) (exh. cat., Paris, Mus. A. Déc., 1970)
Autour de Lévy-Dhurmer (exh. cat., Paris, Grand Pal., 1973)
D. Carter: *Edmond Aman-Jean: A Study of his Life and Works* (Cincinnati, 1974)
Edmond Aman-Jean (exh. cat., London, Ferrers Gal., 1975)

VANINA COSTA

Amapa. Site of Pre-Columbian culture on the coastal plain of Nayarit, Mexico. It was probably an important regional ceremonial centre for the western Mesoamerican cultures. Although it had been extensively studied, notably by Clement Meighan, by the late 1990s an absolute chronology for the site had yet to be established. Some researchers, using obsidian hydration dates, believe that the critical Cerritos phase began *c.* 600 AD, while others, relying on radiocarbon dates and comparative materials from other sites, date this phase several centuries later (Meighan). Early occupation of Amapa may have been more sporadic than in later periods; nonetheless, large quantities of Pre-Classic period (*c.* 2000 BC–*c.* AD 250) material have been found at the site and in its immediate vicinity. Amapa apparently reached its greatest extent during the Post-Classic period (*c.* AD 900–1521), but it had been abandoned by the time of the Spanish conquest of the area by Guzmán's expedition of the 1530s. The boundaries of the site have not been absolutely determined, but a ballcourt formed an important component of the plan. Although TEOTIHUACÁN influences can be noted, the architecture at Amapa is not truly monumental; the most elaborate structures are long ridge-like platforms facing open-ended plazas. Occupation debris has been found on top of these and other platforms, and two cemeteries have also been discovered and explored. The skeletal material recovered displayed cranial deformations and tooth modifications.

Excavations in and around Amapa have given new perspectives on Mesoamerican metal technology, especially from a stylistic point of view (*see* MESOAMERICA, PRE-COLUMBIAN, §IX, 5). A wide range of copper artefacts, described by David Pendergast, were manufactured, of which various bells and thin, axe-shaped ingots are of special interest. Amapa copper-working techniques were sophisticated, and the lost-wax method was employed in the casting of elegant bells. Another highly developed craft reflected in the material culture of Amapa is the graceful polychrome pottery described by Betty Bell. The Cerritos phase saw the greatest elaboration of these widely traded high-status wares. The later Iguanas (or Roblitos) polychrome pottery is noted for its elegance, complex iconography and wide range of colours: the depictions of elaborately costumed Quetzalcóatl-like figures are exceptional. This polychrome ware was traded far into the Central Highlands in exchange for prismatic obsidian blades and other goods. Amapa and the region of Las Cuevas and ETZATLÁN in Jalisco appear to have had a special trading relationship.

For further discussion of Pre-Columbian Mexico *see* MESOAMERICA, PRE-COLUMBIAN.

BIBLIOGRAPHY

D. Pendergast: 'Metal Artifacts from Amapa, Nayarit, Mexico', *Amer. Ant.*, xxvii (1962), pp. 370–79

B. Bell: 'Archaeology of Nayarit, Jalisco and Colima', *Hb. Mid. Amer. Ind.*, xi (1971), pp. 694–753

C. Meighan: *The Archaeology of Amapa, Nayarit*, U. CA Monumenta Archaeologica, ii (Los Angeles, 1976)

PHIL C. WEIGAND

Amaral, Antonio Henrique (*b* São Paulo, 1935). Brazilian painter and printmaker. After studying engraving in São Paulo, in 1959 he moved to New York to complete his studies at the Pratt Graphic Center where his contact with international Pop art merged with his own interest in Brazilian popular imagery, for example in the portfolio of woodcuts *Mine and Yours* (1967). Immediately afterwards he began painting ambiguous and ironic still-lifes collectively titled *Brasíliana*, which use bananas as symbols of underdevelopment and exploitation, for example *BR-1 SP* (1970; São Paulo, Pin. Estado) and *Bananas* (1971; Washington, DC, Mus. Mod. A. Latin America). In 1971 he won a trip abroad in the National Salon of Modern Art (Rio de Janeiro), which took him again to New York between 1972 and 1973. On his return to São Paulo he began the series *Battlegrounds*, in which he submitted the previously reclining bananas to slashing, torture and putrefaction. Subsequently shapes were reorganized into configurations of an undramatic Surrealism, playful, colourful, tumescent and as firmly rooted as ever in his native Brazil and Latin America.

BIBLIOGRAPHY

F. Gullar: 'Antonio Henrique Amaral', *Visão da terra* (exh. cat., Rio de Janeiro, Mus. A. Mod., 1977)

Antonio Henrique Amaral—Obra em processo, 1956–1986 [Antonio Henrique Amaral—work in progress, 1956–1986] (exh. cat. by F. Morais, São Paulo, Mus. A. Mod., 1986)

Art of the Fantastic: Latin America, 1920–1987 (exh. cat. by H. Day and H. Sturges, Indianapolis, IN, Mus. A., 1987)

ROBERTO PONTUAL

Amaral, (Francisco) Keil do (*b* Lisbon, 28 April 1910; *d* Lisbon, 19 Feb 1975). Portuguese architect, theorist and writer. He studied with Carlos Ramos in the early 1930s and his first significant work was a Modernist pavilion (1937; destr.) for the Exposition Internationale des Arts et Techniques dans la Vie Moderne, Paris (1937), a commission he won in competition against Raul Lino. Influenced by contemporary Dutch architecture and urban planning, he designed Lisbon's airport (1943) at Portela and various works in the capital's parks. The latter are intimate, modernist and successfully integrated projects, for example restaurants in the Campo Grande park (1948; destr.), in the Florestal de Monsanto park (1940; altered) and in the Eduardo VII park (altered). He also designed for the same parks a municipal swimming-pool (1965), a tennis club building (1952; with Hernâni Gandra and Alberto Pessoa) and the remodelled Estufa Fria (cold house for plants) respectively. A born teacher, researcher and polemicist, Amaral formed a school of theory and practice of architecture in which he fostered the idea of cultural and social awareness as a determining factor in design. In the years following World War II he was active in politics, adhering firmly to left-wing ideas. He was the main instigator of the survey of vernacular architecture in Portugal (1956–61), carried out collectively by the professional association of architects.

WRITINGS

A arquitetura e a vida (Lisbon, 1942)

A moderna arquitetura Holandesa (Lisbon, 1943)

Lisboa: Uma cidade em transformação (Lisbon, 1970)

BIBLIOGRAPHY

J.-A. França: *A arte em Portugal no século XX* (Lisbon, 1974), pp. 244–5, 449

F. P. K. do Amaral and others: *Keil do Amaral Arquitecto, 1910–1975*, Edição Associação dos Arquitectos Portugueses (Lisbon, 1992)

JOSÉ MANUEL FERNANDES

Amaral, Tarsila do. *See* TARSILA.

Amarante, Carlos Luis Ferreira (*b* Braga, 1748; *d* Oporto, 1815). Portuguese architect and military engineer. He was the most distinguished of the late 18th-century architects of northern Portugal, where he introduced the new spirit of Neo-classicism. He was the son of a musician at the episcopal court at Braga, whose protection and influence were valuable to him. Working in Braga during a period of transition, Amarante ended the architectural tradition inherited from André Ribeiro Soares da Silva, and, although he lacked Soares's creativity, he made an important contribution to the city. Amarante's later work in Oporto was in a more developed Neo-classical style and was an integral part of the new face of that city.

Though he trained as a military engineer, his first activity was designing rocaille ornament. His source for the new aesthetic forms may have been Jacques-François Blondel's *Cours d'architecture* (Paris, 1773), lent to him by the royal archbishop, Dom Gaspar de Braganza (1716–89). His first contract, won in competition with João Bernardes de Silva, was for a design, submitted in 1781, for rebuilding the derelict early 18th-century pilgrimage church of the sanctuary of Bom Jesus do Monte, on a hillside near Braga (for illustration *see* BRAGA). The Baroque project by de Silva was rejected in favour of Amarante's Neo-classical design, indicating the Archbishop's acceptance of the new style. Built between 1784 and 1811, the façade of the church, crowned with a triangular pediment, filled with carved reliefs of the symbols of the Passion, stands at the top of a long pilgrimage garden linked by terraces and staircases, the last stages of which were designed by Amarante.

Amarante designed the façade for the church of the Augustinian Colegio de S Maria do Pópulo, built in Braga between 1775 and 1780. It is notable for its simple lines and panels, and for the effective way in which Ionic columns and pilasters frame the great central arched window. The triangular pediment is placed between the towers, whose cupolas, with their curving forms, are in the Baroque tradition.

The church of S Marcos, Braga, designed in 1787 by Amarante, has a convex curved façade, flanked on either side by connecting buildings, that although elegant shows ambiguities and lack of definition. Amarante's knowledge of Neo-classicism was advanced when he visited Lisbon briefly, some time in the last years of the century, and saw the rebuilding following the 1755 earthquake that had been carried out in the restrained Pombaline style, basic forms of which were the foundation of Neo-classicism in Portugal. It is probable that in Lisbon Amarante met José da Costa e Silva, who was at the time preparing plans for the important Italianate Neo-classical Royal Palace of Ajuda (begun 1802).

From 1801 Carlos Amarante settled in Oporto where, through the presence of the English community, he had access to Neo-classical engravings. The English played a fundamental role in the rebuilding and development taking place in the city, where from 1769 the Palladian building to house the Hospital de Santo António, using plans obtained from John Carr of York, was being constructed. In 1803 Amarante designed the Oporto church and monastery for the Order of Trinitarians. The Igreja da Trinidade was not completed until the end of the century, and Amarante's plan was later altered by João Francisco Guimarães. Some details of the design show Amarante's use of elegant Neo-classical forms, but the completed work appears heavy, with a cupola that is ill-proportioned and a central tower that does not harmonize with the overall horizontality.

In 1807 Amarante modified the 1803 plans of José da Costa e Silva for the Academia Real de Marinha e Comércio (now part of the University of Oporto), his most important Neo-classical work. The lower storey of the façade is rusticated in Palladian style, and the principal storey has a Classical colonnade composed of half columns surmounted by a pediment. In his capacity as military engineer, Amarante built the famous Bridge of Boats across the River Douro at Oporto, which was destroyed during the French invasion in 1809.

BIBLIOGRAPHY

F. Castiço: *Memória histórica do Santuário do Bom Jesus do Monte* (Braga, 1884)

A. Feio: *Uma figura nacional: Carlos Amarante* (Braga, 1951)

J.-A. França: *A arte em Portugal no século XIX* (Lisbon, 1966)

JOSÉ FERNANDES PEREIRA

Amarapura. City in upper Burma on the Irrawaddy River, 11 km south of Mandalay. It was the capital of the Burmese kings of the Konbaung dynasty from 1782, the year of its foundation, to 1823 and again from 1837 to 1860. It was built on a strictly square plan, surrounded by a wall and a moat. Each side of the wall measured 1.6 km and had three gates leading into the main streets that divided the city into equal square blocks, with a great wooden palace at its centre. The palace was dismantled in 1857, and its materials reused to build the new royal capital, Mandalay.

The major monuments of Amarapura are located outside this central square. They include the Naga-yon Temple with its superstructure in the form of a gigantic guardian serpent; the large Kyauk-taw-gyi Temple built in 1847 on the model of the Ananda at Pagan, and famous for its mural paintings depicting scenes of daily life; the tall Pahto-daw-gyi Stupa (1820); the smaller Than-bodde-phaya Stupa built in 1782, with its sides covered by regular tiers of hundreds of small niches, each housing an image of the Buddha (*see* BURMA, fig. 9); and the tombs of the city's founder, King Bodawpaya (*reg* 1781–1819) and his grandson and successor, Bagyidaw (*reg* 1819–38). In addition, numerous small temples and stupas, mostly dating from the 19th century, are scattered around the city. These give a good idea of the architects' various experiments with forms and designs.

BIBLIOGRAPHY

H. Yule: *A Narrative of the Mission Sent by the Governor-General of India to the Court of Ava in 1855* (London, 1858/*R* Kuala Lumpur, 1968)

V. C. Scott O'Connor: *Mandalay and Other Cities of the Past in Burma* (London, 1907/*R* Bangkok, 1987)

Taw Sein Ko: 'The Sangyaung Monasteries of Amarapura', *Archaeol. Surv. India Annu. Rep. 1914–15* (1920), pp. 56–65

U Aung Thaw: *Historical Sites in Burma* (Rangoon, 1972/*R* 1978)

U Kan Hla [S. Ozhegov]: 'Traditional Town Planning in Burma', *J. Soc. Archit. Hist.*, xxxvii/2 (1978), pp. 92–104

PIERRE PICHARD

Amaravati [Amarāvatī]. Site near the ancient city of Dharanikota on the right bank of the Krishna River in Guntur District, Andhra Pradesh, India, that flourished from the 3rd century BC to the 14th century AD. It is also the location of a modern town, but the site is celebrated for its stupa, which may have been the earliest Buddhist foundation in the region and which certainly came to be its largest and most elaborate. It was rediscovered in 1799 as a ruined but largely intact mound by Colonel Colin Mackenzie, first Surveyor General of India. His work in that year and in 1816 led to the excavations conducted in 1845 by Walter Elliot of the Madras Civil Service. Most of the sculptures now in the British Museum, London, were excavated at that time, although part of the Elliot collection remains in the Government Museum, Madras. Unfortunately, between the rediscovery of the stupa and these early excavations, much damage was done to it, with limestone slabs being quarried for building materials by the local residents. The stupa was further excavated in 1877 by Robert Sewell and again in 1881 by James Burgess, following a general clearance of the site ordered by the Governor of Madras in 1880. Alexander Rea also dug at Amaravati in 1889 and in the early 1900s; material from these excavations is for the most part in the Government Museum, Madras. The Archaeological Survey of India conducted excavations from the 1950s to the 1970s, with the results of their work being deposited in the Archaeological Museum, Amaravati.

The Great Stupa (Pkt *mahācētiya*) at Amaravati may have been established during the reign of the emperor Ashoka (*reg c.* 269–*c.* 232 BC). Its simplest and earliest form is illustrated in an engraving on an early railing crossbar from the site (Amaravati, Archaeol. Mus.), which shows a plain dome on a platform surrounded by an undecorated railing. Subsequently, a railing with uprights of polished granite joined by four sets of limestone crossbars and probably capped by a limestone coping was erected. By the 1st and 2nd centuries AD this granite railing seems to have been replaced by a simple limestone railing decorated on the inner side with reliefs similar to those on the verandah pilasters of Cave 3 at Nasik. The name of Sri Vasishthiputra Pulumavi, probably the first king of the SATAVAHANA dynasty who established their rule in the Andhra country in the 1st or 2nd century AD, appears in inscriptions on the Great Stupa. During his time the monument began to be refurbished and rebuilt; in particular, the great railing was increased in size and covered on both faces with elaborate relief sculpture, both narrative and decorative. During this refurbishment, which took place over perhaps two centuries, many relief slabs were reused in various ways: one slab originally carved in a style analogous to the gateways at SANCHI (London, BM, 1880.7–9.79) was subsequently carved with another relief on the reverse side.

In its final and most elaborate form (see fig.) the monument (total diam. 59 m) comprised a large dome-shaped mound set on a platform surrounded by a limestone railing, which created a processional pathway (Skt *pradakṣiṇāpatha*) around the stupa. Four entrances, one at each of the cardinal points, consisted of short passages created by simple extensions of the railing. These entrances were guarded by stone lions mounted at their inner and outer ends, while inside, projecting platforms once carried free-standing pillars (*ayakā stambha*) arranged in groups of five. Depictions of the stupa in its reliefs also indicate that pillars surmounted by stupa models were placed around the circumambulatory path and outside the entrances.

The railing was decorated on the outer face with a complex pattern of lotuses and dancing dwarfs. The inner face had a central series of narrative roundels with lotus medallions above and below; the intervening spaces on the uprights were also carved with narrative vignettes. The crossbars joining the pillars were all carved with lotuses on their outer faces; their inner faces were the same, except that the middle crossbars had narrative scenes. The outer face of the stupa platform was adorned with limestone slabs carved with images of the stupa, each separated from the next by a narrow pilaster. This series was capped by a narrative frieze depicting episodes from the life of the Buddha and tales of his previous incarnations (*jātaka* stories; *see* BUDDHISM, figs 1 and 4). Attached to the lower part of the stupa dome was a series of tall limestone slabs divided into three registers, each containing a depiction of a stupa, tree or wheel. Above these slabs was a row of running animals below a band of *triratna* emblems symbolizing the 'three jewels' of Buddhism: the Buddha, the Dharma (teachings) and the Sangha (spiritual community). At the summit of the dome was a small railed pavilion (*harmikā*) from the centre of which projected a short pillar that may have supported one or more stone parasols. However, the final form of the stupa was not as coherent as the relief depictions would suggest, since a number of early uprights and crossbars were incorporated into the later reconstruction.

No major work on the stupa seems to have been undertaken after the fall of the Satavahanas in the mid-3rd century AD: the last known reference is in an inscription at Gadaladeniya in Sri Lanka, dated to AD 1344, in which the monk Dharmakirtti refers to a donation for the restoration of an image house at the site. Even before that

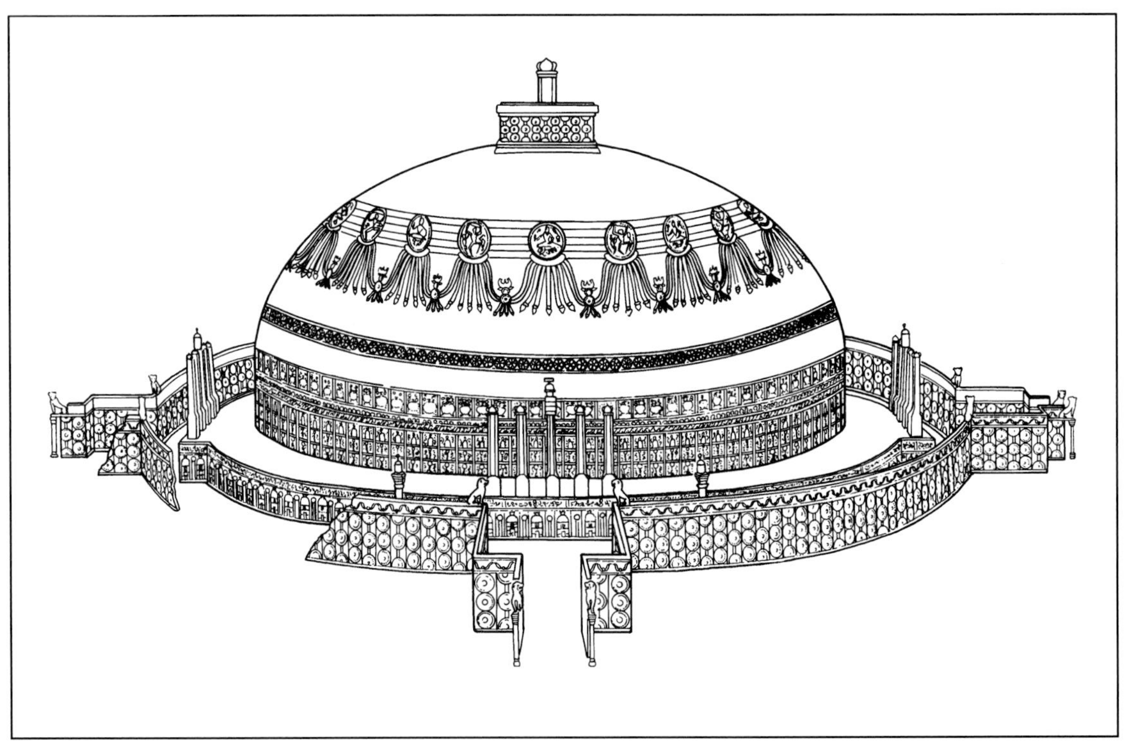

Amaravati, conjectural reconstruction of the Great Stupa, 3rd century BC–14th century AD (London, British Museum)

time, non-Buddhists were present, as evidenced by the late 10th-century Hindu Amareshvara Temple. The modern town of Amaravati was founded in the late 18th century by a local landowner who moved his people to the vicinity of the temple.

See also INDIAN SUBCONTINENT, §IV, 4(v) and 5(vi).

BIBLIOGRAPHY

L. Tripe: *Photographs of the Elliot Marbles and other Subjects in the Central Museum Madras* (Bangalore, 1859)

C. Sivaramamurti: 'Amaravati Sculptures in the Madras Government Museum', *Bull. Madras Govt Mus.*, iv (1942), pp. 1–343

D. Barrett: *Sculptures from Amaravati in the British Museum* (London, 1954)

H. Sarkar and S. P. Nainar: *Amaravati* (New Delhi, 1972, 2/1980)

R. Knox: *Amaravati, Buddhist Sculpture from the Great Stupa* (London, 1992) [cat. of the British Museum col.]

ROBERT KNOX

Amarna, (Tell) el- [anc. Akhetaten]. Site of an Egyptian city of the mid-14th century BC, on the eastern bank of the Nile, *c.* 90 km north of Asyut. The site, which has given its name to the AMARNA STYLE of art, was chosen by the 18th Dynasty king AKHENATEN (*reg c.* 1353–*c.* 1336 BC) for his new capital, which temporarily replaced Memphis and Thebes as the nucleus of the Egyptian empire. It was dedicated to the solar god Aten, thus its ancient name Akhetaten ('Horizon of the Aten'), whose cult was intended to replace worship of the traditional Egyptian pantheon. The city was occupied for no more than 25 years, from the fifth year of Akhenaten's reign until some time in the reign of Tutankhamun (*reg c.* 1332–*c.* 1323 BC). Because of this relatively brief period of occupation and the lack of prior and subsequent settlement, the site is a rare example of ancient Egyptian urban planning. It was excavated by William Flinders Petrie (1891–2), Ludwig von Borchardt (1907 and 1911–14) and a series of British archaeologists in the 1920s and 1930s; work has continued into the 1990s on behalf of the Egyptian Exploration Society. At least a third of the site remains unexcavated, but the 'Workmen's Village'—a small outlying walled settlement perhaps occupied by guards or tomb-workers—and the Temple of Kom el-Nana were meticulously examined in the 1980s (see fig. (a) and (b)).

Akhetaten covers an area of *c.* 10 sq. km, set within a semicircular bay of limestone cliffs; much of its western side lies beneath modern cultivation. The main street, known as Sikket el-Sultan, ran from the administrative buildings at the northern tip of the city to the Maru-Aten, an unusual type of temple incorporating gardens, pools and 'sun-shade' pavilions, in the south (see fig. (c)). The Central City (see fig. (d)), called the 'Island of Aten Distinguished in Jubilees', consisted of two temples (the Per Aten and the Hwt Aten), public administrative buildings and bakeries and a vast palace linked by a bridge across the main street to a building known as the King's House. Under the floor of one of the central administrative blocks were found nearly 350 clay tablets—now scattered among several museum collections (e.g. Cairo, Egyp. Mus.; London, BM; Paris, Louvre)—bearing the cuneiform correspondence between Near Eastern rulers and the Egyptian kings of the Amarna period. These Amarna Letters are one of the most important historical sources for the

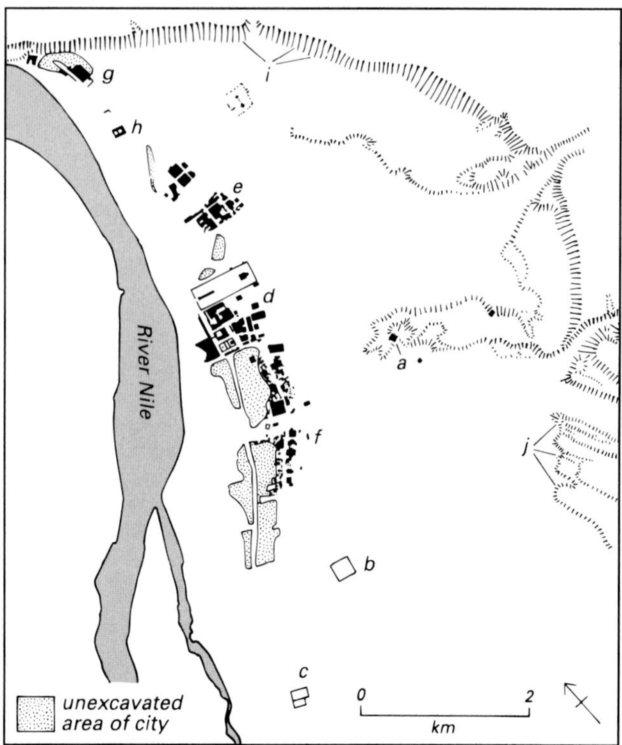

El-Amarna, mid-14th century BC, plan: (a) Workmen's Village; (b) Kom el-Nana; (c) Maru-Aten; (d) Central City; (e) North Suburb; (f) South Suburb; (g) North City; (h) North Palace; (i) North Tombs; (j) South Tombs

study of contemporary foreign policy and diplomacy in the New Kingdom, providing many links between the chronologies of Egypt and the Ancient Near East.

The residential areas of the main city were split into three basic sections, which the excavators called the North and South Suburbs (see fig. (e) and (f)) and the North City (see fig. (g)). The impressive residences of the South Suburb were invariably surrounded by walled gardens with trees, pools, granaries and sometimes a private shrine to the Aten, while the smaller houses of craftsmen and artisans gradually filled up the spaces between them. As the city grew, more specialized areas evolved, particularly in the North Suburb. The Amarna houses and their contents constitute one of the primary archaeological sources of evidence for domestic architecture and daily life in the New Kingdom (*see* EGYPT, ANCIENT, §VIII, 4(vi)).

Many examples of painting and sculpture in the Amarna style have been excavated throughout the city. Inside the King's House, Petrie discovered part of a delicately executed wall painting showing two of Akhenaten's daughters (now Oxford, Ashmolean). Excavations in many of the ceremonial buildings have also revealed numerous fragments of brightly painted walls and floors, including vine-covered pillars in the Coronation Hall and vigorous friezes of plants and birds on the walls of the Green Room in the North Palace (now Cairo, Egyp. Mus., and Oxford, Ashmolean; see fig. (h)). Several sculptors' studios have been excavated, providing some of the finest items of

Amarna statuary. The studio of THUTMOSE, in the South Suburb, contained the famous life-size painted limestone bust of Akhenaten's queen, NEFERTITI (Berlin, Ägyp. Mus.), as well as many fragments of unfinished sculptures and a set of plaster casts of faces, probably used by the sculptors as models.

The stone-built temples in the Central City were dismantled as early as the reign of Horemheb (*c.* 1319–*c.* 1292 BC); many of their distinctive, small relief-carved limestone blocks (*talatat*) were reused as fill in a Ramessid pylon at nearby Hermopolis Magna (e.g. New York, Brooklyn Mus.; Boston, MA, Mus. F.A.; and New York, Schimmel priv. col.). Although only the foundations and a few fragments of sculpture have survived *in situ*, these have been sufficient to allow the buildings' original appearance to be reconstructed (*see* EGYPT, ANCIENT, §VIII, 2(i)(a)).

Two groups of rock-cut private tombs belonging to courtiers, at the northern and southern ends of the cliffs (see fig. (i) and (j); *see also* EGYPT, ANCIENT, fig. 29), were decorated with Amarna-style wall paintings, which have provided numerous details concerning life at Akhetaten. The Royal Tomb, *c.* 6 km east of the Amarna plain, contained a few badly damaged reliefs and fragmentary items of funerary equipment (Cairo, Egyp. Mus.) but no trace of the mummies of the Amarna royal family.

BIBLIOGRAPHY

U. Bouriant: *Deux jours de fouilles à Tell el-Amarna* (Paris, 1884)
W. M. F. Petrie: *Tell el-Amarna* (London, 1894)
N. de G. Davies: *The Rock Tombs of El-Amarna*, 6 vols (London, 1903–08)
T. E. Peet and others: *The City of Akhenaten*, 3 vols (London, 1923–51)
H. Frankfort: *The Mural Painting of El-Amarna* (London, 1929)
S. A. B. Mercer: *The Tell El-Amarna Tablets*, 2 vols (Toronto, 1939)
A. Badawy: 'Maru-Aten: Pleasure Resort or Temple?', *J. Egyp. Archaeol.*, xlii (1956), pp. 58–64
J. D. Cooney: *Amarna Reliefs from Hermopolis in American Collections* (New York, 1965)
L. Moller: *Ägyptische Kunst aus der Zeit des Königs Echnaton* (Hamburg, 1965)
G. Roeder: *Amarna-Reliefs aus Hermopolis* (Hildesheim, 1969)
J. Assmann: 'Palast oder Tempel? Überlegungen zur Architektur und Topographie von Amarna', *J. Nr E. Stud.*, xxxi (1972), pp. 143–55
G. T. Martin: *The Royal Tomb at Amarna*, 2 vols (London, 1974–89)
B. J. Kemp: 'The Window of Appearance at El-Amarna and the Basic Structure of this City', *J. Egyp. Archaeol.*, lxii (1976), pp. 81–99
R. Hanke: *Amarna-Reliefs aus Hermopolis: Neue Veröffentlichungen und Studien* (Hildesheim, 1978)
B. J. Kemp: *Amarna Reports* (London, 1983–)
L. Borchardt and H. Ricke: *Die Wohnhäuser in Tell el-Amarna* (Berlin, 1984)
P. T. Crocker: 'Status-symbols in the Architecture of El-Amarna', *J. Egyp. Archaeol.*, lxxi (1985), pp. 52–65
C. Aldred: *Akhenaten: King of Egypt* (London, 1988)

Amarna style. Ancient Egyptian art style that takes its name from EL-AMARNA, the site of the capital city during the reigns of AKHENATEN (*reg c.* 1353–*c.* 1336 BC) and Smenkhkare (*reg c.* 1335–*c.* 1332 BC). Amarna-style painting and sculpture were characterized by a move away from the traditional idealism of Egyptian art towards a greater realism and artistic freedom. This new sense of vigour and naturalism is most apparent in surviving fragments of paintings from the walls and floors of palaces (Cairo, Egyp. Mus., and Oxford, Ashmolean; *see* EGYPT, ANCIENT, §X, 2). The statuary and reliefs, mainly from el-Amarna, Thebes and Hermopolis Magna, represent the royal family and their subjects in a style that was initially grotesque and often crude, as the artists struggled to come to terms with the new approach (*see* EGYPT, ANCIENT, §IX, 3(viii)). However, they eventually reached a high degree of sophistication and beauty, exemplified by the painted limestone bust of Queen NEFERTITI (Berlin, Ägyp. Mus.) from el-Amarna.

BIBLIOGRAPHY

C. Aldred: *Akhenaten: King of Egypt* (London, 1988)
M. Müller: *Die Kunst Amenophis' III und Echnatons* (Basle, 1988)

IAN M. E. SHAW

Amasis Painter. *See* VASE PAINTERS, §II.

Amastini [Mastini]. Italian family of gem-engravers. Angelo Antonio Amastini (*b* Fossombrone, the Marches, 1754; *d* after 1816) and his son Niccolò Amastini (*b* Rome, 1780; *d* Rome, 1851) worked in Rome; they may also have been active in Florence. A gem-engraver known as Angelo Tesei Mastini could possibly be the same person as Angelo Antonio Amastini. Carlo de Giovanni Amastini (*d* 1824) from Fossombrone was also a gem-engraver, but his relationship to Angelo Antonio Amastini and Niccolò Amastini is unknown. He was active in Berlin, where he taught gem-cutting and was a member of the Akademie der Künste. Surviving examples of work by the Amastini family include onyx cameos of *Cupid and Psyche* and of *Psyche*, signed A. MASTINI (both London, BM), of a woman's head, signed AMASTINI (Vienna, Ksthist. Mus.) and the *Education of Bacchus*, signed N. AMASTINY in Greek letters (New York, Met.). Their workshop in Rome also made series of casts of their own and others' stones, including the work of the Pichler family and Nathaniel Marchant.

BIBLIOGRAPHY

F. Eichler and E. Kris: *Die Kameen im Kunsthistorischen Museum* (Vienna, 1927)
C. G. Bulgari: *Argentieri, gemmari e orafi d'Italia: Notizie storiche e raccolta dei loro contrassegni con la riproduzione grafica dei punzoni individuali e dei punzoni di stato*, 5 vols (Rome, 1958–74)

□

Amasya [anc. Amaseia]. Turkish town in northern Anatolia. Situated in a ravine on both banks of the Yeşilırmak (Iris) River, it served as capital of the kingdom of Pontus during Hellenistic times, and the rock-cut tombs of the Pontic kings are set below the citadel. An important Roman metropolis and a Byzantine bishopric and army base, it fell to the SALJUQ dynasty of Anatolia in 1075. Notable buildings from the medieval period include the Burmalı Minare ('spiral minaret') Mosque (1237–46; derelict); the Gök Madrasa (1266–7) and adjacent tomb (1278), built by the governor Sayf al-Din Turumtay; a hospital (1309); and several other tombs. In the early 14th century the city passed to the Uighur chief Eretna. In 1386 it was conquered by the Ottomans, for whom it served until the end of the 17th century as a princely residence and provincial centre, known for its educational institutions. Buildings from the early Ottoman period include the Sufi convent (Turk. *tekke*) of Pir İlyas (1400–25), the mosques of Bayezid Pasha (1419), Yürgüç Pasha (1428) and Mehmet Pasha (1486) and the covered market (Turk. *bedesten*; 1483). The most important is the complex (1486) built by HAYREDDIN for Bayezid II (*reg* 1481–1512). Built around a small park, it included a U-shaped madrasa, an L-shaped group of buildings containing a soup-kitchen and library, hostels and a mosque covered by two domes. Repeatedly devastated by earthquakes, Amasya nevertheless preserves traditional houses, which make it one of the most picturesque towns in Turkey.

BIBLIOGRAPHY

Enc. Islam/2

A. Gabriel: *Monuments turcs d'Anatolie*, 2 vols (Paris, 1934)

G. Goodwin: *A History of Ottoman Architecture* (London, 1971), pp. 77–83, 151–6, 437–9

P. Kappert: *Die osmanischen Prinzen und ihre Residenz Amasya im 15. und 16. Jahrhundert* (Istanbul, 1976)

LALE H. ULUÇ

Amat (y Junyent), Manuel (de) (*b* Barcelona, 1704; *d* 1782). Spanish architect, engineer and administrator, active in Peru. He was the second son of the Marquis de Castellbell and received military training at an early age. He served as Spanish governor in Chile (1755–61), acquiring a reputation there as a fortifications expert. In 1761 he was appointed Viceroy of Peru, where he launched a vast campaign of public works (*see* PERU, §III, 1). During his administrative term, which lasted until 1776, the city of Lima enjoyed a period of prosperity and splendour marked by the French Baroque taste favoured by the Spanish Court. The evidence strongly suggests that Amat was the designer of several monuments in Lima that were executed by the *alarife* (surveyor and inspector of works) Juan de la Roca, who may have also collaborated in the elaboration of some of the plans. Amat's masterpiece was the church of Las Nazarenas (consecrated 1771; *see* PERU, §III, 1), with a scenographic interior influenced by Ferdinando Galli Bibiena, who had worked in Barcelona. Other major works attributed to him include the *camarín* or chapel of the Virgin (1774) behind the main altar of the church of La Merced, the belfry tower (1775) of the church of S Domingo and a chapel (*c*. 1775) in the convent of Las Mercedarias, all in Lima. In addition, the Paseo de Aguas (begun 1770; formerly La Navona), Lima, which was a rare example of Baroque urban design in the district of Rímac, may have been conceived by Amat himself. He sent designs for the Palacio de la Virreina (begun 1772), Barcelona, back to Spain. It is distinguished by a restrained façade articulated by colossal pilasters over a rusticated base set off by a balustraded roof-line borne on consoles and punctuated by heavy stone vases.

BIBLIOGRAPHY

E. Harth-Terré: '¿Dibujó realmente el Virrey Amat lo que se le atribuye?', *Cult. Peru.*, i (1941), pp. 17–18

V. Rodríguez Casado and F. Pérez Embid: *Construcciones militares del Virrey Amat* (Seville, 1949)

A. Sáenz-Rico Urbina: *El Virrey Amat*, 2 vols (Barcelona, 1967)

HUMBERTO RODRÍGUEZ-CAMILLONI

Amateur Photographic Exchange Club. *See* EXCHANGE CLUB.

Amathus [Amathous]. Site of an ancient city on the south coast of Cyprus, *c*. 10 km east of Limassol, that flourished chiefly from the 11th century BC, when it was founded, to Roman times. Greek sources of the 4th century BC claimed that its inhabitants were descendants of the companions of Kinyras, a semi-legendary Cypriot king, or called them 'autochthons' (that is, neither Greek nor Phoenician settlers). Archaeological discoveries have confirmed that the still undeciphered Eteocypriot language was indeed in use in this small kingdom until the end of the 4th century BC.

In the 10th century BC Amathus established links with the Aegean world, which became stronger, especially in relation to Euboia and Attica, at the end of the 9th century BC and during the 8th. The Phoenicians must have been involved in the development of the town during this period (*see also* CYPRUS, §II, 1(iii)). Amathus seems to have continued to prosper throughout the 7th and 6th centuries BC, reaching its apogee in the 5th century BC after the local king had remained loyal to the Persians during the Ionian Revolt (499–498 BC). The buildings of this period have almost entirely disappeared, but some magnificent tombs built of ashlar masonry show the wealth of the princes of Amathus, as do the sculpted monuments. The two large stone vases that stood in the Sanctuary of Aphrodite Kypria on the acropolis are the most impressive known from Cyprus (7th century BC; one now at Paris, Louvre; one fragment of the other preserved *in situ*). A sculpted sarcophagus (*c*. 480 BC; New York, Met.) is also important for the quality of its workmanship and the originality of its iconography. A large capital bearing a carved and coloured representation of the head of the Egyptian goddess Hathor, who was associated with Aphrodite at Amathus, is another fine example of the adaptation of the Archaic Greek style to local religious traditions (*c*. 480 BC; Limassol, Distr. Mus.). Also of note is a series of vases decorated with scenes that must have had a religious significance, executed in the so-called Amathus style influenced by Greek art.

From the 4th century BC onwards the importance of Amathus declined, although the Sanctuary of Aphrodite was still a centre of worship: in the 2nd century BC the goddess came to be associated with Isis, and a large group of terracotta figurines (Limassol, Distr. Mus.) reveals the various ways in which the two goddesses were represented. Towards the end of the 1st century AD a monumental temple (32×15.5 m) was built in the Sanctuary of Aphrodite, which was then held to be one of the most venerable in Cyprus. It is essentially Greek in appearance, but is remarkable for the form of its capitals, which are of the type known as Nabataean, from their use at Petra and Bosra (*see also* CYPRUS, §II, 2(iv)). In the 3rd century AD a vast complex, probably of a religious nature, was built at the foot of the acropolis. Finds from it include some large statues based on representations of the Egyptian god Bes (Limassol, Distr. Mus.), which, together with a specimen found elsewhere at Amathus (Istanbul, Archaeol. Mus.), are evidence of a last revival of artistic independence.

During the Early Christian period several churches were built in the town but were probably destroyed in the Arab raids of the mid-7th century AD. The site of Amathus appears to have been abandoned towards the end of the 7th century.

BIBLIOGRAPHY

Amathonte, 4 vols (Paris, 1981–8)

V. Karageorghis, O. Picard and C. Tytgat, eds: *La Nécropole d'Amathonte*, 6 vols (Nikosia, 1987–92)

A. Hermary: 'Les Fouilles françaises d'Amathonte/The French Excavations at Amathus', *Kinyras: L'Archéologie française à Chypre/French Archaeology in Cyprus* (Lyon and Paris, 1993), pp. 167–93

A. HERMARY

Amati, Carlo (*b* Monza, 22 Aug 1776; *d* Milan, 23 May 1852). Italian architect and writer. He studied architecture at the Accademia di Brera, Milan, under Giuseppe Zanoia (1752–1817), the Accademia's secretary, and later taught there himself. At the beginning of his career he was involved in the hurried completion (1806–13) of the façade of Milan Cathedral, which was carried out under the direction and with the collaboration of Zanoia. Napoleon's order that the façade should be completed economically determined the execution of the work, which was carried out in a simple Gothic style derived from the cathedral's aisles, and it was later judged to be deficient on a number of counts, including its workmanship. The church of S Carlo al Corso (1838–47) in Milan was Amati's most significant building. Here he grafted 16th-century motifs on to a centralized Roman plan in such a way as to recall both the Pantheon in Rome and the circular Milanese church of S Sebastiano, as well as Bramantesque models and the buildings frequently seen in the backgrounds of Renaissance paintings. The design for the church was part of a proposal (largely unexecuted) to reorder the entire centre of the city. Amati proposed that a vast arcaded square be opened up around the cathedral and that the Corsia dei Servi (now Corso Vittorio Emanuele) should be straightened to lead up to S Carlo, where another piazza, relating architecturally to the church, was proposed. At the time when eclecticism was spreading in Italy and overturning accepted criteria of artistic quality, Amati advocated a return to Vitruvian principles. To this end he produced a series of publications devoted to Vignola, Vitruvius, Roman antiquities in Milan, and on archaeology. The completion of the church of S Carlo and Amati's death, however, marked the end of the Neo-classical movement in Italy.

WRITINGS

Gli ordini di architettura del Barozzi da Vignola (Milan, 1805)
Apologia di Vitruvio Pollione (Milan, 1821)
Dell'architettura di Marco Vitruvio Pollione libri dieci (Milan, 1829–30)

BIBLIOGRAPHY

P. A. Curti: 'Carlo Amati', *G. Ingeg., Architetto & Agron.*, iv (1856–7), pp. 602–14
C. L. V. Meeks: *Italian Architecture, 1750–1914* (New Haven and London, 1966), pp. 174–7
G. Mezzanotte: *Architettura neoclassica in Lombardia* (Naples, 1966), pp. 387–416 [with further bibliography]
R. Middleton and D. Watkin: *Architettura moderna* (Milan, 1977), pp. 300, 303, 417, 449

GIANNI MEZZANOTTE

Amato, Giacomo (*b* Palermo, 1643; *d* Palermo, 1732). Italian architect. He was called to Rome in the 1670s by his Order, the Padri Ministri degl'Infermi, to work first as an assistant to Carlo Bizzaccheri then as supervisor on the enlargement of the convent of the Crociferi. Returning to Palermo by 1685, he produced work that showed Roman influences. His studies for the façade of the monumental church of La Pietà (1678–1723), with which he became associated in the late 1680s, fuse elements from S Andrea della Valle and Girolamo Rainaldi's S Maria in Campitelli, both in Rome. While subduing the horizontal plasticity of the Roman façades, however, Amato intensified the vertical stress of his own: his free-standing superimposed columns are placed at the sides like a partially drawn-back screen, an effect enhanced by his use of the contrasting colours of tufa and Billiemi limestone. The façade's circular window, a clear medieval reference, is characteristically Sicilian and distinguishes the building from contemporary Roman design. The interior decoration (1690s) is striking for its use of vernacular forms and such gilded metalwork as the nun's grille at the west end, which rises like an elaborate fan into the grand barrel vault. The discrepancy between the broad lower and narrow upper storeys of S Teresa alla Kalsa (1686–1706), Palermo, allows the chapel lanterns to appear beside the volutes, an unorthodox idea. The cold and formal interior (begun 1702), on a standard plan for a convent church, shows no concessions to vernacular taste in either architectural articulation or decorative detail. Together with the stuccoist Giacomo Serpotta and the painter Antonio Grano (1660–1718), Amato created the most influential interiors of late 17th- and early 18th-century Palermo. The decoration of the oratory of S Lorenzo (1699–1707) is characteristic in its use of *teatrini*, scenes from the lives of the saints, made with small allegorical figures developed from a Sicilian tradition. He also designed a number of palaces and their interiors, including the Branciforte *Casino* and the Cutò (begun 1705), Tarallo and Spaccaforno palaces. Only drawings and plans of these survive (Palermo, Gal. Reg. Sicilia). The rooms are decorated with gilded and tinted stucco vaults, marble mirrors and gilded wood, producing an overall effect close to that of Amato's church interiors.

UNPUBLISHED SOURCES

Palermo, Gal. Reg. Sicilia [*Studi ed opere fatte in Palermo*, six vols of drawings]

BIBLIOGRAPHY

L. Biagi: 'Giacomo Amato e la sua posizione nell'architettura palermitana', *L'Arte*, xlii (1939), pp. 29–48
A. Blunt: *Sicilian Baroque* (London, 1968)
D. Garstang: *Giacomo Serpotta and the Stuccatori of Palermo* (London, 1984)

Amato, Paolo (*b* Ciminna, 24 Jan 1634; *d* Palermo, 3 July 1714). Italian architect, writer and painter. He trained as a priest in Palermo and entered the Padri Ministri degl'Infermi. Another member of this Order was Giacomo Amato, with whom he worked, although they were not related. While serving as a chaplain Amato studied geometry, architecture, optics and engraving. His earliest known artistic work is a painting on copper of the *Miracle of S Rosalia* (1663), the patron saint of Palermo. After 1686 he created many works of an ephemeral character. For the feasts of S Rosalia and for important political events he provided designs for lavish triumphal chariots, probably developed from those by Jacques Callot, triumphal arches and other ceremonial apparatus set up on principal roads and piazzas, and he painted hangings, papier-mâché models and massive altarpieces for the cathedral. These works influenced Amato's permanent architecture. The spiral columns of the campanile of S Giuseppe dei Teatini, Palermo, recall the festival designs of 1686 for the cathedral (*see* PALERMO, fig. 2); the Garaffo Fountain (1698; moved 1862), the Ramondetta tomb in S Domenico (1691) and the portal and stuccowork of the oratory of SS Pietro e

Paolo (1697–8) share the imagery of the ceremonial designs. Amato's SS Salvatore (1682–1704), for the Basilian Order, is one of the few centrally planned churches in Sicily. Its plan, based on Carlo Rainaldi's S Maria di Montesanto (1661–late 1670s), Rome, is an irregular octagon with deep indentations on each axis. The complexity of the plan dissolves into the simplicity of the oval cupola base. The façade is crammed with an assortment of windows and elaborate niches, terminating in a triple Sicilian belfry. Although he was acquainted with Roman Baroque forms, Amato preferred the intricate complexity of the Sicilian vernacular. In 1687 Amato was elected Architect to the Senate of Palermo, and he designed the portal (1691) and the coronation tablet (1713) of Victor Amadeus II in Palazzo Senatorio. Most of his work, however, was for the Church. Amato began his *La nuova pratica di prospettiva* in 1701, but it was published posthumously by Giuseppe di Miceli in 1736. It was intended for painters and includes practical demonstrations of geometry, reflecting contemporary ideas on optics and perspective. His sources included religious, mathematical and philosophical works and architectural treatises, especially those of Caramuel de Lobkowitz and Juan Bautista Villalpando.

WRITINGS

La nuova pratica di prospettiva, nella quale si spiegano alcune nuove opinioni . . . (Palermo, 1736)

BIBLIOGRAPHY

Meissner

A. Blunt: *Sicilian Baroque* (London, 1968)

M. C. Ruggieri Tricoli: *Paolo Amato: La corona e il serpente* (Palermo, 1983)

HELEN M. HILLS

Amatrice, Cola dell' [dall']. *See* COLA DELL'AMATRICE.

Amaury-Duval [Pineu-Duval], **Eugène-Emmanuel** (*b* Montrouge, Paris, 4 April 1806; *d* Paris, 29 April 1885). French painter and writer. A student of Ingres, he first exhibited at the Salon in 1830 with a portrait of a child. He continued exhibiting portraits until 1868. Such entries as *M. Geoffroy as Don Juan* (1852; untraced), *Rachel, or Tragedy* (1855; Paris, Mus. Comédie-Fr.) and *Emma Fleury* (1861; untraced) from the Comédie-Française indicate an extended pattern of commissions from that institution. His travels in Greece and Italy encouraged the Néo-Grec style that his work exemplifies. Such words as refinement, delicacy, restraint, elegance and charm pepper critiques of both his painting and his sedate, respectable life as an artist, cultural figure and writer in Paris. In contrast to Ingres's success with mature sitters, Amaury-Duval's portraits of young women are his most compelling. In them, clear outlines and cool colours evoke innocence and purity. Though the portraits of both artists were influenced by classical norms, Amaury-Duval's have control and civility in contrast to the mystery and sensuousness of Ingres's.

Amaury-Duval's extant drawings, often of carefully contoured, barely modelled nudes, again link him to Ingres, although the expressions of his figures are often more dreamy than those of his master's. The drawings of nudes were incorporated into such paintings as the *Birth of Venus* (1863; Lille, Mus. B.-A.), using a pose from Ingres's *Venus Anadyomene* (Chantilly, Mus. Condé), and in the fresco decorations for two rooms (one a Pompeian Revival

Eugène-Emmanuel Amaury-Duval: *St Philomena in Prison, Sustained by Two Angels* (1840–44), fresco, chapel of St Philomena, St Merri, Paris

dining-room) of the château at Linières in the Vendée in 1865 (destr. 1912).

Though a religious sceptic, Amaury-Duval was active, along with many of Ingres's other students, in the programme of church decoration pressed on the Second Empire by the conservative Catholic Church. His commissioned works include frescoes for the chapel of the Virgin (1844–66) in St Germain-l'Auxerrois, Paris, the chapel of St Philomena (1844; see fig.) in St Merri, Paris, apse and wall decorations for the church (1849–57) at Saint-Germain-en-Laye, cartoons for two stained-glass windows in Ste Clotilde in Paris (all *in situ*) and a number of large canvases, such as the *Annunciation* (1860; Mâcon, Mus. Mun. Ursulines). The artist's reliance on Perugino and more particularly on Fra Angelico's frescoes for the convent of S Marco in Florence has been noted (Foucart, 1987). Amaury-Duval visited the Nazarenes and admired their Casino Massimo frescoes in Rome in 1836 but, unlike their sophisticated mix of 15th-century Renaissance styles, his religious art is consciously archaic. Angels stand in serried rows as in a 14th-century *Maestà*, air is still and transparent, light casts no shadows (backgrounds are often painted in gold leaf), defined outlines freeze profiles, gestures are repeated as in a chorus, and drapery falls in columnar flutes over Gothic tubular bodies. Visual effects are architecturally severe, although the subjects are more likely to be naive and simple than those of other students of Ingres. Amaury-Duval's writings, such as *Souvenirs de l'atelier d'Ingres* (1878), centre on his connections to the Ingres circle.

WRITINGS

Journal de Voyage (MS.; 1836); ed. B. Foucart (Paris, in preparation)

Souvenirs de l'atelier d'Ingres (Paris, 1878; preface and notes by D. Ternois (Paris, 1986))

Souvenirs de jeunesse, 1829–30 (Paris, 1885)

BIBLIOGRAPHY

Bénézit; Thieme–Becker

E. J. Délécluze: *Les Beaux-arts dans les deux mondes en 1855* (Paris, 1856), pp. 247–9

L. Legrange: 'Salon de 1864', *Gaz. B.-A.*, xxv (1864), p. 510
H. Delaborde: 'Des oeuvres et de la manière de M. Amaury-Duval', *Gaz. B.-A.*, xviii (1865), pp. 419–28
P. Mantz: 'Salon de 1867', *Gaz. B.-A.*, xxii (1867), pp. 517–18
Amaury-Duval, 1806–85 (exh. cat. by V. Noël-Bouton, Montrouge, Hôtel de Ville, 1974)
The Second Empire: Art in France under Napoleon III (exh. cat., ed. G. H. Marcus and J. M. Iandola; Philadelphia, PA, Mus. A.; Detroit, MI, Inst. A.; Paris, Grand Pal.; 1978–9), pp. 249, 362
B. Foucart: *Le Renouveau de la peinture religieuse en France, 1800–1860* (Paris, 1987), pp. 212–14

NANCY DAVENPORT

Ambarnath [anc. Aṁvaranātha, Ambaranātha]. Site of a Shiva temple in Maharashtra, India, some 7 km south-east of Kalyan, a suburb of Bombay. An inscription inside the hall records that it was repaired in 1061 (Shaka year 982) by one Mamvaniraja (Mummuniraja) of the Shilahara dynasty, dating the temple to the early 11th century or before.

Enclosed within a wall (Skt *prakāra*) and facing west, the temple consists of a closed hall (*gūḍha-maṇḍapa*) with three porches, a vestibule and sanctuary (*garbha-gṛha*), the latter placed at a lower level and approached by steps. The exterior walls of the sanctuary and hall are subject to a series of projections and carry niches with divine figures. These include regents of the directions on the corners and themes of Vaishnava and Shaiva mythology: for example Vishnu in his incarnations as Varaha and Narasimha; Durga Slaying the Buffalo Demon (Mahiṣāsuramārdinī); and the marriage of Shiva and Parvati (Kalyanasundara). The main cardinal niches contain Mahakali (north); Gajasurasamhara, Shiva celebrating his victory over the elephant demon, shown dancing and wearing an elephant hide (south); and Hariharapitamaharka, a syncretistic god representing Vishnu, Shiva, Brahma and the Sun (east).

The tower over the sanctuary is a damaged example of the *bhūmija* mode, which is characterized by four spines (*latā*) at the cardinal points springing from large arched windows (*śurasenaka*); the intervening quadrants are filled with superimposed rows of miniature towers (*kūṭa-stambha*). Here the *kūṭa-stambha* are capped with unique bell-shaped elements that appear to represent the *drāviḍa-karma* ('Dravidian decoration') prescribed by architectural texts. The hall carries an elaborate pyramidal roof with bell-shaped finials (*ghaṇṭā-saṁvaraṇa*).

BIBLIOGRAPHY

H. Cousens: *Medieval Temples of the Dakhan* (Calcutta, 1931), pp. 14–18
V. V. Mirashi: *Inscriptions of the Śilāhāras*, Corp. Inscr. Indic., vi (New Delhi, 1960), pp. 110–13
G. B. Deglurkar: *Temple Architecture and Sculpture of Maharashtra* (Nagpur, 1974), pp. 24–7
Krishna Deva: 'Bhūmija Temples', *Studies in Indian Temple Architecture*, ed. P. Chandra (New Delhi, 1975), pp. 90–113

A. P. JAMKHEDKAR

Ambasz, Emilio (*b* Resistencia, June 1943). American architect, industrial designer and museum curator of Argentine birth. He received a Master of Fine Arts degree in architecture from Princeton University, NJ, and then taught at Princeton, at Carnegie Institute of Technology in Pittsburgh and at the Hochschule für Gestaltung in Ulm, Germany. From 1969 to 1976 he was Curator of Design for MOMA in New York. In 1972 he produced the exhibition *Italy: The New Domestic Landscape* and a related book for MOMA. The exhibition offered historical background and a presentation of contemporary Italian avant-garde work and theory. His architectural works include the Lucille Halsell Conservatory at San Antonio, TX (1987); Banque Bruxelles Lambert offices in Milan (1981), Lausanne (1983) and New York (1984); and offices for the Financial Guaranty Insurance Company in New York (1986), for which he won the International Interior Design Award. An innovative designer, Ambasz sought to reinterpret the poetic aspects of Modernism and the relationship between architecture and the landscape. As an industrial designer, he developed furniture, lighting, a diesel engine, and packaging and graphic designs. His work has won many honours and awards.

WRITINGS

with others: *Emilio Ambasz: The Poetics of the Pragmatic* (New York, 1989)

BIBLIOGRAPHY

P. Buchanan: 'Curtains for Ambasz', *Archit. Rev.* [London], clxxxi/1083 (1987), pp. 73–7

JOHN F. PILE

Amber (i). *See* AMER.

Amber (ii). Fossilized, water-insoluble RESIN, 20–120 million years old, which exuded from giant coniferous trees and became buried below them.

1. Material and sources. 2. Working and polishing methods. 3. History and uses.

1. MATERIAL AND SOURCES. Amber is amorphous, of resinous lustre and usually found in small pieces: irregular lumps, grains, drops and stalactites. It feels warm, is lightweight and porous and may fluoresce naturally under daylight, especially when freshly extracted. Inclusions of organic matter—insects, crustacea (some now extinct), flora, bark etc—resulted from these being trapped in the liquid resin as it flowed downwards. When in contact with atmospheric air, its surface becomes oxidized and forms a crust. Transparent, opaque (due to an abundance of tiny bubbles) or osseous, it is commonly yellow to honey-coloured, but approximately 250 different colour varieties including white and black are known, the rarest being red, blue and green. On lengthy exposure to air, golden-yellow amber slowly darkens to red. Green amber is thought to have formed in marshy areas through inclusions of decaying organic material. When burnt or rubbed vigorously amber emits a resinous pine aroma, and friction causes it to produce static sufficient to pick up small particles of paper. It is soft and carves easily but can be brittle, and skill is required to prevent fracturing. It tends to craze when subjected to sustained and extreme heat. Imitations include Chinese dyed sheep's horn and such plastic substitutes as phenolic resin. Amber has been confused with the fossil resins copal, dammar and kauri gum, of more recent date.

The major source of amber in Europe is from the Baltic, where it was formed during the Eocene period. In the Ice Age the geological stratum containing amber, known as Blue Earth, was carried by glaciers and rivers to parts of northern Europe. Some remained on what became the Baltic Sea bed, especially around Kaliningrad and Gdańsk. Until the 19th century, when organized digging, dredging and mining began, all Baltic amber was gathered from the beach or loosened from the sea bed with nets or pronged forks. It was still sought at the end of the 20th century, but the amount collected was comparatively small. It is also deposited along the shores of eastern England and the Netherlands and in Romania along the Carpathian Mountains, where the earliest found piece dates from the Palaeolithic era. 'Simetite' amber from the River Simeto in Sicily, known for its fluorescence and colour range, is *c.* 25 million years old and extremely rare. Amber has been found in 20 states in the USA, frequently associated with coal beds; New Jersey amber is *c.* 100 million years old. Mexican amber occurs in calcareous sandstones and siltstones and in river and stream deposits. The Dominican Republic yields mainly golden-coloured amber with blue fluorescence that is rich in inclusions. Burmite, the major Asian trading amber from Upper Burma, is 38–54 million years old and is mined from pits in the jungle floor.

2. Working and polishing methods. The basic working process consists of removing any outer crust, generally by scraping, then sawing away surplus pieces. Shaping and carving is done with scrapers, files and graving tools. Prior to the advent of metals, amber objects were crudely shaped by means of sandstones or other gritty stones serving as saws or files. Wood with sand could be used for smoothing surfaces, and a paste of wood ashes or chalk smeared on a piece of wood and rubbed on to the surface imparted a polish. A pointed stick revolved against the amber with an abrasive of fine sand was probably used for drilling holes. With bronze and then iron implements, more sophisticated work was achieved, but the methods for shaping, smoothing and polishing remained essentially unchanged, and as late as the 17th century amber was still worked with traditional tools. In the 18th century a spinning wheel was adapted into a crude lathe for turning objects, which were shaped with the aid of a piece of broken glass held against the amber. Industrialization reintroduced lathes and drills (which had been used by the Romans), but hand methods persisted with various saws, files, graving tools, sandpapers and such polishing compounds as tripoli, aluminium oxide and rouge; power-driven lapidary equipment used at slow speeds prevents shattering or melting. In the late 20th century the majority of amber from northern Europe was heated and clarified and underwent block-pressing processes; this made the cutting or moulding of beads or cubes, of uniform colour and composition, efficient for large-scale manufacture. Much of this adulterated amber was produced in Poland and Germany.

3. History and uses. Amber was considered to have remedial and magical properties, and amulets have been found dating from 3500–1800 BC. Trading, mostly by land and river routes, is known from *c.* 2000 BC. Imported amber was found in Mycenaean shaft tombs and in Bronze Age England (*c.* 2000–700 BC; *see* Prehistoric Europe, §V, 8). A wide range of jewellery inlaid with amber has been found in graves from Iron Age Europe (*c.* 1000 BC–*c.* AD 1), and hairpins with large decorated amber heads are known from a number of sites in eastern France (*see* Prehistoric Europe, §VI, 6). It was also used in many

1. Amber group of a woman and a youth reclining with a child, 84×140×31 mm, Etruscan or Greek, 6th century BC (New York, Metropolitan Museum of Art)

Pre-Columbian cultures of North America, Mesoamerica and South America, and for beads in Africa. Alaskan Inuits have traded it possibly from as early as AD 600.

In China amber objects from at least the Shang period (*c.* 1600–*c.* 1050 BC) have been found, although most examples date from the Han period (206 BC–AD 220) and later. It was used in making vessels, especially intricately carved snuff bottles (mainly during the 17th, 18th and 19th centuries), and in jewellery. A find at Qinglongshan, Inner Mongolia, of a tomb of a princess and her consort of the Liao period (AD 907–1125) revealed, among other articles, a small amber flask, amber earrings and a magnificent necklace of multiple strands of spherical and oval beads interspersed with openwork plaques carved with dragons (1018; Hohhot, Inst. Archaeol.). Amber continued to be carved in China into the late 20th century. (*See also* China, §XIII, 11)

The Greeks and Romans journeyed regularly to the Baltic in search of amber; references in Homer to it (e.g. the description of Menelaus' palace resplendent with amber) indicate its treasured status. As well as creating amber jewellery, scarabs and richly carved figural groups (see fig. 1), the Etruscans, like the Greeks, used it for inlays. The Romans made amber toilet vessels, amphorae, mirror handles, sets of game-pieces and portraits of actors (examples in London, BM). There have been Merovingian finds, in addition to extensive examples of Anglo-Saxon strings of beads found in 6th-century graves and such Celtic silver brooches set with cabochon ambers as the Hunterston Brooch (early 8th century; Edinburgh, Royal Mus. Scotland). Evidence exists of 8th-century amber workshops in Schleswig and York. Viking ambers were found in Dublin and game-pieces in Norway, although such evidence in Scandinavia generally is rare.

Amber came into prominence again when paternosters were produced in Bruges and Lübeck in the 14th century; examples are illustrated in such paintings as the *'Arnolfini Wedding'* by Jan van Eyck (1434; London, N.G.). Early 14th-century paternosters have been excavated in London, perhaps originating from workshops near Paternoster Row. Other medieval religious pieces are recorded in French and Burgundian inventories (e.g. a group of the *Holy Family*, 1379, that belonged to Emperor Charles V),

2. Amber *Judgement of Paris* group by Christoph Maucher, 197×195 mm, *c.* 1690–1700 (London, Victoria and Albert Museum)

while surviving examples include small amber reliefs of the *Head of Christ* (1380; Munich, Bayer. Nmus.) and an altar cruet (*c.* 1450–1610; London, V&A). For 200 years Baltic amber supplies were controlled by the Catholic Teutonic Order of Knights, who imposed strict discipline over the valuable raw material. The conversion to Lutheranism in 1525 of the Grand Master of the Teutonic Order, Albert of Hohenzollern-Ansbach, Duke of Prussia (*reg* 1525–68), a patron of amber-carving, encouraged the manufacture of such secular objects as tankards, goblets, caskets, game-boards and candlesticks, some with metalwork mounts. Devotional objects in amber (e.g. Florence, Pitti) continued to be produced in Catholic countries in the 16th century. The Duke of Prussia also lowered the cost of raw amber and expanded the market in Europe. As the craft flourished, guilds were established along the Baltic coast, and amber was distributed from Danzig (now Gdańsk) throughout northern Europe. The market extended to Turkey and India, and Armenians travelled to Königsberg (now Kaliningrad), a leading centre for amber-carving, in order to barter silk carpets for raw amber. One of the most outstanding carvers from Königsberg was GEORG SCHREIBER. An example from Königsberg work is a set of 18 amber and silver-gilt plates (1585; Copenhagen, Rosenberg Slot).

By the mid-17th century Danzig was patronized by the Polish court and flourished as the prime centre for amber working. The technique of 'incrustation' practised in Danzig was a major development: a wooden core was introduced for the construction of larger amber pieces, and slabs of amber were cemented to a wooden carcass to make such large objects as house altars and cabinets. An amber throne commissioned in 1677 for the Habsburg Emperor Leopold I of Austria, of which only fragments (Vienna, Ksthist. Mus.) and drawings (Berlin, Altes Mus.) survive, may have been partly worked by the ivory- and amber-carver Christoph Maucher (*see* MAUCHER, (1)), who also made two fine groups of the *Judgement of Paris* (late 17th century; London, V&A; see fig. 2). Amber veneers in geometric and pictorial designs were used for cabinets and game-boards (e.g. of 1594; Kassel, Hess. Landesmus.). A mosaic effect was achieved with different coloured ambers—as on an altar (*c.* 1650–1700; V&A) from Danzig—with contrasting opaque and clear amber panels, or with a combination of ivory and amber. The last spectacular court commission was an amber room designed for Schloss Charlottenburg near Berlin in 1709; it was presented to Peter the Great in 1717 and reconstructed at Tsarskoye Selo (now Pushkin) in Russia (untraced).

By the mid-18th century the use of amber was waning as fashions changed, patronage was withdrawn and the Baltic guilds declined. In the 19th century it was used chiefly in the Middle East and India for the decoration of horses' saddles and bridles. Ambroid (or Spiller) was made from small chips and offcuts of amber that were pressed hydraulically in a steel mould to form a cake, which was then cut to the required shape. Marketed in Vienna from 1881, Ambroid formed mouthpieces for pipes and cigarette holders. Amber jewellery became fashionable in late Victorian and Edwardian England, with plain round beads and cabochons occasionally set in gold. Georg Jensen and others combined it with silver (e.g. necklace, 1908; Copenhagen, Kstindustmus.), a trend followed on a silver bowl with an amber finial (*c.* 1934; London, V&A). In the 1920s, when amber vied with diamonds as the top gem import to the USA, bead necklaces with insect inclusions and faceted beads of clear amber were eagerly sought (e.g. in Chicago, IL, Field Mus. Nat. Hist.). Imitation and synthetic ambers enjoyed a peak of popularity from 1930 to 1935 for wireless casings, writing sets, table lamps, jewellery and decorative objects. In Poland in the late 20th century amber, sometimes mounted in silver, was used for jewellery.

BIBLIOGRAPHY

W. A. Buffum: *The Tears of the Heliades, or Amber as a Gem* (London, 1898)
G. C. Williamson: *The Book of Amber* (London, 1932)
E. Borglund and J. Flanensgaard: *Working in Plastic, Bone, Amber and Horn* (New York, 1968)
Z. Zalewska: *Amber in Poland* (Warsaw, 1974)
J. Grabowska: *Amber in Polish History* (Edinburgh, 1978)
P. C. Rice: *Amber: The Golden Gem of the Ages* (New York, 1980)
W. Baer: 'Ein Bernsteinstuhl für Kaiser Leopold I: Ein Geschenk des Kurfürsten Friedrich Wilhelm von Brandenburg', *Jb. Ksthist. Samml. Wien*, lxxviii (1982), pp. 91–138
H. Fraquet: *Amber from the Dominican Republic* (London, 1982)
M. Trusted: *Catalogue of European Ambers in the Victoria and Albert Museum* (London, 1985)
H. Fraquet: *Amber* (London, 1987)

□

Amberg, Adolf (*b* Hanau, July 1874; *d* Berlin, 3 July 1913). German silversmith, sculptor and painter. He attended the Zeichenakademie and the Kunstgewerbeschule in Hanau then studied at the Kunstgewerbeschule,

Berlin, and the Académie Julian in Paris, before finally becoming a student of the sculptor Louis Tuaillon at the Kunstakademie, Berlin. From 1894 to 1903 he worked at the renowned silverware factory of Bruckmann & Söhne in Heilbronn, modelling goblets, cutlery, sports prizes and medals etc. In collaboration with Otto Rieth, professor at the Kunstgewerbeschule in Berlin, Amberg made a silver fountain (h. 3.2 m) for the Exposition Universelle, Paris, in 1900.

After designing the silver for the Town Hall of Aachen (1903) and spending a year in Rome (1903–4), Amberg completed his most important work, the design of the *Hochzeitszug* (Berlin, Tiergarten, Kstgewmus.), a table centre for the wedding of Wilhelm (1882–1951), Crown Prince of Germany and Prussia and Herzogin Cecilie von Mecklenburg-Schwerin (1886–1954) in 1905. The designs were, however, rejected by the royal household and sold to the Königliche Porzellan-Manufaktur (KPM) in Berlin, which finally produced them in porcelain (1908–10): an ensemble of twenty figures, two candelabras, one jardinière and several fruit-bowls. Their theme is the homage and presentation of gifts to the bridal couple by representatives of foreign peoples and cultures. The figures were put on sale both unpainted and painted (under- and overglaze).

In 1906 Amberg moved to Berlin and made numerous sculptures, including an equestrian statuette of *Kaiser Wilhelm II as Emperor* for KPM (porcelain, 1910; see 'Jubiläumsausstellung der Königlichen Porzellan-Manufaktur zu Berlin', *Ker. Rundschau*, xliv (1913), pp. 453–5). In 1911 he worked on the Kronprinzensilber, also taking part in the competition for the national monument to the statesman *Otto von Bismarck* in Bingerbrück, near Koblenz. His later work was influenced by elements of Jugendstil and Neo-classicism.

BIBLIOGRAPHY

I. von Treskow: *Die Jugendstilporzellane der KPM* (Munich, 1972), pp. 108–11

Das Kronprinzensilber (exh. cat., W. Berlin, Kolbe Mus., 1982)

W. Baer: 'Adolph Ambergs *Hochzeitszug*', *Weltkunst*, liv/17 (1984), pp. 2224–6

FREYA PROBST

Amberger, Christoph (*b c.* 1505; *d* Augsburg, 1 Nov 1561–19 Oct 1562). German painter and draughtsman. His family came from the Upper Palatinate. He served his apprenticeship in Augsburg, probably with Leonhard Beck, whose daughter Barbara he married. He became a master on 15 May 1530 but rarely signed his work. He was in northern Italy and Venice *c.* 1525–7. His full-length pendant portraits of a husband and wife (both 1525; Vienna, Ksthist. Mus.) show Venetian influence, and the portrait of *Anton Welser* (1527; priv. col., see 1980 exh. cat., p. 98) is in the Italian style. According to Sandrart, during the Imperial Diet of 1530 in Augsburg Amberger painted a portrait of *Emperor Charles V* to the Emperor's satisfaction, but the surviving work (Berlin, Gemäldegal.) dates from 1532, based on the age given. In the decades that followed, Amberger was the favourite portrait painter of ambitious merchant families, such as the Fugger, who belonged to guilds but were connected with the nobility by family or marriage ties.

During the Imperial Diet in Augsburg in 1547–8, Amberger repaired Titian's equestrian portrait of *Emperor Charles V at the Battle of Mühlberg* (Madrid, Prado). He was commissioned by King Ferdinand (subsequently Emperor Ferdinand I) to design ancestral figures for bronze statues on the tomb of *Emperor Maximilian I* (drawings, Vienna, Österreich. Nbib.; statue of *King Clovis*, bronze, Innsbruck, Hofkirche). In 1554 he painted the Italianate *Virgin and SS Ulrich and Afra* (Augsburg Cathedral; drawing, London, BM), commissioned by the chapter of Augsburg Cathedral to replace the *Corpus Christi* altarpiece by Hans Holbein the elder, which had disappeared during the iconoclastic controversy in 1538. In 1549–50 Amberger supplied designs for redecorating a room at the Hofburg in Innsbruck.

Amberger was at his best as a portrait painter. In contrast to German tradition, he preferred physical types that inclined towards placidity. His colours are usually based on browns, and the flesh tones and white linen stand out; occasionally he adopted a heightened, festive brilliance. His sitters included *Jörg Hermann* (1530; Stuttgart, Staatsgal.; drawing, Williamstown, MA, Clark A. Inst.); *Wilhelm Merz* and his wife *Afra Rem* (both 1533; both Augsburg, Schaezlerpal.); *Hieronymus Seiler* and his wife *Felicitas Welser* (1537; Munich, Alte Pin.) and the brothers *Johann Jakob Fugger* (1541; Los Angeles, CA, Co. Mus. A.) and *Christoph Fugger* (1541; Munich, Alte Pin.), who pose aristocratically before shimmering silk curtains. The painting of *Christoph Baumgartner* (1543; Vienna, Ksthist. Mus.; see fig.) is brightly coloured, while the pendants of the Augsburg humanist and town clerk *Conrad Peutinger* and his wife *Margarethe Welser* (1543; Augsburg, Schaezlerpal.) are sober in hue. Amberger's

Christoph Amberger: *Christoph Baumgartner*, oil on panel, 830×623 mm, 1543 (Vienna, Kunsthistorisches Museum)

most mature work, the portrait of the cosmographer *Sebastian Münster* (Berlin, Gemäldegal.), was probably painted *c.* 1543 (notwithstanding the inscribed 1552 on the back of it).

Amberger's ability as an illuminator is revealed in the miniatures in the costume book of Matthäus Schwarz (1538–46; Brunswick, Herzog Anton Ulrich-Mus.; see Fink). In 1549 he made a coloured drawing of the course of the River Lech near the fortified town of Füssen (Munich, Bayer. Hauptstaatsarchv) for Hans Baumgartner. He designed 17 (or 22) woodcuts in a series of pictures of mercenary foot soldiers (pubd Vienna, *c.* 1580).

BIBLIOGRAPHY

Meissner

J. von Sandrart: *Teutsche Academie* (1675–9); ed. A. R. Pelzer (1925), pp. 80–81, 332

E. Haasler: *Der Maler Christoph Amberger* (Königsberg, 1894)

L. Baldass: 'Studien zur Augsburger Porträtmalerei des 16. Jahrhunderts, III: Christoph Amberger als Bildnismaler', *Pantheon*, ix (1932), pp. 177–84

K. Feuchtmayr: 'Christoph Amberger und Jörg Hermann', *Münchn. Jb. Bild. Kst*, xiii (1938–9), pp. 76–86

A. Fink: *Die Schwarzschen Trachtenbücher* (Berlin, 1963), pp. 59–61, 163–71

K. Löcher: 'Ambergers Bildnis Kaiser Karls V.: Repliken und Kopien', *Berlin. Mus.: Ber. Staatl. Mus. Preuss. Kultbes.*, xix (1969), pp. 11–15

——: 'Christoph Amberger als Zeichner', *Münchn. Jb. Bild. Kst*, xxx (1979), pp. 42–80

Welt im Umbruch: Augsburg zwischen Renaissance und Barock (exh. cat., Augsburg, Rathaus and Zeughaus, 1980) [details and some pls of 17 paintings and 13 drawings by Amberger]

KURT LÖCHER

Ambling, Carl Gustav (von). *See* AMLING, CARL GUSTAV.

Ambo. A raised platform for reading and preaching. The term first appears in the Canons of Laodicea (late 4th century AD), Canon 15 of which forbids the laity to ascend the ambo unless they serve as cantor or in the clerical rank of lector. This suggests that an ambo was an elevated platform, accessible by steps, from which scriptural texts were proclaimed and the responsorial psalm between the Epistle and Gospel was sung; the psalm response became known as the *Psalmus gradualis* or gradual, probably derived from the step (Lat. *gradus*) of the ambo. Although the term ambo does not appear before the 4th century AD, there are earlier references to an elevated place, which may also have included a reading stand, reserved for proclaiming scripture. This may have been a simple platform, similar to that described in the account of Ezra the Scribe standing on a wooden platform to proclaim the law of Moses from daybreak to midday (Nehemiah 8:4). The first Latin witness was Cyprian of Carthage (*d* AD 258), who mentions lectors ascending a *pulpitum* so that they might be both seen and heard (*Epistles*, xxxviii.2 and xxxix). A 4th-century collection of church law, the Syrian Apostolic Constitutions, also mentions an elevated place, the bema, reserved for the lector. Other terms used include auditorium, tribunal, exedra and *lectricium*.

There are no examples of ambos in the West before the 6th century. In Syrian and Mesopotamian churches of the 4th–7th centuries, a platform in the centre of the nave functioned as an ambo, related to the *bimah* of the Jewish synagogue (*see* JEWISH ART, §II, 1(ii)) and to the bema of Syrian liturgical texts. Bema is an ambiguous term that may refer to a tribunal or judgement seat, to the sanctuary or apse, or to a platform in the middle of the nave where reading and preaching occurred. In Syria, for example at Qirqbize and Behyo, the bema was a horseshoe-shaped place of assembly from which the liturgy of the catechumens took place. It consisted of a curved bank of stone seats flanking a raised stone platform closed off by a low screen on the side facing the sanctuary.

With the introduction in Eastern Orthodox liturgy during the early 6th century of the Little Entrance, a processional rite of entry by the bishop, a more elaborate architectural arrangement developed that linked the place in the nave for the proclamation of the word with the sanctuary by a long narrow passageway (*solea*) flanked by low walls. In such instances the ambo was located approximately halfway down the nave on the central axis (*see* CHURCH, §§II, 1 and IV, 1). The most notable example of an elaborate ambo connected to the sanctuary by a *solea* was at Hagia Sophia, Constantinople (now Istanbul). The ambo is extensively described in the ekphrasis by Paulos Silentarios, probably recited in AD 563 for the second consecration of the church, in which it is likened to an island rising from the sea. The ambo was inlaid with coloured marbles, ivory and silver plaques and set with hardstones. It was apparently positioned on the main axis, with an elliptical base supported by four pairs of columns. Steps on the east and west sides provided access, and it was surrounded to the north and south by semicircular colonnades. The most renowned of the several large elevated ambos with steps on two sides that were erected in Ravenna at about the same time was commissioned for the cathedral by Archbishop Agnellus (*reg* 556–69). Panels on the stairs and faces of the ambo are decorated with six rows of animal reliefs: lambs, peacocks, deer, doves, ducks and fish.

It is likely that the architectural arrangement of ambo, *solea* and chancel or sanctuary was introduced into the West at the time of Emperor Justinian I's reconquest of the Western empire in the 530s. The arrangement was a suitable response to a similarly elaborate episcopal entrance procession, of imperial derivation, that developed in Western liturgy with the introduction of cantors into the *solea*. The SCHOLA CANTORUM is an elaboration of the *solea* in Eastern churches. The 6th-century *Liber pontificalis* mentions Pope Pelagius (*reg* 555–61) ascending an ambo in his papal basilica. Elected through imperial patronage and no doubt influenced by Eastern practices, Pelagius built what may have been one of the earliest ambos in Rome.

The *Ordo Romanus I*, a description of the stational mass in 7th-century Rome, includes the rubric that the subdeacon ascends the ambo and reads the lesson. Only one ambo is mentioned, a practice that probably extended through the early Middle Ages. No clear indication is made for the ambo's location, which may have been next to the chancel barrier, or in or at the end of the *solea* in the middle of the nave. Surviving Western ambos include the 9th-century example, approached by a single set of eight steps, in the basilica of S Elia at Castel Sant'Elia, near Nepi. Important later examples survive in the Roman basilicas of S Lorenzo fuori le Mura, S Clemente and S Maria in Cosmedin. At S Clemente two ambos face each other midway along the sides of the *schola cantorum* (for illustration *see* SCHOLA CANTORUM). The ambo on the right, for the reading of the Epistle, includes fragments of the 6th-century ambo from the lower basilica. The ambo on the left, reserved for the reading of the Gospel, includes two sets of stairs in the tradition of the 6th-century ambos of Constantinople and Ravenna. The richly decorated Gospel ambo (13th century) at S Lorenzo fuori le Mura survives as an additional example of the 6th-century monumental ambo tradition. Since the Second Vatican Council (1962–5) the term ambo has been used increasingly in Roman Catholic churches, and the liturgy has encouraged the use of a single ambo for both readings and preaching.

For the later development of the ambo *see* PULPIT, §1.

BIBLIOGRAPHY

Reallex. Ant. & Christ.
F. Cabrol and H. Leclercq, OSB: *Dictionnaire d'archéologie chrétienne et de liturgie*, i (Paris, 1903), cols 1330–47
S. G. Xydis: 'The Chancel Barrier, Solea, and Ambo of Hagia Sophia', *A. Bull.*, xxix (1947), pp. 1–24
J. Lassus and G. Tchalenko: 'Ambons syriens', *Cah. Archéol.*, v (1951), pp. 79–81
J. B. Ward Perkins and R. G. Goodchild: 'The Christian Antiquities of Tripolitania', *Archaeologia*, xcv (1953), pp.1–84
W. J. O'Shea: *The Worship of the Church* (Westminster, MD, 1957)
R. Krautheimer: *Early Christian and Byzantine Architecture*, Pelican Hist. A. (Harmondsworth, 1965, rev. 4/1986)
D. Hickley: 'The Ambo in Early Liturgical Planning: A Study with Special Reference to the Syrian *Bema*', *Heythrop J.*, vii/4 (1966), pp. 407–27
G. P. Vrins: 'De ambon: Oorsprong en verspreiding tot 600', *Feestbundel F. van der Meer* (Amsterdam and Brussels, 1966), pp. 11–55
R. Taft, SJ: 'Some Notes on the *Bema* in East and West Syrian Traditions', *Orient. Christ. Period.*, xxxiv (1968), pp. 326–59
J. H. Emminghaus: *Die Gestaltung des Altarraumes*, ed. R. Pacik (Salzburg, 1985)
A. Damblon: *Zwischen Kathedra und Ambo* (Düsseldorf, 1988)

MARCHITA BRADFORD MAUCK

Amboise, d'. French family of patrons. The family, documented from 1100, originally came from Touraine, but in 1469 the line passed to a cadet branch, the Chaumont-d'Amboise. Pierre II Chaumont-d'Amboise (*d* 1473), Counsellor of Charles VII and Louis XI and governor of Touraine, had a large family, several members of which rose to prominence and were active as patrons: his eighth son, (1) Cardinal Georges I d'Amboise and his grandson (2) Charles II d'Amboise, Comte de Chaumont, both resident for a time in Milan, brought Italian artists to work on their projects in France, and they were instrumental in the spread of the Renaissance there.

The patronage of Pierre II's eldest son, Charles I (*d* by 16 March 1503), was centred on the rebuilding of the family château of Chaumont, razed by King Louis XI in 1465. His fourth son, Louis I (*d* 1 July 1503), became Bishop of Albi in 1474 and commissioned various works for the cathedral: the south porch, the Flamboyant rood screen, the tribunes and a *Last Judgement*, painted on the west wall by late followers of Rogier van der Weyden. Louis also ordered a silver antependium and a monumental brass lectern from the Parisian founders Jehan Morant and his son Adam Morant and Regnault Gudeon in 1484. In 1503 Louis was succeeded as Bishop of Albi by his nephew Louis II (1477–1517; Cardinal from 1506), the son of Charles I d'Amboise. He followed King Louis XII to Italy and on his return commissioned wall paintings for the vaults and tribune of the cathedral in the Renaissance style. The large cycle of the *Salvation* (completed 1512), which was intended to promote the French Crown, was produced by a group of unidentified Lombard-Emilian painters working under Giovanni Francesco Donella da Carpi.

Pierre d'Amboise (*d* 1 Sept 1505), the sixth son of Pierre II and Bishop of Poitiers, ordered the completion of the abbey of St Jouin and the cathedral in Poitiers, and commissioned a rural episcopal residence at Dissay; the last contains late 15th-century wall paintings and stained-glass windows of Sibyls, the *Life of Christ* and the *Fountain of Life* in a general style akin to that of Henri de Vulcop. Jacques d'Amboise (*d* 27 Dec 1516), Pierre II's seventh son and Abbot of Jumièges (1475) and Cluny (1485), then Bishop of Clermont-Ferrand (1505), is remembered primarily for the construction of the Parisian residence of the abbots of Cluny (1485–98; now the Musée de Cluny) on the left bank of the Seine, which is the most salient remaining example of Late Gothic secular architecture in the city. The chapel included richly carved stalls, kneeling statues of the d'Amboise family and a *Lamentation*. Jacques also made additions to Clermont-Ferrand Cathedral: colossal statues, rising above new roofs, of the Virgin crowning a Tree of Jesse and of St Michael (1512), stained-glass windows based on xylographs published by Philippe Pigouchet (1496), choir-stalls from the sculptor Gilbert Chapard (*fl* 1506–16) and Flemish tapestries (1516) with Italianate elements, depicting the *Life of Christ and of the Virgin* (now St Petersburg, Hermitage).

BIBLIOGRAPHY

A. de Sainte-Marie: *Histoire généalogique et chronologique de la maison royale de France*, vii (Paris, 1726)
L. Bosseboeuf: *Le Château de Chaumont dans l'histoire et les arts* (Tours, 1906)
H. du Ranquet: *La Cathédrale de Clermont-Ferrand* (Paris, 1913, 2/1928)
P. Lesueur: 'Le Château de Chaumont', *Congr. Archéol. France*, lxxxviii (1925), pp. 454–69
J. Salvini: 'Les Ensembles décoratifs dans le diocèse de Poitiers entre la Guerre de Cent Ans et les Guerres de Religion', *Bull. Soc. Antiqua. Ouest* (1939), pp. 95–125
E. Mâle: *La Cathédrale d'Albi* (Paris, 1950)
F. de Montrémy: 'Le Lieu-dit les Termes et l'Hôtel de Cluny', *Paris & Ile-de-France: Mém.*, vii (1955), pp. 53–148
F. Perrot: 'Un Panneau de la vitrerie de la chapelle de l'Hôtel de Cluny', *Rev. A.* [Paris], x (1970), pp. 66–72
G. Souchal: 'Le Mécénat de la famille d'Amboise', *Bull. Soc. Antiqua. Ouest* (1976), pp. 485–526, 567–612
Congr. Archéol. France, cxl (1982) [issue on Albi]

(1) Cardinal **Georges I d'Amboise** (*b* Chaumont-sur-Loire, 1460; *d* Lyon, 25 May 1510). The eighth son of Pierre II Chaumont-d'Amboise, he was appointed Bishop of Montauban (1484), Archbishop of Narbonne (1492) and Rouen (1494), Cardinal and Prime Minister of Louis XII (1498) and Papal Legate (1501). Georges commissioned substantial extensions (1495–1507) to the episcopal palace of Rouen, including a gallery, a chapel with Italian marbles and gardens (*see* DELORME, PIERRE). He also ordered important hydraulic works and, at Rouen Cathedral, the completion of the Tour de Beurre by Jacques Le Roux (1507) and a new west portal, begun by Jacques and his nephew Roulland in 1509.

In 1502, on his return from Italy, the Cardinal ordered the transformation of the palace of the Rouen archbishops at Gaillon, engaging both French and Italian artists for the work and creating new gardens (*see* GAILLON). The outcome rivalled the most elaborate Renaissance structures in north-central Italy, but it was more than a mere adaptation; Gaillon was unique for its high-pitched roofs, its pinnacles and crockets, recalling those of complex Netherlandish altarpieces, and such elements as the large copper-gilt figure of St George over the lantern of the spiral staircase. The medallion portraits of Roman emperors in the courtyard, the statues of Louis XII in Roman armour and of the Cardinal and his nephew Charles in the gallery of the main façade, and the portal reliefs, reproducing Mantegna's *Triumphs of Caesar* juxtaposed with others by Antonio Giusto Betti, depicting the siege of Genoa by the French in 1507 and Louis XII's triumphal entry into Milan, were intended to bolster the French Crown by associating it with the trappings of antiquity. The Italianate architectural motifs were organized more in the traditions of French Flamboyant than in the Renaissance manner, however, and this eclecticism also characterized the decoration of the château's interior. In the chapel a Florentine-born sculptor referred to in the accounts as Jérôme Pacherot was commissioned to make a Renaissance frame for the altarpiece, a relief, essentially Gothic, of *St George and the Dragon* (1509; Paris, Louvre) by Michel Colombe. The furnishings of the château—panelling, stained glass, carved reliefs *all'antica* and tapestries depicting the Trojan Wars, the god Mars and other Classical subjects—also demonstrate the blend of the new Italian art with more traditional elements.

Tomb of *Georges I and Georges II d'Amboise, Cardinal-Archbishops of Rouen*, designed by Roulland Le Roux, marble and alabaster, 1515–42, Rouen Cathedral

Some of the best paintings of the Cardinal's collection, including works by Perugino, Andrea Solario, Marco d'Oggiono, Andrea Mantegna and, probably, Leonardo da Vinci, were hung in the library, which housed the largest holding of Italian illuminated volumes in France in 1501 (in Naples the Cardinal had purchased the manuscript collection of the kings of Aragon). Georges also commissioned many manuscripts himself. The names of over 12 copyists appear in his accounts, and he employed French illuminators who worked in the style of Jean Bourdichon but incorporated conspicuous Italianate architectural elements, among them Jean Serpin (*fl* 1502–8), Robert Boyvin (*fl* 1501–03; possibly the Master of the Petrarch Triumphs) and Etienne du Monstier (*fl* 1501–22). His books were bound in red and black leather gilded in the Italian style.

The influence of Cardinal Georges's work at Gaillon spread all over western France; it was important both for the development of the French château plan and for the introduction of Italian decorative elements on a large scale. Additional works, including stalls and stained-glass windows, were ordered for Gaillon by George I's nephew, George II d'Amboise (1487–1550), who succeeded him as Archbishop of Rouen, becoming Cardinal in 1545. Georges II was also responsible, in 1515, for commissioning his uncle's prominent marble and alabaster tomb in the choir of Rouen Cathedral, which depicted the deceased kneeling. Completed in 1523, it was transformed in 1525 to serve as a cenotaph for Georges II as well. The monument is profusely carved and includes Virtues, Saints, Apostles, a prominent relief of *St George and the Dragon*, and others with Italianate candelabra, swags and grotesques (see fig.). Roulland Le Roux was overseer, assisted by the sculptors João de Ruão, who began the weepers, Mathieu Laignel (*fl* 1513–25), Regnault Thérouyn, André le Flament (*fl* 1520–21) and Pierre des Aubeaux (*fl* 1500–25). The last executed the statues of Georges I and Georges II (recut, by 1542, by one 'Jean Goujon'). The tomb is the most complex funerary monument in the early Renaissance style in France.

BIBLIOGRAPHY

L. Delisle: *Le Cabinet des manuscrits de la Bibliothèque nationale*, 3 vols (Paris, 1868–81)

Fuzet and Jouen: *Comptes, devis et inventaires du manoir archiépiscopal de Rouen* (Paris and Rouen, 1908)

E. Chirol: *Un Premier Foyer de la Renaissance en France; Le Château de Gaillon* (Rouen, 1952)

R. Weiss: 'The Castle of Gaillon in 1509–10', *J. Warb. & Court. Inst.*, xvi (1953), pp. 1–12, 351

E. Chirol and J. Bailly: *Le Tombeau des cardinaux d'Amboise* (Rouen, 1959)

La Renaissance à Rouen (exh. cat., Rouen, Mus. B.-A., 1980)

(2) Charles II d'Amboise, Comte de Chaumont (*b* 1473; *d* Correggio, 11 Feb 1511). Nephew of (1) Cardinal Georges I d'Amboise and the son of Charles I. He was Governor of Paris (1493–6) and Chamberlain of Louis XII, commanding his armies on the Italian campaign of 1499. He became Governor of Milan, then Marshal of France (1504) and admiral (1508); he was vital in keeping Venice in check at the Battle of Agnadello (1509). In Milan Chaumont commissioned Leonardo da Vinci to provide plans for a palace and a layout of waterways in Lombardy, as well as paintings: the *Virgin of the Rocks* (1483–5; Paris, Louvre) for Louis XII and a *Virgin and*

Child with the Yarnwinder (1501; untraced) for the court official Florimond Robertet. Charles may have brought Leonardo to France in 1505–6. He commissioned Caradosso to produce die-casts for coins of Louis XII as Duke of Milan. The French governor also protected the Solari: he ordered medallions for his castle of Meillant in Berri from Cristoforo Solario (1502) and commissioned Andrea to decorate the Castello Sforzesco in Milan and the chapel of S Maria alla Fontana, and sent him to work for many years at Gaillon. A portrait of Charles by Andrea is in the Louvre, Paris. In 1510 Charles entrusted to a Lombard painter probably identifiable as Antonio, a cousin of the Solari, the fresco decoration of the chapel of Gaglianico, where there is a depiction of Gaillon after a drawing brought by Cardinal Georges I to Italy *c*. 1508. In his château of Chaumont, where he added a new north façade and a tower with reliefs partly in the Lombard Renaissance style, Charles had, it seems, a painting by Mantegna depicting the triumph of the condottiere Castruccio Castracani. He also sent the sculptor Riccardo da Carpi (*fl* 1504–08) to his uncle to carve the chapel stalls of Gaillon. The Chaumont-d'Amboise line became extinct with the death of Charles II's son Georges (1524), and the Amboise line passed to the Bussy-d'Amboise, with Jean, the fifth son of Pierre II Chaumont-d'Amboise.

BIBLIOGRAPHY

M. Rosci and A. Chastel: 'Un Château français en Italie: Un Portrait de Gaillon à Gaglianico', *A. France*, iii (1963), pp. 103–13

F. Girard-Pipau: 'Le Mécénat de Charles d'Amboise 1500–1510', *Inf. Hist. A.*, xvii (1972), pp. 176–81

PATRICK M. DE WINTER

Ambrakia. *See* ARTA.

Ambrogini, Angelo. *See* POLIZIANO, ANGELO.

Ambrogio, Pietro di Giovanni d'. *See* PIETRO DI GIOVANNI D'AMBROGIO.

Ambrogio (d'Antonio) Barocci [da Milano; da Urbino]. *See* BAROCCI, AMBROGIO.

Ambrotype. *See under* PHOTOGRAPHY, §I.

Ambulatory. The extension of the aisles around the sanctuary of a major aisled church to form a passage or walkway. The ambulatory is found throughout western Europe, especially in France, and was particularly popular between the 11th and 13th centuries. It is often provided with radiating chapels that project from its exterior face. Its function was to provide separate access to the radiating chapels and perhaps originally to facilitate the circulation of pilgrims past relics. The ambulatory with radiating chapels was an important innovation of the Romanesque period and is a particularly potent illustration of the style's preoccupation with the articulation of structure (*see* ROMANESQUE, §II).

The origins of the ambulatory are found in Carolingian outer crypts (*see* CRYPT). A good example from England is the simple, barrel-vaulted corridor that runs around the apse at All Saints', Brixworth (Northants), probably built during the 9th century (for illustration *see* BRIXWORTH, ALL SAINTS' CHURCH). The genuine ambulatory, however, surrounds a central space, with which it is interconnected by openings or an arcade. The earliest examples, both crypts, existed at St Pierre-le-Vif (920–40; destr.), Sens, and Thérouanne Cathedral (mid-10th century; destr.). The earliest ambulatory that stood at the principal level as well as below existed at Clermont-Ferrand Cathedral (consecrated 946; rebuilt 13th century). A similar two-storey example survives at St Philibert (*c*. 960–*c*. 979), Tournus (for illustration *see* TOURNUS, ST PHILIBERT); only the crypt remains of St Aignan (989–1029) at Orléans.

The ambulatories at St Aignan and probably Orléans Cathedral were copied throughout France, owing to the great prestige of the Capetian kings, whose headquarters were then at Orléans. The influence of Orléans can be seen in the so-called pilgrimage churches at Tours, Limoges, Conques, Toulouse and Santiago de Compostela. Ste Foy (mid-11th century) at Conques is a well-preserved, typical example: in plan it consists of three semicircular radiating chapels progressing naturally from the single apses projecting from the transept arms, with the sanctuary separated from the ambulatory by a seven-bay arcade of stilted arches on tall, closely spaced columns (see fig.). From the exterior each element of the plan is clearly expressed: the radiating chapels are the smallest compartments, each with a semi-conical roof; at a slightly higher level is the lean-to roof of the ambulatory; the composition is completed by the masonry of the nave space, decorated with a seven-bay blind arcade enclosing the clerestory windows. The other, larger pilgrimage churches have five radiating chapels, and the central or axial chapels are bigger. Very few of the many Romanesque churches in France with similar ambulatories and radiating chapels differ significantly from the example set by Orléans.

Part of the ambulatory, the south radiating chapel and the choir, Ste Foy, Conques, mid-11th century

In Germany an early example of an ambulatory without radiating chapels exists at St Michael (1010–33) at Hildesheim. It is situated around the western apse connecting with a vaulted central space beneath the apse. It is clearly a development of the outer crypt, with only the ambulatory itself standing outside the main body of the church. Nevertheless the ambulatory has a considerable effect on the massing of the building. This effect was exploited dramatically at St Maria im Kapitol (mid-11th century), Cologne, which has a trefoil east end with each apse enveloped by an ambulatory. It is significant that the radiating chapels in the crypt are of a type that is not expressed on the exterior of the building but instead enclosed in masonry.

The French version of the ambulatory with radiating chapels was adopted in Britain after the Norman Conquest of 1066, but with important differences. A major Romanesque church with a normal three-storey elevation would carry the middle storey around the principal apse as well as the aisle, thereby creating a two-storey ambulatory. The radiating chapels would also be of two storeys. The typical French example, as at Ste Foy, Conques, omits the middle storey for the ambulatory, and the radiating chapels are lower still. The English also had a taste for complex and eccentric radiating chapels. These tendencies are illustrated most clearly in the new east end of Canterbury Cathedral and at Norwich Cathedral, both of which were begun in 1096. Owing to its crypt, Canterbury has a three-storey ambulatory. The radiating chapels at Norwich have a curious plan of two intersecting circles, for which the only known precedent is at the collegiate church of Notre-Dame, Mehun-sur-Yèvre, near Bourges, while those at Canterbury consist of rectangles with single apses apparently based on the plan of the chapels at St Maria im Kapitol, Cologne, and Brauweiler Abbey (consecrated 1061). Finally, the radiating chapels at Canterbury were continued upwards to form towers, producing an extraordinary result that may be explained as a fusion between the French taste for protruding chapels and the Germanic liking for flanking towers.

During the Gothic period the principal contribution to the development of the ambulatory was the introduction of the double ambulatory. It occurs at Saint-Denis Abbey (*c.* 1140), where the shallow radiating chapels emerge without subdivision from the outer ambulatory, each chapel and aisle bay covered by a single vault, and at the contemporary church of St Martin-des-Champs, Paris, where the plan is repeated apart from a large axial chapel in the form of a trefoil. Notre-Dame (1163–1250), Paris, was built with a double ambulatory (*see* PARIS, fig. 29). The awkwardly shaped ambulatory bays were vaulted in a particularly ingenious way by increasing both the number of columns that divide the two ambulatories as well as the responds in the outside wall, so that the span of each arch is the same as that of the main or innermost arcade. The vaulting area is consequently divided into almost equal triangles. The double ambulatory at Bourges Cathedral (begun 1190) is a very successful design in which the outer ambulatory is lower than the inner, thereby allowing direct lighting of both ambulatories (*see* BOURGES, §II, 1(i)). This system was adopted in the choir of Le Mans Cathedral (1217–54).

The apse and ambulatory survived in Europe until the end of the Middle Ages other than in Britain, where, except for certain royal foundations, a flat east wall was favoured instead of an apse; this could, however, have a low, aisled extension leading to eastern chapels, as is found at Holy Trinity and St Mary, Abbey Dore (Hereford & Worcs), and Byland Abbey (ruined; N Yorks), both built *c.* 1200.

BIBLIOGRAPHY

E.-E. Viollet-le-Duc: *Dictionnaire raisonné de l'architecture française du XIe au XVIe siècle*, i (Paris, 1854), pp. 4–9

F. Cabrol and H. Leclercq: *Dictionnaire d'archéologie chrétienne et de liturgie*, iv (Paris, 1953), p. 303

K. J. Conant: *Carolingian and Romanesque Architecture, 800–1200*, Pelican Hist. A. (Harmondsworth, 1959, rev. 2/1974)

Monumenta Annonis: Köln und Siegburg: Weltbild und Kunst im hohen Mittelalter (exh. cat., ed. A. Legner; Cologne, Cäcilienkirche, 1975)

E. C. Fernie: 'St Anselm's Crypt', *British Archaeological Association Conference Transactions: Medieval Art and Architecture at Canterbury before 1220: Canterbury, 1979*, pp. 27–38

J. Bony: *French Gothic Architecture of the 12th and 13th Centuries* (Berkeley and London, 1983)

C. Wilson: *The Gothic Cathedral: The Architecture of the Great Church, 1130–1530* (London, 1990)

STEPHEN HEYWOOD

Amedei [Amadei], **Giuliano** (*b* Florence, before 12 March 1446; *d* Lucca, 1496). Italian painter and illuminator. He was a Camaldolite monk; his appointment, from 1470, as Abbot of Agnano, Arezzo, and Val di Castro, Fabriano, was disputed, since he never resided at either abbey. His work is known from a signed triptych of the *Virgin and Child Enthroned with Saints* (1460–67) in SS Martino e Bartolomeo at Tifi, Arezzo (*in situ*). It shows the influence of the most fashionable Florentine artists of the time, such as Neri di Bicci, and such artists from the Marches as Giovanni Boccati and Gerolamo di Giovanni da Camerino. The most noteworthy aspect of the altarpiece, however, is its chromatic quality. This undoubtedly derives from the work of PIERO DELLA FRANCESCA and has made it possible to identify Amedei as the collaborator to whom Piero entrusted the small predella scenes and pilaster figures of the polyptych of the *Misericordia* (Sansepolcro, Pin.), a work that can be dated by the final payments made in 1462. It is also possible to attribute the illuminations in a copy of Plutarch's *Lives* (*c.* 1450; Cesena, Bib. Malatestiana, MSS S.XV.1–2, S.XVII.3) to Amedei on stylistic grounds.

Amedei is documented as a painter in Rome between 1467 and 1472, and a coherent group of miniatures painted in Rome between these dates has been attributed to him, including those in three manuscripts in the Biblioteca Vaticana, Rome (MSS Vat. Burgh. 366, Vat. lat. 7628 and Urb. lat. 261), as well as the illustrations for books xv–xxxvii of a copy of Pliny the elder's *Natural History* (London, V&A, MS. L. 1504–1896). These attributions, however, have been questioned, owing to the lack of firm documentary evidence and to the stylistic variations between these works and the Tifi altarpiece. The illuminations are much closer to the work of Jacopo da Verona (*fl* Pesaro, 1459–60). None of the attempts to identify Amedei's presence at the papal court has proved convincing, while the 19th-century idea that he may have worked on the choirbooks of Lucca Cathedral appears to have come into being simply because he died in that city.

BIBLIOGRAPHY

E. Müntz: *Les Arts à la cour des papes pendant le XVe et le XVIe siècle*, ii (Paris, 1879), pp. 31, 41, 43, 78–81, 108–9

M. Salmi: 'Piero della Francesca e Giuliano Amedei', *Riv. A.*, xxiv (1942), pp. 25–44

——: 'Arte e cultura artistica nella pittura del primo rinascimento a Ferrara', *Rinascimento*, ix (1958), pp. 123–39

J. Ruysschaert: 'Miniaturistes "romains" sous Pie II', *Enea Silvio Piccolomini: Papa Pio II* (Siena, 1968), pp. 245–82

Arte nell'Aretino (exh. cat. by A. M. Maetzke, Arezzo, S Francesco, 1974), no. 34, pp. 94–6

J. I. Whalley: *Pliny the Elder: Historia naturalis*, London, V&A cat. (London, 1982)

ALESSANDRO CONTI

Amedeo di Francesco. *See* MEO DA CAPRINO.

Amelung, John Frederick [Johann Friedrich] (*b* Hettlingen, nr Hannover, Germany, 26 June 1741; *d* Baltimore, MD, 1 Nov 1798). American glass manufacturer of German birth. He was associated with his brother's mirror-glass factory in the town of Grünenplan before his venture to make table wares and utility glass in America began in 1784. With backing from investors in Bremen, Germany, Amelung brought 68 glass craftsmen and furnace equipment to the USA. He purchased an existing glasshouse near Frederick, MD, along with 2100 acres. The factory, which he named the New Bremen Glassmanufactory, had been founded by glassmakers from Henry William Stiegel's defunct operation in Manheim, PA. It was well situated in western Maryland, not far from Baltimore, which offered a fast-growing market. Many settlers in the area were Germans, who were expected to be supportive of the enterprise. During the following decade Amelung built housing for his 400–500 workers. It is believed that he built four glasshouses.

Although Amelung's craftsmen made window glass, bottles and table glass, the most important group of objects associated with the factory are the high-quality, wheel-engraved presentation pieces (e.g. sugar bowl, 1785–95; Winterthur, DE, Du Pont Winterthur Mus.) made as gifts for friends and for such politicians as President George Washington, whom Amelung hoped to impress. These wares shared some of the *Waldglas* lily-pad decoration associated with Caspar Wistar's earlier glassworks, but Amelung's products are more spectacular in conception and execution. They are significant for often being signed and dated; Amelung's was the only American factory doing this at the time.

In 1787 Amelung published a pamphlet entitled *Remarks on Manufactures, Principally on the New Established Glass-house, near Frederick-Town in the State of Maryland*, in which he related the founding of his enterprise and speculated on its future. Its progress, he argued, would be greatly facilitated and the public interest best served by official support of American manufacturers through tax exemptions and interest-free government loans. Although the State of Maryland loaned him £1000 in 1788, additional state or federal government support was not forthcoming. Furthermore, a flood in the autumn of 1786 that damaged one glasshouse, a strong wind in the spring of 1790 that caused the collapse of several houses and mills, and shortly thereafter a fire that destroyed one of his factories and a warehouse, combined to undermine an operation that was already overextended. Amelung's petition to the US Congress for help after the fire was denied for lack of security on a loan. In a second petition he further proposed to build glasshouses in Virginia and the Carolinas to serve the southern USA. Although the second request was rejected, his suggestion that duties be raised on imported glass was executed in several instalments between 1790 and 1794. Amelung's operations virtually ceased following his stroke in 1794, and he went bankrupt in 1795. His son, John Frederick Magnus Amelung, continued to make glass in the glasshouse given to him in 1795 by his father (the site was not included in his father's bankruptcy), but in 1799 he transferred the property to his partners Adam Kohlenberg and George Christian Gabler.

WRITINGS

Remarks on Manufactures, Principally on the New Established Glass-house, near Frederick-Town in the State of Maryland (Frederick-Town, 1787)

BIBLIOGRAPHY

D. P. Lanmon, A. Palmer Schwind and others: *John Frederick Amelung: Early American Glassmaker* (London, 1990)

ELLEN PAUL DENKER

Amenemhet III. *See* AMMENEMES III.

Amenhotpe, son of Hapu (*b* Athribis, nr Benha, *c.* 1440 BC; *d c.* 1350 BC). Ancient Egyptian architect and patron. Amenhotpe rose to prominence in his home town during the reign of Amenophis III (*reg c.* 1391–*c.* 1353 BC) as a royal scribe and chief of the priests of the local god Khentekhtai. About 1390 BC he moved to the royal court at Thebes and was rapidly promoted by Amenophis III to the position of chief royal architect, responsible for the whole process of temple construction, from quarrying to the sculpting of relief decoration, as well as the commissioning of royal statues. The full list of buildings for which Amenhotpe was architect is not known, but he certainly supervised the construction of a huge temple at Soleb near the second cataract of the Nile in Lower Nubia, where several of the reliefs depict him standing alongside the King during the temple consecration ceremony. He also built two tombs and a mortuary temple for himself on the west bank at Thebes (*see* THEBES (i), §VIII). The size of his mortuary temple and the fact that it was located among the royal temples are both indications of the great status that Amenhotpe acquired during his lifetime. He was also granted the exceptional privilege of having several statues of himself placed inside the Karnak temple complex, seven of which have survived (Cairo, Egyp. Mus.; London, BM; and Luxor Mus.). After his death Amenhotpe became increasingly famous for his wisdom and healing powers; like Imhotep, the architect of the 3rd-Dynasty king Djoser (*reg c.* 2630–*c.* 2611 BC), he was deified. In the Ptolemaic period (304–30 BC) chapels dedicated to the worship of Imhotep and Amenhotpe were established in the Temple of Hathor at Deir el-Medina and in the mortuary temple of Hatshepsut at Deir el-Bahri.

BIBLIOGRAPHY

C. Robichon and A. Varille: *Le Temple du scribe royal Amenhotep fils de Hapou* (Cairo, 1936)

A. Varille: *Inscriptions concernant l'architecte Amenhotep fils de Hapou* (Cairo, 1968)

D. Bidoli: 'Zur Lage des Grabes des Amenophis, Sohn des Hapu', *Mitt. Dt. Archäol. Inst.: Abt. Kairo*, xxvi (1970), pp. 12–14

D. Wildung: *Egyptian Saints: Deification in Pharaonic Egypt* (New York, 1977)

H. Sourousian: 'La Statue d'Amenhotep fils de Hapou, âgé, un chef-d'oeuvre de la XVIIIe dynastie', *Mitt. Dt. Archäol. Inst.: Abt. Kairo*, xlvii (1991), pp. 341–55

Amenophis III [Nebmaatre] (*reg c.* 1391–*c.* 1353 BC). Egyptian ruler and patron. He reigned in the late 18th Dynasty (*c.* 1540–*c.* 1292 BC), a time of great national peace and prosperity. Amenophis III was a prolific builder: it was during his reign that AMENHOTPE, SON OF HAPU, the greatest Egyptian architect since Imhotep, rose to a position of power and influence as 'Overseer of all the King's Works'.

Although Amenophis III constructed numerous temples, from Memphis and Bubastis in the north of Egypt to Soleb and Sedeinga in the south (*see* NUBIA, §III), only a small number of these have survived. His mortuary temple, built in fine white limestone on the west bank of the Nile at Thebes, must have been one of the most impressive buildings of the time, but it was systematically dismantled in the 19th Dynasty (*c.* 1292–*c.* 1190 BC). Only a few items of sculpture and stelae have been preserved from it, notably the celebrated 'Colossi of Memnon' (*in situ*; *see* THEBES (i), §V), two massive quartzite seated statues of the King that marked the eastern entrance of the temple. Another colossal statue from the same temple, representing the King, his wife Tiye and three princesses (Cairo, Egyp. Mus., JE 33906), has been reconstructed from limestone fragments discovered in the area. His monuments at Karnak (*see* THEBES (i), §II) include Pylon III, the Temple of Mut and the Temple of Montu; the richness of the decoration in these buildings is indicated by the list of precious materials used for the Temple of Montu, which included 3.25 tonnes of electrum, 2.5 tonnes of gold and over 10 tonnes of copper. Luxor Temple (*see* THEBES (i), §III) is the earliest intact example of the archetypal Egyptian temple design, consisting of a progression from an open columned court to a sanctuary via a series of halls gradually decreasing in size (*see also* TEMPLE, §I, 2). Its walls are carved with the exquisite raised reliefs characteristic of the reign of Amenophis III (*see* EGYPT, ANCIENT, §IX, 3(vii)(b)); further examples survive in the tombs of officials at Thebes, such as those of Kheruef (TT 192), Khaemhat (TT 57) and Ramose (TT 55; *see* RAMOSE, TOMB OF). Elsewhere, private tombs were decorated with superb polychrome paintings executed on plaster (*see* EGYPT, ANCIENT, §X, 2). These are less well preserved, but surviving fragments such as the painting of Amenophis III from TT 226 (now Luxor Mus., J. 134) give some indication of their quality.

Painted wall decorations were also a feature of Amenophis' mud-brick palace complex at Malqata (*see* THEBES (i), §XII). Almost 1 km in length, the complex comprised royal residences and audience halls, a temple, kitchens, workshops, stores and servants' quarters, as well as a vast T-shaped harbour that doubled as a pleasure-lake. The painted decorations of plants and wildfowl (e.g. Cairo, Egyp. Mus., RT 3.5.27.4 and 3.5.27.6) anticipate the naturalistic Amarna style of Amenophis' son and successor, Akhenaten. The King's rock-cut passage tomb (KV 22), in the western annexe of the Valley of the Kings, was excavated by Howard Carter in 1915 and re-examined in the 1990s by a team of archaeologists from Waseda University. Its L-shaped plan, typical of 18th-Dynasty royal tombs, was supplemented by numerous storerooms and an extra burial chamber probably intended for Queen Tiye. The tomb appears to have been dismantled in the 10th century BC, but the surviving fragments of reliefs and equipment show that its decoration and funerary furniture must have been magnificent. The tomb of Tiye's parents, Yuya and Tuya (KV 46), was better preserved and yielded many fine items of furniture and funerary equipment dating from Amenophis' reign (*see* YUYA AND TUYA, TOMB OF).

Working under new artistic influences from the Near East and the Mediterranean region, the artists of the period employed an unusual diversity of styles and materials to produce luxury items for the court (*see* EGYPT, ANCIENT, §XVI, 6 and 8). In sculpture, the colossal statues of Amenophis III's reign were part of a powerful new current of monumentality in Egyptian art, but there was also a clear trend towards greater realism and perhaps even portraiture (*see* EGYPT, ANCIENT, §IX, 3(vii)(a)), exemplified by the gilded ebony statuette of the King from Thebes (New York, Brooklyn Mus., 48.28), the limestone head of a statuette of Queen Tiye from Serabit el-Khadim (Cairo, Egyp. Mus., JE 38257; for illustration *see* SERABIT EL-KHADIM) and a yew-wood female head from Kom Medinet Ghurab, probably also representing Tiye (Berlin, Ägyp. Mus., 21834). The same intimacy is apparent in many surviving funerary statuettes of private individuals, such as the wooden figures of the chantress Mi (New York, Brooklyn Mus., 47.120.3) and the stablemaster Tjay (Cairo, Egyp. Mus., JE 33255), and the steatite statuette of Khaemwas and his wife Manana (Cairo, Egyp. Mus., JE 87911).

BIBLIOGRAPHY

W. Stevenson Smith: *The Art and Architecture of Ancient Egypt*, Pelican Hist. A. (Harmondsworth, 1958, rev. 2/1981), pp. 266–77

L. M. Berman, ed.: *The Art of Amenophis III: Art Historical Analysis* (Cleveland, OH, 1990)

Egypt's Dazzling Sun: Amenophis III and his World (exh. cat. by A. P. Kozloff and B. M. Bryan, Cleveland, OH, Mus. A.; Fort Worth, TX, Kimbell A. Mus.; Paris, Grand Pal.; 1992–3)

IAN M. E. SHAW

Amenophis IV. *See* AKHENATEN.

Amer [Amber]. City in north-west Rajasthan, India, founded by Mina tribesmen in the early 10th century AD and taken by the Kachchhwaha Rajputs *c.* 1150. Amer is dominated by the palace complex located halfway up a hill crowned by massive fortifications. Below, a maze of buildings constitutes the town. The palace complex was built along a north–south axis over a period of *c.* 100 years. Raja Man Singh (*reg c.* 1590–1614) built the original palace at the southernmost end, a central courtyard surrounded by a rectangle of even, uniform structures. Below the palace in a funerary monument are some of the earliest surviving Rajasthani wall paintings. They lack inscriptions but relate formally to late 16th-century miniatures from Mewar and Amer.

Further additions were made to the palace in the 17th and 18th centuries. Two sets of courtyards and structures, showing rich cross-fertilization between the Mughal and Rajput styles, were added along the northern axis by Mirza

Raja Jai Singh (*reg* 1623–67). The third enclosure from the south contains the Diwan-i Am, or hall of public audience (1623–7), while the second enclosure from the south contains the king's private quarters (1635). When these were built, the original palace of Man Singh was converted into women's quarters (*zenana*). The king's quarters contain a hall of private audience and are surmounted by the lavishly decorated Jas Mahal. Gardens are laid out below, adjacent to the Moota Lake. Between the two courts constructed by Jai Singh I, Maharaja Sawai Jai Singh II (*reg* 1699–1744) built the gate known as Ganesha Pol, notable for its mosaic decoration and lattice screens (*see* PALACE, fig. 7). Jai Singh II also added the fourth, northernmost courtyard, its plain, uniform walls adding to the palace's fortifications. In 1727 Jai Singh II founded his new capital at JAIPUR, and Amer was abandoned from 1728. The Archaeological Museum below the palace houses material from Bairat and other nearby sites.

See also INDIAN SUBCONTINENT, §§III, 7(ii)(b) and V, 4(iii)(e).

BIBLIOGRAPHY

K. Khandalavala: *Wall Paintings from Amber* (New Delhi, 1974)

G. H. R. Tillotson: *The Rajput Palaces: The Development of an Architectural Style, 1450–1750* (London, 1987)

C. Tadgell: *The History of Architecture in India* (London, 1990)

WALTER SMITH

Amerbach. Swiss family of collectors of German origin. Johannes Amerbach (*b* ?Amorbach, *c*. 1450; *d* Basle, 25 Dec 1513) gained his MA at the Sorbonne, Paris, and trained as a printer in Nuremberg and Venice. In 1482 he settled in Basle, where in 1484 he founded his own print shop and publishing house. He was in close contact with Albrecht Dürer during the latter's stay in Basle (1491–2). Apart from works of art for personal use, for example ornamental daggers, he probably owned graphic and print blocks for woodcut illustrations by Dürer. Johannes's son, Bonifacius Amerbach (*b* Basle, 11 Oct 1495; *d* Basle, 24 April 1562), a lawyer, professor at the University of Basle and syndic of the Basle council, was the heir and executor of Erasmus and owned paintings by the Holbein family and important gold and silver pieces, for example the well-known 'Globe Cup' (1539; Basle, Hist. Mus.), coins, medals and drawings of Roman antiquities.

Bonifacius's son Basilius Amerbach (*b* Basle, 1 Dec 1533; *d* Basle, 25 April 1591) was also a university professor and syndic in Basle but, unlike his father and grandfather, collected systematically and passionately. In his concept of a universal, humanistic collection, which comprised natural specimens, antiques and curiosities, the fine arts, especially painting, drawing and graphics, had first place. In 1586 he already owned 16 paintings by Hans Holbein (ii) and works by Hans Holbein (i) and Ambrosius Holbein, partly inherited from his father. Basilius concentrated on collecting Upper-Rhine and Swiss art, such as that of Niklaus Manuel Deutsch I and Hans Baldung and of Urs Graf, of whose drawings he acquired the largest number extant (Basle, Kstmus.). A peculiarity of his collection was his acquisition of works bought piecemeal from sales of items in the workshops of painters and goldsmiths, hence the large number of goldsmiths' drawings and models in his possession. Other acquisitions were the result of his extensive correspondence and use of agents. He also owned an outstanding collection of coins and medals, as well as German and Italian plaques, and numerous small antique and Renaissance sculptures. He initiated the earliest excavations in Augusta Raurica, near Basle (1582). His gallery, 'Zum Kaiserstuhl' (1578–82), was built to house the systematic arrangement of his collection, later known as the 'Amerbach-Kabinett', of which he compiled several inventories (1586; Basle, Kstmus.), a testament to his knowledge and critical intellect.

After the death of Basilius Amerbach, his collection and important library passed to his nephew, Ludwig Iselin (1559–1612), from whose estate the city council of Basle acquired it (1661) for the University. An inventory of *c*. 1650 includes 49 paintings, 1866 drawings, 525 woodcuts (without book illustrations) and 3356 copper-engravings. In 1671 the contents of the 'Amerbach-Kabinett' were arranged in the specially reconstructed 'Zur Mücke Haus' on the Münsterplatz, Basle, as a permanent and free exhibition. As such the 'Amerbach-Kabinett' is the oldest public art collection of civic origin owned by a civic body, established 200 years before the secularization of royal collections. It formed the foundation of collections of the Kunstmuseum, Historisches Museum, Naturhistorisches Museum and Universitätsbibliothek in Basle.

See also BASLE, §2(ii).

BIBLIOGRAPHY

P. Ganz and E. Major: 'Die Entstehung des Amerbach'schen Kunstkabinets und die Amerbach'schen Inventare', *Öff. Kstsamml., Basel, Jber.*, n. s. 3, lix (1907)

O. Fischer: 'Geschichte der Öffentlichen Kunstsammlung', *Öffentliche Kstsammlung Basel. Festschrift zur Eröffnung des Kunstmuseums* (Basle, 1936)

T. Falk: *Das 15. Jahrhundert: Hans Holbein der Ältere und Jörg Schweiger, Die Basler Goldschmiederisse*, i of *Katalog der Zeichnungen des 15. und 16. Jahrhunderts im Kupferstichkabinett Basel* (Basle and Stuttgart, 1979), esp. pp. 12–20

H. C. Ackermann: 'The Basle Cabinets of Art and Curiosities in the 16th and 17th Centuries', *Papers of the Ashmolean Tercentenary Symposium: Oxford, 1984*

E. Landolt: *Kabinettstücke der Amerbach im Historischen Museum Basel* (Basle, 1984)

ELISABETH LANDOLT

American Abstract Artists [A.A.A.]. American group of painters and sculptors formed in 1936 in New York. Their aim was to promote American abstract art. Similar to the Abstraction–Création group in Europe, this association introduced the public to American abstraction through annual exhibitions, publications and lectures. It also acted as a forum for abstract artists to share ideas. The group, whose first exhibition was held in April 1937 at the Squibb Galleries in New York, insisted that art should be divorced from political or social issues. Its aesthetics were usually identified with synthetic Cubism, and the majority of its members worked in a geometric Cubist-derived idiom of hard-edged forms, applying flat, strong colours. While the group officially rejected Expressionism and Surrealism, its members actually painted in a number of abstract styles. Almost half of the founding members had studied with Hans Hoffmann and infused their geometric styles with surreal, biomorphic forms, while others experimented with NEO-PLASTICISM.

The first president was Balcomb Greene (*b* 1904). Among the early members were Ilya Bolotowsky, Willem

De Kooning, Burgoyne Diller, A. E. Gallatin, Carl Holty (1900–73), Harry Holtzman (*b* 1912), Lee Krasner, Ibram Lassaw, Ad Reinhardt, David Smith and Albert Swinden (1901–61). The group also included a number of European artists living in the USA, among them Josef Albers, Jean Hélion, László Moholy-Nagy and Piet Mondrian.

The group, which never dissolved, had its heyday from 1937 to 1942, when it established a suitable climate for the formation of Abstract Expressionism.

WRITINGS

American Abstract Artists, Three Yearbooks (1938, 1939, 1946) (New York, 1969)

BIBLIOGRAPHY

G. McNeil: 'American Abstractionists Venerable at Twenty', *Art News*, lv/3 (1956), pp. 34–5, 64–6

S. C. Larsen: 'The American Abstract Artists Group: A History and Evaluation of its Impact upon American Art' (diss., Evanston, IL, Northwestern U., 1975)

Abstract Painting and Sculpture in America, 1927–1944 (exh. cat., ed. J. R. Lane and S. C. Larsen; Pittsburgh, PA, Carnegie Mus. A., 1983)

ILENE SUSAN FORT

American Artists' Congress. Organization founded in 1936 in the USA in response to the call of the Popular Front and the American Communist Party for formations of literary and artistic groups against the spread of Fascism. In May 1935 a group of New York artists met to draw up the 'Call for an American Artists' Congress'; among the initiators were George Ault (1891–1948), Peter Blume, Stuart Davis, Adolph Denn, William Gropper (*b* 1897), Jerome Klein, Louis Lozowick (1892–1973), Moses Soyer, Niles Spencer and Harry Sternberg. Davis became one of the most vociferous promoters of the Congress and was not only the national executive secretary but also the editor of the organization's magazine, *Art Front*, until 1939.

The dual concerns of the American Artists' Congress were the economic distress of artists resulting from the depressions of the 1930s and the effect of Fascism in terms of the use of art as war propaganda and the censorship of art. The Congress endorsed the Works Progress Administration's Federal Art Project (WPA-/FAP) based on the economic needs of artists and lobbied for permanent governmental sponsorship of the arts. In 1939 a book of *Twelve Cartoons Defending WPA by Members of the American Artists' Congress* was published. The Congress supported a policy of museums paying rental fees to artists and called for an exhibition boycott of the Olympic Games in Berlin in 1936.

The first American Artists' Congress against War and Fascism was held in New York at the Town Hall and the New School for Social Research on 14–16 February 1936. About 400 delegates attended, including 'leading American artists, academicians and modernists, purists and social realists' (*American Artists' Congress against War and Fascism*), as well as visiting delegations from Mexico, Cuba, Peru and Canada. The opening address was delivered by Lewis Mumford, then chairman of the American Writers' League, which had been organized in April 1935.

Membership of the American Artists' Congress declined in 1940, when a number of members, concerned at the apparent support by the Communist-orientated organization for the Russians' attack on Finland, seceded to form the politically independent Federation of Modern Painters and Sculptors. By 1943 the Congress was defunct.

WRITINGS

American Artists' Congress against War and Fascism: First American Artists' Congress (New York, 1936)

M. Baigell and J. Williams, eds: *Artists against War and Fascism: Papers of the First American Artists' Congress* (New Brunswick, 1986)

M. SUE KENDALL

American China Manufactory. *See* TUCKER CHINA FACTORY.

American Flint Glass Manufactory. *See under* STIEGEL, HENRY WILLIAM.

American Impressionism. *See under* IMPRESSIONISM.

American Pottery Manufacturing Co. American pottery manufacturer. Beginning in 1828 D. & J. Henderson made award-winning Rockingham in a factory previously occupied by the Jersey Porcelain and Earthenware Co. in Jersey City, NJ, but in 1833 David Henderson (*c*. 1793–1845) took control of the company and changed the name to the American Pottery Manufacturing Co. In addition to the fine Rockingham modelled by the Englishman Daniel Greatbach (*fl* after 1839; *d* after 1866), the company was the first to make transfer-printed pearlware in the USA and in *c*. 1833 reproduced Ridgway's 'Canova' pattern. Many English potters who settled in the USA during the second quarter of the 19th century started their American careers in Henderson's pottery. After Henderson's death in 1845 the firm continued until 1852, when John Owen Rouse (*d* 1896) and Nathaniel Turner (*d* 1884) took over the works for the production of whiteware, which was made there until 1892.

BIBLIOGRAPHY

E. A. Barber: *The Pottery and Porcelain of the United States* (New York, 1893, rev. 3/1909/*R* 1976), pp. 118–25

ELLEN PAUL DENKER

American Scene painting. Term used to describe scenes of typical American life painted in a naturalistic vein from *c*. 1920 until the early 1940s. It applies to both Regionalism and Social Realism in American painting, but its specific boundaries remain ambiguous. The phrase probably derived from Henry James's collection of essays and impressions, *The American Scene* (1907), published upon James's own rediscovery of his native land after 21 years as an expatriate. The term entered the vocabulary of fine arts by the 1920s and was applied to the paintings of Charles Burchfield during 1924.

In the two decades following World War I, American writers and artists began to look for native sources for the aesthetic and spiritual renewal of their modern technological civilization. This search engaged and activated many thoughtful and creative people in the 1920s and 1930s and resulted in that flurry of activity that Waldo Frank (1889–1967) discussed as *The Rediscovery of America* (1929; his personal analysis of American life). The phenomenon blossomed during the 1930s, when a generation of artists struggled to find a form and content for their art that would match their own experiences of America. Traditional boundaries of acceptable subject-matter were broadened to include the everyday lives of average Americans—farmers, office workers, window shoppers and even Franklin D. Roosevelt's 'forgotten man'. From 'ten-cent movies' to fertile farmscapes, factory icons or bathers at Coney Island, images of urban bustle and backwoods folk life were offered up to celebrate and define 'the American Scene' in words and in paint.

Burchfield and Edward Hopper are the names most often associated with American Scene painting in the 1920s. Drawing on memories of his childhood in Salem, OH, Burchfield painted the clapboard houses, Gothic mansions (e.g. *House of Mystery*, 1924; Chicago, IL, A. Inst.), rain-soaked roads and false-fronted shops of provincial America; the art critic Guy Pène du Bois commented on the idea that Burchfield was painting 'the American Scene' in *International Studio* in September, 1924.

In the 1930s the term was closely linked to the art of the Regionalists, Thomas Hart Benton (for illustration *see* BENTON, THOMAS HART), Grant Wood and John Steuart Curry, whose *Baptism in Kansas* (1928; New York, Whitney; see fig.) is a typical example. It has also been applied to the work of Reginald Marsh, Isabel Bishop, Alexander Brook (1898–1980), George Bellows (for illustration *see* BELLOWS, GEORGE) and Moses Soyer and Raphael Soyer. Ben Shahn's paintings, for example that of miners on strike in *Scott's Run, West Virginia* (1937; New York, Whitney), and the work of Stuart Davis also fit the description.

In general, American Scene paintings were characterized by a form of realism that eschewed both radical abstract styles and allegorical academic modes, as in Hopper's *Room in New York* (1932; Lincoln, U. NE A. Gals). As befitted art in a democracy, the subject-matter was both accessible and, as Benton put it, 'arguable in the language of the streets'. Alongside the democratic goal of an 'art for the millions', an interest developed in creating prints for mass distribution. Rooted in the realist tradition of the earlier Ashcan school, American Scene painting was in some ways a reaction against the influence of French modernism that had dominated American art in the early 1920s and it coincided with the growing climate of isolationism during the inter-war years.

See also REGIONALISM (ii).

BIBLIOGRAPHY

A. H. Jones: 'The Search for a Usable American Past in the New Deal Era', *Amer. Q.*, xxiii (1971), pp. 710–24

American Scene painting by John Steuart Curry: *Baptism in Kansas*, oil on canvas, 1.00×1.25 m, 1928 (New York, Whitney Museum of American Art)

F. V. O'Connor, ed.: *Art for the Millions: Essays from the 1930s* (Boston, 1973)
M. Baigell: *The American Scene: American Painting of the 1930s* (New York, 1974)
J. M. Dennis: *Grant Wood: A Study in American Art and Culture* (New York, 1975)
N. Heller and J. Williams: *The Regionalists: Painters of the American Scene* (New York, 1976)
K. A. Marling: *Wall-to-wall America: A Cultural History of Post Office Murals in the Great Depression* (Minneapolis, 1982)
W. M. Corn: *Grant Wood: The Regionalist Vision* (New York, 1983)

M. SUE KENDALL

Americas, Pre-Columbian. *See* MESOAMERICA, PRE-COLUMBIAN; NATIVE NORTH AMERICAN ART; and SOUTH AMERICA, PRE-COLUMBIAN.

Américo de (Figueiredo e) Melo, Pedro (*b* Areia, 1843; *d* Florence, 1905). Brazilian painter. His precocious talent as a draughtsman was recognized as early as 1853, when he accompanied the expedition led by the French naturalist Louis Jacques Brunet to the north-east of Brazil. He then went to Rio de Janeiro, where he entered the Academia Imperial das Belas Artes in 1855. Under the patronage of Emperor Peter II he lived in France from 1859 to 1864, studying with Jean-Auguste-Dominique Ingres and Horace Vernet at the Ecole des Beaux-Arts in Paris. His interests also included physics, philosophy and literature. His essay 'Refutation of the Life of Jesus by Renan' won him the decoration of the papal order of the Holy Sepulchre. He also painted one of his first important pictures at this time, *Carioca* ('Woman from Rio de Janeiro'; 1862; Rio de Janeiro, Mus. N. B.A.). On his return to Brazil he taught drawing (and later art history, aesthetics and archaeology) at the Academia Imperial. When the Republic was proclaimed in 1889, he became a member of the constituent assembly.

Américo de Melo's paintings were firmly rooted in the Neo-classical tradition, later modified by Romantic elements. He produced biblical scenes, allegories, portraits and even caricatures but specialized in historical scenes, notably the *Battle of Avaí* (5×10 m; 1872–7; Rio de Janeiro, Mus. N. B.A.), commissioned by the Brazilian government to commemorate the famous episode in the war against Paraguay (1865–70), and completed in Florence, where he lived from 1873 to the late 1880s. In Florence he painted another of his historical works, the *Cry of Ipiranga* (1886–8; U. São Paulo, Mus. Paulista), depicting the proclamation of Brazilian independence in 1822.

BIBLIOGRAPHY

Pontual
L. Gonzaga Duque: *A arte brasileira* (Rio de Janeiro, 1888)
Pedro Américo no Museu Nacional de Belas Artes, cat. (Rio de Janeiro, 1965)
Q. Campofiorito: *História da pintura brasileira no século XIX* (Rio de Janeiro, 1983)

ROBERTO PONTUAL

Ameringius, Petrus. *See* HEYDEN, PIETER VAN DER.

Amerling, Friedrich von (*b* Vienna, 14 April 1803; *d* Vienna, 14 Jan 1887). Austrian painter. He came from a family of craftsmen and studied (1815–24) at the Akademie der bildenden Künste, Vienna, where one of his teachers was the conservative history painter Hubert Maurer (1738–1818). From 1824 to 1826 he attended the Academy in Prague, where he was taught by Josef Bergler. In 1827 and 1828 Amerling stayed in London, and he met the portrait painter Sir Thomas Lawrence, whose work was to be a strong influence on Amerling's painting during the next two decades. Amerling also travelled to Paris and Rome but was recalled to Vienna on an official commission to paint a life-size portrait of the emperor *Francis I of Austria* (Vienna, Ksthist. Mus.). With this work, Amerling became the most sought-after portrait painter in Vienna, a position he was to retain for about 15 years.

The highpoint of Amerling's work occurred in the 1830s. At that time he was able to combine the stylishness of English portrait painters—both his own contemporaries as well as the older generation such as Reynolds—with the realist traditions of Viennese bourgeois portraiture. Large-scale individual portraits and family or group pictures were equally successful. Among Amerling's most important works are two family pictures with nearly life-size figures, *Graf Breunner and his Family* (1834; priv. col., see Probszt, pl. 40) and *Rudolf von Arthaber with his Children* (1837; Vienna, Belvedere; see fig.). These pictures, particularly the latter, are often seen as the epitome of Viennese Biedermeier culture in their concern for both emotional and material comfort. Among the vast number of portraits by Amerling, many were of important citizens, aristocrats, members of the royal family or artists, as in *The Painter Robert Theer* (1831; Vienna, Belvedere). Amerling also

Friedrich von Amerling: *Rudolf von Arthaber with his Children*, oil on canvas, 2.21×1.56 m, 1837 (Vienna, Belvedere, Österreichische Galerie)

made a large number of spontaneous, often roughly sketched portrait studies that directly capture physiognomy in a manner more independent of the style of the time. These pictures, which show only the subject's head, are among the most striking achievements of European portrait painting of the period. Amerling generally reserved this type of portrait for members of his family, children and artist friends, as in *The Painter Eduard Bendemann* (1837; Vienna, Belvedere). One of Amerling's particular specialities was the 'one-figure genre painting', in which the subjects appear either in a costume alien to the milieu, as in the *Woman Playing a Lute* (1838; Vienna, Belvedere), or in scenes with an implied story-line, as in *The Widow* (1836; Vienna, Hist. Mus.).

His close ties to English painting, his sophistication and his ambition enabled Amerling to go beyond the boundaries of the local Viennese tradition. After 1850 developments caught up with him, however: his painting failed to adapt to changes in taste, though his good reputation remained with him into old age. In spite of his great popularity, Amerling never taught at the Akademie. He had many private pupils, but only one of them, Josef Matthäus Aigner (1805–86), is worthy of mention.

BIBLIOGRAPHY

Kindler; Meissner; Thieme–Becker

Aus dem Nachlasse des vaterländischen Meisters Friedrich von Amerling (exh. cat., Vienna, Kstver., 1888)

L. A. Frankl: *Friedrich von Amerling: Ein Lebensbild* (Vienna, 1889)

H. Tietze: 'Friedrich Amerlings Gruppenporträts', *Alt-Wien. Kal.* (1919), pp. 58ff

G. Probszt: *Friedrich von Amerling: Der Altmeister der Wiener Porträtmalerei* (Zurich, Leipzig and Vienna, 1927) [with cat. rai.]

G. Frodl: *Wiener Malerei der Biedermeierzeit* (Rosenheim, 1987), pp. 243ff

GERBERT FRODL

Amersfoort. Town in the Netherlands, situated *c.* 20 km north-east of Utrecht on the edge of the valley of the River Gelder, where several watercourses join to form the River Eem. Its early history was dominated by that of Utrecht. Amersfoort is known primarily for the survival of its medieval centre, which includes the original street plan, many churches and houses, and parts of the outer ring of fortifications with two watergates.

The early history of Amersfoort is poorly documented, but excavations have provided information about the first canals and parcels of land. The town name first occurs in 1028, when it was a small agricultural settlement on a ford over the Eem. Its growth was closely related to the reclamation of the Gelder valley, and it is mentioned again in the 12th century, when the town had become the seat of an episcopal governor, who may have organized the new development. Early in the 13th century there was an episcopal court with a chapel, which was later enlarged to become the St Joriskerk, the principal church of the town. In 1259 the Bishop of Utrecht granted Amersfoort municipal rights. The main medieval industries were brewing and cloth, but owing to the influence of Utrecht the town never developed as an important trading centre in its own right, and it declined after the 15th century, remaining contained within its medieval walls until the 20th century.

There were two circuits of walls, both built of brick. The inner walls were built *c.* 1300, but the town expanded so quickly in the early 14th century that from 1380 to 1450 an outer circuit was built to enclose the new settlements. Both circuits are shown on a map of *c.* 1560 by Jacob van Deventer (*d* 1575). Once the inner wall was no longer needed as a fortification, prosperous citizens built large houses on its outer face, probably using materials from the wall itself, as traces of it survive elsewhere. These 'Wall Houses', encircling the oldest parts of the inner city, are the most striking features of Amersfoort. The surviving medieval buildings are constructed predominantly of brick and timber, with the occasional use of tufa. Of the inner walls there survive a brick tower, the Plompetoren, built in the late 13th century, and the 14th-century fortified house of Tinnumburg, which was built to defend the original watergate. The watergates of the outer fortifications, the Monnickendam and the Koppelpoort, both date from the 15th century.

In the early 14th century the St Joriskerk was transformed into a cruciform church, but in the 15th it was turned into a hall church, and the unique choir-screen was put in. When Amersfoort was at its most prosperous in the late 14th century and the 15th, many abbeys and chapels were built, of which several survive. Onze Lieve Vrouwe Chapel became a popular place of pilgrimage after a miracle was attributed to the Virgin there in 1444: in the second half of the 15th century a new church was built with the money donated by pilgrims and visitors. The tower, almost 100 m high, survived the explosion that destroyed the church in 1787. Of the St Pieter's and Bloklands hospital (founded 1380) there remain the St Pieter's Chapel and the men's infirmary with, near by, the St Aagten Chapel and the Observantenklooster, all dating from the 15th century. At the Reformation, Amersfoort became and remained strongly Protestant, and many religious buildings fell out of use or were sold. The Observantenklooster and the 15th-century nunnery of Marienhof have been converted to civic use.

BIBLIOGRAPHY

J. van Deventer: *Nederlandsche steden in de 16de eeuw: Plattegronden* [*c.* 1560]; facs., with intro. by R. Fruin, 2 vols (The Hague, 1916–24)

B. J. M. Speet: *Amersfoort*, ii of *Historische stedenatlas van Nederland*, ed. G. van Herwijnen and others (Delft, 1982) [with extensive bibliog.]

MONIQUE KRAUWER

Ames, Ezra (*b* Framingham, MA, 5 May 1768; *d* Albany, NY, 23 Feb 1836). American painter and craftsman. After working briefly in Worcester, MA (1790–93), painting miniatures, chimney-pieces, signs and sleighs, he settled permanently in Albany, NY. There he practised various crafts, including frame-making and painting ornamental clockfaces. Active in the Masonic Temple, he held a high position in the New York chapter from 1802 to 1826. For the Masons he made signs, aprons, urns and carpet designs. Entries in his account books indicate that by 1813 he was primarily painting portraits, improving his technique by copying works by John Singleton Copley and Gilbert Stuart. His first major success was the sale of a portrait of *George Clinton*, Governor of New York and vice-president of the USA, to the Pennsylvania Academy of Fine Arts (1812; destr. 1845). Laudatory reviews generated requests for replicas, including an ambitious but somewhat awkward full-length version (*c.* 1813; Albany, NY, State Capitol). Ames also painted the official portrait of *DeWitt*

Clinton (George Clinton's nephew) *as Governor of New York* for the city of Albany (1817–18; on dep. Albany, NY, Inst. Hist. & A.). It is a half-length portrait and demonstrates his straightforward, factual style. Ames was elected to the American Academy of Fine Arts in 1824 but never exhibited in New York. Nearly 500 of his works, mainly portraits of people in New York state, have been recorded.

BIBLIOGRAPHY

T. Bolton and I. F. Cortelyou: *Ezra Ames of Albany* (New York, 1955)

I. F. Cortelyou: *A Supplement to the Catalogue of Pictures by Ezra Ames of Albany* (New York, 1957)

LEAH LIPTON

Ametller Rotllan, Blas (*b* Barcelona, 1768; *d* Madrid, 20 Oct 1841). Spanish Catalan engraver. He was assistant professor at the Escuela de Artes, Barcelona, in 1787 and received a scholarship from the Junta de Comercio to study engraving in Madrid (1790–95) under Manuel Salvador Carmona. In 1793 he was awarded first prize for engraving by the Real Academia de S Fernando, Madrid, for his portrait of *Ventura Rodríguez* after the painting by Goya (1784; Stockholm, Nmus.), and in 1797 he was made an Academician. In 1803 he made the engraving the *Ostrich Hunt*; he also produced book illustrations, religious engravings and reproductions of paintings. His success led to his appointment as Grabador de Cámara in 1815, in which position he executed a portrait of *Ferdinand VII* (1821) after drawings by Vicente López y Portaña. On the death of Salvador Carmona in 1820, Ametller Rotllan was made Director de Grabado at the Real Academia, a post he held until his death.

BIBLIOGRAPHY

Ceán Bermúdez

P. Sanjuanena: 'Breves noticias de Blas Ametller y sus obras', *A. España*, vi (1867), pp. 137–42

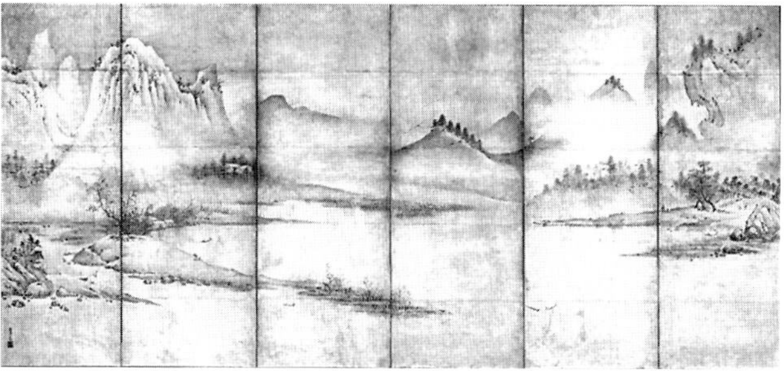

Shinsō Sōami: *Landscape of the Four Seasons*, pair of screens, ink on paper, 380×840 mm, Muromachi period, *c.* 1500 (New York, Metropolitan Museum of Art)

A. Gallego: *Historia del grabado en España* (Madrid, 1979)

J. Carrete, F. Checa and V. Bozal: *El grabado en España: Siglos XV al XVIII*, Summa A., xxxi (Madrid, 1987)

BLANCA GARCÍA VEGA

Amhada. *See under* DAKHLA OASIS.

Ami. Japanese school of ink painting (*suibokuga*; *see* JAPAN, §VI, 4(iii)) active during the Muromachi period (1333–1568). The school is represented by the San'ami ('three Ami'), (1) Shinnō Nōami, his son (2) Shingei Geiami and grandson (3) Shinsō Sōami. The Ami held the post of *karamono bugyō* ('administrator of Chinese things') to the ASHIKAGA shoguns, i.e. curator of their collection of Chinese artworks, and were *dōbōshū* ('comrades'; advisers on artistic matters).

BIBLIOGRAPHY

I. Tanaka: *Shūbun tara Sesshūe* [Shubūn to Sesshū], xii of *Nihon no bijutsu* [Arts of Japan], ed. K. Kamei, S. Takahashi and I. Tanaka (Tokyo, 1964–9); trans. B. Darling as *Japanese Ink Painting: Shubūn to Sesshū* (New York, 1972, rev. Tokyo, 1980), xii of Heibonsha Surv. Jap. Art (Tokyo, 1972–80)

I. Tanaka and Y. Yonezawa: *Suibokuga* [Ink painting] (Tokyo, 1970), xi of *Genshoku Nihon no bijutsu* [Arts of Japan in full colour], ed. T. Akiyama and others (Tokyo, 1966–80)

S. Noma and S. Tani, eds: *Nihon bijutsu jiten* [Encyclopedia of Japanese history of art] (Tokyo, 1987)

MASAMOTO KAWAI

(1) Shinnō Nōami (*b* 1397; *d* Hase, Nara Prefect., 1471). Connoisseur–curator and founder of the Ami school of ink painting (*suibokuga*). Although many paintings are attributed to Nōami, most attributions are questionable. A work widely thought to be by Nōami is the *White-robed Kannon* hanging scroll (ink on silk, 1468; priv. col., see Tanaka, p. 43), and an inscription by the artist indicates that he painted it for his son Shūken. The angular, formal ink-painting of the work blends the Chinese Southern Song (1127–1279) academic styles of XIA GUI and MA YUAN. As a connoisseur, Nōami was responsible for compiling the *Gyomotsu on'e mokuroku* (or *Gyomotsu gyoya mokuroku*), an inventory of the Chinese paintings in the shogunal collection. He may also have been involved in the writing of the *Kundaikan sōchōki* (catalogue of the shogunal collection with display instructions), possibly completed by his grandson (3) Shinsō Sōami.

(2) Shingei Geiami (*b* 1431; *d* 1485). Connoisseur–curator and member of the Ami school of ink painting (*suibokuga*), son of (1) Shinnō Nōami. He served the eighth shogun, Ashikaga Yoshimasa (1436–90), as a painter, artistic adviser and curator. At the age of 50 Geiami painted *Viewing a Waterfall* (hanging scroll, ink and colours on paper, 1480; Tokyo, Nezu A. Mus.) in the angular, formal style of the Chinese Southern Song period (1127–1279) painter XIA GUI, as a farewell present to his student KENKŌ SHŌKEI.

(3) Shinsō Sōami (*d* 1525). Connoisseur–curator and member of the Ami school of ink painting (*suibokuga*), grandson of (1) Shinnō Nōami and son of (2) Shingei Geiami. His extant paintings include a landscape on sliding door panels (ink on paper; Kyoto, Daitokuji, Daisen'in) and *Landscape of the Four Seasons* (pair of screens, ink on paper; New York, Met.; see fig.). He painted in at least two styles: angular, hard-edged ink-painting in the Chinese Southern Song (1127–1279) academic style of the painter

XIA GUI, which his father and grandfather had used; and a new Japanese style, which was a synthesis of the softer, more cursive style of the Southern Song painter MUQI as well as the rich ink washes and dots of the MI FU style and some elements from Korean painting. He incorporated Japanese compositional elements from *Yamatoe* (traditional Japanese painting) into this latter style, and it was adopted by early 16th-century painters, including Kanō Motonobu (*see* KANŌ, (2)).

In addition to his reputation as a painter, Sōami is credited with playing an important part in the writing of the catalogue of the shogunal collection *Kundaikan sō chōki* (or *Kundaikan sauchōki*; 1476–1511), which may have been begun by his grandfather (*see* (1) above). *Kundaikan sō chōki* includes a ranking of Chinese artists into upper, middle and lower categories, with a further three subdivisions of each class, and instructions on the proper way to display works of art, as well as comments on various types of Chinese lacquerwork, ceramics and bronzes.

BRENDA G. JORDAN

Amice. *See under* VESTMENTS, ECCLESIASTICAL, §1(i).

Amidi, Hamid al-. *See* AYTAÇ, HAMID.

Amiens. French city and capital of Picardy in Somme, northern France. It was founded on the River Somme on the site of the Roman city of Samarobriva. Reduced to a fortified *castellum* after the invasions of the 3rd-century AD, the medieval city eventually developed suburbs to the south and east. In 850 the cathedral of Notre-Dame and the church of St Firmin formed a cathedral complex in the old centre. From the 11th century, economic expansion and a growing population revived the city, and a textile industry developed with the production of a blue dye from woad and woollen cloth. The merchant-drapers of Amiens formed a middle class and were affranchized in 1117. A royal city from 1185, Amiens numbered 20,000 inhabitants in the 13th century. Religious foundations multiplied: the Abbey of St Acheul and the churches of St Nicolas, St Martin-aux-Jumeaux and St Martin-du-Bourg, and the cathedral (*see* §1 below). From *c.* 1250 until the late 15th century, manuscript illumination flourished in the city (*see* §2(i) below). The city suffered in the Hundred Years War (1337–1453), but the textile industry subsequently resumed. The Flamboyant churches of St Germain and St Leu were then built and the choir screen and stalls of the cathedral erected, the confraternity of Puy-Notre-Dame commissioning many paintings. In the 16th century and more particularly in the 17th, tapestries were produced in the city (*see* §2(ii) below). Amiens was occupied by the Spanish in 1597 and lost many of its churches in the wake of the Revolution. However, the Société des Antiquaires de Picardie, founded in 1836, endeavoured to protect its artistic heritage. Amiens was the objective of a great battle in 1918 and a bombardment in 1944; it thus lost its medieval character and has been largely rebuilt.

1. Cathedral. 2. Centre of production.

1. CATHEDRAL. The cathedral, dedicated to Notre-Dame, is a classic example of 13th-century architecture and sculpture. Built between 1220 and *c.* 1270, it replaced a complex of episcopal buildings located in the *castrum* of the old city. A cathedral dedicated to the Virgin was already mentioned in AD 850 near the church of St Firmin, and to construct the present cathedral it was necessary to move St Firmin and to extend beyond the Gallo-Roman city walls. The names of the architects are known from the labyrinth (destr. 18th century; reconstructed 1894–7) that in 1288 was set into the floor of the nave: ROBERT DE LUZARCHES, Thomas de Cormont and Regnault de Cormont (*see* CORMONT, DE). The cathedral was built under the patronage of bishops Evrard de Fouilloy (*reg* 1211–22), Geoffroy d'Eu (*reg* 1223–36), Arnoul (*reg* 1236–47), Gérard de Conchy (*reg* 1247–57) and Bernard d'Abbeville (*reg* 1259–78).

The date of 1220 for the beginning of construction was given in the labyrinth. Bishop Evrard de Fouilloy is specified as the founder in his obituary notice, and a charter of Arnoul from 1242 states that the former cathedral was burnt during Evrard's episcopate. In a deed of 31 March 1236 Geoffroy d'Eu affirmed the relocation of St Firmin on to the site of the hospital to enable Notre-Dame to be enlarged; another charter of Arnoul dated 1238 shows that the hospital had been relocated and that St Firmin was being rebuilt. It is accepted that the nave of the cathedral was already finished by this time and that the first church of St Firmin stood on the site of the transept and the first bays of the choir. In 1248 Arnoul was buried in the choir. A fire is recorded in 1258; the restorer, Viollet-le-Duc, noticed traces of it on the vaults of the radiating chapels, so it is thought that the lower parts of the chevet were already built by then. The *Chronicle de Corbie* (Amiens, Bib. Mun., MS. 254) mentions the completion of the cathedral in 1264, the same year as the meeting between Louis IX of France and Henry III of England in Amiens. The axial clerestory window in the apse carries the date 1269 and the name Bernard d'Abbeville: the main fabric of the Cathedral, built from west to east, was thus completed by this time.

The nave chapels were added from 1292, the best-known being that of Jean de La Grange, built *c.* 1375 at the same time as the Beau Pilier intended to reinforce the north tower. The upper storeys of the towers were being built in 1366. Pierre Tarissel, master mason from 1482 to 1510, added extra flying buttreses to the straight bays of the choir, repaired the piers and inserted tie-rods in the triforium to stabilize the crossing vault. The crossing spire was rebuilt after its destruction by lightning in 1528. The French Revolution (1789–95) left the cathedral virtually unscathed, and restoration was undertaken from 1820. Viollet-le-Duc directed work on the upper parts from 1849. The cathedral suffered very little damage in the two World Wars.

(i) Architecture. (ii) Sculpture. (iii) Stained glass.

(i) Architecture. The cathedral has a west façade with two shallow rectangular towers, leading to an aisled nave of six bays (see fig. 1). Each arm of the transept has three bays with east and west aisles. The eastern arm of the church is as long as the nave; the four-bay choir has double aisles, leading to a single ambulatory with seven contiguous, polygonal radiating chapels, the axial chapel being longer

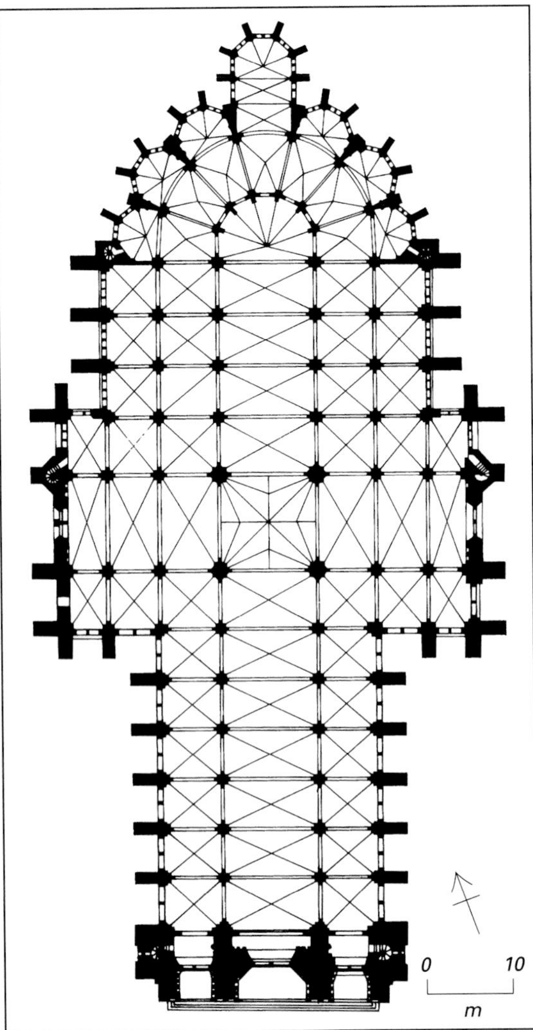

1. Amiens Cathedral, *c.* 1220–70, ground-plan

than the others. This church is one of the largest in France: it measures 145 m in overall length, and the central vessel is nearly 15 m wide. It is also the highest (except for the unfinished Beauvais Cathedral), measuring some 42 m to the vault.

The church has a three-storey elevation: arcades, triforium and clerestory. The tall arcade, reaching nearly half the total height, has *piliers cantonnés.* A foliage string course runs along the base of the triforium. In the nave and on the west side of the transept the triforium is a blind passage with pointed arches opening on to the nave; each bay consists of two sets of triple arches, each under a containing arch with a trilobe piercing the tympanum. On the east side of the transept and in the choir the triforium is more elaborate in design, pierced to the exterior and glazed; on the interior, each straight bay has two gabled arches divided into three lights surmounted by trilobes (see fig. 2). The traceried clerestory windows in the nave have four lights beneath oculi with pierced spandrels. In the straight bays of the choir they are of six lights with more complex tracery; in the narrower apse bays, of four lights surmounted by two trilobes and a larger oculus. The vaults of the church are quadripartite except in the crossing bay, where the vault also includes liernes and tiercerons (*see* FRANCE, §II, 1).

On the west façade there are three portals, sheltered in gabled porches connecting the buttresses. The sculptural decoration of the porches continues around the buttresses, which are decorated above with blind tracery and pinnacles. Behind the gables of the lateral doorways, two windows in the form of curved triangles directly illuminate the aisles. Two superposed galleries run across the façade above the porches. The lower is a passage with an arcade of richly decorated twin arches; the upper consists of a series of niches filled with statues of kings. The central rose is placed above the galleries between the towers, which are open at this level. The Flamboyant tracery of the rose is a later alteration, as are the gallery above it and the top stage of the towers. The rose seems small in relation to the façade as a whole: the extreme height of the nave dictated its position far from the ground.

The transept façades have no towers, and the end walls of the aisles are pierced by windows. Above the central door on each transept, at triforium level on the interior is a row of glazed twin arches below immense traceried windows consisting of two lights beneath a rose. The south rose has Flamboyant tracery, but the Rayonnant north rose is based on the surprising central motif of a five-pointed star. The plain flying buttresses of the nave

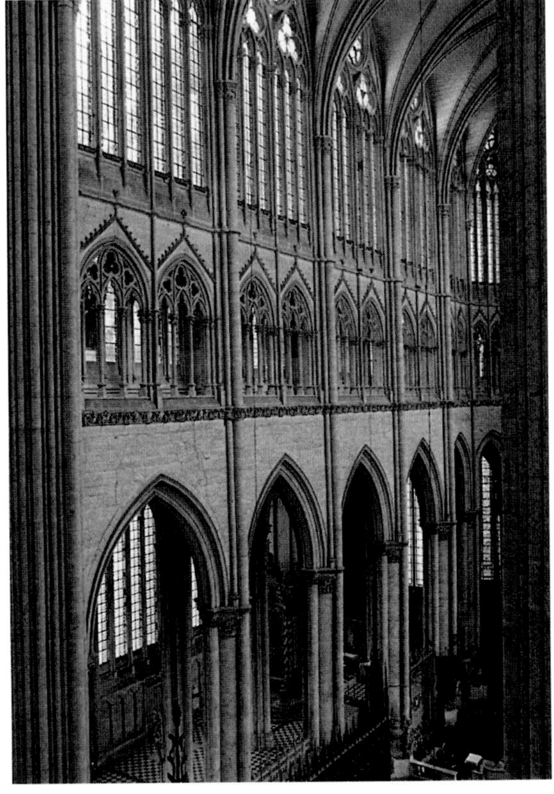

2. Amiens Cathedral, choir, *c.* 1238–64, north elevation

are on two levels, with abutment piers crowned with high pinnacles. They abut the nave wall beneath the upper parapet. Around the chevet (*see* FRANCE, fig. 4) the flyers have a double span in two ranks; the upper rank is made up of twin trilobed arches surmounted by further trilobes. The clerestory windows are crowned with gables, which intersect the parapet with spectacular effect.

The whole structure is built of a white chalky limestone from nearby quarries at Tirancourt, Croissy and elsewhere, on very deep foundations (7.6 m). The coursed piers are made of large blocks of stone. Kimpel has shown that in the choir each course consists of two interchangeable blocks incorporating the engaged shafts. The wall responds were also prefabricated and set first, the wall between being filled in afterwards, as the joints indicate. This shows the concern of the masons' workshop to standardize the moulded elements. The choir piers are held together with iron clamps, and the vaults are thinner than those at Reims Cathedral (about 250 mm compared to 400 mm).

The structure and decoration reveal two principal building campaigns: first the nave and western sides of the transepts, completed *c.* 1236–8, then the eastern parts, the upper transept façades being finished a little later, after 1269. There is a change of design in the nave at clerestory level: the extension of the supports on the interior wall of the façade indicates that the nave was not originally planned to be so high. There may also have been a change in the design of the façade, less evident because of its complexity: the flattened towers and multiple passages at different levels cannot be compared to any other building in France. It is generally thought that the portal zone was completed before 1236, although Erlande-Brandenburg places it between 1236 and 1240 (*see* §(ii) below).

The nave belongs to the classic period of French Gothic (for further discussion *see* HIGH GOTHIC). The plan, the *piliers cantonnés* and the window tracery derive from Reims Cathedral. The porches of the west façade recall Laon Cathedral and the transepts of Chartres Cathedral, but the tall proportions of the arcades and the triforium are inspired rather by Sens Cathedral and are close to Beauvais. The west façade is innovative in continuing its decoration around the buttresses, in its windows on to the aisles, and in its rich ornamentation. The structure of the towers and their passages perhaps reflects lost monuments in northern France, such as Anchin Abbey, but may also have an English origin. The crossing vault and north rose perhaps indicate contacts with contemporary English designs, and the cathedral chevet must have been one of the models for Westminster Abbey.

The nave of Amiens has some Rayonnant characteristics, which are fully apparent in the eastern parts. The radiating chapels are so close in style to the Sainte-Chapelle in Paris that Branner attributed the latter to Thomas de Cormont. The towerless transept façades, the glazed triforium and the gabled treatment of the upper parts of the chevet are linked to the mid-13th-century Parisian style, as at the Sainte-Chapelle and Notre-Dame, Paris. Notre-Dame at Amiens must be regarded as a major work of Rayonnant in the French royal domain, and it influenced the cathedrals of Cambrai, Tournai, Metz and Cologne.

See also MASONRY, figs 7 and 8; for liturgical arrangement *see also* CHURCH, §II, 3(i).

BIBLIOGRAPHY

G. Durand: *Monographie de l'église Notre-Dame, cathédrale d'Amiens*, 2 vols (Amiens, 1901–3)

——: 'Amiens, cathédrale Notre-Dame: Bibliographie', *Congr. Archéol. France*, xci (1936), pp. 10–27

R. Branner: *St Louis and the Court Style in Gothic Architecture* (London, 1965), pp. 138–40

A. Erlande-Brandenburg: 'Le Septième Colloque international de la Société française d'archéologie, 1er et 2 octobre 1974: La Façade de la cathédrale d'Amiens', *Bull. Mnmtl*, cxxv (1977), pp. 253–93

D. Kimpel: 'Le Développement de la taille en série dans l'architecture médiévale et son rôle dans l'histoire économique', *Bull. Mnmtl*, cxxxv (1977), pp. 195–222

H. Kraus: *Gold Was the Mortar: The Economics of Cathedral Building* (London, 1979), pp. 39–59

S. Murray: 'Looking for Robert de Luzarches: The Early Work at Amiens Cathedral', *Gesta*, xxix (1990), pp. 111–31

ANNE PRACHE

(ii) Sculpture. There is figure sculpture on the west façade and the south transept, the main programme being on the west façade. The archaeological and written evidence suggests that contrary to earlier speculation, the unusual west façade, with its rectangular towers and three, deep portals, was constructed integrally with the nave. The lowest levels of the façade belong to the early 1220s; the voussoirs and tympanum of the south portal to *c.* 1225; the north portal to *c.* 1230; and the great central portal to the late 1230s. Work on the column statues started early, and several experimental stages can be detected. As the sculptors carved the portals, the upper façade was rapidly completed to the rose window by around 1240, leaving many of the details temporarily unfinished. Many styles (including Antique Revival) are interwoven in the early work on the voussoirs of the south portal, and certain column statues (*St Ulphia* and *Isaiah*) belong to this early phase. The rigid Byzantinizing style of the *Apostles* (1230s) is closely linked with the north portal of the west façade of Notre-Dame in Paris. The prophets on the front surfaces of the buttresses at Amiens were executed last and embody the elegant style of carving associated mid-century with Reims and Paris.

The high level of coherence in the Amiens portal programme owes much to developments from *c.* 1200 at the cathedrals of Laon, Chartres (transept) and Notre-Dame, Paris. The designers of Laon and Chartres integrated three, deep portals capped by gables with four buttresses that both divide and link the portals. It was at Amiens and Reims that these experiments found their most complete expression. The Reims designer concentrated on vertical integration, while at Amiens horizontal unity was stressed through the emphatic bands of foliate decoration, low-relief scenes framed by quatrefoils and a continuous line of column statues that form the lowest levels.

The size of the undertaking was daunting. Each of the 52 over life-size statues (h. *c.* 2.3 m) is held in place by an ulterior column that engages with an architectural canopy above and an elaborate console below. Three larger trumeau figures (h. *c.* 2.6 m) each have an elaborate base and canopy. Additionally, there are 118 quatrefoil reliefs, as well as 234 curved voussoir units, some with multiple figures. Three tympana are supported by multiple lintels. The Amiens sculptors developed a new technique, carving some of the great figures of the tympana and lintels in stones that were separate from the masonry field behind. The sculpture is executed in the same stone as the cathedral. For the most part the stone is well-preserved, and conservation and cleaning revealed the layers of paint that originally enlivened the figures.

At the axis of the Amiens programme are three images of Christ. In the tip of the central tympanum the apocalyptic *Christ*, face and halo once ablaze with colour, appears in the clouds (Revelation 1:7) with swords issuing from his mouth (Revelation 1:16) and holding two scrolls. Below it the *Second Coming* is depicted. Below this terrible image, framed in the architecture of the New Jerusalem, sits *Christ the Judge*. This resurrected Christ is not a fearsome or godlike creature, but a semi-clad human who has suffered crucifixion. He shows his wounded palms—presumably the marks of the nails and the spear wound in his side were painted. The painted pupils of the eyes lend a highly lifelike appearance. This sacramental Christ is at one end of the cathedral axis that leads to the high altar in the choir, where the transubstantiation of the Eucharist takes place. In the tympanum Christ is flanked by the interceding Virgin and St John the Evangelist, and by angels bearing the Instruments of the Passion.

The *Resurrection of the Dead* is depicted in the lowest lintel, where men and women, either naked or wearing shrouds, force their way out of heavy-lidded sarcophagi. Trumpets are sounded by angels on all sides. In the centre *St Michael and the Weighing of Souls* is depicted. The left scale is weighed down by a Lamb of God with a cross, while the right scale, bearing a devil's head, is raised. A devil underneath interferes with the balance. In the foreground a tiny image of *Synagoga*, blindfolded, slumps under the Devil, while *Ecclesia* (head rest.) sits up and points to her scroll. The division of souls into groups of the elect and the damned in the upper lintel unfolds around the powerful central axis. To the right of Christ a group of naked souls is ushered towards the mouth of hell by devils and angels with flaming swords. The elect (to the left of Christ) are led by a friar wearing a cowled habit with a girdle knotted three times. He covers his hands, hiding the stigmata that suggest that this is St Francis himself. He is welcomed at the gates of heaven by St Peter. Scenes of the triumphant passage of the elect and the anguish of the damned (possibly signifying Purgatory) spill over into the lowest level of the voussoirs, which include two orders of Angels, followed by Martyrs, Confessors, Virgins, the Elders of the Apocalypse, a Tree of Jesse, and the Old Testament Patriarchs.

The binary division of the *Last Judgement* (Matthew 24:29–31) is continued in the door jambs by the *Wise and Foolish Virgins*, who represent types of elect and damned (Matthew 25:1–13). The multiple column statues of the *Apostles* in the embrasures, however, together with the triumphant *Christ* in the trumeau, establish a powerful formal uniformity that overlays the binary left–right division and creates a kind of ideal community. The trumeau *Christ* (*Beau Dieu*) has triumphed over sin and the devil in the form of the two beasts (leonine and serpentine) trampled under his squarely placed feet. His right hand is raised in blessing, and the left, holding a book, hitches up the drapery that swathes his waist. *King Solomon* in the aedicula below, personifying Old Testament wisdom, encourages the interpretation of the third image of Christ not only as the door (John 10:9) but also as the word (John 1:1). The trampling of the beasts signifies Christian triumph as first defined in Constantinian monumental art, and refers to Psalm 91:13: 'Thou shalt tread upon the lion and adder . . .'. This Psalm was often linked with the Temptation of Christ (Matthew 4:1–11), since the Devil quotes it in exhorting Christ to jump from the pinnacle of the Temple. The statues provide a redemptory schema: like the Apostles, the beholder must imitate Christ by eschewing vice and pursuing virtue in order to be deemed worthy of heaven.

The theme of the Last Judgement was first used in Gothic sculpture at Saint-Denis Abbey and developed in the south transept portal at Chartres and in the central portal of Notre-Dame, Paris. The central Christ flanked by his Apostles iconographically recalls the Last Supper and thus the Eucharist, which are connected to the theme of the Last Judgement in John 6:54: 'Whoso eateth my flesh, and drinketh my blood, hath eternal life; and I will raise him up at the last day'. The penitence necessary for the Eucharist is exhorted through the fearful anticipation of the *Last Judgement* experienced in entering. The sacramental *Christ* of the central portal signifies the church in the form of the community gathered for the Eucharist.

The two side portals develop the theme of the church—to the south, the universal church in the form of the *Virgin* (*Mère Dieu*), and to the north, the local church, established through the blood of martyrs physically present in the relics on the altar. The *Dormition* and *Assumption of the Virgin* are shown in the lintel and tympanum of the south portal, surrounded by *Kings* and *Patriarchs* in the voussoirs. The triumphant *Virgin* in the trumeau, the second Eve, tramples the serpent. Scenes from the *Temptation of Adam and Eve* unfold in the trumeau base. Above the Virgin's head, the *Ark of the Covenant*, expressing God's promise to the Israelites, provides a precedent for the church, which expresses God's promise to all penitents. Flanking the Ark are six seated patriarchs, including Moses and Aaron. The column statues depict the *Annunciation*, *Visitation* (see fig. 3) and *Presentation in the Temple* (right embrasure), *Solomon*, *Sheba* and the *Three Magi with Herod*. The quatrefoil images signify the purity of the Nativity (right) and narrate the Epiphany (left).

In the north portal trumeau the image of *St Firminus*, founder of the local church, invites comparison with the trumeau figures of the *Virgin* and *Christ*. St Firminus tramples his murderer, while the tympanum and upper lintel show the miraculous invention of his remains (compare the *Dormition* and *Assumption of the Virgin*) and the triumphant entry of the relics into Amiens (a type of triumphal Entry into Jerusalem). In the lower lintel the six seated patriarchs of the south portal are parelleled by six seated bishops. The column figures depict the founding saints of the local church (left to right: *St Ulphia*; *Angel*; *SS Aceolus*; *Acius*; *Angel*; *SS Honoratus*; *Firminus the Confessor*; *Domitius*; *Salvius*; *Fuscian*; *Warlus*; and *Luxor*; the identification of SS Honoratus, Firminus the Confessor, Salvius, Warlus and Luxor is tentative).

The three portals are bound together by the column statues on the outer surfaces of the buttresses. The

3. Amiens Cathedral, column statues representing the *Annunciation* and *Visitation*, south-west portal, early 1220s

sequence of the 12 minor prophets runs right to left: *Hosea*, *Joel*, *Amos*, *Obadiah*, *Jonah*, *Micah*, *Nahum*, *Habakkuk*, *Zephaniah*, *Haggai*, *Zechariah* and *Malachi*. The scenes in the quatrefoils below illustrate their prophecies, providing balanced contrasts from right to left and leading the viewer's attention inwards from the *Age of Law* to the *Age of Grace* and the *Second Coming*. The centripetal force of the programme is enhanced by the presence of the four major prophets on the inner surfaces of the buttresses flanking the central portal, *Daniel* and *Ezekiel* to the left and *Jeremiah* and *Isaiah* to the right.

On the south transept portal the voussoirs (1230s) depict an encyclopedic programme from *Adam* to the *New Testament*. The tympanum and lintels feature the *Miracles of St Honoratus*, while the embrasures are lined by saints possibly made as an early trial run for the north portal of the west façade. Around 1260 a new trumeau figure was inserted in the location intended for St Honoratus. The elegant *Virgin and Child*, originally brightly painted, was later gilded and consequently known as the *Vierge Dorée*.

Between 1375 and 1378 Cardinal Jean de La Grange added to the chapels he had built from 1373 against the north-west tower a hieratic scheme of nine figure sculptures in three zones, attached to the buttresses and the trumeau between the chapels. The programme, based on that of the staircase (begun 1364) at the Louvre (*see* PARIS, §V, 6(i)), comprises the *Virgin and Child* and *SS John the Baptist* and *Firminus* at the top, *Charles V*, the future *Charles VI* and *Louis, Duke of Orléans*, in the central row, and *Jean de La Grange* himself with two officials of the royal household at the bottom. Standing in niches under canopies, the figures are strongly characterized in pose, facial features and dress, with voluminous draperies. The secular figures, which are flanked by their coats of arms, are individualized to the extent that they might be considered portraits.

BIBLIOGRAPHY

G. Durand: *Monographie de l'église cathédrale Notre-Dame d'Amiens*, 3 vols (Amiens and Paris, 1901–3)

W. Medding: *Die Westportale der Kathedrale von Amiens and ihre Meister* (Augsberg, 1930)

A. Katzenellenbogen: 'The Prophets on the West Façade of Amiens Cathedral', *Gaz. B.-A.*, n. s. 5, xl (1952), pp. 241–60

——: 'Tympanum and Archivolts of the Portal of Saint Honoré at Amiens', *Essays in Honor of Erwin Panofsky*, De Artibus Opuscula, xl (New York, 1961), pp. 280–90

C. R. Sherman: *The Portraits of Charles V of France, 1338–1380* (Paris, 1969)

W. Sauerländer: *Gotische Skulptur in Frankreich, 1140–1270* (Munich, 1970; Eng. trans., London and New York, 1972)

D. Kimpel and R. Suckale: 'Die Skulpturenwerkstatt der Vierge Dorée am Honoratusportal der Kathedrale von Amiens', *Z. Kstgesch.*, xxxvi (1973), pp. 217–65

E. Erlande-Brandenburg: 'La Façade de la cathédrale d'Amiens', *Bull. Mnmtl*, cxxxiv (1977), pp. 253–93

P. Kurmann: 'Nachwirkungen der Amienser Skulptur an den Bildhauerwerkstätten der Kathedrale zu Reims', *Skulptur des Mittelalters*, ed. F. Möbius and E. Schubert (Weimar, 1987), pp. 121–83

——: *La Façade de la cathédrale de Reims*, 2 vols (Lausanne and Paris, 1988)

S. Murray: 'Looking for Robert de Luzarches', *Gesta*, xxix (1990), pp. 111–31

W. Schlink: *Der Beau Dieu von Amiens* (Frankfurt am Main, 1991)

STEPHEN MURRAY

(iii) Stained glass. There is no evidence of the original glazing of the nave, and although many 13th-century windows survived in the choir chapels until 1921, in that year they were heavily damaged or destroyed by fire in the studio where they had been lodged for restoration. The surviving panels and fragments (some now installed in the church; others Champs-sur-Marne, Château) show scenes from the lives of Christ, the Virgin, SS John the Baptist, James, Giles and Leonard, and the Tree of Jesse. Stylistically these windows seem to be related to mid-13th-century Parisian trends and are comparable with glass from St Germain-des-Prés (mostly London, V&A; Baltimore, MD, Walters A.G.; New York, Met.) and the Sainte-Chapelle, Paris.

The best-preserved glass at Amiens, however, is that now in the axial clerestory window, identified by inscription as the gift of Bishop Bernard d'Abbeville and dated 1269. A related series of poorly preserved figures of standing bishops is now installed in the lower gallery of the south rose. A second stylistically distinct but related group of figures, a mutilated series of kings, occupies the galleries under the north rose. A third collection of standing figures, twelve apostles and two sainted bishops, now fill the openings of the choir triforium and seem to date from the last years of the 13th century. It is impossible to determine if these figure groups are in their original locations.

BIBLIOGRAPHY

L. Grodecki and others: *Les Vitraux de Paris, de la région parisienne, de la Picardie, et du Nord-Pas-de-Calais*, Corp. Vitrearum Med. Aevi, Série complémentaire, i (Paris, 1978), pp. 218–22 [reference to earlier bibliog.]

L. Grodecki and C. Brisac: *Le Vitrail gothique au XIIIe siècle* (Fribourg, 1984), pp. 110–12, 146, 241–2

MICHAEL W. COTHREN

2. CENTRE OF PRODUCTION.

(i) Manuscripts. Amiens was an important centre of manuscript production from *c.* 1250. A large group of secular romances dialectally assigned to Picardy may have been produced there, including a richly illuminated *Lancelot* (Bonn, Ubib., MS. 526), which has a colophon stating that it was written in Amiens in 1286. The *Lancelot* and several related manuscripts are characterized by stocky figures and use of heavy black outlines, while other contemporary manuscripts also associated with Amiens, such as the Hours of Yolande de Soissons (New York, Pierpont Morgan Lib., MS. M. 72) and a *Lancelot* (New York, Pierpont Morgan Lib., MSS M. 805–6), have more elegant figures with less reliance on line. Such stylistic variations suggest several active groups of artists or workshops. The latter style continued until *c.* 1350 (e.g. *Bible historiale*, Paris, Bib. N., MS. fr. 152), but from *c.* 1350 to *c.* 1420 few manuscripts can be placed in Amiens. It is not until *c.* 1430 that a considerable group of illuminators were probably active again there. Some, such as the Master of Morgan 453 (*fl c.* 1410–40), seem to have fled from Paris. They mostly produced Books of Hours, which show the influence of the Bedford Master in Paris but are distinguished by heavy, bulky figures with green-tinged faces, a careful observation of light and shadows and the depiction of detailed interiors. This suggests contact with such Netherlandish painters as Jacques Daret, who worked in nearby Arras from 1436. Several Amiens manuscripts from *c.* 1440–50, such as the Hours of Thiebaut de Luxembourg (Brussels, Bib. Royale Albert 1er, MS. 9785), reflect his influence. Late 15th-century manuscripts were often heavily influenced by Rouen models and of a low standard. Indeed, by 1519 the town council had to send a manuscript to Paris to be illuminated.

BIBLIOGRAPHY

R. L. McGrath: 'A Newly Discovered Illustrated Manuscript of Crétien de Troyes: *Yvain* and *Lancelot* in the Princeton University Library', *Speculum*, xxxviii (1963), pp. 583–94

L. M. J. Delaisse, J. Narrow and J. de Wit: *Illuminated Manuscripts in the James A. de Rothschild Collection at Waddesdon Manor* (London, 1977), pp. 106–31

E. S. Greenhill: 'A Fourteenth-century Workshop of Manuscript Illuminators and its Localization', *Z. Kstgesch.*, xl (1977), pp. 1–25

K. Gould: *The Psalter and Hours of Yolande of Soissons*, Cambridge Medieval Academy of America (Cambridge, MA, 1978)

J. Plummer: *The Last Flowering: French Painting in Manuscripts, 1420–1530, from American Collections* (New York, 1982), pp. 9–15

SUSIE NASH

(ii) Tapestry. No tapestry bearing the mark of a double twisted S (for Samarobriva, the Latin name of Amiens) has been found, and it is not possible to identify tapestries woven in Amiens before the beginning of the 17th century. A text of 1491 (see Deharsnes), however, mentions the presence of high-warp tapestry-weavers in the town, and in the inventory of Louis XIV's Garde Meuble, a hanging depicting the *Story of Troy* ('Gothic figures, Amiens factory'; Guiffrey, p. 339) seems to be linked to production of that period. The presence of a workshop subsidized by the town was noted from 1542 to 1547, and there is a possible connection to a tapestry from the collections of Louis XIV that depicts the *Story of Tobias* ('high-warp, factory of Amiens, design by Lucas (van Leyden) or of one of his pupils'; Guiffrey, p. 335). In 1604 Marc de Comans (*d* 1644) and François de La Planche (van den Plancken; 1573–1627) installed in Amiens a branch of their Parisian workshop, where tapestries were woven from the same cartoons as in Paris, for example the *Hunts of Francis I*, mentioned in the inventory of Charles of Lorraine in 1641. The remaining items from Amiens can be identified by their marks (an A and a fleur-de-lis), and all belong to various hangings woven *c.* 1630–60 after Simon Vouet: the *Loves of the Gods* and the *Old Testament* (both Paris, Mobilier National), the *Story of Ulysses* (Besançon, Mus. B.-A. & Archéol.; Riom, Cour d'Appel) and *Rinaldo and Armida* (ex-château de Champchevrier). Although the weave and the border design closely resemble contemporary work produced in the Faubourg St Marcel workshop, the colours—warm browns and reds, deep greens—are notably more subdued than the bright shades that are so characteristic of certain Parisian workshops. It is not known until what date the workshops of Amiens continued their activity. A text of 1683 that describes the presence in the town of some ten high-warp weavers actually refers to weavers hired to make serge.

BIBLIOGRAPHY

J. Deville: *Recueil de documents et de statuts relatifs à la corporation des tapissiers* (Paris, 1875)

J. Guiffrey: *Inventaire général du Mobilier de la Couronne sous Louis XIV* (Paris, 1885)

C. Deharsnes: 'L'Art à Amiens vers la fin du moyen âge', *Rev. A. Chrét.*, xxxiii (1890), p. 27

H. Göbel: *Wandteppiche: Die romanischen Länder* (Leipzig, 1928), pp. 107–9

ISABELLE DENIS

Amiens, Nicholas d'. *See* DIPRE, NICOLAS.

Amiet, Cuno (*b* Solothurn, 28 March 1868; *d* Oschwand, 6 July 1961). Swiss painter and sculptor. From 1884 to 1886 he received irregular lessons from the Swiss painter Frank Buscher (1828–90). In the autumn of 1886 he attended the Akademie der bildenden Künste in Munich and the following year met Giovanni Giacometti, who was to be a lifelong friend. In 1888 he visited the Internationale Kunstausstellung in Munich, where he was particularly impressed by the work of Jules Bastien-Lepage and Whistler. This prompted him to go to Paris to continue his studies, and from 1888 to 1891 he attended the Académie Julian, working under William-Adolphe Bouguereau, Tony Robert-Fleury and Gabriel Ferrier. While in Paris he also met Paul Sérusier, Maurice Denis and other Nabis artists, though his own painting of this period was most influenced by Impressionism. In 1892 he was advised to visit Pont-Aven in Brittany, where he met Emile Bernard, Armand Séguin and Roderic O'Conor, as well as seeing the works of Vincent Van Gogh and Gauguin at first hand. This brief period had a decisive effect upon his work, leading to such Synthetist paintings as *Breton Spinner* (1893; R. Kisling priv. col., see 1982 exh. cat., pl. 5).

In 1893 Amiet returned to Switzerland, where he met Ferdinand Hodler. Hodler was to have a strong influence over his work in the next decade. This is shown in paintings such as the enigmatic *Richness of Evening* (1899; Solothurn, Kstmus.), whose figures and stylized landscape are similar to those in Hodler's work. Amiet participated in a joint exhibition with Giacometti and Hodler in Zurich in 1898 and the same year moved to Oschwand in the canton of Berne, where he lived until his death. He later built and bought property there, making it an important creative centre and attracting artists such as Lovis Corinth and Klee. In 1904 a large exhibition of Hodler and Amiet's work was organized by the Vienna Secession, with 30 works by each artist. Amiet was seen by the critics as merely a follower of Hodler, and this reaction caused him to break from the grip of the older artist. He then returned to the example of Pont-Aven painting, though using brighter colours, as in the *Yellow Girls* (1905; Zurich, Ksthaus).

In May 1905 an exhibition of Amiet's work was held at the Galerie Richter in Dresden and proved an important impetus in the creation of Die Brücke in the city that year. The following year Amiet was invited to join Die Brücke, and he remained in contact with its members thereafter, though his participation was greatest at the beginning. While he had himself initially influenced its members, the situation was reversed after 1907 as the younger artists of Die Brücke turned away from French sources. This change lent Amiet's work a more aggressive, Expressionist style, as shown in *Verschneite Obstbäume* (1909; priv. col., see 1979 exh. cat., pl. 32). In 1917 he completed a series of mural decorations for the Loggia of the Kunsthaus in Zurich. This was the first of several such public projects; later examples included frescoes for the Städtischen Gymnasium in Berne in 1927 and for the conference hall of the Kantonalen Militärdirektion in Berne in 1947. From about 1917 he also started making sculptures, such as the bronze portrait bust of *Alberto Giacometti* (h. 0.36 m, *c.* 1917; Oschwand, see Huggler, p. 57).

Throughout the 1920s Amiet continued the bright Expressionist style of the preceding decade. One of his most striking works of this period was the *Crucifixion* (1927; Lyss, Catholic Church), which used strong reds and greens. In 1931 fifty of his works were destroyed in a fire at the Glaspalast in Munich. During the 1930s and into the early 1950s his painting became more conservative, though as before the subjects remained landscapes, still-lifes and portraits. His palette dulled and his paint handling became more restrained and Impressionist, as in *Boulevard Brune, Paris* (1939; Geneva, Mus. A. & Hist.). In the last years of his life, though dogged by illness, his painting showed another change of style. It became bright in colour again and the objects depicted were dissolved in diffuse light, as in *Paradise* (1958; Oschwand, see Huggler, p. 98).

BIBLIOGRAPHY

G. Charensol: *Cuno Amiet* (Paris, 1932)
A. Baur: *Cuno Amiet* (Basle, 1943)
A. Tatarinoff: *Cuno Amiet: Ein Malerleben* (Solothurn, 1958)
M. Huggler: *Cuno Amiet* (Lausanne, 1971)
Cuno Amiet und die Maler der Brücke (exh. cat. by G. Mauner, G. Krüger and E. D. Bosshard, Zurich, Ksthaus; W. Berlin, Brücke-Mus., 1979)
Cuno Amiet 1868–1961 (exh. cat. by G. Mauner, Pont-Aven, Mus. Pont-Aven, 1982)

□

Amighetti, Francisco (*b* San José, 1 June 1907). Costa Rican engraver, painter, illustrator, draughtsman, writer and critic. He studied for a year from 1931 at the Escuela Nacional de Bellas Artes but was otherwise initially self-taught, using Louis Gonse's *L'Art japonais* (Paris, 1883) as a source. He produced a series of caricature drawings, influenced by Cubism, in the *Album de dibujos de 1926*. During 1929 he met the sculptors Juan Manuel Sánchez and Francisco Zúñiga (the latter was also a printmaker), and through his interest in German and Mexican Expressionist printmakers, he developed a passion for wood-engraving. His first wood-engravings were published in the periodical *Repertorio Americano* (1929). He went on to contribute wood-engravings and drawings to collections of short stories and poetry, educational books, periodicals and newspapers. In 1931 he taught drawing and wood-engraving at the Escuela Normal in Heredia. He exhibited at the Salones Anuales de Artes Plásticas in San José (1931–6). His subject-matter was largely Regionalist, but unlike his peers in the group Círculo de Amigos del Arte, he was able to go beyond a mirror-like reflection of peasant life (e.g. *Burial at Heredia*, 1938; see 1989 exh. cat., p. 21). The dominance of black in his images of this period was especially suited to interiors and night scenes. He visited Argentina, Bolivia and Peru in 1932 and exhibited at the second Sala de Amigos del Arte in Buenos Aires with Raúl Soldi and Antonio Berni.

In 1934, in collaboration with several artists belonging to the Nueva Sensibilidad, including Francisco Zúñiga, Manuel de la Cruz González, Carlos Salazar Herrera, Gilbert Laporte, Teodorico Quirós and Adolfo Sáenz, Amighetti produced a series of engravings collected in the *Album de grabados*, which was to become a valuable art-historical document. From 1936 Amighetti wrote poetry, which he published from time to time. He also taught at the Liceo de Costa Rica. In 1943 he went to the USA to study art at the University of New Mexico in Albuquerque, and from there he went to Taos to study watercolour painting. He taught at the fine arts faculty of the Universidad de Costa Rica in San José in 1944. In 1947 he studied mural painting at the Escuela de Talla Directa 'La Esmeralda' in Mexico with Federico Cantú, a pupil of Diego Rivera. He painted the mural *Agriculture* (1948) in the Casa Presidencial in Costa Rica (now San José, Mus. A. Costarricense) in collaboration with Margarita Bertheau. Two years later he went to Argentina to study engraving. In 1952 he painted murals in the Banco Nacional in Alajuela and the library of the Policlínico de la Caja Costarricense del Seguro Social, San José; in 1954 he completed two murals for the Colegio Lincoln, San José. Amighetti often had one-man shows of oils and watercolours, as well as wood-engravings, until 1968 when he dedicated himself to chromoxylography. After 1970 his works often featured a child as an innocent witness of adult conflict (e.g. *Large Window*, 1981; see 1989 exh. cat., p. 104), and themes of old age and death became more frequent. This later work is characterized by brighter colours and more expressionistic style and abstract composition. Amighetti also published articles on the work of his peers, including Max Jiménez.

WRITINGS

Album de dibujos de 1926 (San José, 1926)
Francisco en Costa Rica (San José, 1966)
La exhibición personal de grabado de Francisco Amighetti (exh. cat., intro.; Taipei, Taiwan Mus., 1989)

BIBLIOGRAPHY

Repert. Amer., xi/470 (1929)
R. Ulloa Barrenechea: *Pintores de Costa Rica* (San José, 1975), pp. 81–8

R. A. Herra: *El desorden del espíritu: Conversaciones con Amighetti* (San José, 1987)

JOSÉ MIGUEL ROJAS

Amigoni [Amiconi], **Jacopo** (*b c.* 1685; *d* Madrid, 21 Aug 1752). Italian painter and etcher, active also in Germany, England and Spain. He was a pioneer of the Venetian Rococo, and his peripatetic career fostered the development of an international decorative style. His oeuvre includes decorative frescoes for churches and palaces, history and mythological paintings and a few etchings. Many of his works were reproduced in prints, and these served as models for tapestries and for the decoration of clocks, wardrobes and porcelain.

Neither the place nor date of Amigoni's birth is known, although it is likely that his parents were Venetian. He was probably taught by Antonio Bellucci and is first recorded in the Venetian painters' guild, the Fraglia, in 1711. Amigoni's one documented work of this early Venetian period (Zanetti), *SS Andrew and Catherine* (Venice, S Stae), was probably painted shortly before this date. His international career began in southern Germany, where his presence is recorded from about 1715 to 1 July 1729. The paintings of this early period, such as *Venus and Pan* (Munich, Residenz) and *St John the Baptist Preaching* (Würzburg Cathedral), reveal a highly accomplished but not completely independent artist. Venetian influences predominate, among them those of Bellucci and of other progressive Rococo painters, especially Sebastiano Ricci and Giovanni Antonio Pellegrini. Yet Amigoni also learnt from Antonio Balestra and from the tenebrists Antonio Zanchi and Johann Carl Loth. The Neapolitan painters Luca Giordano and Francesco Solimena and the Roman art of Pietro da Cortona and Carlo Maratti also contributed to the formation of Amigoni's style. The compact, static treatment of figures, the colour scheme of yellows, reds and blues and the underlying classicism persisted throughout his career. Yet he moved away from Baroque drama and, with a painterly yet delicate palette, created a lighter, more graceful and personal art that made him the most influential Venetian painter in Germany.

From 1719 to 1728 Amigoni painted decorative ceiling frescoes for the Munich court of Maximilian II Emanuel, Elector of Bavaria, and for the Benedictine monastery at Ottobeuren. The ceiling fresco of *Hercules and Selene* (1719) in the vestibule of the library of the monastery, is a slightly awkward work reminiscent of Bellucci and Sebastiano Ricci. His ceiling fresco depicting an *Allegory of Day* in the Badenburg pavilion of the Elector's summer residence at Schloss Nymphenburg similarly looks back to the art of earlier Venetian painters, such as Nicolò Bambini (1651–1736), Giovanni Antonio Fumiani and Louis Dorigny. Yet with the fresco cycle at Schloss Schleissheim, where Amigoni decorated two vast rooms and eight smaller ones on the *piano nobile* with scenes from the *Life of Aeneas*, he created a brilliant new style. He drew on the traditions of Venice (particularly the work of Sebastiano Ricci) and the art of Giordano and of Bolognese decorative painters, but he painted in lighter colours and approached his subjects with less learning; he also depended less on the effects of steep perspective and dramatic foreshortenings than on the fluid arrangement of groups of figures over a vast expanse of sky. Occasionally his composition and colour are reminiscent of Solimena and of Francesco de Mura, while the relaxed elegance anticipates the French Rococo. In 1725 Amigoni again worked at Ottobeuren, where he decorated the abbey chapel with increasingly light and airy frescoes, the *Ascension* and eight lateral scenes, and in 1728 decorated the vestibule of the chapel of St Benedict and the 'Amigoni room'. Here he executed ingenious small ceiling paintings, in oil and tempera, of landscapes and the *Virtues*, as for example the *Allegory of Justice* (see fig.).

In 1729 Amigoni moved to England. He remained there for ten years, interrupted by a visit to France in 1736, enjoying success as a decorative painter. His most accomplished surviving work from this period is the series of large canvases from the *Story of Jupiter and Io* at Moor Park Mansion, Herts. The fashion for ambitious Baroque decoration was ending, however, so Amigoni turned increasingly to portraiture. Such works as the portrait of *Sir Harvey and Lady Smith* (ex-Colnaghi, London; see Palluchini, fig. 60) suggest an awareness of both English and French styles. His greatest successes were portraits of the family and court of George II (*reg* 1727–60), such as that of *Queen Caroline* (1735; Wrest Park House, Beds), and the decoration of Charles Clay's (*d* 1740) famous musical clock with the temple of the four grand monarchies of the world (*c.* 1739; London, Kensington Pal., Royal Col.). His mythological scenes, such as *Diana and Endymion* (Rome, priv. col., see Palluchini, fig. 59) and the *Diana Bathing* (Milan, priv. col., see Palluchini, fig. 58), painted in cool, porcelain-like colours and presented with a frivolity that feigns naivety, are among his most perfect Rococo works. Amigoni was also interested in prints and attempted to set up a print shop with his pupil Joseph Wagner (1706–80). Examples of Amigoni's engravings are the *Virgin and Child* (B. 1), *Jupiter and Callisto* (B. 2) and *Zephyrus and Flora* (B. 3).

Amigoni returned to Venice in August 1739. He responded both to the splendour of contemporary Venetian painting and to older Italian art. Ricci continued to influence him, and at times his style approached that of Tiepolo, though remaining softer and more restrained. New elements became apparent in his work: alongside the search for a greater formal clarity, as in the *Visitation* (Venice, S Maria della Fava), there was the use of shimmering light effects that dissolve form and a melodramatic expression of emotion, elements that anticipate Romanticism. As a fresco painter Amigoni could not compete with Tiepolo, and his *Martyrdom of St Tecla* (*c.* 1745; Este Cathedral) and the *Judgement of Paris* (Stra, Villa Pisani) are unadventurous. Amigoni's pupils of this period, Charles-Joseph Flipart, Michelangelo Morlaiter (1729–1806), Pietro Antonio Novelli (1729–1804) and Antonio Zucchi, developed the classical traits of his art and became exponents of Neo-classicism.

In 1747 Amigoni was appointed court painter to Ferdinand VI of Spain, and his *Immaculate Virgin* (after 1747; Pordenone, Mus. Civ. Pal. Ricchieri) unites the subtlety of his Ottobeuren paintings with the influence of Murillo. His main decorative work for the Spanish court was a large ceiling painting, the *Allegory of the Virtues of the Spanish Monarchy* (1748–50; Aranjuez, Pal. Real, Comedor

Jacopo Amigoni: *Allegory of Justice* (1728), ceiling of the 'Amigoni room', Ottobeuren Abbey

de Gala). His pupil Flipart may have assisted with the decoration, as he is known to have completed two allegorical tondi in the room after Amigoni's death. Amigoni also painted many slightly stiff and pompous portraits, allegorical scenes and mythologies for the court; the *Self-portrait with Friends* (1750–52; Melbourne, N.G. Victoria) has an unusual intimacy and informality. Amigoni died 'overwhelmed with honours and riches, in accordance with his merits' (Longhi).

BIBLIOGRAPHY

Thieme–Becker

A. M. Zanetti: *Descrizione di tutte le pubbliche pitture della città di Venezia* (Venice, 1733/*R* 1980), p. 438

A. Longhi: *Compendio delle vite di pittori veneziani* (Venice, 1762), p. 21

G. Fogolari: 'Dipinti veneziani settecenteschi della galleria del conte F. Algarotti', *Boll. A.*, v (1911), pp. 311–17

J. Woodward: 'Amigoni as Portrait Painter in England', *Burl. Mag.*, ic/646 (1957), pp. 21–3

R. Pallucchini: *La pittura veneziana del trecento* (Venice, 1964)

F. Pilo-Casagrande: 'Documenti per l'attività di Jacopo Amigoni a Ottobeuren', *Atti Ist. Ven. Sci., Lett. & A.*, cxxiv (1965/6), pp. 13–19

H. Wagner: 'Ein Freskenzyklus von Amigoni in Ottobeuren, *Munuscula discipulorum*', *Kunsthistorische Studien Hans Kauffmann zum 70. Geburtstag*, ed. T. Buddensieg and M. Winner (Berlin, 1968), pp. 371–8

E. Croft-Murray: *Decorative Painting in England, 1537–1837*, ii (London, 1970), pp. 17–19, 21, 29–30; figs 20–21

E. Claye: 'A Group of Portrait Drawings by J. Amigoni', *Master Drgs*, ii/1 (1974), pp. 41–8

R. Gualdaroni: 'Un pintor veneciano en la corte de los Borbones de España: Santiago Amiconi', *Archv Esp. A.*, xlvii/186 (1974), pp. 129–47

L. G. Hennessy: 'Jacopo Amigoni and the Myth of Andromeda: Four New Paintings', *A. Ven.*, xxxvii (1982), pp. 233–7

P. Bellini: *Italian Masters of the Seventeenth Century* (1983), 47 [XXI/ii] of *The Illustrated Bartsch*, ed. W. Strauss (New York, 1978–), pp. 457–8 [B.]

L. G. Hennessy: *Jacopo Amigoni (c. 1685–1752): An Artistic Biography with a Catalogue of his Venetian Paintings*, 2 vols (Ann Arbor, 1985)

W. Holler: *Jacopo Amigonis Frühwerk in Süddeutschland* (Zürich and New York, 1986)

WOLFGANG HOLLER

Amio, Domenico. *See* AIMO, DOMENICO.

Amiot [Amyot]**, Laurent** (*b* Quebec, Qué., 10 Aug 1764; *d* Quebec, Qué., 3 June 1839). Canadian metalworker. He studied at the Petit Seminaire du Québec from 1778 to 1780 and began his apprenticeship *c.* 1780 in the silversmith's shop of his elder brother, Jean-Nicolas Amiot (1750–1821); the tradition that he was apprenticed to François Ranvoyzé is unfounded. In 1782 he travelled to Paris to complete his training and remained there for five years, supported by his family. He absorbed the Louis XVI style, then popular in France, and after his return to Quebec in 1787 he set up a workshop to introduce this into Canada.

Amlash region, zebu-shaped ritual pottery vessel, h. 250 mm, from Marlik, late 2nd millennium BC–early 1st (Tehran, Archaeological Museum)

Much of Amiot's work was for the Church, reworking traditional forms in the Louis XVI style. In a sanctuary lamp of 1788 for the church at Repentigny he elongated the standard shape and decorated it with a balanced arrangement of Neo-classical designs. After 1800 his work became formulaic and less innovative, though there are such notable exceptions as the chalice (*c.* 1812) for the church of St Cuthbert at Berthierville. In the realm of domestic silver, Amiot's work tended to be most prominently influenced by English Neo-classicism, as shown by the simple, elegant cream jug and sugar bowl in the Henry Birks Collection in Montreal (see Langdon, pl. 34). Through his introduction of the Louis XVI style, which remained popular until the end of the 19th century, Amiot proved very influential in Lower Canada. He established silversmithing as an art form rather than a craft, as it had been previously conceived. He took at least four apprentices: Paul Morin (1775–1805), Jacques-Richard Filteau, Joseph Babineau and Pierre Lespérance (*fl* 1819–82).

BIBLIOGRAPHY

J. E. Langdon: *Canadian Silversmiths, 1700–1900* (Toronto, 1966)

□

Amiranashvili, Shalva (*b* Oni, 26 March 1899; *d* Tbilisi, 9 Feb 1975). Georgian art historian. He became head of the department of the history and theory of art at Tiflis (now Tbilisi) University in 1925 and was made a professor in 1936. From 1939 to 1975 he was director of the State Museum of Art of the Georgian SSR (now Tbilisi, Mus. A. Georgia). He became a corresponding member of the Georgian Academy of Sciences in 1943 and a member of the USSR Academy of Arts in 1955. His most important publications are on the history of Georgian art, including medieval monumental painting, miniatures and aspects of Niko Pirosmanashvili's work. He also studied the history of Iranian painting.

WRITINGS

Istoriya gruzinskoy monumental'noy zhivopisi [The history of Georgian monumental painting], i (Tbilisi, 1957)
Les Emaux de Géorgie [Georgian enamels] (Paris, 1962)
Istoriya gruzinskogo iskusstva [The history of Georgian art] (Moscow, 1963)
Gruzinskaya miniatyura [The Georgian miniature] (Moscow, 1966)
Pirosmanashvili (Moscow, 1967)

V. YA. PETRUKHIN

Amir Ruhallah. *See* MIRAK.

Amis, Domenico de. *See* AIMO, DOMENICO.

Amlash region. Area in the province of Gilan in northern Iran that has given its name to a series of ancient objects. Since the 1950s the area around the village of Amlash has served as a local market for clandestinely excavated objects from the surrounding valleys. Although the term 'Amlash' should only be used in a geographical sense, to indicate material from Gilan, it has often wrongly been given a chronological meaning. Many objects purporting to come from this area (including fakes) have entered collections and museums, but their dating is often problematic.

Iranian and Japanese archaeological teams explored several sites in Gilan, of which MARLIK, Kaluraz, Dailaman (including Ghalekuti, Nouruz and Hassani Mahaleh) and Tomadjan are the best known. Excavation of the cemeteries provided evidence that the objects belonged to several periods, from the middle of the 2nd millennium BC to the Islamic era. The area was probably inhabited only from the Late Bronze Age or Early Iron Age by nomads, who buried their dead in stone-built tombs or later in vaulted burial chambers cut into the mountain slopes.

Most of the richest material comes from graves of the second half of the 2nd millennium BC and includes numerous decorated gold objects, as well as a variety of bronzes. Highly burnished and thin-walled pottery vessels are typical; most characteristic are zebu-shaped ritual vessels (see fig.). In the 10th to 9th century BC bimetallic objects were produced, but from the 8th century BC utilitarian objects were made of iron, although decorative elements were still of bronze. The Parthian period (*c.* 250 BC–AD 224) is well represented. Numerous decorated gold and silver objects from the following Sasanian period (*c.* AD 225–651) are said to have come from the Amlash area, but unfortunately none has come from a controlled excavation.

BIBLIOGRAPHY

H. Samadi: 'Les Découvertes fortuites', *A. Asiat.*, vi (1959), pp. 175–94
E. Negahban: *A Preliminary Report on Marlik Excavation* (Tehran, 1964)
N. Egami and S. Fukai: *Dailaman*, 4 vols (Tokyo, 1965–71)
S. Fukai and T. Matsutani: *Halimehjan*, 2 vols (Tokyo, 1980–82)
E. Negahban: *Metal Vessels from Marlik* (Munich, 1983)
E. Haerinck: 'The Iron Age in Guilon: Proposal for a Chronology', *Bronze-working Centres of Western Asia, c. 1000 BC–539 BC*, ed. J. Curtis (London, 1988)
——: 'The Achaemenid (Iron Age IV) Period in Gilan, Iran', *Archaeologia Iranica et Orientalis. Miscellanea in Honorem Louis Vanden Berghe*, i (Gent, 1989)

E. HAERINCK

Amling [Ambling], **Carl Gustav (von)** (*b* Nuremberg, *bapt* 25 March 1650; *d* Munich, 1 Jan 1703). German engraver and draughtsman. He mainly produced portraits, in the form of engravings, drawings and grisaille miniatures executed with a brush. From 1671 he was copper-engraver to Ferdinand Maria, Elector of Bavaria, who supported him when he undertook further training in Liège under Michel Natalis (1610–68) and in Paris under Nicolas de Poilly. From the latter Amling learnt how to use and arrange line to produce a very wide range of effects; he also picked up the stiff, two-dimensional look of de Poilly's figures. He must surely have come into contact with Robert Nanteuil in Paris; he shared with him a delight in detail that appears photographic and a veristic style of reproduction.

Amling generally shows his sitters in three-quarter view, following a formulaic composition. Sometimes their features are exaggerated, as for example in the portraits on parchment of *Maximilian II Emanuel, Elector of Bavaria*, and his wife *Maria Antonia of Austria* (1687; Vienna, Albertina), done from preliminary drawings by Johann Andreas Wolff. As well as portraits he produced drawings for *Thesenblätter*. From 1693 onwards he worked on reproducing in engravings the cartoons for tapestries (Munich, Residenzmus.), based on designs (1600–10) by Peter Candid, showing the history of the Wittelsbach family and allegories of the months and seasons.

Amling always relied heavily on models, but his virtuosity in faithfully reproducing what he saw means that he is now regarded as one of the finest portraitists of the later 17th century. Sandrart's praise of Amling's industriousness and his burin technique—criteria then of prime importance in judging art—shows how highly regarded he was in his own lifetime.

BIBLIOGRAPHY

J. von Sandrart: *Teutsche Academie* (1675–9); ed. A. R. Peltzer (1925), pp. 253, 309, 353

MECHTHILD MULLER

Amman [Arab. ʿAmman; anc. Rabbath Ammon, later Philadelphia]. Capital of the kingdom of Jordan and site of a city that flourished between the 2nd millennium BC and the 14th century AD. The site lies in a fertile, well-watered area in the tableland to the east of the River Jordan, on the biblical King's Highway (the ancient Roman Via Nova Traiana), which ran from Bosra in the north to the Red Sea in the south.

The ancient city consisted of the citadel, or acropolis, built in three terraces rising from west to east on a steep-sided, L-shaped hill, and the lower town in the valley of the Wadi ʿAmman to the south. The earliest material found on the citadel dates to the 3rd millennium BC; from *c.* 1100 BC until 582 BC the city was the capital of the kingdom of AMMON. Excavations around the perimeter of the hill have uncovered Ammonite tombs and Hellenistic and early Roman occupation from the 3rd century BC, when the city was renamed Philadelphia in honour of Ptolemy II Philadelphus of Egypt (*reg* 285–246 BC), to the 1st century AD. Older remains were levelled when the citadel was rebuilt after the city's annexation by Rome in AD 106; the Roman fortifications incorporated Ammonite and Hellenistic work.

Of the temples built (or rebuilt) on the citadel during the Roman period, one stood at the northern end on a projecting platform; only the double wall of its enclosure survives. The podium and some of the mouldings remain from another, the Corinthian Temple of Hercules (AD 166–9), which was at the south-east corner, dominating the lower town; fragments of a huge statue, perhaps that of Hercules, have been found. A residential settlement, including a church, occupied the citadel from the 4th century onwards. Below the citadel, along the south bank of the wadi, were the forum, the odeium, the theatre and the nymphaeum, all built under the Roman Empire. The theatre (2nd century) is built into the hill; its auditorium has been restored, and part of the stage building, with Corinthian columns and curved exedra, remains in place.

After its conquest by the Muslims in AD 635, Amman became the seat of a governor and was the market centre for a series of Umayyad castles erected in the desert to the east (*see* QASR KHARANA and MSHATTA). A new citadel was built for the governor *c.* 735. As well as new fortifications, a circular cistern and blocks of houses, it included a large palace within a double enclosure, with a reception hall at the entrance. The hall is extraordinarily well preserved and was traditionally considered to be the tomb of Uriah. It is a square, barrel-vaulted construction of local limestone ashlar, with a number of Iranian features: a four-iwan plan, tiers of blind niches like those in the Taq-i Kisra (Hall of Chosroes) at Ktesiphon, squinches, and stone-carvings derived from Sasanian stuccowork. A second, domed hall was built behind the north iwan.

A congregational mosque measuring 65.8×39.7 m was erected in the lower town in the 8th century (destr. 1924); according to the Palestinian geographer al-Muqaddasi, writing in 985, it was decorated with mosaic. It had a standard plan for the period: a prayer hall with horseshoe arches running perpendicular to the south (qibla) wall and a courtyard built of fine limestone masonry to the north. A square minaret was added, probably in the 12th century. After earthquake damage in 747 and the transfer of the centre of the Islamic caliphate from Syria to Iraq after 750, Amman's prosperity declined, and the citadel became a residential settlement. The site as a whole was abandoned by the end of the 13th century, to be reoccupied by Circassian refugees *c.* 1882. In 1921 the modern settlement on the site became the capital of the new state of Transjordan (now the kingdom of Jordan).

BIBLIOGRAPHY

C. R. Conder: *The Survey of Eastern Palestine* (London, 1889)
H. C. Butler: *Architecture*, 4 vols (1913–19), division II of *Publications of the Princeton University Archaeological Expedition to Syria in 1904–1905, and 1909* (Leiden, 1907–4)
G. L. Harding: *Antiquities of Jordan* (London, 1959), pp. 61–70
F. M. Abel: *Géographie politique: Les Villes de la Palestine*, ii of *Géographie* (Paris, 1938, rev 2/1967)
A. Hadidi: 'The Roman Town-plan of Amman', *Archaeology in the Levant*, ed. P. R. S. Moorey and P. J. Parr (Warminster, 1978), pp. 210–22
A. Almagro and E. Olavarri: 'A New Umayyad Palace at the Citadel of Amman', *Studies in the History and Archaeology of Jordan*, i, ed. A. Hadidi (Amman, 1982), pp. 305–22
R. Dorneman: *The Archaeology of Transjordan in the Bronze and Iron Ages* (Milwaukee, 1983)
A. Northedge, ed.: *Studies on Roman and Islamic ʿAmman I: History, Site and Architecture. The Excavations of Mrs C.-M. Bennett and Other Investigations* (Oxford, 1992)

ADNAN HADIDI, ALASTAIR NORTHEDGE

Amman [Ammann], **Jost** [Jobst, Jos] (*b* Zurich, *bapt* 13 June 1539; *d* Nuremberg, 17 March 1591). Swiss draughtsman, woodcutter, engraver, etcher and painter. He was the youngest son of the noted scholar and Chorherr in Zurich, Johann Jakob Amman, a friend of Ulrich Zwingli and Konrad Gessner. Although a successful pupil at the renowned Collegium Carolinum where his father was a professor, Jost, like his brother Josua (1531–64), who became a goldsmith, did not take up a scholarly career. As early as 1556–7 his copies of prints by other artists, for example Dürer (B. 94) and Virgil Solis (B. 249), show an independent and original approach. For his apprenticeship Amman may have been in Basle or Zurich, but he probably spent some time in Paris or Lyon, since his early works show a close similarity to French book illustrations.

In 1561 Amman was in Nuremberg, where he may have worked with Solis, the chief illustrator for the Frankfurt am Main publisher Sigmund Feyerabend. When Solis died in 1562, Feyerabend probably commissioned Amman to continue the woodcuts for his ambitious Bible projects. The *Biblia* of 1564 (Andresen, no. 181) contains many woodcuts with Amman's initials, which were also partly used for books Feyerabend published later. For the *Livius* (1568; A 201) and the *Tierbuch* (1569; A 238) Amman supplied a great number of woodcuts after drawings by Hans Bocksberger the younger (*fl* 1564–79). His most famous and repeatedly reprinted book of this time is the *Ständebuch* (1568; A 231), with detailed illustrations of the work of various trades (for illustration *see* PARCHMENT; *see also* GILDING, fig. 1). In spite of his extensive work for Feyerabend, Amman found time to produce ornamental designs (see fig.), the woodcuts (with rich ornamental borders) for Philipp Apian's *Bayerische Landtafeln* (1567; A 208) and the etchings for Wenzel Jamnitzer's elaborate *Perspectiva* (1568), with seven complicated ornamental title-pages (A 217), and to finish various commissions for the Nuremberg patrician family Pfinzing, including the Pfinzing Bible (completed 1568) and the Pfinzing *Stammbaum* (1568–70), which was illustrated with more than 100 representations of the family's ancestors. Various portraits

Jost Amman: design for a stained-glass window, pen and ink with wash, diam. 255 mm, 1563 (London, British Museum)

and ex-libris for members of other Nuremberg families were also made before 1570, when Amman recorded the *Firework Display in Nuremberg on 8 June 1570 in Honour of Emperor Maximilian II* in a large etching (A 70) that was sold with printed text as a broadsheet by his own shop.

In 1571 Feyerabend produced yet another Bible (A 182). This time the illustrations (nearly 200) were entirely by Amman, probably his most skilful and attractive work. They show his ability to execute charming and vivacious scenes on a minute scale: each print only measures 58×74 mm, including the ornamental frames, which still betray French influence; most seem to have been cut, in the same block with the frames, by Amman himself. The technique of printing frames and pictures from two separate blocks was used extensively by Feyerabend in 1573 for the new edition of Fronsperger's *Kriegsbuch* (A 226). Amman had provided cuts for the earlier edition (1565) as well as some two dozen etched plates with camp- and battlescenes. In the new edition he contributed more woodcuts, including various new frames (the old ones having been damaged by heavy use). (For an example of a woodcut by Amman *see* WOODCUT, fig. 3.) In 1578 and 1579 Feyerabend produced the works that made Amman famous for the following centuries and which served as pattern books for many other artists: the *Kunst- und Lehrbüchlein* (1578; A 237), the *Wappen- und Stammbuch* (1579; A 230) and the *Stamm- und Gesellenbuch* (1579; A 236), all of which were frequently reprinted.

A contract of 1581 between Count Palatine Ludwig and Feyerabend indicates that by this time Amman was in effect an employee of Feyerabend, who was expected to produce on demand the etched portraits for the *Bayerische Fürsten* (A 15). Within such limits Amman created works full of detailed information about everyday life. The *Kartenspielbuch* of 1588 (A 235) is probably his most charming but least-known work. It was printed in Nuremberg as a book, obviously not meant to be used as playing-cards, and includes a Latin poem in praise of Amman. How well known he was by then is shown by the various commissions he received to do work outside Nuremberg. In 1583 he was in Frankfurt, and in Heidelberg he painted a portrait of the *Elector Ludwig VI* on his deathbed; in 1586–7 in Würzburg he designed the portal for the University Church; he gave drawing lessons to an English earl in Altdorf in 1590. In spite of this fame and enormous productivity, he lived in constant poverty and shortly before his death wrote the last of many letters to his rich relatives in Zurich asking for money and complaining about his illness and the Nuremberg city fathers, whose bankrupting taxes on his property would leave his family in need.

Amman enjoyed a high reputation among his contemporaries and proved an influential source for such later artists as Peter Paul Rubens, Rembrandt and Joshua Reynolds. After his death Amman's reputation declined, and the variable quality of his prolific output was criticized. Yet it was precisely his ability to adapt himself to every task and to change his style according to demand that made him the ideal partner for the most ambitious and prolific publisher of his time. Apparently Amman also produced a few paintings: so far only one is known, the *Portrait of a Bearded Man* (1565; Basle, Öff. Kstsamml.). His collaboration with various goldsmiths (Wenzel Jamnitzer, Hans Keller (1553–1609), Valentin Maler, Abraham Gessner (1552–1613), Hans Petzolt (1551–1633)) has still to be investigated, as has the attribution to him of some 600 drawings, the majority being drawings after his prints. Although Amman had several apprentices, including Alexander Mair (1559–1617) and Georg Keller, none of his followers was able to match his productivity or range.

PRINTS

Biblia . . . Teutsch (Frankfurt am Main, 1564)
Livy: *Von Ankunfft . . . des römischen Reichs* (Frankfurt am Main, 1568)
H. Sachs: *Eygentliche Beschreibung aller Stände auff Erden* (Frankfurt am Main, 1568)
G. Schaller: *Ein neuw Thierbuch* (Frankfurt am Main, 1569)
H. P. Rebenstock: *Neuwe biblische Figuren* (Frankfurt am Main, 1571)
L. Fronsperger: *Kriegsbuch* (Frankfurt am Main, 1573)
Kunst- und Lehrbüchlein (Frankfurt am Main, 1578)
S. Feyerabend: *Wappen- und Stammbuch* (Frankfurt am Main, 1579)
Neuw Jag- und Weydwerck Buch (Frankfurt am Main, 1582) [A 241]
Herr L. V. C.: *Ritterliche Reutterkunst* (Frankfurt am Main, 1584) [A 246]
A. Lonicer: *Stä nd und Order der . . . katholischen Kirchen* (Frankfurt am Main, 1585) [A 232]
Kleidungen und Trachten der Weiber ((Frankfurt am Main, 1586) [A 233]
J. H. Schröter: *Charta Lusoria . . . ein new Kartenspiel* (Nuremberg, 1588)

BIBLIOGRAPHY

Thieme–Becker
J. von Sandrart: *Teutsche Academie* (1675–9); ed. A. R. Peltzer (1925), pp. 104–6
J. G. Doppelmayr: *Historische Nachricht von den nürnbergischen Mathematicis und Künstlern* (Nuremberg, 1730), pp. 207–8
C. Becker: *Jobst Amman: Zeichner und Formschneider, Kupferätzer und Stecher* (Leipzig, 1854)
G. K. Nagler: *Monogrammisten* (1858–1920), i, iii
A. Andresen: *Der deutsche Peintre-Graveur* (Leipzig, 1864–78), i, pp. 99–448 [A]
J. Meyer: *Allgemeines Künstler-Lexikon* (Leipzig, 1872–85), i, pp. 639–51
E. H. Meyer-Zeller: 'Jos Ammann von Zürich, 1539–1591: Ein Beitrag zu seiner Biographie', *Zürch. Taschenb.* (1879), pp. 244–93
T. von Liebenau and A. F. Ammann: *Geschichte der Familie Ammann von Zürich*, 2 vols (Zurich, 1904–13), i, pp. 86–118, 334ff, 358–71, *passim*; ii, pp. 8–10, 85–9, 140ff, 276–81, *passim*
P. Leemann-van Elck: 'Jost Ammans und Tobias Stimmers Beiträge zur Zürcher Buchillustration', *Z. Schweiz. Archäol. & Kstgesch.*, i (1939), pp. 134–7
K. Pilz: 'Jost Ammann', *Mitt. Ver. Gesch. Stadt Nürnberg*, xxxvii (1940), pp. 203–52
P. L. Ganz: *Die Basler Glasmaler der Spätrenaissance und Barockzeit* (Basle, 1966), pp. 40ff
Zeichnung in Deutschland: Deutsche Zeichner, 1540–1640 (exh. cat., ed. H. Geissler; Stuttgart, Staatsgal., 1979–80), i, pp. 194–8
I. O'Dell and A. Szilágyi: 'Jost Amman und Hans Petzolt: Zeichnungsvorlagen für Goldschmiedewerke', *Jb. Ksthist. Samml. Wien*, lxxix (1983), pp. 93–105
I. O'Dell: 'Bemerkungen zu einem Titelblatt von Jost Amman', *Z. Schweiz. Archäol. & Kstgesch.*, xlii/2 (1985), pp. 132–8
J. S. Peters: *Jost Amman*, 2 vols, 20 [IX/i–ii] of *The Illustrated Bartsch*, ed. W. L. Strauss (New York, 1985) [B.]
I. O'Dell-Franke: 'Federkunststücke von und nach Jost Amman', *Kst & Ant.*, vi (1986), pp. 20–25
I. O'Dell: 'Die Nachwirkung von Dürers Tierdarstellungen auf Arbeiten Jost Ammans', *Jb. Ksthist. Samml. Wien*, lxxxii–lxxxiii (1986–7), pp. 91–9
——: 'Etienne Delaune and Jost Amman', *Prt Q.*, vii (Dec 1990), pp. 414–19
——: 'Jost Ammans 'Mummereyen' für Ottavio Strada', *Z. Schweiz. Archäol. & Kstgesch.*, xlvii/3 (1990), pp. 244–51
——: 'Jost Amman and the 'Album Amicorum'', *Prt Q.*, ix (March 1992), pp. 31–6
——: 'Darstellungen der "Zwölf ersten deutschen Könige" von Peter Flötner bis zu Jost Amman', *Z. Schweiz. Archäol. & Kstgesch.* (1993), pp. 357–66
——: *Jost Ammans Buchschmuck-Holzschnitte für Sigmund Feyerabend*, xiii of *Zur Technik der Verwendung von Bild-Holzstöcken in den Drucken von 1563–1599: Repertorien zur Erforschung der frühen Neuzeit* (Wiesbaden, 1993)

ILSE O'DELL-FRANKE

Ammanati [Ammannati], **Bartolomeo** [Bartolommeo] (*b* Settignano, nr Florence, 18 June 1511; *d* Florence, 13 April 1592). Italian sculptor and architect. He was a major figure in Italian art in the second and third quarters of the 16th century. His extensive travels in north and central Italy gave him an unequalled understanding of developments in architecture and sculpture in the era of Mannerism. His style was based inevitably on the example of Michelangelo but was modified by the suaver work of Jacopo Sansovino. In both sculpture and architecture Ammanati was a highly competent craftsman, and his masterpieces, the tombs of *Marco Mantova Benavides* and two members of the del Monte family, the Fountains of Juno and Neptune and the courtyard of the Palazzo Pitti, are among the finest works of the period.

1. Sculpture. 2. Architecture.

1. SCULPTURE. Orphaned at the age of 12, Ammanati earnt his living in the 'Academy' of Baccio Bandinelli *c.* 1523–7, after which time he left Florence, which was in political turmoil, for Venice. Jacopo Sansovino had just arrived there after the Sack of Rome (1527), and Ammanati was probably involved on some of Sansovino's early commissions. Also at this time Ammanati may have executed the life-size stone figure of *Neptune* for the Palazzo Strozzi in Padua, which shows a mixture of influences from Bandinelli and Sansovino as well as from Michelangelo, whom Ammanati strove to emulate. Ammanati left Venice after about five years, perhaps because Sansovino was becoming absorbed with architecture, and returned to Tuscany. He collaborated briefly with Stagio Stagi at Pisa Cathedral, where a lunette of *God the Father* (1536) carved in deep relief is generally accepted as Ammanati's on the evidence of his early biographers (e.g. Borghini). The energetic torsion and bearded head of the large seated figure recall Michelangelo's *Moses* for the tomb of *Julius II* (Rome, S Pietro in Vincoli) as well as Bandinelli's approach to designing reliefs.

Following this work in Pisa, Ammanati returned to Florence, where he carved a statue of *Leda*, possibly for Guidobaldo II, Duke of Urbino: this has been identified (Kinney) as a statue formerly attributed to Vincenzo Danti (London, V&A). It is a variation on a Hellenistic type (e.g. Florence, Uffizi) as well as on an antique *Callipygian Venus* (Naples, Capodimonte). There is a preparatory pen sketch for it (Boston, Mus. F. A.) Ammanati's composition also appears to amalgamate those of two related bronze statuettes made by Bandinelli in 1529–30, a *Leda* and a *Cleopatra* (both Florence, Bargello). From 1536 to 1538 Ammanati worked with Giovanni Angelo Montorsoli on the tomb of the poet *Jacopo Sannazaro* (1457–1530) for S Maria del Parto, Naples, carving statues of *Apollo/David*, *Minerva/Judith*, *St Nazarius* and two putti below. Ammanati's heavy participation in the carving of the figures was due to Montorsoli's absorption with work on the

St Cosmas for the Medici tombs in the New Sacristy of S Lorenzo, Florence. Both sculptors became deeply imbued with the influence of Michelangelo through the statues that he had left behind, some of them not quite finished, for the Medici tombs. Ammanati's seated, yet actively posed figures are obviously indebted to Michelangelo's tomb figures of the Medici, but they exude a greater feeling of calm, classical beauty, and this betrays Ammanati's debt to Jacopo Sansovino. In Ammanati's *St Nazarius*, the head, with its cap of curly hair, aquiline nose and sulky mouth, closely resembles Michelangelo's *Giuliano de' Medici*; its pose is not unlike that of a statue that Ammanati much later admitted admiring, in a letter to the Accademia del Disegno: Jacopo Sansovino's *St James the Greater* (1511–18) in the crossing of Florence Cathedral. Finally, the pair of putti below have the Herculean forms and vigorous poses beloved of Michelangelo. Late in 1538 Ammanati received the commission for the tomb of *Francesco Maria I della Rovere, Duke of Urbino* (*d* Oct 1538) in S Chiara, Urbino, although it may not have been executed until 1542–3 (destr.).

A major commission in Florence intervened, a tomb in SS Annunziata for the soldier *Mario Nari* (*d* Oct 1539). Kinney has shown that Nari was a supporter of Duke Cosimo I de' Medici and a figure of importance, as can be inferred from the remains of his splendid tomb; it was installed by 1550, although not unveiled, as there were religious objections because Nari had died in a duel. The controversy was stirred up by Bandinelli, feigning piety, who was jealous of his pupil's success. This ultimately led to the tomb being dismantled before 1581: the beautiful, although artificially posed allegorical group of *Victory*, modelled on one of Michelangelo's unexecuted groups for the tomb of *Julius II*, Rome, S Pietro in Vincoli, and the recumbent effigy of the deceased, clad in antique Roman armour, are now in the Bargello, Florence. Jacopo Sansovino visited Florence in October 1540, and Ammanati followed him back to Venice shortly after finishing the sculptures for the tomb: his presence there was recorded in Lorenzo Lotto's account book in January/April 1541/2. Ammanati carved a stone statue of *Neptune* for the roofline balustrade on Sansovino's Libreria Marciana (it fell and shattered *c.* 1740); he also collaborated on several river gods on the spandrels and some lion-masks on the keystones of the arches on the short, northern façade.

Ammanati was documented as active in Padua and Vicenza intermittently between 1544 and 1548. He carved a colossal *Hercules* (h. 6.4 m) for the courtyard of the Paduan palazzo of the humanist jurist and antiquarian Marco Mantova Benavides (*in situ*). This was followed by a triumphal arch in the garden of the palazzo, with statues of *Jupiter* and *Apollo* (finished 1547; *in situ*), and by the tomb of *Marco Mantova Benavides* (unveiled 1546) in the church of the Eremitani, Padua. This is reminiscent of Michelangelo's Medici wall tombs (Florence, S Lorenzo, New Sacristy) with a tiered architectural setting. It is topped with a statue of *Immortality* flanked by nude youths. In the middle zone are three pedimented embrasures (like blank windows) framing statues of the deceased flanked by *Honour* and *Fame*. Below stands a sarcophagus with an unusual segmental lid, ending in volutes (again like the Medici tombs), and on either side of this are allegorical

1. Bartolomeo Ammanati: *Juno with her Peacocks*, marble, over life-size, from the Fountain of Juno, late 1550s (Florence, Museo Nazionale del Bargello)

figures of *Work* and *Wisdom*. The figures are solidly built, with bold poses and simple gestures: the torsions of their contrapposti and diagonals of their limbs balance symmetrically to create a visual unity within the sculptural components. They animate the austere, but noble, classical architecture; Ammanati here achieved an exact balance between the two diverse art forms, which makes his tomb a masterpiece. His scheme gives an impression of the balanced grandeur that Michelangelo would have achieved in the New Sacristy, had he completed its sculpture. At Pusterla, near Vicenza, Ammanati designed fountains (1545–6; destr.) for Girolamo Gualdo's garden, and the attempts made to reconstruct them from literary descriptions suggest that they were in an architectural setting (Gualdo).

In Urbino on 17 April 1550 Ammanati married the poetess Laura Battiferri (1523–89), later the subject of an extraordinary portrait by Agnolo Bronzino (*c*. 1555; Florence, Pal. Vecchio). They travelled to Rome to solicit work from the newly elected pope, Julius III. This resulted in a commission for a pair of tombs, for the Pope's uncle, *Cardinal Antonio Maria Ciocchi del Monte*, and for *Fabiano del Monte* (finished *c*. 1553) in S Pietro in Montorio. The arrangement, with allegorical statues (*Religion*, *Justice*) standing in the niches over each effigy, recumbent below, is closer to Ammanati's own earlier monument to Nari than to the design that had been supplied by Vasari. When Julius III died in 1555, Ammanati was summoned by Vasari back to Florence to enter the service of Duke Cosimo I de' Medici. He shortly received a major commission for the spectacular Fountain of Juno for the Sala Grande of the Palazzo Vecchio. The fountain was never erected in the hall but was set up out of doors at Pratolino; a drawing after Ammanati by Giovanni Guerra (Vienna, Albertina) shows six figures mounted around a rainbow, a fantastic design recalling the table decorations made by Mannerist goldsmiths. This was technically ingenious and amusingly erudite in its theme; it was called by Michelangelo 'una bella fantasia' (Heikamp, 1979–80, p. 156, doc. xi). The handsome seated *Juno* (see fig. 1), one of the six over life-size marble fountain figures (all Florence, Bargello), has the active contrapposto pose and *mouvementé* drapery characteristic of Ammanati.

In 1559–60 Ammanati successfully cast in bronze the great terminal group of *Hercules and Antaeus* (h. 2 m) for Niccolò Tribolo's Fountain of Hercules (for illustration *see* TRIBOLO, NICCOLÒ) on the lowest terrace of the gardens behind Cosimo's villa of Il Castello; this technical feat had previously defeated Vincenzo Danti on account of the complexity of the composition. The giant Antaeus is represented as being lifted bodily off the ground by Hercules, his head is thrown back in the throes of death, and from his mouth a great spout of water gushes vertically upwards, symbolizing his last gasp of life. The flow of the fountain is thus rationalized by its iconography, and the water splashing down over the figures into the basins below gives an effect of life and movement to the drily mythological composition. Between 1563 and 1565 Ammanati also modelled and cast a half-length giant in bronze to represent the mountain range of the Apennines. It is the centrepiece of the fishpond on the highest terrace of the gardens of Il Castello: the naked giant, seeming to shiver with cold, appears to rise out of an islet in the centre of the sheet of water. The top of his head is pierced to emit water, which drips down over his shoulders and in winter forms icicles.

Ammanati's best-known sculpture is the Fountain of Neptune (*c*. 1560–75) in the Piazza della Signoria, Florence. The central figure (see fig. 2) was carved out of a colossal block of marble that had been begun by Bandinelli before his death (1560), and this inhibited Ammanati's treatment. Consequently (by general consent) the *Neptune* is neither characteristic nor aesthetically satisfactory. More successful are the surrounding bronze figures of four recumbent deities and a troop of gesticulating fauns and satyrs (all 1571–5), modelled and cast under his supervision by a team of assistants. The general design and character of these figures, as well as an allegorical female nude statuette personifying *Ops* (1572–3), which Ammanati contributed to the Studiolo of Francesco de' Medici, epitomize his mature style, which, while distantly derived from Michelangelo, Bandinelli and Sansovino, concentrated on grace of form and movement at the expense of emotion in a way that was typical of Mannerism.

In 1572 Ammanati was commissioned by Pope Gregory XIII to create a tomb for his nephew, Giovanni Boncompagni, which was erected in the Camposanto of Pisa. It consists of an aedicula framing a central statue of the *Risen*

2. Bartolomeo Ammanati: *Neptune*, marble, over life-size, on the Fountain of Neptune, marble and bronze, h. *c*. 9 m, *c*. 1560–75, Piazza della Signoria, Florence

Christ, draped and showing his wounds. This is derived from a similar statue (1558), wearing only a loincloth, carved by Montorsoli for the high altar of S Maria dei Servi, Bologna. Flanking Christ at a lower level are allegorical statues of *Peace* and *Justice* in the guise of lightly draped females. There is no effigy, only a white marble sarcophagus; the architecture is multicoloured and patterned with variegated marbles, giving a sumptuous appearance and setting off the three white marble statues and the sarcophagus to good effect. By 1582 Ammanati had become so strongly influenced by the Counter-Reformation and the Jesuits, with whom he had been in contact since 1572, that in a famous letter to the Accademia del Disegno in Florence, printed on 22 August 1582, he denounced on moral grounds the public display of nude sculpture (of which he had been most guilty himself in his Fountain of Neptune in the government square of the city and in his Fountain of Juno). In a later letter (*c.* 1590), addressed to Ferdinand I de' Medici (who had been a cardinal), he begged the Grand Duke 'not to allow the sculpting or painting of nude things' (see Holt, 1958).

2. Architecture. As well as being a sculptor, Ammanati was also a gifted architect, generally following the lead of Michelangelo's designs for the Biblioteca Laurenziana and for the New Sacristy in S Lorenzo, both in Florence. Ammanati's tombs and major fountains had involved him in this field from early in his career, and in the 1540s he had worked on Sansovino's Libreria Marciana in Venice and on the Benavides triumphal arch in Padua. In the following decade, in Rome, he began more specifically architectural work for Pope Julius III, in the sunken courtyard and fountain grottoes of the Villa Giulia, alongside Jacopo Vignola and Vasari (1552). He also furnished a wooden model for a classicizing fountain on a street corner in Via dell'Arco Oscuro, which was later modified and installed in the Casino of Pius IV in the Vatican Gardens. Also for Julius III he remodelled the Palazzo Cardelli (now Palazzo di Firenze), which Julius acquired in 1553 for his brother, Baldovino del Monte (*d* 1556).

This experience was valuable to Ammanati when he reached Florence after 1555, for in addition to the various elaborate fountains that Cosimo ordered, he was also commissioned to improve (1560–77) the Palazzo Pitti, which had been acquired (1549) as a residence for the Duchess, Eleonora of Toledo. His masterpiece there is the half-sunken courtyard, with the surrounding building rising a full three storeys on three sides of a rectangle, and, above a fountain grotto on the fourth side, framing a view over the Boboli Gardens, which were being laid out axially up the steep hill that rises towards the Belvedere fortress. It is architecture of a peculiarly sculptural variety, well adapted to make a visual transition between palace and garden on account of its heavily rusticated masonry, which was used in a capricious and deliberately anti-classical way. This recalls the fortress-like building for the Mint (Zecca) in Venice by Sansovino and designs published by Serlio in 1537. The foundations were laid in 1560, and Ammanati was designated sole architect in the following year, succeeding Vasari, who thenceforth had to concentrate on the Uffizi.

Ammanati designed several other palazzi in Florence, including one (1557–74) for Ugolino Grifoni in the Via dei Servi; another for the Giugni in the Via degli Alfani; and another (1568) for the Ramirez di Montalvo family in the Borgo degli Albizzi. Several more are attributed to him, such as the palazzi Mondragone, Pucci, del Nero and Peruzzi–Bagnoli. They are characterized by a continual and inventive variety of forms. Ammanati was inspired by the recently deceased Tribolo and by Bernardo Buontalenti in his use of grotesque elements to enliven the otherwise severe forms of his architecture: he concentrated on the play of solid and void and loved to connect his interiors with exterior surroundings by the employment of wings and porticos. In 1558 the bridge of Santa Trìnita in Florence was destroyed when the River Arno flooded. After an unsuccessful initial approach to Michelangelo in Rome, Ammanati received the commission for its reconstruction to a new design (1567–70). Its arches were derived from chainlike curves and so look long and low, as they spring from substantial and high piers with pointed breakwaters; they are the resolution of complex static and dynamic forces into a whole that displays both energetic robustness and airy lightness.

In Lucca, Ammanati was commissioned to reconstruct the Palazzo degli Anziani (1577–81; now Palazzo della Provincia); he finished the minor façade but left incomplete the Cortile degli Svizzeri and the great courtyard. In Volterra, he designed the cloister of the abbey of SS Giusto e Clemente and the Palazzo Viti; in Arezzo, S Maria in Gradi; and in Seravezza, a project for the palazzo of Cosimo I (1564). Ammanati was in Rome in 1560 and in 1572, designing a palazzo for Lodovico Mattei (Palazzo Caetani; 1564) in the Via delle Botteghe Oscure, and for the Rucellai a palazzo (Palazzo Ruspoli; begun 1586) on the Via del Corso. Cardinal Ferdinand I de' Medici consulted Ammanati when restoring and enlarging the villa of Cardinal Giovanni Ricci (now Villa Medici) on the Pincian Hill. There are two drawings (Florence, Uffizi) related to this scheme, and a model for the villa is documented (Andres, i, p. 440).

Ammanati was in contact with the Jesuit Order from 1572, when they were proposing to enlarge their college in Florence and to reconstruct the neighbouring church of S Giovannino (1579–85). The basic design of the Collegio Romano was also his, according to some authorities, having been chosen by Pope Gregory XIII, but was revised and actually built by a Jesuit, G. Valeriani. (In their wills Ammanati and his wife left all their property to the Jesuits in Florence, as they had no children.) By 1584 he had started to prepare an elaborate treatise on architecture and town planning (untraced). A collection of plans of building types, known as *La città*, is in the Uffizi, some drawings are also in the Uffizi and in the Biblioteca Riccardiana, and papers left to the Jesuits are in the Biblioteca Nazionale Centrale, all in Florence.

BIBLIOGRAPHY

DBI; Thieme–Becker

G. Vasari: *Vite* (1550, rev. 2/1568); ed. G. Milanesi (1878–85)

R. Borghini: *Il riposo* (Florence, 1584); ed. M. Rosci, 2 vols (Milan, 1968), pp. 67, 165, 590–95

G. Gualdo: *Giardino di cà Gualdo* (MS., 1650); ed. L. Poppi (Florence, n.d.)

F. Baldinucci: *Notizie* (1681–1728); ed. F. Ranalli (1845–7), vi (Florence, 1769), pp. 3–132
A. Venturi: *Storia* (1901–40), x/2 (1936), pp. 346–432; xi/2 (1939), pp. 212–350
E. Holt: *Michelangelo and the Mannerists*, ii of *A Documentary History of Art* (Garden City, 1958)
M. G. Ciardi-Dupré: 'La prima attività di Ammanati scultore', *Paragone*, cxxxv (1961), pp. 3–29
H. Keutner: 'Die bronze *Venus* des Bartolommeo Ammanati', *Münchn. Jb. Kstgesch.*, xiv (1963), pp. 79–92
J. Pope-Hennessy: *Italian High Renaissance and Baroque Sculpture*, ii (London, 1963), p. 72
C. Avery: *Florentine Renaissance Sculpture* (London, 1970)
M. Fossi, ed.: *Bartolomeo Ammannati: La città* (Rome, 1970)
H. Utz: 'A Note on Ammannati's Apennine and on the Chronology of the Figures for his Fountain of Neptune', *Burl. Mag.*, cxv (1973), pp. 295–300
G. M. Andres: *The Villa Medici in Rome*, 2 vols (New York, 1976), pp. 438–40
P. Kinney: *The Early Sculpture of Bartolomeo Ammanati* (New York and London, 1976)
F. Bottai: 'Bartolomeo Ammannati: Una reggia per il Granducato di Toscana', *Ant. Viva*, xviii/5–6 (1979), pp. 32–47
D. Coffin: *The Villa in the Life of Renaissance Rome* (Princeton, 1979)
D. Heikamp: 'Ammannati's Fountain for the *Sala Grande* of the Palazzo Vecchio in Florence', *Fons sapientiae: Renaissance Garden Fountains. Fifth Dumbarton Oaks Colloquium on the History, Landscape Architecture: Washington, DC, 1979–80*, pp. 117–73
A. Nova: *The Artistic Patronage of Pope Julius III* (diss., U. London, 1982)
B. Toulier: 'La Villa Médicis', *Mnmts Hist.*, cxxiii (1982), pp. 25–45
A. Nova: 'Bartolomeo Ammannati e Prospero Fontana a Palazzo Firenze', *Ric. Stor. A.*, xxi (1983), pp. 53–76
——: 'The Chronology of the del Monte Chapel in S Pietro in Montorio in Rome', *A. Bull.*, lxvi (1984), pp. 150–54
S. Cocchia, A. Palminteri and L. Petroni: 'Villa Giulia', *Boll. A.*, lxxii/42 (1987), pp. 47–90

CHARLES AVERY

Ammenemes III [Amenemhet III; Nymaatre]. Egyptian ruler. Both architecture and sculpture have survived from his reign in the 12th Dynasty (for chronological chart of Egyptian kings *see* EGYPT, ANCIENT, fig. 2). He built two pyramids, one at DAHSHUR and the other at HAWARA in the Faiyum region, where is also a small temple, finished by Ammenemes III's successor, Ammenemes IV; the reliefs in this temple have not been published in detail. Some reliefs of Ammenemes III were also found at Abydos (Philadelphia, U. PA, Mus.); they display little of the quality and interest of the reliefs of his predecessor, Sesostris III.

There are more than 50 statues and heads of Ammenemes III, easily identifiable because of his distinctive physiognomy. As with the statues of Sesostris III, they appear to correspond to various ages of the King; however, this progression is probably complicated by wider variations of style and dimensions. The characteristic traits of these heads are large eyes (always serious and impassive), exceptionally large ears and a nose that is far less prominent than that of Sesostris III and hooks back into the face after the bump of the nasal bone. His mouth has thick, curled lips, the corners of which turn up to end against fleshy protuberances. The cheek-bones are very high and wide and are cut by a wrinkle leaving the inside corner of the eye at an angle of 45°.

The limestone statue found in his mortuary temple at Hawara (Cairo, Egyp. Mus., CG 385; see fig.) has a smooth, truly juvenile face, but most faces of the King are mature. They are sometimes tense, as in the case of a granite statue (St Petersburg, Hermitage, 729) and a basalt bust (Moscow, Pushkin Mus. F.A., 4757), both of unknown provenance. Some others are brutally dented, such as the series of granite maned sphinxes from Tanis (Cairo, Egyp. Mus., 393–4, 530, 1243) and related works. A granite standing statue from Karnak (Cairo, Egyp. Mus., CG 42014) shows him old and worn. There are also works on a smaller scale, such as the small heads in limestone (Cambridge, Fitzwilliam, E2. 1946), grey granite (London, U. Coll., Petrie Mus.) and grey marble (New York, Met., 29.100.150).

Ammenemes III, limestone, h. 1.6 m, from Hawara, 12th Dynasty, *c.* 1800 BC (Cairo, Egyptian Museum)

BIBLIOGRAPHY

LÄ: 'Amenemhet III', 'Dahshur', 'Hawara'
H. G. Evers: *Staat aus dem Stein: Denkmäler, Geschichte und Bedeutung der ägyptischen Plastik während des Mittleren Reiches*, 2 vols (Munich, 1929)

J. Vandier: *Manuel d'archéologie égyptienne*, iii (Paris, 1958), pp. 195–215
D. Wildung: *Sesostris und Amenemhet: Ägypten im Mittleren Reich* (Munich, 1984)

CLAUDE VANDERSLEYEN

Ammochostos. *See* FAMAGUSTA.

Ammon. Kingdom that flourished from the 11th to the 6th century BC, situated in present-day Jordan. Its capital was at Rabbath-Ammon (AMMAN). The kingdom was in constant contact and conflict with the Israelites to the west and Damascus to the north. Its pottery bears a general similarity to that on the other side of the River Jordan, with some Ammonite idiosyncrasies in the 7th and 6th centuries BC. Most remarkable are the sculptures. More than 30 human heads and statues, up to 850 mm high and carved in limestone or basalt, have been found in the Amman area (e.g. Amman, Jordan Archaeol. Mus.). Six wear the Egyptian *atef* crown (a high headdress with a feather at either side), but other elements indicate Syrian influence. Four double-faced female heads were excavated in Amman (Amman, Jordan Archaeol. Mus.); they are about 260 mm high, with inlaid eyes and beads of a choker around the neck, and can be compared with ivory-carvings from Syria. They are a local adaptation of a widespread theme, derived from the Hathor head of Egyptian art, and probably supported the balustrade of a window. Ammonite metalwork and jewellery are not distinctive. The number of seal-stones identifiable as Ammonite by script or form of name exceeds 50 (e.g. Paris, Bib. N.). While many carry only owners' names and patronyms, like common Hebrew seals, or standard motifs of Egyptian or Babylonian origin, one group has lively animals in the centre (deer, bull, ape).

BIBLIOGRAPHY

La Voie royale: 9000 Ans d'art au royaume de Jordanie (exh. cat., Paris, Pal. Luxembourg, 1986), pp. 91–141
P. Bienkowski, ed.: *The Art of Jordan: Treasures from an Ancient Land* (Liverpool, 1991)

A. R. MILLARD

Amnisos. Minoan site in northern Crete, inhabited *c.* 3500–*c.* 1000 BC. The settlement, a harbour town known as a-mi-ni-so in the Linear B tablets, is 8 km east of Herakleion; it fronts a shallow sandy shore and is backed by a coastal plain. Excavations, chiefly by Spiridon Marinatos in the 1930s and by the German Archaeological Institute, Athens, in 1983–5, have focused on the sides of a low hill and on a cave some 500 m inland. The cave was a sanctuary of Eileithyia, a goddess associated with fertility and childbearing, and is mentioned in the *Odyssey* (XIX.188). Finds cited below are for the most part in the Archaeological Museum, Herakleion.

Traces of occupation dating back to Late Neolithic times (*c.* 4500–*c.* 3800 BC) have been found at the cave, which remained a centre of worship even after the Minoan period. A low wall surrounds a stalagmite, which seems to have been a focus of cultic activity; further activity took place outside the cave mouth. A scattering of house remains near by are of uncertain date. Further west, at Karteros, more Late and Final (*c.* 3800–*c.* 3500/3000 BC) Neolithic material has been recovered.

On the seafront, settlement is recorded in Middle Minoan (MM) I (*c.* 2050–*c.* 1800 BC), although the remains are not architectural. The first surviving structure is the imposing two-storey House of the Lilies, at the eastern foot of the hill. Built in MM III (*c.* 1650 BC), its ground-floor plan reveals the multiple access routes and the division into groups of compartments typical of the Neo-Palatial style of architecture (*see* MINOAN, §II). From a large pier-and-door hall at the north-east, served by a schist-flagged terrace facing the sea, a door leads directly to a shrine and a corridor into a complex at the south-east that includes the main entrance, a possible reception room, stairs to upper levels and what may be a kitchen. The western portion, which is slightly closed off, is dominated by a large flagged hall containing bases for two pillars. Like structures throughout Crete, the house was destroyed by fire at the end of Late Minoan (LM) IB (*c.* 1425 BC). Its apparent isolation is almost certainly misleading, and the suggestion that its occupant was a naval officer is unprovable.

The most notable works of art found in the house were the frescoes in the western hall. The north wall bore a large-scale, repeating design of sea-lilies in formal clumps of three sprays, superimposed on a red and a white background divided by a green band in a stepped arrangement. The naturalistic subject is unexceptional, but its handling and the geometric regularity of the background are less usual. Unusual too is the technique whereby the flowers were cut out of the dry plaster and then refilled with a white or blue mix. The west wall carried designs featuring red irises with bunches of mint and other plants. Further indications of the opulent character of the building are provided by the ashlar masonry of the west façade and by finds that include gold foil, faience and stone vases and perhaps a bronze mirror with a gilt wooden handle. Structures to the west, which probably formed part of the harbour facilities, some of which are now submerged beneath the sea, include buildings of comparable quality to the House of the Lilies.

Occupation of Amnisos continued into the Subminoan period (*c.* 1050–*c.* 1000 BC). Sherds and a cistern have been found on the hill, and a large structure to the west, refurbished in LM IIIA 2 (*c.* 1360–*c.* 1335 BC), contained craft equipment: a potter's wheel, with some LM IIIB (*c.* 1335–*c.* 1190 BC) pottery, a metalworking mould and stone tools. EM and MM burials have been reported on the hill, and EM to LM examples from a cave further inland. A chamber tomb (LM) yielded an ivory comb and a rare glass vessel.

BIBLIOGRAPHY

S. Marinatos: 'Hysterominoikos laxeutos taphos en Kartero Kritis' [LM chamber tomb at Karteros, Crete], *Archaiol. Deltion*, xi (1927–8), pp. 68–90
——: 'Anaskaphe Amnisou Kritis' [Excavations at Amnisos, Crete], *Praktika Athen. Archaiol. Etaireias* (1932), pp. 76–94; (1933), pp. 93–100; (1934), pp. 128–33; (1935), pp. 196–203; (1936), pp. 81–6; (1938), pp. 130–38
S. Marinatos and M. Hirmer: *Crete and Mycenae* (London, 1960), colour pl. xxii
S. G. Spanakis: *Kentriki-anatoliki* [Central and eastern] (1964), i of *I Kriti* [Crete] (Herakleion, 1964–73), pp. 65–70
A. Kanta: *The Late Minoan III Period in Crete: A Survey of Sites, Pottery and their Distribution*, Stud. Medit. Archaeol., lviii (Göteborg, 1980)
J. Schäfer, ed.: *Amnisos: Nach den archäologischen, historischen und epigraphischen Zeugnissen des Altertums und der Neuzeit* (Berlin, 1992)

D. EVELY

Amorgos. Greek island at the south-east extremity of the Aegean Cyclades. Survey work in the 1980s increased the number of known sites of all periods on the island. Most of the Bronze Age finds date from the Early Cycladic (EC) period (*c.* 3500/3000–*c.* 2000 BC) and come from cemeteries, although a settlement at Markiani is being excavated; there is also some Middle Cycladic (MC) and Late Cycladic (LC) pottery from graves at Arkesine, and Mycenaean vases were found at Xilokeratidi. The primary investigations were mainly the work of C. Tsountas, and the more recent of L. Marangou and others, although Dümmler published important material from Amorgos in the 1880s. The small but attractive museum on the island (in Chora) has good prehistoric pottery and (mostly fragmentary) marble objects.

The Dokathismata cemetery on Amorgos has given its name to an important category of Cycladic folded-arm stone figurines (*see* CYCLADIC, §IV, 1). A marble head (Oxford, Ashmolean) is uniquely representational; it must be later than EC and perhaps belongs to the following phase, although no other MC sculpture is known. Fine silver objects from graves at Dokathismata include bowls, a diadem, bracelets (all Oxford, Ashmolean) and a pin (*see* CYCLADIC, fig. 15). A cylinder seal (Oxford, Ashmolean) from Kapros is of Near Eastern type but apparently local manufacture. Important examples of (EC–MC) metalwork from the island (*see also* CYCLADIC, §IX) include spearheads (some slotted and/or 'rat-tailed'), daggers and some of the earliest swords (e.g. London, BM).

BIBLIOGRAPHY

F. Dümmler: 'Mitteilungen von griechischen Inseln', *Mitt. Dt. Archäol. Inst.: Athen. Abt.* (1886), pp. 15–46
C. Tsountas: 'Kykladika', *Archaiol. Ephemeris* (1898), pp. 137–212
E. M. Bossert: 'Zur Datierung der Gräber von Arkesine auf Amorgos', *Festschrift für Peter Goessler* (Stuttgart, 1954), pp. 23–34
C. Renfrew: *The Emergence of Civilisation* (London, 1972), pp. 376–7, 521–3
L. Marangou: 'Amorgos', *Die griechischen Inseln*, ed. E. Melas (Cologne, 1974), pp. 161–6
Archaeol. Rep.: Council Soc. Promotion Hell. Stud. & Managing Ctee Brit. Sch. Archaeol. Athens (1982–3), p. 48; (1983–4), p. 55; (1984–5), pp. 52–3; (1985–6), pp. 74–5; (1986–7), pp. 46–7; (1988–9), p. 88; (1989–90), pp. 69–70; (1990–91), p. 65 [brief notices of recent work]
L. Marangou: 'Evidence for the Early Cycladic Period on Amorgos', *Cycladica: Studies in Memory of N. P. Goulandris*, ed. J. L. Fitton (London, 1984), pp. 99–115

R. L. N. BARBER

Amorini, Antonio Bolognini. *See* BOLOGNINI AMORINI, ANTONIO.

Amorite [Sum. Martu; Akkad. Amurru; Heb. Amori]. Name given to ethnic and political social groups in the Ancient Near East. In its ethnic connotation the term Amorite was used originally to refer to a Semitic, pastoralist and presumably rural population in the Middle Euphrates region in the late 3rd and early 2nd millennium BC. An ethnic connotation may also be recognized behind the biblical use of the term, which is, however, very vague. In its political connotation the term Amorite was used to refer to the kingdom of Babylon under the dynasty of Sumuabum (*reg* 1894–1881 BC), which included Hammurabi (*reg* 1792–1750 BC) as its most famous ruler (Old Babylonian period). By extension, scholars have often used the term to refer to various other dynasties of the early 2nd millennium BC, whose rulers bore 'Amorite' names (e.g. Larsa, Eshnunna, Mari and Aleppo). A distinct use of the political term refers to a territorial state known as the kingdom of Amurru in the late 2nd millennium BC in the inland part of the Syrian steppe.

Evidence is lacking for an artistic tradition associated with the Amorites. Even the evidence for material culture (rather than for artistic production) is extremely limited. No sites have been excavated that may be considered Amorite in the ethnic sense, and no objects found in urban excavations of the Old Babylonian period may be identified as specifically Amorite (or even nomadic or rural) in origin. References in contemporary texts to Amorite artefacts (daggers and garments) are the only indications of a specific manufacturing style. Ethnoarchaeological research has provided some new directions, but the results are minimal.

The term Amorite is most commonly associated in the archaeological literature with the art of the various dynasties of the Old Babylonian period. It is, however, a loose concept that refers not so much to a body of objects or a well-defined style, identifiable as Amorite on the basis of discrete formal traits, as to a chronological period that from convenience encompasses the artistic production of urban centres in Syro-Mesopotamia.

In this sense, for whatever can be defined as Amorite, *see* BABYLON, MARI and TERQA.

BIBLIOGRAPHY

K. Kenyon: *Amorites and Canaanites* (London, 1966)
M. Liverani: 'Per una considerazione storica del problema amorreo', *Oriens Ant.*, ix (1970), pp. 5–27
W. G. Dever: 'New Vistas on the EB IV ('MBI') Horizon in Syria-Palestine', *Bull. Amer. Sch. Orient. Res.*, ccxxxvii (1980), pp. 35–64
K. A. Kamp and N. Yoffee: 'Ethnicity in Ancient Western Asia during the Early Second Millennium BC: Archaeological Assessments and Ethnoarchaeological Prospectives', *Bull. Amer. Sch. Orient. Res.*, ccxxxvii (1980), pp. 85–104
O. Aurenche, ed.: *Nomades et sédentaires: Perspectives ethnoarchéologiques*, Editions recherches sur les civilisations, mém., xl (Paris, 1984)

GIORGIO BUCCELLATI

Amorós, José Alcoverro y. *See* ALCOVERRO Y AMORÓS, JOSÉ.

Amorosi, Antonio (Mercurio) (*b* Comunanza, nr Ascoli Piceno, 1660; *d* 5 Oct 1738). Italian painter. He received public commissions and painted altarpieces for Roman churches, but he was primarily a genre painter, who specialized in paintings of youths and children. He was a pupil of Giuseppe Ghezzi, in whose workshop in Rome, alongside Pier Leone Ghezzi, he received a traditionally academic training between 1676 and 1687. The earliest work attributed to Amorosi is the signed portrait of a child, *Filippo Ricci* (*c.* 1690; New York, Weitzner priv. col., see Battista, 1954, pl. xxxi, fig. 1), and such portraits became a favourite theme. He collaborated with Pier Leone Ghezzi on the *Virgin of Loreto* for S Caterina at Comunanza, the confused composition of which, despite its poor conservation, reveals the artist's immaturity. In 1699 he frescoed the Palazzo Comunale at Civitavecchia with *Innocent XII Receiving the City Fathers* and, opposite, the *Virgin with St Ferma* (both untraced), St Ferma being the patron saint of the city. In 1702 he painted *St Gregory and the Souls in Purgatory* (Civitavecchia, S Maria della Morte), distinguished by the crowding of the figures and by the vortex-like composition; the angel at the centre is indebted to Carlo Maratti. After this date his official commissions became scarce: they include *St Francis of Paola* (1719; Rome, S Rocco) and the altarpiece (1736–8) in S Bernardino, Rome, both undistinguished works.

Early sources state that Amorosi's first genre scenes were commissioned by Juan Francisco Pacheco Tellez, Duke of Uceda (1649–1718), and date from the early 18th century. Amorosi became increasingly attracted to a circle of anti-academic artists, who were excluded from official circles and opposed to the Accademia di S Luca, the Roman painters' guild. In 1715 these specialists in genre, battle pictures and landscapes won a highly important commission, for the decoration (destr.) of the Palazzo Ruspoli in Rome. This was carried out between 20 March and 20 November, under the direction of Domenico Paradisi (*fl* 1691–1721). Among the artists who participated were Pietro Paolo Cennini, Andrea Locatelli and Giulio Solimena (1667–1732); Amorosi was entrusted with the decoration of a room with genre scenes.

During this period Amorosi's numerous portraits of youths and genre scenes were highly successful. The latter belong to a late 17th-century tradition and are conceived on a monumental scale. Nevertheless, they reflect the ideals of the Arcadian movement in 18th-century Roman poetry; they show no awareness of social problems and are characterized by ostentatious simplicity and love of nature. Notable features of these idyllic works include the detailed description of furnishings, the striking depiction of domestic animals and the occasional hint of caricature in the presentation of the otherwise charming figures. Examples include the *Scene in a Tavern* (Rome, Pal. Barberini), the *Portrait of a Youth with a Bunch of Grapes* (Schleissheim, Neues Schloss), the *Little Flute-player* (Nancy, Mus. B.-A.), two half-figures of infants (both Stockholm, Nmus.) and a group of pictures that came from the collection of the historian Lione Pascoli, among them the three-quarter-length *Portrait of a Young Painter* (Deruta, Pin. Com.).

BIBLIOGRAPHY

DBI [with bibliog.]; Thieme–Becker
L. Pascoli: *Vite* (1730–36)
R. Longhi: 'Monsù Bernardo', *Crit. A.*, iii (1938), pp. 121–30
E. Battista: 'Alcune "vite" inedite di Lione Pascoli', *Commentari*, iv/1 (1953), pp. 30–45
——: 'Per la conoscenza di Antonio Amorosi', *Commentari*, iv/2 (1953), pp. 155–64
——: 'Antonio Amorosi e non Monsù Bernardo', *Commentari*, v/1 (1954), pp. 79–80
G. Michel and O. Michel: 'La Décoration du Palais Ruspoli en 1715 et la redécouverte de Monsù Francesco Borgognone', *Mél. Ecole Fr. Rome: Moyen Age, Temps Mod.*, lxxxix (1977), pp. 265–340
A. Lo Bianco: 'Alcune considerazioni sull'attività di Antonio Amorosi', *Ant. B.A.*, ii/7–8 (1978), pp. 286–92
A. M. Rybko: *Amorosi, Antonio Mercurio*, Pitt. Italia, ii (Milan, 1989, rev. 1990), pp. 603–4
E. Donnini: 'Per il '600 nelle Marche', *Not. Pal. Albani*, xix/1 (1990), pp. 45–52

ANA MARIA RYBKO

Ámos, Imre (*b* Nagykálló, nr Debrecen, 7 Dec 1907; *d* Germany, 1944). Hungarian painter. After secondary school he worked in a factory and then attended the Technical University, Budapest, for two years. Between 1929 and 1935 he studied at the Academy of Fine Arts, Budapest. His early works were influenced by József Rippl-Rónai and the NABIS; later he was also influenced by Róbert Berény and Lajos Gulácsy. Ámos combined symbolism with a lyrical interpretation of what he observed (e.g. *Winter: Still-life with a Mask of Ady* (1930; Budapest, N.G.)). He regarded painting as a vision, in which the artist recorded the complexities of his personality: memories, personal experiences and, in his case, his Jewish origins. Pictures painted between 1933 and 1935 have a timeless, cultic significance: dream-like visions of the sense and meaning of the past.

In 1937, after joining the KÚT (Képzőművészek Új Társasága: New Society of Fine Artists), he travelled to Paris with his wife, the painter Margit Anna (*b* 1913). He was strongly influenced by Chagall and Picasso, to whom he felt spiritually related. However, in his own surrealistic works Ámos paid more attention to conventional structures of time and space. From 1938 his works became more dramatic and horror-filled. For a while the friendship of his colleagues at the SZENTENDRE COLONY, where he lived from 1936, helped him bear the situation, but from 1940 onwards he was often dragged away for enforced labour by the Fascists. His experience of this collective and personal tragedy made his art increasingly expressive, and his former pastel tones gave way to fiercer, more contrasting colours, as in his *Painter before a Burning House* (1940; Budapest, N.G.). Further works by Imre Ámos are housed in the Szombathely Picture Gallery, Szombathely.

BIBLIOGRAPHY

Imre Ámos (exh. cat., ed. L. Haulisch; Budapest, N.G., 1958) [retro.]
L. Németh: 'Ámos Imre naplója' [The diary of Imre Ámos], *Magvető Almanach* (Budapest, 1964), pp. 256–82
L. Haulisch: *Ámos* (Budapest, 1966)
M. Egri: *Ámos Imre szolnoki vázlatkönyve* [The artist's sketchbook of Szolnok] (Budapest, 1973) [last works]
K. Passuth: 'Ámos Imre szimbólumrendszere' [Imre Ámos's system of symbols], *Ars Hungarica*, 1 (1975), pp. 65–91
M. Egri: *Ámos Imre* (Budapest, 1980)
K. Petényi: *Ámos Imre* (Budapest, 1982)

ANNA SZINYEI MERSE

Amphiprostyle. Term applied to a temple with columns in porticos at both ends but not along the sides.

□

Amphitheatre. Building or precinct with tiers of seats surrounding a central space used for public spectacles.

1. ROMAN. The Roman amphitheatre differs from a theatre in that it is elliptical in shape, has seats all round the arena and was used either for gladiatorial games or for contests between men and beasts. Under the arena floor were cages for the animals, and rooms and movable platforms for the props and scenery. Spectators were protected from the sun by a canvas awning suspended on ropes that were attached to masts around the top of the outer wall and secured to bollards at ground-level.

During the earlier Republican period gladiatorial games at Rome were held either in the Circus Maximus or in the Forum Romanum, with the spectators seated on temporary wooden benches. The senatorial ban on permanent theatres also applied to amphitheatres, with the result that even during the late Republic only temporary amphitheatres were erected at Rome, such as the one built by the senator Curio in 53 BC. The first permanent amphitheatre at Rome, built by Augustus in 29 BC, the one built by the general T. Statilius Taurus in the Campus Martius and destroyed in the fire of AD 64, the amphitheatre of Caligula (*reg* AD 37–41) and that of Nero (AD 57) were probably mainly of wood. The first securely dated masonry amphitheatre (80 BC) is at Pompeii and measures 140×105 m. Built in the south-east corner of the city where it could utilize the earth embankment of the city walls, its arena was excavated 6 m into the ground, providing additional spoil to support the upper rows of seats. The embankment was supported by a retaining wall reinforced on the outside by radial arches. Access to the upper seats was by external staircases, while four corridors led down to a passage running round the whole amphitheatre. This separated the lowest section of seats from the middle one and was linked to both by several staircases. Though early Imperial amphitheatres (e.g. at Augusta Emerita, 8 BC, and Syracuse, early 1st century AD) were still usually constructed by excavation and embankment, concrete vaults were later increasingly used to support the seating.

In the greatest amphitheatre (188×156 m), the Colosseum (begun AD 75; *see* ROME, §V, 6 and ROME, ANCIENT, fig. 28), the seating was entirely supported by a complex series of annular and radial corridors on three levels, many of which contained staircases. The building's travertine façade is 48.5 m high and contains 80 arched entrances at ground-level, flanked by Doric half-columns and numbered for ticket holders. The middle and upper tiers of arches are flanked by Ionic and Corinthian half-columns respectively, and a fourth storey has alternating square windows and large bronze shields flanked by pilasters. Near the cornice are the brackets that supported the masts for the awning ropes, while at ground-level outside are several of the bollards that secured them. In the middle of the north and south ends of the amphitheatre are elaborate triple entrances, for the emperor and for the consuls and magistrates respectively. Apart from a wooden top gallery, the seating was of stone, and the building's capacity is estimated to between 45,000 and 73,000 spectators. The arena (86×54 m) was surrounded by a high podium wall and a high safety net on wooden poles to protect the spectators. The arena floor, which covered the usual complex of underground chambers, was of wood and so has disappeared.

The arena floors of the amphitheatre at Puteoli and Capua, however, are of concrete, and the underfloor rooms as well as the trapdoors through which the animals entered the arena can be better appreciated. The great amphitheatre at Capua, which measures 170×139 m and is almost as large as the Colosseum, is built entirely on substructures and, though originally Julio-Claudian period (AD 14–68), it was extensively remodelled at the time of Hadrian (*reg* AD 117–38). The amphitheatre at Puteoli (149×116 m; see fig.) was built in Flavian times (AD 69–96) and resembles amphitheatres at Pola (132×105 m) and Verona (152×123 m), all of these being almost entirely supported by substructures. The famous amphitheatres at Nîmes (133×101 m) and Arles (136×107 m; for illustration *see* ARLES) are probably of similar date. Many amphitheatres in the provinces, particularly in military areas, continued to be built largely of timber. In parts of Gaul and

Amphitheatre, annular passage under arena floor, showing *carceres* or animal cages, Puteoli, ?*c*. AD 90

Britain the functions of theatre and amphitheatre were often combined in a building with both an arena, surrounded by a podium wall, and an elevated stage. During the late Empire it became fashionable to adapt existing theatres for gladiatorial use, and comparatively few new amphitheatres were built. The most notable exceptions are the small Amphitheatrum Castrense in Rome (89×79 m; *c*. AD 220) and the large amphitheatre at Thysdrus (El Djem) in Tunisia, which measures nearly 149×124 m and was built towards the mid-3rd century AD.

See also ROME, ANCIENT, §II, 1(i)(e).

BIBLIOGRAPHY

J. R. Mélida: *El teatro y el anfiteatro romanos de Mérida* (Madrid, 1929)
M. della Corte: *Pompei: I nuovi scavi e l'anfiteatro* (Pompeii, 1930)
E. Espérandieu: *L'Amphithéâtre de Nîmes* (Paris, 1933)
M. Girosi: 'L'anfiteatro di Pompei', *Mem. Accad. Archeol., Lett. & B.A. Napoli*, v (1936), pp. 29–55
M. Mirabella Roberti: *L'arena di Pola* (Pola, 1939)
A. Maiuri: *Studi e ricerche sull'anfiteatro flavio puteolano* (Naples, 1955)
A. Neppi Modona: *Gli edifici teatrali grechi e romani* (Florence, 1961)
J. Pearson: *The Story of the Colosseum* (London, 1973)
R. Graefe: *Vela erunt: Die Zeltdächer der römischen Theater und ähnlicher Anlagen* (Mainz, 1979)
J.-C. Laschaux: *Théâtres et amphithéâtres d'Afrique Proconsulaire* (Aix-en-Provence, 1979)
A. Hönle and A. Henze: *Römische Amphitheater und Stadien* (Feldmeilen, 1981)
J.-C. Golvin: *L'Amphithéâtre romain: Essai sur la théorisation de sa forme et de ses fonctions* (Paris, 1988)

F. B. SEAR

2. LATER HISTORY. The Roman elliptical amphitheatre form was not revived until the end of the 18th century in France; a rare earlier example is the Anatomical Theatre (1594), Padua. It was used both in temporary structures

for revolutionary festivals, for example in the Champs de Mars (1790), Paris, and on a monumental scale in a project for a circus (*c*. 1789) by Etienne-Louis Boullée. The Arena (1806–7), Milan, was built at the Foro Buonaparte by Luigi Canonica, as part of the Napoleonic improvements. A circular derivation was used for *plaza de toro* (bullfighting arenas) in Spain and the Spanish Americas from the mid-18th century; the neo-*Mudéjar plaza* (1874; destr. 1934) in Madrid by Emilio Rodríguez Ayuso and Lorenzo Alvarez Capra was an influential model.

Experiments were made in the use of the amphitheatre form for theatrical presentations during the mid-19th century, of which the Cirque d'Hiver (1852; destr.), Paris, by Jacques-Ignace Hittorff, was a pioneer; the Royal Albert Hall (1867–70), London, by Francis Fowke proved unsuitable for music.

As a sports facility—when it is termed stadium (*see* STADIUM, §2)—the amphitheatre form became popular at the end of the 19th century; the revival of the Olympic Games in 1896 provided further stimulus. Its form survived virtually unchanged through the 20th century; the main contemporary technical advances have been the use of steel and reinforced concrete to enable tiers of seats to be cantilevered, the modification of the elliptical geometry to improve sight-lines, and the enclosure of the entire stadium. The earliest uses connected with sport were in the United States, where it became particularly common, for example Madison Square Garden (1890; destr.), New York, which was the first covered stadium, and the Yale University Stadium (1912–14), New Haven, by Ferry & Barber, which with 70,000 spectators was the first to exceed the Colosseum in capacity. The Olympic Stadium (1936), Berlin, by Werner March was a deliberate evocation of Roman grandeur. Distinguished designs after World War II are epitomized by structural virtuosity, such as the National Gymnasia (1963–4; for illustration *see* TANGE, KENZŌ) for the Tokyo Olympics, by Kenzō Tange, with a steel cable roof suspended from concrete towers, and the stadium (1986–90), Bari, by Renzo Piano, in which the elliptical plan geometry and cantilevered tiers of seats have a Roman grandeur, while the fabric roof recalls a *velarium*.

BIBLIOGRAPHY

I. Chierici: *I palazzi dello sport* (Milan, 1960)
F.-J. Verspohl: *Stadionbauten von der Antike bis zur Gegenwart: Regie und Selbsterfahrung der Massen* (Giessen, 1976)
Arquitectura del siglo XIX, del modernismo a 1936 y de 1940 a 1980, Historia de la Arquitectura Española, v (Barcelona and Saragossa, 1980)
V. Gregotti: *Five Necessary Dialogues*, Lotus Documents, 14 (Milan, 1990)
S. san Pietro, ed.: *1990 stadi in Italia* (Milan, 1990)

ZILAH QUEZADO DECKKER

Amphora. Ancient pottery form, used as a storage jar (*see* GREECE, ANCIENT, fig. 71(i)a–d).

Amphoriskos. Ancient form of vessel, used to contain cosmetics, oils and perfumes (*see* GREECE, ANCIENT, fig. 71(v)c). □

Ampurias. *See* EMPORIAE.

ʿAmq. *See* AMUK REGION.

Amritsar. Sikh holy city in Punjab, northern India. Lying on a flat stretch of agricultural land between the rivers Beas and Ravi, close to the Pakistan border, Amritsar (Skt *amrit sarowar*, 'pool of nectar') is the location of the Harmandir, the holiest of Sikh shrines at the heart of the Darbar Sahib temple complex, also referred to as the Golden Temple (*see also* INDIAN SUBCONTINENT, §II, 8(ii) and §III, 7(ii)(a), fig. 106). It was the third Sikh guru, Amar Das (1552–74), who was first drawn to the area by the peace and tranquillity of its forested terrain and the pool where the Harmandir was later built. His successor, Guru Ram Das (1574–81), bought the pool and the surrounding land. Some historians believe that the Mughal emperor Akbar (*reg* 1556–1605) offered the land as a gift, but that Ram Das declined in keeping with the Sikh tradition of self-reliance (*see also* SIKHISM). The two gurus' association with the site made it a place of pilgrimage, which was known by various names, including Guru-ka-Chak, Chak Guru Ram Das and Ramdaspur, before it became known as Amritsar around the beginning of the 18th century. Historians do not always agree on the dates or details of the city's development, but it is accepted that its growth was synchronous with its transformation from a place of pilgrimage into the principal seat of the Sikh religion.

The digging of the larger pool—begun in 1573 by Amar Das—was completed by 1577, and the fifth Guru, Arjan (1581–1606), added the Harmandir during his stewardship. The original modest structure was built in brick and lime in the centre of the pool; a causeway was constructed to reach it. Unlike traditional Hindu temples, which had only one entrance, the Harmandir had four, one on each side. Its doors would thus be open to all the four Hindu castes, for to Arjan, 'the four castes . . . are equal partners in divine instruction'. The holy book of the Sikhs—the *Adi Granth* ('original book') or *Granth Sahib* ('venerable book')—was installed in the Harmandir in 1604, three years after the shrine's completion.

The expansion of the Darbar Sahib complex and the gilding, marble, mirror and inlay work on the Harmandir and other important buildings were carried out in the 19th century, when the Sikhs reached the pinnacle of their power and affluence under Maharaja Ranjit Singh (*reg* 1799–1839). The founder of the Sikh empire, Ranjit Singh encouraged the arts, extending his patronage by bringing some of the best artists, craftsmen and artisans to Amritsar from all over India. Among his many other contributions to Amritsar were the reconstruction of Gobindgarh Fort, his own summer palace set in 80 acres of landscaped gardens known as Ram Bagh, and a massive city wall. By encouraging merchants, traders, bankers and craftsmen he made Amritsar a centre of production, trading and distribution for a wide variety of goods including shawls and carpets, silks, woollen cloth, jewellery and metalwork, woodwork, enamel ware and marble work.

BIBLIOGRAPHY

W. G. Archer: *Paintings of the Sikhs* (London, 1966)
V. N. Datta: *Amritsar: Past and Present* (Amritsar, 1967)
M. R. Anand, ed.: 'Homage to Amritsar', *Marg*, xxx/3 (1977), pp. 2–4
H. Singh: *The Heritage of the Sikhs* (New Delhi, 1983/*R* 1985)
P. Singh: *The Golden Temple* (Hong Kong, 1989)

PATWANT SINGH

Amstel, Jan van [Aertsz., Jan; Hollander, Jan de] (*b* Amsterdam, *c*. 1500; *d* Antwerp, *c*. 1542). South Netherlandish painter of Dutch birth. He was probably the brother of Pieter Aertsen and was married to the sister-in-law of Pieter Coecke van Aelst. He was made a freeman of the Guild of St Luke in Antwerp in 1528 and a citizen of that city in 1536. Lampsonius and van Mander praised him as a landscape artist. According to Lampsonius, he 'enjoyed painting landscapes well, instead of painting portraits, human figures and the Deity badly'. Van Mander described his very large panels, which sold well in the markets of Brabant and Flanders, as well as his unusual technique of painting with a light wash so that the underlying ground colour showed through (apparently influential on Pieter Bruegel the elder).

There are no known documented works by Jan, but he is generally identified (e.g. by Hoogewerff, Genaille, Faggin, Schubert, Wescher and Wallen) as the BRUNSWICK MONOGRAMMIST (*see* MASTERS, ANONYMOUS, AND MONOGRAMMISTS, §III). This attribution is supported by a monogram that can be interpreted as JVAMSL on *The Feeding of the Poor* (Brunswick, Herzog Anton Ulrich-Mus.) and by a painting technique similar at times to that mentioned by van Mander. Some argue that the early descriptions of Jan as a landscape artist seem at odds with the figural emphasis in paintings by the Brunswick Monogrammist, although in 1753 Guarienti mentioned a large painting by 'Gio d'Amstel' of the *Crucifixion*, with more than 200 figures. Bergmans (1957) saw no connection between the two artists and instead gave to Jan (?in collaboration with Pieter Coecke van Aelst) a large, many-figured *Deluge* (Brussels, Sigurd Majorin priv. col., see Bergmans, fig. 2), basing the attribution on a questionable identification of portraits of Jan and certain family members in the painting.

BIBLIOGRAPHY

Thieme–Becker

D. Lampsonius: *Pictorum aliquot celebrium Germaniae Inferioris effigies* [Portraits of famous painters of the Netherlands] (Antwerp, 1572)

K. van Mander: *Schilder-boeck* ([1603]–1604), fol. 215*v*

Guarienti: *Orlandi Abecedario pittorico* (Venice, 1753)

R. Genaille: 'Jan van Amstel, le monogrammiste de Brunswick', *Rev. Belge Archéol. & Hist. A.*, xix (1950), pp. 147–53

S. Bergmans: 'Jan van Amstel, dit Jean de Hollande', *Rev. Belge Archéol. & Hist. A.*, xxvi (1957), pp. 25–36

Le Siècle de Bruegel (exh. cat., Brussels, Mus. Royaux B.-A., 1963), pp. 44–5 [entries by S. Bergmans]

G. T. Faggin: 'Jan van Amstel', *Paragone*, xv (1964), pp. 43–51

P. Wescher: 'Jan van Hemessen und Jan van Amstel', *Jb. Berlin. Mus.*, xii (1970), pp. 34–60

For further bibliography *see* MASTERS, ANONYMOUS, AND MONOGRAMMISTS, §III: BRUNSWICK MONOGRAMMIST.

ELISE L. SMITH

Amsterdam. Capital city of the Netherlands. It has the largest population for a Dutch town (702,731 in 1991) but not the largest area (20,150 ha). The city is located in the province of North Holland on either side of the estuary of the River IJ. The oldest and largest part of the city lies south of the IJ, either side of the River Amstel. An industrial town and port, university and pilgrimage town, Amsterdam is also the country's most important financial and artistic centre, with important museums, galleries, theatres, art dealers and art sales. There are also major educational institutions for professional training in music, the visual arts, applied arts, photography, film, architecture and the theatre.

I. Introduction.

Although the city was traditionally thought to have been founded in 1275, research has revealed that it must have existed much earlier. At the end of the 12th century, the River Amstel was probably dammed, and thus closed off from the IJ, where the present square called the Dam is (hence the city's original name, Amestelledamme). The most important period in Amsterdam's history is the 17th century, also called the 'Golden Age', when the city became the most important trading market in the world. The population explosion that resulted from this economic development led to the enlargement of the city. The famous ring of canals, where mainly rich merchants settled, was laid out at this time. The arts of architecture, painting, sculpture and gold- and silversmithing flourished. Until the end of the 18th century artists were organized in guilds, as were craftsmen. The most important patrons were the patrician regents who from 1477 to 1799 possessed virtually unlimited political strength. Many of the commissions for church interiors and altarpieces disappeared after the iconoclastic riots of 1568 and the replacing of the Catholic patriciate by a mainly Protestant one in 1578 (the *Alteratie*). Other important patrons were guilds, wealthy individuals and the militia companies, who commissioned group portraits called *schuttersstukken* ('militia pieces'). Regents also commissioned group portraits after 1600. Artists worked on speculation for the free market as well, and paintings hung in almost every house, even those of the less well-off.

BIBLIOGRAPHY

A. E. d'Ailly and others: *Historische gids van Amsterdam* (Amsterdam, 1971)

H. Brugmans: *Geschiedenis van Amsterdam*, 6 vols (Utrecht and Antwerp, 1972–3)

M. Jonker, L. Noordegraaf and M. Wagenaar, eds: *Van stadskern tot stadsgewest: Stedebouwkundige geschiedenis van Amsterdam* (Amsterdam, 1984)

D. Carasso: *A Short History of Amsterdam: A Survey of the City's History Illustrated from the Collections of the Amsterdam Historical Museum* (Amsterdam, 1985)

II. History and urban development.

1. BEFORE 1578. At about the same time as the dam was built in the Amstel, dykes were laid down along the banks of the estuary from the dam to the River IJ. These dykes were also used as roads, which still exist: on the east, Warmoesstraat to Nes, and on the west, Nieuwendijk to Kalverstraat. A harbour was created, the Damrak, with open access to the North Sea via the IJ and Zuiderzee (now IJsselmeer). The first houses, built of wood and mud with thatched roofs, were erected inside these dykes on mounds of clay to permit drainage of the waterlogged peatlands. The first stone building was the Oude Kerk or St Nicolaaskerk (*see* §V, 1 below), built from 1300, east of the harbour: the district consequently came to be known

as the Oude Zijde. The Nieuwe Kerk or St Catharinakerk was built at the end of the 14th century on the west side (Nieuwe Zijde) of the harbour in the dam area.

The settlement immediately became an outlet for international trade, such that the harbour was already equipped for storage of goods by 1333. This was the first planned intervention in the city. Land either side of the dam was filled in to build houses with warehouses behind. Later, behind the Nieuwendijk warehouses, a second row of houses was built and a quay laid out called Op 't Water (now Damrak). The merchants settled mostly in Warmoesstraat and by the new quay.

The city's oldest defensive walls (the *voorburgwallen*) were dug parallel to the dykes in 1342. By 1500 second and third walls, parallel to the *voorburgwallen*, had been built on both sides. The city grew inside the third wall, its course now traced by the Singel, Kloveniersburgwal and Gelderse Kade. For the houses built by the walls, the ground was raised with clay in one campaign. The city authorities decreed that houses had to be built in line, thereby creating streets and alleys. The Dam marked the city centre, where goods were traded. The Stadhuis (destr.) and the Waag (Weigh-house) were there. The oldest map of the city (1538; see fig. 1), commissioned by the city authorities from CORNELIS ANTHONISZ., shows the city's various gateways, of which only the St Anthoniespoort survives (converted into a weigh-house in the 17th century). Houses were already packed close together. Between 1300 and 1500 the population increased from 1100 to 10,000. The inner area was completely built up, and houses also became higher. The empty areas still evident on Cornelis Anthonisz.'s map were mainly on the east side and belonged to the many religious houses (mainly nunneries), such as the Begijnhof, founded in 1346.

House-building changed as a result of the city's growth and the authorities' regulations. The first town houses had timber frames and walls. After the great fire of 1453, which burnt most of Amsterdam, the authorities decreed that houses must have a stone side wall and roofs of tiles or slates. Timber frames were used until 1630, so the stone walls did not serve any functional purpose. Since the end of the 14th century, timber frames had rested on brick foundations, reinforced for heavier buildings by a grid foundation (*roosterfundering*): short timber planks held together by a wooden framework. Excavations show that pile foundations made of Norwegian conifer wood were used from the end of the 15th century. The fronts of houses were still made of wood well into the 17th century, because they were easily pulled down in cases of fire.

Interiors changed too. The first houses consisted of a single space with a hearth in the centre. Smoke escaped through the thatched roof. After tiled roofs were introduced, a chimney was installed on one of the side walls. A

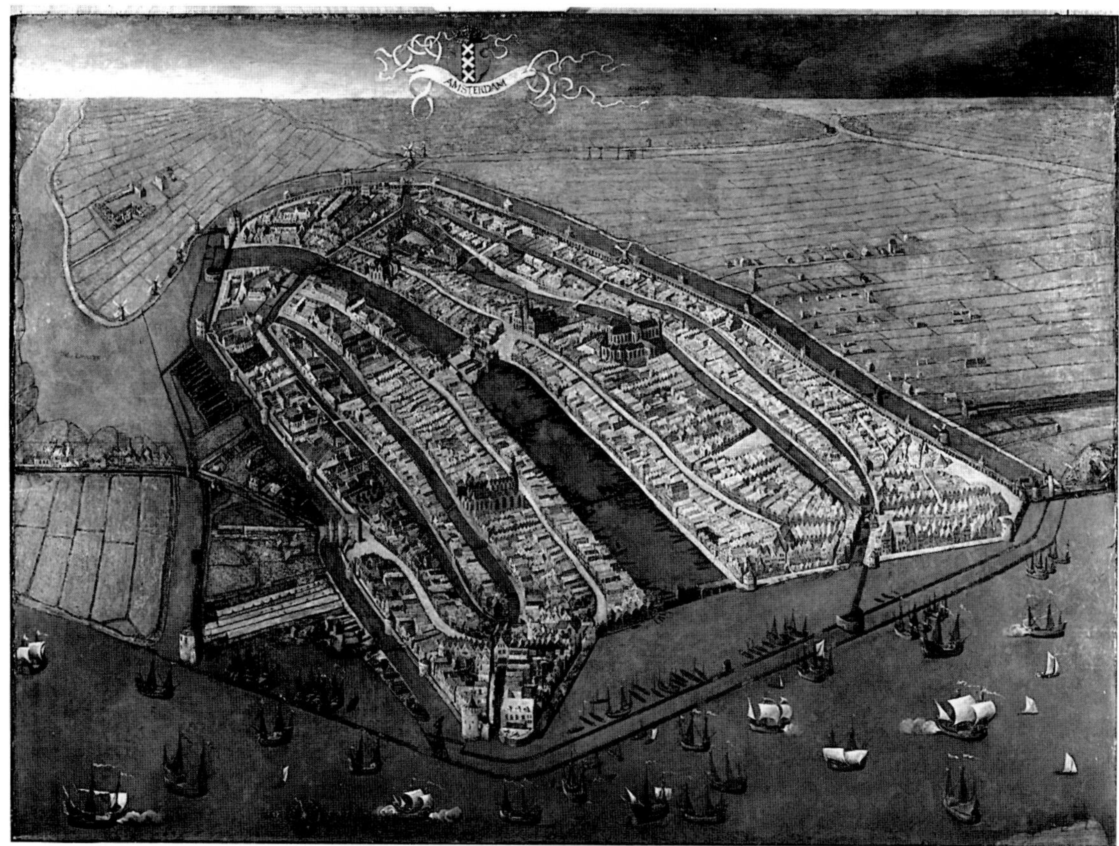

1. *Plan of Amsterdam* by Cornelis Anthonisz., oil on panel, 1.16×1.59 m, *c*. 1538 (Amsterdam, Historisch Museum)

room was built around it called the inside hearth (*binnenhaard*), the first private room in the house. The rest of the house was often used as a shop or workshop. The front room became the living room once a separate fireplace was added. Behind the houses were large fields where increasingly often outhouses (*achterhuizen*) were built.

For bibliography *see* §5 below.

2. 1578–1699. Midway through the 16th century Amsterdam was a medium-sized trading town with *c.* 60,000 inhabitants. The city was crowded, with settlements beyond the city walls, for example Lastage, which had shipyards and ropemaking yards. The regents, who had become an élite dominated by a few Catholic families, prevented further expansion since the landowners among them realized that expansion would decrease the value of their property. The regents' repression of 'heretics' fostered opposition from a growing group of Calvinists, which included many wholesalers, whose economic strength was politically unrepresented. In 1578 Amsterdam chose to support the uprising against the Spanish. A change of government (the *Alteratie*) was enforced, and an overwhelmingly Protestant Reformed city authority was appointed. The regents and their supporters were expelled from the city, and the public practice of Catholicism was forbidden. As a result, Catholics and, to a lesser extent, Jews and certain Protestant groups worshipped in private houses. Clandestine churches (*schuilkerken*) were built behind houses, or behind domestic house-fronts. Existing churches were stripped of their luxurious interiors. The first Reformed church, the Zuiderkerk, was built in 1603 by Hendrick de Keyser I (*see* KEYSER, DE, (1), §2). The city's many monasteries were either designated as accommodation for the poor or demolished to free land for housing. Only the Begijnhof escaped.

After the *Alteratie*, trade and industry developed to such a degree that in the 17th century Amsterdam was the world's most important staple market. The occupation of Antwerp—Amsterdam's most important competitor—by the Spanish in 1585 and the closing of the River Schelde through Holland and Zeeland contributed. Merchant-artisans were replaced by wholesalers who bought goods at the exchange and stored them in warehouses until they could be sold at a profit. From 1608 to 1611 Amsterdam's first exchange (destr.) was built by Hendrick de Keyser I, and soon afterwards the corn exchange (Korenbeurs; destr.) went up west of the Damrak.

The first expansion after the *Alteratie* took place to the east of the city. Adriaen Anthonisz. designed Amsterdam's first defences, which consisted of bastions connected by an earth wall. (From *c.* 1600 many windmills sprang up along the ramparts.) The Lastage area became residential, and shipbuilding was located near the newly reclaimed islands inside the fortifications. The construction of these eastern islands demonstrates that living and working areas were already separate as a result of the extent and nature of new business methods. One of the burgomasters, Willem Baerdesen, designed the urban plan for these islands. At the end of the 17th century they became part of the Jewish district. The Verenigde Oostindische Compagnie (VOC; United East India Company), founded in 1602, established shipyards, ropeyards and other buildings on one of the newly reclaimed islands (Oostenburg) north-east of the city. By 1657 it was the largest industrial complex in Europe. The most important surviving VOC building is the Oostindisch Huis, built in the old city centre in 1605 in a Renaissance style, attributed to Hendrick de Keyser I.

From 1615 the famous semicircle of canals was begun to the west and south of the city. There was no overall plan. First a new defensive wall was constructed from the northern sea dyke (Haarlemmerdijk) up to what is now Leidsestraat, so as to replace the obsolete defensive walls and to create a residential area. New fortifications were built along the Singelgracht, but there was no clear urban plan until one was officially commissioned from the city carpenter, Hendrick Jacobsz. Staets. It filled the area with a network of streets and canals, with a few radial streets cutting through the ring of canals. The land was divided into large lots, and there were few building regulations.

Islands in the IJ were reclaimed to enlarge the western harbour area: Prinseneiland, Realeneiland and Bickerseiland. The merchants J. Bicker and R. Reael bought an island for their shipyards, warehouses and houses for their workers and themselves. The northern part of the ring of canals fell prey to speculators, who divided the large lots and built houses for sale. Private houses were built for rich merchants. The large lots had plenty of space for large gardens, with garden houses, coach houses and sometimes offices. Servants, craftsmen and shopkeepers lived in the smaller, transverse streets. Hendrick de Keyser I built the Westerkerk on the Prinsengracht in 1620.

By 1625 the area was fully developed and an expansion plan was prepared by town planner Cornelis Dankertsz. and Daniël Stalpaert to complete the crescent of canals. The regulations were stricter, particularly concerning the size of lots and commercial development. The increasing wealth of merchants was reflected in the size of the houses. However, after 1670 residential building stagnated, and the district became a leisure area called Plantage, with gardens, avenues and cafés. Meanwhile the district's former inhabitants obtained an area now known as the Jordaan between the Prinsengracht canal and the Singelgracht fortifications. Lucas Sinck prepared a plan using the drainage ditches to establish the layout of roads and the division of lots. Inadequate road connections with the ring of canals was to hinder subsequent expansion. The Jordaan was obviously intended to house the less well-off. Industry came illicitly to the area, driven by a lack of space elewhere in Amsterdam, and so homes and small factories were in close proximity.

Abundant commissions from rich merchants stimulated architecture. In addition to anonymous architects and master masons, trained architects were active in Amsterdam, including Hendrick de Keyser I, Jacob van Campen, Philips Vingboons, Daniël Stalpaert and Adriaen Dorsman. The construction and style of buildings changed during this period. Stone buildings replaced timber structures, and these allowed a basement to be provided for storage of goods or servants' accommodation. Windows remained of the medieval transomed design until the end of the 17th century. The lower halves, often unglazed, could be shuttered, with flaps to allow goods to be displayed for sale. The step gable first appeared in 1500

2. Amsterdam, Huis met de Hoofden, attributed to Pieter de Keyser, 1622

and was a feature of Dutch Renaissance architecture at the end of the 16th century. This was characterized by brick (mostly painted red) with layers of stone (mostly painted yellow) and by façades decorated with masks, cartouches and garlands. This style is seen in De Dolfijn (1605) on the Singel by its most important representative, Hendrick de Keyser I and the Huis met de Hoofden (House with the Heads; 1622) on the Keizersgracht (see fig. 2), attributed to his son Pieter de Keyser.

Stalpaert's and van Campen's classicizing Baroque style was mainly applied to larger buildings and houses. In 1648 van Campen designed the new Stadhuis (now the Royal Palace; *see* §V, 2 below and TOWN HALL, fig. 3) on the Dam, completed by Stalpaert in 1665. In 1655 Stalpaert designed the Admiralty's arsenal (the Zeemagazijn; now the Dutch Maritime Museum) on Kattenburg Island. Van Campen's stately buildings have stone façades and such classical elements as the frame gable with tympanum. His style suits large canal properties, for example Coymanshuizen (1624). Adriaen Dorsman built in the same simple style, as at Keizersgracht 672–4 (1671; altered 18th century; now the Museum van Loon). Van Campen was much imitated, for example by Elias Bouman in his Portuguese Synagogue (1674; *see* §V, 3 below) and the house of the rich Portuguese-Jewish family de Pinto on St Antoniesbreestraat (1651).

For bibliography *see* §5 below.

3. 1700–1812. The 18th century is often seen as one of stagnation and decline for Amsterdam. The VOC's activities promised economic growth, but industrialization lagged behind that of other countries, for example England. Amsterdam was still one of the largest towns in western Europe in 1800 but no longer the world's most important trading centre. It was chiefly important for publishing and finance. The end of the Dutch Republic in 1795 brought the downfall of the regents, who had become all-powerful within its autonomous city-states. During the French period that followed, Amsterdam briefly became the royal seat of Louis Bonaparte, King of Holland. He had the Stadhuis rebuilt as a royal palace (*see* §V, 2 below). Other developments were related to the introduction of religious freedom and improvements in the city's infrastructure. However, a complete reversal in the economy was heralded in 1800 by the VOC's shutdown. The population, which fluctuated around 200,000 in the 18th century, fell by *c.* 40,000 during the French period, chiefly as a result of higher mortality in the poor districts on the east and west islands and in the Jewish district in the east of the city. Although there was no urban expansion from 1780 to 1815, at the end of the 18th century the unregulated construction of mills, factories, gardens and tea houses took place outside the city walls.

French influence, evident in various aspects of culture throughout western Europe since the mid-17th century, was also noticeable in the architecture initiated in Amsterdam by French Protestant refugees. Daniel Marot I, active in Amsterdam in the first and second decades of the century, fostered the adoption of the Louis XIV style. Luxuriantly decorated Rococo gables, sometimes in the form of a large crest, were used on narrow houses with neck gables and Dutch gables as well as on the larger patricians' houses along the canals with frame gables. Reaction against this style is reflected in the adoption of Neo-classicism in Amsterdam, for example for the Roman Catholic Maagdenhuis (1784) by city architect Abraham van der Hart and the Felix Meritis building (1787) by Jacob Otten-Husly.

The main impact of French influence was on interiors, which, until the mid-17th century, were simple, even in the houses of the wealthy, with white plastered walls and scant furnishings. Paintings hung on the white walls, and joists were visible in ceilings, mostly painted red, purple or ochre. Walls, however, began to be hung with cloth, gilt leather or velours d'Utrecht (velvet with embossed reliefs), and were thus less suited to hanging paintings. Ceilings were finely panelled in compartments divided by the joists ('cassette-plafond') and often painted. Richly painted stucco ceilings were introduced at the start of the 18th century. Such painters as GÉRARD DE LAIRESSE and JACOB DE WIT made illusionistic ceiling paintings. Floors were of wood or of marble tiles, covered with Eastern carpets or Spanish mats. Large French sash windows were adopted after 1710, gradually replacing the medieval transomed windows. Interiors thus became much lighter. Entrances and staircases acquired central positions in houses, often emphasized by stucco ornamentation.

For bibliography *see* §5 below.

4. 1813–1901. Amsterdam remained the capital but not the royal seat after the Kingdom of the Netherlands was proclaimed in 1813 under William I. He founded the Nederlandsche Handelmaatschappij (Dutch Trading Company) in 1824, which gave a new impetus to trade, and the Entrepotdok (bonded warehouse) was extended

in 1827–30 by Jan de Greef, but the economy revived only after 1870. The city's prosperity attracted migrants from the agricultural crisis of 1878–95, and between 1870 and 1920 the population rose from 265,000 to 683,000.

New canals and railways increased Amsterdam's accessibility. The Noord-Hollands canal was dug in 1824, and the Noordzeekanaal (1876) gave Amsterdam a shorter link to the North Sea. The first railway in the Netherlands was built in 1838, linking Amsterdam to Haarlem and later to Rotterdam (1871). The line to Utrecht reached Cologne and the Rhine area by 1856. The Centraal Station (1882–9) was built in the Dutch Renaissance Revival style by P. J. H. Cuypers (*see* CUYPERS, (1)), ADOLF LEONARD VAN GENDT and L. J. Eijmer on an artificial island in the IJ.

From the last quarter of the 19th century, the increasing separation of home and workplace affected the old centre: home-based offices, shops and workshops were gradually replaced by large single-purpose buildings. Tourism increased, and the city became a cultural and scientific centre, requiring newer, larger buildings. Department stores, offices, hotels and banks were built at the expense of homes. To increase accessibility a few large through-routes cutting across the canal walls were created, for example Raadhuisstraat, bordered by such large buildings as the Gothic Revival style post office (1899) by Cornelis Hendrik Peters, the gallery in the bend between Herengracht and Keizersgracht (1897) by the van Gendt Brothers, the *Jugendstil* Rotterdamsche Verzekering-Societeiten (Rotterdam Insurance Company) building (1899–1901) by Johannes Verheul and Cornelis Verheul and a rational-style complex combining shops and houses (1897) by H. P. BERLAGE and H. Bonda. The Beursplein, built on land reclaimed from the Damrak, contains Berlage's Koopmansbeurs (Merchants' Exchange; *see* THE NETHERLANDS, fig. 11) begun *c.* 1898, in a rational style, and the new stock exchange (Effectenbeurs). A small coffee-house on the Dam was extended into the Café–Restaurant–Hotel Krasnapolski in 1879 by Gerlof Bartholomeus Salm at the expense of various houses.

Rembrandtsplein, formerly the Botermarkt (Butter market), became an entertainment centre, with the Art Deco Tuschinsky Theatre–cinema (1918–21) by H. L. de Jong (1882–1945). An entertainment district also existed around Leidseplein, with the city theatre (1891–4) by J. L. Springer, J. B. Springer and Adolf Leonard van Gendt and the American Hotel (1902) by Willem Kromhout. After Vijzelstraat was widened in 1916–17, a large bank was erected; the Nederlandsche Handelmaatschappij building (1919–26) by K. P. C. DE BAZEL also later became a bank.

The 19th-century development of Amsterdam is characterized by the large-scale plans of private groups. The involvement of the city authorities was usually confined to guidance, although the creation in 1850 of a spacious residential district for the better-off within the Singelgracht, known as the Plantage, was strictly controlled by the authorities. The Artis Zoo had been established in the area in 1838. Outside the Singelgracht a private group bought a large area in the south-west of the city to create a park, with roads and footpaths, now called the Vondelpark; the first part (by Jan David Zocher and Louis Paul Zocher) was opened in 1864. Because the group owned the land, they could specify the nature of the buildings (houses for the wealthy only), and they retained control of the architecture. Some cultural buildings were established in this district: the privately financed Concertgebouw (1888) by Adolf Leonard van Gendt, the Stedelijk Museum (1893–5) by A. W. Weissman and the Rijksmuseum (1876–85) by P. J. H. Cuypers (*see* THE NETHERLANDS, fig. 10), all in a Renaissance Revival style.

The plan by S. Sarphati (1833–66) proceeded less rapidly. It included a residential district for the wealthy, and middle-class and workers' houses in the area around the junction of the Amstel and Singelgracht. Only a small part of the plan was completed: the Amstel Hotel (1867) by Cornelis Outshoorn (for illustration *see* OUTSHOORN, CORNELIS) and a row of luxury manor houses along the Amstel and Weesperzijde. The Pijp was also built here, an area with multi-storey workers' houses along streets that were narrower than Sarphati had wanted. This district is an example of the 19th-century building revolution in which contractors crowded houses together for profit. The street-plan consists of rectangular blocks with an inner space. Squares and parks were scarce. Yet this neighbourhood was an improvement on living conditions elsewhere. Sometimes an architect was engaged for these houses; for example, Pijp's first houses (1868), built in the middle of fields (now Govert Flinckstraat), are by I. Gosschalk (1838–1907).

In 1867 city engineer J. G. van Niftrik presented his plan for a new ring around the whole city, divided into different residential districts with parks in between, and a separate industrial area. The plan foundered because of its expense and because it took no account of existing property boundaries. The plan of engineer J. Kalff in collaboration with van Niftrik was more acceptable, and Staatsliedenbuurt, Kinkerbuurt, Dapperbuurt and Oosterparkbuurt neighbourhoods were built to its design. These were also of the building revolution type, comprising mainly workers' and middle-class houses in four-storey buildings.

For bibliography *see* §5 below.

5. 1902 AND AFTER. At the start of the 20th century the state acquired increasing influence over urban development and housing for the poor (social housing). Workers' houses had been built by philanthropic institutions in Amsterdam from 1830, but the Housing Act of 1902 removed their philanthropic character by providing government loans and subsidies to housing associations. The Act also required city authorities to make development plans for the whole of their urban areas. From 1915 the Amsterdam authorities took over part of the responsibility for social housing by establishing the municipal Housing Department, and socialists on the city council, notably F. M. Wibaut (1859–1936), encouraged this. Wibaut worked closely with Ary Keppler, who ran the Housing Department and initiated the construction of the garden suburbs in Amsterdam-Noord.

Although the plan by H. P. BERLAGE of 1917 for Amsterdam-Zuid did not include all of the city, it is a significant phase in urban planning. Berlage was a representative of aesthetic urban planning, characterized by spacious layout, wide streets and squares surrounded by large buildings, with blocks as an organizing element.

Because of the expense of the spacious layout, the original plan for a lot of construction by housing associations had to be abandoned. Building was strictly controlled by an aesthetics committee that involved only architects of the AMSTERDAM SCHOOL in order to ensure stylistic unity. The characteristically plastic treatment of the façades was pre-eminently suited to large continuous fronts. Other designs show the Amsterdam school treating the construction of houses or residential complexes as sculpture, using brick and roof tiles as decorative elements, as for the Scheepvaarthuis (1916; see fig. 3) by J. M. VAN DER MEIJ, assisted by M. de Klerk and P. Kramer, and the housing complex and post office (1914–20) in Spaarndammerbuurt by Michel de Klerk (for illustration *see* KLERK, MICHEL DE).

Another architectural movement of the 1920s, the Nieuwe Bouwen, was not involved in Amsterdam-Zuid. The modern, light, open-air school (1930) by Johannes Duiker had to be located in an enclosed area to avoid disturbing its architectural unity. The Amsterdam school of architecture gradually yielded to Nieuwe Bouwen: for example, the studio houses (*atelierwoningen*; 1934) by Piet Zanstra, J. H. L. Giesen and K. L. Sijmons, the 'drive-in' houses (1936) by Willem van Tijen, Mart Stam, L. Stam-Beese and Hugh Aart Maaskant and the Montessori school by van Tijen. The first high-rise housing in Amsterdam was proposed at Victorieplein, the most conspicuous spot in Berlage's plan. In 1929–30 J. F. Staal built 'De Wolkenkrabber' (the skyscraper), a block of flats with stylistic references to Nieuwe Bouwen. However, the best example of Nieuwe Bouwen was in the inner city. In 1935 in Reguliersbreestraat opposite the Art Deco Tuschinsky Theatre–cinema, Duiker built the Cineac, a continuous news cinema with an enormous illuminated advertisement on its pitched roof.

An expansion plan for the whole city was formulated in the 1920s by Keppler and A. W. Bos (Director of Public Works), after the annexation of surrounding localities in 1921, which increased Amsterdam's area from 4630 ha to 17,455 ha. International interest and controversy made the need for a permanent official urban-planning department clear, and so in 1928 the urban-planning division was established within the Public Works department, focusing mainly on research. It was led by T. K. van Lohuizen (1890–1956). CORNELIS VAN EESTEREN was appointed designer and maintained close contact with the Congrès

3. Amsterdam, Scheepvaarthuis by J. M. van der Meij, assisted by Michel de Klerk and P. L. Kramer, 1916

Internationaux d'Architecture Moderne (CIAM), the international organization of Nieuwe Bouwen.

The Algemeen Uitbreidingsplan van Amsterdam (AUP; General Expansion Plan for Amsterdam), presented by the division in 1935, did not draw on the CIAM as has been argued, but concentrated on the development of ordinary city buildings, taking into account Amsterdam's situation. The AUP was the first plan to be presented scientifically, in contrast to Berlage's aesthetic urban planning. Its global zoning scheme provided for spacious living and working districts and green areas, leaving details to a later stage. It represented the definitive future shape of Amsterdam. Although these ideas were superseded by social developments immediately after World War II, the plan was followed in large part until 1970.

The planned ring railway around the existing city was executed, and the parallel ring road was built as a four-lane motorway linking commuter areas in the Randstad via the Coentunnel (1966) in the north and Schiphol airport in the south. The result is an enlarged barrier between the existing city and new extensions. The AUP's expansion areas were filled at a faster rate than had been envisaged as a result of the post-war housing shortage, which led to expansion in Amsterdam-Noord, contrary to the original plan. The pressure to build quickly damaged the quality of these new urban sectors. Nevertheless there are a number of new elements in Amsterdam's post-war architecture, for example the terraced housing in the Westelijke Tuinsteden (Western garden suburbs), which uses the Nieuwe Bouwen idea of building rows of houses transversely to main streets, thus avoiding block construction. Different types of traffic were channelled on to main roads, residential streets, cycle paths and footpaths. Businesses were banned from the housing areas as far as possible, and shops were for the first time concentrated in separate areas.

The Bijlmermeer development in the south-east of Amsterdam has been the source of much controversy since the plan was presented in 1965. Main roads were devoted exclusively to cars and were placed on raised banks, with cycle paths and footpaths at ground-level. The most notable feature of this district is the extended honeycomb of nine-storey blocks above double houses, which accounts for 90% of the development's housing. Escalating costs imposed economies on the plan, and, after completion, the development eventually fell prey to social problems, as a result of which it was decided to demolish it partially .

Although Amsterdam's population fell sharply between 1958 and 1990 from 872,000 to 700,000, there was still a housing shortage, partly because of the demolition of housing in the 1950s and 1960s to make way for offices, shops, businesses and cultural and social institutions. At the end of the 1960s this policy was gradually dropped after public opposition, and the necessity of a place for housing in the existing city was recognized. The concept of urban renewal led to the improvement of Jordaan, the eastern islands and areas developed in the 19th century. Increasingly powerful project groups negotiated between the council and the residents. Instead of completely replacing entire areas, phased development allowed the old structure and livelihood of the neighbourhood to be maintained. Emphasis thus came to rest more on the neighbourhood as a social entity and on the unity of living and working. Squatters occupied empty properties in the inner city, making it clear that housing was necessary there too. Protest action reached its peak in 1975 with resistance to the intended demolition of Nieuwmarkt neighbourhood to make way for the metro to Bijlmermeer and a big motorway. The metro was built, but the neighbourhood was partly spared. In the 1980s and 1990s most new construction comprised social housing that preserved the former street patterns.

BIBLIOGRAPHY

Algemeen Uitbreidingsplan: Grondslagen voor de stedebouwkundige ontwikkeling van Amsterdam [The AUP: the basis of the architectural development of Amsterdam] (n.p., [1934])

J. G. Wattjes and F. A. Warners: *Amsterdams bouwkunst en stadsschoon, 1306–1942* [The architecture and green areas of Amsterdam, 1306–1942] (Amsterdam, 1944)

A. A. Kok: *Amsterdamsche woonhuizen* [Domestic housing in Amsterdam] (Amsterdam, 1946)

Grondslagen voor de Zuid-Oostelijke stadsuitbreiding [The basis of the south-eastern expansion of the city], Afdeling stadsontwikkeling Amsterdam (n.p., 1965)

J. J. van der Velde: *Stadsontwikkeling van Amsterdam, 1939–1967* [The urban development of Amsterdam, 1939–1967] (Amsterdam, 1968)

R. Roegholt: *Amsterdam in de 20e eeuw*, 2 vols (Utrecht and Antwerp, 1976–9)

E. Taverne: *In't land van belofte: In de nieuwe stad: Ideaal en werkelijkheid van de stadsuitleg in de Republiek, 1580–1680* [In the promised land: in the new city: ideal and reality in the expansion of the city in the Republic, 1580–1680] (Maarssen, 1978)

T. Levie and H. Zantkuyl: *Wonen in Amsterdam in de 17de en 18de eeuw* (Purmerend, 1980)

W. Bolte and J. Meijer: *Van Berlage tot Bijlmer* (Nijmegen, 1981)

C. Schade: *Woningbouw voor arbeiders in het 19de-eeuwse Amsterdam* [Labourers' housing in 19th-century Amsterdam] (Amsterdam, 1981)

H. Diederiks: *Een stad in verval: Amsterdam omstreeks 1800* [A city in decline: Amsterdam *c.* 1800] (Amsterdam, 1982)

M. G. Emeis: *Amsterdam buiten de grachten* [Amsterdam beyond the canals] (Amsterdam, 1983)

R. van Gelder and R. Kistemaker: *Amsterdam, 1275–1795: De ontwikkeling van een handelsmetropool* [The development of Amsterdam as a trading metropolis] (Amsterdam, 1983)

H. Hellinga: 'Het algemeen uitbreidingsplan van Amsterdam', *Het nieuwe bouwen Amsterdam, 1920–1960* (Delft, 1983), pp. 52–111

I. Haagsma and H. de Haan: *Stadsvernieuwingsgids van Amsterdam* [A guide to the renewal of Amsterdam] (Amsterdam, 1985)

H. Hellinga and P. de Ruijter, eds: *Algemeen uitbreidingsplan Amsterdam 50 jaar* (Amsterdam, 1985)

W. F. Heinemeijer, M. F. Wagenaar and others: *Amsterdam in kaarten: Verandering van de stad in vier eeuwen cartografie* (Ede and Antwerp, 1987)

G. Kemme, ed.: *Amsterdam Architecture: A Guide* (Amsterdam, 1987)

M. Mentzel: *Bijlmermeer als grensverleggend ideaal* [Bijlmermeer: breaking down barriers to the ideal] (Delft, 1989)

A. van der Valk: *Amsterdam in aanleg: Planvorming en dagelijks handelen, 1850–1900* [Amsterdam in construction: urban planning and daily life, 1850–1900] (Amsterdam, 1989)

M. Wagenaar: *Amsterdam, 1876–1914: Economisch herstel, ruimtelijke expansie en de veranderde ordening van het stedelijk grondgebruik* [Economic recovery, expansion and the changing organization of the city's use of land] (Amsterdam, 1990)

A. Brakenhoff and others: *Hoge bouw, lage status: Overheidsinvloed en bevolkingsdynamiek in de Bijlmermeer* [Tall buildings, low status: governmental influence and population dynamics in Bijlmermeer] (n.p., 1991)

V. van Rossem: *Het algemeen uitbreidingsplan van Amsterdam: Geschiedenis en ontwerp* (Rotterdam, 1993)

HELMA HELLINGA

III. Art life and organization.

1. Before 1578. 2. 1578–1709. 3. 1710–1805. 4. 1806–1899. 5. 1900 and after.

1. BEFORE 1578. During the 14th century Amsterdam developed into an important commercial centre. Very little

survives of the decorations (wall paintings, stained glass, altarpieces and liturgical objects) in the numerous churches and chapels that were built from that period onwards. Patrons were mainly rich merchants. Ten 15th-century painters are mentioned in archival documents, but nothing more is known about their work.

As Amsterdam continued to expand in the 16th century, the number of painters increased considerably, but many paintings from this period still cannot be assigned to particular artists. The first important Amsterdam artist about whom something is known was JACOB CORNELISZ. VAN OOSTSANEN, the founder of an important Amsterdam family of artists. Jacob Cornelisz. designed woodcuts, stained glass and embroidery. His prints, including series of *Passion* scenes, were published by the Amsterdam printer Doen Pietersz. Jacob Cornelisz. was also active as a painter. His portraits were in demand and fetched good prices from the patrician classes of Amsterdam. One of his most important patrons was Pompeius Occo (*c.* 1482–1537), a learned banker who possessed an extensive library. Rich (usually Catholic) merchants were enthusiastic patrons of portraits, and the art of portraiture thus became characteristic of Amsterdam, remaining the major genre until 1578. The group portrait was also developed in the city, although it subsequently flourished in Haarlem. Dirk Jacobsz., the son of Jacob Cornelisz., was one of the first painters to specialize in portraiture. His *Crossbowmen* (1529; Amsterdam, Rijksmus.) is one of the earliest examples of the Dutch militia group portrait. Cornelis Anthonisz., thought to be the grandson of Jacob Cornelisz., also painted a group portrait, the so-called *Braspenningmaaltijd* ('Banquet of the copper coin', 1533; Amsterdam, Hist. Mus.), representing members of the Guild of St George. However, Cornelis Anthonisz. was primarily active as a designer of woodcuts. His subjects were no longer the traditional religious ones, but rather moralistic themes, accompanied by long texts in Dutch and intended for a broad audience; they were published by Jan Ewoutsz. Also important were Anthonisz.'s maps of Amsterdam (see fig. 1 above) and other areas.

Dirck Barendsz., the son of the painter Barend Dircksz., travelled to Italy in 1555–62, where he may have studied with Titian. After his return to Amsterdam, he received commissions for altarpieces; before this, only painters from outside Amsterdam (such as Jan van Scorel and Maarten van Heemskerck) had been commissioned for this type of work. In addition, Dirck Barendsz. also produced individual and group portraits in the Amsterdam tradition: the *Fourteen Guardsmen of Company G* (1562; Amsterdam, Hist. Mus.) and the *Perch Eaters* (1566; Amsterdam, Rijksmus.). Pieter Aertsen was awarded the commission for the altarpiece and stained-glass windows in the Nieuwe Kerk on his return to Amsterdam *c.* 1557 after a time in Antwerp. His sons Aert Pietersz. (1550–1616) and Pieter Pietersz. (1540–1603) became proficient in portraiture and other genres. Pieter settled in Haarlem in 1573 but returned to Amsterdam in 1585.

Art in the churches of Amsterdam suffered particularly badly during the iconoclastic riots of 1566. In the Oude Kerk and the Nieuwe Kerk, in particular, many stained-glass windows and altarpieces were destroyed.

BIBLIOGRAPHY

J. F. M. Sterck: *Onder Amsterdamse humanisten* (Haarlem, 1934)

W. Kloek: *Gewelfschilderingen in de Oude Kerk te Amsterdam* [Vault paintings in the Oude Kerk, Amsterdam] (Amsterdam, 1975)

R. Kistemaker and R. van Gelder: *Amsterdam: The Golden Age, 1275–1795* (New York, 1982)

Kunst voor de beeldenstorm: Noordnederlandse kunst, 1525–1580 [Art before the iconoclastic riots: north Netherlandish art, 1525–80], 2 vols (exh. cat., ed. J. P. Filedt Kok and others; Amsterdam, Rijksmus., 1986)

De smaak van de elite: Amsterdam in de eeuw van de beeldenstorm [The taste of the élite: Amsterdam in the century of the iconoclastic riots] (exh. cat., ed. R. Kistemaker and M. Jonker; Amsterdam, Hist. Mus., 1986)

Woelige tijden: Amsterdam in de eeuw van de beeldenstorm [Turbulent times: Amsterdam in the century of the iconoclastic riots] (exh. cat., Amsterdam, Gemeente Archf, 1986)

ILJA M. VELDMAN

2. 1578–1709. In 1578 Amsterdam sided with William of Orange in the struggle against the Spanish. Many changes took place, including the reorganization of the guilds. Amsterdam painters, engravers and carvers had previously belonged to the masons' and bricklayers' Guild of Our Lady. In 1579 a separate bricklayers' guild was established, while painters, sculptors, glaziers, Delftware potters, embroidery- and tapestry-workers, engravers and carvers formed the Guild of St Luke. The new government was Protestant, and as a result of Catholicism being driven underground, commissions for painters and sculptors declined substantially. Far fewer Protestant commissions could be expected because their churches were more soberly decorated. Catholics commissioned small altarpieces and ornaments for their secret meeting-places. South Netherlanders fleeing the Spanish brought capital and business experience and provided an important cultural stimulus. Among the immigrants were tapestry-weavers, diamond-workers, gilt leather-makers and many painters and art dealers.

Amsterdam's prosperity in the 17th century created a large market for independent painters, and various studios were established where art was produced and pupils were trained. Guild membership was obligatory for painters as it was for most other craftsmen. Guild regulations governed the training of pupils, and guarantees of quality were given. The sale of works imported from outside Amsterdam was prohibited, although the effectiveness of this law is unknown as the guild archive is lost. In 1662 the booksellers and bookbinders ceded from the guild and formed a guild with the hitherto unrepresented book printers. Two years later the print publishers and print sellers were faced with a choice between the guilds, and the Guild of St Luke lost members as a result. In 1688 the Guild of St Luke had 443 registered members, about 10% of whom were painters. The short-lived Broederschap der Schilderkunst (Brotherhood of Painting), a club of painters, poets and patrons, was founded in 1653 on the initiative of the painters Bartholomeus van der Helst and Nicolaas de Helt Stocade (1614–69).

The prodigious production of paintings and prints in the 17th-century Dutch Republic was centred on Amsterdam and reached a peak between 1630 and 1675. The city's increasing prosperity and a population boom contributed to a large demand for works of art, ranging from cheap, easily prepared paintings and popular prints, to expensive paintings to be hung in the houses of the wealthy or in art lovers' collections. The multiplicity of styles and specialities make it difficult to speak of a characteristic 17th-century Amsterdam school of painting, although Rembrandt taught dozens of pupils from 1631 until his death in 1669, and his work inspired many other painters. Amsterdam painters worked for the open market and on commission. Around the mid-17th century demand was so great that painters could be assured of regular sales. Many concentrated on landscapes, marines, genre pieces, still-lifes and portraits. Large commissions from municipal or religious institutions were the exception. Commissions came from orphanages, charitable foundations, the admiralty, the Dutch East India Company, Dutch West India Company, the guilds and the militia companies (see fig. 4). The construction of Amsterdam's Stadhuis (begun 1648; now the Royal Palace; *see* §V, 2 below) also provided important commissions.

In the second half of the 17th century paintings to decorate walls and ceilings were increasingly sought after. Less expensive hangings were painted on cloth. Towards the end of the 17th century two rooms in the Stadhuis were fitted out by the city council as an art gallery. Paintings, drawings, prints and sculptures were displayed there. At the same time sales of works of art were organized. In 1709 the collection was significantly enriched by the legacy of about 7000 prints from Michiel Hinloopen's private collection.

BIBLIOGRAPHY

H. Floerke: *Studien zur niederländischen Kunst- und Kulturgeschichte: Die Formen des Kunsthandels, das Atelier und die Sammler in den Niederlanden vom 15.–18. Jahrhundert* (Munich and Leipzig, 1905/*R* Soest, 1972)

I. H. van Eeghen: 'Het Amsterdamse Sint Lucasgilde in de 17de eeuw', *Jb. Genoot. Amstelodamum*, lxi (1969), pp. 65–102

B. Haak: *The Golden Age: Dutch Painters of the Seventeenth Century* (Amsterdam, 1984), pp. 173–6, 187–204, 273–311, 352–77, 462–99

J. A. VAN DER VEEN

3. 1710–1805. Many of the best-known 18th-century painters in Amsterdam devoted themselves to the decoration of the interiors of houses, notably the design of wallpaper decorations. Jacob de Wit, Jurriaan Andriessen and Jacob Cats (ii) were among the most famous practitioners of this art. One of the most prolific engravers active in Amsterdam at this time was Reinier Vinkeles. Cornelis Troost was the best-known 18th-century painter specializing in genre scenes. Since there was no tradition of sculpture in the Netherlands in the 18th century, there

4. Rembrandt: *'Night Watch' (Militia Company of Capt. Frans Banning Cocq and Lt Willem van Ruytenburch)*, oil on canvas, 3.63×4.37 m, 1642 (Amsterdam, Rijksmuseum)

were relatively few sculptors active in Amsterdam. Netherlandish sculptors of the second half of the 18th century concentrated almost exclusively on decorative sculpture. Among the most important of them were Anthony Ziesenis (1731–1802), who came from Hannover, and his pupil Jan Swart (1754–94). Significant art collectors living in Amsterdam included Lambert Hermansz. ten Kate (1674–1731), Sybrand Feitama II, Cornelis Ploos van Amstel, Johann Goll van Franckenstein and Gerrit Braamcamp.

Before 1718 Amsterdam artists had no communal facilities for drawing. Painters were traditionally trained in a master's studio. Many were members of the Guild of St Luke. In the early 18th century Barent Graat and Gérard de Lairesse ran academies in their houses where artists could draw from the nude model, but, after their deaths, these academies faded away. In 1718 there were many attempts to organize a public place where artists could practise drawing. However, it was not until 1765 that a drawing-course was established outside of the studio-system; in that year, the Amsterdamse Stadstekenacademie (Amsterdam City Drawing School) was founded in a room above the Leidse Poort. It had 18 members. The six directors included Jacobus Buys, Cornelis Ploos van Amstel, Jacob Otten-Husly and Reinier Vinkeles. In 1767 the school moved to a room in the Amsterdam Stadhuis. A decade later, on the initiative of the art dealer C. S. Roos and the painters Jacob Cats (ii) and Jean Grandjean, a department of drawing was opened by the Felix Meritis Society. There, as in the city academy, a live model was used, and lectures on art were given. (Both schools were closed in 1822 to make way for the Koninklijke Academie.) The last of these small academies was founded in 1805 by Jurriaan Andriessen, in his own house; the students there concentrated on the study of nuances of colour in the female nude.

BIBLIOGRAPHY

A. E. d'Ailly: *Zeven eeuwen Amsterdam*, 6 vols (Amsterdam, n.d.)

C. A. van Swighem: 'Beeldhouwers die te Amsterdam de meesterproef hebben afgelegd in de periode 1750–1811', *Jb. Genoot. Amstelodamum*, lvi (1964), pp. 156–63

P. Knolle: 'De Amsterdamse stadstekenacademie: Een 18de-eeuwse "oefenschool" voor modeltekenaars (met een lijst van redevoeringen)', *Ned. Ksthist. Jb.*, xxx (1979), pp. 1–41

——: 'Het departement der tekenkunde van Felix Meritis', *Docbl. Werkgroep 18de Eeuw*, lix–lx (1983), pp. 141–96

Edele eenvoud: Neo-classicisme in Nederland, 1765–1800 (exh. cat. by F. Grijzenhout and C. van Tuyll van Serooskerken, Haarlem, Frans Halsmus. and Teyler, 1989)

TON GEERTS

4. 1806–1899. From 1806 to 1810 Louis Bonaparte, King of Holland, endeavoured to promote the status of Dutch art by organizing exhibitions and a system of grants, and by founding the Koninklijk Museum (1808), predecessor of the Rijksmuseum (renamed as such in 1815). These policies were enthusiastically continued by William I after 1813. Such prominent artists as Jan Willem Pieneman and Cornelis Kruseman were his personal friends and advisers. The state took responsibility for art education, and, following the example of the French Prix de Rome, a travel grant for rising artists was established. Consequently, respect for art increased, as did the number of artists. Societies for the practice of science and the arts continued their activities. The largest of these, the Felix Meritis Society, the Society for the Propagation of General Knowledge (Maatschappij tot Nut van 't Algemeen) and the VW Society, organized discussions of art and provided drawing lessons. There was a widespread effort to return to the golden days of the 17th century. In 1822 the Koninklijke Academie was founded.

After the secession of Belgium in 1830, government spending on the arts dropped. In 1839 a group of private Amsterdam citizens founded a society for artists and art lovers, called Arti et Amicitiae. In contrast to other such societies, policy was determined by artists, and Arti became a dominant institution in the art life of Amsterdam and the Netherlands. Arti supplemented state exhibitions on contemporary artists and had a special exhibition room built (see fig. 5), with an annexe where members could meet and talk formally and informally about the arts. In 1854, because of the current popularity of historical subjects in painting, the society organized an exhibition of objects from the past. Several of the members who lent objects to this exhibition subsequently founded the Koninklijk Oudheidkundig Gezelschap (Royal Antiquarian Society) for the future accommodation and preservation of such art objects. In 1860 exhibitions of drawings and graphic art were introduced in Amsterdam, making it possible for those with limited finances to acquire works of art. Arti's policy was art in the service of the people and the nation, and so in 1862 it commissioned a number of paintings of scenes from Dutch history; these constituted the Historische Galerij (Historical Gallery), which was on view when no special exhibition was taking place. The society also followed artistic developments abroad, heavily influenced by Brussels, and thus Paris.

Three generations later, Arti lost its monopoly because younger members of the society, which had become extremely conservative, began to organize their own groups. Younger artists who came from a student society within the Rijks Academie voor Beeldenden Kunsten (State Academy for the Visual Arts), which had been revitalized in 1870 and rehoused in a new building on the edge of the city, founded the St Luke's Society in 1880. St Luke's organized exhibitions of works by artists from its own circle, including avant-garde works that had been refused elsewhere. Five years later the founders of St Luke's founded the Nederlandsche Etsclub (Dutch Etching Club), partly because of discontent concerning the standard of teaching in the graphic arts. The new group was modelled on the Belgian or French Société des Aquafortistes, although its activities extended beyond the exhibition and publication of etchings. The club was dissolved in 1896, but by the 1990s Arti and St Luke's were still in existence.

Informal discussion groups also existed, often crystallizing around a particular artist. For example, around 1850 the house of Georg Schwartze on the Prinsengracht became such a centre, and in 1878 a group of artists and art collectors gathered around the painter Nicolaas van der Waay (1855–1936); the group (called Michel Angelo Buonarotti) had a social function as well as an interest in art and survived into the 20th century. In the 1880s artistic societies were associated with new literary movements. The painter Willem Witsen's house on the Oosterpark was one such meeting-place for painters and writers at the end

5. J. de Mare after C. Rochussen: *Viewing Art in the Arti et Amicitiae Gallery, Amsterdam*, engraving, 1851 (Amsterdam, Gemeente Archief)

of the 19th century. A few art collectors also formed an exclusive club called Arte et Amicitia (not to be confused with the above-mentioned Arti) to support the visual arts. Some of its members founded the Vereeniging Rembrandt, an organization that purchases works of art (particularly paintings) for museums in order to keep them in the Netherlands.

BIBLIOGRAPHY

G. H. Marius: *De Hollandsche schilderkunst in de negentiende eeuw* (The Hague, 1903, 2/1920; Eng. trans., London, 1908/*R* Woodbridge, 1973)

J. Knoef: 'De genootschapsportretten van Felix Meritis', *Jb. Genoot. Amstelodamum*, xxxv (1938), pp. 203–51

B. Peizel: *Vereniging Sint Lucas: Historisch overzicht, 1880–1940* (Amsterdam, 1940)

A. M. Hammacher: *Amsterdamsche impressionisten en hun kring* [Amsterdam impressionists and their circle] (Amsterdam, 1941)

J. Giltay: 'De Nederlandsche Etsclub (1885–1896)', *Ned. Ksthist. Jb.*, xxvii (1976), pp. 91–125 [Eng. summary]

P. Knolle and A. Martis: 'De Maatschappij tot Nut van 't Algemeen en het tekenonderwijs, 1785–1900', *Om het algemeen volksgeluk, twee eeuwen particulier initiatief, 1784–1984: Gedenkboek ter gelegenheid van het tweehonderdjarig bestaan van de Maatschappij tot Nut van 't Algemeen* (Edam, 1984)

Koning Willem III en Arti: Een kunstenaarsvereniging en haar beschermheer in de 19e eeuw (exh. cat. by E. Fleurbaay and M. van der Wal, Amsterdam, Royal Pal., 1984)

Op zoek naar de Gouden Eeuw: Nederlandse schilderkunst, 1800–1850 (exh. cat., ed. L. van Tilborgh and G. Jansen; Haarlem, Frans Halsmus., 1986)

J. J. Heij and others: *Een vereniging van ernstige kunstenaars: 150 jaar Maatschappij Arti et Amicitiae* (Amsterdam, 1989)

W. Loos: 'Nicolaas van der Waay (1855–1936) en het Amsterdamse genootschap M.A.B. [Michel Angelo Buonarotti]', *19de Eeuw*, xiii (1989), pp. 125–49

M. de Roever and J. Reynaerts: 'Honderdvijftig jaar Arti et Amicitiae: De Kunstzaal en het tentoonstellingsbeleid', *Ons Amsterdam*, xli (1989), pp. 282–6

5. 1900 AND AFTER. Until World War I Amsterdam was a showcase of new ideas and movements. Craftsmen came together in 1904 in the Nederlandsche Vereeniging voor Ambachts- en Nijverheidskunst (VANK; Dutch Association of Arts and Crafts) in reaction to the increasingly industrialized production of formerly handmade utensils, decorations and furniture. From 1901 Catholic artists formed the group called De Violier, whose members tried to link religion and beauty in their work. A group of women, known as the Amsterdamsche Joffers, also pursued flourishing careers as painters at this time. Amsterdam was mainly significant, however, for its encouragement of the international avant-garde movement, which also resulted in the increased importance of the city as a centre of the art trade. From 1906 modern art was on view at St Luke's Society (*see* §4 above), whose young members were influenced by French Cubists in Paris. However, these new ideas met with resistance, and so in 1910 a group of modern artists formed the MODERNE KUNSTKRING. They exhibited Cubist works that had been refused by the

Stedelijk Museum. At the first exhibition in 1911 works by French Cubists were also shown, and works by Germans featured at the second. These shows mark the birth of abstract art in the Netherlands. Members of De Onafhankelijken (Independents Group) created entirely abstract works. The experimentation of these young artists was penalized by juries assessing exhibitions, and so several societies were established that held exhibitions without juries. These included a society founded in 1911, following the example of the Salons des Indépendants in Paris and elsewhere, and the Hollandsche Kunstenaarskring, formed in 1915 from a splinter group of St Luke's.

DE STIJL, begun in 1917, continued to be influential after World War I, although it was less institutionalized and reached beyond Amsterdam. Generally this was a period when great attention to ornament and detail was exchanged for a more functional and practical style. During the occupation of the Netherlands by Germany in World War II artistic freedom was curbed, and German taste was forced on artists. Those who refused to comply were deprived of materials and opportunities to exhibit, and a number did resistance work.

After the war Willem Sandberg, Director of the Stedelijk Museum, took on the task previously performed by the societies of giving exposure to new movements. He obtained the newest art from abroad, and, thanks to him, Amsterdam quickly regained its leading position. Yet the artists' organizations became increasingly traditional. In the summer of 1948, however, a number of experimental artists opposed to traditionalism came together as the Experimentele Groep and exhibited new work. Creativity and spontaneity were valued above rules. Reacting against paternalism, several artists moved that same summer to Paris, where they formed the COBRA group with like-minded Belgian and Danish artists. Sandberg immediately recognized the quality of their work and organized an exhibition of it at the Stedelijk Museum in 1949.

After the war there was renewed contemplation of the position of art and artists. The new Nederlandsche Federatie van Beroepsverenigingen van Kunstenaars (Dutch Federation of Professional Associations of Artists), stemming from the resistance, wanted more power and more government support for the arts. A local arts and cultural policy floundered after a good start, surviving longest in Amsterdam. In 1952 the Kunstraad (Arts Council) was formed to coordinate policy and advise the city council. It consisted of administrators, artists and private individuals. Since then numerous innovative movements have been and continue to be exhibited. Most artists are members of the Beroepsvereniging van Beeldende Kunstenaars (BBK; Professional Association of Visual Artists).

BIBLIOGRAPHY

Gedenkboek, 1901–1911 [van de] Katholieke kunstkring 'De Violier' (Amsterdam, 1912)
L. Kappeyne van de Copello Wijns: *De Amsterdamsche kunstkring* (Amsterdam, 1923)
H. I. C. Jaffé: *De stijl, 1917–1931: The Dutch Contribution to Art* (Amsterdam, 1956/*R* London, 1986)
A. B. Loosjes-Terpstra: *Moderne kunst in Nederland: 1900–1914* (Utrecht, 1959/*R* 1987)
Honderdvijftig jaar Nederlandse kunst, 1813–1963 (exh. cat. by L. C. J. Frerichs, J. W. Niemejer and J. Verbeek, Amsterdam, Stedel. Mus., 1963)
W. Stokvis: *Cobra: Geschiedenis, voorspel en betekenis van een beweging in de kunst van na de tweede wereldoorlog* (Amsterdam, 1974)
A. Venema: *De Amsterdamse Joffers* (Baarn, 1977)
'Kunst en kunstbedrijf: Nederland 1914–1940', *Ned. Ksthist. Jb.*, xxviii (1977) [whole issue]
H. Mulder: *Kunst in crisis en bezetting: Een onderzoek naar de houding van Nederlandse kunstenaars in de periode 1930–45* (Utrecht, 1978)
G. Immanse and others: *Van Gogh tot Cobra: Nederlandse schilderkunst, 1880–1950* (Amsterdam, 1981)
De doorbraak van de moderne kunst in Nederland: De jaren 1945–1951 (exh. cat., ed. W. Stokvis; Leiden, Stedel. Mus. Lakenhal and Ksthist. Inst., 1984)
W. Stokvis: *Cobra: De Internationale van experimentele kunstenaars* (Amsterdam, 1988)
D. Kraaijpoel: *De Nieuwe Salon: Officiële beeldende kunst na 1945* (n. p., 1989)
H. Renders: *Verijdelde dromen: Een surrealistisch avontuur tussen De Stijl en Cobra* (Haarlem, 1989)

MARGRIET DE ROEVER

IV. Centre of production.

1. METALWORK. Amsterdam was the most important centre of pewter production in the Netherlands from the 16th century, and its products were used throughout the country. At least 241 pewterers active in the city in the 16th century have been recorded. At the end of the 16th century autonomous pewterers' guilds, as well as silversmiths' guilds were established, and in the 17th century both pewterers and silversmiths used similar marks based on the city's coat of arms. In the 17th century several types of flagons were produced in Amsterdam, including a bulbous form named after the city (e.g. Amsterdam, Hist. Mus.) The best-known pieces of pewter from Amsterdam are the flagons (*c.* 1651; Amsterdam, Hist. Mus.), each 765 mm high, made for the Stadhuis in the workshop of the widow of Barend Harmensz. (*c.* 1591–1648). The pewterers' guild had 87 masters in 1688, 51 masters in 1751 but only 25 in 1809, and by 1820 the manufacture of pewter in Amsterdam had severely declined.

Amsterdam became an important centre of copper and brass production from the 16th century, when craftsmen emigrated from the southern Netherlands. At this time a system of guilds similar to that found among pewterers evolved, with the two principal trades being the founders and brassworkers. In the 16th century the brassworkers of Amsterdam, such as Hans Rogiers (*fl* end of 16th century) and Caspar the elder (1550–1612), were especially well known for their sconces and chandeliers, and in the 17th century the most prominent craftsmen were Elias van Vliet (*c.* 1609–52), best known for the massive chandelier (?third quarter of the 17th century) in the church of St Nicholas at Kampen, and Gillis Wijbrandts (*c.* 1615–80), who made the brass doors for the Stadhuis in 1659. Prolific founders in Amsterdam in the 17th century were François Hemony (1609–67) and Pieter Hemony (1619–80). In the 18th century the brassworkers of Amsterdam were celebrated for their decorated tobacco-boxes. Several large factories producing brass and copper goods operated in the late 19th century, including those of Jacob van den Bosche (1868–1948), H. P. Berlage (worked 1856–1934, producing domestic objects with Art Nouveau forms) and G. Lautman (1875–1937).

Amsterdam was one of the most important centres of silver production from the 16th century. A system of marking was established in 1572 and remained in force, with modifications, until the adoption of marks based on the French system in 1814. More than 1250 makers' marks for Amsterdam have been identified. The production of silver was at its peak in the 17th century, and more than 300 masters are recorded from this period. One of the most important patrons of silversmiths was the City of Amsterdam, which ordered a set of five large silver-gilt glass holders (1609; Amsterdam, Rijksmus. and Hist. Mus.; see fig. 6). Thomas Boogaert (1597–1653) and Michiel Esselbeeck (1611–71) both specialized in the production of silverware for Roman Catholic churches, while the outstanding exponent of the Auricular style in silver was Johannes Lutma (*see* LUTMA, (1)), who also designed the brass choir-screen in the Nieuwe Kerk. During this period many immigrant German silversmiths, for example the brothers Andries Grill (1604–65), Anthony Grill (1609–75) and Johannes Grill (1614–70) from Augsburg, were active in the city. The prominent silversmiths working in the Rococo and Neo-classical styles in the 18th century were Johannes Schiotling (1730–99) and REYNIER BRANDT; the latter specialized in elaborate salvers and baskets. The French Empire style did not appear in silver made in Amsterdam, and at the end of the 18th century and the beginning of the 19th such silversmiths as Dierderik Lodewijk Bennewitz (1764–1826) and Jacobus Carrenhof (1771–1848) produced classicizing pieces with little or no decoration. Improvements in manufacture *c.* 1900 led to the introduction of forms adapted to machine production, for example a tea-service (1903; priv. col.; *see* THE NETHERLANDS, fig. 58) by JAN EISENLÖFFEL.

6. Silver-gilt glass holder by Leendert Claesz. van Emden, h. 250 mm, 1609 (Amsterdam, Historisch Museum)

For further illustrations *see* THE NETHERLANDS, figs 53 and 55.

BIBLIOGRAPHY

K. A. Citroen: *Amsterdam Silversmiths and their Marks* (New York, 1975)

Keur van tin uit de havensteden Amsterdam, Antwerpen en Rotterdam [A selection of pewter from the ports of Amsterdam, Antwerp and Rotterdam] (exh. cat., Amsterdam, Mus. Willet-Holthuysen, 1979)

Nederlands zilver, 1580–1830/Dutch Silver, 1580–1830 (exh. cat., ed. A. L. den Blaauwen; Amsterdam, Rijksmus., 1979) [bilingual text]

PETER HORNSBY

2. FURNITURE. At the end of the 19th century and beginning of the 20th a number of influential furniture and interior design workshops were established in Amsterdam. The luxury end of the market was catered for by VAN WISSELINGH & CO., while the workshops attached to DE WONING sought to produce good, affordable design for a mass market, a goal sought by 'T BINNENHUIS, whose concept of style was more important, and whose goods in consequence were more costly. The firm of METZ & Co. was also distinguished by its good contacts with designers and commissioned furniture designs from a wide range of international designers until the 1970s.

BIBLIOGRAPHY

L. Gans: *Nieuwe kunst: De Nederlandse bijdrage tot de Art Nouveau: Dekoratieve kunst, kunstnijverheid en architektuur, omstreeks 1900* [Nieuwe Kunst: the Dutch contribution to Art Nouveau: the decorative arts, the applied arts and architecture, *c.* 1900] (Utrecht, 1966)

F. Leidelmeijer and D. van der Cingel: *Art Nouveau en Art Deco in Nederland* (Amsterdam, 1983)

PETRA DUPUITS

V. Buildings.

1. OUDE KERK. The church was founded at the end of the 13th century as a basilica (l. *c.* 40 m) with a square east end. The oldest remaining section is the nucleus of the west tower (*c.* 1300). In 1306 the church was dedicated to St Nicholas, and a new choir was added early in the 14th century. About 1340 the basilica was replaced by a larger hall church to accommodate the rapidly growing population, retaining the earlier choir. The basilica was not demolished until building work was well advanced, resulting in irregularities in the plan. The arcade, piers and west wall survive from this campaign. The choir was enlarged with an ambulatory from *c.* 1380, and work began on the north transept (completed 1412). Fires and financial rivalry with the Nieuwe Kerk, which was also under construction, may have delayed further additions until *c.* 1462, when a side chapel was replaced by the south transept and portal. The baptistery was inserted at the west

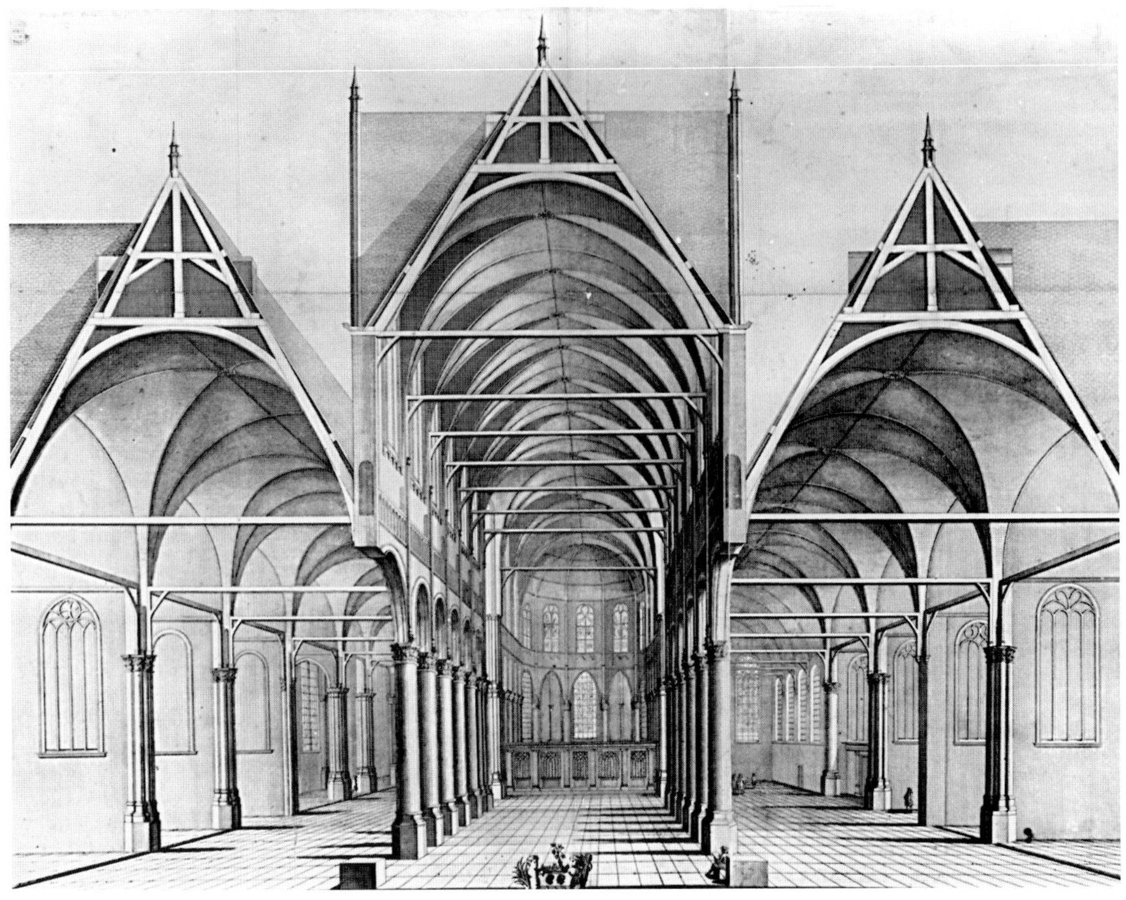

7. Amsterdam, Oude Kerk, cross-section of the nave looking east, *c.* 1681; from an engraving by Justus Vingboons (1620/21–98)

end. Chapels, mostly funded by the guilds and modelled on the transepts, with high gables and large traceried windows, were added along the south and later the north aisles. Even this did not provide sufficient light, however, and the nave was raised in 1512 in order to insert a clerestory (see fig.7). The north portal (1520) and chapel of the Holy Sepulchre (1530), which has a carved wooden *Entombment* covered by a fine stone ciborium, were added west of the north transept, and the Lady chapel (1552–5) was built to the east. By 1558, when a lottery was held to finance the insertion of the choir clerestory (completed 1560), the crossing had been raised and crowned with a spire; plans to raise the transepts remained unexecuted. Another stage was added to the west tower in 1564, raising it to *c.* 70 m. In the following year the timber structure was encased in lead to a design, mostly Gothic in style, though with some Renaissance details, that was probably by Joost Jansz. Bilhamer (1541–90). The carillon was made by François Hemony (1609–67). The outer casing was replaced in 1747. Small houses were built all around the church in the 17th and 18th centuries.

The extensive use of wood throughout the church's structure indicates an economical wish to create the largest space possible for the expenditure (*c.* 70×*c.* 60 m), and the alterations were often intended to maximize light within this area. Some of the decoration, most notably the 15th-century paintings on the wooden vaults of the south aisle (e.g. *c.* 1470; *SS Crispin and Crispinian*), survived iconoclasm in 1566, although they were painted over later. The church was converted to Protestant use after 1578, and most of the furnishings were replaced in accordance with the new liturgical requirements, for example the pulpit (1644) by Jan Pietersz. and N. van Eyckelsbeeck. The 17th-century interior is represented in several paintings by Emanuel de Witte, both before (e.g. 1655; Amsterdam, Oude Kerk) and after the removal of the choir-screen (e.g. *c.* 1659; London, N.G.). The church's condition deteriorated in the 19th century, and a thorough restoration was undertaken from 1955 to 1979.

BIBLIOGRAPHY

W. Kloek: *Gewelfschilderingen in de Oude Kerk te Amsterdam* (Amsterdam, 1975)

Kunstreisboek voor Nederland, Rijksdienst voor Monumentenzorg at Zeist (Antwerp, 1977)

A. van Rooijen: *De Oude Kerk te Amsterdam in vogelvlucht* (Amsterdam, 1985) [with extensive bibliog.]

□

2. ROYAL PALACE. What is now the Royal Palace (Koninklijk Paleis) on the Dam was originally Amsterdam's town hall (Stadhuis; *see* TOWN HALL, fig. 3). It had long been intended to replace the existing town hall with

one more indicative of Amsterdam's power and wealth, and many medieval houses were demolished to make way for it. In 1647 Jacob van Campen designed the monumental building, which was begun in 1648. Daniël Stalpaert was appointed city architect and supervised the building work, taking control of the project when van Campen withdrew in 1654 because of a disagreement with his assistants.

The outbreak of war with England in 1653 imposed financial restrictions on the project, but these were lifted in 1655 when it was decided to carry out the original designs. The front of the building faces the Dam; the ground plan is 80×57.5 m; the height to the top of the dome is 52 m. The building is a rectangular block with two internal courtyards. Three bays project at each corner, together with the seven central bays of the long façades. The corners are emphasized by transverse roofs. Above the basement are two main floors divided by a horizontal cornice. Each of the main floors has two levels of windows, defined by a giant order of pilasters, Composite for the lower and Corinthian for the upper level, following Vincenzo Scamozzi's book of orders *Idea dell'architettura universale* (Venice, 1615). The drum and cupola were built in 1664. The building lacks a grand entrance. The seven small archways in the east front probably symbolize the Seven Provinces. The tribune, where courts were held, is situated behind the middle three. It is unglazed, with open bronze railings, so that the proceedings could be followed from outside. The statues in this room all allude to crime, punishment and justice.

The great hall, also known as the Burgerzaal (Citizens' Hall), is situated in the middle of the building, flanked by the two courtyards. It is the apotheosis of the building, measuring 34×16.75×28 m. Its height is divided by two rows of pilasters. Set into the floor is a marble and copper map of the world and a chart of the heavens, so that a walk from one end of the hall to the other travels through the universe. The most important rooms were situated on the galleries around the courtyards. Fine sculptures allude to the function of each room. Thus the Desolate Boedelkamer (Impounded Property Chamber), where bankruptcy cases were adjudicated, is marked by the *Fall of Icarus*, an empty money box surrounded by rats, poisonous plants and torn money bags. The symbol of the Assurantiekamer (Assurance Chamber) was *Arion*, rescued by the dolphin that had been enchanted by his lyre playing. The Secretariskamer (Secretary's Chamber) was represented by *Duty*, *Fidelity* and *Silence* (the last two *c.* 1655 by Rombout Verhulst), surrounded by seals of the corporation, pens and signet rings. The statues in the galleries represent such planetary gods as *Mars*, *Venus*, *Apollo*, *Jupiter*, *Mercury* and *Diana*.

Although the actual building was completed in 1665, it was several years before all the sculptures and paintings were finished and installed. The sculptures were executed by the Antwerp sculptor Artus Quellinus (i), whose assistants included Artus Quellinus (ii), Rombout Verhulst, Gabriel Grupello, city mason Willem de Keyser and Simon Bosboom (for a discussion of the sculpture *see* QUELLINUS, (3)). Commissions for paintings were given to Govaert Flinck (*see* FLINCK, (1)), JAN LIEVENS, Juriaen Ovens, Ferdinand Bol, Jacob Jordaens and Thomas de Keyser, among others. Jacob de Wit later painted an imitation relief (for illustration *see* WIT, JACOB DE).

In 1808 the city council was more or less forced to give the Stadhuis to Louis Bonaparte, King of Holland, and Barthold W. H. Ziesenis, the city architect, was presented with the difficult task of converting it into a royal palace. He used partitions to divide the galleries and the Burgerzaal into rooms, and concealed much of the symbolism by means of curtains and panelling. The Neo-classical style of the late 18th century and the early 19th had much in common with that of the 17th century, which is probably why the building had such appeal at the time of its remodelling. The alteration was largely sympathetic, although the fine bronze cross-framed windows were replaced by large modern sash windows. Rooms were refurnished in a modern style since all the furniture had been transferred to the Prinsenhof. This replacement furniture remains in the palace and forms Holland's largest collection of Empire furniture.

In 1813 the French left Holland, and William I returned. He gave the building back to the city of Amsterdam, but since the city council did not have the means to redecorate or maintain the enormous building, it was offered again to the King as his official residence in Amsterdam, an arrangement that still continues.

BIBLIOGRAPHY

K. Fremantle: *The Baroque Town Hall of Amsterdam* (Utrecht, 1959)

3. PORTUGUESE SYNAGOGUE. The Portuguese Synagogue was planned from 1671 to amalgamate the three small ones that had been established in Amsterdam during the 17th century. The model by ELIAS BOUMAN was chosen from the various submitted designs, and the foundations were laid in 1671, but building ceased between 1672 and 1674 during the French invasion. The synagogue was ready in 1675. It measures 28×36 m and has a nave and two aisles, each with a wooden barrel vault. The nave is approximately 11 m across and measures 19.5 m to the crown of the vault. The vaults are supported on four sandstone columns with Ionic capitals. The back walls have stuccoed brick pilasters. Access to the aisle galleries was by two flights of stairs from a porch at the rear of the building (altered in the 18th century). The interior dates almost entirely from the 17th century. The Ark or Hechal is rosewood, decorated with columns, cornices, garlands, obelisks and frontons. The Bima or Teba is also made entirely of rosewood.

The stone cornice that runs around the building supports an attic baluster with decorative vases at the angles. The main rank of large arched windows is flanked above and below by smaller square ones; the windows are divided by buttress-like pilasters to form groups of two–three–two on the long sides and one–three–one on the short sides. A similar style is seen in contemporary churches, for example the Oosterkerk (1670), as well as in the nearby High German Synagogue (1670). The Portuguese Synagogue is surrounded by low buildings consisting of a living area, a library and a study. The building is within a walled court and is entered through a gateway. This walled court and the external pilasters at the rear of the building are thought to contain references to Solomon's Temple in Jerusalem.

BIBLIOGRAPHY

H. J. Zantkuijl: 'Reconstructie van een vroeg 17de eeuwse synagoge' [Reconstruction of an early 17th-century synagogue], *Maandbl. Amstelodamum*, lvii (1970), pp. 199–207

J. F. van Agt: *Synagogen in Amsterdam* (The Hague, 1974)

H. J. ZANTKUIJL

Amsterdam, Jacob Cornelisz. von. *See* CORNELISZ. VAN OOSTSANEN, JACOB.

Amsterdam Impressionists. *See* HAGUE SCHOOL.

Amsterdam school. Group of Expressionist architects and craftsworkers active mainly in Amsterdam from *c.* 1915 to *c.* 1930. The term was first used in 1916 by Jan Gratama in an article in a Festschrift for H. P. Berlage. From 1918 the group was loosely centred around the periodical *Wendingen* (1918–31). They were closely involved in attempts to provide architectural solutions for the social and economic problems in Amsterdam during this period.

The acute need for improved housing stock in the Netherlands was greatest in Amsterdam (*see* AMSTERDAM, §II, 5), where the population had more than doubled (reaching half a million) during the last quarter of the 19th century. A growing number of housing associations were founded, and the standard of the dwellings produced under their auspices was enormously improved by the implementation of Amsterdam's first building code in 1905. The greatest need, but the least profits, were to be found in the provision of good housing for the lowest-income groups. Legislation, subsidies and large-scale council ownership of the land scheduled for development allowed close governmental control, with a minimum of speculation by developers. Responsibility for the overall urban plan for the area known as Amsterdam South was given to H. P. Berlage, who produced a number of schemes between 1902 and 1915. The larger parameters were set, but even the architectural infill and its detailing were scrutinized at every stage by the Schoonheidscommissie ('Commission on Beauty'). Membership of this commission was increasingly dominated by architects associated with the Amsterdam school, and from 1918 the architects employed by both government offices and the housing associations were gradually limited to those included on an approved list. The most prominent architects on this list were J. M. van der Meij, Michel de Klerk and P. L. Kramer, all of whom had trained in the office of Eduard Cuypers.

The Amsterdam school was also influenced by the Dutch tradition of 'fantastic' architecture and owed much to the work of Willem Kromhout, architect of the American Hotel (1898–1901), Amsterdam. This building was contemporary with Berlage's Beursgebouw (1898–1903), which exerted the most direct influence on the school. From the earliest mature designs of de Klerk, van der Meij and Kramer, their stylistic debts are clear. In designs of

Amsterdam school architecture by Michel de Klerk and P. L. Kramer: housing block for De Dageraad, P. L. Takstraat, Amsterdam, 1920–23

1910 for a graveyard complex de Klerk displayed an impressive inventiveness and expressiveness in the brick detailing and roof-line. Like Berlage there is the use of traditional materials in a renewed formal language. This approach was exemplified in de Klerk's luxury block of flats (1911–12) for the builder Klaas Hille on the Vermeerplein, Amsterdam, further developed in other commissions for Hille, particularly a series of workers' flats: first the block in the Spaarndammerbuurt (1913–15), and then the two blocks for the Eigen Haard housing association around the Spaarndammerplantsoen (1914–16; 1917–20; for illustration *see* KLERK, MICHEL DE). The second block, one of the most famous works of the Amsterdam school, is on a triangular site. It consists of dwellings, a meeting-hall and a post-office built around the perimeter and containing a central garden. The block has a complicated and picturesque silhouette, culminating in the brick spire over the short façade, intended to alleviate the monotony found in conventional tenement blocks. It is built of variously coloured bricks and tiles laid in different directions and patterns, punctuated by the diverse and idiosyncratic entries and windows.

Between 1912 and 1916 de Klerk and Kramer had worked under van der Meij on the Scheepvaarthuis on the Prins Hendrikkade, a key work of Dutch Expressionism. Highly original brick detailing, stone sculpture and reliefs, ironwork and stained glass are bound together within a strong geometrical framework. No less inventive but certainly cooler and more mature is the work by Kramer and de Klerk for the housing cooperative De Dageraad on the P. L. Takstraat (1920–23; see fig.). Undulations of the brickwork, clear but nuanced articulation of the façade, and the surprising roofscape all confirm the continuous development of the salient stylistic features. Kramer's major body of work was the design of over 400 bridges for the Amsterdam Department of Public Works. The new and renewed quarters of Amsterdam were to a remarkable extent the product of a stylistically unified school.

In 1918 the influence of the Amsterdam school was greatly enhanced by the founding of the periodical *Wendingen* under the editorship of Hendrik Th. Wijdeveld. In 1923, however, de Klerk died and, even more devastating, the Dutch government changed its housing policy by reducing subsidies. With a smaller budget stylistic vigour was sapped. At the Exposition Internationale des Arts Décoratifs et Industriels Modernes, Paris, in 1925, members of the Amsterdam school represented the Netherlands. Major contributions were made by J. F. Staal, Richard Roland Holst and Wijdeveld. The work was in the best tradition of the school but proved to be controversial, partly through the reaction of Theo van Doesburg, who was incensed that De Stijl had not been given equal status. In 1926 Kramer's masterful Bijenkorf department store in The Hague was completed, but in the same year there was also a complete change in the editorial staff of *Wendingen.* By this time the style had been disseminated throughout the Netherlands, but a decline at its centre had already begun. By the end of the decade the social and political circumstances that had provided the original context for the growth of the group had changed, the economic provision had been reduced and the stylistic impetus had been lost. In some subsequent criticism the Amsterdam school was judged in terms of De Stijl and the International Style. This approach, however, underestimates the accomplishments, both practical and stylistic, of the school and ignores the fact that it was concerned with the development of a modern national, not international, style.

BIBLIOGRAPHY

J. Gratama: 'Het werk van Berlage', *Dr H. P. Berlage en zijn werk* (Rotterdam, 1916), p. 49
J. Badovici: 'L'Ecole d'Amsterdam', *Archit. Vivante*, xli (1926), pp. 21–6
R. Banham: *Theory and Design in the First Machine Age* (London, 1960)
G. Fanelli: *Architettura moderna* (1968)
J. J. Vriend: *L'Ecole d'Amsterdam*, Art et Architecture aux Pays-Bas (Amsterdam, 1970)
Amsterdamse school, 1910–1930 (exh. cat. by A. Venema and others, Amsterdam, Stedel. Mus., 1975)
H. Searing: 'With Red Flags Flying: Politics and Architecture in Amsterdam', *Art and Architecture in the Service of Politics*, eds H. A. Millon and L. Nochlin (Cambridge, MA, 1978)
C. Boekraad, ed.: *Architektuur en volkshuisvesting, Nederland 1870–1940* (Nijmegen, 1980)
W. de Wit, ed.: *The Amsterdam School: Dutch Expressionist Architecture, 1915–1930* (New York and London, 1983)
S. S. Frank: *Michel de Klerk, 1884–1923: An Architect of the Amsterdam School* (Ann Arbor, 1984)

ALLAN DOIG

Amuk region ['Amq; Plain of Antioch]. Area in Turkey covered by a rich agricultural plain, watered by the Orontes, Afrin and Kara Su rivers, in a strategic location for routes connecting Syria with Turkey, the coast and Mediterranean maritime trade. In the 1930s a series of ruin mounds of varying date were investigated by the Oriental Institute of the University of Chicago, IL, under the direction of R. J. Braidwood, and a chronological sequence for the region was established, extending back to *c.* 6200 BC (Amuk A, Neolithic). This Amuk sequence is still the basis for the prehistoric chronologies of north Syria and south-east Anatolia. Most of the finds are in the Hatay Museum in Antakya and in the Oriental Institute Museum of the University of Chicago. A further series of sites, of which TELL ATCHANA was the most important, was investigated by a team under C. L. Woolley. Finds from these excavations are mostly in the Hatay Museum, Antakya, the British Museum, London, and the Ashmolean Museum, Oxford.

The earliest evidence for artistic production in the region survives in the elaborately decorated pottery of the Chalcolithic period (Amuk C, from *c.* 5500 BC). Thereafter the emphasis on painted decoration was characteristic of Amuk cultural assemblages. The earliest significant example of artistic expression in a material other than ceramics is a collection of bronze figures found in an early 3rd millennium BC context at Tell Judeideh (Amuk G, Early Bronze Age). The virtually naked human figures, three male and three female (U. Chicago, IL, Orient. Inst. Mus.; Boston, MA, Mus. F.A.), were produced by the lost-wax process. Though fairly flat in profile and with oversized heads and feet, they show excellent modelling and remarkable detail. Other Early Bronze Age (Amuk G-I) representations of humans and animals in the form of clay figurines and seal impressions are simplified or stylized.

However, in the Middle Bronze Age (first half of the 2nd millennium BC) foreign elements from Egypt, the Aegean, Babylonia, Assyria and Anatolia were integrated into a rich local repertory particularly well represented in the seal impressions from Tell Atchana (the ancient Alalakh). A sculptured stone head from that site (for illustration *see* ATCHANA, TELL) is exquisite in detail and modelling. It shows that the smooth, polished, sophisticated style of the seals was also used with equal success on larger works of art.

Evidence for sculpture or relief decoration is rare in the Late Bronze Age (*c.* 1500–*c.* 1200 BC), and the famous statue of Idrimi, King of Alalakh (London, BM, variously dated to *c.* 1500 and *c.* 1250 BC), is the largest surviving excavated piece. Its awkward proportions and rough, simplified style are striking. A high point in ceramic manufacture was reached with the production of Atchana ware. Its elaborate decoration was executed in light paint on a dark background, with floral motifs drawn from local and foreign repertories. Importation of Aegean decorated wares through the port of AL-MINA was most common at the end of the Late Bronze Age, but a rich decorative tradition was sustained throughout the 12th and 11th centuries BC, with a heavy reliance on Greek styles and vessel forms.

The sculptural decoration on the temple at AIN DARA, with its procession of sphinxes and deities, illustrates the artistic production of the early Iron Age (*c.* 1000 BC). At TELL TAYINAT elaborately decorated column bases, lion orthostats, small figural stone orthostats and fragments of monumental sculpture, many of which are covered with 'Hittite' hieroglyphs, represent the artistic traditions from later in the Iron Age. Foreign contacts increased as demonstrated by the Greek wares imported through Al-Mina.

Greek wares continued to be present in the Amuk in Hellenistic times in greater abundance than in most of the surrounding regions. In the Hellenistic and Roman periods the focus shifted from the centre of the plain to its south-western edge. This major change in the history of the Amuk was due to the foundation of Antioch (*see* ANTIOCH (i), §1), present-day Antakya, by Seleucus I (*reg* 305–281 BC) in 300 BC. The wealth of material excavated there illustrates primarily the Roman city of the 2nd to 6th centuries AD, with major documentation of the development of Roman art styles from hundreds of beautifully executed, ornamental mosaic floors. The historian Ammianus Marcellinus was well justified in calling his native city the 'fair crown of the Orient'. The character of the Amuk changed drastically in the 6th century AD when an earthquake blocked the outlet towards the sea of the three rivers that watered the plain. Although the River Orontes eventually found a new channel, the Amuk became a lake and marsh.

BIBLIOGRAPHY

R. J. Braidwood: *Mounds in the Plain of Antioch: An Archaeological Survey*, Oriental Institute Publications 18 (Chicago, 1937)
D. Levi: *Antioch Mosaic Pavements*, 2 vols (Princeton, 1947)
C. L. Woolley: *A Forgotten Kingdom* (Harmondsworth, 1953)
——: *Alalakh: An Account of the Excavations at Tell Atchana in the Hatay, 1937–1949* (Oxford, 1955)
R. J. Braidwood and L. S. Braidwood: *Excavations in the Plain of Antioch*, i, Oriental Institute Publications 61 (Chicago, 1960)
G. Downey: *A History of Antioch in Syria* (Princeton, NJ, 1961)
D. Collon: *The Seal Impressions from Tell Atchana/Alalakh*, Alter Orient und altes Testament 27 (Neukirchen-Vluyn, 1975)
H. Klengel: *Geschichte und Kultur Altsyriens* (Leipzig, 1979)

R. T. H. DORNEMANN

Amulet. Object worn or placed somewhere special in the belief that it has magico-religious powers, such as to protect against danger, cure disease, give strength or promote good fortune. In this sense it is more or less synonymous with 'talisman'. Amulets are commonly worn as jewellery or carried within the clothing, but they may also be incorporated into such objects as weapons or placed within buildings or near crops. They have been treated as goods to trade in several cultures. A charm (i.e. magical formula) may be recited over an amulet, which may then itself be referred to as a charm. The term 'amulet' also denotes a medical or prophylactic treatment and a substance used in medicine.

1. Common themes. 2. Symbolism in ancient cultures. 3. Symbolism in world religions.

1. COMMON THEMES. Scholarly views on how and why amulets are perceived by their users to have power include the theory of 'sympathetic magic' based on similarity and contiguity. The perception here would be that like produces like—that intrinsically connected things act on each other even if the contact is broken. Inuit hunters, for example, use a caribou tail to ensure success in the caribou hunt, and Alaskan whale hunters carry carved flint, whale-shaped amulets round their necks. Another theory is based on the idea that an external, unfixed power or force may affect everything beyond ordinary human power by attaching itself to persons or things—a power outside the common process of nature. A common type of amulet, the gem, would thus fall into this category.

Amuletic materials are often natural substances ranging from bone fragments and plants to gemstones and minerals. Amber, coral, rock crystal and jet have all been considered as having their own magical and medicinal properties, although the properties ascribed vary according to culture. The Greeks and Romans believed that the black colour of jet and its electrostatic qualities gave it the power to attract and combat the dark underworld forces. The early Britons used jet amulets as a protection from, among other things, thunderstorms, devils, poison and snake bite. On the other hand, in antiquity the sapphire was worn to bestow health and preserve chastity chiefly because it was associated with Venus. Natural materials are in many cases used as amulets without much alteration or elaboration, for example the pieces of dried flesh and bone of a deceased relative carried by the Siberian Yukagir in the belief that the ancestors protect them. In other cases the material may be fashioned into an artefact. Such alteration may be simple, for example the piece of rock crystal sculpted into a 'doughnut' shape that was found in an Anglo-Saxon burial, or the material may be embellished with symbols or pictures, for example the jet heart inscribed with a Latin cross that was used in the Middle Ages as an amulet against evil spirits.

The imagery of an amulet may be just as important as the material, or it may be the imagery alone that gives the amulet its significance. Religious and cosmological themes have provided a wealth of amuletic themes—pictures of deities and sacred creatures, and aniconic symbols of creation are common. Lines from sacred texts are also sometimes written on paper, parchment or cloth and placed in a receptacle, which may itself be significant. Other imagery derives from mythical characters and popular symbols of good or evil. The belief in the evil eye and the use of eye amulets as a means of turning back the evil glance is a tradition spanning diverse cultures. In the Mediterranean, the Indian Ocean and the South-east Asian seas, the eyes are painted on the bows of boats, while in the Middle East blue and green beads with painted eyes are incorporated into jewellery or sewn on to children's clothing or animal trappings. The idea here is that the glance of the evil eye is attracted to the artificial eye and away from the wearer. In Europe the brass ornaments that sometimes decorate horse trappings were originally conceived as amulets to avert the evil eye; this was also the case with the long tassels and fringes decorating saddle-bags and harnesses in East Asia.

Another common tradition is the use of medicinal amulets either to wear or ingest. Red stones have been widely associated with blood. In medieval Europe powdered ruby was taken as a medicine to protect against bloody fluxes, while ruby objects were used as amulets against witchcraft, plague and famine. Cornelians and bloodstones have been used as charms to prevent difficult childbirth in Europe and Central and Western Asia, and also in Europe to prevent anger caused by a rush of blood to the head. Silver amulet cases in Central Asia are usually decorated with cornelians, but it is the colour, rather than the stone, that is important, so coral or other red stones can be substituted. Furthermore, medicinal herbs and bark may themselves be used as amuletic objects. In Indonesia a bundle of such vegetation is tied around a Ngaju Dayak child's waist to protect him from disease and evil spirits, while Dayak and Batak warriors and hunters of the island of Sumatra carry specially prepared amuletic medicines within bear or tiger teeth and claws, which are attached to their belts or swords.

2. Symbolism in ancient cultures. Ancient Egypt and the Ancient Near East provide some of the richest and best-documented examples of amulets. It should be pointed out, however, that the identification of individual objects and artefacts as amulets is sometimes conjectural, particularly if there was a tradition of using, for example, a pendant or seal as the amulet. The earliest Egyptian amulets pre-date the 1st Dynasty (*c.* 3000 BC), and they were an important art form, used both as jewellery and funerary equipment (*see* Egypt, ancient, §XVI, 1). Although some people were buried with the amulets they carried in life, many amulets were made specifically to place on the mummified remains of the deceased (*see* Mummy, Egyptian). In Egyptian mythology the dung-beetle symbolized rebirth, and the scarab beetle became a popular model with amuletic properties. A large 'heart-scarab' carved in dark stone was often placed on the mummy (e.g. a human-headed scarab, *c.* 1600 BC; see fig. 1).

In Western Asia amulets may have been used from the 7th millennium BC, most often in the form of seals (*see*

1. Amulet in the shape of a human-headed heart-scarab, green jasper, from the tomb of Nebankh, Egypt, *c.* 1600 BC (London, British Museum)

Ancient Near East, §II, 1). Some early designs were geometric (e.g. a Mesopotamian amulet seal dating from the 5th millennium BC; *see* Ancient Near East, fig. 4), the symbolism of which has not been identified. The seals were in the form of either the stamp seal or the more popular cylinder seal, and many were made with hardstones or stones with symbolic significance. Later designs included animals, deities and astral symbols. The use of seals as amulets subsequently spread to Egypt (*see* Egypt, ancient, §XVI, 15); to complement this, the Egyptian amuletic scarab began to spread to Western Asia *c.* 2000 BC. In Egypt pictures of deities were popular from *c.* 1300 BC (*see* Egypt, ancient, fig. 97). In Hebrew nations, however, in which images of Yaweh were forbidden, the *teraphim* were figures of Assyrian or Babylonian gods and were made from clay or hardstones. The name of God or such symbols as the hexagon of Solomon were inscribed on other Hebrew amulets. The cross was also a common symbol even in these early cultures, for example solar crosses representing the quarters of heaven presided over by the god Anu were used *c.* 2000 BC in Assyria. Furthermore, mathematical ideas about the sacred and mystical properties of numbers were channelled into the amulet. A popular Hebrew amulet was the stone or metal plaque, or a parchment, inscribed with a magical square of numbers related to the Seven Planets.

Ancient Greek and Roman amulets included images of Dionysos/Bacchus or his symbolic attributes of vines, amethysts, panthers and satyrs. Medusa-head amulets, often made of jet, were used to attract, mesmerize and destroy evil powers before they could afflict the wearer. Asklepios, Greek god of medicine, was associated with dogs and snakes, so dogs' teeth and snake images were popular amulets used to ward off illness. Certain gems were believed to channel the beneficent or malevolent powers emanating from the planets to confer wisdom and health on the wearer. Colours were associated with individual planets, so that red rubies, haematites and bloodstones came to be associated with Mars. The iconography of Gnostic engraved amuletic gemstones was often derived from Egyptian solar deities and such underworld figures as Osiris and Anubis. The uterine amulet dating from the 2nd–3rd century AD (*see* GEM-ENGRAVING, fig. 5), which was believed to protect against miscarriage, was derived from Egyptian, Greek and perhaps even Jewish symbols. Away from cultish and cosmological connotations, the amethyst—the colour of wine—was worn in antiquity to protect against the bad effects of wine.

Amulets were important in ancient China and continue to be so today, although the forms may have changed. Jade, endowed with life-preserving properties, was used by the Chinese from at least the 5th millennium BC for a variety of purposes. In modern China, jade amuletic jewellery is widely worn in the belief that it attracts good luck, whereas in ancient China jade amulets were buried with the dead to protect the spirit on its way to the underworld (*see* CHINA, §VIII). Effigies of gods, deified generals and scholars are used to protect a house and family and to attract good luck. Paper images of Zao Jun, the kitchen god, are commonly fixed above the stove. An old Daoist tradition is the written charm, often incorporating pictures of the Five Poisonous Reptiles (viper, scorpion, centipede, toad and spider), placed in a building to scare demons away. Brass amulets of these animals also exist.

Numerous amuletic devices appear to have been used by the Pre-Columbian peoples of the Americas. These took such different forms throughout the different cultures that it is hard to pinpoint trends or make any generalizations. In Central and South America examples range from the written charms strewn by the Aztecs on corpses to protect the deceased against the dangers that might be encountered on the road to the afterlife, to the use of three-pointed *cemis* by the Arawak of the Caribbean and northern coasts of South America. For the peoples of an area now covered by Nicaragua and Costa Rica small, pierced jade amulets of humans, jaguars, monsters and birds may have represented deities (*see* GRAN NICOYA). In North America the amulets ranged from the small sculptures of animals as made by the Canadian Inuit to the use of feathers from birds associated with the Thunderbird by warriors of the Plains region.

3. SYMBOLISM IN WORLD RELIGIONS. A number of amuletic devices are linked with Christianity, although in Europe their use was initially condemned as pagan. The *ankh*, an ancient Egyptian hieroglyph for 'life', was a popular amulet in early Coptic art, used as a symbol of everlasting life through Christ. Bronze, stone, bone, ivory and mother-of-pearl crosses, doves, figures of the Virgin and fish were other popular Coptic amulets. There was widespread use of the cross to keep devils and disease-producing spirits at bay. Christians transformed the Classical symbolism of the sapphire as Venus to an association with the Virgin. Similarly the diamond, originally related to the moon, became a symbol of Christ and was used as an amulet against physical and moral evil. Renaissance Italian paintings sometimes depict the infant Christ wearing a coral amulet around his neck, for example in Piero della Francesca's Senigallia *Madonna* (see fig. 2). Other examples include engravings of St Barbara on rings, which were supposed to protect the wearer from sudden death; pewter pilgrim badges; and Christian texts written on parchment, stones or leather used during the Middle Ages. Christians have also used relics as amulets—a piece of saint's bone or hair carried in a small case, for example.

Hindu amulets may consist of metal lockets depicting the Devi (goddess) or other divinities. Terracotta amulets bearing images of Kubera (Hindu) or Jambhala (Buddhist) and Gaja-Lakshmi were carried to South-east Asia by Indian merchants in the 5th to the 8th centuries. Examples of these and bronze Buddhist figure amulets have been found in Burma, Thailand, Cambodia and Vietnam. A common Buddhist tradition is the use of prayer flags placed near houses, which often depict a flying horse, tiger, lion, dragon or eagle to frighten away demons. Tibetan Buddhists make many amulets, including small metal rings with sacred inscriptions and pictures of deities and amulet boxes (*gau*) for holy relics (*see* TIBET, fig. 20).

Islam forbids the making of images, although the 'hand of Fatima', representing the magical protective hand of the Prophet's daughter, is a popular Muslim amulet, usually carved in jet (*see* JET, §2). Agate, cornelian and sometimes

2. Coral amulet worn by the infant Christ in the Senigallia *Madonna* by Piero della Francesca, tempera on panel, 610×533 mm, 1474–8 (Urbino, Galleria Nazionale delle Marche)

pearl-shell amulets inscribed with the name of God are common. Koranic texts written by a holy man may be carried in a case hung around the neck or tied to the left arm. The material on which they are written may be card, leather or hide (more rarely thin sheets of lead) and may be illuminated with flower and geometric patterns. The case may be silver inscribed with another Koranic text offering further protection. Muslim 'dust amulets'—earth from a saint's tomb or from Mecca that is hung in bags from the neck—are believed at a folk level to work through their contact with the sacred.

BIBLIOGRAPHY

W. M. F. Petrie: *Amulets* (London, 1914)
J. Evans: *Magical Jewels* (Oxford, 1922)
E. Wallis Budge: *Amulets and Superstitions* (Oxford, 1930); *R* as *Amulets and Talismans* (Toronto and London, 1978)
C. Bonner: *Studies in Magical Amulets, Chiefly Graeco-Egyptian* (Ann Arbor, 1950)
T. Schrire: *Hebrew Amulets* (London, 1966)
P. Binder and E. Jones: *Magical Amulets of the World* (London, 1972)
N. Douglas: *Tibetan Tantric Charms and Amulets* (New York, 1978)
A. Knuf and J. Knuf: *Amulette und Talismane: Symbole des magischen Alltags* (Cologne, 1984)
C. Andrews: *Amulets of Ancient Egypt* (London, 1994)

SIAN JAY

Amund (*fl* 1494). Swedish painter. He signed the wall paintings in the nave of the church at Södra Råda, Värmland, in 1494. Wall paintings in some 20 churches in Götaland have been attributed to him on the basis of stylistic comparison with the works at Södra Råda. In 1494 Amund may have been at the end of his career; his style has many features characteristic of the first half of the 15th century, as does the iconographic content of his work, with such didactic themes as the *Creed* and the *Seven Deadly Sins*. His rather naive drawing style and robust sense of humour make his paintings very expressive. It has been suggested that Amund may have been a monk, but this cannot be proved.

BIBLIOGRAPHY

B. G. Söderberg: *Svenska kyrkomålningar från medeltiden* [Swedish church paintings from the Middle Ages] (Stockholm, 1951), pp. 191–200
Å. Nisbeth: *Bildernas predikan* [The pictorial sermon] (Stockholm, 1986), pp. 141–7

ANNA NILSÉN

Amyklai. *See under* SPARTA.

Amyot, Laurent. *See* AMIOT, LAURENT.

Anagni [anc. Anagnia]. Town in Lazio, Italy, situated on a tufaceous outcrop overlooking the Sacco valley and the road from Rome to Naples. It was the sacred city of the Ernici, who founded it in the 8th century BC. After being conquered by the Romans in 306 BC it became a prefecture and then *municipium*. The medieval acropolis stands on the site of the Ernician city, the form of which had determined the layout of the Roman town. This was triangular, fortified by two lines of walls, some impressive sections of which survive, in particular the terraces known as the Arcazzi.

Anagni was first mentioned as the seat of a bishopric in the 5th century AD. It was governed until the 8th century by tribunes appointed by the exarch of Ravenna, in the 9th century by dukes appointed by the Pope, and in the 11th century probably by local lords. In the 12th and 13th centuries Anagni, now a commune, was involved in the struggles between the Papacy and the Empire; during this period the third circuit of walls was constructed, as well as a number of new buildings along the via Maggiore, including the cathedral, the Palazzo Comunale, the palaces of popes Gregory IX (*reg* 1227–41) and Boniface VIII (*reg* 1294–1303), and the tower-houses and porticoed palaces of the local gentry. The 14th century marked the beginning of Anagni's decline, as its links with the papal court weakened. Its vulnerable position led to progressive depopulation and prevented new building. For this reason the town retains its medieval aspect.

Anagni Cathedral, fresco in the crypt depicting *Christ with Four Saints*, 1231

The cathedral, dedicated to St Mary, was erected between 1072 and 1104 by Bishop Pietro di Salerno (*reg* 1062/3–1105) on the site of the former cathedral of St Magnus; some sculptured fragments of the 9th-century church were re-used in the façade of the new. The present building has an aisled nave with alternating square and columnar piers, a transept, and three eastern apses at a higher level to accommodate a crypt beneath. The diaphragm arches supporting the wooden roof of the central vessel and the vaults, ribbed in the transept but groined in the aisles, were added during the mid-13th-century renovations. On the exterior, the construction techniques and the arcading of the east end demonstrate the introduction of Lombard forms into southern Lazio. The apse decoration is attributed to the north Italian craftsmen who built the Palazzo Comunale (1159–63). The Caetani chapel, with the family tombs, opens on the south side of the cathedral. In the presbytery are the episcopal throne (dated 1263), by VASSALLETTUS, the ciborium and the paschal candlestick .

The crypt, consecrated in 1255, has three transverse aisles and is decorated with 13th-century frescoes depicting biblical scenes, allegories of the sciences, Evangelists and saints (see fig.); these are attributed to several artists, the so-called First, Second and Third masters of Anagni. The polychrome mosaic pavement was laid in 1231 by Cosma di Iacopo (*b c.* 1190), of the Cosmatus family, who was also responsible for the pavement (before 1266; largely remade in the 18th century) of the upper church. The free-standing campanile opposite the cathedral façade was completed in 1141 but has been altered by modern restorations.

The plan for the first Palazzo Comunale is attributed to Giacomo da Iseo, who passed through Anagni in 1159 as Brescia's ambassador to Pope Adrian IV (*reg* 1154–9). Rebuilt around the middle of the 13th century, it now comprises a large hall on the ground floor, roofed with wooden beams over diaphragm arches, with the great council chamber on the floor above. Of the papal palaces, the one usually identified as that of Boniface VIII was really the palace of Gregory IX, built during the first quarter of the 13th century. The palace of Boniface VIII was perhaps the building whose remains are incorporated in the 17th-century Palazzo Traietto. Overlooking the Corso is the façade of the Casa Barnekow, probably dating from the 13th century. Its entrance staircase is surmounted by a portico consisting of two large, round-headed arches. Opposite is S Andrea, founded in the 12th century but rebuilt in the 18th; its 13th-century campanile contains fragments of Romanesque sculpture with zoomorphic figures. Inside the church is the 14th-century triptych of the *Saviour*.

BIBLIOGRAPHY

P. Zappasodi: *Anagni attraverso i secoli* (Veroli, 1908)
S. Sibilia: *La cattedrale di Anagni* (Orvieto, 1914)
F. Hermanin: *L'arte a Roma dal secolo VIII al XIV* (Bologna, 1945), p. 406
G. Zander: 'Fasi edilizie e organismo costruttivo del Palazzo di Bonifacio VIII in Anagni', *Palladio*, ii–iii (1951), pp. 112–19
N. Proia: *Anagni monumentale* (Anagni, 1963)
M. Mazzolani: *Anagni: Studi di urbanistica antica* (Rome, 1966), pp. 49–60
S. Sibilia: *Storia di Anagni e breve guida della città* (Anagni, 1967)
M. Mazzolani: *Anagnia*, Forma Italiae, vi (Rome, 1969)
A. Prosperi: *Anagni e i suoi monumenti* (Anagni, 1971)
N. Proia: *Il centro storico di Anagni: Origini e sviluppo attraverso i secoli* (Frosinone, 1976)
A. Panza and R. Ferretti: 'Anagni nel XIII secolo: Iniziative edilizie e politica pontificia', *Stor. Città*, v/18 (1981), pp. 33–76

ROBERTO CORONEO

'Ana Island. *See under* HADITHA REGION.

An Amida Butsu. *See* KAIKEI.

Anamorphosis. *See under* PERSPECTIVE, §II, 3.

Ananauri. *See under* VARDZIA.

Ānandapura. *See* VADNAGAR.

Anant (*fl* 1584–1611). Indian miniature painter. Trained in the studio of the Mughal emperor Akbar (*reg* 1556–1605), he blossomed under Akbar's successor Jahangir (*reg* 1605–27). Anant is known through two sole compositions in the *Tīmūrnāma* ('History of Timur'; 1584; Bankipur, Patna, Khuda Bakhsh Lib., fols 182*r* and 206*v*, and, as colourist, fol. 115*v*)) and as a colourist in the first *Akbarnāma* ('History of Akbar'; *c*. 1590; London, V&A, I.S.2. 1896.117) but eventually specialized in allegorical illustrations. The *'Iyar-i danish* ('Book of fables'; *c*. 1590–95; Dublin, Chester Beatty Lib.) and *Anvār-i Suhaylī* ('Lights of Canopus'; 1596–7; Varanasi, Banaras Hindu U., Bharat Kala Bhavan) were the prelude to his best work in the *Anvār-i Suhaylī* completed for Jahangir in 1610–11 (London, BL, Or. Add. 18579, fols 6*r*, 130*v*, 169*r*, 197*r* and 267*r*). Although he was capable of fine natural history studies, in this manuscript he concentrated on the symbolic function of animals to communicate the moral of the tale. The simple, open compositions reflect the studio style of the early 17th century.

BIBLIOGRAPHY

J. V. S. Wilkinson: *The Lights of Canopus: Anvar-i Suhaili* (London, 1929)
The Grand Mogul: Imperial Painting in India, 1600–1660 (exh. cat. by M. C. Beach, Williamstown, MA, Clark A. Inst., 1978)
The Imperial Image: Paintings for the Mughal Court (exh. cat. by M. C. Beach, Washington, DC, Freer, 1981)

PHILIPPA VAUGHAN

Anantasayanagudi. *See under* HAMPI, §4.

Anasazi [Navajo: 'the ancient ones']. Term applied to the prehistoric 'Basketmakers' (*fl* to *c*. AD 750) of the south-western United States and their successors, the Pueblo tribes, who still live in the region. The Anasazi are famous for their communal buildings, many now ruined, which were known as 'pueblos' by the first Spanish explorers (*see* NATIVE NORTH AMERICAN ART, §II, 2). The most celebrated of these structures were built *c*. 1100–*c*. 1300 and are located at various sites, including MESA VERDE in south-west Colorado and CHACO CANYON in north-west New Mexico. The Anasazi also produced painted pottery, basketry and weaving.

BIBLIOGRAPHY

D. G. Pike: *Anasazi: Ancient People of the Rock* (New York, 1974)
W. M. Ferguson and A. H. Rohn: *Anasazi Ruins of the Southwest in Color* (Albuquerque, 1986)

□

Anastasov, Rodoljub (*b* Skopje, 25 Feb 1935). Macedonian painter. In 1962 he graduated from the Academy of Arts in Belgrade, where he studied under the painter Ljubica Sokić (*b* 1914). After returning to Skopje, Anastasov began to work in the field of non-figurative art. In the 1960s he focused on the structural qualities of the painting's surface, which he rendered with layers of red and black impasto. By the end of the 1960s, stimulated by PHOTOREALISM, he abandoned crude brushwork and the traditional colours of Macedonian embroideries in favour of an urban sensibility. During the 1970s he exhibited works from his series *Man and Skies* (1974–6) and *Man and Time* (1977–9). In the 1980s he produced the series *Man and Space*, a statement on the human condition (e.g. *Man and Space XXVI*, 1981; Skopje, Mus. Contemp. A.), with numerous tiny, alienated human silhouettes populating immense interiors and empty spaces rendered in pale, attenuated colours. Between 1982 and 1986 Anastasov was a member of the international group *Junij*. From 1980 he was a professor at the Academy of Fine Arts in Skopje.

BIBLIOGRAPHY

Rodoljub Anastasov (exh. cat. by S. Abadjieva Dimitrova, Skopje, Mus. Contemp. A., 1970)
B. Petkovski: *Sovremeno Makedonsko slikarstvo* [Contemporary Macedonian painting] (Skopje, 1981), pp. 41, 46, 51

BOJAN IVANOV

Anatolia, ancient. Region roughly equivalent to the modern state of Turkey. The name Anatolia was first used

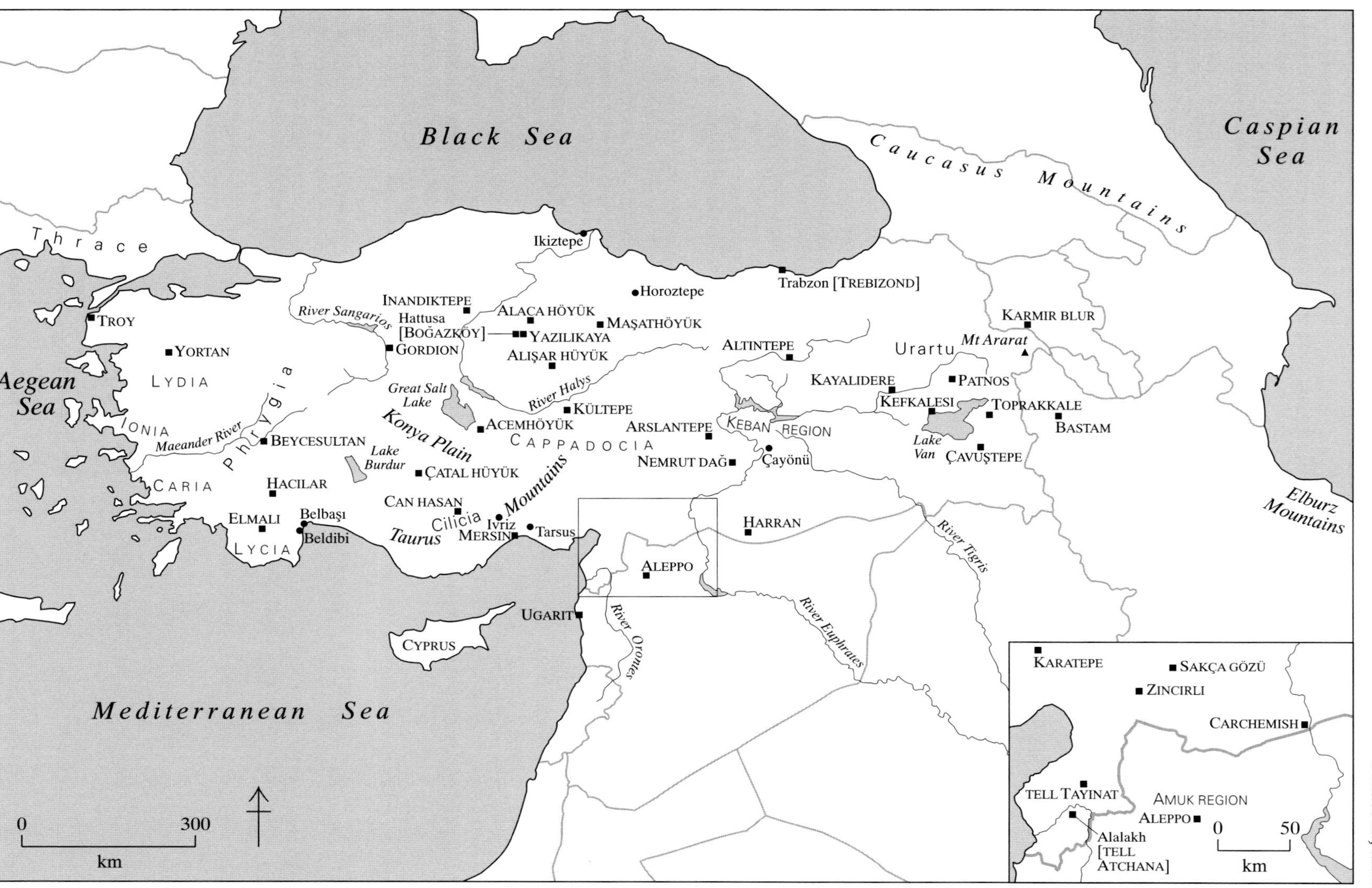

1. Map of ancient Anatolia; those areas with separate entries in this dictionary are distinguished by CROSS-REFERENCE TYPE

by Byzantine writers in the 10th century AD, as an alternative to Asia Minor, and is now often used in its Turkish form, 'Anadolu', to describe Turkey in Asia. In this article the term ancient Anatolia covers the cultures and civilizations that flourished in the region from possibly as early as the 14th millennium BC to the 6th century BC. A wealth of remains from the Neolithic period (*c.* 8000–*c.* 5800 BC) to the Early Bronze Age (*c.* 3400–*c.* 2000 BC) testifies to the advanced prehistoric culture of Anatolia. During the 2nd millennium BC this was succeeded by the civilization of the Hittites (*see* HITTITE), the demise of which was followed by a Dark Age lasting some two centuries. Eastern and south-eastern Anatolia were dominated from the 9th century BC to the early 6th by the Urartians (*see* URARTIAN), while in central and western Anatolia the Phrygians (*see* PHRYGIAN) flourished during the 8th century BC.

In 547/6 BC Anatolia became part of the Persian empire, and the ancient history of the region after that date is discussed elsewhere (*see also* CARIA, IONIA, LYCIA and LYDIA). In several important cases, the influence of later civilizations extended into Anatolia (*see* GREECE, ANCIENT, ROME, ANCIENT, EARLY CHRISTIAN AND BYZANTINE ART and ISLAMIC ART).

This article covers the principal artistic developments in ancient Anatolia, first in a chronological survey (*see* §I, 2 below and ANCIENT NEAR EAST, fig. 2) and then in terms of the major art forms (*see* §§II–VI below). There are extensive cross-references to individual sites that have made a particular contribution at a certain time or in a given field. The development of some types of object, such as seals and jewellery, and the use of some materials (e.g. faience, glass and ivory) are best seen in the wider context of the ANCIENT NEAR EAST. Most of the artefacts discussed are in the Museum of Anatolian Civilizations, Ankara; other principal collections are in the Archaeological Museum, Istanbul. For the modern history of the region, *see* TURKEY.

BIBLIOGRAPHY

H. Frankfort: *The Art and Architecture of the Ancient Orient*, Pelican Hist. A. (Harmondsworth, 1954, rev. 1970)

S. Lloyd: *Early Highland Peoples of Anatolia* (London, 1967)

R. M. Boehmer and H. Hauptmann, eds: *Beiträge zur Altertumskunde Kleinasiens: Festschrift für Kurt Bittel* (Mainz, 1983)

R. W. Ehrich, ed.: *Relative Chronologies in Old World Archaeology*, 2 vols (Chicago, 1985, rev. 1992)

J. V. Canby and others: *Ancient Anatolia: Aspects of Change and Development: Essays in Honor of Machteld J. Mellink* (Wisconsin, 1986)

I. Introduction.

1. GEOGRAPHY AND TRADE. Anatolia has always formed a land-bridge between Asia and Europe (see fig. 1). Throughout its history, peoples have entered Anatolia from the west, by sea or through Thrace, and from Turkestan and the steppes of Central Asia via the Caucasus or Iran. Sometimes they have settled in Anatolia and become assimilated with the local population; sometimes they have moved on into Syria and beyond.

The region is roughly rectangular in shape. In the east the mountains of the Caucasus meet the westward extension of the Elburz Mountains, which border the Caspian Sea in northern Iran, and the mountains of Kurdistan, which extend south-eastwards into northern Iraq and western Iran. These mountain systems are gradually being forced together, and the whole area is prone to violent earthquakes. It is dominated by Mt Ararat—the name preserves that of the ancient kingdom of Urartu—which rises to 5156 m where the borders of Armenia, Iran and Turkey now meet. This area is also a complex system of watersheds, where both the Euphrates and Tigris rivers have their sources. Many rivers drain into Lake Van, which has such a high soda content that it never freezes, although the high altitude means that the whole area is under snow some six months of the year. These severe climatic conditions have nurtured hardy mountaineers, and in the first half of the 1st millennium BC the Urartians produced a vital and distinctive culture, notable for its strategically situated citadels and temples built of fine ashlar masonry. This area is also extremely fertile; wine was exported from at least the early 2nd millennium BC, and horses were another major export. The mines at Ergani Maden were among the main suppliers of copper in antiquity, and Urartian bronzework was highly prized.

Two mountain chains extend from the east to embrace a high central plateau. The northern mountains, known as the Pontic arc, border the Black Sea, and there are semi-tropical forests above Trabzon. Apart from some rich burials, there are few known remains from this area, probably because the inhabitants lived in timber-framed buildings that have not survived. To the west the narrow channel of the Bosporus Strait separates Anatolia from Europe, and to the south, bordering the Mediterranean Sea, the Taurus Mountains form an almost unbroken barrier between a narrow coastal strip and the Anatolian plateau. Only in the north-east corner of the Mediterranean is there a wide coastal plain, known as Cilicia, where many ancient cultures flourished. Cilicia was a vital link in the maritime trade routes that hugged the coast, and there is even evidence at some periods of close contact with Troy on the Ionian coast. The Anatolian plateau was reached through the Cilician Gates, one of the great passes of antiquity. Trade with Syria went through the Beylan Pass to the Amuk region and beyond, and it was in this area, on the borders between Syria and Turkey, that the Neo-Hittite states were established after the collapse of the Hittite empire around 1200 BC.

In the west, where the mountainous arms come together, they are cut by rivers draining from the plateau into the Aegean Sea, and extend in a pattern of islands towards Greece. Harbour towns grew up along this coast, notably those founded by Greek cities in the early 1st millennium BC. Routes along the river valleys, particularly that of the Maeander River (Büyük Menderes), carried trade inland, but the alluvium washed down by the rivers often silted up the harbours: some, like Troy, are now many miles inland.

The central Anatolian plateau lies mostly between 1000 and 1500 m above sea-level. Much of it is arid steppe, particularly in the area round the Great Salt Lake (Tuz Gölü). To the south of this lake lies the Konya Plain, where the prehistoric settlement of Çatal Hüyük traded in obsidian. Another prehistoric site, Hacılar, lay south of Lake Burdur in a more mountainous area at the head of a major trade route through the Taurus Mountains to the coast. Two great rivers cut their way through the plateau in broad curves. In the east the Kızıl Irmak (the River Halys of antiquity) enclosed the homeland of the Hittites, while in the west the River Sankarya (or Sangarios) flowed through the land of the Phrygians. The peoples who passed through Anatolia have left many remains on the plateau. Mud-brick was often used as a building material, and the superimposed remains of mud-brick settlements form ruin-mounds (Turk. *hüyük*, *höyük* or *tepe*), which dot the landscape. Stone was plentiful and was used as a building material, sometimes in the form of orthostats (large vertically set stone slabs) decorated with reliefs. There are also numerous rock reliefs, mostly attributable to the Hittites and Phrygians.

DOMINIQUE COLLON

2. Chronological survey.

(i) Prehistoric period. (ii) Historic period.

(i) Prehistoric period.

(a) Palaeolithic and Mesolithic (before *c.* 8000 BC). (b) Neolithic (*c.* 8000–*c.* 5800 BC). (c) Chalcolithic (*c.* 5800–*c.* 3400 BC). (d) Early Bronze Age (*c.* 3400–*c.* 2000 BC).

(a) Palaeolithic and Mesolithic (before c. *8000* BC*).* There are few published remains from these periods, though a stratified sequence from caves at Beldibi and Belbaşı, near Antalya, helps to document the transition from Middle Palaeolithic to Neolithic. A rock-engraving of two running animals at Beldibi may be of Late Palaeolithic date (*c.* 14,000 BC). Comparable human and animal engravings on pebbles, bone and rock are attested further north at Kara'In and Öküz'In. The engraving at Beldibi is overlaid by paintings in red-brown ochre of cruciform human figures and of an ibex, and these may be contemporary with Mesolithic strata (*c.* 11,000–*c.* 8000 BC) containing red-painted pebbles. Other rock art is known from Adıyaman, Palanlı, Hakkâri and Kobistan but is insecurely dated. The Mesolithic period is also characterized by geometric microliths and, in its later stages, by a crude and crumbly early pottery.

*(b) Neolithic (*c. *8000–*c. *5800* BC*).* During this period settlement in plains and valleys led to the use of mud for building, in pisé or more usually in bricks, with stones sometimes providing foundations. A clay model from level IV at Çayönü, near Ergani, shows a simple rectangular house with flat roof, a low kerb around the base, a doorway at the narrow end and curved doorposts, while excavation of an earlier level (II) at the same site has revealed a more complex house, with a hall, a square room and two rows of subsidiary chambers. At sites in south-central Anatolia, houses abutted immediately on one another, with entry from the roof and a kitchen area inside the structure. Decorative floors were made of pebbles set in clay or plaster (*see also* §II below). A rich tradition of internal decoration existed at the spectacular Neolithic site of ÇATAL HÜYÜK, where both painting and plaster relief were used. The dominant themes of hunting, virility (symbolized by bulls and rams), fertility, pregnancy and childbirth are also reflected in stone and clay figurines, either modelled in the round or in relief (*see also* §III, 1 below). Monumental stone sculpture depicting humans, birds and bird-man has been found at Nevali Çori on the Euphrates. Late Neolithic clay figurines from HACILAR (*c.* 6000–*c.* 5800 BC) show much less interest in bulls and rams, with no adult male figures and no hunting scenes. As at Çatal Hüyük, young and old women were represented with leopards, perhaps with mythological connotations. The images of birth and fertility, however, are more relaxed (see fig. 2a). The art lacked the vivacity and wildness of Çatal Hüyük, but it had grace.

Most Neolithic pottery was monochrome. A few examples from Hacılar have patterns of stripes or net-work,

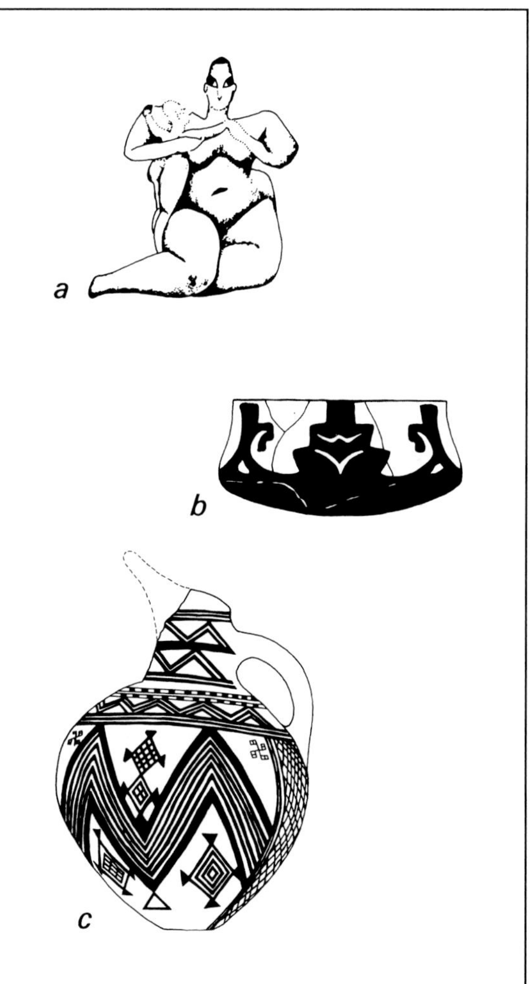

2. Prehistoric artefacts: (a) clay figurine of seated mother and child, h. 66 mm, from Hacılar, Late Neolithic, *c.* 6000–*c.* 5800 BC; (b) bowl in the 'Fantastic' style, diam. 200 mm, from Hacılar, Early Chalcolithic, *c.* 5800–*c.* 5400 BC; (c) Cappadocian ware jug, h. 255 mm, from Kültepe, Early Bronze Age, *c.* 3400–*c.* 2700 BC (Ankara, Museum of Anatolian Civilizations)

and the same site also produced elegant animal-shaped vessels and pottery with applied relief decoration of animal motifs. Tools and vessels of chipped and ground stone were common. Obsidian and, to a lesser extent, tabular flint were prized materials traded over long distances, and sophisticated white marble bowls with three or four feet were carefully kept and mended at Hacılar. From an early level at Çayönü (II) have come over 60 small copper objects, such as beads, hooks, wire and awls. At Çatal Hüyük lead and copper slag provide evidence of smelting. Native copper was also hammered into sheet-metal for use in beads, tubes, pendants and other small objects.

*(c) Chalcolithic (*c. *5800–*c. *3400* BC*).* In the Early Chalcolithic period (*c.* 5800–*c.* 5400 BC) the building traditions of Neolithic south-central Anatolia continued at Can Hasan I (for illustration *see* CAN HASAN). The walls and floors of houses were painted red, grey-blue or, in one case, decorated with a red-on-white meander design. To the west, at Hacılar V–II, quite a different architectural tradition prevailed; the whole village has been uncovered at level II. A later fortress there (level I, *c.* 5700 BC) invites comparison with one at MERSIN XVI (?5300 BC). At Hacılar I narrow gateways led to courtyards, from which staircases led up to a first storey. The houses themselves, the outer walls of which largely comprised the circuit wall, had plans closely resembling those at Can Hasan I. At Mersin XVI a central courtyard at ground-level gave entry through small, private yards into houses built up against the circuit wall. This arrangement anticipated Early Bronze Age fortifications.

The pottery from Hacılar V–II includes examples of a 'Fantastic' style of decoration (see fig. 2b), which uses, in a semi-abstract way, many of the motifs previously found in the Çatal Hüyük wall paintings. Mersin and Cilicia had their own pottery tradition, which during Mersin XXIII–XVI came under the influence of Çatal Hüyük and west Anatolian styles of elaborate geometric design, often resembling textiles or basketry. Monochrome wares were everywhere the norm, but polychrome wares appeared at the same time in Mersin XIX–XVII possibly under Halaf influence (*see* MESOPOTAMIA, §V, 1), and, independently, at Can Hasan I (level 2A3).

The local traditions of figurine making at Hacılar and Can Hasan continued to change. In Hacılar I female figures were shown standing, sitting or lying, but with some stylization towards the later figure-of-eight shape. There were also handsome anthropomorphic and theriomorphic pots, painted and sometimes inlaid with obsidian eyes (for illustration *see* HACILAR).

There are scant Late Chalcolithic (*c.* 4500–*c.* 3400 BC) remains from strata beneath settlements of the Early Bronze Age, which the period anticipates. A Syrian Ubaid influence (*see* SYRIA-PALESTINE, §V, 1) affected many south-eastern Anatolian and Cilician sites, but central and west Anatolia were dominated by dark-burnished wares with simple incised, jabbed or white-painted decoration. Among the earliest examples of skilled Anatolian metalwork are a copper mace-head from Can Hasan, a stamp-seal of tin bronze from Mersin XVI or XVII, and from Beycesultan XXXIV a small hoard of copper tools, a chisel possibly cast in an open mould, and the first attestation of silver, a ring.

*(d) Early Bronze Age (*c. *3400–*c. *2000* BC*).* This period is characterized by a sudden economic and cultural blossoming, perhaps stimulated by Mesopotamian demand for metals, that was made possible by growing Anatolian expertise in metallurgy, the cultivation of grapes and the development of wheeled transport. At ARSLANTEPE the discovery of large numbers of clay seals suggests a control on the movement of goods that permitted the rise of palaces. At Norşuntepe VI (*c.* 2300 BC) a two-storey magazine, a bakery, workshops, simple dwellings and a complex with wall paintings all surrounded a central courtyard and were arranged on terraces and divided by streets. Palaces, towns, villages and even single buildings could be fortified: at Poliochni on Lemnos blocks of megaron-like houses and a rectangular stone council chamber with tiers of stone benches were surrounded by stone walls with squints, and some villages, such as Demirci Hüyük and Sakyol Pulur, were built in a circle, using the outer walls of their radially arranged rectangular houses for defence. Cultic buildings varied: at Arslantepe these comprised a T-shaped sanctuary with relief and painted decoration on the walls; at Beycesultan there were twin megaron-type buildings, each with central circular hearth (for illustration *see* BEYCESULTAN); and Kültepe had a single, large megaron with central hearth and adjoining rooms to one side. At Kırışkal and Gedikli megalithic underground chambers with entrance passages enclosed underground springs and may have been associated with gods of the underworld.

Despite the gradual introduction of the potter's wheel, much pottery was still hand made in the Late Chalcolithic monochrome tradition, sometimes using contrasting colours (red and black) inside and outside the same vessel. Pottery of the periods Early Bronze Age (EB) I–II (*c.* 3400–*c.* 2465 BC) commonly has incision and white-painted decoration, as at YORTAN. In central and south-west Anatolia ribbing and fluting suggest imitations of metalwork. In eastern regions a Transcaucasian influence inspired reliefwork depicting extravagantly moustachioed, semi-abstract faces. Painted wares were common to the Konya Plain and Cilicia in EB II (*c.* 2900–*c.* 2465 BC). In EB III (*c.* 2465–*c.* 2000 BC) the Kültepe and Alişar Hüyük regions developed the strongly geometric, purple-on-orange Cappadocian ware (see fig. 2c), and a contemporary geometric polychrome ware developed independently in the Upper Euphrates region. (*See also* §V below.)

Metalwork is best known from burials, as at Korucutepe, Horoztepe, Ikiztepe and the royal tombs at ALACA HÖYÜK; from burnt strata, as at Arslantepe, Poliochni and TROY; and from chance finds. Ores must have been mined in the mountainous regions and may have been smelted before transport, though further smelting, perhaps for purification, evidently sometimes took place at the metalworking sites themselves. Single-mould and bi-mould casting were common; granulation is attested on earrings from Troy II (?2250 BC); and silver inlay occurs on EB I swords from Arslantepe VIa and on figures of stags from Alaca Höyük (see fig. 8 below), where plating and lost-wax casting are also attested. There is broad uniformity in

3. Bronze figurine of mother and child, h. 203 mm, from Horoztepe, Early Bronze Age, *c.* 3400–*c.* 2000 BC (Ankara, Museum of Anatolian Civilizations)

the more common types of metal tools, such as chisels, awls, adzes and knives. The same applies to many spearheads, daggers and socketed axes, though swords and halberds are rare.

Early Bronze Age metal vessels show more regional variety: almost all the many types of vessels from Troy have local variations in metal or clay. Ritual objects, of uncertain use, are best attested at Alaca Höyük and Horoztepe; and from both sites there is evidence for metal-plated tables with human feet. Jewellery, however, is best represented in west Anatolia (e.g. Troy and Poliochni), where elaborate (?)headdresses, basket earrings with pendent chains, lunate earrings, either segmented and studded or ornamented with granulation, and pins surmounted by birds, vases or rosettes have been found.

The female stone figurines of this period are usually flat, and the shape is sometimes dictated by the form of the stone itself. The west Anatolian tradition favoured figure-of-eight and violin shapes, the head and neck of the latter sometimes dwindling to a pointed stalk. Violin-shaped figurines from central Anatolia often have criss-cross incision suggesting clothes, and similar ornament appears on Cappadocian figurines. An alabaster seated goddess carved in the round is known from Kültepe. A few metal figurines modelled in the round have come from Alaca Höyük and Horoztepe (see fig. 3).

BIBLIOGRAPHY

L. Bernabo-Brea: *Poliochni: Città preistorica nell'isola di Lemnos*, 2 vols (Rome, 1964–76)

Amer. J. Archaeol., lxviii–lxxix (1964–75) (lxix–lxxi) [excavation reports on Karataş-Semayük by M. J. Mellink] and xci–xcvii (1987–93) [excavation reports on Nevali Çori by M. J. Mellink]

E. Anati: 'Anatolia's Earliest Art', *Archaeology* [New York], xxi (1968), pp. 22–35

H. Çambel and R. J. Braidwood: 'An Early Farming Village in Turkey', *Sci. Amer.*, ccxxii/3 (1970), pp. 50–56; also in *Old World Archaeology: Foundations of Civilization: Readings from Scientific American*, ed. C. C. Lamberg-Karlovsky (San Francisco, 1972), pp. 113–19

Keban Projesi Çalısmarı (Ankara, 1970–82) [excavation reports on Norşun-Tepe by H. Hauptmann]

A. Palmieri: 'Scavi nell'area sud-occidentale di Arslantepe', *Origini*, vii (1973), pp. 55–228

U. B. Alkim: 'A Subterranean Construction at Kırışkal', *Mansel'e Armağan* [Mansel miscellany], 3 vols, ed. E. Akurgal and U. B. Alkim (Ankara, 1974), pp. 821–30

M. N. van Loon, ed.: *Korucutepe*, 3 vols (Amsterdam, Oxford and New York, 1975–80)

H. Z. Koşay: *Keban projesi Pulur kazısı 1968–1970* [Keban project Pulur excavations] (Ankara, 1976)

H. Çambel and R. J. Braidwood: *Prehistoric Researches in Southeastern Anatolia*, i (Istanbul, 1980)

P. S. de Jesus: *The Development of Prehistoric Mining and Metallurgy in Anatolia*, 2 vols, Brit. Archaeol. Rep., Int. Ser. (Oxford, 1980)

A. Palmieri: 'Excavations at Arslantepe (Malatya)', *Anatol. Stud.*, xxxi (1981), pp. 101–19

M. Korfmann: *Demirci Hüyük: Die Ergebnisse der Ausgrabungen, 1975–78*, 2 vols (Mainz, 1983–7)

(ii) Historic period.

(a) Middle Bronze Age (*c.* 2000–*c.* 1700 BC). (b) Late Bronze Age (*c.* 1700–*c.* 1200 BC) and Dark Age (*c.* 1200–*c.* 1000 BC). (c) Iron Age (after *c.* 1000 BC).

*(a) Middle Bronze Age (*c. *2000–*c. *1700* BC*).* The earliest historical documents from Anatolia are the thousands of inscribed clay tablets from level II (*c.* 1920–*c.* 1840 BC) of the Lower Town at KÜLTEPE, capital of the kingdom of Kanesh. They come from the business archives of a *karum* (colony) of Assyrian merchants (*see also* ASSYRIAN), present in Anatolia from perhaps as early as *c.* 1920 BC, who retailed tin, clothing and wool to the Anatolians and exported copper and cloth to Assur. The chain of trading stations reached from Assur to the Konya Plain, and the period *c.* 1920–*c.* 1740 BC is often termed the Assyrian Colony period. Local rulers profited greatly from this trade, and the prosperity of Kültepe in particular seems linked to the development of Hittite culture in the early 2nd millennium BC.

The Hittites (*see* HITTITE) are often presumed to have entered central Anatolia from the north, and, since there is no archaeological break at the start of the Middle Bronze Age, a date before *c.* 2000 BC is likely. Their origins, however, remain obscure: the Kültepe texts reveal the occasional use of Indo-European names among the more generally Hattian names of the population and its rulers, and the Hittites later believed that their own Indo-European court-language had been the language of Kanesh. The name of a prince of Kanesh, Anitta, is known from an inscribed spearhead from level Ib of the *karum* (*c.* 1810–*c.* 1740 BC), and it was apparently he who established Kültepe as the principal city in Anatolia. He built up a large territorial state with vassal dependencies, an achievement later enshrined in Hittite tradition. Under Anitta and his successors, however, Assyrian trade declined, perhaps following the conquests of Hammurabi of Babylon (*reg* 1792–1750 BC).

During the Middle Bronze Age there was broad uniformity in domestic architecture. Most houses were of mud-brick and timber, sometimes on stone foundations, and in plan they seem an irregular agglomeration of quadrilateral rooms (*see* KÜLTEPE, fig. 1). In central and eastern Anatolia stone casemate walls with earth fill and a mud-brick superstructure were used for fortification. Citadel gates usually had flanking towers, sometimes also of casemate construction, and two sets of doors. At Korucutepe the citadel walls had regular projecting towers; at Tilmen and Alişar Hüyük there were regular offsets. A palace at Beycesultan V, possibly typical of this period, was an immense two-storey building of mud-brick and timber (*see* BEYCESULTAN). It included a central courtyard, a painted hall, a lustral chamber and light wells; the more elegant rooms had raised floors and sunken air ducts. Shrines have not been identified with certainty but may include megaron-type buildings with subsidiary chambers at Beycesultan and Kültepe.

Central Anatolian pottery was dominated by the vigorous Old Hittite ware. This was brilliantly burnished, usually red, and included animal-shaped rhyta, two-handled cups with quatrefoil rims, and jugs with tall, narrow stems and bearded spouts. Red wares also predominated in west Anatolia, but the shapes were mainly derived from local Early Bronze Age pottery, with limited central Anatolian influence on the south-west and some Middle Helladic influence on the north-west. In Cilicia the Syrian Dark-on-light style was adopted at Tarsus, and sites in the Antitaurus region mainly produced a grey, wheelmade ware.

Middle Bronze Age metalwork is best known from intramural burials at Kültepe, which contained vessels in gold, silver and bronze, weapons, copper ingots, pins, gold skullcaps, seals and a bronze trolley. Numerous lead figurines were made in stone moulds. At Acemhöyük beautifully fluted and ridged drinking cups were carved from rock crystal and obsidian, and there is also evidence for sophisticated ivory-carving.

Cylinder seals, introduced by the Assyrian merchants at Kültepe, depict humans, animals, scenes of war and hunting, and mythological and cultic subjects. Both indigenous and Mesopotamian motifs occur: of the Mesopotamian deities, only the water gods are depicted with real enthusiasm; local gods are shown standing on animals, and goddesses are shown seated and surrounded by attendant animals. In the succeeding level (Ib) stamp seals, the more normal Anatolian form, returned to popularity. These could be of gold, bronze, steatite, serpentine, limestone, ivory or clay, and were decorated with abstract motifs as well as animal heads and heraldic eagles. The style formed the basis for later Hittite seals. (For further discussion of seals *see* ANCIENT NEAR EAST, §II, 1.)

*(b) Late Bronze Age (*c. *1700–*c. *1200* BC*) and Dark Age (*c. *1200–*c. *1000* BC*).* The historical record of Late Bronze Age Anatolia, known from archives at BOĞAZKÖY, Maşathöyük and Ugarit, concerns mainly the Hittites. The Hittite Old Kingdom (*c.* 1650–*c.* 1500 BC) began with the establishment of Boğazköy (anc. Hattusa), instead of Kültepe, as the capital city. For almost five centuries thereafter the Hittites exercised a precarious dominance over central Anatolia, holding at bay Kaska tribes to the north and east, Luwian kingdoms to the west, Hurrians (*see* HURRIAN) to the south-east, and contesting in Syria and north Mesopotamia the claims of, successively, Aleppo, the Mitannians (*see* MITANNIAN), Egyptians and Assyrians. Hittite control was exercised by punitive expeditions, mass deportations, imposition of vassal treaties and tribute, and by diplomatic marriages; and it was tested regularly at the accession of a new king. Several factors contributed to the decline of Hittite power in central Anatolia during the 13th century BC: an increasing Assyrian threat, recurrent famine attested from *c.* 1235 BC onwards, marauders from the Aegean ('Sea Peoples') around 1194 BC, a possible incursion of Phrygians (*see* PHRYGIAN) and other peoples from the Balkans, and doubtless uprisings by subject kingdoms and the Kaska. The extinction of the royal house at Boğazköy *c.* 1200 BC is usually taken to mark the end of the Late Bronze Age, although the lateral line at CARCHEMISH survived, as perhaps did a rival royal line at Tarhuntassa (in or near the Taurus Mountains). Some sites show archaeological continuity to *c.* 1050 BC, indicating that the rupture was incomplete.

Much of the Late Bronze Age material culture derives from the Middle Bronze Age, but central, south and east Anatolia are sharply different from west Anatolia. In military architecture such features as casemate walls, projecting towers, monumental gates with flanking towers, and corbelled subterranean passages (see fig. 6 below) survived from the Middle Bronze Age, though Cyclopean masonry was an innovation. An ornamental vase from Boğazköy indicates that mud-brick battlements topped the stone fortification. The citadel wall at Troy VI–VII, however, was different, with regular offsets and single trapezoidal towers flanking less heavily guarded gates. Hittite palaces, identified at Boğazköy and Alaca Höyük, differed from the Trojan arrangement of free-standing trapezoidal and megaron-type buildings within the citadel of level VI. Similarly, the megaron plan underlay much of the domestic architecture of Beycesultan IVb–I, but was forgotten in central, south and eastern regions, where roughly rectangular rooms clustered irregularly between streets and courtyards. Hittite temples at Boğazköy, Tarsus and Yazılıkaya (*see* YAZILIKAYA (i)) were rectangular, with corridors and side-chambers around a central colonnaded courtyard and an off-centre shrine-room at the far end. At Beycesultan, however, a series of uncertainly identified shrines exhibits the traditional western megaron pattern.

Late Bronze Age Hittite pottery is largely derivative, but the range of shapes is narrower and less inventive than in the Middle Bronze Age, and the wares are dull—except for some Old Hittite polychrome relief vases and animal-shaped cultic vessels. Around 1350 BC Hittite influence was evident both in Cilician pottery and in the Antitaurus region, but Hittite types appeared in the south-west only *c.* 1250. The north-west was strongly influenced by Middle and Late Helladic Grey Minyan ware, but never by central Anatolia. Mycenaean imports occur at coastal sites, especially Troy, and occasionally inland.

Little metalwork survives, but two silver rhyta (New York, Norbert Schimmel Col., on loan to Met. and Boston, MA, Mus. F.A.) show the artistry that could be attained. Amulets and figurines of gold, electrum and bronze show seated goddesses and striding gods and humans in the round, as do others in ivory and rock crystal (Adana, Archaeol. Mus.). From Carchemish come flat gold reliefs of the king and other male figures, inlaid with cloisonné lapis lazuli and steatite (London, BM); a comparable lapis lazuli relief comes from Assur (Berlin, Pergamonmus.).

Stamp seals in metal and stone continued to use Middle Bronze Age motifs, but hieroglyphic inscriptions in Luwian were introduced in the Hittite Old Kingdom period. A fine series of royal seals, known chiefly from impressions, exhibits hieroglyphs and symbols in the central field and, in the later period, surrounding rings of cuneiform legend.

Sculpted designs were applied to architecture and rocky outcrops (*see also* §III, 2 below). Most such sculptures depict one or two divine or royal figures briefly identified by Luwian hieroglyphs; some are associated with perennial springs. The largest compositions are at Alaca Höyük, showing two processions of worshippers and revellers, and at Yazılıkaya, depicting two processions of gods, with unique hieroglyphs conveying Hurrian linguistic forms. Most sculptures are in relief, but lion, sphinx (see fig. 7 below) and human gate-guardians at Boğazköy, Alaca Höyük and Arslantepe are partly in the round. Quarries at Yesemek have revealed many half-finished sculptures of the period.

Around 1200 BC written records ceased and the archaeological evidence shows widespread destruction of Hittite cities. During the ensuing Dark Age (*c.* 1200–*c.* 1000 BC) Anatolia underwent a period of upheaval before the emergence of distinctive Iron Age cultures in Phrygia, Urartia and elsewhere.

BIBLIOGRAPHY

H. T. Bossert: *Altanatolien* (Berlin, 1942)
O. R. Gurney: *The Hittites* (Harmondsworth, 1952, rev. 1990)
E. Akurgal: *The Art of the Hittites* (London, 1962)
P. Garelli: *Les Assyriens en Cappadoce* (Paris, 1963)
S. Alp: *Zylinder- und Stempelsiegel aus Karahöyük bei Konya* (Ankara, 1968)
P. H. J. Houwink ten Cate: *The Records of the Early Hittite Empire, c.* 1450–1380 BC (Istanbul, 1970)
L. L. Orlin: *Assyrian Colonies in Cappadocia* (The Hague, 1970)
K. Emre: *Anadolu Kursun Figurinleri ve Tas Kaliplari/Anatolian Lead Figurines and their Stone Moulds* (Ankara, 1971) [bilingual text]
H. Lewy: 'Anatolia in the Old Assyrian Period', *Early History of the Middle East*, ed. I. E. S. Edwards, C. J. Gadd and N. G. L. Hammond, Cambridge Anc. Hist., I/ii (Cambridge, rev. 3/1971), pp. 707–28
O. R. Gurney: 'Anatolia *c.* 1750–1600 BC', 'Anatolia, *c.* 1600–1380 BC', *History of the Middle East and the Aegean Region, c.* 1800–1380 BC, ed. I. E. S. Edwards, C. J. Gadd and N. G. L. Hammond, Cambridge Anc. Hist., II/i (Cambridge, rev. 3/1973), pp. 228–55, 659–82
O. W. Muscarella: *Ancient Art: The Norbert Schimmel Collection* (Mainz, 1974)
E. Neu: *Der Anitta-Text*, Studien zu den Boğazköy Texten (Wiesbaden, 1974)
A. Goetze: 'Anatolia from Shippiluliumash to the Egyptian War of Muwatallish', 'The Hittites and Syria, 1300–1200 BC', *History of the Middle East and the Aegean Region, c.* 1800–1380 BC, ed. I. E. S. Edwards, C. J. Gadd and N. G. L. Hammond, Cambridge Anc. Hist., II/ii (Cambridge, rev. 3/1975), pp. 117–29, 252–73
J. G. Macqueen: *The Hittites and their Contemporaries in Anatolia* (London, 1975)
K. Bittel: *Die Hethiter* (Munich, 1976)
J. D. Hawkins: 'Kuzi-Tešub and the "Great Kings" of Carchemish', *Anatol. Stud.*, xxxviii (1988), pp. 99–108
H. Otten: *Die Bronzetafel aus Boğazköy: Ein Staatsvertrag Tuthalijas IV* (Wiesbaden, 1988)

DONALD F. EASTON

(c) Iron Age (after c. *1000* BC*).* After the Dark Age that followed the destruction of the Hittite empire, the broad artistic koine suggested by the distribution of Hittite rock reliefs no longer existed. Instead Anatolia can be divided into four regions—Phrygia, Tabal, Urartu and Cilicia—inhabited by at least three new population groups. Although these regions shared some inheritance from Hittite art and were in close political contact, each produced a distinctive art style. Coastal Anatolia was increasingly under Greek domination (*see* IONIA, CARIA and LYCIA), and Greek influence extended inland to include the kingdom of LYDIA. The period covered by this survey ends with the Persian invasion of Anatolia in the mid-6th century BC.

The PHRYGIANS were Indo-European speaking newcomers probably from Thrace, who formed a kingdom in the 9th century BC in the west Anatolian highlands. Their capital at GORDION was surrounded by a magnificent battered city wall of cut stones and by numerous burial tumuli. Inside the citadel, simple rectangular public buildings must together have comprised a palace. Phrygian art is characterized by an animal style, in which natural forms are condensed to create lively, free-spirited creatures. Close-knit geometric motifs, sometimes arranged in mysterious, seemingly haphazard combinations, were used to cover surfaces; they are also seen in the magnificent Phrygian rock-cut tombs between Afyon and Eskişehir.

In eastern Anatolia, the mountainous kingdom of Urartu flourished from the mid-9th century BC until the early 6th century BC. The Urartians made inroads into north-west Iran, north Syria and Cilicia whenever the Assyrians, to the south in Mesopotamia, were weak (*see* URARTIAN). The architectural feats of the Urartians are impressive, particularly their fortifications on rugged peaks and their use of fine ashlar masonry. Some monumental sculpture has survived, as well as a series of wall paintings and a wealth of decorated bronzes (*see* §IV, 2(ii) below). Many Urartian motifs are derived from Assyrian iconography, but they seem to have been used decoratively without, apparently, much underlying meaning.

In the heartland of what had been the Hittite kingdom the new state of Tabal was a federation of small kingdoms that produced rock reliefs accompanied by 'Hittite' hieroglyphic inscriptions, although stylistic details were strongly influenced by Assyria. The rock-cut relief at Ivriz showing *King Warpalawas of Tabal before a Grain God* (see fig. 4), which is among the greatest works of art so far known from Iron Age Anatolia, combines many stylistic currents of the period: the rock relief tradition itself, the hieroglyphs and the turned-up shoes derive from Hittite times; the hairstyle, beard and exaggerated musculature are Assyrian; the patterning of the king's clothes is Phrygian; and the grape clusters and wheat carried by the god refer to a Tabalian deity. The art of this period from most of the kingdoms on the central Anatolian plateau is known only from chance finds, such as the many funerary stelae from Maraş (anc. Marqasi), capital of the state of Gurgum (examples in Paris, Louvre). A city gate decorated

4. Rock relief of *King Warpalawas of Tabal before a Grain God*, h. 4.2 m, Ivriz, late 8th century BC

with lions, sculptures and inscriptions has been excavated at Arslantepe.

Towards the end of the 8th century BC Cimmerian tribes from Turkestan, driven westwards by advancing Scythians, swept through Urartu, Tabal and Phrygia. Urartu survived for another century or so, but the distinctive art of Tabal ceased. According to tradition, King Midas of Phrygia was forced to commit suicide, but Phrygian art survived, under Lydian domination, into the Achaemenid period (5th century BC). Other states came under Assyrian domination and lost their identity.

Hittite culture survived the collapse of the Hittite empire in the new fortified cities of the Neo-Hittites and Semitic Aramaens in Cilicia (*see* ARAMAEAN) and north Syria, where carved stone orthostats and gate guardians were used extensively to decorate city walls and palaces. The language of the inscriptions was generally Luwian, written in 'Hittite' hieroglyphs. Bilingual Luwian and Phoenician inscriptions were found on reliefs at Karatepe (for illustration *see* KARATEPE). Some Hittite traditions lived on, but much was new: the sculptural ensembles are not as coherent as earlier, although richer in fabulous creatures and heraldic scenes, some derived from Mesopotamia. In the last years of the 8th century BC the Neo-Hittite kingdoms fell to the Assyrians, later coming under Neo-Babylonian control. After Anatolia became part of the Persian empire in 547/6 BC, independent artistic traditions continued into the 5th century BC, when the Achaemenid Persians and the Greeks came into conflict in the region. During the second half of the 4th century BC the conquests of Alexander the Great brought Anatolia under Greek influence. The Greeks were later succeeded by the Romans in the 2nd and 1st centuries BC, but some semi-independent kingdoms, such as Commagene in the east (*see* NEMRUT DAĞ), produced syncretic monumental sculpture that combined both oriental and Classical traditions. Anatolian art of this period is discussed elsewhere in terms of the Hellenistic art of ANCIENT GREECE.

BIBLIOGRAPHY

E. Akurgal: *Phrygische Kunst* (Ankara, 1955)
——: *Die Kunst Anatoliens von Homer bis Alexander* (Berlin, 1961)
B. B. Piotrovsky: *The Ancient Civilization of Urartu* (London, 1969)
W. Orthmann: *Untersuchungen zur späthethitischen Kunst* (Bonn, 1971)

JEANNY VORYS CANBY

3. RELIGION AND ICONOGRAPHY. Evidence for the ancient religions of Anatolia comes from the archaeological investigation of shrines and burials, as well as from scattered artefacts such as images, cultic vessels and seals. A further dimension is furnished by written records, which may identify deities and describe mythologies and cults, though this source becomes available only with the cuneiform clay tablets and monumental hieroglyphic inscriptions of the Hittites (*see* §(ii) below).

(i) Prehistoric period to Middle Bronze Age. Prehistoric Anatolian religion has left some striking images. The earliest and most notable of these come from Neolithic shrines of ÇATAL HÜYÜK (7th–6th millennia BC). Their painted and modelled mud-plaster walls provide rich evidence for a cult of fertility, the hunt and death. The figures of the mother goddess and of bulls, leopards and vultures vividly illustrate Neolithic religious concepts. Not until the Early Bronze Age shrines of Beycesultan (3rd millennium BC) is anything comparable known, and even these, with their wealth of cultic equipment, hardly match the Çatal Hüyük paintings. The royal tombs of ALACA HÖYÜK, also Early Bronze Age, yielded rich grave goods, including geometric discs, bulls and stags mounted on 'standards' (see fig. 8 below), and many figures and idols. As in the Çatal Hüyük shrines, bulls' skulls were found in association with the tombs.

In the early part of the Middle Bronze Age (*c.* 2000–*c.* 1700 BC) the Assyrians introduced literacy into Anatolia, but documents from this period do not provide much evidence for contemporary religion, mainly because they are exclusively commercial in character. Their limited information on gods' names and temples is supplemented by finds of figurines, theriomorphic vessels and plaques, but the most substantial sources of religious iconography are the numerous cylinder seals, which bear profuse representations of gods, temples, animals and symbols.

(ii) Hittite. With the advent of the Hittites (*see* §2(ii)(a) above) and their tradition of religious architecture and sculpture, which can be set beside their numerous mythological and cultic texts, knowledge of the Anatolian religion is considerably extended. Several distinct but overlapping pantheons are revealed, connected by varying degrees of syncretism and mutual influence: most notably the pre-Hittite Hattian pantheon, the Hittites' own, the Hurrian and, more distantly, the Semitic pantheon of Syria. The 'thousand gods of Hatti' were organized in a hierarchy

5. *King Sulumeli Making Offerings to Four Deities*, basalt relief, h. 445 mm, from Arslantepe (Malatya), 1050–850 BC (Ankara, Museum of Anatolian Civilizations)

under the supreme Storm God (Hittite Tarhunda, Hurrian Teshub), who was supported by a court of prominent deities, such as the Sun, the Moon, the Grain God and the Stag God, each with their individual sphere of influence. Each prominent god of the 'national' pantheon was represented by many local variations. The gods were conceived anthropomorphically with individual attributes. They had female consorts, organized into their own circle under the chief goddess (Hittite 'Sun goddess of Arinna', Hurrian Hebat) though, apart from an Anatolian version of the Mesopotamian goddess of love and war, Ishtar, these have less pronounced characters than the males.

The gods were housed in temples constituted as their households, and descriptions of rituals, festivals and temple inventories figure prominently among the written texts. They were represented by cult statues of wood, precious metals, stones and ivory, which are themselves inventoried, giving a good idea of their appearance, although none survives. The gods are exhaustively listed in treaty oaths, where they are invoked as witnesses, and in offering lists. Many texts also narrate myths, often embodied in the text of rituals. These can be divided into native Anatolian myths, perhaps of pre-Hittite origin, which are normally simple, folkloristic tales (the Fight of the God and the Dragon, the Disappearance of the Angry God), and imported mythologies, more typically found in the form of sophisticated literary epic (e.g. the Kumarbi cycle).

Sculpture, architecture and artefacts help to illustrate the written sources. The appearance of deities is known from figurines in bronze or precious materials, and from dressed stone and rock reliefs, often colossal. Near the Hittite capital, Hattusa (now Boğazköy), in the great extramural shrine of YAZILIKAYA (i), the rock face is carved with two facing files of male and female deities, representing in lapidary form the Hurrian offering lists. Hittite temples on a standard plan with gatehouse, court-yard and cella are well represented at BOĞAZKÖY. Even the performance of rituals sometimes survives in pictorial representation. The orthostat slabs of the gate at Alaca Höyük show the king and queen praying before an altar, followed by processions of dignitaries, musicians and acrobats. Even more detailed is a polychrome vase from INANDIKTEPE, decorated with bands of reliefs showing similar scenes.

The king was thought to mediate between gods and men, and to be semi-divine, the incarnation of the Sun God. After death he received divine honours: 'to become a god' was a euphemism for a king's dying. As such, kings are usually represented wearing the long robe and skullcap of the Sun God, but also, when associating with the Storm God, wearing his kilt and pointed hat (for illustration *see* BOĞAZKÖY). Kings recognized their personal patron deities, in whose embrace they are shown in monumental representation (for illustration *see* HITTITE) and on seals.

Hittite religious iconography also included a host of minor protective spirits that took the form of mixed creatures: bull-men, mountain-men, griffins and sphinxes (see fig. 7 below). These could be shown in monumental form, particularly as guardians of gateways. The gods also had their own animals, such as the lion, the bull, the leopard, the stag and the eagle. In Hittite hieroglyphic script their names were represented by their symbols, for example the Storm God by a sign for a thunderbolt. The sign for 'god' represents a pair of eyes, symbolizing the divine, all-seeing nature. Another symbol of divinity is the *lituus*, a crooked sceptre, held both by gods and (reversed to indicate the position of deputy) by kings. The winged sun-disc was a symbol imported from Egypt, representing the king as supreme sovereign.

This religious iconography continued without great change into the Iron Age Neo-Hittite period (*c.* 1000–*c.* 700 BC). On a relief from Arslantepe the king is robed and wears the horned headdress of deities (see fig. 5). One innovation was the much greater prominence of the goddess Kubaba, as befitted the chief deity of the city of Carchemish. The nature of the written evidence changed, however, as cuneiform clay tablets were replaced by hieroglyphic stone inscriptions. These are mostly building inscriptions or religious dedications giving details of the foundations of temples and their endowments. Cult statues were commonly in the form of stone stelae with inscriptions, particularly those of the Storm God. Rulers were still deified, and offerings were made to their colossal statues, erected on podia flanked with lions or sphinxes. A further innovation was the practice of setting up tombstones for private individuals. These sometimes show a family seated at a funerary banquet or take the form of castellated towers, and inscriptions often reveal that subjects as well as kings expected to join the gods after death. Much of the iconography of this period was transmitted to the Hittites' neighbours, the Aramaeans, Phoenicians and even the Hebrews. It thus survived the fall of the Hittite empire to reappear in the artistic repertory of the Greek and Roman world.

(iii) Phrygian and Urartian. Early in the Iron Age western Anatolia was occupied by the Phrygians (*see* §2(ii)(c) above), whose surviving alphabetic inscriptions are short and barely understood. They do, however, confirm that, as later Greek sources indicate, the chief Phrygian deity was the mother goddess Kubile, an intermediate figure in the transmission of the old Carchemish goddess Kubaba to the Greeks as Kybele. Her prominence is also emphasized by many rock-cut façades with a central cult niche containing a figure of the goddess (*see* PHRYGIAN, fig. 2). Other Anatolian rock-cut monuments, appparently Phrygian and serving a religious purpose, include hilltop thrones approached by steps and accompanied by carved depressions for libations. These suggest mountain or nature cults. Rock-cut tombs are often decorated with rampant antithetical lions, but the dead were also buried under tumuli, as at the Phrygian capital GORDION.

The Urartian civilization of eastern Anatolia (*fl c.* 850–*c.* 600 BC) produced monumental rock inscriptions in cuneiform script, giving details of the Urartian pantheon. This was headed by the national god Haldi and his consort, and other prominent pairs of deities include the Storm God Teisheba (a form of the Hurrian god Teshub) with his consort, and the Sun God and his consort. Temples were usually built at the highest point of the hilltop cities. They are typically square in plan with a frontal entrance (*see also* §II below). Examples have been found at TOPRAKKALE, Aznavurtepe, KAYALIDERE, ALTINTEPE and Arinberd. Documents relating to the eighth campaign of the Assyrian king Sargon II (*reg* 721–705 BC) give a detailed description of the chief shrine of Haldi at Muṣaṣir and its contents: the temple, which has not been found, was also depicted on reliefs (destr.) excavated in Sargon's palace at Khorsabad. Some sculptured blocks at ADILCEVAZ show winged minor deities standing on animals and performing lustration of the sacred tree. Similar figures formed inlaid bronze decorations on furniture (e.g. London, BM), and were painted on walls at Altıntepe and incised on bronze plaques originally attached to belts. They are paralleled in contemporary Neo-Hittite and Assyrian art. Altogether, the evidence suggests considerable similarities in belief, cult and iconography in Mesopotamia and Anatolia in the early 1st millennium BC.

BIBLIOGRAPHY

F. Naumann: *Die Ikonographie der Kybele in der phrygischen und der griechischen Kunst* (Tübingen, 1983)

M. N. van Loon: *Anatolia in the Second Millennium BC*, Iconography of Religions (Leiden, 1985)

——: *Anatolia in the Early First Millennium BC*, Iconography of Religions (Leiden, 1990)

J. D. HAWKINS

II. Architecture.

1. PREHISTORIC PERIOD TO MIDDLE BRONZE AGE. From the 8th millennium BC new settlement patterns led to the appearance of rectangular structures in the plains and valleys of Neolithic Anatolia. These were built of mud-brick or pisé, often on stone foundations, with internal buttressing and mud-brick walls or wattle-and-daub screens, and roofs constructed of wooden beams, matting, reeds and clay. Impressive architecture already existed in the 8th millennium at Çayönü in eastern Anatolia, where the lower courses of three single-room buildings were found, measuring at least 10×7 m. These buildings had symmetrically placed internal buttresses and floors of large flagstones and in one case a *terrazzo* floor. One building, where human skulls were found stacked in a niche, may have had some cultic use. The architecture of ÇATAL HÜYÜK (7th-6th millennium BC) also differed from that of a normal Neolithic farming village. Here an estimated 1000 houses, covering 13 ha, had continuous outside walls, forming an early kind of fortification. Dwellers entered the two-room houses from the roof. The elaborate decoration of many of these buildings included wall paintings, and plastered reliefs incorporating horn-cores also indicated some cultic use. The houses at Can Hasan I (level IIa, *c.* 5400 BC; for illustration *see* CAN HASAN) were built one against the other with rows of internal buttresses and access from the roof.

A free-standing fortification wall is found at Chalcolithic Hacilar II, in central Anatolia, in the 6th millennium BC (*see* HACILAR). In the 5th millennium BC the village at Mersin XVI, in Cilicia (*see* MERSIN), was turned into a fortress by the addition of gate towers leading to a central courtyard, and a casemate wall.

In eastern Anatolia at ARSLANTEPE small palaces and temples of the Early Bronze Age (*c.* 3400–*c.* 2000 BC) have been found, in some cases with plans influenced by Mesopotamian architecture. By the early 3rd millennium BC, fortified city states had appeared throughout Anatolia. Fortifications, which often had casemate walls, are best preserved at Troy II (*see* TROY), with ramps, towers, buttresses and gates. Public buildings at Troy consisted of neat rows of simple, rectangular units with a front porch and interior hearth, anticipating the later megaron building type used in Greek temple architecture. Megaron-type buildings have also been found at BEYCESULTAN in western Anatolia and at KÜLTEPE in central Anatolia.

In the first three centuries of the 2nd millennium BC (Middle Bronze Age) a large palace with many interior rooms was built at Acemhöyük. Two further palaces at Acemhöyük, one with an exterior portico (for illustration *see* ACEMHÖYÜK), had stone foundations and mud-brick walls incorporating an elaborate wooden framework. This type of construction, also found at Beycesultan and MAŞATHÖYÜK, was possibly intended to give added elasticity to buildings in a region prone to earthquakes. A painted sherd from Acemhöyük shows a view of the wooden railings and columns of the superstructure. In the 18th century BC, TELL ATCHANA (anc. Alalakh) in the Amuk region had a monumental city gate, a large square temple and a palace that contained the elements of a plan that was to be used in that area for more than a millennium.

Buildings of this design, termed *bit hilani*, consisted of a columned entrance with a wide rectangular room behind it and a staircase at one end (*see* SYRIA-PALESTINE, fig. 6b). The use of well-dressed rectangular orthostats at the base of important walls also foreshadowed the extensive use of orthostats, often carved in relief, at sites in the area during the early 1st millennium BC. A large, well-preserved suburb of Assyrian merchants' houses, built around courtyards, lay outside the city wall of Kültepe, and within the citadel a palace has been excavated.

2. HITTITE, PHRYGIAN AND URARTIAN. Monumental Hittite buildings dominate Late Bronze Age architecture (*c.* 1700–*c.* 1200 BC). The 15th-century BC palace at Maşathöyük was planned around a courtyard measuring 40×33 m (for illustration *see* MAŞATHÖYÜK). At the early Hittite site of ALACA HÖYÜK dressed Cyclopean stones carved with reliefs lined the outside façade of an elaborate monumental gate guarded by monolithic sphinxes 2.35 m high. At BOĞAZKÖY, the Hittite capital, the city walls were of Cyclopean polygonal masonry, with gates made of large monoliths and long corbelled posterns (see fig. 6). This strategic circuit ran over rough terrain and bridged a deep chasm below the citadel. A clay model shows that the walls and towers were crenellated and that the latter were provided with windows. Neither the walls nor the processional stairways over the steep, paved glacis at the south end of the city have any parallel in Anatolia. On the citadel itself there were small free-standing buildings, which had various functions, and a large columned hall was surrounded by a series of courts, some of which had columned porticos. These structures combined to create a royal area or palace. They demonstrate an architectural philosophy related to the 3rd-millennium BC megara from Troy, which was later exemplified in the complex of megara at Gordion and perhaps even the groups of *bit hilani* buildings that characterized Neo-Hittite citadels. Excavations at Boğazköy uncovered the massive stone foundations of numerous large temples up to 40 m square. Some had enormous stone socles for the columns of brick and stone, with a wooden frame forming the walls. These temples had standardized plans, with a formal gatehouse leading to a court colonnaded on two sides, and a circuitous route to the projecting cella with deep windows on to the outside. The Temple of the Storm god stood in a compound surrounded by storerooms and living quarters for the temple personnel.

6. Hittite fortifications at Yerkapı, Boğazköy, view down corbelled postern tunnel, h. *c.* 2 m, *c.* 1700–*c.* 1200 BC

From the 9th–7th centuries BC contemporary representations again help to reconstruct the elevations of buildings. From graffiti found at GORDION and from Phrygian rock-cut tomb façades, for example at Yazılıkaya (*see* PHRYGIAN, fig. 1), it is known that the 8th-century BC megara at Gordion had gabled roofs. The interiors sometimes had pillars to support the roof and wooden balconies along the sides. There is also a splendid fortified gateway at Gordion. The depiction on the Assyrian bronze gates from Balawat (9th century BC; London, BM) of the crenellated towers of the great Neo-Hittite city of CARCHEMISH are particularly useful because the excavations there produced little more than the sculptured façades of large buildings and processional ways. Other Neo-Hittite cities, such as KARATEPE, SAKÇA GÖZÜ and ZINCIRLI, provide better plans of monumental gateways decorated with carved orthostats, and the last two sites had well-laid-out citadels incorporating *bit hilani* units. The sculpture and architecture are a blend of Hittite traditions.

During the same period, in the mountains of eastern Anatolia, the Urartians fortified some 75 crags and strategic positions. A bronze model (London, BM; *see* URARTIAN, fig. 1) shows a towered façade with stepped crenellations and three storeys of windows. Some fortresses were built of ashlar masonry on foundations cut out of the living rock. Excavations at such sites as KARMIR BLUR, ÇAVUŞTEPE, KAYALIDERE, Bastam (*see* BASTAM (i)) and TOPRAK KALE have revealed interior details of the fortified sites: long rock-cut water channels, extensive storerooms and workshops and, at Karmir Blur, a row of identical dwellings. Assyrian reliefs of the late 8th century BC provide valuable details of an Urartian temple (destr., but recorded in drawings) with a gabled or pitched roof topped by a giant spearhead, a low façade hung with shields, and a doorway flanked by spears. Excavations have shown, however, that the temples were square towers, with thick walls buttressed at the corners, built of well-dressed ashlar masonry with mud-brick above. They may well have resembled the 6th-century BC Achaemenid Persian towers at Naqsh-i Rustam and Pasargadae (*see* ZOROASTRIANISM, fig. 2), which also had shallow pitched roofs. At ALTINTEPE the temple was surrounded by a colonnade with wall paintings and mosaics. From the 6th century BC onwards Anatolia's indigenous architectural traditions were absorbed into those of her Greek, Persian and, later, Roman rulers (*see also* CARIA, IONIA, LYCIA and LYDIA).

BIBLIOGRAPHY

A. Naumann: *Architektur Kleinasiens von ihren Anfängen bis zum Ende der hethitischen Zeit* (Tübingen, 1955, 2/1971)

R. Young: 'Phrygian Construction and Architecture', *Expedition*, ii (1960), p. 2

——: 'Phrygian Architecture and Construction', *Expedition*, iv (1962), p. 2

T. Özgüç: 'The Art and Architecture of Ancient Kanish', *Anatolia*, viii (1964), pp. 27–48

T. B. Forbes: *Urartian Architecture*, Brit. Archaeol. Rep., Int. Ser. (Oxford, 1983)

P. Neve: 'Die Ausgrabungen in Boğatköy-Ḫattuša 1991', *Archäol. Anz.*, iii (1992), pp. 307–38

III. Sculpture and rock reliefs.

Although the earliest Anatolian sculptures date from *c.* 7000 BC, the archaeological record is patchy, and it is often necessary to rely on isolated objects. It is only in the 2nd millennium BC that a distinctive style appears that can be linked with a historically known people, the Hittites. This article focuses mainly on sculpture and reliefs in either clay or stone, whether small-scale or monumental; works in metal are discussed in §IV below. Unless otherwise stated, all small-scale artefacts are in the Museum of Anatolian Civilizations, Ankara.

1. Small-scale sculpture. 2. Monumental and architectural sculpture and reliefs.

1. SMALL-SCALE SCULPTURE. The excavation of early settlement sites in Anatolia has produced evidence for Neolithic stone reliefs, small sculpture in the round and clay figurines. Relief sculpture is first attested at Çayönü in eastern Anatolia, where a stone slab bears a stylized human face in relief with emphasized nose and eye sockets. The same site also produced roughly modelled clay animal and human figurines, a small stylized human torso of stone and a polished murex seashell, which may have been inlaid with copper or malachite (all in Dıyarbakır, Archaeol. & Ethnog. Mus.). At CATAL HÜYÜK many stone and clay figurines (*c.* 6300–*c.* 6000 BC) were found. The former are of black stone or white marble and include figures of bulky females, thin males and some more elaborate groups—a figure with a leopard, a twin goddess and a plaque with two pairs of figures in high relief (an embracing couple and a mother and child). The carefully modelled clay figurines are mostly of very fat seated women, sometimes decorated with patterns of red paint. One seated figure is supported by double leopards. The nose and eyes are usually emphasized, but the mouth is not indicated. Most of these figurines were found in a succession of shrines decorated with a bizarre series of painted wall reliefs, sculpted in clay over an armature of straw and animal skulls, which depicted women about to give birth, leopards and bulls, and rows of animal heads incorporating real horn-cores. In some cases the thick plaster on the walls was cut away in the shape of animals. Farther west at HACILAR, small figurines from early levels were beautifully modelled. They depict fat women in various recumbent and standing poses (see fig. 2a above). Some seated figures are associated with leopards or embracing youths. Modelled pottery vessels include one shaped like a couchant gazelle with its head turned back. A long-necked figure from Chalcolithic Can Hasan (mid-5th millennium BC), made of burnished clay with painted decoration, has a prominent nose and lug-shaped ears. It wears an elaborate headdress and is seated with hands across the knees.

The ensuing gap in the record of Anatolian sculpture is probably due to the accidents of discovery. Early 3rd-millennium BC sites in western Anatolia have produced flat, stylized clay figurines, some with incised details such as huge eyes and pubic triangles (e.g. at Demircihöyük; Eskişehir, Archaeol. Mus.). A stylized face and a staff were carved on a squared stone found in Troy and anthropomorphic vessels are known from Troy and several other sites of the late 3rd millennium BC (e.g. in Afyon, Archaeol. Mus.). Flat, highly stylized, fiddle-shaped, white stone idols found at several sites, such as Beycesultan, recall Early Bronze Age finds from the Cyclades. Late 3rd millennium BC flat figurines from Kültepe are also made of white marble and have disc-shaped bodies, triangular heads (sometimes several) and drilled and incised decoration.

A lively new style of sculpture, characterized by large, clear, life-like forms, appeared early in the 2nd millennium BC and may be connected with the arrival of the Hittites. It is represented by ivories, found at Kültepe and Acemhöyük (many of the latter in New York, Met.), depicting a nude female figure, a falcon and its prey, couchant gazelles, lions and sphinxes. These and other sites of the Assyrian Colony period (*c.* 1920–*c.* 1740 BC) produced a wealth of modelled clay rhyta (drinking cups) and attachments to pottery, in the shape of well-proportioned animals and parts of animals, birds, fruit, shells, shoes, boats and human figures, as well as little scenes (*see* KÜLTEPE, fig. 2). The walls of some large clay vessels were also decorated with bands of narrative scenes modelled in relief.

2. MONUMENTAL AND ARCHITECTURAL SCULPTURE AND RELIEFS. The earliest known monumental sculpture in the Near East has been found in Neolithic levels (*c.* 7000 BC) at Nevali Çori on the Euphrates. Over life-size figures, both in flat and high relief, were carved on stone stelae and sculptures in the round depicted humans, birds and bird-men. The small ivories and modelled rhyta of the early 2nd millennium BC form the background to the reappearance of monumental sculpture, which belongs to the Hittite empire of the second half of the 2nd millennium BC. Rock reliefs and carved monuments depicting deities, kings or local princes occur throughout Anatolia, sometimes near springs. Sphinx protomes 2.35 m high decorate the gate, possibly 15th-century BC, at ALACA HÖYÜK (*in situ*). A relief on the inside face of one jamb shows a figure standing on a double-headed eagle with hares in its talons. The façade of the gate was decorated with two registers of orthostats depicting lively cultic and hunting scenes and processions, including musicians and acrobats. These were carved in low relief with little interior modelling, yet the figures are always understandable, if sometimes ill-shaped.

The rock faces at the open-air sanctuary of Yazılıkaya (*c.* 1500–1200 BC) outside the Hittite capital were carved with processions of deities and single scenes of the king, either embraced by a god or alone, as well as a composite image interpreted as the Dirk or Dagger god (for illustration *see* YAZILIKAYA (i)). The latter represents a hilt topped with a divine head and lion protomes; on the lower part of the hilt are crouching lions. The gate above the monumental steps on the heights of Yazilikaya has sphinxes with exceptionally sensitive carving of the faces. Gateways at Boğazköy (for illustration *see* BOĞAZKÖY) were carved with giant lion protomes (*in situ*), sphinxes (Istanbul, Mus. Anc. Orient; see fig. 7; and Berlin, Pergamonmus.) and a warrior god in half-round relief (replica *in situ*; original in Ankara). Over life-size sculpture in the round is attested by fragments of human figures. Vases with relief decoration and ornamental rhyta continued to be made, some in architectural shapes. A pair of harnessed bulls (h. 670 mm) was found in Boğazköy. On a smaller scale are deities in gold (Ankara; London, BM; Paris, Louvre; New York, Met.), rock crystal from Tarsus (Adana, Archeol Mus.) and lapis lazuli set in gold from Carchemish (London, BM).

Carved orthostats and gateways protected by lions and sphinxes continued to be a feature of the early 1st millennium BC Neo-Hittite cities east and south-east of the Taurus mountains, such as ARSLANTEPE, which may date still earlier, AIN DARA on the Syrian–Turkish border (*in situ* and Aleppo, N. Mus.), CARCHEMISH (Ankara; London, BM), SAKÇA GÖZÜ, ZINCIRLI (Istanbul, Archaeol. Mus.; Berlin, Pergamonmus.), TELL TAYINAT (U. Chicago, IL, Orient. Inst. Mus.; Antakya, Hatay Mus.) and KARATEPE (*in situ*). A greater variety of scenes was depicted, with banquets, war and mythological subjects added to the earlier hunting, religious and ceremonial scenes. At Maraş several grave stelae show the deceased, often with attributes representing their activities when alive (distaffs and mirrors for women, writing tablets for a young scribe; e.g. Adana, Archaeol. Mus.; Gaziantep Mus.; Paris, Louvre). Each of these cities had its own style of carving. It may be from this area that, in the 9th century BC, the Assyrians adopted the idea of decorating their palaces with reliefs. The Assyrians, in turn, influenced the local styles of the cities they occupied, notably Carchemish and Zincirli. Many of these Neo-Hittite cities also produced sculpture in the round representing kings, deities and pairs of animals or mixed beings, some finely carved and over life-size, others rather crude.

7. Hittite sculptured head of a sphinx, limestone, h. 2 m, from the gate of Yerkapı, Boğazköy, 13th century BC (Istanbul, Museum of the Ancient Orient)

Phrygian sculpture of the first half of the 1st millennium BC includes comical lion protomes from the doorway of a small building at Gordion, and animal-shaped rhyta continued to be made. Architectural tiles from such sites as Gordion and Pazarlı are decorated with foot-soldiers and chariot groups, antithetical lions or goats, and mythological scenes in painted relief. A limestone group, 1.34 m high, of a goddess flanked by two small musicians was found at Boğazköy. It resembles the frontal, robed statues of Kybele carved in numerous rock-cut niches. These include a series shaped like temple façades decorated with geometric designs carved in low relief (*see* PHRYGIAN, figs 1 and 2). A fine Phrygian statuette from Boğazköy may show Greek and Near Eastern influence. Large orthostats found near Ankara were carved with animals and imaginary creatures. At Ivriz a huge scene (h. 4.2 m), executed in high relief on a rock face, blends imperial Hittite, Neo-Hittite and Phrygian elements. It depicts *King Warpalawas of Tabal before a Grain God*: the god holds grapes and wheat (see fig. 4 above). Sculpture in Urartu is best known from small figures of human beings, deities and animals, well made of ivory, bronze or a combination. The style and iconography are clearly dependent on Assyrian art, yet the pieces have a fresh, naive appeal of their own. At Kefkalesi, a column base was decorated in low relief, showing gods on lions beneath turreted city walls. Assyrian reliefs from Khorsabad (destr.), depicting the sack of the Urartian town of Muşaşir, showed monumental figures of the national god Haldi, but no such sculpture survives. In the second half of the 1st millennium BC Anatolia came under Achaemenid Persian and later Hellenistic domination. The monumental figures from Nemrut Dağ show the blending of Greek and Near Eastern styles and iconography. This mixture is well illustrated by a series of reliefs depicting King Antiochus I of Commagene (*reg* 69–34 BC) shaking hands with, among others, Herakles-Veneythragna and Apollo-Mithra (*in situ*).

BIBLIOGRAPHY

B. B. Piotrovskii: *Vanskoi Tsarstvo (Urartu)*, (Moscow, 1959); Eng. trans. as *Urartu: The Kingdom of Van and its Art* (London, 1967)

E. Akurgal: *The Art of the Hittites* (London, 1962)

W. Orthmann: *Untersuchungen zur späthethitischen Kunst* (Bonn, 1971)

K. Bittel: *Die Hethiter: Die Kunst Anatoliens von Ende des 3. bis zum Anfang des 1. Jahrtausends vor Christus* (Munich, 1976)

M. J. Mellink: 'Comments on a Cult Relief of Kybele from Gordion', *Beiträge zur Altertumskunde Kleinasiens: Festschrift für K. Bittel* (Mainz, 1983), pp. 349–60

Amer. J. Archaeol., xci–xcvii (1987–1993) [excavation reports on Nevali Çori by M. J. Mellink]

JEANNY VORYS CANBY

IV. Metalwork.

The study of Anatolian metalwork reveals lively indigenous cultures that interacted with neighbouring areas, such as SYRIA-PALESTINE, MESOPOTAMIA and ANCIENT IRAN, to produce a rich and varied tradition. Using Anatolia's vast mineral resources and polymetallic ore deposits, craftsmen were able to develop an expressive style, employing a variety of different minerals and metals in the production of utilitarian tools and weapons, complex ceremonial artefacts and jewellery. Unless otherwise stated, all the objects mentioned are in the Museum of Anatolian Civilizations in Ankara.

1. Chalcolithic period and Bronze Age (*c.* 5800–*c.* 1000 BC). 2. Iron Age (after *c.* 1000 BC).

1. CHALCOLITHIC PERIOD AND BRONZE AGE (*c.* 5800–*c.* 1000 BC).

(i) Materials and techniques. Skilled metalworking began during the Chalcolithic period and the Early Bronze Age (*c.* 5800–*c.* 2000 BC), although metals had been used in Anatolia in Neolithic settlements as early as *c.* 8000 BC (cold-worked pins and beads of native copper have been found at Çayönü in the east). By *c.* 2000 BC metalworking had progressed beyond the level of a village smithy and was developing into an industry proficient in the arts of smelting, melting, annealing, forging, working sheet-metals, alloying, refining gold and silver, and cupellation of lead sulphides. The earlier dependence on arsenical coppers shifted to the use of bronzes with a 5–15% tin content. Although iron had by then been worked for several centuries, Late Bronze Age metalwork (*c.* 1700–*c.* 1200 BC) shows a marked increase in its use.

Of particular interest are Bronze Age decorative techniques involving the use of silver, gold and electrum. These metals were produced throughout Anatolia from the late 4th millennium BC and occur in jewellery, weapons, vessels (e.g. a silver cup with electrum overlay from Troy; for illustration *see* TROAD), votive objects and ingots. In the Early Bronze Age, vessels, such as those from the tombs at ALACA HÖYÜK, were decorated with swirling, herringbone and concentric circle designs, incised or in repoussé, sometimes with human handles and coiling snakes in relief. The prominence of spiral motifs in Anatolia is reflected by the many variants in different materials appearing from the 4th millennium BC onwards. They had a special meaning at Ikiztepe, where they decorate beads, pins, pendants, idols and blade hilts. Large examples of spiral shapes of unknown function are up to 110 mm in diameter. By the end of the Early Bronze Age (*c.* 2000 BC) metals worked into a spiral shape included pure copper, arsenical copper, bronze, gold, silver and electrum.

During the Early Bronze Age there seems to have been a conscious effort to achieve a silvery colour in weapons and figurines, reflecting the rise of silver as the most important metal in the economies of surrounding areas such as Mesopotamia. In the absence of silver, there is evidence for 'inverse segregation', a technique of using copper with a high arsenic content (up to 12%) to give a shimmering, silvery surface to bull figurines and bronze weapons (examples from Ikiztepe, Horoztepe and north central Anatolia).

In the repertory of solid cast metals there was a trend towards multicoloured and three-dimensional effects and textures in weapons, jewellery, human and animal figurines and votive objects, as in the arsenical copper swords with silver diamond and triangle patterns on the hilt from Arslantepe VIa (late 4th millennium BC; Malatya Mus.). Stoneworking techniques were combined with metals to create polychrome jewellery with a subtle play of colour and texture. Necklaces alternated coloured minerals and stones, while pins were set with cornelians or lapis lazuli, or in patterns of light and dark, such as iron and gold or silver and gold examples from Alaca Höyük (*c.* 2300 BC), and a bronze and iron pin from Alişar Hüyük. Bronze and iron ceremonial weapons in the 3rd millennium BC were often inlaid and overlaid partially with silver, gold or electrum, imparting an interplay of different colours. A silver axe from Alaca Höyük had a gold shaft, while weapons from Troy were encrusted with electrum, silver or gold. A superb example is an iron sword from Tomb K at Alaca Höyük with a gold-covered wooden hilt and crescent shaped top. Hittite inventory texts describe elaborate weapons, such as a dagger with a 'shimmering face' and a 'tail' and pommel of rock crystal.

(ii) Subject-matter. The technical sophistication of Anatolian metalworkers found early artistic expression in female figurines with exaggerated hips and breasts—a tradition going back to the Çatal Hüyük terracottas (*c.* 6300–6000 BC; see fig. 2a above). The earliest metal human representations come from the cache of six tin bronze statuettes from Tell Judeideh G in the AMUK REGION (early 3rd millennium BC; Boston, MA, Mus. F.A.; U. Chicago, IL, Orient. Inst. Mus.). The clenched hands of the three male figures and the articulation of the muscles are realistically portrayed. A multicoloured effect was achieved by the use of a silver-rich alloy, with copper and gold for the accessories. Stylized male and female figures decorate both faces of an arsenical copper blade from Ikiztepe and fit into the artistic conventions of Early Bronze Age idols from central Anatolia. The finest examples, made of bronze, silver or gold (?second half of 3rd millennium BC), come from the Alaca Höyük royal tombs, Horoztepe, Mahmatlar, Göller, Eskiyapar, Kalınkaya, Ikiztepe and Hasanoğlan. These images stress health and wealth: female figures have full hips, and their breasts and feet are often covered in gold or silver. Clothing, head-dresses, weapons and idiosyncratic jewellery were added, recalling the spiral rings, lunate earrings, bracelets, diadems, double and quadruple spiral pins and zoomorphic representations found generally in Bronze Age levels.

In the Early Bronze Age flora, fauna and astrological symbolism were also persistent themes. In the representation of animals the craftsmen combined naturalism with ritual iconography and a richness of detail drawn from both nature and imagination. At Alaca Höyük stags (see fig. 8) and bulls were mounted on 'standards', and openwork geometric discs had separate attached elements, forming musical instruments such as sistra. Although these artefacts can be interpreted as associated with hunting, they were found in graves and also had a ritual meaning. The idea of the untamed power of the animal was achieved by emphasizing the magnificent antlers of stags and the sharp, sweeping horns of wild bulls, while oversimplifying the body and breaking it down into clear geometric forms (such as a cylindrical body, stalk-like legs and tubular muzzle). On the Alaca Höyük standards, an organic coherence is achieved, integrating wild animal imagery with the geometric linear designs of the discs to form a carefully organized semicircular composition, modulated by the sharp angles and the repetitive rhythm of the openwork patterns. Plating in different metals was used to achieve a multicoloured effect.

In the Middle Bronze Age (*c.* 2000–*c.* 1700 BC) both stylized and naturalistic forms of human and divine imagery were employed. The former includes flat, cursive lead figurines cast in stone moulds. At the other extreme are sensitively modelled, gilded faience nude figurines found at Kültepe and gilded ivory furniture fragments from Acemhöyük. This convention of gilding ivory and bone continued into the Iron Age (*see* §2 below). A well-proportioned human image from the Late Bronze Age is provided by a small gold goddess, seated on a feline-pawed throne and holding a child in her lap, a motif current in Anatolia from the Neolithic period (*c.* 1400–1200 BC; New York, Norbert Schimmel Col., on loan to Met.). Her curved legs, the modelling of the face and such details as fingers confer great naturalism and a sense of monumentality on the small figure.

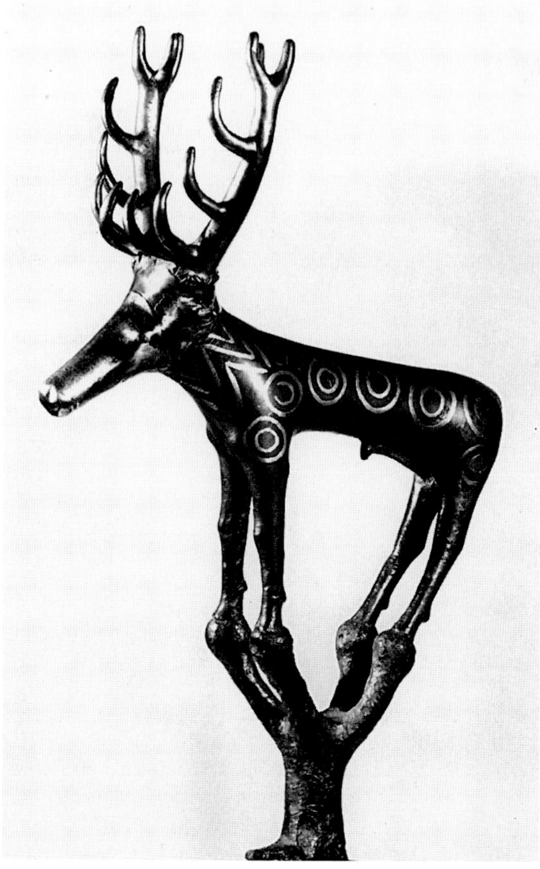

8. Bronze stag with silver decoration, h. 520 mm, from Alaca Höyük, Early Bronze Age, *c.* 2300–*c.* 2100 BC (Ankara, Museum of Anatolian Civilizations)

Hunted in the forests of Anatolia, the stag was a frequent subject. Many examples come from Alaca Höyük and Horoztepe, showing the stag with other forest creatures. It also served as the mount of several deities, and a superb stag-shaped silver rhyton, decorated in repoussé, was probably used in religious ceremonies (New York, Norbert Schimmel Col., on loan to Met.). The bull was associated with mountains and the Storm God, and it occurs frequently in Bronze Age metal artefacts (examples from Alaca Höyük and Horoztepe).

In the Middle and Late Bronze Ages (*c.* 2000–*c.* 1200 BC) swords and axes were decorated with humans, animals and fantastic divine creatures (e.g. shaft-hole axe from Şarkışla). These weapons, which were probably numinous, have a smooth background from which figures stand out in relief. Their forms are recalled in the Hittite relief depicting the *Dagger God* at Yazılıkaya (for illustration *see* YAZILIKAYA (i)), which may have been based on a metal prototype, with its hilt shaped like a god's head framed by four lions. The decoration is an integral part of the weapon and emerges from, rather than being superimposed on, the sword.

After the destruction of the Hittite empire in the 13th century BC, Anatolia entered a Dark Age, and remains of this period from central and eastern Anatolia have yet to be uncovered.

BIBLIOGRAPHY

D. B. Stronach: 'The Development and Diffusion of Metal Types in Early Bronze Anatolia', *Anatol. Stud.*, vii (1957), pp. 90–125

R. F. Tylecote: *Early Metallurgy in the Near East* (London, 1970)

K. Emre: *Anatolian Lead Figurines and their Stone Moulds* (Ankara, 1971)

R. Maxwell-Hyslop: *Western Asiatic Jewellery, c.* 3000–612 BC (London, 1971)

H. Erkanal: *Die Äxte und Beile des 2. Jahrtausends in Zentralanatolian* (Munich, 1977)

R. M. Boehmers: *Die Kleinfunde aus der Unterstadt von Boğazköy* (Berlin, 1979)

P. S. de Jesus: *The Development of Prehistoric Mining and Metallurgy in Anatolia*, 2 vols, Brit. Archaeol. Rep., Int. Ser. (Oxford, 1980)

J. C. Waldbaum: *Metalwork from Sardis: The Finds through 1974* (Cambridge, MA, 1983)

K. A. Yener: 'The Production, Exchange and Utilization of Silver and Lead Metals in Ancient Anatolia: A Source Identification Project', *Anatolica*, x (1983), pp. 1–15

Z. Stós-Gale, N. H. Gale and G. R. Gilmore: 'Early Bronze Age Trojan Metal Sources and Anatolians in the Cyclades', *Oxford J. Archaeol.*, iii (1984), pp. 23–43

J. D. Muhly and others: 'Iron in Anatolia and the Nature of the Hittite Iron Industry', *Anatol. Stud.*, xxxv (1985), pp. 65–84

K. A. Yener: 'The Archaeometry of Silver in Anatolia: The Bolkardağ Mining District', *Amer. J. Archaeol.*, xc (1986), pp. 1–4

K. A. Yener and H. Özbal: 'Tin in the Turkish Taurus Mountains: The Bolkardağ Mining District', *Antiquity*, lxi (1987), pp. 64–71

K. ASLIHAN YENER

2. IRON AGE (AFTER *c.* 1000 BC). Early Iron Age Anatolia was dominated by the Urartians in the east and

the Phrygians, who established cities in central Anatolia either side of the River Halys. Other peoples known to have lived in the central plateau must also have developed their own cultures, including a metal industry, but they remain unidentified.

(i) Phrygian. Evidence for the earliest settlements and artefacts in central Anatolia after the Hittite destruction derives from the Phrygian capital, GORDION. Most Phrygian artefacts have come from excavations, but research is hindered by the lack of inscriptions. Almost all Phrygian bronzes derive from tumulus burials, either at Gordion or at Ankara to the east, and few, except for fibulae, come from the occupation levels at Gordion or other sites, all of which were destroyed *c.* 696 BC. The major sources of material are Tumulus W at Gordion, the earliest (*c.* 740–720 BC), followed by tumuli III, P, and MM (*c.* 720–700 BC). The Ankara tumuli are contemporary with III, P, and MM. The existence of 7th- and 6th-century BC tumuli has revealed that the Phrygian bronze industry continued to function after the destruction of the cities, but with less glory.

Tumulus MM had the largest quantity and variety of bronze artefacts and provides information on the industry at its most developed stage, during the reign of King Midas (*c.* 735–695 BC). The most distinctive Phrygian bronze artefact is the fibula, which has many sub-types. Also typically Phrygian are the belts employing a fibula form as a buckle, omphalos bowls with interior ridges or petals, and plain bowls with a banded rim that held loop handles. There are also many types of jug, and small cauldrons with T-shaped clamps for loop handles. Other small cauldrons with bull protomes may be of Phrygian origin. Distinctive ladles, with tangs connecting the bowl to the handle, found together with cauldrons suggest that they were used together at banquets. Some of the bronze vessels, bowls and jugs were imitated in wood and terracotta.

Both casting and hammering techniques were employed, sometimes on the same vessel, especially bowls and jugs. An apparent innovation was the addition of zinc to copper to make brass, perhaps in imitation of gold. Iron was used in Phrygia to make tools and ring-stands for the cauldrons, and the presence of iron slag and ore at Gordion indicates that an iron industry existed there. Phrygian weapon types and armour have not been recovered. Gold and silver artefacts are extremely rare, but the excavation in 1986–7 of two tumuli at Bayındır near ELMALI produced gold earrings and electrum pin-heads that may be Phrygian. Bronze and silver objects, especially appliqué plaques, belts, fibulae, horse breast plates, omphalos bowls, cauldrons and ladles, are more definitely Phrygian, notably a silver ladle and a small cauldron with Phrygian inscriptions.

(ii) Urartian. The first inscriptions attesting to the Urartian kingdom appeared in the late 9th century BC. Few 9th-century BC sites are known, however, though many exist from the 8th and 7th centuries BC. The quantity and variety of Urartian metal artefacts is enormous. Although much of the material derives from plundering, excavations have yielded a large corpus from tombs and settlements. Inscriptions on a number of objects also allow scholars to chart the progress of Urartian metallurgy.

Iron was used for agricultural and industrial tools, arrows, spears, knives and swords; but iron helmets and vessels are less common. Surviving bronze artefacts, however, typify the range of Urartian metalwork, especially the use of embossed and incised decoration (see fig. 9). Casting was employed for statuettes of humans and deities, fantastic and natural animals, and fittings for furniture and cauldrons. Numerous belts and plaques, many decorated with religious and secular scenes, were produced by hammering, as were shields, quivers, helmets (many also decorated) and vessels. Many objects were clearly horse and chariot equipment: these include bells, armour, blinkers and bits for horses, and plaques and wheel ornaments for chariots. For personal daily use pins and fibulae were worn. Gold jewellery, cast and hammered, some decorated with granulation, includes rings, bracelets, earrings, buttons, beads, spacers and pins. Silver was used to manufacture pins, gorgets, medallions and vessels. Urartian craftsmen were influenced by imported Assyrian metalwork, but they created a characteristic style readily distinguishable from that of neighbouring peoples. (*See also* URARTIAN.)

BIBLIOGRAPHY

E. Akurgal: *Phrygische Kunst* (Ankara, 1955)
——: 'Urtäische Kunst', *Anatolia*, iv (1959), pp. 77–114
M. van Loon: *Urartian Art* (Istanbul, 1966)
G. Arzapay: *Urartian Art and Artifacts* (Berkeley, CA, 1968)
E. Caner: *Fibeln in Anatolien* (Munich, 1983)
L. Van den Berghe and L. De Meyer: *Urartu: Een vergeten cultur het bergland Armenië* (Ghent, 1983)
O. W. Muscarella: 'The Background to the Phrygian Bronze Industry', *Bronzeworking Centres of Western Asia, 1000–539 BC*, ed. J. Curtis (London, 1987), pp. 177–92
Antalya Museum (Ankara, 1988), pp. 32–49

OSCAR WHITE MUSCARELLA

9. Urartian bronze figure standing on back of recumbent bull, h. 146 mm, from eastern Anatolia, *c.* 8th–7th centuries BC (New York, Metropolitan Museum of Art)

V. Pottery.

From the first appearance of pottery in Anatolia in the Mesolithic and Neolithic periods (*c.* 11,000–*c.* 5800 BC), monochrome and coarse wares usually predominated, with variations mostly of interest to the archaeologist. This article, however, concentrates on wares of particular artistic interest.

1. PREHISTORIC PERIOD. Animal-shaped vessels, always common, first appeared in Late Neolithic Hacılar VI. Finely modelled red monochrome fragments survive of a resting doe and a standing boar; a four-legged duck is a less sensitive piece. The Early Chalcolithic levels V–II yielded simple but elegant vessels painted with elaborate red-on-cream designs. The most complex and intriguing are a 'Fantastic' style in which natural motifs, such as flowers, animals, seated human figures, and hands, heads and eyes, were schematized in patterns resembling appliqué work in felt (see fig. 2b above). Human effigy-vases with linear red-on-cream decoration are also known from Hacılar I (*c.* 5700 BC; for illustration *see* HACILAR) and have been extensively faked. A Chalcolithic tradition of dark-on-light linear geometric ornament developed at Çatal Hüyük and Can Hasan I, where a related polychrome ware in combinations of red, purple, chocolate, and black on buff made far less satisfying use of horizontal registers. Chevrons, chequer-boards, crosshatching, thick curved lines and groups of straight or wavy lines are arranged with little sense of the shapes of the vessels.

Although the potter's wheel was introduced during the Early Bronze Age (*c.* 3400–*c.* 2000 BC), much of the best pottery was still handmade. At Beycesultan XIX–XVII (EB I) globular jars, jugs, flasks and cups—all quite simple shapes—in red, buff and black monochrome wares show careful horizontal and vertical fluting, perhaps in imitation of metal prototypes. The fluting continues in levels XVI–XIII (EB II; see fig. 10a) but on more elaborate shapes, and it sometimes undulates diagonally, for example on the bodies of jugs. At YORTAN and related sites, mainly EB II, dark-burnished beak-spouted jugs, tripod jars, funnel-necked jars, pedestalled pyxides and animal vases were attractively decorated with chevrons, hatched lozenges and triangles, and zigzag bands in white paint, or incised and filled with white, and occasionally red, paste. The repertory in Early and Middle Bronze Age Troy shows some borrowings from Yortan, but it is notable for its range of globular jars with funnel necks, which have moulded plastic ornament representing, on the body,

10. Ancient Anatolian pottery: (a) black-burnished jug, h. 115 mm, from Beycesultan, *c.* 2700–*c.* 2400 BC; (b) red-slipped jug, h. 398 mm, from Kültepe, 18th century BC; (c) tankard, with Brown-on-buff decoration, h. 230 mm, from Gordion, late 8th century BC–early 7th (Ankara, Museum of Anatolian Civilizations)

breasts, navel and upraised wings and, on the neck or lid, a stern human face with prominent eyebrows, nose and ears. Also characteristic is the elegant wheelmade *depas amphikypellon*, a tall, two-handled goblet with flaring rim and narrow, rounded base. At Kültepe and Alişar Hüyük a painted ware spans the EB III and Middle Bronze Age (MB) periods. Tall ovoid jugs and jars, small cups with pointed bases, and the inverted rims of shallow bowls were painted in EB III in dark purple-brown on an orange slip, red being added in MB phases to create a polychrome ware. Bold, irregular latticework often encloses lively geometric elaboration in the intervening panels. Similar motifs appear on vessels shaped as shoes, lions and donkeys. This Cappadocian ware is rich in colour and elegant in its shapes (see fig. 2c above).

2. HITTITE, URARTIAN AND PHRYGIAN. The MB red monochrome Old Hittite ware is even more splendid than Cappadocian ware. Its surfaces are highly polished and its shapes adventurous. The repertory includes quatrefoil cups, vessels shaped like grape clusters, biconical teapots with animal-head spouts and chalices with animals and birds modelled on the rim. There is an emphasis on tall, elegant and sharply profiled forms (see fig. 10b). Hittite pottery of the Late Bronze Age (*c*. 1700–*c*. 1200 BC) is mainly descended from the MB Old Hittite ware, but there is a loss of variety and vitality, and little further development occurred over four centuries. The red-brown monochrome ware includes wide flaring bowls, two-handled quatrefoil cups with tall stems, teapots, jugs with 'bearded' spouts, and lentoid 'pilgrim flasks' with flattened circular bodies, tall necks and three handles. There is also a series of finely modelled figures of bulls, rams and lions, some of which, with spouts set in the back, may have been for libations, as may hollow, spouted models of human arms. A rare polychrome ware belongs to the Hittite Old Kingdom (*c*. 1650–*c*. 1500 BC): large jars in red, black and yellow, such as the Inandık Vase (*see* INANDIKTEPE), were decorated with narrative relief friezes of cultic scenes. Stylistically these are related to metal relief vessels and to sculpted stone reliefs as at Alaca Höyük and Yazılıkaya, but, though colourful, they are relatively crude.

Among the uninspiring grey wares of the Iron Age, Urartian and Phrygian pottery stands out. From Urartu the predominant red-burnished Toprakkale or 'Palace' ware is most striking. In colour and shape it seems to imitate copper vessels. There are gourd-shaped goblets, jars, incense burners and kernoi, all on slender stems; and without stems there are grooved bowls, trefoil-mouthed pitchers, long-spouted jugs, tall, waisted two-handled tankards, and horn-shaped rhyta. Rims and shoulders sometimes carry models of animals or animal heads: pithoi from Toprakkale show lions climbing up the inside of the jar to bite bulls on the rim. Elegant cups in a related black ware are shaped like wide-topped leather boots and are decorated with white-filled incision or white paint to suggest stitching or lacing. The rarer painted wares, such as Red-on-buff and Black-and-red-on-buff, generally lack subtlety; but a deep bowl from Patnos has human faces in relief integrated into the design so that the hair streaming out from each face forms part of a multiple-chevron design of wavy black lines. Incised pictographs on coarse-ware storage jars sometimes indicate the contents.

In Phrygia, by contrast, the painted wares are inventive, magnificent and, at their best, meticulously executed. Tight geometric designs in brown-black on cream, occasionally also with red, use zigzags, crosshatching, chequer-boards, chevrons, lozenges, meanders and single dots in small spaces. Sometimes clear panels within the design enclose animal figures, including bulls, deer, lions (see fig. 10c), sphinxes and hawks. Fragments from Boğazköy show a procession of warriors and the goddess Kybele with two lions. Some shapes are traditionally Anatolian: graceful vessels shaped as geese, rams, stags, ducks and birds of prey; animal-head rhyta; jugs with raised spouts; and shallow plates with ring bases. Others, such as kraters and waisted tankards, seem less Anatolian. Most characteristic are jars with long side-spouts. Rims, handles and spouts can all carry animal-shaped attachments. From Pazarlı come terracotta plaques (*c*. 470 mm sq.) with painted relief decoration depicting warriors, centaurs, griffins, feeding goats, and lions attacking cattle. An earlier Brown-on-buff ware attested at Alişar Hüyük and Boğazköy is sometimes regarded as early Phrygian, although no connection has been established. Typically the upper halves of kraters have horizontal registers of geometric ornament framing a frieze of thin-legged, backward-slanting deer, and the background is filled in with small concentric circles.

BIBLIOGRAPHY

H. Schliemann: *Ilios: The City and Country of the Trojans* (London, 1881)
H. H. von der Osten: *The Alishar Hüyük: Seasons of 1930–32*, 3 vols (Chicago, 1937)
C. W. Blegen and others: *Troy: General Introduction: The First and Second Settlements* (1950), i of *Troy: Excavations Conducted by the University of Cincinnati, 1932–1938*, 4 vols (Princeton, 1950–58)
——: *Troy: The Third, Fourth and Fifth Settlements* (1951), ii of *Troy: Excavations Conducted by the University of Cincinnati, 1932–1938*, 4 vols (Princeton, 1950–58)
H. H. von der Osten: 'Die urartäische Töpferei aus Van und die Möglichkeiten ihrer Einordnung in die anatolische Keramik', *Orientalia* [Rome], xxi (1952), pp. 307–28; xxii (1953), pp. 329–54
S. Lloyd and J. Mellaart: *Beycesultan*, i (London, 1962)
Anatol. Stud., xii–xvi (1962–6) [excavation reports on Çatal Hüyük by J. Mellaart]
Anatol. Stud., xii–xviii (1962–8) [excavation reports on Can Hasan by D. H. French]
K. Emre: 'The Pottery of the Assyrian Colony Period According to the Building Levels of the Kaniš Karum', *Anatolia*, vii (1963), pp. 87–99
F. Fischer: *Die hethitische Keramik von Boğazköy* (1963), iv of *Boğazköy-Hattusa: Ergebnisse der Ausgrabungen*, ed. K. Bittel, 5 vols (Berlin, 1952–67)
M. N. van Loon: *Urartian Art: Its Distinctive Traits in the Light of New Excavations* (Istanbul, 1966), pp. 29–37
K. Emre: 'The Urartian Pottery from Altıntepe', *Belleten*, xxxiii (1969), pp. 291–301
J. Mellaart: *Excavations at Hacılar*, 2 vols (Edinburgh, 1970)
T. Kamil: *Yortan Cemetery in the Early Bronze Age of Western Anatolia*, Brit. Archaeol. Rep., Int. Ser. (Oxford, 1982)
F. Prayon: *Phrygische Plastik* (Tübingen, 1987)
T. Özgüç: *Inandıktepe: An Important Cult Center in the Old Hittite Period* (Ankara, 1988)

DONALD F. EASTON

VI. Wall painting.

The decoration of houses with red paint occurred in Anatolia from early times. Neolithic examples come from Aşıklı (*c*. 7000 BC), Hacılar (on lime plaster, *c*. 6700 BC), Can Hasan III (on clay, *c*. 6500 BC) and Erbaba (on clay plaster, *c*. 6000 BC). The outstanding site, however, is

ÇATAL HÜYÜK, where a vast treasure of motifs was painted in a rich palette of organic and mineral colours. The interiors of the houses in levels XIII–IX (*c.* 6300–*c.* 6000 BC) were decorated with wall paintings, with modelled figures and animals cut out of the wall plaster in silhouette. Some of the wall paintings employ 'kilim' motifs, so named because they are reminiscent of carpets. Such motifs include zigzags, dots, 'labyrinth' patterns, nets, flowers, triangles, honeycombs and bands (levels IX–III); hands (before level VIa); vultures (levels VIII–VII); landscapes (levels VII–VI); humans (levels VIII–III, but rare before level VIa); and the figures of 'child-bearing' women (west wall, levels VII–V), which probably represent a mother goddess and a protectress of men and animals. The most astonishing wall paintings are the hunting scenes in levels V and III. One of these shows a bull surrounded by 25 men, of which 15 are wearing loincloths and 7 are armed (for illustration *see* ÇATAL HÜYÜK). In another stags are encircled by men, some clearly agitated and some armed. Boars and a (?)lion also appear, and less important animals include equids and dogs.

The numerous painted buildings in Çatal Hüyük are probably houses rather than shrines. In level V both the relationship between the animal and the number of men surrounding it and the frequency with which the animals occur are shown realistically, while the absence of wounds and the nature of the clothing seem unreal. The hunt is thus neither purely ordinary nor magical, and the paintings are the expression of a people who did not differentiate between daily and religious life. Only the intensity of these scenes varies from house to house.

From the 4th–3rd millennia BC painted buildings occur on the Upper Euphrates, as at Norşun-Tepe, with a stag and some later simple motifs, at Değirmentepe with an awkward assemblage of geometric elements, and at ARSLANTEPE with stylized figures and concentric ovals. In the 2nd millennium BC the 'burnt palace' at Beycesultan and the palace of Maşathöyök were painted in plain colours. Wall paintings found in Temple 9 (13th century BC) at the Hittite capital, Boğazköy, had geometric motifs and palmettes.

Urartian towns of the 8th and 7th centuries BC, such as Van, Aznavurtepe, Çavuştepe and ALTINTEPE, have produced evidence of Assyrian-influenced painting. The motifs of the friezes in the well-preserved reception hall (*apadana*) of Altıntepe include genii on both sides of a sacred tree, hybrid winged beings, kneeling bulls on both sides of a concave quadrangle, palmettes, rosettes, lozenges and battlements. Two scenes of a fighting lion and stag are particularly lively. Glazed decoration is known only from *sikkatu* (glazed terracotta nails) in the 9th-century BC temple-palace at Tell Halaf and from the Temple of the Storm God and the Long Wall of Sculptures at CARCHEMISH (9th century BC), in the form of lozenges and concentric circles on bricks.

BIBLIOGRAPHY

F. Langenegger, K. Müller and R. Naumann: *Die Bauwerke* (1950), ii of *Tell Halaf* (Berlin, 1943–60)

L. Woolley and R. D. Barnett: *The Excavations of the Inner Town* (1952), iii of *Carchemish* (London, 1914–52)

Anatol. Stud., xii (1962), pp. 41–66; xiii (1963), pp. 43–104; xiv (1964), pp. 39–120; xvi (1966), pp. 165–92 [excavation reports on Çatal Hüyük by J. Mellaart]

T. Özgüç: *Altıntepe*, 2 vols (Ankara, 1966–9)

J. Mellaart: *Çatal Hüyük: A Neolithic Town in Anatolia* (London, 1967)

H. Hauptmann: 'Die Grabungen auf dem Norşun-Tepe', *Keban Projesi Çalısmarı 1972* (Ankara, 1976), pp. 71–90

T. Özgüç: *Maşat Höyük kazıları ve cevresindeki araştırmalar/Excavations at Maşat Höyük and Investigations in its Vicinity* (Ankara, 1978) [bilingual text]

P. Neve: 'Die Ausgrabungen in Boğazköy-Hattuša 1982', *Archäol. Anz.* (1983), pp. 427–54

A. Nunn: *Die Wandmalerei und der glasierte Wandschmuck im Alten Orient*, Handbuch der Orientalistik (Leiden, 1988)

A. NUNN

VII. Museums, collections and exhibitions.

The foremost museum of Anatolian antiquities is the Museum of Anatolian Civilizations in Ankara, but most major towns and archaeological sites in Turkey now also have local museums. Collections in foreign museums are small: interest in the pre-Classical archaeological remains of Anatolia developed relatively late, and by the time most foreign expeditions began working there, Turkey had formulated its antiquities laws. There has not been a policy of division of finds excavated by foreign expeditions, as has been the case in other countries of the Near East, so that anything excavated since World War I is now in Turkey.

The few pre-Classical sites excavated before World War I include TROY, but many of the objects from this site disappeared from Berlin during World War II. Some of the finds and reliefs from CARCHEMISH are now in the British Museum in London. Objects from early seasons of excavation at BOĞAZKÖY are preserved in the Vorderasiatisches Museum (Pergamonmuseum) in Berlin. Sites in the AMUK REGION were excavated in the 1930s, when this area was still part of Syria, so that finds were divided between the Hatay Museum in Antakya and the Oriental Institute Museum of the University of Chicago. The same applies to TELL ATCHANA, with finds divided between the Hatay Museum, the British Museum in London and the Ashmolean Museum in Oxford, with a few objects sent to Australian museums.

Since a clampdown in the 1960s on the growing of opium in Turkey, some farmers have, instead, conducted illicit excavations on their land and, despite tight controls, there has been a growing number of Anatolian antiquities on the market. Since major museums are signatories of the UNESCO convention against the purchase of illegally exported antiquities, most such objects are now in private collections. Some private collections have Anatolian objects, particularly the Norbert Schimmel Collection in New York, which frequently lends objects to museums and exhibitions, and the Borowski Collection in Jerusalem. Forgeries have been produced to satisfy a growing demand for Anatolian antiquities; this demand has also led to the theft of antiquities from some regional museums.

Because there were few objects from ancient Anatolia in European collections, little was known about its early culture until, in 1964, the Arts Council in London hosted a small exhibition of some 304 objects of Neolithic to Phrygian origin. Most of these came from Turkish museums, with a few pieces from the British Museum in London and the Ashmolean Museum in Oxford. The exhibition had also been to Darmstadt and Brussels.

Between 1966 and 1968 an exhibition of 282 objects, from the Neolithic period to the 18th century AD, was circulated to ten American cities by the Smithsonian Institution; just over a third of the exhibits were Phrygian or earlier. The first major exhibition of Anatolian antiquities took place in Istanbul in 1983 and was sponsored by the Council of Europe. Almost 900 objects were Phrygian or earlier, and further exhibitions also showed objects from other periods of Turkey's history. A selection of these exhibits later went on tour to Leiden and other European cities.

BIBLIOGRAPHY

Hittite Art and the Antiquities of Anatolia (exh. cat., London, RA, 1964)

Art Treasures of Turkey Circulated by the Smithsonian Institution, 1966–1968 (exh. cat., Washington, DC, Smithsonian Inst., 1966)

O. W. Muscarella: *Ancient Art: The Norbert Schimmel Collection* (Mainz, 1974)

O. W. Muscarella, ed.: *Ladders to Heaven: Art Treasures from the Lands of the Bible* (Toronto, 1981) [cat. of the Elie Borowski Collection]

The Anatolian Civilisations: Prehistoric/Hittite/Early Iron Age (exh. cat., 18th Council of Europe exh.; Istanbul, 1983)

Schatten uit Turkije/Türkiye'nin tarihi zenginlikleri/Treasures from Turkey (exh. cat., Leiden, Rijksmus. Oudhd., 1986) [trilingual]

Anatolia: Immagini di civiltà: Tesori dalla Turchia (exh. cat., Rome, Pal. Venezia; Milan; Catania; 1987)

Treasures of the Bible Lands: The Elie Borowski Collection (exh. cat., ed. R. Merhav; Tel Aviv Mus. A., 1987)

DOMINIQUE COLLON

Anatomical studies. Depictions of the structure of the human body as shown by dissection. The study of anatomy (Gk.: 'cutting apart') has informed and stimulated European artists since the Renaissance and has also led to many remarkable feats of illustration.

1. Ancient and medieval studies. 2. Renaissance developments. 3. Illustration in the Baroque and Enlightment periods. 4. Romanticism, realism and modern illustration. 5. Anatomy books for artists.

1. ANCIENT AND MEDIEVAL STUDIES. Anatomy was being practised at Alexandria *c.* 300 BC, but no images remain from the Classical world. Illustrations demonstrating anatomy occur in European manuscripts from the 12th century onwards. They are sometimes grouped in a series of five or six diagrams of the complete human figure, each showing a frog-like, or squatting, posture. Examples of this series bear a family resemblance, showing that they were copied from earlier examples. It has been suggested that they derive from early Alexandrian originals. Similarly squatting figures occur in many cultures, possibly without connection. The frog-like series in European, and likewise in Persian and Indian manuscripts, include separate figures for representing the skeleton, arteries, veins, nerves and muscles, and often also a pregnant woman. These figures are not observations of bodily structures as seen in dissection but rather symbolic representations of the subject-matter of anatomy, *aides mémoires*. Sometimes highly schematic, almost geometric, diagrams of the male reproductive system, the brain or eye accompany these series. The figures of pregnant women (*gravidae*) occur not only in manuscripts, from the 14th century, but also in early printed works, notably in the Venetian editions of Joannes de Ketham's works and other medical treatises published in Latin as the *Fasciculus medicinae* (1491) and in Italian as the *Fasciculo* (1493). In the *Fasciculus* the woman has a standard frog-like posture; the *Fasciculo* shows greater sophistication, with the squatting stance justified by placing her on a chair. In both the anatomy is symbolic rather than representational.

The *Fasciculo* includes a dissection scene. Such demonstrations began in Bologna *c.* 1300, at first for medico-legal purposes. They became recognized as essential for medical training at not only Bologna but also Montpellier, Padua, Pisa, Paris and eventually, before 1600, in most universities of western and central Europe. They were formal occasions attended by students, university dignitaries and members of the public, who might be charged admission. Meanwhile the late medieval obsession with death continued into the 16th century, illustrated by skulls, whole skeletons and also *lemurs*—figures risen from the grave as wasted, corrupted bodies or skeletons clothed with remnants of skin and ragged flesh. Both skeletons and *lemurs* had correspondences with anatomical diagrams, whether frog-like or upright. Hans Holbein the younger showed many skeletons in his *Dance of Death* woodcut series (drawings 1523–6; pubd Lyon, 1535), but Death sometimes had two bones in the upper arm and only one in the forearm. Hans Baldung showed Death as a *lemur* in his paintings of *Death and the Maiden* (e.g. *c.* 1509/10; Vienna, Kstmus.).

2. RENAISSANCE DEVELOPMENTS.

(i) Alberti and Florentine followers. Renaissance concerns with the structure and functions of the human body were pursued primarily through observations of ancient sculptures, then of posed and moving naked men and finally through anatomical studies. Ancient sculptures had not been based on human dissection. However, Alberti, writing in 1435, provided a theoretical justification (*De pictura*):

> To get the right proportions in painting living creatures, first visualize their bony insides, for bones, being rigid, establish fixed measurements. Then attach tendons and muscles in their places and finally clothe the bones and muscles with flesh and skin. You may object that ... a painter has no concern with what he cannot see. So be it, but if to paint dressed figures you must first draw them nude and then dress them, so to paint nudes you must first situate the bones and muscles before you cover them with flesh and skin in order to show clearly where the muscles are.

These principles may lie behind the evident interest in human anatomy of Florentine artists. Antonio Pollaiuolo's engraving *Battle of the Ten Nudes* (early 1470s; *see* POLLAIUOLO, (1), fig. 3) shows the superficial musculature of five pairs of nude men. The muscles seem contracted, making the figures unbelievable: moreover, they appear weightless. They may have been drawn from sketches of suspended cadavers. Certainly dissection was carried out on corpses pulled up by ropes (often stabilized by two-point attachment: depicted, for example, in Cornelis Cort's engraving *Academy*, 1578, after Joannes Stradanus). Pollaiuolo's figures are shown as *écorchés* (flayed men); Mayor has suggested that they were drawn not from dissection but from wax models specifically constructed. Certainly sculptured *écorchés* of wax, wood, plaster or metal became essential equipment in Italian studios in the early 16th century (*see* ECORCHÉ).

Signorelli's *Last Judgement* frescoes in Orvieto Cathedral (1500–03) show skeletons emerging from the grave and also many naked men and women after their bones have been 'clothed' by flesh. Signorelli was as incompetent as other contemporaries at drawing the pelvis with any degree of verisimilitude. The devils and male damned are essentially *écorchés*; the male blessed are better fed. The women, saints or sinners, owe little to studies of musculature. Indeed, female nudes, whether sculptured or pictured, derived essentially from the Antique and the living model, rather than from the dissecting room.

Alberti's injunction was also followed by Raphael in one of his pen, ink and chalk sketches for the Borghese *Entombment* (1507; London, BM), where a slumped figure held in another's arms is shown as a skeleton. Like Michelangelo and others, Raphael undertook private dissections, emphasizing the skeleton and the superficial musculature. Leonardo dissected in order to understand, for example, the anatomy and behaviour of the shoulder muscles (see fig. 1); he illustrated these from different points of view, so that structures seen in the round could be reconstructed at leisure. (Adequate techniques for preserving anatomical specimens were not devised until the late 17th century.) Leonardo carried his interest in anatomy far beyond any possible use in figure drawing, recording for instance his observations and experiments on the ventricles of the brain.

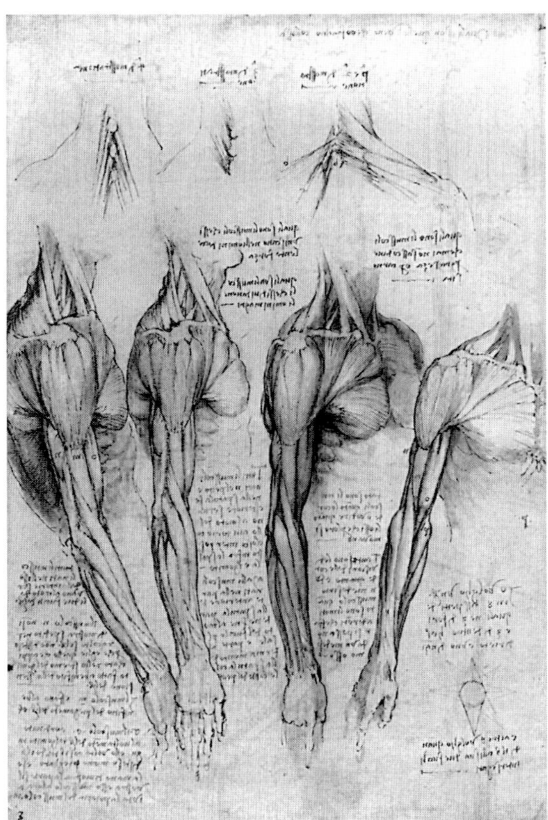

1. Anatomical study by Leonardo da Vinci of shoulder muscles, drawing on paper in pen and ink, with wash modelling over traces of black chalk and small red chalk strokes between the main figures, 289×200 mm, *c.* 1510 (Windsor, Windsor Castle, Royal Library, Leoni vol. 19008*v*)

(ii) Anatomical illustration.

(a) Germany. Although anatomy demonstrated by dissection was part of medical training in German-speaking regions in the 16th century, artists there seem to have been less dedicated to it than those in Italy. Dürer himself saw Leonardo's anatomical notebooks, or at least copies of some of the drawings, but did not himself study anatomy. Other artists of the earlier 16th century did, however, sometimes contribute to academic anatomy. A series of anatomical woodcuts, issued in Strasbourg, Marburg and Paris from 1517, were passed from publisher to publisher, added to and recut. The figures of brain dissections in Dryander's *Anatomia capitis humani* (Marburg, 1536) are particularly dramatic. In Walther Hermann Ryff's *Anatomi* (Strasbourg, 1541), these figures are modified, probably by Hans Baldung. His female figure on a Classical throne is an elegant design—the type of *gravida* familiar from medieval manuscripts and the *Fasciculo*, but clearer and less inaccurate.

Of the many broadsheets issued throughout the 16th century, the most significant early anatomical example was first published by Schott (Strasbourg, 1517) and shows the organs inside the trunk. This and others in the series were the basis of multilayered printed figures in which flaps could be successively lifted to reveal underlying structures—'flap anatomies'. The top layer often showed a male and a female nude, usually seated, sometimes explicitly Adam and Eve, other times figures in a bathhouse etc. The genre culminated in J. Remmelin's *Catoptrum microcosmicum* (Ulm, 1619).

(b) Italy. Berangario da Carpi's *Isagoge brevis* (1522) included illustrations that might 'assist painters in delineating the members'. A remarkable achievement of Venetian artists and craftsmen was the production (1538/9–1543) of hundreds of woodcuts for Andreas Vesalius's *Fabrica* and *Epitome* (both Basle, 1543). These include skeletons and muscle-men dramatically posed against an Italian landscape. The fine cuts in the *Epitome* of a nude woman and of a man, to show surface anatomy, may have been intended, as with da Carpi, to make the book desirable to artists, though Vesalius complained of their presence and arrogance at his demonstrations. Henceforth artists had available an alternative reference source for anatomy: previously many had made use of pattern books that might often contain figures drawn from life, sketches from Classical sculptures and, on occasion, records of dissections. The Vesalian figures were copied commercially many times—sometimes with appropriate acknowledgement (Valderde's woodcuts, Rome, 1556), sometimes without (Thomas Geminus's engravings, London, 1545).

Around 1555 a Roman artist (perhaps Giulio de' Musi) engraved plates for a projected text by Bartolomeo Eustachio (1500–60). These included full-length skeletons, *écorchés* and other muscle-men. The quietly posed figures show none of the energy of the Vesalian woodcuts but would have made an equally important contribution to anatomical studies: however, they were not published until 1714, in Rome.

(c) France. A single-sheet engraving (*c.* 1530) by Domenico del Barbiere is characteristic of the Fontainebleau

school. It shows one skeletal figure from the front and another from the back, both accompanied by *écorchés*. The anatomy book by Charles Estienne and Etienne de La Rivière, *De dissectione* (Paris, 1545/6), was illustrated with woodcuts whose origin, with one or two exceptions, owed nothing to the Vesalian figures. Some came from the workshop of Mercure Jollat. Some of these full-length figures are in the Late Gothic tradition, others in the Fontainebleau style, deriving from illustrations to *Loves of the Gods* by Perino del Vaga.

3. Illustration in the Baroque and Enlightenment periods. In the 17th century, while many illustrations were derived from the Vesalian figures, two wholly original sets of Baroque anatomical drawings were produced. One series of twenty original coloured drawings (*c*. 1618; U. Glasgow, Hunterian A.G.; see fig. 2) has been confidently attributed to Pietro da Cortona; it was engraved about the same time, probably by Luca Ciamberlano, but not published until 1741. The dissected figures were drawn as noble youths posed against Classical masonry in an Italianate landscape. One plate shows a standing young woman holding open the flaps of her own anterior abdominal wall to display the generative organs in the cavity from which the intestines have been removed. The Paduan anatomist Giulio Casserio (*d* 1616) supervised artists, including Odoardo Fialetti, as they drew and then engraved illustrations for a new textbook of anatomy. These were published after Casserio's death, in his and others' names, in 1626/7. The figures are placed, many in extravagant postures, in a detailed landscape. Some images go beyond any concept of reality: for example a pair of dissected legs walks alone towards the viewer, on a hillside with a river scene behind. Also, at the end of the 17th century, a series of large engravings were produced in Paris by the Spanish artist–anatomist Crisostomo Martinez: one, while notably attentive to measurement and proportion, cunningly represents bones and joints as if seen through transparent skin and muscles.

2. Anatomical study attributed to Pietro da Cortona, pen and ink and watercolour, 408×279 mm, *c*. 1618 (Glasgow, University of Glasgow, Hunterian Art Gallery)

Govert Bidloo's *Anatomia humani corporis* (Leiden, 1685) contained over 100 engravings from drawings by Gérard de Lairesse. These were of two kinds: one uses traditional configurations—a skeleton, for example, emerging from a tomb trailing a winding sheet; the other shows dissections realistically in relative close-up—in one case with an accompanying house-fly. Also from the Netherlands came an extraordinary series of engravings illustrating anatomical displays with moral as well as scientific purposes. The displays, for the Amsterdam museum of Frederik Ruysch (1638–1731), were composed of injected and preserved specimens, bones, stuffed birds and so on. One foetal skeleton is shown wiping away tears with an injected omentum as a handkerchief, another holds a miniature sickle—an absurd parody of a grim reaper—another kicks the syphilitic skull of his mother . . . These displays were largely received seriously.

Technical and scientific illustration in the 18th-century Netherlands benefited from the culture's characteristic fascination with appearances. The pre-eminence of the Leiden medical school led to a series of remarkable engravings. The anatomist was Bernard Siegfried Albinus (1697–1770), who worked in the Alberti manner, first displaying the skeleton, which was then 'clothed' with muscles. His patience and that of his artist was immense; from 1725 they implemented a plan to publish an atlas of all human anatomy. The work was still incomplete at Albinus's death. Albinus sought skeletons that met his ideals of anatomical beauty, asking the artist to remove what was less than perfect in the specimen before him. A system of nets was placed before the suspended cadaver: the artist sat drawing square by square. For the plates of the superficial musculature, a thin man stood by in the same posture as the cadaver. Thus a convincing 'life-like' appearance could be given to a figure constructed piecemeal. The artist who stayed with Albinus throughout was Jan Wandelaar (1690–1759). He provided complex backgrounds for his figures, including Classical landscapes with carefully drawn plants in the foreground. Two plates include a rhinoceros (see fig. 3). These plates of 'perfected anatomy' represent a high point in anatomical studies.

In London the surgeon William Cowper contributed to anatomical studies with his illustrations to his *Myotomia reformata* (1724), acknowledging his postures to 'Rafael, Sir Peter Paul Rubens, Guido Reni, Mons. Le Fage; but

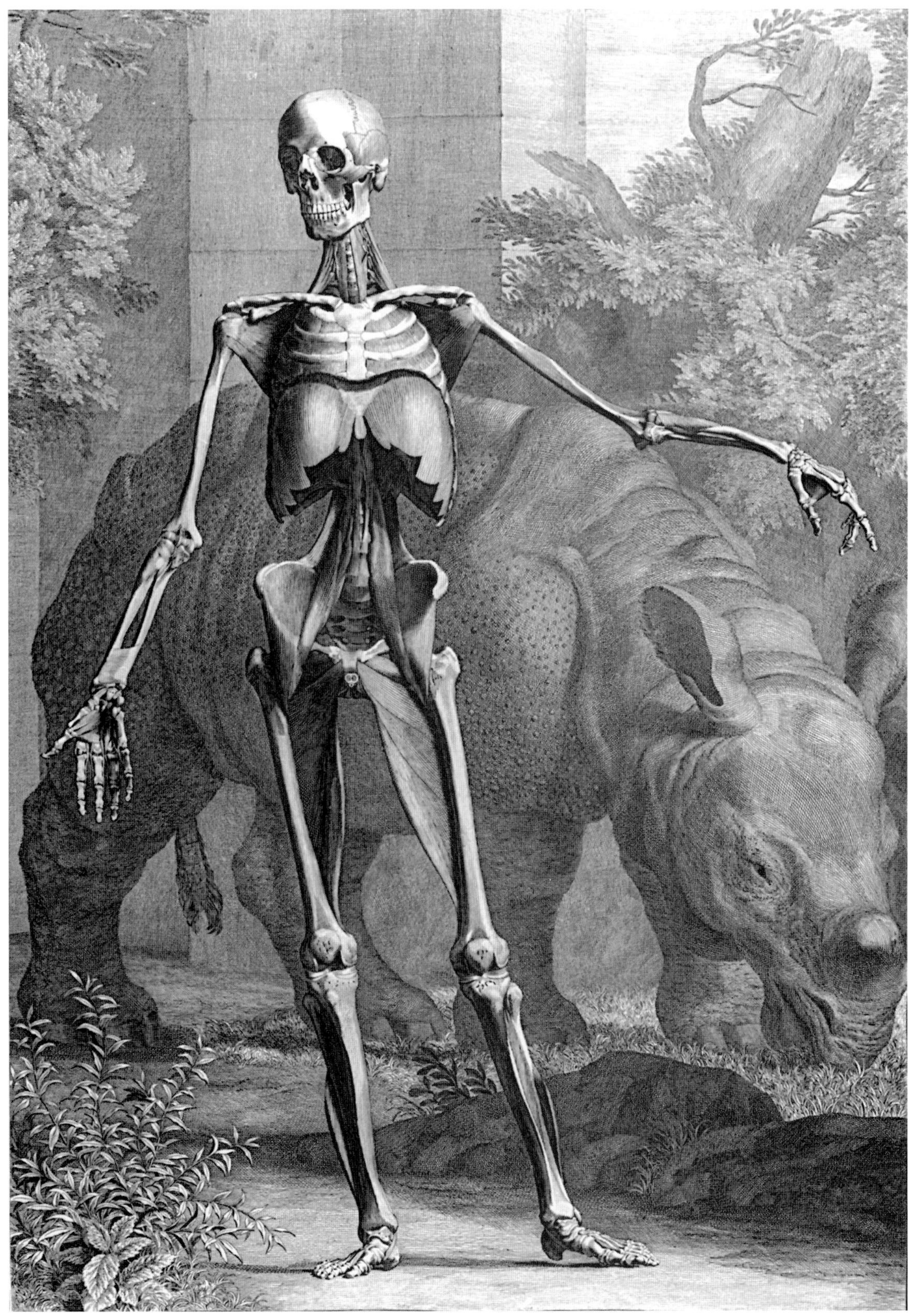

3. Anatomical study by Jan Wandelaar; engraving from B. S. Albinus: *Tabulae sceleti et musculatorum corporis humanis* (Leiden, 1747)

the muscling is done after several human subjects, and not copied from any anatomical book whatever'. William Cheselden's *Osteographia, or the Anatomy of the Bones* (London, 1733) made use of a *camera obscura*; the principal engraver was Gerard Vandergucht. The drawing is careful and sensible, and sometimes affecting as in the skeleton of a praying man—the kneeling position was however chosen to offer a larger scale, rather than for doctrinal reasons. The obstetrical anatomy of 'men-midwives' resulted in a corpus of chalk drawings by a Dutch artist resident in England, Jan van Rymsdyk (many U. Glasgow, Hunterian A.G.), from which engravings were prepared by Charles Grignion, Robert Strange and others: the most important were published in William Smellie's *A Sett of Anatomical Tables* (London, 1754) and William Hunter's *The Anatomy of the Human Gravid Uterus* (London, 1774). Hunter, *accoucheur* to the Queen, was appointed first Professor of Anatomy at the Royal Academy of Arts in 1768. The English painter most outstandingly involved with anatomy at this period was George Stubbs, who, using a methodology similar to Albinus, painstakingly recorded *The Anatomy of the Horse* (London, 1766) and later *The Comparative Anatomical Exposition of the Structure of the Human Body with that of a Tiger, and Common Fowl* (London, 1804–17).

Following Albinus, his pupil Albrecht von Haller (1708–77) collaborated with the draughtsman Joel Paul Kaltenhofer (*d* 1777) to produce a series of fasciculi, *Icones anatomicae* (Göttingen, 1743–56). Among the many illustrated anatomical treatises of Samuel Thomas Soemmerring (1755–1830), one, consisting of a single plate, *Tabula skeleti feminini* (Frankfurt am Main, 1797), was among the few satisfactory engravings of this subject to date, drawn by Christian Koeck of Mainz. Soemmerring had searched for a cadaver of a youthful woman with an 'aptitude for procreation' and 'harmony of her limbs, beauty and elegance of the kind that the ancients use to ascribe to Venus'. This search for a synthesis of scientific accuracy and aesthetic perfection was characteristic of late Enlightenment anatomical studies.

4. ROMANTICISM, REALISM AND MODERN ILLUSTRATION. The Sienese anatomist Paolo Mascagni (1755–1815), collaborating with Antonio Serantoni, prepared large, engraved plates of the whole human body, hand-coloured in thick pigment by Serantoni himself; when three plates are put together they make life-size figures showing particular anatomical structures at different depth of dissection. Many muscles are cut away from their insertions or origins and reflected, sometimes lending the subject strange wing-like projections. Too cumbersome for anatomical reference, the extraordinary enterprise, posthumously printed as *Anatomiae universae . . . icones* (Pisa, 1823), created fantastical images that attracted amazed attention. Mascagni also helped Felice Fontana (1730–1805) on a long-term anatomical project, initiated in 1771, to produce careful, life-size and 'life-like' wax models of dissections (e.g. Florence, Mus. Zool. 'La Specola'), supposedly so as to make the unpleasantness of actual dissections unnecessary. Watercolour drawings were made of each figure, with the parts numbered and, on separate sheets, named. While the style of anatomical representation resembled Cigoli, Eustachio or Albinus, many of the wax models in 'natural' colours appear decadently Romantic and sentimentally funereal. Fontana also supervised the preparation of wooden anatomical sculptures, which could be disassembled into many pieces. In France an anatomical industry was developed in the early 19th century by J.-F. Ameline, Professor of Anatomy at Caen, and by I.-T.-J. Auzoux (1797–1880). The latter devoted himself to developing *papier mâché* anatomical models, influenced by the Italian work. His life-size model of 1830 had 129 major pieces and 1115 numbered details.

Edinburgh and Paris were major international centres for medical study *c.* 1800. In the former, until the Anatomy Acts of 1832, subjects for dissection were often obtained by stealing recently buried bodies from graves, the legal supply from the gallows being insufficient to meet needs. In Paris, however, all bodies of patients who died in the large hospitals could be claimed for anatomical study. John Bell's *Engravings Explaining the Anatomy of the Bones, Muscles and Joints* (Edinburgh, 1784), followed by other volumes, initiated a collection of illustrations of the major bodily systems, drawn by both Bell and his younger brother Charles Bell. The illustrations were certainly not 'perfected anatomy'; rather the actual and disturbing realities of the dissection room were shown. Benjamin Robert Haydon, who made anatomy central to teaching at his London art school, praised these intaglio prints. Charles Bell wrote *Essays on the Anatomy of the Expression in Painting* (London, 1806) and was a candidate for the Professorship of Anatomy at the Royal Academy, supported by members such as Henry Fuseli and John Flaxman who wished to see actual anatomical demonstrations rather than anatomy studied at second hand. The dilemma of anatomical illustration was well expressed by John Bell, writing of the 'continual struggle between the anatomist and the painter; one striving for elegance of form, the other insisting upon accuracy of representation'.

From the 1820s, in Paris first and then elsewhere, numerous atlases of anatomy and surgical anatomy were published with plates printed by lithography: for instance the *Traité complet de l'anatomie de l'homme* (Paris, 1831–54) of Jean-Baptiste-Marc Bourgery (1797–1849) and the artist–anatomist Nicholas-Henry Jacob. Lithography was quicker and less costly than engraving, although the latter had the ability to delineate structures more precisely. In Germany lithography was used to produce large, often life-size monographs such as the folio atlases of Friedrich Tiedemann (1822) on the arteries and of Friedrich Arnold (1834) on the nerves. In London Richard Quain published an elephant folio volume, *Anatomy of the Arteries* (1844), drawn and lithographed by Joseph Maclise (*c.* 1815–*c.* 1880). A realist who imbued his dissected subjects with nobility of face and figure, Maclise issued under his own name *Surgical Anatomy* (1851), commenting in his preface that 'an anatomical illustration enters the understanding at once in a direct passage, and is almost independent of the aid of written language. A picture of form is a proposition which solves itself'. A similar understanding of anatomical studies had been expressed earlier by William Hunter and by Leonardo.

Nineteenth and twentieth-century illustrators of scientific anatomical texts have responded to the challenge of translating the facts of anatomy into a 'universal language' (as Hunter put it) of planar visual representation. Some have used simple, unostentatious wood-engravings to illustrate the topology of regional anatomy—for instance the illustrations to Henry Gray's *Anatomy* (London, 1858). Publishers, particularly in Germany and Austria, have contracted prominent anatomists and teams of artists for many years at a time to make precise drawings summarizing the results of many dissections, resulting in an anatomy 'perfected' by statistical norms rather than by aesthetics. Such drawings were highly coloured in a long-standing convention to differentiate veins, arteries, nerves etc—a useful abstraction, though entirely unlifelike. The text (Vienna, 1937–60) by Eduard Pernkopf (1888–1955) is an example of such methods. The work of Max Brödel (1870–1941) exemplifies the highest traditions of anatomical draughtsmanship. Trained in Leipzig, he moved to Johns Hopkins University in Baltimore.

Photographs of dissected specimens were published from the later 19th century. Stereoscopic atlases were bought by medical schools, but little used by students or teachers. In the 1970s, colour photographic atlases began to appear, pioneered by the coloured atlas of R. M. H. McMinn and the photographer R. T. Hutchings (1977).

5. ANATOMY BOOKS FOR ARTISTS. An early use of the Antique to teach anatomy to artists is found in *Anatomia per uso et intelligenza del disegno* (Rome, 1691) by Bernardino Genga (1655–1734). During the following century a corpus of anatomical work demonstrably of the highest quality was assembled by anatomists collaborating with draughtsmen and engravers. But a problem for artists wishing to refer to such figures was that they were scattered in many expensive books. Large folio publications by J. C. von Loder (Weimar, 1794–1803) and L. M. A. Caldani (Venice, 1801–13) partly resolved this problem, while other books using existing plates included Mascagni's *Anatomia per uso degli studiosi di scultura e pittura* (1816) and J. C. von Mannlich's *Versuch über die Zergliederungskunde für Zöglinge und Liebhaber der bildenden Künste* (Munich, 1812). Lithography was applied by Jules Cloquet in his multi-volume *Anatomie de l'homme* (Paris, 1821–31), which contained classic delineations but added further plates in a Romantic style.

The attempt to provide students studying the Antique with a resolution of the long-standing academic requirement to visualize the skeleton and the muscles beneath the skin was meanwhile pursued by Jean-Galbert Salvage's *Anatomie du gladiateur combattant, applicable aux beaux arts* (Paris, 1812), which was distributed to French art schools. Julien Fau's *Anatomie des formes extérieures du corps humain, à l'usage des peintres et des sculpteurs* (Paris, 1845), was a popular lithographic work in this vein. Other works took an independent approach to artistic anatomy. The remarkable plates by Jacques Gamelin for *Nouveau recueil d'ostéologie et de myologie* (Toulouse, 1779) show skeletons engaged in such activities as reading books. John Flaxman's sketches, engraved by Henry Landseer, in *Anatomical Studies of the Bones and Muscles for the Use of Artists* (London, 1833) owe little to previous work. All these titles represent only a small fraction of artists' anatomy books: this aspect of art history has yet to be investigated in depth.

See also MEDICAL ILLUSTRATED BOOKS, §2.

BIBLIOGRAPHY

A. von Bartsch: *Le Peintre-graveur* (1803–21)
L. Choulant: *Geschichte und Bibliographie der anatomischen Abbildung...* (Leipzig, 1852/*R* 1945), trans. and ed. by M. Frank as *History and Bibliography of Anatomic Illustration in its Relation to Anatomic Science and the Graphic Arts* (Chicago, 1920/*R* New York, 1962)
R. Herrlinger: *Geschichte der medizinischen Abbildung*, i (Munich, 1967), trans. by G. Fulton-Smith as *History of Medical Illustration from Antiquity to AD 1600* (London, 1970)
A. H. Mayor: *Artists and Anatomists* (New York, 1984)
K. F. Russell: *British Anatomy 1525–1800: A Bibliography of Works Published in Britain, America and on the Continent* (Winchester, 1987)
G. D. R. Bridson and J. J. White: *Plant, Animal and Anatomical Illustration in Art and Science: A Bibliographical Guide from the 16th Century to the Present Day* (Winchester, 1990)
I. Bignamini and M. Postle: *The Artist's Model: Its Role in British Art from Lely to Etty* (U. Nottingham, A.G., and London, Kenwood House, 1991)
K. B. Roberts and J. D. W. Tomlinson: *The Fabric of the Body: European Traditions of Anatomical Illustration* (Oxford, 1992)

KENNETH B. ROBERTS

Anaxagoras of Aigina (*fl* first quarter of the 5th century BC). Greek sculptor. The Greek city states that defeated the Persians at Plataia in 479 BC set aside a tithe for Zeus at Olympia from which was made a bronze statue of the god, 10 cubits tall. When Pausanias visited Olympia he saw the statue standing near the Bouleuterion and assigned it to Anaxagoras (*Guide to Greece* V.xxiii.1–3). The base of the statue was inscribed with the names of the dedicating city states. Diogenes Laertius (*History of Philosophy* II.xv) knew the sculptor's name, and Anakreon (*Greek Anthology* I.lv.6) mentioned him in an epigram, but Anaxagoras is otherwise unknown.

BIBLIOGRAPHY

J. Overbeck: *Die antiken Schriftquellen zur Geschichte der bildenden Künste bei den Griechen* (Leipzig, 1868/*R* Hildesheim, 1959), nos 433–6

C. HOBEY-HAMSHER

Anaya, Gustavo Medeiros. *See* MEDEIROS, GUSTAVO.

Ancher. Danish painters. (1) Michael Ancher and his wife (2) Anna Ancher, who were married in 1880, were at the centre of the artists' colony that emerged at SKAGEN in Jutland during the 1870s and 1880s. Their daughter Helga Ancher (1881–1964) was also active as a painter. In 1967 the family home in Skagen was opened as a museum.

(1) Michael (Peter) Ancher (*b* Rutsker, 9 June 1849; *d* Skagen, 19 Sept 1927). He studied at the Kongelige Akademi for de Skønne Kunster, Copenhagen (1871–5), where his teachers Wilhelm Marstrand and Frederik Vermehren encouraged his interest in genre painting. He first visited Skagen in 1874 and settled there in 1880, having found that subject-matter drawn from local scenery was conducive to his artistic temperament. In *Will he Manage to Weather the Point?* (1880; Copenhagen, Kon. Saml.) several fishermen stand on the shore, evidently watching a boat come in. The firmly handled composition focuses on the group of men (the boat itself is invisible); each figure is an individual portrait that captures a response to the moment. Ancher's skill at grouping large numbers of figures with heroic monumentality compensates for his lacklustre colour sense. A change in his use of colour is noticeable in the works produced after an influential visit to Vienna in 1882; he was deeply impressed by the Dutch Old Masters at the Kunsthistorisches Museum, especially the Vermeers. Their effect on his painting can be seen in the *Sick Girl* (1883), a subject he repeated three times (Copenhagen, Stat. Mus. Kst; Skagen, Skagens Mus.; Copenhagen, Hirschsprungske Saml.).

Ancher's eclecticism is also evident in the monumental depiction of his pregnant wife (1884; Copenhagen, Hirschsprungske Saml.; see fig.). Influenced by Dutch and Flemish full-length portraits of the 17th century, he used a black and white colour scheme to enhance the plainness of her gown. The picture also echoes Karel van Mander III's portrait of *Princess Eleanor Christine* (1643–4; Hillerød, Frederiksborg Slot) in its symbolic references: the Princess (daughter of Christian IV) has a tame wolf by her side as an heraldic symbol of her husband; Anna Ancher is accompanied by the family dog, symbolizing conjugal fidelity.

The Brøndum Family, Christmas Day 1900 (1903; Skagen, Skagens Mus.) is Ancher's finest group portrait. Conceived as a modern version of Rembrandt's *Syndics of the Amsterdam Drapers' Guild* (1662; Amsterdam, Rijksmus.; *see* REMBRANDT VAN RIJN, fig. 11), it depicts the female members of his wife's family: his mother-in-law, Ane Hedvig Brøndum, with her daughters Marie, Hulda and Anna and her granddaughter Helga. They are seated around a table, gazing at the same point to the left of the room. Marie has been interrupted in reading from the Bible; the old lady rests her folded hands heavily on the table. The subject is treated with an austere solemnity reminiscent of Rembrandt, together with a keen sense of the character of each member of the family.

Michael Ancher: *Portrait of my Wife*, oil on canvas, 1.80×1.15 m, 1884 (Copenhagen, Hirschsprungske Samling)

(2) Anna (Kirstine) Ancher [née Brøndum] (*b* Skagen, 18 Aug 1859; *d* Skagen, 15 April 1935). Wife of (1) Michael Ancher. She studied drawing at Vilhelm Kyhn's drawing school, Copenhagen (1875–8), and painting under Puvis de Chavannes in Paris (1889). Her genre paintings and portraits are more intimate than those of her husband. Many of her everyday interiors contain a characteristic image of the shadow of window bars on a sunlit wall, displaying her natural skill as a colourist. An exquisite example is the *Blind Woman in her Room* (1883; Copenhagen, Hirschsprungske Saml.), in which the dark, bent figure of an old woman with worn hands is silhouetted against a golden sunlit wall. Women at work, particularly sewing or plucking poultry, are among her favourite subjects, as in the *Girl in the Kitchen* (1883–6; Copenhagen, Hirschsprungske Saml.). The girl stands by the window, turning her back to the viewer and immersed in her daily duties. Her red skirt and black jacket stand out brilliantly against a yellow and orange curtain, enlivened by the sunlight shining on the floor through a half-open door. Like her husband, Anna Ancher was drawn to the work of Vermeer but generally her tastes were not eclectic. She painted several portraits of her mother, one of the last of which dates from 1913 (Skagen, Skagens Mus.); it shows the 87-year-old woman wrapped in blankets and sitting in a chair. The picture may have been influenced by other artists' depictions of the nobility of old age, such as Whistler's famous portrait of his mother (*Arrangement in Grey and Black, No. 1*, Paris, Mus. d'Orsay), but has its own, particularly sensitive handling of the frailty of life.

BIBLIOGRAPHY

K. Madsen: *Skagens malere og Skagens Museum* (Copenhagen, 1929), pp. 21–67

K. Voss: *Friluftsstudie og virkelighedsskildring, 1850–1900* [*Plein-air* studies and representation of real life, 1850–1900], Dansk Kunsthistorie, iv (Copenhagen, 1974), pp. 108–29

——: *Skagensmalerne og deres billeder på Skagens museum* [The painters of Skagen and their pictures at the Skagen Museum] (n.p., 1975, rev. 1986), pp. 53–113

J. Zibrandtsen: *Michael og Anna Anchers Hus Skagen: Kort vejledning gennem samlingerne* [The home of Michael and Anna Ancher: a short guide through the collections] (n.p., 1976)

O. Wivel: *Rejsen til Skagen* [The voyage to Skagen] (Copenhagen, 1977)

M. Loerges: *Et solstrejf i en stue i Skagen: Portræt af Anna Ancher* [A sunfleck in a room: portrait of Anna Ancher] (Copenhagen, 1978)

——: *Michael Ancher* (Copenhagen, 1984)

K. Voss: *Die Maler des Lichts: Nordische Kultur auf Skagen* (Weingarten, 1990)

E. Fabritius: *Michael Anchers ungdom 1865–80* [Michael Ancher's youth] (Skagen, 1992)

JENS PETER MUNK

Ancher, Sydney (Edward Cambrian) (*b* Sydney, 25 Feb 1904; *d* Newcastle, NSW, 8 Dec 1979). Australian architect. After graduation from the Sydney Technical College in 1929, Ancher travelled in Europe. He formed a partnership with Reginald Prevost in Sydney, 1936–9, and in

1946 established Sydney Ancher and Partners. Ancher's most influential work, principally his early houses, combines the visual characteristics of the International Style with a sensitive response to Australia's geography (*see* SYDNEY SCHOOL). These glass-walled houses have flat or concealed low-pitched roofs, and sheltered terraces and courtyards that extend the open-planned interiors, providing convenient areas for outdoor living. Their white geometric forms contrast with and complement their bush settings, for example numbers 1, 2 and 4 Maytone Avenue, Killara, Sydney (1946–8). In later years Ancher experimented with broken roof forms and bright colours: his own houses at Coffs Harbour (1958), and Camden (1972), both NSW, illustrate these characteristics that were, in part, derived from a closer interest in the Australian rural vernacular.

Ancher's architecture, though radical for Australia in the 1930s and 1940s, appears conservative when compared with the work of his younger contemporary, Harry Seidler. He was less interested in the sculptural, structural and functional expressions of modern architecture than in its potential for formal beauty and relaxed planning for pleasant living conditions. Balancing international and regional influences, Ancher's architecture provided a sound basis for modern design appropriate to the Australian environment.

UNPUBLISHED SOURCES

C. Boeson: *Sydney Ancher: A Profile* (diss., U. Sydney, 1979)

BIBLIOGRAPHY

Contemp. Architects

J. Taylor: *An Australian Identity: Houses for Sydney, 1953–63* (Sydney, 1972, rev. 1985)

JENNIFER TAYLOR

Ancheta [Anchieta]**, Juan de** (*b* Azpeitia, Guipúzcoa, *c.* 1540; *d* Pamplona, 30 Nov 1588). Spanish sculptor. His works in alabaster and wood in the north-east region of Spain decisively influenced late 16th-century sculpture in that area. Echoes of major Italian sculptors' works strongly suggest that he trained in Italy, although there is no evidence of this. By 1565 Ancheta was in Valladolid, but shortly after this he is likely to have assisted GASPAR BECERRA on the retable at S Clara, Briviesca. Becerra's grandiose Roman Mannerist style, imbued with the Classicism of ancient Roman and Italian Mannerist sculpture, lies behind Ancheta's art. He probably also worked with Becerra around 1558 on the retable in Astorga Cathedral. He continued to be active in and around Valladolid and at Burgos and was named in Juan de Juni's will as the only sculptor capable of completing Juni's retable at S Maria del Mediavilla in Medina de Ríoseco, although this was actually completed by Esteban Jordán. From about 1575 to 1578 Ancheta worked on the chapel and retable of the Trinity in Jaca Cathedral. The figure of God the Father directly recalls Michelangelo's *Moses* (1510s; Rome, S Pietro in Vincoli).

In 1578 or 1579 Ancheta settled in Pamplona and remained there until his death. The retables on which he worked during the 1580s in Cáseda, Navarre, in the parish church of Aoíz and in the church of S Maria at Tafalla are seminal works that embody his monumental style. In his wood and alabaster retable of *St Michael* (*c.* 1580) at La Seo, Saragossa, the high reliefs of pairs of apostles are dramatic Spanish interpretations of the work of Donatello, Jacopo della Quercia and Michelangelo. Ancheta's pupil, Pedro González de San Pedro (*fl* 1592–6), completed the retable at Tafalla after his master's death, and other local followers perpetuated his style into the early 17th century.

BIBLIOGRAPHY

Ceán Bermúdez

J. Camón Aznar: *El escultor Juan de Ancheta* (Pamplona, 1943)

J. M. Azcárate: *Escultura del siglo XVI*, A. Hisp., xiii (Madrid, 1958), pp. 301–10

F. Checa: *Pintura y escultura del renacimiento en España, 1450–1600* (Madrid, 1983)

MARJORIE TRUSTED

An Ch'i. *See* AN QI.

Anchi. *See* KAIGETSUDŌ, (2).

An Chung-sik [*cha* Uksang, Kongnip; *ho* Shimjŏn, Pulburong, Purija, Purong] (*b* Sunhŭng, 1861; *d* 1919). Korean painter. He excelled in landscapes, figures, flowers and birds, as well as in many styles of calligraphy, and was among the very last court painters of the Bureau of Painting (Tohwasŏ; *see* KOREA, §X, 1) at the end of the Chosŏn period (1392–1910). In 1881 he was sent as a draughtsman to Tianjin in China with a group of men to learn the technique of producing modern weapons. In 1900 he painted the royal portrait of Kojong (*reg* 1864–1907). Perhaps as a reward for this assignment he was appointed magistrate of the county of Yangch'ŏn and T'ongjin in Kyŏnggi Province. In 1911 he and his contemporary Cho Sŏk-chin were the leading teachers at the Sŏhwa misulwŏn (Academy of Calligraphy and Painting), newly established in Seoul to train artists, among whom were Yi Sang-bŏm, Pyŏn Kwan-sik, No Su-hyŏn (1899–1978) and Kim Ŭn-ho. An and Cho were also closely involved in the Sŏhwa misulhoe (Calligraphy and Painting Arts Group). An thus became a bridge between the late Chosŏn and the modern period.

An Chung-sik's *Ch'ungyŏng Sansudo* ('Spring landscape'; 1915; Seoul, N. Mus.) is rendered in his typically decorative and meticulous style. In his vision of a monumental imaginary landscape, in his composition and his fantastic mountain forms, An revealed his indebtedness to his teacher, the court painter CHANG SŬNG-ŎP. As he often did, An built up his imaginary mountain forms with a series of overlapping folds, which are carefully outlined in long lines of light ink. Each mountain fold is coloured vivid green and sprinkled with small dots. Blossoming trees with pink and white flowers dotting the foreground and the middle ground enhance the decorative quality of this work. Although it is an imaginary landscape, the forms used are not as unreal or visionary as in some of An's other works, such as *Asking the Way to The Peach Blossom Land* (hanging scroll, ink and colours on silk, h. 1644 mm, 1913; Seoul, Ho-am A. Mus.; 1979–81 exh. cat., fig. 253). The stylized horizontal bands of clouds in the background and the naturalistic spatial recession can also be seen in his best-known work, *Mt Paegak in Early Spring* (colour on silk, 1.25×0.51 m, 1915; Seoul, N. Mus.), which, however, is not an imaginary scene but an important site in Seoul (the mountain is more generally known as Pugak). The tops of tall trees and the stone image of a mythical beast (*haet'ae*) in the foreground lead the viewer's eye through a long, wide avenue to the Kwanghwa Gate, behind which the Kyŏngbok Palace occupies the middle ground. Mt Paegak looms majestically in the background. This work is significant not only because it depicts the Kwanghwa Gate and many buildings of the Kyŏngbok Palace that were moved or demolished in 1917 to make way for the buildings of the government-general of imperial Japan, but also because An combined traditional brush conventions with Western linear perspective and shading, anticipating an important trend in modern Korean painting.

BIBLIOGRAPHY

E. McCune: *The Arts of Korea: An Illustrated History* (Rutland and Tokyo, 1962)
Yu Pok-yŏl: *Hanguk hoehwa taegwan* [Pageant of Korean painting] (Seoul, 1969), pp. 948–58
Choi Sunu [Ch'oe Sun-u]: *Han'guk misul och'ŏnnyŏn* [5000 years of Korean art] (Seoul, 1979), p. 294
5000 Years of Korean Art (exh. cat., San Francisco, CA, Asian A. Mus.; Seattle, WA, A. Mus.; Chicago, IL, A. Inst., and elsewhere; 1979–81)
Ahn Hwi-joon [An Hwi-jun], ed.: *Sansuhwa* [Landscape painting], ii (1982), xii of *Hanguk-ŭi mi* [Beauties of Korea] (Seoul, 1977–85), pp. 204–8, 263

KIM KUMJA PAIK

Ancient Near East. Area of the ancient world that extends from Turkey in the west to Iran in the east (see fig. 1). Although the term Near East is often synonymous with Middle East, the adjective 'ancient' is always attached to Near East, and 'Ancient Middle East' never occurs. The term Western Asia is sometimes preferred. The ancient history, arts and architecture of the countries in this area are treated elsewhere in this dictionary under the headings ANCIENT ANATOLIA, SYRIA–PALESTINE, MESOPOTAMIA and ANCIENT IRAN. Vast though this area is, the cultures and civilizations that flourished in the Ancient Near East from prehistoric times to the early centuries AD often exerted an influence that reached still further. In general, however, peripheral regions, such as Arabia and Afghanistan, are not included in this survey. From the time of the campaigns of Alexander the Great (*reg* 336–323 BC) to the Islamic conquest in the mid-7th century AD, regions of the Near East came under a succession of influences from the west: the arts of the Hellenistic world are discussed under ANCIENT GREECE, the Roman provinces under ANCIENT ROME and the Christian era under EARLY CHRISTIAN AND BYZANTINE ART.

This article focuses on such topics as trade and the use of writing, which apply to the Ancient Near East as a whole, and on the development of certain arts for which a general view is most revealing.

GENERAL BIBLIOGRAPHY

H. Frankfort: *The Art and Architecture of the Ancient Orient*, Pelican Hist. A. (Harmondsworth, 1954, rev. 4/1970)
J. B. Pritchard: *The Ancient Near East in Pictures Relating to the Old Testament* (Princeton, 1954, rev. 2/1969)
S. Lloyd: *The Art of the Ancient Near East* (London, 1961)
W. Orthmann, ed.: *Der alte Orient*, Propyläen-Kstgesch. (Berlin, 1975)
P. Amiet: *L'Art antique du Proche Orient* (Paris, 1977; Eng. trans., New York, 1980)

I. Introduction. II. Arts. III. Rediscovery.

DETAILED TABLE OF CONTENTS

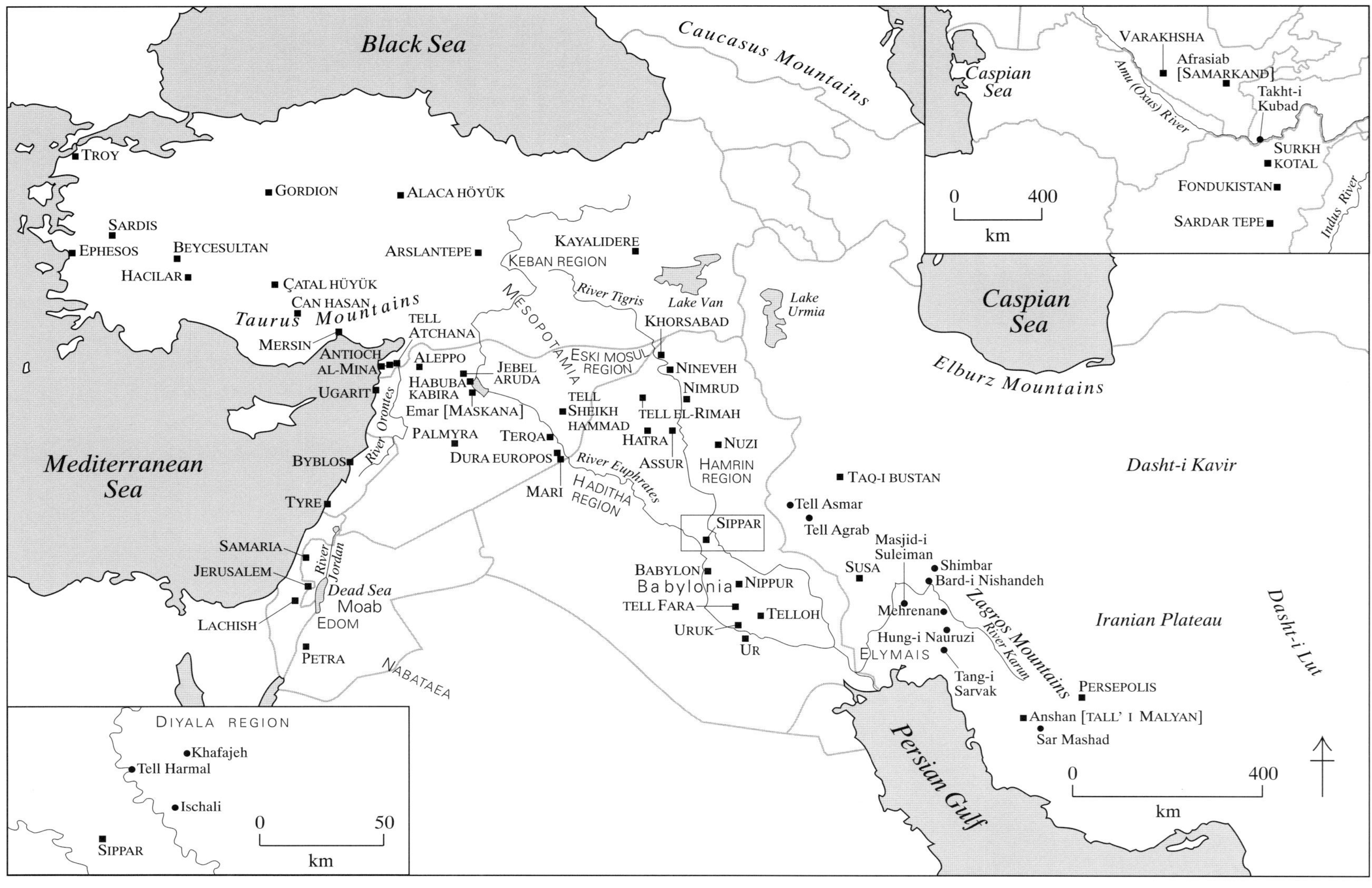

1. Map of the Ancient Near East; those areas and sites with separate entries in this dictionary are distinguished by CROSS-REFERENCE TYPE

I. Introduction.

1. Geography and trade. 2. Archaeology and dating. 3. Development of writing.

1. GEOGRAPHY AND TRADE. The Ancient Near East is considered here in terms of cultural and artistic developments rather than as a geographical entity, and its physical boundaries are in any case ill-defined. The main geographical features of the several distinct regions that comprise the Ancient Near East—Turkey east of the Bosphorus, Syria, Lebanon, Israel, Jordan, Iraq and Iran—are discussed in the articles on those regions, which are also illustrated with maps.

In understanding the development of the Ancient Near East as a whole, one of the most important factors is the existence of extensive trade routes, often indicated archaeologically by the discovery in an unexpected context of artefacts or materials characteristic of another culture or area. A famous example of a trading emporium is the Assyrian merchant colony at KÜLTEPE in central Anatolia, set up in the early 2nd millennium BC. The records of this trade survive, written on clay tablets in the Mesopotamian cuneiform script, which had been developed in the second half of the 4th millennium BC precisely for the purposes of trade and administration (*see* §2(i)(b) below). One of the materials traded at Kültepe was tin for making tin bronzes: the source of this tin may have been northern Afghanistan, which also produced lapis lazuli. This latter was imported into Mesopotamia from as early as the 5th millennium BC onwards and was re-exported, often in the form of scrap lapis lazuli (old seals and pieces of inlay), as hoards found at el-Tod in Egypt (*c.* 1900 BC) and Thebes in Greece (late 13th century BC) testify. Other early imports from the east included barrel-shaped cornelian and agate beads, probably from the region of the Bay of Cambay on the west coast of India, and in about 2600 BC etched cornelian beads were imported into Mesopotamia from India. Beads of amazonite (a pale green stone) may have come from the Urals or Kashmir, and a similar source is probable for a late 8th-century BC fine Neo-Assyrian cylinder seal of green garnet (see fig. 20 below). Cloves from the East Indies were reportedly found in an 18th-century BC context at Terqa on the Middle Euphrates in Syria.

There were two overland routes: one passed through Bactria (now in Afghanistan) and northern Iran, and the second went through Shahr-i Sokhta in eastern Iran and then south of the central Iranian desert via Tepe Yahya (where chlorite vessels were manufactured for export in the mid-3rd millennium BC), Anshan and Susa. A maritime route through the Indus Valley, Makran (the south coast of Iran) and Bahrain or Failaka in the Persian Gulf (referred to in the cuneiform texts respectively as Meluhha, Magan and Dilmun) led up the River Euphrates to the harbours of Ur. Water buffalo represented on seals (see fig. 12 below) suggest that around 2300 BC these animals were being imported from the Indian subcontinent for the zoos of the Akkadian kings of central Mesopotamia. The presence of Indus Valley seals in western Iran and Mesopotamia, in contexts dating to the second half of the 3rd millennium BC, indicates the period when this trade was particularly active. By the beginning of the 2nd millennium BC the islands of the Persian Gulf were handling the trade, and their seals have been found in Bactria, India and southern Mesopotamia and were copied in central Anatolia.

There were also major overland trade routes along the Tigris and Euphrates rivers and across northern Syria. Goods from the east were bartered with imports from the west that reached the ports of the Levant, particularly Byblos, in the 3rd and early 2nd millennia BC, then Minet el Beida (the harbour of Ugarit) and finally, in the 1st millennium BC, the Phoenician harbour towns of Tyre, Sidon and Arvad. In order to handle this foreign trade, the merchants of the Levant developed the alphabet as an alternative to the cumbersome syllabic cuneiform and hieroglyphic scripts of their neighbours (*see* §3 below). The underwater excavation of shipwrecks off the south coast of Turkey illustrates the hazards of such maritime trade, as well as the cargoes carried. These included large quantities of copper, tin and glass ingots, elephant and hippopotamus ivory, pottery—some of intrinsic value and some in the form of containers for wine, oils, perfumes, cereals, textiles and opium—manufactured goods of every description, Baltic amber, lapis lazuli from Afghanistan, Egyptian ebony and gold and cedar-wood from the Lebanon. Trade also went overland through Anatolia: from Europe across the Bosphorus or the Dardanelles and from Turkestan through the Caucasus. Much of this trade was channelled through the narrow pass across the Taurus Mountains, known as the Cilician Gates, and through the Syrian Gates across the Amanus Mountains, reputed as a source for silver.

Finally, it should be remembered that it is only since the invention of steam-propelled boats and trains in the 19th century AD that transport and travel have drastically altered. Such travellers through the Near East as Marco Polo, the Elizabethan ambassadors to the courts of the Tsar, the Shah and the Sultan, or even those who adventurously set out on an extended Grand Tour in the 18th and 19th centuries AD, were undertaking far more perilous ventures than their counterparts in the 19th and 18th centuries BC, when the merchants of Kültepe flourished.

BIBLIOGRAPHY

J. D. Hawkins, ed.: 'Trade in the Ancient Near East: Papers Presented to the XXIII Rencontre Assyriologique Internationale: U. Birmingham, 1976', *Iraq*, 39 (1977)

G. Bass: 'Oldest Known Shipwreck Reveals Splendours of the Bronze Age', *N. Geog.*, clxxii (1987), pp. 692–733

2. Archaeology and dating.

(i) Sources. The two most important archaeological sources for dating in the Anceint Near East are ruin mounds and cuneiform tablets. Ancient ruin mounds, among the most characteristic features of the Near Eastern landscape, are known as *hüyük*, *höyük*, *tepe* or *depe* in Turkish and related languages and as *tell* or *tal* in Arabic. These words linked to a place-name almost invariably mean that there is an ancient site near by. The excavation of these mounds, by both archaeologists and looters, has produced almost all the surviving architectural remains and artefacts from the Ancient Near East. The mounds are generally known in English by the Arabic term *tell*, and they consist of the successive accumulation of building levels and occupational debris. A similar build-up occurs in old towns and cities throughout the world, though the tell formation is unknown outside the Ancient Near East, some parts of Eastern Europe and Egypt (especially the Nile Delta): it is not clear why tells do not occur in other areas, such as Cyprus, where conditions are similar.

Tells are particularly large where wood and stone are scarce and unbaked mud-brick is the principal building material. When a house is rebuilt, the wooden roofing materials, window-frames, lintels and doorjambs are reused (the mud-brick cannot be reused), and the building is flattened to make a platform for the new construction. Within this platform, however, the lower courses of the original building remain intact, and archaeologists can recover its ground-plan. In the case of the wholesale destruction and abandonment of a site, due to attack or fire, the walls of the rubble-filled buildings may survive to a considerable height, and evidence of vaulting or roofing may be preserved. If a site was abandoned in a hurry, and no looting was involved, the archaeologist will find the pottery, furnishings and personal effects of the owners. In the case of a fire, carbonized wood may preserve the form of artefacts, which would otherwise have perished.

Tells are situated near a source of water and the largest are strategically placed near a river crossing or on a main highway. As successive generations build and rebuild their houses, the level of the tell rises, and the slopes become steeper. Thus, although the site becomes easier to defend, the space at the top of the tell becomes smaller and the journey for water and down to the fields more arduous. As a result, houses are terraced into the sides of the mound, and others are built round its base, sometimes forming an abutting tell. The archaeologist therefore has to determine which buildings, at different levels, are in fact contemporary. This problem is compounded by the fact that major buildings, such as palaces and temples, were generally better built, with thicker walls often incorporating baked brick, and therefore outlasted several levels of less substantial housing. Since floors and walls often had to be annually replastered, to ensure that a building remained weather-proof, the number of such replasterings can give an idea of the lifespan of a building.

The approximate range of periods when a site was occupied can be established by examining the sherds of pottery that always litter an ancient site, and the pattern of distribution of tells of different periods gives a clear idea of the density of population in a given area at a given time. Similarly, the distribution of new types of pottery, sometimes associated with new burial customs and occasionally overlying destruction levels, will indicate the arrival and spread of new ethnic groups. The grey wares and cremation burials of the Indo-European tribes, which entered Iran in the second half of the 2nd millennium BC, are a good example.

Tells are still growing today, although the widespread use of concrete may halt the phenomenon. Many modern villages and towns crown the tops of tells, or jostle on their lower slopes. Modern Damascus has completely obscured its ancient tell, whereas the huge tell of Erbil rises in the middle of the modern city, with the fortified old town on its summit. In selecting a tell for excavation, therefore, the archaeologist has to find one where the levels that interest him or her are not only present but are not obscured by too many later levels of occupation.

The cuneiform system of writing on clay tablets (*see* §3(i) and (ii) below), developed in the second half of the 4th millennium BC, has provided a chronological tool of unparalleled accuracy, since these clay tablets have survived when other, more perishable materials have vanished. The earliest readable cuneiform texts are in Sumerian, and the system was subsequently adapted for writing many other languages in different parts of the Ancient Near East, such as Semitic Akkadian, Hurrian, Hittite, Urartian, West Semitic dialects, Elamite and Persian, until it was gradually superseded by alphabetic scripts during the 1st millennium BC (*see* §3(iv) below). Alphabetic scripts, however, were unfortunately often written on perishable materials. Writing was at first primarily used to record trade transactions, and tablets accompanied consignments traded from one area to another, thus helping to establish chronological links. Historical texts appear towards the mid-3rd millennium BC, and these, together with later lists of kings, have produced an extremely accurate sequence of absolute dates (*see* §(ii) below).

(ii) Establishing a chronology. The prehistoric chronologies of the Ancient Near East (see fig. 2) do not differ from prehistoric chronologies elsewhere in the world. Absolute dates are based on radiocarbon techniques and, from *c.* 3500 BC onwards, on dendrochronology (*see* Technical examination, §VII, 3). Such artefacts as flints can be grouped into sequences of development that can be related to typologies in neighbouring areas. In conjunction with the series of levels identified in tells, such data can be used to create a framework for a relative chronology, which may be anchored at various points by reference to absolute dates obtained by other methods.

The most valuable artefact in this context is pottery, much of which was made for everyday use and discarded when broken. Variations in the methods of manufacture,

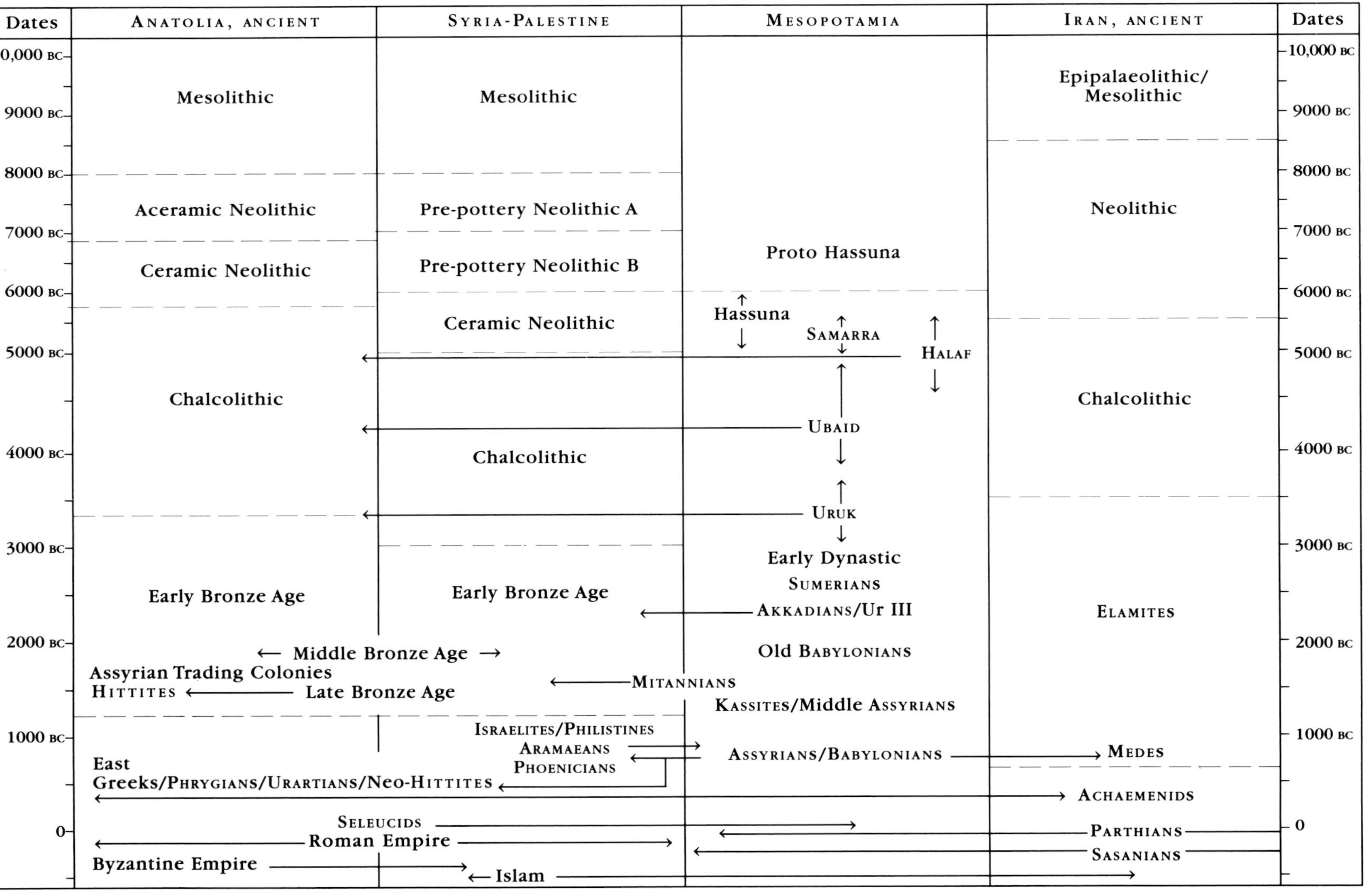

2. Chronological table of the Ancient Near East showing the main periods, cultures and civilizations; those that have separate individual entries in this dictionary are distinguished by CROSS-REFERENCE TYPE

types and sources of clay, shapes and decoration can be recorded and built into sequences, and since many goods were traded in pottery containers, correlations between areas and trade patterns can be established. Burials containing groups of artefacts can also be dated through associated pottery, although some particularly fine objects occasionally buried with the dead as heirlooms can distort a chronology.

The earliest absolute date is provided by records on cuneiform tablets of the sighting of the planet Venus in the reign of the Babylonian king Ammisaduqa. Unfortunately, there are three possible dates for these sightings, and his reign can be dated to 1702–1682 BC, 1646–1626 BC, or 1582–1562 BC, depending on whether the high, middle or low chronology is used. In articles in this dictionary covering the Ancient Near East (*see also* ANATOLIA, ANCIENT; IRAN, ANCIENT; MESOPOTAMIA; and SYRIA-PALESTINE) the middle chronology is used.

Synchronisms with Egypt are also useful, since this was another literate society from which many documents survive and whose sequence of dynasties can also be closely dated. An important synchronism is provided by cuneiform tablets found at El Armana in Egypt and written in Akkadian, the *lingua franca* of diplomacy throughout the Ancient Near East in the 14th century BC: they were sent by the kings of Babylonia, Assyria, Mitanni, Hatti (i.e. the Hittites) and others, and also by the governors of vassal cities in the Levant.

In this way, artefacts occurring in contexts that can be dated by written evidence can be used to date similar objects from contexts that cannot be so dated. One category of object, namely cylinder seals (*see* §II, 1(ii) below), can be particularly well dated, since the use of seals is closely related to writing. As a result, radiocarbon dates in much of the Ancient Near East from *c.* 2500 BC onwards are of limited value: the margin of error is greater than that for absolute dates based on textual evidence.

The development of metalwork has been used since the early 19th century for establishing broad categories in a relative chronology: Chalcolithic (Copper Age); Bronze Age, divided into Early (EB), Middle (MB) and Late (LB) with numerous subdivisions; and Iron Age. These are used in ancient Anatolia, Syria-Palestine and Iran for those periods where more refined chronological systems are unavailable, but the dates assigned to them vary according to the area in question and the scholarly consensus. In the chronological table adopted here an attempt has been made to use convenient absolute dates for the beginnings and ends of periods, without reference to contentious subdivisions.

BIBLIOGRAPHY

S. Lloyd: *Mounds of the Near East* (Edinburgh, 1963)

A. L. Oppenheim: *Ancient Mesopotamia*, app. J. A. Brinkman (Chicago, 1964, rev. 1977), pp. 335–48

W. Hayes, M. B. Rowton and F. H. Stubbings: 'Chronology', *Cambridge Anc. Hist.*, I/i (Cambridge, 1966), pp. 173–285

R. W. Ehrich, ed.: *Chronologies in Old World Archaeology*, 2 vols (Chicago, 1992)

DOMINIQUE COLLON

3. DEVELOPMENT OF WRITING. Unquestionably the most significant craft to originate in the Ancient Near East was writing. It may have been diffused from a single point of origin or independently invented in several different centres, but by the end of the 2nd millennium BC it was used throughout the region, and it played a most important role in all the more advanced societies.

Ancient writing was practised on various materials, the durability of which affects its survival. The use of clay in Mesopotamia and its culturally dependent areas, and the exceptional aridity of the Egyptian climate, which preserves normally perishable materials, have ensured that the formative and subsequent stages of writing in these two important areas are well represented. Elsewhere conditions of survival have been less favourable, but most ancient writing systems have probably left at least scanty traces: there is no reason to suspect the existence of major systems now entirely lost.

(i) Antecedents. The earliest phase of writing seems to have developed in Mesopotamia from a system of clay tokens used for counting, which are found widely distributed from the 4th millennium BC onwards. These were sometimes enclosed in hollow clay balls with seal impressions on the outside, and the advance from this to drawing the tokens with markings of numerals on a solid clay tablet was a short but significant step towards abstraction. It appears that such archaic tablets served as a limited form of accounting, and they have been found at Uruk in levels IV and III, and at Jemdet Nasr (*c.* 3200–*c.* 2800 BC). They range from small tablets with one or two signs to larger ones, divided into compartments with multiple entries. The signs are linear, partly pictographic (i.e. recognizable for what they represent) and partly identifiable as antecedents of later forms in the developed script (see fig. 3). Some are pictograms, such as the signs for 'cow' and 'jar', and some are ideograms (a foot means 'go', 'walk' or 'stand', a star means 'sky' or 'god'): together they are termed logograms (word-signs). Logographic systems provide no evidence in themselves of the language represented by the signs; for instance the pictograms of a cow can be 'read' in any language. Thus there is no firm evidence that tablets from the period termed Protoliterate (late 4th millennium BC–early 3rd) are to be read in Sumerian, so that the invention of writing cannot be ascribed categorically to this people.

(ii) Cuneiform. To the succeeding Early Dynastic period in Mesopotamia (*c.* 2900–*c.* 2340 BC) belong many groups of tablets and inscribed artefacts from such sites as Ur, Telloh, Tell Fara and Abu Salabikh. For the first time it is possible to identify the language of the texts unambiguously as Sumerian, due to the development of a system of syllabograms (sound-signs) alongside the word-signs. This was achieved by divorcing selected word-signs from their meaning and using them simply for their sound, in most cases clearly those of the corresponding Sumerian words: for example the sign *an* ('sky') writes the syllable *an*, and the sign *du* (a foot representing 'go') writes the syllable *du* (see fig. 3a). This made it possible to write undrawable concepts, such as personal names and grammatical elements, and so to write connected sentences clearly.

Concurrently with this internal development, the script underwent external changes. The linear signs came to be rendered by short strokes of the stylus leaving wedge-shaped marks in the clay, giving the script its characteristic appearance and its name, cuneiform (wedge-shaped). For

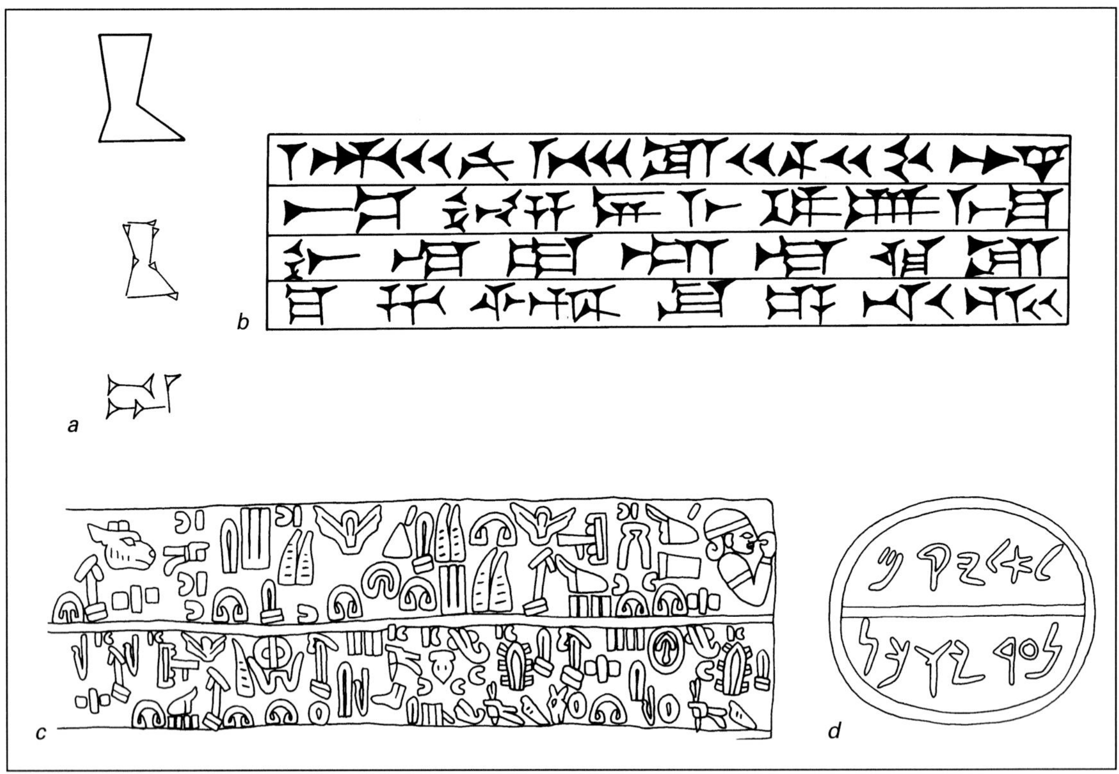

3. Forms of writing in the Ancient Near East: (a) a foot, read in Sumerian as *du* ('go'), *gin* ('walk') and *gub* ('stand'), represented (from top to bottom) in pictogram, *c*. 3000 BC; early cuneiform, *c*. 2400 BC; later cuneiform, *c*. 2000 BC onwards; (b) Neo-Assyrian inscription on a relief of King Sennacherib, *c*. 704–681 BC; (c) parts of two lines of a Hittite hieroglyphic inscription, *c*. 900 BC; (d) seal impression inscribed in the Phoenician alphabet, 6th century BC

practical reasons the direction of the writing was altered to horizontal lines running left to right, which reorientated the signs backwards by 90°. These two developments obliterated any surviving pictorial character in the signs. The script thus evolved was essentially for clay, but was also used from earliest times for formal inscriptions, for example on stone or metal, where the wedge-shapes seen on the clay were imitated. Its use on Assyrian reliefs (see fig. 3b and MESOPOTAMIA, fig. 15) demonstrates this.

During the Early Dynastic period the script began to be adapted for languages other than Sumerian, for instance at Ebla in north Syria, where a large, undisturbed palace archive housed tablets written in Sumerian and in a West Semitic language known as Eblaite. Subsequently, under the Dynasty of Akkad (*c*. 2340–*c*. 2200 BC) the script was fully adapted for writing the East Semitic Akkadian, which henceforth in its two dialects, Assyrian and Babylonian, became the main language of Mesopotamia as Sumerian declined into a 'dead', purely literary language. The cuneiform script was also adapted to write other languages: towards the end of the 3rd millennium BC, Elamite and Hurrian; in the 2nd millennium BC, Hittite and the other Anatolian languages; and in the 1st millennium BC, Urartian.

(iii) Other scripts. From about 3000 BC writing began to appear elsewhere. At Susa, capital of Elam in south-west Iran, and at several sites eastwards across the Iranian plateau, archaic tablets have been found inscribed in a linear script different from that of Uruk. Like the latter, it cannot be read, but the documents also appear to be accounts. Since it is later than Mesopotamian writing, the script is regarded as a short-lived local construct influenced by Mesopotamian developments. In the later 3rd millennium BC Elam used a poorly known linear script alongside a developed version of Mesopotamian cuneiform that became predominant and remained in use for almost 2000 years.

The undeciphered Indus Valley script, represented by many short inscriptions on seals and dockets, occurs in the mid-3rd millennium BC, when contact with Mesopotamia is attested. It too appears to be an indigenous construct made under external influence, either by sea from Sumer or overland through Iran.

Mesopotamian influence is evident in Egypt at the end of the Predynastic period (*c*. 3100 BC), in the form of brick architecture, cylinder seals and distinctive artistic motifs. At this time the earliest Egyptian forms of writing also appear on stone monuments: but although the concept of writing may have derived from Mesopotamia, the hieroglyphic script is of purely indigenous construction, with word-signs pictorially rendered from the world of the Nile and sound-signs based on the Egyptian language (*see* EGYPT, ANCIENT, §XI). Cursive forms for writing on papyrus are known as hieratic and demotic, and documents in these forms circulated widely in the eastern Mediterranean and the Levant, though survivals are sparse. Unlike cuneiform, however, it appears that the Egyptian script was not suitable for writing another language and was never directly borrowed.

Other scripts that appeared in the Mediterranean world during the 2nd millennium BC, such as those of Crete and Cyprus, were probably devised with a knowledge of Egyptian writing. In Anatolia a native hieroglyphic script was developed, apparently by the Luwian people of the west coast, to whose language the script remained tied. This was adopted by the kings of the Hittite empire for their seals and monumental stone inscriptions. After the fall of the empire and the disappearance of the Hittite language, written in cuneiform on clay, hieroglyphic Luwian survived as the script and language of the Neo-Hittite states of south-east Anatolia and north Syria until their destruction *c.* 700 BC. Lengthy inscriptions, with the signs carved in relief (see fig. 3c), are distinctive of this period (for illustration *see* CARCHEMISH).

(iv) The alphabet. Egyptian hieroglyphic also penetrated into Sinai, where many inscriptions dating from *c.* 2700 to *c.* 1000 BC have been found at the turquoise mines of Serabit el-Khadim. Alongside these are a few poorly preserved graffiti in a script designated Proto-Sinaitic, which is of great importance. The signs appear to be modelled on selected forms from the Egyptian hieroglyphic signary, and attempts have been made to identify them with early forms of alphabetic letters and to read them on that basis, though with limited success.

During the course of the 2nd millennium BC the regions surrounding the Levant employed various expanding writing systems, all of which were known in the Levant itself, as has been established by the discovery of stray examples there. One remarkable development was the indigenous script of Ugarit *c.* 1400 to *c.* 1200 BC. This is a signary of external cuneiform appearance, written on clay tablets, but internally an alphabet, arranged in the same order as the later Phoenician–Hebrew alphabet. Stray graffiti on contemporary artefacts across the Levant indicate that a form of alphabet was already in existence, and that alphabetic literacy was widespread in the area in the later 2nd millennium BC. Most of the evidence for this must have been lost on a perishable medium, perhaps papyrus. The origin of this 'Proto-Canaanite' alphabet has been much debated and an ultimate connection with Egyptian hieroglyphic, perhaps through the intermediary of Proto-Sinaitic, looks probable.

The alphabet, even in its earliest forms, is a very different instrument from the cumbersome mixed word- and syllable-sign writing systems with several hundred signs. Its repertory of less than 40 signs of simplified forms makes it much easier to learn and to write, and the numerous graffiti point to a widespread and popular use. By *c.* 1100 BC the Phoenician–Hebrew–Aramaic alphabet had emerged, being attested in its earliest form in a series of stone inscriptions from Byblos. Although it was not bold enough for successful use as a monumental script, some fine carved inscriptions have survived on seals (see fig. 3d) and sarcophagi (*see* SIDON, fig. 1). Thereafter, as transformed by the Greeks, Etruscans and Romans in the early 1st millennium BC, it became the alphabet known today.

BIBLIOGRAPHY

J. D. Hawkins: 'The Origin and Dissemination of Writing in Western Asia', *The Origins of Civilization*, ed. P. R. S. Moorey (Oxford, 1979), pp. 128–66

M. A. Powell, ed.: 'Aspects of Cuneiform Writing', *Visible Lang.*, xv (1981), pp. 319–440

J. Naveh: *Early History of the Alphabet* (Jerusalem, 1982)

J. Oates, ed.: 'Early Writing Systems', *World Archaeol.*, xvii/3 (1986) [whole issue]

J. T. Hooker, ed.: *Reading the Past: Ancient Writing from Cuneiform to the Alphabet* (London, 1990)

D. Schmandt-Besserat: *From Counting to Cuneiform* (Austin, TX, 1992)

J. D. HAWKINS

II. Arts.

1. Seals. 2. Glass. 3. Ivory. 4. Jewellery. 5. Faience. 6. Textiles. 7. Dress. 8. Coins. 9. Mosaics. 10. Furniture. 11. Musical instruments.

1. SEALS. In the context of the Ancient Near East the term 'seal' refers to an object of stone or other hard material, incised with a design (intaglio) that can be impressed on clay to leave the design in relief (the sealing). (In some fields of study the impression itself is also referred to as a 'seal'.) Seals carved in relief (cameo) rather than incised were rarely made in the Near East before the Hellenistic period (323–27 BC). The word 'glyptic' is often used as a general term relating to seals, impressions and sealing practice. Seals were employed to mark ownership, to witness legal transactions and as amulets and charms. Stamp seals may also have been used with dyes or stains as devices for body decoration or textile printing, or as bread stamps, but no evidence has survived. Since seals were made to be impressed, the designs are generally reversed, and it is the design as it appears on the impression that is normally described. There are major published collections of Ancient Near Eastern seals in the Pergamonmuseum in Berlin, the British Museum in London, the Louvre in Paris and the Ashmolean Museum in Oxford.

(i) Stamp. (ii) Cylinder.

(i) Stamp. This type of seal produces an impression from a single incised face stamped into clay, in contrast to cylinder seals, which are rolled (*see* §(ii) below). The restricted carving surface means that isolated motifs and eventually inscriptions, rather than complex imagery, were the norm. Forms were highly varied, and shape is as important as design in the classification of stamp seals.

(a) Early development, before the 4th millennium BC. During the prehistoric period (before *c.* 3400 BC), stamp seals, the use of which for sealing is attested, are best known from north Iraq, north Syria and south-east Anatolia. They evolved from pendants carved with designs that probably originally combined a glyptic and an amuletic role. During the 7th and 6th millennia BC any functional distinction between pendants, amulets and stamp seals and the symbolic interpretation of the motifs on them is conjectural. Mesopotamian pendants of the Halaf to Ubaid periods (*c.* 6000–*c.* 3500 BC) are of simple, mostly geometric forms (hemispheroid, lentoid, lunate and conoid), often with linear markings (see fig. 4). These forms can be linked to the 8th- to 4th-millennia BC clay tokens (the Near

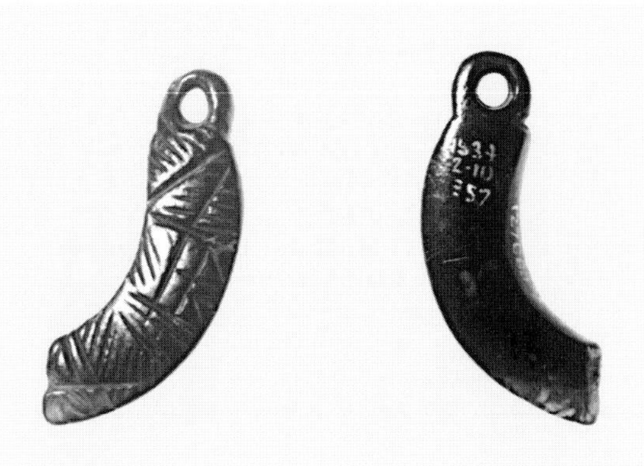

4. Mesopotamian amulet with linear markings (obverse and reverse), black stone, from Arpachiyah, Iraq, 5th millennium BC (London, British Museum)

Eastern recording system that preceded writing) and to the earliest stamp seals with suspension loops. Simple clay tokens, some of which could also be strung, were used for the symbolic representation of commodities (e.g. incised cones for bread); thus early pendants and stamp seals of similar forms may have had a similar symbolism, if not function.

The first attested impressions of geometric and animal motifs made by stamp seals appear in the 7th millennium BC at Buqras in Syria. Prehistoric seals took numerous forms, and the commonest materials were soft stones, such as steatite. In the 6th millennium BC small pebble-like seals are found, with perforated ledge handles and crossed-line or circle-and-dot motifs (Amuk A and B). By the 5th and 4th millennia BC (Ubaid period) there had been a broadening of the repertory to include designs of animals with humans, snakes and birds, and hemispheroid, lentoid and tabloid seal shapes (Değirmentepe; Tepe Gawra, levels XV–XIII). Gable-shaped seals with deeply carved animal motifs became characteristic of north Syria and south-east Anatolia (Amuk E).

(b) Types and distribution, 4th millennium BC *and after.* In the 4th millennium BC indigenous traditions of stamp seals developed, with seals made of steatite, talc, serpentine, marble and chert. In the Khabur at Tell Brak there was a vogue for animal-backed seal amulets (see fig. 5), hemispheroid and kidney-shaped stamps with animal motifs. The animal-shaped seals may have symbolized votive offerings of animals; but they may also be related to later amulets and seals, for which prophylactic and magical properties are attested in texts (for instance bull, lion and goat, symbolizing strength; or fish and frog for fertility). Original, abstract designs were impressed on funerary jars at Byblos in the Levant. In southern Mesopotamia (Uruk, levels VIII–III) hemispheroids and ovoids were drilled with stylized animal motifs. In Iran characteristic button-shaped seals and hemispheroids bore the most vivid imagery in the contemporary stamp repertories (see fig. 6) consisting of geometric, animal, human and demonic motifs (Susa A–B, Tepe Giyan, Parchinah), cultic scenes and heroes with animals (Susa D). From Arslantepe in Anatolia there are circular impressions on bullae with vivid animal subjects.

Stamp seals were generally superseded by the cylinder seal (*see* §(ii) below) in Mesopotamia and southern Iran during the second half of the 4th millennium BC, a development that has been closely linked to the expanding administrations of Uruk and Susa and the apparently greater functional flexibility of sealing with a cylinder. Much later (8th century BC onwards) stamp seals were readopted, under Western influence, by Assyria and Babylonia and used concurrently with cylinders.

During the 3rd millennium BC there was only sporadic use of stamps in Mesopotamia and Iran. Along the Persian Gulf there emerged an important group of steatite dome-backed stamps with animal imagery, possibly related to Indus Valley seals, and later with cultic imagery. In Anatolia stamps served different functions. There are two stone stamps with a square and a lozenge base, tall perforated handles and geometric designs from Beycesultan. Baked clay stamps with deeply incised abstract patterns from Ahlatlibel, Arslantepe and Kusura were probably used for stamping textiles in the continuation of the Neolithic tradition of Çatal Hüyük.

Although in Anatolia the stamp was the dominant seal type from the prehistoric period onwards, the period *c.* 1810 to *c.* 1750 BC was characterized by an unprecedented range and quality of imagery, forms and materials. Proto-Hittite knob- or hammer-handled seals (see fig. 7) have circular, oval or lobed bases carved with geometric or animal designs (Boğazköy, Kültepe, level Ib; and Alişar Hüyük, where soft stones or clay were used), or with ritual and mythological scenes in a modelled style with much use of spiral ornament (Acemhöyük and Karahöyük,

5. Mesopotamian animal-shaped seal amulet (with impression), cream stone, 28×38×17.5 mm, from Tell Brak, *c.* 3500–3000 BC (London, British Museum)

6. Ancient Iranian hemispheroid stamp seal (with impression), black stone, 38.5×39.0×14.0 mm, from Nihavend, *c.* 3500–3000 BC (London, British Museum)

7. Proto-Hittite knob-handled stamp seal (with impression), beige stone, 25×19 mm, from Anatolia, *c.* 1810–1750 BC (London, British Museum)

probably mainly of haematite). Between *c.* 1650 and *c.* 1450 BC the first inscribed stamps appeared: hammer-shaped seals have figural motifs in circular bands around central symbols and Hittite hieroglyphic signs (Boğazköy). From the time of the Hittite empire (*c.* 1450–*c.* 1200 BC) there is an important series of royal seals, sometimes made of metal, with a cuneiform inscription around a central group of Hittite hieroglyphs, and sometimes divine or royal figures and the winged sun-disc (Boğazköy). Soft stone lentoids with hieroglyphs on both sides (generally only a name and title) are numerous.

The use of scarabs as seals in the Near East is attested from *c.* 2000 BC onwards and spread to the Levant *c.* 1900 BC, where the scarab eventually became a major seal form (there are examples from Jericho, Megiddo, Hazor, Tell el Ajjul, Tell Farah South, Ruweise, Byblos). This seal shape, modelled on the dung beetle, derives from Egyptian funerary amulets of the late 3rd millennium BC (*see also* SCARAB). In Egyptian mythology the dung beetle symbolized rebirth, and scarabs were considered talismanic and could be inscribed with good luck wishes. Near Eastern scarab seals were inscribed with royal and personal names and with mazes, scrolls, spirals, floral and hieroglyphic motifs (see fig. 8). They were predominantly made of burnt steatite, but bone, ivory, amethyst and jasper were also used in the Egyptian Second Intermediate Period (*c.* 1630–*c.* 1540 BC). A distinctive linear style of carving known as Hyksos, depicting walking animals, humans, deities and hieroglyphs in broad outline, was characteristic of scarabs from the Nile Delta and Palestine. During the second half of the 2nd millennium BC the introduction of mould-made faience seals led to a progressive decline in quality. The scarab shape was revived in the Levant in the 1st millennium BC, culminating in some particularly fine examples of green jasper, with complex Egyptianizing or Greek-inspired motifs, which were widely distributed in Phoenician colonies throughout the Mediterranean in the 5th and 4th centuries BC.

The scaraboid type was derived from the scarab and retained the beetle shape, while losing details of the original. It is characteristic of Syria–Palestine in the 1st millennium BC. Scaraboids can be divided into two series: common and inscribed/decorated, each with combined sealing and amuletic functions. The former are a popular type, made of bone, steatite or serpentine, and portray simple animal and human motifs (Tell Farah North, 10th–8th centuries BC). The latter are high-quality royal, official or personal seals, made of semi-precious materials (chalcedony, jasper, agate, cornelian, glass), inscribed in various West Semitic scripts, which enable them to be attributed to the kingdoms of Israel and Judah, to Syria (see fig. 9), Ammon (Transjordan), Edom and Moab (east of the Dead Sea) from the 9th to the 6th centuries BC. Motifs are varied, with a marked preference for Egyptianizing themes (winged scarabs, falcons, the child Horus, lions, sphinxes). The scaraboid, with the conoid, became the most common stamp form throughout the Ancient Near East in the 1st millennium BC, carved in a variety of local styles.

The first written references to seal rings occur in Syria in the 18th century BC (*Archives royales de Mari*, xxiii, Paris, 1984, nos 535, 540), and impressions of the inscribed signet ring of King Niqmaddu have been found on tablets of the 14th century BC from Ugarit (Ras Shamra). Simple, non-figured lentoids, made of bone, terracotta, diorite and serpentine, were used in the 1st-millennium BC Neo-Hittite states of north Syria and south-east Anatolia. From the 10th to 8th centuries BC ridge, knob, stud (with and without grooves), pyramid, gable and fist-backed stamps are known, with circular, trefoil, triangular or oval bases. Designs are reminiscent of the prehistoric repertory, with single or multiple animal motifs carved in a deeply incised

8. Scarab seal (with impression), burnt steatite, 24.0×16.5×11.0 mm, from the Levant, mid-2nd millennium BC (London, British Museum)

9. Scaraboid stamp seal (with impression), showing inscription in the Phoenician alphabet ('Elishegub daughter of Elishama'), red jasper, 21×16×10 mm, from Syria, first half of the 1st millennium BC (London, British Museum)

10. Neo-Babylonian pyramidal stamp seal with octagonal base (with impression), grey chalcedony, 29×21×14 mm, 7th–6th centuries BC (London, British Museum)

11. Sasanian domed stamp seal (with impression), grey chalcedony, 20×24×17 mm, 4th–5th centuries AD (London, British Museum)

style (Amuk, Zincirli, Deve Hüyük). In Palestine conoid seals were used, with simple animal motifs (Tell Farah North). By the 7th century BC conoids, scaraboids, scarabs (see above) and, to a lesser extent, tabloids, pyramids, fists and zoomorphic forms, carved in Palestinian, Phoenician, north Syrian and Neo-Assyrian styles, had become standard and widely dispersed throughout the Near East. Materials ranged from bone to soft (steatite, serpentine) and hard stones (chalcedony, agate, jasper) and other materials (bronze, faience, glass). In Mesopotamia the readoption of stamp seals in the 8th century BC in the Assyrian court administration indicates a significant change in sealing practice, probably influenced by Syria. The motif of a king grappling with a lion remained the standard stamp seal device on so-called 'royal' seals until Assur-etil-ilani (*reg c.* 626–623 BC). Ordinary conoid and duck-shaped stamps (the latter also a weight shape), carved in linear, modelled, drilled-and-cut styles and made of chalcedony, rock-crystal and agate, became common from the late 8th century BC onwards and were used concurrently with cylinder seals. Motifs were simple: deities, their symbols (see fig. 10), worshippers and real and imaginary beings. Under the Achaemenid empire, in the 6th to 4th centuries BC, stamps and signets in Iran and Babylonia were reserved for private, non-administrative use. The dominant shape was the conoid, with styles and iconography closely related to those of contemporary Achaemenid cylinders: a royal hero in combat with real or imaginary beasts, hunts, sphinxes. Blue chalcedony and agate were favoured materials. In Anatolia at this time distinctive shapes and designs were developed under Greek influence.

The stamp seals of the Parthians (247 BC–AD 224) are difficult to identify, but the evidence of seal impressions found on Parthian sites indicates the use of signet rings, probably of metal, generally incised with an animal or plant motif. These motifs were also popular on the seals of the Sasanians (AD 224–651). Distinctive domed seals (see fig. 11) and seal-rings carved in hard stones, such as haematite and chalcedony, were produced in large quantities. Ring bezels of cornelian or garnet are also numerous, often carved with a portrait head and an inscription in the Pehlevi script.

BIBLIOGRAPHY

E. Hornung and E. Staehelin: *Skarabäen und andere Siegelamulette aus Basler Sammlungen* (Mainz, 1976)

W. Ward: *Pre 12th-dynasty Scarab Amulets* (1978), i of *Studies on Scarab Seals* (Warminster, 1978–)

B. Buchanan and P. R. S. Moorey, eds: *Catalogue of Ancient Near Eastern Seals in the Ashmolean Museum II: The Prehistoric Stamp Seals* (Oxford, 1984)

O. Tufnell: *Scarab Seals and their Contribution to History in the Early Second Millennium* (1984), ii of *Studies on Scarab Seals* (Warminster, 1978–)

R. M. Boehmer and H. G. Güterbock: *Die Glyptik aus dem Stadtgebiet von Boğazköy*, pt ii (Berlin, 1987)

P. R. S. Moorey: *Catalogue of Ancient Near Eastern Stamp Seals in the Ashmolean Museum III: The Iron Age Stamp Seals* (Oxford, 1988)

M. Rashad: *Die Entwicklung der vor- und frühgeschichtlichen Stempelsiegel in Iran* (Berlin, 1990)

A. von Wickede: *Prähistorische Stempelglyptik in Vorderasien* (Munich, 1990)

H. Keel-Leu: *Vorderasiatische Stempelsiegel*, Orbis Biblicus et Orientalis, cix (Freiburg, 1991)

S. Herbordt: *Neuassyrische Glyptik des 8–7 Jh. v. Chr.*, State Archives of Assyria, i (Helsinki, 1992)

(ii) Cylinder.

(a) Introduction. (b) Types and distribution.

(a) Introduction. A cylinder seal is a small cylinder of stone (see fig. 12), perforated from end to end and carved with a design in intaglio. By rolling it along the clay surface to be sealed, a frieze-like image is produced that proved an ideal medium for the expression of small-scale but immensely varied iconography. Cylinder seals appeared in southern Iraq and south-west Iran in the mid-4th millennium BC. By the beginning of the 3rd millennium BC they had superseded the stamp seal, and they remained the dominant seal shape in Iran, Mesopotamia and Syria until the 1st millennium BC.

12. Cylinder seal (with impression), greenstone, h. 33 mm, *c.* 2250 BC (London, British Museum)

13. Clay envelope of tablet, with seal impressions in Old Assyrian style (bottom) and Anatolian Group style (top), 58×50×26 mm, from Kültepe, 19th century BC (London, British Museum)

Cylinder seals were impressed upon lumps of clay (bullae) used to secure jar-stoppers, door-locks and bales of goods. In conjunction with a person's name, a cylinder seal impression could be used as a signature. From the end of the 3rd millennium BC onwards, letters, administrative and legal texts written on clay tablets, and their clay envelopes (see fig. 13), were the most frequently sealed items. The height and diameter of seals differ according to period and function. Broadly, there was a progression from large, bulky forms to slimmer, more manageable ones. Cylinder seals were often made of attractive or semi-precious stones and could be worn as an adornment that frequently had an amuletic value. Some seals were mounted with gold caps and attached to jewellery or pinned to a garment. Special seals could be inscribed with incantations or used in medical, ritual or prophetic practices. Here the propitious value of different types of stone (e.g. agate, lapis lazuli) was taken into account.

Personal seals are the most common type, and there is no proof of any legal or gender restriction regarding their ownership. The loss of a seal was considered a bad omen and was recorded to prevent illegal use. Official and state seals, including personal royal seals, were used in palace and temple administration, trade and diplomacy. Dynastic seals had often belonged to a ruler's ancestor and thus confirmed the ruler's legitimacy. Special votive seals dedicated to deities were hung round the necks of statues of divinities; often they are very large and carved in relief, for example that dedicated by the Assyrian king Esarhaddon (*reg* 680–669 BC) to the god Marduk (Berlin, Pergamonmus.) was 125×32 mm. Inscriptions are frequently set in vertical panels at one end of the field or are integrated into the design. Most commonly they consist of the owner's name, followed by the father's name, the owner's profession or the formula 'servant of' a given deity or ruler. In some periods there are isolated deities' names and prayers.

Cylinder seals are the most consistent and richest source of knowledge of Ancient Near Eastern iconography. At certain periods they complement other art forms, but at others they are almost uniquely representative. Their repertory is largely religious, with deities and humans in ritual and mythological contexts; secular and decorative subjects are less frequent. Animals and imaginary beings with benevolent or malevolent properties feature prominently, and literary sources or parallels with other art forms are invaluable for interpreting these images. Repertories, like styles, are distinctive, if eclectic, with regions constantly influencing each other. Certain themes are universal (e.g. worshippers being presented before deities, the worship of deities, and ritual meals), while others are symbolic and artistic devices (e.g. combats between heroes and real or imaginary animals) that were often associated with royal or state iconography. Yet other themes were widespread but adapted to suit different ideologies, such as the tree and the winged sun-disc (see fig. 14). Some subjects are specific to certain periods, expressing cultural or geographical traditions or contemporary concerns. Diminutive symbols (divine, astral, votive), often juxtaposed with primary figures, feature to some degree in all periods.

The seal-cutter belonged to a high-ranking professional group of craftsmen, with workshops patronized by the palace or temple. An Achaemenid text states that an

14. Impression from haematite cylinder seal, showing two rulers and suppliant beside tree and winged sun-disc, h. 25 mm, from Syria, 18th century BC (London, British Museum)

15. Impression from white stone cylinder seal, h. 72 mm, from Uruk, second half of the 4th millennium BC (London, British Museum)

16. Impression from gypsum cylinder seal, showing a ritual banquet, h. 41 mm, from Ur, *c.* 2600 BC (London, British Museum)

apprentice took four years to learn his craft. Workshops can be detected by stylistic or iconographic idiosyncrasies, but few records remain of individual artists. Stone, copper or bronze, iron and even wooden gravers, cutting discs and drills (ordinary and tubular, hand-held or powered by the bow) were used for engraving, in conjunction with an abrasive substance. Perforations were drilled from both ends to prevent overheating of the drill and splitting of the stone.

(b) Types and distribution.

Mesopotamia, 4th–3rd millennia BC. Cylinder seals first appeared in the early Uruk period (*c.* 3500 BC) at Uruk and spread northwards along the River Euphrates into Syria and Anatolia soon after. Two styles prevailed in Mesopotamia, each with strong affinities with Iranian glyptic art but with its own iconography. The first consists of modelled, naturalistic and heavily rounded forms carved on large cylinders (*c.* 50–60×20–30 mm). The iconography is dominated by real and imaginary animals (panthers, lions, bulls, antelopes, snakes, griffins) depicted in files being hunted and herded (see fig. 15), and in antithetical heraldic groups. The second group, often given the name Jemdet Nasr, is formed by summarily drilled or incised forms on medium and small squat seals (*c.* 25×20 mm). Characteristic themes are groups of pigtailed figures engaged in domestic or agricultural work, and rows of ovals and schematized fish, scorpions or antelopes. This thematic realism was not repeated in subsequent repertories. The materials used for seals of both types include limestone, serpentine, marble, travertine and lapis lazuli. Some seals are perforated, but some of the larger ones have handles in the form of an animal. In the late Uruk Period (*c.* 3200–*c.* 2900 BC) both these styles continued but with greater iconographic variety. There are also two types of patterns, one being akin to pottery motifs with crosshatching, zigzags and rhombs, and the other having geometric and floral motifs. The latter motifs were deeply incised on burnt steatite seals, which were widely distributed throughout east Mesopotamia, north Syria and south-east Anatolia. In the 3rd millennium BC the use of cylinder seals spread to Egypt (*see* EGYPT, ANCIENT, §XVI, 15), where Mesopotamian cylinders have also been found.

In the succeeding Early Dynastic period (*c.* 2900–*c.* 2334 BC) individual, if connected, styles existed contemporaneously in different regions. This reflected the creation of commercially linked autonomous city states. Seal production was sporadic in the north but prolific in the south. In Early Dynastic I (*c.* 2900–*c.* 2750 BC) the Diyala region north-east of Baghdad produced tall seals in a linear style with patterns of schematic animals and plants (Brocade style), and a delicately modelled style with naturalistic animals. At Ur some seals were deeply carved with abstract designs incorporating human and animal forms with pictograms, while others depict human and animal combats, herding and cultic scenes. On Early Dynastic II (*c.* 2750–*c.* 2600 BC) seals from Tell Fara (for illustration *see* FARA, TELL) slim, linear and loosely grouped figures were later replaced by modelled forms in dense groups showing combats between real and imaginary animals and heroes arranged in friezes. The influence of this glyptic art was widespread and lasted into the succeeding Early Dynastic III period (*c.* 2600–*c.* 2334 BC). Seals from the Royal Tombs at Ur (*c.* 2600–*c.* 2500 BC) are inscribed with royal names (Akalamdug, Meskalamdug, Pu-Abi) and are related in style and composition to the Tell Fara combat seals or depict ritual banquets in a linear style (see fig. 16). Seals of the 1st Dynasty of Ur (*c.* 2500–*c.* 2400 BC), for example those of Mesannipadda or Ninbanda, include heavily modelled combats and a field crowded with diminutive motifs. Seals from Lagash show fully modelled combat scenes, which herald those of the next period. During the Early Dynastic III period inscriptions appear, and a divine iconography is defined with deities distinguished by horned headdresses and solar, vegetal or animal attributes. The cylinders are made of marble, limestone, shell, lapis lazuli and gold, and they have dimensions of 13–25×7–10 mm.

The Akkadian period (*c.* 2334–*c.* 2193 BC) produced some of the most skilfully carved and iconographically varied seals. Their quality made them highly prized, so that inscriptions were often erased (see fig. 12 above) and the seals reused. An early style, dating from the reign of Sargon (*reg* 2334–2279 BC), with stocky, well-defined forms, was replaced by a mature, naturalistically modelled style exemplified by inscribed seals that were produced in court workshops and depict balanced combats between heroes, bull-men, bulls, lions and water buffalo around an inscription. There are also presentation scenes, depicting

17. Impression from Old Babylonian haematite cylinder seal, h. 27 mm, from Sippar, 19th–18th centuries BC (London, British Museum)

18. Impression from Kassite chalcedony cylinder seal, h. 39.5 mm, *c.* 14th century BC (London, British Museum)

worshippers before deities, and mythological scenes, but these are less often inscribed. Regional styles can be identified (e.g. a central Tigris group). Cylinders are large (30–35×15–20 mm), often concave-sided, and made of serpentine, limestone, shell, greenstone, jasper, rock crystal and lapis lazuli.

In the Post-Akkad period (*c.* 2192–*c.* 2112 BC) there was a degeneration in the craft, and seals are small and crudely cut with a narrowed, transitional repertory. The Ur III period (*c.* 2112–*c.* 2004 BC) produced uniform seals distinguished by a delicate, precise carving already apparent in late Akkadian court seals. The iconography is restricted to combats in groups of three, libations before a date-palm altar (a fertility symbol) and presentations to deities or to the king, seated on a stool and distinguished by a round cap. The deification of Ur III kings explains the appearance of royal presentation scenes. Symbols and emblems in the field are limited (lion and eagle standards, dragons, scorpions). Seals are made of chlorite and limestone and measure *c.* 25×15 mm.

Mesopotamia, 2nd–1st millennia BC. In northern, central and southern Mesopotamia during the Old Babylonian period (*c.* 1900–*c.* 1595 BC) different styles, and sometimes iconographies, existed contemporaneously. Sippar had a high standard of carving characterized by modelling and attention to detail. The repertory consists mostly of devotional and supplication scenes involving standing deities (the Sun god and a warrior goddess) and the king, either robed and bearing an offering, or kilted and bearing a mace (see fig. 17). Presentation scenes before seated deities were generally early, and combat scenes are rare. Diminutive symbols are characteristic (fly, monkey, fish, hedgehog, 'ball and staff', sun-disc and crescent, 'bow-legged dwarf'). This iconography was widely diffused through extensive commercial and diplomatic contacts, and it had a strong impact on the repertory of Iran, Syria and Anatolia during the 2nd millennium BC. These seals measure *c.* 25×12 mm, and most are made of haematite. From *c.* 1750 BC the gradual increase in the use of the drill and cutting disc resulted in a deterioration of style.

Most dated seals of the Kassite period (*c.* 1595–*c.* 1155 BC) belong to the 14th to the 12th century BC, although antecedents are found in late Old Babylonian times and in the glyptic art of Hana on the River Euphrates. There were two contemporaneous styles. One is linear, with elongated forms with a supplicant and/or deity and symbols (goat, dog, fly, rosette, cross) beside a lengthy inscription, often a prayer (see fig. 18). The other is more modelled and naturalistic, and scenes have a strong pastoral and mythological bias (birds, floral elements, griffins, genii holding flowing vases). The cylinders are *c.* 35–40×12 mm and made of agate, jasper or chalcedony, often set in gold caps with granulation in triangular patterns. A 12th–10th century BC late or post-Kassite group, carved in a linear style on softer stones or faience, shows predominantly rampant animals beside a sacred tree and has strong affinities with a Middle Elamite group from Khuzistan.

In Assyria, during the Old Assyrian period (*c.* 1920–*c.* 1740 BC), a seal style developed in Assur that was also characteristic of the merchant colonies operating in Anatolia (e.g. at KÜLTEPE). Carving is shallow, angular and linear with schematic elements (nose and hands) and the iconography is a conflation of Mesopotamian and Anatolian subjects (see fig. 13 above). Most common are introductions and the worship of deities, and processions of

19. Impression from Middle Assyrian yellow-brown jasper cylinder seal, h. 28 mm, 13th century BC (London, British Museum)

20. Impression from Neo-Assyrian green garnet cylinder seal, h. 43 mm, *c.* 700 BC (London, British Museum)

21. Impression from Mitannian faience cylinder seal, h. 24 mm, from Tell Atchana, 15th–14th centuries BC (London, British Museum)

supplicants towards the statue of a bull. From *c.* 1810 BC (Kültepe, level Ib) seals are characterized by finer, juxtaposed lines and stronger Old Babylonian influence. In the Old Assyrian period seals measure *c.* 20×8 mm, and haematite is the most common material. Northern Mesopotamia later came under the control of Mitanni and used Mitannian-style seals in the 15th and 14th centuries BC (see below). In the Middle Assyrian period (14th–10th centuries BC) the dated impressions from Assur, Tell el Rimah and Fakhariyah can be divided into three successive groups. Shallow, linear carving of crowded, symmetrical fights between imaginary beasts was replaced in the 13th century BC by delicately modelled carving of animal subjects in lively poses beside trees and bushes (see fig. 19), combats between an armed hero and real or imaginary animals, and rituals before symbols or deities. Seals of the 12th to the 10th century BC are characterized by a heavier but still naturalistic modelling, and the enlarged repertory includes combats, chariot scenes and elaborate rituals. Much of the iconography was transmitted to the repertory of the 1st millennium BC. Seals of the Middle Assyrian period measure 25–30×12 mm and are made of agate, cornelian or marble.

Neo-Assyrian and Neo-Babylonian seals of the 9th to the 7th century BC were cut in four distinctive and partly overlapping styles with regional variations. The linear seals of the 9th and 8th centuries BC varied from shallow outlining to deep gouging in soft materials (steatite, serpentine). The drilled style of the late 9th century BC to the late 8th century BC, in which fine drilling was combined with modelling, was used for high-quality inscribed seals of chalcedony, cornelian and agate belonging to high officials and governors: it continued in a debased, mass-produced form until the 7th century BC. The cut style of Babylonian seals in the 9th and early 8th centuries BC was adopted by Assyria in the late 8th and 7th centuries BC; it was used for both high-quality and mass-produced seals made from hard and soft stones cut with a rotating cutting disc and sometimes enhanced by modelling and by the use of a fine drill. Finally, the modelled style (see fig. 20), which was originally Babylonian, first appeared in Assyria in the mid-9th century BC and lasted there until the 7th century BC. In the four styles outlined here differences between Neo-Assyrian and Neo-Babylonian carving cannot be detected, but there are iconographic distinctions, such as different types of headdress. Themes favoured by, but not exclusive to, one style are: hunts and hunting rituals, banquets (linear); combats (modelled); processions of real and imaginary animals, worship of deities and symbols, and ceremonies beside the sacred tree (all styles). The most common symbols are the spade (representing Marduk), the stylus (Nabu), the fish and goat-fish (Ea), the moon crescent on a pole (Sin) and the star (Ishtar). Cylinders are 15–35×8–12 mm and made of chalcedony, cornelian and serpentine.

Syria–Palestine. Cylinder seals were probably introduced to Syria from Mesopotamia through the Upper Euphrates region and diffused south in the second half of the 4th millennium BC. Syria, and sometimes Lebanon, produced high-quality seals with functions similar to those of Mesopotamia; however, in Palestine they were produced only sporadically, remaining derivative and limited in function. In the 2nd millenniun BC cylinder seals were gradually displaced by stamp seals.

During the late Chalcolithic period and Early Bronze Age (EB) I (*c.* 3500–2750 BC), Euphrates sites, such as Habuba Kabira and Jebel Aruda, adopted a glyptic style similar to that of contemporary Mesopotamia and Elam. Local styles also developed at these sites, in the Amuk region, and at Hama and Byblos. Distinguishing characteristics are angular, low-relief carving, sometimes combined with drilling, V-shaped perforations, looped handles and patterned bases. Surviving cylinders are made of serpentine, marble and bone, but wood was also used. Further south in Palestine, from *c.* 3100 to *c.* 2350 BC, glyptic work is known predominantly from impressions on pottery from Dan to Arad and is mostly concentrated in the north-central zone. Styles are linear and vary in depth of carving, producing different levels of relief. Designs are simple: herringbone, lozenge, ladder and circular patterns, animals in rows or head-to-tail, and rituals with schematic figures joining or raising hands. There are affinities with contemporary glyptic work from Egypt, Syria, Mesopotamia and Elam. This is clearly the result of the commercial interaction that also affected Syria during EB II–III (*c.* 2750–*c.* 2350 BC). Here the themes are broadly derived from the repertory of Early Dynastic Mesopotamia, with the addition of regional characteristics and a greater use of hatched and drilled decoration. The division into registers is often marked by a decorated band. The impressions of seals from Palace G at Tell Mardikh (Ebla) belong to the end of this period and show the survival of Early Dynastic III combat themes combined with original details, including an emphasis on frontality. EB IV (*c.* 2350–*c.* 2000 BC) is poorly represented. Akkadian seals have been found at Mari and Ugarit, but the Ur III style dominated at Mari.

Increased trade led to new styles developing in Middle Bronze Age (MB) I (Old Syrian style, *c.* 2000–*c.* 1850 BC). Earlier themes were revived (rows of animals, banquets) with extensive use of hatching. One distinctively Syrian subject is a single figure drinking from a curved pipe before a bull on a stand. Involvement in Cappadocian trade with Assyria led to the adoption of related styles and iconography. In MB II (Classical Syrian style, *c.* 1850–*c.* 1620 BC) high craftsmanship and iconographic originality combined to make these small haematite seals (15–20×7–9 mm) among the most interesting and appealing of any glyptic group. The discovery of well-dated seal impressions at a number of Anatolian sites, and also at Mari, Chagar Bazar, Tell Mardikh, Carchemish, Ugarit and, for the second part of the period, at Tell Atchana (Alalakh),

22. Impression from quartz cylinder seal, h. 41 mm, from Iran, early 3rd millennium BC (London, British Museum)

has enabled a detailed chronological framework to be established. Syrian iconography is characterized by a blend of original Syrian figures (e.g. the Syrian goddess) with an adaptation of Mesopotamian, Egyptian, Anatolian and Aegean subjects in lively compositions (see fig. 14 above). Royal seals are formalized, the stocky, well-modelled figures gradually being replaced by more elongated ones, but otherwise the repertory is extremely varied. The work of different workshops can be identified, and seals from the Lebanon show strong Egyptian influence. Palestine seems to have imported Syrian seals, though some designs derived from Egyptian scarabs may have been locally manufactured.

After an obscure period, seals of Late Bronze Age (LB) I–II (*c.* 1500–*c.* 1350 BC) show a decline and fragmentation of indigenous production. The overriding influence of foreign styles reflects the political situation. Northern Syria and Mesopotamia were part of the kingdom of Mitanni, whose mass-produced faience seals show varying degrees of modelling and schematization (see fig. 21). The eastern site of Nuzi gradually developed a greater reliance on Sumerian and Akkadian iconographic traditions, and these contributed to a fully autonomous Mitannian style, in which demons and imaginary beings figure prominently: these creatures were to influence Kassite and Middle Assyrian glyptic art. Western workshops at Ugarit and Beth Shan relied more heavily on Syrian iconography, whereas stone seals at these sites betray Egyptian influence. Trade spread the use of cylinder seals to Cyprus, where a distinctive style flourished. From *c.* 1300 BC the growing power of the Hittites in the north (e.g. at Carchemish, Ugarit and Emar) resulted in a modelled court style that included Hittite hieroglyphic and cuneiform inscriptions and a blend of Hittite and Syrian motifs. From the late 2nd millennium BC onwards the stamp seal was predominantly used in Syria–Palestine, but derivative Neo-Assyrian and Achaemenid cylinders also occur.

Anatolia. Stamp seals were the dominant type of seal in Anatolia (*see* §(i) above). Cylinder seals were mostly manufactured to accommodate foreign custom and for commercial reasons, in regions that were in contact with cylinder seal users. The Anatolian Group, the first indigenous style, finely cut in haematite, developed in Cappadocia (Kültepe, *karum*, level II) under the impetus of trade with Assyria *c.* 1920 to *c.* 1840 BC, and it is remarkable for its vivid iconography. The field is filled with irregularly placed multiple scenes and motifs. Much use is made of hatching (see fig. 13 above), and subjects include animals in dynamic poses, processions of deities mounted on animals, armed heroes, and scenes before seated deities. Aspects of this iconography had a strong impact on the contemporary Syrian repertory. In the Hittite Old Kingdom (*c.* 1700–*c.* 1450 BC) cylinder seals with handles and with designs on the base (stamp-cylinders) occur sporadically and are related in style and iconography to contemporary stamp seals. One linear style, with simple animal and guilloche patterns, was present at Boğazköy. There is also an important series, called the Tyszkiewicz group, that has elaborate divine, animal and magical imagery; it is related to the Proto-Hittite stamps from Acemhöyük and has Syrian affinities. (For 13th-century BC Syro-Hittite seals see above.) Stamp-cylinders were also used in Urartu in the 8th and 7th centuries BC.

Iran. The study of glyptic reflects the degree to which Iran was alternately autonomous or subject to foreign influences in different periods. Susa, in the extreme south-west, was at all times most susceptible to Mesopotamian influences but still produced highly original styles.

Between *c.* 3500 and *c.* 3000 BC the styles in south-west Iran were comparable to those at Uruk. Iconographies were also similar, although imaginary animals were favoured in Iran. Between *c.* 3000 and *c.* 2750 BC a highly distinctive style developed, associated with Proto-Elamite tablets. It is characterized by deep, linear carving and heavy, articulated forms (see fig. 22). The iconography is predominantly animal, with bulls, lions and antelopes shown superimposed, rampant, in rows or in human attitudes. This style has a wide distribution from Godin Tepe in the west to Shahr-i Sokhta in the east. Between *c.* 2750 and *c.* 2100 BC Susa was under strong Mesopotamian influence, but a distinctive Elamite iconography developed, depicting deities with a long plait and head-dresses with erect horns. Further east, at Tepe Yahua and Shadad *c.* 2200 BC, there is evidence of an original linear style showing schematic horned deities with sprouting wings and vegetation.

Between *c.* 2100 and *c.* 1450 BC the glyptic of Susa consisted of Mesopotamian imports and locally produced offshoots, often made of bitumen. There are distinctive

23. Impression from Achaemenid blue chalcedony cylinder seal, inscribed 'Seal of Parshandata, son of Artadata', h. 36.5 mm, from Iran, 5th century BC (London, British Museum)

features, such as a hairstyle that bulges out beyond the forehead and a way of holding out both hands with the arms parallel. Royal and official seals show the preservation of a ceremonial weapon and deities seated on coiled serpent thrones. Renewed autonomy is demonstrated at Susa and Chogha Zanbil by Middle Elamite linear, drilled and cut styles on faience or glass seals. These show scenes of banquets, hunting and worship, and rows of animals in an iconography that later influenced Neo-Assyrian glyptic work.

The period *c.* 1000 to *c.* 850 BC is poorly documented. Thereafter Susa imported Mesopotamian seals and produced local imitations favouring the linear style. Between *c.* 625 and *c.* 525 BC a distinctive late Neo-Elamite style developed, with naturalistic, modelled seals depicting hunting scenes, animals and imaginary beings fighting beside a tree. Under the Achaemenid empire stamp seals and signets were generally adopted; the continued use of cylinders was an anachronism peculiar to Achaemenid administration. Modelled carvings on chalcedony, cornelian, agate (often barrel-shaped) and jasper, and a linear style, on dark limestone cylinders, betray a wide range of iconographic influences (late Neo-Elamite, Neo-Assyrian, Greek, Egyptian) that reflect the empire's extent and foreign contacts. A royal hero holding two animals at bay (winged lions, ibexes or sphinxes) was the hallmark of the Achaemenid court style (see fig. 23).

BIBLIOGRAPHY

H. Frankfort: *Cylinder Seals: A Documentary Essay on the Art and Religion of the Ancient Near East* (London, 1939)

E. Porada: *The Collection of the Pierpont Morgan Library* (1948); i of *Corpus of Ancient Near Eastern Seals in North American Collections* (New York, 1948–)

B. Parker: 'Cylinder Seals from Palestine', *Iraq*, xi (1949), pp. 1–43

P. Amiet: *La Glyptique mésopotamienne archaïque* (Paris, 1961, rev. 1980)

D. G. Wiseman: *Uruk—Early Dynastic Period* (1962), i of *Catalogue of the Western Asiatic Seals in the British Museum: Cylinder Seals* (London, 1962–)

R. M. Boehmer: *Die Entwicklung der Glyptik während der Akkad-Zeit* (Berlin, 1965)

N. Özgüç: *The Anatolian Group of Cylinder Seal Impressions from Kültepe* (Ankara, 1965)

B. Buchanan: *Cylinder Seals* (1966), i of *Catalogue of Ancient Near Eastern Seals in the Ashmolean Museum* (Oxford, 1966–)

N. Özgüç: *Seals and Seal Impressions of Level Ib from Karum Kanish* (Ankara, 1968)

P. Amiet: *La Glyptique susienne des origines à l'époque des Perses-Achéménides*, 2 vols, Mémoires de la Délégation Archéologique en Iran (Paris, 1972)

D. Collon: *The Seal Impressions from Tell Atchana/Alalakh*, Alter Orient und altes Testament (Neukirchen-Vlyun, 1975)

M. Gibson and R. D. Biggs, eds: *Seals and Sealing in the Ancient Near East*, Bibliotheca Mesopotamica (Malibu, 1977)

E. Porada, ed.: *Ancient Art in Seals* (Princeton, 1980)

D. Collon: *Akkadian, Post-Akkadian and Ur III Periods* (1982), ii of *Catalogue of the Western Asiatic Seals in the British Museum: Cylinder Seals* (London, 1962–)

——: *The Alalakh Cylinder Seals*, Brit. Archaeol. Rep. (Oxford, 1982)

B. Brentjes: *Alte Siegelkunst des vorderen Orients* (Leipzig, 1983)

C. F. A. Schaeffer-Forrer: *Corpus des cylindres sceaux de Ras Shamra/Ugarit et d'Enkomi-Alasia* (Paris, 1983)

B. Teissier: *Ancient Near Eastern Seals from the Marcopoli Collection* (Berkeley, 1984)

D. Collon: *Isin-Larsa and Old Babylonian Periods* (1986), iii of *Catalogue of the Western Asiatic Seals in the British Museum: Cylinder Seals* (London, 1962–)

R. M. Boehmer and H. G. Güterbock: *Die Glyptik aus dem Stadtgebiet von Boğazköy*, pt ii (Berlin, 1987)

D. Collon: *First Impressions: Cylinder Seals in the Ancient Near East* (London, 1987)

D. M. Matthews: *Principles of Composition in Near Eastern Glyptic of the Later Second Millenium B.C.*, Orbis Biblicus et Orientalis, xviii (Fribourg, 1990)

C. Doumet: *Sceaux et cylindres orientaux: La Collection chiha*, Orbis Biblicus et Orientalis, ix (Fribourg, 1992)

S. Herbordt: *Neuassyrische Glyptik des 8–7. Jh. v. Chr.*, State Archives of Assyria, i (Helsinki, 1992)

D. M. Matthews: *The Kassite Glyptic of Nippur*, Orbis Biblicus et Orientalis, cxvi (Fribourg, 1992)

B. Teissier: *Sealing and Seals on Texts from Kültepe Kārum: Level 2* (The Hague, 1994)

BEATRICE TEISSIER

2. GLASS. The two main periods of glassmaking in the Ancient Near East, the mid-16th century BC to the 13th century BC and the 8th to the 4th century BC, played a leading and decisive role in the early history of glass. The separate development of Near Eastern glass ended with the conquests of Alexander the Great (*reg* 336–323 BC), when glassmaking in most of the area became part of the Hellenistic and, later, Roman tradition.

(i) Before *c.* 1200 BC. (ii) Late 9th century BC and after.

(i) Before c. *1200* BC.

(a) Mesopotamia. Glass was one of the earliest artificial materials; its origin, however, is only vaguely known. Two early glass lumps of uncertain purpose (late 3rd millennium BC) were found at Tell Asmar (anc. Eshnunna) in central Mesopotamia (untraced) and Tell Abu Shahrein (anc. Eridu; London, BM). Glass beads were produced in Egypt (*see* EGYPT, ANCIENT, §XVI, 8) and the Near East during the second half of the 3rd millennium BC and the first half of the 2nd millennium BC, but it seems that glassmaking did not attract much attention during that early stage, and no glass vessels are known from before *c.* 1550 BC. Inventories and word-lists from the late 3rd millennium BC and the first half of the 2nd millennium BC contain Sumerian and Akkadian words that reappear in glassmaking texts of the 14th to the 12th century BC and again in the 7th century BC. At least some of these may refer to glazed materials, if not to glass, being applied later to glass.

Revolutionary changes in glassmaking techniques during the mid-16th century BC were characterized by the invention in the Hurrian areas of north Mesopotamia of elaborate forming techniques and the production of glass in a wide range of colours. The principal innovation was the introduction of core-formed glass vessels: these were manufactured around a metal rod by building up a core in the shape of the hollow space required inside the vessel. The composition of the core was stable enough to allow it to be covered by hot glass and friable enough to be removed after the glass cooled. While still hot and on the core, the vessel was decorated by winding threads or placing blobs of differently coloured glass on its surface and combing them into festoons, feather patterns and the like. The decoration was usually marvered (i.e. embedded) flush with the vessel's surface.

Core-formed pointed bottles and long, straight-sided beakers, with or without button bases (late 16th century BC–early 14th century BC), have been excavated in north Mesopotamian sites such as Nuzi (Cambridge, MA, Harvard U., Semit. Mus.) and Tell al-Fakhar near Kirkuk (Baghdad, Iraq Mus.), Tell el Rimah in the Sinjar region (Baghdad, Iraq Mus.), Tell Brak and Chagar Bazar in the

Khabur Valley (London, U. Coll., Inst. Archaeol.), and Assur (Berlin, Pergamonmus.) and Nineveh (London, BM) in Assyria. Such vessels are usually in blue glass, although white and brown were also used, and decorated with yellow, white, turquoise-blue and red-brown thread decorations or 'eyes' (concentric circlets resembling pupils). The beakers are similar in shape to contemporary, painted pottery in Nuzi ware. The shapes and characteristic decoration employed show that they belong to a homogeneous group produced in north Mesopotamia, probably in the Hurrian kingdom of Mitanni.

A contemporary development is the sudden appearance of objects cast in moulds, such as pendants in the shape of a standing nude female, disc-shaped pendants with an eight-pointed star or plain surface and spacer beads. These were usually made in blue glass and seem also to have come from north Mesopotamia. They remained in vogue until the end of the Late Bronze Age (*c.* 1200 BC). During the 15th century BC marbled and mosaic glass was invented by Mesopotamian glassmakers, possibly Hurrians. A goblet fragment made in marbled red-brown glass, mixed with yellow, dark blue and turquoise-blue segments, was excavated at Nuzi (Cambridge, MA, Harvard U., Semit. Mus.). Mosaic glass involved the building up of a vessel from glass sections of different colours on a core, over which a cover-mould was placed to keep the sections in place during fusion. Hemispherical bowls were made by setting the different sections inside a bowl-shaped mould and inserting a convex mould into it. Fragments of elongated mosaic-glass beakers decorated with chevrons in four colours were discovered at Tell el Rimah (mid-15th century BC–mid-13th century BC; Brussels, Mus. Royaux A. & Hist.; London, BM; Oxford, Ashmolean). Fragments of mosaic-glass bowls decorated with lozenges in three and four different colours (14th century BC; Baghdad, Iraq Mus.) were found in the royal Kassite palace at Aqar Quf. Red glass inlay plaques decorated with birds (?hawks) and geometric patterns in turquoise-blue and white, which were also found in the palace, would appear to be another Mesopotamian innovation.

Fragments of mosaic-glass vessels and inlay plaques adorned with human figures, animals, trees, flowers and geometric patterns, found at Assur in a level dating from the reign of Tukulti-Ninurta I (*reg* 1243–1207 BC), represent the zenith of the technique in Mesopotamia (Berlin, Pergamonmus.). Three fragmentary beakers of this kind have been found as far afield as Hasanlu in north-west Iran (see below).

The imitation of precious materials by this early glass, whether core-formed, cast in moulds, mosaic glass or used for making beads, was considered of greater importance than the achievement of translucency, although such an effect could be produced. The opaque blues are often similar to lapis lazuli or turquoise, while white and red-brown imitate stones in those colours. Yellow may represent an attempt to imitate gold.

Literary sources of the period attest to the flourishing glassmaking activity in Mesopotamia: a few remarkable cuneiform texts give instructions on glassmaking and deal with the composition of different kinds of glass. The earliest date from the Middle Babylonian period (14th–12th century BC; Berlin, Pergamonmus.; London, BM), although unfortunately these cover neither the different uses of glass nor the techniques by which glass objects were made.

The formative and rapid developments in glassmaking in north Mesopotamia from the mid-16th century BC had a direct impact on Egypt and Mycenaean Greece. The introduction of Mesopotamian core-formed vessels in the early 18th Dynasty led to the instigation of the important Egyptian glass industry of the New Kingdom. A few moulded nude female pendants, star-disc pendants, spacer beads and perhaps also blue glass ingots, probably of north Mesopotamian origin, reached Mycenaean Greece and stimulated the appearance of a local industry of moulded glass ornaments (*see* HELLADIC, §IX).

The first period of glassmaking in Mesopotamia ended between the late 13th century BC and the early 12th century BC, following the general upheavals in the Near East. Production ceased for several centuries, as did the associated literary activity. This situation tallies well with the absence of glass from Aegean sites after the collapse of the Mycenaean civilization and in the Levant in the wake of invasions by the Sea Peoples, Aramaeans and the Israelite tribes.

(b) Syria–Palestine. There appears to have been little interest in exported Mesopotamian glass, except perhaps for the nude female pendants, disc-pendants and spacer beads in blue, moulded glass that enjoyed remarkable popularity across Syria and Palestine. Examples have been found as far apart as Maskana, Tell Atchana (London, U. Coll., Inst. Archaeol.), Ebla (Idlib, Archaeol. Mus.), Hama, Byblos (Beirut, Mus. N.), Hazor (Idlib, Archaeol. Mus.), Beth Shan (Jerusalem, Israel Mus.), Megiddo (U. Chicago, IL, Orient. Inst. Mus.), Tell Abu Hawam, Tel Mevorakh (both Jerusalem, Israel Mus.), Gezer, Jerusalem and Lachish (Oxford, Ashmolean).

Mesopotamian core-formed vessels and mosaic-glass objects excavated at Maskana in north-east Syria include a cylindrical vessel in blue glass decorated with yellow sacred trees in yellow-framed rectangular panels. Core-formed vessels reached Tell Atchana further to the west in the plain of Antioch, and numerous fragments have been recovered at various levels (late 16th century BC–13th century BC), including the earliest known example of such a vessel (London, BM) and a pointed bottle decorated with a feather pattern (Oxford, Ashmolean). Similar vessels have not been found at Ugarit or other coastal sites, but a fragmentary long, straight-sided beaker from Megiddo in the shape of Nuzi ware is decorated with rows of white 'eyes' with yellow pupils (U. Chicago, IL, Orient. Inst. Mus.).

(c) Anatolia. Late Bronze Age glass from Anatolian sites is rare. A fragmentary cast nude female pendant, spacer beads and fragments of a Mesopotamian core-formed vessel have been found at the Hittite capital, Boğazköy, which also produced a stone mould for casting spacer beads (Ankara, Mus. Anatol. Civiliz.). A few fragmentary Hittite cuneiform tablets from the same site deal with instructions for glassmaking and seem to be transliterations of contemporary Middle Babylonian texts,

revealing the interest of Hittite scribes in assembling technical information (Berlin, Pergamonmus.).

(d) Iran. Between the 15th century BC and the 13th century BC small quantities of Mesopotamian luxury glass reached Iran. Excavations in the cemetery at Marlik, south-west of the Caspian Sea, produced two splendid mosaic-glass vessels (14th century BC; Tehran, Archaeol. Mus.). The first is a long, straight-sided beaker, resembling Nuzi ware and decorated with red, blue and white lozenges (see fig. 24) in a similar fashion to the 14th-century BC mosaic-glass bowls from Aqar Quf. The second is a cylindrical beaker built up from bichrome twisted threads in white, red, black and yellow glass, which create a herringbone pattern; unpublished examples of similar herringbone ware have been found at Assur (13th century BC; Berlin, Pergamonmus.). Fragments of at least three straight-sided, mosaic-glass beakers from Hasanlu in north-west Iran are decorated in blue, turquoise-blue and white with human figures and pairs of antithetical goats flanking a palm-tree (Tehran, Archaeol. Mus.). Although found in a palace destroyed *c.* 800 BC, close parallels from Assur suggest that they date from the 13th century BC. Other types of

24. Mosaic-glass beaker in red, blue and white glass, h. 163 mm, from Marlik, Iran, 14th century BC (Tehran, Archaeological Museum)

moulded blue glass objects found in Iran include plain and star-disc pendants, demon-mask beads and spacer beads. At Chogha Zanbil, south-east of Susa, the remains of wooden doors (Paris, Louvre) were discovered at the Elamite ziggurat (late 13th century BC). These are ornamented with panels of long tubular glass rods set diagonally. The rods were formed on metal rods and are of opaque dark blue or black glass decorated with a broad white spiral band. They were probably made on the site during its construction, perhaps by craftsmen either of foreign (Mesopotamian) origin or with foreign technical knowledge. A few engraved glass cylinder seals in Elamite style came from the same site.

(ii) Late 9th century BC *and after.* After a hiatus of about four centuries, Near Eastern glassmaking re-emerged in the Neo-Assyrian period with the reappearance of royal courts and of the wealthy society that supported this luxury. Earlier glass objects, such as the mosaic-glass beakers found at Hasanlu (*see* §(i)(d) above) were kept as precious possessions and heirlooms, but it is uncertain whether some glassmaking continued in the intervening period. Various techniques were probably lost and reinvented, but some knowledge was transferred from the Late Bronze Age to the Iron Age glassmakers, although by what means is unknown.

(a) Types and uses. (b) Regions.

(a) Types and uses. The earliest large-scale use of glass in the 1st millennium BC was for glass inlays associated with carved ivories in the North Syrian style, of which numerous examples come from Hasanlu (late 9th century BC; Tehran, Archaeol. Mus.). Carved ivories in the Phoenician style may be divided into two groups. The first (late 9th century BC–first half of the 8th century BC) does not have inlay decoration, but examples from Arslan Tash in north Syria were associated with monochrome and mosaic-glass inlays that were probably used as separate inlays on the same furniture (Aleppo, N. Mus.). The monochrome inlays were cast in moulds, then polished and ground after cooling. Various methods, such as the 'cane technique', were used for mosaic-glass inlays, which include rectangular frames in opaque red or blue glass with a central, square inlay of blue glass decorated with a six-petalled rosette in white. Other inlays are flat semicircular pieces in turquoise-blue or opaque red glass. The sole exceptions are the carved ivories from Arslan Tash showing the 'woman at the window', which are inlaid with a simple strip of colourless to light greenish glass (Aleppo, N. Mus.; Karlsrule, Bad. Landesmus.). Another important collection, similar to examples from Arslan Tash, was found in the palaces of the kings of Israel at Samaria: this includes mosaic-glass inlays with concentric squares and circles, a greenish glass fragment bearing a bird in black and white, and one in blue glass decorated with a floral volute and a lily in white (Jerusalem, Israel Mus.; London, BM).

The second group of Phoenician-style ivories (8th century BC) are richly decorated with glass inlays. Monochrome inlays in various shades of blue, black, red, yellow and green were used for embellishing and accentuating details of figures and flowers, and they contributed considerably to the polychrome appearance of the ivories. In one group the entire design was depicted in champlevé inlays. Examples of Phoenician polychrome inlaid ivories have been found at such sites as SAMARIA, Salamis (Nicosia, Cyprus Mus.) and, unsurpassed in quality and quantity, Nimrud (London, BM). There is a complex association between the ample use of glass inlays in the late 9th century BC and the 8th century BC, the source of the material and its connection with the ivory-carvers. The analysis of inlays from Samaria has established that the glass is of Near Eastern origin (i.e. not Egyptian), thus proving that north Syrian and Phoenician artisans in particular were connected with the reappearance at that time of sophisticated glassmaking. The exact nature of this development, however, is uncertain.

Round cosmetic limestone palettes with a small cavity in the centre, which are commonly found mainly in the kingdoms of Israel and Judah in the 8th and 7th centuries BC, also have plain glass inlays; one example from Megiddo also uses mosaic glass (Jerusalem, Rockefeller Mus.). They are believed to be connected with Phoenicia.

Hellenistic gold-glass (i.e. thin gold foil decorations encased between two layers of colourless or coloured translucent glass) has its forerunners in thin gold foil placed behind the colourless to light greenish glass inlays of Phoenician ivory-inlaid furniture. The elongated strips inlaid in the 'woman at the window' ivories from Arslan Tash are apparently examples of that technique. Rectangular flat and concave inlays in colourless to light greenish glass, bearing painted sphinxes and other designs in Phoenician style, such as those for ivory furniture inlays from Fort Shalmanesser in Nimrud (8th century BC; Baghdad, Iraq Mus.; London, BM; New York, Met.), were probably inlaid with gold foil backing.

The glass bowls that appeared in the second half of the 8th century BC differ considerably from those of the 2nd millennium BC. Although most are simple hemispheres, varying shapes and sizes were also made. These vessels served as costly drinking cups, and closed receptacles are rare. The bowls were cast in moulds, probably using the lost-wax technique, and finished by grinding, cutting, drilling and polishing. The monochrome glass was colourless or light greenish (only rarely blue or purple), and usually translucent, almost clear, in imitation of rock crystal and other translucent stones rather than the opaque turquoise or lapis lazuli that attracted craftsmen of the 2nd millennium BC. The shapes employed are taken from luxury metal and stone vessels.

The largest and most important collection of cast vessels (London, BM) was unearthed in the Assyrian palaces at Nimrud. It includes the Sargon Vase (see fig. 25), a unique translucent, light greenish squat alabastron bearing an engraved inscription, 'Palace of Sargon, King of Assyria' (Sargon II, *reg* 721–705 BC), which was discovered by Austen Henry Layard in 1845–7, and four hemispherical bowls he found in 1851. The full scope and variety of this industry was further demonstrated by Max Mallowan's discovery at the same site of the fragments of some 100 to 140 bowls. Some of these have a diamond-patterned band formed by diagonally cut grooves, and others have square panels cut in relief and engraved figures and flowers similar to Phoenician metal bowls. One bowl was cut, decorated with painted panels and inlaid with a band of

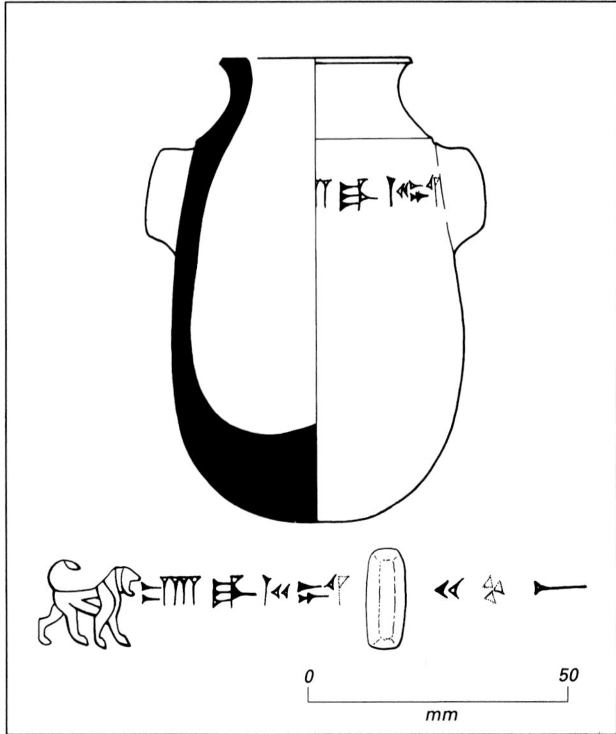

25. Sargon Vase, inscribed 'Palace of Sargon, King of Assyria', cast green glass, h. 88 mm, from Nimrud, Iraq, *c.* 721–705 BC (London, British Museum)

small, square mosaic-glass inlays resembling those with the Phoenician ivories from Arslan Tash. Isolated finds from Nineveh and Khorsabad indicate that such luxury glassware was also used at other Assyrian sites.

Similar glass also reached remote areas. A bowl in colourless glass with radial petals was excavated in a tomb of the late 8th century BC at Gordion in Phrygia (Ankara, Mus. Anatol. Civiliz.). A fragment with a cut diamond pattern (Jerusalem, Rockefeller Mus.) was excavated at Aroer, south-east of Beersheba, and some fragments came from royal tombs (Boston, MA, Mus. F.A.) and royal stores (Oxford, Ashmolean) at Napata-Sanam in Nubia. A colourless hemispherical bowl (Herakleion, Archaeol. Mus.) was found in a tomb (*c.* 735–680 BC) at Fortetsa, near Knossos, and one in blue glass (7th century BC; Rome, Villa Giulia) came from the Bernardini Tomb at Palestrina, Italy.

Some cast and cut vessels have a similar fabric and technique to the glass from Nimrud, but in shapes not found in Mesopotamia. A cut glass jug, for example, from La Aliseda in Spain, which had connections with Phoenicia, is made of light greenish glass and bears a corrupt Egyptian hieroglyphic text (Madrid, Mus. Arqueol. N.); its shape is typical of Phoenician ware from the 7th century BC. Contemporary with this jug are round, moulded and cut cosmetic palettes in light greenish and translucent blue glass, which imitate limestone prototypes and seem to be of Phoenician manufacture. Two examples have been excavated at Megiddo (e.g. U. Chicago, IL, Orient. Inst. Mus.). Elongated cast and cut alabastra, dating from the second half of the 7th century BC or the 6th century BC, have been found at Dali (anc. Idalion), Cyprus (London, BM), and in Italy at, for example, Pozzuoli (anc. Puteoli; London, BM).

The attribution of the manufacture of these cast and cut vessels to Phoenicia, and perhaps to Phoenician craftsmen working in or near the Assyrian palaces, would appear to be fairly strong. As noted above, both the mosaic-glass inlays of the engraved and painted bowl fragments and the bowl fragments with engraved figures from Nimrud have Phoenician parallels in ivories and metalwork respectively. Similarly the shape of the Sargon Vase, which is related to an Egyptian rock-crystal vessel (Paris, Louvre) that bears the name of the pharaoh Amunrud (*reg* 734–731 BC), was more likely to have been copied by a Phoenician craftsman than an Assyrian. It is noteworthy, however, that examples of cast and cut glass, similar to the La Aliseda Jug and made of translucent light green or blue glass, while apparently of Phoenician manufacture, have not been found on Phoenician sites, although they are known from regions with Phoenician connections.

(b) Regions. Core-formed vessels reappeared in Mesopotamia during the late 8th century BC or the early 7th century BC, although the products are rather dull when compared with examples from the 2nd millennium BC. The repertory of shapes includes various small, elongated flasks and globular jars, but no beakers; thread decoration is simple. It would appear that they were not so highly prized as the cast and cut glassware found in the Assyrian palaces, since they have been recovered mostly from private dwellings and graves. During the 7th century BC examples were exported to Iran. Numerous pointed bottles found at Susa indicate a local, short-lived, Neo-Elamite industry of core-formed vessels imitating Mesopotamian types. Isolated examples of Mesopotamian core-formed glassware reached Karmir Blur in Urartu (Erevan, Hist. Mus. Armenia), Syria and Tell Malhata, south-east of Beersheba. The origins of glassmaking on Rhodes may perhaps be connected with the introduction during the late 7th century BC of a Mesopotamian alabastron type with an elongated, almost cylindrical body (*see* GREECE, ANCIENT, §X, 5).

Between the 8th and 7th centuries BC glass parts were made in Mesopotamia for fitting to composite statues of wood and other materials. These include beards and wigs in blue glass from Nimrud, a blue macehead from Nineveh, similar items from Babylon, Dulaim and Ur, and numerous decorative appliqués, mostly using the lost-wax technique (all London, BM). Neither the core-formed vessels nor the parts of composite statues reveal any Phoenician connections. The excavations of the library of Assurbanipal (*reg* 668–627 BC) at Nineveh revealed an important collection of cuneiform tablets with prescriptions for glassmaking (London, BM), demonstrating the revival of the technical literature.

It would appear that glassmaking continued in Mesopotamia after the fall of Assyria in 612 BC. A shallow bowl in greenish glass made by the lost-wax technique and a remarkable core-formed jar in white glass decorated with blue circlets with a central red-brown dot were found in a 6th-century BC tomb at Babylon (Berlin, Pergamonmus.). Typical Mesopotamian core-formed glass vessels, similar to those of the 7th to the 6th century BC, were found in graves of the 5th century BC at Kish (Baghdad, Iraq Mus.; Chicago, IL, Field Mus. Nat. Hist.).

In north-west Iran during the 5th century BC a prolific industry produced square and cylindrical, rod-formed kohl tubes; these were made by covering a circular metal rod with a thin layer of core material. The finest examples of Near Eastern cast and cut glass were made during the Achaemenid period (538–330 BC). These highly prized colourless, light greenish or, more rarely, translucent blue vessels were produced in designs resembling those of popular contemporary metalwork. Most are drinking vessels: shallow or relatively deep phialai, carinated bowls and almost cylindrical beakers with a flaring mouth. Like their metal prototypes, especially silverware (*see* ACHAEMENID, fig. 2), they are decorated with different types of petals in relief, fluting and central rosettes. Receptacles such as alabastra were apparently also made. Cast and cut luxury glassware was used throughout the Achaemenid empire, and many vessels reached the Greek world: examples have been found at the Temple of Artemis, Ephesos (London, BM), on Rhodes and in a Greek tomb (*c.* 430–425 BC) at Aslaia in Cyrenaica (Tolmeita, Archaeol. Mus.). The latter is contemporary with a reference by Aristophanes (*Acharnians*, v. 74) to luxury glass from which the Athenian ambassadors drank wine in the Median court. It is not known where in the Achaemenid empire these fine cut glass vessels were produced.

Glassmakers in the Achaemenid period also produced cylinder, scaraboid and conoid seals, usually in translucent blue or light green glass. Ingots of opaque red glass were discovered in the debris of a workshop at Nimrud (London, BM) and similar material was found at Persepolis.

BIBLIOGRAPHY

A. von Saldern: 'Glass Finds at Gordion', *J. Glass Stud.*, i (1959), pp. 22–49

D. B. Harden: 'Ancient Glass, Part I: Pre-Roman', *Archaeol. J.*, cxxv (1968), pp. 46–72

A. L. Oppenheim and others: *Glass and Glassmaking in Ancient Mesopotamia* (Corning, 1970)

D. Barag: 'Cosmetic Glass Palettes from the Eighth–Seventh Centuries BC', *J. Glass Stud.*, xxiv (1982), pp. 11–19; xxv (1983), p. 280

——: 'Glass Inlays and the Classification and Dating of Ivories in the Ninth–Eighth Centuries BC', *Anatol. Stud.*, xxxiii (1983), pp. 163–7

——: *Catalogue of Western Asiatic Glass in the British Museum*, i (London, 1985)

——: 'The Prelude to Hellenistic Gold-glass', *Annales du 11e congrès de l'Association internationale pour l'histoire du verre: Basle, 1988*, pp. 19–25

——: 'Glass Inlays in Phoenician Ivories, Glass and Stone Vessels', *Annales du 12e congrès de l'Association internationale pour l'histoire du verre: Wien, 1991*, pp. 1–9

D. BARAG

3. IVORY. Only the tusk of the elephant provides true ivory, although alternatives, such as hippopotamus teeth and bone, were also used (*see also* IVORY, §1). African ivory is blond and is harder and more brilliant than the denser, whiter Indian variety. Experts can differentiate between the two when fresh but not, unfortunately, when old. The Syrian elephant, believed to be a sub-species of the Indian elephant, became extinct in the 1st millennium BC. Hippopotamus teeth are harder and whiter than elephant ivory. Both were used from early times and are

often confused in archaeological literature. In this article the word 'ivory' is therefore applied to objects made in either material. Bone is also sometimes confused with ivory, for which it serves as an inferior substitute.

(i) Techniques and uses. (ii) Chronological survey.

(i) Techniques and uses. Ivory is one of the hardest animal substances, uniting strength with flexibility. The tusk is formed of a series of cones within cones, which can be seen in sections cut across the tusk. The worn strata are often even more obvious in ancient ivory, and show how the object was cut from the tusk, either following the grain or across it. The principal limitation of ivory is that of size, and large objects had to be made up from a number of pieces, jointed, tenoned or dowelled together, techniques common in woodworking. Ivory can be worked like a hardwood and is often combined with woods of varying types; it is probable that both materials were worked in the same workshops.

Ivory was used in a variety of ways. Smaller objects, including statuettes and figurines or pyxides and boxes, might be carved from part of a tusk, or occasionally from a complete tusk. More commonly, however, objects were made from several pieces, either jointed together, perhaps to form a statue, or fixed over a wooden form to make a box, chest or piece of furniture. Thin sheets were used as veneer, and small flat pieces as inlay. Demand for ivory usually outstripped supply, and pieces might be reused or patched.

In antiquity ivory was rarely left plain, but was often partly gilded or coloured. Colour was applied as a simple stain or as paint, and in the form of inlays made of glass or stone set in hollows cut in the surface of the ivory. The walls of these hollows or 'cloisons' were sometimes themselves covered with gold, leaving the impression not of an ivory object but of the work of an enameller.

Ivory was highly prized as a symbol of luxury and wealth. Both tusks and finished objects regularly appear in lists of royal gifts and tribute or booty. Indeed, such texts form a valuable source of information, expanding and supplementing the archaeological record. For instance, the 'Amarna letters' (*see* AMARNA, EL-) record exchanges of gifts between the Egyptian Pharaoh and western Asiatic kings in the 14th century BC. These include furniture overlaid with ivory and gold sent to the Kassite kings of Babylonia, and ivories 'carved and coloured in Egypt' specifically requested by the Kassite king Burnaburiash II (*reg* 1359–1333 BC). Pieces of unworked hippopotamus and elephant ivory have been found in the wreck of a ship that sank off Kaş on the south coast of Turkey at about this time. Tablets of the late 3rd millennium BC from Ur record the import of large quantities of ivory, mostly to make tools or sheaths for knives, or furniture feet. Little of this has been found, but texts confirm that this trade continued in the following Isin–Larsa period. The survival of ivory objects gives, therefore, an uneven picture of what must have been a flourishing luxury trade, carried on whenever economic and political conditions permitted.

(ii) Chronological survey.

(a) Before c. *1500* BC. Possibly the earliest example of Near Eastern ivory is a bead found at Qermez Dere in northern Mesopotamia in a context dating to the 7th millennium BC. Statuettes found at Safadi near Beersheba in southern Israel (Jerusalem, Israel Mus.) are among the earliest ivory objects found in the Levant. The settlement at Safadi is dated to the 4th millennium BC and consisted of a complex of small subterranean rooms, one of which, an early workshop complete with tusk and tools, indicates local production, although the figures have affinities with Predynastic Egyptian pieces. Shell seems to have been preferred to ivory in Early Dynastic Mesopotamia (*c.* 2900–2340 BC). Figures were cut out of thin pieces of shell to form silhouettes, and set against a background of pieces of lapis lazuli and cornelian to make a colourful mosaic veneer. A fine example is the 'Royal Standard of Ur' (*c.* 2600 BC, London, BM; *see* UR, fig. 2), which is decorated with scenes of war and a victory banquet. Further north, at Mari in Syria, some of these silhouettes were made of ivory instead of shell (see fig. 26), which may suggest that ivory was not readily available further south. The economical tradition of using ivory only as an inlay continued and can be seen more than a millennium later at Middle Assyrian Assur on the River Tigris and Middle Elamite Chogcha Zanbil in south-western Iran. Ivory was also occasionally used in the round, either for small sculptures, such as a fragmentary bull-man from Kish (*c.* 2500 BC; Baghdad, Iraq Mus.) or an ivory figurine from an Akkadian level at Tell Brak (Dayr al-Zawr Mus.).

26. Sumerian ivory inlays, showing sacrificial scenes, (top) w. 115 mm, (right) h. 67 mm, (bottom) w. 100 mm, from Mari, *c.* 2300 BC (Damascus, National Museum of Damascus)

Significant increases in trade may partly explain the wider distribution of ivory in the early 2nd millennium BC. Clay tablets found at KÜLTEPE in Anatolia indicate a sophisticated trade in metals between Assur and Kültepe in the 19th and 18th centuries BC, and there was a resident Assyrian merchant colony outside the walls of Kültepe. Ivories, notably a nude female figure (Ankara, Mus. Anatol. Civiliz.) have been found there and in contemporary levels at Alaca Höyük and at ACEMHÖYÜK in the Konya Plain. A remarkable box carved from a single piece of ivory came from the latter site (Ankara, Mus. Anatol. Civiliz.). This is cube-shaped with a concave neck, and the sides have panels of delicate incised designs combining Anatolian and Syrian motifs, framed with studs of copper, iron and lapis lazuli. Ivories carved in the round and pieces for inlay, with lions, sphinxes and eagles grasping prey (New York, Met.) were also found at Acemhöyük.

(b) The 'first age of ivory', c. *1500–*c. *1000* BC. In the second half of the 2nd millennium BC there is clear evidence of a 'first age of ivory', once again largely under Egyptian influence. This period was marked by imperial expansion, relative peace and the consequent accumulation of wealth. Egyptian conquests under the rulers of the 18th and 19th dynasties brought Canaan into the Egyptian empire and extended Egyptian influence into Syria. The rise of Mycenaean civilization from *c.* 1600 BC stimulated seaborne trade throughout the eastern Mediterranean.

A plaque, which originally formed the lid of a round box (Paris, Louvre; see fig. 27), was found at Ugarit (Ras Shamra), near Latakia, the ancient Canaanite port that connected Near Eastern kingdoms with the Aegean and Egyptian worlds. It illustrates a favourite oriental motif, the 'mistress of animals', with a goddess between a pair of rampant goats. The goddess, however, is carved in an entirely un-oriental way: her hairstyle, curvaceous body, slender waist and heavy flounced skirt suggest the Great Goddess of the Aegean world. Sixteen panels, found in the palace at Ugarit, formed the double-sided footboard of a bed of Egyptian type (14th or 13th century BC; Damascus, N. Mus.). Each panel is *c.* 240 mm high and is carved in low relief with a variety of scenes, including a man offering a goat, a four-winged sun goddess with Hathor locks suckling two youths, and the familiar motif of a stylized tree. While many of the motifs are Asiatic, the style shows strong Egyptian influence. Other finds in the palace included a circular table, more than 3 m in diameter, inlaid with griffins, and part of an ivory horn carved with a girl with a Hittite hairstyle, flanked by a sphinx with arching wings (both Damascus, N. Mus.). A sensitively carved man's head (h. 150 mm; Damascus, N. Mus.) has a fine nose, deeply excised eyes and eyebrows, and curls on the brow. It belongs to a tradition of Mesopotamian sculpture, going back to the Warka Head (for illustration *see* URUK) of the 4th millennium BC and the Akkadian copper head from Nineveh (*see* AKKADIAN, fig. 2). Many of the smaller pieces of 2nd-millennium BC ivory from the Levant were made of hippopotamus-tooth ivory.

27. Ivory plaque, showing goddess between rampant goats, h. 137 mm, from Ugarit, 14th century BC (Paris, Musée du Louvre)

At Megiddo nearly 300 ivories were recovered, mostly from the treasury: these can probably be dated *c.* 1250 to 1150 BC. They constitute another hybrid assemblage, acquired by gift, exchange or trade, and they demonstrate influences from all the major centres, including Hittite Anatolia, Syria, Mesopotamia, Egypt and Mycenae, and varied origins, including Palestine. Among the Megiddo pieces was a Hittite panel (h. 95 mm; U. Chicago, IL, Orient. Inst. Mus.), carved in low relief and unfortunately rather worn. It shows the meeting of two Hittite 'Great Kings', supported by gods and spirits. A pen-case inscribed in hieroglyphs with the scribe's name (Jerusalem, Rockefeller Mus.) was probably imported from Egypt, although the adaptation of Egyptian objects and motifs is more common. This can be clearly seen in the cosmetic bowls with handles formed of the bodies of elongated 'swimming maidens' (Jerusalem, Rockefeller Mus.), developed from an early Egyptian prototype. Also Egyptian in origin are designs on openwork furniture panels, such as the dancing dwarf Bes, the Megiddo version of which (Jerusalem, Rockefeller Mus.) is shown winged, rather than wingless as in Egypt. A historical event seems to be recorded on a panel (Jerusalem, Rockefeller Mus.), perhaps made locally, showing nude prisoners introduced to a king sitting on a magnificent sphinx throne, which would itself probably have been made of gilded ivory. Mycenaean influence is also particularly strong at Megiddo.

There is an imbalance between Hittite textual references to ivory furniture, images, combs and hairclasps, and actual finds, which include small human figures and an openwork piece from Boğazköy, showing animals circling round a central sphinx (Ankara, Mus. Anatol. Civiliz.), and the worn Hittite plaque from Megiddo.

(c) The 'second age of ivory', c. *1000–*c. *500* BC. The first half of the 1st millennium BC may be regarded as the second and major age of ivory, with the Assyrian city of Nimrud (Calah) as the ivory capital. Huge quantities of ivories have been found there in the palaces, temples and private houses on the acropolis and in the great storehouse in the lower town, known as Fort Shalmaneser. Smaller quantities of ivories have been found elsewhere throughout the area, notably at Tell Halaf, Arslan Tash, Carchemish, Zincirli, Hama and Samaria in Syria and Palestine, at Gordion and Altıntepe in Anatolia, at Hasanlu and Ziwiyeh in north-west Iran, and at Khorsabad near Mosul. The annals of the Assyrian kings often list the campaign booty brought back to Nimrud, including ivories of many types, particularly furniture, beds, couches, chairs and tables, although staves, daggers, cups and dishes are also listed. Sometimes the ivory is described as being overlaid with gold or silver, or inlaid and bejewelled, a reference to the 'cloisonné' ivories.

Three main styles of ivory carving have been recognized at Nimrud: the local Assyrian style (see fig. 28), instantly recognizable both from the stone reliefs and from Assyrian metalwork; the North Syrian style, with strong designs related to the stone carvings of the north Syrian cities and with a marked absence of Egyptian influence; and the 'Phoenician' style, with more graceful designs reflecting some Egyptian influence (*see* PHOENICIAN; for illustration *see* SAMARIA). This tripartite division, while generally adequate, is too simple. Politically the Levant in the early 1st millennium BC seems to have consisted of a series of independent kingdoms, each with its own artistic language,

28. Neo-Assyrian ivory panel, showing winged figure and courtier, h. 260 mm, from Nimrud, 8th–7th centuries BC (London, British Museum)

related to that of its neighbours but in many cases distinct. This is reflected in the Nimrud ivory collections.

Several schools belong to the north Syrian or 'northern' tradition of ivory carving. A magnificent pyxis (Baghdad, Iraq Mus.) from one of these, the 'flame and frond' school, was found in a well in the North-west Palace, complete with its lid, to which were still attached four recumbent calves, carved in the round. The design around the side includes scenes showing sphinxes flanking a stylized tree and a banquet scene, with a woman seated on a sphinx throne similar to that on the much earlier Megiddo panel (see §(b) above). The distinctive flame-like muscle markings on the animals and the frond-like foliage give this school its name. Unusually, gold foil still covers much of the frame and design, indicating how little of the surface of the ivory was intended to be seen.

The elegance of a typical 'Phoenician' ivory, belonging to the southern tradition of ivory carving and closely related to Egyptian art, is well illustrated by a panel, found in Fort Shalmaneser (Baghdad, Iraq Mus.; see fig. 29), portraying a slender goddess wearing the Hathor crown and holding the lotus flail and *ankh*. Beside her are panels of hieroglyphs. The design was richly coloured: the 'cloisons' still contain traces of the Egyptian blue bedding, although nothing survives of the gold foil once covering the 'cloison' walls.

The northern and southern traditions are far apart in spirit and execution, but there are also many ivories from schools transitional between the two. One of these is the fine blinker from a bridle, carved with a nude 'Mistress of Animals' (New York, Met.), who is shown frontally holding up a pair of felines and two lotus flowers. Although slightly more shapely than the typical north Syrian female, she clearly belongs to that tradition, while the winged disc with *uraei* or cobras above her head has links with southern ivories. Three letters, which can be read as 'Lu'ash', a district not far from the city of Hama (Hamath) in Syria, are inscribed on the back. If this reading is correct, and if it identifies the place of manufacture, then this is a rare instance when it is possible to locate an ivory workshop, its transitional style being exactly what might be expected from that area.

The Nimrud ivories were probably deposited there between the mid-9th century BC, when Assurnasirpal II (*reg* 883–859 BC) made it the new capital of Assyria, and the late 8th-century BC, when Sargon II (*reg* 721–705 BC) built a new capital at Khorsabad near Nineveh. Some may also have been brought there during the reign of Sargon's grandson, Esarhaddon (*reg* 680–669 BC). Most were probably produced at the time when the Levantine kingdoms were independent and flourishing, before they were incorporated into the Assyrian empire during the reigns of Tiglath-pileser III (*reg* 744–727 BC) and Sargon II. It is not known when production started, although strong links with the art of the late 2nd millennium BC suggest an early date.

Assyrian pressure on the Phoenicians increased emigration from the Levant to Punic colonies in Cyprus and around the Mediterranean shores of North Africa, Sicily, Italy and Spain. The Phoenicians introduced oriental artefacts to the Greeks and the western Mediterranean, and ivories decorated with a mixture of oriental and

29. Ivory panel (?Phoenician), showing goddess wearing the Hathor crown, h. 159 mm, from Room SW7, Fort Shalmaneser, Nimrud, 8th century BC (Baghdad, Iraq Museum)

Egyptian motifs have been found in Italy in Etruscan tombs of the 7th century BC.

In Anatolia, ivories of Urartian workmanship have been found in the east, at Altıntepe and Toprakkale, while further west at the Phrygian capital Gordion there were imported pieces of bridle harness and others of local manufacture. Tumuli excavated at Emalı in Lycia contained Phrygian metalwork and ivories resembling those found in contemporary levels at Ephesos (*see* EPHESOS, §I, 1(ii)).

This pattern of ivories in a distinctive local style, together with a few imported pieces, also occurred at Hasanlu in north-west Iran, which was sacked by the Urartians in the late 9th century BC. The remains of some wooden objects were stylistically identical to the locally produced ivories. Among the imports were fragments of ivories belonging to the north Syrian 'flame and frond' school. North Syrian exports also reached Greece and contributed to the orientalizing phase of Greek art.

Little is known of ivory working during the period after the fall of Assyria (612 BC), when the Near East was divided between the Lydians, the Medes and the Neo-Babylonian kings, and before the three empires were conquered by the Persian king Cyrus II (*reg* 549–530 BC). The Achaemenid empire, which stretched from northern India to Egypt and Ethiopia, brought the principal sources of supply under its control. Relatively little ivory has been found, but evidence for its continuing popularity and the Achaemenid exploitation of the traditional sources is provided by a foundation inscription from Susa, in which Darius I (*reg* 521–486 BC) lists the materials used in his palace, including ivory from Ethiopia, and Sind (northern India) and Arachosia (western Afghanistan). The Achaemenid empire lasted for more than two centuries before being overwhelmed by the Macedonian army of Alexander the Great. The consequent Hellenizing of western Asia led to new developments in the history of ivory-working (*see* GREECE, ANCIENT, §X, 6).

BIBLIOGRAPHY

T. K. Penniman: *Pictures of Ivory and Other Animal Teeth, Bone and Antlers* (Oxford, 1952)

M. E. L. Mallowan: *Nimrud and its Remains*, 2 vols (London, 1966)

R. D. Barnett: *Ancient Ivories in the Middle East* (Jerusalem, 1982) [detailed site references]

A. MacGregor: *Bone, Antler, Ivory and Horn* (London, 1985)

G. HERRMANN

4. JEWELLERY. Deposits of precious metals and gemstones in the Ancient Near East were relatively sparse and unevenly distributed. Before the beginning of the Bronze Age (*c.* 3400 BC), beads and other ornaments were limited to those made from locally obtained materials, usually soft stones or organic materials, such as bone, teeth and shell. As trade expanded, more sought-after and costly materials could be traded from further afield, and the jewellery produced and worn in the Near East from the Bronze Age to the Islamic period is inextricably linked to extensive trade (*see also* §I, 1 above). Gold, for example, was scarce in Mesopotamia and Iran and was brought from Anatolia, Arabia, and perhaps Afghanistan and even eastern Europe. Some cornelian came from northern India, and lapis lazuli came from Afghanistan. This vast trade in precious materials, combined with the ready portability of jewellery items and the movement of craftsmen, often led to a homogeneity of both design and technique over the huge area of the Ancient Near East.

(i) Bronze Age, before *c.* 1000 BC. (ii) Iron Age, after *c.* 1000 BC.

(i) Bronze Age, before c. *1000* BC.

(a) Before c. *2000* BC. As well as the availability of raw materials, jewellery production requires technical ability.

Except for the simplest of hammering or piercing, goldworking technology relied on copper or bronze tools, and so it is only from the 4th millennium BC onwards that relatively sophisticated goldsmiths' work occurs. At Tepe Gawra in northern Mesopotamia, gold and coloured stone jewellery has been excavated in burials dating to the late 4th millennium BC (Jemdet Nasr period). The coloured stones include beads and inlays of lapis lazuli, reflecting Tepe Gawra's important position on the early trade route between Mesopotamia and Afghanistan. Turquoise also occurs in these burials, although this attractive stone is strangely absent in later Mesopotamian jewellery. Lapis and turquoise are both quite soft and could be shaped or pierced with simple flint or obsidian tools.

The gold in the Tepe Gawra jewellery varies in colour, indicating varying purities. During most of the Bronze Age native gold found in river gravels was employed without refining. Long before the development of more precise assaying techniques, economic and technical distinctions were based on gold colour alone. A gold nugget from a riverbed is never 100% pure, inevitably containing silver as well as traces of copper, iron and other metals. The presence of silver makes the gold pale, and very pale gold containing 25% or more silver is often termed 'electrum'.

Native silver occurring as metallic nuggets or veins was probably not available in the Near East, and the production of silver items depended on the mining and treatment of such silver-bearing ores as the lead mineral galena. There is evidence of the exploitation of silver ores by the early 3rd millennium BC, if not before, and, as with gold, quite elaborate silversmiths' work occurs in the Near East from this period.

Little Mesopotamian jewellery of the first half of the 3rd millennium has survived, although the evidence, for example from Ur, confirms that the earlier range of materials, such as soft stones and animal products, was supplemented by harder stones. The two most popular were lapis lazuli and cornelian, and in jewellery of the Early Dynastic period (*c.* 2900–*c.* 2340 BC) these occur in harmonious combinations with each other and with gold. Sometimes gold forms copy those of stones, for example the biconical shape popular for lapis lazuli beads. In other cases stone forms were based on those first developed in gold, such as the spiral-cone pendants of lapis lazuli that seem to imitate pendant spirals of gold wire. At Ur and other sites there was a huge bead manufacturing industry, evidence for which includes unfinished beads in various stages of production. A typical Sumerian bead shape is the bicone as used for gold, cornelian and, most characteristically, lapis lazuli, which has just the right hardness and lack of directional fracture to allow a mass production of this shape. Pieces of lapis were rolled between two flat abrasive stone blocks with a circular movement, which ground them into perfect bicones. These were then drilled from each end with a bronze bow-driven drill fed with sand or another abrasive.

Almost all the evidence for Near Eastern goldsmiths' work in the 3rd millennium BC comes from Anatolia and Mesopotamia, for example from the Royal Cemetery at UR (see fig. 30). There is little surviving jewellery and few relevant texts of this period from Iran. Like that from most of the ancient world, gold jewellery of the 3rd millennium BC is predominantly made from sheet rather than cast gold. The gold was hammered into thin sheets and cut to shape with a knife or small chisel—some of the earliest Sumerian goldwork is quite crude. The gold sheet may have an embossed design, ranging from scored lines or punched dots to elaborate motifs. Rudimentary composite items were constructed by soldering together two or more sheet-gold components.

30. Jewellery in gold, lapis lazuli and cornelian from the Royal Cemetery at Ur, *c.* 2500 BC (London, British Museum)

Wires of gold, made by hammering or twisting narrow gold strips, were used for applied filigree decoration and for chains, loops and other attachments. From Ur some of the earliest known gold chains are precisely made examples of the loop-in-loop type, and from Ur also come fine early examples of decorative rings with cloisonné inlay. Although intricate goldsmithing techniques, such as applied filigree work, do occur in Early Dynastic jewellery, Sumerian jewellers certainly preferred working sheet-gold.

The designs of 3rd-millennium BC Sumerian goldwork are generally either organic, such as flower-head rosettes, fluted beads and leaves, or simple geometric forms, such as cones, spirals and circles. The overall impression is of simple symmetrical forms consisting of smooth surfaces and curves. In the later 3rd millennium BC, however, an increasing love of bold, often repetitive, designs is evident and is matched by an apparent fashion for banded agates with their strong colouring and pattern. The designs often include applied decoration, mainly filigree wire spirals, which reflect the goldsmiths' increasing skill. Openwork disc pendants in silver and gold from both Mesopotamia and Anatolia are striking evidence for precision soldering and assembly. These contrast strongly with some of the rather clumsily assembled sheet-gold boat earrings from Ur, with their electrum solder alloys, and the crude fusing of some of the Early Dynastic gold wire spirals. These openwork discs also reflect another trait of the later 3rd millennium BC, the love of the negative space: pierced or punched holes were used in designs ranging from simple linear patterns of holes to elaborate lace-like openwork trellises. A consummate example of the latter is the famous gold diadem from Alaca Höyük (Ankara, Mus. Anatol. Civiliz.), which consists of a regular lattice-work design of chisel-cut triangles.

The commonest earring form in the Bronze Age Near East was the boat or leech form, beginning with the often massive examples from Sumeria and including many varieties, from simple wire hoops to multi-lobate and granulated forms.

(b) c. *2000–*c. *1000* BC. The development of skills necessary for the precise handling and assembly of many separate small components culminated in the granulation work that first became popular *c.* 2000 BC, with its designs built up by lines and patterns of minute gold spheres, often under 0.5 mm in diameter. The arguably more barbaric appearance of some of the goldwork of this period, for example pieces from Troy, is partly because irregularity of design is more readily noticeable in filigree and granulation than in undulating smooth gold surfaces.

The art of granulation seems to have spread rapidly throughout the Near East, and by the early 2nd millennium BC had reached a high level of sophistication. Particularly fine examples of goldwork from the 17th and 16th centuries BC come from the royal tombs at Ebla in Syria (Aleppo, N. Mus.). There is also superb granulation on pendants constituting the famous necklet supposedly from Dilbat in Iraq (New York, Met.), and comparable work is also known from Larsa further south in Iraq. The form and precision of the granulated decoration on the jewellery from Ebla, Dilbat and Larsa emphasizes the love of symmetry and regularity characteristic of this period. The designs and techniques of these ornaments, and such common forms as fluted melon beads, point to a wide homogeneity in jewellery forms and techniques through much of the Near East.

An important group of Canaanite gold jewellery from Tell el Ajjul is further evidence for the skills and cosmopolitan nature of the goldsmiths of the mid-2nd millennium BC. This jewellery is now in museums in England and Israel. Apart from a few solid items, the goldwork is mostly of sheet-gold with granulation work, applied twisted wires, filigree and embossing. The decorative techniques, especially the granulation, relate to the pieces from Dilbat and Ebla but are less sophisticated. The forms are often clearly paralleled elsewhere. One ring from Tell el Ajjul showing a sistrum rattle flanked by seated cats is of typical Egyptian New Kingdom style and construction (the type is also well known from Cyprus). Egyptian influence is further evident in gold fly amulets and a pendant of sheet-gold with the head of the Egyptian goddess Hathor. Similar Hathor pendants are also known from Ugarit on the Syrian coast, which, with Alalakh, was an important, international jewellery-producing centre by about 1500 BC. The ring from Tell el Ajjul and other items that can be paralleled with dated examples from Ugarit indicate that the Ajjul goldwork ranges in date to at least the 14th century BC. Egyptian influence is also to be found in the designs on cylinder seals, perhaps mainly those produced on the Syrian coast, and possibly in the use of such gemstones as amethysts, which may have been imported from Egypt. One example is an amulet of Egyptian type in the form of a hippopotamus, found at Tell el Ajjul.

Rings are not typical of Near Eastern jewellery: the ubiquitous cylinder seal was usually too unwieldy to set as a functional signet ring, whereas the Egyptian scarab seal was ideal for setting as a ring. When rings do occur, therefore, they often show either Egyptian origin or inspiration. The scarab ring itself became quite common in the Levant after about 1500 BC. However, surviving Bronze Age rings from the Near East are usually ornamental or apotropaic, rather than signets.

By the mid-2nd millennium BC the leech or boat earring form was joined by a variety of spirals and penannular hoops. These gave far greater possibilities for adornment with pendants, either fixed or free-hanging, and of the new forms that with a pendant cluster of gold spheres became the commonest.

Little mention has so far been made of Iran, since, generally speaking, it has produced little excavated and stratified material in contrast to the relative wealth of goldwork from further west. Unprovenanced material from Iran, however, supplements the meagre archaeological evidence and suggests that during the mid-2nd millennium BC the goldwork produced there was often quite crude and of less pure gold than that of Mesopotamia or the Levant. Towards the end of the 2nd millennium BC better workmanship is evident in some fine jewellery from Iranian burials, for example at Susa (*c.* 12th century BC). This includes precise granulated patterns and filigree work, including guilloche bands. Nearly contemporary jewellery from Tepe Sialk shows similar use of linear and triangular granulated decoration, including some precisely placed granulation, although the gauge of metal used and the simplicity of forms tend to give a rather stolid impression. At Hasanlu some large bipyramidal pendants or earrings have been excavated. These consist of hollow gold spheres, an Iranian form often attested in goldwork from illicit excavations but seldom in provenanced finds: a likely date is *c.* 1000 BC. Also from Hasanlu come quadruple spiral beads made from a central tube with laterally applied wire spirals at each end. This construction contrasts with the one-piece type of quadruple spirals found much earlier in the Near East (and also later, as at Tepe Nush-i Jan). The Hasanlu spirals are paralleled at Troy and Marlik (in general the chronology of the goldwork from Marlik needs further research).

(ii) Iron Age, after c. *1000* BC.

(a) c. *1000*–c. *250* BC. While chronological categories can exaggerate the break between the Bronze Age world of the 3rd and 2nd millennia BC and the flowering of the Iron Age in the early 1st millennium BC, there seems nevertheless to be a discernible break in continuity coupled with a transition period still only hazily discerned.

The gold jewellery of the 1st millennium BC is often not set with stones, and although this period saw the growing use of coloured glass, particularly for beads, glass-set gold jewellery is rare. Little gold jewellery of any kind survives from the 10th and 9th centuries BC, and most of the contemporary literary references to gold and silver consist of descriptions of the spoils of warfare and pillage. Assyrian reliefs from the 9th to the 7th century BC, mainly of male rulers or deities, illustrate a wealth of jewellery, including bracelets, armlets, earrings and necklets. The wearing of earrings by men from the early 1st millennium BC onwards was a Near Eastern trait commented on by Roman writers. The few surviving pieces of Assyrian goldwork of this period, such as earrings, can be closely matched on the reliefs: some are exquisitely made, with minute and precise granulation of a quality not seen earlier in the Near East. Armlets and bracelets with animal heads are among the commonest ornaments depicted on the Assyrian reliefs, and their increasing popularity during the 8th and 7th centuries BC relates to the general fashion for items with animal-head terminals or decorated with animal motifs. Bracelets and other ornaments with animal-head terminals became popular throughout much of the ancient world and are almost a trademark of much Hellenistic Greek jewellery.

The gold jewellery discovered at NIMRUD in the late 1980s has now provided ample evidence for the beauty and skill of goldwork produced in Mesopotamia in the 8th century BC. Ranging from crowns to bracelets, this material provides the basis for a new understanding of early Iron Age goldsmithing techniques and the interconnections between societies of that period. The goldwork includes enamel, a type of broad chain band termed 'strapwork' (previously not attested before the 7th century BC on Rhodes), beautiful inlay work and animal-headed ornaments. Gold vessels include a bowl with a 'Nilotic' scene with naked swimming female figures, a type known from Egypt in the same period.

In Anatolia the kingdom of Urartu flourished between the mid-9th century BC and the early 6th in the highlands between the Caspian and Black seas. The region had gold mines, and its goldsmiths produced beautiful and substantial goldwork. A gold bracelet with lion-head terminals dating to the 7th or early 6th century BC was discovered in the palace at Karmir Blur. Its stark simplicity combined with the representational, animal motif is typical of the region. This is one of the earliest datable examples of a bracelet type well known from the Near East, though seldom from stratified finds. Although animal motifs occur in jewellery before the 1st millennium BC, it is only at this time that they become highly popular in Near Eastern jewellery.

The origins of much of this 'animal-style' work may well lie with the nomads to the north, but by the early 1st millennium BC it had become established in northern Iran, and it continued unabated through the Achaemenid period (538–331 BC). A focal group is the Ziwiyeh Treasure, a large assemblage supposedly from the Hamadan region, which contained much goldwork datable in theory to *c.* 8th and 7th centuries BC. Unfortunately the homogeneity of the find is uncertain, and other works of uncertain origin on the art market acquired a 'Ziwiyeh' provenance from unscrupulous dealers. The appealing 'animal style' of much of the Ziwiyeh Treasure, contrasting with the largely non-representational goldwork of earlier periods, also led to many forgeries, which still confuse the picture of jewellery styles and technology of this period and area. The gold objects that can probably be accepted as authentic, however, show some stylistic homogeneity. They are truly in the 'animal style', and such forms as the couchant stags and antelopes, either appliqué or embossed, on a series of sheet-gold fragments are very similar to Scythian work.

A later hoard, with a more romantic though rather obscure origin, is the OXUS TREASURE (mostly in London, BM). It was recovered from bandits, who had robbed merchants carrying a huge quantity of goldwork discovered in 1877 near the River Oxus. The gold jewellery included two magnificent inlaid gold bracelets with terminals in the form of winged griffins (see fig. 31) and a number of splendid torques and bracelets of twisted or ribbed gold rods with terminals in the form of the heads of lions, gazelles and other animals. The inlays are of turquoise and other stones, recalling Scythian work. There are also finger rings of typical Greek signet form. The jewellery ranges in date from the 5th century BC, if not slightly earlier, to the late 4th century BC. Stylistic links with Greek goldwork can be readily recognized in the rings and animal-headed torques, though they are not actually Hellenistic in either technique or detail. Other pieces are amongst the finest Achaemenid jewels and have close stylistic links with jewels produced in south Russia and Afghanistan. Hoards of this nature might date to the time when the army of Alexander the Great (*reg* 336–323 BC) was advancing eastwards and when many temple authorities were doubtless worried about the precious objects in their care. The numerous partly broken-up items of jewellery in the Oxus Treasure could reflect either its ancient or 19th-century history, both somewhat turbulent, but a detailed scientific examination of the fractures and cuts would help elucidate this question.

The Egyptianizing influences so noticeable in such arts as ivory-carving (*see* §3 above) are also found in goldwork, and an overall homogeneity can be seen between gold jewellery found in Asia Minor, the Levant coast and even Greece. The introduction or in some cases reintroduction

31. Armlet with griffin terminals, gold, originally with coloured stone inlays, from the Oxus Treasure, *c.* 5th–4th centuries BC (London, British Museum)

into these areas of such goldworking techniques as beaded wire may no doubt be ascribed to Phoenician traders, whose importance in the dissemination of jewellery forms and techniques throughout the Mediterranean region cannot be overestimated. There was also considerable mobility of craftsmen within the Persian empire, which included Egypt and Asia Minor. When Darius I (*reg* 521–486 BC) built his palace at Susa his workforce included Egyptian goldsmiths, whose raw material came from western Anatolia and Bactria.

Jewellery from western Anatolia acts as a link between the Near East and the Aegean during the mid-1st millennium BC. Typical products include goldwork with beautiful granulation, though this is of a larger gauge than that of contemporary Etruscan and Hellenistic pieces.

From the time of Alexander the Great, Near Eastern jewellery becomes fairly homogeneous throughout the Hellenistic world, and the same is largely true for the Roman period, though during both periods there are of course some regional variations. The need to conceal treasure in advance of Alexander's armies, suggested for the Oxus Treasure, has also been put forward as the origin of a hoard from Pasargadae in Iran. If this is so, it would open to question the chronology of jewellery of the Hellenistic period (323–27 BC). Some of the Pasargadae items, for example gazelle-headed bracelets, seem so typically Hellenistic that they may have been imported into Iran or made there by Hellenistic craftsmen working for the Achaemenid court or aristocracy: they would thus be of a later date than Alexander the Great's campaigns.

The Pasargadae Treasure also included pearls, which, though apparently mentioned in earlier texts, only begin to occur in surviving jewellery of this period, as well as unworked coral (according to the Babylonian Talmud, coral was obtained in the Persian Gulf in antiquity).

(b) c. *250* BC–c. AD *651: Parthian and Sasanian.* Parthian jewellery is hard to define: little excavated material has been published, and the chronology and typology are largely unexplored. Influence from the Hellenistic and Roman West is often obvious, and some jewels from Iraq and Iran are indistinguishable from products from further west and may indeed be imports. Silver jewellery is not uncommon. Local versions of Hellenistic prototypes include Eros earrings from Iran. The pose of the small winged figures with their hands on their hips is found throughout the Late Hellenistic world, but the Near Eastern examples, often of silver, are distinguished by curiously oversized heads.

A far more elaborate and colourful type of Parthian earring and pendant consists almost entirely of cloisonné-type cells set with garnets, either cabochon or thin and flat-cut, and coloured glass. The edges of the cells are frequently picked out in lines of granulation, and small pendants of a typical flattened bell shape can hang from the earring to complete the ensemble. The overall design is essentially two-dimensional (though sometimes double-sided). The use of flat-cut garnets in cloisonné settings relates to South Russian forms and is ultimately linked to Saxon and other European Dark Age jewels. Garnets were the most popular stones in Parthian gold jewellery, although there was also a love of banded agates and onyxes, sometimes set or encased in gold.

Sasanian jewellery is also a neglected topic, partly because little has been found or published from official excavations. Roman influence is evident in such pieces as intaglio-set signet rings. Though known in the Hellenistic period, stone-set signet rings only became common in Early Christian times. A typical Sasanian form, familiar from Iran and also Syria, consists of a low bezel with a simple, slightly tapered hoop. The intaglio, and hence bezel, is usually of circular or near-circular shape, and the stones are usually onyxes or sometimes garnets and are engraved with representations in the rather rounded Sasanian styles known from stamp seals. There is often a small grain of gold soldered to the bezel at one end of the setting, presumably to indicate the orientation of the seal when stamping its impression in clay. Rings of this type are quite common from Iran and the Transcaucasus region. The elegant simplicity of such rings compares to that of an earring type of the same period. This consists of a plain tapered hoop, to the bottom of which was soldered a vertical wire for threading a pearl or pearl substitute. Other Sasanian jewels show a love for more elaboration, with granulation and filigree work.

Compared to the wealth of plates and vessels of silver that have survived, Sasanian silver jewellery is rare, but extant examples show similar forms to that of the gold jewellery. In general Sasanian gold jewellery seems of paler colour than that from the Roman world, and this might suggest the use of a lower purity alloy.

BIBLIOGRAPHY

G. F. Kunz and C. H. Stevenson: *The Book of the Pearl* (London, 1908)
C. D. Curtis: *Jewelry and Gold Work* (1925), xiii of *Sardis* (Rome)
L. Legrain: 'The Boudoir of Queen Shubad', *U. PA Mus. J.*, xx (1929)
A. Godard: *Le Trésor de Ziwiye* (Haarlem, 1950)

K. R. Maxwell-Hyslop: 'The Ur Jewellery', *Iraq*, xx (1960), pp. 105–15
O. Dalton: *The Treasure of the Oxus, with Other Examples of Early Oriental Metal-work* (London, 1964)
O. Tufnell and W. A. Ward: 'Relations between Byblos, Egypt and Mesopotamia at the End of the Third Millennium BC', *Syria*, xliii (1966), pp. 165–241
M. I. Artamonov: *Treasures from Scythian Tombs in the Hermitage Museum, Leningrad* (London, 1969)
J. Boardman: *Greek Gems and Finger Rings: Early Bronze Age to Late Classical* (London, 1970)
O. Negbi: *The Hoards of Goldwork from Tell el-'Ajjul*, Stud. Medit. Archaeol. (1970)
K. R. Maxwell-Hyslop: *Western Asiatic Jewellery* (London, 1971)
B. Zouhdi: 'Les Influences réciproques entre l'orient et l'occident d'après les bijoux du Musée national de Damas', *An. Archéol. Arabes, Syr.*, xxi (1971), pp. 95–103
M. S. Ruxer and J. Kubczak: *Naszyjnik grecki w okresach, hellenistycznym i rzymskim* [The Greek necklace in the Hellenistic and Roman periods] (Warsaw, 1972)
G. Q. Pisano: *I gioielli ferici di Tharros nel Museo Nazionale di Cagliari* (Rome, 1974)
M. A. R. Colledge: *The Art of Palmyra* (London, 1976)
D. Arnaud, Y. Calvet and J.-L. Huot: 'Ilsu-ibnisu orfèvre de l'E. Babbar de Larsa', *Syria*, lvi (1979), pp. 1–64
R. G. Chandra: *Indo-Greek Jewellery* (New Delhi, 1979)
T. Dothan: 'Excavations of the Cemetery of Deir el-Balah', *Quedem*, x (1979)
P. Mattiae: *Studi Eblaiti*, i (1979)
Jewellery, Ancient to Modern (exh. cat., Baltimore, MD, Walters A.G., 1980)
J. Ogden: *Jewellery of the Ancient World* (London, 1982)
J. Wolters: *Die Granulation* (Munich, 1983)
B. Deppert-Lippitz: *Goldschmuck der Römerzeit* (Mainz, 1984)
——: *Griechischer Goldschmuck* (Mainz, 1985)
K. R. Maxwell-Hyslop: 'Recent Discoveries of Western Asiatic Jewellery', *Jewel. Stud.*, ii (1985), pp. 3–10

JACK OGDEN

5. Faience.

(i) Definition. (ii) Uses.

(i) Definition. Strictly speaking, in Ancient Near East scholarship the word 'faience' refers to a siliceous composition based on quartz dust or sand, which could be modelled or moulded to form objects or vessels, and which was covered with a glaze. This glaze, an alkaline vitreous substance, was coloured by adding metal oxides: copper oxides (blue to pale green), lead antimonate (yellow) and ferrous manganese oxides (brown to black) were the most common. Faience seems to have been invented principally as a substitute for precious stones, such as lapis lazuli and turquoise. It first appeared in Egypt and Mesopotamia in the 5th millennium BC, and later spread throughout the Levant and Iran, where the art was perfected between the 14th and 12th centuries BC. Faience was also produced in the ancient Aegean.

There are a number of related techniques, which produced artefacts resembling those made of true faience. Glassworking began at the beginning of the 2nd millennium BC, derived from the glazing techniques used by the faience makers. The composition of the frit employed was similar to that of faience, but it was not covered with a glaze. 'Egyptian blue', a variety of blue frit, was obtained by using an artificial blue pigment (calcium and copper silicates), which was powdered and baked in a mould. Objects in 'Egyptian blue' were common in Egypt during the New Kingdom and were also produced in workshops in Mesopotamia, the Levant and Iran at the end of the Bronze Age and during the Assyrian and Achaemenid periods. Objects in glazed clay cannot always be distinguished from faience without careful examination. The process of glazing clay involved causing an alkaline glaze identical to that of faience to adhere to a clay object. Some of the earliest examples, which date from the 15th century BC, were found in northern Mesopotamia, for instance at Nuzi. They are large figures of guardian animals in terracotta (Baghdad, Iraq Mus.) on to which a glaze has been poured. During the 14th century BC a revolutionary process enabled thrown vessels to be glazed. This process, which made them not only more pleasing to the eye but also watertight, was perfected in the workshops of Cyprus and Syria and spread to Mesopotamia, where it survived until the Achaemenid period. In the Parthian period, from the 3rd century BC, this process was used for most fine earthenware. It is found in southern Mesopotamia, southwest Iran, the Persian Gulf and as far as the mouth of the River Indus, where it encountered competition from polished grey ceramics. Production was widespread in Syria as far as the Middle Euphrates, beyond which the polished wares of the Greek tradition had become established. In the late 8th century BC around Al-Mina and Rhodes, however, multi-coloured pear-shaped glazed vessels appeared. These are decorated with orange, possibly yellow, green and blue petals perhaps under Babylonian influence. The tradition of monochrome glazed ceramics persisted along the Euphrates, in Mesopotamia and in Iran until the Islamic period; at certain sites, such as Raqqa, the tradition was almost uninterrupted.

(ii) Uses.

(a) Small artefacts.

Beads, pendants and seals. It appears that the earliest use of faience was for jewellery. In Mesopotamia beads and pendant earrings, probably intended to replace coloured stones, were produced from the end of the 5th millennium BC. This common use of faience was without competition until the 2nd millennium BC, when glass beads appeared. Most monochrome faience beads were probably produced locally, but some were traded over considerable distances, such as the lantern-shaped beads, decorated with openwork, that have been identified by chemical analysis as made in Egypt and subsequently exported to the Levant (Ugarit, Lachish), the Aegean and as far as the Black Sea. A particular category of jewellery consists of small pendants in the form of female masks. Bitumen and shell inlay in the glaze give these faces the appearance of wearing make-up. Ties passing through small holes in the ears enabled these pendants to be hung round the wearer's neck, as suggested by a 13th-century BC example from a tomb at Mari in Syria (Paris, Louvre). They are comparable with metal jewellery bearing the stylized images of 'fertility goddesses'. These masks have been found from Cyprus to Iran (Susa), and in large numbers at Ugarit in the Euphrates Valley and in Babylonia. It appears that they were produced around the 13th and 12th centuries BC.

The art of stamp seals and cylinder seals (*see* §1 above) was also an important medium for the faience makers of the Ancient Near East. Among the earliest examples are the seals of Tepe Gawra (late 5th millennium BC) and the cylinders of Susa, which were light green or light yellow with wickerwork decorations. Thousands of faience seals in the Mitannian style, which was widespread from the north Syrian coast to northern Mesopotamia, are known from the mid-2nd millennium BC. Their iconographic repertory includes reclining horned animals, stylized trees and human figures. The shapes made up of juxtaposed globules were obtained by working the siliceous clay with a tool analogous to a ball drill before applying the glaze.

Boxes, small vessels and figurines. Local production of these items appeared along the Syrian and Palestinian coast from the Middle Bronze Age onwards. Their inspiration is Egyptian, both in the forms (the closed bottle and the pilgrim flask) and in the decoration in black lines on a blue background. Only laboratory analysis can distinguish the Syrian and Palestinian artefacts from the Egyptian, by establishing which manganese ore was used for the black pigment. The Egyptian influence became more diffuse the further north the articles were made; forms and decoration progressively freed themselves from the Egyptian models, and an entirely local style emerged. A small goblet (Aleppo, N. Mus.) made at Ebla in the 17th century BC is an example of such a local style: it takes the form of a woman's face, framed by heavy locks of plaited hair with eyes accentuated by circumflex eyebrows. A type of make-up spoon, the handle of which ends in a duck's head, with the bowl of the spoon supported by a hand in relief was found at Ugarit (Damascus, N. Mus.; Aleppo, N. Mus.).

During the Late Bronze Age (14th–13th centuries BC), workshops on the Syrian coast continued to make objects in an Egyptian-influenced style, including chalices in the shape of a lotus with plant decoration, and dishes showing Nilotic motifs, such as papyri and a lotus in water accompanied by hieroglyphic signs (e.g. Paris, Louvre). During the same period a technique was used to juxtapose alternate areas of yellow or orange, white, blue, green and black on boxes or dishes with a decoration of petals in relief, and on gadrooned pyxides with horizontal pegs and lids. Goblets decorated with a woman's face in relief may have borrowed their type of feminine beauty from Crete: made-up eyes are set in a face framed by tresses in kiss-curls (Paris, Louvre; see fig. 32). The blue-frit or 'Egyptian blue' technique was used at this time to make small objects, such as beads or amulets, as well as for 'make-up' pots from Ugarit (Damascus, N. Mus.) and Assur (Berlin, Pergamonmus.). Workshops in inner Syria or Mesopotamia were probably responsible for a range of small containers, which were distributed over an area from the Syrian coast (Ugarit) to Elam (Susa). The most distinctive of these containers are 'tubs' or cylindrical goblets with little basket handles, glazed in pale blue with a horizontal band or a row of dots around the rim. Many of these were found in tombs in the Euphrates Valley (Mari and Emar (now Maskana)), the Hamrin region and at Ur. Small hemispherical dishes (diam. 100–120 mm max.) were also decorated with a black horizontal band or row of blue or yellow dots around the rim. There were many variations: some have a lateral spout, others have incised floral decoration in imitation of the bowls made on the Syrian coast with petals in relief.

Large bowls with linear decoration in yellow, green or bright blue on a pale green background were also made in the 13th century BC. Their motifs represent stylized plants

32. Faience goblet, with relief decoration of a woman's face, h. 165 mm, from Ugarit, Syria, 13th century BC (Paris, Musée du Louvre)

in the form of cypress trees radiating from the centre (Mari) and concentric or intersecting circles and festoons (Emar). These polychrome vessels have been found from the Middle Euphrates to Ur and probably came from Mesopotamian workshops. The Elamite workshops of the 12th century BC are important for their abundant production of maces and figurines of worshippers that were consecrated in the sanctuaries of Susa and Chogha Zanbil. These workshops continued production into the 1st millennium BC, including handsome vases of the 8th century BC with incised decoration showing confronted winged monsters or bulls on either side of stylized trees, set within frames of plaited or spiral lines and covered with a thick blue glaze. Pegs in relief often show the forequarters of an animal or a human head. From the 7th century BC vessels and figurines were produced with geometric decoration comprising juxtaposed panels of ochre and green on a blue ground: these are stylistically similar to those from Al-Mina and Rhodes. From the Achaemenid period (late 6th century BC) onwards, the tradition of faience gave way to the production of ordinary pottery in glazed clay.

During the 1st millennium BC Egyptian influence became pre-eminent in the Levant, as in the use of blue background with brown-black markings, and in the repertory of forms and decoration. Egyptian-style amulets represented *wedjat*-eyes and *shabti* figures, and there were small anthropomorphic vases, like those in the form of the Nile god, kneeling genies wearing tall feather headdresses and holding jars before them, and hedgehogs. Such artefacts have been found throughout the Mediterranean, and workshops were probably set up in Phoenicia, in the Nile Delta (perhaps at Naukratis), in East Greece, on Rhodes and as far as Carthage and Italy.

(b) Architectural decoration. Faience had long been a part of architectural decoration: examples include the wall rosettes from Tell al Rimah and Ugarit (14th–13th century BC). From the mid-2nd millennium BC onwards, the walls of some sanctuaries were covered with moulded-brick decoration showing figures in relief. Each motif comprised a particular arrangement of bricks, making the creation of large decorated surfaces quite straightforward.

At Susa in the 12th century BC the Elamites replaced these simple clay bricks with blocks of moulded and glazed faience, the brilliant and colourful appearance of which must have created a remarkable effect. Only a few fragments remain of a sanctuary decorated in this way by order of the Elamite king Kutir Nahhunte (Paris, Louvre). The panels show figures, including the royal couple, with bodies shown frontally, clothed in green, with hands clasped at the waist and brown faces presented in profile. A dedicatory inscription is impressed on a brick course across the clothing, running from one figure to the next. Wall decoration in coloured bricks developed considerably during the 1st millennium BC. At Babylon new colours were added to the range available to eastern faience workers, including the bright blue of cobalt, the red-brown of copper and iron and the opaque whites of tin. The Ishtar Gate, the Processional Way and part of the palace were decorated with panels framed with stylized plant motifs (reconstructed in Berlin, Pergamonmus.) recalling the 'palace of the palm trees' mentioned in contemporary texts. Processions in static lines of monsters or symbolic animals, such as lions, dragons and bulls, alternate with abstract symbols, in contrast with the narrative art of the stone reliefs in the Assyrian palaces. This tradition survived for a long time, and is found in the Seleucid period (311–64 BC) in the temple of Anu-Antum at Uruk. It prefigures the Islamic ornamental system of faience tiles. Local craftsmen in Elam remained faithful to their traditional techniques.

Wall plaques were fixed to the wall by pommels, the heads of which were also covered with faience. They were probably designed to hide the ends of beams, like the antefixes of Greek architecture. A series inscribed with the name of the Elamite king Untash-Napirisha (e.g. Paris, Louvre) decorated the 'Upper Temple' erected on the summit of the ziggurat at Chogha Zanbil in the mid-13th century BC. This means of decoration was also used in the 1st millennium BC in Assyria, for example in the palace of Assurnasirpal at Nimrud (9th century BC), but here it is in glazed clay (Baghdad, Iraq Mus.). At Susa the Elamites still made use of siliceous faience: the small sanctuary constructed by Shutruk-Nahhunte II on the acropolis in the 7th century BC has plaques fixed by pegs decorated with the projecting protomes of bull-men or of a goddess with the ears of a cow or the forequarters of a horse (e.g. Paris, Louvre).

During the Achaemenid period (538–331 BC), Elamite craftsmen took the use of faience bricks to the limits of virtuosity. A procession of Persian archers and spear-carriers from the *apadana* (columned hall) of Susa stands out against a blue-green background (Paris, Louvre). Their costume is purple, decorated with fine rows of rosettes or stylized motifs in the form of tiny white and blue fortresses. The faces and hands are dark brown, while the jewels and weapons are yellow. All these colours are arranged within a network of partitions made of grey-blue clay, which indicates at least two firings.

BIBLIOGRAPHY

A. Lucas: *Ancient Egyptian Materials and Industries* (London, 1926, rev. J. Harris, 1962)

P. Amiet: *Elam* (Auvers-sur-Oise, 1966)

——: 'Eléments émaillés du décor architectural néo-élamite', *Syria*, xliv (1967), pp. 27–46

E. J. Peltenburg: 'Al Mina Glazed Pottery and its Relations', *Levant*, i (1969), pp. 73–96

——: 'On the Classification of Faience Vases from the Late Bronze Age Cyprus', *Praktika tou Protou Diethnous Kyprologikou Synedriou* [Proceedings of the first international Cypriological symposium]: *Nicosia, 1972*, pp. 129–36

P. Amiet: 'Disjecta Membra Aelamica: Le Décor architectural en briques émaillées à Suse', *A. Asiatiques*, xxxii (1976), pp. 13–28

E. J. Peltenburg: 'A Faience from Hala Sultan Tekke and Second Millennium BC Western Asiatic Pendants Depicting Females', *Hala Sultan Tekke*, ed. P. Aström, G. Hult and M. S. Olofsson, Stud. Medit. Archaeol. (Göteborg, 1977), pp. 177–200

A. Kaczmarczyk and R. E. M. Hedges: *Ancient Egyptian Faience* (Warminster, 1983)

P. R. S. Moorey: *Materials and Manufacture in Ancient Mesopotamia: The Evidence of Archaeology and Art: Metals and Metalwork, Glazed Materials and Glass*, Brit. Archaeol. Rep., Int. Ser. (Oxford, 1985)

ANNIE CAUBET

6. Textiles.

(i) Introduction. (ii) Chronological survey.

(i) Introduction. Sewing, basketry, mat-making and weaving developed early, before even pottery, but fragile textiles are rarely preserved, except in dry, sterile soils like that of Egypt, and often the only evidence is provided by tools of imperishable materials. Many important sites were excavated before the development of modern conservation methods and have not been reworked, so that textile evidence was lost. Modern techniques are able to preserve textiles, and excavations in Anatolia, Israel, Turkmenistan and Europe have challenged the traditional view that the Fertile Crescent was the only cradle of textile technology.

(a) Fibres. The chief fibres of antiquity were flax and sheep's wool. Other plants used included hemp, rush, reed and palm, sometimes mixed; animal fibres from goat, deer, horse and camel have also been found.

The wild flax of the *Linum* genus, *L. angustifolium*, and the chief domesticated species, *L. humile* and *L. usitatissimum*, originated in the Near East as far east as Armenia. Large seed flax was found on sites dating from the 6th millennium BC, including Ramad near Damascus (*c.* 6000 BC), and in the Samarran villages of Tel es Sawwan and Chogha Mami, north-east of Baghdad *c.* 5600 BC. It requires a sandy soil, and the irrigation which presupposes settled communities; but it is not known whether it was cultivated for food or fibre. It flourished in Egypt and the Levant, where large linen industries developed in Palestine and the Jordan Valley.

Sheep, goats and dogs were domesticated in the upland areas of the Near East between *c.* 9000 BC and the 6th millennium BC. Sheep-breeding was an important activity in south Mesopotamia by *c.* 3500 BC. Sheep appear in Sumerian art by *c.* 3000 BC, principally on seals, and both hairy and woolly sheep, with either spiralling or curled, Amon-type, horns were known (e.g. on the Royal Standard of Ur, London, BM; *see* UR, fig. 2). Sheep and goats were plucked until the Roman period, but the invention in around 1000 BC of shears that yielded a whole fleece encouraged further selective breeding for softer wool. Texts show that wool was a major Mesopotamian export, especially in the late 3rd and 2nd millennia BC. Plentiful evidence of sheep-rearing and textile technology occurs in biblical texts.

Cotton, from trees of the *Gossypium* genus, is native to India, the Sudan and Ethiopia, and is first mentioned in the *Annals* of Sennacherib of Assyria (*reg* 705–681 BC) as 'trees bearing wool'. The fibre was sheared and woven into garments, though it was not important before the Islamic conquest. According to Aristotle, 'wild' or *tussore* silk was woven in Kos in the 4th century BC. True silk from the *Bombex Mori* moth was developed exclusively in China, though it was probably known in India and Iran by the 6th century BC.

(b) Manufacture. It is possible to spin with the fingers, but a slender wooden stick (or spindle) and a whorl were used over a wide area from the Upper Palaeolithic period onwards. Spindles have largely perished, but whorls of stone and clay are common finds on settlement sites and in the graves of women, whose work it was to spin. Whorls vary from early flat shapes to conical, and in weight according to thread weight. Hand-spinning was used throughout the Ancient Near East. Egyptian-style 'spinning' bowls, with loops in the base, were excavated at Deir el-Balah, Israel, but these were probably used for plying groups of spun thread.

The earliest apparatus for weaving was the horizontal or ground loom, which pre-dates the vertical loom. Used throughout the period, it is easily transported and is still favoured by nomads. Loom-weights, required for even warp tension, indicate the use of the vertical warp-weighted loom with no lower beam. Perforated lumps of stone or clay have been found in quantity, but their identification has been controversial. The earliest firm evidence comes from Troy II (*c.* 2300 BC), where post-holes were found in the same context as loom-weights. At Lachish (13th–12th centuries BC) a platform with one upright post and groups of loom-weights was identified as a weaving workshop, and at Tell Beit Mirsim, destroyed in the 10th century BC, vertical stones were found that may have supported loom beams, together with hundreds of loom-weights. The vertical two-beam loom, suited to tapestry-weaving, was used by the Greeks and became popular in the Roman Empire. All three looms use the same system of rod-heddle and shed-rod, permitting simple weaves with one warp system. The draw-loom harness apparatus, however, which developed in the eastern Mediterranean or on the Iranian Plateau (?3rd century AD), allowed several sets of warps and wefts, resulting in compound cloths and precise repeats.

Early weaves were of plainweave tabby, varying from tent-cloth to gauze, and were plain, striped or checked. Decoration with beads or embroidery was known, but the first woven patterned fabrics were of tapestry, which became the principal pattern weave. The earliest examples, with the name of Pharaoh Amenophis II (*reg c.* 1438–1412 BC), were found in the tomb of his successor, Tuthmosis IV (*reg* 1412–1402 BC), and were possibly Syrian.

The use of plant dyes must have been ubiquitous, and cloth dyed red, blue and yellow was found at Çatal Hüyük in Turkey (*c.* 6500–5500 BC). Leonard Woolley found red wool at Ur (*c.* 2600 BC), and traces of dyeplants were excavated at Tell Beit Mirsim. Red was obtained from madder, yellow from weld and safflower, blue from a Near Eastern variety of indigo, and black from gall-nuts. Red and blue were mixed to produce a cheap purple. Alum, urine and iron salt mordants were used. More expensive reds came from the insect dyes kermes and cochineal. 'Tyrian purple', the most costly and a prerogative of royalty, came from molluscs found off the Syria-Palestine coast. Crushed shells have been found in the Levant at Ugarit (*c.* 1450–1365 BC) and Byblos. Purple dyeing was developed by the Phoenicians in the 1st millennium BC, chiefly at Tyre, which produced dark reds from the *murex bandaris*, and Sidon, which specialized in the true purple from *murex trunculus.* At Tell Beit Mirsim in Israel 30 dyeshops were uncovered (8th century BC) with up to 90 cylindrical vats. Tell Mor, near Ashdod (*c.* 400–200 BC) had a tiered installation of two spring-fed lined basins. Most dyed material is wool, which was fleece-dyed. Later cotton and silk were dyed, but linen does not take dye well.

(c) Trade. From the 7th millennium BC Neolithic peoples conducted long-distance trade. Wool and cloth, being lightweight specialist products, were undoubtedly important trade goods and were exchanged for raw materials. There is documentary evidence of textile trade from the 3rd millennium BC onwards. Between *c.* 2400 and *c.* 1900 BC Ur exported cloth and oil to the Indus Valley. Records list 'ten talents [*c.* 300 kg] of different kinds of wool of ordinary quality' and 'sixty talents of wool, seventy garments and one hundred and eighty skeins for buying copper from Makan' (probably Oman). Tablets from Ur also mention trade up the River Euphrates to Babylon and Mari, in Syria. From *c.* 1900 BC Assyrian merchants at Kültepe in Anatolia traded cloth and garments for metals. From *c.* 1700 BC Canaanites traded dyed wool. Later, Jewish kings engaged in the lucrative caravan trade, controlling the 'King's Highway' north from the Gulf of Aqaba. According to Ezekiel 27:21, 18, 7, sheep and goats from Arabia, white wool from Hebron and Egyptian linen were marketed in Damascus. In the Hellenistic period (323–27 BC) the caravan cities of Petra, Palmyra and Dura Europos handled overland trade from

China, India and Iran, sending goods on to Antioch, Alexandria and Rome.

(ii) Chronological survey.

(a) Before the 1st century AD.

Anatolia. Among the earliest surviving textiles are those from the Neolithic town of Çatal Hüyük, occupied from *c.* 6500 to *c.* 5500 BC. Considerable textile activity is indicated by finds of fine-spun single and two-plied thread, plainweave cloth in several weights, including a gauze shawl fabric, darned clothing fragments and plain and knotted fringes. A young woman buried under a house floor was wearing a string skirt, the ends terminating in copper weights. First identified as wool, the fibres may in fact be linen (see Ryder, 1983), although there are remains of sheep but none of flax. Cloth was dyed red, blue and yellow with local dyeplants. Baskets and mats of rush and straw were also found. Wall paintings in rooms identified as shrines show nets of varying thickness and designs strongly resembling much later Turkish kilims (wool tapestries), with spirals and paired hooks, triangular and diamond-lattice patterns, segmented in blocks of colour that are outlined in black and white in kilim fashion. These paintings may have been derived from textiles, since border stitches are represented, and they have been cited as evidence for kilim weaving at Çatal Hüyük. Further excavation here and at other early Anatolian sites could revolutionize knowledge of Neolithic textile production. In the Phrygian capital Gordion up to 20 layers of linen and wool cloth on a burial bed (*c.* 700 BC) were discovered in 1957, and traces of purple wool were discovered on a throne. Hemp and mohair were also present.

Mesopotamia. Sumerian male statues of the early 3rd millennium BC show a fleece kilt worn with a mantle, while a fleece tunic was worn by women. The 'War' panel of the Royal Standard of Ur (*c.* 2600 BC; London, BM) shows the later woven male version, a kilt with four overlapping looped fringes for dignitaries and a plain kilt with only one hem fringe for the others. It is possible that the latter may have been of plainweave wool with a starting-fringe and the former of plainweave with regular rows of weft-loops. The Burial Pits of this period at Ur were described by Woolley as mat-lined and, although much textile material perished on excavation, he recorded that Queen Pu-Abi's ladies wore sleeved coats, of which the red woollen, bead-decorated cuffs survived. In the later 3rd millennium BC the chief industry at Nanna's temple at Ur was weaving, and tablets refer to one building that housed 165 women weavers, slaves and freewomen, some of them specialist weavers. Doubtless cottage industries also existed.

Palestine. Widespread excavation has widened knowledge of ancient textiles in Israel. At Nahal Hemar in the Judaean desert (*c.* 7160–6150 BC), textiles include cordage, matting, netting, spun and plied yarns, chiefly of flax, and plainweave tabby cloth, among which was blue-dyed fabric decorated with beads and shells (Jerusalem, Israel Mus.). At nearby Nahal Mishmar (4th millennium BC) similar material with undecorated plainweave was excavated. The urban settlement of Arad (*c.* 3500–2650 BC) yielded whorls, spun linen thread wrapped round tool-handles, and pottery impressions of fine plainweave (Jerusalem, Israel Mus.). Rock-cut tombs at Jerico (*c.* 1800–1650 BC) preserved rush baskets, matting and linen plainweave fragments. Rare fragments of a large tent-shrine of thick red and yellow wool (*c.* 1300 BC) were excavated at the copper-mine site of Timna. Tools and textiles have also been found in the towns of Tell el-Hamah (10th–8th centuries BC) and Tell Beit Mirsim, evidently a textile centre until destroyed by the Egyptians in the 10th century BC. At Kuntillet Ajrud, a trading settlement in the Negev region (9th–8th centuries BC), more than 100 cloth fragments, chiefly of linen, were found.

(b) 1st century AD *to Islamic conquest.*

The Roman Empire. Textile evidence from the Greco-Roman world before the 1st century BC is negligible outside Egypt. Hellenistic and Roman rulers in the Near East had annexed existing industries, and the eastern provinces provided most of the Empire's textile requirements. From the 3rd century AD to the 5th state-controlled industries produced remarkable pattern uniformity in domestic fabrics, tunics and cloaks woven in one piece from linen and wool, with inset wool tapestry, in polychrome or in monochrome blue. Patterns closely resemble the mosaic repertory, with geometric and plant ornament, portrait figures, and dancing and bucolic scenes of Hellenistic origin, all of which persisted until the 7th century AD. Eastern influences also appeared, however, for example the 'inhabited scroll' motif from Syria and the mounted huntsman from Iran. International trade brought Chinese silks and Indian cotton muslins to Rome.

Syria is known to have supported textile industries and trade. Damasks and twills were probably woven there, in wool and silk, using Chinese yarn and unravelled thread from Chinese cloth. The caravan city of Palmyra, destroyed in AD 273, yielded only textiles of the 1st to the 3rd centuries AD: Han Chinese silks, Syrian damasks, a rare diamond twill from the Elahbel Tomb and fine tapestry of local and Egyptian manufacture (Syrian tapestry has a more even weave and smoother texture than Egyptian). Wool and linen tunics woven in one piece were found at Palmyra and at Dura Europos on the River Euphrates, where an early weft-faced compound cloth with a reversible meander pattern was excavated.

Jewish textiles, although conforming with contemporary trends, adhered to the 'Law of Diverse Kinds' (*shaatnez*), prohibiting the mixing of animal and vegetable fibres. Scrolls from Dead Sea sites (mid-3rd century BC) were wrapped in plain linen cloth. In the Cave of Letters (132 BC–AD 35) spun yarn included cheap indigo and cochineal-dyed purple wool and tent-fabric yarn of white wool. Cloth included medium and fine wool plainweave and tapestry, some in simple coloured stripes, fragments of tunics and cloaks woven in one piece and scroll wrappers. Blended yarns were not used here or at Masada.

The excavation of burials in the At Tar Caves in Iraq (3rd century BC–3rd century AD) has revealed some 4000 textiles. One-piece tunics, mantles and fragments, predominantly of wool with some flax, hemp and cotton, are of plainweave and basket weave. Patterned tapestry textiles show geometric and plant designs technically and icono-

33. Textile of silk woven weft-faced compound twill, depicting a Semourv, 350×525 mm, from Iran or Trans-Oxiana, 7th–8th centuries AD (London, Victoria and Albert Museum)

graphically close to the Dura Europos textiles, with local variations, and there is a group of portraits. Pile fragments from rugs placed beneath and over the bodies are of exceptional importance. Techniques include weft-loop pile, symmetric and asymmetric knots, and the type with single knot rows and long pile between numerous weft rows. The latter is found on pile fragments excavated at sites on the Silk Road.

Iran. Chinese silks reached the West by the 6th century BC. Little is known of the earliest overland trade routes, but Iran is known to have played a crucial role during the Parthian and Sasanian dynasties (3rd century BC–7th century AD) and the intermittent wars with Rome and Byzantium hinged on control of the western trade routes. The introduction of silk-weaving into Iran is obscure. Later Arab accounts of captive Syrian weavers settled in Khuzistan by Shapur I (*reg* AD 241–72) are suspect but may contain some truth. Secondary evidence of Parthian textiles from statues in the Iraq Museum in Baghdad and reliefs at Palmyra show decoration consisting of small lozenges or roundels of metal plaques or embroidery. Woven patterns are not documented until the late Sasanian period (6th century AD).

Rock-reliefs showing King Chosroes II Parviz (*reg* AD 591–628) at Taq-i Bustan provide the only contemporary evidence for Sasanian textiles in Iran. The King appears on horseback and in a boat at a boar-hunt. His clothing is embellished with a mythical creature, the Semourv, which slightly resembles the griffins of ancient Mesopotamia and Iran (in Avestan texts it brings rain and has healing powers). A Semourv is depicted on silk that was possibly woven in the 7th or 8th century AD in Iran or Trans-Oxiana (London, V&A; see fig. 33). The pearl roundel-frame, joined by smaller ones with crescents, is not found at Taq-i Bustan, but appears in wall paintings at Afrasiab (Samarkand) of the 6th to 8th centuries AD.

At Taq-i Bustan the Semourv is worn only by the king; cocks, ducks and water-birds appear on courtiers' clothing. A silk with cocks standing on jewelled plinths, and a pearl-collared pheasant with a vine-stem in its beak (Rome, Vatican, Mus. Sacro Bib. Apostolica) is possibly a Byzantine copy and closely resembles a wall painting at Varakhsha, near Bokhara. Cocks and other long-legged birds are depicted on a rare group of red wool and white cotton compound reversible cloths, perhaps woven for domestic use in post-Sasanian Iran or Mesopotamia (e.g. New York, Brooklyn Mus. and Met.; Washington, DC, Textile Mus.). There is no evidence at Taq-i Bustan of textiles with human figures, though these are common in post-Sasanian silks, occurring singly or in confronted pairs, often hunting or in combat, and confronted figures also occur on contemporary reliefs and silver artefacts.

Patterned silks with animals in roundels, associated with Sasanian Iran, were first excavated in 1896–7 at Antinoë in Egypt (e.g. Lyon, Mus. Hist. Tissus; Paris, Louvre). Others have come from European church treasuries (e.g.

Rome, Vatican, Mus. Sacro Bib. Apostolica) and Central Asian burials (e.g. New Delhi, N. Mus.; Urumqi, Mus. Xinjiang Uygur Auton. Reg.). None has been found in Iran. Attribution and dating are controversial, but surviving textiles, which are chiefly compound weft-faced tabby or twill, drawloom woven, are now thought to be of post-Sasanian date and woven outside Iran.

Sasanian textiles, of which seemingly only Central Asian versions survive, were much copied. Byzantine and early Islamic silks, and wool tapestry from Egypt and Mesopotamia demonstrate their profound influence for centuries after the dynasty's fall, and their motifs entered the iconography of medieval Europe.

BIBLIOGRAPHY

A. F. Kendrick: *Catalogue of Early Medieval Fabrics*, London, V&A cat. (London, 1925)
R. Pfister: *Les Textiles de Palmyre*, 3 vols (Paris, 1934–40)
G. M. Crowfoot: 'The Vertical Loom in Palestine and Syria', *Palestine Explor. Q.* (1941), pp. 141–51
R. Pfister and L. Bellinger: *The Textiles* (1945), IV/ii of *The Excavations at Dura-Europos, Final Report* (New Haven, CT)
G. M. Crowfoot: 'Textiles, Matting and Basketry', *Qumran Cave I*, ed. D. Barthélemy and J. T.Milik (1955), i of *Discoveries in the Judaean Desert* (Oxford, 1955–), pp. 18–38
R. S. Young: 'The 1961 Campaign at Gordion', *Amer. J. Archaeol.*, lxiv (1962), pp. 153–68
T. Dothan: 'Spinning Bowls', *Israel Explor. J.*, xiii (1963), pp. 97–112
Y. Yadin: *The Finds from the Bar Kokhba Period in the Cave of Letters* (Jerusalem, 1963)
R. J. Forbes: *Textiles*, iv of *Studies in Ancient Technology* (Leiden, 1964)
M. Hoffman: *The Warp-weighted Loom* (Kragero, 1964)
M. L. Ryder: 'Report on the Textiles from Çatal Hüyük', *Anatol. Stud.*, xv (1965), pp. 175–6
T. Talbot-Rice: *Ancient Arts of Central Asia* (London, 1965)
P. Horn: 'Textiles in Biblical Times', *Ciba Z.* (1968)
K. Riboud: 'Some Remarks on the Face-covers (fu-mien), Discovered in the Tombs of Astana', *Orient. A.*, xxiii (1977), pp. 438–54
A. Geijer: *A History of Textile Art* (London, 1979)
Fabrics from the Silk Road: The Stein Collection (exh. cat., New Delhi, N. Mus., 1979)
D. K. Burnham: *Warp and Weft: A Textile Terminology* (Toronto, 1980)
A. Sheffer: 'The Use of Perforated Clay Balls on the Warp-weighted Loom', *Tel Aviv. U. Inst. Archaeol., J.*, viii (1981), pp. 81–3
H. Fujii and others: 'Textile(s) from At-Tar Caves, Iraq', *Al-Rāfidān*, iii–iv (1982–3), pp. 89–96
M. L. Ryder: *Sheep and Man* (London, 1983)

JOAN ALLGROVE MCDOWELL

7. DRESS. Since few textiles survive (*see* §6(i) above), information on dress comes mostly from secondary sources, in particular designs on seals, but also sculpture, metalwork, and occasionally paintings. Such information relates largely to the rich, influential and well-born, and to men rather than women and children. Some geographical areas, such as Mesopotamia, are well represented for most periods; for other areas documentation is sporadic. It should also be noted that the dress of deities and the ceremonial costume of kings was probably traditional and may not have reflected current fashions. In general dress consisted of lengths of material draped in different ways with varied borders and fringing, sometimes using macramé techniques. At some periods elaborate tailoring and dressmaking skills are apparent, for example in the fitted dresses worn by women in Mesopotamia and south-western Iran at the end of the 3rd millennium BC and the beginning of the 2nd (*see* §(i) below), or the hunting costume of the Assyrian king Assurbanipal on reliefs of the mid-7th century BC (e.g. London, BM). Most people went barefoot regardless of class, but sandals, embroidered slippers and boots with upturned toes are sometimes represented.

(i) Before *c.* 2000 BC. (ii) *c.* 2000–*c.* 1000 BC. (iii) After *c.* 1000 BC.

(i) Before c. *2000* BC. The earliest evidence for personal adornment consists of strings of beads made of shells, stones of different colours, copper, bone and animal teeth. These are found at sites throughout the Ancient Near East from the 10th millennium BC onwards. At El-Wad in Israel a body was buried in the 10th millennium BC with a cap of dentalium shells and a necklace of gazelle phalanges (Jerusalem, Rockefeller Mus.). Wall paintings of the early 6th millennium BC from Çatal Hüyük in Anatolia (finds in Ankara, Mus. Anatol. Civiliz.) show figures wearing animal skins for hunting (for illustration *see* ÇATAL HÜYÜK). The painted designs on some of the figurines from this site may be evidence of body paint, and it has been suggested that the baked clay 'seals' bearing geometric designs may have been used for printing the skin, leather and textile remains that were also found. A polished bone belt-clasp indicates some sophistication in dress. A figurine, possibly male from Can Hasan of the first half of the 5th millennium BC (Ankara, Mus. Anatol. Civiliz.) wears an elaborate spotted headdress. Stamp seals of the first half of the 4th millennium BC from Susa (e.g. Paris, Louvre) depict figures in long skirts, with animal heads or horns (see fig. 34a). Whether these are masked priests or priestesses, deities or demons is not clear, but the patterning of the skirts, with chevrons, squares or grids, indicates some elaboration in textiles. Necklaces, often with a large pendant, are also shown. Sculptures and seals of the late 4th millennium BC (e.g. Baghdad, Iraq Mus.) frequently depict a bearded man wearing a calf-length kilt that is diagonally crosshatched and a fillet around his head. A tall vase from Uruk (the Warka Vase; *see* MESOPOTAMIA, fig. 12) depicts figures in short or long bordered kilts, one in an elaborate, cross-hatched, fringed skirt with a tasselled train, and a female figure in a long, bordered dress, which is draped over one shoulder.

During the Early Dynastic period in Mesopotamia (*c.* 2900–*c.* 2340 BC) the skins of sheep and goats seem to have been used as skirts for men and robes for women. In the earlier part of the period the fleece may have been removed, leaving a long, tufted fringe round the bottom (*see* DIYALA REGION, fig. 1), but later the fleece was retained and worn outwards. Women also wore plain, bordered, calf-length robes, draped over one shoulder, or shawls fastened by pierced pins (toggle pins) from which hung beads or seals. Domed hats were worn by women at Mari (Paris, Louvre; Damascus, N. Mus.), while carved heads from Khafajeh in the Diyala region (Baghdad, Iraq Mus.) show that women had wimple-like headdresses or wore their hair in elaborate, plaited styles. Silver pins topped with jewelled flowers were worn in the hair of women buried in the Royal Cemetery of UR (Baghdad, Iraq Mus.; London, BM; Philadelphia, U. PA, Mus.), as well as other elaborate jewellery (*see* §4 above) and toggle pins. A gold helmet from one grave (Baghdad, Iraq Mus.) is shaped like a wig with plaited hair and a bun: this seems to have been a form of royal headdress and is depicted on the statue of a Mari king (Aleppo, N. Mus.), on the copper

34. Forms of dress in the Ancient Near East (line drawings of examples depicted on seals and in sculpture and wall painting): (a) Iranian, from a stamp seal from Susa, early 4th millennium BC (Paris, Musée du Louvre); (b)–(e) Mesopotamian, from cylinder seals, 19th–17th centuries BC (London, British Museum); (f) and (g) Syrian, from seal impressions from Tell Atchana, *c.* 1720 BC (Antakya, Hatay Museum); (h) Syrian, from a painting in the Tomb of Huy, Qurnat Mara ʿi, Egypt, *c.* 1320 BC (*in situ*); (i) Hittite, from a relief from Alaca Höyük, 14th century BC (Ankara, Museum of Anatolian Civilizations); (j) Neo-Assyrian, from a relief from the palace of Sargon II at Khorsabad, *c.* 721–705 BC (Paris, Musée du Louvre); (k) Neo-Babylonian, from a stele depicting King Marduk-apla-iddina II, *c.* 714 BC (Berlin, Pergamonmuseum); (l) Achaemenid, from a relief at Persepolis, 5th century BC (*in situ*); (m) Parthian, from a statue from Hatra, 2nd–3rd centuries AD (Mosul, Museum); (n) and (o) Sasanian, from a relief of Bahram II, from Sar Mashad, *c.* AD 276–93 (*in situ*)

head of an Akkadian king (Baghdad, Iraq Mus.; *see* AKKADIAN, fig. 2) and, in a simpler form, on the Stele of the Vultures (Paris, Louvre; *see* MESOPOTAMIA, fig. 3).

The Akkadian king Naram-Sin (*reg* 2254–2218 BC) adopted two different types of royal headdress: one was beehive-shaped (on the Pir Husein Stele; Istanbul, Mus. Anc. Orient), while the other (on his stele; Paris, Louvre; *see* AKKADIAN, fig. 1), was horned, like the headdresses of deities. On the Paris stele Naram-Sin also wears a short garment that is draped over his left shoulder, knotted over the opposite hip and has a fringed end hanging down. This type of dress (see fig. 34b) symbolized the king as a warrior from the Akkadian period (*c.* 2340–*c.* 2180 BC) until the end of the Old Babylonian period (1595 BC) and even later. An even longer-lasting innovation of the period was the flounced robe adopted by important figures and deities. This may have derived from the Early Dynastic tufted skin but was made of a lighter material, perhaps with threads of wool hanging down or with close pleats draped in layers (see fig. 34c). Some male deities are shown wearing pleated skirts, sometimes hitched up in front to allow freedom of movement. A plain robe with fringed border and hem (later replaced by a rolled hem) was worn by both sexes. In the later 3rd millennium BC a plain robe wrapped around the body, under the right armpit and over the left shoulder, with a vertical fringed border hanging over the left arm and a fringed edge drawn around the body and tucked in under the armpit, is depicted on the many statues of Gudea of Lagash (*c.* 2140 BC; e.g. Paris, Louvre); it was worn by kings and laymen for several centuries. Women also wore a version of this garment, generally draped over both shoulders, or close-fitting round-necked dresses, with or without a shawl over the shoulders. Gudea probably also introduced the royal headdress of a round, probably fur, cap with upturned brim, which continued in use until the end of the Old Babylonian period (for illustration *see* TELLOH). Throughout the 3rd millennium BC men might be either clean-shaven or bearded, but priests generally seem to have been clean-shaven and to have had their heads shaved. (Later, in the Old Babylonian period, priests grew a forelock or wore a forehead ornament.)

In Anatolia there is little evidence for dress, but finds from Alaca Höyük (*c.* 2300 BC) include toggle pins for fastening garments, a diadem and jewellery. Toggle pins are also frequently found on Syrian and Palestinian sites.

(ii) c. *2000*–c. *1000* BC. All the types of garment developed in Mesopotamia in the Akkadian period continued to be depicted during the first half of the 2nd millennium BC. Kings officiating at religious ceremonies or sitting, deified, on thrones wore the long fringed robe and the fur hat. Sometimes the robe hangs open over a kilt (see fig. 34d), revealing more of the male torso than previously

or even passing under both armpits, with only the loose end hanging over the shoulder. Worshippers also wore the long fringed robe but not the fur hat: in Babylonia they were shaven-headed and beardless, but in outlying regions they wore a cap-like hairstyle (possibly a cap is represented). Women, though seldom depicted, wore a kerchief and a plain dress with decorated borders, of a kind worn for centuries (see fig. 34e). This dress was also adopted for goddesses from *c.* 1700 BC, replacing the flounced robe associated with them since Akkadian times. The choker necklaces worn were so heavy as to need a necklace counterweight hanging at the back.

Similar types of dress seem to have been the fashion in Elam in south-western Iran during the first half of the 2nd millennium BC, but there men wore their hair short, bulging out over the forehead in a distinctive style that lasted into the 1st millennium BC. A female figurine from Susa (mid-2nd millennium BC; Tehran, Archaeol. Mus.) is shown in a robe with its lappet edges appearing at the hem, in an inverted V-shape across the skirt, and around the hips; a shawl is pinned to the bodice on either side, and there is an elaborate hairstyle with fillets and a veil hanging behind, and a necklace with a large round pendant and bracelets.

In Syria, and probably Palestine, during the first half of the 2nd millennium BC a type of dress with lappet borders, later replaced by rolled, possibly fur-trimmed, borders, was worn over a kilt or wrapped several times around the body. Kings were beardless and wore a tall, oval headdress sometimes referred to as a *polos* (see fig. 34f). Round, brimmed hats were worn by bearded men with a distinctive, elaborately patterned robe that enclosed one arm. Kilts were often horizontally ridged. Women are not represented, but goddesses wore either the Babylonian flounced robe and multiple-horned headdress or a plain robe with fringed or rolled borders, wrapped around the body and draped over both shoulders, with a square-topped headdress with a single pair of horns (see fig. 34g). Judging from a wall painting from a tomb at Beni Hasan in Egypt (*c.* 1890 BC), the textiles used were brightly patterned, and this is reflected in the biblical account of Joseph's 'coat of many colours' (Genesis 37:3). In the 15th century BC Syrians with small, pointed beards are generally depicted on Egyptian tomb paintings (e.g. London, BM) in close-fitting, long-sleeved robes with the edges and seams decorated with patterned braid, and small tassels at the hem. In the 14th century BC they are shown with fuller beards, wearing a long-sleeved undergarment and a brightly patterned, wrapped dress, forming capes over the shoulders (see fig. 34h). Porters wore tasselled kilts (e.g. Thebes, Tomb 40). Women are occasionally depicted wearing a dress with a many-tiered skirt.

In the second half of the 2nd millennium BC the Kassites in southern Mesopotamia wore a garment that was draped so that a heavy, often ladder-patterned, border ran over one shoulder and down the skirt. In some cases Mitannians in the north wore a similar type of dress, but it is not attested in Assyria, although it was current in all the surrounding regions. In Elam, where it continued in use in the 1st millennium BC, it was draped so that the border ran vertically and often diagonally as well, and the end, with its heavy fringe, ran round the bottom. Instead of being wrapped round the legs, the length of cloth could also be looped up over an arm to reveal a knee-length kilt. Often the ends of the kilt's tasselled belt hung down to below the knees, and sometimes, particularly in Assyria, only the kilt was worn. Metal statuettes from Susa (Paris, Louvre) and wall paintings in Egyptian tombs indicate patterning of textiles with stars and dots. With the arrival of the Hittites there is more evidence for dress from Anatolia. Horizontally patterned kilts were worn with wide belts with rounded ends (for illustration *see* BOĞAZKÖY). Ceremonial dress ended in a train behind (see fig. 34i). In Egypt Hittites are depicted wearing brightly patterned textiles, and a cape tied under the chin is also shown.

(iii) *After* c. *1000* BC.

(a) Neo-Assyrian and Neo-Babylonian. (b) Achaemenid. (c) Parthian and Sasanian.

(a) Neo-Assyrian and Neo-Babylonian. After a gap of several centuries (*c.* 1200–*c.* 900 BC) from which little has survived, Neo-Assyrian reliefs (e.g. London, BM; Paris, Louvre; *see also* MESOPOTAMIA, §III, 6(i)) provide a rich source of information, both for Assyrian dress and for that of subject peoples. Short- or long-skirted tunics were ubiquitous, with fringes for the more important members of society. On ceremonial occasions the Assyrian king wore a fringed robe with patterned borders, wrapped diagonally around the body; it is first attested on an altar (Berlin, Pergamonmus.) of King Tukulti-Ninurta I (*reg* 1243–1207 BC). The king's headdress was tall and conical, possibly a turban wrapped round a pointed core, while the crown prince wore a headband that was broader in front. Ethnic groups were distinguished by the type of headband, fillet or headdress they wore, and by the cut of their beards. In addition Syrians wore large fringed shawls over their tunics and tall, domed headdresses or turbans; the tribes of the Zagros Mountains wore animal-skin cloaks; an Elamite king is depicted in a fringed robe and a round crown with a feather hanging down the back. At Carchemish in the 8th century BC the royal family were represented wearing plain, short-sleeved, ankle-length tunics, which, for the adults, had pleats at the back; Araras, the regent, was distinguished by a shawl with a pointed end falling over his right shoulder, while the young king had a broad belt with a webbing end; the younger princes had headbands and straps across their chests linked by a large pectoral ornament; the queen (or possibly a nursemaid) wore a broad headband and the baby had a pocket (Ankara, Mus. Anatol. Civiliz.). Other women are shown with a shawl draped over their heads.

A type of textile with a grid pattern was an innovation of the 8th century BC that became popular throughout the Ancient Near East. It was worn by the soldiers of Tiglath-pileser III of Assyria (*reg* 744–727 BC) and is also shown on the divine statues they carried off from a Levantine town (relief in London, BM). Anatolian examples of this pattern include the dress of bronze figures from Urartu (e.g. London, BM) and the figure of King Warpalawas on a rock relief at Ivriz (*see* ANATOLIA, ANCIENT, fig. 4): in the latter a Greek key motif is shown around the hem; the King wears a shawl over the shoulders, fastened by a fibula and a round hat with horizontal bands of decoration. From Tiglath-pileser's reign onwards Assyrian officials also wore over their tunics a wrap made of long strands of wool, or perhaps of fur, which went diagonally across the torso and then around the waist to leave a straight lower edge (see fig. 34j). Kilts with a fringed end hanging below the hemline were also popular. The hunting reliefs of Assurbanipal (*reg* 668–627 BC; London, BM) show the King wearing elaborately decorated tunics on which rosettes figured prominently, although it is not clear whether this decoration was woven, embroidered or embossed on metal plates, or a combination of all these. Sometimes the tunic was shorter in front to allow greater freedom of movement. One of the rare occurrences in Assyrian art of a high-born lady, in the 'Garden Party' relief (London, BM; for illustration *see* ASSYRIAN), shows the King feasting with his queen, who wears a crenellated crown and a patterned robe, the ornamental borders of which are draped diagonally across her knees and over her shoulder.

Military uniform varied according to period and the part of the Assyrian empire from which soldiers were recruited. Scale armour worn over kilts or tunics, pointed helmets, crested helmets and laced boots are all attested. Priests wore feathered or beaded headdresses, or tall oval tiaras; for special ceremonies they may have worn fish-cloaks and lion masks and skins.

There is less evidence for Neo-Babylonian dress. A *kudurru* (boundary stone) of King Marduk-nadin-ahhe (*reg* 1099–1082 BC; London, BM) shows him wearing a patterned tunic closer to that of Assurbanipal than to the wrapped garments of his predecessors, a belt and crossed straps, a tall cylindrical hat with feathered top similar to that worn by Babylonian deities during the 1st millennium BC, and quilted slippers. Reliefs of Nabu-apla-iddina (9th century BC; London, BM), Marduk-zakir-shumi I (9th century BC; Paris, Louvre) and Marduk-apla-iddina II (Bibl. Merodach-Baladan; 8th century BC; Berlin, Pergamonmus.; see fig. 34k and *see also* BABYLONIAN) show the king wearing a long, fringed tunic, with pleats at the back, a belt and straps across the chest, and a pointed helmet with a streamer down the back. On a stele (London, BM) King Nabonidus (*reg* 555–539 BC) is shown in a similar headdress, belt and crossed straps but wearing a shawl with lappets and a tiered skirt with lappet decoration and a fringed hem. In mythological scenes on seals of the 8th century BC (e.g. New York, Pierpont Morgan Lib.) figures wear long, open, sometimes many-tiered, fringed skirts lined with material patterned with hexagons. This patterning already occurs on the 11th-century BC *kudurru* mentioned above and was adopted for Assyrian dress in the late 8th century BC (see fig. 20 above). On seals of the 6th century BC priests wear belted, wrap-around skirts with fringed hems.

BIBLIOGRAPHY

M. G. Houston: *Ancient Egyptian, Mesopotamian and Persian Costume and Decoration* (London, 1954)

R. M. Boehmer: 'Phrygische Prunkgewänder des 8. Jahrhunderts v. Chr.: Herkunft und Export', *Archäol. Anz.* (1973), pp. 149–72

I. Siebert: *Woman in* [the] *Ancient Near East* (Leipzig, 1974)

M.-T. Barrelet: 'Un Inventaire de Kar-Tukulti-Ninurta: Textiles décorés assyriens et autres', *Rev. Assyriol.*, xli (1975), pp. 51–92

S. Mazzoni: 'Nota sull'evoluzione del costume paleosiriano', *Egitto & Vicino Oriente*, ii (1979), pp. 111–38

E. Andersen: *Makramee als Kunst und Hobby* (Niederhausen, 1980)

J. Asher-Greve: *Frauen in altsumerischer Zeit*, Bibliotheca Mesopotamica (Malibu, 1985)

D. Collon: *Isin-Larsa and Old Babylonian Periods* (1986), iii of *Catalogue of the Western Asiatic Seals in the British Museum: Cylinder Seals* (London, 1962–) [esp. pp. 21–40]

——: *First Impressions: Cylinder Seals in the Ancient Near East* (London, 1987) [esp. pp. 148–50]

DOMINIQUE COLLON

(b) Achaemenid. The Achaemenid empire (538–331 BC) stretched from the Nile to the Oxus, from the Danube to the Indus, encompassing a wide variety of peoples who wore many different forms of dress. The principal evidence comes from the Achaemenid royal reliefs, in particular the reliefs on the palaces and tombs at Persepolis, the Canal Stelae (fragments, Cairo, Pal. Isma'il Pasha and Paris, Louvre) and the Egyptian statue of *Darius* found at Susa (Tehran, Iran Bastan Mus.), and the relief of Darius at Bisitun. Other works of art and literary sources (particularly Herodotus: *Histories*) give valuable additional information. The royal reliefs were a form of political propaganda, and their representations of costumes appear to have been devised to differentiate between the different peoples. In some cases the identities of these peoples are certain or nearly so, but in others their identity cannot be determined. The dress shown on royal Achaemenid monumental art presumably reflects the dress of the foreign nobility who were summoned to the Achaemenid court and of the Persians who served the king. The dress of the common people, priests, women and other groups is not shown at Persepolis. The costumes worn by the peoples of the Achaemenid empire can be divided into five main categories, which reflect ethnic, cultural and geographically defined groups.

The Persians shown on the monuments wore a garment with wide sleeves and a long skirt (see fig. 34l). The details of this garment have been much discussed, but it is not certain whether it was made out of two pieces or, as seems more probable, out of a single piece. A similar dress was worn by the Elamites, but it is not clear whether the Persians adopted an Elamite dress or vice versa. A further complication is that in Greek descriptions and representations Persians wore the same dress as the Medes. The Persian kings wore a form of cylindrical crown, while other Persians wore a cylindrical fluted headdress, a fillet, or a form of turban that covered their chins. The Elamites wore a fillet tied at the back of the head. From the evidence of seals and minor arts it seems that Persian women wore a similar type of gown to that worn by the Persian and Elamite men.

The Medes wore a long-sleeved knee-length tunic, trousers or hose, and sometimes a coat was draped over the shoulders. Similar dress was worn by Persians, Armenians, Cappadocians, Arians, Bactrians, Parthians, Arachosians and Drangianans. The trousers might be either tight-fitting or loose, and sometimes coats with sleeves or simple cloaks are shown. Such dress is typical of Iranian riding peoples. Both Medes and Persians who wore this costume also wore either a smooth rounded hat with a tail hanging behind or a type of bonnet with earflaps. Other peoples went bareheaded, or wore fillets, turbans or bonnets.

A similar costume was worn by the Saka or Scythian peoples—Scythians, Sogdians, Chorasmians, Skudrians (Thracians)—but they are shown with a long-sleeved belted jacket with a cut-away front lower edge over their trousers. These peoples normally wore a variation of the Median bonnet. One tall pointed type of bonnet, shown both at Persepolis and at Bisitun, has been recognized as typical of the Saka Tigrakhauda or 'pointed-hat Scythians'.

A group of Indic peoples—Indian (Sind), Gandhara, Sattagydian and Makan—are shown wearing a short kilt, sometimes with a cloak. Sometimes these figures are shown bareheaded and sometimes with a fillet.

Finally, a miscellaneous group of plains dwellers wore knee-length or ankle-length gowns, often with a cloak. They included Babylonians, Assyrians, Arabians, Egyptians, Libyans, Nubians, Lydians, Ionians and Carians. Most of these peoples went bareheaded, though the Assyrians were shown with a fillet and the Babylonians with a bell-shaped headdress of a type worn by earlier Babylonian kings, and the Lydians wore a tall turban.

BIBLIOGRAPHY

G. Walser: *Die Völkerschaften auf den Reliefs von Persepolis: Historische Studien über den sogenannten Tributzug an der Apadanatreppe* (Berlin, 1966)

M. Roaf: 'The Subject Peoples on the Base of the Statue of Darius', *Cah. Dél. Archéol. Fr. Iran*, iv (1974), pp. 73–160

MICHAEL ROAF

(c) Parthian and Sasanian. The costume of the Parthians (*c.* 250 BC–*c.* AD 224), as known from monuments, is a type of trouser suit for male figures (*see* PARTHIAN, fig. 2), while the few female representations known from within the Parthian empire are either in Greek dress or in the nude or semi-nude. The trouser suit consisted of a round-necked, long-sleeved and belted tunic, which ended above or below the knees. Sometimes a short crossed-over jacket was worn instead. Combined with either the tunic or the jacket were trousers, which were usually baggy and tapered, but could also be of cylindrical shape. Sometimes a pair of leggings or over-trousers, probably of leather, was worn, either over the ordinary trousers or combined with a pair of short trousers. This is best seen on the large bronze statue from Shami (Tehran, Archaeol. Mus.; for illustration *see* ELYMAIS). The leggings were usually attached at the sides to a suspender-belt, which was hidden by the jacket or tunic. The wide leggings fell over the shoes, but the trousers were often worn inside ankle shoes or tucked into boots. Sometimes a shoulder-cloak or, more often, a long-sleeved coat, open at the front, were added to the trouser suit. Royal Arsacid coins clearly show on their reverse a figure with the long-sleeved coat draped over his shoulders. The royal headgear consisted of a diadem, either on its own or tied around a tall pointed tiara with earflaps and neck-guard. A loose sword strap could be tied below the waistband. A torque and a wide elaborate necklace were often worn, the latter particularly in the late Parthian period.

Sculptures from Nysa, the first capital of the Parthian empire, provide the earliest representations of the trouser suit; it remained popular throughout the Parthian period and became one of the hallmarks of Parthian art. The costume became highly elaborate, particularly during the late Parthian period, with geometric and floral motifs often decorating the tunic and trousers. Good examples occur on reliefs from sites in ancient Elymais, such as Tang-i Sarvak, Masjid-i Suleiman and Bard-i Nishandeh, but the most securely dated and elaborate examples of Parthian costume come from outside the Parthian empire. At Palmyra religious and funerary art represent many male figures, including deities, priests and wealthy men wearing various combinations of the Parthian trouser suit and other items of clothing. For example, the god Aglibol on the Bel Temple relief of the early 1st century AD wears a Parthian tunic and leggings with the Hellenistic cuirass. Priests, particularly in the 1st century AD, wore the trouser suit with the draped *himation* (a rectangular outer garment). The costumes of these wealthy inhabitants are often decorated with elaborate designs, particularly in the 2nd and early 3rd centuries AD. A similar pattern can be observed in sculpture from Hatra in Mesopotamia where, among the statues and reliefs of worshippers set up in various shrines and temples (see fig. 34m), all the combinations of the trouser suit are depicted. It is worn by royals, non-royals, some deities and prosperous members of the city. The beautifully designed tunics, trousers, leggings and long-sleeved coats were often embroidered with elaborate floral and geometric designs. At Dura Europos figures clad in the Parthian costume appear on the stone sculptures and in wall paintings in the Bel Temple, the Mithraeum, private houses and particularly the synagogue (e.g. Damascus, N. Mus.). Most of the paintings date from the Roman occupation of the city. Finds of textiles from Dura Europos and Palmyra indicate that wool was probably used for the tunic, trousers and the long-sleeved coat.

The dress of the Sasanian period (*c.* AD 224–*c.* 651) generally consisted of the same items as in the Parthian period. The trouser suit continued to be the official and ceremonial outfit in which the king of kings (see fig. 34n), princes, deities and nobles were depicted. Female figures wore a long dress (see fig. 34o). Figures were also depicted in heavy armour. This is well illustrated during the early period on the relief of Ardashir I (*reg* AD 224–41) at FIRUZABAD and the commemoration of his victory over the last Parthian king Artabanus IV (*reg* AD 213–24).

The round-necked, long-sleeved tunic is usually slit at the sides, and in addition to the belt there is again a loose strap for supporting the sword in its scabbard. Wide leggings, falling over the shoes and attached by a button to suspender-belts, cover the legs. These leggings are held tight by straps that pass under the foot. Also common are baggy trousers, sometimes tucked into boots and usually combined with a straight tunic. A crossed-over belted tunic or jacket can replace the round-necked tunic, as on the colossal statue of *Shapur I* (*reg* AD 241–72) from a cave near Bishapur (*see* IRAN, ANCIENT, fig. 10). Over the round-necked tunic, a flowing shoulder-cloak or a long-sleeved coat were common. Both types of overgarment were usually secured by two circular brooches on the upper part of the chest. The long-sleeved coat is worn not only by the king, gods, priests and other dignitaries but also by some female figures, such as the goddess Anahita on the rock carving associated with Chosroes II Parviz (*reg* AD 590–628) at Taq-i Bustan. Here the long overcoat is hung over the shoulders with the sleeves left empty, recalling depictions of this garment on the reverse of Parthian coins. In the late Sasanian period, particularly after the end of the 4th century AD, the long-sleeved tunic apparently underwent some minor changes. Reliefs, hunting bowls and stamp seals of this time depict a type of tunic that is no longer loose and wide, but is narrow at the bottom and has a U-shaped hem at the front. A halter, consisting of straps over the shoulders and around the chest and secured in the centre by a round clasp, is worn over the tunic. A thick necklace of large beads or precious stones is often worn.

The most striking and typical item of Sasanian clothing is the headgear. Each Sasanian king had his personal crown—a reliable means of identifying the various rulers. Although Ardashir I still wore the bejewelled headgear of the Parthian ruler Mithradates II (*reg* 123–88 BC) on some of his coins, both he and his successors preferred the combination of the crown, diadem and *korymbos* (a ball of hair covered with a silk cloth; see fig. 35). The ends of the diadem were left loose like ribbons. A tall tiara-like hat, rounded at the top and sometimes ending in an animal head, was worn both with and without a diadem by princes, dignitaries and nobles. It often bore at the side a personal device, sometimes enabling identification of the owner. Altogether the dress of the Sasanian period is much more elaborate than the Parthian, being full of folds, frills and bows, recalling the description by Ammianus Marcellinus (*c.* AD 330–95): 'most of them are . . . covered with clothes gleaming with many shimmering colours . . . they have their robes open in the front and on the sides, and let them flutter in the wind, yet from their head to their shoes no part of the body is seen uncovered'.

BIBLIOGRAPHY

R. Ghirshman: *Iran: Parthians and Sasanians* (London, 1962)
D. Schlumberger: *L'Orient hellénisé* (Paris, 1970)
A. Perkins: *The Art of Dura Europos* (Oxford, 1973)
F. Safar and M. A. Mustafa: *Al-Ḥaḍr: Madīnat al-shams* [Hatra: the city of the sun god] (Baghdad, 1974)
M. A. R. Colledge: *The Art of Palmyra* (London, 1976)
R. Ghirshman: *Terrasses sacrées de Bard-é Nechandeh et de Masjid-i Solaiman*, 2 vols (Leiden, 1976)
M. A. R. Colledge: *Parthian Art* (London, 1977)
G. Herrmann: *The Iranian Revival*, The Making of the Past (Oxford, 1977)
P. O. Harper and P. Meyers: *Royal Imagery* (1981), i of *Silver Vessels of the Sasanian Period* (New York, 1981–)

VESTA SARKHOSH CURTIS

8. COINS. Coinage was invented in Asia Minor around 600 BC. It is not certain whether the first coins were made by Greek settlers in Ionia or by their Lydian overlords, but there is no doubt that the Greeks quickly became the principal coin producers: coinage rapidly spread west into Europe, but its progress eastward into the heartlands of the Ancient Near East was much slower. The most important issuers of the earliest phase of coinage were the kings of Lydia, whose small white gold coins were decorated with a lion's head or, on fractional pieces, a lion's paw, presumably heraldic symbols of the kingdom. The last and best-known Lydian king, Croesus (*reg* 560–546 BC), is usually credited with introducing the first bimetallic coinage, consisting of gold and silver staters and fractions decorated with confronting foreparts of a lion and bull. These coins are known as 'Croeseids', though most of the issues were probably produced after the overthrow of the Lydian kingdom by the Achaemenid Persians.

(i) Achaemenid. The lion and bull coins were succeeded by gold darics and silver sigloi, first issued towards the end of the 6th century BC. These are the definitive Achaemenid coins, mass-produced and circulating until the conquest of the Persian empire in 331 BC by Alexander the Great (*reg* 336–323 BC). On one side they depict a crowned figure, armed with a bow, and sometimes also with a spear or dagger (see fig. 35a); while the other shows only the imprint of a punch, continuing an earlier Lydian tradition at a time when most other coinages were struck with designs on both sides (*see* GREECE, ANCIENT, §X, 2(i) and (ii)). The 'royal archer' figure symbolized the authority of the Persian Great King. The Greeks, who called the coins 'darics', may have seen in the figure a portrait of King Darius I (*reg* 521–486 BC).

Other, local, coinages were also produced within the Persian empire. In coastal areas of Asia Minor, Cyprus and Cyrenaica coins with Greek-style designs were issued by the predominantly Greek populations. In Phoenicia the coastal cities such as Aradus, Sidon and Tyre issued coins with designs influenced by Achaemenid royal art, though with an emphasis on maritime subjects. Client kings, such as the Hekatomnids of Caria, and Persian satraps (provincial governors) also produced their own issues in the 4th century BC. Designs on Greek coins were often imitated, notably the ubiquitous 'owls' of Athens, which were copied as far as southern Arabia; but there were also innovations, for instance portraiture, which first developed on coins in the issues of local dynasts in Lycia and the Persian satraps.

(ii) Parthian. Alexander the Great's conquest of the Persian empire brought great changes to the coinages of

35. Coins from the Ancient Near East: (a) Achaemenid silver siglos, struck at Sardis, *c.* 500 BC; (b) Parthian silver drachm of King Mithridates II, 123–88 BC (obverse and reverse); (c) Sasanian silver drachm of King Shapur I, AD 241–70 (all in London, British Museum)

the Ancient Near East. His mass-produced coinage was minted further east than any Achaemenid issues, and the Greek designs and script on the coins of Alexander and his Macedonian successors in the east, the Seleucid kings, had a lasting impact on the native issues of coinage which eventually emerged (*see* GREECE, ANCIENT, §X, 2(iii)). The Parthian kingdom, traditionally founded in 247 BC, rose to become the dominant power in the region. Its principal coins were silver drachms (see fig. 35b) issued from numerous mints in the Iranian Plateau, and silver four-drachm pieces minted in Mesopotamia. Portraits of the Arsacid dynasty of Parthian kings dominate the coinage. They depict bearded Iranian monarchs in Parthian royal dress, but they belong to the Greek tradition of portraiture developed in the Hellenistic kingdoms. The designs that accompany the portraits, featuring a seated Iranian bowman or standing figures surrounded by legends in Greek, also follow Hellenistic prototypes. The early issues have a style that suggests the employment of Greek die-cutters; later Parthian coins developed their own, more linear, style, and the Greek legends degenerated and were eventually replaced by Pehlevi inscriptions.

Portrait coins in the Hellenistic Greek tradition were issued by the other native kingdoms of Persis, Elymais and Characene, which emerged in the region to the north of the Persian Gulf during the long decline of the Seleucid kingdom. On the coins of Elymais and Characene, Seleucid coin designs were also copied for the reverses, and Greek lettering was employed; but in Persis a design depicting the priest-king before a fire altar was used, together with inscriptions in Aramaic. The Nabataean kings of northern Arabia issued portrait coins in the first centuries BC and AD, but in the same period their neighbours, the Hasmonaean and later Herodian kings of Judaea, studiously avoided portraits. Their coins were decorated mostly with inanimate objects, such as palms, vessels and anchors, and Hebrew inscriptions.

(iii) Sasanian. In AD 224 the Arsacid dynasty was overthrown by Ardashir, ruler of Persis. The Sasanian empire that he founded dominated the Near East until the Arab conquest of 651. The standard Sasanian coin was the silver drachm, which was larger in diameter but much thinner and flatter than the Parthian drachm. The same coin designs were used throughout the history of the Sasanian empire: the king's head and the Zoroastrian fire altar, as on the earlier coins of Persis. Each king was distinguished by a different crown (see fig. 35c), which stated his religious affinities. Two figures, usually either the king and his heir or the king and a patron deity, frequently appeared beside the fire altar on the reverse design.

BIBLIOGRAPHY

R. Gobl: *Sasanian Numismatics* (Brunswick, 1971)
D. G. Sellwood: *An Introduction to the Coinage of Parthia* (London, 1971, rev. 1980)
M. Alram: *Iranisches Personennamenbuch* (Vienna, 1986)
I. Carradice: 'The "Regal" Coinage of the Persian Empire', *The Ninth Oxford Symposium on Coinage and Monetary History: Oxford 1986*, pp. 73–108

IAN CARRADICE

9. MOSAICS. The decoration of buildings using mosaic-like techniques began as early as the 4th millennium BC, when walls, pilasters and columns at URUK were embellished with cones of coloured limestone or clay dipped in paint and set in bitumen. The cones were arranged in geometric patterns, often based on zigzags and perhaps intended to reproduce the patterns on the trunk of the date-palm (e.g. London, BM). In the mid-3rd millennium BC panels were decorated with designs in shell, lapis lazuli and coloured limestone set in bitumen. Such panels have been found at several Mesopotamian sites, especially Mari and Ur (e.g. the 'Royal Standard' of Ur; *see* UR, fig. 2). The antecedents of the Greek and Roman tradition of floor mosaics, however, are to be found in the geometric floors made from river pebbles in Assyria and Phrygia during the 8th and 7th centuries BC.

(i) Assyrian. All the known Assyrian examples come from unroofed areas and are simple black and white chequerwork designs, sometimes embellished with solid circles or rosettes within squares, or squares of red pebbles. Squares of pebble mosaic may be interspersed with terracotta floor tiles. Individual rows of the designs were first laid out with lines of setting stones in one or both directions. Where the floor area was not a true rectangle, the mosaicists distorted the pattern in order to accommodate it.

Two pebble mosaics were excavated at Assur by the German archaeologist Walter Andrae. One, of simple chequerwork design, paved an open area north-west of the *Junge West-Zikurrat* in the Anu-Adad temple complex and was perhaps in the courtyard of a building that encroached on the temple area in the later Neo-Assyrian period. The other Assur mosaic, in which long pebbles were set radially within each square to form rosettes, covered the north-east side of the courtyard in the 'caravanserai'; to the north-west it degenerated into a coarse cobbled floor. French excavations by F. Thureau-Dangin and M. Dunand in the palace of the provincial Neo-Assyrian city of Til-Barsip in north Syria revealed mosaics in a room apparently connected with a bath complex and also along a corridor. These have a regular geometric pattern of white circles in black squares alternating with white squares containing black circles. A double row of squares ran down the centre of the corridor, separated from rows along either edge by large terracotta floor tiles, which were commonly used by Neo-Assyrian architects. These striking mosaics were laid only in relatively unimportant unroofed areas, such as the corridor, or where water was being used, for example next to a bathroom; water and bright sunlight brought out the vividness of the designs that would have appeared dull in the dark, lofty rooms of the palace, which were adorned with paintings.

The House of Ivories at Arslan Tash in north Syria was a two-storey residential building comprising ranges of long, narrow rooms arranged around an internal courtyard, which was floored with a pebble mosaic in a plain chequerwork pattern. An almost identical building has been excavated at Tille Höyük on the west bank of the River Euphrates in south-east Turkey. The Tille mosaic, also in an internal courtyard, consisted of 238 squares (*c.* 750 mm sq.), mostly black and white but with 4 symmetrically spaced red squares in the axial row leading to the door of the main reception room and 16 squares in one corner, which, like the Til-Barsip examples, have solid circles in opposing colours. Tille was a settlement in the Neo-Hittite state of Kummukh, which was conquered in 708 BC by Sargon II of Assyria (*reg* 721–705 BC). This would appear to indicate that the Tille building and, by implication, the House of Ivories at Arslan Tash were built at the end of the 8th century BC.

(ii) Phrygian. Gordion, the capital city of Phrygia, was richly adorned with pebble mosaics from the late 8th century BC onwards. Three of these floors were in megaron buildings that were destroyed by the Cimmerians in the late 8th century BC or the early 7th century BC. They are thus roughly contemporary with the mosaics in Assyria, although they are different in function, design and quality. The best-preserved, from Megaron 2 (10.85×9.7 m; Yassıhöyük, Gordion Mus.; *see* GORDION, fig. 1), was made from small river pebbles of various colours. The design consisted of several randomly placed and orientated geometric patterns. The other early mosaics from Gordion belonged to the same tradition but were poorly preserved. Unlike those at Til-Barsip, the pebble mosaic floors at Gordion were laid in the most important rooms and display outstanding craftsmanship.

BIBLIOGRAPHY

W. Andrae: *Der Anu-Adad Tempel in Assur*, Wiss. Veröff. Dt. Orient-Ges., x (Leipzig, 1909)

F. Thureau-Dangin and others: *Arslan-Tash*, 2 vols (Paris, 1931)

F. Thureau-Dangin and M. Dunand: *Til-Barsip* (Paris, 1936), p. 25, pl. xlii

T. Özgüç: *Altıntepe* (Ankara, 1966), p. 8, pls 4, 16

G. Turner: 'The Palace and Bâtiment aux Ivoires at Arslan Tash: A Reappraisal', *Iraq*, xxx (1968), pp. 62–8

D. Salzmann: *Untersuchungen zu den antiken Kieselmosaiken*, Archäologische Forschungen (Berlin, 1982)

D. H. French: 'Tille, 1984', *VII. Kazı Sonuçları Toplantısı* (Ankara, 1985), pp. 211–15

G. D. SUMMERS

10. FURNITURE. Few pieces of wooden furniture survive, but exceptional conditions in sealed tombs at JERICO in Palestine (*c*. 1800–1650 BC; e.g. London, BM) and at GORDION in Phrygia (late 8th–early 7th century BC; Ankara, Mus. Anatol. Civiliz.) preserved some pieces, including, in both cases, tripod tables. At Jerico there were also stools and a bed with caned tops; the feet are mostly of a distinctive shape, derived from the lions' paws on Egyptian furniture but cut out of flat wood. The Phrygian tombs contained boxwood and yew tripod stands (*see* GORDION, fig. 2) and tables, which are elaborately carved with openwork and inlaid geometric patterns or bronze studs. One, the 'Pagoda Table', is exceptionally elaborate with lace-like openwork lattices and struts. Decorated beds (including four-posters), chairs, footstools, screens and chests were also found. The grain of the wood follows the bent legs of the tables, possibly indicating a bentwood technique. Mortice and tenon joints were used and the workmanship is of remarkable quality.

The Phrygian finds were a revelation because they represent types of furniture that are never depicted on reliefs and seal engravings, which show relatively simple furniture, generally using straight elements. Stools were apparently the most common form of seat, and chairs were generally low-backed. In the 3rd millennium BC furniture had vertical struts, of which one pair was shaped like bulls' legs on the more elaborate examples (e.g. London, BM). Towards the end of the 3rd millennium BC padded stools with plain feet and horizontal stretchers appeared, and these remained popular for several centuries. Bentwood legs for tables are depicted on seals and seal impressions of the early 2nd millennium BC (e.g. from Kültepe; Ankara, Mus. Anatol. Civiliz.), and on an ivory of the same period from Ebla in Syria (Damascus, N. Mus.). In Neo-Assyrian times the king often sat on a stool with palmette feet, the seat of which was decorated with animal heads, and used a footstool with lions' feet. Reliefs of the 8th century BC onwards depict straight-backed thrones with arm-rests sometimes supported by figures with raised arms (e.g. London, BM); an example of such a figure in bronze has survived (Baghdad, Iraq Mus.). The bronze decoration of a throne of this date was discovered in the temple at Toprakkale in Urartu; in this case some of the supporting figures were winged monsters originally covered in gold leaf, with inlaid faces and eyes (London, BM; St Petersburg, Hermitage). Beds had bulls' legs, and incurving bedheads are depicted from the early 3rd millennium BC until Neo-Assyrian times, as on the 'Garden Party' relief of Assurbanipal (*reg* 668–627) from Nineveh (*c*. 650 BC; London, BM; *see* ASSYRIAN). Beds supported by figures of subject peoples are depicted on Achaemenid funerary monuments (*see* ZOROASTRIANISM, fig. 1). Representations of tables on Neo-Assyrian reliefs show them to have had three legs, and stone examples survive (e.g. London, BM). Finds of bronze and ivory sheathing struts and stretchers are often decorated with palmettes and scrolls. Carved ivory panels for chair-backs and bedheads occur from the 2nd millennium BC onwards (e.g. from Ugarit; Damascus, N. Mus.). Many were found stacked in the storerooms of the palaces at Nimrud in Assyria (*see also* §3(ii)(c) above), where they had been taken as booty from parts of the Assyrian empire before its collapse in 612 BC (e.g. London, BM). Although the Persepolis reliefs show that Achaemenid furniture continued in the Assyrian tradition, the furniture of Seleucid, Parthian and Sasanian times is poorly documented.

BIBLIOGRAPHY

H. S. Baker: *Furniture in the Ancient World* (London, 1966), pp. 157–232

E. Simpson: 'Reconstructing an Ancient Table', *Expedition* (Summer 1983), pp. 11–27

E. Simpson and R. Payton: 'Royal Wooden Furniture from Gordion', *Archaeology* [New York], xxxix/6 (1986), pp. 40–47

E. Simpson: 'The Phrygian Artistic Intellect', *Source*, vii/3–4 (1988), pp. 24–42

The Furniture of Western Asia: Proceedings of a Conference Held at the Institute of Archaeology, University College, London: London, 1993

11. MUSICAL INSTRUMENTS. As with textiles, dress and furniture, knowledge of musical instruments in the Ancient Near East is largely derived from their depiction in art. There are, however, some notable exceptions. During the excavation of burials of *c*. 2600 BC in the Royal Cemetery at Ur, the excavators found hollow areas into which they poured plaster and recovered the casts of at least eight lyres and two harps. The wooden parts had rotted, but the decoration in silver and gold, and inlays of shell, limestone and lapis lazuli set in bitumen were still preserved. The lyres (London, BM; Baghdad, Iraq Mus.; Philadelphia, U. PA, Mus.) were generally portable, with approximately 11 strings, and the soundboxes were decorated with the head of a bull, which, in some cases, had a

silver, gold or lapis lazuli beard fastened over the muzzle. One particularly fine inlaid panel (Philadelphia, U. PA, Mus.) from the front of a soundbox depicts scenes in four registers: these show a nude hero clasping two bison with human faces; a hyena, lion and goat bearing a table of food, and a jar and cups of drink for a banquet, with a scorpion-man as master of ceremonies; and an orchestra consisting of a donkey plucking the strings of a large, free-standing bull-headed lyre and a small quadruped with a sistrum playing for a dancing bear. One boat-shaped lyre was decorated with the figure of a stag. Silver double pipes were also found in the Royal Cemetery (Philadelphia, U. PA, Mus.).

Other surviving instruments of various periods include bone pipes or whistles and clay rattles, sometimes in the shape of animals and birds. Clappers of *c.* 3000 BC were found at Kish (U. Chicago, IL, Orient. Inst. Mus.) and are depicted from the 3rd millennium BC onwards (e.g. London, BM). Some cymbals also survive (London, BM).

Among the earliest representations of musical instruments may be a design scratched on a stone from Megiddo in Palestine just before 3000 BC, which possibly depicts a man with a lyre. Lyres seem to have been popular in Syria, where symmetrical and asymmetrical types are known and were transmitted to Egypt in the 15th century BC. Both types appear together on an 8th-century BC relief from Karatepe in south-east Turkey, and lyres of different sizes are shown on the Inandık Vase (16th century BC; Ankara, Mus. Anatol. Civiliz.). It was the symmetrical lyre or cithara that was adopted in Greece, via Cyprus and Crete. Some lyres had ducks' heads decorating the uprights, while others had bulls' heads, and this probably reflected the type of sound the instruments produced. Harps seem to have been less common except in Elam: a vertical and a horizontal variety are depicted together on an Assyrian relief from Nineveh (*c.* 650 BC; London, BM); the upright of the horizontal variety was shaped like a human arm.

Lutes are first attested on two Akkadian cylinder seals, one of them belonging to a singer (*c.* 2300 BC; London, BM). From then on they appear sporadically on monuments, including some early 2nd-millennium BC terracottas of small nude musicians. They were transmitted to Egypt via Syria in the 15th century BC. Tambourines and frame-drums often accompany erotic scenes of the early 2nd millennium BC onwards, and huge drums are depicted on several stelae of the late 3rd millennium BC (e.g. the Ur-Nammu Stele; Philadelphia, U. PA, Mus.). Reed instruments in the form of double pipes appear on Assyrian reliefs of the 7th century BC and are also played by a small figure that forms part of a terracotta group from Boğazköy (Ankara, Mus. Anatol. Civiliz.). Bells appear in Neo-Assyrian times, and the first dated examples are inscribed with the names of Urartian kings of about 800 BC.

An orchestra consisting of a harp, clappers and a singer appears on a seal impression dating to *c.* 3100 BC. Lyres and, more rarely, harps are depicted on inlaid panels and seals of the 3rd millennium BC, as parts of orchestras accompanying singers at banquets (e.g. from Ur; London, BM), and the statue of a singer, sitting cross-legged, was found at Mari (Damascus, N. Mus.). Lutes, horizontal harps and handclapping accompany a macabre dance by 9th-century BC Assyrian soldiers, who hold the decapitated heads of their enemies (from Nimrud; London, BM). Ivory boxes and bronze bowls of Syrian manufacture (9th–8th century BC; London, BM) and reliefs, such as the 'Garden Party' relief from Nineveh of Assurbanipal in his harem (*c.* 650 BC; London, BM; for illustration *see* ASSYRIAN), depict processions of musicians playing lutes, tambourines, frame-drums, double pipes, harps and lyres.

BIBLIOGRAPHY

RLA: 'Laute', 'Leier', 'Musik'

J. Rimmer: *Ancient Musical Instruments of Western Asia in the British Museum* (London, 1969)

T. C. Mitchell, ed.: *Music and Civilisation* (London, 1980), pp. 13–42

S. A. Rashid: *Mesopotamien* (1984), II/ii of *Musikgeschichte in Bildern* (Leipzig, 1965–)

D. Collon: *First Impressions: Cylinder Seals in the Ancient Near East* (London, 1987), pp. 151–3

DOMINIQUE COLLON

III. Rediscovery.

1. Excavation and research. 2. Collecting and dealing. 3. Forgeries.

1. Excavation and research.

(i) Early investigations, before 1853. (ii) 1853–1918. (iii) 1919–45. (iv) After 1945.

(i) Early investigations, before 1853. Until the mid-19th century most countries in the Near East were subject to the rule of the Ottoman empire. Knowledge of their historical geography among Europeans depended largely on the Bible and Classical literature, while interest in their antiquities was stimulated only by the accounts of a few enterprising travellers. The sites of Nineveh and Babylon had been tentatively located, but more reliable information was not available until the arrival of Claudius James Rich (1787–1821), who was appointed British Resident in Baghdad in 1808. Rich's closer examination of the mounds and the modest collection of inscribed objects that he sent to the British Museum seemed temporarily to exhaust the possibility of further research without excavation.

The first attempt at excavation was made in 1842 by Paul-Emile Botta (1802–70) at a site called KHORSABAD, 23 km north-east of Mosul, where he uncovered the short-lived capital of Assyria, which was built and occupied by Sargon II (*reg* 721–705 BC). He encountered the heavy mud-brick walls of a palace and temples, which were lined with relief sculptures in stone and portal figures in the form of winged bulls. Botta believed that he had discovered Nineveh, and the publication of his finds, subsidized by the Louvre, was entitled *Monument de Ninive* (London, 1850). Soon afterwards AUSTEN HENRY LAYARD concentrated on the huge mound beside the River Tigris, 32 km south-west of Mosul, that marked the remains of NIMRUD (Calah), an earlier Assyrian capital built by Assurnasirpal II (*reg* 883–859 BC). Like Botta, Layard (who also thought that he had discovered ancient Nineveh) recovered many hundred metres of relief sculptures and portal figures, often by tunnelling along the bases of the massive walls. There were also inscriptions in the cuneiform writing of ancient Mesopotamia, which scholars were beginning to understand (*see* §I, 3(ii) above).

Forty years earlier, attempts at deciphering this script had been made by the German scholar Georg Friedrich Grötefend (1775–1853), while studying similar inscriptions from sites in Persia. His conclusions, however, were still unpublished when, in 1835, Sir Henry Creswicke Rawlinson (1810–95) recorded the great trilingual inscription of the Achaemenid king Darius I (*reg* 521–486 BC) on a high rock-face at BISITUN near Kirmanshah in Iran. Rawlinson's decipherment, in collaboration with other orientalists, was already far advanced in 1843 when Layard discovered at Nimrud the 'Black Obelisk' (London, BM) of Shalmaneser III (*reg* 858–824 BC), on which certain biblical names could be recognized. Together with other sensational material from Layard's site, the stele reached London in 1848, just before the publication of his own popular account of his work, *Nineveh and its Remains* (London, 1849; at that time he still thought Nimrud was Nineveh).

More volumes of drawings appeared in 1853 after Layard's second excavation, this time in the Küyünjik mound across the river from Mosul. This proved to be the ruins of NINEVEH itself, where he uncovered the palace of Sargon II's successor, Sennacherib (*reg* 704–681 BC), which contained a library of cuneiform tablets, including the *Epic of Creation* and a flood story similar to that in Genesis. After his finds had been published and installed in the British Museum, Layard withdrew from archaeology. His work was continued by his principal assistant, Hormuzd Rassam (1826–1910), who discovered at Küyünjik a second palace, built by Assurbanipal (*reg* 668–627 BC), which also contained a library. It was here also that he recovered the famous sequence of reliefs known as the *Lion Hunt* (London, BM).

At Khorsabad, meanwhile, Botta's work had been resumed by Victor Place (1818–75), and in 1855 a large consignment of antiquities was loaded on to country boats for transport by river to Basra. Unfortunately, at al-Qurna near the confluence with the River Euphrates, this 'armada' was set upon by hostile tribesmen, and its freight, including some 240 cases of sculpture, sank irretrievably beneath the waters of the Tigris. This disastrous loss included finds accumulated by French scholars engaged in examining city-mounds in the alluvial region of southern Iraq. For some years, British archaeologists too had been investigating major sites in this area, though without encouraging results. Among others, William Kennett Loftus (1820–56) succeeded in locating several important cities, including UR and ERIDU, where ineffectual soundings were made. Much inscribed material had been collected, but to those expecting sculpture and other treasures like those found in Assyria, the tangled remains of mud-brick foundations proved incomprehensible.

(ii) 1853–1918. During and after the Crimean War (1853–6) there was a lull in excavations in the Near East. When they were resumed in the final decades of the 19th century, some change in the ethics and methods of those taking part was clearly overdue. In Iraq, an undignified scramble for removable antiquities was the order of the day. In 1878, at Balawat near Nimrud, Rassam discovered and partly removed the bronze gates of Shalmaneser III (London, BM); at the same time Edmond de Sarzec (1837–1901) was digging for the Louvre at TELLOH, where fine archaic (22nd century BC) statues had appeared, depicting the governors of Lagash (Paris, Louvre). Six years later, an American expedition from Pennsylvania under Hermann V. Hilprecht (1859–1925) arrived at the neighbouring site of NIPPUR. After an initial disaster, in 1900 he literally 'made history' by discovering a vast library of tablets, many of them in Sumerian. In other respects his excavation methods were still imperfect, and much was lost. From 1897, beyond the Iranian border in the Dezful region, Jacques de Morgan (1857–1924) undertook the excavation of a gigantic mound covering the remains of SUSA, the Elamite capital. Among buildings of the 2nd and 3rd millennia BC he recovered priceless monuments looted from Mesopotamian cities during their many wars, including the Stele of Naram-Sin and Hammurabi's Code of Laws (Paris, Louvre; *see* AKKADIAN, fig. 1 and MESOPOTAMIA, fig. 14 respectively). In 1897 he acquired the official monopoly of Iranian archaeology, and his expedition was given the title Délégation française en Perse. However, de Morgan's excavations showed few signs of effective strategy or technique.

It was in the more accessible countries to the west that the great change was already taking place. Here, the purpose of archaeology had become better understood and the objective of excavators more clearly defined. In Asia Minor, for instance, it would be fair to credit HEINRICH SCHLIEMANN and Wilhelm Dörpfeld (1853–1940) with the first attempt to excavate a mound in depth, at Hisarlık in Turkey, unguided by major buildings, and to approve their rudimentary attempts to record the provenance of minor objects (*see* TROY (i)). The work of FLINDERS PETRIE in Egypt and Palestine from 1881 onwards first established the guiding principles of scientific excavation, introducing techniques during the next four decades that created new standards of procedural requirements. The forms of observation that he advocated included studies of ceramic chronology and analysis of artefacts, which were later to become common practice. At the end of the 19th century some order was at last brought into the method and conduct of excavation in Mesopotamia. By then no excavator had truly laid bare the actual buildings of an Assyrian or Babylonian city. The newly founded Deutsche Orient Gesellschaft remedied this situation through excavations between 1899 and 1913 by Robert Koldewey (1855–1925) and Walter Andrae (1875–1956), first at the site of BABYLON itself and later at ASSUR, cradle of the Assyrian empire. Their success was based on a new skill in tracing walls and the elucidation of mud-brick architecture by trained architects. At Babylon the results can be seen in the revelation of the city planning, in their reconstructions of major buildings with their glazed-brick ornament and, at Assur, their stratified records of the Temple of Ishtar, which dated from Sumerian times. Their methods and industry set a standard of procedure that their colleagues could no longer ignore and established new standards in regional archaeology.

While the Germans were concentrating on Mesopotamia, others were paying attention to the Levant. In Palestine they were at first concerned with biblical topography and the identification of ancient sites. Many major cities such as MEGIDDO, JERICO, Bethel and HAZOR had already been located. Some excavation was in progress, and the pre-Israelite history of the country was beginning to be understood, though the regional characteristics of its art and architecture could as yet hardly be recognized.

In coastal Syria, products of Phoenician craftsmanship and relics of luxury trade among the great trading centres could hardly escape notice. Further inland, however, one class of find had led to a much wider field of enquiry. From HAMA, Aleppo and elsewhere came stones bearing an unknown form of pictographic writing, which was soon also found in association with crude reliefs on rock-faces in southern Anatolia (*see* §I, 3(iii) above). Provisionally attributed by Archibald Henry Sayce (1845–1933) to the Hittites of the Old Testament, these could also be identified as the work of the inhabitants of certain ruined cities on the Syrian–Turkish border, where excavation became imperative. During the two decades preceding World War I, ZINCIRLI (anc. Sam'al) was revealed by the German Institute, SAKÇA GÖZÜ by John Garstang (1876–1956) and CARCHEMISH by archaeologists from the British Museum, including LEONARD WOOLLEY. These excavations exposed much elaborate architecture and a collection of sculptured reliefs and statues, slightly inferior to those of the late Assyrian palaces with which they proved to be contemporary. It now became apparent that the builders of these cities were not the true imperial Hittites ('Kheta' of the Egyptian annals). Far to the north-east, within the bend of the River Halys, German excavations at BOĞAZKÖY in 1906–8 revealed a vast fortified city, ancient Hattusa, capital of an empire whose rulers corresponded and fought with pharaohs of the 18th and 19th dynasties. Their gods were depicted in classically refined relief carvings at Yazılıkaya (*see* YAZILIKAYA (i)), a cave-sanctuary outside its walls, and the national archives were stored in its citadel; more than 10,000 tablets in the cuneiform script of the true Hittite language, which was soon translated by Bedřich Hrozný (1879–1952) and others. The term Neo-Hittite is now usually applied to the art of the Iron Age cities mentioned above, whose populations, after the fall of the Hittite empire (*c.* 1200 BC), included both fugitives from the Hittite homeland and a Luwian element to whom the hieroglyphic script has been attributed.

(iii) 1919–45. The return of peace after World War I inspired a wide range of archaeological activity throughout the Near East. Large-scale excavations during the next 20 years provided the basis for future research and the choice of sites. The focus of interest seemed to be shifting towards earlier periods, particularly in Mesopotamia, where the Sumerians now monopolized the attention of historians. Cities whose dynastic rulers featured by name in their literature became a prime target for investigation. The early discovery by Woolley at Ur of 'royal tombs', with their incomparable treasure and widespread exposure of public buildings, provided an initial stimulus, soon supplemented by the excavation by Louis Christian Watelin (1874–1934) of the palace of the rulers of Kish. An expedition from Chicago, under the direction of HENRI FRANKFORT, dealt methodically with the minor cities of Tell Asmar, Khafajeh and Tell Agrab in the DIYALA REGION and clarified the stratigraphic and chronological progression, concentrating on the enigma of Sumerian origins. They found themselves concerned with a vital phase in the evolution of pre-dynastic civilization, notable above all for the invention of pictographic writing. The complex of building remains, articulated with consummate skill, and the changing designs in pottery and carved artefacts, which they observed during many seasons of work, together created the basis from which the chronology of the Early Dynastic period (2900–2340 BC) was deduced.

Important Bronze Age discoveries were made in the years between the two world wars in other parts of the Near East. In the Levant, for instance, much had already been learnt about the Canaanite and Phoenician cities from the correspondence of the 18th dynasty between the 'great powers', found at EL-AMARNA in Egypt in Petrie's time. The great seaport of UGARIT (Ras Shamra) on the Syrian coast, often mentioned in these letters, was first excavated from 1929 by Claude Schaeffer (1898–1982). Its most important contribution was a library of tablets written in the first alphabetic cuneiform script. At Jerico, Garstang exposed buildings and fortifications relevant to biblical history. The failure of many Levantine sites to throw much light on contemporary art was partly compensated for during the late 1930s by the re-excavation by Gordon Loud of Megiddo, where the beginnings of Syrian ivory-carving were magnificently represented. At this time, however, art historians were perhaps better served by the excavations of small state-capitals of northern principalities, contemporary with Hammurabi's reign in Babylon (*c.* 1750 BC). These included palace ruins, such as the splendid metropolis at MARI (Tell Hariri) on the Middle Euphrates, excavated by André Parrot (1901–80), two palaces at TELL ATCHANA (Alalakh) on the River Orontes, excavated by Woolley, and others in Syria with a longer history, such as EBLA (Tell Mardikh) and TELL BRAK.

During the late 1930s the discovery at ALACA HÖYÜK, 32 km north of Boğazköy, of a pre-Hittite treasure comparable with the Royal Tombs at Ur gave a new impetus to Bronze Age research. Deep beneath the ruins of a walled city with a palace and sculpture attributable to an early Hittite régime, Hamit Koşay came upon a group of tombs (*c.* 2300 BC), structures of stone and wood, richly provided with funerary ornaments of gold and bronze. Smaller excavations, mostly aiming at stratigraphical determination, were carried out at sites on the Anatolian Plateau, while in the south more ambitious soundings, such as Garstang's successful enterprise at MERSIN in Cilicia, linked the antecedents of the Bronze Age with contemporary cultures in neighbouring countries.

(iv) After 1945. The British Institute of Archaeology at Ankara opened in 1948 and initiated a sequence of projects, culminating in a prolonged investigation of a major mound at BEYCESULTAN, to the west of the Hittite frontiers, revealing the spectacular remains of a burnt palace of the early 2nd millennium BC. Excavations at Boğazköy resumed in 1952, under Kurt Bittel (1907–91), and its citadel and temples have been intensively studied. However, initiative in excavation passed increasingly into the hands of Turkish archaeologists. Tahsin Özgüc and Nimet Özgüc returned to KÜLTEPE, the site of ancient Kanesh. During the 1920s Hrozný had traced the 'Cappadocian tablets' to this location, identifying them with a colony of Assyrian merchants, annexed to the pre-Hittite city. This dual setting produced a wealth of sealed clay documents and ceramic

objects (Ankara, Mus. Anatol. Civiliz.). Later discoveries have included a late Hittite palace at MAŞATHÖYÜK and the site of ACEMHÖYÜK, identified with the trading colony of Burushhanda. Other Turkish scholars interested themselves in Iron Age sites. One group, led by Halet Çambel and Bahadır Alkım, excavated Karatepe (Azatiwataya; *see* TERMEZ, §2(i)) on the River Ceyhan in Cilicia, discovering a bilingual inscription in Luwian hieroglyphics and Phoenician, and crude reliefs. From the 1960s most attention was focused on the Urartian cities of eastern Anatolia, a source of fine architecture, sculpture and inscriptions. Apart from the citadel at Lake Van itself (TOPRAKKALE), fortress cities and tombs have been excavated at ALTINTEPE, ADILCEVAZ, ÇAVUSTEPE and KAYALIDERE.

The art of Iran in the Bronze Age and Iron Age is known less from legitimate excavation than from chance finds and standing monuments. The work of the Délégation française en Perse at Susa, the capital of the Elamites in the mid-2nd millennium BC, has been supplemented by the discovery by Roman Ghirshman (1895–1979), at a neighbouring site called CHOGHA ZANBIL, of a well-dated architectural complex surrounding a colossal ziggurat temple with many unusual characteristics. Most of the distinctively Iranian works of art that have accumulated in museums and other collections throughout the world are derived from cemeteries, which were discovered and rifled from 1928 onwards. These seem to be an inexhaustible repository of Iranian craftsmanship, now collectively known as the 'Luristan bronzes'. Individual finds from further north, even richer in gold and silver ornament, included the famous Ziwiyeh Treasure and material from the AMLASH REGION. Such finds have been coordinated chronologically, first by the American excavation of a richly equipped palace (*c.* 900 BC) at HASANLU, south of Lake Urmia, and by the patient work of the Iranian scholar Ezat O. Negahban in a rich necropolis at MARLIK, near the Caspian coast. The metalwork and pottery from all these sources made an important contribution to the tradition of early Iranian art, which culminated in the palaces and rock-carvings of the Achaemenid Persians, transformed in their time by influences from Mesopotamia and contacts with Classical Greece.

After World War II the objectives of archaeological research in the Near East showed signs of a notable reorientation, largely replacing the predominant concern with the accomplishments of literate peoples with an interest in their prehistoric antecedents. This has resulted in the proliferation of stratigraphical soundings, some beneath the foundations of historical habitations, others at sites no longer occupied in later times. The progressive sophistication of communal living has been traced back to its origins in semi-barbarism, and the results of such research, often dependent on multi-disciplinary collaboration, have been voluminously published: architecture, wall painting, stone-carving, modelling in clay, metalwork and, especially, pottery design have been extensively studied in relation to chronology.

German research at URUK in Mesopotamia revealed the advanced architectural practices perfected by pre- or proto-Sumerian people in the late 4th millennium BC, and the head of a life-size statue and a variety of finely carved cylinder seals revealed additional features of the 'Uruk' culture. Woolley's soundings at Ur, beneath traces of the Uruk period, had produced the first evidence for an 'Ubaid' phase of prehistory, distinguished by its monochrome painted pottery. At nearby Eridu in 1946–7, Seton Lloyd (1902–) and Fuad Safar (1913–78) found a small tripartite temple of this period, its ruins incorporated in the platform of a more complicated 'Uruk' shrine. Earlier rebuildings were exposed down to a primitive chapel on virgin soil, revealing a long architectural sequence and varying pottery designs. These have since been correlated with other settlements in the southern provinces, including TELL ES-SAWWAN, with its interesting secular architecture, Hajji Muhammad, near Uruk, and CHOGA MAMI. Comparable developments in the prehistory of northern Iraq included the finds of MAX MALLOWAN at ARPACHIYAH and of Ephraim A. Speiser (1902–65) at TEPE GAWRA, where a pre-Ubaidian phase was characterized by superbly designed polychrome pottery, first found at TELL HALAF. Mallowan, in a deep sounding at Nineveh, had also found this pottery 24 m beneath the surface, separated from the basal rock only by a brief and enigmatic occupation, which was later identified by the Iraqi discoveries at Hassuna, where Neolithic nomads first settled. Few traces of primitive art were found in these upper Mesopotamian soundings, apart from significant variations of pottery designs. Some new examples were added to the category of clay figurines, found throughout the Near East from the Late Neolithic period onwards.

The sequence of cultural phases in Mesopotamian prehistory had next to be related to similar discoveries in neighbouring countries. In Iran a point of departure was created by de Morgan's findings in the deepest levels at Susa itself, and Ghirshman's at TEPE SIALK, near Kashan. Great interest was created by de Morgan's discovery in his level I of a painted ware more elegant than any then known. When, in 1957, the whole Iranian sequence was coordinated by Louis Le Breton (1909–57), this beautiful pottery was relabelled Susa A and dated to the early Uruk period (*c.* 4000 BC). The excavation of Early Bronze Age sites, such as Godin Tepe, the Elamite capital of Anshan (TALL'I MALYAN), TEPE YAHYA and SHAHR-I SOKHTA, has thrown further light on the early trade routes linking Elam with Afghanistan.

Excavations in countries nearer to the Mediterranean have extended the history of applied arts. KATHLEEN MARY KENYON, during her meticulous study of Jericho stratigraphy in the 1950s, had already reached a level described as 'Pre-pottery Neolithic' (7th millennium BC), when she came upon the 'portrait heads' modelled in plaster over human skulls. At HACILAR in Anatolia, James Mellaart found pottery vessels, in shape and ornament comparable in perfection to Susa A, and beneath them a new and lively repertory of clay figurines. His most important revelation, however, was at ÇATAL HÜYÜK in the Konya Plain, where, in rapid cultural advancement, a township of contiguous dwellings (*c.* 6000 BC) produced flint implements, textiles and wooden counterparts of pottery vessels; human and animal figures were modelled in clay or carved in stone, and chambers were decorated with wall paintings. Another major discovery took place at Ebla, where Italian excavations under Paolo Matthiae uncovered palaces, rich tombs, ivories and jewellery, which have revealed the hitherto unsuspected wealth of north Syrian cities in the late 3rd and early 2nd millennia BC.

The construction of hydroelectric dams and irrigation projects, canals and motorways has resulted in government sponsorship of rescue archaeology. Huge areas of Turkey, Syria and Iraq have been investigated by teams of archaeologists, anthropologists, botanists, zoologists and geologists, before they were flooded as a result of dam-building on the Euphrates (Keban, Tabqa, Haditha), Tigris (Eski Mosul), Zab and Hamrin rivers. Both major and minor sites and patterns of settlement have been recorded in areas for which there had previously been little or no archaeological information, as part of an inter-disciplinary study.

BIBLIOGRAPHY

A. U. Pope and P. Ackerman, eds: *Survey of Persian Art*, i–iv (1938–9)
S. Lloyd: *Foundations in the Dust* (Harmondsworth, 1947; rev. London, 1980)
A. Godard: *Le Trésor de Ziwiyé* (Haarlem, 1950)
H. Frankfort: *Art and Architecture of the Ancient Orient*, Pelican Hist. A. (Harmondsworth, 1954, rev. 4/1979)
E. Akurgal: *The Art of the Hittites* (London, 1962)
S. Piggott: *The Dawn of Civilization* (London, 1962)
E. Strommenger and M. Hirmer: *Fünf Jahrtausende Mesopotamien: Die Kunst von den Anfängen um 5000 v. Chr. bis zu Alexander dem Grossem* (Munich, 1962); Eng. trans. as *The Art of Mesopotamia* (London, 1964)
R. Ghirshman: *Persia from the Origins to Alexander the Great* (London, 1964)
W. Culican: *The Medes and Persians* (London, 1965)
S. Lloyd: *The Art of the Ancient Near East* (London, 1965)
J. Mellaart: *Çatal Hüyük: A Neolithic Town in Anatolia* (London, 1967)
——: *The Neolithic of the Near East* (London, 1975)
S. Lloyd: *The Archaeology of Mesopotamia* (London, 1978, rev. 1984)
J. Mellaart: *The Archaeology of Ancient Turkey* (London, 1978)

SETON LLOYD

2. Collecting and dealing.

(i) Before 1900. Interest in Near Eastern antiquities was probably first shown in the early 17th century. In England Thomas Howard (*see* HOWARD (i), (1)), the 2nd Earl of Arundel, acquired ancient sculptures from Asiatic Turkey, but these were of Greco-Roman date and thus are of significance here only as to their provenance. In 1620–21 PIETRO DELLA VALLE, an Italian nobleman, travelled in Mesopotamia and Persia (Iran), where he copied and collected cuneiform inscriptions in Babylon and Persepolis. The German scholar CARSTEN NIEBUHR spent about a month at Persepolis in 1765 making extensive plans and drawings of the architecture, reliefs and inscriptions. The first sizeable group of antiquities to be brought back to Europe was probably that of Claudius James Rich (1787–1821), British Resident in Baghdad from 1808 (*see also* §1(i) above), which his widow sold to the British Museum in 1825 for the considerable sum of £7000.

Real interest in Near Eastern antiquities was inspired by the excavations of the Assyrian capitals by Paul-Emile Botta (1802–70) and Victor Place (1818–75) at Khorsabad and by AUSTEN HENRY LAYARD at Nineveh and Nimrud. The latter's discoveries, with their proven Old Testament connections, aroused interest in religious circles, especially in America. In the North-west Palace of King Assurnasirpal II at Nimrud, Layard unearthed numerous orthostats of 'Mosul marble' (gypsum), many carved in relief with repetitive scenes, unlike those from Nineveh and Khorsabad, which mostly illustrated narrative scenes. A selection of the Nimrud reliefs was dispatched to the British Museum, leaving behind many duplicates (*see also* MESOPOTAMIA, §III, 6(i)). In 1851 and 1855 Dwight Whitney Marsh (1823–90), an American missionary based in Mosul, obtained a series of reliefs and sent them to American seminaries at Williamstown (Williamstown, MA, Williams Coll. Mus. A.), St Louis, MO (now in Kansas City, MO, Nelson-Atkins Mus. A.), and Hartford, CT (now in Hartford, CT, Wadsworth Atheneum). In the following decade other American missionaries in Mosul acquired from Sir Henry Creswicke Rawlinson (1810–95) at least 55 slabs from the North-west Palace, and at least another 43 slabs from the same palace were later sent to America. European institutions were also active: for example in 1864 Julius Weber-Locher (1838–1906) sent 14 large slabs to Zurich, and in 1864–5 the French consul in Baghdad, Pacifique Delaporte, presented further Nimrud reliefs to the Louvre.

This early interest in collecting Neo-Assyrian sculptures, which inspired an art style known as ASSYRIAN REVIVAL, was primarily religious rather than aesthetic: the reliefs provided the first authentication of the Old Testament and were thus intended to fire the enthusiasm of young missionaries. At the same time Layard and his successors had sent to the British Museum a huge quantity of cuneiform tablets, mostly from the library of King Assurbanipal at Kuyunjik (Nineveh). Following the rapid decipherment of cuneiform and the translation of Akkadian and then Sumerian (*see* §I, 3(ii) above), interest was focused almost entirely on inscriptions. Excavations in southern Iraq, for instance by the French at Telloh and by the Americans at Nippur (and also by unofficial diggers), produced further vast quantities of tablets, which found their way into European and American collections, both public and private. Some artefacts of great importance were also discovered, but as yet they were little sought after.

To the east antiquities were also appearing from Iran, and to the west from Syria and Turkey. In the Levant interest focused on objects from the Greco-Roman periods, although earlier pieces were also acquired, for example those in the De Clercq collection (now dispersed). In Aleppo the hereditary Italian consuls, the Marcopoli family, were active collectors, perhaps from as early as the 18th century, although the main collection was made much later, in the mid-20th century, by Paolo Marcopoli. (He accumulated cylinder and stamp seals, as well as acquiring or inheriting many other Syrian and Mesopotamian antiquities, dating from the earliest periods to Classical and Islamic times.)

(ii) 1900 and after. In the 20th century the main interest of both private collectors and museums remained centred on Egyptian and Classical antiquities. This was probably due both to aesthetic reasons and to lack of knowledge of the diversity of Near Eastern civilizations, a situation to some extent remedied by increased scientific archaeological work in this area (*see* §1 above). Since World War II an increasing quantity of objects has appeared on the open market, especially from Iran, but also from Turkey and Syria.

Until the overthrow of the Shah in 1979, Iran proved an extremely productive source of antiquities dating from prehistoric times to the Islamic period. The best-known objects are probably Early Iron Age bronzes from Luristan and the Amlash region and, to a lesser extent, the associated terracottas and pottery. These have been avidly collected both in Iran and in the West, where there are representative groups in almost all museums that cover the Ancient Near East. Far more spectacular, however, are the gold and silver objects of the Achaemenid, Parthian and Sasanian periods, many of which are in the Metropolitan Museum of Art, New York. The illicit export of antiquities from Iraq has been much curtailed following the establishment of an antiquities service and national museum in the early 1920s; however, many objects from Syria, both Classical and earlier, have appeared on the market, mostly via Beirut. Before the political troubles in Lebanon in the 1970s and 1980s, there was a free trade in antiquities with controlled exports, the Musée National in Beirut selecting objects of Lebanese provenance that it considered of national importance. This excluded Syrian antiquities, which were thus freely exported. This system has changed little, except that after 1975 there was no control whatsoever on exports. Surprisingly, the Lebanese collectors remained active during the civil war. In Turkey there were few restrictions on the export of antiquities. Again the principal emphasis has been on objects of Greco-Roman or Byzantine date, but latterly earlier pieces have appeared in increasing numbers, for example Chalcolithic pottery and terracottas of Hacılar type, Yortan pottery and Urartian bronzes. Since the mid-1960s export controls have been far stricter and, although fewer objects have left Turkey, these tended to be of greater importance and of higher value. Distinctive alabaster sculptures were acquired by British military and colonial officials in Aden and the Protectorate of South Yemen until independence in 1967. Since then a few have reached Europe via Saudi Arabia, but Saudi museums and collectors began showing an interest, and by the late 1980s hardly any fresh objects were appearing on the open market.

Although there is still a considerable European interest in Near Eastern antiquities, with important collections being formed especially of 'Luristan' bronzes, for example those of Bröckelschen (Berlin), David-Weill (Paris) and Peter Adam (now dispersed), the international trade is dominated by Japanese and American buyers, both public and private. In Japan the Mr and Mrs Ishiguro Collection of Ancient Art is one of the more notable and scholarly collections, and the many new museums are also active buyers: the number of Japanese travellers in the Middle East is doubtless one reason for this interest. In America the better-known private collections are those of Schimmel, Pommerance and Leon Levy. The collection of the Bible Lands Museum in Jerusalem was formed by a retired dealer of international repute, Elie Borowski, formerly based in Basle and Toronto: it is an outstanding collection of antiquities, covering all the principal cultures and civilizations of the Near East. There remains a host of private owners of Near Eastern archaeological objects, both specialized collections and those with objects from other cultures.

See also ANATOLIA, ANCIENT, §VII; IRAN, ANCIENT, §VIII; MESOPOTAMIA, §VII; SYRIA-PALESTINE, §VII.

3. FORGERIES. Wherever there is an interest in collecting, and obvious profit to be gained therefrom, an industry in forgeries will appear. It is not known when the first Near Eastern fake was produced, but by the second half of the 19th century forgery was a thriving business. In the early stages objects were manufactured in Baghdad in imitation of recent discoveries, especially cylinder seals, cuneiform tablets, other inscribed objects and, on a larger scale, the Gudea-type sculptures of ancient Lagash (for illustration *see* TELLOH). Many spectacular objects and items of jewellery in precious metals have come from Iran in the 20th century, copying those of the Achaemenid, Parthian and Sasanian periods. These are often intended for tourists and are of poor workmanship, but an alarmingly large number of others are exceptionally well made, and are probably in several important private and public collections. Many fakes have also been produced of the 'Amlash' terracotta rhyta and idols, and, to a lesser extent although much publicized, of 'Luristan' bronzes and 'Ziwiyeh' jewellery. In the Levant, both in Beirut and in Syria, antiquities of all types, periods and materials have been extensively reproduced. Syrian craftsmen are also skilled in restoring in full objects of which only fragments have been discovered, especially in terracotta and bronze. In Palmyra a well-known local artist has occasionally devoted his talent to carving an 'ancient' funerary stele.

The quantity of Turkish antiquities has generally limited the opportunities for manufacturing fakes; yet they have been reproduced when intense interest has focused on a certain group of objects. Following Mellaart's discoveries at Hacılar in 1957–60, many terracotta figurines of mother-goddess type appeared on the market. Museums and collectors were prepared to pay extremely high prices for them, but most were subsequently proved by the thermoluminescence test to be modern fabrications, and the value of Hacılar objects dropped.

BIBLIOGRAPHY

Collection De Clercq: Catalogue méthodique et raisonné, 3 vols (Paris, 1888–1912)
S. Lloyd: *Foundations in the Dust* (Harmondsworth, 1947, rev. London, 1980)
J. B. Stearns: *Reliefs from the Palace of Ashurnaṣirpal II* (Graz, 1961)
P. Calmeyer: *Altiranische Bronzen der Sammlung Bröckelschen* (Berlin, 1964)
The Pommerance Collection of Ancient Art (exh. cat., New York, Brooklyn Mus., 1966)
E. Leichty: 'A Remarkable Forger', *Expedition*, xii/3 (1970), pp. 17–21
P. R. S. Moorey: *Catalogue of the Ancient Persian Bronzes in the Ashmolean Museum* (Oxford, 1971)
——: *Ancient Persian Bronzes in the Adam Collection* (London, 1974)
D. E. L. Haynes: *The Arundel Marbles* (Oxford, 1975)
K. Ishiguro: *The Mr and Mrs Ishiguro Collection of Ancient Art* (Tokyo, 1975)
P. Amiet: *Collection David-Weill: Les Antiquités du Luristan* (Paris, 1976)
Ancient Art: The Norbert Schimmel Collection (exh. cat., ed. O. W. Muscarella; Mainz, Landesmus., 1978)
Ladders to Heaven: Art Treasures from Lands of the Bible (exh. cat., ed. O. W. Muscarella; Toronto, Royal Ont. Mus., 1981)
A Guide to the Oriental Institute Museum, University of Chicago (Chicago, 1982)
'Ancient Near Eastern Art: The Metropolitan Museum of Art', *Bull. Met. Mus. A.*, xli/4 (1984)
B. Teissier: *Ancient Near Eastern Cylinder Seals from the Marcopoli Collection* (Berkeley, CA, 1984)
C. Trillin: 'American Chronicles: Frenchy and the Persians', *New Yorker* (29 June 1987), pp. 44–67

Das Vorderasiatische Museum, Berlin, Staatl. Museen cat. (Berlin, 1987)
Treasures of the Bible Lands: The Elie Borowski Collection (exh. cat., ed. R. Merhav; Tel Aviv Mus. A., 1987)

GEOFFREY TURNER

Ancients. Group of British painters and engravers active in the 1820s and 1830s. Samuel Palmer, the central figure of the group, first referred to 'the Ancients' in a letter to George Richmond in May 1827. They were drawn together by their admiration for William Blake and for 'the grand old men'—artists of the Renaissance, especially Dürer and Michelangelo—in preference to 'the moderns', the naturalistic landscape painters of the day. They met at Blake's house in London, stayed with Palmer in Shoreham, Kent, and continued their association with monthly meetings in London in the 1830s. The work of Palmer, Richmond and Edward Calvert in the 1820s and early 1830s represents their aesthetic ideals most fully: it is generally small in scale and elaborately worked, employing archaic media and a primitive, linear style. Their subject-matter was drawn from the Bible, or from a vision of a golden age of pastoral innocence and abundance that had both Christian and Vergilian overtones.

Characteristic examples are Palmer's *Valley Thick with Corn* (gum and wash, varnished, 1825; Oxford, Ashmolean; *see* PALMER, SAMUEL, fig. 1), Richmond's *Christ and the Woman of Samaria* (tempera, 1828; London, Tate) and Calvert's *Chamber Idyll* (wood-engraving, 1831). The other Ancients were Francis Oliver Finch (1802–62), who painted landscape watercolours in the style of Claude Lorrain; Welby Sherman (*fl* 1827–34), whose engravings were after, or closely indebted to, Palmer, Richmond and Calvert; Henry Walter (1799–1849), a portrait and animal painter; Frederick Tatham (1805–78), a sculptor and miniaturist; his brother, Arthur Tatham; and Palmer's cousin, John Giles. John Linnell was on the fringes of the group. All set a high value on imagination and visionary experience: their watchwords, according to Palmer's son Alfred H. Palmer, were 'Poetry and Sentiment' and most were intensely religious, though of varying persuasions.

BIBLIOGRAPHY

L. Binyon: *The Followers of William Blake* (London, 1925)
Samuel Palmer and his Circle: The Shoreham Period (exh. cat., ACGB, 1956)
H. Meltzer: *The Ancients* (diss., New York, Columbia U., 1975)
R. Wark, ed.: *Essays on the Blake Followers* (San Marino, 1983)
Samuel Palmer and 'the Ancients' (exh. cat., ed. R. Lister; Cambridge, Fitzwilliam, 1984)

CHRISTIANA PAYNE

Ancients and Moderns, Quarrel of the [Fr. *Querelle des Anciens et des Modernes*]. Name given to a debate that involved both the arts and the sciences, concerning the notion of progressive improvement since Classical antiquity. Reaching its apogee in 17th-century France, it marked a move away from belief in the supreme authority of antique tradition and example, towards a readiness to question and challenge the accepted norms and propose new approaches. The idea that the modern age might surpass the Antique originated with the 15th-century Florentine humanists and was fuelled by the growth of scientific knowledge in the 16th century; but the Quarrel of the Ancients and Moderns as such erupted in literary circles in late 17th-century France. It essentially concerned the status of writers of the ancient Greek and Roman world: whether they had reached a state of perfection that could not be bettered, as the so-called 'Ancients' believed; or whether, as the 'Moderns' asserted, the absolute authority of the Antique was open to challenge from later authors.

The immediate cause of the Quarrel concerned the relative merits of using French or Latin to inscribe a triumphal arch for Louis XIV in 1670. When Charles Perrault first published his *Parallèles des anciens et des modernes* in 1688, he widened the debate in two ways. First, the *Parallèles*, by being written in a more popular style, addressed a wider audience. Second, it concerned itself not just with literary matters, but also with artistic matters. Perrault asserted that the Moderns could not only equal the Ancients, but could in many cases surpass them. He believed in the idea of progress, arguing that knowledge was amassed with time: if Raphael, Titian and Veronese were all great men, they appeared more so because of the lack of talent that surrounded them. Perrault argued that the painters of his day surpassed their art, as well as the art of the painters of antiquity; only in sculpture in the round could the Ancients be admitted to have excelled. Perrault extended to the arts the argument that had been made earlier in the 17th century in relation to science: namely, that the authority of rules was appropriate only to the Church and the Monarchy, and that judgement on all other matters should be based on reason. In other words, the Ancient authors should be subjected to critical analysis based on experiment and experience. Perrault pointed to what he claimed were advances in each of the three arts. In architecture, he claimed, the Ancients had not known how to build suspended staircases; in relief sculpture they had been unable to convey any idea of perspective; and in painting they had not understood composition. Whether or not Perrault was correct is immaterial. What was significant was that he questioned the idea of the arts being subject to rules of absolute authority, whether that was the authority of the Antique, or that of Raphael. In the field of architecture, the support for the Ancients was led by FRANÇOIS BLONDEL in his admiration for Roman masterpieces (*see also* PARIS, §VI, 2).

It is difficult to assign precise effects on the arts to this phase of the Quarrel. Insofar as the Moderns questioned rules based on tradition, the Quarrel can be seen as symptomatic of a broader movement in French society, away from dogmatic forms and towards more discursive ones, in which improvisation and spontaneity were important. It would be too simplistic to say, for example, that the paintings of Watteau were a consequence of the Quarrel, or that the Quarrel resulted in some stylistic change. Nevertheless, the relative lack of sympathy for Poussin from around the second decade of the 18th century and the rise of Watteau's reputation from that period to *c.* 1750 can be seen as parallel developments, away from appreciation of the authoritative 'statements' of the former towards a welcome for the more open-ended 'comments' of the latter.

In diminishing the rule of previously accepted authority, the Quarrel left a vacuum. The increasing appreciation during the early 18th century in France of the unfinished work of art suggests that this vacuum was being filled by the imagination and the aesthetic response. This change in the manner of exercising taste was given theoretical expression by Jean-Baptiste Dubos, who argued (*Réflexions critiques sur la poésie et la peinture*, Paris, 1719) that sentiment, rather than reason, was the judge of painting. As Antoine Coypel said, when Director of the Académie Royale de Peinture et de Sculpture: 'It is always necessary to give the spectator [of a painting] some occasion to allow his imagination to work' (*Discours*, 1721). In other words, a certain open-endedness in the content of a painting, and perhaps in the manner of interpreting it, was permissible. Nevertheless, for both Dubos and Coypel the space for the imagination was still limited by the bounds of the taste of the educated man. The Quarrel itself had posited a contrast not between authority and imagination, but between authority and reason. The Ancients had upheld authority that was traditional; the Moderns, that which was rationally verifiable. Rationalism was, however, insufficient to account for the aesthetic response of the beholder of a painting. Both Coypel and Dubos acknowledged the role of the spectator but could not legislate for it: hence Dubos, being unable to limit the spectator's response, put limits on the type of spectator whose response was relevant.

The Moderns implicitly acknowledged change, but change was bound to undermine rules, whether they were based on tradition or on reason. The Quarrel can be said, therefore, to have indirectly created space for the imagination; and the debate then changed to the question of defining the respective boundaries of authority, reason and imagination, both of artists and of their patrons. For example, one point of debate was the relative contributions to the making of a good artist of inborn talent on the one hand, and of learning and experience on the other. Another was the relative roles of sentiment and reason in judging a work of art. This was a hotly disputed point around 1750, when French artists argued that works of art should be judged by the rules of art, of which they—but not the Salon critics—were cognizant.

These points can be seen as indirect results of the Quarrel but were not part of the Quarrel itself. That emerged again around 1740 with writers, including the Comte de CAYLUS, arguing that the painters of antiquity were as competent as their modern counterparts. This position was undermined during the 1750s, following publication of engravings after the recently discovered Roman frescoes at Herculaneum, when even Caylus was forced to acknowledge their mediocrity. From the later 1750s Caylus promoted what he interpreted as the characteristics of antique painting, on the basis of ancient texts, such as Pliny the elder's *Questiones naturales*: simplicity of composition, unity of light and clear colouring. Caylus argued that the ancient technique of encaustic painting, details of which he published in 1755 with the chemist Majault, was superior to oil or fresco. He also published suggestions for artistic subject-matter drawn from Virgil and Homer, among other authors. Few painters took up encaustic painting; as regards style, however, Joseph-Marie Vien's *Cupid Seller* (exh. Salon 1763; Fontainebleau, Château; *see* VIEN, JOSEPH-MARIE, fig. 2) was an attempt to adapt an antique ideal to the modern world. By the late 1770s, when the movement toward the Antique had gathered sufficient force to regard Vien's *Cupid Seller* as too fancy, the Quarrel had ceased. Ironically, it was those who believed in progress, the Moderns of the Quarrel, who were now promoting the perceived values of the Antique.

BIBLIOGRAPHY

B. Le Bovier de Fontenelle: *Digression sur les anciens et les modernes* (Paris, 1688); ed. R. Shackleton (Oxford, 1955)
C. Perrault: *Parallèles des anciens et des modernes en ce qui regarde les arts et les sciences* (Paris, 1688)
A. Félibien: *Entretiens sur les vies et sur les ouvrages des plus excellens peintres* (Paris, 1696); Eng. trans. (part), ed. C. Pace as *Life of Poussin* (London, 1981)
H. Rigault: *Histoire de la querelle des anciens et des modernes* (Paris, 1856)
A. Coypel: *Conférences de l'Académie royale de peinture et de sculpture, recueilliés...et précédés d'une étude sur les artistes écrivains par [Henry Jouin]* (Paris, 1883)
W. Folkierski: *Entre le classicisme et le romantisme* (Paris, 1925)
B. Teyssèdre: *Roger de Piles et les débats sur le coloris au siècle de Louis XIV* (Paris, 1957)
H. Baron: 'The Querelle of the Ancients and Moderns as a Problem for Renaissance Scholarship', *J. Hist. Ideas*, xx/1 (1959), pp. 3–22
R. C. Saisselin: *The Rule of Reason and the Rules of the Heart* (Cleveland, OH, 1970)
C. Michel: 'Les Peintures d'Herculanum et la querelle des anciens et des modernes (1740–1760)', *Bull. Soc. Hist. A. Fr.* (1984), pp. 105–17
M. Vidal: 'Conversation as Literary and Painted Form: Madeleine de Scudéry, Roger de Piles, and Watteau', *Antoine Watteau (1684–1721): Le Peintre, son temps et sa légende*, ed. F. Moureau and M. M. Grasselli (Paris and Geneva, 1987), p. 173
J. Dewald: *Aristocratic Experience and the Origin of Modern Culture: France, 1570–1715* (Berkeley, CA, and Oxford, 1993)

HUMPHREY WINE

Anckerman [Anckermann]**, Daniel** (*b* Germany, *fl* 1620–56; *d* Mecklenburg). German stuccoist and sculptor. His few surviving works provide fine examples from a period that is sparsely represented in the history of stucco decoration in parts of middle and northern Europe. Anckerman's first known work is in Mecklenburg, where he decorated the ceilings in the castles of Dargun (destr.) and Güstrow. In the latter a vast expanse of his relief panels (1620) survives, although some of them are 20th-century free reconstructions. His other identified works are in Sweden, where he worked for several patrons, including Queen Christina. In the 1640s he decorated the funerary chapel of General Herman Wrangel (*d* 1645) in Skokloster (Uppland) parish church. In this tower-like chapel he provided three stucco wall reliefs: the *Battle of Gorzno (1629)* (depicting the battle in which the Swedes defeated the Poles), a family tree and a decorative landscape. The Gothic vault is decorated with leaves, entwined along the ribs, a central floral motif and four figures of angels, sculpted in such high relief as to seem almost in the round. In addition there are two life-size figures representing General Wrangel, one reposing on the tomb, the other an equestrian monument set against a wall. None of the stucco is painted or gilded, and the effect of so much decoration in a small room is somewhat overcrowded; however, it succeeds in communicating the patron's martial pride. Although there is no documentation to support identification of Anckerman as the sculptor of these works, the stylistic similarity to the documented ones in Strängnäs Cathedral strongly suggests such an attribution.

In Strängnäs Cathedral, Daniel Anckerman decorated a mortuary chapel for Admiral Carl Carlsson Gyllenhielm

(1574–1650). The vault shows scenes from the *Life of Christ*, most particularly the *Resurrection*, with a complementary decorative motif of angels' heads and clouds. Around the chapel's tall window are ornamental urns and tendrils of acanthus, while the arch between the chapel and the body of the church is festooned with flowers and clusters of fruit. On opposing walls of the chapel are two large maplike panoramas illustrating two of the admiral's exploits: one on land—the *Battle of Kokenhusen* (in Livonia), fought in 1601 against the Poles, and one at sea—the *Blockade of Danzig Harbour* (1626). These scenes, surrounded by rich, rather heavy scrollwork, garlands and decorative figures, are rendered with careful attention to accuracy (of costume, weapons, equipment and ships) and realism (tiny ropes and metal strands represent spars and rigging, and some of the faces are astonishingly individualized). The overall effect is of a world in miniature. There is some use of gilding and colour, but the white surfaces predominate. It is recorded that Anckerman attempted to abandon this project before it had been completed, but he was persuaded to return (from Denmark) and to continue the work until 1656, when he once again left, this time for good. Another of Anckerman's Swedish patrons was Magnus Gabriel De la Gardie, but none of his decorations for the family's palace in Stockholm have survived.

After 1656 nothing is known of Anckerman except that he returned to Mecklenburg. As to his stylistic models, he obviously knew the stucco decorations executed by the Parr family in Güstrow Castle, which are outstanding examples of 16th-century stuccowork. He could also have been familiar with the royal chapel in Uppsala Cathedral, decorated in the 1590s by Antonius Watz, the Parrs' Swedish collaborator. Arent Passer's relief (1589–93) on Pontus De la Gardie's funerary monument in Reval Cathedral (Estonia) may well have inspired his battle panoramas, whether he knew it at first hand or through prints. While there is a similarity with all these earlier models, Anckerman's work is characterized by the stylistic features of his time: heavy scrolls, garlands, fruit and flowers, angels with bulky foreheads and scroll-like hair. The style is familiar from contemporary stone and wood carvings, but stucco examples are comparatively rare.

BIBLIOGRAPHY

SVKL

W. Nisser: 'Daniel Anckermans stuckaturer i de Gyllenhielmska och Wrangelska gravkoren', *Fornvännen*, xxxiv (1939), pp. 129–53

R. Bennet and E. Bohrn: *Strängnäs domkyrka*, II/1: *Gravminnen*, Sveriges Kyrkor Södermanland (Stockholm, 1974)

TORBJÖRN FULTON

Illustration Acknowledgements

We are grateful to those listed below for permission to reproduce copyright illustrative material and to those contributors who supplied photographs or helped us to obtain them. The word 'Photo:' precedes the names of large commercial or archival sources who have provided us with photographs, as well as the names of individual photographers (where known). It has generally not been used before the names of owners of works of art, such as museums and civic bodies. Every effort has been made to contact copyright holders and to credit them appropriately; we apologize to anyone who may have been omitted from the acknowledgements or cited incorrectly. Any error brought to our attention will be corrected in subsequent editions. Where illustrations have been taken from books, publication details are provided in the acknowledgements below.

Line drawings, maps, plans, chronological tables and family trees commissioned by the *Dictionary of Art* are not included in the list below. All of the maps in the dictionary were produced by Oxford Illustrators Ltd, who were also responsible for some of the line drawings. Most of the line drawings and plans, however, were drawn by the following artists: Diane Fortenberry, Lorraine Hodghton, Chris Miners, Amanda Patton, Mike Pringle, Jo Richards, Miranda Schofield, John Tiernan, John Wilson and Philip Winton. The chronological tables and family trees were prepared initially by Kate Boatfield and finalized by John Johnson.

Aachen, Hans von *1* Kunsthistorisches Museum, Vienna; *2* Bayerische Staatsgemäldesammlungen, Munich

Aalto, Alvar *1* Museum of Finnish Architecture, Helsinki; *2* Museum of Finnish Architecture, Helsinki/Photo: Heikki Havas

Abate, Nicolò dell' *1* Photo: Scala, Florence; *2* Trustees of the National Gallery, London

Abbey, Edwin Austin Trustees of the Boston Public Library, Boston, MA

ʿAbd al-Samad Freer Gallery of Art, Smithsonian Institution, Washington, DC (no. 63.41-l)

Aberdeen Royal Commission on Ancient Monuments, Scotland/© Crown Copyright

Abildgaard, Nicolai Abraham *1–2* Statens Museum for Kunst, Copenhagen

Abondio: (1) Antonio Abondio Syndics of the Fitzwilliam Museum, Cambridge

Aboriginal Australia *2* Photo: Andrée Rosenfeld; *3* Photo: Paul Tacon, Canberra; *4* Pictorial Collection, A.I.A.T.S.I.S./Photo: Fred McCarthy, 1962; *5* South Australian Museum, Adelaide/Photo: Michal Kluvanek; *6* Photo: Ian Keen; *7* Anthropology Research Museum, University of Western Australia, Perth/Photo: J.E. Stanton; *8* Anthropology Research Museum, University of Western Australia, Perth/Photo: M. Brandl; *10, 16* Photo: Howard Morphy; *11* Photo: Peter Brokensha; *12* Pitt Rivers Museum, Oxford; *13* Trustees of the British Museum, London; *14* Photo: Pictorial Collection, A.I.A.T.S.I.S.; *15* Photo: Luke Taylor; *17* South Australian Museum, Adelaide; *18* National Gallery of Australia, Canberra/© Paddy Jupurrurla Nelson, Paddy Japaljarri Sims, Kumanjayi Jungarrayi Spencer; *19–20* Flinders University Art Museum, Bedford Park, SA/Photo: Aboriginal Artist Agency, Sydney

Abramtsevo Photo: VAAP, Moscow

Abstract art *1* Hamburger Kunsthalle, Hamburg/© ADAGP, Paris, and DACS, London, 1996; *2* Öffentliche Kunstsammlung Basel, Kunstmuseum, Basle; *3* Art Gallery of Ontario, Toronto (Gift of Mr and Mrs Roger Davidson, 1970, donated by the Ontario Heritage Foundation, 1970)/© DACS, 1996

Abstract Expressionism *1* Munson–Williams–Proctor Institute, Museum of Art, Utica, NY; *2* Art Institute of Chicago, IL/© 1996

Abstraction-Création © ADAGP, Paris, and DACS, London, 1996

Abu'l-Hasan Freer Gallery of Art, Smithsonian Institution, Washington, DC (no. 45.9)

Abu Simbel Photo: Walter Emery

Abydos *2* Photo: Werner Forman Archive, London; *3* Committee of the Egypt Exploration Society

Academy *1* Photo: © RMN, Paris; *2* British Library, London (no. N.L.15.c)

Acanthus *2* Ancient Art and Architecture Collection, London/Photo: C. Hellier; *3* Board of Trustees of the Victoria and Albert Museum, London

Achaemenid *1* Photo: Margaret Cool Root; *2* Freer Gallery of Art, Smithsonian Institution, Washington, DC (no. 74.30-1)

Acoustics *1* Bibliothèque de l'Institut de France, Paris; *2* Photo: British Architectural Library, RIBA, London

Acquarossa Swedish Institute of Classical Studies, Rome

Acrylic painting Tate Gallery, London

Adam (ii): (2) Lambert-Sigisbert Adam Photo: © RMN, Paris

Adam (ii): (3) Robert Adam *1*, 3 Photo: Anthony Kersting, London; *2* Board of Trustees of the Victoria and Albert Museum, London; *4* Photo: British Architectural Library, RIBA, London

Adams, Ansel Photo: Ansel Adams Publishing Rights Trust, Carmel, CA

Adams, Mark Fine Arts Museums of San Francisco, CA (Gift of Mark Adams; no. 1977.3)

Addaura Soprintendenza delle Antichità, Palermo

Adelaide Mortlock Library, State Library of South Australia, Adelaide

Adena Mound Ohio Historical Society, Columbus, OH

Adler, Dankmar Photo: Rochelle Berger Elstein

Adriano Fiorentino Philadelphia Museum of Art, Philadelphia, PA (Given by Mr and Mrs George D. Widener)

Aelst, Willem van Mauritshuis, The Hague

Aertgen van Leyden Photo: © RMN, Paris

Aertsen, Pieter Museum Boymans–van Beuningen, Rotterdam

Aesthetic Movement *1* Board of Trustees of the Victoria and Albert Museum, London

Afghanistan *2–3, 5–6, 9, 12* Photo: © RMN, Paris; *4, 7, 10–11* Photo: Mme Tissot; *8* Photo: Dr P.H.B. Baker; *13–14* Trustees of the British Museum, London; *15* Photo: Kickan Hansen, Copenhagen

Africa *2* Trustees of the National Museums of Scotland, Edinburgh; *3, 9, 44, 52, 54, 76, 101, 104–5, 132–3, 136, 142* Trustees of the British Museum, London; *4* Photo: Dr K.H. Striedeter; *5* Photo: Werner Forman Archive, London; *6* South African Museum, Cape Town/Photo: P. Davison; *7* Museum for African Art, New York (from the exhibition *Africa Explores: 20th-century African Art*); *8, 137* Staatliche Museen zu Berlin, Preussischer Kulturbesitz/Museum für Völkerkunde, Berlin; *10* Archives Musée Dapper, Paris/Photo: Hugo Dubois; *11* National Museum of African Art, Washington, DC (Anonymous gift; Eliot Elisofon Photographic Archives)/Photo: Franko Khoury; *12* National Museum of African Art, Washington, DC (Gift of Helen and Dr Robert Kuhn; Eliot Elisofon Photographic Archives)/Photo: Franko Khoury; *13, 45* Photo: Rebecca Busselle, New York; *14, 61, 159* Photo: Jeremy Coote; *15–16* Photo: H.J. Drewal; *17* Photo: Kano State Information Ministry; *18, 42, 49* Photo: Herbert M. Cole; *19* Photo: Simon Ottenberg; *20* Photo: Monni Adams; *21* Photo: Sokari Douglas Camp; *22, 47, 60, 90* Photo: Marla C. Berns; *23* Photo: Harold

W. Turner, Auckland; *24* Phoebe A. Hearst Museum of Anthropology, University of California, Berkeley, CA; *25* Photo: Philip and Miep Palmer; *27* Photo: Corinne A. Kratz; *28* Williams College Museum of Art, Williamstown, MA/Photo: Dr Ernie Wolfe; *29* Swedish Missionary Association, Stockholm; *30* Photo: Frederick Lamp; *31* Paul and Ruth Tishman Collection/Photo: Jerry Thompson; *32* Collection of Dr Theo Dobbelmann, Amsterdam/Photo: © Walter Dräyer, Zurich; *33, 36, 81* Photo: Jean M. Borgatti; *34* Brooklyn Museum, New York (Purchased with funds given by Mr and Mrs Alastair Bradley Martin, Mrs Donald M. Oenslager, Mr and Mrs Robert E. Blum, Mrs Florence A. Blum Fund); *35, 46, 139, 154* Fowler Museum of Cultural History, UCLA, Los Angeles, CA; *37* Indianapolis Museum of Art, Indianapolis, IN (Gift of Dr Wally Zollman); *38* Photo: Mr Itzikovitz, Paris; *39* Linden-Museum, Stuttgart; *40* National Museum of African Art, Washington, DC (Museum purchase with funds provided by the Smithsonian Collections Acquisition Program, 1983; no. 83-3-6)/Photo: Jeffrey Ploskonka; *41, 97* Art Gallery of Ontario, Toronto (Barbara and Murray Frum Collection); *43, 78, 99* Musée de l'Homme, Paris; *48* Photo: Carlyn Saltman; *50* Photo: Fred T. Smith, Kent State University, Kent, OH; *51* Museum Rietberg, Zurich/Photo: Eberhard Fischer; *53, 100, 138, 146, 150* Koninklijk Museum voor Midden-Afrika, Tervuren; *55* Museum of Archaeology and Anthropology, Cambridge University; *56* Fowler Museum of Cultural History, UCLA, Los Angeles, CA (Wellcome Collection); *57* Photo: Barbara E. Frank; *58* National Museum of African Art, Washington, DC (Bequest of Eliot Elisofon; no. 73-7-440)/Photo: Ken Heinen, 1984; *62* Hutchison Library, London/Photo: S. Robertshaw; *63–4, 94* Photo: Robert Estall Photo Agency, Sudbury, Suffolk/© Angela Fisher; *65, 67* Photo: Heinemann, 1978 (from Susan Denyer: *African Traditional Architecture*); *66* Photo: Elizabeth Schneider; *68* Hutchison Library, London/Photo: Mick Csaky; *69* Photo: Prof. J.C. Moughtin; *70* Aga Khan Trust for Culture, Geneva; *71, 73* Museum for African Art, New York (Private Collection, USA)/Photo: Jerry L. Thompson; *72, 74* Museum for African Art, New York (W. and U. Horstmann, Switzerland)/Photo: Jerry L. Thompson; *75* Laboratorio Fotografico, Museo Nazionale Preistorico ed Etnografico 'Luigi Pigorini', Rome; *77* Department of Library Services, American Museum of Natural History, New York (neg. no. 90.1/4693); *79* Photo: Doran H. Ross; *80* Musée d'Art Contemporain, Lyon; *82, 84* Photo: © Michel Huet; *83, 85* Photo: David A. Binkley; *86, 95* Photoarchiv, Rautenstrauch-Joest-Museum für Völkerkunde, Cologne; *87* Photo: René A. Bravmann; *88* Department of Library Services, American Museum of Natural History, New York (neg. no. 224507); *89* Photo: James C. Faris; *91* Photo: Dr Allen F. Roberts; *92* Photo: Prof. Joanne Eicher; *93* Department of Ethnography, Nationalmuseet, Copenhagen/Photo: Lennart Larsen; *96* National Museum of African Art, Washington, DC/Photo: Eliot Elisofon; *98* Department of Library Services, American Museum of Natural History, New York (neg. no. 123187)/Photo: Alex Rota; *102* Department of Anthropology, Smithsonian Institution, Washington, DC (cat. no. 20600K); *106* University of East Anglia, Norwich (Robert and Lisa Sainsbury Collection)/Photo: James Austin, Cambridge; *107* National Museum of African Art, Smithsonian Institution, Washington, DC (neg. no. 82-6-2); *109* Photo: Jean-Dominique Lajoux, Paris; *115* Musée National du Bardo, Tunis; *117* British Library, London (MS. OR. 516, fol. 64*v*); *119* Indiana University Art Museum, Bloomington, IN/Photo: Michael Cavanagh/Kevin Montague; *120, 122* Indiana University Art Museum, Bloomington, IN; *121* Photo: Christopher D. Roy; *124, 143–4* Pitt Rivers Museum, Oxford; *125* National Museum of African Art, Washington, DC (Eliot Elisofon Photographic Archives)/Photo: Eliot Elisofon; *126* Baltimore Museum of Art, Baltimore, MD; *127* Museum Rietberg, Zurich/Photo: Wettstein and Kauf; *129, 162* Museum für Völkerkunde, Frankfurt am Main; *130* Musée Carnavalet, Paris/© Musées de la Ville de Paris, and DACS, London, 1996; *131* Dwight and Blossom Strong Collection/Photo: Kaz Tsuruta; *135* Náprstek Museum of Asian, African and American Culture, Prague; *141* Photo: Robert Estall Photo Agency, Sudbury, Suffolk/© F.K.J. Nielsen; *147–8* University of the Witwatersrand Art Galleries, Johannesburg (Standard Bank Collection of African Art); *149* University of the Witwatersrand Art Galleries, Johannesburg (Standard Bank Collection of African Art)/Photo: B. Cnoops; *151* Photo: J.M. Vlach; *152* New York State Historical Association, Cooperstown, NY; *153* Department of Library Services, American Museum of Natural History, New York; *155* Museum of Fine Arts, Boston, MA (Bequest of Maxim Karolik); *156* National Museum of American History, Smithsonian Institution, Washington, DC; *157* National Museum of American Art, Washington, DC/Photo: Art Resource, New York; *158* Photo: Prof. Marshall W. Mount; *160* B. Jewsiewicki Collection, Quebec City; *161* African Art Centre, Durban, South Africa; *163* University of Bremen (Bremen African Archives)

African American art *1* National Museum of American Art, Washington, DC (Gift of Delta Sigma Theta Sorority, Inc.)/Photo: Art Resource, New York; *2* Photo: Art Resource, New York; *3* Photo: Regenia A. Perry; *4* Corcoran Gallery of Art (Gift of the Women's Committee)/Photo: Robert Grove/Chris Middendorf, Washington, DC

Agasse, Jacques-Laurent Royal Collection, Windsor Castle/© Her Majesty Queen Elizabeth II

Agostino di Duccio National Gallery of Art, Washington, DC (Andrew W. Mellon Collection)

Agra *1–2* Photo: R. Nath

Ahmadabad Photo: George Michell

Aigina *1* Photo: R.A. Tomlinson; *2* Staatliche Antikensammlungen und Glyptothek, Munich

Aigues-Mortes Comité Départemental du Tourisme du Gard, Nîmes

Aihole *1–2* Photo: Gary Michael Tartakov

Ai Khanum *2* Photo: F. Tissot

Ain Ghazal Photo: Peter Dorrell

Ainu Museum für Völkerkunde, Hamburg

Airport Photo: Peter Sanders

Aix-en-Provence Photo: Arch. Phot. Paris/© DACS, 1996

Ajanta *2* Photo: Gary Michael Tartakov

Ajmer Photo: Wim Swaan, London

Akan Seattle Art Museum, Seattle, WA (Gift of Katherine White and the Boeing Company)

Akkadian *1* Photo: © RMN, Paris; *2* Photo: Hirmer Fotoarchiv, Munich

Aksum Photo: Francis Anfray

Akye Photo: Dr M.B. Visonq

Alabaster *1* Trustees of Sir John Soane's Museum, London; *2* Photo: RCHME/© Crown Copyright; *3* Board of Trustees of the Victoria and Albert Museum, London

Alaca Höyük Photo: Hirmer Fotoarchiv, Munich

Alahan Monastery From M. Gough, ed.: *Alahan* (Toronto, 1985)/© 1985

Alba Hispanic Society of America, New York

Alba, Macrino d' Photo: Archivi Alinari, Florence

Albani, Francesco *1* Photo: Arch. Phot. Paris/© DACS, 1996; *2* Photo: Archivi Alinari, Florence

Albania *2, 4* Photo: G. Frashëri; *3, 6* Galeria Kombetare e Arteve Figurative, Tiranë/Photo: G. Frashëri; *5* Instituti Monumenteve te Kultures, Tiranë/Photo: G. Frashëri

Albers: (2) Josef Albers Josef Albers Museum, Bottrop/© DACS, 1996

Alberti: (2) Cherubino Alberti Photo: Archivio Fotografico Vasari, Rome

Alberti, Antonio Museo Civico, Carpi

Alberti, Leon Battista *1* National Gallery of Art, Washington, DC (Samuel H. Kress Collection); *2* Photo: AKG Ltd, London; *3* Photo: Scala, Florence; *5, 8* Photo: Archivi Alinari, Florence; *7* Photo: Bildarchiv Foto Marburg

Albertinelli, Mariotto *1, 2* Photo: Archivi Alinari, Florence

Albertolli: (1) Giocondo Albertolli British Library, London (no. 1899.p.24)

Albi Photo: Anthony Kersting, London

Album *1–2* Trustees of the British Museum, London

Album amicorum Koninklijke Bibliotheek, The Hague

Alcalá de Henares Photo: Prof. M. Castillo

Alcobaça Abbey Photo: Conway Library, Courtauld Institute of Art, London

Aldegrever, Heinrich *1* Westfälisches Landesmuseum für Kunst und Kulturgeschichte, Münster; *2* Kunstsammlungen der Veste Coburg

Alekseyev, Fyodor Tret'yakov Gallery, Moscow

Aleotti, Giovanni Battista Photo: Archivi Alinari, Florence

Aleppo Photo: Warwick Ball

Alessi, Galeazzo *1* Photo: Publifoto, Genoa; *2–3* Photo: Archivi Alinari, Florence

Alexandria *1, 3* Graeco-Roman Museum, Alexandria; *2* Forschungszentrum Griechisch-Römisches Ägypten, Trier University/Photo: Dieter Johannes, Deutsches Archäologisches Institut, Cairo

Alfieri, Benedetto Innocente Photo: Archivi Alinari, Florence

Algardi, Alessandro *1* Photo: K. Fremantle; *2* Photo: Archivi Alinari, Florence; *3–4* Photo: Gabinetto Fotografico Nazionale, Istituto Centrale per il Catalogo e la Documentazione, Rome

Algeria *1* Jordan National Gallery of Fine Arts, Amman; *2* Institut du Monde Arabe, Paris/Photo: Philippe Maillard

'Ali Board of Trustees of the Victoria and Albert Museum, London

Alighieri, Dante British Library, London (MS. 19587)

Aligny, Théodore Caruelle d' Musée des Beaux-Arts de Bordeaux/Photo: Alain Danvers
Allebé, August Museum Boymans–van Beuningen, Rotterdam
Allegory *1, 3* Bibliothèque Nationale de France, Paris; *2* British Library, London (no. 1703.d.7); *4, 6, 10* Photo: © RMN, Paris; *5, 7* Trustees of the National Gallery, London; *8* Rijksmuseum Paleis Het Loo, Apeldoorn/Photo: A.A.W. Meine Jansen; *9* Bildarchiv, Österreichische Nationalbibliothek, Vienna
Allegory of art Governing Body, Christ Church, Oxford
Allori: (1) Alessandro Allori Photo: Archivi Alinari, Florence
Allori: (2) Cristofano Allori *1–2* Photo: Archivi Alinari, Florence
Allston, Washington Harvard University Art Museums, Cambridge, MA
Alma-Tadema: (1) Lawrence Alma-Tadema Manchester City Art Galleries, Manchester
Alt, Rudolf Staatliche Graphische Sammlung, Munich
Altamira Photo: Romain Robert
Altar *1* Pergamon Museum, Berlin/Photo: AKG Ltd, London; *3* Photo: Bildarchiv Foto Marburg; *4* Photo: Archivi Alinari, Florence; *5* British Library, London (no. 3475.g.31); *6* South American Pictures, Woodbridge, Suffolk/Photo: Tony Morrison; *7* Photo: Ann Paludan; *8* Photo: Werner Forman Archive, London
Altarpiece *1* Photo: © RMN, Paris; *2, 5* Photo: Archivi Alinari, Florence; *3, 6* Photo: Bildarchiv Foto Marburg; *4* Photo: Osvaldo Böhm, Venice
Altdorfer: (1) Albrecht Altdorfer *1* Syndics of the Fitzwilliam Museum, Cambridge; *2* Staatliche Museen zu Berlin, Preussischer Kulturbesitz; *3* Photo: Bundesdenkmalamt, Vienna; *4* Bayerische Staatsbibliothek, Munich
Altdorfer: (2) Erhard Altdorfer Museum für Kunst und Kulturgeschichte, Lübeck
Alternating system Photo: Bildarchiv Foto Marburg
Altichiero *1* Photo: Archivi Alinari, Florence; *2* Photo: Overseas Agenzia Fotografica, Milan
Altıntepe *2* Museum of Anatolian Civilizations, Ankara/Photo: Prof. Tahsin Özgüç
Altomonte: (1) Martino Altomonte Österreichische Galerie im Belvedere, Vienna
Aluminium *1* Architectural Association, London/Photo: Peter Cook; *2* Nantenshi Gallery, Tokyo
Alvares: (2) Baltazar Alvares Photo: Eduardo Duarte
Alvarez: (1) José Alvarez Cubero *1* Photo: Ampliaciones y Reproducciones MAS, Barcelona; *2* Museo del Prado, Madrid
Amadeo, Giovanni Antonio *1–2* Photo: Archivi Alinari, Florence
Amaravati Trustees of the British Museum, London
Amaury-Duval, Eugène-Emmanuel Photo: Nancy Davenport
Amber (ii) *1* Metropolitan Museum of Art, New York (Gift of J. Pierpont Morgan, 1917; no. 17.190.2067); *2* Board of Trustees of the Victoria and Albert Museum, London
Amberger, Christoph Kunsthistorisches Museum, Vienna
Amboise, d': (1) Georges I d'Amboise Photo: Conway Library, Courtauld Institute of Art, London
Ambulatory Photo: James Austin, Cambridge
American Scene painting Whitney Museum of American Art, New York (Gift of Gertrude Vanderbilt Whitney)/Photo: Geoffrey Clements
Amerling, Friedrich von Österreichische Galerie im Belvedere, Vienna
Ami: (3) Shinsō Sōami Metropolitan Museum of Art, New York (Gift of John D. Rockefeller, 1941; no. 41.59.1–2)
Amiens *2–3* Photo: James Austin, Cambridge
Amigoni, Jacopo Photo: Bildarchiv Foto Marburg
Amlash region Iran Bastan Museum, Tehran/Photo: Ezat O. Negahban
Amman, Jost Trustees of the British Museum, London
Ammanati, Bartolomeo *1* Photo: Scala, Florence; *2* Photo: Charles Avery
Ammenemes III Photo: Hirmer Fotoarchiv, Munich
Amphitheatre Photo: Fototeca Unione, American Academy in Rome
Amsterdam *1, 6* Amsterdams Historisch Museum, Amsterdam; *2–3* Photo: Jan Derwig, Architectuur Fotografie, Amsterdam; *4* Rijksmuseum, Amsterdam; *5, 7* Gemeentelijke Archiefdienst, Amsterdam
Amsterdam school Photo: Frank den Oudsten, Amsterdam
Amulet *1* Trustees of the British Museum, London; *2* Photo: Oscar Savio, Rome
Anagni Photo: Archivi Alinari, Florence
Anatolia, ancient *3* Photo: Tahsin Özgüç; *4–6, 8* Photo: Hirmer Fotoarchiv, Munich; *7* Archaeological Museums of Istanbul; *9* Metropolitan Museum of Art, New York (no. 50.163)
Anatomical studies *1* Royal Collection, Windsor Castle/© Her Majesty Queen Elizabeth II; *2* Hunterian Art Gallery, University of Glasgow; *3* British Library, London
Ancher: (1) Michael Ancher Hirschsprungske Samling, Copenhagen
Ancient Near East *4–23, 28, 30–31, 35* Trustees of the British Museum, London; *24* Iran Bastan Museum, Tehran; *26* Photo: La Mission Archéologique de Mari; *27* Photo: © RMN, Paris; *29* Department of Antiquities and Heritage, Baghdad; *32* Photo: Annie Caubet; *33* Board of Trustees of the Victoria and Albert Museum, London